PLATO

COMPLETE WORKS

PLATO

COMPLETE WORKS

Edited, with
Introduction and Notes, by
JOHN M. COOPER

Associate Editor
D. S. HUTCHINSON

HACKETT PUBLISHING COMPANY
Indianapolis/Cambridge

KH

For further information, please address

Hackett Publishing Company, Inc.
P. O. Box 44937
Indianapolis, Indiana 46244-0937

www.hackettpublishing.com

Jacket design by Chris Hammill Paul
Text design by Dan Kirklin

Library of Congress Cataloging-in-Publication Data
Plato.
[Works. English. 1997]
Complete works/Plato;
edited, with introduction and notes, by
John M. Cooper;
associate editor, D. S. Hutchinson.
p.   cm.
Includes bibliographical references and index.
ISBN 0-87220-349-2 (cloth: alk. paper)
1. Philosophy, Ancient.
2. Socrates.
I. Cooper, John M. (John Madison).
II. Hutchinson, D. S.
III. Title.
B358.C3   1997
184—dc21
96-53280
CIP

12/13/05

CONTENTS

v

Names listed are those of the translators.

*It is generally agreed by scholars that Plato is not the author of this work.

†It is not generally agreed by scholars whether Plato is the author of this work.

‡As to Plato's authorship of the individual Letters and Epigrams, consult the respective introductory notes.

INTRODUCTION

Since they were written nearly twenty-four hundred years ago, Plato's dialogues have found readers in every generation. Indeed, in the major centers of Greek intellectual culture, beginning in the first and second centuries of our era, Plato's works gradually became the central texts for the study and practice of philosophy altogether: in later antiquity, a time when Greek philosophy was struggling to maintain itself against Christianity and other eastern 'wisdoms', Platonist philosophy *was* philosophy itself. Even after Christianity triumphed in the Roman Empire, Platonism continued as the dominant philosophy in the Greek-speaking eastern Mediterranean. As late as the fifteenth century, in the last years of the Byzantine empire, the example of George Gemistos Plethon shows how strong this traditional concentration on Plato could be among philosophically educated Greeks.[1] When Plethon, the leading Byzantine scholar and philosopher of the time, accompanied the Byzantine Emperor to Ferrara and Florence in 1438–39 for the unsuccessful Council of Union between the Catholic and Orthodox churches, he created a sensation among Italian humanists with his elevation of Plato as the first of philosophers—above the Latin scholastics' hero, Aristotle. Plato's works had been unavailable for study in the Latin west for close to a millennium, except for an incomplete Latin translation of *Timaeus*,[2] but from the fifteenth century onwards, through the revived knowledge of Greek and from translations into Latin and then into the major modern European languages, Plato's dialogues resumed their central place in European culture as a whole. They have held it without interruption ever since.

In presenting this new edition of Plato's dialogues in English translation, we hope to help readers of the twenty-first century carry this tradition forward. In this introduction I explain our presentation of these works (Section I), discuss questions concerning the chronology of their composition (II), comment on the dialogue form in which Plato wrote (III), offer some advice on how to approach the reading and study of his works (IV),

---

1. 'Plethon' is a pseudonym George Gemistos adopted toward the end of his life—in Greek it has essentially the same meaning as 'Gemistos' itself does—apparently to mark, by its resemblance to Plato's own name, his authoritative sponsorship of Platonist doctrines. See *George Gemistos Plethon: The Last of the Hellenes*, by C. M. Woodhouse (Oxford: Clarendon Press, 1986); for the change of name, see pp. 186–88.

2. Translations of *Phaedo* and *Meno*, made in Sicily, were also available from about 1160.

and describe the principles on which the translations in the volume have been prepared (V). But first, a few basic facts about Plato's life and career.

Plato, a native Athenian, was born in 427 B.C. and died at the age of eighty-one in 347.[3] He belonged, on both his mother's and father's side, to old and distinguished aristocratic families. At some point in his late teens or early twenties (we do not know when or under what circumstances), he began to frequent the circle around Socrates, the Athenian philosopher who appears as the central character in so many of his dialogues and whose trial and death he was to present so eloquently in his *Apology* and his *Phaedo*. In the dozen years or so following Socrates' death in 399, Plato, then nearly thirty years old, may have spent considerable time away from Athens, for example, in Greek-inhabited southern Italy, where he seems to have met philosophers and scientists belonging to the indigenous "Pythagorean" philosophical school, some of whose ideas were taken up in several of his own dialogues, most notably, perhaps, in the *Phaedo*. In about 388 he visited Syracuse, in Sicily—the first of three visits to the court of the "tyrants" Dionysius I and II during his thirty-odd-year-long engagement in Syracusan politics. This involvement is reported on at length in the Platonic *Letters*, included in this edition. At some point, presumably in the 'eighties, Plato opened a school of higher education in the sacred grove of Academus, in the Attic countryside near Athens, apparently offering formal instruction in mathematical, philosophical, and political studies. He seems to have spent the rest of his life (except for the visits to Syracuse) teaching, researching, and writing there. Under his leadership, the Academy became a major center of research and intellectual exchange, gathering to itself philosophers and mathematicians from all over the Greek world. Among its members was Aristotle, who came as a student in about 367 at the age of eighteen and remained there as teacher, researcher, and writer himself, right up to the time of Plato's death twenty years later.

I. The 'Canon' of Thrasyllus

These *Complete Works* make available a single collection of all the works that have come down to us from antiquity under Plato's name. We include all the texts published in the early first century A.D. in what became the definitive edition of Plato's works, that by Thrasyllus, an astrologer and Platonist philosopher from the Greek city of Alexandria, in Egypt.[4] From Thrasyllus' edition derive all our medieval manuscripts of Plato—and so almost all our own knowledge of his texts. Apparently following earlier

---

3. Several 'lives' of Plato have survived from antiquity, of which the earliest, that by Diogenes Laertius (translated by R. D. Hicks, Cambridge, Mass.: Loeb Classical Library, 1925), dates perhaps from the third century A.D.

4. For the sake of completeness, we also print translations of the short poems ('Epigrams') that have come down to us from antiquity with Plato's name attached.

precedent, Thrasyllus arranged the works of Plato (thirty-five dialogues, plus a set of thirteen 'Letters' as a thirty-sixth entry) in nine 'tetralogies'— groups of four works each—reminiscent of the ancient tragedies, which were presented in trilogies (such as the well-known *Oresteia* of Aeschylus) followed by a fourth, so-called satyr play, preserving a link to the origins of tragedy in rituals honoring the god Dionysus. In addition to these, he included in an appendix a group of 'spurious' works, presumably ones that had been circulating under Plato's name, but that he judged were later accretions. We follow Thrasyllus in our own presentation: first the nine tetralogies, then the remaining works that he designated as spurious.[5] With one exception, earlier translations into English of Plato's collected works have actually been only selections from this traditional material:[6] usually they have omitted all the Thrasyllan 'spurious' works, plus a certain number of others that were included in his tetralogies, since the editors of the collections judged them not in fact Plato's work. In their widely used collection,[7] Edith Hamilton and Huntington Cairns include none of the 'spuria' and only twenty-nine of the thirty-six other works.[8] From Thrasyllus' tetralogies they omit *Alcibiades, Second Alcibiades, Hipparchus, Rival Lovers, Theages, Clitophon,* and *Minos.* Even if these dialogues are not by Plato himself (and at least *Clitophon* and *Alcibiades* could very well be), they are all valuable works, casting interesting light on Socrates and the Socratic legacy. They also deserve attention as important documents in the history of Platonism: it is worthy of note that teachers of Platonist philosophy in later antiquity standardly organized their instruction through lectures on ten 'major' dialogues, beginning with *Alcibiades*— omitted by Hamilton and Cairns, presumably as not by Plato. The dialogues classified by Thrasyllus as spurious also deserve attention, even though in their case there are strong reasons for denying Plato's authorship; and the *Definitions* are a valuable record of work being done in Plato's Academy

5. Since our manuscripts standardly present the thirty-six 'tetralogical' works in the order that ancient evidence indicates was Thrasyllus', it is reasonable to think that their order for the spuria goes back to Thrasyllus' edition too. We present these in the order of our oldest manuscript that contains them, the famous ninth- or tenth-century Paris manuscript of the complete works. (In some other manuscripts *Axiochus* is placed at the front of the list, instead of the back.)

6. The only previous comparably complete translation (it does however omit one small work of disputed authorship, the *Halcyon,* included here, and the Epigrams as well) is *The Works of Plato,* edited by George Burges, in six volumes, for the Bohn Classical Library, London: G. Bell and Sons, 1861–70. This is a 'literal' translation, not easy to read or otherwise use.

7. *The Collected Dialogues of Plato including the Letters,* Bollingen Foundation (Princeton University Press, 1961).

8. In its ten Plato volumes, the Loeb Classical Library (Cambridge: Harvard University Press, various dates) does include translations (with facing Greek text) of all thirty-six works in Thrasyllus' tetralogies, but none of the 'spuria'.

in his lifetime and the immediately following decades.[9] (For further details see the respective introductory notes to each of the translations.)

Especially given the often inevitably subjective character of judgments about authenticity, it is inappropriate to allow a modern editor's judgment to determine what is included in a comprehensive collection of Plato's work. The only viable policy is the one followed here, to include the whole corpus of materials handed down from antiquity. At the same time, it should be frankly emphasized that this corpus—both the works it includes as genuine and the text itself of the works—derives from the judgment of one ancient scholar, Thrasyllus. His edition of Plato's work, prepared nearly four hundred years after Plato's death, was derived from no doubt differing texts of the dialogues (and *Letters*) in libraries and perhaps in private hands, not at all from anything like a modern author's 'autograph'. No doubt also, both in its arrangement and in decisions taken as to the genuineness of items and the text to be inscribed, it may have reflected the editor's own understanding of Plato's philosophy (perhaps a tendentious one) and his views on how it ought to be organized for teaching purposes.[10] So, since the present editor has exercised his own judgment only to the extent of deciding to follow the edition of Thrasyllus, we are thrown back on Thrasyllus' judgment in the works included and in their order and arrangement. Since Thrasyllus included all the genuine works of Plato that any surviving ancient author refers to, plus some disputed ones, we apparently have the good fortune to possess intact all of Plato's published writings.

Thrasyllus' order appears to be determined by no single criterion but by several sometimes conflicting ones, though his arrangement may represent some more or less unified idea about the order in which the dialogues should be read and taught. For example, the first four works (*Euthyphro, Apology, Crito, Phaedo*) manifestly follow internal evidence establishing a chronological order for the events related in them—the 'Last Days of Socrates'. The conversation in *Euthyphro* is marked as taking place shortly before Socrates' trial; his speech at his trial is then given in the *Apology*, while *Crito* presents a visit to Socrates in prison, three days before his execution, which is the culminating event of the *Phaedo*. Somewhat similar internal linkages explain the groups *Republic-Timaeus-Critias* and *Theaetetus-Sophist-Statesman* (although the conversation in *Theaetetus* seems to present itself as taking place earlier on the same day as that of *Euthyphro*—a key to grouping that Thrasyllus quite reasonably opted to ignore). But topical and other, more superficial connections play a role as well. *Clitophon* is placed before *Republic*, and *Minos* before *Laws* to serve as brief introduc-

9. In the table of contents works whose Platonic authorship has plausibly been questioned in antiquity or modern times are marked, either as ones which no one reasonably thinks are by Plato or as ones as to which there is no consensus that they are by him.

10. For a somewhat speculative, rather alarmist, view of the extent of Thrasyllus' editorial work, see H. Tarrant, *Thrasyllan Platonism* (Ithaca, N.Y.: Cornell University Press, 1993).

tions to the central themes of these two major works, justice and legislation respectively, and the two *Alcibiades* dialogues are grouped together, as are the *Greater* and *Lesser Hippias*. Even the presumed order of composition seems responsible for the last tetralogy's bringing the series to a conclusion with *Laws* and its appendix *Epinomis* (followed by *Letters*): we have evidence that *Laws* was left unpublished at Plato's death, presumably because he had not finished working on it.

Most readers will have little need to attend to such details of Thrasyllus' arrangement, but one point is important. Except for *Laws*, as just noted, Thrasyllus' tetralogies do not claim to present the dialogues in any supposed order of their composition by Plato. Indeed, given the enormous bulk of *Laws*, different parts of it could well have been written before or contemporaneously with other dialogues—so Thrasyllus' order need not indicate even there that *Laws* was *the* last work Plato composed. Thrasyllus' lack of bias as regards the order of composition is one great advantage that accrues to us in following his presentation of the dialogues. Previous editors (for example, both Hamilton and Cairns and Benjamin Jowett[11]) imposed their own view of the likely order of composition upon their arrangement of the dialogues. But judgments about the order of composition are often as subjective as judgments about Platonic authorship itself. In modern times, moreover, the chronology of composition has been a perennial subject of scholarly debate, and sometimes violent disagreement, in connection with efforts to establish the outline of Plato's philosophical 'development', or the lack of any. We have solid scholarly arguments and a consensus about some aspects of the chronology of Plato's writings (I return to this below), but this is much too slight a basis on which conscientiously to fix even an approximate ordering of all the dialogues. Speaking

---

11. *The Dialogues of Plato* (London: Macmillan, 1st ed. 1871, 3rd 1892; 4th ed., revised, by D. J. Allan and H. E. Dale, Oxford: Clarendon Press, 1953, four vols.). Allan and Dale claim explicitly that theirs is the approximate order of composition; Jowett left his own order unexplained, but it is not very different from Allan and Dale's. Of Thrasyllus' thirty-six 'genuine' works Jowett[1] prints twenty-seven dialogues (no *Letters*); Jowett[3] adds a twenty-eighth (*Second Alcibiades*), plus one of Thrasyllus' eight 'spurious' works (*Eryxias*), both translated by his secretary Matthew Knight; Jowett[4] shrinks back to twenty-eight (adding *Greater Hippias*, translated by Allan and Dale themselves, but omitting *Second Alcibiades* as nongenuine). The earliest comprehensive English translation, that of Thomas Taylor (except that F. Sydenham is credited with the translation of nine dialogues) (London, 1804, five vols.) is organized on a fanciful 'systematic' basis, in which the dialogues judged by him to establish the 'comprehensive' Platonic views respectively in ethics and politics and in natural philosophy and metaphysics come first, followed by the various more 'partial' treatments of specific questions. The title page to each of Taylor's five volumes claims to present '[Plato's] Fifty-five Dialogues and Twelve Epistles', a surprising way of referring to the thirty-five Thrasyllan 'genuine' dialogues that the collection actually contains (he omits the thirteenth *Letter* as obviously spurious): presumably he counts each book of *Republic* and *Laws* as a separate 'dialogue', in which case the total is indeed fifty-five.

generally, issues of chronology should be left to readers to pursue or not, as they see fit, and it would be wrong to bias the presentation of Plato's works in a translation intended for general use by imposing on it one's own favorite chronological hypotheses. Thrasyllus' order does not do that, and it has the additional advantage of being for us the traditional one, common ground for all contemporary interpreters.[12] Such interpretative biases as it may contain do not concern any writer nowadays, so it can reasonably be considered a neutral basis on which to present these works to contemporary readers.

II. Chronological vs. Thematic Groupings of the Platonic Dialogues

In teaching and writing about Plato, it is almost customary nowadays (in my view unfortunately so: see below) to divide the dialogues into groups on the basis of a presumed rough order of their composition: People constantly speak of Plato's 'early', 'middle' (or 'middle-period'), and 'late' dialogues—though there is no perfect unanimity as to the membership of the three groups, and finer distinctions are sometimes marked, of 'early-middle' dialogues or 'transitional' ones at either end of the intermediate group.[13] Although this terminology announces itself as marking chronologically distinct groups, it is in reality based only in small part on anything like hard facts about when Plato composed given dialogues. (For these facts, see the next paragraph.) For the most part, the terminology encapsulates a certain interpretative thesis about the evolving character of Plato's authorship, linked to the development of his philosophical thought. This authorship began, it is assumed, sometime after 399 B.C., the year of Socrates' death, and continued until his own death some fifty years later. According to this thesis, Plato began as the author of dialogues setting forth his 'teacher' conversing much as we presume he typically actually did when discussing his favorite philosophical topics—morality, virtue, the best human life—with the young men who congregated round him and other intellectuals in Athens, where he spent his entire life. These, then, would constitute the 'early' dialogues, sometimes also thematically described as the 'Socratic' dialogues; they are all relatively short works. Only gradually, on this view, did Plato grow into a fully independent philosopher, with new ideas and interests of his own, as outgrowths from and supplements to his 'Socratic heritage'. In his writings presumed to postdate the founding of the Academy, we see new ideas and interests first and primarily in the

---

12. Modern editions of Plato in Greek (for example, that of J. Burnet in the Oxford Classical Texts series of Clarendon Press, Oxford, 1900–1907, in five volumes: a revised edition is underway) regularly present the Thrasyllan corpus in Thrasyllus' order.

13. For one influential version of this division, see G. Vlastos, *Socrates: Ironist and Moral Philosopher* (Ithaca, N.Y.: Cornell University Press, 1991), pp. 46–47.

introduction of his celebrated theory of 'Forms'—eternal, nonphysical, quintessentially unitary entities, knowledge of which is attainable by abstract and theoretical thought, standing immutably in the nature of things as standards on which the physical world and the world of moral relationships among human beings are themselves grounded. This happens in the 'middle' dialogues: *Symposium, Phaedo,* and *Republic,* most notably—much longer and philosophically more challenging works. The 'middle' dialogues are usually construed to include also *Parmenides,* with its critical reflections on the theory of Forms, and *Theaetetus.* Finally—still according to this interpretative thesis—the 'late' period comprises a new series of investigations into logic, metaphysics, the philosophy of physics, and ethics and political theory, from which these 'Forms' either are absent altogether or else at least the principal theoretical work is accomplished without direct and simple appeal to their authoritative status. These include *Timaeus, Sophist, Statesman, Philebus,* and *Laws.* Along with these philosophical developments, Plato's manner of writing dialogues was evolving, too. In the 'middle' dialogues, where Socrates continues to be the principal speaker, he is no longer limited to questioning and commenting upon the views of his fellow discussants, as in the 'early' dialogues, but branches out into the development of elaborate, positive philosophical theses of his own. In the 'late' dialogues, however (with the understandable exception of *Philebus*—see the introductory note to that work), Socrates ceases altogether to be an active participant in the discussion. Moreover, the conversation takes on the character of a dogmatic exposition of doctrine by the main speaker to an audience. One of these may play virtually the sole role of nodding assent from time to time or requesting further explanations, so as to register acceptance and provide an easy means of noting and dividing—and highlighting the importance of—the principal topics as they successively arise.

Now, in its broad outlines, such a division of Plato's works into three chronological periods could be correct—the interpretative thesis, or rather theses, on which it rests do have some plausibility, though they are obviously not compelling. But in fact we have really only two bits of reliable, hard information about the chronology of Plato's writings. One of these I have already mentioned: *Laws* was left unpublished at Plato's death. The other derives from the fact that *Theaetetus* seems to present itself as a memorial honoring its namesake, a famous mathematician and longtime associate of Plato's in his Academy, who died an untimely death in 369 B.C.: that seems to date the dialogue to about 369–365 or so. Since internal evidence links *Theaetetus* to *Sophist* and *Statesman* as its two successors, that would suggest (though of course it does not prove) that those three dialogues were written in that order, after about 367—therefore in the last two decades of Plato's life, his sixties and seventies. Useful as that information may be, it is obviously not sufficient basis for fixing any complete chronological guide to the reading and teaching of the dialogues. As for *Laws,* however, it began to be noticed already in the nineteenth century that its sentences are characterized by the frequency and constancy of a number of stylistic features that it shares with only a few other dialogues: the four that I listed above as 'late'—*Timaeus, Sophist, Statesman, Philebus*—plus *Critias*. On the obviously not perfectly secure assumption that, at least cumulatively, such stylistic affiliation, setting these works off strongly from all the others, must fix a chronological grouping, exhaustive 'stylometric' investigations have led to a consensus in favor of adding these five works to *Laws*—independently known to be a late composition—as constituting Plato's last period.[14] Thus one might claim substantial hard evidence in favor at least of recognizing these six works (plus *Epinomis*, if it is by Plato) as constituting a separate, late group. But stylometry does not strongly support any particular order among the six, nor can it establish any particular ordering of the remaining dialogues among themselves—though some do claim that it establishes a second group of four dialogues as the latest of the nonlate group: *Republic, Parmenides, Theaetetus*, and *Phaedrus* in some undetermined order. So, even if we accept the somewhat insecure assumption noted just above, no hard data support the customary division of the dialogues into chronological groups, except with respect to the last of the three—the 'late' dialogues *Timaeus, Critias, Sophist, Statesman, Philebus*, and *Laws*. The classifications of 'early' and 'middle-period' dialogues rest squarely on the interpretative theses concerning the progress of Plato's work, philosophically and literarily, outlined above. As such, they are an unsuitable basis for bringing anyone to the reading of these works. To use them in that way is to announce in advance the results of a certain interpretation of the dialogues and to canonize that interpretation under the guise of a presumably objective order of composition—when in fact no such order *is* objectively known. And it thereby risks prejudicing an unwary reader against the fresh, individual reading that these works demand.

For these reasons, I urge readers not to undertake the study of Plato's works holding in mind the customary chronological groupings of 'early', 'middle', and 'late' dialogues. It is safe to recognize only the group of six late dialogues. Even for these, it is better to relegate thoughts about chronology to the secondary position they deserve and to concentrate on the literary and philosophical content of the works, taken on their own and in relation to the others. In some cases it may indeed seem desirable to begin with a preliminary idea about the place of a given dialogue in the series (*Gorgias* and *Protagoras* earlier than *Republic*, say, or *Theaetetus* before *Sophist*, or *Symposium* before *Phaedo*). Certainly, a study of such sets of dialogues might lead one to argue that the philosophical ideas they contain show an evolution in some particular direction. But chronological hypotheses must not preclude the independent interpretation and evalua-

---

14. For a survey of these investigations and references to recent and older stylometric studies of Plato, see Charles M. Young, 'Plato and Computer Dating' in *Oxford Studies in Ancient Philosophy*, XII, ed. C. C. W. Taylor (Oxford: Clarendon Press, 1994), pp. 227–50.

tion of the philosophical arguments the dialogues contain; so far as possible, the individual texts must be allowed to speak for themselves. However, in reading the dialogues, it may help to be aware from the outset of certain thematic groupings among them. In our introductory notes to the individual works, we inform readers about such links from the work in question to others and provide other information that may help in placing the work in the proper context within Plato's writings and in the Athens of the fifth and fourth centuries B.C. One very large group of dialogues can usefully be identified here. These are what we may call the Socratic dialogues—provided that the term is understood to make no chronological claims, but rather simply to indicate certain broad thematic affinities. In these works, not only is Socrates the principal speaker, but also the topics and manner of the conversation conform to what we have reason to think, both from Plato's own representations in the *Apology* and from other contemporary literary evidence, principally that of the writer Xenophon,[15] was characteristic of the historical Socrates' own philosophical conversations. Included here are fully twenty of the thirty-six works in Thrasyllus' tetralogies and (allowance made for their post-Platonic authorship) all seven of the dialogues that he classified as spurious: from the tetralogies, *Euthyphro, Apology, Crito, Alcibiades, Second Alcibiades, Hipparchus, Rival Lovers, Theages, Charmides, Laches, Lysis, Euthydemus, Protagoras, Gorgias, Greater* and *Lesser Hippias, Ion, Menexenus, Clitophon,* and *Minos.*

One can think of these works, in part, as presenting a portrait of Socrates—Socrates teaching young men by challenging them to examine critically their own ideas, Socrates as moral exemplar and supreme philosophical dialectician, Socrates seeking after moral knowledge, while always disclaiming the final possession of any, through subjecting his own and others' ideas to searching rational scrutiny. But just as there is no reason to think that these dialogues are or derive in any way from records of actual conversations of the historical Socrates, so there is also no reason to suppose that in writing them[16] Plato intended simply to reconstruct from memory actual arguments, philosophical distinctions, etc., that Socrates had used, or views that he had become persuaded of through his lifelong practice of philosophical dialectic. To be sure, one evident feature of these dialogues is that in them Socrates does philosophize in the way the historical Socrates, according to the rest of our evidence, did. He seeks the opinions of his interlocutors on moral, political, and social questions

---

15. Xenophon's Socratic writings include his own *Apology,* a *Symposium,* and four books of *Memoirs of Socrates* (often referred to by its Latin title, *Memorabilia*); these are translated by H. Tredennick and R. Waterfield (Penguin Books, 1990), and are available in Greek and English in the Loeb Classical Library series (Cambridge, Mass.: Harvard University Press, various dates).

16. That is, the ones he did write: there are reasonable doubts as to the Platonic origins of several of the dialogues included in the tetralogies, and a few are generally held not to be his work.

and subjects them to searching critical examination. It is true that, in some of them, such as *Gorgias*, he also comes forward with distinctive moral and political ideas of his own, to which he attempts to show his interlocutors, despite their overt denials, are logically committed since these ideas follow from propositions that the other speakers have themselves granted. But, by contrast with dialogues such as *Phaedo* and *Republic*, he does not engage here in elaborate positive philosophical construction, putting forward ambitious philosophical theses of his own and offering independent philosophical argument and other considerations in their favor. In particular, Socrates says nothing about the theory of Forms. That is a sign that in these dialogues Plato intends not to depart, as he does elsewhere, from Socratic methods of reasoning or from the topics to which Socrates devoted his attention, and no doubt he carries over into these portraits much of the substance of Socrates' own philosophizing, as Plato himself understood it.

But Plato was not the only or even the first of Socrates' companions to write Socratic dialogues. Though, with the exception of Xenophon's, no other such dialogues have survived complete, we know enough about the contents of some of them to be sure that no convention of the genre forbade the author to write freely and from his own head about philosophical and other matters that interested him. Indeed, quite to the contrary, as we can see from Xenophon's dialogue *Oeconomicus*, in which Socrates discourses knowledgeably and at great length about estate management, a subject we have good reason to think he never knew or cared anything about— though Xenophon himself certainly did. So we have good reason to expect that at least some of what Plato makes Socrates say in his Socratic dialogues expresses new ideas developed in his own philosophical reflections, not mere elaborations of historically Socratic thoughts. This is perhaps particularly clearly the case, though in different ways, in *Charmides, Lysis, Euthydemus*, and *Gorgias*, but it is an open possibility in them all, to be decided in the light of a full interpretation of their contents, in relation to that of other dialogues. It is worth saying again that classifying these along with the rest as Socratic dialogues carries no implication whatsoever of an early date of composition or an early stage of the author's philosophical development. As I am using the term, it is a thematic classification only. We know no reason to conclude that Plato wrote dialogues of this genre during only one phase of his career as an author, whether early or late. Though it is reasonable to suppose that Plato's earliest writings were in fact Socratic dialogues, there is no reason to suppose that, just because a dialogue is a Socratic one, it must have been written before all the dialogues of other types—except, of course, that if we were right to accept a special group of late dialogues, the Socratic dialogues must predate all of these. The decision about the relative chronology of any of these dialogues, if one wishes to reach a decision on that secondary question at all, must be reached only after a careful and complete study of their philosophical content, in comparison with the contents of Plato's other works.

There are eight dialogues other than the Socratic and the late dialogues: *Phaedo, Cratylus, Theaetetus, Parmenides, Symposium, Phaedrus, Meno,* and *Republic*. It is not easy to identify a common theme unifying this whole group. As it happens, however, they correspond closely to the putative classification of 'middle-period' dialogues. In these Socrates remains a principal speaker, although in *Parmenides* not Socrates but Parmenides sets and directs the philosophical agenda. As noted above, these stand apart from the Socratic dialogues in that here Socrates takes and argues directly for ambitious, positive philosophical positions of his own. However, those considerations do not set them cleanly apart from the late dialogues as a whole, since Socrates is the main speaker again in *Philebus,* and he appears in the introductory conversations of *Timaeus* and *Critias,* more briefly in those of *Sophist* and *Statesman,* and those dialogues are just as philosophically ambitious, even if in somewhat different ways. In all but two of the dialogues of this group (*Theaetetus* and *Meno*), the Platonic theory of Forms plays a prominent and crucial role: Indeed, it is these dialogues that establish and define the 'classical' theory of Forms, as that has been understood by later generations of philosophers. Were it not for *Theaetetus* and *Meno,* one might be tempted to classify this group simply as the 'Classical Theory of Forms' dialogues. On the other hand, *Phaedrus,* despite Socrates' use of the classical theory in his second speech on *erōs,* foreshadows the revised conception of a Form as some sort of divided whole—no longer a simple unity—known about by the method of 'collection and division' that the late dialogues *Sophist, Statesman,* and *Philebus* set out and employ at length. And it seems that one important lesson Parmenides wishes to teach Socrates in the *Parmenides* also goes in the same direction. Moreover, *Theaetetus* is marked by Plato as some sort of successor to *Parmenides* and predecessor of *Sophist* and *Statesman.* (See the introductory notes to these dialogues.) Thus *Phaedrus, Parmenides,* and *Theaetetus* all have clear forward connections to the late dialogues.

For all these reasons, it would be a mistake to claim any unifying single common theme for this group. At the most, one could say that this group develops the positive philosophical theories in ethics and politics and in metaphysics and theory of knowledge that we normally associate with Plato, centering on the classical theory of Forms, while including several dialogues which point forward to the innovations worked out in the late group. Accordingly, no thematic name for the group seems available, and we must make do simply by referring to a 'second' group of Plato's dialogues, alongside the Socratic works, both groups to be placed chronologically before the late dialogues. As before, this classification must be understood as having no chronological implications whatsoever of its own, as regards their relationship to the Socratic dialogues. Any decision as to relative dates of composition, either within the second group itself or with respect to the various members of the Socratic group, must be reached only after comparative study of the philosophical contents of the individual dialogues themselves. While one might reasonably suppose that, in general, the dialogues of the second group were written later than the Socratic group, it is not safe to rule out some chronological overlapping in composition.

III. Plato and the Dialogue Form

Why did Plato write dialogues? What does it mean for the reader of his works that they take this form? Philosophers of earlier generations expounded their views and developed their arguments either in the meters of epic poetry (Xenophanes, Parmenides, Empedocles, for example), or in short prose writings or collections of remarks (Anaximander, Heraclitus, Anaxagoras, Philolaus, Democritus), or in rhetorical display pieces (the Sophists Gorgias, Protagoras, and Prodicus). Socrates himself, of course, was not a writer at all but engaged in philosophy only orally, in face-to-face question-and-answer discussions. It is clear that the dialogue form for philosophical writing began within the circle of those for whom philosophy meant in the first instance the sort of inquiry Socrates was engaged in. I mentioned above that Plato was not the first or only Socratic to write philosophical dialogues, but he certainly elaborated and expanded the genre far beyond what anyone else ever attempted. He not only wrote Socratic dialogues, as we have seen, but he developed the genre also to the point where, eventually, Socrates dropped out of the cast of characters altogether—in the magnum opus of his old age, the *Laws*. Plato's younger associate Aristotle also wrote dialogues (all of which have perished), as well as the lectures and treatises that we know him for, but, significantly, they seem not to have had Socrates among their characters:[17] Socrates had been dead for fifteen years at Aristotle's birth, and he could not have had the personal attachment to him as a philosophical model that Plato and the others in the first generation of dialogue writers obviously did.[18] But, as already with Aristotle, the medium of choice for later philosophers—Theophrastus and other Peripatetics, Epicurus and his followers, the Stoic philosophers, Sextus Empiricus, late Platonists—was the prose discourse or treatise (sometimes a commentary on a work of Plato's or Aristotle's or some other 'ancient' philosopher).[19] There, the author spoke directly to his readers in his own voice. The close association of the dialogue form with the Socratic conception of philosophy as face-to-face discussion is

17. According to Cicero (*Letters to Atticus* XIII xix 4), Aristotle appeared as the main speaker in his own dialogues.

18. At least one other Academic of Aristotle's generation, Plato's nephew and successor as head of the school, Speusippus, also wrote dialogues, along with philosophical works of other genres. We know nothing substantial about them.

19. Epicurus also seems to have written at least one dialogue, and there is evidence of dialogues written by some Peripatetics.

borne out in the principal exception to this rule, the Latin philosophical works of Cicero (first century B.C.): the plurality of voices and the author's capacity to stand back from and question what these voices say made the dialogue format suit perfectly a nondogmatic or 'skeptical' Platonist like Cicero. (On 'skeptical' Platonism, see further below.)

It was characteristic of philosophy before Socrates and Plato that philosophers usually put themselves forward as possessors of special insight and wisdom: *they* had the truth, and everyone else should just listen to them and learn. Thus Parmenides' poem tells how he was brought in a chariot to a goddess at the borders of night and day—the very center of the truth—and then sets out that truth and the arguments on which it rests, while also revealing the errors of everyone else's ways. Similarly Heraclitus, in his prose book, claims to have discovered in one big thought—essentially, the unity of opposites—the key to all reality, and he excoriates other thinkers—several by name—as having missed it by wasting their time learning up all sorts of arcane details. These philosophers hoped and expected to win fame for themselves personally, as the authors (among humans) of their own 'truth'. The genres in which they wrote suited this intellectual stance and these authorial ambitions perfectly: they could speak directly to their readers, as the authors of the poetry or prose in which they were handing down the truth.

Socrates was a totally new kind of Greek philosopher. He denied that he had discovered some new wisdom, indeed that he possessed any wisdom at all, and he refused to hand anything down to anyone as his personal 'truth', his claim to fame. All that he knew, humbly, was how to reason and reflect, how to improve himself and (if they would follow him in behaving the same way) help others to improve themselves, by doing his best to make his own moral, practical opinions, and his life itself, rest on appropriately tested and examined reasons—not on social authority or the say-so of esteemed poets (or philosophers) or custom or any other kind of intellectual laziness. At the same time, he made this self-improvement and the search for truth in which it consisted a common, joint effort, undertaken in discussion together with similarly committed other persons—even if it sometimes took on a rather combative aspect. The truth, if achieved, would be a truth attained by and for all who would take the trouble to think through on their own the steps leading to it: it could never be a personal 'revelation' for which any individual could claim special credit.

In writing Socratic dialogues and, eventually, dialogues of other types, Plato was following Socrates in rejecting the earlier idea of the philosopher as wise man who hands down the truth to other mortals for their grateful acceptance and resulting fame for himself. It is important to realize that whatever is stated in his works is stated by one or another of his characters, *not* directly by Plato the author; in his writings he is not presenting his 'truth' and himself as its possessor, and he is not seeking glory for having it. If there is new wisdom and ultimate truth in his works, this is not served up on a plate. Plato does not formulate his own special 'truth' for his readers, for them to learn and accept. You must work hard even to find out what the author of a Platonic dialogue is saying to the reader— it is in the writing as a whole that the author speaks, not in the words of any single speaker—and the dialogue form demands that you think for yourself in deciding what, if anything, in it or suggested by it is really the truth. So you have to read and think about what each speaker says to the others (and also, sometimes, what he does not say), notice what may need further defense than is actually given it, and attend to the author's manner in presenting each character, and the separate speeches, for indications of points on which the author thinks some further thought is required. And, beyond that, you must think for yourself, reasoning on the basis of the text, to see whether or not there really are adequate grounds in support of what it may appear to you the text as a whole *is* saying. In all this, Plato is being faithful to Socrates' example: the truth must be arrived at by each of us for ourselves, in a cooperative search, and Plato is only inviting others to do their own intellectual work, in cooperation with him, in thinking through the issues that he is addressing.

One might attend here to what Plato has Socrates say at the end of *Phaedrus* about written discourses. Socrates is speaking in the first instance of speeches written for oral delivery, but he applies his remarks to all writing on political or other serious philosophical subjects. Actual knowledge of the truth on any of these matters requires a constant capacity to express and re-express it in relation to varying circumstances and needs and in response to new questions or challenges that may arise. Knowledge is a limitless ability to interpret and reinterpret itself—it cannot be set down exhaustively in any single set of formulas, for universal, once-for-all use. Accordingly, no book can actually embody the knowledge of anything of philosophical importance; only a mind can do that, since only a mind can have this capacity to interpret and reinterpret its own understandings. A book must keep on saying the same words to whoever picks it up. Most books—perhaps those of Parmenides and some other early philosophers among them—attempt the impossible task of telling the reader the truth, with the vain idea that, through putting their words into their heads, they will come to possess knowledge of it.[20] Plato's dialogues are writings—books—too; like all books, once written, their words are

---

20. *Letter VII* (341c–d, 344c–e) speaks rather similarly about philosophical writings, emphasizing the impossibility of *writing down* the content of any state of mind that might constitute true knowledge of philosophical truth. *Letter II* (314b–c) limits itself to a very different, much less interesting, complaint about such writing—and recommends a remedy that actually contradicts the main idea here: it will inevitably fall into the wrong hands, so that any sensible philosopher will have his pupils commit his oral teaching to memory instead of writing down on paper the words to be memorized! In both *Letters* the author (whether Plato or someone impersonating him) gives these considerations as Plato's reasons for never having written a philosophical treatise.

fixed for all time and all readers. But because they demand that the reader interpret and reinterpret the meaning of what is said, going ever deeper in their own questioning and their own understanding both of the writings themselves and of the truth about the subjects addressed in them, these writings speak in a unique new way to the reader. It may remain true that only a mind, and no book, can contain the knowledge of anything important. But a Platonic dialogue makes a unique claim to do what a book *can* do to engage a person effectively in the right sort of search for truth.

IV. Reading Plato

Despite this inherent open-endedness and the fact that Plato speaks only through the writing as a whole, all Plato's dialogues do have a principal speaker, one who establishes the topic of discussion and presides over it. In the Socratic works and the second group of dialogues, with the exception of *Parmenides*, this is Socrates. In the late dialogues, except *Philebus*, where Socrates reappears to discuss the nature of the human good, it is the anonymous visitor from Elea, in *Sophist* and *Statesman*, or the equally anonymous Athenian of *Laws* and *Epinomis*, or else Timaeus or Critias, in the dialogues named after them. In each dialogue Plato focuses the reader's attention on what the principal speaker says. Indeed, in the late dialogues, though again *Philebus* is something of an exception, the other speakers put up so little opposition and their comments introduce into the proceedings so little of the sort of fertile nuance that one finds in the other dialogues, that for long stretches there is little else that could claim the reader's attention at all. In fact, the substance of *Timaeus* and *Critias* is contained in uninterrupted discourses that the main speaker delivers to the others present, with no indication even at the end of how they received it: there is no return to the conversational context in which it was originally introduced. Can one not take these principal speakers as Plato's mouthpieces, handing straight out as their own opinions what Plato himself believed at the time he wrote and what he wished his readers to understand as such—both as the truth and as what Plato *thought* was the truth?

If what I have said about the dialogue form and Plato's commitment to it—right to the end of his writer's career—is correct, the *strict* answer to this question must be in the negative, in all cases. However much his principal speakers really do, in some way, speak on his behalf, he must also, in some way, be holding back from arguing and asserting personally the things that he has any of them say. What, then, are we to make of Plato's relation to what they do say? Each dialogue has to be read individually, but the three different groups—the Socratic dialogues, the second group, and the late dialogues—plainly do place the author in different sorts of relationship to his main speaker. Without going into the individual differences, here is some general orientation on the author's relationships to the leading speakers in each of the three groups.

First, there is a matter of literary form that applies to all the dialogues. As I have emphasized, Plato never speaks in his own author's voice but puts all his words into a particular speaker's mouth. This means that, although everything any speaker says is Plato's creation, he also stands before it all as the reader does: he puts before us, the readers, and before himself as well, ideas, arguments, theories, claims, etc. for all of us to examine carefully, reflect on, follow out the implications of—in sum, to use as a springboard for our own further philosophical thought. Authors writing in their own voices can, of course, do the same: they do not always have to be straightforwardly advocating the positions they develop and argue for, though that is what Greek authors usually did, and with passionate self-promotion. But they must take special steps to make the reader aware that that is what they are doing, for example by saying it in so many words. In his dialogues, Plato adopts that stance automatically.[21] However much he may himself believe everything that, say, the Athenian visitor puts forward in *Laws* X about the existence of the gods and the importance for human life of accepting their providential relationship to us and the physical world, he stands to it, even though he is its author, as his readers also stand. To finally understand all this *as* the truth requires further work—one must sift and develop and elevate the thoughts expressed there into the kind of self-sufficient, self-interpreting total grasp that I referred to above in drawing on what *Phaedrus* says about writing. Certainly, we should not think that Plato had already attained that Elysian condition and was writing from its perspective through the Athenian's mouth. Much less should we think that he was pretending to himself or to his readers that he had attained it. That would be a malicious and unprincipled abuse of the very dialogue form that Plato was so obviously determined to uphold. So even in the late dialogues, where, as noted, there is often little else before us but the arguments of the principal speaker, Plato stands back—everything needs further thought; what we have before us is partial and provisional at best, however decisive it might be about particular points under discussion.

In the dialogues of the second group, the role of the interlocutors is much more substantial, and the main speaker himself, usually Socrates, expresses more reservations, more caution and tentativeness, about what he is putting forward. Accordingly, even though readers always and understandably speak of the theories adumbrated by Socrates here as 'Plato's theories', one ought not to speak of them so without some compunction—the writing itself, and also Plato the author, present these always in a spirit of open-ended exploration, and sometimes there are contextual clues

---

21. I should emphasize that I am speaking here simply of Plato's handling of the dialogue form. Another author (perhaps Berkeley in his *Three Dialogues between Hylas and Philonous* is one of these) might use the form simply for expository convenience, making it clear that he is using one of the speakers to present his own ideas and arguments and using the others as a means of countering certain sorts of resistance to them.

indicating that Socrates exaggerates or goes beyond what the argument truly justifies, and so on. Finally, in the Socratic dialogues, all these cautionary points hold good, and others too. To the extent that Plato is providing a portrait of his friend Socrates, it is only common sense not to assume that Plato accepts as valid everything philosophical that he makes Socrates say. Even beyond that, and however much one knows Plato admired Socrates and, indeed, regarded him as the very model of how a philosopher should live, one should remain open to the possibility that a Socratic dialogue, when read fully and properly, may actually indicate some criticisms and point to some shortcomings of positions or methods of argument that it attributes to Socrates. Here one might especially mention *Gorgias* and *Protagoras* as dialogues that may demand interpretation along those lines, but the same applies in principle to all the Socratic dialogues.

Reading a Platonic dialogue in the spirit in which it was written is therefore a dauntingly complex task. It is in the entire writing that the author speaks to us, not in the remarks made by the individual speakers. To find out what the writing itself is saying—equivalently, what Plato is saying *as its author*—one must work constantly to question everything that any speaker says, to ask what reasons he may have or what reasons might be provided to support it and what might tend to speak against it; one must never simply take, as if on Plato's authority, a claim made by any speaker as one that, from the perspective of the dialogue as a whole, constitutes an established philosophical truth—certainly not in the form in which it is stated and not without qualification, expansion, taking into account wider perspectives, and so on. Especially in the Socratic dialogues and those of the second group, one must be alert to contextual indicators of all sorts—the particular way in which an interlocutor agrees to or dissents from something, the more or less explicit characterization provided and other indicators about the personal qualities and commitments of the speakers, as well as hesitations and reservations and qualifications expressed by one or another of them.

Those, then, are my own suggestions about the significance of the dialogue form in Plato's writings. The dialogues have not always been read in the way I have suggested, and not all scholars today share this approach to them: many would not hesitate simply to identify the positions and arguments stated or suggested by Socrates, or whoever the principal speaker is in any given dialogue, as those of the author at the time of composition. Already in antiquity Aristotle usually treats them in that 'dogmatic' way, except for the Socratic dialogues, which he seems to have taken as depicting (equally 'dogmatically') the historical Socrates' philosophy. However, in Plato's own Academy, beginning only a couple of generations after Aristotle's death, the dialogues were read differently. They were taken to express a skeptical philosophy, one that raises questions about everything, examining the reasons pro and con on each issue, but always holds back from asserting anything as definitely established, as known to be the case. This reading works best, of course, for the Socratic dialogues, in which Socrates makes much of the fact that he does not actually know anything himself and can only examine and criticize the well-groundedness of other people's opinions who think that they do. But Arcesilaus (third century B.C.), one of Plato's successors as head of the Academy, who first adopted such a skeptical mode of philosophizing and defended it as genuinely Platonic, is reported to have owned a complete set of Plato's writings—apparently that was an unusual thing in those days—so apparently he studied them all. And indeed, even the last of Plato's works can sustain the skeptical reading if one takes account of the fact that, formally at least, as I have emphasized myself, Plato never speaks in his own person when any of his characters does: even a main character like the Athenian in *Laws* or the visitor from Elea, who does not hesitate to speak dogmatically himself, as if he had full possession of the truth on the matters he discourses upon, can still be read as putting something forward that Plato the author is presenting merely for examination and criticism. This 'skeptical' Platonism held the field in the Academy for the best part of two centuries, until Antiochus of Ascalon early in the first century B.C. refused any longer to accept the skeptical interpretation of Plato's own dialogues.

After Antiochus, Plato was interpreted again, in the way Aristotle and his contemporaries had understood him, as a systematic philosopher with a whole system of doctrine, both about human life and about metaphysical and scientific principles for interpreting and relating to one another all the facts of experience. This system could be found expounded and argued for especially in the dialogues of the second and the late groups—one just had to take each dialogue's main character as Plato's mouthpiece. In Roman imperial times, this dogmatic interpretation was expanded and consolidated, as Platonist philosophers came to regard Plato's writings as the repository of the ultimate and permanent highest truths about the universe—the equivalent for rationalist pagans of the Jews' Books of Moses or the Christians' Gospels. For them, Plato himself had gained a complete and totally adequate insight into the nature and structure of the world and of the divine principles upon which it is organized. All that anyone need do is to read the dialogues correctly in order to discover the truth about every important question of philosophy. It is as if, for Plotinus and the other Platonists of late antiquity (the ones we usually refer to as 'Neoplatonists'), Plato was speaking to us in his writings in the same way that Parmenides or Heraclitus had done, as possessor of his own 'truth'— the *real* truth—handing that down to other mortals in his own somewhat cryptic way, in dialogues. It is quite an irony that, in treating Plato thus as a superwise authority on all philosophical subjects, himself in direct intellectual touch with the highest and most divine principles on which the universe depends, these late Platonists set Plato upon the pedestal of wisdom, traditional among earlier philosophers, the very pedestal that, if I am right, his own commitment to the dialogue form for his writings was intended to renounce.

My suggested approach to the reading of Plato pays full respect to this renunciation. But—with the reservations already noted about Plato's openness and experimental spirit—it also accepts the overwhelming impression, not just of Antiochus, but of every modern reader of at least many of his dialogues, that Platonism nonetheless constitutes a systematic body of 'philosophical doctrine'—about the soul and its immortality; the nature of human happiness and its dependence on the perfection of mind and character that comes through the virtues of wisdom, justice, temperance, and courage; the eternal and unaltering Forms whose natures structure our physical world and the world of decent human relations within it; the nature of love and the subservience of love in its genuine form to a vision of that eternal realm. These and many other substantive philosophical ideas to be explored in Plato's dialogues are his permanent contribution to our Western philosophical culture. But we would fail to heed his own warnings if we did not explore these in a spirit of open-ended inquiry, seeking to expand and deepen our own understandings as we interrogate his texts, and ourselves through them.

V. The Translations

Hackett Publishing Company began bringing out the works of Plato in modern, readable English translations in 1974, with G.M.A. Grube's *Republic*. By 1980 I was advising first William Hackett and then James Hullett, his successor, in the commissioning of, and providing editorial oversight over, the new translations that the company published during the next decade and a half, looking toward an eventual *Complete Works*. In 1991 D. S. Hutchinson joined the project. In completing the process we now add to the twenty dialogues already published twenty new works commissioned specially for this volume, taking over five additional translations from other sources (two of them extensively revised by the translators for publication here).

In overseeing the preparation of the translations, I have had constantly in mind two principal objectives, not often combined, that I was convinced could be achieved simultaneously. First, I wanted them to be as correct as was humanly possible. Taking Plato's to be first and foremost works of philosophy, for me that meant not just that the meaning of the Greek sentences should be correctly grasped and rendered, with any significant, genuine alternative renderings indicated, but, equally important, that everything establishing the flow and connection of philosophical ideas in the Greek be somehow preserved in the English. Variances and continuities in philosophically significant terminology within a single work should so far as possible be preserved or otherwise indicated in the translation. Where logical relationships are precisely defined in the Greek, they have to be rendered equally precisely in the English. And so on. Many older translations, smooth-reading though they sometimes are, fail signally in these crucial respects. On the other hand, I saw no need, in the name of 'philosophical accuracy', to introduce indiscriminately neologisms and technical language and to resort to other odd and unnatural terminology or turns of phrase or to torture normal English syntax and patterns of prose composition. Plato's Greek is straightforward and elegant, most of the time, though in order to express novel and complex theoretical ideas, it must sometimes strain the powers of ordinary language.

The aim should be to find a way, while adhering to normal English word order and sentence construction, to say as precisely as possible, in ordinary English—where necessary, ordinary philosophical English—just what an educated contemporary of Plato's would have taken the Greek being translated to be saying. It is neither necessary nor appropriate to produce 'English' encrusted with esoteric code-formations that no one could make good use of except by consulting the Greek text. Hence, we have to reject the ideal some recent translators of Greek philosophy into English have held aloft, to produce a version as 'close' to the Greek text in syntax, word order, and terminology as were the medieval Latin Aristotle translations of William of Moerbeke. For one thing, Latin grammar and normal sentence construction are vastly closer to the Greek than our contemporary English has any chance of being. And, in any case, the scholastic study of Aristotle that Moerbeke's translations were intended to facilitate is nothing we should wish ourselves or our students to emulate in reading Plato (or, for that matter, Aristotle, either). When we English-speaking readers turn to Plato's texts, we want to find a Plato who speaks in English—our English—and communicates to us as accurately as possible all the details of his thought and artistry. I know that these translations achieve this aim in varying degrees and no doubt none of them as fully as one might realistically wish. But I hope they will be found a durable basis on which both general readers and students can rely in carrying forward into the new millennium the twenty-four-hundred-year tradition of reading and studying these classics of Western philosophy.

John M. Cooper
July 1996

EDITORIAL NOTES

Marginal references   In order to facilitate comparison between this edition and others, in Greek or in translation, we print in the margins of the translations the 'Stephanus numbers' that are commonly used in scholarly references to the works of Plato. These numbers and letters indicate the corresponding page and section on that page of the relevant volume of the Greek text of Plato as edited (Paris, 1578) by the French scholar Henri Estienne (in Latin, Stephanus). (These are omitted in the case of *Halcyon* and *Epigrams* because Stephanus did not include those works in his edition.)

Footnotes   It has been our intention to provide in footnotes all the basic information the general reader might need in order to follow the discussion in the texts. This includes the identification of persons, places, events, etc., in Greek history and culture, insofar as these are not explained sufficiently in the context where the references to them occur. We have also identified the sources of all Plato's quotations from other authors, so far as those are known; any that are not identified should be presumed to be from now unidentifiable authors or works. In general, we have not attempted to provide any guidance or commentary as regards issues of philosophical interpretation, apart from that contained in the introductory notes to the individual works. But we have sometimes given alternative translations, where some point of philosophical significance may be at issue and the Greek is ambiguous or otherwise subject to differing construals. In all cases the editor bears ultimate responsibility for the footnotes to the translations: usually these incorporate material that was in the footnotes in the original place of publication or was provided by those responsible for translations here published for the first time, but the editor has decided when a footnote is needed, and when not, and he has borne the responsibility of editing and otherwise preparing the footnotes as they appear here, including providing most of the alternative translations himself. Responsibility for any errors or omissions in the footnotes rests with the editor.

Greek text   In general the Greek text translated is that of John Burnet, in *Platonis Opera*, Oxford Classical Texts, five volumes (Oxford: Clarendon Press, 1900–1907). Where the translation of a given work is based on a different text from Burnet's, this is recorded in a note at the beginning of the work in question. For each work, every effort has been made to register in footnotes all variances in the translation from the basic Greek text, Burnet's or another. Such departures, as indicated in the notes, often select alternative readings contained in the manuscripts, or else follow emendations proposed by other editors or in scholarly articles: we do not record the details, beyond saying that a given reading is found in "some manuscripts," or else that a given emendation "is accepted," or the like. Those who wish to know the details may usually find them in the *apparatus criticus* of a critical edition of the dialogue in question. In a few places the translator has opted for a new conjectural treatment in the text translated; there we simply record the conjectured reading without further elaboration.

Translations Many of the translations in this book have been published before, either by Hackett Publishing Company or by another publisher (details are given in the Acknowledgments). In all cases the version appearing here reflects revisions, of varying quantity and significance, made by the translators on the advice of the editor. While no general effort has been made to ensure consistency in the translation of recurrent words or phrases across the vast extent of Plato's works (that would intrude too greatly on the prerogatives and the individual judgment of the translators to whose scholarly expertise we are indebted for these *Complete Works*), we have adopted a policy of keeping to a single spelling for each of the proper nouns and adjectives that occur in the book.

Editorial responsibilities As editor, John M. Cooper has had editorial oversight over the preparation for publication of all the translations in this volume, as well as for the introductions and notes. He is the author of all the introductory notes except those noted just below, signing them *J.M.C.* In addition to advising the editor generally, D. S. Hutchinson's special responsibilities as associate editor concerned a set of fifteen works—the ones marked as spurious by the first-century-A.D. editor Thrasyllus, plus eight further dialogues whose Platonic authorship has been at least doubted in modern times: *Definitions, On Justice, On Virtue, Demodocus, Sisyphus, Eryxias, Axiochus, Halcyon, Alcibiades, Second Alcibiades, Hipparchus, Rival Lovers, Theages, Clitophon,* and *Minos.* He recruited the translators (translating two of the works, *Definitions* and *Alcibiades,* himself) and worked closely with them in the preparation and revision of their versions. He wrote the introductory notes to these fifteen works, signing them *D.S.H.*

ACKNOWLEDGMENTS

The editor would like to acknowledge the assistance of Sean Kelsey, who as research assistant read through all the translations at the penultimate stage, offering many excellent suggestions for improvement, identifying the sources of Plato's quotations, and indicating where footnotes were needed, as well as preparing the texts for submission to the publisher. For advice and help on the introduction and introductory notes he would like to thank Rachel Barney, Christopher Bobonich, Panos Dimas, D. S. Hutchinson, George Kateb, Alexander Nehamas, C.D.C. Reeve, J. B. Schneewind, and David Sedley. Discussion with Øyvind Rabbås was helpful in preparing the introductory notes for the Socratic dialogues, especially *Laches*. Paul Woodruff gave good advice on the revision of the *Epigrams* translation. For Hackett Publishing Company Deborah Wilkes and Dan Kirklin gave steady, reliable, and invariably intelligent advice and assistance on all aspects of the production of the book.

The associate editor would like to thank Nicholas Denyer, Rudolf Kassel, and Carl Werner Müller (whose book *Die Kurzdialoge der Appendix Platonica* sheds invaluable light on the spurious works in the Platonic corpus), as well as John Cooper, whose critical eye improved every introductory note.

The index was prepared by Paul Coppock. The editors would also like to thank him for his work at earlier stages of the project in overseeing the preparation of the translations on behalf of the publisher. Thanks also go to Jonathan Beere for verifying typographical errors and other corrections for the second printing, and to Adam Kissel for invaluable help in bringing some of these to the editors' attention. Further corrections in the third printing were suggested by Rachel Barney, Alfonso Gomez-Lobo, Charles Kahn, Henry R. Mendell, and Donald Morrison. The editors are grateful for these, as well as for the continued interest of the translators in the improvement of their earlier work.

Many of the translations appearing (in revised form) in this book have previously been published separately by Hackett Publishing Company: *Euthyphro, Apology, Crito, Phaedo, Theaetetus, Sophist, Parmenides, Philebus, Symposium, Phaedrus, Charmides, Laches, Lysis, Euthydemus, Protagoras, Gorgias, Meno, Greater Hippias, Ion,* and *Republic.*

Published here for the first time are the translations of *Cratylus, Alcibiades, Second Alcibiades, Hipparchus, Rival Lovers, Theages, Lesser Hippias, Menexenus, Clitophon, Timaeus, Critias, Minos, Epinomis, Definitions, On Justice, On Virtue, Demodocus, Sisyphus, Halcyon,* and *Eryxias.*

Translations previously published by other publishers are

Statesman, translated by C. J. Rowe, Warminster: 1995, reprinted here by permission of Aris & Phillips Ltd., UK.

Laws, translated by Trevor J. Saunders, reprinted here by permission of Penguin Books Ltd. First published in Great Britain by Penguin Books Ltd., 1970. Reprinted with minor revisions, 1975.

Letters, translated by Glenn R. Morrow, from Plato, *Epistles,* 1962, Library of Liberal Arts, Bobbs-Merrill Co., Inc.

Axiochus, translated by Jackson P. Hershbell, 1981, The Society of Biblical Literature. Reprinted here by permission of Jackson P. Hershbell.

Epigrams, reprinted as revised by John M. Cooper by permission of the publishers of the Loeb Classical Library from *Elegy and Iambus with the Anacreontea,* Vol. II, edited by J. M. Edmonds, Cambridge, Mass.: Harvard University Press, 1931.

Over the twenty years and more that Hackett Publishing Company has been bringing out new translations of Plato, including the work done on the translations appearing here for the first time, many scholars have generously offered their advice as line-by-line readers and consultants on the translations-in-progress of individual works—in some cases, a single reader has worked on more than one such project. The publisher gratefully acknowledges the invaluable assistance of:

William Arrowsmith	J.M.E. Moravcsik
Malcolm Brown	Alexander Nehamas
Eve Browning Cole	Martha Nussbaum
John M. Cooper	C.D.C. Reeve
Daniel Devereux	Jean Roberts
Cynthia Freeland	T. M. Robinson
Marjorie Grene	Allan Silverman
Richard Hogan	Simon Slings
D. S. Hutchinson	Nicholas P. White
Mark Joyal	Paul Woodruff
Richard Kraut	Donald J. Zeyl
M. M. McCabe	

EUTHYPHRO

The scene is the agora or central marketplace of Athens, before the offices of the magistrate who registers and makes preliminary inquiries into charges brought under the laws protecting the city from the gods' displeasure. There Socrates meets Euthyphro—Socrates is on his way in to answer the charges of 'impiety' brought against him by three younger fellow citizens, on which he is going to be condemned to death, as we learn in the Apology. Euthyphro has just deposed murder charges against his own father for the death of a servant. Murder was a religious offense, since it entailed 'pollution' which if not ritually purified was displeasing to the gods; but equally, a son's taking such action against his father might well itself be regarded as 'impious'. Euthyphro professes to be acting on esoteric knowledge about the gods and their wishes, and so about the general topic of 'piety'. Socrates seizes the opportunity to acquire from Euthyphro this knowledge of piety so that he can rebut the accusations against himself. However, like all his other interlocutors in Plato's 'Socratic' dialogues, Euthyphro cannot answer Socrates' questions to Socrates' satisfaction, or ultimately to his own. So he cannot make it clear what piety is—though he continues to think that he does know it. Thus, predictably, Socrates' hopes are disappointed; just when he is ready to press further to help Euthyphro express his knowledge, if indeed he does possess it, Euthyphro begs off on the excuse of business elsewhere.

Though Socrates does not succeed in his quest, we readers learn a good deal about the sort of thing Socrates is looking for in asking his question 'What is piety?' and the other 'What is . . . ?' questions he pursues in other dialogues. He wants a single 'model' or 'standard' he can look to in order to determine which acts and persons are pious, one that gives clear, unconflicting, and unambiguous answers. He wants something that can provide such a standard all on its own—as one of Euthyphro's proposals, that being pious is simply being loved by the gods, cannot do, since one needs to know first what the gods do love. Pious acts and people may indeed be loved by the gods, but that is a secondary quality, not the 'essence' of piety—it is not that which serves as the standard being sought.

There seems no reason to doubt the character Socrates' sincerity in probing Euthyphro's statements so as to work out an adequate answer—he has in advance no answer of his own to test out or to advocate. But does the dialogue itself suggest to the attentive reader an answer of its own? Euthyphro frustrates Socrates by his inability to develop adequately his final suggestion, that piety is justice in relation to the gods, in serving and assisting them in some purpose

1

or enterprise of their own. Socrates seems to find that an enticing idea. Does Plato mean to suggest that piety may be shown simply in doing one's best to become as morally good as possible—something Socrates claims in the Apology the gods want more than anything else? If so, can piety remain an independent virtue at all, with its own separate standard for action? These are among the questions this dialogue leaves us to ponder.

J.M.C.

2   EUTHYPHRO: What's new, Socrates, to make you leave your usual haunts in the Lyceum and spend your time here by the king-archon's court? Surely you are not prosecuting anyone before the king-archon as I am?

SOCRATES: The Athenians do not call this a prosecution but an indictment, Euthyphro.

b   EUTHYPHRO: What is this you say? Someone must have indicted you, for you are not going to tell me that you have indicted someone else.

SOCRATES: No indeed.

EUTHYPHRO: But someone else has indicted you?

SOCRATES: Quite so.

EUTHYPHRO: Who is he?

SOCRATES: I do not really know him myself, Euthyphro. He is apparently young and unknown. They call him Meletus, I believe. He belongs to the Pitthean deme, if you know anyone from that deme called Meletus, with long hair, not much of a beard, and a rather aquiline nose.

EUTHYPHRO: I don't know him, Socrates. What charge does he bring against you?

c   SOCRATES: What charge? A not ignoble one I think, for it is no small thing for a young man to have knowledge of such an important subject. He says he knows how our young men are corrupted and who corrupts them. He is likely to be wise, and when he sees my ignorance corrupting

d   his contemporaries, he proceeds to accuse me to the city as to their mother. I think he is the only one of our public men to start out the right way, for it is right to care first that the young should be as good as possible, just as a good farmer is likely to take care of the young plants first, and of the

3   others later. So, too, Meletus first gets rid of us who corrupt the young shoots, as he says, and then afterwards he will obviously take care of the older ones and become a source of great blessings for the city, as seems likely to happen to one who started out this way.

EUTHYPHRO: I could wish this were true, Socrates, but I fear the opposite may happen. He seems to me to start out by harming the very heart of

Translated by G.M.A. Grube.

the city by attempting to wrong you. Tell me, what does he say you do to corrupt the young?

SOCRATES: Strange things, to hear him tell it, for he says that I am a maker of gods, and on the ground that I create new gods while not believing in the old gods, he has indicted me for their sake, as he puts it.

EUTHYPHRO: I understand, Socrates. This is because you say that the divine sign keeps coming to you.[1] So he has written this indictment against you as one who makes innovations in religious matters, and he comes to court to slander you, knowing that such things are easily misrepresented to the crowd. The same is true in my case. Whenever I speak of divine matters in the assembly and foretell the future, they laugh me down as if I were crazy; and yet I have foretold nothing that did not happen. Nevertheless, they envy all of us who do this. One need not worry about them, but meet them head-on.

SOCRATES: My dear Euthyphro, to be laughed at does not matter perhaps, for the Athenians do not mind anyone they think clever, as long as he does not teach his own wisdom, but if they think that he makes others to be like himself they get angry, whether through envy, as you say, or for some other reason.

EUTHYPHRO: I have certainly no desire to test their feelings towards me in this matter.

SOCRATES: Perhaps you seem to make yourself but rarely available, and not be willing to teach your own wisdom, but I'm afraid that my liking for people makes them think that I pour out to anybody anything I have to say, not only without charging a fee but even glad to reward anyone who is willing to listen. If then they were intending to laugh at me, as you say they laugh at you, there would be nothing unpleasant in their spending their time in court laughing and jesting, but if they are going to be serious, the outcome is not clear except to you prophets.

EUTHYPHRO: Perhaps it will come to nothing, Socrates, and you will fight your case as you think best, as I think I will mine.

SOCRATES: What is your case, Euthyphro? Are you the defendant or the prosecutor?

EUTHYPHRO: The prosecutor.

SOCRATES: Whom do you prosecute?

EUTHYPHRO: One whom I am thought crazy to prosecute.

SOCRATES: Are you pursuing someone who will easily escape you?

EUTHYPHRO: Far from it, for he is quite old.

SOCRATES: Who is it?

EUTHYPHRO: My father.

SOCRATES: My dear sir! Your own father?

EUTHYPHRO: Certainly.

---

1. See *Apology* 31d.

SOCRATES: What is the charge? What is the case about?

EUTHYPHRO: Murder, Socrates.

SOCRATES: Good heavens! Certainly, Euthyphro, most men would not
b know how they could do this and be right. It is not the part of anyone to
do this, but of one who is far advanced in wisdom.

EUTHYPHRO: Yes, by Zeus, Socrates, that is so.

SOCRATES: Is then the man your father killed one of your relatives? Or
is that obvious, for you would not prosecute your father for the murder
of a stranger.

EUTHYPHRO: It is ridiculous, Socrates, for you to think that it makes any
difference whether the victim is a stranger or a relative. One should only
watch whether the killer acted justly or not; if he acted justly, let him go,
c but if not, one should prosecute, if, that is to say, the killer shares your
hearth and table. The pollution is the same if you knowingly keep company
with such a man and do not cleanse yourself and him by bringing him to
justice. The victim was a dependent of mine, and when we were farming
in Naxos he was a servant of ours. He killed one of our household slaves
in drunken anger, so my father bound him hand and foot and threw him
d in a ditch, then sent a man here to inquire from the priest what should
be done. During that time he gave no thought or care to the bound man,
as being a killer, and it was no matter if he died, which he did. Hunger
and cold and his bonds caused his death before the messenger came back
from the seer. Both my father and my other relatives are angry that I am
prosecuting my father for murder on behalf of a murderer when he hadn't
even killed him, they say, and even if he had, the dead man does not
e deserve a thought, since he was a killer. For, they say, it is impious for a
son to prosecute his father for murder. But their ideas of the divine attitude
to piety and impiety are wrong, Socrates.

SOCRATES: Whereas, by Zeus, Euthyphro, you think that your knowledge
of the divine, and of piety and impiety, is so accurate that, when those
things happened as you say, you have no fear of having acted impiously
in bringing your father to trial?

EUTHYPHRO: I should be of no use, Socrates, and Euthyphro would not
5 be superior to the majority of men, if I did not have accurate knowledge
of all such things.

SOCRATES: It is indeed most important, my admirable Euthyphro, that I
should become your pupil, and as regards this indictment, challenge Meletus about these very things and say to him: that in the past too I considered
knowledge about the divine to be most important, and that now that he
b says that I am guilty of improvising and innovating about the gods I
have become your pupil. I would say to him: "If, Meletus, you agree that
Euthyphro is wise in these matters, consider me, too, to have the right
beliefs and do not bring me to trial. If you do not think so, then prosecute
that teacher of mine, not me, for corrupting the older men, me and his
own father, by teaching me and by exhorting and punishing him." If he

is not convinced, and does not discharge me or indict you instead of me, I shall repeat the same challenge in court.

EUTHYPHRO: Yes, by Zeus, Socrates, and, if he should try to indict me, I think I would find his weak spots and the talk in court would be about him rather than about me. c

SOCRATES: It is because I realize this that I am eager to become your pupil, my dear friend. I know that other people as well as this Meletus do not even seem to notice you, whereas he sees me so sharply and clearly that he indicts me for ungodliness. So tell me now, by Zeus, what you just now maintained you clearly knew: what kind of thing do you say that godliness and ungodliness are, both as regards murder and other things; d or is the pious not the same and alike in every action, and the impious the opposite of all that is pious and like itself, and everything that is to be impious presents us with one form or appearance in so far as it is impious?

EUTHYPHRO: Most certainly, Socrates.

SOCRATES: Tell me then, what is the pious, and what the impious, do you say?

EUTHYPHRO: I say that the pious is to do what I am doing now, to prosecute the wrongdoer, be it about murder or temple robbery or anything else, whether the wrongdoer is your father or your mother or anyone else; e not to prosecute is impious. And observe, Socrates, that I can cite powerful evidence that the law is so. I have already said to others that such actions are right, not to favor the ungodly, whoever they are. These people themselves believe that Zeus is the best and most just of the gods, yet they agree that 6 he bound his father because he unjustly swallowed his sons, and that he in turn castrated his father for similar reasons. But they are angry with me because I am prosecuting my father for his wrongdoing. They contradict themselves in what they say about the gods and about me.

SOCRATES: Indeed, Euthyphro, this is the reason why I am a defendant in the case, because I find it hard to accept things like that being said about the gods, and it is likely to be the reason why I shall be told I do wrong. Now, however, if you, who have full knowledge of such things, share b their opinions, then we must agree with them, too, it would seem. For what are we to say, we who agree that we ourselves have no knowledge of them? Tell me, by the god of friendship, do you really believe these things are true?

EUTHYPHRO: Yes, Socrates, and so are even more surprising things, of which the majority has no knowledge.

SOCRATES: And do you believe that there really is war among the gods, and terrible enmities and battles, and other such things as are told by the c poets, and other sacred stories such as are embroidered by good writers and by representations of which the robe of the goddess is adorned when it is carried up to the Acropolis? Are we to say these things are true, Euthyphro?

EUTHYPHRO: Not only these, Socrates, but, as I was saying just now, I will, if you wish, relate many other things about the gods which I know will amaze you.

SOCRATES: I should not be surprised, but you will tell me these at leisure some other time. For now, try to tell me more clearly what I was asking
d   just now, for, my friend, you did not teach me adequately when I asked you what the pious was, but you told me that what you are doing now, in prosecuting your father for murder, is pious.

EUTHYPHRO: And I told the truth, Socrates.

SOCRATES: Perhaps. You agree, however, that there are many other pious actions.

EUTHYPHRO: There are.

SOCRATES: Bear in mind then that I did not bid you tell me one or two of the many pious actions but that form itself that makes all pious actions pious, for you agreed that all impious actions are impious and all pious
e   actions pious through one form, or don't you remember?

EUTHYPHRO: I do.

SOCRATES: Tell me then what this form itself is, so that I may look upon it, and using it as a model, say that any action of yours or another's that is of that kind is pious, and if it is not that it is not.

EUTHYPHRO: If that is how you want it, Socrates, that is how I will tell you.

SOCRATES: That is what I want.

7   EUTHYPHRO: Well then, what is dear to the gods is pious, what is not is impious.

SOCRATES: Splendid, Euthyphro! You have now answered in the way I wanted. Whether your answer is true I do not know yet, but you will obviously show me that what you say is true.

EUTHYPHRO: Certainly.

SOCRATES: Come then, let us examine what we mean. An action or a man dear to the gods is pious, but an action or a man hated by the gods is impious. They are not the same, but quite opposite, the pious and the impious. Is that not so?

EUTHYPHRO: It is indeed.

SOCRATES: And that seems to be a good statement?
b   EUTHYPHRO: I think so, Socrates.

SOCRATES: We have also stated that the gods are in a state of discord, that they are at odds with each other, Euthyphro, and that they are at enmity with each other. Has that, too, been said?

EUTHYPHRO: It has.

SOCRATES: What are the subjects of difference that cause hatred and anger? Let us look at it this way. If you and I were to differ about numbers as to which is the greater, would this difference make us enemies and
c   angry with each other, or would we proceed to count and soon resolve our difference about this?

EUTHYPHRO: We would certainly do so.

SOCRATES: Again, if we differed about the larger and the smaller, we would turn to measurement and soon cease to differ.

EUTHYPHRO: That is so.

SOCRATES: And about the heavier and the lighter, we would resort to weighing and be reconciled.

EUTHYPHRO: Of course.

SOCRATES: What subject of difference would make us angry and hostile to each other if we were unable to come to a decision? Perhaps you do not have an answer ready, but examine as I tell you whether these subjects are the just and the unjust, the beautiful and the ugly, the good and the bad. Are these not the subjects of difference about which, when we are unable to come to a satisfactory decision, you and I and other men become hostile to each other whenever we do?

EUTHYPHRO: That is the difference, Socrates, about those subjects.

SOCRATES: What about the gods, Euthyphro? If indeed they have differences, will it not be about these same subjects?

EUTHYPHRO: It certainly must be so.

SOCRATES: Then according to your argument, my good Euthyphro, different gods consider different things to be just, beautiful, ugly, good, and bad, for they would not be at odds with one another unless they differed about these subjects, would they?

EUTHYPHRO: You are right.

SOCRATES: And they like what each of them considers beautiful, good, and just, and hate the opposites of these?

EUTHYPHRO: Certainly.

SOCRATES: But you say that the same things are considered just by some gods and unjust by others, and as they dispute about these things they are at odds and at war with each other. Is that not so?

EUTHYPHRO: It is.

SOCRATES: The same things then are loved by the gods and hated by the gods, and would be both god-loved and god-hated.

EUTHYPHRO: It seems likely.

SOCRATES: And the same things would be both pious and impious, according to this argument?

EUTHYPHRO: I'm afraid so.

SOCRATES: So you did not answer my question, you surprising man. I did not ask you what same thing is both pious and impious, and it appears that what is loved by the gods is also hated by them. So it is in no way surprising if your present action, namely punishing your father, may be pleasing to Zeus but displeasing to Cronus and Uranus, pleasing to Hephaestus but displeasing to Hera, and so with any other gods who differ from each other on this subject.

EUTHYPHRO: I think, Socrates, that on this subject no gods would differ from one another, that whoever has killed anyone unjustly should pay the penalty.

c   SOCRATES: Well now, Euthyphro, have you ever heard any man maintaining that one who has killed or done anything else unjustly should not pay the penalty?

EUTHYPHRO: They never cease to dispute on this subject, both elsewhere and in the courts, for when they have committed many wrongs they do and say anything to avoid the penalty.

SOCRATES: Do they agree they have done wrong, Euthyphro, and in spite of so agreeing do they nevertheless say they should not be punished?

EUTHYPHRO: No, they do not agree on that point.

SOCRATES: So they do not say or do just anything. For they do not venture to say this, or dispute that they must not pay the penalty if they have
d   done wrong, but I think they deny doing wrong. Is that not so?

EUTHYPHRO: That is true.

SOCRATES: Then they do not dispute that the wrongdoer must be punished, but they may disagree as to who the wrongdoer is, what he did and when.

EUTHYPHRO: You are right.

SOCRATES: Do not the gods have the same experience, if indeed they are at odds with each other about the just and the unjust, as your argument maintains? Some assert that they wrong one another, while others deny
e   it, but no one among gods or men ventures to say that the wrongdoer must not be punished.

EUTHYPHRO: Yes, that is true, Socrates, as to the main point.

SOCRATES: And those who disagree, whether men or gods, dispute about each action, if indeed the gods disagree. Some say it is done justly, others unjustly. Is that not so?

EUTHYPHRO: Yes, indeed.

9   SOCRATES: Come now, my dear Euthyphro, tell me, too, that I may become wiser, what proof you have that all the gods consider that man to have been killed unjustly who became a murderer while in your service, was bound by the master of his victim, and died in his bonds before the one who bound him found out from the seers what was to be done with him, and that it is right for a son to denounce and to prosecute his father on
b   behalf of such a man. Come, try to show me a clear sign that all the gods definitely believe this action to be right. If you can give me adequate proof of this, I shall never cease to extol your wisdom.

EUTHYPHRO: This is perhaps no light task, Socrates, though I could show you very clearly.

SOCRATES: I understand that you think me more dull-witted than the jury, as you will obviously show them that these actions were unjust and that all the gods hate such actions.

EUTHYPHRO: I will show it to them clearly, Socrates, if only they will listen to me.

c   SOCRATES: They will listen if they think you show them well. But this thought came to me as you were speaking, and I am examining it, saying to myself: "If Euthyphro shows me conclusively that all the gods consider such a death unjust, to what greater extent have I learned from him the nature of piety and impiety? This action would then, it seems, be hated by the gods, but the pious and the impious were not thereby now defined, for what is hated by the gods has also been shown to be loved by them." So I will not insist on this point; let us assume, if you wish, that all the gods consider this unjust and that they all hate it. However, is this the d correction we are making in our discussion, that what all the gods hate is impious, and what they all love is pious, and that what some gods love and others hate is neither or both? Is that how you now wish us to define piety and impiety?

EUTHYPHRO: What prevents us from doing so, Socrates?

SOCRATES: For my part nothing, Euthyphro, but you look whether on your part this proposal will enable you to teach me most easily what you promised.

EUTHYPHRO: I would certainly say that the pious is what all the gods e love, and the opposite, what all the gods hate, is the impious.

SOCRATES: Then let us again examine whether that is a sound statement, or do we let it pass, and if one of us, or someone else, merely says that something is so, do we accept that it is so? Or should we examine what the speaker means?

EUTHYPHRO: We must examine it, but I certainly think that this is now a fine statement.

SOCRATES: We shall soon know better whether it is. Consider this: Is the 10 pious being loved by the gods because it is pious, or is it pious because it is being loved by the gods?

EUTHYPHRO: I don't know what you mean, Socrates.

SOCRATES: I shall try to explain more clearly: we speak of something carried and something carrying, of something led and something leading, of something seen and something seeing, and you understand that these things are all different from one another and how they differ?

EUTHYPHRO: I think I do.

SOCRATES: So there is also something loved and—a different thing— something loving.

EUTHYPHRO: Of course.

SOCRATES: Tell me then whether the thing carried is a carried thing b because it is being carried, or for some other reason?

EUTHYPHRO: No, that is the reason.

SOCRATES: And the thing led is so because it is being led, and the thing seen because it is being seen?

EUTHYPHRO: Certainly.

SOCRATES: It is not being seen because it is a thing seen but on the contrary it is a thing seen because it is being seen; nor is it because it is something led that it is being led but because it is being led that it is something led; nor is something being carried because it is something carried, but it is something carried because it is being carried. Is what I want to say clear, c Euthyphro? I want to say this, namely, that if anything is being changed

or is being affected in any way, it is not being changed because it is
something changed, but rather it is something changed because it is being
changed; nor is it being affected because it is something affected, but it is
something affected because it is being affected.[2] Or do you not agree?

EUTHYPHRO: I do.

SOCRATES: Is something loved either something changed or something
affected by something?

EUTHYPHRO: Certainly.

SOCRATES: So it is in the same case as the things just mentioned; it is not
being loved by those who love it because it is something loved, but it is
something loved because it is being loved by them?

EUTHYPHRO: Necessarily.

d   SOCRATES: What then do we say about the pious, Euthyphro? Surely that
it is being loved by all the gods, according to what you say?

EUTHYPHRO: Yes.

SOCRATES: Is it being loved because it is pious, or for some other reason?

EUTHYPHRO: For no other reason.

SOCRATES: It is being loved then because it is pious, but it is not pious
because it is being loved?

EUTHYPHRO: Apparently.

SOCRATES: And yet it is something loved and god-loved because it is
being loved by the gods?

EUTHYPHRO: Of course.

SOCRATES: Then the god-loved is not the same as the pious, Euthyphro,
nor the pious the same as the god-loved, as you say it is, but one differs
from the other.

e   EUTHYPHRO: How so, Socrates?

SOCRATES: Because we agree that the pious is being loved for this reason,
that it is pious, but it is not pious because it is being loved. Is that not so?

EUTHYPHRO: Yes.

SOCRATES: And that the god-loved, on the other hand, is so because it
is being loved by the gods, by the very fact of being loved, but it is not
being loved because it is god-loved.

EUTHYPHRO: True.

SOCRATES: But if the god-loved and the pious were the same, my dear
Euthyphro, then if the pious was being loved because it was pious, the
11   god-loved would also be being loved because it was god-loved; and if the
god-loved was god-loved because it was being loved by the gods, then

2. Here Socrates gives the general principle under which, he says, the specific cases
already examined—those of leading, carrying, and seeing—all fall. It is by being changed
by something that changes *it* (e.g. by carrying it somewhere) that anything is a changed
thing—not vice versa: it is not by something's being a changed thing that something
else then changes it so that it comes to be being changed (e.g. by carrying it somewhere).
Likewise for "affections" such as being seen by someone: it is by being "affected" by
something that "affects" it that anything is an "affected" thing, not vice versa. It is not
by being an "affected" thing (e.g., a thing seen) that something else then "affects" it.

the pious would also be pious because it was being loved by the gods. But now you see that they are in opposite cases as being altogether different from each other: the one is such as to be loved because it is being loved, the other is being loved because it is such as to be loved. I'm afraid, Euthyphro, that when you were asked what piety is, you did not wish to make its nature clear to me, but you told me an affect or quality of it, that the pious has the quality of being loved by all the gods, but you have not yet told me what the pious is. Now, if you will, do not hide things from me but tell me again from the beginning what piety is, whether being loved by the gods or having some other quality—we shall not quarrel about that—but be keen to tell me what the pious and the impious are.

EUTHYPHRO: But Socrates, I have no way of telling you what I have in mind, for whatever proposition we put forward goes around and refuses to stay put where we establish it.

SOCRATES: Your statements, Euthyphro, seem to belong to my ancestor, Daedalus. If I were stating them and putting them forward, you would perhaps be making fun of me and say that because of my kinship with him my conclusions in discussion run away and will not stay where one puts them. As these propositions are yours, however, we need some other jest, for they will not stay put for you, as you say yourself.

EUTHYPHRO: I think the same jest will do for our discussion, Socrates, for I am not the one who makes them go round and not remain in the same place; it is you who are the Daedalus; for as far as I am concerned they would remain as they were.

SOCRATES: It looks as if I was cleverer than Daedalus in using my skill, my friend, in so far as he could only cause to move the things he made himself, but I can make other people's move as well as my own. And the smartest part of my skill is that I am clever without wanting to be, for I would rather have your statements to me remain unmoved than possess the wealth of Tantalus as well as the cleverness of Daedalus. But enough of this. Since I think you are making unnecessary difficulties, I am as eager as you are to find a way to teach me about piety, and do not give up before you do. See whether you think all that is pious is of necessity just.

EUTHYPHRO: I think so.

SOCRATES: And is then all that is just pious? Or is all that is pious just, but not all that is just pious, but some of it is and some is not?

EUTHYPHRO: I do not follow what you are saying, Socrates.

SOCRATES: Yet you are younger than I by as much as you are wiser. As I say, you are making difficulties because of your wealth of wisdom. Pull yourself together, my dear sir, what I am saying is not difficult to grasp. I am saying the opposite of what the poet said who wrote:

You do not wish to name Zeus, who had done it, and who made
all things grow, for where there is fear there is also shame.[3]

---

3. Author unknown.

I disagree with the poet. Shall I tell you why?

EUTHYPHRO: Please do.

SOCRATES: I do not think that "where there is fear there is also shame," for I think that many people who fear disease and poverty and many other such things feel fear, but are not ashamed of the things they fear. Do you not think so?

EUTHYPHRO: I do indeed.

c SOCRATES: But where there is shame there is also fear. For is there anyone who, in feeling shame and embarrassment at anything, does not also at the same time fear and dread a reputation for wickedness?

EUTHYPHRO: He is certainly afraid.

SOCRATES: It is then not right to say "where there is fear there is also shame," but that where there is shame there is also fear, for fear covers a larger area than shame. Shame is a part of fear just as odd is a part of number, with the result that it is not true that where there is number there is also oddness, but that where there is oddness there is also number. Do you follow me now?

EUTHYPHRO: Surely.

d SOCRATES: This is the kind of thing I was asking before, whether where there is piety there is also justice, but where there is justice there is not always piety, for the pious is a part of justice. Shall we say that, or do you think otherwise?

EUTHYPHRO: No, but like that, for what you say appears to be right.

SOCRATES: See what comes next: if the pious is a part of the just, we must, it seems, find out what part of the just it is. Now if you asked me something of what we mentioned just now, such as what part of number is the even, and what number that is, I would say it is the number that is divisible into two equal, not unequal, parts. Or do you not think so?

EUTHYPHRO: I do.

e SOCRATES: Try in this way to tell me what part of the just the pious is, in order to tell Meletus not to wrong us any more and not to indict me for ungodliness, since I have learned from you sufficiently what is godly and pious and what is not.

EUTHYPHRO: I think, Socrates, that the godly and pious is the part of the just that is concerned with the care of the gods, while that concerned with the care of men is the remaining part of justice.

SOCRATES: You seem to me to put that very well, but I still need a bit of 13 information. I do not know yet what you mean by care, for you do not mean the care of the gods in the same sense as the care of other things, as, for example, we say, don't we, that not everyone knows how to care for horses, but the horse breeder does.

EUTHYPHRO: Yes, I do mean it that way.

SOCRATES: So horse breeding is the care of horses.

EUTHYPHRO: Yes.

SOCRATES: Nor does everyone know how to care for dogs, but the hunter does.

EUTHYPHRO: That is so.

SOCRATES: So hunting is the care of dogs.

EUTHYPHRO: Yes.

SOCRATES: And cattle raising is the care of cattle.

EUTHYPHRO: Quite so.

SOCRATES: While piety and godliness is the care of the gods, Euthyphro. Is that what you mean?

EUTHYPHRO: It is.

SOCRATES: Now care in each case has the same effect; it aims at the good and the benefit of the object cared for, as you can see that horses cared for by horse breeders are benefited and become better. Or do you not think so?

EUTHYPHRO: I do.

SOCRATES: So dogs are benefited by dog breeding, cattle by cattle raising, and so with all the others. Or do you think that care aims to harm the object of its care?

EUTHYPHRO: By Zeus, no.

SOCRATES: It aims to benefit the object of its care?

EUTHYPHRO: Of course.

SOCRATES: Is piety then, which is the care of the gods, also to benefit the gods and make them better? Would you agree that when you do something pious you make some one of the gods better?

EUTHYPHRO: By Zeus, no.

SOCRATES: Nor do I think that this is what you mean—far from it—but that is why I asked you what you meant by the care of gods, because I did not believe you meant this kind of care.

EUTHYPHRO: Quite right, Socrates, that is not the kind of care I mean.

SOCRATES: Very well, but what kind of care of the gods would piety be?

EUTHYPHRO: The kind of care, Socrates, that slaves take of their masters.

SOCRATES: I understand. It is likely to be a kind of service of the gods.

EUTHYPHRO: Quite so.

SOCRATES: Could you tell me to the achievement of what goal service to doctors tends? Is it not, do you think, to achieving health?

EUTHYPHRO: I think so.

SOCRATES: What about service to shipbuilders? To what achievement is it directed?

EUTHYPHRO: Clearly, Socrates, to the building of a ship.

SOCRATES: And service to housebuilders to the building of a house?

EUTHYPHRO: Yes.

SOCRATES: Tell me then, my good sir, to the achievement of what aim does service to the gods tend? You obviously know since you say that you, of all men, have the best knowledge of the divine.

EUTHYPHRO: And I am telling the truth, Socrates.

SOCRATES: Tell me then, by Zeus, what is that excellent aim that the gods achieve, using us as their servants?

EUTHYPHRO: Many fine things, Socrates.

14   SOCRATES: So do generals, my friend. Nevertheless you could easily tell
me their main concern, which is to achieve victory in war, is it not?

EUTHYPHRO: Of course.

SOCRATES: The farmers too, I think, achieve many fine things, but the
main point of their efforts is to produce food from the earth.

EUTHYPHRO: Quite so.

SOCRATES: Well then, how would you sum up the many fine things that
the gods achieve?

EUTHYPHRO: I told you a short while ago, Socrates, that it is a considerable
b   task to acquire any precise knowledge of these things, but, to put it simply,
I say that if a man knows how to say and do what is pleasing to the gods
at prayer and sacrifice, those are pious actions such as preserve both private
houses and public affairs of state. The opposite of these pleasing actions
are impious and overturn and destroy everything.

SOCRATES: You could tell me in far fewer words, if you were willing, the
c   sum of what I asked, Euthyphro, but you are not keen to teach me, that
is clear. You were on the point of doing so, but you turned away. If you
had given that answer, I should now have acquired from you sufficient
knowledge of the nature of piety. As it is, the lover of inquiry must follow
his beloved wherever it may lead him. Once more then, what do you say
that piety and the pious are? Are they a knowledge of how to sacrifice
and pray?

EUTHYPHRO: They are.

SOCRATES: To sacrifice is to make a gift to the gods, whereas to pray is
to beg from the gods?

EUTHYPHRO: Definitely, Socrates.

d   SOCRATES: It would follow from this statement that piety would be a
knowledge of how to give to, and beg from, the gods.

EUTHYPHRO: You understood what I said very well, Socrates.

SOCRATES: That is because I am so desirous of your wisdom, and I
concentrate my mind on it, so that no word of yours may fall to the ground.
But tell me, what is this service to the gods? You say it is to beg from
them and to give to them?

EUTHYPHRO: I do.

SOCRATES: And to beg correctly would be to ask from them things that
we need?

EUTHYPHRO: What else?

e   SOCRATES: And to give correctly is to give them what they need from
us, for it would not be skillful to bring gifts to anyone that are in no
way needed.

EUTHYPHRO: True, Socrates.

SOCRATES: Piety would then be a sort of trading skill between gods
and men?

EUTHYPHRO: Trading yes, if you prefer to call it that.

SOCRATES: I prefer nothing, unless it is true. But tell me, what benefit do
the gods derive from the gifts they receive from us? What they give us is

obvious to all. There is for us no good that we do not receive from them, but how are they benefited by what they receive from us? Or do we have such an advantage over them in the trade that we receive all our blessings from them and they receive nothing from us?

EUTHYPHRO: Do you suppose, Socrates, that the gods are benefited by what they receive from us?

SOCRATES: What could those gifts from us to the gods be, Euthyphro?

EUTHYPHRO: What else, do you think, than honor, reverence, and what I mentioned just now, gratitude?

SOCRATES: The pious is then, Euthyphro, pleasing to the gods, but not beneficial or dear to them?

EUTHYPHRO: I think it is of all things most dear to them.

SOCRATES: So the pious is once again what is dear to the gods.

EUTHYPHRO: Most certainly.

SOCRATES: When you say this, will you be surprised if your arguments seem to move about instead of staying put? And will you accuse me of being Daedalus who makes them move, though you are yourself much more skillful than Daedalus and make them go round in a circle? Or do you not realize that our argument has moved around and come again to the same place? You surely remember that earlier the pious and the god-loved were shown not to be the same but different from each other. Or do you not remember?

EUTHYPHRO: I do.

SOCRATES: Do you then not realize now that you are saying that what is dear to the gods is the pious? Is this not the same as the god-loved? Or is it not?

EUTHYPHRO: It certainly is.

SOCRATES: Either we were wrong when we agreed before, or, if we were right then, we are wrong now.

EUTHYPHRO: That seems to be so.

SOCRATES: So we must investigate again from the beginning what piety is, as I shall not willingly give up before I learn this. Do not think me unworthy, but concentrate your attention and tell the truth. For you know it, if any man does, and I must not let you go, like Proteus,[4] before you tell me. If you had no clear knowledge of piety and impiety you would never have ventured to prosecute your old father for murder on behalf of a servant. For fear of the gods you would have been afraid to take the risk lest you should not be acting rightly, and would have been ashamed before men, but now I know well that you believe you have clear knowledge of piety and impiety. So tell me, my good Euthyphro, and do not hide what you think it is.

EUTHYPHRO: Some other time, Socrates, for I am in a hurry now, and it is time for me to go.

---

4. See *Odyssey* iv.382 ff.

SOCRATES: What a thing to do, my friend! By going you have cast me
down from a great hope I had, that I would learn from you the nature of
the pious and the impious and so escape Meletus' indictment by showing
him that I had acquired wisdom in divine matters from Euthyphro, and
my ignorance would no longer cause me to be careless and inventive about
such things, and that I would be better for the rest of my life.

APOLOGY

This work is universally known as Plato's 'Apology' of Socrates, in deference to the word apologia that stands in its Greek title. Actually, the word means not an apology but a defense speech in a legal proceeding, and that is what we get—certainly, Socrates does not apologize for anything! This is not really a dialogue. Except for an interlude when he engages one of his accusers in the sort of question-and-answer discussion characteristic of Plato's 'Socratic' dialogues, we see Socrates delivering a speech before his jury of 501 fellow male Athenians. At the age of seventy he had been indicted for breaking the law against 'impiety'—for offending the Olympian gods (Zeus, Apollo, and the rest) recognized in the city's festivals and other official activities. The basis of the charge, such as it was, lay in the way that, for many years, Socrates had been carrying on his philosophical work in Athens. It has often been thought that the real basis for it lay in 'guilt by association': several of Socrates' known associates had been prominent malfeasants in Athens' defeat in the Peloponnesian War only a few years earlier and the oligarchic reign of terror that followed; but an amnesty had forbidden suits based on political offenses during that time. However much those associations may have been in the minds of his accusers—and his jurors, too—Plato makes him respond sincerely to the charges as lodged. After all, these would be the ultimate basis on which he should or should not be found guilty of anything. So he takes the occasion to explain and defend his devotion to philosophy, and the particular ways he has pursued that in discussions with select young men and with people prominent in the city—discussions like those we see in Plato's other 'Socratic' works. He argues that, so far from offending the gods through his philosophizing, or showing disbelief in them, he has piously followed their lead (particularly that of Apollo, through his oracle at Delphi) in making himself as good a person as he can and encouraging (even goading) others to do the same. The gods want, more than anything else, that we shall be good, and goodness depends principally upon the quality of our understanding of what to care about and how to behave in our lives: philosophy, through Socratic discussion, is the pursuit of that understanding.

This is, of course, no record of the actual defense Socrates mounted at his trial in 399 B.C., but a composition of Plato's own—we have no way of knowing how closely, if at all, it conforms to Socrates' real speech. In it Plato gives us the best, most serious, response to the charges that, on his own knowledge of Socrates, Socrates was entitled to give. Was Socrates nonetheless guilty as charged? In deciding this, readers should notice that, however sincere Plato's

Socrates may be in claiming a pious motivation for his philosophical work, he does set up human reason in his own person as the final arbiter of what is right and wrong, and so of what the gods want us to do: he interprets Apollo, through his oracle at Delphi, to have told him to do that! As we see also from Euthyphro, he has no truck with the authority of myths or ancient poets or religious tradition and 'divination' to tell us what to think about the gods and their commands or wishes as regards ourselves.

In democratic Athens, juries were randomly selected subsets—representatives—of the whole people. Hence, as Socrates makes clear, he is addressing the democratic people of Athens, and when the jury find him guilty and condemn him to death, they act as and for the Athenian people. Did Socrates bring on his own condemnation, whether wittingly or not, by refusing to say the sorts of things and to comport himself in the sort of way that would have won his acquittal? Perhaps. True to his philosophical calling, he requires that the Athenians think, honestly and dispassionately, and decide the truth of the charges by reasoning from the facts as they actually were. This was his final challenge to them to care more for their souls—their minds, their power of reason—than for their peace and comfort, undisturbed by the likes of him. Seen in that light, as Plato wants us to see it, the failure was theirs.

J.M.C.

17   I do not know, men of Athens, how my accusers affected you; as for me, I was almost carried away in spite of myself, so persuasively did they speak. And yet, hardly anything of what they said is true. Of the many lies they told, one in particular surprised me, namely that you should be

b   careful not to be deceived by an accomplished speaker like me. That they were not ashamed to be immediately proved wrong by the facts, when I show myself not to be an accomplished speaker at all, that I thought was most shameless on their part—unless indeed they call an accomplished speaker the man who speaks the truth. If they mean that, I would agree that I am an orator, but not after their manner, for indeed, as I say,

c   practically nothing they said was true. From me you will hear the whole truth, though not, by Zeus, gentlemen, expressed in embroidered and stylized phrases like theirs, but things spoken at random and expressed in the first words that come to mind, for I put my trust in the justice of what I say, and let none of you expect anything else. It would not be fitting at my age, as it might be for a young man, to toy with words when I appear before you.

        One thing I do ask and beg of you, gentlemen: if you hear me making my defense in the same kind of language as I am accustomed to use in the marketplace by the bankers' tables, where many of you have heard

d   me, and elsewhere, do not be surprised or create a disturbance on that

Translated by G.M.A. Grube.

account. The position is this: this is my first appearance in a lawcourt, at the age of seventy; I am therefore simply a stranger to the manner of speaking here. Just as if I were really a stranger, you would certainly excuse me if I spoke in that dialect and manner in which I had been brought up, so too my present request seems a just one, for you to pay no attention to my manner of speech—be it better or worse—but to concentrate your attention on whether what I say is just or not, for the excellence of a judge lies in this, as that of a speaker lies in telling the truth.

It is right for me, gentlemen, to defend myself first against the first lying accusations made against me and my first accusers, and then against the later accusations and the later accusers. There have been many who have accused me to you for many years now, and none of their accusations are true. These I fear much more than I fear Anytus and his friends, though they too are formidable. These earlier ones, however, are more so, gentlemen; they got hold of most of you from childhood, persuaded you and accused me quite falsely, saying that there is a man called Socrates, a wise man, a student of all things in the sky and below the earth, who makes the worse argument the stronger. Those who spread that rumor, gentlemen, are my dangerous accusers, for their hearers believe that those who study these things do not even believe in the gods. Moreover, these accusers are numerous, and have been at it a long time; also, they spoke to you at an age when you would most readily believe them, some of you being children and adolescents, and they won their case by default, as there was no defense.

What is most absurd in all this is that one cannot even know or mention their names unless one of them is a writer of comedies.[1] Those who maliciously and slanderously persuaded you—who also, when persuaded themselves then persuaded others—all those are most difficult to deal with: one cannot bring one of them into court or refute him; one must simply fight with shadows, as it were, in making one's defense, and crossexamine when no one answers. I want you to realize too that my accusers are of two kinds: those who have accused me recently, and the old ones I mention; and to think that I must first defend myself against the latter, for you have also heard their accusations first, and to a much greater extent than the more recent.

Very well then, men of Athens. I must surely defend myself and attempt to uproot from your minds in so short a time the slander that has resided there so long. I wish this may happen, if it is in any way better for you and me, and that my defense may be successful, but I think this is very difficult and I am fully aware of how difficult it is. Even so, let the matter proceed as the god may wish, but I must obey the law and make my defense.

Let us then take up the case from its beginning. What is the accusation from which arose the slander in which Meletus trusted when he wrote

---

1. This is Aristophanes. Socrates refers below (19c) to the character Socrates in his *Clouds* (225 ff.), first produced in 423 B.C.

out the charge against me? What did they say when they slandered me? I must, as if they were my actual prosecutors, read the affidavit they would have sworn. It goes something like this: Socrates is guilty of wrongdoing in that he busies himself studying things in the sky and below the earth; he makes the worse into the stronger argument, and he teaches these same

c   things to others. You have seen this yourself in the comedy of Aristophanes, a Socrates swinging about there, saying he was walking on air and talking a lot of other nonsense about things of which I know nothing at all. I do not speak in contempt of such knowledge, if someone is wise in these things—lest Meletus bring more cases against me—but, gentlemen, I have no part in it, and on this point I call upon the majority of you as witnesses. I think it right that all those of you who have heard me conversing, and

d   many of you have, should tell each other if anyone of you has ever heard me discussing such subjects to any extent at all. From this you will learn that the other things said about me by the majority are of the same kind.

   Not one of them is true. And if you have heard from anyone that I undertake to teach people and charge a fee for it, that is not true either.

e   Yet I think it a fine thing to be able to teach people as Gorgias of Leontini does, and Prodicus of Ceos, and Hippias of Elis.[2] Each of these men can go to any city and persuade the young, who can keep company with

20   anyone of their own fellow citizens they want without paying, to leave the company of these, to join with themselves, pay them a fee, and be grateful to them besides. Indeed, I learned that there is another wise man from Paros who is visiting us, for I met a man who has spent more money on Sophists than everybody else put together, Callias, the son of Hipponicus. So I asked him—he has two sons—"Callias," I said, "if your sons were colts or calves, we could find and engage a supervisor for them

b   who would make them excel in their proper qualities, some horse breeder or farmer. Now since they are men, whom do you have in mind to supervise them? Who is an expert in this kind of excellence, the human and social kind? I think you must have given thought to this since you have sons. Is there such a person," I asked, "or is there not?" "Certainly there is," he said. "Who is he?" I asked, "What is his name, where is he from? and what is his fee?" "His name, Socrates, is Evenus, he comes from Paros,

c   and his fee is five minas." I thought Evenus a happy man, if he really possesses this art, and teaches for so moderate a fee. Certainly I would pride and preen myself if I had this knowledge, but I do not have it, gentlemen.

   One of you might perhaps interrupt me and say: "But Socrates, what is your occupation? From where have these slanders come? For surely if you did not busy yourself with something out of the common, all these rumors and talk would not have arisen unless you did something other than most

d   people. Tell us what it is, that we may not speak inadvisedly about you." Anyone who says that seems to be right, and I will try to show you what

---

2. These were all well-known Sophists. For Gorgias and Hippias see Plato's dialogues named after them; both Hippias and Prodicus appear in *Protagoras*.

has caused this reputation and slander. Listen then. Perhaps some of you will think I am jesting, but be sure that all that I shall say is true. What has caused my reputation is none other than a certain kind of wisdom. What kind of wisdom? Human wisdom, perhaps. It may be that I really possess this, while those whom I mentioned just now are wise with a wisdom more than human; else I cannot explain it, for I certainly do not possess it, and whoever says I do is lying and speaks to slander me. Do not create a disturbance, gentlemen, even if you think I am boasting, for the story I shall tell does not originate with me, but I will refer you to a trustworthy source. I shall call upon the god at Delphi as witness to the existence and nature of my wisdom, if it be such. You know Chaerephon. He was my friend from youth, and the friend of most of you, as he shared your exile and your return. You surely know the kind of man he was, how impulsive in any course of action. He went to Delphi at one time and ventured to ask the oracle—as I say, gentlemen, do not create a disturbance—he asked if any man was wiser than I, and the Pythian replied that no one was wiser. Chaerephon is dead, but his brother will testify to you about this.

Consider that I tell you this because I would inform you about the origin of the slander. When I heard of this reply I asked myself: "Whatever does the god mean? What is his riddle? I am very conscious that I am not wise at all; what then does he mean by saying that I am the wisest? For surely he does not lie; it is not legitimate for him to do so." For a long time I was at a loss as to his meaning; then I very reluctantly turned to some such investigation as this; I went to one of those reputed wise, thinking that there, if anywhere, I could refute the oracle and say to it: "This man is wiser than I, but you said I was." Then, when I examined this man—there is no need for me to tell you his name, he was one of our public men—my experience was something like this: I thought that he appeared wise to many people and especially to himself, but he was not. I then tried to show him that he thought himself wise, but that he was not. As a result he came to dislike me, and so did many of the bystanders. So I withdrew and thought to myself: "I am wiser than this man; it is likely that neither of us knows anything worthwhile, but he thinks he knows something when he does not, whereas when I do not know, neither do I think I know; so I am likely to be wiser than he to this small extent, that I do not think I know what I do not know." After this I approached another man, one of those thought to be wiser than he, and I thought the same thing, and so I came to be disliked both by him and by many others.

After that I proceeded systematically. I realized, to my sorrow and alarm, that I was getting unpopular, but I thought that I must attach the greatest importance to the god's oracle, so I must go to all those who had any reputation for knowledge to examine its meaning. And by the dog, men of Athens—for I must tell you the truth—I experienced something like this: in my investigation in the service of the god I found that those who had the highest reputation were nearly the most deficient, while those

e

21

b

c

d

e

22

who were thought to be inferior were more knowledgeable. I must give
you an account of my journeyings as if they were labors I had undertaken
to prove the oracle irrefutable. After the politicians, I went to the poets,
b   the writers of tragedies and dithyrambs and the others, intending in their
case to catch myself being more ignorant than they. So I took up those
poems with which they seemed to have taken most trouble and asked
them what they meant, in order that I might at the same time learn something from them. I am ashamed to tell you the truth, gentlemen, but I
must. Almost all the bystanders might have explained the poems better
c   than their authors could. I soon realized that poets do not compose their
poems with knowledge, but by some inborn talent and by inspiration, like
seers and prophets who also say many fine things without any understanding of what they say. The poets seemed to me to have had a similar
experience. At the same time I saw that, because of their poetry, they
thought themselves very wise men in other respects, which they were not.
So there again I withdrew, thinking that I had the same advantage over
them as I had over the politicians.

d   Finally I went to the craftsmen, for I was conscious of knowing practically
nothing, and I knew that I would find that they had knowledge of many
fine things. In this I was not mistaken; they knew things I did not know,
and to that extent they were wiser than I. But, men of Athens, the good
craftsmen seemed to me to have the same fault as the poets: each of them,
because of his success at his craft, thought himself very wise in other most
e   important pursuits, and this error of theirs overshadowed the wisdom
they had, so that I asked myself, on behalf of the oracle, whether I should
prefer to be as I am, with neither their wisdom nor their ignorance, or to
have both. The answer I gave myself and the oracle was that it was to my
advantage to be as I am.

        As a result of this investigation, men of Athens, I acquired much unpopu-
23   larity, of a kind that is hard to deal with and is a heavy burden; many
slanders came from these people and a reputation for wisdom, for in each
case the bystanders thought that I myself possessed the wisdom that I
proved that my interlocutor did not have. What is probable, gentlemen,
is that in fact the god is wise and that his oracular response meant that
b   human wisdom is worth little or nothing, and that when he says this man,
Socrates, he is using my name as an example, as if he said: "This man
among you, mortals, is wisest who, like Socrates, understands that his
wisdom is worthless." So even now I continue this investigation as the
god bade me—and I go around seeking out anyone, citizen or stranger,
whom I think wise. Then if I do not think he is, I come to the assistance
of the god and show him that he is not wise. Because of this occupation,
I do not have the leisure to engage in public affairs to any extent, nor
indeed to look after my own, but I live in great poverty because of my
service to the god.

c   Furthermore, the young men who follow me around of their own free
will, those who have most leisure, the sons of the very rich, take pleasure

in hearing people questioned; they themselves often imitate me and try to question others. I think they find an abundance of men who believe they have some knowledge but know little or nothing. The result is that those whom they question are angry, not with themselves but with me. They say: "That man Socrates is a pestilential fellow who corrupts the young." If one asks them what he does and what he teaches to corrupt them, they are silent, as they do not know, but, so as not to appear at a loss, they mention those accusations that are available against all philosophers, about "things in the sky and things below the earth," about "not believing in the gods" and "making the worse the stronger argument"; they would not want to tell the truth, I'm sure, that they have been proved to lay claim to knowledge when they know nothing. These people are ambitious, violent and numerous; they are continually and convincingly talking about me; they have been filling your ears for a long time with vehement slanders against me. From them Meletus attacked me, and Anytus and Lycon, Meletus being vexed on behalf of the poets, Anytus on behalf of the craftsmen and the politicians, Lycon on behalf of the orators, so that, as I started out by saying, I should be surprised if I could rid you of so much slander in so short a time. That, men of Athens, is the truth for you. I have hidden or disguised nothing. I know well enough that this very conduct makes me unpopular, and this is proof that what I say is true, that such is the slander against me, and that such are its causes. If you look into this either now or later, this is what you will find.

Let this suffice as a defense against the charges of my earlier accusers. After this I shall try to defend myself against Meletus, that good and patriotic man, as he says he is, and my later accusers. As these are a different lot of accusers, let us again take up their sworn deposition. It goes something like this: Socrates is guilty of corrupting the young and of not believing in the gods in whom the city believes, but in other new spiritual things. Such is their charge. Let us examine it point by point.

He says that I am guilty of corrupting the young, but I say that Meletus is guilty of dealing frivolously with serious matters, of irresponsibly bringing people into court, and of professing to be seriously concerned with things about none of which he has ever cared, and I shall try to prove that this is so. Come here and tell me, Meletus. Surely you consider it of the greatest importance that our young men be as good as possible?—Indeed I do.

Come then, tell these men who improves them. You obviously know, in view of your concern. You say you have discovered the one who corrupts them, namely me, and you bring me here and accuse me to these men. Come, inform them and tell them who it is. You see, Meletus, that you are silent and know not what to say. Does this not seem shameful to you and a sufficient proof of what I say, that you have not been concerned with any of this? Tell me, my good sir, who improves our young men?—The laws.

That is not what I am asking, but what person who has knowledge of the laws to begin with?—These jurymen, Socrates.

How do you mean, Meletus? Are these able to educate the young and improve them?—Certainly.

All of them, or some but not others?—All of them.

25   Very good, by Hera. You mention a great abundance of benefactors. But what about the audience? Do they improve the young or not?—They do, too.

What about the members of Council?—The Councillors, also.

But, Meletus, what about the assembly? Do members of the assembly corrupt the young, or do they all improve them?—They improve them.

All the Athenians, it seems, make the young into fine good men, except me, and I alone corrupt them. Is that what you mean?—That is most definitely what I mean.

b   You condemn me to a great misfortune. Tell me: does this also apply to horses do you think? That all men improve them and one individual corrupts them? Or is quite the contrary true, one individual is able to improve them, or very few, namely, the horse breeders, whereas the majority, if they have horses and use them, corrupt them? Is that not the case, Meletus, both with horses and all other animals? Of course it is, whether you and Anytus say so or not. It would be a very happy state of affairs if only one person corrupted our youth, while the others improved them.

c   You have made it sufficiently obvious, Meletus, that you have never had any concern for our youth; you show your indifference clearly; that you have given no thought to the subjects about which you bring me to trial.

And by Zeus, Meletus, tell us also whether it is better for a man to live among good or wicked fellow citizens. Answer, my good man, for I am not asking a difficult question. Do not the wicked do some harm to those who are ever closest to them, whereas good people benefit them?—Certainly.

d   And does the man exist who would rather be harmed than benefited by his associates? Answer, my good sir, for the law orders you to answer. Is there any man who wants to be harmed?—Of course not.

Come now, do you accuse me here of corrupting the young and making them worse deliberately or unwillingly?—Deliberately.

What follows, Meletus? Are you so much wiser at your age than I am

e   at mine that you understand that wicked people always do some harm to their closest neighbors while good people do them good, but I have reached such a pitch of ignorance that I do not realize this, namely that if I make one of my associates wicked I run the risk of being harmed by him so that I do such a great evil deliberately, as you say? I do not believe you, Meletus,

26   and I do not think anyone else will. Either I do not corrupt the young or, if I do, it is unwillingly, and you are lying in either case. Now if I corrupt them unwillingly, the law does not require you to bring people to court for such unwilling wrongdoings, but to get hold of them privately, to instruct them and exhort them; for clearly, if I learn better, I shall cease to do what I am doing unwillingly. You, however, have avoided my company and were unwilling to instruct me, but you bring me here, where

the law requires one to bring those who are in need of punishment, not of instruction.

And so, men of Athens, what I said is clearly true: Meletus has never   b
been at all concerned with these matters. Nonetheless tell us, Meletus, how you say that I corrupt the young; or is it obvious from your deposition that it is by teaching them not to believe in the gods in whom the city believes but in other new spiritual things? Is this not what you say I teach and so corrupt them?—That is most certainly what I do say.

Then by those very gods about whom we are talking, Meletus, make this   c
clearer to me and to these men: I cannot be sure whether you mean that I teach the belief that there are some gods—and therefore I myself believe that there are gods and am not altogether an atheist, nor am I guilty of that—not, however, the gods in whom the city believes, but others, and that this is the charge against me, that they are others. Or whether you mean that I do not believe in gods at all, and that this is what I teach to others.—This is what I mean, that you do not believe in gods at all.

You are a strange fellow, Meletus. Why do you say this? Do I not believe,   d
as other men do, that the sun and the moon are gods?—No, by Zeus, gentlemen of the jury, for he says that the sun is stone, and the moon earth.

My dear Meletus, do you think you are prosecuting Anaxagoras? Are you so contemptuous of these men and think them so ignorant of letters as not to know that the books of Anaxagoras of Clazomenae are full of those theories, and further, that the young men learn from me what they   e
can buy from time to time for a drachma, at most, in the bookshops, and ridicule Socrates if he pretends that these theories are his own, especially as they are so absurd? Is that, by Zeus, what you think of me, Meletus, that I do not believe that there are any gods?—That is what I say, that you do not believe in the gods at all.

You cannot be believed, Meletus, even, I think, by yourself. The man appears to me, men of Athens, highly insolent and uncontrolled. He seems to have made this deposition out of insolence, violence and youthful zeal.   27
He is like one who composed a riddle and is trying it out: "Will the wise Socrates realize that I am jesting and contradicting myself, or shall I deceive him and others?" I think he contradicts himself in the affidavit, as if he said: "Socrates is guilty of not believing in gods but believing in gods," and surely that is the part of a jester!

Examine with me, gentlemen, how he appears to contradict himself, and   b
you, Meletus, answer us. Remember, gentlemen, what I asked you when I began, not to create a disturbance if I proceed in my usual manner.

Does any man, Meletus, believe in human activities who does not believe in humans? Make him answer, and not again and again create a disturbance. Does any man who does not believe in horses believe in horsemen's activities? Or in flute-playing activities but not in flute-players? No, my good sir, no man could. If you are not willing to answer, I will tell you   c
and these men. Answer the next question, however. Does any man believe in spiritual activities who does not believe in spirits?—No one.

Thank you for answering, if reluctantly, when these gentlemen made you. Now you say that I believe in spiritual things and teach about them, whether new or old, but at any rate spiritual things according to what you say, and to this you have sworn in your deposition. But if I believe in spiritual things I must quite inevitably believe in spirits. Is that not so? It is indeed. I shall
d   assume that you agree, as you do not answer. Do we not believe spirits to be either gods or the children of gods? Yes or no?—Of course.

Then since I do believe in spirits, as you admit, if spirits are gods, this is what I mean when I say you speak in riddles and in jest, as you state that I do not believe in gods and then again that I do, since I do believe in spirits. If on the other hand the spirits are children of the gods, bastard children of the gods by nymphs or some other mothers, as they are said to be, what man would believe children of the gods to exist, but not gods?
e   That would be just as absurd as to believe the young of horses and asses, namely mules, to exist, but not to believe in the existence of horses and asses. You must have made this deposition, Meletus, either to test us or because you were at a loss to find any true wrongdoing of which to accuse me. There is no way in which you could persuade anyone of even small intelligence that it is possible for one and the same man to believe in
28   spiritual but not also in divine things, and then again for that same man to believe neither in spirits nor in gods nor in heroes.

I do not think, men of Athens, that it requires a prolonged defense to prove that I am not guilty of the charges in Meletus' deposition, but this is sufficient. On the other hand, you know that what I said earlier is true, that I am very unpopular with many people. This will be my undoing, if I am undone, not Meletus or Anytus but the slanders and envy of many
b   people. This has destroyed many other good men and will, I think, continue to do so. There is no danger that it will stop at me.

Someone might say: "Are you not ashamed, Socrates, to have followed the kind of occupation that has led to your being now in danger of death?" However, I should be right to reply to him: "You are wrong, sir, if you think that a man who is any good at all should take into account the risk of life or death; he should look to this only in his actions, whether what
c   he does is right or wrong, whether he is acting like a good or a bad man." According to your view, all the heroes who died at Troy were inferior people, especially the son of Thetis who was so contemptuous of danger compared with disgrace.[3] When he was eager to kill Hector, his goddess mother warned him, as I believe, in some such words as these: "My child, if you avenge the death of your comrade, Patroclus, and you kill Hector, you will die yourself, for your death is to follow immediately after Hector's." Hearing this, he despised death and danger and was much more afraid
d   to live a coward who did not avenge his friends. "Let me die at once," he said, "when once I have given the wrongdoer his deserts, rather than

---

3. See *Iliad* xviii.94 ff.

remain here, a laughingstock by the curved ships, a burden upon the earth." Do you think he gave thought to death and danger?

This is the truth of the matter, men of Athens: wherever a man has taken a position that he believes to be best, or has been placed by his commander, there he must I think remain and face danger, without a thought for death or anything else, rather than disgrace. It would have been a dreadful way to behave, men of Athens, if, at Potidaea, Amphipolis and Delium, I had, at the risk of death, like anyone else, remained at my post where those you had elected to command had ordered me, and then, when the god ordered me, as I thought and believed, to live the life of a philosopher, to examine myself and others, I had abandoned my post for fear of death or anything else. That would have been a dreadful thing, and then I might truly have justly been brought here for not believing that there are gods, disobeying the oracle, fearing death, and thinking I was wise when I was not. To fear death, gentlemen, is no other than to think oneself wise when one is not, to think one knows what one does not know. No one knows whether death may not be the greatest of all blessings for a man, yet men fear it as if they knew that it is the greatest of evils. And surely it is the most blameworthy ignorance to believe that one knows what one does not know. It is perhaps on this point and in this respect, gentlemen, that I differ from the majority of men, and if I were to claim that I am wiser than anyone in anything, it would be in this, that, as I have no adequate knowledge of things in the underworld, so I do not think I have. I do know, however, that it is wicked and shameful to do wrong, to disobey one's superior, be he god or man. I shall never fear or avoid things of which I do not know, whether they may not be good rather than things that I know to be bad. Even if you acquitted me now and did not believe Anytus, who said to you that either I should not have been brought here in the first place, or that now I am here, you cannot avoid executing me, for if I should be acquitted, your sons would practice the teachings of Socrates and all be thoroughly corrupted; if you said to me in this regard: "Socrates, we do not believe Anytus now; we acquit you, but only on condition that you spend no more time on this investigation and do not practice philosophy, and if you are caught doing so you will die;" if, as I say, you were to acquit me on those terms, I would say to you: "Men of Athens, I am grateful and I am your friend, but I will obey the god rather than you, and as long as I draw breath and am able, I shall not cease to practice philosophy, to exhort you and in my usual way to point out to any one of you whom I happen to meet: Good Sir, you are an Athenian, a citizen of the greatest city with the greatest reputation for both wisdom and power; are you not ashamed of your eagerness to possess as much wealth, reputation and honors as possible, while you do not care for nor give thought to wisdom or truth, or the best possible state of your soul?" Then, if one of you disputes this and says he does care, I shall not let him go at once or leave him, but I shall question him, examine him and test him, and if I do not think he has attained the goodness that he says he

e

29

b

c

d

e

30   has, I shall reproach him because he attaches little importance to the most
      important things and greater importance to inferior things. I shall treat in
      this way anyone I happen to meet, young and old, citizen and stranger,
      and more so the citizens because you are more kindred to me. Be sure
      that this is what the god orders me to do, and I think there is no greater
      blessing for the city than my service to the god. For I go around doing
      nothing but persuading both young and old among you not to care for
b   your body or your wealth in preference to or as strongly as for the best
      possible state of your soul, as I say to you: "Wealth does not bring about
      excellence, but excellence makes wealth and everything else good for men,
      both individually and collectively."[4]

         Now if by saying this I corrupt the young, this advice must be harmful,
      but if anyone says that I give different advice, he is talking nonsense. On
      this point I would say to you, men of Athens: "Whether you believe Anytus
c   or not, whether you acquit me or not, do so on the understanding that
      this is my course of action, even if I am to face death many times." Do
      not create a disturbance, gentlemen, but abide by my request not to cry
      out at what I say but to listen, for I think it will be to your advantage to
      listen, and I am about to say other things at which you will perhaps cry
      out. By no means do this. Be sure that if you kill the sort of man I say I
      am, you will not harm me more than yourselves. Neither Meletus nor
d   Anytus can harm me in any way; he could not harm me, for I do not think
      it is permitted that a better man be harmed by a worse; certainly he might
      kill me, or perhaps banish or disfranchise me, which he and maybe others
      think to be great harm, but I do not think so. I think he is doing himself
      much greater harm doing what he is doing now, attempting to have a
      man executed unjustly. Indeed, men of Athens, I am far from making a
      defense now on my own behalf, as might be thought, but on yours, to
e   prevent you from wrongdoing by mistreating the god's gift to you by
      condemning me; for if you kill me you will not easily find another like
      me. I was attached to this city by the god—though it seems a ridiculous
      thing to say—as upon a great and noble horse which was somewhat
      sluggish because of its size and needed to be stirred up by a kind of gadfly.
      It is to fulfill some such function that I believe the god has placed me in
      the city. I never cease to rouse each and every one of you, to persuade and
31   reproach you all day long and everywhere I find myself in your company.
         Another such man will not easily come to be among you, gentlemen,
      and if you believe me you will spare me. You might easily be annoyed
      with me as people are when they are aroused from a doze, and strike out
      at me; if convinced by Anytus you could easily kill me, and then you
      could sleep on for the rest of your days, unless the god, in his care for
      you, sent you someone else. That I am the kind of person to be a gift of
b   the god to the city you might realize from the fact that it does not seem

---

4. Alternatively, this sentence could be translated: "Wealth does not bring about excellence, but excellence brings about wealth and all other public and private blessings
for men."

like human nature for me to have neglected all my own affairs and to have tolerated this neglect now for so many years while I was always concerned with you, approaching each one of you like a father or an elder brother to persuade you to care for virtue. Now if I profited from this by charging a fee for my advice, there would be some sense to it, but you can see for yourselves that, for all their shameless accusations, my accusers have not been able in their impudence to bring forward a witness to say that I have ever received a fee or ever asked for one. I, on the other hand, have a convincing witness that I speak the truth, my poverty.

It may seem strange that while I go around and give this advice privately and interfere in private affairs, I do not venture to go to the assembly and there advise the city. You have heard me give the reason for this in many places. I have a divine or spiritual sign which Meletus has ridiculed in his deposition. This began when I was a child. It is a voice, and whenever it speaks it turns me away from something I am about to do, but it never encourages me to do anything. This is what has prevented me from taking part in public affairs, and I think it was quite right to prevent me. Be sure, men of Athens, that if I had long ago attempted to take part in politics, I should have died long ago, and benefited neither you nor myself. Do not be angry with me for speaking the truth; no man will survive who genuinely opposes you or any other crowd and prevents the occurrence of many unjust and illegal happenings in the city. A man who really fights for justice must lead a private, not a public, life if he is to survive for even a short time.

I shall give you great proofs of this, not words but what you esteem, deeds. Listen to what happened to me, that you may know that I will not yield to any man contrary to what is right, for fear of death, even if I should die at once for not yielding. The things I shall tell you are commonplace and smack of the lawcourts, but they are true. I have never held any other office in the city, but I served as a member of the Council, and our tribe Antiochis was presiding at the time when you wanted to try as a body the ten generals who had failed to pick up the survivors of the naval battle.[5] This was illegal, as you all recognized later. I was the only member of the presiding committee to oppose your doing something contrary to the laws, and I voted against it. The orators were ready to prosecute me and take me away, and your shouts were egging them on, but I thought I should run any risk on the side of law and justice rather than join you, for fear of prison or death, when you were engaged in an unjust course.

This happened when the city was still a democracy. When the oligarchy was established, the Thirty[6] summoned me to the Hall, along with four others, and ordered us to bring Leon from Salamis, that he might be

5. This was the battle of Arginusae (south of Lesbos) in 406 B.C., the last Athenian victory of the Peloponnesian war. A violent storm prevented the Athenian generals from rescuing their survivors.

6. This was the harsh oligarchy that was set up after the final defeat of Athens in 404 B.C. and ruled Athens for some nine months in 404–3 before the democracy was restored.

d   executed. They gave many such orders to many people, in order to impli-
cate as many as possible in their guilt. Then I showed again, not in words
but in action, that, if it were not rather vulgar to say so, death is something
I couldn't care less about, but that my whole concern is not to do anything
unjust or impious. That government, powerful as it was, did not frighten
me into any wrongdoing. When we left the Hall, the other four went to
Salamis and brought in Leon, but I went home. I might have been put to
e   death for this, had not the government fallen shortly afterwards. There
are many who will witness to these events.

Do you think I would have survived all these years if I were engaged
in public affairs and, acting as a good man must, came to the help of justice
and considered this the most important thing? Far from it, men of Athens,
33   nor would any other man. Throughout my life, in any public activity I
may have engaged in, I am the same man as I am in private life. I have
never come to an agreement with anyone to act unjustly, neither with
anyone else nor with any one of those who they slanderously say are my
pupils. I have never been anyone's teacher. If anyone, young or old, desires
to listen to me when I am talking and dealing with my own concerns, I
have never begrudged this to anyone, but I do not converse when I receive
b   a fee and not when I do not. I am equally ready to question the rich and
the poor if anyone is willing to answer my questions and listen to what
I say. And I cannot justly be held responsible for the good or bad conduct
of these people, as I never promised to teach them anything and have not
done so. If anyone says that he has learned anything from me, or that he
heard anything privately that the others did not hear, be assured that he
is not telling the truth.

c   Why then do some people enjoy spending considerable time in my
company? You have heard why, men of Athens; I have told you the whole
truth. They enjoy hearing those being questioned who think they are wise,
but are not. And this is not unpleasant. To do this has, as I say, been
enjoined upon me by the god, by means of oracles and dreams, and in
every other way that a divine manifestation has ever ordered a man to
do anything. This is true, gentlemen, and can easily be established.

d   If I corrupt some young men and have corrupted others, then surely
some of them who have grown older and realized that I gave them bad
advice when they were young should now themselves come up here to
accuse me and avenge themselves. If they were unwilling to do so themselves, then some of their kindred, their fathers or brothers or other relations
should recall it now if their family had been harmed by me. I see many
e   of these present here, first Crito, my contemporary and fellow demesman,
the father of Critobulus here; next Lysanias of Sphettus, the father of
Aeschines here; also Antiphon the Cephisian, the father of Epigenes; and
others whose brothers spent their time in this way; Nicostratus, the son
of Theozotides, brother of Theodotus, and Theodotus has died so he could
34   not influence him; Paralius here, son of Demodocus, whose brother was
Theages; there is Adeimantus, son of Ariston, brother of Plato here; Aeantodorus, brother of Apollodorus here.

I could mention many others, some one of whom surely Meletus should have brought in as witness in his own speech. If he forgot to do so, then let him do it now; I will yield time if he has anything of the kind to say. You will find quite the contrary, gentlemen. These men are all ready to come to the help of the corruptor, the man who has harmed their kindred, as Meletus and Anytus say. Now those who were corrupted might well have reason to help me, but the uncorrupted, their kindred who are older men, have no reason to help me except the right and proper one, that they know that Meletus is lying and that I am telling the truth.

Very well, gentlemen. This, and maybe other similar things, is what I have to say in my defense. Perhaps one of you might be angry as he recalls that when he himself stood trial on a less dangerous charge, he begged and implored the jurymen with many tears, that he brought his children and many of his friends and family into court to arouse as much pity as he could, but that I do none of these things, even though I may seem to be running the ultimate risk. Thinking of this, he might feel resentful toward me and, angry about this, cast his vote in anger. If there is such a one among you—I do not deem there is, but if there is—I think it would be right to say in reply: My good sir, I too have a household and, in Homer's phrase, I am not born "from oak or rock" but from men, so that I have a family, indeed three sons, men of Athens, of whom one is an adolescent while two are children. Nevertheless, I will not beg you to acquit me by bringing them here. Why do I do none of these things? Not through arrogance, gentlemen, nor through lack of respect for you. Whether I am brave in the face of death is another matter, but with regard to my reputation and yours and that of the whole city, it does not seem right to me to do these things, especially at my age and with my reputation. For it is generally believed, whether it be true or false, that in certain respects Socrates is superior to the majority of men. Now if those of you who are considered superior, be it in wisdom or courage or whatever other virtue makes them so, are seen behaving like that, it would be a disgrace. Yet I have often seen them do this sort of thing when standing trial, men who are thought to be somebody, doing amazing things as if they thought it a terrible thing to die, and as if they were to be immortal if you did not execute them. I think these men bring shame upon the city so that a stranger, too, would assume that those who are outstanding in virtue among the Athenians, whom they themselves select from themselves to fill offices of state and receive other honors, are in no way better than women. You should not act like that, men of Athens, those of you who have any reputation at all, and if we do, you should not allow it. You should make it very clear that you will more readily convict a man who performs these pitiful dramatics in court and so makes the city a laughing-stock, than a man who keeps quiet.

Quite apart from the question of reputation, gentlemen, I do not think it right to supplicate the jury and to be acquitted because of this, but to teach and persuade them. It is not the purpose of a juryman's office to give justice as a favor to whoever seems good to him, but to judge according to law, and this he has sworn to do. We should not accustom you to perjure yourselves, nor should you make a habit of it. This is irreverent conduct for either of us.

d   Do not deem it right for me, men of Athens, that I should act towards you in a way that I do not consider to be good or just or pious, especially, by Zeus, as I am being prosecuted by Meletus here for impiety; clearly, if I convinced you by my supplication to do violence to your oath of office, I would be teaching you not to believe that there are gods, and my defense would convict me of not believing in them. This is far from being the case, gentlemen, for I do believe in them as none of my accusers do. I leave it to you and the god to judge me in the way that will be best for me and for you.

> [*The jury now gives its verdict of guilty, and Meletus asks for the penalty of death.*]

e   There are many other reasons for my not being angry with you for
36   convicting me, men of Athens, and what happened was not unexpected. I am much more surprised at the number of votes cast on each side for I did not think the decision would be by so few votes but by a great many. As it is, a switch of only thirty votes would have acquitted me. I think
b   myself that I have been cleared on Meletus' charges, and not only this, but it is clear to all that, if Anytus and Lycon had not joined him in accusing me, he would have been fined a thousand drachmas for not receiving a fifth of the votes.

He assesses the penalty at death. So be it. What counter-assessment should I propose to you, men of Athens? Clearly it should be a penalty I deserve, and what do I deserve to suffer or to pay because I have deliberately not led a quiet life but have neglected what occupies most people: wealth, household affairs, the position of general or public orator or the other offices, the political clubs and factions that exist in the city? I thought
c   myself too honest to survive if I occupied myself with those things. I did not follow that path that would have made me of no use either to you or to myself, but I went to each of you privately and conferred upon him what I say is the greatest benefit, by trying to persuade him not to care for any of his belongings before caring that he himself should be as good and as wise as possible, not to care for the city's possessions more than
d   for the city itself, and to care for other things in the same way. What do I deserve for being such a man? Some good, men of Athens, if I must truly make an assessment according to my deserts, and something suitable. What is suitable for a poor benefactor who needs leisure to exhort you? Nothing is more suitable, gentlemen, than for such a man to be fed in the Prytaneum,[7] much more suitable for him than for any one of you who has won a victory at Olympia with a pair or a team of horses. The Olympian

---

7. The Prytaneum was the magistrates' hall or town hall of Athens in which public entertainments were given, particularly to Olympian victors on their return home.

victor makes you think yourself happy; I make you be happy. Besides, he   e
does not need food, but I do. So if I must make a just assessment of what
I deserve, I assess it as this: free meals in the Prytaneum.   37

When I say this you may think, as when I spoke of appeals to pity and
entreaties, that I speak arrogantly, but that is not the case, men of Athens;
rather it is like this: I am convinced that I never willingly wrong anyone,
but I am not convincing you of this, for we have talked together but a
short time. If it were the law with us, as it is elsewhere, that a trial for life   b
should not last one but many days, you would be convinced, but now it
is not easy to dispel great slanders in a short time. Since I am convinced
that I wrong no one, I am not likely to wrong myself, to say that I deserve
some evil and to make some such assessment against myself. What should
I fear? That I should suffer the penalty Meletus has assessed against me,
of which I say I do not know whether it is good or bad? Am I then to
choose in preference to this something that I know very well to be an evil
and assess the penalty at that? Imprisonment? Why should I live in prison,   c
always subjected to the ruling magistrates, the Eleven? A fine, and imprisonment until I pay it? That would be the same thing for me, as I have no
money. Exile? for perhaps you might accept that assessment.

I should have to be inordinately fond of life, men of Athens, to be so
unreasonable as to suppose that other men will easily tolerate my company
and conversation when you, my fellow citizens, have been unable to endure   d
them, but found them a burden and resented them so that you are now
seeking to get rid of them. Far from it, gentlemen. It would be a fine life
at my age to be driven out of one city after another, for I know very well
that wherever I go the young men will listen to my talk as they do here.   e
If I drive them away, they will themselves persuade their elders to drive
me out; if I do not drive them away, their fathers and relations will drive
me out on their behalf.

Perhaps someone might say: But Socrates, if you leave us will you not
be able to live quietly, without talking? Now this is the most difficult point
on which to convince some of you. If I say that it is impossible for me to   38
keep quiet because that means disobeying the god, you will not believe
me and will think I am being ironical. On the other hand, if I say that it
is the greatest good for a man to discuss virtue every day and those other
things about which you hear me conversing and testing myself and others,
for the unexamined life is not worth living for men, you will believe me
even less.

What I say is true, gentlemen, but it is not easy to convince you. At the   b
same time, I am not accustomed to think that I deserve any penalty. If I
had money, I would assess the penalty at the amount I could pay, for that
would not hurt me, but I have none, unless you are willing to set the
penalty at the amount I can pay, and perhaps I could pay you one mina
of silver.[8] So that is my assessment.

---

8. One mina was the equivalent of 100 drachmas. In the late fifth century one drachma
was the standard daily wage of a laborer. A mina, then, was a considerable sum.

Plato here, men of Athens, and Crito and Critobulus and Apollodorus bid me put the penalty at thirty minas, and they will stand surety for the money. Well then, that is my assessment, and they will be sufficient guarantee of payment.

[The jury now votes again and sentences Socrates to death.]

c   It is for the sake of a short time, men of Athens, that you will acquire the reputation and the guilt, in the eyes of those who want to denigrate the city, of having killed Socrates, a wise man, for they who want to revile you will say that I am wise even if I am not. If you had waited but a little while, this would have happened of its own accord. You see my age, that

d   I am already advanced in years and close to death. I am saying this not to all of you but to those who condemned me to death, and to these same ones I say: Perhaps you think that I was convicted for lack of such words as might have convinced you, if I thought I should say or do all I could to avoid my sentence. Far from it. I was convicted because I lacked not words but boldness and shamelessness and the willingness to say to you what you would most gladly have heard from me, lamentations and tears

e   and my saying and doing many things that I say are unworthy of me but that you are accustomed to hear from others. I did not think then that the danger I ran should make me do anything mean, nor do I now regret the nature of my defense. I would much rather die after this kind of defense than live after making the other kind. Neither I nor any other man should,

39   on trial or in war, contrive to avoid death at any cost. Indeed it is often obvious in battle that one could escape death by throwing away one's weapons and by turning to supplicate one's pursuers, and there are many ways to avoid death in every kind of danger if one will venture to do or

b   say anything to avoid it. It is not difficult to avoid death, gentlemen; it is much more difficult to avoid wickedness, for it runs faster than death. Slow and elderly as I am, I have been caught by the slower pursuer, whereas my accusers, being clever and sharp, have been caught by the quicker, wickedness. I leave you now, condemned to death by you, but they are condemned by truth to wickedness and injustice. So I maintain my assessment, and they maintain theirs. This perhaps had to happen, and I think it is as it should be.

c   Now I want to prophesy to those who convicted me, for I am at the point when men prophesy most, when they are about to die. I say gentlemen, to those who voted to kill me, that vengeance will come upon you immediately after my death, a vengeance much harder to bear than that which you took in killing me. You did this in the belief that you would avoid giving an account of your life, but I maintain that quite the opposite will

d   happen to you. There will be more people to test you, whom I now held back, but you did not notice it. They will be more difficult to deal with as they will be younger and you will resent them more. You are wrong if you believe that by killing people you will prevent anyone from reproaching you for not living in the right way. To escape such tests is neither possible nor good, but it is best and easiest not to discredit others but to prepare oneself to be as good as possible. With this prophecy to you who convicted me, I part from you.

I should be glad to discuss what has happened with those who voted   e
for my acquittal during the time that the officers of the court are busy and I do not yet have to depart to my death. So, gentlemen, stay with me awhile, for nothing prevents us from talking to each other while it is allowed. To you, as being my friends, I want to show the meaning of what   40
has occurred. A surprising thing has happened to me, jurymen—you I would rightly call jurymen. At all previous times my familiar prophetic power, my spiritual manifestation, frequently opposed me, even in small matters, when I was about to do something wrong, but now that, as you can see for yourselves, I was faced with what one might think, and what is generally thought to be, the worst of evils, my divine sign has not opposed me, either when I left home at dawn, or when I came into court,   b
or at any time that I was about to say something during my speech. Yet in other talks it often held me back in the middle of my speaking, but now it has opposed no word or deed of mine. What do I think is the reason for this? I will tell you. What has happened to me may well be a good thing, and those of us who believe death to be an evil are certainly mistaken. I have convincing proof of this, for it is impossible that my   c
familiar sign did not oppose me if I was not about to do what was right.

Let us reflect in this way, too, that there is good hope that death is a blessing, for it is one of two things: either the dead are nothing and have no perception of anything, or it is, as we are told, a change and a relocating for the soul from here to another place. If it is complete lack of perception,   d
like a dreamless sleep, then death would be a great advantage. For I think that if one had to pick out that night during which a man slept soundly and did not dream, put beside it the other nights and days of his life, and then see how many days and nights had been better and more pleasant than that night, not only a private person but the great king would find them easy to count compared with the other days and nights. If death is   e
like this I say it is an advantage, for all eternity would then seem to be no more than a single night. If, on the other hand, death is a change from here to another place, and what we are told is true and all who have died are there, what greater blessing could there be, gentlemen of the jury? If   41
anyone arriving in Hades will have escaped from those who call themselves jurymen here, and will find those true jurymen who are said to sit in judgment there, Minos and Rhadamanthus and Aeacus and Triptolemus and the other demi-gods who have been upright in their own life, would that be a poor kind of change? Again, what would one of you give to keep company with Orpheus and Musaeus, Hesiod and Homer? I am willing to die many times if that is true. It would be a wonderful way for me to spend my time whenever I met Palamedes and Ajax, the son of Telamon,   b
and any other of the men of old who died through an unjust conviction,

to compare my experience with theirs. I think it would be pleasant. Most important, I could spend my time testing and examining people there, as I do here, as to who among them is wise, and who thinks he is, but is not.

c What would one not give, gentlemen of the jury, for the opportunity to examine the man who led the great expedition against Troy, or Odysseus, or Sisyphus, and innumerable other men and women one could mention? It would be an extraordinary happiness to talk with them, to keep company with them and examine them. In any case, they would certainly not put one to death for doing so. They are happier there than we are here in other respects, and for the rest of time they are deathless, if indeed what we are told is true.

d You too must be of good hope as regards death, gentlemen of the jury, and keep this one truth in mind, that a good man cannot be harmed either in life or in death, and that his affairs are not neglected by the gods. What has happened to me now has not happened of itself, but it is clear to me that it was better for me to die now and to escape from trouble. That is why my divine sign did not oppose me at any point. So I am certainly not angry with those who convicted me, or with my accusers. Of course that was not their purpose when they accused and convicted me, but they

e thought they were hurting me, and for this they deserve blame. This much I ask from them: when my sons grow up, avenge yourselves by causing them the same kind of grief that I caused you, if you think they care for money or anything else more than they care for virtue, or if they think they are somebody when they are nobody. Reproach them as I reproach you, that they do not care for the right things and think they are worthy

42 when they are not worthy of anything. If you do this, I shall have been justly treated by you, and my sons also.

Now the hour to part has come. I go to die, you go to live. Which of us goes to the better lot is known to no one, except the god.

CRITO

As the beginning of the Phaedo relates, Socrates did not die until a month after his trial, which followed by a day the sailing of the Athenian state galley on an annual religious mission to the island of Delos; no executions were permitted during its absence. Crito comes to tell Socrates of its anticipated arrival later that day and to make one last effort to persuade him to allow his friends to save him by bribing his jailers and bundling him off somewhere beyond the reach of Athenian law. Crito indicates that most people expect his friends to do this—unless (dishonorably) they value their money more than their friend. Socrates, however, refuses. Even if people do expect it, to do that would be grossly unjust.

Both Crito's arguments in favor of his plan and Socrates' in rejecting it are rather jumbled—as perhaps befits the pressure and excitement of the moment. Crito cites the damage to his and Socrates' other friends' reputations and delicately minimizes any financial loss he might suffer, in case Socrates might be unwilling to accept any great sacrifice from a friend. Socrates witheringly dismisses the first consideration and ignores the second. But Crito also claims that it would actually be unjust of Socrates to stay. That would allow his enemies to triumph over him and his friends, including his young sons, whom he will abandon by going docilely to his death: a person ought not to take lying down an attack on the things he holds most dear, including philosophy itself and the philosophical life to which he and (presumably) his friends are devoted. Here we hear strains of the time-honored Greek idea that justice is helping one's friends and harming one's enemies, cited by Polemarchus in Republic I. (But Crito does not propose harming their enemies—only preventing them from having their way.) As to his children, Socrates responds that they will be as well or better cared for after his death than if he resisted it and went into exile. But ironically, considering his own subsequent arguments for accepting his death, he seems not to hear the larger claim of injustice that Crito lodges. Crito's jumbled presentation of his case facilitates this.

Unmoved by the claims of justice grounded in his private relationships to friends and family, Socrates appeals to the standards of civic justice imbedded in his relations as a citizen to the Athenian people and to the Athenian system of law. He claims that a citizen is necessarily, given the benefits he has enjoyed under the laws of the city, their slave, justly required to do whatever they ask, and more forbidden to attack them than to violate his own parents. That would be retaliation—rendering a wrong for the wrong received in his unjust condemnation—and retaliation is never just. But what if he chose to depart not in an

37

unjust spirit of retaliation, but only in order to evade the ill consequences of the unjust condemnation for himself and his friends and family? As if recognizing that loophole, Socrates also develops a celebrated early version of the social contract—a 'contract' between the laws or the city and each citizen, not among the citizens themselves—with the argument that now, after he is condemned by an Athenian court and has exhausted all legal appeals, he must, in justice to his implicit promise, abide by the laws' final judgment and accept his death sentence.

It is clear where Socrates stands; he is committed, as a public figure known for pleading the preeminent value of the civic virtues, to honoring them in his personal life—and death. But the dialogue itself, through Crito's ignored appeal to justice in the private sphere, invites the reader to reflect on a wider range of issues about justice than Socrates himself addresses. Did justice really require that Socrates stay to accept his death?

J.M.C.

43   SOCRATES: Why have you come so early, Crito? Or is it not still early?
       CRITO: It certainly is.
       SOCRATES: How early?
       CRITO: Early dawn.
       SOCRATES: I am surprised that the warder was willing to listen to you.
       CRITO: He is quite friendly to me by now, Socrates. I have been here often and I have given him something.
       SOCRATES: Have you just come, or have you been here for some time?
       CRITO: A fair time.
  b   SOCRATES: Then why did you not wake me right away but sit there in silence?
       CRITO: By Zeus no, Socrates. I would not myself want to be in distress and awake so long. I have been surprised to see you so peacefully asleep. It was on purpose that I did not wake you, so that you should spend your time most agreeably. Often in the past throughout my life, I have considered the way you live happy, and especially so now that you bear your present misfortune so easily and lightly.
       SOCRATES: It would not be fitting at my age to resent the fact that I must die now.
  c   CRITO: Other men of your age are caught in such misfortunes, but their age does not prevent them resenting their fate.
       SOCRATES: That is so. Why have you come so early?
       CRITO: I bring bad news, Socrates, not for you, apparently, but for me and all your friends the news is bad and hard to bear. Indeed, I would count it among the hardest.

Translated by G.M.A. Grube.

SOCRATES: What is it? Or has the ship arrived from Delos, at the arrival   d
of which I must die?

CRITO: It has not arrived yet, but it will, I believe, arrive today, according
to a message some men brought from Sunium, where they left it. This makes
it obvious that it will come today, and that your life must end tomorrow.

SOCRATES: May it be for the best. If it so please the gods, so be it. However,
I do not think it will arrive today.

CRITO: What indication have you of this?   44

SOCRATES: I will tell you. I must die the day after the ship arrives.

CRITO: That is what those in authority say.

SOCRATES: Then I do not think it will arrive on this coming day, but on
the next. I take to witness of this a dream I had a little earlier during this
night. It looks as if it was the right time for you not to wake me.

CRITO: What was your dream?

SOCRATES: I thought that a beautiful and comely woman dressed in white
approached me. She called me and said: "Socrates, may you arrive at fertile   b
Phthia[1] on the third day."

CRITO: A strange dream, Socrates.

SOCRATES: But it seems clear enough to me, Crito.

CRITO: Too clear it seems, my dear Socrates, but listen to me even now
and be saved. If you die, it will not be a single misfortune for me. Not
only will I be deprived of a friend, the like of whom I shall never find
again, but many people who do not know you or me very well will think   c
that I could have saved you if I were willing to spend money, but that I
did not care to do so. Surely there can be no worse reputation than to be
thought to value money more highly than one's friends, for the majority
will not believe that you yourself were not willing to leave prison while
we were eager for you to do so.

SOCRATES: My good Crito, why should we care so much for what the
majority think? The most reasonable people, to whom one should pay
more attention, will believe that things were done as they were done.

CRITO: You see, Socrates, that one must also pay attention to the opinion   d
of the majority. Your present situation makes clear that the majority can
inflict not the least but pretty well the greatest evils if one is slandered
among them.

SOCRATES: Would that the majority could inflict the greatest evils, for
they would then be capable of the greatest good, and that would be fine,
but now they cannot do either. They cannot make a man either wise or
foolish, but they inflict things haphazardly.

---

1. A quotation from *Iliad* ix.363. Achilles has rejected all the presents Agamemnon
offered him to get him to return to the battle, and threatens to go home. He says his
ships will sail in the morning, and with good weather he might arrive on the third day
"in fertile Phthia" (which is his home). The dream means that Socrates' soul, after death,
will find its home on the third day (counting, as usual among the Greeks, both the first
and the last member of the series).

e   CRITO: That may be so. But tell me this, Socrates, are you anticipating that I and your other friends would have trouble with the informers if you escape from here, as having stolen you away, and that we should be compelled to lose all our property or pay heavy fines and suffer other
45   punishment besides? If you have any such fear, forget it. We would be justified in running this risk to save you, and worse, if necessary. Do follow my advice, and do not act differently.

SOCRATES: I do have these things in mind, Crito, and also many others.

CRITO: Have no such fear. It is not much money that some people require to save you and get you out of here. Further, do you not see that those informers are cheap, and that not much money would be needed to deal
b   with them? My money is available and is, I think, sufficient. If, because of your affection for me, you feel you should not spend any of mine, there are those strangers here ready to spend money. One of them, Simmias the Theban, has brought enough for this very purpose. Cebes, too, and a good many others. So, as I say, do not let this fear make you hesitate to save yourself, nor let what you said in court trouble you, that you would not
c   know what to do with yourself if you left Athens, for you would be welcomed in many places to which you might go. If you want to go to Thessaly, I have friends there who will greatly appreciate you and keep you safe, so that no one in Thessaly will harm you.

Besides, Socrates, I do not think that what you are doing is just, to give up your life when you can save it, and to hasten your fate as your enemies would hasten it, and indeed have hastened it in their wish to destroy you.
d   Moreover, I think you are betraying your sons by going away and leaving them, when you could bring them up and educate them. You thus show no concern for what their fate may be. They will probably have the usual fate of orphans. Either one should not have children, or one should share with them to the end the toil of upbringing and education. You seem to me to choose the easiest path, whereas one should choose the path a good and courageous man would choose, particularly when one claims throughout one's life to care for virtue.
e   I feel ashamed on your behalf and on behalf of us, your friends, lest all that has happened to you be thought due to cowardice on our part: the fact that your trial came to court when it need not have done so, the handling of the trial itself, and now this absurd ending which will be thought to have got beyond our control through some cowardice and
46   unmanliness on our part, since we did not save you, or you save yourself, when it was possible and could be done if we had been of the slightest use. Consider, Socrates, whether this is not only evil, but shameful, both for you and for us. Take counsel with yourself, or rather the time for counsel is past and the decision should have been taken, and there is no further opportunity, for this whole business must be ended tonight. If we delay now, then it will no longer be possible; it will be too late. Let me persuade you on every count, Socrates, and do not act otherwise.

SOCRATES: My dear Crito, your eagerness is worth much if it should have   b
some right aim; if not, then the greater your keenness the more difficult
it is to deal with. We must therefore examine whether we should act in
this way or not, as not only now but at all times I am the kind of man
who listens to nothing within me but the argument that on reflection seems
best to me. I cannot, now that this fate has come upon me, discard the
arguments I used; they seem to me much the same. I value and respect   c
the same principles as before, and if we have no better arguments to bring
up at this moment, be sure that I shall not agree with you, not even if the
power of the majority were to frighten us with more bogeys, as if we were
children, with threats of incarcerations and executions and confiscation of
property. How should we examine this matter most reasonably? Would
it be by taking up first your argument about the opinions of men, whether   d
it is sound in every case that one should pay attention to some opinions,
but not to others? Or was that well-spoken before the necessity to die came
upon me, but now it is clear that this was said in vain for the sake of
argument, that it was in truth play and nonsense? I am eager to examine
together with you, Crito, whether this argument will appear in any way
different to me in my present circumstances, or whether it remains the
same, whether we are to abandon it or believe it. It was said on every
occasion by those who thought they were speaking sensibly, as I have just   e
now been speaking, that one should greatly value some people's opinions,
but not others. Does that seem to you a sound statement?

You, as far as a human being can tell, are exempt from the likelihood
of dying tomorrow, so the present misfortune is not likely to lead you   47
astray. Consider then, do you not think it a sound statement that one must
not value all the opinions of men, but some and not others, nor the opinions
of all men, but those of some and not of others? What do you say? Is this
not well said?

CRITO: It is.

SOCRATES: One should value the good opinions, and not the bad ones?

CRITO: Yes.

SOCRATES: The good opinions are those of wise men, the bad ones those
of foolish men?

CRITO: Of course.

SOCRATES: Come then, what of statements such as this: Should a man
professionally engaged in physical training pay attention to the praise and   b
blame and opinion of any man, or to those of one man only, namely a
doctor or trainer?

CRITO: To those of one only.

SOCRATES: He should therefore fear the blame and welcome the praise
of that one man, and not those of the many?

CRITO: Obviously.

SOCRATES: He must then act and exercise, eat and drink in the way the
one, the trainer and the one who knows, thinks right, not all the others?

CRITO: That is so.

c SOCRATES: Very well. And if he disobeys the one, disregards his opinion and his praises while valuing those of the many who have no knowledge, will he not suffer harm?

CRITO: Of course.

SOCRATES: What is that harm, where does it tend, and what part of the man who disobeys does it affect?

CRITO: Obviously the harm is to his body, which it ruins.

SOCRATES: Well said. So with other matters, not to enumerate them all, and certainly with actions just and unjust, shameful and beautiful, good

d and bad, about which we are now deliberating, should we follow the opinion of the many and fear it, or that of the one, if there is one who has knowledge of these things and before whom we feel fear and shame more than before all the others. If we do not follow his directions, we shall harm and corrupt that part of ourselves that is improved by just actions and destroyed by unjust actions. Or is there nothing in this?

CRITO: I think there certainly is, Socrates.

SOCRATES: Come now, if we ruin that which is improved by health and corrupted by disease by not following the opinions of those who know,

e is life worth living for us when that is ruined? And that is the body, is it not?

CRITO: Yes.

SOCRATES: And is life worth living with a body that is corrupted and in bad condition?

CRITO: In no way.

SOCRATES: And is life worth living for us with that part of us corrupted that unjust action harms and just action benefits? Or do we think that part

48 of us, whatever it is, that is concerned with justice and injustice, is inferior to the body?

CRITO: Not at all.

SOCRATES: It is more valuable?

CRITO: Much more.

SOCRATES: We should not then think so much of what the majority will say about us, but what he will say who understands justice and injustice, the one, that is, and the truth itself. So that, in the first place, you were wrong to believe that we should care for the opinion of the many about what is just, beautiful, good, and their opposites. "But," someone might say, "the many are able to put us to death."

b CRITO: That too is obvious, Socrates, and someone might well say so.

SOCRATES: And, my admirable friend, that argument that we have gone through remains, I think, as before. Examine the following statement in turn as to whether it stays the same or not, that the most important thing is not life, but the good life.

CRITO: It stays the same.

SOCRATES: And that the good life, the beautiful life, and the just life are the same; does that still hold, or not?

CRITO: It does hold.

SOCRATES: As we have agreed so far, we must examine next whether it is just for me to try to get out of here when the Athenians have not acquitted me. If it is seen to be just, we will try to do so; if it is not, we will abandon the idea. As for those questions you raise about money, reputation, the upbringing of children, Crito, those considerations in truth belong to those people who easily put men to death and would bring them to life again if they could, without thinking; I mean the majority of men. For us, however, since our argument leads to this, the only valid consideration, as we were saying just now, is whether we should be acting rightly in giving money and gratitude to those who will lead me out of here, and ourselves helping with the escape, or whether in truth we shall do wrong in doing all this. If it appears that we shall be acting unjustly, then we have no need at all to take into account whether we shall have to die if we stay here and keep quiet, or suffer in another way, rather than do wrong.

CRITO: I think you put that beautifully, Socrates, but see what we should do.

SOCRATES: Let us examine the question together, my dear friend, and if you can make any objection while I am speaking, make it and I will listen to you, but if you have no objection to make, my dear Crito, then stop now from saying the same thing so often, that I must leave here against the will of the Athenians. I think it important to persuade you before I act, and not to act against your wishes. See whether the start of our inquiry is adequately stated, and try to answer what I ask you in the way you think best.

CRITO: I shall try.

SOCRATES: Do we say that one must never in any way do wrong willingly, or must one do wrong in one way and not in another? Is to do wrong never good or admirable, as we have agreed in the past, or have all these former agreements been washed out during the last few days? Have we at our age failed to notice for some time that in our serious discussions we were no different from children? Above all, is the truth such as we used to say it was, whether the majority agree or not, and whether we must still suffer worse things than we do now, or will be treated more gently, that nonetheless, wrongdoing or injustice is in every way harmful and shameful to the wrongdoer? Do we say so or not?

CRITO: We do.

SOCRATES: So one must never do wrong.

CRITO: Certainly not.

SOCRATES: Nor must one, when wronged, inflict wrong in return, as the majority believe, since one must never do wrong.

CRITO: That seems to be the case.

SOCRATES: Come now, should one mistreat anyone or not, Crito?

CRITO: One must never do so.

SOCRATES: Well then, if one is oneself mistreated, is it right, as the majority say, to mistreat in return, or is it not?

CRITO: It is never right.

SOCRATES: Mistreating people is no different from wrongdoing.

CRITO: That is true.

SOCRATES: One should never do wrong in return, nor mistreat any man,
d   no matter how one has been mistreated by him. And Crito, see that you do
not agree to this, contrary to your belief. For I know that only a few people
hold this view or will hold it, and there is no common ground between those
who hold this view and those who do not, but they inevitably despise each
other's views. So then consider very carefully whether we have this view in
common, and whether you agree, and let this be the basis of our deliberation,
that neither to do wrong nor to return a wrong is ever right, nor is bad treatment in return for bad treatment. Or do you disagree and do not share this
e   view as a basis for discussion? I have held it for a long time and still hold it
now, but if you think otherwise, tell me now. If, however, you stick to our
former opinion, then listen to the next point.

CRITO: I stick to it and agree with you. So say on.

SOCRATES: Then I state the next point, or rather I ask you: when one has
come to an agreement that is just with someone, should one fulfill it or
cheat on it?

CRITO: One should fulfill it.

SOCRATES: See what follows from this: if we leave here without the city's
50   permission, are we mistreating people whom we should least mistreat?
And are we sticking to a just agreement, or not?

CRITO: I cannot answer your question, Socrates. I do not know.

SOCRATES: Look at it this way. If, as we were planning to run away from
here, or whatever one should call it, the laws and the state came and
confronted us and asked: "Tell me, Socrates, what are you intending to
do? Do you not by this action you are attempting intend to destroy us,
b   the laws, and indeed the whole city, as far as you are concerned? Or do
you think it possible for a city not to be destroyed if the verdicts of
its courts have no force but are nullified and set at naught by private
individuals?" What shall we answer to this and other such arguments?
For many things could be said, especially by an orator on behalf of this
law we are destroying, which orders that the judgments of the courts shall
c   be carried out. Shall we say in answer, "The city wronged me, and its
decision was not right." Shall we say that, or what?

CRITO: Yes, by Zeus, Socrates, that is our answer.

SOCRATES: Then what if the laws said: "Was that the agreement between
us, Socrates, or was it to respect the judgments that the city came to?"
And if we wondered at their words, they would perhaps add: "Socrates,
do not wonder at what we say but answer, since you are accustomed to
d   proceed by question and answer. Come now, what accusation do you
bring against us and the city, that you should try to destroy us? Did we
not, first, bring you to birth, and was it not through us that your father
married your mother and begat you? Tell you, do you find anything to
criticize in those of us who are concerned with marriage?" And I would
say that I do not criticize them. "Or in those of us concerned with the

nurture of babies and the education that you too received? Were those assigned to that subject not right to instruct your father to educate you in the arts and in physical culture?" And I would say that they were right. "Very well," they would continue, "and after you were born and nurtured and educated, could you, in the first place, deny that you are our offspring and servant, both you and your forefathers? If that is so, do you think that we are on an equal footing as regards the right, and that whatever we do to you it is right for you to do to us? You were not on an equal footing with your father as regards the right, nor with your master if you had one, so as to retaliate for anything they did to you, to revile them if they reviled you, to beat them if they beat you, and so with many other things. Do you think you have this right to retaliation against your country and its laws? That if we undertake to destroy you and think it right to do so, you can undertake to destroy us, as far as you can, in return? And will you say that you are right to do so, you who truly care for virtue? Is your wisdom such as not to realize that your country is to be honored more than your mother, your father and all your ancestors, that it is more to be revered and more sacred, and that it counts for more among the gods and sensible men, that you must worship it, yield to it and placate its anger more than your father's? You must either persuade it or obey its orders, and endure in silence whatever it instructs you to endure, whether blows or bonds, and if it leads you into war to be wounded or killed, you must obey. To do so is right, and one must not give way or retreat or leave one's post, but both in war and in courts and everywhere else, one must obey the commands of one's city and country, or persuade it as to the nature of justice. It is impious to bring violence to bear against your mother or father; it is much more so to use it against your country." What shall we say in reply, Crito, that the laws speak the truth, or not?

CRITO: I think they do.

SOCRATES: "Reflect now, Socrates," the laws might say, "that if what we say is true, you are not treating us rightly by planning to do what you are planning. We have given you birth, nurtured you, educated you; we have given you and all other citizens a share of all the good things we could. Even so, by giving every Athenian the opportunity, once arrived at voting age and having observed the affairs of the city and us the laws, we proclaim that if we do not please him, he can take his possessions and go wherever he pleases. Not one of our laws raises any obstacle or forbids him, if he is not satisfied with us or the city, if one of you wants to go and live in a colony or wants to go anywhere else, and keep his property. We say, however, that whoever of you remains, when he sees how we conduct our trials and manage the city in other ways, has in fact come to an agreement with us to obey our instructions. We say that the one who disobeys does wrong in three ways, first because in us he disobeys his parents, also those who brought him up, and because, in spite of his agreement, he neither obeys us nor, if we do something wrong, does he try to persuade us to do better. Yet we only propose things, we do not

issue savage commands to do whatever we order; we give two alternatives, either to persuade us or to do what we say. He does neither. We do say that you too, Socrates, are open to those charges if you do what you have in mind; you would be among, not the least, but the most guilty of the Athenians." And if I should say "Why so?" they might well be right to upbraid me and say that I am among the Athenians who most definitely
b   came to that agreement with them. They might well say: "Socrates, we have convincing proofs that we and the city were congenial to you. You would not have dwelt here most consistently of all the Athenians if the city had not been exceedingly pleasing to you. You have never left the city, even to see a festival, nor for any other reason except military service; you have never gone to stay in any other city, as people do; you have had
c   no desire to know another city or other laws; we and our city satisfied you.
      "So decisively did you choose us and agree to be a citizen under us. Also, you have had children in this city, thus showing that it was congenial to you. Then at your trial you could have assessed your penalty at exile if you wished, and you are now attempting to do against the city's wishes what you could then have done with her consent. Then you prided yourself that you did not resent death, but you chose, as you said, death in prefer-ence to exile. Now, however, those words do not make you ashamed, and
d   you pay no heed to us, the laws, as you plan to destroy us, and you act like the meanest type of slave by trying to run away, contrary to your commitments and your agreement to live as a citizen under us. First then, answer us on this very point, whether we speak the truth when we say that you agreed, not only in words but by your deeds, to live in accordance with us." What are we to say to that, Crito? Must we not agree?
      CRITO: We must, Socrates.
      SOCRATES: "Surely," they might say, "you are breaking the commitments
e   and agreements that you made with us without compulsion or deceit, and under no pressure of time for deliberation. You have had seventy years during which you could have gone away if you did not like us, and if
53   you thought our agreements unjust. You did not choose to go to Sparta or to Crete, which you are always saying are well governed, nor to any other city, Greek or foreign. You have been away from Athens less than the lame or the blind or other handicapped people. It is clear that the city has been outstandingly more congenial to you than to other Athenians, and so have we, the laws, for what city can please without laws? Will you then not now stick to our agreements? You will, Socrates, if we can persuade you, and not make yourself a laughingstock by leaving the city.
      "For consider what good you will do yourself or your friends by breaking our agreements and committing such a wrong. It is pretty obvious that
b   your friends will themselves be in danger of exile, disfranchisement and loss of property. As for yourself, if you go to one of the nearby cities—Thebes or Megara, both are well governed—you will arrive as an enemy to their government; all who care for their city will look on you with suspicion, as a destroyer of the laws. You will also strengthen the conviction

of the jury that they passed the right sentence on you, for anyone who   c
destroys the laws could easily be thought to corrupt the young and the
ignorant. Or will you avoid cities that are well governed and men who
are civilized? If you do this, will your life be worth living? Will you have
social intercourse with them and not be ashamed to talk to them? And
what will you say? The same as you did here, that virtue and justice are
man's most precious possession, along with lawful behavior and the laws?   d
Do you not think that Socrates would appear to be an unseemly kind of
person? One must think so. Or will you leave those places and go to Crito's
friends in Thessaly? There you will find the greatest license and disorder,
and they may enjoy hearing from you how absurdly you escaped from
prison in some disguise, in a leather jerkin or some other things in which
escapees wrap themselves, thus altering your appearance. Will there be
no one to say that you, likely to live but a short time more, were so greedy
for life that you transgressed the most important laws? Possibly, Socrates, e
if you do not annoy anyone, but if you do, many disgraceful things will
be said about you.

"You will spend your time ingratiating yourself with all men, and be
at their beck and call. What will you do in Thessaly but feast, as if you
had gone to a banquet in Thessaly? As for those conversations of yours
about justice and the rest of virtue, where will they be? You say you want 54
to live for the sake of your children, that you may bring them up and
educate them. How so? Will you bring them up and educate them by
taking them to Thessaly and making strangers of them, that they may
enjoy that too? Or not so, but they will be better brought up and educated
here, while you are alive, though absent? Yes, your friends will look after
them. Will they look after them if you go and live in Thessaly, but not if
you go away to the underworld? If those who profess themselves your
friends are any good at all, one must assume that they will.   b

"Be persuaded by us who have brought you up, Socrates. Do not value
either your children or your life or anything else more than goodness, in
order that when you arrive in Hades you may have all this as your defense
before the rulers there. If you do this deed, you will not think it better or
more just or more pious here, nor will any one of your friends, nor will
it be better for you when you arrive yonder. As it is, you depart, if you
depart, after being wronged not by us, the laws, but by men; but if you   c
depart after shamefully returning wrong for wrong and mistreatment for
mistreatment, after breaking your agreements and commitments with us,
after mistreating those you should mistreat least—yourself, your friends,
your country and us—we shall be angry with you while you are still alive,
and our brothers, the laws of the underworld, will not receive you kindly,
knowing that you tried to destroy us as far as you could. Do not let Crito
persuade you, rather than us, to do what he says."   d

Crito, my dear friend, be assured that these are the words I seem to
hear, as the Corybants seem to hear the music of their flutes, and the echo
of these words resounds in me, and makes it impossible for me to hear

anything else. As far as my present beliefs go, if you speak in opposition to them, you will speak in vain. However, if you think you can accomplish anything, speak.

CRITO: I have nothing to say, Socrates.

SOCRATES: Let it be then, Crito, and let us act in this way, since this is the way the god is leading us.

54e

PHAEDO

Phaedo, *known to the ancients also by the descriptive title* On the Soul, *is a drama about Socrates' last hours and his death in the jail at Athens. On the way back home to Elis, one of his intimates, Phaedo, who was with him then, stops off at Phlius, in the Peloponnese. There he reports it all to a group of Pythagoreans settled there since their expulsion from Southern Italy. The Pythagorean connection is carried further in the dialogue itself, since Socrates' two fellow discussants, Simmias and Cebes—from Thebes, the other city where expelled members of the brotherhood settled—are associates of Philolaus, the leading Pythagorean there. Pythagoreans were noted for their belief in the immortality of the soul and its reincarnation in human or animal form and for the consequent concern to keep one's soul pure by avoiding contamination with the body, so as to win the best possible next life. Socrates weaves all these themes into his own discussion of the immortality of the soul.*

It is noteworthy that these Pythagorean elements are lacking from the Apology, where Socrates expresses himself noncommittally and unconcernedly about the possibility of immortality—and from Crito, *as well as the varied discussions of the soul's virtues in such dialogues as* Euthyphro, Laches, *and* Protagoras. *Those dialogues are of course not records of discussions the historical Socrates actually held, but Plato seems to take particular pains to indicate that* Phaedo *does not give us Socrates' actual last conversation or even one that fits at all closely his actual views. He takes care to tell us that he was not present on the last day: Phaedo says he was ill. Socrates makes much of the human intellect's affinity to eternal Forms of Beauty, Justice, and other normative notions, and of mathematical properties and objects, such as Oddness and Evenness and the integers Two, Three, and the rest, as well as physical forces such as Hot and Cold, all existing in a nonphysical realm accessible only to abstract thought. None of this comports well with Socrates' description of his philosophical interests in the* Apology *or with the way he conducts his inquiries in Plato's 'Socratic' dialogues. It is generally agreed that both the Pythagorean motifs of immortality and purification and the theory of eternal Forms that is linked with them in this dialogue are Plato's own contribution. Indeed, the Phaedo's affinities in philosophical theory go not toward the Socratic dialogues, but to* Symposium *and* Republic. *There is an unmistakable reference to* Meno's *theory of theoretical knowledge (of geometry, and also of the nature of human virtue) as coming by recollection of objects known before birth. But now the claim is made that this recollection is of Forms.*

Phaedo *concludes with a myth, describing the fate of the soul after death. Concluding myths in other dialogues, with which this one should be compared, are those in* Gorgias *and* Republic. *It should also be compared with the myth in Socrates' second speech in the* Phaedrus.

Despite the Platonic innovations in philosophical theory, the Phaedo *presents a famously moving picture of Socrates' deep commitment to philosophy and the philosophical life even, or especially, in the face of an unjustly imposed death.*

J.M.C.

57   ECHECRATES: Were you with Socrates yourself, Phaedo, on the day when he drank the poison in prison, or did someone else tell you about it?

PHAEDO: I was there myself, Echecrates.

ECHECRATES: What are the things he said before he died? And how did he die? I should be glad to hear this. Hardly anyone from Phlius visits
b Athens nowadays, nor has any stranger come from Athens for some time who could give us a clear account of what happened, except that he drank the poison and died, but nothing more.

58   PHAEDO: Did you not even hear how the trial went?

ECHECRATES: Yes, someone did tell us about that, and we wondered that he seems to have died a long time after the trial took place. Why was that, Phaedo?

PHAEDO: That was by chance, Echecrates. The day before the trial, as it happened, the prow of the ship that the Athenians send to Delos had been crowned with garlands.

ECHECRATES: What ship is that?

PHAEDO: It is the ship in which, the Athenians say, Theseus once sailed to Crete, taking with him the two lots of seven victims.[1] He saved them
b and was himself saved. The Athenians vowed then to Apollo, so the story goes, that if they were saved they would send a mission to Delos every year. And from that time to this they send such an annual mission to the god. They have a law to keep the city pure while it lasts, and no execution may take place once the mission has begun until the ship has made its journey to Delos and returned to Athens, and this can sometimes take a
c long time if the winds delay it. The mission begins when the priest of Apollo crowns the prow of the ship, and this happened, as I say, the day before Socrates' trial. That is why Socrates was in prison a long time between his trial and his execution.

Translated by G.M.A. Grube.

1. Legend says that Minos, king of Crete, compelled the Athenians to send seven youths and seven maidens every year to be sacrificed to the Minotaur until Theseus saved them and killed the monster.

ECHECRATES: What about his actual death, Phaedo? What did he say? What did he do? Who of his friends were with him? Or did the authorities not allow them to be present and he died with no friends present?

PHAEDO: By no means. Some were present, in fact, a good many.

d

ECHECRATES: Please be good enough to tell us all that occurred as fully as possible, unless you have some pressing business.

PHAEDO: I have the time and I will try to tell you the whole story, for nothing gives me more pleasure than to call Socrates to mind, whether talking about him myself, or listening to someone else do so.

ECHECRATES: Your hearers will surely be like you in this, Phaedo. So do try to tell us every detail as exactly as you can.

PHAEDO: I certainly found being there an astonishing experience. Although I was witnessing the death of one who was my friend, I had no feeling of pity, for the man appeared happy both in manner and words as he died nobly and without fear, Echecrates, so that it struck me that even in going down to the underworld he was going with the gods' blessing and that he would fare well when he got there, if anyone ever does. That is why I had no feeling of pity, such as would seem natural in my sorrow, nor indeed of pleasure, as we engaged in philosophical discussion as we were accustomed to do—for our arguments were of that sort—but I had a strange feeling, an unaccustomed mixture of pleasure and pain at the same time as I reflected that he was just about to die. All of us present were affected in much the same way, sometimes laughing, then weeping; especially one of us, Apollodorus—you know the man and his ways.

e

59

ECHECRATES: Of course I do.

b

PHAEDO: He was quite overcome; but I was myself disturbed, and so were the others.

ECHECRATES: Who, Phaedo, were those present?

PHAEDO: Among the local people there was Apollodorus, whom I mentioned, Critobulus and his father,[2] also Hermogenes, Epigenes, Aeschines and Antisthenes. Ctesippus of Paeania was there, Menexenus and some others. Plato, I believe, was ill.

ECHECRATES: Were there some foreigners present?

PHAEDO: Yes, Simmias from Thebes with Cebes and Phaedondes, and from Megara, Euclides and Terpsion.

c

ECHECRATES: What about Aristippus and Cleombrotus? Were they there?

PHAEDO: No. They were said to be in Aegina.

---

2. The father of Critobulus is Crito, after whom the dialogue *Crito* is named. Several of the other friends of Socrates mentioned here also appear in other dialogues. Hermogenes is one of the speakers in *Cratylus*. Epigenes is mentioned in *Apology* 33d, as is Aeschines, who was a writer of Socratic dialogues. Menexenus has a part in *Lysis* and has a dialogue named after him; Ctesippus appears in both *Lysis* and *Euthydemus*. Euclides and Terpsion are speakers in the introductory conversation of *Theaetetus*, and Euclides too wrote Socratic dialogues. Simmias and Cebes are mentioned in *Crito*, 45b, as having come to Athens with enough money to secure Socrates' escape.

ECHECRATES: Was there anyone else?

PHAEDO: I think these were about all.

ECHECRATES: Well then, what do you say the conversation was about?

PHAEDO: I will try to tell you everything from the beginning. On the
d   previous days also both the others and I used to visit Socrates. We foregath-
ered at daybreak at the court where the trial took place, for it was close
to the prison, and each day we used to wait around talking until the prison
should open, for it did not open early. When it opened we used to go in
to Socrates and spend most of the day with him. On this day we gathered
e   rather early, because when we left the prison on the previous evening we
were informed that the ship from Delos had arrived, and so we told each
other to come to the usual place as early as possible. When we arrived
the gatekeeper who used to answer our knock came out and told us to
wait and not go in until he told us to. "The Eleven,"[3] he said, "are freeing
Socrates from his bonds and telling him how his death will take place
60   today." After a short time he came and told us to go in. We found Socrates
recently released from his chains, and Xanthippe—you know her—sitting
by him, holding their baby. When she saw us, she cried out and said the
sort of thing that women usually say: "Socrates, this is the last time your
friends will talk to you and you to them." Socrates looked at Crito. "Crito,"
he said, "let someone take her home." And some of Crito's people led her
b   away lamenting and beating her breast.

Socrates sat up on the bed, bent his leg and rubbed it with his hand,
and as he rubbed he said: "What a strange thing that which men call
pleasure seems to be, and how astonishing the relation it has with what
is thought to be its opposite, namely pain! A man cannot have both at the
same time. Yet if he pursues and catches the one, he is almost always
bound to catch the other also, like two creatures with one head. I think
c   that if Aesop had noted this he would have composed a fable that a god
wished to reconcile their opposition but could not do so, so he joined their
two heads together, and therefore when a man has the one, the other
follows later. This seems to be happening to me. My bonds caused pain
in my leg, and now pleasure seems to be following."

Cebes intervened and said: "By Zeus, yes, Socrates, you did well to
remind me. Evenus[4] asked me the day before yesterday, as others had
d   done before, what induced you to write poetry after you came to prison,
you who had never composed any poetry before, putting the fables of
Aesop into verse and composing the hymn to Apollo. If it is of any concern
to you that I should have an answer to give to Evenus when he repeats
his question, as I know he will, tell me what to say to him."

Tell him the truth, Cebes, he said, that I did not do this with the idea
of rivaling him or his poems, for I knew that would not be easy, but I

---

3. The Eleven were the police commissioners of Athens.

4. Socrates refers to Evenus as a Sophist and teacher of the young in *Apology* 20a, c.

tried to find out the meaning of certain dreams and to satisfy my conscience   e
in case it was this kind of art they were frequently bidding me to practice.
The dreams were something like this: the same dream often came to me
in the past, now in one shape now in another, but saying the same thing:
"Socrates," it said, "practice and cultivate the arts." In the past I imagined
that it was instructing and advising me to do what I was doing, such as
those who encourage runners in a race, that the dream was thus bidding   61
me do the very thing I was doing, namely, to practice the art of philosophy,
this being the highest kind of art, and I was doing that.

But now, after my trial took place, and the festival of the god was
preventing my execution, I thought that, in case my dream was bidding
me to practice this popular art, I should not disobey it but compose poetry.
I thought it safer not to leave here until I had satisfied my conscience by   b
writing poems in obedience to the dream. So I first wrote in honor of the
god of the present festival. After that I realized that a poet, if he is to be
a poet, must compose fables, not arguments. Being no teller of fables
myself, I took the stories I knew and had at hand, the fables of Aesop,
and I versified the first ones I came across. Tell this to Evenus, Cebes, wish
him well and bid him farewell, and tell him, if he is wise, to follow me
as soon as possible. I am leaving today, it seems, as the Athenians so order it.   c

Said Simmias: "What kind of advice is this you are giving to Evenus,
Socrates? I have met him many times, and from my observation he is not
at all likely to follow it willingly."

How so, said he, is Evenus not a philosopher?

I think so, Simmias said.

Then Evenus will be willing, like every man who partakes worthily of
philosophy. Yet perhaps he will not take his own life, for that, they say,
is not right. As he said this, Socrates put his feet on the ground and   d
remained in this position during the rest of the conversation.

Then Cebes asked: "How do you mean Socrates, that it is not right to
do oneself violence, and yet that the philosopher will be willing to follow
one who is dying?"

Come now, Cebes, have you and Simmias, who keep company with
Philolaus,[5] not heard about such things?

Nothing definite, Socrates.

Indeed, I too speak about this from hearsay, but I do not mind telling
you what I have heard, for it is perhaps most appropriate for one who is
about to depart yonder to tell and examine tales about what we believe   e
that journey to be like. What else could one do in the time we have
until sunset?

But whatever is the reason, Socrates, for people to say that it is not right
to kill oneself? As to your question just now, I have heard Philolaus say
this when staying in Thebes and I have also heard it from others, but I
have never heard anyone give a clear account of the matter.

---

5. See Introductory Note.

62   Well, he said, we must do our best, and you may yet hear one. And it
may well astonish you if this subject, alone of all things, is simple, and it
is never, as with everything else, better at certain times and for certain
people to die than to live. And if this is so, you may well find it astonishing
that those for whom it is better to die are wrong to help themselves, and
that they must wait for someone else to benefit them.

And Cebes, lapsing into his own dialect, laughed quietly and said: "Zeus
knows it is."

b   Indeed, said Socrates, it does seem unreasonable when put like that, but
perhaps there is reason to it. There is the explanation that is put in the
language of the mysteries, that we men are in a kind of prison, and that
one must not free oneself or run away. That seems to me an impressive
doctrine and one not easy to understand fully. However, Cebes, this seems
to me well expressed, that the gods are our guardians and that men are
one of their possessions. Or do you not think so?

I do, said Cebes.

And would you not be angry if one of your possessions killed itself
c   when you had not given any sign that you wished it to die, and if you
had any punishment you could inflict, you would inflict it?

Certainly, he said.

Perhaps then, put in this way, it is not unreasonable that one should
not kill oneself before a god had indicated some necessity to do so, like
the necessity now put upon us.

d   That seems likely, said Cebes. As for what you were saying, that philosophers should be willing and ready to die, that seems strange, Socrates, if
what we said just now is reasonable, namely, that a god is our protector
and that we are his possessions. It is not logical that the wisest of men
should not resent leaving this service in which they are governed by the
best of masters, the gods, for a wise man cannot believe that he will look
after himself better when he is free. A foolish man might easily think so,
e   that he must escape from his master; he would not reflect that one must
not escape from a good master but stay with him as long as possible,
because it would be foolish to escape. But the sensible man would want
always to remain with one better than himself. So, Socrates, the opposite
of what was said before is likely to be true; the wise would resent dying,
whereas the foolish would rejoice at it.

I thought that when Socrates heard this he was pleased by Cebes' argu-
63   mentation. Glancing at us, he said: "Cebes is always on the track of some
arguments; he is certainly not willing to be at once convinced by what
one says."

Said Simmias: "But actually, Socrates, I think myself that Cebes has a
point now. Why should truly wise men want to avoid the service of masters
better than themselves, and leave them easily? And I think Cebes is aiming
his argument at you, because you are bearing leaving us so lightly, and
leaving those good masters, as you say yourself, the gods."

You are both justified in what you say, and I think you mean that I   b
must make a defense against this, as if I were in court.

You certainly must, said Simmias.

Come then, he said, let me try to make my defense to you more convincing than it was to the jury. For, Simmias and Cebes, I should be wrong
not to resent dying if I did not believe that I should go first to other wise
and good gods, and then to men who have died and are better than men
are here. Be assured that, as it is, I expect to join the company of good   c
men. This last I would not altogether insist on, but if I insist on anything
at all in these matters, it is that I shall come to gods who are very good
masters. That is why I am not so resentful, because I have good hope that
some future awaits men after death, as we have been told for years, a
much better future for the good than for the wicked.

Well now, Socrates, said Simmias, do you intend to keep this belief to
yourself as you leave us, or would you share it with us? I certainly think   d
it would be a blessing for us too, and at the same time it would be your
defense if you convince us of what you say.

I will try, he said, but first let us see what it is that Crito here has, I
think, been wanting to say for quite a while.

What else, Socrates, said Crito, but what the man who is to give you
the poison has been telling me for some time, that I should warn you to
talk as little as possible. People get heated when they talk, he says, and
one should not be heated when taking the poison, as those who do must   e
sometimes drink it two or three times.

Socrates replied: "Take no notice of him; only let him be prepared to
administer it twice or, if necessary, three times."

I was rather sure you would say that, Crito said, but he has been bothering me for some time.

Let him be, he said. I want to make my argument before you, my judges,
as to why I think that a man who has truly spent his life in philosophy is
probably right to be of good cheer in the face of death and to be very
hopeful that after death he will attain the greatest blessings yonder. I will   64
try to tell you, Simmias and Cebes, how this may be so. I am afraid that other
people do not realize that the one aim of those who practice philosophy in
the proper manner is to practice for dying and death. Now if this is true,
it would be strange indeed if they were eager for this all their lives and
then resent it when what they have wanted and practiced for a long time
comes upon them.

Simmias laughed and said: "By Zeus, Socrates, you made me laugh,
though I was in no laughing mood just now. I think that the majority, on   b
hearing this, will think that it describes the philosophers very well, and
our people in Thebes would thoroughly agree that philosophers are nearly
dead and that the majority of men is well aware that they deserve to be.

And they would be telling the truth, Simmias, except for their being
aware. They are not aware of the way true philosophers are nearly dead,

c   nor of the way they deserve to be, nor of the sort of death they deserve. But never mind them, he said, let us talk among ourselves. Do we believe that there is such a thing as death?

Certainly, said Simmias.

Is it anything else than the separation of the soul from the body? Do we believe that death is this, namely, that the body comes to be separated by itself apart from the soul, and the soul comes to be separated by itself apart from the body? Is death anything else than that?

No, that is what it is, he said.

Consider then, my good sir, whether you share my opinion, for this will
d   lead us to a better knowledge of what we are investigating. Do you think it is the part of a philosopher to be concerned with such so-called pleasures as those of food and drink?

By no means.

What about the pleasures of sex?

Not at all.

What of the other pleasures concerned with the service of the body? Do you think such a man prizes them greatly, the acquisition of distinguished clothes and shoes and the other bodily ornaments? Do you think he values
e   these or despises them, except in so far as one cannot do without them?

I think the true philosopher despises them.

Do you not think, he said, that in general such a man's concern is not with the body but that, as far as he can, he turns away from the body towards the soul?

I do.

65   So in the first place, such things show clearly that the philosopher more than other men frees the soul from association with the body as much as possible?

Apparently.

A man who finds no pleasure in such things and has no part in them is thought by the majority not to deserve to live and to be close to death; the man, that is, who does not care for the pleasures of the body.

What you say is certainly true.

Then what about the actual acquiring of knowledge? Is the body an obstacle when one associates with it in the search for knowledge? I mean,
b   for example, do men find any truth in sight or hearing, or are not even the poets forever telling us that we do not see or hear anything accurately, and surely if those two physical senses are not clear or precise, our other senses can hardly be accurate, as they are all inferior to these. Do you not think so?

I certainly do, he said.

When then, he asked, does the soul grasp the truth? For whenever it attempts to examine anything with the body, it is clearly deceived by it.
c   True.

Is it not in reasoning if anywhere that any reality becomes clear to the soul?

Yes.

And indeed the soul reasons best when none of these senses troubles it, neither hearing nor sight, nor pain nor pleasure, but when it is most by itself, taking leave of the body and as far as possible having no contact or association with it in its search for reality.

That is so.

And it is then that the soul of the philosopher most disdains the body,   d
flees from it and seeks to be by itself?

It appears so.

What about the following, Simmias? Do we say that there is such a thing as the Just itself, or not?

We do say so, by Zeus.

And the Beautiful, and the Good?

Of course.

And have you ever seen any of these things with your eyes?

In no way, he said.

Or have you ever grasped them with any of your bodily senses? I am speaking of all things such as Bigness, Health, Strength and, in a word, the reality of all other things, that which each of them essentially is. Is what is most true in them contemplated through the body, or is this the   e
position: whoever of us prepares himself best and most accurately to grasp that thing itself which he is investigating will come closest to the knowledge of it?

Obviously.

Then he will do this most perfectly who approaches the object with thought alone, without associating any sight with his thought, or dragging   66
in any sense perception with his reasoning, but who, using pure thought alone, tries to track down each reality pure and by itself, freeing himself as far as possible from eyes and ears, and in a word, from the whole body, because the body confuses the soul and does not allow it to acquire truth and wisdom whenever it is associated with it. Will not that man reach reality, Simmias, if anyone does?

What you say, said Simmias, is indeed true.

All these things will necessarily make the true philosophers believe and   b
say to each other something like this: "There is likely to be something such as a path to guide us out of our confusion, because as long as we have a body and our soul is fused with such an evil we shall never adequately attain what we desire, which we affirm to be the truth. The body keeps us busy in a thousand ways because of its need for nurture. Moreover, if certain diseases befall it, they impede our search for the truth. It fills us   c
with wants, desires, fears, all sorts of illusions and much nonsense, so that, as it is said, in truth and in fact no thought of any kind ever comes to us from the body. Only the body and its desires cause war, civil discord and battles, for all wars are due to the desire to acquire wealth, and it is the body and the care of it, to which we are enslaved, which compel us to   d
acquire wealth, and all this makes us too busy to practice philosophy.

Worst of all, if we do get some respite from it and turn to some investigation, everywhere in our investigations the body is present and makes for confusion and fear, so that it prevents us from seeing the truth.

e   "It really has been shown to us that, if we are ever to have pure knowledge, we must escape from the body and observe things in themselves with the soul by itself. It seems likely that we shall, only then, when we are dead, attain that which we desire and of which we claim to be lovers, namely, wisdom, as our argument shows, not while we live; for if it is impossible to attain any pure knowledge with the body, then one of two things is true: either we can never attain knowledge or we can do so after

67   death. Then and not before, the soul is by itself apart from the body. While we live, we shall be closest to knowledge if we refrain as much as possible from association with the body and do not join with it more than we must, if we are not infected with its nature but purify ourselves from it until the god himself frees us. In this way we shall escape the contamination of the body's folly; we shall be likely to be in the company of people of the same kind, and by our own efforts we shall know all that is pure, which is

b   presumably the truth, for it is not permitted to the impure to attain the pure."

Such are the things, Simmias, that all those who love learning in the proper manner must say to one another and believe. Or do you not think so?

I certainly do, Socrates.

And if this is true, my friend, said Socrates, there is good hope that on arriving where I am going, if anywhere, I shall acquire what has been our

c   chief preoccupation in our past life, so that the journey that is now ordered for me is full of good hope, as it is also for any other man who believes that his mind has been prepared and, as it were, purified.

It certainly is, said Simmias.

And does purification not turn out to be what we mentioned in our argument some time ago, namely, to separate the soul as far as possible from the body and accustom it to gather itself and collect itself out of

d   every part of the body and to dwell by itself as far as it can both now and in the future, freed, as it were, from the bonds of the body?

Certainly, he said.

And that freedom and separation of the soul from the body is called death?

That is altogether so.

It is only those who practice philosophy in the right way, we say, who always most want to free the soul; and this release and separation of the soul from the body is the preoccupation of the philosophers?

So it appears.

Therefore, as I said at the beginning, it would be ridiculous for a man to train himself in life to live in a state as close to death as possible, and

e   then to resent it when it comes?

Ridiculous, of course.

In fact, Simmias, he said, those who practice philosophy in the right way are in training for dying and they fear death least of all men. Consider it from this point of view: if they are altogether estranged from the body and desire to have their soul by itself, would it not be quite absurd for them to be afraid and resentful when this happens? If they did not gladly set out for a place, where, on arrival, they may hope to attain that for which they had yearned during their lifetime, that is, wisdom, and where they would be rid of the presence of that from which they are estranged?

68

Many men, at the death of their lovers, wives or sons, were willing to go to the underworld, driven by the hope of seeing there those for whose company they longed, and being with them. Will then a true lover of wisdom, who has a similar hope and knows that he will never find it to any extent except in Hades, be resentful of dying and not gladly undertake the journey thither? One must surely think so, my friend, if he is a true philosopher, for he is firmly convinced that he will not find pure knowledge anywhere except there. And if this is so, then, as I said just now, would it not be highly unreasonable for such a man to fear death?

b

It certainly would, by Zeus, he said.

Then you have sufficient indication, he said, that any man whom you see resenting death was not a lover of wisdom but a lover of the body, and also a lover of wealth or of honors, either or both.

c

It is certainly as you say.

And, Simmias, he said, does not what is called courage belong especially to men of this disposition?

Most certainly.

And the quality of moderation which even the majority call by that name, that is, not to get swept off one's feet by one's passions, but to treat them with disdain and orderliness, is this not suited only to those who most of all despise the body and live the life of philosophy?

d

Necessarily so, he said.

If you are willing to reflect on the courage and moderation of other people, you will find them strange.

In what way, Socrates?

You know that they all consider death a great evil?

Definitely, he said.

And the brave among them face death, when they do, for fear of greater evils?

That is so.

Therefore, it is fear and terror that make all men brave, except the philosophers. Yet it is illogical to be brave through fear and cowardice.

It certainly is.

e

What of the moderate among them? Is their experience not similar? Is it license of a kind that makes them moderate? We say this is impossible, yet their experience of this unsophisticated moderation turns out to be similar: they fear to be deprived of other pleasures which they desire, so

they keep away from some pleasures because they are overcome by others. Now to be mastered by pleasure is what they call license, but what happens
69   to them is that they master certain pleasures because they are mastered by others. This is like what we mentioned just now, that in some way it is a kind of license that has made them moderate.

That seems likely.

My good Simmias, I fear this is not the right exchange to attain virtue, to exchange pleasures for pleasures, pains for pains and fears for fears,
b   the greater for the less like coins, but that the only valid currency for which all these things should be exchanged is wisdom. With this we have real courage and moderation and justice and, in a word, true virtue, with wisdom, whether pleasures and fears and all such things be present or absent. Exchanged for one another without wisdom such virtue is only an illusory appearance of virtue; it is in fact fit for slaves, without soundness or truth, whereas, in truth, moderation and courage and justice are a
c   purging away of all such things, and wisdom itself is a kind of cleansing or purification. It is likely that those who established the mystic rites for us were not inferior persons but were speaking in riddles long ago when they said that whoever arrives in the underworld uninitiated and unsanctified will wallow in the mire, whereas he who arrives there purified and initiated will dwell with the gods. There are indeed, as those concerned
d   with the mysteries say, many who carry the thyrsus but the Bacchants are few.[6] These latter are, in my opinion, no other than those who have practiced philosophy in the right way. I have in my life left nothing undone in order to be counted among these as far as possible, as I have been eager to be in every way. Whether my eagerness was right and we accomplished anything we shall, I think, know for certain in a short time, god willing, on arriving yonder.

This is my defense, Simmias and Cebes, that I am likely to be right to
e   leave you and my masters here without resentment or complaint, believing that there, as here, I shall find good masters and good friends. If my defense is more convincing to you than to the Athenian jury, it will be well.

When Socrates finished, Cebes intervened: Socrates, he said, everything
70   else you said is excellent, I think, but men find it very hard to believe what you said about the soul. They think that after it has left the body it no longer exists anywhere, but that it is destroyed and dissolved on the day the man dies, as soon as it leaves the body; and that, on leaving it, it is dispersed like breath or smoke, has flown away and gone and is no longer anything anywhere. If indeed it gathered itself together and existed by itself and escaped those evils you were recently enumerating, there
b   would then be much good hope, Socrates, that what you say is true; but to believe this requires a good deal of faith and persuasive argument, to

---

6. That is, the true worshippers of Dionysus, as opposed to those who only carry the external symbols of his worship.

believe that the soul still exists after a man has died and that it still possesses some capability and intelligence.

What you say is true, Cebes, Socrates said, but what shall we do? Do you want to discuss whether this is likely to be true or not?

Personally, said Cebes, I should like to hear your opinion on the subject.

I do not think, said Socrates, that anyone who heard me now, not even a comic poet, could say that I am babbling and discussing things that do not concern me, so we must examine the question thoroughly, if you think we should do so. Let us examine it in some such a manner as this: whether the souls of men who have died exist in the underworld or not. We recall an ancient theory that souls arriving there come from here, and then again that they arrive here and are born here from the dead. If that is true, that the living come back from the dead, then surely our souls must exist there, for they could not come back if they did not exist, and this is a sufficient proof that these things are so if it truly appears that the living never come from any other source than from the dead. If this is not the case we should need another argument.

Quite so, said Cebes.

Do not, he said, confine yourself to humanity if you want to understand this more readily, but take all animals and all plants into account, and, in short, for all things which come to be, let us see whether they come to be in this way, that is, from their opposites if they have such, as the beautiful is the opposite of the ugly and the just of the unjust, and a thousand other things of the kind. Let us examine whether those that have an opposite must necessarily come to be from their opposite and from nowhere else, as for example when something comes to be larger it must necessarily become larger from having been smaller before.

Yes.

Then if something smaller comes to be, it will come from something larger before, which became smaller?

That is so, he said.

And the weaker comes to be from the stronger, and the swifter from the slower?

Certainly.

Further, if something worse comes to be, does it not come from the better, and the juster from the more unjust?

Of course.

So we have sufficiently established that all things come to be in this way, opposites from opposites?

Certainly.

There is a further point, something such as this, about these opposites: between each of those pairs of opposites there are two processes: from the one to the other and then again from the other to the first; between the larger and the smaller there is increase and decrease, and we call the one increasing and the other decreasing?

Yes, he said.

c

d

e

71

b

And so too there is separation and combination, cooling and heating, and all such things, even if sometimes we do not have a name for the process, but in fact it must be everywhere that they come to be from one another, and that there is a process of becoming from each into the other?

Assuredly, he said.

c   Well then, is there an opposite to living, as sleeping is the opposite of being awake?

Quite so, he said.

What is it?

Being dead, he said.

Therefore, if these are opposites, they come to be from one another, and there are two processes of generation between the two?

Of course.

I will tell you, said Socrates, one of the two pairs I was just talking about, the pair itself and the two processes, and you will tell me the other.

d   I mean, to sleep and to be awake; to be awake comes from sleeping, and to sleep comes from being awake. Of the two processes one is going to sleep, the other is waking up. Do you accept that, or not?

Certainly.

You tell me in the same way about life and death. Do you not say that to be dead is the opposite of being alive?

I do.

And they come to be from one another?

Yes.

What comes to be from being alive?

Being dead.

And what comes to be from being dead?

One must agree that it is being alive.

Then, Cebes, living creatures and things come to be from the dead?

e   So it appears, he said.

Then our souls exist in the underworld.

That seems likely.

Then in this case one of the two processes of becoming is clear, for dying is clear enough, is it not?

It certainly is.

What shall we do then? Shall we not supply the opposite process of becoming? Is nature to be lame in this case? Or must we provide a process of becoming opposite to dying?

We surely must.

And what is that?

Coming to life again.

72   Therefore, he said, if there is such a thing as coming to life again, it would be a process of coming from the dead to the living?

Quite so.

It is agreed between us then that the living come from the dead in this way no less than the dead from the living and, if that is so, it seems to be a sufficient proof that the souls of the dead must be somewhere whence they can come back again.

I think, Socrates, he said, that this follows from what we have agreed on.

Consider in this way, Cebes, he said, that, as I think, we were not wrong to agree. If the two processes of becoming did not always balance each other as if they were going round in a circle, but generation proceeded from one point to its opposite in a straight line and it did not turn back again to the other opposite or take any turning, do you realize that all things would ultimately be in the same state, be affected in the same way, and cease to become?

How do you mean? he said.

It is not hard to understand what I mean. If, for example, there was such a process as going to sleep, but no corresponding process of waking up, you realize that in the end everything would show the story of Endymion[7] to have no meaning. There would be no point to it because everything would have the same experience as he, be asleep. And if everything were combined and nothing separated, the saying of Anaxagoras[8] would soon be true, "that all things were mixed together." In the same way, my dear Cebes, if everything that partakes of life were to die and remain in that state and not come to life again, would not everything ultimately have to be dead and nothing alive? Even if the living came from some other source, and all that lived died, how could all things avoid being absorbed in death?

It could not be, Socrates, said Cebes, and I think what you say is altogether true.

I think, Cebes, said he, that this is very definitely the case and that we were not deceived when we agreed on this: coming to life again in truth exists, the living come to be from the dead, and the souls of the dead exist.

Furthermore, Socrates, Cebes rejoined, such is also the case if that theory is true that you are accustomed to mention frequently, that for us learning is no other than recollection. According to this, we must at some previous time have learned what we now recollect. This is possible only if our soul existed somewhere before it took on this human shape. So according to this theory too, the soul is likely to be something immortal.

Cebes, Simmias interrupted, what are the proofs of this? Remind me, for I do not quite recall them at the moment.

There is one excellent argument, said Cebes, namely that when men are interrogated in the right manner, they always give the right answer of their own accord, and they could not do this if they did not possess the knowledge and the right explanation inside them. Then if one shows them

---

7. Endymion was granted eternal sleep by Zeus.

8. Anaxagoras of Clazomenae was born at the beginning of the fifth century B.C. He came to Athens as a young man and spent most of his life there in the study of natural philosophy. He is quoted later in the dialogue (97c ff.) as claiming that the universe is directed by Mind (*Nous*). The reference here is to his statement that in the original state of the world all its elements were thoroughly commingled.

a diagram or something else of that kind, this will show most clearly that such is the case.[9]

If this does not convince you, Simmias, said Socrates, see whether you agree if we examine it in some such way as this, for do you doubt that what we call learning is recollection?

It is not that I doubt, said Simmias, but I want to experience the very thing we are discussing, recollection, and from what Cebes undertook to say, I am now remembering and am pretty nearly convinced. Nevertheless, I should like to hear now the way you were intending to explain it.

c   This way, he said. We surely agree that if anyone recollects anything, he must have known it before.

Quite so, he said.

Do we not also agree that when knowledge comes to mind in this way, it is recollection? What way do I mean? Like this: when a man sees or hears or in some other way perceives one thing and not only knows that thing but also thinks of another thing of which the knowledge is not the same but different, are we not right to say that he recollects the second thing that comes into his mind?

d   How do you mean?

Things such as this: to know a man is surely a different knowledge from knowing a lyre.

Of course.

Well, you know what happens to lovers: whenever they see a lyre, a garment or anything else that their beloved is accustomed to use, they know the lyre, and the image of the boy to whom it belongs comes into their mind. This is recollection, just as someone, on seeing Simmias, often recollects Cebes, and there are thousands of other such occurrences.

Thousands indeed, said Simmias.

Is this kind of thing not recollection of a kind? he said, especially so
e   when one experiences it about things that one had forgotten, because one had not seen them for some time?—Quite so.

Further, he said, can a man seeing the picture of a horse or a lyre recollect a man, or seeing a picture of Simmias recollect Cebes?—Certainly.

Or seeing a picture of Simmias, recollect Simmias himself?—He certainly can.

74   In all these cases the recollection can be occasioned by things that are similar, but it can also be occasioned by things that are dissimilar?—It can.

When the recollection is caused by similar things, must one not of necessity also experience this: to consider whether the similarity to that which one recollects is deficient in any respect or complete?—One must.

Consider, he said, whether this is the case: we say that there is something that is equal. I do not mean a stick equal to a stick or a stone to a stone,

---

9. Cf. *Meno* 81e ff., where Socrates does precisely that.

or anything of that kind, but something else beyond all these, the Equal itself. Shall we say that this exists or not?

Indeed we shall, by Zeus, said Simmias, most definitely.   b

And do we know what this is?—Certainly.

Whence have we acquired the knowledge of it? Is it not from the things we mentioned just now, from seeing sticks or stones or some other things that are equal we come to think of that other which is different from them? Or doesn't it seem to you to be different? Look at it also this way: do not equal stones and sticks sometimes, while remaining the same, appear to one to be equal and to another to be unequal?—Certainly they do.

But what of the equals themselves? Have they ever appeared unequal   c
to you, or Equality to be Inequality?

Never, Socrates.

These equal things and the Equal itself are therefore not the same?

I do not think they are the same at all, Socrates.

But it is definitely from the equal things, though they are different from that Equal, that you have derived and grasped the knowledge of equality?

Very true, Socrates.

Whether it be like them or unlike them?

Certainly.

It makes no difference. As long as the sight of one thing makes you think of another, whether it be similar or dissimilar, this must of necessity be recollection?   d

Quite so.

Well then, he said, do we experience something like this in the case of equal sticks and the other equal objects we just mentioned? Do they seem to us to be equal in the same sense as what is Equal itself? Is there some deficiency in their being such as the Equal, or is there not?

A considerable deficiency, he said.

Whenever someone, on seeing something, realizes that that which he now sees wants to be like some other reality but falls short and cannot be   e
like that other since it is inferior, do we agree that the one who thinks this must have prior knowledge of that to which he says it is like, but deficiently so?

Necessarily.

Well, do we also experience this about the equal objects and the Equal itself, or do we not?

Very definitely.

We must then possess knowledge of the Equal before that time when we first saw the equal objects and realized that all these objects strive to   75
be like the Equal but are deficient in this.

That is so.

Then surely we also agree that this conception of ours derives from seeing or touching or some other sense perception, and cannot come into our mind in any other way, for all these senses, I say, are the same.

They are the same, Socrates, at any rate in respect to that which our argument wishes to make plain.

b   Our sense perceptions must surely make us realize that all that we perceive through them is striving to reach that which is Equal but falls short of it; or how do we express it?

Like that.

Then before we began to see or hear or otherwise perceive, we must have possessed knowledge of the Equal itself if we were about to refer our sense perceptions of equal objects to it, and realized that all of them were eager to be like it, but were inferior.

That follows from what has been said, Socrates.

But we began to see and hear and otherwise perceive right after birth?

Certainly.

c   We must then have acquired the knowledge of the Equal before this.

Yes.

It seems then that we must have possessed it before birth.

It seems so.

Therefore, if we had this knowledge, we knew before birth and immediately after not only the Equal, but the Greater and the Smaller and all such things, for our present argument is no more about the Equal than about

d   the Beautiful itself, the Good itself, the Just, the Pious and, as I say, about all those things which we mark with the seal of "what it is," both when we are putting questions and answering them. So we must have acquired knowledge of them all before we were born.

That is so.

If, having acquired this knowledge in each case, we have not forgotten it, we remain knowing and have knowledge throughout our life, for to know is to acquire knowledge, keep it and not lose it. Do we not call the losing of knowledge forgetting?

e   Most certainly, Socrates, he said.

But, I think, if we acquired this knowledge before birth, then lost it at birth, and then later by the use of our senses in connection with those objects we mentioned, we recovered the knowledge we had before, would not what we call learning be the recovery of our own knowledge, and we are right to call this recollection?

Certainly.

76   It was seen to be possible for someone to see or hear or otherwise perceive something, and by this to be put in mind of something else which he had forgotten and which is related to it by similarity or difference. One of two things follows, as I say: either we were born with the knowledge of it, and all of us know it throughout life, or those who later, we say, are learning, are only recollecting, and learning would be recollection.

That is certainly the case, Socrates.

Which alternative do you choose, Simmias? That we are born with

b   this knowledge or that we recollect later the things of which we had knowledge previously?

I have no means of choosing at the moment, Socrates.

Well, can you make this choice? What is your opinion about it? A man who has knowledge would be able to give an account of what he knows, or would he not?

He must certainly be able to do so, Socrates, he said.

And do you think everybody can give an account of the things we were mentioning just now?

I wish they could, said Simmias, but I'm afraid it is much more likely that by this time tomorrow there will be no one left who can do so adequately.

So you do not think that everybody has knowledge of those things?   c

No indeed.

So they recollect what they once learned?

They must.

When did our souls acquire the knowledge of them? Certainly not since we were born as men.

Indeed no.

Before that then?

Yes.

So then, Simmias, our souls also existed apart from the body before they took on human form, and they had intelligence.

Unless we acquire the knowledge at the moment of birth, Socrates, for that time is still left to us.

Quite so, my friend, but at what other time do we lose it? We just now   d
agreed that we are not born with that knowledge. Do we then lose it at the very time we acquire it, or can you mention any other time?

I cannot, Socrates. I did not realize that I was talking nonsense.

So this is our position, Simmias? he said. If those realities we are always talking about exist, the Beautiful and the Good and all that kind of reality, and we refer all the things we perceive to that reality, discovering that it existed before and is ours, and we compare these things with it, then, just   e
as they exist, so our soul must exist before we are born. If these realities do not exist, then this argument is altogether futile. Is this the position, that there is an equal necessity for those realities to exist, and for our souls to exist before we were born? If the former do not exist, neither do the latter?

I do not think, Socrates, said Simmias, that there is any possible doubt that it is equally necessary for both to exist, and it is opportune that our argument comes to the conclusion that our soul exists before we are born,   77
and equally so that reality of which you are now speaking. Nothing is so evident to me personally as that all such things must certainly exist, the Beautiful, the Good, and all those you mentioned just now. I also think that sufficient proof of this has been given.

Then what about Cebes? said Socrates, for we must persuade Cebes also.

He is sufficiently convinced I think, said Simmias, though he is the most difficult of men to persuade by argument, but I believe him to be fully convinced that our soul existed before we were born. I do not think myself,   b
however, that it has been proved that the soul continues to exist after

death; the opinion of the majority which Cebes mentioned still stands, that when a man dies his soul is dispersed and this is the end of its existence. What is to prevent the soul coming to be and being constituted from some other source, existing before it enters a human body and then, having done so and departed from it, itself dying and being destroyed?

c   You are right, Simmias, said Cebes. Half of what needed proof has been proved, namely, that our soul existed before we were born, but further proof is needed that it exists no less after we have died, if the proof is to be complete.

It has been proved even now, Simmias and Cebes, said Socrates, if you are ready to combine this argument with the one we agreed on before, that every living thing must come from the dead. If the soul exists before,
d   it must, as it comes to life and birth, come from nowhere else than death and being dead, so how could it avoid existing after death since it must be born again? What you speak of has then even now been proved. However, I think you and Simmias would like to discuss the argument more fully. You seem to have this childish fear that the wind would really dissolve
e   and scatter the soul, as it leaves the body, especially if one happens to die in a high wind and not in calm weather.

Cebes laughed and said: Assuming that we were afraid, Socrates, try to change our minds, or rather do not assume that we are afraid, but perhaps there is a child in us who has these fears; try to persuade him not to fear death like a bogey.

You should, said Socrates, sing a charm over him every day until you have charmed away his fears.

78   Where shall we find a good charmer for these fears, Socrates, he said, now that you are leaving us?

Greece is a large country, Cebes, he said, and there are good men in it; the tribes of foreigners are also numerous. You should search for such a charmer among them all, sparing neither trouble nor expense, for there is nothing on which you could spend your money to greater advantage. You must also search among yourselves, for you might not easily find people who could do this better than yourselves.

b   That shall be done, said Cebes, but let us, if it pleases you, go back to the argument where we left it.

Of course it pleases me.

Splendid, he said.

We must then ask ourselves something like this: what kind of thing is likely to be scattered? On behalf of what kind of thing should one fear this, and for what kind of thing should one not fear it? We should then examine to which class the soul belongs, and as a result either fear for the soul or be of good cheer.

What you say is true.

c   Is not anything that is composite and a compound by nature liable to be split up into its component parts, and only that which is noncomposite, if anything, is not likely to be split up?

I think that is the case, said Cebes.

Are not the things that always remain the same and in the same state most likely not to be composite, whereas those that vary from one time to another and are never the same are composite?

I think that is so.

Let us then return to those same things with which we were dealing earlier, to that reality of whose existence we are giving an account in our d
questions and answers; are they ever the same and in the same state, or do they vary from one time to another; can the Equal itself, the Beautiful itself, each thing in itself, the real, ever be affected by any change whatever? Or does each of them that really is, being uniform by itself, remain the same and never in any way tolerate any change whatever?

It must remain the same, said Cebes, and in the same state, Socrates.

What of the many beautiful particulars, be they men, horses, clothes, or e
other such things, or the many equal particulars, and all those which bear the same name as those others? Do they remain the same or, in total contrast to those other realities, one might say, never in any way remain the same as themselves or in relation to each other?

The latter is the case, they are never in the same state.

These latter you could touch and see and perceive with the other senses, 79
but those that always remain the same can only be grasped by the reasoning power of the mind? They are not seen but are invisible?

That is altogether true, he said.

Do you then want us to assume two kinds of existences, the visible and the invisible?

Let us assume this.

And the invisible always remains the same, whereas the visible never does?

Let us assume that too.

Now one part of ourselves is the body, another part is the soul? b

Quite so.

To which class of existence do we say the body is more alike and akin?

To the visible, as anyone can see.

What about the soul? Is it visible or invisible?

It is not visible to men, Socrates, he said.

Well, we meant visible and invisible to human eyes; or to any others, do you think?

To human eyes.

Then what do we say about the soul? Is it visible or not visible?

Not visible.

So it is invisible?—Yes.

So the soul is more like the invisible than the body, and the body more c
like the visible?—Without any doubt, Socrates.

Haven't we also said some time ago that when the soul makes use of the body to investigate something, be it through hearing or seeing or some other sense—for to investigate something through the body is to do it through the senses—it is dragged by the body to the things that are never the same, and the soul itself strays and is confused and dizzy, as if it were drunk, in so far as it is in contact with that kind of thing?

Certainly.

d   But when the soul investigates by itself it passes into the realm of what is pure, ever existing, immortal and unchanging, and being akin to this, it always stays with it whenever it is by itself and can do so; it ceases to stray and remains in the same state as it is in touch with things of the same kind, and its experience then is what is called wisdom?

Altogether well said and very true, Socrates, he said.

e   Judging from what we have said before and what we are saying now, to which of these two kinds do you think that the soul is more alike and more akin?

I think, Socrates, he said, that on this line of argument any man, even the dullest, would agree that the soul is altogether more like that which always exists in the same state rather than like that which does not.

What of the body?

That is like the other.

80   Look at it also this way: when the soul and the body are together, nature orders the one to be subject and to be ruled, and the other to rule and be master. Then again, which do you think is like the divine and which like the mortal? Do you not think that the nature of the divine is to rule and to lead, whereas it is that of the mortal to be ruled and be subject?

I do.

Which does the soul resemble?

Obviously, Socrates, the soul resembles the divine, and the body resembles the mortal.

Consider then, Cebes, whether it follows from all that has been said that

b   the soul is most like the divine, deathless, intelligible, uniform, indissoluble, always the same as itself, whereas the body is most like that which is human, mortal, multiform, unintelligible, soluble and never consistently the same. Have we anything else to say to show, my dear Cebes, that this is not the case?

We have not.

Well then, that being so, is it not natural for the body to dissolve easily, and for the soul to be altogether indissoluble, or nearly so?

c   Of course.

You realize, he said, that when a man dies, the visible part, the body, which exists in the visible world, and which we call the corpse, whose natural lot it would be to dissolve, fall apart and be blown away, does not immediately suffer any of these things but remains for a fair time, in fact, quite a long time if the man dies with his body in a suitable condition and at a favorable season? If the body is emaciated or embalmed, as in Egypt, it remains almost whole for a remarkable length

d   of time, and even if the body decays, some parts of it, namely bones and sinews and the like, are nevertheless, one might say, deathless. Is that not so?—Yes.

Will the soul, the invisible part which makes its way to a region of the same kind, noble and pure and invisible, to Hades in fact, to the good and wise god whither, god willing, my soul must soon be going—will the soul, being of this kind and nature, be scattered and destroyed on leaving the body, as the majority of men say? Far from it, my dear Cebes and Simmias, but what   e
happens is much more like this: if it is pure when it leaves the body and drags nothing bodily with it, as it had no willing association with the body in life, but avoided it and gathered itself together by itself and always practiced this, which is no other than practising philosophy in the right way, in fact,   81
training to die easily. Or is this not training for death?

It surely is.

A soul in this state makes its way to the invisible, which is like itself, the divine and immortal and wise, and arriving there it can be happy, having rid itself of confusion, ignorance, fear, violent desires and the other human ills and, as is said of the initiates, truly spend the rest of time with the gods. Shall we say this, Cebes, or something different?

This, by Zeus, said Cebes.

But I think that if the soul is polluted and impure when it leaves the   b
body, having always been associated with it and served it, bewitched by physical desires and pleasures to the point at which nothing seems to exist for it but the physical, which one can touch and see or eat and drink or make use of for sexual enjoyment, and if that soul is accustomed to hate and fear and avoid that which is dim and invisible to the eyes but intelligible and to be grasped by philosophy—do you think such a soul will escape pure and by itself?

Impossible, he said.   c

It is no doubt permeated by the physical, which constant intercourse and association with the body, as well as considerable practice, has caused to become ingrained in it?

Quite so.

We must believe, my friend, that this bodily element is heavy, ponderous, earthy and visible. Through it, such a soul has become heavy and is dragged back to the visible region in fear of the unseen and of Hades. It wanders, as we are told, around graves and monuments, where shadowy phantoms,   d
images that such souls produce, have been seen, souls that have not been freed and purified but share in the visible, and are therefore seen.

That is likely, Socrates.

It is indeed, Cebes. Moreover, these are not the souls of good but of inferior men, which are forced to wander there, paying the penalty for their previous bad upbringing. They wander until their longing for that   e
which accompanies them, the physical, again imprisons them in a body, and they are then, as is likely, bound to such characters as they have practiced in their life.

What kind of characters do you say these are, Socrates?

Those, for example, who have carelessly practiced gluttony, violence and drunkenness are likely to join a company of donkeys or of similar animals. Do you not think so?   82

Very likely.

Those who have esteemed injustice highly, and tyranny and plunder will join the tribes of wolves and hawks and kites, or where else shall we say that they go?

Certainly to those, said Cebes.

And clearly, the destination of the others will conform to the way in which they have behaved?

Clearly, of course.

b   The happiest of these, who will also have the best destination, are those who have practiced popular and social virtue, which they call moderation and justice and which was developed by habit and practice, without philosophy or understanding?

How are they the happiest?

Because it is likely that they will again join a social and gentle group, either of bees or wasps or ants, and then again the same kind of human group, and so be moderate men.

That is likely.

No one may join the company of the gods who has not practiced philoso-

c   phy and is not completely pure when he departs from life, no one but the lover of learning. It is for this reason, my friends Simmias and Cebes, that those who practice philosophy in the right way keep away from all bodily passions, master them and do not surrender themselves to them; it is not at all for fear of wasting their substance and of poverty, which the majority and the money-lovers fear, nor for fear of dishonor and ill repute, like the ambitious and lovers of honors, that they keep away from them.

That would not be natural for them, Socrates, said Cebes.

d   By Zeus, no, he said. Those who care for their own soul and do not live for the service of their body dismiss all these things. They do not travel the same road as those who do not know where they are going but, believing that nothing should be done contrary to philosophy and their deliverance and purification, they turn to this and follow wherever philosophy leads.

How so, Socrates?

I will tell you, he said. The lovers of learning know that when philosophy

e   gets hold of their soul, it is imprisoned in and clinging to the body, and that it is forced to examine other things through it as through a cage and not by itself, and that it wallows in every kind of ignorance. Philosophy sees that the worst feature of this imprisonment is that it is due to desires, so that the prisoner himself is contributing to his own incarceration most

83   of all. As I say, the lovers of learning know that philosophy gets hold of their soul when it is in that state, then gently encourages it and tries to free it by showing them that investigation through the eyes is full of deceit, as is that through the ears and the other senses. Philosophy then persuades the soul to withdraw from the senses in so far as it is not compelled to use them and bids the soul to gather itself together by itself, to trust only

b   itself and whatever reality, existing by itself, the soul by itself understands, and not to consider as true whatever it examines by other means, for this is different in different circumstances and is sensible and visible, whereas what the soul itself sees is intelligible and invisible. The soul of the true philosopher thinks that this deliverance must not be opposed and so keeps away from pleasures and desires and pains as far as he can; he reflects that violent pleasure or pain or passion does not cause merely such evils as one might expect, such as one suffers when one has been sick or extravagant through desire, but the greatest and most extreme evil, though one does not reflect on this.

What is that, Socrates? asked Cebes.

That the soul of every man, when it feels violent pleasure or pain in connection with some object, inevitably believes at the same time that what causes such feelings must be very clear and very true, which it is not. Such objects are mostly visible, are they not?

Certainly.

And doesn't such an experience tie the soul to the body most completely?

How so?

Because every pleasure and every pain provides, as it were, another nail to rivet the soul to the body and to weld them together. It makes the soul corporeal, so that it believes that truth is what the body says it is. As it shares the beliefs and delights of the body, I think it inevitably comes to share its ways and manner of life and is unable ever to reach Hades in a pure state; it is always full of body when it departs, so that it soon falls back into another body and grows with it as if it had been sewn into it. Because of this, it can have no part in the company of the divine, the pure and uniform.

What you say is very true, Socrates, said Cebes.

This is why genuine lovers of learning are moderate and brave, or do you think it is for the reasons the majority says they are?

I certainly do not.

Indeed no. This is how the soul of a philosopher would reason: it would not think that while philosophy must free it, it should while being freed surrender itself to pleasures and pains and imprison itself again, thus laboring in vain like Penelope at her web. The soul of the philosopher achieves a calm from such emotions; it follows reason and ever stays with it contemplating the true, the divine, which is not the object of opinion. Nurtured by this, it believes that one should live in this manner as long as one is alive and, after death, arrive at what is akin and of the same kind, and escape from human evils. After such nurture there is no danger, Simmias and Cebes, that one should fear that, on parting from the body, the soul would be scattered and dissipated by the winds and no longer be anything anywhere.

When Socrates finished speaking there was a long silence. He appeared to be concentrating on what had been said, and so were most of us. But Cebes and Simmias were whispering to each other. Socrates observed them and questioned them. Come, he said, do you think there is something lacking in my argument? There are still many doubtful points and many objections for anyone who wants a thorough discussion of these matters. If you are discussing some other subject, I have nothing to say, but if you have some difficulty about this one, do not hesitate to speak for yourselves and expound it if you think the argument could be improved, and if you

d   think you will do better, take me along with you in the discussion.

I will tell you the truth, Socrates, said Simmias. Both of us have been in difficulty for some time, and each of us has been urging the other to question you because we wanted to hear what you would say, but we hesitated to bother you, lest it be displeasing to you in your present misfortune.

When Socrates heard this he laughed quietly and said: "Really, Simmias,

e   it would be hard for me to persuade other people that I do not consider my present fate a misfortune if I cannot persuade even you, and you are afraid that it is more difficult to deal with me than before. You seem to think me inferior to the swans in prophecy. They sing before too, but when they realize that they must die they sing most and most beautifully, as

85   they rejoice that they are about to depart to join the god whose servants they are. But men, because of their own fear of death, tell lies about the swans and say that they lament their death and sing in sorrow. They do not reflect that no bird sings when it is hungry or cold or suffers in any other way, neither the nightingale nor the swallow nor the hoopoe, though they do say that these sing laments when in pain. Nor do the swans, but

b   I believe that as they belong to Apollo, they are prophetic, have knowledge of the future and sing of the blessings of the underworld, sing and rejoice on that day beyond what they did before. As I believe myself to be a fellow servant with the swans and dedicated to the same god, and have received from my master a gift of prophecy not inferior to theirs, I am no more despondent than they on leaving life. Therefore, you must speak and ask whatever you want as long as the authorities allow it."

Well spoken, said Simmias. I will tell you my difficulty, and then Cebes

c   will say why he does not accept what was said. I believe, as perhaps you do, that precise knowledge on that subject is impossible or extremely difficult in our present life, but that it surely shows a very poor spirit not to examine thoroughly what is said about it, and to desist before one is exhausted by an all-round investigation. One should achieve one of these things: learn the truth about these things or find it for oneself, or, if that

d   is impossible, adopt the best and most irrefutable of men's theories, and, borne upon this, sail through the dangers of life as upon a raft, unless someone should make that journey safer and less risky upon a firmer vessel of some divine doctrine. So even now, since you have said what you did, I will feel no shame at asking questions, and I will not blame myself in the future because I did not say what I think. As I examine what we said, both by myself and with Cebes, it does not seem to be adequate.

e   Said Socrates: "You may well be right, my friend, but tell me how it is inadequate."

In this way, as it seems to me, he said: "One might make the same argument about harmony, lyre and strings, that a harmony is something invisible, without body, beautiful and divine in the attuned lyre, whereas the lyre itself and its strings are physical, bodily, composite, earthy and akin to what is mortal. Then if someone breaks the lyre, cuts or breaks the strings and then insists, using the same argument as you, that the harmony must still exist and is not destroyed because it would be impossible for the lyre and the strings, which are mortal, still to exist when the strings are broken, and for the harmony, which is akin and of the same nature as the divine and immortal, to be destroyed before that which is mortal; he would say that the harmony itself still must exist and that the wood and the strings must rot before the harmony can suffer. And indeed Socrates, I think you must have this in mind, that we really do suppose the soul to be something of this kind; as the body is stretched and held together by the hot and the cold, the dry and the moist and other such things, and our soul is a mixture and harmony of those things when they are mixed with each other rightly and in due measure. If then the soul is a kind of harmony or attunement, clearly, when our body is relaxed or stretched without due measure by diseases and other evils, the soul must immediately be destroyed, even if it be most divine, as are the other harmonies found in music and all the works of artists, and the remains of each body last for a long time until they rot or are burned. Consider what we shall say in answer to one who deems the soul to be a mixture of bodily elements and to be the first to perish in the process we call death."

Socrates looked at us keenly, as was his habit, smiled and said: "What Simmias says is quite fair. If one of you is more resourceful than I am, why did he not answer him, for he seems to have handled the argument competently. However, I think that before we answer him, we should hear Cebes' objection, in order that we may have time to deliberate on an answer. When we have heard him we should either agree with them, if we think them in tune with us or, if not, defend our own argument. Come then, Cebes. What is troubling you?"

I tell you, said Cebes, the argument seems to me to be at the same point as before and open to the same objection. I do not deny that it has been very elegantly and, if it is not offensive to say so, sufficiently proved that our soul existed before it took on this present form, but I do not believe the same applies to its existing somewhere after our death. Not that I agree with Simmias' objection that the soul is not stronger and much more lasting than the body, for I think it is superior in all these respects. "Why then," the argument might say, "are you still unconvinced? Since you see that when the man dies, the weaker part continues to exist, do you not think that the more lasting part must be preserved during that time?" On this point consider whether what I say makes sense.

Like Simmias, I too need an image, for I think this argument is much as if one said at the death of an old weaver that the man had not perished but was safe and sound somewhere, and offered as proof the fact that the

c   cloak the old man had woven himself and was wearing was still sound
and had not perished. If one was not convinced, he would be asked whether
a man lasts longer than a cloak which is in use and being worn, and if
the answer was that a man lasts much longer, this would be taken as proof
that the man was definitely safe and sound, since the more temporary
thing had not perished. But Simmias, I do not think that is so, for consider
what I say. Anybody could see that the man who said this was talking
nonsense. That weaver had woven and worn out many such cloaks. He

d   perished after many of them, but before the last. That does not mean that
a man is inferior and weaker than a cloak. The image illustrates, I think,
the relationship of the soul to the body, and anyone who says the same
thing about them would appear to me to be talking sense, that the soul
lasts a long time while the body is weaker and more short-lived. He might
say that each soul wears out many bodies, especially if it lives many years.
If the body were in a state of flux and perished while the man was still

e   alive, and the soul wove afresh the body that is worn out, yet it would
be inevitable that whenever the soul perished it would be wearing the last
body it wove and perish only before this last. Then when the soul perished,
the body would show the weakness of its nature by soon decaying and
disappearing. So we cannot trust this argument and be confident that our

88   soul continues to exist somewhere after our death. For, if one were to
concede, even more than you do, to a man using that argument, if one
were to grant him not only that the soul exists in the time before we are
born, but that there is no reason why the soul of some should not exist
and continue to exist after our death, and thus frequently be born and die
in turn; if one were to grant him that the soul's nature is so strong that it
can survive many bodies, but if, having granted all this, one does not
further agree that the soul is not damaged by its many births and is not,
in the end, altogether destroyed in one of those deaths, he might say that

b   no one knows which death and dissolution of the body brings about the
destruction of the soul, since not one of us can be aware of this. And in
that case, any man who faces death with confidence is foolish, unless he
can prove that the soul is altogether immortal. If he cannot, a man about
to die must of necessity always fear for his soul, lest the present separation
of the soul from the body bring about the complete destruction of the soul.

c   When we heard what they said we were all depressed, as we told each
other afterwards. We had been quite convinced by the previous argument,
and they seemed to confuse us again, and to drive us to doubt not only
what had already been said but also what was going to be said, lest we
be worthless as critics or the subject itself admitted of no certainty.

ECHECRATES: By the gods, Phaedo, you have my sympathy, for as I listen

d   to you now I find myself saying to myself: "What argument shall we trust?
That of Socrates, which was extremely convincing, has now fallen into
discredit; the statement that the soul is some kind of harmony has a
remarkable hold on me, now and always, and when it was mentioned it

reminded me that I had myself previously thought so. And now I am again quite in need, as if from the beginning, of some other argument to convince me that the soul does not die along with the man. Tell me then, by Zeus, how Socrates tackled the argument. Was he obviously distressed, as you say you people were, or was he not, but quietly came to the rescue e of his argument, and did he do so satisfactorily or inadequately? Tell us everything as precisely as you can.

PHAEDO: I have certainly often admired Socrates, Echecrates, but never more than on this occasion. That he had a reply was perhaps not strange. 89 What I wondered at most in him was the pleasant, kind and admiring way he received the young men's argument, and how sharply he was aware of the effect the discussion had on us, and then how well he healed our distress and, as it were, recalled us from our flight and defeat and turned us around to join him in the examination of their argument.

ECHECRATES: How did he do this?

PHAEDO: I will tell you. I happened to be sitting on his right by the couch on a low stool, so that he was sitting well above me. He stroked my head b and pressed the hair on the back of my neck, for he was in the habit of playing with my hair at times. "Tomorrow, Phaedo," he said, "you will probably cut this beautiful hair."

Likely enough, Socrates, I said.

Not if you take my advice, he said.

Why not? said I.

It is today, he said, that I shall cut my hair and you yours, if our argument dies on us, and we cannot revive it. If I were you, and the argument c escaped me, I would take an oath, as the Argives did, not to let my hair grow before I fought again and defeated the argument of Simmias and Cebes.

But, I said, they say that not even Heracles could fight two people.

Then call on me as your Iolaus, as long as the daylight lasts.

I shall call on you, but in this case as Iolaus calling on Heracles.

It makes no difference, he said, but first there is a certain experience we must be careful to avoid.

What is that? I asked.

That we should not become misologues, as people become misanthropes. d There is no greater evil one can suffer than to hate reasonable discourse. Misology and misanthropy arise in the same way. Misanthropy comes when a man without knowledge or skill has placed great trust in someone and believes him to be altogether truthful, sound and trustworthy; then, a short time afterwards he finds him to be wicked and unreliable, and then this happens in another case; when one has frequently had that experience, especially with those whom one believed to be one's closest e friends, then, in the end, after many such blows, one comes to hate all men and to believe that no one is sound in any way at all. Have you not seen this happen?

I surely have, I said.

This is a shameful state of affairs, he said, and obviously due to to an attempt to have human relations without any skill in human affairs, for such skill would lead one to believe, what is in fact true, that the very
90   good and the very wicked are both quite rare, and that most men are between those extremes.

How do you mean? said I.

The same as with the very tall and the very short, he said. Do you think anything is rarer than to find an extremely tall man or an extremely short one? Or a dog or any thing else whatever? Or again, one extremely swift or extremely slow, ugly or beautiful, white or black? Are you not aware that in all those cases the most extreme at either end are rare and few, but those in between are many and plentiful?

Certainly, I said.

b   Therefore, he said, if a contest of wickedness were established, there too the winners, you think, would be very few?

That is likely, said I.

Likely indeed, he said, but arguments are not like men in this particular. I was merely following your lead just now. The similarity lies rather in this: it is as when one who lacks skill in arguments puts his trust in an argument as being true, then shortly afterwards believes it to be false— as sometimes it is and sometimes it is not—and so with another argument and then another. You know how those in particular who spend their time
c   studying contradiction in the end believe themselves to have become very wise and that they alone have understood that there is no soundness or reliability in any object or in any argument, but that all that exists simply fluctuates up and down as if it were in the Euripus[10] and does not remain in the same place for any time at all.

What you say, I said, is certainly true.

It would be pitiable, Phaedo, he said, when there is a true and reliable argument and one that can be understood, if a man who has dealt with
d   such arguments as appear at one time true, at another time untrue, should not blame himself or his own lack of skill but, because of his distress, in the end gladly shift the blame away from himself to the arguments, and spend the rest of his life hating and reviling reasonable discussion and so be deprived of truth and knowledge of reality.

Yes, by Zeus, I said, that would be pitiable indeed.

e   This then is the first thing we should guard against, he said. We should not allow into our minds the conviction that argumentation has nothing sound about it; much rather we should believe that it is we who are not yet sound and that we must take courage and be eager to attain soundness,
91   you and the others for the sake of your whole life still to come, and I for the sake of death itself. I am in danger at this moment of not having a

10. The Euripus is the straits between the island of Euboea and Boeotia on the Greek mainland; its currents were both violent and variable.

philosophical attitude about this, but like those who are quite uneducated, I am eager to get the better of you in argument, for the uneducated, when they engage in argument about anything, give no thought to the truth about the subject of discussion but are only eager that those present will accept the position they have set forth. I differ from them only to this extent: I shall not be eager to get the agreement of those present that what I say is true, except incidentally, but I shall be very eager that I should myself be thoroughly convinced that things are so. For I am thinking— see in how contentious a spirit—that if what I say is true, it is a fine thing to be convinced; if, on the other hand, nothing exists after death, at least for this time before I die I shall distress those present less with lamentations and my folly will not continue to exist along with me—that would be a bad thing—but will come to an end in a short time. Thus prepared, Simmias and Cebes, he said, I come to deal with your argument. If you will take my advice, you will give but little thought to Socrates but much more to the truth. If you think that what I say is true, agree with me; if not, oppose it with every argument and take care that in my eagerness I do not deceive myself and you and, like a bee, leave my sting in you when I go.

We must proceed, he said, and first remind me of what you said if I do not appear to remember it. Simmias, as I believe, is in doubt and fear that the soul, though it is more divine and beautiful than the body, yet predeceases it, being a kind of harmony. Cebes, I thought, agrees with me that the soul lasts much longer than the body, but that no one knows whether the soul often wears out many bodies and then, on leaving its last body, is now itself destroyed. This then is death, the destruction of the soul, since the body is always being destroyed. Are these the questions, Simmias and Cebes, which we must investigate?

They both agreed that they were.

Do you then, he asked, reject all our previous statements, or some but not others?

Some, they both said, but not others.

What, he said, about the statements we made that learning is recollection and that, if this was so, our soul must of necessity exist elsewhere before us, before it was imprisoned in the body?

For myself, said Cebes, I was wonderfully convinced by it at the time and I stand by it now also, more than by any other statement.

That, said Simmias, is also my position, and I should be very surprised if I ever changed my opinion about this.

But you must change your opinion, my Theban friend, said Socrates, if you still believe that a harmony is a composite thing, and that the soul is a kind of harmony of the elements of the body in a state of tension, for surely you will not allow yourself to maintain that a composite harmony existed before those elements from which it had to be composed, or would you?

Never, Socrates, he said.

Do you realize, he said, that this is what you are in fact saying when you state that the soul exists before it takes on the form and body of a

man and that it is composed of elements which do not yet exist? A harmony
is not like that to which you compare it; the lyre and the strings and the
c   notes, though still unharmonized, exist; the harmony is composed last of
all, and is the first to be destroyed. How will you harmonize this statement
with your former one?

In no way, said Simmias.

And surely, he said, a statement about harmony should do so more than
any other.

It should, said Simmias.

So your statement is inconsistent? Consider which of your statements
you prefer, that learning is recollection or that the soul is a harmony?
d   I much prefer the former, Socrates. I adopted the latter without proof,
because of a certain probability and plausibility, which is why it appeals
to most men. I know that arguments of which the proof is based on
probability are pretentious and, if one does not guard against them, they
certainly deceive one, in geometry and everything else. The theory of
recollection and learning, however, was based on an assumption worthy
of acceptance, for our soul was said to exist also before it came into the
body, just as the reality does that is of the kind that we qualify by the
e   words "what it is," and I convinced myself that I was quite correct to
accept it. Therefore, I cannot accept the theory that the soul is a harmony
either from myself or anyone else.

What of this, Simmias? Do you think it natural for a harmony, or any
93   other composite, to be in a different state from that of the elements of
which it is composed?

Not at all, said Simmias.

Nor, as I think, can it act or be acted upon in a different way than
its elements?

He agreed.

One must therefore suppose that a harmony does not direct its components, but is directed by them.

He accepted this.

A harmony is therefore far from making a movement, or uttering a
sound, or doing anything else, in a manner contrary to that of its parts.

Far from it indeed, he said.

Does not the nature of each harmony depend on the way it has been harmonized?

I do not understand, he said.
b   Will it not, if it is more and more fully harmonized, be more and more
fully a harmony, and if it is less and less fully harmonized, it will be less
and less fully a harmony?

Certainly.

Can this be true about the soul, that one soul is more and more fully a
soul than another, or is less and less fully a soul, even to the smallest extent?

Not in any way.

Come now, by Zeus, he said. One soul is said to have intelligence and virtue and to be good, another to have folly and wickedness and to be bad. Are those things truly said?

They certainly are.

What will someone who holds the theory that the soul is a harmony say that those things are which reside in the soul, that is, virtue and wickedness? Are these some other harmony and disharmony? That the good soul is harmonized and, being a harmony, has within itself another harmony, whereas the evil soul is both itself a lack of harmony and has no other within itself?

I don't know what to say, said Simmias, but one who holds that assumption must obviously say something of that kind.

We have previously agreed, he said, that one soul is not more and not less a soul than another, and this means that one harmony is not more and more fully, or less and less fully, a harmony than another. Is that not so?

Certainly.

Now that which is no more and no less a harmony is not more or less harmonized. Is that so?

It is.

Can that which is neither more nor less harmonized partake more or less of harmony, or does it do so equally?

Equally.

Then if a soul is neither more nor less a soul than another, it has been harmonized to the same extent?

This is so.

If that is so, it would have no greater share of disharmony or of harmony?

It would not.

That being the case, could one soul have more wickedness or virtue than another, if wickedness is disharmony and virtue harmony?

It could not.

But rather, Simmias, according to correct reasoning, no soul, if it is a harmony, will have any share of wickedness, for harmony is surely altogether this very thing, harmony, and would never share in disharmony.

It certainly would not.

Nor would a soul, being altogether this very thing, a soul, share in wickedness?

How could it, in view of what has been said?

So it follows from this argument that all the souls of all living creatures will be equally good, if souls are by nature equally this very thing, souls.

I think so, Socrates.

Does our argument seem right, he said, and does it seem that it should have come to this, if the hypothesis that the soul is a harmony was correct?

Not in any way, he said.

Further, of all the parts of a man, can you mention any other part that rules him than his soul, especially if it is a wise soul?

82   *Phaedo*

I cannot.

Does it do so by following the affections of the body or by opposing
them? I mean, for example, that when the body is hot and thirsty the soul
draws him to the opposite, to not drinking; when the body is hungry, to
c   not eating, and we see a thousand other examples of the soul opposing
the affections of the body. Is that not so?

It certainly is.

On the other hand we previously agreed that if the soul were a harmony,
it would never be out of tune with the stress and relaxation and the striking
of the strings or anything else done to its composing elements, but that it
would follow and never direct them?

We did so agree, of course.

Well, does it now appear to do quite the opposite, ruling over all the
d   elements of which one says it is composed, opposing nearly all of them
throughout life, directing all their ways, inflicting harsh and painful punishment on them, at times in physical culture and medicine, at other times
more gently by threats and exhortations, holding converse with desires
and passions and fears as if it were one thing talking to a different one,
as Homer wrote somewhere in the *Odyssey* where he says that Odysseus
"struck his breast and rebuked his heart saying, 'Endure, my heart, you
have endured worse than this.' "[11]

e   Do you think that when he composed this the poet thought that his soul
was a harmony, a thing to be directed by the affections of the body? Did
he not rather regard it as ruling over them and mastering them, itself a
much more divine thing than a harmony?

Yes, by Zeus, I think so, Socrates.

95   Therefore, my good friend, it is quite wrong for us to say that the soul
is a harmony, and in saying so we would disagree both with the divine
poet Homer and with ourselves.

That is so, he said.

Very well, said Socrates. Harmonia of Thebes seems somehow reasonably propitious to us. How and by what argument, my dear Cebes, can
we propitiate Cadmus?[12]

I think, Cebes said, that you will find a way. You dealt with the argument
about harmony in a manner that was quite astonishing to me. When
b   Simmias was speaking of his difficulties I was very much wondering
whether anyone would be able to deal with his argument, and I was quite
dumbfounded when right away he could not resist your argument's first
onslaught. I should not wonder therefore if that of Cadmus suffered the
same fate.

11. *Odyssey* xx.17–18.

12. Harmonia was in legend the wife of Cadmus, the founder of Thebes. Socrates'
punning joke is simply that, having dealt with Harmonia (harmony), we must now deal
with Cadmus (i.e., Cebes, the other Theban).

My good sir, said Socrates, do not boast, lest some malign influence upset the argument we are about to make. However, we leave that to the care of the god, but let us come to grips with it in the Homeric fashion, to see if there is anything in what you say. The sum of your problem is this: you consider that the soul must be proved to be immortal and indestructible before a philosopher on the point of death, who is confident that he will fare much better in the underworld than if he had led any other kind of life, can avoid being foolish and simple-minded in this confidence. To prove that the soul is strong, that it is divine, that it existed before we were born as men, all this, you say, does not show the soul to be immortal but only long-lasting. That it existed for a very long time before, that it knew much and acted much, makes it no more immortal because of that; indeed, its very entering into a human body was the beginning of its destruction, like a disease; it would live that life in distress and would in the end be destroyed in what we call death. You say it makes no difference whether it enters a body once or many times as far as the fear of each of us is concerned, for it is natural for a man who is no fool to be afraid, if he does not know and cannot prove that the soul is immortal. This, I think, is what you maintain, Cebes; I deliberately repeat it often, in order that no point may escape us, and that you may add or subtract something if you wish.

And Cebes said: "There is nothing that I want to add or subtract at the moment. That is what I say."

Socrates paused for a long time, deep in thought. He then said: "This is no unimportant problem that you raise, Cebes, for it requires a thorough investigation of the cause of generation and destruction. I will, if you wish, give you an account of my experience in these matters. Then if something I say seems useful to you, make use of it to persuade us of your position."

I surely do wish that, said Cebes.

Listen then, and I will, Cebes, he said. When I was a young man I was wonderfully keen on that wisdom which they call natural science, for I thought it splendid to know the causes of everything, why it comes to be, why it perishes and why it exists. I was often changing my mind in the investigation, in the first instance, of questions such as these: Are living creatures nurtured when heat and cold produce a kind of putrefaction, as some say? Do we think with our blood, or air, or fire, or none of these, and does the brain provide our senses of hearing and sight and smell, from which come memory and opinion, and from memory and opinion which has become stable, comes knowledge? Then again, as I investigated how these things perish and what happens to things in the sky and on the earth, finally I became convinced that I have no natural aptitude at all for that kind of investigation, and of this I will give you sufficient proof. This investigation made me quite blind even to those things which I and others thought that I clearly knew before, so that I unlearned what I thought I knew before, about many other things and specifically about how men grew. I thought before that it was obvious to anybody that men grew

d   through eating and drinking, for food adds flesh to flesh and bones to
     bones, and in the same way appropriate parts were added to all other
     parts of the body, so that the man grew from an earlier small bulk to a
     large bulk later, and so a small man became big. That is what I thought
     then. Do you not think it was reasonable?

     I do, said Cebes.

     Then further consider this: I thought my opinion was satisfactory, that
e   when a large man stood by a small one he was taller by a head, and so a
     horse was taller than a horse. Even clearer than this, I thought that ten
     was more than eight because two had been added, and that a two-cubit
     length is larger than a cubit because it surpasses it by half its length.

     And what do you think now about those things?

     That I am far, by Zeus, from believing that I know the cause of any of
     those things. I will not even allow myself to say that where one is added
     to one either the one to which it is added or the one that is added becomes
97   two, or that the one added and the one to which it is added become two
     because of the addition of the one to the other. I wonder that, when each
     of them is separate from the other, each of them is one, nor are they then
     two, but that, when they come near to one another, this is the cause of
     their becoming two, the coming together and being placed closer to one
     another. Nor can I any longer be persuaded that when one thing is divided,
b   this division is the cause of its becoming two, for just now the cause of
     becoming two was the opposite. At that time it was their coming close
     together and one was added to the other, but now it is because one is
     taken and separated from the other.

     I do not any longer persuade myself that I know why a unit or anything
     else comes to be, or perishes or exists by the old method of investigation,
     and I do not accept it, but I have a confused method of my own. One day
c   I heard someone reading, as he said, from a book of Anaxagoras, and
     saying that it is Mind that directs and is the cause of everything. I was
     delighted with this cause and it seemed to me good, in a way, that Mind
     should be the cause of all. I thought that if this were so, the directing Mind
     would direct everything and arrange each thing in the way that was best.
     If then one wished to know the cause of each thing, why it comes to be
d   or perishes or exists, one had to find what was the best way for it to be,
     or to be acted upon, or to act. On these premises then it befitted a man to
     investigate only, about this and other things, what is best. The same man
     must inevitably also know what is worse, for that is part of the same
     knowledge. As I reflected on this subject I was glad to think that I had
     found in Anaxagoras a teacher about the cause of things after my own
e   heart, and that he would tell me, first, whether the earth is flat or round,
     and then would explain why it is so of necessity, saying which is better,
     and that it was better to be so. If he said it was in the middle of the
     universe, he would go on to show that it was better for it to be in the
     middle, and if he showed me those things I should be prepared never to
98   desire any other kind of cause. I was ready to find out in the same way

about the sun and the moon and the other heavenly bodies, about their relative speed, their turnings and whatever else happened to them, how it is best that each should act or be acted upon. I never thought that Anaxagoras, who said that those things were directed by Mind, would bring in any other cause for them than that it was best for them to be as they are. Once he had given the best for each as the cause for each and   b the general cause of all, I thought he would go on to explain the common good for all, and I would not have exchanged my hopes for a fortune. I eagerly acquired his books and read them as quickly as I could in order to know the best and the worst as soon as possible.

This wonderful hope was dashed as I went on reading and saw that the man made no use of Mind, nor gave it any responsibility for the management of things, but mentioned as causes air and ether and water and many   c other strange things. That seemed to me much like saying that Socrates' actions are all due to his mind, and then in trying to tell the causes of everything I do, to say that the reason that I am sitting here is because my body consists of bones and sinews, because the bones are hard and are separated by joints, that the sinews are such as to contract and relax, that they surround the bones along with flesh and skin which hold them   d together, then as the bones are hanging in their sockets, the relaxation and contraction of the sinews enable me to bend my limbs, and that is the cause of my sitting here with my limbs bent.

Again, he would mention other such causes for my talking to you: sounds and air and hearing, and a thousand other such things, but he would neglect to mention the true causes, that, after the Athenians decided it was better to condemn me, for this reason it seemed best to me to sit here   e and more right to remain and to endure whatever penalty they ordered. For by the dog, I think these sinews and bones could long ago have been in Megara or among the Boeotians, taken there by my belief as to the best   99 course, if I had not thought it more right and honorable to endure whatever penalty the city ordered rather than escape and run away. To call those things causes is too absurd. If someone said that without bones and sinews and all such things, I should not be able to do what I decided, he would be right, but surely to say that they are the cause of what I do, and not that I have chosen the best course, even though I act with my mind, is to speak very lazily and carelessly. Imagine not being able to distinguish the   b real cause from that without which the cause would not be able to act as a cause. It is what the majority appear to do, like people groping in the dark; they call it a cause, thus giving it a name that does not belong to it. That is why one man surrounds the earth with a vortex to make the heavens keep it in place, another makes the air support it like a wide lid. As for   c their capacity of being in the best place they could possibly be put, this they do not look for, nor do they believe it to have any divine force, but they believe that they will some time discover a stronger and more immortal Atlas to hold everything together more, and they do not believe that the truly good and "binding" binds and holds them together. I would gladly become the disciple of any man who taught the workings of that kind of cause. However, since I was deprived and could neither discover

d it myself nor learn it from another, do you wish me to give you an explanation of how, as a second best, I busied myself with the search for the cause, Cebes?

I would wish it above all else, he said.

After this, he said, when I had wearied of investigating things, I thought that I must be careful to avoid the experience of those who watch an eclipse of the sun, for some of them ruin their eyes unless they watch its

e reflection in water or some such material. A similar thought crossed my mind, and I feared that my soul would be altogether blinded if I looked at things with my eyes and tried to grasp them with each of my senses. So I thought I must take refuge in discussions and investigate the truth of things by means of words. However, perhaps this analogy is inadequate,

100 for I certainly do not admit that one who investigates things by means of words is dealing with images any more than one who looks at facts. However, I started in this manner: taking as my hypothesis in each case the theory that seemed to me the most compelling, I would consider as true, about cause and everything else, whatever agreed with this, and as untrue whatever did not so agree. But I want to put my meaning more clearly for I do not think that you understand me now.

No, by Zeus, said Cebes, not very well.

b This, he said, is what I mean. It is nothing new, but what I have never stopped talking about, both elsewhere and in the earlier part of our conversation. I am going to try to show you the kind of cause with which I have concerned myself. I turn back to those oft-mentioned things and proceed from them. I assume the existence of a Beautiful, itself by itself, of a Good and a Great and all the rest. If you grant me these and agree that they exist, I hope to show you the cause as a result, and to find the soul to be immortal.

c Take it that I grant you this, said Cebes, and hasten to your conclusion.

Consider then, he said, whether you share my opinion as to what follows, for I think that, if there is anything beautiful besides the Beautiful itself, it is beautiful for no other reason than that it shares in that Beautiful, and I say so with everything. Do you agree to this sort of cause?—I do.

d I no longer understand or recognize those other sophisticated causes, and if someone tells me that a thing is beautiful because it has a bright color or shape or any such thing, I ignore these other reasons—for all these confuse me—but I simply, naively and perhaps foolishly cling to this, that nothing else makes it beautiful other than the presence of, or the sharing in, or however you may describe its relationship to that Beautiful we mentioned, for I will not insist on the precise nature of the relationship, but that all beautiful things are beautiful by the Beautiful. That, I think,

e is the safest answer I can give myself or anyone else. And if I stick to this I think I shall never fall into error. This is the safe answer for me or anyone else to give, namely, that it is through Beauty that beautiful things are made beautiful. Or do you not think so too?—I do.

And that it is through Bigness that big things are big and the bigger are bigger, and that smaller things are made small by Smallness?—Yes.

And you would not accept the statement that one man is taller than another by a head and the shorter man shorter by the same, but you would bear witness that you mean nothing else than that everything that is bigger is made bigger by nothing else than by Bigness, and that is the cause of its being bigger, and the smaller is made smaller only by Smallness and this is why it is smaller. I think you would be afraid that some opposite argument would confront you if you said that someone is bigger or smaller by a head, first, because the bigger is bigger and the smaller smaller by the same, then because the bigger is bigger by a head which is small, and this would be strange, namely, that someone is made bigger by something small. Would you not be afraid of this?

I certainly would, said Cebes, laughing.

Then you would be afraid to say that ten is more than eight by two, and that this is the cause of the excess, and not magnitude and because of magnitude, or that two cubits is bigger than one cubit by half and not by Bigness, for this is the same fear.—Certainly.

Then would you not avoid saying that when one is added to one it is the addition and when it is divided it is the division that is the cause of two? And you would loudly exclaim that you do not know how else each thing can come to be except by sharing in the particular reality in which it shares, and in these cases you do not know of any other cause of becoming two except by sharing in Twoness, and that the things that are to be two must share in this, as that which is to be one must share in Oneness, and you would dismiss these additions and divisions and other such subtleties, and leave them to those wiser than yourself to answer. But you, afraid, as they say, of your own shadow and your inexperience, would cling to the safety of your own hypothesis and give that answer. If someone then attacked your hypothesis itself, you would ignore him and would not answer until you had examined whether the consequences that follow from it agree with one another or contradict one another.[13] And when you must give an account of your hypothesis itself you will proceed in the same way: you will assume another hypothesis, the one which seems to you best of the higher ones until you come to something acceptable, but you will not jumble the two as the debaters do by discussing the hypothesis and its consequences at the same time, if you wish to discover any truth. This they do not discuss at all nor give any thought to, but their wisdom enables them to mix everything up and yet to be pleased with themselves, but if you are a philosopher I think you will do as I say.

What you say is very true, said Simmias and Cebes together.

ECHECRATES: Yes, by Zeus, Phaedo, and they were right, I think he made these things wonderfully clear to anyone of even small intelligence.

---

13. Alternatively: "If someone should cling to your hypothesis itself, you would dismiss him and would not answer until you had examined whether the consequences that follow from it agree with one another or contradict one another."

PHAEDO: Yes indeed, Echecrates, and all those present thought so too.

ECHECRATES: And so do we who were not present but hear of it now. What was said after that?

PHAEDO: As I recall it, when the above had been accepted, and it was
b   agreed that each of the Forms existed, and that other things acquired their name by having a share in them, he followed this up by asking: If you say these things are so, when you then say that Simmias is taller than Socrates but shorter than Phaedo, do you not mean that there is in Simmias both tallness and shortness?—I do.

But, he said, do you agree that the words of the statement 'Simmias is
c   taller than Socrates' do not express the truth of the matter? It is not, surely, the nature of Simmias to be taller than Socrates because he is Simmias but because of the tallness he happens to have? Nor is he taller than Socrates because Socrates is Socrates, but because Socrates has smallness compared with the tallness of the other?—True.

Nor is he shorter than Phaedo because Phaedo is Phaedo, but because Phaedo has tallness compared with the shortness of Simmias?—That is so.
d   So then Simmias is called both short and tall, being between the two, presenting his shortness to be overcome by the tallness of one, and his tallness to overcome the shortness of the other. He smilingly added, I seem to be going to talk like a book, but it is as I say. The other agreed.

My purpose is that you may agree with me. Now it seems to me that not only Tallness itself is never willing to be tall and short at the same time, but also that the tallness in us will never admit the short or be
e   overcome, but one of two things happens: either it flees and retreats whenever its opposite, the short, approaches, or it is destroyed by its approach. It is not willing to endure and admit shortness and be other than it was, whereas I admit and endure shortness and still remain the same person and am this short man. But Tallness, being tall, cannot venture to be small.
103 In the same way, the short in us is unwilling to become or to be tall ever, nor does any other of the opposites become or be its opposite while still being what it was; either it goes away or is destroyed when that happens.— I altogether agree, said Cebes.

When he heard this, someone of those present—I have no clear memory of who it was—said: "By the gods, did we not agree earlier in our discussion[14] to the very opposite of what is now being said, namely, that the larger came from the smaller and the smaller from the larger, and that this simply was how opposites came to be, from their opposites, but now I think we are saying that this would never happen?"

On hearing this, Socrates inclined his head towards the speaker and said: "You have bravely reminded us, but you do not understand the
b   difference between what is said now and what was said then, which was that an opposite thing came from an opposite thing; now we say that the

---

14. The reference is to 70d–71a above.

opposite itself could never become opposite to itself, neither that in us nor that in nature. Then, my friend, we were talking of things that have opposite qualities and naming these after them, but now we say that these opposites themselves, from the presence of which in them things get their name, never can tolerate the coming to be from one another." At the same time he looked to Cebes and said: "Does anything of what this man says also disturb you?"

Not at the moment, said Cebes, but I do not deny that many things do disturb me.

We are altogether agreed then, he said, that an opposite will never be opposite to itself.—Entirely agreed.

Consider then whether you will agree to this further point. There is something you call hot and something you call cold.—There is.

Are they the same as what you call snow and fire?—By Zeus, no.

So the hot is something other than fire, and the cold is something other than snow?—Yes.

You think, I believe, that being snow it will not admit the hot, as we said before, and remain what it was and be both snow and hot, but when the hot approaches it will either retreat before it or be destroyed.—Quite so.

So fire, as the cold approaches, will either go away or be destroyed; it will never venture to admit coldness and remain what it was, fire and cold.—What you say is true.

It is true then about some of these things that not only the Form itself deserves its own name for all time, but there is something else that is not the Form but has its character whenever it exists. Perhaps I can make my meaning clearer: the Odd must always be given this name we now mention. Is that not so?—Certainly.

Is it the only one of existing things to be called odd?—this is my question—or is there something else than the Odd which one must nevertheless also always call odd, as well as by its own name, because it is such by nature as never to be separated from the Odd? I mean, for example, the number three and many others. Consider three: do you not think that it must always be called both by its own name and by that of the Odd, which is not the same as three? That is the nature of three, and of five, and of half of all the numbers; each of them is odd, but it is not the Odd. Then again, two and four and the whole other column of numbers; each of them, while not being the same as the Even, is always even. Do you not agree?—Of course.

Look now. What I want to make clear is this: not only do those opposites not admit each other, but this is also true of those things which, while not being opposite to each other yet always contain the opposites, and it seems that these do not admit that Form which is opposite to that which is in them; when it approaches them, they either perish or give way. Shall we not say that three will perish or undergo anything before, while remaining three, becoming even?—Certainly, said Cebes.

Yet surely two is not the opposite of three?—Indeed it is not.

c

d

e

104

b

c

It is then not only opposite Forms that do not admit each other's approach, but also some other things that do not admit the onset of opposites.—Very true.

Do you then want us, if we can, to define what these are?—I surely do.

d   Would they be the things that are compelled by whatever occupies them not only to contain that thing's Form but also always that of some opposite?—How do you mean?

As we were saying just now, you surely know that what the Form of three occupies must not only be three but also odd.—Certainly.

And we say that the opposite Form to the Form that achieves this result could never come to it.—It could not.

Now it is Oddness that has done this?—Yes.

And opposite to this is the Form of the Even?—Yes.

e   So then the Form of the Even will never come to three?—Never.

Then three has no share in the Even?—Never.

So three is uneven?—Yes.

As for what I said we must define, that is, what kind of things, while not being opposites to something, yet do not admit the opposite, as for example the triad, though it is not the opposite of the Even, yet does not
105   admit it because it always brings along the opposite of the Even, and so the dyad in relation to the Odd, fire to the Cold, and very many other things, see whether you would define it thus: Not only does the opposite not admit its opposite, but that which brings along some opposite into that which it occupies, that which brings this along will not admit the opposite to that which it brings along. Refresh your memory, it is no worse for being heard often. Five does not admit the form of the Even, nor will ten, its double, admit the form of the Odd. The double itself is an opposite of something else, yet it will not admit the form of the Odd. Nor do one-
b   and-a-half and other such fractions admit the form of the Whole, nor will one-third, and so on, if you follow me and agree to this.

I certainly agree, he said, and I follow you.

Tell me again from the beginning, he said, and do not answer in the words of the question, but do as I do. I say that beyond that safe answer, which I spoke of first, I see another safe answer. If you should ask me
c   what, coming into a body, makes it hot, my reply would not be that safe and ignorant one, that it is heat, but our present argument provides a more sophisticated answer, namely, fire, and if you ask me what, on coming into a body, makes it sick, I will not say sickness but fever. Nor, if asked the presence of what in a number makes it odd, I will not say oddness but oneness, and so with other things. See if you now sufficiently understand what I want.—Quite sufficiently.

Answer me then, he said, what is it that, present in a body, makes it living?—A soul.

d   And is that always so?—Of course.

Whatever the soul occupies, it always brings life to it?—It does.

Is there, or is there not, an opposite to life?—There is.

What is it?—Death.

So the soul will never admit the opposite of that which it brings along, as we agree from what has been said?

Most certainly, said Cebes.

Well, and what do we call that which does not admit the form of the even?—The uneven.

What do we call that which will not admit the just and that which will not admit the musical?

The unmusical, and the other the unjust.   e

Very well, what do we call that which does not admit death?

The deathless, he said.

Now the soul does not admit death?—No.

So the soul is deathless?—It is.

Very well, he said. Shall we say that this has been proved, do you think?

Quite adequately proved, Socrates.

Well now, Cebes, he said, if the uneven were of necessity indestructible, surely three would be indestructible?—Of course.   106

And if the non-hot were of necessity indestructible, then whenever anyone brought heat to snow, the snow would retreat safe and unthawed, for it could not be destroyed, nor again could it stand its ground and admit the heat?—What you say is true.

In the same way, if the non-cold were indestructible, then when some cold attacked the fire, it would neither be quenched nor destroyed, but retreat safely.—Necessarily.

Must then the same not be said of the deathless? If the deathless is also   b indestructible, it is impossible for the soul to be destroyed when death comes upon it. For it follows from what has been said that it will not admit death or be dead, just as three, we said, will not be even nor will the odd; nor will fire be cold, nor the heat that is in the fire. But, someone might say, what prevents the odd, while not becoming even as has been agreed,   c from being destroyed, and the even to come to be instead? We could not maintain against the man who said this that it is not destroyed, for the uneven is not indestructible. If we had agreed that it was indestructible we could easily have maintained that at the coming of the even, the odd and the three have gone away and the same would hold for fire and the hot and the other things.—Surely.

And so now, if we are agreed that the deathless is indestructible, the soul,   d besides being deathless, is indestructible. If not, we need another argument.

—There is no need for one as far as that goes, for hardly anything could resist destruction if the deathless, which lasts forever, would admit destruction.

All would agree, said Socrates, that the god, and the Form of life itself, and anything that is deathless, are never destroyed.—All men would agree, by Zeus, to that, and the gods, I imagine, even more so.

If the deathless is indestructible, then the soul, if it is deathless, would   e also be indestructible?—Necessarily.

Then when death comes to man, the mortal part of him dies, it seems, but his deathless part goes away safe and indestructible, yielding the place to death.—So it appears.

107   Therefore the soul, Cebes, he said, is most certainly deathless and inde-structible and our souls will really dwell in the underworld.

I have nothing more to say against that, Socrates, said Cebes, nor can I doubt your arguments. If Simmias here or someone else has something to say, he should not remain silent, for I do not know to what further occasion other than the present he could put it off if he wants to say or to hear anything on these subjects.

Certainly, said Simmias, I myself have no remaining grounds for doubt after what has been said; nevertheless, in view of the importance of our
b   subject and my low opinion of human weakness, I am bound still to have some private misgivings about what we have said.

You are not only right to say this, Simmias, Socrates said, but our first hypotheses require clearer examination, even though we find them con-vincing. And if you analyze them adequately, you will, I think, follow the argument as far as a man can and if the conclusion is clear, you will look no further.—That is true.

c   It is right to think then, gentlemen, that if the soul is immortal, it requires our care not only for the time we call our life, but for the sake of all time, and that one is in terrible danger if one does not give it that care. If death were escape from everything, it would be a great boon to the wicked to get rid of the body and of their wickedness together with their soul. But
d   now that the soul appears to be immortal, there is no escape from evil or salvation for it except by becoming as good and wise as possible, for the soul goes to the underworld possessing nothing but its education and upbringing, which are said to bring the greatest benefit or harm to the dead right at the beginning of the journey yonder.

We are told that when each person dies, the guardian spirit who was allotted to him in life proceeds to lead him to a certain place, whence those
e   who have been gathered together there must, after being judged, proceed to the underworld with the guide who has been appointed to lead them thither from here. Having there undergone what they must and stayed there the appointed time, they are led back here by another guide after
108   long periods of time. The journey is not as Aeschylus' Telephus[15] describes it. He says that only one single path leads to Hades, but I think it is neither one nor simple, for then there would be no need of guides; one could not make any mistake if there were but one path. As it is, it is likely to have many forks and crossroads; and I base this judgment on the sacred rites and customs here.

The well-ordered and wise soul follows the guide and is not without familiarity with its surroundings, but the soul that is passionately attached

---

15. The *Telephus* of Aeschylus is not extant.

to the body, as I said before, hovers around it and the visible world for a   b
long time, struggling and suffering much until it is led away by force and
with difficulty by its appointed spirit. When the impure soul which has
performed some impure deed joins the others after being involved in
unjust killings, or committed other crimes which are akin to these and are
actions of souls of this kind, everybody shuns it and turns away, unwilling
to be its fellow traveller or its guide; such a soul wanders alone completely   c
at a loss until a certain time arrives and it is forcibly led to its proper
dwelling place. On the other hand, the soul that has led a pure and moderate
life finds fellow travellers and gods to guide it, and each of them dwells
in a place suited to it.

There are many strange places upon the earth, and the earth itself is not
such as those who are used to discourse upon it believe it to be in nature
or size, as someone has convinced me.

Simmias said: "What do you mean, Socrates? I have myself heard many   d
things said about the earth, but certainly not the things that convince you.
I should be glad to hear them."

Indeed, Simmias, I do not think it requires the skill of Glaucus[16] to tell
you what they are, but to prove them true requires more than that skill,
and I should perhaps not be able to do so. Also, even if I had the knowledge,
my remaining time would not be long enough to tell the tale. However,   e
nothing prevents my telling you what I am convinced is the shape of the
earth and what its regions are.

Even that is sufficient, said Simmias.

Well then, he said, the first thing of which I am convinced is that if the   109
earth is a sphere in the middle of the heavens, it has no need of air or any
other force to prevent it from falling. The homogeneous nature of the
heavens on all sides and the earth's own equipoise are sufficient to hold
it, for an object balanced in the middle of something homogeneous will
have no tendency to incline more in any direction than any other but will
remain unmoved. This, he said, is the first point of which I am persuaded.

And rightly so, said Simmias.

Further, the earth is very large, and we live around the sea in a small
portion of it between Phasis and the pillars of Heracles, like ants or frogs   b
around a swamp; many other peoples live in many such parts of it. Everywhere about the earth there are numerous hollows of many kinds and
shapes and sizes into which the water and the mist and the air have
gathered. The earth itself is pure and lies in the pure sky where the stars
are situated, which the majority of those who discourse on these subjects   c
call the ether. The water and mist and air are the sediment of the ether
and they always flow into the hollows of the earth. We, who dwell in the
hollows of it, are unaware of this and we think that we live above, on the
surface of the earth. It is as if someone who lived deep down in the middle

16. A proverbial expression whose origin is obscure.

of the ocean thought he was living on its surface. Seeing the sun and the
d   other heavenly bodies through the water, he would think the sea to be
the sky; because he is slow and weak, he has never reached the surface
of the sea or risen with his head above the water or come out of the sea
to our region here, nor seen how much purer and more beautiful it is than
his own region, nor has he ever heard of it from anyone who has seen it.

Our experience is the same: living in a certain hollow of the earth, we
believe that we live upon its surface; the air we call the heavens, as if the
stars made their way through it; this too is the same: because of our
e   weakness and slowness we are not able to make our way to the upper
limit of the air; if anyone got to this upper limit, if anyone came to it or
reached it on wings and his head rose above it, then just as fish on rising
from the sea see things in our region, he would see things there and, if
his nature could endure to contemplate them, he would know that there
110   is the true heaven, the true light and the true earth, for the earth here,
these stones and the whole region, are spoiled and eaten away, just as
things in the sea are by the salt water.

Nothing worth mentioning grows in the sea, nothing, one might say, is
fully developed; there are caves and sand and endless slime and mud
wherever there is earth—not comparable in any way with the beauties of
our region. So those things above are in their turn far superior to the things
b   we know. Indeed, if this is the moment to tell a tale, Simmias, it is worth
hearing about the nature of things on the surface of the earth under the
heavens.

At any rate, Socrates, said Simmias, we should be glad to hear this story.

Well then, my friend, in the first place it is said that the earth, looked
at from above, looks like those spherical balls made up of twelve pieces
of leather; it is multi-colored, and of these colors those used by our painters
c   give us an indication; up there the whole earth has these colors, but much
brighter and purer than these; one part is sea-green and of marvelous
beauty, another is golden, another is white, whiter than chalk or snow;
the earth is composed also of the other colors, more numerous and beautiful
than any we have seen. The very hollows of the earth, full of water and
d   air, gleaming among the variety of other colors, present a color of their
own so that the whole is seen as a continuum of variegated colors. On the
surface of the earth the plants grow with corresponding beauty, the trees
and the flowers and the fruits, and so with the hills and the stones, more
beautiful in their smoothness and transparency and color. Our precious
e   stones here are but fragments, our cornelians, jaspers, emeralds and the
rest. All stones there are of that kind, and even more beautiful. The reason
is that there they are pure, not eaten away or spoiled by decay and brine,
or corroded by the water and air which have flowed into the hollows here
and bring ugliness and disease upon earth, stones, the other animals and
111   plants. The earth itself is adorned with all these things, and also with gold
and silver and other metals. These stand out, being numerous and massive
and occurring everywhere, so that the earth is a sight for the blessed. There

are many other living creatures upon the earth, and also men, some living inland, others at the edge of the air, as we live on the edge of the sea, others again live on islands surrounded by air close to the mainland. In a word, what water and the sea are to us, the air is to them and the ether is to them what the air is to us. The climate is such that they are without disease, and they live much longer than people do here; their eyesight, hearing and intelligence and all such are as superior to ours as air is superior to water and ether to air in purity; they have groves and temples dedicated to the gods, in which the gods really dwell, and they communicate with them by speech and prophecy and by the sight of them; they see the sun and moon and stars as they are, and in other ways their happiness is in accord with this.

This then is the nature of the earth as a whole and of its surroundings; around the whole of it there are many regions in the hollows; some are deeper and more open than that in which we live; others are deeper and have a narrower opening than ours, and there are some that have less depth and more width. All these are connected with each other below the surface of the earth in many places by narrow and broader channels, and thus have outlets through which much water flows from one to another as into mixing bowls; huge rivers of both hot and cold water thus flow beneath the earth eternally, much fire and large rivers of fire, and many of wet mud, both more pure and more muddy, such as those flowing in advance of the lava and the stream of lava itself in Sicily. These streams then fill up every and all regions as the flow reaches each, and all these places move up and down with the oscillating movement of the earth. The natural cause of the oscillation is as follows: one of the hollows of the earth, which is also the biggest, pierces through the whole earth; it is that which Homer mentioned when he said: "Far down where is the deepest pit below the earth . . . ,"[17] and which he elsewhere, and many other poets, call Tartarus; into this chasm all the rivers flow together, and again flow out of it, and each river is affected by the nature of the land through which it flows. The reason for their flowing into and out of Tartarus is that this water has no bottom or solid base but it oscillates up and down in waves, and the air and wind about it do the same, for they follow it when it flows to this or that part of the earth. Just as when people breathe, the flow of air goes in and out, so here the air oscillates with the water and creates terrible winds as it goes in and out. Whenever the water retreats to what we call the lower part of the earth, it flows into those parts and fills them up as if the water were pumped in; when it leaves that part for this, it fills these parts again, and the parts filled flow through the channels and through the earth and in each case arrive at the places to which the channels lead and create seas and marshes and rivers and springs. From there the waters flow under the earth again, some flowing around larger and more

b

c

d

e

112

b

c

d

17. *Iliad* viii.14; cf. viii.481.

numerous regions, some round smaller and shallower ones, then flow back into Tartarus, some at a point much lower than where they issued forth, others only a little way, but all of them at a lower point, some of them at the opposite side of the chasm, some on the same side; some flow in a wide circle round the earth once or many times like snakes, then go as far down as possible, then go back into the chasm of Tartarus. From each side

e   it is possible to flow down as far as the center, but not beyond, for this part that faces the river flow from either side is steep.

There are many other large rivers of all kinds, and among these there are four of note; the biggest which flows on the outside (of the earth) in a circle is called Oceanus; opposite it and flowing in the opposite direction

113 is the Acheron; it flows through many other deserted regions and further underground makes its way to the Acherusian lake to which the souls of the majority come after death and, after remaining there for a certain appointed time, longer for some, shorter for others, they are sent back to birth as living creatures. The third river issues between the first two, and close to its source it falls into a region burning with much fire and makes

b   a lake larger than our sea, boiling with water and mud. From there it goes in a circle, foul and muddy, and winding on its way it comes, among other places, to the edge of the Acherusian lake but does not mingle with its waters; then, coiling many times underground it flows lower down into Tartarus; this is called the Pyriphlegethon, and its lava streams throw off

c   fragments of it in various parts of the earth. Opposite this the fourth river issues forth, which is called Stygion, and it is said to flow first into a terrible and wild region, all of it blue-gray in color, and the lake that this river forms by flowing into it is called the Styx. As its waters fall into the lake they acquire dread powers; then diving below and winding round it flows in the opposite direction from the Pyriphlegethon and into the opposite side of the Acherusian lake; its waters do not mingle with any other; it too flows in a circle and into Tartarus opposite the Pyriphlegethon. The name of that fourth river, the poets tell us, is Cocytus.[18]

d   Such is the nature of these things. When the dead arrive at the place to which each has been led by his guardian spirit, they are first judged as to whether they have led a good and pious life. Those who have lived an average life make their way to the Acheron and embark upon such vessels as there are for them and proceed to the lake. There they dwell and are

e   purified by penalties for any wrongdoing they may have committed; they are also suitably rewarded for their good deeds as each deserves. Those who are deemed incurable because of the enormity of their crimes, having committed many great sacrileges or wicked and unlawful murders and other such wrongs—their fitting fate is to be hurled into Tartarus never to emerge from it. Those who are deemed to have committed great but curable crimes, such as doing violence to their father or mother in a fit of

18. For these features of the underworld, see *Odyssey* x.511 ff, xi.157.

temper but who have felt remorse for the rest of their lives, or who have   114
killed someone in a similar manner, these must of necessity be thrown
into Tartarus, but a year later the current throws them out, those who are
guilty of murder by way of Cocytus, and those who have done violence
to their parents by way of the Pyriphlegethon. After they have been carried
along to the Acherusian lake, they cry out and shout, some for those they
have killed, others for those they have maltreated, and calling them they
then pray to them and beg them to allow them to step out into the lake   b
and to receive them. If they persuade them, they do step out and their
punishment comes to an end; if they do not, they are taken back into
Tartarus and from there into the rivers, and this does not stop until they
have persuaded those they have wronged, for this is the punishment which
the judges imposed on them.

Those who are deemed to have lived an extremely pious life are freed   c
and released from the regions of the earth as from a prison; they make
their way up to a pure dwelling place and live on the surface of the earth.
Those who have purified themselves sufficiently by philosophy live in the
future altogether without a body; they make their way to even more
beautiful dwelling places which it is hard to describe clearly, nor do we
now have the time to do so. Because of the things we have enunciated,
Simmias, one must make every effort to share in virtue and wisdom in
one's life, for the reward is beautiful and the hope is great.

No sensible man would insist that these things are as I have described   d
them, but I think it is fitting for a man to risk the belief—for the risk is a
noble one—that this, or something like this, is true about our souls and
their dwelling places, since the soul is evidently immortal, and a man
should repeat this to himself as if it were an incantation, which is why I
have been prolonging my tale. That is the reason why a man should be
of good cheer about his own soul, if during life he has ignored the pleasures   e
of the body and its ornamentation as of no concern to him and doing
him more harm than good, but has seriously concerned himself with the
pleasures of learning, and adorned his soul not with alien but with its
own ornaments, namely, moderation, righteousness, courage, freedom and   115
truth, and in that state awaits his journey to the underworld.

Now you, Simmias, Cebes and the rest of you, Socrates continued, will
each take that journey at some other time but my fated day calls me now,
as a tragic character might say, and it is about time for me to have my
bath, for I think it better to have it before I drink the poison and save the
women the trouble of washing the corpse.

When Socrates had said this Crito spoke. Very well, Socrates, what are   b
your instructions to me and the others about your children or anything
else? What can we do that would please you most?—Nothing new, Crito,
said Socrates, but what I am always saying, that you will please me and
mine and yourselves by taking good care of your own selves in whatever
you do, even if you do not agree with me now, but if you neglect your
own selves, and are unwilling to live following the tracks, as it were, of   c

what we have said now and on previous occasions, you will achieve nothing even if you strongly agree with me at this moment.

We shall be eager to follow your advice, said Crito, but how shall we bury you?

In any way you like, said Socrates, if you can catch me and I do not escape you. And laughing quietly, looking at us, he said: I do not convince
d   Crito that I am this Socrates talking to you here and ordering all I say, but he thinks that I am the thing which he will soon be looking at as a corpse, and so he asks how he shall bury me. I have been saying for some time and at some length that after I have drunk the poison I shall no longer be with you but will leave you to go and enjoy some good fortunes of the blessed, but it seems that I have said all this to him in vain in an attempt to reassure you and myself too. Give a pledge to Crito on my behalf, he said, the opposite pledge to that he gave the jury. He pledged that I would
e   stay; you must pledge that I will not stay after I die, but that I shall go away, so that Crito will bear it more easily when he sees my body being burned or buried and will not be angry on my behalf, as if I were suffering terribly, and so that he should not say at the funeral that he is laying out, or carrying out, or burying Socrates. For know you well, my dear Crito, that to express oneself badly is not only faulty as far as the language goes, but does some harm to the soul. You must be of good cheer, and say
116   you are burying my body, and bury it in any way you like and think most customary.

After saying this he got up and went to another room to take his bath, and Crito followed him and he told us to wait for him. So we stayed, talking among ourselves, questioning what had been said, and then again talking of the great misfortune that had befallen us. We all felt as if we
b   had lost a father and would be orphaned for the rest of our lives. When he had washed, his children were brought to him—two of his sons were small and one was older—and the women of his household came to him. He spoke to them before Crito and gave them what instructions he wanted. Then he sent the women and children away, and he himself joined us. It was now close to sunset, for he had stayed inside for some time. He came and sat down after his bath and conversed for a short while, when the
c   officer of the Eleven came and stood by him and said: "I shall not reproach you as I do the others, Socrates. They are angry with me and curse me when, obeying the orders of my superiors, I tell them to drink the poison. During the time you have been here I have come to know you in other ways as the noblest, the gentlest and the best man who has ever come here. So now too I know that you will not make trouble for me; you know who is responsible and you will direct your anger against them. You know what message I bring. Fare you well, and try to endure what you must
d   as easily as possible." The officer was weeping as he turned away and went out. Socrates looked up at him and said: "Fare you well also; we shall do as you bid us." And turning to us he said: "How pleasant the man is! During the whole time I have been here he has come in and

conversed with me from time to time, a most agreeable man. And how genuinely he now weeps for me. Come, Crito, let us obey him. Let someone bring the poison if it is ready; if not, let the man prepare it."

But Socrates, said Crito, I think the sun still shines upon the hills and has not yet set. I know that others drink the poison quite a long time after they have received the order, eating and drinking quite a bit, and some of them enjoy intimacy with their loved ones. Do not hurry; there is still some time.

It is natural, Crito, for them to do so, said Socrates, for they think they derive some benefit from doing this, but it is not fitting for me. I do not expect any benefit from drinking the poison a little later, except to become ridiculous in my own eyes for clinging to life, and be sparing of it when there is none left. So do as I ask and do not refuse me.

Hearing this, Crito nodded to the slave who was standing near him; the slave went out and after a time came back with the man who was to administer the poison, carrying it made ready in a cup. When Socrates saw him he said: "Well, my good man, you are an expert in this; what must one do?"—"Just drink it and walk around until your legs feel heavy, and then lie down and it will act of itself." And he offered the cup to Socrates, who took it quite cheerfully, Echecrates, without a tremor or any change of feature or color, but looking at the man from under his eyebrows as was his wont, asked: "What do you say about pouring a libation from this drink? It is allowed?"—"We only mix as much as we believe will suffice," said the man.

I understand, Socrates said, but one is allowed, indeed one must, utter a prayer to the gods that the journey from here to yonder may be fortunate. This is my prayer and may it be so.

And while he was saying this, he was holding the cup, and then drained it calmly and easily. Most of us had been able to hold back our tears reasonably well up till then, but when we saw him drinking it and after he drank it, we could hold them back no longer; my own tears came in floods against my will. So I covered my face. I was weeping for myself, not for him—for my misfortune in being deprived of such a comrade. Even before me, Crito was unable to restrain his tears and got up. Apollodorus had not ceased from weeping before, and at this moment his noisy tears and anger made everybody present break down, except Socrates. "What is this," he said, "you strange fellows. It is mainly for this reason that I sent the women away, to avoid such unseemliness, for I am told one should die in good omened silence. So keep quiet and control yourselves."

His words made us ashamed, and we checked our tears. He walked around, and when he said his legs were heavy he lay on his back as he had been told to do, and the man who had given him the poison touched his body, and after a while tested his feet and legs, pressed hard upon his foot and asked him if he felt this, and Socrates said no. Then he pressed his calves, and made his way up his body and showed us that it was cold and stiff. He felt it himself and said that when the cold reached his heart

e

117

b

c

d

e

118

118a   he would be gone. As his belly was getting cold Socrates uncovered his head—he had covered it—and said—these were his last words—"Crito, we owe a cock to Asclepius;[19] make this offering to him and do not forget."—"It shall be done," said Crito, "tell us if there is anything else." But there was no answer. Shortly afterwards Socrates made a movement; the man uncovered him and his eyes were fixed. Seeing this Crito closed his mouth and his eyes.

Such was the end of our comrade, Echecrates, a man who, we would say, was of all those we have known the best, and also the wisest and the most upright.

19. A cock was sacrificed to Asclepius by the sick people who slept in his temples, hoping for a cure. Socrates apparently means that death is a cure for the ills of life.

CRATYLUS

This dialogue is on a topic of great interest to Plato's contemporaries that figures little in our own discussions in philosophy of language: the 'correctness of names'. When a name (or, for that matter, any other word or phrase) is the correct one for naming a given thing or performing another linguistic function, what is the source of this correctness? Socrates canvasses two opposed positions. The first is defended by his close friend Hermogenes (Hermogenes was in Socrates' entourage on the day of his death), the impecunious brother of Callias, the rich patron of sophists at Athens in whose house the drama of Protagoras is set. Hermogenes adopts the minimalist position that correctness is by convention: whatever is agreed in a community to be the name to use for a thing is the correct one in that community. The other position is defended by Cratylus, a historical person mentioned also by Aristotle, whose own information about him may however derive from what the character Cratylus says in this dialogue. Cratylus adopts the obscure 'naturalist' position that each name names only whatever it does 'by nature'—no matter what the conventions in any community may be. As a first approximation, this means that under expert etymological examination each name can be reduced to a disguised description correctly revealing the nature of the thing named by it—and that revelatory capacity is what makes it the correct name for that thing. Socrates examines the views of each disputant and attempts to resolve the conflict between them. But he concludes that the knowledge of names—the etymological art professing to reveal the true nature of things by working out the ultimate descriptive meanings of the words we use—is of no real importance. All it can ever reveal is what those who first introduced our words thought was the nature of reality, and that might well be wrong—indeed, Socrates employs etymological principles themselves to argue that the Greek language indicates, falsely, that the nature of reality is constant change and flux. To learn the truth we have to go behind words altogether, to examine with our minds, and grasp directly the permanent, unchanging natures of things as they are in themselves: Platonic Forms.

Readers are always puzzled at the fact that Plato has Socrates devote more than half his discussion to proposing etymological analyses of a whole series of names, beginning with the names of the gods. We should bear in mind that, when Plato was writing, expertise in etymology was highly regarded, precisely as a means of discovering the ultimate truth about things through coming to possess knowledge of names. At least part of Plato's purpose seems to be to establish Socrates' credentials as a first-rate practitioner of the art of etymology *as then practiced, better than the 'experts' themselves. When Socrates then also argues that knowledge of names is an unimportant thing, he can be taken to speak with the authority not just of philosophy but even of etymological science itself—as an insider, not an outsider looking in. Somewhat similarly, in Phaedrus and Menexenus philosophy is credited with the unique ability actually to do well what rhetoric, another prestigious contemporary expertise, professed to be able to do on its own.*

J.M.C.

383   HERMOGENES: Shall we let Socrates here join our discussion?

CRATYLUS: If you like.

HERMOGENES: Cratylus says, Socrates, that there is a correctness of name for each thing, one that belongs to it by nature. A thing's name isn't whatever people agree to call it—some bit of their native language that applies to it—but there is a natural correctness of names, which is the

b   same for everyone, Greek or foreigner. So, I ask him whether his own name is truly 'Cratylus'. He agrees that it is. "What about Socrates?" I say. "His name is 'Socrates'." "Does this also hold for everyone else? Is the name we call him his name?" "It certainly doesn't hold of you. Your name isn't 'Hermogenes', not even if everyone calls you by it." Eagerly, I ask him to tell me what he means. He responds sarcastically and makes nothing

384   clear. He pretends to possess some private knowledge which would force me to agree with him and say the very things about names that he says himself, were he to express it in plain terms. So, if you can somehow interpret Cratylus' oracular utterances, I'd gladly listen. Though I'd really rather find out what you yourself have to say about the correctness of names, if that's all right with you.

SOCRATES: Hermogenes, son of Hipponicus, there is an ancient proverb

b   that "fine things are very difficult" to know about, and it certainly isn't easy to get to know about names. To be sure, if I'd attended Prodicus' fifty-drachma lecture course, which he himself advertises as an exhaustive treatment of the topic, there'd be nothing to prevent you from learning the precise truth about the correctness of names straightaway. But as

c   I've heard only the one-drachma course, I don't know the truth about it. Nonetheless, I am ready to investigate it along with you and Cratylus. As for his denying that your real name is 'Hermogenes', I suspect he's making fun of you. Perhaps he thinks you want to make money but fail every time you try.[1] In any case, as I was saying, it's certainly difficult to know

Translated by C.D.C. Reeve.

1. Hermes is the god of profit and 'Hermogenes' means 'son of Hermes.' A different account of the name is given at 407e–408b.

about these matters, so we'll have to conduct a joint investigation to see who is right, you or Cratylus.

HERMOGENES: Well, Socrates, I've often talked with Cratylus—and with lots of other people, for that matter—and no one is able to persuade me that the correctness of names is determined by anything besides convention and agreement. I believe that any name you give a thing is its correct   d
name. If you change its name and give it another, the new one is as correct as the old. For example, when we give names to our domestic slaves, the new ones are as correct as the old. No name belongs to a particular thing by nature, but only because of the rules and usage of those who establish the usage and call it by that name. However, if I'm wrong about this, I'm ready to listen not just to Cratylus but to anyone, and to learn from him too.   e

SOCRATES: Perhaps you're on to something, Hermogenes, let's see. Are   385
you saying that whatever anyone decides to call[2] a particular thing is its name?

HERMOGENES: I am.

SOCRATES: Whether it is a private individual or a community that does so?

HERMOGENES: Yes.

SOCRATES: What about this? Suppose I call one of the things that are— for instance, the one we now call 'man'—suppose I give *that* the name 'horse' and give the one we now call 'horse' the name 'man'. Will the same thing have the public name 'man' but the private name 'horse'? Is that what you mean?

HERMOGENES: Yes.[3]   385b1

SOCRATES: So whatever each person says is the name of something, for   d
him, that is its name?

HERMOGENES: Yes.

SOCRATES: And however many names someone says there are for each thing, it will really have that number at whatever time he says it?

HERMOGENES: Yes, Socrates, for I can't conceive of any other way in which names could be correct. I call a thing by the name I gave it; you call it by the different name you gave it. In the same way, I see that different communities have different names for the same things—Greeks differing   e
from other Greeks, and Greeks from foreigners.

SOCRATES: Let's see, Hermogenes, whether the same also seems to you to hold of the things that are. Is the being or essence of each of them something private for each person, as Protagoras tells us? He says that man is "the measure of all things," and that things are to me as they appear to me, and are to you as they appear to you. Do you agree, or do you   386
believe that things have some fixed being or essence of their own?

---

2. Reading *ho ean thēi kalein* in a2.

3. Following Schofield, *Classical Quarterly* 22 (1972), we transfer 385b2–d1 to follow 387c5.

HERMOGENES: There have been times, Socrates, when I have been so puzzled that I've been driven to take refuge in Protagoras' doctrine, even though I don't believe it at all.

SOCRATES: What's that? Have you actually been driven to believe that

b   there is no such thing as a bad man?

HERMOGENES: No, by god, I haven't. Indeed, I've often found myself believing that there are *very* bad ones, and plenty of them.

SOCRATES: What? Have you never believed that there are any who are very good?

HERMOGENES: Not many.

SOCRATES: But you did believe that there were *some* good ones?

HERMOGENES: I did.

SOCRATES: And what do you hold about such people? Or is it this: the very good are very wise, while the very bad are very foolish?

c   HERMOGENES: Yes, that's what I believe.

SOCRATES: But if Protagoras is telling the truth—if it *is* the *Truth*[4] that things are for each person as he believes them to be, how is it possible for one person to be wise and another foolish?

HERMOGENES: It isn't possible.

SOCRATES: You strongly believe, it seems to me, that if wisdom exists, and foolishness likewise, then Protagoras cannot be telling the truth. After all, if what each person believes to be true *is* true for him, no one can truly

d   be wiser than anyone else.

HERMOGENES: That's right.

SOCRATES: But you also reject Euthydemus' doctrine that everything always has every attribute simultaneously. For if virtue and vice always belong to everything simultaneously, it follows once again that it is impossible for some people to be good and others to be bad.

HERMOGENES: That's true.

SOCRATES: But if neither is right, if it isn't the case that everything always has every attribute simultaneously or that each thing has a being or essence privately for each person, then it is clear that things have some fixed being

e   or essence of their own. They are not in relation to us and are not made to fluctuate by how they appear to us. They are by themselves, in relation to their own being or essence, which is theirs by nature.

HERMOGENES: I agree, Socrates.

SOCRATES: And if things are of such a nature, doesn't the same hold of actions performed in relation to them? Or aren't actions included in some one class of the things that are?

HERMOGENES: Of course they are.

SOCRATES: So an action's performance accords with the action's own

387 nature, and not with what we believe. Suppose, for example, that we undertake to cut something. If we make the cut in whatever way *we* choose and with whatever tool *we* choose, we will not succeed in cutting. But if

---

4. Plato is making a pun on the title of Protagoras' book.

in each case we choose to cut in accord with the nature of cutting and being cut and with the natural tool for cutting, we'll succeed and cut correctly. If we try to cut contrary to nature, however, we'll be in error and accomplish nothing.

HERMOGENES: That's my view, at least. b

SOCRATES: So, again, if we undertake to burn something, our burning mustn't accord with every belief but with the correct one—that is to say, with the one that tells us how that thing burns and is burned naturally, and what the natural tool for burning it is?

HERMOGENES: That's right.

SOCRATES: And the same holds of all other actions?

HERMOGENES: Certainly.

SOCRATES: Now isn't speaking or saying one sort of action?

HERMOGENES: Yes.

SOCRATES: Then will someone speak correctly if he speaks in whatever way he believes he should speak? Or isn't it rather the case that he will accomplish something and succeed in speaking if he says things in the natural way to say them, in the natural way for them to be said, and with c the natural tool for saying them? But if he speaks in any other way he will be in error and accomplish nothing?

HERMOGENES: I believe so.[5] 387c5

SOCRATES: Tell me this. Is there something you call speaking the truth 385b2 and something you call speaking a falsehood?

HERMOGENES: Indeed, there is.

SOCRATES: Then some statements are true, while others are false?

HERMOGENES: Certainly.

SOCRATES: And those that say of the things that are that they are, are true, while those that say of the things that are that they are not, are false?

HERMOGENES: Yes.

SOCRATES: So it is possible to say both things that are and things that are not in a statement?

HERMOGENES: Certainly.

SOCRATES: Is a whole true statement true but not its parts? c

HERMOGENES: No, the parts are also true.

SOCRATES: Are the large parts true but not the small ones, or are all of them true?

HERMOGENES: In my view, they are all true.

SOCRATES: Is there a part of a statement that's smaller than a name?

HERMOGENES: No, it is the smallest.

SOCRATES: In a true statement, is this smallest part something that's said?

HERMOGENES: Yes.

SOCRATES: And, on your view, this part is then true.

HERMOGENES: Yes.

SOCRATES: And a part of a false statement is false?

---

5. Here we insert 385b2–d1; see note to 385b above.

HERMOGENES: That's right.

SOCRATES: So isn't it possible to say a true or a false name, since true or false statements are possible?

d HERMOGENES: Certainly.

387c6 SOCRATES: Now using names is a part of saying; since it is by using names that people say things.

HERMOGENES: Certainly.

SOCRATES: And if speaking or saying is a sort of action, one that is about things, isn't using names also a sort of action?

HERMOGENES: Yes.

d SOCRATES: And didn't we see that actions aren't in relation to us but have a special nature of their own?

HERMOGENES: We did.

SOCRATES: So if we are to be consistent with what we said previously, we cannot name things as we choose; rather, we must name them in the natural way for them to be named and with the natural tool for naming them. In that way we'll accomplish something and succeed in naming, otherwise we won't.

HERMOGENES: So it seems.

SOCRATES: Again, what one has to cut, one must cut with something?

HERMOGENES: Yes.

SOCRATES: And what one has to weave, one must weave with something?

e And what one has to drill, one must drill with something?

HERMOGENES: Certainly.

SOCRATES: And what one has to name, one must name with something?

388 HERMOGENES: That's right.

SOCRATES: What must drilling be done with?

HERMOGENES: A drill.

SOCRATES: Weaving?

HERMOGENES: A shuttle.

SOCRATES: And naming?

HERMOGENES: A name.

SOCRATES: Well done! So a name is also a sort of tool?

HERMOGENES: That's right.

SOCRATES: And suppose I ask, "What sort of tool is a shuttle?" Isn't the answer, "One we weave with"?

b HERMOGENES: Yes.

SOCRATES: What do we do when we weave? Don't we divide the warp and woof that are mixed together?

HERMOGENES: Yes.

SOCRATES: Would you answer in the same way about drills and other tools?

HERMOGENES: Certainly.

SOCRATES: And you'd also answer in the same way about names, since they are tools. What do we do when we name?

HERMOGENES: I don't know what to answer.

SOCRATES: Don't we instruct each other, that is to say, divide things according to their natures?

HERMOGENES: Certainly.

SOCRATES: So just as a shuttle is a tool for dividing warp and woof, a name is a tool for giving instruction, that is to say, for dividing being.   c

HERMOGENES: Yes.

SOCRATES: Isn't a shuttle a weaver's tool?

HERMOGENES: Of course.

SOCRATES: So a weaver will use shuttles well; and to use a shuttle well is to use it as a weaver does. By the same token, an instructor will use names well; and to use a name well is to use it as an instructor does.

HERMOGENES: Yes.

SOCRATES: When a weaver uses a shuttle well, whose product is he using?

HERMOGENES: A carpenter's.

SOCRATES: Is everyone a carpenter or only those who possess the craft of carpentry?

HERMOGENES: Only those who possess the craft.

SOCRATES: And whose product does a driller use well when he uses a drill?   d

HERMOGENES: A blacksmith's.

SOCRATES: And is everyone a blacksmith or only those who possess the craft?

HERMOGENES: Only those who possess the craft.

SOCRATES: Good. So whose product does an instructor use when he uses a name?

HERMOGENES: I don't know.

SOCRATES: Can you at least tell me this? Who or what provides us with the names we use?

HERMOGENES: I don't know that either.

SOCRATES: Don't you think that rules[6] provide us with them?

HERMOGENES: I suppose they do.

SOCRATES: So, when an instructor uses a name, he's using the product of a rule-setter.   e

HERMOGENES: I believe he is.

SOCRATES: Do you think that every man is a rule-setter or only the one who possesses the craft?

HERMOGENES: Only the one who possesses the craft.

SOCRATES: It follows that it isn't every man who can give names, Hermogenes, but only a namemaker, and he, it seems, is a rule-setter—the kind   389 of craftsman most rarely found among human beings.

HERMOGENES: I suppose so.

---

6. The Greek here is *ho nomos:* law or customary usage—itself established, as Socrates immediately goes on to say, by a *nomothetēs,* usually a legislator or law-giver, but here someone who establishes the rules of usage that give significance to names, a 'rule-setter.'

SOCRATES: Come now, consider where a rule-setter looks in giving names. Use the previous discussion as your guide. Where does a carpenter look in making a shuttle? Isn't it to that sort of thing whose nature is to weave?

HERMOGENES: Certainly.

b   SOCRATES: Suppose the shuttle breaks while he's making it. Will he make another looking to the broken one? Or will he look to the very form to which he looked in making the one he broke?

HERMOGENES: In my view, he will look to the form.

SOCRATES: Then it would be absolutely right to call that what a shuttle itself is.

HERMOGENES: I suppose so.

SOCRATES: Hence whenever he has to make a shuttle for weaving garments of any sort, whether light or heavy, linen or woolen, mustn't it possess the form of a shuttle? And mustn't he put into it the nature that

c   naturally best suits it to perform its own work?

HERMOGENES: Yes.

SOCRATES: And the same holds of all other tools. When a craftsman discovers the type of tool that is naturally suited for a given type of work, he must embody it in the material out of which he is making the tool. He mustn't make the tool in whatever way he happens to choose, but in the natural way. So it seems that a blacksmith must know how to embody in iron the type of drill naturally suited for each type of work.

HERMOGENES: Certainly.

SOCRATES: And a carpenter must embody in wood the type of shuttle naturally suited for each type of weaving.

HERMOGENES: That's right.

SOCRATES: Because it seems that there's a type of shuttle that's naturally

d   suited to each type of weaving. And the same holds of tools in general.

HERMOGENES: Yes.

SOCRATES: So mustn't a rule-setter also know how to embody in sounds and syllables the name naturally suited to each thing? And if he is to be an authentic giver of names, mustn't he, in making and giving each name, look to what a name itself is? And if different rule-setters do not make

e   each name out of the same syllables, we mustn't forget[7] that different blacksmiths, who are making the same tool for the same type of work, don't all make it out of the same iron. But as long as they give it the same form—even if that form is embodied in different iron—the tool will be

390 correct, whether it is made in Greece or abroad. Isn't that so?

HERMOGENES: Certainly.

SOCRATES: Don't you evaluate Greek and foreign rule-setters in the same way? Provided they give each thing the form of name suited to it, no matter what syllables it is embodied in, they are equally good rule-setters, whether they are in Greece or abroad.

7. Reading *agnoein* in e1.

HERMOGENES: Certainly.

SOCRATES: Now, who is likely to know whether the appropriate form of shuttle is present in any given bit of wood? A carpenter who makes it or a weaver who uses it?

HERMOGENES: In all likelihood, Socrates, it is the one who uses it.

SOCRATES: So who uses what a lyre-maker produces? Isn't he the one who would know best how to supervise the manufacture of lyres and would also know whether what has been made has been well made or not?

HERMOGENES: Certainly.

SOCRATES: Who is that?

HERMOGENES: A lyre-player.

SOCRATES: And who will supervise a ship-builder?

HERMOGENES: A ship's captain.

SOCRATES: And who can best supervise the work of a rule-setter, whether here or abroad, and judge its products? Isn't it whoever will use them?

HERMOGENES: Yes.

SOCRATES: And isn't that the person who knows how to ask questions?

HERMOGENES: Certainly.

SOCRATES: And he also knows how to answer them?

HERMOGENES: Yes.

SOCRATES: And what would you call someone who knows how to ask and answer questions? Wouldn't you call him a dialectician?

HERMOGENES: Yes, I would.

SOCRATES: So it's the work of a carpenter to make a rudder. And if the rudder is to be a fine one, a ship-captain must supervise him.

HERMOGENES: Evidently.

SOCRATES: But it's the work of a rule-setter, it seems, to make a name. And if names are to be given well, a dialectician must supervise him.

HERMOGENES: That's right.

SOCRATES: It follows that the giving of names can't be as inconsequential a matter as you think, Hermogenes, nor can it be the work of an inconsequential or chance person. So Cratylus is right in saying that things have natural names, and that not everyone is a craftsman of names, but only someone who looks to the natural name of each thing and is able to put its form into letters and syllables.

HERMOGENES: I don't know how to oppose you, Socrates. It isn't easy for me suddenly to change my opinion, though. I think you would be more likely to persuade me if you showed me just what this natural correctness of names you're talking about consists in.

SOCRATES: My dear Hermogenes, I don't have a position on this. You have forgotten what I told you a while ago, namely that I didn't know about names but that I would investigate them with you. And now that we *are* investigating them, you and I, at least this much is clearer than before, that names do possess some sort of natural correctness and that it isn't every man who knows how to name things well. Isn't that right?

HERMOGENES: Certainly.

SOCRATES: So our next task is to try to discover what this correctness is, if indeed you want to know.

HERMOGENES: Of course I do.

SOCRATES: Then investigate the matter.

HERMOGENES: How am I to do that?

SOCRATES: The most correct way is together with people who already know, but you must pay them well and show gratitude besides—these are the sophists. Your brother Callias got his reputation for wisdom from
c them in return for a lot of money. So you had better beg and implore him to teach you what he learned from Protagoras about the correctness of names, since you haven't yet come into any money of your own.

HERMOGENES: But it would be absurd for me to beg for Protagoras' "Truth," Socrates, as if I desired the things contained in it and thought them worthwhile, when I totally reject them.

SOCRATES: Well, if that doesn't suit you, you'll have to learn from Homer
d and the other poets.

HERMOGENES: And where does Homer say anything about names, Socrates, and what does he say?

SOCRATES: In lots of places. The best and most important are the ones in which he distinguishes between the names humans call things and those the gods call them. Or don't you think that these passages tell us something remarkable about the correctness of names? Surely, the gods call things
e by their naturally correct names—or don't you think so?

HERMOGENES: I certainly know that if they call them by any names at all, it's by the correct ones. But what passages are you referring to?

SOCRATES: Do you know where he says that the Trojan river that had single combat with Hephaestus is "called 'Xanthos' by the gods and 'Skamandros' by men"?[8]

HERMOGENES: I certainly do.

392 SOCRATES: And don't you think it's an awe-inspiring thing to know that the river is more correctly called 'Xanthos' than 'Skamandros'? Or consider, if you like, when he says about a certain bird that

> The gods call it 'chalcis' but men call it 'cymindis'.[9]

Do you think it's an inconsequential matter to learn that it is far more correct to call this bird 'chalcis' than to call it 'cymindis'? What about all the similar things that Homer and the other poets tell us? For example,
b that it is more correct to call a certain hill 'Murine' than 'Batieia'?[10] But perhaps these examples are too hard for you and me to figure out. It is

8. *Iliad* xxi.332–80 and xx.74.

9. *Iliad* xiv.291.

10. *Iliad* ii.813 ff.

easier and more within human power, I think, to investigate the kind of
correctness Homer ascribes to 'Skamandrios' and 'Astyanax', which he
says are the names of Hector's son. You know, of course, the lines to which
I refer.[11]

HERMOGENES: Certainly.

SOCRATES: Which of the names given to the boy do you suppose Homer
thought was more correct, 'Astyanax' or 'Skamandrios'?

HERMOGENES: I really can't say.   c

SOCRATES: Look at it this way. If you were asked who gives names more
correctly, those who are wiser or those who are more foolish, what would
you answer?

HERMOGENES: That it is clearly those who are wiser.

SOCRATES: And which class do you think is wiser on the whole, a city's
women or its men?

HERMOGENES: Its men.

SOCRATES: Now you know, don't you, that Homer tells us that Hector's
son was called 'Astyanax' by the men of Troy?[12] But if the men called him   d
'Astyanax', isn't it clear that 'Skamandrios' must be what the women
called him?

HERMOGENES: Probably so.

SOCRATES: And didn't Homer also think that the Trojans were wiser than
their women?

HERMOGENES: I suppose he did.

SOCRATES: So mustn't he have thought that 'Astyanax' was a more correct
name for the boy than 'Skamandrios'?

HERMOGENES: Evidently.

SOCRATES: Well, let's investigate why it is more correct. Doesn't Homer
himself suggest a very good explanation when he says

He alone defended their city and long walls?[13]   e

For because of this, you see, it seems correct to call the son of the defender
'Astyanax' or lord of the city (*astu, anax*) which, as Homer says, his father
was defending.

HERMOGENES: That seems right to me.

SOCRATES: It does? You understand it, Hermogenes? For I don't understand it yet myself.

HERMOGENES: Then *I* certainly don't.

SOCRATES: But, my good friend, didn't Homer also give Hector his name?   393

HERMOGENES: What if he did?

11. *Iliad* vi.402–3.
12. *Iliad* xxii.506.
13. *Iliad* xxii.507, referring to Hector.

SOCRATES: Well, it seems to me that 'Hector' is more or less the same as 'Astyanax', since both names seem to be Greek. After all, 'lord' (*'anax'*) and 'possessor' (*'hektōr'*) signify pretty much the same, since both are names for a king. Surely, a man possesses that of which he is lord, since it is clear that he controls, owns, and has it. But perhaps you think I'm

b   talking nonsense, and that I'm wrong to suppose that I've found a clue to Homer's beliefs about the correctness of names.

HERMOGENES: No, I don't think you're wrong. You may well have found a clue.

SOCRATES: At any rate, it seems to me that it is right to call a lion's offspring a 'lion' and a horse's offspring a 'horse'. I'm not talking about some monster other than a horse that happens to be born from a horse

c   but one that is a natural offspring of its kind. If, contrary to nature, a horse gave birth to a calf, it should be called a 'calf', not a 'colt'. And if something that isn't a human offspring is born to a human, I don't think it should be called a 'human'. And the same applies to trees and all the rest. Don't you agree?

HERMOGENES: I agree.

SOCRATES: Good. But you had better watch out in case I trick you, for by the same argument any offspring of a king should be called a 'king'. But it doesn't matter whether the same thing is signified by the same

d   syllables or by different ones. And if a letter is added or subtracted, that doesn't matter either, so long as the being or essence of the thing is in control and is expressed in its name.

HERMOGENES: How do you mean?

SOCRATES: It's something fairly simple. You know that when we speak of the elements or letters of the alphabet, it is their names we utter, not the letters themselves, except in the case of these four *e, u, o,* and *ō*.[14] We make names for all the other vowels and consonants, as you know, by

e   uttering additional letters together with them. But as long as we include the force or power of the letter, we may correctly call it by that name, and it will express it for us. Take *'bēta'*, for example. The addition of *'ē'*, *'t'*, and *'a'* does no harm and doesn't prevent the whole name from expressing the nature of that element or letter which the rule-setter wished to name, so well did he know how to give names to the letters.

HERMOGENES: I believe you're right.

SOCRATES: Doesn't the same argument apply to 'king'? For a king will

394 probably be the son of a king, a good man the son of a good man, a fine man the son of a fine one, and so on. So, unless a monster is born, the offspring of a kind will be of the same kind and should be called by the same name. But because of variation in their syllables, names that are really the same seem different to the uninitiated. Similarly, a doctor's medicines, which have different colors and perfumes added to them, ap-

---

14. The names 'epsilon', 'upsilon', 'omicron' (short *o*), and 'omega' (long *o*) were not used in Plato's time; one simply pronounced the sound.

pear different to us, although they are really the same and appear the same to a doctor, who looks only to their power to cure and isn't disconcerted by the additives. Similarly, someone who knows about names looks to their force or power and isn't disconcerted if a letter is added, transposed, or subtracted, or even if the force a name possesses is embodied in different letters altogether. So, for example, in the names 'Hector' and 'Astyanax', which we were discussing just now, none of the letters is the same, except 't', but they signify the same anyway. And what letters does 'Archepolis'— 'Ruler-of-a-city'—have in common with them? Yet, it expresses the same thing. Many other names signify simply king; others signify general, for example, 'Agis' ('Leader'), 'Polemarchus' ('War-lord'), 'Eupolemus' ('Good-warrior'); and still others signify doctor, for example, 'Iatrocles' ('Famous-healer') and 'Acesimbrotus' ('Healer-of-mortals'). And we might perhaps find many others, which differ in their letters and syllables, but which have the same force or power when spoken. Is that plain to you or not?

HERMOGENES   Certainly.

SOCRATES: Then those that are born according to nature should be given the same names as their fathers.

HERMOGENES: Yes.

SOCRATES: What about the ones that are born contrary to nature, those that are some form of monster? For instance, when a good and pious man has an impious son, the latter shouldn't have his father's name but that of the kind to which he belongs, just as in our earlier example of a horse having a calf as offspring?

HERMOGENES: Yes.

SOCRATES: Therefore the impious son of a pious father should be given the name of the kind to which he belongs.

HERMOGENES: That's right.

SOCRATES: Then he shouldn't be called 'Theophilus' ('God-beloved') or 'Mnesitheus' ('Mindful-of-god'), or anything of that sort, but something that signifies the opposite, if indeed names are to be actually correct.

HERMOGENES: That's absolutely right, Socrates.

SOCRATES: Thus the name 'Orestes' ('Mountain-man') is surely correct, Hermogenes, whether it was given to him by chance or by some poet, who displayed in his name the brutality, savagery, and ruggedness of his nature.

HERMOGENES: It seems so, Socrates.

SOCRATES: And his father's name also seems to accord with nature.

HERMOGENES: It does.

SOCRATES: Yes, for Agamemnon is someone who worked hard and perse-vered, bringing his plans to completion because of his virtue or excellence. The stay of his army in Troy and his perseverance there is a sign of this. And thus the name 'Agamemnon' signifies that this man is admirable (*agastos*) for holding his ground (*epimonē*). The name 'Atreus' also seems to be correct; for both his murder of Chrysippus and his cruelty to Thyestes

b

c

d

e

395

b

were damaging and destructive (*atēra*) to his virtue. However, the meaning of his name is somewhat distorted and obscure, so that it doesn't express his nature to everyone. But to those who understand about names it adequately expresses what 'Atreus' means. For whether the name accords with his stubbornness (*ateires*), or his boldness (*atrestos*), or his destructiveness (*at-*

c   *ēros*), it is correctly given to him. I think Pelops also has a fitting name; for 'Pelops' signifies he who sees only what is near at hand (*pelas, opsis*).

HERMOGENES: How is that?

SOCRATES: Because, according to legend, he didn't think about or foresee what the long-term consequences of murdering Myrtilus would be for his entire family, or all the misery that would overwhelm them. In his eagerness to win Hippodameia by any available means, he saw only what was ready

d   to hand and on the spot—that is to say, what was nearby (*pelas*). Everyone would agree, too, that 'Tantalus' was given correctly and according to nature, if what's said about its bearer is true.

HERMOGENES: What's that?

SOCRATES: They say that many terrible misfortunes happened to him in his life—the last of which was the total overthrow of his country—and that, in Hades, after his death, he had a stone suspended (*talanteia*) over

e   his head, in wondrous harmony with his name. It's exactly as if someone had wished to name him 'Talantatos' ('Most-weighed-upon') but had disguised the name and said 'Tantalus' instead. In some such way, in any case, the chance of legend supplied him with this name. His father, who is said to have been Zeus, also seems to have had an altogether fine name

396 given to him—but it isn't easy to figure out. That's because the name 'Zeus' is exactly like a phrase that we divide into two parts, 'Zēna' and 'Dia', some of us using one of them and some the other.[15] But these two names, reunited into one, express the nature of the god—which is just what we said a name should do. Certainly, no one is more the cause of life (*zēn*), whether for us or for anything else, than the ruler and king of all things. Thus 'Zēna' and 'Dia' together correctly name the god that is

b   always the cause of life (*di' hon zēn*) for all creatures. But, as I say, his name, which is really one, is divided in two, 'Dia' and 'Zēna'. When one hears that Zeus is the son of Cronus, one might find that offensive at first, and it might seem more reasonable to say that he is the offspring of a great intellect. But in fact Cronus' name signifies not a child (*koros*), but the purity and clarity of his intellect or understanding.[16] According to legend, he was the son of Uranus (Heaven), whose name is also correctly given, for the sight of what is above is well called by the name 'ourania' ('heavenly')—looking at the things above (*horōsa ta anō*)—and astronomers

15. 'Zeus' (nominative) has two declensions, one of which (a poetical one) has 'Zēna' in the accusative, the other (the ordinary one) 'Dia'.

16. Socrates is treating Cronus' name as deriving not from 'koros' but from 'korein' ('to sweep'). Cronus' character is spotless and his intelligence clear because both have been well swept.

say, Hermogenes, that that results in purity of intellect. If I could remember   c
Hesiod's genealogy, and the even earlier ancestors of the gods he mentions,
I wouldn't have stopped explaining the correctness of the names he gives
them, until I had tested this wisdom which has suddenly come upon me—
I do not know from where—to see whether or not it holds up till the end.   d

HERMOGENES: Indeed, Socrates, you do seem to me to be exactly like a
prophet who has suddenly been inspired to deliver oracles.

SOCRATES: Yes, Hermogenes, and I, for my part, mostly blame Euthyphro,
of the deme of Prospalta,[17] for its coming upon me. I was with him at
dawn, lending an ear to his lengthy discussion. He must have been inspired,
because it looks as though he has not only filled my ears with his superhuman wisdom but taken possession of my soul as well. So it seems to me
that this is what we ought to do: Today, we'll use this wisdom and finish   e
our examination of names, but tomorrow, if the rest of you agree, we'll
exorcise it and purify ourselves, as soon as we've found someone—whether
priest or wise man—who is clever at that kind of purification.   397

HERMOGENES: That's fine with me. I'd be very glad to hear what remains
to be said about names.

SOCRATES: Then that's what we must do. Since we now have some sort
of outline to follow, which names do you want us to begin with, in order
to find out whether names themselves will testify to us that they are not
given by chance, but have some sort of correctness? The names that heroes
and men are said to have might perhaps deceive us. After all, as we saw   b
at the beginning, they are often given because they are the names of
ancestors, and some of them are wholly inappropriate. Many, too, are
given in the hope that they will prove appropriate, such as 'Eutychides'
('Son-of-good-fortune'), 'Sosias' ('Saviour'), 'Theophilus' ('God-beloved'),
and many others. In my view, we must leave such names aside. We are
most likely to find correctly given names among those concerned with the
things that by nature always are, since it is proper for their names to be
given with the greatest care, and some may even be the work of a more   c
than human power.

HERMOGENES: I think that's sensible, Socrates.

SOCRATES: So isn't it right to begin by seeing why the name '*theoi*' ('gods')
is itself one that the gods are correctly called?

HERMOGENES: It probably is.

SOCRATES: I suspect something like this. It seems to me that the first
inhabitants of Greece believed only in those gods in which many foreigners   d
still believe today—the sun, moon, earth, stars, and sky. And, seeing that
these were always moving or running, they gave them the name '*theoi*'
because it was their nature to run (*thein*). Later, when they learned about
the other gods, they called them all by that name. Does that seem likely—
or am I talking nonsense?

---

17. This is probably the Euthyphro who appears in the dialogue of that name, where he
is described as claiming authority on Uranus, Cronus, and Zeus (*Euthyphro* 4e–5a, 5e–6a).

HERMOGENES: It's very likely.

SOCRATES: What shall we investigate next? Clearly, it's daemons,[18] then heroes, then humans, isn't it?[19]

e   HERMOGENES: Yes, daemons are next.[20]

SOCRATES: And what is the correct meaning of the name 'daemons', Hermogenes? See if you think there's anything in what I'm about to say.

HERMOGENES: Say it, and I will.

SOCRATES: Do you know what Hesiod says daemons are?

HERMOGENES: No, I don't remember.

SOCRATES: Do you remember that he speaks of a golden race, which was the first race of human beings to be born?

HERMOGENES: Yes, I remember that.

SOCRATES: He says this about it:

> *Since this race has been eclipsed by fate,*
398 > *They are called sacred daemons;*
> *They live on earth and are good,*
> *Warding off evil and guarding mortal men.*[21]

HERMOGENES: So what?

SOCRATES: Well, I don't think he's saying that the golden race is by nature made of gold, but that it is good and fine. I consider it a proof of this that he calls us a race of iron.

HERMOGENES: That's true.

SOCRATES: So don't you think that if someone who presently exists were
b   good, Hesiod would say that he too belonged to the golden race?

HERMOGENES: He probably would.

SOCRATES: Are good people any different from wise ones?

HERMOGENES: No, they aren't.

SOCRATES: It is principally because daemons are wise and knowing (*daēmones*), I think, that Hesiod says they are named 'daemons' ('*daimones*'). In our older Attic dialect, we actually find the word '*daēmones*'. So, Hesiod and many other poets speak well when they say that when a good man dies, he has a great destiny and a great honor and becomes a 'daemon',
c   which is a name given to him because it accords with wisdom. And I myself assert, indeed, that every good man, whether alive or dead, is daemonic, and is correctly called a 'daemon'.

---

18. Daemons are gods or children of the gods (*Apology* 27d–e) or messengers from the gods (*Symposium* 202e).

19. Reading *ē dēlon dē hoti daimonas te kai hērōas kai anthrōpous?* in d9–e1, attributing these words to Socrates.

20. Attributing *daimonas* in e1 to Hermogenes.

21. *Works and Days*, 121–23, with minor variations.

HERMOGENES: And I think that I completely agree with you, Socrates. But what about the name 'hero' (*'hērōs'*)? What is it?

SOCRATES: That one isn't so hard to understand because the name has been little altered. It expresses the fact that heroes were born out of love (*erōs*).

HERMOGENES: How do you mean?

SOCRATES: Don't you know that the heroes are demigods?

HERMOGENES: So what?

SOCRATES: So all of them sprang from the love of a god for a mortal woman or of a mortal man for a goddess. And if, as before, you investigate the matter by relying on old Attic, you will get a better understanding, since it will show you that the name 'hero' (*'hērōs'*) is only a slightly altered form of the word 'love' (*'erōs'*)—the very thing from which the heroes sprang. And either this is the reason they were called 'heroes' or else because they were sophists, clever speech-makers (*rhētores*) and dialecticians, skilled questioners (*erōtan*)—for *'eirein'* is the same as *'legein'* ('to speak'). And therefore, as we were saying just now, in the Attic dialect, the heroes turn out to be speech-makers and questioners. Hence the noble breed of heroes turns out be a race of speech-makers and sophists. That isn't hard to understand. But can you tell me why members of the human race are called 'humans' (*'anthrōpoi'*)? That's much harder to understand.

HERMOGENES: How could *I* do that, Socrates? I wouldn't strain myself to find it even if I could, because I think you're much more likely to find it than I am.

SOCRATES: You really do have faith in Euthyphro's inspiration, it seems.

HERMOGENES: Clearly.

SOCRATES: And you're certainly right to have faith in it. Indeed, I seem to have had such a clever insight just now, that, if I'm not careful, I'll be in danger of becoming altogether *too* wise before the day is out. So pay attention. First of all, we must bear in mind the following point about names: we often add letters or take them out and change the accents as well, thus swerving aside from what we want to name. For instance, take *'Dii philos'* ('Friend-to-Zeus'). In order for us to have a name instead of a phrase, we took out the second *'i'*, and pronounced the second syllable with a grave accent instead of an acute (*'Diphilos'*). In other cases, we do the opposite, inserting letters and pronouncing a syllable with an acute accent instead of a grave.

HERMOGENES: That's true.

SOCRATES: Now, I think our name for human beings is a case of just this sort. It was a phrase but became a name. One letter—*'a'*—has been taken away and the accent on the final syllable has become a grave.

HERMOGENES: What do you mean?

SOCRATES: The name 'human' signifies that the other animals do not investigate or reason about anything they see, nor do they observe anything closely. But a human being no sooner sees something—that is to say, *'opōpe'*—than he observes it closely and reasons about it. Hence human

d

e

399

b

c

beings alone among the animals are correctly named *'anthrōpos'*—one who observes closely what he has seen (*anathrōn ha opōpe*).

HERMOGENES: What comes next? May I tell you what I'd like to have explained?

SOCRATES: Of course.

d HERMOGENES: It seems to me to be next in order. We speak of the body and soul of a human being.

SOCRATES: Certainly.

HERMOGENES: Then let's try to analyze their names as we did the previous ones.

SOCRATES: Are you saying that we should investigate whether soul and then body are reasonably named?

HERMOGENES: Yes.

SOCRATES: Speaking off the top of my head, I think that those who gave soul its name had something like this in mind. They thought that when the soul is present in the body, it causes it to live and gives it the power

e to breathe the air and be revitalized (*anapsuchon*), and that when this revitalization fails, the body dies and is finished. It's for this reason, I think, that they called it 'soul' (*'psuchē'*). But hold on a minute, if you don't mind, for I imagine that the followers of Euthyphro would despise this

400 analysis and think it crude. But I think I glimpse one they will find more persuasive. Have a look and see whether it pleases you.

HERMOGENES: Tell it to me and I will.

SOCRATES: When you consider the nature of every body, what, besides the soul, do you think sustains and supports it, so that it lives and moves about?

HERMOGENES: There isn't anything.

SOCRATES: What about when you consider the nature of everything else? Don't you agree with Anaxagoras that it is ordered and sustained by mind or soul?

HERMOGENES: I do.

b SOCRATES: So a fine name to give this power, which supports and sustains (*ochei kai echei*) the whole of nature (*phusis*), would be 'nature-sustainer' (*'phusechē'*). This may also be pronounced more elegantly, *'psuchē'*.

HERMOGENES: Absolutely, and I also think this *is* a more scientific explanation than the other.

SOCRATES: Yes, it is. Nevertheless, it sounds funny when it's named in the true way, with its actual name (i.e., *'phusechē'*).

HERMOGENES: What are we going to say about the next one?

SOCRATES: Are you referring to the name 'body'?

HERMOGENES: Yes.

SOCRATES: There's a lot to say, it seems to me—and if one distorted the name a little, there would be even more. Thus some people say that the

c body (*sōma*) is the tomb (*sēma*) of the soul, on the grounds that it is entombed in its present life, while others say that it is correctly called 'a sign' (*'sēma'*) because the soul signifies whatever it wants to signify by means of the body. I think it is most likely the followers of Orpheus who gave the body its name, with the idea that the soul is being punished for something, and that the body is an enclosure or prison in which the soul is securely kept (*sōzetai*)—as the name '*sōma*' itself suggests—until the penalty is paid; for, on this view, not even a single letter of the word needs to be changed.

HERMOGENES: I think we've adequately examined these names, Socrates. But could we investigate the names of the other gods along the lines of your earlier discussion of 'Zeus', to see with what kind of correctness they have been given?

SOCRATES: By Zeus, we certainly can, Hermogenes. The first and finest line of investigation, which as intelligent people we must acknowledge, is this, that we admit that we know nothing about the gods themselves or about the names they call themselves—although it is clear that they call themselves by true ones. The second best line on the correctness of names is to say, as is customary in our prayers, that we hope the gods are pleased by the names we give them, since we know no others. I think this is an excellent custom. So, if it's all right with you, let's begin our investigation by first announcing to the gods that we will not be investigating *them*—since we do not regard ourselves as worthy to conduct such an investigation—but rather human beings, and the beliefs they had in giving the gods their names. After all, there's no offense in doing that.

HERMOGENES: What you say seems reasonable to me, Socrates, so let's proceed as you suggest.

SOCRATES: Shall we begin, as is customary, with Hestia?[22]

HERMOGENES: All right.

SOCRATES: What do you think the person who gave Hestia her name had in mind by naming her that?

HERMOGENES: That's no easy question to answer, in my opinion.

SOCRATES: At any rate, Hermogenes, the first name-givers weren't ordinary people, but lofty thinkers and subtle reasoners.

HERMOGENES: What of it?

SOCRATES: Well, it's obvious to me that it was people of this sort who gave things names, for even if one investigates names foreign to Attic Greek, it is equally easy to discover what they mean. In the case of what we in Attic call '*ousia*' ('being'), for example, some call it '*essia*' and others '*ōsia*'. First, then, it is reasonable, according to the second of these names, to call the being or essence (*ousia*) of things 'Hestia'. Besides, we ourselves say that what partakes of being 'is' ('*estin*'), so being is also correctly called 'Hestia' for this reason. We even seem to have called being '*essia*' in ancient times. And, if one has sacrifices in mind, one will realize that the name-givers themselves understood matters in this way, for anyone who called the being or essence of all things '*essia*' would naturally sacrifice to Hestia before all the other gods. On the other hand, those who use the name '*ōsia*' seem to agree pretty much with Heraclitus' doctrine that the things that are

22. Hestia, the goddess of the hearth, usually received the first part of a sacrifice and was named first in prayers and (often) in oaths.

are all flowing and that nothing stands fast—for the cause and originator of
them is then the pusher (*ōthoun*), and so is well named '*ōsia*'. But that's
e   enough for us to say about this, since we know nothing. After Hestia, it
is right to investigate Rhea and Cronus, though we've already discussed
the latter's name. Now, maybe what I'm about to tell you is nonsense.

HERMOGENES: Why do you say that, Socrates?

SOCRATES: Because I've got a whole swarm of wisdom in my mind!

HERMOGENES: What sort of wisdom?

SOCRATES: It sounds completely absurd, yet it seems to me to have some-
402   thing very plausible about it.

HERMOGENES: How so?

SOCRATES: I seem to see Heraclitus spouting some ancient bits of wisdom
that Homer also tells us—wisdom as old as the days of Cronus and Rhea.

HERMOGENES: What are you referring to?

SOCRATES: Heraclitus says somewhere that "everything gives way and
nothing stands fast," and, likening the things that are to the flowing (*rhoē*)
of a river, he says that "you cannot step into the same river twice."[23]

HERMOGENES: So he does.

SOCRATES: Well, then, don't you think that whoever gave the names
'Rhea' and 'Cronus' to the ancestors of the other gods understood things
b   in the same way as Heraclitus? Or do you think he gave them both the
names of streams (*rheumata*) merely by chance?[24] Similarly, Homer speaks of

Ocean, origin of the gods, and their mother Tethys;[25]

I think Hesiod says much the same. Orpheus, too, says somewhere that

Fair-flowing Ocean was the first to marry,
c   *And he wedded his sister, the daughter of his mother.*[26]

See how they agree with each other, and how they all lean towards the
doctrines of Heraclitus.

HERMOGENES: I think there's something in what you say, Socrates, but I
don't understand what the name 'Tethys' means.

SOCRATES: But it practically tells you itself that it is the slightly disguised
name of a spring! After all, what is strained (*diattōmenon*) and filtered
d   (*ēthoumenon*) is like a spring, and the name 'Tethys' is a compound of these
two names.

23. Frg. 91 (Diels-Kranz).

24. 'Rhea' sounds a lot like '*rheuma*' ('stream'); apparently Socrates expects Hermogenes
to hear 'Cronus' as connected with '*krounos*' ('spring').

25. *Iliad* xiv.201, 302.

26. Frg. 15 (Kern).

HERMOGENES: That's elegant, Socrates.

SOCRATES: Indeed, it is. But what comes next? We've already talked about Zeus.

HERMOGENES: Yes, we have.

SOCRATES: So let's discuss his brothers, Posidon and Pluto (whether we call him 'Pluto' or by his other name).

HERMOGENES: Certainly.

SOCRATES: It seems to me that whoever first gave Posidon his name, gave it to him because he saw that the force of the waves stopped him from walking and prevented him from going any further, just like a shackle around his feet (*desmos tōn podōn*). So he called this god, who is the ruler of the sea's power, 'Posidon', because his 'feet were shackled' ('*poside-smon*')—the '*e*' was probably added for the sake of euphony. But perhaps this isn't what it says. Perhaps, instead of the '*s*' the name was originally pronounced with a double '*l*', because many things are known (*poll' eidōs*) to the god. Or maybe he was called 'The Shaker' ('*ho seiōn*'), because he shook (*seiein*) the earth, and the '*p*' and '*d*' were added on. As for Pluto, he was given that name because it accords with his being the source of wealth (*ploutos*), since wealth comes up from below the ground. It seems to me that most people call him by the name 'Pluto', because they are afraid of what they can't see (*aeides*), and they assume that his other name, 'Hades', associates him with that.

HERMOGENES: And what do you think yourself, Socrates?

SOCRATES: I think people have lots of mistaken opinions about the power of this god and are unduly afraid of him. They are afraid because once we are dead we remain in his realm forever. They are terrified because the soul goes there stripped of the body. But I think that all these things, together with the name and office of the god, point in the same direction.

HERMOGENES: How so?

SOCRATES: I'll tell you how it looks to me. But first answer me this: Of the shackles that bind a living being and keep him in a place, which is stronger, force or desire?

HERMOGENES: Desire is far stronger, Socrates.

SOCRATES: Don't you think then that many people would escape from Hades, if he didn't bind those who come to him with the strongest of shackles?

HERMOGENES: Clearly.

SOCRATES: So, if he is to bind them with the strongest of shackles, rather than holding them by force, he must, it seems, bind them with some sort of desire.

HERMOGENES: Evidently.

SOCRATES: Now, there are lots of desires, aren't there?

HERMOGENES: Yes.

SOCRATES: So, if he is really going to hold them with the greatest shackles, he has to bind them with the greatest desire.

HERMOGENES: Yes.

SOCRATES: Is any desire greater than the desire to associate with someone whose company one believes will make one a better man?

HERMOGENES: No, there certainly isn't, Socrates.

SOCRATES: So let's say that it is for these reasons, Hermogenes, that hitherto no one has wished to come back here from there. The words
e   Hades knows how to speak are so beautiful, it seems, that everyone—even the Sirens—has been overcome by his enchantments. On this account, therefore, this god is a perfect sophist, and a great benefactor to those who are with him. So great is the wealth that surrounds him there below, indeed, that he even sends many good things to us from it. This is how he got the name 'Pluto'. On the other hand, because he is unwilling to associate with human beings while they have their bodies, but converses with them only when their souls are purified of all the desires and evils
404 of the body, doesn't he seem to you to be a philosopher? For hasn't he well understood that when people are free of their bodies he can bind them with the desire for virtue, but that while they feel the agitation and madness of the body not even the famous shackles of his father Cronus could keep them with him?[27]

HERMOGENES: Probably so, Socrates.

b   SOCRATES: It's much more likely then, Hermogenes, that Hades derives his name not from what cannot be seen (*aeides*), but from the fact that he knows (*eidenai*) everything fine and beautiful, and that that is why the rule-setter called him 'Hades'.

HERMOGENES: All right. But what about Demeter, Hera, Apollo, Athena, Hephaestus, and all the other gods? What are we to say about them?

SOCRATES: Demeter seems to have been so called because she gives (*didousa*) nourishment just like a mother (*mētēr*); Hera is a loveable one (*eratē*),
c   and, indeed, Zeus is said to have married her for love. But perhaps the rule-setter, being a lofty thinker, called her 'Hera' as a disguised name for air (*aēr*), putting the end of her name at the beginning—you'll get the idea if you repeat the name 'Hera' over and over. As for '*pherrephatta*': it seems that many people dread the names 'Pherrephatta' and 'Apollo' because they are ignorant about the correctness of names, for they change the first name to 'Phersephone', and then it seems terrifying to them.[28] But really the name 'Pherrephatta' indicates that the goddess is wise—for since things
d   are being swept along, wisdom is the power to grasp (*ephaptomenon*), comprehend (*epaphōn*), and follow (*epakolouthein*) them. Thus it would be correct to call this goddess 'Pherepapha', or something like that, because of her wisdom, that is to say, her power to comprehend what is being swept along (*epaphē tou pheromenou*)—this is also the reason that Hades, since he is himself wise, associates with her. But people nowadays attach

27. Cronus, the father of Posidon and Zeus, was dethroned by the latter and chained by him in Tartarus, the deepest part of Hades. See *Iliad* xiv.203–4.

28. Presumably because they see it as meaning 'who brings carnage' (*pherein phonon*).

more importance to euphony than to truth, so they distort her name and call her 'Pherrephatta'. And, as I said, the same thing has happened to Apollo. Many people are afraid of his name because they think it indicates something terrifying.[29] Haven't you noticed this?

HERMOGENES: I certainly have, and what you say is true.

SOCRATES: In my view, however, the name is most beautifully suited to the power of the god.

HERMOGENES: How so?

SOCRATES: I'll try to say how it seems to me, at least. I think no single name could be more in keeping with the four powers of the god. It comprehends each of them, expressing his power in music, prophecy, medicine, and archery.

HERMOGENES: It's a pretty remarkable name you're talking about; so go ahead and explain it.

SOCRATES: It's certainly a harmonious one. After all, it's the name of the god of music. To begin with, the purgations and purifications that doctors and prophets use, the fumigations with medicinal and magical drugs, and the various washings and sprinklings that are involved in these processes, all have the same effect, don't they, namely, to make a person pure in body and soul?

HERMOGENES: Certainly.

SOCRATES: But isn't Apollo the purifying god who washes away (*apolouōn*) such evil impurities and releases (*apoluōn*) us from them?

HERMOGENES: Certainly.

SOCRATES: Since he washes and releases and is a doctor for our evil impurities, he might correctly be called '*Apolouōn*' ('The Washer'). On the other hand, it may well be most correct to call him by the name the Thessalians use, since it accords with his prophecy, that is to say, with his single-mindedness (*haploun*) or truthfulness (these being the same thing), for all the Thessalians call this god '*Aploun*'. And since he always (*aei*) makes his shots (*bolōn*), because of his skill in archery, he is also '*Aeiballōn*' ('Always-shooting'). To understand how his name accords with his musical powers, we have to understand that the letter '*a*' often signifies togetherness (*to homou*), as it does in '*akolouthos*' ('follower' or 'attendant') and '*akoitis*' ('bed-fellow', 'spouse', 'husband').[30] In this case, it signifies moving together (*homou polēsis*), whether the moving together of the heavens around what we call the 'poles' ('*poloi*'), or the harmonious moving together in music, which we call 'being in concert' ('*sumphonia*'); for, as those who are clever in astronomy and music say, all these things move together simultaneously by a kind of harmony. Apollo is the god who directs the harmony, and makes all things move together (*homopolōn*), whether for gods or human beings. So, just as the names '*akolouthos*' and '*akoitis*' are derived from

---

29. They connect 'Apollo' with '*apolluōn*' ('who destroys').
30. Removing the brackets in c7.

'homokolouthos' and *'homokoitis'* by replacing *'homo'* with *'a'*, we called him 'Apollo', though he was really *'Homopolon'* ('the one who makes things move together'). We inserted the second *'l'* lest his name become an oppressive one.[31] Even as it is, indeed, some people, who haven't correctly investigated the force or power of his name, are afraid of it, because they suspect that it does signify some kind of destructiveness. But, as we said earlier, it really comprehends each of the powers of the god, who is a single-minded, always shooting washer, who makes things move together. As for the Muses and music and poetry in general, they seem to have derived their name from their eager desire (*mōsthai*) to investigate and do philosophy. Leto is so-called because of being very gentle (*pra(i)otētos*) and willing (*ethelēmos*) to do whatever is asked of her. Or perhaps her name derives from the one used by those who speak dialects other than Attic, many of whom call her 'Letho'—apparently on account of the fact that her character isn't rough but gentle and smooth (*leion*). Artemis appears to have been so-called because of her soundness (*artemes*) and orderliness, and because of her desire for virginity (*parthenia*). Or perhaps the one who gave her that name was calling her 'an investigator of virtue' (*'aretēs histōr'*) or 'a hater of sexual intercourse between men and women' (*'aroton misēsasēs'*). It is for some one of these reasons or for all of them that the one who gave this name to the goddess gave it to her.

HERMOGENES: What about 'Dionysos' and 'Aphrodite'?

SOCRATES: You're asking great things of me, son of Hipponicus, because there is not only a serious way of explaining the names of these divinities but a playful one as well. You'll have to ask others for the serious one, but there's nothing to prevent us from going through the playful one—even the gods love play. Dionysos, the giver of wine (*ho didous ton oinon*), might playfully be called *'Didoinusos'*; while wine (*oinos*) would most justly be called *'oionous'*, since it makes most drinkers think they understood (*oiesthai noun echein*) when they don't. As far as Aphrodite is concerned, there's no point in contradicting Hesiod—we should agree with him that she is called 'Aphrodite' because she was born from foam (*aphros*).[32]

HERMOGENES: Being an Athenian, Socrates, you surely aren't going to forget Athena, or Hephaestus and Ares either, for that matter.

SOCRATES: Not likely.

HERMOGENES: No, indeed.

SOCRATES: It isn't hard to explain how Athena got her other name.

HERMOGENES: Which one?

SOCRATES: 'Pallas'—you know we call her that.

HERMOGENES: Of course.

SOCRATES: In my view, we would be correct to think that this name derives from her dancing in arms and armor, for lifting oneself or anything

---

31. *'Apolōn'* means 'destroying utterly', 'killing', 'slaying'.
32. *Theogony* 195–97.

else up, whether from the ground or in one's hands, is called 'shaking' ('*pallein*') and 'dancing' or 'being shaken' ('*pallesthai*') and 'being danced'.   407

HERMOGENES: Certainly.

SOCRATES: She's called 'Pallas' because of this.

HERMOGENES: And correctly so. But how do you explain her other name?

SOCRATES: You mean 'Athena'?

HERMOGENES: Yes.

SOCRATES: That's a much weightier issue, my friend. The ancients seem to have had the same opinion about Athena as do contemporary experts on Homer. Many of them say in their interpretations of the poet that he   b represents Athena as Understanding or Thought. The maker of names seems to think the same sort of thing about the goddess. Indeed, he speaks of her in still grander terms, saying she is the very mind of god (*theou noēsis*), as if she is '*ha theonoa*'—using '*a*' in the non-Attic style in place of '*ē*' and deleting '*i*' and '*s*'.[33] But perhaps this isn't the explanation. Perhaps what he called her was '*Theonoē*', because of her unparalleled knowledge of divine things (*ta theia noousa*). Nor would we be far off the mark if we supposed that what he called her was '*Ēthonoē*', because he wanted to identify the goddess with her understanding character (*hē en tōi ēthei noēsis*). Then he himself or others after him made the name more beautiful, as   c they thought, and called her '*Athēnaa*'.

HERMOGENES: What about Hephaestus? How do you explain him?

SOCRATES: Are you asking me about the noble judge of light (*phaeos histōr*)?

HERMOGENES: It seems so.

SOCRATES: Isn't it clear to everyone then that he is 'Phaestus' with an '*ē*' added on?

HERMOGENES: It probably is—unless you happen to have yet another opinion on the matter. And you probably do.

SOCRATES: Then to prevent me from giving it, ask me about Ares.

HERMOGENES: Consider yourself asked!

SOCRATES: All right, if that's what you want. It is proper for a god who is in every way warlike to be called 'Ares', for 'Ares' accords with virility (*arren*) and courage (*andreia*), or with a hard and unbending nature, the   d one that is called '*arratos*'.

HERMOGENES: It certainly is.

SOCRATES: Then for god's sake let's leave the subject of the gods, because it frightens me to talk about them. But ask me about anything else you like, "until we see what the horses" of Euthyphro "can do."[34]

HERMOGENES: I'll do that, but there is still one god I want to ask you about, and that's Hermes, since Cratylus says that I am no Hermogenes   e

---

33. I.e., '*ha theonoa*' or 'Athena' is derived thus: delete '*sis*' from '*theou noēsis*', yielding a single word '*theounoē*'; add the feminine article in its non-Attic style and change '*ē*' to '*a*' to get '*ha theounoa*'. Since at this time there was not the distinction we now make between '*o*' and '*ou*', we get '*ha theonoa*'.

34. *Iliad* v.221–22. For Euthyphro, see 396d.

(Son-of-Hermes). So let's examine the name 'Hermes' and its meaning, to see whether there's anything in what he says.

SOCRATES: Well, the name 'Hermes' seems to have something to do with speech: he is an interpreter (*hermēneus*), a messenger, a thief and a deceiver in words, a wheeler-dealer—and all these activities involve the power of speech. Now, as we mentioned before,[35] '*eirein*' means 'to use words', and the other part of the name says—as Homer often does—'*emēsato*' ('he contrived'), which means 'to devise'. And it was out of these two words that the rule-setter established the name of the god who devised speech (*legein*) and words, since '*eirein*' means the same as '*legein*' ('to speak'). It's just as if he had told us: "Humans, it would be right for you to call the god who has contrived speech (*to eirein emēsato*) '*Eiremēs*'." But we, beautifying the name, as we suppose, call him 'Hermes' nowadays.

HERMOGENES: I'm certain that Cratylus was right when he said that I'm no Hermogenes then, since I'm no good at devising speeches.

SOCRATES: But it *is* reasonable for Pan to be Hermes' double-natured son.

HERMOGENES: How so?

SOCRATES: You know speech signifies all things (*to pan*) and keeps them circulating and always going about, and that it has two forms—true and false?

HERMOGENES: Certainly.

SOCRATES: Well, the true part is smooth and divine and dwells among the gods above, while the false part dwells below among the human masses, and is rough and goatish (*tragikon*); for it is here, in the tragic (*tragikon*) life, that one finds the vast majority of myths and falsehoods.

HERMOGENES: Certainly.

SOCRATES: Therefore the one who expresses all things (*pan*) and keeps them always in circulation (*aei polōn*) is correctly called 'Pan-the-goat-herd' ('*Pan aipolos*'). The double-natured son of Hermes, he is smooth in his upper parts, and rough and goatish in the ones below. He is either speech itself or the brother of speech, since he is the son of Hermes. And it's not a bit surprising that a brother resembles his brother. But, as I said, let's leave the gods.

HERMOGENES: That sort of gods, Socrates, if that's what you want. But what keeps you from discussing these gods: the sun and moon, and stars, earth, aether, air, fire, water, and the seasons and the year?

SOCRATES: That's a lot you're asking of me! All the same, if it will please you, I am willing.

HERMOGENES: Of course, it will.

SOCRATES: Which one do you want me to take up first? Or, since you mentioned the sun (*hēlios*) first, shall we begin with it?

HERMOGENES: Certainly.

SOCRATES: If we use the Doric form of the name, I think matters will become clearer, for the Dorians call the sun '*halios*'. So '*halios*' might accord

35. See 398d.

with the fact that the sun collects (*halizein*) people together when it rises, or with the fact that it is always rolling (*aei heilein iōn*) in its course around the earth, or with the fact that it seems to color (*poikillei*) the products of the earth, for '*poikillein*' means the same as '*aiolein*' ('to shift rapidly to and fro').

HERMOGENES: What about the moon (*selēnē*)?

SOCRATES: The name certainly seems to put Anaxagoras in an awkward position.

HERMOGENES: Why is that?

SOCRATES: It seems to reveal that his recent theory about the moon deriving its light from the sun is in fact quite old.

HERMOGENES: In what way?

SOCRATES: *Selas* (bright light) and *phōs* (light) are the same thing.

HERMOGENES: Yes.

SOCRATES: Now, if what the Anaxagoreans say is true, the light of the moon (*selēnē*) is always both new (*neon*) and old (*henon*), for they say that as the sun circles around the moon it always casts new light on it, but that the light from the previous month also remains there.

HERMOGENES: Certainly.

SOCRATES: But many people call the moon '*Selanaia*'.

HERMOGENES: Yes, they do.

SOCRATES: And, since its light is always both new and old (*selas neon kai enon echei aei*), the right name to call it is '*Selaenoneoaeia*', and this is the one that has been compressed into '*Selanaia*'.

HERMOGENES: And a dithyrambic[36] name it is too, Socrates! But what have you to say about the month and the stars?

SOCRATES: The correct name to call a month (*meis*) is '*meiēs*' from '*meiousthai*' ('to grow smaller'). And the stars (*astra*) seem to get their name given to them from '*astrapē*' ('lightning'), for lightning is what causes the eyes to turn upward (*anastrephei ta ōpa*). Hence, it should really be called '*anastrōpē*', but nowadays the name is beautified and it is called '*astrapē*'.

HERMOGENES: What about fire and water?

SOCRATES: I'm really puzzled about fire (*pur*). So either Euthyphro's muse has abandoned me or this really is very hard. But notice the device I use in all such puzzling cases.

HERMOGENES: What is that?

SOCRATES: I'll tell you. But first answer me this. Could you say in what way *pur* (fire) comes to be so called?

HERMOGENES: I certainly can't.

SOCRATES: Here's what I suspect. I think that the Greeks, especially those who live abroad, have adopted many names from foreign tongues.

HERMOGENES: What of it?

---

36. A dithyramb is a choral song to the god Dionysus, noted for its complex and pompous language.

SOCRATES: Well, if someone were trying to discover whether these names had been reasonably given, and he treated them as belonging to the Greek language rather than the one they really come from, you know that he would be in a quandary.

HERMOGENES: He very probably would.

410   SOCRATES: Now, look at 'fire' (*'pur'*) and see whether it isn't a foreign name—for it certainly isn't easy to connect it with the Greek language. Besides, it's obvious that the Phrygians use the same name slightly altered. And the same holds for 'water' (*'hudōr'*) and 'dog' (*'kuōn'*), and lots of others.

HERMOGENES: So it does.

SOCRATES: Consequently, though one might say something about these names, one mustn't push them too far. That, then, is how I get rid of 'fire' (*'pur'*) and 'water' (*'hudōr'*). But what about air, Hermogenes? Is it called
b   *'aēr'* because it raises (*airei*) things from the earth? Or because it is always flowing (*aei rhei*)? Or because wind (*pneuma*) arises from its flow? For the poets call the winds (*pneumata*) 'gales' (*aētai*), don't they? So, perhaps a poet says *'aētorrous'* ('gale flow') in place of *'pneumatorrous'* ('wind flow'), thereby indicating that what he is talking about is air.[37] As for aether, I'd explain it as follows: it is right to call it *'aeitheēr'*, because it is always running and flowing (*aei thei rheōn*) about the air. The earth (*gē*) is better
c   signified by the name *'gaia'*; for *gaia* is correctly called a 'mother', as Homer tells us by using *'gegaasi'* for 'to be born'. All right, what was to come next?

HERMOGENES: 'Seasons' (*'Hōrai'*), Socrates, and the two names for the year, *'eniautos'* and *'etos'*.

SOCRATES: If you want to know the probable truth about the name *'hōrai'* ('seasons'), you must look to the fact that it is spelled *'horai'* in old Attic. The seasons are rightly called *'horai'* ('things that distinguish or mark off one thing from another'), because they distinguish (*horizein*) the weathers of winter and summer, the winds, and the fruits of the earth. As for
d   *'eniautos'* and *'etos'*, they are actually one name. We saw earlier that Zeus' name was divided in two—some called him *'Zēna'*, some *'Dia'* in the accusative.[38] Well, exactly the same is true of the name of the year. It is the year by itself that brings the plants and animals of the earth to light, each in its proper season, and passes them in review within itself (*en heautōi exetazei*). Hence, some people call it *'etos'*, because it passes things in review (*etazei*), while others call it *'eniautos'*, because it does this within itself (*en heautōi*). The whole phrase is 'passing things in review within itself' (*'en heautōi etazon'*), but this single phrase results in the year being called these two different names. Thus, the two names, *'eniautos'* and *'etos'*, derive from
e   a single phrase.

HERMOGENES: I say, Socrates, you *are* making great progress!

SOCRATES: I think I'm driving my apparent wisdom pretty hard at present.

37. Removing the brackets in b5–6.
38. See 395e ff.

HERMOGENES: You certainly are.

SOCRATES: You'll be even more certain in a second.

HERMOGENES: Now that we've examined that sort of name, I'd next like 411 to see with what correctness the names of the virtues are given. I mean 'wisdom' (*phronēsis*), 'comprehension' (*sunesis*), 'justice' (*dikaiosunē*), and all the other fine names of that sort.

SOCRATES: That's no inconsequential class of names you're stirring up, Hermogenes, but, since I have put on the lion's skin,[39] I mustn't lose heart. So, it seems I must investigate 'wisdom', 'comprehension', 'judgment' (*gnōmē*), 'knowledge' (*epistēmē*), and all those other fine names of which you speak. b

HERMOGENES: We certainly mustn't stop until we've done so.

SOCRATES: By the dog, I think that's a pretty good inspiration—what popped into my mind just now! Most of our wise men nowadays get so dizzy going around and around in their search for the nature of the things that are, that the things themselves appear to them to be turning around and moving every which way. Well, I think that the people who gave things their names in very ancient times are exactly like these wise men. c They don't blame this on their own internal condition, however, but on the nature of the things themselves, which they think are never stable or steadfast, but flowing and moving, full of every sort of motion and constant coming into being. I say this, because the names you just mentioned put me in mind of it.

HERMOGENES: How did they do that, Socrates?

SOCRATES: Perhaps you didn't notice that they are given on the assumption that the things they name are moving, flowing, and coming into being.

HERMOGENES: No, I didn't think of that at all.

SOCRATES: Well, to begin with, the first name we mentioned is undoubt- d edly like this.

HERMOGENES: What name was that?

SOCRATES: 'Wisdom' (*phronēsis*). Wisdom is the understanding of motion (*phoras noēsis*) and flow. Or it might be interpreted as taking delight in motion (*phoras onēsis*). In either case, it has to do with motion. If you want another example, the name 'judgment' (*gnōmē*) expresses the fact that to judge is to examine or study whatever is begotten (*gonēs nōmēsis*); for 'studying' (*nōman*) and 'examining' (*skopein*) are the same. And if you want yet another example, understanding (*noēsis*) itself is the longing for the new (*neou hesis*). But to say that the things that are are new is to signify that they are always coming into being. And such things are what the soul longs for, as the giver of the name, 'neoesis' expressed, for the ancient name e wasn't 'noēsis' but 'noesis', but an '*ē*' took the place of the double '*e*'. Moderation (*sōphrosunē*) is the saviour (*sōteria*) of the wisdom (*phronēsis*) we just looked at. 'Knowledge' (*epistēmē*) indicates that a worthwhile soul 412 follows (*hepetai*) the movement of things, neither falling behind nor running

39. The skin of the Nemean lion worn by Heracles.

on ahead. So we ought to insert an *'e'* in the name and spell it *'hepeïstēmē'*. Comprehension (*sunesis*), in turn, seems to be a kind of summing up (*sullogismos*), and whenever one says 'comprehends' (*'sunienai'*), it's exactly as if one has said 'knows' (*'epistasthai'*), for *'sunienai'* (literally, 'goes along with') means that the soul 'journeys together' with things. As for 'wisdom'
b   (*'sophia'*), it signifies the grasp of motion. But it is rather obscure and non-Attic. Nonetheless, we must remember that the poets often say of something that begins to advance quickly that it "rushed" (*"esuthē"*). Indeed, there was a famous Spartan man named *'Sous'*, for this is what the Spartans call a rapid advance. 'Wisdom' signifies the grasping (*epaphē*) of this motion, on the assumption that the things that are are moving. The
c   name 'good' (*'agathon'*) is intended to signify everything in nature that is admirable (*agaston*). The things that are are moving, but some are moving quickly, others slowly. So what moves quickly is not all there is, but the admirable part of it. Hence this name *'tagathon'* ('the good') is applied to what is admirable (*agaston*) about the fast (*thoon*).

It's easy to figure out that 'justice' (*'dikaiosunē'*) is the name given to the comprehension of the just (*dikaiou sunesis*), but the just itself is hard to understand. It seems that many people agree with one another about it up to a point, but beyond that they disagree. Those who think that the
d   universe is in motion believe that most of it is of such a kind as to do nothing but give way, but that something penetrates all of it and generates everything that comes into being. This, they say, is the fastest and smallest thing of all; for if it were not the smallest, so that nothing could keep it out, or not the fastest, so that it could treat all other things as though they were standing still, it wouldn't be able to travel through everything. However, since it is governor and penetrator (*diaïon*) of everything else,
e   it is rightly called 'just' (*'dikaïon'*)—the *'k'*-sound is added for the sake of euphony. As I was saying before, many people agree about the just up to
413 this point. As for myself, Hermogenes, because I persisted at it, I learned all about the matter in secret—that this is the just and the cause, since that through which (*di' ho*) a thing comes to be is the cause. Indeed, someone told me that it is correct to call this *'Dia'* ('Zeus') for that reason. Even when I'd heard this, however, I persisted in gently asking, "If all this is true, my friend, what actually *is* the just?" Thereupon, they think I am
b   asking too many questions and demanding the impossible, and they tell me that I have already learned enough. Then they try to satisfy me by having each tell me his own view. But they disagree with each other. One says that the just is the sun, since only the sun governs all of the things that are, penetrating (*diaïon*) and burning (*kaon*) them. Well-satisfied, I tell this fine answer to one of the others, but he ridicules me by asking if I think nothing just ever happens in human affairs once the sun has set. So
c   I persist, and ask him to tell me what *he* thinks the just is, and he says that it is fire (*to pur*)—but that isn't easy to understand. Another says that it isn't fire, but the heat itself that is in fire. Another says that all these explanations are ridiculous, and that the just is what Anaxagoras talks

about, namely, mind; for he says that mind is self-ruling, mixes with nothing else, orders the things that are, and travels through everything.[40] Thereupon, my friend, I am even more perplexed than when I set out to learn what the just is. However, the goal of our investigation was the *name*   d 'just', and it seems to have been given for the reasons we mentioned.

HERMOGENES: I think you really must have heard this from someone, Socrates, rather than making it up as you went along.

SOCRATES: What about the other explanations I've mentioned?

HERMOGENES: I certainly don't think you heard those.

SOCRATES: Listen, then, and perhaps I'll be able to deceive you into thinking that I haven't heard the remaining ones either. After justice what's left? I don't think we've discussed courage—but it's clear that injustice (*adikia*) is really nothing more than a hindering of that which penetrates (*diaïon*). 'Courage' ('*andreia*') signifies that this virtue was given its name   e in battle. And if indeed the things that are are flowing, then a battle cannot be anything but an opposing flow. If we remove the '*d*' from '*andreia*' to get '*anreia*' ('flowing back'), the name itself indicates this fact. Of course, it is clear that courage doesn't oppose every flow, but only the one that is contrary to justice; otherwise, courage wouldn't be praiseworthy. Similarly,   414 'male' ('*arren*') and 'man' ('*anēr*') indicate upward flow (*anō rhoē*). It seems to me that '*gunē*' ('woman') wants to be '*gonē*' ('womb'), that '*thēlus*' ('female') comes from '*thēlē*' ('nipple'), and that a nipple (*thēlē*) is so-called, Hermogenes, because it makes things flourish (*tethēlenai*) in just the way that watering makes plants flourish.

HERMOGENES: Probably so, Socrates.

SOCRATES: Yes, '*thallein*' itself seems to me to be like the sudden and rapid growth of the young, for the name-giver has imitated something like this in the name, which he put together from '*thein*' ('to run') and   b '*hallesthai*' ('to jump'). Notice how I go off course, when I get on the flat. But there are still plenty of names left that seem important.

HERMOGENES: That's true.

SOCRATES: And one of them is to see what the name '*technē*' ('craft') means.

HERMOGENES: Certainly.

SOCRATES: If you remove the '*t*' and insert an '*o*' between the '*ch*' and the '*n*' and the '*n*' and the '*ē*',[41] doesn't it signify the possession of understanding (*hexis nou*)?   c

HERMOGENES: Yes, Socrates, but getting it to do so is like trying to haul a boat up a very sticky ramp!

SOCRATES: But then you know, Hermogenes, that the first names given to things have long since been covered over by those who wanted to dress them up, and that letters were added or subtracted to make them sound good in the mouth, resulting in distortions and ornamentation of every

---

40. Frg. 12 (Diels-Kranz).
41. Resulting in '*echonoē*'.

kind. You know, too, that time has had a share in this process. Take
'*katoptron* ('mirror'), for example, don't you think that the '*r*' is an absurd
addition?[42] In my view, this sort of thing is the work of people who think

d   nothing of the truth, but only of the sounds their mouths make. Hence,
they keep embellishing the first names, until finally a name is reached that
no human being can understand. One example, among many others, is
that they call the Sphinx by that name instead of '*Phix*'.[43]

HERMOGENES: That's right, Socrates.

SOCRATES: And yet, if we can add whatever we like to names, or subtract
whatever we like from them, it will be far too easy to fit any name to

e   any thing.

HERMOGENES: That's true.

SOCRATES: Yes, it is true. So, I think a wise supervisor,[44] like yourself,
will have to keep a close watch, to preserve balance and probability.

HERMOGENES: That's what I want to do.

SOCRATES: And I want to do it along with you, Hermogenes, but don't

415   demand too much precision, in case

> *You enfeeble my strength.*[45]

Now that '*technē*' is out of the way, I'm about to come to the summit of
our inquiries. But first I'll investigate '*mēchanē*' ('device'). It seems to me
that '*mēchanē*' signifies great accomplishment (*anein epi polu*); for '*mēkos*'
signifies some sort of greatness, and these two, '*mēkos*' and '*anein*' make
up the name '*mēchanē*'. But, as I was saying just now, we must go on to
the summit of our inquiries, and investigate the names '*aretē*' ('virtue')

b   and '*kakia*' ('vice'). I don't yet understand the first of them, but the other
seems clear enough, since it is in harmony with everything we said before.
To the degree that things are in motion, all that is moving badly (*kakōs
ion*) should be called '*kakia*', but the name for all such things is mostly
given to a soul in which this bad movement in relation to things resides.
It seems to me that the name '*deilia*' ('cowardice'), which we haven't discussed, expresses what this bad movement is.—We ought to have discussed

c   '*deilia*' after '*andreia*' ('courage'), but we passed it by, as I believe we have
passed by lots of other names.—Now, '*deilia*' signifies the soul's being
bound with a strong shackle (*desmos*), for *lian* (too much) is a degree of
strength. Therefore, '*deilia*' signifies the strongest of the soul's shackles.

---

42. Because it interrupts the sequence '*opto*', suggesting a verb for seeing.

43. Hesiod uses the latter form of the name at *Theogony* 326. Popular etymology inappropriately connects '*Sphinx*' with a verb meaning 'to torture'. '*Phix*', the Boeotian form of
the word, connects it more appropriately with Mount Phikion in Boeotia, because of the
special association of the Sphinx with Thebes.

44. See 390b ff.

45. *Iliad* vi.265.

Aporia (perplexity, inability to move on) is a vice of the same sort, and so, it seems, is everything else that hinders movement and motion. This makes it clear that the bad movement in question is a restrained or hindered motion, whose possession by a soul causes it to become filled with vice. And, if '*kakia*' is the name of that sort of thing, '*aretē*' is the opposite. It signifies, first, lack of perplexity (*euporia*, ease of movement), and, second, that the flow of a good soul is always unimpeded; for it seems that it is given this name '*aretē*' because it is unrestrained and unhindered and so is always flowing (*aei rheon*). Thus it is correct to call it '*aeirheitē*', but this has been contracted, and it is called '*aretē*'. Now, maybe you'll say that I'm inventing things again, but I think that if what I just said about '*kakia*' is correct, then so is what I said about the name '*aretē*'.

HERMOGENES: What about '*kakon*' ('bad'), which has been involved in many of the previous inquiries? What's the meaning of it?

SOCRATES: It's a strange word, by god! At least, that's what I think. And one that's hard to interpret. So I'll use the device I introduced earlier on it as well.

HERMOGENES: Which one?

SOCRATES: That of attributing a foreign origin to it.[46]

HERMOGENES: And you may well be correct. So suppose we leave these inquiries, and try to see what rationale there is for '*kalon*' ('fine', 'beautiful') and '*aischron*' ('disgraceful', 'ugly').

SOCRATES: The meaning of '*aischron*' seems clear to me, and it is also in harmony with what we said before. It seems to me that the giver of names reviles everything that hinders or restrains the flowing of the things that are. In particular, he gave this name '*aeischoroun*' to what always restrains their flowing (*aei ischei ton rhoun*). But nowadays it is contracted and pronounced '*aischron*'.

HERMOGENES: What about '*kalon*'?

SOCRATES: It's harder to understand. Indeed, it is pronounced like this only because it sounds harmonious to shorten the '*ou*' to '*o*'.

HERMOGENES: How so?

SOCRATES: In my view, this name derives from a sort of thought (*dianoia*).

HERMOGENES: What do you mean?

SOCRATES: Tell me. What caused each of the things that are to be called by a name? Isn't it whatever gave them their names?

HERMOGENES: Certainly.

SOCRATES: And wasn't it thought—whether divine or human or both—that did this?

HERMOGENES: Yes.

SOCRATES: And isn't what originally named them the same as what names (*kaloun*) them now, that is to say, thought?

HERMOGENES: Evidently.

46. See 409d.

SOCRATES: Aren't all the works performed by thought and understanding praiseworthy, while those that aren't are blameworthy?

HERMOGENES: Certainly.

SOCRATES: Now, medicine performs medical works and carpentry performs works of carpentry? Do you agree?

HERMOGENES: I do.

SOCRATES: And to name things (*kaloun*) is to perform beautiful (*kalon*) works?

HERMOGENES: Necessarily.

SOCRATES: And we say that it is thought that does this?

HERMOGENES: Certainly.

SOCRATES: Therefore wisdom (*phronēsis*) is correctly given the name '*kalon*' ('beautiful'), since it performs the works that we say are beautiful and welcome as such.

HERMOGENES: Evidently.

SOCRATES: What other such names still remain for us to examine?

HERMOGENES: Those related to the good and the beautiful, such as '*sumpheron*' ('advantageous'), '*lusiteloun*' ('profitable'), '*ōphelimon*' ('beneficial'), '*kerdaleon*' ('gainful'), and their opposites.

SOCRATES: In light of the previous investigations, you should now be able to explain '*sumpheron*' ('advantageous') for yourself, since it is obviously a close relative of '*epistēmē*' ('knowledge'). It expresses the fact that what is advantageous is nothing other than the movement (*phora*) of a soul in accord with the movement of things.[47] The things that are done as a result of this movement are probably called '*sumphora*' or '*sumpheronta*' because they are being moved in harmony with things (*sumperipheresthai*). But '*kerdaleon*' ('gainful') derives from '*kerdos*' ('gain'). If you replace the '*d*' in '*kerdos*' with a '*n*', the name expresses its meaning clearly; it names the good, but in another way. Because the good penetrates everything, it has the power to regulate (*kerannutai*) everything, and the one who gave it its name named it after this power. But he put a '*d*' instead of the '*n*' and pronounced it '*kerdos*'.

HERMOGENES: What about '*lusiteloun*' ('profitable')?

SOCRATES: I don't think, Hermogenes, that he uses the name '*lusiteloun*' to mean the profit that releases (*apoluei*) a capital sum for reinvestment, which is what retailers use it to mean. The namer-giver calls the good by that name because it is the fastest of the things that are, it doesn't allow things to remain at rest, or permit their motion to stop, pause, or reach an end. Instead, it always does away with (*luei*) any attempt to let motion end, making it unceasing and immortal. In my view, it is for this reason that the good is said to be '*lusiteloun*', because it does away with (*luon*) any end (*telos*) to motion. '*Ōphelimon*' ('beneficial') is a non-Attic name. Homer often uses it in the form '*ophellein*', which derives from '*auxein*' ('to increase') and '*poiein*' ('to make').

HERMOGENES: And what are we to say about their opposites?

47. See 412a ff.

SOCRATES: Those that are mere negations don't need any discussion, in my view.

HERMOGENES: Which ones are they?

SOCRATES: '*Asumpheron*' ('disadvantageous'), '*anōpheles*' ('nonbeneficial'), '*alusiteles*' ('unprofitable'), and '*akerdes*' ('non-gainful').

HERMOGENES: It's true, they don't need discussion.

SOCRATES: But '*blaberon*' ('harmful') and '*zēmiōdes*' ('hurtful') do.

HERMOGENES: Yes.

SOCRATES: '*Blaberon*' ('harmful') means that which is harming (*blapton*) the flow (*rhoun*). '*Blapton*', in turn, signifies wanting to grasp (*boulomenon haptein*). But grasping is the same as shackling, and the name-giver always finds fault with that. Now what wants to grasp the flow (*to boulomenon haptein rhoun*) would be most correctly called '*boulapteroun*', but this has been beautified, as it seems to me, and so it is called '*blaberon*'. e

HERMOGENES: What intricate names you come up with, Socrates! When you uttered the name '*boulapteroun*' just now, you looked just as if you were whistling the flute-prelude of the Hymn to Athena! 418

SOCRATES: I'm not responsible for them, Hermogenes; the name-givers are.

HERMOGENES: That's true. But what about '*zēmiōdes*' ('hurtful')? What does it mean?

SOCRATES: What does '*zēmiōdes*' mean? See how right I was to say, Hermogenes, that people make huge changes in the meaning of names by adding or subtracting letters, and how even a very slight alteration of this sort can make a name signify the opposite of what it used to signify. '*Deon*' ('obligation') is an example that has just occurred to me, and it reminds me of what I was about to say to you about '*zēmiōdes*'. Our fine modern language has obliterated the true meaning of these names by so twisting them around that they now mean the opposite of what they used to, whereas the ancient language expresses clearly what they mean. b

HERMOGENES: What do you mean?

SOCRATES: I'll tell you. You know that our ancestors made great use of '*i*' and '*d*' (especially the women, who are the best preservers of the ancient language). But nowadays people change '*i*' to '*ē*' or '*e*', which are supposed to sound more grandiose. c

HERMOGENES: They do?

SOCRATES: Yes. For example, people now call the day '*hēmera*', but in very ancient times they called it '*himera*' or '*hemera*'.

HERMOGENES: That's true.

SOCRATES: You know then that only the ancient name expresses the name-giver's meaning clearly? People welcome the daylight that comes out of the darkness and long for (*himeirousin*) it, and that's why they named it '*himera*'. d

HERMOGENES: Evidently.

SOCRATES: But nowadays the name is so dressed up that no one can understand what it means. Although there are some who think the day is called '*hēmera*' because it makes things gentle (*hēmera*).

HERMOGENES: So it seems.

SOCRATES: Do you also know that the ancients called a yoke *'duogon'* not *'zugon'*?

HERMOGENES: Of course.

SOCRATES: Now, *'zugon'* expresses nothing clearly, but the name *'duogon'*, on the other hand, is quite rightly given to whatever binds two animals
e   together so that they can pull a plough or cart (*duoin agōgēn*). Nonetheless, nowadays *'zugon'* it is. And there are plenty of other examples.

HERMOGENES: Evidently.

SOCRATES: Similarly, *'deon'* ('obligation'), when pronounced in this way, seems at first to signify the opposite of all the other names for the good. After all, even though an obligation is a kind of good, *'deon'* plainly signifies a shackle (*desmos*) and obstacle to motion, and so is closely akin to *'blaberon'* ('harmful').

HERMOGENES: Yes, Socrates, it does plainly signify that.

SOCRATES: But not if you use the ancient name, which is much more likely to have been correctly given than the present one. If you replace
419   the *'e'* with an *'i'*, as in the ancient name, it agrees with the earlier names of good things—for *'dion'* ('passing through'), not *'deon'*, signifies a good, and is a term of praise. So the name-giver didn't contradict himself, and *'deon'* ('obligation') is plainly the same as *'ōphelimon'* ('beneficial'), *'lusiteloun'* ('profitable'), *'kerdaleon'* ('gainful'), *'agathon'* ('good'), *'sumpheron'* ('advantageous'), and *'euporon'* ('lack of perplexity'), which are different names signifying what orders and moves. This is always praised, while what
b   restrains and shackles is found fault with. Likewise, in the case of *'zēmiōdes'* ('hurtful'), if you replace the *'z'* with a *'d'*, as in the ancient language, it will be plain to you that the name was given to what shackles motion (*doun to ion*), since *'dēmiōdes'* derives from that.

HERMOGENES: What about *'hēdonē'* ('pleasure'), *'lupē'* ('pain'), and *'epithumia'* ('appetite'), Socrates, and others like them?

SOCRATES: I don't think there is any great difficulty about them, Hermogenes. *Hēdonē* (pleasure) seems to have been given its name because it is an activity that tends towards enjoyment (*hē onēsis*), but a *'d'* has been inserted and we call it *'hēdonē'* instead of *'hēonē'*. *'Lupē'* ('pain') seems to
c   derive from the weakening (*dialusis*) the body suffers when in pain. *'Ania'* ('sorrow') signifies what hinders (*hienai*) motion. *'Algēdōn'* ('distress') seems to me to be a foreign name deriving from *'algeinos'* ('distressing'). *'Odunē'* ('grief') seems to be named after the entering in (*endusis*) of pain. It is clear to everyone that pronouncing the name *'achthēdōn'* ('affliction') is like giving motion a burden (*achthos*) to carry. *Chara* (joy) seems to have been so called because it is an outpouring (*diachusis*) or good movement of the soul's flow (*rhoē*). *'Terpsis'* ('delight') comes from *'terpnon'* ('delightful'),
d   which, in turn, comes from that which glides (*herpsis*) through the soul like a breath (*pnoē*). By rights it is called *'herpnoun'*, but over time its name has been changed to *'terpnon'*. *Euphrosunē* (lightheartedness) needs no explanation, since it is clear to everyone that it derives its name from

the movement of the soul that well accords (*eu sumpheresthai*) with that of things. By rights it is called *'eupherosunē'*, but we call it *'euphrosunē'*. Nor is there any difficulty about *epithumia* ('appetite'), for it is clear that its name derives from the power that opposes the spirited part of the soul (*epi ton thumon iousa*), while *'thumos'* ('spirit', 'anger') derives from the raging (*thusis*) and boiling of the soul. The name *'himeros'* ('desire') derives from what most drives the soul's flow. It flows with a rush (*hiemenos rhei*) and sets on (*ephiemenos*) things, thus violently dragging the soul because of the rush of its flow. And so, because it has all this power, it is called *'himeros'*. *'Pothos'* ('longing'), on the other hand, signifies that it isn't a desire (or flow) for what is present but for what is elsewhere (*pou*) or absent. So, when its object is absent, it is given the name *'pothos'*, and, when its object is present, it is called *'himeros'*. *Erōs* (erotic love) is so called because it flows in from outside, that is to say, the flow doesn't belong to the person who has it, but is introduced into him through his eyes. Because of this it was called *'esros'* ('influx') in ancient times, when they used *'o'* for *'ō'*, but now that *'o'* is changed to *'ō'*, it is called *'erōs'*. So, what other names do you think are left for us to examine?

HERMOGENES: What do you think about *'doxa'* ('opinion') and the like?

SOCRATES: *'Doxa'* ('opinion) either derives from the pursuit (*diōxis*) the soul engages in when it hunts for the knowledge of how things are, or it derives from the shooting of a bow (*toxon*). But the latter is more likely. At any rate, *'oiēsis'* ('thinking') is in harmony with it. It seems to express the fact that thinking is the motion (*oisis*) of the soul towards every thing, towards how each of the things that are really is. In the same way, *'boulē'* ('planning') has to do with trying to hit (*bolē*) some target, and *'boulesthai'* ('wishing') and *'bouleuesthai'* ('deliberating') signify aiming at something (*ephiesthai*). All these names seem to go along with *'doxa'* in that they're all like *'bolē'*, like trying to hit some target. Similarly, the opposite, *'aboulia'* ('lack of planning'), seems to signify a failure to get something (*atuchia*), as when someone fails to hit or get what he shot at, wished for, planned, or desired.

HERMOGENES: The pace of investigating seems to be quickening, Socrates!

SOCRATES: That's because I'm coming to the finishing post! But I still want to investigate *'anankē'* ('compulsion') and *'hekousion'* ('voluntary'), since they're next. The name *'hekousion'* expresses the fact that it signifies yielding and not resisting, but yielding, as I said before, to the motion (*eikon tōi ionti*)—the one that comes into being in accord with our wish. *'Anankaion'* ('compulsory') and *'antitupnon'* ('resistant'), on the other hand, since they signify motion contrary to our wish, are associated with 'error' and 'ignorance'. Indeed, saying *'anankaion'* is like trying to get through a ravine (*ankē*), for ravines restrain motion, since they are rough-going, filled with bushes, and hard to get through. It's probably for this reason that we use *'anankaion'* in the way we do—because saying it is like trying to get through a ravine. Nonetheless, while my strength lasts, let's not stop using it. Don't you stop, either, but keep asking your questions.

421 HERMOGENES: Well, then, let me ask about the finest and most important names, *'alētheia'* ('truth'), *'pseudos'* ('falsehood'), *'on'* ('being'), and—the subject of our present conversation—*'onoma'* ('name'), and why it is so named.

SOCRATES: Do you know what *'maiesthai'* means?

HERMOGENES: Yes, it means 'to search' (*'zētein'*).

SOCRATES: Well, *'onoma'* ('name') seems to be a compressed statement which says: "this is a being for which there is a search." You can see this more easily in *'onomaston'* ('thing named'), since it clearly says: "this is a being for which there is a search (*on hou masma estin*)." *'Alētheia'* ('truth')

b is like these others in being compressed, for the divine motion of being is called *'alētheia'* because *'alētheia'* is a compressed form of the phrase "a wandering that is divine (*alē theia*)." *'Pseudos'* ('falsehood') is the opposite of this motion, so that, once again, what is restrained or compelled to be inactive is reviled by the name-giver, and likened to people asleep (*katheudousi*)—but the meaning of the name is concealed by the addition of *'ps'*. *'On'* ('being') or *'ousia'* ('being') says the same as *'alētheia'* once an *'i'* is added, since it signifies going (*ion*). *'Ouk on'* ('not being'), in turn, is

c *'ouk ion'* ('not going'), and indeed some people actually use that name for it.

HERMOGENES: I think you've hammered these into shape manfully, Socrates. But suppose someone were to ask you about the correctness of the names *'ion'* ('going'), *'rheon'* ('flowing'), and *'doun'* ('shackling') . . .

SOCRATES: "How should we answer him?" Is that what you were going to say?

HERMOGENES: Yes, exactly.

SOCRATES: One way of giving the semblance of an answer has been suggested already.[48]

HERMOGENES: What way is that?

SOCRATES: To say that a name has a foreign origin when we don't know what it signifies. Now, it may well be true that some of these names are

d foreign, but it is also possible that the basic or 'first' names are Greek, but not recoverable because they are so old. Names have been twisted in so many ways, indeed, that it wouldn't be surprising if the ancient Greek word was the same as the modern foreign one.

HERMOGENES: At any rate, it wouldn't be at all inappropriate for you to respond that way.

SOCRATES: No, it probably wouldn't. Nevertheless, it seems to me that "once we're in the competition, we're allowed no excuses,"[49] but must investigate these names vigorously. We should remember this, however: if someone asks about the terms from which a name is formed, and then about the ones from which those terms are formed, and keeps on doing

e this indefinitely, the answerer must finally give up. Mustn't he?

---

48. See 409d, 416a.

49. A proverbial expression. See *Laws* 751d.

HERMOGENES: That's my view, at any rate.

SOCRATES: At what point would he be right to stop? Wouldn't it be when he reaches the names that are as it were the elements of all the other statements and names? For, if these are indeed elements, it cannot be right to suppose that *they* are composed out of other names. Consider *'agathos'* ('good'), for example; we said it is composed out of *'agaston'* ('admirable') and *'thoon'* ('fast').[50] And probably *'thoon'* is composed out of other names, and those out of still other ones. But if we ever get hold of a name that isn't composed out of other names, we'll be right to say that at last we've reached an element, which cannot any longer be carried back to other names.

HERMOGENES: That seems right to me, at least.

SOCRATES: And if the names you're asking about now turn out to be elements, won't we have to investigate their correctness in a different manner from the one we've been using so far?

HERMOGENES: Probably so.

SOCRATES: It is certainly probable, Hermogenes. At any rate, it's obvious that all the earlier ones were resolved into these. So, if they are indeed elements, as they seem to me to be, join me again in investigating them, to ensure that I don't talk nonsense about the correctness of the first names.

HERMOGENES: You have only to speak, and I will join in the investigation so far as I'm able.

SOCRATES: I think you agree with me that there is only one kind of correctness in all names, primary as well as derivative, and that considered simply as names there is no difference between them.

HERMOGENES: Certainly.

SOCRATES: Now, the correctness of every name we analyzed was intended to consist in its expressing the nature of one of the things that are.

HERMOGENES: Of course.

SOCRATES: And this is no less true of primary names than derivative ones, if indeed they are names.

HERMOGENES: Certainly.

SOCRATES: But it seems that the derivative ones were able to accomplish this by means of the primary ones.

HERMOGENES: Apparently.

SOCRATES: And if the primary names are indeed names, they must make the things that are as clear as possible to us. But how can they do this when they aren't based on other names? Answer me this: If we hadn't a voice or a tongue, and wanted to express things to one another, wouldn't we try to make signs by moving our hands, head, and the rest of our body, just as dumb people do at present?

HERMOGENES: What other choice would we have, Socrates?

SOCRATES: So, if we wanted to express something light in weight or above us, I think we'd raise our hand towards the sky in imitation of the very

50. See 412b–c.

nature of the thing. And if we wanted to express something heavy or below us, we'd move our hand towards the earth. And if we wanted to express a horse (or any other animal) galloping, you know that we'd make our bodies and our gestures as much like theirs as possible.

HERMOGENES: I think we'd have to.

SOCRATES: Because the only way to express anything by means of our
b body is to have our body imitate whatever we want to express.

HERMOGENES: Yes.

SOCRATES: So, if we want to express a particular fact by using our voice, tongue, and mouth, we will succeed in doing so, if we succeed in imitating it by means of them?

HERMOGENES: That must be right, I think.

SOCRATES: It seems to follow that a name is a vocal imitation of what it imitates, and that someone who imitates something with his voice names what he imitates.

HERMOGENES: I think so.

c SOCRATES: Well, *I* don't. I don't think this is a fine thing to say at all.

HERMOGENES: Why not?

SOCRATES: Because then we'd have to agree that those who imitate sheep, cocks, or other animals are naming the things they imitate.

HERMOGENES: That's true, we would.

SOCRATES: And do you think that's a fine conclusion?

HERMOGENES: No, I don't. But then what sort of imitation is a name, Socrates?

SOCRATES: In the first place, if we imitate things the way we imitate them
d in music, we won't be naming them, not even if the imitation in question is vocal. And the same holds if we imitate the things music imitates. What I mean is this: each thing has a sound and a shape, and many of them have a color. Don't they?

HERMOGENES: Certainly.

SOCRATES: It doesn't seem to be the craft of naming that's concerned with imitating these qualities, however, but rather the crafts of music and painting. Isn't that so?

HERMOGENES: Yes.

e SOCRATES: And what about this? Don't you think that just as each thing has a color or some of those other qualities we mentioned, it also has a being or essence? Indeed, don't color and sound each have a being or essence, just like every other thing that we say "is"?

HERMOGENES: Yes, I think they do.

SOCRATES: So if someone were able to imitate in letters and syllables this being or essence that each thing has, wouldn't he express what each thing itself is?

424 HERMOGENES: He certainly would.

SOCRATES: And if you were to identify the person who is able to do this, in just the way that you said the first was a musician and the second a painter, what would you say he is?

HERMOGENES: I think he's the namer, Socrates, the one we've been looking for from the beginning.

SOCRATES: If that's true, doesn't it seem that we are now in a position to investigate each of the names you were asking about—'*rhoē*' ('flowing'), '*ienai*' ('going'), and '*schesis*' ('restraining')—to see whether or not he has grasped the being or essence of each of the things they signify by imitating its being or essence in the letters and syllables of its name. Isn't that so?   b

HERMOGENES: Certainly.

SOCRATES: Come, then, let's see if these are the only primary names or if there are many others.

HERMOGENES: For my part, I think there are others.

SOCRATES: Yes, there probably are. But how are we to divide off the ones with which the imitator begins his imitation? Since an imitation of a thing's being or essence is made out of letters and syllables, wouldn't it be most correct for us to divide off the letters or elements first, just as those who set to work on speech rhythms first divide off the forces or powers of   c the letters or elements, then those of syllables, and only then investigate rhythms themselves?

HERMOGENES: Yes.

SOCRATES: So mustn't we first divide off the vowels and then the others in accordance with their differences in kind, that is to say, the "consonants" and "mutes" (as I take it they're called by specialists in these matters) and the semivowels, which are neither vowels nor mutes? And, as to the vowels themselves, mustn't we also divide off those that differ in kind from one another? Then when we've also well divided off the things that are—the things to which we have to give names—if there are some things to which   d they can all be carried back, as names are to the letters, and from which we can see that they derive, and if different kinds of being are found among them, in just the way that there are among the letters—once we've done all this well, we'll know how to apply each letter to what it resembles, whether one letter or a combination of many is to be applied to one thing. It's just the same as it is with painters. When they want to produce a resemblance, they sometimes use only purple, sometimes another color,   e and sometimes—for example, when they want to paint human flesh or something of that sort—they mix many colors, employing the particular color, I suppose, that their particular subject demands. Similarly, we'll apply letters to things, using one letter for one thing, when that's what seems to be required, or many letters together, to form what's called a syllable, or many syllables combined to form names and verbs. From   425 names and verbs, in turn, we shall finally construct something important, beautiful, and whole. And just as the painter painted an animal, so—by means of the craft of naming or rhetoric or whatever it is—we shall construct sentences. Of course, I don't really mean *we ourselves*—I was carried away by the discussion. It was *the ancients* who combined things in this way. Our job—if indeed we are to examine all these things with scientific knowledge—is to divide where they put together, so as to see whether or

b   not both the primary and derivative names are given in accord with nature.
      For, any other way of connecting names to things, Hermogenes, is inferior
      and unsystematic.

          HERMOGENES: By god, Socrates, it probably is.

          SOCRATES: Well, then, do you think you could divide them in that way?
      I don't think I could.

          HERMOGENES: Then it's even less likely that I could.

          SOCRATES: Shall we give up then? Or do you want us to do what we
      can, and try to see a little of what these names are like? Aren't we in a
c   similar situation to the one we were in a while ago with the gods?[51] We
      prefaced that discussion by saying that we were wholly ignorant of the
      truth, and were merely describing human beliefs about the gods. So,
      shouldn't we now say this to ourselves before we proceed: If anyone,
      whether ourselves or someone else, divides names properly, he will divide
      them in the way we have just described, but, given our present situation,
      we must follow the proverb and "do the best we can" to work at them?
      Do you agree or not?

          HERMOGENES: Of course, I agree completely.

d   SOCRATES: Perhaps it will seem absurd, Hermogenes, to think that things
      become clear by being imitated in letters and syllables, but it is absolutely
      unavoidable. For we have nothing better on which to base the truth of
      primary names. Unless you want us to behave like tragic poets, who
      introduce a *deus ex machina* whenever they're perplexed. For we, too, could
      escape our difficulties by saying that the primary names are correct because
      they were given by the gods. But is that the best account we can give? Or
e   is it this one: that we got them from foreigners, who are more ancient than
      we are? Or this: that just as it is impossible to investigate foreign names,
      so it is impossible to investigate the primary ones because they are too
426   ancient? Aren't all these merely the clever excuses of people who have
      no account to offer of how primary names are correctly given? And yet
      regardless of what kind of excuse one offers, if one doesn't know about
      the correctness of primary names, one cannot know about the correctness
      of derivative ones, which can only express something by means of those
      others about which one knows nothing. Clearly, then, anyone who claims
      to have a scientific understanding of derivative names must first and
b   foremost be able to explain the primary ones with perfect clarity. Otherwise
      he can be certain that what he says about the others will be worthless. Or
      do you disagree?

          HERMOGENES: No, Socrates, not in the least.

          SOCRATES: Well, my impressions about primary names seem to me to be
      entirely outrageous and absurd. Nonetheless, I'll share them with you, if you
      like. But if you have something better to offer, I hope you'll share it with me.

          HERMOGENES: Have no fear, I will.

c   SOCRATES: First off, 'r' seems to me to be a tool for copying every sort
      of motion (*kinēsis*).—We haven't said why motion has this name, but it's

      51. See 401a.

clear that it means *'hesis'* ('a going forth'), since in ancient times we used *'e'* in place of *'ē'*. The first part comes from *'kiein'*, a non-Attic name equivalent to *'ienai'* ('moving'). So if you wanted to find an ancient name corresponding to the present *'kinēsis'*, the correct answer would be *'hesis'*. But nowadays, what with the non-Attic word *'kiein'*, the change from *'e'* to *'ē'*, and the insertion of *'n'*, we say *'kinēsis'*, though it ought to be *'kieinēsis'*. *'Stasis'* ('rest') is a beautified version of a name meaning the opposite of *'ienai'* ('moving').—In any case, as I was saying, the letter *'r'* seemed to the name-giver to be a beautiful tool for copying motion, at any rate he often uses it for this purpose. He first uses this letter to imitate motion in the name *'rhein'* ('flowing') and *'rhoē'* ("flow") themselves. Then in *'tromos'* ('trembling') and *'trechein'* ('running'), and in such verbs as *'krouein'* ('striking'), *'thrauein'* ('crushing'), *'ereikein'* ('rending'), *'thruptein'* ('breaking'), *'kermatizein'* ('crumbling'), *'rhumbein'* ('whirling'), it is mostly *'r'* he uses to imitate these motions. He saw, I suppose, that the tongue was most agitated and least at rest in pronouncing this letter, and that's probably why he used it in these names. He uses *'i'*, in turn, to imitate all the small things that can most easily penetrate everything. Hence, in *'ienai'* ('moving') and *'hiesthai'* ('hastening'), he uses *'i'* to do the imitating. Similarly, he uses *'phi'*, *'psi'*, *'s'*, and *'z'* to do the imitating in such names as *'psuchron'* ('chilling'), *'zeon'* ('seething'), *'seiesthai'* ('shaking'), and *'seismos'* ('quaking'), because all these letters are pronounced with an expulsion of breath. Indeed, whenever the name-giver wants to imitate some sort of blowing or hard breathing (*phusōdes*), he almost always seems to employ them. He also seems to have thought that the compression and stopping of the power of the tongue involved in pronouncing *'d'* and *'t'* made such names as *'desmos'* ('shackling') and *'stasis'* ('rest') appropriately imitative. And because he observed that the tongue glides most of all in pronouncing *'l'*, he uses it to produce a resemblance in *'olisthanein'* ('glide') itself, and in such names as *'leion'* ('smooth'), *'liparon'* ('sleek'), *'kollōdes'* ('viscous'), and the like. But when he wants to imitate something cloying, he uses names, such as *'glischron'* ('gluey'), *'gluku'* ('sweet'), and *'gloiōdes'* ('clammy'), in which the gliding of the tongue is stopped by the power of the *'g'*. And because he saw that *'n'* is sounded inwardly, he used it in *'endon'* ('within') and *'entos'* ('inside'), in order to make the letters copy the things. He put an *'a'* in *'mega'* ('large') and an *'ē'* in *'mēkos'* ('length') because these letters are both pronounced long. He wanted *'o'* to signify roundness, so he mixed lots of it into the name *'gongulon'* ('round'). In the same way, the rule-setter apparently used the other letters or elements as likenesses in order to make a sign or name for each of the things that are, and then compounded all the remaining names out of these, imitating the things they name. That, Hermogenes, is my view of what it means to say that names are correct—unless, of course, Cratylus disagrees.

HERMOGENES: Well, Socrates, as I said at the beginning, Cratylus confuses me a lot of the time. He *says* that there is such a thing as the correctness of names, but he never explains clearly what it is. Consequently, I'm never able to determine whether his lack of clarity is intentional or unintentional.

e   So tell me now, Cratylus, here in the presence of Socrates, do you agree
     with what he has been saying about names, or do you have something
     better to say? If you have, tell it to us, and either you'll learn about your
     errors from Socrates or become our teacher.

          CRATYLUS: But, Hermogenes, do you really think that any subject can be
     taught or learned so quickly, not to mention one like this, which seems
     to be among the most important?

428   HERMOGENES: No, by god, I don't. But I think that Hesiod is right in
     saying that

            If you can add even a little to a little, it's worthwhile.[52]

     So, if you can add even a little more, don't shrink from the labor, but assist
     Socrates—he deserves it—and assist me, too.

          SOCRATES: Yes, Cratylus, please do. As far as I'm concerned, nothing I've
     said is set in stone. I have simply been saying what seems right to me as
     a result of my investigations with Hermogenes. So, don't hesitate to speak,
b   and if your views are better than mine, I'll gladly accept them. And it
     wouldn't surprise me if they were better, for you've both investigated
     these matters for yourself and learned about them from others. So, if indeed
     you do happen to have something better to offer, you may sign me up as
     a student in your course on the correctness of names.

          CRATYLUS: Yes, Socrates, I have, as you say, occupied myself with these
     matters, and it's possible that you might have something to learn from
c   me. But I fear the opposite is altogether more likely. So much so, indeed,
     that it occurs to me to say to you what Achilles says to Ajax in the "Prayers":

            Ajax, son of Telamon, seed of Zeus, lord of the people,
            All you have said to me seems spoken after my own mind.[53]

     The same is true of me where you're concerned, Socrates: your oracular
     utterances—whether inspired by Euthyphro or by some other Muse who
     has long inhabited your own mind without your knowing about it—seem
     to be pretty much spoken after *my* own mind.

d   SOCRATES: But, Cratylus, *I* have long been surprised at my own wisdom—
     and doubtful of it, too. That's why I think it's necessary to keep re-investi-
     gating whatever I say, since self-deception is the worst thing of all. How
     could it not be terrible, indeed, when the deceiver never deserts you even
     for an instant but is always right there with you? Therefore, I think we
     have to turn back frequently to what we've already said, in order to
     test it by looking at it "backwards and forwards simultaneously," as the

52. *Works and Days*, 361.
53. *Iliad* ix.644–45.

aforementioned poet puts it.[54] So, let's now see what we *have* said. We said that the correctness of a name consists in displaying the nature of the thing it names. And is that statement satisfactory?

CRATYLUS: In my view, Socrates, it is entirely satisfactory.

SOCRATES: So names are spoken in order to give instruction?

CRATYLUS: Certainly.

SOCRATES: Is there a craft for that and are there craftsmen who practice it?

CRATYLUS: Certainly.

SOCRATES: Who are they?

CRATYLUS: As you said at the beginning, they're the rule-setters.[55]

SOCRATES: Is this craft attributed to human beings in the same way as other crafts or not? What I mean is this: aren't some painters better or worse than others?

CRATYLUS: Certainly.

SOCRATES: And the better painters produce finer products or paintings, while the others produce inferior ones? Similarly with builders—some build finer houses, others build inferior ones?

CRATYLUS: Yes.

SOCRATES: What about rule-setters? Do some of them produce finer products, others inferior ones?

CRATYLUS: No, there I no longer agree with you.

SOCRATES: So you don't think that some rules are better, others inferior?

CRATYLUS: Certainly not.

SOCRATES: Nor names either, it seems. Or do you think that some names have been better given, others worse?

CRATYLUS: Certainly not.

SOCRATES: So all names have been correctly given?

CRATYLUS: Yes, as many of them as are names at all.

SOCRATES: What about the case of Hermogenes, which we mentioned earlier? Has he not been given this name at all, unless he belongs to the family of Hermes? Or has he been given it, only not correctly?

CRATYLUS: I think he hasn't been given it at all, Socrates. People take it to have been given to him, but it is really the name of someone else, namely, the very one who also has the nature.

SOCRATES: What about when someone says that our friend here is Hermogenes? Is he speaking falsely or is he not even managing to do that much? Is it even possible to say that he *is* Hermogenes, if he isn't?

CRATYLUS: What do you mean?

SOCRATES: That false speaking is in every way impossible, for isn't that what *you* are trying to say? Certainly, many people do say it nowadays, Cratylus, and many have said it in the past as well.

CRATYLUS: But, Socrates, how can anyone say the thing he says and not say something that is? Doesn't speaking falsely consist in not saying things that are?

54. *Iliad* i.343.

55. See 388d ff.

SOCRATES: Your argument is too subtle for me at my age. All the same, tell me this. Do you think it is possible to say something falsely, although not possible to speak it falsely?

CRATYLUS: In my view, one can neither speak nor say anything falsely.

SOCRATES: What about announcing something falsely or addressing someone falsely? For example, suppose you were in a foreign country and someone meeting you took your hand and said, "Greetings! Hermogenes, son of Smicrion, visitor from Athens," would he be speaking, saying, announcing, or addressing these words not to you but to Hermogenes— or to no one?

CRATYLUS: In my view, Socrates, he is not articulating them as he should.

SOCRATES: Well, that's a welcome answer. But are the words he articulates true or false, or partly true and partly false? If you tell me that, I'll be satisfied.

CRATYLUS: For my part, I'd say he's just making noise and acting pointlessly, as if he were banging a brass pot.

SOCRATES: Let's see, Cratylus, if we can somehow come to terms with one another. You agree, don't you, that it's one thing to be a name and another to be the thing it names?

CRATYLUS: Yes, I do.

SOCRATES: And you also agree that a name is an imitation of a thing?

CRATYLUS: Absolutely.

SOCRATES: And that a painting is a different sort of imitation of a thing?

CRATYLUS: Yes.

SOCRATES: Well, perhaps what you're saying is correct and I'm misunderstanding you, but can both of these imitations—both paintings and names—be assigned and applied to the things of which they are imitations, or not?

CRATYLUS: They can.

SOCRATES: Then consider this. Can we assign a likeness of a man to a man and that of a woman to a woman, and so on?

CRATYLUS: Certainly.

SOCRATES: What about the opposite? Can we assign the likeness of a man to a woman and that of a woman to a man?

CRATYLUS: Yes, we can.

SOCRATES: And are both these assignments correct, or only the first?

CRATYLUS: Only the first.

SOCRATES: That is to say, the one that assigns to each thing the painting or name that is appropriate to it or like it?

CRATYLUS: That's my view, at least.

SOCRATES: Since you and I are friends, we don't want to mince words, so here's what I think. I call the first kind of assignment correct, whether it's an assignment of a painting or a name, but if it's an assignment of a name, I call it both correct and *true*. And I call the other kind of assignment, the one that assigns and applies unlike imitations, incorrect, and, in the case of names, *false* as well.

CRATYLUS: But it may be, Socrates, that it's possible to assign paintings incorrectly, but not names, which must always be correctly assigned.

SOCRATES: What do you mean? What's the difference between them? Can't I step up to a man and say "This is your portrait," while showing him what happens to be his own likeness, or what happens to be the likeness of a woman? And by "show" I mean bring before the sense of sight.

CRATYLUS: Certainly.

SOCRATES: Well, then, can't I step up to the same man a second time and say, "This is your name"? Now, a name is an imitation, just as a painting or portrait is. So, can't I say to him, "This is your name," and after that put before his sense of hearing what happens to be an imitation of himself, saying "Man," or what happens to be an imitation of a female of the human species, saying "Woman"? Don't you think that all this is possible and sometimes occurs?

CRATYLUS: I'm willing to go along with you, Socrates, and say that it occurs.

SOCRATES: It's good of you to do so, Cratylus, provided you really are willing, since then we don't have to argue any further about the matter. So if some such assignments of names take place, we may call the first of them speaking truly and the second speaking falsely. But if that is so, it is sometimes possible to assign names incorrectly, to give them not to things they fit but to things they don't fit. The same is true of verbs. But if verbs and names can be assigned in this way, the same must be true of statements, since statements are, I believe, a combination of names and verbs. What do you think, Cratylus?

CRATYLUS: The same as you, since I think you're right.

SOCRATES: Further, primary names may be compared to paintings, and in paintings it's possible to present all the appropriate colors and shapes, or not to present them all. Some may be left out, or too many included, or those included may be too large. Isn't that so?

CRATYLUS: It is.

SOCRATES: So doesn't someone who presents all of them, present a fine painting or likeness, while someone who adds some or leaves some out, though he still produces a painting or likeness, produces a bad one?

CRATYLUS: Yes.

SOCRATES: What about someone who imitates the being or essence of things in syllables and letters? According to this account, if he presents all the appropriate things, won't the likeness—that is to say, the name—be a fine one? But if he happens to add a little or leave a little out, though he'll still have produced an image, it won't be fine? Doesn't it follow that some names are finely made, while others are made badly?

CRATYLUS: Presumably.

SOCRATES: So presumably one person will be a good craftsman of names and another a bad one?

CRATYLUS: Yes.

SOCRATES: And this craftsman is named a rule-setter.

CRATYLUS: Yes.

SOCRATES: By god, presumably some rule-setters are good and others bad then, especially if what we agreed to before is true, and they are just like other craftsmen.

CRATYLUS: That's right. But you see, Socrates, when we assign '*a*', '*b*', and each of the other letters to names by using the craft of grammar, if we add, subtract, or transpose a letter, we don't simply write the name incorrectly, we don't write *it* at all, for it immediately becomes a different name, if any of those things happens.

432

SOCRATES: That's not a good way for us to look at the matter, Cratylus.

CRATYLUS: Why not?

SOCRATES: What you say may well be true of numbers, which have to be a certain number or not be at all. For example, if you add anything to the number ten or subtract anything from it, it immediately becomes a different number, and the same is true of any other number you choose. But this isn't the sort of correctness that belongs to things with sensory qualities, such as images in general. Indeed, the opposite is true of them—an image cannot remain an image if it presents all the details of what it represents. See if I'm right. Would there be two things—Cratylus and an image of Cratylus—in the following circumstances? Suppose some god didn't just represent your color and shape the way painters do, but made all the inner parts like yours, with the same warmth and softness, and put motion, soul, and wisdom like yours into them—in a word, suppose he made a duplicate of everything you have and put it beside you. Would there then be two Cratyluses or Cratylus and an image of Cratylus?

b

c

CRATYLUS: It seems to me, Socrates, that there would be two Cratyluses.

SOCRATES: So don't you see that we must look for some other kind of correctness in images and in the names we've been discussing, and not insist that if a detail is added to an image or omitted from it, it's no longer an image at all. Or haven't you noticed how far images are from having the same features as the things of which they are images?

d

CRATYLUS: Yes, I have.

SOCRATES: At any rate, Cratylus, names would have an absurd effect on the things they name, if they resembled them in every respect, since all of them would then be duplicated, and no one would be able to say which was the thing and which was the name.

CRATYLUS: That's true.

SOCRATES: Take courage then and admit that one name may be well-given while another isn't. Don't insist that it have all the letters and exactly resemble the thing it names, but allow that an inappropriate letter may be included. But if an inappropriate letter may be included in a name, an inappropriate name may be included in a phrase. And if an inappropriate name may be included in a phrase, a phrase which is inappropriate to the things may be employed in a statement. Things are still named and described when this happens, provided the phrases include the pattern of

e

the things they're about. Remember that this is just what Hermogenes and
I claimed earlier about the names of the elements.[56]

CRATYLUS: I remember.

SOCRATES: Good. So even if a name doesn't include all the appropriate
letters, it will still describe the thing if it includes its pattern—though it
will describe the thing well, if it includes all the appropriate letters, and
badly, if it includes few of them. I think we had better accept this, Cratylus,
or else, like men lost on the streets of Aegina late at night, we, too, may
incur the charge of truly seeming to be the sort of people who arrive at
things later than they should. For if you deny it, you cannot agree that a
name is correct if it expresses things by means of letters and syllables and
you'll have to search for some other account of the correctness of names,
since if you both deny it and accept this account of correctness, you'll
contradict yourself.

CRATYLUS: You seem to me to be speaking reasonably, Socrates, and I
take what you've said as established.

SOCRATES: Well, then, since we agree about that, let's consider the next
point. If a name is well given, don't we say that it must have the appropriate letters?

CRATYLUS: Yes.

SOCRATES: And the appropriate letters are the ones that are like the things?

CRATYLUS: Certainly.

SOCRATES: Therefore that's the way that well-given names are given. But
if a name isn't well given, it's probable that most of its letters are appropriate
or like the thing it names, if indeed it is a likeness of it, but that some are
inappropriate and prevent the name from being good or well given. Is
that our view or is it something different?

CRATYLUS: I don't suppose there's anything to be gained by continuing
to quarrel, Socrates, but I'm not satisfied that something is a name if it
isn't well given.

SOCRATES: But you *are* satisfied that a name is a way of expressing a thing?

CRATYLUS: I am.

SOCRATES: And you think it's true that some names are composed out
of more primitive ones, while others are primary?

CRATYLUS: Yes, I do.

SOCRATES: But if the primary names are to be ways of expressing things
clearly, is there any better way of getting them to be such than by making
each of them as much like the thing it is to express as possible? Or do you
prefer the way proposed by Hermogenes and many others, who claim
that names are conventional signs that express things to those who already
knew the things before they established the conventions? Do you think
that the correctness of names is conventional, so that it makes no difference
whether we accept the present convention or adopt the opposite one,

b

c

d

e

56. See 393d–e.

calling 'big' what we now call 'small', and 'small' what we now call 'big'? Which of these two ways of getting names to express things do you prefer?

434   CRATYLUS: A name that expresses a thing by being like it is in every way superior, Socrates, to one that is given by chance.

SOCRATES: That's right. But if a name is indeed to be like a thing, mustn't the letters or elements out of which primary names are composed be naturally like things? Let me explain by returning to our earlier analogy with painting. Could a painting ever be made like any of the things that are, if it were not composed of pigments that were by nature like the

b   things that the art of painting imitates? Isn't that impossible?

CRATYLUS: Yes, it's impossible.

SOCRATES: Then by the same token can names ever be like anything unless the things they're composed out of have some kind of likeness to the things they imitate? And aren't they composed of letters or elements?

CRATYLUS: Yes.

SOCRATES: Now, consider what I said to Hermogenes earlier. Tell me,

c   do you think I was right to say that 'r' is like motion, moving, and hardness or not?

CRATYLUS: You were right.

SOCRATES: And 'l' is like smoothness, softness, and the other things we mentioned.

CRATYLUS: Yes.

SOCRATES: Yet you know that the very thing that we call '*sklērotēs*' ('hardness') is called '*sklērotēr*' by the Eretrians?

CRATYLUS: Certainly.

SOCRATES: Then are both 'r' and 's' like the same thing, and does the name ending in 'r' express the same thing to them as the one ending in 's' does to us, or does one of them fail to express it?

d   CRATYLUS: They both express it.

SOCRATES: In so far as 'r' and 's' are alike, or in so far as they are unlike?

CRATYLUS: In so far as they are alike.

SOCRATES: Are they alike in all respects?

CRATYLUS: They are presumably alike with respect to expressing motion, at any rate.

SOCRATES: What about the 'l' in these names? Doesn't it express the opposite of hardness?

CRATYLUS: Perhaps it is incorrectly included in them, Socrates. Maybe it's just like the examples you cited to Hermogenes a while ago in which you added or subtracted letters. You were correct to do so, in my view. So, too, in the present case perhaps we ought to replace 'l' with 'r'.

SOCRATES: You have a point. But what about when someone says '*sklēron*'

e   ('hard'), and pronounces it the way we do at present? Don't we understand him? Don't you yourself know what *I* mean by it?

CRATYLUS: I do, but that's because of usage.

SOCRATES: When you say 'usage', do you mean something other than convention? Do you mean something by 'usage' besides this: when I utter this name and mean hardness by it, you know that this is what I mean? Isn't that what you're saying?

CRATYLUS: Yes. 435

SOCRATES: And if when I utter a name, you know what I mean, doesn't that name become a way for me to express it to you?

CRATYLUS: Yes.

SOCRATES: Even though the name I utter is unlike the thing I mean— since '*l*' is unlike hardness (to revert to your example). But if that's right, surely you have entered into a convention with yourself, and the correctness of names has become a matter of convention for you, for isn't it the chance of usage and convention that makes both like and unlike letters express things? And even if usage is completely different from convention, still you must say that expressing something isn't a matter of likeness but b of usage, since usage, it seems, enables both like and unlike names to express things. Since we agree on these points, Cratylus, for I take your silence as a sign of agreement, both convention and usage must contribute something to expressing what we mean when we speak. Consider numbers, Cratylus, since you want to have recourse to them.[57] Where do you think you'll get names that are like each one of the numbers, if you don't allow this agreement and convention of yours to have some control over the correctness of names? I myself prefer the view that names should be as c much like things as possible, but I fear that defending this view is like hauling a ship up a sticky ramp, as Hermogenes suggested,[58] and that we have to make use of this worthless thing, convention, in the correctness of names. For probably the best possible way to speak consists in using names all (or most) of which are like the things they name (that is, are appropriate to them), while the worst is to use the opposite kind of names. But let me next ask you this. What power do names have for us? What's d the good of them?

CRATYLUS: To give instruction, Socrates. After all, the simple truth is that anyone who knows a thing's name also knows the thing.

SOCRATES: Perhaps you mean this, Cratylus, that when you know what a name is like, and it is like the thing it names, then you also know the thing, since it is like the name, and all like things fall under one and the e same craft. Isn't that why you say that whoever knows a thing's name also knows the thing?

CRATYLUS: Yes, you're absolutely right.

SOCRATES: Then let's look at that way of giving instruction about the things that are. Is there also another one, but inferior to this, or is it the only one? What do you think?

CRATYLUS: I think that it is the best and only way, and that there are no others. 436

57. See 432a.
58. At 414c.

SOCRATES: Is it also the best way to *discover* the things that are? If one discovers something's name has one also discovered the thing it names? Or are names only a way of getting people to learn things, and must investigation and discovery be undertaken in some different way?

CRATYLUS: They must certainly be undertaken in exactly the same way and by means of the same things.

SOCRATES: But don't you see, Cratylus, that anyone who investigates
b things by taking names as his guides and looking into their meanings runs no small risk of being deceived?

CRATYLUS: In what way?

SOCRATES: It's clear that the first name-giver gave names to things based on his conception of what those things were like. Isn't that right?

CRATYLUS: Yes.

SOCRATES: And if his conception was incorrect and he gave names based on it, what do you suppose will happen to us if we take him as our guide? Won't we be deceived?

CRATYLUS: But it wasn't that way, Socrates. The name-giver had to know
c the things he was naming. Otherwise, as I've been saying all along, his names wouldn't be names at all. And here's a powerful proof for you that the name-giver didn't miss the truth: His names are entirely consistent with one another. Or haven't you noticed that all the names you utter are based on the same assumption and have the same purpose?

SOCRATES: But surely that's no defense, Cratylus. The name-giver might have made a mistake at the beginning and then forced the other names
d to be consistent with it. There would be nothing strange in that. Geometrical constructions often have a small unnoticed error at the beginning with which all the rest is perfectly consistent. That's why every man must think a lot about the first principles of any thing and investigate them thoroughly to see whether or not it's correct to assume them. For if they have been adequately examined, the subsequent steps will plainly follow from them.
e However, I'd be surprised if names *are* actually consistent with one another. So let's review our earlier discussion. We said that names signify the being or essence of things to us on the assumption that all things are moving and flowing and being swept along.[59] Isn't that what you think names express?

437   CRATYLUS: Absolutely. Moreover, I think they signify correctly.

SOCRATES: Of those we discussed, let's reconsider the name *'epistēmē'* ('knowledge') first and see how ambiguous it is. It seems to signify that it stops (*histēsi*) the movement of our soul towards (*epi*) things, rather than that it accompanies them in their movement, so that it's more correct to pronounce the beginning of it as we now do than to insert an *'e'* and get *'hepeïstēmē'*[60]—or rather, to insert an *'i'* instead of an *'e'*.[61] Next, consider

---

59. See 411c.

60. As was suggested at 412a, yielding something to do with "following" things.

61. To get *'epihistēmē'*, revealing more clearly the derivation from *'epi'* and *'histēsi'*.

'bebaion' ('certain'), which is an imitation of being based (*basis*) or resting (*stasis*), not of motion. *'Historia'* ('inquiry'), which is somewhat the same, signifies the stopping (*histēsi*) of the flow (*rhous*). *'Piston'* ('confidence'), b too, certainly signifies stopping (*histan*). Next, anyone can see that *'mnēmē'* ('memory') means a staying (*monē*) in the soul, not a motion. Or consider *'hamartia'* ('error') and *'sumphora'* ('mishap'), if you like. If we take names as our guides, they seem to signify the same as *'sunesis'* ('comprehension') and *'epistēmē'* ('knowledge') and other names of excellent things.[62] Moreover, *'amathia'* ('ignorance') and *'akolasia'* ('licentiousness') also seem to be closely akin to them. For *'amathia'* seems to mean the journey of someone who accompanies god (*hama theōi iōn*), and *'akolasia'* seems precisely to c mean movement guided by things (*akolouthia tois pragmasin*). Thus names of what we consider to be the very worst things seem to be exactly like those of the very best. And if one took the trouble, I think one could find many other names from which one could conclude that the name-giver intended to signify not that things were moving and being swept along, but the opposite, that they were at rest.

CRATYLUS: But observe, Socrates, that most of them signify motion. d

SOCRATES: What if they do, Cratylus? Are we to count names like votes and determine their correctness that way? If more names signify motion, does that make *them* the true ones?

CRATYLUS: No, that's not a reasonable view.

SOCRATES: It certainly isn't, Cratylus. So let's drop this topic, and return to the one that led us here. A little while ago, you said, if you remember, 438 that the name-giver had to know the things he named.[63] Do you still believe that or not?

CRATYLUS: I still do.

SOCRATES: Do you think that the giver of the first names also knew the things he named?

CRATYLUS: Yes, he did know them.

SOCRATES: What names did he learn or discover those things from? After all, the first names had not yet been given. Yet it's impossible, on our b view, to learn or discover things except by learning their names from others or discovering them for ourselves?

CRATYLUS: You have a point there, Socrates.

SOCRATES: So, if things cannot be learned except from their names, how can we possibly claim that the name-givers or rule-setters had knowledge before any names had been given for them to know?

CRATYLUS: I think the truest account of the matter, Socrates, is that a c more than human power gave the first names to things, so that they are necessarily correct.

---

62. *'Hamartia'* is like *'homartein'* ('to accompany'), and *'sumphora'* is like *'sumpheresthai'* ('to move together with').

63. At 435d.

SOCRATES: In your view then this name-giver contradicted himself, even though he's either a daemon or a god? Or do you think we were talking nonsense just now?

CRATYLUS: But one of the two apparently contradictory groups of names that we distinguished aren't names at all.

SOCRATES: Which one, Cratylus? Those which point to rest or those which point to motion? As we said just now, this cannot be settled by majority vote.

d   CRATYLUS: No, that wouldn't be right, Socrates.

SOCRATES: But since there's a civil war among names, with some claiming that they are like the truth and others claiming that *they* are, how then are we to judge between them, and what are we to start from? We can't start from other different names because there are none. No, it's clear we'll have to look for something other than names, something that will make plain to us without using names which of these two kinds of names are the true ones—that is to say, the ones that express the truth about the
e   things that are.

CRATYLUS: I think so, too.

SOCRATES: But if that's right, Cratylus, then it seems it must be possible to learn about the things that are, independently of names.

CRATYLUS: Evidently.

SOCRATES: How else would you expect to learn about them? How else than in the most legitimate and natural way, namely, learning them through one another, if they are somehow akin, and through themselves? For something different, something that was other than they, wouldn't signify them, but something different, something other.

CRATYLUS: That seems true to me.

439   SOCRATES: But wait a minute! Haven't we often agreed that if names are well given, they are like the things they name and so are likenesses of them?

CRATYLUS: Yes.

SOCRATES: So if it's really the case that one can learn about things through names and that one can also learn about them through themselves, which would be the better and clearer way to learn about them? Is it better to learn from the likeness both whether it itself is a good likeness and also the truth it is a likeness of? Or is it better to learn from the truth both the
b   truth itself and also whether the likeness of it is properly made?

CRATYLUS: I think it is certainly better to learn from the truth.

SOCRATES: How to learn and make discoveries about the things that are is probably too large a topic for you or me. But we should be content to have agreed that it is far better to investigate them and learn about them through themselves than to do so through their names.

CRATYLUS: Evidently so, Socrates.

SOCRATES: Still, let's investigate one further issue so as to avoid being deceived by the fact that so many of these names seem to lean in the same
c   direction—as we will be if, as seems to me to be the case, the name-givers really did give them in the belief that everything is always moving and

flowing, and as it happens things aren't really that way at all, but the name-givers themselves have fallen into a kind of vortex and are whirled around in it, dragging us with them. Consider, Cratylus, a question that I for my part often dream about: Are we or aren't we to say that there is a beautiful itself, and a good itself, and the same for each one of the things that are?

CRATYLUS: I think we are, Socrates.

SOCRATES: Let's not investigate whether a particular face or something of that sort is beautiful then, or whether all such things seem to be flowing, but let's ask this instead: Are we to say that the beautiful itself is always such as it is?

CRATYLUS: Absolutely.

SOCRATES: But if it is always passing away, can we correctly say of it first that it is *this*, and then that it is *such and such*? Or, at the very instant we are speaking, isn't it inevitably and immediately becoming a different thing and altering and no longer being as it was?

CRATYLUS: It is.

SOCRATES: Then if it never stays the same, how can it *be* something? After all, if it ever stays the same, it clearly isn't changing—at least, not during that time; and if it always stays the same and is always the same thing, so that it never departs from its own form, how can it ever change or move?

CRATYLUS: There's no way.

SOCRATES: Then again it can't even be known by anyone. For at the very instant the knower-to-be approaches, what he is approaching is becoming a different thing, of a different character, so that he can't yet come to know either what sort of thing it is or what it is like—surely, no kind of knowledge is knowledge of what isn't in any way.

CRATYLUS: That's right.

SOCRATES: Indeed, it isn't even reasonable to say that there is such a thing as knowledge, Cratylus, if all things are passing on and none remain. For if that thing itself, knowledge, did not pass on from being knowledge, then knowledge would always remain, and there would *be* such a thing as knowledge. On the other hand, if the very form of knowledge passed on from being knowledge, the instant it passed on into a different form than that of knowledge, there would be no knowledge. And if it were always passing on, there would always be no knowledge. Hence, on this account, no one could know anything and nothing could be known either. But if there is always that which knows and that which is known, if there are such things as the beautiful, the good, and each one of the things that are, it doesn't appear to me that these things can be at all like flowings or motions, as we were saying just now they were. So whether I'm right about these things or whether the truth lies with Heraclitus and many others[64] isn't an easy matter to investigate. But surely no one with any understanding will commit himself or the cultivation of his soul to names,

64. See 402a.

or trust them and their givers to the point of firmly stating that he knows something—condemning both himself and the things that are to be totally unsound like leaky sinks—or believe that things are exactly like people with runny noses, or that all things are afflicted with colds and drip over everything. It's certainly possible that things are that way, Cratylus, but it is also possible that they are not. So you must investigate them courageously and thoroughly and not accept anything easily—you are still young and in your prime, after all. Then after you've investigated them, if you happen to discover the truth, you can share it with me.

CRATYLUS: I'll do that. But I assure you, Socrates, that I have already investigated them and have taken a lot of trouble over the matter, and things seem to me to be very much more as Heraclitus says they are.

SOCRATES: Instruct me about it another time, Cratylus, after you get back. But now go off into the country, as you were planning to do, and Hermogenes here will see you on your way.[65]

CRATYLUS: I'll do that, Socrates, but I hope that you will also continue to think about these matters yourself.

---

65. 'See on your way' (*propempsei*): as a good son of Hermes *pompaios* (who conducts souls of the dead to Hades) would do. Hermogenes is thus correctly named after all. See 384c, 408b.

THEAETETUS

Plato has much to say in other dialogues about knowledge, but this is his only sustained inquiry into the question 'What is knowledge?' As such, it is the founding document of what has come to be known as 'epistemology', as one of the branches of philosophy; its influence on Greek epistemology—in Aristotle and the Stoics particularly—is strongly marked. Theaetetus was a famous mathematician, Plato's associate for many years in the Academy; the dialogue's prologue seems to announce the work as published in his memory, shortly after his early death on military service in 369 B.C. We can therefore date the publication of Theaetetus fairly precisely, to the few years immediately following Theaetetus' death. Plato was then about sixty years of age, and another famous longtime associate, Aristotle, was just joining the Academy as a student (367).

Though it is not counted as a 'Socratic' dialogue—one depicting Socrates inquiring into moral questions by examining and refuting the opinions of his fellow discussants—Theaetetus depicts a Socrates who makes much of his own ignorance and his subordinate position as questioner, and the dialogue concludes inconclusively. Socrates now describes his role, however, as he does not in the 'Socratic' dialogues, as that of a 'midwife': he brings to expression ideas of clever young men like Theaetetus, extensively develops their presuppositions and consequences so as to see clearly what the ideas amount to, and then establishes them as sound or defective by independent arguments of his own. The first of Theaetetus' three successive definitions of knowledge—that knowledge is 'perception'—is not finally 'brought to birth' until Socrates has linked it to Protagoras' famous 'man is the measure' doctrine of relativistic truth, and also to the theory that 'all is motion and change' that Socrates finds most Greek thinkers of the past had accepted, and until he has fitted it out with an elaborate and ingenious theory of perception and how it works. He then examines separately the truth of these linked doctrines—introduced into the discussion by him, not Theaetetus—and, in finally rejecting Theaetetus' idea as unsound, he advances his own positive analysis of perception and its role in knowledge. This emphasis on the systematic exploration of ideas before finally committing oneself to them or rejecting them as unsound is found in a different guise in Parmenides, with its systematic exploration of hypotheses about unity as a means of working hard toward an acceptable theory of Forms. Socrates establishes a clear link between the two dialogues when, at 183e, he drags in a reference back to the conversation reported in Parmenides.

Theaetetus has a unique format among Plato's dialogues. The prologue gives a brief conversation between Euclides and Terpsion, Socratics from

*nearby Megara (they are among those present for the discussion on Socrates'
last day in* Phaedo). *For the remainder, a slave reads out a book composed by
Euclides containing a conversation of Socrates, Theodorus, and Theaetetus that
took place many years previously. Since ancient sources tell us of Socratic dialogues actually published by Euclides, it is as if, except for the prologue, Plato
is giving us under his own name one of* Euclides' *dialogues! The last line of
the work establishes it as the first of a series, with* Sophist *and* Statesman *to
follow—as noted above,* Parmenides *precedes. In* Theaetetus *Socrates tests
Theaetetus' mettle with the geometer Theodorus' aid and in the presence of his
namesake Socrates, another associate of Plato's in the Academy; in the other
two works, first Theaetetus, then young Socrates will be discussion partners
with an unnamed visitor from Elea, in Southern Italy, home to Parmenides
and Zeno—a very different type of partner. Socrates and his midwifery are su-
perseded.*

*Despite its lively and intellectually playful Socrates, reminiscent of the 'So-
cratic' dialogues,* Theaetetus *is a difficult work of abstract philosophical theory. The American logician and philosopher C. S. Peirce counted it, along with*
Parmenides, *as Plato's greatest work, and more recently it has attracted favorable attention from such major philosophers as Ludwig Wittgenstein and Gil-
bert Ryle.*

J.M.C.

142   EUCLIDES: Are you only just in from the country, Terpsion? Or have you
been here some time?

TERPSION: I've been here a good while. In fact, I have been looking for
you in the market-place and wondering that I couldn't find you.

EUCLIDES: Well, you couldn't, because I was not in the city.

TERPSION: Where have you been, then?

EUCLIDES: I went down to the harbor; and as I was going, I met Theaetetus,
being taken to Athens from the camp at Corinth.

TERPSION: Alive or dead?

b   EUCLIDES: Alive; but that's about all one could say. Badly wounded for
one thing; but the real trouble is this sickness that has broken out in
the army.

TERPSION: Dysentery?

EUCLIDES: Yes.

TERPSION: What a man to lose!

EUCLIDES: Yes. A fine man, Terpsion. Only just now I was listening to
some people singing his praises for the way he behaved in the battle.

TERPSION: Well, there's nothing extraordinary about that. Much more to
c   be wondered at if he hadn't distinguished himself. But why didn't he put
up here at Megara?

Translated by M. J. Levett, revised by Myles Burnyeat.

EUCLIDES: He was in a hurry to get home. I kept asking him myself, and advising him; but he wouldn't. So I saw him on his way. And as I was coming back, I thought of Socrates and what a remarkably good prophet he was—as usual—about Theaetetus. It was not long before his death, if I remember rightly, that he came across Theaetetus, who was a boy at the time. Socrates met him and had a talk with him, and was very much struck with his natural ability; and when I went to Athens, he repeated to me the discussion they had had, which was well worth listening to. And he said to me then that we should inevitably hear more of Theaetetus, if he lived to grow up.

TERPSION: Well, he appears to have been right enough.—But what was this discussion? Could you tell it to me?

EUCLIDES: Good Lord, no. Not from memory, anyway. But I made some notes of it at the time, as soon as I got home; then afterwards I recalled it at my leisure and wrote it out, and whenever I went to Athens, I used to ask Socrates about the points I couldn't remember, and correct my version when I got home. The result is that I have got pretty well the whole discussion in writing.

TERPSION: Yes, of course. I have heard you say that before, and I have always been meaning to ask you to show it to me, though I have been so long about it. But is there any reason why we shouldn't go through it now? I want a rest, in any case, after my journey in from the country.

EUCLIDES: Well, I shouldn't mind sitting down either. I saw Theaetetus as far as Erineum. Come along. We will get the slave to read it to us while we rest.

TERPSION: Right.

EUCLIDES: This is the book, Terpsion. You see, I have written it out like this: I have not made Socrates relate the conversation as he related it to me, but I represent him as speaking directly to the persons with whom he said he had this conversation. (These were, he told me, Theodorus the geometer and Theaetetus.) I wanted, in the written version, to avoid the bother of having the bits of narrative in between the speeches—I mean, when Socrates, whenever he mentions his own part in the discussion, says 'And I maintained' or 'I said,' or, of the person answering, 'He agreed' or 'He would not admit this.' That is why I have made him talk directly to them and have left out these formulae.

TERPSION: Well, that's quite in order, Euclides.

EUCLIDES: Now, boy, let us have it.

SOCRATES: If Cyrene were first in my affections, Theodorus, I should be asking you how things are there, and whether any of your young people are taking up geometry or any other branch of philosophy. But, as it is, I love Athens better than Cyrene, and so I'm more anxious to know which of our young men show signs of turning out well. That, of course, is what I am always trying to find out myself, as best I can; and I keep asking other people too—anyone round whom I see the young men are inclined to gather. Now you, of course, are very much sought after, and with good

e   reason; your geometry alone entitles you to it, and that is not your only
    claim. So if you have come across anyone worth mentioning, I should be
    glad to hear.

    THEODORUS: Well, Socrates, I think you ought to be told, and I think I
    ought to tell you, about a remarkable boy I have met here, one of your
    fellow countrymen. And if he were beautiful, I should be extremely nervous
    of speaking of him with enthusiasm, for fear I might be suspected of being
    in love with him. But as a matter of fact—if you'll excuse my saying such
    a thing—he is not beautiful at all, but is rather like you, snub-nosed, with
    eyes that stick out; though these features are not quite so pronounced in
144 him. I speak without any qualms; and I assure you that among all the
    people I have ever met—and I have got to know a good many in my
    time—I have never yet seen anyone so amazingly gifted. Along with a
    quickness beyond the capacity of most people, he has an unusually gentle
    temper; and, to crown it all, he is as manly a boy as any of his fellows. I
    never thought such a combination could exist; I don't see it arising else-
    where. People as acute and keen and retentive as he is are apt to be very
b   unbalanced. They get swept along with a rush, like ships without ballast;
    what stands for courage in their makeup is a kind of mad excitement;
    while, on the other hand, the steadier sort of people are apt to come to
    their studies with minds that are sluggish, somehow—freighted with a
    bad memory. But this boy approaches his studies in a smooth, sure, effective
    way, and with great good temper; it reminds one of the quiet flow of a
    stream of oil. The result is that it is astonishing to see how he gets through
    his work, at his age.

    SOCRATES: That is good news. And he is an Athenian—whose son is he?
c   THEODORUS: I have heard the name, but I don't remember it. But he is
    the middle one of this group coming toward us. He and his companions
    were greasing themselves outside just now; it looks as if they have finished
    and are coming in here. But look and see if you recognize him.

    SOCRATES: Yes, I know him. He's the son of Euphronius of Sunium—
    very much the kind of person, my friend, that you tell me his son is. A
    distinguished man in many ways; he left a considerable property too. But
    I don't know the boy's name.
d   THEODORUS: His name, Socrates, is Theaetetus. As for the property, that, I
    think, has been made away with by trustees. All the same, he is wonderfully
    open-handed about money, Socrates.

    SOCRATES: A thoroughbred, evidently. I wish you would ask him to come
    and sit with us over here.

    THEODORUS: All right. Theaetetus, come here beside Socrates.

    SOCRATES: Yes, come along, Theaetetus. I want to see for myself what
e   sort of a face I have. Theodorus says I am like you. But look. If you and
    I had each had a lyre, and Theodorus had told us that they were both
    similarly tuned, should we have taken his word for it straightaway? Or
    should we have tried to find out if he was speaking with any expert
    knowledge of music?

THEAETETUS: Oh, we should have inquired into that.

SOCRATES: And if we had found that he was a musician, we should have believed what he said; but if we found he had no such qualification, we should have put no faith in him.

THEAETETUS: Yes, that's true.

SOCRATES: And now, I suppose, if we are interested in this question of our faces being alike, we ought to consider whether he is speaking with any knowledge of drawing or not?

145

THEAETETUS: Yes, I should think so.

SOCRATES: Then is Theodorus an artist?

THEAETETUS: No, not so far as I know.

SOCRATES: Nor a geometer, either?

THEAETETUS: Oh, there's no doubt about his being that, Socrates.

SOCRATES: And isn't he also a master of astronomy and arithmetic and music—of all that an educated man should know?

THEAETETUS: Well, he seems to me to be.

SOCRATES: Then if he asserts that there is some physical resemblance between us—whether complimenting us or the reverse—one ought not to pay much attention to him?

THEAETETUS: No, perhaps not.

SOCRATES: But supposing it were the soul of one of us that he was praising? Suppose he said one of us was good and wise? Oughtn't the one who heard that to be very anxious to examine the object of such praise? And oughtn't the other to be very willing to show himself off?

b

THEAETETUS: Yes, certainly, Socrates.

SOCRATES: Then, my dear Theaetetus, now is the time for you to show yourself and for me to examine you. For although Theodorus often gives me flattering testimonials for people, both Athenians and foreigners, I assure you I have never before heard him praise anybody in the way he has just praised you.

c

THEAETETUS: That's all very well, Socrates; but take care he wasn't saying that for a joke.

SOCRATES: That is not Theodorus' way. Now don't you try to get out of what we have agreed upon with the pretence that our friend is joking, or you may make it necessary for him to give his evidence—since no charge of perjury is ever likely to be brought against him. So have the pluck to stand by your agreement.

THEAETETUS: All right, I must, then, if that's what you've decided.

SOCRATES: Tell me now. You are learning some geometry from Theodorus, I expect?

THEAETETUS: Yes, I am.

SOCRATES: And some astronomy and music and arithmetic?

d

THEAETETUS: Well, I'm very anxious to, anyway.

SOCRATES: And so am I, my son—from Theodorus or from anyone who seems to me to know about these things. But although I get on with them pretty well in most ways, I have a small difficulty, which I think ought to

be investigated, with your help and that of the rest of the company.—
Now isn't it true that to learn is to become wiser[1] about the thing one
is learning?

THEAETETUS: Yes, of course.

SOCRATES: And what makes men wise, I take it, is wisdom?

THEAETETUS: Yes.

e   SOCRATES: And is this in any way different from knowledge?

THEAETETUS: What?

SOCRATES: Wisdom. Isn't it the things which they know that men are
wise about?

THEAETETUS: Well, yes.

SOCRATES: So knowledge and wisdom will be the same thing?

THEAETETUS: Yes.

SOCRATES: Now this is just where my difficulty comes in. I can't get a
146   proper grasp of what on earth knowledge really is. Could we manage to
put it into words? What do all of you say? Who'll speak first? Anyone
who makes a mistake shall sit down and be Donkey, as the children say
when they are playing ball; and anyone who comes through without a
miss shall be King and make us answer any question he likes.—Well, why
this silence? Theodorus, I hope my love of argument is not making me
forget my manners—just because I'm so anxious to start a discussion and
get us all friendly and talkative together?

b   THEODORUS: No, no, Socrates—that's the last thing one could call forgetting your manners. But do make one of the young people answer you. I
am not used to this kind of discussion, and I'm too old to get into the way
of it. But it would be suitable enough for them and they would profit more
by it. For youth can always profit, that's true enough. So do go on; don't
let Theaetetus off but ask him some more questions.

SOCRATES: Well, Theaetetus, you hear what Theodorus says. You won't
c   want to disobey him, I'm sure; and certainly a wise man shouldn't be
disobeyed by his juniors in matters of this kind—it wouldn't be at all the
proper thing. Now give me a good frank answer. What do you think
knowledge is?

THEAETETUS: Well, I ought to answer, Socrates, as you and Theodorus
tell me to. In any case, you and he will put me right, if I make a mistake.

SOCRATES: We certainly will, if we can.

THEAETETUS: Then I think that the things Theodorus teaches are knowl-
d   edge—I mean geometry and the subjects you enumerated just now. Then
again there are the crafts such as cobbling, whether you take them together
or separately. They must be knowledge, surely.

SOCRATES: That is certainly a frank and indeed a generous answer, my
dear lad. I asked you for one thing and you have given me many; I wanted
something simple, and I have got a variety.

1. The words 'wise' and 'wisdom' in the argument which begins here represent the
Greek *sophos* and *sophia*. The point of the argument will come across more naturally in
English if readers substitute in their mind the words 'expert' and 'expertise'.

THEAETETUS: And what does that mean, Socrates?

SOCRATES: Nothing, I dare say. But I'll tell you what I think. When you talk about cobbling, you mean just knowledge of the making of shoes?

THEAETETUS: Yes, that's all I mean by it.

SOCRATES: And when you talk about carpentering, you mean simply the knowledge of the making of wooden furniture?

THEAETETUS: Yes, that's all I mean, again.

SOCRATES: And in both cases you are putting into your definition what the knowledge is of?

THEAETETUS: Yes.

SOCRATES: But that is not what you were asked, Theaetetus. You were not asked to say what one may have knowledge of, or how many branches of knowledge there are. It was not with any idea of counting these up that the question was asked; we wanted to know what knowledge itself is.— Or am I talking nonsense?

THEAETETUS: No, you are perfectly right.

SOCRATES: Now think about this too. Supposing we were asked about some commonplace, everyday thing; for example, what is clay? And supposing we were to answer, 'clay of the potters' and 'clay of the stovemakers' and 'clay of the brickmakers', wouldn't that be absurd of us?

THEAETETUS: Well, perhaps it would.

SOCRATES: Absurd to begin with, I suppose, to imagine that the person who asked the question would understand anything from our answer when we say 'clay', whether we add that it is dollmakers' clay or any other craftsman's. Or do you think that anyone can understand the name of a thing when he doesn't know what the thing is?

THEAETETUS: No, certainly not.

SOCRATES: And so a man who does not know what knowledge is will not understand 'knowledge of shoes' either?

THEAETETUS: No, he won't.

SOCRATES: Then a man who is ignorant of what knowledge is will not understand what cobbling is, or any other craft?

THEAETETUS: That is so.

SOCRATES: So when the question raised is 'What is knowledge?', to reply by naming one of the crafts is an absurd answer; because it points out something that knowledge is of when this is not what the question was about.

THEAETETUS: So it seems.

SOCRATES: Again, it goes no end of a long way round, in a case where, I take it, a short and commonplace answer is possible. In the question about clay, for example, it would presumably be possible to make the simple, commonplace statement that it is earth mixed with liquid, and let the question of whose clay it is take care of itself.

THEAETETUS: That seems easier, Socrates, now you put it like that. But I believe you're asking just the sort of question that occurred to your namesake Socrates here and myself, when we were having a discussion a little while ago.

SOCRATES: And what was that, Theaetetus?

THEAETETUS: Theodorus here was demonstrating to us with the aid of diagrams a point about powers.[2] He was showing us that the power of three square feet and the power of five square feet are not commensurable in length with the power of one square foot; and he went on in this way, taking each case in turn till he came to the power of seventeen square feet; there for some reason he stopped. So the idea occurred to us that, since the powers were turning out to be unlimited in number, we might try to collect the powers in

e   question under one term, which would apply to them all.

SOCRATES: And did you find the kind of thing you wanted?

THEAETETUS: I think we did. But I'd like you to see if it's all right.

SOCRATES: Go on, then.

THEAETETUS: We divided all numbers into two classes. Any number which can be produced by the multiplication of two equal numbers, we compared to a square in shape, and we called this a square or equilateral number.

SOCRATES: Good, so far.

148   THEAETETUS: Then we took the intermediate numbers, such as three and five and any number which can't be produced by multiplication of two equals but only by multiplying together a greater and a less; a number such that it is always contained by a greater and a less side. A number of this kind we compared to an oblong figure, and called it an oblong number.

SOCRATES: That's excellent. But how did you go on?

THEAETETUS: We defined under the term 'length' any line which produces in square an equilateral plane number; while any line which produces in square an oblong number we defined under the term 'power', for the

b   reason that although it is incommensurable with the former in length, it is commensurable in the plane figures which they respectively have the

---

2. 'Powers' is a mathematical term for squares. By contrast, at 148a–b 'power' is given a new, specially defined use to denominate a species of line, viz. the incommensurable lines for which the boys wanted a general account. It may be useful to give a brief explanation of the mathematics of the passage.

Two lines are incommensurable if and only if they have no common measure; that is, no unit of length will measure both without remainder. Two squares are incommensurable *in length* if and only if their sides are incommensurable lines; the areas themselves may still be commensurable, i.e., both measurable by some unit of area, as is mentioned at 148b. When Theodorus showed for a series of powers (squares) that each is incommensurable in length with the one foot (unit) square, we can think of him as proving case by case the irrationality of $\sqrt{3}, \sqrt{5}, \ldots \sqrt{17}$. But this was not how he thought of it himself. Greek mathematicians did not recognize irrational *numbers* but treated of irrational quantities as geometrical entities: in this instance, lines identified by the areas of the squares that can be constructed on them. Similarly, we can think of the boys' formula for powers or square lines at 148a–b as making the point that, for any positive integer n, $\sqrt{n}$ is irrational if and only if there is no positive integer m such that $n = m \times m$. But, once again, a Greek mathematician would think of this generalization in the geometrical terms in which Theaetetus expounds it.

power to produce. And there is another distinction of the same sort with regard to solids.

SOCRATES: Excellent, my boys. I don't think Theodorus is likely to be had up for false witness.

THEAETETUS: And yet, Socrates, I shouldn't be able to answer your question about knowledge in the same way that I answered the one about lengths and powers—though you seem to me to be looking for something of the same sort. So Theodorus turns out a false witness after all.

SOCRATES: Well, but suppose now it was your running he had praised; suppose he had said that he had never met anyone among the young people who was such a runner as you. And then suppose you were beaten by the champion runner in his prime—would you think Theodorus' praise had lost any of its truth?

THEAETETUS: No, I shouldn't.

SOCRATES: But do you think the discovery of what knowledge is is really what I was saying just now—a small thing? Don't you think that's a problem for the people at the top?

THEAETETUS: Yes, rather, I do; and the very topmost of them.

SOCRATES: Then do have confidence in yourself and try to believe that Theodorus knew what he was talking about. You must put your whole heart into what we are doing—in particular into this matter of getting a statement of what knowledge really is.

THEAETETUS: If putting one's heart into it is all that is required, Socrates, the answer will come to light.

SOCRATES: Go on, then. You gave us a good lead just now. Try to imitate your answer about the powers. There you brought together the many powers within a single form; now I want you in the same way to give one single account of the many branches of knowledge.

THEAETETUS: But I assure you, Socrates, I have often tried to think this out, when I have heard reports of the questions you ask. But I can never persuade myself that anything I say will really do; and I never hear anyone else state the matter in the way that you require. And yet, again, you know, I can't even stop worrying about it.

SOCRATES: Yes; those are the pains of labor, dear Theaetetus. It is because you are not barren but pregnant.

THEAETETUS: I don't know about that, Socrates. I'm only telling you what's happened to me.

SOCRATES: Then do you mean to say you've never heard about my being the son of a good hefty midwife, Phaenarete?[3]

THEAETETUS: Oh, yes, I've heard that before.

SOCRATES: And haven't you ever been told that I practice the same art myself?

THEAETETUS: No, I certainly haven't.

3. The name means 'She who brings virtue to light'.

SOCRATES: But I do, believe me. Only don't give me away to the rest of the world, will you? You see, my friend, it is a secret that I have this art. That is not one of the things you hear people saying about me, because they don't know; but they do say that I am a very odd sort of person, always causing people to get into difficulties. You must have heard that, surely?

b   THEAETETUS: Yes, I have.

SOCRATES: And shall I tell you what is the explanation of that?

THEAETETUS: Yes, please do.

SOCRATES: Well, if you will just think of the general facts about the business of midwifery, you will see more easily what I mean. You know, I suppose, that women never practice as midwives while they are still conceiving and bearing children themselves. It is only those who are past child-bearing who take this up.

THEAETETUS: Oh, yes.

SOCRATES: They say it was Artemis who was responsible for this custom;

c   it was because she, who undertook the patronage of childbirth, was herself childless. She didn't, it's true, entrust the duties of midwifery to barren women, because human nature is too weak to acquire skill where it has no experience. But she assigned the task to those who have become incapable of child-bearing through age—honoring their likeness to herself.

THEAETETUS: Yes, naturally.

SOCRATES: And this too is very natural, isn't it?—or perhaps necessary? I mean that it is the midwives who can tell better than anyone else whether women are pregnant or not.

THEAETETUS: Yes, of course.

d   SOCRATES: And then it is the midwives who have the power to bring on the pains, and also, if they think fit, to relieve them; they do it by the use of simple drugs, and by singing incantations. In difficult cases, too, they can bring about the birth; or, if they consider it advisable, they can promote a miscarriage.

THEAETETUS: Yes, that is so.

SOCRATES: There's another thing too. Have you noticed this about them, that they are the cleverest of match-makers, because they are marvellously knowing about the kind of couples whose marriage will produce the best children?

THEAETETUS: No, that is not at all familiar to me.

SOCRATES: But they are far prouder of this, believe me, than of cutting

e   the umbilical cord. Think now. There's an art which is concerned with the cultivation and harvesting of the crops. Now is it the same art which prescribes the best soil for planting or sowing a given crop? Or is it a different one?

THEAETETUS: No, it is all the same art.

SOCRATES: Then applying this to women, will there be one art of the sowing and another of the harvesting?

THEAETETUS: That doesn't seem likely, certainly.

SOCRATES: No, it doesn't. But there is also an unlawful and unscientific practice of bringing men and women together, which we call procuring; and because of that the midwives—a most august body of women—are very reluctant to undertake even lawful matchmaking. They are afraid that if they practice this, they may be suspected of the other. And yet, I suppose, reliable matchmaking is a matter for no one but the true midwife.

THEAETETUS: Apparently.

SOCRATES: So the work of the midwives is a highly important one; but it is not so important as my own performance. And for this reason, that there is not in midwifery the further complication, that the patients are sometimes delivered of phantoms and sometimes of realities, and that the two are hard to distinguish. If there were, then the midwife's greatest and noblest function would be to distinguish the true from the false offspring—don't you agree?

THEAETETUS: Yes, I do.

SOCRATES: Now my art of midwifery is just like theirs in most respects. The difference is that I attend men and not women, and that I watch over the labor of their souls, not of their bodies. And the most important thing about my art is the ability to apply all possible tests to the offspring, to determine whether the young mind is being delivered of a phantom, that is, an error, or a fertile truth. For one thing which I have in common with the ordinary midwives is that I myself am barren of wisdom. The common reproach against me is that I am always asking questions of other people but never express my own views about anything, because there is no wisdom in me; and that is true enough. And the reason of it is this, that God compels me to attend the travail of others, but has forbidden me to procreate. So that I am not in any sense a wise man; I cannot claim as the child of my own soul any discovery worth the name of wisdom. But with those who associate with me it is different. At first some of them may give the impression of being ignorant and stupid; but as time goes on and our association continues, all whom God permits are seen to make progress—a progress which is amazing both to other people and to themselves. And yet it is clear that this is not due to anything they have learned from me; it is that they discover within themselves a multitude of beautiful things, which they bring forth into the light. But it is I, with God's help, who deliver them of this offspring. And a proof of this may be seen in the many cases where people who did not realize this fact took all the credit to themselves and thought that I was no good. They have then proceeded to leave me sooner than they should, either of their own accord or through the influence of others. And after they have gone away from me they have resorted to harmful company, with the result that what remained within them has miscarried; while they have neglected the children I helped them to bring forth, and lost them, because they set more value upon lies and phantoms than upon the truth; finally they have been set down for ignorant fools, both by themselves and by everybody else. One of these people was

Aristides the son of Lysimachus;[4] and there have been very many others. Sometimes they come back, wanting my company again, and ready to move heaven and earth to get it. When that happens, in some cases the divine sign that visits me forbids me to associate with them; in others, it permits me, and then they begin again to make progress.

There is another point also in which those who associate with me are like women in child-birth. They suffer the pains of labor, and are filled day and night with distress; indeed they suffer far more than women. And this pain my art is able to bring on, and also to allay.

b   Well, that's what happens to them; but at times, Theaetetus, I come across people who do not seem to me somehow to be pregnant. Then I realize that they have no need of me, and with the best will in the world I undertake the business of match-making; and I think I am good enough— God willing—at guessing with whom they might profitably keep company. Many of them I have given away to Prodicus;[5] and a great number also to other wise and inspired persons.

Well, my dear lad, this has been a long yarn; but the reason was that I have a suspicion that you (as you think yourself) are pregnant and in

c   labor. So I want you to come to me as to one who is both the son of a midwife and himself skilled in the art; and try to answer the questions I shall ask you as well as you can. And when I examine what you say, I may perhaps think it is a phantom and not truth, and proceed to take it quietly from you and abandon it. Now if this happens, you mustn't get savage with me, like a mother over her first-born child. Do you know, people have often before now got into such a state with me as to be literally ready to bite when I take away some nonsense or other from them. They never believe that I am doing this in all goodwill; they are so far from

d   realizing that no God can wish evil to man, and that even I don't do this kind of thing out of malice, but because it is not permitted to me to accept a lie and put away truth.

So begin again, Theaetetus, and try to say what knowledge is. And don't on any account tell me that you can't. For if God is willing, and you play the man, you can.

THEAETETUS: Well, Socrates, after such encouragement from *you*, it would

e   hardly be decent for anyone not to try his hardest to say what he has in him. Very well then. It seems to me that a man who knows something perceives what he knows, and the way it appears at present, at any rate, is that knowledge is simply perception.

SOCRATES: There's a good frank answer, my son. That's the way to speak one's mind. But come now, let us look at this thing together, and see whether what we have here is really fertile or a mere wind-egg. You hold that knowledge is perception?

4. Aristides is one of the two young men whose education Socrates discusses in *Laches* (see 178a–179b).

5. A famous Sophist. See *Protagoras* 315d, 337a–c, 340e–341c, 358a–b.

THEAETETUS: Yes.

SOCRATES: But look here, this is no ordinary account of knowledge you've come out with: it's what Protagoras used to maintain. He said the very 152 same thing, only he put it in rather a different way. For he says, you know, that 'Man is the measure of all things: of the things which are, that they are, and of the things which are not, that they are not.' You have read this, of course?

THEAETETUS: Yes, often.

SOCRATES: Then you know that he puts it something like this, that as each thing appears to me, so it is for me, and as it appears to you, so it is for you—you and I each being a man?

THEAETETUS: Yes, that is what he says.

SOCRATES: Well, it is not likely that a wise man would talk nonsense. So b let us follow him up. Now doesn't it sometimes happen that when the same wind is blowing, one of us feels cold and the other not? Or that one of us feels rather cold and the other very cold?

THEAETETUS: That certainly does happen.

SOCRATES: Well then, in that case are we going to say that the wind itself, by itself, is cold or not cold? Or shall we listen to Protagoras, and say it is cold for the one who feels cold, and for the other, not cold?

THEAETETUS: It looks as if we must say that.

SOCRATES: And this is how it appears to each of us?

THEAETETUS: Yes.

SOCRATES: But this expression 'it appears' means 'he perceives it'?

THEAETETUS: Yes, it does.

SOCRATES: The appearing of things, then, is the same as perception, in c the case of hot and things like that. So it results, apparently, that things are for the individual such as he perceives them.

THEAETETUS: Yes, that seems all right.

SOCRATES: Perception, then, is always of what is, and unerring—as befits knowledge.

THEAETETUS: So it appears.

SOCRATES: But, I say, look here. Was Protagoras one of those omniscient people? Did he perhaps put this out as a riddle for the common crowd of us, while he revealed the *Truth*[6] as a secret doctrine to his own pupils?

THEAETETUS: What do you mean by that, Socrates? d

SOCRATES: I'll tell you; and this, now, is certainly no ordinary theory— I mean the theory that there is nothing which in itself is just one thing: nothing which you could rightly call anything or any kind of thing. If you call a thing large, it will reveal itself as small, and if you call it heavy, it is liable to appear as light, and so on with everything, because nothing is one or anything or any kind of thing. What is really true, is this: the things of which we naturally say that they 'are', are in process of coming to be, e

6. Protagoras of Abdera was a fifth century B.C. philosopher and sophist; this appears to have been the title of his book.

as the result of movement and change and blending with one another. We are wrong when we say they 'are', since nothing ever is, but everything is coming to be.

And as regards this point of view, let us take it as a fact that all the wise men of the past, with the exception of Parmenides, stand together. Let us take it that we find on this side Protagoras and Heraclitus and Empedocles; and also the masters of the two kinds of poetry, Epicharmus in comedy and Homer in tragedy.[7] For when Homer talked about 'Ocean, begetter of gods, and Tethys their mother', he made all things the offspring of flux and motion.[8]—Or don't you think he meant that?

THEAETETUS: Oh, I think he did.

153   SOCRATES: And if anyone proceeded to dispute the field with an army like that—an army led by Homer—he could hardly help making a fool of himself, could he?

THEAETETUS: It would not be an easy matter, Socrates.

SOCRATES: It would not, Theaetetus. You see, there is good enough evidence for this theory that being (what passes for such) and becoming are a product of motion, while not-being and passing-away result from a state of rest. There is evidence for it in the fact that heat or fire, which presumably generates and controls everything else, is itself generated out of movement and friction—these being motions.—Or am I wrong in saying these are the original sources of fire?

b   THEAETETUS: Oh no, they certainly are.

SOCRATES: Moreover, the growth of living creatures depends upon these same sources?

THEAETETUS: Yes, certainly.

SOCRATES: And isn't it also true that bodily condition deteriorates with rest and idleness? While by exertion and motion it can be preserved for a long time?

THEAETETUS: Yes.

SOCRATES: And what about the condition of the soul? Isn't it by learning and study, which are motions, that the soul gains knowledge and is pre-
c   served[9] and becomes a better thing? Whereas in a state of rest, that is, when it will not study or learn, it not only fails to acquire knowledge but forgets what it has already learned?

7. Heraclitus was famous for holding that 'everything flows' (cf. 179d ff.). Empedocles described a cosmic cycle in which things are constituted and dissolved by the coming together and separating of the four elements earth, air, fire, and water. Epicharmus made humorous use of the idea that everything is always changing by having a debtor claim he is not the same person as incurred the debt. Parmenides remains outside the chorus of agreement because he held that the only reality is one single, completely changeless thing (cf. 183e).

8. *Iliad* xiv.201, 302.

9. The Greek could equally be translated 'that the soul gains and preserves knowledge'; the reader may perhaps be expected to hear the clause both ways.

THEAETETUS: That certainly is so.

SOCRATES: And so we may say that the one thing, that is, motion, is beneficial to both body and soul, while the other has the opposite effect?

THEAETETUS: Yes, that's what it looks like.

SOCRATES: Yes, and I might go on to point out to you the effect of such conditions as still weather on land and calms on the sea. I might show you how these conditions rot and destroy things, while the opposite conditions make for preservation. And finally, to put the crown on my argument, I might bring in Homer's golden cord,[10] and maintain that he means by this simply the sun; and is here explaining that so long as the revolution continues and the sun is in motion, all things are and are preserved, both in heaven and in earth, but that if all this should be 'bound fast', as it were, and come to a standstill, all things would be destroyed and, as the saying goes, the world would be turned upside down. Do you agree with this?

THEAETETUS: Yes, Socrates, I think that is the meaning of the passage.

SOCRATES: Then, my friend, you must understand our theory in this way. In the sphere of vision, to begin with, what you would naturally call a white color is not itself a distinct entity, either outside your eyes or in your eyes. You must not assign it any particular place; for then, of course it would be standing at its post; it wouldn't be in process of becoming.

THEAETETUS: But what do you mean?

SOCRATES: Let us follow what we stated a moment ago, and posit that there is nothing which is, in itself, one thing. According to this theory, black or white or any other color will turn out to have come into being through the impact of the eye upon the appropriate motion; and what we naturally call a particular color is neither that which impinges nor that which is impinged upon, but something which has come into being between the two, and which is private to the individual percipient.—Or would you be prepared to insist that every color appears to a dog, or to any other animal, the same as it appears to you?

THEAETETUS: No, I most certainly shouldn't.

SOCRATES: Well, and do you even feel sure that anything appears to another human being like it appears to you? Wouldn't you be much more disposed to hold that it doesn't appear the same even to yourself because you never remain like yourself?

THEAETETUS: Yes, that seems to me nearer the truth than the other.

SOCRATES: Well now, supposing such things as size or warmth or whiteness really belonged to the object we measure ourselves against or touch, it would never be found that this object had become different simply by coming into contact with another thing and without any change in itself. On the other hand, if you suppose them to belong to what is measuring

10. *Iliad* viii.17–27. Zeus boasts that if he pulled on a golden cord let down from heaven, he could haul up earth, sea and all, bind the cord fast round the peak of Mt. Olympus, and leave the lot dangling in mid-air.

or touching, this again could never become different simply because something else had come into its neighborhood, or because something had
happened to the first thing—nothing having happened to itself. As it is,
you see, we may easily find ourselves forced into saying the most astonishing and ridiculous things, as Protagoras would point out or anyone who
undertook to expound the same views.

THEAETETUS: What do you mean? What sort of ridiculous things?

c   SOCRATES: Let me give you a simple example of what I mean, and you
will see the rest for yourself. Here are six dice. Put four beside them, and
they are more, we say, than the four, that is, half as many again; but put
twelve beside them, and we say they are less, that is, half the number.
And there is no getting out of that—or do you think there is?

THEAETETUS: No, I don't.

SOCRATES: Well now, supposing Protagoras or anyone else were to ask
you this question: 'Is it possible, Theaetetus, for any thing to become bigger
d   or more in number in any other way than by being increased?' What is
your answer to that?

THEAETETUS: Well, Socrates, if I answer what seems true in relation to
the present question, I shall say 'No, it is not possible'; but if I consider
it in relation to the question that went before, then in order to avoid
contradicting myself, I say 'Yes, it is.'

SOCRATES: That's a good answer, my friend, by Jove it is; you are inspired.
But, I think, if you answer 'Yes', it will be like that episode in Euripides—
the tongue will be safe from refutation but the mind will not.[11]

THEAETETUS: That's true.

SOCRATES: Now if you and I were professional savants, who had already
analyzed all the contents of our minds, we should now spend our super-
e   fluous time trying each other out; we should start a regular Sophists' set-
to, with a great clashing of argument on argument. But, as it is, we are
only plain men; and so our first aim will be to look at our thoughts
themselves in relation to themselves, and see what they are—whether, in
our opinion, they agree with one another or are entirely at variance.

THEAETETUS: That would certainly be my aim, anyway.

SOCRATES: And mine. That being so, as we are not in any way pressed
155   for time, don't you think the thing to do is to reconsider this matter quietly
and patiently, in all seriousness 'analyzing' ourselves, and asking what
are these apparitions within us?—And when we come to review them, I
suppose we may begin with the statement that nothing can possibly have
become either greater or less, in bulk or in number, so long as it is equal
to itself. Isn't that so?

THEAETETUS: Yes.

SOCRATES: Secondly, we should say that a thing to which nothing is added
and from which nothing is taken away neither increases nor diminishes but
remains equal.

11. Cf. *Hippolytus* 612.

THEAETETUS: Yes, certainly.

SOCRATES: Thirdly, that it is impossible that a thing should ever be   b
what it was not before without having become and without any process
of becoming?

THEAETETUS: Yes, I think so.

SOCRATES: Now it seems to me that these three statements that we have
admitted are fighting one another in our souls when we speak of the
example of the dice; or when we say that, within the space of a year, I (a
full-grown man) without having been either increased or diminished, am
now bigger than you (who are only a boy) and, later on, smaller—though
I have lost nothing and it is only that you have grown. For this means   c
that I am, at a later stage, what I was not before, and that, too, without
having become—for without becoming it is not possible to have become,
and without suffering any loss in size I could never become less. And
there are innumerable other examples of the same thing if once we admit
these. You follow me, I take it, Theaetetus—I think you must be familiar
with this kind of puzzle.

THEAETETUS: Oh yes, indeed, Socrates, I often wonder like mad what
these things can mean; sometimes when I'm looking at them I begin to
feel quite giddy.

SOCRATES: I dare say you do, my dear boy. It seems that Theodorus was   d
not far from the truth when he guessed what kind of person you are. For
this is an experience which is characteristic of a philosopher, this wondering: this is where philosophy begins and nowhere else. And the man who
made Iris the child of Thaumas was perhaps no bad genealogist.[12]—But
aren't you beginning to see now what is the explanation of these puzzles,
according to the theory which we are attributing to Protagoras?

THEAETETUS: I don't think I am, yet.

SOCRATES: Then I dare say you will be grateful to me if I help you to   e
discover the veiled truth in the thought of a great man—or perhaps I
should say, of great men?

THEAETETUS: Of course I shall be, Socrates, very grateful.

SOCRATES: Then you have a look round, and see that none of the uninitiated are listening to us—I mean the people who think that nothing exists
but what they can grasp with both hands; people who refuse to admit
that actions and processes and the invisible world in general have any
place in reality.

THEAETETUS: They must be tough, hard fellows, Socrates.   156

SOCRATES: They are, my son—very crude people. But these others, whose
mysteries I am going to tell you, are a much more subtle type. These
mysteries begin from the principle on which all that we have just been
saying also depends, namely, that everything is really motion, and there
is nothing but motion. Motion has two forms, each an infinite multitude,

---

12. *Theogony* 265. 'Thaumas' means wonder, while Iris, the messenger of the gods, is
the rainbow which passes between earth and heaven.

but distinguished by their powers, the one being active and the other passive. And through the intercourse and mutual friction of these two
b there comes to be an offspring infinite in multitude but always twin births, on the one hand what is perceived, on the other, the perception of it, the perception in every case being generated together with what is perceived and emerging along with it. For the perceptions we have such names as sight, hearing, smelling, feeling cold and feeling hot; also what are called pleasures and pains, desires and fears; and there are others besides, a great number which have names, an infinite number which have not. And on the other side there is the race of things perceived, for each of these
c perceptions perceived things born of the same parentage, for all kinds of visions all kinds of colors, for all kinds of hearings all kinds of sounds; and so on, for the other perceptions the other things perceived, that come to be in kinship with them.

Now what does this tale really mean, from our point of view, Theaetetus? How does it bear on what we were saying before? Do you see?

THEAETETUS: Not really, Socrates.

SOCRATES: Look here, then, let us see if we can somehow round it off. What it is trying to express, presumably, is this. All these things are in motion, just as we say; and their motion is distinguished by its swiftness or slowness. What is slow has its motion in one and the same place, and
d in relation to the things in the immediate neighborhood; in this way it generates and the offspring are swifter, as they move through space, and their motion takes the form of spatial movement.

Thus the eye and some other thing—one of the things commensurate with the eye—which has come into its neighborhood, generate both whiteness and the perception which is by nature united with it (things which would never have come to be if it had been anything else that eye or object
e approached). In this event, motions arise in the intervening space, sight from the side of the eye and whiteness from the side of that which cooperates in the production of the color. The eye is filled with sight; at that moment it sees, and becomes not indeed sight, but a seeing eye; while its partner in the process of producing color is filled with whiteness, and becomes not whiteness but white, a white stick or stone or whatever it is that happens to be colored this sort of color.

157   We must understand this account as applying in the same way to hard and hot and everything else: nothing, as we were saying before, *is* in itself any of these. All of them, of all kinds whatsoever, are what things become through association with one another, as the result of motion. For even in the case of the active and passive motions it is impossible, as they say, for thought, taking them singly, to pin them down to being anything. There is no passive till it meets the active, no active except in conjunction with the passive; and what, in conjunction with one thing, is active, reveals itself as passive when it falls in with something else.

And so, wherever you turn, there is nothing, as we said at the outset,
b which in itself is just one thing; all things become relatively to something.

The verb 'to be' must be totally abolished—though indeed we have been led by habit and ignorance into using it ourselves more than once, even in what we have just been saying. That is wrong, these wise men tell us, nor should we allow the use of such words as 'something', 'of something', or 'mine', 'this' or 'that', or any other name that makes things stand still. We ought, rather, to speak according to nature and refer to things as 'becoming', 'being produced', 'passing away', 'changing'; for if you speak in such a way as to make things stand still, you will easily be refuted. And this applies in speaking both of the individual case and of many aggregated together—such an aggregate, I mean, as people call 'man' or 'stone', or to which they give the names of the different animals and sorts of thing.

—Well, Theaetetus, does this look to you a tempting meal and could you take a bite of the delicious stuff?

THEAETETUS: I really don't know, Socrates. I can't even quite see what you're getting at—whether the things you are saying are what you think yourself, or whether you are just trying me out.

SOCRATES: You are forgetting, my friend. I don't know anything about this kind of thing myself, and I don't claim any of it as my own. I am barren of theories; my business is to attend you in your labor. So I chant incantations over you and offer you little tidbits from each of the wise till I succeed in assisting you to bring your own belief forth into the light. When it has been born, I shall consider whether it is fertile or a wind-egg. But you must have courage and patience; answer like a man whatever appears to you about the things I ask you.

THEAETETUS: All right, go on with the questions.

SOCRATES: Tell me again, then, whether you like the suggestion that good and beautiful and all the things we were just speaking of cannot be said to 'be' anything, but are always 'coming to be'.[13]

THEAETETUS: Well, as far as I'm concerned, while I'm listening to your exposition of it, it seems to me an extraordinarily reasonable view; and I feel that the way you have set out the matter has got to be accepted.

SOCRATES: In that case, we had better not pass over any point where our theory is still incomplete. What we have not yet discussed is the question of dreams, and of insanity and other diseases; also what is called mishearing or misseeing or other cases of misperceiving. You realize, I suppose, that it would be generally agreed that all these cases appear to provide a refutation of the theory we have just expounded. For in these conditions, we surely have false perceptions. Here it is far from being true that all things which appear to the individual also are. On the contrary, no one of the things which appear to him really is.

THEAETETUS: That is perfectly true, Socrates.

---

13. An alternative translation would be: 'the suggestion that nothing is, but rather becomes, good, beautiful or any of the things we were speaking of just now'.

SOCRATES: Well then, my lad, what argument is left for the person who maintains that knowledge is perception and that what appears to any individual also is, for him to whom it appears to be?

THEAETETUS: Well, Socrates, I hardly like to tell you that I don't know
b what to say, seeing I've just got into trouble with you for that. But I really shouldn't know how to dispute the suggestion that a madman believes what is false when he thinks he is a god; or a dreamer when he imagines he has wings and is flying in his sleep.

SOCRATES: But there's a point here which *is* a matter of dispute, especially as regards dreams and real life—don't you see?

THEAETETUS: What do you mean?

SOCRATES: There's a question you must often have heard people ask— the question what evidence we could offer if we were asked whether in
c the present instance, at this moment, we are asleep and dreaming all our thoughts, or awake and talking to each other in real life.

THEAETETUS: Yes, Socrates, it certainly is difficult to find the proof we want here. The two states seem to correspond in all their characteristics. There is nothing to prevent us from thinking when we are asleep that we are having the very same discussion that we have just had. And when we dream that we are telling the story of a dream, there is an extraordinary likeness between the two experiences.

SOCRATES: You see, then, it is not difficult to find matter for dispute,
d when it is disputed even whether this is real life or a dream. Indeed we may say that, as our periods of sleeping and waking are of equal length, and as in each period the soul contends that the beliefs of the moment are preeminently true, the result is that for half our lives we assert the reality of the one set of objects, and for half that of the other set. And we make our assertions with equal conviction in both cases.

THEAETETUS: That certainly is so.

SOCRATES: And doesn't the same argument apply in the cases of disease and madness, except that the periods of time are not equal?

THEAETETUS: Yes, that is so.

SOCRATES: Well now, are we going to fix the limits of truth by the clock?
e THEAETETUS: That would be a very funny thing to do.

SOCRATES: But can you produce some other clear indication to show which of these beliefs are true?

THEAETETUS: I don't think I can.

SOCRATES: Then you listen to me and I'll tell you the kind of thing that might be said by those people who propose it as a rule that whatever a man thinks at any time is the truth for him. I can imagine them putting their position by asking you this question: 'Now, Theaetetus, suppose you have something which is an entirely different thing from something else. Can it have in any respect the same powers as the other thing?' And observe, we are not to understand the question to refer to something which is the same in some respects while it is different in others, but to that which is wholly different.

THEAETETUS: In that case, then, it is impossible that it should have any- 159
thing the same, either as regards its powers or in any other respect, if it
is a completely different thing.

SOCRATES: And aren't we obliged to admit that such a thing is also unlike
the other?

THEAETETUS: Yes, I think so.

SOCRATES: Now supposing a thing is coming to be like or unlike to
something, whether to itself or to something else; are we to say that when
it is growing like it is coming to be the same, and when it is growing
unlike it is coming to be a different thing?

THEAETETUS: Yes, that must be so.

SOCRATES: Now weren't we saying, at an earlier stage, that there is a
number—indeed an infinite number—of both active and passive factors?

THEAETETUS: Yes.

SOCRATES: Also this, that when a thing mixes now with one thing and
now with another, it will not generate the same things each time but
different things?

THEAETETUS: Yes, certainly.   b

SOCRATES: Well, now let us apply this same statement to you and me
and things in general. Take, for example, Socrates ill and Socrates well.
Shall we say Socrates in health is like or unlike Socrates in sickness?

THEAETETUS: You mean the ill Socrates as a whole compared with the
well Socrates as a whole?

SOCRATES: You get my point excellently; that is just what I mean.

THEAETETUS: Unlike, then, I suppose.

SOCRATES: And different also, in so far as he is unlike?

THEAETETUS: Yes, that follows.

SOCRATES: Similarly, you would say, when he is asleep or in any of the   c
conditions we enumerated just now?

THEAETETUS: Yes, I should.

SOCRATES: Then it must surely be true that, when any one of the naturally
active factors finds Socrates well, it will be dealing with one me, and when
it finds Socrates ill, with a different me?

THEAETETUS: Yes, surely.

SOCRATES: Then in these two events the combination of myself as passive
and it as the active factor will generate different things?

THEAETETUS: Of course.

SOCRATES: Now if I drink wine when I am well, it appears to me pleasant
and sweet?

THEAETETUS: Yes.   d

SOCRATES: Going by what we earlier agreed, that is so because the active
and passive factors, moving simultaneously, generate both sweetness and a
perception; on the passive side, the perception makes the tongue percipient,
while on the side of the wine, sweetness moving about it makes it both
be and appear sweet to the healthy tongue.

THEAETETUS: That's certainly the sense of what we agreed to before.

SOCRATES: But when the active factor finds Socrates ill, then, to begin with, it is not in strict truth the same man that it gets hold of, is it? Because here, as we saw, it has come upon an unlike.

THEAETETUS: Yes.

e SOCRATES: Then this pair, Socrates ill and the draft of wine, generates, presumably, different things again: a perception of bitterness in the region of the tongue, and bitterness coming to be and moving in the region of the wine. And then the wine becomes, not bitterness, but bitter; and I become, not perception, but percipient.

THEAETETUS: Yes, quite.

SOCRATES: And I shall never again become *thus* percipient of anything
160 else. A perception of something else is another perception, and makes another and a changed percipient. Nor again, in the case of that which acts on me, will it ever, in conjunction with something else, generate the same thing and itself become such as it now is. From something else it will generate something else, and itself become a changed thing.

THEAETETUS: That is so.

SOCRATES: Nor will I become such for myself or it such for itself.

THEAETETUS: No.

SOCRATES: But I must necessarily become percipient of something when
b I become percipient; it is impossible to become percipient, yet percipient of nothing. And it again, when it becomes sweet or bitter or anything of that kind, must become so for somebody, because it is impossible to become sweet and yet sweet for no one.

THEAETETUS: Quite impossible.

SOCRATES: It remains, then, that I and it, whether we are or whether we become, are or become for each other. For our being is, by Necessity's decree, tied to a partner; yet we are tied neither to any other thing in the world nor to our respective selves. It remains, then, that we are tied to each other. Hence, whether you apply the term 'being' to a thing or the term 'becoming', you must always use the words 'for somebody' or 'of something' or 'relatively to something'. You must not speak of anything
c as in itself either being or becoming nor let anyone else use such expressions. That is the meaning of the theory we have been expounding.

THEAETETUS: Yes, that's certainly true, Socrates.

SOCRATES: Then since that which acts on me is for me, and not for anyone else, it is I who perceive it too, and nobody else?

THEAETETUS: Undoubtedly.

SOCRATES: Then my perception is true for me—because it is always a perception of that being which is peculiarly mine; and I am judge, as Protagoras said, of things that are, that they are, for me; and of things that are not, that they are not.

THEAETETUS: So it seems.

d SOCRATES: How then, if I am thus unerring and never stumble in my thought about what is—or what is coming to be—how can I fail to be a knower of the things of which I am a perceiver?

THEAETETUS: There is no way you could fail.

SOCRATES: Then that was a grand idea of yours when you told us that knowledge is nothing more or less than perception. So we find the various theories have converged to the same thing: that of Homer and Heraclitus and all their tribe, that all things flow like streams; of Protagoras, wisest of men, that man is the measure of all things; and of Theaetetus that, these things being so, knowledge proves to be perception. What about it, Theaetetus? Shall we say we have here your first-born child, the result of my midwifery? Or what would you say?

THEAETETUS: Oh, there's no denying it, Socrates.

SOCRATES: This, then, it appears, is what our efforts have at last brought forth—whatever it really is. And now that it has been born, we must perform the rite of running round the hearth with it; we must make it in good earnest go the round of discussion. For we must take care that we don't overlook some defect in this thing that is entering into life; it may be something not worth bringing up, a wind-egg, a falsehood. What do you say? Is it your opinion that your child ought in any case to be brought up and not exposed to die? Can you bear to see it found fault with, and not get into a rage if your first-born is stolen away from you?

THEODORUS: Theaetetus will put up with it, Socrates. He is not at all one to lose his temper. But tell me, in Heaven's name, in what way is it not as it should be?

SOCRATES: You are the complete lover of discussion, Theodorus, and it is too good of you to think that I am a sort of bag of arguments, and can easily pick one out which will show you that this theory is wrong. But you don't realize what is happening. The arguments never come from me; they always come from the person I am talking to. All that I know, such as it is, is how to take an argument from someone else—someone who *is* wise—and give it a fair reception. So, now, I propose to try to get our answer out of Theaetetus, not to make any contribution of my own.

THEODORUS: That's a better way of putting it, Socrates; do as you say.

SOCRATES: Well then, Theodorus, do you know what astonishes me about your friend Protagoras?

THEODORUS: No—what is it?

SOCRATES: Well, I was delighted with his general statement of the theory that a thing is for any individual what it seems to him to be; but I was astonished at the way he began. I was astonished that he did not state at the beginning of the *Truth* that 'Pig is the measure of all things' or 'Baboon' or some yet more out-of-the-way creature with the power of perception. That would have made a most imposing and disdainful opening. It would have made it clear to us at once that, while we were standing astounded at his wisdom as though he were a god, he was in reality no better authority than a tadpole—let alone any other man.

Or what are we to say, Theodorus? If whatever the individual judges by means of perception is true for him; if no man can assess another's experience better than he, or can claim authority to examine another man's judgment and see if it be right or wrong; if, as we have repeatedly said,

only the individual himself can judge of his own world, and what he judges is always true and correct: how could it ever be, my friend, that
e   Protagoras was a wise man, so wise as to think himself fit to be the teacher of other men and worth large fees; while we, in comparison with him the ignorant ones, needed to go and sit at his feet—we who are ourselves each the measure of his own wisdom? Can we avoid the conclusion that Protagoras was just playing to the crowd when he said this? I say nothing about my own case and my art of midwifery and how silly we look. So too, I think, does the whole business of philosophical discussion. To examine and try to refute each other's appearances and judgments, when each
162 person's are correct—this is surely an extremely tiresome piece of nonsense, if the *Truth* of Protagoras is true, and not merely an oracle speaking in jest from the impenetrable sanctuary of the book.

THEODORUS: Protagoras was my friend, Socrates, as you have just remarked. I could not consent to have him refuted through my admissions; and yet I should not be prepared to resist you against my own judgment. So take on Theaetetus again. He seemed to be following you very sympathetically just now.

b   SOCRATES: Now, Theodorus, supposing you went to Sparta and were visiting the wrestling-schools. Would you think it right to sit and watch other men exercising naked—some of them not much to look at—and refuse to strip yourself alongside of them, and take your turn of letting people see what you look like?

THEODORUS: Why not, if I could persuade them to leave the choice to me? Similarly I am hoping to persuade you to allow me to be a spectator and not drag me into the arena now that I am grown stiff; but to take on someone who is younger and more supple.

SOCRATES: Well, Theodorus, what you like I'll not dislike, as the saying
c   goes. So we must again resort to our wise Theaetetus. Come, Theaetetus. Think, to begin with, of what we have just been saying, and tell me if you are not yourself astonished at suddenly finding that you are the equal in wisdom of any man or even a god?—Or do you think the Protagorean measure isn't meant to be applied to gods as much as to men?

THEAETETUS: I most certainly don't. And, to answer your question, yes,
d   I am very much astonished. When we were working out the meaning of the principle that a thing is for each man what it seems to him to be, it appeared to me a very sound one. But now, all in a minute, it is quite the other way round.

SOCRATES: Yes, because you are young, dear lad; and so you lend a ready ear to mob-oratory and let it convince you. For Protagoras, or anyone speaking on his behalf, will answer us like this: 'My good people, young
e   and old,' he will say, 'you sit here orating; you drag in gods, whose existence or nonexistence I exclude from all discussion, written or spoken;[14]

---

14. A reference to a notorious declaration by Protagoras (Diog. Laert. 9.51): 'Concerning gods I am unable to know whether they exist or do not exist, or what they are like in

you keep on saying whatever is likely to be acceptable to the mob, telling them that it would be a shocking thing if no man were wiser than any cow in a field; but of proof or necessity not a word. You just rely on plausibility; though if Theodorus or any other geometer were to do that in his branch of science, it's a good-for-nothing geometer he would be'. So you and Theodorus had better consider whether, in matters of such importance, you are going to accept arguments which are merely persua- 163 sive or plausible.

THEAETETUS: You wouldn't say we had any business to do that, Socrates; and neither should we.

SOCRATES: Then, it seems, you and Theodorus say our criticism should take a different line?

THEAETETUS: Yes, it certainly should.

SOCRATES: Here, then, is another way in which we might consider whether knowledge and perception are the same or different things—for that is the question which our argument has held in view throughout, isn't it? And it was for its sake that we have unearthed all this extraordinary stuff?

THEAETETUS: Undoubtedly.

SOCRATES: Well, now, are we going to agree that when we perceive things b by seeing or hearing them, we always at the same time *know* them? Take, for example, the case of hearing people speaking a foreign language which we have not yet learned. Are we going to say that we do not hear the sound of their voices when they speak? Or that we both hear it and know what they are saying? Again, supposing we do not know our letters, are we going to insist that we do not see them when we look at them? Or shall we maintain that, if we see them, we know them?

THEAETETUS: We shall say, Socrates, that we know just that in them which we see and hear. We both see and know the shape and the color of the letters; and with the spoken words we both hear and know the rise and c fall of the voice. But what schoolmasters and interpreters tell us about them, we don't perceive by seeing or hearing, and we don't know, either.

SOCRATES: Very good indeed, Theaetetus; and it would not be right for me to stand in the way of your progress by raising objections to what you say. But look, there is another difficulty coming upon us. You must think now how we are going to fend it off.

THEAETETUS: What kind of difficulty?

SOCRATES: I mean something like this. Supposing you were asked, 'If a d man has once come to know a certain thing, and continues to preserve the memory of it, is it possible that, at the moment when he remembers it, he doesn't know this thing that he is remembering?' But I am being long-winded, I'm afraid. What I am trying to ask is, 'Can a man who has learned something not know it when he is remembering it?'

THEAETETUS: How could that happen, Socrates? That would be a most extraordinary thing.

form; for there are many hindrances to knowledge, the obscurity of the subject and the brevity of human life'.

SOCRATES: Then am I perhaps talking nonsense? But think now. You say that seeing is perceiving and sight is perception?

THEAETETUS: Yes.

e   SOCRATES: Then a man who has seen something has come to know that which he saw, according to the statement you made just now?

THEAETETUS: Yes.

SOCRATES: But you do say—don't you?—that there is such a thing as memory?

THEAETETUS: Yes.

SOCRATES: Memory of nothing? Or of something?

THEAETETUS: Of something, surely.

SOCRATES: That is to say, of things which one has learned, that is, perceived—that kind of 'something'?

THEAETETUS: Of course.

SOCRATES: And what a man has once seen, he recalls, I take it, from time to time?

THEAETETUS: He does.

SOCRATES: Even if he shuts his eyes? Or does he forget it if he does this?

THEAETETUS: That would be a strange thing to say, Socrates.

164   SOCRATES: Yet it is what we must say, if we are to save our previous statement. Otherwise, it's all up with it.

THEAETETUS: Yes, by Jove, I begin to have my suspicions too; but I don't quite see it yet. You explain.

SOCRATES: This is why. According to us, the man who sees has acquired knowledge of what he sees, as sight, perception and knowledge are agreed to be the same thing.

THEAETETUS: Yes, certainly.

SOCRATES: But the man who sees and has acquired knowledge of the thing he saw, if he shuts his eyes remembers but does not see it. Isn't that so?

THEAETETUS: Yes.

b   SOCRATES: But to say 'He doesn't see' is to say 'He doesn't know', if 'sees' is 'knows'?

THEAETETUS: True.

SOCRATES: Then we have this result, that a man who has come to know something and still remembers it doesn't know it because he doesn't see it? And that's what we said would be a most extraordinary thing to happen.

THEAETETUS: That's perfectly true.

SOCRATES: Then apparently we get an impossible result when knowledge and perception are identified?

THEAETETUS: It looks like it.

SOCRATES: Then we have got to say that perception is one thing and knowledge another?

THEAETETUS: Yes, I'm afraid so.

c   SOCRATES: Then what *is* knowledge? We shall have to begin again at the beginning, it seems. And yet—whatever are we thinking about, Theaetetus?

THEAETETUS: What do you mean?

SOCRATES: We appear to be behaving like a base-born fighting-cock, jumping away off the theory, and crowing before we have the victory over it.

THEAETETUS: How are we doing that?

SOCRATES: We seem to have been adopting the methods of professional controversialists: we've made an agreement aimed at getting words to agree consistently; and we feel complacent now that we have defeated the theory by the use of a method of this kind. We profess to be philosophers, not champion controversialists; and we don't realize that we are doing just what those clever fellows do.   d

THEAETETUS: I still don't quite see what you mean.

SOCRATES: Well, I will try to explain what I have in mind here. We were enquiring into the possibility that a man should not know something that he has learned and remembers. And we showed that a man who has seen something, and then shuts his eyes, remembers but does not see it; and that showed that he does not know the thing at the very time that he remembers it. We said that this was impossible. And so the tale of Protagoras comes to an untimely end; yours too, your tale about the identity of knowledge and perception.

THEAETETUS: So it appears.   e

SOCRATES: But I don't think this would have happened, my friend, if the father of the other tale were alive. He would find plenty of means of defending it. As things are, it is an orphan we are trampling in the mud. Not even the people Protagoras appointed its guardians are prepared to come to its rescue; for instance, Theodorus here. In the interests of justice, it seems that we shall have to come to the rescue ourselves.

THEODORUS: I think you must. It is not I, you know, Socrates, but Callias,   165 the son of Hipponicus,[15] who is the guardian of Protagoras' relics. As it happened, I very soon inclined away from abstract discussion to geometry. But I shall be very grateful if you can rescue the orphan.

SOCRATES: Good, Theodorus. Now will you give your mind to this rescue work of mine—what little I can do? Because one might be driven into making even more alarming admissions than we have just made, if one paid as little attention to the words in which we express our assertions and denials as we are for the most part accustomed to doing. Shall I tell you how this might happen? Or shall I tell Theaetetus?

THEODORUS: Tell us both, Socrates; but the younger had better answer. It will not be so undignified for him to get tripped up.   b

SOCRATES: Well, then, here is the most alarming poser of all. It goes something like this, I think: 'Is it possible for a man who knows something not to know this thing which he knows?'

---

15. A wealthy Athenian famous for his patronage of the sophists: 'a man who has spent more money on sophists than everyone else put together' (*Apology* 20a). The discussion of Plato's *Protagoras* is set in his house, where Protagoras and other visiting sophists are staying.

THEODORUS: What are we going to answer now, Theaetetus?

THEAETETUS: That it is impossible, I should think.

SOCRATES: But it is not, if you are going to premise that seeing is knowing. For what are you going to do when some intrepid fellow has you 'trapped in the well-shaft', as they say, with a question that leaves you no way out:

c clapping his hand over one of your eyes, he asks you whether you see his cloak with the eye that is covered—how will you cope with that?

THEAETETUS: I shall say that I don't see it with this one, but I do with the other.

SOCRATES: So you both see and do not see the same thing at the same time?

THEAETETUS: Well, yes, in that sort of way I do.

SOCRATES: 'That's not the question I'm setting you,' he will say, 'I was not asking you in what way it happened. I was asking you "*Does* it happen that you don't know what you know?" You now appear to be seeing what you don't see; and you have actually admitted that seeing is knowing, and not to see is not to know. I leave you to draw your conclusion.'

d THEAETETUS: Well, I draw a conclusion that contradicts my original suppositions.

SOCRATES: And that is the kind of thing that might have happened to you more than once, you wonderful fellow. It might have happened if someone had gone on asking you whether it was possible to know sometimes clearly and sometimes dimly; or to know near at hand and not from a distance; or to know the same thing both intensely and slightly. And there are a million other questions with which one of the mercenary skirmishers of debate might ambush you, once you had proposed that knowledge and perception are the same thing. He would lay into hearing and smelling and other perceptions of that kind; and would keep on refuting

e you and not let you go till you had been struck with wonder at his wisdom—that 'answer to many prayers'—and had got yourself thoroughly tied up by him. Then, when he had you tamed and bound, he would set you free for a ransom—whatever price seemed appropriate to the two of you.

But perhaps you'll ask, what argument would Protagoras himself bring to the help of his offspring. Shall we try to state it?

THEAETETUS: Yes, surely.

SOCRATES: Well, he will say all the things that we are saying in our

166 attempt to defend him; and then, I imagine, he will come to grips with us, and in no respectful spirit either. I imagine him saying: 'This good Socrates here—what he did was to frighten a small boy by asking him if it were possible that the same man should at once remember and not know the same thing; and when the boy in his fright answered "No," because he couldn't see what was coming, then, according to Socrates, the laugh was against *me* in the argument. You are too easy-going, Socrates. The true position is this. When you are examining any doctrine of mine by the method of question and answer, if the person being questioned answers as I myself would answer, and gets caught, then it is I who am refuted;

but if his answers are other than I should give, then it is he who is put in   b
the wrong.

  'Now, to begin with, do you expect someone to grant you that a man's
present memory of something which he has experienced in the past but
is no longer experiencing is the same sort of experience as he then had?
That is very far from being true. Again, do you suppose he will hesitate
to admit that it is possible for the same man to know and not know the
same thing? Or—if he has misgivings about this—do you expect him to
concede to you that the man, who is in process of becoming unlike, is the
same as he was before the process began? Do you expect him even to
speak of "the man" rather than of "the men," indeed of an infinite number
of these men coming to be in succession, assuming this process of becoming
unlike? Not if we really must take every precaution against each other's   c
verbal traps. Show a little more spirit, my good man,' he will say, 'and
attack my actual statement itself, and refute it, if you can, by showing that
each man's perceptions are not his own private events; or that, if they are
his own private events, it does not follow that the thing which appears
"becomes" or, if we may speak of being, "is" only for the man to whom
it appears. You keep talking about pigs and baboons; you show the mental-
ity of a pig yourself, in the way you deal with my writings, and you
persuade your audience to follow your example. That is not the way   d
to behave.

  'I take my stand on the truth being as I have written it. Each one of us
is the measure both of what is and of what is not; but there are countless
differences between men for just this very reason, that different things
both are and appear to be to different subjects. I certainly do not deny the
existence of both wisdom and wise men: far from it. But the man whom
I call wise is the man who can change the appearances—the man who in
any case where bad things both appear and are for one of us, works a
change and makes good things appear and be for him.

  'And I must beg you, this time, not to confine your attack to the letter   e
of my doctrine. I am now going to make its meaning clearer to you. For
instance, I would remind you of what we were saying before, namely,
that to the sick man the things he eats both appear and are bitter, while
to the healthy man they both appear and are the opposite. Now what we
have to do is not to make one of these two wiser than the other—that is   167
not even a possibility—nor is it our business to make accusations, calling
the sick man ignorant for judging as he does, and the healthy man wise,
because he judges differently. What we have to do is to make a change
from the one to the other, because the other state is *better*. In education,
too, what we have to do is to change a worse state into a better state; only
whereas the doctor brings about the change by the use of drugs, the
professional teacher[16] does it by the use of words. What never happens is
that a man who judges what is false is made to judge what is true. For it

---

16. Literally, 'the sophist'.

is impossible to judge what is not, or to judge anything other than what one
b is immediately experiencing; and what one is immediately experiencing is
always true. This, in my opinion, is what really happens: when a man's
soul is in a pernicious state, he judges things akin to it, but giving him a
sound state of the soul causes him to think different things, things that
are good. In the latter event, the things which appear to him are what
some people, who are still at a primitive stage, call "true"; my position,
however, is that the one kind are *better* than the others, but in no way *truer*.

'Nor, my dear Socrates, should I dream of suggesting that we might
look for wisdom among frogs. I look for wisdom, as regards animal bodies,
in doctors; as regards plant-life, in gardeners—for I am quite prepared to
c maintain that gardeners too, when they find a plant sickly, proceed by
causing it to have good and healthy, that is, "true" perceptions, instead
of bad ones. Similarly, the wise and efficient politician is the man who
makes wholesome things seem just to a city instead of pernicious ones.
Whatever in any city is regarded as just and admirable *is* just and admirable,
in that city and for so long as that convention maintains itself; but the
wise man replaces each pernicious convention by a wholesome one, making
this both be and seem just. Similarly the professional teacher who is able
d to educate his pupils on these lines is a wise man, and is worth his large
fees to them.

'In this way we are enabled to hold both that some men are wiser than
others, and also that no man judges what is false. And you, too, whether
you like it or not, must put up with being a "measure." For this is the line
we must take if we are to save the theory.

'If you feel prepared to go back to the beginning, and make a case against
this theory, let us hear your objections set out in a connected argument.
Or, if you prefer the method of question and answer, do it that way; there
is no reason to try to evade that method either, indeed an intelligent person
might well prefer it to any other. Only I beg that you will observe this
e condition: do not be unjust in your questions. It is the height of unreason-
ableness that a person who professes to care for moral goodness should
be consistently unjust in discussion. I mean by injustice, in this connection,
the behavior of a man who does not take care to keep controversy distinct
from discussion; a man who forgets that in controversy he may play about
and trip up his opponent as often as he can, but that in discussion he must
be serious, he must keep on helping his opponent to his feet again, and
168 point out to him only those of his slips which are due to himself or to the
intellectual society which he has previously frequented. If you observe
this distinction, those who associate with you will blame themselves for
their confusion and their difficulties, not you. They will seek your company,
and think of you as their friend; but they will loathe themselves, and seek
refuge from themselves in philosophy, in the hope that they may thereby
become different people and be rid forever of the men that they once were.
But if you follow the common practice and do the opposite, you will

get the opposite results. Instead of philosophers, you will make your   b
companions grow up to be the enemies of philosophy.

'So, if you take my advice, as I said before, you will sit down with us
without ill will or hostility, in a kindly spirit. You will genuinely try to
find out what our meaning is when we maintain (*a*) that all things are in
motion and (*b*) that for each person and each city, things are what they seem
to them to be. And upon this basis you will inquire whether knowledge and
perception are the same thing or different things. But you will not proceed
as you did just now. You will not base your argument upon the use and
wont of language; you will not follow the practice of most men, who drag   c
words this way and that at their pleasure, so making every imaginable
difficulty for one another.'

Well, Theodorus, here is my contribution to the rescue of your friend—
the best I can do, with my resources, and little enough that is. If he were
alive himself, he would have come to the rescue of his offspring in a
grander style.

THEODORUS: That must be a joke, Socrates. It was a very spirited rescue.

SOCRATES: You are kind, my friend. Tell me now, did you notice that
Protagoras was complaining of us, in the speech that we have just heard,   d
for addressing our arguments to a small boy and making the child's ner-
vousness a weapon against his ideas? And how he disparaged our method
of arguments as merely an amusing game, and how solemnly he upheld
his 'measure of all things' and commanded us to be serious when we dealt
with his theory?

THEODORUS: Yes, of course I noticed that, Socrates.

SOCRATES: Then do you think we should obey his commands?

THEODORUS: Most certainly I do.

SOCRATES: Look at the company then. They are all children but you. So
if we are to obey Protagoras, it is you and I who have got to be serious   e
about his theory. It is you and I who must question and answer one
another. Then he will not have *this* against us, at any rate, that we turned
the criticism of his philosophy into sport with boys.

THEODORUS: Well, isn't our Theaetetus better able to follow the investigation of a theory than many an old fellow with a long beard?

SOCRATES: But not better than *you*, Theodorus. Do not go on imagining
that it is my business to be straining every nerve to defend your dead   169
friend while you do nothing. Come now, my very good Theodorus, come
a little way with me. Come with me at any rate until we see whether in
questions of geometrical proofs it is really you who should be the measure
or whether all men are as sufficient to themselves as you are in astronomy
and all the other sciences in which you have made your name.

THEODORUS: Socrates, it is not easy for a man who has sat down beside
you to refuse to talk. That was all nonsense just now when I was pretending
that you were going to allow me to keep my coat on, and not use compulsion like the Spartans. So far from that, you seem to me to have leanings

b towards the methods of Sciron.[17] The Spartans tell one either to strip or to go away; but you seem rather to be playing the part of Antaeus.[18] You don't let any comer go till you have stripped him and made him wrestle with you in an argument.

SOCRATES: That, Theodorus, is an excellent simile to describe what is the matter with me. But I am more of a fiend for exercise than Sciron and Antaeus. I have met with many and many a Heracles and Theseus in my time, mighty men of words; and they have well battered me. But for all

c that I don't retire from the field, so terrible a lust has come upon me for these exercises. *You* must not grudge me this, either; try a fall with me and we shall both be the better.

THEODORUS: All right. I resign myself; take me with you where you like. In any case, I see, I have got to put up with the fate you spin for me, and submit to your inquisition. But not further than the limits you have laid down; beyond that I shall not be able to offer myself.

SOCRATES: It will do if you will go with me so far. Now there is one kind of mistake I want you to be specially on your guard against, namely, that

d we do not unconsciously slip into some childish form of argument. We don't want to get into disgrace for this again.

THEODORUS: I will do my best, I promise you.

SOCRATES: The first thing, then, is to tackle the same point that we were dealing with before. We were making a complaint. Now let us see whether we were right or wrong in holding it to be a defect in this theory that it made every man self-sufficient in wisdom; and whether we were right or wrong when we made Protagoras concede that some men are superior to others in questions of better and worse, these being 'the wise'. Do you agree?

THEODORUS: Yes.

SOCRATES: It would be a different matter if Protagoras were here in person

e and agreed with us, instead of our having made this concession on his behalf in our attempt to help him. In that case, there would be no need to take this question up again and make sure about it. In the circumstances, however, it might be decided that we had no authority on his behalf, and so it is desirable that we should come to a clearer agreement on this point; for it makes no small difference whether this is so or not.

THEODORUS: True.

170 SOCRATES: Then don't let us obtain this concession through anybody else. Let us take the shortest way, an appeal to his own statement.

THEODORUS: How?

17. A legendary highwayman who attacked travellers on the coast between Megara and Corinth. His most famous 'method' was to compel them to wash his feet, and kick them over the cliff into the sea while they were so doing.

18. Antaeus was said to have lived in a cave and compelled all passers-by to wrestle with him, with results invariably fatal to them.

SOCRATES: In this way. He says, does he not, that things are for every man what they seem to him to be?

THEODORUS: Yes, that is what he says.

SOCRATES: Well, then, Protagoras, we too are expressing the judgments of a man—I might say, of all men—when we say that there is no one in the world who doesn't believe that in some matters he is wiser than other men; while in other matters, they are wiser than he. In emergencies—if at no other time—you see this belief. When they are in distress, on the battlefield, or in sickness or in a storm at sea, all men turn to their leaders in each sphere as to gods and look to them for salvation because they are superior in precisely this one thing—knowledge. And wherever human life and work goes on, you find everywhere men seeking teachers and masters, for themselves and for other living creatures and for the direction of all human works. You find also men who believe that they are able to teach and to take the lead. In all these cases, what else can we say but that men do believe in the existence of both wisdom and ignorance among themselves?

THEODORUS: There can be no other conclusion.

SOCRATES: And they believe that wisdom is true thinking? While ignorance is a matter of false judgment?

THEODORUS: Yes, of course.

SOCRATES: What then, Protagoras, are we to make of your argument? Are we to say that all men, on every occasion, judge what is true? Or that they judge sometimes truly and sometimes falsely? Whichever we say, it comes to the same thing, namely, that men do not always judge what is true; that human judgments are both true and false. For think, Theodorus. Would you, would anyone of the school of Protagoras be prepared to contend that no one ever thinks his neighbor is ignorant or judging falsely?

THEODORUS: No, that's not a thing one could believe, Socrates.

SOCRATES: And yet it is to this that our theory has been driven—this theory that man is the measure of all things.

THEODORUS: How is that?

SOCRATES: Well, suppose you come to a decision in your own mind and then express a judgment about something to me. Let us assume with Protagoras that your judgment is true for *you*. But isn't it possible that the rest of us may criticize your verdict? Do we always agree that your judgment is true? Or does there rise up against you, every time, a vast army of persons who think the opposite, who hold that your decisions and your thoughts are false?

THEODORUS: Heaven knows they do, Socrates, in their 'thousands and tens of thousands', as Homer says,[19] and give me all the trouble that is humanly possible.

19. *Odyssey* xvi.121.

SOCRATES: Then do you want us to say that you are then judging what is true for yourself, but false for the tens of thousands?

THEODORUS: It looks as if that is what we must say, according to the theory, at any rate.

SOCRATES: And what of Protagoras himself? Must he not say this, that supposing he himself did not believe that man is the measure, any more than the majority of people (who indeed do not believe it), then this *Truth* which he wrote is true for no one? On the other hand, suppose he believed it himself, but the majority of men do not agree with him; then you see— to begin with—the more those to whom it does not seem to be the truth outnumber those to whom it does, so much the more it isn't than it is?

THEODORUS: That must be so, if it is going to be or not be according to the individual judgment.

SOCRATES: Secondly, it has this most exquisite feature: Protagoras admits, I presume, that the contrary opinion about his own opinion (namely, that it is false) must be true, seeing he agrees that all men judge what is.

THEODORUS: Undoubtedly.

SOCRATES: And in conceding the truth of the opinion of those who think him wrong, he is really admitting the falsity of his own opinion?

THEODORUS: Yes, inevitably.

SOCRATES: But for their part the others do not admit that they are wrong?

THEODORUS: No.

SOCRATES: But Protagoras again admits *this* judgment to be true, according to his written doctrine?

THEODORUS: So it appears.

SOCRATES: It will be disputed, then, by everyone, beginning with Protagoras—or rather, it will be admitted by him, when he grants to the person who contradicts him that he judges truly—when he does that, even Protagoras himself will be granting that neither a dog nor the 'man in the street' is the measure of anything at all which he has not learned. Isn't that so?

THEODORUS: It is so.

SOCRATES: Then since it is disputed by everyone, the *Truth* of Protagoras is not true for anyone at all, not even for himself?

THEODORUS: Socrates, we are running my friend too hard.

SOCRATES: But it is not at all clear, my dear Theodorus, that we are running off the right track. Hence it is likely that Protagoras, being older than we are, really is wiser as well; and if he were to stick up his head from below as far as the neck just here where we are, he would in all likelihood convict me twenty times over of talking nonsense, and show you up too for agreeing with me, before he ducked down to rush off again. But we have got to take ourselves as we are, I suppose, and go on saying the things which seem to us to be. At the moment, then, mustn't we maintain that any man would admit at least this, that some men are wiser than their fellows and others more ignorant?

THEODORUS: So it seems to me, at any rate.

SOCRATES: We may also suggest that the theory would stand firm most successfully in the position which we sketched out for it in our attempt to bring help to Protagoras. I mean the position that most things are for the individual what they seem to him to be; for instance, warm, dry, sweet and all this type of thing. But if the theory is going to admit that there is any sphere in which one man is superior to another, it might perhaps be prepared to grant it in questions of what is good or bad for one's health. Here it might well be admitted that it is not true that every creature— woman or child or even animal—is competent to recognize what is good for it and to heal its own sickness; that here, if anywhere, one person is better than another. Do you agree?

THEODORUS: Yes, that seems so to me.

SOCRATES: Then consider political questions. Some of these are questions of what may or may not fittingly be done, of just and unjust, of what is sanctioned by religion and what is not; and here the theory may be prepared to maintain that whatever view a city takes on these matters and establishes as its law or convention, is truth and fact for that city. In such matters neither any individual nor any city can claim superior wisdom. But when it is a question of laying down what is to the interest of the state and what is not, the matter is different. The theory will again admit that here, if anywhere, one counsellor is better than another; here the decision of one city may be more in conformity with the truth than that of another. It would certainly not have the hardihood to affirm that when a city decides that a certain thing is to its own interest, that thing will undoubtedly turn out to be to its interest. It is in those other questions I am talking about— just and unjust, religious and irreligious—that men are ready to insist that no one of these things has by nature any being of its own; in respect of these, they say, what seems to people collectively to be so is true, at the time when it seems that way and for just as long as it so seems. And even those who are not prepared to go all the way with Protagoras take some such view of wisdom. But I see, Theodorus, that we are becoming involved in a greater discussion emerging from the lesser one.

THEODORUS: Well, we have plenty of time, haven't we, Socrates?

SOCRATES: We appear to . . . That remark of yours, my friend, reminds me of an idea that has often occurred to me before—how natural it is that men who have spent a great part of their lives in philosophical studies make such fools of themselves when they appear as speakers in the law courts.

THEODORUS: How do you mean now?

SOCRATES: Well, look at the man who has been knocking about in law courts and such places ever since he was a boy; and compare him with the man brought up in philosophy, in the life of a student. It is surely like comparing the upbringing of a slave with that of a free man.

THEODORUS: How is that, now?

SOCRATES: Because the one man always has what you mentioned just now—plenty of time. When he talks, he talks in peace and quiet, and his

time is his own. It is so with us now: here we are beginning on our third
new discussion; and he can do the same, if he is like us, and prefers the
newcomer to the question in hand. It does not matter to such men whether
they talk for a day or a year, if only they may hit upon that which is. But
e   the other—the man of the law courts—is always in a hurry when he is
talking; he has to speak with one eye on the clock. Besides, he can't make
his speeches on any subject he likes; he has his adversary standing over
him, armed with compulsory powers and with the sworn statement, which
is read out point by point as he proceeds, and must be kept to by the
speaker. The talk is always about a fellow-slave, and is addressed to a
master, who sits there holding some suit or other in his hand. And the
struggle is never a matter of indifference; it always directly concerns the
speaker, and sometimes life itself is at stake.

173   Such conditions make him keen and highly strung, skilled in flattering
the master and working his way into favor; but cause his soul to be small
and warped. His early servitude prevents him from making a free, straight
growth; it forces him into doing crooked things by imposing dangers and
alarms upon a soul that is still tender. He cannot meet these by just and
honest practice, and so resorts to lies and to the policy of repaying one
b   wrong with another; thus he is constantly being bent and distorted, and
in the end grows up to manhood with a mind that has no health in it,
having now become—in his own eyes—a man of ability and wisdom.

There is your practical man, Theodorus. What about our own set? Would
you like us to have a review of them, or shall we let them be, and return
to the argument? We don't want to abuse this freedom to change our
subject of which we were speaking just now.

c   THEODORUS: No, no, Socrates. Let us review the philosophers. What you
said just now was quite right; we who move in such circles are not the
servants but the masters of our discussions. Our arguments are our own,
like slaves; each one must wait about for us, to be finished whenever we
think fit. We have no jury, and no audience (as the dramatic poets have),
sitting in control over us, ready to criticize and give orders.

SOCRATES: Very well, then; we must review them, it seems, since you
have made up your mind. But let us confine ourselves to the leaders;
why bother about the second-rate specimens? To begin with, then, the
d   philosopher grows up without knowing the way to the market-place, or
the whereabouts of the law courts or the council chambers or any other
place of public assembly. Laws and decrees, published orally or in writing,
are things he never sees or hears. The scrambling of political cliques for
office; social functions, dinners, parties with flute-girls—such doings never
enter his head even in a dream. So with questions of birth—he has no
more idea whether a fellow citizen is high-born or humble, or whether he
has inherited some taint from his forebears, male or female, than he has
e   of the number of pints in the sea, as they say. And in all these matters,
he knows not even that he knows not; for he does not hold himself aloof
from them in order to get a reputation, but because it is in reality only his

body that lives and sleeps in the city. His mind, having come to the conclusion that all these things are of little or no account, spurns them and pursues its wingéd way, as Pindar says,[20] throughout the universe, 'in the deeps below the earth' and 'in the heights above the heaven'; geometrizing upon earth, measuring its surfaces, astronomizing in the heavens; tracking down by every path the entire nature of each whole among the things that are, and never condescending to what lies near at hand.

174

THEODORUS: What do you mean by that, Socrates?

SOCRATES: Well, here's an instance: they say Thales[21] was studying the stars, Theodorus, and gazing aloft, when he fell into a well; and a witty and amusing Thracian servant-girl made fun of him because, she said, he was wild to know about what was up in the sky but failed to see what was in front of him and under his feet. The same joke applies to all who spend their lives in philosophy. It really is true that the philosopher fails to see his next-door neighbor; he not only doesn't notice what he is doing; he scarcely knows whether he is a man or some other kind of creature. The question he asks is, What is Man? What actions and passions properly belong to human nature and distinguish it from all other beings? This is what he wants to know and concerns himself to investigate. You see what I mean, Theodorus, don't you?

b

THEODORUS: Yes, and what you say is true.

SOCRATES: This accounts, my friend, for the behavior of such a man when he comes into contact with his fellows, either privately with individuals or in public life, as I was saying at the beginning. Whenever he is obliged, in a law court or elsewhere, to discuss the things that lie at his feet and before his eyes, he causes entertainment not only to Thracian servant-girls but to all the common herd, by tumbling into wells and every sort of difficulty through his lack of experience. His clumsiness is awful and gets him a reputation for fatuousness. On occasions when personal scandal is the topic of conversation, he never has anything at all of his own to contribute; he knows nothing to the detriment of anyone, never having paid any attention to this subject—a lack of resource which makes him look very comic. And again, when compliments are in order, and self-laudation, his evident amusement—which is by no means a pose but perfectly genuine—is regarded as idiotic. When he hears the praises of a despot or a king being sung, it sounds to his ears as if some stock-breeder were being congratulated—some keeper of pigs or sheep, or cows that are giving him plenty of milk; only he thinks that the rulers have a more difficult and treacherous animal to rear and milk, and that such a man, having no spare time, is bound to become quite as coarse and uncultivated as the stock-farmer; for the castle of the one is as much a prison as the

c

d

e

20. This quotation from a lost poem of Pindar's is listed as his frag. 292 (Snell).

21. The first founder of Greek natural philosophy (sixth century B.C.), about whom we have anecdotes but little solid information.

mountain fold of the other. When he hears talk of land—that so-and-so has a property of ten thousand acres or more, and what a vast property that is, it sounds to him like a tiny plot, used as he is to envisage the whole earth. When his companions become lyric on the subject of great families, and exclaim at the noble blood of one who can point to seven wealthy ancestors, he thinks that such praise comes of a dim and limited
175 vision, an inability, through lack of education, to take a steady view of the whole, and to calculate that every single man has countless hosts of ancestors, near and remote, among whom are to be found, in every instance, rich men and beggars, kings and slaves, Greeks and foreigners, by the thousand. When men pride themselves upon a pedigree of twenty-five ancestors, and trace their descent back to Heracles the son of Amphitryon,
b   they seem to him to be taking a curious interest in trifles. As for the twenty-fifth ancestor of Amphitryon, what *he* may have been is merely a matter of luck, and similarly with the fiftieth before him again. How ridiculous, he thinks, not to be able to work that out, and get rid of the gaping vanity of a silly mind.

On all these occasions, you see, the philosopher is the object of general derision, partly for what men take to be his superior manner, and partly for his constant ignorance and lack of resource in dealing with the obvious.

THEODORUS: What you say exactly describes what does happen, Socrates.

SOCRATES: But consider what happens, my friend, when he in his turn draws someone to a higher level, and induces him to abandon questions
c   of 'My injustice towards you, or yours towards me' for an examination of justice and injustice themselves—what they are, and how they differ from everything else and from each other; or again, when he gets him to leave such questions as 'Is a king happy?' or 'a man of property?' for an inquiry into kingship, and into human happiness and misery in general—what these two things are, and what, for a human being, is the proper method by which the one can be obtained and the other avoided. When it is an
d   account of matters like all these that is demanded of our friend with the small, sharp, legal mind, the situation is reversed; his head swims as, suspended at such a height, he gazes down from his place among the clouds; disconcerted by the unusual experience, he knows not what to do next, and can only stammer when he speaks. And that causes great entertainment, not to Thracian servant-girls or any other uneducated persons—they do not see what is going on—but to all men who have not been brought up like slaves.

e   These are the two types, Theodorus. There is the one who has been brought up in true freedom and leisure, the man you call a philosopher; a man to whom it is no disgrace to appear simple and good-for-nothing when he is confronted with menial tasks, when, for instance, he doesn't know how to make a bed, or how to sweeten a sauce or a flattering speech. Then you have the other, the man who is keen and smart at doing all these jobs, but does not know how to strike up a song in his turn like a

free man, or how to tune the strings of common speech to the fitting praise   176
of the life of gods and of the happy among men.

THEODORUS: Socrates, if your words convinced everyone as they do me,
there would be more peace and less evil on earth.

SOCRATES: But it is not possible, Theodorus, that evil should be destroyed—for there must always be something opposed to the good; nor
is it possible that it should have its seat in heaven. But it must inevitably
haunt human life, and prowl about this earth. That is why a man should
make all haste to escape from earth to heaven; and escape means becoming   b
as like God as possible; and a man becomes like God when he becomes
just and pure, with understanding. But it is not at all an easy matter, my
good friend, to persuade men that it is not for the reasons commonly
alleged that one should try to escape from wickedness and pursue virtue.
It is not in order to avoid a bad reputation and obtain a good one that
virtue should be practiced and not vice; that, it seems to me, is only what   c
men call 'old wives' talk'.

Let us try to put the truth in this way. In God there is no sort of wrong
whatsoever; he is supremely just, and the thing most like him is the man
who has become as just as it lies in human nature to be. And it is here
that we see whether a man is truly able, or truly a weakling and a nonentity;
for it is the realization of this that is genuine wisdom and goodness, while
the failure to realize it is manifest folly and wickedness. Everything else
that passes for ability and wisdom has a sort of commonness—in those
who wield political power a poor cheap show, in the manual workers a
matter of mechanical routine. If, therefore, one meets a man who practices   d
injustice and is blasphemous in his talk or in his life, the best thing for
him by far is that one should never grant that there is any sort of ability
about his unscrupulousness; such men are ready enough to glory in the
reproach, and think that it means not that they are mere rubbish, cumbering
the ground to no purpose, but that they have the kind of qualities that
are necessary for survival in the community. We must therefore tell them
the truth—that their very ignorance of their true state fixes them the more
firmly therein. For they do not know what is the penalty of injustice, which
is the last thing of which a man should be ignorant. It is not what they
suppose—scourging and death—things which they may entirely evade in
spite of their wrongdoing. It is a penalty from which there is no escape.   e

THEODORUS: And what is that?

SOCRATES: My friend, there are two patterns set up in reality. One is
divine and supremely happy; the other has nothing of God in it, and is
the pattern of the deepest unhappiness. This truth the evildoer does not
see; blinded by folly and utter lack of understanding, he fails to perceive   177
that the effect of his unjust practices is to make him grow more and more
like the one, and less and less like the other. For this he pays the penalty
of living the life that corresponds to the pattern he is coming to resemble.
And if we tell him that, unless he is delivered from this 'ability' of his,

when he dies the place that is pure of all evil will not receive him; that he will forever go on living in this world a life after his own likeness—a bad man tied to bad company: he will but think, 'This is the way fools talk to a clever rascal like me.'

THEODORUS: Oh, yes, Socrates, sure enough.

b   SOCRATES: I know it, my friend. But there is one accident to which the unjust man is liable. When it comes to giving and taking an account in a private discussion of the things he disparages; when he is willing to stand his ground like a man for long enough, instead of running away like a coward, then, my friend, an odd thing happens. In the end the things he says do not satisfy even himself; that famous eloquence of his somehow dries up, and he is left looking nothing more than a child.

c   But we had better leave it there; all this is really a digression; and if we go on, a flood of new subjects will pour in and overwhelm our original argument. So, if you don't mind, we will go back to what we were saying before.

THEODORUS: As a matter of fact, Socrates, *I* like listening to this kind of talk; it is easier for a man of my years to follow. Still, if you like, let us go back to the argument.

SOCRATES: Well, then, we were at somewhere about this point in the argument, weren't we? We were speaking of the people who assert a being that is in motion, and who hold that for every individual things always are whatever they seem to him to be; and we said that they were prepared to stand upon their principle in almost every case—not least in questions of what is just and right. Here they are perfectly ready to maintain that

d   whatever any community decides to be just and right, and establishes as such, actually is what is just and right for that community and for as long as it remains so established. On the other hand, when it is a question of what things are good, we no longer find anyone so heroic that he will venture to contend that whatever a community thinks useful, and establishes, really is useful, so long as it is the established order—unless, of course, he means that it is *called* 'useful'; but that would be making a game of our argument, wouldn't it?

THEODORUS: It would indeed.

e   SOCRATES: Let us suppose, then, that he is not talking about the name 'useful' but has in view the thing to which it is applied.

THEODORUS: Agreed.

SOCRATES: It is surely this that a government aims at when it legislates, whatever name it calls it. A community always makes such laws as are most useful to it—so far as the limits of its judgment and capacity permit.— Or do you think legislation may have some other object in view?

178   THEODORUS: Oh no, not at all.

SOCRATES: And does a community always achieve this object? Or are there always a number of failures?

THEODORUS: It seems to me that there are failures.

SOCRATES: Now we might put this matter in a rather different way and be still more likely to get people generally to agree with our conclusions. I mean, one might put a question about the whole class of things to which 'what is useful' belongs. These things are concerned, I take it, with future time; thus when we legislate, we make laws that are going to be useful in the time to come. This kind of thing we may properly call 'future'.

THEODORUS: Yes, certainly.   b

SOCRATES: Come then, let's put a question to Protagoras (or to anyone who professes the same views): 'Now, Protagoras, "Man is the measure of all things" as you people say—of white and heavy and light and all that kind of thing without exception. He has the criterion of these things within himself; so when he thinks that they are as he experiences them, he thinks what is true and what really is for him.' Isn't that so?

THEODORUS: It is.

SOCRATES: 'Then, Protagoras,' we shall say, 'what about things that are going to be in the future? Has a man the criterion of these within himself?   c
When he thinks certain things *will be*, do they actually happen, for him, as he thought they would? Take heat, for example. Suppose the ordinary man thinks he is going to take a fever, and that his temperature will go up to fever point; while another man, this time a doctor, thinks the opposite. Do we hold that the future will confirm either the one judgment or the other? Or are we to say that it will confirm both; that is, that for the doctor the man will not have a temperature or be suffering from fever, while for himself he will?'

THEODORUS: That would be absurd.

SOCRATES: But, when there is a question of the sweetness and dryness of the next vintage, I presume it would always be the grower's judgment   d
that would carry authority, rather than that of a musician?

THEODORUS: Of course.

SOCRATES: Nor again, in any question of what will be in tune or out of tune, would the judgment of a teacher of gymnastic be superior to that of a musician—even about what is going to seem to be in tune to the gymnastic master himself?

THEODORUS: No, never.

SOCRATES: Or suppose a dinner is being prepared. Even the guest who is going to eat it, if he has no knowledge of cooking, will not be able to pronounce so authoritative a verdict as the professional cook on how nice it is going to be. I say 'going to be', because we had better not at this stage   e
press our point as regards what is *now* pleasant to any individual, or what has been in the past. Our question for the moment is, whether the individual himself is the best judge, for himself, of what is going to seem and be for him in the future. 'Or,' we will ask, 'would not you, Protagoras, predict better than any layman about the persuasive effect that speeches in a law court will have upon any one of us?'

THEODORUS: And in fact, Socrates, this at any rate is a point on which Protagoras used to make strong claims to superiority over other people.

SOCRATES: Of course he did, my dear good fellow. No one would have
179   paid large fees for the privilege of talking with him if he had not been in the habit of persuading his pupils that he was a better judge than any fortune-teller—or anyone else—about what was going to be and seem to be in the future.[22]

THEODORUS: That's true enough.

SOCRATES: Legislation also and 'what is useful' is concerned with the future; and it would be generally admitted to be inevitable that a city when it legislates often fails to achieve what is the most useful.

THEODORUS: Yes, surely.

SOCRATES: Then we shall be giving your master fair measure if we tell
b   him that he has now got to admit that one man is wiser than another, and that it is such a man who is 'the measure'; but that I, the man with no special knowledge, have not by any means got to be a measure—a part which the recent speech in his defense was trying to force upon me, whether I liked it or not.

THEODORUS: Now that, Socrates, seems to me to be the chief point on which the theory is convicted of error—though it stands convicted also when it makes other men's judgments carry authority and these turn out to involve thinking that Protagoras' statements are completely untrue.

c   SOCRATES: There is more than one point besides these, Theodorus, on which a conviction might be secured—at least so far as it is a matter of proving that not every man's judgment is true. But so long as we keep within the limits of that immediate present experience of the individual which gives rise to perceptions and to perceptual judgments, it is more difficult to convict these latter of being untrue—but perhaps I'm talking nonsense. Perhaps it is not possible to convict them at all; perhaps those who profess that they are perfectly evident and are always knowledge may be saying what really is. And it may be that our Theaetetus was not
d   far from the mark with his proposition that knowledge and perception are the same thing. We shall have to come to closer grips with the theory, as the speech on behalf of Protagoras required us to do. We shall have to consider and test this moving Being, and find whether it rings true or sounds as if it had some flaw in it. There is no small fight going on about it, anyway—and no shortage of fighting men.

THEODORUS: No, indeed; but in Ionia it seems to be even growing, and assuming vast dimensions. On the side of this theory, the Heraclitean party is conducting a most vigorous campaign.

22. An alternative text (accepting the conjecture of *dē* for *mē* at 179a1 and retaining the mss' *hautōi* at a3) yields: 'if he really was in the habit of persuading his pupils that, even about the future, neither a fortune-teller nor anyone else can judge better than one can for oneself'.

SOCRATES: The more reason, then, my dear Theodorus, why we should examine it by going back to its first principle,[23] which is the way they present it themselves.

THEODORUS: I quite agree. You know, Socrates, these Heraclitean doctrines (or, as you say, Homeric or still more ancient)—you can't discuss them in person with any of the people at Ephesus who profess to be adepts, any more than you could with a maniac. They are just like the things they say in their books—always on the move. As for abiding by what is said, or sticking to a question, or quietly answering and asking questions in turn, there is less than nothing of that in their capacity. That's an exaggeration, no doubt. I mean there isn't so much as a tiny bit of repose in these people. If you ask any one of them a question, he will pull out some little enigmatic phrase from his quiver and shoot it off at you; and if you try to make him give an account of what he has said, you will only get hit by another, full of strange turns of language. You will never reach any conclusion with any of them, ever; indeed they never reach any conclusion with each other, they are so very careful not to allow anything to be stable, either in an argument or in their own souls. I suppose they think that if they did it would be something that stands still—this being what they are totally at war with, and what they are determined to banish from the universe, if they can.

SOCRATES: I dare say, Theodorus, you have seen these men only on the field of battle, and never been with them in times of peace—as you don't belong to their set. I expect they keep such matters to be explained at leisure to their pupils whom they want to make like themselves.

THEODORUS: *Pupils*, my good man? There are no pupils and teachers among these people. They just spring up on their own, one here, one there, wherever they happen to catch their inspiration; and no one of them will credit another with knowing anything. As I was just going to say, you will never get these men to give an account of themselves, willingly or unwillingly. What we must do is to take their doctrine out of their hands and consider it for ourselves, as we should a problem in geometry.

SOCRATES: What you say is very reasonable. This problem now, we have inherited it, have we not, from the ancients? They used poetical forms which concealed from the majority of men their real meaning, namely, that Ocean and Tethys, the origin of all things, are actually flowing streams, and nothing stands still. In more modern times, the problem is presented to us by men who, being more accomplished in these matters, plainly demonstrate their meaning so that even shoemakers may hear and assimilate their wisdom, and give up the silly idea that some things in this world stand still while others move, learn that all things are in motion, and recognize the greatness of their instructors.

23. I.e., the principle that everything is really motion (156a).

But I was almost forgetting, Theodorus, that there are other thinkers
e   who have announced the opposite view; who tell us that 'Unmoved is the
Universe',[24] and other similar statements which we hear from a Melissus[25]
or a Parmenides as against the whole party of Heracliteans. These philosophers insist that all things are One, and that this One stands still, itself
within itself, having no place in which to move.

What are we to do with all these people, my friend? We have been
gradually advancing till, without realizing it, we have got ourselves in
181   between the two parties; and if we don't in some way manage to put up
a fight and make our escape, we shall pay for it, like the people who play
that game on the line in the wrestling schools, and get caught by both
parties and pulled in opposite directions.

Now I think we ought to begin by examining the other party, the fluent
fellows we started to pursue. If they appear to us to be talking sense, we
will help them to drag us over to their side, and try to escape the others.
But if those who make their stand for the whole appear to be nearer the
b   truth, we will take refuge with them from the men who 'move what should
not be moved'. And if it appears that neither party has a reasonable theory,
then we shall be very absurd if we think that insignificant people like
ourselves can have anything to say, after we have rejected the views of men
who lived so long ago and possessed all wisdom. Think now, Theodorus, is
it of any use for us to go forward upon such a dangerous venture?

THEODORUS: We can't refuse to examine the doctrines of these two schools,
Socrates; that couldn't be allowed.

c   SOCRATES: Then we must examine them, if *you* feel so strongly about it.
Now it seems to me that the proper starting point of our criticism is the
nature of motion; what is this thing that they are talking about when they
say that all things are in motion? I mean, for example, are they referring
to one form of motion only, or, as I think, to two—but don't let this be
only what *I* think. You commit yourself as well, so that we may come to
grief together, if need be. Tell me, do you call it 'motion' when a thing
changes from one place to another or turns round in the same place?

THEODORUS: I do, yes.

SOCRATES: Here then is one form of motion. Then supposing a thing
d   remains in the same place, but grows old, or becomes black instead of
white, or hard instead of soft, or undergoes any other alteration; isn't it
right to say that here we have motion in another form?

THEODORUS: Unquestionably.

SOCRATES: Then I now have two forms of motion, alteration and spatial movement.

THEODORUS: Yes; and that's quite correct.

SOCRATES: Then now that we have made this distinction, let us have a
talk with the people who allege that all things are in motion. Let us ask

24. Both the text and the sense of this quotation are uncertain.
25. Melissus of Samos was a fifth-century follower of Parmenides.

them, 'Do you hold that everything is in motion in both ways, that is, that   e
it both moves through space and undergoes alteration? Or do you suggest
that some things are in motion in both ways, and some only in one or
the other?'

THEODORUS: Heaven knows, *I* can't answer that. I suppose they would
say, in both ways.

SOCRATES: Yes; otherwise, my friend, it will turn out that, in their view,
things are both moving and standing still; and it will be no more correct
to say that all things are in motion than to say that all things stand still.

THEODORUS: That's perfectly true.

SOCRATES: Then since they must be in motion, and there is no such thing
anywhere as absence of motion, it follows that all things are always in   182
every kind of motion.

THEODORUS: Yes, that must be so.

SOCRATES: Then I want you to consider this point in their theory. As we
were saying, they hold that the genesis of things such as warmth and
whiteness occurs when each of them is moving, together with a perception,
in the space between the active and passive factors: the passive factor
thereby becoming percipient, but not a perception, while the active factor
becomes such or such, but not a quality—isn't that so? But perhaps 'quality'
seems a strange word to you; perhaps you don't quite understand it as a
general expression.[26] So I will talk about particular cases. What I mean is
that the active factor becomes not warmth or whiteness, but warm and   b
white; and so on. You will remember, perhaps, that we said in the earlier
stages of the argument that there is nothing which in itself is just one
thing; and that this applies also to the active and passive factors. It is by
the association of the two with one another that they generate perceptions
and the things perceived; and in so doing, the active factor becomes such
and such, while the passive factor becomes percipient.

THEODORUS: Yes, I remember that, of course.

SOCRATES: Then we need not concern ourselves about other points in   c
their doctrine, whether they mean what we say or something else. We
must keep our eyes simply upon the object of our discussion. We must
ask them this question: 'According to you, all things move and flow; isn't
that so?'

THEODORUS: Yes.

SOCRATES: And they have both the motions that we distinguished, that
is to say, they both move and alter?

THEODORUS: That must be so, if they are to be wholly and completely
in motion.

SOCRATES: Now if they were only moving through space and not altering,
we should presumably be able to say *what* the moving things flow? Or
how do we express it?

26. This is the first occurrence in Greek of the word *poiotēs*, 'quality' or 'what-sort-ness',
coined by Plato from the interrogative adjective *poios*, 'of what sort?'.

THEODORUS: That's all right.

d   SOCRATES: But since not even this abides, that what flows flows white, but rather it is in process of change, so that there is flux of this very thing also, the whiteness, and it is passing over into another color, lest it be convicted of standing still in this respect—since that is so, is it possible to give any name to a color which will properly apply to it?

THEODORUS: I don't see how one could, Socrates; nor yet surely to anything else of that kind, if, being in flux, it is always quietly slipping away as you speak?

SOCRATES: And what about any particular kind of perception; for example,
e   seeing or hearing? Does it ever abide, and remain seeing or hearing?

THEODORUS: It ought not to, certainly, if all things are in motion.

SOCRATES: Then we may not call anything seeing rather than not-seeing; nor indeed may we call it any other perception rather than not—if it be admitted that all things are in motion in every way?

THEODORUS: No, we may not.

SOCRATES: Yet Theaetetus and I said that knowledge was perception?

THEODORUS: You did.

SOCRATES: And so our answer to the question, 'What is knowledge?' gave something which is no more knowledge than not.

183   THEODORUS: It seems as if it did.

SOCRATES: A fine way this turns out to be of making our answer right. We were most anxious to prove that all things are in motion, in order to make that answer come out correct; but what has really emerged is that, if all things are in motion, every answer, on whatever subject, is equally correct, both 'it is thus' and 'it is not thus'—or if you like 'becomes', as we don't want to use any expressions which will bring our friends to a standstill.

THEODORUS: You are quite right.

b   SOCRATES: Well, yes, Theodorus, except that I said 'thus' and 'not thus'. One must not use even the word 'thus'; for this 'thus' would no longer be in motion; nor yet 'not thus' for here again there is no motion. The exponents of this theory need to establish some other language; as it is, they have no words that are consistent with their hypothesis—unless it would perhaps suit them best to use 'not at all thus' in a quite indefinite sense.

THEODORUS: That would at least be an idiom most appropriate to them.

c   SOCRATES: Then we are set free from your friend, Theodorus. We do not yet concede to him that every man is the measure of all things, if he be not a man of understanding. And we are not going to grant that knowledge is perception, not at any rate on the line of inquiry which supposes that all things are in motion; we are not going to grant it unless Theaetetus here has some other way of stating it.

THEODORUS: That's very good hearing, Socrates, for when these matters were concluded I was to be set free from my task of answering you, according to our agreement, which specified the end of the discussion of Protagoras' theory.

THEAETETUS: Oh, no, indeed, Theodorus! Not till you and Socrates have done what you proposed just now, and dealt with the other side, the people who say that the Universe stands still.

THEODORUS: What's this, Theaetetus? You at your age teaching your elders to be unjust and break their agreements? What you have got to do is to prepare to render account to Socrates yourself for the rest of the discussion.

THEAETETUS: All right, if he likes. But I would rather have listened to a discussion of these views.

THEODORUS: Well, challenging Socrates to an argument is like inviting 'cavalry into the plain'. So ask your questions and you shall hear.

SOCRATES: But I don't think, Theodorus, that I am going to be persuaded by Theaetetus to do what he demands.

THEODORUS: But what is it makes you unwilling?

SOCRATES: Shame. I am afraid our criticism might be a very cheap affair. And if I feel like this before the many who have made the universe one and unmoved, Melissus and the rest of them, I feel it still more in the face of the One—Parmenides. Parmenides seems to me, in the words of Homer, to be 'reverend' and 'awful'.[27] I met him when I was very young and he was a very old man; and he seemed to me to have a wholly noble depth.[28] So I am afraid we might not understand even what he says; still less should we attain to his real thought. Above all, I am afraid that the very object of our discussion, the nature of knowledge, might be left unexamined amid the crowd of theories that will rush in upon us if we admit them; especially as the theory we have now brought up is one which involves unmanageably vast issues. To treat it as a sideshow would be insult and injury; while if it is adequately discussed, it is likely to spread out until it completely eclipses the problems of knowledge. We must not do either. What we must do is to make use of our midwife's art to deliver Theaetetus of the thoughts which he has conceived about the nature of knowledge.*

THEODORUS: Well, if that is what you think proper, it must be done.

SOCRATES: Now, Theaetetus, I want you to think about one point in what has been said. Your answer was that knowledge is perception, wasn't it?

THEAETETUS: Yes.

SOCRATES: Now supposing you were asked: 'With what does a man see white and black things, and with what does he hear high and low notes?' You would reply, I imagine, 'With his eyes and ears.'

THEAETETUS: I should, yes.

27. *Iliad* iii.172.

28. A reference probably to the discussion between Socrates and Parmenides in *Parmenides*.

*Alternatively, this sentence could be translated: 'What we must do is to make use of our midwife's art to set Theaetetus free from the thoughts which he has conceived about the nature of knowledge'.

c SOCRATES: Now as a rule it is no sign of ill-breeding to be easy in the use of language and take no particular care in one's choice of words; it is rather the opposite that gives a man away. But such exactness is sometimes necessary; and it is necessary here, for example, to fasten upon something in your answer that is not correct. Think now. Is it more correct to say that the eyes are that *with* which we see, or that *through* which we see? Do we hear *with* the ears or *through* the ears?

THEAETETUS: Well, I should think, Socrates, that it is '*through* which' we perceive in each case, rather than '*with* which.'

d SOCRATES: Yes, my son. It would be a very strange thing, I must say, if there were a number of perceptions sitting inside us as if we were Wooden Horses, and there were not some single form, soul or whatever one ought to call it, to which all these converge—something *with* which, *through* those things,[29] as if they were instruments, we perceive all that is perceptible.

THEAETETUS: That sounds to me better than the other way of putting it.

SOCRATES: Now the reason why I am being so precise with you is this. I want to know if it is with one and the same part of ourselves that we e reach, through our eyes to white and black things, and through the other means to yet further things; and whether, if asked, you will be able to refer all these to the body. But perhaps it would be better if you stated the answers yourself, rather than that I should busy myself on your behalf. Tell me: the instruments through which you perceive hot, hard, light, sweet things—do you consider that they all belong to the body? Or can they be referred elsewhere?

THEAETETUS: No, they all belong to the body.

SOCRATES: And are you also willing to admit that what you perceive 185 through one power, you can't perceive through another? For instance, what you perceive through hearing, you couldn't perceive through sight, and similarly what you perceive through sight you couldn't perceive through hearing?

THEAETETUS: I could hardly refuse to grant that.

SOCRATES: Then suppose you think something about both; you can't possibly be having a perception about both, either through one of these instruments or through the other?

THEAETETUS: No.

SOCRATES: Now take a sound and a color. First of all, don't you think this same thing about both of them, namely, that they both are?

THEAETETUS: I do.

SOCRATES: Also that each of them is different from the other and the same as itself?

b THEAETETUS: Of course.

SOCRATES: And that both together are two, and each of them is one?

THEAETETUS: Yes, I think that too.

---

29. Viz., the eyes and ears.

SOCRATES: Are you also able to consider whether they are like or unlike each other?

THEAETETUS: Yes, I may be.

SOCRATES: Now what is it through which you think all these things about them? It is not possible, you see, to grasp what is common to both either through sight or through hearing. Let us consider another thing which will show the truth of what we are saying. Suppose it were possible to inquire whether both are salty or not. You can tell me, of course, with what you would examine them. It would clearly be neither sight nor hearing, but something else.

THEAETETUS: Yes, of course; the power which functions through the tongue.

SOCRATES: Good. Now through what does that power function which reveals to you what is common in the case both of all things and of these two—I mean that which you express by the words 'is' and 'is not' and the other terms used in our questions about them just now? What kind of instruments will you assign for all these? Through what does that which is percipient in us perceive all of them?

THEAETETUS: You mean being and not-being, likeness and unlikeness, same and different; also one, and any other number applied to them. And obviously too your question is about odd and even, and all that is involved with these attributes; and you want to know through what bodily instruments we perceive all these with the soul.

SOCRATES: You follow me exceedingly well, Theaetetus. These are just the things I am asking about.

THEAETETUS: But *I* couldn't possibly say. All I can tell you is that it doesn't seem to me that for these things there is any special instrument at all, as there is for the others. It seems to me that in investigating the common features of everything the soul functions through itself.

SOCRATES: Yes, Theaetetus, you would say that, because you are handsome and not ugly as Theodorus would have it.[30] For handsome is as handsome says. And besides being handsome, you have done me a good turn; you have saved me a vast amount of talk if it seems to you that, while the soul considers some things through the bodily powers, there are others which it considers alone and through itself. This was what I thought myself, but I wanted you to think it too.

THEAETETUS: Well, it does seem to me to be so.

SOCRATES: Now in which class do you put being? For that, above all, is something that accompanies everything.

THEAETETUS: I should put it among the things which the soul itself reaches out after by itself.

SOCRATES: Also like and unlike, same and different?

THEAETETUS: Yes.

SOCRATES: What about beautiful and ugly, good and bad?

c

d

e

186

---

30. Cf. 143e.

THEAETETUS: Yes, these too; in these, above all, I think the soul examines
their being in comparison with one another. Here it seems to be making
a calculation within itself of past and present in relation to future.

SOCRATES: Not so fast, now. Wouldn't you say that it is through touch
that the soul perceives the hardness of what is hard, and similarly the
softness of what is soft?

THEAETETUS: Yes.

SOCRATES: But as regards their being—the fact that they are—their opposition to one another, and the being, again, of this opposition, the matter
is different. Here the soul itself attempts to reach a decision for us by
rising to compare them with one another.

THEAETETUS: Yes, undoubtedly.

SOCRATES: And thus there are some things which all creatures, men and
animals alike, are naturally able to perceive as soon as they are born; I mean,
the experiences which reach the soul through the body. But calculations
regarding their being and their advantageousness come, when they do,
only as the result of a long and arduous development, involving a good
deal of trouble and education.

THEAETETUS: Yes, that certainly is so.

SOCRATES: Now is it possible for someone who does not even get at being
to get at truth?

THEAETETUS: No; it's impossible.

SOCRATES: And if a man fails to get at the truth of a thing, will he ever
be a person who knows that thing?

THEAETETUS: I don't see how, Socrates.

SOCRATES: Then knowledge is to be found not in the experiences but in
the process of reasoning about them; it is here, seemingly, not in the
experiences, that it is possible to grasp being and truth.

THEAETETUS: So it appears.

SOCRATES: Then in the face of such differences, would you call both by
the same name?

THEAETETUS: One would certainly have no right to.

SOCRATES: Now what name do you give to the former—seeing, hearing,
smelling, feeling cold or warm?

THEAETETUS: I call that perceiving—what else could I call it?

SOCRATES: So the whole lot taken together you call perception?

THEAETETUS: Necessarily.

SOCRATES: Which, we say, has no share in the grasping of truth, since it
has none in the grasping of being.

THEAETETUS: No, it has none.

SOCRATES: So it has no share in knowledge either.

THEAETETUS: No.

SOCRATES: Then, Theaetetus, perception and knowledge could never be
the same thing.

THEAETETUS: No, apparently not, Socrates; we have now got the clearest
possible proof that knowledge is something different from perception.

SOCRATES: But our object in beginning this discussion was not to find 187 out what knowledge is not, but to find out what it is. However, we have made a little progress. We shall not now look for knowledge in sense-perception at all, but in whatever we call that activity of the soul when it is busy by itself about the things which are.

THEAETETUS: Well, the name, Socrates, I suppose is judgment.

SOCRATES: Your opinion, my dear lad, is correct. Now look back to the beginning. Wipe out all that we have said hitherto, and see if you can see b any better from where you have now progressed to. Tell me again, what is knowledge?

THEAETETUS: Well, Socrates, one can't say that it is judgment in general, because there is also false judgment—but true judgment may well be knowledge. So let that be my answer. If the same thing happens again, and we find, as we go on, that it turns out not to be so, we'll try something else.

SOCRATES: And even so, Theaetetus, you have answered me in the way one ought—with a good will, and not reluctantly, as you did at first. If c we continue like this, one of two things will happen. Either we shall find what we are going out after; or we shall be less inclined to think we know things which we don't know at all—and even that would be a reward we could not fairly be dissatisfied with. Now what is this that you say? There are two forms of judgment, true and false; and your definition is that true judgment is knowledge?

THEAETETUS: Yes. That is how it looks to me now.

SOCRATES: Now I wonder if it's worth while, at this stage, to go back to an old point about judgment—

THEAETETUS: What point do you mean?

SOCRATES: I have something on my mind which has often bothered me d before, and got me into great difficulty, both in my own thought and in discussion with other people—I mean, I can't say what it is, this experience we have, and how it arises in us.

THEAETETUS: What experience?

SOCRATES: Judging what is false. Even now, you know, I'm still considering; I'm in two minds whether to let it go or whether to look into it in a different manner from a short while ago.

THEAETETUS: Why not, Socrates, if this appears for any reason to be the right thing to do? As you and Theodorus were saying just now, and quite rightly, when you were talking about leisure, we are not pressed for time in talk of this kind.

SOCRATES: A very proper reminder. Perhaps it would not be a bad mo- e ment to go back upon our tracks. It is better to accomplish a little well than a great deal unsatisfactorily.

THEAETETUS: Yes, it certainly is.

SOCRATES: Now how are we to proceed? And actually what is it that we are saying? We claim, don't we, that false judgment repeatedly occurs and one of us judges falsely, the other truly, as if it was in the nature of things for this to happen?

THEAETETUS: That is what we claim.

188   SOCRATES: Now isn't it true about all things, together or individually, that we must either know them or not know them? I am ignoring for the moment the intermediate conditions of learning and forgetting, as they don't affect the argument here.

THEAETETUS: Of course, Socrates, in that case there is no alternative. With each thing we either know it or we do not.

SOCRATES: Then when a man judges, the objects of his judgment are necessarily either things which he knows or things which he doesn't know?

THEAETETUS: Yes, that must be so.

SOCRATES: Yet if he knows a thing, it is impossible that he should not
b   know it; or if he does not know it, he cannot know it.

THEAETETUS: Yes, of course.

SOCRATES: Now take the man who judges what is false. Is he thinking that things which he knows are not these things but some other things which he knows—so that knowing both he is ignorant of both?

THEAETETUS: But that would be impossible, Socrates.

SOCRATES: Then is he imagining that things which he doesn't know are other things which he doesn't know? Is it possible that a man who knows neither Theaetetus nor Socrates should take it into his head that Socrates is Theaetetus or Theaetetus Socrates?

c   THEAETETUS: I don't see how that could happen.

SOCRATES: But a man certainly doesn't think that things he knows are things he does not know, or again that things he doesn't know are things he knows.

THEAETETUS: No, that would be a very odd thing.

SOCRATES: Then in what way is false judgment still possible? There is evidently no possibility of judgment outside the cases we have mentioned, since everything is either a thing we know or a thing we don't know; and within these limits there appears to be no place for false judgment to be possible.

THEAETETUS: That's perfectly true.

SOCRATES: Then perhaps we had better take up a different line of inquiry;
d   perhaps we should proceed not by way of knowing and not-knowing, but by way of being and not-being?

THEAETETUS: How do you mean?

SOCRATES: Perhaps the simple fact is this: it is when a man judges about anything things which are not, that he is inevitably judging falsely, no matter what may be the nature of his thought in other respects.

THEAETETUS: That again is very plausible, Socrates.

SOCRATES: Now how will that be? What are we going to say, Theaetetus, if somebody sets about examining us, and we are asked, 'Is what these words express possible for anyone? Can a man judge what is not, either
e   about one of the things which are, or just by itself?' I suppose we shall reply, 'Yes, when he is thinking, but thinking what is not true.' Or how shall we answer?

THEAETETUS: That's our answer.

SOCRATES: Now does this kind of thing happen elsewhere?

THEAETETUS: What kind of thing?

SOCRATES: Well, for instance, that a man sees something, yet sees nothing.

THEAETETUS: How could he?

SOCRATES: On the contrary, in fact, if he is seeing any one thing, he must be seeing a thing which is. Or do you think that a 'one' can be found among the things which are not?

THEAETETUS: I certainly don't.

SOCRATES: Then a man who is seeing any one thing is seeing something which is?

THEAETETUS: Apparently.

SOCRATES: It also follows that a man who is hearing anything is hearing some one thing and something which is.

189

THEAETETUS: Yes.

SOCRATES: And a man who is touching anything is touching some one thing, and a thing which is, if it is one?

THEAETETUS: Yes, that also follows.

SOCRATES: And a man who is judging is judging some one thing, is he not?

THEAETETUS: Necessarily.

SOCRATES: And a man who is judging some one thing is judging something which is?

THEAETETUS: I grant that.

SOCRATES: Then that means that a man who is judging something which is not is judging nothing?

THEAETETUS: So it appears.

SOCRATES: But a man who is judging nothing is not judging at all.

THEAETETUS: That seems clear.

SOCRATES: And so it is not possible to judge what is not, either about the things which are or just by itself.

b

THEAETETUS: Apparently not.

SOCRATES: False judgment, then, is something different from judging things which are not?

THEAETETUS: It looks as if it were.

SOCRATES: Then neither on this approach nor on the one we followed just now does false judgment exist in us.

THEAETETUS: No, indeed.

SOCRATES: Then is it in this way that the thing we call by that name arises?

THEAETETUS: How?

SOCRATES: We say that there is false judgment, a kind of 'other-judging', when a man, in place of one of the things that are, has substituted in his thought another of the things that are and asserts that it is.[31] In this way,

c

31. Reading [*anti tinos*] for Burnet's [*ti*] at 189c1; the latter reading would yield: 'when a man asserts that one of the things which are is another of the things which are, having substituted one for the other in his thought'.

he is always judging something which is, but judges one thing in place of
another; and having missed the thing which was the object of his consideration, he might fairly be called one who judges falsely.

THEAETETUS: Now you seem to me to have got it quite right. When a
man judges 'ugly' instead of 'beautiful', or 'beautiful' instead of 'ugly',
then he is truly judging what is false.

SOCRATES: Evidently, Theaetetus, you have not much opinion of me; you
don't find me at all alarming.

THEAETETUS: What in particular makes you say that?

d   SOCRATES: Well, I suppose you don't think me capable of taking up your
'truly false', and asking you whether it is possible that a thing should be
slowly swift, or heavily light, or whether anything else can possibly occur
in a way not in accordance with its own nature but in accordance with
that of its opposite and contrary to itself. But let that pass; I don't want
your boldness to go unrewarded. You like the suggestion, you say, that
false judgment is 'other-judging'?

THEAETETUS: Yes, I do.

SOCRATES: Then, according to your judgment, it is possible to set down
a thing in one's thought as another thing and not itself?

THEAETETUS: Surely it is.

e   SOCRATES: Now when a man's thought is accomplishing this, isn't it
essential that he should be thinking of either one or both of these two
things?

THEAETETUS: It is essential; either both together, or each in turn.

SOCRATES: Very good. Now by 'thinking' do you mean the same as I do?

THEAETETUS: What do you mean by it?

SOCRATES: A talk which the soul has with itself about the objects under
its consideration. Of course, I'm only telling you my idea in all ignorance;
but this is the kind of picture I have of it. It seems to me that the soul
190   when it thinks is simply carrying on a discussion in which it asks itself
questions and answers them itself, affirms and denies. And when it arrives
at something definite, either by a gradual process or a sudden leap, when
it affirms one thing consistently and without divided counsel, we call this
its judgment. So, in my view, to judge is to make a statement, and a
judgment is a statement which is not addressed to another person or
spoken aloud, but silently addressed to oneself. And what do you think?

THEAETETUS: I agree with that.

SOCRATES: So that when a man judges one thing to be another, what he
is doing, apparently, is to say to himself that the one thing is the other.

b   THEAETETUS: Yes, of course.

SOCRATES: Now try to think if you have ever said to yourself 'Surely the
beautiful is ugly',[32] or 'The unjust is certainly just'. Or—to put it in the
most general terms—have you ever tried to persuade yourself that 'Surely

32. The Greek idiom here could be used to say either that some particular beautiful
thing is ugly, or that beauty is ugliness.

one thing is another'? Wouldn't the very opposite of this be the truth? Wouldn't the truth be that not even in your sleep have you ever gone so far as to say to yourself 'No doubt the odd is even', or anything of that kind?

THEAETETUS: Yes, that's so.

SOCRATES: And do you think that anyone else, in his right mind or out   c
of it, ever ventured seriously to tell himself, with the hope of winning his own assent, that 'A cow must be a horse' or 'Two must be one'?

THEAETETUS: No, indeed I don't.

SOCRATES: Well, then, if to make a statement to oneself is to judge, no one who makes a statement, that is, a judgment, about both things, getting hold of both with his soul, can state, or judge, that one is the other. And you, in your turn, must let this form of words pass.[33] What I mean by it is this: no one judges 'The ugly is beautiful' or makes any other such   d
judgment.

THEAETETUS: All right, Socrates, I pass it; and I think you're right.

SOCRATES: Thus a man who has both things before his mind when he judges cannot possibly judge that one is the other.

THEAETETUS: So it seems.

SOCRATES: But if he has only one of them before his mind in judging, and the other is not present to him at all, he will never judge that one is the other.

THEAETETUS: That's true. For he would have to have hold also of the one that is not present to his judgment.

SOCRATES: Then 'other-judging' is not possible for anyone either when he has both things present to him in judgment or when he has one only.   e
So, if anyone is going to define false judgment as 'heterodoxy',[34] he will be saying nothing. The existence of false judgment in us cannot be shown in this way any more than by our previous approaches.

THEAETETUS: It seems not.

SOCRATES: And yet, Theaetetus, if it is not shown to exist, we shall be driven into admitting a number of absurdities.

THEAETETUS: And what would they be?

SOCRATES: I am not going to tell you until I have tried every possible way of looking at this matter. I should be ashamed to see us forced into   191
making the kind of admissions I mean while we are still in difficulties. If we find what we're after, and become free men, then we will turn round and talk about how these things happen to other people—having secured our own persons against ridicule. While if we can't find any way of

---

33. In the Greek the opposition here between 'one' and 'the other' is expressed by the repetition of the word meaning 'other'—thus yielding, literally, the unparadoxical tautology 'the other is other'. As Socrates refrained at 189c–d from taking up the paradoxical construal of Theaetetus' 'truly false', so Theaetetus must refrain from taking up this unparadoxical construal of Socrates' 'one is the other'.

34. A transliteration of a variant Greek expression for 'other-judging' that Socrates uses here.

extricating ourselves, then I suppose we shall be laid low, like seasick passengers, and give ourselves into the hands of the argument and let it trample all over us and do what it likes with us. And now let me tell you where I see a way still open to this inquiry.

THEAETETUS: Yes, do tell me.

SOCRATES: I am going to maintain that we were wrong to agree that it
b   is impossible for a man to be in error through judging that things he knows are things he doesn't know. In a way, it is possible.

THEAETETUS: Now I wonder if you mean the same thing as I too suspected at the time when we suggested it was like that—I mean, that sometimes I, who know Socrates, have seen someone else in the distance whom I don't know and thought it to be Socrates whom I do know. In a case like that, the sort of thing you are referring to does happen.

SOCRATES : But didn't we recoil from this suggestion because it made us not know, when we do know, things which we know?

THEAETETUS: Yes, we certainly did.

SOCRATES: Then don't let us put the case in that way; let's try another
c   way. It may prove amenable or it may be obstinate; but the fact is we are in such an extremity that we need to turn every argument over and over and test it from all sides. Now see if there is anything in this. Is it possible to learn something you didn't know before?

THEAETETUS: Surely it is.

SOCRATES: And again another and yet another thing?

THEAETETUS: Well, why not?

SOCRATES: Now I want you to suppose, for the sake of the argument, that we have in our souls a block of wax, larger in one person, smaller in
d   another, and of purer wax in one case, dirtier in another; in some men rather hard, in others rather soft, while in some it is of the proper consistency.

THEAETETUS: All right, I'm supposing that.

SOCRATES: We may look upon it, then, as a gift of Memory, the mother of the Muses. We make impressions upon this of everything we wish to remember among the things we have seen or heard or thought of ourselves; we hold the wax under our perceptions and thoughts and take a stamp from them, in the way in which we take the imprints of signet rings. Whatever is impressed upon the wax we remember and know so long as
e   the image remains in the wax; whatever is obliterated or cannot be impressed, we forget and do not know.

THEAETETUS: Let that be our supposition.

SOCRATES: Then take the case of a man who knows these things, but is also considering something he is seeing or hearing; and see if he might judge falsely in this way.

THEAETETUS: In what kind of way?

SOCRATES: In thinking, of things which he knows, sometimes that they are things which he knows and sometimes that they are things which he doesn't know—these cases being what at an earlier stage we wrongly admitted to be impossible.

THEAETETUS: And what do you say now?

SOCRATES: We must begin this discussion by making certain distinctions. We must make it clear that it is impossible to think (1) that a thing you know, because you possess the record of it in your soul, but which you are not perceiving, is another thing which you know—you have its imprint too—but are not perceiving, (2) that a thing you know is something you do not know and do not have the seal of, (3) that a thing you don't know is another thing you don't know, (4) that a thing you don't know is a thing you know.

Again, it is impossible to think (1) that a thing you are perceiving is another thing that you are perceiving, (2) that a thing you are perceiving is a thing which you are not perceiving, (3) that a thing you are not perceiving is another thing you are not perceiving, (4) that a thing you are not perceiving is a thing you are perceiving.

Yet again, it is impossible to think (1) that a thing you both know and are perceiving, when you are holding its imprint in line with your perception of it, is another thing which you know and are perceiving, and whose imprint you keep in line with the perception (this indeed is even more impossible than the former cases, if that can be), (2) that a thing which you both know and are perceiving, and the record of which you are keeping in its true line, is another thing you know, (3) that a thing you both know and are perceiving and of which you have the record correctly in line as before, is another thing you are perceiving, (4) that a thing you neither know nor are perceiving is another thing you neither know nor perceive, (5) that a thing you neither know nor perceive is another thing you don't know, (6) that a thing you neither know nor perceive is another thing you are not perceiving.

In all these cases, it is a sheer impossibility that there should be false judgment. It remains that it arises, if anywhere, in the cases I am just going to tell you.

THEAETETUS: What are they? Perhaps I may understand a little better from them; at present, I don't follow.

SOCRATES: In these cases of things you know: when you think (1) that they are other things you know and are perceiving, (2) that they are things you don't know but are perceiving, (3) that things you both know and are perceiving are other things you both know and are perceiving.

THEAETETUS: Well, now you have left me further behind than ever.

SOCRATES: I'll go over it again in another way. I know Theodorus and remember within myself what he is like; and in the same way I know Theaetetus. But sometimes I am seeing them and sometimes not; sometimes I am touching them, and sometimes not; or I may hear them or perceive them through some other sense, while at other times I have no perception about you two at all, but remember you none the less, and know you within myself—isn't that so?

THEAETETUS: Yes, certainly.

SOCRATES: Now please take this first point that I want to make clear to you—that we sometimes perceive and sometimes do not perceive the things that we know.

b

c

d

e

THEAETETUS: That's true.

SOCRATES: Then as regards the things we don't know, we often don't perceive them either, but often we only perceive them.

THEAETETUS: That is so, also.

193   SOCRATES: Now see if you can follow me a little better. Supposing Socrates knows both Theodorus and Theaetetus, but is not seeing either of them, or having any other perception about them: he could never in that case judge within himself that Theaetetus was Theodorus. Is that sense or not?

THEAETETUS: Yes, that's quite true.

SOCRATES: This, then, was the first of the cases I was speaking of.

THEAETETUS: It was.

SOCRATES: Secondly then. Supposing I am acquainted with one of you and not the other, and am perceiving neither of you: in that case, I could never think the one I do know to be the one I don't know.

THEAETETUS: That is so.

b   SOCRATES: Thirdly, supposing I am not acquainted with either of you, and am not perceiving either of you: I could not possibly think that one of you, whom I don't know, is another of you whom I don't know. Now will you please take it that you have heard all over again in succession the other cases described before—the cases in which I shall never judge falsely about you and Theodorus, either when I am familiar or when I am unfamiliar with both of you; or when I know one and not the other. And similarly with perceptions, you follow me.

THEAETETUS: I follow.

SOCRATES: So there remains the possibility of false judgment in this case.

c   I know both you and Theodorus; I have your signs upon that block of wax, like the imprints of rings. Then I see you both in the distance, but cannot see you well enough; but I am in a hurry to refer the proper sign to the proper visual perception, and so get this fitted into the trace of itself, that recognition may take place. This I fail to do; I get them out of line, applying the visual perception of the one to the sign of the other. It is like people putting their shoes on the wrong feet, or like what happens when

d   we look at things in mirrors, when left and right change places. It is then that 'heterodoxy' or false judgment arises.

THEAETETUS: Yes, that seems very likely, Socrates; it is an awfully good description of what happens to the judgment.

SOCRATES: Then, again, supposing I know both of you, and am also perceiving one of you, and not the other, but am not keeping my knowledge of the former in line with my perception—that's the expression I used before and you didn't understand me then.

THEAETETUS: No, I certainly didn't.

SOCRATES: Well, I was saying that if you know one man and perceive

e   him as well, and keep your knowledge of him in line with your perception, you will never take him for some other person whom you know and are perceiving, and the knowledge of whom you are holding straight with the perception. Wasn't that so?

THEAETETUS: Yes.

SOCRATES: There remained, I take it, the case we have just mentioned where false judgment arises in the following manner: you know both men 194 and you are looking at both, or having some other perception of them; and you don't hold the two signs each in line with its own perception, but like a bad archer you shoot beside the mark and miss—which is precisely what we call falsehood.

THEAETETUS: Naturally so.

SOCRATES: And when for one of the signs there is also a present perception but there is not for the other, and you try to fit to the present perception the sign belonging to the absent perception, in all such cases thought is in error.

We may sum up thus: it seems that in the case of things we do not b know and have never perceived, there is no possibility of error or of false judgment, if what we are saying is at all sound; it is in cases where we both know things and are perceiving them that judgment is erratic and varies between truth and falsity. When it brings together the proper stamps and records directly and in straight lines, it is true; when it does so obliquely and crosswise, it is false.

THEAETETUS: Well, isn't that beautiful, Socrates?

SOCRATES: Ah, when you've heard what is coming next, you will say so c all the more. For true judgment is beautiful, right enough, and error is ugly.

THEAETETUS: No doubt about that.

SOCRATES: Well, this, then, they say, is why the two things occur. In some men, the wax in the soul is deep and abundant, smooth and worked to the proper consistency; and when the things that come through the senses are imprinted upon this 'heart' of the soul—as Homer calls it, hinting at the likeness to the wax[35]—the signs that are made in it are lasting, because d they are clear and have sufficient depth. Men with such souls learn easily and remember what they learn; they do not get the signs out of line with the perceptions, but judge truly. As the signs are distinct and there is plenty of room for them, they quickly assign each thing to its own impress in the wax—the things in question being, of course, what we call the things that are and these people being the ones we call wise.

Or do you feel any doubts about this?

THEAETETUS: No, I find it extraordinarily convincing.

SOCRATES: But it is a different matter when a man's 'heart' is 'shaggy' e (the kind of heart our marvellously knowing poet praises), or when it is dirty and of impure wax; or when it is very soft or hard. Persons in whom the wax is soft are quick to learn but quick to forget; when the wax is hard, the opposite happens. Those in whom it is 'shaggy' and rugged, a stony thing with earth or filth mixed all through it, have indistinct impressions. So too if the wax is hard, for then the impressions have no depth; similarly they are indistinct if the wax is soft, because they quickly run 195 together and are blurred. If, in addition to all this, the impresses in the wax are crowded upon each other for lack of space, because it is only

35. *Iliad* ii.851, xvi.554. The word for 'heart' attributed to Homer here is *kear*, which has a superficial resemblance to the word for wax, *kēros*.

some little scrap of a soul, they are even more indistinct. All such people are liable to false judgment. When they see or hear or think of anything, they can't quickly allot each thing to each impress; they are slow and allot things to impresses which do not belong to them, misseeing, mishearing and misthinking most of them—and these in turn are the ones we describe as in error about the things that are and ignorant.

b   THEAETETUS: That's exactly it, Socrates; no man could improve on your account.

SOCRATES: Then are we to say that false judgments do exist in us?

THEAETETUS: Yes, most emphatically.

SOCRATES: And true ones, of course?

THEAETETUS: And true ones.

SOCRATES: And we think we have now reached a satisfactory agreement, when we say that these two kinds of judgment certainly exist?

THEAETETUS: There's no earthly doubt about it, Socrates.

SOCRATES: Theaetetus, I'm afraid a garrulous man is really an awful nuisance.

THEAETETUS: Why, what are you talking about?

c   SOCRATES: I'm annoyed at my own stupidity—my own true garrulousness. What else could you call it when a man will keep dragging arguments up and down, because he is too slow-witted to reach any conviction, and will not be pulled off any of them?

THEAETETUS: But why should *you* be annoyed?

SOCRATES: I am not only annoyed; I am alarmed. I am afraid of what I may say if someone asks me: 'So, Socrates, you've discovered false judgment, have you? You have found that it arises not in the relation of

d   perceptions to one another, or of thoughts to one another, but in the connecting of perception with thought?' I believe I am very likely to say 'Yes', with an air of flattering myself upon our having made some beautiful discovery.

THEAETETUS: Well, Socrates, what you have just shown us looks to me quite a presentable thing anyway.

SOCRATES: 'You mean', he goes on, 'that we would never suppose that a man we are merely thinking of but not seeing is a horse which again we are not seeing or touching, but just thinking of and not perceiving anything else about it?' I suppose I shall agree that we do mean this.

THEAETETUS: Yes, and quite rightly.

e   SOCRATES: 'Well then,' he goes on, 'doesn't it follow from this theory that a man couldn't possibly suppose that eleven, which he is merely thinking about, is twelve, which again he is merely thinking about?' Come now, you answer.

THEAETETUS: Well, my answer will be that someone who is seeing or touching them could suppose that eleven are twelve, but not with those that he has in his thought: he would never judge this in that way about them.

196   SOCRATES: Well, now, take the case where a man is considering five and seven within himself—I don't mean seven men and five men, or anything

of that sort, but five and seven themselves; the records, as we allege, in that waxen block, things among which it is not possible that there should be false judgment. Suppose he is talking to himself about them, and asking himself how many they are. Do you think that in such a case it has ever happened that one man thought they were eleven and said so, while another thought and said that they were twelve? Or do all men say and all men think that they are twelve?

THEAETETUS: Oh, good Heavens, no; lots of people would make them eleven. And with larger numbers they go wrong still more often—for I suppose what you say is intended to apply to all numbers.

SOCRATES: Quite right. And I want you to consider whether what happens here is not just this, that a man thinks that twelve itself, the one on the waxen block, is eleven.

THEAETETUS: It certainly looks as if he does.

SOCRATES: Then haven't we come back to the things we were saying at the outset? You see, anyone to whom this happens is thinking that one thing he knows is another thing he knows. And this we said was impossible; in fact, it was just this consideration which led us to exclude the possibility of false judgment, because, if admitted, it would mean that the same man must, at one and the same time, both know and not know the same objects.

THEAETETUS: That's perfectly true.

SOCRATES: Then we shall have to say that false judgment is something other than a misapplication of thought to perception; because if this were so, we could never be in error so long as we remained within our thoughts themselves. But as the matter now stands, either there is no such thing as false judgment; or a man may not know what he knows. Which do you choose?

THEAETETUS: You are offering me an impossible choice, Socrates.

SOCRATES: But I'm afraid the argument will not permit both. Still— we must stop at nothing; supposing now we were to set about being quite shameless?

THEAETETUS: How?

SOCRATES: By consenting to say what knowing is like.

THEAETETUS: And why should that be shameless?

SOCRATES: You don't seem to realize that our whole discussion from the beginning has been an inquiry about knowledge, on the assumption that we do not yet know what it is.

THEAETETUS: Oh but I do.

SOCRATES: Well, then, don't you think it is a shameless thing that we, who don't know what knowledge is, should pronounce on what knowing is like? But as a matter of fact, Theaetetus, for some time past our whole method of discussion has been tainted. Time and again we have said 'we are acquainted with' and 'we are not acquainted with', 'we know' and 'we do not know', as if we could to some extent understand one another while we are still ignorant of what knowledge is. Or here's another example, if you like: at this very moment, we have again used the words 'to be ignorant of', and 'to understand', as if these were quite proper expressions for us when we are deprived of knowledge.

THEAETETUS: But how are you going to carry on the discussion at all, Socrates, if you keep off these words?

197   SOCRATES: Quite impossible, for a man like me; but if I were one of the experts in contradiction, I might be able to. If one of those gentlemen were present, he would have commanded us to refrain from them, and would keep coming down upon us heavily for the faults I'm referring to. But since we are no good anyway, why don't I make bold to tell you what knowing is like? It seems to me that this might be of some help.

THEAETETUS: Then do be bold, please. And if you don't keep from using these words, we'll forgive you all right.

SOCRATES: Well, then, have you heard what people are saying nowadays that knowing is?

THEAETETUS: I dare say I have; but I don't remember it at the moment.

b   SOCRATES: Well, they say, of course, that it is 'the having of knowledge'.

THEAETETUS: Oh, yes, that's true.

SOCRATES: Let us make a slight change; let us say 'the possession of knowledge'.

THEAETETUS: And how would you say that was different from the first way of putting it?

SOCRATES: Perhaps it isn't at all; but I will tell you what I think the difference is, and then you must help me to examine it.

THEAETETUS: All right—if I can.

SOCRATES: Well, then, to 'possess' doesn't seem to me to be the same as to 'have'. For instance, suppose a man has bought a coat and it is at his disposal but he is not wearing it; we would not say that he 'has' it on, but we would say he 'possesses' it.

THEAETETUS: Yes, that would be correct.

c   SOCRATES: Now look here: is it possible in this way to possess knowledge and not 'have' it? Suppose a man were to hunt wild birds, pigeons or something, and make an aviary for them at his house and look after them there; then, in a sense, I suppose, we might say he 'has' them all the time, because of course he possesses them. Isn't that so?

THEAETETUS: Yes.

SOCRATES: But in another sense he 'has' none of them; it is only that he has acquired a certain power in respect of them, because he has got them

d   under his control in an enclosure of his own. That is to say, he has the power to hunt for any one he likes at any time, and take and 'have' it whenever he chooses, and let it go again; and this he can do as often as he likes.

THEAETETUS: That is so.

SOCRATES: Well a little while ago we were equipping souls with I don't know what sort of a waxen device. Now let us make in each soul a sort of aviary of all kinds of birds; some in flocks separate from the others, some in small groups, and others flying about singly here and there among all the rest.

THEAETETUS: All right, let us suppose it made. What then? e

SOCRATES: Then we must say that when we are children this receptacle is empty; and by the birds we must understand pieces of knowledge. When anyone takes possession of a piece of knowledge and shuts it up in the pen, we should say that he has learned or has found out the thing of which this is the knowledge; and knowing, we should say, is this.

THEAETETUS: That's given, then.

SOCRATES: Now think: when he hunts again for any one of the pieces of 198 knowledge that he chooses, and takes it and 'has' it, then lets it go again, what words are appropriate here? The same as before, when he took possession of the knowledge, or different ones?—You will see my point more clearly in this way. There is an art you call arithmetic, isn't there?

THEAETETUS: Yes.

SOCRATES: Now I want you to think of this as a hunt for pieces of knowledge concerning everything odd and even.

THEAETETUS: All right, I will.

SOCRATES: It is by virtue of this art, I suppose, that a man both has under b his control pieces of knowledge concerning numbers and also hands them over to others?

THEAETETUS: Yes.

SOCRATES: And we call it 'teaching' when a man hands them over to others, and 'learning' when he gets them handed over to him; and when he 'has' them through possessing them in this aviary of ours, we call that 'knowing'.

THEAETETUS: Yes, certainly.

SOCRATES: Now you must give your attention to what is coming next. It must surely be true that a man who has completely mastered arithmetic knows all numbers? Because there are pieces of knowledge covering all numbers in his soul.

THEAETETUS: Of course.

SOCRATES: And a man so trained may proceed to do some counting, c either counting to himself the numbers themselves, or counting something else, one of the external things which have number?

THEAETETUS: Yes, surely.

SOCRATES: And counting we shall take to be simply a matter of considering how large a number actually is?

THEAETETUS: Yes.

SOCRATES: Then it looks as if this man were considering something which he knows as if he did not know it (for we have granted that he knows all numbers). I've no doubt you've had such puzzles put to you.

THEAETETUS: I have, yes.

SOCRATES: Then using our image of possessing and hunting for the pi- d geons, we shall say that there are two phases of hunting; one before you have possession in order to get possession, and another when you already possess in order to catch and have in your hands what you previously acquired. And in this way even with things you learned and got the knowledge of long ago and have known ever since, it is possible to learn them—these same things—all over again. You can take up again and 'have' that knowledge of each of them which you acquired long ago but had not ready to hand in your thought, can't you?

THEAETETUS: True.

e SOCRATES: Now this is what I meant by my question a moment ago. What terms ought we to use about them when we speak of what the arithmetician does when he proceeds to count, or the scholar when he proceeds to read something? Here, it seems, a man who knows something is setting out to learn again from himself things which he already knows.

THEAETETUS: But that would be a very odd thing, Socrates.

SOCRATES: But are we to say that it is things which he does not know
199 that such a man is going to read and count—remembering that we have granted him knowledge of all letters and all numbers?

THEAETETUS: That wouldn't be reasonable, either.

SOCRATES: Then would you like us to take this line? Suppose we say we do not mind at all about the names; let people drag around the terms 'knowing' and 'learning' to their heart's content. We have determined that to 'possess' knowledge is one thing and to 'have' it is another; accordingly we maintain that it is impossible for anyone not to possess that which he has possession of, and thus, it never happens that he does not know something he knows. But he may yet make a false judgment about it. This
b is because it is possible for him to 'have', not the knowledge of this thing, but another piece of knowledge instead. When he is hunting for one piece of knowledge, it may happen, as they fly about, that he makes a mistake and gets hold of one instead of another. It was this that happened when he thought eleven was twelve. He got hold of the knowledge of eleven that was in him, instead of the knowledge of twelve, as you might catch a ring-dove instead of a pigeon.

THEAETETUS: Yes; that is reasonable, now.

SOCRATES: But when he gets hold of the one he is trying to get hold of, then he is free from error; when he does that, he is judging what is. In
c this way, both true and false judgment exist; and the things that worried us before no longer stand in our way. I daresay you'll agree with me? Or, if not, what line will you take?

THEAETETUS: I agree.

SOCRATES: Yes; we have now got rid of this 'not knowing what one knows'. For we now find that at no point does it happen that we do not possess what we possess, whether we are in error about anything or not. But it looks to me as if something else more alarming is by way of coming upon us.

THEAETETUS: What's that?

SOCRATES: I mean, what is involved if false judgment is going to become a matter of an interchange of pieces of knowledge.

THEAETETUS: What do you mean?

SOCRATES: To begin with, it follows that a man who has knowledge of   d
something is ignorant of this very thing not through want of knowledge but actually in virtue of his knowledge. Secondly, he judges that this is something else and that the other thing is it. Now surely this is utterly unreasonable; it means that the soul, when knowledge becomes present to it, knows nothing and is wholly ignorant. According to this argument, there is no reason why an accession of ignorance should not make one know something, or of blindness make one see something, if knowledge is ever going to make a man ignorant.

THEAETETUS: Well, perhaps, Socrates, it wasn't a happy thought to make   e
the birds only pieces of knowledge. Perhaps we ought to have supposed that there are pieces of ignorance also flying about in the soul along with them, and what happens is that the hunter sometimes catches a piece of knowledge and sometimes a piece of ignorance concerning the same thing; and the ignorance makes him judge falsely, while the knowledge makes him judge truly.

SOCRATES: I can hardly refrain from expressing my admiration of you, Theaetetus; but do think again about that. Let us suppose it is as you say: then, you maintain, the man who catches a piece of ignorance will judge   200
falsely. Is that it?

THEAETETUS: Yes.

SOCRATES: But presumably he will not think he is judging falsely?

THEAETETUS: No, of course he won't.

SOCRATES: He will think he is judging what is true; and his attitude towards the things about which he is in error will be as if he knew them.

THEAETETUS: Of course.

SOCRATES: He will think he has hunted down and 'has' a piece of knowledge and not a piece of ignorance.

THEAETETUS: Yes, that's clear.

SOCRATES: So, after going a long way round, we are back at our original difficulty. Our friend the expert in refutation will laugh. 'My very good   b
people,' he will say, 'do you mean that a man who knows both knowledge and ignorance is thinking that one of them which he knows is the other which he knows? Or is it that he knows neither, and judges the one he doesn't know to be the other which he doesn't know? Or is it that he knows one and not the other, and judges that the one he knows is the one he doesn't know? Or does he think that the one he doesn't know is the one he does? Or are you going to start all over again and tell me that there's another set of pieces of knowledge concerning pieces of knowledge and ignorance, which a man may possess shut up in some other ridiculous aviaries or waxen devices, which he knows so long as he possesses them   c
though he may not have them ready to hand in his soul—and in this way

end up forced to come running round to the same place over and over again and never get any further?' What are we going to say to that, Theaetetus?

THEAETETUS: Oh, dear me, Socrates, I don't know what one ought to say.

SOCRATES: Then don't you think, my boy, that the argument is perhaps dealing out a little proper chastisement, and showing us that we were

d wrong to leave the question about knowledge and proceed to inquire into false judgment first? While as a matter of fact it's impossible to know this until we have an adequate grasp of what knowledge is.

THEAETETUS: Well, at the moment, Socrates, I feel bound to believe you.

SOCRATES: Then, to go back to the beginning, what are we going to say knowledge is?—We are not, I suppose, going to give up yet?

THEAETETUS: Certainly not, unless you give up yourself.

SOCRATES: Tell me, then, how could we define it with the least risk of contradicting ourselves?

e THEAETETUS: In the way we were attempting before, Socrates; I can't think of any other.

SOCRATES: In what way do you mean?

THEAETETUS: By saying that knowledge is true judgment. Judging truly is at least something free of mistakes, I take it, and everything that results from it is admirable and good.

SOCRATES: Well, Theaetetus, as the man who was leading the way across

201 the river said, 'It will show you.'[36] If we go on and track this down, perhaps we may stumble on what we are looking for; if we stay where we are, nothing will come clear.

THEAETETUS: You're right; let's go on and consider it.

SOCRATES: Well, this won't take long to consider, anyway; there is a whole art indicating to you that knowledge is not what you say.

THEAETETUS: How's that? What art do you mean?

SOCRATES: The art of the greatest representatives of wisdom—the men called orators and lawyers. These men, I take it, use their art to produce conviction not by teaching people, but by making them judge whatever they themselves choose. Or do you think there are any teachers so clever

b that within the short time allowed by the clock they can teach adequately to people who were not eye-witnesses the truth of what happened to people who have been robbed or assaulted?

THEAETETUS: No, I don't think they possibly could; but they might be able to *persuade* them.

SOCRATES: And by 'persuading them', you mean 'causing them to judge', don't you?

THEAETETUS: Of course.

SOCRATES: Then suppose a jury has been justly persuaded of some matter which only an eye-witness could know, and which cannot otherwise be

---

36. According to the scholiast the story was: some travellers came to the bank of a river, which they wished to cross at the ford; one of them asked the guide, 'Is the water deep?' He said, 'It will show you', i.e., you must try it for yourself.

known; suppose they come to their decision upon hearsay, forming a c
true judgment: then they have decided the case without knowledge, but,
granted they did their job well, being correctly persuaded?

THEAETETUS: Yes, certainly.

SOCRATES: But, my dear lad, they couldn't have done that if true judgment
is the same thing as knowledge; in that case the best juryman in the world
couldn't form a correct judgment without knowledge. So it seems they
must be different things.

THEAETETUS: Oh, yes, Socrates, that's just what I once heard a man say;
I had forgotten, but now it's coming back to me. He said that it is true d
judgment with an account[37] that is knowledge; true judgment without an
account falls outside of knowledge. And he said that the things of which
there is no account are not knowable (yes, he actually called them that),[38]
while those which have an account are knowable.

SOCRATES: Very good indeed. Now tell me, how did he distinguish these
knowables and unknowables? I want to see if you and I have heard the
same version.

THEAETETUS: I don't know if I can find that out; but I think I could follow
if someone explained it.

SOCRATES: Listen then to a dream in return for a dream. In my dream,
too, I thought I was listening to people saying that the primary elements, e
as it were, of which we and everything else are composed, have no account.
Each of them, in itself, can only be named; it is not possible to say anything
else of it, either that it is or that it is not. That would mean that we were 202
adding being or not-being to it; whereas we must not attach anything, if
we are to speak of that thing itself alone. Indeed we ought not to apply
to it even such words as 'itself' or 'that', 'each', 'alone', or 'this', or any
other of the many words of this kind; for these go the round and are
applied to all things alike, being other than the things to which they are
added, whereas if it were possible to express the element itself and it had
its own proprietary account, it would have to be expressed without any
other thing. As it is, however, it is impossible that any of the primaries b
should be expressed in an account; it can only be named, for a name is
all that it has. But with the things composed of these, it is another matter.
Here, just in the same way as the elements themselves are woven together,
so their names may be woven together and become an account of something—an account being essentially a complex of names. Thus the elements
are unaccountable and unknowable, but they are perceivable, whereas the

---

37. 'Account' translates *logos*, which can also mean 'statement,' 'argument', 'speech',
and 'discourse'.

38. The parenthesis may alternatively be translated: '(that was the word he used)'. The
translation in the text expresses surprise about the claim that some things are not knowable at all. The alternative translation calls attention to the particular Greek word used
for 'knowable'.

complexes are both knowable and expressible and can be the objects of true judgment.

c Now when a man gets a true judgment about something without an account, his soul is in a state of truth as regards that thing, but he does not know it; for someone who cannot give and take an account of a thing is ignorant about it. But when he has also got an account of it, he is capable of all this and is made perfect in knowledge. Was the dream you heard the same as this or a different one?

THEAETETUS: No, it was the same in every respect.

SOCRATES: Do you like this then, and do you suggest that knowledge is true judgment with an account?

THEAETETUS: Yes, certainly.

d SOCRATES: Theaetetus, can it be that all in a moment, you and I have today laid hands upon something which many a wise man has searched for in the past—and gone gray before he found it?

THEAETETUS: Well, it does seem to me anyway, Socrates, that what has just been said puts the matter very well.

SOCRATES: And it seems likely enough that the matter is really so; for what knowledge could there be apart from an account and correct judgment? But there is one of the things said which I don't like.

THEAETETUS: And what's that?

SOCRATES: What looks like the subtlest point of all—that the elements

e are unknowable and the complexes knowable.

THEAETETUS: And won't that do?

SOCRATES: We must make sure; because, you see, we do have as hostages for this theory the original models that were used when all these statements were made.

THEAETETUS: What models?

SOCRATES: Letters—the elements of language—and syllables.[39] It must have been these, mustn't it, that the author of our theory had in view— it couldn't have been anything else?

THEAETETUS: No, he must have been thinking of letters and syllables.

203 SOCRATES: Let's take and examine them then. Or rather let us examine ourselves, and ask ourselves whether we really learned our letters in this way or not. Now, to begin with, one can give an account of the syllables but not of the letters—is that it?

THEAETETUS: Well, perhaps.

SOCRATES: It most certainly looks like that to me. At any rate, supposing you were asked about the first syllable of 'Socrates': 'Tell me, Theaetetus, what is SO?' What would you answer to that?

THEAETETUS: That it's S and O.

SOCRATES: And there you have an account of the syllable?

---

39. 'Letters' translates *stoicheia*, which can also mean 'elements' more generally (and is so translated sometimes below). 'Syllables': in Greek *sullabai*, also translated below as 'complexes.'

THEAETETUS: Yes.

SOCRATES: Come along then, and let us have the account of S in the same way.   b

THEAETETUS: How *can* anyone give the letters of a letter? S is just one of the voiceless letters, Socrates, a mere sound like a hissing of the tongue. B again has neither voice nor sound, and that's true of most letters. So the statement that they themselves are unaccountable holds perfectly good. Even the seven clearest have only voice; no sort of account whatever can be given of them.[40]

SOCRATES: So here, my friend, we have established a point about knowledge.

THEAETETUS: We do appear to have done so.

SOCRATES: Well then: we have shown that the syllable is knowable but not the letter—is that all right?   c

THEAETETUS: It seems the natural conclusion, anyway.

SOCRATES: Look here, what do we mean by 'the syllable'? The two letters (or if there are more, all the letters)? Or do we mean some single form produced by their combination?

THEAETETUS: I think we mean all the letters.

SOCRATES: Then take the case of the two letters, S and O; these two are the first syllable of my name. If a man knows the syllable, he must know both the letters?

THEAETETUS: Of course.   d

SOCRATES: So he knows S and O.

THEAETETUS: Yes.

SOCRATES: But can it be that he is ignorant of each one, and knows the two of them without knowing either?

THEAETETUS: That would be a strange and unaccountable thing, Socrates.

SOCRATES: And yet, supposing it is necessary to know each in order to know both, then it is absolutely necessary that anyone who is ever to know a syllable must first get to know the letters. And in admitting this, we shall find that our beautiful theory has taken to its heels and got clean away from us.

THEAETETUS: And very suddenly too.   e

SOCRATES: Yes; we are not keeping a proper watch on it. Perhaps we ought not to have supposed the syllable to be the letters; perhaps we ought to have made it some single form produced out of them, having its own single nature—something different from the letters.

THEAETETUS: Yes, certainly; that might be more like it.

SOCRATES: We must look into the matter; we have no right to betray a great and imposing theory in this faint-hearted manner.

THEAETETUS: Certainly not.

---

40. I.e., the seven vowels of ancient Greek, as contrasted with two classes of consonant: mutes like B, which cannot be pronounced without a vowel, and semivowels like S, which can.

204 SOCRATES: Then let it be as we are now suggesting. Let the complex be a single form resulting from the combination of the several elements when they fit together; and let this hold both of language and of things in general.

THEAETETUS: Yes, certainly.

SOCRATES: Then it must have no parts.

THEAETETUS: Why is that, now?

SOCRATES: Because when a thing has parts, the whole is necessarily all the parts. Or do you mean by 'the whole' also a single form arising out of the parts, yet different from all the parts?

THEAETETUS: I do.

b SOCRATES: Now do you call 'sum'[41] and 'whole' the same thing or different things?

THEAETETUS: I don't feel at all certain; but as you keep telling me to answer up with a good will, I will take a risk and say they are different.

SOCRATES: Your good will, Theaetetus, is all that it should be. Now we must see if your answer is too.

THEAETETUS: We must, of course.

SOCRATES: As the argument stands at present, the whole will be different from the sum?

THEAETETUS: Yes.

SOCRATES: Well now, is there any difference between all the things and c the sum? For instance, when we say 'one, two, three, four, five, six'; or, 'twice three', or 'three times two', 'four and two', 'three and two and one'; are we speaking of the same thing in all these cases or different things?

THEAETETUS: The same thing.

SOCRATES: That is, six?

THEAETETUS: Precisely.

SOCRATES: Then with each expression have we not spoken of all the six?

THEAETETUS: Yes.

SOCRATES: And when we speak of them all, aren't we speaking of a sum?

THEAETETUS: We must be.

SOCRATES: That is, six?

THEAETETUS: Precisely.

d SOCRATES: Then in all things made up of number, at any rate, by 'the sum' and 'all of them' we mean the same thing?

THEAETETUS: So it seems.

SOCRATES: Now let us talk about them in this way. The number of an acre is the same thing as an acre, isn't it?

THEAETETUS: Yes.

SOCRATES: Similarly with a mile.

THEAETETUS: Yes.

41. The word translated 'sum' (*pan*) and the word translated 'all' (*panta*) in the phrase 'all the parts' are singular and plural forms of the same Greek word.

SOCRATES: And the number of an army is the same as the army? And so always with things of this sort; their total number is the sum that each of them is.

THEAETETUS: Yes.

SOCRATES: But is the number of each anything other than its parts? e

THEAETETUS: No.

SOCRATES: Now things which have parts consist of parts?

THEAETETUS: That seems true.

SOCRATES: And it is agreed that all the parts are the sum, seeing that the total number is to be the sum.

THEAETETUS: That is so.

SOCRATES: Then the whole does not consist of parts. For if it did, it would be all the parts and so would be a sum.

THEAETETUS: It looks as if it doesn't.

SOCRATES: But can a part, as such, be a part of anything but the whole?

THEAETETUS: Yes; of the sum.

SOCRATES: You are putting up a good fight anyway, Theaetetus. But this 205 sum now—isn't it just when there is nothing lacking that it is a sum?

THEAETETUS: Yes, necessarily.

SOCRATES: And won't this very same thing—that from which nothing anywhere is lacking—be a whole? While a thing from which something is absent is neither a whole nor a sum—the same consequence having followed from the same condition in both cases at once?

THEAETETUS: Well, it doesn't seem to me now that there can be any difference between whole and sum.

SOCRATES: Very well. Now were we not saying[42] that in the case of a thing that has parts, both the whole and the sum will be all the parts?

THEAETETUS: Yes, certainly.

SOCRATES: Now come back to the thing I was trying to get at just now.[43] Supposing the syllable is not just its letters, doesn't it follow that it cannot b contain the letters as parts of itself? Alternatively, if it is the same as the letters, it must be equally knowable with them?

THEAETETUS: That is so.

SOCRATES: Well, wasn't it just in order to avoid this result that we supposed it different from the letters?

THEAETETUS: Yes.

SOCRATES: Well then, if the letters are not parts of the syllable, can you tell me of any other things, not its letters, which are?

THEAETETUS: No, indeed. If I were to admit that it had component parts, Socrates, it would be ridiculous, of course, to set aside the letters and look for other components.

42. At 204a.
43. See 203d–e.

c   SOCRATES: Then, Theaetetus, according to our present argument, a syllable is an absolutely single form, indivisible into parts.

THEAETETUS: It looks like it.

SOCRATES: Now, my friend, a little while ago, if you remember, we were inclined to accept a certain proposition which we thought put the matter very well—I mean the statement that no account can be given of the primaries of which other things are constituted, because each of them is in itself incomposite; and that it would be incorrect to apply even the term 'being' to it when we spoke of it or the term 'this', because these terms signify different and alien things; and that is the reason why a primary is an unaccountable and unknowable thing. Do you remember?

THEAETETUS: I remember.

d   SOCRATES: And is that the reason also why it is single in form and indivisible into parts or is there some other reason for that?[44] I can see no other myself.

THEAETETUS: No, there really doesn't seem to be any other.

SOCRATES: And hasn't the complex now fallen into the same class as the primary, seeing it has no parts and is a single form?

THEAETETUS: Yes, it certainly has.

SOCRATES: Well now, if the complex is both many elements and a whole, with them as its parts, then both complexes and elements are equally capable of being known and expressed, since all the parts turned out to be the same thing as the whole.

e   THEAETETUS: Yes, surely.

SOCRATES: But if, on the other hand, the complex is single and without parts, then complexes and elements are equally unaccountable and unknowable—both of them for the same reason.

THEAETETUS: I can't dispute that.

SOCRATES: Then if anyone tries to tell us that the complex can be known and expressed, while the contrary is true of the element, we had better not listen to him.

THEAETETUS: No, we'd better not, if we go along with the argument.

206   SOCRATES: And, more than this, wouldn't you more easily believe somebody who made the contrary statement, because of what you know of your own experience in learning to read and write?

THEAETETUS: What kind of thing do you mean?

SOCRATES: I mean that when you were learning you spent your time just precisely in trying to distinguish, by both eye and ear, each individual letter in itself so that you might not be bewildered by their different positions in written and spoken words.

THEAETETUS: That's perfectly true.

---

44. Alternatively (accepting the conjecture of *to* for *touto* at 205d): 'And is there any other reason for this than that it is single in form and indivisible into parts?'

SOCRATES: And at the music-teacher's, wasn't the finished pupil the one who would follow each note and tell to which string it belonged—the notes being generally admitted to be the elements in music?   b

THEAETETUS: Yes, that's just what it amounted to.

SOCRATES: Then if the proper procedure is to take such elements and complexes as we ourselves have experience of, and make an inference from them to the rest, we shall say that the elements are much more clearly known, and the knowledge of them is more decisive for the mastery of any branch of study than knowledge of the complex. And if anyone maintains that the complex is by nature knowable, and the element unknowable, we shall regard this as tomfoolery, whether it is intended to be or not.

THEAETETUS: Oh, quite.

SOCRATES: I think that might be proved in other ways too. But we mustn't   c
let them distract us from the problem before us. We wanted to see what can be meant by the proposition that it is in the addition of an account to a true judgment that knowledge is perfected.

THEAETETUS: Well yes, we must try to see that.

SOCRATES: Come then, what are we intended to understand by an 'account'? I think it must be one of three meanings.

THEAETETUS: What are they?

SOCRATES: The first would be, making one's thought apparent vocally   d
by means of words and verbal expressions—when a man impresses an image of his judgment upon the stream of speech, like reflections upon water or in a mirror. Don't you think this kind of thing is an account?

THEAETETUS: Yes, I do. At least, a man who does this is said to be giving an account.[45]

SOCRATES: But isn't that a thing that everyone is able to do more or less readily—I mean, indicate what he thinks about a thing, if he is not deaf or dumb to begin with? And that being so, anyone at all who makes a correct judgment will turn out to have it 'together with an account'; correct   e
judgment without knowledge will no longer be found anywhere.

THEAETETUS: True.

SOCRATES: Well then, we mustn't be too ready to condemn the author of the definition of knowledge now before us for talking nonsense. Perhaps he didn't mean this; perhaps he meant being able, when questioned about   207
what a thing is, to give an answer by reference to its elements.

THEAETETUS: As for example, Socrates?

SOCRATES: As for example, what Hesiod is doing when he says, 'One hundred are the timbers of a wagon.'[46] Now I couldn't say what they are; and I don't suppose you could either. If you and I were asked what a

---

45. 'Giving an account' here translates *legein*, the ordinary Greek word for 'say, speak, speak of,' which corresponds to *logos* in its wider meanings 'speech, discourse, statement'.

46. *Works and Days* 456.

wagon is, we should be satisfied if we could answer, 'Wheels, axle, body, rails, yoke.'

THEAETETUS: Yes, surely.

SOCRATES: But he might think us ridiculous, just as he would if we were asked what your name is, and replied by giving the syllables. In that case,

b   he would think us ridiculous because although we might be correct in our judgment and our expression of it, we should be fancying ourselves as scholars, thinking we knew and were expressing a scholar's account of Theaetetus' name. Whereas in fact no one gives an account of a thing with knowledge till, in addition to his true judgment, he goes right through the thing element by element—as I think we said before.

THEAETETUS: We did, yes.

SOCRATES: In the same way, in the example of the wagon, he would say

c   that we have indeed correct judgment; but it is the man who can explore its being by going through those hundred items who has made the addition which adds an account to his true judgment. It is this man who has passed from mere judgment to expert knowledge of the being of a wagon; and he has done so in virtue of having gone over the whole by means of the elements.

THEAETETUS: And doesn't that seem sound to you, Socrates?

SOCRATES: Well, tell me if it seems sound to you, my friend. Tell me if you are prepared to accept the view that an account is a matter of going through a thing element by element, while going through it by 'syllables'

d   or larger divisions falls short of being an account. Then we shall be able to discuss it.

THEAETETUS: I'm certainly prepared to accept that.

SOCRATES: And do you at the same time think that a man has knowledge of anything when he believes the same thing now to be part of one thing and now part of something else? Or when he judges that now one thing and now something different belongs to one and the same object?

THEAETETUS: No, indeed I don't.

SOCRATES: Then have you forgotten that at first when you were learning to read and write that is just what you and the other boys used to do?

THEAETETUS: You mean we used to think that sometimes one letter

e   and sometimes another belonged to the same syllable, and used to put the same letter sometimes into its proper syllable and sometimes into another?

SOCRATES: Yes, that is what I mean.

THEAETETUS: Well, I certainly haven't forgotten; and I don't think people at that stage can be said to have knowledge yet.

SOCRATES: Well, suppose now that someone who is at this sort of stage is writing the name 'Theaetetus'; he thinks he ought to write THE and

208 does so. Then suppose another time he is trying to write 'Theodorus', and this time he thinks he should write TE and proceeds to do so. Are we going to say that he knows the first syllable of your names?

THEAETETUS: No. We've admitted that anyone who is at that stage has not yet knowledge.

SOCRATES: And is there anything to prevent the same person being in that situation as regards the second and third and fourth syllables?

THEAETETUS: No, nothing.

SOCRATES: Now at the time when he does this, he will be writing 'Theaetetus' not only with correct judgment, but with command of the way through its letters; that must be so whenever he writes them out one after another in their order.

THEAETETUS: Yes, clearly.

SOCRATES: And still without knowledge though with correct judgment—   b
isn't that our view?

THEAETETUS: Yes.

SOCRATES: Yet possessing an account of it along with his correct judgment. He was writing it, you see, with command of the way through its letters; and we agreed that that is an account.

THEAETETUS: True.

SOCRATES: So here, my friend, we have correct judgment together with an account, which we are not yet entitled to call knowledge.

THEAETETUS: Yes, I'm afraid that's so.

SOCRATES: So it was only the poor man's dream of gold that we had when we thought we had got the truest account of knowledge. Or is it early days to be harsh? Perhaps this is not the way in which one is to   c
define 'account'. We said that the man who defines knowledge as correct judgment together with an account would choose one of three meanings for 'account'. Perhaps the last is the one to define it by.

THEAETETUS: Yes, you're right to remind me; there is one possibility still left. The first was, a kind of vocal image of thought; the one we have just discussed was the way to the whole through the elements. Now what's your third suggestion?

SOCRATES: What the majority of people would say—namely, being able to tell some mark by which the object you are asked about differs from all other things.

THEAETETUS: Can you give me an example of such an 'account' of something?

SOCRATES: Well, take the sun, if you like. You would be satisfied, I   d
imagine, with the answer that it is the brightest of the bodies that move round the earth in the heavens.

THEAETETUS: Oh yes, quite.

SOCRATES: Now I want you to get hold of the principle that this illustrates. It is what we were just saying—that if you get hold of the difference that distinguishes a thing from everything else, then, so some people say, you will have got an account of it. On the other hand, so long as it is some common feature that you grasp, your account will be about all those things which have this in common.

e   THEAETETUS: I see; I think it's very good to call this kind of thing an account.

SOCRATES: Then if a man with correct judgment about any one of the things that are grasps in addition its difference from the rest, he has become a knower of the thing he was a judger of before.

THEAETETUS: That's our present position, anyway.

SOCRATES: Well, at this point, Theaetetus, as regards what we are saying, I'm for all the world like a man looking at a shadow-painting;[47] when I'm close up to it I can't take it in in the least, though when I stood well back from it, it appeared to me to have some meaning.

THEAETETUS: How's that?

209   SOCRATES: I'll see if I can explain. Suppose I have formed a correct judgment about you; if I can grasp your account in addition, I know you, but if not, I am merely judging you.

THEAETETUS: Yes.

SOCRATES: And an account was to be a matter of expounding your differentness?

THEAETETUS: That is so.

SOCRATES: Then when I was merely judging, my thought failed to grasp any point of difference between you and the rest of mankind?

THEAETETUS: Apparently.

SOCRATES: What I had in mind, it seems, was some common characteristic—something that belongs no more to you than to anybody else.

b   THEAETETUS: Yes, that must be so.

SOCRATES: Then tell me, in Heaven's name how, if that was so, did it come about that you were the object of my judgment and nobody else? Suppose my thought is that 'This is Theaetetus—one who is a human being, and has a nose and eyes and mouth', and so on through the whole list of limbs. Will this thought cause me to be thinking of Theaetetus rather than of Theodorus, or of the proverbial 'remotest Mysian'?

THEAETETUS: No, how could it?

SOCRATES: But suppose I think not merely of 'the one with nose and eyes', but of 'the one with a snub nose and prominent eyes'. Shall I even then be judging you any more than myself or anyone who is like that?

THEAETETUS: Not at all.

SOCRATES: It will not, I take it, be Theaetetus who is judged in my mind until this snub-nosedness of yours has left imprinted and established in me a record that is different in some way from the other snub-nosednesses I have seen; and so with the other details of your makeup. And this will remind me, if I meet you tomorrow, and make me judge correctly about you.

---

47. The pictorial technique referred to (*skiagraphia*) seems to have been one which depended on contrasts between light and shade to create the appearance of form and volume. A more familiar comparison for modern readers would be a pointilliste painting by Seurat.

THEAETETUS: That's perfectly true.

SOCRATES: Then correct judgment also must be concerned with the differentness of what it is about?   d

THEAETETUS: So it seems, anyway.

SOCRATES: Then what more might this 'adding an account to correct judgment' be? If, on the one hand, it means that we must make another judgment about the way in which a thing differs from the rest of things, we are being required to do something very absurd.

THEAETETUS: How's that?

SOCRATES: Because we already have a correct judgment about the way a thing differs from other things; and we are then directed to add a correct judgment about the way it differs from other things. At that rate, the way a roller goes round or a pestle or anything else proverbial would be nothing   e
compared with such directions; they might be more justly called a matter of 'the blind leading the blind'. To tell us to add what we already have, in order to come to know what we are judging about, bears a generous resemblance to the behavior of a man benighted.

THEAETETUS: Whereas if, on the other hand, ... ?[48] What else were you going to suggest when you started this inquiry just now?

SOCRATES: Well, if 'adding an account' means that we are required to get to *know* the differentness, not merely judge it, this most splendid of our accounts of knowledge turns out to be a very amusing affair. For   210
getting to know of course is acquiring knowledge, isn't it?

THEAETETUS: Yes.

SOCRATES: So, it seems, the answer to the question 'What is knowledge?' will be 'Correct judgment accompanied by *knowledge* of the differentness'— for this is what we are asked to understand by the 'addition of an account.'

THEAETETUS: Apparently so.

SOCRATES: And it is surely just silly to tell us, when we are trying to discover what knowledge is, that it is correct judgment accompanied by *knowledge*, whether of differentness or of anything else? And so, Theaetetus, knowledge is neither perception nor true judgment, nor an account added   b
to true judgment.

THEAETETUS: It seems not.

SOCRATES: Well now, dear lad, are we still pregnant, still in labor with any thoughts about knowledge? Or have we been delivered of them all?

THEAETETUS: As far as I'm concerned, Socrates, you've made me say far more than ever was in me, Heaven knows.

SOCRATES: Well then, our art of midwifery tells us that all of these offspring are wind-eggs and not worth bringing up?

THEAETETUS: Undoubtedly.

SOCRATES: And so, Theaetetus, if ever in the future you should attempt to conceive or should succeed in conceiving other theories, they will be   c
better ones as the result of this inquiry. And if you remain barren, your

48. Reading *Ei ge dē* . . . for *Eipe dē* at 209e5.

companions will find you gentler and less tiresome; you will be modest and not think you know what you don't know. This is all my art can achieve—nothing more. I do not know any of the things that other men know—the great and inspired men of today and yesterday. But this art of midwifery my mother and I had allotted to us by God; she to deliver women, I to deliver men that are young and generous of spirit, all that have any beauty. And now I must go to the King's Porch to meet the indictment that Meletus has brought against me; but let us meet here again in the morning, Theodorus.

210d

SOPHIST

The day following their conversation in Theaetetus, *the geometer Theodorus, together with his Athenian pupils Theaetetus and Socrates' young namesake, rejoins Socrates for further discussion. They bring with them a philosopher visiting from Elea, a Greek town of Southern Italy famous as home to the great philosopher Parmenides and his pupil, the logician Zeno—both of whom Socrates had encountered in yet another dialogue closely linked to this one,* Parmenides. *Socrates asks whether this visitor and the others at Elea treat the philosopher, the statesman, and the sophist as actually being just one thing—a single sort of person, though appearing to different people as falling under just one or another of these headings—or rather as having three distinct intellectual capacities, as their three names indicate. Hearing that the latter is the Eleatics' view, he thus initiates two successive, complex discussions. First, in* Sophist, *the visitor, opting to use Socrates' favorite procedure of question and answer, displays in full detail his own conception of the sophist. In* Statesman *he then continues in a similar way with the statesman. There is no third discussion of the philosopher, despite occasional suggestions that the initial agenda calls for one. The visitor, after all, is a distinguished philosopher. Perhaps Plato's intention is to mark the philosopher off for us from these other two through showing a supreme philosopher at work defining them and therein demonstrating his own devotion to truth, and the correct method of analysis for achieving it: for Plato these together define the philosopher.*

In defining the sophist, the visitor employs the 'method of division'—or, more accurately, of 'collection and division'—described in Phaedrus *265d ff. and early on in* Philebus; *this also underlies the latter's discussion of the varieties of pleasure and knowledge. He first offers six distinct routes for understanding the sophist, by systematically demarcating specific classes within successively smaller, nested, more inclusive classes of practitioners; these specific subclasses are then identified as the sophists. Apparently 'sophistry' is a somewhat loosely associated set of distinct capacities—it hunts rich, prominent young men so as to receive a wage for speaking persuasively to them about virtue, it sells (in several different circumstances) items of alleged knowledge on this same subject, it is expert at winning private debates about right and wrong, it cleanses people's souls by refuting their false or poorly supported ideas. Yet in a final accounting—whose long-delayed completion is reached only at the very end of the dialogue—the sophist is 'penned in' as one who,*

*though aware that he does not know anything, produces in words totally inade-
quate 'copies' of the truth on important subjects, ones he makes appear to others to be the truth, even though, being false, they are hardly even like it. The
relation of this final definition to the six first ones is not fully explored. The visitor may be intimating the general principle that sometimes a 'nature' or real
'kind' has no single place in a systematic division; it unifies a set of differently
located functions, each with its own differences from its more immediate intellectual neighbors. In any case, the essential idea of the 'method of collection
and division' is that each thing is to be understood through a full, lively awareness of its similarities and differences in relation to other things—the sort of
awareness that the varied divisions encourage us to reach. Much other general
instruction on how to make proper use of the 'method' is given in* Statesman.

*The visitor delays completing his final accounting because he sees the need
first to show how it is even possible for anyone to do what he wants to say the
sophist does do—speak words that appear to be true but in fact are false. The
trouble is that he understands speaking falsely as saying 'what is not', while
his teacher Parmenides famously maintained that that is impossible: so he is required to engage in 'parricide'—in showing how Parmenides was wrong. There
ensues an elaborate discussion of the meaning of 'what is' as well as of 'what
is not', in which we can see Plato working out a new theory of the nature of
the Form of being, and its relations to other 'greatest' or most comprehensive
Forms: such a theory is needed to make saying 'what is not'—speaking
falsely—intelligible after all. Much of the interest of the dialogue has always
been found in this metaphysical excursion into the topic of being—and not being—in general.*

J.M.C.

216   THEODORUS: We've come at the proper time by yesterday's agreement,
Socrates. We're also bringing this man who's visiting us. He's from Elea
and he's a member of the group who gather around Parmenides and Zeno.
And he's very much a philosopher.

SOCRATES: Are you bringing a visitor, Theodorus? Or are you bringing
a god without realizing it instead, like the ones Homer mentions? He says
b   gods accompany people who are respectful and just.[1] He also says the god
of visitors—who's at least as much a god as any other—is a companion
who keeps an eye on people's actions, both the criminal and the lawful
ones. So your visitor might be a greater power following along with you,

Translated by Nicholas P. White.

1. See *Odyssey* ix.270–71.

a sort of god of refutation to keep watch on us and show how bad we are at speaking—and to refute us.

THEODORUS: That's not our visitor's style, Socrates. He's more moderate than the enthusiasts for debating are. And he doesn't seem to me to be a god at all. He *is* divine—but then I call all philosophers that.   c

SOCRATES: And that's the right thing for you to do, my friend. But probably it's no easier, I imagine, to distinguish that kind of person than it is to distinguish gods. Certainly the genuine philosophers who "haunt our cities"[2]—by contrast to the fake ones—take on all sorts of different appearances just because of other people's ignorance. As philosophers look down from above at the lives of those below them, some people think they're worthless and others think they're worth everything in the world. Sometimes they take on the appearance of statesmen, and sometimes of sophists.   d
Sometimes, too, they might give the impression that they're completely insane. But if it's all right with our visitor I'd be glad to have him tell us what the people where he comes from used to apply the following names to, and what they thought about these things?   217

THEODORUS: What things?

SOCRATES: *Sophist, statesman,* and *philosopher.*

THEODORUS: What, or what kind of thing, especially makes you consider asking that question? What special problem about them do you have in mind?

SOCRATES: This: did they think that sophists, statesmen, and philosophers make up one kind of thing or two? Or did they divide them up into three kinds corresponding to the three names and attach one name to each of them?

THEODORUS: I don't think it would offend him to tell us about it. Or would it, sir?

VISITOR: No, Theodorus, it wouldn't offend me. I don't have any objection.   b
And the answer is easy: they think there are three kinds. Distinguishing clearly what each of them is, though, isn't a small or easy job.

THEODORUS: Luckily, Socrates, you've gotten hold of words that are very much like the ones we happened to be asking him about. And he made the same excuse to us that he made to you just now—since he's heard a lot about the issue, after all, and hasn't forgotten it.

SOCRATES: In that case, sir, don't refuse our very first request. Tell us   c
this. When you want to explain something to somebody, do you usually prefer to explain it by yourself in a long speech, or to do it with questions? That's the way Parmenides did it one time, when he was very old and I was young.[3] He used questions to generate a very fine discussion.

---

2. See *Odyssey* xvii.483–87. . . . gods go from town to town disguised as visitors of varied appearance, just like Odysseus on this occasion, to observe the deeds of just and unjust people.

3. The reference is to the conversation in the *Parmenides.*

d   VISITOR: It's easier to do it the second way, Socrates, if you're talking with someone who's easy to handle and isn't a trouble-maker. Otherwise it's easier to do it alone.

    SOCRATES: You can pick anyone here you want. They'll all answer you politely. But if you take my advice you'll choose one of the young ones— Theaetetus here or for that matter any of the others you prefer.

    VISITOR: As long as I'm here with you for the first time, Socrates, I'd be
e embarrassed not to make our meeting a conversational give-and-take, but instead to stretch things out and give a long continuous speech by myself or even to someone else, as if I were delivering an oration. A person wouldn't expect the issue you just mentioned to be as small as your question suggests. In fact it needs a very long discussion. On the other hand, it certainly seems rude and uncivilized for a visitor not to oblige you and these people here, especially when you've spoken the way you
218 have. So I'll accept Theaetetus as the person to talk with, on the basis of your urging, and because I've talked with him myself before.

    THEAETETUS: Then please do that, sir, and you'll be doing us all a favor, just as Socrates said.

    VISITOR: We probably don't need to say anything more about that, then, Theaetetus. From now on you're the one I should have the rest of our talk with. But if you're annoyed at how long the job takes, you should blame your friends here instead of me.

b   THEAETETUS: I don't think I'll give out now, but if anything like that does happen we'll have to use this other Socrates over here as a substitute. He's Socrates' namesake, but he's my age and exercises with me and he's used to sharing lots of tasks with me.

    VISITOR: Good. As the talk goes along you'll think about that on your own. But with me I think you need to begin the investigation from the
c sophist—by searching for him and giving a clear account of what he is. Now in this case you and I only have the name in common, and maybe we've each used it for a different thing. In every case, though, we always need to be in agreement about the thing itself by means of a verbal explanation, rather than doing without any such explanation and merely agreeing about the name. But it isn't the easiest thing in the world to grasp the tribe we're planning to search for—I mean, the sophist—or say what it is. But if an important issue needs to be worked out well, then as everyone
d has long thought, you need to practice on unimportant, easier issues first. So that's my advice to us now, Theaetetus: since we think it's hard to hunt down and deal with the kind, *sophist*, we ought to practice our method of hunting on something easier first—unless you can tell us about another way that's somehow more promising.

    THEAETETUS: I can't.

    VISITOR: Do you want us to focus on something trivial and try to use it as a model for the more important issue?

THEAETETUS: Yes.

VISITOR: What might we propose that's unimportant and easy to understand, but can have an account given of it just as much as more important things can? For example, *an angler*: isn't that recognizable to everybody, but not worth being too serious about?

THEAETETUS: Yes.

VISITOR: That, I expect, will provide an appropriate method of hunting and way of talking for what we want.

THEAETETUS: That would be fine.

VISITOR: Well then, let's go after the angler from this starting point. Tell me, shall we take him to be an expert at something, or a nonexpert with another sort of capacity?

THEAETETUS: He's definitely not a nonexpert.

VISITOR: But expertise as a whole falls pretty much into two types.

THEAETETUS: How?

VISITOR: There's farming, or any sort of caring for any mortal body; and there's also caring for things that are put together or fabricated, which we call equipment; and there's imitation. The right thing would be to call all those things by a single name.

THEAETETUS: How? What name?

VISITOR: When you bring anything into being that wasn't in being before, we say you're a producer and that the thing you've brought into being is produced.

THEAETETUS: That's right.

VISITOR: And all the things we went through just now have their own capacity for that.

THEAETETUS: Yes.

VISITOR: Let's put them under the heading of production.

THEAETETUS: All right.

VISITOR: Next, consider the whole type that has to do with learning, recognition, commerce, combat, and hunting. None of these creates anything. They take things that are or have come into being, and they take possession of some of them with words and actions, and they keep other things from being taken possession of. For that reason it would be appropriate to call all the parts of this type acquisition.

THEAETETUS: Yes, that would be appropriate.

VISITOR: If every expertise falls under acquisition or production, Theaetetus, which one shall we put angling in?

THEAETETUS: Acquisition, obviously.

VISITOR: Aren't there two types of expertise in acquisition? Is one type mutually willing exchange, through gifts and wages and purchase? And would the other type, which brings things into one's possession by actions or words, be expertise in taking possession?

THEAETETUS: It seems so, anyway, given what we've said.

e

219

b

c

d

VISITOR: Well then, shouldn't we cut possession-taking in two?

THEAETETUS: How?

e   VISITOR: The part that's done openly we label combat, and the part that's secret we call hunting.

THEAETETUS: Yes.

VISITOR: And furthermore it would be unreasonable not to cut hunting in two.

THEAETETUS: How?

VISITOR: We divide it into the hunting of living things and the hunting of lifeless things.

THEAETETUS: Yes, if there are both kinds.

220   VISITOR: How could there not be? But we should let the part involving lifeless things go. It doesn't have a name, except for some kinds of diving and other trivial things like that. The other part—namely the hunting of living animals—we should call animal-hunting.

THEAETETUS: All right.

VISITOR: And isn't it right to say that animal-hunting has two types? One is land-hunting, the hunting of things with feet, which is divided into many types with many names. The other is aquatic hunting, which hunts animals that swim.

THEAETETUS: Of course.

b   VISITOR: And things that swim, we see, fall into things with wings and things living underwater.

THEAETETUS: Of course.

VISITOR: And all hunting of things that have wings, I suppose, is called bird-catching.

THEAETETUS: Yes.

VISITOR: And all hunting of underwater things is fishing.

THEAETETUS: Yes.

VISITOR: Well then, this kind of hunting might be divided into two main parts.

THEAETETUS: What are they?

VISITOR: One of them does its hunting with stationary nets and the other one does it by striking.

THEAETETUS: What do you mean? How are you dividing them?

c   VISITOR: The first one is whatever involves surrounding something and enclosing it to prevent it from escaping, so it's reasonable to call it enclosure.

THEAETETUS: Of course.

VISITOR: Shouldn't baskets, nets, slipknots, creels, and so forth be called enclosures?

THEAETETUS: Yes.

VISITOR: So we'll call this part of hunting enclosure-hunting or something like that.

THEAETETUS: Yes.

VISITOR: But the kind that's done by striking with hooks or three-pronged spears is different, and we should call it by one word, strike-hunting. Or what term would be better?

d

THEAETETUS: Let's not worry about the name. That one will do.

VISITOR: Then there's a part of striking that's done at night by firelight, and as it happens is called torch-hunting by the people who do it.

THEAETETUS: Of course.

VISITOR: But the whole daytime part is called hooking, since even the three-pronged spears have hooks on their points.

THEAETETUS: Yes, that's what it's called.

e

VISITOR: Then one part of the hooking part of striking is done by striking downward from above. And since you usually use a three-pronged spear that way, I think it's called spearing.

THEAETETUS: Some people do call it that.

VISITOR: And I suppose there's only one type left.

THEAETETUS: What?

VISITOR: It's the type of striking contrary to the previous one. It's done with a hook, not to just any part of the fish's body but always to the prey's head and mouth, and pulls it upward from below with rods or reeds. What are we going to say its name should be, Theaetetus?

221

THEAETETUS: I think we've now found what we said we aimed to find.

VISITOR: So now we're in agreement about the angler's expertise, not just as to its name; in addition we've also sufficiently grasped a verbal explanation concerning the thing itself. Within expertise as a whole one half was acquisitive; half of the acquisitive was taking possession; half of possession-taking was hunting; half of hunting was animal-hunting; half of animal-hunting was aquatic hunting; all of the lower portion of aquatic hunting was fishing; half of fishing was hunting by striking; and half of striking was hooking. And the part of hooking that involves a blow drawing a thing upward from underneath is called by a name that's derived by its similarity to the action itself, that is, it's called draw-fishing or angling— which is what we're searching for.

b

c

THEAETETUS: We've got a completely adequate demonstration of that, anyway.

VISITOR: Well then, let's use that model to try and find the sophist, and see what he is.

THEAETETUS: Fine.

VISITOR: The first question, then, was whether we should suppose the angler is a nonexpert, or that he's an expert at something?

THEAETETUS: Yes.

VISITOR: Well, shall we suppose the sophist is a layman, or completely and truly an expert?

d

THEAETETUS: He's not a layman at all. I understand what you're saying: he has to be the kind of person that the name *sophist* indicates.[4]

VISITOR: So it seems we need to take him to have a kind of expertise.

THEAETETUS: But what is it?

VISITOR: For heaven's sake, don't we recognize that the one man belongs to the same kind as the other?

THEAETETUS: Which men?

VISITOR: The angler and the sophist.

THEAETETUS: In what way?

VISITOR: To me they both clearly appear to be hunters.

e   THEAETETUS: We said which kind of hunting the angler does. What kind does the sophist do?

VISITOR: We divided all hunting into two parts, one for land animals and one for swimming animals.

THEAETETUS: Yes.

VISITOR: We went through one part, about the animals that swim underwater. But we left the land part undivided, though we noted that it contains many types.

222   THEAETETUS: Of course.

VISITOR: Up till that point the sophist and the angler go the same way, beginning from expertise in acquisition.

THEAETETUS: They seem to, anyway.

VISITOR: Starting from animal hunting, though, they turn away from each other. One goes to ponds, rivers, and the sea, and hunts for the animals there.

THEAETETUS: Of course.

VISITOR: The other one goes to the land and to different kinds of rivers, which are like plentiful meadows of wealthy youths, to take possession of the things living there.

b   THEAETETUS: What do you mean?

VISITOR: There are two main kinds of things to hunt on land.

THEAETETUS: What are they?

VISITOR: Tame things and wild ones.

THEAETETUS: Is there any such thing as hunting tame animals?

VISITOR: There is if human beings are tame animals, at any rate. Make whichever assumption you like: either there are no tame animals, or there are tame animals but humans are wild, or else, you'll say, humans are tame but aren't hunted. Specify whichever you prefer to say.

c   THEAETETUS: I think we're tame animals and I'll say that humans are in fact hunted.

---

4. The word "sophist" (*sophistēs*) is etymologically related to the word "wise" (*sophos*), and so can be taken to connote knowledge and expertise.

VISITOR: Then let's say that the hunting of tame animals falls into two parts.

THEAETETUS: How?

VISITOR: Let's take piracy, enslavement, tyranny, along with everything that has to do with war, and let's define them all together as hunting by force.

THEAETETUS: Fine.

VISITOR: And we'll also take legal oratory, political oratory, and conversation all together in one whole, and call them all one single sort of expertise, expertise in persuasion.

d

THEAETETUS: Right.

VISITOR: Let's say that there are two kinds of persuasion.

THEAETETUS: What are they?

VISITOR: One is done privately, and the other is done in public.

THEAETETUS: Yes, each of those is one type.

VISITOR: And doesn't one part of private hunting earn wages, while the other part gives gifts?

THEAETETUS: I don't understand.

VISITOR: It seems you aren't paying attention to the way lovers hunt.

THEAETETUS: In what connection?

VISITOR: The fact that when they hunt people they give presents to them too.

e

THEAETETUS: Very true.

VISITOR: Let's call this type expertise in love.

THEAETETUS: All right.

VISITOR: One part of the wage-earning type approaches people by being agreeable, uses only pleasure as its bait, and earns only its own room and board. I think we'd all call it flattery, or expertise in pleasing people.

223

THEAETETUS: Of course.

VISITOR: But doesn't the kind of wage-earning that actually earns money, though it claims to deal with people for the sake of virtue, deserve to be called by a different name?

THEAETETUS: Of course.

VISITOR: What name? Try and tell me.

THEAETETUS: It's obvious. I think we've found the sophist. I think that's the name that would be suitable for him.

VISITOR: So according to our account now, Theaetetus, it seems that this sort of expertise belongs to appropriation, taking possession, hunting, animal-hunting, hunting on land, human hunting, hunting by persuasion, hunting privately, and money-earning.[5] It's the hunting of rich, prominent young men. And according to the way our account has turned out, it's what should be called the expertise of the sophist.

b

---

5. In addition to the words bracketed by Burnet, we bracket *doxopaideutikēs* also.

THEAETETUS: Absolutely.

c   VISITOR: Still, let's look at it this way too, since what we're looking for isn't a trivial sort of expertise but quite a diverse one. And even in what we've just said earlier it actually presents the appearance of being not what we're now saying, but a different type.

THEAETETUS: How?

VISITOR: Expertise in acquisition had two parts, hunting and exchanging.

THEAETETUS: Yes.

VISITOR: And let's say there are two types of exchanging, giving and selling.

THEAETETUS: All right.

VISITOR: And we're also going to say that selling divides in two.

d   THEAETETUS: How?

VISITOR: One part is the sale of things that the seller himself makes. The other is purveying, that is, the purveying of things other people make.

THEAETETUS: Of course.

VISITOR: Then what? Isn't the part of purveying that's done within the city—about half of it—called retailing?

THEAETETUS: Yes.

VISITOR: And isn't wholesaling the part that buys and sells things for exchange between one city and another?

THEAETETUS: Of course.

e   VISITOR: And can't we see that one part of wholesaling sells things for the nourishment and use of the body in exchange for cash, and the other sells things for the soul?

THEAETETUS: What do you mean by that?

VISITOR: Maybe we don't understand the one for the soul—since certainly we understand the other kind.

THEAETETUS: Yes.

224   VISITOR: Let's consider every kind of music that's carried from one city to another and bought here and sold there, as well as painting and shows and other things for the soul. Some of them are transported and sold for amusement and others for serious purposes. We can use the word *wholesaler* for the transporter and seller of these things just as well as for someone who sells food and beverages.

THEAETETUS: That's absolutely true.

b   VISITOR: Wouldn't you use the same name for somebody who bought and exchanged items of knowledge for money from city to city?

THEAETETUS: Definitely.

VISITOR: Wouldn't the right thing to say be that the art of display is one part of that soul-wholesaling? And don't we have to call the other part of it, the part that consists in selling knowledge, by a name that's similar and also equally ridiculous?

THEAETETUS: Definitely.

VISITOR: And one name should be used for the part of this knowledge-selling that deals with knowledge of virtue, and another name for the part c that deals with knowledge of other things?

THEAETETUS: Of course.

VISITOR: "Expertise-selling" would fit the second one. You try and tell me the name of the first one.

THEAETETUS: What other name could you mention that would fit, except for the kind, *sophist*, which we're looking for right now?

VISITOR: I couldn't mention any other one. Come on now and let's collect it all together. We'll say that the expertise of the part of acquisition, exchange, selling, wholesaling, and soul-wholesaling, dealing in words and learning d that have to do with virtue—that's sophistry in its second appearance.

THEAETETUS: Definitely.

VISITOR: In the third place I think you'd call somebody just the same thing if he settled here in the city and undertook to make his living selling those same things, both ones that he'd bought and ones that he'd made himself.

THEAETETUS: Yes, I would.

VISITOR: So apparently you'll still say that sophistry falls under acquisi- e tion, exchange, and selling, either by retailing things that others make or by selling things that he makes himself. It's the retail sale of any learning that has to do with the sorts of things we mentioned.

THEAETETUS: It has to be, since we need to stay consistent with what we said before.

VISITOR: Now let's see whether the type we're chasing is something like the following.

THEAETETUS: What? 225

VISITOR: Combat was one part of acquisition.[6]

THEAETETUS: Yes.

VISITOR: And it makes sense to divide it in two.

THEAETETUS: How?

VISITOR: We'll take one part to be competition and the other part to be fighting.

THEAETETUS: Yes.

VISITOR: And it would be fitting and proper to give a name like *violence* to the part of fighting in which one body fights against another.

THEAETETUS: Yes.

VISITOR: And as for the part that pits words against words, what else would you call it other than controversy? b

THEAETETUS: Nothing else.

---

6. The word here translated by "debating," *eristikon,* is sometimes translated (or translit-erated) "eristic." It refers to a practice of competitive debating which the sophists made popular in Athens. Plato's use of the term stigmatizes the practice as not directed at truth.

VISITOR: But we have to have two types of controversy.

THEAETETUS: In what way?

VISITOR: So far as it involves one long public speech directed against another and deals with justice and injustice, it's forensic.

THEAETETUS: Yes.

VISITOR: But if it goes on in private discussions and is chopped up into questions and answers, don't we usually call it disputation?

THEAETETUS: Yes.

c   VISITOR: One part of disputation involves controversy about contracts and isn't carried on in any systematic or expert way. We should take that to be a type of disputation, since we can express what makes it different. But it hasn't been given a name before and it doesn't deserve to get one from us.

THEAETETUS: That's true. Its subtypes are too small and varied.

VISITOR: But what about disputation that's done expertly and involves controversy about general issues, including what's just and what's unjust? Don't we normally call that debating?

THEAETETUS: Of course.

d   VISITOR: Part of debating, it turns out, wastes money and the other part makes money.

THEAETETUS: Absolutely.

VISITOR: Let's try and say what each of them ought to be called.

THEAETETUS: We have to.

VISITOR: I think one type of debating is a result of the pleasure a person gets from the activity, and involves neglecting his own livelihood. But its style is unpleasant to most people who hear it, and in my view it's right to call it chatter.

THEAETETUS: That's pretty much what people do call it.

e   VISITOR: You take a turn now. Say what its contrary is, which makes money from debates between individuals.

THEAETETUS: How could anyone go wrong in saying that the amazing sophist we've been after has turned up once again for the fourth time.

226   VISITOR: It seems his type is precisely the money-making branch of expertise in debating, disputation, controversy, fighting, combat, and acquisition. According to what our account shows us now, that's the sophist.

THEAETETUS: Absolutely.

VISITOR: So you see how true it is that the beast is complex and can't be caught with one hand, as they say.

THEAETETUS: It does take both hands.

b   VISITOR: Yes, and you need all your capacity to follow his tracks in what's to come. Tell me: don't we call some things by names that house-servants use?

THEAETETUS: A lot of things. But what are you asking about?

VISITOR: For example things like filtering, straining, winnowing.

THEAETETUS: Of course.

VISITOR: And also we know about carding, spinning, weaving, and a million other things like that which are involved in experts' crafts. Is that right?

THEAETETUS: What general point are you trying to make with these ex-   c
amples?

VISITOR: All the things I've mentioned are kinds of dividing.

THEAETETUS: Yes.

VISITOR: Since there's a single kind of expertise involved in all of them, then according to what I've said we'll expect it to have a single name.

THEAETETUS: What shall we call it?

VISITOR: Discrimination.

THEAETETUS: All right.

VISITOR: Think about whether we can see two types in it.

THEAETETUS: You're asking me to do some quick thinking.

VISITOR: In fact in what we've called discriminations one kind separates   d
what's worse from what's better and the other separates like from like.

THEAETETUS: That's obvious—now that you've said it.

VISITOR: I don't have an ordinary name for one of them, but I do have a name for the kind of discrimination that leaves what's better and throws away what's worse.

THEAETETUS: What? Tell me.

VISITOR: I think everyone says that that kind of discrimination is cleansing.

THEAETETUS: Yes.

VISITOR: Won't everyone see that cleansing has two types?   e

THEAETETUS: Yes, maybe, if they had time, but I don't see now.

VISITOR: Many kinds of cleansing that have to do with the body can appropriately be included under a simple name.

THEAETETUS: Which ones? What name?

VISITOR: There's the cleansing of the inside part of living bodies, which is done by gymnastics and medicine. And there's the cleansing of the   227
insignificant outside part that's done by bathing. And also there's the cleansing of nonliving bodies, which fulling and all kinds of furbishing take care of and which have lots of specialized and ridiculous-seeming names.

THEAETETUS: Very ridiculous.

VISITOR: Of course, Theaetetus. But our method of dealing with words doesn't care one way or the other whether cleansing by sponging or by taking medicine does a lot of good or only a little. The method aims at acquiring intelligence, so it tries to understand how all kinds of expertise   b
belong to the same kind or not. And so for that it values them all equally without thinking that some of them are more ridiculous than others, as far as their similarity is concerned. And it doesn't consider a person more impressive because he exemplifies hunting by military expertise rather

than by picking lice. Instead it usually considers him more vapid. Moreover you just asked about what name we call all the capacities that are assigned

c   to living or nonliving bodies. As far as that's concerned, it doesn't matter to our method which name would seem to be the most appropriate, just so long as it keeps the cleansing of the soul separate from the cleansing of everything else. For the time being, the method has only tried to distinguish the cleansing that concerns thinking from the other kinds—if, that is, we understand what its aim is.

THEAETETUS: I do understand, and I agree that there are two types of cleansing, one dealing with the soul and a separate one dealing with the body.

VISITOR: Fine. Next listen and try to cut the one we've mentioned in two.

d   THEAETETUS: I'll try to follow your lead and cut it however you say.

VISITOR: Do we say that wickedness in the soul is something different from virtue?

THEAETETUS: Of course.

VISITOR: And to cleanse something was to leave what's good and throw out whatever's inferior.

THEAETETUS: Yes.

VISITOR: So insofar as we can find some way to remove what's bad in the soul, it will be suitable to call it cleansing.

THEAETETUS: Of course.

VISITOR: We have to say that there are two kinds of badness that affect the soul.

THEAETETUS: What are they?

228   VISITOR: One is like bodily sickness, and the other is like ugliness.

THEAETETUS: I don't understand.

VISITOR: Presumably you regard sickness and discord as the same thing, don't you?

THEAETETUS: I don't know what I should say to that.

VISITOR: Do you think that discord is just dissension among things that are naturally of the same kind, and arises out of some kind of corruption?

THEAETETUS: Yes.

VISITOR: And ugliness is precisely a consistently unattractive sort of disproportion?

b   THEAETETUS: Yes.

VISITOR: Well then, don't we see that there's dissension in the souls of people in poor condition, between beliefs and desires, anger and pleasures, reason and pains, and all of those things with each other?

THEAETETUS: Absolutely.

VISITOR: But all of them do have to be akin to each other.

THEAETETUS: Of course.

VISITOR: So we'd be right if we said that wickedness is discord and sickness of the soul.

THEAETETUS: Absolutely right.

VISITOR: Well then, suppose something that's in motion aims at a target   c
and tries to hit it, but on every try passes by it and misses. Are we going
to say that it does this because it's properly proportioned or because it's
out of proportion?

THEAETETUS: Out of proportion, obviously.

VISITOR: But we know that no soul is willingly ignorant of anything.

THEAETETUS: Definitely.

VISITOR: But ignorance occurs precisely when a soul tries for the truth,   d
but swerves aside from understanding and so is beside itself.

THEAETETUS: Of course.

VISITOR: So we have to take it that an ignorant soul is ugly and out
of proportion.

THEAETETUS: It seems so.

VISITOR: Then there are, it appears, these two kinds of badness in the
soul. Most people call one of them wickedness, but it's obviously a disease
of the soul.

THEAETETUS: Yes.

VISITOR: They call the other one ignorance, but if it occurs only in a
person's soul they aren't willing to agree that it's a form of badness.

THEAETETUS: One thing absolutely must be granted—the point I was in   e
doubt about when you made it just now—that there are two kinds of
deficiency in the soul. We need to say that cowardice, licentiousness, and
injustice are a disease in us, and that to be extremely ignorant of all sorts
of things is a kind of ugliness.

VISITOR: In the case of the body, weren't there two kinds of expertise
dealing with those two conditions?

THEAETETUS: What were they?

VISITOR: Gymnastics for ugliness and medicine for sickness.   229

THEAETETUS: Apparently.

VISITOR: And isn't correction the most appropriate of all kinds of expertise
for treating insolence, injustice, and cowardice?[7]

THEAETETUS: So it seems, to judge by what people think.

VISITOR: Well then, for all kinds of ignorance wouldn't teaching be the
right treatment to mention?

THEAETETUS: Yes.

VISITOR: Now should we say that there's only one kind of expertise in   b
teaching or more than one, with two of them being the most important
ones? Think about it.

THEAETETUS: I am.

VISITOR: I think we'll find it quickest this way.

THEAETETUS: How?

7. The text seems faulty here. The general sense, however, is clear.

VISITOR: By seeing whether ignorance has a cut down the middle of it. If it has two parts, that will force teaching to have two parts too, one for each of the parts of ignorance.

THEAETETUS: Well, do you see what we're looking for?

c   VISITOR: I think I see a large, difficult type of ignorance marked off from the others and overshadowing all of them.

THEAETETUS: What's it like?

VISITOR: Not knowing, but thinking that you know. That's what probably causes all the mistakes we make when we think.

THEAETETUS: That's true.

VISITOR: And furthermore it's the only kind of ignorance that's called lack of learning.

THEAETETUS: Certainly.

VISITOR: Well then, what should we call the part of teaching that gets rid of it?

d   THEAETETUS: The other part consists in the teaching of crafts, I think, but here in Athens we call this one education.

VISITOR: And just about all other Greeks do too, Theaetetus. But we still have to think about whether education is indivisible or has divisions that are worth mentioning.

THEAETETUS: We do have to think about that.

VISITOR: I think it can be cut somehow.

THEAETETUS: How?

e   VISITOR: One part of the kind of teaching that's done in words is a rough road, and the other part is smoother.

THEAETETUS: What do you mean by these two parts?

VISITOR: One of them is our forefathers' time-honored method of scolding or gently encouraging. They used to employ it especially on their sons, 230   and many still use it on them nowadays when they do something wrong. Admonition would be the right thing to call all of this.

THEAETETUS: Yes.

VISITOR: As for the other part, some people seem to have an argument to give to themselves that lack of learning is always involuntary, and that if someone thinks he's wise, he'll never be willing to learn anything about what he thinks he's clever at. These people think that though admonition is a lot of work, it doesn't do much good.

THEAETETUS: They're right about that.

b   VISITOR: So they set out to get rid of the belief in one's own wisdom in another way.

THEAETETUS: How?

VISITOR: They cross-examine someone when he thinks he's saying something though he's saying nothing. Then, since his opinions will vary inconsistently, these people will easily scrutinize them. They collect his opinions together during the discussion, put them side by side, and show that they conflict with each other at the same time on the same subjects in relation to the same things and in the same respects. The people who are being examined see this, get angry at themselves, and become calmer toward others. They lose their inflated and rigid beliefs about themselves that way, and no loss is pleasanter to hear or has a more lasting effect on them. Doctors who work on the body think it can't benefit from any food that's offered to it until what's interfering with it from inside is removed. The people who cleanse the soul, my young friend, likewise think the soul, too, won't get any advantage from any learning that's offered to it until someone shames it by refuting it, removes the opinions that interfere with learning, and exhibits it cleansed, believing that it knows only those things that it does know, and nothing more.

THEAETETUS: That's the best and most healthy-minded way to be.

VISITOR: For all these reasons, Theaetetus, we have to say that refutation is the principal and most important kind of cleansing. Conversely we have to think that even the king of Persia, if he remains unrefuted, is uncleansed in the most important respect. He's also uneducated and ugly, in just the ways that anyone who is going to be really happy has to be completely clean and beautiful.

THEAETETUS: Absolutely.

VISITOR: Well then, who are we going to say the people who apply this form of expertise are? I'm afraid to call them sophists.

THEAETETUS: Why?

VISITOR: So we don't pay sophists too high an honor.

THEAETETUS: But there's a similarity between a sophist and what we've been talking about.

VISITOR: And between a wolf and a dog, the wildest thing there is and the gentlest. If you're going to be safe, you have to be especially careful about similarities, since the type we're talking about is very slippery. Anyway, let that description of them stand. I certainly don't think that when the sophists are enough on their guard the dispute will be about an unimportant distinction.

THEAETETUS: That seems right.

VISITOR: So let it be the cleansing part of the expertise of discriminating things; and let it be marked off as the part of that which concerns souls; and within that it's teaching; and within teaching it's education. And let's say that within education, according to the way the discussion has turned now, the refutation of the empty belief in one's own wisdom is nothing other than our noble sophistry.

THEAETETUS: Let's say that. But the sophist has appeared in lots of different ways. So I'm confused about what expression or assertion could convey the truth about what he really is.

VISITOR: You're right to be confused. But we have to think that he's extremely confused, too, about where he can go to escape from our account of him. The saying that you can't escape all your pursuers is right. So now we really have to go after him.

THEAETETUS: Right.

VISITOR: But let's stop first and catch our breath, so to speak. And while
d   we're resting let's ask ourselves, "Now, how many different appearances has the sophist presented to us?" I think we first discovered him as a hired hunter of rich young men.

THEAETETUS: Yes.

VISITOR: Second, as a wholesaler of learning about the soul.

THEAETETUS: Right.

VISITOR: Third, didn't he appear as a retailer of the same things?

THEAETETUS: Yes, and fourth as a seller of his own learning?

VISITOR: Your memory's correct. I'll try to recall the fifth way: he was
e   an athlete in verbal combat, distinguished by his expertise in debating.

THEAETETUS: Yes.

VISITOR: The sixth appearance was disputed, but still we made a concession to him and took it that he cleanses the soul of beliefs that interfere with learning.

THEAETETUS: Definitely.

232   VISITOR: Well then, suppose people apply the name of a single sort of expertise to someone, but he appears to have expert knowledge of lots of things. In a case like that don't you notice that something's wrong with the way he appears? Isn't it obvious that if somebody takes him to be an expert at many things, then that observer can't be seeing clearly what it is in his expertise that all of those many pieces of learning focus on—which is why he calls him by many names instead of one?

THEAETETUS: That definitely does seem to be the nature of the case.

b   VISITOR: So let's not let laziness make that happen to us. First let's take up one of the things we said about the sophist before, which seemed to me to exhibit him especially clearly.

THEAETETUS: What is it?

VISITOR: We said that he engages in disputes, didn't we?

THEAETETUS: Yes.

VISITOR: And also that he teaches other people to do the same thing too?

THEAETETUS: Of course.

VISITOR: Then let's think: what subject do people like him claim to make others able to engage in disputes about? Let's start with something like
c   this: do sophists make people competent to dispute about issues about the gods, which are opaque to most people?

THEAETETUS: Well, people say they do.

VISITOR: And also things that are open to view, on the earth and in the sky, and related matters?

THEAETETUS: Of course.

VISITOR: And when people make general statements in private discussions about being and coming-to-be, we know that sophists are clever at contradicting them and they also make other people able to do the same thing?

THEAETETUS: Absolutely.

VISITOR: And what about laws and all kinds of political issues? Don't   d
sophists promise to make people capable of engaging in controversies about them?

THEAETETUS: If they didn't promise that, practically no one would bother to discuss anything with them.

VISITOR: As a matter of fact you can find anything you need to say to contradict any expert himself, both in general and within each particular field, laid out published and written down for anybody who wants to learn it.

THEAETETUS: Apparently you're talking about Protagoras' writings on wrestling and other fields of expertise.   e

VISITOR: And on many other things, too, my friend. In fact, take expertise in disputation as a whole. Doesn't it seem like a capacity that's sufficient for carrying on controversies about absolutely everything?

THEAETETUS: It doesn't seem to leave much of anything out, anyway.

VISITOR: But for heaven's sake, my boy, do you think that's possible? Or maybe you young people see into this issue more keenly than we do.

THEAETETUS: Into what? What are you getting at? I don't fully understand   233
what you're asking.

VISITOR: Whether it's possible for any human being to know everything.

THEAETETUS: If it were, sir, we'd be very well off.

VISITOR: But how could someone who didn't know about a subject make a sound objection against someone who knew about it?

THEAETETUS: He couldn't.

VISITOR: Then what is it in the sophist's capacity that's so amazing?

THEAETETUS: About what?

VISITOR: How the sophists can ever make young people believe they're   b
wiser than everyone else about everything. It's obvious that they didn't make correct objections against anyone, or didn't appear so to young people. Or if they did appear to make correct objections, but their controversies didn't make them look any the wiser for it, then—just as you say—people would hardly be willing to pay them money to become their students.

THEAETETUS: Right.

VISITOR: But people are willing to?

THEAETETUS: They certainly are.

VISITOR: Since sophists do seem, I think, to know about the things they   c
dispute about.

THEAETETUS: Of course.

VISITOR: And they do it, we say, about every subject?

THEAETETUS: Yes.

VISITOR: So to their students they appear wise about everything?

THEAETETUS: Of course.

VISITOR: But without actually being wise—since that appeared impossible.

THEAETETUS: Of course it's impossible.

VISITOR: So the sophist has now appeared as having a kind of belief-knowledge about everything, but not truth.

d   THEAETETUS: Absolutely. What you've said about them is probably just right.

VISITOR: But let's consider a pattern that will exhibit them more clearly.

THEAETETUS: What pattern is that?

VISITOR: This one. Pay attention to me, and try to do a good job of answering my questions.

THEAETETUS: Which questions?

VISITOR: If someone claimed that by a single kind of expertise he could know, not just how to say things or to contradict people, but how to make and do everything, then . . .

e   THEAETETUS: What do you mean, *everything*?

VISITOR: You don't understand the first thing I say! Seemingly you don't understand *everything*!

THEAETETUS: No, I don't.

VISITOR: Well, I mean everything to include you and me and also the other animals and plants . . .

THEAETETUS: What are you talking about?

VISITOR: If someone claimed that he'd make you and me and all the other living things . . .

234   THEAETETUS: What kind of making are you talking about? You're not talking about some kind of gardener—after all, you did say he made animals.

VISITOR: Yes, and also I mean the sea and earth and heaven and gods and everything else. And furthermore he makes them each quickly and sells them at a low price.

THEAETETUS: You're talking about some kind of game for schoolchildren.

VISITOR: Well, if someone says he knows everything and would teach it to someone else cheaply and quickly, shouldn't we think it's a game?

THEAETETUS: Of course.

b   VISITOR: Do you know of any game that involves more expertise than imitation does, and is more engaging?

THEAETETUS: No, not at all, since you've collected everything together and designated a very broad, extremely diverse type.

VISITOR: So think about the man who promises he can make everything by means of a single kind of expertise. Suppose that by being expert at drawing he produces things that have the same names as real things. Then we know that when he shows his drawings from far away he'll be able to fool the more mindless young children into thinking that he can actually produce anything he wants to.

THEAETETUS: Of course.

VISITOR: Well then, won't we expect that there's another kind of expertise—this time having to do with words—and that someone can use it to trick young people when they stand even farther away from the truth about things? Wouldn't he do it by putting words in their ears, and by showing them spoken copies of everything, so as to make them believe that the words are true and that the person who's speaking to them is the wisest person there is?

THEAETETUS: Yes, why shouldn't there be that kind of expertise too?

VISITOR: So, Theaetetus, suppose enough time has passed and the sophist's hearers have gotten older, and that they approach closer to real things and are forced by their experiences to touch up palpably against them. Won't most of them inevitably change their earlier beliefs, which made large things appear small and easy things appear hard? And won't the facts they've encountered in the course of their actions completely overturn all the appearances that had come to them in the form of words?

THEAETETUS: Yes—at least as far as what someone my age can tell. But I think I'm one of the young people who are still standing far away from real things.

VISITOR: That's why all of us here will keep trying to take you as close to them as possible, but without your needing those experiences to force you. But tell me about the sophist. Is it obvious by now that he's a kind of cheat who imitates real things? Or are we still in any doubt about whether he truly knows all the things that he seems to be able to engage in controversies about?

THEAETETUS: But, sir, how could we be in any doubt? By this time it's pretty obvious from what we've said that he's one of those people who play games.

VISITOR: So we have to regard him as a cheat and an imitator.

THEAETETUS: How could we avoid it?

VISITOR: Well, now it's our job not to let the beast escape. We've almost hemmed him in with one of those net-like devices that words provide for things like this. So anyway he won't get away from this next point.

THEAETETUS: What is it?

VISITOR: From being taken to be a kind of magician.

THEAETETUS: That's what he seems to me to be too.

VISITOR: So it's settled. We'll divide the craft of copy-making as quickly as we can and we'll go down into it. Then if the sophist gives up right away we'll obey the royal command and we'll capture him and hand our

catch over to the king. But if the sophist slips down somewhere into the
parts of the craft of imitation, we'll follow along with him and we'll divide
each of the parts that contain him until we catch him. Anyway, neither
he nor any other kind will ever be able to boast that he's escaped from
the method of people who are able to chase a thing through both the
particular and the general.

THEAETETUS: Good. That's how we have to do it.

d VISITOR: Going by the method of division that we've used so far, I think
I see two types of imitation here too. But I don't think I can clearly tell
yet which one the type or form we're looking for is in.

THEAETETUS: Well, first tell us what distinction you mean.

VISITOR: One type of imitation I see is the art of likeness-making. That's
the one we have whenever someone produces an imitation by keeping to
e the proportions of length, breadth, and depth of his model, and also by
keeping to the appropriate colors of its parts.

THEAETETUS: But don't all imitators try to do that?

VISITOR: Not the ones who sculpt or draw very large works. If they
reproduced the true proportions of their beautiful subjects, you see, the
236 upper parts would appear smaller than they should, and the lower parts
would appear larger, because we see the upper parts from farther away
and the lower parts from closer.

THEAETETUS: Of course.

VISITOR: So don't those craftsmen say goodbye to truth, and produce
in their images the proportions that seem to be beautiful instead of the
real ones?

THEAETETUS: Absolutely.

VISITOR: So can't the first sort of image be called a likeness, since it's like
the thing?

THEAETETUS: Yes.

b VISITOR: And as we said before, the part of imitation that deals with that
should be called likeness-making.

THEAETETUS: Yes.

VISITOR: Now, what are we going to call something that appears to be
like a beautiful thing, but only because it's seen from a viewpoint that's
not beautiful, and would seem unlike the thing it claims to be like if you
came to be able to see such large things adequately? If it appears the way
the thing does but in fact isn't like it, isn't it an appearance?

THEAETETUS: Of course.

c VISITOR: And this part of imitation covers a great deal of painting and
of the rest of imitation.

THEAETETUS: Of course.

VISITOR: Wouldn't appearance-making be the right thing to call expertise
in producing appearances that aren't likenesses?

THEAETETUS: Yes, definitely.

VISITOR: Well, these are the two types of copy-making I meant, likeness-making and appearance-making.

THEAETETUS: You were right about that.

VISITOR: But still I can't see clearly the thing I was in doubt about then, namely, which type we should put the sophist in. He's really an amazing man—very hard to make out. He's still escaped neatly into an impossibly confusing type to search through.   d

THEAETETUS: It seems that way.

VISITOR: Are you agreeing with me because you know that, or is the current dragging you, so to speak, into agreement so quickly because the discussion has given you a habit of agreeing?

THEAETETUS: What do you mean? Why do you say that?

VISITOR: Really, my young friend, this is a very difficult investigation we're engaged in. This appearing, and this seeming but not being, and   e
this saying things but not true things—all these issues are full of confusion, just as they always have been. It's extremely hard, Theaetetus, to say what form of speech we should use to say that there really is such a thing as false saying or believing, and moreover to utter this without being caught   237
in a verbal conflict.

THEAETETUS: Why?

VISITOR: Because this form of speech of ours involves the rash assumption that that which is not is, since otherwise falsity wouldn't come into being. But when we were boys, my boy, the great Parmenides testified to us from start to finish, speaking in both prose and poetic rhythms, that

> Never shall this force itself on us, that that which is not may be;
> While you search, keep your thought far away from this path.[8]

So we have his testimony to this. And our own way of speaking itself   b
would make the point especially obvious if it we examined it a little. So if it's all the same to you, let's look at that first.

THEAETETUS: As far as I'm concerned you can do what you want. But as far as our way of speaking is concerned, think about how it will go best, and follow along with it and take me along the road with you.

VISITOR: That's what we have to do. Tell me: do we dare to utter the sound *that which in no way is*?

THEAETETUS: Of course.

VISITOR: But suppose one of our listeners weren't debating or playing a game but had to think seriously and answer the following question: What   c
should the name, *that which is not*, be applied to? Why do we think he'd

---

8. See Parmenides, frg. 7, ll.1–2. The same lines reoccur, with one slight textual difference, at 258d.

use it, and in what connection, and for what kind of purpose? And what would he indicate by it to someone else who wanted to find out about it?

THEAETETUS: That's a hard question. In fact, it's just about completely, impossibly confusing for someone like me to answer.

VISITOR: But anyway this much is obvious to us, that *that which is not* can't be applied to any of those which are.

THEAETETUS: Of course not.

VISITOR: So if you can't apply it to that which is, it wouldn't be right either to apply it to *something*.

THEAETETUS: Why not?

d VISITOR: It's obvious to us that we always apply this *something* to a being, since it's impossible to say it by itself, as if it were naked and isolated from all beings. Isn't that right?

THEAETETUS: Yes.

VISITOR: Are you agreeing because you're thinking that a person who says *something* has to be saying some *one* thing?

THEAETETUS: Yes.

VISITOR: Since you'd say that *something* is a sign of *one*, and that *a couple of things* is a sign of *two*, and *somethings* is a sign of a *plurality*?

THEAETETUS: Of course.

e VISITOR: And it's absolutely necessary, it seems, that someone who does not say *something* says *nothing*⁹ at all.

THEAETETUS: Yes.

VISITOR: Therefore don't we have to refuse to admit that a person like that speaks but says nothing? Instead, don't we have to deny that anyone who tries to utter *that which is not* is even speaking?

THEAETETUS: Then our way of speaking would have reached the height of confusion.

238 VISITOR: Don't do any boasting yet. There are still more confusions to come, including the primary and most fundamental one, which actually happens to be at the source of the whole problem.

THEAETETUS: What do you mean? Don't hold back. Tell me.

VISITOR: To that which is there might belong some other of those which are.

THEAETETUS: Of course.

VISITOR: But shall we say that any of those which are can ever belong to that which is not?

THEAETETUS: How could they?

VISITOR: Now then, we take all the numbers to be beings.

b THEAETETUS: Yes, if we take anything else to be.

VISITOR: Then let's not even try to apply either plurality of number or one to that which is not.

---

9. Note that the Greek word for "nothing," *mēden*, literally means something like "not even one" (*mēde hen*).

THEAETETUS: Our way of speaking itself tells us that it would be wrong to try to.

VISITOR: Then how would anyone try either to say *those which are not* or *that which is not* out loud, or even grasp them in thought, apart from number?

THEAETETUS: Tell me.

VISITOR: Whenever we speak of *those which are not*, aren't we trying to apply numerical plurality to them?   c

THEAETETUS: Of course.

VISITOR: And when we speak of *that which is not* aren't we applying *one* to it?

THEAETETUS: Obviously.

VISITOR: But we say it isn't either right or correct to try to attach *that which is* to that which is not.

THEAETETUS: That's absolutely true.

VISITOR: Do you understand, then, that it's impossible to say, speak, or think *that which is not* itself correctly by itself? It's unthinkable, unsayable, unutterable, and unformulable in speech.

THEAETETUS: Absolutely.

VISITOR: So was I wrong just now when I said that I would formulate   d the biggest confusion about it, when we have this other one to state which is even bigger?

THEAETETUS: What is it?

VISITOR: My good young friend, don't you notice on the basis of the things we said that *that which is not* even confuses the person who's refuting it in just this way, that whenever someone tries to refute it, he's forced to say mutually contrary things about it?

THEAETETUS: What do you mean? Say it more clearly.

VISITOR: You shouldn't expect more clarity from me. I was the one who made the statement that *that which is not* should not share either in *one* or   e in *plurality*. But even so I've continued after all that to speak of it as *one*, since I say *that which is not*. You understand?

THEAETETUS: Yes.

VISITOR: And again a little earlier I said that it *is* unutterable, unsayable, and inexpressible in speech. Do you follow?

THEAETETUS: I follow, of course.

VISITOR: So in trying to attach *being* to it wasn't I saying things that were   239 the contrary of what I'd said before?

THEAETETUS: Apparently.

VISITOR: And in attaching *that which*,[10] wasn't I speaking of it as *one*?

THEAETETUS: Yes.

10. Accepting the conjecture *to* "to," translated by "that which" on the view that it is part of the phrase *to mē on*, which is generally translated by "that which is not." In Greek the form is singular (in contrast with *ta*, for example, "those which").

VISITOR: And also in speaking of it as something inexpressible in speech, unsayable, and unutterable, I was speaking of it as one thing.

THEAETETUS: Of course.

VISITOR: But we say that if someone speaks correctly he shouldn't definitely fix it as either one or plural. He shouldn't even call it *it* at all, since even calling it by that label he'd be addressing it by means of the form, *one*.

THEAETETUS: Absolutely.

b   VISITOR: Then what would somebody say about me? He'd find that the refutation of that which is not has been defeating me for a long time. So, as I said, let's not use what I say to help us think of how to speak correctly about that which is not. Come on, let's use what you say instead.

THEAETETUS: What do you mean?

VISITOR: Come on, pull yourself together for us as well as you can and try it—since you're young. Try to say something correct about that which is not, without attaching either *being*, *one*, or numerical *plurality* to it.

c   THEAETETUS: I'd have to have a strangely large amount of enthusiasm for the project to try it myself after seeing what you've gone through.

VISITOR: Well, let's give up on both you and me, if you prefer. But until we meet someone who can do it let's say that the sophist has stopped at nothing. He's escaped down into inaccessible confusion.

THEAETETUS: He certainly seems to have.

VISITOR: So if we say he has some expertise in appearance-making, it

d   will be easy for him to grab hold of our use of words in return and twist our words in the contrary direction. Whenever we call him a copy-maker he'll ask us what in the world we mean by a "copy." We need to think, Theaetetus, about how to answer the young man's question.

THEAETETUS: Obviously we'll say we mean copies in water and mirrors, and also copies that are drawn and stamped and everything else like that.

e   VISITOR: Evidently, Theaetetus, you haven't seen a sophist.

THEAETETUS: Why do you say that?

VISITOR: He'll seem to you to have his eyes shut, or else not to have any eyes at all.

THEAETETUS: How?

VISITOR: He'll laugh at what you say when you answer him that way, with talk about things in mirrors or sculptures, and when you speak

240   to him as if he could see. He'll pretend he doesn't know about mirrors or water or even sight, and he'll put his question to you only in terms of words.

THEAETETUS: What sort of question?

VISITOR: He'll ask about what runs through all those things which you call many, but which you thought you should call by the one name, *copy*, to cover them all, as if they were all one thing. Say something, then, and defend yourself, and don't give any ground to him.

THEAETETUS: What in the world would we say a copy is, sir, except something that's made similar to a true thing and is another thing that's like it?   b

VISITOR: You're saying it's another *true* thing like it? Or what do you mean by *like it*?

THEAETETUS: Not that it's *true* at all, but that it resembles the true thing.

VISITOR: Meaning by *true*, really being?

THEAETETUS: Yes.

VISITOR: And meaning by *not true*, contrary of true?

THEAETETUS: Of course.

VISITOR: So you're saying that that which is like is not really that which is, if you speak of it as not true.

THEAETETUS: But it *is*, in a way.

VISITOR: But not truly, you say.

THEAETETUS: No, except that it really is a likeness.

VISITOR: So it's not really what is, but it really is what we call a likeness?

THEAETETUS: Maybe *that which is not* is woven together with *that which*   c
is in some way like that—it's quite bizarre.

VISITOR: Of course it's strange. Anyway, you can see that the many-headed sophist is still using this interweaving to force us to agree unwillingly that that which is not in a way is.

THEAETETUS: I definitely do see it.

VISITOR: Well then, how can we define his field of expertise, so as to be consistent?

THEAETETUS: What do you mean? What kind of problem are you afraid of?

VISITOR: When we say that he deceives us about appearances and that   d
he's an expert at deception, are we saying so because his expertise makes our souls believe what is false? Or what shall we say?

THEAETETUS: Just that. What else would we say?

VISITOR: Again, a false belief will be a matter of believing things that are contrary to those which are? Or what?

THEAETETUS: Yes, contrary.

VISITOR: So you're saying that a false belief is believing those which are not.

THEAETETUS: Necessarily.

VISITOR: Believing that those which are not are not, or that those which   e
in no way are in a way are?

THEAETETUS: That those which are not are in a way, it has to be, if anyone is ever going to be even a little bit wrong.

VISITOR: Well, doesn't a false belief also believe that those which completely are in no way are?

THEAETETUS: Yes.

VISITOR: And this is false too?

THEAETETUS: Yes.

241   VISITOR: And I think we'll also regard false speaking the same way, as saying that those which are are not, and that those which are not are.

THEAETETUS: How else would it be false?

VISITOR: I don't suppose there's any other way. The sophist, though, is going to deny that this way is possible. And how could any sensible person accept it, now that what we agreed to earlier has been reinforced.[11] Do we understand what he's saying, Theaetetus?

THEAETETUS: How could we not understand that when we dare to say that falsity is in beliefs and words contain falsity, we're saying what is

b   contrary to what we said just before. We're forced to attach that which is to that which is not, even though we agreed just now that that's completely impossible.

VISITOR: Your memory's correct. But think about what we need to do about the sophist. You see how many and easily available his supply of objections and confusions is if we assume, as we search for him, that he's an expert at cheating and falsehood-making.

THEAETETUS: Definitely.

c   VISITOR: He's got a practically infinite supply of them, and we've gone through only a small fraction.

THEAETETUS: If so, then it seems it would be impossible to catch him.

VISITOR: What, then? Are we going to go soft and give up?

THEAETETUS: I say we shouldn't, if there's even the smallest chance that we can catch him.

VISITOR: So you'll be forgiving and, as you said, happy if we can somehow extricate ourselves even slightly from such a powerful argument?

THEAETETUS: Of course.

d   VISITOR: Then I've got something even more urgent to request.

THEAETETUS: What?

VISITOR: Not to think that I'm turning into some kind of patricide.

THEAETETUS: What do you mean?

VISITOR: In order to defend ourselves we're going to have to subject father Parmenides' saying to further examination, and insist by brute force both that *that which is not* somehow is, and then again that *that which is* somehow is not.

THEAETETUS: It does seem that in what we're going to say, we'll to have to fight through that issue.

e   VISITOR: That's obvious even to a blind man, as they say. We'll never be able to avoid having to make ourselves ridiculous by saying conflicting things whenever we talk about false statements and beliefs, either as copies or likenesses or imitations or appearances, or about whatever sorts of expertise there are concerning those things—unless, that is, we either refute Parmenides' claims or else agree to accept them.

11. I.e., 237a–238c, reinforced by 238d–239c.

THEAETETUS: That's true.

VISITOR: So that's why we have to be bold enough to attack what our 242
father says. Or, if fear keeps us from doing that, then we'll have to leave
it alone completely.

THEAETETUS: Fear, anyway, isn't going to stop us.

VISITOR: Well then, I've got a third thing to ask you, something small.

THEAETETUS: Just tell me what it is.

VISITOR: When I was talking a minute ago I said that I've always given
up whenever I've tried to refute what Parmenides said, just the way I did
this time.

THEAETETUS: Yes, you did say that.

VISITOR: I'm afraid I'll seem insane to you if I'm always shifting my
position back and forth, given what I've said. It's for your sake that we'll b
be trying to refute what Parmenides said—*if* we can do it.

THEAETETUS: Go ahead, then. Don't worry about that. I won't think you're
behaving inappropriately in any way if you go right ahead with your
refutation and demonstration.

VISITOR: Well then, how shall I begin this dangerous discussion? The
path we absolutely have to turn onto, my boy, is this.

THEAETETUS: Namely, . . . ?

VISITOR: We have to reconsider whether we may not be somehow confused about things that now seem to be clear, and whether over-hasty c
judgment may make us agree too easily.

THEAETETUS: Say what you mean more clearly.

VISITOR: Parmenides' way of talking to us has been rather easygoing, it
seems to me. So does the way of talking that everyone uses who has ever
urged us to specify just how many beings there are and what they're like.

THEAETETUS: How?

VISITOR: They each appear to me to tell us a myth, as if we were children.
One tells us that there are three beings, and that sometimes they're somehow at war with each other, while at other times they become friendly, d
marry, give birth, and bring up their offspring. Another one says that there
are two beings, wet and dry or hot and cold. He marries them off and
makes them set up house together. And our Eleatic tribe, starting from
Xenophanes and even people before him, tells us their myth on the assumption that what they call "all things" are just one.[12] Later on, some Ionian
and Sicilian muses both had the idea that it was safer to weave the two e
views together. They say that *that which is* is both many and one, and is
bound by both hatred and friendship. According to the terser of these
muses, in being taken apart they're brought together.[13] The more relaxed

12. This group includes Parmenides of Elea (the Visitor, of course, comes from there).

13. The reference here is to Heraclitus, who was Ionian. See frg. 51 (cf. Plato, *Symp.* 187a).

muses, though, allow things to be free from that condition sometimes. They say that all that there is alternates, and that sometimes it's one and friendly under Aphrodite's influence, but at other times it's many and at war with itself because of some kind of strife.[14] It's hard to say whether any one of these thinkers has told us the truth or not, and it wouldn't be appropriate for us to be critical of such renowned and venerable men. But it wouldn't be offensive to note the following thing, either.

THEAETETUS: What?

VISITOR: That they've been inconsiderate and contemptuous toward us. They've simply been talking their way through their explanations, without paying any attention to whether we were following them or were left behind.

THEAETETUS: What do you mean?

VISITOR: For heaven's sake, Theaetetus, do you understand anything of what they mean each time one of them says that many or one or two things *are* or *have become* or *are becoming*, or when another one speaks of hot mixed with cold and supposes that there are separations and combinations?[15] Earlier in my life I used to think I understood exactly what someone meant when he said just what we're confused about now, namely, this *is not*. You do see what confusion we're in about it?

THEAETETUS: Yes, I do.

VISITOR: But just perhaps the very same thing has happened to us equally about *is*. We say we're in the clear about it, and that we understand when someone says it, but that we don't understand *is not*. But maybe we're in the same state about both.

THEAETETUS: Maybe.

VISITOR: And let's suppose the same thing may be true of the other expressions we've just used.

THEAETETUS: All right.

VISITOR: We can look into most of them later, if that seems to be the best thing to do. Now we'll think about the most fundamental and most important expression.

THEAETETUS: Which one? Oh, obviously you're saying that *being* is the one we have to explore first—that we have to ask what people who say it think they're indicating by it.

VISITOR: You understand exactly, Theaetetus. I'm saying we have to follow the track this way. Let's ask—as if they were here—"Listen, you people who say that all things are just some two things, hot and cold or some such pair. What are you saying about them both when you say that they both *are* and each one *is*? What shall we take this *being* to be? Is it a

14. Here Plato refers to Empedocles, who lived in Sicily.

15. Accepting the emendation of *allos eipēi* for *allothi pēi* in b5.

third thing alongside those two beings, so that according to you everything is no longer two but three? Surely in calling one or the other of the two of them *being*, you aren't saying that they both are, since then in either case they'd be one and not two."

THEAETETUS: That's true.

VISITOR: "But you do want to call both of them *being*?"

THEAETETUS: Probably.

VISITOR: "But," we'll say, "if you did that, friends, you'd also be saying very clearly that the two are one."

THEAETETUS: That's absolutely right.

VISITOR: "Then clarify this for us, since we're confused about it. What do you want to signify when you say *being*? Obviously you've known for a long time. We thought we did, but now we're confused about it. So first teach it to us, so we won't think we understand what you're saying when just the contrary is the case." Would it be the least bit inappropriate for us to ask them this, and anyone else who says that everything is more than one?

THEAETETUS: Not at all.

VISITOR: Well, then, shouldn't we do our best to find out from the people who say that everything is one what they mean by *being*?

THEAETETUS: Of course.

VISITOR: Then they should answer this question: "Do you say that only one thing is?" "We do," they'll say, won't they?

THEAETETUS: Yes.

VISITOR: "Well then, you call something *being*?"

THEAETETUS: Yes.

VISITOR: "Is that just what you call *one*, so that you use two names for the same thing? Or what?"

THEAETETUS: How will they answer that question?

VISITOR: Obviously it's not the easiest thing in the world to answer that question—or any other question, either—for someone who makes the supposition that they do.

THEAETETUS: Why not?

VISITOR: Surely it's absurd for someone to agree that there are two names when he maintains that there's only one thing.

THEAETETUS: Of course.

VISITOR: And it's completely absurd, and unacceptable, for someone to say that there's a name if there's no account of it.

THEAETETUS: What do you mean?

VISITOR: If he supposes that a thing is different from its name, then surely he's mentioning two things.

THEAETETUS: Yes.

VISITOR: And moreover if he supposes that the name is the same as the thing, he'll either be forced to say that the name is the name of nothing,

244

b

c

d

or else, if he says that it's the name of something, then it's the name of nothing other than itself and so will turn out to be only the name of a name and nothing else.

THEAETETUS: Yes.

VISITOR: And also *the one*, being the name of *the one*, will also be the one of the name.[16]

THEAETETUS: It will have to be.

VISITOR: Well then, will they say that *the whole* is different from *the one being*, or the same as it?

e THEAETETUS: Of course they'll say it's the same, and they do.

VISITOR: But suppose a whole is, as even Parmenides says,

> *All around like the bulk of a well-formed sphere,*
> *Equal-balanced all ways from the middle, since neither anything*
>   *more*
> *Must it be, this way or that way, nor anything less.*

If it's like that, then *that which is* will have a middle and extremities. And if it has those then it absolutely has to have parts, doesn't it?

THEAETETUS: Yes.

245 VISITOR: But if a thing has parts then nothing keeps it from having the characteristic of being one in all its parts, and in that way it's all being and it's also one whole.

THEAETETUS: Of course.

VISITOR: But something with that characteristic can't be just the one itself, can it?

THEAETETUS: Why not?

VISITOR: Surely a thing that's truly one, properly speaking, has to be completely without parts.

THEAETETUS: Yes.

b VISITOR: But a thing like what we've described, which consists of many parts, won't fit that account.

THEAETETUS: I understand.

VISITOR: Now if that which is has the characteristic of the one in this way, will it be one and a whole? Or shall we simply deny it's a whole at all?

THEAETETUS: That's a hard choice.

VISITOR: You're right. If it has the characteristic of somehow being one, it won't appear to be the same as the one. Moreover, everything will then be more than one.

THEAETETUS: Yes.

16. Plato is relying on the thought that if the terms "one" and "name" designate one thing (in the sense that he assumes is relevant), then they are interchangeable, even to the point of generating the strange phrase "the one of the name."

VISITOR: Further if *that which is* is not a whole by possessing that as a   c
characteristic, but rather just is *the whole* itself, *that which is* will turn out
to be less than itself.

THEAETETUS: Certainly.

VISITOR: And because it's deprived of itself, *that which is* will be *not being*,
according to that account.

THEAETETUS: Yes.

VISITOR: And everything will be more than one, since *that which is* and
the whole will each have its own separate nature.

THEAETETUS: Yes.

VISITOR: But if *the whole* is not at all, then the very same things are true
of *that which is*, and in addition to not being, it would not even become   d
a being.

THEAETETUS: Why not?

VISITOR: Invariably whatever becomes has at some point become as a
whole. So we can't label either *being* or *becoming* as being without taking
the whole to be among the beings too.

THEAETETUS: That seems entirely right.

VISITOR: And moreover something that isn't a whole can't be of any
quantity at all, since something that's of a certain quantity has to be a
whole of that quantity, whatever it may be.

THEAETETUS: Exactly.

VISITOR: And millions of other issues will also arise, each generating
indefinitely many confusions, if you say that being is only two or one.   e

THEAETETUS: The ones that just turned up show that. One problem led
to another, and at each step there was more and more difficulty and
uncertainty about what we'd just said at the previous stage.

VISITOR: We haven't gone through all the detailed accounts that people
give of *that which is* and *that which is not*, but this is enough. Now we have
to look at the people who discuss the issue in another way. Our aim is to
have them all in view and that way to see that saying what *that which is*   246
is isn't a bit easier than saying what *that which is not* is.

THEAETETUS: So we need to go on to these people too.

VISITOR: It seems that there's something like a battle of gods and giants
among them, because of their dispute with each other over being.[17]

THEAETETUS: How?

VISITOR: One group drags everything down to earth from the heavenly
region of the invisible, actually clutching rocks and trees with their hands.
When they take hold of all these things they insist that only what offers
tangible contact is, since they define being as the same as body. And if   b
any of the others say that something without a body is, they absolutely
despise him and won't listen to him any more.

17. See *Theogony*, esp. 675–715.

THEAETETUS: These are frightening men you're talking about. I've met quite a lot of them already.

VISITOR: Therefore the people on the other side of the debate defend their position very cautiously, from somewhere up out of sight. They insist violently that true being is certain nonbodily forms that can be thought about. They take the bodies of the other group, and also what they call

c   the truth, and they break them up verbally into little bits and call them a process of coming-to-be instead of being. There's a never-ending battle going on constantly between them about this issue.

THEAETETUS: That's true.

VISITOR: Let's talk with each of these groups about the being that they posit.

THEAETETUS: How shall we do it?

VISITOR: It's easier to talk with the ones who put being in the forms. They're gentler people. It's harder—and perhaps just about impossible—

d   with the ones who drag everything down to body by force. It seems to me that we have to deal with them this way.

THEAETETUS: Namely . . . ?

VISITOR: Mainly by making them actually better than they are—if we somehow could. But if we can't do that in fact, then let's do it in words, by supposing that they're willing to answer less wildly than they actually do. Something that better people agree to is worth more than what worse ones agree to. Anyway we're not concerned with the people; we're looking for what's true.

e   THEAETETUS: That's absolutely right.

VISITOR: Then tell the better people to answer you and interpret what they say.

THEAETETUS: All right.

VISITOR: Then let them tell us this: do they say that anything is a mortal animal?

THEAETETUS: Of course they do.

VISITOR: And they agree that a mortal animal is an ensouled body?

THEAETETUS: Of course.

247   VISITOR: And so they're placing soul among the beings?

THEAETETUS: Yes.

VISITOR: What then? Do they say that this soul is just and that soul is unjust, and that this one's intelligent and that one isn't?

THEAETETUS: Of course.

VISITOR: But isn't a soul just by the possession and presence of justice, and isn't another soul contrary to it by the possession and presence of the contrary?

THEAETETUS: Yes, they agree with that.

VISITOR: But they'll say further that at any rate what can be present to a thing or absent from it is something.

THEAETETUS: Yes.

VISITOR: So since there is justice and intelligence and the rest of virtue,   b
and also their contraries, and moreover since there is a soul in which those
things come to be present, do they say that any of these are visible or
touchable, or that they all are invisible?

THEAETETUS: They can hardly say any of them is visible.

VISITOR: And what about these invisible things? Do they say that they
have bodies?

THEAETETUS: They don't give one single answer to that question. They
do say that the soul seems to them to have a kind of body. But as far as
intelligence and the other things you've asked about are concerned, they're
ashamed and don't dare either to agree that they are not beings or to insist   c
that everything is a body.

VISITOR: Obviously this breed of men has improved, Theaetetus. The
native earthborn giants would never have been ashamed to hold the line
for their position, that anything they can't squeeze in their hands is absolutely nothing.

THEAETETUS: That pretty much describes their thinking.

VISITOR: Then let's go back to questioning them. It's enough if they admit
that even a small part of *that which is* doesn't have body. They need to   d
say something about what's common to both it and the things that do
have body, which they focus on when they say that they both *are*. Maybe
that will raise some confusion for them. If it does, then think about whether
they'd be willing to accept our suggestion that *that which is* is something
like the following.

THEAETETUS: Like what? Tell me and maybe we'll know.

VISITOR: I'm saying that a thing really is if it has any capacity at all,   e
either by nature to do something to something else or to have even the
smallest thing done to it by even the most trivial thing, even if it only
happens once. I'll take it as a definition that *those which are* amount to
nothing other than *capacity*.

THEAETETUS: They accept that, since they don't have anything better to
say right now.

VISITOR: Fine. Maybe something else will occur to them later, and to us
too. For now let's agree with them on this much.   248

THEAETETUS: All right.

VISITOR: Let's turn to the other people, the friends of the forms. You
serve as their interpreter for us.

THEAETETUS: All right.

VISITOR: You people distinguish coming-to-be and being and say that
they are separate? Is that right?

THEAETETUS: "Yes."

VISITOR: And you say that by our bodies and through perception we
have dealings with coming-to-be, but we deal with real being by our souls

and through reasoning. You say that being always stays the same and in the same state, but coming-to-be varies from one time to another.

b   THEAETETUS: "We do say that."

VISITOR: And what shall we say this *dealing with* is that you apply in the two cases? Doesn't it mean what we said just now?

THEAETETUS: "What?"

VISITOR: What happens when two things come together, and by some capacity one does something to the other or has something done to it. Or maybe you don't hear their answer clearly, Theaetetus. But I do, probably because I'm used to them.

THEAETETUS: Then what account do they give?

c   VISITOR: They don't agree with what we just said to the earth people about being.

THEAETETUS: What's that?

VISITOR: We took it as a sufficient definition of *beings* that the capacity be present in a thing to do something or have something done to it, to or by even the smallest thing or degree.

THEAETETUS: Yes.

VISITOR: In reply they say that coming-to-be has the capacity to do something or have something done to it, but that this capacity doesn't fit with being.

THEAETETUS: Is there anything to that?

d   VISITOR: We have to reply that we need them to tell us more clearly whether they agree that the soul knows and also that *being* is known.

THEAETETUS: "Yes," they say.

VISITOR: Well then, do you say that knowing and being known are cases of doing, or having something done, or both? Is one of them doing and the other having something done? Or is neither a case of either?

THEAETETUS: Obviously that neither is a case of either, since otherwise they'd be saying something contrary to what they said before.

e   VISITOR: Oh, I see. You mean that if knowing is doing something, then necessarily what is known has something done to it. When being is known by knowledge, according to this account, then insofar as it's known it's changed by having something done to it—which we say wouldn't happen to something that's at rest.

THEAETETUS: That's correct.

VISITOR: But for heaven's sake, are we going to be convinced that it's true that change, life, soul, and intelligence are not present in *that which*
249   *wholly is*, and that it neither lives nor thinks, but stays changeless, solemn, and holy, without any understanding?

THEAETETUS: If we did, sir, we'd be admitting something frightening.

VISITOR: But are we going to say that it has understanding but doesn't have life?

THEAETETUS: Of course not.

VISITOR: But are we saying that it has both those things in it while denying that it has them in its soul?

THEAETETUS: How else would it have them?

VISITOR: And are we saying that it has intelligence, life, and soul, but that it's at rest and completely changeless even though it's alive?

THEAETETUS: All that seems completely unreasonable.

b

VISITOR: Then both *that which changes* and also *change* have to be admitted as being.

THEAETETUS: Of course.

VISITOR: And so, Theaetetus, it turns out that if no beings change then nothing anywhere possesses any intelligence about anything.[18]

THEAETETUS: Absolutely not.

VISITOR: But furthermore if we admit that everything is moving and changing, then on that account we take the very same thing away from those which are.

THEAETETUS: Why?

VISITOR: Do you think that without rest anything would be the same, in the same state in the same respects?

c

THEAETETUS: Not at all.

VISITOR: Well then, do you see any case in which intelligence is or comes-to-be anywhere without these things?

THEAETETUS: Not in the least.

VISITOR: And we need to use every argument we can to fight against anyone who does away with knowledge, understanding, and intelligence but at the same time asserts anything at all about anything.

THEAETETUS: Definitely.

VISITOR: The philosopher—the person who values these things the most—absolutely has to refuse to accept the claim that everything is at rest, either from defenders of the one or from friends of the many forms. In addition he has to refuse to listen to people who say that *that which is* changes in every way. He has to be like a child begging for "both," and say that *that which is*—everything—is both the unchanging and that which changes.

d

THEAETETUS: True.

VISITOR: Well now, apparently we've done a fine job of making our account pull together *that which is*, haven't we?

THEAETETUS: Absolutely.

VISITOR: But for heaven's sake, Theaetetus, ... Now I think we'll recognize how confused our investigation about it is.

THEAETETUS: Why, though? What do you mean?

e

VISITOR: Don't you notice, my young friend, that we're now in extreme ignorance about it, though it appears to us that we're saying something.

18. Accepting the emendation of inserting *pantōn* after *ontōn*.

THEAETETUS: It does to me anyway. But I don't completely understand how we got into this situation without noticing.

VISITOR: Then think more clearly about it. Given what we've just agreed to, would it be fair for someone to ask us the same question we earlier asked the people who say that everything is just *hot* and *cold*?

THEAETETUS: What was it? Remind me.

VISITOR: Certainly. And I'll try, at any rate, to do it by asking you in just the same way as I asked them, so that we can move forward at the same pace.

THEAETETUS: Good.

VISITOR: Now then, wouldn't you say that change and rest are completely contrary to each other?

THEAETETUS: Of course.

VISITOR: And you'd say they both equally are, and that each of them equally is?

THEAETETUS: Yes.

VISITOR: When you admit that they are, are you saying that both and each of them change?

THEAETETUS: Not at all.

VISITOR: And are you signifying that they rest when you say that they both are?

THEAETETUS: Of course not.

VISITOR: So do you conceive *that which is* as a third thing alongside them which encompasses rest and change? And when you say that they both are, are you taking the two of them together and focusing on their association with being?

THEAETETUS: It does seem probably true that when we say change and rest are, we do have a kind of omen of *that which is* as a third thing.

VISITOR: So *that which is* isn't both change and rest; it's something different from them instead.

THEAETETUS: It seems so.

VISITOR: Therefore by its own nature *that which is* doesn't either rest or change.

THEAETETUS: I suppose it doesn't.

VISITOR: Which way should someone turn his thoughts if he wants to establish for himself something clear about it?

THEAETETUS: I don't know.

VISITOR: I don't think any line is easy. If something isn't changing, how can it not be resting? And how can something not change if it doesn't in any way rest? But now *that which is* appears to fall outside both of them. Is that possible?

THEAETETUS: Absolutely not.

VISITOR: In this connection we ought to remember the following.

THEAETETUS: What?

VISITOR: When we were asked what we should apply the name *that which is not* to, we became completely confused. Do you remember?

THEAETETUS: Of course.

VISITOR: And now aren't we in just as much confusion about *that which is?* e

THEAETETUS: We seem to be in even more confusion, if that's possible.

VISITOR: Then we've now given a complete statement of our confusion. But there's now hope, precisely because both *that which is* and *that which is not* are involved in equal confusion. That is, in so far as one of them is clarified, either brightly or dimly, the other will be too. And if we can't 251 see either of them, then anyway we'll push our account of both of them forward as well as we can.

THEAETETUS: Fine.

VISITOR: Let's give an account of how we call the very same thing, whatever it may be, by several names.

THEAETETUS: What, for instance? Give me an example.

VISITOR: Surely we're speaking of a man even when we name him several things, that is, when we apply colors to him and shapes, sizes, defects, and virtues. In these cases and a million others we say that he's not only a man but also is good and indefinitely many different things. And similarly b on the same account we take a thing to be one, and at the same time we speak of it as many by using many names for it.

THEAETETUS: That's true.

VISITOR: Out of all this we've prepared a feast for young people and for old late-learners. They can grab hold of the handy idea that it's impossible for that which is many to be one and for that which is one to be many. They evidently enjoy forbidding us to say that a man is good, and only c letting us say that that which is good is good, or that the man is a man. You've often met people, I suppose, who are carried away by things like that. Sometimes they're elderly people who are amazed at this kind of thing, because their understanding is so poor and they think they've discovered something prodigiously wise.

THEAETETUS: Of course.

VISITOR: Then let's direct our questions now both to these people and d also to the others we were talking with before. That way our account will be addressed to everyone who's ever said anything at all about being.

THEAETETUS: What questions do you mean?

VISITOR: Shall we refuse to apply being to change or to rest, or anything to anything else? Shall we take these things to be unblended and incapable of having a share of each other in the things we say? Or shall we pull them all together and treat them all as capable of associating with each other? Or shall we say that some can associate and some can't? Which of these options shall we say they'd choose, Theaetetus? e

THEAETETUS: I don't know how to answer for them.

VISITOR: Why don't you reply to the options one by one by thinking about what results from each of them?

THEAETETUS: Fine.

VISITOR: First, if you like, let's take them to say that nothing has any capacity at all for association with anything. Then change and rest won't have any share in being.

252   THEAETETUS: No, they won't.

VISITOR: Well then, will either of them be, if they have no association with being?

THEAETETUS: No.

VISITOR: It seems that agreeing to that destroys everything right away, both for the people who make everything change, for the ones who make everything an unchanging unit, and for the ones who say that beings are forms that always stay the same and in the same state. All of these people apply *being*. Some do it when they say that things really are changing, and others do it when they say that things really are at rest.

THEAETETUS: Absolutely.

b   VISITOR: Also there are people who put everything together at one time and divide them at another.[19] Some put them together into one and divide them into indefinitely many, and others divide them into a finite number of elements and put them back together out of them. None of these people, regardless of whether they take this to happen in stages or continuously, would be saying anything if there isn't any blending.

THEAETETUS: Right.

VISITOR: But furthermore the most ridiculous account is the one that's adopted by the people who won't allow anything to be called by a name that it gets by association with something else.

c   THEAETETUS: Why?

VISITOR: They're forced to use *being* about everything, and also *separate*, *from others*, *of itself*, and a million other things. They're powerless to keep from doing it—that is, from linking them together in their speech. So they don't need other people to refute them, but have an enemy within, as people say, to contradict them, and they go carrying him around talking in an undertone inside them like the strange ventriloquist Eurycles.[20]

d   THEAETETUS: That's a very accurate comparison.

VISITOR: Well then, what if we admit that everything has the capacity to associate with everything else?

THEAETETUS: I can solve that one.

VISITOR: How?

THEAETETUS: Because if change and rest belonged to each other then change would be completely at rest and conversely rest itself would be changing.

19. These thinkers were introduced at 242c–d, e–243a.

20. See Aristophanes, *Wasps*, 1017–20.

VISITOR: But I suppose it's ruled out by very strict necessity that change should be at rest and that rest should change.

THEAETETUS: Of course.

VISITOR: So the third option is the only one left.

THEAETETUS: Yes.

VISITOR: Certainly one of the following things has to be the case: either everything is willing to blend, or nothing is, or some things are and some are not.

THEAETETUS: Of course.

VISITOR: And we found that the first two options were impossible.

THEAETETUS: Yes.

VISITOR: So everyone who wants to give the right answer will choose the third.

THEAETETUS: Absolutely.

VISITOR: Since some will blend and some won't, they'll be a good deal like letters of the alphabet. Some of them fit together with each other and some don't.

THEAETETUS: Of course.

VISITOR: More than the other letters the vowels run through all of them like a bond, linking them together, so that without a vowel no one of the others can fit with another.

THEAETETUS: Definitely.

VISITOR: So does everyone know which kinds of letters can associate with which, or does it take an expert?

THEAETETUS: It takes an expert.

VISITOR: What kind?

THEAETETUS: An expert in grammar.

VISITOR: Well then, isn't it the same with high and low notes? The musician is the one with the expertise to know which ones mix and which ones don't, and the unmusical person is the one who doesn't understand that.

THEAETETUS: Yes.

VISITOR: And in other cases of expertise and the lack of it we'll find something similar.

THEAETETUS: Of course.

VISITOR: Well then, we've agreed that kinds mix with each other in the same way. So if someone's going to show us correctly which kinds harmonize with which and which kinds exclude each other, doesn't he have to have some kind of knowledge as he proceeds through the discussion? And in addition doesn't he have to know whether there are any kinds that run through all of them and link them together to make them capable of blending, and also, when there are divisions, whether certain kinds running through wholes are always the cause of the division?

THEAETETUS: Of course that requires knowledge—probably just about the most important kind.

VISITOR: So, Theaetetus, what shall we label this knowledge? Or for heaven's sake, without noticing have we stumbled on the knowledge that free people have? Maybe we've found the philosopher even though we were looking for the sophist?

THEAETETUS: What do you mean?

d   VISITOR: Aren't we going to say that it takes expertise in dialectic to divide things by kinds and not to think that the same form is a different one or that a different form is the same?

THEAETETUS: Yes.

VISITOR: So if a person can do that, he'll be capable of adequately discriminating a single form spread out all through a lot of other things, each of which stands separate from the others. In addition he can discriminate forms that are different from each other but are included within a single form that's outside them, or a single form that's connected as a unit throughout many wholes, or many forms that are completely separate

e   from others.[21] That's what it is to know how to discriminate by kinds how things can associate and how they can't.

THEAETETUS: Absolutely.

VISITOR: And you'll assign this dialectical activity only to someone who has a pure and just love of wisdom.

THEAETETUS: You certainly couldn't assign it to anyone else.

VISITOR: We'll find that the philosopher will always be in a location like

254   this if we look for him. He's hard to see clearly too, but not in the same way as the sophist.

THEAETETUS: Why not?

VISITOR: The sophist runs off into the darkness of *that which is not*, which he's had practice dealing with, and he's hard to see because the place is so dark. Isn't that right?

THEAETETUS: It seems to be.

VISITOR: But the philosopher always uses reasoning to stay near the form, *being*. He isn't at all easy to see because that area is so bright and the eyes

b   of most people's souls can't bear to look at what's divine.

THEAETETUS: That seems just as right as what you just said before.

VISITOR: We'll think about the philosopher more clearly soon if we want to. But as far as the sophist is concerned we obviously shouldn't give up until we've gotten a good enough look at him.

THEAETETUS: Fine.

---

21. Alternatively, the two previous sentences can be translated: "So if a person can do that, he'll adequately discriminate a single form spread out all through many, each of which stands separate from the others, and many forms that are different from each other but are included within a single form that's outside them; and another single form connected as a unit through many wholes, and many forms that are all marked off in separation."

VISITOR: We've agreed on this: some kinds will associate with each other and some won't, some will to a small extent and others will associate a great deal, nothing prevents still others from being all-pervading—from being associated with every one of them. So next let's pursue our account together this way. Let's not talk about every form. That way we won't be thrown off by dealing with too many of them. Instead let's choose some of the most important ones. First we'll ask what they're like, and next we'll ask about their ability to associate with each other. Even if our grasp of *that which is* and *that which is not* isn't completely clear, our aim will be to avoid being totally without an account of them—so far as that's allowed by our present line of inquiry—and see whether we can get away with saying that *that which is not* really is that which is not.

THEAETETUS: That's what we have to do.

VISITOR: The most important kinds we've just been discussing are *that which is, rest*, and *change.*

THEAETETUS: Yes, by far.

VISITOR: And we say that two of them don't blend with each other.

THEAETETUS: Definitely not.

VISITOR: But *that which is* blends with both of them, since presumably both of them are.

THEAETETUS: Of course.

VISITOR: We do have three of them.

THEAETETUS: Yes.

VISITOR: So each of them is different from two of them, but is the same as itself.

THEAETETUS: Yes.

VISITOR: But what in the world are *the same* and *the different* that we've been speaking of? Are they two kinds other than those three but necessarily always blending with them? And do we have to think of them all as being five and not three? Or have what we've been calling *the same* and *the different* turned out, without our realizing it, to be among those three?

THEAETETUS: Maybe.

VISITOR: But change and rest are certainly not *different* or *the same.*

THEAETETUS: Why not?

VISITOR: Whatever we call change and rest in common can't be either one of them.

THEAETETUS: Why not?

VISITOR: Then change would rest and rest would change. In both cases, if either change or rest comes to be either same or different, then it will force the other to change to the contrary of its own nature, since it will share in its contrary.

THEAETETUS: Absolutely.

VISITOR: And both do share in the same and in the different.

THEAETETUS: Yes.

VISITOR: Then anyway let's not say that change is the same or the different, nor that rest is.

THEAETETUS: All right.

VISITOR: But do we have to think of *that which is* and the same as one thing?

THEAETETUS: Maybe.

VISITOR: But if *that which is* and the same don't signify distinct things,
c   then when we say that change and rest both are, we'll be labeling both of them as being the same.

THEAETETUS: But certainly that's impossible.

VISITOR: So it's impossible for *the same* and *that which is* to be one.

THEAETETUS: I suppose so.

VISITOR: Shall we take *the same* as a fourth in addition to the other three forms?

THEAETETUS: Of course.

VISITOR: Well then, do we have to call *the different* a fifth? Or should we think of it and *that which is* as two names for one kind?

THEAETETUS: Maybe.

VISITOR: But I think you'll admit that some of those which are are said by themselves, but some are always said in relation to other things.

THEAETETUS: Of course.

d   VISITOR: But *the different* is always said in relation to another, isn't it?

THEAETETUS: Yes.

VISITOR: But it wouldn't be if *that which is* and the different weren't completely distinct. If the different shared in both kinds the way *that which is* does, then some of the things that are different would be different without being different in relation to anything different. In fact, though, it turns out that whatever is different definitely has to be what it is *from* something that's different.

THEAETETUS: That's exactly the way it is.

e   VISITOR: And we do have to call the nature of the different a fifth among the forms we're choosing.

THEAETETUS: Yes.

VISITOR: And we're going to say that it pervades all of them, since each of them is different from the others, not because of its own nature but because of sharing in the type of the different.

THEAETETUS: Absolutely.

VISITOR: Let's take up each of the five one by one and say this.

THEAETETUS: What?

VISITOR: First let's say that change is completely different from rest. Shall we say that?

THEAETETUS: Yes.

VISITOR: So it is not rest.

THEAETETUS: Not at all.

256 VISITOR: But it is, because it shares in *that which is*.

THEAETETUS: Yes.

VISITOR: Then again change is different from the same.

THEAETETUS: Pretty much.

VISITOR: So it is not the same.

THEAETETUS: No.

VISITOR: But still it was the same, we said,[22] because everything has a share of that.

THEAETETUS: Definitely.

VISITOR: We have to agree without any qualms that change is the same and not the same. When we say that it's the same and not the same, we aren't speaking the same way. When we say it's the same, that's because it shares in the same in relation to itself. But when we say it's not the same, that's because of its association with the different. Because of its association with the different, change is separated from the same, and so becomes not it but different. So that it's right to say that it's not *the same*.

THEAETETUS: Of course.

VISITOR: So if change itself ever somehow had a share in rest, there would be nothing strange about labeling it resting?

THEAETETUS: That's absolutely right, as long as we admit that some kinds will blend with each other and some won't.

VISITOR: That, though, we demonstrated earlier, before we came to this point, and we showed that by nature it has to be so.[23]

THEAETETUS: Of course.

VISITOR: To repeat,[24] change is different from *different*, just as it's other than both the same and rest.

THEAETETUS: It has to be.

VISITOR: So in a way it is different and not different, according to what we've said.

THEAETETUS: Right.

VISITOR: So what next? Are we going to say that *change* is different from the first three but not from the fourth, in spite of the fact that we've agreed that there were five things we were going to investigate?

THEAETETUS: How could we do that? We can't admit that there are fewer of them than there appeared to be just now.

VISITOR: So shall we go on fearlessly contending that *change* is different from *that which is*?

22. Cf. 255a.

23. At 251a–252c.

24. Alternatively: "Let's continue, then:" (On this translation, the Visitor is here taking the next step in his plan announced at 255e8; he has said how change relates to rest and to the same, and now proceeds to say how it relates to the different—after which, c11 ff., he completes the plan by saying how it relates to being. Thus he is not repeating anything already said previously.)

THEAETETUS: Yes, we should be absolutely fearless.

VISITOR: So it's clear that *change* really is both something that is not, but also a thing that is since it partakes in *that which is*?

THEAETETUS: That's absolutely clear.

VISITOR: So it has to be possible for *that which is not* to be, in the case of change and also as applied to all the kinds. That's because as applied to

e all of them the nature of *the different* makes each of them not be, by making it different from that which is. And we're going to be right if we say that all of them *are not* in this same way. And on the other hand we're also going to be right if we call them beings, because they have a share in that which is.

THEAETETUS: It seems that way.

VISITOR: So as concerning each of the forms that which is is extensive, and that which is not is indefinite in quantity.

THEAETETUS: That seems right.

257 VISITOR: So we have to say that *that which is* itself is different from the others.

THEAETETUS: Necessarily.

VISITOR: So even *that which is* is not, in as many applications as there are of the others, since, not being them, it is one thing, namely itself, and on the other hand it is not those others, which are an indefinite number.

THEAETETUS: I suppose so.

VISITOR: So then we shouldn't even be annoyed about this conclusion, precisely because it's the nature of kinds to allow association with each other. And if somebody doesn't admit that, then he needs to win us over from our earlier line of argument for it, in order to win us over from its consequences.

THEAETETUS: That's entirely fair.

b VISITOR: Now let's look at this.

THEAETETUS: What?

VISITOR: It seems that when we say *that which is not*, we don't say something contrary to *that which is*, but only something different from it.

THEAETETUS: Why?

VISITOR: It's like this. When we speak of something as not large, does it seem to you that we indicate the small rather than the equal?

THEAETETUS: Of course not.

VISITOR: So we won't agree with somebody who says that negation

c signifies a contrary. We'll only admit this much: when "not" and "non-" are prefixed to names that follow them, they indicate something *other* than the names, or rather, other than the things to which the names following the negation are applied.

THEAETETUS: Absolutely.

VISITOR: If you don't mind, though, let's think about this.

THEAETETUS: What?

VISITOR: The nature of the different appears to be chopped up, just like knowledge.

THEAETETUS: Why?

VISITOR: Knowledge is a single thing, too, I suppose. But each part of it that has to do with something is marked off and has a name peculiar to itself. That's why there are said to be many expertises and many kinds of knowledge.

THEAETETUS: Of course.

VISITOR: And so the same thing happens to the parts of the nature of the different, too, even though it's one thing.

THEAETETUS: Maybe. But shall we say how?

VISITOR: Is there a part of the different that's placed over against the beautiful?

THEAETETUS: Yes.

VISITOR: Shall we say that it's nameless, or does it have a name?

THEAETETUS: It has a name. What we call *not beautiful* is the thing that's different from nothing other than the nature of the beautiful.

VISITOR: Now go ahead and tell me this.

THEAETETUS: What?

VISITOR: Isn't it in the following way that *the not beautiful* turns out to be, namely, by being both marked off within one kind of *those that are*, and also set over against one of *those that are*?

THEAETETUS: Yes.

VISITOR: Then it seems that *the not beautiful* is a sort of setting of a being over against a being.

THEAETETUS: That's absolutely right.

VISITOR: Well then, according to this account, is the beautiful more a being than the not beautiful?

THEAETETUS: Not at all.

VISITOR: So we have to say that both the not large and the large equally *are*.

THEAETETUS: Yes.

VISITOR: So we also have to put the not just on a par with the just, in that neither *is* any more than the other.

THEAETETUS: Of course.

VISITOR: And we'll speak about the others in the same way too, since the nature of the different appeared as being one of *those that are*. And because it *is*, we have to posit its parts as no less beings.

THEAETETUS: Of course.

VISITOR: So it seems that the setting against each other of the nature of a part of the different and the nature of *that which is* is not any less being— if we're allowed to say such a thing—than *that which is* itself. And it does not signify something contrary to *that which is* but only something different from it.

THEAETETUS: Clearly.

VISITOR: So what shall we call it?

THEAETETUS: Obviously *that which is not*—which we were looking for because of the sophist—is just exactly this.

VISITOR: Then does it have just as much being as any of the others, as you said it did? Should we work up the courage now to say that *that which is not* definitely is something that has its own nature? Should we say that

c just as *the large* was large, *the beautiful* was beautiful, *the not large* was not large, and *the not beautiful* was not beautiful, in the same way *that which is not* also was and is not being, and is one form among the many *that are*? Do we, Theaetetus, still have any doubts about that?

THEAETETUS: No.

VISITOR: You know, our disbelief in Parmenides has gone even farther than his prohibition.

THEAETETUS: How?

VISITOR: We've pushed our investigation ahead and shown him something even beyond what he prohibited us from even thinking about.

THEAETETUS: In what way?

d VISITOR: Because he says, remember,

Never shall it force itself on us, that that which is not may be;
Keep your thought far away from this path of searching.

THEAETETUS: That's what he says.

VISITOR: But we've not only shown that *those which are not* are. We've also caused what turns out to be the form of *that which is not* to appear.

e Since we showed that the nature of *the different* is, chopped up among all beings in relation to each other, we dared to say that *that which is not* really is just this, namely, each part of the nature of the different that's set over against *that which is*.

THEAETETUS: And what we've said seems to me completely and totally true.

VISITOR: Nobody can say that this *that which is not*, which we've made to appear and now dare to say is, is the contrary of *that which is*. We've

259 said good-bye long ago to any contrary of *that which is*, and to whether it is or not, and also to whether or not an account can be given of it. With regard to *that which is not*, which we've said is, let someone refute us and persuade us that we've made a mistake—or else, so long as he can't do that, he should say just what we say. He has to say that the kinds blend with each other, that *that which is* and *the different* pervade all of them and each other, that *the different* shares in *that which is* and so, because of that sharing, is. But he won't say that it is that which it shares in, but that it is different from it, and necessarily, because it *is* different from *that which*

b *is*, it clearly can be *what is not*. On the other hand *that which is* has a share in *the different*, so, being different from all of the others, it is not each of them and it is not all of the others except itself. So *that which is* indisputably is not millions of things, and all of the others together, and also each of them, are in many ways and also are not in many ways.

THEAETETUS: True.

VISITOR: And if anyone doesn't believe these contrarieties, he has to think about them himself and say something better than what we've said. But if he thinks he's recognized a problem in it and enjoys dragging the argument back and forth, then he's been carried away by something that's not worth much of anyone's attention—to go by what we've just been saying, anyway. A thing like that isn't clever or hard to discover, but the other thing is both difficult and at the same time beautiful.

THEAETETUS: What other thing?

VISITOR: The thing we said earlier. That is, we should leave pointless things like this alone. Instead we should be able to follow what a person says and scrutinize it step by step. When he says that what's different is the same in a certain way or that what's the same is different in a certain way, we should understand just what way he means, and the precise respect in which he's saying that the thing is the same or different. But when someone makes that which is the same appear different in just any old way, or vice versa, or when he makes what's large appear small or something that's similar appear dissimilar—well, if someone enjoys constantly trotting out contraries like that in discussion, that's not true refutation. It's only the obvious new-born brain-child of someone who just came into contact with *those which are*.[25]

THEAETETUS: Definitely.

VISITOR: In fact, my friend, it's inept to try to separate everything from everything else. It's the sign of a completely unmusical and unphilosophical person.

THEAETETUS: Why?

VISITOR: To dissociate each thing from everything else is to destroy totally everything there is to say. The weaving together of forms is what makes speech possible for us.

THEAETETUS: That's true.

VISITOR: Think about what a good moment we picked to fight it out against people like that, and to force them further to let one thing blend with another.

THEAETETUS: Why a good moment?

VISITOR: For speech's being one kind among *those that are*. If we were deprived of that, we'd be deprived of philosophy—to mention the most important thing. Besides, now we have to agree about what speech is, but we'd be able to say nothing if speech were taken away from us and weren't

25. See 234d–e.

b   anything at all. And it would be taken away if we admitted that there's
no blending of anything with anything else.

THEAETETUS: This last thing is right, anyway. But I don't understand why
we have to agree about speech.

VISITOR: Well, perhaps you'll understand if you follow me this way.

THEAETETUS: Where?

VISITOR: *That which is not* appeared to us to be one kind among others,
but scattered over all *those which are*.

THEAETETUS: Yes.

VISITOR: So next we have to think about whether it blends with belief
and speech.

THEAETETUS: Why?

c   VISITOR: If it doesn't blend with them then everything has to be true.
But if it does then there will be false belief and false speech, since falsity
in thinking and speaking amount to believing and saying *those that are not*.

THEAETETUS: Yes.

VISITOR: And if there's falsity then there's deception.

THEAETETUS: Of course.

VISITOR: And if there's deception then necessarily the world will be full
of copies, likenesses, and appearances.

THEAETETUS: Of course.

VISITOR: We said that the sophist had escaped into this region, but that
d   he denied that there has come to be or is such a thing as falsity. For he
denied that anyone either thinks or says *that which is not*, on the ground
that *that which is not* never in any way has a share in being.

THEAETETUS: That's what he said.

VISITOR: But now it apparently does share in *that which is*, so he probably
wouldn't still put up a fight about that. Perhaps, though, he might say
that some forms share in *that which is not* and some don't, and that speech
and belief are ones that don't. So he might contend again that copy-making
e   and appearance-making—in which we said he was contained—totally are
not. His ground would be that belief and speech don't associate with *that
which is not*, and that without this association falsity totally is not. That's
why we have to search around for speech, belief, and appearance, and
first discover what they are, so that when they appear we see their associa-
261   tion with *that which is not* clearly. Then when we've seen that clearly we
can show that falsity is, and when we've shown that we can tie the sophist
up in it, if we can keep hold of him—or else we'll let him go and look for
him in another kind.

THEAETETUS: What you said at the start seems absolutely true. The sophist
is a hard kind to hunt down. He seems to have a whole supply of road-
blocks, and whenever he throws one down in our way we have to fight
through it before we can get to him. But now when we've barely gotten
through the one about how *that which is not* is not, he's thrown another
b   one down and we have to show that falsity is present in both speech and

belief. And next, it seems, there will be another and another after that. A limit, it seems, never appears.

VISITOR: Even if you can only make a little progress, Theaetetus, you should cheer up. If you give up in this situation, what will you do some other time when you don't get anywhere or even are pushed back? A person like that would hardly capture a city, as the saying goes. But since we've done what you just said, my friend, the largest wall may already have been captured and the rest of them may be lower and easier.

THEAETETUS: Fine.

VISITOR: Then let's take up speech and belief, as we said just now. That way we can calculate whether *that which is not* comes into contact with them, or whether they're both totally true and neither one is ever false.

THEAETETUS: All right.

VISITOR: Come on, then. Let's think about names again, the same way as we spoke about forms and letters of the alphabet. What we're looking for seems to lie in that direction.

THEAETETUS: What kind of question about them do we have to answer?

VISITOR: Whether they all fit with each other, or none of them do, or some of them will and some of them won't.

THEAETETUS: Anyway it's clear that some will and some won't.

VISITOR: Maybe you mean something like this: names that indicate something when you say them one after another fit together, and names that don't signify anything when you put them in a row don't fit.

THEAETETUS: What do you mean?

VISITOR: The same thing I thought you were assuming when you agreed with me just now—since there are two ways to use your voice to indicate something about being.

THEAETETUS: What are they?

VISITOR: One kind is called names, and the other is called verbs.

THEAETETUS: Tell me what each of them is.

VISITOR: A verb is the sort of indication that's applied to an action.

THEAETETUS: Yes.

VISITOR: And a name is the kind of spoken sign that's applied to things that perform the actions.

THEAETETUS: Definitely.

VISITOR: So no speech is formed just from names spoken in a row, and also not from verbs that are spoken without names.

THEAETETUS: I didn't understand that.

VISITOR: Clearly you were focusing on something else when you agreed with me just now. What I meant was simply this: things don't form speech if they're said in a row like this.

THEAETETUS: Like what?

VISITOR: For example, "walks runs sleeps," and other verbs that signify actions. Even if somebody said all of them one after another that wouldn't be speech.

THEAETETUS: Of course not.

VISITOR: Again, if somebody said "lion stag horse," and whatever names
c   there are of things that perform actions, the series wouldn't make up
speech. The sounds he uttered in the first or second way wouldn't indicate
either an action or an inaction or the being of something that is or of
something that is not—not until he mixed verbs with nouns. But when he
did that, they'd fit together and speech—the simplest and smallest kind
of speech, I suppose—would arise from that first weaving of name and
verb together.

THEAETETUS: What do you mean?

VISITOR: When someone says "man learns," would you say that's the
shortest and simplest kind of speech?

d   THEAETETUS: Yes.

VISITOR: Since he gives an indication about what is, or comes to be, or
has come to be, or is going to be. And he doesn't just name, but *accomplishes*
something, by weaving verbs with names. That's why we said he speaks
and doesn't just name. In fact this weaving is what we use the word
"speech" for.

THEAETETUS: Right.

VISITOR: So some things fit together and some don't. Likewise some vocal
e   signs don't fit together, but the ones that do produce speech.

THEAETETUS: Absolutely.

VISITOR: But there's still this small point.

THEAETETUS: What?

VISITOR: Whenever there's speech it has to be about something. It's
impossible for it not to be about something.

THEAETETUS: Yes.

VISITOR: And speech also has to have some particular quality.

THEAETETUS: Of course.

VISITOR: Now let's turn our attention to ourselves.

THEAETETUS: All right.

VISITOR: I'll produce some speech by putting a thing together with an
action by means of a name and a verb. You have to tell me what it's about.

263   THEAETETUS: I'll do it as well as I can.

VISITOR: "Theaetetus sits." That's not a long piece of speech, is it?

THEAETETUS: No, not too long.

VISITOR: Your job is to tell what it's about, what it's of.

THEAETETUS: Clearly it's about me, of me.

VISITOR: Then what about this one?

THEAETETUS: What one?

VISITOR: "Theaetetus (to whom I'm now talking) flies."

THEAETETUS: No one would ever deny that it's of me and about me.

VISITOR: We also say that each piece of speech has to have some particular quality.

THEAETETUS: Yes.

VISITOR: What quality should we say each one of these has?

THEAETETUS: The second one is false, I suppose, and the other one is true.

VISITOR: And the true one says *those that are*, as they are, about you.[26]

THEAETETUS: Of course.

VISITOR: And the false one says things different from *those that are*.

THEAETETUS: Yes.

VISITOR: So it says *those that are not*, but that they are.

THEAETETUS: I suppose so.

VISITOR: But they're different things that are from the things that are about you—since we said that concerning each thing many beings are and many are not.[27]

THEAETETUS: Absolutely.

VISITOR: In the first place, the second piece of speech I said about you must be one of the shortest there is, according to our definition of speech.

THEAETETUS: We agreed to that just now, anyway.

VISITOR: And we agreed that it's of something.

THEAETETUS: Yes.

VISITOR: And if it is not of you, it isn't of anything else.

THEAETETUS: Of course not.

VISITOR: And if it were not of anything it would not be speech at all, since we showed that it was impossible for speech that is, to be speech that is of nothing.

THEAETETUS: Absolutely right.

VISITOR: But if someone says things about you, but says different things as the same or not beings as beings, then it definitely seems that false speech really and truly arises from that kind of putting together of verbs and names.

THEAETETUS: Yes, very true.

VISITOR: Well then, isn't it clear by now that both true and false thought and belief and appearance can occur in our souls?

THEAETETUS: How?

VISITOR: The best way for you to know how is for you first to grasp what they are and how they're different from each other.

THEAETETUS: Then just tell me.

VISITOR: Aren't thought and speech the same, except that what we call thought is speech that occurs without the voice, inside the soul in conversation with itself?

26. This sentence is ambiguous. First, the Greek here uses an idiom which could mean either "says those that are, as they are" or "says those that are, that they are" (cf. 263d). Secondly, the additional explanatory phrase, "about you," could be taken with "says," with "are," or with both.

27. See 256e5–6.

THEAETETUS: Of course.

VISITOR: And the stream of sound from the soul that goes through the mouth is called speech?

THEAETETUS: Right.

VISITOR: And then again we know that speech contains . . .

THEAETETUS: What?

VISITOR: Affirmation and denial.

THEAETETUS: Yes.

264 VISITOR: So when affirmation or denial occurs as silent thought inside the soul, wouldn't you call that belief?

THEAETETUS: Of course.

VISITOR: And what if that doesn't happen on its own but arises for someone through perception? When that happens, what else could one call it correctly, besides appearance?

THEAETETUS: Yes.

VISITOR: So since there is true and false speech, and of the processes just mentioned, thinking appeared to be the soul's conversation with itself,

b belief the conclusion of thinking, and what we call appearing the blending of perception and belief, it follows that since these are all the same kind of thing as speech, some of them must sometimes be false.

THEAETETUS: Of course.

VISITOR: So you realize we've found false belief and speech sooner than we expected to just now. Then we were afraid that to look for it would be to attack a completely hopeless project.

THEAETETUS: Yes.

VISITOR: So let's not be discouraged about what's still left. Since these

c other things have come to light, let's remember the divisions by types that we made earlier.

THEAETETUS: Which ones?

VISITOR: We divided copy-making into two types, likeness-making and appearance-making.

THEAETETUS: Yes.

VISITOR: And we said we were confused about which one to put the sophist in.

THEAETETUS: Yes.

VISITOR: And in our confusion about that we plunged into even greater bewilderment, when an account emerged that disagreed with everyone, by denying that there are likenesses or copies or appearances at all, on

d the ground that there isn't ever any falsity in any way anywhere.

THEAETETUS: That's right.

VISITOR: But now since false speech and false belief both appear to be, it's possible for imitations of *those that are* to be, and for expertise in deception to arise from that state of affairs.

THEAETETUS: Yes.

VISITOR: And we agreed before that the sophist does fall under one of the two types we just mentioned.

THEAETETUS: Yes.

VISITOR: Then let's try again to take the kind we've posited and cut it in two. Let's go ahead and always follow the righthand part of what we've cut, and hold onto things that the sophist is associated with until we strip away everything that he has in common with other things. Then when we've left his own peculiar nature, let's display it, especially to ourselves but also to people to whom this sort of procedure is naturally congenial.

e

265

THEAETETUS: All right.

VISITOR: Didn't we begin by dividing expertise into productive and acquisitive?

THEAETETUS: Yes.

VISITOR: And under the acquisitive part the sophist appeared in hunting, combat, wholesaling, and types of that sort.[28]

THEAETETUS: Of course.

VISITOR: But now, since he's included among experts in imitation, first we obviously have to divide productive expertise in two. We say imitation is a sort of production, but of copies and not of the things themselves. Is that right?

b

THEAETETUS: Absolutely.

VISITOR: First of all, production has two parts.

THEAETETUS: What are they?

VISITOR: Divine and human.

THEAETETUS: I don't understand yet.

VISITOR: If you remember how we started,[29] we said production was any capacity that causes things to come to be that previously were not.

THEAETETUS: I remember.

VISITOR: Take animals and everything mortal, including plants and everything on the earth that grows from seeds and roots, and also all lifeless bodies made up inside the earth, whether fusible or not. Are we going to say that anything besides the craftsmanship of a god makes them come to be after previously not being? Or shall we rely on the saying and the widespread belief that . . . ?

c

THEAETETUS: That what?

VISITOR: Are we going to say that nature produces them by some spontaneous cause that generates them without any thought, or by a cause that works by reason and divine knowledge derived from a god?

THEAETETUS: I often shift back and forth on that from one view to the other, maybe because of my age. When I'm focusing on you now, and

d

28. See 221c–225a.
29. See 219b.

supposing that you think they come to be by the agency of a god, that's what I think too.

VISITOR: Fine, Theaetetus. If we thought you were the kind of person who might believe something different in the future we'd try to use some cogent, persuasive argument to make you agree. But since I know what

e   your nature is and I know, too, that even without arguments from us it will tend in the direction that it's pulled toward now, I'll let the issue go. It would take too much time. I'll assume divine expertise produces the things that come about by so-called nature, and that human expertise produces the things that humans compound those things into. According to this account there are two kinds of production, human and divine.

THEAETETUS: Right.

VISITOR: Since there are two of them, cut each of them in two again.

THEAETETUS: How?

266   VISITOR: It's as if you'd already cut production all the way along its width, and now you'll cut it along its length.

THEAETETUS: All right.

VISITOR: That way there are four parts of it all together, two human ones related to us and two divine ones related to the gods.

THEAETETUS: Yes.

VISITOR: Then if we take the division we made the first way, one part of each of those parts is the production of originals. Just about the best thing to call the two parts that are left might be "copy-making." That way, production is divided in two again.

b   THEAETETUS: Tell me again how each of them is divided.

VISITOR: We know that we human beings and the other living things, and also fire, water, and things like that, which natural things come from, are each generated and produced by a god. Is that right?

THEAETETUS: Yes.

VISITOR: And there are copies of each of these things, as opposed to the things themselves, that also come about by divine workmanship.

THEAETETUS: What kinds of things?

VISITOR: Things in dreams, and appearances that arise by themselves during the day. They're shadows when darkness appears in firelight, and

c   they're reflections when a thing's own light and the light of something else come together around bright, smooth surfaces and produce an appearance that looks the reverse of the way the thing looks from straight ahead.

THEAETETUS: Yes, those are two products of divine production—the things themselves and the copies corresponding to each one.

VISITOR: And what about human expertise? We say housebuilding makes a house itself and drawing makes a different one, like a human dream made for people who are awake.

d   THEAETETUS: Of course.

VISITOR: And just the same way in other cases, too, there are pairs of products of human production, that is, the thing itself, we say, and the copy.

THEAETETUS: Now I understand better and I take it that there are two kinds of double production, divine and human in each division. One kind produces things themselves, and the other kind produces things similar to them.

VISITOR: Let's recall that one part of copy-making is likeness-making. The other kind was going to be appearance-making, if falsity appeared to be truly falsity and by nature one of *those that are*.

THEAETETUS: Yes, it was.

VISITOR: But falsity did turn out that way, so are we going to count likeness-making and appearance-making as indisputably two forms?

THEAETETUS: Yes.

VISITOR: Then let's divide appearance-making in two again.

THEAETETUS: How?

VISITOR: Into one sort that's done with tools and one that uses one's own self as the tool of the person making the appearance.

THEAETETUS: What do you mean?

VISITOR: When somebody uses his own body or voice to make something similar to your body or voice, I think the best thing to call this part of appearance-making is "imitating."

THEAETETUS: Yes.

VISITOR: Let's set this part off by calling it imitation, and let's be lazy and let the other part go. We'll leave it to someone else to bring it together into a unit and give it a suitable name.

THEAETETUS: All right, let's take the one and let the other go.

VISITOR: But the right thing, Theaetetus, is still to take imitation to have two parts. Think about why.

THEAETETUS: Tell me.

VISITOR: Some imitators know what they're imitating and some don't. And what division is more important than the one between ignorance and knowledge?

THEAETETUS: None.

VISITOR: Wasn't the imitation that we just mentioned the kind that's associated with knowledge? Someone who knew you and your character might imitate you, mightn't he?

THEAETETUS: Of course.

VISITOR: What about the character of justice and all of virtue taken together? Don't many people who are ignorant of it, but have some beliefs about it, try hard to cause what they believe it is to appear to be present in them. And don't they imitate it in their words and actions as much as they can?

THEAETETUS: Very many people do that.

VISITOR: And are they all unsuccessful at seeming to be just without being just at all? Or is the opposite true?

THEAETETUS: Yes, the opposite.

d   VISITOR: I think we have to say that this person, who doesn't know, is a very different imitator from the previous one, who does.

THEAETETUS: Yes.

VISITOR: Where would you get a suitable name for each of them? Isn't it obviously hard to, just because the people who came before us were thoughtless and lazy about dividing kinds into types, and so they never even tried to divide them. That's why we necessarily lack a good supply of names. Still, even though it sounds daring let's distinguish them by

e   calling imitation accompanied by belief "belief-mimicry" and imitation accompanied by knowledge "informed mimicry."

THEAETETUS: All right.

VISITOR: Then we need to use the former term, since the sophist isn't one of the people who know but is one of the people who imitate.

THEAETETUS: He certainly is.

VISITOR: Let's examine the belief-mimic the way people examine iron, to see whether it's sound or has a crack in it.

THEAETETUS: All right.

268   VISITOR: Well, it has a big one. One sort of belief-mimic is foolish and thinks he knows the things he only has beliefs about. The other sort has been around a lot of discussions, and so by temperament he's suspicious and fearful that he doesn't know the things that he pretends in front of others to know.

THEAETETUS: There definitely are both types that you've mentioned.

VISITOR: Shall we take one of these to be a sort of sincere imitator and the other to be an insincere one?

THEAETETUS: That seems right.

VISITOR: And are there one or two kinds of insincere ones?

THEAETETUS: You look and see.

b   VISITOR: I'm looking, and there clearly appear to be two. I see that one sort can maintain his insincerity in long speeches to a crowd, and the other uses short speeches in private conversation to force the person talking with him to contradict himself.

THEAETETUS: You're absolutely right.

VISITOR: How shall we show up the long-winded sort, as a statesman or as a demagogue?

THEAETETUS: A demogogue.

VISITOR: And what shall we call the other one? Wise, or a sophist?

THEAETETUS: We can't call him wise, since we took him not to know

c   anything. But since he imitates the wise man he'll obviously have a name derived from the wise man's name. And now at last I see that we have to call him the person who is really and truly a *sophist*.

VISITOR: Shall we weave his name together from start to finish and tie it up the way we did before?

THEAETETUS: Of course.

VISITOR: Imitation of the contrary-speech-producing, insincere and unknowing sort, of the appearance-making kind of copy-making, the word-juggling part of production that's marked off as human and not divine. 268d Anyone who says the sophist is of this "blood and family"[30] will be saying, it seems, the complete truth.

THEAETETUS: Absolutely.

---

30. See *Iliad* vi.211.

STATESMAN

This dialogue is a sequel to Sophist. *Here the unnamed philosopher from Elea
continues his project of expounding his own conceptions of the natures of sophistry and statesmanship, as intellectual capacities distinct both from one another and from that of the philosopher. Now, for his account of the statesman,
he takes as his discussion partner—the respondent to the questions he asks in
developing and displaying his views—Socrates' namesake, a pupil, with
Theaetetus, of the visiting geometer Theodorus, from Cyrene, an important
Greek city on the North African coast. As in* Sophist, *neither Socrates nor
Theodorus takes part in the discussion, except for the brief introductory conversation.*

The 'statesman'—in Greek the politikos, *whence the Latinized title* Poli-
ticus *by which the dialogue is alternatively known—is understood from the
outset as the possessor of the specialist, expert knowledge of how to rule justly
and well—to the citizens' best interests—in a 'city' or* polis, *directing all its
public institutions and affairs. (It is assumed that such knowledge is not only
possible, but that politics should be led by it—assumptions that could be questioned, of course.) In constructing his 'divisions,' the visitor looks simply to
the demand for, and the demands of, this knowledge: he is not defining the capacities needed in their work by any actual persons whom we (or Greeks of the
time) would ordinarily describe as 'statesmen'. In fact, a central thesis of the
visitor is that no current city is ruled by such expert statesmen at all. And
since no actual person ruling in a city possesses this knowledge, the best current government could (paradoxically) only be that directed by an imitator—a
'sophist', one who as* Sophist *has explained is aware that he does not* know
*the right thing to do, but makes it appear to others that he does; such a govern-
ment would have good laws and would enforce them, under this 'sophist's' direction, but the knowledge of statesmanship itself would only be weakly reflected in these laws and in the 'sophist's' behavior—it would not actually
reside anywhere in the community.*

*The visitor repeatedly makes plain that, in presenting his views on states-
manship, he is not concerned merely with questions of political theory. In fact,
his chief concern is to teach us how to improve ourselves in philosophy itself—
to become expert in precisely this 'method of division' that he is employing to
make the statesman's nature clear. So he pauses in his exposition several times
to point up errors being made along the way, and say how to correct them, as
well as to indicate special features of the method and the reasons why they are
needed. Thus we are treated to excursuses on what it is to divide a class at*

294

places where there are real subclasses marked off by their own specific natures, not in some arbitrary and merely conventional way; on which sorts of things require the preliminary study of 'models' in order to understand them fully— and on the precise nature of such a 'model'; on the often neglected but crucially important science of measuring things by reference to 'due measure' and not relatively to given other things exceeding or falling short of them in the relevant respect—length, weight, size, etc. And we get an elaborate and brilliant 'myth' about rule in a former era when gods were personally in charge of human affairs—necessarily different from the statesmanship we are trying to define, since that is an expertise possessed, if at all, by human beings. In their contribution to our understanding of Plato's later metaphysics, these digressions can usefully be compared to the long digression in Sophist on the natures of being and not being.

Modern readers are often impatient with the visitor's use of lengthy 'divisions' in expounding his views on the nature of statesmanship. Nonetheless, this brilliant dialogue presents a fascinating set of ideas about human affairs— 'second thoughts' about politics quite different from the theory of philosopher-kings recommended in Republic, *and looking forward to the system of laws, and government under them, set out in* Laws. *It richly repays any effort needed to read it.*

J.M.C.

SOCRATES: I'm really much indebted to you, Theodorus, for introducing   257
me to Theaetetus, and also to our visitor.

THEODORUS: And perhaps,[1] Socrates, your debt will be three times as great, when they complete both the statesman and the philosopher for you.

SOCRATES: Well, yes and no: shall we say, my dear Theodorus, that we've heard the best arithmetician and geometer putting it like that?

THEODORUS: How do you mean, Socrates?   b

SOCRATES: Because you assumed that each of the three were to be assigned equal worth, when in fact they differ in value by more than can be expressed in terms of mathematical proportion.

THEODORUS: Well said, Socrates, by our god Ammon;[2] a just rebuke— you've remembered your arithmetic very well,[3] to bring me up on my mistake like that. As for you, I'll get my own back for this on another occasion. But turning to our guest—don't you give up at all on obliging   c

Translated by C. J. Rowe.

1. Reading *de ge* at a3.

2. Ammon, a great god of the Egyptians, had a famous oracle at Siwah, not far from Theodorus' home city of Cyrene.

3. Reading *panu mnēmonikōs* at b6.

us, but, whether you choose the statesman first or the philosopher, make your choice and go through him in his turn.

VISITOR: That, Theodorus, is what we must do, since we have tried our hand once, and[4] we must not desist until we come to the end of what we have in hand. But I have a question: what should I do about Theaetetus here?

THEODORUS: In what respect?

VISITOR: Should we give him a rest and substitute for him young Socrates here, who trains with him? Or what's your advice?

THEODORUS: As you say, make the substitution; since they are young, they'll put up with any sort of exertion more easily if they take a rest.

d   [OLDER] SOCRATES: What's more, my friend, both of them seem somehow to have a certain kinship with me. One of them you all say is like me in
258   the way he looks; as for the other, he is called and designated by the same name as I am, and that produces a certain relatedness. Well, we must always be eager to recognize those akin to us by talking to them. With Theaetetus I myself got together in discussion yesterday, and I have just now heard him[5] answering questions, whereas neither applies in Socrates' case; we must take a look at him too. He'll answer me on another occasion; for now let him answer you.

VISITOR: I'll go along with that. Socrates, do you hear what Socrates says?

YOUNG SOCRATES: Yes.

VISITOR: Then do you agree to it?

YOUNG SOCRATES: Absolutely.

b   VISITOR: It seems there is no obstacle on your side, and perhaps there should be even less on mine. Well then, after the sophist, it seems to me that the two of us must search for the statesman.[6] Now tell me: should we posit in the case of this person too that he is one of those who possess knowledge,[7] or what assumption should we make?

YOUNG SOCRATES: That's what we should assume.

VISITOR: In that case we must divide the various sorts of knowledge, as we did when we were considering the previous individual?

YOUNG SOCRATES: Perhaps so.

VISITOR: But it's not in the same place, Socrates, that I think I see a cut.

YOUNG SOCRATES: Why not?

c   VISITOR: It's in a different place.

YOUNG SOCRATES: Yes, apparently.

4. Reading *kai* at c3.

5. 'Yesterday' refers to the (fictional) occasion of the *Theaetetus*, 'just now' to that of the *Sophist*.

6. Reading *ton politikon andra* at b3.

7. In Greek, *epistēmē*. 'Knowledge' or 'expert knowledge' in this translation normally indicates the presence of this noun or of words deriving from the same root. The term 'expertise' by itself is reserved for *technē*. Where Plato speaks e.g. of the 'kingly' or 'political' *epistēmē* or *technē*, the translation shifts to 'art,' the traditional rendering.

VISITOR: So in what direction will one discover the path that leads to the statesman? For we must discover it, and after having separated it from the rest we must impress one character on it; and having stamped a single different form on the other turnings we must make our minds think of all sorts of knowledge there are as falling into two classes.[8]

YOUNG SOCRATES: That, I think, is actually for you to do, visitor, not for me.

VISITOR: But, Socrates, it must also be a matter for you, when it becomes   d
clear to us what it is.

YOUNG SOCRATES: You're right.

VISITOR: Well then: isn't it the case that arithmetic and some other sorts of expertise that are akin to it don't involve any practical actions, but simply provide knowledge?

YOUNG SOCRATES: That's so.

VISITOR: Whereas for their part the sorts of expertise involved in carpentry and manufacture as a whole have their knowledge as it were naturally bound up with practical actions, and use it to complete those material   e
objects they cause to come into being from not having been before?

YOUNG SOCRATES: What of that?

VISITOR: Well, divide all cases of knowledge in this way, calling the one sort practical knowledge, the other purely theoretical.

YOUNG SOCRATES: I grant you these as two classes of that single thing, knowledge, taken as a whole.

VISITOR: Then shall we posit the statesman and king and slave-master, and the manager of a household as well, as one thing, when we refer to them by all these names, or are we to say that they are as many sorts of expertise as the names we use to refer to them? Or rather, let me take this way, and you follow me.

YOUNG SOCRATES: What way is that?

---

8. 'Class', or occasionally 'real class', are reserved in this translation for *eidos* (as here), or *genos*, which is used synonymously in this role. (In the *Sophist* translation, *eidos* generally appears as 'form' or 'type,' *genos* as 'kind.') What the Visitor and Young Socrates appear to be doing when they 'divide' in each case—as here, with knowledge— is to divide a more generic grouping or 'class' into more specific sub-groups or '(sub-) classes' (the claim being in each case that the 'cut' is made in accordance with actual divisions, existing in things themselves). A third, related, term is *idea*. It can be used to refer to what distinguishes a given class of things from others—its 'character'—but can also substitute for *eidos* and *genos* as 'class'/'real class'. Conversely, *eidos* itself can be used synonymously with *idea* in the sense of 'character'. Other terms that can play something like the role of *eidos/genos* as 'class' are *phulon*, literally 'tribe' (260d7), and *phusis* (306e11; cf. 278b2), which more usually serves as the standard term for 'nature'. Puns on *genos* in the two senses of 'family'/'race' and 'class' call for special measures: at 260d6, 266b1, it is 'family or class', at 310b10 ff., 'family-type'. Other related terms used in the translation, like 'category' (as at 263d8) or 'sort' (as in 'sort of expertise'), do not indicate the presence of any of these key Greek terms, but are supplied by the translator, simply to find natural English phrases to fill out elliptical Greek ones.

259   VISITOR: This one. If someone who is himself in private practice is capable
of advising a doctor in public employment, isn't it necessary for him to
be called by the same professional title as the person he advises?

YOUNG SOCRATES: Yes.

VISITOR: Well then, won't we say that the person who is clever at giving
advice to a king of a country, although he is himself a private individual,
himself has the expert knowledge that the ruler himself ought to have possessed?

YOUNG SOCRATES: We will.

b   VISITOR: But the knowledge that belongs to the true king is the knowledge
of kingship?

YOUNG SOCRATES: Yes.

VISITOR: And isn't it the case that the person who possesses this, whether
he happens to be a ruler or a private citizen, in all circumstances, in virtue
of his possession of the expertise itself, will correctly be addressed as an
expert in kingship?

YOUNG SOCRATES: That's fair.

VISITOR: Next, a household manager and a slave-master are the same
thing.

YOUNG SOCRATES: Of course.

VISITOR: Well then, surely there won't be any difference, so far as ruling
is concerned, between the character of a large household, on the one hand,
and the bulk of a small city on the other?

YOUNG SOCRATES: None.

c   VISITOR: So, in answer to the question we were asking ourselves just
now, it's clear that there is one sort of expert knowledge concerned with
all these things; whether someone gives this the name of expertise in
kingship, or statesmanship, or household management, let's not pick any
quarrel with him.

YOUNG SOCRATES: I agree—why should we?

VISITOR: But this much is clear, that the power of any king to maintain
his rule has little to do with the use of his hands or his body in general
in comparison with the understanding and force of his mind.

YOUNG SOCRATES: Clearly.

VISITOR: Then do you want us to assert that the king is more closely
d   related to the theoretical sort of knowledge than to the manual or generally
practical sort?

YOUNG SOCRATES: Of course.

VISITOR: In that case we shall put all these things together—the statesman's knowledge and the statesman, the king's knowledge and the king—
as one, and regard them as the same?[9]

9. Alternatively: "In that case we shall take all these things together—the statesman's
knowledge and the statesman, the king's knowledge and the king—as one, and put
them into the same category?"

YOUNG SOCRATES: Clearly.

VISITOR: Well, would we be proceeding in the right order, if after this we divided theoretical knowledge?

YOUNG SOCRATES: Certainly.

VISITOR: So look closely to see if we can detect some break in it.

YOUNG SOCRATES: Of what sort? Tell me.

VISITOR: Of this sort. We agreed, I think, that there is such a thing as an art of calculation?   e

YOUNG SOCRATES: Yes.

VISITOR: And I suppose it belongs absolutely among the theoretical sorts of expertise.

YOUNG SOCRATES: Quite.

VISITOR: Because once it recognizes that there is a difference between numbers, there surely isn't any further job we'll assign to it than judging what it has recognized?

YOUNG SOCRATES: No, certainly not.

VISITOR: And all master-builders too[10]—they don't act as workers themselves, but manage workers.

YOUNG SOCRATES: Yes.

VISITOR: In so far—I suppose—as what the master-builder provides is understanding rather than manual labor.

YOUNG SOCRATES: Just so.

VISITOR: It would be right to say, then, that he has a share in the theoretical   260
sort of knowledge?

YOUNG SOCRATES: Certainly.

VISITOR: But it belongs to him, I think, once he has given his professional judgment, not to be finished or to take his leave, in the way that the expert in calculation took his, but to assign whatever is the appropriate task to each group of workers until they complete what has been assigned to them.

YOUNG SOCRATES: That's correct.

VISITOR: So both all sorts of knowledge like this and all those that go along with the art of calculation are theoretical, but these two classes of   b
knowledge differ from each other in so far as one makes judgments, while the other directs?

YOUNG SOCRATES: They appear to do so.

VISITOR: So if we divided off two parts of theoretical knowledge as a whole, referring to one as directive and the other as making judgments, would we say that it had been divided suitably?

YOUNG SOCRATES: Yes, at least according to my view.

VISITOR: But if people are doing something together, it is enough if they agree with one another.

YOUNG SOCRATES: Quite.

10. Reading *kai mēn* for *kai gar* at e9.

VISITOR: So for as long as we are sharing in the present task, we should say goodbye to what everybody else may think.

YOUNG SOCRATES: Of course.

c   VISITOR: So tell me: in which of these two sorts of expertise should we locate the expert in kingship? In the one concerned with making judgments, as if he were some sort of spectator, or shall we rather locate him as belonging to the directive sort of expertise, seeing that he is master of others?

YOUNG SOCRATES: In the second, of course.

VISITOR: Then we should need to look at directive expertise in its turn, to see if it divides somewhere. And to me it seems that it does so somewhere in this direction: in the way that the expertise of the retail-dealer is distinguished from that of the 'self-seller' or producer who sells

d   his own products, so the class of kings appears set apart from the class of heralds.

YOUNG SOCRATES: How so?

VISITOR: The retailer, I think, takes over someone else's products, which have previously been sold, and sells them on, for a second time.

YOUNG SOCRATES: Absolutely.

VISITOR: Well then, the class of heralds takes over directions that have been thought up by someone else, and itself issues them for a second time to another group.

YOUNG SOCRATES: Very true.

VISITOR: So—shall we mix together the expertise of the king with that

e   of the interpreter, the person who gives the time to the rowers, the seer, the herald, and many other sorts of expertise related to these, just because they all have the feature of issuing directions? Or do you want us to make up a name in line with the analogy we were using just now, since in fact the class of 'self-directors' happens pretty much to be without a name of its own? Should we divide these things this way, locating the class of kings as belonging to the 'self-directing' sort of expertise, and taking no notice of all the rest, leaving someone else to propose another name for them?

261 For we set up our investigation in order to find the person who rules, not his opposite.

YOUNG SOCRATES: Absolutely.

VISITOR: Well then, since this[11] is at a certain distance from those others, distinguished by difference in relation to kinship, we must in turn divide it too, if we still find some cut yielding to us in it?

YOUNG SOCRATES: Certainly.

VISITOR: And what's more, we seem to have one: follow on and make the cut with me.

YOUNG SOCRATES: Where?

11. I.e., the 'self-directing' sort of expertise.

VISITOR: All those in control of others that we can think of as employing   b
directions—we shall find them issuing their directions, won't we, for the
sake of something's coming into being?

YOUNG SOCRATES: Of course.

VISITOR: And it's not at all difficult to separate into two all of those things
that come into being.

YOUNG SOCRATES: How?

VISITOR: I imagine that, of all of them taken together, some are inanimate
and some are animate.

YOUNG SOCRATES: Yes.

VISITOR: And it's by these very things that we'll cut the part of the
theoretical which is directive, if indeed we wish to cut it.

YOUNG SOCRATES: How?

VISITOR: By assigning part of it to the production of inanimate things,   c
part to that of animate things; and in this way it will all immediately be
divided into two.

YOUNG SOCRATES: I agree absolutely.

VISITOR: So then let's leave one of these parts to one side, and take up
the other; and then let's divide the whole of it into two parts.

YOUNG SOCRATES: Which of the two parts do you say we should take up?

VISITOR: I suppose it must be the one that issues directions in relation
to living creatures. For surely it is not the case that the expert knowledge
that belongs to a king is ever something that oversees inanimate things,
as if it were the knowledge of the master-builder; it is something nobler,
which always has its power among living creatures and in relation to   d
just these.

YOUNG SOCRATES: Correct.

VISITOR: Now, as one can observe, either the production and rearing of
living creatures is done singly, or it is a caring for creatures together[12]
in herds.

YOUNG SOCRATES: Correct.

VISITOR: But we'll certainly not find the statesman rearing individual
creatures, like some ox-driver or groom, but rather resembling a horse-
breeder or cowherd.

YOUNG SOCRATES: It certainly seems so, now you say it.

VISITOR: Well then: when it comes to rearing living creatures, are we to   e
call[13] the shared rearing of many creatures together a sort of 'herd-rearing'
or 'collective rearing'?

YOUNG SOCRATES: Whichever turns out to fit, in the course of the argument.

VISITOR: Well said, Socrates; and if you persevere in not paying serious
attention to names, you will be seen to be richer in wisdom as you advance

12. Reading *koinēi* at d4.
13. Reading *onomazōmen* at 2–3.

to old age. But now we must do just as you instruct. Do you see how by
262   showing the collective rearing of herds to be twin in form one will make
what is now being sought in double the field then be sought in half of that?

YOUNG SOCRATES: I shall try my hardest. It seems to me that there is a
different sort of rearing of human beings, and in turn another sort where
animals are concerned.

VISITOR: Yes, absolutely, you've made a very keen and courageous division! But let's try to avoid *this* happening to us again.

YOUNG SOCRATES: What sort of thing?

b   VISITOR: Let's not take off one small part on its own, leaving many large
ones behind, and without reference to real classes; let the part bring a real
class along with it. It's a really fine thing to separate off immediately what
one is searching for from the rest, if one gets it right—as you thought you
had the right division, just before, and hurried the argument on, seeing it
leading to human beings; but in fact, my friend, it's not safe to make thin
cuts; it's safer to go along cutting through the middle of things, and that
way one will be more likely to encounter real classes. This makes all the
c   difference in relation to philosophical investigations.

YOUNG SOCRATES: What do you mean by this, visitor?

VISITOR: I must try to tell you still more clearly, Socrates, out of good
will towards your natural endowments. In the present circumstances, I
have to say, it is impossible to show what I mean with absolute completeness; but I must bring it just a little further forward for the sake of clarity.

YOUNG SOCRATES: Well then, what sort of thing are you saying we weren't
doing right just now in our divisions?

VISITOR: This sort of thing: it's as if someone tried to divide the human
d   race into two and made the cut in the way that most people here carve
things up, taking the Greek race away as one, separate from all the rest,
and to all the other races together, which are unlimited in number, which
don't mix with one another, and don't share the same language—calling
this collection by the single appellation 'barbarian'. Because of this single
appellation, they expect it to be a single family or class too. Another
example would be if someone thought that he was dividing number into
e   two real classes by cutting off the number ten-thousand from all the rest,
separating it off as a single class, and in positing a single name for all the
rest supposed here too that through getting the name this class too came
into existence, a second single one apart from the other. But I imagine the
division would be done better, more by real classes and more into two, if
one cut number by means of even and odd, and the human race in its
turn by means of male and female, and only split off Lydians or Phrygians
or anyone else and ranged them against all the rest when one was at a
263   loss as to how to split in such a way that each of the halves split off was
simultaneously a real class and a part.

YOUNG SOCRATES: Quite right; but this very thing—how is one to see it
more plainly, that class and part are not the same but different from
each other?

VISITOR: An excellent response, Socrates, but what you demand is no light thing. We have already wandered far away from the discussion we proposed, and you are telling us to wander even more. Well, as for now, let's go back to where we were, which seems the reasonable thing to do; b and these other things we'll pursue like trackers on another occasion, when we have the time. However, there is one thing you must absolutely guard against, and that is ever to suppose that you have heard from me a plain account of the matter.

YOUNG SOCRATES: Which?

VISITOR: That class and part are different from each other.

YOUNG SOCRATES: What should I say I have heard from you?

VISITOR: That whenever there is a class of something, it is necessarily also a part of whatever thing it is called a class of, but it is not at all necessary that a part is a class. You must always assert, Socrates, that this is what I say rather than the other way round.[14]

YOUNG SOCRATES: I shall do just that.

VISITOR: Tell me, then, about the next thing.   c

YOUNG SOCRATES: What's that?

VISITOR: The point from which our digression brought us to where we are now. I think it was pretty much the point at which you were asked how to divide herd-rearing, and you said with great keenness that there were two classes of living creatures, one human, and a second single one consisting of all the rest—the animals—together.

YOUNG SOCRATES: True.

VISITOR: And to me you appeared then to think that in taking away a part you had left behind the rest as in its turn a single class, consisting of all of them, because you had the same name, 'animals', to apply to them all.   d

YOUNG SOCRATES: This too was as you say.

VISITOR: And yet, my courageous friend, maybe, if by chance there is some other animal which is rational, as for example the crane seems to be, or some other such creature, and which perhaps distributes names on the same principles as you, it might oppose cranes as one class to all other living creatures and give itself airs, taking all the rest together with human beings and putting them into the same category, which it would call by no other name except—perhaps—'animals'. So let's try to be very wary   e of everything of this sort.

YOUNG SOCRATES: How?

VISITOR: By not dividing the class of living creatures as a whole, in order to lessen the risk of its happening to us.

YOUNG SOCRATES: Yes, we must certainly avoid it.

VISITOR: Yes; and we were going wrong in this way just at that point.

YOUNG SOCRATES: How so?

---

14. Alternatively: "You must always assert, Socrates, that this is what I say, rather than that other thing."

VISITOR: Of that theoretical knowledge which was directive we had a part, I think, of the class concerned with rearing living creatures, one which was concerned with creatures living in herds. True?

YOUNG SOCRATES: Yes.

264   VISITOR: Well then, living creatures as a whole together had in effect already at that point been divided by the categories of domesticated and wild; for those that have a nature amenable to domestication are called tame, and those who resist it[15] are called wild.

YOUNG SOCRATES: Right.

VISITOR: But the knowledge we are hunting had to be and still is concerned with tame things, and must be looked for with reference to herd animals.

YOUNG SOCRATES: Yes.

b   VISITOR: Well then, let's not divide in the way we did then, looking at everything, or in a hurry, just in order to get quickly to statesmanship. It has already put us in the proverbial situation.

YOUNG SOCRATES: What situation is that?

VISITOR: That by not quietly getting on with dividing properly we have got to our destination more slowly.

YOUNG SOCRATES: Yes, visitor, and a fine situation it is!

VISITOR: If you say so. In any case, let's go back and try again from the beginning to divide collective rearing; perhaps, as we go through it in detail, the argument itself will be better able to reveal to you what you are so keen to find. Tell me this.

YOUNG SOCRATES: What?

VISITOR: This—I wonder if perhaps you've heard about it from others?
c   You certainly haven't yourself any direct acquaintance, I know, with the instances of domesticated fish-rearing in the Nile and in the King's[16] ponds. In ornamental fountains, at any rate, you may perhaps have seen them.

YOUNG SOCRATES: Absolutely—I've both seen these and heard about the others from many people.

VISITOR: And again, examples of goose-rearing and crane-rearing—even if you haven't travelled over the plains of Thessaly, you've certainly heard about these and believe that they exist.

YOUNG SOCRATES: Of course.

d   VISITOR: Look, it's for this purpose that I've asked you all this: of the rearing of herd animals, some has to do with creatures living in water, some also with creatures that live on dry land.

YOUNG SOCRATES: It does.

VISITOR: Do you agree, then, that we must split the expert knowledge of collective rearing into two in this way, allocating one of its two parts to each of these, calling one aquatic rearing, the other dry-land rearing?

15. Reading *echonta* for *'thelonta* at a3.
16. I.e., the King of Persia.

YOUNG SOCRATES: I do.

VISITOR: And we certainly shan't ask, in this case, to which of the two sorts of expertise kingship belongs; it's quite clear[17] to anyone.

YOUNG SOCRATES: Quite.

VISITOR: Everybody would divide the dry-land rearing sort of herd-rearing.

YOUNG SOCRATES: How?

VISITOR: By separating it by reference to the winged and what goes on foot.

YOUNG SOCRATES: Very true.

VISITOR: Well then—mustn't we[18] look for statesmanship in relation to what goes on foot? Or don't you think that practically even the simplest of minds supposes so?

YOUNG SOCRATES: I do.

VISITOR: And the expertise to do with the management of creatures that go on foot—we must show it being cut into two, like an even[19] number.

YOUNG SOCRATES: Clearly.

VISITOR: Now it seems that there are two routes to be seen stretching out in the direction of the part towards which our argument has hurried, one of them quicker, dividing a small part off against a large one, while the other more closely observes the principle we were talking about earlier, that one should cut in the middle as much as possible, but is longer. We can go down whichever of the two routes we like.

YOUNG SOCRATES: What if I were to ask if it is impossible to follow both?

VISITOR: An extraordinary suggestion, if you mean both at once; but clearly it is possible to take each in turn.

YOUNG SOCRATES: Then I opt for taking both, in turn.

VISITOR: That's easy, since the part that remains is short; if we had been at the beginning or in the middle of our journey, the instruction would have been difficult to carry out. As it is, since you think we should take this option, let's go down the longer route first; while we are fresher we'll travel it more easily. Observe the division.

YOUNG SOCRATES: Tell me what it is.

VISITOR: Of tame things that live in herds, we find those that go on foot naturally divided into two.

YOUNG SOCRATES: By what?

VISITOR: By the fact that some of them come into being without horns, some with horns.

YOUNG SOCRATES: Evidently.

VISITOR: Well then, divide the management of creatures that go on foot by assigning it to each of these two parts, using a descriptive phrase for

---

17. Reading *gar dē* at e1.
18. Reading *ou peri* at e8.
19. Reading *artion* at e11.

the results of the division. For if you want to give them names, it will be more complicated than necessary.

YOUNG SOCRATES: How then should it be put?

VISITOR: Like this: by saying that when the knowledge that has to do with the management of creatures that go by foot is divided into two, one part is allocated to the horned part of the herd, the other to the hornless part.

d   YOUNG SOCRATES: Let it be put like that; in any case it's sufficiently clear.

VISITOR: Now, as for the next step, it's perfectly obvious to us that the king tends a sort of docked herd—of hornless creatures.[20]

YOUNG SOCRATES: How couldn't it be clear?

VISITOR: So by breaking this up let's try to assign what falls to him.

YOUNG SOCRATES: Yes, certainly.

VISITOR: Well, do you want to divide it by the split-hooved and the so-called 'single-hooved', or by interbreeding and non-interbreeding? I think you grasp the point.

YOUNG SOCRATES: What's that?

e   VISITOR: That horses and donkeys are naturally such as to breed from one another.

YOUNG SOCRATES: Yes.

VISITOR: Whereas what is still left of the smooth-headed herd of tame creatures is unmixed in breeding, one with another.

YOUNG SOCRATES: Quite.

VISITOR: So: does the statesman, then, seem to take care of an interbreeding or of some non-interbreeding sort?

YOUNG SOCRATES: Clearly, of the non-mixing sort.

VISITOR: This, then, it seems, we must separate into two, as we did in the previous cases.

YOUNG SOCRATES: Indeed we must.

266   VISITOR: Now those creatures that are tame and live in herds have pretty well all now been cut into their pieces, except for two classes. For it is not worth our while to count the class of dogs as among creatures living in herds.

YOUNG SOCRATES: No indeed. But what are we to use to divide[21] the two classes?

VISITOR: Something that is absolutely appropriate for Theaetetus and you to use in your distributions, since it's geometry the two of you engage in.[22]

YOUNG SOCRATES: What is it?

VISITOR: The diagonal, one could say, and then again the diagonal of the diagonal.

YOUNG SOCRATES: What do you mean?

---

20. Reading *kolobon tina agelēn akeratōn* at d4.

21. Reading *diairōmen* at a5.

22. See *Theaetetus* 147c ff.

VISITOR: The nature which the family or class of us humans possesses   b
surely isn't endowed for the purpose of going from place to place any
differently from the diagonal that has the power of two feet?[23]

YOUNG SOCRATES: No.

VISITOR: And what's more the nature of the remaining class has in its
turn the power of the diagonal of our power, if indeed it is endowed with
two times two feet.

YOUNG SOCRATES: Of course it is—and I actually almost understand what
you want to show.

VISITOR: And there's more—do we see, Socrates, that there's something
else resulting in our divisions that would itself have done well as a   c
comic turn?

YOUNG SOCRATES: What's that?

VISITOR: That our human class has shared the field and run together
with the noblest and also most easy-going class of existing things?[24]

YOUNG SOCRATES: I see it turning out very oddly indeed.

VISITOR: Well, isn't it reasonable to expect the slowest—or sow-est—to
come in last?

YOUNG SOCRATES: Yes, I can agree with that.

VISITOR: And don't we notice that the king looks even more ridiculous,
when he continues to run, along with his herd, and has traversed conver-
gent paths, with the man who for his part is best trained of all for the   d
easy-going life?[25]

YOUNG SOCRATES: Absolutely right.

VISITOR: Yes, Socrates, and what we said before, in our inquiry about
the sophist, is now plainer.[26]

YOUNG SOCRATES: What was that?

VISITOR: That such a method of argument as ours is not more concerned
with what is more dignified than with what is not, and neither does it at
all despise the smaller more than the greater, but always reaches the truest
conclusion by itself.

---

23. In Greek mathematical parlance, 'having the power of two feet' is the way of
expressing the length of the diagonal of a one-foot square (i.e., in modern terms,
$\sqrt{2}$); the expression reflects the fact that a square formed on this line will have an
area of two square feet. The diagonal of this square will then 'have the power' of
four feet—the 'power of the diagonal of our power' in the Visitor's next remark. All
this is for the sake of the pun on 'power' and 'feet': we humans are enabled to
move by having two feet, while the members of 'the remaining class' from which
we are being distinguished—pigs—have four. (On the mathematical use of 'power'
see *Theaetetus* 147d–148b and n.)

24. I.e., pigs, as the Visitor makes clear in his next question, by punning on the Greek
word for 'pig'.

25. The swineherd.

26. See *Sophist* 227b.

YOUNG SOCRATES: It seems so.

VISITOR: Well then, after this, so that you don't get in before me and ask
e   what the shorter way is—the one we spoke of earlier—to the definition
of the king, shall I go first and show you the way?

YOUNG SOCRATES: Very much so.

VISITOR: Then I say that in this case one must immediately distribute
what goes on foot by opposing the two-footed to the four-footed class,
and when one sees the human still sharing the field with the winged alone,
one must go on to cut the two-footed herd by means of the non-feathered
and the feathered; and when it has been cut, and the expertise of human-
herding has then and there been brought into the light, one must lift the
expert in statesmanship and kingship like a charioteer into it and instal
him there, handing over the reins of the city as belonging to him, and
because this expert knowledge is his.

267   YOUNG SOCRATES: That's well done, and you've paid me the account I
asked for as if it were a debt, adding the digression as a kind of interest,
making up the sum.

VISITOR: Come on, then: let's go back to the beginning and gather together
from there to the end our account of the name of the expertise of the
statesman.

YOUNG SOCRATES: Absolutely.

VISITOR: Well then: of theoretical knowledge, we had at the beginning
b   a directive part; and of this, the section we wanted was by analogy said
to be 'self-directing'. Then again, rearing of living creatures, not the smallest
of the classes of self-directing knowledge, was split off from it; then a
herd-rearing form from rearing of living creatures, and from that, in turn,
rearing of what goes on foot; and from that, as the relevant part, was cut
off the expertise of rearing the hornless sort. Of this in turn the part must
be woven together as not less than triple, if one wants to bring it together
into a single name, calling it expert knowledge of rearing of non-interbreed-
c   ing creatures. The segment from this, a part relating to a two-footed flock,
concerned with rearing of human beings, still left on its own—this very
part is now what we were looking for, the same thing we call both kingly
and statesmanlike.

YOUNG SOCRATES: Absolutely.

VISITOR: Is it really the case, Socrates, that we have actually done this,
as you have just said?

YOUNG SOCRATES: Done what?

VISITOR: Given a completely adequate response to the matter we raised.
Or is our search lacking especially in just this respect, that our account of
d   the matter has been stated in a certain way, but has not been finished off
to complete perfection?

YOUNG SOCRATES: How do you mean?

VISITOR: I shall try now to show, for both of us, still more clearly just
what I am thinking of.

YOUNG SOCRATES: Please go ahead.

VISITOR: Well then, of the many sorts of expertise to do with rearing herds that appeared in our view just now, statesmanship was one, and was care of some one sort of herd?

YOUNG SOCRATES: Yes.

VISITOR: And our account defined it not as rearing of horses, or of other animals, but as knowledge of the collective rearing of human beings.

YOUNG SOCRATES: Just so.

VISITOR: Then let us look at the difference between all herdsmen, on the one hand, and kings on the other.

YOUNG SOCRATES: What's that?

VISITOR: Let us see if in the case of any other herdsman anyone who has the title of another expertise claims or pretends to share the rearing of the herd with him.

YOUNG SOCRATES: How do you mean?

VISITOR: Like this: that merchants, farmers, millers and bakers, all of them, and gymnastic trainers too, and doctors as a class—all of these, as you well know, would loudly contend against the herdsmen concerned with things human whom we called statesmen that *they* care for human rearing, not merely for that of human beings in the herd, but for that of the rulers as well.

YOUNG SOCRATES: Well, would they be right?

VISITOR: Perhaps. That we'll consider, but what we know is that with a cowherd no one will dispute about any of these things, but the herdsman is by himself rearer of the herd, by himself its doctor, by himself its matchmaker, as it were, and sole expert in the midwife's art when it comes to the births of offspring and confinements. Again, to the extent that the nature of his charges allows them to partake in play and music, no one else is more capable of comforting them and soothing them with his incantations, performing best, as he does, the music that belongs to his flock with instruments or with unaccompanied voice. And it's the same way with all other herdsmen. True?

YOUNG SOCRATES: Quite right.

VISITOR: So how will our account of the king appear to us right and complete, when we posit him as sole herdsman and rearer of the human herd, singling him out on his own from among tens of thousands of others who dispute the title with him?

YOUNG SOCRATES: There's no way in which it can.

VISITOR: Then our fears a little earlier were right, when we suspected that we should prove in fact to be describing some kingly figure, but not yet accurately to have finished the statesman off, until we remove those who crowd round him, pretending to share his herding function with him, and having separated him from them, we reveal him on his own, uncontaminated with anyone else?

YOUNG SOCRATES: Yes, absolutely right.

VISITOR: Well then, Socrates, this is what we must do, if we are not going to bring disgrace on our argument at its end.

YOUNG SOCRATES: That is something we must certainly avoid doing at all costs.

VISITOR: Then we must travel some other route, starting from another point.

YOUNG SOCRATES: What route is that?

VISITOR: By mixing in, as one might put it, an element of play: we must bring in a large part of a great story, and as for the rest, we must then—

e   as in what went before—take away part from part in each case and so arrive at the furthest point of the object of our search. So should we do it?

YOUNG SOCRATES: Absolutely.

VISITOR: In that case, pay complete attention to my story, as children do; you certainly haven't left childish games behind for more than a few years.

YOUNG SOCRATES: Please go ahead.

VISITOR: Then I'll begin. There have occurred in the past, and will occur in the future, many of the things that have been told through the ages; one is the portent relating to the quarrel between Atreus and Thyestes. I imagine you remember hearing what people say happened then.[27]

YOUNG SOCRATES: You're referring, perhaps, to the sign of the golden lamb.

269   VISITOR: Not at all; rather to that of the changing of the setting and rising of the sun and the other stars—it's said that they actually began setting in the region from which they now rise, and rising from the opposite region, and that then after having given witness in favor of Atreus the god changed everything to its present configuration.

YOUNG SOCRATES: Yes indeed, they do say this as well.

VISITOR: And what's more, we've also heard from many about the kingship exercised by Cronus.[28]

b   YOUNG SOCRATES: Yes, from a great many.

VISITOR: And what of the report that earlier men were born from the earth and were not reproduced from each other?

YOUNG SOCRATES: This too is one of the things that have been told through the ages.

VISITOR: Well, all these things together are consequences of the same state of affairs, and besides these thousands of others still more astonishing than they; but through the great lapse of time since then some have been obliterated, while others have been reported in a scattered way, each separate from one another. But as for the state of affairs that is responsible

c   for all of these things, no one has related it, and we should relate it now; for once it has been described, it will be a fitting contribution towards our exposition of the king.

YOUNG SOCRATES: I very much like what you say; go on, and leave nothing out.

27. Cf. Euripides, *Orestes* 986 ff.

28. A 'golden age' (cf. Hesiod, *Works and Days* 111–22), when everything necessary for the survival of human beings was provided without their having to work for it.

VISITOR: Listen then. This universe the god himself sometimes accompanies, guiding it on its way and helping it move in a circle, while at other times he lets it go, when its circuits have completed the measure of the time allotted to it; then it revolves back in the opposite direction, of its own accord, being a living creature and having had intelligence assigned   d
to it by the one who fitted it together in the beginning. This backward movement is inborn in it from necessity, for the following reason.

YOUNG SOCRATES: What reason, exactly?

VISITOR: Remaining permanently in the same state and condition, and being permanently the same, belongs only to the most divine things of all, and by its nature body is not of this order. Now the thing to which we have given the name of 'heavens' and 'cosmos'[29] certainly has a portion of many blessed things from its progenitor, but on the other hand it also has its share of *body*. In consequence it is impossible for it to be altogether   e
exempt from change, although as far as is possible, given its capacities, it moves in the same place, in the same way, with a single motion; and this is why it has reverse rotation as its lot, which is the smallest possible variation of its movement. To turn itself by itself forever is, I dare say, impossible for anything except the one who guides all the things which, unlike him, are in movement; and for him to cause movement now in one way, now in the opposite way is not permitted. From all of these considerations, it follows that one must neither say that the cosmos is always itself responsible for its own turning, nor say at all[30] that it is turned by god in a pair of opposed revolutions, nor again that it is turned by   270
some pair of gods whose thoughts are opposed to each other; it is rather what was said just now, which is the sole remaining possibility, that at times it is helped by the guidance of another, divine, cause, acquiring life once more and receiving a restored immortality from its craftsman, while at other times, when it is let go, it goes on its own way under its own power, having been let go at such a time as to travel backwards for many tens of thousands of revolutions because of the very fact that its movement combines the effects of its huge size, perfect balance, and its resting on the smallest of bases.

YOUNG SOCRATES: It certainly seems that everything you have gone   b
through is very reasonable.

VISITOR: Then drawing on what's just been said, let's reflect on the state of affairs we said was responsible for all those astonishing things. In fact it's just this very thing.

YOUNG SOCRATES: What's that?

VISITOR: That the movement of the universe is now in the direction of its present rotation, now in the opposite direction.

YOUNG SOCRATES: How do you mean?

29. Alternatively, 'world-order'; the idea of order is central to the Greek term.
30. Reading *mēth' holon* at e9.

c   VISITOR: We must suppose that this change is, of the turnings that occur
in the heavens, the greatest and the most complete turning of all.

YOUNG SOCRATES: Yes, it certainly seems so.

VISITOR: We must suppose, then, that at that time the greatest changes
also occur for us who live within the universe?

YOUNG SOCRATES: That too seems likely.

VISITOR: And don't we recognize that living creatures by their nature
have difficulty in tolerating changes that are at once large, great in number,
and of all different sorts?

YOUNG SOCRATES: Certainly we do.

VISITOR: Necessarily, then, there occur at that time cases of destruction
d   of other living creatures on a very large scale, and humankind itself survives only in small numbers. Many new and astonishing things happen
to them, but the greatest is the one I shall describe, one that is in accordance
with the retrogradation of the universe, at the time when its turning becomes the opposite of the one that now obtains.

YOUNG SOCRATES: What kind of thing do you mean?

VISITOR: First, the visible age of each and every creature, whatever it
was, stopped increasing, and everything that was mortal ceased moving
e   in the direction of looking older; instead it changed back in the opposite
direction, and grew as it were younger, more tender. The white hairs of
the older men became black, and in turn the cheeks of those who had
their beards became smooth again, returning each to his past bloom; the
bodies of those in their puberty, becoming smoother and smaller each day
and night, went back to the form of new-born children, which they came
to resemble both in mind and in body, and from then on they proceeded
to waste away until they simply disappeared altogether. As for those who
271   died a violent death at that time, the body of the dead person underwent
the same effects and quickly dissolved to nothing in a few days.

YOUNG SOCRATES: But, visitor, how did living creatures come into being
in that time? And in what way were they produced from each other?

VISITOR: Clearly, Socrates, reproduction from one another was not part
of the nature of things then. It was the earth-born race, the one said to
have existed once, that existed then, returning to life again from the earth;
it was remembered by our first ancestors, who lived in the succeeding
b   time but bordered on the ending of the previous period, growing up at
the beginning of this one. They became our messengers for the accounts
of the earth-born, which are nowadays wrongly disbelieved by many
people. For I think we must reflect on what is implied by what we have
said. If old men went back to being children, it follows that people should
be put together again from the dead, there in the earth, and come back to
life; they would be following the reversal of things, with coming-into-
being turning round with it to the opposite direction, and since they would
c   according to this argument necessarily come into existence as earth-born,
they would thus acquire that name and have that account given of them—
all those of them, that is, whom god did not take off to another destiny.

YOUNG SOCRATES: Yes, quite; this does seem to follow on what went before. But as for the life which you say there was in the time of Cronus' power—was it in that period of rotation or in this one? For it clearly turns out that the change affecting the stars and the sun occurs in each period.[31]

VISITOR: You have been keeping up with the argument well. As for what you asked, about everything's springing up of its own accord for human beings, it belongs least to the period that now obtains; it too belonged to the one before. For then the god began to rule and take care of the rotation itself as a whole, and as for[32] the regions, in their turn, it was just the same, the parts of the world-order having everywhere[33] been divided up by gods ruling over them. As for living things, divine spirits had divided them between themselves, like herdsmen, by kind and by herd, each by himself providing independently for all the needs of those he tended, so that none of them was savage, nor did they eat each other, and there was no war or internal dissent at all; and as for all the other things that belong as consequences to such an arrangement, there would be tens of thousands of them to report. But to return to what we have been told about a human life without toil, the origin of the report is something like this. A god tended them, taking charge of them himself, just as now human beings, themselves living creatures, but different and more divine, pasture other kinds of living creatures more lowly than themselves; and given his tendance, they had no political constitutions,

d

e

---

31. Alternatively: "at each of the two turnings." (The word tr. 'period' in the text is elsewhere tr. 'turning,' i.e., reversal of the direction of rotation.) The translation in the text is based on the assumption that in the myth as a whole the Visitor envisages two eras during *both* of which the cosmos rotates, as it now does, from east to west (one era when it is under god's control, one under its own inherent power), separated by a relatively brief period of rotation in the reverse direction (so that then the sun rises in the west and sets in the east). This reverse rotation begins immediately after the god releases control, i.e., at the outset of the time when the cosmos rules itself, and it ends when the cosmos gains sufficient self-possession to return to rotating in the normal, east-to-west direction. On this interpretation, the Visitor has just been describing the 'earth-born' people as existing during the relatively brief period of reverse-rotation, and Young Socrates now asks whether the golden age of Cronus also occurred during that time, or instead in the era that preceded it. The alternative translation fits with a different interpretation of the myth, which is that of most scholars. According to this prevailing interpretation the Visitor envisages, more simply, two alternating eras, one of west-to-east rotation (under god's control) and one of the east-to-west rotation we are familiar with: this latter, for us normal, direction of rotation occupies the *whole* of the time when the cosmos is under self-rule. On this interpretation there is no intervening, brief period of reverse-rotation, so the Visitor's description of the 'earth-born' people has placed them in the era of god's control. Accordingly, Young Socrates is now asking whether the golden age of Cronus existed in that same era, or instead during the era we now live in.

32. Reading *hōs d'au kata* at d4.

33. Reading *pantēi ta* at d5.

272   nor acquired wives and children, for all of them came back to life from
       the earth, remembering nothing of the past.[34] While they lacked things of
       this sort, they had an abundance of fruits from trees and many other plants,
       which grew not through cultivation but because the earth sent them up
       of its own accord. For the most part they would feed outdoors, naked and
       without bedding; for the blend of the seasons was without painful extremes,
  b   and they had soft beds from abundant grass that sprang from the earth.
       What you are hearing about, then, Socrates, is the life of those who lived
       in the time of Cronus; as for this one, which they say is in the time of
       Zeus, the present one, you are familiar with it from personal experience.
       Would you be able and willing to judge which of the two is the more for-
       tunate?
          YOUNG SOCRATES: Not at all.
          VISITOR: Then do you want me to make some sort of decision for you?
          YOUNG SOCRATES: Absolutely.
          VISITOR: Well then, if, with so much leisure available to them, and so
       much opportunity to get together in conversation not only with human
  c   beings but also with animals—if the nurslings of Cronus used all these
       advantages to do philosophy, talking both with animals and with each
       other, and inquiring from all sorts of creatures whether any one of them
       had some capacity of its own that enabled it to see better in some way
       than the rest with respect to the gathering of wisdom, the judgment is
       easy, that those who lived then were far, far more fortunate than those
       who live now. But if they spent their time gorging themselves with food
       and drink and exchanging stories with each other and with the animals
  d   of the sort that[35] even now are told about them, this too, if I may reveal
       how it seems to me, at least, is a matter that is easily judged. But however
       that may be, let us leave it to one side, until such time as someone appears
       who is qualified to inform us in which of these two ways the desires of
       men of that time were directed in relation to the different varieties of
       knowledge and the need for talk; we must now state the point of our
       rousing our story into action, in order to move forward and bring what
       follows to its end. When the time of all these things had been completed
  e   and the hour for change had come, and in particular all the earth-born
       race had been used up, each soul having rendered its sum of births, falling
       to the earth as seed as many times as had been laid down for each, at that
       point the steersman of the universe, let go—as it were—of the bar of the
       steering-oars and retired to his observation-post; and as for the cosmos,

---

34. On the interpretation assumed in the translation (see n. 31 above) these must be a
different kind of 'earth-born' people from the previous ones (perhaps they are to be
considered as produced from the earth instead as babies: cf. 272e, 274a). On the prevalent
interpretation this is a second reference to the same earth-born people as before: we
now learn that being born from the earth full grown was characteristic of human life
for the whole period of god's control of the cosmos.

35. Reading *muthous hoioi* at c7.

its allotted and innate desire turned it back again in the opposite direction. So all the gods who ruled over the regions together with the greatest divinity, seeing immediately what was happening, let go in their turn the parts of the cosmos that belonged to their charge; and as it turned about 273 and came together with itself, impelled with opposing movements, both the one that was beginning and the one that was now ending, it produced a great tremor in itself, which in its turn brought about another destruction of all sorts of living things. After this, when sufficient time had elapsed, it began to cease from noise and confusion and attained calm from its tremors; it set itself in order, into the accustomed course that belongs to b it, itself taking charge of and mastering both the things within it and itself, because it remembered so far as it could the teaching of its craftsman and father. At the beginning it fulfilled his teaching more accurately, but in the end less keenly; the cause of this was the bodily element in its mixture, its companion since its origins long in the past, because this element was marked by a great disorder before it entered into the present world-order. For from the one who put it together the world possesses all fine things; from its previous condition, on the other hand, it both has for itself from c that source everything that is bad and unjust in the heavens, and produces it in its turn in living things. So while it reared living things in itself in company with the steersman, it created only slight evils, and great goods; but in separation from him, during all the time closest to the moment of his letting go, it manages everything very well, but as time moves on and forgetfulness increases in it, the condition of its original disharmony also d takes greater control of it, and, as this time ends, comes to full flower. Then the goods it mixes in are slight, but the admixture it causes of the opposite is great, and it reaches the point where it is in danger of destroying both itself and the things in it. It is for this reason that now the god who ordered it, seeing it in difficulties, and concerned that it should not, storm-tossed as it is, be broken apart in confusion and sink into the boundless sea of unlikeness, takes his position again at its steering-oars, and having e turned round what had become diseased and been broken apart in the previous rotation, when the world was left to itself, orders it and by setting it straight renders it immortal and ageless. What has been described, then, is the end-point of everything; as for what is relevant to our showing the nature of the king, it is sufficient if we take up the account from what went before. When the cosmos had been turned back again on the course that leads to the sort of coming-into-being which obtains now, the movement of the ages of living creatures once again stopped and produced new effects which were the opposite of what previously occurred. For those living creatures that were close to disappearing through smallness began to increase in size, while those bodies that had just been born from the earth already gray-haired began to die again and return into the earth. And everything else changed, imitating and following on the condition of 274 the universe, and in particular, there was a change to the mode of conception, birth and rearing, which necessarily imitated and kept pace with the

change to everything; for it was no longer possible for a living creature to grow within the earth under the agency of others' putting it together, but just as the world-order had been instructed to be master of its own motion, so too in the same way its parts were instructed themselves to perform the functions of begetting, birth and rearing so far as possible by
b   themselves, under the agency of a similar impulse. We are now at the point that our account has all along been designed to reach. To go through the changes that have occurred in relation to the other animals, and from what causes, would involve a description of considerable length; those that relate to human beings will be shorter to relate and more to the point. Since we had been deprived of the god who possessed and pastured us, and since for their part the majority of animals—all those who had an aggressive nature—had gone wild, human beings, by themselves weak
c   and defenseless, were preyed on by them, and in those first times were still without resources and without expertise of any sort; their spontaneous supply of food was no longer available to them, and they did not yet know how to provide for themselves, having had no shortage to force them to do so before. As a result of all of this they were in great difficulties. This is why the gifts from the gods, of which we have ancient reports, have been given to us, along with an indispensable requirement for teaching and education: fire from Prometheus, crafts from Hephaestus and his
d   fellow craftworker, seeds and plants from others. Everything that has helped to establish human life has come about from these things, once care from the gods, as has just been said, ceased to be available to human beings, and they had to live their lives through their own resources and take care for themselves, just like the cosmos as a whole, which we imitate
e   and follow for all time, now living and growing in this way, now in the way we did then. As for the matter of our story, let it now be ended, and we shall put it to use in order to see how great our mistake was when we gave our account of the expert in kingship and statesmanship in our preceding argument.

YOUNG SOCRATES: So how do you say we made a mistake, and how great was it?

VISITOR: In one way it was lesser, in another it was very high-minded, and much greater and more extensive than in the other case.

YOUNG SOCRATES: How so?

VISITOR: In that when asked for the king and statesman from the period of the present mode of rotation and generation we replied with the shep-
275   herd from the opposite period, who cared for the human herd that existed then, and at that a god instead of a mortal—in that way we went very greatly astray. But in that we revealed him as ruling over the whole city together, without specifying in what manner he does so, in this way, by contrast, what we said was true, but incomplete and unclear, which is why our mistake was lesser than in the respect just mentioned.

YOUNG SOCRATES: True.

VISITOR: So we should define the manner of his rule over the city; it's in this way that we should expect our discussion of the statesman to reach its completion.

YOUNG SOCRATES: Right.

VISITOR: It was just for these reasons that we introduced our story, in order that it might demonstrate, in relation to herd-rearing, not only that as things now stand everyone disputes this function with the person we are looking for, but also in order that we might see more plainly that other person himself whom alone, in accordance with the example of shepherds and cowherds, because he has charge of human rearing, it is appropriate to think worthy of this name, and this name alone.[36]

YOUNG SOCRATES: Correct.

VISITOR: But in my view, Socrates, this figure of the divine herdsman is still greater than that of a king, and the statesmen who belong to our present era are much more like their subjects in their natures and have shared in an education and nurture closer to theirs.

YOUNG SOCRATES: I suppose you must be right.

VISITOR: Yet they will be neither less nor more worth looking for, whether their natures are of the latter or of the former sort.

YOUNG SOCRATES: Quite.

VISITOR: Then let's go back by the following route. The sort of expertise we said was 'self-directing' in the case of living creatures, but which took its care of them not as individuals but in groups, and which we then went on immediately to call herd-rearing—you remember?[37]

YOUNG SOCRATES: Yes.

VISITOR: Well, in a way we missed in our aim at this expertise; for we did not at all succeed in grasping the statesman along with the rest or name him, but he eluded us in our naming, and we did not notice.

YOUNG SOCRATES: How so?

VISITOR: All the other sorts of herdsmen, I think, share the feature of rearing their several herds, but although the statesman does not we still applied the name to him, when we should have applied to all of them one of the names that belongs in common to them.

YOUNG SOCRATES: What you say is true, if indeed there is such a name.

VISITOR: And how would—perhaps—'looking after' not have been common to them all, without any specification of it as 'rearing', or any other sort of activity? By calling it some sort of expertise in 'herd-keeping' or 'looking after', or 'caring for', as applying to them all, we could have covered the statesman too as well as the rest, given that this was the requirement our argument indicated.

36. Alternatively: "... whom alone, because only he has charge of human rearing in accordance with the example of shepherd and cowherd, it is appropriate to think worthy of this name."

37. See 261d.

276   YOUNG SOCRATES: Correct. But in what way would the division following this be made?

VISITOR: In the same way as we previously divided herd-rearing by footed and wingless, and non-interbreeding and hornless—by dividing herd-keeping too by these same things, I think, we would have included in our account to the same degree both the present sort of kingship and that in the time of Cronus.

YOUNG SOCRATES: It seems so; but again I ask what step follows this.

b   VISITOR: It's clear that if we had used the name 'herd-keeping' like this, no one would ever have contended with us on the grounds that there is no such thing as *caring* at all, in the way that it was then justly contended that there was no sort of expertise available that deserved this appellation of 'rearing', but that if there really were such a thing, many people had a prior and better claim to it than any of our kings.

YOUNG SOCRATES: Correct.

VISITOR: But care of the whole human community together—no other sort of expertise would be prepared to say that it had a better and prior claim to being *that* than kingly rule, which is over all human beings.

c

YOUNG SOCRATES: What you say is correct.

VISITOR: But after that, Socrates, do we see that at the very end of our account we again made a large mistake?

YOUNG SOCRATES: What sort of mistake?

VISITOR: It was this, that even if we had been quite convinced that there was some expertise concerned with the rearing of the two-footed herd, we should certainly not for that reason immediately have called it the expertise of the king and statesman, as if that were the end of the matter.

YOUNG SOCRATES: What should we have done?

VISITOR: First of all, as we are saying, we should have altered the name, aligning it more with caring for things than with rearing, and then we should have cut this; for it would still offer room for cuts of no small size.

d

YOUNG SOCRATES: Where would they be?

VISITOR: I imagine, where we would have divided off the divine herdsman, on one side, and the human carer on the other.

YOUNG SOCRATES: Correct.

VISITOR: But again we ought to have cut into two the art of the carer resulting from this apportionment.

YOUNG SOCRATES: By using what distinction?

VISITOR: That between the enforced and the voluntary.

YOUNG SOCRATES: Why so?

e   VISITOR: I think we made a mistake before in this way too, by behaving more simple-mindedly than we should have. We put king and tyrant into the same category, when both they themselves and the manner of their rule are very unlike one another.

YOUNG SOCRATES: True.

VISITOR: But now should we set things to rights again, and, as I said, should we divide the expertise of the human carer into two, by using the categories of the enforced and the voluntary?

YOUNG SOCRATES: Absolutely.

VISITOR: And should we perhaps call tyrannical the expertise that relates to subjects who are forced, and the herd-keeping that is voluntary and relates to willing two-footed living things that expertise which belongs to statesmanship, displaying, in his turn, the person who has this expertise and cares for his subjects in this way as being genuinely king and statesman?

YOUNG SOCRATES: Yes, visitor, and it's likely that in this way our exposi-   277
tion concerning the statesman would reach completion.

VISITOR: It would be a fine thing for us, Socrates. But this mustn't be just your view alone; I too have got to share it in common with you. And as it is, according to my view our discussion does not yet seem to have given a complete shape to the king. Just as sculptors sometimes hurry when it is not appropriate to do so and actually lose time by making additions and increasing the size of the various parts of their work[38] beyond   b
what is necessary, so too in our case—I suppose that in order to give a grand as well as a quick demonstration of the mistake in the route we previously took, we thought it was appropriate to the king to give large-scale illustrations. We took upon ourselves an astonishing mass of material in the story we told, so forcing ourselves to use a greater part of it than necessary; thus we have made our exposition longer, and have in every way failed to apply a finish to our story, and our account, just like a portrait, seems adequate in its superficial outline, but not yet to have   c
received its proper clarity, as it were with paints and the mixing together of colors. But it is not painting or any other sort of manual craft, but speech and discourse, that constitute the more fitting medium for exhibiting all living things, for those who are able to follow; for the rest, it will be through manual crafts.

YOUNG SOCRATES: That much is correct; but show me how you say we have not yet given an adequate account.

VISITOR: It's a hard thing, my fine friend, to demonstrate any of the more   d
important subjects without using models. It looks as if each of us knows everything in a kind of dreamlike way, and then again is ignorant of everything when as it were awake.

YOUNG SOCRATES: What do you mean?

VISITOR: I do seem rather oddly now to have stirred up the subject of what happens to us in relation to knowledge.

YOUNG SOCRATES: How so?

VISITOR: It has turned out, my dear fellow, that the idea of a 'model' itself in its turn also has need of a model to demonstrate it.

38. Reading *tōi ergōi* at a7.

e   YOUNG SOCRATES: How so? Explain, and don't hold back for *my* sake.

         VISITOR: Explain I must, in view of your own readiness to follow. I suppose we recognize that when children are just acquiring skill in reading and writing—

         YOUNG SOCRATES: Recognize what?

         VISITOR: That they distinguish each of the individual letters well enough in the shortest and easiest syllables, and come to be capable of indicating what is true in relation to them.

278   YOUNG SOCRATES: Of course.

         VISITOR: But then once again they make mistakes about these very same letters in other syllables, and think and say what is false.

         YOUNG SOCRATES: Absolutely.

         VISITOR: Well then, isn't this the easiest and best way of leading them on to the things they're not yet recognizing?

         YOUNG SOCRATES: What way?

         VISITOR: To take them first back to those cases in which they were getting these same things right, and having done that, to put these beside what

b   they're not yet recognizing. By comparing them, we demonstrate that there is the same kind of thing with similar features in both combinations, until the things that they are getting right have been shown set beside all the ones that they don't know; once the things in question have been shown like this, and so become models, they bring it about that each of all the individual letters is called both different, on the basis that it is different from the others, and the same, on the basis that it is always the same as

c   and identical to itself, in all syllables.

         YOUNG SOCRATES: Absolutely right.

         VISITOR: Well then, have we grasped this point adequately, that we come to be using a *model* when a given thing, which is the same in something different and distinct, is correctly identified there, and having been brought together with the original thing, brings about a single true judgment about each separately and both together?[39]

         YOUNG SOCRATES: It seems so.

         VISITOR: Then would we be surprised if our minds by their nature experi-

d   enced this same thing in relation to the individual 'letters' of everything, now, in some cases, holding a settled view with the aid of truth in relation to each separate thing, now, in others, being all at sea in relation to all of them—somehow or other getting the constituents of the combinations themselves right, but once again not knowing these same things when they are transferred into the long 'syllables' of things and the ones that are not easy?

         YOUNG SOCRATES: There would be absolutely nothing surprising in it.

e   VISITOR: Right, my friend: how could anyone begin from false belief and get to even a small part of the truth, and so acquire wisdom?

         YOUNG SOCRATES: I dare say it's impossible.

         39. Reading *kai sunamphō* at c7.

VISITOR: Well, if that's the way it is, the two of us would not at all be in the wrong in having first attempted to see the nature of models as a whole in the specific case of a further insignificant model, with the intention then of bringing to the case of the king, which is of the greatest importance, something of the same form from less significant things somewhere, in an attempt once more through the use of a model to recognize in an expert, systematic way what looking after people in the city is, so that it may be present to us in our waking state instead of in a dream?

YOUNG SOCRATES: Absolutely right.

VISITOR: Then we must take up once again what we were saying before,[40]   279 to the effect that since tens of thousands of people dispute the role of caring for cities with the kingly class, what we have to do is to separate all these off and leave the king on his own; and it was just for this purpose that we said we needed a model.

YOUNG SOCRATES: Very much so.

VISITOR: So what model, involving the same activities as statesmanship, on a very small scale, could one compare with it, and so discover in a satisfactory way what we are looking for? By Zeus, Socrates, what do you   b think? If there isn't anything else to hand, well, what about weaving? Do you want us to choose that? Not all of it, if you agree, since perhaps the weaving of cloth from wool will suffice; maybe it is this part of it, if we choose it, which would provide the testimony we want.

YOUNG SOCRATES: I've certainly no objection.

VISITOR: Why then don't we now do the very same thing with weaving that we did in what preceded, dividing each thing by cutting it into parts,   c and then cutting them? We'll get back to what is useful in the present context after covering everything as briefly and quickly as we can.

YOUNG SOCRATES: What do you mean?

VISITOR: I shall make my answer to you by just going through it.

YOUNG SOCRATES: An excellent suggestion.

VISITOR: Well then: all the things we make and acquire are either for the sake of our doing something, or they prevent something's happening to us. Of preventives, some are charms, whether divine or human, warding   d things off, others forms of defense. Of forms of defense some are ways of arming for war, others forms of protection. Of forms of protection some are screens, others means of warding off cold and hot weather. Of the latter type of protectives some are shelters, others coverings; of coverings one sort consists of things spread under, a different sort of things put round. Of things put round, some are cut out in one piece, while a different sort are compound; of the compound some are perforated, others bound   e together without perforation; of the unperforated some are made of the 'sinews' of things growing from the earth, others of hair. Of those made of hair, some are stuck together by means of water and earth, others are bound together with themselves. It is to these preventives and coverings

40. See 268c1, and also 267e ff., 275b, 276b.

manufactured from materials that are being bound together with themselves that we give the name 'clothes'; as for the expertise that especially
280   has charge of clothes—just as before we gave the name of 'statesmanship'
to the sort of expertise that especially had charge of the state, so too now
shall we call this sort 'the art of clothes-making', from the thing itself?
And shall we say that weaving too, in so far as it represented the largest
part of the manufacture of clothes, does not differ at all, except in name,
from this art of clothes-making, just as in that other case we said that the
art of kingship did not differ from that of statesmanship?[41]

YOUNG SOCRATES: Yes; absolutely correct.

VISITOR: As for what comes next, let's reflect that someone might perhaps
b   suppose that weaving had been adequately described when put like this,
being unable to grasp that it had not yet been divided off from those co-
operative arts that border on it, while it had been parcelled off from many
other related ones.

YOUNG SOCRATES: Tell me—which related ones?

VISITOR: You didn't follow what's been said, it seems; so it looks as if
we must go back again, starting from the end. If you grasp the kinship in
this case, we cut off one 'related' expertise from weaving just now, separating off the putting together of blankets by means of the distinction between
putting round and putting under.

YOUNG SOCRATES: I understand.

c   VISITOR: What's more, we took away all craftwork out of flax, esparto,
and what we just now by analogy called 'sinews' of plants; again we
divided off both the art of felting and the sort of putting together that
uses perforation and sewing, of which the largest is the art of cobbling.

YOUNG SOCRATES: Absolutely.

VISITOR: Still further, working with skins, which looks after coverings
cut in a single piece, and those sorts of activities that look after shelters,
all those involved in building and carpentry in general and, in other sorts
d   of expertise, contriving shelter from inflowing water—all of these we took
away. Also, all those sorts of expertise in forms of protection that offer
preventive products in relation to thefts and violent acts, and those that
have to do with carrying out the work of lid-making, and fixings to door-
ways, which are assigned as parts of the art of joinery. And we cut away
the art of arms-manufacture, a segment of that great and varied capacity
which is defense-production. Then again our first and immediate move
e   was to divide off the whole of the art of magic which is concerned with
protective charms, and we have left behind—as we might suppose—the
very expertise we looked for, which protects us against cold weather,
productive of a woollen defense, and called by the name of weaving.

YOUNG SOCRATES: Yes, that seems to be so.

41. See 258e ff.

VISITOR: But put like this, my boy, it is not yet complete. The person who puts his hand first to the production of clothes seems to do the opposite of weaving.

281

YOUNG SOCRATES: How so?

VISITOR: The business of weaving, I suppose, is a sort of intertwining.

YOUNG SOCRATES: Yes.

VISITOR: But in fact what I'm talking about is a matter of breaking apart things that are combined or matted together.

YOUNG SOCRATES: What is it you're referring to?

VISITOR: The function of the art of the carder. Or shall we dare to call the art of carding the art of weaving, and treat the carder as if he were a weaver?

YOUNG SOCRATES: Certainly not.

VISITOR: And then too if someone calls the art of manufacturing warp and woof 'weaving', he is using a name that is not only odd but false.

b

YOUNG SOCRATES: Quite.

VISITOR: And what about these cases? Are we to put down the whole of the art of fulling, and clothes-mending, as being no sort of care for clothes, nor as any sort of looking after them, or shall we refer to all of these too as arts of weaving?

YOUNG SOCRATES: Certainly not.

VISITOR: Yet all of these will dispute the role of looking after and producing clothes with the capacity which is the art of weaving, conceding a very large part to it, but assigning large shares to themselves too.

YOUNG SOCRATES: Certainly.

c

VISITOR: Then again, in addition to these, we must suppose that the sorts of expertise responsible for making the tools through which the products of weaving are completed will also lay claim to being at least a contributory cause of every woven article.

YOUNG SOCRATES: Quite correct.

VISITOR: So will our account of that part of the art of weaving that we selected be sufficiently definite, if we proceed to set it down as finest and greatest of all those sorts of care that exist in relation to woollen clothing? Or would we be saying something true, but not clear or complete, until such time as we remove all of these too from around it?

d

YOUNG SOCRATES: Correct.

VISITOR: Then after this we must do what we're saying we should do, in order that our account may proceed in due order.

YOUNG SOCRATES: Quite.

VISITOR: Well then, let's look at two sorts of expertise that there are in relation to all the things that people do.

YOUNG SOCRATES: Which are they?

VISITOR: One which is a contributory cause of production, one which is itself a cause.

YOUNG SOCRATES: How so?

e   VISITOR: Those which do not make the thing itself, but which provide
tools for those that do—tools which, if they were not present, what has
been assigned to each expertise would never be accomplished: these are
what I mean by contributory causes, while those that bring the thing itself
to completion are causes.

YOUNG SOCRATES: That seems to make sense.

VISITOR: Then as a next step shall we call contributory causes all those
that are concerned with spindles and shuttles and whatever other tools
share in the process of production in relation to garments, calling those
that look after and make garments themselves causes?

YOUNG SOCRATES: Quite correct.

282   VISITOR: Then among the causes, washing and mending and the whole
business of looking after clothes in these sorts of ways—it's perfectly
reasonable to encompass this part of the extensive field covered by the art
of preparation by calling it all 'the art of the fuller'.

YOUNG SOCRATES: Right.

VISITOR: Again, carding and spinning and everything relating to the
making of clothes itself—which is the thing whose parts we're talking
about—all constitute a single expertise among those everybody recognizes,
namely wool-working.

YOUNG SOCRATES: Of course.

b   VISITOR: Next, there are two segments of wool-working, and each of
these is a part of two sorts of expertise at once.

YOUNG SOCRATES: How so?

VISITOR: What has to do with carding, and half of the art of the shuttle,
and all those activities that set apart from each other things that are together—all of this we can, I suppose, declare as one and as belonging to
wool-working itself? And there were, we agreed, two great sorts of expertise in every sphere, that of combination and that of separation.[42]

YOUNG SOCRATES: Yes.

VISITOR: Well then, it's to the art of separation that belong that of carding
c   and all the things just mentioned; for separation in the case of wool and
the warp, which happens in different ways, in the first case through the
shuttle, in the second through use of the hands, has acquired as many
names as we referred to a moment ago.

YOUNG SOCRATES: Absolutely.

VISITOR: Then again, by contrast, let's take a part that is simultaneously
a part of combination and of wool-working and takes place in the latter;
and whatever parts of separation there were here, let's let all of them go,
cutting wool-working into two by means of the cut between separation
and combination.

YOUNG SOCRATES: Count it as divided.

---

42. See perhaps *Sophist* 226b ff.

VISITOR: Then in its turn, Socrates, you should divide the part that is simultaneously combination and wool-working, if indeed we are going to capture the aforesaid art of weaving.   d

YOUNG SOCRATES: Then I must.

VISITOR: Indeed you must: and let's say that part of it is twisting, part intertwining.

YOUNG SOCRATES: Do I understand correctly? By twisting, you seem to me to be talking about what relates to the manufacture of the warp.

VISITOR: Not only of the warp, but of the woof too; or are we going to find some origin for the woof which doesn't involve twisting?

YOUNG SOCRATES: Certainly not.

VISITOR: Well, define each of these two things too; perhaps you might   e
find defining them timely.

YOUNG SOCRATES: Define them how?

VISITOR: Like this: among the products of carding, when its material is drawn out to a certain length and has acquired breadth, do we say that there's a 'flock' of wool?

YOUNG SOCRATES: Yes.

VISITOR: Of this, then, the yarn that has been twisted by the spindle and been made firm you'll call the warp, and the expertise that guides its production 'warp-spinning'.

YOUNG SOCRATES: Correct.

VISITOR: But those threads that in their turn get a loose twisting, and have a softness appropriate to the twining in of the warp, but also to what is needed for drawing out in the dressing process, you'll call these—the products of the spinning—the woof, and the expertise that is set over their production—let's call it 'woof-spinning'.[43]   283

YOUNG SOCRATES: Quite correct.

VISITOR: And as for the part of weaving that we put forward for investigation, I suppose that's now clear to anyone. When the part of combination which is contained in wool-working produces something intertwined, by the regular intertwining of woof and warp, the whole product of the intertwining we refer to as a piece of woollen clothing, and we refer to the expertise that is over this as weaving.

YOUNG SOCRATES: Quite correct.

VISITOR: Good; so why ever, then, didn't we immediately reply that   b
weaving was an intertwining of woof and warp, instead of going round in a circle defining a whole collection of things to no purpose?

YOUNG SOCRATES: To me at least, visitor, nothing of what we have said seemed to have been said to no purpose.

VISITOR: And that isn't at all surprising, I may say; but perhaps, my dear fellow, it might seem so. So against such a malady, in case it should come

---

43. Reading *technēn krokonētikēn* at 282e14–283a1.

c   upon you later (that wouldn't be at all surprising), listen to a point which
it's appropriate to make in all cases like this.

YOUNG SOCRATES: Do make it.

VISITOR: First, then, let's look at excess and deficiency in general, so that
we may distribute praise and censure proportionately on each occasion,
when things are said at greater length than necessary and when the opposite occurs in discussions like the present one.

YOUNG SOCRATES: That's what we must do, then.

VISITOR: If we talked about these very things, I think we'd be proceeding correctly.

YOUNG SOCRATES: What things?

d   VISITOR: About length and brevity, and excess and deficiency in general.
I suppose the art of measurement relates to all of these.

YOUNG SOCRATES: Yes.

VISITOR: Then let's divide it into two parts; that's what we need towards
our present objective.

YOUNG SOCRATES: Please tell me how we should divide it.

VISITOR: This way: one part will relate to the association of greatness
and smallness with each other, the other to what coming into being necessarily is.[44]

YOUNG SOCRATES: What do you mean?

VISITOR: Does it not seem to you that by its nature the greater has to be
said to be greater than nothing other than the less, and the less in its turn
e   less than the greater, and than nothing else?

YOUNG SOCRATES: It does.

VISITOR: What about this: shan't we also say that there really is such
a thing as what exceeds what is in due measure, and everything of
that sort, in what we say or indeed in what we do? Isn't it just in that
respect that those of us who are bad and those who are good[45] most
differ?

YOUNG SOCRATES: It seems so.

VISITOR: In that case we must lay it down that the great and the small
exist and are objects of judgment in these twin ways. It is not as we said
just before, that we must suppose them to exist only in relation to each
other, but rather as we have now said, that we should speak of their
existing in one way in relation to each other, and in another in relation to
what is in due measure. Do we want to know why?

YOUNG SOCRATES: Of course.

---

44. The Greek here is obscure. The Visitor will immediately explain—in d11–e1—the
first of the two 'parts' of the expertise of measurement; the second emerges gradually
at 284a5–b2, e2–8. See also 284c1 and d6, 'the coming into being of what is in due
measure', and the reference at 285a1–2 to 'an art of measurement relating to everything
that comes into being'.

45. Reading *hoi agathoi* at e6.

VISITOR: If someone will admit the existence of the greater and everything   284
of the sort in relation to nothing other than the less, it will never be in
relation to what is in due measure—you agree?

YOUNG SOCRATES: That's so.

VISITOR: Well, with this account of things we shall destroy—shan't we?—
both the various sorts of expertise themselves and their products, and in
particular we shall make the one we're looking for now, statesmanship,
disappear, and the one we said was weaving. For I imagine all such sorts
of expertise guard against what is more and less than what is in due
measure, not as something which is not, but as something which is and
is troublesome in relation to what they do. It is by preserving measure in
this way that they produce all the good and fine things they do produce.   b

YOUNG SOCRATES: Of course.

VISITOR: If, then, we make the art of statesmanship disappear, our search
after that for the knowledge of kingship will lack any way forward?

YOUNG SOCRATES: Very much so.

VISITOR: Is it the case then that just as with the sophist we compelled
what is not into being as well as what is, when our argument escaped us
down that route,[46] so now we must compel the more and less, in their
turn, to become measurable not only in relation to each other but also in   c
relation to the coming into being of what is in due measure? For if this
has not been agreed, it is certainly not possible for either the statesman
or anyone else who possesses knowledge of practical subjects to acquire
an undisputed existence.

YOUNG SOCRATES: Then now too we must do the same as much as we can.

VISITOR: This task, Socrates, is even greater than the former one—and
we remember what the length of *that* was. Still, it's very definitely fair to
propose the following hypothesis about the subject in question.

YOUNG SOCRATES: What's that?

VISITOR: That at some time we shall need what I referred to just now[47]   d
for the sort of demonstration that would be commensurate with the precise
truth itself. But so far as concerns what is presently being shown, quite
adequately for our immediate purposes, the argument we are using seems
to me to come to our aid in magnificent fashion. Namely, we should surely
suppose that it is similarly the case that all the various sorts of expertise
exist, and at the same time that greater and less are measured not only in
relation to each other but also in relation to the coming into being of what
is in due measure. For if the latter is the case, then so is the former, and
also if it is the case that the sorts of expertise exist, the other is the case
too. But if one or the other is not the case, then neither of them will ever be.

YOUNG SOCRATES: This much is right; but what's the next move after this?   e

---

46. I.e., in the *Sophist*.

47. I.e., probably, a way of 'compelling the more and the less . . . to become measurable
. . . in relation to the coming into being of what is in due measure' (284b–c).

VISITOR: It's clear that we would divide the art of measurement, cutting it in two in just the way we said, positing as one part of it all those sorts of expertise that measure the number, lengths, depths, breadths and speeds of things in relation to what is opposed to them, and as the other, all those that measure in relation to what is in due measure, what is fitting, the right moment, what is as it ought to be—everything that removes itself from the extremes to the middle.

YOUNG SOCRATES: Each of the two sections you refer to is indeed a large one, and very different from the other.

VISITOR: Yes, Socrates; and what many sophisticated people sometimes
285   say, supposing themselves to be expressing something clever, to the effect that there is in fact an art of measurement relating to everything that comes into being—that's actually the very thing we have just said. For it is indeed the case, in a certain way, that all the products of the various sorts of expertise share in measurement. But because of their not being accustomed to carrying on their investigations by dividing according to real classes, the people in question throw these things together at once, despite the degree of difference between them, thinking them alike—and then again they also do the opposite of this by dividing other things not according
b   to parts, when the rule is that when one perceives first the community between the members of a group of many things, one should not desist until one sees in it all those differences that are located in classes, and conversely, with the various unlikenesses, when they are seen in multitudes, one should be incapable of pulling a face and stopping before one has penned all the related things within one likeness and actually surrounded them in some real class. So let this be enough for us to say about these things, and about modes of defect and excess; and let's just
c   keep hold of the fact that two distinct classes of measurement have been discovered in relation to them, and remember what we say they are.

YOUNG SOCRATES: We'll remember.

VISITOR: Well then, after this point, let's admit another one that relates both to the very things we are inquiring into and to the whole business of discussions of this sort.

YOUNG SOCRATES: What's that?

VISITOR: What if someone put the following question about our pupils sitting together learning their letters. When one of them is asked what letters make up some word or other, are we to say that for him on that
d   occasion the inquiry takes place more for the sake of the single question set before him, or for the sake of his becoming more able to answer all questions relating to letters?

YOUNG SOCRATES: Clearly for the sake of his being able to answer all.

VISITOR: What then about our inquiry now about the statesman? Has it been set before us more for the sake of that very thing, or for the sake of our becoming better dialecticians in relation to all subjects?

YOUNG SOCRATES: That's clear too—for the sake of our becoming better dialecticians generally.

VISITOR: I certainly don't suppose that anyone with any sense would want to hunt down the definition of *weaving* for the sake of weaving itself. But I think the majority of people fail to recognize that for some of the things there are, there are certain perceptible likenesses which are there to be easily understood, and which it is not at all hard to point out when one wants to make an easy demonstration, involving no trouble and without recourse to verbal means, to someone who asks for an account of one of these things. Conversely, for those things that are greatest and most valuable, there is no image at all which has been worked in plain view for the use of mankind, the showing of which will enable the person who wants to satisfy the mind of an inquirer to satisfy it adequately, just by fitting it to one of the senses. That is why one must practice at being able to give and receive an account of each thing; for the things that are without body, which are finest and greatest, are shown clearly only by verbal means and by nothing else, and everything that is now being said is for the sake of these things. But practice in everything is easier in smaller things, rather than in relation to the greater.

YOUNG SOCRATES: Very well said.

VISITOR: Well then, let's remind ourselves of the reasons why we've said all this on these subjects.

YOUNG SOCRATES: Why did we say it all?

VISITOR: Not least because of the difficulty we found in accepting the length of our talk about weaving—and about the reversal of the universe, and about the being of the non-being which is the sphere of the sophist; we reflected that it had a rather great length, and in all these cases we rebuked ourselves, out of fear that what we were saying would turn out to be superfluous as well as long. So, the thing for you to say is that the foregoing was for the sake of all those cases, in order that we shan't suffer any of this sort of misgiving on any future occasion.

YOUNG SOCRATES: I shall do as you say. Tell me what comes next.

VISITOR: Well, I say that you and I must be careful to remember what we have now said, and to distribute censure and praise of both shortness and length, whatever subjects we happen to be talking about on each occasion, by judging lengths not in relation to each other but, in accordance with the part of the art of measurement we previously said we must remember, in relation to what is fitting.

YOUNG SOCRATES: Correct.

VISITOR: Well, that's right, but we mustn't refer *everything* to this. For one thing, we shan't have any need for a length that fits in relation to pleasure, except perhaps as an incidental consideration. And again, as for what contributes towards the inquiry into the subject set before us, what we have said commits us to making a second and not a first priority of the question how we might find it most easily and quickly, and to give by far the greatest and primary value to the pursuit itself of the ability to divide by classes. In particular, if an account is very long but renders the hearer better at discovering things, our business is to take this one seriously

and not feel at all irritated at its length, and similarly if a shorter one, in its turn, has the same effect. Then again, over and above this, if in relation to such discussions someone finds fault with the length of what is said and will not put up with going round in circles, we must not let such a
287   person go just like that[48] without a backward glance—with his having made the simple complaint that what has been said has taken a long time. We should think it right that he should also demonstrate, in addition, that if it had been shorter it would make the partners in the discussion better dialecticians and better at discovering how to display in words the things there are. We shall take no notice at all of the other sorts of censure and praise, relating to some other criteria, nor even seem to hear such things at all when they are said. Now enough of these things, if I have your
b   agreement too; let's go back again to the statesman, and bring the model of weaving, which we talked about before, to bear on it.

YOUNG SOCRATES: Well said—let's do what you say.

VISITOR: Well then, the king has been separated off from the many sorts of expertise that share his field—or rather from all of them concerned with herds; there remain, we are saying, those sorts of expertise in the city itself that are contributory causes and those that are causes, which we must first divide from each other.

YOUNG SOCRATES: Correct.

VISITOR: So do you recognize that it is difficult to cut them into two?
c   The cause, I think, will become more evident if we proceed.

YOUNG SOCRATES: Well, then that's what we should do.

VISITOR: Then let's divide them limb by limb, like a sacrificial animal, since we can't do it into two. For we must always cut into the nearest number so far as we can.

YOUNG SOCRATES: So how are we to do it in this case?

VISITOR: Just as before: the sorts of expertise that provided tools relating to weaving—all of these, of course, we put down then as contributory causes.

YOUNG SOCRATES: Yes.

d   VISITOR: We must do the same thing now too, but to a still greater degree than we did then. For we must put down as being contributory causes all the sorts of expertise that produce any tool in the city, whether small or large. Without these there would never come to be a city, nor statesmanship, but on the other hand we shan't, I think, put down any of them as the product of the expertise of the king.

YOUNG SOCRATES: No, we shan't.

VISITOR: And yet we're trying to do a difficult thing in separating this class of things from the rest; in fact it is possible for someone to treat anything you like as a tool of *something* and seem to have said something
e   credible. Nevertheless, among the things people possess in a city, let's treat the following as being of a different sort.

YOUNG SOCRATES: Different in what way?

48. Reading *panu* at e6.

VISITOR: Because it does not have the same capacity that tools have. For it is not put together with the purpose of causing the coming into being of something, as a tool is, but for the sake of preserving what craftsmen have produced.

YOUNG SOCRATES: What do you mean?

VISITOR: That varied class of things which is worked for things liquid and solid, and for things that are prepared on the fire and things that are not—what we refer to with the single name of 'vessel': a common class, and one that, I think, simply does not belong at all to the sort of expert knowledge we are looking for.

288

YOUNG SOCRATES: Certainly not.

VISITOR: We must then observe a third very extensive class of things that people possess, different from these others, which is found on land and on water, moves about a lot and is fixed, and is accorded high value and none, but has a single name, because it is all for the sake of some supporting or other, always being a seat for something.

YOUNG SOCRATES: What do you mean?

VISITOR: I suppose we call it by the name of 'vehicle'; not at all a product of the art of statesmanship, but much more of those of carpentry, pottery, and bronze-working.

YOUNG SOCRATES: I see.

VISITOR: And what is fourth? Should we say that it is something different from these, something that includes the larger part of the things we mentioned before, all clothing, most armor, and walls, all those encirclements made out of earth, or out of stone, and tens of thousands of other things? Since all of them together are worked for the purpose of defending, it would be most apposite to call the whole class that of 'defense', and it would be thought to be a product much more of the expertise of the builder and the weaver, most of it, more correctly than it would be thought to belong to that of the statesman.

b

YOUNG SOCRATES: Absolutely.

VISITOR: Would we want to put down as a fifth class things to do with decoration, painting, and those representations that are completed by the use of painting, and of music, which have been executed solely to give us pleasures, and which would appropriately be embraced by a single name?

c

YOUNG SOCRATES: What name?

VISITOR: I think we talk about something we call a 'plaything'.

YOUNG SOCRATES: Of course.

VISITOR: Well, this one name will be fittingly given to all of them; for not one of them is for the sake of a serious purpose, but all are done for amusement.

YOUNG SOCRATES: This too I pretty well understand.

d

VISITOR: And what provides materials for all these things, from which and in which all of the sorts of expertise that have now been mentioned work, a varied class that is itself the offspring of many other sorts of expertise—shall we not put it down as a sixth?

YOUNG SOCRATES: What exactly are you referring to?

VISITOR: Gold and silver, and everything that is mined, and all that the art of tree-felling and any lopping cuts and provides for the art of the carpenter and the basket-weaver—and again the art of stripping off the

e   outer covering of plants, and the one that removes skins from bodies of living things, the art of the skinner; and all the sorts of expertise there are in relation to such things, which by producing cork, and papyrus, and materials for bindings make possible the working up of classes of composite things from classes of things that are not put together. Let us call[49] it all one thing, the first-born and incomposite possession of mankind, which is in no way a product of the knowledge of kingship.

YOUNG SOCRATES: Right.

VISITOR: Then again that sort of possession that consists in nutrition, and all those things which when they are blended into the body, their own

289   parts with parts of the body, have a capacity for promoting its care, we must say is a seventh, calling it all together 'nurture', unless we have some more attractive term to propose. And if we place it under the arts of the farmer, the hunter, the trainer in the gymnasium, the doctor and the cook, we shall be assigning it more correctly than if we give it to the art of the statesman.

YOUNG SOCRATES: Of course.

VISITOR: Well then, we have, I think, pretty well dealt, in these seven classes, with all the things that have to do with possessions, with the exception of tame living creatures. Look at our list: it would be most

b   appropriate if we put down the 'first-born' class of things at the beginning, and after this 'tool', 'vessel', 'vehicle', 'defense', 'plaything', 'nourishment'. If anything of no great importance has escaped us, we leave it to one side,[50] because it is capable of fitting into one or other of these, for example the class consisting of currency, seals, and any sort of engraving. For these do not have any great shared class among them, but if some of them are dragged off into decoration, others into tools, it will be forcibly done, but nevertheless they'll wholly agree to it. As for what relates to possession

c   of tame living creatures, apart from slaves, the art of herd-rearing which we divided into its parts before will clearly be seen to have caught them all.

YOUNG SOCRATES: Absolutely.

VISITOR: Then what remains is the class of slaves and all those people who are subordinate to others, among whom, I strongly suspect, those who dispute with the king about the 'woven fabric' itself will come into view, just as in the case of weaving we found those concerned with spinning and carding and all the other things we mentioned disputing with the weavers over their product.[51] All the others, who have been described as

49. Reading *prosagoreuōmen* at e4.
50. Reading *thremma. paraleipomen de* at b2.
51. Cf. 281b.

'contributory causes', have been disposed of along with the products we have just listed, as each was separated off from the practical activity which is the sphere of the art of kingship and statesmanship.

YOUNG SOCRATES: So it seems, at any rate.

VISITOR: Come along, then: let's get up close to those people that are left and take a look at them, so that we may get a firmer knowledge of them.

YOUNG SOCRATES: That's what we should do.

VISITOR: Well, those who are subordinate to the greatest degree, looked at from our present perspective, we find possessing a function and condition which are the opposite of what we suspected just now.

YOUNG SOCRATES: Who are they?

VISITOR: Those who are bought, and acquired as possessions by this means; people whom we can indisputably call slaves, and who least pretend to kingly expertise.

YOUNG SOCRATES: Quite.

VISITOR: What then of all those among free men who voluntarily place themselves in the service of those we have been discussing, conveying their products—the products of farming and the other sorts of expertise—between them, and establishing equality between these products; some in market-places, others moving from one city to another, whether by sea or by land, exchanging currency both for everything else and for itself—people to whom we give the names of 'money-changers', 'merchants', 'ship-owners', and 'retailers': surely they won't lay claim at all to the art of statesmanship?

YOUNG SOCRATES: It may be, perhaps, that they will—to the sort that has to do with commercial matters.

VISITOR: But those we see placing themselves with complete readiness at the service of all, for hire, as day-laborers—these we shall never find pretending to kingly expertise.

YOUNG SOCRATES: Quite so.

VISITOR: What in that case are we to say about those who perform services of the following sorts for us whenever we need them?

YOUNG SOCRATES: What services do you mean, and who is it you're talking about?

VISITOR: Among others, the tribe of heralds, and all those who become accomplished at writing by having repeatedly given their services in this respect, and certain others who are very clever at working through many different tasks relating to public offices: what shall we call these?

YOUNG SOCRATES: What you called them just now—subordinates, and not themselves rulers in cities.

VISITOR: But I certainly wasn't dreaming, I think, when I said that somewhere here there would appear those who particularly lay claim to the art of statesmanship. And yet it would seem very odd indeed to look for them in some portion of the subordinate arts.

YOUNG SOCRATES: Yes, quite.

VISITOR: Then let's get still closer to those we haven't yet cross-examined. There are those who have a part of a subordinate sort of expert knowledge in relation to divination; for they are, I believe, considered to be interpreters from gods to men.

YOUNG SOCRATES: Yes.

VISITOR: And then too the class of priests, in its turn, has—as custom tells us—expert knowledge about the giving through sacrifices of gifts
d   from us to the gods which are pleasing to them, and about asking from them through prayers for the acquisition of good things for us. I imagine that both of these things are parts of a subordinate art.

YOUNG SOCRATES: It appears so, at any rate.

VISITOR: Well now, it seems to me that at this point we are, as it were, getting close to some sort of trail leading to our destination. For the type of priests and seers is filled full of self-importance and gets a lofty reputation because of the magnitude of what they undertake, so that in Egypt it is
e   not even permitted for a king to hold office without also exercising that of priest. If in fact he happens to have acceded to power at the beginning by force from another class, it is later necessary for him to be initiated into the class of priests. And again among the Greeks too, in many places, it is to the greatest offices that one would find being assigned the performance of the greatest of the sacrifices in relation to such things. And in fact what I'm saying receives the clearest illustration in your case; for they say that the most solemn and ancestral of the ancient sacrifices are assigned here to the person who becomes king by lot.[52]

YOUNG SOCRATES: Most certainly.

291   VISITOR: Well then, we must look both at these king-priests by lot, and their subordinates, and also at a certain other very large crowd of people which has just become visible to us,[53] now that the previous ones have been separated off.

YOUNG SOCRATES: But who are the people you mean?

VISITOR: Some very odd people indeed.

YOUNG SOCRATES: How, exactly?

VISITOR: It's a class mixed out of all sorts, or so it seems to me as I look
b   at it just now. For many of the men resemble lions and centaurs and other such things, and very many resemble satyrs and those animals that are weak but versatile; and they quickly exchange their shapes and capacity for action for each other's. And yet *now*, Socrates, I think I have identified the men in question.

YOUNG SOCRATES: Please explain; you seem to have something odd in view.

VISITOR: Yes; it's a universal experience that not recognizing something makes it odd. And this is exactly what happened to me just now: at the

52. At Athens, one of the 'archons' or chief magistrates had the title of King Archon.
53. Reading *katadēlos hēmin* at a3.

moment when I first saw the chorus of those concerned with the affairs   c
of cities I failed to recognize them.

YOUNG SOCRATES: What chorus?

VISITOR: That of the greatest magician of all the sophists, and the most
versed in their expertise. Although removing him from among those who
really are in possession of the art of statesmanship and kingship is a very
difficult thing to do, remove him we must if we are going to see plainly
what we are looking for.

YOUNG SOCRATES: We must certainly not let this slip.

VISITOR: Certainly not, if you ask my view. So tell me this.

YOUNG SOCRATES: What?

VISITOR: We recognize monarchy, don't we, as one of the varieties of   d
rule in cities?

YOUNG SOCRATES: Yes.

VISITOR: After monarchy one would, I think, list the holding of power
by the few.

YOUNG SOCRATES: Of course.

VISITOR: And isn't a third type of constitution rule by the mass of the
people, called by the name of 'democracy'?

YOUNG SOCRATES: Most certainly.

VISITOR: So there are three of them—but don't they in a certain way
become five, giving birth from among them to two other names in addition
to themselves?

YOUNG SOCRATES: What are these?

VISITOR: I think that as things are people refer to the aspects of force   e
and consent, poverty and wealth, and law and lawlessness as they occur
in them, and use these to divide each of the first two types into two. So
they call monarchy by two names, on the grounds that it exhibits two
forms, the one 'tyrannical', the other 'kingly' monarchy.

YOUNG SOCRATES: Of course.

VISITOR: And any city which has come to be controlled by a few people
they call by the names of 'aristocracy' and 'oligarchy'.

YOUNG SOCRATES: Most certainly.

VISITOR: With democracy, on the other hand, whether in fact it's by force
or with their consent that the mass rules over those who possess the wealth,   292
and whether by accurately preserving the laws or not, in all these cases
no one is in the habit of changing its name.

YOUNG SOCRATES: True.

VISITOR: What then? Do we suppose that any of these constitutions is
correct, when it is defined by these criteria—one, few and many, wealth
and poverty, force and consent, and whether it turns out to be accompanied
by written laws or without laws?

YOUNG SOCRATES: Why, what actually prevents it?

VISITOR: Look at it more clearly, following this way.   b

YOUNG SOCRATES: Which?

VISITOR: Shall we abide by what we said when we first began, or shall we be in discord with it?

YOUNG SOCRATES: What was that?

VISITOR: We said, I think, that kingly rule was one of the sorts of expert knowledge.

YOUNG SOCRATES: Yes.

VISITOR: And not just one of them all, but we chose out from the rest particularly one that was concerned in a sense with making judgments and controlling.

YOUNG SOCRATES: Yes.

c VISITOR: And then from the controlling sort, we took one that was set over inanimate products, and one set over living creatures; and it's by splitting things up in just this way that we have been progressing all the time to the point where we are now. We haven't forgotten that it's knowledge, but as for what sort of knowledge it is, we're not yet able to give a sufficiently accurate answer.

YOUNG SOCRATES: Your account is correct.

VISITOR: Then do we see just this very point, that the criterion in the things in question must not be few, nor many, nor consent nor the lack of it, nor poverty nor wealth, but some sort of knowledge, if indeed we are going to be consistent with what we said before?

d YOUNG SOCRATES: But *that* we can't possibly fail to do.

VISITOR: Necessarily, then, we must now consider in which, if any, of these types of rule expert knowledge about ruling human beings turns out to occur—practically the most difficult and the most important thing of which to acquire knowledge. For we must catch sight of it, in order to consider which people we must remove from the wise king's company, who pretend to possess of the art of statesmanship, and persuade many people that they do, but in fact do not have it at all.

YOUNG SOCRATES: Yes, we must indeed do this, as our argument has already told us.

e VISITOR: Well, does it seem that a mass of people in the city are capable of acquiring this expertise?

YOUNG SOCRATES: How could they?

VISITOR: But in a city of a thousand men, is it possible for a hundred or so, or again fifty, to acquire it adequately?

YOUNG SOCRATES: In that case, it would be quite the easiest of all the sorts of expertise there are; for we know that among a thousand men there would never be so many top *petteia*-players[54] in relation to those among the rest of the Greeks, let alone kings. For it is that man who actually possesses the expert knowledge of kingship, whether he rules or not, who
293 must in any case be called an expert in kingship, according to what we said before.[55]

54. *Petteia* was a board game, resembling draughts or checkers.
55. 259b.

VISITOR: You've remembered well. As a consequence of this, I think, we must look for correct rule in relation to some one person, or two, or altogether few—when it *is* correct.

YOUNG SOCRATES: We certainly must.

VISITOR: Yes, but these people, whether they rule over willing or unwilling subjects, whether according to written laws or without them, and whether they rule as rich men or poor, we must suppose—as is now our view—to be carrying out whatever sort of rule they do on the basis of expertise. Doctors provide the clearest parallel. We believe in them whether they cure us with our consent or without it, by cutting or burning or applying some other painful treatment, and whether they do so according to written rules or apart from written rules, and whether as poor men or rich. In all these cases we are no less inclined at all to say they are doctors, so long as they are in charge of us on the basis of expertise, purging or otherwise reducing us, or else building us up—it is no matter, if only each and every one of those who care for our bodies acts for our bodies' good, making them better than they were, and so preserves what is in their care. It's in this way, as I think, and in no other that we'll lay down the criterion of medicine and of any other sort of rule whatsoever; it is the only correct criterion.

YOUNG SOCRATES: Yes, just so.

VISITOR: It must then be the case, it seems, that of constitutions too the one that is correct in comparison with the rest, and alone a constitution, is the one in which the rulers would be found truly possessing expert knowledge, and not merely seeming to do so, whether they rule according to laws or without laws, over willing or unwilling subjects, and whether the rulers are poor or wealthy—there is no principle of correctness according to which any of these must be taken into any account at all.

YOUNG SOCRATES: Right.

VISITOR: And whether they purge the city for its benefit by putting some people to death or else by exiling them, or whether again they make it smaller by sending out colonies somewhere like swarms of bees, or build it up by introducing people from somewhere outside and making them citizens—so long as they act to preserve it on the basis of expert knowledge and what is just, making it better than it was so far as they can, *this* is the constitution which alone we must say is correct, under these conditions and in accordance with criteria of this sort. All the others that we generally say are constitutions we must say are not genuine, and not really constitutions at all, but imitations of this one; those we say are 'law-abiding' have imitated[56] it for the better, the others for the worse.

YOUNG SOCRATES: The rest of it, visitor, seems to have been said in due measure; but that ideal rule may exist even without laws was something harder for a hearer to accept.

56. Retaining *memimēsthai* at e5.

VISITOR: You got in just a little before me with your question, Socrates.
294   For I was about to ask you whether you accept all of this, or whether in
fact you find any of the things we have said difficult to take. But as it is
it's already apparent that we'll want a discussion of this matter of the
correctness of those who rule without laws.

YOUNG SOCRATES: Quite.

VISITOR: Now in a certain sense[57] it is clear that the art of the legislator
belongs to that of the king; but the best thing is not that the laws should
prevail, but rather the kingly man who possesses wisdom. Do you
know why?

YOUNG SOCRATES: What then is the reason?

b   VISITOR: That law could never accurately embrace what is best and most
just for all at the same time, and so prescribe what is best. For the dissimilar-
ities between human beings and their actions, and the fact that practically
nothing in human affairs ever remains stable, prevent any sort of expertise
whatsoever from making any simple decision in any sphere that covers all
cases and will last for all time. I suppose this is something we agree about?

YOUNG SOCRATES: Certainly.

c   VISITOR: But we see law bending itself more or less towards this very
thing; it resembles some self-willed and ignorant person, who allows no
one to do anything contrary to what he orders, nor to ask any questions
about it, not even if, after all, something new turns out for someone which
is better, contrary to the prescription which he himself has laid down.

YOUNG SOCRATES: True; the law does absolutely as you have just said
with regard to each and every one of us.

VISITOR: Then it is impossible for what is perpetually simple to be useful
in relation to what is never simple?

YOUNG SOCRATES: Very likely.

d   VISITOR: Why then is it ever necessary to make laws, given that law is
not something completely correct? We must find out the cause of this.

YOUNG SOCRATES: Certainly.

VISITOR: Now with you, too, people train in groups in the way they do
in other cities, whether for running or for anything else, for competitive purposes?

YOUNG SOCRATES: Yes, very frequently.

VISITOR: Well, now let's recall to mind the instructions that expert trainers
give when they're in charge of people in such circumstances.

YOUNG SOCRATES: What are you thinking of?

VISITOR: That they don't suppose there is room for them to make their
prescriptions piece by piece to suit each individual, giving the instruction
e   appropriate to the physical condition of each; they regard it as necessary
to make rougher prescriptions about what will bring physical benefit, as
suits the majority of cases and a large number of people.

YOUNG SOCRATES: Right.

---

57. Reading *mentoi tina* at a6.

VISITOR: And it's just for this reason that, as it is, they give equally heavy exercises to the group as a whole, starting them off together and stopping them together in their running, wrestling, and the rest of their physical exercises.

YOUNG SOCRATES: That's so.

VISITOR: Then let's suppose the same about the legislator too, the person who will direct his herds in relation to justice and their contracts with one   295
another: he will never be capable, in prescribing for everyone together, of assigning accurately to each individual what is appropriate for him.

YOUNG SOCRATES: What you say certainly sounds reasonable.

VISITOR: Instead he will, I think, set down the law for each and every one according to the principle of 'for the majority of people, for the majority of cases, and roughly, somehow, like this', whether expressing it in writing or in unwritten form, legislating by means of ancestral customs.

YOUNG SOCRATES: Correct.

VISITOR: Yes, it certainly is. For how would anyone ever be capable, Socrates, of sitting beside each individual perpetually throughout his life   b
and accurately prescribing what is appropriate to him? Since in my view, if he were capable of this, any one of those who had really acquired the expert knowledge of kingship would hardly put obstacles in his own way by writing down these laws we talked about.

YOUNG SOCRATES: It certainly follows from what we have now said, visitor.

VISITOR: Yes, but more, my good friend, from the things that are going to be said.

YOUNG SOCRATES: And what are they?

VISITOR: Things like the following. Are we to say—that is, between us— that if a doctor, or else some gymnastic trainer, were going to be out of   c
the country and away from his charges for what he thought would be a long time, and thought that the people being trained, or his patients, would not remember the instructions he had given them, he would want to write down reminders for them—or what are we to say?

YOUNG SOCRATES: As you suggested.

VISITOR: But what if he came back unexpectedly, having been away for less time than he thought he would be? Do you think he wouldn't propose other prescriptions, contrary to the ones he had written down, when things   d
turned out to be different, and better, for his patients because of winds or else some other of the things that come from Zeus which had come about contrary to expectation, in some way differently from the usual pattern? Would he obstinately think that neither he nor the patient should step outside those ancient laws that had once been laid down—he himself by giving other instructions, the patient by daring to do different things contrary to what was written down—on the grounds that these were the rules of the art of medicine and of health, and that things that happened differently were unhealthy and not part of his expertise? Or would all such things, if they happened in the context of truly expert knowledge,

e   cause altogether the greatest ridicule, in all spheres, for acts of legislation
     of this sort?

     YOUNG SOCRATES: Absolutely right.

     VISITOR: And as for the person who has written down what is just and
     unjust, fine and shameful, good and bad, or has laid down unwritten laws
     on these subjects, for all those herds of human beings that graze, city by
     city, according to the laws of those who wrote them down in each case—
     if the person who wrote them on the basis of expertise, or someone else
296 resembling him, arrives, is it really not to be permitted to him to give
     different instructions contrary to these? Or wouldn't this prohibition ap-
     pear in truth no less ridiculous than the other one?

     YOUNG SOCRATES: Of course.

     VISITOR: Well then, do you know what the majority of people say in
     such a case?

     YOUNG SOCRATES: It doesn't come to mind for the moment, just like that.

     VISITOR: Well, it sounds fine enough. What they say is that if someone
     recognizes laws that are better, contrary to those established by people
     before him, then he must introduce them by persuading his city to accept
     them in each case, but not otherwise.

     YOUNG SOCRATES: Well then? Is that not a correct view?

b   VISITOR: Perhaps. But first things first: if someone forces through what
     is better without the use of persuasion, tell me, what will be the name to
     give to the use of force in this case? No—not yet; answer me first in relation
     to the previous cases.

     YOUNG SOCRATES: What do you mean?

     VISITOR: If then—to continue with our example—someone does not per-
     suade his patient, but has a correct grasp of the relevant expertise, and
     forces child, or man, or woman, to do what is better, contrary to what has
     been written down, what will be the name to give to this use of force?
     Surely anything rather than what we called an unhealthy mistake contrary
c   to the expertise in question? And the last thing the person who was the
     object of such force can correctly say about such a thing is that he had
     unhealthy things done to him by the doctors who used force on him, things
     that did not belong to their expertise?

     YOUNG SOCRATES: What you say is very true.

     VISITOR: And what do we really suppose to be the sort of mistake we're
     talking about, the one in contravention of the expertise of the statesman?
     Isn't it what is shameful, what is bad,[58] and unjust?

     YOUNG SOCRATES: I agree, absolutely.

     VISITOR: Then those who have been forced, contrary to what has been
     written down and to ancestral custom, to do different things that are more
d   just, better and finer than the things they did before—tell me, if people in
     this kind of situation for their part censure this kind of use of force, isn't
     it true that, if their censure isn't to be the most laughable of all, they must

58. Reading *kai to* at c5.

say anything on each occasion rather than that those who have been forced have had shameful, unjust and bad things done to them by those who did the forcing?

YOUNG SOCRATES: What you say is very true.

VISITOR: But are the things forced on them just, if the person who did the forcing is rich, and unjust if he happens to be poor? Or if, whether by using persuasion or not, whether as a rich or a poor man, or according to written law or contrary to it, he does what is not to the benefit of the citizens[59] or what is to their benefit, must that be the criterion, and must it have to do with these things—the truest criterion of correct government of a city, the one according to which the wise and good man will govern the interests of the ruled? Just as a steersman, always watching out for what is to the benefit of the ship and the sailors, preserves his fellow sailors not by putting things down in writing but offering his expertise as law, so too in this same manner a constitution would be correct, would it not, if it issued from those who are able to rule in this way, offering the strength of their expertise as more powerful than the laws? And there is no mistake, is there, for wise rulers, whatever they do, provided that they watch for one great thing, that by always distributing to those in the city what is most just, as judged by the intelligent application of their expertise, they are able both to preserve them and so far as they can to bring it about that they are better than they were?

YOUNG SOCRATES: It is certainly not possible to contradict what has just been said.

VISITOR: And neither should one contradict those other things we said.

YOUNG SOCRATES: What are you referring to?

VISITOR: That a mass of any people whatsoever would never be able to acquire this sort of expert knowledge and so govern a city with intelligence; and that we must look for that one constitution, the correct one, in relation to a small element in the population, few in number, or even a single individual, putting down the other constitutions as imitations, as was said a little earlier, some of them imitating this one for the better, the others for the worse.

YOUNG SOCRATES: What do you mean by this? What are you saying? For I did not understand the point about imitations when it was made just now[60] either.

VISITOR: And it's no small matter, if one stirs up this subject and then proceeds to leave it where it is instead of going through it and showing the mistake that now occurs in relation to it.

YOUNG SOCRATES: What mistake is that?

VISITOR: This sort of thing we must hunt for, since it is not altogether what we are used to or easy to see; but all the same let's try to get hold

e

297

b

c

d

---

59. Retaining *mē sumphora ē* at e1.

60. Reading *arti rhēthen* at c5. The reference is to 293e.

of it. Tell me: given that this constitution we have talked about is on our view the only correct one, do you recognize that the others ought to employ the written documents that belong to this one, and save themselves in that way, doing what is now praised, although it is not the most correct thing to do?

YOUNG SOCRATES: What are you referring to?

e   VISITOR: The principle that no one in the city should dare to do anything contrary to the laws, and that the person who dares to do so should be punished by death and all the worst punishments. This is very correct and fine as a second choice, when one changes the principle we discussed just now,[61] which is our first choice; but let us go over the way in which what we have called 'second-best' has come about. Do you agree?

YOUNG SOCRATES: Absolutely.

VISITOR: Well then, let's go back to the likenesses to which we must always compare our kingly rulers.

YOUNG SOCRATES: Which likenesses?

VISITOR: The noble steersman and the doctor who is 'worth many others'.[62] Let us look at the matter by fashioning a kind of figure, using these as material.

YOUNG SOCRATES: A figure of what kind?

298   VISITOR: Of the following sort: let's suppose that we all thought of them as doing the most terrible things to us. For the one as much as the other saves whichever of us he wishes to save; and whichever of us they wish to mutilate, they do it by cutting and burning us and directing us to pay them expenses as if they were taxes, of which they spend little or none on the patient, while they themselves and their household use the rest;

b   and the final step is for them to take money from relatives or some enemies of the patient as pay for killing him. And steersmen, in their turn, bring about thousands of other things of a similar sort, leaving people stranded on voyages because of some conspiracy or other, causing shipwrecks on the seas and throwing people overboard, and doing other malicious things. Let's suppose then that we thought this, and came to a conclusion about

c   them in a sort of council, no longer to allow either of these sorts of expertise to have autonomous control either of slaves or of free men, but to call together an assembly with ourselves as members, consisting either of the people all together or only of the rich. The rule would be that both laymen and craftsmen other than steersmen and doctors would be permitted to contribute an opinion, whether about sailing or about diseases, as to the basis on which drugs and the tools of the doctor's art should be used on

d   patients, and even how to employ ships themselves, and the tools of the sailor's art for operating them, for facing not only the dangers affecting the voyage itself from winds and sea, but encounters with pirates, and

61. Cf. 293c–d.
62. *Iliad* xi.514.

perhaps, if it should turn out to be necessary, for fighting a sea battle with long ships against others of the same type. And once there was a record, on *kurbeis*[63] or blocks of stone of some sort, of what the majority had decided, whether with the advice of some doctors and steersmen or of those who had no specialized knowledge of medicine or steersmanship, then all our sailing and caring for patients for all future time would have to be done according to this, along with certain other rules established as unwritten ancestral customs.

YOUNG SOCRATES: What you've described is distinctly odd.

VISITOR: Yes—and let's suppose that a further conclusion was that we should set up officers annually who belong to the mass of people, whether from the rich or from the whole people, whoever has office assigned to him by lot; and that those who take office should execute it by steering the ships and healing patients according to the written rules.

YOUNG SOCRATES: This is even harder to take.

VISITOR: Then consider too what follows after this. When the year ends for each and every one of the officers, there will be a requirement to set up courts, either of the rich on the basis of preselection or again those chosen by lot from the whole people together, and to bring before these judges those who have held office, in order to examine their conduct. Anyone who wishes will be permitted to charge an officer that he failed to steer the ships during the year according to the written rules or according to the ancient customs of our ancestors. There will be these same requirements also in the case of those healing the sick, and for any officers condemned by the vote, the judges will have to assess what penalty they should suffer or what financial restitution they should make.

YOUNG SOCRATES: Well, anyone who willingly and voluntarily undertakes to hold office under such conditions would fully deserve to suffer any penalty whatever and to pay back any amount.

VISITOR: And further still it will be necessary to establish a law against all the following things. Suppose anyone is found inquiring into steersmanship and seafaring, or health and truth in the doctor's art, in relation to winds and heat and cold, above and beyond the written rules, and making clever speculations of any kind in relation to such things. In the first place one must not call him an expert doctor or an expert steersman, but a stargazer, some babbling sophist. The next provision will be that anyone who wishes from among those permitted to do so shall indict him and bring him before some court or other as corrupting other people younger than himself and inducing them to engage in the arts of the steersman and the doctor not in accordance with the laws, but instead by taking autonomous control of ships and patients. If he is found guilty of persuading anyone, whether young or old, contrary to the laws and the written rules, the most extreme penalties shall be imposed on him. For (so the law will say) there must be nothing wiser than the laws; no one is ignorant about what belongs

e

299

b

c

63. Revolving columns on which the laws were traditionally inscribed at Athens.

to the art of the doctor, or about health, or what belongs to the art of the
d   steersman, or seafaring, since it is possible for anyone who wishes to
understand things that are written down and things established as ancestral
customs. Suppose then these things came about, Socrates, in the way we
say, both in relation to these sorts of expert knowledge, and to generalship,
and all the art of hunting, of whatever kind; to painting, or any part
whatever of all the art of imitation; to carpentry, the whole of tool-making,
of whatever kind, or again farming and the whole of the expertise that
deals with plants. Or again, suppose we imagined a sort of horse-rearing
e   that took place according to written rules, or all of herd-keeping, or the
art of divination, or every part included in the art of the subordinate, or
petteia, or all the science of numbers, whether perhaps dealing with them
on their own, or in two dimensions, or in solids, or in speeds. If all of
these were practiced in this way, and they were done on the basis of
written rules and not on the basis of expertise, what on earth would be
the result?

YOUNG SOCRATES: It's clear both that we should see all the various sorts
of expertise completely destroyed, and that they would never be restored,
either, because of this law prohibiting inquiry; so that life, which even
300   now is difficult, in such a time would be altogether unliveable.

VISITOR: But what about the following consideration? Suppose we required each of the things mentioned to be done according to written rules,
and we required the person elected or appointed to office by lot, on the
basis of chance, to oversee these written rules of ours: what then if this
person were to take no notice of what is written down, in order either to
profit in some way or to do some personal favor, and were to take it upon
himself to do different things, contrary to these, when he possesses no
knowledge? Would this not be an evil still greater than the previous one?

YOUNG SOCRATES: Yes, very true.[64]

b   VISITOR: Yes, for if, I imagine, contrary to the laws that have been established on the basis of much experiment, with some advisers or other having
given advice on each subject in an attractive way, and having persuaded
the majority to pass them—if someone were brazen enough to act contrary
to these, he would be committing a mistake many times greater than the
other, and would overturn all expert activity to a still greater degree than
do the written rules.

YOUNG SOCRATES: Yes—how would he not?

VISITOR: For these reasons, then, the second-best method of proceeding,
c   for those who establish laws and written rules about anything whatever,
is to allow neither individual nor mass ever to do anything contrary to
these—anything whatsoever.

YOUNG SOCRATES: Correct.

64. Reading *alēthestata ge* at a8.

VISITOR: Well, imitations of the truth of each and every thing would be these, wouldn't they—the things issuing from those who know which have been written down so far as they can be?[65]

YOUNG SOCRATES: Of course.

VISITOR: Now we said—if we remember—that the knowledgeable person, the one who really possesses the art of statesmanship, would do many things in relation to his own activity by using his expertise, without taking any notice of the written laws, when other things appear to him to be   d better, contrary to those that have been written down by him and given as orders to people who are not currently with him.

YOUNG SOCRATES: Yes, that's what we said.

VISITOR: Well, any individual whatever or any large collection of people whatever, for whom there are actually written laws established, who undertake to do anything at all that is different, contrary to these, on the grounds that it is better, will be doing, won't they, the same thing as that true expert, so far as they can?

YOUNG SOCRATES: Absolutely.

VISITOR: Well then, if they were to do such a thing without having expert knowledge, they would be undertaking to imitate what is true, but would   e imitate it altogether badly; but if they did it on the basis of expertise, this is no longer imitation but that very thing that is most truly what it sets out to be?

YOUNG SOCRATES: I agree completely—I think.

VISITOR: But it is established as agreed between us—we agreed to it before, at any rate—that no large collection of people is capable of acquiring any sort of expertise whatever.[66]

YOUNG SOCRATES: Yes, it remains agreed.

VISITOR: Then if some sort of kingly expertise exists, neither the collection of people that consists of the rich, nor all the people together, could ever acquire this expert knowledge of statesmanship.

YOUNG SOCRATES: How could they?

VISITOR: The requirement, then, as it seems, for all constitutions of this sort, if they are going to produce a good imitation of that true constitution of one man ruling with expertise, so far as they can, is that—given that   301 they have their laws—they must never do anything contrary to what is written or to ancestral customs.

YOUNG SOCRATES: Very well said.

VISITOR: In that case, when the rich imitate it, then we shall call such a constitution an 'aristocracy'; when they take no notice of the laws, we shall call it an 'oligarchy'.

YOUNG SOCRATES: Possibly.

65. Alternatively: "Well, wouldn't those laws—written with the advice of people who know so far as is possible—be imitations of the truth on each subject?"

66. See 292e.

b   VISITOR: And, in turn, when one person rules according to laws, so imitating the person with expert knowledge, we shall call him a king, not distinguishing by name the one ruling on his own with expert knowledge or the one doing so on the basis of opinion, according to laws.

YOUNG SOCRATES: Possibly we shall.

VISITOR: Well then, if in fact some one person rules who really possesses expert knowledge, in every case he will be called by the same name of king and not by any other one. As a result of this the five names of what are now called constitutions have become only one.

YOUNG SOCRATES: It seems so, at any rate.

VISITOR: And what of the case when some one ruler acts neither according
c   to laws nor according to customs, but pretends to act like the person with expert knowledge, saying that after all one must do what is contrary to what has been written down if it is *best*, and there is some desire or other combined with ignorance controlling this imitation? Surely in those circumstances we must call every such person a tyrant?

YOUNG SOCRATES: Of course.

VISITOR: Then it is in this way that the tyrant has come about, we say, and the king, and oligarchy, and aristocracy, and democracy—because people found themselves unable to put up with the idea of that single individual of ours as monarch, and refused to believe that there would
d   ever come to be anyone who deserved to rule in such a way, so as to be willing and able to rule with virtue and expert knowledge, distributing what is just and right correctly to all. They think that a person in such a position always mutilates, kills and generally maltreats whichever of us he wishes; although if there were to come to be someone of the sort we are describing, he would be prized and would govern a constitution that would alone be correct in the strict sense, steering it through in happiness.

YOUNG SOCRATES: Quite.

VISITOR: But as things are, when—as we say—a king does not come to be
e   in cities as a king-bee is born in a hive, one individual immediately superior in body and mind, it is necessary—so it seems—for people to come together and write things down, chasing after the traces of the truest constitution.

YOUNG SOCRATES: Possibly.

VISITOR: Do we wonder, then, Socrates, at all the evils that turn out to occur in such constitutions, and all those that will turn out for them, when a foundation of this sort underlies them, one of carrying out their functions
302   according to written rules and customs without knowledge—which if used by another expertise would manifestly destroy everything that comes about through it? Or should we rather wonder at something else, namely at how strong a thing a city is by its nature? For in fact cities have suffered such things now for time without limit, but nevertheless some particular ones among them are enduring and are not overturned. Yet many from time to time sink like[67] ships, and perish, and have perished, and will perish

67. Reading *eniote kathaper* at a6.

in the future through the depravity of their steersmen and sailors, who have acquired the greatest ignorance about the greatest things—although they have no understanding at all about what belongs to the art of statesmanship, they think they have completely acquired this sort of expert knowledge, most clearly of them all.

YOUNG SOCRATES: Very true.

VISITOR: So which of these 'incorrect' constitutions is least difficult to live with, given that they are all difficult, and which the heaviest to bear? Should we take a brief look at this, although a discussion of it will be a side-issue in relation to the subject now set before us? And yet, at any rate in general, perhaps everything that all of us do is for the sake of this sort of thing.

YOUNG SOCRATES: We should certainly look at it.

VISITOR: Well then, what you should say is that, if there are three sorts of constitution, the same one is at the same time exceptionally difficult and easiest.

YOUNG SOCRATES: What are you saying?

VISITOR: Just this: monarchy, I'm saying, rule by a few and rule by many—there were these three sorts of constitution we were talking about at the beginning of the discussion with which we have now been deluged.

YOUNG SOCRATES: Yes, there were.

VISITOR: Well then, let's divide these, each single one into two, and make six, separating off the correct one from these on its own, as a seventh.

YOUNG SOCRATES: How so?

VISITOR: Out of monarchy let's make kingly and tyrannical rule; out of the sort that doesn't involve many, we said there was[68] the auspiciously named aristocracy, and oligarchy, while out of the sort that does involve many, there was democracy, which we then called single and put it down as such, but now in turn we must put this too down as double.

YOUNG SOCRATES: How, then? And dividing it by what criterion?

VISITOR: By one that is no different from the other cases, even if *its* name, 'democracy', is now double; but certainly ruling according to laws and contrary to laws belongs both to this and to the others.

YOUNG SOCRATES: Yes, it does.

VISITOR: Well, at the time when we were looking for the correct constitution, this cut was not useful, as we demonstrated in what we said before; but since we have now set that correct constitution to one side, and have put down the rest as necessary, in the case of these, certainly, the criterion of contrary to and abiding by laws cuts each of them in two.

YOUNG SOCRATES: It seems so, given what has now been said.

VISITOR: Well then, when monarchy is yoked in good written rules, which we call laws, it is best of all six; but if it is without laws, it is difficult and heaviest to live with.

YOUNG SOCRATES: Possibly.

303

---

68. Reading *ephamen einai* at d2.

VISITOR: And as for the rule of those who are not many, just as few is in the middle between one and a large number, let's suppose it to be middling in both ways; while that of the mass, in its turn, we may suppose to be weak in all respects and capable of nothing of any importance either for good or for bad as judged in relation to the others, because under it offices are distributed in small portions among many people. For this reason, if all the types of constitution are law-abiding, it turns out to be

b   the worst of them, but if all are contrary to law, the best; and if all are uncontrolled, living in a democracy takes the prize, but if they are ordered, life in it is least liveable, and in first place and best by far will be life in the first, except for the seventh. For of all of them, *that* one we must separate out from the other constitutions, like a god from men.

YOUNG SOCRATES: This seems both to follow, and to be, as you say; and we must do as you suggest.

c   VISITOR: So then we must also remove those who participate in all these constitutions, except for the one based on knowledge, as being, not states- men, but experts in faction; we must say that, as presiding over insubstan- tial images, on the largest scale, they are themselves of the same sort, and that as the greatest imitators and magicians they turn out the be the greatest sophists among sophists.[69]

YOUNG SOCRATES: This term 'sophist' looks as if it has been only too correctly turned round against the so-called experts in statesmanship.

VISITOR: So: this is our play, as it were—as we said just now that there

d   was some band of centaurs and satyrs in view, one that we had to set apart from the expertise of the statesman; and now it has been set apart, as we have seen, with great difficulty.

YOUNG SOCRATES: It appears so.

VISITOR: Yes, but there is something else remaining that is still more difficult than this, by reason of its being both more akin to the kingly class, and closer to it, and harder to understand; and we seem to me to be in a situation similar to that of those who refine gold.

YOUNG SOCRATES: How so?

VISITOR: I imagine that these craftsmen also begin by separating out earth, and stones, and many different things; and after these, there remain

e   commingled with the gold those things that are akin to it, precious things and only removable with the use of fire: copper, silver, and sometimes adamant, the removal of which through repeated smelting and testing leaves the 'unalloyed' gold that people talk about there for us to see, itself alone by itself.

YOUNG SOCRATES: Yes, they certainly do say these things happen in this way.

VISITOR: Well, it seems that in the same way we have now separated off those things that are different from the expert knowledge of statesmanship, and those that are alien and hostile to it, and that there remain those that

69. See 291c.

are precious and related to it. Among these, I think, are generalship, the art of the judge, and that part of rhetoric which in partnership with kingship persuades people of what is just and so helps in steering through the business of cities. As for these, in what way will one most easily portion them off and show, stripped and alone by himself, that person we are looking for? 304

YOUNG SOCRATES: It's clear that we must try to do this somehow.

VISITOR: Well, if it depends on our trying, we'll find him; music will help us reveal him. Answer me this.

YOUNG SOCRATES: What?

VISITOR: I imagine we recognize such a thing as the learning of music, and in general of the sorts of expert knowledge involving work with the hands? b

YOUNG SOCRATES: We do.

VISITOR: And what of this—the matter of whether we should learn any one of these or not? Shall we say that this too, in its turn, is a sort of knowledge, concerned with these very things, or what shall we say?

YOUNG SOCRATES: Yes, we'll say that it is.

VISITOR: Then shall we agree that this sort of knowledge is distinct from those?

YOUNG SOCRATES: Yes.

VISITOR: And shall we agree that no one of them should control any other, or that the others should control this one, or that this one should manage and control all the others together? c

YOUNG SOCRATES: This one should control them.

VISITOR: In that case you, at any rate, declare it to be your opinion that the one that decides whether one should learn or not should be in control, so far as we are concerned, over the one that is the object of learning and does the teaching?

YOUNG SOCRATES: Very much so.

VISITOR: And also, in that case, that the one which decides whether one should persuade or not should control the one which is capable of persuading?

YOUNG SOCRATES: Of course.

VISITOR: Well then: to which sort of expert knowledge shall we assign what is capable of persuading mass and crowd, through the telling of stories, and not through teaching? d

YOUNG SOCRATES: This too is clear, I think: it must be given to rhetoric.

VISITOR: And the matter of whether to do through persuasion whatever it may be in relation to some people or other, or else by the use of some sort of force, or indeed to do nothing at all: to what sort of expert knowledge shall we attach this?

YOUNG SOCRATES: To the one that controls the art of persuasion and speaking.

VISITOR: This would be none other, I think, than the capacity of the statesman.

YOUNG SOCRATES: Very well said.

VISITOR: This matter of rhetoric too seems to have been separated quickly
e from statesmanship, as a distinct class, but subordinate to it.

YOUNG SOCRATES: Yes.

VISITOR: What should we think about the following sort of capacity, in
its turn?

YOUNG SOCRATES: Which one?

VISITOR: The one that decides how to make war against each group of
people against whom we choose to make war. The question is whether
we shall say that this is or is not a matter of expertise.

YOUNG SOCRATES: And how could we suppose it not to involve expertise:
that capacity which is exercised by generalship and all activity concerned
with war?

VISITOR: And are we to understand as different from this the expertise
that is able and knows how to reach a considered decision about whether
we should make war, or whether we should withdraw in friendly fashion?
Or are we to take it to be the same as this one?

YOUNG SOCRATES: Anyone who was following what was said before must
suppose that it is distinct.

305   VISITOR: Shall we then declare our view that it controls it, if in fact we
are going to take things in line with what we said before?

YOUNG SOCRATES: I say yes.

VISITOR: Then what mistress will we even try to propose for so terrifying
and important an expertise, the whole of that concerned with war, except
the true art of kingship?

YOUNG SOCRATES: No other.

VISITOR: In that case we shall not set down the expert knowledge of
generals as statesmanship, since it is subordinate.

YOUNG SOCRATES: It seems unlikely that we shall.

b   VISITOR: Come on then; let's look at the capacity that belongs to those
judges who judge correctly.

YOUNG SOCRATES: Absolutely.

VISITOR: Well then, does its capacity extend to anything more than taking
over from the legislator-king all those things that are established as lawful
in relation to contracts, and judging by reference to these the things that
have been prescribed as just and unjust, providing its own individual
excellence by virtue of the fact that it would not be willing to decide the
c   complaints of one citizen against another contrary to the prescription of
the legislator through being overcome by presents of some sort, or fears,
or feelings of compassion, or again by any enmity or friendship?

YOUNG SOCRATES: No, the function of this capacity extends, roughly
speaking, to what you have said.

VISITOR: In that case we discover the power of judges too not to be that
belonging to the king, but to be a guardian of the laws and a subordinate
of that other capacity.

YOUNG SOCRATES: It seems so, at any rate.

VISITOR: If then one looks at all the sorts of expert knowledge that have been discussed, it must be observed that none of them has been declared to be statesmanship. For what is really kingship must not itself perform   d
practical tasks, but control those with the capacity to perform them, because it knows when it is the right time to begin and set in motion the most important things in cities, and when it is the wrong time; and the others must do what has been prescribed for them.

YOUNG SOCRATES: Correct.

VISITOR: For this reason, then, the sorts of expertise we have just examined control neither each other nor themselves, but each is concerned with some individual practical activity of its own, and in accordance with the individual nature of the activities in question has appropriately acquired a name that is individual to it.

YOUNG SOCRATES: That seems so, at any rate.   e

VISITOR: Whereas the one that controls all of these, and the laws, and cares for every aspect of things in the city, weaving everything together in the most correct way—this, embracing its capacity with the appellation belonging to the whole,[70] we would, it seems, most appropriately call statesmanship.

YOUNG SOCRATES: Yes, absolutely.

VISITOR: At this point we'll want, won't we, to pursue it further by reference to the model of the art of weaving, now that all the classes of things in the city have become clear to us?

YOUNG SOCRATES: Yes, very much so.

VISITOR: Then it seems that we should discuss the intertwining that   306
belongs to kingship—of what kind it is, and in what way it intertwines to render us what sort of fabric.

YOUNG SOCRATES: Clearly.

VISITOR: What it seems we have to deal with, in that case, is certainly a difficult thing to show.

YOUNG SOCRATES: But in any case we have to discuss it.

VISITOR: To say that part of virtue is in a certain sense different in kind from virtue provides an all too easy target for those expert in disputing statements, if we view things in relation to what the majority of people think.

YOUNG SOCRATES: I don't understand.

VISITOR: I'll put it again, like this. I imagine you think that courage, for us, constitutes one part of virtue.   b

YOUNG SOCRATES: Certainly.

VISITOR: And also that moderation is something distinct from courage, but at the same time that this too is one part of what the other is part of.

YOUNG SOCRATES: Yes.

VISITOR: Well, we must take our courage in our hands and declare something astonishing in relation to these two.

70. That is, the appellation *polis* or 'city' gives rise to that of 'statesmanship', *politikē*.

YOUNG SOCRATES: What?

VISITOR: That, in some sort of way, they are extremely hostile to each other and occupy opposed positions in many things.[71]

YOUNG SOCRATES: What do you mean?

c   VISITOR: Not in any way the sort of thing people are used to saying. For certainly, I imagine, all the parts of virtue are said to be amicably disposed towards each other, if anything is.

YOUNG SOCRATES: Yes.

VISITOR: Then should we look, with extremely close attention, to see whether this is unqualifiedly the case, or whether emphatically some aspects of them admit of dissent in some respect with what is related to them?

YOUNG SOCRATES: Yes; please say how we should do so.

VISITOR: We should look at the matter in relation to all those things that we call fine, but then go on to place them in two classes which are opposed to each other.

YOUNG SOCRATES: Put it still more clearly.

d   VISITOR: Sharpness and speed, whether in bodies, or in minds, or in the movement of the voice,[72] whether belonging to the things themselves or as represented in images of them—all those imitations that music, and painting too, provide: have you ever either praised any of these yourself, or been present to hear someone else praising them?

YOUNG SOCRATES: Of course.

VISITOR: And do you remember how they do it in every one of such cases?

YOUNG SOCRATES: I don't at all.

VISITOR: Then would I be able, I wonder, to show it to you in words just as I have it before my mind?

e   YOUNG SOCRATES: Why not?

VISITOR: You seem to think this kind of thing easy; but in any case let's consider it in the two opposite sorts of case. Often, and in many activities, whenever we admire speed and vigour and sharpness, of mind and body, and again of voice, we speak in praise of it by using a single appellation, that of 'courage'.[73]

YOUNG SOCRATES: How so?

VISITOR: I think we say 'sharp and courageous'—that's a first example; and 'fast and courageous', and similarly with 'vigorous'. In every case it's by applying the name I'm talking about in common to all these sorts of thing that we praise them.

YOUNG SOCRATES: Yes.

307   VISITOR: But again—in many activities, don't we often praise the class of things that happen gently?

---

71. Reading *echthra . . . echeton* at b10.

72. The word translated 'sharpness' can also refer to high pitch in sound.

73. Greek *andreia*, literally 'manliness'. Bearing the literal meaning in mind helps to make more intelligible some of the applications of 'courage' suggested here and below.

YOUNG SOCRATES: Yes, very much so.

VISITOR: Well then, don't we express this by saying the opposite of what we say of the other things?

YOUNG SOCRATES: How?

VISITOR: In that, I think, we say on each occasion that they are 'quiet and moderate', admiring things done in the mind, and in the sphere of actions themselves, that are slow and soft, and also things the voice does that turn out smooth and deep—and all rhythmic movement, and the whole of music when it employs slowness at the right time. We apply to them all the name, not of courage, but of orderliness.

b

YOUNG SOCRATES: Very true.

VISITOR: And when, conversely, both of these sets of qualities occur at the wrong time, we change round and censure each of them, assigning them to opposite effect by the names we use.

YOUNG SOCRATES: How?

VISITOR: By calling them 'excessive and manic' when they turn out sharper than is timely, and appear too fast and hard, and calling things that are too deep and slow and soft 'cowardly and lethargic'. It's pretty much a general rule that we find that these qualities, and the moderate type as a whole, and the 'courage' of the opposite qualities do not mix with each other in the relevant activities, as if they were sorts of thing that had a warring stance allotted to them. Moreover we shall see that those who possess them in their souls are at odds with each other, if we go looking for them.

c

YOUNG SOCRATES: Where do you mean us to look?

VISITOR: Both in all the spheres we mentioned just now, and no doubt in many others. For I think because of their affinity to either set of qualities, they praise some things as belonging to their own kin, and censure those of their opponents as alien, engaging in a great deal of hostility towards each other, about a great many things.

d

YOUNG SOCRATES: Very likely.

VISITOR: Well, this disagreement, of these classes of people, is a sort of play; but in relation to the most important things, it turns out to be a disease which is the most hateful of all for cities.

YOUNG SOCRATES: In relation to what, do you mean?

VISITOR: In relation to the organization of life as a whole. For those who are especially orderly are always ready to live the quiet life, carrying on their private business on their own by themselves. They both associate with everyone in their own city on this basis, and similarly with cities outside their own, being ready to preserve peace of some sort in any way they can. As a result of this passion of theirs, which is less timely than it should be, when they do what they want nobody notices that they are being unwarlike and making the young men the same, and that they are perpetually at the mercy of those who attack them. The consequence is that within a few years they themselves, their children, and the whole city together often become slaves instead of free men before they have noticed it.

e

308

YOUNG SOCRATES: What you describe is a painful and terrifying thing to go through.

VISITOR: But what about those who incline more towards courage? Isn't it the case that they are always drawing their cities into some war or other because of their desire for a life of this sort, which is more vigorous than it should be, and that they make enemies of people who are both numerous and powerful, and so either completely destroy their own fatherlands, or else make them slaves and subjects of their enemies?

b   YOUNG SOCRATES: This too is true.

VISITOR: How then can we deny that in these things both of these classes of people always admit of much hostility and dissent between them, even to the greatest degree?

YOUNG SOCRATES: There's no way we shall deny it.

VISITOR: Then we have found, haven't we, what we were originally looking into, that parts of virtue of no small importance are by nature at odds with each other, and moreover cause those who possess them to be in this same condition?

YOUNG SOCRATES: Very likely they do.

VISITOR: Then let's take the following point in its turn.

YOUNG SOCRATES: What's that?

c   VISITOR: Whether, I suppose, any of the sorts of expert knowledge that involve putting things together voluntarily puts together any at all of the things it produces, even of the lowliest kind, out of bad and good things, or whether every sort of expert knowledge everywhere throws away the bad so far as it can, and takes what is suitable and good[74], bringing all of this—both like and unlike—together into one, and so producing some single kind of thing with a single capacity.

YOUNG SOCRATES: Of course.

d   VISITOR: In that case, neither will what we have decided is by nature truly the art of statesmanship ever voluntarily put together a city out of good and bad human beings. It's quite clear that it will first put them to the test in play, and after the test it will in turn hand them over to those with the capacity to educate them and serve it towards this particular end. It will itself lay down prescriptions for the educators and direct them, in the same way that weaving follows along with the carders, and those who prepare the other things it needs for its own work, prescribing for and directing them, giving indications to each group to finish their products

e   in whatever way it thinks suitable for its own interweaving.

YOUNG SOCRATES: Yes, absolutely.

VISITOR: In just this very way, it seems to me, the art of kingship—since it is this that itself possesses the capacity belonging to the directing art—will not permit the educators and tutors, who function according to law, to do anything in the exercise of their role that will not ultimately result in some disposition which is appropriate to its own mixing role. It calls

74. Reading *kai ta chrēsta* at c5.

on them to teach these things alone; and those of their pupils that are
unable to share in a disposition that is courageous and moderate, and
whatever else belongs to the sphere of virtue, but are thrust forcibly away   309
by an evil nature into godlessness, excess and injustice, it throws out by
killing them, sending them into exile, and punishing them with the most
extreme forms of dishonor.

YOUNG SOCRATES: At least it is put something like that.

VISITOR: And again those who wallow in great ignorance and baseness
it brings under the yoke of the class of slaves.

YOUNG SOCRATES: Quite correct.

VISITOR: Then as for the others, whose natures are capable of becoming
composed and stable in the direction of nobility, if they acquire education,   b
and, with the help of expertise, of admitting commingling with each other—
of these, it tries to bind together and intertwine the ones who strain more
towards courage, its view being that their firm disposition is as it were
like the warp, and the ones who incline towards the moderate, who produce
an ample, soft, and—to continue the image—wooflike thread, two natures
with opposite tendencies; and it does so in something like the following
way.

YOUNG SOCRATES: What way is that?

VISITOR: First, by fitting together that part of their soul that is eternal   c
with a divine bond, in accordance with its kinship with the divine, and after
the divine, in turn fitting together their mortal aspect with human bonds.

YOUNG SOCRATES: Again, what do you mean by this?

VISITOR: I call divine, when it comes to be in souls,[75] that opinion about
what is fine, just and good, and the opposites of these, which is really true
and is guaranteed; it belongs to the class of the more than human.

YOUNG SOCRATES: That's certainly a fitting view to take.

VISITOR: Then do we recognize that it belongs to the statesman and the   d
good legislator alone to be capable of bringing this very thing about, by
means of the music that belongs to the art of kingship, in those who have
had their correct share of education—the people we were speaking of
just now?

YOUNG SOCRATES: That's certainly reasonable.

VISITOR: Yes, and let's never call anyone who is incapable of doing this
sort of thing by the names we are now investigating.

YOUNG SOCRATES: Quite correct.

VISITOR: Well then—is a 'courageous' soul that grasps this sort of truth   e
not tamed, and wouldn't it be especially willing, as a result, to share in
what is just, whereas if it fails to get a share of it, doesn't it rather slide
away[76] towards becoming like some kind of beast?

YOUNG SOCRATES: Quite.

75. Reading *en tais psuchais* at c7.
76. Reading *apoklinei* at e2.

VISITOR: And what of the case of the 'moderate' sort of nature? If it gets a share of these opinions, doesn't it become genuinely moderate and wise, so far as wisdom goes in the context of life in a city, while if it fails to get a portion of the things we're talking about, doesn't it very appropriately acquire a disgraceful reputation, for simplemindedness?

YOUNG SOCRATES: Absolutely.

VISITOR: And let's not say, shall we, that this sort of interweaving and bonding, in the case of vicious men in relation to each other and good men in relation to the vicious, ever turns out to be lasting, nor that any sort of expert knowledge would ever seriously use it in relation to people like this?

YOUNG SOCRATES: No; how would it?

310   VISITOR: What I propose we should say is that it only takes root, through laws, in those dispositions that were both born noble in the first place and have been nurtured in accordance with their nature; and that it is for these that this remedy exists, by virtue of expertise. As we said, this bonding together is more divine, uniting parts of virtue that are by nature[77] unlike each other, and tend in opposite directions.

YOUNG SOCRATES: Very true.

VISITOR: Yes, and the remaining bonds, which are human, once this divine one exists, are perhaps not difficult at all either to understand, or to effect once one has understood them.

b   YOUNG SOCRATES: How then, and what are they?

VISITOR: Those that consist in intermarriages and the sharing of children,[78] and in those matters relating to private giving-away in marriage. For most people, in the way they handle these things, do not bind themselves together correctly with respect to the procreation of children.

YOUNG SOCRATES: Why so?

VISITOR: Is there any reason why anyone should seriously concern themselves with censuring the pursuit of wealth and forms of influence in such contexts, as if it were worth discussing?

YOUNG SOCRATES: None.

VISITOR: No; it would be more appropriate for us to discuss those people
c   who pay attention to family-types, and ask whether they are acting erroneously in some way.

YOUNG SOCRATES: Yes, that's reasonable.

VISITOR: Well, they act out of entirely the wrong sort of consideration: they go for what is immediately easiest, welcoming those who are much like them, and not liking those who are unlike them, assigning the largest part of their decisions to their feelings of antipathy.

YOUNG SOCRATES: How?

VISITOR: The moderate, I think, look out for people with the disposition they themselves possess, and so far as they can they both marry from

77. Reading *phusei* at a5.
78. I.e., between families, through marriage.

among these and marry off the daughters they are giving away back to   d
people of this sort.[79] The type related to courage does just the same thing,
seeking after the nature that belongs to itself, when both types ought to
do completely the opposite of this.

YOUNG SOCRATES: How, and why?

VISITOR: Because it is in the nature of courage that when it is reproduced
over many generations without being mixed with a moderate nature, it
comes to a peak of power at first, but in the end it bursts out completely
in fits of madness.

YOUNG SOCRATES: That's likely.

VISITOR: And in its turn the soul that is too full of reserve and has no
admixture of courageous initiative, and is reproduced over many genera-   e
tions in this way, by nature grows more sluggish than is timely and then
in the end is completely crippled.

YOUNG SOCRATES: It's likely that this too turns out as you say.

VISITOR: It was these bonds that I meant when I said that there was no
difficulty at all in tying them together once the situation existed in which
both types had a single opinion about what was fine and good. For this
is the single and complete task of kingly weaving-together, never to allow
moderate dispositions to stand away from the courageous. Rather, by
working them closely into each other as if with a shuttle, through sharing
of opinions, through honors, dishonor, esteem, and the giving of pledges
to one another, it draws together a smooth and 'fine-woven' fabric out of   311
them, as the expression is, and always entrusts offices in cities to these
in common.

YOUNG SOCRATES: How?

VISITOR: By choosing the person who has both qualities to put in charge
wherever there turns out to be a need for a single officer, and by mixing
together a part of each of these groups where there is a need for more
than one. For the dispositions of moderate people when in office are
markedly cautious, just, and conservative, but they lack bite, and a certain
sharp and practical keenness.

YOUNG SOCRATES: This too certainly seems to be the case.

VISITOR: And the dispositions of the courageous, in their turn, are inferior   b
to the others in relation to justice and caution, but have an exceptional
degree of keenness when it comes to action. Everything in cities cannot
go well, either on the private or on the public level, unless both of these
groups are there to give their help.

YOUNG SOCRATES: Quite.

VISITOR: Then let us say that this marks the completion of the fabric
which is the product of the art of statesmanship: the weaving together,
with regular intertwining, of the dispositions of brave and moderate people—when the expertise belonging to the king brings their life together in   c
agreement and friendship and makes it common between them, completing

---

79. Reading *toioutous* at d1.

311c   the most magnificent and best of all fabrics and covering with it all the other inhabitants of cities, both slave and free; and holds them together with this twining and rules and directs without, so far as it belongs to a city to be happy, falling short of that in any respect.

[OLDER] SOCRATES:[80] Another most excellent portrait, visitor, this one that you have completed for us, of the man who possesses the art of kingship: the statesman.

---

80. The final words are attributed by many editors to the younger Socrates, but they seem perhaps a little authoritative for him, and it was after all old Socrates himself who set up the whole discussion in the beginning—both in the *Sophist* and in the *Statesman*.

PARMENIDES

The great philosopher Parmenides is the central figure of this dialogue. He, not Socrates, directs the philosophical discussion—if Plato has a 'spokesman' here, it is Parmenides. Socrates is portrayed as a very bright and promising young philosopher—he is virtually a teenager, only just beginning his career in the subject—who needs to think a lot harder and longer before he will have an adequate grasp of the nature of reality: this Socrates is a budding metaphysician, not the purely ethical thinker of Apology *and other 'Socratic' dialogues.*

Accompanied by his disciple Zeno (originator of Zeno's paradoxes), Parmenides has come on a visit to Athens. At Pythodorus' house, after Zeno has read out his book (now lost) attacking the intelligibility of any 'plurality' of real things, Socrates questions Zeno and is then questioned by Parmenides about his own conception of reality as consisting of nonphysical, nonperceptible 'Forms' in which perceptible, physical entities 'participate'. Parmenides raises six difficulties that Socrates' view entails, including the celebrated 'third man' argument to which twentieth-century analytical philosophers have paid much attention. Concluding the first part of the dialogue, he explains the method of analysis which Socrates must now use in order to resolve them—Socrates' efforts to articulate a theory of Forms have been premature. One must consider systematically not just the consequences of any hypothesis, but also those of its denial, and the method involves other complexities as well: one must systematically consider eight different trains of consequences, in order to decide finally what the right way of putting one's thesis will be. In the second part of the dialogue, occupying more than two-thirds of its total length, Parmenides demonstrates this new method, using as his respondent not Socrates but one of the other young men present, Aristotle. (In choosing this name, Plato may have been alluding to the philosopher Aristotle, who began his own metaphysical work as a member of Plato's Academy.) Considering the 'hypothesis' of 'one being', he works out a series of eight conflicting 'deductions' (plus a ninth, 155e–157b, added as an appendix to the first two) as to its metaphysically significant properties—its being, unity, sameness and difference, similarity and dissimilarity, motion and rest, place, time, and so on. It is left to Socrates, and to the reader, to infer just what use to make of these deductions in determining how best to formulate an adequate theory of Forms. Since the theory that Socrates presented at the beginning of the dialogue is plainly the one developed in Symposium, Phaedo, *and* Republic, *this dialogue seems to be implying that that theory of Forms needs refurbishing and that, in demonstrating his method,*

Parmenides has shown us how to do that. Parmenides *thus points forward to* Sophist, Statesman, *and* Philebus, *where Forms are further rethought.*

The meeting of Socrates with the Eleatic philosophers (an invention of Plato's) is reported in a way unparalleled in the other dialogues. The narrator, Cephalus—a different Cephalus from the one in whose house the Republic's *conversation takes place—speaks directly to the reader (as Socrates himself does in* Republic*), telling of his visit to Athens from his home in Clazomenae, accompanied by a group of Clazomenian philosophers. (Clazomenae was famous as the birthplace of the pre-Socratic 'physical' philosopher Anaxagoras.) They have come specially to hear Antiphon, in fact Plato's younger half brother, recite from memory the record of this conversation: he had heard it from Pythodorus. Cephalus now reports what Antiphon said, in himself reporting what Pythodorus had told him the various speakers on the original occasion had said to one another: four levels of conversation, counting the one Cephalus is having now with an undetermined group—us, the readers. The effect is twofold: to emphasize the extraordinary philosophical value of this conversation and to put us hearers at a great intellectual distance from it—as if to say that we could barely be expected to assimilate and learn properly from it. The situation in* Symposium *is in some ways comparable—except that the meeting there is reported at only two removes and its fame apparently extends only to those with a personal interest in Socrates (one intimate of Socrates has just reported it to a second and is now reporting it to another friend). This* conversation *is marked as having truly universal significance.*

J.M.C.

Cephalus

126   When we arrived in Athens from home in Clazomenae, we ran into Adeimantus and Glaucon in the marketplace. Adeimantus took me by the hand and said, "Welcome, Cephalus. If there is anything you want here that we can do for you, please tell us."

"In fact that's the very reason I'm here," I replied, "to ask a favor of you."

"Tell us what you want," he said.

b   And I replied, "Your half brother on your mother's side – what was his name? I've forgotten. He would have been a child when I came here from Clazomenae to stay before – and that's a long time ago now. I think his father's name was Pyrilampes."

"It was, indeed," he said.

"And his?"

"Antiphon. But why do you ask?"

"These men are fellow citizens of mine," I said, "keen philosophers, and they have heard that this Antiphon met many times with a friend of Zeno's

Translated by Mary Louise Gill and Paul Ryan.

called Pythodorus and can recite from memory the discussion that Socrates   c
and Zeno and Parmenides once had, since he heard it often from Pythodorus."

"That's true," he said.

"Well, we want to hear that discussion," I replied.

"Nothing hard about that," he said. "When Antiphon was a young man,
he practiced it to perfection, although these days, just like the grandfather
he's named for, he devotes most of his time to horses. But if that's what's
called for, let's go to his house. He left here to go home just a short time
ago, but he lives close by in Melite."

After this exchange, we set off walking and found Antiphon at home   127
engaging a smith to work on a bit of some kind. When he had finished
with the smith, and his brothers told him why we were there, he recognized
me from my earlier visit and greeted me. We asked him to go through
the discussion, and he balked at first – it was, he said, a lot of work. But
finally he narrated it in detail.

Antiphon said that Pythodorus said that Zeno and Parmenides once
came to the Great Panathenaea. Parmenides was already quite venerable,   b
very gray but of distinguished appearance, about sixty-five years old. Zeno
was at that time close to forty, a tall, handsome man who had been, as
rumor had it, the object of Parmenides' affections when he was a boy.
Antiphon said that the two of them were staying with Pythodorus, outside   c
the city wall in the Potters' Quarter, and that Socrates had come there,
along with a number of others, because they were eager to hear Zeno read
his book, which he and Parmenides had just brought to Athens for the
first time. Socrates was then quite young.

Zeno was reading to them in person; Parmenides happened to be out.
Very little remained to be read when Pythodorus, as he related it, came   d
in, and with him Parmenides and Aristotle – the man who later became
one of the Thirty. They listened to a little of the book at the very end. But
not Pythodorus himself; he had heard Zeno read it before.

Then Socrates, after he had heard it, asked Zeno to read the first hypothesis of the first argument again; and when he had read it, Socrates said,   e
"Zeno, what do you mean by this: if things[1] are many, they must then be
both like and unlike, but that is impossible, because unlike things can't
be like or like things unlike? That's what you say, isn't it?"

"It is," said Zeno.

"If it's impossible for unlike things to be like and like things unlike,
isn't it then also impossible for them to be many? Because, if they were
many, they would have incompatible properties. Is this the point of your
arguments – simply to maintain, in opposition to everything that is commonly said, that things are not many? And do you suppose that each of
your arguments is proof for this position, so that you think you give as

---

1. Lit., "the things that are."

128 many proofs that things are not many as your book has arguments? Is that what you're saying – or do I misunderstand?"

"No," Zeno replied. "On the contrary, you grasp the general point of the book splendidly."

"Parmenides," Socrates said, "I understand that Zeno wants to be on intimate terms with you not only in friendship but also in his book. He has, in a way, written the same thing as you, but by changing it round he tries to fool us into thinking he is saying something different. You say in

b your poem that the all is one, and you give splendid and excellent proofs for that; he, for his part, says that it is not many and gives a vast array of very grand proofs of his own. So, with one of you saying 'one,' and the other 'not many,' and with each of you speaking in a way that suggests that you've said nothing the same – although you mean practically the same thing – what you've said you appear to have said over the heads of the rest of us."

"Yes, Socrates," said Zeno. "Still, you haven't completely discerned the truth about my book, even though you chase down its arguments and

c follow their spoor as keenly as a young Spartan hound. First of all, you have missed this point: the book doesn't at all preen itself on having been written with the intent you described, while disguising it from people, as if that were some great accomplishment. You have mentioned something that happened accidentally. The truth is that the book comes to the defense of Parmenides' argument against those who try to make fun of it by

d claiming that, if it² is one, many absurdities and self-contradictions result from that argument. Accordingly, my book speaks against those who assert the many and pays them back in kind with something for good measure, since it aims to make clear that their hypothesis, if it is many,³ would, if someone examined the matter thoroughly, suffer consequences even more absurd than those suffered by the hypothesis of its being one. In that competitive spirit, then, I wrote the book when I was a young man. Some-one made an unauthorized copy, so I didn't even have a chance to decide

e for myself whether or not it should see the light. So in this respect you missed the point, Socrates: you think it was written not out of a young man's competitiveness, but out of a mature man's vainglory. Still, as I said, your portrayal was not bad."

"I take your point," Socrates said, "and I believe it was as you say. But

129 tell me this: don't you acknowledge that there is a form, itself by itself,⁴

---

2. I.e., the all (cf. 128a8–b1).

3. In English we normally speak of a hypothesis *that* something is the case. Instead, Zeno here, and later Socrates and Parmenides, regularly place the content of a hypothesis within an "if" clause, ready for us to draw out its implications and consequences: e.g., "if the all is one, then . . . ," or "if the all is many, then. . . ."

4. According to the usage of this dialogue, something is "itself by itself," first, if it is separate from other things or is considered on its own, apart from other things. When the phrase is construed in this way, "by itself" means "apart, on its own." Second,

of likeness, and another form, opposite to this, which is what unlike is? Don't you and I and the other things we call 'many' get a share of those two entities? And don't things that get a share of likeness come to be like in that way and to the extent that they get a share, whereas things that get a share of unlikeness come to be unlike, and things that get a share of both come to be both? And even if all things get a share of both, though they are opposites, and by partaking of them are both like and unlike themselves, what's astonishing about that?

"If someone showed that the likes themselves come to be unlike or the   b
unlikes like – that, I think, would be a marvel; but if he shows that things that partake of both of these have both properties, there seems to me nothing strange about that, Zeno – not even if someone shows that all things are one by partaking of oneness,[5] and that these same things are many by partaking also of multitude. But if he should demonstrate this thing itself, what one is, to be many, or, conversely, the many to be one – at this I'll be astonished.

"And it's the same with all the others: if he could show that the kinds   c
and forms[6] themselves have in themselves these opposite properties, that would call for astonishment. But if someone should demonstrate that I am one thing and many, what's astonishing about that? He will say, when he wants to show that I'm many, that my right side is different from my left, and my front from my back, and likewise with my upper and lower parts – since I take it I do partake of multitude. But when he wants to show that I'm one, he will say I'm one person among the seven of us,   d
because I also partake of oneness. Thus he shows that both are true.

"So if – in the case of stones and sticks and such things – someone tries to show that the same thing is many and one, we'll say that he is demonstrating *something* to be many and one, not the one to be many or the many one – and we'll say that he is saying nothing astonishing, but just what all of us would agree to. But if someone first distinguishes as separate the forms, themselves by themselves, of the things I was talking about a moment ago – for example, likeness and unlikeness, multitude and oneness, rest and motion, and everything of that sort – and then shows   e
that in themselves they can mix together and separate, I for my part," he said, "would be utterly amazed, Zeno. I think these issues have been

something is "itself by itself," if it is itself responsible for its own proper being, independently of other things. When the phrase is understood in this way, "by itself" means "in virtue of, or because of, itself." Both of these meanings should be kept in mind whenever this phrase recurs in the translation.

5. In this dialogue Plato uses the expression *to hen* in several ways. It is variously translated as "the one," "oneness," and "one" depending on the context.

6. In this dialogue Plato uses three different abstract expressions to specify these entities, two of which occur here: *genos* (a term restricted to the part of the dialogue preceding the "Deductions"), rendered as "kind," and *eidos*, rendered as "form." Later he will use a third term, *idea*, rendered as "character."

handled with great vigor in your book; but I would, as I say, be much more impressed if someone were able to display this same difficulty, which you and Parmenides went through in the case of visible things, also
130   similarly entwined in multifarious ways in the forms themselves – in things that are grasped by reasoning."

Pythodorus said that, while Socrates was saying all this, he himself kept from moment to moment expecting Parmenides and Zeno to get annoyed; but they both paid close attention to Socrates and often glanced at each other and smiled, as though they admired him. In fact, what Parmenides said when Socrates had finished confirmed this impression. "Socrates," he
b   said, "you are much to be admired for your keenness for argument! Tell me. Have you yourself distinguished as separate, in the way you mention, certain forms themselves, and also as separate the things that partake of them? And do you think that likeness itself is something, separate from the likeness we have? And one and many and all the things you heard Zeno read about a while ago?"

"I do indeed," Socrates answered.

"And what about these?" asked Parmenides. "Is there a form, itself by itself, of just, and beautiful, and good, and everything of that sort?"

"Yes," he said.

c   "What about a form of human being, separate from us and all those like us? Is there a form itself of human being, or fire, or water?"

Socrates said, "Parmenides, I've often found myself in doubt whether I should talk about those in the same way as the others or differently."

"And what about these, Socrates? Things that might seem absurd, like hair and mud and dirt, or anything else totally undignified and worthless? Are
d   you doubtful whether or not you should say that a form is separate for each of these, too, which in turn is other than anything we touch with our hands?"

"Not at all," Socrates answered. "On the contrary, these things are in fact just what we see. Surely it's too outlandish to think there is a form for them. Not that the thought that the same thing might hold in all cases hasn't troubled me from time to time. Then, when I get bogged down in that, I hurry away, afraid that I may fall into some pit of nonsense and come to harm; but when I arrive back in the vicinity of the things we agreed a moment ago have forms, I linger there and occupy myself with them."

e   "That's because you are still young, Socrates," said Parmenides, "and philosophy has not yet gripped you as, in my opinion, it will in the future, once you begin to consider none of the cases beneath your notice. Now, though, you still care about what people think, because of your youth.

"But tell me this: is it your view that, as you say, there are certain forms from which these other things, by getting a share of them, derive their
131   names – as, for instance, they come to be like by getting a share of likeness, large by getting a share of largeness, and just and beautiful by getting a share of justice and beauty?"

"It certainly is," Socrates replied.

"So does each thing that gets a share get as its share the form as a whole or a part of it? Or could there be some other means of getting a share apart from these two?"

"How could there be?" he said.

"Do you think, then, that the form as a whole – one thing – is in each of the many? Or what do you think?"

"What's to prevent its being one,[7] Parmenides?" said Socrates.

"So, being one and the same, it will be at the same time, as a whole, in   b
things that are many and separate; and thus it would be separate from itself."

"No it wouldn't," Socrates said. "Not if it's like one and the same day. That is in many places at the same time and is none the less not separate from itself. If it's like that, each of the forms might be, at the same time, one and the same in all."

"Socrates," he said, "how neatly you make one and the same thing be in many places at the same time! It's as if you were to cover many people with a sail, and then say that one thing as a whole is over many. Or isn't that the sort of thing you mean to say?"

"Perhaps," he replied.   c

"In that case would the sail be, as a whole, over each person, or would a part of it be over one person and another part over another?"

"A part."

"So the forms themselves are divisible, Socrates," he said, "and things that partake of them would partake of a part; no longer would a whole form, but only a part of it, be in each thing."

"It does appear that way."

"Then are you willing to say, Socrates, that our one form is really divided? Will it still be one?"

"Not at all," he replied.

"No," said Parmenides. "For suppose you are going to divide largeness itself. If each of the many large things is to be large by a part of largeness   d
smaller than largeness itself, won't that appear unreasonable?"

"It certainly will," he replied.

"What about this? Will each thing that has received a small part of the equal have something by which to be equal to anything, when its portion is less than the equal itself?"

"That's impossible."

"Well, suppose one of us is going to have a part of the small. The small will be larger than that part of it, since the part is a part of it: so the small itself will be larger! And that to which the part subtracted is added will   e
be smaller, not larger, than it was before."

"That surely couldn't happen," he said.

---

7. Removing the brackets in a10–11.

"Socrates, in what way, then, will the other things get a share of your forms, if they can do so neither by getting parts nor by getting wholes?"

"By Zeus!" Socrates exclaimed. "It strikes me that's not at all easy to determine!"

"And what do you think about the following?"

"What's that?"

132   "I suppose you think each form is one on the following ground: whenever some number of things seem to you to be large, perhaps there seems to be some one character, the same as you look at them all, and from that you conclude that the large is one."

"That's true," he said.

"What about the large itself and the other large things? If you look at them all in the same way with the mind's eye, again won't some one thing appear large, by which all these appear large?"[8]

"It seems so."

"So another form of largeness will make its appearance, which has emerged alongside largeness itself and the things that partake of it, and
b   in turn another over all these, by which all of them will be large. Each of your forms will no longer be one, but unlimited in multitude."

"But, Parmenides, maybe each of these forms is a thought,"[9] Socrates said, "and properly occurs only in minds. In this way each of them might be one and no longer face the difficulties mentioned just now."

"What do you mean?" he asked. "Is each of the thoughts one, but a thought of nothing?"

"No, that's impossible," he said.

"Of something, rather?"

"Yes."

c   "Of something that is, or of something that is not?"

"Of something that is."

"Isn't it of some one thing, which that thought thinks is over all the instances, being some one character?"

"Yes."

"Then won't this thing that is thought to be one, being always the same over all the instances, be a form?"

"That, too, appears necessary."

"And what about this?" said Parmenides. "Given your claim that other things partake of forms, won't you necessarily think either that each thing is composed of thoughts and all things think, or that, although they are thoughts, they are unthinking?"[10]

"That isn't reasonable either, Parmenides," he said. "No, what appears
d   most likely to me is this: these forms are like patterns set in nature, and

8. Alternatively: "If you look at them all in the same way with the mind's eye, won't some one large again appear, by which all these appear large?"

9. Alternatively: "But, Parmenides, maybe each of the forms is a thought of these things."

10. Alternatively: "or that, although they are thoughts, they are not thought?"

other things resemble them and are likenesses; and this partaking of the forms is, for the other things, simply being modeled on them."

"If something resembles the form," he said, "can that form not be like what has been modeled on it, to the extent that the thing has been made like it? Or is there any way for something like to be like what is not like it?"

"There is not."

"And isn't there a compelling necessity for that which is like to partake of the same one form as what is like it?"[11]   e

"There is."

"But if like things are like by partaking of something, won't that be the form itself?"

"Undoubtedly."

"Therefore nothing can be like the form, nor can the form be like anything else. Otherwise, alongside the form another form will always make its appearance, and if that form is like anything, yet another; and if the form   133 proves to be like what partakes of it, a fresh form will never cease emerging."

"That's very true."

"So other things don't get a share of the forms by likeness; we must seek some other means by which they get a share."

"So it seems."

"Then do you see, Socrates," he said, "how great the difficulty is if one marks things off as forms, themselves by themselves?"

"Quite clearly."

"I assure you," he said, "that you do not yet, if I may put it so, have an inkling of how great the difficulty is if you are going to posit one form   b in each case every time you make a distinction among things."

"How so?" he asked.

"There are many other reasons," Parmenides said, "but the main one is this: suppose someone were to say that if the forms are such as we claim they must be, they cannot even be known. If anyone should raise that objection, you wouldn't be able to show him that he is wrong, unless the objector happened to be widely experienced and not ungifted, and consented to pay attention while in your effort to show him you dealt with many distant considerations. Otherwise, the person who insists that they are necessarily unknowable would remain unconvinced."   c

"Why is that, Parmenides?" Socrates asked.

"Because I think that you, Socrates, and anyone else who posits that there is for each thing some being, itself by itself, would agree, to begin with, that none of those beings is in us."

"Yes – how could it still be itself by itself?" replied Socrates.

"Very good," said Parmenides. "And so all the characters that are what they are in relation to each other have their being in relation to themselves but not in relation to things that belong to us. And whether one posits the   d

11. Removing the brackets in e1.

latter as likenesses or in some other way, it is by partaking of them that we come to be called by their various names. These things that belong to us, although they have the same names as the forms, are in their turn what they are in relation to themselves but not in relation to the forms; and all the things named in this way are *of* themselves but not *of* the forms."

"What do you mean?" Socrates asked.

e

"Take an example," said Parmenides. "If one of us is somebody's master or somebody's slave, he is surely not a slave of master itself – of what a master is – nor is the master a master of slave itself – of what a slave is. On the contrary, being a human being, he is a master or slave of a human being. Mastery itself, on the other hand, is what it is of slavery itself; and, in the same way, slavery itself is slavery of mastery itself. Things in us do not have their power in relation to forms, nor do they have theirs in relation to us; but, I repeat, forms are what they are *of* themselves and in relation

134

to themselves, and things that belong to us are, in the same way, what they are in relation to themselves. You do understand what I mean?"

"Certainly," Socrates said, "I understand."

"So too," he said, "knowledge itself, what knowledge is, would be knowledge of that truth itself, which is what truth is?"

"Certainly."

"Furthermore, each particular knowledge, what it is, would be knowledge of some particular thing, of what that thing is. Isn't that so?"

"Yes."

"But wouldn't knowledge that belongs to us be of the truth that belongs to our world? And wouldn't it follow that each particular knowledge that

b

belongs to us is in turn knowledge of some particular thing in our world?"

"Necessarily."

"But, as you agree, we neither have the forms themselves nor can they belong to us."

"Yes, you're quite right."

"And surely the kinds themselves, what each of them is, are known by the form of knowledge itself?"

"Yes."

"The very thing that we don't have."

"No, we don't."

"So none of the forms is known by us, because we don't partake of knowledge itself."

"It seems not."

"Then the beautiful itself, what it is, cannot be known by us, nor can the

c

good, nor, indeed, can any of the things we take to be characters themselves."

"It looks that way."

"Here's something even more shocking than that."

"What's that?"

"Surely you would say that if in fact there is knowledge – a kind itself – it is much more precise than is knowledge that belongs to us. And the same goes for beauty and all the others."

"Yes."

"Well, whatever else partakes of knowledge itself, wouldn't you say that god more than anyone else has this most precise knowledge?"

"Necessarily."

"Tell me, will god, having knowledge itself, then be able to know things   d
that belong to our world?"

"Yes, why not?"

"Because we have agreed, Socrates," Parmenides said, "that those forms do not have their power in relation to things in our world, and things in our world do not have theirs in relation to forms, but that things in each group have their power in relation to themselves."

"Yes, we did agree on that."

"Well then, if this most precise mastery and this most precise knowledge belong to the divine, the gods' mastery could never master us, nor could their knowledge know us or anything that belongs to us. No, just as we   e
do not govern them by our governance and know nothing of the divine by our knowledge, so they in their turn are, for the same reason, neither our masters nor, being gods, do they know human affairs."

"If god is to be stripped of knowing," he said, "our argument may be getting too bizarre."

"And yet, Socrates," said Parmenides, "the forms inevitably involve these objections and a host of others besides – if there are those characters   135
for things, and a person is to mark off each form as 'something itself.' As a result, whoever hears about them is doubtful and objects that they do not exist, and that, even if they *do*, they must by strict necessity be unknowable to human nature; and in saying this he seems to have a point; and, as we said, he is extraordinarily hard to win over. Only a very gifted man can come to know that for each thing there is some kind, a being itself by   b
itself; but only a prodigy more remarkable still will discover that and be able to teach someone else who has sifted all these difficulties thoroughly and critically for himself."

"I agree with you, Parmenides," Socrates said. "That's very much what I think too."

"Yet on the other hand, Socrates," said Parmenides, "if someone, having an eye on all the difficulties we have just brought up and others of the same sort, won't allow that there are forms for things and won't mark off a form for each one, he won't have anywhere to turn his thought, since he doesn't allow that for each thing there is a character that is always the   c
same. In this way he will destroy the power of dialectic[12] entirely. But I think you are only too well aware of that."

"What you say is true," Socrates said.

"What then will you do about philosophy? Where will you turn, while these difficulties remain unresolved?"

---

12. The Greek word is *dialegesthai*, which could instead be translated as "discourse," or untechnically as "conversation."

"I don't think I have anything clearly in view, at least not at present."

"Socrates, that's because you are trying to mark off something beautiful, and just, and good, and each one of the forms, too soon," he said, "before

d   you have been properly trained. I noticed that the other day too, as I listened to you conversing with Aristotle here. The impulse you bring to argument is noble and divine, make no mistake about it. But while you are still young, put your back into it and get more training through something people think useless – what the crowd call idle talk. Otherwise, the truth will escape you."

"What manner of training is that, Parmenides?" he asked.

"The manner is just what you heard from Zeno," he said. "Except I was

e   also impressed by something you had to say to him: you didn't allow him to remain among visible things and observe their wandering between opposites. You asked him to observe it instead among those things that one might above all grasp by means of reason and might think to be forms."

"I did that," he said, "because I think that here, among visible things, it's not at all hard to show that things are both like and unlike and anything else you please."

"And you are quite right," he said. "But you must do the following in addition to that: if you want to be trained more thoroughly, you must not

136   only hypothesize, if each thing is, and examine the consequences of that hypothesis; you must also hypothesize, if that same thing is not."

"What do you mean?" he asked.

"If you like," said Parmenides, "take as an example this hypothesis that Zeno entertained: if many are,[13] what must the consequences be both for the many themselves in relation to themselves and in relation to the one, and for the one in relation to itself and in relation to the many? And, in turn, on the hypothesis, if many are not, you must again examine what the consequences will be both for the one and for the many in relation

b   to themselves and in relation to each other. And again, in turn, if you hypothesize, if likeness is or if it is not, you must examine what the consequences will be on each hypothesis, both for the things hypothesized themselves and for the others, both in relation to themselves and in relation to each other. And the same method applies to unlike, to motion, to rest, to generation and destruction, and to being itself and not-being. And, in a word, concerning whatever you might ever hypothesize as being or as not being or as having any other property, you must examine the

c   consequences for the thing you hypothesize in relation to itself and in relation to each one of the others, whichever you select, and in relation to several of them and to all of them in the same way; and, in turn, you must examine the others, both in relation to themselves and in relation to whatever other thing you select on each occasion, whether what you hypothesize you hypothesize as being or as not being. All this you must

13. Alternatively: "if [things] are many," or "if there are many."

do if, after completing your training, you are to achieve a full view of the truth."

"Scarcely manageable, Parmenides, this task you describe! And besides, I don't quite understand," he said. "To help me understand more fully, why don't you hypothesize something and go through the exercise for me yourself?"

"For a man my age that's a big assignment, Socrates," he said.

"Well then," said Socrates, "you, Zeno – why don't you go through it for us?"

And Antiphon said that Zeno laughed and said, "Let's beg Parmenides to do it himself, Socrates. What he's proposing won't be easy, I'm afraid. Or don't you recognize what a big assignment it is? Indeed, if there were more of us here, it wouldn't be right to ask him – it's not fitting, especially for a man his age, to engage in such a discussion in front of a crowd. Ordinary people don't know that without this comprehensive and circuitous treatment we cannot hit upon the truth and gain insight. And so, Parmenides, I join with Socrates in begging you, so that I too may become your pupil again after all this time."

When Zeno had finished speaking, Antiphon said that Pythodorus said that he too, along with Aristotle and the others, begged Parmenides not to refuse, but to give a demonstration of what he was recommending. In the end Parmenides said: "I am obliged to go along with you. And yet I feel like the horse in the poem of Ibycus.[14] Ibycus compares himself to a horse – a champion but no longer young, on the point of drawing a chariot in a race and trembling at what experience tells him is about to happen – and says that he himself, old man that he is, is being forced against his will to compete in Love's game. I too, when I think back, feel a good deal of anxiety as to how at my age I am to make my way across such a vast and formidable sea of words. Even so, I'll do it, since it is right for me to oblige you; and besides, we are, as Zeno says, by ourselves.

"Well then, at what point shall we start? What shall we hypothesize first? I know: since we have in fact decided to play this strenuous game, is it all right with you if I begin with myself and my own hypothesis? Shall I hypothesize about the one itself and consider what the consequences must be, if it is one or if it is not one?"

"By all means," said Zeno.

"Then who will answer my questions?" he asked. "The youngest, surely? For he would give the least trouble and would be the most likely to say what he thinks. At the same time his answer would allow me a breathing space."

"I'm ready to play this role for you, Parmenides," Aristotle said. "Because you mean me when you say the youngest. Ask away – you can count on me to answer."

14. Ibycus frg. 6 (Page 1962). Ibycus of Rhegium (sixth century B.C.) was best known for his love poems.

"Very good," he said. "If it is one,[15] the one would not be many, would it?"—"No, how could it?"—"Then there cannot be a part of it nor can it be a whole."—"Why?"—"A part is surely part of a whole."—"Yes."— "But what is the whole? Wouldn't that from which no part is missing be a whole?"—"Certainly."—"In both cases, then, the one would be composed of parts, both if it is a whole and if it has parts."—"Necessarily."—"So in

d   both cases the one would thus be many rather than one."—"True."—"Yet it must be not many but one."—"It must."—"Therefore, if the one is to be one, it will neither be a whole nor have parts."—"No, it won't."

"Well, then, if it doesn't have a part, it could have neither a beginning nor an end nor a middle; for those would in fact be parts of it."—"That's right."—"Furthermore, end and beginning are limits of each thing."— "Doubtless."—"So the one is unlimited if it has neither beginning nor end."—"Unlimited."—"So it is also without shape; for it partakes of neither

e   round nor straight."—"How so?"—"Round is surely that whose extremities are equidistant in every direction from the middle."—"Yes."—"Furthermore, straight is that whose middle stands in the way of the two extremities."—"Just so."—"So the one would have parts and be many if it partook of either a straight or a curved shape."—"Of course."—"There-

138 fore it is neither straight nor curved, since in fact it doesn't have parts."— "That's right."

"Furthermore, being like that, it would be nowhere, because it could be neither in another nor in itself."—"How is that?"—"If it were in another, it would surely be contained all around by the thing it was in and would touch it in many places with many parts; but since it is one and without parts and does not partake of circularity, it cannot possibly touch in many places all around."—"It can't."—"Yet, on the other hand, if it were in itself, its container would be none other than itself, if in fact it were in itself; for

b   a thing can't be in something that doesn't contain it."—"No, it can't."— "So the container itself would be one thing, and the thing contained something else, since the same thing will not, as a whole at any rate, undergo and do both at once. And in that case the one would be no longer one but two."—"Yes, you're quite right."—"Therefore, the one is not anywhere, if it is neither in itself nor in another."—"It isn't."

"Then consider whether, since it is as we have said, it can be at rest or in motion."—"Yes, why not?"—"Because if it moves, it would either move

c   spatially or be altered, since these are the only motions."—"Yes."—"But the one surely can't be altered from itself and still be one."—"It can't."— "Then it doesn't move by alteration at least."—"Apparently not."—"But by moving spatially?"—"Perhaps."—"And if the one moved spatially, it surely would either spin in a circle in the same location or change from one place to another."—"Necessarily."—"Well then, if it spins in a circle, it must be poised on its middle and have other parts of itself that move

15. The hypothesis could also be rendered "if one is." But cf. Parmenides' statement above at 137b.

round the middle. But how will a thing that has nothing to do with middle or parts manage to be moved in a circle round its middle?"—"Not at all."—"But by changing places does it come to be here at one time, there at another, and move in this way?"—"If in fact it moves at all."—"Wasn't it shown that it cannot be anywhere in anything?"—"Yes."—"Then is it not even more impossible for it to *come* to be?"—"I don't see why."—"If something comes to be in something, isn't it necessary that it not yet be in that thing – since it is still coming to be in it – and that it no longer be entirely outside it, if in fact it is already coming to be in it?"—"Necessarily."—"So if anything is to undergo this, only that which has parts could do so, because some of it would already be in that thing, while some, at the same time, would be outside. But a thing that doesn't have parts will not by any means be able to be, at the same time, neither wholly inside nor wholly outside something."—"True."—"But isn't it much more impossible still for a thing that has no parts and is not a whole to come to be in something somewhere, if it does so neither part by part nor as a whole?"— "Apparently."—"Therefore it doesn't change places by going somewhere and coming to be in something, nor does it move by spinning in the same location or by being altered."—"It seems not."—"The one, therefore, is unmoved by every sort of motion."—"Unmoved."

"Yet, on the other hand, we also say that it cannot be in anything."— "Yes, we do."—"Then it is also never in the *same* thing."—"Why?"— "Because it would then be *in* that – in that same thing it is in."—"Of course."—"But it was impossible for it to be either in itself or in another."— "Yes, you're quite right."—"So the one is never in the same thing."—"It seems not."—"But what is never in the same thing neither enjoys repose nor is at rest."—"No, it cannot."—"Therefore the one, as it seems, is neither at rest nor in motion."—"It certainly does appear not."

"Furthermore, it won't be the same as another thing or itself; nor, again, could it be different from itself or another thing."—"Why is that?"—"If it were different from itself, it would surely be different from one, and would not be one."—"True."—"On the other hand, if it were the same as another, it would be that thing, and not itself. So in this way, too, it would not be just what it is – one – but would be different from one."—"Yes, you're quite right."—"Therefore, it won't be the same as another or different from itself."—"No, it won't."

"And it won't be different from another, as long as it is one; for it is not proper to one to be different from something, but proper to different-from-another alone, and to nothing else."—"That's right."—"Therefore it won't be different by being one. Or do you think it will?"—"No indeed."— "Yet if it isn't different by being one, it will not be so by itself; and if it isn't so by itself, it will not itself be so. And if it is itself in no way different, it will be different from nothing."—"That's right."

"Nor will it be the same as itself."—"Why not?"—"The nature of the one is not, of course, also that of the same."—"Why?"—"Because it is not the case that, whenever a thing comes to be the same as something, it comes to be one."—"But why?"—"If it comes to be the same as the many, it must come to be many, not one."—"True."—"But if the one and the same in no way differ, whenever something came to be the same, it would always come to be one; and whenever it came to be one, it would always

e   come to be the same."—"Certainly."—"Therefore, if the one is to be the same as itself, it won't be one with itself; and thus it will be one and not one. But this surely is impossible. Therefore the one can't be either different from another or the same as itself."—"It can't."—"Thus the one could neither be different from nor the same as itself or another."—"Yes, you're quite right."

    "Furthermore, it will be neither like nor unlike anything, either itself or another."—"Why?"—"Because whatever has a property the same is surely like."—"Yes."—"But it was shown that the same is separate in its nature

140   from the one."—"Yes, it was."—"But if the one has any property apart from being one, it would be more than one; and that is impossible."— "Yes."—"Therefore, the one can in no way have a property the same as another or itself."—"Apparently not."—"So it cannot be like another or itself either."—"It seems not."

    "Nor does the one have the property of being different; for in this way too it would be more than one."—"Yes, it would be more."—"Surely that which has a property different from itself or another would be unlike itself

b   or another, if in fact what has a property the same is like."—"That's right."—"But the one, as it seems, since it in no way has a property different, is in no way unlike itself or another thing."—"Yes, you're quite right."— "Therefore the one could be neither like nor unlike another or itself."— "Apparently not."

    "Furthermore, being like that, it will be neither equal nor unequal to itself or another."—"How?"—"If it is equal, it will be of the same measures as that to which it is equal."—"Yes."—"But surely if it is greater or less,

c   it will, in the case of things with which it is commensurate, have more measures than those that are less, and fewer than those that are greater."— "Yes."—"And in the case of things with which it is not commensurate, it will be of smaller measures in the one case, and of larger measures in the other."—"No doubt."—"Well, if a thing doesn't partake of the same, it can't be of the same measures or of the same anything else at all, can it?"— "It can't."—"So it couldn't be equal to itself or another, if it is not of the same measures."—"It certainly appears not."—"Yet if it is, on the other

d   hand, of more measures or fewer, it would have as many parts as measures; and thus, again, it will be no longer one, but just as many as are its measures."—"That's right."—"And if it were of one measure, it would prove to be equal to its measure; but it was shown that it couldn't be equal to anything."—"Yes, it was."—"Therefore, since it doesn't partake of one measure or many or few, and since it doesn't partake of the same at all, it will, as it seems, never be equal to itself or another; nor again will it be greater or less than itself or another."—"That's absolutely so."

e   "What about this? Do you think that the one can be older or younger than, or the same age as, anything?"—"Yes, why not?"—"Because if it is the same age as itself or another, it will surely partake of likeness and of equality of time, of which – likeness and equality – we said the one has no share."—"Yes, we did say that."—"And we also said that it does not partake of unlikeness and inequality."—"Of course."—"Then, being like that, how will it be able to be older or younger than, or the same age as, anything?"—"In no way."—"Therefore, the one could not be younger or older than, or the same age as, itself or another."—"Apparently not."

141

"So if it is like that, the one could not even be in time at all, could it? Or isn't it necessary, if something is in time, that it always come to be older than itself?"—"Necessarily."—"Isn't the older always older than a younger?"—"To be sure."—"Therefore, that which comes to be older than itself comes to be, at the same time, younger than itself, if in fact it is to have something it comes to be older than."—"What do you mean?"—"I mean this: there is no need for a thing to come to be different from a thing that is already different; it must, rather, already be different from what is already different, have come to be different from what has come to be different, and be going to be different from what is going to be different; but it must not have come to be, be going to be, or be different from what comes to be different: it must come to be different, and nothing else."— "Yes, that's necessary."—"But surely older is a difference from younger and from nothing else."—"Yes, it is."—"So that which comes to be older than itself must also, at the same time, come to be younger than itself."— "So it seems."—"But it must also not come to be for more or less time than itself; it must come to be and be and have come to be and be going to be for a time equal to itself."—"Yes, that too is necessary."—"Therefore it is necessary, as it seems, that each thing that is in time and partakes of time be the same age as itself and, at the same time, come to be both older and younger than itself."—"It looks that way."—"But the one surely had no share of any of that."—"No, it didn't."—"Therefore, it has no share of time, nor is it *in* any time."—"It certainly isn't, as the argument proves."

b

c

d

"Now, don't you think that 'was' and 'has come to be' and 'was coming to be' signify partaking of time past?"—"By all means."—"And again that 'will be' and 'will come to be' and 'will be coming to be' signify partaking of time hereafter?"—"Yes."—"And that 'is' and 'comes to be' signify partaking of time now present?"—"Of course."—"Therefore, if the one partakes of no time at all, it is not the case that it has at one time come to be, was coming to be, or was; or has now come to be, comes to be, or is; or will hereafter come to be, will be coming to be, or will be."—"Very true."— "Could something partake of being except in one of those ways?"—"It couldn't."—"Therefore the one in no way partakes of being."—"It seems not."—"Therefore the one in no way is."—"Apparently not."—"Therefore neither *is* it in such a way as to be one, because it would then, by being and partaking of being, be. But, as it seems, the one neither is one nor is, if we are obliged to trust this argument."—"It looks that way."

e

142

"If something is not, could anything belong *to* this thing that is not, or be *of* it?"—"How could it?"—"Therefore, no name belongs to it, nor is there an account or any knowledge or perception or opinion of it."—

"Apparently not."—"Therefore it is not named or spoken of, nor is it the object of opinion or knowledge, nor does anything that is perceive it."—"It seems not."—"Is it possible that these things are so for the one?"—"I certainly don't think so."

b   "Do you want to return to the hypothesis from the beginning, in the hope that another kind of result may come to light as we go back over it?"—"I do indeed."—"If one is, we are saying, aren't we, that we must agree on the consequences for it, whatever they happen to be?"—"Yes."— "Consider from the beginning: if one is, can it *be*, but not partake of being?"—"It cannot."—"So there would also be the being of the one, and that is not the same as the one. For if it were, it couldn't be the being of

c the one, nor could the one partake of it. On the contrary, saying that one is would be like saying that one is one. But this time that is not the hypothesis, namely, what the consequences must be, if one is one, but if one is. Isn't that so?"—"Of course."—"Is that because 'is' signifies something other than 'one'?"—"Necessarily."—"So whenever someone, being brief, says 'one is,' would this simply mean that the one partakes of being?"—"Certainly."

"Let's again say what the consequences will be, if one is. Consider

d whether this hypothesis must not signify that the one is such as to have parts."—"How so?"—"In this way: if we state the 'is' of the one that is, and the 'one' of that which is one, and if being and oneness are not the same, but both belong to that same thing that we hypothesized, namely, the one that is, must it not itself, since it is one being, be a whole, and the parts of this whole be oneness and being?"—"Necessarily."—"Shall we call each of these two parts a part only, or must the part be called part of the whole?"—"Of the whole."—"Therefore whatever is one both is a whole and has a part."—"Certainly."

"Now, what about each of these two parts of the one that is, oneness

e and being? Is oneness ever absent from the being part or being from the oneness part?"—"That couldn't be."—"So again, each of the two parts possesses oneness and being; and the part, in its turn, is composed of at least two parts; and in this way always, for the same reason, whatever part turns up always possesses these two parts, since oneness always possesses being and being always possesses oneness. So, since it always

143 proves to be two, it must never be one."—"Absolutely."—"So, in this way, wouldn't the one that is be unlimited in multitude?"—"So it seems."

"Come, let's proceed further in the following way."—"How?"—"Do we say that the one partakes of being, and hence is?"—"Yes."—"And for this reason the one that is was shown to be many."—"Just so."—"And what about the one itself, which we say partakes of being? If we grasp it in thought alone by itself, without that of which we say it partakes, will it appear to be only one, or will this same thing also appear to be many?"—

b "One, I should think."—"Let's see. Must not its being be something and it itself something different, if in fact the one is not being but, as one, partakes of being?"—"Necessarily."—"So if being is something and the one is something different, it is not by its being one that the one is different from being, nor by its being being that being is other than the one. On the contrary, they are different from each other by difference and otherness."—"Of course."—"And so difference is not the same as oneness or being."—"Obviously not."

"Now, if we select from them, say, being and difference, or being and oneness, or oneness and difference, do we not in each selection choose a certain pair that is correctly called 'both'?"—"How so?"—"As follows: we can say 'being'?"—"We can."—"And, again, we can say 'one'?"—"That too."—"So hasn't each of the pair been mentioned?"—"Yes."—"What about when I say 'being and oneness'? Haven't both been mentioned?"—"Certainly."—"And if I say 'being and difference' or 'difference and oneness,' and so on – in each case don't I speak of both?"—"Yes."—"Can things that are correctly called 'both' be both, but not two?"—"They cannot."—"If there are two things, is there any way for each member of the pair not to be one?"—"Not at all."—"Therefore, since in fact each pair taken together turns out to be two, each member would be one."—"Apparently."—"And if each of them is one, when any one is added to any couple, doesn't the total prove to be three?"—"Yes."—"And isn't three odd, and two even?"—"Doubtless."

"What about this? Since there are two, must there not also be twice, and since there are three, thrice, if in fact two is two times one and three is three times one?"—"Necessarily."—"Since there are two and twice, must there not be two times two? And since there are three and thrice, must there not be three times three?"—"Doubtless."—"And again: if there are three and they are two times, and if there are two and they are three times, must there not be two times three and three times two?"—"There certainly must."—"Therefore, there would be even times even, odd times odd, odd times even, and even times odd."—"That's so."—"Then if that is so, do you think there is any number that need not be?"—"In no way at all."—"Therefore, if one is, there must also be number."—"Necessarily."—"But if there is number, there would be many, and an unlimited multitude of beings. Or doesn't number, unlimited in multitude, also prove to partake of being?"—"It certainly does."—"So if all number partakes of being, each part of number would also partake of it?"—"Yes."

"So has being been distributed to all things, which are many, and is it missing from none of the beings, neither the smallest nor the largest? Or is it unreasonable even to ask that question? How could being be missing from any of the beings?"—"In no way."—"So being is chopped up into beings of all kinds, from the smallest to the largest possible, and is the most divided thing of all; and the parts of being are countless."—"Quite so."—"Therefore its parts are the most numerous of things."—"The most numerous indeed."

"Now, is there any of them that is part of being, yet not one part?"—"How could that happen?"—"I take it, on the contrary, that if in fact it *is*,

it must always, as long as it is, be some one thing; it cannot be nothing."—
"Necessarily."—"So oneness is attached to every part of being and is not
absent from a smaller or a larger, or any other, part."—"Just so."—"So,
d   being one, is it, as a whole, in many places at the same time? Look at this
carefully."—"I am – and I see that it's impossible."—"Therefore as divided,
if in fact not as a whole; for surely it will be present to all the parts of
being at the same time only as divided."—"Yes."—"Furthermore, a divided
thing certainly must be as numerous as its parts."—"Necessarily."—"So
we were not speaking truly just now, when we said that being had been
distributed into the most numerous parts. It is not distributed into more
e   parts than oneness, but, as it seems, into parts equal to oneness, since
neither is being absent from oneness, nor is oneness absent from being.
On the contrary, being two, they are always equal throughout all things."—
"It appears absolutely so."—"Therefore, the one itself, chopped up by
being, is many and unlimited in multitude."—"Apparently."—"So not
only is it the case that the one being is many, but also the one itself,
completely distributed by being, must be many."—"Absolutely."

"Furthermore, because the parts are parts of a whole, the one, as the
145   whole, would be limited. Or aren't the parts contained by the whole?"—
"Necessarily."—"But surely that which contains would be a limit."—
"Doubtless."—"So the one that is is surely both one and many, a whole
and parts, and limited and unlimited in multitude."—"Apparently."

"So, since in fact it is limited, does it not also have extremities?"—
"Necessarily."—"And again: if it is a whole, would it not have a beginning,
a middle, and an end? Or can anything be a whole without those three?
And if any one of them is missing from something, will it still consent to
be a whole?"—"It won't."—"The one, as it seems, would indeed have
b   a beginning, an end, and a middle."—"It would."—"But the middle is
equidistant from the extremities – otherwise, it wouldn't be a middle."—
"No, it wouldn't."—"Since the one is like that, it would partake of some
shape, as it seems, either straight or round, or some shape mixed from
both."—"Yes, it would partake of a shape."

"Since it is so, won't it be both in itself and in another?"—"How so?"—
"Each of the parts is surely in the whole, and none outside the whole."—
c   "Just so."—"And are all the parts contained by the whole?"—"Yes."—
"Furthermore, the one is all the parts of itself, and not any more or less
than all."—"No, it isn't."—"The one is also the whole, is it not?"—"Doubtless."—"So if all its parts are actually in a whole, and the one is both all
the parts and the whole itself, and all the parts are contained by the whole,
the one would be contained by the one; and thus the one itself would,
then, be in itself."—"Apparently."

d   "Yet, on the other hand, the whole is not in the parts, either in all or in
some one. For if it were in all, it would also have to be in one, because if
it were not in some one, it certainly could not be in all. And if this one is
among them all, but the whole is not in it, how will the whole still be in
all?"—"In no way."—"Nor is it in some of the parts: for if the whole were

in some, the greater would be in the less, which is impossible."—"Yes, impossible."—"But if the whole is not in some or one or all the parts, must it not be in something different or be nowhere at all?"—"Necessarily."— "If it were nowhere, it would be nothing; but since it is a whole, and is not in itself, it must be in another. Isn't that so?"—"Certainly."—"So the one, insofar as it is a whole, is in another; but insofar as it is all the parts, it is in itself. And thus the one must be both in itself and in a different thing."—"Necessarily."

"Since that is the one's natural state, must it not be both in motion and at rest?"—"How?"—"It is surely at rest, if in fact it is in itself. For being in one thing and not stirring from that, it would be in the same thing, namely, itself."—"Yes, it is."—"And that which is always in the same thing must, of course, always be at rest."—"Certainly."—"What about this? Must not that which is always in a different thing be, on the contrary, never in the same thing? And since it is never in the same thing, also not at rest? And since not at rest, in motion?"—"Just so."—"Therefore the one, since it is itself always both in itself and in a different thing, must always be both in motion and at rest."—"Apparently."

"Furthermore, it must be the same as itself and different from itself, and, likewise, the same as and different from the others, if in fact it has the aforesaid properties."—"How so?"—"Everything is surely related to everything as follows: either it is the same or different; or, if it is not the same or different, it would be related as part to whole or as whole to part."—"Apparently."

"Is the one itself part of itself?"—"In no way."—"So neither could it be a whole in relation to itself as part of itself, because then it would be a part in relation to itself."—"No, it could not."—"But is the one different from one?"—"No indeed."—"So it couldn't be different from itself."— "Certainly not."—"So if it is neither different nor whole nor part in relation to itself, must it not then be the same as itself?"—"Necessarily."

"What about this? Must not that which is in something different from itself – the self that is in the same thing as itself – be different from itself, if in fact it is also to be in something different?"—"It seems so to me."— "In fact the one was shown to be so, since it is, at the same time, both in itself and in a different thing."—"Yes, it was."—"So in this way the one, as it seems, would be different from itself."—"So it seems."

"Now, if anything is different from something, won't it be different from something that is different?"—"Necessarily."—"Aren't all the things that are not-one different from the one, and the one from the things not-one?"— "Doubtless."—"Therefore the one would be different from the others."—"Different."

"Consider this: aren't the same itself and the different opposite to each other?"—"Doubtless."—"Then will the same ever consent to be in the different, or the different in the same?"—"It won't."—"So if the different is never to be in the same, there is no being that the different is in for any time; for if it were in anything for any time whatsoever, for that time the

e

146

b

c

d

e

different would be in the same. Isn't that so?"—"Just so."—"But since it is never in the same, the different would never be in any being."—"True."—"So the different wouldn't be in the things not-one or in the one."—"Yes, you're quite right."—"So not by the different would the one be different from the things not-one or they different from it."—"No, it wouldn't."—"Nor by themselves would they be different from each other, if they don't

147 partake of the different."—"Obviously not."—"But if they aren't different by themselves or by the different, wouldn't they in fact entirely avoid being different from each other?"—"They would."—"But neither do the things not-one partake of the one; otherwise they would not be not-one, but somehow one."—"True."—"So the things not-one could not be a number either; for in that case, too, they would not be absolutely not-one, since they would at least have number."—"Yes, you're quite right."—"And again: are the things not-one parts of the one? Or would the things not-one in that case, too, partake of the one?"—"They would."—"So if it is in

b every way one, and they are in every way not-one, the one would be neither a part of the things not-one nor a whole with them as parts; and, in turn, the things not-one would be neither parts of the one nor wholes in relation to the one as part."—"No, they wouldn't."—"But in fact we said that things that are neither parts nor wholes nor different from each other will be the same as each other."—"Yes, we did."—"So are we to say that the one, since it is so related to the things not-one, is the same as they are?"—"Let's say so."—"Therefore the one, as it seems, is both different from the others and itself, and the same as the others and itself."—"It certainly looks that way from our argument."

c "Would the one then also be both like and unlike itself and the others?"—"Perhaps."—"At any rate, since it was shown to be different from the others, the others would surely also be different from it."—"To be sure."—"Wouldn't it be different from the others just as they are different from it, and neither more nor less?"—"Yes, why not?"—"So if neither more nor less, in like degree."—"Yes."—"Accordingly, insofar as it has the property of being different from the others and they, likewise, have the property of being different from it, in this way the one would have a property the same as the others, and they would have a property the same as it."—"What do you mean?"

d "As follows: don't you apply to something each name you use?"—"I do."—"Now, could you use the same name either more than once or once?"—"I could."—"So if you use it once, do you call by name that thing whose name it is, but not that thing, if you use it many times? Or whether you utter the same name once or many times, do you quite necessarily always also speak of the same thing?"—"To be sure."—"Now 'different'

e in particular is a name for something, isn't it?"—"Certainly."—"So when you utter it, whether once or many times, you don't apply it to another thing or name something other than that thing whose name it is."—"Necessarily."—"Whenever we say 'the others are different from the one' and 'the one is different from the others,' although we use 'different' twice, we don't apply it to another nature, but always to that nature whose name it is."—"Of course."—"So insofar as the one is different from the others, and the others from the one, on the basis of having the property difference itself, the one would have a property not other, but the same as the others. And that which has a property the same is surely like, isn't it?"—"Yes."— "Indeed, insofar as the one has the property of being different from the others, owing to that property itself it would be altogether like them all, because it is altogether different from them all."—"So it seems." 148

"Yet, on the other hand, the like is opposite to the unlike."—"Yes."— "Isn't the different also opposite to the same?"—"That too."—"But this was shown as well: that the one is the same as the others."—"Yes, it was."—"And being the same as the others is the property opposite to being different from the others."—"Certainly."—"Insofar as the one is different, it was shown to be like."—"Yes."—"So insofar as it is the same, it will be unlike, owing to the property opposite to that which makes it like. And surely the different made it like?"—"Yes."—"So the same will make it unlike; otherwise it won't be opposite to the different."—"So it seems."—"Therefore the one will be like and unlike the others – insofar as it is different, like, and insofar as it is the same, unlike."—"Yes, it admits of this argument too, as it seems." b

c

"It also admits of the following."—"What is that?"—"Insofar as it has a property the same, it has a property that is not of another kind; and if it has a property that is not of another kind, it is not unlike; and if not unlike, it is like. But insofar as it has a property other, it has a property that is of another kind; and if it has a property that is of another kind, it is unlike."—"That's true."—"So because the one is the same as the others and because it is different, on both grounds and either, it would be both like and unlike the others."—"Certainly." d

"So, in the same way, it will be like and unlike itself as well. Since in fact it was shown to be both different from itself and the same as itself, on both grounds and either, won't it be shown to be both like and unlike itself?"—"Necessarily."

"And what about this? Consider the question whether the one touches or does not touch itself and the others."—"Very well."—"Surely the one was shown to be in itself as a whole."—"That's right."—"Isn't the one also in the others?"—"Yes."—"Then insofar as it is in the others, it would touch the others; but insofar as it is in itself, it would be kept from touching the others, and being in itself, would touch itself."—"Apparently."—"Thus the one would touch itself and the others."—"It would." e

"And again, in this way: must not everything that is to touch something lie next to that which it is to touch, occupying the position adjacent to that occupied by what it touches?"—"Necessarily."—"So, too, the one, if it is to touch itself, must lie directly adjacent to itself, occupying a place next to that in which it itself is."—"Yes, it must."—"Now if the one were two it could do that and turn out to be in two places at the same time; but 149 won't it refuse as long as it is one?"—"Yes, you're quite right."—"So the same necessity that keeps the one from being two keeps it from touching itself."—"The same."

"But it won't touch the others either."—"Why?"—"Because, we say, that which is to touch must, while being separate, be next to what it is to touch, and there must be no third thing between them."—"True."—"So there must be at least two things if there is to be contact."—"There must."—"But if to the two items a third is added in a row, they themselves will

b   be three, their contacts two."—"Yes."—"And thus whenever one item is added, one contact is also added, and it follows that the contacts are always fewer by one than the multitude of the numbers. For in regard to the number being greater than the contacts, every later number exceeds all the contacts by an amount equal to that by which the first two exceeded

c   their contacts, since thereafter one is added to the number and, at the same time, one contact to the contacts."—"That's right."—"So however many the things are in number, the contacts are always fewer than they are by one."—"True."—"But if there is only one, and not two, there could not be contact."—"Obviously not."—"Certainly the things other than the one, we say, are not one and do not partake of it, if in fact they are other."—"No, they don't."—"So number is not in the others, if one is not in them."—"Obviously not."—"So the others are neither one nor two, nor do they

d   have a name of any other number."—"No."—"So the one alone is one, and there could not be two."—"Apparently not."—"So there is no contact, since there aren't two items."—"There isn't."—"Therefore, the one doesn't touch the others nor do the others touch the one, since in fact there is no contact."—"Yes, you're quite right."—"Thus, to sum up, the one both touches and does not touch the others and itself."—"So it seems."

"Is it then both equal and unequal to itself and the others?"—"How

e   so?"—"If the one were greater or less than the others, or they in turn greater or less than it, they wouldn't be in any way greater or less than each other by the one being one and the others being other than one – that is, by their own being – would they? But if they each had equality in addition to their own being, they would be equal to each other. And if the others had largeness and the one had smallness, or vice versa, whichever form had largeness attached would be greater, and whichever had smallness attached would be less?"—"Necessarily."

"Then aren't there these two forms, largeness and smallness? For certainly, if there weren't, they couldn't be opposite to each other and couldn't

150   occur in things that are."—"No. How could they?"—"So if smallness occurs in the one, it would be either in the whole of it or in part of it."—"Necessarily."—"What if it were to occur in the whole? Wouldn't it be in the one either by being stretched equally throughout the whole of it, or by containing it?"—"Quite clearly."—"Wouldn't smallness, then, if it were in the one equally throughout, be equal to it, but if it contained the one, be larger?"—"Doubtless."—"So can smallness be equal to or larger than some-

b   thing, and do the jobs of largeness and equality, but not its own?"—"It can't."—"So smallness could not be in the one as a whole; but if in fact it is in the one, it would be in a part."—"Yes."—"But, again, not in all the part. Otherwise, it will do exactly the same thing as it did in relation to the whole: it will be equal to or larger than whatever part it is in."—"Necessarily."—"Therefore smallness will never be in any being, since it occurs neither in a part nor in a whole. Nor will anything be small except smallness itself."—"It seems not."

"So largeness won't be in the one either. For if it were, something else, apart from largeness itself, would be larger than something, namely, that which the largeness is in – and that too, although there is for it no small thing, which it must exceed, if in fact it is large. But this is impossible, since smallness is nowhere in anything."—"True."

"But largeness itself is not greater than anything other than smallness itself, nor is smallness less than anything other than largeness itself."—"No, they aren't."—"So the others aren't greater than the one, nor are they less, because they have neither largeness nor smallness. Nor do these two themselves – largeness and smallness – have, in relation to the one, their power of exceeding and being exceeded; they have it, rather, in relation to each other. Nor could the one, in its turn, be greater or less than these two or the others, since it has neither largeness nor smallness."—"It certainly appears not."—"So if the one is neither greater nor less than the others, it must neither exceed them nor be exceeded by them?"—"Necessarily."—"Now, it is quite necessary that something that neither exceeds nor is exceeded be equally matched, and if equally matched, equal."—"No doubt."

"Furthermore, the one would also itself be so in relation to itself: having neither largeness nor smallness in itself, it would neither be exceeded by nor exceed itself, but, being equally matched, would be equal to itself."—"Of course."—"Therefore the one would be equal to itself and the others."—"Apparently."

"And yet, since it is in itself, it would also be around itself on the outside, and as container it would be greater than itself, but as contained it would be less. And thus the one would be greater and less than itself."—"Yes, it would be."

"Isn't this necessary too, that there be nothing outside the one and the others?"—"No doubt."—"But surely what is must always be somewhere."—"Yes."—"Then won't that which is in something be in something greater as something less? For there is no other way that something could be in something else."—"No, there isn't."—"Since there is nothing else apart from the others and the one, and since they must be in something, must they not in fact be in each other – the others in the one and the one in the others – or else be nowhere?"—"Apparently."—"So, on the one hand, because the one is in the others, the others would be greater than the one, since they contain it, and the one would be less than the others, since it is contained. On the other hand, because the others are in the one, by the same argument the one would be greater than the others and they less than it."—"So it seems."—"Therefore the one is both equal to, and greater and less than, itself and the others."—"Apparently."

    "And if in fact it is greater and less and equal, it would be of measures
c equal to, and more and fewer than, itself and the others; and since of measures, also of parts."—"Doubtless."—"So, since it is of equal and more and fewer measures, it would also be fewer and more than itself and the others in number, and, correspondingly, equal to itself and the others."—"How so?"—"It would surely be of more measures than those things it is greater than, and of as many parts as measures; and likewise it would be of fewer measures and parts than those things it is less than; and correspondingly for the things it is equal to."—"Just so."—"Since it is,
d then, greater and less than, and equal to, itself, would it not be of measures more and fewer than, and equal to, itself? And since of measures, also of parts?"—"Doubtless."—"So, since it is of parts equal to itself, it would be equal to itself in multitude, but since it is of more and fewer parts, it would be more and fewer than itself in number."—"Apparently."—"Now won't the one be related in the same way also to the others? Because it appears larger than they, it must also be more than they are in number; and because it appears smaller, fewer; and because it appears equal in largeness, it must also be equal to the others in multitude."—"Necessarily."—"Thus,
e in turn, as it seems, the one will be equal to, and more and fewer than, itself and the others in number."—"It will."

    "Does the one also partake of time? And, in partaking of time, is it and does it come to be both younger and older than, and neither younger nor older than, itself and the others?"—"How so?"—"If in fact one is, being surely belongs to it."—"Yes."—"But is *to be* simply partaking of being
152 with time present, just as *was* is communion with being together with time past, and, in turn, *will be* is communion with being together with time future?"—"Yes, it is."—"So the one partakes of time, if in fact it partakes of being."—"Certainly."

    "Of time advancing?"—"Yes."—"So the one always comes to be older than itself, if in fact it goes forward in step with time."—"Necessarily."—"Do we recall that the older comes to be older than something that comes to be younger?"—"We do."—"So, since the one comes to be older than itself, wouldn't it come to be older than a self that comes to be younger?"—
b "Necessarily."—"Thus it indeed comes to be both younger and older than itself."—"Yes."

    "But it *is* older, isn't it, whenever, in coming to be, it is at the now time, between *was* and *will be*? For as it proceeds from the past to the future, it certainly won't jump over the now."—"No, it won't."—"Doesn't it stop
c coming to be older when it encounters the now? It doesn't come to be, but is then already older, isn't it? For if it were going forward, it could never be grasped by the now. A thing going forward is able to lay hold of both the now and the later – releasing the now and reaching for the

later, while coming to be between the two, the later and the now."— "True."—"But if nothing that comes to be can sidestep the now, whenever a thing *is* at this point, it always stops its coming-to-be and then is whatever it may have come to be."—"Apparently."—"So, too, the one: whenever, in coming to be older, it encounters the now, it stops its coming-to-be and is then older."—"Of course."—"So it also is older than that very thing it was coming to be older than – and wasn't it coming to be older than itself?"—"Yes."—"And the older is older than a younger?"—"It is."—"So the one is then also younger than itself, whenever, in its coming-to-be older, it encounters the now."—"Necessarily."—"Yet the now is always present to the one throughout its being; for the one always is now, when- ever it is."—"No doubt."—"Therefore the one always both is and comes to be older and younger than itself."—"So it seems."

"Is it or does it come to be for more time than itself or an equal time?"— "An equal."—"But if it comes to be or is for an equal time, it is the same age."—"Doubtless."—"And that which is the same age is neither older nor younger."—"No, it isn't."—"So the one, since it comes to be and is for a time equal to itself, neither is nor comes to be younger or older than itself."—"I think not."

"And again: what of the others?"—"I can't say."— "This much, surely,   153 you can say: things other than the one, if in fact they are different things and not *a* different thing, are more than one. A different thing would be one, but different things are more than one and would have multitude."— "Yes, they would."—"And, being a multitude, they would partake of a greater number than the one."—"Doubtless."—"Now, shall we say in connection with number that things that are more or things that are less come to be and have come to be earlier?"—"Things that are less."—"So, the least thing first; and this is the one. Isn't that so?"—"Yes."—"So of all   b the things that have number the one has come to be first. And the others, too, all have number, if in fact they are others and not an other."—"Yes, they do."—"But that which has come to be first, I take it, has come to be earlier, and the others later; and things that have come to be later are younger than what has come to be earlier. Thus the others would be younger than the one, and the one older than they."—"Yes, it would."

"What about the following? Could the one have come to be in a way contrary to its own nature, or is that impossible?"—"Impossible."—"Yet   c the one was shown to have parts, and if parts, a beginning, an end, and a middle."—"Yes."—"Well, in the case of all things – the one itself and each of the others – doesn't a beginning come to be first, and after the beginning all the others up to the end?"—"To be sure."—"Furthermore, we shall say that all these others are parts of some one whole, but that it itself has come to be one and whole at the same time as the end."—"Yes, we shall."—"An end, I take it, comes to be last, and the one naturally   d comes to be at the same time as it. And so if in fact the one itself must not come to be contrary to nature, it would naturally come to be later

than the others, since it has come to be at the same time as the end."—
"Apparently."—"Therefore the one is younger than the others, and the
others are older than it."—"That, in turn, appears to me to be so."

"But again: must not a beginning or any other part of the one or of
anything else, if in fact it is a part and not parts, be one, since it is *a*
part?"—"Necessarily."—"Accordingly, the one would come to be at the
e   same time as the first part that comes to be, and at the same time as the
second; and it is absent from none of the others that come to be – no matter
what is added to what – until, upon arriving at the last part, it comes to
be one whole, having been absent at the coming-to-be of neither the middle
nor the first nor the last nor any other part."—"True."—"Therefore the
one is the same age as all the others. And so, unless the one itself is
naturally contrary to nature, it would have come to be neither earlier nor
154 later than the others, but at the same time. And according to this argument
the one would be neither older nor younger than the others, nor the others
older or younger than it. But according to our previous argument, it was
both older and younger than they, and likewise they were both older and
younger than it."—"Of course."

"That's how it is and has come to be. But what about its coming-to-be
both older and younger, and neither older nor younger, than the others
and they than it? Is the case with coming-to-be just as it is with being, or
b   is it different?"—"I can't say."—"But I can say this much, at least: if
something is indeed older than another thing, it could not come to be still
older by an amount greater than the original difference in age. Nor, in
turn, could the younger come to be still younger. For equals added to
unequals, in time or anything else at all, always make them differ by an
amount equal to that by which they differed at first."—"No doubt."—"So
c   what is older or younger could never come to be older or younger than
what is older or younger, if in fact they always differ in age by an equal
amount. On the contrary, something is and has come to be older, and
something younger, but they do not come to be so."—"True."—"So also
the one, since it is older or younger, never comes to be older or younger than
the others that are older or younger than it."—"Yes, you're quite right."

"But consider whether it comes to be older and younger in this way."—
"In what way?"—"In the way that the one was shown to be older than
the others and they older than it."—"What of that?"—"When the one is
d   older than the others, it has surely come to be for more time than they."—
"Yes."—"Go back and consider: if we add an equal time to more and less
time, will the more differ from the less by an equal or a smaller fraction?"[16]—
"A smaller."—"So the one's difference in age in relation to the others will
not be in the future just what it was at first. On the contrary, by getting
an increment of time equal to the others, it will differ from them in age
always less than it did before. Isn't that so?"—"Yes."—"Wouldn't that
e   which differs from anything in age less than before come to be younger

16. The word translated here and below as "fraction" is elsewhere translated as "part."

than before in relation to those things it was previously older than?"—
"Younger."—"And if the one comes to be younger, don't those others, in
turn, come to be older than before in relation to it?"—"Certainly."—"So
what is younger comes to be older in relation to what has come to be
earlier and is older, but it never is older. On the contrary, it always comes
to be older than that thing. For the older advances toward the younger,
while the younger advances toward the older. And, in the same way, the   155
older, in its turn, comes to be younger than the younger. For both, by
going toward their opposites, come to be each other's opposite, the younger
coming to be older than the older, and the older younger than the younger.
But they could not come to *be* so. For if they came to be, they would no
longer *come* to be, but would be so. But as it is they come to be older and
younger than each other. The one comes to be younger than the others,
because it was shown to be older and to have come to be earlier, whereas
the others come to be older than the one, because they have come to be later.   b

"And by the same argument the others, too, come to be younger in
relation to the one, since in fact they were shown to be older than it and
to have come to be earlier."—"Yes, it does appear so."

"Well then, insofar as nothing comes to be older or younger than a
different thing, owing to their always differing from each other by an
equal number, the one would not come to be older or younger than the
others, and they would not come to be older or younger than it. But insofar
as things that came to be earlier must differ from things that come to be
later by a fraction that is always different, and vice versa, in this way they   c
must come to be older and younger than each other – both the others than
the one and the one than the others."—"Of course."—"To sum up all this,
the one itself both is and comes to be older and younger than itself and
the others, and it neither is nor comes to be older or younger than itself
or the others."—"Exactly."

"And since the one partakes of time and of coming to be older and   d
younger, must it not also partake of time past, future, and present – if in
fact it partakes of time?"—"Necessarily."—"Therefore, the one was and
is and will be, and was coming to be and comes to be and will come to
be."—"To be sure."—"And something could belong to it and be of it, in
the past, present, and future."—"Certainly."—"And indeed there would
be knowledge and opinion and perception of it, if in fact even now we
are engaging in all those activities concerning it."—"You're right."—"And
a name and an account belong to it, and it is named and spoken of. And   e
all such things as pertain to the others also pertain to the one."—"That's
exactly so."

"Let's speak of it yet a third time. If the one is as we have described
it – being both one and many and neither one nor many, and partaking
of time – must it not, because it is one, sometimes partake of being, and in
turn because it is not, sometimes not partake of being?"—"Necessarily."—
"When it partakes, can it at that time not partake, or partake when it

doesn't?"—"It cannot."—"So it partakes at one time, and doesn't partake at another; for only in this way could it both partake and not partake of the same thing."—"That's right."—"Isn't there, then, a definite time when it gets a share of being and when it parts from it? Or how can it at one time have and at another time not have the same thing, if it never gets and releases it?"—"In no way."

"Don't you in fact call getting a share of being 'coming-to-be'?"—"I do."—"And parting from being 'ceasing-to-be'?"—"Most certainly."—"Indeed the one, as it seems, when it gets and releases being, comes to be and ceases to be."—"Necessarily."—"And since it is one and many and comes to be and ceases to be, doesn't its being many cease to be whenever it comes to be one, and doesn't its being one cease to be whenever it comes to be many?"—"Certainly."—"Whenever it comes to be one and many, must it not separate and combine?"—"It certainly must."—"Furthermore, whenever it comes to be like and unlike, must it not be made like and unlike?"—"Yes."—"And whenever it comes to be greater and less and equal, must it not increase and decrease and be made equal?"—"Just so."

"And whenever, being in motion, it comes to a rest, and whenever, being at rest, it changes to moving, it must itself, presumably, be in no time at all."—"How is that?"—"It won't be able to undergo being previously at rest and later in motion or being previously in motion and later at rest without changing."—"Obviously not."—"Yet there is no time in which something can, simultaneously, be neither in motion nor at rest."—"Yes, you're quite right."—"Yet surely it also doesn't change without changing."—"Hardly."—"So when does it change? For it does not change while it is at rest or in motion, or while it is in time."—"Yes, you're quite right."

"Is there, then, this queer thing in which it might be, just when it changes?"—"What queer thing?"—"The instant. The instant seems to signify something such that changing occurs from it to each of two states. For a thing doesn't change from rest while rest continues, or from motion while motion continues. Rather, this queer creature, the instant, lurks between motion and rest – being in no time at all – and to it and from it the moving thing changes to resting and the resting thing changes to moving."—"It looks that way."—"And the one, if in fact it both rests and moves, could change to each state – for only in this way could it do both. But in changing, it changes at an instant, and when it changes, it would be in no time at all, and just then it would be neither in motion nor at rest."—"No, it wouldn't."

"Is it so with the other changes too? Whenever the one changes from being to ceasing-to-be, or from not-being to coming-to-be, isn't it then between certain states of motion and rest? And then it neither is nor is not, and neither comes to be nor ceases to be?"—"It seems so, at any rate."—"Indeed, according to the same argument, when it goes from one to many and from many to one, it is neither one nor many, and neither separates nor combines. And when it goes from like to unlike and from unlike to like, it is neither like nor unlike, nor is it being made like or

unlike. And when it goes from small to large and to equal and vice versa,   b
it is neither small nor large nor equal; nor would it be increasing or
decreasing or being made equal."—"It seems not."—"The one, if it is,
could undergo all that."—"Doubtless."

"Must we not examine what would be proper for the others to undergo,
if one is?"—"We must."—"Are we to say, then, what properties things
other than the one must have, if one is?"—"Let's do."—"Well then, since
in fact they are other than the one, the others are not the one. For if they
were, they would not be other than the one."—"That's right."   c
"And yet the others are not absolutely deprived of the one, but somehow
partake of it."—"In what way?"—"In that things other than the one are
surely other because they have parts; for if they didn't have parts, they
would be altogether one."—"That's right."—"And parts, we say, are parts
of that which is a whole."—"Yes, we do."—"Yet the whole of which the
parts are to be parts must be one thing composed of many, because each
of the parts must be part, not of many, but of a whole."—"Why is that?"—
"If something were to be part of many, in which it itself is, it will, of   d
course, be both part of itself, which is impossible, and of each one of the
others, if in fact it is part of all of them. For if it is not part of one, it will
be part of the others, that one excepted, and thus it will not be part of
each one. And if it is not part of each, it will be part of none of the many.
But if something is part of none, it cannot be a part, or anything else at
all, of all those things of which it is no part of any."—"It certainly appears
so."—"So the part would not be part of many things or all, but of some
one character and of some one thing, which we call a 'whole,' since it has   e
come to be one complete thing composed of all. This is what the part
would be part of."—"Absolutely."—"So if the others have parts, they
would also partake of some one whole."—"Certainly."—"So things other
than the one must be one complete whole with parts."—"Necessarily."
"Furthermore, the same account applies also to each part, since it too   158
must partake of the one. For if each of them is a part, 'each,' of course,
signifies that it is one thing, detached from the others and being by itself,
if in fact it is to be *each*."—"That's right."—"But clearly it would partake
of the one, while being something other than one. Otherwise, it wouldn't
partake, but would itself be one. But as it is, it is surely impossible for
anything except the one itself to be one."—"Impossible."
"But both the whole and the part must partake of the one; for the whole
will be one thing of which the parts are parts, and in turn each thing that
is part of a whole will be one part of the whole."—"Just so."—"Well, then,   b
won't things that partake of the one partake of it, while being different
from it?"—"Doubtless."—"And things different from the one would surely
be many; for if things other than the one were neither one nor more than
one, they would be nothing."—"Yes, you're quite right."
"Since both things that partake of the oneness of a part and things that
partake of the oneness of a whole are more than one, must not those things

themselves that get a share of the one in fact be unlimited in multitude?"—
"How so?"—"Let's observe the following: isn't it the case that, at the time
when they get a share of the one, they get a share, while not being one
and not partaking of the one?"—"Quite clearly."—"While being multi-
c   tudes, then, in which oneness is not present?"—"Certainly, multitudes."—
"Now, if we should be willing to subtract, in thought, the very least we
can from these multitudes, must not that which is subtracted, too, be a
multitude and not one, if in fact it doesn't partake of the one?"—"Necessarily."—"So always, as we examine in this way its nature, itself by itself,
different from the form, won't as much of it as we ever see be unlimited
in multitude?"—"Absolutely."

d   "Furthermore, whenever each part comes to be one part, the parts then
have a limit in relation to each other and in relation to the whole, and the
whole has a limit in relation to the parts."—"Quite so."—"Accordingly,
it follows for things other than the one that from the one and themselves
gaining communion with each other, as it seems, something different comes
to be in them, which affords a limit for them in relation to each other; but
their own nature, by themselves, affords unlimitedness."—"Apparently."—"In this way, indeed, things other than the one, taken both as
wholes and part by part, both are unlimited and partake of a limit."—"Certainly."

e   "Well, aren't they both like and unlike each other and themselves?"—
"In what way?"—"On the one hand, insofar as they are all unlimited by
their own nature, they would in this way have a property the same."—
"Certainly."—"Furthermore, insofar as they all partake of a limit, in this
way, too, they would all have a property the same."—"Doubtless."—"On
the other hand, insofar as they are both limited and unlimited, they have
159 these properties, which are opposite to each other."—"Yes."—"And opposite properties are as unlike as possible."—"To be sure."—"So in respect
of either property they would be like themselves and each other, but in
respect of both properties they would be utterly opposite and unlike both
themselves and each other."—"It looks that way."—"Thus the others
would be both like and unlike themselves and each other."—"Just so."

        "And indeed we will have no further trouble in finding that things other
than the one are both the same as and different from each other, both in
motion and at rest, and have all the opposite properties, since in fact they
b   were shown to have those we mentioned."—"You're right."

        "Well, then, suppose we now concede those results as evident and
examine again, if one is: Are things other than the one also not so, or only
so?"—"Of course."—"Let's say from the beginning, what properties things
other than the one must have, if one is."—"Yes, let's do."—"Must not the
one be separate from the others, and the others separate from the one?"—
"Why?"—"Because surely there is not something else in addition to them
c   that is both other than the one and other than the others; for all things
have been mentioned, once the one and the others are mentioned."—"Yes,

all things."—"So there is no further thing, different from them, in which same thing the one and the others could be."—"No, there isn't."—"So the one and the others are never in the same thing."—"It seems not."—"So they are separate?"—"Yes."

"Furthermore, we say that what is really one doesn't have parts."— "Obviously not."—"So the one could not be in the others as a whole, nor could parts of it be in them, if it is separate from the others and doesn't have parts."—"Obviously not."—"So the others could in no way partake   d of the one, if they partake neither by getting some part of it nor by getting it as a whole."—"It seems not."—"In no way, then, are the others one, nor do they have any oneness in them."—"Yes, you're quite right."

"So the others aren't many either; for each of them would be one part of a whole, if they were many. But as it is, things other than the one are neither one nor many nor a whole nor parts, since they in no way partake of the one."—"That's right."—"Therefore, the others are not themselves two or three, nor are two or three in them, if in fact they are entirely   e deprived of the one."—"Just so."

"So the others aren't themselves like and unlike the one, and likeness and unlikeness aren't in them. For if they were themselves like and unlike, or had likeness and unlikeness in them, things other than the one would surely have in themselves two forms opposite to each other."—"Apparently."—"But it was impossible for things that couldn't partake even of one to partake of any two."—"Impossible."—"So the others are neither like nor unlike nor both. If they were like or unlike, they would partake   160 of one of the two forms, and if they were both, they would partake of two opposite forms. But these alternatives were shown to be impossible."— "True."

"So they are neither the same nor different, neither in motion nor at rest, neither coming to be nor ceasing to be, neither greater nor less nor equal. Nor do they have any other such properties. For if the others submit to having any such property, they will partake of one and two and three and odd and even, of which it was shown they could not partake, since   b they are in every way entirely deprived of the one."—"Very true."

"Thus if one is, the one is all things and is not even one, both in relation to itself and, likewise, in relation to the others."[17] "Exactly."

"So far so good. But must we not next examine what the consequences must be, if the one is not?"—"Yes, we must."—"What, then, would this hypothesis be: 'if one is not'? Does it differ at all from this hypothesis: 'if not-one is not'?"—"Of course it differs."—"Does it merely differ, or is saying 'if not-one is not' the complete opposite of saying, 'if one is not'?"—   c

17. Alternatively, accepting a plausible emendation at b3: "Thus if one is, the one is all things and is not even one, both in relation to itself and in relation to the others, and likewise for the others." With this emended text, the sentence describes the contents of all four deductions, instead of only the first two.

"The complete opposite."—"What if someone were to say, 'if largeness is not' or 'if smallness is not' or anything else like that, would it be clear in each case that what he is saying is not is something different?"—"Certainly."—"So now, too, whenever he says, 'if one is not,' isn't it clear that what he says is not is different from the others, and don't we recognize what he means?"—"We do."—"So he speaks of something, in the first place, knowable, and in the second, different from the others, whenever he says 'one,' whether he attaches being or not-being to it; for we still know what thing is said not to be, and that it is different from the others. Isn't that so?"—"Necessarily."

"Then we must state from the beginning as follows what must be the case, if one is not. First, as it seems, this must be so for it, that there is knowledge of it; otherwise we don't even know what is meant when someone says, 'if one is not'."—"True."—"And it must be the case that the others are different from it – or else it isn't said to be different from them?"—"Certainly."—"Therefore difference in kind pertains to it in addition to knowledge. For someone doesn't speak of the difference in kind of the others when he says that the one is different from the others, but of *that* thing's difference in kind."—"Apparently."

"Furthermore, the one that is not partakes of *that* and of *something, this, to this, these,* and so on; for the one could not be mentioned, nor could things be different from the one, nor could anything belong to it or be of it, nor could it be said to be anything, unless it had a share of *something* and the rest."—"That's right."—"The one can't *be,* if in fact it is not, but nothing prevents it from partaking of many things. Indeed, it's even necessary, if in fact it's that one and not another that is not. If, however, neither the one nor *that* is not to be, but the account is about something else, we shouldn't even utter a sound. But if that one and not another is posited not to be, it must have a share of *that* and of many other things."— "Quite certainly."

"So it has unlikeness, too, in relation to the others. For things other than the one, since they are different, would also be different in kind."—"Yes."— "And aren't things different in kind other in kind?"—"Doubtless."— "Aren't things other in kind unlike?"—"Unlike, certainly."—"Well, then, if in fact they are unlike the one, clearly things unlike would be unlike an unlike."—"Clearly."—"So the one would also have unlikeness, in relation to which the others are unlike it."—"So it seems."

"But, then, if it has unlikeness to the others, must it not have likeness to itself?"—"How so?"—"If the one has unlikeness to one, the argument would surely not be about something of the same kind as the one, nor would the hypothesis be about one, but about something other than one."— "Certainly."—"But it must not be."—"No indeed."—"Therefore the one must have likeness of itself to itself."—"It must."

"Furthermore, it is not equal to the others either; for if it were equal, it would then both be, and be like them in respect of equality. But those are both impossible, if in fact one is not."—"Impossible."—"Since it is not equal to the others, must not the others, too, be not equal to it?"—"Necessarily."—"Aren't things that are not equal unequal?"—"Yes."—"And aren't things unequal unequal to something unequal?"—"Doubtless."—"So the one par-   d takes also of inequality, in relation to which the others are unequal to it."—"It does."

"But largeness and smallness are constitutive of inequality."—"Yes, they are."—"So do largeness and smallness, too, belong to this one?"—"It looks that way."—"Yet largeness and smallness always stand apart from each other."—"Certainly."—"So there is always something between them."—"There is."—"Then can you mention anything between them other than equality?"—"No, just that."—"Therefore whatever has largeness and smallness also has equality, since it is between them."—"Apparently."—"The one, if it is not, would have, as it seems, a share of equality, largeness,   e and smallness."—"So it seems."

"Furthermore, it must also somehow partake of being."—"How is that?"—"It must be in the state we describe; for if it is not so, we wouldn't speak truly when we say that the one is not. But if we do speak truly, it is clear that we say things that are. Isn't that so?"—"It is indeed so."—"And since we claim to speak truly, we must claim also to speak of things   162 that are."—"Necessarily."—"Therefore, as it seems, the one *is* a not-being; for if it is not to *be* a not-being, but is somehow to give up its being in relation to not-being, it will straightway be a being."—"Absolutely."—"So if it is not to be, it must have *being* a not-being as a bond in regard to its not-being, just as, in like manner, what is must have *not-being* what is not, in order that it, in its turn, may completely be. This is how what is would most of all be and what is not would not be: on the one hand, by what is, if it is completely to be, partaking of being in regard to being a being   b and of not-being in regard to being a not-being; and, on the other hand, by what is not, if in its turn what is not is completely not to be, partaking of not-being in regard to not-being a not-being and of being in regard to being a not-being."[18]—"Very true."—"Accordingly, since in fact what is has a share of not-being and what is not has a share of being, so, too, the one, since it is not, must have a share of being in regard to its not-being."—"Necessarily."—"Then the one, if it is not, appears also to have being."—"Apparently."—"And of course not-being, if in fact it is not."—"Doubtless."

"Can something that is in some state not be so, without changing from that state?"—"It cannot."—"So everything of the sort we've described,   c which is both so and not so, signifies a change."—"Doubtless."—"And a change is a motion – or what shall we call it?"—"A motion."—"Now wasn't the one shown both to be and not to be?"—"Yes."—"Therefore, it appears both to be so and not so."—"So it seems."—"Therefore the one that is not has been shown also to move, since in fact it has been shown to change from being to not-being."—"It looks that way."

18. Dropping the supplement in 162a8 and removing the brackets in b2.

"Yet, on the other hand, if it is nowhere among the things that are – as it isn't, if in fact it is not – it couldn't travel from one place to another."—

d "Obviously not."—"So it couldn't move by switching place."—"No, it couldn't."—"Nor could it rotate in the same thing, because it nowhere touches the same thing. For that which is the same is a being, and what is not cannot be in anything that is."—"No, it can't."—"Therefore the one, if it is not, would be unable to rotate in that in which it is not."—"Yes, you're quite right."—"And, surely, the one isn't altered from itself either, whether as something that is or as something that is not. For the argument would no longer be about the one, but about something else, if in fact the one were altered from itself."—"That's right."—"But if it isn't altered and doesn't rotate in the same thing or switch place, could it still move

e somehow?"—"Obviously not."—"Yet what is unmoved must enjoy repose, and what reposes must be at rest."—"Necessarily."—"Therefore the one, as it seems, since it is not, is both at rest and in motion."—"So it seems."

163 "Furthermore, if in fact it moves, it certainly must be altered; for however something is moved, by just so much it is no longer in the same state as it was, but in a different state."—"Just so."—"Then because it moves, the one is also altered."—"Yes."—"And yet, because it in no way moves, it could in no way be altered."—"No, it couldn't."—"So insofar as the one that is not moves, it is altered, but insofar as it doesn't move, it is not altered."—"No, it isn't.—"Therefore the one, if it is not, is both altered and not altered."—"Apparently."

"Must not that which is altered come to be different from what it was

b before, and cease to be in its previous state; and must not that which is not altered neither come to be nor cease to be?"—"Necessarily."—"Therefore also the one, if it is not, comes to be and ceases to be, if it is altered, and does not come to be or cease to be, if it is not altered. And thus the one, if it is not, both comes to be and ceases to be, and does not come to be or cease to be."—"Yes, you're quite right."

"Let's go back again to the beginning to see whether things will appear

c the same to us as they do now, or different."—"Indeed, we must."— "Aren't we saying, if one is not, what the consequences must be for it?"— "Yes."—"When we say 'is not,' the words don't signify anything other than absence of being for whatever we say is not, do they?"—"Nothing other."—"When we say that something is not, are we saying that in a way it is not, but in a way it is? Or does this 'is not' signify without qualification that what is not is in no way at all and does not in any way partake of being?"—"Absolutely without qualification."—"Therefore what is not

d could neither be nor partake of being in any other way at all."—"No, it couldn't."

"Can coming-to-be and ceasing-to-be possibly be anything other than getting a share of being and losing it?"—"Nothing other."—"But what has no share of being could neither get nor lose it."—"Obviously not."—"So the one, since it in no way is, must in no way have, release, or get a share

of, being."—"That's reasonable."—"So the one that is not neither ceases
to be nor comes to be, since in fact it in no way partakes of being."—
"Apparently not."—"So it also isn't altered in any way. For if it were to   e
undergo this, it would then come to be and cease to be."—"True."—"And
if it isn't altered, it must not move either?"—"Necessarily."—"And surely
we won't say that what in no way is is at rest, since what is at rest must
always be in some same thing."—"In the same thing, no doubt."—"Thus,
let's say that what is not is, in turn, never at rest or in motion."—"Yes,
you're quite right."

"But in fact nothing that is belongs to it; for then, by partaking of   164
that, it would partake of being."—"Clearly."—"So neither largeness nor
smallness nor equality belongs to it."—"No, they don't."—"Furthermore,
it would have neither likeness nor difference in kind in relation to itself
or in relation to the others."—"Apparently not."

"What about this? Can the others be related to it, if, necessarily, nothing
belongs to it?"—"They can't."—"So the others are neither like nor unlike
it, and they are neither the same as nor different from it."—"No, they
aren't."—"And again: will *of that, to that, something, this, of this, of another,
to another,* or time past, hereafter, or now, or knowledge, opinion, percep-   b
tion, an account, a name, or anything else that is be applicable to what is
not?"—"It will not."—"Thus one, since it is not, is not in any state at
all."—"At any rate, it certainly seems to be in no state at all."

"Let's go on and say what properties the others must have, if one is
not."—"Yes, let's do."—"They must surely be other; for if they weren't
even other, we wouldn't be talking about the others."—"Just so."—"But
if the argument is about the others, the others are different. Or don't you
apply the names 'other' and 'different' to the same thing?"—"I do."—   c
"And surely we say that the different is different from a different thing,
and the other is other than another thing?"—"Yes."—"So the others, too,
if they are to be other, have something they will be other than."—"Necessarily."—"What would it be then? For they won't be other than the one,
if it is indeed not."—"No, they won't."—"So they are other than each
other, since that alternative remains for them, or else to be other than
nothing."—"That's right."

"So they each are other than each other as multitudes; for they couldn't
be so as ones, if one is not. But each mass of them, as it seems, is unlimited   d
in multitude, and if you take what seems to be smallest, in an instant, just
as in a dream, instead of seeming to be one, it appears many, and instead
of very small, immense in relation to the bits chopped from it."—"That's
quite right."—"The others would be other than each other as masses of
this sort, if they are other, and if one is not."—"Quite so."

"Well then, won't there be many masses, each appearing, but not being,
one, if in fact one is not to be?"—"Just so."—"And there will seem to be
a number of them, if in fact each seems to be one, although being many."—   e
"Certainly."—"And among them some appear even and some odd,

although not really being so, if in fact one is not to be."—"Yes, you're quite right."

"Furthermore, a smallest too, we say, will seem to be among them; but 165 this appears many and large in relation to each of its many, because they are small."—"Doubtless."—"And each mass will be conceived to be equal to its many small bits. For it could not, in appearance, shift from greater to less, until it seems to come to the state in between, and this would be an appearance of equality."—"That's reasonable."

"Now won't it appear to have a limit in relation to another mass, but itself to have no beginning, limit, or middle in relation to itself?"—"Why is that?"—"Because whenever you grasp any bit of them in thought as b being a beginning, middle, or end, before the beginning another beginning always appears, and after the end a different end is left behind, and in the middle others more in the middle than the middle but smaller, because you can't grasp each of them as one, since the one is not."—"Very true."— "So every being that you grasp in thought must, I take it, be chopped up and dispersed, because surely, without oneness, it would always be grasped as a mass."—"Of course."—"So must not such a thing appear one to a person c dimly observing from far off; but to a person considering it keenly from up close, must not each one appear unlimited in multitude, if in fact it is deprived of the one, if it is not?"—"Indeed, most necessarily."—"Thus the others must each appear unlimited and as having a limit, and one and many, if one is not, but things other than the one are."—"Yes, they must."

"Won't they also seem to be both like and unlike?"—"Why is that?"— "Just as, to someone standing at a distance, all things in a painting,[19] appearing one, appear to have a property the same and to be like."— d "Certainly."—"But when the person comes closer, they appear many and different and, by the appearance of the different, different in kind and unlike themselves."—"Just so."—"So the masses must also appear both like and unlike themselves and each other."—"Of course."

"Accordingly, if one is not and many are, the many must appear both the same as and different from each other, both in contact and separate from themselves, both moving with every motion and in every way at rest, both coming to be and ceasing to be and neither, and surely everything e of that sort, which it would now be easy enough for us to go through."— "Very true indeed."

"Let's go back to the beginning once more and say what must be the case, if one is not, but things other than the one are."—"Yes, let's do."— "Well, the others won't be one."—"Obviously not."—"And surely they won't be many either, since oneness would also be present in things that are many. For if none of them is one, they are all nothing – so they also

19. Plato's word here refers specifically to painting that aims at the illusion of volume through the contrast of light and shadow.

couldn't be many."—"True."—"If oneness isn't present in the others, the others are neither many nor one."—"No, they aren't."

"Nor even do they appear one or many."—"Why?"—"Because the others 166
have no communion in any way at all with any of the things that are not, and none of the things that are not belongs to any of the others, since things that are not have no part."—"True."—"So no opinion or any appearance of what is not belongs to the others, nor is not-being conceived in any way at all in the case of the others."—"Yes, you're quite right."—"So if one is not, none of the others is conceived to be one or many, since, without   b
oneness, it is impossible to conceive of many."—"Yes, impossible."—"Therefore, if one is not, the others neither are nor are conceived to be one or many."—"It seems not."

"So they aren't like or unlike either."—"No, they aren't."—"And indeed, they are neither the same nor different, neither in contact nor separate, nor anything else that they appeared to be in the argument we went through before. The others neither are nor appear to be any of those things, if one is not."—"True."—"Then if we were to say, to sum up, 'if one is   c
not, nothing is,' wouldn't we speak correctly?"—"Absolutely."

"Let us then say this – and also that, as it seems, whether one is or is not, it and the others both are and are not, and both appear and do not appear all things in all ways, both in relation to themselves and in relation to each other."—"Very true."

PHILEBUS

Scholars universally agree that this is one of Plato's last works, along with at least Laws *(about which we have independent testimony that it was a work of his old age), plus* Sophist *and* Statesman. *It was written after* Phaedo, Republic, *and* Phaedrus, *and also after* Parmenides *and* Theaetetus. *In those other latest works (as well as* Timaeus *and* Critias, *whatever their place in the order of composition may have been), the principal speaker who directs the discussion's agenda is not Socrates, but the Athenian visitor (*Laws*), or the visitor from Elea (*Sophist *and* Statesman*), or* Timaeus *or* Critias *themselves. Indeed, although he participates actively in the first part of* Parmenides, *Socrates is already made to yield center stage there to the dialogue's namesake—Parmenides calls the tunes. Here, however, Socrates is again fully in charge. Naturally enough: the topic is again one we readily associate with Socrates in Plato's 'Socratic' dialogues, as well as in* Phaedo, Republic, *and* Phaedrus: *what is 'the human good'? how will a human being lead the best life possible? Yet this is a Socrates very sure of his ground, ready to expound at length difficult metaphysical doctrines, and possessed of a whole theory about the ingredients of the best life and their proper ordering. He pursues the discussion much more in the manner of the Visitor of* Sophist *or* Statesman *than in his own manner in either the 'Socratic' dialogues or the* Republic— *though his fellow discussant is much more ready to throw up opposition to his ideas than the Visitor's are in* Sophist *and* Statesman.

We pick up the thread in mediis rebus. In the presence of a company of young men, Socrates has been disputing with one of them, Philebus, about what constitutes the good in human life. Is it pleasure, as Philebus had maintained, or knowledge—Socrates' candidate? (We know nothing of Philebus, apart from this dialogue: his name means "youth lover" and so pleasure seeker, and he is presented as himself an attractive young man. He may be purely fictional.) They had ended at loggerheads. Now another young man, Protarchus, takes over Philebus' side. (He is addressed at 19b as "son of Callias," the very rich Athenian said in Apology *20a to have spent more than anyone else on the sophists, and at 58a–b he seems to speak as a respectful admirer of Gorias.) The discussion now takes a new tack. Socrates will argue, not that the good in human life is knowledge (not pleasure), but that it is some third thing, in fact the principle for the proper mixture of knowledge and pleasure—both together—within a life. Knowledge, he will argue, though not the good itself, is vastly closer and more akin to it than pleasure is. Thus knowledge wins second prize in the contest, coming far ahead of pleasure in the final accounting.*

398

*Socrates first insists that neither pleasure nor knowledge is a simple unity;
there are significantly different varieties of each—different ways of being a pleasure or an instance of knowledge—which must be examined first before one
can determine the value of pleasure and knowledge, and so resolve the question
of their respective places in the best life. This leads to a lengthy defense of the
basic philosophical method of looking to unity-in-plurality in coming to understand the nature of anything and to a metaphysical division (not easy to understand) of 'everything that actually exists now in the universe' into four basic
categories: the 'unlimited', 'limit', the 'mixture' of these two, and the 'cause' of
the mixture. These methodological and metaphysical passages should be studied
alongside the* Sophist's *theories about being and not being, and the method of
division exemplified and discussed in* Sophist *and* Statesman. *There follows a
delineation and examination of various genera of pleasure and then of knowledge, including a controversial discussion of some pleasures as 'false' ones. Finally, we reach the 'mixed' life and its ordering principle.*

The dialogue ends, as it began, in mediis rebus: Protarchus *is not ready to
let Socrates off; more points require to be dealt with. But which ones? That is
left for the reader to ponder.*

J.M.C.

SOCRATES: Well, then, Protarchus, consider just what the thesis is that   11
you are now taking over from Philebus—and what *our* thesis is that you
are going to argue against, if you find that you do not agree with it. Shall   b
we summarize them both?

PROTARCHUS: Yes, let's do that.

SOCRATES: Philebus holds that what is good for all creatures is to enjoy
themselves, to be pleased and delighted, and whatever else goes together
with that kind of thing. We contend that not these, but knowing, understanding, and remembering, and what belongs with them, right opinion
and true calculations, are better than pleasure and more agreeable to all   c
who can attain them; those who can, get the maximum benefit possible
from having them, both those now alive and future generations. Isn't that
how we present our respective positions, Philebus?

PHILEBUS: Absolutely, Socrates.

SOCRATES: Do you agree, Protarchus, to take over this thesis that's now
offered you?

PROTARCHUS: I am afraid I have to. Fair Philebus has given up on us.

SOCRATES: So we must do everything possible to get through somehow
to the truth about these matters?

PROTARCHUS: We certainly must.   d

SOCRATES: Come on, then. Here is a further point we need to agree on.

Translated by Dorothea Frede.

PROTARCHUS: What is that?

SOCRATES: That each of us will be trying to prove some possession or state of the soul to be the one that can render life happy for all human beings. Isn't that so?

PROTARCHUS: Quite so.

SOCRATES: You, that it is pleasure; we, that it is knowledge?

PROTARCHUS: That is so.

e   SOCRATES: What if it should turn out that there is another possession, better than either of them? Would the result not be that, if it turns out to be more closely related to pleasure, we will both lose out against a life
12 that firmly possesses that, but the life of pleasure will defeat the life of knowledge?

PROTARCHUS: Yes.

SOCRATES: And if it is closer to knowledge, then knowledge wins over pleasure, and pleasure loses? Do you accept this as agreed?

PROTARCHUS: It seems agreeable to me.

SOCRATES: But also to Philebus? Philebus, what do you say?

PHILEBUS: To my mind pleasure wins and always will win, no matter what. But you must see for yourself, Protarchus.

PROTARCHUS: But now you have handed over the argument to us, Philebus, you can no longer control the agreements we make with Socrates nor our disagreements.

b   PHILEBUS: You are right. I absolve myself of all responsibility and now call the goddess herself as my witness.

PROTARCHUS: We will be your witnesses, too,—that you did say what you are now saying. As to what follows, Socrates, let us go ahead and try to push through to a conclusion, with Philebus' consent or not.

SOCRATES: We must do our best, making our start with the goddess herself—this fellow claims that though she is called Aphrodite her truest name is pleasure.

PROTARCHUS: Certainly.

c   SOCRATES: I always feel a more than human dread over what names to use for the gods—it surpasses the greatest fear.[1] So now I address Aphrodite by whatever title pleases her. But as to pleasure, I know that it is complex and, just as I said, we must make it our starting point and consider carefully what sort of nature it has. If one just goes by the name it is one single thing, but in fact it comes in many forms that are in some way even quite unlike each other. Think about it: we say that a debauched person gets
d   pleasure, as well as that a sober-minded person takes pleasure in his very sobriety. Again, we say that a fool, though full of foolish opinions and hopes, gets pleasure, but likewise a wise man takes pleasure in his wisdom. But surely anyone who said in either case that these pleasures are like one another would rightly be regarded as a fool.

1. Cf. *Cratylus* 400d–401a.

PROTARCHUS: Well, yes, Socrates—the pleasures come from opposite things. But *they* are not at all opposed to one another. For how could pleasure not be, of all things, most like pleasure? How could that thing not be most like itself?

SOCRATES: Just as color is most like color! Really, you surprise me: Colors certainly won't differ insofar as every one of them is a color; but we all know that black is not only different from white but is in fact its very opposite. And shape is most like shape in the same way. For shape is all one in genus, but some of its parts are absolutely opposite to one another, and others differ in innumerable ways. And we will discover many other such cases. So don't rely on this argument which makes a unity of all the things that are most opposed. I am afraid we will find there are some pleasures that are contrary to others.

PROTARCHUS: Maybe so. But how will this harm our thesis?

SOCRATES: Because you call these unlike things, we will say, by a different name. For you say that all pleasant things are *good*. Now, no one contends that pleasant things are not pleasant. But while most of them are bad but some good, as we hold, you nevertheless call them all good, even though you would admit that they are unlike one another if someone pressed the point. What is the common element in the good and bad pleasures that allows you to call them all good?

PROTARCHUS: What are you saying, Socrates? Do you think anyone will agree to this who begins by laying it down that pleasure is the good? Do you think he will accept it when you say that some pleasures are good but others are bad?

SOCRATES: But you will grant that they are *unlike* each other and that some are opposites?

PROTARCHUS: Not insofar as they are pleasures.

SOCRATES: But really, Protarchus, this takes us back to the same old point. Are we, then, to say that pleasure does not differ from pleasure, but all are alike? Don't the examples just given make the slightest impression on us? Are we to behave and speak in just the same way as those who are the most incompetent and at the same time newcomers in such discussions?

PROTARCHUS: What way do you mean?

SOCRATES: This: Suppose I imitate you and dare to say, in defense of my thesis, that the most unlike thing is of all things most *like* the most unlike; then I could say the same thing as you did. But this would make us look quite childish, and our discussion would founder on the rock. Let us therefore set it afloat again. Perhaps we can reach a mutual accommodation if each side accepts a similar stance toward its candidate.

PROTARCHUS: Just tell me how.

SOCRATES: Let me be the one questioned in turn by you.

PROTARCHUS: About what?

SOCRATES: About wisdom, knowledge, understanding, and all the things that I laid down at the beginning as good, when I tried to answer the question what is good. Won't my answer suffer the same consequences as your thesis did?

PROTARCHUS: How so?

SOCRATES: Taken all together, the branches of knowledge will seem to be a plurality, and some will seem quite unlike others. And if some of them turn out in some way actually to be opposites, would I be a worthy partner in a discussion if I dreaded this so much that I would deny that one kind of knowledge can be unlike another? That way our whole discussion would come to an end like that of a fairy tale—with us kept safe and sound through some absurdity.

PROTARCHUS: We must not let that happen, except the part about our being kept safe and sound. But I am rather pleased by the fact that our theses are on the same footing. So let it be agreed that there can be many and unlike kinds of pleasures, but also many and different kinds of knowledge.

SOCRATES: Well, then, let us not cover up the difference between your good and mine, Protarchus, but put it right in the middle and brave the possibility that, when put to a closer scrutiny, it will come to light whether pleasure should be called the good, or wisdom, or yet a third thing. For we are not contending here out of love of victory for my suggestion to win or for yours. We ought to act together as allies in support of the truest one.

PROTARCHUS: We certainly ought to.

SOCRATES: Let us then give even stronger support to our principle by an agreement.

PROTARCHUS: What principle?

SOCRATES: The one that creates difficulties for everyone, for some willingly, for some, sometimes, against their will.

PROTARCHUS: Explain this more clearly.

SOCRATES: It is this principle that has turned up here, which somehow has an amazing nature. For that the many are one and the one many are amazing statements, and can easily be disputed, whichever side of the two one may want to defend.

PROTARCHUS: Do you mean this in the sense that someone says that I, Protarchus, am one by nature but then also says that there are many 'me's' and even contrary ones, when he treats me, who am one and the same, as tall and short, heavy and light, and endless other such things?

SOCRATES: You, dear Protarchus, are speaking about those puzzles about the one and many that have become commonplace. They are agreed by everybody, so to speak, to be no longer even worth touching; they are considered childish and trivial but a serious impediment to argument if one takes them on. No more worthy is the following quibble: when someone who first distinguishes a person's limbs and parts asks your agreement that all these parts are identical with that unity, but then exposes you to ridicule because of the monstrosities you have to admit, that the one is many and indefinitely many, and again that the many are only one thing.

PROTARCHUS: But what other kinds of such puzzles with respect to the same principle do you have in mind, Socrates, that have not yet admittedly become commonplace?

SOCRATES: When, my young friend, the *one* is not taken from the things that come to be or perish, as we have just done in our example. For that is where the sort of one belongs that we were just discussing, which we agreed is not worthy of scrutiny. But when someone tries to posit man as one, or ox as one, or the beautiful as one, and the good as one, zealous concern with divisions of these unities and the like gives rise to controversy. 15

PROTARCHUS: In what sense?

SOCRATES: Firstly, whether one ought to suppose that there are any such b unities truly in existence. Then again, how they are supposed to be: whether each one of them is always one and the same, admitting neither of generation nor of destruction; and whether it remains most definitely one and the same, even though it is afterwards found again among the things that come to be and are unlimited, so that it finds itself as one and the same in one and many things at the same time.[2] And must it be treated as dispersed and multiplied or as entirely separated from itself, which would seem most impossible of all? It is these problems of the one and many, c but not those others, Protarchus, that cause all sorts of difficulties if they are not properly settled, but promise progress if they are.

PROTARCHUS: Is this the first task we should try our hands at right now, Socrates?

SOCRATES: So I would say at least.

PROTARCHUS: Take it, then, that we all here are agreed with you about this. As for Philebus, it might be best not to bother him with questions any further, but let sleeping dogs lie.

SOCRATES: Quite so. Now, where should we make our entry into that d complex and wide-ranging battle about this controversial issue? Is it not best to start here?

PROTARCHUS: Where?

SOCRATES: By making the point that it is through *discourse* that the same thing flits around, becoming one and many in all sorts of ways, in whatever it may be that is said at any time, both long ago and now. And this will never come to an end, nor has it just begun, but it seems to me that this is an "immortal and ageless" condition[3] that comes to us with discourse. Whoever among the young first gets a taste of it is as pleased as if he had e found a treasure of wisdom. He is quite beside himself with pleasure and

---

2. Reading Burnet's text, but replacing his interrogation mark at b4 with a comma, on the assumption that there are two rather than three problems addressed.

3. Socrates uses the customary epithet of the gods (cf. *Iliad* viii.539) to show how serious the problem is. The ambiguity of language, whether words have a unitary and unchangeable meaning, is a serious problem with a flip side that is exploited by the boys who make fun of it.

revels in moving every statement, now turning it to one side and rolling it all up into one, then again unrolling it and dividing it up. He thereby involves first and foremost himself in confusion, but then also whatever others happen to be nearby, be they younger or older or of the same age,

16   sparing neither his father nor his mother nor anyone else who might listen to him. He would almost try it on other creatures, not only on human beings, since he would certainly not spare any foreigner if only he could find an interpreter somewhere.[4]

PROTARCHUS: Careful, Socrates, don't you see what a crowd we are and that we are all young? And are you not afraid that we will gang up against you with Philebus if you insult us? Still, we know what you want to say, and if there are some ways and means to remove this kind of disturbance

b   from our discussion in a peaceful way, and to show us a better solution to the problem, then just go ahead, and we will follow you as best we can. For the present question is no mean thing, Socrates.

SOCRATES: It certainly is not, my boys, as Philebus is wont to address you. Indeed, there is not, nor could there be, any way that is finer than the one I have always admired, although it has often escaped me and left me behind, alone and helpless.

PROTARCHUS: What is this way? Let us have it.

c   SOCRATES: It is not very difficult to describe it, but extremely difficult to use. For everything in any field of art that has ever been discovered has come to light because of this. See what way I have in mind.

PROTARCHUS: Please do tell us.

SOCRATES: It is a gift of the gods to men, or so it seems to me, hurled down from heaven by some Prometheus along with a most dazzling fire. And the people of old, superior to us and living in closer proximity to the

d   gods, have bequeathed us this tale, that whatever is said to be consists of one and many, having in its nature limit and unlimitedness. Since this is the structure of things, we have to assume that there is in each case always one form for every one of them, and we must search for it, as we will indeed find it there. And once we have grasped it, we must look for two, as the case would have it, or if not, for three or some other number. And we must treat every one of those further unities in the same way, until it is not only established of the original unit that it is one, many and unlimited, but also how many kinds it is. For we must not grant the form of the unlimited to the plurality before we know the exact number of every

e   plurality that lies between the unlimited and the one. Only then is it permitted to release each kind of unity into the unlimited and let it go. The gods, as I said, have left us this legacy of how to inquire and learn

---

4. This description of the exploitation of the problem by naughty boys recalls strikingly (even in the words used) Socrates' explanation of why boys should not have access to dialectic (*R.* 539b). The image there is of a dog tearing around and shredding things to pieces, while here Socrates seems to be thinking of the spreading out or rolling together

and teach one another. But nowadays the clever ones among us make a
one, haphazardly, and a many, faster or slower than they should; they go   17
straight from the one to the unlimited and omit the intermediates. It is
these, however, that make all the difference as to whether we are engaged
with each other in dialectical or only in eristic discourse.

PROTARCHUS: Some of what you said I think I understand in some way,
Socrates, but of some I still need further clarification.

SOCRATES: What I mean is clear in the case of letters, and you should
take your clue from them, since they were part of your own education.   b

PROTARCHUS: How so?

SOCRATES: The sound that comes out of the mouth is one for each and
every one of us, but then it is also unlimited in number.

PROTARCHUS: No doubt.

SOCRATES: Neither of these two facts alone yet makes us knowledgeable,
neither that we know its unlimitedness nor its unity. But if we know how
many kinds of vocal sounds there are and what their nature is, that makes
every one of us literate.

PROTARCHUS: Very true.

SOCRATES: And the very same thing leads to the knowledge of music.

PROTARCHUS: How is that?

SOCRATES: Sound is also the unit in this art, just as it was in writing.   c

PROTARCHUS: Yes, right.

SOCRATES: We should posit low and high pitch as two kinds, and equal
pitch as a third kind. Or what would you say?

PROTARCHUS: Just that.

SOCRATES: But you could not yet claim knowledge of music if you knew
only this much, though if you were ignorant even about that, you would
be quite incompetent in these matters, as one might say.

PROTARCHUS: Certainly.

SOCRATES: But you will be competent, my friend, once you have learned
how many intervals there are in high pitch and low pitch, what character
they have, by what notes the intervals are defined, and the kinds of   d
combinations they form—all of which our forebears have discovered and
left to us, their successors, together with the names of these modes of
harmony. And again the motions of the body display other and similar
characteristics of this kind, which they say should be measured by numbers
and called rhythms and meters. So at the same time they have made us
realize that every investigation should search for the one and many. For
when you have mastered these things in this way, then you have acquired   e
expertise there, and when you have grasped the unity of any of the other
things there are, you have become wise about that. The boundless multitude, however, in any and every kind of subject leaves you in boundless

---

of dough (or perhaps wool). Cf. also the remarks on the feasts for young boys and late-
learners in *Sophist* 252a–c.

ignorance, and makes you count for nothing and amount to nothing, since you have never worked out the amount and number of anything at all.

PROTARCHUS: For my part, I think that Socrates has explained all this very well, Philebus.

18   PHILEBUS: I agree as far as this question itself goes. But of what use is all this talk to us, and what is its purpose?

SOCRATES: Philebus is right, Protarchus, when he asks us this question.

PROTARCHUS: Good, so please answer him.

SOCRATES: I will do so when I have gone a little further into the subject matter. Just as someone who has got hold of some unity or other should not, as we were saying, immediately look for the unlimited kind but first look for some number, so the same holds for the reverse case. For if he is forced to start out with the unlimited, then he should not head straight

b   for the one, but should in each case grasp some number that determines every plurality whatever, and from all of those finally reach the one. Let us again make use of letters to explain what this means.

PROTARCHUS: In what way?

SOCRATES: The way some god or god-inspired man discovered that vocal sound is unlimited, as tradition in Egypt claims for a certain deity called Theuth. He was the first to discover that the vowels in that unlimited

c   variety are not one but several, and again that there are others that are not voiced, but make some kind of noise, and that they, too, have a number. As a third kind of letters he established the ones we now call mute. After this he further subdivided the ones without sound or mutes down to every single unit. In the same fashion he also dealt with the vowels and the intermediates, until he had found out the number for each one of them, and then he gave all of them together the name "letter." And as he realized that none of us could gain any knowledge of a single one of them, taken

d   by itself without understanding them all, he considered that the one link that somehow unifies them all and called it the art of literacy.

PHILEBUS: Protarchus, I understood this even better than what came before, at least how it hangs together. But I still find that this explanation now suffers from the same defect as your earlier one.

SOCRATES: You are wondering again what the relevance of it all is, Philebus?

PHILEBUS: Right, that is what I and Protarchus have been wanting to see for quite a while.

SOCRATES: But have you not already under your nose what you both, as

e   you say, have long wanted to see?

PHILEBUS: How could that be?

SOCRATES: Did we not embark on an investigation of knowledge and pleasure, to find out which of the two is preferable?

PHILEBUS: Yes, indeed.

SOCRATES: And we do say that each of them is one.

PHILEBUS: Right.

SOCRATES: This is the very point in question to which our preceding discussion obliges us to give an answer: to show how each of them is one

and many, and how instead of becoming unlimited straightaway, each   19
one of them acquires some definite number before it becomes unlimited.

PROTARCHUS: Socrates has plunged us into a considerable problem, Philebus, by leading us around, I don't know how, in some kind of circle. But
make up your mind which of us should answer the present question. It
would seem quite ridiculous that I, who had volunteered to take over the
thesis from you as your successor, should now hand it back to you because
I don't have an answer to this question. But it would be even more ridiculous if neither of us could answer it. So what do you think we should do?   b
Socrates seems to be asking whether there are *kinds* of pleasures or not,
and how many there are, and of what sort they are. And the same set of
questions applies to knowledge.

SOCRATES: You speak the truth, son of Callias. Unless we are able to do
this for every kind of unity, similarity, sameness, and their opposite, in
the way that our recent discussion has indicated, none of us will ever turn
out to be any good at anything.

PROTARCHUS: I am afraid that this is so. But while it is a great thing for   c
the wise man to know everything, the second best is not to be mistaken
about oneself, it seems to me. What prompts me to say that at this point?
I will tell you. You, Socrates, have granted this meeting to all of us, and
yourself to boot, in order to find out what is the best of all human possessions. Now, Philebus advocated that it is pleasure, amusement, enjoyment,
and whatever else there is of this kind. You on the contrary denied this
for all of them, but rather proposed those other goods we willingly and   d
with good reason keep reminding ourselves of, so that they can be tested
as they are lying side by side in our memory. You claim, it seems, that
the good that should by right be called superior to pleasure, at least, is
reason, as well as knowledge, intelligence, science, and everything that is
akin to them, which must be obtained, rather than Philebus' candidates.
Now, after both these conflicting positions have been set up against each   e
other, we threatened you in jest that we would not let you go home before
the deliberation of these questions had reached its satisfactory limit. But
since you made a promise and committed yourself to us, we therefore
insist, like children, that there is no taking back a gift properly given. So
give up this way of turning against us in the discussion here.

SOCRATES: What way are you talking about?

PROTARCHUS: Your way of plunging us into difficulties and repeating   20
questions to which we have at present no proper answer to give you. But
we should not take it that the aim of our meeting is universal confusion;
if we cannot solve the problem, you must do it, for you promised. It is
up to you to decide whether for this purpose you need to divide off
different kinds of pleasure and knowledge or can leave that out, if you
are able and willing to show some other way to settle the issues of our controversy.

SOCRATES: At least there is no longer anything terrible in store for poor   b
me, since you said it this way. For the clause "if you are willing" takes

away all further apprehension. In addition, some memory has come to my mind that one of the gods seems to have sent me to help us.

PROTARCHUS: How is that and what about?

SOCRATES: It is a doctrine that once upon a time I heard in a dream—or perhaps I was awake—that I remember now, concerning pleasure and knowledge, that neither of the two is the good, but that there is some third

c thing which is different from and superior to both of them. But if we can clearly conceive now that this is the case, then pleasure has lost its bid for victory. For the good could no longer turn out to be identical with it. Right?

PROTARCHUS: Right.

SOCRATES: So we will not have to worry any longer, I think, about the division of the kinds of pleasure. But further progress will show this more clearly.

PROTARCHUS: Very well said; just push on.

SOCRATES: There are some small matters we ought to agree on first, though.

PROTARCHUS: What are they?

d SOCRATES: Whether the good is necessarily bound to be perfect or not perfect.

PROTARCHUS: But surely it must be the most perfect thing of all, Socrates!

SOCRATES: Further: must the good be sufficient?

PROTARCHUS: How could it fail to be that? This is how it is superior to everything else there is.

SOCRATES: Now, this point, I take it, is most necessary to assert of the good: that everything that has any notion of it hunts for it and desires to get hold of it and secure it for its very own, caring nothing for anything else except for what is connected with the acquisition of some good.

PROTARCHUS: There is no way of denying this.

e SOCRATES: So let us put the life of pleasure and the life of knowledge on trial, and reach some verdict by looking at them separately.

PROTARCHUS: In what way do you mean?

SOCRATES: Let there be neither any knowledge in a life of pleasure, nor any pleasure in that of knowledge. For if either of the two is the good, then it must have no need of anything in addition. But if one or the other

21 should turn out to be lacking anything, then this can definitely no longer be the real good we are looking for.

PROTARCHUS: How could it be?

SOCRATES: So shall we then use *you* as our test case to try both of them?

PROTARCHUS: By all means.

SOCRATES: Then answer me.

PROTARCHUS: Go ahead.

SOCRATES: Would you find it acceptable to live your whole life in enjoyment of the greatest pleasures?

PROTARCHUS: Why, certainly!

SOCRATES: And would you see yourself in need of anything else if you had secured this altogether?

PROTARCHUS: In no way.

SOCRATES: But look, might you not have some need of knowledge, intelligence, and calculation, or anything else that is related to them?[5]

PROTARCHUS: How so? If I had pleasure I would have all in all!

SOCRATES: And living like that you could enjoy the greatest pleasures throughout your life?

PROTARCHUS: Why should I not?

SOCRATES: Since you would not be in possession of either reason, memory, knowledge, or true opinion, must you not be in ignorance, first of all, about this very question, whether you were enjoying yourself or not, given that you were devoid of any kind of intelligence?

PROTARCHUS: Necessarily.

SOCRATES: Moreover, due to lack of memory, it would be impossible for you to remember that you ever enjoyed yourself, and for any pleasure to survive from one moment to the next, since it would leave no memory. But, not possessing right judgment, you would not realize that you are enjoying yourself even while you do, and, being unable to calculate, you could not figure out any future pleasures for yourself. You would thus not live a human life but the life of a mollusk or of one of those creatures in shells that live in the sea. Is this what would happen, or can we think of any other consequences besides these?

PROTARCHUS: How could we?

SOCRATES: But is this a life worth choosing?

PROTARCHUS: Socrates, this argument has left me absolutely speechless for the moment.

SOCRATES: Even so, let us not give in to weakness; let us in turn rather inspect the life of reason.

PROTARCHUS: What kind of life do you have in mind?

SOCRATES: Whether any one of us would choose to live in possession of every kind of intelligence, reason, knowledge, and memory of all things, while having no part, neither large nor small, of pleasure or of pain, living in total insensitivity of anything of that kind.

PROTARCHUS: To me at least neither of these two forms of life seems worthy of choice, nor would it to anyone else, I presume.

SOCRATES: But what about a combination of both, Protarchus, a life that results from a mixture of the two?

PROTARCHUS: You mean a mixture of pleasure with reason and intelligence?

SOCRATES: Right, those are the ingredients I mean.

PROTARCHUS: Everybody would certainly prefer this life to either of the other two, without exception.

SOCRATES: Do we realize what the upshot of this new development in our discussion is?

5. Accepting the deletion of *ta deonta*.

PROTARCHUS: Certainly, that of the three lives offered to us, two are not
b   sufficient or worthy of choice for either man or animal.

SOCRATES: As far as they are concerned, is it then not clear at least, that
neither the one nor the other contained the good, since otherwise it would
be sufficient, perfect, and worthy of choice for any of the plants and animals
that can sustain them, throughout their lifetime? And if anyone among us
should choose otherwise, then he would do so involuntarily, in opposition
to what is by nature truly choiceworthy, from ignorance or some unfortunate necessity.

PROTARCHUS: It certainly looks that way.

c   SOCRATES: Enough has been said, it seems to me, to prove that Philebus'
goddess and the good cannot be regarded as one.[6]

PHILEBUS: Nor is your reason the good, Socrates, and the same complaint
applies to it.

SOCRATES: It may apply to *my* reason, Philebus, but certainly not to the
true, the divine reason, I should think. It is in quite a different condition.
But now I am not arguing that reason ought to get first prize over and
d   against the combined life; we have rather to look and make up our minds
about the second prize, how to dispose of it. One of us may want to give
credit for the combined life to reason, making it responsible, the other to
pleasure. Thus neither of the two would be the good, but it could be
assumed that one or the other of them is its *cause*. But I would be even
more ready to contend against Philebus that, whatever the ingredient in
the mixed life may be that makes it choiceworthy and good, reason is
more closely related to that thing and more like it than pleasure; and if
e   this can be upheld, neither first nor second prize could really ever be
claimed for pleasure. She will in fact not even get as much as third prize,
if we can put some trust in my insight for now.

PROTARCHUS: By now it seems to me indeed that pleasure has been
defeated as if knocked down by your present arguments, Socrates. In her
23   fight for victory, she has fallen. And as for reason, we may say that it
wisely did not compete for first prize, for it would have suffered the
same fate. But if pleasure were also deprived of second prize, she would
definitely be somewhat dishonored in the eyes of her own lovers, nor
would she seem as fair to them as before.

SOCRATES: What, then? Had we not better leave her alone now, rather
than subject her to the most exacting test and give her pain by such
an examination?

PROTARCHUS: You talk nonsense, Socrates.

b   SOCRATES: Why, because I said the impossible, "giving pain to pleasure"?

PROTARCHUS: Not only that, but because you don't realize that not one
among us would let you go before you have carried the discussion of these
questions to its end.

---

6. See 12b ff.

SOCRATES: Oh dear, Protarchus, then a long discussion lies ahead of us, and not exactly an easy one either at this point. For it seems that, in the battle about the second prize for reason, a different device will be needed, different armament as it were, from that used in our previous discussion, though it may partly be the same. Are we to proceed?

PROTARCHUS: Of course.

SOCRATES: Let us be very careful about the starting point we take.   c

PROTARCHUS: What kind of starting point?

SOCRATES: Let us make a division of everything that actually exists now in the universe into two kinds, or if this seems preferable, into three.

PROTARCHUS: Could you explain on what principle?

SOCRATES: By taking up some of what has been said before.

PROTARCHUS: Like what?

SOCRATES: We agreed earlier that the god had revealed a division of what is into the unlimited and the limit.[7]

PROTARCHUS: Certainly.

SOCRATES: Let us now take these as two of the kinds, while treating the one that results from the mixture of these two as our third kind. But I must   d look like quite a fool with my distinctions into kinds and enumerations!

PROTARCHUS: What are you driving at?

SOCRATES: That we seem to be in need of yet a fourth kind.

PROTARCHUS: Tell us what it is.

SOCRATES: Look at the cause of this combination of those two together, and posit it as my fourth kind in addition to those three.

PROTARCHUS: Might you not also be in need of a fifth kind that provides for their separation?

SOCRATES: Perhaps, but I do not think so, at least for now. But if it turns out that I need it, I gather you will bear with me if I should search for a   e fifth kind.

PROTARCHUS: Gladly.

SOCRATES: Let us first take up three of the four, and since we observe that of two of them, both are split up and dispersed into many, let's make an effort to collect those into a unity again, in order to study how each of them is in fact one and many.

PROTARCHUS: If you could explain all that more clearly, I might be able to follow you.

SOCRATES: What I mean is this: The two kinds are the ones I referred to   24 just now, the unlimited and what has limit. That the unlimited in a way is many I will try to explain now. The treatment of what has limit will have to wait a little longer.

PROTARCHUS: Let it wait.

SOCRATES: Attention, then. The matter I am asking you to attend to is difficult and controversial, but attend to it nevertheless. Check first in the case of the hotter and the colder whether you can conceive of a limit, or

---

7. See 16c.

b whether the 'more and less' do not rather reside in these kinds, and while they reside in them do not permit the attainment of any end. For once an end has been reached, they will both have been ended as well.

PROTARCHUS: Very true.

SOCRATES: We are agreed, then, that the hotter and the colder always contain the more and less.

PROTARCHUS: Quite definitely.

SOCRATES: Our argument forces us to conclude that these things never have an end. And since they are endless, they turn out to be entirely unlimited.

PROTARCHUS: Quite strongly so, Socrates.

SOCRATES: You have grasped this rather well, Protarchus, and remind
c me rightly with your pronouncement of 'strongly' that it and equally its counterpart 'gently' are of the same caliber as the more and less. Wherever they apply, they prevent everything from adopting a definite quantity; by imposing on all actions the qualification 'stronger' relative to 'gentler' or the reverse, they procure a 'more and less' while doing away with all definite quantity. We are saying now, in effect, that if they do not abolish definite quantity, but let quantity and measurement take a foothold in the
d domain of the more and less, the strong and mild, they will be driven out of their own territory. For once they take on a definite quantity, they would no longer be hotter and colder. The hotter and equally the colder are always in flux and never remain, while definite quantity means standstill and the end of all progression. The upshot of this argument is that the hotter, together with its opposite, turn out to be unlimited.

PROTARCHUS: That seems to be its result, Socrates, although, as you said yourself, it is difficult to follow in these matters. But if they are repeated
e again and again, perhaps both questioner and respondent may end up in a satisfactory state of agreement.

SOCRATES: A good idea; let us carry it out. But consider whether, to avoid the needless length of going through a complete survey of all cases, the following indication may serve to mark out the nature of the unlimited.

PROTARCHUS: What indication do you have in mind?

SOCRATES: Whatever seems to us to become 'more and less', or susceptible to 'strong and mild' or to 'too much' and all of that kind, all that we
25 ought to subsume under the genus of the unlimited as its unity. This is in compliance with the principle we agreed on before, that for whatever is dispersed and split up into a multitude, we must try to work out its unifying nature as far as we can, if you remember.

PROTARCHUS: I do remember.

SOCRATES: But look now at what does not admit of these qualifications but rather their opposites, first of all 'the equal' and 'equality' and, after
b the equal, things like 'double', and all that is related as number to number or measure to measure: If we subsume all these together under the heading of 'limit', we would seem to do a fair job. Or what do you say?

PROTARCHUS: A very fair job, Socrates.

SOCRATES: Very well, then. But what nature shall we ascribe to the third kind, the one that is the mixture of the two?

PROTARCHUS: You will have to answer that question for me, I think.

SOCRATES: A god rather, if any of them should listen to my prayers.

PROTARCHUS: So say your prayer, and wait for the result.

SOCRATES: I am waiting, and indeed I have the feeling that one of the gods is favorably disposed to us now, Protarchus.

PROTARCHUS: What do you mean by that, and what evidence have you?   c

SOCRATES: I certainly will tell you, but you follow closely what I say.

PROTARCHUS: Just go on.

SOCRATES: We called something hotter and colder just now, didn't we?

PROTARCHUS: Yes.

SOCRATES: Now add dryer and wetter to them, and more and less, faster and slower, taller and shorter, and whatever else we have previously collected together as the one kind that has the nature of taking on the 'more and less'.

PROTARCHUS: You mean the nature of the unlimited?   d

SOCRATES: Yes. Now take the next step and mix with it the class of the limit.

PROTARCHUS: Which one?

SOCRATES: The very one we have so far omitted to collect together, the class that has the character of limit, although we ought to have given unity to it, just as we collected together the unlimited kind. But perhaps it will come to the same thing even now if, through the collection of these two kinds, the unity of the former kind becomes conspicuous too.

PROTARCHUS: What kind do you mean, and how is this supposed to work?

SOCRATES: The kind that contains equal and double, and whatever else puts an end to the conflicts there are among opposites, making them   e
commensurate and harmonious by imposing a definite number on them.

PROTARCHUS: I understand. I have the impression that you are saying that, from such mixture in each case, certain generations result?

SOCRATES: Your impression is correct.

PROTARCHUS: Then go on with your explanation.

SOCRATES: Is it not true that in sickness the right combination of the opposites establishes the state of health?

PROTARCHUS: Certainly.   26

SOCRATES: And does not the same happen in the case of the high and the low, the fast and the slow, which belong to the unlimited? Is it not the presence of these factors in them[8] which forges a limit and thereby creates the different kinds of music in their perfection?

PROTARCHUS: Beautiful!

SOCRATES: And once engendered in frost and heat, limit takes away their excesses and unlimitedness, and establishes moderation and harmony in that domain?

---

8. Retaining *eggignomena* in the text at 26a3, and leaving out the colon after *tauta*.

PROTARCHUS: Quite.

b   SOCRATES: And when the unlimited and what has limit are mixed together, we are blessed with seasons and all sorts of fine things of that kind?

PROTARCHUS: Who could doubt it?

SOCRATES: And there are countless other things I have to pass by in
silence: With health there come beauty and strength, and again in our soul
there is a host of other excellent qualities. It is the goddess herself, fair
Philebus, who recognizes how excess and the overabundance of our wickedness allow for no limit in our pleasures and their fulfillment, and she

c   therefore imposes law and order as a limit on them. And while you may
complain that this ruins them, I by contrast call it their salvation. How
does this strike you, Protarchus?

PROTARCHUS: This fits my own intuitions, Socrates.

SOCRATES: These, then, are the three kinds I spoke of, if you see what
I mean.

PROTARCHUS: I think I've got it. It seems to me that you are referring to
the unlimited as one kind, to the limit within things as the other, second
kind. But I still do not sufficiently understand what you mean by the third.

SOCRATES: You are simply overwhelmed by the abundance of the third

d   kind,[9] my admirable friend. Although the class of the unlimited also displays a multiplicity, it preserved at least the appearance of unity, since it
was marked out by the common character of the more and less.

PROTARCHUS: That is true.

SOCRATES: About limit, on the other hand, we did not trouble ourselves,[10]
neither that it has plurality nor whether it is one by nature.

PROTARCHUS: Why should we have done so?

SOCRATES: No reason. But see what I mean by the third kind: I treat all
the joint offspring of the other two kinds as a unity, a coming-into-being
created through the measures imposed by the limit.

PROTARCHUS: I understand.

e   SOCRATES: But now we have to look at the fourth kind we mentioned
earlier, in addition to these three. Let this be our joint investigation. See
now whether you think it necessary that everything that comes to be comes
to be through some cause?

PROTARCHUS: Certainly, as far as I can see. How could anything come
to be without one?

SOCRATES: And is it not the case that there is no difference between the
nature of what *makes* and the *cause*, except in name, so that the maker and
the cause would rightly be called one?

PROTARCHUS: Right.

---

9. Lit., "of the genesis of the third [kind]": The third kind is described just below as a
"coming-into-being," lit. "genesis into [a?] being." See further 53c–55d below, where the
word for "genesis" is translated "(process of) generation."

10. Adopting the insertion of *hoti* before *polla* at d4.

SOCRATES: But what about what is made and what comes into being, will we not find the same situation, that they also do not differ except in name?

PROTARCHUS: Exactly.

SOCRATES: And isn't it the case that what makes is always leading in the order of nature, while the thing made follows since it comes into being through it?

PROTARCHUS: Right.

SOCRATES: Therefore the cause and what is subservient to the cause in a process of coming to be are also different and not the same?

PROTARCHUS: How should they be?

SOCRATES: It follows, then, that what comes to be and that from which it is produced represent all three kinds?

PROTARCHUS: Very true.

SOCRATES: We therefore declare that the craftsman who produces all these must be the fourth kind, the cause, since it has been demonstrated sufficiently that it differs from the others?

PROTARCHUS: It certainly is different.

SOCRATES: Now that the four kinds have been distinguished, it seems right to go through them one by one, for memory's sake.

PROTARCHUS: Of course.

SOCRATES: As the first I count the unlimited, limit as the second, afterwards in third place comes the being which is mixed and generated out of those two. And no mistake is made if the cause of this mixture and generation is counted as number four?

PROTARCHUS: How could there be one?

SOCRATES: Now, let's see, what is going to be our next point after this, and what concern of ours got us to this point? Was it not this? We were wondering whether second prize should be awarded to pleasure or to knowledge, wasn't that it?[11]

PROTARCHUS: It was indeed.

SOCRATES: On the basis of our fourfold distinction we may now perhaps be in a better position to come to a decision about the first and the second prize, the issue that started our whole debate.

PROTARCHUS: Perhaps.

SOCRATES: Let us continue, then. We declared the life that combines pleasure and knowledge the winner. Didn't we?

PROTARCHUS: We did.

SOCRATES: Should we not take a look at this life and see what it is and to which kind it belongs?

PROTARCHUS: Nothing to prevent us.

SOCRATES: We will, I think, assign it to the third kind, for it is not a mixture of just two elements but of the sort where all that is unlimited is

27

b

c

d

11. See 22a ff.

tied down by limit.[12] It would seem right, then, to make our victorious form of life part of that kind.

PROTARCHUS: Very right.

e   SOCRATES: That is settled, then. But how about your kind of life, Philebus, which is pleasant and unmixed? To which of the established kinds should it by right be assigned? But before you make your pronouncement, answer me the following question.

PHILEBUS: Just tell me!

SOCRATES: Do pleasure and pain have a limit, or are they of the sort that admit the more and less?

PHILEBUS: Certainly the sort that admit the more, Socrates! For how could pleasure be all that is good if it were not by nature boundless in plenty and increase?

28   SOCRATES: Nor would, on the other hand, pain be all that is bad, Philebus! So we have to search for something besides its unlimited character that would bestow on pleasures a share of the good. But take note that pleasure[13] is thereby assigned to the boundless. As to assigning intelligence, knowledge, and reason to one of our aforesaid kinds, how can we avoid the danger of blasphemy, Protarchus and Philebus? A lot seems to hinge on whether or not we give the right answer to this question.

b   PHILEBUS: Really now, you are extolling your own god, Socrates.

SOCRATES: Just as you extoll that goddess of yours, Philebus. But the question needs an answer, nevertheless.

PROTARCHUS: Socrates is right in this, Philebus; we must obey him.

PHILEBUS: Didn't you choose to speak instead of me?

PROTARCHUS: Quite. But now I am at a loss, and I entreat you, Socrates, to act as our spokesman, so that we do not misstate the case of your candidate and thus introduce a false note into the discussion.

c   SOCRATES: Your obedient servant, Protarchus, especially since it is not a very difficult task. But did my playful exaltation really confuse you, as Philebus claims, when I asked to what kind reason and knowledge belonged?

PROTARCHUS: It certainly did, Socrates.

SOCRATES: It is easy to settle, nevertheless. For all the wise are agreed, in true self-exaltation, that reason is our king, both over heaven and earth. And perhaps they are justified. But let us go into the discussion of this class itself at greater length, if you have no objections.

d   PROTARCHUS: Discuss it in whichever way you like, Socrates, and don't be apologetic about longwindedness; we will not lose patience.

SOCRATES: Well said. Let us proceed by taking up this question.

PROTARCHUS: What question?

SOCRATES: Whether we hold the view that the universe and this whole world order are ruled by unreason and irregularity, as chance would have

---

12. Reading *mikton ekeino*.

13. Accepting the correction of *touto* at 28a3 and retaining the mss. reading of *estō*.

it, or whether they are not rather, as our forebears taught us, governed by reason and by the order of a wonderful intelligence.

PROTARCHUS: How can you even think of a comparison here, Socrates? What you suggest now is downright impious, I would say. The only account that can do justice to the wonderful spectacle presented by the cosmic order of sun, moon, and stars and the revolution of the whole heaven, is that reason arranges it all, and I for my part would never waver in saying or believing it.

SOCRATES: Is this what you want us to do, that we should not only conform to the view of earlier thinkers who professed this as the truth, repeating without any risk what others have said, but that we should share their risk and blame if some formidable opponent denies it and argues that disorder rules?

PROTARCHUS: How could I fail to want it?

SOCRATES: Well, then, now face up to the consequences of this position that we have to come to terms with.

PROTARCHUS: Please tell me.

SOCRATES: We somehow discern that what makes up the nature of the bodies of all animals—fire, water, and air, "and earth!," as storm-battered sailors say—are part of their composition.

PROTARCHUS: Very much so. We are indeed battered by difficulties in our discussion.

SOCRATES: Come, now, and realize that the following applies to all constituents that belong to us.

PROTARCHUS: What is it?

SOCRATES: That the amount of each of these elements in us is small and insignificant, that it does not possess in the very least the purity or the power that is worthy of its nature. Take one example as an illustration representative for all. There is something called fire that belongs to us, and then again there is fire in the universe.

PROTARCHUS: No doubt.

SOCRATES: And is not the fire that belongs to us small in amount, feeble and poor, while the fire in the universe overwhelms us by its size and beauty and by the display of all its power?

PROTARCHUS: What you say is very true.

SOCRATES: But what about this? Is the fire in the universe generated, nourished, and ruled by the fire that belongs to us, or is it not quite the reverse, that your heat and mine, and that in every animal, owe all this to the cosmic fire?

PROTARCHUS: It is not even worth answering that question.

SOCRATES: Right. And I guess you will give the same answer about the earth here in the animals when it is compared to earth in the universe, and likewise about the other elements I mentioned a little earlier. Is that your answer?

PROTARCHUS: Who could answer differently without seeming insane?

SOCRATES: No one at all. But now see what follows. To the combination of all these elements taken as a unit we give the name "body," don't we?

PROTARCHUS: Certainly.

e   SOCRATES: Now, realize that the same holds in the case of what we call the ordered universe. It will turn out to be a body in the same sense, since it is composed of the same elements.

PROTARCHUS: What you say is undeniable.

SOCRATES: Does the body of the universe as a whole provide for the sustenance of what is body in our sphere, or is it the reverse, and the universe possesses and derives all the goods enumerated from ours?

PROTARCHUS: That too is a question not worth asking, Socrates.

30   SOCRATES: But what about the following, is this also a question not worth asking?

PROTARCHUS: Tell me what the question is.

SOCRATES: Of the body that belongs to us, will we not say that it has a soul?

PROTARCHUS: Quite obviously that is what we will say.

SOCRATES: But where does it come from, unless the body of the universe which has the same properties as ours, but more beautiful in all respects, happens to possess a soul?

PROTARCHUS: Clearly from nowhere else.

SOCRATES: We surely cannot maintain this assumption, with respect to

b   our four classes (limit, the unlimited, their mixture, and their cause—which is present in everything): that this cause is recognized as all-encompassing wisdom, since among us it imports the soul and provides training for the body and medicine for its ailments and in other cases order and restitution, but that it should fail to be responsible for the same things on a large scale in the whole universe (things that are, in addition, beautiful and pure), for the contrivance of what has so fair and wonderful a nature.

c   PROTARCHUS: That would make no sense at all.

SOCRATES: But if that is inconceivable, we had better pursue the alternative account and affirm, as we have said often, that there is plenty of the unlimited in the universe as well as sufficient limit, and that there is, above them, a certain cause, of no small significance, that orders and coordinates the years, seasons, and months, and which has every right to the title of wisdom and reason.

PROTARCHUS: The greatest right.

SOCRATES: But there could be no wisdom and reason without a soul.

PROTARCHUS: Certainly not.

d   SOCRATES: You will therefore say that in the nature of Zeus there is the soul of a king, as well as a king's reason, in virtue of this power displayed by the cause, while paying tribute for other fine qualities in the other divinities, in conformity with the names by which they like to be addressed.

PROTARCHUS: Very much so.

SOCRATES: Do not think that we have engaged in an idle discussion here, Protarchus, for it comes as a support for the thinkers of old who held the view that reason is forever the ruler over the universe.

PROTARCHUS: It certainly does.

SOCRATES: It also has provided an answer to my query, that reason

e   belongs to that kind which is the cause of everything. But that was one of our four kinds. So there you already have the solution to our problem in your hands.

PROTARCHUS: I have indeed, and quite to my satisfaction, although at first I did not realize that you were answering.

SOCRATES: Sometimes joking is a relief from seriousness.

PROTARCHUS: Well said.

SOCRATES: By now, dear friend, we have arrived at a satisfactory explana-   31
tion of the class that reason belongs to and what power it has.

PROTARCHUS: Quite so.

SOCRATES: And as to pleasure, it became apparent quite a while ago what class it belongs to.

PROTARCHUS: Definitely.

SOCRATES: Let us firmly keep it in mind about both of them, that reason is akin to cause and is part of that family, while pleasure itself is unlimited and belongs to the kind that in and by itself neither possesses nor will ever possess a beginning, middle, or end.

PROTARCHUS: We will keep it in mind, how could we help it?   b

SOCRATES: After this we must next find out in what kind of thing each of them resides and what kind of condition makes them come to be when they do. Let us take pleasure first, for just as we searched for the class it belongs to first, so we start our present investigation with it. But again, we will not be able to provide a satisfactory examination of pleasure if we do not study it together with pain.

PROTARCHUS: If that is the direction we have to take, then let's go that way.

SOCRATES: Do you share my view about their generation?

PROTARCHUS: What view?   c

SOCRATES: Pleasure and pain seem to me by nature to arise together in the common kind.

PROTARCHUS: Could you remind us once again, Socrates, which of those you mentioned you called the common kind?

SOCRATES: As far as I can, my most esteemed friend.

PROTARCHUS: That is noble of you.

SOCRATES: By the common kind, we meant the one that was number three on our list of four.

PROTARCHUS: You mean the one you introduced after the unlimited and the limited, the one that included health, and also harmony, I believe?

SOCRATES: Excellently stated. But now try to put your mind to this as   d
much as possible.

PROTARCHUS: Just go on.

SOCRATES: What I claim is that when we find the harmony in living creatures disrupted, there will at the same time be a disintegration of their nature and a rise of pain.

PROTARCHUS: What you say is very plausible.

SOCRATES: But if the reverse happens, and harmony is regained and the former nature restored, we have to say that pleasure arises, if we must pronounce only a few words on the weightiest matters in the shortest possible time.

e   PROTARCHUS: I believe that you are right, Socrates, but why don't we try
to be more explicit about this very point?

SOCRATES: Well, is it not child's play to understand the most ordinary
and well-known cases?

PROTARCHUS: What cases do you mean?

SOCRATES: Hunger, I take it, is a case of disintegration and pain?

PROTARCHUS: Yes.

SOCRATES: And eating, the corresponding refilling, is a pleasure?

PROTARCHUS: Yes.

SOCRATES: But thirst is, once again, a destruction and pain, while the
32   process that fills what is dried out with liquid is pleasure? And, further,
unnatural separation and dissolution, the affection caused by heat, is pain,
while the natural restoration of cooling down is pleasure?

PROTARCHUS: Very much so.

SOCRATES: And the unnatural coagulation of the fluids in an animal
through freezing is pain, while the natural process of their dissolution or
redistribution is pleasure. To cut matters short, see whether the following
b   account seems acceptable to you. When the natural combination of limit
and unlimitedness that forms a live organism, as I explained before, is
destroyed, this destruction is pain, while the return towards its own nature,
this general restoration, is pleasure.

PROTARCHUS: So be it, for it seems to provide at least an outline.

SOCRATES: Shall we then accept this as one kind of pleasure and pain,
what happens in either of these two kinds of processes?

PROTARCHUS: Accepted.

SOCRATES: But now accept also the anticipation by the *soul* itself of these
c   two kinds of experiences; the hope before the actual pleasure will be
pleasant and comforting, while the expectation of pain will be frightening
and painful.

PROTARCHUS: This turns out then to be a different kind of pleasure and
pain, namely the *expectation* that the soul experiences by itself, without
the body.

SOCRATES: Your assumption is correct. In both these cases, as I see it at least,
pleasure and pain will arise pure and unmixed with each other, so that it
will become apparent as far as pleasure is concerned whether its whole class
d   is to be welcomed or whether this should rather be the privilege of one of
the other classes which we have already discussed. Pleasure and pain may
rather turn out to share the predicament of hot and cold and other such things
that are welcome at one point but unwelcome at another, because they are
not good, but it happens that some of them do occasionally assume a beneficial nature.

PROTARCHUS: You are quite right if you suggest that this must be the
direction to take if we want to find a solution to what we are looking
for now.

SOCRATES: First, then, let us take a look together at the following point.
e   If it truly holds, as we said, that their disintegration constitutes pain, but
restoration is pleasure, what kind of state should we ascribe to animals

when they are neither destroyed nor restored; what kind of condition is this? Think about it carefully, and tell me: Is there not every necessity that the animal will at that time experience neither pain nor pleasure, neither large nor small?

PROTARCHUS: That is indeed necessary.

SOCRATES: There is, then, such a condition, a third one, besides the one in which one is pleased or in which one is in pain?   33

PROTARCHUS: Obviously.

SOCRATES: Make an effort to keep this fact in mind. For it makes quite a difference for our judgment of pleasure whether we remember that there is such a state or not. But we had better give it a little more consideration, if you don't mind.

PROTARCHUS: Just tell me how.

SOCRATES: You realize that nothing prevents the person who has chosen the life of reason from living in this state.

PROTARCHUS: You mean without pleasure and pain?   b

SOCRATES: It was one of the conditions agreed on in our comparison of lives that the person who chooses the life of reason and intelligence must not enjoy pleasures either large or small.

PROTARCHUS: That was indeed agreed on.

SOCRATES: He may then live in this fashion, and perhaps there would be nothing absurd if this life turns out to be the most godlike.

PROTARCHUS: It is at any rate not likely that the gods experience either pleasure or the opposite.

SOCRATES: It is certainly not likely. For either of these states would be quite unseemly in their case. But this is a question we had better take up again later if it should be relevant to our discussion, but let us count it as   c an additional point in favor of reason in the competition for second prize, even if we cannot count it in that for first prize.

PROTARCHUS: A very good suggestion.

SOCRATES: But now as for the other kind of pleasure, of which we said that it belongs to the soul itself. It depends entirely on memory.

PROTARCHUS: In what way?

SOCRATES: It seems we have first to determine what kind of a thing memory is; in fact I am afraid that we will have to determine the nature of perception even before that of memory, if the whole subject matter is to become at all clear to us in the right way.

PROTARCHUS: How do you mean?   d

SOCRATES: You must realize that some of the various affections of the body are extinguished within the body before they reach the soul, leaving it unaffected. Others penetrate through both body and soul and provoke a kind of upheaval that is peculiar to each but also common to both of them.

PROTARCHUS: I realize that.

SOCRATES: Are we fully justified if we claim that the soul remains oblivious of those affections that do not penetrate both, while it is not oblivious of those that penetrate both?

PROTARCHUS: Of course we are justified.   e

SOCRATES: But you must not so misunderstand me as to suppose I meant that this 'obliviousness' gave rise to any kind of forgetting. Forgetting is rather the loss of memory, but in the case in question here no memory has yet arisen. It would be absurd to say that there could be the process of losing something that neither is nor was in existence, wouldn't it?

PROTARCHUS: Quite definitely.

SOCRATES: You only have to make some change in names, then.

PROTARCHUS: How so?

SOCRATES: Instead of saying that the soul is oblivious when it remains unaffected by the disturbances of the body, now change the name of what
34   you so far called obliviousness to that of *nonperception.*

PROTARCHUS: I understand.

SOCRATES: But when the soul and body are jointly affected and moved by one and the same affection, if you call this motion *perception,* you would say nothing out of the way.

PROTARCHUS: You are right.

SOCRATES: And so we know by now what we mean by perception?

PROTARCHUS: Certainly.

SOCRATES: So if someone were to call memory the 'preservation of perception', he would be speaking correctly, as far as I am concerned.

b   PROTARCHUS: Rightly so.

SOCRATES: And do we not hold that recollection differs from memory?

PROTARCHUS: Perhaps.

SOCRATES: Does not their difference lie in this?

PROTARCHUS: In what?

SOCRATES: Do we not call it 'recollection' when the soul recalls as much as possible by itself, without the aid of the body, what she had once experienced together with the body? Or how would you put it?

PROTARCHUS: I quite agree.

SOCRATES: But on the other hand, when, after the loss of memory of
c   either a perception or again a piece of knowledge, the soul calls up this memory for itself, we also call all these events recollection.

PROTARCHUS: You are right.

SOCRATES: The point for the sake of which all this has been said is the following.

PROTARCHUS: What is it?

SOCRATES: That we grasp as fully and clearly as possible the pleasure that the soul experiences without the body, as well as the desire. And through a clarification of these states, the nature of both pleasure and desire will somehow be revealed.

PROTARCHUS: Let us now discuss this as our next issue, Socrates.

d   SOCRATES: It seems that in our investigation we have to discuss many points about the origin of pleasure and about all its different varieties. For it looks as if we will first have to determine what desire is and on what occasion it arises.

PROTARCHUS: Let us determine that, then. We have nothing to lose.

SOCRATES: We will certainly lose something, Protarchus; by discovering what we are looking for now, we will lose our ignorance about it.

PROTARCHUS: You rightly remind us of that fact. But now let us try to return to the further pursuit of our subject.

SOCRATES: Are we agreed now that hunger and thirst and many other things of this sort are desires?

PROTARCHUS: Quite in agreement.

SOCRATES: But what is the common feature whose recognition allows us to address all these phenomena, which differ so much, by the same name?

PROTARCHUS: Heavens, that is perhaps not an easy thing to determine, Socrates, but it must be done nevertheless.

SOCRATES: Shall we go back to the same point of departure?

PROTARCHUS: What point?

SOCRATES: When we say "he is thirsty," we always have something in mind?

PROTARCHUS: We do.

SOCRATES: Meaning that he is getting empty?

PROTARCHUS: Certainly.

SOCRATES: But thirst is a desire?

PROTARCHUS: Yes, the desire for drink.

SOCRATES: For drink or for the filling with drink?

PROTARCHUS: For the filling with drink, I think.

SOCRATES: Whoever among us is emptied, it seems, desires the opposite of what he suffers. Being emptied, he desires to be filled.

PROTARCHUS: That is perfectly obvious.

SOCRATES: But what about this problem? If someone is emptied for the first time, is there any way he could be in touch with filling, either through sensation or memory, since he has no experience of it, either in the present or ever in the past?

PROTARCHUS: How should he?

SOCRATES: But we do maintain that he who has a desire desires something?

PROTARCHUS: Naturally.

SOCRATES: He does, then, not have a desire for what he in fact experiences. For he is thirsty, and this is a process of emptying. His desire is rather of filling.

PROTARCHUS: Yes.

SOCRATES: Something in the person who is thirsty must necessarily somehow be in contact with filling.

PROTARCHUS: Necessarily.

SOCRATES: But it is impossible that this should be the body, for the body is what is emptied out.

PROTARCHUS: Yes.

SOCRATES: The only option we are left with is that the soul makes contact with the filling, and it clearly must do so through memory. Or could it make contact through anything else?

PROTARCHUS: Clearly through nothing else.

e

35

b

c

SOCRATES: Do we understand, then, what conclusions we have to draw from what has been said?

PROTARCHUS: What are they?

SOCRATES: Our argument forces us to conclude that desire is not a matter of the body.

PROTARCHUS: Why is that?

SOCRATES: Because it shows that every living creature always strives towards the opposite of its own experience.

PROTARCHUS: And very much so.

SOCRATES: This impulse, then, that drives it towards the opposite of its own state signifies that it has memory of that opposite state?

PROTARCHUS: Certainly.

d   SOCRATES: By pointing out that it is this memory that directs it towards the objects of its desires, our argument has established that every impulse, and desire, and the rule over the whole animal is the domain of the soul.

PROTARCHUS: Very much so.

SOCRATES: Our argument will, then, never allow that it is our body that experiences thirst, hunger, or anything of that sort.

PROTARCHUS: Absolutely not.

SOCRATES: There is yet a further point we have to consider that is connected with these same conditions. For our discussion seems to me to indicate that there is a form of life that consists of these conditions.

e   PROTARCHUS: What does it consist of, and what form of life are you talking about?

SOCRATES: It consists of filling and emptying and all such processes as are related to both the preservation and the destruction of animals. And when one of us is in either of the two conditions, he is in pain, or again he experiences pleasure, depending on the nature of these changes.

PROTARCHUS: That is indeed what happens.

SOCRATES: But what if someone finds himself in between these two affections?

PROTARCHUS: What do you mean by "in between"?

SOCRATES: When he is pained by his condition and remembers the pleasant things that would put an end to the pain, but is not yet being filled.

36   What about this situation? Should we claim that he is then in between these two affections, or not?

PROTARCHUS: We should claim that.

SOCRATES: And should we say that the person is altogether in pain or pleasure?

PROTARCHUS: By heaven, he seems to me to be suffering a twofold pain; one consists in the body's condition, the other in the soul's desire caused by the expectation.

SOCRATES: How do you mean that there is a twofold pain, Protarchus? Does it not sometimes happen that one of us is emptied at one particular

b   time, but is in clear hope of being filled, while at another time he is, on the contrary, without hope?

PROTARCHUS: It certainly happens.

SOCRATES: And don't you think that he enjoys this hope for replenishment when he remembers, while he is simultaneously in pain because he has been emptied at that time?

PROTARCHUS: Necessarily.

SOCRATES: This is, then, the occasion when a human being and other animals are simultaneously undergoing pain and pleasure.

PROTARCHUS: It seems so.

SOCRATES: But what if he is without hope of attaining any replenishment when he is emptied? Is not that the situation where this twofold pain occurs, which you have just come across and simply taken to be twofold?   c

PROTARCHUS: That is quite undeniable, Socrates.

SOCRATES: Now let us apply the results of our investigation of these affections to this purpose.

PROTARCHUS: What is it?

SOCRATES: Shall we say that these pains and pleasures are true or false, or rather that some of them are true, but not others?

PROTARCHUS: But how could there be false pleasures or pains, Socrates?

SOCRATES: Well, how could there be true or false fears, true or false expectations, true or false judgments, Protarchus?

PROTARCHUS: For judgments I certainly would be ready to admit it, but   d
not for the other cases.

SOCRATES: What is that you are saying? I am afraid we are stirring up a weighty controversy here.

PROTARCHUS: You are right.

SOCRATES: But if it is relevant to what we were discussing before, you worthy son of that man, it ought to be taken up.

PROTARCHUS: Perhaps, in that case.

SOCRATES: We have to forego any excursions here or any discussion of whatever side issues are not directly relevant to our topic.

PROTARCHUS: Right.

SOCRATES: But tell me this, for I have lived in continued perplexity about   e
the difficulty we have come across now. What is your view? Are there not false pleasures, as well as true ones?

PROTARCHUS: How should there be?

SOCRATES: Do you really want to claim that there is no one who, either in a dream or awake, either in madness or any other delusion, sometimes believes he is enjoying himself, while in reality he is not doing so, or believes he is in pain while he is not?

PROTARCHUS: We all assume that this is indeed the case, Socrates.

SOCRATES: But rightly so? Should we not rather take up the question whether or not this claim is justified?

PROTARCHUS: We should take it up, as I at least would say.

SOCRATES: Let us try to achieve more clarity about what we said concern-   37
ing pleasure and judgment. Is there something we call judging?

PROTARCHUS: Yes.

SOCRATES: And is there also taking pleasure?

PROTARCHUS: Yes.

SOCRATES: But there is also what the judgment is about?

PROTARCHUS: Certainly.

SOCRATES: And also what the pleasure is about?

PROTARCHUS: Very much so.

SOCRATES: But what makes a judgment, whether it judges rightly or not, cannot be deprived of really making a judgment.

b   PROTARCHUS: How should it?

SOCRATES: And what takes pleasure, whether it is rightly pleased or not, can obviously never be deprived of really taking pleasure.

PROTARCHUS: Yes, that is also the case.

SOCRATES: But what we have to question is how it is that judgment is usually either true or false, while pleasure admits only truth, even though in both cases there is equally real judgment and real pleasure.

PROTARCHUS: We have to question that.

SOCRATES: Is it that judgment takes on the additional qualification of true

c   and false and is thus not simply judgment, but also has either one of these two qualities? Would you say that is a point we have to look into?

PROTARCHUS: Yes.

SOCRATES: And furthermore, whether quite generally certain things allow extra qualifications, while pleasure and pain are simply what they are and do not take on any qualifications. About that we also have to come to an agreement.

PROTARCHUS: Obviously.

SOCRATES: But at least it is not difficult to see that they, too, take on qualifications. For we said earlier that both of them, pleasures as well as pains, can be great and small, and also have intensity.

d   PROTARCHUS: We certainly did.

SOCRATES: But if some bad state should attach itself to any of them, then we would say that the judgment becomes a bad one, and the pleasure becomes bad too, Protarchus?

PROTARCHUS: Naturally, Socrates.

SOCRATES: But what if some rightness or the opposite of rightness are added to something, would we not call the judgment right, if it were right, and the pleasure too?

PROTARCHUS: Necessarily.

e   SOCRATES: And if a mistake is made about the object of judgment, then we say that the judgment that makes that mistake is not right and does not judge rightly?

PROTARCHUS: How could it?

SOCRATES: But what if we notice that a pain or pleasure is mistaken in what it is pleased or pained about, shall we then call it right or proper or give it other names of praise?

PROTARCHUS: That would be impossible, if indeed pleasure should be mistaken.

SOCRATES: As to pleasure, it certainly often seems to arise in us not with a right, but with a false, judgment.

PROTARCHUS: Of course. But what we call false in this case at that point   38
is the judgment, Socrates; nobody would dream of calling the pleasure
itself false.

SOCRATES: You certainly put up a spirited defense for pleasure now, Protarchus!

PROTARCHUS: Not at all; I only repeat what I hear.

SOCRATES: Is there no difference between the pleasure that goes with
right judgment and knowledge and the kind that often comes to any of
us with false judgment and ignorance?

PROTARCHUS: There's probably no small difference.   b

SOCRATES: So let us turn to inspect the difference between them.

PROTARCHUS: Lead on where you like.

SOCRATES: I lead you this way.

PROTARCHUS: What way?

SOCRATES: Of our judgment we say that it is sometimes false, and sometimes true?

PROTARCHUS: It is.

SOCRATES: And as we said just now, these are often accompanied by
pleasure and pain. I am talking of true and false judgment.

PROTARCHUS: That's right.

SOCRATES: And is it not memory and perception that lead to judgment
or the attempt to come to a definite judgment, as the case may be?

PROTARCHUS: Indeed.   c

SOCRATES: Do we agree that the following must happen here?

PROTARCHUS: What?

SOCRATES: Wouldn't you say that it often happens that someone who
cannot get a clear view because he is looking from a distance wants to
make up his mind about what he sees?

PROTARCHUS: I would say so.

SOCRATES: And might he then not again raise another question for
himself?

PROTARCHUS: What question?

SOCRATES: "What could that be that appears to stand near that rock under
a tree?"—Do you find it plausible that someone might say these words to   d
himself when he sets his eyes on such appearances?

PROTARCHUS: Certainly.

SOCRATES: And might he not afterwards, as an answer to his own
question, say to himself, "It is a man," and in so speaking, would get it
right?

PROTARCHUS: No doubt.

SOCRATES: But he might also be mistaken and say that what he sees is
a statue, the work of some herdsmen?

PROTARCHUS: Very likely.

SOCRATES: But if he were in company, he might actually say out loud to   e
his companion what he had told himself, and so what we earlier called
judgment would turn into an assertion?

PROTARCHUS: To be sure.

SOCRATES: Whereas if he is alone, he entertains this thought by himself, and sometimes he may even resume his way for quite a long time with the thought in his mind?

PROTARCHUS: No doubt.

SOCRATES: But look, do you share my view on this?

PROTARCHUS: What view?

SOCRATES: That our soul in such a situation is comparable to a book?

PROTARCHUS: How so?

39 SOCRATES: If memory and perceptions concur with other impressions at a particular occasion, then they seem to me to inscribe words in our soul, as it were. And if what is written is true, then we form a true judgment and a true account of the matter. But if what our scribe writes is false, then the result will be the opposite of the truth.

b PROTARCHUS: I quite agree, and I accept this way of putting it.

SOCRATES: Do you also accept that there is another craftsman at work in our soul at the same time?

PROTARCHUS: What kind of craftsman?

SOCRATES: A painter who follows the scribe and provides illustrations to his words in the soul.

PROTARCHUS: How and when do we say he does this work?

SOCRATES: When a person takes his judgments and assertions directly from sight or any other sense-perception and then views the images he

c has formed inside himself, corresponding to those judgments and assertions. Or is it not something of this sort that is going on in us?

PROTARCHUS: Quite definitely.

SOCRATES: And are not the pictures of the true judgments and assertions true, and the pictures of the false ones false?

PROTARCHUS: Certainly.

SOCRATES: If we have been right with what we have said so far, let us in addition come to terms about this question.

PROTARCHUS: What about?

SOCRATES: Whether these experiences are necessarily confined to the past and the present, but are not extended into the future.

PROTARCHUS: They should apply equally to all the tenses: past, present, and future.

d SOCRATES: Now, did we not say before, about the pleasures and pains that belong to the soul alone, that they might precede those that go through the body? It would therefore be possible that we have anticipatory pleasures and pains about the future.

PROTARCHUS: Undeniably.

SOCRATES: And are those writings and pictures which come to be in us,

e as we said earlier, concerned only with the past and the present, but not with the future?

PROTARCHUS: Decidedly with the future.

SOCRATES: If you say 'decidedly', is it because all of them are really hopes for future times, and we are forever brimful of hopes, throughout our lifetime?

PROTARCHUS: Quite definitely.

SOCRATES: Well, then, in addition to what has been said now, also answer this question.

PROTARCHUS: Concerning what?

SOCRATES: Is not a man who is just, pious, and good in all respects, also loved by the gods?

PROTARCHUS: How could he fail to be?

SOCRATES: But what about someone who is unjust and in all respects evil? Isn't he that man's opposite?

PROTARCHUS: Of course.

SOCRATES: And is not everyone, as we just said, always full of many hopes?

PROTARCHUS: Certainly.

SOCRATES: There are, then, assertions in each of us that we call hopes?

PROTARCHUS: Yes.

SOCRATES: But there are also those painted images. And someone often envisages himself in the possession of an enormous amount of gold and of a lot of pleasures as a consequence. And in addition, he also sees, in this inner picture himself, that he is beside himself with delight.

PROTARCHUS: What else!

SOCRATES: Now, do we want to say that in the case of good people these pictures are usually true, because they are dear to the gods, while quite the opposite usually holds in the case of wicked ones, or is this not what we ought to say?

PROTARCHUS: That is just what we ought to say.

SOCRATES: And wicked people nevertheless have pleasures painted in their minds, even though they are somehow false?

PROTARCHUS: Right.

SOCRATES: So wicked people as a rule enjoy false pleasures, but the good among mankind true ones?

PROTARCHUS: Quite necessarily so.

SOCRATES: From what has now been said, it follows that there are false pleasures in human souls that are quite ridiculous imitations of true ones, and also such pains.

PROTARCHUS: There certainly are.

SOCRATES: Now, it was agreed that whoever judges anything at all is always *really* judging, even if it is not about anything existing in the present, past, or future.

PROTARCHUS: Right.

SOCRATES: And these were, I think, the conditions that produce a false judgment and judging falsely, weren't they?

PROTARCHUS: Yes.

40

b

c

d

SOCRATES: But should we not also grant to pleasures and pains a condition that is analogous in these ways?

PROTARCHUS: In what ways?

SOCRATES: In the sense that whoever has any pleasure at all, however ill-founded it may be, really does have pleasure, even if sometimes it is not about anything that either is the case or ever was the case, or often (or perhaps most of the time) refers to anything that ever will be the case.

e PROTARCHUS: That also must necessarily be so.

SOCRATES: And the same account holds in the case of fear, anger, and everything of that sort, namely that all of them can at times be false?

PROTARCHUS: Certainly.

SOCRATES: Well, then, do we have any other way of distinguishing between bad and good judgments than their falsity?

PROTARCHUS: We have no other.

SOCRATES: Nor, I presume, will we find any other way to account for badness in the case of pleasures unless they are false.

41 PROTARCHUS: What you say is quite the opposite of the truth, Socrates! It is not at all because they are false that we regard pleasures or pains as bad, but because there is some other grave and wide-ranging kind of badness involved.

SOCRATES: But let us discuss bad pleasures and what badness there is in their case a little later, if we still feel like it. Now we have to take up false pleasures in another sense and show that there is a great variety that arise and are at work in us. This argument will perhaps come in handy later, b when we have to make our decisions.

PROTARCHUS: That may well be so, at least if there are any such pleasures.

SOCRATES: There certainly are, Protarchus; I at least am convinced. But until this is our accepted opinion, we cannot leave this conviction unexamined.

PROTARCHUS: Right.

SOCRATES: So let us get ready like athletes to form a line of attack around this problem.

PROTARCHUS: Here we go.

SOCRATES: We did say a short while ago in our discussion, as we may c recall, that when what we call desires are in us, then body and soul part company and have each their separate experiences.

PROTARCHUS: We do remember, that was said before.

SOCRATES: And wasn't it the soul that had desires, desires for conditions opposite to the actual ones of the body, while it was the body that undergoes the pain or the pleasure of some affection?

PROTARCHUS: That was indeed so.

SOCRATES: Draw your conclusions as to what is going on here.

PROTARCHUS: You tell me.

d SOCRATES: What happens is this: Under these circumstances pains and pleasures exist side by side, and there are simultaneously opposite perceptions of them, as we have just made clear.

PROTARCHUS: Yes, that is clear.

SOCRATES: But did we not also discuss this point and come to an agreement how to settle it earlier?

PROTARCHUS: What point?

SOCRATES: That the two of them, both pleasure and pain, admit the more and less and belong to the unlimited kind?

PROTARCHUS: That was what we said. What about it?

SOCRATES: Do we have any means of making a right decision about these matters?

PROTARCHUS: Where and in what respect?

e

SOCRATES: In the case where we intend to come to a decision about any of them in such circumstances, which one is greater or smaller, or which one is more intensive or stronger: pain compared to pleasure, or pain compared to pain, or pleasure to pleasure.

PROTARCHUS: Yes, these questions do arise, and that is what we want to decide.

SOCRATES: Well, then, does it happen only to eyesight that seeing objects from afar or close by distorts the truth and causes false judgments? Or does not the same thing happen also in the case of pleasure and pain?

42

PROTARCHUS: Much more so, Socrates.

SOCRATES: But this is the reverse of the result we reached a little earlier.

PROTARCHUS: What are you referring to?

SOCRATES: Earlier it was true and false *judgments* which affected the respective pleasures and pains with their own condition.

PROTARCHUS: Quite right.

b

SOCRATES: But now it applies to pleasures and pains themselves; it is because they are alternately looked at from close up or far away, or simultaneously put side by side, that the pleasures seem greater compared to pain and more intensive, and pains seem, on the contrary, moderate in comparison with pleasures.

PROTARCHUS: It is quite inevitable that such conditions arise under these circumstances.

SOCRATES: But if you take that portion of them by which they appear greater or smaller than they really are, and cut it off from each of them as a mere appearance and without real being, you will neither admit that this appearance is right nor dare to say that anything connected with this portion of pleasure or pain is right and true.

c

PROTARCHUS: Certainly not.

SOCRATES: Next in order after these, we will find pleasures and pains in animals that are even falser than these, both in appearance and reality, if we approach them in this way.

PROTARCHUS: What are they, and what is the way?

SOCRATES: It has by now been said repeatedly that it is a destruction of the nature of those entities through combinations and separations, through processes of filling and emptying, as well as certain kinds of growth and decay, that gives rise to pain and suffering, distress, and whatever else comes to pass that goes under such a name.

d

PROTARCHUS: Yes, that has often been said.

SOCRATES: But when things are restored to their own nature again, this restoration, as we established in our agreement among ourselves, is pleasure.

PROTARCHUS: Correct.

SOCRATES: But what if nothing of that sort happens to our body, what then?

PROTARCHUS: When could that ever happen, Socrates?

e   SOCRATES: Your objection is not to the point, Protarchus.

PROTARCHUS: How so?

SOCRATES: Because you do not prevent me from putting my question to you again.

PROTARCHUS: What question?

SOCRATES: If in fact nothing of that sort took place, I will ask you, what would necessarily be the consequence of this for us?

PROTARCHUS: You mean if the body is not moved in either direction, Socrates?

SOCRATES: That is my question.

PROTARCHUS: This much is clear, Socrates, that in such a case there would not be either any pleasure or pain at all.

43   SOCRATES: Very well put. But I guess what you meant to say is that we necessarily are always experiencing one or the other, as the wise men say. For everything is in an eternal flux, upward and downward.

PROTARCHUS: They do say that, and what they say seems important.

SOCRATES: How else, since they themselves are important people? But I do want to avoid this argument which now assails us. I plan to escape it in this way, and you'd better make your escape with me.

PROTARCHUS: Just tell me how.

SOCRATES: "So be it," we will reply to them. But as for you, answer me

b   this question: whether all living creatures in all cases notice it whenever they are affected in some way, so that we notice when we grow or experience anything of that sort, or whether it is quite otherwise.

PROTARCHUS: It is indeed quite otherwise. Almost all of these processes totally escape our notice.

SOCRATES: But then what we just agreed to was not well spoken, that the changes 'upwards and downwards' evoke pleasures and pains.

PROTARCHUS: How could it?

c   SOCRATES: But if it is stated in this way, it will be better and become unobjectionable.

PROTARCHUS: In what way?

SOCRATES: That great changes cause pleasures and pains in us, while moderate or small ones engender neither of the two effects.

PROTARCHUS: That is more correct than the other statement, Socrates.

SOCRATES: But if this is correct, then we are back with the same kind of life we discussed before.

PROTARCHUS: What kind?

SOCRATES: The life that we said was painless, but also devoid of charm.

PROTARCHUS: Undeniably.

SOCRATES: So we end up with three kinds of life, the life of pleasure, the   d
life of pain, and the neutral life. Or what would you say about these matters?

PROTARCHUS: I would put it in the same way, that there are three kinds of life.

SOCRATES: But to be free of pain would not be the same thing as to have pleasure?

PROTARCHUS: How could it be the same?

SOCRATES: If you hear someone say that it is the most pleasant thing of all to live one's whole life without pain, how do you understand the speaker's intention?

PROTARCHUS: To my understanding he seems to identify pleasure with freedom from pain.

SOCRATES: Now, imagine three sorts of things, whichever you may like,   e
and because these are high-sounding names, let us call them gold, silver, and what is neither of the two.

PROTARCHUS: Consider it done.

SOCRATES: Is there any way conceivable in which this third kind could turn out to be the same as one of our other two sorts, gold or silver?

PROTARCHUS: How could it?

SOCRATES: That the middle kind of life could turn out to be either pleasant or painful would be the wrong thing to think, if anyone happened to think so, and it would be the wrong thing to say, if anyone should say so, according to the proper account of the matter?

PROTARCHUS: No doubt.

SOCRATES: But we do find people who both think so and say so, my friend.   44

PROTARCHUS: Certainly.

SOCRATES: And do they really believe they experience pleasure when they are not in pain?

PROTARCHUS: They say so, at any rate.

SOCRATES: They believe therefore that they are pleased at that time. Otherwise they would not say that they are.

PROTARCHUS: It looks that way.

SOCRATES: But they hold a false judgment about pleasure, if in fact freedom from pain and pleasure each have a nature of their own.

PROTARCHUS: But they do have their own.

SOCRATES: What decision shall we make? That there are three states in us, as we said just now, or that there are only two: pain being an evil in human   b
life, and liberation from pain, also called pleasure, being the good as such?

PROTARCHUS: But why is it that we are asking ourselves this question now, Socrates? I don't get the point.

SOCRATES: That is because you don't really understand who the enemies of our Philebus here are.

PROTARCHUS: What enemies do you mean?

SOCRATES: I mean people with a tremendous reputation in natural science who say that there are no such things as pleasures at all.

PROTARCHUS: How so?

c   SOCRATES: They hold that everything the followers of Philebus call pleasures are nothing but escape from pain.

PROTARCHUS: Do you suggest we should believe them, Socrates, or what
is it you want us to do?

SOCRATES: Not that, but to use them as seers who make their prophecies,
not in virtue of any art but in virtue of a certain harshness in their nature. It
is a nature not without nobility, but out of an inordinate hatred that they
have conceived against the power of pleasure, they refuse to acknowledge
anything healthy in it, even to the point that they regard its very attractiveness itself as witchcraft rather than pleasure. You may now make use of them
d   for our purposes, taking notice of the rest of their complaints that result from
their harshness. After that you will hear what I, for my part, regard as true
pleasures, so that through an examination of these two opposed points of
view, we can reach a decision about the power of pleasure.

PROTARCHUS: A fair proposal.

SOCRATES: Let us attach ourselves to them as to allies and follow their
traces in the direction in which their dour arguments point us. I think they
employ reasoning of this kind, starting from some such basic principle: If
e   we wanted to know the nature of any character, like that of hardness,
would we get a better understanding if we looked at the hardest kinds of
things rather than at what has a low degree of hardness? Now, it is your
task, Protarchus, to answer these difficult people, just as you answered me.

PROTARCHUS: Gladly, and my answer to them will be that I would look
at hardness of the first degree.

SOCRATES: But again if we wanted to study the form of pleasure, to see
45   what kind of nature it has, in that case we ought not to look at low-level
pleasures, but at those that are said to be the strongest and most intensive.

PROTARCHUS: Everyone would grant you this point.

SOCRATES: Now, aren't the most immediate and greatest among the pleasures the ones connected with the body, as we have often said?

PROTARCHUS: No doubt.

SOCRATES: And is it the case that pleasures are more intensive or set in
with greater intensity when people suffer from an illness than when they are
healthy? We have to beware of a hasty answer here, lest we get tripped up.
b   Perhaps we might be inclined to affirm this rather for the healthy people?

PROTARCHUS: Quite likely.

SOCRATES: But what about this? Are not those pleasures overwhelming
which are also preceded by the greatest desires?

PROTARCHUS: That is certainly true.

SOCRATES: And when people suffer from fever or any such disease, aren't
they more subject to thirst, chill, and whatever else continues to affect
them through the body? Do they not feel greater deprivations, and also
greater pleasures at their replenishment? Or shall we deny that this is true?

PROTARCHUS: It seems undeniable as you explained it now.

c   SOCRATES: Very well. Are we justified, then, if we claim that whoever
wants to study the greatest pleasures should turn to sickness, not to health?

Now, mind you, my question was not whether the very sick have *more* pleasures than healthy people; my concern is rather with the *size* and *intensity* of the condition when it takes place. Our task, as we said, is to comprehend both what its true nature is and how those conceive of it who deny that there is any such thing as pleasure at all.

PROTARCHUS: I am following quite well what you say.   d

SOCRATES: You might as well be its guide, Protarchus. Now, tell me. Do you recognize greater pleasures in a life given to excesses—I do not say more pleasures, but pleasures that exceed by their force and intensity— than in a moderate life? Think carefully about it before you answer.

PROTARCHUS: I quite understand what you are after; I see indeed a huge difference. The moderate people somehow always stand under the guidance of the proverbial maxim "nothing too much" and obey it. But as to   e foolish people and those given to debauchery, the excesses of their pleasures drive them near madness and to shrieks of frenzy.

SOCRATES: Good. But if this is how it stands, then it is obvious that it is in some vicious state of soul and body and not in virtue that the greatest pleasures as well as the greatest pains have their origin.

PROTARCHUS: Obviously.

SOCRATES: So we must pick out some of them to find out what characteristic of theirs made us call them the greatest.

PROTARCHUS: Necessarily.   46

SOCRATES: Now, look at the pleasures that go with these types of maladies, what kinds of conditions they are.

PROTARCHUS: What types do you mean?

SOCRATES: Those pleasures of a rather repugnant type, which our harsh friends hate above all.

PROTARCHUS: What kinds?

SOCRATES: For example, the relief from itching by rubbing, and all of that sort that needs no other remedy. But if this condition should befall us, what in heaven's name should we call it, pleasure or pain?

PROTARCHUS: That really would seem to be a mixed experience, with a bad component, Socrates.

SOCRATES: I did not raise this question with the intention of alluding to   b Philebus. But without a clarification of these pleasures and of those who cultivate them, we could hardly come to any resolution of our problem.

PROTARCHUS: Then let us take up the whole tribe of these pleasures.

SOCRATES: You mean the ones that have that mixed nature?

PROTARCHUS: Right.

SOCRATES: There are mixtures that have their origin in the body and are confined to the body; then, there are mixtures found in the soul, and they   c are confined to the soul. But then we will also find mixtures of pleasures and pains in both soul and body, and at one time the combination of both will be called pleasure; at other times it will be called pain.

PROTARCHUS: How so?

SOCRATES: When someone undergoes restoration or destruction he experiences two opposed conditions at once. He may feel hot while shivering or

feel chilled while sweating. I suppose he will then want to retain one of these
d   conditions and get rid of the other. But if this so called bittersweet condition is
hard to shake, it first causes irritation and later on turns into wild excitement.

PROTARCHUS: A very accurate description.

SOCRATES: Now, isn't it the case that some of those mixtures contain an
even amount of pleasures and pain, while there is a preponderance of
either of the two in others?

PROTARCHUS: Right.

SOCRATES: Take the case that we just mentioned, of itching and scratching,
as an example where the pains outweigh the pleasures. Now, when the
e   irritation and infection are inside and cannot be reached by rubbing and
scratching, there is only a relief on the surface.[14] In case they treat these
parts by exposing them to fire or its opposite—they go from one extreme
to the other in their distress—they sometimes procure enormous pleasures.
But sometimes this leads to a state inside that is opposite to that outside,
with a mixture of pains and pleasures, whichever way the balance may
turn, because this treatment disperses by force what was mixed together or
47 mixes together what was separate, so that pains arise besides the pleasures.

PROTARCHUS: Necessarily.

SOCRATES: Now, in all those cases where the mixture contains a surplus
of pleasure, the small admixture of pain gives rise only to a tickle and a
mild irritation, while the predominant part of pleasure causes contractions
of the body to the point of leaping and kicking, color changes of all sorts,
distortion of features, and wild palpitations; it finally drives the person
totally out of his mind, so that he shouts aloud like a madman.

b   PROTARCHUS: Very much so.

SOCRATES: And this state causes him and others to say of him that he is
almost dying of these pleasures. And the more profligate and mindless
he is, the more will he pursue them by any means possible, and he calls
them supreme and considers as the happiest of all mortals whoever lives
in continuous enjoyment of them, as much as that is possible.

PROTARCHUS: Your description fits exactly the preconceptions of the common run of people, Socrates.

c   SOCRATES: Yes, as far as concerns the pleasures that arise when there is
a mixture of the external and internal state of the body, Protarchus. But
take now the cases where the soul's contributions are opposed to the
body's: When there is pain over and against pleasures, or pleasure against
pain, both are finally joined in a mixed state. We have talked about them
earlier and agreed that in these cases it is the deprivation that gives rise
to the desire for replenishment, and while the expectation is pleasant, the
deprivation itself is painful. When we discussed this we did not make any
d   special mention, as we do now, of the fact that, in the vast number of
cases where soul and body are not in agreement, the final result is a single
mixture that combines pleasure and pain.

14. Leaving out Burnet's insertion of *en tois*.

PROTARCHUS: I suspect that you are right.

SOCRATES: But here we are still left with one further kind of mixture of pleasure and pain.

PROTARCHUS: Tell me what it is.

SOCRATES: The case, a common one, where the mixture is the product of affections within the soul itself, as we said before.

PROTARCHUS: What was it again that we said?

SOCRATES: Take wrath, fear, longing, lamentations, love, jealousy, malice, and other things like that; don't you regard them as a kind of pain within the soul itself?

PROTARCHUS: I certainly do.

SOCRATES: And don't we find that they are full of marvellous pleasures? Or do we need the famous lines as a reminder about wrath:

> ... *That can embitter even the wise*
> ... *But much sweeter than soft-flowing honey* ...[15]

Similarly, in the case of lamentations and longing, aren't there also pleasures mixed in with the pain?

PROTARCHUS: No need for further reminders; in all these cases it must be just as you said.

SOCRATES: And the same happens in those who watch tragedies: There is laughter mixed with the weeping, if you remember.

PROTARCHUS: How could I forget?

SOCRATES: Now, look at our state of mind in comedy. Don't you realize that it also involves a mixture of pleasure and pain?

PROTARCHUS: I don't quite see that yet.

SOCRATES: It is indeed not quite so easy to see that this condition applies under those circumstances.

PROTARCHUS: It certainly is not to me!

SOCRATES: Since it is such an obscure matter, let us be all the more careful. For this will help us to recognize more easily when there is a mixture of pain and pleasure in other cases as well.

PROTARCHUS: Please tell me.

SOCRATES: Since we just mentioned the word "malice": Do you treat malice as a pain of the soul, or what?

PROTARCHUS: I do.

SOCRATES: On the other hand, will not the malicious person display pleasure at his neighbor's misfortunes?

PROTARCHUS: Very much so.

SOCRATES: Now, ignorance is a vice, and so is what we call stupidity?

PROTARCHUS: Decidedly!

15. *Iliad* xviii.108–9.

SOCRATES: What conclusions do you draw from this about the nature of the ridiculous?

PROTARCHUS: You tell me.

SOCRATES: It is, in sum, a kind of vice that derives its name from a special disposition; it is, among all the vices, the one with a character[16] that stands in direct opposition to the one recommended by the famous inscription in Delphi.

PROTARCHUS: You mean the one that says "Know thyself," Socrates?

d   SOCRATES: I do. The opposite recommendation would obviously be that we not know ourselves at all.[17]

PROTARCHUS: No doubt.

SOCRATES: Go on and make a subdivision of this disposition into three, Protarchus.

PROTARCHUS: What do you mean? I am afraid I don't know how to.

SOCRATES: Are you saying that it is up to me to make this division now?

PROTARCHUS: That is indeed what I am saying, but in addition I beg you to do so.

SOCRATES: Are there not necessarily three ways in which it is possible not to know oneself?

PROTARCHUS: What are they?

e   SOCRATES: The first way concerns money, if someone thinks himself richer than he in fact is.

PROTARCHUS: Many people certainly share that condition.

SOCRATES: Even more consider themselves taller and handsomer than they in fact are, and believe they have other such physical advantages.

PROTARCHUS: Definitely.

SOCRATES: But an overwhelming number are mistaken about the third kind, which belongs to the soul, namely virtue, and believe that they are superior in virtue, although they are not.

PROTARCHUS: Very much so.

49   SOCRATES: And, again, among the virtues, is it not especially to wisdom that the largest number of people lay claim, puffing themselves up with quarrels and false pretensions to would-be knowledge?

PROTARCHUS: Undeniably so.

SOCRATES: It would therefore be quite justified to say that all these conditions are bad.

PROTARCHUS: Quite justified.

SOCRATES: So we must continue with our division of ignorance, Protarchus, if we want to find out what a strange mixture of pleasure and pain this comic malice is. How would you suggest that we should further

b   subdivide? In the case of all those who have such a false opinion about

16. Inserting *to* before *tounantion* in 48c8.
17. Accepting the deletion of *legomenon hupo tou grammatos* at d2.

themselves, is it not most necessary, as it is for all mankind, that it be combined either with strength and power, or with its opposite?

PROTARCHUS: Necessarily.

SOCRATES: So make this the point of division. All those who combine this delusion with weakness and are unable to avenge themselves when they are laughed at, you are justified in calling ridiculous. But as for those who do have the power and strength to take revenge, if you call them dangerous and hateful, you are getting exactly the right conception about them. For ignorance on the side of the strong and powerful is odious and ugly; it is harmful even for their neighbors, both the ignorance itself and its imitations, whatever they may be. Ignorance on the side of the weak, by contrast, deserves to be placed among the ridiculous in rank and nature.

PROTARCHUS: You are right about this division. But I am still not quite clear about where there is a mixture of pleasure and pain in these cases.

SOCRATES: So take first the nature of malice.

PROTARCHUS: Please explain.

SOCRATES: It contains a kind of unjust pain and pleasure.

PROTARCHUS: Necessarily.

SOCRATES: Now, if you rejoice about evils that happen to your enemy, is there any injustice or malice in your pleasure?

PROTARCHUS: How should there be?

SOCRATES: But is there any occasion when it is not unjust to be pleased rather than pained to see bad things happen to your friends?

PROTARCHUS: Clearly not.

SOCRATES: But we just agreed that ignorance is bad for everyone?

PROTARCHUS: Right.

SOCRATES: Let us take now the ignorance of friends which we said came in three versions, would-be wisdom and would-be beauty, and the other sort we just mentioned, each of which is ridiculous if weak, but odious if strong. Now, are we ready to affirm of our friends' state what we just said, namely, that it is ridiculous if it is harmless to others?

PROTARCHUS: Very much so.

SOCRATES: But did we not agree that it is bad if it is ignorance?

PROTARCHUS: We certainly did.

SOCRATES: But if we laugh about it, are we pleased or pained by it?

PROTARCHUS: We are pleased, obviously.

SOCRATES: But this pleasure in the face of the misfortunes of friends— did we not say that it was the product of malice?

PROTARCHUS: Necessarily.

SOCRATES: Our argument leads to the conclusion that if we laugh at what is ridiculous about our friends, by mixing pleasure with malice, we thereby mix pleasure with pain. For we had agreed earlier that malice is a pain in the soul, that laughing is a pleasure, and that both occur together on those occasions.

PROTARCHUS: True.

b   SOCRATES: The upshot of our discussion, then, is that in lamentations as well as in tragedies and comedies, not only on stage but also in all of life's tragedies and comedies, pleasures are mixed with pains, and so it is on infinitely other occasions.

PROTARCHUS: It would be impossible not to agree with this, even for the most ambitious defense of the opposite position, Socrates.

SOCRATES: Now, we had on our list of examples wrath, longing, lamenta-
c   tions, fear, love, jealousy, malice, and whatever else, and we said that in these cases we would discern the mixture that we have already mentioned so frequently, right?

PROTARCHUS: Right.

SOCRATES: So we understand, then, that our whole explanation also applies to longing, malice, and wrath?

PROTARCHUS: How could we fail to understand that?

SOCRATES: And there are many other such cases to which it applies?

PROTARCHUS: A great many.

SOCRATES: Now, what precisely do you think was the purpose for which I pointed out to you this mixture in comedy? Don't you see that it was
d   designed to make it easier to persuade you that there is such a mixture in fear and love and other cases? I hoped that once you had accepted this you would release me from a protracted discussion of the rest—once the main point was understood, that there exists the possibility, for the body without the soul, for the soul without the body, and for both of them in a joint affection, to contain a mixture of pleasure and pain.

Now, tell me whether you will let me go now or whether you will keep us up till midnight. One further remark will gain me my release, I
e   hope. I will gladly give you a full account of the rest tomorrow, but for now I want to steer towards the remaining points needed to make the decision Philebus demands of us.

PROTARCHUS: Well spoken, Socrates. Discuss the rest any way you like.

SOCRATES: It seems natural, somehow, that we must proceed from the mixed pleasures to the discussion of the *unmixed* ones.

51   PROTARCHUS: A very good point.

SOCRATES: I will now try to explain them in turn. Although I am not really in agreement with those who hold that all pleasures are merely release from pain, I nevertheless treat them as witnesses, as I said before, to prove that there are certain kinds that only seem to be pleasures, but are not so in reality, and furthermore, that there are others that have the appearance of enormous size and great variety, but which are in truth commingled with pain or with respite from severe pains suffered by soul and body.

b   PROTARCHUS: But, Socrates, what are the kinds of pleasures that one could rightly regard as true?

SOCRATES: Those that are related to so-called pure colors and to shapes and to most smells and sounds and in general all those that are based on imperceptible and painless lacks, while their fulfilllments are perceptible and pleasant.

PROTARCHUS: But really, Socrates, what are you talking about?

SOCRATES: What I am saying may not be entirely clear straightaway, but I'll try to clarify it. By the beauty of a shape, I do not mean what the many might presuppose, namely that of a living being or of a picture. What I mean, what the argument demands, is rather something straight or round and what is constructed out of these with a compass, rule, and square, such as plane figures and solids. Those things I take it are not beautiful in a relative sense, as others are, but are by their very nature forever beautiful by themselves. They provide their own specific pleasures that are not at all comparable to those of rubbing! And colors are beautiful in an analogous way and import their own kinds of pleasures. Do we now understand it better, or how do you feel?

PROTARCHUS: I am really trying to understand, Socrates, but will you also try to say this more clearly?

SOCRATES: What I am saying is that those among the smooth and bright sounds that produce one pure note are not beautiful in relation to anything else but in and by themselves and that they are accompanied by their own pleasures, which belong to them by nature.

PROTARCHUS: That much is true.

SOCRATES: Then there is also the less divine tribe of pleasures connected with smells. But because there is no inevitable pain mixed with them, in whatever way or wherever we may come by them, for this reason I regard them as the counterpart to those others. So, if you get my point, we will then treat those as two species of the kinds of pleasures we are looking for.

PROTARCHUS: I do get your point.

SOCRATES: Then let us also add to these the pleasures of learning, if indeed we are agreed that there is no such thing as hunger for learning connected with them, nor any pains that have their source in a hunger for learning.

PROTARCHUS: Here, too, I agree with you.

SOCRATES: Well, then, if after such filling with knowledge, people lose it again through forgetting, do you notice any kinds of pain?

PROTARCHUS: None that could be called inherent by nature, but in our reflections on this loss when we need it, we experience it as a painful loss.

SOCRATES: But, my dear, we are here concerned only with the natural affections themselves, apart from reflection on them.

PROTARCHUS: Then you are right in saying that the lapse of knowledge never causes us any pain.

SOCRATES: Then we may say that the pleasures of learning are unmixed with pain and belong, not to the masses, but only to a very few?

PROTARCHUS: How could one fail to agree?

SOCRATES: But now that we have properly separated the pure pleasures and those that can rightly be called impure, let's add to our account the attribution of immoderation to the violent pleasures, but moderation, in contrast, to the others. That is to say, we will assign those pleasures which display high intensity and violence, no matter whether frequently or rarely, to the class of the unlimited, the more and less, which affects both body and soul.

d   The other kinds of pleasures we will assign to the class of things that possess measurement.

PROTARCHUS: Quite right, Socrates.

SOCRATES: But we have also to look into the following question about
them.

PROTARCHUS: What question?

SOCRATES: The question of their relation to truth. What is closer to it: the pure,
unadulterated, and sufficient[18] or the violent, multiform, and enormous?

PROTARCHUS: Just what are you after in asking this question, Socrates?

e   SOCRATES: I want to omit nothing in the investigation of both pleasure
and knowledge. I want to ask if one part of them is pure, another impure,
so that both of them may come to trial in their pure form, and so make
it easier for you and me and all those present to come to a verdict in this trial.

PROTARCHUS: Quite right.

SOCRATES: Then let us go on and see whether all items that belong in
the pure kind display the following qualification. But let us first pick out
one of them and study it.

53   PROTARCHUS: Which one shall we choose?

SOCRATES: Let us take whiteness first, if you have no objection.

PROTARCHUS: That is fine with me.

SOCRATES: Now, how can there be purity in the case of whiteness, and
what sort of thing is it? Is it the greatest quantity or amount, or is it rather
the complete lack of any admixture, that is, where there is not the slightest
part of any other kind contained in this color?

PROTARCHUS: It will obviously be the perfectly unadulterated color.

SOCRATES: Right. But shall we not also agree that this is the truest and
b   the most beautiful of all instances of white, rather than what is greatest
in quantity or amount?

PROTARCHUS: Certainly.

SOCRATES: So we are perfectly justified if we say that a small portion of
pure white is to be regarded as whiter than a larger quantity of an impure
whiteness, and at the same time more beautiful and possessed of more truth?

PROTARCHUS: Perfectly justified.

SOCRATES: Well, now, we don't need to run through many more examples
to justify our account of pleasure, but this example suffices to prove that
c   in the case of pleasure, too, every small and insignificant pleasure that is
unadulterated by pain will turn out to be pleasanter, truer, and more
beautiful than a greater quantity and amount of the impure kind.

PROTARCHUS: Quite definitely so, and the example is sufficient.

SOCRATES: But what about the following point? Have we not been told
that pleasure is always a process of *becoming*, and that there is no *being* at
all of pleasure? There are some subtle thinkers who have tried to pass on
this doctrine to us, and we ought to be grateful to them.

PROTARCHUS: What does it mean?

18. Accepting the transposition of *kai to hikanon* from d8 to after *eilikrines* in d7.

SOCRATES: I will indeed try to explain it to you, my friend Protarchus, by resuming my questioning.   d

PROTARCHUS: You have only to keep on asking.

SOCRATES: Suppose there are two kinds of things, one kind sufficient to itself, the other in need of something else.

PROTARCHUS: How and what sort of things do you mean?

SOCRATES: The one kind by nature possesses supreme dignity; the other is inferior to it.

PROTARCHUS: Express this more clearly, please.

SOCRATES: We must have met handsome and noble youths, together with their courageous lovers.

PROTARCHUS: Certainly.

SOCRATES: Now, try to think of another set of two items that corresponds to this pair in all the relevant features that we just mentioned.   e

PROTARCHUS: Do I have to repeat my request for the third time? Please express more clearly what it is you want to say, Socrates!

SOCRATES: Nothing fanciful at all, Protarchus; this is just a playful manner of speaking. What is really meant is that all things are either for the sake of something else or they are that for whose sake the other kind comes to be in each case.

PROTARCHUS: I finally managed to understand it, thanks to the many repetitions.

SOCRATES: Perhaps, my boy, we will understand better as the argument proceeds.   54

PROTARCHUS: No doubt.

SOCRATES: So let's take another pair.

PROTARCHUS: Of what kind?

SOCRATES: Take on the one hand the *generation* of all things, on the other their *being*.

PROTARCHUS: I also accept this pair from you, being and generation.

SOCRATES: Excellent. Now, which of the two do you think exists for the other's sake? Shall we say that generation takes place for the sake of being, or does being exist for the sake of generation?

PROTARCHUS: Whether what is called being is what it is for the sake of generation, is that what you want to know?

SOCRATES: Apparently.

PROTARCHUS: By heavens, what a question to ask me! You might as well   b
ask: "Tell me, Protarchus, whether shipbuilding goes on for the sake of ships or whether ships are for the sake of shipbuilding," or some such thing.

SOCRATES: That is precisely what I am talking about, Protarchus.

PROTARCHUS: What keeps you from answering your questions yourself, Socrates?

SOCRATES: Nothing, provided you take your share in the argument.

PROTARCHUS: I am quite determined to.

SOCRATES: I hold that all ingredients, as well as all tools, and quite   c
generally all materials, are always provided for the sake of some process

of generation. I further hold that every process of generation in turn always takes place for the sake of some particular being, and that all generation taken together takes place for the sake of being as a whole.

PROTARCHUS: Nothing could be clearer.

SOCRATES: Now, pleasure, since it is a process of generation, necessarily comes to be for the sake of some being.

PROTARCHUS: Of course.

SOCRATES: But that for the sake of which what comes to be for the sake of something comes to be in each case, ought to be put into the class of the things good in themselves, while that which comes to be for the sake of something else belongs in another class, my friend.

PROTARCHUS: Undeniably.

d   SOCRATES: But if pleasure really is a process of generation, will we be placing it correctly, if we put it in a class different from that of the good?

PROTARCHUS: That too is undeniable.

SOCRATES: It is true, then, as I said at the beginning of this argument, that we ought to be grateful to the person who indicated to us that there is always only generation of pleasure and that it has no being whatsoever. And it is obvious that he will just laugh at those who claim that pleasure is good.

PROTARCHUS: Certainly.

e   SOCRATES: But this same person will also laugh at those who find their fulfillment in processes of generation.

PROTARCHUS: How so, and what sort of people are you alluding to?

SOCRATES: I am talking of those who cure their hunger and thirst or anything else that is cured by processes of generation. They take delight in generation as a pleasure and proclaim that they would not want to live if they were not subject to hunger and thirst and if they could not experience all the other things one might want to mention in connection with such conditions.

55   PROTARCHUS: That is very like them.

SOCRATES: But would we not all say that destruction is the opposite of generation?

PROTARCHUS: Necessarily.

SOCRATES: So whoever makes this choice would choose generation and destruction in preference to that third life which consists of neither pleasure nor pain, but is a life of thought in the purest degree possible.

PROTARCHUS: So a great absurdity seems to appear, Socrates, if we posit pleasure as good.

SOCRATES: An absurdity indeed, especially if we go on to look at it this way.

PROTARCHUS: In what way?

b   SOCRATES: How is this not absurd: that there should be nothing good or noble in bodies or anywhere else except in the soul, but in the soul pleasure should be the only good thing, so that courage or moderation or reason or any of the other goods belonging to the soul would be neither good nor noble? In addition, we would have to call the person who experiences not pleasure but pain *bad* while he is in pain, even if he were the best of all men. By contrast, we would have to say of whoever is pleased that the greater his pleasure whenever he is pleased, the more he excels in virtue!   c

PROTARCHUS: All that is as absurd as possible, Socrates.

SOCRATES: Now, let us not undertake to give pleasure every possible test, while going very lightly with reason and knowledge. Let us rather strike them valiantly all around, to see if there is some fault anywhere. So we'll learn what is by nature purest in them. And seeing this, we can use the truest parts of these, as well as of pleasure, to make our joint decision.

PROTARCHUS: Fair enough.

SOCRATES: Among the disciplines to do with knowledge, one part is   d productive, the other concerned with education and nurture, right?

PROTARCHUS: Just so.

SOCRATES: But let us first find out whether within the manual arts there is one side more closely related to knowledge itself, the other less closely; secondly, whether we should treat the one as quite pure, as far as it goes, the other as less pure.

PROTARCHUS: That is what we ought to do.

SOCRATES: So let us sort out the leading disciplines among them.

PROTARCHUS: Which disciplines, and how are we to do it?

SOCRATES: If someone were to take away all counting, measuring, and   e weighing from the arts and crafts, the rest might be said to be worthless.

PROTARCHUS: Worthless, indeed!

SOCRATES: All we would have left would be conjecture and the training of our senses through experience and routine. We would have to rely on our ability to make the lucky guesses that many people call art, once it has acquired some proficiency through practice and hard work.   56

PROTARCHUS: Undeniably so.

SOCRATES: This is clear, to start with, in the case of flute-playing.[19] The harmonies are found not by measurement but by the hit and miss of training, and quite generally music tries to find the measure by observing the vibrating strings. So there is a lot of imprecision mixed up in it and very little reliability.

PROTARCHUS: Very true.

SOCRATES: And will we not discover that medicine, agriculture, naviga-   b tion, and strategy are in the same condition?

PROTARCHUS: Definitely.

SOCRATES: But as to building, I believe that it owes its superior level of craftsmanship over other disciplines to its frequent use of measures and instruments, which give it high accuracy.

PROTARCHUS: In what way?

---

19. Accepting the interchange of *mousikē* in a3 with *autēs aulētikē* in a5.

SOCRATES: In shipbuilding and housebuilding, but also in many other
c woodworking crafts. For it employs straightedge and compass, as well as
a mason's rule, a line, and an ingenious gadget called a carpenter's square.

PROTARCHUS: You are quite right, Socrates.

SOCRATES: Let us, then, divide the so-called arts into two parts, those
like music, with less precision in their practice, and those like building,
with more precision.

PROTARCHUS: Agreed.

SOCRATES: And let's take those among them as most accurate that we
called primary just now.

PROTARCHUS: I suppose you mean arithmetic and the other disciplines
you mentioned after it.

d SOCRATES: That's right. But don't you think we have to admit that they,
too, fall into two kinds, Protarchus?

PROTARCHUS: What two kinds do you mean?

SOCRATES: Don't we have to agree, first, that the arithmetic of the many
is one thing, and the philosophers' arithmetic is quite another?

PROTARCHUS: How could anyone distinguish these two kinds of arithmetic?

SOCRATES: The difference is by no means small, Protarchus. First there
are those who compute sums of quite unequal units, such as two armies
e or two herds of cattle, regardless whether they are tiny or huge. But then
there are the others who would not follow their example, unless it were
guaranteed that none of those infinitely many units differed in the least
from any of the others.

PROTARCHUS: You explain very well the notable difference among those
who make numbers their concern, so it stands to reason that there are
those two different kinds of arithmetic.

SOCRATES: Well, then, what about the art of calculating and measuring as
builders and merchants use them and the geometry and calculations prac-
57 ticed by philosophers—shall we say there is one sort of each of them or two?

PROTARCHUS: Going by what was said before, I ought to vote for the
option that they are two of each sort.

SOCRATES: Right. But do you realize why we have brought up this question here?

PROTARCHUS: Possibly, but I would appreciate it if you answered the
question yourself.

SOCRATES: The aim of our discussion now seems to be, just as it was
b when we first set out, to find an analogue here to the point we made about
pleasure. So now we ought to find out whether there is a difference in
purity between different kinds of knowledge in the same way as there
was between different kinds of pleasures.

PROTARCHUS: This obviously was the purpose of our present question.

SOCRATES: But what next? Have we not discovered before that different
subject matters require different arts and that they have different degrees
of certainty?

PROTARCHUS: Yes, we did.

SOCRATES: It is questionable, then, whether an art that goes under one name and is commonly treated as one should not rather be treated as two, depending on the difference in certainty and purity. And if this is so, we must also ask whether the art has more precision in the hands of the philosopher than its counterpart in the hands of the nonphilosopher.   c

PROTARCHUS: That is indeed the question here.

SOCRATES: So what answer shall we give to it, Protarchus?

PROTARCHUS: Socrates, we have come across an amazing difference between the sciences, as far as precision is concerned.

SOCRATES: Will that facilitate our answer?

PROTARCHUS: Obviously. And let it be said that these sciences are far superior to the other disciplines, but that those among them that are animated by the spirit of the true philosophers are infinitely superior yet in precision and truth in their use of measure and number.   d

SOCRATES: Let us settle for this doctrine, and trusting you, we will confidently answer those powerful makers of word traps.[20]

PROTARCHUS: What answer shall we give them?

SOCRATES: That there are two kinds of arithmetic and two kinds of geometry, and a great many other sciences following in their lead, which have the same twofold nature while sharing one name.

PROTARCHUS: Let us give our answer, with best wishes, to those powerful people, as you call them, Socrates.   e

SOCRATES: Do we maintain that these kinds of sciences are the most precise?

PROTARCHUS: Certainly.

SOCRATES: But the power of dialectic would repudiate us if we put any other science ahead of her.

PROTARCHUS: What science do we mean by that again?

SOCRATES: Clearly everybody would know what science I am referring to now! For I take it that anyone with any share in reason at all would consider the discipline concerned with being and with what is really and forever in every way eternally self-same by far the truest of all kinds of knowledge. But what is your position? How would you decide this question, Protarchus?   58

PROTARCHUS: On many occasions, Socrates, I have heard Gorgias insist that the art of persuasion is superior to all others because it enslaves all the rest, with their own consent, not by force, and is therefore by far the best of all the arts. Now I am reluctant to take up a position against either him or you.   b

SOCRATES: I suspect that at first you wanted to say "take up arms," but then suppressed it in embarrassment.[21]

PROTARCHUS: You may take this whatever way pleases you.

---

20. Cf. 15a–16a and 16c ff.

21. Since the claim is that rhetoric persuades and does not use force.

SOCRATES: But am I to blame for a misunderstanding on your part?

PROTARCHUS: In what respect?

c   SOCRATES: What I wanted to find out here, my dear friend Protarchus, was not what art or science excels all others by its grandeur, by its nobility, or by its usefulness to us. Our concern here was rather to find which one aims for clarity, precision, and the highest degree of truth, even if it is a minor discipline and our benefit is small. Look at it this way: You can avoid making an enemy of Gorgias so long as you let his art win as far as the actual profit for human life is concerned.

But as to the discipline I am talking about now, what I said earlier about the white also applies in this case: Even in a small quantity it can

d   be superior in purity and truth to what is large in quantity but impure and untrue. We must look for this science without concern for its actual benefit or its prestige, but see whether it is by its nature a capacity in our soul to love the truth and to do everything for its sake. And if thorough reflection and sufficient discussion confirms this for our art, then we can say that it is most likely to possess purity of mind and reason. Otherwise we would have to look for a higher kind of knowledge than this.

e   PROTARCHUS: Well, thinking it over, I agree that it would be difficult to find any other kind of art or any other science that is closer to the truth than this one.

SOCRATES: When you gave this answer now, did you realize that most of the arts and sciences and those who work at them are in the first place

59   only concerned with opinions and make opinions the center of their search? For even if they think they are studying nature, you must realize that all their lives they are merely dealing with this world order, how it came to be, how it is affected, and how it acts? Is that our position or not?

PROTARCHUS: Quite so.

SOCRATES: So such a person assumes the task of dealing, not with things eternal, but with what comes to be, will come to be, or has come to be?

PROTARCHUS: Undeniably.

SOCRATES: So how could we assert anything definite about these matters

b   with exact truth if it never did possess nor will possess nor now possesses any kind of sameness?

PROTARCHUS: Impossible.

SOCRATES: And how could we ever hope to achieve any kind of certainty about subject matters that do not in themselves possess any certainty?

PROTARCHUS: I see no way.

SOCRATES: Then there can be no reason or knowledge that attains the highest truth about these subjects!

PROTARCHUS: At least it does not seem likely.

SOCRATES: We must therefore dismiss entirely you and me and also Gorgias and Philebus, but must make this declaration about our investigation.

c   PROTARCHUS: What declaration?

SOCRATES: Either we will find certainty, purity, truth, and what we may call integrity among the things that are forever in the same state, without anything mixed in it, or we will find it in what comes as close as possible to it. Everything else has to be called second-rate and inferior.

PROTARCHUS: Very true.

SOCRATES: Would not strict justice demand that we call the noblest things by the noblest names?

PROTARCHUS: That's only fair.

SOCRATES: And aren't reason and knowledge names that deserve the highest honor?   d

PROTARCHUS: Yes.

SOCRATES: So, in their most accurate sense and appropriate use, they are applied to insights into true reality?

PROTARCHUS: Definitely.

SOCRATES: But these were the very names that I put forward at the beginning for our verdict.

PROTARCHUS: The very ones, Socrates.

SOCRATES: Good. But as to the *mixture* of intelligence and pleasure, if one likened our situation to that of builders with ingredients or materials to use in construction, this would be a fitting comparison.   e

PROTARCHUS: Very fitting.

SOCRATES: So next we ought to try our hands at the mixture?

PROTARCHUS: Definitely.

SOCRATES: But had we not better repeat and remind ourselves of certain points?

PROTARCHUS: What are they?

SOCRATES: Those we kept reminding ourselves of before. The proverb fits well here that says that good things deserve repeating 'twice or even thrice'.   60

PROTARCHUS: Definitely.

SOCRATES: On, then, by the heavens! This is, I think, the general drift of what we said.

PROTARCHUS: What was it?

SOCRATES: Philebus says that pleasure is the right aim for all living beings and that all should try to strive for it, that it is at the same time the good for all things, so that good and pleasant are but two names that really belong to what is by nature one and the same. Socrates, by contrast, affirms   b
that these are not one and the same thing but two, just as they are two in name, that the good and the pleasant have a different nature, and that intelligence has a greater share in the good than pleasure. Isn't that the matter at issue now, just as it was before, Protarchus?[22]

PROTARCHUS: Very much so.

SOCRATES: And are we also agreed on this point now, just as we were before?

PROTARCHUS: What point?

SOCRATES: That the difference between the nature of the good and everything else is this?

22. See 11b–c, and, for the references just below, 20d–23b.

c   PROTARCHUS: What is it?

SOCRATES: Any creature that was in permanent possession of it, entirely and in every way, would never be in need of anything else, but would live in perfect self-sufficiency. Is that right?

PROTARCHUS: It is right.

SOCRATES: But didn't we try to give them a separate trial in our discussion, assigning each of them a life of its own, so that pleasure would remain unmixed with intelligence, and, again, intelligence would not have the tiniest bit of pleasure?

PROTARCHUS: That's what we did.

d   SOCRATES: Did either of the two seem to us self-sufficient at that time for anyone?

PROTARCHUS: How could it?

SOCRATES: If some mistake was made then, anyone now has the opportunity to take it up again and correct it. Let him put memory, intelligence, knowledge, and true opinion into one class, and ask himself whether anybody would choose to possess or acquire anything else without that class. Most particularly, whether he would want pleasure, as much and

e   as intensive as it can be, without the true opinion that he enjoys it, without recognizing what kind of experience it is he has, without memory of this affection for any length of time. And let him put reason to the same test, whether anyone would prefer to have it without any kind of pleasure, even a very short-lived one, rather than with some pleasures, provided that he does not want all pleasures without intelligence rather than with some fraction of it.

PROTARCHUS: Neither of them will do, Socrates, and there is no need to raise the same question so often.

61   SOCRATES: So neither of these two would be perfect, worthy of choice for all, and the supreme good?

PROTARCHUS: How could they?

SOCRATES: The good therefore must be taken up precisely or at least in outline, so that, as we said before, we know to whom we will give the second prize.

PROTARCHUS: You are right.

SOCRATES: Have we not discovered at least a road that leads towards the good?

PROTARCHUS: What road?

SOCRATES: It's as if, when you are looking for somebody, you first find out

b   where he actually lives. That would be a major step towards finding him.

PROTARCHUS: No doubt.

SOCRATES: Similarly here. There is this argument which has now indicated to us, just as it did at the beginning of our discussion, that we ought not to seek the good in the unmixed life but in the mixed one.

PROTARCHUS: Quite.

SOCRATES: But there is more hope that what we are looking for will show itself in a well-mixed life rather than in a poorly mixed one?

PROTARCHUS: Much more.

SOCRATES: So let us pray to the gods for assistance when we perform our mixture, Protarchus, whether it be Dionysus or Hephaestus or any other deity who is in charge of presiding over such mixtures. c

PROTARCHUS: By all means.

SOCRATES: We stand like cup-bearers before the fountains—the fountain of pleasure, comparable to honey, and the sobering fountain of intelligence, free of wine, like sober, healthy water—and we have to see how to make a perfect mixture of the two.

PROTARCHUS: Certainly.

SOCRATES: But let's look first into this: Will our mixture be as good as it d
can be if we mix every kind of pleasure with every kind of intelligence?

PROTARCHUS: Maybe.

SOCRATES: It is not without risk, however. But now I have an idea how we might procure a safer mixture.

PROTARCHUS: Tell us what it is.

SOCRATES: Didn't we find that one pleasure turned out to be truer than another, just as one art was more precise than the other?

PROTARCHUS: Definitely.

SOCRATES: But there was also a difference between different sciences, since one kind deals with a subject matter that comes to be and perishes, the other e
is concerned with what is free of that, the eternal and self-same. Since we made truth our criterion, the latter kind appeared to be the truer one.

PROTARCHUS: That was certainly so.

SOCRATES: If we took from each sort the segments that possess most truth and mixed them together, would this mixture provide us with the most desirable life, or would we also need less-true ones?

PROTARCHUS: We should do it this way, it seems to me. 62

SOCRATES: Suppose, then, there is a person who understands what justice itself is and can give the appropriate definitions and possesses the same kind of comprehension about all the rest of what there is.

PROTARCHUS: Let that be presupposed.

SOCRATES: Will he be sufficiently versed in science if he knows the definition of the circle and of the divine sphere itself but cannot recognize the human sphere and these our circles, using even in housebuilding those b
other yardsticks and those circles?

PROTARCHUS: We would find ourselves in a rather ridiculous position if we were confined entirely to those divine kinds of knowledge, Socrates!

SOCRATES: What are you saying? Ought we at the same time to include the inexact and impure science of the false yardstick and circle, and add it to the mixture?

PROTARCHUS: Yes, necessarily so, if any one of us ever wants to find his own way home.

SOCRATES: But how about music: Ought we also to mix in the kind of c
which we said a little earlier that it is full of lucky hits and imitation but lacks purity?

PROTARCHUS: It seems necessary to me, if in fact our life is supposed to be at least some sort of *life*.

SOCRATES: Do you want me, then, to yield like a doorkeeper to the pushing and shoving of a crowd and to throw open the doors and let the flood of all sorts of knowledge in, the inferior kind mingling with the pure?

d   PROTARCHUS: I for my part can't see what damage it would do to accept all the other kinds of knowledge, as long as we have those of the highest kind.

SOCRATES: Shall I, then, let the lot of them flow into the vessel like Homer's very poetical "commingling of mountain glens"?[23]

PROTARCHUS: Absolutely.

SOCRATES: In they go! But now we have to return again to the fountain of pleasure. We cannot any longer carry out our original intention of first mixing only the true parts of each of them together. Our love for every

e   kind of knowledge has made us let them all in together, before any of the pleasures.

PROTARCHUS: What you say is true.

SOCRATES: Now it is time for us to decide about pleasures, too, whether we ought to admit the whole tribe in their cases or whether we should at first admit the true ones only.

PROTARCHUS: It is much safer if we let the true in first!

SOCRATES: Let them in, then. But what next? If some turn out to be necessary, should we not mix them in also, as we did in the other case?

PROTARCHUS: No reason why not, at least if they really are necessary.

63   SOCRATES: But having decided that it was innocuous or even beneficial to spend our lives in the pursuit of all the arts and crafts, we may now come to the same conclusion about the pleasures. If it is beneficial and harmless to live our lives enjoying all the pleasures, then we should mix them all in.

PROTARCHUS: So what are we to say in their case, and what are we to do?

SOCRATES: We should not turn to ourselves with this question, Protarchus, but to the pleasures themselves, as well as to the different kinds of knowledge, and find out how they feel about each other by putting the question in this way.

b   PROTARCHUS: What way?

SOCRATES: "My friends, whether you ought to be called 'pleasures' or some other name,[24] would you prefer to live together with every kind of knowledge or rather to live without it entirely?"—To this I think they cannot help giving this answer.

PROTARCHUS: What answer?

SOCRATES: What has been said already: "It is neither possible nor beneficial

c   for one tribe to remain alone, in isolation and unmixed. We would prefer to live side by side with that best kind of knowledge, the kind that understands not only all other things but also each one of us, as far as that is possible."

PROTARCHUS: "An excellent answer," we will reply to them.

---

23. Cf. *Iliad* iv.452. The picture in Homer is not nearly as cheerful as Plato's; it is the mixture of the uproar in a fierce battle that is there described.

24. See 11b.

SOCRATES: With justice. But after that we have to raise the question with intelligence and reason. "Do you have any need for any association with the pleasures?" That is how we would address reason and knowledge. "What kinds of pleasures?" they might ask in return.

PROTARCHUS: Very likely.

SOCRATES: Our discussion would then continue as follows: "Will you have any need to associate with the strongest and most intensive pleasures in addition to the true pleasures?" we will ask them. "Why on earth should we need them, Socrates?" they might reply, "They are a tremendous impediment to us, since they infect the souls in which they dwell with madness or even prevent our own development altogether. Furthermore, they totally destroy most of our offspring, since neglect leads to forgetfulness. But as to the true and pure pleasures you mentioned, those regard as our kin. And besides, also add the pleasures of health and of temperance and all those that commit themselves to virtue as to their deity and follow it around everywhere. But to forge an association between reason and those pleasures that are forever involved with foolishness and other kinds of vice would be totally unreasonable for anyone who aims at the best and most stable mixture or blend. This is true particularly if he wants to discover in this mixture what the good is in man and in the universe and to get some vision of the nature of the good itself." When reason makes this defense for herself, as well as for memory and right opinion, shall we not admit that she has spoken reasonably and in accord with her own standards?

PROTARCHUS: Absolutely.

SOCRATES: But see whether the following is also necessary and without it not a single thing could come to be.

PROTARCHUS: What is it?

SOCRATES: Wherever we do not mix in truth nothing could truly come to be nor remain in existence once it had come to be.

PROTARCHUS: How should it?

SOCRATES: In no way. But now, if there is anything else missing in our mixture, it is up to you and Philebus to say so. To me at least it seems that our discussion has arrived at the design of what might be called an incorporeal order that rules harmoniously over a body possessed by a soul.

PROTARCHUS: Count me as one who shares that opinion, Socrates.

SOCRATES: Would there be some justification to our claim that we are by now standing on the very threshold of the good and of the house[25] of every member of its family?[26]

PROTARCHUS: It would seem so, to me at least.

SOCRATES: What ingredient in the mixture ought we to regard as most valuable and at the same time as the factor that makes it precious to all mankind? Once we have found it, we will inquire further whether it is more closely related and akin to pleasure or to reason, in nature as a whole.

25. For the house, see 61b.
26. Keeping the reading of the manuscripts.

d PROTARCHUS: You are right. This would certainly be very useful in bringing us closer to our final verdict.

SOCRATES: But it is certainly not difficult to see what factor in each mixture it is that makes it either most valuable or worth nothing at all.

PROTARCHUS: What do you mean?

SOCRATES: There is not a single human being who does not know it.

PROTARCHUS: Know what?

SOCRATES: That any kind of mixture that does not in some way or other possess measure or the nature of proportion will necessarily corrupt its

e ingredients and most of all itself. For there would be no blending in such cases at all but really an unconnected medley, the ruin of whatever happens to be contained in it.

PROTARCHUS: Very true.

SOCRATES: But now we notice that the force of the good has taken refuge in an alliance with the nature of the beautiful. For measure and proportion manifest themselves in all areas as beauty and virtue.

PROTARCHUS: Undeniably.

SOCRATES: But we did say that truth is also included along with them in our mixture?

PROTARCHUS: Indeed.

65 SOCRATES: Well, then, if we cannot capture the good in *one* form, we will have to take hold of it in a conjunction of three: beauty, proportion, and truth. Let us affirm that these should by right be treated as a unity and be held responsible for what is in the mixture, for its goodness is what makes the mixture itself a good one.

PROTARCHUS: Very well stated.

SOCRATES: Anyone should by now be able to judge between pleasure

b and intelligence, which of the two is more closely related to the supreme good and more valuable among gods and men.

PROTARCHUS: Even if it is obvious, it is better to make it explicit in our discussion.

SOCRATES: So now let us judge each one of the three in relation to pleasure and reason. For we have to see for which of those two we want to grant closer kinship to each of them.

PROTARCHUS: You mean to beauty, truth, and measure?

SOCRATES: Yes. Take up truth first, Protarchus, and, holding it in front

c of you, look at all three: reason, truth, and pleasure. Then, after withholding judgment for a long time, give your answer, whether for you pleasure or reason is more akin to truth.

PROTARCHUS: What need is there for any length of time? I think there is an enormous difference. For pleasure is the greatest impostor of all, by general account, and in connection with the pleasures of love, which seem to be the greatest of all, even perjury is pardoned by the gods. Pleasures are perhaps rather like children who don't possess the least bit of reason.

d Reason, by contrast, either is the same as truth or of all things it is most like it and most true.

SOCRATES: Next look at measure in the same way, and see whether pleasure possesses more of it than intelligence or intelligence more than pleasure.

PROTARCHUS: Once again you are setting me a task I am well prepared for. I don't think that one could find anything that is more outside all measure than pleasure and excessive joy, while nothing more measured than reason and knowledge could ever be found.

SOCRATES: Well argued. But now go on to the third criterion. Does reason contain more beauty than the tribe of pleasures in our estimate, so that reason is more beautiful than pleasure, or is it the other way round?

PROTARCHUS: Why, Socrates, no one, awake or dreaming, could ever see intelligence and reason to be ugly; no one could ever have conceived of them as becoming or being ugly, or that they ever will be.

SOCRATES: Right.

PROTARCHUS: In the case of pleasures, by contrast, when we see anyone actively engaged in them, especially those that are most intense, we notice that their effect is quite ridiculous, if not outright obscene; we become quite ashamed ourselves and hide them as much as possible from sight, and we confine such activities to the night, as if daylight must not witness such things.

SOCRATES: So you will announce everywhere, both by sending messengers and saying it in person to those present, that pleasure is not a property of the first rank, nor again of the second, but that first comes what is somehow connected with measure, the measured and the timely, and whatever else is to be considered similar.[27]

PROTARCHUS: That seems at least to be the upshot of our discussion now.

SOCRATES: The second rank goes to the well-proportioned and beautiful, the perfect, the self-sufficient, and whatever else belongs in that family.

PROTARCHUS: That seems right.

SOCRATES: If you give the third rank, as I divine, to reason and intelligence, you cannot stray far from the truth.

PROTARCHUS: Perhaps.

SOCRATES: Nor again if, beside these three, you give fourth place to those things that we defined as the soul's own properties, to the sciences and the arts, and what we called right opinions, since they are more closely related to the good than pleasure at least.

PROTARCHUS: Maybe so.

SOCRATES: The fifth kind will be those pleasures we set apart and defined as painless; we called them the soul's own pure pleasures, since they are attached to the sciences, some of them even to sense-perception.

PROTARCHUS: Perhaps.

SOCRATES: "With the sixth generation the well-ordered song may find its end," says Orpheus. So it seems that our discussion, too, has found its

e

66

b

c

---

27. In our mss this sentence ends with a hopelessly corrupt and meaningless phrase, which has therefore been omitted in the translation.

d   end at the determination of the sixth ranking. There remains nothing
further to do for us except to give a final touch to what has been said.

PROTARCHUS: We have to do that.

SOCRATES: Come on, then, "the third libation goes to Zeus the Savior,"
let us call the same argument to witness for the third time.

PROTARCHUS: Which one?

SOCRATES: Philebus declares that every pleasure of any kind is the
good. . . .

PROTARCHUS: By the "third libation" you appear to mean, as you just
stated, that we have to repeat the argument all over from the beginning!

e   SOCRATES: Yes, but let's also hear what follows. In view of all the considerations laid out here and out of distaste for Philebus' position pronounced
by countless others on many occasions, I maintained that reason is far
superior to pleasure and more beneficial for human life.

PROTARCHUS: That is correct.

SOCRATES: Suspecting that there are many other goods, I said that if
something turned out to be better than these two, then I would fight on
the side of reason for the second prize against pleasure, so that pleasure
would be deprived even of the second rank.

67   PROTARCHUS: You did say that.

SOCRATES: Afterwards it became most sufficiently clear that neither of
those two would suffice.

PROTARCHUS: Very true.

SOCRATES: And did it not become clear at this point in our discussion
that both reason and pleasure had lost any claim that one or the other
would be the good itself, since they were lacking in autonomy and in the
power of self-sufficiency and perfection?

PROTARCHUS: Exactly.

SOCRATES: Then, when a third competitor showed up, superior to either
of them, it became apparent that reason was infinitely more closely related
and akin to the character of the victor.

PROTARCHUS: Undeniably.

SOCRATES: And did not pleasure turn out to receive fifth position, according to the verdict we reached in our discussion?

PROTARCHUS: Apparently.

b   SOCRATES: But not first place, even if all the cattle and horses and the rest
of the animals gave testimony by following pleasure. Now, many people
accept their testimony, as the seers do that of the birds, and judge that pleasures are most effective in securing the happy life; they even believe that the
animal passions are more authoritative witnesses than is the love of argument that is constantly revealed under the guidance of the philosophic muse.

PROTARCHUS: We are all agreed now that what you said is as true as
possible, Socrates.

SOCRATES: So will you let me go now?

PROTARCHUS: There is still a little missing, Socrates. Surely you will not
give up before we do. But I will remind you of what is left!

SYMPOSIUM

This dialogue, Plato's poetic and dramatic masterpiece, relates the events of a 'symposium' or formal drinking party held in honor of the tragedian Agathon's first victorious production. To gratify Phaedrus (the passionate admirer of speeches and rhetoric in the dialogue named after him), who indignantly regrets the neglect by Greek poets and writers of the god of Love, the company agree to give speeches in turn, while they all drink, in praise of Love. 'Love' (Greek erôs) covers sexual attraction and gratification between men and women and between men and teenage boys, but the focus here is also and especially on the adult male's role as ethical and intellectual educator of the adolescent that was traditional among the Athenians in the latter sort of relationship, whether accompanied by sex or not. There are six speeches—plus a seventh delivered by an uninvited and very drunk latecomer, the Athenian statesman and general Alcibiades. In his youth Alcibiades had been one of Socrates' admiring followers, and he now reports in gripping detail the fascinating reversal Socrates worked upon him in the erotic roles of the older and the younger man usual among the Greeks in a relationship of 'love': Socrates became the pursued, Alcibiades the pursuer. Appropriately enough, all the speakers, with the interesting exception of the comic poet Aristophanes, are mentioned in Protagoras as among those who flocked to Callias' house to attend the sophists gathered there (all experts on speaking): as he enters Callias' house, Socrates spots four of the Symposium speakers—Phaedrus and Eryximachus in a crowd round Hippias, and Agathon and Pausanias (his lover) hanging on the words of Prodicus; Alcibiades joins the company shortly afterwards.

Socrates' own speech is given over to reporting a discourse on love he says he once heard from Diotima, a wise woman from Mantinea. This Diotima seems an invention, contrived by Socrates (and Plato) to distance Socrates in his report of it from what she says. In any event, Diotima herself is made to say that Socrates can probably not follow her in the 'final and highest mystery' of the 'rites of love'—her account of the ascent in love, beginning with love for individual young men, ending with love for the Form of Beauty, which 'always is and neither comes to be nor passes away, neither waxes nor wanes', and is 'not beautiful this way and ugly that way, nor beautiful at one time and ugly at another, nor beautiful in relation to one thing and ugly in relation to another' but is 'just what it is to be beautiful'. In this way Plato lets us know that this theory of the Beautiful is his own contrivance, not really an idea of Socrates (whether the historical philosopher or the philosopher of the 'Socratic' dialogues). Readers will want to compare Diotima's speech on Love with those *of Socrates in* Phaedrus, *and also with Socrates' discussion on friendship with the boys in the* Lysis.

The events of this evening at Agathon's house are all reported long afterward by a young friend of Socrates' in his last years, Apollodorus. Apparently they had become famous among Socrates' intimates and others who were interested in hearing about him. That, at any rate, is the impression Apollodorus leaves us with: he has himself taken the trouble to learn about it all from Aristodemus, who was present on the occasion, and he has just reported on it to Glaucon (Socrates' conversation partner in the Republic). *He now reports again to an unnamed friend who has asked to hear about it all—and to us readers of Plato's dialogue.*

J.M.C.

172   APOLLODORUS: In fact, your question does not find me unprepared. Just the other day, as it happens, I was walking to the city from my home in Phaleron when a man I know, who was making his way behind me, saw me and called from a distance:

"The gentleman from Phaleron!" he yelled, trying to be funny. "Hey, Apollodorus, wait!"

So I stopped and waited.

b   "Apollodorus, I've been looking for you!" he said. "You know there once was a gathering at Agathon's when Socrates, Alcibiades, and their friends had dinner together; I wanted to ask you about the speeches they made on Love. What were they? I heard a version from a man who had it from Phoenix, Philip's son, but it was badly garbled, and he said you were the one to ask. So please, will you tell me all about it? After all, Socrates is your friend—who has a better right than you to report his conversation? But before you begin," he added, "tell me this: were you there yourself?"

c   "Your friend must have really garbled his story," I replied, "if you think this affair was so recent that I could have been there."

"I did think that," he said.

"Glaucon, how could you? You know very well Agathon hasn't lived in Athens for many years, while it's been less than three that I've been Socrates' companion and made it my job to know exactly what he says

173   and does each day. Before that, I simply drifted aimlessly. Of course, I used to think that what I was doing was important, but in fact I was the most worthless man on earth—as bad as you are this very moment: I used to think philosophy was the last thing a man should do."

"Stop joking, Apollodorus," he replied. "Just tell me when the party took place."

Translated by A. Nehamas and P. Woodruff.

"When we were still children, when Agathon won the prize with his first tragedy. It was the day after he and his troupe held their victory celebration."

"So it really was a long time ago," he said. "Then who told you about it? Was it Socrates himself?"

"Oh, for god's sake, of course not!" I replied. "It was the very same man   b
who told Phoenix, a fellow called Aristodemus, from Cydatheneum, a real runt of a man, who always went barefoot. He went to the party because, I think, he was obsessed with Socrates—one of the worst cases at that time. Naturally, I checked part of his story with Socrates, and Socrates agreed with his account."

"Please tell me, then," he said. "You speak and I'll listen, as we walk to the city. This is the perfect opportunity."

So this is what we talked about on our way; and that's why, as I said   c
before, I'm not unprepared. Well, if I'm to tell *you* about it too—I'll be glad to. After all, my greatest pleasure comes from philosophical conversation, even if I'm only a listener, whether or not I think it will be to my advantage. All other talk, especially the talk of rich businessmen like you, bores me to tears, and I'm sorry for you and your friends because you think your affairs are important when really they're totally trivial. Perhaps,   d
in your turn, you think I'm a failure, and, believe me, I think that what you think is true. But as for all of you, I don't just *think* you are failures— I know it for a fact.

FRIEND: You'll never change, Apollodorus! Always nagging, even at yourself! I do believe you think everybody—yourself first of all—is totally worthless, except, of course, Socrates. I don't know exactly how you came to be called "the maniac," but you certainly talk like one, always furious with everyone, including yourself—but not with Socrates!

APOLLODORUS: Of course, my dear friend, it's perfectly obvious why I   e
have these views about us all: it's simply because I'm a maniac, and I'm raving!

FRIEND: It's not worth arguing about this now, Apollodorus. Please do as I asked: tell me the speeches.

APOLLODORUS: All right . . . Well, the speeches went something like this— but I'd better tell you the whole story from the very beginning, as Aristode-   174
mus told it to me.

He said, then, that one day he ran into Socrates, who had just bathed and put on his fancy sandals—both very unusual events. So he asked him where he was going, and why he was looking so good.

Socrates replied, "I'm going to Agathon's for dinner. I managed to avoid yesterday's victory party—I really don't like crowds—but I promised to be there today. So, naturally, I took great pains with my appearance: I'm going to the house of a good-looking man; I had to look my best. But let me ask you this," he added, "I know you haven't been invited to the dinner; how would you like to come anyway?"   b

And Aristodemus answered, "I'll do whatever you say."

"Come with me, then," Socrates said, "and we shall prove the proverb wrong; the truth is, 'Good men go uninvited to Goodman's feast.'[1] Even Homer himself, when you think about it, did not much like this proverb;

c he not only disregarded it, he violated it. Agamemnon, of course, is one of his great warriors, while he describes Menelaus as a 'limp spearman.' And yet, when Agamemnon offers a sacrifice and gives a feast, Homer has the weak Menelaus arrive uninvited at his superior's table."[2]

Aristodemus replied to this, "Socrates, I am afraid Homer's description is bound to fit me better than yours. Mine is a case of an obvious inferior arriving uninvited at the table of a man of letters. I think you'd better figure out a good excuse for bringing me along, because, you know, I

d won't admit I've come without an invitation. I'll say I'm your guest."

"Let's go," he said. "We'll think about what to say 'as we proceed the two of us along the way.' "[3]

With these words, they set out. But as they were walking, Socrates began to think about something, lost himself in thought, and kept lagging behind. Whenever Aristodemus stopped to wait for him, Socrates would urge him

e to go on ahead. When he arrived at Agathon's he found the gate wide open, and that, Aristodemus said, caused him to find himself in a very embarrassing situation: a household slave saw him the moment he arrived and took him immediately to the dining room, where the guests were already lying down on their couches, and dinner was about to be served.

As soon as Agathon saw him, he called:

"Welcome, Aristodemus! What perfect timing! You're just in time for dinner! I hope you're not here for any other reason—if you are, forget it. I looked all over for you yesterday, so I could invite you, but I couldn't find you anywhere. But where is Socrates? How come you didn't bring him along?"

So I turned around (Aristodemus said), and Socrates was nowhere to be seen. And I said that it was actually Socrates who had brought *me* along as his guest.

175   "I'm delighted he did," Agathon replied. "But where is he?"

"He was directly behind me, but I have no idea where he is now."

"Go look for Socrates," Agathon ordered a slave, "and bring him in. Aristodemus," he added, "you can share Eryximachus' couch."

A slave brought water, and Aristodemus washed himself before he lay down. Then another slave entered and said: "Socrates is here, but he's gone off to the neighbor's porch. He's standing there and won't come in even though I called him several times."

---

1. Agathon's name could be translated "Goodman." The proverb is, "Good men go uninvited to an inferior man's feast" (Eupolis fr. 289 Kock).

2. Menelaus calls on Agamemnon at *Iliad* ii.408. Menelaus is called a limp spearman at xvii.587–88.

3. An allusion to *Iliad* x.224, "When two go together, one has an idea before the other."

"How strange," Agathon replied. "Go back and bring him in. Don't leave him there."

But Aristodemus stopped him. "No, no," he said. "Leave him alone. It's one of his habits: every now and then he just goes off like that and stands motionless, wherever he happens to be. I'm sure he'll come in very soon, so don't disturb him; let him be."

"Well, all right, if you really think so," Agathon said, and turned to the slaves: "Go ahead and serve the rest of us. What you serve is completely up to you; pretend nobody's supervising you—as if I ever did! Imagine that we are all your own guests, myself included. Give us good reason to praise your service."

So they went ahead and started eating, but there was still no sign of Socrates. Agathon wanted to send for him many times, but Aristodemus wouldn't let him. And, in fact, Socrates came in shortly afterward, as he always did—they were hardly halfway through their meal. Agathon, who, as it happened, was all alone on the farthest couch, immediately called: "Socrates, come lie down next to me. Who knows, if I touch you, I may catch a bit of the wisdom that came to you under my neighbor's porch. It's clear *you've* seen the light. If you hadn't, you'd still be standing there."

Socrates sat down next to him and said, "How wonderful it would be, dear Agathon, if the foolish were filled with wisdom simply by touching the wise. If only wisdom were like water, which always flows from a full cup into an empty one when we connect them with a piece of yarn—well, then I would consider it the greatest prize to have the chance to lie down next to you. I would soon be overflowing with your wonderful wisdom. My own wisdom is of no account—a shadow in a dream—while yours is bright and radiant and has a splendid future. Why, young as you are, you're so brilliant I could call more than thirty thousand Greeks as witnesses."

"Now you've gone *too* far, Socrates," Agathon replied. "Well, eat your dinner. Dionysus will soon enough be the judge of our claims to wisdom!"[4] 176

Socrates took his seat after that and had his meal, according to Aristodemus. When dinner was over, they poured a libation to the god, sang a hymn, and—in short—followed the whole ritual. Then they turned their attention to drinking. At that point Pausanias addressed the group:

"Well, gentlemen, how can we arrange to drink less tonight? To be honest, I still have a terrible hangover from yesterday, and I could really use a break. I daresay most of you could, too, since you were also part of the celebration. So let's try not to overdo it."

Aristophanes replied: "Good idea, Pausanias. We've got to make a plan for going easy on the drink tonight. I was over my head last night myself, like the others."

After that, up spoke Eryximachus, son of Acumenus: "Well said, both of you. But I still have one question: How do *you* feel, Agathon? Are you strong enough for serious drinking?"

---

4. Dionysus was the god of wine and drunkenness.

"Absolutely not," replied Agathon. "I've no strength left for anything."

c   "What a lucky stroke for us," Eryximachus said, "for me, for Aristodemus, for Phaedrus, and the rest—that you large-capacity drinkers are
already exhausted. Imagine how weak drinkers like ourselves feel after
last night! Of course I don't include Socrates in my claims: he can drink
or not, and will be satisfied whatever we do. But since none of us seems
particularly eager to overindulge, perhaps it would not be amiss for me

d   to provide you with some accurate information as to the nature of intoxica-
tion. If I have learned anything from medicine, it is the following point:
inebriation is harmful to everyone. Personally, therefore, I always refrain
from heavy drinking; and I advise others against it—especially people
who are suffering the effects of a previous night's excesses."

       "Well," Phaedrus interrupted him, "I always follow your advice, espe-
cially when you speak as a doctor. In this case, if the others know what's
good for them, they too will do just as you say."

e   At that point they all agreed not to get drunk that evening; they decided
to drink only as much as pleased them.

       "It's settled, then," said Eryximachus. "We are resolved to force no one
to drink more than he wants. I would like now to make a further motion:
let us dispense with the flute-girl who just made her entrance; let her play
for herself or, if she prefers, for the women in the house. Let us instead
spend our evening in conversation. If you are so minded, I would like to

177   propose a subject."

       They all said they were quite willing, and urged him to make his pro-
posal. So Eryximachus said:

       "Let me begin by citing Euripides' *Melanippe*: 'Not mine the tale.' What
I am about to tell belongs to Phaedrus here, who is deeply indignant on
this issue, and often complains to me about it:

       "'Eryximachus,' he says, 'isn't it an awful thing! Our poets have com-
posed hymns in honor of just about any god you can think of; but has a

b   single one of them given one moment's thought to the god of love, ancient
and powerful as he is? As for our fancy intellectuals, they have written
volumes praising Heracles and other heroes (as did the distinguished
Prodicus). Well, perhaps *that's* not surprising, but I've actually read a book

c   by an accomplished author who saw fit to extol the usefulness of salt!
How *could* people pay attention to such trifles and never, not even once,
write a proper hymn to Love? How could anyone ignore so great a god?'

       "Now, Phaedrus, in my judgment, is quite right. I would like, therefore,
to take up a contribution, as it were, on his behalf, and gratify his wish.

d   Besides, I think this a splendid time for all of us here to honor the god. If
you agree, we can spend the whole evening in discussion, because I propose
that each of us give as good a speech in praise of Love as he is capable
of giving, in proper order from left to right. And let us begin with Phaedrus,
who is at the head of the table and is, in addition, the father of our subject."

       "No one will vote against that, Eryximachus," said Socrates. "How could

e   *I* vote 'No,' when the only thing I say I understand is the art of love?

Could Agathon and Pausanias? Could Aristophanes, who thinks of nothing but Dionysus and Aphrodite? No one I can see here now could vote against your proposal.

"And though it's not quite fair to those of us who have to speak last, if the first speeches turn out to be good enough and to exhaust our subject, I promise we won't complain. So let Phaedrus begin, with the blessing of Fortune; let's hear his praise of Love."

They all agreed with Socrates, and pressed Phaedrus to start. Of course, Aristodemus couldn't remember exactly what everyone said, and I myself don't remember everything he told me. But I'll tell you what he remembered best, and what I consider the most important points.

As I say, he said Phaedrus spoke first, beginning more or less like this:

Love is a great god, wonderful in many ways to gods and men, and most marvelous of all is the way he came into being. We honor him as one of the most ancient gods, and the proof of his great age is this: the parents of Love have no place in poetry or legend. According to Hesiod, the first to be born was Chaos,

> . . . but then came
> *Earth, broad-chested, a seat for all, forever safe,*
> *And Love.*[5]

And Acusilaus agrees with Hesiod: after Chaos came Earth and Love, these two.[6] And Parmenides tells of this beginning:

> *The very first god [she] designed was Love.*[7]

All sides agree, then, that Love is one of the most ancient gods. As such, he gives to us the greatest goods. I cannot say what greater good there is for a young boy than a gentle lover, or for a lover than a boy to love. There is a certain guidance each person needs for his whole life, if he is to live well; and nothing imparts this guidance—not high kinship, not public honor, not wealth—nothing imparts this guidance as well as Love. What guidance do I mean? I mean a sense of shame at acting shamefully, and a sense of pride in acting well. Without these, nothing fine or great can be accomplished, in public or in private.

What I say is this: if a man in love is found doing something shameful, or accepting shameful treatment because he is a coward and makes no defense, then nothing would give him more pain than being seen by the boy he loves—not even being seen by his father or his comrades. We see

5. *Theogony* 116–120, 118 omitted.
6. Acusilaus was an early-fifth-century writer of genealogies.
7. Parmenides, B 13 Diels-Kranz.

the same thing also in the boy he loves, that he is especially ashamed before his lover when he is caught in something shameful. If only there were a way to start a city or an army made up of lovers and the boys they love! Theirs would be the best possible system of society, for they would
179   hold back from all that is shameful, and seek honor in each other's eyes.[8] Even a few of them, in battle side by side, would conquer all the world, I'd say. For a man in love would never allow his loved one, of all people, to see him leaving ranks or dropping weapons. He'd rather die a thousand deaths! And as for leaving the boy behind, or not coming to his aid in danger—why, no one is so base that true Love could not inspire him with
b   courage, and make him as brave as if he'd been born a hero. When Homer says a god 'breathes might' into some of the heroes, this is really Love's gift to every lover.[9]

       Besides, no one will die for you but a lover, and a lover will do this even if she's a woman. Alcestis is proof to everyone in Greece that what
c   I say is true.[10] Only she was willing to die in place of her husband, although his father and mother were still alive. Because of her love, she went so far beyond his parents in family feeling that she made them look like outsiders, as if they belonged to their son in name only. And when she did this her deed struck everyone, even the gods, as nobly done. The gods were so delighted, in fact, that they gave her the prize they reserve for a handful
d   chosen from the throngs of noble heroes—they sent her soul back from the dead. As you can see, the eager courage of love wins highest honors from the gods.

       Orpheus, however, they sent unsatisfied from Hades, after showing him only an image of the woman he came for. They did not give him the woman herself, because they thought he was soft (he was, after all, a cithara-player) and did not dare to die like Alcestis for Love's sake, but contrived to enter living into Hades. So they punished him for that, and
e   made him die at the hands of women.[11]

       The honor they gave to Achilles is another matter. They sent him to the Isles of the Blest because he dared to stand by his lover Patroclus and
180   avenge him, even after he had learned from his mother that he would die if he killed Hector, but that if he chose otherwise he'd go home and end his life as an old man. Instead he chose to die for Patroclus, and more than that, he did it for a man whose life was already over. The gods were highly delighted at this, of course, and gave him special honor, because he made so much of his lover. Aeschylus talks nonsense when he claims

---

8. Accepting the deletion of *ē* in e5.

9. Cf. *Iliad* x.482, xv.262; *Odyssey* ix.381.

10. Alcestis was the self-sacrificing wife of Admetus, whom Apollo gave a chance to live if anyone would go to Hades in his place.

11. Orpheus was a musician of legendary powers, who charmed his way into the underworld in search of his dead wife, Eurydice.

Achilles was the lover;[12] he was more beautiful than Patroclus, more beautiful than all the heroes, and still beardless. Besides he was much younger,
as Homer says.

In truth, the gods honor virtue most highly when it belongs to Love.   b
They are more impressed and delighted, however, and are more generous
with a loved one who cherishes his lover, than with a lover who cherishes
the boy he loves. A lover is more godlike than his boy, you see, since he
is inspired by a god. That's why they gave a higher honor to Achilles than
to Alcestis, and sent him to the Isles of the Blest.

Therefore I say Love is the most ancient of the gods, the most honored,
and the most powerful in helping men gain virtue and blessedness, whether
they are alive or have passed away.

That was more or less what Phaedrus said according to Aristodemus.   c
There followed several other speeches which he couldn't remember very
well. So he skipped them and went directly to the speech of Pausanias.

Phaedrus (Pausanias began), I'm not quite sure our subject has been
well defined. Our charge has been simple—to speak in praise of Love.
This would have been fine if Love himself were simple, too, but as a matter
of fact, there are two kinds of Love. In view of this, it might be better to
begin by making clear which kind of Love we are to praise. Let me therefore   d
try to put our discussion back on the right track and explain which kind
of Love ought to be praised. Then I shall give him the praise he deserves,
as the god he is.

It is a well-known fact that Love and Aphrodite are inseparable. If,
therefore, Aphrodite were a single goddess, there could also be a single
Love; but, since there are actually two goddesses of that name, there also
are two kinds of Love. I don't expect you'll disagree with me about the
two goddesses, will you? One is an older deity, the motherless daughter
of Uranus, the god of heaven: she is known as Urania, or Heavenly Aphrodite. The other goddess is younger, the daughter of Zeus and Dione: her
name is Pandemos, or Common Aphrodite. It follows, therefore, that there   e
is a Common as well as a Heavenly Love, depending on which goddess
is Love's partner. And although, of course, all the gods must be praised,
we must still make an effort to keep these two gods apart.

The reason for this applies in the same way to every type of action:
considered in itself, no action is either good or bad, honorable or shameful.   181
Take, for example, our own case. We had a choice between drinking,
singing, or having a conversation. Now, in itself none of these is better
than any other: how it comes out depends entirely on how it is performed.
If it is done honorably and properly, it turns out to be honorable; if it is
done improperly, it is disgraceful. And my point is that exactly this principle applies to being in love: Love is not in himself noble and worthy of

---

12. In his play, *The Myrmidons*. In Homer there is no hint of sexual attachment between
Achilles and Patroclus.

praise; that depends on whether the sentiments he produces in us are themselves noble.

b   Now the Common Aphrodite's Love is himself truly common. As such, he strikes wherever he gets a chance. This, of course, is the love felt by the vulgar, who are attached to women no less than to boys, to the body more than to the soul, and to the least intelligent partners, since all they care about is completing the sexual act. Whether they do it honorably or not is of no concern. That is why they do whatever comes their way, sometimes good, sometimes bad; and which one it is is incidental to their purpose. For the Love who moves them belongs to a much younger god-

c   dess, who, through her parentage, partakes of the nature both of the female and the male.

        Contrast this with the Love of Heavenly Aphrodite. This goddess, whose descent is purely male (hence this love is for boys), is considerably older and therefore free from the lewdness of youth. That's why those who are inspired by her Love are attracted to the male: they find pleasure in what is by nature stronger and more intelligent. But, even within the group that

d   is attracted to handsome boys, some are not moved purely by this Heavenly Love; those who are do not fall in love with little boys; they prefer older ones whose cheeks are showing the first traces of a beard—a sign that they have begun to form minds of their own. I am convinced that a man who falls in love with a young man of this age is generally prepared to share everything with the one he loves—he is eager, in fact, to spend the rest of his own life with him. He certainly does not aim to deceive him— to take advantage of him while he is still young and inexperienced and

e   then, after exposing him to ridicule, to move quickly on to someone else.

        As a matter of fact, there should be a law forbidding affairs with young boys. If nothing else, all this time and effort would not be wasted on such an uncertain pursuit—and what is more uncertain than whether a particular boy will eventually make something of himself, physically or mentally? Good men, of course, are willing to make a law like this for themselves, but those other lovers, the vulgar ones, need external restraint.

182   For just this reason we have placed every possible legal obstacle to their seducing our own wives and daughters. These vulgar lovers are the people who have given love such a bad reputation that some have gone so far as to claim that taking *any* man as a lover is in itself disgraceful. Would anyone make this claim if he weren't thinking of how hasty vulgar lovers are, and therefore how unfair to their loved ones? For nothing done prop- erly and in accordance with our customs would ever have provoked such righteous disapproval.

        I should point out, however, that, although the customs regarding Love in most cities are simple and easy to understand, here in Athens (and in

b   Sparta as well) they are remarkably complex. In places where the people are inarticulate, like Elis or Boeotia, tradition straightforwardly approves taking a lover in every case. No one there, young or old, would ever consider it shameful. The reason, I suspect, is that, being poor speakers, they want to save themselves the trouble of having to offer reasons and arguments in support of their suits.

By contrast, in places like Ionia and almost every other part of the Persian empire, taking a lover is always considered disgraceful. The Persian empire is absolute; that is why it condemns love as well as philosophy and sport. It is no good for rulers if the people they rule cherish ambitions for themselves or form strong bonds of friendship with one another. That these are precisely the effects of philosophy, sport, and especially of Love is a lesson the tyrants of Athens learned directly from their own experience: Didn't their reign come to a dismal end because of the bonds uniting Harmodius and Aristogiton in love and affection?[13]

So you can see that plain condemnation of Love reveals lust for power in the rulers and cowardice in the ruled, while indiscriminate approval testifies to general dullness and stupidity.

Our own customs, which, as I have already said, are much more difficult to understand, are also far superior. Recall, for example, that we consider it more honorable to declare your love rather than to keep it a secret, especially if you are in love with a youth of good family and accomplishment, even if he isn't all that beautiful. Recall also that a lover is encouraged in every possible way; this means that what he does is not considered shameful. On the contrary, conquest is deemed noble, and failure shameful. And as for *attempts* at conquest, our custom is to praise lovers for totally extraordinary acts—so extraordinary, in fact, that if they performed them for any other purpose whatever, they would reap the most profound contempt. Suppose, for example, that in order to secure money, or a public post, or any other practical benefit from another person, a man were willing to do what lovers do for the ones they love. Imagine that in pressing his suit he went to his knees in public view and begged in the most humiliating way, that he swore all sorts of vows, that he spent the night at the other man's doorstep, that he were anxious to provide services even a slave would have refused—well, you can be sure that everyone, his enemies no less than his friends, would stand in his way. His enemies would jeer at his fawning servility, while his friends, ashamed on his behalf, would try everything to bring him back to his senses. But let a lover act in any of these ways, and everyone will immediately say what a charming man he is! No blame attaches to his behavior: custom treats it as noble through and through. And what is even more remarkable is that, at least according to popular wisdom, the gods will forgive a lover even for breaking his vows—a lover's vow, our people say, is no vow at all. The freedom given to the lover by both gods and men according to our custom is immense.

In view of all this, you might well conclude that in our city we consider the lover's desire and the willingness to satisfy it as the noblest things in

13. Harmodius and Aristogiton attempted to overthrow the tyrant Hippias in 514 B.C. Although their attempt failed, the tyranny fell three years later, and the lovers were celebrated as tyrannicides.

the world. When, on the other hand, you recall that fathers hire attendants for their sons as soon as they're old enough to be attractive, and that an attendant's main task is to prevent any contact between his charge and his suitors; when you recall how mercilessly a boy's own friends tease him if they catch him at it, and how strongly their elders approve and
d   even encourage such mocking—when you take all this into account, you're bound to come to the conclusion that we Athenians consider such behavior the most shameful thing in the world.

In my opinion, however, the fact of the matter is this. As I said earlier, love is, like everything else, complex: considered simply in itself, it is neither honorable nor a disgrace—its character depends entirely on the behavior it gives rise to. To give oneself to a vile man in a vile way is truly disgraceful behavior; by contrast, it is perfectly honorable to give oneself honorably to the right man. Now you may want to know who counts as vile in this context. I'll tell you: it is the common, vulgar lover,
e   who loves the body rather than the soul, the man whose love is bound to be inconstant, since what he loves is itself mutable and unstable. The moment the body is no longer in bloom, "he flies off and away,"[14] his promises and vows in tatters behind him. How different from this is a man who loves the right sort of character, and who remains its lover for
184   life, attached as he is to something that is permanent.

We can now see the point of our customs: they are designed to separate the wheat from the chaff, the proper love from the vile. That's why we do everything we can to make it as easy as possible for lovers to press their suits and as difficult as possible for young men to comply; it is like a competition, a kind of test to determine to which sort each belongs. This explains two further facts: First, why we consider it shameful to yield too quickly: the passage of time in itself provides a good test in these matters.
b   Second, why we also consider it shameful for a man to be seduced by money or political power, either because he cringes at ill-treatment and will not endure it or because, once he has tasted the benefits of wealth and power, he will not rise above them. None of these benefits is stable or permanent, apart from the fact that no genuine affection can possibly be based upon them.

Our customs, then, provide for only one honorable way of taking a man
c   as a lover. In addition to recognizing that the lover's total and willing subjugation to his beloved's wishes is neither servile nor reprehensible, we allow that there is one—and only one—further reason for willingly subjecting oneself to another which is equally above reproach: that is subjection for the sake of virtue. If someone decides to put himself at another's disposal because he thinks that this will make him better in wisdom or in any other part of virtue, we approve of his voluntary subjection: we consider it neither shameful nor servile. Both these principles— that is, both the principle governing the proper attitude toward the lover

14. *Iliad* ii.71.

of young men and the principle governing the love of wisdom and of   d
virtue in general—must be combined if a young man is to accept a lover
in an honorable way. When an older lover and a young man come together
and each obeys the principle appropriate to him—when the lover realizes
that he is justified in doing anything for a loved one who grants him favors,
and when the young man understands that he is justified in performing any
service for a lover who can make him wise and virtuous—and when the   e
lover *is* able to help the young man become wiser and better, and the
young man *is* eager to be taught and improved by his lover—then, and only
then, when these two principles coincide absolutely, is it ever honorable for
a young man to accept a lover.

Only in this case, we should notice, is it never shameful to be deceived;
in every other case it is shameful, both for the deceiver and the person he   185
deceives. Suppose, for example, that someone thinks his lover is rich and
accepts him for his money; his action won't be any less shameful if it turns
out that he was deceived and his lover was a poor man after all. For the
young man has already shown himself to be the sort of person who will
do anything for money—and that is far from honorable. By the same token,
suppose that someone takes a lover in the mistaken belief that this lover
is a good man and likely to make him better himself, while in reality the
man is horrible, totally lacking in virtue; even so, it is noble for him to   b
have been deceived. For he too has demonstrated something about himself:
that he is the sort of person who will do anything for the sake of virtue—
and what could be more honorable than that? It follows, therefore, that
giving in to your lover for virtue's sake is honorable, whatever the outcome.
And this, of course, is the Heavenly Love of the heavenly goddess. Love's
value to the city as a whole and to the citizens is immeasurable, for he
compels the lover and his loved one alike to make virtue their central   c
concern. All other forms of love belong to the vulgar goddess.

Phaedrus, I'm afraid this hasty improvisation will have to do as my
contribution on the subject of Love.

When Pausanias finally came to a pause (I've learned this sort of fine
figure from our clever rhetoricians), it was Aristophanes' turn, according
to Aristodemus. But he had such a bad case of the hiccups—he'd probably
stuffed himself again, though, of course, it could have been anything—
that making a speech was totally out of the question. So he turned to the
doctor, Eryximachus, who was next in line, and said to him: d

"Eryximachus, it's up to you—as well it should be. Cure me or take
my turn."

"As a matter of fact," Eryximachus replied, "I shall do both. I shall take
your turn—you can speak in my place as soon as you feel better—and I
shall also cure you. While I am giving my speech, you should hold your
breath for as long as you possibly can. This may well eliminate your   e
hiccups. If it fails, the best remedy is a thorough gargle. And if even this
has no effect, then tickle your nose with a feather. A sneeze or two will
cure even the most persistent case."

"The sooner you start speaking, the better," Aristophanes said. "I'll follow your instructions to the letter."

This, then, was the speech of Eryximachus:

Pausanias introduced a crucial consideration in his speech, though in my opinion he did not develop it sufficiently. Let me therefore try to carry 186 his argument to its logical conclusion. His distinction between the two species of Love seems to me very useful indeed. But if I have learned a single lesson from my own field, the science of medicine, it is that Love does not occur only in the human soul; it is not simply the attraction we feel toward human beauty: it is a significantly broader phenomenon. It b certainly occurs within the animal kingdom, and even in the world of plants. In fact, it occurs everywhere in the universe. Love is a deity of the greatest importance: he directs everything that occurs, not only in the human domain, but also in that of the gods.

Let me begin with some remarks concerning medicine—I hope you will forgive my giving pride of place to my own profession. The point is that our very bodies manifest the two species of Love. Consider for a moment the marked difference, the radical dissimilarity, between healthy and diseased constitutions and the fact that dissimilar subjects desire and love objects that are themselves dissimilar. Therefore, the love manifested in health is fundamentally distinct from the love manifested in disease. And c now recall that, as Pausanias claimed, it is as honorable to yield to a good man as it is shameful to consort with the debauched. Well, my point is that the case of the human body is strictly parallel. Everything sound and healthy in the body must be encouraged and gratified; that is precisely the object of medicine. Conversely, whatever is unhealthy and unsound must be frustrated and rebuffed: that's what it is to be an expert in medicine.

d   In short, medicine is simply the science of the effects of Love on repletion and depletion of the body, and the hallmark of the accomplished physician is his ability to distinguish the Love that is noble from the Love that is ugly and disgraceful. A good practitioner knows how to affect the body and how to transform its desires; he can implant the proper species of Love when it is absent and eliminate the other sort whenever it occurs. The physician's task is to effect a reconciliation and establish mutual love between the most basic bodily elements. Which are those elements? They are, of course, those that are most opposed to one another, as hot is to e cold, bitter to sweet, wet to dry, cases like those. In fact, our ancestor Asclepius first established medicine as a profession when he learned how to produce concord and love between such opposites—that is what those poet fellows say, and—this time—I concur with them.

187   Medicine, therefore, is guided everywhere by the god of Love, and so are physical education and farming as well. Further, a moment's reflection suffices to show that the case of poetry and music, too, is precisely the same. Indeed, this may have been just what Heraclitus had in mind, though

his mode of expression certainly leaves much to be desired. The one, he says, "being at variance with itself is in agreement with itself" "like the attunement of a bow or a lyre."[15] Naturally, it is patently absurd to claim that an attunement or a harmony is in itself discordant or that its elements are still in discord with one another. Heraclitus probably meant that an expert musician creates a harmony by resolving the prior discord between high and low notes. For surely there can be no harmony so long as high and low are still discordant; harmony, after all, is consonance, and consonance is a species of agreement. Discordant elements, as long as they are still in discord, cannot come to an agreement, and they therefore cannot produce a harmony. Rhythm, for example, is produced only when fast and slow, though earlier discordant, are brought into agreement with each other. Music, like medicine, creates agreement by producing concord and love between these various opposites. Music is therefore simply the science of the effects of Love on rhythm and harmony.

These effects are easily discernible if you consider the constitution of rhythm and harmony in themselves; Love does not occur in both his forms in this domain. But the moment you consider, in their turn, the effects of rhythm and harmony on their audience—either through composition, which creates new verses and melodies, or through musical education, which teaches the correct performance of existing compositions—complications arise directly, and they require the treatment of a good practitioner. Ultimately, the identical argument applies once again: the love felt by good people or by those whom such love might improve in this regard must be encouraged and protected. This is the honorable, heavenly species of Love, produced by the melodies of Urania, the Heavenly Muse. The other, produced by Polyhymnia, the muse of many songs, is common and vulgar. Extreme caution is indicated here: we must be careful to enjoy his pleasures without slipping into debauchery—this case, I might add, is strictly parallel to a serious issue in my own field, namely, the problem of regulating the appetite so as to be able to enjoy a fine meal without unhealthy aftereffects.

In music, therefore, as well as in medicine and in all the other domains, in matters divine as well as in human affairs, we must attend with the greatest possible care to these two species of Love, which are, indeed, to be found everywhere. Even the seasons of the year exhibit their influence. When the elements to which I have already referred—hot and cold, wet and dry—are animated by the proper species of Love, they are in harmony with one another: their mixture is temperate, and so is the climate. Harvests are plentiful; men and all other living things are in good health; no harm can come to them. But when the sort of Love that is crude and impulsive controls the seasons, he brings death and destruction. He spreads the

15. Heraclitus of Ephesus, a philosopher of the early fifth century, was known for his enigmatic sayings. This one is quoted elsewhere in a slightly different form, frg. B 51 Diels-Kranz.

plague and many other diseases among plants and animals; he causes frost and hail and blights. All these are the effects of the immodest and disordered species of Love on the movements of the stars and the seasons of the year, that is, on the objects studied by the science called astronomy.

c   Consider further the rites of sacrifice and the whole area with which the art of divination is concerned, that is, the interaction between men and gods. Here, too, Love is the central concern: our object is to try to maintain the proper kind of Love and to attempt to cure the kind that is diseased. For what is the origin of all impiety? Our refusal to gratify the orderly kind of Love, and our deference to the other sort, when we should have been guided by the former sort of Love in every action in connection with our parents, living or dead, and with the gods. The task of divination is to keep watch over these two species of Love and to doctor them as
d   necessary. Divination, therefore, is the practice that produces loving affection between gods and men; it is simply the science of the effects of Love on justice and piety.

Such is the power of Love—so varied and great that in all cases it might be called absolute. Yet even so it is far greater when Love is directed, in temperance and justice, toward the good, whether in heaven or on earth: happiness and good fortune, the bonds of human society, concord with the gods above—all these are among his gifts.

e   Perhaps I, too, have omitted a great deal in this discourse on Love. If so, I assure you, it was quite inadvertent. And if in fact I have overlooked certain points, it is now your task, Aristophanes, to complete the argument—unless, of course, you are planning on a different approach. In any
189   case, proceed; your hiccups seem cured.

Then Aristophanes took over (so Aristodemus said): "The hiccups have stopped all right—but not before I applied the Sneeze Treatment to them. Makes me wonder whether the 'orderly sort of Love' in the body calls for the sounds and itchings that constitute a sneeze, because the hiccups stopped immediately when I applied the Sneeze Treatment."

"You're good, Aristophanes," Eryximachus answered. "But watch what you're doing. You are making jokes before your speech, and you're forcing me to prepare for you to say something funny, and to put up my guard
b   against you, when otherwise you might speak at peace."

Then Aristophanes laughed. "Good point, Eryximachus. So let me 'unsay what I have said.' But don't put up your guard. I'm not worried about saying something funny in my coming oration. That would be pure profit, and it comes with the territory of my Muse. What I'm worried about is that I might say something ridiculous."

"Aristophanes, do you really think you can take a shot at me, and then escape? Use your head! Remember, as you speak, that you will be called
c   upon to give an account. Though perhaps, if I decide to, I'll let you off."

"Eryximachus," Aristophanes said, "indeed I do have in mind a different approach to speaking than the one the two of you used, you and Pausanias.

You see, I think people have entirely missed the power of Love, because, if they had grasped it, they'd have built the greatest temples and altars to him and made the greatest sacrifices. But as it is, none of this is done for him, though it should be, more than anything else! For he loves the human race more than any other god, he stands by us in our troubles, and he cures those ills we humans are most happy to have mended. I shall, therefore, try to explain his power to you; and you, please pass my teaching on to everyone else."

    First you must learn what Human Nature was in the beginning and what has happened to it since, because long ago our nature was not what it is now, but very different. There were three kinds of human beings, that's my first point—not two as there are now, male and female. In addition to these, there was a third, a combination of those two; its name survives, though the kind itself has vanished. At that time, you see, the word "androgynous" really meant something: a form made up of male and female elements, though now there's nothing but the word, and that's used as an insult. My second point is that the shape of each human being was completely round, with back and sides in a circle; they had four hands each, as many legs as hands, and two faces, exactly alike, on a rounded neck. Between the two faces, which were on opposite sides, was one head with four ears. There were two sets of sexual organs, and everything else was the way you'd imagine it from what I've told you. They walked upright, as we do now, whatever direction they wanted. And whenever they set out to run fast, they thrust out all their eight limbs, the ones they had then, and spun rapidly, the way gymnasts do cartwheels, by bringing their legs around straight.

    Now here is why there were three kinds, and why they were as I described them: The male kind was originally an offspring of the sun, the female of the earth, and the one that combined both genders was an offspring of the moon, because the moon shares in both. They were spherical, and so was their motion, because they were like their parents in the sky.

    In strength and power, therefore, they were terrible, and they had great ambitions. They made an attempt on the gods, and Homer's story about Ephialtes and Otus was originally about them: how they tried to make an ascent to heaven so as to attack the gods.[16] Then Zeus and the other gods met in council to discuss what to do, and they were sore perplexed. They couldn't wipe out the human race with thunderbolts and kill them all off, as they had the giants, because that would wipe out the worship they receive, along with the sacrifices we humans give them. On the other hand, they couldn't let them run riot. At last, after great effort, Zeus had an idea.

    "I think I have a plan," he said, "that would allow human beings to exist and stop their misbehaving: they will give up being wicked when

d

e

190

b

c

d

16. *Iliad* v.385, *Odyssey* xi.305 ff.

they lose their strength. So I shall now cut each of them in two. At one stroke they will lose their strength and also become more profitable to us, owing to the increase in their number. They shall walk upright on two legs. But if I find they still run riot and do not keep the peace," he said, "I will cut them in two again, and they'll have to make their way on one leg, hopping."

e   So saying, he cut those human beings in two, the way people cut sorb-apples before they dry them or the way they cut eggs with hairs. As he cut each one, he commanded Apollo to turn its face and half its neck towards the wound, so that each person would see that he'd been cut and keep better order. Then Zeus commanded Apollo to heal the rest of the wound, and Apollo did turn the face around, and he drew skin from all sides over what is now called the stomach, and there he made one mouth, as in a pouch with a drawstring, and fastened it at the center of the stomach.

191   This is now called the navel. Then he smoothed out the other wrinkles, of which there were many, and he shaped the breasts, using some such tool as shoemakers have for smoothing wrinkles out of leather on the form. But he left a few wrinkles around the stomach and the navel, to be a reminder of what happened long ago.

Now, since their natural form had been cut in two, each one longed for its own other half, and so they would throw their arms about each other, weaving themselves together, wanting to grow together. In that condition

b   they would die from hunger and general idleness, because they would not do anything apart from each other. Whenever one of the halves died and one was left, the one that was left still sought another and wove itself together with that. Sometimes the half he met came from a woman, as we'd call her now, sometimes it came from a man; either way, they kept on dying.

Then, however, Zeus took pity on them, and came up with another plan: he moved their genitals around to the front! Before then, you see, they

c   used to have their genitals outside, like their faces, and they cast seed and made children, not in one another, but in the ground, like cicadas. So Zeus brought about this relocation of genitals, and in doing so he invented interior reproduction, *by* the man *in* the woman. The purpose of this was so that, when a man embraced a woman, he would cast his seed and they would have children; but when male embraced male, they would at least have the satisfaction of intercourse, after which they could stop embracing,

d   return to their jobs, and look after their other needs in life. This, then, is the source of our desire to love each other. Love is born into every human being; it calls back the halves of our original nature together; it tries to make one out of two and heal the wound of human nature.

Each of us, then, is a "matching half" of a human whole, because each was sliced like a flatfish, two out of one, and each of us is always seeking the half that matches him. That's why a man who is split from the double sort (which used to be called "androgynous") runs after women. Many

e   lecherous men have come from this class, and so do the lecherous women who run after men. Women who are split from a woman, however, pay no attention at all to men; they are oriented more towards women, and lesbians come from this class. People who are split from a male are male-oriented. While they are boys, because they are chips off the male block, they love men and enjoy lying with men and being embraced by men; those are the best of boys and lads, because they are the most manly in their nature. Of course, some say such boys are shameless, but they're lying. It's not because they have no shame that such boys do this, you see, but because they are bold and brave and masculine, and they tend to cherish what is like themselves. Do you want me to prove it? Look, these are the only kind of boys who grow up to be real men in politics. When they're grown men, they are lovers of young men, and they naturally pay no attention to marriage or to making babies, except insofar as they are required by local custom. They, however, are quite satisfied to live their lives with one another unmarried. In every way, then, this sort of man grows up as a lover of young men and a lover of Love, always rejoicing in his own kind.

And so, when a person meets the half that is his very own, whatever his orientation, whether it's to young men or not, then something wonderful happens: the two are struck from their senses by love, by a sense of belonging to one another, and by desire, and they don't want to be separated from one another, not even for a moment.

These are the people who finish out their lives together and still cannot say what it is they want from one another. No one would think it is the intimacy of sex—that mere sex is the reason each lover takes so great and deep a joy in being with the other. It's obvious that the soul of every lover longs for something else; his soul cannot say what it is, but like an oracle it has a sense of what it wants, and like an oracle it hides behind a riddle. Suppose two lovers are lying together and Hephaestus[17] stands over them with his mending tools, asking, "What is it you human beings really want from each other?" And suppose they're perplexed, and he asks them again: "Is this your heart's desire, then—for the two of you to become parts of the same whole, as near as can be, and never to separate, day or night? Because if that's your desire, I'd like to weld you together and join you into something that is naturally whole, so that the two of you are made into one. Then the two of you would share one life, as long as you lived, because you would be one being, and by the same token, when you died, you would be one and not two in Hades, having died a single death. Look at your love, and see if this is what you desire: wouldn't this be all the good fortune you could want?"

Surely you can see that no one who received such an offer would turn it down; no one would find anything else that he wanted. Instead, everyone would think he'd found out at last what he had always wanted: to come together and melt together with the one he loves, so that one person

17. Cf. *Odyssey* viii.266 ff.

emerged from two. Why should this be so? It's because, as I said, we used
to be complete wholes in our original nature, and now "Love" is the name
193   for our pursuit of wholeness, for our desire to be complete.

Long ago we were united, as I said; but now the god has divided us as
punishment for the wrong we did him, just as the Spartans divided the
Arcadians.[18] So there's a danger that if we don't keep order before the
gods, we'll be split in two again, and then we'll be walking around in the
condition of people carved on gravestones in bas-relief, sawn apart between
the nostrils, like half dice. We should encourage all men, therefore, to treat
b   the gods with all due reverence, so that we may escape this fate and find
wholeness instead. And we will, if Love is our guide and our commander.
Let no one work against him. Whoever opposes Love is hateful to the
gods, but if we become friends of the god and cease to quarrel with him,
then we shall find the young men that are meant for us and win their
love, as very few men do nowadays.

c   Now don't get ideas, Eryximachus, and turn this speech into a comedy.
Don't think I'm pointing this at Pausanias and Agathon. Probably, they
both do belong to the group that are entirely masculine in nature. But I
am speaking about everyone, men and women alike, and I say there's just
one way for the human race to flourish: we must bring love to its perfect
conclusion, and each of us must win the favors of his very own young
man, so that he can recover his original nature. If that is the ideal, then,
of course, the nearest approach to it is best in present circumstances, and
that is to win the favor of young men who are naturally sympathetic to us.

d   If we are to give due praise to the god who can give us this blessing,
then, we must praise Love. Love does the best that can be done for the
time being: he draws us towards what belongs to us. But for the future,
Love promises the greatest hope of all: if we treat the gods with due
reverence, he will restore to us our original nature, and by healing us, he
will make us blessed and happy.

"That," he said, "is my speech about Love, Eryximachus. It is rather
different from yours. As I begged you earlier, don't make a comedy of it.
e   I'd prefer to hear what all the others will say—or, rather, what each of
them will say, since Agathon and Socrates are the only ones left."

"I found your speech delightful," said Eryximachus, "so I'll do as you
say. Really, we've had such a rich feast of speeches on Love, that if I
couldn't vouch for the fact that Socrates and Agathon are masters of the
art of love, I'd be afraid that they'd have nothing left to say. But as it is,
I have no fears on this score."

194   Then Socrates said, "That's because *you* did beautifully in the contest,
Eryximachus. But if you ever get in my position, or rather the position I'll

18. Arcadia included the city of Mantinea, which opposed Sparta, and was rewarded
by having its population divided and dispersed in 385 B.C. Aristophanes seems to be
referring anachronistically to those events; such anachronisms are not uncommon in
Plato.

be in after Agathon's spoken so well, then you'll really be afraid. You'll be at your wit's end, as I am now."

"You're trying to bewitch me, Socrates," said Agathon, "by making me think the audience expects great things of my speech, so I'll get flustered."   b

"Agathon!" said Socrates, "How forgetful do you think I am? I saw how brave and dignified you were when you walked right up to the theater platform along with the actors and looked straight out at that enormous audience. You were about to put your own writing on display, and you weren't the least bit panicked. After seeing that, how could I expect you to be flustered by us, when we are so few?"

"Why, Socrates," said Agathon. "You must think I have nothing but theater audiences on my mind! So you suppose I don't realize that, if you're intelligent, you find a few sensible men much more frightening than a senseless crowd?"

"No," he said, "It wouldn't be very handsome of me to think you crude   c
in any way, Agathon. I'm sure that if you ever run into people you consider wise, you'll pay more attention to them than to ordinary people. But you can't suppose we're in that class; we were at the theater too, you know, part of the ordinary crowd. Still, if you did run into any wise men, other than yourself, you'd certainly be ashamed at the thought of doing anything ugly in front of them. Is that what you mean?"

'That's true," he said.

"On the other hand, you wouldn't be ashamed to do something ugly   d
in front of ordinary people. Is that it?"

At that point Phaedrus interrupted: "Agathon, my friend, if you answer Socrates, he'll no longer care whether we get anywhere with what we're doing here, so long as he has a partner for discussion. Especially if he's handsome. Now, like you, I enjoy listening to Socrates in discussion, but it is my duty to see to the praising of Love and to exact a speech from every one of this group. When each of you two has made his offering to the god, then you can have your discussion."   e

"You're doing a beautiful job, Phaedrus," said Agathon. "There's nothing to keep me from giving my speech. Socrates will have many opportunities for discussion later."

I wish first to speak of how I ought to speak, and only then to speak. In my opinion, you see, all those who have spoken before me did not so much celebrate the god as congratulate human beings on the good things that come to them from the god. But who it is who gave these gifts, what he is like—no one has spoken about that. Now, only one method is correct   195
for every praise, no matter whose: you must explain what qualities in the subject of your speech enable him to give the benefits for which we praise him. So now, in the case of Love, it is right for us to praise him first for what he is and afterwards for his gifts.

I maintain, then, that while all the gods are happy, Love—if I may say so without giving offense—is the happiest of them all, for he is the most

beautiful and the best. His great beauty lies in this: First, Phaedrus, he is
b the youngest of the gods.[19] He proves my point himself by fleeing old age
in headlong flight, fast-moving though it is (that's obvious—it comes after
us faster than it should). Love was born to hate old age and will come
nowhere near it. Love always lives with young people and is one of them:
the old story holds good that like is always drawn to like. And though
on many other points I agree with Phaedrus, I do not agree with this: that
c Love is more ancient than Cronus and Iapetus. No, I say that he is the
youngest of the gods and stays young forever.

Those old stories Hesiod and Parmenides tell about the gods—those
things happened under Necessity, not Love, if what they say is true. For
not one of all those violent deeds would have been done—no castrations,
no imprisonments—if Love had been present among them. There would
have been peace and brotherhood instead, as there has been now as long
as Love has been king of the gods.

d So he is young. And besides being young, he is delicate. It takes a poet
as good as Homer to show how delicate the god is. For Homer says that
Mischief is a god and that she is delicate—well, that her feet are delicate,
anyway! He says:

> . . . hers are delicate feet: not on the ground
> Does she draw nigh; she walks instead upon the heads of men.[20]

e A lovely proof, I think, to show how delicate she is: she doesn't walk on
anything hard; she walks only on what is soft. We shall use the same proof
about Love, then, to show that he is delicate. For he walks not on earth,
not even on people's skulls, which are not really soft at all, but in the
softest of all the things that are, there he walks, there he has his home.
For he makes his home in the characters, in the souls, of gods and men—
and not even in every soul that comes along: when he encounters a soul
with a harsh character, he turns away; but when he finds a soft and gentle
character, he settles down in it. Always, then, he is touching with his feet
196 and with the whole of himself what is softest in the softest places. He
must therefore be most delicate.

He is youngest, then, and most delicate; in addition he has a fluid, supple
shape. For if he were hard, he would not be able to enfold a soul completely
or escape notice when he first entered it or withdrew. Besides, his graceful
good looks prove that he is balanced and fluid in his nature. Everyone
knows that Love has extraordinary good looks, and between ugliness and
Love there is unceasing war.

And the exquisite coloring of his skin! The way the god consorts with
b flowers shows that. For he never settles in anything, be it a body or a soul,

---

19. Contrast 178b.
20. *Iliad* xix.92–93. "Mischief" translates *Atē*.

that cannot flower or has lost its bloom. His place is wherever it is flowery and fragrant; there he settles, there he stays.

Enough for now about the beauty of the god, though much remains still to be said. After this, we should speak of Love's moral character.[21] The main point is that Love is neither the cause nor the victim of any injustice; he does no wrong to gods or men, nor they to him. If anything has an effect on him, it is never by violence, for violence never touches Love. And the effects he has on others are not forced, for every service we give to love we give willingly. And whatever one person agrees on with another, when both are willing, that is right and just; so say "the laws that are kings of society."[22]

And besides justice, he has the biggest share of moderation.[23] For moderation, by common agreement, is power over pleasures and passions, and no pleasure is more powerful than Love! But if they are weaker, they are under the power of Love, and *he* has the power; and because he has power over pleasures and passions, Love is exceptionally moderate.

And as for manly bravery, "Not even Ares can stand up to" Love![24] For Ares has no hold on Love, but Love does on Ares—love of Aphrodite, so runs the tale.[25] But he who has hold is more powerful than he who is held; and so, because Love has power over the bravest of the others, he is bravest of them all.

Now I have spoken about the god's justice, moderation, and bravery; his wisdom remains.[26] I must try not to leave out anything that can be said on this. In the first place—to honor *our* profession as Eryximachus did his[27]—the god is so skilled a poet that he can make others into poets: once Love touches him, *anyone* becomes a poet,

. . . howe'er uncultured he had been before.[28]

21. "Moral character": *aretē*, i.e., virtue.

22. A proverbial expression attributed by Aristotle (*Rhetoric* 1406a17–23) to the fourth-century liberal thinker and rhetorician Alcidamas.

23. *Sōphrosunē*. The word can be translated also as "temperance" and, most literally, "sound-mindedness." (Plato and Aristotle generally contrast *sōphrosunē* as a virtue with self-control: the person with *sōphrosunē* is naturally well-tempered in every way and so does not need to control himself, or hold himself back.)

24. From Sophocles, fragment 234b Dindorf: "Even Ares cannot withstand Necessity." Ares is the god of war.

25. See *Odyssey* viii.266–366. Aphrodite's husband Hephaestus made a snare that caught Ares in bed with Aphrodite.

26. "Wisdom" translates *sophia*, which Agathon treats as roughly equivalent to *technē* (professional skill); he refers mainly to the ability to produce things. Accordingly "wisdom" translates *sophia* in the first instance; afterwards in this passage it is "skill" or "art."

27. At 186b.

28. Euripides, *Stheneboea* (frg. 666 Nauck).

This, we may fittingly observe, testifies that Love is a good poet, good, in sum, at every kind of artistic production. For you can't give to another what you don't have yourself, and you can't teach what you don't know.

197

And as to the production of animals—who will deny that they are all born and begotten through Love's skill?

And as for artisans and professionals—don't we know that whoever has this god for a teacher ends up in the light of fame, while a man untouched by Love ends in obscurity? Apollo, for one, invented archery,

b medicine, and prophecy when desire and love showed the way. Even he, therefore, would be a pupil of Love, and so would the Muses in music, Hephaestus in bronze work, Athena in weaving, and Zeus in "the governance of gods and men."

That too is how the gods' quarrels were settled, once Love came to be among them—love of beauty, obviously, because love is not drawn to ugliness. Before that, as I said in the beginning, and as the poets say, many dreadful things happened among the gods, because Necessity was king.

c But once this god was born, all goods came to gods and men alike through love of beauty.

This is how I think of Love, Phaedrus: first, he is himself the most beautiful and the best; after that, if anyone else is at all like that, Love is responsible. I am suddenly struck by a need to say something in poetic meter,[29] that it is he who—

> *Gives peace to men and stillness to the sea,*
d > *Lays winds to rest, and careworn men to sleep.*

Love fills us with togetherness and drains all of our divisiveness away. Love calls gatherings like these together. In feasts, in dances, and in ceremonies, he gives the lead. Love moves us to mildness, removes from us wildness. He is giver of kindness, never of meanness. Gracious, kindly[30]— let wise men see and gods admire! Treasure to lovers, envy to others, father of elegance, luxury, delicacy, grace, yearning, desire. Love cares

e well for good men, cares not for bad ones. In pain, in fear, in desire, or speech, Love is our best guide and guard; he is our comrade and our savior. Ornament of all gods and men, most beautiful leader and the best! Every man should follow Love, sing beautifully his hymns, and join with him in the song he sings that charms the mind of god or man.

This, Phaedrus, is the speech I have to offer. Let it be dedicated to the

198 god, part of it in fun, part of it moderately serious, as best I could manage.

When Agathon finished, Aristodemus said, everyone there burst into applause, so becoming to himself and to the god did they think the young man's speech.

29. After these two lines of poetry, Agathon continues with an extremely poetical prose peroration.
30. Accepting the emendation *aganos* at d5.

Then Socrates glanced at Eryximachus and said, "Now do you think I was foolish to feel the fear I felt before? Didn't I speak like a prophet a while ago when I said that Agathon would give an amazing speech and I would be tongue-tied?"

"You were prophetic about one thing, I think," said Eryximachus, "that Agathon would speak well. But you, tongue-tied? No, I don't believe that."   b

"Bless you," said Socrates. "How am I not going to be tongue-tied, I or anyone else, after a speech delivered with such beauty and variety? The other parts may not have been so wonderful, but that at the end! Who would not be struck dumb on hearing the beauty of the words and phrases? Anyway, I was worried that I'd not be able to say anything that came close to them in beauty, and so I would almost have run away and escaped,   c
if there had been a place to go. And, you see, the speech reminded me of Gorgias, so that I actually experienced what Homer describes: I was afraid that Agathon would end by sending the Gorgian head,[31] awesome at speaking in a speech, against my speech, and this would turn me to stone by striking me dumb. Then I realized how ridiculous I'd been to agree to join   d
with you in praising Love and to say that I was a master of the art of love, when I knew nothing whatever of this business, of how anything whatever ought to be praised. In my foolishness, I thought you should tell the truth about whatever you praise, that this should be your basis, and that from this a speaker should select the most beautiful truths and arrange them most suitably. I was quite vain, thinking that I would talk well and that I knew the truth about praising anything whatever. But now it appears that this is not what it is to praise anything whatever; rather, it is to apply   e
to the object the grandest and the most beautiful qualities, whether he actually has them or not. And if they are false, that is no objection; for the proposal, apparently, was that everyone here make the rest of us think he is praising Love—and not that he actually praise him. I think that is why you stir up every word and apply it to Love; your description of him and   199
his gifts is designed to make him look better and more beautiful than anything else—to ignorant listeners, plainly, for of course he wouldn't look that way to those who knew. And your praise did seem beautiful and respectful. But I didn't even know the method for giving praise; and it was in ignorance that I agreed to take part in this. So "the tongue" promised, and "the mind" did not.[32] Goodbye to that! I'm not giving another eulogy using that method, not at all—I wouldn't be able to do   b
it!—but, if you wish, I'd like to tell the truth my way. I want to avoid any comparison with your speeches, so as not to give you a reason to laugh at me. So look, Phaedrus, would a speech like this satisfy your requirement?

---

31. "Gorgian head" is a pun on "Gorgon's head." In his peroration Agathon had spoken in the style of Gorgias, and this style was considered to be irresistibly powerful. The sight of a Gorgon's head would turn a man to stone.

32. The allusion is to Euripides, *Hippolytus* 612.

You will hear the truth about Love, and the words and phrasing will take care of themselves."

Then Aristodemus said that Phaedrus and the others urged him to speak in the way he thought was required, whatever it was.

c "Well then, Phaedrus," said Socrates, "allow me to ask Agathon a few little questions, so that, once I have his agreement, I may speak on that basis."

"You have my permission," said Phaedrus. "Ask away."

After that, said Aristodemus, Socrates began: "Indeed, Agathon, my friend, I thought you led the way beautifully into your speech when you said that one should first show the qualities of Love himself, and only then those of his deeds. I must admire that beginning. Come, then, since

d you have beautifully and magnificently expounded his qualities in other ways, tell me this, too, about Love. Is Love such as to be a love of something or of nothing? I'm not asking if he is born *of* some mother or father, (for the question whether Love is love of mother or of father would really be ridiculous), but it's as if I'm asking this about a father—whether a father is the father *of* something or not. You'd tell me, of course, if you wanted to give me a good answer, that it's *of* a son or a daughter that a father is the father. Wouldn't you?"

"Certainly," said Agathon.

"Then does the same go for the mother?"

e He agreed to that also.

"Well, then," said Socrates, "answer a little more fully, and you will understand better what I want. If I should ask, 'What about this: a brother, just insofar as he *is* a brother, is he the brother of something or not?' "

He said that he was.

"And he's of a brother or a sister, isn't he?"

He agreed.

"Now try to tell me about love," he said. "Is Love the love of nothing or of something?"

200 "Of something, surely!"

"Then keep this object of love in mind, and remember what it is.[33] But tell me this much: does Love desire that of which it is the love, or not?"

"Certainly," he said.

"At the time he desires and loves something, does he actually have what he desires and loves at that time, or doesn't he?"

"He doesn't. At least, that wouldn't be likely," he said.

"Instead of what's *likely*," said Socrates, "ask yourself whether it's *neces-*

b *sary* that this be so: a thing that desires desires something of which it is in need; otherwise, if it were not in need, it would not desire it. I can't tell you, Agathon, how strongly it strikes me that this is necessary. But how about you?"

"I think so too."

33. Cf. 197b.

"Good. Now then, would someone who is tall, want to be tall? Or someone who is strong want to be strong?"

"Impossible, on the basis of what we've agreed."

"Presumably because no one is in need of those things he already has."

"True."

"But maybe a strong man could want to be strong," said Socrates, "or a fast one fast, or a healthy one healthy: in cases like these, you might think people really do want to be things they already are and do want to have qualities they already have—I bring them up so they won't deceive us. But in these cases, Agathon, if you stop to think about them, you will see that these people are what they are at the present time, whether they want to be or not, by a logical necessity. And who, may I ask, would ever bother to desire what's necessary in any event? But when someone says 'I am healthy, but that's just what I want to be,' or 'I am rich, but that's just what I want to be,' or 'I desire the very things that I have,' let us say to him: 'You already have riches and health and strength in your possession, my man, what you want is to possess these things in time to come, since in the present, whether you want to or not, you have them. Whenever you say, *I desire what I already have*, ask yourself whether you don't mean this: *I want the things I have now to be mine in the future as well.*' Wouldn't he agree?"

c

d

According to Aristodemus, Agathon said that he would.

So Socrates said, "Then this is what it is to love something which is not at hand, which the lover does not have: it is to desire the preservation of what he now has in time to come, so that he will have it then."

e

"Quite so," he said.

"So such a man or anyone else who has a desire desires what is not at hand and not present, what he does not have, and what he is not, and that of which he is in need; for such are the objects of desire and love."

"Certainly," he said.

"Come, then," said Socrates. "Let us review the points on which we've agreed. Aren't they, first, that Love is the love of something, and, second, that he loves things of which he has a present need?"

201

"Yes," he said.

"Now, remember, in addition to these points, what you said in your speech about what it is that Love loves. If you like, I'll remind you. I think you said something like this: that the gods' quarrels were settled by love of beautiful things, for there is no love of ugly ones.[34] Didn't you say something like that?"

"I did," said Agathon.

"And that's a suitable thing to say, my friend," said Socrates. "But if this is so, wouldn't Love have to be a desire for beauty, and never for ugliness?"

He agreed.

b

34. 197b3–5.

"And we also agreed that he loves just what he needs and does not have."

"Yes," he said.

"So Love needs beauty, then, and does not have it."

"Necessarily," he said.

"So! If something needs beauty and has got no beauty at all, would you still say that it is beautiful?"

"Certainly not."

"Then do you still agree that Love is beautiful, if those things are so?"

c   Then Agathon said, "It turns out, Socrates, I didn't know what I was talking about in that speech."

"It was a beautiful speech, anyway, Agathon," said Socrates. "Now take it a little further. Don't you think that good things are always beautiful as well?"

"I do."

"Then if Love needs beautiful things, and if all good things are beautiful, he will need good things too."

"As for me, Socrates," he said, "I am unable to contradict you. Let it be as you say."

"Then it's the truth, my beloved Agathon, that you are unable to contradict," he said. "It is not hard at all to contradict Socrates."

d   Now I'll let you go. I shall try to go through for you the speech about Love I once heard from a woman of Mantinea, Diotima—a woman who was wise about many things besides this: once she even put off the plague for ten years by telling the Athenians what sacrifices to make. She is the one who taught me the art of love, and I shall go through her speech as best I can on my own, using what Agathon and I have agreed to as a basis.

Following your lead, Agathon, one should first describe who Love is

e   and what he is like, and afterwards describe his works—I think it will be easiest for me to proceed the way Diotima did and tell you how she questioned me.

You see, I had told her almost the same things Agathon told me just now: that Love is a great god and that he belongs to beautiful things.[35] And she used the very same arguments against me that I used against Agathon; she showed how, according to my very own speech, Love is neither beautiful nor good.

So I said, "What do you mean, Diotima? Is Love ugly, then, and bad?"

202   But she said, "Watch your tongue! Do you really think that, if a thing is not beautiful, it has to be ugly?"

"I certainly do."

35. The Greek is ambiguous between "Love loves beautiful things" and "Love is one of the beautiful things." Agathon had asserted the former (197b5, 201a5), and this will be a premise in Diotima's argument, but he asserted the latter as well (195a7), and this is what Diotima proceeds to refute.

"And if a thing's not wise, it's ignorant? Or haven't you found out yet that there's something in between wisdom and ignorance?"

"What's that?"

"It's judging things correctly without being able to give a reason. Surely you see that this is not the same as knowing—for how could knowledge be unreasoning? And it's not ignorance either—for how could what hits the truth be ignorance? Correct judgment, of course, has this character: it is *in between* understanding and ignorance."

"True," said I, "as you say."　　　　　　　　　　　　　　　　　　　b

"Then don't force whatever is not beautiful to be ugly, or whatever is not good to be bad. It's the same with Love: when you agree he is neither good nor beautiful, you need not think he is ugly and bad; he could be something in between," she said.

"Yet everyone agrees he's a great god," I said.

"Only those who don't know?" she said. "Is that how you mean 'every-one'? Or do you include those who do know?"

"Oh, everyone together."

And she laughed. "Socrates, how could those who say that he's not a　　c
god at all agree that he's a great god?"

"Who says that?" I asked.

"You, for one," she said, "and I for another."

"How can you say this!" I exclaimed.

"That's easy," said she. "Tell me, wouldn't you say that all gods are beautiful and happy? Surely you'd never say a god is not beautiful or happy?"

"Zeus! Not I," I said.

"Well, by calling anyone 'happy,' don't you mean they possess good and beautiful things?"

"Certainly."　　　　　　　　　　　　　　　　　　　　　　　　　d

"What about Love? You agreed he needs good and beautiful things, and that's why he desires them—because he needs them."

"I certainly did."

"Then how could he be a god if he has no share in good and beauti-ful things?"

"There's no way he could, apparently."

"Now do you see? You don't believe Love is a god either!"

"Then, what could Love be?" I asked. "A mortal?"

"Certainly not."

"Then, what is he?"

"He's like what we mentioned before," she said. "He is in between mortal and immortal."

"What do you mean, Diotima?"

"He's a great spirit, Socrates. Everything spiritual, you see, is in between　　e
god and mortal."

"What is their function?" I asked.

"They are messengers who shuttle back and forth between the two, conveying prayer and sacrifice from men to gods, while to men they bring commands from the gods and gifts in return for sacrifices. Being in the middle of the two, they round out the whole and bind fast the all to all. Through them all divination passes, through them the art of priests in sacrifice and ritual, in enchantment, prophecy, and sorcery. Gods do not mix with men; they mingle and converse with us through spirits instead, whether we are awake or asleep. He who is wise in any of these ways is a man of the spirit, but he who is wise in any other way, in a profession or any manual work, is merely a mechanic. These spirits are many and various, then, and one of them is Love."

203

b   "Who are his father and mother?" I asked.

"That's rather a long story," she said. "I'll tell it to you, all the same."

"When Aphrodite was born, the gods held a celebration. Poros, the son of Metis, was there among them.[36] When they had feasted, Penia came begging, as poverty does when there's a party, and stayed by the gates. Now Poros got drunk on nectar (there was no wine yet, you see) and, feeling drowsy, went into the garden of Zeus, where he fell asleep. Then

c   Penia schemed up a plan to relieve her lack of resources: she would get a child from Poros. So she lay beside him and got pregnant with Love. That is why Love was born to follow Aphrodite and serve her: because he was conceived on the day of her birth. And that's why he is also by nature a lover of beauty, because Aphrodite herself is especially beautiful.

"As the son of Poros and Penia, his lot in life is set to be like theirs. In the first place, he is always poor, and he's far from being delicate and

d   beautiful (as ordinary people think he is); instead, he is tough and shriveled and shoeless and homeless, always lying on the dirt without a bed, sleeping at people's doorsteps and in roadsides under the sky, having his mother's nature, always living with Need. But on his father's side he is a schemer after the beautiful and the good; he is brave, impetuous, and intense, an awesome hunter, always weaving snares, resourceful in his pursuit of intelligence, a lover of wisdom[37] through all his life, a genius with enchantments, potions, and clever pleadings.

e   "He is by nature neither immortal nor mortal. But now he springs to life when he gets his way; now he dies—all in the very same day. Because he is his father's son, however, he keeps coming back to life, but then anything he finds his way to always slips away, and for this reason Love is never completely without resources, nor is he ever rich.

204   "He is in between wisdom and ignorance as well. In fact, you see, none of the gods loves wisdom or wants to become wise—for they are wise— and no one else who is wise already loves wisdom; on the other hand, no

36. *Poros* means "way," "resource." His mother's name, *Mētis*, means "cunning." *Penia* means "poverty."

37. I.e., a philosopher.

one who is ignorant will love wisdom either or want to become wise. For what's especially difficult about being ignorant is that you are content with yourself, even though you're neither beautiful and good nor intelligent. If you don't think you need anything, of course you won't want what you don't think you need."

"In that case, Diotima, who *are* the people who love wisdom, if they are neither wise nor ignorant?" b

"That's obvious," she said. "A child could tell you. Those who love wisdom fall in between those two extremes. And Love is one of them, because he is in love with what is beautiful, and wisdom is extremely beautiful. It follows that Love *must* be a lover of wisdom and, as such, is in between being wise and being ignorant. This, too, comes to him from his parentage, from a father who is wise and resourceful and a mother who is not wise and lacks resource.

"My dear Socrates, that, then, is the nature of the Spirit called Love. c Considering what you thought about Love, it's no surprise that you were led into thinking of Love as you did. On the basis of what you say, I conclude that you thought Love was *being loved*, rather than *being a lover*. I think that's why Love struck you as beautiful in every way: because it is what is really beautiful and graceful that deserves to be loved, and this is perfect and highly blessed; but being a lover takes a different form, which I have just described."

So I said, "All right then, my friend. What you say about Love is beautiful, but if you're right, what use is Love to human beings?" d

"I'll try to teach you that, Socrates, after I finish this. So far I've been explaining the character and the parentage of Love. Now, according to you, he is love for beautiful things. But suppose someone asks us, 'Socrates and Diotima, what is the point of loving beautiful things?'

"It's clearer this way: 'The lover of beautiful things has a desire; what does he desire?' "

"That they become his own," I said.

"But that answer calls for still another question, that is, 'What will this man have, when the beautiful things he wants have become his own?' "

I said there was no way I could give a ready answer to that question. e

Then she said, "Suppose someone changes the question, putting 'good' in place of 'beautiful,' and asks you this: 'Tell me, Socrates, a lover of good things has a desire; what does he desire?' "

"That they become his own," I said.

"And what will he have, when the good things he wants have become his own?"

"This time it's easier to come up with the answer," I said. "He'll have hap- 205 piness."[38]

---

38. *Eudaimonia*: no English word catches the full range of this term, which is used for the whole of well-being and the good, flourishing life.

"That's what makes happy people happy, isn't it—possessing good things. There's no need to ask further, 'What's the point of wanting happiness?' The answer you gave seems to be final."

"True," I said.

"Now this desire for happiness, this kind of love—do you think it is common to all human beings and that everyone wants to have good things forever and ever? What would you say?"

"Just that," I said. "It is common to all."

b   "Then, Socrates, why don't we say that everyone is in love," she asked, "since everyone always loves the same things? Instead, we say some people are in love and others not; why is that?"

"I wonder about that myself," I said.

"It's nothing to wonder about," she said. "It's because we divide out a special kind of love, and we refer to it by the word that means the whole—'love'; and for the other kinds of love we use other words."

"What do you mean?" I asked.

"Well, you know, for example, that 'poetry' has a very wide range.[39] After all, everything that is responsible for creating something out of
c   nothing is a kind of poetry; and so all the creations of every craft and profession are themselves a kind of poetry, and everyone who practices a craft is a poet."

"True."

"Nevertheless," she said, "as you also know, these craftsmen are not called poets. We have other words for them, and out of the whole of poetry we have marked off one part, the part the Muses give us with melody and rhythm, and we refer to this by the word that means the whole. For this alone is called 'poetry,' and those who practice this part of poetry are called poets."

d   "True."

"That's also how it is with love. The main point is this: every desire for good things or for happiness is 'the supreme and treacherous love' in everyone. But those who pursue this along any of its many other ways—through making money, or through the love of sports, or through philosophy—we don't say that *these* people are in love, and we don't call them lovers. It's only when people are devoted exclusively to one special kind of love that we use these words that really belong to the whole of it: 'love' and 'in love' and 'lovers.' "

"I am beginning to see your point," I said.

e   "Now there is a certain story," she said, "according to which lovers are those people who seek their other halves. But according to my story, a lover does not seek the half or the whole, unless, my friend, it turns out to be good as well. I say this because people are even willing to cut off

---

39. "Poetry" translates *poiēsis*, lit. 'making', which can be used for any kind of production or creation. However, the word *poiētēs*, lit. 'maker', was used mainly for poets—writers of metrical verses that were actually set to music.

their own arms and legs if they think they are diseased. I don't think an individual takes joy in what belongs to him personally unless by 'belonging to me' he means 'good' and by 'belonging to another' he means 'bad.' That's because what everyone loves is really nothing other than the good. Do you disagree?"

"Zeus! Not I," I said.

"Now, then," she said. "Can we simply say that people love the good?"

"Yes," I said.

"But shouldn't we add that, in loving it, they want the good to be theirs?"

"We should."

"And not only that," she said. "They want the good to be theirs forever, don't they?"

"We should add that too."

"In a word, then, love is wanting to possess the good forever."

"That's very true," I said.

"This, then, is the object of love,"[40] she said. "Now, how do lovers pursue it? We'd rightly say that when they are in love they do something with eagerness and zeal. But what is it precisely that they do? Can you say?"

"If I could," I said, "I wouldn't be your student, filled with admiration for your wisdom, and trying to learn these very things."

"Well, I'll tell you," she said. "It is giving birth in beauty,[41] whether in body or in soul."

"It would take divination to figure out what you mean. I can't."

"Well, I'll tell you more clearly," she said. "All of us are pregnant, Socrates, both in body and in soul, and, as soon as we come to a certain age, we naturally desire to give birth. Now no one can possibly give birth in anything ugly; only in something beautiful. That's because when a man and a woman come together in order to give birth, this is a godly affair. Pregnancy, reproduction—this is an immortal thing for a mortal animal to do, and it cannot occur in anything that is out of harmony, but ugliness is out of harmony with all that is godly. Beauty, however, is in harmony with the divine. Therefore the goddess who presides at childbirth—she's called Moira or Eilithuia—is really Beauty.[42] That's why, whenever pregnant animals or persons draw near to beauty, they become gentle and joyfully disposed and give birth and reproduce; but near ugliness they are foulfaced and draw back in pain; they turn away and shrink back and do not reproduce, and because they hold on to what they carry inside them,

206

b

c

d

---

40. Accepting the emendation *toutou* in b1.

41. The preposition is ambiguous between "within" and "in the presence of." Diotima may mean that the lover causes the newborn (which may be an idea) to come to be within a beautiful person; or she may mean that he is stimulated to give birth to it in the presence of a beautiful person.

42. Moira is known mainly as a Fate, but she was also a birth goddess (*Iliad* xxiv.209), and was identified with the birth-goddess Eilithuia (Pindar, *Olympian Odes* vi.42, *Nemean Odes* vii.1).

the labor is painful. This is the source of the great excitement about beauty
e   that comes to anyone who is pregnant and already teeming with life:
beauty releases them from their great pain. You see, Socrates," she said,
"what Love wants is not beauty, as you think it is."

"Well, what is it, then?"

"Reproduction and birth in beauty."

"Maybe," I said.

"Certainly," she said. "Now, why reproduction? It's because reproduc-
207   tion goes on forever; it is what mortals have in place of immortality. A
lover must desire immortality along with the good, if what we agreed
earlier was right, that Love wants to possess the good forever. It follows
from our argument that Love must desire immortality."

All this she taught me, on those occasions when she spoke on the art
of love. And once she asked, "What do you think causes love and desire,
Socrates? Don't you see what an awful state a wild animal is in when it
b   wants to reproduce? Footed and winged animals alike, all are plagued by
the disease of Love. First they are sick for intercourse with each other,
then for nurturing their young—for their sake the weakest animals stand
ready to do battle against the strongest and even to die for them, and they
may be racked with famine in order to feed their young. They would do
anything for their sake. Human beings, you'd think, would do this because
c   they understand the reason for it; but what causes wild animals to be in
such a state of love? Can you say?"

And I said again that I didn't know.

So she said, "How do you think you'll ever master the art of love, if
you don't know that?"

"But that's why I came to you, Diotima, as I just said. I knew I needed
a teacher. So tell me what causes this, and everything else that belongs to
the art of love."

"If you really believe that Love by its nature aims at what we have often
d   agreed it does, then don't be surprised at the answer," she said. "For
among animals the principle is the same as with us, and mortal nature
seeks so far as possible to live forever and be immortal. And this is possible
in one way only: by reproduction, because it always leaves behind a new
young one in place of the old. Even while each living thing is said to be
alive and to be the same—as a person is said to be the same from childhood
till he turns into an old man—even then he never consists of the same
things, though he is called the same, but he is always being renewed and
e   in other respects passing away, in his hair and flesh and bones and blood
and his entire body. And it's not just in his body, but in his soul, too, for
none of his manners, customs, opinions, desires, pleasures, pains, or fears
ever remains the same, but some are coming to be in him while others
are passing away. And what is still far stranger than that is that not only
208   does one branch of knowledge come to be in us while another passes away
and that we are never the same even in respect of our knowledge, but
that each single piece of knowledge has the same fate. For what we call

studying exists because knowledge is leaving us, because forgetting is the departure of knowledge, while studying puts back a fresh memory in place of what went away, thereby preserving a piece of knowledge, so that it seems to be the same. And in that way everything mortal is preserved, not, like the divine, by always being the same in every way, but because   b
what is departing and aging leaves behind something new, something such as it had been. By this device, Socrates," she said, "what is mortal shares in immortality, whether it is a body or anything else, while the immortal has another way. So don't be surprised if everything naturally values its own offspring, because it is for the sake of immortality that everything shows this zeal, which is Love."

Yet when I heard her speech I was amazed, and spoke: "Well," said I,   c
"Most wise Diotima, is this really the way it is?"

And in the manner of a perfect sophist she said, "Be sure of it, Socrates. Look, if you will, at how human beings seek honor. You'd be amazed at their irrationality, if you didn't have in mind what I spoke about and if you hadn't pondered the awful state of love they're in, wanting to become famous and 'to lay up glory immortal forever,' and how they're ready to brave any danger for the sake of this, much more than they are for their children; and they are prepared to spend money, suffer through all sorts of ordeals, and even die for the sake of glory. Do you really think that   d
Alcestis would have died for Admetus," she asked, "or that Achilles would have died after Patroclus, or that your Codrus would have died so as to preserve the throne for his sons,[43] if they hadn't expected the memory of their virtue—which we still hold in honor—to be immortal? Far from it," she said. "I believe that anyone will do anything for the sake of immortal virtue and the glorious fame that follows; and the better the people, the   e
more they will do, for they are all in love with immortality.

"Now, some people are pregnant in body, and for this reason turn more to women and pursue love in that way, providing themselves through childbirth with immortality and remembrance and happiness, as they think, for all time to come; while others are pregnant in soul—because there   209
surely *are* those who are even more pregnant in their souls than in their bodies, and these are pregnant with what is fitting for a soul to bear and bring to birth. And what is fitting? Wisdom and the rest of virtue, which all poets beget, as well as all the craftsmen who are said to be creative. But by far the greatest and most beautiful part of wisdom deals with the proper ordering of cities and households, and that is called moderation and justice. When someone has been pregnant with these in his soul from   b
early youth, while he is still a virgin, and, having arrived at the proper age, desires to beget and give birth, he too will certainly go about seeking the beauty in which he would beget; for he will never beget in anything

43. Codrus was the legendary last king of Athens. He gave his life to satisfy a prophecy that promised victory to Athens and salvation from the invading Dorians if their king was killed by the enemy.

ugly. Since he is pregnant, then, he is much more drawn to bodies that are beautiful than to those that are ugly; and if he also has the luck to find a soul that is beautiful and noble and well-formed, he is even more drawn

c to this combination; such a man makes him instantly teem with ideas and arguments about virtue—the qualities a virtuous man should have and the customary activities in which he should engage; and so he tries to educate him. In my view, you see, when he makes contact with someone beautiful and keeps company with him, he conceives and gives birth to what he has been carrying inside him for ages. And whether they are together or apart, he remembers that beauty. And in common with him he nurtures the newborn; such people, therefore, have much more to share than do the parents of human children, and have a firmer bond of friendship, because the children in whom they have a share are more

d beautiful and more immortal. Everyone would rather have such children than human ones, and would look up to Homer, Hesiod, and the other good poets with envy and admiration for the offspring they have left behind—offspring, which, because they are immortal themselves, provide their parents with immortal glory and remembrance. "For example," she said, "those are the sort of children Lycurgus[44] left behind in Sparta as the saviors of Sparta and virtually all of Greece. Among you the honor goes

e to Solon for his creation of your laws. Other men in other places everywhere Greek or barbarian, have brought a host of beautiful deeds into the light and begotten every kind of virtue. Already many shrines have sprung up to honor them for their immortal children, which hasn't happened yet to anyone for human offspring.

210 "Even you, Socrates, could probably come to be initiated into these rites of love. But as for the purpose of these rites when they are done correctly— that is the final and highest mystery, and I don't know if you are capable of it. I myself will tell you," she said, "and I won't stint any effort. And you must try to follow if you can."

"A lover who goes about this matter correctly must begin in his youth to devote himself to beautiful bodies. First, if the leader[45] leads aright, he should love one body and beget beautiful ideas there; then he should

b realize that the beauty of any one body is brother to the beauty of any other and that if he is to pursue beauty of form he'd be very foolish not to think that the beauty of all bodies is one and the same. When he grasps this, he must become a lover of all beautiful bodies, and he must think that this wild gaping after just one body is a small thing and despise it.

"After this he must think that the beauty of people's souls is more valuable than the beauty of their bodies, so that if someone is decent in

c his soul, even though he is scarcely blooming in his body, our lover must be content to love and care for him and to seek to give birth to such ideas

44. Lycurgus was supposed to have been the founder of the oligarchic laws and stern customs of Sparta.

45. The leader: Love.

as will make young men better. The result is that our lover will be forced
to gaze at the beauty of activities and laws and to see that all this is akin
to itself, with the result that he will think that the beauty of bodies is a
thing of no importance. After customs he must move on to various kinds
of knowledge. The result is that he will see the beauty of knowledge and   d
be looking mainly not at beauty in a single example—as a servant would
who favored the beauty of a little boy or a man or a single custom (being
a slave, of course, he's low and small-minded)—but the lover is turned to
the great sea of beauty, and, gazing upon this, he gives birth to many
gloriously beautiful ideas and theories, in unstinting love of wisdom,[46]
until, having grown and been strengthened there, he catches sight of such   e
knowledge, and it is the knowledge of such beauty . . .

"Try to pay attention to me," she said, "as best you can. You see, the
man who has been thus far guided in matters of Love, who has beheld
beautiful things in the right order and correctly, is coming now to the goal
of Loving: all of a sudden he will catch sight of something wonderfully
beautiful in its nature; that, Socrates, is the reason for all his earlier labors: 211

"First, it always *is* and neither comes to be nor passes away, neither
waxes nor wanes. Second, it is not beautiful this way and ugly that way,
nor beautiful at one time and ugly at another, nor beautiful in relation to
one thing and ugly in relation to another; nor is it beautiful here but ugly
there, as it would be if it were beautiful for some people and ugly for
others. Nor will the beautiful appear to him in the guise of a face or hands
or anything else that belongs to the body. It will not appear to him as one
idea or one kind of knowledge. It is not anywhere in another thing, as in   b
an animal, or in earth, or in heaven, or in anything else, but itself by itself
with itself, it is always one in form; and all the other beautiful things share
in that, in such a way that when those others come to be or pass away,
this does not become the least bit smaller or greater nor suffer any change.
So when someone rises by these stages, through loving boys correctly, and
begins to see this beauty, he has almost grasped his goal. This is what it   c
is to go aright, or be led by another, into the mystery of Love: one goes
always upwards for the sake of this Beauty, starting out from beautiful
things and using them like rising stairs: from one body to two and from
two to all beautiful bodies, then from beautiful bodies to beautiful customs,
and from customs to learning beautiful things, and from these lessons he
arrives[47] in the end at this lesson, which is learning of this very Beauty,
so that in the end he comes to know just what it is to be beautiful.   d

"And there in life, Socrates, my friend," said the woman from Mantinea,
"there if anywhere should a person live his life, beholding that Beauty. If
you once see that, it won't occur to you to measure beauty by gold or
clothing or beautiful boys and youths—who, if you see them now, strike

---

46. I.e., philosophy.
47. Reading *teleutēsēi* at c7.

you out of your senses, and make you, you and many others, eager to be
with the boys you love and look at them forever, if there were any way
to do that, forgetting food and drink, everything but looking at them and
e   being with them. But how would it be, in our view," she said, "if someone
got to see the Beautiful itself, absolute, pure, unmixed, not polluted by
human flesh or colors or any other great nonsense of mortality, but if he
212 could see the divine Beauty itself in its one form? Do you think it would
be a poor life for a human being to look there and to behold it by that
which he ought, and to be with it? Or haven't you remembered," she said,
"that in that life alone, when he looks at Beauty in the only way that
Beauty can be seen—only then will it become possible for him to give
birth not to images of virtue (because he's in touch with no images), but
to true virtue (because he is in touch with the true Beauty). The love of the
gods belongs to anyone who has given birth to true virtue and nourished it,
b   and if any human being could become immortal, it would be he."

   This, Phaedrus and the rest of you, was what Diotima told me. I was
persuaded. And once persuaded, I try to persuade others too that human
nature can find no better workmate for acquiring this than Love. That's
why I say that every man must honor Love, why I honor the rites of Love
myself and practice them with special diligence, and why I commend them
to others. Now and always I praise the power and courage of Love so far
c   as I am able. Consider this speech, then, Phaedrus, if you wish, a speech
in praise of Love. Or if not, call it whatever and however you please to
call it.

   Socrates' speech finished to loud applause. Meanwhile, Aristophanes
was trying to make himself heard over their cheers in order to make a
response to something Socrates had said about his own speech.[48] Then, all
of a sudden, there was even more noise. A large drunken party had arrived
at the courtyard door and they were rattling it loudly, accompanied by
the shrieks of some flute-girl they had brought along. Agathon at that
point called to his slaves:
d   "Go see who it is. If it's people we know, invite them in. If not, tell them
the party's over, and we're about to turn in."
   A moment later they heard Alcibiades shouting in the courtyard, very
drunk and very loud. He wanted to know where Agathon was, he demanded to see Agathon at once. Actually, he was half-carried into the
e   house by the flute-girl and by some other companions of his, but, at the
door, he managed to stand by himself, crowned with a beautiful wreath
of violets and ivy and ribbons in his hair.
   "Good evening, gentlemen. I'm plastered," he announced. "May I join
your party? Or should I crown Agathon with this wreath—which is all I
came to do, anyway—and make myself scarce? I really couldn't make it
yesterday," he continued, "but nothing could stop me tonight! See, I'm

48. Cf. 205d–e.

wearing the garland myself. I want this crown to come directly from my
head to the head that belongs, I don't mind saying, to the cleverest and
best looking man in town. Ah, you laugh; you think I'm drunk! Fine, go   213
ahead—I know I'm right anyway. Well, what do you say? May I join you
on these terms? Will you have a drink with me or not?"

Naturally they all made a big fuss. They implored him to join them,
they begged him to take a seat, and Agathon called him to his side. So
Alcibiades, again with the help of his friends, approached Agathon. At
the same time, he kept trying to take his ribbons off so that he could crown
Agathon with them, but all he succeeded in doing was to push them
further down his head until they finally slipped over his eyes. What with
the ivy and all, he didn't see Socrates, who had made room for him on
the couch as soon as he saw him. So Alcibiades sat down between Socrates   b
and Agathon and, as soon as he did so, he put his arms around Agathon,
kissed him, and placed the ribbons on his head.

Agathon asked his slaves to take Alcibiades' sandals off. "We can all
three fit on my couch," he said.

"What a good idea!" Alcibiades replied. "But wait a moment! Who's
the third?"

As he said this, he turned around, and it was only then that he saw
Socrates. No sooner had he seen him than he leaped up and cried:

"Good lord, what's going on here? It's Socrates! You've trapped me   c
again! You always do this to me—all of a sudden you'll turn up out of
nowhere where I least expect you! Well, what do you want now? Why
did you choose this particular couch? Why aren't you with Aristophanes
or anyone else we could tease you about? But no, you figured out a way
to find a place next to the most handsome man in the room!"

"I beg you, Agathon," Socrates said, "protect me from this man! You   d
can't imagine what it's like to be in love with him: from the very first
moment he realized how I felt about him, he hasn't allowed me to say
two words to anybody else—what am I saying, I can't so much as look
at an attractive man but he flies into a fit of jealous rage. He yells; he
threatens; he can hardly keep from slapping me around! Please, try to
keep him under control. Could you perhaps make him forgive me? And
if you can't, if he gets violent, will you defend me? The fierceness of his
passion terrifies me!"

"I shall never forgive you!" Alcibiades cried. "I promise you, you'll pay   e
for this! But for the moment," he said, turning to Agathon, "give me some
of these ribbons. I'd better make a wreath for him as well—look at that
magnificent head! Otherwise, I know, he'll make a scene. He'll be grumbling that, though I crowned you for your first victory, I didn't honor him
even though he has never lost an argument in his life."

So Alcibiades took the ribbons, arranged them on Socrates' head, and
lay back on the couch. Immediately, however, he started up again:

"Friends, you look sober to me; we can't have that! Let's have a drink!
Remember our agreement? We need a master of ceremonies; who should
it be? . . . Well, at least till you are all too drunk to care, I elect . . . myself!

Who else? Agathon, I want the largest cup around ... No! Wait! You!
214   Bring me that cooling jar over there!"

He'd seen the cooling jar, and he realized it could hold more than two
quarts of wine. He had the slaves fill it to the brim, drained it, and ordered
them to fill it up again for Socrates.

"Not that the trick will have any effect on *him*," he told the group.
"Socrates will drink whatever you put in front of him, but no one yet has
seen him drunk."

The slave filled the jar and, while Socrates was drinking, Eryximachus
said to Alcibiades:

b   "This is certainly most improper. We cannot simply pour the wine down
our throats in silence: we must have some conversation, or at least a song.
What we are doing now is hardly civilized."

What Alcibiades said to him was this:

"O Eryximachus, best possible son to the best possible, the most temperate father: Hi!"

"Greetings to you, too," Eryximachus replied. "Now what do you suggest we do?"

"Whatever you say. Ours to obey you, 'For a medical mind is worth a
million others'.[49] Please prescribe what you think fit."

c   "Listen to me," Eryximachus said. "Earlier this evening we decided to
use this occasion to offer a series of encomia of Love. We all took our
turn—in good order, from left to right—and gave our speeches, each
according to his ability. You are the only one not to have spoken yet,
though, if I may say so, you have certainly drunk your share. It's only
proper, therefore, that you take your turn now. After you have spoken,
you can decide on a topic for Socrates on your right; he can then do the
same for the man to his right, and we can go around the table once again."

"Well said, O Eryximachus," Alcibiades replied. "But do you really think
it's fair to put my drunken ramblings next to your sober orations? And
d   anyway, my dear fellow, I hope you didn't believe a single word Socrates
said: the truth is just the opposite! He's the one who will most surely beat
me up if I dare praise anyone else in his presence—even a god!"

"Hold your tongue!" Socrates said.

"By god, don't you dare deny it!" Alcibiades shouted. "I would never—
never—praise anyone else with you around."

e   "Well, why not just do that, if you want?" Eryximachus suggested. "Why
don't you offer an encomium to Socrates?"

"What do you mean?" asked Alcibiades. "Do you really think so, Eryximachus? Should I unleash myself upon him? Should I give him his punishment in front of all of you?"

"Now, wait a minute," Socrates said. "What do you have in mind? Are
you going to praise me only in order to mock me? Is that it?"

"I'll only tell the truth—please, let me!"

49. *Iliad* xi.514.

"I would certainly like to hear the truth from you. By all means, go ahead," Socrates replied.

"Nothing can stop me now," said Alcibiades. "But here's what you can do: if I say anything that's not true, you can just interrupt, if you want, and correct me; at worst, there'll be mistakes in my speech, not lies. But you can't hold it against me if I don't get everything in the right order—I'll say things as they come to mind. It is no easy task for one in my condition to give a smooth and orderly account of your bizarreness!" 215

I'll try to praise Socrates, my friends, but I'll have to use an image. And though he may think I'm trying to make fun of him, I assure you my image is no joke: it aims at the truth. Look at him! Isn't he just like a statue of Silenus? You know the kind of statue I mean; you'll find them in any shop in town. It's a Silenus sitting, his flute[50] or his pipes in his hands, and it's hollow. It's split right down the middle, and inside it's full of tiny statues of the gods. Now look at him again! Isn't he also just like the satyr Marsyas?[51] b

Nobody, not even you, Socrates, can deny that you *look* like them. But the resemblance goes beyond appearance, as you're about to hear.

You are impudent, contemptuous, and vile! No? If you won't admit it, I'll bring witnesses. And you're quite a fluteplayer, aren't you? In fact, you're much more marvelous than Marsyas, who needed instruments to cast his spells on people. And so does anyone who plays his tunes today—for even the tunes Olympus[52] played are Marsyas' work, since Olympus learned everything from him. Whether they are played by the greatest flautist or the meanest flute-girl, his melodies have in themselves the power to possess and so reveal those people who are ready for the god and his mysteries. That's because his melodies are themselves divine. The only difference between you and Marsyas is that you need no instruments; you do exactly what he does, but with words alone. You know, people hardly ever take a speaker seriously, even if he's the greatest orator; but let anyone—man, woman, or child—listen to you or even to a poor account of what you say—and we are all transported, completely possessed. c

If I were to describe for you what an extraordinary effect his words have always had on me (I can feel it this moment even as I'm speaking), you might actually suspect that I'm drunk! Still, I swear to you, the moment e

50. This is the conventional translation of the word, but the *aulos* was in fact a reed instrument and not a flute. It was held by the ancients to be the instrument that most strongly arouses the emotions.

51. Satyrs had the sexual appetites and manners of wild beasts and were usually portrayed with large erections. Sometimes they had horses' tails or ears, sometimes the traits of goats. Marsyas, in myth, dared to compete in music with Apollo and was skinned alive for his impudence.

52. Olympus was a legendary musician who was said to be loved by Marsyas (*Minos* 318b5) and to have made music that moved its listeners out of their senses.

he starts to speak, I am beside myself: my heart starts leaping in my chest, the tears come streaming down my face, even the frenzied Corybantes[53] seem sane compared to me—and, let me tell you, I am not alone. I have heard Pericles and many other great orators, and I have admired their speeches. But nothing like this ever happened to me: they never upset me so deeply that my very own soul started protesting that my life—*my* life!— was no better than the most miserable slave's. And yet that is exactly how

216   this Marsyas here at my side makes me feel all the time: he makes it seem that my life isn't worth living! You can't say that isn't true, Socrates. I know very well that you could make me feel that way this very moment if I gave you half a chance. He always traps me, you see, and he makes me admit that my political career is a waste of time, while all that matters is just what I most neglect: my personal shortcomings, which cry out for the closest attention. So I refuse to listen to him; I stop my ears and tear

b   myself away from him, for, like the Sirens, he could make me stay by his side till I die.

Socrates is the only man in the world who has made me feel shame— ah, you didn't think I had it in me, did you? Yes, he makes me feel ashamed: I know perfectly well that I can't prove he's wrong when he tells me what I should do; yet, the moment I leave his side, I go back to my old ways: I cave in to my desire to please the crowd. My whole life has become one constant effort to escape from him and keep away, but when I see him, I

c   feel deeply ashamed, because I'm doing nothing about my way of life, though I have already agreed with him that I should. Sometimes, believe me, I think I would be happier if he were dead. And yet I know that if he dies I'll be even more miserable. I can't live with him, and I can't live without him! What *can* I do about him?

That's the effect of this satyr's music—on me and many others. But that's the least of it. He's like these creatures in all sorts of other ways; his powers are really extraordinary. Let me tell you about them, because,

d   you can be sure of it, none of you really understands him. But, now I've started, I'm going to show you what he really is.

To begin with, he's crazy about beautiful boys; he constantly follows them around in a perpetual daze. Also, he likes to say he's ignorant and knows nothing. Isn't this just like Silenus? Of course it is! And all this is just on the surface, like the outsides of those statues of Silenus. I wonder, my fellow drinkers, if you have any idea what a sober and temperate man he proves to be once you have looked inside. Believe me, it couldn't matter less to him whether a boy is beautiful. You can't imagine how little he

e   cares whether a person is beautiful, or rich, or famous in any other way that most people admire. He considers all these possessions beneath contempt, and that's exactly how he considers all of us as well. In public, I tell you, his whole life is one big game—a game of irony. I don't know if

---

53. Legendary worshippers of Cybele, who brought about their own derangement through music and dance.

any of you have seen him when he's really serious. But I once caught him when he was open like Silenus' statues, and I had a glimpse of the figures he keeps hidden within: they were so godlike—so bright and beautiful, so utterly amazing—that I no longer had a choice—I just had to do whatever he told me.

What I thought at the time was that what he really wanted was *me*, and that seemed to me the luckiest coincidence: all I had to do was to let him have his way with me, and he would teach me everything he knew— believe me, I had a lot of confidence in my looks. Naturally, up to that time we'd never been alone together; one of my attendants had always been present. But with this in mind, I sent the attendant away, and met Socrates alone. (You see, in this company I must tell the whole truth: so pay attention. And, Socrates, if I say anything untrue, I want you to correct me.)

So there I was, my friends, alone with him at last. My idea, naturally, was that he'd take advantage of the opportunity to tell me whatever it is that lovers say when they find themselves alone; I relished the moment. But no such luck! Nothing of the sort occurred. Socrates had his usual sort of conversation with me, and at the end of the day he went off.

My next idea was to invite him to the gymnasium with me. We took exercise together, and I was sure that this would lead to something. He took exercise and wrestled with me many times when no one else was present. What can I tell you? I got nowhere. When I realized that my ploy had failed, I decided on a frontal attack. I refused to retreat from a battle I myself had begun, and I needed to know just where matters stood. So what I did was to invite him to dinner, as if *I* were his lover and he my young prey! To tell the truth, it took him quite a while to accept my invitation, but one day he finally arrived. That first time he left right after dinner: I was too shy to try to stop him. But on my next attempt, I started some discussion just as we were finishing our meal and kept him talking late into the night. When he said he should be going, I used the lateness of the hour as an excuse and managed to persuade him to spend the night at my house. He had had his meal on the couch next to mine, so he just made himself comfortable and lay down on it. No one else was there.

Now you must admit that my story so far has been perfectly decent; I could have told it in any company. But you'd never have heard me tell the rest of it, as you're about to do, if it weren't that, as the saying goes, 'there's truth in wine when the slaves have left'—and when they're present, too. Also, would it be fair to Socrates for me to praise him and yet to fail to reveal one of his proudest accomplishments? And, furthermore, you know what people say about snakebite—that you'll only talk about it with your fellow victims: only they will understand the pain and forgive you for all the things it made you do. Well, something much more painful than a snake has bitten me in my most sensitive part—I mean my heart, or my soul, or whatever you want to call it, which has been struck and bitten by philosophy, whose grip on young and eager souls is much more

217

b

c

d

e

218

vicious than a viper's and makes them do the most amazing things. Now,
b all you people here, Phaedrus, Agathon, Eryximachus, Pausanias, Aristodemus, Aristophanes—I need not mention Socrates himself—and all the rest,
have all shared in the madness, the Bacchic frenzy of philosophy. And
that's why you will hear the rest of my story; you will understand and
forgive both what I did then and what I say now. As for the house slaves
and for anyone else who is not an initiate, my story's not for you: block
your ears!

c   To get back to the story. The lights were out; the slaves had left; the
time was right, I thought, to come to the point and tell him freely what I
had in mind. So I shook him and whispered:
"Socrates, are you asleep?"
"No, no, not at all," he replied.
"You know what I've been thinking?"
"Well, no, not really."
"I think," I said, "you're the only worthy lover I have ever had—and
yet, look how shy you are with me! Well, here's how I look at it. It would
d be really stupid not to give you anything you want: you can have me, my
belongings, anything my friends might have. Nothing is more important
to me than becoming the best man I can be, and no one can help me more
than you to reach that aim. With a man like you, in fact, I'd be much more
ashamed of what wise people would say if I did *not* take you as my lover,
than I would of what all the others, in their foolishness, would say if I did."

He heard me out, and then he said in that absolutely inimitable ironic
manner of his:
e   "Dear Alcibiades, if you are right in what you say about me, you are
already more accomplished than you think. If I really have in me the
power to make you a better man, then you can see in me a beauty that is
really beyond description and makes your own remarkable good looks
pale in comparison. But, then, is this a fair exchange that you propose?
You seem to me to want more than your proper share: you offer me the
merest appearance of beauty, and in return you want the thing itself, 'gold
219 in exchange for bronze.'[54]

"Still, my dear boy, you should think twice, because you could be wrong,
and I may be of no use to you. The mind's sight becomes sharp only when
the body's eyes go past their prime—and you are still a good long time
away from that."
When I heard this I replied:
"I really have nothing more to say. I've told you exactly what I think.
Now it's your turn to consider what you think best for you and me."
b   "You're right about that," he answered. "In the future, let's consider
things together. We'll always do what seems the best to the two of us."

---

54. *Iliad* vi.232–36 tells the famous story of the exchange by Glaucus of golden armor
for bronze.

His words made me think that my own had finally hit their mark, that he was smitten by my arrows. I didn't give him a chance to say another word. I stood up immediately and placed my mantle over the light cloak which, though it was the middle of winter, was his only clothing. I slipped underneath the cloak and put my arms around this man—this utterly unnatural, this truly extraordinary man—and spent the whole night next to him. Socrates, you can't deny a word of it. But in spite of all my efforts, this hopelessly arrogant, this unbelievably insolent man—he turned me down! He spurned my beauty, of which I was so proud, members of the jury—for this is really what you are: you're here to sit in judgment of Socrates' amazing arrogance and pride. Be sure of it, I swear to you by all the gods and goddesses together, my night with Socrates went no further than if I had spent it with my own father or older brother!

    How do you think I felt after that? Of course, I was deeply humiliated, but also I couldn't help admiring his natural character, his moderation, his fortitude—here was a man whose strength and wisdom went beyond my wildest dreams! How could I bring myself to hate him? I couldn't bear to lose his friendship. But how could I possibly win him over? I knew very well that money meant much less to him than enemy weapons ever meant to Ajax,[55] and the only trap by means of which I had thought I might capture him had already proved a dismal failure. I had no idea what to do, no purpose in life; ah, no one else has ever known the real meaning of slavery!

    All this had already occurred when Athens invaded Potidaea,[56] where we served together and shared the same mess. Now, first, he took the hardships of the campaign much better than I ever did—much better, in fact, than anyone in the whole army. When we were cut off from our supplies, as often happens in the field, no one else stood up to hunger as well as he did. And yet he was the one man who could really enjoy a feast; and though he didn't much want to drink, when he had to, he could drink the best of us under the table. Still, and most amazingly, no one ever saw him drunk (as we'll straightaway put to the test).

    Add to this his amazing resistance to the cold—and, let me tell you, the winter there is something awful. Once, I remember, it was frightfully cold; no one so much as stuck his nose outside. If we absolutely had to leave our tent, we wrapped ourselves in anything we could lay our hands on and tied extra pieces of felt or sheepskin over our boots. Well, Socrates went out in that weather wearing nothing but this same old light cloak, and even in bare feet he made better progress on the ice than the other

---

55. Ajax, a hero of the Greek army at Troy, carried an enormous shield and so was virtually invulnerable to enemy weapons.

56. Potidaea, a city in Thrace allied to Athens, was induced by Corinth to revolt in 432 B.C. The city was besieged by the Athenians and eventually defeated in a bloody local war, 432–430 B.C.

c soldiers did in their boots. You should have seen the looks they gave him; they thought he was only doing it to spite them!

So much for that! But you should hear what else he did during that same campaign,

The exploit our strong-hearted hero dared to do.[57]

One day, at dawn, he started thinking about some problem or other; he just stood outside, trying to figure it out. He couldn't resolve it, but he wouldn't give up. He simply stood there, glued to the same spot. By midday, many soldiers had seen him, and, quite mystified, they told everyone that Socrates had been standing there all day, thinking about something. He was still there when evening came, and after dinner some Ionians

d moved their bedding outside, where it was cooler and more comfortable (all this took place in the summer), but mainly in order to watch if Socrates was going to stay out there all night. And so he did; he stood on the very same spot until dawn! He only left next morning, when the sun came out, and he made his prayers to the new day.

And if you would like to know what he was like in battle—this is a tribute he really deserves. You know that I was decorated for bravery dur-

e ing that campaign: well, during that very battle, Socrates single-handedly saved my life! He absolutely did! He just refused to leave me behind when I was wounded, and he rescued not only me but my armor as well. For my part, Socrates, I told them right then that the decoration really belonged to you, and you can blame me neither for doing so then nor for saying so now. But the generals, who seemed much more concerned with my social position, insisted on giving the decoration to me, and, I must say, you were more eager than the generals themselves for me to have it.

221   You should also have seen him at our horrible retreat from Delium.[58] I was there with the cavalry, while Socrates was a foot soldier. The army had already dispersed in all directions, and Socrates was retreating together with Laches. I happened to see them just by chance, and the moment I did I started shouting encouragements to them, telling them I was never going to leave their side, and so on. That day I had a better opportunity

b to watch Socrates than I ever had at Potidaea, for, being on horseback, I wasn't in very great danger. Well, it was easy to see that he was remarkably more collected than Laches. But when I looked again I couldn't get your words, Aristophanes, out of my mind: in the midst of battle he was making his way exactly as he does around town,

---

57. *Odyssey* iv.242, 271.

58. At Delium, a town on the Boeotian coastline just north of Attica, a major Athenian expeditionary force was routed by a Boeotian army in 424 B.C. For another description of Socrates' action during the retreat, see *Laches* 181b.

. . . with swagg'ring gait and roving eye.[59]

He was observing everything quite calmly, looking out for friendly troops and keeping an eye on the enemy. Even from a great distance it was obvious that this was a very brave man, who would put up a terrific fight if anyone approached him. This is what saved both of them. For, as a rule, you try to put as much distance as you can between yourself and such men in battle; you go after the others, those who run away helter-skelter.   c

You could say many other marvelous things in praise of Socrates. Perhaps he shares some of his specific accomplishments with others. But, as a whole, he is unique; he is like no one else in the past and no one in the present—this is by far the most amazing thing about him. For we might be able to form an idea of what Achilles was like by comparing him to Brasidas or some other great warrior, or we might compare Pericles with Nestor or Antenor or one of the other great orators.[60] There is a parallel   d
for everyone—everyone else, that is. But this man here is so bizarre, his ways and his ideas are so unusual, that, search as you might, you'll never find anyone else, alive or dead, who's even remotely like him. The best you can do is not to compare him to anything human, but to liken him, as I do, to Silenus and the satyrs, and the same goes for his ideas and arguments.

Come to think of it, I should have mentioned this much earlier: even his ideas and arguments are just like those hollow statues of Silenus. If   e
you were to listen to his arguments, at first they'd strike you as totally ridiculous; they're clothed in words as coarse as the hides worn by the most vulgar satyrs. He's always going on about pack asses, or blacksmiths, or cobblers, or tanners; he's always making the same tired old points in the same tired old words. If you are foolish, or simply unfamiliar with him, you'd find it impossible not to laugh at his arguments. But if you   222
see them when they open up like the statues, if you go behind their surface, you'll realize that no other arguments make any sense. They're truly worthy of a god, bursting with figures of virtue inside. They're of great—no, of the greatest—importance for anyone who wants to become a truly good man.

Well, this is my praise of Socrates, though I haven't spared him my   b
reproach, either; I told you how horribly he treated me—and not only me but also Charmides, Euthydemus, and many others. He has deceived us all: he presents himself as your lover, and, before you know it, you're in love with him yourself! I warn you, Agathon, don't let him fool you!

59. Cf. Aristophanes, *Clouds* 362.

60. Brasidas, among the most effective Spartan generals during the Peloponnesian War, was mortally wounded while defeating the Athenians at Amphipolis in 422 B.C. Antenor (for the Trojans) and Nestor (for the Greeks) were legendary wise counsellors during the Trojan War.

Remember our torments; be on your guard: don't wait, like the fool in the
c   proverb, to learn your lesson from your own misfortune.[61]

Alcibiades' frankness provoked a lot of laughter, especially since it was
obvious that he was still in love with Socrates, who immediately said to him:
"You're perfectly sober after all, Alcibiades. Otherwise you could never
have concealed your motive so gracefully: how casually you let it drop,
almost like an afterthought, at the very end of your speech! As if the real
d   point of all this has not been simply to make trouble between Agathon
and me! You think that I should be in love with you and no one else,
while you, and no one else, should be in love with Agathon—well, we
were *not* deceived; we've seen through your little satyr play. Agathon, my
friend, don't let him get away with it: let no one come between us!"
      Agathon said to Socrates:
e   "I'm beginning to think you're right; isn't it proof of that that he literally
came between us here on the couch? Why would he do this if he weren't
set on separating us? But he won't get away with it; I'm coming right over
to lie down next to you."
      "Wonderful," Socrates said. "Come here, on my other side."
      "My god!" cried Alcibiades. "How I suffer in his hands! He kicks me
when I'm down; he never lets me go. Come, don't be selfish, Socrates; at
least, let's compromise: let Agathon lie down between us."
      "Why, that's impossible," Socrates said. "You have already delivered
your praise of me, and now it's my turn to praise whoever's on my right.
But if Agathon were next to you, he'd have to praise me all over again
223 instead of having me speak in his honor, as I very much want to do in
any case. Don't be jealous; let me praise the boy."
      "Oh, marvelous," Agathon cried. "Alcibiades, nothing can make me stay
next to you now. I'm moving no matter what. I simply *must* hear what
Socrates has to say about me."
      "There we go again," said Alcibiades. "It's the same old story: when
Socrates is around, nobody else can get close to a good-looking man. Look
b   how smoothly and plausibly he found a reason for Agathon to lie down
next to him!"
      And then, all of a sudden, while Agathon was changing places, a large
drunken group, finding the gates open because someone was just leaving,
walked into the room and joined the party. There was noise everywhere,
and everyone was made to start drinking again in no particular order.
      At that point, Aristodemus said, Eryximachus, Phaedrus, and some
c   others among the original guests made their excuses and left. He himself
fell asleep and slept for a long time (it was winter, and the nights were
quite long). He woke up just as dawn was about to break; the roosters
were crowing already. He saw that the others had either left or were asleep

61. Cf. *Iliad* xvii.32.

on their couches and that only Agathon, Aristophanes, and Socrates were
still awake, drinking out of a large cup which they were passing around   d
from left to right. Socrates was talking to them. Aristodemus couldn't
remember exactly what they were saying—he'd missed the first part of
their discussion, and he was half-asleep anyway—but the main point was
that Socrates was trying to prove to them that authors should be able to
write both comedy and tragedy: the skillful tragic dramatist should also
be a comic poet. He was about to clinch his argument, though, to tell the
truth, sleepy as they were, they were hardly able to follow his reasoning.
In fact, Aristophanes fell asleep in the middle of the discussion, and very
soon thereafter, as day was breaking, Agathon also drifted off.

But after getting them off to sleep, Socrates got up and left, and Aristodemus followed him, as always. He said that Socrates went directly to the
Lyceum, washed up, spent the rest of the day just as he always did, and
only then, as evening was falling, went home to rest.

PHAEDRUS

Phaedrus is commonly paired on the one hand with Gorgias *and on the other with* Symposium—*with the former in sharing its principal theme, the nature and limitations of rhetoric, with the latter in containing speeches devoted to the nature and value of erotic love. Here the two interests combine in manifold ways. Socrates, a city dweller little experienced in the pleasures of the country, walks out from Athens along the river Ilisus, alone with his friend Phaedrus, an impassioned admirer of oratory, for a private conversation: in Plato most of his conversations take place in a larger company, and no other in the private beauty of a rural retreat. There he is inspired to employ his knowledge of philosophy in crafting two speeches on the subject of erotic love, to show how paltry is the best effort on the same subject of the best orator in Athens, Lysias, who knows no philosophy. In the second half of the dialogue he explains to Phaedrus exactly how philosophical understanding of the truth about any matter discoursed upon, and about the varieties of human soul and their rhetorical susceptibilities, is an indispensable basis for a rhetorically accomplished speech— such as he himself delivered in the first part of the dialogue. By rights, Phaedrus' passionate admiration for oratory ought therefore to be transformed into an even more passionate love of philosophical knowledge, fine oratory's essential prerequisite. Socrates' own speeches about erotic love and his dialectical presentation of rhetoric's subservience to philosophy are both aimed at persuading Phaedrus to this transformation.*

In his great second speech Socrates draws upon the psychological theory of the Republic *and the metaphysics of resplendent Forms common to that dialogue and several others (notably* Phaedo *and* Symposium*) to inspire in Phaedrus a love for philosophy. By contrast, the philosophy drawn upon in the second, dialectical, half of the dialogue is linked closely to the much more austere, logically oriented investigations via the 'method of divisions' that we find in* Sophist, Statesman, *and* Philebus—*where the grasp of any important philosophical idea (any Form) proceeds by patient, detailed mapping of its relations to other concepts and to its own subvarieties, not through an awe-inspiring vision of a self-confined, single brilliant entity. One of Socrates' central claims in the second part of the dialogue is that a rhetorical composition, of which his second speech is a paragon, must construct in words mere resemblances of the real truth, ones selected to appeal to the specific type of 'soul' that its hearers possess, so as to draw them on toward knowledge of the truth—or else to disguise it! A rhetorical composition does not actually convey the truth; the truth*

506

is known only through philosophical study—of the sort whose results are presented in the second half of the dialogue. So Socrates himself warns us that the 'philosophical theories' embodied in his speech are resemblances only, motivated in fact by his desire to win Phaedrus away from an indiscriminate love of rhetoric to a controlled but elevated love of philosophical study.

Phaedrus is one of Plato's most admired literary masterpieces. Yet toward its end Socrates criticizes severely those who take their own writing seriously—any writing, not just orators' speeches. Writings cannot contain or constitute knowledge of any important matter. Knowledge can only be lodged in a mind, and its essential feature there is an endless capacity to express, interpret, and reinterpret itself suitably, in response to every challenge—something a written text once let go by its author plainly lacks: it can only keep on repeating the same words to whoever picks it up. But does not a Platonic dialogue, in engaging its reader in a creative, multilayered intellectual encounter, have a similar capacity for ever-deeper reading, for the discovery of underlying meaning beyond the simple presentation of its surface ideas? Knowledge is only in souls, but, despite the Phaedrus' own critique of writing, reading such a dialogue may be a good way of working to attain it.

J.M.C.

SOCRATES: Phaedrus, my friend! Where have you been? And where are   227
you going?

PHAEDRUS: I was with Lysias, the son of Cephalus,[1] Socrates, and I am going for a walk outside the city walls because I was with him for a long time, sitting there the whole morning. You see, I'm keeping in mind the advice of our mutual friend Acumenus,[2] who says it's more refreshing to   b
walk along country roads than city streets.

SOCRATES: He is quite right, too, my friend. So Lysias, I take it, is in the city?

PHAEDRUS: Yes, at the house of Epicrates, which used to belong to Morychus,[3] near the temple of the Olympian Zeus.

SOCRATES: What were you doing there? Oh, I know: Lysias must have been entertaining you with a feast of eloquence.

PHAEDRUS: You'll hear about it, if you are free to come along and listen.

Translated by A. Nehamas and P. Woodruff.

1. Cephalus is prominent in the opening section of Plato's *Republic*, which is set in his home in Piraeus, the port of Athens. His sons Lysias, Polemarchus, and Euthydemus were known for their democratic sympathies.

2. Acumenus was a doctor and a relative of the doctor Eryximachus who speaks in the *Symposium*.

3. Morychus is mentioned for his luxurious ways in a number of Aristophanes' plays.

SOCRATES: What? Don't you think I would consider it "more important than the most pressing engagement," as Pindar says, to hear how you and Lysias spent your time?[4]

PHAEDRUS: Lead the way, then.

c SOCRATES: If only you will tell me.

PHAEDRUS: In fact, Socrates, you're just the right person to hear the speech that occupied us, since, in a roundabout way, it was about love. It is aimed at seducing a beautiful boy, but the speaker is not in love with him—this is actually what is so clever and elegant about it: Lysias argues that it is better to give your favors to someone who does not love you than to someone who does.

SOCRATES: What a wonderful man! I wish he would write that you should

d give your favors to a poor rather than to a rich man, to an older rather than to a younger one—that is, to someone like me and most other people: then his speeches would be really sophisticated, and they'd contribute to the public good besides! In any case, I am so eager to hear it that I would follow you even if you were walking all the way to Megara, as Herodicus recommends, to touch the wall and come back again.[5]

PHAEDRUS: What on earth do you mean, Socrates? Do you think that a

228 mere dilettante like me could recite from memory in a manner worthy of him a speech that Lysias, the best of our writers, took such time and trouble to compose? Far from it—though actually I would rather be able to do that than come into a large fortune!

SOCRATES: Oh, Phaedrus, if I don't know my Phaedrus I must be forgetting who I am myself—and neither is the case. I know very well that he did not hear Lysias' speech only once: he asked him to repeat it over and over again, and Lysias was eager to oblige. But not even that was enough for

b him. In the end, he took the book himself and pored over the parts he liked best. He sat reading all morning long, and when he got tired, he went for a walk, having learned—I am quite sure—the whole speech by heart, unless it was extraordinarily long. So he started for the country, where he could practice reciting it. And running into a man who is sick with passion for hearing speeches, seeing him—just seeing him—he was filled with delight: he had found a partner for his frenzied dance, and he

c urged him to lead the way. But when that lover of speeches asked him to recite it, he played coy and pretended that he did not want to. In the end, of course, he was going to recite it even if he had to force an unwilling audience to listen. So, please, Phaedrus, beg him to do it right now. He'll do it soon enough anyway.

PHAEDRUS: Well, I'd better try to recite it as best I can: you'll obviously not leave me in peace until I do so one way or another.

SOCRATES: You are absolutely right.

---

4. Pindar, *Isthmian* I.2, adapted by Plato.

5. Herodicus was a medical expert whose regimen Socrates criticizes in *Republic* 406a–b.

PHAEDRUS: That's what I'll do, then. But, Socrates, it really is true that I did not memorize the speech word for word; instead, I will give a careful summary of its general sense, listing all the ways he said the lover differs from the non-lover, in the proper order.

SOCRATES: Only if you first show me what you are holding in your left hand under your cloak, my friend. I strongly suspect you have the speech itself. And if I'm right, you can be sure that, though I love you dearly, I'll never, as long as Lysias himself is present, allow you to practice your own speechmaking on me. Come on, then, show me.

PHAEDRUS: Enough, enough. You've dashed my hopes of using you as my training partner, Socrates. All right, where do you want to sit while we read?

SOCRATES: Let's leave the path here and walk along the Ilisus; then we can sit quietly wherever we find the right spot.

PHAEDRUS: How lucky, then, that I am barefoot today—you, of course, are always so. The easiest thing to do is to walk right in the stream; this way, we'll also get our feet wet, which is very pleasant, especially at this hour and season.

SOCRATES: Lead the way, then, and find us a place to sit.

PHAEDRUS: Do you see that very tall plane tree?

SOCRATES: Of course.

PHAEDRUS: It's shady, with a light breeze; we can sit or, if we prefer, lie down on the grass there.

SOCRATES: Lead on, then.

PHAEDRUS: Tell me, Socrates, isn't it from somewhere near this stretch of the Ilisus that people say Boreas carried Orithuia away?[6]

SOCRATES: So they say.

PHAEDRUS: Couldn't this be the very spot? The stream is lovely, pure and clear: just right for girls to be playing nearby.

SOCRATES: No, it is two or three hundred yards farther downstream, where one crosses to get to the district of Agra. I think there is even an altar to Boreas there.

PHAEDRUS: I hadn't noticed it. But tell me, Socrates, in the name of Zeus, do you really believe that that legend is true?

SOCRATES: Actually, it would not be out of place for me to reject it, as our intellectuals do. I could then tell a clever story: I could claim that a gust of the North Wind blew her over the rocks where she was playing with Pharmaceia; and once she was killed that way people said she had been carried off by Boreas—or was it, perhaps, from the Areopagus? The story is also told that she was carried away from there instead. Now, Phaedrus, such explanations are amusing enough, but they are a job for a man I cannot envy at all. He'd have to be far too ingenious and work

6. According to legend, Orithuia, daughter of the Athenian king Erechtheus, was abducted by Boreas while she was playing with Nymphs along the banks of the Ilisus River. Boreas personifies the north wind.

too hard—mainly because after that he will have to go on and give a rational account of the form of the Hippocentaurs, and then of the Chimera;
e   and a whole flood of Gorgons and Pegasuses and other monsters, in large numbers and absurd forms, will overwhelm him. Anyone who does not believe in them, who wants to explain them away and make them plausible by means of some sort of rough ingenuity, will need a great deal of time.

But I have no time for such things; and the reason, my friend, is this. I
230   am still unable, as the Delphic inscription orders, to know myself; and it really seems to me ridiculous to look into other things before I have understood that. This is why I do not concern myself with them. I accept what is generally believed, and, as I was just saying, I look not into them but into my own self: Am I a beast more complicated and savage than Typhon,[7] or am I a tamer, simpler animal with a share in a divine and gentle nature? But look, my friend—while we were talking, haven't we reached the tree you were taking us to?

b   PHAEDRUS: That's the one.

SOCRATES: By Hera, it really is a beautiful resting place. The plane tree is tall and very broad; the chaste-tree, high as it is, is wonderfully shady, and since it is in full bloom, the whole place is filled with its fragrance. From under the plane tree the loveliest spring runs with very cool water—our feet can testify to that. The place appears to be dedicated to Achelous and some of the Nymphs, if we can judge from the statues and votive
c   offerings.[8] Feel the freshness of the air; how pretty and pleasant it is; how it echoes with the summery, sweet song of the cicadas' chorus! The most exquisite thing of all, of course, is the grassy slope: it rises so gently that you can rest your head perfectly when you lie down on it. You've really been the most marvelous guide, my dear Phaedrus.

PHAEDRUS: And you, my remarkable friend, appear to be totally out of
d   place. Really, just as you say, you seem to need a guide, not to be one of the locals. Not only do you never travel abroad—as far as I can tell, you never even set foot beyond the city walls.

SOCRATES: Forgive me, my friend. I am devoted to learning; landscapes and trees have nothing to teach me—only the people in the city can do that. But you, I think, have found a potion to charm me into leaving. For
e   just as people lead hungry animals forward by shaking branches of fruit before them, you can lead me all over Attica or anywhere else you like simply by waving in front of me the leaves of a book containing a speech. But now, having gotten as far as this place this time around, I intend to lie down; so choose whatever position you think will be most comfortable for you, and read on.

7. Typhon is a fabulous multiform beast with a hundred heads resembling many different animal species.

8. Achelous is a river god. The Nymphs are benevolent female deities associated with natural phenomena such as streams, woods, and mountains.

PHAEDRUS: Listen, then:

"You understand my situation: I've told you how good it would be for us, in my opinion, if this worked out. In any case, I don't think I should lose the chance to get what I am asking for, merely because I don't happen to be in love with you.

"A man in love will wish he had not done you any favors once his desire dies down, but the time will never come for a man who's not in love to change his mind. That is because the favors he does for you are not forced but voluntary; and he does the best that he possibly can for you, just as he would for his own business.

"Besides, a lover keeps his eye on the balance sheet—where his interests have suffered from love, and where he has done well; and when he adds up all the trouble he has taken, he thinks he's long since given the boy he loved a fair return. A non-lover, on the other hand, can't complain about love's making him neglect his own business; he can't keep a tab on the trouble he's been through, or blame you for the quarrels he's had with his relatives. Take away all those headaches and there's nothing left for him to do but put his heart into whatever he thinks will give pleasure.

"Besides, suppose a lover does deserve to be honored because, as they say, he is the best friend his loved one will ever have, and he stands ready to please his boy with all those words and deeds that are so annoying to everyone else. It's easy to see (if he is telling the truth) that the next time he falls in love he will care more for his new love than for the old one, and it's clear he'll treat the old one shabbily whenever that will please the new one.

"And anyway, what sense does it make to throw away something like that on a person who has fallen into such a miserable condition that those who have suffered it don't even try to defend themselves against it? A lover will admit that he's more sick than sound in the head. He's well aware that he is not thinking straight; but he'll say he can't get himself under control. So when he does start thinking straight, why would he stand by decisions he had made when he was sick?

"Another point: if you were to choose the best of those who are in love with you, you'd have a pretty small group to pick from; but you'll have a large group if you don't care whether he loves you or not and just pick the one who suits you best; and in that larger pool you'll have a much better hope of finding someone who deserves your friendship.

"Now suppose you're afraid of conventional standards and the stigma that will come to you if people find out about this. Well, it stands to reason that a lover—thinking that everyone else will admire him for his success as much as he admires himself—will fly into words and proudly declare to all and sundry that his labors were not in vain. Someone who does not love you, on the other hand, can control himself and will choose to do what is best, rather than seek the glory that comes from popular reputation.

"Besides, it's inevitable that a lover will be found out: many people will see that he devotes his life to following the boy he loves. The result is that

[margin: 231]
[margin: b]
[margin: c]
[margin: d]
[margin: e]
[margin: 232]

b whenever people see you talking with him they'll think you are spending time together just before or just after giving way to desire. But they won't even begin to find fault with people for spending time together if they are not lovers; they know one has to talk to someone, either out of friendship or to obtain some other pleasure.

"Another point: have you been alarmed by the thought that it is hard for friendships to last? Or that when people break up, it's ordinarily just

c as awful for one side as it is for the other, but when you've given up what is most important to you already, then your loss is greater than his? If so, it would make more sense for you to be afraid of lovers. For a lover is easily annoyed, and whatever happens, he'll think it was designed to hurt him. That is why a lover prevents the boy he loves from spending time with other people. He's afraid that wealthy men will outshine him with their money, while men of education will turn out to have the advantage of greater intelligence. And he watches like a hawk everyone who may

d have any other advantage over him! Once he's persuaded you to turn those people away, he'll have you completely isolated from friends; and if you show more sense than he does in looking after your own interests, you'll come to quarrel with him.

"But if a man really does not love you, if it is only because of his excellence that he got what he asked for, then he won't be jealous of the people who spend time with you. Quite the contrary! He'll hate anyone who does not want to be with you; he'll think they look down on him while those who spend time with you do him good; so you should expect

e friendship, rather than enmity, to result from this affair.

"Another point: lovers generally start to desire your body before they know your character or have any experience of your other traits, with the result that even they can't tell whether they'll still want to be friends with

233 you after their desire has passed. Non-lovers, on the other hand, are friends with you even before they achieve their goal, and you've no reason to expect that benefits received will ever detract from their friendship for you. No, those things will stand as reminders of more to come.

"Another point: you can expect to become a better person if you are won over by me, rather than by a lover. A lover will praise what you say and what you do far beyond what is best, partly because he is afraid of

b being disliked, and partly because desire has impaired his judgment. Here is how love draws conclusions: When a lover suffers a reverse that would cause no pain to anyone else, love makes him think he's accursed! And when he has a stroke of luck that's not worth a moment's pleasure, love compels him to sing its praises. The result is, you should feel sorry for lovers, not admire them.

"If my argument wins you over, I will, first of all, give you my time with no thought of immediate pleasure; I will plan instead for the benefits

c that are to come, since I am master of myself and have not been overwhelmed by love. Small problems will not make me very hostile, and big ones will make me only gradually, and only a little, angry. I will forgive you for unintentional errors and do my best to keep you from going wrong intentionally. All this, you see, is the proof of a friendship that will last a long time.

"Have you been thinking that there can be no strong friendship in the absence of erotic love? Then you ought to remember that we would not care so much about our children if that were so, or about our fathers and mothers. And we wouldn't have had any trustworthy friends, since those relationships did not come from such a desire but from doing quite different things.

"Besides, if it were true that we ought to give the biggest favor to those who need it most, then we should all be helping out the very poorest people, not the best ones, because people we've saved from the worst troubles will give us the most thanks. For instance, the right people to invite to a dinner party would be beggars and people who need to sate their hunger, because they're the ones who'll be fond of us, follow us, knock on our doors,[9] take the most pleasure with the deepest gratitude, and pray for our success. No, it's proper, I suppose, to grant your favors to those who are best able to return them, not to those in the direst need— that is, not to those who merely desire the thing, but to those who really deserve it—not to people who will take pleasure in the bloom of your youth, but to those who will share their goods with you when you are older; not to people who achieve their goal and then boast about it in public, but to those who will keep a modest silence with everyone; not to people whose devotion is short-lived, but to those who will be steady friends their whole lives; not to the people who look for an excuse to quarrel as soon as their desire has passed, but to those who will prove their worth when the bloom of your youth has faded. Now, remember what I said and keep this in mind: friends often criticize a lover for bad behavior; but no one close to a non-lover ever thinks that desire has led him into bad judgment about his interests.

"And now I suppose you'll ask me whether I'm urging you to give your favors to everyone who is not in love with you. No. As I see it, a lover would not ask you to give in to all your lovers either. You would not, in that case, earn as much gratitude from each recipient, and you would not be able to keep one affair secret from the others in the same way. But this sort of thing is not supposed to cause any harm, and really should work to the benefit of both sides.

"Well, I think this speech is long enough. If you are still longing for more, if you think I have passed over something, just ask."

How does the speech strike you, Socrates? Don't you think it's simply superb, especially in its choice of words?

SOCRATES: It's a miracle, my friend; I'm in ecstasy. And it's all your doing, Phaedrus: I was looking at you while you were reading and it seemed to me the speech had made you radiant with delight; and since I

---

9. This is classic behavior in ancient Greek literature of a lovesick man pursuing his prey.

believe you understand these matters better than I do, I followed your lead, and following you I shared your Bacchic frenzy.

PHAEDRUS: Come, Socrates, do you think you should joke about this?

SOCRATES: Do you really think I am joking, that I am not serious?

e   PHAEDRUS: You are not at all serious, Socrates. But now tell me the truth, in the name of Zeus, god of friendship: Do you think that any other Greek could say anything more impressive or more complete on this same subject?

SOCRATES: What? Must we praise the speech even on the ground that its author has said what the situation demanded, and not instead simply on the ground that he has spoken in a clear and concise manner, with a precise turn of phrase? If we must, I will have to go along for your sake,

235 since—surely because I am so ignorant—that passed me by. I paid attention only to the speech's style. As to the other part, I wouldn't even think that Lysias himself could be satisfied with it. For it seemed to me, Phaedrus—unless, of course, you disagree—that he said the same things two or even three times, as if he really didn't have much to say about the subject, almost as if he just weren't very interested in it. In fact, he seemed to me to be showing off, trying to demonstrate that he could say the same thing in two different ways, and say it just as well both times.

b   PHAEDRUS: You are absolutely wrong, Socrates. That is in fact the best thing about the speech: He has omitted nothing worth mentioning about the subject, so that no one will ever be able to add anything of value to complete what he has already said himself.

SOCRATES: You go too far: I can't agree with you about that. If, as a favor to you, I accept your view, I will stand refuted by all the wise men and women of old who have spoken or written about this subject.

c   PHAEDRUS: Who are these people? And where have you heard anything better than this?

SOCRATES: I can't tell you offhand, but I'm sure I've heard better somewhere; perhaps it was the lovely Sappho or the wise Anacreon or even some writer of prose. So, what's my evidence? The fact, my dear friend, that my breast is full and I feel I can make a different speech, even better than Lysias'. Now I am well aware that none of these ideas can have come from me—I know my own ignorance. The only other possibility, I think,

d   is that I was filled, like an empty jar, by the words of other people streaming in through my ears, though I'm so stupid that I've even forgotten where and from whom I heard them.

PHAEDRUS: But, my dear friend, you couldn't have said a better thing! Don't bother telling me when and from whom you've heard this, even if I ask you—instead, do exactly what you said: You've just promised to make another speech making more points, and better ones, without repeating a word from my book. And I promise you that, like the Nine Archons, I shall set up in

e   return a life-sized golden statue at Delphi, not only of myself but also of you.[10]

10. The archons were magistrates chosen by lot in classical Athens. On taking office they swore an oath to set up a golden statue if they violated the laws.

SOCRATES: You're a real friend, Phaedrus, good as gold, to think I'm claiming that Lysias failed in absolutely every respect and that I can make a speech that is different on every point from his. I am sure that that couldn't happen even to the worst possible author. In our own case, for example, do you think that anyone could argue that one should favor the non-lover rather than the lover without praising the former for keeping his wits about him or condemning the latter for losing his—points that are essential to make—and still have something left to say? I believe we must allow these points, and concede them to the speaker. In their case, we cannot praise their novelty but only their skillful arrangement; but we can praise both the arrangement and the novelty of the nonessential points that are harder to think up.

236

PHAEDRUS: I agree with you; I think that's reasonable. This, then, is what I shall do. I will allow you to presuppose that the lover is less sane than the non-lover—and if you are able to add anything of value to complete what we already have in hand, you will stand in hammered gold beside the offering of the Cypselids in Olympia.[11]

b

SOCRATES: Oh, Phaedrus, I was only criticizing your beloved in order to tease you—did you take me seriously? Do you think I'd really try to match the product of his wisdom with a fancier speech?

PHAEDRUS: Well, as far as that goes, my friend, you've fallen into your own trap. You have no choice but to give your speech as best you can: otherwise you will force us into trading vulgar jibes the way they do in comedy. Don't make me say what you said: "Socrates, if I don't know my Socrates, I must be forgetting who I am myself," or "He wanted to speak, but he was being coy." Get it into your head that we shall not leave here until you recite what you claimed to have "in your breast." We are alone, in a deserted place, and I am younger and stronger. From all this, "take my meaning"[12] and don't make me force you to speak when you can do so willingly.

c

d

SOCRATES: But, my dear Phaedrus, I'll be ridiculous—a mere dilettante, improvising on the same topics as a seasoned professional!

PHAEDRUS: Do you understand the situation? Stop playing hard to get! I know what I can say to make you give your speech.

SOCRATES: Then please don't say it!

PHAEDRUS: Oh, yes, I will. And what I say will be an oath. I swear to you—by which god, I wonder? How about this very plane tree?—I swear in all truth that, if you don't make your speech right next to this tree here, I shall never, never again recite another speech for you—I shall never utter another word about speeches to you!

e

11. The Cypselids were rulers of Corinth in the seventh century B.C.; an ornate chest in which Cypselus was said to have been hidden as an infant was on display at Olympia, perhaps along with other offerings of theirs.

12. A line of Pindar's (Snell 105).

SOCRATES: My oh my, what a horrible man you are! You've really found the way to force a lover of speeches to do just as you say!

PHAEDRUS: So why are you still twisting and turning like that?

SOCRATES: I'll stop—now that you've taken this oath. How could I possibly give up such treats?

237   PHAEDRUS: Speak, then.

SOCRATES: Do you know what I'll do?

PHAEDRUS: What?

SOCRATES: I'll cover my head while I'm speaking. In that way, as I'm going through the speech as fast as I can, I won't get embarrassed by having to look at you and lose the thread of my argument.

PHAEDRUS: Just give your speech! You can do anything else you like.

SOCRATES: Come to me, O you clear-voiced Muses, whether you are called so because of the quality of your song or from the musical people of Liguria,[13] "come, take up my burden" in telling the tale that this fine fellow forces upon me so that his companion may now seem to him even

b   more clever than he did before:

There once was a boy, a youth rather, and he was very beautiful, and had very many lovers. One of them was wily and had persuaded him that he was not in love, though he loved the lad no less than the others. And once in pressing his suit to him, he tried to persuade him that he ought to give his favors to a man who did not love him rather than to one who did. And this is what he said:

"If you wish to reach a good decision on any topic, my boy, there is

c   only one way to begin: You must know what the decision is about, or else you are bound to miss your target altogether. Ordinary people cannot see that they do not know the true nature of a particular subject, so they proceed as if they did; and because they do not work out an agreement at the start of the inquiry, they wind up as you would expect—in conflict with themselves and each other. Now you and I had better not let this happen to us, since we criticize it in others. Because you and I are about to discuss whether a boy should make friends with a man who loves him

d   rather than with one who does not, we should agree on defining what love is and what effects it has. Then we can look back and refer to that as we try to find out whether to expect benefit or harm from love. Now, as everyone plainly knows, love is some kind of desire; but we also know that even men who are not in love have a desire for what is beautiful. So how shall we distinguish between a man who is in love and one who is not? We must realize that each of us is ruled by two principles which we follow wherever they lead: one is our inborn desire for pleasures, the other is our acquired judgment that pursues what is best. Sometimes these two

e   are in agreement; but there are times when they quarrel inside us, and

---

13. Socrates here suggests a farfetched etymology for a common epithet of the Muses, as the "clear-voiced" ones, on the basis of its resemblance to the Greek name for the Ligurians, who lived in what is now known as the French Riviera.

then sometimes one of them gains control, sometimes the other. Now when judgment is in control and leads us by reasoning toward what is best, that sort of self-control is called 'being in your right mind'; but when desire   238
takes command in us and drags us without reasoning toward pleasure, then its command is known as 'outrageousness'.[14] Now outrageousness has as many names as the forms it can take, and these are quite diverse.[15] Whichever form stands out in a particular case gives its name to the person who has it—and that is not a pretty name to be called, not worth earning at all. If it is desire for food that overpowers a person's reasoning about what is best and suppresses his other desires, it is called gluttony and it   b
gives him the name of a glutton, while if it is desire for drink that plays the tyrant and leads the man in that direction, we all know what name we'll call him then! And now it should be clear how to describe someone appropriately in the other cases: call the man by that name—sister to these others—that derives from the sister of these desires that controls him at the time. As for the desire that has led us to say all this, it should be obvious already, but I suppose things said are always better understood than things unsaid: The unreasoning desire that overpowers a person's considered impulse to do right and is driven to take pleasure in beauty,   c
its force reinforced by its kindred desires for beauty in human bodies— this desire, all-conquering in its forceful drive, takes its name from the word for force (*rhōmē*) and is called *erōs*."

There, Phaedrus my friend, don't you think, as I do, that I'm in the grip of something divine?

PHAEDRUS: This is certainly an unusual flow of words for you, Socrates.

SOCRATES: Then be quiet and listen. There's something really divine about this place, so don't be surprised if I'm quite taken by the Nymphs' madness   d
as I go on with the speech. I'm on the edge of speaking in dithyrambs[16] as it is.

PHAEDRUS: Very true!

SOCRATES: Yes, and you're the cause of it. But hear me out; the attack may yet be prevented. That, however, is up to the god; what we must do is face the boy again in the speech:

"All right then, my brave friend, now we have a definition for the subject of our decision; now we have said what it really is; so let us keep that in   e
view as we complete our discussion. What benefit or harm is likely to come from the lover or the non-lover to the boy who gives him favors? It is surely necessary that a man who is ruled by desire and is a slave to pleasure will turn his boy into whatever is most pleasing to himself. Now a sick man takes pleasure in anything that does not resist him, but sees

14. I.e., *hubris*, which ranges from arrogance to the sort of crimes to which arrogance gives rise, sexual assault in particular.

15. Reading *polumeles kai polueides* at a3 (lit., "multilimbed and multiformed").

16. A dithyramb was a choral poem originally connected with the worship of Dionysus. In classical times it became associated with an artificial style dominated by music.

239   anyone who is equal or superior to him as an enemy. That is why a lover
       will not willingly put up with a boyfriend who is his equal or superior,
       but is always working to make the boy he loves weaker and inferior to
       himself. Now, the ignorant man is inferior to the wise one, the coward to
       the brave, the ineffective speaker to the trained orator, the slow-witted to
       the quick. By necessity, a lover will be delighted to find all these mental
       defects and more, whether acquired or innate in his boy; and if he does
       not, he will have to supply them or else lose the pleasure of the moment.
  b   The necessary consequence is that he will be jealous and keep the boy
       away from the good company of anyone who would make a better man
       of him; and that will cause him a great deal of harm, especially if he keeps
       him away from what would most improve his mind—and that is, in fact,
       divine philosophy, from which it is necessary for a lover to keep his boy
       a great distance away, out of fear the boy will eventually come to look
       down on him. He will have to invent other ways, too, of keeping the boy
       in total ignorance and so in total dependence on himself. That way the
  c   boy will give his lover the most pleasure, though the harm to himself will
       be severe. So it will not be of any use to your intellectual development to
       have as your mentor and companion a man who is in love.
           "Now let's turn to your physical development. If a man is bound by
       necessity to chase pleasure at the expense of the good, what sort of shape
       will he want you to be in? How will he train you, if he is in charge? You
       will see that what he wants is someone who is soft, not muscular, and not
       trained in full sunlight but in dappled shade—someone who has never
       worked out like a man, never touched hard, sweaty exercise. Instead, he
  d   goes for a boy who has known only a soft unmanly style of life, who
       makes himself pretty with cosmetics because he has no natural color at
       all. There is no point in going on with this description: it is perfectly
       obvious what other sorts of behavior follow from this. We can take up
       our next topic after drawing all this to a head: the sort of body a lover
       wants in his boy is one that will give confidence to the enemy in a war
       or other great crisis while causing alarm to friends and even to his lovers.
       Enough of that; the point is obvious.
  e   "Our next topic is the benefit or harm to your possessions that will come
       from a lover's care and company. Everyone knows the answer, especially
       a lover: His first wish will be for a boy who has lost his dearest, kindliest
       and godliest possessions—his mother and father and other close relatives.
       He would be happy to see the boy deprived of them, since he would
240   expect them either to block him from the sweet pleasure of the boy's
       company or to criticize him severely for taking it. What is more, a lover
       would think any money or other wealth the boy owns would only make
       him harder to snare and, once snared, harder to handle. It follows by
       absolute necessity that wealth in a boyfriend will cause his lover to envy
       him, while his poverty will be a delight. Furthermore, he will wish for the
       boy to stay wifeless, childless, and homeless for as long as possible, since
       that's how long he desires to go on plucking his sweet fruit.

"There are other troubles in life, of course, but some divinity has mixed most of them with a dash of immediate pleasure. A flatterer, for example, may be an awful beast and a dreadful nuisance, but nature makes flattery rather pleasant by mixing in a little culture with its words. So it is with a mistress—for all the harm we accuse her of causing—and with many other creatures of that character, and their callings: at least they are delightful company for a day. But besides being harmful to his boyfriend, a lover is simply disgusting to spend the day with. 'Youth delights youth,' as the old proverb runs—because, I suppose, friendship grows from similarity, as boys of the same age go after the same pleasures. But you can even have too much of people your own age. Besides, as they say, it is miserable for anyone to be forced into anything by necessity—and this (to say nothing of the age difference) is most true for a boy with his lover. The older man clings to the younger day and night, never willing to leave him, driven by necessity and goaded on by the sting that gives him pleasure every time he sees, hears, touches, or perceives his boy in any way at all, so that he follows him around like a servant, with pleasure.

"As for the boy, however, what comfort or pleasure will the lover give to him during all the time they spend together? Won't it be disgusting in the extreme to see the face of that older man who's lost his looks? And everything that goes with that face—why, it is a misery even to hear them mentioned, let alone actually handle them, as you would constantly be forced to do! To be watched and guarded suspiciously all the time, with everyone! To hear praise of yourself that is out of place and excessive! And then to be falsely accused—which is unbearable when the man is sober and not only unbearable but positively shameful when he is drunk and lays into you with a pack of wild barefaced insults!

"While he is still in love he is harmful and disgusting, but after his love fades he breaks his trust with you for the future, in spite of all the promises he has made with all those oaths and entreaties which just barely kept you in a relationship that was troublesome at the time, in hope of future benefits. So, then, by the time he should pay up, he has made a change and installed a new ruling government in himself: right-minded reason in place of the madness of love. The boy does not even realize that his lover is a different man. He insists on his reward for past favors and reminds him of what they had done and said before—as if he were still talking to the same man! The lover, however, is so ashamed that he does not dare tell the boy how much he has changed or that there is no way, now that he is in his right mind and under control again, that he can stand by the promises he had sworn to uphold when he was under that old mindless regime. He is afraid that if he acted as he had before he would turn out the same and revert to his old self. So now he is a refugee, fleeing from those old promises on which he must default by necessity; he, the former lover, has to switch roles and flee, since the coin has fallen the other way, while the boy must chase after him, angry and cursing. All along he has been completely unaware that he should never have given

b

c

d

e

241

b

c   his favors to a man who was in love—and who therefore had by necessity
lost his mind. He should much rather have done it for a man who was
not in love and had his wits about him. Otherwise it follows necessarily
that he'd be giving himself to a man who is deceitful, irritable, jealous,
disgusting, harmful to his property, harmful to his physical fitness, and
absolutely devastating to the cultivation of his soul, which truly is, and
will always be, the most valuable thing to gods and men.

      "These are the points you should bear in mind, my boy. You should
know that the friendship of a lover arises without any good will at all.

d   No, like food, its purpose is to sate hunger. 'Do wolves love lambs? That's
how lovers befriend a boy!'"

      That's it, Phaedrus. You won't hear another word from me, and you'll
have to accept this as the end of the speech.

      PHAEDRUS: But I thought you were right in the middle—I thought you
were about to speak at the same length about the non-lover, to list his
good points and argue that it's better to give one's favors to him. So why
are you stopping now, Socrates?

e   SOCRATES: Didn't you notice, my friend, that even though I am criticizing
the lover, I have passed beyond lyric into epic poetry?[17] What do you
suppose will happen to me if I begin to praise his opposite? Don't you
realize that the Nymphs to whom you so cleverly exposed me will take
complete possession of me? So I say instead, in a word, that every shortcom-
ing for which we blamed the lover has its contrary advantage, and the
non-lover possesses it. Why make a long speech of it? That's enough about

242   them both. This way my story will meet the end it deserves, and I will
cross the river and leave before you make me do something even worse.

      PHAEDRUS: Not yet, Socrates, not until this heat is over. Don't you see
that it is almost exactly noon, "straight-up" as they say? Let's wait and
discuss the speeches, and go as soon as it turns cooler.

      SOCRATES: You're really superhuman when it comes to speeches, Phae-
drus; you're truly amazing. I'm sure you've brought into being more of

b   the speeches that have been given during your lifetime than anyone else,
whether you composed them yourself or in one way or another forced
others to make them; with the single exception of Simmias the Theban,
you are far ahead of the rest.[18] Even as we speak, I think, you're managing
to cause me to produce yet another one.

      PHAEDRUS: Oh, how wonderful! But what do you mean? What speech?

      SOCRATES: My friend, just as I was about to cross the river, the familiar

c   divine sign came to me which, whenever it occurs, holds me back from
something I am about to do. I thought I heard a voice coming from this
very spot, forbidding me to leave until I made atonement for some offense

---

17. The overheated choral poems known as dithyrambs (see 238d) were written in lyric
meters. The meter of the last line of Socrates' speech, however, was epic, and it is the
tradition in epic poetry to glorify a hero, not to attack him.

18. Simmias, a companion of Socrates, was evidently a lover of discussion (cf. *Phaedo* 85c).

against the gods. In effect, you see, I am a seer, and though I am not particularly good at it, still—like people who are just barely able to read and write—I am good enough for my own purposes. I recognize my offense clearly now. In fact, the soul too, my friend, is itself a sort of seer; that's why, almost from the beginning of my speech, I was disturbed by a very   d
uneasy feeling, as Ibycus puts it, that "for offending the gods I am honored by men."[19] But now I understand exactly what my offense has been.

PHAEDRUS: Tell me, what is it?

SOCRATES: Phaedrus, that speech you carried with you here—it was horrible, as horrible as the speech you made me give.

PHAEDRUS: How could that be?

SOCRATES: It was foolish, and close to being impious. What could be more horrible than that?

PHAEDRUS: Nothing—if, of course, what you say is right.

SOCRATES: Well, then? Don't you believe that Love is the son of Aphrodite? Isn't he one of the gods?

PHAEDRUS: This is certainly what people say.

SOCRATES: Well, Lysias certainly doesn't and neither does your speech, which you charmed me through your potion into delivering myself. But if Love is a god or something divine—which he is—he can't be bad in   e
any way; and yet our speeches just now spoke of him as if he were. That is their offense against Love. And they've compounded it with their utter foolishness in parading their dangerous falsehoods and preening them-   243
selves over perhaps deceiving a few silly people and coming to be admired by them.

And so, my friend, I must purify myself. Now for those whose offense lies in telling false stories about matters divine, there is an ancient rite of purification—Homer did not know it, but Stesichorus did. When he lost his sight for speaking ill of Helen, he did not, like Homer, remain in the dark about the reason why. On the contrary, true follower of the Muses that he was, he understood it and immediately composed these lines:

> *There's no truth to that story:*
> *You never sailed that lovely ship,*
> *You never reached the tower of Troy.*[20]   b

And as soon as he completed the poem we call the Palinode, he immediately regained his sight. Now I will prove to be wiser than Homer and Stesichorus to this small extent: I will try to offer my Palinode to Love before I am punished for speaking ill of him—with my head bare, no longer covered in shame.

PHAEDRUS: No words could be sweeter to my ears, Socrates.

19. Ibycus was a sixth-century poet, most famous for his passionate love poetry.
20. Frg. 18 (Edmonds).

c   SOCRATES: You see, my dear Phaedrus, you understand how shameless
the speeches were, my own as well as the one in your book. Suppose a
noble and gentle man, who was (or had once been) in love with a boy of
similar character, were to hear us say that lovers start serious quarrels for
trivial reasons and that, jealous of their beloved, they do him harm—don't
you think that man would think we had been brought up among the most
d   vulgar of sailors, totally ignorant of love among the freeborn? Wouldn't
he most certainly refuse to acknowledge the flaws we attributed to Love?

PHAEDRUS: Most probably, Socrates.

SOCRATES: Well, that man makes me feel ashamed, and as I'm also afraid
of Love himself, I want to wash out the bitterness of what we've heard
with a more tasteful speech. And my advice to Lysias, too, is to write as
soon as possible a speech urging one to give similar favors to a lover rather
than to a non-lover.

PHAEDRUS: You can be sure he will. For once you have spoken in praise
e   of the lover, I will most definitely make Lysias write a speech on the
same topic.

SOCRATES: I do believe you will, so long as you are who you are.

PHAEDRUS: Speak on, then, in full confidence.

SOCRATES: Where, then, is the boy to whom I was speaking? Let him
hear this speech, too. Otherwise he may be too quick to give his favors to
the non-lover.

PHAEDRUS: He is here, always right by your side, whenever you want him.

244   SOCRATES: You'll have to understand, beautiful boy, that the previous
speech was by Phaedrus, Pythocles' son, from Myrrhinus, while the one
I am about to deliver is by Stesichorus, Euphemus' son, from Himera.[21]
And here is how the speech should go:

"'There's no truth to that story'—that when a lover is available you
should give your favors to a man who doesn't love you instead, because
he is in control of himself while the lover has lost his head. That would
have been fine to say if madness were bad, pure and simple; but in fact
the best things we have come from madness, when it is given as a gift of
the god.

b   "The prophetess of Delphi and the priestesses at Dodona are out of their
minds when they perform that fine work of theirs for all of Greece, either
for an individual person or for a whole city, but they accomplish little or
nothing when they are in control of themselves. We will not mention the
Sybil or the others who foretell many things by means of god-inspired
prophetic trances and give sound guidance to many people—that would
take too much time for a point that's obvious to everyone. But here's some
evidence worth adding to our case: The people who designed our language
in the old days never thought of madness as something to be ashamed of
or worthy of blame; otherwise they would not have used the word 'manic'

21. Etymologically: "Stesichorus son of Good Speaker, from the Land of Desire."
Myrrhinus was one of the demes of ancient Athens.

for the finest experts of all—the ones who tell the future—thereby weaving   c
insanity into prophecy. They thought it was wonderful when it came as
a gift of the god, and that's why they gave its name to prophecy; but
nowadays people don't know the fine points, so they stick in a 't' and call
it '*mantic*.' Similarly, the clear-headed study of the future, which uses birds
and other signs, was originally called *oionoïstic*, since it uses reasoning to
bring intelligence (*nous*) and learning (*historia*) into human thought; but
now modern speakers call it *oiōnistic*, putting on airs with their long '*ō*'.   d
To the extent, then, that prophecy, *mantic*, is more perfect and more admirable than sign-based prediction, *oiōnistic*, in both name and achievement,
madness (*mania*) from a god is finer than self-control of human origin,
according to the testimony of the ancient language givers.

"Next, madness can provide relief from the greatest plagues of trouble
that beset certain families because of their guilt for ancient crimes: it turns
up among those who need a way out; it gives prophecies and takes refuge   e
in prayers to the gods and in worship, discovering mystic rites and purifications that bring the man it touches[22] through to safety for this and all
time to come. So it is that the right sort of madness finds relief from present
hardships for a man it has possessed.

"Third comes the kind of madness that is possession by the Muses,   245
which takes a tender virgin soul and awakens it to a Bacchic frenzy of
songs and poetry that glorifies the achievements of the past and teaches
them to future generations. If anyone comes to the gates of poetry and
expects to become an adequate poet by acquiring expert knowledge of the
subject without the Muses' madness, he will fail, and his self-controlled
verses will be eclipsed by the poetry of men who have been driven out
of their minds.

"There you have some of the fine achievements—and I could tell you   b
even more—that are due to god-sent madness. We must not have any fear
on this particular point, then, and we must not let anyone disturb us or
frighten us with the claim that you should prefer a friend who is in control
of himself to one who is disturbed. Besides proving that point, if he is to
win his case, our opponent must show that love is not sent by the gods
as a benefit to a lover and his boy. And we, for our part, must prove the
opposite, that this sort of madness is given us by the gods to ensure our
greatest good fortune. It will be a proof that convinces the wise if not   c
the clever.

"Now we must first understand the truth about the nature of the soul,
divine or human, by examining what it does and what is done to it. Here
begins the proof:

"Every soul[23] is immortal. That is because whatever is always in motion
is immortal, while what moves, and is moved by, something else stops

22. Retaining *heautēs* at e3.
23. Alternatively, "All soul."

living when it stops moving. So it is only what moves itself that never
desists from motion, since it does not leave off being itself. In fact, this
self-mover is also the source and spring of motion in everything else that
d   moves; and a source has no beginning. That is because anything that has
a beginning comes from some source, but there is no source for this, since
a source that got its start from something else would no longer be the
source. And since it cannot have a beginning, then necessarily it cannot
be destroyed. That is because if a source were destroyed it could never
get started again from anything else and nothing else could get started
from it—that is, if everything gets started from a source. This then is why
a self-mover is a source of motion. And *that* is incapable of being destroyed
e   or starting up; otherwise all heaven and everything that has been started
up[24] would collapse, come to a stop, and never have cause to start moving
again. But since we have found that a self-mover is immortal, we should
have no qualms about declaring that this is the very essence and principle
of a soul, for every bodily object that is moved from outside has no soul,
while a body whose motion comes from within, from itself, does have a
soul, that being the nature of a soul; and if this is so—that whatever moves
itself is essentially a soul—then it follows necessarily that soul should have
neither birth nor death.

246   "That, then, is enough about the soul's immortality. Now here is what
we must say about its structure. To describe what the soul actually is
would require a very long account, altogether a task for a god in every
way; but to say what it is like is humanly possible and takes less time. So
let us do the second in our speech. Let us then liken the soul to the natural
union of a team of winged horses and their charioteer. The gods have
horses and charioteers that are themselves all good and come from good
b   stock besides, while everyone else has a mixture. To begin with, our driver
is in charge of a pair of horses; second, one of his horses is beautiful and
good and from stock of the same sort, while the other is the opposite and
has the opposite sort of bloodline. This means that chariot-driving in our
case is inevitably a painfully difficult business.

        "And now I should try to tell you why living things are said to include
both mortal and immortal beings. All soul looks after all that lacks a soul,
c   and patrols all of heaven, taking different shapes at different times. So
long as its wings are in perfect condition it flies high, and the entire universe
is its dominion; but a soul that sheds its wings wanders until it lights on
something solid, where it settles and takes on an earthly body, which
then, owing to the power of this soul, seems to move itself. The whole
combination of soul and body is called a living thing, or animal, and has
the designation 'mortal' as well. Such a combination cannot be immortal,
not on any reasonable account. In fact it is pure fiction, based neither on
d   observation nor on adequate reasoning, that a god is an immortal living
thing which has a body and a soul, and that these are bound together by

24. Reading *pasan te genesin* at e1.

nature for all time—but of course we must let this be as it may please the gods, and speak accordingly.

"Let us turn to what causes the shedding of the wings, what makes them fall away from a soul. It is something of this sort: By their nature wings have the power to lift up heavy things and raise them aloft where the gods all dwell, and so, more than anything that pertains to the body, they are akin to the divine, which has beauty, wisdom, goodness, and everything of that sort. These nourish the soul's wings, which grow best in their presence; but foulness and ugliness make the wings shrink and disappear.

"Now Zeus, the great commander in heaven, drives his winged chariot first in the procession, looking after everything and putting all things in order. Following him is an army of gods and spirits arranged in eleven sections. Hestia is the only one who remains at the home of the gods; all the rest of the twelve are lined up in formation, each god in command of the unit to which he is assigned. Inside heaven are many wonderful places from which to look and many aisles which the blessed gods take up and back, each seeing to his own work, while anyone who is able and wishes to do so follows along, since jealousy has no place in the gods' chorus. When they go to feast at the banquet they have a steep climb to the high tier at the rim of heaven; on this slope the gods' chariots move easily, since they are balanced and well under control, but the other chariots barely make it. The heaviness of the bad horse drags its charioteer toward the earth and weighs him down if he has failed to train it well, and this causes the most extreme toil and struggle that a soul will face. But when the souls we call immortals reach the top, they move outward and take their stand on the high ridge of heaven, where its circular motion carries them around as they stand while they gaze upon what is outside heaven.

"The place beyond heaven—none of our earthly poets has ever sung or ever will sing its praises enough! Still, this is the way it is—risky as it may be, you see, I must attempt to speak the truth, especially since the truth is my subject. What is in this place is without color and without shape and without solidity, a being that really is what it is, the subject of all true knowledge, visible only to intelligence, the soul's steersman. Now a god's mind is nourished by intelligence and pure knowledge, as is the mind of any soul that is concerned to take in what is appropriate to it, and so it is delighted at last to be seeing what is real and watching what is true, feeding on all this and feeling wonderful, until the circular motion brings it around to where it started. On the way around it has a view of Justice as it is; it has a view of Self-control; it has a view of Knowledge—not the knowledge that is close to change, that becomes different as it knows the different things which we consider real down here. No, it is the knowledge of what really is what it is. And when the soul has seen all the things that are as they are and feasted on them, it sinks back inside heaven and goes home. On its arrival, the charioteer stables the horses by the manger, throws in ambrosia, and gives them nectar to drink besides.

248   "Now that is the life of the gods. As for the other souls, one that follows
a god most closely, making itself most like that god, raises the head of its
charioteer up to the place outside and is carried around in the circular
motion with the others. Although distracted by the horses, this soul does
have a view of Reality, just barely. Another soul rises at one time and falls
at another, and because its horses pull it violently in different directions,
it sees some real things and misses others. The remaining souls are all
eagerly straining to keep up, but are unable to rise; they are carried around
below the surface, trampling and striking one another as each tries to get
b   ahead of the others. The result is terribly noisy, very sweaty, and disorderly.
Many souls are crippled by the incompetence of the drivers, and many
wings break much of their plumage. After so much trouble, they all leave
without having seen reality, uninitiated, and when they have gone they
will depend on what they think is nourishment—their own opinions.

        "The reason there is so much eagerness to see the plain where truth
c   stands is that this pasture has the grass that is the right food for the best
part of the soul, and it is the nature of the wings that lift up the soul to
be nourished by it. Besides, the law of Destiny is this: If any soul becomes
a companion to a god and catches sight of any true thing, it will be
unharmed until the next circuit; and if it is able to do this every time, it
will always be safe. If, on the other hand, it does not see anything true
because it could not keep up, and by some accident takes on a burden of
forgetfulness and wrongdoing, then it is weighed down, sheds its wings
d   and falls to earth. At that point, according to the law, the soul is not born
into a wild animal in its first incarnation; but a soul that has seen the most
will be planted in the seed of a man who will become a lover of wisdom[25]
or of beauty, or who will be cultivated in the arts and prone to erotic love.
The second sort of soul will be put into someone who will be a lawful king
or warlike commander; the third, a statesman, a manager of a household, or
a financier; the fourth will be a trainer who loves exercise or a doctor who
e   cures the body; the fifth will lead the life of a prophet or priest of the
mysteries. To the sixth the life of a poet or some other representational
artist is properly assigned; to the seventh the life of a manual laborer or
farmer; to the eighth the career of a sophist or demagogue, and to the
ninth a tyrant.

        "Of all these, any who have led their lives with justice will change to a
better fate, and any who have led theirs with injustice, to a worse one. In
fact, no soul returns to the place from which it came for ten thousand
249   years, since its wings will not grow before then, except for the soul of a
man who practices philosophy without guile or who loves boys philosophically. If, after the third cycle of one thousand years, the last-mentioned
souls have chosen such a life three times in a row, they grow their wings
back, and they depart in the three-thousandth year. As for the rest, once
their first life is over, they come to judgment; and, once judged, some are

25. I.e., a philosopher.

condemned to go to places of punishment beneath the earth and pay the full penalty for their injustice, while the others are lifted up by justice to a place in heaven where they live in the manner the life they led in human   b
form has earned them. In the thousandth year both groups arrive at a choice and allotment of second lives, and each soul chooses the life it wants. From there, a human soul can enter a wild animal, and a soul that was once human can move from an animal to a human being again. But a soul that never saw the truth cannot take a human shape, since a human being must understand speech in terms of general forms, proceeding to   c
bring many perceptions together into a reasoned unity.[26] That process is the recollection of the things our soul saw when it was traveling with god, when it disregarded the things we now call real and lifted up its head to what is truly real instead.

"For just this reason it is fair that only a philosopher's mind grows wings, since its memory always keeps it as close as possible to those realities by being close to which the gods are divine. A man who uses reminders of these things correctly is always at the highest, most perfect level of initiation, and he is the only one who is perfect as perfect can be. He stands outside human concerns and draws close to the divine; ordinary   d
people think he is disturbed and rebuke him for this, unaware that he is possessed by god. Now this takes me to the whole point of my discussion of the fourth kind of madness—that which someone shows when he sees the beauty we have down here and is reminded of true beauty; then he takes wing and flutters in his eagerness to rise up, but is unable to do so; and he gazes aloft, like a bird, paying no attention to what is down below— and that is what brings on him the charge that he has gone mad. This is   e
the best and noblest of all the forms that possession by god can take for anyone who has it or is connected to it, and when someone who loves beautiful boys is touched by this madness he is called a lover. As I said, nature requires that the soul of every human being has seen reality; other- wise, no soul could have entered this sort of living thing. But not every   250
soul is easily reminded of the reality there by what it finds here—not souls that got only a brief glance at the reality there, not souls who had such bad luck when they fell down here that they were twisted by bad company into lives of injustice so that they forgot the sacred objects they had seen before. Only a few remain whose memory is good enough; and they are startled when they see an image of what they saw up there. Then they are beside themselves, and their experience is beyond their comprehension because they cannot fully grasp what it is that they are seeing.   b

"Justice and self-control do not shine out through their images down here, and neither do the other objects of the soul's admiration; the senses are so murky that only a few people are able to make out, with difficulty, the original of the likenesses they encounter here. But beauty was radiant

26. Accepting the emendation *iont'* at b7.

to see at that time when the souls, along with the glorious chorus (we[27] were with Zeus, while others followed other gods), saw that blessed and spectacular vision and were ushered into the mystery that we may rightly

c call the most blessed of all. And we who celebrated it were wholly perfect and free of all the troubles that awaited us in time to come, and we gazed in rapture at sacred revealed objects that were perfect, and simple, and unshakeable and blissful. That was the ultimate vision, and we saw it in pure light because we were pure ourselves, not buried in this thing we are carrying around now, which we call a body, locked in it like an oyster in its shell.

"Well, all that was for love of a memory that made me stretch out my
d speech in longing for the past. Now beauty, as I said, was radiant among the other objects; and now that we have come down here we grasp it sparkling through the clearest of our senses. Vision, of course, is the sharpest of our bodily senses, although it does not see wisdom. It would awaken a terribly powerful love if an image of wisdom came through our sight as clearly as beauty does, and the same goes for the other objects of inspired
e love. But now beauty alone has this privilege, to be the most clearly visible and the most loved. Of course a man who was initiated long ago or who has become defiled is not to be moved abruptly from here to a vision of Beauty itself when he sees what we call beauty here; so instead of gazing at the latter reverently, he surrenders to pleasure and sets out in the manner of a four-footed beast, eager to make babies; and, wallowing in vice, he
251 goes after unnatural pleasure too, without a trace of fear or shame. A recent initiate, however, one who has seen much in heaven—when he sees a godlike face or bodily form that has captured Beauty well, first he shudders and a fear comes over him like those he felt at the earlier time; then he gazes at him with the reverence due a god, and if he weren't afraid people would think him completely mad, he'd even sacrifice to his boy
b as if he were the image of a god. Once he has looked at him, his chill gives way to sweating and a high fever, because the stream of beauty that pours into him through his eyes warms him up and waters the growth of his wings. Meanwhile, the heat warms him and melts the places where the wings once grew, places that were long ago closed off with hard scabs to keep the sprouts from coming back; but as nourishment flows in, the feather shafts swell and rush to grow from their roots beneath every part of the soul (long ago, you see, the entire soul had wings). Now the whole
c soul seethes and throbs in this condition. Like a child whose teeth are just starting to grow in, and its gums are all aching and itching—that is exactly how the soul feels when it begins to grow wings. It swells up and aches and tingles as it grows them. But when it looks upon the beauty of the boy and takes in the stream of particles flowing into it from his beauty

27. I.e., we philosophers; cf. 252e.

(that is why this is called 'desire'[28]), when it is watered and warmed by this, then all its pain subsides and is replaced by joy. When, however, it $\quad$ d is separated from the boy and runs dry, then the openings of the passages in which the feathers grow are dried shut and keep the wings from sprouting. Then the stump of each feather is blocked in its desire and it throbs like a pulsing artery while the feather pricks at its passageway, with the result that the whole soul is stung all around, and the pain simply drives it wild—but then, when it remembers the boy in his beauty, it recovers its joy. From the outlandish mix of these two feelings—pain and joy— comes anguish and helpless raving: in its madness the lover's soul cannot $\quad$ e sleep at night or stay put by day; it rushes, yearning, wherever it expects to see the person who has that beauty. When it does see him, it opens the sluice-gates of desire and sets free the parts that were blocked up before. And now that the pain and the goading have stopped, it can catch its breath and once more suck in, for the moment, this sweetest of all pleasures. This it is not at all willing to give up, and no one is more important to it $\quad$ 252 than the beautiful boy. It forgets mother and brothers and friends entirely and doesn't care at all if it loses its wealth through neglect. And as for proper and decorous behavior, in which it used to take pride, the soul despises the whole business. Why, it is even willing to sleep like a slave, anywhere, as near to the object of its longing as it is allowed to get! That is because in addition to its reverence for one who has such beauty, the $\quad$ b soul has discovered that the boy is the only doctor for all that terrible pain.

"This is the experience we humans call love, you beautiful boy (I mean the one to whom I am making this speech).[29] You are so young that what the gods call it is likely to strike you as funny. Some of the successors of Homer, I believe, report two lines from the less well known poems, of which the second is quite indecent and does not scan very well. They praise love this way:

> Yes, mortals call him powerful winged 'Love';
> But because of his need to thrust out the wings,
> $\qquad$ the gods call him 'Shove.'[30]

You may believe this or not as you like. But, seriously, the cause of love $\quad$ c is as I have said, and this is how lovers really feel.

"If the man who is taken by love used to be an attendant on Zeus, he will be able to bear the burden of this feathered force with dignity. But if

---

28. "Desire" is *himeros*: the derivation is from *merē* ("particles"), *ienai* ("go") and *rhein* ("flow").

29. Cf. 237b, 238d, 243e.

30. The lines are probably Plato's invention, as the language is not consistently Homeric. The pun in the original is on *erōs* and *pterōs* ("the winged one").

it is one of Ares' troops who has fallen prisoner of love—if that is the god with whom he took the circuit—then if he has the slightest suspicion that the boy he loves has done him wrong, he turns murderous, and he is ready to make a sacrifice of himself as well as the boy.

d   "So it is with each of the gods: everyone spends his life honoring the god in whose chorus he danced, and emulates that god in every way he can, so long as he remains undefiled and in his first life down here. And that is how he behaves with everyone at every turn, not just with those he loves. Everyone chooses his love after his own fashion from among
e   those who are beautiful, and then treats the boy like his very own god, building him up and adorning him as an image to honor and worship. Those who followed Zeus, for example, choose someone to love who is a Zeus himself in the nobility of his soul. So they make sure he has a talent for philosophy and the guidance of others, and once they have found him and are in love with him they do everything to develop that talent. If any lovers have not yet embarked on this practice, then they start to learn, using any source they can and also making progress on their own. They are well equipped to track down their god's true nature with their own
253   resources because of their driving need to gaze at the god, and as they are in touch with the god by memory they are inspired by him and adopt his customs and practices, so far as a human being can share a god's life. For all of this they know they have the boy to thank, and so they love him all the more; and if they draw their inspiration from Zeus, then, like the Bacchants,[31] they pour it into the soul of the one they love in order to
b   help him take on as much of their own god's qualities as possible. Hera's followers look for a kingly character, and once they have found him they do all the same things for him. And so it is for followers of Apollo or any other god: They take their god's path and seek for their own a boy whose nature is like the god's; and when they have got him they emulate the god, convincing the boy they love and training him to follow their god's pattern and way of life, so far as is possible in each case. They show no envy, no mean-spirited lack of generosity, toward the boy, but make every
c   possible effort to draw him into being totally like themselves and the god to whom they are devoted. This, then, is any true lover's heart's desire: if he follows that desire in the manner I described, this friend who has been driven mad by love will secure a consummation[32] for the one he has befriended that is as beautiful and blissful as I said—if, of course, he captures him. Here, then, is how the captive is caught:

"Remember how we divided each soul in three at the beginning of our
d   story—two parts in the form of horses and the third in that of a charioteer? Let us continue with that. One of the horses, we said, is good, the other not; but we did not go into the details of the goodness of the good horse

---

31. Bacchants were worshippers of Dionysus who gained miraculous abilities when possessed by the madness of their god.

32. Reading *teleutē* at c3.

or the badness of the bad. Let us do that now. The horse that is on the right, or nobler, side is upright in frame and well jointed, with a high neck and a regal nose; his coat is white, his eyes are black, and he is a lover of honor with modesty and self-control; companion to true glory, he needs no whip, and is guided by verbal commands alone. The other horse is a crooked great jumble of limbs with a short bull-neck, a pug nose, black skin, and bloodshot white eyes; companion to wild boasts and indecency, he is shaggy around the ears—deaf as a post—and just barely yields to horsewhip and goad combined. Now when the charioteer looks in the eye of love, his entire soul is suffused with a sense of warmth and starts to fill with tingles and the goading of desire. As for the horses, the one who is obedient to the charioteer is still controlled, then as always, by its sense of shame, and so prevents itself from jumping on the boy. The other one, however, no longer responds to the whip or the goad of the charioteer; it leaps violently forward and does everything to aggravate its yokemate and its charioteer, trying to make them go up to the boy and suggest to him the pleasures of sex. At first the other two resist, angry in their belief that they are being made to do things that are dreadfully wrong. At last, however, when they see no end to their trouble, they are led forward, reluctantly agreeing to do as they have been told. So they are close to him now, and they are struck by the boy's face as if by a bolt of lightning. When the charioteer sees that face, his memory is carried back to the real nature of Beauty, and he sees it again where it stands on the sacred pedestal next to Self-control. At the sight he is frightened, falls over backwards awestruck, and at the same time has to pull the reins back so fiercely that both horses are set on their haunches, one falling back voluntarily with no resistance, but the other insolent and quite unwilling. They pull back a little further; and while one horse drenches the whole soul with sweat out of shame and awe, the other—once it has recovered from the pain caused by the bit and its fall—bursts into a torrent of insults as soon as it has caught its breath, accusing its charioteer and yokemate of all sorts of cowardice and unmanliness for abandoning their position and their agreement. Now once more it tries to make its unwilling partners advance, and gives in grudgingly only when they beg it to wait till later. Then, when the promised time arrives, and they are pretending to have forgotten, it reminds them; it struggles, it neighs, it pulls them forward and forces them to approach the boy again with the same proposition; and as soon as they are near, it drops its head, straightens its tail, bites the bit, and pulls without any shame at all. The charioteer is now struck with the same feelings as before, only worse, and he's falling back as he would from a starting gate; and he violently yanks the bit back out of the teeth of the insolent horse, only harder this time, so that he bloodies its foul-speaking tongue and jaws, sets its legs and haunches firmly on the ground, and 'gives it over to pain.'[33] When the bad horse has suffered this same thing

e

254

b

c

d

e

33. Cf. *Iliad* v.397 and *Odyssey* xvii.567.

time after time, it stops being so insolent; now it is humble enough to follow the charioteer's warnings, and when it sees the beautiful boy it dies of fright, with the result that now at last the lover's soul follows its boy in reverence and awe.

255   "And because he is served with all the attentions due a god by a lover who is not pretending otherwise but is truly in the throes of love, and because he is by nature disposed to be a friend of the man who is serving him (even if he has already been set against love by schoolfriends or others who say that it is shameful to associate with a lover, and initially rejects the lover in consequence), as time goes forward he is brought by his

b   ripening age and a sense of what must be to a point where he lets the man spend time with him. It is a decree of fate, you see, that bad is never friends with bad, while good cannot fail to be friends with good. Now that he allows his lover to talk and spend time with him, and the man's good will is close at hand, the boy is amazed by it as he realizes that all the friendship he has from his other friends and relatives put together is nothing compared to that of this friend who is inspired by a god.

      "After the lover has spent some time doing this, staying near the boy (and even touching him during sports and on other occasions), then the

c   spring that feeds the stream Zeus named 'Desire' when he was in love with Ganymede begins to flow mightily in the lover and is partly absorbed by him, and when he is filled it overflows and runs away outside him. Think how a breeze or an echo bounces back from a smooth solid object to its source; that is how the stream of beauty goes back to the beautiful boy and sets him aflutter. It enters through his eyes, which are its natural

d   route to the soul; there it waters the passages for the wings, starts the wings growing, and fills the soul of the loved one with love in return. Then the boy is in love, but has no idea what he loves. He does not understand, and cannot explain, what has happened to him. It is as if he had caught an eye disease from someone else, but could not identify the cause; he does not realize that he is seeing himself in the lover as in a mirror. So when the lover is near, the boy's pain is relieved just as the lover's is, and when they are apart he yearns as much as he is yearned

e   for, because he has a mirror image of love in him—'backlove'—though he neither speaks nor thinks of it as love, but as friendship. Still, his desire is nearly the same as the lover's, though weaker: he wants to see, touch, kiss, and lie down with him; and of course, as you might expect, he acts on these desires soon after they occur.

      "When they are in bed, the lover's undisciplined horse has a word to

256   say to the charioteer—that after all its sufferings it is entitled to a little fun. Meanwhile, the boy's bad horse has nothing to say, but swelling with desire, confused, it hugs the lover and kisses him in delight at his great good will. And whenever they are lying together it is completely unable, for its own part, to deny the lover any favor he might beg to have. Its yokemate, however, along with its charioteer, resists such requests with modesty and reason. Now if the victory goes to the better elements in both

their minds, which lead them to follow the assigned regimen of philosophy, their life here below is one of bliss and shared understanding. They are modest and fully in control of themselves now that they have enslaved the part that brought trouble into the soul and set free the part that gave it virtue. After death, when they have grown wings and become weightless, they have won the first of three rounds in these, the true Olympic Contests. There is no greater good than this that either human self-control or divine madness can offer a man. If, on the other hand, they adopt a lower way of living, with ambition in place of philosophy, then pretty soon when they are careless because they have been drinking or for some other reason, the pair's undisciplined horses will catch their souls off guard and together bring them to commit that act which ordinary people would take to be the happiest choice of all; and when they have consummated it once, they go on doing this for the rest of their lives, but sparingly, since they have not approved of what they are doing with their whole minds. So these two also live in mutual friendship (though weaker than that of the philosophical pair), both while they are in love and after they have passed beyond it, because they realize they have exchanged such firm vows that it would be forbidden for them ever to break them and become enemies. In death they are wingless when they leave the body, but their wings are bursting to sprout, so the prize they have won from the madness of love is considerable, because those who have begun the sacred journey in lower heaven may not by law be sent into darkness for the journey under the earth; their lives are bright and happy as they travel together, and thanks to their love they will grow wings together when the time comes.

"These are the rewards you will have from a lover's friendship, my boy, and they are as great as divine gifts should be. A non-lover's companionship, on the other hand, is diluted by human self-control; all it pays are cheap, human dividends, and though the slavish attitude it engenders in a friend's soul is widely praised as virtue, it tosses the soul around for nine thousand years on the earth and leads it, mindless, beneath it.

"So now, dear Love, this is the best and most beautiful palinode[34] we could offer as payment for our debt, especially in view of the rather poetical choice of words Phaedrus made me use.[35] Forgive us our earlier speeches in return for this one; be kind and gracious toward my expertise at love, which is your own gift to me: do not, out of anger, take it away or disable it; and grant that I may be held in higher esteem than ever by those who are beautiful. If Phaedrus and I said anything that shocked you in our earlier speech, blame it on Lysias, who was its father, and put a stop to his making speeches of this sort; convert him to philosophy like his brother Polemarchus so that his lover here may no longer play both sides as he does now, but simply devote his life to Love through philosophical discussions."

34. Cf. 243b.
35. Cf. 234c, 238c.

c   PHAEDRUS: I join you in your prayer, Socrates. If this is really best for us, may it come to pass. As to your speech, I admired it from the moment you began: You managed it much better than your first one. I'm afraid that Lysias' effort to match it is bound to fall flat, if of course he even dares to try to offer a speech of his own. In fact, my marvelous friend, a politician I know was only recently taking Lysias to task for just that reason: All through his invective, he kept calling him a "speech writer." So perhaps his pride will keep him from writing this speech for us.

d   SOCRATES: Ah, what a foolish thing to say, young man. How wrong you are about your friend: he can't be intimidated so easily! But perhaps you thought the man who was taking him to task meant what he said as a reproach?

PHAEDRUS: He certainly seemed to, Socrates. In any case, you are surely aware yourself that the most powerful and renowned politicians are ashamed to compose speeches or leave any writings behind; they are afraid that in later times they may come to be known as "sophists."

SOCRATES: Phaedrus, you don't understand the expression "Pleasant

e   Bend"—it originally referred to the long bend of the Nile.[36] And, besides the bend, you also don't understand that the most ambitious politicians love speechwriting and long for their writings to survive. In fact, when they write one of their speeches, they are so pleased when people praise it that they add at the beginning a list of its admirers everywhere.

PHAEDRUS: What do you mean? I don't understand.

258   SOCRATES: Don't you know that the first thing politicians put in their writings[37] is the names of their admirers?

PHAEDRUS: How so?

SOCRATES: "Resolved," the author often begins, "by the Council" or "by the People" or by both, and "So-and-so said"[38]—meaning himself, the writer, with great solemnity and self-importance. Only then does he go on with what he has to say, showing off his wisdom to his admirers, often composing a very long document. Do you think there's any difference between that and a written speech?

b   PHAEDRUS: No, I don't.

SOCRATES: Well, then, if it remains on the books, he is delighted and leaves the stage a poet. But if it is struck down, if he fails as a speech writer and isn't considered worthy of having his work written down, he goes into deep mourning, and his friends along with him.

PHAEDRUS: He certainly does.

SOCRATES: Clearly, then, they don't feel contempt for speechwriting; on the contrary, they are in awe of it.

36. Apparently this was a familiar example of something named by language that means the opposite—though called "pleasant" it was really a long, nasty bend.

37. Reading *suggramatos* at a1.

38. This is the standard form for decisions, including legislation, made by the assembly of Athens, though it is not the standard beginning for even the most political of speeches.

PHAEDRUS: Quite so.

SOCRATES: There's this too. What of an orator or a king who acquires   c
enough power to match Lycurgus, Solon, or Darius as a lawgiver[39] and
acquires immortal fame as a speech writer in his city? Doesn't he think
that he is equal to the gods while he is still alive? And don't those who
live in later times believe just the same about him when they behold
his writings?

PHAEDRUS: Very much so.

SOCRATES: Do you really believe then that any one of these people,
whoever he is and however much he hates Lysias, would reproach him
for being a writer?

PHAEDRUS: It certainly isn't likely in view of what you said, for he would
probably be reproaching his own ambition as well.

SOCRATES: This, then, is quite clear: Writing speeches is not in itself a   d
shameful thing.

PHAEDRUS: How could it be?

SOCRATES: It's not speaking or writing well that's shameful; what's really
shameful is to engage in either of them shamefully or badly.

PHAEDRUS: That is clear.

SOCRATES: So what distinguishes good from bad writing? Do we need
to ask this question of Lysias or anyone else who ever did or will write
anything—whether a public or a private document, poetic verse or
plain prose?

PHAEDRUS: You ask if we need to? Why else should one live, I say, if   e
not for pleasures of this sort? Certainly not for those you cannot feel unless
you are first in pain, like most of the pleasures of the body, and which
for this reason we call the pleasures of slaves.

SOCRATES: It seems we clearly have the time. Besides, I think that the
cicadas, who are singing and carrying on conversations with one another   259
in the heat of the day above our heads, are also watching us. And if they
saw the two of us avoiding conversation at midday like most people,
diverted by their song and, sluggish of mind, nodding off, they would
have every right to laugh at us, convinced that a pair of slaves had come
to their resting place to sleep like sheep gathering around the spring in
the afternoon. But if they see us in conversation, steadfastly navigating   b
around them as if they were the Sirens, they will be very pleased and
immediately give us the gift from the gods they are able to give to mortals.

PHAEDRUS: What is this gift? I don't think I have heard of it.

SOCRATES: Everyone who loves the Muses should have heard of this.
The story goes that the cicadas used to be human beings who lived before
the birth of the Muses. When the Muses were born and song was created

---

39. Lycurgus was the legendary lawgiver of Sparta. Solon reformed the constitution of
Athens in the early sixth century B.C. and was revered by both democrats and their
opponents. Darius was king of Persia (521–486 B.C.). None of these was famous as a
speech writer.

for the first time, some of the people of that time were so overwhelmed
c with the pleasure of singing that they forgot to eat or drink; so they died
without even realizing it. It is from them that the race of the cicadas came
into being; and, as a gift from the Muses, they have no need of nourishment
once they are born. Instead, they immediately burst into song, without
food or drink, until it is time for them to die. After they die, they go to
the Muses and tell each one of them which mortals have honored her. To
d Terpsichore they report those who have honored her by their devotion to
the dance and thus make them dearer to her. To Erato, they report those
who honored her by dedicating themselves to the affairs of love, and so
too with the other Muses, according to the activity that honors each. And
to Calliope, the oldest among them, and Urania, the next after her, who
preside over the heavens and all discourse, human and divine, and sing
with the sweetest voice, they report those who honor their special kind of
music by leading a philosophical life.

There are many reasons, then, why we should talk and not waste our
afternoon in sleep.

PHAEDRUS: By all means, let's talk.

e SOCRATES: Well, then, we ought to examine the topic we proposed just
now: When is a speech well written and delivered, and when is it not?

PHAEDRUS: Plainly.

SOCRATES: Won't someone who is to speak well and nobly have to have
in mind the truth about the subject he is going to discuss?

PHAEDRUS: What I have actually heard about this, Socrates, my friend,
260 is that it is not necessary for the intending orator to learn what is really
just, but only what will seem just to the crowd who will act as judges.
Nor again what is really good or noble, but only what will seem so. For
that is what persuasion proceeds from, not truth.

SOCRATES: Anything that wise men say, Phaedrus, "is not lightly to be
cast aside";[40] we must consider whether it might be right. And what you
just said, in particular, must not be dismissed.

PHAEDRUS: You're right.

SOCRATES: Let's look at it this way, then.

PHAEDRUS: How?

b SOCRATES: Suppose I were trying to convince you that you should fight
your enemies on horseback, and neither one of us knew what a horse is,
but I happened to know this much about you, that Phaedrus believes a
horse is the tame animal with the longest ears—

PHAEDRUS: But that would be ridiculous, Socrates.

SOCRATES: Not quite yet, actually. But if I were seriously trying to convince
you, having composed a speech in praise of the donkey in which I called
it a horse and claimed that having such an animal is of immense value

---

40. *Iliad* ii.361.

both at home and in military service, that it is good for fighting and for carrying your baggage and that it is useful for much else besides—   c

PHAEDRUS: Well, that would be totally ridiculous.

SOCRATES: Well, which is better? To be ridiculous and a friend? Or clever and an enemy?

PHAEDRUS: The former.

SOCRATES: And so, when a rhetorician who does not know good from bad addresses a city which knows no better and attempts to sway it, not praising a miserable donkey as if it were a horse, but bad as if it were good, and, having studied what the people believe, persuades them to do something bad instead of good—with that as its seed, what sort of crop   d do you think rhetoric can harvest?

PHAEDRUS: A crop of really poor quality.

SOCRATES: But could it be, my friend, that we have mocked the art of speaking more rudely than it deserves? For it might perhaps reply, "What bizarre nonsense! Look, I am not forcing anyone to learn how to make speeches without knowing the truth; on the contrary, my advice, for what it is worth, is to take me up only after mastering the truth. But I do make this boast: even someone who knows the truth couldn't produce conviction on the basis of a systematic art without me."

PHAEDRUS: Well, is that a fair reply?   e

SOCRATES: Yes, it is—if, that is, the arguments now advancing upon rhetoric testify that it is an art. For it seems to me as if I hear certain arguments approaching and protesting that that is a lie and that rhetoric is not an art but an artless practice.[41] As the Spartan said, there is no genuine art of speaking without a grasp of truth, and there never will be.

PHAEDRUS: We need to hear these arguments, Socrates. Come, produce   261 them, and examine them: What is their point? How do they make it?

SOCRATES: Come to us, then, noble creatures; convince Phaedrus, him of the beautiful offspring,[42] that unless he pursues philosophy properly he will never be able to make a proper speech on any subject either. And let Phaedrus be the one to answer.

PHAEDRUS: Let them put their questions.

SOCRATES: Well, then, isn't the rhetorical art, taken as a whole, a way of directing the soul by means of speech, not only in the lawcourts and on other public occasions but also in private? Isn't it one and the same art whether its subject is great or small, and no more to be held in esteem—   b if it is followed correctly—when its questions are serious than when they are trivial? Or what have you heard about all this?

PHAEDRUS: Well, certainly not what *you* have! Artful speaking and writing is found mainly in the lawcourts; also perhaps in the Assembly. That's all I've heard.

41. For a criticism of rhetoric as not an art, see *Gorgias* 462b–c.
42. Cf. 242a–b; *Symposium* 209b–e.

SOCRATES: Well, have you only heard of the rhetorical treatises of Nestor and Odysseus—those they wrote in their spare time in Troy? Haven't you also heard of the works of Palamedes?[43]

c PHAEDRUS: No, by Zeus, I haven't even heard of Nestor's—unless by Nestor you mean Gorgias, and by Odysseus, Thrasymachus or Theodorus.[44]

SOCRATES: Perhaps. But let's leave these people aside. Answer this question yourself: What do adversaries do in the lawcourts? Don't they speak on opposite sides? What else can we call what they do?

PHAEDRUS: That's it, exactly.

SOCRATES: About what is just and what is unjust?

PHAEDRUS: Yes.

d SOCRATES: And won't whoever does this artfully make the same thing appear to the same people sometimes just and sometimes, when he prefers, unjust?

PHAEDRUS: Of course.

SOCRATES: And when he addresses the Assembly, he will make the city approve a policy at one time as a good one, and reject it—the very same policy—as just the opposite at another.

PHAEDRUS: Right.

SOCRATES: Now, don't we know that the Eleatic Palamedes is such an artful speaker that his listeners will perceive the same things to be both similar and dissimilar, both one and many, both at rest and also in motion?[45]

PHAEDRUS: Most certainly.

SOCRATES: We can therefore find the practice of speaking on opposite

e sides not only in the lawcourts and in the Assembly. Rather, it seems that one single art—if, of course, it is an art in the first place—governs all speaking. By means of it one can make out as similar anything that can be so assimilated, to everything to which it can be made similar, and expose anyone who tries to hide the fact that that is what he is doing.

PHAEDRUS: What do you mean by that?

SOCRATES: I think it will become clear if we look at it this way. Where is deception most likely to occur—regarding things that differ much or things that differ little from one another?

262 PHAEDRUS: Regarding those that differ little.

SOCRATES: At any rate, you are more likely to escape detection, as you shift from one thing to its opposite, if you proceed in small steps rather than in large ones.

---

43. Nestor and Odysseus are Homeric heroes known for their speaking ability. Palamedes, who does not figure in Homer, was proverbial for his cunning.

44. Gorgias of Leontini was the most famous teacher of rhetoric to visit Athens. About Thrasymachus of Chalcedon (cf. 267c) we know little beyond what we can infer from his appearance in Book 1 of the *Republic*. On Theodorus of Byzantium (not to be confused with the geometer who appears in the *Theaetetus*) see 266e and Aristotle *Rhetoric* 3.13.5.

45. The Eleatic Palamedes is presumably Zeno of Elea, the author of the famous paradoxes about motion.

PHAEDRUS: Without a doubt.

SOCRATES: Therefore, if you are to deceive someone else and to avoid deception yourself, you must know precisely the respects in which things are similar and dissimilar to one another.

PHAEDRUS: Yes, you must.

SOCRATES: And is it really possible for someone who doesn't know what each thing truly is to detect a similarity—whether large or small—between something he doesn't know and anything else?

PHAEDRUS: That is impossible.

SOCRATES: Clearly, therefore, the state of being deceived and holding beliefs contrary to what is the case comes upon people by reason of certain similarities.

PHAEDRUS: That is how it happens.

SOCRATES: Could someone, then, who doesn't know what each thing is ever have the art to lead others little by little through similarities away from what is the case on each occasion to its opposite? Or could he escape this being done to himself?

PHAEDRUS: Never.

SOCRATES: Therefore, my friend, the art of a speaker who doesn't know the truth and chases opinions instead is likely to be a ridiculous thing— not an art at all!

PHAEDRUS: So it seems.

SOCRATES: So, shall we look for instances of what we called the artful and the artless in the speech of Lysias you carried here and in our own speeches?

PHAEDRUS: That's the best thing to do—because, as it is, we are talking quite abstractly, without enough examples.

SOCRATES: In fact, by some chance the two speeches do, as it seems, contain an example of the way in which someone who knows the truth can toy with his audience and mislead them. For my part, Phaedrus, I hold the local gods responsible for this—also, perhaps, the messengers of the Muses who are singing over our heads may have inspired me with this gift: certainly *I* don't possess any art of speaking.

PHAEDRUS: Fine, fine. But explain what you mean.

SOCRATES: Come, then—read me the beginning of Lysias' speech.

PHAEDRUS: "You understand my situation: I've told you how good it would be for us, in my opinion, if we could work this out. In any case, I don't think I should lose the chance to get what I am asking for, merely because I don't happen to be in love with you. A man in love will wish he had not done you any favors—"

SOCRATES: Stop. Our task is to say how he fails and writes artlessly. Right?

PHAEDRUS: Yes.

SOCRATES: Now isn't this much absolutely clear: We are in accord with one another about some of the things we discourse about and in discord about others?

PHAEDRUS: I think I understand what you are saying; but, please, can you make it a little clearer?

b

c

d

e

263

SOCRATES: When someone utters the word "iron" or "silver," don't we all think of the same thing?

PHAEDRUS: Certainly.

SOCRATES: But what happens when we say "just" or "good"? Doesn't each one of us go in a different direction? Don't we differ with one another and even with ourselves?

PHAEDRUS: We certainly do.

b   SOCRATES: Therefore, we agree about the former and disagree about the latter.

PHAEDRUS: Right.

SOCRATES: Now in which of these two cases are we more easily deceived? And when does rhetoric have greater power?

PHAEDRUS: Clearly, when we wander in different directions.

SOCRATES: It follows that whoever wants to acquire the art of rhetoric must first make a systematic division and grasp the particular character of each of these two kinds of thing, both the kind where most people wander in different directions and the kind where they do not.

c   PHAEDRUS: What a splendid thing, Socrates, he will have understood if he grasps *that!*

SOCRATES: Second, I think, he must not be mistaken about his subject; he must have a sharp eye for the class to which whatever he is about to discuss belongs.

PHAEDRUS: Of course.

SOCRATES: Well, now, what shall we say about love? Does it belong to the class where people differ or to that where they don't?

PHAEDRUS: Oh, surely the class where they differ. Otherwise, do you think you could have spoken of it as you did a few minutes ago, first saying that it is harmful both to lover and beloved and then immediately afterward that it is the greatest good?

d   SOCRATES: Very well put. But now tell me this—I can't remember at all because I was completely possessed by the gods: Did I define love at the beginning of my speech?

PHAEDRUS: Oh, absolutely, by Zeus, you most certainly did.

SOCRATES: Alas, how much more artful with speeches the Nymphs, daughters of Achelous, and Pan, son of Hermes, are, according to what you say, than Lysias, son of Cephalus! Or am I wrong? Did Lysias too, at

e   the start of his love-speech, compel us to assume that love is the single thing that he himself wanted it to be? Did he then complete his speech by arranging everything in relation to that? Will you read its opening once again?

PHAEDRUS: If you like. But what you are looking for is not there.

SOCRATES: Read it, so that I can hear it in his own words.

PHAEDRUS: "You understand my situation: I've told you how good it would be for us, in my opinion, if we could work this out. In any case, I don't think I should lose the chance to get what I am asking for, merely

264   because I don't happen to be in love with you. A man in love will wish he had not done you any favors, once his desire dies down—"

SOCRATES: He certainly seems a long way from doing what we wanted. He doesn't even start from the beginning but from the end, making his speech swim upstream on its back. His first words are what a lover would say to his boy as he was concluding his speech. Am I wrong, Phaedrus, dear heart?

PHAEDRUS: Well, Socrates, that was the end for which he gave the speech!   b

SOCRATES: And what about the rest? Don't the parts of the speech appear to have been thrown together at random? Is it evident that the second point had to be made second for some compelling reason? Is that so for any of the parts? I at least—of course I know nothing about such matters—thought the author said just whatever came to mind next, though not without a certain noble willfulness. But you, do you know any principle of speech-composition compelling him to place these things one after another in this order?

PHAEDRUS: It's very generous of you to think that I can understand his   c
reasons so clearly.

SOCRATES: But surely you will admit at least this much: Every speech must be put together like a living creature, with a body of its own; it must be neither without head nor without legs; and it must have a middle and extremities that are fitting both to one another and to the whole work.

PHAEDRUS: How could it be otherwise?

SOCRATES: But look at your friend's speech: Is it like that or is it otherwise? Actually, you'll find that it's just like the epigram people say is inscribed on the tomb of Midas the Phrygian.

PHAEDRUS: What epigram is that? And what's the matter with it?   d

SOCRATES: It goes like this:

> *A maid of bronze am I, on Midas' tomb I lie*
> *As long as water flows, and trees grow tall*
> *Shielding the grave where many come to cry*
> *That Midas rests here I say to one and all.*

I'm sure you notice that it makes no difference at all which of its verses   e
comes first, and which last.

PHAEDRUS: You are making fun of our speech, Socrates.

SOCRATES: Well, then, if that upsets you, let's leave that speech aside—even though I think it has plenty of very useful examples, provided one tries to emulate them as little as possible—and turn to the others. I think it is important for students of speechmaking to pay attention to one of their features.

PHAEDRUS: What do you mean?   265

SOCRATES: They were in a way opposite to one another. One claimed that one should give one's favors to the lover; the other, to the non-lover.

PHAEDRUS: Most manfully, too.

SOCRATES: I thought you were going to say "madly," which would have been the truth, and is also just what I was looking for: We did say, didn't we, that love is a kind of madness?

PHAEDRUS: Yes.

SOCRATES: And that there are two kinds of madness, one produced by human illness, the other by a divinely inspired release from normally accepted behavior?

b   PHAEDRUS: Certainly.

SOCRATES: We also distinguished four parts within the divine kind and connected them to four gods. Having attributed the inspiration of the prophet to Apollo, of the mystic to Dionysus, of the poet to the Muses, and the fourth part of madness to Aphrodite and to Love, we said that the madness of love is the best. We used a certain sort of image to describe love's passion; perhaps it had a measure of truth in it, though it may also have led us astray. And having whipped up a not altogether implausible

c   speech, we sang playfully, but also appropriately and respectfully, a story-like hymn to my master and yours, Phaedrus—to Love, who watches over beautiful boys.

PHAEDRUS: And I listened to it with the greatest pleasure.

SOCRATES: Let's take up this point about it right away: How was the speech able to proceed from censure to praise?

PHAEDRUS: What exactly do you mean by that?

SOCRATES: Well, everything else in it really does appear to me to have been spoken in play. But part of it was given with Fortune's guidance,

d   and there were in it two kinds of things the nature of which it would be quite wonderful to grasp by means of a systematic art.

PHAEDRUS: Which things?

SOCRATES: The first consists in seeing together things that are scattered about everywhere and collecting them into one kind, so that by defining each thing we can make clear the subject of any instruction we wish to give. Just so with our discussion of love: Whether its definition was or was not correct, at least it allowed the speech to proceed clearly and consistently with itself.

PHAEDRUS: And what is the other thing you are talking about, Socrates?

e   SOCRATES: This, in turn, is to be able to cut up each kind according to its species along its natural joints, and to try not to splinter any part, as a bad butcher might do. In just this way, our two speeches placed all

266 mental derangements into one common kind. Then, just as each single body has parts that naturally come in pairs of the same name (one of them being called the right-hand and the other the left-hand one), so the speeches, having considered unsoundness of mind to be by nature one single kind within us, proceeded to cut it up—the first speech cut its left-hand part, and continued to cut until it discovered among these parts a sort of love that can be called "left-handed," which it correctly denounced; the second speech, in turn, led us to the right-hand part of madness; discovered a love that shares its name with the other but is actually divine; set it out

b   before us, and praised it as the cause of our greatest goods.

PHAEDRUS: You are absolutely right.

SOCRATES: Well, Phaedrus, I am myself a lover of these divisions and collections, so that I may be able to think and to speak; and if I believe that someone else is capable of discerning a single thing that is also by nature capable of encompassing many,[46] I follow "straight behind, in his tracks, as if he were a god."[47] God knows whether this is the right name for those who can do this correctly or not, but so far I have always called them "dialecticians." But tell me what I must call them now that we have learned all this from Lysias and you. Or is it just that art of speaking that Thrasymachus and the rest of them use, which has made them masters of speechmaking and capable of producing others like them—anyhow those who are willing to bring them gifts and to treat them as if they were kings?

PHAEDRUS: They may behave like kings, but they certainly lack the knowledge you're talking about. No, it seems to me that you are right in calling the sort of thing you mentioned dialectic; but, it seems to me, rhetoric still eludes us.

SOCRATES: What are you saying? Could there be anything valuable which is independent of the methods I mentioned and is still grasped by art? If there is, you and I must certainly honor it, and we must say what part of rhetoric it is that has been left out.

PHAEDRUS: Well, there's quite a lot, Socrates: everything, at any rate, written up in the books on the art of speaking.

SOCRATES: You were quite right to remind me. First, I believe, there is the Preamble with which a speech must begin. This is what you mean, isn't it—the fine points of the art?

PHAEDRUS: Yes.

SOCRATES: Second come the Statement of Facts and the Evidence of Witnesses concerning it; third, Indirect Evidence; fourth, Claims to Plausibility. And I believe at least that excellent Byzantine word-wizard adds Confirmation and Supplementary Confirmation.

PHAEDRUS: You mean the worthy Theodorus?[48]

SOCRATES: Quite. And he also adds Refutation and Supplementary Refutation, to be used both in prosecution and in defense. Nor must we forget the most excellent Evenus of Paros,[49] who was the first to discover Covert Implication and Indirect Praise and who—some say—has even arranged Indirect Censures in verse as an aid to memory: a wise man indeed! And Tisias[50] and Gorgias? How can we leave them out when it is they who realized that what is likely must be held in higher honor than what is true; they who, by the power of their language, make small things appear great and great things small; they who express modern ideas in ancient garb, and ancient ones in modern dress; they who have discovered how to argue

c

d

e

267

b

---

46. Reading *pephukos* at b6.

47. *Odyssey* ii.406.

48. Cf. 261c.

49. Evenus of Paros was active as a sophist toward the end of the fifth century B.C. Only a few tiny fragments of his work survive.

50. Tisias of Syracuse, with Corax, is credited with the founding of the Sicilian school of rhetoric, represented by Gorgias and Polus.

both concisely and at infinite length about any subject? Actually, when I told Prodicus[51] this last, he laughed and said that only he had discovered the art of proper speeches: What we need are speeches that are neither long nor short but of the right length.

PHAEDRUS: Brilliantly done, Prodicus!

SOCRATES: And what about Hippias?[52] How can we omit him? I am sure our friend from Elis would cast his vote with Prodicus.

PHAEDRUS: Certainly.

SOCRATES: And what shall we say of the whole gallery of terms Polus[53]
c   set up—speaking with Reduplication, Speaking in Maxims, Speaking in Images—and of the terms Licymnius gave him as a present to help him explain Good Diction?[54]

PHAEDRUS: But didn't Protagoras actually use similar terms?[55]

SOCRATES: Yes, Correct Diction, my boy, and other wonderful things. As to the art of making speeches bewailing the evils of poverty and old age, the prize, in my judgment, goes to the mighty Chalcedonian.[56] He it is also
d   who knows best how to inflame a crowd and, once they are inflamed, how to hush them again with his words' magic spell, as he says himself. And let's not forget that he is as good at producing slander as he is at refuting it, whatever its source may be.

As to the way of ending a speech, everyone seems to be in agreement, though some call it Recapitulation and others by some other name.

PHAEDRUS: You mean, summarizing everything at the end and reminding the audience of what they've heard?

SOCRATES: That's what I mean. And if you have anything else to add about the art of speaking—

PHAEDRUS: Only minor points, not worth making.

268   SOCRATES: Well, let's leave minor points aside. Let's hold what we do have closer to the light so that we can see precisely the power of the art these things produce.

PHAEDRUS: A very great power, Socrates, especially in front of a crowd.

SOCRATES: Quite right. But now, my friend, look closely: Do you think, as I do, that its fabric is a little threadbare?

51. Prodicus of Ceos, who lived from about 470 till after 400 B.C., is frequently mentioned by Plato in connection with his ability to make fine verbal distinctions.

52. Hippias of Elis was born in the mid-fifth century and traveled widely teaching a variety of subjects, including mathematics, astronomy, harmony, mnemonics, ethics, and history as well as public speaking.

53. Polus was a pupil of Gorgias; Plato represents him in the *Gorgias*, esp. at 448c and 471a–c. He was said to have composed an *Art of Rhetoric* (*Gorgias*, 462b).

54. Licymnius of Chios was a dithyrambic poet and teacher of rhetoric.

55. Protagoras of Abdera, whose life spanned most of the fifth century B.C., was the most famous of the early sophists. We have a vivid portrayal of him in Plato's *Protagoras* and an intriguing reconstruction of his epistemology in the *Theaetetus*.

56. Literally, "the might of the Chalcedonian": a Homeric figure referring to Thrasymachus, who came from Chalcedon. Cf. 261c.

PHAEDRUS: Can you show me?

SOCRATES: All right, tell me this. Suppose someone came to your friend Eryximachus or his father Acumenus and said: "I know treatments to raise or lower (whichever I prefer) the temperature of people's bodies; if I decide to, I can make them vomit or make their bowels move, and all sorts of things. On the basis of this knowledge, I claim to be a physician; and I claim to be able to make others physicians as well by imparting it to them." What do you think they would say when they heard that?

PHAEDRUS: What could they say? They would ask him if he also knew to whom he should apply such treatments, when, and to what extent.

SOCRATES: What if he replied, "I have no idea. My claim is that whoever learns from me will manage to do what you ask on his own"?

PHAEDRUS: I think they'd say the man's mad if he thinks he's a doctor just because he read a book or happened to come across a few potions; he knows nothing of the art.

SOCRATES: And suppose someone approached Sophocles and Euripides and claimed to know how to compose the longest passages on trivial topics and the briefest ones on topics of great importance, that he could make them pitiful if he wanted, or again, by contrast, terrifying and menacing, and so on. Suppose further that he believed that by teaching this he was imparting the knowledge of composing tragedies—

PHAEDRUS: Oh, I am sure they too would laugh at anyone who thought a tragedy was anything other than the proper arrangement of these things: They have to fit with one another and with the whole work.

SOCRATES: But I am sure they wouldn't reproach him rudely. They would react more like a musician confronted by a man who thought he had mastered harmony because he was able to produce the highest and lowest notes on his strings. The musician would not say fiercely, "You stupid man, you are out of your mind!" As befits his calling, he would speak more gently: "My friend, though that too is necessary for understanding harmony, someone who has gotten as far as you have may still know absolutely nothing about the subject. What you know is what it's necessary to learn before you study harmony, but not harmony itself."

PHAEDRUS: That's certainly right.

SOCRATES: So Sophocles would also tell the man who was showing off to them that he knew the preliminaries of tragedy, but not the art of tragedy itself. And Acumenus would say his man knew the preliminaries of medicine, but not medicine itself.

PHAEDRUS: Absolutely.

SOCRATES: And what if the "honey-tongued Adrastus" (or perhaps Pericles)[57] were to hear of all the marvelous techniques we just discussed—Speaking Concisely and Speaking in Images and all the rest we listed and

57. Pericles, who dominated Athens from the 450s until his death in 429 B.C., was famous as the most successful orator-politician of his time. The quotation is from the early Spartan poet Tyrtaeus, fragment 12.8 (Edmonds). Adrastus is a legendary warrior hero of Argos, one of the main characters in Euripides' *Suppliants*.

b proposed to examine under the light? Would he be angry or rude, as you and I were, with those who write of those techniques and teach them as if they are rhetoric itself, and say something coarse to them? Wouldn't he—being wiser than we are—reproach us as well and say, "Phaedrus and Socrates, you should not be angry with these people—you should be sorry for them. The reason they cannot define rhetoric is that they are ignorant of dialectic. It is their ignorance that makes them think they have discovered what rhetoric is when they have mastered only what it is

c necessary to learn as preliminaries. So they teach these preliminaries and imagine their pupils have received a full course in rhetoric, thinking the task of using each of them persuasively and putting them together into a whole speech is a minor matter, to be worked out by the pupils from their own resources"?

PHAEDRUS: Really, Socrates, the art these men present as rhetoric in their courses and handbooks is no more than what you say. In my judgment, at least, your point is well taken. But how, from what source, could one

d acquire the art of the true rhetorician, the really persuasive speaker?

SOCRATES: Well, Phaedrus, becoming good enough to be an accomplished competitor is probably—perhaps necessarily—like everything else. If you have a natural ability for rhetoric, you will become a famous rhetorician, provided you supplement your ability with knowledge and practice. To the extent that you lack any one of them, to that extent you will be less than perfect. But, insofar as there is an art of rhetoric, I don't believe the right method for acquiring it is to be found in the direction Lysias and Thrasymachus have followed.

PHAEDRUS: Where can we find it then?

e SOCRATES: My dear friend, maybe we can see now why Pericles was in all likelihood the greatest rhetorician of all.

PHAEDRUS: How is that?

270 SOCRATES: All the great arts require endless talk and ethereal speculation about nature: This seems to be what gives them their lofty point of view and universal applicability. That's just what Pericles mastered—besides having natural ability. He came across Anaxagoras, who was just that sort of man, got his full dose of ethereal speculation, and understood the nature of mind and mindlessness[58]—just the subject on which Anaxagoras had the most to say. From this, I think, he drew for the art of rhetoric what was useful to it.

PHAEDRUS: What do you mean by that?

b SOCRATES: Well, isn't the method of medicine in a way the same as the method of rhetoric?

PHAEDRUS: How so?

SOCRATES: In both cases we need to determine the nature of something— of the body in medicine, of the soul in rhetoric. Otherwise, all we'll have will be an empirical and artless practice. We won't be able to supply, on

58. Reading *anoias* at a5.

the basis of an art, a body with the medicines and diet that will make it healthy and strong, or a soul with the reasons and customary rules for conduct that will impart to it the convictions and virtues we want.

PHAEDRUS: That is most likely, Socrates.

SOCRATES: Do you think, then, that it is possible to reach a serious under- c standing of the nature of the soul without understanding the nature of the world as a whole?

PHAEDRUS: Well, if we're to listen to Hippocrates, Asclepius' descendant,[59] we won't even understand the body if we don't follow that method.

SOCRATES: He speaks well, my friend. Still, Hippocrates aside, we must consider whether argument supports that view.

PHAEDRUS: I agree.

SOCRATES: Consider, then, what both Hippocrates and true argument say about nature. Isn't this the way to think systematically about the nature d of anything? First, we must consider whether the object regarding which we intend to become experts and capable of transmitting our expertise is simple or complex. Then, if it is simple, we must investigate its power: What things does it have what natural power of acting upon? By what things does it have what natural disposition to be acted upon? If, on the other hand, it takes many forms, we must enumerate them all and, as we did in the simple case, investigate how each is naturally able to act upon what and how it has a natural disposition to be acted upon by what.

PHAEDRUS: It seems so, Socrates.

SOCRATES: Proceeding by any other method would be like walking with e the blind. Conversely, whoever studies anything on the basis of an art must never be compared to the blind or the deaf. On the contrary, it is clear that someone who teaches another to make speeches as an art will demonstrate precisely the essential nature of that to which speeches are to be applied. And that, surely, is the soul.

PHAEDRUS: Of course.

SOCRATES: This is therefore the object toward which the speaker's whole 271 effort is directed, since it is in the soul that he attempts to produce convic- tion. Isn't that so?

PHAEDRUS: Yes.

SOCRATES: Clearly, therefore, Thrasymachus and anyone else who teaches the art of rhetoric seriously will, first, describe the soul with absolute precision and enable us to understand what it is: whether it is one and homogeneous by nature or takes many forms, like the shape of bodies, since, as we said, that's what it is to demonstrate the nature of some- thing.

PHAEDRUS: Absolutely.

---

59. Hippocrates, a contemporary of Socrates, is the famous doctor whose name is given to the Hippocratic Oath. None of the written works that have come down to us under his name express the view attributed to him in what follows. All doctors were said to be descendants of Asclepius, hero and god of healing.

SOCRATES: Second, he will explain how, in virtue of its nature, it acts and is acted upon by certain things.

PHAEDRUS: Of course.

b SOCRATES: Third, he will classify the kinds of speech and of soul there are, as well as the various ways in which they are affected, and explain what causes each. He will then coordinate each kind of soul with the kind of speech appropriate to it. And he will give instructions concerning the reasons why one kind of soul is necessarily convinced by one kind of speech while another necessarily remains unconvinced.

PHAEDRUS: This, I think, would certainly be the best way.

SOCRATES: In fact, my friend, no speech will ever be a product of art, whether it is a model or one actually given, if it is delivered or written in

c any other way—on this or on any other subject. But those who now write *Arts of Rhetoric*—we were just discussing them—are cunning people: they hide the fact that they know very well everything about the soul. Well, then, until they begin to speak and write in this way, we mustn't allow ourselves to be convinced that they write on the basis of the art.

PHAEDRUS: What way is that?

SOCRATES: It's very difficult to speak the actual words, but as to how one should write in order to be as artful as possible—that I am willing to tell you.

PHAEDRUS: Please do.

d SOCRATES: Since the nature of speech is in fact to direct the soul, whoever intends to be a rhetorician must know how many kinds of soul there are. Their number is so-and-so many; each is of such-and-such a sort; hence some people have such-and-such a character and others have such-and-such. Those distinctions established, there are, in turn, so-and-so many kinds of speech, each of such-and-such a sort. People of such-and-such a character are easy to persuade by speeches of such-and-such a sort in connection with such-and-such an issue for this particular reason, while people of such-and-such another sort are difficult to persuade for those particular reasons.

The orator must learn all this well, then put his theory into practice and

e develop the ability to discern each kind clearly as it occurs in the actions of real life. Otherwise he won't be any better off than he was when he was still listening to those discussions in school. He will now not only be able to say what kind of person is convinced by what kind of speech; on

272 meeting someone he will be able to discern what he is like and make clear to himself that the person actually standing in front of him is of just this particular sort of character he had learned about in school—to that he must now apply speeches of such-and-such a kind in this particular way in order to secure conviction about such-and-such an issue. When he has learned all this—when, in addition, he has grasped the right occasions for speaking and for holding back; and when he has also understood when the time is right for Speaking Concisely or Appealing to Pity or Exaggeration or for any other of the kinds of speech he has learned and when it is not—then,

and only then, will he have finally mastered the art well and completely. But if his speaking, his teaching, or his writing lacks any one of these elements and he still claims to be speaking with art, you'll be better off if you don't believe him.

"Well, Socrates and Phaedrus," the author of this discourse might say, "do you agree? Could we accept an art of speaking presented in any other terms?"

PHAEDRUS: That would be impossible, Socrates. Still, it's evidently rather a major undertaking.

SOCRATES: You're right. And that's why we must turn all our arguments every which way and try to find some easier and shorter route to the art: we don't want to follow a long rough path for no good reason when we can choose a short smooth one instead.

Now, try to remember if you've heard anything helpful from Lysias or anybody else. Speak up.

PHAEDRUS: It's not for lack of trying, but nothing comes to mind right now.

SOCRATES: Well, then, shall I tell you something I've heard people say who care about this topic?

PHAEDRUS: Of course.

SOCRATES: We do claim, after all, Phaedrus, that it is fair to give the wolf's side of the story as well.

PHAEDRUS: That's just what you should do.

SOCRATES: Well, these people say that there is no need to be so solemn about all this and stretch it out to such lengths. For the fact is, as we said ourselves at the beginning of this discussion,[60] that one who intends to be an able rhetorician has no need to know the truth about the things that are just or good or yet about the people who are such either by nature or upbringing. No one in a lawcourt, you see, cares at all about the truth of such matters. They only care about what is convincing. This is called "the likely," and that is what a man who intends to speak according to art should concentrate on. Sometimes, in fact, whether you are prosecuting or defending a case, you must not even say what actually happened, if it was not likely to have happened—you must say something that is likely instead. Whatever you say, you should pursue what is likely and leave the truth aside: the whole art consists in cleaving to that throughout your speech.

PHAEDRUS: That's an excellent presentation of what people say who profess to be expert in speeches, Socrates. I recall that we raised this issue briefly earlier on, but it seems to be their single most important point.

SOCRATES: No doubt you've churned through Tisias' book quite carefully. Then let Tisias tell us this also: By "the likely" does he mean anything but what is accepted by the crowd?

PHAEDRUS: What else?

60. At 259e ff.

SOCRATES: And it's likely it was when he discovered this clever and artful technique that Tisias wrote that if a weak but spunky man is taken to court because he beat up a strong but cowardly one and stole his cloak or something else, neither one should tell the truth. The coward must say that the spunky man didn't beat him up all by himself, while the latter

c   must rebut this by saying that only the two of them were there, and fall back on that well-worn plea, "How could a man like me attack a man like him?" The strong man, naturally, will not admit his cowardice, but will try to invent some other lie, and may thus give his opponent the chance to refute him. And in other cases, speaking as the art dictates will take similar forms. Isn't that so, Phaedrus?

PHAEDRUS: Of course.

SOCRATES: Phew! Tisias—or whoever else it was and whatever name he pleases to use for himself[61]—seems[62] to have discovered an art which he has disguised very well! But now, my friend, shall we or shall we not say to him—

d   PHAEDRUS: What?

SOCRATES: This: "Tisias, some time ago, before you came into the picture, we were saying that people get the idea of what is likely through its similarity to the truth. And we just explained that in every case the person who knows the truth knows best how to determine similarities. So, if you have something new to say about the art of speaking, we shall listen. But if you don't, we shall remain convinced by the explanations we gave just before: No one will ever possess the art of speaking, to the extent that any

e   human being can, unless he acquires the ability to enumerate the sorts of characters to be found in any audience, to divide everything according to its kinds, and to grasp each single thing firmly by means of one form. And no one can acquire these abilities without great effort—a laborious effort a sensible man will make not in order to speak and act among human beings, but so as to be able to speak and act in a way that pleases the gods as much as possible. Wiser people than ourselves, Tisias, say that a reasonable man must put his mind to being pleasant not to his fellow

274   slaves (though this may happen as a side effect) but to his masters, who are wholly good. So, if the way round is long, don't be astonished: we must make this detour for the sake of things that are very important, not for what you have in mind. Still, as our argument asserts, if that is what you want, you'll get it best as a result of pursuing our own goal.

PHAEDRUS: What you've said is wonderful, Socrates—if only it could be done!

b   SOCRATES: Yet surely whatever one must go through on the way to an honorable goal is itself honorable.

PHAEDRUS: Certainly.

---

61. Socrates may be referring to Corax, whose name is also the Greek word for "crow."
62. Literally, "is likely."

SOCRATES: Well, then, that's enough about artfulness and artlessness in connection with speaking.

PHAEDRUS: Quite.

SOCRATES: What's left, then, is aptness and ineptness in connection with writing: What feature makes writing good, and what inept? Right?

PHAEDRUS: Yes.

SOCRATES: Well, do you know how best to please god when you either use words or discuss them in general?

PHAEDRUS: Not at all. Do you?

SOCRATES: I can tell you what I've heard the ancients said, though they alone know the truth. However, if we could discover that ourselves, would we still care about the speculations of other people?

PHAEDRUS: That's a silly question. Still, tell me what you say you've heard.

SOCRATES: Well, this is what I've heard. Among the ancient gods of Naucratis[63] in Egypt there was one to whom the bird called the ibis is sacred. The name of that divinity was Theuth,[64] and it was he who first discovered number and calculation, geometry and astronomy, as well as the games of checkers and dice, and, above all else, writing.

Now the king of all Egypt at that time was Thamus,[65] who lived in the great city in the upper region that the Greeks call Egyptian Thebes; Thamus they call Ammon.[66] Theuth came to exhibit his arts to him and urged him to disseminate them to all the Egyptians. Thamus asked him about the usefulness of each art, and while Theuth was explaining it, Thamus praised him for whatever he thought was right in his explanations and criticized him for whatever he thought was wrong.

The story goes that Thamus said much to Theuth, both for and against each art, which it would take too long to repeat. But when they came to writing, Theuth said: "O King, here is something that, once learned, will make the Egyptians wiser and will improve their memory; I have discovered a potion for memory and for wisdom." Thamus, however, replied: "O most expert Theuth, one man can give birth to the elements of an art, but only another can judge how they can benefit or harm those who will use them. And now, since you are the father of writing, your affection for it has made you describe its effects as the opposite of what they really are. In fact, it will introduce forgetfulness into the soul of those who learn it: they will not practice using their memory because they will put their trust in writing, which

c

d

e

275

---

63. Naucratis was a Greek trading colony in Egypt. The story that follows is probably an invention of Plato's (see 275b3) in which he reworks elements from Egyptian and Greek mythology.

64. Theuth (or Thoth) is the Egyptian god of writing, measuring, and calculation. The Greeks identified Thoth with Hermes, perhaps because of his role in weighing the soul. Thoth figures in a related story about the alphabet at *Philebus* 18b.

65. As king of the Egyptian gods, Ammon (Thamus) was identified by Egyptians with the sun god Ra and by the Greeks with Zeus.

66. Accepting the emendation of *Thamoun* at d4.

is external and depends on signs that belong to others, instead of trying to remember from the inside, completely on their own. You have not discovered a potion for remembering, but for reminding; you provide your students with the appearance of wisdom, not with its reality. Your invention will enable them to hear many things without being properly taught, and they will

b   imagine that they have come to know much while for the most part they will know nothing. And they will be difficult to get along with, since they will merely appear to be wise instead of really being so."

PHAEDRUS: Socrates, you're very good at making up stories from Egypt or wherever else you want!

SOCRATES: But, my friend, the priests of the temple of Zeus at Dodona say that the first prophecies were the words of an oak. Everyone who lived at that time, not being as wise as you young ones are today, found it rewarding enough in their simplicity to listen to an oak or even a stone,

c   so long as it was telling the truth, while it seems to make a difference to you, Phaedrus, who is speaking and where he comes from. Why, though, don't you just consider whether what he says is right or wrong?

PHAEDRUS: I deserved that, Socrates. And I agree that the Theban king was correct about writing.

SOCRATES: Well, then, those who think they can leave written instructions for an art, as well as those who accept them, thinking that writing can yield results that are clear or certain, must be quite naive and truly ignorant of Ammon's prophetic judgment: otherwise, how could they possibly think

d   that words that have been written down can do more than remind those who already know what the writing is about?

PHAEDRUS: Quite right.

SOCRATES: You know, Phaedrus, writing shares a strange feature with painting. The offsprings of painting stand there as if they are alive, but if anyone asks them anything, they remain most solemnly silent. The same is true of written words. You'd think they were speaking as if they had some understanding, but if you question anything that has been said because you want to learn more, it continues to signify just that very same thing forever. When it has once been written down, every discourse roams

e   about everywhere, reaching indiscriminately those with understanding no less than those who have no business with it, and it doesn't know to whom it should speak and to whom it should not. And when it is faulted and attacked unfairly, it always needs its father's support; alone, it can neither defend itself nor come to its own support.

PHAEDRUS: You are absolutely right about that, too.

276   SOCRATES: Now tell me, can we discern another kind of discourse, a legitimate brother of this one? Can we say how it comes about, and how it is by nature better and more capable?

PHAEDRUS: Which one is that? How do you think it comes about?

SOCRATES: It is a discourse that is written down, with knowledge, in the soul of the listener; it can defend itself, and it knows for whom it should speak and for whom it should remain silent.

PHAEDRUS: You mean the living, breathing discourse of the man who knows, of which the written one can be fairly called an image.

SOCRATES: Absolutely right. And tell me this. Would a sensible farmer, who cared about his seeds and wanted them to yield fruit, plant them in all seriousness in the gardens of Adonis in the middle of the summer and enjoy watching them bear fruit within seven days? Or would he do this as an amusement and in honor of the holiday, if he did it at all?[67] Wouldn't he use his knowledge of farming to plant the seeds he cared for when it was appropriate and be content if they bore fruit seven months later?

PHAEDRUS: That's how he would handle those he was serious about, Socrates, quite differently from the others, as you say.

SOCRATES: Now what about the man who knows what is just, noble, and good? Shall we say that he is less sensible with his seeds than the farmer is with his?

PHAEDRUS: Certainly not.

SOCRATES: Therefore, he won't be serious about writing them in ink, sowing them, through a pen, with words that are as incapable of speaking in their own defense as they are of teaching the truth adequately.

PHAEDRUS: That wouldn't be likely.

SOCRATES: Certainly not. When he writes, it's likely he will sow gardens of letters for the sake of amusing himself, storing up reminders for himself "when he reaches forgetful old age" and for everyone who wants to follow in his footsteps, and will enjoy seeing them sweetly blooming. And when others turn to different amusements, watering themselves with drinking parties and everything else that goes along with them, he will rather spend his time amusing himself with the things I have just described.

PHAEDRUS: Socrates, you are contrasting a vulgar amusement with the very noblest—with the amusement of a man who can while away his time telling stories of justice and the other matters you mentioned.

SOCRATES: That's just how it is, Phaedrus. But it is much nobler to be serious about these matters, and use the art of dialectic. The dialectician chooses a proper soul and plants and sows within it discourse accompanied by knowledge—discourse capable of helping itself as well as the man who planted it, which is not barren but produces a seed from which more discourse grows in the character of others. Such discourse makes the seed forever immortal and renders the man who has it as happy as any human being can be.

PHAEDRUS: What you describe is really much nobler still.

SOCRATES: And now that we have agreed about this, Phaedrus, we are finally able to decide the issue.

PHAEDRUS: What issue is that?

SOCRATES: The issue which brought us to this point in the first place: We wanted to examine the attack made on Lysias on account of his writing

b

c

d

e

277

b

---

67. Gardens of Adonis were pots or window boxes used for forcing plants during the festival of Adonis.

speeches, and to ask which speeches are written artfully and which not. Now, I think that we have answered that question clearly enough.

PHAEDRUS: So it seemed; but remind me again how we did it.

SOCRATES: First, you must know the truth concerning everything you are speaking or writing about; you must learn how to define each thing in itself; and, having defined it, you must know how to divide it into kinds until you reach something indivisible. Second, you must understand the nature of the soul, along the same lines; you must determine which kind

c of speech is appropriate to each kind of soul, prepare and arrange your speech accordingly, and offer a complex and elaborate speech to a complex soul and a simple speech to a simple one. Then, and only then, will you be able to use speech artfully, to the extent that its nature allows it to be used that way, either in order to teach or in order to persuade. This is the whole point of the argument we have been making.

PHAEDRUS: Absolutely. That is exactly how it seemed to us.

d SOCRATES: Now how about whether it's noble or shameful to give or write a speech—when it could be fairly said to be grounds for reproach, and when not? Didn't what we said just a little while ago make it clear—

PHAEDRUS: What was that?

SOCRATES: That if Lysias or anybody else ever did or ever does write— privately or for the public, in the course of proposing some law—a political document which he believes to embody clear knowledge of lasting importance, then this writer deserves reproach, whether anyone says so or not. For to be unaware of the difference between a dream-image and the reality

e of what is just and unjust, good and bad, must truly be grounds for reproach even if the crowd praises it with one voice.

PHAEDRUS: It certainly must be.

SOCRATES: On the other hand, take a man who thinks that a written discourse on any subject can only be a great amusement, that no discourse worth serious attention has ever been written in verse or prose, and that those that are recited in public without questioning and explanation, in

278 the manner of the rhapsodes, are given only in order to produce conviction. He believes that at their very best these can only serve as reminders to those who already know. And he also thinks that only what is said for the sake of understanding and learning, what is truly written in the soul concerning what is just, noble, and good can be clear, perfect, and worth serious attention: Such discourses should be called his own legitimate children, first the discourse he may have discovered already within himself

b and then its sons and brothers who may have grown naturally in other souls insofar as these are worthy; to the rest, he turns his back. Such a man, Phaedrus, would be just what you and I both would pray to become.

PHAEDRUS: I wish and pray for things to be just as you say.

SOCRATES: Well, then: our playful amusement regarding discourse is complete. Now you go and tell Lysias that we came to the spring which is sacred to the Nymphs and heard words charging us to deliver a message

c to Lysias and anyone else who composes speeches, as well as to Homer and anyone else who has composed poetry either spoken or sung, and third, to Solon and anyone else who writes political documents that he calls laws: If any one of you has composed these things with a knowledge of the truth, if you can defend your writing when you are challenged, and if you can yourself make the argument that your writing is of little worth, then you must be called by a name derived not from these writings but rather from those things that you are seriously pursuing.

d

PHAEDRUS: What name, then, would you give such a man?

SOCRATES: To call him wise, Phaedrus, seems to me too much, and proper only for a god. To call him wisdom's lover—a philosopher—or something similar would fit him better and be more seemly.

PHAEDRUS: That would be quite appropriate.

SOCRATES: On the other hand, if a man has nothing more valuable than what he has composed or written, spending long hours twisting it around, pasting parts together and taking them apart—wouldn't you be right to call him a poet or a speech writer or an author of laws?

e

PHAEDRUS: Of course.

SOCRATES: Tell that, then, to your friend.

PHAEDRUS: And what about you? What shall you do? We must surely not forget your own friend.

SOCRATES: Whom do you mean?

PHAEDRUS: The beautiful Isocrates.[68] What are you going to tell him, Socrates? What shall we say he is?

SOCRATES: Isocrates is still young, Phaedrus. But I want to tell you what I foresee for him.

279

PHAEDRUS: What is that?

SOCRATES: It seems to me that by his nature he can outdo anything that Lysias has accomplished in his speeches; and he also has a nobler character. So I wouldn't be at all surprised if, as he gets older and continues writing speeches of the sort he is composing now, he makes everyone who has ever attempted to compose a speech seem like a child in comparison. Even more so if such work no longer satisfies him and a higher, divine impulse leads him to more important things. For nature, my friend, has placed the love of wisdom in his mind.

b

That is the message I will carry to my beloved, Isocrates, from the gods of this place; and you have your own message for your Lysias.

PHAEDRUS: So it shall be. But let's be off, since the heat has died down a bit.

SOCRATES: Shouldn't we offer a prayer to the gods here before we leave?

PHAEDRUS: Of course.

SOCRATES: O dear Pan and all the other gods of this place, grant that I may be beautiful inside. Let all my external possessions be in friendly harmony with what is within. May I consider the wise man rich. As for

c

---

68. Isocrates (436–338 B.C.) was an Athenian teacher and orator whose school was more famous in its day than Plato's Academy.

279c   gold, let me have as much as a moderate man could bear and carry with him.

    Do we need anything else, Phaedrus? I believe my prayer is enough for me.

    PHAEDRUS: Make it a prayer for me as well. Friends have everything in common.

    SOCRATES: Let's be off.

ALCIBIADES

Socrates feels that the time has come to approach Alcibiades and bring him into his intellectual and moral orbit. It is Alcibiades' lust for power that Socrates appeals to, promising that Alcibiades will never amount to anything without his help. In the discussion that follows, Alcibiades is brought to see, very reluctantly, that he knows nothing about moral values or political expediency and that he needs to cultivate himself assiduously in order to realize his enormous ambitions.

But what is this "self" that he needs to cultivate? It is his soul, the ruler of his body. The virtues of the soul that he needs to acquire are the intellectual skills that give it the authority to rule, over its body and over other people as well. Alcibiades is dismayed to recognize that he has no knowledge of himself and is currently fit to be ruled, not to rule. He attaches himself to Socrates to cultivate the knowledge of virtue and pledges undying devotion to Socrates and his values, a pledge which Socrates presciently distrusts, for Alcibiades was notorious in later life for his unprincipled conduct. He became a brilliant Athenian politician and general in the Peloponnesian War, but he defected to the Spartan side when accused of capital crimes in Athens and later became a double agent in the war between Athens and Persia.

Socrates wins Alcibiades over, but their affair remains on a Platonic level; in fact, their love affair gave us the term 'Platonic love'. Many of Socrates' followers wrote versions of this love story: Euclides, Antisthenes, and Aeschines each wrote an Alcibiades dialogue—some fragments of Aeschines' survive, in which Alcibiades eventually weeps with humiliation. Plato's Symposium also contributes to this genre, in an inventive way, in the speech in praise of Socrates by the drunken Alcibiades. Platonic love is an intensely affectionate, but not a sexual, relationship; but with Socrates and Alcibiades it was also a teaching relationship, in which Socrates tried to help Alcibiades make the transition to manhood by his stimulating conversation.

Because of its emphasis on self-knowledge as the necessary foundation of any other worthwhile knowledge, Alcibiades held pride of place in later antiquity as the ideal work with which to begin the study of Platonic philosophy. We have extensive commentaries from Olympiodorus (complete) and Proclus (first half only) and fragments of commentaries by Iamblichus, Damascius, and others. Proclus says, "Let this then be the start of philosophy and of the teaching of Plato, viz., the knowledge of ourselves."

Until the nineteenth century Alcibiades was assumed to be the work of Plato, but the ascription to Plato is now a minority view. It resembles Plato's

'Socratic' dialogues in its plain conversational quality, but it reflects later Aca-
demic doctrine as well. The clearest argument against Plato's authorship is
probably that Plato never wrote a work whose interpretation was as simple and
straightforward as that of Alcibiades. *That very quality makes it an excellent*
introduction to philosophy.

  If Plato is not the author, the signs point to an Academic philosopher writ-
ing in the 350s or soon after (116d). The anthropology implicit in Alcibiades
is similar to Aristotle's, and the Aristotelian Magna Moralia *(1213a20–24)*
takes up the striking idea that self-knowledge is best gained through a philo-
sophical friendship in which we see ourselves, as if in a mirror (132c–133c).

D.S.H.

103   SOCRATES: I was the first man to fall in love with you, son of Clinias,
and now that the others have stopped pursuing you I suppose you're
wondering why I'm the only one who hasn't given up—and also why,
when the others pestered you with conversation, I never even spoke to
you all these years. Human causes didn't enter into it; I was prevented
by some divine being, the effect of which you'll hear about later on. But
b   now it no longer prevents me, so here I am. I'm confident it won't prevent
me in future either.

    I've been observing you all this time, and I've got a pretty good idea
how you treated all those men who pursued you: they held themselves
in high esteem, but you were even more arrogant and sent them packing,
104   every single one of them. I'd like to explain the reason why you felt yourself
so superior.

    You say you don't need anybody for anything, since your own qualities,
from your body right up to your soul, are so great there's nothing you
lack. In the first place, you fancy yourself the tallest and best-looking man
around—and it's quite plain to see you're not wrong about that. Next,
you think that yours is the leading family in your city, which is the greatest
b   city in Greece: on your father's side you have plenty of aristocratic friends
and relations, who would be of service to you if there was any need; and
on your mother's side your connections are no worse and no fewer. And
you have Pericles son of Xanthippus,[1] whom your father left as a guardian
to you and your brother; you think he's a more powerful ally than all
those people I mentioned put together—he can do whatever he likes, not
only in this city, but anywhere in Greece, and also in many important

Translated by D. S. Hutchinson. Except where noted, the translation follows the edition
of J. Burnet; I have also consulted the edition of Antonio Carlini, *Platone: Alcibiade,
Alcibiade Secondo, Ipparco, Rivali* (Turin, 1964).—D.S.H.

  1. Pericles was the most influential Athenian politician of the mid-fifth century B.C.

foreign countries. I will also mention your wealth, but I think that's the   c
least of the reasons you hold yourself in high esteem. You bragged about
all those things and got the better of your suitors; they didn't measure up
and came off the worse. You knew what was going on.

And so I'm sure you're wondering what I could possibly have in mind—
why don't I give up on you? The others have all been sent packing, so
what do I hope to achieve by persisting?

ALCIBIADES: Yes, Socrates, perhaps you don't realize that you've just
taken the words out of my mouth. I had already decided to come and ask   d
you that very question: what could you have in mind? What do you hope
to achieve by bothering me, always making so sure you're there wherever
I am? Yes, I really do wonder what you might be up to, and I'd be very
glad to find out.

SOCRATES: So then you'll probably be eager to give me your full attention,
since, as you say, you're keen to know what I have in mind. I take it that
you'll listen carefully?

ALCIBIADES: Yes, of course—just tell me.

SOCRATES: Watch out—I wouldn't be at all surprised if I found it as hard   e
to stop as it was to start.

ALCIBIADES: Tell me, please. I will pay attention.

SOCRATES: Speak I must, then. It's not easy to play the role of suitor with
a man who doesn't give in to them; nevertheless, I must summon up my
courage and say what's on my mind.

Alcibiades, if I saw that you were content with the advantages I just
mentioned and thought that this was the condition in which you should
live out the rest of your life, I would have given up on you long ago; at   105
least that's what I persuade myself. But I'm going to prove to you in person
what very different plans you actually have in mind. Then you'll realize
how constantly I've been thinking about you.

Suppose one of the gods asked you, "Alcibiades, would you rather live
with what you now have, or would you rather die on the spot if you
weren't permitted to acquire anything greater?" I think you'd choose to
die. What then *is* your real ambition in life? I'll tell you. You think that
as soon as you present yourself before the Athenian people—as indeed   b
you expect to in a very few days—by presenting yourself you'll show
them that you deserve to be honored more than Pericles or anyone else
who ever was. Having shown that, you'll be the most influential man in
the city, and if you're the greatest here, you'll be the greatest in the rest
of Greece, and not only in Greece, but also among the foreigners who live
on the same continent as we do.

And if that same god were then to tell you that you should have absolute
power in Europe, but that you weren't permitted to cross over into Asia   c
or get mixed up with affairs over there, I think you'd rather not live with
only that to look forward to; you want your reputation and your influence
to saturate all mankind, so to speak. I don't think you regard anybody as

ever having been much to speak of, except perhaps Cyrus and Xerxes.[2] I'm not guessing that this is your ambition—I'm sure of it.

d   Since you know that what I say is true, maybe you'll say, "Well then, Socrates, what's this got to do with your point? You said you were going to tell me why you haven't given up on me."[3] Yes, I will tell you, my dear son of Clinias and Dinomache. It is impossible to put any of these ideas of yours into effect without me—that's how much influence I think I have over you and your business. I think this is why the god hasn't allowed me to talk to you all this time; and I've been waiting for the day he allows me.

e   I'm hoping for the same thing from you[4] as you are from the Athenians: I hope to exert great influence over you by showing you that I'm worth the world to you and that nobody is capable of providing you with the influence you crave, neither your guardian nor your relatives, nor anybody else except me—with the god's help, of course. When you were younger, before you were full of such ambitions, I think the god didn't let me talk
106   to you because the conversation would have been pointless. But now he's told me to, because now you will listen to me.

ALCIBIADES: Really, Socrates, now that you've started talking you seem much more bizarre to me than when you followed me in silence, though you were very bizarre to look at then, too. Well, on the question of whether or not these are my ambitions, you seem to have made up your mind already, and no denial of mine will do anything to convince you otherwise. Fine. But supposing I really do have these ambitions, how will you help me achieve them? What makes you indispensable? Have you got something to say?

b   SOCRATES: Are you asking if I can say some long speech like the ones you're used to hearing? No, that sort of thing's not for me. But I do think I'd be able to show you that what I said is true, if only you were willing to grant me just one little favor.

ALCIBIADES: Well, as long as you mean a favor that's not hard to grant, I'm willing.

SOCRATES: Do you think it's hard to answer questions?

ALCIBIADES: No, I don't.

SOCRATES: Then answer me.

ALCIBIADES: Ask me.

SOCRATES: My question is whether you have in mind what I say you have in mind.

c   ALCIBIADES: Let's say I do, if you like, so I can find out what you're going to say.

SOCRATES: Right then; you plan, as I say, to come forward and advise the Athenians some time soon. Suppose I stopped you as you were about to take the podium and asked, "Alcibiades, what are the Athenians propos-

2. Great empire-building kings of Persia in the sixth and fifth centuries B.C.

3. Retaining the bracketed phrase in d1.

4. Omitting d7–e2 *endeixasthai . . . dunēsesthai*.

ing to discuss? You're getting up to advise them because it's something you know better than they do, aren't you?" What would you reply?

ALCIBIADES: Yes, I suppose I would say it was something that I know   d
better than they do.

SOCRATES: So it's on matters you know about that you're a good adviser.

ALCIBIADES: Of course.

SOCRATES: Now the only things you know are what you've learned from others or found out for yourself; isn't that right?

ALCIBIADES: What else could I know?

SOCRATES: Could you ever have learned or found out anything without wanting to learn it or work it out for yourself?

ALCIBIADES: No, I couldn't have.

SOCRATES: Is that right? Would you have wanted to learn or work out something that you thought you understood?

ALCIBIADES: Of course not.

SOCRATES: So there was a time when you didn't think you knew what   e
you now understand.

ALCIBIADES: There must have been.

SOCRATES: But I've got a pretty good idea what you've learned. Tell me if I've missed anything: as far as I remember, you learned writing and lyre-playing and wrestling, but you didn't want to learn aulos-playing.[5] These are the subjects that you understand—unless perhaps you've been learning something while I wasn't looking; but I don't think you have been, either by night or by day, on your excursions from home.

ALCIBIADES: No, those are the only lessons I took.

SOCRATES: Well then, is it when the Athenians are discussing how to   107
spell a word correctly that you'll stand up to advise them?

ALCIBIADES: Good God, I'd never do that!

SOCRATES: Then is it when they're discussing the notes on the lyre?

ALCIBIADES: No, never.

SOCRATES: But surely they're not in the habit of discussing wrestling in the Assembly.

ALCIBIADES: Certainly not.

SOCRATES: Then what will they be discussing? I presume it won't be building.

ALCIBIADES: Of course not.

SOCRATES: Because a builder would give better advice on these matters than you.

ALCIBIADES: Yes.   b

SOCRATES: Nor will they be discussing divination, will they?

ALCIBIADES: No.

SOCRATES: Because then a diviner would be better at giving advice than you.

ALCIBIADES: Yes.

5. The *aulos*, conventionally translated 'flute', was actually a reed instrument.

SOCRATES: Regardless of whether he's tall or short, or handsome or ugly, or even noble or common.

ALCIBIADES: Of course.[6]

SOCRATES: And when the Athenians are discussing measures for public
c   health, it will make no difference to them if their counsellor is rich or poor, but they will make sure that their adviser is a doctor.

ALCIBIADES: Of course.

SOCRATES: I suppose that's because advice on any subject is the business not of those who are rich but of those who know it.

ALCIBIADES: Quite reasonably so.

SOCRATES: Then what *will* they be considering when you stand up to advise them, assuming you're right to do so?

ALCIBIADES: They'll be discussing their own business, Socrates.

SOCRATES: You mean their shipbuilding business—what sorts of ships they should be building?

ALCIBIADES: No, Socrates, I don't.

SOCRATES: I suppose that's because you don't understand shipbuilding. Am I right, or is there some other reason?

ALCIBIADES: No, that's it.

d   SOCRATES: So what kind of 'their own business' do you think they'll be discussing?

ALCIBIADES: War, Socrates, or peace, or anything else which is the business of the city.

SOCRATES: Do you mean they'll be discussing who they should make peace with and who they should go to war with and how?

ALCIBIADES: Yes.

SOCRATES: But shouldn't they do that with the ones with whom it's better to?

ALCIBIADES: Yes.

e   SOCRATES: And when it's better?

ALCIBIADES: Certainly.

SOCRATES: And for as long a time as it's better?

ALCIBIADES: Yes.

SOCRATES: Now supposing the Athenians were discussing who they should wrestle with and who they should spar with and how, who would be a better adviser, you or the trainer?

ALCIBIADES: The trainer, I guess.

SOCRATES: And can you tell me what the trainer has in view when he advises you who you should or shouldn't wrestle with, and when, and how? I mean, for example, that one should wrestle with those with whom it's better to wrestle, isn't that right?

ALCIBIADES: Yes.

---

6. In the manuscripts, Alcibiades' reply and the next speech of Socrates are preceded by the following reply-speech pair; the translation follows a conjectural transposition of b8–10 with b11–c2.

108

SOCRATES: And as much as is better?

ALCIBIADES: That's right.

SOCRATES: And when it's better, right?

ALCIBIADES: Certainly.

SOCRATES: Let's take another example: when you're singing, you should sometimes accompany the song with lyre-playing and dancing.

ALCIBIADES: Yes, you should.

SOCRATES: You should do so when it's better to, right?

ALCIBIADES: Yes.

SOCRATES: And as much as is better.

ALCIBIADES: I agree.

SOCRATES: Really? Since you used the term 'better' in both cases—in wrestling and in playing the lyre while singing—what do you call what's better in lyre-playing, as I call what's better in wrestling 'athletic'? What do you call that?

ALCIBIADES: I don't get it.

SOCRATES: Then try to follow my example. My answer was, I think, 'what is correct in every case'—and what is correct, I presume, is what takes place in accordance with the skill, isn't it?

ALCIBIADES: Yes.

SOCRATES: Wasn't the skill athletics?

ALCIBIADES: Of course.

SOCRATES: I said that what's better in wrestling, was 'athletic'.

ALCIBIADES: That's what you said.

SOCRATES: Wasn't that well said?

ALCIBIADES: I think so, anyway.

SOCRATES: Come on then, it's your turn; it's partly up to you, surely, to keep our conversation going well. First of all, tell me what the skill is for singing and dancing and playing the lyre correctly. What is it called as a whole? . . . Aren't you able to tell me yet?

ALCIBIADES: No, I can't.

SOCRATES: Well, try it this way. Who are the goddesses to whom the skill belongs?

ALCIBIADES: Do you mean the Muses, Socrates?

SOCRATES: I do indeed. Don't you see? What's the name of the skill that's named after them?

ALCIBIADES: I think you mean music.

SOCRATES: Yes, I do. Now what is "correctly" for what takes place in accordance with this skill? In the other case I told you what "correctly" is for what takes place in accordance with the skill, so now it's your turn to say something similar in this case. *How* does it take place?

ALCIBIADES: Musically, I think.

SOCRATES: A good answer. Come on now, what do you call what's better in both going to war and keeping the peace? In these last two examples you said that what was better was more musical and more athletic, respectively. Now try to tell me what's better in this case, too.

ALCIBIADES: I really can't do it.

SOCRATES: But surely it's disgraceful if when you're speaking and giving advice about food—saying that a certain kind is better than another, and better at a certain time and in a certain quantity—and someone should ask you, "What do you mean by 'better', Alcibiades?" you could tell him in that case that 'better' was 'healthier', though you don't even pretend to be a doctor; and yet in a case where you do pretend to understand and are going to stand up and give advice as though you knew, if you aren't able, as seems likely, to answer the question in this case, won't you be embarrassed? Won't that seem disgraceful?

109

ALCIBIADES: Yes, certainly.

SOCRATES: Then think about it, and try to tell me what the better tends towards, in keeping the peace or in waging war with the right people.

ALCIBIADES: I'm thinking, but I can't get it.

SOCRATES: But suppose we're at war with somebody—surely you know what treatment we accuse each other of when we enter into a war, and what we call it.

b   ALCIBIADES: I do—we say that they're playing some trick on us, or attacking us or taking things away from us.

SOCRATES: Hold on—*how* do we suffer from each of these treatments? Try to tell me how one way differs from another way.

ALCIBIADES: When you say 'way', Socrates, do you mean 'justly' or 'unjustly'?

SOCRATES: Precisely.

ALCIBIADES: But surely that makes all the difference in the world.

SOCRATES: Really? Who will you advise the Athenians to wage war on? Those who are treating us unjustly, or those who are treating us justly?

c   ALCIBIADES: That's a hard question you're asking. Even if someone thought it was necessary to wage war on people who were treating us justly, he wouldn't admit it.

SOCRATES: Because I think that wouldn't be lawful.

ALCIBIADES: It certainly wouldn't.

SOCRATES: Nor would it be considered a proper thing to do.

ALCIBIADES: No.[7]

SOCRATES: So you would also frame your speech in these terms.

ALCIBIADES: I'd have to.

SOCRATES: Then this 'better' I was just asking you about—when it comes to waging war or not, on whom to wage war and on whom not to, and when and when not to—this 'better' turns out to be the same as 'more just', doesn't it?

ALCIBIADES: It certainly seems so.

d   SOCRATES: But how could it, my dear Alcibiades? Don't you realize that this is something you don't understand? Or perhaps, when I wasn't look-

---

7. Attributing *oude ge kalon dokei einai* in c5 to Socrates, and accepting the conjectured reply *ou* from Alcibiades.

ing, you've been seeing some teacher who taught you how to tell the difference between the more just and the less just. Have you? . . . Well, who is he? Tell me who he is so that you can sign me up with him as well.

ALCIBIADES: Stop teasing me, Socrates.

SOCRATES: I'm not—I'll swear by Friendship,[8] yours and mine. I'd never perjure myself by him. So tell me who he is, if you can.

ALCIBIADES: And what if I can't? Don't you think I might know about justice and injustice some other way?

SOCRATES: Yes, you might—if you found it out.

ALCIBIADES: Well, don't you think I might find it out?

SOCRATES: Yes, of course—if you investigate the matter.

ALCIBIADES: And don't you think I might investigate it?

SOCRATES: Yes, I do—if you thought you didn't know.

ALCIBIADES: And didn't I once think that?

SOCRATES: A fine answer. Can you tell me when this was, when you didn't think you knew about justice and injustice . . . Well, was it last year that you were looking into it and didn't think you knew? Or did you think you knew? . . . Answer me truthfully, or else our conversation will be a waste of time.

ALCIBIADES: Yes, I thought I knew.

SOCRATES: Didn't you think the same thing two years ago, and three years ago, and four?

ALCIBIADES: I did.

SOCRATES: But surely before that you were a boy, weren't you?

ALCIBIADES: Yes.

SOCRATES: Well now, at that point I'm sure you thought you knew.

ALCIBIADES: How can you be sure of that?

SOCRATES: When you were a boy I often observed you, at school and other places, and sometimes when you were playing knucklebones or some other game, you'd say to one or another of your playmates, very loudly and confidently—not at all like someone who was at a loss about justice and injustice—that he was a lousy cheater and wasn't playing fairly. Isn't that true?

ALCIBIADES: But what was I to do, Socrates, when somebody cheated me like that?

SOCRATES: Do you mean, what should you have done if you didn't actually know then whether or not you were being cheated?

ALCIBIADES: But I *did* know, by Zeus! I saw clearly that they were cheating me.

SOCRATES: So it seems that even as a child you thought you understood justice and injustice.

ALCIBIADES: Yes, and I *did* understand.

SOCRATES: At what point did you find it out? Surely it wasn't when you thought you knew.

8. One of the aspects under which Zeus was worshipped was as the god of friendship.

ALCIBIADES: Of course not.

SOCRATES: Then when did you think you didn't know? Think about it—you won't find any such time.

ALCIBIADES: By Zeus, Socrates, I really can't say.

d   SOCRATES: So it isn't by finding it out that you know it.

ALCIBIADES: That's not very likely.

SOCRATES: But surely you just finished saying that it wasn't by being taught, either, that you knew it. So if you neither found it out nor were taught it, how and where did you come to know it?

ALCIBIADES: Maybe I gave you the wrong answer when I said I knew it by finding it out myself.

SOCRATES: Then how did it happen?

ALCIBIADES: I suppose I learned it in the same way as other people.

SOCRATES: That brings us back to the same argument: from whom? Do tell me.

e   ALCIBIADES: From people in general.

SOCRATES: When you give the credit to 'people in general', you're falling back on teachers who are no good.

ALCIBIADES: What? Aren't they capable of teaching?

SOCRATES: No, they can't even teach you what moves to make or not make in knucklebones. And yet that's a trivial matter, I suppose, compared with justice . . . What? Don't you agree?

ALCIBIADES: Yes.

SOCRATES: So although they can't teach trivial things, you say they can teach more serious things.

ALCIBIADES: *I* think so; at any rate, they can teach a lot of things that are more important than knucklebones.

SOCRATES: Like what?

111   ALCIBIADES: Well, for example, I learned how to speak Greek from them; I couldn't tell you who my teacher was, but I give the credit to the very people you say are no good at teaching.

SOCRATES: Yes, my noble friend, people in general are good teachers of that, and it would be only fair to praise them for their teaching.

ALCIBIADES: Why?

SOCRATES: Because they have what it takes to be good teachers of the subject.

ALCIBIADES: What do you mean by that?

SOCRATES: Don't you see that somebody who is going to teach anything must first know it himself? Isn't that right?

b   ALCIBIADES: Of course.

SOCRATES: And don't people who know something agree with each other, not disagree?

ALCIBIADES: Yes.

SOCRATES: If people disagree about something, would you say that they know it?

ALCIBIADES: Of course not.

SOCRATES: Then how could they be teachers of it?

ALCIBIADES: They couldn't possibly.

SOCRATES: Well then, do you think that people in general disagree about what wood or stone is? If you ask them, don't they give the same answers? Don't they reach for the same things when they want to get some wood c or some stone? And similarly for all other such cases; I suppose this is pretty much what you mean by understanding Greek, isn't it?

ALCIBIADES: Yes.

SOCRATES: So they agree with each other in these cases, as we said, and with themselves when acting privately. But don't they also agree in public? Cities don't disagree with each other and use different words for the same thing, do they?

ALCIBIADES: No.

SOCRATES: So it's likely that they would make good teachers of these things.

ALCIBIADES: Yes. d

SOCRATES: So if we wanted somebody to know these things, we'd be right to send him to lessons given by these people in general.

ALCIBIADES: Certainly.

SOCRATES: Now if we wanted to know not just what men or horses are like, but which of them could and couldn't run, would people in general be able to teach this as well?

ALCIBIADES: Of course not.

SOCRATES: Isn't the fact that they disagree with each other about these things enough to show you that they don't understand them, and are not e 'four-square teachers' of them?

ALCIBIADES: Yes, it is.

SOCRATES: Now if we wanted to know not just what men are like, but what sick and healthy men are like, would people in general be able to teach us?

ALCIBIADES: Of course not.

SOCRATES: And if you saw them disagreeing about it, that would show you that they were bad teachers of it.

ALCIBIADES: Yes, it would.

SOCRATES: Very well, then—does it seem to you that people in general actually agree among themselves or with each other about just and unjust people and actions?

ALCIBIADES: Not in the slightest, Socrates. 112

SOCRATES: Really? Do they disagree a huge amount about these things?

ALCIBIADES: Very much so.

SOCRATES: I don't suppose you've ever seen or heard people disagreeing so strongly about what is healthy and unhealthy that they fight and kill each other over it, have you?

ALCIBIADES: Of course not.

SOCRATES: But I know you've seen this sort of dispute over questions of justice and injustice; or even if you haven't seen it, at least you've heard b about it from many other people—especially Homer, since you've heard the *Iliad* and the *Odyssey*, haven't you?

ALCIBIADES: I certainly have, of course, Socrates.

SOCRATES: Aren't these poems all about disagreements over justice and injustice?

ALCIBIADES: Yes.

SOCRATES: It was over this sort of disagreement that the Achaeans and the Trojans fought battles and lost their lives, as did Odysseus and the suitors of Penelope.

c   ALCIBIADES: You're right.

SOCRATES: I suppose the same is true of those Athenians and Spartans and Boeotians who died at Tanagra, and later at Coronea, including your own father. The disagreement that caused those battles and those deaths was none other than a disagreement over justice and injustice, wasn't it?

ALCIBIADES: You're right.

SOCRATES: Are we to say that people understand something if they dis-
d   agree so much about it that in their disputes with each other they resort to such extreme measures?

ALCIBIADES: Obviously not.

SOCRATES: But aren't you giving credit to teachers of this sort who, as you yourself admit, have no knowledge?

ALCIBIADES: I guess I am.

SOCRATES: Well then, given that your opinion wavers so much, and given that you obviously neither found it out yourself nor learned it from anyone else, how likely is it that you know about justice and injustice?

ALCIBIADES: From what you say anyway, it's not very likely.

e   SOCRATES: See, there you go again, Alcibiades, that's not well said!

ALCIBIADES: What do you mean?

SOCRATES: You say that *I* say these things.

ALCIBIADES: What? Aren't you saying that I don't understand justice and injustice?

SOCRATES: No, not at all.

ALCIBIADES: Well, am *I*?

SOCRATES: Yes.

ALCIBIADES: How?

SOCRATES: Here's how. If I asked you which is more, one or two, would you say two?

ALCIBIADES: I would.

SOCRATES: By how much?

ALCIBIADES: By one.

SOCRATES: Then which of us is saying that two is one more than one?

ALCIBIADES: I am.

SOCRATES: Wasn't I asking and weren't you answering?

ALCIBIADES: Yes.

113   SOCRATES: Who do you think is saying these things—me, the questioner, or you, the answerer?

ALCIBIADES: I am.

SOCRATES: And what if I asked you how to spell 'Socrates', and you told me? Which of us would be saying it?

ALCIBIADES: I would.

SOCRATES: Come then, give me the general principle. When there's a question and an answer, who is the one saying things—the questioner or the answerer?

ALCIBIADES: The answerer, I think, Socrates.

SOCRATES: Wasn't I the questioner in everything just now?   b

ALCIBIADES: Yes.

SOCRATES: And weren't you the answerer?

ALCIBIADES: I certainly was.

SOCRATES: Well then, which of us said what was said?

ALCIBIADES: From what we've agreed, Socrates, it seems that I did.

SOCRATES: And what was said was that Alcibiades, the handsome son of Clinias, doesn't understand justice and injustice—though he thinks he does—and that he is about to go to the Assembly to advise the Athenians on what he doesn't know anything about. Wasn't that it?

ALCIBIADES: Apparently.   c

SOCRATES: Then it's just like in Euripides, Alcibiades; 'you heard it from yourself, not from me.'[9] I'm not the one who says these things—*you* are—don't try to blame me. And furthermore, you're quite right to say so. This scheme you have in mind—teaching what you don't know and haven't bothered to learn—your scheme, my good fellow, is crazy.

ALCIBIADES: Actually, Socrates, I think the Athenians and the other Greeks   d
rarely discuss which course is more just or unjust. They think that sort of thing is obvious, so they skip over it and ask which one would be advantageous to do. In fact, though, what's just is not the same, I think, as what's advantageous; many people have profited by committing great injustices, and others, I think, got no advantage from doing the right thing.

SOCRATES: So? Even if just and advantageous things happen to be completely different, surely you don't think you know what's advantageous   e
for people, and why, do you?

ALCIBIADES: What's to stop me, Socrates?—unless you're going to ask me all over again who I learned it from or how I found it out myself.

SOCRATES: What a way of carrying on! If you say something wrong, and if there's a previous argument that can prove that it was wrong, you think you ought to be given some new and different proof, as if the previous one were a worn-out scrap of clothing that you refuse to wear again. No, you want an immaculate, brand-new proof.

I'll pass over your anticipation of my argument and ask you, all the   114
same, 'How did you come to understand what is advantageous? Who was your teacher?', and in my one question ask everything I asked you before. Clearly this will put you in the same position again—you won't be able

9. Cf. Euripides, *Hippolytus* 350–53.

to prove that you know what is advantageous, either by finding it out or by learning it.

But since you've got a delicate stomach and wouldn't enjoy another taste of the same argument, I'll pass over this question of whether or not
b you know what is advantageous for the Athenians. But why don't you prove whether the just and the advantageous are the same or different? You can question me, if you like, as I questioned you—or else work it out yourself, in your own argument.

ALCIBIADES: No, Socrates, I don't think I'd be able to work it out in front of you.

SOCRATES: Well then, my good sir, imagine that I'm the Assembly and the people gathered there; even there, you know, you'll have to persuade them one by one. Isn't that right?

ALCIBIADES: Yes.

SOCRATES: If somebody knows something, don't you think he can per-
c suade people about it one by one, as well as all together? Take the school-teacher—don't you think he persuades people about letters individually, as well as collectively?

ALCIBIADES: Yes.

SOCRATES: And won't the same person be able to persuade people about numbers individually, as well as in groups?

ALCIBIADES: Yes.

SOCRATES: He would be a mathematician, someone who knows about numbers.

ALCIBIADES: Certainly.

SOCRATES: So won't you also be able to persuade an individual person about the things you can persuade a group of people about?

ALCIBIADES: Probably.

SOCRATES: Obviously these are things you know about.

ALCIBIADES: Yes.

SOCRATES: Is there any difference between an orator speaking to the
d people and an orator speaking in this sort of conversation, except insofar as the former persuades them all together while the latter persuades them one by one?

ALCIBIADES: I guess not.

SOCRATES: Well then, since it's plain that the same person can persuade individuals as well as groups, practice on me, and try to prove that what is just is sometimes not advantageous.

ALCIBIADES: Stop pushing me around, Socrates!

SOCRATES: No, in fact I'm going to push you around and persuade you of the *opposite* of what you're not willing to show me.

ALCIBIADES: Just try it!

SOCRATES: Just answer my questions.
e ALCIBIADES: No, you do the talking yourself.

SOCRATES: What?! Don't you want to be completely convinced?

ALCIBIADES: Absolutely, I'm sure.

SOCRATES: Wouldn't you be completely convinced if you yourself said, 'Yes, that's how it is'?

ALCIBIADES: Yes, I think so.

SOCRATES: Then answer my questions. And if you don't hear yourself say that just things are also advantageous, then don't believe anything else I say.

ALCIBIADES: No, I'm sure I won't. But I'd better answer—I don't think I'll come to any harm.

SOCRATES: You're quite a prophet. Now tell me—are you saying that some just things are advantageous while others are not?

ALCIBIADES: Yes.

SOCRATES: Really? Are some of them admirable and others not admirable?

ALCIBIADES: What do you mean by that question?

SOCRATES: Have you ever thought that someone was doing something that was both just and contemptible?

ALCIBIADES: No, I haven't.

SOCRATES: So all just things are admirable.

ALCIBIADES: Yes.

SOCRATES: Now what about admirable things? Are they all good, or are some good and others not good?

ALCIBIADES: What I think, Socrates, is that some admirable things are bad.

SOCRATES: And some contemptible things are good?

ALCIBIADES: Yes.

SOCRATES: Are you thinking of this sort of case? Many people get wounded and killed trying to rescue their friends and relatives in battle, while those who don't go to rescue them, as they should, escape safe and sound. Is this what you're referring to?

ALCIBIADES: Exactly.

SOCRATES: Now you call a rescue of this sort admirable, in that it's an attempt to help the people whom you should help, and this is what courage is; isn't that what you're saying?

ALCIBIADES: Yes.

SOCRATES: But you call it bad, in that it involves wounds and death, don't you?

ALCIBIADES: Yes.

SOCRATES: Now courage is one thing, and death is something else, right?

ALCIBIADES: Certainly.

SOCRATES: So it's not on the same basis that rescuing your friends is admirable and bad, is it?

ALCIBIADES: Apparently not.

SOCRATES: Now let's see whether, insofar as it's admirable, it's also good, as indeed it is. You agreed that the rescue is admirable, in that it's courageous. Now consider this very thing—courage. Is it good or bad? Look at it like this: which would you rather have, good things or bad things?

ALCIBIADES: Good things.

SOCRATES: Namely the greatest goods?

ALCIBIADES: Very much so.[10]

SOCRATES: And wouldn't you be least willing to be deprived of such things?

ALCIBIADES: Of course.

SOCRATES: What would you say about courage? How much would you have to be offered to be deprived of that?

ALCIBIADES: I wouldn't even want to go on living if I were a coward.

SOCRATES: So you think that cowardice is the worst thing in the world.

ALCIBIADES: I do.

SOCRATES: On a par with death, it would seem.

ALCIBIADES: That's what I say.

SOCRATES: Aren't life and courage the extreme opposites of death and cowardice?

ALCIBIADES: Yes.

e   SOCRATES: And wouldn't you want the former most and the latter least?

ALCIBIADES: Yes.

SOCRATES: Is that because you think that the former are best and the latter are worst?

ALCIBIADES: Certainly.

SOCRATES: Would you say that courage ranks among the best things and death among the worst?

ALCIBIADES: I would say so.

SOCRATES: So you called rescuing your friends in battle admirable, insofar as it is admirable, in that it does something good, being courageous.

ALCIBIADES: I think so, anyway.

SOCRATES: But you called it bad, in that it does something bad, being fatal.[11]

ALCIBIADES: Yes.

116   SOCRATES: Now since you call this act bad insofar as it produces something bad, wouldn't you also, in all fairness, have to call it good insofar as it produces something good?

ALCIBIADES: I think so.

SOCRATES: Isn't it also admirable insofar as it's good, and contemptible insofar as it's bad?

ALCIBIADES: Yes.

SOCRATES: Then when you say that rescuing one's friends in battle is admirable but bad, you mean exactly the same as if you'd called it good but bad.

ALCIBIADES: I suppose you're right, Socrates.

SOCRATES: So nothing admirable, to the extent that it's admirable, is bad, and nothing contemptible, to the extent that it's contemptible, is good.

ALCIBIADES: Apparently not.

10. Assigning *malista* (d1) to Alcibiades, and rejecting the supplement *nai* (d2).

11. Omitting *ge* in e13.

SOCRATES: Now then, let's take a new approach. People who do what's   b
admirable do things well, don't they?

ALCIBIADES: Yes.

SOCRATES: And don't people who do things well live successful lives?

ALCIBIADES: Of course.

SOCRATES: Aren't they successful because they've got good things?

ALCIBIADES: Certainly.

SOCRATES: And they get good things by acting properly and admirably.

ALCIBIADES: Yes.

SOCRATES: So it is good to act properly.

ALCIBIADES: Of course.

SOCRATES: And good conduct is admirable.

ALCIBIADES: Yes.

SOCRATES: So we've seen once again that the very thing that is admirable   c
is also good.

ALCIBIADES: Apparently.

SOCRATES: So if we find that something is admirable, we'll also find that
it's good—according to this argument, at least.

ALCIBIADES: We'll have to.

SOCRATES: Well then, are good things advantageous, or not?

ALCIBIADES: Advantageous.

SOCRATES: Do you remember what we agreed about doing just things?

ALCIBIADES: I think we agreed that someone who does what's just must
also be doing what's admirable.

SOCRATES: And didn't we also agree that someone who does what's
admirable must also be doing what's good?

ALCIBIADES: Yes.

SOCRATES: And that what's good is advantageous?   d

ALCIBIADES: Yes.

SOCRATES: So, Alcibiades, just things are advantageous.

ALCIBIADES: So it seems.

SOCRATES: Well then, am I not the questioner and are you not the answerer?

ALCIBIADES: It appears I am.

SOCRATES: So if someone who believed that he knew what is just and
unjust were to stand up to advise the Athenians, or even the Peparethians,[12]
and said that sometimes just things are bad,[13] what could you do but laugh
at him? After all, as you yourself say, the same things are just and also   e
advantageous.

ALCIBIADES: I swear by the gods, Socrates, I have no idea what I mean—
I must be in some absolutely bizarre condition! When you ask me questions,
first I think one thing, and then I think something else.

12. Peparethus, an otherwise insignificant Aegean island, was embroiled in conflict in
the late 360s.

13. As Alcibiades did at 113d.

SocRATES: And are you unaware, my dear fellow, of what this feeling is?

ALCIBIADES: Completely.

SocRATES: Well, if someone asked you whether you had two eyes or three eyes, or two hands or four hands, or something else like that, do you think you'd give different answers at different times, or would you always give the same answer?

117   ALCIBIADES: I'm quite unsure of myself at this point, but I think I'd give the same answer.

SocRATES: Because you know it—isn't that the reason?

ALCIBIADES: I think so.

SocRATES: So if you gave conflicting answers about something, without meaning to, then it would be obvious that you didn't know it.

ALCIBIADES: Probably.

SocRATES: Well then, you tell me that you're wavering about what is just and unjust, admirable and contemptible, good and bad, and advantageous and disadvantageous. Isn't it obvious that the reason you waver about them is that you don't know about them?

b   ALCIBIADES: Yes, it is.

SocRATES: Would you also say that whenever someone doesn't know something, his soul will necessarily waver about it?

ALCIBIADES: Of course.

SocRATES: Really? Do you know any way of ascending to the stars?

ALCIBIADES: I certainly don't.

SocRATES: Does your opinion waver on this question, too?

ALCIBIADES: Of course not.

SocRATES: Do you know the reason, or shall I tell you?

ALCIBIADES: Tell me.

SocRATES: It's because, my friend, you don't understand it and you don't think you understand it.

c   ALCIBIADES: And what do you mean by that?

SocRATES: Let's look at it together. Do you waver about what you realize you don't understand? For example, you know, I think, that you don't know how to prepare a fine meal, right?

ALCIBIADES: Quite right.

SocRATES: So do you have your own opinions about how to prepare it, and waver about it; or do you leave it to someone who knows how?

ALCIBIADES: The latter.

SocRATES: Well, if you were sailing in a ship, would you be out there wondering whether to put the helm to port or starboard, and wavering because you didn't know? Or would you leave it to the skipper and take it easy?

ALCIBIADES: I'd leave it to the skipper.

SocRATES: So you don't waver about what you don't know, if in fact you know that you don't know.

ALCIBIADES: Apparently not.

SocRATES: Don't you realize that the errors in our conduct are caused by this kind of ignorance, of thinking that we know when we don't know?

ALCIBIADES: What do you mean by that?

SOCRATES: Well, we don't set out to do something unless we think we know what we're doing, right?

ALCIBIADES: Right.

SOCRATES: But when people don't think they know how to do something, they hand it over to somebody else, right?

ALCIBIADES: Of course.

SOCRATES: So the sort of people who don't think they know how to do things make no mistakes in life, because they leave those things to other people.

ALCIBIADES: You're right.

SOCRATES: Well, who are the ones making the mistakes? Surely not the ones who know?

ALCIBIADES: Of course not.

SOCRATES: Well, since it's not those who know, and it's not those who don't know and know they don't know, is there anyone left except those who don't know but think they do know?

ALCIBIADES: No, they're the only ones left.

SOCRATES: So this is the ignorance that causes bad things; this is the most disgraceful sort of stupidity.

ALCIBIADES: Yes.

SOCRATES: And isn't it most harmful and most contemptible when it is ignorance of the most important things?

ALCIBIADES: Very much so.

SOCRATES: Well, can you name anything more important than what's just and admirable and good and advantageous?

ALCIBIADES: No, I really can't.

SOCRATES: But aren't those the things you say you're wavering about?

ALCIBIADES: Yes.

SOCRATES: So, if you're wavering, it's obvious from what we've said that not only are you ignorant about the most important things, but you also think you know what you don't know.

ALCIBIADES: I guess that's right.

SOCRATES: Good God, Alcibiades, what a sorry state you're in! I hesitate to call it by its name, but still, since we're alone, it must be said. You are wedded to stupidity, my good fellow, stupidity in the highest degree— our discussion and your own words convict you of it. This is why you're rushing into politics before you've got an education. You're not alone in this sad state—you've got most of our city's politicians for company. There are only a few exceptions, among them, perhaps, your guardian, Pericles.

ALCIBIADES: Yes, Socrates, and people do say that he didn't acquire his expertise all by himself; he kept company with many experts like Pythoclides and Anaxagoras. Even now, despite his advanced age, he consults with Damon[14] for the same purpose.

14. Pythoclides of Ceos and Damon of Athens were musicians and philosophers; Anaxagoras of Clazomenae was a philosopher; all taught in Athens in the fifth century B.C.

SOCRATES: Really? Have you ever seen any expert who is unable to make others expert in what he knows? The person who taught you how to read and write—he had expertise in his field, and he made you and anybody else he liked expert as well, didn't he?

ALCIBIADES: Yes.

d   SOCRATES: And will you, having learned from him, be able to teach somebody else?

ALCIBIADES: Yes.

SOCRATES: And isn't it the same with the music teacher and the gymnastics teacher?

ALCIBIADES: Certainly.

SOCRATES: I think we can be pretty sure that someone understands something when he can show that he has made someone else understand it.

ALCIBIADES: I agree.

SOCRATES: Well then, can you tell me who Pericles has made into an expert? Shall we start with his sons?

e   ALCIBIADES: But Socrates, both of his sons turned out to be idiots!

SOCRATES: What about Clinias, your brother?

ALCIBIADES: There's no point talking about *him*—he's a madman!

SOCRATES: Well then, since Clinias is mad and Pericles' sons were idiots, what shall we say is the reason that he allowed *you* to be in the state you're in?

ALCIBIADES: I suppose it's because I didn't really pay attention.

119   SOCRATES: But can you name any other Athenian or any foreigner—slave or free—who became any more of an expert by keeping company with Pericles? After all, I can name Pythodorus, son of Isolochus, and Callias, son of Calliades, who became wise through their association with Zeno;[15] they paid him a hundred minas each and became famous experts.

ALCIBIADES: I can't think of anyone, by Zeus.

SOCRATES: Very well. What do you propose for yourself? Do you intend to remain in your present condition, or practice some self-cultivation?

b   ALCIBIADES: Let's discuss it together, Socrates. You know, I do see what you're saying and actually I agree—it seems to me that none of our city's politicians has been properly educated, except for a few.

SOCRATES: And what does that mean?

ALCIBIADES: Well, if they were educated, then anyone who wanted to compete with them would have to get some knowledge and go into training, like an athlete. But as it is, since they entered politics as amateurs, there's no need for me to train and go to the trouble of learning. I'm sure

c   my natural abilities will be far superior to theirs.

SOCRATES: Good God, my dear boy, what a thing to say—how unworthy of your good looks and your other advantages!

---

15. Zeno of Elea was a philosopher; Pythodorus and Callias were both prominent politicians in Athens in the fifth century B.C. See *Parmenides* 126e–128e.

ALCIBIADES: What in the world do you mean, Socrates? What are you getting at?

SOCRATES: I'm furious with you and with my infatuation for you!

ALCIBIADES: Why?

SOCRATES: Because you stoop to compete with these people.

ALCIBIADES: Who else have I got to compete with?

SOCRATES: That's a fine sort of question, from a man who thinks he holds   d
himself in high esteem!

ALCIBIADES: What do you mean? Aren't they my competitors?

SOCRATES: Look here, if you were intending to steer a ship into battle, would you be content to be the best sailor at steering? Granted that's necessary, but wouldn't you keep your eye on your real opponents and not on your comrades, as you're doing now? Surely you ought to be so far superior to them that they're happy to be your humble comrades in the struggle, and wouldn't dream of competing with you. I'm assuming   e
that you do really intend to distinguish yourself with some splendid deed worthy of you and your city.

ALCIBIADES: Yes, that's certainly what I intend to do.

SOCRATES: Dear me, how very proper it is for you to be satisfied with being better than the soldiers—how proper not to keep an eye on the leaders of the opposing camp, so that you can some day become better than them by training and scheming against them!

ALCIBIADES: Who are you talking about, Socrates?   120

SOCRATES: Don't you know that our city is at war from time to time with the Spartans and with the Great King of Persia?

ALCIBIADES: You're right.

SOCRATES: So since you plan to be leader of this city, wouldn't it be right to think that your struggle is with the kings of Sparta and Persia?

ALCIBIADES: That may well be true.

SOCRATES: But no sir, you've got to keep an eye on Midias the cockfighter and such people—people who try to run the city's affairs with their 'slave-   b
boy hair styles' (as the women say) still showing on their boorish minds. They set out to flatter the city with their outlandish talk, not to rule it. These are the people, I'm telling you, you've got to keep your eyes on. So relax, don't bother to learn what needs to be learned for the great struggle to come, don't train yourself for what needs training—go ahead and go   c
into politics with your complete and thorough preparation.

ALCIBIADES: No, Socrates, I think you're right. But still I don't think the Spartan generals or the Persian king are any different from anybody else.

SOCRATES: But what sort of a notion is that? Think about it.

ALCIBIADES: About what?

SOCRATES: In the first place, when do you think you'd cultivate yourself: if you feared them and thought they were formidable, or if you didn't?   d

ALCIBIADES: Obviously if I thought they were formidable.

SOCRATES: Surely you don't think that cultivating yourself will do you any harm, do you?

ALCIBIADES: Not at all. In fact, it would be a big help.

SOCRATES: So that's one flaw in this notion of yours, a big flaw, isn't it?

ALCIBIADES: You're right.

SOCRATES: Now the second flaw is that it's also false, judging by the probabilities.

ALCIBIADES: What do you mean?

SOCRATES: Is it likely that natural talents will be greatest among noble families, or in other families?

e   ALCIBIADES: In noble families, obviously.

SOCRATES: Those who are well born will turn out to be perfectly virtuous, if they're well brought up, won't they?

ALCIBIADES: They certainly will.

SOCRATES: So let's compare our situation with theirs, and consider, first of all, whether the Spartan and Persian kings are of humbler descent. We know, of course, that the Spartan kings are descended from Heracles, and the Persian kings are descended from Achaemenes, and that the families of Heracles and Achaemenes go right back to Perseus, son of Zeus.

121   ALCIBIADES: Mine too, Socrates—my family goes back to Eurysaces and Eurysaces' goes back to Zeus.

SOCRATES: So does mine too, noble Alcibiades, mine goes back to Daedalus and Daedalus' goes back to Hephaestus,[16] son of Zeus. Starting with those kings, though, and tracing backwards, every one of them is a king all the way back to Zeus—kings of Argos and Sparta, and kings of Persia in eternity, and sometimes of Asia, too, as they are now. But you and I

b   are private citizens, as were our fathers. And if you had to show off your ancestors and Salamis, the native land of Eurysaces, to Artaxerxes, son of Xerxes—or Aegina, the native land of Aeacus the ancestor of Eurysaces— don't you realize how much you'd be laughed at? But you think we're the equal of those men in the dignity of our descent, as well as in our up- bringing.

Haven't you noticed what a commanding position the Spartan kings enjoy? Their wives are guarded at public expense by the ephors, so as to ensure, as far as possible, that their kings are descended from the family

c   of the Heraclidae alone. And as for the Persian king, his position is so supreme that nobody so much as *suspects* his heir of being fathered by anybody but him; that's why his queen is left unguarded except by fear. When the eldest son and heir to the throne is born, all the king's subjects have a feast day. Then, in the years that follow, the whole of Asia celebrates that day, the king's birthday, with further sacrifice and feasting. But when

d   *we* are born, Alcibiades, "even the neighbors hardly notice it," as the comic poet[17] says.

---

16. Socrates' father was a sculptor; sculptors recognized Daedalus as their patron and legendary ancestor. Hephaestus was the artisan among the Olympian gods.

17. A line of the comic poet Plato, frg. 204 Kock.

Then the boy is brought up—not by some nanny of no account, but by the most highly respected eunuchs in the royal household. They attend to all the needs of the infant child, and are especially concerned to make him as handsome as possible, shaping and straightening his infant limbs; and for this they are held in great esteem. When the boys reach seven years of age they take up horseback riding with their instructors, and begin to hunt wild game.

When he is twice seven years, the boy is entrusted to people called the "royal tutors." These are four Persians of mature age who have been selected as the best: the wisest, the justest, and most self-controlled, and the bravest. The first of them instructs him in the worship of their gods, the Magian lore of Zoroaster, son of Horomazes, and also in what a king should know. The justest man teaches him to be truthful his whole life long. The most self-controlled man teaches him not to be mastered by even a single pleasure, so that he can get accustomed to being a free man and a real king, whose first duty is to rule himself, not be a slave to himself. The bravest man trains him to be fearless and undaunted, because fear is slavery.

But for you, Alcibiades, Pericles chose from among his household Zopyrus the Thracian, a tutor so old he was perfectly useless. I could tell you about all the rest of the upbringing and education of your competitors, but it would be a long story and, besides, you can probably imagine the later stages from what I've told you so far. But, Alcibiades, your birth, your upbringing, and your education—or that of any other Athenian—is of no concern to anybody, to tell the truth—nobody, that is, except perhaps some man who may happen to be in love with you.

Again, if you care to consider the wealth of the Persians, the splendor, the clothes and trailing robes, the anointings with myrrh, the throng of servants-in-waiting, and all their other luxuries, you'd be ashamed of your circumstances, because you'd see how inferior they are to theirs.

Again, if you care to consider the self-control and the decorum of the Spartans, their confidence and their composure, their self-esteem and their discipline, their courage and their fortitude, and their love of hardship, victory, and honor, you'd consider yourself a mere child in all these respects.

Again, we'd better discuss your wealth, Alcibiades, if you're to see where you stand. *You* may devote yourself to it and think it makes you something, but if you care to look at the wealth of the Spartans you'd realize that it greatly exceeds ours in Athens. They have land of their own and in Messene that not a single one of our estates could compete with—not in size, nor in quality, nor in slaves—especially Helots—nor even in horses, nor in the other livestock grazing in Messene. But I'll pass over all that.

There is more gold and silver in Sparta in private hands than in the rest of Greece put together. It's been coming in to them for many generations, pouring in from all of Greece's cities, and often from foreign cities, too, and it never goes out again. It's just like what the fox says to the lion in

Aesop's fable[18]—you can clearly see the tracks of the money going in toward Sparta, but the tracks coming out are nowhere to be seen. So you can be sure that the Spartans are the richest of the Greeks in gold and silver, and that the king is the richest of all the Spartans, because the greatest share of these revenues goes to him. Furthermore, he receives a considerable sum from the Spartans by way of royal tribute.

b   But great as they are when compared with other Greek cities, the Spartan fortunes are nothing compared with the fortunes of the Persians and their king. I once spoke with a reliable man who travelled over to the Persian court, and he told me that he crossed a very large and rich tract of land, nearly a day's journey across, which the locals called "the Queen's girdle."

c   There's another one called "the Queen's veil," as well as many others, all fine and rich properties, each one named for a part of the Queen's wardrobe, because each one is set aside to pay for the Queen's finery.

      Now suppose someone were to say to Amestris, the king's mother and the widow of Xerxes, "The son of Dinomache intends to challenge your son; her wardrobe is worth only fifty minas at best, and her son has less than three hundred acres[19] of land at Erchia." I think she'd be wondering

d   what this Alcibiades had up his sleeve to think of competing against Artaxerxes. I think she'd say, "I don't see what this fellow could be relying on, except diligence and wisdom—the Greeks don't have anything else worth mentioning."

      But if she heard that this Alcibiades who is making this attempt is, in the first place, hardly twenty years old yet, and, secondly, entirely uneducated, and furthermore, when his lover tells him to study and culti-

e   vate himself and discipline himself so that he can compete with the king, he says he doesn't want to and that he's happy with the way he is—if she heard all that, I think she'd ask in amazement, "What in the world could this youngster be relying on?" Suppose we were to reply, "Good looks, height, birth, wealth, and native intelligence." Then, Alcibiades, consider-ing all that they have of these things as well, she'd conclude that we were stark raving mad. Again, I think that Lampido, the daughter of Leotychides,

124   wife of Archidamus and mother of Agis, who were all Spartan kings, would be similarly amazed if you, with your bad upbringing, proposed to compete with her son, considering all his advantages.

      And yet, don't you think it's disgraceful that even our enemies' *wives* have a better appreciation than we do of what it would take to challenge them? No, my excellent friend, trust in me and in the Delphic inscription

b   and 'know thyself'. These are the people we must defeat, not the ones you think, and we have no hope of defeating them unless we act with both diligence and skill. If you fall short in these, then you will fall short

---

18. No. 142 (Perry), 147 (Hausrath).

19. The Attic 'acre' was 874 square meters, so Alcibiades' holding was less than 26 hectares (65 modern acres).

of achieving fame in Greece as well as abroad; and that is what I think you're longing for, more than anyone else ever longed for anything.

ALCIBIADES: Well, Socrates, what kind of self-cultivation do I need to practice? Can you show me the way? What you said really sounded true.

SOCRATES: Yes—but let's discuss together how we can become as good as possible. You know, what I've said about the need for education applies   c
to me as well as to you—we're in the same condition, except in one respect.

ALCIBIADES: What?

SOCRATES: My guardian is better and wiser than Pericles, your guardian.

ALCIBIADES: Who's that, Socrates?

SOCRATES: God, Alcibiades; it was a god who prevented me from talking with you before today. I put my faith in him, and I say that your glory will be entirely my doing.

ALCIBIADES: You're teasing me, Socrates.   d

SOCRATES: Maybe; but I'm right in saying that we stand in need of self-cultivation. Actually, every human being needs self-cultivation, but *especially* the two of us.

ALCIBIADES: You're right about me.

SOCRATES: And about me.

ALCIBIADES: So what should we do?

SOCRATES: There must be no giving up, my friend, and no slacking off.

ALCIBIADES: No, Socrates, that really wouldn't do.

SOCRATES: No it wouldn't. So let's work it out together. Tell me—we say   e
that we want to be as good as possible, don't we?

ALCIBIADES: Yes.

SOCRATES: In what respect?

ALCIBIADES: In what good men do, obviously.

SOCRATES: Good at what?

ALCIBIADES: Taking care of things, obviously.

SOCRATES: What sorts of things? Horses?

ALCIBIADES: Of course not.

SOCRATES: In that case, we'd consult a horse expert.

ALCIBIADES: Yes.

SOCRATES: Well, do you mean sailing?

ALCIBIADES: No.

SOCRATES: In that case, we'd consult a sailing expert.

ALCIBIADES: Yes.

SOCRATES: Well, what sorts of things? Whose business is it?

ALCIBIADES: The leading citizens of Athens.

SOCRATES: By 'leading citizens' do you mean clever men or stupid men?   125

ALCIBIADES: Clever.

SOCRATES: But isn't everybody good at what they're clever at?

ALCIBIADES: Yes.

SOCRATES: And bad at what they're not?

ALCIBIADES: Of course.

SOCRATES: And is the shoemaker clever at making shoes?

ALCIBIADES: Certainly.

SOCRATES: Then he's good at it.

ALCIBIADES: That's right.

SOCRATES: Well now, isn't the shoemaker stupid at making clothes?

ALCIBIADES: Yes.

b   SOCRATES: So he's bad at that.

ALCIBIADES: Yes.

SOCRATES: So the same person is both good and bad, at least by this argument.

ALCIBIADES: Apparently.

SOCRATES: Do you mean to say that *good men* are also bad?

ALCIBIADES: Of course not.

SOCRATES: So which ones *do* you say are good men?

ALCIBIADES: I mean those with the ability to rule in the city.

SOCRATES: But not, I presume, over horses.

ALCIBIADES: No, of course not.

SOCRATES: Over people?

ALCIBIADES: Yes.

SOCRATES: When they're sick?

ALCIBIADES: No.

SOCRATES: When they're at sea?

ALCIBIADES: No.

SOCRATES: When they're harvesting?

ALCIBIADES: No.

c   SOCRATES: When they're doing nothing? Or when they're doing something?

ALCIBIADES: Doing something.

SOCRATES: Doing what? Try to make it clear for me.

ALCIBIADES: It's when they're helping each other and dealing with each other, as we do in our urban way of life.

SOCRATES: So you mean ruling over men who deal with men.

ALCIBIADES: Yes.

SOCRATES: Over the boatswains who deal with rowers?

ALCIBIADES: Of course not.

SOCRATES: That's what the pilot is good at.

ALCIBIADES: Yes.

d   SOCRATES: Do you mean ruling over flute-players, who direct the singers and deal with the dancers?

ALCIBIADES: Of course not.

SOCRATES: Again, that's what the chorus-master is good at.

ALCIBIADES: Certainly.

SOCRATES: So what *do* you mean by being able to 'rule over men who deal with men'?

ALCIBIADES: I mean ruling over the men in the city who take part in citizenship and who make a mutual contribution.

SOCRATES: Well, what skill is this? Suppose I asked you the same thing again—what skill makes men understand how to rule over men who take part in sailing?

ALCIBIADES: The pilot's.

SOCRATES: And what knowledge did we say enables them to rule over those who take part in singing?

e

ALCIBIADES: The chorus-master's, as you just said.

SOCRATES: Well now, what do you call the knowledge that enables you to rule over those who take part in citizenship?

ALCIBIADES: I call it the knowledge of good advice, Socrates.

SOCRATES: But then do you think the pilot's advice is bad advice?

ALCIBIADES: Of course not.

SOCRATES: Then is it good advice?

ALCIBIADES: I should think so; he has to ensure the safety of his passengers.

126

SOCRATES: You're right. Well then, what's the purpose of this good advice you're talking about?

ALCIBIADES: The safety and better management of the city.

SOCRATES: But what is present or absent when the city is safe and better managed? If, for example, you asked me, "What is present or absent in the body when it is safe and better managed?" I'd reply, "Health is present and disease is absent." Wouldn't you agree?

ALCIBIADES: Yes.

b

SOCRATES: And if you asked me again, "What is present in our eyes when they are better cared for?" I'd say the same sort of thing—"Sight is present and blindness is absent." Again, with our ears, deafness is absent and hearing is present when they're in better condition and getting better treatment.

ALCIBIADES: You're right.

SOCRATES: Well then, what about a city? What is it that's present or absent when it's in a better condition and getting better management and treatment?

ALCIBIADES: The way I look at it, Socrates, mutual friendship will be present, and hatred and insurrection will be absent.

c

SOCRATES: When you say 'friendship', do you mean agreement or disagreement?

ALCIBIADES: Agreement.

SOCRATES: What skill is it that makes cities agree about numbers?

ALCIBIADES: Arithmetic.

SOCRATES: What about private citizens? Isn't it the same skill?

ALCIBIADES: Yes.

SOCRATES: And doesn't it also make each person agree with himself?

ALCIBIADES: Yes.

SOCRATES: And what skill is it that makes each of us agree with himself about whether a hand's-width is larger than an arm's-length? It's measuring, isn't it?

d

ALCIBIADES: Of course.

SOCRATES: Doesn't it make both cities and private citizens agree?

ALCIBIADES: Yes.

SOCRATES: And isn't it the same with weighing?

ALCIBIADES: It is.

SOCRATES: Well, this agreement you're talking about, what is it? What's it about? What skill provides it? Doesn't the same skill make both a city and a private citizen agree, both with themselves and with others?

ALCIBIADES: That does seem quite likely.

e   SOCRATES: What is it then? Don't give up. . . . Try your best to tell me.

ALCIBIADES: I suppose I mean the sort of friendship and agreement you find when a mother and father agree with a son they love, and when a brother agrees with his brother, and a woman agrees with her husband.

SOCRATES: Well, Alcibiades, do you think that a husband is able to agree with his wife about wool-working, when he doesn't understand it and she does?

ALCIBIADES: Of course not.

SOCRATES: Nor does he have any need to, because that's for a woman to know about.

ALCIBIADES: That's right.

127   SOCRATES: And is a woman able to agree with her husband about military tactics, without having learned about it?

ALCIBIADES: Of course not.

SOCRATES: I suppose you'd say that that's for a man to know about.

ALCIBIADES: I would.

SOCRATES: So, according to your argument, some subjects are women's subjects and some are men's subjects.

ALCIBIADES: Of course.

SOCRATES: So, in these areas at least, there's no agreement between men and women.

ALCIBIADES: No.

SOCRATES: Nor is there any friendship, since friendship was agreement.

ALCIBIADES: Apparently not.

SOCRATES: So women are not loved by men, insofar as they do their own work.

b   ALCIBIADES: It seems not.

SOCRATES: Nor are men loved by women, insofar as they do theirs.

ALCIBIADES: No.

SOCRATES: So neither are cities well governed when the different groups each do their own work.

ALCIBIADES: But I think they *are*, Socrates.

SOCRATES: What do you mean? In that case there's no friendship in cities, but we said friendship was present when cities are well governed, and not otherwise.

ALCIBIADES: But I think it's when each person does his own work that mutual friendship results.

SOCRATES: You've just changed your mind. What do you mean now?   c
Can there be friendship without agreement? Can there be any agreement
when some know about the matter and others don't?

ALCIBIADES: There can't possibly.

SOCRATES: But when everyone does his own work, is everyone being
just, or unjust?

ALCIBIADES: Just, of course.

SOCRATES: So when the citizens do what is just in the city, there is no
friendship between them.

ALCIBIADES: Again, Socrates, I think there must be.

SOCRATES: Then what *do* you mean by this 'friendship' and 'agreement'   d
that we must be wise and good advisers in if we're to be good men? I
can't figure out what it is, or who's got it. According to your argument,
it seems that sometimes certain people have it and sometimes they don't.

ALCIBIADES: Well, Socrates, I swear by the gods that I don't even know
what I mean. I think I must have been in an appalling state for a long
time, without being aware of it.

SOCRATES: But don't lose heart. If you were fifty when you realized it,   e
then it would be hard for you to cultivate yourself, but now you're just
the right age to see it.

ALCIBIADES: Now that I've seen it, Socrates, what should I do about it?

SOCRATES: Answer my questions, Alcibiades. If you do that, then, God
willing,—if we are to trust in my divination—you and I will be in a
better state.

ALCIBIADES: Then we will be, if it depends on my answering.

SOCRATES: Well then, what does it mean to cultivate oneself?—I'm afraid   128
we often think we're cultivating ourselves when we're not. When does a
man do that? Is he cultivating himself when he cultivates what he has?

ALCIBIADES: *I* think so, anyway.

SOCRATES: Really? When does a man cultivate or care for his feet? Is it
when he's caring for what belongs to his feet?

ALCIBIADES: I don't understand.

SOCRATES: Is there anything you'd say belonged to a hand? Take a ring,
for example—could it belong anywhere else on a man but on his finger?

ALCIBIADES: Of course not.

SOCRATES: Similarly a shoe belongs nowhere but on the feet.

ALCIBIADES: Yes.

SOCRATES: Likewise cloaks and bedclothes belong to the rest of the
body.

ALCIBIADES: Yes.   b

SOCRATES: So when we cultivate or care for our shoes, are we caring for
our feet?

ALCIBIADES: I don't really understand, Socrates.

SOCRATES: Surely, Alcibiades, you talk about taking proper care of one
thing or another, don't you?

ALCIBIADES: Yes, I do.

SOCRATES: And when you make something better, you say you're taking proper care of it.

ALCIBIADES: Yes.

SOCRATES: What skill is it that makes shoes better?

ALCIBIADES: Shoemaking.

SOCRATES: So shoemaking is the skill by which we take care of shoes.

c   ALCIBIADES: Yes.

SOCRATES: Do we use shoemaking to take care of our feet, too? Or do we use the skill that makes our feet better?

ALCIBIADES: The latter.

SOCRATES: Isn't the skill that makes the feet better the same as what makes the rest of the body better?

ALCIBIADES: I think so.

SOCRATES: Isn't this skill athletics?

ALCIBIADES: Yes, absolutely.

SOCRATES: So while we take care of our feet with athletics, we take care of what belongs to our feet with shoemaking.

ALCIBIADES: Certainly.

SOCRATES: And while we take care of our hands with athletics, we take care of what belongs to our hands with ring-making.

ALCIBIADES: Yes.

SOCRATES: And while we cultivate our bodies with athletics, we take care

d   of what belongs to our bodies with weaving and other skills.

ALCIBIADES: That's absolutely right.

SOCRATES: So while we cultivate each thing with one skill, we cultivate what belongs to it with another skill.

ALCIBIADES: Apparently so.

SOCRATES: And so when you're cultivating what belongs to you, you're not cultivating yourself.

ALCIBIADES: Not at all.

SOCRATES: For it seems that cultivating yourself and cultivating what belongs to you require different skills.

ALCIBIADES: Apparently.

SOCRATES: Well then, what sort of skill could we use to cultivate ourselves?

ALCIBIADES: I couldn't say.

e   SOCRATES: But we've agreed on this much, at least—it's a skill that won't make anything that belongs to us better, but it will make *us* better.

ALCIBIADES: You're right.

SOCRATES: Now if we didn't know what a shoe was, would we have known what skill makes a shoe better?

ALCIBIADES: No, we couldn't have.

SOCRATES: Nor would we have known what skill makes a ring better if we didn't know what a ring was.

ALCIBIADES: True.

SOCRATES: Well then, could we ever know what skill makes us better if we didn't know what *we* were?

ALCIBIADES: We couldn't.

129

SOCRATES: Is it actually such an easy thing to know oneself? Was it some simpleton who inscribed those words on the temple wall at Delphi? Or is it difficult, and not for everybody?

ALCIBIADES: Sometimes I think, Socrates, that anyone can do it, but then sometimes I think it's extremely difficult.

SOCRATES: But Alcibiades, whether it's easy or not, nevertheless this is the situation we're in: if we know ourselves, then we might be able to know how to cultivate ourselves, but if we don't know ourselves, we'll never know how.

ALCIBIADES: I agree.

SOCRATES: Tell me, how can we find out what 'itself' is, in itself?[20] Maybe this is the way to find out what we ourselves might be—maybe it's the only possible way.

b

ALCIBIADES: You're right.

SOCRATES: Hold on, by Zeus—who are you speaking with now? Anybody but me?

ALCIBIADES: No.

SOCRATES: And I'm speaking with you.

ALCIBIADES: Yes.

SOCRATES: Is Socrates doing the talking?

ALCIBIADES: He certainly is.

SOCRATES: And is Alcibiades doing the listening?

ALCIBIADES: Yes.

SOCRATES: And isn't Socrates talking with words?

ALCIBIADES: Of course.

c

SOCRATES: I suppose you'd say that talking is the same as using words?

ALCIBIADES: Certainly.

SOCRATES: But the thing being used and the person using it—they're different, aren't they?

ALCIBIADES: What do you mean?

SOCRATES: A shoemaker, for example, cuts with a knife and a scraper, I think, and with other tools.

ALCIBIADES: Yes, he does.

SOCRATES: So isn't the cutter who uses the tools different from the tools he's cutting with?

ALCIBIADES: Of course.

SOCRATES: And likewise isn't the lyre-player different from what he's playing with?

ALCIBIADES: Yes.

20. Reading *auto to auto* in b1.

d   SOCRATES: This is what I was just asking—doesn't the user of a thing always seem to be different from what he's using?

ALCIBIADES: It seems so.

SOCRATES: Let's think about the shoemaker again. Does he cut with his tools only, or does he also cut with his hands?

ALCIBIADES: With his hands, too.

SOCRATES: So he uses his hands, too.

ALCIBIADES: Yes.

SOCRATES: And doesn't he use his eyes, too, in shoemaking?

ALCIBIADES: Yes.

SOCRATES: Didn't we agree that the person who uses something is different from the thing that he uses?

ALCIBIADES: Yes.

SOCRATES: So the shoemaker and the lyre-player are different from the hands and eyes they use in their work.

e   ALCIBIADES: So it seems.

SOCRATES: Doesn't a man use his whole body, too?

ALCIBIADES: Certainly.

SOCRATES: And we agreed that the user is different from the thing being used.

ALCIBIADES: Yes.

SOCRATES: So a man is different from his own body.

ALCIBIADES: So it seems.

SOCRATES: Then what *is* a man?

ALCIBIADES: I don't know what to say.

SOCRATES: Yes, you do—say that it's what uses the body.

ALCIBIADES: Yes.

130   SOCRATES: What else uses it but the soul?

ALCIBIADES: Nothing else.

SOCRATES: And doesn't the soul rule the body?

ALCIBIADES: Yes.

SOCRATES: Now here's something I don't think anybody would disagree with.

ALCIBIADES: What?

SOCRATES: Man is one of three things.

ALCIBIADES: What things?

SOCRATES: The body, the soul, or the two of them together, the whole thing.

ALCIBIADES: Of course.

SOCRATES: But we agreed that man is that which rules the body.

b   ALCIBIADES: Yes, we did agree to that.

SOCRATES: Does the body rule itself?

ALCIBIADES: It couldn't.

SOCRATES: Because we said it was ruled.

ALCIBIADES: Yes.

SOCRATES: So *this* can't be what we're looking for.

ALCIBIADES: Not likely.

SOCRATES: Well then, can the two of them together rule the body? Is this what man is?

ALCIBIADES: Yes, maybe that's it.

SOCRATES: No, that's the least likely of all. If one of them doesn't take part in ruling, then surely no combination of the two of them could rule.

ALCIBIADES: You're right.

SOCRATES: Since a man is neither his body, nor his body and soul together, what remains, I think, is either that he's nothing, or else, if he *is* something, he's nothing other than his soul.

ALCIBIADES: Quite so.

SOCRATES: Do you need any clearer proof that the soul is the man?

ALCIBIADES: No, by Zeus, I think you've given ample proof.

SOCRATES: Well, if we've proven it fairly well, although perhaps not rigorously, that will do for us. We'll have a rigorous proof when we find out what we skipped over, because it would have taken quite a lot of study.

ALCIBIADES: What was that?

SOCRATES: What we mentioned just now, that we should first consider what 'itself' is, in itself. But in fact, we've been considering what an individual self[21] is, instead of what 'itself' is. Perhaps that was enough for us, for surely nothing about us has more authority than the soul, wouldn't you agree?

ALCIBIADES: Certainly.

SOCRATES: So the right way of looking at it is that, when you and I talk to each other, one soul uses words to address another soul.

ALCIBIADES: Very true.

SOCRATES: That's just what we were saying a little while ago—that Socrates converses with Alcibiades not by saying words to his face, apparently, but by addressing his words to *Alcibiades*, in other words, to his soul.

ALCIBIADES: I see it now.

SOCRATES: So the command that we should know ourselves means that we should know our souls.

ALCIBIADES: So it seems.

SOCRATES: And someone who knows certain things[22] about his body knows about what belongs to him, not himself.

ALCIBIADES: That's right.

SOCRATES: So no doctor, to the extent he's a doctor, knows himself, and neither does any trainer, to the extent he's a trainer.

ALCIBIADES: It seems not.

SOCRATES: So farmers and other tradesmen are a long way from knowing themselves. It seems *they* don't even know what belongs to them; their skills are about what's even further away than what belongs to them. They only know what belongs to the body and how to take care of it.

21. Reading *auton hekaston* at d4.
22. Conjecturing *atta* before *tōn* in a2, and omitting *ti*.

ALCIBIADES: You're right.

SOCRATES: If being self-controlled is knowing yourself, then their skills don't make any of them self-controlled.

ALCIBIADES: I don't think so.

SOCRATES: That's why we consider these skills to be beneath us, and not suitable for a gentleman to learn.

ALCIBIADES: You're quite right.

SOCRATES: Furthermore, if someone takes care of his body, then isn't he caring for something that belongs to him, and not for himself?

ALCIBIADES: That seems likely.

SOCRATES: And isn't someone who takes care of his wealth caring neither
c   for himself nor for what belongs to him, but for something even further away?

ALCIBIADES: I agree.

SOCRATES: So the money-earner is not, in fact, doing his own work.

ALCIBIADES: Right.

SOCRATES: Now if there was someone who loved Alcibiades' body, he wouldn't be loving Alcibiades, only something that belonged to Alcibiades.

ALCIBIADES: That's right.

SOCRATES: But someone who loved you would love your soul.

ALCIBIADES: By our argument, I think he'd have to.

SOCRATES: Wouldn't someone who loves your body go off and leave you when your beauty is no longer in full bloom?

ALCIBIADES: Obviously.
d   SOCRATES: But someone who loves your soul will not leave you, as long as you're making progress.

ALCIBIADES: That's probably right.

SOCRATES: Well, I'm the one who won't leave you—I'm the one who will stay with you, now that your body has lost its bloom and everyone else has gone away.

ALCIBIADES: I'm glad you are, Socrates, and I hope you never leave me.

SOCRATES: Then you must try to be as attractive as possible.

ALCIBIADES: I'll certainly try.
e   SOCRATES: So this is your situation: you, Alcibiades, son of Clinias, have no lovers and never have had any, it seems, except for one only, and he is your darling[23] Socrates, son of Sophroniscus and Phaenarete.

ALCIBIADES: True.

SOCRATES: Remember when I first spoke to you? You said that you were just about to say something; you wanted to ask me why I was the only one who hadn't given up on you.[24]

ALCIBIADES: That's right.

SOCRATES: Well, this is the reason: I was your only lover—the others were only lovers of what you had. While your possessions are passing

23. An echo of *Odyssey* ii.365.
24. At 104c–d.

their prime, *you* are just beginning to bloom. I shall never forsake you
now, never, unless the Athenian people make you corrupt and ugly. And
that is my greatest fear, that a love of the common people might corrupt
you, for many Athenian gentlemen have suffered that fate already. "The
people of great-hearted Erechtheus"[25] might look attractive on the outside,
but you need to scrutinize them in their nakedness, so take the precaution
I urge.

ALCIBIADES: What precaution?

SOCRATES: Get in training first, my dear friend, and learn what you need   b
to know *before* entering politics. That will give you an antidote against the
terrible dangers.

ALCIBIADES: I think you're right, Socrates. But try to explain how exactly
we should cultivate ourselves.

SOCRATES: Well, we've made one step forward anyway—we've pretty
well agreed what we are; we were afraid that we might make a mistake
about that and unwittingly cultivate something other than ourselves.

ALCIBIADES: That's right.

SOCRATES: And the next step is that we have to cultivate our soul and   c
look to that.

ALCIBIADES: Obviously.

SOCRATES: And let others take care of our bodies and our property.

ALCIBIADES: Quite so.

SOCRATES: Now, how can we get the clearest knowledge of our soul? If
we knew that, we'd probably know ourselves as well . . . By the gods—
that admirable Delphic inscription we just mentioned[26]—didn't we understand it?

ALCIBIADES: What's the point of bringing that up again, Socrates?

SOCRATES: I'll tell you what I suspect that inscription means, and what   d
advice it's giving us. There may not be many examples of it, except the
case of sight.

ALCIBIADES: What do you mean by that?

SOCRATES: You think about it, too. If the inscription took our eyes to be
men and advised them, "See thyself," how would we understand such
advice? Shouldn't the eye be looking at something in which it could see
itself?

ALCIBIADES: Obviously.

SOCRATES: Then let's think of something that allows us to see both it and
ourselves when we look at it.

ALCIBIADES: Obviously, Socrates, you mean mirrors and that sort of thing.   e

SOCRATES: Quite right. And isn't there something like that in the eye,
which we see with?

ALCIBIADES: Certainly.

25. An epithet for the people of Athens, in Homer, *Iliad* ii.547.

26. "Know Thyself"; cf. 129a.

133   SOCRATES: I'm sure you've noticed that when a man looks into an eye his face appears in it, like in a mirror. We call this the 'pupil', for it's a sort of miniature of the man who's looking.[27]

ALCIBIADES: You're right.

SOCRATES: Then an eye will see itself if it observes an eye and looks at the best part of it, the part with which it can see.

ALCIBIADES: So it seems.

SOCRATES: But it won't see itself if it looks at anything else in a man, or anything else at all, unless it's similar to the eye.

b   ALCIBIADES: You're right.

SOCRATES: So if an eye is to see itself, it must look at an eye, and at that region of it in which the good activity of an eye actually occurs, and this, I presume, is seeing.

ALCIBIADES: That's right.

SOCRATES: Then if the soul, Alcibiades, is to know itself, it must look at a soul, and especially at that region in which what makes a soul good, wisdom, occurs, and at anything else which is similar to it.

ALCIBIADES: I agree with you, Socrates.

c   SOCRATES: Can we say that there is anything about the soul which is more divine than that where knowing and understanding take place?

ALCIBIADES: No, we can't.

SOCRATES: Then that region in it resembles the divine,[28] and someone who looked at that and grasped everything divine—vision[29] and under-standing—would have the best grasp of himself as well.

ALCIBIADES: So it seems.[30]

SOCRATES: But we agreed that knowing oneself was the same as being self-controlled.

ALCIBIADES: Certainly.

SOCRATES: So if we didn't know ourselves and weren't self-controlled, would we be able to know which of the things that belong to us were good and which were bad?

ALCIBIADES: How could we know that, Socrates?

d   SOCRATES: No; I suppose it would seem impossible to you to know that what belongs to Alcibiades belongs to him, without knowing Alcibiades.

27. The Greek word for 'pupil' also means 'doll'.

28. Reading *theiōi* in c4.

29. Accepting the emendation *thean* (vision) for *theon* (god) in c5.

30. Omitting 133c8–17 (which seem to have been added by a later neo-Platonist scholar). The lines read:
SOCRATES: Just as mirrors are clearer, purer, and brighter than the reflecting surface of the eye, isn't God both purer and brighter than the best part of our soul?
ALCIBIADES: I would certainly think so, Socrates.
SOCRATES: So the way that we can best see and know ourselves is to use the finest mirror available and look at God and, on the human level, at the virtue of the soul.
ALCIBIADES: Yes.

ALCIBIADES: Quite impossible, I'm sure.

SOCRATES: And similarly we couldn't know that what belongs to us belongs to us, without knowing ourselves.

ALCIBIADES: How could we?

SOCRATES: And if we didn't even know what belongs to us, how could we possibly know what belongs to our belongings?

ALCIBIADES: We couldn't.

SOCRATES: Then it wasn't quite right to agree, as we did a few minutes ago,[31] that some people know what belongs to them without knowing themselves, while others know what belongs to their belongings. It seems that it's the job of one man, and one skill, to know all these things: himself, his belongings, and his belongings' belongings.

ALCIBIADES: That seems likely.

SOCRATES: And it follows that anyone who doesn't know his own belongings probably won't know other people's belongings either.

ALCIBIADES: Quite so.

SOCRATES: And if he doesn't know other people's belongings, nor will he know what belongs to the city.

ALCIBIADES: He couldn't.

SOCRATES: So such a man couldn't become a statesman.

ALCIBIADES: Of course not.

SOCRATES: Nor could he even manage a household estate.

ALCIBIADES: Of course not.

SOCRATES: Nor indeed will he know what he's doing.

ALCIBIADES: Certainly not.

SOCRATES: And if he doesn't know what he's doing, won't he make mistakes?

ALCIBIADES: Certainly.

SOCRATES: Since he makes mistakes, won't he conduct himself badly, both publicly and privately?

ALCIBIADES: Of course.

SOCRATES: Since he conducts himself badly, won't he be a failure?

ALCIBIADES: Absolutely.

SOCRATES: What about the people he's working for?

ALCIBIADES: They will be too.

SOCRATES: Then it's impossible for anyone to prosper unless he is self-controlled and good.

ALCIBIADES: Impossible.

SOCRATES: So it's the bad men who are failures.

ALCIBIADES: Absolutely.

SOCRATES: And so the way to avoid being a failure is not by getting rich, but by being self-controlled.

ALCIBIADES: Apparently.

e

134

b

31. At 131a–c.

SOCRATES: So it's not walls or war-ships or shipyards that cities need, Alcibiades, if they are to prosper, nor is it numbers or size, without virtue.

ALCIBIADES: Definitely.

SOCRATES: So if you are to manage the city's business properly and well,
c   you must impart virtue to the citizens.

ALCIBIADES: Of course.

SOCRATES: Is it possible to impart something you haven't got?

ALCIBIADES: How could you?

SOCRATES: Then you, or anyone else who is to be ruler and trustee, not only of himself and his private business, but also the city and the city's business, must first acquire virtue himself.

ALCIBIADES: You're right.

SOCRATES: So what you need to get for yourself and for the city isn't political power, nor the authority to do what you like; what you need is justice and self-control.

ALCIBIADES: Apparently.[32]

e   SOCRATES: Because my dear Alcibiades, when an individual or a city with no intelligence is at liberty to do what he or it wants, what do you think the likely result will be? For example, if he's sick and has the power
135 to do whatever he likes—without any medical insight but with such a dictator's power that nobody criticizes him—what's going to happen? Isn't it likely his health will be ruined?

ALCIBIADES: You're right.

SOCRATES: And in a ship, if someone were free to do what he liked, but was completely lacking in insight and skill in navigation, don't you see what would happen to him and his fellow sailors?

ALCIBIADES: I do indeed; they would all die.

---

32. Accepting a conjectural deletion of 134d1–e7 (which seem to have been added by a later neo-Platonist scholar). The lines read:

SOCRATES: And if you and the city act with justice and self-control, you and the city will be acting in a way that pleases God.

ALCIBIADES: That seems likely.

SOCRATES: And, as we were saying before, you will be acting with a view to what is divine and bright.

ALCIBIADES: Apparently.

SOCRATES: Of course, if you keep that in view, you will see and understand yourselves and your own good.

ALCIBIADES: Yes.

SOCRATES: And you will act properly and well.

ALCIBIADES: Yes.

SOCRATES: And if you act that way, I'm prepared to guarantee your prosperity.

ALCIBIADES: And I trust your guarantee.

SOCRATES: But if you act unjustly, with your eyes on what is dark and godless, as is likely, your conduct will also be dark and godless, because you don't know yourself.

ALCIBIADES: That's likely.

SOCRATES: Likewise, if a city, or any ruler or administrator, is lacking in   b
virtue, then bad conduct will result.

ALCIBIADES: It must.

SOCRATES: Well then, my good Alcibiades, if you are to prosper, it isn't
supreme power you need to get for yourself or the city, but virtue.

ALCIBIADES: You're right.

SOCRATES: But before one acquires virtue it's better to be ruled by somebody superior than to rule; this applies to men as well as to boys.

ALCIBIADES: So it seems.

SOCRATES: And isn't what is better also more admirable?

ALCIBIADES: Yes.

SOCRATES: And isn't what is more admirable more appropriate?

ALCIBIADES: Of course.   c

SOCRATES: So it's appropriate for a bad man to be a slave, since it's better.

ALCIBIADES: Yes.

SOCRATES: And vice is appropriate for a slave.

ALCIBIADES: Apparently.

SOCRATES: And virtue is appropriate for a free man.

ALCIBIADES: Yes.

SOCRATES: Well, my friend, shouldn't we avoid whatever is appropriate
for slaves?

ALCIBIADES: Yes, as much as possible, Socrates.

SOCRATES: Can you see what condition you're now in? Is it appropriate
for a free man or not?

ALCIBIADES: I think I see only too clearly.

SOCRATES: Then do you know how to escape from your present state?—
let's not call a handsome young man by *that* name.

ALCIBIADES: I do.   d

SOCRATES: How?

ALCIBIADES: It's up to you, Socrates.

SOCRATES: That's not well said, Alcibiades.

ALCIBIADES: Well, what should I say?

SOCRATES: That it's up to God.

ALCIBIADES: Then that's what I say. And furthermore I say this as well:
we're probably going to change roles, Socrates. I'll be playing yours and
you'll be playing mine, for from this day forward I will never fail to attend
on you, and you will always have me as your attendant.

SOCRATES: Then my love for you, my excellent friend, will be just like a   e
stork: after hatching a winged love in you, it will be cared for by it in return.

ALCIBIADES: Yes, that's right. I'll start to cultivate justice in myself
right now.

SOCRATES: I should like to believe that you will persevere, but I'm afraid—
not because I distrust your nature, but because I know how powerful the
city is—I'm afraid it might get the better of both me and you.

SECOND ALCIBIADES

Alcibiades, full of ambition, encounters Socrates, who engages him in conversation and makes him realize how little he understands of what he needs to understand; at the end Alcibiades is humiliated and begs Socrates to be his teacher and lover. To this schematic extent Second Alcibiades *tells the same story as the* Alcibiades *also preserved in the Platonic corpus. Certain other parallels suggest that the author of* Second Alcibiades *adapted* Alcibiades: *141a–b ≈ 105a–c; 145b–c ≈ 107d–108a. But perhaps the similarities between the two dialogues are to be explained by their common derivation from the celebrated* Alcibiades *of Aeschines of Sphettus, or from one of the other dialogues called* Alcibiades. *We cannot determine this question, because Aeschines' dialogue survives only in fragments, and the* Alcibiades *dialogues of Euclides and Antisthenes, other students of Socrates and writers of Socratic dialogues, are lost.*

In most respects Socrates in Second Alcibiades *is a figure familiar from other Socratic literature. He uses analogies taken from humble occupations; he argues that sometimes ignorance is better than knowledge; he argues that the only truly valuable knowledge is the knowledge of the good, an authoritative knowledge that will correctly advise us when to use the other goods and skills in our possession; he believes that the gods hold the virtues of the soul in higher regard than expensive gifts and sacrifices. Most important is the main theme of the dialogue: Socrates argues that it would be better not to pray for anything in particular, so fallible is our human knowledge of what is good for us; best would be to follow the example of the Spartans, who simply pray to the gods for what is good and what is noble. This coheres well with what is known of Socrates' view of prayer (cf. Xenophon's* Memoirs of Socrates *I.iii.2).*

But the author of Second Alcibiades *seems also to be writing against a different branch of the Socratic legacy, Cynicism. The Cynics regarded all ignorance as madness, whereas Socrates in* Second Alcibiades *takes care to distinguish madmen from people with lesser forms of ignorance. The latter he calls fools and asses, or (euphemistically) innocent, naive, simple, or even bighearted* (megalopsychos). *Why does the author use this word? Megalopsychia, the ability to rise above and be unaffected by the events in life that are normally thought to be bad—pain, poverty, bad treatment by other people, and so on—was a cardinal virtue for the Cynics. But here Socrates applies the term to people who stupidly don't know or care about what's good for them (140c, 150c). This curious negative connotation of megalopsychia—not found elsewhere in ancient Greek—is another sign that* Second Alcibiades *is arguing against the Cynics.*

The author of Second Alcibiades *had a notable predilection (shared with Plato, but with few of the other authors in the Platonic corpus) to quote and adapt Greek poetry. Certain features of his language tell us that he came from Northern Greece and suggest that he wrote in the third century B.C., but the evidence is not strong and the dialogue might well date from the end of the fourth century B.C.*

D.S.H.

SOCRATES: Alcibiades, are you on your way to say your prayers? 138

ALCIBIADES: Yes, indeed, Socrates.

SOCRATES: You have a depressed and downcast look; you seem preoccupied.

ALCIBIADES: And what might preoccupy me, Socrates?

SOCRATES: The most serious of all questions, in my view. Tell me, in b
God's name, what you think. In public and private prayer we make requests to the gods: don't they sometimes grant some of them and not all of them, and don't they say yes to some people and no to others?

ALCIBIADES: Indeed they do.

SOCRATES: So don't you agree that there is a great need for caution, for fear you might, all unawares, be praying for great evils when you think you are asking for great goods? Suppose the gods were in a mood to give whatever was asked; it might be just like the case of Oedipus who blurted out the prayer that his sons might take arms to settle their inheritance.[1] c
He could have prayed for relief from the ills which beset him without begging for others in addition! But in fact, what he asked for came to pass, with many terrible consequences which there is no need to enumerate.

ALCIBIADES: But you're talking about a madman, Socrates: do you think any person of sound mind would have dared to make such a prayer?

SOCRATES: Do you take madness to be the opposite of wisdom?

ALCIBIADES: Yes, indeed.

SOCRATES: Do you think there are some people who are wise and some d
who are stupid?

ALCIBIADES: So it seems.

SOCRATES: Well, then, let's see which are which. We have agreed that there are some people who are stupid, some who are wise, and others who are mad.

ALCIBIADES: Agreed.

Translated by Anthony Kenny.

1. Socrates refers to *The Thebans* (frg. 2 Davies), an epic poem in the style of Homer about the travails of unfortunate King Oedipus of Thebes and his family. Oedipus' prayer was granted—and his sons killed one another.

SOCRATES: Are there some people who are healthy?

ALCIBIADES: Yes.

SOCRATES: And others who are sick?

139   ALCIBIADES: Indeed.

SOCRATES: Not the same people?

ALCIBIADES: Of course not.

SOCRATES: Are there any other people who are neither one thing nor the other?

ALCIBIADES: No.

SOCRATES: Because a person has to be either sick or not sick?

ALCIBIADES: That's what I think.

SOCRATES: Well now, do you have the same view about wisdom and stupidity?

ALCIBIADES: How do you mean?

SOCRATES: Do you think it is only possible either to be wise or stupid,
b   or is there also a third state in between in which a person is neither wise nor stupid?

ALCIBIADES: No, there isn't.

SOCRATES: So you have to be one or the other?

ALCIBIADES: So I believe.

SOCRATES: Now do you remember that you agreed that madness is the opposite of wisdom?

ALCIBIADES: Yes, I did.

SOCRATES: And that there is no third state in which a person is neither wise nor stupid?

ALCIBIADES: Yes.

SOCRATES: And can one thing have two distinct opposites?

ALCIBIADES: No.

c   SOCRATES: So it looks as if stupidity and madness are one and the same thing.

ALCIBIADES: It does.

SOCRATES: So would it be correct to say that all stupid people are mad—not just any of your contemporaries who are stupid, as some of them certainly are, but even older people? Tell me, in God's name, don't you think that in our city the wise are in a minority, and most people are stupid, or, as you would say, mad?

ALCIBIADES: I do.

d   SOCRATES: But do you think we could live comfortably in a city of so many madmen? Would we not have met our fate long ago, and been punched and beaten and subjected to every madman's trick? Things aren't quite like that, are they?

ALCIBIADES: No, not at all; it looks as if I've not got the matter quite right.

SOCRATES: I don't think so either. Try looking at it another way.

ALCIBIADES: What way do you mean?

SOCRATES: I'll tell you. We take it that some people are sick, don't we?

ALCIBIADES: Yes, indeed.

SOCRATES: Do you think that anyone who is sick must necessarily have   e
gout, or fever, or eye ache? Or can a person be sick in some other way
without having any of these? Surely there are many other diseases besides these?

ALCIBIADES: Surely.

SOCRATES: Eye ache is always a sickness, don't you think?

ALCIBIADES: Yes.

SOCRATES: But is sickness always eye ache?

ALCIBIADES: No; but I'm not sure what to say.

SOCRATES: But if you pay attention to me, we may find out; for two heads   140
are better than one.

ALCIBIADES: I am paying attention, Socrates, as well as I can.

SOCRATES: Well, we have agreed that while eye ache is always a sickness,
not every sickness is eye ache, have we not?

ALCIBIADES: Yes, we have.

SOCRATES: And rightly. Anyone with a fever is sick, but not everyone
who is sick has a fever—nor gout, I take it, nor eye ache. Each of these is   b
a disease, but they present quite different symptoms, to use the doctors'
term. They are not all alike, and they do not have like effects; each of them
works according to its own nature, but they are all none the less diseases.
Similarly, we classify some people as workmen, don't we?

ALCIBIADES: Of course.

SOCRATES: There are shoemakers, and carpenters, and sculptors, and very
many others whom we needn't enumerate. They all have their own share
of work, and they are all workmen; but they are not all carpenters or   c
shoemakers or sculptors even though they are all workmen.

ALCIBIADES: No.

SOCRATES: Well now, in the same way people have shared out stupidity
among themselves; those who have the largest share we call madmen,
those with a smaller share we call fools or asses. People who prefer euphe-
misms call them big-hearted or simple, or perhaps innocent, naive, or   d
dumb: you will come across many other names if you look for them. But
all these things are stupidity, and differ from each other in the way one
kind of work and one kind of disease differs from another. Isn't that right?

ALCIBIADES: Absolutely.

SOCRATES: Let's go back, then. At the beginning of our discussion we set
out to discover which people were wise and which were stupid, because
we had agreed that some were one and some were the other.

ALCIBIADES: We had indeed.

SOCRATES: Is it your view that the wise are those who know what should   e
be done and said?

ALCIBIADES: Yes.

SOCRATES: And who are the stupid? Those who know neither of these
things?

ALCIBIADES: Just so.

SOCRATES: And those who know neither of these things will say and do what they ought not, without knowing that this is what they are saying and doing?

ALCIBIADES: So it seems.

141 SOCRATES: And just such a person—I said—was Oedipus. And in our own time you will find many such people—not in a rage as he was—who pray for things that are bad for them in the belief that they are good for them. He did not think so, or pray so; but there are others who are in a very different case. Suppose that the god to whom you are about to pray were to appear to you and ask you, before you began praying, whether you would be happy to be sole ruler of the city of Athens—or, if that

b seemed mean and tiny, were to offer you all the Greeks as well—or, if he saw that you regarded that too as insignificant unless the whole of Europe were included, were to promise you all of that plus simultaneous acknowledgment by the whole human race of the rule of Alcibiades son of Clinias. If that happened, I imagine, you would go home very happy and think you had come into possession of the greatest of goods.

ALCIBIADES: So would anyone else, I imagine, Socrates, if he were given the same promise.

c SOCRATES: But you would not give your own life in exchange for the territory and sole rule of all the Greeks and all the barbarians?

ALCIBIADES: I should think not, since they would be no use to me.

SOCRATES: But suppose you were going to use them, but were going to make a bad and harmful use of them? Would you want them then?

ALCIBIADES: No.

SOCRATES: So you see, it is not safe to accept without thinking what one

d is given, nor to pray for something which is going to injure one or take away one's life altogether. We could name many people who set their hearts on obtaining sole rulership, and strove to achieve this goal as a great good, and then had their lives taken by plotters against their rule. I think you are not unaware of the events of the last few days: Archelaus of Macedon was in love with a man whose love for Archelaus' kingship was greater than Archelaus' love for him, and who killed his lover in order

e to make himself a king and a happy man. He had only ruled for three or four days when he in his turn fell victim to a plot and was killed himself.

Among our own citizens too—as we know not just by hearsay, but as

142 eye-witnesses—we see some who have longed to command armies, and having got what they wanted are now exiled from the city or have lost their lives altogether. And even those who seem to have done best have lived amidst dangers and fears; not only during their campaigns, but when they have returned home where they have been besieged by informers as tightly as they were by the enemy, so that some of them wished to heaven

b that they had stayed privates rather than generals. Of course, it would make some sense if these dangers and burdens brought any benefit; but in fact it's quite the contrary.

You will find the same in the matter of children: some people pray to have them, and when they have them they bring them utter disaster and grief. Some people's children are so thoroughly bad that they make their whole life a misery; other people have good children and lose them in some calamity and end up no less miserable than the others, wishing they had never had children at all.

However, in spite of all these and similar dire examples, you rarely find anyone who declines a gift or who refrains from praying for what he hopes to be granted. Most people, if given the chance to become a ruler or a general, or any of the other things which bring more harm than good, will not hesitate to take the opportunity; and they will even pray for such things before they are on offer. After a while, however, they change their tune and pray away their former prayers.

I wonder, then, if humans are not wrong in "placing the blame" for their ills on the gods, when "they themselves by their own presumption"— or stupidity, should we say?—"have brought sorrows on themselves beyond their destined lot."[2] There was a poet who composed a prayer for all his friends to say in common, more or less like this:

> King Zeus, whether we pray or not, give us what is good for us
> What is bad for us, give us not, however hard we pray for it.[3]

He certainly seems to have been a wise man: I expect he had stupid friends whom he had seen working and praying for things that it was better for them not to have, no matter what they thought. That is what he recommended, and in my view he spoke well and soundly; but if you have anything against what he said, speak up.

ALCIBIADES: It is hard, Socrates, to speak against what has been well spoken. One thing I do observe is that the cause of very many human evils is ignorance: it is ignorance which deceives us into doing and—what is worse—praying for the greatest evils. No one, however, thinks thus about himself; each of us thinks himself quite capable of praying not for the worst but for the best. For such a prayer would really seem to be more like a curse than a prayer!

SOCRATES: Well said! But perhaps someone even wiser than you and I might say that we were wrong to blame ignorance in such general terms; we should specify what it is ignorance *of*. Indeed, just as ignorance is an evil to some people, there are other people, in certain states, to whom it is a good.

ALCIBIADES: How do you mean? Can there be anything of which it is better for people to have ignorance than knowledge, no matter what state they are in?

2. Socrates adapts *Odyssey* i.32–34.
3. An epigram in the *Palatine Anthology*, X.108, modified.

SOCRATES: I think there can; don't you?

ALCIBIADES: No, I don't; not on your life.

SOCRATES: But surely I am not to judge that you would ever want to
d commit against your mother crimes like those of Orestes and Alcmaeon[4]
and anyone else like them?

ALCIBIADES: Spare me, for God's sake, Socrates!

SOCRATES: It isn't the person who says that you would not ever want to
behave like that whom you should ask to spare you, but rather anyone
who contradicted him; for the act seems to you so horrendous that you
do not like to hear it spoken of even by way of example. But do you think
that Orestes, if he had been of sound mind and known what was best for
him to do, would have dared to commit any such crime?

ALCIBIADES: No, I don't.

e SOCRATES: Nor, I think, would anyone else.

ALCIBIADES: Certainly not.

SOCRATES: It seems then that it is ignorance of the best, failing to know
what is best, that is a bad thing.

ALCIBIADES: So it seems.

SOCRATES: And not only for the person himself, but also for everyone else?

ALCIBIADES: I agree.

SOCRATES: Let's consider a further point. Suppose the thought sprang
into your mind that it would be an excellent thing to kill your friend and
mentor Pericles,[5] and you took a dagger and went to his door and asked
144 if he were at home, with the intention of killing him and him alone, and
they said he was at home. I don't mean to say that you would wish to do
any such thing; but just suppose that you were to think that the worst
thing was the best thing—that's a thought that might at any time occur
to someone who is ignorant of what is really best—or don't you think so?

ALCIBIADES: Absolutely.

b SOCRATES: Well then, if you went inside and saw Pericles, but did not
recognize him and thought he was someone else, would you still go on
to kill him?

ALCIBIADES: I should think not, in God's name.

SOCRATES: For your intention surely was to kill not just anyone you came
across, but only that particular person. Isn't that right?

ALCIBIADES: Yes.

SOCRATES: And if, having tried several times, you always failed, when
it came to the point, to recognize Pericles, you would never lay a hand
on him.

ALCIBIADES: Certainly not.

---

4. According to legend, they murdered their mothers to avenge the deaths of their fathers.

5. Alcibiades' father died early and left his two sons in the care of Pericles, the most influential Athenian politician of the mid-fifth century.

SOCRATES: Well then, do you think that Orestes would ever have laid a hand on his mother if he had failed to recognize her?

ALCIBIADES: I don't think so.

c

SOCRATES: For presumably he too had no intention of killing the first woman he came across, or killing just anyone's mother, but only his own.

ALCIBIADES: That's right.

SOCRATES: Then for those in that state, with such intentions, these are things which it is better not to know.

ALCIBIADES: Very likely.

SOCRATES: So you see that there are some things which, for certain people in certain states, it is better not to know than to know.

ALCIBIADES: So it seems.

SOCRATES: Now if you care to look at what follows from this, you may find that you're in for a surprise.

d

ALCIBIADES: What surprise, Socrates?

SOCRATES: I mean that, in general, it seems that if someone lacks knowledge of what is best, the possession of other skills will only rarely help, but in most cases will harm, their possessor. Consider it this way. When we are about to say or do something, mustn't we first of all know, or at least believe we know, what we are so keen to say and do?

e

ALCIBIADES: I believe so.

SOCRATES: Orators, for instance, are bound to know, or at least to think they know, how to give us advice on various topics—whether it is about war and peace, or about the construction of walls or the equipment of harbors. Altogether, whatever a state does in foreign or domestic matters is done on the advice of the orators.

145

ALCIBIADES: As you say.

SOCRATES: See then what follows.

ALCIBIADES: If I can.

SOCRATES: You call some people wise and others stupid?

ALCIBIADES: I do.

SOCRATES: And you call most people stupid, and a few wise?

ALCIBIADES: Exactly.

SOCRATES: In each case you make use of a criterion?

ALCIBIADES: Yes.

SOCRATES: Well, do you call a man wise who knows how to give advice, but not what advice is best to give or when it is best to give it?

b

ALCIBIADES: Certainly not.

SOCRATES: Nor, I imagine, a man who knows how to make war, without knowing when or for how long war should best be made? Isn't that right?

ALCIBIADES: Yes.

SOCRATES: Nor again a man who knows how to kill or steal or banish people without knowing when it is better to do this, or to whom?

ALCIBIADES: No.

c   SOCRATES: So what we want is the person who knows one or other of
these things but also has the knowledge of what is best—which no doubt
is the same as knowledge of utility.

ALCIBIADES: Yes.

SOCRATES: And this is the person whom we shall call wise, a reliable
counsellor for himself and for the state. But someone who is not like this
we shall call the opposite. What do you think?

ALCIBIADES: I agree.

SOCRATES: Now suppose we have a person who knows how to ride or
d   shoot, or box, or wrestle, or compete in any other sport or exhibit any
other skill. What do you call the person who knows how best to exercise
a particular skill? If it is the skill of riding, I expect you will call him a
good rider.

ALCIBIADES: I will.

SOCRATES: And if it is boxing, you will call him a good boxer, and if it
is flute-playing you will call him a good flute-player, and so in other cases.
Or do you disagree?

ALCIBIADES: No, not at all.

SOCRATES: Now do you think that knowing about these things suffices
e   to make a person wise, or is more needed?

ALCIBIADES: Much more, upon my life.

SOCRATES: Suppose there were a state in which there were good archers
and flute-players, good athletes and craftsmen, and among them the kind
of people we have been talking about, who know only how to make war
and only how to kill, and also fine orators who know how to sound off
about politics, but none of them had the knowledge of what is best, and
146   none of them knew when or on whom it was better for them to exercise
their skills—what sort of state do you think that would be?

ALCIBIADES: A miserable one, Socrates.

SOCRATES: I'm sure you would if you saw them all competing with each
other for honors, "each one assigning precedence in political matters to
his own sphere of excellence"[6]—I mean, what is best according to the
scope of his own skill—while he may be much mistaken about what is
best for the state and for himself, since he has not used his intelligence
b   but put his trust in mere seeming. If that's the situation, wouldn't we be
right to describe such a state as a hotbed of dissension and lawlessness?

ALCIBIADES: Indeed we would.

SOCRATES: Did we not think that if you are on the point of saying or
doing something, you must first know, or at least think you know what
you are doing or saying?

ALCIBIADES: We did.

SOCRATES: So if someone does what he knows, or thinks he knows, and
c   has in addition knowledge of utility, we will judge him a boon both to
the state and to himself?

6. Socrates adapts some lines from Euripides' *Antiope* (frg. 183 Nauck²).

ALCIBIADES: Absolutely.

SOCRATES: But if he does the contrary, he will be no good to the state or to himself?

ALCIBIADES: No good.

SOCRATES: Well, then: are you still of the same mind, or have you changed it?

ALCIBIADES: Still the same.

SOCRATES: You said that you called most people stupid, and only a few wise?

ALCIBIADES: I did.

SOCRATES: So, to repeat, most people have been mistaken about what is best because they have not used their intelligence but put their trust in mere seeming.

ALCIBIADES: Yes.   d

SOCRATES: For most people, then, it is an advantage neither to know nor to think they know anything, if they are going to do themselves more harm than good by rushing to do what they know or think they know.

ALCIBIADES: Very true.

SOCRATES: So you see it seems that I was quite right when I said that it looked as if other skills, if not combined with the knowledge of what is   e best, are more often than not harmful to their possessors.

ALCIBIADES: I may not have thought so then, but I do now, Socrates.

SOCRATES: So if the life of a soul or a state is to go aright, this knowledge of what is best must be embraced with exactly the kind of trust a patient has in his doctor or a seafarer in his good ship's captain. For without this, the stronger the winds of fortune blow towards the acquisition of wealth   147 or health and strength or anything else of that kind, the greater the errors to which these things will necessarily lead. Someone may have acquired so many skills as to deserve the name of polymath, but if he lets himself be led by one or other of these skills and lacks this true knowledge he will, as he indeed deserves, run into very rough weather, "alone on the   b high seas with no helmsman and with not long to live." There is a verse which fits his case, where the poet complains of someone that "he knew a lot of things but knew them all wrong."[7]

ALCIBIADES: Whatever has that verse got to do with the matter, Socrates? It does not seem at all to the point.

SOCRATES: It is very much to the point; but you are right that he speaks enigmatically, just like a poet. All poetry, by its nature, is enigmatic, and not everyone can take it in; but when, in addition, it is housed in a poet   c who is miserly and wishes so far as possible to conceal rather than exhibit his wisdom, it may be quite remarkably difficult to find out what each of them might mean. For you don't think that Homer, the divinest and wisest of poets—for it is he who says that Margites knew a lot of things but knew   d

---

7. Socrates quotes from the mock epic *Margites* (frg. 3 Allen), which was generally (but incorrectly) attributed to Homer in the ancient world.

them all wrong—didn't know that it was impossible to know a thing wrong. He is riddling, I think; he meant "wrong" as an adjective, not as an adverb; and he meant "to know" rather than "knew." So, if we forget about the original meter we can put together his meaning as this: he knew a lot of things, but it was wrong for him to know them all. Clearly, if it was wrong for him to know a lot of things, he must have been a bad man, if we are to trust our previous arguments.

e   ALCIBIADES: I agree Socrates; if we cannot trust these arguments I really don't know which ones we can trust.

SOCRATES: You are right to think so.

ALCIBIADES: But perhaps I should think again.

SOCRATES: Oh, for God's sake! You see what a terrible great muddle we are in, and it is partly your fault; for you change incessantly from side to side. No sooner are you convinced of something than you give it up again

148   and change your mind. Well, if the god to whom you are on your way should appear to you at this very moment, before you start praying, and ask whether you would be happy to get one of the things we spoke of earlier, or whether he should leave the choice of prayer to you, which do you think offers the best prospect: accepting his offers or making your own prayer?

ALCIBIADES: By the gods, Socrates, I would have to take time to answer

b   your question; an impromptu response would be folly. You really have to take a great deal of care to make sure that you are not, all unawares, praying for evil in the belief that it is good, and that after a little while you won't, as you said a moment ago, change your tune and call back all your prayers.

SOCRATES: That poet I mentioned at the beginning of our discussion, who told us to pray to be saved from the evils we pray for—he was wiser than us, wasn't he?

ALCIBIADES: I guess so.

SOCRATES: Whether in admiration of this poet, or because they have

c   worked it out for themselves, the Spartans take the same course in their public and private prayers. They pray the gods to give them first what is good and then what is noble; no one ever hears them asking anything more. They have not, so far, been any less fortunate in consequence than any other people; and even if they have not invariably enjoyed good

d   fortune it has not been because of their prayers. Whether we are given what we pray for or the reverse is in the lap of the gods.

I would like to tell you another story which I once heard from some of my elders. There was a quarrel between the Athenians and the Spartans, and whenever there was a battle, whether by land or sea, our city always came off worse and could never win a victory. The Athenians took this

e   hard, and cast about to discover how they could find relief from their troubles. After discussion they decided to send a delegation to consult Ammon,[8] to ask in particular why the gods granted victory to the Spartans

---

8. An Egyptian god with an oracle in the Libyan desert.

rather than themselves. "We" they said "offer more and finer sacrifices than the rest of the Greeks, and we surpass all others in adorning the temples with emblems, and every year we organize for the gods' benefit the most solemn and sumptuous processions, spending more money than all the other Greeks put together. But the Spartans have never taken any such pains, and they are so mean to the gods that they regularly sacrifice blemished animals and fall well behind us in the quality of their worship, in spite of being no less wealthy than ourselves." Having said that, they also asked what they should do to be relieved from the evils that beset them. The prophet, no doubt under divine instruction, called them to him and said simply this. "Thus saith Ammon to the Athenians: I prefer the terse Laconic utterance to all the sacrifices of the Greeks." That was all he said; not a word more. By their "terse utterance" I expect the god meant their prayer, for it is indeed very different from other prayers. Other Greeks offer bulls with gilded horns, and others present the gods with votive emblems, and pray for whatever comes into their heads, good or bad. But when the gods hear their profanities they scorn these magnificent processions and sacrifices. We should, I believe, be very careful and cautious when we consider what should be said and what should not.

In Homer you will find other similar stories. He tells how the Trojans, when they pitched camp, "sacrificed to the immortals perfect hecatombs" and how

> The winds carried the delicious smell from the plain up to heaven.
> But the blessed gods took none of it, and had no pleasure in it;
> So deep was their hatred of holy Ilium, and Priam,
> And the people of Priam of the ashen spear.[9]

So it was no help to them to sacrifice and offer vain gifts, when they were out of favor with the gods. For I don't imagine that it is like the gods to be swayed by gifts, like some low moneylender; we make ourselves sound very silly when we boast that we do better than the Spartans on this score.

It would be a strange and sorry thing if the gods took more account of our gifts and sacrifices than of our souls and whether there is holiness and justice to be found in them. Yes, that is what they care about, I believe, far more than about these extravagant processions and sacrifices offered year by year by states and individuals who may, for all we know, have sinned greatly against gods and men. The gods are not venal, and scorn all these things, as Ammon and his prophet told us. Gods and men of sound mind are more likely to hold justice and wisdom in especial honor; and none are wise and just but those who know how to behave and speak to gods and men. But now I would like to hear what your opinion may be about all this.

9. Cf. *Iliad* viii.548–52.

ALCIBIADES: No different from yours and the god's, Socrates; it would hardly be fitting for me to take sides against the god.

SOCRATES: But you remember that you said you were very worried that

c without knowing it you might pray for evil, thinking it to be good?

ALCIBIADES: I do.

SOCRATES: You see, then, how dangerous it is for you to go to pray to the god, in case he hears you speaking amiss, rejects your sacrifice altogether, and perhaps adds some further penalty. I think you would do best to hold your peace; for I expect you are rather too big-hearted (to use the

d favorite euphemism for stupidity) to be willing to use the Laconian prayer. It takes time to learn how to behave towards gods and men.

ALCIBIADES: How long will it take, Socrates, and who will teach me? I would very much like to see the man who could do it.

SOCRATES: It is the man who has his eye on you. But you remember how

e Homer says that Athena took away the fog from the eyes of Diomedes, "so that he could clearly see both god and man."[10] You too need to get rid of the fog which is wrapped around your soul, so as to prepare you to receive the means of telling good from evil. At present I don't think you could do so.

ALCIBIADES: Let him remove the fog, or whatever else it is; I am prepared to do whatever he tells me, whoever he may be, so long as it will make me better.

151 SOCRATES: He too is more than anxious to help.

ALCIBIADES: Then I think it is better to put off the sacrifice for the time being.

SOCRATES: You're quite right; it is much safer than running such a big risk.

ALCIBIADES: Here's an idea, Socrates; I'll put this garland on *your* head,

b for giving me such good advice. Only when there comes the day of which you have spoken will we give the gods their garlands and their customary dues. God willing, that day will not be too far off.

SOCRATES: I am glad to accept, and I look forward to seeing myself receiving other gifts from you. In Euripides' play, when Creon sees Tiresias crowned with garlands and learns that he has been given them by the enemy as trophies to reward his skill, he says

> Good as an omen are your victor's wreaths
> For we, you know, are battered by the waves.[11]

c Just so, I regard the honor you have paid me as a good omen. For I am just as tempest-tossed as Creon, and I look forward to victory over your lovers.

---

10. Cf. *Iliad* v.127–28.
11. *Phoenician Women* 858–59.

HIPPARCHUS

Socrates and a friend try to find a definition of greed. The friend feels that he understands the concept perfectly well: isn't greed an inclination to profit from things which a gentleman shouldn't exploit, things of no value? Socrates replies that insofar as greed is an intention to profit from worthless things, it's a foolish intention, and no sensible man is greedy; but insofar as it's a desire for profit, it's a desire for the good, and everyone is greedy. The latter conclusion is especially hard to accept, but the friend cannot get the better of Socrates and accuses him of deceiving him somehow in the argument. Socrates protests that deceiving a friend would be contrary to the teaching of Hipparchus, a ruler of Athens in the late sixth century B.C. who was keen to learn from the poets and bestow his wisdom upon the Athenian people. Although Socrates offers to take back any disputable premise of the argument, the friend cannot escape the dialogue's paradoxical conclusion that everyone is greedy.

Plato called the irrational part of the soul 'greedy' (Republic 581a, 586d). The sketch of the greedy man in the Characters of Theophrastus (§30) is vivid and witty; Theophrastus knew well what he was talking about. So when the speakers in Hipparchus seem unable to avoid the idea that everyone, even a good person, is greedy, many readers will agree with Socrates' friend that he has been tricked somehow. This is the other main theme of the dialogue: intellectual honesty and fair play in the conduct of dialectical discussion. Socrates tells an implausibly revisionist history of Hipparchus, whom he represents as wise and cultivated, whereas his regime was generally regarded by Athenians of later generations as tyranny, and his assassins Harmodius and Aristogiton were celebrated as national heroes. Socrates protests that he would never disobey Hipparchus' wise injunction and deceive a friend. To no avail: right to the end of the dialogue the friend is unpersuaded by Socrates' arguments, though he cannot say what is wrong with them, just as many modern readers of Socratic dialogues feel that the wool has somehow been pulled over their eyes. But has it?

From the formal point of view, Hipparchus is composed of dry Academic dialectic together with a literary-historical excursus on Hipparchus. The classic example of such an excursus is the Atlantis myth in Plato's Timaeus and Critias, and there are other examples in Alcibiades, Second Alcibiades, Minos, and probably in the (now mostly lost) Socratic dialogues of Antisthenes and Aeschines. The academic dialectic of Hipparchus is a good example of the way questions were discussed in the mid-fourth-century Academy, the dialectic studied in Aristotle's Topics and Sophistical Refutations. The combination of

609

dialectic and excursus is similar to that in Minos, *as is the scepticism toward the values implicit in Athenian popular culture and history; many scholars conclude that they are the work of the same author, probably writing soon after the middle of the fourth century* B.C.

D.S.H.

225   SOCRATES: What is greed? What can it be, and who are greedy people?

FRIEND: In my opinion, they're the ones who think it's a good idea to profit from things of no value.

SOCRATES: Do you think they know these things are of no value, or do they not know? For if they don't know, you mean that greedy people are stupid.

FRIEND: No, I don't mean they're stupid. What I mean is this: they're

b   unscrupulous and wicked people who are overcome by profit, knowing that the things from which they dare to profit are of no value; yet their shamelessness makes them dare to be greedy.

SOCRATES: So, then, do you mean that the greedy person is, for example, like a farmer who plants, knowing his plant is of no value, and thinks it's a good idea to profit from the plant when fully grown? Is this the sort of person you mean?

FRIEND: The greedy person, at any rate, Socrates, thinks he ought to profit from everything.

SOCRATES: Don't let me make you give in like that, as if you had somehow

c   been tricked by something; pay attention and answer as if I were asking again from the beginning. Don't you agree that the greedy person knows about the value of the thing from which he thinks it is a good idea to profit?

FRIEND: I do.

SOCRATES: So who knows about the value of plants, in what seasons and soils it's a good idea to plant them—if we may throw in one of those clever phrases with which legal experts beautify their speeches?[1]

d   FRIEND: The farmer, I think.

SOCRATES: By "thinking it's a good idea to profit" do you mean anything but thinking one ought to profit?

FRIEND: That's what I mean.

226   SOCRATES: Well then, don't try to deceive me—I'm already an old man and you're so very young—by answering as you did just now, saying what you yourself don't think; tell the truth. Do you think there is any man who takes up farming, and expects to profit from planting crops that he knows to be of no value?

FRIEND: By Zeus, I don't!

Translated by Nicholas D. Smith.

1. The Greek words for "seasons and soils" rhyme.

SOCRATES: Well then, do you think that a horseman who knowingly gives his horse food that is of no value is unaware that he is harming his horse?

FRIEND: I don't.

SOCRATES: So *he* doesn't expect to profit from food that is of no value.   b

FRIEND: No.

SOCRATES: Well then, do you think that a ship's captain who has rigged his ship with sails and rudders that are of no value is unaware that he will suffer loss, and risks being lost himself and losing the ship and all it carries?

FRIEND: No, I don't.

SOCRATES: So *he* doesn't expect to profit from equipment that is of no   c value.

FRIEND: Not at all.

SOCRATES: Or does a general who knows that his army has arms that are of no value expect to profit, or think it's a good idea to profit from them?

FRIEND: Certainly not.

SOCRATES: Or does a flute-player who has flutes that are of no value, or a lyre-player with a lyre, or an archer with a bow, or, in short, does any other craftsman, or any other sensible man who has worthless tools, or any other sort of equipment, expect to profit from them?

FRIEND: Obviously not.   d

SOCRATES: Then who *do* you say the greedy people are? For surely the ones just mentioned are not the ones who expect to profit from what they know has no value.[2] But in that case, my wonderful friend, there aren't any greedy people at all, according to what you say.

FRIEND: What I mean, Socrates, is this: greedy people are those whose greed gives them an insatiable desire to profit even from things that are actually quite petty, and of little or no value.   e

SOCRATES: Not, of course, knowing that they are of no value, my very good friend; for we have just proved to ourselves in our argument that this is impossible.

FRIEND: I believe so.

SOCRATES: And if they don't know this, plainly they're ignorant of it, thinking instead that the things of no value are very valuable.

FRIEND: Apparently.

SOCRATES: Now, of course, greedy people love to make a profit.

FRIEND: Yes.

SOCRATES: And by profit, you mean the opposite of loss?

FRIEND: I do.   227

SOCRATES: Is there anyone for whom it is a good thing to suffer loss?

FRIEND: No one.

SOCRATES: It's a bad thing?

FRIEND: Yes.

SOCRATES: So people are harmed by loss?

2. Omitting *all'* in d4.

FRIEND: Yes, harmed.

SOCRATES: So loss is bad?

FRIEND: Yes.

SOCRATES: And profit is the opposite of loss?

FRIEND: Yes, the opposite.

SOCRATES: So profit is good?

FRIEND: Yes.

SOCRATES: So it is those who love the good whom you call greedy.

FRIEND: So it seems.

b   SOCRATES: Well, my friend, at least you don't call greedy people lunatics. But you yourself, do you or don't you love what's good?

FRIEND: I do.

SOCRATES: Is there something good that you don't love? Or something bad that you do?

FRIEND: By Zeus, no!

SOCRATES: So presumably you love all good things?

FRIEND: Yes.

SOCRATES: And you can ask me, too, if I'm not the same; for I will also agree with you that I love good things. But besides you and me, don't

c   you believe that all other people love what's good and hate what's bad?

FRIEND: So it appears to me.

SOCRATES: And we agreed that profit is good?

FRIEND: Yes.

SOCRATES: Well, then, in this way of looking at it, everyone appears to be greedy; whereas, according to what we said earlier, no one was greedy. So which of these approaches would it be safe to rely on?

FRIEND: I think, Socrates, we have to get the right conception of the greedy person. The right conception is that the greedy person is the one

d   who is concerned with and thinks it's a good idea to profit from things which virtuous people would never dare to profit from.

SOCRATES: But you see, my dear sweet fellow, that we have already agreed that to profit is to be benefited.

FRIEND: Well, what of it?

SOCRATES: We also agreed that everyone always wants good things.

FRIEND: Yes.

SOCRATES: Therefore, even good people want every kind of profit, at least if they're good.

e   FRIEND: But not profits from which they're going to suffer harm, Socrates.

SOCRATES: By "suffer harm," do you mean "suffer loss," or something else?

FRIEND: No; I mean "suffer loss."

SOCRATES: Do people suffer loss from profit, or from loss?

FRIEND: From both; for they suffer loss from loss and from wicked profit.

SOCRATES: Well, do you believe that anything virtuous and good is wicked?

FRIEND: I don't.

SOCRATES: And we agreed a little while ago that profit is the opposite   228
of loss, which is bad?

FRIEND: I would say so.

SOCRATES: And being the opposite of bad, it's good?

FRIEND: We agreed to that.

SOCRATES: So you see, you're trying to deceive me, deliberately saying
the opposite of what we just agreed to.

FRIEND: No, by Zeus, Socrates! Quite the opposite: it's you who's deceiving me, and turning me upside down in these arguments—I don't know
how you do it!

SOCRATES: Be careful what you say; it wouldn't be right for me not to   b
obey a good and wise man.

FRIEND: Who is that? What are you talking about?

SOCRATES: I mean my and your fellow citizen: Pisistratus' son, Hipparchus, of Philaedae, who was the eldest and wisest of Pisistratus' children. In addition to the many other fine deeds in which he displayed his
wisdom, it was he who first brought the works of Homer to this land, and
compelled the rhapsodes at the Panathenaea to recite them in relays—one
following another—as they still do now. He also sent a fifty-oared ship   c
for Anacreon of Teos, and brought him to the city. He also entreated
Simonides of Ceos always to be around, with large fees and gifts.[3] He did
these things with a view to educating the citizens, so that he could govern
the best possible people; like the gentleman he was, he didn't think it right
to begrudge wisdom to anyone.

And when the citizens from the city had been educated by him and
were impressed by his wisdom, he decided to educate the country-people,
as well, setting up Herms[4] for them along the roads between the middle   d
of the city and each deme.[5] And then, selecting from his store of wisdom—
both what he had learned and what he had found out by himself—what
he thought were the wisest he put into elegiac verse and inscribed them
(his own poetry and examples of his wisdom) on the Herms. He did this
in order that, first, his citizens would not be impressed by those wise
Delphic inscriptions, "Know Thyself," and "Nothing in Excess," and other   e
things of this sort, but would instead regard the words of Hipparchus as
wiser. And, second, he did this so that when they travelled back and forth
they would read and acquire a taste for his wisdom and would come in
from the country to complete their education. There are two sides to the
inscriptions: on the left side of each Herm, it is inscribed that the Herm   229
stands in the middle of the city or the deme, whereas on the right it says:
"This is a monument of Hipparchus: walk with justice in mind." There

---

3. Anacreon and Simonides were lyric poets of the sixth and early fifth centuries.

4. Herms were statues with full heads of Hermes, the god of travellers, on rectangular
pillars, often placed along roadways.

5. The local districts into which Attica was divided.

are many other fine inscriptions of his poetry on other Herms. There is one
in particular—on the Stiria road—on which it says: "This is a monument of

b Hipparchus: do not deceive a friend." So, since I am your friend, I would
never dare to deceive you and disobey so great a man.

After his death the Athenians were ruled under tyranny by his brother,
Hippias, for three years, and you would have heard from all of those of
earlier days that there was tyranny in Athens only for those three years,
and that during the other times the Athenians lived almost as when Cronus
was King.[6] In fact, the more sophisticated people claim that his death did

c not come about in the way that the common people think—that it was
because his sister was dishonored in the carrying of the basket,[7] for that's
silly—but because Harmodius had become the boyfriend of Aristogiton
and was educated by him. Aristogiton also prided himself on educating
this fellow, and regarded himself as a rival of Hipparchus. At that time,

d Harmodius himself happened to be a lover of one of the handsome and
noble youths of that era. (They say what his name was, but I don't remember
it.) In any case, this youth was for a while impresssed by Harmodius and
Aristogiton as wise men, but later—after associating with Hipparchus—
he disdained them, and they were so hurt by this dishonor that they killed
Hipparchus for it.

FRIEND: Well now, Socrates, it seems likely that either you don't regard
me as your friend, or if you do, you don't obey Hipparchus. For you

e will never be able to persuade me that you aren't deceiving me in these
arguments, though I don't know how you do it.

SOCRATES: Very well, just like in a friendly game of checkers, I'm willing
to let you take back anything you want of what's been said in the discussion,
so you won't think you're being deceived. So should I take this back for
you, that all men desire good things?

FRIEND: No, not that.

SOCRATES: Well, how about that suffering loss, or loss, is bad?

FRIEND: No, not that.

SOCRATES: Well, how about that profit and profiting are opposite to loss
and suffering loss?

230   FRIEND: Not that, either.

SOCRATES: Well, how about that profiting, as the opposite of bad, is good?

FRIEND: It's not always good; take that back for me.

SOCRATES: So you believe, it seems, that some profit is good, and some
is bad.

FRIEND: I do.

SOCRATES: All right, I'll take this back for you; let's say that some profit
is good and some other profit is bad. And neither one is more profit, the
good or the bad. Right?

---

6. A mythical golden age when Cronus, the father of Zeus, ruled.

7. A ritual in the Panathenaic procession.

FRIEND: What are you asking me?

SOCRATES: I'll explain. Is some food good and some bad?

FRIEND: Yes.   b

SOCRATES: Then is one of them more food than the other, or are they both the same thing, food, and in this respect, at least, the one is no different from the other in so far as being food, but only in so far as one is good, and one is bad?

FRIEND: Yes.

SOCRATES: And so with drink and everything else; when some things of the same sort come to be good and others bad, the one does not differ from the other in that respect by which they are the same? For example with people, I suppose: one is virtuous, and one is wicked.   c

FRIEND: Yes.

SOCRATES: But neither of them is more or less a person than the other, I think—neither the virtuous person more than the wicked, nor vice versa.

FRIEND: That's true.

SOCRATES: Then are we to think this way about profit, too, that both the wicked and the virtuous sort alike are profit?

FRIEND: They have to be.

SOCRATES: So, then, one who makes virtuous profit doesn't profit more than one who makes the wicked sort—it appears that neither one is more   d profit than the other, as we agree.

FRIEND: Yes.

SOCRATES: For neither "more" nor "less" is added to either of them.

FRIEND: Not at all.

SOCRATES: And how could one ever do or suffer anything more or less with this sort of thing, to which neither of these things is added?

FRIEND: Impossible.

SOCRATES: Therefore, because both alike are profits and profitable, we must now investigate what it is in virtue of which you call both of them profit—what do you see that's the same in both of them? For example, if   e you were to ask me, about the examples I just gave, "what is it, in virtue of which you call both good and bad food alike, 'food'," I would tell you that both are solid nourishment for the body—this is why. For surely you would agree that this is what food is, wouldn't you?

FRIEND: I would.

SOCRATES: And with regard to drink, the answer would be the same, that the liquid nourishment of the body, whether virtuous or wicked, has this name: "drink," and similarly in other cases. Try, therefore, to imitate   231 me by answering in this way. When you say that virtuous profit and wicked profit are both profit, what do you see in both that's the same— that which is actually profit? If you yourself are again unable to answer, consider what I say: do you call a profit every possession that one has acquired either by spending nothing, or by spending less and receiving more?

FRIEND: Yes, I believe I'd call that profit.   b

SOCRATES: Do you mean cases like this—when you are given a feast, spending nothing but eating your fill, and getting sick?

FRIEND: By Zeus, I do not!

SOCRATES: If you became healthy from the feast, would you be profiting or losing?

FRIEND: Profiting.

SOCRATES: So this, at least, is not profit: acquiring just any possession at all.

FRIEND: Certainly not.

SOCRATES: Not if it's bad, right? But if one acquires anything good at all, doesn't one acquire a profit?

FRIEND: Apparently, if it's good.

c   SOCRATES: And if it's bad, won't one suffer a loss?

FRIEND: I believe so.

SOCRATES: Don't you see that you are coming around back again to the same place? Profit appears to be good, and loss bad.

FRIEND: I'm at a loss for what to say.

SOCRATES: At least you're not at an unfair loss. But answer this: when one acquires more than one has spent, do you say it's profit?

FRIEND: At least I don't mean when it's bad, but if one acquires more gold or silver than one has spent.

SOCRATES: I'm just about to ask you that: if someone spends half a measure
d   of gold and gets double that in silver, has he profited or lost?

FRIEND: Lost, surely, Socrates, for then his gold is worth only double, instead of twelve times as much as silver.

SOCRATES: But still he's acquired more; or isn't double more than half?

FRIEND: Not in value, at least, with silver and gold.

SOCRATES: So it looks like we must add the notion of *value* to profit. At least, now you say that silver, though there is more of it than gold, is not as valuable, and that gold, although there's less, is of equal value.

e   FRIEND: Of course, for that is indeed the case.

SOCRATES: Value, then, is what brings profit, whether it's small or large, and what has no value brings no profit.

FRIEND: Yes.

SOCRATES: And by "value," do you mean anything other than "valuable to possess"?

FRIEND: Yes, "valuable to possess."

SOCRATES: Moreover, by "valuable to possess," do you mean the unbeneficial or the beneficial?

FRIEND: The beneficial, surely.

SOCRATES: Well, isn't the beneficial good?

FRIEND: Yes.

232   SOCRATES: And so, my valiant warrior, haven't we once again, for the third or fourth time, come to the agreement that what's profitable is good?

FRIEND: So it seems.

SOCRATES: Do you remember the point from which this discussion of ours arose?

FRIEND: I think so.

SOCRATES: If not, I'll remind you. You disagreed with me, claiming that good people do not want to make just any sort of profit, but only those that are good ones, and not the wicked ones.

FRIEND: Yes indeed.

SOCRATES: And doesn't the argument now force us to agree that all gains, small and large, are good?

FRIEND: It forces me, Socrates, rather than persuades me.

SOCRATES: Well, perhaps later it will also persuade you. But for now, whatever condition you're in—persuaded or not—you do at least agree with us that all profits are good, both small and large.

FRIEND: I do agree.

SOCRATES: And do you agree that all virtuous people want all good things, or not?

FRIEND: I agree.

SOCRATES: Well now, you yourself said that wicked people love profits, both small and large.

FRIEND: I did.

SOCRATES: So according to your argument, all people would be greedy, both the virtuous and the wicked.

FRIEND: Apparently.

SOCRATES: So, therefore, it is not a correct reproach, if someone reproaches another as being greedy—for it turns out that he who makes this reproach is greedy himself.

RIVAL LOVERS

Socrates encounters a young man who is keen to learn something about every-thing and who sneers at his rival, a young man whose strength is not knowl-edge but athletic discipline. The young polymath supposes that in pursuing universal general knowledge he is pursuing philosophy. Socrates rejects this conception of philosophy. Since no generalist can master a number of subjects to the same standard as a specialist can master his speciality, no one with gen-eral knowledge can ever excel in any field, but must be like the pentathlete who may win overall but be only a runner-up in each individual competition. No generalist can therefore ever claim any right to authority, not even over mere workmen—as the true philosopher must. For Socrates, philosophy is essentially a discipline of authority—the authority to evaluate, improve, and discipline one-self and others, an authority based on justice, good sense, and self-knowledge.

The dialogue's charming setting and amusing touches invite comparison with Plato's Charmides, *where the Socratic ideal of self-control and good sense through self-knowledge is shown to involve subtleties that need exploring in a deeper philosophical investigation. Elsewhere Plato argued that the (very few) people who are capable of intelligent self-control and authority over others should enjoy a highly focused and disciplined education (Republic 521c–535a; Laws 965a–968a); the wide learning favored by the young polymath of* Rival Lovers *is rejected (Laws 817e–819a). The author of* Rival Lovers *also agrees with Plato in recognizing only one kind of authority, whether practiced by poli-tician, king, head of household, or master of slaves (Statesman 258a–259d).*

Standing on the other side of these issues was Aristotle, a student of Plato who embraced a research project to search for the general principles of every branch of knowledge, including those of humble workmen (Parts of Animals 639a1–12; Metaphysics 982a8–983a10). Aristotle held (especially in his lost dialogue On Justice*) that there are many kinds of authority and justice, which differ according to the context in which they are exercised (Politics 1278b30–79a21; Eudemian Ethics 1231b27–40; Nicomachean Ethics 1160b22–61a9). "Those who think it is the same thing to be able to be a politician, a king, a head of a household, or a master of slaves, are mistaken" (Politics 1252a7–9).*

There was probably a lively debate along these lines within the Academy while Aristotle was still a member, and Rival Lovers *might have been a contri-bution to that debate in the years before Plato's death in 347 B.C. Or else it might be a diatribe aimed by one of his former Academic colleagues against Ar-istotle's way of thinking, written after he began teaching in the Lyceum in Ath-ens, in which case it dates from the last third of the fourth century. It was*

618

probably someone familiar with Rival Lovers *who gave the nicknames "Pent-athlete" and "Runner-up" to Eratosthenes of Cyrene, an accomplished scholar and polymath who studied philosophy in Athens in the early third century* B.C.

A note on the title: in an ancient list of the works of Plato, the title is Rival Lovers *(and the word for 'rival lover' introduces the young polymath at 132c), but the manuscripts carry the title* Lovers, *as do many editions and transla-tions.*

D.S.H.

I walked into the school of Dionysius the grammarian and saw there 132 some extremely attractive young men of good family; their lovers were there too. Two of the boys happened to be arguing about something, but I couldn't quite make out what it was. They appeared, however, to be arguing about Anaxagoras or Oenopides; in any event, they appeared to b be drawing circles and holding their hands at angles to depict certain astronomical inclinations, and they were very serious about it.[1] And I— I'd sat down next to the lover of one of them—I nudged him with my elbow and asked him what it could be that the boys were arguing about so seriously and said, "It must be something important and admirable for them to be putting such serious effort into it."

"What?!" he said. "Important and admirable? Those guys are just bab-bling about things up in the sky and talking philosophical nonsense."

Astonished at his reply, I asked him, "Young man, does the pursuit of c philosophy seem to you to be contemptible? Why do you speak of it so harshly?"

And the other one—a rival lover of the boy, you see, happened to be sitting next to him—the other one heard my question and his reply and said, "You're wasting your time, Socrates, asking *him* whether he thinks philosophy is a contemptible pursuit. Don't you realize that he's spent his whole life wrestling, stuffing himself and sleeping? How could you expect him to give any answer *other* than that philosophy is contemptible?"

Of the two lovers, this one spent all his time pursuing the liberal studies,[2] d while the other, the one he'd just insulted, spent all his time on athletics. And it seemed to me that I ought to leave off questioning the one I'd just asked—as he didn't claim to be any good with words, but only with deeds—and instead direct my questions to the one who claimed to be the wiser, on the chance that I might somehow be able to benefit from him.

Translated by Jeffrey Mitscherling. In preparing this translation we have consulted, in addition to Burnet's edition, that of Antonio Carlini, *Platone: Alcibiade, Alcibiade Secondo, Ipparco, Rivali* (Turin, 1964).

1. Anaxagoras of Clazomenae, the fifth century B.C. philosopher of nature, is reported to have worked on problems of geometry; Oenopides of Chios, a younger contemporary, was a mathematical astronomer.

2. The activities over which the Muses presided, especially music, poetry, literature, and philosophy.

So then I said, "My question was addressed to everybody, and if you think you can give a better answer, then I'll ask you the same thing: do you think the pursuit of philosophy is admirable, or not?"

133   At about this point in our conversation, the two boys overheard us and fell silent, and, putting aside their argument, came over to listen to us. Now, I don't know what their lovers were feeling, but I was struck senseless—as always happens to me when I'm around beautiful young men. It did seem to me, however, that the other lover was struggling no less than I was. And yet he did manage to answer me, and in a very self-important manner.

b   "Socrates," he said, "if I ever came to regard philosophy as contemptible, I would no longer consider myself a human being, nor anybody else who felt that way!" As he said this he gestured toward his rival and raised his voice so that his young favorite would be sure to get the message.

"So," I said, "you think philosophy is an admirable pursuit."

"Certainly," he said.

"Well then," I said, "do you think it's possible for someone to know whether a thing is admirable or contemptible unless he first knows what it is?"

"No," he said.

c   "So you know what philosophy is," I went on.

"Certainly," he said.

"What is it, then?" I asked.

"What else but what Solon says it is? He says somewhere, 'I continue to learn many things as I grow old.'[3] And I agree with him that someone who wants to pursue philosophy, whether young or old, should always be learning one thing or another in order to learn as many things as possible in life."

Now at first I thought there was something to this, but after I thought it over a bit I asked him if he thought philosophy consisted in learning many things.

d   "Precisely that," he said.

"And do you believe," I went on, "that philosophy is only admirable, or that it's also good?"

"It's also good," he said, "of course it is."

"Do you regard this property as something peculiar to philosophy, or do you think it belongs to other things as well? For example, do you believe athletics to be not only admirable but also good, or don't you?"

e   Very sarcastically, he gave me two answers: "To *him* I would say that it is neither. But with you, Socrates, I agree that it is both admirable and good, for I believe this to be correct."

Then I asked him, "And do you think athletics consists in doing lots of exercise?"

---

3. This verse (frg. 18 Edmonds, *Elegy and Iambus*, Loeb, vol. I) is also quoted at *Laches* 189a5 and alluded to at *Republic* 536d.

"Indeed," he said, "just as I think philosophy consists in learning many things."

And then I said, "Do you think that athletes desire anything other than what will bring about their good physical condition?"

"Just that," he said.

"And is it true," I went on, "that it's by doing lots of exercise that one gets into good physical condition?"

"Obviously," he said, "for how could anyone get into good physical condition by doing only a little exercise?"

It seemed to me appropriate at this point to get the athlete going, so that he might offer me some assistance drawn from his experience in athletics. So I asked him, "How can you sit there so quietly, my friend, with this man saying these things? Does it seem to you too that people get into good physical condition by exercising a lot, or by exercising moderately?"

"As far as I'm concerned, Socrates," he said, "I thought even a pig would know, as they say, that it's moderate exercise that produces good physical condition, so why shouldn't a man who doesn't sleep or eat know this, somebody who's out of shape and scrawny from sitting around meditating?" The boys were amused by what he said, and they snickered, while the other lover blushed.

And I said, "Well then, do *you* now grant that it's neither lots of exercise nor a little, but a moderate amount, that produces good physical condition? Or do you want to fight out the argument against the two of us?"

Then he said, "With *him* I would very happily fight it out, and I'm sure that I would be able to support the claim I made, even if my position were far weaker than it is—for he's no competition. But there's no need to compete with you about my opinion. I agree that it's not lots of athletics but a moderate amount that produces good physical condition in people."

"And what about food?" I said. "A moderate amount or a lot?"

He agreed about food as well.

And then I also made him agree that with everything else concerning the body the moderate is the most beneficial, neither a large nor a small amount; and he agreed with me about that.

"And what about the soul?" I said. "Does it benefit most from having moderate or immoderate amounts of things administered to it?"

"Moderate amounts," he said.

"And isn't learning something that's administered to the soul?"

He agreed.

"And so a moderate amount of learning is beneficial, but not a great deal of learning?"

He agreed.

"Now suppose we wanted to ask which exercises and which foods are moderate for the body; who would be the right man to ask?"

All three of us agreed that it would be either a doctor or an athletic trainer.

"And who would we ask about the moderate amount of seed to sow?"

134

b

c

d

e

The farmer, is what we agreed this time.

"And what about sowing and planting the seeds of learning in the soul? Suppose we wanted to ask which ones and how many were moderate; who would be the right man to ask?"

135 At this point we all found ourselves completely at a loss. So I asked them, in fun, "Since we're all at a loss, would you like it if we asked these boys here? Or perhaps we're ashamed to do that, like the suitors in Homer, who didn't expect anybody else to be able to string the bow?"[4]

At this point they seemed to me to be losing enthusiasm for the argument, so I tried a different approach, and I said, "What would you guess are the main sorts of subjects that a philosopher needs to learn, since he doesn't need to learn them all, or even a lot of them?"

b The wiser one now took up the question and said, "The most admirable and proper sorts of learning are those from which one derives the most fame as a philosopher, and one acquires the most fame by appearing to be an expert in all the skills, or if not in all of them, in most of the really important ones, learning as much of them as is proper for a free man— that is, their theory, not their actual practice."

c "Do you mean," I said, "something like in the building trade? You can buy a workman for five or six minas, but a master architect will cost you thousands of drachmas, and indeed there are few of them in all of Greece. Do you perhaps mean something like that?" He agreed that what I said was something like what he meant.

Then I asked him if it wasn't impossible to learn even two of the skills so thoroughly, let alone several important ones.

"You mustn't think I'm saying, Socrates," he replied, "that the philoso-
d pher needs to understand each skill as thoroughly as the man who makes it his profession. He needs to understand it only as far as is reasonable for a free and educated man, so that he can follow the explanations offered by the tradesman better than everyone else present, and can add his own opinion; that way, he always appears to be the most accomplished and the wisest of those present whenever the skills are discussed or practiced."

e But since I still wasn't sure what he meant, I asked him, "Am I understanding what sort of man you suppose the philosopher to be? It seems to me that you mean someone like the pentathlon athletes who compete against runners or wrestlers. They lose to the latter in their respective sports and are runners-up behind them, but they place first among the other athletes and defeat them. Perhaps you're suggesting something along
136 those lines, that philosophy produces this result in those who devote themselves to it. In knowledge of the skills, they rank behind those who place first, but as runners-up they remain superior to the rest; and so a man who has studied philosophy becomes a strong competitor in all subjects. You seem to be describing someone like that."

4. Cf. *Odyssey* xxi.285 ff.: Penelope's suitors, ashamed at having proven unable to string Odysseus' bow, are reluctant to permit Odysseus (disguised as a beggar) to attempt it.

"You appear to me, Socrates," he said, "to have just the right conception of the philosopher, when you compare him with the pentathlete. He is just the sort of man not to be enslaved to any one thing, nor to have worked anything out in such detail that, by concentrating on only that one thing, as do the tradesmen, he is left behind in all the others, but has touched on everything to a moderate extent."

b

After he'd offered this answer, I was eager to know exactly what he meant, so I asked him whether he supposed that good people were useful or useless.

"Useful, surely, Socrates," he said.

"So, if good people are useful, then bad people are useless?"

He agreed.

"Well then, do you think that philosophers are useful men, or not?"

He agreed that they were useful, and he added that he held them to be extremely useful.

c

"Let's see, then. Supposing what you're saying is true, when are these people, these runners-up, of any use to us? For it's obvious that the philosopher is inferior to each of the skilled professionals."

He agreed.

"And what about you?" I went on. "If it happened that you, or one of your friends about whom you cared a great deal, were to become sick, and you were looking for a cure, would you call that runner-up, the philosopher,[5] to your house, or would you call the doctor?"

"I'd call both," he said.

d

"No, don't tell me you'd call both of them; tell me which you'd rather call first."

"No one would have any doubt," he said, "about calling the doctor first."

"Well then, on a ship in stormy weather, to whom would you rather entrust you and your possessions, the pilot or the philosopher?"

"I would prefer the pilot."

"And isn't it the same in every other case, that as long as there's a tradesman, the philosopher is of no use?"

"So it appears," he said.

e

"Then isn't the philosopher actually useless to us? For surely we always have tradesmen. We agreed, however, that good men are useful, and bad men useless."

He was forced to agree.

"So what follows? Should I question you further, or would that be rude?"

"Ask whatever you like."

"All I'm trying to do," I said, "is sum up what's been said. It was something like this: we agreed that philosophy is admirable,[6] that philosophers are good, that good men are useful, and that bad men are useless;

137

5. Reading *ton philosophon* at c10.
6. Accepting a conjectural deletion of *kai autoi philosophoi einai* at a2.

on the other hand, we agreed that philosophers are of no use whenever there are tradesmen, and that tradesmen are always to be found. Isn't that what we agreed?"

"It is indeed," he said.

b   "We agreed then, it seems, at least according to *your* argument, that if philosophy consists, as you suggest, in knowledge of skills, then philosophers are bad and useless, as long as there are men with skills.

"But no, my friend, philosophers are *not* like that, and philosophy does *not* consist in stooping to a concern with skills nor in learning many things,[7] but in something quite different—in fact, I thought that was actually dishonorable, and that people who pursued the skills were called vulgar. But we'll be able to see more clearly whether what I say is true if you will

c   answer this: who understands how to discipline horses properly, those who make them better[8] horses, or someone else?"

"Those who make them better."

"And as it is with horses, so it is with every other animal?"

"That's correct."[9]

"Well then, aren't those who know how to make dogs better also those who know how to discipline them properly?"

"Yes."

"Then it's the same skill which both makes better and properly disciplines?"

"That's how it seems to me," he said.

"Well then, is the skill that makes them better and properly disciplines them the same as that which distinguishes between the good ones and the bad ones, or is it a different skill?"

"It's the same," he said.

d   "And are you prepared to agree to this point concerning people, that the skill which makes them better is the same as that which disciplines them and that which distinguishes between the good ones and the bad?"

"Certainly," he said.

"And a skill that can do this with one can also do it with many, and vice versa?"

"Yes."

"Now what kind of knowledge is it that properly disciplines the undisciplined and lawless people in cities? Is it not knowledge of the law?"

"Yes."

"Now is what you call justice the same as this or is it different?"

"No, it's the same."

e   "Isn't the knowledge used in disciplining people properly the same as that used in knowing the good ones from the bad?"

7. Accepting a conjectural deletion of *espoudakenai, oude polupragmonounta* at b3.

8. Reading *beltious* rather than *beltistous* at c1, c2, c3, c6, c9, and d1.

9. Moving this and the preceding line (137d8-9), so as to make them follow c2 (a conjectural transposition).

"It's the same."

"And whoever has such knowledge with regard to one person will also have it with regard to many?"

"Yes."

"And whoever is ignorant with regard to many is also ignorant with regard to one?"

"That's correct."

"So if one were a horse and didn't know good horses from bad horses, then one also wouldn't know what sort of horse one was oneself?"

"That's right."

"And if one were an ox and didn't know bad oxen from good ones, then one also wouldn't know what sort of ox one was?"

"Yes," he said.

"Likewise if one were a dog?"

He agreed.

"Well then, if a human being didn't know good human beings from   138
bad ones, wouldn't he fail to know whether he himself was good or bad, since he is in fact a human being?"

He conceded that.

"And not knowing yourself, is that being sensible, or is it not being sensible?"

"Not being sensible."

"Then knowing yourself is being sensible?"

"It is," he said.

"So it is this, it seems, which is prescribed in the Delphic inscription, to exercise good sense and justice."

"It would seem so."

"And this is how we understand how to discipline properly?"

"Yes."

"So the way we understand how to discipline properly is justice, and   b
the way we evaluate ourselves and others is good sense."

"It would seem so," he said.

"So justice and good sense are one and the same."

"Apparently."

"And isn't it also the case that cities are well governed when the unjust are punished?"

"That's true," he said.

"And this is political skill."

He agreed.

"Well then, when one man properly governs a city, isn't he called a tyrant or a king?"

"He is."

"And isn't it by means of kingly or tyrannical skill that he governs?"

"That's right."

"These skills, then, are the same as the previous ones?"

"So they seem."

c   "Well then, when one man governs a household properly, what's the name for him? Isn't it 'head of the household', and 'master of slaves'?"

        "Yes."

        "And isn't it also by means of justice that he governs his household well, or is it through some other skill?"

        "It's through justice."

        "So they are all the same, it seems: king, tyrant, politician, head of the household, master of slaves, sensible man, and just man. And they are all one skill: kingly, tyrannical, political, managerial and household skills, and justice and good sense."

d   "So it seems," he said.

        "Now if it is contemptible for the philosopher to be unable to follow what the doctor says when he talks about sick people or to add any opinion of his own regarding what's being said or done, and to be in the same situation whenever any other tradesman does or says something—when it's a judge speaking or a king or any of those others we've just been talking about—wouldn't it be contemptible for him to be able neither to follow what is said nor to add his own opinion?"

        "How could it not be contemptible, Socrates, for him to be incapable of contributing an opinion concerning such matters?"

e   "So," I said, "are we to say that he needs to be a pentathlete and a runner-up in these areas as well?[10] To begin with, surely he shouldn't hand over control of his own household to anybody else or take second place in it, but should himself administer justice and discipline, if his household is to be well governed?"

        He conceded this point to me.

        "And furthermore, if his friends entrust him with the settling of some

139   dispute, or if the city commissions him to investigate or pass judgment on something, wouldn't it surely be contemptible in these cases, my friend, for him to appear second or third and not to take the lead?"

        "I think it would."

        "So for us to say, my friend, that philosophy consists in learning many things and busying oneself with skills, would be very far from the truth."

        When I said this, the wise fellow was ashamed at what he'd said before and fell silent, while the unlearned one said that I was right; and the others approved of what I'd said.

---

10. Accepting a conjectural deletion of *kai tautēs . . . toutōn tis ēi* (e2–4).

THEAGES

Theages tells the story of the first encounter between Socrates and the young Theages, who hoped to fulfill his political ambitions by learning whatever Socrates had to teach him. We also hear about Theages in Plato's Republic, *where we learn that his poor health (the 'bridle of Theages') frustrated his political ambitions, and in Plato's* Apology, *where we learn that he died before Socrates.* Theages *provides a vivid and distinctive account of what was unusual about Socrates: his divine inner voice and the magical effect he had on his students.*

*At unpredictable times Socrates would experience an inner premonition which he interpreted as a voice from the gods. In Plato this premonition always held him back from something he was about to do. In Xenophon we read of similar incidents (*Symposium viii.5, Apology 4 = Memoirs of Socrates IV.viii.5*), as well as cases where the voice warned him against what his companions were about to do (*Memoirs of Socrates I.i.4*). In* Theages *we are told of four cases in which the premonition was ignored, with disastrous consequences to others. In Plato's* Theaetetus *Socrates says that the voice prevents him from accepting back some of his students who had strayed (151b), but in* Theages *the spiritual power that speaks to him not only prohibits Socrates sometimes from taking new students, it also exerts itself for some of his students rather than others.* Theages *is under the impression that this divine power can be propitiated by prayer and sacrifice, an almost superstitious idea that has no parallel in any other surviving Socratic dialogue.*

In Plato's Symposium, *Socrates said that he was an expert in nothing except love (177e), and in* Theages *Socrates says something similar. In his (now mostly lost) dialogue* Alcibiades, *Aeschines has Socrates say, "Although I know no subject with which I might help a man by teaching it to him, still I thought that if I was with Alcibiades my loving him would make him better" (frg. 11c). Although he has nothing to teach his students, his affection and conversation make them improve. Unlike in other Socratic dialogues, the only improvement mentioned in* Theages *is intellectual and dialectical skill, not progress in moral virtue.*

But not all his students made permanent progress. Alcibiades reverted to his former dissolute ways when he stayed away from Socrates (Plato, Symposium *216b), and others, including young Aristides, reverted to being the incompetent fools they had been before Socrates began to improve their minds (*Theaetetus *150d–151a).* Theages *tells a remarkable version of the lapse of Aristides: now that Aristides has gone away from Socrates, the impressive skill in argument he formerly had has deserted him; better was to be in his presence; but*

627

best of all was to be right beside him, touching him, feeling his mysterious power flowing out of him. Plato argued against such a conception of Socrates' pedagogical gifts (Symposium 175c–e), whereas for the author of Theages *the magical effect of Socrates on his students was another aspect of the divine power that dwelled in him.*

The arguments against Plato being the author are circumstantial but convincing enough that there is virtual unanimity among modern scholars on the issue. In the decades after 350 B.C., several philosophers in Plato's Academy pursued an interest in the miraculous and the supernormal; the author of Theages *may have been among them.*

D.S.H.

121   DEMODOCUS: Oh, Socrates, I've been needing to have a talk with you in private, if you've got the time—even if you *are* busy—still, please make some time, for my sake.

SOCRATES: Well, it so happens that I do have some time, lots of time, in fact, if it's for *your* sake. If there's something you want to talk about, go ahead.

DEMODOCUS: Do you mind if we move back out of the way into the portico of Zeus the Liberator?

SOCRATES: If you like.

b   DEMODOCUS: Then let's go.

Socrates, all living things tend to follow the same course—particularly man, but also the other animals and the plants that grow in the earth. It's an easy thing, for us farmers, to prepare the ground for planting, and the planting is easy, too. But after the plants come up, there's a great deal of hard and difficult work in tending to them. It seems the same goes for

c   people, if others have the same problems I've had. I found the planting, or procreation—whatever you're supposed to call it—of this son of mine the easiest thing in the world. But his upbringing has been difficult, and I've always been anxious about him.

There are many things I could mention, but his current passion really scares me—not that it's beneath him, but it *is* dangerous. Here we have

d   him, Socrates, saying that he wants to become wise. What I think is that some other boys from his district who go into town have got him all worked up by telling him about certain discussions they've heard. He envies them and he's been pestering me for a long time—he's demanding that I take his ambition seriously, and pay money to some expert who'll make him wise. The money is actually the least of my concerns, but I think

122   what he's up to is very risky.

Translated by Nicholas D. Smith.

For a while I held him back with reassurances. But since I can't hold him back any longer, I think I'd better give in to him, so that he won't get corrupted, as he might by associating with someone behind my back. This is why I've come to town, to place this boy with one of those so-called experts. And then you appeared before us at just the right moment, and I'd be very glad to have your advice about what to do next. If you've got any advice to give based on what I've said, you're welcome to give it, please.   b

SOCRATES: Well, you know, Demodocus, they say that advice is a sacred thing, and if it's ever sacred, then it surely is in this case. There's nothing more divine for a man to take advice about than the education of himself and his family.

First, then, let's settle exactly what it is that you and I intend to discuss.   c
I might perhaps be taking it to be one thing, and you another, and then, after we'd discussed it a while, we'd both feel silly because I, the one giving advice, and you, the one taking advice, would be thinking about entirely different matters.

DEMODOCUS: I think you're right, Socrates—that's the way it should be done.

SOCRATES: I *am* right, but not completely—I have one little change to make. It occurs to me that this youngster may not really want what we think he wants, but something else. In that case our thinking would be even more absurd and irrelevant. So it seems best for us to start with the   d
boy himself, and ask what exactly it is that he wants.

DEMODOCUS: Well, it does seem that it would be best to do as you say.

SOCRATES: Then tell me, what's the fine name of the young man? How should we address him?

DEMODOCUS: Theages is his name, Socrates.

SOCRATES: It *is* a fine name you've given your son, Demodocus, and godly.[1] Tell us, then, Theages, do you say you want to become wise; are   e
you demanding that your father here arrange to have you associate with some man who'll make you wise?

THEAGES: Yes.

SOCRATES: Whom do you call wise—those who know (whatever they know about), or those who don't?

THEAGES: Those who know.

SOCRATES: Well, didn't your father have you taught and trained in what others of your age—the sons of gentlemen—are taught, such as reading and writing, and playing the lyre, and wrestling, and other sports?

THEAGES: Yes, he did.

SOCRATES: Yet you think that you're lacking some knowledge, which it's   123
appropriate for your father to provide you?

THEAGES: I do.

---

1. The name seems to mean either "guided by god" or "revered by god" or "revering god."

SOCRATES: What is it? Tell us, so we can oblige you.

THEAGES: *He* knows it, Socrates, because I've often told him. But in front of you he talks as if he didn't know what I want. In fact, he argues with me about these things, and other things, too,[2] and refuses to place me with anyone.

b   SOCRATES: But what you said before was said without witnesses, as it were. Now make me your witness, and state in my presence what this wisdom is that you want. Come on; if you desired that wisdom by which people steer ships, and I asked you: "Theages, what wisdom do you lack? Why do you criticize your father for refusing to place you with someone who could make you wise?" What would you answer me? What is it? Isn't it the helmsman's skill?

THEAGES: Yes.

c   SOCRATES: And if you criticized your father because you desired the wisdom by which people steer chariots, and again I asked what this wisdom is, what would you say it is? Isn't it the charioteer's skill?

THEAGES: Yes.

SOCRATES: And the object of your current desire; is it some nameless thing, or does it have a name?

THEAGES: I think it has.

SOCRATES: Then do you know it, but not the name, or do you know the name, as well?

THEAGES: I know the name, too.

SOCRATES: So what is it? Tell me!

d   THEAGES: What other name, Socrates, would anyone give it but wisdom?

SOCRATES: But isn't the charioteer's skill also a kind of wisdom? Or do you think it's ignorance?

THEAGES: I don't.

SOCRATES: So it's wisdom.

THEAGES: Yes.

SOCRATES: What do we use it for? Isn't it what we use in knowing how to direct a team of horses?

THEAGES: Yes.

SOCRATES: Isn't the helmsman's skill also a kind of wisdom?

THEAGES: I think it is.

SOCRATES: And isn't that the skill we use in knowing how to direct ships?

THEAGES: Yes, that's right.

SOCRATES: And the one that you desire, what sort of wisdom is that?
e   What would it give us the knowledge to direct?

THEAGES: People, I think.

SOCRATES: Sick people?

THEAGES: Of course not!

SOCRATES: That would be medicine, wouldn't it?

THEAGES: Yes.

2. Reading *eti kai hetera* in a7.

SOCRATES: Well is it what we use in knowing how to direct the singers in choruses?

THEAGES: No.

SOCRATES: That would be music?

THEAGES: Obviously.

SOCRATES: Well is it what we use in knowing how to direct athletes?

THEAGES: No.

SOCRATES: Because that's physical education?

THEAGES: Yes.

SOCRATES: Well then, to direct those who are doing what? Try your best to tell me, following the examples I've just given.

THEAGES: Those in the city, that's what *I* think.   124

SOCRATES: But aren't the sick people in the city, too?

THEAGES: Yes, but I don't mean just those people, but also everyone else in the city, too.

SOCRATES: Let's see if I understand the skill you're talking about. I don't think you're talking about the skill by which we know how to direct harvesters and pickers and planters and seeders and threshers, for it's the farmer's skill by which we direct these isn't it?

THEAGES: Yes.

SOCRATES: Nor, I suppose, do you mean the skill by which we know   b
how to direct sawyers and drillers and planers and turners, and so on, because that would be carpentry.

THEAGES: Yes.

SOCRATES: Perhaps it's the skill by which we know how to direct or rule over all of these—the farmers and the carpenters, and all the workers and ordinary people, both women and men. Is this, perhaps, the sort of wisdom you mean?

THEAGES: That's what I've been trying to say all along, Socrates.

SOCRATES: So, can you say whether Aegisthus, who killed Agamemnon   c
in Argos, ruled over those you mean—the workers and the ordinary people, both men and women, all together, or over other people?

THEAGES: No; just those.

SOCRATES: Really? Didn't Peleus (son of Aeacus) rule over the same sorts of people in Phthia?

THEAGES: Yes.

SOCRATES: And have you heard about how Periander (son of Cypselus) ruled in Corinth?

THEAGES: I have.

SOCRATES: Weren't these the people he ruled over in his city?

THEAGES: Yes.   d

SOCRATES: Well, then. Don't you think that Archelaus (son of Perdiccas), who recently ruled in Macedonia, ruled over the same sorts of people?

THEAGES: I do.

SOCRATES: And whom do you suppose did Hippias (son of Pisistratus) rule over when he ruled this city? Weren't they the same sort of people?

THEAGES: Of course.

SOCRATES: Tell me next, then, what name do Bakis, and Sibyl, and our own Amphilytus have?

THEAGES: "Oracle-givers," Socrates. What else?

e   SOCRATES: Right. Now try to answer me in the same way about these: what name do Hippias and Periander have, considering their style of ruling?

THEAGES: "Tyrants," I suppose. What else could we call them?

SOCRATES: When someone wants to rule over all the people in the city together, doesn't he want the same sort of rule as these people had— tyranny, and to be a tyrant?

THEAGES: Apparently.

SOCRATES: Isn't this what you claim to desire?

THEAGES: It seems so, from what I said.

SOCRATES: You rascal! So you want to be a tyrant over us, and that's
125   why you criticized your father all along for refusing to send you to some tyrant-teacher! And you, Demodocus, aren't you ashamed for having known all along what he wants, and though you knew where you could have sent him to make him skilled in the wisdom he wants, you begrudge it to him and refuse to send him! But look here; now that he has accused you right in front of me, don't you think you and I had better discuss this together? To whom should we send him? Whose company will make him a wise tyrant?

b   DEMODOCUS: Yes, by Zeus, Socrates, let's do it. It seems to me that this issue requires careful consideration.

SOCRATES: Not now, my good man; let's first finish our examination of him.

DEMODOCUS: Let's do that.

SOCRATES: Well now, what if we were to bring in Euripides, Theages? For Euripides somewhere says, "Wise company makes wise tyrants." So if someone were to ask Euripides, "Euripides, in *what* are these men wise, whose company, you say, makes tyrants wise? For example, if he said,
c   "Wise company makes wise farmers," and we asked: "Wise in *what*?," what would his answer be? Wouldn't it be: "in what's pertinent to farming"?

THEAGES: Right.

SOCRATES: And what if he said, "Wise company makes wise cooks?" If we asked "wise in *what*?," what would his answer be? Wouldn't it be: "in what's pertinent to cooking"?[3]

THEAGES: Yes.

SOCRATES: And what if "Wise company makes wise wrestlers" were what
d   he said? If we asked "Wise in *what*?," wouldn't he say, "in wrestling"?

THEAGES: Yes.

---

3. Accepting the emendation to *tōn ta mageirika* in c10.

SOCRATES: But since he said: "Wise company makes wise tyrants," we are asking, "What do you mean, Euripides, those who are wise in *what*?" What would he reply? What would he say it was this time?[4]

THEAGES: Well, by Zeus, I don't know!

SOCRATES: Well, do you want me to tell you?

THEAGES: If you want to.

SOCRATES: These are the kinds of things that Anacreon said that Callicrite knew. Or don't you know the song?

THEAGES: I do.

SOCRATES: Well, now, do you, too, desire to get together with some man who has the same skill as Callicrite (daughter of Cyane), and knows what   e
is pertinent to tyranny, as the poet said, so that you, too, may become a tyrant over us and the city?

THEAGES: All along, Socrates, you've been joking and playing games with me.

SOCRATES: Really? Don't you claim to desire that wisdom by which you might rule over all the citizens? If you did this, would you be anything other than a tyrant?

THEAGES: I would pray, no doubt, to become a tyrant, over all people if possible, but if not, over as many as possible. And so would you, I think,   126
and everyone else. Or perhaps even to become a god. But that's not what I said I wanted.

SOCRATES: Well, what is it you want, then? Didn't you claim to want to rule over the citizens?

THEAGES: But not by *violence*, the way tyrants do. I want to rule over those who voluntarily submit. This is the way other people—men of good repute in the city—rule over people.

SOCRATES: So you mean you want to rule over people in the way Themistocles and Pericles and Cimon did,[5] and whoever else was an outstanding politician.

THEAGES: Yes, by Zeus, *that's* what I mean!

SOCRATES: Well, then, what if you wanted to become wise in horsemanship? To whom do you suppose you'd have to go, in order to become an   b
outstanding horseman? To the horsemen, right?

THEAGES: Right, by Zeus!

SOCRATES: Moreover, you'd go to those who are themselves outstanding at these things, and who have horses and work with them all the time, both their own horses and many other people's, too?

THEAGES: Obviously.

SOCRATES: And what if you wanted to become wise in javelin-throwing? Don't you suppose that you'd become wise by going to the javelin-

---

4. Accepting an emendation to *poia au* in d6.
5. Three of the most famous leaders of democratic Athens.

c throwers, who have javelins, and work with them all the time, many of
   them, both others' and their own?[6]

   THEAGES: I think so.

   SOCRATES: Then tell me: since you want to become wise in politics, do
   you suppose that you'll become wise by going to anyone else than the
   politicians, the ones who are outstanding at politics, and work with their
   own city all the time, and many others, conducting business with both
   Greek and foreign cities? Or do you believe you'll become wise in what
   these men do by associating with other people and not with the politicians themselves?

d   THEAGES: I've heard, Socrates, about the arguments they say you offer,
   that the sons of the politicians are no better than the sons of the shoemakers.[7]
   And I believe that what you say is really true, from what I've been able
   to see. So I'd be foolish if I thought that one of these men would give his
   wisdom to me, but wouldn't be of any help to his own son, if indeed he
   could have been helpful to anyone else at all in these matters.

   SOCRATES: Well, then, my dear sir, how would *you* deal with it, if, when
   you came to have a son, he pestered you like this, and said that he wanted

e to become a good painter, and criticized you, his father, for refusing to
   spend money on him for this, and yet he didn't respect those who practiced
   this very thing, the painters, and refused to learn from them? Or the flute-
   players, if he wanted to become a flute-player, or the lyre-players? Would
   you know what to do with him and where else to send him, if he refused
   to learn from them?

   THEAGES: By Zeus, I wouldn't.

127   SOCRATES: So now, when you yourself are acting like this with your
   father, how can you be surprised and criticize him if he's at a loss as to
   what to do with you and where to send you? And yet we'll place you
   with any of the gentlemen in politics you want, of the Athenians at least,
   who'll associate with you without charge. You won't waste any money,
   and you'll also gain a much better reputation among the general public
   than if you associate with someone else.

   THEAGES: Well, then, Socrates—aren't *you* one of these gentlemen? If
   you'll agree to associate with me, that satisfies me, and I won't look for
   anyone else.

b SOCRATES: What do you mean by that, Theages?

   DEMODOCUS: Oh, Socrates, that's not a bad idea at all! And you would
   oblige me as well; for there's nothing I'd consider a greater stroke of luck
   than if he were content to associate with you and you agreed to associate
   with him. Indeed, I'm even ashamed to say how much I want it! I beg
   you both: you—to agree to associate with this boy, and you—not to seek

c to associate with anyone other than Socrates. You'll thereby relieve me of

---

6. Accepting the conjectural deletion of *akontiois* in c1.

7. Cf. *Alcibiades* 118d–119a; *Meno* 93a–94e; *Protagoras* 319e–320b.

a great load of worry. As it is now, I'm very afraid that he might fall in with some other person who'll corrupt him.

THEAGES: Don't worry any more about me now, father, if you're able to persuade him to accept me!

DEMODOCUS: Excellent! Socrates, what I have to say from here on is now *your* business: to be brief, I'm prepared to make available to you both myself and what I own, as freely as I can, pretty well whatever you might need—if you'll welcome Theages here and be of whatever service you can.

SOCRATES: Demodocus, I'm not surprised at your seriousness, if you think that I could really help this boy of yours—for I don't know what a sensible person should be more serious about than that his own son become the best he can be. But I *do* wonder where you got the idea that I would be better able than you yourself to help your son become a good citizen— and how he imagined that I'd help him more than you could. In the first place, you're older than I am, and moreover you've served in many of the highest offices for the Athenians, and are held in the highest esteem by those of the Anagyrus district, as well as by the rest of the city. You don't see this in my case.

Moreover, if Theages here refuses to associate with the politicians and seeks some other men, who claim to be able to educate young people, there are a number of such men here: Prodicus of Ceos, and Gorgias of Leontini, and Polus of Acragas, and many others, who are so wise that they go from city to city and persuade the most aristocratic and wealthiest of the young men—who can associate with any of the citizens they want without charge—these men persuade them to desert the others and associate only with them instead, to pay a great deal of money up front,[8] and, on top of that, to be grateful! It would be reasonable for your son and you to choose one of these men, but it wouldn't be reasonable to choose me. I know none of these magnificent and splendid subjects. I wish I did! I am always saying, indeed, that I know virtually nothing, except a certain small subject—love, although on this subject, I'm thought to be amazing, better than anyone else, past or present.

THEAGES: You see, father? I really don't think that Socrates is actually willing to associate with me, and yet I'd be prepared to if he were willing. But he's only playing games with us. I know some people my age, and some a little older, who were nothing before they associated with him, but after associating even for a very short time with him became obviously better than all of those they had been worse than before.

SOCRATES: Do you know how that's possible, son of Demodocus?

THEAGES: Yes, by Zeus, I do: if you agree, I will become like them, too.

SOCRATES: No, sir; you don't understand. I'll have to explain it to you. There's a certain spiritual thing which, by divine dispensation, has been with me from childhood. It's a voice that, when it comes, always signals me to turn away from what I'm about to do, but never prescribes anything.

8. Accepting an emendation to *prokatatithentas* in a6.

And if some one of my friends consults with me and the voice comes, it's the same: it prohibits him and won't allow him to act.

e   I have witnesses for this: Surely you know Charmides (son of Glaucon) who's become so good-looking. He once happened to be consulting with me when he was just about to train for the race at Nemea. As soon as he began to tell me that he was going to train, the voice came and I tried to stop him and said, "As you were speaking, the voice of the spiritual thing came to me. Don't train!"

"Maybe," he said, "its significance is that I won't win; but even if I'm not going to win, I'll benefit from the exercise I'll get." Saying this, he

129   trained; it would be worthwhile to ask him what happened to him as a result of his training.

Or if you want, ask Clitomachus, the brother of Timarchus, what Timarchus said to him when he was on his way to his death together with Euathlus the runner,[9] who harbored Timarchus as a fugitive. This is what Timarchus said, according to him . . .

THEAGES: What?

SOCRATES: "Clitomachus," he said, "I'm going off to die now, because I refused to trust Socrates."

You might wonder why Timarchus would say that. I'll explain. When

b   Timarchus and Philemon (son of Philemonides) got up to leave the banquet, they were planning to kill Nicias (son of Heroscamandrus). Only those two knew the plot.

But Timarchus, as he got up to leave, said to me, "What do you say, Socrates? You guys go on drinking, but I have to get up and go somewhere. I'll be back a little later, perhaps."

And then the voice came to me and I said to him, "No! Don't get up!

c   For my familiar spiritual sign has come to me." And he stayed.

But after a while he again started to go and said, "Well, I'm going, Socrates."

Again the voice came, and so again I compelled him to stay. The third time, wanting me not to notice, he got up without saying anything more to me, watching until I had my attention elsewhere. Thus it was that he went off and did what led him to his death. And this is why he spoke to his brother in the way I just told you—he was going to his death because he hadn't trusted me.

d   Moreover, many people can tell you what I said about the destruction of the army in Sicily.[10] You can hear about past events from those who know the details, but it's still possible to test the sign, to see if it means anything. For when the good-looking Sannio went out on campaign, the sign came to me; and he's now with Thrasyllus on an expedition to Ephesus

9. Accepting a conjectural deletion of *euthu tou daimoniou* in a3.

10. Socrates refers to the ill-fated Sicilian expedition of 415–413 B.C., in which the Athenian invasion force was almost totally lost.

and the rest of Ionia. So I suppose he'll either die or else come close to it, and I'm really afraid about the rest of that business.[11]

I've told you all these things because this spiritual thing has absolute power in my dealings with those who associate with me. On the one hand, it opposes many, and it's impossible for them to be helped by associating with me, so I can't associate with them. On the other hand, it does not prevent my associating with many others, but it is of no help to them. Those whose association with me the power of the spiritual thing assists, however—these are the ones you've noticed, for they make rapid progress right away. And of these, again, who make progress, some are helped in a secure and permanent way, whereas many make wonderful progress as long as they're with me, but when they go away from me they're again no different from anyone else.

This is what happened to Aristides (son of Lysimachus, grandson of Aristides). While he was associating with me he made tremendous progress in a short time; but then there was some military expedition and he sailed away. On his return he learned that Thucydides (son of Melesias, grandson of Thucydides)[12] was associating with me. Thucydides had quarrelled with me the day before about some arguments that had come up.

When Aristides saw me, after greeting me and talking of other things, he said, "I hear, Socrates, that Thucydides is rather indignant and irritated with you, as if he were someone important."

"Yes, that's right," I said.

"Doesn't he know," he said, "what a slave[13] he was before he began associating with you?"

"Apparently not, by the gods," I said.

"You know, Socrates, he said, "I am also in a ridiculous situation!"

"Why?" I said.

"Because," he said, "before I sailed away, I was able to discuss things with anyone, and never came off worse than anyone in arguments; I even tried to associate with the cleverest people. But now, on the contrary, whenever I even *see* anybody with any education, I avoid them. That's how ashamed I am of my incompetence."

"Did you lose your ability all of a sudden," I asked, "or little by little?"

"Little by little," he said.

"And when you had your ability," I said, "Did you have it by learning something from me, or some other way?"

"By the gods, Socrates, you're not going to believe this, but it's true! I've never learned anything from you, as you know. But I made progress whenever I was with you, even if I was only in the same house and not in the same room—but more when I was in the same room. And it seemed,

---

11. Reading *pragmateias* in d8.

12. On Aristides and Thucydides see *Laches* 178a ff. and *Theaetetus* 150d ff.

13. Accepting the conjectural deletion of *to* in b7.

to me at least, that when I was in the same room and looked at you when you were speaking, I made much more progress than when I looked away.

e   And I made by far the most and greatest progress when I sat right beside you, and physically held on to you or touched you. But now," he said, "all that condition has trickled away."

So this is how it is when you associate with me, Theages. If it's favored by the god, you'll make great and rapid progress; if not, you won't. So think about it; wouldn't it be safer for you to become educated in the company of somebody who has control over the way he benefits people rather than taking your chances with me?

131   THEAGES: It seems to me, Socrates, that we should do this: let's test this spiritual thing by associating with one another. If it allows us, then that's what's best; if not, then we'll immediately think about what we should do—whether to go and associate with someone else, or try to appease the divine thing that comes to you with prayers and sacrifices and any other way the diviners might suggest.

DEMODOCUS: Don't oppose the boy any more in these things, Socrates; for Theages is right.

SOCRATES: Well, if it seems that this is what we ought to do, then let's do it.

CHARMIDES

Charmides was Plato's uncle, on his mother's side. He is seen here as a teenager in conversation with Socrates in 432 B.C. on the latter's return to Athens from service in the battle at Potidaea, the battle that initiated the Peloponnesian War. Socrates' other interlocutor is an older kinsman, first cousin of both Charmides and Plato's mother—Critias. It was a very distinguished family, tracing its descent from Solon, the great poet and statesman of the beginning of the sixth century, with distinguished forebears even before that. The subject of discussion is the virtue of 'sōphrosunē', here translated 'temperance'—but there is no adequate translation in modern European languages. Sōphrosunē means a well-developed consciousness of oneself and one's legitimate duties in relation to others (where it will involve self-restraint and showing due respect) and in relation to one's own ambitions, social standing, and the relevant expectations as regards one's own behavior. It is an aristocrat's virtue par excellence, involving a sense of dignity and self-command. At the time Plato was writing, both Charmides and Critias were notorious for involvement with the Thirty Tyrants (Critias was their leader). These were rich antidemocrats appointed by the Spartan king in 404 B.C. to draw up a new constitution after the defeat of Athens in the Peloponnesian War, who however seized power and established a reign of terror against their political and class enemies (Socrates alludes in Apology to his own behavior during this sorry episode). They both died in 403 in the fighting that overthrew them and restored the democracy. Their behavior was the antithesis of what could be expected of 'temperate' (sōphrōn) gentlemen.

For an ancient reader, these historic overtones would have played vividly against the bright surface of the dialogue. Charmides comes on stage here as a beautiful, thoughtful, much-admired youth, very modest and self-possessed—for Critias and the others present, the model of aristocratic excellence in the making. Only at the very end of the dialogue does Plato, very delicately, reveal another side of his character: advised by Critias to attach himself to Socrates so as to learn sōphrosunē through repeated discussion with him, Charmides tells Socrates he will do that by force, since his guardian Critias has commanded it, without allowing Socrates to say yea or nay. That ominous sour note aside, we get here a rich and subtle portrait of Socrates in conversation with an adolescent male, beautiful in body, but (infinitely more important) giving signs of beauty of soul and character—just the sort of person he was so constantly attracted to. Equally rich and subtle is the complementary portrayal in Lysis, on friendship, with which this dialogue should be compared.

Questioned by Socrates, Charmides attempts to say what this virtue of 'temperance' is, of which Critias and others think him a paragon. He offers three successive accounts, the last being something he has gathered from some respected adult (Critias, it turns out), but without being able to explain it satisfactorily either to himself or to Socrates. That by itself should suggest (anyhow to Socrates) that he does not possess the virtue, but out of consideration for his age, Socrates does not press the point. Instead, Critias takes over the defense of this last account—that 'temperance' is (equivalently) 'minding one's own business', or behaving in a way that suits the person who one is, or behaving with self-knowledge. Critias, too, is unable to develop and defend this idea satisfactorily, and the dialogue ends, as usual with Plato's 'Socratic' dialogues, in perplexity. Both Charmides' and Critias' proposals, and some of Socrates' criticisms, may strike us as oddly off base as accounts of whatever it is we mean by temperance; matters may be put to rights if we bear in mind the wider scope of the Greek virtue, as explained above.

J.M.C.

153   We got back the preceding evening from the camp at Potidaea, and since I was arriving after such a long absence I sought out my accustomed haunts with special pleasure. To be more specific, I went straight to the palaestra of Taureas (the one directly opposite the temple of Basile), and there I found a good number of people, most of whom were familiar,
b   though there were some, too, whom I didn't know. When they saw me coming in unexpectedly, I was immediately hailed at a distance by people coming up from all directions, and Chaerephon,[1] like the wild man he is, sprang up from the midst of a group of people and ran towards me and, seizing me by the hand, exclaimed, "Socrates! how did you come off in the battle?" (A short time before we came away there had been a battle at Potidaea and the people at home had only just got the news.)

And I said in reply, "Exactly as you see me."
c   "The way we heard it here," he said, "the fighting was very heavy and many of our friends were killed."

"The report is pretty accurate," I said.

"Were you actually in the battle?" he said.

"Yes, I was there."

"Well, come sit down and give us a complete account, because we've had very few details so far." And while he was still talking he brought me over to Critias, the son of Callaeschrus, and sat me down there.

Translated by Rosamond Kent Sprague.

1. Socrates' devoted friend, who put the question to the Delphic Oracle reported at *Apology* 21a.

When I took my seat I greeted Critias and the rest and proceeded to   d
relate the news from the camp in answer to whatever questions anyone
asked, and they asked plenty of different ones.

When they had had enough of these things, I in my turn began to
question them with respect to affairs at home, about the present state of
philosophy and about the young men, whether there were any who had
become distinguished for wisdom or beauty or both. Whereupon Critias,
glancing towards the door and seeing several young men coming in and   154
laughing with each other, with a crowd of others following behind, said
"As far as beauty goes, Socrates, I think you will be able to make up your
mind straight away, because those coming in are the advance party and
the admirers of the one who is thought to be the handsomest young man
of the day, and I think that he himself cannot be far off."

"But who is he," I said, "and who is his father?"

"You probably know him," he said, "but he was not yet grown up when   b
you went away. He is Charmides, the son of my mother's brother Glaucon,
and my cousin."

"Good heavens, of course I know him," I said, "because he was worth
noticing even when he was a child. By now I suppose he must be pretty
well grown up."

"It won't be long," he said, "before you discover how grown up he is
and how he has turned out." And while he was speaking Charmides
came in.

You mustn't judge by me, my friend. I'm a broken yardstick as far as
handsome people are concerned, because practically everyone of that age
strikes me as beautiful. But even so, at the moment Charmides came in   c
he seemed to me to be amazing in stature and appearance, and everyone
there looked to me to be in love with him, they were so astonished and
confused by his entrance, and many other lovers followed in his train.
That men of my age should have been affected this way was natural
enough, but I noticed that even the small boys fixed their eyes upon him
and no one of them, not even the littlest, looked at anyone else, but all
gazed at him as if he were a statue. And Chaerephon called to me and
said, "Well, Socrates, what do you think of the young man? Hasn't he a   d
splendid face?"

"Extraordinary," I said.

"But if he were willing to strip," he said, "you would hardly notice his
face, his body is so perfect."

Well, everyone else said the same things as Chaerephon, and I said, "By
Heracles, you are describing a man without an equal—if he should happen
to have one small thing in addition."

"What's that?" asked Critias.

"If he happens to have a well-formed soul," I said. "It would be appropriate if he did, Critias, since he comes from your family."

"He is very distinguished in that respect, too," he said.

"Then why don't we undress this part of him and have a look at it before we inspect his body? Surely he has already reached the age when he is willing to discuss things."

"Very much so," said Critias, "since he is not only a philosopher but
155   also, both in his own opinion and that of others, quite a poet."

"This is a gift, my dear Critias," I said, "which has been in your family as far back as Solon. But why not call the young man over and put him through his paces? Even though he is still so young, there can be nothing wrong in talking to him when you are here, since you are both his guardian and his cousin."

b   "You are right," he said; "we'll call him." And he immediately spoke to his servant and said, "Boy, call Charmides and tell him I want him to meet a doctor for the weakness he told me he was suffering from yesterday." Then Critias said to me, "You see, just lately he's complained of a headache when he gets up in the morning. Why not pretend to him that you know a remedy for it?"

"No reason why not," I said, "if he will only come."

"Oh, he will come," he said.

c   Which is just what happened. He did come, and his coming caused a lot of laughter, because every one of us who was already seated began pushing hard at his neighbor so as to make a place for him to sit down. The upshot of it was that we made the man sitting at one end get up, and the man at the other end was toppled off sideways. In the end he came and sat down between me and Critias. And then, my friend, I really was in difficulties, and although I had thought it would be perfectly easy to talk to him, I found my previous brash confidence quite gone. And when
d   Critias said that I was the person who knew the remedy and he turned his full gaze upon me in a manner beyond description and seemed on the point of asking a question, and when everyone in the palaestra surged all around us in a circle, my noble friend, I saw inside his cloak and caught on fire and was quite beside myself. And it occurred to me that Cydias[2] was the wisest love-poet when he gave someone advice on the subject of beautiful boys and said that "the fawn should beware lest, while taking a look at the lion, he should provide part of the lion's dinner," because I felt as if I had been snapped up by such a creature. All the same, when he asked me if I knew the headache remedy, I managed somehow to answer that I did.

"What exactly is it?" he said.

e   And I said that it was a certain leaf, and that there was a charm to go with it. If one sang the charm while applying the leaf, the remedy would bring about a complete cure, but without the charm the leaf was useless.
156   And he said, "Well, then I shall write down the charm at your dictation."

"With my permission," I said, "or without it?"

"With it, of course, Socrates," he said, laughing.

***

2. Cydias: an obscure lyric poet.

"Very well," I said. "And are you quite sure about my name?"

"It would be disgraceful if I were not," he said, "because you are no small topic of conversation among us boys, and besides, I remember you being with Critias here when I was a child."

"Good for you," I said. "Then I shall speak more freely about the nature b of the charm. Just now I was in difficulties about what method I would adopt in order to demonstrate its power to you. Its nature, Charmides, is not such as to be able to cure the head alone. You have probably heard this about good doctors, that if you go to them with a pain in the eyes, they are likely to say that they cannot undertake to cure the eyes by themselves, but that it will be necessary to treat the head at the same time if things are also to go well with the eyes. And again it would be very c foolish to suppose that one could ever treat the head by itself without treating the whole body. In keeping with this principle, they plan a regime for the whole body with the idea of treating and curing the part along with the whole. Or haven't you noticed that this is what they say and what the situation is?"

"Yes, I have," he said.

"Then what I have said appears true, and you accept the principle?"

"Absolutely," he said.

And when I heard his approval, I took heart and, little by little, my d former confidence revived, and I began to wake up. So I said, "Well Charmides, it is just the same with this charm. I learned it while I was with the army, from one of the Thracian doctors of Zalmoxis, who are also said to make men immortal. And this Thracian said that the Greek doctors were right to say what I told you just now. 'But our king Zalmoxis,' he said, 'who is a god, says that just as one should not attempt to cure e the eyes apart from the head, nor the head apart from the body, so one should not attempt to cure the body apart from the soul. And this, he says, is the very reason why most diseases are beyond the Greek doctors, that they do not pay attention to the whole as they ought to do, since if the whole is not in good condition, it is impossible that the part should be. Because,' he said, 'the soul is the source both of bodily health and bodily disease for the whole man, and these flow from the soul in the same way that the eyes are affected by the head. So it is necessary first 157 and foremost to cure the soul if the parts of the head and of the rest of the body are to be healthy. And the soul,' he said, 'my dear friend, is cured by means of certain charms, and these charms consist of beautiful words. It is a result of such words that temperance arises in the soul, and when the soul acquires and possesses temperance, it is easy to provide health both for the head and for the rest of the body.' So when he taught me the b remedy and the charms, he also said, 'Don't let anyone persuade you to treat his head with this remedy who does not first submit his soul to you for treatment with the charm. Because nowadays,' he said, 'this is the mistake some doctors make with their patients. They try to produce health of body apart from health of soul.' And he gave me very strict instructions

c   that I should be deaf to the entreaties of wealth, position, and personal
beauty. So I (for I have given him my promise and must keep it) shall
be obedient, and if you are willing, in accordance with the stranger's
instructions, to submit your soul to be charmed with the Thracian's charms
first, then I shall apply the remedy to your head. But if not, there is nothing
we can do for you, my dear Charmides."

When Critias heard me saying this, he said, "The headache will turn
out to have been a lucky thing for the young man, Socrates, if, because of
d   his head, he will be forced to improve his wits. Let me tell you, though,
that Charmides not only outstrips his contemporaries in beauty of form
but also in this very thing for which you say you have the charm; it was
temperance, wasn't it?"

"Yes, indeed it was," I said.

"Then you must know that not only does he have the reputation of
being the most temperate young man of the day, but that he is second to
none in everything else appropriate to his age."

e   "And it is quite right, Charmides, that you should be superior to the
rest in all such things," I replied, "because I don't suppose that anyone
else here could so readily point to two Athenian families whose union
would be likely to produce a more aristocratic lineage than that from
which you are sprung. Your father's family, that of Critias, the son of
158 Dropides,[3] has been praised for us by Anacreon, Solon, and many other
poets for superior beauty, virtue, and everything else called happiness.
It's the same on your mother's side. Your maternal uncle Pyrilampes has
the reputation of being the finest and most influential man in the country
because of his numerous embassies to the Great King and others, so that
this whole side of the family is not a bit inferior to the other. As the
offspring of such forebears, it is likely that you hold pride of place. In the
b   matter of visible beauty, dear son of Glaucon, you appear to me to be in
no respect surpassed by those who come before. But if, in addition, you
have a sufficient share of temperance and the other attributes mentioned
by your friend here, then your mother bore a blessed son in you, my dear
Charmides. Now this is the situation: if temperance is already present in
you, as Critias here asserts, and if you are sufficiently temperate, you have
no need of the charms either of Zalmoxis or of Abaris the Hyperborean,
c   and you may have the remedy for the head straightaway. But if you still
appear to lack these things, you must be charmed before you are given
the remedy. So tell me yourself: do you agree with your friend and assert
that you already partake sufficiently of temperance, or would you say that
you are lacking in it?"

At first Charmides blushed and looked more beautiful than ever, and
his bashfulness was becoming at his age. Then he answered in a way that
was quite dignified: he said that it was not easy for him, in the present
circumstances, either to agree or to disagree with what had been asked.

3. This Critias is the grandfather of our Critias. (See *Timaeus* 20e.)

"Because," he said, "if I should deny that I am temperate, it would not
only seem an odd thing to say about oneself, but I would at the same time
make Critias here a liar, and so with the many others to whom, by his
account, I appear to be temperate. But if, on the other hand, I should agree
and should praise myself, perhaps that would appear distasteful. So I do
not know what I am to answer."

And I said, "What you say appears to me to be reasonable, Charmides.
And I think," I said, "we ought to investigate together the question whether
you do or do not possess the thing I am inquiring about, so that you will
not be forced to say anything against your will and I, on the other hand,
shall not turn to doctoring in an irresponsible way. If this is agreeable to
you, I would like to investigate the question with you, but if not, we can
give it up."

"Oh, I should like it above all things," he said, "so go ahead and investigate the matter in whatever way you think best."

"Well then," I said, "in these circumstances, I think the following method
would be best. Now it is clear that if temperance is present in you, you
have some opinion about it. Because it is necessary, I suppose, that if it
really resides in you, it provides a sense of its presence, by means of which
you would form an opinion not only that you have it but of what sort it
is. Or don't you think so?"

"Yes," he said, "I do think so."

"Well, then, since you know how to speak Greek," I said, "I suppose
you could express this impression of yours in just the way it strikes you?"

"Perhaps," he said.

"Well, to help us decide whether it resides in you or not, say what, in
your opinion, temperance is," I said.

At first he shied away and was rather unwilling to answer. Finally,
however, he said that in his opinion temperance was doing everything in
an orderly and quiet way—things like walking in the streets, and talking,
and doing everything else in a similar fashion. "So I think," he said, "taking
it all together, that what you ask about is a sort of quietness."

"Perhaps you are right," I said, "at least they do say, Charmides, that the
quiet are temperate. Let's see if there is anything in it. Tell me, temperance is
one of the admirable things, isn't it?"

"Yes indeed," he said.

"Now when you are at the writing master's, is it more admirable to
copy the letters quickly or quietly?"[4]

"Quickly."

"What about reading? Quickly or quietly?"

"Quickly."

"And certainly to play the lyre quickly and to wrestle in a lively fashion
is much more admirable than to do these things quietly and slowly?"

"Yes."

4. The Greek word *hēsuchei* ("quietly") connotes slowness as well.

"Well, isn't the same thing true about boxing and the pancration?"

"Yes indeed."

d   "And with running and jumping and all the movements of the body, aren't the ones that are performed briskly and quickly the admirable ones, and those performed with difficulty and quietly the ugly ones?"

"It seems so."

"And it seems to us that, in matters of the body, it is not the quieter movement but the quickest and most lively which is the most admirable. Isn't it so?"

"Yes indeed."

"But temperance was something admirable?"

"Yes."

"Then in the case of the body it would not be quietness but quickness which is the more temperate, since temperance is an admirable thing."

"That seems reasonable," he said.

e   "Well then," I said, "is facility in learning more admirable or difficulty in learning?"

"Facility."

"But facility in learning is learning quickly? And difficulty in learning is learning quietly and slowly?"

"Yes."

"And to teach another person quickly—isn't this far more admirable than to teach him quietly and slowly?"

"Yes."

"Well then, to recall and to remember quietly and slowly—is this more admirable, or to do it vehemently and quickly?"

"Vehemently," he said, "and quickly."

160   "And isn't shrewdness a kind of liveliness of soul, and not a kind of quietness?"

"True."

"And again this is also true of understanding what is said, at the writing master's and at the lyre teacher's and everywhere else: to act not as quietly but as quickly as possible is the most admirable."

"Yes."

"And, further, in the operations of thought and in making plans, it is not the quietest man, I think, and the man who plans and finds out things b   with difficulty who appears to be worthy of praise but the one who does these things most easily and quickly."

"Exactly so," he said.

"Therefore, Charmides," I said, "in all these cases, both of soul and body, we think that quickness and speed are more admirable than slowness and quietness?"

"It seems likely," he said.

"We conclude then that temperance would not be a kind of quietness, nor would the temperate life be quiet, as far as this argument is concerned at any rate, since the temperate life is necessarily an admirable thing. There

are two possibilities for us: either no quiet actions in life appear to be more   c
admirable than the swift and strong ones, or very few. If then, my friend,
even quite a few quiet actions should turn out to be more admirable than
the violent and quick ones, not even on this assumption would temperance
consist in doing things quietly rather than in doing them violently and
quickly, neither in walking nor in speech nor in anything else; nor would
the quiet life be more temperate than its opposite, since in the course of   d
the argument we placed temperance among the admirable things, and the
quick things have turned out to be no less admirable than the quiet ones."

"What you say seems to me quite right, Socrates," he said.

"Then start over again, Charmides," I said, "and look into yourself with
greater concentration, and when you have decided what effect the presence
of temperance has upon you and what sort of thing it must be to have
this effect, then put all this together and tell me clearly and bravely, what   e
does it appear to you to be?"

He paused and, looking into himself very manfully, said, "Well, temperance seems to me to make people ashamed and bashful, and so I think
modesty must be what temperance really is."

"But," I said, "didn't we agree just now that temperance was an admirable thing?"

"Yes, we did," he said.

"And it would follow that temperate men are good?"

"Yes."

"And could a thing be good that does not produce good men?"

"Of course not."

"Then not only is temperance an admirable thing, but it is a good thing."

"I agree."   161

"Well then," I said, "you don't agree with Homer when he said that
'modesty is not a good mate for a needy man'?"[5]

"Oh, but I do," he said.

"So it seems to be the case that modesty both is and is not a good."

"Yes, it does."

"But temperance must be a good if it makes those good in whom it is
present and makes bad those in whom it is not."

"Why yes, it seems to me to be exactly as you say."

"Then temperance would not be modesty if it really is a good and if   b
modesty is no more good than bad."

"What you say has quite convinced me, Socrates," he said. "But give
me your opinion of the following definition of temperance: I have just
remembered having heard someone say that temperance is minding one's
own business. Tell me if you think the person who said this was right."

And I said, "You wretch, you've picked this up from Critias or from   c
some other wise man."

5. *Odyssey* xvii.347.

"I guess it was from some other," said Critias, "because it was certainly not from me."

"What difference does it make, Socrates," said Charmides, "from whom I heard it?"

"None at all," I answered, "since the question at issue is not who said it, but whether what he said is true or not."

"Now I like what you say," he said.

"Good for you," I replied, "but if we succeed in finding out what it means, I should be surprised, because it seems to be a sort of riddle."

"In what way?" he asked.

d "I mean," I said, "that when he uttered the words, I don't suppose the person speaking really meant that temperance was minding your own business. Or do you consider that the writing master does nothing when he writes or reads?"

"On the contrary, I do think he does something."

"And do you think the writing master teaches you to read and write your own name only or those of the other boys as well? And do you write the names of your enemies just as much as your own names and those of your friends?"

"Just as much," he said.

e "And are you a busybody and intemperate when you do this?"

"Not at all."

"But aren't you doing other people's business if to read and write are to do something?"

"I suppose I am."

"And then healing, my friend, is doing something, I suppose, and so is housebuilding and weaving and engaging in any one of the arts."

"Yes indeed."

"Well then," I said, "do you think a city would be well governed by a law commanding each man to weave and wash his own cloak, make his 162 own shoes and oil flask and scraper, and perform everything else by this same principle of keeping his hands off of other people's things and making and doing his own?"

"No, I don't think it would," he said.

"But," said I, "if a city is going to be temperately governed, it must be governed well."

"Of course," he said.

"Then if temperance is 'minding your own business', it can't be minding things of this sort and in this fashion."

"Apparently not."

"Then the person who said that temperance was 'minding your own business' must, apparently, have been riddling, as I pointed out just now, b because I don't suppose he was quite so simpleminded. Or was it some silly fellow you heard saying this, Charmides?"

"Far from it," he said, "he seemed very wise indeed."

"Then I think he must certainly have tossed off a riddle, since it is difficult to know what in the world this 'minding your own business' can be."

"Perhaps it is," he said.

"Then what in the world is 'minding your own business'? Are you able to say?"

"I'm at a total loss," he said. "But perhaps the one who said it didn't know what he meant either." And when he said this he smiled and looked at Critias.

It was clear that Critias had been agitated for some time and also that he was eager to impress Charmides and the rest who were there. He had held himself in with difficulty earlier, but now he could do so no longer. In my opinion, what I suspected earlier was certainly true, that Charmides had picked up this saying about temperance from Critias. And then Charmides, who wanted the author of the definition to take over the argument rather than himself, tried to provoke him to it by going on pointing out that the cause was lost. Critias couldn't put up with this but seemed to me to be angry with Charmides just the way a poet is when his verse is mangled by the actors. So he gave him a look and said, "Do you suppose, Charmides, that just because *you* don't understand what in the world the man meant who said that temperance was 'minding your own business', the man himself doesn't understand either?"

"Well, my dear Critias," said I, "there would be nothing remarkable in his being ignorant of the matter at his age, but you, because of your age and experience, are very likely to understand it. So if you agree that temperance is what the man said it was and take over the argument, I would be very happy to investigate with you the question whether what was said is true or not."

"I am quite ready to agree," he said, "and to take over the argument."

"I admire you for it," I said. "Now tell me: do you also agree with what I was just saying, that all craftsmen make something?"

"Yes I do."

"And do they seem to you to make their own things only, or those of other people as well?"

"Those of others as well."

"And are they temperate in not making their own things only?"

"Is there any objection?" he asked.

"None for me," I said, "but see whether there may not be one for the man who defines temperance as 'minding your own business' and then says there is no objection if those who do other people's business are temperate too."

"But," said he, "have I agreed that those who *do* other people's business are temperate by admitting that those *making* other people's things are temperate?"

"Tell me," I said, "don't you call making and doing the same thing?"

c

d

e

163

b

"Not at all," he said, "nor do I call working and making the same. I have learned this from Hesiod, who said 'work is no disgrace'.[6] Do you suppose that Hesiod, if he referred to the sort of things you mentioned just now by both the term 'work' and the term 'do', would have said there was no disgrace in cobbling or selling salt fish or prostitution? One ought not to think this, Socrates, but rather believe, as I do, that he supposed
c   making to be something other than doing and working, and that a 'made' or created thing became a disgrace on those occasions when it was not accompanied by the admirable, but that work is never any sort of disgrace. Because he gave the name 'works' to things done admirably and usefully, and it is creations of this sort which are 'works' and 'actions'. We ought to represent him as thinking that only things of this sort are 'one's own' and that all the harmful ones belong to other people. The result is that we must suppose that Hesiod and any other man of sense calls the man who minds his own business temperate."

d   "Critias," I said, "I understood the beginning of your speech pretty well, when you said that you called things that were 'one's own' and 'of oneself' good and called the doing of good things actions, because I have heard Prodicus discourse upon the distinction in words a hundred times. Well, I give you permission to define each word the way you like just so long as you make clear the application of whatever word you use. Now start
e   at the beginning and define more clearly: the doing of good things or the making of them or whatever you want to call it—is this what you say temperance is?"

"Yes, it is," he said.

"And the man who performs evil actions is not temperate, but the man who performs good ones?"

"Doesn't it seem so to you, my friend?"

"Never mind that," I said; "we are not investigating what I think but rather what you now say."

"Well then, I," he said, "deny that the man who does things that are not good but bad is temperate, and assert that the man who does things that are good but not bad *is* temperate. So I give you a clear definition of temperance as the doing of good things."

164   "And there is no reason why you should not be speaking the truth. But it certainly does surprise me," I said, "if you believe that temperate men are ignorant of their temperance."

"I don't think so at all," he said.

"But didn't you say just a moment ago," said I, "that there was nothing to prevent craftsmen, even while they do other people's business, from being temperate?"

"Yes, I did say that," he said. "But what about it?"

6. *Works and Days* 311.

"Nothing, but tell me if you think that a doctor, when he makes someone healthy, does something useful both for himself and for the person he cures."

"Yes, I agree."

"And the man who does these things does what he ought?"

"Yes."

"And the man who does what he ought is temperate, isn't he?"

"Of course he is temperate."

"And does a doctor have to know when he cures in a useful way and when he does not? And so with each of the craftsmen: does he have to know when he is going to benefit from the work he performs and when he is not?"

"Perhaps not."

"Then sometimes," I said, "the doctor doesn't know himself whether he has acted beneficially or harmfully. Now if he has acted beneficially, then, according to your argument, he has acted temperately. Or isn't this what you said?"

"Yes, it is."

"Then it seems that on some occasions he acts beneficially and, in so doing, acts temperately and is temperate, but is ignorant of his own temperance?"

"But this," he said, "Socrates, would never happen. And if you think it necessary to draw this conclusion from what I admitted before, then I would rather withdraw some of my statements, and would not be ashamed to admit I had made a mistake, in preference to conceding that a man ignorant of himself could be temperate. As a matter of fact, this is pretty much what I say temperance is, to know oneself, and I agree with the inscription to this effect set up at Delphi. Because this inscription appears to me to have been dedicated for the following purpose, as though it were a greeting from the god to those coming in in place of the usual 'Hail', as though to say 'hail' were an incorrect greeting, but we should rather urge one another to 'be temperate'. It is in this fashion, then, that the god greets those who enter his temple, not after the manner of man—or so I suppose the man thought who dedicated the inscription. What he says to the person entering is nothing else than 'be temperate'; this is what he says. Now in saying this he speaks very darkly, as a seer would do. That 'know thyself' and 'be temperate' are the same (as the inscription claims, and so do I) might be doubted by some, and this I think to be the case with those who dedicated the later inscriptions 'Nothing too much' and 'Pledges lead to perdition'. Because these people thought that 'Know thyself' was a piece of advice and not the god's greeting to those who enter, so, with the idea of dedicating some admonitions which were no less useful, they wrote these things and put them up. But here's the reason why I say all this, Socrates: I concede to you everything that was said before—perhaps you said something more nearly right on the subject and perhaps I did, but nothing of what we said was really clear—but now I wish to give you an explanation of this definition, unless of course you already agree that temperance is to know oneself."

"But Critias," I replied, "you are talking to me as though I professed to know the answers to my own questions and as though I could agree with you if I really wished. This is not the case—rather, because of my own

c ignorance, I am continually investigating in your company whatever is put forward. However, if I think it over, I am willing to say whether I agree or not. Just wait while I consider."

"Well, think it over," he said.

"Yes, I'm thinking," said I. "Well, if knowing is what temperance is, then it clearly must be some sort of science and must be of something, isn't that so?"

"Yes—of oneself," he said.

"Then medicine, too," I said, "is a science and is of health?"

"Certainly."

"Now," I said, "if you should ask me, 'If medicine is a science of health,

d what benefit does it confer upon us and what does it produce?' I would answer that it conferred no small benefit. Because health is a fine result for us, if you agree that this is what it produces."

"I agree."

"And if you should ask me about housebuilding, which is a science of building houses, and ask what I say that it produces, I would say that it produces houses, and so on with the other arts. So you ought to give an answer on behalf of temperance, since you say it is a science of self, in case

e you should be asked, 'Critias, since temperance is a science of self, what fine result does it produce which is worthy of the name?' Come along, tell me."

"But, Socrates," he said, "you are not conducting the investigation in the right way. This science does not have the same nature as the rest, any more than they have the same nature as each other, but you are carrying on the investigation as though they were all the same. For instance," he said, "in the arts of calculation and geometry, tell me what is the product corresponding to the house in the case of housebuilding and the cloak in

166 the case of weaving and so on—one could give many instances from many arts. You ought to point out to me a similar product in these cases, but you won't be able to do it."

And I said, "You are right. But I can point out to you in the case of each one of these sciences what it is a science *of*, this being distinct from the science itself. For instance, the art of calculation, of course, is of the odd and even—how many they are in themselves and with respect to other numbers—isn't that so?"

"Yes indeed," he said.

"Now aren't the odd and even distinct from the art of calculation itself?"

"Of course."

b "And again, the art of weighing is an art concerned with the heavier and lighter; and the heavy and light are distinct from the art of weighing. Do you agree?"

"Yes, I do."

"Then, since temperance is also a science of something, state what that something is which is distinct from temperance itself."

"This is just what I mean, Socrates," he said. "You arrive at the point of investigating the respect in which temperance differs from all the other sciences, and then you start looking for some way in which it resembles all the others. It's not like this; but rather, all the others are sciences of something else, not of themselves, whereas this is the only science which is both of other sciences *and* of itself. And I think you are quite consciously doing what you denied doing a moment ago—you are trying to refute me and ignoring the real question at issue."

"Oh come," I said, "how could you possibly think that even if I were to refute everything you say, I would be doing it for any other reasons than the one I would give for a thorough investigation of my own statements—the fear of unconsciously thinking I know something when I do not. And this is what I claim to be doing now, examining the argument for my own sake primarily, but perhaps also for the sake of my friends. Or don't you believe it to be for the common good, or for that of most men, that the state of each existing thing should become clear?"

"Very much so, Socrates," he said.

"Pluck up courage then, my friend, and answer the question as seems best to you, paying no attention to whether it is Critias or Socrates who is being refuted. Instead, give your attention to the argument itself to see what the result of its refutation will be."

"All right, I will do as you say, because you seem to me to be talking sense."

"Then remind me," I asked, "what it is you say about temperance."

"I say," he replied, "that it is the only science that is both a science of itself and of the other sciences."

"Would it then," I said, "also be a science of the absence of science, if it is a science of science?"

"Of course," he said.

"Then only the temperate man will know himself and will be able to examine what he knows and does not know, and in the same way he will be able to inspect other people to see when a man does in fact know what he knows and thinks he knows, and when again he does not know what he thinks he knows, and no one else will be able to do this. And being temperate and temperance and knowing oneself amount to this, to knowing what one knows and does not know. Or isn't this what you say?"

"Yes, it is," he said.

"Then for our third libation, the lucky one,[7] let us investigate, as though from the beginning, two points: first, whether it is possible or not to know that one knows and does not know what he knows and does not know

----

7. Literally, "the third [cup] to [Zeus] the Savior." The third cup was regularly drunk thus, especially at the start of a voyage, and became thought of as lucky.

and second, should this be perfectly possible, what benefit there would be for those who know this."

"Yes, we ought to look into this," he said.

"Then, come on, Critias," said I, "and consider whether you appear better off than I in these matters, because I am in difficulties. Shall I tell you where my difficulty lies?"

"Yes, do."

c   "Well," I said, "wouldn't the whole thing amount to this, if what you said just now is true, that there is one science which is not of anything except itself and the other sciences and that this same science is also a science of the absence of science?"

"Yes indeed."

"Then see what an odd thing we are attempting to say, my friend— because if you look for this same thing in other cases, you will find, I think, that it is impossible."

"How is that, and what cases do you mean?"

"Cases like the following: consider, for instance, if you think there could be a kind of vision that is not the vision of the thing that other visions are of but is the vision of itself and the other visions and also of the lack of

d   visions, and, although it is a type of vision, it sees no color, only itself and the other visions. Do you think there is something of this kind?"

"Good heavens, no, not I."

"And what about a kind of hearing that hears no sound but hears itself and the other hearings and nonhearings?"

"Not this either."

"Then take all the senses together and see if there is any one of them that is a sense of the senses and of itself but that senses nothing which the other senses sense."

"I can't see that there is."

e   "And do you think there is any desire that is a desire for no pleasure but for itself and the other desires?"

"Certainly not."

"Nor indeed any wish, I think, that wishes for no good but only for itself and the other wishes."

"No, that would follow."

"And would you say there was a love of such a sort as to be a love of no fine thing but of itself and the other loves?"

"No," he said, "I would not."

168   "And have you ever observed a fear that fears itself and the other fears, but of frightful things fears not a one?"

"I have never observed such a thing," he said.

"Or an opinion that is of itself and other opinions but opines nothing that other opinions do?"

"Never."

"But we are saying, it seems, that there is a science of this sort, which is a science of no branch of learning but is a science of itself and the other sciences."

"Yes, we are saying that."

"But isn't it strange if there really is such a thing? However, we ought not yet to state categorically that there is not, but still go on investigating whether there is."

"You are right."

"Come on then: is this science a science of something and does it have a certain faculty of being 'of something'? What about it?" b

"Yes, it does."

"And do we say the greater has a certain faculty of being greater than something?"

"Yes, it has."

"Presumably than something less, if it is going to be greater."

"Necessarily."

"Then if we should discover something greater that is greater than the greater things and than itself, but greater than nothing than which the other greater things are greater, surely what would happen to it is that, c if it were actually greater than itself, it would also be less than itself, wouldn't it?"

"That would certainly have to be the case, Socrates," he said.

"It would follow, too, that anything that was the double of the other doubles and of itself would, I suppose, be half of itself and of the other doubles—because I don't suppose there is a double of anything else except a half."

"That's true."

"And something that is more than itself will also be less, and the heavier, lighter and the older, younger, and so with all the other cases—the very d thing which has its own faculty applied to itself will have to have that nature towards which the faculty was directed, won't it? I mean something like this: in the case of hearing don't we say that hearing is of nothing else than sound?"

"Yes."

"Then if it actually hears itself, it will hear itself possessing sound? Because otherwise it would not do any hearing."

"Necessarily so."

"And vision, I take it, O best of men, if it actually sees itself, will have to have some color? Because vision could certainly never see anything that e has no color."

"No, that would follow."

"You observe then, Critias, that of the cases we have gone through, some appear to us to be absolutely impossible, whereas in others it is very doubtful if they could ever apply their own faculties to themselves? And that magnitude and number and similar things belong to the absolutely impossible group, isn't that so?"

"Certainly."

"Again, that hearing or vision or, in fact, any sort of motion should move itself, or heat burn itself—all cases like this also produce disbelief in some, though perhaps there are some in whom it does not. What 169 we need, my friend, is some great man to give an adequate interpretation of this point in every detail, whether no existing thing can by nature apply its own faculty to itself but only towards something else, or whether some can, but others cannot. We also need him to determine whether, if there are things that apply to themselves, the science which we call temperance is among them. I do not regard myself as competent

b   to deal with these matters, and this is why I am neither able to state categorically whether there might possibly be a science of science nor, if it definitely were possible, able to accept temperance as such a science before I investigate whether such a thing would benefit us or not. Now I divine that temperance is something beneficial and good. Do you then, O son of Callaeschrus, since the definition of temperance as the science of science and, more especially, of the absence of science belongs to you, first clear up this point, that what I just mentioned is possible

c   and then, after having shown its possibility, go on to show that it is useful. And so, perhaps, you will satisfy me that you are right about what temperance is."

When Critias heard this and saw that I was in difficulties, then, just as in the case of people who start yawning when they see other people doing it, he seemed to be affected by my troubles and to be seized by difficulties himself. But since his consistently high reputation made him feel ashamed in the eyes of the company and he did not wish to admit to me that he

d   was incapable of dealing with the question I had asked him, he said nothing clear but concealed his predicament. So I, in order that our argument should go forward, said, "But if it seems right, Critias, let us now grant this point, that the existence of a science of science is possible—we can investigate on some other occasion whether this is really the case or not. Come then, if this is perfectly possible, is it any more possible to know what one knows and does not know? We did say, I think, that knowing oneself and being temperate consisted in this?"

e   "Yes indeed," he said, "and your conclusion seems to me to follow, Socrates, because if a man has a science which knows itself, he would be the very same sort of man as the science which he has. For instance, whenever a person has speed he is swift, and when he has beauty he is beautiful, and when he has knowledge he is knowing. So when a person has a knowledge which knows itself, then I imagine he will be a person who knows himself."

"It is not this point," I said, "on which I am confused, that whenever someone possesses this thing which knows itself he will know himself, but how the person possessing it will necessarily know what he knows and what he does not know."

170   "But this is the same thing as the other, Socrates."

"Perhaps," I said, "but I'm in danger of being as confused as ever, because I still don't understand how knowing what one knows and does not know is the same thing as knowledge of self."

"How do you mean?" he said.

"It's like this," I said. "Supposing that there is a science of science, will it be anything more than the ability to divide things and say that one is science and the other not?"

"No, it amounts to this."

"And is it the same thing as the science and absence of science of health, b and as the science and absence of science of justice?"

"Not at all."

"One is medicine, I think, and the other politics, but we are concerned with science pure and simple."

"What else?"

"Therefore, when a person lacks this additional science of health and justice but knows science only, seeing that this is the only knowledge he has, then he will be likely, both in his own case and in that of others, to know that he knows something and has a certain science, won't he?"

"Yes."

"And how will he know whatever he knows by means of this science? c Because he will know the healthy by medicine, but not by temperance, and the harmonious by music, but not by temperance, and housebuilding by that art, but not by temperance, and so on—isn't it so?"

"It seems so."

"But by temperance, if it is merely a science of science, how will a person know that he knows the healthy or that he knows housebuilding?"

"He won't at all."

"Then the man ignorant of this won't know *what* he knows, but only *that* he knows."

"Very likely."

"Then this would not be being temperate and would not be temperance: d to know what one knows and does not know, but only *that* one knows and does not know—or so it seems."

"Probably."

"Nor, when another person claims to know something, will our friend be able to find out whether he knows what he says he knows or does not know it. But he will only know this much, it seems, that the man has some science; yes, but of what, temperance will fail to inform him."

"Apparently so."

"So neither will he be able to distinguish the man who pretends to be e a doctor, but is not, from the man who really is one, nor will he be able to make this distinction for any of the other experts. And let's see what follows: if the temperate man or anyone else whatsoever is going to tell the real doctor from the false, how will he go about it? He won't, I suppose, engage him in conversation on the subject of medicine, because what the doctor knows, we say, is nothing but health and disease, isn't that so?"

"Yes, that is the case."

"But about science the doctor knows nothing, because we have allotted precisely this function to temperance alone."

"Yes."

171   "Neither will the doctor know anything about medicine since medicine
is a science."

"True."

"However, the temperate man will know that the doctor has some science, but in order to try and grasp what sort it is, won't he have to examine
what it is of? Because hasn't each science been defined, not just as science,
but also by that which it is of?"

"By that, certainly."

"Now medicine is distinguished from the other sciences by virtue of its
definition as science of health and disease."

"Yes."

b   "It follows that the man who wants to examine medicine should look
for it where it is to be found, because I don't suppose he will discover it
where it is *not* to be found, do you?"

"Certainly not."

"Then the man who conducts the examination correctly will examine
the doctor in those matters in which he is a medical man, namely health
and disease."

"So it seems."

"And he will look into the manner of his words and actions to see if
what he says is truly spoken and what he does is correctly done?"

"Necessarily."

"But, without the medical art, would anyone be able to follow up either
of these things?"

"Certainly not."

c   "No one, in fact, could do this, it seems, except the doctor—not even
the temperate man himself. If he could, he would be a doctor in addition
to his temperance."

"That is the case."

"The upshot of the matter is, then, that if temperance is only the science
of science and absence of science, it will not be able to distinguish the
doctor who knows the particulars of his art from the one who does not
know them but pretends or supposes he does, nor will it recognize any
other genuine practitioner whatsoever, except the man in its own field,
the way other craftsmen do."

"It seems so," he said.

d   "Then, Critias," I replied, "what benefit would we get from temperance
if it is of this nature? Because if, as we assumed in the beginning[8] the
temperate man knew what he knew and what he did not know (and that
he knows the former but not the latter) and were able to investigate another
man who was in the same situation, then it would be of the greatest benefit
to us to be temperate. Because those of us who had temperance would

e   live lives free from error and so would all those who were under our
rule. Neither would we ourselves be attempting to do things we did not

8. See 167a.

understand—rather we would find those who did understand and turn
the matter over to them—nor would we trust those over whom we ruled
to do anything except what they would do correctly, and this would be
that of which they possessed the science. And thus, by means of temperance, every household would be well-run, and every city well-governed,
and so in every case where temperance reigned. And with error rooted   172
out and rightness in control, men so circumstanced would necessarily fare
admirably and well in all their doings and, faring well, they would be
happy. Isn't this what we mean about temperance, Critias," I said, "when
we say what a good thing it would be to know what one knows and what
one does not know?"

"This is certainly what we mean," he said.

"But now you see," I replied, "that no science of this sort has put in
an appearance."

"I see that," he said.

"Well then," I said, "is this the advantage of the knowledge of science   b
and absence of science, which we are now finding out to be temperance—
that the man who has this science will learn whatever he learns more
easily, and everything will appear to him in a clearer light since, in addition
to what he learns, he will perceive the science? And he will examine others
on the subjects he himself knows in a more effective fashion, whereas
those without the science will conduct their examinations in a weaker and
less fruitful way. And are not these, my friend, the kind of benefits we   c
shall reap from temperance? Or are we regarding it as something greater,
and demanding that it be greater than it really is?"

"Perhaps that may be so," he said.

"Perhaps," I said, "and perhaps we have been demanding something
useless. I say this because certain odd things become clear about temperance if it has this nature. If you are willing, let us investigate the matter
by admitting both that it is possible to know a science and also what we
assumed temperance to be in the beginning: to know what one knows and   d
does not know—let us grant this and not deny it. And, having granted
all these things, let us investigate more thoroughly whether, if it is like
this, it will benefit us in any way. Because what we were saying just now,
about temperance being regarded as of great benefit (if it were like this)
in the governing of households and cities, does not seem to me, Critias,
to have been well said."

"In what way?" he asked.

"Because," I said, "we carelessly agreed that it would be a great good
for men if each of us should perform the things he knows and should
hand over what he does not know to those others who do."

"And weren't we right in agreeing on this?" he said.   e

"I don't think we were," I replied.

"You certainly say some queer things, Socrates," he said.

"By the dog," I said, "they seem queer to me too, and that is why, when
I became aware of this a moment ago, I said that some strange things

would come to light and that I was afraid we were not conducting the examination correctly. Because truly, even if there were no doubt that 173 temperance is like this, it appears in no way clear to me that it does us any good."

"How so?" he said. "Tell me, so that we can both understand what you are saying."

"I think I am making a fool of myself," I said, "but all the same it is necessary to investigate what occurs to us and not to proceed at random, if we are going to have the least care for ourselves."

"You are right," he said.

"Listen then," I said, "to my dream, to see whether it comes through horn or through ivory.[9] If temperance really ruled over us and were as b we now define it, surely everything would be done according to science: neither would anyone who says he is a pilot (but is not) deceive us, nor would any doctor or general or anyone else pretending to know what he does not know escape our notice. This being the situation, wouldn't we have greater bodily health than we do now, and safety when we are in danger at sea or in battle, and wouldn't we have dishes and all our clothes c and shoes and things skillfully made for us, and many other things as well, because we would be employing true craftsmen? And, if you will, let us even agree that the mantic art is knowledge of what is to be and that temperance, directing her, keeps away deceivers and sets up the true d seers as prophets of the future. I grant that the human race, if thus equipped, would act and live in a scientific way—because temperance, watching over it, would not allow the absence of science to creep in and become our accomplice. But whether acting scientifically would make us fare well and be happy, this we have yet to learn, my dear Critias."

"But on the other hand," he said, "you will not readily gain the prize of faring well by any other means if you eliminate scientific action."

"Instruct me on just one more small point," I said. "When you say that e something is scientifically done, are you talking about the science of cutting out shoes?"

"Good heavens no!"

"Of bronze working, then?"

"Certainly not."

"Then of wool or wood or some similar thing?"

"Of course not."

"Then," I said, "we no longer keep to the statement that the man who lives scientifically is happy. Because those who live in the ways we mentioned are not admitted by you to be happy, but rather you seem to me to define the happy man as one who lives scientifically concerning certain specific things. And perhaps you mean the person I mentioned a moment

9. The reference is to *Odyssey* xix.564–67. True dreams come through the horn gate, deceitful ones through the gate of ivory.

ago, the man who knows what all future events will be, namely the seer. Are you referring to this man or some other?"

"Both to this one," he said, "and another."

"Which one?" I said. "Isn't it the sort of man who, in addition to the future, knows everything that has been and is now and is ignorant of nothing? Let us postulate the existence of such a man. Of this man I think you would say that there was no one living who was more scientific."

"Certainly not."

"There is one additional thing I want to know: which one of the sciences makes him happy? Do all of them do this equally?"

"No, very unequally," he said.

"Well, which one in particular makes him happy? The one by which he knows which one of the things are and have been and are to come? Will it be the one by which he knows checker playing?"

"Oh for heaven's sake," he said.

"Well, the one by which he knows calculation?"

"Of course not."

"Well, will it be that by which he knows health?"

"That's better," he said.

"But the most likely case," I said, "is that by which he knows what?"

"By which he knows good," he said, "and evil."

"You wretch," said I, "all this time you've been leading me right round in a circle and concealing from me that it was not living scientifically that was making us fare well and be happy, even if we possessed all the sciences put together, but that we have to have this one science of good and evil. Because, Critias, if you consent to take away this science from the other sciences, will medicine any the less produce health, or cobbling produce shoes, or the art of weaving produce clothes, or will the pilot's art any the less prevent us from dying at sea or the general's art in war?"

"They will do it just the same," he said.

"But my dear Critias, our chance of getting any of these things well and beneficially done will have vanished if this is lacking."

"You are right."

"Then this science, at any rate, is not temperance, as it seems, but that one of which the function is to benefit us. For it is not a science of science and absence of science but of good and evil. So that, if this latter one is beneficial, temperance would be something else for us."

"But why should not temperance be beneficial?" he said. "Because if temperance really is a science of sciences and rules over the other sciences, then I suppose it would rule over this science of the good and would benefit us."

"And would this science make us healthy," I said, "and not the art of medicine? And would it perform the tasks of the other arts rather than each of them performing its own task? Didn't we protest solemnly just a moment ago that it is a science of science and absence of science only and of nothing else? We did, didn't we?"

"It seems so, at any rate."

"Then it will not be the craftsman of health?"

"Certainly not."

175   "Because health belonged to some other art, didn't it?"

"Yes, to another."

"Then it will be of no benefit, my friend. Because we have just awarded this work to another art, isn't that so?"

"Yes indeed."

"Then how will temperance be beneficial when it is the craftsman of no beneficial thing?"

"Apparently it won't be any benefit at all, Socrates."

"You see then, Critias, that my earlier fears were reasonable and that I was right to blame myself for discerning nothing useful in temperance?

b   Because I don't suppose that the thing we have agreed to be the finest of all would have turned out to be of no benefit if I had been of any use in making a good search. But now we have got the worst of it in every way and are unable to discover to which one of existing things the lawgiver gave this name, temperance. Furthermore, we gave our joint assent to many things which did not follow from our argument.[10] For instance, we conceded that there was a science of science when the argument did not allow us to make this statement. Again, we conceded that this science knew the tasks of the other sciences, when the argument did not allow us to say this either, so that our temperate man should turn out to be knowing, both that he knows things he knows and does not know things he does

c   not know. And we made this concession in the most prodigal manner, quite overlooking the impossibility that a person should in some fashion know what he does not know at all—because our agreement amounts to saying he knows things he does not know. And yet, I think, there could

d   be nothing more irrational than this. But in spite of the fact that the inquiry has shown us to be both complacent and easy, it is not a whit more capable of discovering the truth. It has, in fact, made fun of the truth to this extent, that it has very insolently exposed as useless the definition of temperance which we agreed upon and invented earlier. I am not so much vexed on my own account, but on yours, Charmides," I said, "I am very vexed

e   indeed, if, with such a body and, in addition, a most temperate soul, you should derive no benefit from this temperance nor should it be of any use to you in this present life. And I am still more vexed on behalf of the charm I took so much trouble to learn from the Thracian, if it should turn out to be worthless. I really do not believe this to be the case; rather I

176   think that I am a worthless inquirer. Because I think that temperance is a great good, and if you truly have it, that you are blessed. So see whether you do have it and are in no need of the charm—because if you do have it, my advice to you would rather be to regard me as a babbler, incapable

10. Socrates recalls the assumptions granted hypothetically at 169d and 173a–d.

of finding out anything whatsoever by means of argument, and yourself as being exactly as happy as you are temperate."

And Charmides said, "But good heavens, Socrates, I don't know whether I have it or whether I don't—because how would I know the nature of a thing when neither you nor Critias is able to discover it, as you say? However, I don't really believe you, Socrates, but I think I am very much in need of the charm, and as far as I am concerned I am willing to be charmed by you every day until you say I have had enough."

"Very well, Charmides," said Critias, "if you do this, it will convince me of your temperance—if you submit yourself to be charmed by Socrates and let nothing great or small dissuade you from it."

"This is the course I shall follow," he said, "and I shall not give it up. I would be acting badly if I failed to obey my guardian and did not carry out your commands."

"Well then," said Critias, "these are my instructions."

"And I shall execute them," he said, "from this day forward."

"Look here," I said, "what are you two plotting?"

"Nothing," said Charmides—"our plotting is all done."

"Are you going to use force," I asked, "and don't I get a preliminary hearing?"

"We shall have to use force," said Charmides, "seeing that this fellow here has given me my orders. So you had better take counsel as to your own procedure."

"What use is counsel?" said I. "Because when you undertake to do anything by force, no man living can oppose you."

"Well then," he said, "don't oppose me."

"Very well, I shan't," said I.

LACHES

In Greek, the subject of this dialogue is andreia, *literally 'manliness', a personal quality of wide scope, covering all the sorts of unwavering, active leadership in and on behalf of the community that were traditionally expected in Greek cities of true men. Its special connotation of military prowess makes 'courage' a suitable, even inevitable, translation, but its broader scope should be borne in mind. Here Socrates probes the traditional conception of such courage as the primary quality a young man should be brought up to possess. His fellow discussants include two distinguished Athenian generals, Laches and Nicias, active in the Peloponnesian War (Nicias was captured and put to death in the disastrous Athenian withdrawal from Sicily in 413). The other two parties to the discussion are elderly and undistinguished sons of distinguished statesmen and generals of earlier times—Lysimachus, son of Aristides 'the Just', a famous leader during the Persian War, and Melesias, son of Thucydides, son of Melesias, a principal early opponent of Pericles in his policy of imperial expansion. Laches has an unusually full and extensive 'prologue' before Socrates takes over the reins of the discussion and seeks and refutes first Laches' and then Nicias' ideas about the nature of courage. Its function is at least in part to provide opportunities for these four representatives of the traditional conception to give it some preliminary articulation, thus bringing out some of the tensions and divergent ways of thinking about courage and related matters that the tradition harbors and that Socrates exploits in his own questioning later on.*

As always in Plato's 'Socratic' dialogues, neither general's answers to Socrates' question 'What is courage?' prove satisfactory. Much of the discussion focuses upon the element of knowledge—of reasoned, nuanced responsiveness to the detailed circumstances for action—that on reflection Laches and Nicias both agree is an essential, though perhaps somewhat submerged, part of the traditional conception to which they themselves are committed. It is because of this that Nicias and Socrates agree (Laches is slow to accept the point, but it is clearly implied in what he has already said about courage's involving 'wisdom') that no dumb animal, and not even children, can correctly be called courageous—however much people may ordinarily speak that way. Nicias, indeed, wants to define courage simply as a kind of wisdom—wisdom about what is to be feared and what, on the contrary, to be buoyed up by and made hopeful as one pursues one's objectives. He intimates that this fits well with things he has heard Socrates say on other occasions, and in fact toward the end of Protagoras *Socrates does adopt just this formulation of courage. Here, however,*

whether this was a genuinely 'Socratic' idea or not, he and the two generals
find difficulties in it that they seem to see no immediate way to resolve, and
the discussion breaks off.

J.M.C.

LYSIMACHUS: You have seen the man fighting in armor, Nicias and Laches. 178
When Melesias and I invited you to see him with us, we neglected to give
the reason why, but now we shall explain, because we think it especially
right to be frank with you. Now there are some people who make fun of
frankness and if anyone asks their advice, they don't say what they think, b
but they make a shot at what the other man would like to hear and say
something different from their own opinion. But you we considered capable not only of forming a judgment but also, having formed one, of saying
exactly what you think, and this is why we have taken you into our
confidence about what we are going to communicate to you. Now the 179
matter about which I have been making such a long preamble is this: we
have these two sons here—this one is the son of my friend Melesias here,
and he is called Thucydides after his grandfather, and this one is my son,
who also goes by his grandfather's name—we call him Aristides after my
father. We have made up our minds to take as good care of them as we
possibly can and not to behave like most parents, who, when their children
start to grow up, permit them to do whatever they wish. No, we think
that now is the time to make a real beginning, so far as we can. Since we b
knew that both of you had sons too, we thought that you, if anyone, would
have been concerned about the sort of training that would make the best
men of them. And if by any chance you have not turned your attention
to this kind of thing very often, let us remind you that you ought not to
neglect it, and let us invite you to care for your sons along with ours. How
we reached this conclusion, Nicias and Laches, you must hear, even if it
means my talking a bit longer. Now you must know that Melesias and I c
take our meals together, and the boys eat with us. We shall be frank with
you, exactly as I said in the beginning: each of us has a great many fine
things to say to the young men about his own father, things they achieved
both in war and in peace in their management of the affairs both of their
allies and of the city here. But neither of us has a word to say about his
own accomplishments. This is what shames us in front of them, and we d
blame our fathers for allowing us to take things easy when we were
growing up, while they were busy with other people's affairs. And we
point these same things out to the young people here, saying that if they
are careless of themselves and disobedient to us, they will turn out to be
nobodies, but if they take pains, perhaps they may become worthy of the

Translated by Rosamond Kent Sprague.

names they bear.[1] Now the boys promise to be obedient, so we are looking into the question what form of instruction or practice would make them

e   turn out best. Somebody suggested this form of instruction to us, saying that it would be a fine thing for a young man to learn fighting in armor. And he praised this particular man whom you have just seen giving a display and proceeded to encourage us to see him. So we thought we ought to go to see the man and to take you with us, not only as fellow spectators but also as fellow counsellors and partners, if you should be

180 willing, in the care of our sons. This is what we wanted to share with you. So now is the time for you to give us your advice, not only about this form of instruction—whether you think it should be learned or not—but also about any other sort of study or pursuit for a young man which you admire. Tell us too, what part you will take in our joint enterprise.

NICIAS: I, for one, Lysimachus and Melesias, applaud your plan and am ready to take part in it. And I think Laches here is ready too.

b   LACHES: You are quite right, Nicias. As for what Lysimachus said just now about his father and Melesias' father, I think that what he said applied very well to them and to us and to everyone engaged in public affairs, because this is pretty generally what happens to them—that they neglect their private affairs, children as well as everything else, and manage them

c   carelessly. So you were right on this point, Lysimachus. But I am astonished that you are inviting us to be your fellow counsellors in the education of the young men and are not inviting Socrates here! In the first place, he comes from your own deme, and in the second, he is always spending his time in places where the young men engage in any study or noble pursuit of the sort you are looking for.

LYSIMACHUS: What do you mean, Laches? Has our friend Socrates concerned himself with any things of this kind?

LACHES: Certainly, Lysimachus.

NICIAS: This is a point I can vouch for no less than Laches, since he only

d   recently recommended a man to me as music teacher for my son. The man's name is Damon, a pupil of Agathocles, and he is the most accomplished of men, not only in music, but in all the other pursuits in which you would think it worthwhile for boys of his age to spend their time.

LYSIMACHUS: People at my time of life, Socrates, Nicias, and Laches, are no longer familiar with the young because our advancing years keep us

e   at home so much of the time. But if you, son of Sophroniscus, have any good advice to give your fellow demesman, you ought to give it. And you have a duty to do so, because you are my friend through your father. He and I were always comrades and friends, and he died without our ever having had a single difference. And this present conversation reminds me of something—when the boys here are talking to each other at home, they

---

1. On the boys' future see *Theaetetus* 150e ff., where we are told that Aristides became an associate of Socrates but left his company too soon. Both Aristides and the young Thucydides are mentioned in *Theages* 130a ff.

often mention Socrates and praise him highly, but I've never thought to ask if they were speaking of the son of Sophroniscus. Tell me, boys, is this 181
the Socrates you spoke of on those occasions?

BOYS: Certainly, father, this is the one.

LYSIMACHUS: I am delighted, Socrates, that you keep up your father's good reputation, for he was the best of men, and I am especially pleased at the idea that the close ties between your family and mine will be renewed.

LACHES: Don't under any circumstances let the man get away, Lysima- b
chus—because I have seen him elsewhere keeping up not only his father's reputation but that of his country. He marched with me in the retreat from Delium,[2] and I can tell you that if the rest had been willing to behave in the same manner, our city would be safe and we would not then have suffered a disaster of that kind.

LYSIMACHUS: Socrates, the praise you are receiving is certainly of a high order, both because it comes from men who are to be trusted and because of the qualities for which they praise you. Be assured that I am delighted to hear that you are held in such esteem, and please consider me among those most kindly disposed towards you. You yourself ought to have c
visited us long before and considered us your friends—that would have been the right thing to do. Well, since we have recognized each other, resolve now, starting today, to associate both with us and the young men here and to make our acquaintance, so that you may preserve the family friendship. So do what I ask, and we in turn shall keep you in mind of your promise. But what have you all to say about our original question? What is your opinion? Is fighting in armor a useful subject for young men to learn or not?

SOCRATES: Well, I shall try to advise you about these things as best I can, d
Lysimachus, in addition to performing all the things to which you call my attention. However, it seems to me to be more suitable, since I am younger than the others and more inexperienced in these matters, for me to listen first to what they have to say and to learn from them. But if I should have something to add to what they say, then will be the time for me to teach and persuade both you and the others. Come, Nicias, why doesn't one of you two begin?

NICIAS: Well, there is no reason why not, Socrates. I think that knowledge e
of this branch of study is beneficial for the young in all sorts of ways. For one thing, it is a good idea for the young not to spend their time in the pursuits in which they normally do like to spend it when they are at leisure, but rather in this one, which necessarily improves their bodies, 182
since it is in no way inferior to gymnastics exercises and no less strenuous, and, at the same time, this and horsemanship are forms of exercise especially suited to a free citizen. For in the contest in which we are the

2. The Athenians were defeated by the Boeotians at Delium in November of 424, the eighth year of the Peloponnesian War. Alcibiades refers to the conduct of Socrates in the retreat (to the detriment of Laches) at *Symposium* 220e ff.

contestants and in the matters on which our struggle depends, only those are practiced who know how to use the instruments of war. And again, there is a certain advantage in this form of instruction even in an actual battle, whenever one has to fight in line with a number of others. But the greatest advantage of it comes when the ranks are broken and it then

b becomes necessary for a man to fight in single combat, either in pursuit when he has to attack a man who is defending himself, or in flight, when he has to defend himself against another person who is attacking him. A man who has this skill would suffer no harm at the hands of a single opponent, nor even perhaps at the hands of a larger number, but he would have the advantage in every way. Then again, such a study arouses in us the desire for another fine form of instruction, since every man who learns to fight in armor will want to learn the subject that comes next, that is,

c the science of tactics; and when he has mastered this and taken pride in it, he will press on to the whole art of the general. So it has already become clear that what is connected with this latter art, all the studies and pursuits which are fine and of great value for a man to learn and to practice, have this study as a starting point. And we shall add to this an advantage which is not at all negligible, that this knowledge will make every man much bolder and braver in war than he was before. And let us not omit to mention, even if to some it might seem a point not worth making, that

d this art will give a man a finer-looking appearance at the very moment when he needs to have it, and when he will appear more frightening to the enemy because of the way he looks. So my opinion, Lysimachus, is just as I say, that young men should be taught these things, and I have given the reasons why I think so. But if Laches has anything to say on the other side, I would be glad to hear it.

LACHES: But the fact is, Nicias, that it is difficult to maintain of any study whatsoever that it ought not to be learned, because it seems to be a good

e idea to learn everything. So as far as this fighting in armor is concerned, if it is a genuine branch of study, as those who teach it claim, and as Nicias says, then it ought to be learned, but if it is not a real subject and the people who propose to teach it are deceiving us, or if it is a real subject but not a very important one, what need is there to learn it? The reason I say these things about it is that I consider that, if there were anything in it, it would not have escaped the attention of the Lacedaemonians, who

183 have no other concern in life than to look for and engage in whatever studies and pursuits will increase their superiority in war. And if the Lacedaemonians had overlooked the art, the teachers of it would certainly not have overlooked this fact, that the Lacedaemonians are the most concerned with such matters of any of the Greeks and that anyone who was honored among them in these matters would make a great deal of money just as is the case when a tragic poet is honored among us. The result is

b that whenever anyone fancies himself as a good writer of tragedy, he does not go about exhibiting his plays in the other cities round about Athens but comes straight here and shows his work to our people, as is the natural thing to do. But I observe that those who fight in armor regard Lacedaemon as forbidden ground and keep from setting foot in it. They give it a wide berth and prefer to exhibit to anyone rather than the Spartans—in fact they take pains to select people who themselves admit that plenty of others surpass them in warfare. Then again, Lysimachus, I have encountered quite a few of these gentlemen on the actual field of battle and I have seen what they are like. This makes it possible for us to consider the matter at first hand. In a manner which seems almost deliberate, not a single practitioner of the art of fighting in armor has ever become renowned in war. And yet in all the other arts, those who are well-known in each are those who have practiced the various ones. But the men who practice this art seem to be those who have the worst luck at it. For instance, this very man Stesilaus, whom you and I have witnessed giving a display before such a large crowd and praising himself the way he did, I once saw in the quite different circumstances of actual warfare giving a much finer demonstration against his will. On an occasion when a ship on which he was serving as a marine rammed a transport-vessel, he was armed with a combination scythe and spear, as singular a weapon as he was singular a man. His other peculiarities are not worth relating, but let me tell you how his invention of a scythe plus a spear turned out. In the course of the fight it somehow got entangled in the rigging of the other ship and there it stuck. So Stesilaus dragged at the weapon in an attempt to free it, but he could not, and meanwhile his ship was going by the other ship. For a time he kept running along the deck holding fast to the spear. But when the other ship was actually passing his and was dragging him after it while he still held onto the weapon, he let it slide through his hand until he just had hold of the ferule at the end. There was laughter and applause from the men on the transport at the sight of him, and when somebody hit the deck at his feet with a stone and he let go the shaft, then even the men on the trireme could no longer keep from laughing when they saw that remarkable scythe-spear dangling from the transport. Now perhaps these things may be of value, as Nicias maintains, but my own experience has been of the sort I describe. So, as I said in the beginning, either it is an art but has little value, or it is not an art but people say and pretend that it is, but in any case it is not worth trying to learn. And then it seems to me that if a cowardly man should imagine he had mastered the art, he would, because of his increasing rashness, show up more clearly the sort of man he was, whereas in the case of a brave man, everyone would be watching him and if he made the smallest mistake, he would incur a great deal of criticism. The reason for this is that a man who pretends to knowledge of this sort is the object of envy, so that unless he is outstandingly superior to the rest, there is no way in which he can possibly avoid becoming a laughingstock when he claims to have this knowledge. So the study of this art seems to me to be of this sort, Lysimachus. But, as I said before, we ought not to let Socrates here escape, but we ought to consult him as to his opinion on the matter in hand.

d   LYSIMACHUS: Well, I do ask your opinion, Socrates, since what might be called our council seems to me to be still in need of someone to cast the deciding vote. If these two had agreed, there would be less necessity of such a procedure, but as it is, you perceive that Laches has voted in opposition to Nicias. So we would do well to hear from you too, and find out with which of them you plan to vote.

SOCRATES: What's that, Lysimachus? Do you intend to cast your vote for whatever position is approved by the majority of us?

LYSIMACHUS: Why, what else could a person do, Socrates?

e   SOCRATES: And do you, Melesias, plan to act in the same way? Suppose there should be a council to decide whether your son ought to practice a particular kind of gymnastic exercise, would you be persuaded by the greater number or by whoever has been educated and exercised under a good trainer?

MELESIAS: Probably by the latter, Socrates.

SOCRATES: And you would be persuaded by him rather than by the four of us?

MELESIAS: Probably.

SOCRATES: So I think it is by knowledge that one ought to make decisions, if one is to make them well, and not by majority rule.

MELESIAS: Certainly.

SOCRATES: So in this present case it is also necessary to investigate first
185 of all whether any one of us is an expert in the subject we are debating, or not. And if one of us is, then we should listen to him even if he is only one, and disregard the others. But if no one of us is an expert, then we must look for someone who is. Or do you and Lysimachus suppose that the subject in question is some small thing and not the greatest of all our possessions? The question is really, I suppose, that of whether your sons turn out to be worthwhile persons or the opposite—and the father's whole estate will be managed in accordance with the way the sons turn out.

MELESIAS: You are right.

SOCRATES: So we ought to exercise great forethought in the matter.

MELESIAS: Yes, we should.

b   SOCRATES: Then, in keeping with what I said just now, how would we investigate if we wanted to find out which of us was the most expert with regard to gymnastics? Wouldn't it be the man who had studied and practiced the art and who had had good teachers in that particular subject?

MELESIAS: I should think so.

SOCRATES: And even before that, oughtn't we to investigate what art it is of which we are looking for the teachers?

MELESIAS: What do you mean?

SOCRATES: Perhaps it will be more clear if I put it this way: I do not think we have reached any preliminary agreement as to what in the world we are consulting about and investigating when we ask which of us is expert
c   in it and has acquired teachers for this purpose, and which of us is not.

NICIAS: But, Socrates, aren't we investigating the art of fighting in armor and discussing whether young men ought to learn it or not?

SOCRATES: Quite so, Nicias. But when a man considers whether or not he should use a certain medicine to anoint his eyes, do you think he is at that moment taking counsel about the medicine or about the eyes?

NICIAS: About the eyes.

SOCRATES: Then too, whenever a man considers whether or not and when he should put a bridle on a horse, I suppose he is at that moment taking counsel about the horse and not about the bridle?

NICIAS: That is true.

SOCRATES: So, in a word, whenever a man considers a thing for the sake of another thing, he is taking counsel about that thing for the sake of which he was considering, and not about what he was investigating for the sake of something else.

NICIAS: Necessarily so.

SOCRATES: Then the question we ought to ask with respect to the man who gives us advice, is whether he is expert in the care of that thing for the sake of which we are considering when we consider.

NICIAS: Certainly.

SOCRATES: So do we now declare that we are considering a form of study for the sake of the souls of young men?

NICIAS: Yes.

SOCRATES: Then the question whether any one of us is expert in the care of the soul and is capable of caring for it well, and has had good teachers, is the one we ought to investigate.

LACHES: What's that, Socrates? Haven't you ever noticed that in some matters people become more expert without teachers than with them?

SOCRATES: Yes, I have, Laches, but you would not want to trust them when they said they were good craftsmen unless they should have some well-executed product of their art to show you—and not just one but more than one.

LACHES: What you say is true.

SOCRATES: Then what we ought to do, Laches and Nicias, since Lysimachus and Melesias called us in to give them advice about their two sons out of a desire that the boys' souls should become as good as possible— if we say we have teachers to show, is to point out to them the ones who in the first place are good themselves and have tended the souls of many young men, and in the second place have manifestly taught us. Or, if any one of us says that he himself has had no teacher but has works of his own to tell of, then he ought to show which of the Athenians or foreigners, whether slave or free, is recognized to have become good through his influence. But if this is not the case with any of us, we should give orders that a search be made for others and should not run the risk of ruining the sons of our friends and thus incurring the greatest reproach from their nearest relatives. Now I, Lysimachus and Melesias, am the first to say,

c   concerning myself, that I have had no teacher in this subject. And yet I
have longed after it from my youth up. But I did not have any money to
give the sophists, who were the only ones who professed to be able to
make a cultivated man of me, and I myself, on the other hand, am unable
to discover the art even now. If Nicias or Laches had discovered it or
learned it, I would not be surprised, because they are richer than I and so
may have learned it from others, and also older, so they may have discov-
d   ered it already. Thus they seem to me to be capable of educating a man,
because they would never have given their opinions so fearlessly on the
subject of pursuits which are beneficial and harmful for the young if they
had not believed themselves to be sufficiently informed on the subject. In
other matters I have confidence in them, but that they should differ with
each other surprises me. So I make this counter-request of you, Lysimachus:
just as Laches was urging you just now not to let me go but to ask me
questions, so I now call on you not to let Laches go, or Nicias, but to
e   question them, saying that Socrates denies having any knowledge of the
matter or being competent to decide which of you speaks the truth, because
he denies having been a discoverer of such things or having been anyone's
pupil in them. So, Laches and Nicias, each of you tell us who is the cleverest
person with whom you have associated in this matter of educating young
men, and whether you acquired your knowledge of the art from another
person or found it out for yourselves, and, if you learned it from some
187 one, who were your respective teachers, and what other persons share the
same art with them. My reason for saying all this is that, if you are too
busy because of your civic responsibilities, we can go to these men and
persuade them, either by means of gifts or favors or both, to look after
both our boys and yours too so that they won't put their ancestors to
shame by turning out to be worthless. But if you yourselves have been
the discoverers of such an art, give us an example of what other persons you
have already made into fine men by your care when they were originally
b   worthless. Because if you are about to begin educating people now for the
first time, you ought to watch out in case the risk is being run, not by a
guinea-pig, but by your own sons and the children of your friends, and
you should keep from doing just what the proverb says not to do—to
begin pottery on a wine jar.[3] So state which of these alternatives you would
select as being appropriate and fitting for you and which you would reject.
Find out these things from them, Lysimachus, and don't let the men escape.
c   LYSIMACHUS: I like what Socrates has said, gentlemen. But whether you
are willing to be questioned about such matters and to give account of
them, you must decide for yourselves, Nicias and Laches. As far as Melesias
here and I are concerned, we would certainly be pleased if the two of you
were willing to give complete answers to all of Socrates' questions. Because,
as I started to say right at the beginning, the reason we invited you to

_____

3. The same proverb appears at *Gorgias* 514e. A wine jar is the largest pot; one ought
to learn pottery on something smaller.

advise us on these matters was that we supposed that you would naturally have given some thought to such things—especially so since your sons, like ours, are very nearly of an age to be educated. So, if you have no objection, speak up and look into the subject along with Socrates, exchanging arguments with each other. Because he is right in saying that it is about the most important of our affairs that we are consulting. So decide if you think this is what ought to be done.

NICIAS: It is quite clear to me, Lysimachus, that your knowledge of Socrates is limited to your acquaintance with his father and that you have had no contact with the man himself, except when he was a child—I suppose he may have mingled with you and your fellow demesmen, following along with his father at the temple or at some other public gathering. But you are obviously still unacquainted with the man as he is now he has grown up.

LYSIMACHUS: What exactly do you mean, Nicias?

NICIAS: You don't appear to me to know that whoever comes into close contact with Socrates and associates with him in conversation must necessarily, even if he began by conversing about something quite different in the first place, keep on being led about by the man's arguments until he submits to answering questions about himself concerning both his present manner of life and the life he has lived hitherto. And when he does submit to this questioning, you don't realize that Socrates will not let him go before he has well and truly tested every last detail. I personally am accustomed to the man and know that one has to put up with this kind of treatment from him, and further, I know perfectly well that I myself will have to submit to it. I take pleasure in the man's company, Lysimachus, and don't regard it as at all a bad thing to have it brought to our attention that we have done or are doing wrong. Rather I think that a man who does not run away from such treatment but is willing, according to the saying of Solon, to value learning as long as he lives,[4] not supposing that old age brings him wisdom of itself, will necessarily pay more attention to the rest of his life. For me there is nothing unusual or unpleasant in being examined by Socrates, but I realized some time ago that the conversation would not be about the boys but about ourselves, if Socrates were present. As I say, I don't myself mind talking with Socrates in whatever way he likes—but find out how Laches here feels about such things.

LACHES: I have just one feeling about discussions, Nicias, or, if you like, not one but two, because to some I might seem to be a discussion-lover and to others a discussion-hater. Whenever I hear a man discussing virtue or some kind of wisdom, then, if he really is a man and worthy of the words he utters, I am completely delighted to see the appropriateness and harmony existing between the speaker and his words. And such a man seems to me to be genuinely musical, producing the most beautiful

---

4. Here (see also *Republic* 536d) Plato refers to a verse of Solon (Athenian poet and lawgiver of the early sixth century): "I grow old ever learning many things" (frg. 18 Bergk).

harmony, not on the lyre or some other pleasurable instrument, but actually rendering his own life harmonious by fitting his deeds to his words in a truly Dorian mode, not in the Ionian, nor even, I think, in the Phrygian or Lydian, but in the only harmony that is genuinely Greek. The discourse

e   of such a man gladdens my heart and makes everyone think that I am a discussion-lover because of the enthusiastic way in which I welcome what is said; but the man who acts in the opposite way distresses me, and the better he speaks, the worse I feel, so that his discourse makes me look like a discussion-hater. Now I have no acquaintance with the words of Socrates, but before now, I believe, I have had experience of his deeds, and there I found him a person privileged to speak fair words and to indulge in every

189 kind of frankness. So if he possesses this ability too, I am in sympathy with the man, and I would submit to being examined by such a person with the greatest pleasure, nor would I find learning burdensome, because I too agree with Solon, though with one reservation—I wish to grow old learning many things, but from good men only. Let Solon grant me this point, that the teacher should himself be good, so that I may not show myself a stupid pupil taking no delight in learning. Whether my teacher

b   is to be younger than I am or not yet famous or has any other such peculiarity troubles me not at all. To you then, Socrates, I present myself as someone for you to teach and to refute in whatever manner you please, and, on the other hand, you are welcome to any knowledge I have myself. Because this has been my opinion of your character since that day on which we shared a common danger and you gave me a sample of your valor—the sort a man must give if he is to render a good account of himself. So say whatever you like and don't let the difference in our ages concern you at all.

c   SOCRATES: We certainly can't find fault with you for not being ready both to give advice and to join in the common search.

        LYSIMACHUS: But the task is clearly ours, Socrates (for I count you as one of ourselves), so take my place and find out on behalf of the young men what we need to learn from these people, and then, by talking to the boys, join us in giving them advice. Because, on account of my age, I very often forget what questions I was going to ask, and I forget the answers as well.

d   Then, if fresh arguments start up in the middle, my memory is not exactly good. So you do the talking and examine among yourselves the topics we proposed. And I will listen, and when I have heard your conversation, I will do whatever you people think best and so will Melesias here.

        SOCRATES: Let us do what Lysimachus and Melesias suggest, Nicias and Laches. Perhaps it won't be a bad idea to ask ourselves the sort of question which we proposed to investigate just now: what teachers have we had

e   in this sort of instruction, and what other persons have we made better? However, I think there is another sort of inquiry that will bring us to the same point and is perhaps one that begins somewhat more nearly from the beginning. Suppose we know, about anything whatsoever, that if it is added to another thing, it makes that thing better, and furthermore, we are able to make the addition, then clearly we know the very thing about which we should be consulting as to how one might obtain it most easily and best. Perhaps you don't understand what I mean, but will do so more easily this way: suppose we know that sight, when added to the eyes, makes better those eyes to which it is added, and furthermore, we are able to add it to the eyes, then clearly we know what this very thing sight is, about which we should be consulting as to how one might obtain it most easily and best. Because if we didn't know what sight in itself was, nor hearing, we would hardly be worthy counsellors and doctors about either the eyes or the ears as to the manner in which either sight or hearing might best be obtained.

190

b

LACHES: You are right, Socrates.

SOCRATES: Well then, Laches, aren't these two now asking our advice as to the manner in which virtue might be added to the souls of their sons to make them better?

LACHES: Yes, indeed.

SOCRATES: Then isn't it necessary for us to start out knowing what virtue is? Because if we are not absolutely certain what it is, how are we going to advise anyone as to the best method of obtaining it?

c

LACHES: I do not think that there is any way in which we can do this, Socrates.

SOCRATES: We say then, Laches, that we know what it is.

LACHES: Yes, we do say so.

SOCRATES: And what we know, we must, I suppose, be able to state?

LACHES: Of course.

SOCRATES: Let us not, O best of men, begin straightaway with an investigation of the whole of virtue—that would perhaps be too great a task—but let us first see if we have a sufficient knowledge of a part. Then it is likely that the investigation will be easier for us.

d

LACHES: Yes, let's do it the way you want, Socrates.

SOCRATES: Well, which one of the parts of virtue should we choose? Or isn't it obvious that we ought to take the one to which the technique of fighting in armor appears to lead? I suppose everyone would think it leads to courage, wouldn't they?

LACHES: I think they certainly would.

SOCRATES: Then let us undertake first of all, Laches, to state what courage is. Then after this we will go on to investigate in what way it could be added to the young, to the extent that the addition can be made through occupations and studies. But try to state what I ask, namely, what courage is.

e

LACHES: Good heavens, Socrates, there is no difficulty about that: if a man is willing to remain at his post and to defend himself against the enemy without running away, then you may rest assured that he is a man of courage.

SOCRATES: Well spoken, Laches. But perhaps I am to blame for not making myself clear; the result is that you did not answer the question I had in mind but a different one.

LACHES: What do you mean, Socrates?

191   SOCRATES: I will tell you if I can. That man, I suppose, is courageous whom you yourself mention, that is, the man who fights the enemy while remaining at his post?

LACHES: Yes, that is my view.

SOCRATES: And I agree. But what about this man, the one who fights with the enemy, not holding his ground, but in retreat?

LACHES: What did you mean, in retreat?

SOCRATES: Why, I mean the way the Scythians are said to fight, as much retreating as pursuing; and then I imagine that Homer is praising the
b   horses of Aeneas when he says they know how "to pursue and fly quickly this way and that," and he praises Aeneas himself for his knowledge of fear and he calls him "counsellor of fright."

LACHES: And Homer is right, Socrates, because he was speaking of chariots, and it was the Scythian horsemen to which you referred. Now cavalry do fight in this fashion, but the hoplites in the manner I describe.

c   SOCRATES: Except perhaps the Spartan hoplites, Laches. Because they say that at Plataea the Spartans, when they were up against the soldiers carrying wicker shields, were not willing to stand their ground and fight against them but ran away. Then when the ranks of the Persians were broken, they turned and fought, just like cavalrymen, and so won that particular battle.

LACHES: You are right.

SOCRATES: So as I said just now, my poor questioning is to blame for
d   your poor answer, because I wanted to learn from you not only what constitutes courage for a hoplite but for a horseman as well and for every sort of warrior. And I wanted to include not only those who are courageous in warfare but also those who are brave in dangers at sea, and the ones who show courage in illness and poverty and affairs of state; and then again I wanted to include not only those who are brave in the face of pain
e   and fear but also those who are clever at fighting desire and pleasure, whether by standing their ground or running away—because there are some men, aren't there, Laches, who are brave in matters like these?

LACHES: Very much so, Socrates.

SOCRATES: So all these men are brave, but some possess courage in pleasures, some in pains, some in desires, and some in fears. And others, I think, show cowardice in the same respects.

LACHES: Yes, they do.

SOCRATES: Then what are courage and cowardice? This is what I wanted to find out. So try again to state first what is the courage that is the same in all these cases. Or don't you yet have a clear understanding of what I mean?

LACHES: Not exactly.

SOCRATES: Well, I mean something like this: suppose I asked what speed 192
was, which we find in running and in playing the lyre and in speaking and
in learning and in many other instances—in fact we may say we display the
quality, so far as it is worth mentioning, in movements of the arms or legs
or tongue or voice or thought? Or isn't this the way you too would express it?

LACHES: Yes, indeed.

SOCRATES: Then if anyone should ask me, "Socrates, what do you say it
is which you call swiftness in all these cases," I would answer him that   b
what I call swiftness is the power of accomplishing a great deal in a short
time, whether in speech or in running or all the other cases.

LACHES: And you would be right.

SOCRATES: Then make an effort yourself, Laches, to speak in the same
way about courage. What power is it which, because it is the same in
pleasure and in pain and in all the other cases in which we were just
saying it occurred, is therefore called courage?

LACHES: Well then, I think it is a sort of endurance of the soul, if it is   c
necessary to say what its nature is in all these cases.

SOCRATES: But it is necessary, at any rate if we are to give an answer to
our question. Now this is what appears to me: I think that you don't regard
every kind of endurance as courage. The reason I think so is this: I am
fairly sure, Laches, that you regard courage as a very fine thing.

LACHES: One of the finest, you may be sure.

SOCRATES: And you would say that endurance accompanied by wisdom
is a fine and noble thing?

LACHES: Very much so.

SOCRATES: Suppose it is accompanied by folly? Isn't it just the opposite,   d
harmful and injurious?

LACHES: Yes.

SOCRATES: And you are going to call a thing fine which is of the injurious
and harmful sort?

LACHES: No, that wouldn't be right, Socrates.

SOCRATES: Then you won't allow this kind of endurance to be courage,
since it is not fine, whereas courage *is* fine.

LACHES: You are right.

SOCRATES: Then, according to your view, it would be wise endurance
which would be courage.

LACHES: So it seems.

SOCRATES: Let us see then in what respect it is wise—is it so with respect   e
to everything both great and small? For instance, if a man were to show
endurance in spending his money wisely, knowing that by spending it he
would get more, would you call this man courageous?

LACHES: Heavens no, not I.

SOCRATES: Well, suppose a man is a doctor, and his son or some other
patient is ill with inflammation of the lungs and begs him for something
to eat or drink, and the man doesn't give in but perseveres in refusing?   193

LACHES: No, this would certainly not be courage either, not at all.

SOCRATES: Well, suppose a man endures in battle, and his willingness to fight is based on wise calculation because he knows that others are coming to his aid and that he will be fighting men who are fewer than those on his side, and inferior to them, and in addition his position is stronger: would you say that this man, with his kind of wisdom and preparation, endures more courageously or a man in the opposite camp who is willing to remain and hold out?

b   LACHES: The one in the opposite camp, Socrates, I should say.

SOCRATES: But surely the endurance of this man is more foolish than that of the other.

LACHES: You are right.

SOCRATES: And you would say that the man who shows endurance in a cavalry attack and has knowledge of horsemanship is less courageous than the man who lacks this knowledge.

LACHES: Yes, I would.

SOCRATES: And the one who endures with knowledge of slinging or archery or some other art is the less courageous.

c   LACHES: Yes indeed.

SOCRATES: And as many as would be willing to endure in diving down into wells without being skilled, or to endure in any other similar situation, you say are braver than those who are skilled in these things.

LACHES: Why, what else would anyone say, Socrates?

SOCRATES: Nothing, if that is what he thought.

LACHES: Well, this is what I think at any rate.

SOCRATES: And certainly, Laches, such people run risks and endure more foolishly than those who do a thing with art.

LACHES: They clearly do.

d   SOCRATES: Now foolish daring and endurance was found by us to be not only disgraceful but harmful, in what we said earlier.

LACHES: Quite so.

SOCRATES: But courage was agreed to be a noble thing.

LACHES: Yes, it was.

SOCRATES: But now, on the contrary, we are saying that a disgraceful thing, foolish endurance, is courage.

LACHES: Yes, we seem to be.

SOCRATES: And do you think we are talking sense?

LACHES: Heavens no, Socrates, I certainly don't.

e   SOCRATES: Then I don't suppose, Laches, that according to your statement you and I are tuned to the Dorian mode, because our deeds are not harmonizing with our words. In deeds I think anyone would say that we partook of courage, but in words I don't suppose he would, if he were to listen to our present discussion.

LACHES: You are absolutely right.

SOCRATES: Well then: is it good for us to be in such a state?

LACHES: Certainly not, in no way whatsoever.

SOCRATES: But are you willing that we should agree with our statement to a certain extent?

LACHES: To what extent and with what statement?

SOCRATES: With the one that commands us to endure. If you are willing, let us hold our ground in the search and let us endure, so that courage itself won't make fun of us for not searching for it courageously—if endurance should perhaps be courage after all.

LACHES: I am ready not to give up, Socrates, although I am not really accustomed to arguments of this kind. But an absolute desire for victory has seized me with respect to our conversation, and I am really getting annoyed at being unable to express what I think in this fashion. I still think I know what courage is, but I can't understand how it has escaped me just now so that I can't pin it down in words and say what it is.

SOCRATES: Well, my friend, a good hunter ought to pursue the trail and not give up.

LACHES: Absolutely.

SOCRATES: Then, if you agree, let's also summon Nicias here to the hunt—he might get on much better.

LACHES: I am willing—why not?

SOCRATES: Come along then, Nicias, and, if you can, rescue your friends who are storm-tossed by the argument and find themselves in trouble. You see, of course, that our affairs are in a bad way, so state what you think courage is and get us out of our difficulties as well as confirming your own view by putting it into words.

NICIAS: I have been thinking for some time that you are not defining courage in the right way, Socrates. And you are not employing the excellent observation I have heard you make before now.

SOCRATES: What one was that, Nicias?

NICIAS: I have often heard you say that every one of us is good with respect to that in which he is wise and bad in respect to that in which he is ignorant.

SOCRATES: By heaven, you are right, Nicias.

NICIAS: Therefore, if a man is really courageous, it is clear that he is wise.

SOCRATES: You hear that, Laches?

LACHES: I do, but I don't understand exactly what he means.

SOCRATES: Well, I think I understand him, and the man seems to me to be saying that courage is some kind of wisdom.

LACHES: Why, what sort of wisdom is he talking about, Socrates?

SOCRATES: Why don't you ask him?

LACHES: All right.

SOCRATES: Come, Nicias, tell him what sort of wisdom courage would be according to your view. I don't suppose it is skill in flute playing.

NICIAS: Of course not.

SOCRATES: And not in lyre playing either.

NICIAS: Far from it.

SOCRATES: But what is this knowledge and of what?

LACHES: You are questioning him in just the right way.

SOCRATES: Let him state what kind of knowledge it is.

195   NICIAS: What I say, Laches, is that it is the knowledge of the fearful and the hopeful in war and in every other situation.

LACHES: How strangely he talks, Socrates.

SOCRATES: What do you have in mind when you say this, Laches?

LACHES: What do I have in mind? Why, I take wisdom to be quite a different thing from courage.

SOCRATES: Well, Nicias, at any rate, says it isn't.

LACHES: He certainly does—that's the nonsense he talks.

SOCRATES: Well, let's instruct him instead of making fun of him.

b   NICIAS: Very well, but it strikes me, Socrates, that Laches wants to prove that I am talking nonsense simply because he was shown to be that sort of person himself a moment ago.

LACHES: Quite so, Nicias, and I shall try to demonstrate that very thing, because you *are* talking nonsense. Take an immediate example: in cases of illness, aren't the doctors the ones who know what is to be feared? Or do you think the courageous are the people who know? Perhaps you call the doctors the courageous?

NICIAS: No, of course not.

LACHES: And I don't imagine you mean the farmers either, even though I do suppose they are the ones who know what is to be feared in farming. And all the other craftsmen know what is to be feared and hoped for in

c   their particular arts. But these people are in no way courageous all the same.

SOCRATES: What does Laches mean, Nicias? Because he does seem to be saying something.

NICIAS: Yes, he is saying something, but what he says is not true.

SOCRATES: How so?

NICIAS: He thinks a doctor's knowledge of the sick amounts to something more than being able to describe health and disease whereas I think their knowledge is restricted to just this. Do you suppose, Laches, that when a man's recovery is more to be feared than his illness, the doctors know this? Or don't you think there are many cases in which it would be better

d   not to get up from an illness? Tell me this: do you maintain that in all cases to live is preferable? In many cases, is it not better to die?

LACHES: Well, I agree with you on this point at least.

NICIAS: And do you suppose that the same things are to be feared by those for whom it is an advantage to die as by those for whom it is an advantage to live?

LACHES: No, I don't.

NICIAS: But do you grant this knowledge to the doctors or to any other craftsmen except the one who knows what is and what is not to be feared, who is the one I call courageous?

SOCRATES: Do you understand what he is saying, Laches?

e   LACHES: Yes I do—he is calling the seers the courageous. Because who else will know for whom it is better to live than to die? What about you,

Nicias—do you admit to being a seer, or, if you are not a seer, to not being courageous?

NICIAS: Well, what of it? Don't you, for your part, think it is appropriate for a seer to know what is to be feared and what is to be hoped?

LACHES: Yes, I do, because I don't see for what other person it would be.

NICIAS: Much more for the man I am talking about, my friend, because the seer needs to know only the signs of what is to be, whether a man will experience death or illness or loss of property, or will experience victory or defeat, in battle or in any other sort of contest. But why is it more suitable for the seer than for anyone else to judge for whom it is better to suffer or not to suffer these things?

196

LACHES: It isn't clear to me from this, Socrates, what he is trying to say. Because he doesn't select either the seer or the doctor or anyone else as the man he calls courageous, unless some god is the person he means. Nicias appears to me unwilling to make a gentlemanly admission that he is talking nonsense, but he twists this way and that in an attempt to cover up his difficulty. Even you and I could have executed a similar twist just now if we had wanted to avoid the appearance of contradicting ourselves. If we were making speeches in a court of law, there might be some point in doing this, but as things are, why should anyone adorn himself sense-lessly with empty words in a gathering like this?

b

SOCRATES: I see no reason why he should, Laches. But let us see if Nicias thinks he is saying something and is not just talking for the sake of talking. Let us find out from him more clearly what it is he means, and if he is really saying something, we will agree with him, but if not, we will instruct him.

c

LACHES: You go ahead and question him, Socrates, if you want to find out. I think perhaps I have asked enough.

SOCRATES: I have no objection, since the inquiry will be a joint effort on behalf of us both.

LACHES: Very well.

SOCRATES: Then tell me, Nicias, or rather tell us, because Laches and I are sharing the argument: you say that courage is knowledge of the grounds of fear and hope?

d

NICIAS: Yes, I do.

SOCRATES: Then this knowledge is something possessed by very few indeed if, as you say, neither the doctor nor the seer will have it and won't be courageous without acquiring this particular knowledge. Isn't that what you're saying?

NICIAS: Just so.

SOCRATES: Then, as the proverb says, it is true that this is not something "every sow would know," and she would not be courageous?

NICIAS: I don't think so.

SOCRATES: Then it is obvious, Nicias, that you do not regard the Crom-myon sow[5] as having been courageous. I say this not as a joke, but because

e

5. The famous sow of Crommyon (near Corinth) was killed by Theseus. See Plutarch *Theseus* 9.

I think that anyone taking this position must necessarily deny courage to any wild beast or else admit that some wild beast, a lion or a leopard or some sort of wild boar, is wise enough to know what is so difficult that very few men understand it. And the man who defines courage as you define it would have to assert that a lion and a stag, a bull and a monkey are all equally courageous by nature.

197   LACHES: By heaven, you talk well, Socrates. Give us an honest answer to this, Nicias—whether you say that these wild beasts, whom we all admit to be courageous, are wiser than we in these respects, or whether you dare to oppose the general view and say that they are not courageous.

NICIAS: By no means, Laches, do I call courageous wild beasts or anything else that, for lack of understanding, does not fear what should be feared. Rather, I would call them rash and mad. Or do you really suppose I call

b   all children courageous, who fear nothing because they have no sense? On the contrary, I think that rashness and courage are not the same thing. My view is that very few have a share of courage and foresight, but that a great many, men and women and children and wild animals, partake in boldness and audacity and rashness and lack of foresight. These cases,

c   which you and the man in the street call courageous, I call rash, whereas the courageous ones are the sensible people I was talking about.

LACHES: You see, Socrates, how the man decks himself out in words and does it well in his own opinion. Those whom everyone agrees to be courageous he attempts to deprive of that distinction.

NICIAS: I'm not depriving you of it, Laches, so cheer up. I declare that you are wise, and Lamachus[6] too, so long as you are courageous, and I say the same of a great many other Athenians.

LACHES: I shan't say anything about that—though I could—in case you should call me a typical Aexonian.[7]

d   SOCRATES: Never mind him, Laches, I don't think you realize that he has procured this wisdom from our friend Damon, and Damon spends most of his time with Prodicus, who has the reputation of being best among the sophists at making such verbal distinctions.

LACHES: Well, Socrates, it is certainly more fitting for a sophist to make such clever distinctions than for a man the city thinks worthy to be its leader.

e   SOCRATES: Well, I suppose it would be fitting, my good friend, for the man in charge of the greatest affairs to have the greatest share of wisdom. But I think it worthwhile to ask Nicias what he has in mind when he defines courage in this way.

LACHES: Well then, you ask him, Socrates.

SOCRATES: This is just what I intend to do, my good friend. But don't therefore suppose that I shall let you out of your share of the argument. Pay attention and join me in examining what is being said.

6. Lamachus shared the command of the Sicilian expedition with Nicias and Alcibiades; he died at Syracuse.

7. The people of the deme Aexone were regarded as abusive speakers.

LACHES: Very well, if that seems necessary.

SOCRATES: Yes, it does. And you, Nicias, tell me again from the beginning—you know that when we were investigating courage at the beginning of the argument, we were investigating it as a part of virtue?

NICIAS: Yes, we were.

SOCRATES: And didn't you give your answer supposing that it was a part, and, as such, one among a number of other parts, all of which taken together were called virtue?

NICIAS: Yes, why not?

SOCRATES: And do you also speak of the same parts that I do? In addition to courage, I call temperance and justice and everything else of this kind parts of virtue. Don't you?

NICIAS: Yes, indeed.

SOCRATES: Stop there. We are in agreement on these points, but let us investigate the grounds of fear and confidence to make sure that you don't regard them in one way and we in another. We will tell you what we think about them, and if you do not agree, you shall instruct us. We regard as fearful things those that produce fear, and as hopeful things those that do not produce fear; and fear is produced not by evils which have happened or are happening but by those which are anticipated. Because fear is the expectation of a future evil—or isn't this your opinion too, Laches?

LACHES: Very much so, Socrates.

SOCRATES: You hear what we have to say, Nicias: that fearful things are future evils, and the ones inspiring hope are either future non-evils or future goods. Do you agree with this or have you some other view on the subject?

NICIAS: I agree with this one.

SOCRATES: And you declare that knowledge of just these things is courage?

NICIAS: Exactly so.

SOCRATES: Let us find out if we all agree on still a third point.

NICIAS: What one is that?

SOCRATES: I will explain. It seems to me and my friend here that of the various things with which knowledge is concerned, there is not one kind of knowledge by which we know how things have happened in the past, and another by which we know how they are happening at the present time, and still another by which we know how what has not yet happened might best come to be in the future, but that the knowledge is the same in each case. For instance, in the case of health, there is no other art related to the past, the present, and the future except that of medicine, which, although it is a single art, surveys what is, what was, and what is likely to be in the future. Again, in the case of the fruits of the earth, the art of farming conforms to the same pattern. And I suppose that both of you could bear witness that, in the case of the affairs of war, the art of generalship is that which best foresees the future and the other times—nor does this art consider it necessary to be ruled by the art of the seer, but to rule *it*, as being better acquainted with both present and future in the affairs of war.

In fact, the law decrees, not that the seer should command the general, but that the general should command the seer. Is this what we shall say, Laches?

LACHES: Yes, it is.

SOCRATES: Well then, do you agree with us, Nicias, that the same knowledge has understanding of the same things, whether future, present, or past?

NICIAS: Yes, that is how it seems to me, Socrates.

b   SOCRATES: Now, my good friend, you say that courage is the knowledge of the fearful and the hopeful, isn't that so?

NICIAS: Yes, it is.

SOCRATES: And it was agreed that fearful and hopeful things were future goods and future evils.

NICIAS: Yes, it was.

SOCRATES: And that the same knowledge is of the same things—future ones and all other kinds.

NICIAS: Yes, that is the case.

SOCRATES: Then courage is not knowledge of the fearful and the hopeful

c   only, because it understands not simply future goods and evils, but those of the present and the past and all times, just as is the case with the other kinds of knowledge.

NICIAS: So it seems, at any rate.

SOCRATES: Then you have told us about what amounts to a third part of courage, Nicias, whereas we asked you what the whole of courage was. And now it appears, according to your view, that courage is the knowledge not just of the fearful and the hopeful, but in your own opinion, it would

d   be the knowledge of practically all goods and evils put together. Do you agree to this new change, Nicias, or what do you say?

NICIAS: That seems right to me, Socrates.

SOCRATES: Then does a man with this kind of knowledge seem to depart from virtue in any respect if he really knows, in the case of all goods whatsoever, what they are and will be and have been, and similarly in the case of evils? And do you regard that man as lacking in temperance or justice and holiness to whom alone belongs the ability to deal circum-

e   spectly with both gods and men with respect to both the fearful and its opposite, and to provide himself with good things through his knowledge of how to associate with them correctly?

NICIAS: I think you have a point, Socrates.

SOCRATES: Then the thing you are now talking about, Nicias, would not be a part of virtue but rather virtue entire.

NICIAS: So it seems.

SOCRATES: And we have certainly stated that courage is one of the parts of virtue.

NICIAS: Yes, we have.

SOCRATES: Then what we are saying now does not appear to hold good.

NICIAS: Apparently not.

Socrates: Then we have not discovered, Nicias, what courage is.

Nicias: We don't appear to.

Laches: But I, my dear Nicias, felt sure you would make the discovery 200 after you were so scornful of me while I was answering Socrates. In fact, I had great hopes that with the help of Damon's wisdom you would solve the whole problem.

Nicias: That's a fine attitude of yours, Laches, to think it no longer to be of any importance that you yourself were just now shown to be a person who knows nothing about courage. What interests you is whether I will turn out to be a person of the same kind. Apparently it will make no difference to you to be ignorant of those things which a man of any pretensions ought to know, so long as you include me in your ignorance. b Well, you seem to me to be acting in a thoroughly human fashion by noticing everybody except yourself. As far as I am concerned I think enough has been said on the topic for the present, and if any point has not been covered sufficiently, then later on I think we can correct it both with the help of Damon—whom you think it right to laugh at, though you have never seen the man—and with that of others. And when I feel secure on these points, I will instruct you too and won't begrudge the c effort—because you seem to me to be sadly in need of learning.

Laches: You are a clever man, Nicias, I know. All the same, I advise Lysimachus here and Melesias to say good-bye to you and me as teachers of the young men and to retain the services of this man Socrates, as I said in the beginning. If my boys were the same age, this is what I would do.

Nicias: And I agree: if Socrates is really willing to undertake the supervision of the boys, then don't look for anyone else. In fact I would gladly d entrust Niceratus to him, if he is willing. But whenever I bring up the subject in any way, he always recommends other people to me but is unwilling to take on the job himself. But see if Socrates might be more willing to listen to you, Lysimachus.

Lysimachus: Well, he should, Nicias, since I myself would be willing to do a great many things for him which I would not be willing to do for practically anyone else. What do you say, Socrates? Will you comply with our request and take an active part with us in helping the young men to become as good as possible?

Socrates: Well, it would be a terrible thing, Lysimachus, to be unwilling e to join in assisting any man to become as good as possible. If in the conversations we have just had I had seemed to be knowing and the other two had not, then it would be right to issue a special invitation to me to perform this task; but as the matter stands, we were all in the same difficulty. Why then should anybody choose one of us in preference to another? 201 What I think is that he ought to choose none of us. But as things are, see whether the suggestion I am about to make may not be a good one: what I say we ought to do, my friends—since this is just between ourselves— is to join in searching for the best possible teacher, first for ourselves—we really need one—and then for the young men, sparing neither money nor

anything else. What I don't advise is that we remain as we are. And if
anyone laughs at us because we think it worthwhile to spend our time in
school at our age, then I think we should confront him with the saying of
Homer, "Modesty is not a good mate for a needy man."[8] And, not paying
any attention to what anyone may say, let us join together in looking after
both our own interests and those of the boys.

LYSIMACHUS: I like what you say, Socrates, and the fact that I am the
oldest makes me the most eager to go to school along with the boys. Just
do this for me: come to my house early tomorrow—don't refuse—so that
we may make plans about these matters, but let us make an end of our
present conversation.

SOCRATES: I shall do what you say, Lysimachus, and come to you tomorrow, God willing.

8. *Odyssey* xvii.347.

LYSIS

Lysis, *together with* Charmides, *gives a rich and subtle portrayal of Socrates in one of his favorite pursuits—engaging in conversation with bright, cultivated, good-looking teenage boys from distinguished Athenian families.* Lysis *and Menexenus are best friends, in their early teens, still overseen by family servants (slaves) as 'tutors'. (Menexenus later became one of Socrates' close associates: there is a dialogue named after him, and he was present at the conversation in* Phaedo.) *Hippothales is an older teenage boy, infatuated with Lysis to the point of boring to death Ctesippus (another close associate of Socrates later on, also with him on his last day) and the other boys of his own age, with his poems and prose discourses on Lysis' and his ancestors' excellences. For Socrates, however, this is the wrong way to draw such a young person to you. Poetry and rhetorical praises will play to their pride and encourage arrogance. The right way is by engaging them in philosophical discussion. If they are worth attention at all, it is by turning them toward the improvement of their souls, that is, their minds, that you will attract their sober interest and grateful affection. Readers should compare what Alcibiades says about his own love for Socrates in the* Symposium, *and Socrates' dithyramb to love for boys in his second speech in* Phaedrus.

Socrates exhibits this right approach by engaging Lysis, and then also his friend Menexenus, in an extended discussion about the nature of friendship: who are friends to whom (or what), and on what ground? His first question to Lysis fixes the theme, before it is clearly announced: 'Am I right in assuming that your father and mother love you very much?' The Greek word for love here is philein, *cognate to the word for 'friendship',* philia: *'friendship' in this discussion includes the love of parents and children and other relatives, as well as the close elective attachments of what we understand as personal friendship. It also covers impassioned, erotic fixations like Hippothales' for Lysis. What is friendship, so understood, and under what conditions does it actually exist?*

Socrates does not really seek and examine the boys' opinions on this topic (as he does with other interlocutors, including Charmides, in Plato's 'Socratic' dialogues). Rather, he confronts them with a carefully constructed series of conceptual problems that arise when one tries to think seriously about friends and friendships. Is the friend the one who loves or the one loved? Or are there friends only where each loves the other? Difficulties arise for each solution. Or is it rather that good people are friends of other good people? But wait: since good people are so much like one another, can they do each other any good at all, as friends must do (if friendship is a good thing)? Poets such as Hesiod

687

have pointed to an inherent enmity between people of the same kind (people of the same profession, for example): what is one to make of that idea? Finally, what is the basis of a friendship: what does the friend ultimately love in loving his friend, and how does the love of that relate to the love of the friend? These philosophical ('logical') problems, Socrates seems to be saying, must be worked through in a systematic way before one can claim to understand what friendship is. But he only poses the problems, bringing the boys to see the difficulty they face in understanding the relationship they have entered into in being best friends.

Some of these issues recur in the Symposium, *in Socrates' questions to Agathon and in Diotima's remarks. Aristotle's celebrated theory of friendship in* Eudemian *and* Nicomachean Ethics *is visibly constructed in part out of solutions proposed on these issues.*

J.M.C.

203   I was on my way from the Academy straight to the Lyceum, following the road just outside and beneath the wall; and when I got to the little gate by Panops spring, I happened to meet Hippothales, Hieronymus' son, and Ctesippus of Paeania, and with them some other young men standing together in a group. Seeing me coming, Hippothales said,

"Hey, Socrates, where are you coming from and where are you going?"

"From the Academy," I said, "straight to the Lyceum."

"Well, come straight over here to us, why don't you? You won't come? It's worth your while, I assure you."

"Where do you mean, and who all are you?"

"Over here," he said, showing me an open door and an enclosed area just facing the wall. "A lot of us spend our time here. There are quite a

204   few besides ourselves—and they're all good-looking."

"What is this, and what do you do here?"

"This is a new wrestling-school," he said, "just built. But we spend most of our time discussing things, and we'd be glad to have you join in."

"How very nice," I said. "And who is the teacher here?"

"Your old friend and admirer, Mikkos."

"Well, God knows, he's a serious person and a competent instructor."

"Well, then, won't you please come in and see who's here?"

b   "First I'd like to hear what I'm coming in for—and the name of the best-looking member."

"Each of us has a different opinion on who that is, Socrates."

"So tell me, Hippothales, who do you think it is?"

He blushed at the question, so I said, "Aha! You don't have to answer that, Hippothales, for me to tell whether you're in love with any of these boys or not—I can see that you are not only in love but pretty far gone too. I may not

Translated by Stanley Lombardo.

be much good at anything else, but I have this god-given ability to tell pretty quickly when someone is in love, and who he's in love with."

When he heard this he really blushed, which made Ctesippus say, "O very cute, Hippothales, blushing and too embarrassed to tell Socrates the name. But if he spends any time at all with you he'll be driven to distraction hearing you say it so often. We're all just about deaf, Socrates, from all the 'Lysis' he's poured into our ears. And if he's been drinking, odds are we'll wake up in the middle of the night thinking we hear Lysis' name. As bad as all this is in normal conversation, it's nothing compared to when he drowns us with his poems and prose pieces. And worst of all, he actually sings odes to his beloved in a weird voice, which we have to put up with listening to. And now when you ask him the name he blushes!"

"Lysis must be pretty young," I said. "I say that because the name doesn't register with me."

"That's because they don't call him by his own name much. He still goes by his father's name, because his father is so famous. I'm sure you know what the boy looks like; his looks are enough to know him by."

"Tell me whose son he is," I said.

"He's the oldest son of Democrates of Aexone."

"Well, congratulations, Hippothales, on finding someone so spirited and noble to love! Now come on and perform for me what you've performed for your friends here, so that I can see if you know what a lover ought to say about his boyfriend to his face, or to others."

"Do you think what *he* says really counts for anything, Socrates?"

"Are you denying that you are in love with the one he says you are?"

"No, but I am denying that I write love poems about him and all."

"The man's not well, he's raving," Ctesippus hooted.

"O.K., Hippothales," I said. "I don't need to hear any poems or songs you may or may not have composed about the boy. Just give me the general sense, so I'll know how you deal with him."

"Well why don't you ask Ctesippus? He must have total recall of it all, from what he says about it being drummed into his head from listening to me."

"You bet I do," Ctesippus said, "and it's pretty ridiculous too, Socrates. I mean, here he is, completely fixated on this boy and totally unable to say anything more original to him than any child could say. How ridiculous can you get? All he can think of to say or write is stuff the whole city goes around singing—poems about Democrates and the boy's grandfather Lysis and all his ancestors, their wealth and their stables and their victories at the Pythian, Isthmian, and Nemean Games in the chariot races and the horseback races. And then he gets into the really ancient history. Just the day before yesterday he was reciting some poem to us about Heracles being entertained by one of their ancestors because he was related to the hero—something about him being a son of Zeus and the daughter of their deme's founding father—old women's spinning-songs, really. This is the sort of thing he recites and sings, Socrates, and forces us to listen to."

When I heard that I said, "Hippothales, you deserve to be ridiculed. Do you really compose and sing your own victory-ode before you've won?"

"I don't compose or sing victory-odes for myself, Socrates."

"You only think you don't."

"How is that?" he asked.

e   "You are really what these songs are all about," I said. "If you make a conquest of a boy like this, then everything you've said and sung turns out to eulogize yourself as victor in having won such a boyfriend. But if he gets away, then the greater your praise of his beauty and goodness,

206   the more you will seem to have lost and the more you will be ridiculed. This is why the skilled lover doesn't praise his beloved until he has him: he fears how the future may turn out. And besides, these good-looking boys, if anybody praises them, get swelled heads and start to think they're really somebody. Doesn't it seem that way to you?"

"It certainly does," he said.

"And the more swell-headed they get, the harder they are to catch."

"So it seems."

"Well, what do you think of a hunter who scares off his game and makes it harder to catch?"

"He's pretty poor."

b   "And isn't it a gross misuse of language and music to drive things wild rather than to soothe and charm?"

"Well, yes."

"Then be careful, Hippothales, that you don't make yourself guilty of all these things through your poetry. I don't imagine you would say that a man who hurts himself, by his poetry, is at all a good poet—after all, he does hurt himself."

c   "No, of course not," he said. "That wouldn't make any sense at all. But that's just why I'm telling you all this, Socrates. What different advice can you give me about what one should say or do so his prospective boyfriend will like him?"

"That's not easy to say. But if you're willing to have him talk with me, I might be able to give you a demonstration of how to carry on a conversation with him instead of talking and singing the way your friends here say you've been doing."

"That's easy enough," he said. "If you go in with Ctesippus here and

d   sit down and start a conversation, I think he will come up to you by himself. He really likes to listen, Socrates. And besides, they're celebrating the festival of Hermes, so the younger and older boys are mingled together. Anyway, he'll probably come up to you; but if he doesn't, he and Ctesippus know one another because Ctesippus' nephew is Menexenus, and Menexenus is Lysis' closest companion. So have Ctesippus call him if he doesn't come by himself."

e   "That's what I'll have to do," I said, and, taking Ctesippus with me, I went into the wrestling-school, followed by the others. When we got inside we found that the boys had finished the sacrifice and the ritual and, still all dressed up, were starting to play knucklebones. Most of them were playing in the courtyard outside, but some of them were over in a corner of the dressing-room playing with a great many knucklebones, which they drew from little baskets. Still others were standing around watching this group, and among them was Lysis. He stood out among the boys and older youths, a garland on his head, and deserved to be called not only a beautiful boy but a well-bred young gentleman. We went over to the other side of the room, where it was quiet, sat down, and started up a conversation among ourselves. Lysis kept turning around and looking at us, obviously wanting to come over, but too shy to do so alone. After a while Menexenus, taking a break from his game in the court, came in, and, when he saw Ctesippus and me, he came to take a seat beside us. Lysis saw him and followed over, sitting down together with Menexenus next to him, and then all the others came too. When Hippothales (let's not forget about him) saw that a small crowd had gathered, he took up a position in the rear where he thought Lysis wouldn't see him—afraid he might annoy him—and listened from his outpost.

Then I looked at Menexenus and asked him, "Son of Demophon, which of you two is older?"

"We argue about that," he said.

"Then you probably disagree about which one has the nobler family too," I said.

"Very much so," he said.

"And likewise about which one is better looking." They both laughed.

"Naturally, I won't ask which of you two is richer. For you two are friends, isn't that so?"

"Definitely," they said.

"And friends have everything in common, as the saying goes; so in this respect the two of you won't differ, that is, if what you said about being friends is true."

They agreed.

I was about to ask them next which of them was juster and wiser when somebody came in to get Menexenus, saying that the trainer was calling him. It seemed he still had some part to play in the ceremony, and so off he went. I asked Lysis then, "Am I right in assuming, Lysis, that your father and mother love you very much?"

"Oh, yes," he said.

"Then they would like you to be as happy as possible, right?"

"Naturally."

"Well, do you think a man is happy if he's a slave and is not permitted to do whatever he likes?"

"No, by Zeus, I don't think so."

"Well, then, if your father and mother love you and want you to be happy, it's clear that they must be extremely concerned to make sure that you *are* happy."

"Well, of course," he said.

"So they allow you to do as you please, and they never scold you or stop you from doing whatever you want to do."

"Not true, Socrates. There are a whole lot of things they don't let me do."

208   "What do you mean?" I said. "They want you to be happy but they stop you from doing what you want? Well, tell me this. Suppose you have your heart set on driving one of your father's chariots and holding the reins in a race. You mean they won't let you?"

"That's right," he said. "They won't let me."

"Well, whom do they let drive it?"

"There's a charioteer who gets a salary from my father."

"What? They trust a hired hand instead of you to do whatever he likes with the horses, and they actually pay him for doing that?"

b   "Well, yes."

"But I suppose they trust you to drive the mule-team, and if you wanted to take the whip and lash them, they would let you?"

"Why ever would they?" he said.

"Is anyone allowed to whip them?"

"Sure," he said, "the muleteer."

"A slave or free?"

"A slave."

"It seems, then, that your parents think more even of a slave than their own son and trust him rather than you with their property and let him

c   do what he wants, but prevent you. But tell me one more thing. Do they allow you to be in charge of your own life, or do they not trust you even that far?"

"Are you kidding?"

"Who is in charge of you, then?"

"My guardian here."

"He's a slave, isn't he?"

"What else? He's ours, anyway."

"Pretty strange, a free man directed by a slave. How does this guardian direct you; I mean, what does he do?"

"Mostly he takes me to school."

"And your schoolteachers, they're not in charge of you too, are they?"

"They sure are!"

d   "It looks like your father has decided to put quite a few masters and dictators over you. But what about when you come home to your mother, does she let you do whatever it takes to make you happy, like playing with her wool or her loom when she's weaving? She doesn't stop you from touching the blade or the comb or any of her other wool-working tools, does she?"

e   "Stop me?" he laughed. "She would beat me if I laid a finger on them."

"Good gracious!" I said. "You must have committed some kind of terrible offense against your father or mother."

"No, I swear!"

"Then why in the world do they so strangely prevent you from being happy and doing what you like? And why are they raising you in a perpetual condition of servitude to someone or other, day in and day out? Why do you hardly ever get to do what you want to do? The upshot is, it seems, that your many and varied possessions do you no good at all. Everybody but you has charge of them, and this extends to your own person, which, well-born though it is, somebody else tends and takes care of—while you, Lysis, control nothing, and get to do nothing you want to do."

"Well, Socrates, that's because I haven't come of age yet."

"That can't be it, son of Democrates, since there are *some* things, I imagine, that your father and mother trust you with without waiting for you to come of age. For instance, when they want someone to read or write for them, I'll bet that you, of everyone in the household, are their first choice for the job. Right?"

"Right."

"And nobody tells you which letter to write first and which second, and the same goes for reading. And when you take up your lyre, I'll bet neither your father nor mother stop you from tightening or loosening whatever string you wish, or from using a plectrum or just your fingers to play."

"No, they don't."

"Then what's going on? What's the reason they let you have your way here, but not in all the cases we've been talking about?"

"I suppose it's because I understand these things but not those."

"Aha!" I said. "So your father isn't waiting for you to come of age before he trusts you with everything; but come the day when he thinks that you know more than he does, he'll trust you with himself and everything that belongs to him."

"I guess so," he said.

"Well, then," I said, "what about your neighbor? Would he use the same rule of thumb as your father about you? When he thinks you know more about managing his estate than he does, will he trust you to do it, or will he manage it himself?"

"I suppose he will trust me to do it."

"And how about the Athenians? Do you think they will trust you with their affairs when they perceive that you know enough?"

"I sure do."

"Well, by Zeus, let's not stop here," I said. "What about the Great King? Would he trust his eldest son, crown prince of Asia, to add whatever he likes to the royal stew, or would he trust us, provided we went before him and gave him a convincing demonstration of our superior culinary acumen?"

"Why, us, of course."

"And he wouldn't let his son put the least little bit into the pot, but we could throw in fistfuls of salt if we wanted to."

"Right."

210   "What about if his son had something wrong with his eyes, would he let him treat his own eyes, knowing he wasn't a doctor, or would he prevent him?"

"Prevent him."

"But, if he thought we were doctors, he wouldn't stop us even if we pried his eyes open and smeared ashes in them, because he would think we knew what we were doing."

"True."

"So . . . he would trust us, rather than himself or his son, with all his business, as long as we seemed to him more skilled than either of them."

"He would have to, Socrates," he said.

"Then this is the way it is, my dear Lysis: in those areas where we
b   really understand something everybody—Greeks and barbarians, men and women—will trust us, and there we will act just as we choose, and nobody will want to get in our way. There we will be free ourselves, and in control of others. There things will belong to us, because we will derive some advantage from them. But in areas where we haven't got any understanding, no one will trust us to act as we judge best, but everybody will do
c   their best to stop us, and not only strangers, but also our mother and father and anyone else even more intimate. And there we are going to be subject to the orders of others; there things are not going to be ours because we are not going to derive any advantage from them. Do you agree this is how it is?"

"I agree."

"Well, then, are we going to be anyone's friend, or is anyone going to love us as a friend in those areas in which we are good for nothing?"

"Not at all," he said.

"So it turns out that your father does not love you, nor does anyone love anyone else, so far as that person is useless."

"It doesn't look like it."

d   "But if you become wise, my boy, then everybody will be your friend, everybody will feel close to you, because you will be useful and good. If you don't become wise, though, nobody will be your friend, not even your father or mother or your close relatives."

"Now, tell me, Lysis, is it possible to be high-minded in areas where one hasn't yet had one's mind trained?"

"How could anyone?" he said.

"And if *you* need a teacher, *your* mind is not yet trained."

"True."

"Then you're not high-minded either—since you don't have a mind of your own."

"You've got me there, Socrates!"

e   Hearing his last answer I glanced over at Hippothales and almost made the mistake of saying: "This is how you should talk with your boyfriends, Hippothales, cutting them down to size and putting them in their place, instead of swelling them up and spoiling them, as you do." But when I saw how anxious and upset he was over what we were saying, I remembered how he had positioned himself so as to escape Lysis' notice, so I bit my tongue. In the middle of all this, Menexenus came back and sat down 211 next to Lysis, where he had been before. Then Lysis turned to me with a good deal of boyish friendliness and, unnoticed by Menexenus, whispered in my ear: "Socrates, tell Menexenus what you've been saying to me."

I said to him: "Why don't you tell him yourself, Lysis? You gave it your complete attention."

"I certainly did," he said.

"Then try as hard as you can to remember it, so that you can tell it all b to him clearly. But if you forget any of it, ask me about it again the next time you run into me."

"I will, Socrates; you can count on it. But talk to him about something else, so I can listen too until it's time to go home."

"Well, I guess I'll have to, since it's you who ask. But you've got to come to my rescue if he tries to refute me. Or don't you know what a debater he is?"

"Sure I do—he's very much one. That's why I want you to have a discussion with him."

"So that I can make a fool of myself?" c

"No, so you can teach him a lesson!"

"What are you talking about? He's very clever, and Ctesippus' student at that. And look, Ctesippus himself is here!"

"Never mind about anybody else, Socrates. Just go on and start discussing with him."

"Discuss we shall," I said.

Our little tête-à-tête was interrupted by Ctesippus' asking: "Is this a private party between you two, or do we get a share of the conversation?"

"Of course you get a share!" I said. "Lysis here doesn't quite understand d something I've been saying, but he says he thinks Menexenus knows and wants me to ask him."

"Why don't you ask him then?"

"That's just what I'm going to do," I said. "So, Menexenus, tell me something. Ever since I was a boy there's a certain thing I've always wanted to possess. You know how it is, everybody is different: one person wants to own horses, another dogs, another wants money, and another fame. e Well, I'm pretty lukewarm about those things, but when it comes to having friends I'm absolutely passionate, and I would rather have a good friend than the best quail or gamecock known to man, and, I swear by Zeus above, more than any horse or dog. There's no doubt in my mind, by the Dog, that I would rather possess a friend than all Darius' gold, or even than Darius himself. That's how much I value friends and companions. 212 And that's why, when I see you and Lysis together, I'm really amazed; I think it's wonderful that you two have been able to acquire this possession so quickly and easily while you're still so young. Because you have in fact, each of you, gotten the other as a true friend—and quickly too. And here I am, so far from having this possession that I don't even know how one person becomes the friend of another, which is exactly what I want to question you about, since you have experience of it.

b   "So tell me: when someone loves someone else, which of the two becomes the friend of the other, the one who loves or the one who is loved? Or is there no difference?"

"I don't see any difference," he said.

"Do you mean," I said, "that they both become each other's friend when only one of them loves the other?"

"It seems so to me," he said.

"Well, what about this: Isn't it possible for someone who loves somebody not to be loved by him in return?"

"Yes, it's possible."

"And isn't it possible for him even to be hated? Isn't this how men are

c   often treated by the young boys they are in love with? They are deeply in love, but they feel that they are not loved back, or even that they are hated. Don't you think this is true?"

"Very true," he said.

"In a case like this, one person loves and the other is loved. Right?"

"Yes."

"Then which is the friend of the other? Is the lover the friend of the loved, whether he is loved in return or not, or is even hated? Or is the loved the friend of the lover? Or in a case like this, when the two do not both love each other, is neither the friend of the other?"

d   "That's what it looks like anyway," he said.

"So our opinion now is different from what it was before. First we thought that if one person loved another, they were both friends. But now, unless they both love each other, neither is a friend."

"Perhaps."

"So nothing is a friend of the lover unless it loves him in return."

"It doesn't look like it."

"So there are no horse-lovers unless the horses love them back, and no quail-lovers, dog-lovers, wine-lovers, or exercise-lovers. And no lovers of

e   wisdom, unless wisdom loves them in return. But do people really love them even though these things are not their friends, making a liar of the poet who said,

> *Happy the man who has as friends his children and*
> *solid-hoofed horses,*
> *his hunting hounds and a host abroad?*"[1]

"I don't think so," he said.

"Then you think he spoke the truth?"

1. Solon frg. 23 Edmonds.

"Yes."

"So what is loved is a friend to the person who loves it, or so it seems, Menexenus, whether it loves him or hates him. Babies, for example, who are too young to show love but not too young to hate, when they are disciplined by their mother or father, are at that moment, even though they hate their parents then, their very dearest friends." 213

"It seems so to me."

"So by this line of reasoning it is not the lover who is a friend, but the loved."

"It looks like it."

"And so the hated is the enemy, not the hater."

"Apparently so."

"Then many people are loved by their enemies and hated by their friends, and are friends to their enemies and enemies to their friends—if the object b of love rather than the lover is a friend. But this doesn't make any sense at all, my dear friend, in fact I think it is simply impossible to be an enemy to one's friend and a friend to one's enemy."

"True, Socrates, I think you're right."

"Then if this is impossible, that would make the lover the friend of the loved."

"Apparently so."

"And the hater the enemy of the hated."

"That must be."

"Then we are going to be forced to agree to our previous statement, c that one is frequently a friend of a nonfriend, and even of an enemy. This is the case when you love someone who does not love you, or even hates you. And frequently one is an enemy to a nonenemy, or even to a friend, as happens when you hate someone who does not hate you, or even loves you."

"Perhaps," he said.

"Then what are we going to do," I said, "if friends are not those who love, nor those who are loved, nor those who love and are loved? Are there any other besides these of whom we can say that they become each other's friends?"

"By Zeus," he said, "I certainly can't think of any, Socrates."

"Do you think, Menexenus," I said, "that we may have been going about d our inquiry in entirely the wrong way?"

"I certainly think so, Socrates," said Lysis. And as he said it, he blushed. I had the impression that the words just slipped out unintentionally because he was paying such close attention to what was being said, which he clearly had been all along.

Well, I wanted to give Menexenus a break anyway, and I was pleased with the other's fondness for philosophy, so I turned the conversation e towards Lysis, and said: "I think you're right, Lysis, to say that if we were looking at things in the right way, we wouldn't be so far off course. Let's not go in that direction any longer. That line of inquiry looks like a rough

214   road to me. I think we'd better go back to where we turned off, and look
       for guidance to the poets, the ancestral voices of human wisdom. What
       they say about who friends are is by no means trivial: that God himself
       makes people friends, by drawing them together. What they say goes
       something like this:

God always draws the like unto the like[2]

b   and makes them acquainted. Or haven't you come across these lines?"
       He said he had.
       "And haven't you also come across writings of very wise men saying
       the same thing, that the like must always be friend to the like? You know,
       the authors who reason and write about Nature and the Universe?"
       "Yes, I have," he said.
       "And do you think what they say is right?" I asked.
       "Maybe," he said.
       "Maybe half of it," I said, "maybe even all of it, but we don't understand
c   it. To our way of thinking, the closer a wicked man comes to a wicked
       man and the more he associates with him, the more he becomes his enemy.
       Because he does him an injustice. And it's impossible for those who do
       an injustice and those who suffer it to be friends. Isn't that so?"
       "Yes," he said.
       "Then that would make half the saying untrue, if we assume the wicked
       are like each other."
       "You're right," he said.
       "But what I think they're saying is that the good are like each other and
d   are friends, while the bad—as another saying goes—are never alike, not
       even to themselves. They are out of kilter and unstable. And when some-
       thing is not even like itself and is inconsistent with itself, it can hardly be
       like something else and be a friend to it. Don't you agree?"
       "Oh, I do," he said.
       "Well, my friend, it seems to me that the hidden meaning of those who
       say 'like is a friend to like' is that only the good is a friend, and only to
       the good, while the bad never enters into true friendship with either the
       good or the bad. Do you agree?"
       He nodded yes.
e   "So now we've got it. We know what friends are. Our discussion indicates
       to us that whoever are good are friends."
       "That seems altogether true to me."
       "To me also," I said. "But I'm still a little uneasy with it. By Zeus, let's
       see why I'm still suspicious. Is like friend to like insofar as he is like, and
       as such is he useful to his counterpart? I can put it better this way: When
       something, anything at all, is like something else, how can it benefit or

2. *Odyssey* xvii.218.

harm its like in a way that it could not benefit or harm itself? Or what
could be done to it by its like that could not be done to it by itself? Can   215
such things be prized by each other when they cannot give each other
assistance? Is there any way?"

"No, there isn't."

"And how can anything be a friend if it is not prized?"

"It can't."

"All right, then, like is not friend to like. But couldn't the good still be
friend to the good insofar as he is good, not insofar as he is like?"

"Maybe."

"What about this, though? Isn't a good person, insofar as he is good,
sufficient to himself?"

"Yes."

"And a self-sufficient person has no need of anything, just because of   b
his self-sufficiency?"

"How could he?"

"And the person who needs nothing wouldn't prize anything."

"No, he wouldn't."

"What he didn't prize he wouldn't love."

"Definitely not."

"And whoever doesn't love is not a friend."

"It appears not."

"Then how in the world are the good going to be friends to the good?
They don't yearn for one another when apart, because even then they are
sufficient to themselves, and when together they have no need of one
another. Is there any way people like that can possibly value each other?"

"No."

"But people who don't place much value on each other couldn't be
friends."

"True."

"Now, Lysis, consider how we have been knocked off course. Are we   c
somehow completely mistaken here?"

"How?" he asked.

"Once I heard someone say—I just now remembered this—that like is
most hostile to like, and good men to good men. And he cited Hesiod
as evidence:

> Potter is angry with potter, poet with poet
> And beggar with beggar.[3]

And he said that it had to be the same with everything else: things that   d
are most like are filled with envy, contentiousness, and hatred for each
other, and things most unlike with friendship. The poor man is forced to

---

3. Hesiod, *Works and Days* 25–26.

be friends with the rich, and the weak with the strong—for the sake of assistance—and the sick man with the doctor, and in general every ignorant person has to prize the man who knows and love him. Then he went on

e   to make a very impressive point indeed, saying that the like is totally unqualified to be friend to the like; that just the opposite is true; that things that are completely in opposition to each other are friends in the highest degree, since everything desires its opposite and not its like. Dry desires wet, cold hot, bitter sweet, sharp blunt, empty full, full empty, and so forth on the same principle. For the opposite, he said, is food for its opposite, whereas the like has no enjoyment of its like. Well, my friend,

216 I thought he was quite clever as he said this, for he put it all so well. But you two, what do you think of what he said?"

"It sounds fine," said Menexenus, "at least when you hear it put like that."

"Then should we say that the opposite is its opposite's best friend?"

"Absolutely."

"But Menexenus," I said, "this is absurd. In no time at all those virtuosos,

b   the contradiction mongers, are going to jump on us gleefully and ask us whether enmity is not the thing most opposite to friendship. How are we going to answer them? Won't we have to admit that what they say is true?"

"Yes, we will."

"So then, they will continue, is the enemy a friend to the friend, or the friend a friend to the enemy?"

"Neither," he answered.

"Is the just a friend to the unjust, or the temperate to the licentious, or the good to the bad?"

"I don't think so."

"But if," I said, "something is a friend to something because it is its opposite, then these things must be friends."

"You're right, they must."

"So like is not friend to like, nor is opposite friend to opposite."

"Apparently not."

c   "But there's this too we still ought to consider. We may have overlooked something else, the possibility that the friend is none of these things, but something that is neither bad nor good but becomes the friend of the good just for that reason."

"What do you mean?" he asked.

"By Zeus," I said, "I hardly know myself. I'm getting downright dizzy with the perplexities of our argument. Maybe the old proverb is right, and the beautiful is a friend. It bears a resemblance, at any rate, to something

d   soft and smooth and sleek, and maybe that's why it slides and sinks into us so easily, because it's something like that. Now I maintain that the good is beautiful. What do you think?"

"I agree."

"All right, now, I'm going to wax prophetic and say that what is neither good nor bad is a friend of the beautiful and the good. Listen to the motive for my mantic utterance. It seems to me that there are three kinds of things: the good, the bad, and the neither good nor bad. What about you?"

"It seems so to me too," he said.

"And the good is not a friend to the good, nor the bad to the bad, nor the good to the bad. Our previous argument disallows it. Only one possibility remains. If anything is a friend to anything, what is neither good nor bad is a friend either to the good or to something like itself. For I don't suppose anything could be a friend to the bad."

"True."

"But we just said that like is not friend to like."

"Yes."

"So what is neither good nor bad cannot be a friend to something like itself."

"Apparently not."

"So it turns out that only what is neither good nor bad is friend to the good, and only to the good."

"It seems it must be so."

"Well, then, boys, are we on the right track with our present statement? Suppose we consider a healthy body. It has no need of a doctor's help. It's fine just as it is. So no one in good health is friend to a doctor, on account of his good health. Right?"

"Right."

"But a sick man is, I imagine, on account of his disease."

"Naturally."

"Now, disease is a bad thing, and medicine is beneficial and good."

"Yes."

"And the body, as body, is neither good nor bad."

"True."

"And because of disease, a body is forced to welcome and love medicine."

"I think so."

"So what is neither good nor bad becomes a friend of the good because of the presence of something bad."

"It looks like it."

"But clearly this is before it becomes bad itself by the bad it is in contact with. Because once it has become bad, it can no longer desire the good or be its friend. Remember we said it was impossible for the bad to befriend the good."

"It *is* impossible."

"Now consider what I'm going to say. I say that some things are of the same sort as what is present with them, and some are not. For example, if you paint something a certain color, the paint is somehow present with the thing painted."

"Definitely."

"Then is the thing painted of the same sort, as far as color goes, as the applied paint?"

"I don't understand," he said.

e

217

b

c

d   "Look at it this way," I said. "If someone smeared your blond hair with white lead, would your hair then *be* white or *appear* white?"

"Appear white," he said.

"And yet whiteness would surely be present with it."

"Yes."

"But all the same your hair would not yet be white. Though whiteness would be present, your hair would not be white any more than it is black."

"True."

e   "But when, my friend, old age introduces this same color to your hair, then it will become of the same sort as what is present, white by the presence of white."

"Naturally."

"Here at last is my question, then. When a thing has something present with it, will it be of the same sort as what is present? Or only when that thing is present in a certain way?"

"Only then," he said.

"And what is neither good nor bad sometimes has not yet become bad by the presence with it of bad, but sometimes it has."

"Certainly."

"And when it is not yet bad although bad is present, that presence makes it desire the good. But the presence that makes it be bad deprives

218   it of its desire as well as its love for the good. For it is no longer neither good nor bad, but bad. And the bad can't be friend to the good."

"No, it can't."

"From this we may infer that those who are already wise no longer love wisdom,[4] whether they are gods or men. Nor do those love it who are so ignorant that they are bad, for no bad and stupid man loves wisdom. There remain only those who have this bad thing, ignorance, but have not yet been made ignorant and stupid by it. They are conscious of not knowing

b   what they don't know. The upshot is that those who are as yet neither good nor bad love wisdom, while all those who are bad do not, and neither do those who are good. For our earlier discussion made it clear that the opposite is not friend to the opposite, nor is like friend to like. Remember?"

"Of course," they both answered.

"So now, Lysis and Menexenus, we have discovered for sure what is a

c   friend and what it is friend to. For we maintain that in the soul and in the body and everywhere, that which is neither good nor bad itself is, by the presence of evil, a friend of the good."

The two of them heartily agreed that this was the case, and I was pretty happy myself. I had the satisfied feeling of a successful hunter and was basking in it, when a very strange suspicion, from where I don't know, came over me. Maybe what we had all agreed to wasn't true after all. What an awful thought. "Oh, no!" I screamed out. "Lysis and Menexenus, our wealth has all been a dream!"

---

4. I.e., "philosophize," "engage in philosophy."

"But why?" said Menexenus.   d

"I'm afraid we've fallen in with arguments about friendship that are no better than con artists."

"How?" he asked.

"Let's look at it this way," I said. "Whoever is a friend, is he a friend to someone or not?"

"He has to be a friend to someone," he said.

"For the sake of nothing and on account of nothing, or for the sake of something and on account of something?"

"For the sake of something and on account of something."

"And that something for the sake of which he is a friend, is it a friend, or is it neither friend nor foe?"

"I don't get it," he said.

"Naturally enough," I said. "But perhaps you will if we try it this way—   e
and I think I might better understand what I am saying myself. A sick man, we were just now saying, is a friend to the doctor. Right?"

"Yes."

"And isn't he a friend on account of disease and for the sake of health?"

"Yes."

"And disease is a bad thing?"

"Of course."

"And what about health?" I asked. "Is it a good thing or a bad thing or neither?"

"A good thing," he said.

"I believe we also said that the body, which is neither good nor bad, is   219
a friend of medicine on account of disease, that is, on account of something bad. And medicine is a good thing. It is for the sake of health that medicine has received the friendship. And health is a good thing. All right so far?"

"Yes."

"Is health a friend or not a friend?"

"A friend."

"And disease is an enemy?"

"Certainly."

"So what is neither good nor bad is friend of the good on account of   b
what is bad and an enemy, for the sake of what is good and a friend."

"It appears so."

"So the friend is friend of its friend for the sake of a friend, on account of its enemy."

"It looks like it."

"Well, then," I said, "since we have come this far, boys, let's pay close attention so that we won't be deceived. The fact that the friend has become friend of the friend, and so like has become friend of like, which we said was impossible—I'm going to let that pass by. But there is another point that we must examine, so that what is now being said won't deceive us.   c
Medicine, we say, is a friend for the sake of health."

"Yes."

"Health, then, is also a friend?"

"Very much a friend."

"If, therefore, it is a friend, it is for the sake of something."

"Yes."

"And that something is a friend, if it is going to accord with our previous agreement."

"Very much so."

"Will that too, then, also be a friend for the sake of a friend?"

"Yes."

d "Aren't we going to have to give up going on like this? Don't we have to arrive at some first principle which will no longer bring us back to another friend, something that goes back to the first friend, something for the sake of which we say that all the rest are friends too?"

"We have to."

"This is what I am talking about, the possibility that all the other things that we have called friends for the sake of that thing may be deceiving us, like so many phantoms of it, and that it is that first thing which is truly a friend. Let's think of it in this way. Suppose a man places great value on something, say, a father who values his son more highly than all his other possessions. Would such a man, for the sake of his supreme

e regard for his son, also value something else? If, for example, he learned that his son had drunk hemlock, would he value wine if he thought it could save his son?"

"Why, certainly," he said.

"And also the container the wine was in?"

"Very much."

"At that time would he place the same value on the ceramic cup or the three pints of wine as on his son? Or is it the case that all such concern is expended not for things that are provided for the sake of something

220 else, but for that something else for whose sake all the other things are provided? Not that we don't often talk about how much we value gold and silver. But that's not so and gets us no closer to the truth, which is that we value above all else that for which gold and all other provisions are provided, whatever it may turn out to be. Shall we put it like that?"

"Most certainly."

"And isn't the same account true of the friend? When we talk about all

b the things that are our friends for the sake of another friend, it is clear that we are merely using the word 'friend'. The real friend is surely that in which all these so-called friendships terminate."

"Yes, surely," he said.

"Then the real friend is not a friend for the sake of a friend."

"True."

"So much, then, for the notion that it is for the sake of some friend that the friend is a friend. But then is the good a friend?"

"It seems so to me," he said.

"And it is on account of the bad that the good is loved. Look, this is how it stands. There are three things of which we have just been speaking— good, bad, and what is neither good nor bad. Suppose there remained only two, and bad were eliminated and could affect no one in body or soul or anything else that we say is neither good nor bad in and of itself. Would the good then be of any use to us, or would it have become useless? For if nothing could still harm us, we would have no need of any assistance, and it would be perfectly clear to us that it was on account of the bad that we prized and loved the good—as if the good is a drug against the bad, and the bad is a disease, so that without the disease there is no need for the drug. Isn't the good by nature loved on account of the bad by those of us who are midway between good and bad, but by itself and for its own sake it has no use at all?"

"It looks like that's how it is," he said.

"Then that friend of ours, the one which was the terminal point for all the other things that we called 'friends for the sake of another friend,' does not resemble them at all. For they are called friends for the sake of a friend, but the real friend appears to have a nature completely the opposite of this. It has become clear to us that it was a friend for the sake of an enemy. Take away the enemy and it seems it is no longer a friend."

"It seems it isn't," he said, "not, at least, by what we are saying now."

"By Zeus," I said, "I wonder, if the bad is eliminated, whether it will be possible to be hungry or thirsty or anything like that. Or if there will be hunger as long as human beings and other animals exist, but it won't do harm. Thirst, too, and all the other desires, but they won't be bad, because the bad will have been abolished. Or is it ridiculous to ask what will be then and what will not? Who knows? But we do know this: that it is possible for hunger to do harm, and also possible for it to help. Right?"

"Certainly."

"And isn't it true that thirst or any other such desires can be felt sometimes to one's benefit, sometimes to one's harm, and sometimes to neither?"

"Absolutely."

"And if bad things are abolished, does this have anything to do with things that aren't bad being abolished along with them?"

"No."

"So the desires that are neither good nor bad will continue to exist, even if bad things are abolished."

"It appears so."

"And is it possible to desire and love something passionately without feeling friendly towards it?

"It doesn't seem so to me."

"So there will still be some friendly things even if the bad is abolished."

"Yes."

"It is impossible, if bad were the cause of something's being a friend, that with the bad abolished one thing could be another's friend. When a cause is abolished, the thing that it was the cause of can no longer exist."

"That makes sense."

"Haven't we agreed that the friend loves something, and loves it on account of something, and didn't we think then that it was on account of bad that what was neither good nor bad loved the good?"

"True."

d   "But now it looks like some other cause of loving and being loved has appeared."

"It does look like it."

"Then can it really be, as we were just saying, that desire is the cause of friendship, and that what desires is a friend to that which it desires, and is so whenever it does so? And that what we were saying earlier about being a friend was all just chatter, like a poem that trails on too long?"

"There's a good chance," he said.

e   "But still," I said, "a thing desires what it is deficient in. Right?"

"Yes."

"And the deficient is a friend to that in which it is deficient."

"I think so."

"And it becomes deficient where something is taken away from it."

"How couldn't it?"

"Then it is what belongs to oneself, it seems, that passionate love and friendship and desire are directed towards, Menexenus and Lysis."

They both agreed.

"And if you two are friends with each other, then in some way you naturally belong to each other."

"Absolutely," they said together.

222   "And if one person desires another, my boys, or loves him passionately, he would not desire him or love him passionately or as a friend unless he somehow belonged to his beloved either in his soul or in some characteristic, habit, or aspect of his soul."

"Certainly," said Menexenus, but Lysis was silent.

"All right," I said, "what belongs to us by nature has shown itself to us as something we must love."

"It looks like it," he said.

b   "Then the genuine and not the pretended lover must be befriended by his boy."

Lysis and Menexenus just managed a nod of assent, but Hippothales beamed every color in the rainbow in his delight.

Wanting to review the argument, I said, "It seems to me, Lysis and Menexenus, that if there is some difference between belonging and being like, then we might have something to say about what a friend is. But if belonging and being like turn out to be the same thing, it won't be easy to toss out our former argument that like is useless to like insofar as they

c   are alike. And to admit that the useless is a friend would strike a sour note. So if it's all right with you, I said, since we are a little groggy from this discussion, why don't we agree to say that what belongs is something different from what is like?"

"Certainly."

"And shall we suppose that the good belongs to everyone, while the bad is alien? Or does the bad belong to the bad, the good to the good, and what is neither good nor bad to what is neither good nor bad?"

They both said they liked this latter correlation.

"Well, here we are again, boys," I said. "We have fallen into the same   d
arguments about friendship that we rejected at first. For the unjust will be no less a friend to the unjust, and the bad to the bad, as the good will be to the good."

"So it seems," he said.

"Then what? If we say that the good is the same as belonging, is there any alternative to the good being a friend only to the good?"

"No."

"But we thought we had refuted ourselves on this point. Or don't you remember?"

"We remember."

"So what can we still do with our argument? Or is it clear that there is   e
nothing left? I do ask, like the able speakers in the law courts, that you think over everything that has been said. If neither the loved nor the loving, nor the like nor the unlike, nor the good, nor the belonging, nor any of the others we have gone through—well, there have been so many I certainly don't remember them all any more, but if none of these is a friend, then I have nothing left to say."

Having said that, I had a mind to get something going with one of the   223
older men there. But just then, like some kind of divine intermediaries, the guardians of Menexenus and Lysis were on the scene. They had the boys' brothers with them and called out to them that it was time to go home. It actually was late by now. At first our group tried to drive them off, but they didn't pay any attention to us and just got riled up and went on calling in their foreign accents. We thought they had been drinking too   b
much at the Hermaea and might be difficult to handle, so we capitulated and broke up our party. But just as they were leaving I said, "Now we've done it, Lysis and Menexenus—made fools of ourselves, I, an old man, and you as well. These people here will go away saying that we are friends of one another—for I count myself in with you—but what a friend is we have not yet been able to find out."

EUTHYDEMUS

Socrates meets his good friend Crito, recounts and discusses with him a public encounter he had the previous day with a pair of sophists, and urges him to join him in enrolling—old men though they are!—as the sophists' pupils. That is a bare summary of this exquisitely accomplished dialogue. Euthydemus and his older brother Dionysodorus (real people, though hardly known except here) have been in Athens previously. But now they have abandoned their former teaching of lawyer's oratory and military science for instruction in a different sort of combat: the combat of words in question-and-answer discussion of the basic type to which Socrates himself is devoted, and of which we get especially well defined instances in Protagoras. They promise to 'refute whatever may be said, no matter whether it is true or false'; by teaching the same 'eristic' wisdom to their pupils (it doesn't take long, they say), they will make them paragons of human virtue. Socrates forestalls the formal sophistic 'exhibition' of their skill that they have brought with them (as he similarly avoids or silently endures Gorgias' and Hippias' exhibitions in the dialogues named after them), and gets them instead to converse with the young boy Clinias, to persuade him to devote himself to 'philosophy and the practice of virtue'—under their tutelage, it goes without saying. Though it is not their prepared exhibition, their questioning of Clinias (and, later on, Ctesippus and Socrates himself) does give a clear demonstration of their methods. Thus readers, together with Crito, can form their own opinion of the value of this new brand of the sophist's art, so different from that of Protagoras, or Prodicus, or Hippias. Socrates twice interposes extended question-and-answer conversations of his own with Clinias, offering a very different picture of how one might draw a young boy on to devote himself to philosophy and the practice of virtue.

Crito is not nearly so enthusiastic as Socrates himself claims to be about these new sophists' 'wisdom', and hesitates to accept his invitation to join him in enrolling as their students. As emerges at the very end of the dialogue, he had got an earlier report on yesterday's proceedings from an unnamed acquaintance, which was much less laudatory than Socrates'. Plato makes it plain to his contemporary readers that this person is the orator and teacher of 'philosophy' Isocrates, head of a very successful school at Athens in the decades after Socrates' death, rival to Plato's own Academy. (Plato has Socrates compliment him by name in carefully qualified ways toward the end of Phaedrus.) Accepting Crito's description of the sophists' activities as 'philosophy', this person denounces it as 'of no value whatsoever', as 'worthless' and 'ridiculous'. Do Socrates, and Plato, agree? It seems not—that at least is the implication of

Socrates' praise, no doubt ironically overdrawn, and of his refusal to join in the denunciation. True philosophy, and real devotion to it, require an interest in logic and argument for its own sake, whether or not it is used correctly or yields valid support for true conclusions. Even the misuse of reason has its gripping appeal to one who would model his life on the proper use of it. Socrates is himself no 'eristic'—his approach to Clinias is fostering, not refutatory, and his firm interest throughout is in the truth, not mere verbal victory. But he (or Plato) refuses to reject, dismiss, and denounce the arguments of the eristics, Euthydemus and Dionysodorus, as 'of no value whatsoever', as 'worthless' and 'ridiculous'. They have their own power, as all uses of reason do, and must be respectfully examined and analyzed—even while one does not accept their conclusions.

J.M.C.

CRITO: Who was it, Socrates, you were talking to in the Lyceum yester-   271
day? There was such a crowd standing around you that when I came up and wanted to listen, I couldn't hear anything distinctly. But by craning my neck I did get a look, and I thought it was some stranger you were talking to. Who was it?

SOCRATES: Which one are you asking about, Crito? There was not just one, but two.

CRITO: The person I mean was sitting next but one to you on your right—   b
between you was Axiochus' young son.[1] He seemed to me, Socrates, to have grown tremendously, and to be almost of a size with our Critobulus. But Critobulus is thin, whereas this boy has come on splendidly and is extremely good-looking.

SOCRATES: Euthydemus is the man you mean, Crito, and the one sitting next to me on my left was his brother, Dionysodorus—he, too, takes part in the discussions.

CRITO: I don't know either of them, Socrates. They are another new kind of sophist, I suppose. Where do they come from, and what is their   c
particular wisdom?

SOCRATES: By birth, I think, they are from this side, from Chios. They went out as colonists to Thurii but were exiled from there and have already spent a good many years in this region. As to your question about the wisdom of the pair, it is marvelous, Crito! The two are absolutely omniscient, so much so that I never knew before what pancratiasts really were. They are both absolutely all-round fighters, not like the two battling brothers from Acarnania who could only fight with their bodies.[2] These two   d

Translated by Rosamond Kent Sprague.

1. Clinias: see below, 273a–b.
2. The pancration (lit., "all-round fighting") was a combination of wrestling and boxing.

are first of all completely skilled in body, being highly adept at fighting
272   in armor and able to teach this skill to anyone else who pays them a fee;
and then they are the ones best able to fight the battle of the law court
and to teach other people both how to deliver and how to compose the
sort of speeches suitable for the courts. Previously these were their only
skills, but now they have put the finishing touch to pancratistic art. They
have now mastered the one form of fighting they had previously left
untried; as a result, not a single man can stand up to them, they have
b   become so skilled in fighting in arguments and in refuting whatever may
be said, no matter whether it is true or false. So that I, Crito, have a mind
to hand myself over to these men, since they say that they can make any
other person clever at the same things in a short time.

CRITO: What's that, Socrates? Aren't you afraid that, at your age, you
are already too old?

SOCRATES: Far from it, Crito—I have enough example and encouragement
to keep me from being afraid. The two men themselves were pretty well
advanced in years when they made a start on this wisdom I want to get;
I mean the eristic sort. Last year or the year before they were not yet wise.
c   My only anxiety is that I may disgrace the two strangers just as I have
already disgraced Connus the harpist, Metrobius' son, who is still trying
to teach me to play. The boys who take lessons with me laugh at the sight
and call Connus the "Old Man's Master." So I am afraid that someone may
reproach the strangers on the same score; perhaps they may be unwilling to
take me as a pupil for fear that this should happen. So, Crito, I have
persuaded some other old men to go along with me as fellow pupils to
d   the harp lessons, and I shall attempt to persuade some others for this
project. Why don't you come along yourself? We will take your sons as
bait to catch them—I feel sure that their desire to get the boys will make
them give us lessons too.

CRITO: I have no objection, Socrates, if you really think well of the plan.
But first explain to me what the wisdom of the two men is, to give me
some idea of what we are going to learn.

SOCRATES: You shall hear at once, since I can't pretend that I paid no
attention to the pair. As a matter of fact, I did just that and remember
e   what was said and will try to recount the whole thing from the beginning.
As good luck would have it, I was sitting by myself in the undressing-
room just where you saw me and was already thinking of leaving. But
when I got up, my customary divine sign put in an appearance. So I
273   sat down again, and in a moment the two of them, Euthydemus and
Dionysodorus, came in, and some others with them, disciples of theirs,
who seemed to me pretty numerous. When the pair came in, they walked
around the cloister, and they had not yet made more than two or three
turns when in came Clinias, who, as you rightly say, has grown a lot.
Following him were a good many others, lovers of his, and among them
Ctesippus, a young man from Paeania—he's a well-bred fellow except for
b   a certain youthful brashness. From the doorway Clinias caught sight of

me sitting alone and came straight up and sat down on my right, just as you describe it. When Dionysodorus and Euthydemus saw him, at first they stood talking to each other and glancing at us every so often (I was keeping a good eye on them) but after a while they came over and one of them, Euthydemus, sat down next to the boy, and his brother next to me on my left, and the rest found places where they could. Since I hadn't   c
seen the two for quite a time, I gave them a good welcome, and then I said to Clinias, You know, Clinias, that the wisdom of these two men, Euthydemus and Dionysodorus, has to do with important matters and not mere trivia. They know all about war, that is, the things a man ought to know who means to be a good general, such as the formations of troops and their command and how to fight in armor; and besides this, they can make a man capable of looking out for himself in court if anyone should do him an injury.

They obviously thought little of me for saying this, because they both   d
laughed and glanced at each other, and Euthydemus said, We are not any longer in earnest about these things, Socrates—we treat them as diversions.

I was astonished and said, Your serious occupation must certainly be splendid if you have important things like these for your diversions! For heaven's sake, tell me what this splendid occupation is!

Virtue, Socrates, is what it is, he said, and we think we can teach it better than anyone else and more quickly.

Good heavens, I said, what a claim you make! Wherever did you find   e
this godsend? I was still thinking of you, as I just said, as men particularly skilled in fighting in armor, and so I spoke of you in this way. When you visited us before, I remember that this was what you claimed to be. But now if you really have this other wisdom, be propitious—you see, I am addressing you exactly as though you were gods because I want you to forgive me for what I said earlier. But make sure, Euthydemus and   274
Dionysodorus, that you are telling the truth—the magnitude of your claim certainly gives me some cause for disbelief.

Rest assured, Socrates, that things are as we say.

Then I count you much happier in your possession of this wisdom than the Great King in that of his empire! But tell me just this: do you plan to give a demonstration of this wisdom, or what do you mean to do?

We are here for that very purpose, Socrates: to give a demonstration,   b
and to teach, if anyone wants to learn.

I give you my word that everyone who does not have this wisdom will wish to have it: first myself, then Clinias here, and, in addition to us, this fellow Ctesippus and these others, I said, pointing to the lovers of Clinias who were already grouped around us. This had come about because Ctesippus had taken a seat a long way from Clinias, and when Euthydemus leaned forward in talking to me, he apparently obscured Ctesippus' view   c
of Clinias, who was sitting between us. So Ctesippus, who wanted to look at his darling, as well as being interested in the discussion, sprang up first and stationed himself right in front of us. When the others saw him doing

d this, they gathered around too, not only Clinias' lovers but the followers of Euthydemus and Dionysodorus as well. These were the ones I pointed to when I told Euthydemus that everyone was ready to learn. Then Ctesippus agreed very eagerly and so did all the rest, and all together they besought the pair to demonstrate the power of their wisdom.

So I said, Euthydemus and Dionysodorus, do your absolute best to gratify these people and give a demonstration—and do it for my sake too. To give a complete one would obviously be a lengthy business; but tell

e me just this: are you able to make only that man good who is already persuaded that he ought to take lessons from you, or can you also make the man good who is not yet persuaded on this point, either because he believes that this thing, virtue, cannot be taught at all, or because he thinks that you two are not its teachers? Come tell me, does the task of persuading a man in this frame of mind both that virtue can be taught, and that you are the ones from whom he could learn it best, belong to this same art or to some other one?

It belongs to this same art, Socrates, said Dionysodorus.

275   Then, Dionysodorus, I said, you and your brother are the men of the present day best able to exhort a man to philosophy and the practice of virtue?

This is exactly what we think, Socrates.

Then put off the rest of your display to another time and give us a demonstration of this one thing: persuade this young man here that he ought to love wisdom and have a care for virtue, and you will oblige both me and all the present company. The boy's situation is this: both I and all these people want him to become as good as possible. He is the son of

b Axiochus (son of the old Alcibiades) and is cousin to the present Alcibiades—his name is Clinias. He is young, and we are anxious about him, as one naturally is about a boy of his age, for fear that somebody might get in ahead of us and turn his mind to some other interest and ruin him. So you two have arrived at the best possible moment. If you have no objection, make trial of the boy and converse with him in our presence.

When I had spoken, in almost these exact words, Euthydemus answered,

c with a mixture of bravery and confidence. It makes no difference to us, Socrates, so long as the young man is willing to answer.

As a matter of fact, he is quite used to that, I said, since these people here are always coming to ask him all sorts of questions and to converse with him. So he is pretty brave at answering.

As to what happened next, Crito, how shall I give you an adequate description of it? It is no small task to be able to recall such wisdom in

d detail, it was so great. So I ought to begin my account as the poets do, by invoking the Muses and Memory. Well, Euthydemus, as I remember, began something like this: Clinias, which are the men who learn, the wise or the ignorant?

Being confronted with this weighty question, the boy blushed and looked at me in doubt. And I, seeing that he was troubled, said, Cheer up, Clinias,

and choose bravely whichever seems to you to be the right answer—he   e
may be doing you a very great service.

Just at this moment Dionysodorus leaned a little toward me and, smiling
all over his face, whispered in my ear and said, I may tell you beforehand,
Socrates, that whichever way the boy answers he will be refuted.

While he was saying this, Clinias gave his answer, so that I had no   276
chance to advise the boy to be careful; and he answered that the wise were
the learners.

Then Euthydemus said, Are there some whom you call teachers, or not?

He agreed that there were.

And the teachers are teachers of those who learn, I suppose, in the same
way that the music master and the writing master were teachers of you
and the other boys when you were pupils?

He agreed.

And when you were learning, you did not yet know the things you
were learning, did you?

No, he said.

And were you wise when you did not know these things?   b

By no means, he said.

Then if not wise, ignorant?

Very much so.

Then in the process of learning what you did not know, you learned
while you were ignorant?

The boy nodded.

Then it is the ignorant who learn, Clinias, and not the wise, as you
suppose.

When he said this, the followers of Dionysodorus and Euthydemus   c
broke into applause and laughter, just like a chorus at a sign from their
director. And before the boy could well recover his breath, Dionysodorus
took up the argument and said, Well then, Clinias, when the writing
master gave you dictation, which of the boys learned the piece, the wise
or the ignorant?

The wise, said Clinias.

Then it is the wise who learn, and not the ignorant, and you gave
Euthydemus a wrong answer just now.

Whereupon the supporters of the pair laughed and cheered very loudly   d
indeed, in admiration of their cleverness. We, on the other hand, were
panic-struck and kept quiet. Euthydemus, observing our distress, and in
order to confound us further, would not let the boy go but went on
questioning him and, like a skillful dancer, gave a double twist to his
questions on the same point, saying, Do those who learn learn the things
they know or the things they do not know?

And Dionysodorus again whispered to me in a low voice, This is another,   e
Socrates, just like the first.

Mercy on us, I said, the first question certainly seemed good enough!

All our questions are of this same inescapable sort, Socrates, he said.

And this, no doubt, is the reason why your pupils admire you so much, I said.

Just then Clinias answered Euthydemus that the learners learned what they do not know, whereupon Euthydemus put him through the same course of questions as before.

277   What then, he said, don't you know your letters?

Yes, he said.

Then you know them all?

He agreed.

Whenever anyone dictates anything, doesn't he dictate letters?

He agreed.

b   Then doesn't he dictate something you know, if you really know them all?

He agreed to this too.

Well then, he said, you are not the one who learns what someone dictates, are you, but the one who doesn't know his letters is the one who learns?

No, he said, I am the one who learns.

Then you learn what you know, he said, if you in fact do know all your letters.

He agreed.

Then your answer was wrong, he said.

Euthydemus had barely said this when Dionysodorus picked up the argument as though it were a ball and aimed it at the boy again, saying, Euthydemus is completely deceiving you, Clinias. Tell me, isn't learning the acquisition of the knowledge of what one learns?

Clinias agreed.

And what about knowing? he said. Is it anything except having knowledge already?

c   He agreed.

Then not knowing is not yet having knowledge?

He agreed with him.

And are those who acquire something those who have it already or those who do not?

Those who do not.

And you have admitted, haven't you, that those who do not know belong to the group of those who do not have something?

He nodded.

Then the learners belong to those who acquire and not to those who have?

He agreed.

Then it is those who do not know who learn, Clinias, and not those who know.

d   Euthydemus was hastening to throw the young man for the third fall when I, seeing that he was going down and wanting to give him a chance to breathe so that he should not turn coward and disgrace us, encouraged him, saying, Don't be surprised, Clinias, if these arguments seem strange to you, since perhaps you don't take in what the visitors are doing with you. They are doing exactly what people do in the Corybantic mysteries when they enthrone a person they intend to initiate. If you have been initiated you know that there is dancing and sport on these occasions; and now these two are doing nothing except dancing around you and making sportive leaps with a view to initiating you presently. So you must now imagine yourself to be hearing the first part of the sophistic mysteries. In the first place, as Prodicus says, you must learn about the correct use of words; and our two visitors are pointing out this very thing, that you did not realize that people use the word "learn" not only in the situation in which a person who has no knowledge of a thing in the beginning acquires it later, but also when he who has this knowledge already uses it to inspect the same thing, whether this is something spoken or something done. (As a matter of fact, people call the latter "understand" rather than "learn," but they do sometimes call it "learn" as well.) Now this, as they are pointing out, had escaped your notice—that the same word is applied to opposite sorts of men, to both the man who knows and the man who does not. There was something similar to this in the second question, when they asked you whether people learn what they know or what they do not know. These things are the frivolous part of study (which is why I also tell you that the men are jesting); and I call these things "frivolity" because even if a man were to learn many or even all such things, he would be none the wiser as to how matters stand but would only be able to make fun of people, tripping them up and overturning them by means of the distinctions in words, just like the people who pull the chair out from under a man who is going to sit down and then laugh gleefully when they see him sprawling on his back. So you must think of their performance as having been mere play. But after this they will doubtless show you serious things, if anyone will, and I shall give them a lead to make sure they hand over what they promised me. They said they would give a demonstration of hortatory skill, but now it seems to me that they must have thought it necessary to make fun of you before beginning. So, Euthydemus and Dionysodorus, put an end to this joking; I think we have had enough of it. The next thing to do is to give an exhibition of persuading the young man that he ought to devote himself to wisdom and virtue. But first I shall give you two a demonstration of the way in which I conceive the undertaking and of the sort of thing I want to hear. And if I seem to you to be doing this in an unprofessional and ridiculous way, don't laugh at me—it is out of a desire to hear your wisdom that I have the audacity to improvise in front of you. Therefore, you and your disciples restrain yourselves and listen without laughing; and you, son of Axiochus, answer me:

Do all men wish to do well? Or is this question one of the ridiculous ones I was afraid of just now? I suppose it is stupid even to raise such a question, since there could hardly be a man who would not wish to do well.

No, there is no such person, said Clinias.

Well then, I said, the next question is, since we wish to do well, how are we to do so? Would it be through having many good things? Or is this question still more simple-minded than the other, since this must obviously be the case too?

He agreed.

279   Well then, what kinds of existing things are good for us? Or perhaps this isn't a difficult question and we don't need an important personage to supply the answer because everybody would tell us that to be rich is a good—isn't that so?

Very much so, he said.

b   And so with being healthy, and handsome, and having a sufficient supply of the other things the body needs?

He agreed.

And, again, it is clear that noble birth, and power, and honor in one's country are goods.

He agreed.

Then which goods do we have left? I said. What about being self-controlled and just and brave? For heaven's sake tell me, Clinias, whether you think we will be putting these in the right place if we class them as goods or if we refuse to do so? Perhaps someone might quarrel with us on this point—how does it seem to you?

They are goods, said Clinias.

c   Very well, said I. And where in the company shall we station wisdom? Among the goods, or what shall we do with it?

Among the goods.

Now be sure we do not leave out any goods worth mentioning.

I don't think we are leaving out any, said Clinias.

But I remembered one and said, Good heavens, Clinias, we are in danger of leaving out the greatest good of all!

Which one is that? He said.

Good fortune, Clinias, which everybody, even quite worthless people, says is the greatest of the goods.

You are right, he said.

d   And I reconsidered a second time and said, son of Axiochus, you and I have nearly made ourselves ridiculous in front of our visitors.

How so? he said.

Because in putting good fortune in our previous list we are now saying the same thing all over again.

What do you mean?

Surely it is ridiculous, when a thing has already been brought up, to bring it up again and say the same things twice.

What do you mean by that?

Wisdom is surely good fortune, I said—this is something even a child would know.

He was amazed—he is still so young and simple-minded.

I noticed his surprise and said, You know, don't you, Clinias, that flute   e
players have the best luck when it comes to success in flute music?

He agreed.

And the writing masters at reading and writing?

Certainly.

What about the perils of the sea—surely you don't think that, as a general
rule, any pilots have better luck than the wise ones?

Certainly not.

And again, if you were on a campaign, with which general would you   280
prefer to share both the danger and the luck, a wise one or an ignorant one?

With a wise one.

And if you were sick, would you rather take a chance with a wise doctor
or with an ignorant one?

With a wise one.

Then it is your opinion, I said, that it is luckier to do things in the
company of wise men than ignorant ones?

He agreed.

So wisdom makes men fortunate in every case, since I don't suppose
she would ever make any sort of mistake but must necessarily do right
and be lucky—otherwise she would no longer be wisdom.

We finally agreed (I don't know quite how) that, in sum, the situation   b
was this: if a man had wisdom, he had no need of any good fortune in
addition. When we had settled this point, I went back and asked him how
our former statements might be affected. We decided, I said, that if we
had many good things, we should be happy and do well.

He agreed.

And would the possession of good things make us happy if they were   c
of no advantage to us, or if they were of some?

If they were of some advantage, he said.

And would they be advantageous to us if we simply had them and did
not use them? For instance, if we had a great deal of food but didn't eat
any, or plenty to drink but didn't drink any, would we derive any advantage from these things?

Certainly not, he said.

Well then, if every workman had all the materials necessary for his
particular job but never used them, would he do well by reason of possessing all the things a workman requires? For instance, if a carpenter were
provided with all his tools and plenty of wood but never did any carpentry,
could he be said to benefit from their possession?   d

Not at all, he said.

Well then, if a man had money and all the good things we were mentioning just now but made no use of them, would he be happy as a result of
having these good things?

Clearly not, Socrates.

So it seems, I said, that the man who means to be happy must not only have such goods but must use them too, or else there is no advantage in having them.

You are right.

e   Then are these two things, the possession of good things and the use of them, enough to make a man happy, Clinias?

They seem so to me, at any rate.

If, I said, he uses them rightly, or if he does not?

If he uses them rightly.

Well spoken, I said. Now I suppose there is more harm done if someone uses a thing wrongly than if he lets it alone—in the first instance there is

281 evil, but in the second neither evil nor good. Or isn't this what we maintain?

He agreed that it was.

Then what comes next? In working and using wood there is surely nothing else that brings about right use except the knowledge of carpentry, is there?

Certainly not.

And, again, I suppose that in making utensils, it is knowledge that produces the right method.

He agreed.

And also, I said, with regard to using the goods we mentioned first—

b   wealth and health and beauty—was it knowledge that ruled and directed our conduct in relation to the right use of all such things as these, or some other thing?

It was knowledge, he said.

Then knowledge seems to provide men not only with good fortune but also with well-doing, in every case of possession or action.

He agreed.

Then in heaven's name, I said, is there any advantage in other possessions without good sense and wisdom? Would a man with no sense profit more if he possessed and did much or if he possessed and did little?[3] Look at

c   it this way: if he did less, would he not make fewer mistakes; and if he made fewer mistakes, would he not do less badly, and if he did less badly, would he not be less miserable?

Yes, indeed, he said.

And in which case would one do less, if one were poor or if one were rich?

Poor, he said.

And if one were weak or strong?

Weak.

If one were held in honor or in dishonor?

In dishonor.

And if one were brave and self-controlled would one do less, or if one were a coward?

A coward.

3. Omitting *noun echōn* at b8.

Then the same would be true if one were lazy rather than industrious? He agreed.

And slow rather than quick, and dull of sight and hearing rather than   d
keen?

We agreed with each other on all points of this sort.

So, to sum up, Clinias, I said, it seems likely that with respect to all the things we called good in the beginning, the correct account is not that in themselves they are good by nature, but rather as follows: if ignorance controls them, they are greater evils than their opposites, to the extent that they are more capable of complying with a bad master; but if good sense and wisdom are in control, they are greater goods. In themselves, however,   e
neither sort is of any value.

It seems, he said, to be just as you say.

Then what is the result of our conversation? Isn't it that, of the other things, no one of them is either good or bad, but of these two, wisdom is good and ignorance bad?

He agreed.

Then let us consider what follows: since we all wish to be happy, and   282
since we appear to become so by using things and using them rightly, and since knowledge was the source of rightness and good fortune, it seems to be necessary that every man should prepare himself by every means to become as wise as possible—or isn't this the case?

Yes, it is, he said.

And for a man who thinks he ought to get this from his father much more than money, and not only from his father but also from his guardians   b
and friends (especially those of his city and elsewhere who claim to be his lovers), and who begs and beseeches them to give him some wisdom, there is nothing shameful, Clinias, nor disgraceful if, for the sake of this, he should become the servant or the slave of a lover or of any man, being willing to perform any honorable service in his desire to become wise. Or don't you think so? I said.

You seem to me to be absolutely right, said he.

But only if wisdom can be taught, Clinias, I said, and does not come to   c
men of its own accord. This point still remains for us to investigate and is not yet settled between you and me.

As far as I am concerned, Socrates, he said, I think it can be taught.

I was pleased and said, I like the way you talk, my fine fellow, and you have done me a good turn by relieving me of a long investigation of this very point, whether or not wisdom can be taught. Now then, since you believe both that it can be taught and that it is the only existing thing which makes a man happy and fortunate, surely you would agree that it   d
is necessary to love wisdom and you mean to do this yourself.

This is just what I mean to do, Socrates, as well as ever I can.

When I heard this I was delighted and said, There, Dionysodorus and Euthydemus, is my example of what I want a hortatory argument to be, though amateurish, perhaps, and expressed at length and with some difficulty. Now let either of you who wishes give us a demonstration of the same thing in a professional manner. Or if you do not wish to do that,

e then start where I left off and show the boy what follows next: whether he ought to acquire every sort of knowledge, or whether there is one sort that he ought to get in order to be a happy man and a good one, and what it is. As I said in the beginning, it is of great importance to us that this young man should become wise and good.

283   This is what I said, Crito, and I paid particular attention to what should come next and watched to see just how they would pick up the argument and where they would start persuading the young man to practice wisdom and virtue. The elder of the two, Dionysodorus, took up the argument first and we all gazed at him in expectation of hearing some wonderful words immediately. And this is just what happened, since the man began

b an argument which was certainly wonderful, in a way, Crito, and worth your while to hear, since it was an incitement to virtue.

Tell me, Socrates, he said, and all you others who say you want this young man to become wise—are you saying this as a joke or do you want it truly and in earnest?

This gave me the idea that they must have thought we were joking earlier when we asked them to talk to the boy, and that this was why they

c made a joke of it and failed to take it seriously. When this idea occurred to me, I insisted all the more that we were in dead earnest.

And Dionysodorus said, Well, take care, Socrates, that you don't find yourself denying these words.

I have given thought to the matter, I said, and I shall never come to deny them.

Well then, he said, you say you want him to become wise?

Very much so.

And at the present moment, he said, is Clinias wise or not?

He says he is not yet, at least—he is a modest person, I said.

d   But you people wish him to become wise, he said, and not to be ignorant?

We agreed.

Therefore, you wish him to become what he is not, and no longer to be what he is now?

When I heard this I was thrown into confusion, and he broke in upon me while I was in this state and said, Then since you wish him no longer to be what he is now, you apparently wish for nothing else but his death. Such friends and lovers must be worth a lot who desire above all things that their beloved should utterly perish!

e   When Ctesippus heard this he became angry on his favorite's account and said, Thurian stranger, if it were not a rather rude remark, I would say "perish yourself" for taking it into your head to tell such a lie about me and the rest, which I think is a wicked thing to say—that I could wish this person to die!

Why Ctesippus, said Euthydemus, do you think it possible to tell lies?

Good heavens yes, he said, I should be raving if I didn't.

When one speaks the thing one is talking about, or when one does not speak it?

When one speaks it, he said.   284

So that if he speaks this thing, he speaks no other one of things that are except the very one he speaks?

Of course, said Ctesippus.

And the thing he speaks is one of those that are, distinct from the rest?

Certainly.

Then the person speaking that thing speaks what is, he said.

Yes.

But surely the person who speaks what is and things that are speaks the truth—so that Dionysodorus, if he speaks things that are, speaks the truth and tells no lies about you.

Yes, said Ctesippus, but a person who speaks these things, Euthydemus,   b
does not speak things that are.

And Euthydemus said, But the things that are not surely do not exist, do they?

No, they do not exist.

Then there is nowhere that the things that are not are?

Nowhere.

Then there is no possibility that any person whatsoever could do anything to the things that are not so as to make them be[4] when they are nowhere?

It seems unlikely to me, said Ctesippus.

Well then, when the orators speak to the people, do they do nothing?

No, they do something, he said.

Then if they do something, they also make something?   c

Yes.

Speaking, then, is doing and making?

He agreed.

Then nobody speaks things that are not, since he would then be making something, and you have admitted that no one is capable of making something that is not. So according to your own statement, nobody tells lies; but if Dionysodorus really does speak, he speaks the truth and things that are.

Yes indeed, Euthydemus, said Ctesippus, but he speaks things that are only in a certain way and not as really is the case.

What do you mean, Ctesippus? said Dionysodorus. Are there some   d
persons who speak of things as they are?

There certainly are, he said—gentlemen and those who speak the truth.

Now then, he said, are not good things well and bad things ill?

He agreed.

And you admit that gentlemen speak of things as they are?

Yes, I do.

4. Reading *hōste kai einai* at b6.

Then good men speak ill of bad things, Ctesippus, if they do in fact speak of them as they are.

They certainly do, he said—at any rate they speak ill of bad men. If you
e take my advice you will take care not to be one of them in case the good speak ill of *you*. For rest assured that the good speak ill of the bad.

And do they speak greatly of the great and hotly of the hot? asked Euthydemus.

Very much so, said Ctesippus, and what is more, they speak coldly of persons who argue in a frigid fashion.

You, Ctesippus, said Dionysodorus, are being abusive, very abusive indeed.

I am certainly doing no such thing, Dionysodorus, he said, since I like you, I am merely giving you a piece of friendly advice and endeavouring
285 to persuade you never to say, so rudely and to my face, that I want my most cherished friends to die.

Since they seemed to be getting pretty rough with each other, I started to joke with Ctesippus and said, Ctesippus, I think we ought to accept what the strangers tell us, if they are willing to be generous, and not to quarrel over a word. If they really know how to destroy men so as to make good and sensible people out of bad and stupid ones, and the two
b of them have either found out for themselves or learned from someone else a kind of ruin or destruction by which they do away with a bad man and render him good, if, as I say, they know how to do this—well, they clearly do, since they specifically claimed that the art they had recently discovered was that of making good men out of bad ones—then let us concede them the point and permit them to destroy the boy for us and make him wise—and do the same to the rest of us as well. And if you
c young men are afraid, let them "try it on the Carian,"[5] as they say, and I will be the victim. Being elderly, I am ready to run the risk, and I surrender myself to Dionysodorus here just as I might to Medea of Colchis.[6] Let him destroy me, or if he likes, boil me, or do whatever else he wants, but he must make me good.

And Ctesippus said, I too, Socrates, am ready to hand myself over to the visitors; and I give them permission to skin me even more thoroughly than they are doing now so long as my hide will in the end become not
d a wineskin (which is what happened to Marsyas),[7] but a piece of virtue. And yet Dionysodorus here thinks I am cross with him. It's not that I'm cross—I'm simply contradicting the things he said which I find objectionable. So, my fine Dionysodorus, don't call contradiction abuse—abuse is something quite different.

5. That is, try it on the dog or on a guinea pig.

6. Medea persuaded the daughters of Pelias to cut up their father and boil him in a cauldron, telling them that in this way they would renew his youth.

7. Marsyas, a satyr, challenged Apollo to a musical contest. Apollo, having won the contest, flayed his opponent alive. Cf. Herodotus, vii.26.

And Dionysodorus answered, Are you making your speech on the assumption that there exists such a thing as contradiction, Ctesippus?

I certainly am, he said, decidedly so. And do you think there is none, Dionysodorus?

Well you, at any rate, could not prove that you have ever heard one person contradicting another.

Do you really mean that? he answered. Well then, just listen to Ctesippus contradicting Dionysodorus, if you want to hear my proof.[8]

And do you undertake to back that up?

I certainly do, he said.

Well then, he went on, are there words to describe each thing that exists?

Certainly.

And do they describe it as it is or as it is not?

As it is.

Now if you remember, Ctesippus, he said, we showed a moment ago that no one speaks of things as they are not, since it appeared that no one speaks what does not exist.

Well, what about it? said Ctesippus. Are you and I contradicting each other any the less?

Now would we be contradicting, he said, if we were both to speak the[9] description of the same thing? I suppose we would be saying the same things in that case.

He agreed.

But when neither of us speaks the description of the thing, would we be contradicting then? Or wouldn't it be the case that neither of us had the thing in mind at all?

He agreed to this too.

But when I speak the description of the thing whereas you speak another description of another thing, do we contradict then? Or is it the case that I speak it but that you speak nothing at all? And how would a person who does not speak contradict one who does?

Ctesippus fell silent at this, but I was astonished at the argument and said, How do you mean, Dionysodorus? The fact is that I have heard this particular argument from many persons and at many times, and it never ceases to amaze me. The followers of Protagoras made considerable use of it, and so did some still earlier. It always seems to me to have a wonderful way of upsetting not just other arguments, but itself as well. But I think I shall learn the truth about it better from you than from anyone else. The argument amounts to claiming that there is no such thing as false speaking, doesn't it? And the person speaking must either speak the truth or else not speak?

He agreed.

---

8. Reading *akouōmen nun ei* at e5.

9. Accepting the addition of ⟨*ton*⟩ before *tou* at a5.

d   Now would you say it was impossible to speak what is false, but possible to think it?

No, thinking it is not possible either, he said.

Then there is absolutely no such thing as false opinion, I said.

There is not, he said.

Then is there no ignorance, nor are there any ignorant men? Or isn't this just what ignorance would be, if there should be any—to speak falsely about things?

It certainly would, he said.

And yet there is no such thing, I said.

He said there was not.

Are you making this statement just for the sake of argument, Dionysodorus—to say something startling—or do you honestly believe that there is no such thing as an ignorant man?

e   Your business is to refute me, he said.

Well, but is there such a thing as refutation if one accepts your thesis that nobody speaks falsely?

No, there is not, said Euthydemus.

Then it can't be that Dionysodorus ordered me to refute him just now, can it? I said.

How would anyone order a thing which doesn't exist? Are you in the habit of giving such orders?

The reason I've raised the point, Euthydemus, is that I'm rather thickwitted and don't understand these fine clever things. And perhaps I'm about to ask a rather stupid question, but bear with me. Look at it this way: if
287   it is impossible to speak falsely, or to think falsely, or to be ignorant, then there is no possibility of making a mistake when a man does anything? I mean that it is impossible for a man to be mistaken in his actions—or isn't this what you are saying?

Certainly it is, he said.

This is just where my stupid question comes in, I said. If no one of us makes mistakes either in action or in speech or in thought—if this really is the case—what in heaven's name do you two come here to teach? Or
b   didn't you say just now that if anyone wanted to learn virtue, you would impart it best?

Really, Socrates, said Dionysodorus, interrupting, are you such an old Cronus[10] as to bring up now what we said in the beginning? I suppose if I said something last year, you will bring that up now and still be helpless in dealing with the present argument.

Well you see, I said, these arguments are very difficult (as is natural, since they come from wise men) and this last one you mention turns out to be particularly difficult to deal with. Whatever in the world do you mean by the expression "be helpless in dealing with," Dionysodorus?
c   Doesn't it clearly mean that I am unable to refute the argument? Just tell

---

10. As the father of Zeus whom Zeus dethroned, Cronus is a symbol of the out-of-date.

me, what else is the sense of this phrase "I am helpless in dealing with the argument"?

But at least it is not very difficult to deal with *your* phrase,[11] he said, so go ahead and answer.

Before you answer me, Dionysodorus? I said.

You refuse to answer then? he said.

Well, is it fair?

Perfectly fair, he said.

On what principle? I said. Or isn't it clearly on this one, that you have come here on the present occasion as a man who is completely skilled in arguments, and you know when an answer should be given and when it should not? So now you decline to give any answer whatsoever because you realize you ought not to?

You are babbling instead of being concerned about answering, he said. But, my good fellow, follow my instructions and answer, since you admit that I am wise.

I must obey then, I said, and it seems I am forced to do so, since you are in command, so ask away.

Now are the things that have sense those that have soul, or do things without soul have sense too?

It is the ones with soul that have sense.

And do you know any phrase that has soul? he asked.

Heavens no, not I.

Then why did you ask me just now what was the sense of my phrase?

I suppose, I said, for no other reason than that I made a mistake on account of being so stupid. Or perhaps I did not make a mistake but was right when I spoke as if phrases had sense? Are you saying that I made a mistake or not? Because if I did not make one you will not refute me no matter how wise you are, and you will be "helpless in dealing with the argument." And if I did make one, you said the wrong thing when you claimed it was impossible to make mistakes—and I'm not talking about things you said last year. So, Dionysodorus and Euthydemus, I said, it looks as if this argument has made no progress and still has the old trouble of falling down itself in the process of knocking down others. And your art has not discovered how to prevent this from happening in spite of your wonderful display of precision in words.

And Ctesippus said, Your manner of speech is certainly remarkable, O men of Thurii or Chios, or from wherever and however you like to be styled, because it matters nothing to you if you talk complete nonsense.

I was worried in case there might be hard words, and started to pacify Ctesippus once again, saying, Ctesippus, let me say to you the same things I was just saying to Clinias, that you fail to recognize how remarkable the strangers' wisdom is. It's just that the two of them are unwilling to give us a serious demonstration, but are putting on conjuring tricks in imitation

d

e

288

b

---

11. Removing the brackets in c3 and accepting the emendation of *g'ou* for *tōi*.

c   of that Egyptian sophist, Proteus.[12] So let us imitate Menelaus and refuse to release the pair until they have shown us their serious side. I really think some splendid thing in them will appear whenever they begin to be in earnest, so let us beg and exhort and pray them to make it known. As for me, I think I ought once again to take the lead and give an indication

d   of what sort of persons I pray they will show themselves to be. Beginning where I left off earlier, I shall do my best to go through what comes next so as to spur them to action and in hopes that out of pity and commiseration for my earnest exertions they may be earnest themselves.

   So, Clinias, I said, remind me where we left off. As far as I can remember it was just about at the point where we finally agreed that it was necessary to love wisdom, wasn't it?

   Yes, he said.

   Now the love of wisdom, or philosophy, is the acquisition of knowledge, isn't that so? I said.

   Yes, he said.

e   Well, what sort of knowledge would we acquire if we went about it in the right way? Isn't the answer simply this, that it would be one which will benefit us?

   Certainly, he said.

   And would it benefit us in any way if we knew how to go about and discover where in the earth the greatest quantities of gold are buried?

   Perhaps, he said.

   But earlier,[13] I said, we gave a thorough demonstration of the point that even if all the gold in the world should be ours with no trouble and without digging for it, we should be no better off—no, not even if we knew how

289   to make stones into gold would the knowledge be worth anything. For unless we also knew how to use the gold, there appeared to be no value in it. Or don't you remember? I said.

   Yes, I remember very well, he said.

   Nor does there seem to be any value in any other sort of knowledge which knows how to make things, whether money making or medicine or any other such thing, unless it knows how to use what it makes—isn't this the case?

   He agreed.

b   And again, if there exists the knowledge of how to make men immortal, but without the knowledge of how to use this immortality, there seems to be no value in it, if we are to conclude anything from what has already been settled.

   We agreed on all this.

---

12. In *Odyssey* iv.456 ff. Proteus, a sea deity, refuses to assume his proper shape until he has transformed himself into a lion, a dragon, a panther, an enormous pig, into water, and into a tree.

13. At 280d, although the point made was more general.

Then what we need, my fair friend, I said, is a kind of knowledge which combines making and knowing how to use the thing which it makes.

So it appears, he said.

Then it seems not at all needful for us to become lyre makers and skilled in some such knowledge as that. For there the art which makes is one thing and that which uses is another; they are quite distinct although they deal with the same thing. There is a great difference between lyre making and lyre playing, isn't there?

He agreed.

And it is equally obvious that we stand in no need of the art of flute making, since this is another of the same kind.

He said yes.

Seriously then, said I, if we were to learn the art of writing speeches, is this the art which we would have to get if we are going to be happy?

I don't think so, said Clinias in answer.

On what ground do you say this? I asked.

Well, he said, I notice that certain speech writers have no idea of how to use the particular speeches they themselves have written, in the same way that the lyre makers have no idea of how to use their lyres. And in the former case too, there are other people who are capable of using what the speech writers have composed but are themselves unable to write. So it is clear that in regard to speeches too, there is one art of making and another of using.

You seem to me, I said, to have sufficient ground for stating that the art of speech writing is not the one a man would be happy if he acquired. And yet it was in this connection that I expected the very knowledge we have been seeking all this time would put in an appearance. Because, as far as I am concerned, whenever I have any contact with these same men who write speeches, they strike me as being persons of surpassing wisdom, Clinias; and this art of theirs seems to me something marvelous and lofty. Though after all there is nothing remarkable in this, since it is part of the enchanters' art and but slightly inferior to it. For the enchanters' art consists in charming vipers and spiders and scorpions and other wild things, and in curing diseases, while the other art consists in charming and persuading the members of juries and assemblies and other sorts of crowds. Or do you have some other notion of it? I said.

No, he said, it seems to me to be just as you say.

Where should we turn next, then? I asked. To which one of the arts?

I find myself at a loss, he said.

But I think I have discovered it, said I.

Which one is it? said Clinias.

The art of generalship seems to me, I said, to be the one which, more than any other, a man would be happy if he acquired.

It doesn't seem so to me, he said.

How is that? said I.

Well, this art is a kind of man hunting.

What then? I said.

No art of actual hunting, he said, extends any further than pursuing and capturing: whenever the hunters catch what they are pursuing they are incapable of using it, but they and the fishermen hand over their prey
c   to the cooks. And again, geometers and astronomers and calculators (who are hunters too, in a way, for none of these make their diagrams; they simply discover those which already exist), since they themselves have no idea of how to use their prey but only how to hunt it, hand over the task of using their discoveries to the dialecticians—at least, those of them do so who are not completely senseless.

Well done, I said, most handsome and clever Clinias! And is this really the case?
d   Very much so. And the same is true of the generals, he said. Whenever they capture some city, or a camp, they hand it over to the statesmen—for they themselves have no idea of how to use the things they have captured—just in the same way, I imagine, that quail hunters hand theirs over to quail keepers. So, he said, if we are in need of that art which will itself know how to use what it acquires through making or capturing, and if it is an art of this sort which will make us happy, then, he said, we must look for some other art besides that of generalship.
e   CRITO: What do you mean, Socrates? Did that boy utter all this?
SOCRATES: You're not convinced of it, Crito?
CRITO: Good heavens no! Because, in my opinion, if he spoke like that, he needs no education, either from Euthydemus or anyone else.
SOCRATES: Dear me, then perhaps after all it was Ctesippus who said this, and I am getting absent-minded.
291   CRITO: Not my idea of Ctesippus!
SOCRATES: But I'm sure of one thing at least, that it was neither Euthydemus nor Dionysodorus who said it. Do you suppose, my good Crito, that some superior being was there and uttered these things—because I am positive I heard them.
CRITO: Yes, by heaven, Socrates, I certainly think it was some superior being, very much so. But after this did you still go on looking for the art? And did you find the one you were looking for or not?
b   SOCRATES: Find it, my dear man—I should think not! We were really quite ridiculous—just like children running after crested larks; we kept thinking we were about to catch each one of the knowledges, but they always got away. So why should I recount the whole story? When we got to the kingly art and were giving it a thorough inspection to see whether it might be the one which both provided and created happiness, just there we got into a sort of labyrinth: when we thought we had come to the end,
c   we turned round again and reappeared practically at the beginning of our search in just as much trouble as when we started out.
CRITO: And how did this come about, Socrates?
SOCRATES: I shall tell you. We had the idea that the statesman's art and the kingly art were the same.

CRITO: And then what?

SOCRATES: It was due to this art that generalship and the others handed over the management of the products of which they themselves were the craftsmen, as if this art alone knew how to use them. It seemed clear to us that this was the art we were looking for, and that it was the cause of right action in the state, and, to use the language of Aeschylus, that this art alone sits at the helm of the state, governing all things, ruling all things, and making all things useful.[14]

d

CRITO: And wasn't your idea a good one, Socrates?[15]

SOCRATES: You will form an opinion, Crito, if you like to hear what happened to us next. We took up the question once again in somewhat this fashion: Well, does the kingly art, which rules everything, produce some result for us, or not? Certainly it does, we said to each other. Wouldn't you say so too, Crito?

e

CRITO: Yes, I would.

SOCRATES: Then what would you say its result was? For instance, if I should ask you what result does medicine produce, when it rules over all the things in its control, would you not say that this result was health?

CRITO: Yes, I would.

SOCRATES: And what about your own art of farming, when it rules over all the things in its control—what result[16] does it produce? Wouldn't you say that it provides us with nourishment from the earth?

292

CRITO: Yes, I would.

SOCRATES: Now what about the kingly art; when it rules over all the things in its control—what does it produce? Perhaps you won't find the answer quite so easy in this case.

CRITO: No, I certainly don't, Socrates.

SOCRATES: Nor did we, Crito. But you are aware of this point at least, that if this is to be the art we are looking for, it must be something useful.

CRITO: Yes indeed.

SOCRATES: And it certainly must provide us with something good?

CRITO: Necessarily, Socrates.

SOCRATES: And Clinias and I of course agreed that nothing is good except some sort of knowledge.

b

CRITO: Yes, you said that.

SOCRATES: Then the other results which a person might attribute to the statesman's art—and these, of course, would be numerous, as for instance, making the citizens rich and free and not disturbed by faction—all these appeared to be neither good nor evil;[17] but this art had to make them wise

---

14. The reference is probably to *Seven Against Thebes*, 2.

15. Writing *Oukoun* with acute accent on the first syllable rather than circumflex on the second in d4.

16. Removing the brackets in a1.

17. Cf. 281d–e.

c   and to provide them with a share of knowledge if it was to be the one that benefited them and made them happy.

CRITO: True enough. So you agreed on this for the moment at any rate, according to your account.

SOCRATES: And does the kingly art make men wise and good?

CRITO: Why not, Socrates?

SOCRATES: But does it make all people good, and in every respect? And is it the art which conveys every sort of knowledge, shoe making and carpentry and all the rest?

CRITO: I don't think so, Socrates.

d   SOCRATES: Then what knowledge does it convey? And what use are we to make of it? It must not be the producer of any of those results which are neither good nor bad, but it must convey a knowledge which is none other than itself. Now shall we try to say what in the world this is, and what use we are to make of it? Is it agreeable to you if we say it is that by which we shall make others good?

CRITO: Certainly.

SOCRATES: And in what respect will they be good and in what respect useful, as far as we are concerned? Or shall we go on to say that they will

e   make others good and that these others will do the same to still others? But in what conceivable way they are good is in no way apparent to us, especially since we have discredited what are said to be the results of the statesman's art. It is altogether a case of the proverbial "Corinthus, son of Zeus";[18] and, as I was saying, we are in just as great difficulties as ever, or even worse, when it comes to finding out what that knowledge is which will make us happy.

CRITO: Mercy on us, Socrates, you seem to have got yourselves into a frightful tangle.

293   SOCRATES: As far as I was concerned, Crito, when I had fallen into this difficulty, I began to exclaim at the top of my lungs and to call upon the two strangers as though they were the Heavenly Twins to rescue both myself and the boy from the third wave[19] of the argument and to endeavor in every conceivable way to make plain what this knowledge can be which we ought to have if we are going to spend the remainder of our lives in the right way.

CRITO: And what about it? Was Euthydemus willing to reveal anything to you?

b   SOCRATES: Of course! And he began his account, my friend, in this generous manner: Would you prefer, Socrates, to have me teach you this knowledge you have been in difficulties over all this time, or to demonstrate that you possess it?

O marvellous man, I said, is this in your power?

18. The expression was proverbial for any sort of vain repetition.

19. For the first two, see 292a and 292d–e. The Heavenly Twins (Dioscuri) were regarded as protectors of seamen.

Very much so, he said.

Then for heaven's sake demonstrate that I possess it! I said. That will be much easier than learning for a man of my age.

Then come answer me this, he said: Is there anything you know?

Oh, yes, I said, many things, though trivial ones.

That will serve the purpose, he said. Now do you suppose it possible for any existing thing not to be what it is?

Heavens no, not I.

And do you know something? he said.   c

Yes, I do.

Then you are knowing, if you really know?

Of course, as far as concerns that particular thing.

That doesn't matter, because mustn't you necessarily know everything, if you are knowing?

How in heaven's name can that be, said I, when there are many other things I don't know?

Then if there is anything you don't know, you are not knowing.

In just that matter, my friend, I said.

Are you any the less not knowing for all that? said he. And just now you said you were knowing, with the result that you are the man you are, and then again you are not, at the same time and in respect to the   d
same things.

Very good, Euthydemus—according to the proverb, "whatever you say is well said."[20] But how do I know that knowledge we were looking for? Since it is impossible both to be and not to be the same thing, if I know one thing I know absolutely everything—because I could not be both knowing and not knowing at the same time—and since I know everything, I also have this knowledge. Is this what you mean, and is this your piece of wisdom?

You are refuted out of your own mouth, Socrates, he said.   e

But Euthydemus, I said, aren't you in the same condition? Because I would not be at all vexed at anything I might suffer in company with you and this dear man Dionysodorus. Tell me, don't you two know some existing things, and aren't there others you don't know?

Far from it, Socrates, said Dionysodorus.

What's that? I said. Do you know nothing at all?

On the contrary, he said.

Then you know everything, I said, since you know something?   294

Yes, everything, he said, and you also know everything if you really know even one thing.

O heavens, said I, how marvellous! And what a great blessing has come to light! But it can't be true that all the rest of mankind either know everything or nothing?

---

20. Reading *panta legeis* at d3.

Well, he said, I don't suppose they know some things and not others and are thus knowing and not knowing at the same time.

But what follows? I asked.

Everyone, he said, knows everything, if he really knows something.

b   By the gods, Dionysodorus, I said—for I realize that you are both now in earnest, although I have provoked you to it with some difficulty—do you two really know everything? Carpentry and shoe making, for instance?

Yes indeed, he said.

So you are both able to do leather stitching?

Heavens yes, and we can do cobbling, he said.

And do you also have the sort of information which tells the number of the stars and of the sands?

Of course, he said. Do you think we would fail to agree to that too?

c   Here Ctesippus interrupted: For goodness' sake, Dionysodorus, give me some evidence of these things which will convince me that you are both telling the truth.

What shall I show you? he asked.

Do you know how many teeth Euthydemus has, and does he know how many you have?

Aren't you satisfied, he said, with being told that we know everything?

Not at all, he answered, but tell us just this one thing in addition and prove that you speak the truth. Because if you say how many each of you has, and you turn out to be right when we have made a count, then we shall trust you in everything else.

d   Well, they weren't willing to do it, since they thought they were being laughed at, but they claimed to know every single thing they were questioned about by Ctesippus. And there was practically nothing Ctesippus did not ask them about in the end, inquiring shamelessly whether they knew the most disgraceful things. The two of them faced his questions very manfully, claiming to know in each case, just like boars when they are driven up to the attack. The result was that even I myself, Crito, was

e   finally compelled, out of sheer disbelief, to ask whether Dionysodorus even knew how to dance, to which he replied that he certainly did.

I don't suppose, I said, that at your age you are so far advanced in wisdom as to somersault over swords or be turned about on a wheel?

There is nothing I cannot do, he said.

And do you know everything just at the present moment, I asked, or is your knowledge also a permanent thing?

It is permanent as well, he said.

And when you were children and had just been born, did you know everything?

They both answered yes at the same moment.

295   Now the thing struck us as unbelievable; and Euthydemus asked, Are you incredulous, Socrates?

Well, I would be, I said, except for the probability that you are both wise men.

But if you are willing to answer my questions, he said, I will prove that you agree to these remarkable things too.

But, said I, there is nothing I would like better than to be refuted on these points. Because if I am unaware of my own wisdom, but you are going to demonstrate that I know everything and know it forever, what greater godsend than this would I be likely to come across my whole life long?

Then answer, he said.

Ask away, I am ready.

Well then, Socrates, he said, when you have knowledge, do you have it of something, or not?

I have it of something.

And do you know by means of that by which you have knowledge, or by means of something else?

By means of that by which I have knowledge. I suppose you mean the soul, or isn't this what you have in mind?

Aren't you ashamed, Socrates, he said, to be asking a question of your own when you ought to be answering?

Very well, said I, but how am I to act? I will do just what you tell me. Now whenever I don't understand your question, do you want me to answer just the same, without inquiring further about it?

You surely grasp something of what I say, don't you? he said.

Yes, I do, said I.

Then answer in terms of what you understand.

Well then, I said, if you ask a question with one thing in mind and I understand it with another and then answer in terms of the latter, will you be satisfied if I answer nothing to the purpose?

I shall be satisfied, he said, although I don't suppose *you* will.

Then I'm certainly not going to answer, said I, until I understand the question.

You are evading a question you understand all along, he said, because you keep talking nonsense and are practically senile.

I realized he was angry with me for making distinctions in his phrases, because he wanted to surround me with words and so hunt me down. Then I remembered that Connus, too, is vexed with me whenever I don't give in to him, and that as a result, he takes fewer pains with me because he thinks I am stupid. And since I had made up my mind to attend this man's classes too, I thought I had better give in for fear he might think me too uncouth to be his pupil. So I said, Well, Euthydemus, if you think this is how to do things, we must do them your way, because you are far more of an expert at discoursing than I, who have merely a layman's knowledge of the art. So go back and ask your questions from the beginning.

And you answer again from the beginning, he said. Do you know what you know by means of something, or not?

I know it by means of the soul, I said.

b

c

d

e

296   There he is again, he said, adding on something to the question! I didn't
ask you by what you know, but whether you know by means of something.
    Yes, I did give too much of an answer again, I said, because I am so
uneducated. Please forgive me and I shall answer simply that I know what
I know by means of something.
    And do you always know by this same means, said he, or is it rather the
case that you know sometimes by this means and sometimes by another?
    Always, whenever I know, I said, it is by this means.
    Won't you stop adding things on again? he said.
    But I'm afraid that this word "always" may trip us up.

b   It won't do it to us, he said, but to you, if anyone. Come along and
answer: do you always know by this means?
    Always, I said, since I have to withdraw the "whenever."
    Then you always know, by this means. And since you are always know-
ing, the next question is, do you know some things by this means by which
you know and others by some other means, or everything by this one?
    Absolutely everything by this one, said I—those that I know, that is.
    There it is again, he said—here comes the same qualification.
    Well I take back the "those that I know," I said.
    No, don't take back a single thing, he said—I'm not asking you any

c   favors. Just answer me this: would you be capable of knowing "absolutely
everything," if you did not know everything?
    It would be remarkable if I did, said I.
    And he said, Then add on everything you like now, because you admit
that you know absolutely everything.
    It seems I do, I said, especially since my "those that I know" has no
effect, and I know everything.
    And you have also admitted that you always know (by means of that
by which you know), whenever you know, or however else you like to
put it, because you have admitted that you always know and know all
things at the same time. It is obvious that you knew even when you were

d   a child and when you were being born and when you were being conceived.
And before you yourself came into being and before the foundation of
heaven and earth, you knew absolutely everything, if it is true that you
always know. And, by heaven, he said, you always will know, and will
know everything, if I want it that way.
    I hope you will want it that way, most honorable Euthydemus, said I,
if you are genuinely telling the truth. But I don't quite believe in your
ability to bring it off unless your brother Dionysodorus here should lend
a helping hand—perhaps the two of you might be able to do it. Tell me,

e   I went on: with respect to other things I see no possibility of disputing
with men of such prodigious wisdom by saying that I do not know everything, since you have stated that I do; but what about things of this sort,
Euthydemus—how shall I say I know that good men are unjust? Come
tell me, do I know this, or not?
    Oh yes, you know it, he said.

Know what? said I.

That the good are not unjust.

Yes, I've always known that, I said. But this isn't my question—what I'm asking is, where did I learn that the good *are* unjust?							297

Nowhere, said Dionysodorus.

Then this is something I do not know, I said.

You are ruining the argument, said Euthydemus to Dionysodorus, and this fellow here will turn out to be not knowing, and then he will be knowing and not knowing at the same time. And Dionysodorus blushed.

But you, I said, what do you say, Euthydemus? Your all-knowing brother							b
doesn't appear to be making a mistake, does he?

Am I a brother of Euthydemus? said Dionysodorus, interrupting quickly.

And I said, Let that pass, my good friend, until Euthydemus instructs me as to how I know that good men are unjust, and don't begrudge me this piece of information.

You are running away, Socrates, said Dionysodorus, and refusing to answer.

And with good reason, said I, because I am weaker than either of you, so that I do not hesitate to run away from you both together. I am much							c
more worthless than Heracles, who was unable to fight it out with both the Hydra, a kind of lady-sophist who was so clever that if anyone cut off one of her heads of argument, she put forth many more in its place, and with another sort of sophist, a crab arrived on shore from the sea—rather recently, I think. And when Heracles was in distress because this creature was chattering and biting on his left, he called for his nephew Iolaus to come and help him, which Iolaus successfully did. But if my							d
Iolaus should come, he would do more harm than good.

And when you have finished this song and story, said Dionysodorus, will you tell me whether Iolaus is any more Heracles' nephew than yours?

Well, I suppose it will be best for me if I answer you, Dionysodorus, I said, because you will not stop asking questions—I am quite convinced of that—out of an envious desire to prevent Euthydemus from teaching me that piece of wisdom.

Then answer, he said.

Well, I said, my answer is that Iolaus was the nephew of Heracles, but							e
as for being mine, I don't see that he is, in any way whatsoever. Because my brother, Patrocles, was not his father, although Heracles' brother, Iphicles, does have a name which is somewhat similar.

And Patrocles, he said, is your brother?

Yes indeed, said I—we have the same mother, though not the same father.

Then he both is and is not your brother.

Not by the same father, my good friend, I said, because his father was Chaeredemus and mine was Sophroniscus.

But Sophroniscus and Chaeredemus were both fathers? he asked.

Certainly, I said—the former was mine and the latter his.							298

Then was Chaeredemus other than a father? he said.

Other than mine at any rate, said I.

Then he was a father while he was other than a father? Or are you the same as a stone?

I'm afraid you will show that I am, I said, although I don't feel like one.

Then are you other than a stone? he said.

Yes, quite other.

Then isn't it the case that if you are other than a stone, you are not a stone, he said, and if you are other than gold, you are not gold?

That's true.

Then Chaeredemus is not a father if he is other than a father, he said.

So it seems that he is not a father, said I.

b   Because if Chaeredemus *is* a father, said Euthydemus, interrupting, then, on the other hand, Sophroniscus, being other than a father, is not a father, so that you, Socrates, are without a father.

Here Ctesippus took up the argument, saying, Well, isn't your father in just the same situation? Isn't he other than my father?

Far from it, said Euthydemus.

What! Is he the same? he asked.

The same, certainly.

c   I should not agree with that. But tell me, Euthydemus, is he just my father, or the father of everyone else as well?

Of everyone else as well, he replied. Or do you think the same man is both a father and not a father?

I was certainly of that opinion, said Ctesippus.

What, he said—do you think that a thing can be both gold and not gold? Or both a man and not a man?

But perhaps, Euthydemus, said Ctesippus, you are not uniting flax with flax, as the proverb has it. Because you are making an alarming statement if you say your father is the father of all.

But he is, he replied.

Just of men, said Ctesippus, or of horses and all the other animals?

d   All of them, he said.

And is your mother their mother?

Yes, she is.

And is your mother the mother of sea urchins?

Yes, and so is yours, he said.

So you are the brother of gudgeons and puppies and piglets.

Yes, and so are you, he said.

And your father turns out to be a boar and a dog.

And so does yours, he said.

You will admit all this in a moment, Ctesippus, if you answer my questions, said Dionysodorus. Tell me, have you got a dog?

Yes, and a brute of a one too, said Ctesippus.

e   And has he got puppies?

Yes indeed, and they are just like him.

And so the dog is their father?

Yes, I saw him mounting the bitch myself, he said.

Well then: isn't the dog yours?

Certainly, he said.

Then since he is a father and is yours, the dog turns out to be your father, and you are the brother of puppies, aren't you?

And again Dionysodorus cut in quickly to keep Ctesippus from making some reply first and said, Just answer me one more small question: Do you beat this dog of yours?

And Ctesippus laughed and said, Heavens yes, since I can't beat you!

Then do you beat your own father? he asked.

There would certainly be much more reason for me to beat yours, he said, for taking it into his head to beget such clever sons. But I suppose, Euthydemus, that the father of you and the puppies has benefited greatly from this wisdom of yours!

But he has no need of a lot of good things, Ctesippus—he does not, and neither do you.

Nor you either, Euthydemus? he asked.

Nor any other man. Tell me, Ctesippus, do you think it a good thing for a sick man to drink medicine whenever he needs it, or does it seem to you not a good thing? And do you think it good for a man to be armed when he goes to war rather than to go unarmed?

It seems good to me, he said. And yet I think you are about to play one of your charming tricks.

The best way to find out is to go ahead and answer, he said. Since you admit that it is a good thing for a man to drink medicine whenever he needs it, then oughtn't he to drink as much as possible? And won't it be fine if someone pounds up and mixes him a wagon load of hellebore?[21]

And Ctesippus said, Very true indeed, Euthydemus, if the man drinking is as big as the statue at Delphi!

It also follows, he said, that since it is a good thing to be armed in war, a man ought to have as many spears and shields as possible, if it really is a good thing?

It really does seem to be so, said Ctesippus. But surely you don't believe this yourself, Euthydemus? Wouldn't you prefer one shield and one spear?

Yes, I would.

And would you also arm Geryon and Briareus[22] in this fashion? he asked. I thought you and your companion here were cleverer than that, considering that you both fight in armor.

---

21. A plant with both poisonous and medicinal properties, a proverbial treatment for mental disorders.

22. Briareus was a hundred-handed monster who aided Zeus against the Titans. Geryon was a three-headed or three-bodied monster whose cattle were stolen by Heracles.

d   Euthydemus was silent, but Dionysodorus went back to the answers
Ctesippus had given earlier and asked, And what about gold, then? In
your opinion is it a good thing to have?

Yes indeed, and, in this case, lots of it, said Ctesippus.

Well then, oughtn't one to have good things always and everywhere?
Very much so, he said.

And you admit that gold is also one of the good things?

Yes, I have admitted that already, he said.

Then one should have it always and everywhere, and especially in
e   oneself? And wouldn't a man be happiest of all if he had three talents of
gold in his stomach, and a talent in his skull, and a stater of gold in each eye?

Well, they do say, Euthydemus, said Ctesippus, that among the Scythians
the happiest and best are the men who have a lot of gold in their own
skulls (the same way that you were talking a moment ago about the dog
being my father); and, what is still more remarkable, the story is that they
also drink out of their own gilded skulls and gaze at the insides of them,
having their own heads in their hands![23]

300   Tell me, said Euthydemus, do the Scythians and the rest of mankind
see things capable of sight or incapable?[24]

Capable, I suppose.

And do you do so too? he asked.

Yes, so do I.

And do you see our cloaks?

Yes.

Then these same cloaks are capable of sight.

Remarkably so, said Ctesippus.

Well, what do they see? he said.

Nothing at all. And you, perhaps, don't suppose you see *them*,[25] you are
such a sweet innocent. But you strike me, Euthydemus, as having fallen
asleep with your eyes open; and if it is possible to speak and say nothing,
you are doing exactly that.

b   But surely it is not possible for there to be a speaking of the silent, said
Dionysodorus.[26]

Entirely impossible, said Ctesippus.

Then neither is there a silence of the speaking?

Still less so, he answered.

---

23. The Scythians' habit of using the gilded skulls of their enemies as cups is described
by Herodotus, iv.65.

24. The Greek phrase translated "capable of sight" here can be understood as either
active (capable of seeing) or passive (capable of being seen). The argument to follow
exploits this ambiguity.

25. Reading *horan auta* in that order at a6.

26. The "speaking of the silent" here, like the "silence of the speaking" just below, must
be heard as ambiguous between "speaking done by the silent" and "speaking about
silent things." The argument to follow exploits this ambiguity.

But whenever you mention stones and wood and pieces of iron, are you not speaking of the silent?

Not if I go by the blacksmiths' shops, he said, because there the pieces of iron are said to speak out and cry aloud if anyone handles them. So here, thanks to your wisdom, you were talking nonsense without being aware of it. But prove me the other point, how there can be a silence of the speaking.

(I had the notion that Ctesippus was very much keyed up on account of his favorite being there.)

Whenever you are silent, said Euthydemus, are you not silent with respect to all things?

Yes, I am, he said.

Therefore, you are also silent with respect to the speaking, if "the speaking" is included in all things.

What, said Ctesippus, all things are not silent, are they?

I imagine not, said Euthydemus.

Well then, my good friend, do all things speak?

All the speaking ones, I suppose.

But, he said, this is not my question—I want to know, are all things silent, or do they speak?

Neither and both, said Dionysodorus, breaking in, and I'm convinced you will be helpless in dealing with that answer.

Ctesippus gave one of his tremendous laughs and said, Euthydemus, your brother has made the argument sit on both sides of the fence and it is ruined and done for! Clinias was very pleased and laughed too, which made Ctesippus swell to ten times his normal size. It is my opinion that Ctesippus, who is a bit of a rogue, had picked up these very things by overhearing these very men, because there is no wisdom of a comparable sort among any other person of the present day.

And I said, Clinias, why are you laughing at such serious and beautiful things?

Why Socrates, have you ever yet seen a beautiful thing? asked Dionysodorus.

Yes indeed, Dionysodorus, I said, and many of them.

And were they different from the beautiful, he asked, or were they the same as the beautiful?

This put me in a terrible fix, which I thought I deserved for my grumbling. All the same I answered that they were different from the beautiful itself, but at the same time there was some beauty present with each of them.

Then if an ox is present with you, you are an ox? And because I am present with you now, you are Dionysodorus?

Heaven forbid, said I.

But in what way, he said, can the different be different just because the different is present with the different?

Are you in difficulties there? I said. (I was so eager to have the wisdom of the pair that I was already trying to copy it.)

How can I not be in difficulties? he said. Not only I but everyone else must be, when a thing is impossible.

What are you saying, Dionysodorus? I said. Isn't the beautiful beautiful and the ugly ugly?

Yes, if I like, he said.

And do you like?

Certainly, he said.

c   Then isn't it also the case that the same is the same and the different different? Because I don't imagine that the different is the same, but I thought even a child would hardly doubt that the different is different. But you must have neglected this point deliberately, Dionysodorus, since in every other respect you and your brother strike me as bringing the art of argument to a fine pitch of excellence, like craftsmen who bring to completion whatever work constitutes their proper business.

You know then, he said, what the proper business of each craftsman is? For instance, you know whose business it is to work metal?

Yes, I do—the blacksmith's.

Well then, what about making pots?

The potter's.

And again, to slaughter and skin, and to boil and roast the pieces after cutting them up?

d   The cook's, I said.

Now if a man does the proper business, he said, he will do rightly?

Very much so.

And the proper business in the case of the cook is, as you say, to cut up and skin?[27] You did agree to that didn't you?

Yes, I did, I said, but forgive me.

Then it is clear, he said, that if someone kills the cook and cuts him up, and then boils him and roasts him, he will be doing the proper business. And if anyone hammers the blacksmith himself, and puts the potter on

e   the wheel, he will also be doing the proper business.

By Posidon, I exclaimed, you are putting the finishing touches on your wisdom! And do you think that such skill will ever be mine?

And would you recognize it, Socrates, he asked, if it did become yours?

If only you are willing, I said, I clearly would.

What's that, said he—do you think you know your own possessions?

Yes, unless you forbid it—for all my hopes must begin with you and end with Euthydemus here.

And do you consider those things to be yours over which you have

302   control and which you are allowed to treat as you please? For instance, an ox or a sheep: do you regard these as yours because you are free to

---

27. The Greek here is ambiguous between "it's proper for a cook to cut up and skin" and "it's proper to cut up and skin a cook." This English must be heard as having the same two readings.

sell them or give them away or sacrifice them to any god you please? And if you could not treat them in this fashion, then they would not be yours?

And because I knew that some fine thing would emerge from their questions, and, at the same time, because I wanted to hear it as quickly as possible, I said, This is exactly the case—it is only things like these which are mine.

Very well, he said. You give the name of living beings to all things that have a soul, don't you?

Yes, I said.

And you admit that only those living beings are yours over which you have power to do all these things I mentioned just now? b

I admit it.

And he pretended to pause as though he were contemplating some weighty matter, and then said, Tell me, Socrates, do you have an ancestral Zeus?[28]

I had a suspicion (a correct one as it turned out) of the way in which the argument would end, and I began to make a desperate effort to escape, twisting about as though I were already caught in the net.

No, I have not, Dionysodorus, I said.

Then you are a miserable sort of fellow, and not even an Athenian, if c you have no ancestral gods nor shrines, nor any of the other things of this sort which befit a gentleman.

Enough of that, Dionysodorus—mind your tongue and don't give me a lecture which is prematurely harsh. I certainly do have altars; and I have shrines, both domestic and ancestral, and everything else of the kind, just like the other Athenians.

Well, what about the other Athenians? he said. Doesn't each of them have an ancestral Zeus?

None of the Ionians use that expression, I said, neither those who are colonists from the city nor we ourselves. We do have an ancestral Apollo because of Ion's parentage,[29] but Zeus is not given the name of "ancestral" d by us. Rather we call him "defender of the house" or "of the tribe," and we also have an Athena "of the tribe."

Oh, that will do, said Dionysodorus, since you do appear to have an Apollo and a Zeus and an Athena.

Certainly, said I.

Then these would be your gods? he said.

My ancestors, I said, and my masters.

28. The Greek word translated "ancestral" here and in the following was applied in different parts of the Greek world to the specific divinities worshipped there as "hereditary" protectors, the "fathers" of the people. But it also had a different application to Zeus in particular, as protector of the rights of ancestors. The argument to follow exploits this ambiguity.

29. Ion was the son of Apollo by Creusa. (Cf. Euripides, *Ion* 61–75.)

But at any rate they are yours, he said. Or didn't you admit that they were?

Yes, I admitted it, I said. What is going to happen to me?

e   Then these gods, he said, are also living beings? Because you have admitted that everything which has a soul is a living being. Or don't these gods have a soul?

Oh yes, they do, I said.

Then they are living beings?

Yes, living beings, I said.

And you have agreed that those living beings are yours which you have a right to give away and to sell and to sacrifice to any god you please.

Yes, I agreed to that, I said—there is no retreat for me, Euthydemus.

303   Then come tell me straightway, he said: since you admit that Zeus and the other gods are yours, then do you have the right to sell them or give them away or treat them in any way you like, as you do with the other living creatures?

Then I, Crito, lay speechless, just as if the argument had struck me a blow. But Ctesippus ran to my aid, saying, Bravo, Heracles, what a fine argument! And Dionysodorus said, Is Heracles a bravo, or is a bravo Heracles? And Ctesippus said, By Posidon, what marvelous arguments! I give up—the pair are unbeatable.

b   Whereupon, my dear Crito, there was no one there who did not praise to the skies the argument and the two men, laughing and applauding and exulting until they were nearly exhausted. In the case of each and every one of the previous arguments, it was only the admirers of Euthydemus who made such an enthusiastic uproar; but now it almost seemed as if the pillars of the Lyceum applauded the pair and took pleasure in their

c   success. Even I myself was so affected by it as to declare that I had never in my life seen such wise men; and I was so absolutely captivated by their wisdom that I began to praise and extol them and said, O happy pair, what miraculous endowment you possess to have brought such a thing to perfection in so short a time! Among the many other fine things which belong to your arguments, Euthydemus and Dionysodorus, there is one which is the most magnificent of all, that you care nothing for the many,

d   or in fact, for men of consequence or reputation, but only for persons of your own sort. And I am convinced that there are very few men like you who would appreciate these arguments, but that the majority understand them so little that I feel sure they would be more ashamed to refute others with arguments of this sort than to be refuted by them. And then there is this other public-spirited and kindly aspect of your performance; whenever you deny that there is anything beautiful or good or white, and that the

e   different is in any way different, you do in fact completely stitch up men's mouths, as you say. But since you would appear to stitch up your own as well, you are behaving in a charming fashion and the harshness of your words is quite removed. But the greatest thing of all is that your skill is such, and is so skillfully contrived, that anyone can master it in a very short time. I myself found this out by watching Ctesippus and seeing how quickly he was able to imitate you on the spur of the moment. This ability of your technique to be picked up rapidly is a fine thing,[30] but not something which lends itself well to public performance. If you will take my advice, be careful not to talk in front of a large group; the listeners are likely to master it right away and give you no credit. Better just talk to each other in private, or, if you must have an audience, then let no one come unless he gives you money. And if you are sensible you will give your disciples the same advice, never to argue with anyone but yourselves and each other. For it is the rare thing, Euthydemus, which is the precious one, and water is cheapest, even though, as Pindar said, it is the best.[31] But come, said I, and see to admitting Clinias and me to your classes.

After saying these things, Crito, and making a few other brief remarks, we separated. Now figure out a way to join us in attending their classes, since they claim to be able to instruct anyone who is willing to pay, and say that neither age nor lack of ability prevents anyone whatsoever from learning their wisdom easily. And, what is specially relevant for you to hear, they say that their art is in no way a hindrance to the making of money.

CRITO: Well, Socrates, I am indeed a person who loves listening and who would be glad to learn something; but all the same I am afraid that I also am not one of Euthydemus' sort. Instead I am one of those you mentioned who would rather be refuted by arguments of this kind than use them to refute. Now it seems ridiculous to me to give you advice, but I want to tell you what I heard. When I was taking a walk one of the men who was leaving your discussion came up to me (someone who has a high opinion of himself for wisdom and is one of those clever people who write speeches for the law courts) and he said, Crito, aren't you a disciple of these wise men? Heavens no, I said—there was such a crowd that I was unable to hear, even though I stood quite close. And yet, he said, it was worth hearing. What was it? I asked. You would have heard men conversing who are the wisest of the present day in this kind of argument. And I said, what did they show you? Nothing else, said he, than the sort of thing one can hear from such people at any time—chattering and making a worthless fuss about matters of no consequence. (These are his approximate words.) But surely, I said, philosophy is a charming thing. Charming, my innocent friend? he said—why it is of no value whatsoever! And if you had been present, I think you would have been embarrassed on your friend's account, he acted so strangely in his willingness to put himself at the disposal of men who care nothing about what they say, but just snatch at every word. And these men, as I was just saying, are among the most influential people of the present day. But the fact is, Crito, he said, that both the activity itself and the men who engage in it are worthless and

30. Omitting *to sophon* at a1.
31. *Olympian* I.1.

b   ridiculous. Now as far as I am concerned, Socrates, the man is wrong to criticize the activity and so is anyone else who does so. But to be willing to argue with such people in front of a large crowd does seem to me worthy of reproach.

    SOCRATES: Crito, men like these are very strange. Still, I don't yet know what to say in return. What sort of man was this who came up and attacked philosophy? Was he one of those clever persons who contend in the law courts, an orator? Or was he one of those who equip such men for battle, a writer of the speeches which the orators use?

c   CRITO: He was certainly not an orator, no indeed. Nor do I think he has ever appeared in court. But they say he understands the business—very much so—and that he is a clever man and can compose clever speeches.

    SOCRATES: Now I understand—it was about this sort of person that I was just going to speak myself. These are the persons, Crito, whom Prodicus describes as occupying the no-man's-land between the philosopher and the statesman. They think that they are the wisest of men, and that they not only are but also seem to be so in the eyes of a great many, so that

d   no one else keeps them from enjoying universal esteem except the followers of philosophy. Therefore, they think that if they place these persons in the position of appearing to be worth nothing, then victory in the contest for the reputation of wisdom will be indisputably and immediately theirs, and in the eyes of all. They think they really are the wisest, and whenever they are cut short in private conversation, they attribute this to Euthydemus and his crew. They regard themselves as very wise, and reasonably so, since they think they are not only pretty well up in philosophy but also

e   in politics. Yes, their conceit of wisdom is quite natural because they think they have as much of each as they need; and, keeping clear of both risk and conflict, they reap the fruits of wisdom.

    CRITO: And so, Socrates, do you think there is anything in what they say? For surely it can't be denied that their argument has a certain plausibility.

306   SOCRATES: Plausibility is just what it does have, Crito, rather than truth. It is no easy matter to persuade them that a man or anything else which is between two things and partakes of both is worse than one and better than the other in the case where one of the things is good and the other evil; and that in the case where it partakes of two distinct goods, it is worse than either of them with respect to the end for which each of the two (of which it is composed) is useful. It is only in the case where the

b   thing in the middle partakes of two distinct evils that it is better than either of those of which it has a share. Now if philosophy is a good, and so is the activity of a statesman (and each has a different end), and those partaking of both are in between, then these men are talking nonsense, since they are inferior to both. If one is good and the other bad, then they are better than the practitioners of the latter and worse than those of the former; while if both are bad, there is some truth in what they say, but

c   otherwise none at all. I don't suppose they would agree that both [philosophy and politics] are bad, nor that one is bad and the other good. The fact of the matter is that, while partaking of both, they are inferior to both with respect to the object for which either politics or philosophy is of value; and that whereas they are actually in the third place, they want to be regarded as being in the first. However, we ought to forgive them their ambition and not feel angry, although we still ought to see these men for what they are. After all, we ought to admire every man who says anything sensible, and who labors bravely in its pursuit.

CRITO: All the same, Socrates, as I keep telling you, I am in doubt about what I ought to do with my sons. The younger one is still quite small, but Critobulus is at an age when he needs someone who will do him good. Now whenever I am in your company your presence has the effect of leading me to think it madness to have taken such pains about my children in various other ways, such as marrying to make sure that they would be of noble birth on the mother's side, and making money so that they would be as well off as possible, and then to give no thought to their education. But on the other hand, whenever I take a look at any of those persons who set up to educate men, I am amazed; and every last one of them strikes me as utterly grotesque, to speak frankly between ourselves. So the result is that I cannot see how I am to persuade the boy to take up philosophy.

SOCRATES: My dear Crito, don't you realize that in every pursuit most of the practitioners are paltry and of no account whereas the serious men are few and beyond price? For instance, doesn't gymnastics strike you as a fine thing? And money making and rhetoric and the art of the general?

CRITO: Yes, of course they do.

SOCRATES: Well then, in each of these cases don't you notice that the majority give a laughable performance of their respective tasks?

CRITO: Yes indeed—you are speaking the exact truth.

SOCRATES: And just because this is so, do you intend to run away from all these pursuits and entrust your son to none of them?

CRITO: No, this would not be reasonable, Socrates.

SOCRATES: Then don't do what you ought not to, Crito, but pay no attention to the practitioners of philosophy, whether good or bad. Rather give serious consideration to the thing itself: if it seems to you negligible, then turn everyone from it, not just your sons. But if it seems to you to be what I think it is, then take heart, pursue it, practice it, both you and yours, as the proverb says.

PROTAGORAS

This is the dramatic masterpiece among Plato's 'Socratic' dialogues. It depicts Socrates debating the great sophist Protagoras, with Hippias and Prodicus, two other very famous sophists, in active attendance. An excited flock of students and admirers looks on. Plato gives us deep and sympathetic portraits of both his principal speakers—and neither comes off unscathed.

A sophist is an educator. Protagoras offers to teach young men 'sound deliberation' and the 'art of citizenship'—in other words, as Socrates puts it, human 'virtue', what makes someone an outstandingly good person. But can this really be taught? Is virtue—as it ought to be if it can be taught—an expertise, a rationally based way of understanding, deliberating about and deciding things for the best? Socrates doubts that virtue can be taught at all, and all the more that Protagoras can teach it. Protagoras is committed to holding that it can be—by him—and he expounds an extremely attractive myth about the original establishment of human societies to show how there is room for him to do it. But he is also deeply cautious in the practice of his educator's art—almost his first words in the dialogue are a long oration on the importance to a sophist of caution as he offers himself publicly as the teacher of a city's youth. Can he then be bold enough to answer Socrates' questions about human virtue in such a way as to articulate an account that will sustain his claims to teach it? In the protracted dialectical exchange that follows, Protagoras distinguishes several virtues, all parts of that human virtue that he teaches, and insists, against Socrates' urging, that not all of these (in particular, not courage) are to be thought of as knowledge or wisdom. That, after all, is the popular view of the matter—so, in his caution, Protagoras sticks with that, or tries to, to the bitter end, resisting as long as he can Socrates' elaborate efforts to show that courage, too, like the rest of virtue, is nothing but wisdom. But if Protagoras is right, how can virtue in general, and courage in particular, be the sort of rationally based expertise that it has to be if it can be taught? It appears that Protagoras would have done better to follow his own convictions about virtue—that all of it is teachable—riding roughshod over popular opinion where necessary to show how all the parts of human virtue are wisdom or knowledge. In fact, Socrates shows himself to be much more an ally of Protagoras on the question of the nature of human virtue than at first appears. He is deeply committed, more deeply indeed than Protagoras, to Protagoras' initial claim that virtue is a rationally based expertise at deliberation and decision. But how, then, can he have been right to doubt whether virtue is teachable? Aren't all rationally based expertises acquired by teaching? (In reflecting on this question, readers will want to consult also the Meno.)

Thus both speakers get their comeuppance—Socrates for denying that virtue is teachable, Protagoras for denying that it is wisdom. The whole matter has to be rethought. At the end, we are sent back to the beginning, to go over the old ground once more, as Socrates himself has just done in retelling the events of the day to his unnamed friend and to us readers. One thing has been established, though—precisely what Socrates set out to discover in accompanying his friend Hippocrates to Callias' house to confront Protagoras: even if virtue can be taught, no one should entrust himself to Protagoras to learn it, since he does not even have a coherent view of what it is.

This Socrates, like that of Gorgias, *has more substantial theoretical commitments than the Socrates of other 'Socratic' dialogues. He does not limit himself to examining the opinions of others, but argues, as something he is committed to, however revisably, that all virtue is one, namely a single knowledge, that acting against one's own convictions—'weakness of will'—is impossible, and that our 'salvation in life' depends upon an 'art of measurement' that will overcome the power of appearance and get us to act rightly always. The dialogue invites us to ponder these theses, to work out for ourselves Socrates' reasons for holding to them—and to question whether he is right to do so.*

J.M.C.

FRIEND: Where have you just come from, Socrates? No, don't tell me. 309 It's pretty obvious that you've been hunting the ripe and ready Alcibiades.[1] Well, I saw him just the other day, and he is certainly still a beautiful man—and just between the two of us, 'man' is the proper word, Socrates: his beard is already filling out.

SOCRATES: Well, what of it? I thought you were an admirer of Homer, b who says that youth is most charming when the beard is first blooming[2]— which is just the stage Alcibiades is at.

FRIEND: So what's up? Were you just with him? And how is the young man disposed towards you?

SOCRATES: Pretty well, I think, especially today, since he rallied to my side and said a great many things to support me.[3] You're right, of course: I *was* just with him. But there's something really strange I want to tell you

Translated by Stanley Lombardo and Karen Bell.

1. Alcibiades (c. 450–404 B.C.), Athenian general, noted in his youth for his beauty and intellectual promise. See his encomium of Socrates in *Symposium* 215a ff. for more details on their relationship, as Plato understood it.

2. *Iliad* xxiv.348; *Odyssey* x.279.

3. See below, 336b and 347b.

about. Although we were together, I didn't pay him any mind; in fact, I forgot all about him most of the time.

c   FRIEND: How could anything like that have happened to the two of you? You surely haven't met someone else more beautiful, at least not in this city.

SOCRATES: Much more beautiful.

FRIEND: What are you saying? A citizen or a foreigner?

SOCRATES: A foreigner.

FRIEND: From where?

SOCRATES: Abdera.

FRIEND: And this foreigner seems to you more beautiful than the son of Clinias?

SOCRATES: How could superlative wisdom not seem surpassingly beautiful?

FRIEND: What! Have you been in the company of some wise man, Socrates?

d   SOCRATES: The wisest man alive, if you think the wisest man is—Protagoras.

FRIEND: What are you saying? Is Protagoras in town?

SOCRATES: And has been for two days.

FRIEND: And you've just now come from being with him?

310   SOCRATES: That's right, and took part in quite a long conversation.

FRIEND: Well, sit right down, if you're free now, and tell us all about it. Let the boy make room for you here.

SOCRATES: By all means. I'd count it a favor if you'd listen.

FRIEND: And vice versa, if you'd tell us.

SOCRATES: That would make it a double favor then. Well, here's the story.

b   This morning just before daybreak, while it was still dark, Hippocrates,[4] son of Apollodorus and Phason's brother, banged on my door with his stick, and when it was opened for him he barged right in and yelled in that voice of his, "Socrates, are you awake or asleep?"

Recognizing his voice, I said, "Is that Hippocrates? No bad news, I hope."

"Nothing but good news," he said.

"I'd like to hear it," I said. "What brings you here at such an hour?"

"Protagoras has arrived," he said, standing next to me.

"Day before yesterday," I said. "Did you just find out?"

c   "Yes! Just last evening." As he said this he felt around for the bed and sat at my feet and continued: "That's right, late yesterday evening, after I got back from Oenoë. My slave Satyrus had run away from me. I meant to tell you that I was going after him, but something else came up and made me forget. After I got back and we had eaten dinner and were about to get some rest, *then* my brother tells me Protagoras has arrived. I was

d   getting ready to come right over to see you even then, until I realized it was just too late at night. But as soon as I had slept some and wasn't dead-tired any more, I got up and came over here right away."

---

4. This Hippocrates is known to us only from this one dialogue.

Recognizing his fighting spirit and his excitement, I asked him: "So what's it to you? Has Protagoras done anything wrong to you?"

He laughed and said, "You bet he has, Socrates. He has a monopoly on wisdom and won't give me any."

"But look," I said, "if you meet his price he'll make you wise too."

"If only it were as simple as that," he said, "I'd bankrupt myself and   e
my friends too. But that's why I'm coming to you, so you will talk to him for me. I'm too young myself, and besides, I've never even seen Protagoras or heard him speak. I was still just a child the last time he was in town. He's such a celebrity, Socrates, and everyone says he's a terribly clever   311
speaker. Why don't we walk over now, to be sure to catch him in? I've heard he's staying with Callias, son of Hipponicus. Come on, let's go."

"Let's not go there just yet," I said. "It's too early. Why don't we go out here into the courtyard and stroll around until it's light? Then we can go. Protagoras spends most of his time indoors, so don't worry; we're likely to catch him in."

So we got up and walked around the courtyard. I wanted to see what   b
Hippocrates was made of, so I started to examine him with a few questions. "Tell me, Hippocrates," I said. "You're trying to get access to Protagoras, prepared to pay him a cash fee for his services to you. But what is he, and what do you expect to become? I mean, suppose you had your mind set on going to your namesake, Hippocrates of Cos, the famous physician, to   c
pay him a fee for his services to you, and if someone asked you what this Hippocrates is that you were going to pay him, what would you say?"

"I would say a physician," he said.

"And what would you expect to become?"

"A physician."

"And if you had a mind to go to Polyclitus of Argos or Phidias of Athens to pay them a fee, and if somebody were to ask you what kind of professionals you had in mind paying, what would you say?"

"I would say sculptors."

"And what would you expect to become?"

"A sculptor, obviously."

"All right," I said. "Here we are, you and I, on our way to Protagoras,   d
prepared to pay him cash as a fee on your behalf, spending our own money, and if that's not enough to persuade him, our friends' money as well. Suppose someone notices our enthusiasm and asks us: 'Tell me, Socrates and Hippocrates, what is your idea in paying Protagoras? What   e
is he?' What would we say to him? What other name do we hear in reference to Protagoras? Phidias is called a sculptor and Homer a poet. What do we hear Protagoras called?"

"A sophist is what they call him, anyway, Socrates."

"Then it is as a sophist that we are going to pay him?"

"Yes."

"And if somebody asks you what you expect to become in going to   312
Protagoras?"

He blushed in response—there was just enough daylight now to show him up—and said, "If this is at all like the previous cases, then, obviously, to become a sophist."

"What? You? Wouldn't you be ashamed to present yourself to the Greek world as a sophist?"

"Yes, I would, Socrates, to be perfectly honest."

b "Well, look, Hippocrates, maybe this isn't the sort of education you expect to get from Protagoras. Maybe you expect to get the kind of lessons you got from your grammar instructor or music teacher or wrestling coach. You didn't get from them technical instruction to become a professional, but a general education suitable for a gentleman."

"That's it exactly! That's just the sort of education you get from Protagoras."

"Then do you know what you are about to do now, or does it escape you?" I said.

"What do you mean?"

c "That you are about to hand over your soul for treatment to a man who is, as you say, a sophist. As to what exactly a sophist is, I would be surprised if you really knew. And yet, if you are ignorant of this, you don't know whether you are entrusting your soul to something good or bad."

"But I think I do know," he said.

"Then tell me what you think a sophist is."

"I think," he said, "that, as the name suggests, he is someone who has an understanding of wise things."

d "Well, you could say the same thing about painters and carpenters, that they understand wise things. But if someone asked us 'wise in what respect?' we would probably answer, for painters, 'wise as far as making images is concerned,' and so on for the other cases. And if someone asked, 'What about sophists? What wise things do they understand?'—what would we answer? What are they expert at making?"

"What else, Socrates, should we say a sophist is expert at than making people clever speakers?"

"Our answer would then be true, but not sufficient, for it requires another
e question: On what subject does the sophist make you a clever speaker? For example, a lyre-player makes you a clever speaker on his subject of expertise, the lyre. Right?"

"Yes."

"All right then. On what subject does a sophist make you a clever speaker?"

"It's clear that it's the same subject that he understands."

"Likely enough. And what is this subject that the sophist understands and makes his student understand?"

"By God," he said, "I really don't know what to say."

313 I went on to my next point: "Do you see what kind of danger you are about to put your soul in? If you had to entrust your body to someone

and risk its becoming healthy or ill, you would consider carefully whether
you should entrust it or not, and you would confer with your family and
friends for days on end. But when it comes to something you value more
than your body, namely your soul, and when everything concerning   b
whether you do well or ill in your life depends on whether it becomes
worthy or worthless, I don't see you getting together with your father or
brother or a single one of your friends to consider whether or not to entrust
your soul to this recently arrived foreigner. No, you hear about him in
the evening—right?—and the next morning, here you are, not to talk about
whether it's a good idea to entrust yourself to him or not, but ready to
spend your own money and your friends' as well, as if you had thought
it all through already and, no matter what, you had to be with Protagoras,   c
a man whom you admit you don't know and have never conversed with,
and whom you call a sophist although you obviously have no idea what
this sophist is to whom you are about to entrust yourself."

"I guess so, Socrates, from what you say."

"Am I right, then, Hippocrates, that a sophist is a kind of merchant who
peddles provisions upon which the soul is nourished? That's what he
seems like to me."

"But what is the soul nourished on, Socrates?"

"Teachings, I would say. And watch, or the sophist might deceive us   d
in advertising what he sells, the way merchants who market food for the
body do. In general, those who market provisions don't know what is
good or bad for the body—they just recommend everything they sell—
nor do those who buy (unless one happens to be a trainer or doctor). In
the same way, those who take their teachings from town to town and sell
them wholesale or retail to anybody who wants them recommend all their
products, but I wouldn't be surprised, my friend, if some of these people
did not know which of their products are beneficial and which detrimental   e
to the soul. Likewise those who buy from them, unless one happens to be
a physician of the soul. So if you are a knowledgeable consumer, you can
buy teachings safely from Protagoras or anyone else. But if you're not,
please don't risk what is most dear to you on a roll of the dice, for there   314
is a far greater risk in buying teachings than in buying food. When you
buy food and drink from the merchant you can take each item back home
from the store in its own container and before you ingest it into your body
you can lay it all out and call in an expert for consultation as to what
should be eaten or drunk and what not, and how much and when. So   b
there's not much risk in your purchase. But you cannot carry teachings
away in a separate container. You put down your money and take the
teaching away in your soul by having learned it, and off you go, either
helped or injured. Anyway, these are the questions we should look into,
with the help of our elders. You and I are still a little too young to get to
the bottom of such a great matter. Well, let's do what we had started out
to do and go hear this man; and after we have heard him, we can talk
with some others also. Protagoras isn't the only one there. There's Hippias   c

of Elis too, and also Prodicus of Ceos, I believe. And many others as well, wise men all."

Having agreed on this, we set out. When we got to the doorway we stood there discussing some point which had come up along the road and which we didn't want to leave unsettled before we went in. So we were standing there in the doorway discussing it until we reached an agreement,

d   and I think the doorman, a eunuch, overheard us. He must have been annoyed with all the traffic of sophists in and out of the house, because when we knocked he opened the door, took one look at us and said, "Ha! More sophists! He's busy." Then he slammed the door in our faces with both hands as hard as he could. We knocked again, and he answered through the locked door, "Didn't you hear me say he's busy?" "My good

e   man," I said, "we haven't come to see Callias, and we are not sophists. Calm down. We want to see Protagoras. That's why we've come. So please announce us." Eventually he opened the door for us.

When we went in we found Protagoras walking in the portico flanked by two groups. On one side were Callias, son of Hipponicus, and his

315 brother on his mother's side, Paralus, son of Pericles, and Charmides,[5] son of Glaucon. On the other side were Pericles' other son, Xanthippus, Philippides, son of Philomelus, and Antimoerus of Mende, Protagoras' star pupil who is studying professionally to become a sophist. Following behind and trying to listen to what was being said were a group of what seemed to be mostly foreigners, men whom Protagoras collects from the

b   various cities he travels through. He enchants them with his voice like Orpheus, and they follow the sound of his voice in a trance. There were some locals also in this chorus, whose dance simply delighted me when I saw how beautifully they took care never to get in Protagoras' way. When he turned around with his flanking groups, the audience to the rear would split into two in a very orderly way and then circle around to either side and form up again behind him. It was quite lovely.

c   And then I perceived (as Homer[6] says) Hippias of Elis, on a high seat in the other side of the colonnade. Seated on benches around him were Eryximachus,[7] son of Acumenus, Phaedrus of Myrrhinus, Andron, son of Androtion, a number of Elians and a few other foreigners. They seemed to be asking Hippias questions on astronomy and physics, and he, from his high seat, was answering each of their questions point by point.

d   And not only that, but I saw Tantalus too, for Prodicus of Ceos was also in town. He was in a room which Hipponicus had formerly used for storage, but because of the number of visitors Callias had cleared it out

---

5. For Charmides (d. 403 B.C.), see the *Charmides* and its Introductory Note.

6. *Odyssey* xi.601. Socrates' reference below to "seeing Tantalus" is another quotation from the same passage, in which Odysseus reports what he saw in his descent into the underworld.

7. Eryximachus is a doctor; he appears in Plato's *Symposium*, as does his friend Phaedrus, on whom see also the dialogue *Phaedrus*.

and made it into a guest room. Prodicus was still in bed and looked to be bundled up in a pile of sheepskin fleeces and blankets. Seated on couches next to him were Pausanias[8] from Cerames, and with Pausanias a fairly young boy, well-bred I would say, and certainly good-looking. I think I heard his name is Agathon, and I wouldn't be surprised if he were Pausanias' young love. So this boy was there, and the two Adeimantuses,[9] sons of Cepis and Leucolophides, and there seemed to be some others. What they were talking about I couldn't tell from outside, even though I really wanted to hear Prodicus, a man who in my opinion is godlike in his universal knowledge. But his voice is so deep that it set up a reverberation in the room that blurred what was being said.

We had just arrived when along came Alcibiades the Beautiful (as you call him, and I'm not arguing) and Critias son of Callaeschrus.[10] So when we were inside and had spent a little more time looking at everything, we went up to Protagoras, and I said, "Protagoras, Hippocrates here and I have come to see you."

"Do you want to talk with me alone or with others present?" he said.

"It doesn't make any difference to us," I said. "Listen to what we've come for, and decide for yourself."

"Well, then, what have you come for?" he asked.

"Hippocrates is from here, a son of Apollodorus and a member of a great and well-to-do family. His own natural ability ranks him with the best of anyone his age. It's my impression that he wants to be a man of respect in the city, and he thinks this is most likely to happen if he associates himself with you. So now you must decide. Should we discuss this alone or in the presence of others?"

"Your discretion on my behalf is appropriate, Socrates. Caution is in order for a foreigner who goes into the great cities and tries to persuade the best of the young men in them to abandon their associations with others, relatives and acquaintances, young and old alike, and to associate with him instead on the grounds that they will be improved by this association. Jealousy, hostility, and intrigue on a large scale are aroused by such activity. Now, I maintain that the sophist's art is an ancient one, but that the men who practiced it in ancient times, fearing the odium attached to it, disguised it, masking it sometimes as poetry, as Homer and Hesiod and Simonides did, or as mystery religions and prophecy, witness Orpheus and Musaeus, and occasionally, I've noticed, even as athletics, as with Iccus of Tarentum and, in our own time, Herodicus of Selymbria (originally of Megara), as great a sophist as any. Your own Agathocles, a great sophist, used music as a front, as did Pythoclides of Ceos, and many others. All

8. Pausanias and Agathon are among those who give speeches in praise of love in the *Symposium*.

9. The first of these is unknown, the second was later an Athenian general in the Peloponnesian War.

10. For Critias (c. 460–403) see the *Charmides* and its Introductory Note.

of them, as I say, used these various arts as screens out of fear of ill will. And this is where I part company with them all, for I do not believe that they accomplished their end; I believe they failed, in fact, to conceal from the powerful men in the cities the true purpose of their disguises. The b masses, needless to say, perceive nothing, but merely sing the tune their leaders announce. Now, for a runaway not to succeed in running away, but to be caught in the open, is sheer folly from the start and inevitably makes men even more hostile than they were before, for on top of everything else they perceive him as a real rogue. So I have come down the completely opposite road. I admit that I am a sophist and that I educate c men, and I consider this admission to be a better precaution than denial. And I have given thought to other precautions as well, so as to avoid, God willing, suffering any ill from admitting I am a sophist. I have been in the profession many years now, and I'm old enough to be the father of any of you here. So, if you do have a request, it would give me the greatest pleasure by far to deliver my lecture in the presence of everyone in the house."

d It looked to me that he wanted to show off in front of Prodicus and Hippias, and to bask in glory because we had come as his admirers, so I said, "Well, why don't we call Prodicus and Hippias over, and their companions, so that they can listen to us?"

"By all means!" said Protagoras.

"Then you want to make this a general session and have everyone take seats for a discussion?" Callias proposed this, and it seemed like the only thing to do. We were all overjoyed at the prospect of listening to wise men, and we laid hold of the benches and couches ourselves and arranged e them over by Hippias, since that's where the benches were already. Meanwhile Callias and Alcibiades had gotten Prodicus up and brought him over with his group.

When we had all taken our seats, Protagoras said, "Now, then, Socrates, since these gentlemen also are present, would you please say what it was you brought up to me a little while ago on the young man's behalf."

318 "Well, Protagoras," I said, "as to why we have come, I'll begin as I did before. Hippocrates here has gotten to the point where he wants to be your student, and, quite naturally, he would like to know what he will get out of it if he does study with you. That's really all we have to say."

Protagoras took it from there and said, "Young man, this is what you will get if you study with me: The very day you start, you will go home b a better man, and the same thing will happen the day after. Every day, day after day, you will get better and better."

When I heard this I said, "What you're saying, Protagoras, isn't very surprising, but quite likely. Why, even you, though you are so old and wise, would get better if someone taught you something you didn't happen to know already. But what if the situation were a little different, and Hippocrates here all of a sudden changed his mind and set his heart on c studying with this young fellow who has just come into town, Zeuxippus

of Heraclea, and came to him, as he now comes to you, and heard from
him the very same thing as from you—that each day he spent with him
he would become better and make progress. If Hippocrates asked him in
what way he would become better, and toward what he would be making
progress, Zeuxippus would say at painting. And if he were studying with
Orthagoras of Thebes and he heard from him the same thing as he hears
from you and asked him in what he would be getting better every day he
studied with him, Orthagoras would say at flute-playing. It is in this way   d
that you must tell me and the young man on whose behalf I am asking
the answer to this question: If Hippocrates studies with Protagoras, exactly
how will he go away a better man and in what will he make progress
each and every day he spends with you?"

Protagoras heard me out and then said, "You put your question well,
Socrates, and I am only too glad to answer those who pose questions well.
If Hippocrates comes to me he will not experience what he would if he
studied with some other sophist. The others abuse young men, steering   e
them back again, against their will, into subjects the likes of which they
have escaped from at school, teaching them arithmetic, astronomy, geometry, music, and poetry"—at this point he gave Hippias a significant look—
"but if he comes to me he will learn only what he has come for. What I
teach is sound deliberation, both in domestic matters—how best to manage   319
one's household, and in public affairs—how to realize one's maximum
potential for success in political debate and action."

"Am I following what you are saying?" I asked. "You appear to be
talking about the art of citizenship, and to be promising to make men
good citizens."

"This is exactly what I claim, Socrates."

"Well, this is truly an admirable technique you have developed, if indeed
you have. There is no point in my saying to you anything other than   b
exactly what I think. The truth is, Protagoras, I have never thought that
this could be taught, but when you say it can be, I can't very well doubt
it. It's only right that I explain where I got the idea that this is not teachable,
not something that can be imparted from one human being to another. I
maintain, along with the rest of the Greek world, that the Athenians are
wise. And I observe that when we convene in the Assembly and the city
has to take some action on a building project, we send for builders to
advise us; if it has to do with the construction of ships, we send for
shipwrights; and so forth for everything that is considered learnable and   c
teachable. But if anyone else, a person not regarded as a craftsman, tries
to advise them, no matter how handsome and rich and well-born he might
be, they just don't accept him. They laugh at him and shout him down
until he either gives up trying to speak and steps down himself, or the
archer-police remove him forcibly by order of the board. This is how they
proceed in matters which they consider technical. But when it is a matter   d
of deliberating on city management, anyone can stand up and advise them,
carpenter, blacksmith, shoemaker, merchant, ship-captain, rich man, poor

man, well-born, low-born—it doesn't matter—and nobody blasts him for
presuming to give counsel without any prior training under a teacher. The
e   reason for this is clear: They do not think that this can be taught. Public
life aside, the same principle holds also in private life, where the wisest
and best of our citizens are unable to transmit to others the virtues that
they possess. Look at Pericles,[11] the father of these young men here. He
320   gave them a superb education in everything that teachers can teach, but
as for what he himself is really wise in, he neither teaches them that himself
nor has anyone else teach them either, and his sons have to browse like
stray sacred cattle and pick up virtue on their own wherever they might
find it. Take a good look at Clinias, the younger brother of Alcibiades
here. When Pericles became his guardian he was afraid that he would be
corrupted, no less, by Alcibiades. So he separated them and placed Clinias
in Ariphron's house and tried to educate him there. Six months later he
b   gave him back to Alcibiades because he couldn't do anything with him.
I could mention a great many more, men who are good themselves but have
never succeeded in making anyone else better, whether family members or
total strangers. Looking at these things, Protagoras, I just don't think that
virtue can be taught. But when I hear what you have to say, I waver; I
think there must be something in what you are talking about. I consider
you to be a person of enormous experience who has learned much from
others and thought through a great many things for himself. So if you can
clarify for us how virtue is teachable, please don't begrudge us your explanation."

c   "I wouldn't think of begrudging you an explanation, Socrates," he replied. "But would you rather that I explain by telling you a story, as an
older man to a younger audience, or by developing an argument?"

The consensus was that he should proceed in whichever way he wished.
"I think it would be more pleasant," he said, "if I told you a story.

d   "There once was a time when the gods existed but mortal races did not.
When the time came for their appointed genesis, the gods molded them
inside the earth, blending together earth and fire and various compounds
of earth and fire. When they were ready to bring them to light the gods
put Prometheus and Epimetheus in charge of decking them out and assigning to each its appropriate powers and abilities.

"Epimetheus begged Prometheus for the privilege of assigning the abilities himself. 'When I've completed the distribution,' he said, 'you can
inspect it.' Prometheus agreed, and Epimetheus started distributing abilities.

e   "To some he assigned strength without quickness; the weaker ones he
made quick. Some he armed; others he left unarmed but devised for them
321   some other means for preserving themselves. He compensated for small
size by issuing wings for flight or an underground habitat. Size was itself
a safeguard for those he made large. And so on down the line, balancing

11. The great Athenian statesman and general (c. 495–429).

his distribution, making adjustments, and taking precautions against the possible extinction of any of the races.

"After supplying them with defenses against mutual destruction, he devised for them protection against the weather. He clothed them with thick pelts and tough hides capable of warding off winter storms, effective against heat, and serving also as built-in, natural bedding when they went to sleep. He also shod them, some with hooves, others with thick pads of bloodless skin. Then he provided them with various forms of nourishment, plants for some, fruit from trees for others, roots for still others. And there were some to whom he gave the consumption of other animals as their sustenance. To some he gave the capacity for few births; to others, ravaged by the former, he gave the capacity for multiple births, and so ensured the survival of their kind.

"But Epimetheus was not very wise, and he absentmindedly used up all the powers and abilities on the nonreasoning animals; he was left with the human race, completely unequipped. While he was floundering about at a loss, Prometheus arrived to inspect the distribution and saw that while the other animals were well provided with everything, the human race was naked, unshod, unbedded, and unarmed, and it was already the day on which all of them, human beings included, were destined to emerge from the earth into the light. It was then that Prometheus, desperate to find some means of survival for the human race, stole from Hephaestus and Athena wisdom in the practical arts together with fire (without which this kind of wisdom is effectively useless) and gave them outright to the human race. The wisdom it acquired was for staying alive; wisdom for living together in society, political wisdom, it did not acquire, because that was in the keeping of Zeus. Prometheus no longer had free access to the high citadel that is the house of Zeus, and besides this, the guards there were terrifying. But he did sneak into the building that Athena and Hephaestus shared to practice their arts, and he stole from Hephaestus the art of fire and from Athena her arts, and he gave them to the human race. And it is from this origin that the resources human beings needed to stay alive came into being. Later, the story goes, Prometheus was charged with theft, all on account of Epimetheus.

"It is because humans had a share of the divine dispensation that they alone among animals worshipped the gods, with whom they had a kind of kinship, and erected altars and sacred images. It wasn't long before they were articulating speech and words and had invented houses, clothes, shoes, and blankets, and were nourished by food from the earth. Thus equipped, human beings at first lived in scattered isolation; there were no cities. They were being destroyed by wild beasts because they were weaker in every way, and although their technology was adequate to obtain food, it was deficient when it came to fighting wild animals. This was because they did not yet possess the art of politics, of which the art of war is a part. They did indeed try to band together and survive by founding cities. The outcome when they did so was that they wronged each other, because

b

c

d

e

322

b

c they did not possess the art of politics, and so they would scatter and
again be destroyed. Zeus was afraid that our whole race might be wiped
out, so he sent Hermes to bring justice and a sense of shame to humans,
so that there would be order within cities and bonds of friendship to unite
them. Hermes asked Zeus how he should distribute shame and justice to
humans. 'Should I distribute them as the other arts were? This is how the
others were distributed: one person practicing the art of medicine suffices
for many ordinary people; and so forth with the other practitioners. Should

d I establish justice and shame among humans in this way, or distribute it
to all?' 'To all,' said Zeus, 'and let all have a share. For cities would never
come to be if only a few possessed these, as is the case with the other arts.
And establish this law as coming from me: Death to him who cannot
partake of shame and justice, for he is a pestilence to the city.'

"And so it is, Socrates, that when the Athenians (and others as well)
are debating architectural excellence, or the virtue proper to any other
professional specialty, they think that only a few individuals have the right

e to advise them, and they do not accept advice from anyone outside these
select few. You've made this point yourself, and with good reason, I might
add. But when the debate involves political excellence, which must proceed

323 entirely from justice and temperance, they accept advice from anyone, and
with good reason, for they think that this particular virtue, political or
civic virtue, is shared by all, or there wouldn't be any cities. This must be
the explanation for it, Socrates.

"And so you won't think you've been deceived, consider this as further
evidence for the universal belief that all humans have a share of justice
and the rest of civic virtue. In the other arts, as you have said, if someone
claims to be a good flute-player or whatever, but is not, people laugh at

b him or get angry with him, and his family comes round and remonstrates
with him as if he were mad. But when it comes to justice or any other
social virtue, even if they know someone is unjust, if that person publicly
confesses the truth about himself, they will call this truthfulness madness,
whereas in the previous case they would have called it a sense of decency.

c They will say that everyone ought to claim to be just, whether they are
or not, and that it is madness not to pretend to justice, since one must
have some trace of it or not be human.

"This, then, is my first point: It is reasonable to admit everyone as an
adviser on this virtue, on the grounds that everyone has some share of it.
Next I will attempt to show that people do *not* regard this virtue as natural
or self-generated, but as something taught and carefully developed in
those in whom it is developed.

d "In the case of evils that men universally regard as afflictions due to
nature or bad luck, no one ever gets angry with anyone so afflicted or
reproves, admonishes, punishes, or tries to correct them. We simply pity
them. No one in his right mind would try to do anything like this to
someone who is ugly, for example, or scrawny or weak. The reason is, I
assume, that they know that these things happen to people as a natural

process or by chance, both these ills and their opposites. But in the case of the good things that accrue to men through practice and training and teaching, if someone does not possess these goods but rather their corresponding evils, he finds himself the object of anger, punishment, and reproof. Among these evils are injustice, impiety, and in general everything that is opposed to civic virtue. Offenses in this area are always met with anger and reproof, and the reason is clearly that this virtue is regarded as something acquired through practice and teaching. The key, Socrates, to the true significance of punishment lies in the fact that human beings consider virtue to be something acquired through training. For no one punishes a wrong-doer in consideration of the simple fact that he has done wrong, unless one is exercising the mindless vindictiveness of a beast. Reasonable punishment is not vengeance for a past wrong—for one cannot undo what has been done—but is undertaken with a view to the future, to deter both the wrong-doer and whoever sees him being punished from repeating the crime. This attitude towards punishment as deterrence implies that virtue is learned, and this is the attitude of all those who seek requital in public or in private. All human beings seek requital from and punish those who they think have wronged them, and the Athenians, your fellow citizens, especially do so. Therefore, by my argument, the Athenians are among those who think that virtue is acquired and taught. So it is with good reason that your fellow citizens accept a blacksmith's or a cobbler's advice in political affairs. And they do think that virtue is acquired and taught. It appears to me that both these propositions have been sufficiently proved, Socrates.

"Now, on to your remaining difficulty, the problem you raise about good men teaching their sons everything that can be taught and making them wise in these subjects, but not making them better than anyone else in the particular virtue in which they themselves excel. On this subject, Socrates, I will abandon story for argument. Consider this: Does there or does there not exist one thing which all citizens must have for there to be a city? Here and nowhere else lies the solution to your problem. For if such a thing exists, and this one thing is not the art of the carpenter, the blacksmith, or the potter, but justice, and temperance, and piety—what I may collectively term the virtue of a man, and if this is the thing which everyone should share in and with which every man should act whenever he wants to learn anything or do anything, but should not act without it, and if we should instruct and punish those who do not share in it, man, woman, and child, until their punishment makes them better, and should exile from our cities or execute whoever doesn't respond to punishment and instruction; if this is the case, if such is the nature of this thing, and good men give their sons an education in everything but this, then we have to be amazed at how strangely our good men behave. For we have shown that they regard this thing as teachable both in private and public life. Since it is something that can be taught and nurtured, is it possible that they have their sons taught everything in which there is no death

c penalty for not understanding it, but when their children are faced with
the death penalty or exile if they fail to learn virtue and be nurtured in it—
and not only death but confiscation of property and, practically speaking,
complete familial catastrophe—do you think they do not have them taught
this or give them all the attention possible? We must think that they
do, Socrates.

d "Starting when they are little children and continuing as long as they
live, they teach them and correct them. As soon as a child understands
what is said to him, the nurse, mother, tutor, and the father himself fight
for him to be as good as he possibly can, seizing on every action and word
to teach him and show him that this is just, that is unjust, this is noble,
that is ugly, this is pious, that is impious, he should do this, he should
not do that. If he obeys willingly, fine; if not, they straighten him out with
threats and blows as if he were a twisted, bent piece of wood. After this

e they send him to school and tell his teachers to pay more attention to his
good conduct than to his grammar or music lessons. The teachers pay
attention to these things, and when the children have learned their letters
and are getting to understand writing as well as the spoken language,
they are given the works of good poets to read at their desks and have to

326 learn them by heart, works that contain numerous exhortations, many
passages describing in glowing terms good men of old, so that the child
is inspired to imitate them and become like them. In a similar vein, the
music teachers too foster in their young pupils a sense of moral decency
and restraint, and when they learn to play the lyre they are taught the

b works of still more good poets, the lyric and choral poets. The teachers
arrange the scores and drill the rhythms and scales into the children's
souls, so that they become gentler, and their speech and movements become
more rhythmical and harmonious. For all of human life requires a high
degree of rhythm and harmony. On top of all this, they send their children
to an athletic trainer so that they may have sound bodies in the service

c of their now fit minds and will not be forced to cowardice in war or other
activities through physical deficiencies.

d "This is what the most able, i.e., the richest, do. Their sons start going
to school at the earliest age and quit at the latest age. And when they quit
school, the city in turn compels them to learn the laws and to model their
lives on them. They are not to act as they please. An analogy might be
drawn from the practice of writing-teachers, who sketch the letters faintly
with a pen in workbooks for their beginning students and have them write
the letters over the patterns they have drawn. In the same way the city
has drawn up laws invented by the great lawgivers in the past and compels
them to govern and be governed by them. She punishes anyone who goes
beyond these laws, and the term for this punishment in your city and

e others is, because it is a corrective legal action, 'correction.'

"When so much care and attention is paid to virtue, Socrates, both in
public and private, are you still puzzled about virtue being teachable? The
wonder would be if it were not teachable.

"Why, then, do many sons of good fathers never amount to anything? I want you to understand this too, and in fact it's no great wonder, if what I've just been saying is true about virtue being something in which no one can be a layman if there is to be a city. For if what I am saying is true— and nothing could be more true: Pick any other pursuit or study and reflect upon it. Suppose, for instance, there could be no city unless we were all flute-players, each to the best of his ability, and everybody were teaching everybody else this art in public and private and reprimanding the poor players and doing all this unstintingly, just as now no one begrudges or conceals his expertise in what is just and lawful as he does his other professional expertise. For it is to our collective advantage that we each possess justice and virtue, and so we all gladly tell and teach each other what is just and lawful. Well, if we all had the same eagerness and generosity in teaching each other flute-playing, do you think, Socrates, that the sons of good flute-players would be more likely to be good flute-players than the sons of poor flute-players? I don't think so at all. When a son happened to be naturally disposed toward flute-playing, he would progress and become famous; otherwise, he would remain obscure. In many cases the son of a good player would turn out to be a poor one, and the son of a poor player would turn out to be good. But as flute-players, they would all turn out to be capable when compared with ordinary people who had never studied the flute. Likewise you must regard the most unjust person ever reared in a human society under law as a paragon of justice compared with people lacking education and lawcourts and the pervasive pressure to cultivate virtue, savages such as the playwright Pherecrates brought on stage at last year's Lenaean festival. There's no doubt that if you found yourself among such people, as did the misanthropes in that play's chorus, you would be delighted to meet up with the likes of Eurybatus and Phrynondas[12] and would sorely miss the immorality of the people here. As it is, Socrates, you affect delicate sensibilities, because everyone here is a teacher of virtue, to the best of his ability, and you can't see a single one. You might as well look for a teacher of Greek; you wouldn't find a single one of those either. Nor would you be any more successful if you asked who could teach the sons of our craftsmen the very arts which they of course learned from their fathers, to the extent that their fathers were competent, and their friends in the trade. It would be difficult to produce someone who could continue their education, whereas it would be easy to find a teacher for the totally unskilled. It is the same with virtue and everything else. If there is someone who is the least bit more advanced in virtue than ourselves, he is to be cherished.

"I consider myself to be such a person, uniquely qualified to assist others in becoming noble and good, and worth the fee that I charge and even more, so much so that even my students agree. This is why I charge according to the following system: a student pays the full price only if he

327

b

c

d

e

328

b

c

12. Historical persons, conventional paradigms of viciousness.

wishes to; otherwise, he goes into a temple, states under oath how much he thinks my lessons are worth, and pays that amount.

"There you have it, Socrates, my mythic story and my argument that virtue is teachable and that the Athenians consider it to be so, and that it is no wonder that worthless sons are born of good fathers and good sons of worthless fathers, since even the sons of Polyclitus, of the same age as

d   Paralus and Xanthippus here, are nothing compared to their father, and the same is true for the sons of other artisans. But it is not fair to accuse these two yet; there is still hope for them, for they are young."

Protagoras ended his virtuoso performance here and stopped speaking. I was entranced and just looked at him for a long time as if he were going to say more. I was still eager to listen, but when I perceived that he had really stopped I pulled myself together and, looking at Hippocrates, barely

e   managed to say: "Son of Apollodorus, how grateful I am to you for suggesting that I come here. It is marvelous to have heard from Protagoras what I have just heard. Formerly I used to think there was no human practice by which the good become good, but now I am persuaded that there is, except for one small obstacle which Protagoras will explain away, I am

329 sure, since he has explained away so much already. Now, you could hear a speech similar to this from Pericles or some other competent orator if you happened to be present when one of them was speaking on this subject. But try asking one of them something, and they will be as unable to answer your question or to ask one of their own as a book would be. Question the least little thing in their speeches and they will go on like bronze bowls that keep ringing for a long time after they have been struck and prolong the sound indefinitely unless you dampen them. That's how

b   these orators are: Ask them one little question and they're off on another long-distance speech. But Protagoras here, while perfectly capable of delivering a beautiful long speech, as we have just seen, is also able to reply briefly when questioned, and to put a question and then wait for and accept the answer—rare accomplishments these.

"Now, then, Protagoras, I need one little thing, and then I'll have it all, if you'll just answer me this. You say that virtue is teachable, and if there's

c   any human being who could persuade me of this, it's you. But there is one thing you said that troubles me, and maybe you can satisfy my soul. You said that Zeus sent justice and a sense of shame to the human race. You also said, at many points in your speech, that justice and temperance[13] and piety and all these things were somehow collectively one thing: virtue.

d   Could you go through this again and be more precise? Is virtue a single thing, with justice and temperance and piety its parts, or are the things I have just listed all names for a single entity? This is what still intrigues me."

---

13. The Greek term is *sōphrosunē*. For Plato, *sōphrosunē* was a complex virtue involving self-control and moderation of the physical appetites, as well as good sense and self-knowledge.

"This is an easy question to answer, Socrates," he replied. "Virtue is a single entity, and the things you are asking about are its parts."

"Parts as in the parts of a face: mouth, nose, eyes, and ears? Or parts as in the parts of gold, where there is no difference, except for size, between parts or between the parts and the whole?"

"In the former sense, I would think, Socrates: as the parts of the face are to the whole face."   e

"Then tell me this. Do some people have one part and some another, or do you necessarily have all the parts if you have any one of them?"

"By no means, since many are courageous but unjust, and many again are just but not wise."

"Then these also are parts of virtue—wisdom and courage?"

"Absolutely, and wisdom is the greatest part."   330

"Is each of them different from the others?"

"Yes."

"And does each also have its own unique power or function? In the analogy to the parts of the face, the eye is not like the ear, nor is its power or function the same, and this applies to the other parts as well: They are not like each other in power or function or in any other way. Is this how it is with the parts of virtue? Are they unlike each other, both in themselves   b
and in their powers or functions? Is it not clear that this must be the case, if our analogy is valid?"

"Yes, it must be the case, Socrates."

"Then, none of the other parts of virtue is like knowledge, or like justice, or like courage, or like temperance, or like piety?"

"Agreed."

"Come on, then, and let's consider together what kind of thing each of   c
these is. Here's a good first question: Is justice a thing or is it not a thing? I think it is. What about you?"

"I think so too."

"The next step, then: Suppose someone asked us, 'Protagoras and Socrates, tell me about this thing you just named, justice. Is it itself just or unjust?' My answer would be that it is just. What would your verdict be? The same as mine or different?"

"The same."

"Then justice is the sort of thing that is just. That's how I would reply to the questioner. Would you also?"

"Yes."

"Suppose he questioned us further: 'Do you also say there is a thing   d
called piety?' We would say we do, right?"

"Right."

" 'Do you say this too is a thing?' We would say we do, wouldn't we?"

"That too."

" 'Do you say that this thing is by nature impious or pious?' Myself, I would be irritated with this question and would say, 'Quiet, man! How   e could anything else be pious if piety itself is not?' What about you? "Wouldn't you answer in the same way?"

"Absolutely."

"Suppose he asked us next: 'Then what about what you said a little while ago? Maybe I didn't hear you right. I thought you two said that the parts of virtue are related to each other in such a way that no part resembles any other.' I would answer, 'There's nothing wrong with your hearing, except that I didn't say that. Protagoras here said that in answer to my question.' If he were to say then, 'Is he telling the truth, Protagoras? Are you the one who says that one part of virtue is not like another? Is this dictum yours?' how would you answer him?"

"I would have to admit it, Socrates."

"Well, if we accept that, Protagoras, what are we going to say if he asks next, 'Isn't piety the sort of thing that is just, and isn't justice the sort of thing that is pious? Or is it the sort of thing which is not pious? Is piety the sort of thing to be not just, and therefore unjust, and justice impious?' What are we going to say to him? Personally, I would answer both that justice is pious and piety is just, and I would give the same answer on your behalf (if you would let me), that justice is the same thing as piety, or very similar, and, most emphatically, that justice is the same kind of thing as piety, and piety as justice. What do you think? Will you veto this answer, or are you in agreement with it?"

"It's not so absolutely clear a case to me, Socrates, as to make me grant that justice is pious, and piety just. It seems a distinction is in order here. But what's the difference? If you want, we'll let justice be pious and piety just."

"Don't do that to me! It's not this 'if you want' or 'if you agree' business I want to test. It's you and me I want to put on the line, and I think the argument will be tested best if we take the 'if' out."

"Well, all right. Justice does have some resemblance to piety. Anything at all resembles any other thing in some way. There is a certain way in which white resembles black, and hard soft, and so on for all the usual polar opposites. And the things we were just talking about as having different powers or functions and not being the same kinds of things— the parts of the face—these resemble each other in a certain way, and they are like each other. So by this method you could prove, if you wanted to, that these things too are all like each other. But it's not right to call things similar because they resemble each other in some way, however slight, or to call them dissimilar because there is some slight point of dissimilarity."

I was taken aback, and said to him, "Do you consider the relationship between justice and piety really only one of some slight similarity?"

"Not exactly, but not what you seem to think it is either."

"Well, then, since you seem to me to be annoyed about this, let's drop it and consider another point that you raised. Do you acknowledge that there is such a thing as folly?"

"Yes."

"And diametrically opposed to it is wisdom?"

"It seems so to me."

"And when people act correctly and beneficially, do they seem to you to be acting temperately or the opposite?"

"Temperately."

"Then it is by temperance that they act temperately?"

"It has to be."   b

"And those who do not act correctly act foolishly, and those who act this way do not act temperately?"

"I agree."

"And the opposite of acting foolishly is acting temperately?"

"Yes."

"And foolish behavior is done with folly, just as temperate behavior is done with temperance?"

"Yes."

"And if something is done with strength, it is done strongly; if done with weakness, it is done weakly?"

"I agree."

"If it is done with quickness, it is done quickly, and if with slowness, slowly?"

"Yes."

"So whatever is done in a certain way is done from a certain quality,   c
and whatever is done in the opposite way is done from its opposite?"

"I agree."

"Then let's go. Is there such a thing as beauty?"

"Yes."

"Is there any opposite to it except ugliness?"

"There is not."

"Is there such a thing as goodness?"

"There is."

"Is there any opposite to it except badness?"

"There is not."

"Is there such a thing as a shrill tone?"

"There is."

"Is there any opposite to it except a deep tone?"

"No, there is not."

"So for each thing that can have an opposite, there is only one opposite,   d
not many?"

"I agree."

"Suppose we now count up our points of agreement. Have we agreed that there is one opposite for one thing, and no more?"

"Yes, we have."

"And that what is done in an opposite way is done from opposites?"

"Yes."

"And have we agreed that what is done foolishly is done in a way opposite to what is done temperately?"

"We have."

"And that what is done temperately is done from temperance, and what is done foolishly is done from folly?"

"Agreed."

e   "And it's true that if it's done in an opposite way, it is done from an opposite?"

"Yes."

"And one is done from temperance, the other from folly?"

"Yes."

"In an opposite way?"

"Yes."

"From opposites?"

"Yes."

"Then folly is the opposite of temperance?"

"It seems so."

"Well, then, do you recall our previous agreement that folly is the opposite of wisdom?"

"Yes, I do."

"And that one thing has only one opposite?"

"Of course."

333   "Then which of these propositions should we abandon, Protagoras? The proposition that for one thing there is only one opposite, or the one stating that wisdom is different from temperance and that each is a part of virtue, and that in addition to being distinct they are dissimilar, both in themselves and in their powers or functions, just like the parts of a face? Which should we abandon? The two statements are dissonant; they

b   are not in harmony with one another. How could they be, if there is one and only one opposite for each single thing, while folly, which is a single thing, evidently has two opposites, wisdom and temperance? Isn't this how it stands, Protagoras?"

He assented, although very grudgingly, and I continued:

"Wouldn't that make wisdom and temperance one thing? And a little while ago it looked like justice and piety were nearly the same thing. Come on, Protagoras, we can't quit now, not before we've tied up these loose ends. So, does someone who acts unjustly seem temperate to you in that he acts unjustly?"

c   "I would be ashamed to say that is so, Socrates, although many people do say it."

"Then shall I address myself to them or to you?"

"If you like, why don't you debate the majority position first?"

"It makes no difference to me, provided you give the answers, whether it is your own opinion or not. I am primarily interested in testing the argument, although it may happen both that the questioner, myself, and my respondent wind up being tested."

At first Protagoras played it coy, claiming the argument was too hard   d
for him to handle, but after a while he consented to answer.

"Let's start all over, then," I said, "with this question. Do you think
some people are being sensible[14] when they act unjustly?"

"Let us grant it," he said.

"And by 'sensible' you mean having good sense?"

"Yes."

"And having good sense means having good judgment in acting unjustly?"

"Granted."

"Whether or not they get good results by acting unjustly?"

"Only if they get good results."

"Are you saying, then, that there are things that are good?"

"I am."

"These good things constitute what is advantageous to people?"

"Good God, yes! And even if they are not advantageous to people, I   e
can still call them good."

I could see that Protagoras was really worked up and struggling by now
and that he was dead set against answering any more. Accordingly, I
carefully modified the tone of my questions.

"Do you mean things that are advantageous to no human being, Protago-   334
ras, or things that are of no advantage whatsoever? Do you call things
like that good?"

"Of course not," he said. "But I know of many things that are disadvantageous to humans, foods and drinks and drugs and many other things, and
some that are advantageous; some that are neither to humans but one or
the other to horses; some that are advantageous only to cattle; some only
to dogs; some that are advantageous to none of these but are so to trees;
some that are good for the roots of a tree, but bad for its shoots, such as   b
manure, which is good spread on the roots of any plant but absolutely
ruinous if applied to the new stems and branches. Or take olive oil, which
is extremely bad for all plants and is the worst enemy of the hair of all
animals except humans, for whose hair it is beneficial, as it is for the rest
of their bodies. But the good is such a multifaceted and variable thing
that, in the case of oil, it is good for the external parts of the human body   c
but very bad for the internal parts, which is why doctors universally forbid
their sick patients to use oil in their diets except for the least bit, just
enough to dispel a prepared meal's unappetizing aroma."

When the applause for this speech of Protagoras had died down, I said,
"Protagoras, I tend to be a forgetful sort of person, and if someone speaks   d
to me at length I tend to forget the subject of the speech. Now, if I happened
to be hard of hearing and you were going to converse with me, you would
think you had better speak louder to me than to others. In the same way,

14. The Greek term is *sōphronein*, a verb related to the noun *sōphrosunē* (temperance).

now that you have fallen in with a forgetful person, you will have to cut your answers short if I am going to follow you."

"How short are you ordering me to make my answers? Shorter than necessary?"

"By no means."

"As long as necessary?"

e   "Yes."

"Then should I answer at the length I think necessary or the length you think necessary?"

335   "Well, I have heard, anyway, that when you are instructing someone in a certain subject, you are able to speak at length, if you choose, and never get off the subject, or to speak so briefly that no one could be briefer. So if you are going to converse with me, please use the latter form of expression, brevity."

"Socrates, I have had verbal contests with many people, and if I were to accede to your request and do as my opponent demanded, I would not be thought superior to anyone, nor would Protagoras be a name to be reckoned with among the Greeks."

b   I could see he was uncomfortable with his previous answers and that he would no longer be willing to go on answering in a dialectical discussion, so I considered my work with him to be finished, and I said so: "You know, Protagoras, I'm not exactly pleased myself that our session has not gone the way you think it should. But if you are ever willing to hold a discussion in such a way that I can follow, I will participate in it with you. People say of you—and you say yourself—that you are able to discuss

c   things speaking either at length or briefly. You are a wise man, after all. But I don't have the ability to make those long speeches: I only wish I did. It was up to you, who have the ability to do both, to make this concession, so that the discussion could have had a chance. But since you're not willing, and I'm somewhat busy and unable to stay for your extended speeches—there's somewhere I have to go—I'll be leaving now. Although I'm sure it would be rather nice to hear them."

d   Having had my say, I stood up to go, but as I was getting up, Callias took hold of my wrist with his right hand and grasped this cloak I'm wearing with his left. "We won't let you go, Socrates," he said. "Our discussions wouldn't be the same without you, so please stay here with us, I beg you. There's nothing I would rather hear than you and Protagoras in debate. Please do us all a favor."

e   By now I was on my feet and really making as if to leave. I said, "Son of Hipponicus, I have always admired your love of wisdom, and I especially honor and hold it dear now. I would be more than willing to gratify you, if you would ask me something that is possible for me. As it is, you might as well be asking me to keep up with Crison of Himera, the champion sprinter, or to compete with the distance runners, or match strides with the couriers who run all day long. What could I say, except that I want it

336   for myself more than you want it for me, but I simply cannot match these

runners' pace, and if you want to watch me running in the same race with
Crison, you must ask him to slow down to my speed, since I am not able
to run fast, but he is able to run slowly. So if you have your heart set on
hearing me and Protagoras, you must ask him to answer my questions
now as he did at the outset—briefly. If he doesn't, what turn will our   b
dialogue take? To me, the mutual exchange of a dialogue is something
quite distinct from a public address."

"But you see, Socrates, Protagoras has a point when he says that he
ought to be allowed, no less than you, to conduct the discussion as he
sees fit."

At this point Alcibiades jumped in and said: "You're not making sense,
Callias. Socrates admits that long speeches are beyond him and concedes   c
to Protagoras on that score. But when it comes to dialectical discussion
and understanding the give and take of argument, I would be surprised
if he yields to anyone. Now, if Protagoras admits that he is Socrates' inferior
in dialectic, that should be enough for Socrates. But if he contests the point,
let him engage in a question-and-answer dialogue and not spin out a long
speech every time he answers, fending off the issues because he doesn't
want to be accountable, and going on and on until most of the listeners   d
have forgotten what the question was about, although I guarantee you
Socrates won't forget, no matter how he jokes about his memory. So I
think that Socrates has a stronger case. Each of us ought to make clear his
own opinion."

After Alcibiades it was Critias, I think, who spoke next: "Well, Prodicus
and Hippias, it seems to be that Callias is very much on Protagoras' side,   e
while Alcibiades as usual wants to be on the winning side of a good fight.
But there's no need for any of us to lend partisan support to either Socrates
or Protagoras. We should instead join in requesting them both not to break
up our meeting prematurely."

Prodicus spoke up next: "That's well said, Critias. Those who attend   337
discussions such as this ought to listen impartially, but not equally, to
both interlocutors. There is a distinction here. We ought to listen impartially
but not divide our attention equally: More should go to the wiser speaker
and less to the more unlearned. For my part, I think that the two of you   b
ought to debate the issues, but dispense with eristics. Friends debate each
other on good terms; eristics are for enemies at odds. In this way our
meeting would take a most attractive turn, for you, the speakers, would
then most surely earn the good opinion, rather than the praise, of those
of us listening to you. For a good opinion is guilelessly inherent in the
souls of the listeners, but praise is all too often merely a deceitful verbal
expression. And then, too, we, your audience, would be most cheered, but   c
not pleased, for to be cheered is to learn something, to participate in some
intellectual activity, and is a mental state; but to be pleased has to do with
eating or experiencing some other pleasure in one's body."

Prodicus' remarks were enthusiastically received by the majority of us,
and then the wise Hippias spoke: "Gentlemen, I regard all of you here

d   present as kinsmen, intimates, and fellow citizens by nature, not by convention. For like is akin to like by nature, but convention, which tyrannizes
the human race, often constrains us contrary to nature. Therefore it would
be disgraceful for us to understand the nature of things and not—being
as we are the wisest of the Greeks and gathered here together in this
veritable hall of wisdom, in this greatest and most august house of the
e   city itself—not, I say, produce anything worthy of all this dignity, but
bicker with each other as if we were the dregs of society. I therefore
implore and counsel you, Protagoras and Socrates, to be reconciled and
to compromise, under our arbitration, as it were, on some middle course.
338   You, Socrates, must not insist on that precise, excessively brief form of
discussion if it does not suit Protagoras, but rather allow free rein to the
speeches, so that they might communicate to us more impressively and
elegantly. And you, Protagoras, must not let out full sail in the wind and
leave the land behind to disappear into the Sea of Rhetoric. Both of you
b   must steer a middle course. So that's what you shall do, and take my
advice and choose a referee or moderator or supervisor who will monitor
for you the length of your speeches."

Everyone there thought this was a fine idea and gave it their approval.
Callias said he wouldn't let me go, and they requested me to choose a
moderator. I said it would be unseemly to choose someone to umpire our
speeches. "If the person chosen is going to be our inferior, it is not right
for an inferior to supervise his superiors. If he's our peer that's no good
c   either, because he will do the same as we would and be superfluous.
Choose someone who's our superior? I honestly think it's impossible for
you to choose someone wiser than Protagoras. And if you choose someone
who is not his superior but claim that he is, then you're insulting him.
Protagoras is just not the insignificant sort of person for whom you appoint
a supervisor. For myself, I don't care one way or another. But you have
your heart set on this conference and these discussions proceeding, and
d   if that's going to happen, this is what I want to do. If Protagoras is not
willing to answer questions, let him ask them, and I will answer, and at
the same time I will try to show him how I think the answerer ought to
answer. When I've answered all the questions he wishes to ask, then it's
his turn to be accountable to me in the same way. So if he doesn't seem
ready and willing to answer the actual question asked, you and I will
unite in urgently requesting him, as you have requested me, not to ruin
e   our conference. This will not require any one supervisor, since you will
all supervise together."

Everyone agreed this was the thing to do. Protagoras wanted no part
of it, but he had to agree to ask questions, and when he had asked enough,
to respond in turn with short answers.

339   So he began to ask questions something like this: "I consider, Socrates,
that the greatest part of a man's education is to be in command of poetry,
by which I mean the ability to understand the words of the poets, to know
when a poem is correctly composed and when not, and to know how to

analyze a poem and to respond to questions about it. So my line of questioning now will still concern the subject of our present discussion, namely virtue, but translated into the sphere of poetry. Now, Simonides somewhere says to Scopas, the son of Creon of Thessaly:

> *For a man to become good truly is hard,*
> *in hands and feet and mind foursquare,*
> *blamelessly built . . .*

b

Do you know this lyric ode, or shall I recite it all for you?"

I told him there was no need, for I knew the poem, and it happened to be one to which I had given especially careful attention.

"Good," he said. "So, do you think it's well made or not?"

"Very well made."

"And do you think it's well made if the poet contradicts himself?"

"No."

"Take a better look then."

c

"As I've said, I'm already familiar enough with it."

"Then you must know that at some point later in the ode he says:

> *Nor is Pittacus' proverb in tune*
> *however wise a man he was.*
> *Hard it is to be good, he said.*

"You do recognize that both these things are said by the same person?"

"I do."

"Well, do you think that the latter is consistent with the former?"

"It seems so to me," I said (but as I said it I was afraid he had a point there). "Doesn't it seem so to you?"

"How can anyone who says both these things be consistent? First, he asserts himself that it is hard for a man truly to become good, and then, a little further on in his poem he forgets and criticizes Pittacus for saying the same thing as he did, that it is hard for a man to be good, and refuses to accept from him the same thing that he himself said. And yet, when he criticizes him for saying the same thing as himself, he obviously criticizes himself as well, so either the earlier or the later must not be right."

d

Protagoras got a noisy round of applause for this speech. At first I felt as if I had been hit by a good boxer. Everything went black and I was reeling from Protagoras' oratory and the others' clamor. Then, to tell you the truth, to stall for time to consider what the poet meant, I turned to Prodicus and, calling on him, "Prodicus," I said, "Simonides was from your hometown, wasn't he? It's your duty to come to the man's rescue, so I don't mind calling for your help, just as Homer says Scamander called Simoïs to help him when he was besieged by Achilles:

e

340

Dear brother, let's buck this hero's strength together.[15]

So also do I summon your aid, lest to our dismay Protagoras destroy
b   Simonides. But really, Prodicus, Simonides' rehabilitation does require
your special art, by which you distinguish 'wanting' from 'desiring' and
make all the other fine distinctions that you did just a while ago. So tell
me if you agree with me, because it's not clear to me that Simonides does
in fact contradict himself. Just give us your offhand opinion. Are becoming
and being the same or different?"

"Good heavens, different."

"All right. Now, in the first passage, Simonides declared as his own
opinion that it is hard for a man truly to become good."

c   "That's right," Prodicus said.

"Then he criticizes Pittacus not for saying the same thing as himself, as
Protagoras thinks, but for saying something different. Because Pittacus did
not say that it is hard to *become* good, as Simonides said, but to *be* good.
As Prodicus here says, being and becoming are not the same thing, Protago-
d   ras. And if being is not the same as becoming, Simonides does not contradict
himself. Perhaps Prodicus and many others might agree with Hesiod that
it is difficult to become good:

> *The gods put Goodness where we have to sweat*
> *To get at her. But once you reach the top*
> *She's as easy to have as she was hard at first.*"[16]

Prodicus applauded me when he heard this, but Protagoras said, "Your
rehabilitation, Socrates, has a crippling error greater than the one you
are correcting."

"Then I've done my work badly," I said, "and I am the ridiculous sort
of physician whose cure is worse than the disease."

"That's exactly right," he said.

e   "How so?" said I.

"The poet's ignorance would be monumental if he says the possession
of virtue is so trivial when everyone agrees it is the hardest thing in
the world."

Then I said, "By heaven, Prodicus' participation in our discussion
341   couldn't be more timely. It may well be, Protagoras, that Prodicus' wisdom
is of ancient and divine origin, dating back to the time of Simonides or
even earlier. But although your experience is very broad, it does not seem
to extend to this branch of wisdom, which I have been schooled in as a
pupil of Prodicus. And now it appears that you do not understand that
Simonides may well have not conceived of the word 'hard' as you do. In

15. *Iliad* xxi.308.
16. *Works and Days* 289, 291–92.

much the same way Prodicus corrects me each time I use the word 'terrible' to praise you or someone else, as, for example, 'Protagoras is a terribly wise man.' When I say that, he asks me if I am not ashamed to call good things terrible. For terrible, he says, is bad. No one ever speaks of terrible wealth, or terrible peace, or terrible well-being, but we do hear of terrible disease, terrible war, and terrible poverty, 'terrible' here being 'bad.' So perhaps the Ceans and Simonides conceived of 'hard' as 'bad' or something else that you do not understand. Let's ask Prodicus. He's just the right person to consult on Simonides' dialect. Prodicus, what did Simonides mean by 'hard'?"

"Bad."

"Then this is why he criticizes Pittacus for saying it is hard to be good, just as if he had heard him say it is bad to be good. Right, Prodicus?"

"What else do you think Simonides meant, Socrates? He was censuring Pittacus, a man from Lesbos brought up in a barbarous dialect, for not distinguishing words correctly."

"Well, Protagoras, you hear Prodicus. Do you have anything to say in response?"

"You've got it all wrong, Prodicus," Protagoras said. "I am positive that Simonides meant by 'hard' the same thing we do: not 'bad,' but whatever is not easy and takes a lot of effort."

"Oh, but I think so too, Protagoras," I said. "This is what Simonides meant, and Prodicus knows it. He was joking and thought he would test your ability to defend your own statement. The best proof that Simonides did not mean that 'hard' is 'bad' is found in the very next phrase, which says:

God alone can have this privilege.

He cannot very well mean that it is bad to be good if he then says that God alone has this privilege. Prodicus would call Simonides a reprobate for that and no Cean at all. But I would like to tell you what I think Simonides' purpose is in this ode, if you would like to test my command (to use your term) of poetry. If you'd rather, though, I'll listen to you."

Protagoras heard me out and said, "If you please, Socrates," and then Prodicus, Hippias, and the others urged me on.

"All right, then," I said, "I will try to explain to you what I think this poem is about. Philosophy, first of all, has its most ancient roots and is most widespread among the Greeks in Crete and Lacedaemon, and those regions have the highest concentration of sophists in the world. But the natives deny it and pretend to be ignorant in order to conceal the fact that it is by their wisdom that they are the leaders of the Greek world, something like those sophists Protagoras was talking about. Their public image is that they owe their superiority to their brave fighting men, and their reason for promoting this image is that if the real basis for their superiority were discovered, i.e., wisdom, everyone else would start cultivating it. This is

top secret; not even the Spartanizing cults in the other cities know about
c   it, and so you have all these people getting their ears mangled aping the
Spartans, lacing on leather gloves, exercising fanatically and wearing short
capes, as if Sparta's political power depended on these things. And when
the citizens in Sparta want some privacy to have free and open discussions
with their sophists, they pass alien acts against any Spartanizers and other
foreigners in town, and conceal their meetings from the rest of the world.
d   And so that their young men won't unlearn what they are taught, they
do not permit any of them to travel to other cities (the Cretans don't either).
Crete and Sparta are places where there are not only men but women also
who take pride in their education. You know how to test the truth of my
contention that the Spartans have the best education in philosophy and
e   debate? Pick any ordinary Spartan and talk with him for a while. At first
you will find he can barely hold up his end of the conversation, but at
some point he will pick his spot with deadly skill and shoot back a terse
remark you'll never forget, something that will make the person he's
talking with (in this case you) look like a child. Acute observers have
known this for a long time now: To be a Spartan is to be a philosopher
343 much more than to be an athlete. They know that to be able to say something
like that is the mark of a perfectly educated man. We're talking about men
like Thales of Miletus, Pittacus of Mytilene, Bias of Priene, our own Solon,
Cleobulus of Lindus, Myson of Chen, and, the seventh in the list, Chilon
of Sparta. All of these emulated, loved, and studied Spartan culture. You
b   can see that distinctive kind of Spartan wisdom in their pithy, memorable
sayings, which they jointly dedicated as the first fruits of their wisdom to
Apollo in his temple at Delphi, inscribing there the maxims now on everyone's lips: 'Know thyself' and 'Nothing in excess.'

"What is my point? That the characteristic style of ancient philosophy
c   was laconic brevity. It was in this context that the saying of Pittacus—*It
is hard to be good*—was privately circulated with approval among the sages.
Then Simonides, ambitious for philosophical fame, saw that if he could
score a takedown against this saying, as if it were a famous wrestler, and
get the better of it, he would himself become famous in his own lifetime.
So he composed this poem as a deliberate attack against this maxim. That's
how it seems to me.

"Let's test my hypothesis together, to see whether what I say is true. If
d   all the poet wanted to say was that it is hard to become good, then the
beginning of the poem would be crazy, for he inserted there an antithetical
particle.[17] It doesn't make any sense to insert this unless one supposes that
Simonides is addressing the Pittacus maxim as an opponent. Pittacus says
it is hard to be good; Simonides rebuts this by saying, 'No, but it is hard

17. The first line of Simonides' ode, "For a man to become good truly is hard," is in
fact introduced with a contrasting particle, not translated here. Socrates does not quote
the continuation (and the lines have not survived elsewhere), so we do not know what
sort of contrast was intended.

for a man to become good, Pittacus, truly.' Notice that he does not say truly good; he is not talking about truth in the context of some things being truly good and other things being good but not truly so. This would create an impression of naivete very unlike Simonides. The position of 'truly' in the verse must be a case of hyperbaton. We have to approach this maxim of Pittacus by imagining him speaking and Simonides replying, something like this: Pittacus: 'Gentlemen, it is hard to be good.' Simonides: 'What you say is not true, Pittacus, for it is not being but becoming good, in hands and feet and mind foursquare, blamelessly built—that is hard truly.' This way the insertion of the antithetical particle makes sense, and the 'truly' feels correct in its position at the end. Everything that comes after is evidence for this interpretation. The poem is full of details that testify to its excellent composition; indeed, it is a lovely and exquisitely crafted piece, but it would take a long time to go through it from that point of view. Let's review instead the overall structure and intention of the ode, which is from beginning to end a refutation of Pittacus' maxim.

"A few lines later he states (imagine he is making a speech): 'To become good truly is hard, and although it may be possible for a short period of time, to persist in that state and to be a good man, as you put it, Pittacus, is not humanly possible. God alone can have this privilege,

> But that man inevitably is bad
> whom incapacitating misfortune throws down.

" 'Whom does incapacitating misfortune throw down when it comes to, say, the command of a ship? Clearly not the ordinary passenger, who is always susceptible. You can't knock down someone already supine; you can only knock down someone standing up and render him supine. In the same way, incapacitating misfortune would overthrow only someone who is capable, not the chronically incapable. A hurricane striking a pilot would incapacitate him, a bad season will do it to a farmer, and the same thing applies to a doctor. For the good is susceptible to becoming bad, as another poet testifies:

> The good man is at times bad, at times good.

" 'But the bad is not susceptible to becoming bad; it must always be bad. So that when incapacitating misfortune throws down a man who is capable, wise, and good, he must "inevitably be bad." You say, Pittacus, that it is hard to be good; in fact, to become good is hard, though possible, but to be good is impossible.

> Faring well, every man is good;
> Bad, faring ill.

" 'What does it mean to fare well in letters; what makes a man good at
345 them? Clearly, the learning of letters. What kind of faring well makes a
good doctor? Clearly, learning how to cure the sick. 'Bad, faring ill': who
could become a bad doctor? Clearly, someone who is, first, a doctor and,
second, a good doctor. He could in fact become a bad doctor, but we who
are medical laymen could never by faring ill become doctors or carpenters
b or any other kind of professional. And if one cannot become a doctor by
faring ill, clearly one cannot become a bad one either. In the same way a
good man may eventually become bad with the passage of time, or through
hardship, disease, or some other circumstance that involves the only real
kind of faring ill, which is the loss of knowledge. But the bad man can
never become bad, for he is so all the time. If he is to become bad, he must
c first become good. So the tenor of this part of the poem is that it is
impossible to be a good man and continue to be good, but possible for
one and the same person to become good and also bad, and those are best
for the longest time whom the gods love.'

"All this is directed at Pittacus, as the next few lines of the poem make
even clearer:

Therefore never shall I seek for the impossible,
cast away my life's lot on empty hope, a quixotic quest
for a blameless man among those who reap
the broad earth's fruit,
d   *but if I find him you will have my report.*

This is strong language, and he keeps up his attack on Pittacus' maxim
throughout the poem:

All who do no wrong willingly
I praise and love.
Necessity not even the gods resist.

This is spoken to the same end. For Simonides was not so uneducated as
e to say that he praised all who did nothing bad willingly, as if there were
anyone who willingly did bad things. I am pretty sure that none of the
wise men thinks that any human being willingly makes a mistake or
willingly does anything wrong or bad. They know very well that anyone
who does anything wrong or bad does so involuntarily. So also Simonides,
346 who does not say that he praises those who willingly do nothing bad;
rather he applies the term 'willingly' to himself. He perceived that a good
man, an honorable man, often forces himself to love and praise someone
utterly different from himself, one's alienated father perhaps, or mother,
or country. Scoundrels in a similar situation are almost happy to see their
parents' or country's trouble and viciously point it out and denounce it
b so that their own dereliction of duty toward them will not be called into
question. They actually exaggerate their complaints and add gratuitous to

unavoidable hostility, whereas good men conceal the trouble and force themselves to give praise, and if they are angry because their parents or country wronged them, they calm themselves down and reconcile themselves to it, and they force themselves to love and praise their own people. I think that Simonides reflected that on more than one occasion he himself had eulogized some tyrant or other such person, not willingly but because   c
he had to. So he is saying to Pittacus: 'Pittacus, it is not because I am an overcritical person that I am criticizing you, since,

> *enough for me a man who is not bad*
> *nor too intractable, who knows civic Right, a sound man.*
> *I shall not blame him,*
> *for I am not fond of blame.*
> *Infinite the tribe of fools,'*

the implication being that a censorious person would have his hands full blaming them.

> *'All is fair in which foul is not mixed.'*

The sense here is not that all is white in which black is not mixed, which   d
would be ludicrous in many ways, but rather that he himself accepts without any objection what is in between. 'I do not seek,' he says,

> *'for a blameless man among those who reap*
> *the broad earth's fruit,*
> *but if I find him you will have my report.'*

The meaning is that 'on those terms I will never praise anyone, but I am happy with an average man who does no wrong, since I willingly

> *praise and love all'*—

—note the Lesbian dialect form of the verb 'praise,' since he is addressing   e
Pittacus—

> *'all who do no wrong'*

(this is where the pause should be, before 'willingly')

> *'willingly*
> *I praise and love*

but there are some whom I praise and love unwillingly. So if you spoke something even moderately reasonable and true, Pittacus, I would never

347   censure you. But the fact is that you have lied blatantly yet with verisimili-
      tude about extremely important issues, and for that I do censure you.'
          "And that, Prodicus and Protagoras," I concluded, "is what I think was
      going through Simonides' mind when he composed this ode."

b   Then Hippias said, "I am favorably impressed by your analysis of this
      ode, Socrates. I have quite a nice talk on it myself, which I will present to
      you if you wish."
          "Yes, Hippias," Alcibiades said, "some other time, though. What should
      be done now is what Socrates and Protagoras agreed upon, which is for
      Socrates to answer any questions Protagoras may still have to ask, or if
      he so chooses, to answer Socrates' questions."

c   Then I said, "I leave it up to Protagoras, but if it's all right with him,
      why don't we say good-bye to odes and poetry and get back to what I
      first asked him, a question, Protagoras, which I would be glad to settle in
      a joint investigation with you. Discussing poetry strikes me as no different
      from the second-rate drinking parties of the agora crowd. These people,
      largely uneducated and unable to entertain themselves over their wine by

d   using their own voices to generate conversation, pay premium prices for
      flute-girls and rely on the extraneous voice of the reed flute as background
      music for their parties. But when well-educated gentlemen drink together,
      you will not see girls playing the flute or the lyre or dancing, but a group
      that knows how to get together without these childish frivolities, convers-

e   ing civilly no matter how heavily they are drinking. Ours is such a group,
      if indeed it consists of men such as most of us claim to be, and it should
      require no extraneous voices, not even of poets, who cannot be questioned
      on what they say. When a poet is brought up in a discussion, almost
      everyone has a different opinion about what he means, and they wind up
      arguing about something they can never finally decide. The best people

348   avoid such discussions and rely on their own powers of speech to entertain
      themselves and test each other. These people should be our models. We
      should put the poets aside and converse directly with each other, testing
      the truth and our own ideas. If you have more questions to ask, I am ready
      to answer them; or, if you prefer, you can render the same service to me,
      and we can resume where we broke off and try to reach a conclusion."

b   I went on in this vein, but Protagoras would not state clearly which
      alternative he preferred. So Alcibiades looked over at Callias and said,
      "Callias, do you think Protagoras is behaving well in not making it
      clear whether he will participate in the discussion or not? I certainly
      don't. He should either participate or say he is not going to, so we
      will know how he stands, and Socrates, or whoever, can start a discussion
      with someone else."

c   It looked to me that Protagoras was embarrassed by Alcibiades' words,
      not to mention the insistence of Callias and practically the whole company.
      In the end he reluctantly brought himself to resume our dialogue and
      indicated he was ready to be asked questions.

"Protagoras," I said, "I don't want you to think that my motive in talking with you is anything else than to take a good hard look at things that continually perplex me. I think that Homer said it all in the line,

Going in tandem, one perceives before the other.[18]   d

Human beings are simply more resourceful this way in action, speech, and thought. If someone has a private perception, he immediately starts going around and looking until he finds somebody he can show it to and have it corroborated. And there is a particular reason why I would rather talk with you than anyone else: I think you are the best qualified to investigate the sort of things that decent and respectable individuals ought   e
to examine, and virtue especially. Who else but you? Not only do you consider yourself to be noble and good but, unlike others who are themselves decent and respectable individuals yet unable to make others so, you are not only good yourself but able to make others good as well, and you have so much self-confidence that instead of concealing this skill, as others do, you advertise it openly to the whole Greek world, calling yourself   349
a sophist, highlighting yourself as a teacher of virtue, the first ever to have deemed it appropriate to charge a fee for this. How could I not solicit your help in a joint investigation of these questions? There is no way I could not.

"So right now I want you to remind me of some of the questions I first asked, starting from the beginning. Then I want to proceed together to   b
take a good hard look at some other questions. I believe the first question was this: Wisdom, temperance, courage, justice, and piety—are these five names for the same thing, or is there underlying each of these names a unique thing, a thing with its own power or function, each one unlike any of the others? You said that they are not names for the same thing, that   c
each of these names refers to a unique thing, and that all these are parts of virtue, not like the parts of gold, which are similar to each other and to the whole of which they are parts, but like the parts of a face, dissimilar to the whole of which they are parts and to each other, and each one having its own unique power or function. If this is still your view, say so; if it's changed in any way, make your new position clear, for I am certainly not going to hold you accountable for what you said before if you want   d
to say something at all different now. In fact, I wouldn't be surprised if you were just trying out something on me before."

"What I am saying to you, Socrates, is that all these are parts of virtue, and that while four of them are reasonably close to each other, courage is completely different from all the rest. The proof that what I am saying is true is that you will find many people who are extremely unjust, impious, intemperate, and ignorant, and yet exceptionally courageous."

18. *Iliad* x.224.

e   "Hold it right there," I said. "This is worth looking into. Would you say courageous men are confident, or something else?"

         "Confident, yes, and ready for action where most men would be afraid."

         "Well, then, do you agree that virtue is something fine, and that you offer yourself as a teacher of it because it is fine?"

         "The finest thing of all, unless I am quite out of my mind."

         "Then is part of it worthless and part of it fine, or all of it fine?"

         "Surely it is all as fine as can be."

350   "Do you know who dives confidently into wells?"

         "Of course, divers."

         "Is this because they know what they are doing, or for some other reason?"

         "Because they know what they are doing."

         "Who are confident in fighting from horseback? Riders or nonriders?"

         "Riders."

         "And in fighting with shields? Shieldmen or nonshieldmen?"

         "Shieldmen, and so on down the line, if that's what you're getting at. Those with the right kind of knowledge are always more confident than those without it, and a given individual is more confident after he acquires it than he was before."

b   "But haven't you ever seen men lacking knowledge of all of these things yet confident in each of them?"

         "I have, all too confident."

         "Is their confidence courage?"

         "No, because courage would then be contemptible. These men are out of their minds."

         "Then what do you mean by courageous men? Aren't they those who are confident?"

c   "I still hold by that."

         "Then *these* men who are so confident turn out to be not courageous but mad? And, on the other side, the wisest are the most confident and the most confident are the most courageous? And the logical conclusion would be that wisdom is courage?"

         "You are doing a poor job of remembering what I said when I answered your questions, Socrates. When I was asked if the courageous are confident, I agreed. I was not asked if the confident are courageous. If you had asked

d   me that, I would have said, 'Not all of them.' You have nowhere shown that my assent to the proposition that the courageous are confident was in error. What you did show next was that knowledge increases one's confidence and makes one more confident than those without knowledge. In consequence of this you conclude that courage and wisdom are the same thing. But by following this line of reasoning you could conclude that strength and wisdom are the same thing. First you would ask me if

e   the strong are powerful, and I would say yes. Then, if those who know how to wrestle are more powerful than those who do not, and if individual wrestlers became more powerful after they learn than they were before.

Again I would say yes. After I had agreed to these things, it would be open to you to use precisely these points of agreement to prove that wisdom is strength. But nowhere in this process do I agree that the powerful are strong, only that the strong are powerful. Strength and power are not 351 the same thing. Power derives from knowledge and also from madness and passionate emotion. Strength comes from nature and proper nurture of the body. So also confidence and courage are not the same thing, with the consequence that the courageous are confident, but not all those who are confident are courageous. For confidence, like power, comes from skill (and from passionate emotion and madness as well); courage, from nature and the proper nurture of the soul."

"Would you say, Protagoras, that some people live well and others b live badly?"

"Yes."

"But does it seem to you that a person lives well, if he lives distressed and in pain?"

"No, indeed."

"Now, if he completed his life, having lived pleasantly, does he not seem to you to have lived well?"

"It seems that way to me."

"So, then, to live pleasantly is good, and unpleasantly, bad?" c

"Yes, so long as he lived having taken pleasure in honorable things."

"What, Protagoras? Surely you don't, like most people, call some pleasant things bad and some painful things good? I mean, isn't a pleasant thing good just insofar as it is pleasant, that is, if it results in nothing other than pleasure; and, on the other hand, aren't painful things bad in the same way, just insofar as they are painful?"

"I don't know, Socrates, if I should answer as simply as you put the d question—that everything pleasant is good and everything painful is bad. It seems to me to be safer to respond not merely with my present answer in mind but from the point of view of my life overall, that on the one hand, there are pleasurable things which are not good, and on the other hand, there are painful things which are not bad but some which are, and a third class which is neutral—neither bad nor good."

"You call pleasant things those which partake of pleasure or produce e pleasure?"

"Certainly."

"So my question is this: Just insofar as things are pleasurable are they good? I am asking whether pleasure itself is not a good."

"Just as you always say, Socrates, let us inquire into this matter, and if your claim seems reasonable and it is established that pleasure and the good are the same, then we will come to agreement; otherwise we will disagree."

"Do you wish to lead this inquiry, or shall I?"

"It is fitting for you to lead, for it is you who brought up the idea."

"All right, will this help to make it clear? When someone evaluates a 352 man's health or other functions of the body through his appearance, he looks at the face and extremities, and might say: 'Show me your chest and back too, so that I can make a better examination.' That's the kind of investigation I want to make. Having seen how you stand on the good and the pleasant, I need to say something like this to you: Come now,

b   Protagoras, and reveal this about your mind: What do you think about knowledge? Do you go along with the majority or not? Most people think this way about it, that it is not a powerful thing, neither a leader nor a ruler. They do not think of it in that way at all; but rather in this way: while knowledge is often present in a man, what rules him is not knowledge but rather anything else—sometimes anger, sometimes pleasure, some-

c   times pain, at other times love, often fear; they think of his knowledge as being utterly dragged around by all these other things as if it were a slave. Now, does the matter seem like that to you, or does it seem to you that knowledge is a fine thing capable of ruling a person, and if someone were to know what is good and bad, then he would not be forced by anything to act otherwise than knowledge dictates, and intelligence would be sufficient to save a person?"

"Not only does it seem just as you say, Socrates, but further, it would

d   be shameful indeed for me above all people to say that wisdom and knowledge are anything but the most powerful forces in human activity."

"Right you are. You realize that most people aren't going to be convinced by us. They maintain that most people are unwilling to do what is best, even though they know what it is and are able to do it. And when I have asked them the reason for this, they say that those who act that way do

e   so because they are overcome by pleasure or pain or are being ruled by one of the things I referred to just now."

"I think people say a lot of other things erroneously too, Socrates."

353   "Come with me, then, and let's try to persuade people and to teach them what is this experience which they call being overcome by pleasure, because of which they fail to do the best thing when they know what it is. For perhaps if we told them that what they were saying isn't true, but is demonstrably false, they would ask us: 'Protagoras and Socrates, if this is not the experience of being overcome by pleasure, but something other than that, what do you two say it is? Tell us.' "

"Socrates, why is it necessary for us to investigate the opinion of ordinary people, who will say whatever occurs to them?"

b   "I think this will help us find out about courage, how it is related to the other parts of virtue. If you are willing to go along with what we agreed just now, that I will lead us toward what I think will turn out to be the best way to make things clear, then fine; if you are not willing, I will give it up."

"No, you are right; proceed as you have begun."

c   "Going back, then; if they should ask us: 'We have been speaking of "being overcome by pleasure." What do you say this is?' I would reply to them this way: 'Listen. Protagoras and I will try to explain it to you. Do you hold, gentlemen, that this happens to you in circumstances like these—you are often overcome by pleasant things like food or drink or sex, and you do those things all the while knowing they are ruinous?' They would say yes. Then you and I would ask them again: 'In what sense do you call these things ruinous? Is it that each of them is pleasant in itself and produces immediate pleasure, or is it that later they bring about diseases and poverty and many other things of that sort? Or even if it doesn't bring about these things later, but gives only enjoyment, would it still be a bad thing, just because it gives enjoyment in whatever way?' Can we suppose then, Protagoras, that they would make any other answer than that bad things are bad not because they bring about immediate pleasure, but rather because of what happens later, disease and things like that?"

"I think that is how most people would answer."

" 'And in bringing about diseases and poverty, do they bring about pain?' I think they would agree."

"Yes."

" 'Does it not seem to you, my good people, as Protagoras and I maintain, that these things are bad on account of nothing other than the fact that they result in pain and deprive us of other pleasures?' Would they agree?"

Protagoras concurred.

"Then again, suppose we were to ask them the opposite question: 'You who say that some painful things are good, do you not say that such things as athletics and military training and treatments by doctors such as cautery, surgery, medicines, and starvation diet are good things even though painful?' Would they say so?"

"Yes."

" 'Would you call these things good for the reason that they bring about intense pain and suffering, or because they ultimately bring about health and good condition of bodies and preservation of cities and power over others and wealth?' Would they agree?"

"Yes."

" 'These things are good only because they result in pleasure and in the relief and avoidance of pain? Or do you have some other criterion in view, other than pleasure and pain, on the basis of which you would call these things good?' They say no, I think."

"And I would agree with you."

" 'So then you pursue pleasure as being good and avoid pain as bad?' "

"Yes."

" 'So this you regard as bad, pain, and pleasure, you regard as good, since you call the very enjoying of something bad whenever it deprives us of greater pleasures than it itself provides, or brings about greater pains than the very pleasures inherent in it? But if you call the very enjoying of something bad for some other reason and with some other criterion in view than the one I have suggested, you could tell us what it is; but you won't be able to.' "

"I don't think they'll be able to either."

" 'And likewise concerning the actual state of being in pain? Do you call the actual condition of being in pain good, whenever it relieves pains greater than the ones it contains or brings about greater pleasures than its attendant pains? Now, if you are using some other criterion than the one I have suggested, when you call the very condition of being pained good, you can tell us what it is; but you won't be able to.' "

"Truly spoken."

"Now, again, gentlemen, if you asked me: 'Why are you going on so much about this and in so much detail?' I would reply, forgive me. First of all, it is not easy to show what it is that you call 'being overcome by pleasure,' and then, it is upon this very point that all the arguments rest. But even now it is still possible to withdraw, if you are able to say that the good is anything other than pleasure or that the bad is anything other than pain. Or is it enough for you to live life pleasantly without pain? If it is enough, and you are not able to say anything else than that the good and the bad are that which result in pleasure and pain, listen to this. For I say to you that if this is so, your position will become absurd, when you say that frequently a man, knowing the bad to be bad, nevertheless does that very thing, when he is able not to do it, having been driven and overwhelmed by pleasure; and again when you say that a man knowing the good is not willing to do it, on account of immediate pleasure, having been overcome by it. Just how absurd this is will become very clear, if we do not use so many names at the same time, 'pleasant' and 'painful,' 'good' and 'bad'; but since these turned out to be only two things, let us instead call them by two names, first, 'good' and 'bad,' then later, 'pleasant' and 'painful.' On that basis, then, let us say that a man knowing bad things to be bad, does them all the same. If then someone asks us: 'Why?' 'Having been overcome,' we shall reply. 'By what?' he will ask us. We are no longer able to say 'by pleasure,'—for it has taken on its other name, 'the good' instead of 'pleasure'—so we will say and reply that 'he is overcome . . .' 'By what?' he will ask. 'By the good,' we will say, 'for heaven's sake!' If by chance the questioner is rude he might burst out laughing and say: 'What you're saying is ridiculous—someone does what is bad, knowing that it is bad, when it is not necessary to do it, having been overcome by the good. So,' he will say, 'within yourself, does the good outweigh the bad or not?' We will clearly say in reply that it does not; for if it did, the person who we say is overcome by pleasure would not have made any mistake. 'In virtue of what,' he might say, 'does the good *outweigh* the bad or the bad the good? Only in that one is greater and one is smaller, or more and less.' We could not help but agree. 'So clearly then' he will say, 'by "being overcome" you mean getting more bad things for the sake of fewer good things.'[19] That settles that, then.

---

19. The Greek translated "for the sake of" here is *anti*: it might alternatively be translated "in exchange for."

"So let's now go back and apply the names 'the pleasant' and 'the painful' to these very same things. Now let us say that a man does what before we called 'bad' things and now shall call 'painful' ones, knowing they are painful things, but being overcome by pleasant things, although it is clear that they do not outweigh them. But how else does pleasure outweigh pain, except in relative excess or deficiency? Isn't it a matter (to use other terms) of larger and smaller, more or fewer, greater or lesser degree?

356

"For if someone were to say: 'But Socrates, the immediate pleasure is very much different from the pleasant and the painful at a later time,' I would reply, 'They are not different in any other way than by pleasure and pain, for there is no other way that they could differ. Weighing is a good analogy; you put the pleasures together and the pains together, both the near and the remote, on the balance scale, and then say which of the two is more. For if you weigh pleasant things against pleasant, the greater and the more must always be taken; if painful things against painful, the fewer and the smaller. And if you weigh pleasant things against painful, and the painful is exceeded by the pleasant—whether the near by the remote or the remote by the near—you have to perform that action in which the pleasant prevails; on the other hand, if the pleasant is exceeded by the painful, you have to refrain from doing that. Does it seem any different to you, my friends?' I know that they would not say otherwise."

b

c

Protagoras assented.

"Since this is so, I will say to them: 'Answer me this: Do things of the same size appear to you larger when seen near at hand and smaller when seen from a distance, or not?' They would say they do. 'And similarly for thicknesses and pluralities? And equal sounds seem louder when near at hand, softer when farther away?' They would agree. 'If then our well-being depended upon this, doing and choosing large things, avoiding and not doing the small ones, what would we see as our salvation in life? Would it be the art of measurement or the power of appearance? While the power of appearance often makes us wander all over the place in confusion, often changing our minds about the same things and regretting our actions and choices with respect to things large and small, the art of measurement in contrast, would make the appearances lose their power by showing us the truth, would give us peace of mind firmly rooted in the truth and would save our life.' Therefore, would these men agree, with this in mind, that the art of measurement would save us, or some other art?"

d

e

"I agree, the art of measurement would."

"What if our salvation in life depended on our choices of odd and even, when the greater and the lesser had to be counted correctly, either the same kind against itself or one kind against the other, whether it be near or remote? What then would save our life? Surely nothing other than knowledge, specifically some kind of measurement, since that is the art of the greater and the lesser? In fact, nothing other than arithmetic, since it's a question of the odd and even? Would these men agree with us or not?"

357

Protagoras thought they would agree.

"Well, then, my good people: Since it has turned out that our salvation
b   in life depends on the right choice of pleasures and pains, be they more
or fewer, greater or lesser, farther or nearer, doesn't our salvation seem,
first of all, to be measurement, which is the study of relative excess and
deficiency and equality?"

"It must be."

"And since it is measurement, it must definitely be an art, and
knowledge."

"They will agree."

"What exactly this art, this knowledge is, we can inquire into later;
that it is knowledge of some sort is enough for the demonstration which
c   Protagoras and I have to give in order to answer the question you asked
us. You asked it, if you remember, when we were agreeing that nothing
was stronger or better than knowledge, which always prevails, whenever
it is present, over pleasure and everything else. At that point you said that
pleasure often rules even the man who knows; since we disagreed, you
went on to ask us this: 'Protagoras and Socrates, if this experience is not
d   being overcome by pleasure, what is it then; what do you say it is? Tell
us.' If immediately we had said to you 'ignorance,' you might have laughed
at us, but if you laugh at us now, you will be laughing at yourselves. For
you agreed with us that those who make mistakes with regard to the
choice of pleasure and pain, in other words, with regard to good and bad,
do so because of a lack of knowledge, and not merely a lack of knowledge
e   but a lack of that knowledge you agreed was measurement. And the
mistaken act done without knowledge you must know is one done from
ignorance. So this is what "being overcome by pleasure" is—ignorance in
the highest degree, and it is this which Protagoras and Prodicus and
Hippias claim to cure. But you, thinking it to be something other than
ignorance, do not go to sophists yourselves, nor do you send your children
to them for instruction, believing as you do that we are dealing with
something unteachable. By worrying about your money and not giving it
to them, you all do badly in both private and public life.'

358   "This is how we would have answered the many. Now, I ask you,
Hippias and Prodicus, as well as Protagoras—this is your conversation
also—to say whether you think what I say is true or false." They all thought
that what I said was marvelously true.

"So you agree that the pleasant is good, the painful bad. I beg indulgence
of Prodicus who distinguishes among words; for whether you call it 'pleas-
b   ant' or 'delightful' or 'enjoyable,' or whatever way or manner you please
to name this sort of thing, my excellent Prodicus, please respond to the
intent of my question." Prodicus, laughing, agreed, as did the others.

"Well, then, men, what about this? Are not all actions leading toward
living painlessly and pleasantly honorable and beneficial? And isn't honorable activity good and beneficial?"

They agreed.

"Then if the pleasant is the good, no one who knows or believes there   c
is something else better than what he is doing, something possible, will
go on doing what he had been doing when he could be doing what is
better. To give in to oneself is nothing other than ignorance, and to control
oneself is nothing other than wisdom."

They all agreed.

"Well, then, do you say that ignorance is to have a false belief and to
be deceived about matters of importance?"

They all agreed on this.

"Now, no one goes willingly toward the bad or what he believes to be   d
bad; neither is it in human nature, so it seems, to want to go toward what
one believes to be bad instead of to the good. And when he is forced to
choose between one of two bad things, no one will choose the greater if
he is able to choose the lesser."

They agreed with all of that too.

"Well, then, is there something you call dread or fear? And I address
this to you, Prodicus. I say that whether you call it fear or dread, it is an
expectation of something bad."

Protagoras and Hippias thought that this was true of both dread and   e
fear, but Prodicus thought it applied to dread, but not to fear.

"Well, it does not really matter, Prodicus. This is the point. If what I
have said up to now is true, then would anyone be willing to go toward
what he dreads, when he can go toward what he does not? Or is this
impossible from what we have agreed? For it was agreed that what one
fears one holds to be bad; no one goes toward those things which he holds
to be bad, or chooses those things willingly."

They all agreed.   359

"Well, Prodicus and Hippias, with this established, let Protagoras defend
for us the truth of his first answer. I don't mean his very first answer, for
then he said that while there are five parts of virtue, none is like any other,
but each one has its own unique power or function. I'm not talking about
this now, but about what he said later. For later he said that four of them   b
are very similar to each other, but one differs very much from the others,
namely courage. And he said that I would know this by the following
evidence: 'You will find, Socrates, many people who are extremely impious,
unjust, intemperate, and ignorant, and yet exceptionally courageous; by
this you will recognize that courage differs very much from all the other
parts of virtue.' I was very surprised at his answer then, and even more
so now that I have gone over these things with you. I asked him then if
he said that the courageous were confident. And he said, 'Yes, and ready   c
for action too.' Do you remember giving this answer?"

He said he did.

"Well, then, tell us, for what actions are the courageous ready? The same
actions as the cowardly?"

"No."

"Different actions?"

"Yes."

"Do the cowardly go forward to things which inspire confidence, and the courageous toward things to be feared?"

"So it is said by most people."

d   "Right, but I am not asking that. Rather, what do *you* say the courageous go boldly toward: toward things to be feared, believing them to be fearsome, or toward things not to be feared?"

"By what you have just said, the former is impossible."

"Right again; so, if our demonstration has been correct, then no one goes toward those things he considers to be fearsome, since not to be in control of oneself was found to be ignorance."

He agreed.

e   "But all people, both the courageous and the cowardly, go toward that about which they are confident; both the cowardly and the courageous go toward the same things."

"But, Socrates, what the cowardly go toward is completely opposite to what the courageous go toward. For example, the courageous are willing to go to war, but the cowardly are not."

"Is going to war honorable or is it disgraceful?"

"Honorable."

"Then, if it is honorable, we have agreed before, it is also good, for we agreed that all honorable actions were good."

"Very true, and I always believed this."

360   "And rightly; but who would you say are not willing to go to war, war being honorable and good?"

"The cowardly."

"If a thing is noble and good, is it also pleasant?"

"That was definitely agreed upon."

"So, the cowardly, with full knowledge, are not willing to go toward the more honorable, the better, and more pleasant?"

"If we agree to that, we will undermine what we agreed on earlier."

"What about the courageous man: Does he go toward the more honorable, the better, and more pleasant?"

"We must agree to that."

"So, generally, when the courageous fear, their fear is not disgraceful; nor when they are confident is their confidence disgraceful."

b   "True."

"If not disgraceful, is it honorable?"

He agreed.

"If honorable, then also good?"

"Yes."

"Whereas the fear and confidence of the cowardly, the foolhardy, and madmen are disgraceful?"

He agreed.

"Is their confidence disgraceful and bad for any reason other than ignorance and stupidity?"

"No, it isn't."   c

"Now then; that through which cowardly people are cowardly, do you call it cowardice or courage?"

"Cowardice."

"And aren't cowards shown to be so through their ignorance of what is to be feared?"

"Absolutely."

"So they are cowards because of that ignorance?"

He agreed.

"You agreed that it is through cowardice that they are cowards?"

He said he did.

"So, can we conclude that cowardice is ignorance of what is and is not to be feared?"

He nodded.

"Now, courage is the opposite of cowardice."   d

He said yes.

"So then, wisdom about what is and is not to be feared is the opposite of this ignorance?"

He nodded again.

"And this ignorance is cowardice?"

He nodded again, very reluctantly.

"So the wisdom about what is and is not to be feared is courage and is the opposite of this ignorance?"

He would not even nod at this; he remained silent.

And I said, "What's this, Protagoras? Will you not say yes or no to my question?"

"Answer it yourself."

"I have only one more question to ask you. Do you still believe, as you   e
did at first, that some men are extremely ignorant and yet still very courageous?"

"I think that you just want to win the argument, Socrates, and that is why you are forcing me to answer. So I will gratify you and say that, on the basis of what we have agreed upon, it seems to me to be impossible."

"I have no other reason for asking these things than my desire to answer these questions about virtue, especially what virtue is in itself. For I know   361
that if we could get clear on that, then we would be able to settle the question about which we both have had much to say, I—that virtue cannot be taught, you—that it can.

"It seems to me that our discussion has turned on us, and if it had a voice of its own, it would say, mockingly, 'Socrates and Protagoras, how ridiculous you are, both of you. Socrates, you said earlier that virtue cannot   b
be taught, but now you are arguing the very opposite and have attempted to show that everything is knowledge—justice, temperance, courage—in

which case, virtue would appear to be eminently teachable. On the other hand, if virtue is anything other than knowledge, as Protagoras has been trying to say, then it would clearly be unteachable. But, if it turns out to be wholly knowledge, as you now urge, Socrates, it would be very surprising indeed if virtue could not be taught. Now, Protagoras maintained at first

c   that it could be taught, but now he thinks the opposite, urging that hardly any of the virtues turn out to be knowledge. On that view, virtue could hardly be taught at all.'

"Now, Protagoras, seeing that we have gotten this topsy-turvy and

d   terribly confused, I am most eager to clear it all up, and I would like us, having come this far, to continue until we come through to what virtue is in itself, and then to return to inquire about whether it can or cannot be taught, so that Epimetheus might not frustrate us a second time in this inquiry, as he neglected us in the distribution of powers and abilities in your story. I liked the Prometheus character in your story better than Epimetheus. Since I take promethean forethought over my life as a whole, I pay attention to these things, and if you are willing, as I said at the beginning, I would be pleased to investigate them along with you."

e   "Socrates, I commend your enthusiasm and the way you find your way through an argument. I really don't think I am a bad man, certainly the last man to harbor ill will. Indeed, I have told many people that I admire you more than anyone I have met, certainly more than anyone in your generation. And I say that I would not be surprised if you gain among men high repute for wisdom. We will examine these things later, whenever you wish; now it is time to turn our attention elsewhere."

362   "That is what we should do, if it seems right to you. It is long since time for me to keep that appointment I mentioned. I stayed only as a favor to our noble colleague Callias."

Our conversation was over, and so we left.

GORGIAS

Gorgias was a famous teacher of oratory and the author of oratorical display pieces. He had served his native Leontini in Greek Sicily on embassies, including one to Athens in 427 B.C., when his artistically elaborate prose style made a great and lasting impression. We loosely consider him a 'sophist', like the intellectuals whom Plato gathers together at Callias' house in Protagoras, but Plato pointedly reports Gorgias' teaching as restricted to the art of public speaking: he did not offer to instruct young people in 'virtue'—the qualities, whatever they were, that made a good person overall and a good citizen. Nonetheless, as Plato also makes clear, he praised so highly the speaking abilities that his own teaching imparted that one could pardon ambitious young Athenians like Callicles if they thought that, by learning oratory from him, they would know everything a man needs in order to secure for himself the best life possible. And, as we learn from Meno, he did have striking things to say about the nature of, and differences between, virtue in men and women, old persons and young, and so on. So in the end not much separates him from the other itinerant teachers that, with him, we classify as 'sophists'.

Socrates begins by skeptically seeking clarification from the elderly, respected Gorgias about the nature and power of his 'craft'—the skill at persuading people massed in assemblies and juries about what is good and what is right. Gorgias is trapped in a contradiction when he admits that the true, skilled orator must know (and not merely speak persuasively on) his most particular subjects—right and wrong, justice and injustice in the lawcourts. When Gorgias bows out, a fellow rhetorician takes over his side of the argument—the young and rambunctious Polus, a real person. His name means 'colt'—almost too good to be true! Polus is intoxicated with the thought that rhetoric gives the power to do what one pleases, even injustice if that suits the situation. Against him, Socrates insists that in fact it is better to suffer injustice than to do it—and, unable to deny this consistently, Polus in his turn falls to Socrates' dialectic. In the remainder of the dialogue—more than half—Socrates contends with Callicles, apparently also a real person, though we hear nothing about him outside this dialogue. The discussion develops into a contentious and sometimes bitter dispute about which way of life is best—the selfish, domineering, pleasure-seeking one that Callicles associates with his own unbounded admiration for rhetorical skill, or the philosophical life that Socrates champions, committed to the objective existence of justice and the other virtues and devoted to learning about and living in accordance with them. Socrates struggles and struggles to undermine Callicles' views. He tries to bring Callicles to admit that some of *his own deepest convictions commit him to agreeing with Socrates: Socrates thinks he knows better than Callicles what Callicles really believes. In giving vent to strongly worded assertions of his own moral commitments, he seems to adopt a conception of 'irrational' desires like that of* Republic *IV, incompatible with the views he works with in the other 'Socratic' dialogues. Callicles, though personally well disposed, is equally vehement and contemptuous in rejecting Socrates' outlook—he refuses to succumb to the toils of Socratic logic. If the methods of argument Socrates employs here produce at best an uneasy standoff, the different methods of* Republic *II–IX may seem to Plato to offer a resolution.*

Gorgias *is so long, complex, and intellectually ambitious that it strains the confines of a simple 'Socratic' dialogue—a portrait of Socrates carrying out moral inquiries by his customary method of questioning others and examining their opinions. Here Socrates is on the verge of becoming the take-charge, independent philosophical theorist that he is in such dialogues as* Phaedo *and* Republic. *Like those two works,* Gorgias *concludes with an eschatological myth, affirming the soul's survival after our death and its punishment or reward in the afterlife for a life lived unjustly or the reverse.*

In Phaedrus *Socrates makes connected but different arguments about the nature and value of rhetoric. Whereas in* Gorgias *Socrates paints an unrelievedly negative picture of the practice of rhetoric, in* Phaedrus *he finds legitimate uses for it, so long as it is kept properly subordinate to philosophy.*

J.M.C.

447   CALLICLES: This, they say, is how you're supposed to do your part in a war or a battle, Socrates.

SOCRATES: Oh? Did we "arrive when the feast was over," as the saying goes? Are we late?[1]

CALLICLES: Yes, and a very urbane one it was! Gorgias gave us an admirable, varied presentation[2] just a short while ago.

SOCRATES: But that's Chaerephon's fault, Callicles. He kept us loitering about in the marketplace.

Translated by Donald J. Zeyl. Text: E. R. Dodds, Oxford (1959).

1. The setting of the dialogue is not clear. We may suppose that the conversation takes place outside a public building in Athens such as the gymnasium (see the reference to persons "inside" at 447c and 455c).

In the exchange that opens the dialogue, Callicles and Socrates are evidently alluding to a Greek saying, unknown to us, the equivalent of the English phrase, "first at a feast, last at a fray." Cf. Shakespeare, *Henry IV, Part 1*, Act 4, Sc. 2.

2. Gk. *epideiknusthai*. An *epideixis* was a lecture regularly given by sophists as a public display of their oratorical prowess.

CHAEREPHON: That's no problem, Socrates. I'll make up for it, too. Gorgias   b
is a friend of mine, so he'll give us a presentation—now, if you see fit, or
else some other time, if you like.

CALLICLES: What's this, Chaerephon? Is Socrates eager to hear Gorgias?

CHAEREPHON: Yes. That's the very thing we're here for.

CALLICLES: Well then, come to my house any time you like. Gorgias is
staying with me and will give you a presentation there.

SOCRATES: Very good, Callicles. But would he be willing to have a discussion with us? I'd like to find out from the man what his craft can accomplish,   c
and what it is that he both makes claims about and teaches. As for the other
thing, the presentation, let him put that on another time, as you suggest.

CALLICLES: There's nothing like asking him, Socrates. This was, in fact,
one part of his presentation. Just now he invited those inside to ask him
any question they liked, and he said that he'd answer them all.

SOCRATES: An excellent idea. Ask him, Chaerephon.

CHAEREPHON: Ask him what?

SOCRATES: What he is.   d

CHAEREPHON: What do you mean?

SOCRATES: Well, if he were a maker of shoes, he'd answer that he was
a cobbler, wouldn't he? Or don't you see what I mean?

CHAEREPHON: I do. I'll ask him. Tell me, Gorgias, is Callicles right in
saying that you make claims about answering any question anyone might
put to you?

GORGIAS: He is, Chaerephon. In fact I just now made that very claim,   448
and I say that no one has asked me anything new in many a year.

CHAEREPHON: In that case I'm sure you'll answer this one quite easily,
Gorgias.

GORGIAS: Here's your chance to try me, Chaerephon.

POLUS: By Zeus, Chaerephon! Try me, if you like! I think Gorgias is quite
worn out. He's only just now finished a long discourse.

CHAEREPHON: Really, Polus? Do you think you'd give more admirable
answers than Gorgias?

POLUS: What does it matter, as long as they're good enough for you?   b

CHAEREPHON: Nothing at all! You answer us then, since that's what
you want.

POLUS: Ask your questions.

CHAEREPHON: I will. Suppose that Gorgias were knowledgeable in his
brother Herodicus' craft. What would be the right name for us to call him
by then? Isn't it the same one as his brother's?

POLUS: Yes, it is.

CHAEREPHON: So we'd be right in saying that he's a doctor?

POLUS: Yes.

CHAEREPHON: And if he were experienced in the craft of Aristophon the
son of Aglaophon or his brother, what would be the correct thing to
call him?

POLUS: A painter, obviously.

CHAEREPHON: Now then, since he's knowledgeable in a craft, what is it, and what would be the correct thing to call him?

POLUS: Many among men are the crafts experientially devised by experience, Chaerephon. Yes, it is experience that causes our times to march along the way of craft, whereas inexperience causes them to march along the way of chance. Of these various crafts various men partake in various ways, the best men partaking of the best of them. Our Gorgias is indeed in this group; he partakes of the most admirable of the crafts.

SOCRATES: Polus certainly appears to have prepared himself admirably for giving speeches, Gorgias. But he's not doing what he promised Chaerephon.

GORGIAS: How exactly isn't he, Socrates?

SOCRATES: He hardly seems to me to be answering the question.

GORGIAS: Why don't you question him then, if you like?

SOCRATES: No, I won't, not as long as you yourself may want to answer. I'd much rather ask you. It's clear to me, especially from what he has said, that Polus has devoted himself more to what is called oratory than to discussion.

POLUS: Why do you say that, Socrates?

SOCRATES: Because, Polus, when Chaerephon asks you what craft Gorgias is knowledgeable in, you sing its praises as though someone were discrediting it. But you haven't answered what it is.

POLUS: Didn't I answer that it was the most admirable one?

SOCRATES: Very much so. No one, however, asked you what Gorgias' craft is like, but what craft it is, and what one ought to call Gorgias. So, just as when Chaerephon put his earlier questions to you and you answered him in such an admirably brief way, tell us now in that way, too, what his craft is, and what we're supposed to call Gorgias. Or rather, Gorgias, why don't you tell us yourself what the craft you're knowledgeable in is, and hence what we're supposed to call you?

GORGIAS: It's oratory, Socrates.

SOCRATES: So we're supposed to call you an orator?

GORGIAS: Yes, and a good one, Socrates, if you really want to call me "what I boast myself to be," as Homer puts it.[3]

SOCRATES: Of course I do.

GORGIAS: Call me that then.

SOCRATES: Aren't we to say that you're capable of making others orators too?

GORGIAS: That's exactly the claim I make. Not only here, but elsewhere, too.

SOCRATES: Well now, Gorgias, would you be willing to complete the discussion in the way we're having it right now, that of alternately asking questions and answering them, and to put aside for another

3. *Iliad* vi.211.

time this long style of speechmaking like the one Polus began with? Please don't go back on your promise, but be willing to give a brief answer to what you're asked.

GORGIAS: There are some answers, Socrates, that must be given by way of long speeches. Even so, I'll try to be as brief as possible. This, too, in fact, is one of my claims. There's no one who can say the same things more briefly than I.   c

SOCRATES: That's what we need, Gorgias! Do give me a presentation of this very thing, the short style of speech, and leave the long style for some other time.

GORGIAS: Very well, I'll do that. You'll say you've never heard anyone make shorter speeches.

SOCRATES: Come then. You claim to be knowledgeable in the craft of oratory and to be able to make someone else an orator, too. With which   d of the things there are is oratory concerned? Weaving, for example, is concerned with the production of clothes, isn't it?

GORGIAS: Yes.

SOCRATES: And so, too, music is concerned with the composition of tunes?

GORGIAS: Yes.

SOCRATES: By Hera, Gorgias, I do like your answers. They couldn't be shorter!

GORGIAS: Yes, Socrates, I daresay I'm doing it quite nicely.

SOCRATES: And so you are. Come and answer me then that way about oratory, too. About which, of the things there are, is *it* knowledge?

GORGIAS: About speeches.   e

SOCRATES: What sort of speeches, Gorgias? Those that explain how sick people should be treated to get well?

GORGIAS: No.

SOCRATES: So oratory isn't concerned with all speeches.

GORGIAS: Oh, no.

SOCRATES: But it does make people capable of speaking.

GORGIAS: Yes.

SOCRATES: And also to be wise in what they're speaking about?

GORGIAS: Of course.

SOCRATES: Now does the medical craft, the one we were talking about   450 just now, make people able both to have wisdom about and to speak about the sick?

GORGIAS: Necessarily.

SOCRATES: This craft, then, is evidently concerned with speeches too.

GORGIAS: Yes.

SOCRATES: Speeches about diseases, that is?

GORGIAS: Exactly.

SOCRATES: Isn't physical training also concerned with speeches, speeches about good and bad physical condition?

GORGIAS: Yes, it is.

SOCRATES: In fact, Gorgias, the same is true of the other crafts, too. Each
b of them is concerned with those speeches that are about the object of the
particular craft.

GORGIAS: Apparently.

SOCRATES: Then why don't you call the other crafts oratory, since you
call any craft whatever that's concerned with speeches oratory? They're
concerned with speeches, too!

GORGIAS: The reason, Socrates, is that in the case of the other crafts the
knowledge consists almost completely in working with your hands and
activities of that sort. In the case of oratory, on the other hand, there
isn't any such manual work. Its activity and influence depend entirely on
c speeches. That's the reason I consider the craft of oratory to be concerned
with speeches. And I say that I'm right about this.

SOCRATES: I'm not sure I understand what sort of craft you want to call
it. I'll soon know more clearly. Tell me this. There are crafts for us to
practice, aren't there?

GORGIAS: Yes.

SOCRATES: Of all the crafts there are, I take it that there are those that
consist for the most part of making things and that call for little speech,
and some that call for none at all, ones whose task could be done even
silently. Take painting, for instance, or sculpture, or many others. When
d you say that oratory has nothing to do with other crafts, it's crafts of this
sort I think you're referring to. Or aren't you?

GORGIAS: Yes, Socrates. You take my meaning very well.

SOCRATES: And then there are other crafts, the ones that perform their
whole task by means of speeches and that call for practically no physical
work besides, or very little of it. Take arithmetic or computation or geometry, even checkers and many other crafts. Some of these involve speeches
to just about the same degree as they do activity, while many involve
speeches more. All their activity and influence depend entirely on speeches.
e I think you mean that oratory is a craft of this sort.

GORGIAS: True.

SOCRATES: But you certainly don't want to call any of *these* crafts oratory,
do you, even though, as you phrase it, oratory is the craft that exercises
its influence through speech. Somebody might take you up, if he wanted
to make a fuss in argument, and say, "So you're saying that arithmetic is
oratory, are you, Gorgias?" I'm sure, however, that you're not saying that
either arithmetic or geometry is oratory.

451   GORGIAS: Yes, you're quite correct, Socrates. You take my meaning
rightly.

SOCRATES: Come on, then. Please complete your answer in the terms of
my question. Since oratory is one of those crafts which mostly uses speech,
and since there are also others of that sort, try to say *what* it is that oratory,
which exercises its influence through speeches, is about. Imagine someone
asking me about any of the crafts I mentioned just now, "Socrates, what
b is the craft of arithmetic?" I'd tell him, just as you told me, that it's one of

those that exercise their influence by means of speech. And if he continued, "What are they crafts about?" I'd say that they're about even and odd, however many of each there might be. If he then asked, "What is the craft you call computation?" I'd say that this one, too, is one of those that exercise their influence entirely by speech. And if he then continued, "What is it about?" I'd answer in the style of those who draw up motions in the Assembly that in other respects computation is like arithmetic—for it's   c
about the same thing, even and odd—yet it differs from arithmetic insofar as computation examines the quantity of odd and even, both in relation to themselves and in relation to each other. And if someone asked about astronomy and I replied that it, too, exercises its influence by means of speech, then if he asked, "What are the speeches of astronomy about, Socrates?" I'd say that they're about the motions of the stars, the sun and the moon, and their relative velocities.

GORGIAS: And you'd be quite right to say so, Socrates.

SOCRATES: Come, Gorgias, you take your turn. For oratory is in fact one   d
of those crafts that carry out and exercise their influence entirely by speech, isn't it?

GORGIAS: That's right.

SOCRATES: Tell us then: what are they crafts about? Of the things there are, which is the one that these speeches used by oratory are concerned with?

GORGIAS: The greatest of human concerns, Socrates, and the best.

SOCRATES: But that statement, too, is debatable, Gorgias. It isn't at all clear yet, either. I'm sure that you've heard people at drinking parties   e
singing that song in which they count out as they sing that "to enjoy good health is the best thing; second is to have turned out good looking; and third"—so the writer of the song puts it—"is to be honestly rich."

GORGIAS: Yes, I've heard it. Why do you mention it?

SOCRATES: Suppose that the producers of the things the songwriter   452
praised were here with you right now: a doctor, a physical trainer, and a financial expert. Suppose that first the doctor said, "Socrates, Gorgias is telling you a lie. It isn't his craft that is concerned with the greatest good for humankind, but mine." If I then asked him, "What are you, to say that?" I suppose he'd say that he's a doctor. "What's this you're saying? Is the product of your craft really the greatest good?" "Of course, Socrates," I suppose he'd say, "seeing that its product is health. What greater good for humankind is there than health?" And suppose that next in his turn   b
the trainer said, "I too would be amazed, Socrates, if Gorgias could present you with a greater good derived from his craft than the one I could provide from mine." I'd ask this man, too, "What are you, sir, and what's your product?" "I'm a physical trainer," he'd say, "and my product is making people physically good-looking and strong." And following the trainer the financial expert would say, I'm sure with an air of considerable scorn for all, "Do consider, Socrates, whether you know of any good, Gorgias'   c
or anyone else's, that's a greater good than wealth." We'd say to him, "Really? Is that what you produce?" He'd say yes. "As what?" "As a

financial expert." "Well," we'll say, "is wealth in your judgment the greatest good for humankind?" "Of course," he'll say. "Ah, but Gorgias here disputes that. He claims that his craft is the source of a good that's greater than yours," we'd say. And it's obvious what question he'd ask next. "And

d   what is this good, please? Let Gorgias answer me that!" So come on, Gorgias. Consider yourself questioned by both these men and myself, and give us your answer. What is this thing that you claim is the greatest good for humankind, a thing you claim to be a producer of?

GORGIAS: The thing that is in actual fact the greatest good, Socrates. It is the source of freedom for humankind itself and at the same time it is for each person the source of rule over others in one's own city.

SOCRATES: And what is this thing you're referring to?

e   GORGIAS: I'm referring to the ability to persuade by speeches judges in a law court, councillors in a council meeting, and assemblymen in an assembly or in any other political gathering that might take place. In point of fact, with this ability you'll have the doctor for your slave, and the physical trainer, too. As for this financial expert of yours, he'll turn out to be making more money for somebody else instead of himself; for you, in fact, if you've got the ability to speak and to persuade the crowds.

453 SOCRATES: *Now* I think you've come closest to making clear what craft you take oratory to be, Gorgias. If I follow you at all, you're saying that oratory is a producer of persuasion. Its whole business comes to that, and that's the long and short of it. Or can you mention anything else oratory can do besides instilling persuasion in the souls of an audience?

GORGIAS: None at all, Socrates. I think you're defining it quite adequately. That is indeed the long and short of it.

b   SOCRATES: Listen then, Gorgias. You should know that I'm convinced I'm one of those people who in a discussion with someone else really want to have knowledge of the subject the discussion's about. And I consider you one of them, too.

GORGIAS: Well, what's the point, Socrates?

SOCRATES: Let me tell you now. You can know for sure that I don't know what this persuasion derived from oratory that you're talking about is, or what subjects it's persuasion about. Even though I do have my suspicions about which persuasion I think you mean and what it's about, I'll still ask

c   you just the same what you say this persuasion produced by oratory is, and what it's about. And why, when I have my suspicions, do I ask you and refrain from expressing them myself? It's not you I'm after, it's our discussion, to have it proceed in such a way as to make the thing we're talking about most clear to us. Consider, then, whether you think I'm being fair in resuming my questions to you. Suppose I were to ask you which of the painters Zeuxis is. If you told me that he's the one who paints pictures, wouldn't it be fair for me to ask, "Of what sort of pictures is he the painter, and where?"

GORGIAS: Yes, it would.

d   SOCRATES: And isn't the reason for this the fact that there are other painters, too, who paint many other pictures?

GORGIAS: Yes.

SOCRATES: But if no one besides Zeuxis were a painter, your answer would have been a good one?

GORGIAS: Of course.

SOCRATES: Come then, and tell me about oratory. Do you think that oratory alone instills persuasion, or do other crafts do so too? This is the sort of thing I mean: Does a person who teaches some subject or other persuade people about what he's teaching, or not?

GORGIAS: He certainly does, Socrates. He persuades most of all.

SOCRATES: Let's talk once more about the same crafts we were talking about just now. Doesn't arithmetic or the arithmetician teach us everything that pertains to number?

GORGIAS: Yes, he does.

SOCRATES: And he also persuades?

GORGIAS: Yes.

SOCRATES: So arithmetic is also a producer of persuasion.

GORGIAS: Apparently.

SOCRATES: Now if someone asks us what sort of persuasion it produces and what it's persuasion about, I suppose we'd answer him that it's the persuasion through teaching about the extent of even and odd. And we'll be able to show that all the other crafts we were just now talking about are producers of persuasion, as well as what the persuasion is and what it's about. Isn't that right?

GORGIAS: Yes.

SOCRATES: So oratory isn't the only producer of persuasion.

GORGIAS: That's true.

SOCRATES: In that case, since it's not the only one to produce this product but other crafts do it too, we'd do right to repeat to our speaker the question we put next in the case of the painter: "Of what sort of persuasion is oratory a craft, and what is its persuasion about?" Or don't you think it's right to repeat that question?

GORGIAS: Yes, I do.

SOCRATES: Well then, Gorgias, since you think so too, please answer.

GORGIAS: The persuasion I mean, Socrates, is the kind that takes place in law courts and in those other large gatherings, as I was saying a moment ago. And it's concerned with those matters that are just and unjust.

SOCRATES: Yes, Gorgias, I suspected that this was the persuasion you meant, and that these are the matters it's persuasion about. But so you won't be surprised if in a moment I ask you again another question like this, about what seems to be clear, and yet I go on with my questioning— as I say, I'm asking questions so that we can conduct an orderly discussion. It's not you I'm after; it's to prevent our getting in the habit of second-guessing and snatching each other's statements away ahead of time. It's to allow you to work out your assumption in any way you want to.

GORGIAS: Yes, I think that you're quite right to do this, Socrates.

SOCRATES: Come then, and let's examine this point. Is there something you call "to have learned"?

GORGIAS: There is.

SOCRATES: Very well. And also something you call "to be convinced"?

d   GORGIAS: Yes, there is.

SOCRATES: Now, do you think that to have learned, and learning, are the same as to be convinced and conviction, or different?

GORGIAS: I certainly suppose that they're different, Socrates.

SOCRATES: You suppose rightly. This is how you can tell: If someone asked you, "Is there such a thing as true and false conviction, Gorgias?" you'd say yes, I'm sure.

GORGIAS: Yes.

SOCRATES: Well now, is there such a thing as true and false knowledge?

GORGIAS: Not at all.

SOCRATES: So it's clear that they're not the same.

GORGIAS: That's true.

e   SOCRATES: But surely both those who have learned and those who are convinced have come to be persuaded?

GORGIAS: That's right.

SOCRATES: Would you like us then to posit two types of persuasion, one providing conviction without knowledge, the other providing knowledge?

GORGIAS: Yes, I would.

SOCRATES: Now which type of persuasion does oratory produce in law courts and other gatherings concerning things that are just and unjust? The one that results in being convinced without knowing or the one that results in knowing?

GORGIAS: It's obvious, surely, that it's the one that results in conviction.

SOCRATES: So evidently oratory produces the persuasion that comes from being convinced, and not the persuasion that comes from teaching, concern-

455   ing what's just and unjust.

GORGIAS: Yes.

SOCRATES: And so an orator is not a teacher of law courts and other gatherings about things that are just and unjust, either, but merely a persuader, for I don't suppose that he could teach such a large gathering about matters so important in a short time.

GORGIAS: No, he certainly couldn't.

SOCRATES: Well now, let's see what we're really saying about oratory.

b   For, mind you, even I myself can't get clear yet about what I'm saying. When the city holds a meeting to appoint doctors or shipbuilders or some other variety of craftsmen, that's surely not the time when the orator will give advice, is it? For obviously it's the most accomplished craftsman who should be appointed in each case. Nor will the orator be the one to give advice at a meeting that concerns the building of walls or the equipping of harbors or dockyards, but the master builders will be the ones. And when there is a deliberation about the appointment of generals or an

c   arrangement of troops against the enemy or an occupation of territory, it's not the orators but the generals who'll give advice then. What do you say about such cases, Gorgias? Since you yourself claim both to be an orator and to make others orators, we'll do well to find out from you the characteristics of your craft. You must think of me now as eager to serve your interests, too. Perhaps there's actually someone inside who wants to become your pupil. I notice some, in fact a good many, and they may well be embarrassed to question you. So, while you're being questioned by me, consider yourself being questioned by them as well: "What will we get if d we associate with you, Gorgias? What will we be able to advise the city on? Only about what's just and unjust or also about the things Socrates was mentioning just now?" Try to answer them.

GORGIAS: Well, Socrates, I'll try to reveal to you clearly everything oratory can accomplish. You yourself led the way nicely, for you do know, don't you, that these dockyards and walls of the Athenians and the equipping e of the harbor came about through the advice of Themistocles and in some cases through that of Pericles, but not through that of the craftsmen?[4]

SOCRATES: That's what they say about Themistocles, Gorgias. I myself heard Pericles when he advised us on the middle wall.

GORGIAS: And whenever those craftsmen you were just now speaking 456 of are appointed, Socrates, you see that the orators are the ones who give advice and whose views on these matters prevail.

SOCRATES: Yes, Gorgias, my amazement at that led me long ago to ask what it is that oratory can accomplish. For as I look at it, it seems to me to be something supernatural in scope.

GORGIAS: Oh yes, Socrates, if only you knew all of it, that it encompasses and subordinates to itself just about everything that can be accomplished. b And I'll give you ample proof. Many a time I've gone with my brother or with other doctors to call on some sick person who refuses to take his medicine or allow the doctor to perform surgery or cauterization on him. And when the doctor failed to persuade him, I succeeded, by means of no other craft than oratory. And I maintain too that if an orator and a doctor came to any city anywhere you like and had to compete in speaking in the assembly or some other gathering over which of them should be appointed doctor, the doctor wouldn't make any showing at all, but the c one who had the ability to speak would be appointed, if he so wished. And if he were to compete with any other craftsman whatever, the orator more than anyone else would persuade them that they should appoint him, for there isn't anything that the orator couldn't speak more persuasively about to a gathering than could any other craftsman whatever. That's how great the accomplishment of this craft is, and the sort of accomplishment it is! One should, however, use oratory like any other competitive skill, Socrates. In other cases, too, one ought not to use a competitive skill d against any and everybody, just because he has learned boxing, or boxing and wrestling combined, or fighting in armor, so as to make himself be superior to his friends as well as to his enemies. That's no reason to strike, stab, or kill one's own friends! Imagine someone who after attending

4. Themistocles and Pericles were Athenian statesmen of the fifth century B.C.

wrestling school, getting his body into good shape and becoming a boxer, went on to strike his father and mother or any other family member or friend. By Zeus, that's no reason to hate physical trainers and people who

e   teach fighting in armor, and to exile them from their cities! For while these people imparted their skills to be used justly against enemies and wrongdoers, and in defense, not aggression, their pupils pervert their

457   strength and skill and misuse them. So it's not their teachers who are wicked, nor does that make the craft guilty or wicked; those who misuse it, surely, are the wicked ones. And the same is true for oratory as well. The orator has the ability to speak against everyone on every subject, so as in gatherings to be more persuasive, in short, about

b   anything he likes, but the fact that he has the ability to rob doctors or other craftsmen of their reputations doesn't give him any more of a reason to do it. He should use oratory justly, as he would any competitive skill. And I suppose that if a person who has become an orator goes on with this ability and this craft to commit wrongdoing, we shouldn't hate his teacher and exile him from our cities. For while the teacher

c   imparted it to be used justly, the pupil is making the opposite use of it. So it's the misuser whom it's just to hate and exile or put to death, not the teacher.

SOCRATES: Gorgias, I take it that you, like me, have experienced many discussions and that you've observed this sort of thing about them: it's not easy for the participants to define jointly what they're undertaking to

d   discuss, and so, having learned from and taught each other, to conclude their session. Instead, if they're disputing some point and one maintains that the other isn't right or isn't clear, they get irritated, each thinking the other is speaking out of spite. They become eager to win instead of investigating the subject under discussion. In fact, in the end some have a most shameful parting of the ways, abuse heaped upon them, having given and gotten to hear such things that make even the bystanders upset with themselves for having thought it worthwhile to come to listen to such

e   people. What's my point in saying this? It's that I think you're now saying things that aren't very consistent or compatible with what you were first saying about oratory. So, I'm afraid to pursue my examination of you, for fear that you should take me to be speaking with eagerness to win against

458   you, rather than to have our subject become clear. For my part, I'd be pleased to continue questioning you if you're the same kind of man I am, otherwise I would drop it. And what kind of man am I? One of those who would be pleased to be refuted if I say anything untrue, and who would be pleased to refute anyone who says anything untrue; one who, however, wouldn't be any less pleased to be refuted than to refute. For I count being refuted a greater good, insofar as it is a greater good for oneself to be delivered from the worst thing there is than to deliver someone else from it. I don't suppose there's anything quite so bad for a person as having false belief about the things we're discussing right now. So if you say

b   you're this kind of man, too, let's continue the discussion; but if you think we should drop it, let's be done with it and break it off.

GORGIAS: Oh yes, Socrates, I say that I myself, too, am the sort of person you describe. Still, perhaps we should keep in mind the people who are present here, too. For quite a while ago now, even before you came, I gave them a long presentation, and perhaps we'll stretch things out too long if   c we continue the discussion. We should think about them, too, so as not to keep any of them who want to do something else.

CHAEREPHON: You yourselves hear the commotion these men are making, Gorgias and Socrates. They want to hear anything you have to say. And as for myself, I hope I'll never be so busy that I'd forego discussions such as this, conducted in the way this one is, because I find it more practical to do something else.

CALLICLES: By the gods, Chaerephon, as a matter of fact I, too, though   d I've been present at many a discussion before now, don't know if I've ever been so pleased as I am at the moment. So if you're willing to discuss, even if it's all day long, you'll be gratifying me.

SOCRATES: For my part there's nothing stopping me, Callicles, as long as Gorgias is willing.

GORGIAS: It'll be to my shame ever after, Socrates, if I weren't willing, when I myself have made the claim that anyone may ask me anything he wants. All right, if it suits these people, carry on with the discussion, and   e ask what you want.

SOCRATES: Well then, Gorgias, let me tell you what surprises me in the things you've said. It may be that what you said was correct and that I'm not taking your meaning correctly. Do you say that you're able to make an orator out of anyone who wants to study with you?

GORGIAS: Yes.

SOCRATES: So that he'll be persuasive in a gathering about all subjects, not by teaching but by persuading?

GORGIAS: Yes, that's right.   459

SOCRATES: You were saying just now, mind you, that the orator will be more persuasive even about health than a doctor is.

GORGIAS: Yes I was, more persuasive in a gathering, anyhow.

SOCRATES: And doesn't "in a gathering" just mean "among those who don't have knowledge"? For, among those who do have it, I don't suppose that he'll be more persuasive than the doctor.

GORGIAS: That's true.

SOCRATES: Now if he'll be more persuasive than a doctor, doesn't he prove to be more persuasive than the one who has knowledge?

GORGIAS: Yes, that's right.

SOCRATES: Even though he's not a doctor, right?   b

GORGIAS: Yes.

SOCRATES: And a non-doctor, I take it, isn't knowledgeable in the thing in which a doctor is knowledgeable.

GORGIAS: That's obvious.

SOCRATES: So when an orator is more persuasive than a doctor, a non-knower will be more persuasive than a knower among non-knowers. Isn't this exactly what follows?

GORGIAS: Yes it is, at least in this case.

SOCRATES: The same is true about the orator and oratory relative to the other crafts, too, then. Oratory doesn't need to have any knowledge of the
c   state of their subject matters; it only needs to have discovered some device to produce persuasion in order to make itself appear to those who don't have knowledge that it knows more than those who actually do have it.

GORGIAS: Well, Socrates, aren't things made very easy when you come off no worse than the craftsmen even though you haven't learned any other craft but this one?

SOCRATES: Whether the orator does or does not come off worse than the others because of this being so, we'll examine in a moment if it has any
d   bearing on our argument. For now, let's consider this point first. Is it the case that the orator is in the same position with respect to what's just and unjust, what's shameful and admirable, what's good and bad, as he is about what's healthy and about the subjects of the other crafts? Does he lack knowledge, that is, of what these are, of what is good or what is bad, of what is admirable or what is shameful, or just or unjust? Does he employ devices to produce persuasion about them, so that—even though he doesn't know—he seems, among those who don't know either, to know more than
e   someone who actually does know? Or is it necessary for him to know, and must the prospective student of oratory already be knowledgeable in these things before coming to you? And if he doesn't, will you, the oratory teacher, not teach him any of these things when he comes to you—for that's not your job—and will you make him seem among most people to have knowledge of such things when in fact he doesn't have it, and to seem good when in fact he isn't? Or won't you be able to teach him oratory at all, unless he knows the truth about these things to begin with? How
460   do matters such as these stand, Gorgias? Yes, by Zeus, do give us your revelation and tell us what oratory can accomplish, just as you just now said you would.

GORGIAS: Well, Socrates, I suppose that if he really doesn't have this knowledge, he'll learn these things from me as well.

SOCRATES: Hold it there. You're right to say so. If you make someone an orator, it's necessary for him to know what's just and what's unjust, either beforehand, or by learning it from you afterwards.

GORGIAS: Yes, it is.

b   SOCRATES: Well? A man who has learned carpentry is a carpenter, isn't he?

GORGIAS: Yes.

SOCRATES: And isn't a man who has learned music a musician?

GORGIAS: Yes.

SOCRATES: And a man who has learned medicine a doctor? And isn't this so too, by the same reasoning, with the other crafts? Isn't a man who has learned a particular subject the sort of man his knowledge makes him?

GORGIAS: Yes, he is.

SOCRATES: And, by this line of reasoning, isn't a man who has learned what's just a just man too?

GORGIAS: Yes, absolutely.

SOCRATES: And a just man does just things, I take it?

GORGIAS: Yes.

SOCRATES: Now isn't an orator necessarily just, and doesn't a just man   c
necessarily want to do just things?

GORGIAS: Apparently so.

SOCRATES: Therefore an orator will never want to do what's unjust.

GORGIAS: No, apparently not.

SOCRATES: Do you remember saying a little earlier that we shouldn't
complain against physical trainers or exile them from our cities if the boxer   d
uses his boxing skill to do what's unjust, and that, similarly, if an orator
uses his oratorical skill unjustly we shouldn't complain against his teacher
or banish him from the city, but do so to the one who does what's unjust,
the one who doesn't use his oratorical skill properly? Was that said or not?

GORGIAS: Yes, it was.

SOCRATES: But now it appears that this very man, the orator, would never   e
have done what's unjust, doesn't it?

GORGIAS: Yes, it does.

SOCRATES: And at the beginning of our discussion, Gorgias, it was said
that oratory would be concerned with speeches, not those about even and
odd, but those about what's just and unjust. Right?

GORGIAS: Yes.

SOCRATES: Well, at the time you said that, I took it that oratory would
never be an unjust thing, since it always makes its speeches about justice.
But when a little later you were saying that the orator could also use   461
oratory unjustly, I was surprised and thought that your statements weren't
consistent, and so I made that speech in which I said that if you, like me,
think that being refuted is a profitable thing, it would be worthwhile to
continue the discussion, but if you don't, to let it drop. But now, as we
subsequently examine the question, you see for yourself too that it's agreed
that, quite to the contrary, the orator is incapable of using oratory unjustly
and of being willing to do what's unjust. By the Dog, Gorgias, it'll take   b
more than a short session to go through an adequate examination of how
these matters stand!

POLUS: Really, Socrates? Is what you're now saying about oratory what
you actually think of it? Or do you really think, just because Gorgias was
too ashamed not to concede your further claim that the orator also knows
what's just, what's admirable, and what's good, and that if he came to
him without already having this knowledge to begin with, he said that he
would teach him himself, and then from this admission maybe some   c
inconsistency crept into his statements—just the thing that gives you delight, you're the one who leads him on to face such questions—who do
you think would deny that he himself knows what's just and would teach
others? To lead your arguments to such an outcome is a sign of great
rudeness.

SOCRATES: Most admirable Polus, it's not for nothing that we get ourselves
companions and sons. It's so that, when we ourselves have grown older
and stumble, you younger men might be on hand to straighten our lives

up again, both in what we do and what we say. And if Gorgias and I are
d   stumbling now in what we say—well, you're on hand, straighten us up
again. That's only right. And if you think we were wrong to agree on it,
I'm certainly willing to retract any of our agreements you like, provided
that you're careful about just one thing.

POLUS: What do you mean?

SOCRATES: That you curb your long style of speech, Polus, the style you
tried using at first.

POLUS: Really? Won't I be free to say as much as I like?

e   SOCRATES: You'd certainly be in a terrible way, my good friend, if upon
coming to Athens, where there's more freedom of speech than anywhere
else in Greece, you alone should miss out on it here. But look at it the
other way. If you spoke at length and were unwilling to answer what
you're asked, wouldn't I be in a terrible way if I'm not to have the freedom
462   to stop listening to you and leave? But if you care at all about the discussion
we've had and want to straighten it up, please retract whatever you think
best, as I was saying just now. Take your turn in asking and being asked
questions the way Gorgias and I did, and subject me and yourself to
refutation. You say, I take it, that you know the same craft that Gorgias
knows? Or don't you?

POLUS: Yes, I do.

SOCRATES: And don't you also invite people to ask you each time whatever
they like, because you believe you'll answer as one who has knowledge?

POLUS: Certainly.

b   SOCRATES: So now please do whichever of these you like: either ask
questions or answer them.

POLUS: Very well, I shall. Tell me, Socrates, since you think Gorgias is
confused about oratory, what do you say it is?

SOCRATES: Are you asking me what *craft* I say it is?

POLUS: Yes, I am.

SOCRATES: To tell you the truth, Polus, I don't think it's a craft at all.

POLUS: Well then, what do you think oratory is?

c   SOCRATES: In the treatise that I read recently, it's the thing that you say
has produced craft.[5]

POLUS: What do you mean?

SOCRATES: I mean a knack.[6]

POLUS: So you think oratory's a knack?

SOCRATES: Yes, I do, unless you say it's something else.

POLUS: A knack for what?

SOCRATES: For producing a certain gratification and pleasure.

POLUS: Don't you think that oratory's an admirable thing, then, to be
able to give gratification to people?

5. Alternatively, " . . . it's something of which you claim to have made a craft."
6. Gk. *empeiria*, translated "experience" at 448c.

SOCRATES: Really, Polus! Have you already discovered from me what I say it is, so that you go on to ask me next whether I don't think it's admirable?   d

POLUS: Haven't I discovered that you say it's a knack?

SOCRATES: Since you value gratification, would you like to gratify me on a small matter?

POLUS: Certainly.

SOCRATES: Ask me now what craft I think pastry baking is.

POLUS: All right, I will. What craft is pastry baking?

SOCRATES: It isn't one at all, Polus. Now say, "What is it then?"

POLUS: All right.

SOCRATES: It's a knack. Say, "A knack for what?"

POLUS: All right.

SOCRATES: For producing gratification and pleasure, Polus.   e

POLUS: So oratory is the same thing as pastry baking?

SOCRATES: Oh no, not at all, although it *is* a part of the same practice.

POLUS: What practice do you mean?

SOCRATES: I'm afraid it may be rather crude to speak the truth. I hesitate to do so for Gorgias' sake, for fear that he may think I'm satirizing what he practices. I don't know whether this is the kind of oratory that Gorgias practices—in fact in our discussion a while ago we didn't get at all clear   463
on just what he thinks it is. But what *I* call oratory is a part of some business that isn't admirable at all.

GORGIAS: Which one's that, Socrates? Say it, and don't spare my feelings.

SOCRATES: Well then, Gorgias, I think there's a practice that's not craftlike, but one that a mind given to making hunches takes to, a mind that's bold and naturally clever at dealing with people. I call it flattery, basically. I   b
think that this practice has many other parts as well, and pastry baking, too, is one of them. This part *seems* to be a craft, but in my account of it it isn't a craft but a knack and a routine. I call oratory a part of this, too, along with cosmetics and sophistry. These are four parts, and they're directed to four objects. So if Polus wants to discover them, let him do so.   c
He hasn't discovered yet what sort of part of flattery I say oratory is. Instead, it's escaped him that I haven't answered that question yet, and so he goes on to ask whether I don't consider it to be admirable. And I won't answer him whether I think it's admirable or shameful until I first tell what it is. That wouldn't be right, Polus. If, however, you do want to discover this, ask me what sort of part of flattery I say oratory is.

POLUS: I shall. Tell me what sort of part it is.

SOCRATES: Would you understand my answer? By my reasoning, oratory   d
is an image of a part of politics.

POLUS: Well? Are you saying that it's something admirable or shameful?

SOCRATES: I'm saying that it's a shameful thing—I call bad things shameful—since I must answer you as though you already know what I mean.

GORGIAS: By Zeus, Socrates, I myself don't understand what you mean, either!

e   SOCRATES: Reasonably enough, Gorgias. I'm not saying anything clear yet. This colt here is youthful and impulsive.

GORGIAS: Never mind him. Please tell me what you mean by saying that oratory is an image of a part of politics.

SOCRATES: All right, I'll try to describe my view of oratory. If this isn't 464 what it actually is, Polus here will refute me. There is, I take it, something you call *body* and something you call *soul*?

GORGIAS: Yes, of course.

SOCRATES: And do you also think that there's a state of fitness for each of these?

GORGIAS: Yes, I do.

SOCRATES: All right. Is there also an apparent state of fitness, one that isn't real? The sort of thing I mean is this. There are many people who *appear* to be physically fit, and unless one is a doctor or one of the fitness experts, one wouldn't readily notice that they're not fit.

GORGIAS: That's true.

SOCRATES: I'm saying that this sort of thing exists in the case of both the body and the soul, a thing that makes the body and the soul seem fit when b   in fact they aren't any the more so.

GORGIAS: That's so.

SOCRATES: Come then, and I'll show you more clearly what I'm saying, if I can. I'm saying that of this pair of subjects there are two crafts. The one for the soul I call politics; the one for the body, though it is one, I can't give you a name for offhand, but while the care of the body is a single craft, I'm saying it has two parts: gymnastics and medicine. And in politics, the counterpart of gymnastics is legislation, and the part that c   corresponds to medicine is justice. Each member of these pairs has features in common with the other, medicine with gymnastics and justice with legislation, because they're concerned with the same thing. They do, how-ever, differ in some way from each other. These, then, are the four parts, and they always provide care, in the one case for the body, in the other for the soul, with a view to what's best. Now flattery takes notice of them, and—I won't say by *knowing*, but only by *guessing*—divides itself into four, d   masks itself with each of the parts, and then pretends to be the characters of the masks. It takes no thought at all of whatever is best; with the lure of what's most pleasant at the moment, it sniffs out folly and hoodwinks it, so that it gives the impression of being most deserving. Pastry baking has put on the mask of medicine, and pretends to know the foods that are best for the body, so that if a pastry baker and a doctor had to compete in front of children, or in front of men just as foolish as children, to determine which of the two, the doctor or the pastry baker, had expert knowledge of good food and bad, the doctor would die of starvation. I 465   call this flattery, and I say that such a thing is shameful, Polus—it's you I'm saying this to—because it guesses at what's pleasant with no consider-ation for what's best. And I say that it isn't a craft, but a knack, because it has no account of the nature of whatever things it applies by which it applies them,[7] so that it's unable to state the cause of each thing. And I refuse to call anything that lacks such an account a craft. If you have any quarrel with these claims, I'm willing to submit them for discussion.

So pastry baking, as I say, is the flattery that wears the mask of medicine.   b
Cosmetics is the one that wears that of gymnastics in the same way; a mischievous, deceptive, disgraceful and ill-bred thing, one that perpetrates deception by means of shaping and coloring, smoothing out and dressing up, so as to make people assume an alien beauty and neglect their own, which comes through gymnastics. So that I won't make a long-style speech, I'm willing to put it to you the way the geometers do—for perhaps you   c
follow me now—that what cosmetics is to gymnastics, pastry baking is to medicine; or rather, like this: what cosmetics is to gymnastics, sophistry is to legislation, and what pastry baking is to medicine, oratory is to justice. However, as I was saying, although these activities are naturally distinct in this way, yet because they are so close, sophists and orators tend to be mixed together as people who work in the same area and concern themselves with the same things. They don't know what to do with themselves, and other people don't know what to do with them. In fact, if the soul didn't govern the body but the body governed itself, and if pastry baking   d
and medicine weren't kept under observation and distinguished by the soul, but the body itself made judgments about them, making its estimates by reference to the gratification it receives, then the world according to Anaxagoras would prevail, Polus my friend—you're familiar with these views—all things would be mixed together in the same place, and there would be no distinction between matters of medicine and health, and matters of pastry baking.[8]

You've now heard what I say oratory is. It's the counterpart in the soul to pastry baking, its counterpart in the body. Perhaps I've done an absurd   e
thing: I wouldn't let you make long speeches, and here I've just composed a lengthy one myself. I deserve to be forgiven, though, for when I made my statements short you didn't understand and didn't know how to deal with the answers I gave you, but you needed a narration. So if I don't know how to deal with your answers either, you must spin out a speech,   466
too. But if I do, just let me deal with them. That's only fair. And if you now know how to deal with my answer, please deal with it.

POLUS: What is it you're saying, then? You think oratory is flattery?

SOCRATES: I said that it was a *part* of flattery. Don't you remember, Polus, young as you are? What's to become of you?

POLUS: So you think that good orators are held in low regard in their cities, as flatterers?

SOCRATES: Is this a question you're asking, or some speech you're be-   b
ginning?

7. The translation here follows the mss, rejecting Dodds' emendation.

8. Anaxagoras' book began with the words "All things were together," describing the primordial state of the universe.

POLUS: I'm asking a question.

SOCRATES: I don't think they're held in any regard at all.

POLUS: What do you mean, they're not held in any regard? Don't they have the greatest power in their cities?

SOCRATES: No, if by "having power" you mean something that's good for the one who has the power.

POLUS: That's just what I do mean.

SOCRATES: In that case I think that orators have the least power of any in the city.

POLUS: Really? Don't they, like tyrants, put to death anyone they want,
c and confiscate the property and banish from their cities anyone they see fit?

SOCRATES: By the Dog, Polus! I can't make out one way or the other with each thing you're saying whether you're saying these things for yourself and revealing your own view, or whether you're questioning me.

POLUS: I'm questioning you.

SOCRATES: Very well, my friend. In that case, are you asking me two questions at once?

POLUS: What do you mean, two?

SOCRATES: Weren't you just now saying something like "Don't orators,
d like tyrants, put to death anyone they want, don't they confiscate the property of anyone they see fit, and don't they banish them from their cities?"

POLUS: Yes, I was.

SOCRATES: In that case I say that these are two questions, and I'll answer you both of them. I say, Polus, that both orators and tyrants have the least
e power in their cities, as I was saying just now. For they do just about nothing they want to, though they certainly do whatever they see most fit to do.

POLUS: Well, isn't this having great power?

SOCRATES: No; at least Polus says it isn't.

POLUS: I say it isn't? I certainly say it is!

SOCRATES: By . . . , you certainly don't! since you say that having great power is good for the one who has it.

POLUS: Yes, I do say that.

SOCRATES: Do you think it's good, then, if a person does whatever he sees most fit to do when he lacks intelligence? Do you call this "having great power" too?

POLUS: No, I do not.

SOCRATES: Will you refute me, then, and prove that orators do have
467 intelligence, and that oratory is a craft, and not flattery? If you leave me unrefuted, then the orators who do what they see fit in their cities, and the tyrants, too, won't have gained any good by this. Power is a good thing, you say, but you agree with me that doing what one sees fit without intelligence is bad. Or don't you?

POLUS: Yes, I do.

SOCRATES: How then could it be that orators or tyrants have great power in their cities, so long as Socrates is not refuted by Polus to show that they do what they want?

POLUS: This fellow—

SOCRATES: —denies that they do what they want. Go ahead and refute me.

POLUS: Didn't you just now agree that they do what they see fit?

SOCRATES: Yes, and I still do.

POLUS: Don't they do what they want, then?

SOCRATES: I say they don't.

POLUS: Even though they do what they see fit?

SOCRATES: That's what I say.

POLUS: What an outrageous thing to say, Socrates! Perfectly monstrous!

SOCRATES: Don't attack me, my peerless Polus, to address you in your own style. Instead, question me if you can, and prove that I'm wrong. Otherwise you must answer me.

POLUS: All right, I'm willing to answer, to get some idea of what you're saying.

SOCRATES: Do you think that when people do something, they want the thing they're doing at the time, or the thing for the sake of which they do what they're doing? Do you think that people who take medicines prescribed by their doctors, for instance, want what they're doing, the act of taking the medicine, with all its discomfort, or do they want to be healthy, the thing for the sake of which they're taking it?

POLUS: Obviously they want their being healthy.

SOCRATES: With seafarers, too, and those who make money in other ways, the thing they're doing at the time is not the thing they want—for who wants to make dangerous and troublesome sea voyages? What they want is their being wealthy, the thing for the sake of which, I suppose, they make their voyages. It's for the sake of wealth that they make them.

POLUS: Yes, that's right.

SOCRATES: Isn't it just the same in all cases, in fact? If a person does anything for the sake of something, he doesn't want this thing that he's doing, but the thing for the sake of which he's doing it?

POLUS: Yes.

SOCRATES: Now is there any thing that isn't either *good*, or *bad*, or, what is between these, *neither good nor bad*?

POLUS: There can't be, Socrates.

SOCRATES: Do you say that wisdom, health, wealth and the like are good, and their opposites bad?

POLUS: Yes, I do.

SOCRATES: And by things which are neither good nor bad you mean things which sometimes partake of what's good, sometimes of what's bad, and sometimes of neither, such as sitting or walking, running or making sea voyages, or stones and sticks and the like? Aren't these the ones you mean? Or are there any others that you call things neither good nor bad?

POLUS: No, these are the ones.

SOCRATES: Now whenever people do things, do they do these intermediate things for the sake of good ones, or the good things for the sake of the intermediate ones?

b   POLUS: The intermediate things for the sake of the good ones, surely.

SOCRATES: So it's because we pursue what's good that we walk whenever we walk; we suppose that it's better to walk. And conversely, whenever we stand still, we stand still for the sake of the same thing, what's good. Isn't that so?

POLUS: Yes.

SOCRATES: And don't we also put a person to death, if we do, or banish him and confiscate his property because we suppose that doing these things is better for us than not doing them?

POLUS: That's right.

SOCRATES: Hence, it's for the sake of what's good that those who do all these things do them.

POLUS: I agree.

SOCRATES: Now didn't we agree that we want, not those things that we
c   do for the sake of something, but that thing for the sake of which we do them?

POLUS: Yes, very much so.

SOCRATES: Hence, we don't simply want to slaughter people, or exile them from their cities and confiscate their property as such; we want to do these things if they are beneficial, but if they're harmful we don't. For we want the things that are good, as you agree, and we don't want those that are neither good nor bad, nor those that are bad. Right? Do you think that what I'm saying is true, Polus, or don't you? Why don't you answer?

POLUS: I think it's true.

d   SOCRATES: Since we're in agreement about that then, if a person who's a tyrant or an orator puts somebody to death or exiles him or confiscates his property because he supposes that doing so is better for himself when actually it's worse, this person, I take it, is doing what he sees fit, isn't he?

POLUS: Yes.

SOCRATES: And is he also doing what he wants, if these things are actually bad? Why don't you answer?

POLUS: All right, I don't think he's doing what he wants.

e   SOCRATES: Can such a man possibly have great power in that city, if in fact having great power is, as you agree, something good?

POLUS: He cannot.

SOCRATES: So, what I was saying is true, when I said that it is possible for a man who does in his city what he sees fit not to have great power, nor to be doing what he wants.

POLUS: Really, Socrates! As if *you* wouldn't welcome being in a position to do what you see fit in the city, rather than not! As if *you* wouldn't be envious whenever you'd see anyone putting to death some person he saw fit, or confiscating his property or tying him up!

SOCRATES: Justly, you mean, or unjustly?

POLUS: Whichever way he does it, isn't he to be envied either way?   469

SOCRATES: Hush, Polus.

POLUS: What for?

SOCRATES: Because you're not supposed to envy the unenviable or the miserable. You're supposed to pity them.

POLUS: Really? Is this how you think it is with the people I'm talking about?

SOCRATES: Of course.

POLUS: So, you think that a person who puts to death anyone he sees fit, and does so justly, is miserable and to be pitied?

SOCRATES: No, I don't, but I don't think he's to be envied either.

POLUS: Weren't you just now saying that he's miserable?

SOCRATES: Yes, the one who puts someone to death unjustly is, my friend,   b
and he's to be pitied besides. But the one who does so justly isn't to be envied.

POLUS: Surely the one who's put to death unjustly is the one who's both to be pitied and miserable.

SOCRATES: Less so than the one putting him to death, Polus, and less than the one who's justly put to death.

POLUS: How can that be, Socrates?

SOCRATES: It's because doing what's unjust is actually the worst thing there is.

POLUS: Really? Is *that* the worst? Isn't suffering what's unjust still worse?

SOCRATES: No, not in the least.

POLUS: So you'd rather want to suffer what's unjust than do it?

SOCRATES: For my part, I wouldn't want either, but if it had to be one   c
or the other, I would choose suffering over doing what's unjust.

POLUS: You wouldn't welcome being a tyrant, then?

SOCRATES: No, if by being a tyrant you mean what I do.

POLUS: I mean just what I said a while ago, to be in a position to do whatever you see fit in the city, whether it's putting people to death or exiling them, or doing any and everything just as you see fit.

SOCRATES: Well, my wonderful fellow! I'll put you a case, and you criticize   d
it. Imagine me in a crowded marketplace, with a dagger up my sleeve, saying to you, "Polus, I've just got myself some marvelous tyrannical power. So, if I see fit to have any one of these people you see here put to death right on the spot, to death he'll be put. And if I see fit to have one of them have his head bashed in, bashed in it will be, right away. If I see fit to have his coat ripped apart, ripped it will be. That's how great my power in this city is!" Suppose you didn't believe me and I showed you   e
the dagger. On seeing it, you'd be likely to say, "But Socrates, *everybody* could have great power that way. For this way any house you see fit might be burned down, and so might the dockyards and triremes of the Athenians, and all their ships, both public and private." But then *that's* not what having great power is, doing what one sees fit. Or do you think it is?

POLUS: No, at least not like that.

470   SOCRATES: Can you then tell me what your reason is for objecting to this sort of power?

POLUS: Yes, I can.

SOCRATES: What is it? Tell me.

POLUS: It's that the person who acts this way is necessarily punished.

SOCRATES: And isn't being punished a bad thing?

POLUS: Yes, it really is.

SOCRATES: Well then, my surprising fellow, here again you take the view that as long as acting as one sees fit coincides with acting beneficially, it is good, and this, evidently, is having great power. Otherwise it is a bad

b   thing, and is having little power. Let's consider this point, too. Do we agree that sometimes it's better to do those things we were just now talking about, putting people to death and banishing them and confiscating their property, and at other times it isn't?

POLUS: Yes, we do.

SOCRATES: This point is evidently agreed upon by you and me both?

POLUS: Yes.

SOCRATES: When do you say that it's better to do these things then? Tell me where you draw the line.

POLUS: Why don't you answer that question yourself, Socrates.

c   SOCRATES: Well then, Polus, if you find it more pleasing to listen to me, I say that when one does these things justly, it's better, but when one does them unjustly, it's worse.

POLUS: How hard it is to refute you, Socrates! Why, even a child could refute you and show that what you're saying isn't true!

SOCRATES: In that case, I'll be very grateful to the child, and just as grateful to you if you refute me and rid me of this nonsense. Please don't falter now in doing a friend a good turn. Refute me.

POLUS: Surely, Socrates, we don't need to refer to ancient history to refute

d   you. Why, current events quite suffice to do that, and to prove that many people who behave unjustly are happy.

SOCRATES: What sorts of events are these?

POLUS: You can picture this man Archelaus, the son of Perdiccas, ruling Macedonia, I take it?

SOCRATES: Well, if I can't picture him, I do hear things about him.

POLUS: Do you think he's happy or miserable?

SOCRATES: I don't know, Polus. I haven't met the man yet.

e   POLUS: Really? You'd know this if you had met him, but without that you don't know straight off that he's happy?

SOCRATES: No, I certainly don't, by Zeus!

POLUS: It's obvious, Socrates, that you won't even claim to know that the Great King⁹ is happy.

9. The King of Persia, whose riches and imperial power embodied the popular idea of supreme happiness.

SOCRATES: Yes, and that would be true, for I don't know how he stands in regard to education and justice.

POLUS: Really? Is happiness determined entirely by that?

SOCRATES: Yes, Polus, so I say anyway. I say that the admirable and good person, man or woman, is happy, but that the one who's unjust and wicked is miserable.

POLUS: So on your reasoning this man Archelaus is miserable? 471

SOCRATES: Yes, my friend, if he is in fact unjust.

POLUS: Why of course he's unjust! The sovereignty which he now holds doesn't belong to him at all, given the fact that his mother was a slave of Alcetas, Perdiccas' brother. By rights he was a slave of Alcetas, and if he wanted to do what's just, he'd still be a slave to Alcetas, and on your reasoning would be happy. As it is, how marvelously "miserable" he's turned out to be, now that he's committed the most heinous crimes. First he sends for this man, his very own master and uncle, on the pretext of b restoring to him the sovereignty that Perdiccas had taken from him. He entertains him, gets him drunk, both him and his son Alexander, his own cousin and a boy about his own age. He then throws them into a wagon, drives it away at night, and slaughters and disposes of them both. And although he's committed these crimes, he remains unaware of how "miserable" he's become, and feels no remorse either. He refuses to become "happy" by justly bringing up his brother and conferring the sovereignty upon him, the legitimate son of Perdiccas, a boy of about seven to whom c the sovereignty was by rights due to come. Instead, not long afterward, he throws him into a well and drowns him, telling the boy's mother Cleopatra that he fell into the well chasing a goose and lost his life. For this very reason now, because he's committed the most terrible of crimes of any in Macedonia, he's the most "miserable" of all Macedonians instead of the happiest, and no doubt there are some in Athens, beginning with yourself, who'd prefer being any other Macedonian at all to being Arch- d elaus.

SOCRATES: Already at the start of our discussions, Polus, I praised you because I thought you were well educated in oratory. But I also thought that you had neglected the practice of discussion. And now is *this* all there is to the argument by which even a child could refute me, and do you suppose that when I say that a person who acts unjustly is not happy, I now stand refuted by you by means of *this* argument? Where did you get that idea, my good man? As a matter of fact, I disagree with every single thing you say!

POLUS: You're just unwilling to admit it. You really do think it's the way e I say it is.

SOCRATES: My wonderful man, you're trying to refute me in oratorical style, the way people in law courts do when they think they're refuting some claim. There, too, one side thinks it's refuting the other when it produces many reputable witnesses on behalf of the arguments it presents, while the person who asserts the opposite produces only one witness, or

472 none at all. This "refutation" is worthless, as far as truth is concerned, for it might happen sometimes that an individual is brought down by the false testimony of many reputable people. Now too, nearly every Athenian and alien will take your side on the things you're saying, if it's witnesses you want to produce against me to show that what I say isn't true. Nicias the son of Niceratus will testify for you, if you like, and his brothers along with him, the ones whose tripods are standing in a row in the precinct of

b Dionysus. Aristocrates the son of Scellias will too, if you like, the one to whom that handsome votive offering in the precinct of Pythian Apollo belongs. And so will the whole house of Pericles, if you like, or any other local family you care to choose. Nevertheless, though I'm only one person, I don't agree with you. You don't compel me; instead you produce many false witnesses against me and try to banish me from my property, the truth. For my part, if I don't produce you as a single witness to agree with what I'm saying, then I suppose I've achieved nothing worth mentioning

c concerning the things we've been discussing. And I suppose you haven't either, if I don't testify on your side, though I'm just one person, and you disregard all these other people.

There is, then, this style of refutation, the one you and many others accept. There's also another, one that I accept. Let's compare the one with the other and see if they'll differ in any way. It's true, after all, that the matters in dispute between us are not at all insignificant ones, but pretty nearly those it's most admirable to have knowledge about, and most shameful not to. For the heart of the matter is that of recognizing or failing to

d recognize who is happy and who is not. To take first the immediate question our present discussion's about: you believe that it's possible for a man who behaves unjustly and who is unjust to be happy, since you believe Archaelaus to be both unjust and happy. Are we to understand that this is precisely your view?

POLUS: That's right.

SOCRATES: And I say that that's impossible. This is one point in dispute between us. Fair enough. Although he acts unjustly, he'll be happy—that is, if he gets his due punishment?

POLUS: Oh no, certainly not! That's how he'd be the most miserable!

e SOCRATES: But if a man who acts unjustly doesn't get his due, then, on your reasoning, he'll be happy?

POLUS: That's what I say.

SOCRATES: On my view of it, Polus, a man who acts unjustly, a man who is unjust, is thoroughly miserable, the more so if he doesn't get his due punishment for the wrongdoing he commits, the less so if he pays and receives what is due at the hands of both gods and men.

473 POLUS: What an absurd position you're trying to maintain, Socrates!

SOCRATES: Yes, and I'll try to get you to take the same position too, my good man, for I consider you a friend. For now, these are the points we differ on. Please look at them with me. I said earlier, didn't I, that doing what's unjust is worse than suffering it?

POLUS: Yes, you did.

SOCRATES: And you said that suffering it is worse.

POLUS: Yes.

SOCRATES: And I said that those who do what's unjust are miserable, and was "refuted" by you.

POLUS: You certainly were, by Zeus!

SOCRATES: So you think, Polus.

POLUS: So I *truly* think.

SOCRATES: Perhaps. And again, you think that those who do what's unjust are happy, so long as they don't pay what is due.

POLUS: I certainly do.

SOCRATES: Whereas I say that they're the most miserable, while those who pay their due are less so. Would you like to refute this too?

POLUS: Why, that's even more "difficult" to refute than the other claim, Socrates!

SOCRATES: Not difficult, surely, Polus. It's impossible. What's true is never refuted.

POLUS: What do you mean? Take a man who's caught doing something unjust, say, plotting to set himself up as tyrant. Suppose that he's caught, put on the rack, castrated, and has his eyes burned out. Suppose that he's subjected to a host of other abuses of all sorts, and then made to witness his wife and children undergo the same. In the end he's impaled or tarred. Will he be happier than if he hadn't got caught, had set himself up as tyrant, and lived out his life ruling in his city and doing whatever he liked, a person envied and counted happy by fellow citizens and aliens alike? Is *this* what you say is impossible to refute?

SOCRATES: This time you're spooking me, Polus, instead of refuting me. Just before, you were arguing by testimony. Still, refresh my memory on a small point: if the man plots to set himself up as tyrant *unjustly*, you said?

POLUS: Yes, I did.

SOCRATES: In that case neither of them will ever be the happier one, neither the one who gains tyrannical power unjustly, nor the one who pays what is due, for of two miserable people one could not be happier than the other. But the one who avoids getting caught and becomes a tyrant is the more miserable one. What's this, Polus? You're laughing? Is this now some further style of refutation, to laugh when somebody makes a point, instead of refuting him?

POLUS: Don't you think you've been refuted already, Socrates, when you're saying things the likes of which no human being would maintain? Just ask any one of these people.

SOCRATES: Polus, I'm not one of the politicians. Last year I was elected to the Council by lot, and when our tribe was presiding and I had to call for a vote, I came in for a laugh. I didn't know how to do it. So please don't tell me to call for a vote from the people present here. If you have no better "refutations" than these to offer, do as I suggested just now: let me have my turn, and you try the kind of refutation I think is called for.

b

c

d

e

474

For I do know how to produce one witness to whatever I'm saying, and that's the man I'm having a discussion with. The majority I disregard. And I do know how to call for a vote from one man, but I don't even

b discuss things with the majority. See if you'll be willing to give me a refutation, then, by answering the questions you're asked. For I do believe that you and I and everybody else consider doing what's unjust worse than suffering it, and not paying what is due worse than paying it.

POLUS: And I do believe that I don't, and that no other person does, either. So you'd take suffering what's unjust over doing it, would you?

SOCRATES: Yes, and so would you and everyone else.

POLUS: Far from it! I wouldn't, you wouldn't, and nobody else would, either.

c SOCRATES: Won't you answer, then?

POLUS: I certainly will. I'm eager to know what you'll say, in fact.

SOCRATES: So that you'll know, answer me as though this were my first question to you. Which do you think is worse, Polus, doing what's unjust or suffering it?

POLUS: I think suffering it is.

SOCRATES: You do? Which do you think is more shameful, doing what's unjust or suffering it? Tell me.

POLUS: Doing it.

SOCRATES: Now if doing it is in fact more shameful, isn't it also worse?

POLUS: No, not in the least.

d SOCRATES: I see. Evidently you don't believe that *admirable* and *good* are the same, or that *bad* and *shameful* are.

POLUS: No, I certainly don't.

SOCRATES: Well, what about this? When you call all admirable things admirable, bodies, for example, or colors, shapes and sounds, or practices, is it with nothing in view that you do so each time? Take admirable bodies first. Don't you call them admirable either in virtue of their usefulness, relative to whatever it is that each is useful for, or else in virtue of some pleasure, if it makes the people who look at them get enjoyment from looking at them? In the case of the admirability of a body, can you mention anything other than these?

e POLUS: No, I can't.

SOCRATES: Doesn't the same hold for all the other things? Don't you call shapes and colors admirable on account of either some pleasure or benefit or both?

POLUS: Yes, I do.

SOCRATES: Doesn't this also hold for sounds and all things musical?

POLUS: Yes.

SOCRATES: And certainly things that pertain to laws and practices—the admirable ones, that is—don't fall outside the limits of being either pleasant or beneficial, or both, I take it.

475 POLUS: No, I don't think they do.

SOCRATES: Doesn't the same hold for the admirability of the fields of learning, too?

POLUS: Yes indeed. Yes, Socrates, your present definition of the admirable in terms of pleasure and good is an admirable one.

SOCRATES: And so is my definition of the shameful in terms of the opposite, pain and bad, isn't it?

POLUS: Necessarily so.

SOCRATES: Therefore, whenever one of two admirable things is more admirable than the other, it is so because it surpasses the other either in one of these, pleasure or benefit, or in both.

POLUS: Yes, that's right.

SOCRATES: And whenever one of two shameful things is more shameful than the other, it will be so because it surpasses the other either in pain or in badness. Isn't that necessarily so? b

POLUS: Yes.

SOCRATES: Well now, what were we saying a moment ago about doing what's unjust and suffering it? Weren't you saying that suffering it is worse, but doing it more shameful?

POLUS: I was.

SOCRATES: Now if doing what's unjust is in fact more shameful than suffering it, wouldn't it be so either because it is more painful and surpasses the other in pain, or because it surpasses it in badness, or both? Isn't that necessarily so, too?

POLUS: Of course it is.

SOCRATES: Let's look at this first: does doing what's unjust surpass suffering it in pain, and do people who do it hurt more than people who suffer it? c

POLUS: No, Socrates, that's not the case at all!

SOCRATES: So it doesn't surpass it in pain, anyhow.

POLUS: Certainly not.

SOCRATES: So, if it doesn't surpass it in pain, it couldn't at this point surpass it in both.

POLUS: Apparently not.

SOCRATES: This leaves it surpassing it only in the other thing.

POLUS: Yes.

SOCRATES: In badness.

POLUS: Evidently.

SOCRATES: So, because it surpasses it in badness, doing what's unjust would be worse than suffering it.

POLUS: That's clear.

SOCRATES: Now didn't the majority of mankind, and you earlier, agree with us that doing what's unjust is more shameful than suffering it? d

POLUS: Yes.

SOCRATES: And now, at least, it's turned out to be worse.

POLUS: Evidently.

SOCRATES: Would you then welcome what's worse and what's more shameful over what is less so? Don't shrink back from answering, Polus. You won't get hurt in any way. Submit yourself nobly to the argument, as you would to a doctor, and answer me. Say yes or no to what I ask you.

POLUS: No, I wouldn't, Socrates. e

SOCRATES: And would any other person?

POLUS: No, I don't think so, not on this reasoning, anyhow.

SOCRATES: I was right, then, when I said that neither you nor I nor any other person would take doing what's unjust over suffering it, for it really is something worse.

POLUS: So it appears.

SOCRATES: So you see, Polus, that when the one refutation is compared with the other, there is no resemblance at all. Whereas everyone but me agrees with you, you are all I need, although you're just a party of one, for your agreement and testimony. It's you alone whom I call on for a vote; the others I disregard. Let this be our verdict on this matter, then. Let's next consider the second point in dispute between us, that is whether a wrongdoer's paying what is due is the worst thing there is, as you were supposing, or whether his not paying it is even worse, as I was.

Let's look at it this way. Are you saying that paying what is due and being justly disciplined for wrongdoing are the same thing?

POLUS: Yes, I do.

SOCRATES: Can you say, then, that all just things aren't admirable, insofar as they are just? Think carefully and tell me.

POLUS: Yes, I think they are.

SOCRATES: Consider this point, too. If somebody acts upon something, there also has to be something that has something done to it by the one acting upon it?

POLUS: Yes, I think so.

SOCRATES: And that it has done to it what the thing acting upon it does, and in the sort of way the thing acting upon it does it? I mean, for example, that if somebody hits, there has to be something that's being hit?

POLUS: There has to be.

SOCRATES: And if the hitter hits hard or quickly, the thing being hit is hit that way, too?

POLUS: Yes.

SOCRATES: So the thing being hit gets acted upon in whatever way the hitting thing acts upon it?

POLUS: Yes, that's right.

SOCRATES: So, too, if somebody performs surgical burning, then there has to be something that's being burned?

POLUS: Of course.

SOCRATES: And if he burns severely or painfully, the thing that's being burned is burned in whatever way the burning thing burns it?

POLUS: That's right.

SOCRATES: Doesn't the same account also hold if a person makes a surgical cut? For something is being cut.

POLUS: Yes.

SOCRATES: And if the cut is large or deep or painful, the thing being cut is cut in whatever way the cutting thing cuts it?

POLUS: So it appears.

SOCRATES: Summing it up, see if you agree with what I was saying just now, that in all cases, in whatever way the thing acting upon something acts upon it, the thing acted upon is acted upon in just that way.

POLUS: Yes, I do agree.

SOCRATES: Taking this as agreed, is paying what is due a case of being acted upon or of acting upon something?

POLUS: It must be a case of being acted upon, Socrates.

SOCRATES: By someone who acts?

POLUS: Of course. By the one administering discipline.

SOCRATES: Now one who disciplines correctly disciplines justly?   e

POLUS: Yes.

SOCRATES: Thereby acting justly, or not?

POLUS: Yes, justly.

SOCRATES: So the one being disciplined is being acted upon justly when he pays what is due?

POLUS: Apparently.

SOCRATES: And it was agreed, I take it, that just things are admirable?

POLUS: That's right.

SOCRATES: So one of these men does admirable things, and the other, the one being disciplined, has admirable things done to him.

POLUS: Yes.

SOCRATES: If they're admirable, then, aren't they good? For they're either   477 pleasant or beneficial.

POLUS: Necessarily so.

SOCRATES: Hence, the one paying what is due has good things being done to him?

POLUS: Evidently.

SOCRATES: Hence, he's being benefited?

POLUS: Yes.

SOCRATES: Is his benefit the one I take it to be? Does his soul undergo improvement if he's justly disciplined?

POLUS: Yes, that's likely.

SOCRATES: Hence, one who pays what is due gets rid of something bad in his soul?

POLUS: Yes.

SOCRATES: Now, is the bad thing he gets rid of the most serious one? Consider it this way: in the matter of a person's financial condition, do   b you detect any bad thing other than poverty?

POLUS: No, just poverty.

SOCRATES: What about that of a person's physical condition? Would you say that what is bad here consists of weakness, disease, ugliness, and the like?

POLUS: Yes, I would.

SOCRATES: Do you believe that there's also some corrupt condition of the soul?

POLUS: Of course.

SOCRATES: And don't you call this condition injustice, ignorance, cowardice, and the like?

POLUS: Yes, certainly.

SOCRATES: Of these three things, one's finances, one's body, and one's soul, you said there are three states of corruption, namely poverty, disease, and injustice?

POLUS: Yes.

SOCRATES: Which of these states of corruption is the most shameful? Isn't it injustice, and corruption of one's soul in general?

POLUS: Very much so.

SOCRATES: And if it's the most shameful, it's also the worst?

POLUS: What do you mean, Socrates?

SOCRATES: I mean this: What we agreed on earlier implies that what's most shameful is so always because it's the source either of the greatest pain, or of harm, or of both.

POLUS: Very much so.

SOCRATES: And now we've agreed that injustice, and corruption of soul as a whole, is the most shameful thing.

POLUS: So we have.

SOCRATES: So either it's most painful and is most shameful because it surpasses the others in pain, or else in harm, or in both?

POLUS: Necessarily so.

SOCRATES: Now is being unjust, undisciplined, cowardly, and ignorant more painful than being poor or sick?

POLUS: No, I don't think so, Socrates, given what we've said, anyhow.

SOCRATES: So the reason that corruption of one's soul is the most shameful of them all is that it surpasses the others by some monstrously great harm and astounding badness, since it doesn't surpass them in pain, according to your reasoning.

POLUS: So it appears.

SOCRATES: But what is surpassing in greatest harm would, I take it, certainly be the worst thing there is.

POLUS: Yes.

SOCRATES: Injustice, then, lack of discipline and all other forms of corruption of soul are the worst thing there is.

POLUS: Apparently so.

SOCRATES: Now, what is the craft that gets rid of poverty? Isn't it that of financial management?

POLUS: Yes.

SOCRATES: What's the one that gets rid of disease? Isn't it that of medicine?

POLUS: Necessarily.

SOCRATES: What's the one that gets rid of corruption and injustice? If you're stuck, look at it this way: where and to whom do we take people who are physically sick?

POLUS: To doctors, Socrates.

SOCRATES: Where do we take people who behave unjustly and without discipline?

POLUS: To judges, you mean?

SOCRATES: Isn't it so they'll pay what's due?

POLUS: Yes, I agree.

SOCRATES: Now don't those who administer discipline correctly employ a kind of justice in doing so?

POLUS: That's clear.

SOCRATES: It's financial management, then, that gets rid of poverty, medicine that gets rid of disease, and justice that gets rid of injustice and indiscipline.   b

POLUS: Apparently.

SOCRATES: Which of these, now, is the most admirable?

POLUS: Of which, do you mean?

SOCRATES: Of financial management, medicine, and justice.

POLUS: Justice is by far, Socrates.

SOCRATES: Doesn't it in that case provide either the most pleasure, or benefit, or both, if it really is the most admirable?

POLUS: Yes.

SOCRATES: Now, is getting medical treatment something pleasant? Do people who get it enjoy getting it?

POLUS: No, I don't think so.

SOCRATES: But it *is* beneficial, isn't it?

POLUS: Yes.

SOCRATES: Because they're getting rid of something very bad, so that it's   c
worth their while to endure the pain and so get well.

POLUS: Of course.

SOCRATES: Now, would a man be happiest, as far as his body goes, if he's under treatment, or if he weren't even sick to begin with?

POLUS: If he weren't even sick, obviously.

SOCRATES: Because happiness evidently isn't a matter of getting rid of something bad; it's rather a matter of not even contracting it to begin with.

POLUS: That's so.

SOCRATES: Very well. Of two people, each of whom has something bad   d
in either body or soul, which is the more miserable one, the one who is treated and gets rid of the bad thing or the one who doesn't but keeps it?

POLUS: The one who isn't treated, it seems to me.

SOCRATES: Now, wasn't paying what's due getting rid of the worst thing there is, corruption?

POLUS: It was.

SOCRATES: Yes, because such justice makes people self-controlled, I take it, and more just. It proves to be a treatment against corruption.

POLUS: Yes.

SOCRATES: The happiest man, then, is the one who doesn't have any badness in his soul, now that this has been shown to be the most serious kind of badness.

POLUS: That's clear.

SOCRATES: And second, I suppose, is the man who gets rid of it.   e

POLUS: Evidently.

SOCRATES: This is the man who gets lectured and lashed, the one who pays what is due.

POLUS: Yes.

SOCRATES: The man who keeps it, then, and who doesn't get rid of it, is the one whose life is the worst.

POLUS: Apparently.

479   SOCRATES: Isn't this actually the man who, although he commits the most serious crimes and uses methods that are most unjust, succeeds in avoiding being lectured and disciplined and paying his due, as Archelaus according to you, and the other tyrants, orators, and potentates have put themselves in a position to do?

POLUS: Evidently.

SOCRATES: Yes, my good man, I take it that these people have managed to accomplish pretty much the same thing as a person who has contracted very serious illnesses, but, by avoiding treatment manages to avoid paying what's due to the doctors for his bodily faults, fearing, as would a child,

b   cauterization or surgery because they're painful. Don't you think so, too?

POLUS: Yes, I do.

SOCRATES: It's because he evidently doesn't know what health and bodily excellence are like. For on the basis of what we're now agreed on, it looks as though those who avoid paying what is due also do the same sort of thing, Polus. They focus on its painfulness, but are blind to its benefit and are ignorant of how much more miserable it is to live with an unhealthy

c   soul than with an unhealthy body, a soul that's rotten with injustice and impiety. This is also the reason they go to any length to avoid paying what is due and getting rid of the worst thing there is. They find themselves funds and friends, and ways to speak as persuasively as possible. Now if what we're agreed on is true, Polus, are you aware of what things follow from our argument? Or would you like us to set them out?

POLUS: Yes, if you think we should anyhow.

SOCRATES: Does it follow that injustice, and doing what is unjust, is the worst thing there is?

d   POLUS: Yes, apparently.

SOCRATES: And it has indeed been shown that paying what is due is what gets rid of this bad thing?

POLUS: So it seems.

SOCRATES: And that if it isn't paid, the bad thing is retained?

POLUS: Yes.

SOCRATES: So, doing what's unjust is the second worst thing. Not paying what's due when one has done what's unjust is by its nature the first worst thing, the very worst of all.

POLUS: Evidently.

SOCRATES: Now wasn't this the point in dispute between us, my friend?

e   You considered Archelaus happy, a man who committed the gravest crimes without paying what was due, whereas I took the opposite view, that whoever avoids paying his due for his wrongdoing, whether he's Archelaus or any other man, is and deserves to be miserable beyond all other men, and that one who does what's unjust is always more miserable than the one who suffers it, and the one who avoids paying what's due always more miserable than the one who does pay it. Weren't these the things I said?

POLUS: Yes.

SOCRATES: Hasn't it been proved that what was said is true?

POLUS: Apparently.

SOCRATES: Fair enough. If these things are true then, Polus, what is the great use of oratory? For on the basis of what we're agreed on now, what a man should guard himself against most of all is doing what's unjust, knowing that he will have trouble enough if he does. Isn't that so? 480

POLUS: Yes, that's right.

SOCRATES: And if he or anyone else he cares about acts unjustly, he should voluntarily go to the place where he'll pay his due as soon as possible; he should go to the judge as though he were going to a doctor, b anxious that the disease of injustice shouldn't be protracted and cause his soul to fester incurably. What else can we say, Polus, if our previous agreements really stand? Aren't these statements necessarily consistent with our earlier ones in only this way?

POLUS: Well yes, Socrates. What else are we to say?

SOCRATES: So, if oratory is used to defend injustice, Polus, one's own or that of one's relatives, companions, or children, or that of one's country when it acts unjustly, it is of no use to us at all, unless one takes it to be c useful for the opposite purpose: that he should accuse himself first and foremost, and then too his family and anyone else dear to him who happens to behave unjustly at any time; and that he should not keep his wrongdoing hidden but bring it out into the open, so that he may pay his due and get well; and compel himself and the others not to play the coward, but to grit his teeth and present himself with grace and courage as to a doctor for cauterization and surgery, pursuing what's good and admirable without taking any account of the pain. And if his unjust behavior merits flogging, he should present himself to be whipped; if it merits imprisonment, to be d imprisoned; if a fine, to pay it; if exile, to be exiled; and if execution, to be executed. He should be his own chief accuser, and the accuser of other members of his family, and use his oratory for the purpose of getting rid of the worst thing there is, injustice, as the unjust acts are being exposed. Are we to affirm or deny this, Polus?

POLUS: I think these statements are absurd, Socrates, though no doubt e you think they agree with those expressed earlier.

SOCRATES: Then either we should abandon those, or else these necessarily follow?

POLUS: Yes, that's how it is.

SOCRATES: And, on the other hand, to reverse the case, suppose a man had to harm someone, an enemy or anybody at all, provided that he didn't suffer anything unjust from this enemy himself—for this is something to be on guard against—if the enemy did something unjust against another

481 person, then our man should see to it in every way, both in what he does and what he says, that his enemy does not go to the judge and pay his due. And if he does go, he should scheme to get his enemy off without paying what's due. If he's stolen a lot of gold, he should scheme to get him not to return it but to keep it and spend it in an unjust and godless way both on himself and his people. And if his crimes merit the death penalty, he should scheme to keep him from being executed, preferably never to die at all but to live forever in corruption, but failing that, to have

b him live as long as possible in that condition. Yes, this is the sort of thing I think oratory is useful for, Polus, since for the person who has no intention of behaving unjustly it doesn't seem to me to have much use—if in fact it has any use at all—since its usefulness hasn't in any way become apparent so far.

CALLICLES: Tell me, Chaerephon, is Socrates in earnest about this or is he joking?

CHAEREPHON: I think he's in dead earnest about this, Callicles. There's nothing like asking him, though.

CALLICLES: By the gods! Just the thing I'm eager to do. Tell me, Socrates,

c are we to take you as being in earnest now, or joking? For if you *are* in earnest, and these things you're saying are really true, won't this human life of ours be turned upside down, and won't everything we do evidently be the opposite of what we should do?

SOCRATES: Well, Callicles, if human beings didn't share common experiences, some sharing one, others sharing another, but one of us had some

d unique experience not shared by others, it wouldn't be easy for him to communicate what he experienced to the other. I say this because I realize that you and I are both now actually sharing a common experience: each of the two of us is a lover of two objects, I of Alcibiades, Clinias' son,[10] and of philosophy, and you of the *demos* [people] of Athens, and the Demos who's the son of Pyrilampes. I notice that in each case you're unable to contradict your beloved, clever though you are, no matter what he says

e or what he claims is so. You keep shifting back and forth. If you say anything in the Assembly and the Athenian *demos* denies it, you shift your ground and say what it wants to hear. Other things like this happen to you when you're with that good-looking young man, the son of Pyrilampes. You're unable to oppose what your beloveds say or propose, so that if somebody heard you say what you do on their account and was amazed at how absurd that is, you'd probably say—if you were minded to tell

482 him the truth—that unless somebody stops your beloveds from saying what they say, you'll never stop saying these things either. In that case you must believe that you're bound to hear me say things like that, too, and instead of being surprised at my saying them, you must stop my beloved, philosophy, from saying them. For she always says what you now hear me say, my dear friend, and she's by far less fickle than my

10. See *Symposium* 215a–219d.

other beloved. As for that son of Clinias, what he says differs from one time to the next, but what philosophy says always stays the same, and she's saying things that now astound you, although you were present when they were said. So, either refute her and show that doing what's unjust without paying what is due for it is *not* the ultimate of all bad things, as I just now was saying it is, or else, if you leave this unrefuted, then by the Dog, the god of the Egyptians, Callicles will not agree with you, Callicles, but will be dissonant with you all your life long. And yet for my part, my good man, I think it's better to have my lyre or a chorus that I might lead out of tune and dissonant, and have the vast majority of men disagree with me and contradict me, than to be out of harmony with myself, to contradict myself, though I'm only one person.

CALLICLES: Socrates, I think you're grandstanding in these speeches, acting like a true crowd pleaser. Here you are, playing to the crowd now that Polus has had the same thing happen to him that he accused Gorgias of letting you do to him. For he said, didn't he, that when Gorgias was asked by you whether he would teach anyone who came to him wanting to learn oratory but without expertise in what's just, Gorgias was ashamed and, out of deference to human custom, since people would take it ill if a person refused, said that he'd teach him. And because Gorgias agreed on this point, he said, he was forced to contradict himself, just the thing you like. He ridiculed you at the time, and rightly so, as I think anyhow. And now the very same thing has happened to him. And for this same reason *I* don't approve of Polus: he agreed with you that doing what's unjust is more shameful than suffering it. As a result of this admission he was bound and gagged by you in the discussion, too ashamed to say what he thought. Although you claim to be pursuing the truth, you're in fact bringing the discussion around to the sort of crowd-pleasing vulgarities that are admirable only by law and not by nature. And these, nature and law, are for the most part opposed to each other, so if a person is ashamed and doesn't dare to say what he thinks, he's forced to contradict himself. This is in fact the clever trick you've thought of, with which you work mischief in your discussions: if a person makes a statement in terms of law, you slyly question him in terms of nature; if he makes it in terms of nature, you question him in terms of law. That's just what happened here, on the question of doing what's unjust versus suffering it. While Polus meant that doing it is more shameful by law, you pursued the argument as though he meant by nature. For by nature all that is worse is also more shameful, like suffering what's unjust, whereas by law doing it is more shameful. No, no man would put up with suffering what's unjust; only a slave would do so, one who is better dead than alive, who when he's treated unjustly and abused can't protect himself or anyone else he cares about. I believe that the people who institute our laws are the weak and the many. So they institute laws and assign praise and blame with themselves and their own advantage in mind. As a way of frightening the more powerful among men, the ones who are capable of having a greater share,

out of getting a greater share than they, they say that getting more than one's share is "shameful" and "unjust," and that doing what's unjust is nothing but trying to get more than one's share. I think they like getting an equal share, since they are inferior.

These are the reasons why trying to get a greater share than most is said to be unjust and shameful by law and why they call it doing what's unjust. But I believe that nature itself reveals that it's a just thing for the better man and the more capable man to have a greater share than the worse man and the less capable man. Nature shows that this is so in many places; both among the other animals and in whole cities and races of men, it shows that this is what justice has been decided to be: that the superior rule the inferior and have a greater share than they. For what sort of justice did Xerxes go by when he campaigned against Greece, or his father when he campaigned against Scythia? Countless other such examples could be mentioned. I believe that these men do these things in accordance with the nature of what's just—yes, by Zeus, in accordance with the law of nature, and presumably not with the one we institute. We mold the best and the most powerful among us, taking them while they're still young, like lion cubs, and with charms and incantations we subdue them into slavery, telling them that one is supposed to get no more than his fair share, and that that's what's admirable and just. But surely, if a man whose nature is equal to it arises, he will shake off, tear apart, and escape all this, he will trample underfoot our documents, our tricks and charms, and all our laws that violate nature. He, the slave, will rise up and be revealed as our master, and here the justice of nature will shine forth. I think Pindar, too, refers to what I'm saying in that song in which he says that

> *Law, the king of all,*
> *Of mortals and the immortal gods*

—this, he says,

> *Brings on and renders just what is most violent*
> *With towering hand. I take as proof of this*
> *The deeds of Heracles. For he ... unbought ...*

His words are something like that—I don't know the song well—he says that Heracles drove off Geryon's cattle, even though he hadn't paid for them and Geryon hadn't given them to him, on the ground that this is what's just by nature, and that cattle and all the other possessions of those who are worse and inferior belong to the one who's better and superior.

This is the truth of the matter, as you will acknowledge if you abandon philosophy and move on to more important things. Philosophy is no doubt a delightful thing, Socrates, as long as one is exposed to it in moderation at the appropriate time of life. But if one spends more time with it than he should, it's a man's undoing. For even if one is naturally well favored but engages in philosophy far beyond that appropriate time of life, he can't help but turn out to be inexperienced in everything a man who's to be admirable and good and well thought of is supposed to be experienced in. Such people turn out to be inexperienced in the laws of their city or in the kind of speech one must use to deal with people on matters of business, whether in public or private, inexperienced also in human pleasures and appetites and, in short, inexperienced in the ways of human beings altogether. So, when they venture into some private or political activity, they become a laughingstock, as I suppose men in politics do when they venture into your pursuits and your kind of speech. What results is Euripides' saying, where he says that "each man shines" in this and "presses on to this,

> *allotting the greatest part of the day to this,*
> *where he finds himself at his best."*

And whatever a man's inferior in, he avoids and rails against, while he praises the other thing, thinking well of himself and supposing that in this way he's praising himself. I believe, however, that it's most appropriate to have a share of both. To partake of as much philosophy as your education requires is an admirable thing, and it's not shameful to practice philosophy while you're a boy, but when you still do it after you've grown older and become a man, the thing gets to be ridiculous, Socrates! My own reaction to men who philosophize is very much like that to men who speak haltingly and play like children. When I see a child, for whom it's still quite proper to make conversation this way, halting in its speech and playing like a child, I'm delighted. I find it a delightful thing, a sign of good breeding, and appropriate for the child's age. And when I hear a small child speaking clearly, I think it's a harsh thing; it hurts my ears. I think it is something fit for a slave. But when one hears a man speaking haltingly or sees him playing like a child, it strikes me as ridiculous and unmanly, deserving of a flogging. Now, I react in the same way to men who engage in philosophy, too. When I see philosophy in a young boy, I approve of it; I think it's appropriate and consider such a person well-bred, whereas I consider one who doesn't engage in philosophy ill-bred, one who'll never count himself deserving of any admirable or noble thing. But when I see an older man still engaging in philosophy and not giving it up, I think such a man by this time needs a flogging. For, as I was just now saying, it's typical that such a man, even if he's naturally very well favored, becomes unmanly and avoids the centers of his city and the marketplaces—in which, according to the poet,[11] men attain "preeminence"—and, instead, lives the rest

---

11. Homer, *Iliad* ix.441.

e   of his life in hiding, whispering in a corner with three or four boys, never uttering anything well-bred, important, or apt.

    Socrates, I do have a rather warm regard for you. I find myself feeling what Zethus, whose words I recalled just now, felt toward Amphion in Euripides' play. In fact, the sorts of things he said to his brother come to my mind to say to you. "You're neglecting the things you should devote yourself to, Socrates, and though your spirit's nature is so noble, you show yourself to the world in the shape of a boy. You couldn't put a speech

486   together correctly before councils of justice or utter any plausible or persuasive sound. Nor could you make any bold proposal on behalf of anyone else." And so then, my dear Socrates—please don't be upset with me, for it's with good will toward you that I'll say this—don't you think it's shameful to be the way I take you to be, and others who ever press on too far in philosophy? As it is, if someone got hold of you or of anyone else like you and took you off to prison on the charge that you're doing something unjust when in fact you aren't, be assured that you wouldn't have any use for yourself. You'd get dizzy, your mouth would hang open

b   and you wouldn't know what to say. You'd come up for trial and face some no good wretch of an accuser and be put to death, if death is what he'd want to condemn you to. And yet, Socrates, "how can this be a wise thing, the craft which took a well-favored man and made him worse," able neither to protect himself nor to rescue himself or anyone else from the gravest dangers, to be robbed of all of his property by his enemies,

c   and to live a life with absolutely no rights in his city? Such a man one could knock on the jaw without paying what's due for it, to put it rather crudely. Listen to me, my good man, and stop this refuting. "Practice the sweet music of an active life and do it where you'll get a reputation for being intelligent. Leave these subtleties to others"—whether we should call them just silly or outright nonsense—"which will cause you to live in empty houses,"[12] and envy not those men who refute such trivia, but those

d   who have life and renown, and many other good things as well.

    SOCRATES: If I actually had a soul made of gold, Callicles, don't you think I'd be pleased to find one of those stones on which they test gold? And if this stone to which I intended to take my soul were the best stone and it agreed that my soul had been well cared for, don't you think I could know well at that point that I'm in good shape and need no further test?

e   CALLICLES: What's the point of your question, Socrates?

    SOCRATES: I'll tell you. I believe that by running into you, I've run into just such a piece of luck.

    CALLICLES: Why do you say that?

    SOCRATES: I know well that if you concur with what my soul believes,

487   then that is the very truth. I realize that a person who is going to put a soul to an adequate test to see whether it lives rightly or not must have three qualities, all of which you have: knowledge, good will, and frankness.

---

12. Here and just above Callicles again quotes or adapts Euripides' *Antiope*.

I run into many people who aren't able to test me because they're not wise like you. Others are wise, but they're not willing to tell me the truth, because they don't care for me the way you do. As for these two visitors, Gorgias and Polus, they're both wise and fond of me, but rather more lacking in frankness, and more ashamed than they should be. No wonder! They've come to such a depth of shame that, because they are ashamed, each of them dares to contradict himself, face to face with many people, and on topics of the greatest importance. You have all these qualities, which the others don't. You're well-enough educated, as many of the Athenians would attest, and you have good will toward me. What's my proof of this? I'll tell you. I know, Callicles, that there are four of you who've become partners in wisdom, you, Teisander of Aphidnae, Andron the son of Androtion, and Nausicydes of Cholarges. Once I overheard you deliberating on how far one should cultivate wisdom, and I know that some such opinion as this was winning out among you: you called on each other not to enthusiastically pursue philosophizing to the point of pedantry but to be careful not to become wiser than necessary and so inadvertently bring yourselves to ruin. So, now that I hear you giving me the same advice you gave your closest companions, I have sufficient proof that you really do have good will toward me. And as to my claim that you're able to speak frankly without being ashamed, you yourself say so and the speech you gave a moment ago bears you out. It's clear, then, that this is how these matters stand at the moment. If there's any point in our discussions on which you agree with me, then that point will have been adequately put to the test by you and me, and it will not be necessary to put it to any further test, for you'd never have conceded the point through lack of wisdom or excess of shame, and you wouldn't do so by lying to me, either. You are my friend, as you yourself say, too. So, our mutual agreement will really lay hold of truth in the end. Most admirable of all, Callicles, is the examination of those issues about which you took me to task, that of what a man is supposed to be like, and of what he's supposed to devote himself to and how far, when he's older and when he's young. For my part, if I engage in anything that's improper in my own life, please know well that I do not make this mistake intentionally but out of my ignorance. So don't leave off lecturing me the way you began, but show me clearly what it is I'm to devote myself to, and in what way I might come by it; if you catch me agreeing with you now but at a later time not doing the very things I've agreed upon, then take me for a very stupid fellow and don't bother ever afterward with lecturing me, on the ground that I'm a worthless fellow.

Please restate your position for me from the beginning. What is it that you and Pindar hold to be true of what's just by nature? That the superior should take by force what belongs to the inferior, that the better should rule the worse and the more worthy have a greater share than the less worthy? You're not saying anything else, are you? I do remember correctly?

CALLICLES: Yes, that's what I was saying then, and I still say so now, too.

SOCRATES: Is it the same man you call both "better" and "superior"? I
c   wasn't able then, either, to figure out what you meant. Is it the stronger
ones you call superior, and should those who are weaker take orders from
the one who's stronger? That's what I think you were trying to show then
also, when you said that large cities attack small ones according to what's
just by nature, because they're superior and stronger, assuming that *superior*, *stronger* and *better* are the same. Or is it possible for one to be better
d   and also inferior and weaker, or greater but more wretched? Or do "better"
and "superior" have the same definition? Please define this for me clearly.
Are *superior*, *better* and *stronger* the same or are they different?

CALLICLES: Very well, I'm telling you clearly that they're the same.

SOCRATES: Now aren't the many superior by nature to the one? They're
the ones who in fact impose the laws upon the one, as you were saying
yourself a moment ago.

CALLICLES: Of course.

SOCRATES: So the rules of the many are the rules of the superior.

CALLICLES: Yes, they are.

e   SOCRATES: Aren't they the rules of the better? For by your reasoning, I
take it, the superior are the better.

CALLICLES: Yes.

SOCRATES: And aren't the rules of these people admirable by nature,
seeing that they're the superior ones?

CALLICLES: That's my view.

SOCRATES: Now, isn't it a rule of the many that it's just to have an equal
share and that doing what's unjust is more shameful than suffering it, as
489   you yourself were saying just now? Is this so or not? Be careful that you
in your turn don't get caught being ashamed now. Do the many observe
or do they not observe the rule that it's just to have an equal and not a
greater share, and that doing what's unjust is more shameful than suffering
it? Don't grudge me your answer to this, Callicles, so that if you agree with
me I may have my confirmation from you, seeing that it's the agreement of
a man competent to pass judgment.

CALLICLES: All right, the many do have that rule.

b   SOCRATES: It's not only by law, then, that doing what's unjust is more
shameful than suffering it, or just to have an equal share, but it's so by
nature, too. So it looks as though you weren't saying what's true earlier
and weren't right to accuse me when you said that nature and law were
opposed to each other and that I, well aware of this, am making mischief
in my statements, taking any statement someone makes meant in terms
of nature, in terms of law, and any statement meant in terms of law, in
terms of nature.

CALLICLES: This man will not stop talking nonsense! Tell me, Socrates,
aren't you ashamed, at your age, of trying to catch people's words and of
c   making hay out of someone's tripping on a phrase? Do you take me to
mean by people being *superior* anything else than their being *better*? Haven't

I been telling you all along that by "better" and "superior" I mean the same thing? Or do you suppose that I'm saying that if a rubbish heap of slaves and motley men, worthless except perhaps in physical strength, gets together and makes any statements, then these are the rules?

SOCRATES: Fair enough, wisest Callicles. Is this what you're saying?

CALLICLES: It certainly is.

SOCRATES: Well, my marvelous friend, I guessed some time ago that it's   d
some such thing you mean by "superior," and I'm questioning you because I'm intent upon knowing clearly what you mean. I don't really suppose that you think two are better than one or that your slaves are better than you just because they're stronger than you. Tell me once more from the beginning, what *do* you mean by the *better*, seeing that it's not the stronger? And, my wonderful man, go easier on me in your teaching, so that I won't quit your school.

CALLICLES: You're being ironic, Socrates.   e

SOCRATES: No I'm not, Callicles, by Zethus—the character you were invoking in being ironic with me so often just now! But come and tell me: whom do you mean by *the better*?

CALLICLES: I mean the worthier.

SOCRATES: So do you see that you yourself are uttering words, without making anything clear? Won't you say whether by *the better* and *the superior* you mean *the more intelligent*, or some others?

CALLICLES: Yes, by Zeus, they're very much the ones I mean.

SOCRATES: So on your reasoning it will often be the case that a single   490
intelligent person is superior to countless unintelligent ones, that this person should rule and they be ruled, and that the one ruling should have a greater share than the ones being ruled. This is the meaning I think you intend—and I'm not trying to catch you with a phrase—if the one is superior to these countless others.

CALLICLES: Yes, that's what I do mean. This is what I take the just by nature to be: that the better one, the more intelligent one, that is, both rules over and has a greater share than his inferiors.

SOCRATES: Hold it right there! What can your meaning be this time?   b
Suppose we were assembled together in great numbers in the same place, as we are now, and we held in common a great supply of food and drink, and suppose we were a motley group, some strong and some weak, but one of us, being a doctor, was more intelligent about these things. He would, very likely, be stronger than some and weaker than others. Now this man, being more intelligent than we are, will certainly be better and superior in these matters?

CALLICLES: Yes, he will.

SOCRATES: So should he have a share of this food greater than ours   c
because he's better? Or should he be the one to distribute everything because he's in charge, but not to get a greater share to consume and use up on his own body if he's to escape being punished for it? Shouldn't he,

instead, have a greater share than some and a lesser one than others, and if he should happen to be the weakest of all, shouldn't the best man have the least share of all, Callicles? Isn't this so, my good man?

d   CALLICLES: You keep talking of food and drink and doctors and such nonsense. That's not what I mean!

SOCRATES: Don't you mean that the more intelligent one is the better one? Say yes or no.

CALLICLES: Yes, I do.

SOCRATES: But not that the better should have a greater share?

CALLICLES: Not of food or drink, anyhow.

SOCRATES: I see. Of clothes, perhaps? Should the weaver have the biggest garment and go about wearing the greatest number and the most beautiful clothes?

CALLICLES: What do you mean, clothes?

SOCRATES: But when it comes to shoes, obviously the most intelligent,

e   the best man in that area should have the greater share. Perhaps the cobbler should walk around with the largest and greatest number of shoes on.

CALLICLES: What do you mean, shoes? You keep on with this nonsense!

SOCRATES: Well, if that's not the sort of thing you mean, perhaps it's this. Take a farmer, a man intelligent and admirable and good about land. Perhaps he should have the greater share of seed and use the largest possible quantity of it on his own land.

CALLICLES: How you keep on saying the same things, Socrates!

SOCRATES: Yes, Callicles, not only the same things, but also about the same subjects.

491   CALLICLES: By the gods! You simply don't let up on your continual talk of shoemakers and cleaners, cooks and doctors, as if our discussion were about them!

SOCRATES: Won't you say whom it's about, then? What does the superior, the more intelligent man have a greater share of, and have it justly? Will you neither bear with my promptings nor tell me yourself?

CALLICLES: I've been saying it all along. First of all, by the ones who are the superior I don't mean cobblers or cooks, but those who are intelligent

b   about the affairs of the city, about the way it's to be well managed. And not only intelligent, but also brave, competent to accomplish whatever they have in mind, without slackening off because of softness of spirit.

SOCRATES: Do you see, my good Callicles, that you and I are not accusing each other of the same thing? You claim that I'm always saying the same things, and you criticize me for it, whereas I, just the opposite of you, claim that you never say the same things about the same subjects. At one

c   time you were defining the better and the superior as the stronger, then again as the more intelligent, and now you've come up with something else again: the superior and the better are now said by you to be the braver. But tell me, my good fellow, once and for all, whom you mean by the better and the superior, and what they're better and superior in.

CALLICLES: But I've already said that I mean those who are intelligent in the affairs of the city, and brave, too. It's fitting that they should be the ones who rule their cities, and what's just is that they, as the rulers, should have a greater share than the others, the ruled.

SOCRATES: But what of themselves, my friend?

CALLICLES: What of *what*?

SOCRATES: Ruling or being ruled?

CALLICLES: What do you mean?

SOCRATES: I mean each individual ruling himself. Or is there no need at all for him to rule himself, but only to rule others?

CALLICLES: What do you mean, rule himself?

SOCRATES: Nothing very subtle. Just what the many mean: being self-controlled and master of oneself, ruling the pleasures and appetites within oneself.

CALLICLES: How delightful you are! By the self-controlled you mean the stupid ones!

SOCRATES: How so? There's no one who'd fail to recognize that I mean no such thing.

CALLICLES: Yes you do, Socrates, very much so. How could a man prove to be happy if he's enslaved to anyone at all? Rather, this is what's admirable and just by nature—and I'll say it to you now with all frankness—that the man who'll live correctly ought to allow his own appetites to get as large as possible and not restrain them. And when they are as large as possible, he ought to be competent to devote himself to them by virtue of his bravery and intelligence, and to fill them with whatever he may have an appetite for at the time. But this isn't possible for the many, I believe; hence, they become detractors of people like this because of the shame they feel, while they conceal their own impotence. And they say that lack of discipline is shameful, as I was saying earlier, and so they enslave men who are better by nature, and while they themselves lack the ability to provide for themselves fulfillment for their pleasures, their own lack of courage leads them to praise self-control and justice. As for all those who were either sons of kings to begin with or else naturally competent to secure some position of rule for themselves as tyrants or potentates, what in truth could be more shameful and worse than self-control and justice for these people who, although they are free to enjoy good things without any interference, should bring as master upon themselves the law of the many, their talk, and their criticism? Or how could they exist without becoming miserable under that "admirable" regime of justice and self-control, allotting no greater share to their friends than to their enemies, and in this way "rule" in their cities? Rather, the truth of it, Socrates—the thing you claim to pursue—is like this: wantonness, lack of discipline, and freedom, if available in good supply, are excellence and happiness; as for these other things, these fancy phrases, these contracts of men that go against nature, they're worthless nonsense!

d   SOCRATES: The way you pursue your argument, speaking frankly as you do, certainly does you credit, Callicles. For you are now saying clearly what others are thinking but are unwilling to say. I beg you, then, not to relax in any way, so that it may really become clear how we're to live. Tell me: are you saying that if a person is to be the kind of person he should be, he shouldn't restrain his appetites but let them become as large as possible and then should procure their fulfillment from some source or

e   other, and that this is excellence?

CALLICLES: Yes, that's what I'm saying.

SOCRATES: So then those who have no need of anything are wrongly said to be happy?

CALLICLES: Yes, for in that case stones and corpses would be happiest.

SOCRATES: But then the life of those people you call happiest is a strange one, too. I shouldn't be surprised that Euripides' lines are true when he says:

> But who knows whether being alive is being dead
> And being dead is being alive?

493   Perhaps in reality we're dead. Once I even heard one of the wise men say that we are now dead and that our bodies are our tombs, and that the part of our souls in which our appetites reside is actually the sort of thing to be open to persuasion and to shift back and forth. And hence some clever man, a teller of stories, a Sicilian, perhaps, or an Italian, named this part a jar [*pithos*], on account of its being a persuadable [*pithanon*] and

b   suggestible thing, thus slightly changing the name. And fools [*anoētoi*] he named uninitiated [*amuētoi*], suggesting that that part of the souls of fools where their appetites are located is their undisciplined part, one not tightly closed, a leaking jar, as it were. He based the image on its insatiability. Now this man, Callicles, quite to the contrary of your view, shows that of the people in Hades—meaning the unseen [*aïdes*]—these, the uninitiated ones, would be the most miserable. They would carry water into the leaking jar using another leaky thing, a sieve. That's why by the sieve he means

c   the soul (as the man who talked with me claimed). And because they leak, he likened the souls of fools to sieves; for their untrustworthiness and forgetfulness makes them unable to retain anything. This account is on the whole a bit strange; but now that I've shown it to you, it does make clear what I want to persuade you to change your mind about if I can: to choose the orderly life, the life that is adequate to and satisfied with its circumstances at any given time instead of the insatiable, undisciplined

d   life. Do I persuade you at all, and are you changing your mind to believe that those who are orderly are happier than those who are undisciplined, or, even if I tell you many other such stories, will you change it none the more for that?

CALLICLES: The latter thing you said is the truer, Socrates.

SOCRATES: Come then, and let me give you another image, one from the same school as this one. Consider whether what you're saying about each life, the life of the self-controlled man and that of the undisciplined one, is like this: Suppose there are two men, each of whom has many jars. The jars belonging to one of them are sound and full, one with wine, another   e with honey, a third with milk, and many others with lots of other things. And suppose that the sources of each of these things are scarce and difficult to come by, procurable only with much toil and trouble. Now the one man, having filled up his jars, doesn't pour anything more into them and gives them no further thought. He can relax over them. As for the other one, he too has resources that can be procured, though with difficulty, but his containers are leaky and rotten. He's forced to keep on filling them,   494 day and night, or else he suffers extreme pain. Now since each life is the way I describe it, are you saying that the life of the undisciplined man is happier than that of the orderly man? When I say this, do I at all persuade you to concede that the orderly life is better than the undisciplined one, or do I not?

CALLICLES: You do not, Socrates. The man who has filled himself up has no pleasure any more, and when he's been filled up and experiences neither joy nor pain, that's living like a stone, as I was saying just now. Rather,   b living pleasantly consists in this: having as much as possible flow in.

SOCRATES: Isn't it necessary, then, that if there's a lot flowing in, there should also be a lot going out and that there should be big holes for what's passed out?

CALLICLES: Certainly.

SOCRATES: Now you're talking about the life of a stonecurlew[13] instead of that of a corpse or a stone. Tell me, do you say that there is such a thing as hunger, and eating when one is hungry?

CALLICLES: Yes, there is.

SOCRATES: And thirst, and drinking when one is thirsty?   c

CALLICLES: Yes, and also having all other appetites and being able to fill them and enjoy it, and so live happily.

SOCRATES: Very good, my good man! Do carry on the way you've begun, and take care not to be ashamed. And I evidently shouldn't shrink from being ashamed, either. Tell me now first whether a man who has an itch and scratches it and can scratch to his heart's content, scratch his whole life long, can also live happily.

CALLICLES: What nonsense, Socrates. You're a regular crowd pleaser.   d

SOCRATES: That's just how I shocked Polus and Gorgias and made them be ashamed. You certainly won't be shocked, however, or be ashamed, for you're a brave man. Just answer me, please.

CALLICLES: I say that even the man who scratches would have a pleasant life.

SOCRATES: And if a pleasant one, a happy one, too?

CALLICLES: Yes indeed.

13. Dodds: "A bird of messy habits and uncertain identity."

e   SOCRATES: What if he scratches only his head—or what am I to ask you further? See what you'll answer if somebody asked you one after the other every question that comes next. And isn't the climax of this sort of thing, the life of a catamite,[14] a frightfully shameful and miserable one? Or will you have the nerve to say that they are happy as long as they have what they need to their hearts' content?

CALLICLES: Aren't you ashamed, Socrates, to bring our discussion to such matters?

SOCRATES: Is it I who bring them there, my splendid fellow, or is it the man who claims, just like that, that those who enjoy themselves, however
495   they may be doing it, are happy, and doesn't discriminate between good kinds of pleasures and bad? Tell me now too whether you say that the pleasant and the good are the same or whether there is some pleasure that isn't good.

CALLICLES: Well, to keep my argument from being inconsistent if I say that they're different, I say they're the same.

SOCRATES: You're wrecking your earlier statements, Callicles, and you'd no longer be adequately inquiring into the truth of the matter with me if you speak contrary to what you think.

b   CALLICLES: And you're wrecking yours, too, Socrates.

SOCRATES: In that case, it isn't right for me to do it, if it's what I do, or for you either. But consider, my marvelous friend, surely the good isn't just unrestricted enjoyment. For both those many shameful things hinted at just now obviously follow if this is the case, and many others as well.

CALLICLES: That's your opinion, Socrates.

SOCRATES: Do you really assert these things, Callicles?

CALLICLES: Yes, I do.

c   SOCRATES: So we're to undertake the discussion on the assumption that you're in earnest?

CALLICLES: Most certainly.

SOCRATES: All right, since that's what you think, distinguish the following things for me: There is something you call knowledge, I take it?

CALLICLES: Yes.

SOCRATES: Weren't you also saying just now that there is such a thing as bravery with knowledge?

CALLICLES: Yes, I was.

SOCRATES: Was it just on the assumption that bravery is distinct from knowledge that you were speaking of them as two?

CALLICLES: Yes, very much so.

SOCRATES: Well now, do you say that pleasure and knowledge are the same or different?

d   CALLICLES: Different of course, you wisest of men.

SOCRATES: And surely that bravery is different from pleasure, too?

14. Catamite: passive partner (esp. boy) in homosexual practices (*Oxford Dictionary of Current English*).

CALLICLES: Of course.

SOCRATES: All right, let's put this on the record: Callicles from Acharnae says that *pleasant* and *good* are the same, and that *knowledge* and *bravery* are different both from each other and from what's good.

CALLICLES: And Socrates from Alopece doesn't agree with us about this. Or does he?

SOCRATES: He does not. And I believe that Callicles doesn't either when   e
he comes to see himself rightly. Tell me: don't you think that those who do well have the opposite experience of those who do badly?

CALLICLES: Yes, I do.

SOCRATES: Now since these experiences are the opposites of each other, isn't it necessary that it's just the same with them as it is with health and disease? For a man isn't both healthy and sick at the same time, I take it, nor does he get rid of both health and disease at the same time.

CALLICLES: What do you mean?

SOCRATES: Take any part of the body you like, for example, and think   496
about it. A man can have a disease of the eyes, can't he, to which we give the name "eye disease"?

CALLICLES: Of course.

SOCRATES: But then surely his eyes aren't also healthy at the same time?

CALLICLES: No, not in any way.

SOCRATES: What if he gets rid of his eye disease? Does he then also get rid of his eyes' health and so in the end he's rid of both at the same time?

CALLICLES: No, not in the least.

SOCRATES: For that, I suppose, is an amazing and unintelligible thing to   b
happen, isn't it?

CALLICLES: Yes, it very much is.

SOCRATES: But he acquires and loses each of them successively, I suppose.

CALLICLES: Yes, I agree.

SOCRATES: Isn't it like this with strength and weakness, too?

CALLICLES: Yes.

SOCRATES: And with speed and slowness?

CALLICLES: Yes, that's right.

SOCRATES: Now, does he acquire and get rid of good things and happiness, and their opposites, bad things and misery, successively too?

CALLICLES: No doubt he does.

SOCRATES: So if we find things that a man both gets rid of and keeps at   c
the same time, it's clear that these things wouldn't be what's good and what's bad. Are we agreed on that? Think very carefully about it and tell me.

CALLICLES: Yes, I agree most emphatically.

SOCRATES: Go back, now, to what we've agreed on previously. You mentioned hunger—as a pleasant or a painful thing? I mean the hunger itself.

CALLICLES: As a painful thing. But for a hungry man to eat is pleasant.

d   SOCRATES: I agree. I understand. But the hunger itself is painful, isn't it?

CALLICLES: So I say.

SOCRATES: And thirst is, too?

CALLICLES: Very much so.

SOCRATES: Am I to ask any further, or do you agree that every deficiency and appetite is painful?

CALLICLES: I do. No need to ask.

SOCRATES: Fair enough. Wouldn't you say that, for a thirsty person, to drink is something pleasant?

CALLICLES: Yes, I would.

SOCRATES: And in the case you speak of, "a thirsty person" means "a person who's in pain," I take it?

e   CALLICLES: Yes.

SOCRATES: And drinking is a filling of the deficiency, and is a pleasure?

CALLICLES: Yes.

SOCRATES: Now, don't you mean that insofar as a person is drinking, he's feeling enjoyment?

CALLICLES: Very much so.

SOCRATES: Even though he's thirsty?

CALLICLES: Yes, I agree.

SOCRATES: Even though he's in pain?

CALLICLES: Yes.

SOCRATES: Do you observe the result, that when you say that a thirsty person drinks, you're saying that a person who's in pain simultaneously feels enjoyment? Or doesn't this happen simultaneously in the same place, in the soul or in the body as you like? I don't suppose it makes any difference which. Is this so or not?

CALLICLES: It is.

SOCRATES: But you do say that it's impossible for a person who's doing
497 well to be doing badly at the same time.

CALLICLES: Yes, I do.

SOCRATES: Yet you did agree that it's possible for a person in pain to feel enjoyment.

CALLICLES: Apparently.

SOCRATES: So, feeling enjoyment isn't the same as doing well, and being in pain isn't the same as doing badly, and the result is that what's pleasant turns out to be different from what's good.

CALLICLES: I don't know what your clever remarks amount to, Socrates.

SOCRATES: You do know. You're just pretending you don't, Callicles. Go just a bit further ahead.

CALLICLES: Why do you keep up this nonsense?

b   SOCRATES: So you'll know how wise you are in scolding me. Doesn't each of us stop being thirsty and stop feeling pleasure at the same time as a result of drinking?

CALLICLES: I don't know what you mean.

GORGIAS: Don't do that, Callicles! Answer him for our benefit too, so that the discussion may be carried through.

CALLICLES: But Socrates is always like this, Gorgias. He keeps questioning people on matters that are trivial, hardly worthwhile, and refutes them!

GORGIAS: What difference does that make to you? It's none of your business to appraise them, Callicles. You promised Socrates that he could try to refute you in any way he liked.

CALLICLES: Go ahead, then, and ask these trivial, petty questions, since that's what pleases Gorgias.   c

SOCRATES: You're a happy man, Callicles, in that you've been initiated into the greater mysteries before the lesser. I didn't think it was permitted. So answer where you left off, and tell me whether each of us stops feeling pleasure at the same time as he stops being thirsty.

CALLICLES: That's my view.

SOCRATES: And doesn't he also stop having pleasures at the same time as he stops being hungry or stops having the other appetites?

CALLICLES: That's so.

SOCRATES: Doesn't he then also stop having pains and pleasures at the   d
same time?

CALLICLES: Yes.

SOCRATES: But, he certainly doesn't stop having good things and bad things at the same time, as you agree. Don't you still agree?

CALLICLES: Yes I do. Why?

SOCRATES: Because it turns out that good things are not the same as pleasant ones, and bad things not the same as painful ones. For pleasant and painful things come to a stop simultaneously, whereas good things and bad ones do not, because they are in fact different things. How then could pleasant things be the same as good ones and painful things the same as bad ones?

Look at it this way, too, if you like, for I don't suppose that you agree with that argument, either. Consider this. Don't you call men good because   e
of the presence of good things in them, just as you call them good-looking because of the presence of good looks?

CALLICLES: Yes, I do.

SOCRATES: Well then, do you call foolish and cowardly men good? You didn't a while ago; you were then calling brave and intelligent ones good. Or don't you call these men good?

CALLICLES: Oh yes, I do.

SOCRATES: Well then, have you ever seen a foolish child feel enjoyment?

CALLICLES: Yes, I have.

SOCRATES: But you've never yet seen a foolish man feel enjoyment?

CALLICLES: Yes, I suppose I have. What's the point?

SOCRATES: Nothing. Just answer me.   498

CALLICLES: Yes, I've seen it.

SOCRATES: Well now, have you ever seen an intelligent man feel pain or enjoyment?

CALLICLES: Yes, I daresay I have.

SOCRATES: Now who feels pain or enjoyment more, intelligent men or foolish ones?

CALLICLES: I don't suppose there's a lot of difference.

SOCRATES: Good enough. Have you ever seen a cowardly man in combat?

CALLICLES: Of course I have.

SOCRATES: Well then, when the enemy retreated, who do you think felt enjoyment more, the cowards or the brave men?

b CALLICLES: Both felt it, I think; maybe the cowards felt it more. But if not, they felt it to pretty much the same degree.

SOCRATES: It makes no difference. So cowards feel enjoyment too?

CALLICLES: Oh yes, very much so.

SOCRATES: Fools do too, evidently.

CALLICLES: Yes.

SOCRATES: Now when the enemy advances, are the cowards the only ones to feel pain, or do the brave men do so too?

CALLICLES: They both do.

SOCRATES: To the same degree?

CALLICLES: Maybe the cowards feel it more.

SOCRATES: And when the enemy retreats, don't they feel enjoyment more?

CALLICLES: Maybe.

SOCRATES: So don't foolish men and intelligent ones, and cowardly men c and brave ones feel enjoyment and pain to pretty much the same degree, as you say, or cowardly men feel them more than brave ones?

CALLICLES: That's my view.

SOCRATES: But surely the intelligent and brave men are good and the cowardly and foolish are bad?

CALLICLES: Yes.

SOCRATES: Hence the degree of enjoyment and pain that good and bad men feel is pretty much the same.

CALLICLES: I agree.

SOCRATES: Now are good and bad men pretty much equally both good and bad, or are the bad ones even better?

d CALLICLES: By Zeus! I don't know what you mean.

SOCRATES: Don't you know that you say that the good men are good and the bad men bad because of the presence of good or bad things in them, and that the good things are pleasures and the bad ones pains?

CALLICLES: Yes, I do.

SOCRATES: Aren't good things, pleasures, present in men who feel enjoyment, if in fact they do feel it?

CALLICLES: Of course.

SOCRATES: Now aren't men who feel enjoyment good men, because good things are present in them?

CALLICLES: Yes.

SOCRATES: Well then, aren't bad things, pains, present in men who feel pain?

CALLICLES: They are.

e SOCRATES: And you do say that it's because of the presence of bad things that bad men are bad. Or don't you say this any more?

CALLICLES: Yes, I do.

SOCRATES: So all those who feel enjoyment are good, and all those who feel pain are bad.

CALLICLES: Yes, that's right.

SOCRATES: And those feeling them more are more so, those feeling them less are less so, and those feeling them to pretty much the same degree are good or bad to pretty much the same degree.

CALLICLES: Yes.

SOCRATES: Now aren't you saying that intelligent men and foolish ones, and cowardly and courageous ones, experience pretty much the same degree of enjoyment and pain, or even that cowardly ones experience more of it?

CALLICLES: Yes, I am.

SOCRATES: Join me, then, in adding up what follows for us from our agreements. They say it's an admirable thing to speak of and examine what's admirable "twice and even thrice." We say that the intelligent and brave man is good, don't we?

499

CALLICLES: Yes.

SOCRATES: And that the foolish and cowardly man is bad?

CALLICLES: Yes, that's right.

SOCRATES: And again, that the man who feels enjoyment is good?

CALLICLES: Yes.

SOCRATES: And the one experiencing pain is bad?

CALLICLES: Necessarily.

SOCRATES: And that the good and the bad man feel pain and enjoyment to the same degree, and that perhaps the bad man feels them even more?

CALLICLES: Yes.

SOCRATES: Doesn't it then turn out that the bad man is both good and bad to the same degree as the good man, or even that he's better? Isn't this what follows, along with those earlier statements, if one holds that pleasant things are the same as good things? Isn't this necessarily the case, Callicles?

b

CALLICLES: I've been listening to you for quite some time now, Socrates, and agreeing with you, while thinking that even if a person grants some point to you in jest, you gladly fasten on it, the way boys do. As though you really think that I or anybody else at all don't believe that some pleasures are better and others worse.

SOCRATES: Oh, Callicles! What a rascal you are. You treat me like a child. At one time you say that things are one way and at another that the same things are another way, and so you deceive me. And yet I didn't suppose at the beginning that I'd be deceived intentionally by you, because I assumed you were a friend. Now, however, I've been misled, and evidently have no choice but to "make the best with what I have," as the ancient proverb has it, and to accept what I'm given by you. The thing you're saying now, evidently, is that some pleasures are good while others are bad. Is that right?

c

d   CALLICLES: Yes.

SOCRATES: Are the good ones the beneficial ones, and the bad ones the harmful ones?

CALLICLES: Yes, that's right.

SOCRATES: And the beneficial ones are the ones that produce something good while the bad ones are those that produce something bad?

CALLICLES: That's my view.

SOCRATES: Now, do you mean pleasures like the ones we were just now mentioning in connection with the body, those of eating and drinking? Do some of these produce health in the body, or strength, or some other bodily excellence, and are these pleasures good, while those that produce

e   the opposites of these things are bad?

CALLICLES: That's right.

SOCRATES: And similarly, aren't some pains good and others bad, too?

CALLICLES: Of course.

SOCRATES: Now, shouldn't we both choose and act to have the good pleasures and pains?

CALLICLES: Yes, we should.

SOCRATES: But not the bad ones?

CALLICLES: Obviously.

SOCRATES: No, for Polus and I both thought, if you recall, that we should, surely, do all things for the sake of what's good.[15] Do you also think as we do that the end of all action is what's good, and that we should do all

500   other things for its sake, but not it for their sake? Are you voting on our side to make it three?

CALLICLES: Yes, I am.

SOCRATES: So we should do the other things, including pleasant things, for the sake of good things, and not good things for the sake of pleasant things.

CALLICLES: That's right.

SOCRATES: Now, is it for every man to pick out which kinds of pleasures are good ones and which are bad ones, or does this require a craftsman in each case?

CALLICLES: It requires a craftsman.

SOCRATES: Let's recall what I was actually saying to Polus and Gorgias.[16]

b   I was saying, if you remember, that there are some practices that concern themselves with nothing further than pleasure and procure only pleasure, practices that are ignorant about what's better and worse, while there are other practices that do know what's good and what's bad. And I placed the "knack" (not the craft) of pastry baking among those that are concerned with pleasure, and the medical craft among those concerned with what's good. And by Zeus, the god of friendship, Callicles, please don't think that you should jest with me either, or answer anything that comes to

15. At 468b.

16. At 464b–465a.

mind, contrary to what you really think, and please don't accept what you get from me as though I'm jesting! For you see, don't you, that our discussion's about this (and what would even a man of little intelligence take more seriously than this?), about the way we're supposed to live. Is it the way you urge me toward, to engage in these manly activities, to make speeches among the people, to practice oratory, and to be active in the sort of politics you people engage in these days? Or is it the life spent in philosophy? And in what way does this latter way of life differ from the former? Perhaps it's best to distinguish them, as I just tried to do; having done that and having agreed that these are two distinct lives, it's best to examine how they differ from each other, and which of them is the one we should live. Now perhaps you don't yet know what I'm talking about.

CALLICLES: No, I certainly don't.

SOCRATES: Well, I'll tell you more clearly. Given that we're agreed, you and I, that there is such a thing as *good* and such a thing as *pleasant* and that the pleasant is different from the good, and that there's a practice of each of them and a procedure for obtaining it, the quest for the pleasant on the one hand and that for the good on the other—give me first your assent to this point or withhold it. Do you assent to it?

CALLICLES: Yes, I do.

SOCRATES: Come then, and agree further with me about what I was saying to them too, if you think that what I said then was true. I was saying, wasn't I, that I didn't think that pastry baking is a craft, but a knack, whereas medicine is a craft. I said that the one, medicine, has investigated both the nature of the object it serves and the cause of the things it does, and is able to give an account of each of these. The other, the one concerned with pleasure, to which the whole of its service is entirely devoted, proceeds toward its object in a quite uncraftlike way, without having at all considered either the nature of pleasure or its cause. It does so completely irrationally, with virtually no discrimination. Through routine and knack it merely preserves the memory of what customarily happens, and that's how it also supplies its pleasures. So, consider first of all whether you think that this account is an adequate one and whether you think that there are also other, similar preoccupations in the case of the soul. Do you think that some of the latter are of the order of crafts and possess forethought about what's best for the soul, while others slight this and have investigated only, as in the other case, the soul's way of getting its pleasure, without considering which of the pleasures is better or worse, and without having any concerns about anything but mere gratification, whether for the better or for the worse? For my part, Callicles, I think there are such preoccupations, and I say that this sort of thing is flattery, both in the case of the body and that of the soul and in any other case in which a person may wait upon a pleasure without any consideration of what's better or worse. As for you, do you join us in subscribing to the same opinion on these matters or do you dissent from it?

CALLICLES: No, I won't dissent. I'm going along with you, both to expedite your argument and to gratify Gorgias here.

d   SOCRATES: Now is this the case with one soul only, and not with two or many?

CALLICLES: No, it's also the case with two or many.

SOCRATES: Isn't it also possible to gratify a group of souls collectively at one and the same time, without any consideration for what's best?

CALLICLES: Yes, I suppose so.

SOCRATES: Can you tell me which ones are the practices that do this? Better yet, if you like I'll ask you and you say yes for any which you think

e   falls in this group, and no for any which you think doesn't. Let's look at fluteplaying first. Don't you think that it's one of this kind, Callicles? That it merely aims at giving us pleasure without giving thought to anything else?

CALLICLES: Yes, I think so.

SOCRATES: Don't all such practices do that, too? Lyreplaying at competitions, for example?

CALLICLES: Yes.

SOCRATES: What about training choruses and composing dithyrambs? Doesn't that strike you as being something of the same sort? Do you think that Cinesias the son of Meles gives any thought to saying anything of a sort that might lead to the improvement of his audience, or to what is

502   likely to gratify the crowd of spectators?

CALLICLES: Clearly the latter, Socrates, at least in Cinesias' case.

SOCRATES: What about his father Meles? Do you think he sang to the lyre with a regard for what's best? Or did he fail to regard even what's most pleasant? For he inflicted pain upon his spectators with his singing. But consider whether you don't think that all singing to the lyre and composing of dithyrambs has been invented for the sake of pleasure.

CALLICLES: Yes, I do think so.

b   SOCRATES: And what about that majestic, awe-inspiring practice, the composition of tragedy? What is it after? Is the project, the intent of tragic composition merely the gratification of spectators, as you think, or does it also strive valiantly not to say anything that is corrupt, though it may be pleasant and gratifying to them, and to utter in both speech and song anything that might be unpleasant but beneficial, whether the spectators enjoy it or not? In which of these ways do you think tragedy is being composed?

c   CALLICLES: This much is obvious, Socrates, that it's more bent upon giving pleasure and upon gratifying the spectators.

SOCRATES: And weren't we saying just now that this sort of thing is flattery?

CALLICLES: Yes, we were.

SOCRATES: Well then, if one stripped away from the whole composition both melody, rhythm, and meter, does it turn out that what's left is only speeches?

CALLICLES: Necessarily.

SOCRATES: Aren't these speeches given to a large gathering of people?

CALLICLES: I agree.

SOCRATES: So poetry is a kind of popular harangue.[17]

CALLICLES: Apparently.   d

SOCRATES: And such popular harangue would be oratory, then. Or don't you think that poets practice oratory in the theatres?

CALLICLES: Yes, I do.

SOCRATES: So now we've discovered a popular oratory of a kind that's addressed to men, women, and children, slave and free alike. We don't much like it; we say that it's a flattering sort.

CALLICLES: Yes, that's right.

SOCRATES: Very well. What about the oratory addressed to the Athenian people and to those in other cities composed of free men? What is our   e
view of this kind? Do you think that orators always speak with regard to what's best? Do they always set their sights on making the citizens as good as possible through their speeches? Or are they also bent upon the gratification of the citizens and do they slight the common good for the sake of their own private good, and so keep company with the people trying solely to gratify them, without any thought at all for whether this will make them be better or worse?   503

CALLICLES: This issue you're asking about isn't just a simple one, for there are those who say what they do because they do care for the citizens, and there are also those like the ones you're talking about.

SOCRATES: That's good enough. For if this matter really has two parts to it, then one part of it would be flattery, I suppose, and shameful public harangue, while the other—that of getting the souls of the citizens to be as good as possible and of striving valiantly to say what is best, whether the audience will find it more pleasant or more unpleasant—is something admirable. But you've never seen this type of oratory—or, if you can   b
mention any orator of this sort, why haven't you let me also know who he is?

CALLICLES: No, by Zeus! I certainly can't mention any of our contemporary orators to you.

SOCRATES: Well then, can you mention anyone from former times through whom the Athenians are reputed to have become better after he began his public addresses, when previously they had been worse? I certainly don't know who this could be.

CALLICLES: What? Don't they tell you that Themistocles proved to be a   c
good man, and so did Cimon, Miltiades and Pericles who died just recently, and whom you've heard speak, too?

SOCRATES: Yes, Callicles, if the excellence you were speaking of earlier, the filling up of appetites, both one's own and those of others, is the true kind. But if this is not, and if what we were compelled to agree on in our subsequent discussion is the true kind instead—that a man should satisfy

---

17. Gk. *dēmēgoria*. A cognate noun, *dēmēgoros*, was translated "crowd pleaser" at 482c, where the cognate verb *dēmēgorein* was translated "playing to the crowd."

d   those of his appetites that, when they are filled up, make him better, and
not those that make him worse, and that this is a matter of craft—I don't
see how I can say that any of these men has proved to be such a man.

CALLICLES: But if you'll look carefully, you'll find that they were.[18]

SOCRATES: Let's examine the matter calmly and see whether any of these
men has proved to be like that. Well then, won't the good man, the man
e   who speaks with regard to what's best, say whatever he says not randomly
but with a view to something, just like the other craftsmen, each of whom
keeps his own product in view and so does not select and apply randomly
what he applies, but so that he may give his product some shape? Take
a look at painters for instance, if you would, or housebuilders or shipwrights or any of the other craftsmen you like, and see how each one
504 places what he does into a certain organization, and compels one thing to
be suited for another and to fit to it until the entire object is put together
in an organized and orderly way. The other craftsmen, too, including the
ones we were mentioning just lately, the ones concerned with the body,
physical trainers and doctors, no doubt give order and organization to the
body. Do we agree that this is so or not?

CALLICLES: Let's take it that way.

SOCRATES: So if a house gets to be organized and orderly it would be a
good one, and if it gets to be disorganized it would be a terrible one?

CALLICLES: I agree.

SOCRATES: This holds true for a boat, too?

b   CALLICLES: Yes.

SOCRATES: And we surely take it to hold true for our bodies, too?

CALLICLES: Yes, we do.

SOCRATES: What about the soul? Will it be a good one if it gets to be
disorganized, or if it gets to have a certain organization and order?

CALLICLES: Given what we said before, we must agree that this is so, too.

SOCRATES: What name do we give to what comes into being in the body
as a result of organization and order?

CALLICLES: You mean health and strength, presumably.

c   SOCRATES: Yes, I do. And which one do we give to what comes into
being in the soul as a result of organization and order? Try to find and
tell me its name, as in the case of the body.

CALLICLES: Why don't you say it yourself, Socrates?

SOCRATES: All right, if that pleases you more, I'll do so. And if you think
I'm right, give your assent. If not, refute me and don't give way. I think

18. There are variances in the mss in the text of the last two lines of Socrates' previous
speech and this response. The translation follows one ms, while the other mss, with a
conjectural addition of Dodds', would yield this: "SOCRATES: . . . and not those that
make him worse—and this seemed to us to be a matter of craft—can you say that any
of these men has proved to be such a man? CALLICLES: For my part, I don't know
what I would say. SOCRATES: But if you look carefully you'll find out. Let's examine
the matter calmly, then, and . . ."

that the name for the states of organization of the body is "healthy," as a result of which health and the rest of bodily excellence comes into being in it. Is this so or isn't it?

CALLICLES: It is.

SOCRATES: And the name for the states of organization and order of the soul is "lawful" and "law," which lead people to become law-abiding and orderly, and these are justice and self-control. Do you assent to this or not?

CALLICLES: Let it be so.

SOCRATES: So this is what that skilled and good orator will look to when he applies to people's souls whatever speeches he makes as well as all of his actions, and any gift he makes or any confiscation he carries out. He will always give his attention to how justice may come to exist in the souls of his fellow citizens and injustice be gotten rid of, how self-control may come to exist there and lack of discipline be gotten rid of, and how the rest of excellence may come into being there and badness may depart. Do you agree or not?

CALLICLES: I do.

SOCRATES: Yes, for what benefit is there, Callicles, in giving a body that's sick and in wretched shape lots of very pleasant food or drink or anything else when it won't do the man a bit more good, or, quite to the contrary, when by a fair reckoning it'll do him less good? Is that so?

CALLICLES: Let it be so.

SOCRATES: Yes, for I don't suppose that it profits a man to be alive with his body in a terrible condition, for this way his life, too, would be necessarily a wretched one. Or wouldn't it be?

CALLICLES: Yes.

SOCRATES: Now, isn't it also true that doctors generally allow a person to fill up his appetites, to eat when he's hungry, for example, or drink when he's thirsty as much as he wants to when he's in good health, but when he's sick they practically never allow him to fill himself with what he has an appetite for? Do you also go along with this point, at least?

CALLICLES: Yes, I do.

SOCRATES: And isn't it just the same way with the soul, my excellent friend? As long as it's corrupt, in that it's foolish, undisciplined, unjust and impious, it should be kept away from its appetites and not be permitted to do anything other than what will make it better. Do you agree or not?

CALLICLES: I agree.

SOCRATES: For this is no doubt better for the soul itself?

CALLICLES: Yes, it is.

SOCRATES: Now isn't keeping it away from what it has an appetite for, disciplining it?

CALLICLES: Yes.

SOCRATES: So to be disciplined is better for the soul than lack of discipline, which is what you yourself were thinking just now.

CALLICLES: I don't know what in the world you mean, Socrates. Ask somebody else.

SOCRATES: This fellow won't put up with being benefited and with his undergoing the very thing the discussion's about, with being disciplined.

CALLICLES: And I couldn't care less about anything you say, either. I gave you these answers just for Gorgias' sake.

SOCRATES: Very well. What'll we do now? Are we breaking off in the midst of the discussion?

CALLICLES: That's for you to decide.

SOCRATES: They say that it isn't permitted to give up in the middle of
d telling stories, either. A head must be put on it, so that it won't go about headless. Please answer the remaining questions, too, so that our discussion may get its head.

CALLICLES: How unrelenting you are, Socrates! If you'll listen to me, you'll drop this discussion or carry it through with someone else.

SOCRATES: Who else is willing? Surely we mustn't leave the discussion incomplete.

CALLICLES: Couldn't you go through the discussion by yourself, either by speaking in your own person or by answering your own questions?
e SOCRATES: In that case Epicharmus' saying applies to me: I prove to be sufficient, being "one man, for what two men were saying before."[19] But it looks as though I have no choice at all. Let's by all means do it that way then. I suppose that all of us ought to be contentiously eager to know what's true and what's false about the things we're talking about. That it should become clear is a good common to all. I'll go through the discussion,
506 then, and say how I think it is, and if any of you thinks that what I agree to with myself isn't so, you must object and refute me. For the things I say I certainly don't say with any knowledge at all; no, I'm searching together with you so that if my opponent clearly has a point, I'll be the first to concede it. I'm saying this, however, in case you think the discussion ought to be carried through to the end. If you don't want it to be, then let's drop it now and leave.
b GORGIAS: No, Socrates, I don't think we should leave yet. You must finish the discussion. It seems to me that the others think so, too. I myself certainly want to hear you go through the rest of it by yourself.

SOCRATES: All right, Gorgias. I myself would have been glad to continue my discussion with Callicles here, until I returned him Amphion's speech for that of Zethus. Well, Callicles, since you're not willing to join me in carrying the discussion through to the end, please do listen to me and
c interrupt if you think I'm saying anything wrong. And if you refute me, I shan't be upset with you as you were with me; instead you'll go on record as my greatest benefactor.

CALLICLES: Speak on, my good friend, and finish it up by yourself.

SOCRATES: Listen, then, as I pick up the discussion from the beginning. Is the pleasant the same as the good?—It isn't, as Callicles and I have agreed.—Is the pleasant to be done for the sake of the good, or the good

19. Epicharmus was a comic poet; the source of the line is not known.

for the sake of the pleasant?—The pleasant for the sake of the good.— And *pleasant* is that by which, when it's come to be present in us, we feel   d pleasure, and *good* that by which, when it's present in us, we are good?— That's right.—But surely we are good, both we and everything else that's good, when some excellence has come to be present in us?—Yes, I do think that that's necessarily so, Callicles.—But the best way in which the excellence of each thing comes to be present in it, whether it's that of an artifact or of a body or a soul as well, or of any animal, is not just any old way, but is due to whatever organization, correctness, and craftsmanship is bestowed on each of them. Is that right?—Yes, I agree.—So it's due to   e organization that the excellence of each thing is something which is organized and has order?—Yes, I'd say so.—So it's when a certain order, the proper one for each thing, comes to be present in it that it makes each of the things there are, good?—Yes, I think so.—So also a soul which has its own order is better than a disordered one?—Necessarily so.—But surely one that has order is an orderly one?—Of course it is.—And an orderly soul is a self-controlled one?—Absolutely.—So a self-controlled soul is a   507 good one. I for one can't say anything else beyond that, Callicles my friend; if you can, please teach me.

CALLICLES: Say on, my good man.

SOCRATES: I say that if the self-controlled soul is a good one, then a soul that's been affected the opposite way of the self-controlled one is a bad one. And this, it's turned out, is the foolish and undisciplined one.—That's right.—And surely a self-controlled person would do what's appropriate with respect to both gods and human beings. For if he does what's inappropriate, he wouldn't be self-controlled.—That's necessarily how it is.—And   b of course if he did what's appropriate with respect to human beings, he would be doing what's just, and with respect to gods he would be doing what's pious, and one who does what's just and pious must necessarily be just and pious.—That's so.—Yes, and he would also necessarily be brave, for it's not like a self-controlled man to either pursue or avoid what isn't appropriate, but to avoid and pursue what he should, whether these are things to do, or people, or pleasures and pains, and to stand fast and endure them where he should. So, it's necessarily very much the case,   c Callicles, that the self-controlled man, because he's just and brave and pious, as we've recounted, is a completely good man, that the good man does well and admirably whatever he does, and that the man who does well is blessed and happy, while the corrupt man, the one who does badly, is miserable. And this would be the one who's in the condition opposite to that of the self-controlled one, the undisciplined one whom you were praising.

So this is how I set down the matter, and I say that this is true. And if it is true, then a person who wants to be happy must evidently pursue and practice self-control. Each of us must flee away from lack of discipline   d as quickly as his feet will carry him, and must above all make sure that he has no need of being disciplined, but if he does have that need, either he himself or anyone in his house, either a private citizen or a whole city, he must pay his due and must be disciplined, if he's to be happy. This is the target which I think one should look to in living, and in his actions he should direct all of his own affairs and those of his city to the end that

e justice and self-control will be present in one who is to be blessed. He should not allow his appetites to be undisciplined or undertake to fill them up—that's interminably bad—and live the life of a marauder. Such a man could not be dear to another man or to a god, for he cannot be a partner, and where there's no partnership there's no friendship. Yes, Callicles, wise

508 men claim that partnership and friendship, orderliness, self-control, and justice hold together heaven and earth, and gods and men, and that is why they call this universe a *world order*, my friend, and not an undisciplined world-disorder. I believe that you don't pay attention to these facts, even though you're a wise man in these matters. You've failed to notice that proportionate equality has great power among both gods and men, and you suppose that you ought to practice getting the greater share. That's because you neglect geometry.

b   Very well. We must either refute this argument and show that it's not the possession of justice and self-control that makes happy people happy and the possession of badness that makes miserable people miserable, or else, if this is true, we must consider what the consequences are. These consequences are all those previous things, Callicles, the ones about which you asked me whether I was speaking in earnest when I said that a man should be his own accuser, or his son's or his friend's, if he's done anything unjust, and should use oratory for that purpose. Also what you thought Polus was ashamed to concede is true after all, that doing what's unjust

c is as much worse than suffering it as it is more shameful, and that a person who is to be an orator the right way should be just and be knowledgeable in what is just, the point Polus in his turn claimed Gorgias to have agreed to out of shame.

That being so, let's examine what it is you're taking me to task for, and whether it's right or not. You say that I'm unable to protect either myself or any of my friends or relatives or rescue them from the gravest dangers, and that I'm at the mercy of the first comer, just as people without rights are,

d whether he wants to knock me on the jaw, to use that forceful expression of yours, or confiscate my property, or exile me from the city, or ultimately put me to death. To be in that position is, by your reasoning, the most shameful thing of all. As for what my own reasoning is, that's been told many times by now, but there's nothing to stop its being told once again. I deny, Callicles, that being knocked on the jaw unjustly is the most shameful

e thing, or that having my body or my purse cut is, and I affirm that to knock or cut me or my possessions unjustly is both more shameful and worse, and at the same time that to rob or enslave me or to break into my house or, to sum up, to commit any unjust act at all against me and my possessions is both worse and more shameful for the one who does these unjust acts than it is for me, the one who suffers them. These conclusions, at which we arrived earlier in our previous discussions are, I'd say, held down and bound by arguments of iron and adamant, even if it's rather rude to say so. So it would seem, anyhow. And if you or someone more forceful than you won't undo them, then anyone who says anything other than what I'm now saying cannot be speaking well. And yet for my part, my account is ever the same: I don't know how these things are, but no one I've ever met, as in this case, can say anything else without being ridiculous. So once more I set it down that these things are so. And if they are—if injustice is the worst thing there is for the person committing it and if that person's failure to pay what's due is something even worse, if possible, than this one that's the greatest—what is the protection which would make a man who's unable to provide it for himself truly ridiculous? Isn't it the one that will turn away what harms us most? Yes, it's necessarily very much the case that this is the most shameful kind of protection not to be able to provide, either for oneself or for one's friends or relatives. And the second kind's the one that turns away the second worst thing, the third kind the one against the third worst, and so on. The greater by its nature each bad thing is, the more admirable it is to be able to provide protection against it, too, and the more shameful not to be able to. Is this the way it is, Callicles, or is it some other way?

CALLICLES: No, it's not any other way.

SOCRATES: Of these two things, then, of doing what's unjust and suffering it, we say that doing it is worse and suffering it is less bad. With what, then, might a man provide himself to protect himself so that he has both these benefits, the one that comes from not doing what's unjust and the one that comes from not suffering it? Is it power or wish? What I mean is this: Is it when a person doesn't wish to suffer what's unjust that he will avoid suffering it, or when he procures a power to avoid suffering it?

CALLICLES: When he procures a power. That is obvious, at least.

SOCRATES: And what about doing what's unjust? Is it when he doesn't wish to do it, is that sufficient—for he won't do it—or should he procure a power and a craft for this, too, so that unless he learns and practices it, he will commit injustice? Why don't you answer at least this question, Callicles? Do you think Polus and I were or were not correct in being compelled to agree in our previous discussion when we agreed that no one does what's unjust because he wants to, but that all who do so do it unwillingly?[20]

CALLICLES: Let it be so, Socrates, so you can finish up your argument.

SOCRATES: So we should procure a certain power and craft against this too, evidently, so that we won't do what's unjust.

CALLICLES: That's right.

SOCRATES: What, then, is the craft by which we make sure that we don't suffer anything unjust, or as little as possible? Consider whether you think it's the one I do. This is what I think it is: that one ought either to be a

20. Cf. 467c–468e.

ruler himself in his city or even be a tyrant, or else to be a partisan of the regime in power.

CALLICLES: Do you see, Socrates, how ready I am to applaud you when-

b ever you say anything right? I think that this statement of yours is right on the mark.

SOCRATES: Well, consider whether you think that the following statement of mine is a good one, too. I think that the one man who's a friend of another most of all is the one whom the men of old and the wise call a friend, the one who's like the other. Don't you think so, too?

CALLICLES: Yes, I do.

SOCRATES: Now, if in the case of a tyrant who's a savage, uneducated ruler, there were in his city someone much better than he, wouldn't the tyrant no doubt be afraid of him and never be able to be a friend to him

c with all his heart?

CALLICLES: That's so.

SOCRATES: Nor would he, the tyrant, be a friend to a man much his inferior, if there were such a man, for the tyrant would despise him and would never take a serious interest in him as a friend.

CALLICLES: That's true, too.

SOCRATES: This leaves only a man of like character, one who approves and disapproves of the same thing and who is willing to be ruled by and be subject to the ruler, to be to such a man a friend worth mentioning.

d This man will have great power in that city, and no one will do him any wrong and get away with it. Isn't that so?

CALLICLES: Yes.

SOCRATES: So, if some young person in that city were to reflect, "In what way would I be able to have great power and no one treat me unjustly?" this, evidently, would be his way to go: to get himself accustomed from childhood on to like and dislike the same things as the master, and to make sure that he'll be as like him as possible. Isn't that so?

CALLICLES: Yes.

SOCRATES: Now won't this man have achieved immunity to unjust treat-

e ment and great power in his city, as you people say?

CALLICLES: Oh, yes.

SOCRATES: And also immunity to unjust action? Or is that far from the case, since he'll be like the ruler who's unjust, and he'll have his great power at the ruler's side? For my part, I think that, quite to the contrary, in this way he'll be making sure he'll have the ability to engage in as much unjust action as possible and to avoid paying what's due for acting so. Right?

CALLICLES: Apparently.

511 SOCRATES: So he'll have incurred the worst thing there is, when his soul is corrupt and mutilated on account of his imitation of the master and on account of his "power."

CALLICLES: I don't know how you keep twisting our discussion in every direction, Socrates. Or don't you know that this "imitator" will put to death, if he likes, your "non-imitator," and confiscate his property?

SOCRATES: I do know that, Callicles. I'm not deaf. I hear you say it, and   b
heard Polus just now say it many times, and just about everyone else in
the city. But now you listen to me, too. I say that, yes, he'll kill him, if he
likes, but it'll be a wicked man killing one who's admirable and good.

CALLICLES: And isn't that just the most irritating thing about it?

SOCRATES: No, not for an intelligent person, anyway, as our discussion
points out. Or do you think that a man ought to make sure that his life
be as long as possible and that he practice those crafts that ever rescue us
from dangers, like the oratory that you tell me to practice, the kind that   c
preserves us in the law courts?

CALLICLES: Yes, and by Zeus, that's sound advice for you!

SOCRATES: Well, my excellent fellow, do you think that expertise in swimming is a grand thing?

CALLICLES: No, by Zeus, I don't.

SOCRATES: But it certainly does save people from death whenever they
fall into the kind of situation that requires this expertise. But if you think
this expertise is a trivial one, I'll give you one more important than it, that   d
of helmsmanship, which saves not only souls but also bodies and valuables
from the utmost dangers, just as oratory does. This expertise is unassuming
and orderly, and does not make itself grand, posturing as though its
accomplishment is so magnificent. But while its accomplishment is the
same as that of the expertise practiced in the courts, it has earned two
obols, I suppose, if it has brought people safely here from Aegina; and if
it has brought them here from Egypt or the Pontus,[21] then, for that great   e
service, having given safe passage to those I was mentioning just now,
the man himself, his children, valuables, and womenfolk, and setting them
ashore in the harbor, it has earned two drachmas, if that much.[22] And
the man who possesses the craft and who has accomplished these feats,
disembarks and goes for a stroll along the seaside and beside his ship,
with a modest air. For he's enough of an expert, I suppose, to conclude
that it isn't clear which ones of his fellow voyagers he has benefited by
not letting them drown in the deep, and which ones he has harmed,
knowing that they were no better in either body or soul when he set them   512
ashore than they were when they embarked. So he concludes that if a man
afflicted with serious incurable physical diseases did not drown, this man
is miserable for not dying and has gotten no benefit from him. But if a
man has many incurable diseases in what is more valuable than his body,
his soul, life for that man is not worth living, and he won't do him any
favor if he rescues him from the sea or from prison or from anywhere
else. He knows that for a corrupt person it's better not to be alive, for he   b
necessarily lives badly.

21. A region along the southern shore of the Black Sea.

22. A drachma is six obols. In 409–406 B.C. the standard daily wage of a laborer was
one drachma.

That is why it's not the custom for the helmsman to give himself glory even though he preserves us, and not the engineer either, who sometimes can preserve us no less well than a general or anyone else, not to mention a helmsman. For there are times when he preserves entire cities. You don't think that he's on a level with the advocate, do you? And yet if he wanted

c   to say what you people do, Callicles, glorifying his occupation, he would smother you with speeches, telling you urgently that people should become engineers, because nothing else amounts to anything. And the speech would make his point. But you nonetheless despise him and his craft, and you'd call him "engineer" as a term of abuse. You'd be unwilling either to give your daughter to his son, or take his daughter yourself. And yet, given your grounds for applauding your own activities, what just reason

d   do you have for despising the engineer and the others whom I was mentioning just now? I know that you'd say that you're a better man, one from better stock. But if "better" does not mean what I take it to mean, and if instead to preserve yourself and what belongs to you, no matter what sort of person you happen to be, is what excellence is, then your reproach against engineer, doctor, and all the other crafts which have been devised to preserve us will prove to be ridiculous. But, my blessed man, please see whether what's noble and what's good isn't something other than

e   preserving and being preserved. Perhaps one who is truly a man should stop thinking about how long he will live. He should not be attached to life but should commit these concerns to the god and believe the women who say that not one single person can escape fate. He should thereupon give consideration to how he might live the part of his life still before him

513   as well as possible. Should it be by becoming like the regime under which he lives? In that case you should now be making yourself as much like the Athenian people as possible if you expect to endear yourself to them and have great power in the city. Please see whether this profits you and me, my friend, so that what they say happens to the Thessalian witches when they pull down the moon[23] won't happen to us. Our choice of this kind of civic power will cost us what we hold most dear. If you think that some person or other will hand you a craft of the sort that will give you

b   great power in this city while you are unlike the regime, whether for better or for worse, then in my opinion, Callicles, you're not well advised. You mustn't be their imitator but be naturally like them in your own person if you expect to produce any genuine result toward winning the friendship of the Athenian people [*demos*] and, yes, by Zeus, of Demos the son of Pyrilampes to boot. Whoever then turns you out to be most like these men, he'll make you a politician in the way you desire to be one, and an

c   orator, too. For each group of people takes delight in speeches that are given in its own character, and resents those given in an alien manner— unless you say something else, my dear friend. Can we say anything in reply to this, Callicles?

23. That is, causing an eclipse.

CALLICLES: I don't know, Socrates—in a way you seem to me to be right, but the thing that happens to most people has happened to me: I'm not really persuaded by you.

SOCRATES: It's your love for the people, Callicles, existing in your soul, that stands against me. But if we closely examine these same matters often and in a better way, you'll be persuaded. Please recall that we said that there are two practices for caring for a particular thing, whether it's the body or the soul.[24] One of them deals with pleasure and the other with what's best and doesn't gratify it but struggles against it. Isn't this how we distinguished them then?

CALLICLES: Yes, that's right.

SOCRATES: Now one of them, the one dealing with pleasure, is ignoble and is actually nothing but flattery, right?

CALLICLES: Let it be so, if you like.

SOCRATES: Whereas the other one, the one that aims to make the thing we're caring for, whether it's a body or a soul, as good as possible, is the more noble one?

CALLICLES: Yes, that's so.

SOCRATES: Shouldn't we then attempt to care for the city and its citizens with the aim of making the citizens themselves as good as possible? For without this, as we discovered earlier, it does no good to provide any other service if the intentions of those who are likely to make a great deal of money or take a position of rule over people or some other position of power aren't admirable and good. Are we to put this down as true?

CALLICLES: Certainly, if that pleases you more.

SOCRATES: Suppose, then, Callicles, that you and I were about to take up the public business of the city, and we called on each other to carry out building projects—the major works of construction: walls, or ships, or temples—would we have to examine and check ourselves closely, first, to see if we are or are not experts in the building craft, and whom we've learned it from? Would we have to, or wouldn't we?

CALLICLES: Yes, we would.

SOCRATES: And, second, we'd have to check, wouldn't we, whether we've ever built a work of construction in private business, for a friend of ours, say, or for ourselves, and whether this structure is admirable or disgraceful. And if we discovered on examination that our teachers have proved to be good and reputable ones, and that the works of construction built by us under their guidance were numerous and admirable, and those built by us on our own after we left our teachers were numerous, too, then, if that were our situation, we'd be wise to proceed to public projects. But if we could point out neither teacher nor construction works, either none at all or else many worthless ones, it would surely be stupid to undertake public projects and to call each other on to them. Shall we say that this point is right, or not?

24. At 500b.

CALLICLES: Yes, we shall.

SOCRATES: Isn't it so in all cases, especially if we attempted to take up public practice and called on each other, thinking we were capable doctors? I'd have examined you, and you me, no doubt: "Well now, by the gods! What is Socrates' own physical state of health? Has there ever been anyone else, slave or free man, whose deliverance from illness has been due to Socrates?" And I'd be considering other similar questions about you, I

e   suppose. And if we found no one whose physical improvement has been due to us, among either visitors or townspeople, either a man or a woman, then by Zeus, Callicles, wouldn't it be truly ridiculous that people should advance to such a height of folly that, before producing many mediocre as well as many successful results in private practice and before having had sufficient exercise at the craft, they should attempt to "learn pottery on the big jar," as that saying goes, and attempt both to take up public practice themselves and to call on others like them to do so as well? Don't you think it would be stupid to proceed like that?

CALLICLES: Yes, I do.

515   SOCRATES: But now, my most excellent fellow, seeing that you yourself are just now beginning to be engaged in the business of the city and you call on me and take me to task for not doing so, shall we not examine each other? "Well now, has Callicles ever improved any of the citizens? Is there anyone who was wicked before, unjust, undisciplined, and foolish, a visitor or townsman, a slave or free man, who because of Callicles has turned out admirable and good?" Tell me, Callicles, what will you say if

b   somebody asks you these scrutinizing questions? Whom will you say you've made a better person through your association with him? Do you shrink back from answering—if there even *is* anything you produced while still in private practice before attempting a public career?

CALLICLES: You love to win, Socrates.

SOCRATES: But it's not for love of winning that I'm asking you. It's rather because I really do want to know the way, whatever it is, in which you

c   suppose the city's business ought to be conducted among us. Now that you've advanced to the business of the city, are we to conclude that you're devoted to some objective other than that we, the citizens, should be as good as possible? Haven't we agreed many times already that this is what a man active in politics should be doing? Have we or haven't we? Please answer me. Yes we have. (I'll answer for you.) So, if this is what a good man should make sure about for his own city, think back now to those men whom you were mentioning a little earlier and tell me whether you

d   still think that Pericles, Cimon, Miltiades, and Themistocles have proved to be good citizens.

CALLICLES: Yes, I do.

SOCRATES: So if they were good ones, each of them was obviously making the citizens better than they were before. Was he or wasn't he?

CALLICLES: Yes.

SOCRATES: So when Pericles first began giving speeches among the people, the Athenians were worse than when he gave his last ones?

CALLICLES: Presumably.

SOCRATES: Not "presumably," my good man. It necessarily follows from what we've agreed, if he really was a good citizen.

CALLICLES: So what?

SOCRATES: Nothing. But tell me this as well. Are the Athenians said to have become better because of Pericles, or, quite to the contrary, are they said to have been corrupted by him? That's what *I* hear, anyhow, that Pericles made the Athenians idle and cowardly, chatterers and money-grubbers, since he was the first to institute wages for them.

CALLICLES: The people you hear say this have cauliflower ears, Socrates.

SOCRATES: Here, though, is something I'm not just hearing. I do know clearly and you do, too, that at first Pericles had a good reputation, and when they were worse, the Athenians never voted to convict him in any shameful deposition. But after he had turned them into "admirable and good" people, near the end of his life, they voted to convict Pericles of embezzlement and came close to condemning him to death, because they thought he was a wicked man, obviously.

CALLICLES: Well? Did that make Pericles a bad man?

SOCRATES: A man like that who cared for donkeys or horses or cattle would at least look bad if he showed these animals kicking, butting, and biting him because of their wildness, when they had been doing none of these things when he took them over. Or don't you think that any caretaker of any animal is a bad one who will show his animals to be wilder than when he took them over, when they were gentler? Do you think so or not?

CALLICLES: Oh yes, so I may gratify you.

SOCRATES: In that case gratify me now with your answer, too. Is man one of the animals, too?

CALLICLES: Of course he is.

SOCRATES: Wasn't Pericles a caretaker of men?

CALLICLES: Yes.

SOCRATES: Well? Shouldn't he, according to what we agreed just now, have turned them out more just instead of more unjust, if while he cared for them he really was good at politics?

CALLICLES: Yes, he should have.

SOCRATES: Now as Homer says, the just are gentle.[25] What do you say? Don't you say the same?

CALLICLES: Yes.

SOCRATES: But Pericles certainly showed them to be wilder than they were when he took them over, and that toward himself, the person he'd least want this to happen to.

25. Apparently a reference to the formulaic expression, "wild and not just," which occurs three times in the *Odyssey* (vi.120; ix.175; xiii.201).

860

CALLICLES: Do you want me to agree with you?

SOCRATES: Yes, if you think that what I say is true.

CALLICLES: So be it, then.

SOCRATES: And if wilder, then both more unjust and worse?

d   CALLICLES: So be it.

SOCRATES: So on this reasoning Pericles wasn't good at politics.

CALLICLES: You at least deny that he was.

SOCRATES: By Zeus, you do, too, given what you were agreeing to. Let's go back to Cimon. Tell me: didn't the people he was serving ostracize him so that they wouldn't hear his voice for ten years? And didn't they do the very same thing to Themistocles, punishing him with exile besides? And didn't they vote to throw Miltiades, of Marathon fame, into the pit, and

e   if it hadn't been for the prytanis he would have been thrown in?[26] And yet these things would not have happened to these men if they were good men, as you say they were. At least it's not the case that good drivers are the ones who at the start don't fall out of their chariots but who do fall out after they've cared for their horses and become better drivers themselves. This doesn't happen either in driving or in any other work. Or do you think it does?

CALLICLES: No, I don't.

517 SOCRATES: So it looks as though our earlier statements were true, that we don't know any man who has proved to be good at politics in this city. You were agreeing that none of our present-day ones has, though you said that some of those of times past had, and you gave preference to these men. But these have been shown to be on equal footing with the men of today. The result is that if these men were orators, they practiced neither the true oratory—for in that case they wouldn't have been thrown out—nor the flattering kind.

CALLICLES: But surely, Socrates, any accomplishment that any of our present-day men produces is a far cry from the sorts of accomplishments

b   produced by any one of the others you choose.

SOCRATES: No, my strange friend, I'm not criticizing these men either, insofar as they were servants of the city. I think rather that they proved to be better servants than the men of today, and more capable than they of satisfying the city's appetites. But the truth is that in redirecting its appetites and not giving in to them, using persuasion or constraint to get

c   the citizens to become better, they were really not much different from our contemporaries. That alone is the task of a good citizen. Yes, I too agree with you that they were more clever than our present leaders at supplying ships and walls and dockyards and many other things of the sort.

Now you and I are doing an odd thing in our conversation. The whole time we've been discussing, we constantly keep drifting back to the same point, neither of us recognizing what the other is saying. For my part, I

26. The *prytanis* was that member of the officiating tribe in the Council chosen daily by lot to preside over the Council and the Assembly.

believe you've agreed many times and recognized that after all this subject of ours has two parts, both in the case of the body and the soul. The one part of it is the servient one, enabling us to provide our bodies with food whenever they're hungry or with drink whenever they're thirsty, and whenever they're cold, with clothes, wraps, shoes, and other things our bodies come to have an appetite for. I'm purposely using the same examples in speaking to you, so that you'll understand more easily. For these, I think you agree, are the very things a shopkeeper, importer, or producer can provide, a breadbaker or pastrychef, a weaver or cobbler or tanner, so it isn't at all surprising that such a person should think himself and be thought by others to be a caretaker of the body—by everyone who doesn't know that over and above all these practices there's a craft, that of gymnastics and medicine, that really does care for the body and is entitled to rule all these crafts and use their products because of its knowledge of what food or drink is good or bad for bodily excellence, a knowledge which all of the others lack. That's why the other crafts are slavish and servient and ill-bred, and why gymnastics and medicine are by rights mistresses over them. Now, when I say that these same things hold true of the soul, too, I think you sometimes understand me, and you agree as one who knows what I'm saying. But then a little later you come along saying that there have been persons who've proved to be admirable and good citizens in the city, and when I ask who they are, you seem to me to produce people who in the area of politics are very much the same sort you would produce if I asked you, "Who have proved to be or are good caretakers of bodies?" and you replied in all seriousness, "Thearion the breadbaker, and Mithaecus the author of the book on Sicilian pastry baking, and Sarambus the shopkeeper, because these men have proved to be wonderful caretakers of bodies, the first by providing wonderful loaves of bread, the second pastry, and the third wine."

Perhaps you'd be upset if I said to you, "My man, you don't have the slightest understanding of gymnastics. The men you're mentioning to me are servants, satisfiers of appetites! They have no understanding whatever of anything that's admirable and good in these cases. They'll fill and fatten people's bodies, if they get the chance, and besides that, destroy their original flesh as well, all the while receiving their praise! The latter, in their turn, thanks to their inexperience, will lay the blame for their illnesses and the destruction of their original flesh not on those who threw the parties, but on any people who happen to be with them at the time giving them advice. Yes, when that earlier stuffing has come bringing sickness in its train much later, then, because it's proved to be unhealthy, they'll blame these people and scold them and do something bad to them if they can, and they'll sing the praises of those earlier people, the ones responsible for their ills. Right now you're operating very much like that, too, Callicles. You sing the praises of those who threw parties for these people, and who feasted them lavishly with what they had an appetite for. And they say that *they* have made the city great! But that the city is swollen and festering,

d

e

518

b

c

d

e

519

thanks to those early leaders, that they don't notice. For they filled the city with harbors and dockyards, walls, and tribute payments and such trash as that, but did so without justice and self-control. So, when that fit of sickness comes on, they'll blame their advisers of the moment and sing the praises of Themistocles and Cimon and Pericles, the ones who are to blame for their ills. Perhaps, if you're not careful, they'll lay their hands

b   on you, and on my friend Alcibiades, when they lose not only what they gained but what they had originally as well, even though you aren't responsible for their ills but perhaps accessories to them.

And yet there's a foolish business that I, for one, both see happening now and hear about in connection with our early leaders. For I notice that whenever the city lays its hands on one of its politicians because he does what's unjust, they resent it and complain indignantly that they're suffering terrible things. They've done many good things for the city, and so they're

c   being unjustly brought to ruin by it, so their argument goes. But that's completely false. Not a single city leader could ever be brought to ruin by the very city he's the leader of. It looks as though those who profess to be politicians are just like those who profess to be sophists. For sophists, too, even though they're wise in other matters, do this absurd thing: while they claim to be teachers of excellence, they frequently accuse their students of doing them wrong, depriving them of their fees and withholding other forms of thanks from them, even though the students have been well served by them. Yet what could be a more illogical business than this

d   statement, that people who've become good and just, whose injustice has been removed by their teacher and who have come to possess justice, should wrong him—something they can't do? Don't you think that's absurd, my friend? You've made me deliver a real popular harangue, Callicles, because you aren't willing to answer.

CALLICLES: And you couldn't speak unless somebody answered you?

e   SOCRATES: Evidently I could. Anyhow I *am* stretching my speeches out at length now, since you're unwilling to answer me. But, my good man, tell me, by the god of friendship: don't you think it's illogical that someone who says he's made someone else good should find fault with that person, charging that he, whom he himself made to become and to be good, is after all wicked?

CALLICLES: Yes, I do think so.

SOCRATES: Don't you hear people who say they're educating people for excellence saying things like that?

520   CALLICLES: Yes, I do. But why would you mention completely worthless people?

SOCRATES: Why would you talk about those people who, although they say they're the city's leaders and devoted to making it as good as possible, turn around and accuse it, when the time comes, of being the most wicked? Do you think they're any different from those others? Yes, my blessed man, they are one and the same, the sophist and the orator, or nearly so and pretty similar, as I was telling Polus. But because you don't see this,

you suppose that one of them, oratory, is something wonderful, while you   b
sneer at the other. In actuality, however, sophistry is more to be admired
than oratory, insofar as legislation is more admirable than the administration of justice, and gymnastics more than medicine. And I, for one, should
have supposed that public speakers and sophists are the only people not
in a position to charge the creature they themselves educate with being
wicked to them, or else they simultaneously accuse themselves as well,
by this same argument, of having entirely failed to benefit those whom
they say they benefit. Isn't this so?

CALLICLES: Yes, it is.   c

SOCRATES: And if what I was saying is true, then they alone, no doubt,
are in a position to offer on terms of honor the benefit they provide—
without charge, as is reasonable. For somebody who had another benefit
conferred on him, one who, for example, had been turned into a fast runner
by a physical trainer, could perhaps deprive the man of his compensation
if the trainer offered him that benefit on his honor, instead of agreeing on
a fixed fee and taking his money as closely as possible to the time he   d
imparts the speed. For I don't suppose that it's by slowness that people
act unjustly, but by injustice. Right?

CALLICLES: Yes.

SOCRATES: So if somebody removes that very thing, injustice, he shouldn't
have any fear of being treated unjustly. For him alone is it safe to offer
this benefit on terms of honor, if it's really true that one can make people
good. Isn't that so?

CALLICLES: I agree.

SOCRATES: This, then, is evidently why there's nothing shameful in taking
money for giving advice concerning other matters such as housebuilding
or the other crafts.

CALLICLES: Yes, evidently.   e

SOCRATES: But as for this activity, which is concerned with how a person
might be as good as possible and manage his own house or his city in
the best possible way, it's considered shameful to refuse to give advice
concerning it unless somebody pays you money. Right?

CALLICLES: Yes.

SOCRATES: For it's clear that what accounts for this is the fact that of all
the benefits this one alone makes the one who has had good done to him
have the desire to do good in return, so that we think it's a good sign of
someone's having done good by conferring this benefit that he'll have
good done to him in return, and not a good sign if he won't. Is this how
it is?

CALLICLES: It is.   521

SOCRATES: Now, please describe for me precisely the type of care for the
city to which you are calling me. Is it that of striving valiantly with the
Athenians to make them as good as possible, like a doctor, or is it like
one ready to serve them and to associate with them for their gratification?
Tell me the truth, Callicles. For just as you began by speaking candidly

to me, it's only fair that you should continue speaking your mind. Tell me now, too, well and nobly.

CALLICLES: In that case I say it's like one ready to serve.

b SOCRATES: So, noblest of men, you're calling on me to be ready to flatter.

CALLICLES: Yes, if you find it more pleasant not to mince words, Socrates. Because if you don't do this—

SOCRATES: I hope you won't say what you've said many times, that anyone who wants to will put me to death. That way I, too, won't repeat my claim that it would be a wicked man doing this to a good man. And don't say that he'll confiscate any of my possessions, either, so I won't reply that when he's done so he won't know how to use them. Rather, just as he unjustly confiscated them from me, so, having gotten them, he'll

c use them unjustly too, and if unjustly, shamefully, and if shamefully, badly.

CALLICLES: How sure you seem to me to be, Socrates, that not even one of these things will happen to you! You think that you live out of their way and that you wouldn't be brought to court perhaps by some very corrupt and mean man.

SOCRATES: In that case I really am a fool, Callicles, if I don't suppose that anything might happen to anybody in this city. But I know this well: that

d if I do come into court involved in one of those perils which you mention, the man who brings me in will be a wicked man—for no good man would bring in a man who is not a wrongdoer—and it wouldn't be at all strange if I were to be put to death. Would you like me to tell you my reason for expecting this?

CALLICLES: Yes, I would.

SOCRATES: I believe that I'm one of a few Athenians—so as not to say I'm the only one, but the only one among our contemporaries—to take up the true political craft and practice the true politics. This is because the speeches I make on each occasion do not aim at gratification but at what's

e best. They don't aim at what's most pleasant. And because I'm not willing to do those clever things you recommend, I won't know what to say in court. And the same account I applied to Polus comes back to me. For I'll be judged the way a doctor would be judged by a jury of children if a pastry chef were to bring accusations against him. Think about what a man like that, taken captive among these people, could say in his defense, if somebody were to accuse him and say, "Children, this man has worked many great evils on you, yes, on you. He destroys the youngest among

522 you by cutting and burning them, and by slimming them down and choking them he confuses them. He gives them the most bitter potions to drink and forces hunger and thirst on them. He doesn't feast you on a great variety of sweets the way I do!" What do you think a doctor, caught in such an evil predicament, could say? Or if he should tell them the truth and say, "Yes, children, I was doing all those things in the interest of health," how big an uproar do you think such "judges" would make? Wouldn't it be a loud one?

CALLICLES: Perhaps so.

SOCRATES: I should think so! Don't you think he'd be at a total loss as   b
to what he should say?

CALLICLES: Yes, he would be.

SOCRATES: That's the sort of thing I know would happen to me, too, if
I came into court. For I won't be able to point out any pleasures that I've
provided for them, ones they believe to be services and benefits, while I
envy neither those who provide them nor the ones for whom they're
provided. Nor will I be able to say what's true if someone charges that I
ruin younger people by confusing them or abuse older ones by speaking
bitter words against them in public or private. I won't be able to say, that
is, "Yes, I say and do all these things in the interest of justice, my 'honored   b
judges' "—to use that expression you people use—nor anything else. So
presumably I'll get whatever comes my way.

CALLICLES: Do you think, Socrates, that a man in such a position in his
city, a man who's unable to protect himself, is to be admired?

SOCRATES: Yes, Callicles, as long as he has that one thing that you've
often agreed he should have: as long as he has protected himself against
having spoken or done anything unjust relating to either men or gods.
For this is the self-protection that you and I often have agreed avails the   d
most. Now if someone were to refute me and prove that I am unable to
provide *this* protection for myself or for anyone else, I would feel shame
at being refuted, whether this happened in the presence of many or of a
few, or just between the two of us; and if I were to be put to death for
lack of this ability, I really would be upset. But if I came to my end because
of a deficiency in flattering oratory, I know that you'd see me bear my
death with ease. For no one who isn't totally bereft of reason and courage   e
is afraid to die; doing what's unjust is what he's afraid of. For to arrive
in Hades with one's soul stuffed full of unjust actions is the ultimate of
all bad things. If you like, I'm willing to give you an account showing that
this is so.

CALLICLES: All right, since you've gone through the other things, go
through this, too.

SOCRATES: Give ear then—as they put it—to a very fine account. You'll   523
think that it's a mere tale, I believe, although I think it's an account, for
what I'm about to say I will tell you as true. As Homer tells it, after Zeus,
Posidon, and Pluto took over the sovereignty from their father, they divided
it among themselves. Now there was a law concerning human beings
during Cronus' time, one that gods even now continue to observe, that
when a man who has lived a just and pious life comes to his end, he goes
to the Isles of the Blessed, to make his abode in complete happiness, beyond   b
the reach of evils, but when one who has lived in an unjust and godless
way dies, he goes to the prison of payment and retribution, the one
they call Tartarus. In Cronus' time, and even more recently during Zeus'
tenure of sovereignty, these men faced living judges while they were still
alive, who judged them on the day they were going to die. Now the cases
were badly decided, so Pluto and the keepers from the Isles of the Blessed

came to Zeus and told him that people were undeservingly making their
c   way in both directions. So Zeus said, "All right, I'll put a stop to that. The
cases are being badly decided at this time because those being judged are
judged fully dressed. They're being judged while they're still alive. Many,"
he said, "whose souls are wicked are dressed in handsome bodies, good
stock and wealth, and when the judgment takes place they have many
witnesses appear to testify that they have lived just lives. Now the judges
d   are awestruck by these things and pass judgment at a time when they
themselves are fully dressed, too, having put their eyes and ears and their
whole bodies up as screens in front of their souls. All these things, their
own clothing and that of those being judged, have proved to be obstructive
to them. What we must do first," he said, "is to stop them from knowing
their death ahead of time. Now they do have that knowledge. This is
e   something that Prometheus has already been told to put a stop to. Next,
they must be judged when they're stripped naked of all these things, for
they should be judged when they're dead. The judge, too, should be naked,
and dead, and with only his soul he should study only the soul of each
person immediately upon his death, when he's isolated from all his kinsmen and has left behind on earth all that adornment, so that the judgment
may be a just one. Now I, realizing this before you did, have already
appointed my sons as judges, two from Asia, Minos and Rhadamanthus,
524   and one from Europe, Aeacus. After they've died, they'll serve as judges
in the meadow, at the three-way crossing from which the two roads go
on, the one to the Isles of the Blessed and the other to Tartarus. Rhadamanthus will judge the people from Asia and Aeacus those from Europe.
I'll give seniority to Minos to render final judgment if the other two are
at all perplexed, so that the judgment concerning the passage of humankind
may be as just as possible."

b   This, Callicles, is what I've heard, and I believe that it's true. And on
the basis of these accounts I conclude that something like this takes place:
Death, I think, is actually nothing but the separation of two things from
each other, the soul and the body. So, after they're separated, each of them
stays in a condition not much worse than what it was in when the person
was alive. The body retains its nature, and the care it had received as well
c   as the things that have happened to it are all evident. If a man had a body,
for instance, which was large (either by nature or through nurture, or both)
while he was alive, his corpse after he has died is large, too. And if it was
fat, so is the corpse of the dead man, and so on. And if a man took care
to grow his hair long, his corpse will have long hair, too. And again, if a
man had been a criminal whipped for his crime and showed scars, traces
of beatings on his body inflicted by whips or other blows while he was
alive, his body can be seen to have these marks, too, when he is dead.
And if a man's limbs were broken or twisted while he was alive, these
d   very things will be evident, too, when he is dead. In a word, however a
man treated his body while he was alive, all the marks of that treatment,
or most of them, are evident for some time even after he is dead. And I

think that the same thing, therefore, holds true also for the soul, Callicles. All that's in the soul is evident after it has been stripped naked of the body, both things that are natural to it and things that have happened to it, things that the person came to have in his soul as a result of his pursuit of each objective. So when they arrive before their judge—the people from Asia before Rhadamanthus—Rhadamanthus brings them to a halt and studies each person's soul without knowing whose it is. He's often gotten hold of the Great King, or some other king or potentate, and noticed that there's nothing sound in his soul but that it's been thoroughly whipped and covered with scars, the results of acts of perjury and of injustice, things that each of his actions has stamped upon his soul. Everything was warped as a result of deception and pretense, and nothing was straight, all because the soul had been nurtured without truth. And he saw that the soul was full of distortion and ugliness due to license and luxury, arrogance and incontinence in its actions. And when he had seen it, he dismissed this soul in dishonor straight to the guardhouse, where it went to await suffering its appropriate fate.

It is appropriate for everyone who is subject to punishment rightly inflicted by another either to become better and profit from it, or else to be made an example for others, so that when they see him suffering whatever it is he suffers, they may be afraid and become better. Those who are benefited, who are made to pay their due by gods and men, are the ones whose errors are curable; even so, their benefit comes to them, both here and in Hades, by way of pain and suffering, for there is no other possible way to get rid of injustice. From among those who have committed the ultimate wrongs and who because of such crimes have become incurable come the ones who are made examples of. These persons themselves no longer derive any profit from their punishment, because they're incurable. Others, however, do profit from it when they see them undergoing for all time the most grievous, intensely painful and frightening sufferings for their errors, simply strung up there in the prison in Hades as examples, visible warnings to unjust men who are ever arriving. I claim that Archelaus, too, will be one of their number, if what Polus says is true, and anyone else who's a tyrant like him. I suppose that in fact the majority of these examples have come from the ranks of tyrants, kings, potentates, and those active in the affairs of cities, for these people commit the most grievous and impious errors because they're in a position to do so. Homer, too, is a witness on these matters, for he has depicted those undergoing eternal punishment in Hades as kings and potentates: Tantalus, Sisyphus and Tityus. As for Thersites and any other private citizen who was wicked, no one has depicted him as surrounded by the most grievous punishments, as though he were incurable; he wasn't in that position, I suppose, and for that reason he's also happier than those who were. The fact is, Callicles, that those persons who become extremely wicked do come from the ranks of the powerful, although there's certainly nothing to stop good men from turning up even among the powerful, and those who do turn up there deserve to be enthusiastically admired. For it's a difficult thing, Callicles, and one that merits much praise, to live your whole life justly when you've found yourself having ample freedom to do what's unjust. Few are those who prove to be like that. But since there *have* proved to be such people, both here and elsewhere, I suppose that there'll be others, too, men admira-

b ble and good in that excellence of justly carrying out whatever is entrusted to them. One of these, Aristides the son of Lysimachus, has proved to be very illustrious indeed, even among the rest of the Greeks. But the majority of our potentates, my good man, prove to be bad.

So as I was saying, when Rhadamanthus the judge gets hold of someone like that, he doesn't know a thing about him, neither who he is nor who his people are, except that he's somebody wicked. And once he's noticed that, he brands the man as either curable or incurable, as he sees fit, and dismisses the man to Tartarus, and once the man has arrived there, he

c undergoes the appropriate sufferings. Once in a while he inspects another soul, one who has lived a pious life, one devoted to truth, the soul of a private citizen or someone else, especially—and I at any rate say this, Callicles—that of a philosopher who has minded his own affairs and hasn't been meddlesome in the course of his life. He admires the man and sends him off to the Isles of the Blessed. And Aeacus, too, does the very same things. Each of them with staff in hand renders judgments. And Minos is seated to oversee them. He alone holds the golden scepter the way Homer's

d Odysseus claims to have seen him,

> *holding his golden scepter, decreeing right among the dead.*[27]

For my part, Callicles, I'm convinced by these accounts, and I think about how I'll reveal to the judge a soul that's as healthy as it can be. So I disregard the things held in honor by the majority of people, and by practicing truth I really try, to the best of my ability, to be and to live as

e a very good man, and when I die, to die like that. And I call on all other people as well, as far as I can—and you especially I call on in response to your call—to this way of life, this contest, that I hold to be worth all the other contests in this life. And I take you to task, because you won't be able to come to protect yourself when you appear at the trial and judgment I was talking about just now. When you come before that judge,

527 the son of Aegina, and he takes hold of you and brings you to trial, your mouth will hang open and you'll get dizzy there just as much as I will here, and maybe somebody'll give you a demeaning knock on the jaw and throw all sorts of dirt at you.

Maybe you think this account is told as an old wives' tale, and you feel contempt for it. And it certainly wouldn't be a surprising thing to feel contempt for it if we could look for and somehow find one better and

---

27. *Odyssey* xi.569.

truer than it. As it is, you see that there are three of you, the wisest of the Greeks of today—you, Polus, and Gorgias—and you're not able to prove that there's any other life one should live than the one which will clearly turn out to be advantageous in that world, too. But among so many arguments this one alone survives refutation and remains steady: that doing what's unjust is more to be guarded against than suffering it, and that it's not *seeming* to be good but *being* good that a man should take care of more than anything, both in his public and his private life; and that if a person proves to be bad in some respect, he's to be disciplined, and that the second best thing after being just is to become just by paying one's due, by being disciplined; and that every form of flattery, both the form concerned with oneself and that concerned with others, whether they're few or many, is to be avoided, and that oratory and every other activity is always to be used in support of what's just.

So, listen to me and follow me to where I am, and when you've come here you'll be happy both during life and at its end, as the account indicates. Let someone despise you as a fool and throw dirt on you, if he likes. And, yes, by Zeus, confidently let him deal you that demeaning blow. Nothing terrible will happen to you if you really are an admirable and good man, one who practices excellence. And then, after we've practiced it together, then at last, if we think we should, we'll turn to politics, or then we'll deliberate about whatever subject we please, when we're better at deliberating than we are now. For it's a shameful thing for us, being in the condition we appear to be in at present—when we never think the same about the same subjects, the most important ones at that—to sound off as though we're somebodies. That's how far behind in education we've fallen. So let's use the account that has now been disclosed to us as our guide, one that indicates to us that this way of life is the best, to practice justice and the rest of excellence both in life and in death. Let us follow it, then, and call on others to do so, too, and let's not follow the one that you believe in and call on me to follow. For that one is worthless, Callicles.

MENO

Meno's is one of the leading aristocratic families of Thessaly, traditionally friendly to Athens and Athenian interests. Here he is a young man, about to embark on an unscrupulous military and political career, leading to an early death at the hands of the Persian king. To his aristocratic 'virtue' (Plato's ancient readers would know what that ultimately came to) he adds an admiration for ideas on the subject he has learned from the rhetorician Gorgias (about whom we learn more in the dialogue named after him). What brings him to Athens we are not told. His family's local sponsor is the democratic politician Anytus, one of Socrates' accusers at his trial, and apparently Anytus is his host. The dialogue begins abruptly, without stage-setting preliminaries of the sort we find in the 'Socratic' dialogues, and with no context of any kind being provided for the conversation. Meno wants to know Socrates' position on the then much-debated question whether virtue can be taught, or whether it comes rather by practice, or else is acquired by one's birth and nature, or in some other way? Socrates and Meno pursue that question, and the preliminary one of what virtue indeed is, straight through to the inconclusive conclusion characteristic of 'Socratic' dialogues. (Anytus joins the conversation briefly. He bristles when, to support his doubts that virtue can be taught, Socrates points to the failure of famous Athenian leaders to pass their own virtue on to their sons, and he issues a veiled threat of the likely consequences to Socrates of such 'slanderous' attacks.)

The dialogue is best remembered, however, for the interlude in which Socrates questions Meno's slave about a problem in geometry—how to find a square double in area to any given square. Having determined that Meno does not know what virtue is, and recognizing that he himself does not know either, Socrates has proposed to Meno that they inquire into this together. Meno protests that that is impossible, challenging Socrates with the 'paradox' that one logically cannot inquire productively into what one does not already know—nor of course into what one already does! Guided by Socrates' questions, the slave (who has never studied geometry before) comes to see for himself, to recognize, what the right answer to the geometrical problem must be. Socrates argues that this confirms something he has heard from certain wise priests and priestesses—that the soul is immortal and that at our birth we already possess all theoretical knowledge (he includes here not just mathematical theory but moral knowledge as well). Prodded by Socrates' questions, the slave was 'recollecting' this prior knowledge, not drawing new conclusions from data being presented to him for the first time. So in moral inquiry, as well, there is hope that, if we question ourselves rightly, 'recollection' can progressively improve our under-standing of moral truth and eventually lead us to full knowledge of it.

The examination of the slave assuages Meno's doubt about the possibility of such inquiry. He and Socrates proceed to inquire together what virtue is—but now they follow a new method of 'hypothesis', introduced by Socrates again by analogy with procedures in geometry. Socrates no longer asks Meno for his views and criticizes those. Among other 'hypotheses' that he now works with, he advances and argues for an hypothesis of his own, that virtue is knowledge (in which case it must be teachable). But he also considers weaknesses in his own argument, leading to the alternative possible hypothesis, that virtue is god-granted right opinion (and so, not teachable). In the second half of the dialogue we thus see a new Socrates, with new methods of argument and inquiry, not envisioned in such 'Socratic' dialogues as Euthyphro, Laches, *and* Charmides. Meno *points forward to* Phaedo, *where the thesis that theoretical knowledge comes by recollection is discussed again, with a clear reference back to the* Meno, *but now expanded by the addition of Platonic Forms as objects of recollection and knowledge.*

J.M.C.

MENO: Can you tell me, Socrates, can virtue be taught? Or is it not   70
teachable but the result of practice, or is it neither of these, but men possess
it by nature or in some other way?

SOCRATES: Before now, Meno, Thessalians had a high reputation among
the Greeks and were admired for their horsemanship and their wealth,
but now, it seems to me, they are also admired for their wisdom, not least   b
the fellow citizens of your friend Aristippus of Larissa. The responsibility
for this reputation of yours lies with Gorgias, for when he came to your
city he found that the leading Aleuadae, your lover Aristippus among
them, loved him for his wisdom, and so did the other leading Thessalians.
In particular, he accustomed you to give a bold and grand answer to any
question you may be asked, as experts are likely to do. Indeed, he himself   c
was ready to answer any Greek who wished to question him, and every
question was answered. But here in Athens, my dear Meno, the opposite
is the case, as if there were a dearth of wisdom, and wisdom seems to
have departed hence to go to you. If then you want to ask one of us that   71
sort of question, everyone will laugh and say: "Good stranger, you must
think me happy indeed if you think I know whether virtue can be taught
or how it comes to be; I am so far from knowing whether virtue can be
taught or not that I do not even have any knowledge of what virtue itself is."

I myself, Meno, am as poor as my fellow citizens in this matter, and I   b
blame myself for my complete ignorance about virtue. If I do not know

Translated by G.M.A. Grube.

what something is, how could I know what qualities it possesses? Or do you think that someone who does not know at all who Meno is could know whether he is good-looking or rich or well-born, or the opposite of these? Do you think that is possible?

MENO: I do not; but, Socrates, do you really not know what virtue is? Are we to report this to the folk back home about you?

SOCRATES: Not only that, my friend, but also that, as I believe, I have never yet met anyone else who did know.

MENO: How so? Did you not meet Gorgias when he was here?

SOCRATES: I did.

MENO: Did you then not think that he knew?

SOCRATES: I do not altogether remember, Meno, so that I cannot tell you now what I thought then. Perhaps he does know; you know what he used to say, so you remind me of what he said. You tell me yourself, if you are willing, for surely you share his views.—I do.

SOCRATES: Let us leave Gorgias out of it, since he is not here. But Meno, by the gods, what do you yourself say that virtue is? Speak and do not begrudge us, so that I may have spoken a most unfortunate untruth when I said that I had never met anyone who knew, if you and Gorgias are shown to know.

MENO: It is not hard to tell you, Socrates. First, if you want the virtue of a man, it is easy to say that a man's virtue consists of being able to manage public affairs and in so doing to benefit his friends and harm his enemies and to be careful that no harm comes to himself; if you want the virtue of a woman, it is not difficult to describe: she must manage the home well, preserve its possessions, and be submissive to her husband; the virtue of a child, whether male or female, is different again, and so is that of an elderly man, if you want that, or if you want that of a free man or a slave. And there are very many other virtues, so that one is not at a loss to say what virtue is. There is virtue for every action and every age, for every task of ours and every one of us—and Socrates, the same is true for wickedness.

SOCRATES: I seem to be in great luck, Meno; while I am looking for one virtue, I have found you to have a whole swarm of them. But, Meno, to follow up the image of swarms, if I were asking you what is the nature of bees, and you said that they are many and of all kinds, what would you answer if I asked you: "Do you mean that they are many and varied and different from one another in so far as they are bees? Or are they no different in that regard, but in some other respect, in their beauty, for example, or their size or in some other such way?" Tell me, what would you answer if thus questioned?

MENO: I would say that they do not differ from one another in being bees.

SOCRATES: If I went on to say: "Tell me, what is this very thing, Meno, in which they are all the same and do not differ from one another?" Would you be able to tell me?

MENO: I would.

SOCRATES: The same is true in the case of the virtues. Even if they are many and various, all of them have one and the same form which makes them virtues, and it is right to look to this when one is asked to make clear what virtue is. Or do you not understand what I mean? d

MENO: I think I understand, but I certainly do not grasp the meaning of the question as fully as I want to.

SOCRATES: I am asking whether you think it is only in the case of virtue that there is one for man, another for woman and so on, or is the same true in the case of health and size and strength? Do you think that there is one health for man and another for woman? Or, if it is health, does it have the same form everywhere, whether in man or in anything else whatever? e

MENO: The health of a man seems to me the same as that of a woman.

SOCRATES: And so with size and strength? If a woman is strong, that strength will be the same and have the same form, for by "the same" I mean that strength is no different as far as being strength, whether in a man or a woman. Or do you think there is a difference?

MENO: I do not think so.

SOCRATES: And will there be any difference in the case of virtue, as far as being virtue is concerned, whether it be in a child or an old man, in a woman or in a man? 73

MENO: I think, Socrates, that somehow this is no longer like those other cases.

SOCRATES: How so? Did you not say that the virtue of a man consists of managing the city well, and that of a woman of managing the household?—I did.

SOCRATES: Is it possible to manage a city well, or a household, or anything else, while not managing it moderately and justly?—Certainly not.

SOCRATES: Then if they manage justly and moderately, they must do so b with justice and moderation?—Necessarily.

SOCRATES: So both the man and the woman, if they are to be good, need the same things, justice and moderation.—So it seems.

SOCRATES: What about a child and an old man? Can they possibly be good if they are intemperate and unjust?—Certainly not.

SOCRATES: But if they are moderate and just?—Yes.

SOCRATES: So all human beings are good in the same way, for they become c good by acquiring the same qualities.—It seems so.

SOCRATES: And they would not be good in the same way if they did not have the same virtue.—They certainly would not be.

SOCRATES: Since then the virtue of all is the same, try to tell me and to remember what Gorgias, and you with him, said that that same thing is.

MENO: What else but to be able to rule over people, if you are seeking d one description to fit them all.

SOCRATES: That is indeed what I am seeking, but Meno, is virtue the same in the case of a child or a slave, namely, for them to be able to rule over a master, and do you think that he who rules is still a slave?—I do not think so at all, Socrates.

SOCRATES: It is not likely, my good man. Consider this further point: you say that virtue is to be able to rule. Shall we not add to this *justly and not unjustly?*

MENO: I think so, Socrates, for justice is virtue.

e   SOCRATES: Is it virtue, Meno, or a virtue?—What do you mean?

SOCRATES: As with anything else. For example, if you wish, take roundness, about which I would say that it is a shape, but not simply that it is shape. I would not so speak of it because there are other shapes.

MENO: You are quite right. So I too say that not only justice is a virtue but there are many other virtues.

74   SOCRATES: What are they? Tell me, as I could mention other shapes to you if you bade me do so, so do you mention other virtues.

MENO: I think courage is a virtue, and moderation, wisdom, and munificence, and very many others.

SOCRATES: We are having the same trouble again, Meno, though in another way; we have found many virtues while looking for one, but we cannot find the one which covers all the others.

b   MENO: I cannot yet find, Socrates, what you are looking for, one virtue for them all, as in the other cases.

SOCRATES: That is likely, but I am eager, if I can, that we should make progress, for you understand that the same applies to everything. If someone asked you what I mentioned just now: "What is shape, Meno?" and you told him that it was roundness, and if then he said to you what I did: "Is roundness shape or a shape?" you would surely tell him that it is a shape?—I certainly would.

c   SOCRATES: That would be because there are other shapes?—Yes.

SOCRATES: And if he asked you further what they were, you would tell him?—I would.

SOCRATES: So too, if he asked you what color is, and you said it is white, and your questioner interrupted you, "Is white color or a color?" you would say that it is a color, because there are also other colors?—I would.

SOCRATES: And if he bade you mention other colors, you would mention

d   others that are no less colors than white is?—Yes.

SOCRATES: Then if he pursued the argument as I did and said: "We always arrive at the many; do not talk to me in that way, but since you call all these many by one name, and say that no one of them is not a shape even though they are opposites, tell me what this is which applies

e   as much to the round as to the straight and which you call shape, as you say the round is as much a shape as the straight." Do you not say that?—I do.

SOCRATES: When you speak like that, do you assert that the round is no more round than it is straight, and that the straight is no more straight than it is round?

MENO: Certainly not, Socrates.

SOCRATES: Yet you say that the round is no more a shape than the straight is, nor the one more than the other.—That is true.

SOCRATES: What then is this to which the name shape applies? Try to tell me. If then you answered the man who was questioning about shape or color: "I do not understand what you want, my man, nor what you mean," he would probably wonder and say: "You do not understand that I am seeking that which is the same in all these cases?" Would you still have nothing to say, Meno, if one asked you: "What is this which applies to the round and the straight and the other things which you call shapes and which is the same in them all?" Try to say, that you may practice for your answer about virtue.

MENO: No, Socrates, but you tell me.

SOCRATES: Do you want me to do you this favor?

MENO: I certainly do.

SOCRATES: And you will then be willing to tell me about virtue?

MENO: I will.

SOCRATES: We must certainly press on. The subject is worth it.

MENO: It surely is.

SOCRATES: Come then, let us try to tell you what shape is. See whether you will accept that it is this: Let us say that shape is that which alone of existing things always follows color. Is that satisfactory to you, or do you look for it in some other way? I should be satisfied if you defined virtue in this way.

MENO: But that is foolish, Socrates.

SOCRATES: How do you mean?

MENO: That shape, you say, always follows color. Well then, if someone were to say that he did not know what color is, but that he had the same difficulty as he had about shape, what do you think your answer would be?

SOCRATES: A true one, surely, and if my questioner was one of those clever and disputatious debaters, I would say to him: "I have given my answer; if it is wrong, it is your job to refute it." Then, if they are friends as you and I are, and want to discuss with each other, they must answer in a manner more gentle and more proper to discussion. By this I mean that the answers must not only be true, but in terms admittedly known to the questioner. I too will try to speak in these terms. Do you call something "the end?" I mean such a thing as a limit or boundary, for all those are, I say, the same thing. Prodicus[1] might disagree with us, but you surely call something "finished" or "completed"—that is what I want to express, nothing elaborate.

MENO: I do, and I think I understand what you mean.

SOCRATES: Further, you call something a plane, and something else a solid, as in geometry?

MENO: I do.

SOCRATES: From this you may understand what I mean by shape, for I say this of every shape, that a shape is that which limits a solid; in a word, a shape is the limit of a solid.

1. Prodicus was a well-known sophist who was especially keen on the exact meaning of words.

MENO: And what do you say color is, Socrates?

SOCRATES: You are outrageous, Meno. You bother an old man to answer
b questions, but you yourself are not willing to recall and to tell me what
Gorgias says that virtue is.

MENO: After you have answered this, Socrates, I will tell you.

SOCRATES: Even someone who was blindfolded would know from your
conversation that you are handsome and still have lovers.

MENO: Why so?

SOCRATES: Because you are forever giving orders in a discussion, as
spoiled people do, who behave like tyrants as long as they are young. And
c perhaps you have recognized that I am at a disadvantage with handsome
people, so I will do you the favor of an answer.

MENO: By all means do me that favor.

SOCRATES: Do you want me to answer after the manner of Gorgias, which
you would most easily follow?

MENO: Of course I want that.

SOCRATES: Do you both say there are effluvia of things, as Empedocles[2]
does?— Certainly.

SOCRATES: And that there are channels through which the effluvia make
their way?—Definitely.

d SOCRATES: And some effluvia fit some of the channels, while others are
too small or too big?—That is so.

SOCRATES: And there is something which you call sight?—There is.

SOCRATES: From this, "comprehend what I state," as Pindar said;[3] for
color is an effluvium from shapes which fits the sight and is perceived.

MENO: That seems to me to be an excellent answer, Socrates.

SOCRATES: Perhaps it was given in the manner to which you are accustomed. At the same time I think that you can deduce from this answer
e what sound is, and smell, and many such things.—Quite so.

SOCRATES: It is a theatrical answer so it pleases you, Meno, more than
that about shape.—It does.

SOCRATES: It is not better, son of Alexidemus, but I am convinced that
the other is, and I think you would agree, if you did not have to go away
before the mysteries as you told me yesterday, but could remain and
be initiated.

MENO: I would stay, Socrates, if you could tell me many things like
77 these.

SOCRATES: I shall certainly not be lacking in eagerness to tell you such
things, both for your sake and my own, but I may not be able to tell you
many. Come now, you too try to fulfill your promise to me and tell me
the nature of virtue as a whole and stop making many out of one, as jokers
say whenever someone breaks something; but allow virtue to remain whole
b and sound, and tell me what it is, for I have given you examples.

2. Empedocles (c. 493–433 B.C.) of Acragas in Sicily was a philosopher famous for his
theories about the world of nature and natural phenomena (including sense-perception).

3. Frg. 105 (Snell).

MENO: I think, Socrates, that virtue is, as the poet says, "to find joy in beautiful things and have power." So I say that virtue is to desire beautiful things and have the power to acquire them.

SOCRATES: Do you mean that the man who desires beautiful things desires good things?—Most certainly.

SOCRATES: Do you assume that there are people who desire bad things, and others who desire good things? Do you not think, my good man, that all men desire good things?

MENO: I do not.

SOCRATES: But some desire bad things?—Yes.

SOCRATES: Do you mean that they believe the bad things to be good, or that they know they are bad and nevertheless desire them?—I think there are both kinds.

SOCRATES: Do you think, Meno, that anyone, knowing that bad things are bad, nevertheless desires them?—I certainly do.

SOCRATES: What do you mean by desiring? Is it to secure for oneself?—What else?

SOCRATES: Does he think that the bad things benefit him who possesses them, or does he know they harm him?

MENO: There are some who believe that the bad things benefit them, others who know that the bad things harm them.

SOCRATES: And do you think that those who believe that bad things benefit them know that they are bad?

MENO: No, that I cannot altogether believe.

SOCRATES: It is clear then that those who do not know things to be bad do not desire what is bad, but they desire those things that they believe to be good but that are in fact bad. It follows that those who have no knowledge of these things and believe them to be good clearly desire good things. Is that not so?—It is likely.

SOCRATES: Well then, those who you say desire bad things, believing that bad things harm their possessor, know that they will be harmed by them?—Necessarily.

SOCRATES: And do they not think that those who are harmed are miserable to the extent that they are harmed?—That too is inevitable.

SOCRATES: And that those who are miserable are unhappy?—I think so.

SOCRATES: Does anyone wish to be miserable and unhappy?—I do not think so, Socrates.

SOCRATES: No one then wants what is bad, Meno, unless he wants to be such. For what else is being miserable but to desire bad things and secure them?

MENO: You are probably right, Socrates, and no one wants what is bad.

SOCRATES: Were you not saying just now that virtue is to desire good things and have the power to secure them?—Yes, I was.

SOCRATES: The desiring part of this statement is common to everybody, and one man is no better than another in this?—So it appears.

SOCRATES: Clearly then, if one man is better than another, he must be better at securing them.—Quite so.

SOCRATES: This then is virtue according to your argument, the power of
c   securing good things.

MENO: I think, Socrates, that the case is altogether as you now understand it.

SOCRATES: Let us see then whether what you say is true, for you may
well be right. You say that the capacity to acquire good things is virtue?—
I do.

SOCRATES: And by good things you mean, for example, health and wealth?

MENO: Yes, and also to acquire gold and silver, also honors and offices
in the city.

SOCRATES: By good things you do not mean other goods than these?

MENO: No, but I mean all things of this kind.

d   SOCRATES: Very well. According to Meno, the hereditary guest friend of
the Great King, virtue is the acquisition of gold and silver. Do you add
to this acquiring, Meno, the words justly and piously, or does it make no
difference to you but even if one secures these things unjustly, you call it
virtue none the less?

MENO: Certainly not, Socrates.

SOCRATES: You would then call it wickedness?—Indeed I would.

SOCRATES: It seems then that the acquisition must be accompanied by
e   justice or moderation or piety or some other part of virtue; if it is not, it
will not be virtue, even though it provides good things.

MENO: How could there be virtue without these?

SOCRATES: Then failing to secure gold and silver, whenever it would not
be just to do so, either for oneself or another, is not this failure to secure
them also virtue?

MENO: So it seems.

SOCRATES: Then to provide these goods would not be virtue any more
79 than not to provide them, but apparently whatever is done with justice
will be virtue, and what is done without anything of the kind is wickedness.

MENO: I think it must necessarily be as you say.

SOCRATES: We said a little while ago that each of these things was a part
of virtue, namely, justice and moderation and all such things?—Yes.

SOCRATES: Then you are playing with me, Meno.—How so, Socrates?

SOCRATES: Because I begged you just now not to break up or fragment
virtue, and I gave examples of how you should answer. You paid no
b   attention, but you tell me that virtue is to be able to secure good things
with justice, and justice, you say, is a part of virtue.

MENO: I do.

SOCRATES: It follows then from what you agree to, that to act in whatever
you do with a part of virtue is virtue, for you say that justice is a part of
virtue, as are all such qualities. Why do I say this? Because when I begged
you to tell me about virtue as a whole, you are far from telling me what
it is. Rather, you say that every action is virtue if it is performed with a
c   part of virtue, as if you had said what virtue is as a whole, so I would
already know that, even if you fragment it into parts. I think you must

face the same question from the beginning, my dear Meno, namely, what is virtue, if every action performed with a part of virtue is virtue? For that is what one is saying when he says that every action performed with justice is virtue. Do you not think you should face the same question again, or do you think one knows what a part of virtue is if one does not know virtue itself?—I do not think so.

SOCRATES: If you remember, when I was answering you about shape, we rejected the kind of answer that tried to answer in terms still being the subject of inquiry and not yet agreed upon.—And we were right to reject them.

SOCRATES: Then surely, my good sir, you must not think, while the nature of virtue as a whole is still under inquiry, that by answering in terms of the parts of virtue you can make its nature clear to anyone or make anything else clear by speaking in this way, but only that the same question must be put to you again—what do you take the nature of virtue to be when you say what you say? Or do you think there is no point in what I am saying?—I think what you say is right.

SOCRATES: Answer me again then from the beginning: What do you and your friend say that virtue is?

MENO: Socrates, before I even met you I used to hear that you are always in a state of perplexity and that you bring others to the same state, and now I think you are bewitching and beguiling me, simply putting me under a spell, so that I am quite perplexed. Indeed, if a joke is in order, you seem, in appearance and in every other way, to be like the broad torpedo fish, for it too makes anyone who comes close and touches it feel numb, and you now seem to have had that kind of effect on me, for both my mind and my tongue are numb, and I have no answer to give you. Yet I have made many speeches about virtue before large audiences on a thousand occasions, very good speeches as I thought, but now I cannot even say what it is. I think you are wise not to sail away from Athens to go and stay elsewhere, for if you were to behave like this as a stranger in another city, you would be driven away for practising sorcery.

SOCRATES: You are a rascal, Meno, and you nearly deceived me.

MENO: Why so particularly, Socrates?

SOCRATES: I know why you drew this image of me.

MENO: Why do you think I did?

SOCRATES: So that I should draw an image of you in return. I know that all handsome men rejoice in images of themselves; it is to their advantage, for I think that the images of beautiful people are also beautiful, but I will draw no image of you in turn. Now if the torpedo fish is itself numb and so makes others numb, then I resemble it, but not otherwise, for I myself do not have the answer when I perplex others, but I am more perplexed than anyone when I cause perplexity in others. So now I do not know what virtue is; perhaps you knew before you contacted me, but now you are certainly like one who does not know. Nevertheless, I want to examine and seek together with you what it may be.

MENO: How will you look for it, Socrates, when you do not know at all what it is? How will you aim to search for something you do not know at all? If you should meet with it, how will you know that this is the thing that you did not know?

e   SOCRATES: I know what you want to say, Meno. Do you realize what a debater's argument you are bringing up, that a man cannot search either for what he knows or for what he does not know? He cannot search for what he knows—since he knows it, there is no need to search—nor for what he does not know, for he does not know what to look for.

81   MENO: Does that argument not seem sound to you, Socrates?

SOCRATES: Not to me.

MENO: Can you tell me why?

SOCRATES: I can. I have heard wise men and women talk about divine matters . . .

MENO: What did they say?

SOCRATES: What was, I thought, both true and beautiful.

MENO: What was it, and who were they?

SOCRATES: The speakers were among the priests and priestesses whose

b   care it is to be able to give an account of their practices. Pindar too says it, and many others of the divine among our poets. What they say is this; see whether you think they speak the truth: They say that the human soul is immortal; at times it comes to an end, which they call dying, at times it is reborn, but it is never destroyed, and one must therefore live one's life as piously as possible:

> *Persephone will return to the sun above in the ninth year*
> *the souls of those from whom*
> *she will exact punishment for old miseries,*
c   > *and from these come noble kings,*
> *mighty in strength and greatest in wisdom,*
> *and for the rest of time men will call them sacred heroes.*[4]

As the soul is immortal, has been born often and has seen all things here and in the underworld, there is nothing which it has not learned; so it is in no way surprising that it can recollect the things it knew before, both

d   about virtue and other things. As the whole of nature is akin, and the soul has learned everything, nothing prevents a man, after recalling one thing only—a process men call learning—discovering everything else for himself, if he is brave and does not tire of the search, for searching and learning are, as a whole, recollection. We must, therefore, not believe that debater's argument, for it would make us idle, and fainthearted men like to hear it,

e   whereas my argument makes them energetic and keen on the search. I

4. Frg. 133 (Snell).

trust that this is true, and I want to inquire along with you into the nature of virtue.

MENO: Yes, Socrates, but how do you mean that we do not learn, but that what we call learning is recollection? Can you teach me that this is so?

SOCRATES: As I said just now, Meno, you are a rascal. You now ask me if I can teach you, when I say there is no teaching but recollection, in order to show me up at once as contradicting myself.

MENO: No, by Zeus, Socrates, that was not my intention when I spoke, but just a habit. If you can somehow show me that things are as you say, please do so.

SOCRATES: It is not easy, but I am nevertheless willing to do my best for your sake. Call one of these many attendants of yours, whichever you like, that I may prove it to you in his case.

MENO: Certainly. You there come forward.

SOCRATES: Is he a Greek? Does he speak Greek?

MENO: Very much so. He was born in my household.

SOCRATES: Pay attention then whether you think he is recollecting or learning from me.

MENO: I will pay attention.

SOCRATES: Tell me now, boy, you know that a square figure is like this?—I do.

SOCRATES: A square then is a figure in which all these four sides are equal?—Yes indeed.

SOCRATES: And it also has these lines through the middle equal?[5]—Yes.

---

5. Socrates draws a square ABCD. The "lines through the middle" are the lines joining the middle of these sides, which also go through the center of the square, namely EF and GH.

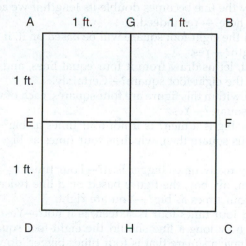

82

b

c

Socrates: And such a figure could be larger or smaller?—Certainly.

Socrates: If then this side were two feet, and this other side two feet, how many feet would the whole be? Consider it this way: if it were two feet this way, and only one foot that way, the figure would be once two feet?—Yes.

d   Socrates: But if it is two feet also that way, it would surely be twice two feet?—Yes.

Socrates: How many feet is twice two feet? Work it out and tell me.— Four, Socrates.

Socrates: Now we could have another figure twice the size of this one, with the four sides equal like this one.—Yes.

Socrates: How many feet will that be?—Eight.

Socrates: Come now, try to tell me how long each side of this will be. The side of this is two feet. What about each side of the one which is its
e   double?—Obviously, Socrates, it will be twice the length.

Socrates: You see, Meno, that I am not teaching the boy anything, but all I do is question him. And now he thinks he knows the length of the line on which an eight-foot figure is based. Do you agree?

Meno: I do.

Socrates: And does he know?

Meno: Certainly not.

Socrates: He thinks it is a line twice the length?

Meno: Yes.

Socrates: Watch him now recollecting things in order, as one must recollect. Tell me, boy, do you say that a figure double the size is based
83   on a line double the length? Now I mean such a figure as this, not long on one side and short on the other, but equal in every direction like this one, and double the size, that is, eight feet. See whether you still believe that it will be based on a line double the length.—I do.

Socrates: Now the line becomes double its length if we add another of the same length here?—Yes indeed.

Socrates: And the eight-foot square will be based on it, if there are four lines of that length?—Yes.

b   Socrates: Well, let us draw from it four equal lines, and surely that is what you say is the eight-foot square?—Certainly.

Socrates: And within this figure are four squares, each of which is equal to the four-foot square?—Yes.

Socrates: How big is it then? Is it not four times as big?—Of course.

Socrates: Is this square then, which is four times as big, its double?— No, by Zeus.

Socrates: How many times bigger is it?—Four times.

c   Socrates: Then, my boy, the figure based on a line twice the length is not double but four times as big?—You are right.

Socrates: And four times four is sixteen, is it not?—Yes.

Socrates: On how long a line should the eight-foot square be based? On *this* line we have a square that is four times bigger, do we not?—Yes.

SOCRATES: Now this four-foot square is based on this line here, half the length?—Yes.

SOCRATES: Very well. Is the eight-foot square not double this one and half that one?[6]—Yes.

SOCRATES: Will it not be based on a line longer than this one and shorter than that one? Is that not so?—I think so. d

SOCRATES: Good, you answer what you think. And tell me, was this one not two-feet long, and that one four feet?—Yes.

SOCRATES: The line on which the eight-foot square is based must then be longer than this one of two feet, and shorter than that one of four feet?—It must be.

SOCRATES: Try to tell me then how long a line you say it is.—Three e feet.

SOCRATES: Then if it is three feet, let us add the half of this one, and it will be three feet? For these are two feet, and the other is one. And here, similarly, these are two feet and that one is one foot, and so the figure you mention comes to be?—Yes.

SOCRATES: Now if it is three feet this way and three feet that way, will the whole figure be three times three feet?—So it seems.

SOCRATES: How much is three times three feet?—Nine feet.

SOCRATES: And the double square was to be how many feet?—Eight.

SOCRATES: So the eight-foot figure cannot be based on the three-foot line?—Clearly not.

SOCRATES: But on how long a line? Try to tell us exactly, and if you do 84 not want to work it out, show me from what line.—By Zeus, Socrates, I do not know.

SOCRATES: You realize, Meno, what point he has reached in his recollection. At first he did not know what the basic line of the eight-foot square was; even now he does not yet know, but then he thought he knew, and answered confidently as if he did know, and he did not think himself at a loss, but now he does think himself at a loss, and as he does not know, b neither does he think he knows.

MENO: That is true.

SOCRATES: So he is now in a better position with regard to the matter he does not know?

MENO: I agree with that too.

SOCRATES: Have we done him any harm by making him perplexed and numb as the torpedo fish does?

MENO: I do not think so.

SOCRATES: Indeed, we have probably achieved something relevant to finding out how matters stand, for now, as he does not know, he would be glad to find out, whereas before he thought he could easily make many

---

6. I.e., the eight-foot square is double the four-foot square and half the sixteen-foot square—double the square based on a line two feet long, and half the square based on a four-foot side.

c   fine speeches to large audiences about the square of double size and said that it must have a base twice as long.

MENO: So it seems.

SOCRATES: Do you think that before he would have tried to find out that which he thought he knew though he did not, before he fell into perplexity and realized he did not know and longed to know?

MENO: I do not think so, Socrates.

SOCRATES: Has he then benefitted from being numbed?

MENO: I think so.

SOCRATES: Look then how he will come out of his perplexity while searching along with me. I shall do nothing more than ask questions and not

d   teach him. Watch whether you find me teaching and explaining things to him instead of asking for his opinion.

SOCRATES: You tell me, is this not a four-foot figure? You understand?— I do.

SOCRATES: We add to it this figure which is equal to it?—Yes.

SOCRATES: And we add this third figure equal to each of them?—Yes.

SOCRATES: Could we then fill in the space in the corner?—Certainly.[7]

SOCRATES: So we have these four equal figures?—Yes.

e   SOCRATES: Well then, how many times is the whole figure larger than this one?[8]—Four times.

SOCRATES: But we should have had one that was twice as large, or do you not remember?—I certainly do.

7. Socrates now builds up his sixteen-foot square by joining two four-foot squares, then a third, like this:

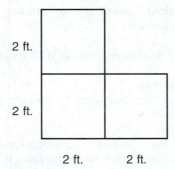

Filling "the space in the corner" will give another four-foot square, which completes the sixteen-foot square containing four four-foot squares.

8. "This one" is any one of the inside squares of four feet.

SOCRATES: Does not this line from one corner to the other cut each of these figures in two?[9]—Yes.

SOCRATES: So these are four equal lines which enclose this figure?[10]—They are.

SOCRATES: Consider now: how large is the figure?—I do not understand.

SOCRATES: Within these four figures, each line cuts off half of each, does it not?—Yes.

SOCRATES: How many of this size are there in this figure?[11]—Four.

SOCRATES: How many in this?[12]—Two.

SOCRATES: What is the relation of four to two?—Double.   b

SOCRATES: How many feet in this?[13]—Eight.

SOCRATES: Based on what line?—This one.

SOCRATES: That is, on the line that stretches from corner to corner of the four-foot figure?—Yes.—Clever men call this the diagonal, so that if diagonal is its name, you say that the double figure would be that based on the diagonal?—Most certainly, Socrates.

SOCRATES: What do you think, Meno? Has he, in his answers, expressed any opinion that was not his own?   c

MENO: No, they were all his own.

SOCRATES: And yet, as we said a short time ago, he did not know?—That is true.

SOCRATES: So these opinions were in him, were they not?—Yes.

9. Socrates now draws the diagonals of the four inside squares, namely, FH, HE, EG, and GF, which together form the square GFHE.

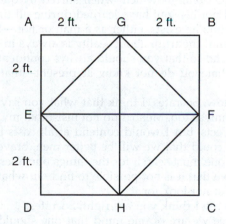

A   2 ft.   G   2 ft.   B

2 ft.

E   F

2 ft.

D   H   C

10. I.e., GFHE.

11. Again, GFHE: Socrates is asking how many of the triangles "cut off from inside" there are inside GFHE.

12. I.e., any of the interior squares.

13. GFHE again.

SOCRATES: So the man who does not know has within himself true opinions about the things that he does not know?—So it appears.

SOCRATES: These opinions have now just been stirred up like a dream, but if he were repeatedly asked these same questions in various ways, you know that in the end his knowledge about these things would be as accurate as anyone's.—It is likely.

SOCRATES: And he will know it without having been taught but only questioned, and find the knowledge within himself?—Yes.

SOCRATES: And is not finding knowledge within oneself recollection?—Certainly.

SOCRATES: Must he not either have at some time acquired the knowledge he now possesses, or else have always possessed it?—Yes.

SOCRATES: If he always had it, he would always have known. If he acquired it, he cannot have done so in his present life. Or has someone taught him geometry? For he will perform in the same way about all geometry, and all other knowledge. Has someone taught him everything? You should know, especially as he has been born and brought up in your house.

MENO: But I know that no one has taught him.

SOCRATES: Yet he has these opinions, or doesn't he?

MENO: That seems indisputable, Socrates.

SOCRATES: If he has not acquired them in his present life, is it not clear that he had them and had learned them at some other time?—It seems so.

SOCRATES: Then that was the time when he was not a human being?—Yes.

SOCRATES: If then, during the time he exists and is not a human being he will have true opinions which, when stirred by questioning, become knowledge, will not his soul have learned during all time? For it is clear that during all time he exists, either as a man or not.—So it seems.

SOCRATES: Then if the truth about reality is always in our soul, the soul would be immortal so that you should always confidently try to seek out and recollect what you do not know at present—that is, what you do not recollect?

MENO: Somehow, Socrates, I think that what you say is right.

SOCRATES: I think so too, Meno. I do not insist that my argument is right in all other respects, but I would contend at all costs both in word and deed as far as I could that we will be better men, braver and less idle, if we believe that one must search for the things one does not know, rather than if we believe that it is not possible to find out what we do not know and that we must not look for it.

MENO: In this too I think you are right, Socrates.

SOCRATES: Since we are of one mind that one should seek to find out what one does not know, shall we try to find out together what virtue is?

MENO: Certainly. But Socrates, I should be most pleased to investigate and hear your answer to my original question, whether we should try on the assumption that virtue is something teachable, or is a natural gift, or in whatever way it comes to men.

SOCRATES: If I were directing you, Meno, and not only myself, we would not have investigated whether virtue is teachable or not before we had investigated what virtue itself is. But because you do not even attempt to rule yourself, in order that you may be free, but you try to rule me and do so, I will agree with you—for what can I do? So we must, it appears, inquire into the qualities of something the nature of which we do not yet know. However, please relax your rule a little bit for me and agree to investigate whether it is teachable or not by means of a hypothesis. I mean the way geometers often carry on their investigations. For example, if they are asked whether a specific area can be inscribed in the form of a triangle within a given circle, one of them might say: "I do not yet know whether that area has that property, but I think I have, as it were, a hypothesis that is of use for the problem, namely this: If that area is such that when one has applied it as a rectangle to the given straight line in the circle it is deficient by a figure similar to the very figure which is applied, then I think one alternative results, whereas another results if it is impossible for this to happen. So, by using this hypothesis, I am willing to tell you what results with regard to inscribing it in the circle— that is, whether it is impossible or not."[14] So let us speak about virtue also, since we do not know either what it is or what qualities it possesses, and let us investigate whether it is teachable or not by means of a hypothesis, and say this: Among the things existing in the soul, of what sort is virtue, that it should be teachable or not? First, if it is another sort than knowledge, is it teachable or not, or, as we were just saying, recollectable? Let it make no difference to us which term we use: is it teachable? Or is it plain to anyone that men cannot be taught anything but knowledge?—I think so.

SOCRATES: But, if virtue is a kind of knowledge, it is clear that it could be taught.—Of course.

SOCRATES: We have dealt with that question quickly, that if it is of one kind it can be taught, if it is of a different kind, it cannot.—We have indeed.

SOCRATES: The next point to consider seems to be whether virtue is knowledge or something else.—That does seem to be the next point to consider.

SOCRATES: Well now, do we say that virtue is itself something good, and will this hypothesis stand firm for us, that it is something good?—Of course.

SOCRATES: If then there is anything else good that is different and separate from knowledge, virtue might well not be a kind of knowledge; but if there is nothing good that knowledge does not encompass, we would be right to suspect that it is a kind of knowledge.—That is so.

SOCRATES: Surely virtue makes us good?—Yes.

SOCRATES: And if we are good, we are beneficent, for all that is good is beneficial. Is that not so?—Yes.

SOCRATES: So virtue is something beneficial?

MENO: That necessarily follows from what has been agreed.

14. The translation here follows the interpretation of T. L. Heath, *A History of Greek Mathematics* (Oxford: Clarendon Press, 1921), vol. I pp. 298 ff.

SOCRATES: Let us then examine what kinds of things benefit us, taking them up one by one: health, we say, and strength, and beauty, and also wealth. We say that these things, and others of the same kind, benefit us, do we not?— We do.

SOCRATES: Yet we say that these same things also sometimes harm one.

88   Do you agree or not?—I do.

SOCRATES: Look then, what directing factor determines in each case whether these things benefit or harm us? Is it not the right use of them that benefits us, and the wrong use that harms us?—Certainly.

SOCRATES: Let us now look at the qualities of the soul. There is something you call moderation, and justice, courage, intelligence, memory, munificence, and all such things?—There is.

b   SOCRATES: Consider whichever of these you believe not to be knowledge but different from it; do they not at times harm us, at other times benefit us? Courage, for example, when it is not wisdom but like a kind of recklessness: when a man is reckless without understanding, he is harmed; when with understanding, he is benefitted.—Yes.

SOCRATES: The same is true of moderation and mental quickness; when they are learned and disciplined with understanding they are beneficial, but without understanding they are harmful?—Very much so.

c   SOCRATES: Therefore, in a word, all that the soul undertakes and endures, if directed by wisdom, ends in happiness, but if directed by ignorance, it ends in the opposite?—That is likely.

SOCRATES: If then virtue is something in the soul and it must be beneficial, it must be knowledge, since all the qualities of the soul are in themselves

d   neither beneficial nor harmful, but accompanied by wisdom or folly they become harmful or beneficial. This argument shows that virtue, being beneficial, must be a kind of wisdom.—I agree.

SOCRATES: Furthermore, those other things we were mentioning just now, wealth and the like, are at times good and at times harmful. Just as for the rest of the soul the direction of wisdom makes things beneficial, but harmful

e   if directed by folly, so in these cases, if the soul uses and directs them right it makes them beneficial, but bad use makes them harmful?—Quite so.

SOCRATES: The wise soul directs them right, the foolish soul wrongly?— That is so.

SOCRATES: So one may say this about everything; all other human activities depend on the soul, and those of the soul itself depend on wisdom if

89   they are to be good. According to this argument the beneficial would be wisdom, and we say that virtue is beneficial?—Certainly.

SOCRATES: Then we say that virtue is wisdom, either the whole or a part of it?

MENO: What you say, Socrates, seems to me quite right.

SOCRATES: Then, if that is so, the good are not so by nature?—I do not think they are.

b   SOCRATES: For if they were, this would follow: if the good were so by nature, we would have people who knew which among the young were by nature good; we would take those whom they had pointed out and guard them in the Acropolis, sealing them up there much more carefully than gold so that no one could corrupt them, and when they reached maturity they would be useful to their cities.—Reasonable enough, Socrates.

SOCRATES: Since the good are not good by nature, does learning make them so?

MENO: Necessarily, as I now think, Socrates, and clearly, on our hypothesis, if virtue is knowledge, it can be taught.

SOCRATES: Perhaps, by Zeus, but may it be that we were not right to agree to this?

MENO: Yet it seemed to be right at the time.

SOCRATES: We should not only think it right at the time, but also now and in the future if it is to be at all sound.

MENO: What is the difficulty? What do you have in mind that you do not like about it and doubt that virtue is knowledge?

SOCRATES: I will tell you, Meno. I am not saying that it is wrong to say that virtue is teachable if it is knowledge, but look whether it is reasonable of me to doubt whether it is knowledge. Tell me this: if not only virtue but anything whatever can be taught, should there not be of necessity people who teach it and people who learn it?—I think so.

SOCRATES: Then again, if on the contrary there are no teachers or learners of something, we should be right to assume that the subject cannot be taught?

MENO: Quite so, but do you think that there are no teachers of virtue?

SOCRATES: I have often tried to find out whether there were any teachers of it, but in spite of all my efforts I cannot find any. And yet I have searched for them with the help of many people, especially those whom I believed to be most experienced in this matter. And now, Meno, Anytus[15] here has opportunely come to sit down by us. Let us share our search with him. It would be reasonable for us to do so, for Anytus, in the first place, is the son of Anthemion, a man of wealth and wisdom, who did not become rich automatically or as the result of a gift like Ismenias the Theban, who recently acquired the possessions of Polycrates, but through his own wisdom and efforts. Further, he did not seem to be an arrogant or puffed up or offensive citizen in other ways, but he was a well-mannered and well-behaved man. Also he gave our friend here a good upbringing and education, as the majority of Athenians believe, for they are electing him to the highest offices. It is right then to look for the teachers of virtue with the help of men such as he, whether there are any and if so who they are. Therefore, Anytus, please join me and your guest friend Meno here, in our inquiry as to who are the teachers of virtue. Look at it in this way: if we wanted Meno to become a good physician, to what teachers would we send him? Would we not send him to the physicians?

---

15. Anytus was one of Socrates' accusers at his trial. See *Apology* 23e.

ANYTUS: Certainly.

SOCRATES: And if we wanted him to be a good shoemaker, to shoemakers?—Yes.

SOCRATES: And so with other pursuits?—Certainly.

SOCRATES: Tell me again on this same topic, like this: we say that we would be right to send him to the physicians if we want him to become

d   a physician; whenever we say that, we mean that it would be reasonable to send him to those who practice the craft rather than to those who do not, and to those who exact fees for this very practice and have shown themselves to be teachers of anyone who wishes to come to them and learn. Is it not with this in mind that we would be right to send him? —Yes.

SOCRATES: And the same is true about flute-playing and the other crafts?

e   It would be very foolish for those who want to make someone a flute-player to refuse to send him to those who profess to teach the craft and make money at it, but to send him to make trouble for others by seeking to learn from those who do not claim to be teachers or have a single pupil in that subject which we want the one we send to learn from them? Do you not think it very unreasonable to do so?—By Zeus I do, and also very ignorant.

SOCRATES: Quite right. However, you can now deliberate with me about our guest friend Meno here. He has been telling me for some time, Anytus,

91   that he longs to acquire that wisdom and virtue which enables men to manage their households and their cities well, to take care of their parents, to know how to welcome and to send away both citizens and strangers

b   as a good man should. Consider to whom we should be right to send him to learn this virtue. Or is it obvious in view of what was said just now that we should send him to those who profess to be teachers of virtue and have shown themselves to be available to any Greek who wishes to learn, and for this fix a fee and exact it?

ANYTUS: And who do you say these are, Socrates?

SOCRATES: You surely know yourself that they are those whom men call sophists.

c   ANYTUS: By Heracles, hush, Socrates. May no one of my household or friends, whether citizen or stranger, be mad enough to go to these people and be harmed by them, for they clearly cause the ruin and corruption of their followers.

SOCRATES: How do you mean, Anytus? Are these people, alone of those who claim the knowledge to benefit one, so different from the others that they not only do not benefit what one entrusts to them but on the contrary

d   corrupt it, even though they obviously expect to make money from the process? I find I cannot believe you, for I know that one man, Protagoras, made more money from this knowledge of his than Phidias who made such notably fine works, and ten other sculptors. Surely what you say is extraordinary, if those who mend old sandals and restore clothes would

be found out within the month if they returned the clothes and sandals   e
in a worse state than they received them; if they did this they would soon
die of starvation, but the whole of Greece has not noticed for forty years
that Protagoras corrupts those who frequent him and sends them away
in a worse moral condition than he received them. I believe that he was
nearly seventy when he died and had practiced his craft for forty years.
During all that time to this very day his reputation has stood high; and
not only Protagoras but a great many others, some born before him and
some still alive today. Are we to say that you maintain that they deceive   92
and harm the young knowingly, or that they themselves are not aware of
it? Are we to deem those whom some people consider the wisest of men
to be so mad as that?

ANYTUS: They are far from being mad, Socrates. It is much rather those
among the young who pay their fees who are mad, and even more the
relatives who entrust their young to them and most of all the cities who   b
allow them to come in and do not drive out any citizen or stranger who
attempts to behave in this manner.

SOCRATES: Has some sophist wronged you, Anytus, or why are you so
hard on them?

ANYTUS: No, by Zeus, I have never met one of them, nor would I allow
any one of my people to do so.

SOCRATES: Are you then altogether without any experience of these men?

ANYTUS: And may I remain so.

SOCRATES: How then, my good sir, can you know whether there is any   c
good in their instruction or not, if you are altogether without experience
of it?

ANYTUS: Easily, for I know who they are, whether I have experience of
them or not.

SOCRATES: Perhaps you are a wizard, Anytus, for I wonder, from what
you yourself say, how else you know about these things. However, let us
not try to find out who the men are whose company would make Meno   d
wicked—let them be the sophists if you like—but tell us, and benefit your
family friend here by telling him, to whom he should go in so large a city
to acquire, to any worthwhile degree, the virtue I was just now describing.

ANYTUS: Why did you not tell him yourself?

SOCRATES: I did mention those whom I thought to be teachers of it, but
you say I am wrong, and perhaps you are right. You tell him in your turn   e
to whom among the Athenians he should go. Tell him the name of anyone
you want.

ANYTUS: Why give him the name of one individual? Any Athenian
gentleman he may meet, if he is willing to be persuaded, will make him
a better man than the sophists would.

SOCRATES: And have these gentlemen become virtuous automatically,
without learning from anyone, and are they able to teach others what they   93
themselves never learned?

ANYTUS: I believe that these men have learned from those who were gentlemen before them; or do you not think that there are many good men in this city?

SOCRATES: I believe, Anytus, that there are many men here who are good at public affairs, and that there have been as many in the past, but have they been good teachers of their own virtue? That is the point we are discussing, not whether there are good men here or not, or whether there

b have been in the past, but we have been investigating for some time whether virtue can be taught. And in the course of that investigation we are inquiring whether the good men of today and of the past knew how to pass on to another the virtue they themselves possessed, or whether a man cannot pass it on or receive it from another. This is what Meno and I have been investigating for some time. Look at it this way, from what

c you yourself have said. Would you not say that Themistocles[16] was a good man?—Yes. Even the best of men.

SOCRATES: And therefore a good teacher of his own virtue if anyone was?

ANYTUS: I think so, if he wanted to be.

SOCRATES: But do you think he did not want some other people to be worthy men, and especially his own son? Or do you think he begrudged

d him this, and deliberately did not pass on to him his own virtue? Have you not heard that Themistocles taught his son Cleophantus to be a good horseman? He could remain standing upright on horseback and shoot javelins from that position and do many other remarkable things which his father had him taught and made skillful at, all of which required good teachers. Have you not heard this from your elders?—I have.

SOCRATES: So one could not blame the poor natural talents of the son

e for his failure in virtue?—Perhaps not.

SOCRATES: But have you ever heard anyone, young or old, say that Cleophantus, the son of Themistocles, was a good and wise man at the same pursuits as his father?—Never.

SOCRATES: Are we to believe that he wanted to educate his son in those other things but not to do better than his neighbors in that skill which he himself possessed, if indeed virtue can be taught?—Perhaps not, by Zeus.

SOCRATES: And yet he was, as you yourself agree, among the best teachers

94 of virtue in the past. Let us consider another man, Aristides, the son of Lysimachus. Do you not agree that he was good?—I very definitely do.

SOCRATES: He too gave his own son Lysimachus the best Athenian education in matters which are the business of teachers, and do you think he made him a better man than anyone else? For you have been in his company

b and seen the kind of man he is. Or take Pericles, a man of such magnificent wisdom. You know that he brought up two sons, Paralus and Xanthippus?—I know.

16. Famous Athenian statesman and general of the early fifth century, a leader in the victorious war against the Persians.

SOCRATES: You also know that he taught them to be as good horsemen as any Athenian, that he educated them in the arts, in gymnastics, and in all else that was a matter of skill not to be inferior to anyone, but did he not want to make them good men? I think he did, but this could not be taught. And lest you think that only a few most inferior Athenians are incapable in this respect, reflect that Thucydides[17] too brought up two sons, Melesias and Stephanus, that he educated them well in all other things. They were the best wrestlers in Athens—he entrusted the one to Xanthias and the other to Eudorus, who were thought to be the best wrestlers of the day, or do you not remember?

ANYTUS: I remember I have heard that said.

SOCRATES: It is surely clear that he would not have taught his boys what it costs money to teach, but have failed to teach them what costs nothing— making them good men—if that could be taught? Or was Thucydides perhaps an inferior person who had not many friends among the Athenians and the allies? He belonged to a great house; he had great influence in the city and among the other Greeks, so that if virtue could be taught he would have found the man who could make his sons good men, be it a citizen or a stranger, if he himself did not have the time because of his public concerns. But, friend Anytus, virtue can certainly not be taught.

ANYTUS: I think, Socrates, that you easily speak ill of people. I would advise you, if you will listen to me, to be careful. Perhaps also in another city, and certainly here, it is easier to injure people than to benefit them. I think you know that yourself.

SOCRATES: I think, Meno, that Anytus is angry, and I am not at all surprised. He thinks, to begin with, that I am slandering those men, and then he believes himself to be one of them. If he ever realizes what slander is, he will cease from anger, but he does not know it now. You tell me, are there not worthy men among your people?—Certainly.

SOCRATES: Well now, are they willing to offer themselves to the young as teachers? Do they agree they are teachers, and that virtue can be taught?

MENO: No, by Zeus, Socrates, but sometimes you would hear them say that it can be taught, at other times, that it cannot.

SOCRATES: Should we say that they are teachers of this subject, when they do not even agree on this point?—I do not think so, Socrates.

SOCRATES: Further, do you think that these sophists, who alone profess to be so, are teachers of virtue?

MENO: I admire this most in Gorgias, Socrates, that you would never hear him promising this. Indeed, he ridicules the others when he hears them making this claim. He thinks one should make people clever speakers.

SOCRATES: You do not think then that the sophists are teachers?

MENO: I cannot tell, Socrates; like most people, at times I think they are, at other times I think that they are not.

17. Not the historian but Thucydides the son of Melesias, an Athenian statesman who was an opponent of Pericles and who was ostracized in 440 B.C.

SOCRATES: Do you know that not only you and the other public men at
d   times think that it can be taught, at other times that it cannot, but that the
poet Theognis[18] says the same thing?—Where?

SOCRATES: In his elegiacs: "Eat and drink with these men, and keep their
company. Please those whose power is great, for you will learn goodness
e   from the good. If you mingle with bad men you will lose even what wit
you possess." You see that here he speaks as if virtue can be taught?—So
it appears.

SOCRATES: Elsewhere, he changes somewhat: "If this could be done" he
says, "and intelligence could be instilled," somehow those who could do
this "would collect large and numerous fees," and further: "Never would
a bad son be born of a good father, for he would be persuaded by wise
96   words, but you will never make a bad man good by teaching." You realize
that the poet is contradicting himself on the same subject?—He seems to be.

SOCRATES: Can you mention any other subject of which those who claim
to be teachers not only are not recognized to be teachers of others but are
not recognized to have knowledge of it themselves, and are thought to be
b   poor in the very matter which they profess to teach? Or any other subject
of which those who are recognized as worthy teachers at one time say it
can be taught and at other times that it cannot? Would you say that people
who are so confused about a subject can be effective teachers of it?—No,
by Zeus, I would not.

SOCRATES: If then neither the sophists nor the worthy people themselves
are teachers of this subject, clearly there would be no others?—I do not
think there are.

c   SOCRATES: If there are no teachers, neither are there pupils?—As you say.

SOCRATES: And we agreed that a subject that has neither teachers nor
pupils is not teachable?—We have so agreed.

SOCRATES: Now there seem to be no teachers of virtue anywhere?—That
is so.

SOCRATES: If there are no teachers, there are no learners?—That seems so.

SOCRATES: Then virtue cannot be taught?

d   MENO: Apparently not, if we have investigated this correctly. I certainly
wonder, Socrates, whether there are no good men either, or in what way
good men come to be.

SOCRATES: We are probably poor specimens, you and I, Meno. Gorgias
has not adequately educated you, nor Prodicus me. We must then at all
costs turn our attention to ourselves and find someone who will in some
e   way make us better. I say this in view of our recent investigation, for it
is ridiculous that we failed to see that it is not only under the guidance
of knowledge that men succeed in their affairs, and that is perhaps why
the knowledge of how good men come to be escapes us.

MENO: How do you mean, Socrates?

18. Theognis was a poet of the mid-sixth century B.C. The quotations below are of lines
33–36 and 434–38 (Diehl) of his elegies.

SOCRATES: I mean this: we were right to agree that good men must be beneficent, and that this could not be otherwise. Is that not so?—Yes.

SOCRATES: And that they will be beneficent if they give us correct guidance in our affairs. To this too we were right to agree?—Yes. 97

SOCRATES: But that one cannot guide correctly if one does not have knowledge; to this our agreement is likely to be incorrect.—How do you mean?

SOCRATES: I will tell you. A man who knew the way to Larissa, or anywhere else you like, and went there and guided others would surely lead them well and correctly?—Certainly.

SOCRATES: What if someone had had a correct opinion as to which was b the way but had not gone there nor indeed had knowledge of it, would he not also lead correctly?—Certainly.

SOCRATES: And as long as he has the right opinion about that of which the other has knowledge, he will not be a worse guide than the one who knows, as he has a true opinion, though not knowledge.—In no way worse.

SOCRATES: So true opinion is in no way a worse guide to correct action than knowledge. It is this that we omitted in our investigation of the nature of virtue, when we said that only knowledge can lead to correct action, c for true opinion can do so also.—So it seems.

SOCRATES: So correct opinion is no less useful than knowledge?

MENO: Yes, to this extent, Socrates. But the man who has knowledge will always succeed, whereas he who has true opinion will only succeed at times.

SOCRATES: How do you mean? Will he who has the right opinion not always succeed, as long as his opinion is right?

MENO: That appears to be so of necessity, and it makes me wonder, Socrates, this being the case, why knowledge is prized far more highly d than right opinion, and why they are different.

SOCRATES: Do you know why you wonder, or shall I tell you?—By all means tell me.

SOCRATES: It is because you have paid no attention to the statues of Daedalus, but perhaps there are none in Thessaly.

MENO: What do you have in mind when you say this?

SOCRATES: That they too run away and escape if one does not tie them down but remain in place if tied down.—So what? e

SOCRATES: To acquire an untied work of Daedalus is not worth much, like acquiring a runaway slave, for it does not remain, but it is worth much if tied down, for his works are very beautiful. What am I thinking of when I say this? True opinions. For true opinions, as long as they remain, are a fine thing and all they do is good, but they are not willing to remain 98 long, and they escape from a man's mind, so that they are not worth much until one ties them down by (giving) an account of the reason why. And that, Meno my friend, is recollection, as we previously agreed. After they are tied down, in the first place they become knowledge, and then they remain in place. That is why knowledge is prized higher than correct opinion, and knowledge differs from correct opinion in being tied down.

MENO: Yes, by Zeus, Socrates, it seems to be something like that.

b   SOCRATES: Indeed, I too speak as one who does not have knowledge but is guessing. However, I certainly do not think I am guessing that right opinion is a different thing from knowledge. If I claim to know anything else—and I would make that claim about few things—I would put this down as one of the things I know.—Rightly so, Socrates.

SOCRATES: Well then, is it not correct that when true opinion guides the course of every action, it does no worse than knowledge?—I think you are right in this too.

c   SOCRATES: Correct opinion is then neither inferior to knowledge nor less useful in directing actions, nor is the man who has it less so than he who has knowledge.—That is so.

SOCRATES: And we agreed that the good man is beneficent.—Yes.

SOCRATES: Since then it is not only through knowledge but also through right opinion that men are good, and beneficial to their cities when they

d   are, and neither knowledge nor true opinion come to men by nature but are acquired—or do you think either of these comes by nature?—I do not think so.

SOCRATES: Then if they do not come by nature, men are not so by nature either.—Surely not.

SOCRATES: As goodness does not come by nature, we inquired next whether it could be taught.—Yes.

SOCRATES: We thought it could be taught, if it was knowledge?—Yes.

SOCRATES: And that it was knowledge if it could be taught?—Quite so.

e   SOCRATES: And that if there were teachers of it, it could be taught, but if there were not, it was not teachable?—That is so.

SOCRATES: And then we agreed that there were no teachers of it?—We did.

SOCRATES: So we agreed that it was neither teachable nor knowledge?—Quite so.

SOCRATES: But we certainly agree that virtue is a good thing?—Yes.

SOCRATES: And that which guides correctly is both useful and good?—Certainly.

99   SOCRATES: And that only these two things, true belief and knowledge, guide correctly, and that if a man possesses these he gives correct guidance. The things that turn out right by some chance are not due to human guidance, but where there is correct human guidance it is due to two things, true belief or knowledge.—I think that is so.

SOCRATES: Now because it cannot be taught, virtue no longer seems to be knowledge?—It seems not.

b   SOCRATES: So one of the two good and useful things has been excluded, and knowledge is not the guide in public affairs.—I do not think so.

SOCRATES: So it is not by some kind of wisdom, or by being wise, that such men lead their cities, those such as Themistocles and those mentioned by Anytus just now? That is the reason why they cannot make others be like themselves, because it is not knowledge which makes them what they are.

MENO: It is likely to be as you say, Socrates.

SOCRATES: Therefore, if it is not through knowledge, the only alternative is that it is through right opinion that statesmen follow the right course for their cities. As regards knowledge, they are no different from soothsayers and prophets. They too say many true things when inspired, but they have no knowledge of what they are saying.—That is probably so.

SOCRATES: And so, Meno, is it right to call divine these men who, without any understanding, are right in much that is of importance in what they say and do?—Certainly.

SOCRATES: We should be right to call divine also those soothsayers and prophets whom we just mentioned, and all the poets, and we should call no less divine and inspired those public men who are no less under the gods' influence and possession, as their speeches lead to success in many important matters, though they have no knowledge of what they are saying.—Quite so.

SOCRATES: Women too, Meno, call good men divine, and the Spartans, when they eulogize someone, say "This man is divine."

MENO: And they appear to be right, Socrates, though perhaps Anytus here will be annoyed with you for saying so.

SOCRATES: I do not mind that; we shall talk to him again, but if we were right in the way in which we spoke and investigated in this whole discussion, virtue would be neither an inborn quality nor taught, but comes to those who possess it as a gift from the gods which is not accompanied by understanding, unless there is someone among our statesmen who can make another into a statesman. If there were one, he could be said to be among the living as Homer said Tiresias was among the dead, namely, that "he alone retained his wits while the others flitted about like shadows."[19] In the same manner such a man would, as far as virtue is concerned, here also be the only true reality compared, as it were, with shadows.

MENO: I think that is an excellent way to put it, Socrates.

SOCRATES: It follows from this reasoning, Meno, that virtue appears to be present in those of us who may possess it as a gift from the gods. We shall have clear knowledge of this when, before we investigate how it comes to be present in men, we first try to find out what virtue in itself is. But now the time has come for me to go. You convince your guest friend Anytus here of these very things of which you have yourself been convinced, in order that he may be more amenable. If you succeed, you will also confer a benefit upon the Athenians.

19. *Odyssey* x.494–95.

GREATER HIPPIAS

This dialogue presents a conversation apparently held in private between Socrates and the sophist Hippias—no company of bystanders is indicated, as they are in Protagoras *and all Socrates' other confrontations with those itinerant educators, the sophists. There is another, shorter dialogue also called* Hippias—*whence this one gets the addition* Greater. *Near the beginning of our dialogue, Hippias invites Socrates to come the next day but one to hear and admire him giving an exhibition speech—the very one which gives the occasion for his and Socrates' discussion in the* Lesser Hippias. *On that later occasion Socrates is plainly not impressed with what he has heard—he stands pointedly silent while the others give it their praises. But here in* Greater Hippias *the invitation reminds him that he has often before praised some parts of other speeches as fine, criticized others as poor, but could never, when challenged, say satisfactorily what it is that makes something fine in the first place—as he ought to have done, if he was entitled to issue those judgments. He wishes to make up this deficiency now, by hearing from the wise Hippias (a self-professed know-everything) 'what the fine is itself'. The Greek word here translated 'fine' is* kalon, *a widely applicable term of highly favorable evaluation, covering our 'beautiful' (in physical, aesthetic, and moral senses), 'noble,' 'admirable', 'excellent', and the like—it is the same term translated 'beautiful' in Diotima's speech about love and its object in* Symposium. *What Socrates is asking for, then, is a general explanation of what feature any object, or action, or person, or accomplishment of any kind, has to have in order correctly to be characterized as highly valued or worth valuing in this broad way. Hippias, of course, fails to deliver himself of an answer that stands up to scrutiny in discussion with Socrates: Socrates now sees clearly that he does not know what the 'fine' is—accordingly, he ought to refrain from issuing judgments about which speeches, or parts of speeches, are fine or the reverse. As a result we have an explanation for Socrates' unexplained silence at the beginning of* Lesser Hippias: *not knowing what the 'fine' itself is, he cannot legitimately evaluate some parts of Hippias' exhibition as 'fine' and others as 'foul' and must simply hold his peace—thinking, perhaps, but not saying, that it is no good at all.*

Hippias himself offers in succession three definitions of the 'fine'. Then, following up on things Hippias has said, Socrates initiates a line of questioning that leads to three or four other suggestions. His procedures here, and the objections he finds against the various answers canvassed, should be compared closely with his similar search for definitions in Euthyphro, Charmides, Laches, *and others of Plato's 'Socratic' dialogues.*

The Platonic authenticity of this dialogue has been both attacked and defended by scholars since the beginning of modern scholarship in the early nineteenth century. It is not cited by Aristotle, though in a few passages he may perhaps be referring to things that Socrates says in it. The neat—perhaps too neat—way it connects itself with Lesser Hippias *might be thought to have its best explanation in an imitator's exploitation of an opening left by Plato in* Lesser Hippias *for a further* Hippias *dialogue. But its philosophical content seems genuinely Platonic, and scholars have studied it respectfully in exploring the development of Plato's own theory of Forms out of reflection on Socrates' search for definitions of moral and other evaluative terms.*

J.M.C.

SOCRATES: Here comes Hippias, fine and wise! How long it's been since 281
you put in to Athens!

HIPPIAS: No spare time, Socrates. Whenever Elis[1] has business to work out with another city, they always come first to me when they choose an ambassador. They think I'm the citizen best able to judge and report b
messages from the various cities. I've often been on missions to other cities, but most often and on the most and greatest affairs to Sparta. That, to answer your question, is why I don't exactly haunt these parts.

SOCRATES: That is what it is like to be truly wise, Hippias, a man of complete accomplishments: in private you are able to make a lot of money from young people (and to give still greater benefits to those from whom you take it); while in public you are able to provide your own city with c
good service (as is proper for one who expects not to be despised, but admired by ordinary people).

But Hippias, how in the world do you explain this: in the old days people who are still famous for wisdom—Pittacus and Bias and the school of Thales of Miletus, and later ones down to Anaxagoras—that all or most of those people, we see, kept away from affairs of state?[2]

HIPPIAS: What do you think, Socrates? Isn't it that they were weak and d
unable to carry their good sense successfully into both areas, the public and the private?

SOCRATES: Then it's really like the improvements in other skills, isn't it, where early craftsmen are worthless compared to modern ones? Should

Translated by Paul Woodruff.

1. Elis was an independent city-state in the northwest Peloponnesus, not far from Olympia. Although geographically close to Sparta, Elis was tilting toward Athens in the contest for leadership between the two.

2. Pittacus ruled in Mytilene for ten years, about 600 B.C., and was famous as a lawgiver; Bias was a statesman of Priene, active in the mid–sixth century B.C.; and Thales is said to have predicted the eclipse of 585 B.C. All three were included in the "Seven Sages." Anaxagoras (c. 500–c. 428) was a philosopher active in Athens in Socrates' youth.

we say that your skill—the skill of the sophists—has been improved in the same way, and that the ancients are worthless compared to you in wisdom?

HIPPIAS: Yes, certainly, you're right.

SOCRATES: So if Bias came to life again in our time, Hippias, he would
282   make himself a laughingstock compared with you people, just as Daedalus[3] also, according to the sculptors, would be laughable if he turned up now doing things like the ones that made him famous.

HIPPIAS: That's right, Socrates, just as you say. However *I* usually praise the ancients who came before us before and more highly than I praise people of our own day, for while I take care to avoid the envy of the living, I fear the wrath of the dead.

b   SOCRATES: You're putting fine thoughts in fine words, Hippias; that's what I think. I can support the truth of your claim; the skill you people have has really been improved in its ability to handle public business as well as private.

Why, Gorgias of Leontini, the well-known sophist, came here on public business as ambassador from his hometown—because he was best qualified in Leontini to handle community affairs. In the assembly, he won his case,
c   and in private, by giving displays and tutorials to young people, he made a lot of money and took it out of the city. Or, another case, our colleague Prodicus came often enough on public business; but just this last time, when he came on public business from Ceos, he made a great impression with his speech in the council, and in private he earned a wonderful sum of money giving displays and tutoring the young. But none of these early
d   thinkers thought fit to charge a monetary fee or give displays of his wisdom for all comers. They were so simple they didn't realize the great value of money. But Gorgias and Prodicus each made more money from wisdom than any craftsman of any kind ever made from his skill. And Protagoras did the same even earlier.

HIPPIAS: Socrates, you haven't the slightest idea how fine this can be. If
e   you knew how much money *I've* made, you'd be amazed. Take one case: I went to Sicily once, when Protagoras was visiting there (he was famous then, and an older man); though I was younger I made much more than a hundred and fifty minas in a short time—and from one very small place, Inycon, more than twenty minas. When I went home with this I gave it to my father, so that he and the other citizens were amazed and thunderstruck. And I almost think I've made more money than any other two sophists you like put together.

283   SOCRATES: That's a fine thing you say, Hippias, strong evidence of your own and modern wisdom, and of the superiority of men nowadays over the ancients. There was a lot of ignorance among our predecessors down to Anaxagoras, according to you. People say the opposite of what happened to you happened to Anaxagoras: he inherited a large sum, but lost every-

---

3. Daedalus was praised in legend as an inventor of lifelike statues for King Minos of Crete.

thing through neglect—there was so little *intelligence*[4] in his wisdom. And they tell stories like that about other early wise men. You make me see there's fine evidence, here, I think, for the superiority of our contemporaries over those who came before; and many will have the same opinion, that a wise man needs to be wise primarily for his own sake. The mark of being wise, I see, is when someone makes the most money. Enough said about that.

Tell me this: from which of the cities you visit did you make the most money? From Sparta, obviously, where you visited most often.

HIPPIAS: Lord no, Socrates.

SOCRATES: Really? Did you make the least?

HIPPIAS: Nothing at all, ever.

SOCRATES: That's weird, Hippias, and amazing! Tell me, isn't the wisdom you have the sort that makes those who study and learn it stronger in virtue?

HIPPIAS: Very much so, Socrates.

SOCRATES: But while you were able to make the sons of Inycans better, you were powerless for the sons of Spartans?

HIPPIAS: Far from it.

SOCRATES: But then do Sicilians want to become better, but not Spartans?

HIPPIAS: Certainly the Spartans want to, as well, Socrates.

SOCRATES: Well, did they stay away from you for lack of money?

HIPPIAS: No. They have enough.

SOCRATES: How could it be that they have money and the desire, and you have the ability to give them the greatest benefits, but they didn't send you away loaded with money? Could it be this, that the Spartans educate their own children better than you would? Should we say this is so, do you agree?

HIPPIAS: Not at all.

SOCRATES: Then weren't you able to persuade the young men in Sparta that if they studied with you they would make more progress in virtue than if they stayed with their own teachers? Or couldn't you persuade their fathers they should entrust the matter to you, rather than look after it themselves, if they cared at all for their sons? Surely they didn't enviously begrudge their own sons the chance to become as good as possible.

HIPPIAS: I don't think they begrudged it.

SOCRATES: But Sparta really is law-abiding.

HIPPIAS: Of course.

SOCRATES: And what's most highly prized in law-abiding cities is virtue.

HIPPIAS: Of course.

SOCRATES: And you, you know most finely of men how to pass virtue on to other people.

HIPPIAS: Very much so, Socrates.

---

4. "Intelligence" (*nous*) was said to be prominent in Anaxagoras' philosophy as the source of order for the entire universe.

SOCRATES: Well, a man who knew most finely how to teach skill with horses would be most honored, and get the most money, in Thessaly, or wherever else in Greece that skill is seriously studied.

HIPPIAS: That's likely.

b SOCRATES: Then won't a man who can teach lessons of the greatest value for virtue be given the highest honor, and make the most money, if he wishes, in Sparta, or in any other law-abiding Greek city? But you think it will be more in Sicily, more in Inycon? Should we believe all this, Hippias? If *you* give the order, it has to be believed.

HIPPIAS: An ancestral tradition of the Spartans, Socrates, forbids them to change their laws, or to give their sons any education contrary to established customs.

c SOCRATES: What do you mean? The Spartans have an ancestral tradition of not doing right, but doing wrong?

HIPPIAS: I wouldn't say so, Socrates.

SOCRATES: But they would do right to educate their young men better, not worse?

HIPPIAS: Right, indeed. But foreign education is not lawful for them: because, mind you, if anybody else had ever taken money from there for education, I would have taken by far the most—they love my lectures and applaud—but, as I say, it's against the law.

d SOCRATES: Do you call law harmful or beneficial to the city, Hippias?

HIPPIAS: I think it is made to be beneficial, but sometimes it does harm, too, if the law is made badly.

SOCRATES: But look here. Don't lawmakers make law to be the greatest good to the city? Without that, law-abiding civilized life is impossible.

HIPPIAS: True.

SOCRATES: So when people who are trying to make laws fail to make them good, they have failed to make them lawful—indeed, to make them law. What do you say?

e HIPPIAS: In precise speech, Socrates, that is so. But men are not accustomed to use words in that manner.

SOCRATES: Do you mean those who know, Hippias, or those who don't?

HIPPIAS: Ordinary people.

SOCRATES: Are *they* the ones who know the truth—ordinary people?

HIPPIAS: Of course not.

SOCRATES: But I suppose people who know, at least, believe that what is more beneficial is more lawful in truth for all men. Do you agree?

HIPPIAS: Yes, I grant it's that way in truth.

SOCRATES: Then it is and stays just the way those who know believe it to be?

HIPPIAS: Quite.

285 SOCRATES: But, as you say, it would be more beneficial for the Spartans to be educated by your teaching, though it's foreign—more beneficial than the local education?

HIPPIAS: And what I say is true.

SOCRATES: And that what is more beneficial is more lawful—do you say that too, Hippias?

HIPPIAS: I did say it.

SOCRATES: By your account it is more lawful for the sons of the Spartans to be educated by Hippias and less lawful by their fathers, if they will really be more benefited by you.

HIPPIAS: They certainly will be benefited, Socrates.   b

SOCRATES: Then the Spartans are breaking the law by not giving you money and entrusting their sons to you.

HIPPIAS: I grant that. I think you said your say on my behalf, and there's no need for me to oppose it.

SOCRATES: So we find the Spartans to be lawbreakers, and that on the most important issue, though they appear to be most lawful. So when they applaud you, really, Hippias, and enjoy your speech, what sort of things have they heard? Surely they're those things you know most finely, things   c about stars and movements in the sky?

HIPPIAS: Not at all. They can't stand the subject.

SOCRATES: Then do they enjoy hearing about geometry?

HIPPIAS: No. Many of them can't even, well, *count.*

SOCRATES: Then they're a long way from putting up with your displays of arithmetic.

HIPPIAS: Good god, yes. A long way.

SOCRATES: Well, do they like those things on which you know how to   d make the sharpest distinctions of anybody—the functions of letters, syllables, rhythms, and harmonies?

HIPPIAS: Harmonies and letters, indeed!

SOCRATES: Well just what is it they love to hear about from you, and applaud? Tell me yourself; I can't figure it out.

HIPPIAS: The genealogies of heroes and men, Socrates, and the settlements (how cities were founded in ancient times), and in a word all ancient   e history—that's what they most love to hear about. So because of them I have been forced to learn up on all such things and to study them thoroughly.

SOCRATES: Good lord, Hippias, you're lucky the Spartans don't enjoy it when someone lists our archons from the time of Solon.[5] Otherwise, you'd have had a job learning them.

HIPPIAS: How come, Socrates? Let me hear them once and I'll memorize fifty names.

SOCRATES: That's right. I forgot you had the art of memory. So I under-   286 stand: the Spartans enjoy you, predictably, because you know a lot of things, and they use you the way children use old ladies, to tell stories for pleasure.

HIPPIAS: Yes—and, good lord, actually about fine activities, Socrates. Just now I made a great impression there speaking about the activities a young

5. The chief elected magistrates of Athens were called archons. Solon was a lawgiver, political reformer, and poet (c. 640/635 to soon after 561/560 B.C.).

man should take up. I have a speech about that I put together really finely, and I put the words particularly well. My setting and the starting point

b   of the speech are something like this: After Troy was taken, the tale is told that Neoptolemus asked Nestor[6] what sort of activities are fine—the sort of activities that would make someone most famous if he adopted them while young. After that the speaker is Nestor, who teaches him a very great many very fine customs. I displayed that there and I expect to display it here the day after tomorrow, in Phidostratus' schoolroom—with many

c   other fine things worth hearing. Eudicus,[7] Apemantus' son, invited me. But why don't you come too, and bring some more people, if they are capable of hearing and judging what is said?

SOCRATES: Certainly, Hippias, if all goes well. But now answer me a short question about that; it's a fine thing you reminded me. Just now someone got me badly stuck when I was finding fault with parts of some speeches for being foul, and praising other parts as fine. He questioned me this

d   way, really insultingly: "Socrates, how do *you* know what sorts of things are fine and foul? Look, would you be able to say what the fine is?" And I, I'm so worthless, I was stuck and I wasn't able to answer him properly. As I left the gathering I was angry and blamed myself, and I made a threatening resolve, that whomever of you wise men I met *first*, I would listen and learn and study, then return to the questioner and fight the argument back. So, as I say, it's a fine thing you came now. Teach me

e   enough about what the fine is itself, and try to answer me with the greatest precision possible, so I won't be a laughingstock again for having been refuted a second time. Of course you know it clearly; it would be a pretty small bit of learning out of the many things *you* know.

HIPPIAS: Small indeed, Socrates, and not worth a thing, as they say.

SOCRATES: Then I'll learn it easily, and no one will ever refute me again.

287   HIPPIAS: No one will. Or what I do would be crude and amateurish.

SOCRATES: Very well said, Hippias—*if* we defeat the man! Will it hurt if I act like him and take the other side of the argument when you answer, so that you'll give me the most practice? I have some experience of the other side. So if it's the same to you I'd like to take the other side, to learn more strongly.

b   HIPPIAS: Take the other side. And, as I just said, the question is not large. I could teach you to answer much harder things than that so no human being could refute you.

SOCRATES: That's amazingly well said! Now, since it's your command, let me become the man as best I can and try to question you. If you displayed that speech to him, the one you mentioned about the fine activities, he'd listen, and when you stopped speaking he'd ask not about anything else

---

6. Neoptolemus, son of Achilles, is the type of the young hero; Nestor, the oldest of the Greeks in the expedition against Troy, is a proverbial wise old man.

7. Eudicus was probably Hippias' host in Athens (*Lesser Hippias* 363b). Nothing is known about Phidostratus.

but about the fine—that's a sort of habit with him—and he'd say: "O c
visitor from Elis, is it not by justice that just people are just?" Answer,
Hippias, as if *he* were the questioner.

HIPPIAS: I shall answer that it is by justice.

SOCRATES: "And is this justice *something*?"

HIPPIAS: Very much so.

SOCRATES: "And by wisdom wise people are wise, and by the good all
good things are good?"

HIPPIAS: How could they be otherwise?

SOCRATES: ". . . by these each *being* something? Of course, it can't be that
they're not."

HIPPIAS: They are.

SOCRATES: "Then all fine things, too, are fine by the fine, isn't that so?"

HIPPIAS: Yes, by the fine. d

SOCRATES: ". . . by that being *something*?"

HIPPIAS: It is. Why not?

SOCRATES: "Tell me then, visitor," he'll say, "what is that, the fine?"

HIPPIAS: Doesn't the person who asks this want to find out what is a
fine thing?

SOCRATES: I don't think so, Hippias. What is *the* fine.

HIPPIAS: And what's the difference between the one and the other?

SOCRATES: You don't think there is any?

HIPPIAS: There's no difference.

SOCRATES: Well, clearly your knowledge is finer. But look here, he's e
asking you not what is a fine thing, but what is the fine.

HIPPIAS: My friend, I understand. I will indeed tell him what the fine is,
and never will I be refuted. Listen, Socrates, to tell the truth, a fine girl is
a fine thing.

SOCRATES: That's fine, Hippias; by Dog you have a glorious answer. So
you really think, if *I* gave that answer, I'd be answering what was asked, 288
and correctly, and never will I be refuted?

HIPPIAS: Socrates, how could you be refuted when you say what everyone
thinks, when everyone who hears you will testify that you're right?

SOCRATES: Very well. Certainly. Now, look, Hippias, let me go over what
you said for myself. *He* will question me somewhat like this: "Come now,
Socrates, give me an answer. All those things you say are fine, will they
be fine if the fine itself is *what*?" Shall I say that if a fine girl is a fine thing,
those things will be fine because of that?

HIPPIAS: Then do you think that man will still try to refute you—that what b
you say is not a fine thing—or if he does try, he won't be a laughingstock?

SOCRATES: You're wonderful! But I'm sure he'll try. Whether trying will
make him a laughingstock—we'll see about that. But I want to tell you
what he'll say.

HIPPIAS: Tell me.

SOCRATES: "How sweet you are, Socrates," he'll say. "Isn't a fine Elean c
mare a fine thing? The god praised mares in his oracle." What shall we

say, Hippias? Mustn't we say that the mare is a fine thing? At least if it's a fine one. How could we dare deny that the fine thing is a fine thing?

HIPPIAS: That's true, Socrates. And the god was right to say that too. We breed very fine mares in our country.

SOCRATES: "Very well," he'll say. "What about a fine lyre? Isn't it a fine thing?" Shouldn't we say so, Hippias?

HIPPIAS: Yes.

SOCRATES: Then after that he'll ask—I know fairly well, judging from the way he is—"Then what about a fine pot, my good fellow? Isn't it a fine thing?"

d HIPPIAS: Who is the man, Socrates? What a boor he is to dare in an august proceeding to speak such vulgar speech that way!

SOCRATES: He's like that, Hippias, not refined. He's garbage, he cares about nothing but the truth. Still the man must have an answer; so here's my first opinion: *If* the pot should have been turned by a good potter, smooth and round and finely fired, like some of those fine two-handled

e pots that hold six choes, very fine ones—*if* he's asking about a pot like that, we have to agree it's fine. How could we say that what is fine is not a fine thing?

HIPPIAS: We couldn't, Socrates.

SOCRATES: "Then is a fine pot a fine thing too? Answer me!" he'll say.

HIPPIAS: But I think that's so, Socrates. Even that utensil is fine if finely

289 made. But on the whole that's not worth judging fine, compared to a horse and a girl and all the other fine things.

SOCRATES: Very well. Then I understand how we'll have to answer him when he asks this question, here: "Don't you know that what Heraclitus said holds good—'the finest of monkeys is foul put together with another class',[8] and the finest of pots is foul put together with the class of girls, so says Hippias the wise." Isn't that so, Hippias?

HIPPIAS: Of course, Socrates. Your answer's right.

b SOCRATES: Then listen. I'm sure of what he'll say next. "What? If you put the class of girls together with the class of gods, won't the same thing happen as happened when the class of pots was put together with that of girls? Won't the finest girl be seen to be foul? And didn't Heraclitus (whom you bring in) say the same thing too, that 'the wisest of men is seen to be a monkey compared to god in wisdom and fineness and everything else?' " Should we agree, Hippias, that the finest girl is foul compared to the class of gods?

HIPPIAS: Who would object to that, Socrates?

c SOCRATES: Then if we agreed to that, he'd laugh and say, "Socrates, do you remember what you were asked?" "Yes," I'll say: "Whatever is the fine itself?" "Then," he'll say, "when you were asked for the fine, do you answer with something that turns out to be no more fine than foul, as you

8. Reading *allōi* at a4; Heraclitus B82 Diels-Kranz.

say yourself?" "Apparently," I'll say. Or what do you advise me to say, my friend?

HIPPIAS: That's what I'd say. Because compared to gods, anyway, the human race is not fine—that's true.

SOCRATES: He'll say: "If I had asked you from the beginning what is both   d
fine and foul, and you had given me the answer you just gave, then wouldn't you have given the right answer? Do you *still* think that the fine itself by which everything else is beautified and seen to be fine when that form is added to it—that *that* is a girl or a horse or a lyre?"

HIPPIAS: But if *that's* what he's looking for, it's the easiest thing in the world to answer him and tell him what the fine (thing) is by which everything else is beautified and is seen to be fine when it is added. The man's   e
quite simple; he has no feeling at all for fine possessions. If you answer him that this thing he's asking for, the fine, is just *gold*, he'll be stuck and won't try to refute you. Because we all know, don't we, that wherever that is added, even if it was seen to be foul before, it will be seen to be fine when it has been beautified with gold.

SOCRATES: You have no experience of this man, Hippias. He stops at nothing, and he never accepts anything easily.

HIPPIAS: So what? He *must* accept what's said correctly, or, if not, be a   290
laughingstock.

SOCRATES: Well, *that* answer he certainly will not accept, my friend. And what's more, he'll jeer at me, and say, "Are you crazy? Do you think Phidias[9] is a bad workman?" And I think I'll say, "No, not at all."

HIPPIAS: And you'll be right about that.

SOCRATES: Right enough. Then when I agree that Phidias is a good   b
workman, this person will say, "Next, do you think Phidias didn't know about this fine thing you mention?" "What's the point?" I'll say. "The point is," he'll say, "that Phidias didn't make Athena's eyes out of gold, nor the rest of her face, nor her feet, nor her hands—as he would have done if gold would really have made them be seen to be finest—but he made them out of ivory. Apparently he went wrong through ignorance; he didn't know gold was what made everything fine, wherever it is added." What shall we answer when he says that, Hippias?

HIPPIAS: It's not hard. We'll say he made the statue right. Ivory's fine   c
too, I think.

SOCRATES: "Then why didn't he work the middles of the eyes out of ivory? He used stone, and he found stone that resembled ivory as closely as possible. Isn't a stone a fine thing too, if it's a fine one?" Shall we agree?

HIPPIAS: Yes, at least when it's appropriate.

SOCRATES: "But when it's not appropriate it's foul?" Do I agree or not?

HIPPIAS: Yes, when it's not appropriate anyway.

---

9. Phidias (b. ca. 490 B.C.), an Athenian sculptor, was best known as designer of the Parthenon sculptures. The statue of Athena mentioned in Socrates' next speech was fashioned of ivory and gold for the Parthenon.

d   SOCRATES: "Well," he'll say. "You're a wise man! Don't ivory and gold make things be seen to be fine when they're appropriate, but foul when they're not?" Shall we be negative? Or shall we agree with him that he's right?

HIPPIAS: We'll agree to *this:* whatever is appropriate to each thing makes that particular thing fine.

SOCRATES: "Then," he'll say, "when someone boils the pot we just mentioned, the fine one, full of fine bean soup, is a gold stirring spoon or a figwood one more appropriate?"

e   HIPPIAS: Heracles! What kind of man is this! Won't you tell me who he is?

SOCRATES: You wouldn't know him if I told you the name.

HIPPIAS: But I know right now he's an ignoramus.

SOCRATES: Oh, he's a real plague, Hippias. Still, what shall we say? Which of the two spoons is appropriate to the soup and the pot? Isn't it clearly the wooden one? It makes the soup smell better, and at the same time, my friend, it won't break our pot, spill out the soup, put out the fire, and make us do without a truly noble meal, when we were going to have a

291   banquet. That gold spoon would do all these things; so *I* think we should say the figwood spoon is more appropriate than the gold one, unless you say otherwise.

HIPPIAS: Yes, it's more appropriate. But *I* wouldn't talk with a man who asked things like that.

SOCRATES: Right you are. It wouldn't be appropriate for you to be filled up with words like that, when you're so finely dressed, finely shod, and

b   famous for wisdom all over Greece. But it's nothing much for me to mix with him. So help me get prepared. Answer for my sake. "If the figwood is really more appropriate than the gold," the man will say, "wouldn't it be finer? Since you agreed, Socrates, that the appropriate is finer than the not appropriate?"

Hippias, don't we agree that the figwood spoon is finer than the gold one?

HIPPIAS: Would you like me to tell you what you can say the fine is— and save yourself a lot of argument?

c   SOCRATES: Certainly. But not before you tell me how to answer. Which of those two spoons I just mentioned is appropriate and finer?

HIPPIAS: Answer, if you'd like, that it's the one made of fig.

SOCRATES: Now tell me what you were going to say. Because by *that* answer, if I say the fine is gold, apparently I'll be made to see that gold is no finer than wood from a figtree. So what do you say the fine is this time?

d   HIPPIAS: I'll tell you. I think you're looking for an answer that says the fine is the sort of thing that will never be seen to be foul for anyone, anywhere, at any time.

SOCRATES: Quite right, Hippias. Now you've got a fine grasp of it.

HIPPIAS: Listen now, if anyone has anything to say against *this,* you can certainly say I'm not an expert on anything.

SOCRATES: Tell me quickly, for god's sake.

HIPPIAS: I say, then, that it is always finest, both for every man and in every place, to be rich, healthy, and honored by the Greeks, to arrive at old age, to make a fine memorial to his parents when they die, and to have a fine, grand burial from his own children.

SOCRATES: Hurray, Hippias! What a wonderful long speech, worthy of yourself! I'm really delighted at the kind way in which—to the best of your ability—you've helped me out. But we didn't hit the enemy, and now he'll certainly laugh at us harder than ever.

HIPPIAS: That laughter won't do him any good, Socrates. When he has nothing to say in reply, but laughs anyway, he'll be laughing at himself, and he'll be a laughingstock to those around.

SOCRATES: That may be so. But maybe, as I suspect, he'll do more than laugh at me for that answer.

HIPPIAS: What do you mean?

SOCRATES: If he happens to have a stick, and I don't run and run away from him, he'll try to give me a thrashing.

HIPPIAS: What? Is the man your owner or something? Do you mean he could do that and not be arrested and convicted? Or don't you have any laws in this city, but people are allowed to hit each other without any right?

SOCRATES: No, that's not allowed at all.

HIPPIAS: Then he'll be punished for hitting you without any right.

SOCRATES: I don't think so, Hippias. No, if I gave *that* answer he'd have a right—in *my* opinion anyway.

HIPPIAS: Then I think so too, seeing that you yourself believe it.

SOCRATES: Should I tell you why *I* believe he'd have a right to hit me if I gave that answer? Or will you hit me without trial too? Will you hear my case?

HIPPIAS: It would be awful if I wouldn't. What do you have to say?

SOCRATES: I'll tell you the same way as before. I'll be acting out his part—so the words I use are not directed against you; they're like what he says to me, harsh and grotesque. "Tell me, Socrates," you can be sure he'll say, "do you think it's wrong for a man to be whipped when he sings such a dithyramb[10] as that, so raucously, way out of tune with the question?" "How?" I'll say. "How!" he'll say. "Aren't you capable of remembering that I asked for the fine itself? For what when added to anything—whether to a stone or a plank or a man or a god or any action or any lesson—*anything* gets to be fine? I'm asking you to tell me what fineness is itself, my man, and I am no more able to make you hear me than if you were sitting here in stone—and a millstone at that, with no ears and no brain!"

Hippias, wouldn't you be upset if I got scared and came back with this: "But that's what Hippias said the fine was. And I asked him the way you asked me, for that which is fine always and for everyone." So what do you say? Wouldn't you be upset if I said that?

10. A dithyramb is a sort of choral ode heavily embellished with music.

HIPPIAS: Socrates, I know perfectly well that what I said is fine for everyone—everyone will think so.

SOCRATES: "And *will* be fine?" he'll ask. "I suppose the fine is always fine."

HIPPIAS: Certainly.

SOCRATES: "Then it *was* fine, too," he'll say.

HIPPIAS: It was.

SOCRATES: "For Achilles as well?" he'll ask. "Does the visitor from Elis 293 say it is fine for *him* to be buried after his parents? And for his grandfather Aeacus? And for the other children of the gods? And for the gods themselves?"[11]

HIPPIAS: What's that? Go to blessedness. These questions the man asks, Socrates, they're sacrilegious!

SOCRATES: What? Is it a sacrilege to say that's so when someone else asks the question?

HIPPIAS: Maybe.

SOCRATES: "Then maybe you're the one who says that it is fine for everyone, always, to be buried by his children, and to bury his parents? And isn't Heracles included in 'everyone' as well as everybody we mentioned a moment ago?"

HIPPIAS: But I didn't mean it for the *gods*.

b SOCRATES: "Apparently you didn't mean it for the heroes either."

HIPPIAS: Not if they're children of gods.

SOCRATES: "But if they're not?"

HIPPIAS: Certainly.

SOCRATES: "Then according to your latest theory, I see, what's awful and unholy and foul for some heroes—Tantalus and Dardanus and Zethus— is fine for Pelops and those with similar parentage."

HIPPIAS: That's my opinion.

SOCRATES: "Then what you think is what you did not say a moment c ago—that being buried by your children and burying your parents is foul sometimes, and for some people. Apparently it's still more impossible for that to become and be fine for everyone; so that has met the same fate as the earlier ones, the girl and the pot, and a more laughable fate besides; it is fine for some, not fine for others. And to this very day, Socrates, you aren't able to answer the question about the fine, what it is."

That's how he'll scold me—and he's right if I give him such an answer. d Most of what he says to me is somewhat like that. But sometimes, as if he took pity on my inexperience and lack of education, he himself makes me a suggestion. He asks if I don't think such and such is the fine, or whatever else he happens to be investigating and the discussion is about.

HIPPIAS: How do you mean?

11. Achilles' mother, Thetis, was a goddess. His grandfather, Aeacus, was a son of Zeus. Heracles, Tantalus, Dardanus, and Zethus (below) were all said to be sons of Zeus. Pelops, son of Tantalus, was of human parentage.

SOCRATES: I'll show you. "You're a strange man, Socrates," he'll say, "giving answers like that, in that way. You should stop that. They're very simple and easy to refute. But see if you think this sort of answer is fine. We had a grip on it just now when we replied that gold is fine for things it's appropriate to, but not for those it's not. And anything else is fine if *this* has been added to it: this, the appropriate itself—the nature of the appropriate itself. See if it turns out to be the fine."

e

I'm used to agreeing with such things every time, because I don't know what to say. What do you think? Is the appropriate fine?

HIPPIAS: In every way, Socrates.

SOCRATES: Let's look it over. We'd better not be deceived.

HIPPIAS: We have to look it over.

SOCRATES: See here, then. What do we say about the appropriate: Is it what makes—by coming to be present—each thing to which it is present *be seen to be fine*, or *be fine*, or neither?

294

HIPPIAS: I think it's what makes things be seen to be fine. For example, when someone puts on clothes and shoes that suit him, even if he's ridiculous, he is seen to be finer.

SOCRATES: Then if the appropriate makes things be seen to be finer than they are, it would be a kind of deceit about the fine, and it wouldn't be what we are looking for, would it, Hippias? I thought we were looking for that by which all fine things are fine. For example, what all large things are large by is *the projecting*. For by that all large things—even if they are not seen to be so—if they project they are necessarily large. Similarly, we say the fine is what all things are fine by, whether or not they are seen to be fine. What would it be? It wouldn't be the appropriate. Because that makes things be seen to be finer than they are—so you said—and it won't let things be seen to be as they are. We must try to say what it is that makes things fine, whether they are seen to be fine or not, just as I said a moment ago. That's what we're looking for, if we're really looking for the fine.

b

c

HIPPIAS: But Socrates, the appropriate makes things both be fine and be seen to be fine, when it's present.

SOCRATES: Is it impossible for things that are really fine not to be seen to be fine, since what makes them be seen is present?

HIPPIAS: It's impossible.

SOCRATES: Then shall we agree to this, Hippias: that everything really fine—customs and activities both—are both thought to be, and seen to be, fine always, by everybody? Or just the opposite, that they're unknown, and individuals in private and cities in public both have more strife and contention about them than anything?

d

HIPPIAS: Much more the latter, Socrates. They are unknown.

SOCRATES: They wouldn't be, if "being seen to be" had been added to them. And that would have been added if the appropriate were fine and made things not only be but be seen to be fine. Therefore, if the appropriate e is what makes things fine, it would be the fine we're looking for, but it would not be what makes things be seen to be fine. Or, if the appropriate is what makes things be seen to be fine, it wouldn't be the fine we're looking for. Because *that* makes things be; but by itself it could not make things be seen to be and be, nor could anything else. Let's choose whether we think the appropriate is what makes things be seen to be, or be, fine.

HIPPIAS: It's what makes things be seen to be, in my opinion, Socrates.

SOCRATES: Oh dear! It's gone and escaped from us, our chance to know what the fine is, since the appropriate has been seen to be something other than fine.

HIPPIAS: God yes, Socrates. And I think that's very strange.

295 SOCRATES: But we shouldn't let it go yet, my friend. I still have some hope that the fine will make itself be seen for what it is.

HIPPIAS: Of course it will. It's not hard to find. I'm sure if I went off and looked for it by myself—in quiet—I would tell it to you more precisely than any preciseness.

SOCRATES: Ah, Hippias! Don't talk big. You see how much trouble it has

b given us already; and if it gets mad at us I'm afraid it will run away still harder. But that's nonsense. You'll easily find it, I think, when you're alone. But for god's sake, find it in front of me, or look for it with me if you want, as we've been doing. If we find it, that would be the finest thing; but if not, I will content myself with my fate, while you go away and find it easily. And if we find it now, of course I won't be a nuisance to you

c later, trying to figure out what it was you found on your own. Now see what you think the fine is: I'm saying that it's—pay attention now, be careful I'm not raving—let this be fine for us: whatever is useful. What I had in mind when I said that was this. We say eyes are fine not when we think they are in such a state they're unable to see, but whenever they *are able*, and are useful for seeing. Yes?

HIPPIAS: Yes.

SOCRATES: And that's how we call the whole body fine, sometimes for

d running, sometimes for wrestling. And the same goes for all animals—a fine horse, rooster, or quail—and all utensils and means of transport on land and sea, boats and warships, and the tools of every skill, music and all the others; and, if you want, activities and laws—virtually all these are called fine in the same way. In each case we look at the nature it's got, its

e manufacture, its condition; then we call what is useful "fine" in respect of *the way* it is useful, *what* it is useful *for*, and *when* it is useful; but anything useless in all those respects we call "foul." Don't you think that way too, Hippias?

HIPPIAS: Yes, I do.

SOCRATES: So then are we right to say now that the useful more than anything turns out to be fine?

HIPPIAS: Right, Socrates.

SOCRATES: So what's *able* to accomplish a particular thing is useful for that for which it is able; and what's unable is useless.

HIPPIAS: Certainly.

SOCRATES: Then is ability[12] fine, but inability foul?

HIPPIAS: Very much so. Many things give us evidence for the truth of that, especially politics. The finest thing of all is to be able politically in your own city, and to be unable is the foulest of all. 296

SOCRATES: Good! Then doesn't it follow from these points that, by god, wisdom is really the finest thing of all, and ignorance the foulest?

HIPPIAS: What are you thinking?

SOCRATES: Keep quiet, my friend. I'm frightened. What on earth are we saying now?

HIPPIAS: Why should you be frightened now? The discussion has gone really well for you this time. b

SOCRATES: I wish it had! Look this over with me: could anyone do something he doesn't know how to do, and isn't at all able to do?

HIPPIAS: Not at all. How could he do what he isn't able to do?

SOCRATES: Then when people make mistakes, do bad work, even when they do it unintentionally—if they aren't able to do things, they wouldn't ever do them, would they?

HIPPIAS: That's clear.

SOCRATES: But people who are able are able by ability? I don't suppose it's by inability. c

HIPPIAS: Of course not.

SOCRATES: And everyone who does things is able to do the things he does.

HIPPIAS: Yes.

SOCRATES: And all men do much more bad work than good, starting from childhood—and make mistakes unintentionally.

HIPPIAS: That's right.

SOCRATES: So? We don't call that ability and that sort of useful thing fine, do we? The sort that's useful for doing some bad piece of work? Far from it. d

HIPPIAS: Far indeed, Socrates. That's what I think.

SOCRATES: Then this able and useful of ours is apparently not the fine, Hippias.

HIPPIAS: It is, Socrates, if it's able to do good, if it's useful for that sort of thing.

SOCRATES: Then here's what got away from us: the able-and-useful without qualification is fine. And this is what our mind wanted to say, Hippias: the useful-and-able for making some good—*that* is the fine. e

HIPPIAS: I think so.

SOCRATES: But that is beneficial. Isn't it?

HIPPIAS: Certainly.

SOCRATES: Then that's the way fine bodies and fine customs and wisdom and everything we mentioned a moment ago are fine—because they're beneficial.

12. Alternatively, "power."

HIPPIAS: That's clear.

SOCRATES: So the beneficial appears to be the fine we wanted.

HIPPIAS: Certainly, Socrates.

SOCRATES: But the beneficial is the maker of good.

HIPPIAS: It is.

SOCRATES: And the maker is nothing else but the cause, isn't it?

HIPPIAS: That's so.

SOCRATES: Then the fine is a cause of the good.

297   HIPPIAS: It is.

SOCRATES: But the cause is different from what it's a cause of. I don't suppose the cause would be a cause of a cause. Look at it this way: isn't the cause seen to be a maker?

HIPPIAS: Certainly.

SOCRATES: Then what is made by the maker is the thing that comes to be; it's not the maker.

HIPPIAS: That's right.

SOCRATES: Then the thing that comes to be and the maker are different things.

HIPPIAS: Yes.

b   SOCRATES: So the cause isn't a cause of a cause, but of the thing that comes to be because of it.

HIPPIAS: Certainly.

SOCRATES: So if the fine is a cause of the good, the good should come to be from the fine. And apparently this is why we're eager to have intelligence and all the other fine things: because their product, their child—the good—is worth being eager about. It would follow that the fine is a kind of father of the good.

HIPPIAS: Certainly. You're talking fine, Socrates.

c   SOCRATES: Then see if this is fine as well: the father is not a son and the son is not a father.

HIPPIAS: Fine.

SOCRATES: The cause is not a thing that comes to be, and the thing that comes to be is not a cause.

HIPPIAS: That's true.

SOCRATES: Good god! Then the fine is not good, nor the good fine. Or do you think they could be, from what we've said?

HIPPIAS: Good god, no. I don't think so.

SOCRATES: So are we happy with that? Would you like to say that the fine is not good, nor the good fine?

HIPPIAS: Good god, no. I'm not at all happy with it.

d   SOCRATES: Good god, yes, Hippias. Nothing we've said so far makes me less happy.

HIPPIAS: So it seems.

SOCRATES: Then it doesn't turn out to be the finest account, as we thought a moment ago, that the beneficial—the useful and the able for making some good—is fine. It's not that way at all, but if possible it's more laughable than the first accounts, when we thought the girl, or each one of those things mentioned earlier, was the fine.

HIPPIAS: Apparently.

SOCRATES: And *I* don't know where to turn, Hippias. I'm stuck. Do you have anything to say?

HIPPIAS: Not at present; but as I said a little while ago, I'm sure I'll find it when I've looked.

SOCRATES: But I don't think I can wait for you to do that, I have such a desire to know. And besides I think I just got clear. Look. If whatever makes us be glad, not with all the pleasures, but just through hearing and sight—if we call *that* fine, how do you suppose we'd do in the contest?

Men, when they're fine anyway—and everything decorative, pictures and sculptures—these all delight us when we see them, if they're fine. Fine sounds and music altogether, and speeches and storytelling have the same effect. So if we answered that tough man, "Your honor, the fine is what is pleasant through hearing and sight," don't you think we'd curb his toughness?

HIPPIAS: This time, Socrates, I think what the fine is has been well said.

SOCRATES: What? shall we say that fine activities and laws are fine by being pleasant through hearing and sight? Or that they have some other form?

HIPPIAS: Those things might slip right past the man.

SOCRATES: By Dog, Hippias, not past the person I'd be most ashamed to babble at, or pretend to say something when I'm not saying anything.

HIPPIAS: Who's that?

SOCRATES: Sophroniscus' son.[13] He wouldn't easily let me say those things without testing them, any more than he'd let me talk as if I knew what I didn't know.

HIPPIAS: Well for my part, since you say so, I think that's something else in the case of the laws.

SOCRATES: Keep quiet, Hippias. We could well be thinking we're in the clear again, when we've gotten stuck on the same point about the fine as we did a moment ago.

HIPPIAS: What do you mean, Socrates?

SOCRATES: I'll show you what's become obvious to me, if I'm saying anything. In the case of laws and activities, those could easily be seen not to be outside the perception we have through hearing and sight. But let's stay with this account, that what is pleasing through them is fine, and not bring that about the laws into the center. But if someone should ask—whether he's the one I mentioned or anyone else—"What, Hippias and Socrates? Are you marking off the sort of pleasant you call fine from the pleasant, and not calling what is pleasant to the other senses fine—food and drink, what goes with making love, and all the rest of that sort of

13. Sophroniscus' son is Socrates himself.

thing? Aren't they pleasant? Do you say there's altogether no pleasure in such things? Not in anything but seeing and hearing?"

What shall we say, Hippias?

HIPPIAS: Of course we'll say there are very great pleasures in those others, Socrates.

SOCRATES: "What?" he'll say. "Though they're no less pleasures than these, would you strip them of this word, and deprive them of being fine?"

"Yes," we'll say, "because anyone in the world would laugh at us if we called it not *pleasant to eat* but *fine*, or if we called a pleasant smell not *pleasant* but *fine*. And as for making love, everybody would fight us; they'd say it is most pleasant, but that one should do it, if he does it at all, where no one will see, because it is the foulest thing to be seen." When we've said that, Hippias, he'd probably reply, "I understand that too. You're ashamed, you've been ashamed a long time, to call those pleasures fine, because men don't think they are. But I didn't ask for that—what ordinary people think is fine—but for what *is* fine."

I think we'll repeat our hypothesis: "This is what we say is fine, the part of the pleasant that comes by sight and hearing." What else would you do with the argument? What should we say, Hippias?

HIPPIAS: We must say that and nothing else, in view of what's been said.

SOCRATES: "That's fine," he'll say. "Then if the pleasant through sight and hearing is fine, whatever is not pleasant in that way clearly would not be fine."

Shall we agree?

HIPPIAS: Yes.

SOCRATES: "Then is the pleasant through sight pleasant through sight and hearing? Or is the pleasant through hearing pleasant through hearing and through sight?"

"By no means," we'll say. "In that case what comes through one would be what comes through both—I think that's what you mean—but *we* said that each of these pleasant things taken itself by itself is fine, and both are fine as well."

Isn't that our answer?

HIPPIAS: Certainly.

SOCRATES: "Then," he'll say, "does one pleasant thing differ from another in *this:* in being pleasant? I'm not asking whether one pleasure can be greater or lesser than another, or more or less, but whether one can differ in this very way—in being a pleasure—and one of the pleasures not be a pleasure."

We don't think so, do we?

HIPPIAS: We don't think so.

SOCRATES: "So," he'll say. "You selected those pleasures from the other pleasures because of something different from their being pleasures. You saw some quality in the pair of them, something that differentiates them from the others, and you say they are fine by looking at that. I don't suppose pleasure through sight is fine because of *that*—that it is through sight. Because if that were the cause of its being fine, the other—the one through hearing—wouldn't ever be fine. It's not a pleasure through sight."

That's true. Shall we say that's true?

HIPPIAS: We'll say it.

SOCRATES: "And again, pleasure through hearing turns out not to be fine   300 because of *that*—that it is through hearing. Otherwise, pleasure through sight would never be fine, because it is not a pleasure through hearing."

Shall we say that the man who says this is saying the truth, Hippias?

HIPPIAS: It's true.

SOCRATES: "But both are fine, as you say." We do say that.

HIPPIAS: We do.

SOCRATES: "Then they have some thing that itself makes them be fine, that common thing that belongs to both of them in common and to each   b privately. Because I don't suppose there's any other way they would both and each be fine."

Answer me as you would him.

HIPPIAS: I think it's as he says, and that's my answer.

SOCRATES: Then if something is attributed to both pleasures but not to each one, they would not be fine by that attribute.

HIPPIAS: And how could that be, Socrates? That when neither has an attribute, whatever it may be, this attribute—which belongs to neither—could belong to both?

SOCRATES: Don't you think it could happen?   c

HIPPIAS: If it did I'd be in the grip of a lot of inexperience about the nature of these things and the terms of the present terminology.

SOCRATES: Pleasantly put, Hippias. But maybe I'm turning out to think I can see something that's the way you say it can't be, or I'm not seeing anything.

HIPPIAS: It turns out that you're not, Socrates. You're quite readily mis-seeing.

SOCRATES: And yet a lot of things like that are seen plainly in my mind; but I don't believe them if they're not imagined in yours, since you're a   d man who's made the most money by wisdom of anyone alive, and I'm one who never made anything. And I wonder, my friend, if you're not playing with me and deliberately fooling me, so many and so clear are the examples I see.

HIPPIAS: Socrates, no one will know finer than you whether I'm playing or not, if you try to say what these things are that are seen by you plainly. You'll be seen to be saying nothing. Because never shall you find what is attributed to neither me nor you, but is attributed to both of us.

SOCRATES: What do you mean, Hippias? Maybe you're saying something   e I don't understand. But listen more clearly to what I want to say. Because I see what is not attributed to me to be, and what neither I am nor you are, and this can be attributed to both of us. And there are others besides, which are attributed to both of us to be, things neither of us is.

HIPPIAS: Your answers seem weird again, Socrates, more so than the ones you gave a little earlier. Look. If both of us were just, wouldn't each
301   of us be too? Or if each of us were unjust, wouldn't both of us? Or if we were healthy, wouldn't each be? Or if each of us had some sickness or were wounded or stricken or had any other tribulation, again, wouldn't both of us have that attribute? Similarly, if we happened to be gold or silver or ivory, or, if you like, noble or wise or honored or even old or young or anything you like that goes with human beings, isn't it really necessary that each of us be that as well?

b   SOCRATES: Of course.

HIPPIAS: But Socrates, *you* don't look at the entireties of things, nor do the people you're used to talking with. You people knock away at the fine and the other beings by taking each separately and cutting it up with words. Because of that you don't realize how great they are—naturally continuous bodies of being. And now you're so far from realizing it that
c   you think there's some attribute or being that is true of these both but not of each, or of each but not of both. That's how unreasonably and unobservantly and foolishly and uncomprehendingly you operate.

SOCRATES: That's the way things are for us, Hippias. "They're not the way a person wants"—so runs the proverb people often quote—"but the way he can get them." But your frequent admonitions are a help to us. This time, for example, before these admonitions from you about the stupid way we operate. . . . Shall I make a still greater display, and tell you what
d   we had in mind about them? Or not tell?

HIPPIAS: You're telling someone who already knows, Socrates. I know how everybody who's involved in speeches operates. All the same, if it's more pleasant for you, speak on.

SOCRATES: It really is more pleasant. We were so foolish, my friend, before you said what you did, that we had an opinion about me and you that *each* of us is *one*, but that we wouldn't *both* be *one* (which is what *each*
e   of us would be) because we're not *one* but *two*—we were so stupid-like. But now, we have been instructed by you that if two is what we both are, two is what each of us must be as well; and if each is one, then both must be one as well. The continuous theory of *being*, according to Hippias, does not allow it to be otherwise; but whatever both are, that each is as well; and whatever each is, both are. Right now I sit here persuaded by you. First, however, remind me, Hippias. Are you and I one? Or are you two and I two?

HIPPIAS: What do you mean, Socrates?

302   SOCRATES: Just what I say. I'm afraid of you, afraid to speak clearly, because you get angry at me whenever you think you've said anything. All the same, tell me more. Isn't each of us one, and *that*—being one—is attributed to him?

HIPPIAS: Certainly.

SOCRATES: Then if each of us is one, wouldn't he also be odd-numbered? Or don't you consider *one* to be odd?

HIPPIAS: I do.

SOCRATES: Then will both of us be odd-numbered, being two?

HIPPIAS: It couldn't be, Socrates.

SOCRATES: But both are even-numbered. Yes?

HIPPIAS: Certainly.

SOCRATES: Then because both are even-numbered, on account of *that*, each of us is even-numbered as well. Right?

HIPPIAS: Of course not.   b

SOCRATES: Then it's not entirely necessary, as you said it was a moment ago, that whatever is true of both is also true of each, and that whatever is true of each is also true of both.

HIPPIAS: Not that sort of thing, but the sort I said earlier.

SOCRATES: They're enough, Hippias. We have to accept them too, because we see that some are this way, and others are not this way. I said (if you remember how this discussion got started) that pleasure through sight and hearing was not fine by *this*—that each of them turned out to have   c
an attribute but not both, or that both had it but not each—but by that by which both and each are fine, because you agreed that they are both and each fine. That's why I thought it was by the being that adheres to both, if both are fine—it was by *that* they had to be fine, and not by what falls off one or the other. And I still think so now. But let's make a fresh start. Tell me, if the pleasure through sight and the one through hearing are   d
both and each fine, doesn't what makes them fine adhere in both and in each of them?

HIPPIAS: Certainly.

SOCRATES: Then is it because each and both are *pleasure*—would they be fine because of that? Or would that make all other pleasures no less fine than these? Remember, we saw that they were no less pleasures.

HIPPIAS: I remember.

SOCRATES: But is it because they are through sight and hearing—are they   e
called *fine* because of that?

HIPPIAS: That's the way it was put.

SOCRATES: See if this is true. It was said, I'm remembering, that the pleasant was fine this way: not all the pleasant, but whatever is through sight and hearing.

HIPPIAS: True.

SOCRATES: Doesn't that attribute adhere in both, but not in each? I don't suppose each of them is through both (as we said earlier), but both through both, not each. Is that right?

HIPPIAS: Yes.

SOCRATES: Then *that's* not what makes each of them fine; it doesn't adhere in each (because "both" doesn't adhere in each). So the hypothesis lets us call both of them fine, but it doesn't let us call each of them fine.

What else should we say? Isn't it necessarily so?   303

HIPPIAS: So we see.

SOCRATES: Then should we call both fine, but not call each fine?

HIPPIAS: What's to stop us?

SOCRATES: *This* stops us, friend, in my opinion. We had things that come to belong to particular things in this way: if they come to belong to both, they do to each also; and if to each, to both—all the examples you gave. Right?

HIPPIAS: Yes.

SOCRATES: But the examples *I* gave were not that way. Among them were "each" itself and "both." Is that right?

HIPPIAS: It is.

b   SOCRATES: With which of these do you put the fine, Hippias? With those you mentioned? If I am strong and so are you, we're both strong too; and if I am just and so are you, we both are too. And if both, then each. In the same way, if I am fine and so are you, we both are too; and if both, then each. Or does nothing stop them from being like the things I said I saw clearly: when both of anything are even-numbered, each may be either odd- or possibly even-numbered. And again, when each of them is
c   inexpressible, both together may be expressible, or possibly inexpressible.[14] And millions of things like that. With which do you place the fine? Do you see the matter the way I do? I think it's a great absurdity for both of us to be fine, but each not; or each fine, but both not, or anything else like that.

Do you choose the way I do, or the other way?

HIPPIAS: The first way is for me, Socrates.

d   SOCRATES: Well done, Hippias! We've saved ourselves a longer search. Because if the fine is with *those*, then the pleasant through sight and hearing is not fine anymore. "Through sight and hearing" makes both fine, but not each. But that's impossible, as you and I agree, Hippias.

HIPPIAS: We do agree.

SOCRATES: Then it's impossible for the pleasant through sight and hearing to be fine, since if it becomes fine it presents one of the impossibilities.

HIPPIAS: That's right.

e   SOCRATES: "Tell me again from the beginning," he'll say; "since you were quite wrong with that. What do you say that is—the fine in both pleasures, which made you value them above the others and call them fine?" Hippias, I think we have to say that they are the most harmless pleasures and the best, both and each as well. Or can you mention something else that distinguishes them from all the others?

HIPPIAS: Not at all. They really are best.

SOCRATES: He'll say, "Then this is what you say is the fine—beneficial pleasure?"

"Apparently so," I'll say. And you?

HIPPIAS: Me too.

---

14. By "inexpressible number" is probably meant an irrational surd (square root of a non-square number). If so, the claim is false. The sum of two such numbers is irrational.

SOCRATES: He'll say: "The maker of good is beneficial, but we just saw   304
that the maker and what is made are different. Your account comes down
to the earlier account. The good would not be fine, or the fine good, if
each of these were different."

"Absolutely," we'll say, if we have any sense. It's not proper to disagree
with a man when he's right.

HIPPIAS: But Socrates, really, what do you think of all that? It's flakings
and clippings of speeches, as I told you before, divided up small. But
here's what is fine and worth a lot: to be able to present a speech well   b
and finely, in court or council or any other authority to whom you give
the speech, to convince them and go home carrying not the smallest but
the greatest of prizes, the successful defense of yourself, your property,
and friends. One should stick to that.

He should give up and abandon all that small-talking, so he won't be
thought a complete fool for applying himself, as he is now, to babbling nonsense.

SOCRATES: Hippias, my friend, you're a lucky man, because you know
which activities a man should practice, and you've practiced them too—   c
successfully, as you say. But I'm apparently held back by my crazy luck.
I wander around and I'm always getting stuck. If I make a display of how
stuck I am to you wise men, I get mud-spattered by your speeches when
I display it. You all say what you just said, that I am spending my time
on things that are silly and small and worthless. But when I'm convinced
by you and say what you say, that it's much the most excellent thing to
be able to present a speech well and finely, and get things done in court   d
or any other gathering, I hear every insult from that man (among others
around here) who has always been refuting me. He happens to be a close
relative of mine, and he lives in the same house. So when I go home to
my own place and he hears me saying those things, he asks if I'm not
ashamed that I dare discuss fine activities when I've been so plainly refuted
about the fine, and it's clear I don't even know at all what *that* is itself!
"Look," he'll say. "How will you know whose speech—or any other ac-   e
tion—is finely presented or not, when you are ignorant of the fine? And
when you're in a state like that, do you think it's any better for you to
live than die?" That's what I get, as I said. Insults and blame from you,
insults from him. But I suppose it is necessary to bear all that. It wouldn't
be strange if it were good for me. I actually think, Hippas, that associating
with both of you has done me good. The proverb says, "What's fine is
hard"—I think I know *that*.

LESSER HIPPIAS

The great sophist Hippias, who has come to Athens on his rounds of the Greek cities, has just exhibited his talents in a discourse on Homer. Socrates asks Hippias to explain further his view on Achilles and Odysseus, the heroes of the two Homeric poems. In the poems, says Hippias, Achilles is 'best and bravest' of the Greek heroes at Troy, and truthful, while Odysseus is 'wily and a liar'— he speaks untruths. Homer implies, and Hippias agrees, that being truthful and being a liar (speaking untruths) are two distinct, contrasting things—one and the same person cannot be both truthful and a 'liar'. But is that so, Socrates wants to know? Isn't the one who has the truth about some matter the best able to tell an untruth? After all, only he is in a position even to know what would be an untruth to say! So the good and truthful man—Achilles, according to Hippias—would also be a liar, one accomplished at telling untruths. On this account, it could not be right to contrast Achilles, as a truthful person, with Odysseus as a liar—they would both have to be both. Hippias proves unable to sort these questions out satisfactorily, and so to explain adequately his own view about the differences between the two Homeric heroes: his self-proclaimed wisdom about the interpretation of Homer and indeed about everything else is thus shown up as no wisdom at all.

Toward the end of this short dialogue Socrates presses Hippias to admit that those who make moral errors 'voluntarily'—e.g., the just person, who knows what the just thing to do is, but precisely through knowing that does the unjust thing instead—are better people than those who act unjustly 'involuntarily', from ignorance and by being unjust. Given his earlier inability to show how the good, knowledgeable, truthful person is not also the liar—the person most adept at telling untruths—Hippias is in no position to reject this suggestion, however unpalatable the thought may be that just people are exquisitely good at doing injustice! Nonetheless, he resists—no doubt correctly, however illogically, given his own earlier statements. As usual, in pressing him to accept this conclusion, Socrates is arguing only on the basis of assertions Hippias has made, not his own personal views. Indeed, Socrates indicates his own disavowal of this conclusion when he introduces at the end of the dialogue his own 'if': if there is anyone who voluntarily does what is unjust, then perhaps that person would be a 'good' doer of injustice. So we have no good reason to doubt, as some scholars have done, fearing for Socrates' moral reputation, that this dialogue is Plato's work. It is cited by Aristotle under the simple title Hippias (we call it Lesser to distinguish it from the longer or Greater Hippias dialogue). As often in citing Plato, Aristotle names no author, but—provided,

as seems reasonable, that he means the reader to know it as Plato's—his cita-
tion seems to assure its genuineness.

Elsewhere in Plato we hear nothing about Eudicus, the third speaker of the
dialogue, except in Greater Hippias, *where Hippias says Eudicus has invited*
him to give the exhibition on Homer that provides the occasion for our dia-
logue. From this evidence he would appear to be Hippias' host in Athens, and
so one of his more prominent Athenian admirers—though he is not mentioned
in Protagoras *among those attending him.*

J.M.C.

EUDICUS: Why are you silent, Socrates, after Hippias has given such an   363
exhibition? Why don't you either join us in praising some point or other
in what he said, or else put something to the test, if it seems to you anything
was not well said—especially since we who most claim to have a share
in the practice of philosophy are now left to ourselves?

SOCRATES: Indeed, Eudicus, there *are* some things in what Hippias said
just now about Homer that I'd like to hear more about. For your father   b
Apemantus used to say that the *Iliad* of Homer is a finer poem than the
Odyssey, to just the extent that Achilles is a better man than Odysseus; for,
he said, one of these poems is about Odysseus and the other about Achilles.
I'd like to ask about that, then, if Hippias is willing. What does he think
about these two men? Which of them does he say is the better? For in his   c
exhibition he's told us all sorts of other things both about other poets and
about Homer.

EUDICUS: It's plain that Hippias won't object to answering any question
you ask him. Right, Hippias? If Socrates asks you something, will you
answer, or what will you do?

HIPPIAS: Well, it would be strange behavior if I didn't, Eudicus. I always
go from my home at Elis to the festival of the Greeks at Olympia when it   d
is held and offer myself at the temple to speak on demand about any
subject I have prepared for exhibition, and to answer any questions anyone
wants to ask. I can hardly flee now from answering the questions of Socrates.

SOCRATES: What a godlike state of mind you're in, Hippias, if you go to   364
the temple at every Olympiad so confident about your soul's wisdom! I'd
be amazed if any of the athletes of the body goes there to take part in the
contests as fearless and trusting about his body as you say you are about
your intellect!

HIPPIAS: It is reasonable for me to be in that state of mind, Socrates. Ever
since I began taking part in the contests at the Olympic games, I have
never met anyone superior to me in anything.

Translated by Nicholas D. Smith.

b   Socrates: A fine reply, Hippias. Your fame is a monument for wisdom to the city of Elis and to your parents. But what do you say to us about Achilles and about Odysseus? Which do you say is the better man, and in what respect? When there were many of us inside, and you were giving your exhibition, I couldn't keep up with what you were saying, but I hesitated to keep asking questions. There were so many people inside, and I didn't want to hinder your display by raising questions. But now, since there are fewer of us and Eudicus here urges me to question you,

c speak, and instruct us clearly. What were you saying about these two men? How were you distinguishing them?

     Hippias: Well, I am glad to explain to you even more clearly than before what I say about these men and others, too. I say that Homer made Achilles the "best and bravest" man of those who went to Troy, and Nestor the wisest, and Odysseus the wiliest.

     Socrates: What? Hippias, will you do me the favor of not laughing at

d me if I have difficulty understanding what you are saying and often repeat my questions? But try to answer me gently and in a good–natured way.

     Hippias: It would be shameful, Socrates, if I, who teach others to do that very thing and demand a fee for it, should not myself be lenient when questioned by you and answer gently.

     Socrates: Finely put. But really, when you said that the poet made Achilles the "best and bravest," and when you said that he made Nestor

e the wisest, I thought I understood you. But when you said that he made Odysseus the wiliest—well, to tell you the truth, I don't know in the least what you mean by that. But tell me this; maybe it'll make me understand better. Doesn't Homer make Achilles wily?

     Hippias: Not in the least, Socrates, but most simple and truthful; for in the "Prayers," when he has them conversing, he has Achilles say to Odysseus:

365
> *Son of Laertes, sprung from Zeus, resourceful Odysseus,*
> *I must speak the word bluntly,*
> *How I will act and how I think it shall be accomplished,*
> *For as hateful to me as the gates of Hades*

b
> *Is he who hides one thing in his mind, and says another.*
> *As for me, I will speak as it shall also be accomplished.*[1]

In these lines he clearly shows the way of each man, that Achilles is truthful and simple, and Odysseus is wily and a liar;[2] for he presents Achilles as saying these words to Odysseus.

     Socrates: Now, Hippias, it may be that I understand what you mean. You mean that the wily person is a liar, or so it appears.

---

1. *Iliad* ix.308–10, 12–14. The "Prayers" is the embassy scene in which Odysseus, Phoenix, and Ajax plead with Achilles to give up his anger and return to the fighting.

2. Or rather, "one who says what is false," whether or not their intent is to deceive. In what follows "liar" should be understood in that broad sense.

HIPPIAS: Certainly, Socrates. Homer presents Odysseus as that kind of   c
person in many places, both in the *Iliad* and in the *Odyssey*.

SOCRATES: So Homer, it seems, thought the truthful man was one kind
of person, and the liar another, and not the same.

HIPPIAS: How could he not, Socrates?

SOCRATES: And do you yourself think so, Hippias?

HIPPIAS: Certainly, Socrates. It would be very strange if it were otherwise.

SOCRATES: Let's dismiss Homer, then, since it's impossible to ask him   d
what he had in mind when he wrote these lines. But since you're evidently
taking up the cause, and agree with what you say he meant, answer for
both Homer and yourself.

HIPPIAS: So be it. Ask briefly what you wish.

SOCRATES: Do you say that liars, like sick people, don't have the power
to do anything, or that they do have the power to do something?

HIPPIAS: I say they very much have the power to do many things, and
especially to deceive people.

SOCRATES: So according to your argument they are powerful, it would   e
seem, and wily. Right?

HIPPIAS: Yes.

SOCRATES: Are they wily and deceivers from dimwittedness and foolishness, or by cunning and some kind of intelligence?

HIPPIAS: From cunning, absolutely, and intelligence.

SOCRATES: So they are intelligent, it seems.

HIPPIAS: Yes, by Zeus. Too much so.

SOCRATES: And being intelligent, do they not know what they are doing,
or do they know?

HIPPIAS: They know very well. That's how they do their mischief.

SOCRATES: And knowing the things that they know, are they ignorant,
or wise?

HIPPIAS: Wise, surely, in just these things: in deception.   366

SOCRATES: Stop. Let us recall what it is that you are saying. You claim
that liars are powerful and intelligent and knowledgeable and wise in
those matters in which they are liars?

HIPPIAS: That's what I claim.

SOCRATES: And that the truthful and the liars are different, complete
opposites of one another?

HIPPIAS: That's what I say.

SOCRATES: Well, then. The liars are among the powerful and wise, according to your argument.

HIPPIAS: Certainly.

SOCRATES: And when you say that the liars are powerful and wise in   b
these very matters, do you mean that they have the power to lie if they
want, or that they are without power in the matters in which they are liars?

HIPPIAS: I mean they are powerful.

SOCRATES: To put it in a nutshell, then, liars are wise and have the power
to lie.

HIPPIAS: Yes.

SOCRATES: So a person who did not have the power to lie and was ignorant would not be a liar.

HIPPIAS: That's right.

c   SOCRATES: But each person who can do what he wishes when he wishes is powerful. I mean someone who is not prevented by disease or other such things, someone like you with regard to writing my name. You have the power to do this whenever you wish to. That's what I mean. Or don't you say that one in such a condition is powerful?

HIPPIAS: I do.

SOCRATES: Now tell me, Hippias: aren't you experienced in calculating and arithmetic?

HIPPIAS: Most experienced of all, Socrates.

SOCRATES: So if someone were to ask you what three times seven hundred is, couldn't you tell him the truth about this most quickly and best of all, if you wished?

d   HIPPIAS: Of course.

SOCRATES: Because you are most powerful and wisest in these matters?

HIPPIAS: Yes.

SOCRATES: Are you, then, merely wisest and most powerful, or are you also best in those things in which you are most powerful and wisest, that is, in arithmetic?

HIPPIAS: Best also, for sure, Socrates.

SOCRATES: Then would you tell the truth most powerfully about these things?

e   HIPPIAS: *I* think so.

SOCRATES: But what about falsehoods about these same things? Please answer with the same nobility and grandeur you showed before, Hippias. If someone were to ask you what three times seven hundred is, could you lie the best, always consistently say falsehoods about these things, if you
367 wished to lie and never to tell the truth? Or would one who is ignorant of calculations have more power than you to lie if he wished to? Don't you think the ignorant person would often involuntarily tell the truth when he wished to say falsehoods, if it so happened, because he didn't know; whereas you, the wise person, if you should wish to lie, would always consistently lie?

HIPPIAS: Yes, it is just as you say.

SOCRATES: Is the liar, then, a liar about other things but not about number—he wouldn't lie about numbers?

HIPPIAS: But yes, by Zeus, about numbers, too.

b   SOCRATES: So we should also maintain this, Hippias, that there is such a person as a liar about calculation and number.

HIPPIAS: Yes.

SOCRATES: Who would this person be? Mustn't he have the power to lie, as you just now agreed, if he is going to be a liar? If you remember, you said that one who did not have the power to lie could never become a liar.

HIPPIAS: I remember. I said that.

SOCRATES: And were you not just now shown to have the most power to lie about calculations?

HIPPIAS: Yes. I said that, too.

SOCRATES: Do you, therefore, have the most power to tell the truth   c
about calculations?

HIPPIAS: Of course.

SOCRATES: Then the same person has the most power both to say falsehoods and to tell the truth about calculations. And this person is the one who is good with regard to these things, the arithmetician?

HIPPIAS: Yes.

SOCRATES: Then who becomes a liar about calculations, Hippias, other than the good person? For the same person is also powerful, and truthful, as well.

HIPPIAS: Apparently.

SOCRATES: Do you see, then, that the same person is both a liar and truthful about these things, and the truthful person is no better than the   d
liar? For, indeed, he is the same person and the two are not complete opposites, as you supposed just now.

HIPPIAS: He does not appear to be, at least in this field.

SOCRATES: Do you wish to investigate some other field, then?

HIPPIAS: If you wish.

SOCRATES: All right. Are you not also experienced in geometry?

HIPPIAS: I am.

SOCRATES: Well, then. Isn't it the same way in geometry? Doesn't the same person have the most power to lie and to tell the truth about geometrical diagrams, namely, the geometer?

HIPPIAS: Yes.

SOCRATES: Is anyone else good at these things, or the geometer?

HIPPIAS: No one else.   e

SOCRATES: The good and wise geometer, then, is the most powerful in both respects, isn't he? And if anyone could be a liar about diagrams, it would be this person, the good geometer? For he has the power to lie, but the bad one is powerless; and one who does not have the power to lie cannot become a liar, as you agreed.

HIPPIAS: That's right.

SOCRATES: Let us investigate a third person, the astronomer, whose craft you think you know even better than the preceding ones. Right, Hippias?   368

HIPPIAS: Yes.

SOCRATES: Aren't the same things true in astronomy, also?

HIPPIAS: Probably, Socrates.

SOCRATES: In astronomy, too, if anyone is a liar, it will be the good astronomer, he who has the power to lie. Certainly it won't be the one who does not have the power; for he is ignorant.

HIPPIAS: That's the way it appears.

SOCRATES: So the same person will be truthful and a liar in astronomy.

HIPPIAS: So it seems.

b   SOCRATES: Come then, Hippias. Examine all the sciences similarly. Is there any that's different from these, or are they all like this? You are the wisest of people in the greatest number of crafts, as I once heard you boasting. In the marketplace, next to the tables of the bankers, you told of your great and enviable wisdom. You said that you had once gone to Olympia with everything you had on your body the product of your own work. First, the ring you were wearing— you began with that—was your

c   own work, showing that you knew how to engrave rings. And another signet, too, was your work, and a strigil[3] and an oil bottle, which you had made. Then you said that you yourself had cut from leather the sandals you were wearing, and had woven your cloak and tunic. And what seemed to everyone most unusual and an exhibition of the greatest wisdom was when you said that the belt you wore around your tunic was like the very expensive Persian ones, and that you had plaited it yourself. In addition to these things, you said that you brought poems with you—epic, tragic,

d   and dithyrambs, and many writings of all sorts in prose. You said you came with knowledge that distinguished you from all others on the subjects I was just now speaking of, and also about rhythms, and harmony, and the correctness of letters, and many other things besides, as I seem to remember. But I've forgotten to mention your artful technique (as it seems) of memory, in which you think you are most brilliant. I suppose I have

e   forgotten a great many other things, as well. But, as I say, look both at your own crafts—for they are sufficient—and also those of others, and tell me, in accordance with what you and I have agreed upon, if you find any case in which one person is truthful and another (distinct, not the same)

369   person is a liar. Look for one in whatever sort of wisdom or villainy you like, or whatever you want to call it; but you will not find it, my friend, for none exists. So tell me!

HIPPIAS: But I can't, Socrates; at least not offhand.

SOCRATES: And you never will, I think. But if what I say is true, you will remember what follows from our argument.

HIPPIAS: I don't entirely understand what you mean, Socrates.

SOCRATES: Presumably that's because you are not using your memory technique; plainly, you don't think you need it. But I will remind you.

b   You realize that you said that Achilles was truthful, whereas Odysseus was a liar and wily?

HIPPIAS: Yes.

SOCRATES: You are now aware, then, that the same person has been discovered to be a liar and truthful, so that if Odysseus was a liar, he also becomes truthful, and if Achilles was truthful, he also becomes a liar, and these two men are not different from one another, nor opposites, but similar?

---

3. The strigil was a tool used to scrape from the skin the residue of olive oil used to wash off perspiration and soil after athletic exercise.

HIPPIAS: Oh, Socrates! You're always weaving arguments of this kind. You pick out whatever is the most difficult part of the argument, and fasten on to it in minute detail, and don't dispute about the whole subject under discussion. So now, if you wish, I'll prove to you by sufficient argument, based upon much evidence, that Homer made Achilles better than Odysseus and not a liar, whereas he made the latter deceitful, a teller of many lies, and worse than Achilles. If you wish, you may then offer counterarguments to mine, to the effect that the other is better. That way, these people here will know more which of us speaks better.

SOCRATES: Hippias, I don't dispute that you are wiser than I, but it is always my custom to pay attention when someone is saying something, especially when the speaker seems to me to be wise. And because I desire to learn what he means, I question him thoroughly and examine and place side-by-side the things he says, so I can learn. If the speaker seems to me to be some worthless person, I neither ask questions nor do I care what he says. This is how you'll recognize whom I consider wise. You'll find me being persistent about what's said by this sort of person, questioning him so that I can benefit by learning something. And so now I noticed as you were speaking, that in the lines you just now recited—to show that Achilles speaks to Odysseus as if Odysseus were a fraud—it seems ridiculous to me, if you speak truly, that Odysseus (the wily one), is nowhere portrayed as lying, whereas Achilles is portrayed as a wily person according to your argument. In any case, he lies. For he begins by saying the lines which you just now recited:

> For as hateful to me as the gates of Hades
> Is he who hides one thing in his mind, and says another.

A little later he says he wouldn't be persuaded by Odysseus and Agamemnon, and wouldn't stay in Troy at all. But, he says,

> Tomorrow, when I have sacrificed to Zeus and all the gods,
> And loaded my ships, having dragged them to the sea,
> You will see, if you want to, and if you care about such things,
> My ships sailing very early on the fish-filled Hellespont,
> And in them, the men eagerly rowing.
> And if the glorious Earth-shaker should grant a fair voyage,
> On the third day I should come to fertile Phthia.[4]

And before that, when he was insulting Agamemnon, he said,

4. *Iliad* ix.357–63; the Earth-shaker is the god Posidon.

> *Now I am going to Phthia, because it is much better*
> *To go home with my curved ships. I do not think*
d   *I will stay here dishonored, and pile up riches and wealth for you.*[5]

Although he said these things—once before the entire army and once before his colleagues—nowhere is he shown to have prepared or tried to drag down the ships to sail home. Rather, he shows quite a noble contempt for telling the truth. So, Hippias, I've been questioning you from the
e   beginning because I'm confused as to which of these two men was represented as better by the poet, thinking that both were "best and bravest" and that it's hard to discern which is better, with regard both to lying and to truth, and to virtue, as well; for in this, also, the two are quite similar.

HIPPIAS: That's because you don't look at it right, Socrates. When Achilles lies, he's portrayed as lying not on purpose but involuntarily, forced to stay and help by the misfortune of the army. But the lies of Odysseus are voluntary and on purpose.

SOCRATES: You're deceiving me, my dear Hippias, and are yourself imitating Odysseus!

371   HIPPIAS: Not at all, Socrates! What do you mean? What are you referring to?

SOCRATES: To your saying that Achilles didn't lie on purpose—he, who was also such a cheat and a schemer in addition to his fraudulence, as Homer has represented him. He's shown to be so much more intelligent than Odysseus in easily defrauding him without being noticed, that right in front of the other, he dared to contradict himself and Odysseus didn't notice. In any case, Odysseus isn't portrayed as saying anything to him
b   which shows that he perceived his lying.

HIPPIAS: What are you talking about, Socrates?

SOCRATES: Don't you know that after he said to Odysseus that he would sail away at dawn, he doesn't say again that he's going to sail away when he speaks to Ajax, but says something different?

HIPPIAS: Where?

SOCRATES: In the lines in which he says,

> *I will not think of bloody war*
c   > *Until the son of thoughtful Priam, noble Hector*
> *Comes to the tents and the ships of the Myrmidons,*
> *Killing Argives, and burns the ships with blazing fire.*
> *But at my tent and my black ship*
> *I think Hector himself, though eager for battle, will stop.*[6]

d   So, Hippias; do you think the son of Thetis, who was taught by the most wise Chiron, was so forgetful that—though a little earlier he had insulted

5. *Iliad* i.169–71.
6. *Iliad* ix.650–55.

fraudulent people with the most extreme insults—he himself said to Odysseus that he was going to sail away, and to Ajax that he was going to stay? And he wasn't doing this on purpose, supposing that Odysseus was an old fool, and that he himself could get the better of him by precisely such conniving and lying?

HIPPIAS: It doesn't seem that way to me, Socrates. Rather, in these things, too, it was because of his guilelessness[7] that he was led to say something different to Ajax and to Odysseus. But when Odysseus tells the truth, he always has a purpose, and when he lies, it's the same.

SOCRATES: Then it seems that Odysseus is better than Achilles after all.

HIPPIAS: Not at all, surely, Socrates.

SOCRATES: Why not? Didn't it emerge just now that the voluntary liars are better than the involuntary ones?

HIPPIAS: But Socrates, how could those who are voluntarily unjust, and are voluntary and purposeful evil-doers, be better than those who act that way involuntarily? For these people, there seems to be much lenience, when they act unjustly without knowing, or lie, or do some other evil. The laws, too, are surely much harsher towards those who do evil and lie voluntarily than towards those who do so involuntarily.

SOCRATES: You see, Hippias, that I am telling the truth when I say that I'm persistent in questioning wise people? It may be that this is the only good trait I have and that all the others I have are quite worthless. I make mistakes as to the way things are, and don't know how they are—I find it sufficient evidence of this that when I am with one of you who are highly regarded for wisdom, and to whose wisdom all the Greeks bear witness, I show myself to know nothing. For I think pretty well none of the same things as you do; yet what greater evidence of ignorance is there than when someone disagrees with wise men? But I have one wonderfully good trait, which saves me: I'm not ashamed to learn. I inquire and ask questions and I'm very grateful to the one who answers, and I've never failed in gratitude to anyone. I've never denied it when I've learned anything, pretending that what I learned was my own discovery. Instead, I sing the praises of the one who taught me as a wise person, and proclaim what I learned from him. So indeed now, I don't agree with what you are saying but disagree very strongly. But I know very well that this is my fault—it's because I'm the sort of person I am, not to say anything better of myself than I deserve. To me, Hippias, it appears entirely the opposite to what you say: those who harm people and commit injustice and lie and cheat and go wrong voluntarily, rather than involuntarily, are better than those who do so involuntarily. However, sometimes I believe the opposite, and I go back and forth about all this—plainly because I don't know. But now at this moment a fit of lightheadedness has come over me, and I think those who voluntarily go wrong regarding something are better than those who do so involuntarily. I blame the preceding arguments for my present

---

7. Reading *euētheias* in e1.

condition, making it appear to me now that those who do any of these things involuntarily are more worthless than those who do them voluntarily. So please be nice and don't refuse to cure my soul. You'll do me a much greater good if you give my soul relief from ignorance, than if you gave my body relief from disease. But if you wish to give a long speech, I tell you in advance that you wouldn't cure me, for I couldn't follow you. If you are willing to answer me as you did just now, you'll benefit me a great deal, and I think you yourself won't be harmed. I might justly call for *your* help, too, son of Apemantus, for you goaded me into a discussion with Hippias. So now, if Hippias isn't willing to answer me, ask him for me.

EUDICUS: Well, Socrates, I don't think Hippias will need us to plead with him. For that's not what he said earlier; he said that he wouldn't flee from any man's questioning. Right, Hippias? Isn't that what you said?

HIPPIAS: I did. But Socrates always creates confusion in arguments, and seems to argue unfairly.

SOCRATES: Oh excellent Hippias, I don't do that voluntarily, for then I'd be wise and awesome, according to your argument, but involuntarily. So please be lenient with me, for you say that one who acts unfairly involuntarily should be treated leniently.

EUDICUS: By all means don't do otherwise, Hippias. For our sakes and for the sake of what you said earlier, answer what Socrates asks you.

HIPPIAS: I will answer, then, since you beg me to. Ask whatever you wish.

SOCRATES: I want very much, Hippias, to investigate what we were just now saying: whether those who go wrong voluntarily, or those who go wrong involuntarily are better. I think the most correct way to pursue our investigation is as follows. You answer. Do you call one sort of runner a good one?

HIPPIAS: I do.

SOCRATES: And one sort bad?

HIPPIAS: Yes.

SOCRATES: You think one who runs well is a good runner; one who runs badly, a bad one?

HIPPIAS: Yes.

SOCRATES: And one who runs slowly runs badly, and one who runs quickly runs well?

HIPPIAS: Yes.

SOCRATES: In a race, then, and in running, quickness is a good thing, and slowness, bad?

HIPPIAS: What else would it be?

SOCRATES: Which one is the better runner, then: the one who runs slowly voluntarily, or the one who does so involuntarily?

HIPPIAS: The one who does so voluntarily.

SOCRATES: And isn't running doing something?

HIPPIAS: Doing something, of course.

SOCRATES: If doing, doesn't it also accomplish something?

HIPPIAS: Yes.

SOCRATES: So one who runs badly accomplishes something bad and shameful in a race?

HIPPIAS: Bad; how else?

SOCRATES: One who runs slowly runs badly?

HIPPIAS: Yes.

SOCRATES: So the good runner voluntarily accomplishes this bad and shameful thing, and the bad runner, involuntarily?

HIPPIAS: So it seems, at least.

SOCRATES: In a race, then, one who accomplishes bad things involuntarily is more worthless than one who does them voluntarily?

HIPPIAS: In a race, at least.

SOCRATES: What about in wrestling? Which is the better wrestler, one who falls down voluntarily, or involuntarily?

HIPPIAS: One who does so voluntarily, it seems.

SOCRATES: Is it more worthless and shameful in wrestling to fall down or to knock down the opponent?

HIPPIAS: To fall down.

SOCRATES: So also in wrestling, one who voluntarily has worthless and shameful accomplishments is a better wrestler than one who has them involuntarily.

HIPPIAS: So it seems.

SOCRATES: What about in other physical activities? Isn't the physically better person able to accomplish both sorts of things: the strong *and* the weak, the shameful *and* the fine? So whenever he accomplishes worthless physical results, the one who is physically better does them voluntarily, whereas the one who is worse does them involuntarily?

HIPPIAS: That how it seems to be in matters of strength, also.

SOCRATES: What about gracefulness, Hippias? Doesn't the better body strike shameful and worthless poses voluntarily, and the worse body involuntarily? What do you think?

HIPPIAS: That's right.

SOCRATES: So awkwardness, when voluntary, counts toward virtue, but when involuntary, toward worthlessness.

HIPPIAS: Apparently.

SOCRATES: What do you say about the voice? Which do you say is better, one that sings out of tune voluntarily, or involuntarily?

HIPPIAS: One that does so voluntarily.

SOCRATES: And the one that does so involuntarily is in a worse condition?

HIPPIAS: Yes.

SOCRATES: Would you prefer to possess good or bad things?

HIPPIAS: Good.

SOCRATES: Then would you prefer to possess feet that limp voluntarily, or involuntarily?

HIPPIAS: Voluntarily.

SOCRATES: But doesn't having a limp mean having worthless and awkward feet?

374

b

c

d

HIPPIAS: Yes.

SOCRATES: Well, again; doesn't dullness of sight mean having worthless eyes?

HIPPIAS: Yes.

SOCRATES: Which sort of eyes, then, would you wish to possess and live with: those with which you would see dully and incorrectly voluntarily, or involuntarily?

HIPPIAS: Those with which one would do so voluntarily.

SOCRATES: So you regard organs that voluntarily accomplish worthless results as better than those that do so involuntarily?

HIPPIAS: Yes, in these sorts of cases.

SOCRATES: So then one statement embraces them all, ears, nose, mouth
e   and all the senses: those that involuntarily accomplish bad results aren't worth having because they're worthless, whereas those that do so voluntarily are worth having because they're good.

HIPPIAS: I think so.

SOCRATES: Well, then. Which tools are better to work with? Those with which one accomplishes bad results voluntarily, or involuntarily? For example, is a rudder with which one will involuntarily steer badly better, or one with which one will do so voluntarily?

HIPPIAS: One with which one will do so voluntarily.

SOCRATES: Isn't it the same with a bow, a lyre, flutes, and all the rest?
375 HIPPIAS: What you say is true.

SOCRATES: Well, then. Is it better to possess a horse with such a soul that one could ride it badly voluntarily, or involuntarily?

HIPPIAS: Voluntarily.

SOCRATES: So that's a better one.

HIPPIAS: Yes.

SOCRATES: With the better horse's soul, then, one would voluntarily do the worthless acts of this soul, but with the soul of the worthless mare one would do them involuntarily.

HIPPIAS: Certainly.

SOCRATES: And so also with a dog and all other animals?

HIPPIAS: Yes.

SOCRATES: Well now, then. For an archer, is it better to possess a soul
b   which voluntarily misses the target, or one which does so involuntarily?

HIPPIAS: One which does so voluntarily.

SOCRATES: So this sort of soul is better also for archery?

HIPPIAS: Yes.

SOCRATES: A soul which involuntarily misses the mark is more worthless than one which does so voluntarily.

HIPPIAS: In archery, anyway.

SOCRATES: How about in medicine? Isn't one that voluntarily accomplishes bad things for the body better at medicine?

HIPPIAS: Yes.

SOCRATES: Then this sort of soul is better at this craft than the other.

HIPPIAS: Yes.

SOCRATES: Well, then. As to the soul that plays the lyre and the flute better and does everything else better in the crafts and the sciences— c doesn't it accomplish bad and shameful things and miss the mark voluntarily, whereas the more worthless does this involuntarily?

HIPPIAS: Apparently.

SOCRATES: And perhaps we would prefer to have slaves with souls that voluntarily miss the mark and act badly, rather than those which do so involuntarily, as being better at these things.

HIPPIAS: Yes.

SOCRATES: Well, then. Would we not wish to possess our own soul in the best condition?

HIPPIAS: Yes.

SOCRATES: So, will it be better if it acts badly and misses the mark d voluntarily or involuntarily?

HIPPIAS: But it would be terrible, Socrates, if those who commit injustice voluntarily are to be better than those who do it involuntarily!

SOCRATES: But nonetheless they appear to be, at least given what's been said.

HIPPIAS: Not to me.

SOCRATES: But I thought, Hippias, that they appeared to be so to you, too. But answer again: isn't justice either some sort of power or knowledge, or both? Or isn't justice necessarily one of these things?

HIPPIAS: Yes.   e

SOCRATES: So if justice is a power of the soul, isn't the more powerful soul the more just? For, my excellent friend, it appeared to us, didn't it, that one of this sort was better?

HIPPIAS: Yes, it did.

SOCRATES: And if it's knowledge? Then isn't the wiser soul more just and the more ignorant more unjust?

HIPPIAS: Yes.

SOCRATES: And if it's both? Then isn't the soul which has both—knowledge and power—more just, and the more ignorant more unjust? Isn't that necessarily so?

HIPPIAS: It appears so.

SOCRATES: This more powerful and wiser soul was seen to be better and to have more power to do both fine and shameful in everything it accomplishes?   376

HIPPIAS: Yes.

SOCRATES: Whenever it accomplishes shameful results, then, it does so voluntarily, by power and craft, and these things appear to be attributes of justice, either both or one of them.

HIPPIAS: So it seems.

SOCRATES: And to do injustice is to do bad, whereas to refrain from injustice is to do something fine.

HIPPIAS: Yes.

SOCRATES: So the more powerful and better soul, when it does injustice, will do injustice voluntarily, and the worthless soul involuntarily?

HIPPIAS: Apparently.

376b   SOCRATES: And isn't the good man the one who has a good soul, and the bad man the one who has a bad soul?

HIPPIAS: Yes.

SOCRATES: Therefore, it's up to the good man to do injustice voluntarily, and the bad man to do it involuntarily; that is, if the good man has a good soul.

HIPPIAS: But surely he has.

SOCRATES: So the one who voluntarily misses the mark and does what is shameful and unjust, Hippias—that is, if there is such a person—would be no other than the good man.

HIPPIAS: I can't agree with you in that, Socrates.

c   SOCRATES: Nor I with myself, Hippias. But given the argument, we can't help having it look that way to us, now, at any rate. However, as I said before, on these matters I waver back and forth and never believe the same thing. And it's not surprising at all that I or any other ordinary person *should* waver. But if you wise men are going to do it, too—that means something terrible for us, if we can't stop our wavering even after we've put ourselves in your company.

ION

A 'rhapsode' is a professional reciter of the poetry of Homer and certain other prestigious early poets of Greece. In Athens the prize-winning rhapsode Ion from Ephesus (we do not know whether he is a historical personage or Plato's invention) runs into Socrates, who expresses admiration for his profession and questions him about it. Theirs is a private conversation, apparently with no others present (as in Euthyphro). Ion professes not just to recite superbly Homer's poetry (his specialty) but also to speak beautifully in his own right about Homer—in interpreting and explaining his poetry and its excellences. Socrates is more interested in this second aspect of Ion's professional expertise than in the first. He wants to know whether Ion speaks about Homer 'on the basis of knowledge or mastery': is he the master of some body of knowledge, which he employs and expresses in speaking about Homer?

The chief interest of this short dialogue, apart from its comical portrayal of Ion's enthusiasm for his own skills, lies in the way Socrates develops his own view—which Ion in the end blithely accepts!—that Ion speaks not from knowledge but from inspiration, his thoughts being 'breathed into' him without the use of his own understanding at all. Using the analogy of a magnet, with the power to draw one iron ring to itself, and through that another, and another, Socrates suggests that Homer himself—the greatest of the Greek poets—had no knowledge of his own in writing his poetry, but was divinely possessed. Ion and other expert rhapsodes are also divinely possessed—as it were, 'magnetized'—through him, both when they recite his poetry and when they speak about it—and they pass on the inspiration to their hearers, who are in a state of divine possession in opening themselves to the poetry. Neither poets nor rhapsodes have any knowledge or mastery of anything: their work, with all its beauty, is the product of the gods working through them, not of any human intelligence and skill. Thus these minor characters, the rhapsodes, provide Socrates entrée to much bigger game, the poet Homer himself, the great 'teacher' of the Greeks. Readers should compare (and contrast) Socrates' criticisms of Homer here with those in Republic II and III, and his critique of poetry in X, along with the views about poetic 'madness' that he advances in Phaedrus and elsewhere.

J.M.C.

530   SOCRATES: Ion! Hello. Where have you come from to visit us this time? From your home in Ephesus?

ION: No, no, Socrates. From Epidaurus, from the festival of Asclepius.

SOCRATES: Don't tell me the Epidaurians hold a contest for *rhapsodes* in honor of the god?

ION: They certainly do! They do it for every sort of poetry and music.

SOCRATES: Really! Did you enter the contest? And how did it go for you?

b   ION: First prize, Socrates! We carried it off.

SOCRATES: That's good to hear. Well, let's see that we win the big games at Athens, next.

ION: We'll do it, Socrates, god willing.

SOCRATES: You know, Ion, many times I've envied you rhapsodes your profession. Physically, it is always fitting for you in your profession to be dressed up to look as beautiful as you can; and at the same time it is necessary for you to be at work with poets—many fine ones, and with

c   Homer above all, who's the best poet and the most divine—and you have to learn his thought, not just his verses! Now that is something to envy! I mean, no one would ever get to be a good rhapsode if he didn't understand what is meant by the poet. A rhapsode must come to present the poet's thought to his audience; and he can't do that beautifully unless he knows what the poet means. So this all deserves to be envied.

ION: That's true, Socrates. And that's the part of my profession that took the most work. I think I speak more beautifully than anyone else about

d   Homer; neither Metrodorus of Lampsacus nor Stesimbrotus of Thasos nor Glaucon nor anyone else past or present could offer as many beautiful thoughts about Homer as I can.

SOCRATES: That's good to hear, Ion. Surely you won't begrudge me a demonstration?

ION: Really, Socrates, it's worth hearing how well I've got Homer dressed up. I think I'm worthy to be crowned by the Sons of Homer[1] with a golden crown.

531   SOCRATES: Really, I shall make time to hear that later. Now I'd just like an answer to this: Are you so wonderfully clever about Homer alone—or also about Hesiod and Archilochus?

ION: No, no. Only about Homer. That's good enough, I think.

SOCRATES: Is there any subject on which Homer and Hesiod both say the same things?

ION: Yes, I think so. A good many.

SOCRATES: Then, on those subjects, would you explain Homer's verse better and more beautifully than Hesiod's?

b   ION: Just the same Socrates, on those subjects, anyway, where they say the same things.

Translated by Paul Woodruff.

1. The sons of Homer were a guild of rhapsodes who originally claimed to be descendants of Homer.

SOCRATES: And how about the subjects on which they do not say the same things? Divination, for example. Homer says something about it and so does Hesiod.

ION: Certainly.

SOCRATES: Well. Take all the places where those two poets speak of divination, both where they agree and where they don't: who would explain those better and more beautifully, you, or one of the diviners if he's good?

ION: One of the diviners.

SOCRATES: Suppose *you* were a diviner: if you were really able to explain the places where the two poets agree, wouldn't you also know how to explain the places where they disagree?

ION: That's clear.

SOCRATES: Then what in the world is it that you're clever about in Homer but not in Hesiod and the other poets? Does Homer speak of any subjects that differ from those of *all* the other poets? Doesn't he mainly go through tales of war, and of how people deal with each other in society—good people and bad, ordinary folks and craftsmen? And of the gods, how *they* deal with each other and with men? And doesn't he recount what happens in heaven and in hell, and tell of the births of gods and heroes? Those are the subjects of Homer's poetry-making, aren't they?

ION: That's true, Socrates.

SOCRATES: And how about the other poets? Did they write on the same subjects?

ION: Yes, but Socrates, they didn't do it the way Homer did.

SOCRATES: How, then? Worse?

ION: Much worse.

SOCRATES: And Homer does it better?

ION: *Really* better.

SOCRATES: Well now, Ion, dear heart, when a number of people are discussing arithmetic, and one of them speaks best, I suppose *someone* will know how to pick out the good speaker.

ION: Yes.

SOCRATES: Will it be the same person who can pick out the bad speakers, or someone else?

ION: The same, of course.

SOCRATES: And that will be someone who has mastered arithmetic, right?

ION: Yes.

SOCRATES: Well. Suppose a number of people are discussing healthy nutrition, and one of them speaks best. Will one person know that the best speaker speaks best, and another that an inferior speaker speaks worse? Or will the same man know both?

ION: Obviously, the same man.

SOCRATES: Who is he? What do we call him?

ION: A doctor.

SOCRATES: So, to sum it up, this is what we're saying: when a number
532   of people speak on the same subject, it's always the same person who will
know how to pick out good speakers and bad speakers. If he doesn't know
how to pick out a bad speaker, he certainly won't know a good speaker—
on the same subject, anyway.

ION: That's so.

SOCRATES: Then it turns out that the same person is "wonderfully clever"
about both speakers.

ION: Yes.

SOCRATES: Now *you* claim that Homer and the other poets (including
Hesiod and Archilochus) speak on the same subjects, but not equally well.
He's good, and they're inferior.

ION: Yes, and it's true.

b   SOCRATES: Now if you really do know who's speaking well, you'll know
that the inferior speakers are speaking worse.

ION: Apparently so.

SOCRATES: You're superb! So if we say that Ion is equally clever about
Homer and the other poets, we'll make no mistake. Because you agree
yourself that the same person will be an adequate judge of all who speak
on the same subjects, and that almost all the poets *do* treat the same subjects.

ION: Then how in the world do you explain what *I* do, Socrates? When
c   someone discusses another poet I pay no attention, and I have no power
to contribute anything worthwhile: I simply doze off. But let someone
mention Homer and right away I'm wide awake and I'm paying attention
and I have plenty to say.

SOCRATES: *That's* not hard to figure out, my friend. Anyone can tell that
you are powerless to speak about Homer on the basis of knowledge or
mastery. Because if your ability came by mastery, you would be able to
speak about all the other poets as well. Look, there is an art of poetry as
a whole, isn't there?

ION: Yes.

d   SOCRATES: And now take the whole of *any* other subject: won't it have
the same discipline throughout? And this goes for every subject that can
be mastered. Do you need me to tell you what I mean by this, Ion?

ION: Lord, yes, I do, Socrates. I love to hear you wise men talk.

SOCRATES: I wish that were true, Ion. But wise? Surely you are the wise
men, you rhapsodes and actors, you and the poets whose work you sing.
As for me, I say nothing but the truth, as you'd expect from an ordinary
e   man. I mean, even this question I asked you—look how commonplace
and ordinary a matter it is. Anybody could understand what I meant:
don't you use the same discipline throughout whenever you master the
whole of a subject? Take this for discussion—painting is a subject to be
mastered as a whole, isn't it?

ION: Yes.

SOCRATES: And there are many painters, good and bad, and there have
been many in the past.

ION: Certainly.

SOCRATES: Have you ever known anyone who is clever at showing what's well painted and what's not in the work of Polygnotus, but who's powerless to do that for other painters? Someone who dozes off when the work of 533 other painters is displayed, and is lost, and has nothing to contribute—but when he has to give judgment on Polygnotus or any other painter (so long as it's just *one*), he's wide awake and he's paying attention and he has plenty to say—have you ever known anyone like that?

ION: Good lord no, of course not!

SOCRATES: Well. Take sculpture. Have you ever known anyone who is clever at explaining which statues are well made in the case of Daedalus, b son of Metion, or Epeius, son of Panopeus, or Theodorus of Samos, or any other *single* sculptor, but who's lost when he's among the products of other sculptors, and he dozes off and has nothing to say?

ION: Good lord no. I haven't.

SOCRATES: And further, it is my opinion, you've never known anyone ever—not in flute-playing, not in cithara-playing, not in singing to the cithara, and not in rhapsodizing—you've never known a man who is clever at explaining Olympus or Thamyrus or Orpheus or Phemius, the rhapsode c from Ithaca, but who has nothing to contribute about Ion, the rhapsode from Ephesus, and cannot tell when he does his work well and when he doesn't—you've never known a man like that.

ION: I have nothing to say against you on that point, Socrates. But *this* I know about myself: I speak about Homer more beautifully than anybody else and I have lots to say; and everybody says I do it well. But about the other poets I do not. Now see what that means.

SOCRATES: I do see, Ion, and I'm going to announce to you what I think d that is. As I said earlier, that's not a subject you've mastered—speaking well about Homer; it's a divine power that moves you, as a "Magnetic" stone moves iron rings. (That's what Euripides called it; most people call it "Heraclean.")[2] This stone not only pulls those rings, if they're iron, it also puts power *in* the rings, so that they in turn can do just what the e stone does—pull other rings—so that there's sometimes a very long chain of iron pieces and rings hanging from one another. And the power in all of them depends on this stone. In the same way, the Muse makes some people inspired herself, and then through those who are inspired a chain of other enthusiasts is suspended. You know, none of the epic poets, if they're good, are masters of their subject; they are inspired, possessed, and that is how they utter all those beautiful poems. The same goes for lyric poets if they're good: just as the Corybantes are not in their right 534 minds when they dance, lyric poets, too, are not in their right minds when they make those beautiful lyrics, but as soon as they sail into harmony and

2. Natural magnets apparently came from Magnesia and Heraclea in Caria in Asia Minor, and were called after those places.

rhythm they are possessed by Bacchic frenzy. Just as Bacchus worshippers[3] when they are possessed draw honey and milk from rivers, but not when they are in their right minds—the soul of a lyric poet does this too, as

b   they say themselves. For of course poets tell us that they gather songs at honey-flowing springs, from glades and gardens of the Muses, and that they bear songs to us as bees carry honey, flying like bees. And what they say is true. For a poet is an airy thing, winged and holy, and he is not able to make poetry until he becomes inspired and goes out of his mind and his intellect is no longer in him. As long as a human being has his intellect in his possession he will always lack the power to make poetry

c   or sing prophecy. Therefore because it's not by mastery that they make poems or say many lovely things about their subjects (as you do about Homer)—but because it's by a divine gift—each poet is able to compose beautifully only that for which the Muse has aroused him: one can do dithyrambs, another encomia, one can do dance songs, another, epics, and yet another, iambics; and each of them is worthless for the other types of poetry. You see, it's not mastery that enables them to speak those verses, but a divine power, since if they knew how to speak beautifully on one type of poetry by mastering the subject, they could do so for all the others

d   also. That's why the god takes their intellect away from them when he uses them as his servants, as he does prophets and godly diviners, so that we who hear should know that *they* are not the ones who speak those verses that are of such high value, for their intellect is not in them: the god himself is the one who speaks, and he gives voice through them to us. The best evidence for this account is Tynnichus from Chalcis, who never made a poem anyone would think worth mentioning, *except* for the praise-song everyone sings, almost the most beautiful lyric-poem there is,

e   and simply, as he says himself, "an invention of the Muses." In this more than anything, then, I think, the god is showing us, so that we should be in no doubt about it, that these beautiful poems are not human, not even *from* human beings, but are divine and from gods; that poets are nothing but representatives of the gods, possessed by whoever possesses them. To

535 show *that*, the god deliberately sang the most beautiful lyric poem through the most worthless poet. Don't you think I'm right, Ion?

ION: Lord yes, *I* certainly do. Somehow you touch my soul with your words, Socrates, and I do think it's by a divine gift that good poets are able to present these poems to us from the gods.

SOCRATES: And you rhapsodes in turn present what the poets say.

ION: That's true too.

SOCRATES: So you turn out to be representatives of representatives.

ION: Quite right.

b   SOCRATES: Hold on, Ion; tell me this. Don't keep any secrets from *me*. When you recite epic poetry well and you have the most stunning effect

---

3. Bacchus worshippers apparently danced themselves into a frenzy in which they found streams flowing with honey and milk (Euripides, *Bacchae* 708–11).

on your spectators, either when you sing of Odysseus—how he leapt into the doorway, his identity now obvious to the suitors, and he poured out arrows at his feet—or when you sing of Achilles charging at Hector, or when you sing a pitiful episode about Andromache or Hecuba or Priam, are you at that time in your right mind, or do you get beside yourself? And doesn't your soul, in its enthusiasm, believe that it is present at the actions you describe, whether they're in Ithaca or in Troy or wherever the epic actually takes place?

c

ION: What a vivid example you've given me, Socrates! I won't keep secrets from *you*. Listen, when *I* tell a sad story, my eyes are full of tears; and when I tell a story that's frightening or awful, my hair stands on end with fear and my heart jumps.

SOCRATES: Well, Ion, should we say this man is in his right mind at times like these: when he's at festivals or celebrations, all dressed up in fancy clothes, with golden crowns, and he weeps, though he's lost none of his finery—or when he's standing among millions of friendly people and he's frightened, though no one is undressing him or doing him any harm? Is he in his right mind then?

d

ION: Lord no, Socrates. Not at all, to tell the truth.

SOCRATES: And you know that you have the same effects on most of your spectators too, don't you?

ION: I know very well that we do. I look down at them every time from up on the rostrum, and they're crying and looking terrified, and as the stories are told they are filled with amazement. You see I must keep my wits and pay close attention to them: if I start them crying, *I* will laugh as I take their money, but if *they* laugh, I shall cry at having lost money.

e

SOCRATES: And you know that this spectator is the last of the rings, don't you—the ones that I said take their power from each other by virtue of the Heraclean stone [the magnet]? The middle ring is you, the rhapsode or actor, and the first one is the poet himself. The god pulls people's souls through all these wherever he wants, looping the power down from one to another. And just as if it hung from that stone, there's an enormous chain of choral dancers and dance teachers and assistant teachers hanging off to the sides of the rings that are suspended from the Muse. One poet is attached to one Muse, another to another (we say he is "possessed," and that's near enough, for he is *held*). From these first rings, from the poets, *they* are attached in their turn and inspired, some from one poet, some from another: some from Orpheus, some from Musaeus, and many are possessed and held from Homer. You are one of *them*, Ion, and you are possessed from Homer. And when anyone sings the work of another poet, you're asleep and you're lost about what to say; but when any song of that poet is sounded, you are immediately awake, your soul is dancing, and you have plenty to say. You see it's not because you're a master of knowledge about Homer that you can say what you say, but because of a divine gift, because you are possessed. That's how it is with the Corybantes, who have sharp ears only for the specific song that belongs to whatever

536

b

c

god possesses them; they have plenty of words and movements to go with *that* song; but they are quite lost if the music is different. That's how it is with you, Ion: when anyone mentions Homer, you have plenty to say, but

d   if he mentions the others you are lost; and the explanation of this, for which you ask me—why it is that you have plenty to say about Homer but not about the others—is that it's not mastering the subject, but a divine gift, that makes you a wonderful singer of Homer's praises.

ION: You're a good speaker, Socrates. Still, I would be amazed if you could speak well enough to convince me that I am possessed or crazed when I praise Homer. I don't believe you'd think so if you heard me speaking on Homer.

e   SOCRATES: And I really do want to hear you, but not before you answer me this: on which of Homer's subjects do you speak well? I don't suppose you speak well on *all* of them.

ION: I do, Socrates, believe me, on every single one!

SOCRATES: Surely not on those subjects you happen to know nothing about, even if Homer does speak of them.

ION: And these subjects Homer speaks of, but I don't know about— what are they?

537   SOCRATES: But doesn't Homer speak about professional subjects in many places, and say a great deal? Chariot driving, for example, I'll show you, if I can remember the lines.

ION: No, I'll recite them. I *do* remember.

SOCRATES: Then tell me what Nestor says to his son Antilochus, when he advises him to take care at the turning post in the horse race they held for Patroclus' funeral.

ION: "Lean," he says,

> Lean yourself over on the smooth-planed chariot
b   > Just to the left of the pair. Then the horse on the right—
> Goad him, shout him on, easing the reins with your hands.
> At the post let your horse on the left stick tight to the turn
> So you seem to come right to the edge, with the hub
> Of your welded wheel. But escape cropping the stone . . .[4]

c   SOCRATES: That's enough. Who would know better, Ion, whether Homer speaks correctly or not in these particular verses—a doctor or a charioteer?

ION: A charioteer, of course.

SOCRATES: Is that because he is a master of that profession, or for some other reason?

---

4. *Iliad* xxiii.335–40.

ION: No. It's because he's a master of it.

SOCRATES: Then to each profession a god has granted the ability to know a certain function. I mean, the things navigation teaches us—we won't learn them from medicine as well, will we?

ION: Of course not.

SOCRATES: And the things medicine teaches us we won't learn from architecture.

ION: Of course not.   d

SOCRATES: And so it is for every other profession: what we learn by mastering one profession we won't learn by mastering another, right? But first, answer me this. Do you agree that there are different professions—that one is different from another?

ION: Yes.

SOCRATES: And is this how you determine which ones are different? When *I* find that the knowledge [involved in one case] deals with different subjects from the knowledge [in another case], then I claim that one is a   e different profession from the other. Is that what you do?

ION: Yes.

SOCRATES: I mean if there is some knowledge of the same subjects, then why should we say there are two different professions?—Especially when each of them would allow us to know the same subjects! Take these fingers: I know there are five of them, and you know the same thing about them that I do. Now suppose I asked you whether it's the same profession—arithmetic—that teaches you and me the same things, or whether it's two different ones. Of course you'd say it's the same one.

ION: Yes.

SOCRATES: Then tell me now what I was going to ask you earlier. Do   538 you think it's the same way for every profession—the same profession must teach the same subjects, and a different profession, if it *is* different, must teach not the same subjects, but different ones?

ION: That's how I think it is, Socrates.

SOCRATES: Then a person who has not mastered a given profession will not be able to be a good judge of the things which belong to that profession, whether they are things said or things done.

ION: That's true.   b

SOCRATES: Then who will know better whether or not Homer speaks beautifully and well in the lines you quoted? You, or a charioteer?

ION: A charioteer.

SOCRATES: That's because you're a rhapsode, of course, and not a charioteer.

ION: Yes.

SOCRATES: And the rhapsode's profession is different from the charioteer's.

ION: Yes.

SOCRATES: If it's different, then its knowledge is of different subjects also.

ION: Yes.

c   SOCRATES: Then what about the time Homer tells how Hecamede, Nestor's woman, gave barley-medicine to Machaon to drink? He says something like this—

> *Over wine of Pramnos she grated goat's milk cheese*
> *With a brazen grater. . . . And onion relish for the drink . . .*[5]

Is Homer right or not: would a fine diagnosis here come from a doctor's profession or a rhapsode's?

ION: A doctor's.

SOCRATES: And what about the time Homer says:

d   > *Leaden she plunged to the floor of the sea like a weight*
> *That is fixed to a field cow's horn. Given to the hunt*
> *It goes among ravenous fish, carrying death.*[6]

Should we say it's for a fisherman's profession or a rhapsode's to tell whether or not he describes this beautifully and well?

ION: That's obvious, Socrates. It's for a fisherman's.

e   SOCRATES: All right, look. Suppose you were the one asking questions, and you asked me, "Socrates, since you're finding out which passages belong to each of the professions Homer treats—which are the passages that each profession should judge—come tell me this: which are the passages that belong to a diviner and to divination, passages he should be able to judge as to whether they're well or badly composed?" Look how easily I can give you a true answer. Often, in the *Odyssey*, he says things like what Theoclymenus says—the prophet of the sons of Melampus:

539 > *Are you mad? What evil is this that's upon you? Night*
> *Has enshrouded your hands, your faces, and down to your knees.*
> *Wailing spreads like fire, tears wash your cheeks.*
> *Ghosts fill the dooryard, ghosts fill the hall, they rush*
> *To the black gate of hell, they drop below darkness. Sunlight*
b   > *Has died from a sky run over with evil mist.*[7]

And often in the *Iliad*, as in the battle at the wall. There he says:

---

5. *Iliad* xi.639–40 with 630.

6. *Iliad* xxiv.80–82.

7. *Odyssey* xx.351–57; line 354 is omitted by Plato.

There came to them a bird as they hungered to cross over.
An eagle, a high-flier, circled the army's left
With a blood-red serpent carried in its talons, a monster,
Alive, still breathing, it has not yet forgotten its warlust,
For it struck its captor on the breast, by the neck;
It was writhing back, but the eagle shot it groundwards
In agony of pain, and dropped it in the midst of the throng,
Then itself, with a scream, soared on a breath of the wind.[8]

I shall say that these passages and those like them belong to a diviner. They are for him to examine and judge.

ION: That's a true answer, Socrates.

SOCRATES: Well, *your* answers are true, too, Ion. Now *you* tell me—just as I picked out for you, from the *Odyssey* and the *Iliad*, passages that belong to a diviner and ones that belong to a doctor and ones that belong to a fisherman—in the same way, Ion, since you have more experience with Homer's work than I do, you pick out for me the passages that belong to the rhapsode and to his profession, the passages a rhapsode should be able to examine and to judge better than anyone else.

ION: My answer, Socrates, is "all of them."

SOCRATES: That's not *your* answer, Ion. Not "all of them." Or are you really so forgetful? But no, it would not befit a *rhapsode* to be forgetful.

ION: What do you think I'm forgetting?

SOCRATES: Don't you remember you said that a rhapsode's profession is different from a charioteer's?

ION: I remember.

SOCRATES: And didn't you agree that because they are different they will know different subjects?

ION: Yes.

SOCRATES: So a rhapsode's profession, on *your* view, will not know everything, and neither will a rhapsode.

ION: But things like that are exceptions, Socrates.

SOCRATES: By "things like that" you mean that almost all the subjects of the other professions are exceptions, don't you? But then what sort of thing *will* a rhapsode know, if not everything?

ION: My opinion, anyhow, is that he'll know what it's fitting for a man or a woman to say—or for a slave or a freeman, or for a follower or a leader.

SOCRATES: So—what should a leader say when he's at sea and his ship is hit by a storm—do you mean a rhapsode will know better than a navigator?

ION: No, no. A navigator will know *that*.

SOCRATES: And when he is in charge of a sick man, what should a leader say—will a rhapsode know better than a doctor?

ION: Not that, either.

---

8. *Iliad* xii.200–207.

SOCRATES: But he *will* know what a slave should say. Is that what you mean?

ION: Yes.

SOCRATES: For example, what should a slave who's a cowherd say to calm down his cattle when they're going wild—will a rhapsode know what a cowherd does not?

ION: Certainly not.

SOCRATES: And what a woman who spins yarn should say about working

d   with wool?

ION: No.

SOCRATES: And what a man should say, if he's a general, to encourage his troops?

ION: Yes! That's the sort of thing a rhapsode will know.

SOCRATES: What? Is a rhapsode's profession the same as a general's?

ION: Well, *I* certainly would know what a general should say.

SOCRATES: Perhaps that's because you're also a general by profession, Ion. I mean, if you were somehow both a horseman and a cithara-player

e   at the same time, you would know good riders from bad. But suppose I asked you: "Which profession teaches you good horsemanship—the one that makes you a horseman, or the one that makes you a cithara-player?"

ION: The horseman, I'd say.

SOCRATES: Then if you also knew good cithara-players from bad, the profession that taught you *that* would be the one which made you a cithara-player, not the one that made you a horseman. Wouldn't you agree?

ION: Yes.

SOCRATES: Now, since you know the business of a general, do you know this by being a general or by being a good rhapsode?

ION: I don't think there's any difference.

541   SOCRATES: What? Are you saying there's no difference? On your view is there one profession for rhapsodes and generals, or two?

ION: One, I think.

SOCRATES: So anyone who is a good rhapsode turns out to be a good general too.

ION: Certainly, Socrates.

SOCRATES: It also follows that anyone who turns out to be a good general is a good rhapsode too.

ION: No. This time I don't agree.

b   SOCRATES: But you do agree to this: anyone who is a good rhapsode is a good general too.

ION: I quite agree.

SOCRATES: And aren't you the best rhapsode in Greece?

ION: By far, Socrates.

SOCRATES: Are you also a general, Ion? Are you the best in Greece?

ION: Certainly, Socrates. That, too, I learned from Homer's poetry.

SOCRATES: Then why in heaven's name, Ion, when you're both the best general *and* the best rhapsode in Greece, do you go around the country

giving rhapsodies but not commanding troops? Do you think Greece really   c
needs a rhapsode who is crowned with a golden crown? And does not
need a general?

ION: Socrates, *my* city is governed and commanded by you [by Athens];
we don't need a general. Besides, neither your city nor Sparta would choose
me for a general. You think you're good enough for that yourselves.

SOCRATES: Ion, you're superb. Don't you know Apollodorus of Cyzicus?

ION: What does *he* do?

SOCRATES: He's a foreigner who has often been chosen by Athens to be   d
their general. And Phanosthenes of Andros and Heraclides of Clazomenae—they're also foreigners; they've demonstrated that they are worth
noticing, and Athens appoints them to be generals or other sorts of officials.
And do you think that *this* city, that makes such appointments, would not
select Ion of Ephesus and honor him, if they thought he was worth noticing?
Why? Aren't you people from Ephesus Athenians of long standing? And   e
isn't Ephesus a city that is second to none?

But *you*, Ion, you're doing me wrong, if what you say is true that what
enables you to praise Homer is knowledge or mastery of a profession. You
assured me that you knew many lovely things about Homer, you promised
to give a demonstration; but you're cheating me, you're a long way from
giving a demonstration. You aren't even willing to tell me what it is that
you're so wonderfully clever *about*, though I've been begging you for ages.
Really, you're just like Proteus,[9] you twist up and down and take many
different shapes, till finally you've escaped me altogether by turning your-   542
self into a general, so as to avoid proving how wonderfully wise you are
about Homer.

If you're really a master of your subject, and if, as I said earlier, you're
cheating me of the demonstration you promised about Homer, then you're
doing me wrong. But if you're not a master of your subject, if you're
possessed by a divine gift from Homer, so that you make many lovely
speeches about the poet without knowing anything—as *I* said about you—
then you're not doing me wrong. So choose, how do you want us to think
of you—as a *man* who does wrong, or as someone *divine*?

ION: There's a great difference, Socrates. It's much lovelier to be   b
thought divine.

SOCRATES: Then *that* is how we think of you, Ion, the lovelier way: it's
as someone divine, and not as master of a profession, that you are a singer
of Homer's praises.

---

9. Proteus was a servant of Posidon. He had the power to take whatever shape he
wanted in order to avoid answering questions (*Odyssey* iv.385 ff.).

MENEXENUS

Menexenus *was also known in antiquity as* Funeral Oration; *Aristotle cites it once in his* Rhetoric *under that title. Here Socrates recites to Menexenus an oration for the annual ceremony when Athens praised itself and its citizens fallen in battle for the city. Several such speeches survive, including the celebrated oration of Pericles in Thucydides, Book II. Socrates himself alludes to this famous speech, claiming that its true author was none other than Aspasia, Pericles' intellectually accomplished mistress. He also claims her as his own rhetoric teacher—not that rhetoric ever was her profession!—and in fact as the author of the speech he is about to recite. Knowing that the time was at hand for the selection of this year's speaker, Aspasia, in the usual manner of rhetoric teachers in ancient Greece, had her pupil commit to memory her own composition, as a model of what a funeral orator ought to say. The rest of the dialogue is then occupied with Socrates' recitation.*

It is usual in Plato for Socrates to disclaim personal responsibility, as here with Aspasia, for his excursions outside philosophy. One could compare especially Cratylus, *where he playfully attributes his brilliant etymologizing to instruction and inspiration from Euthyphro (whose expert knowledge about the gods reported in* Euthyphro *thus included expert knowledge of the meanings of their names), and* Phaedrus, *with its appeal to the magical effects of the locale and to Socrates' retentive recall of others' speeches to explain his unaccustomed oratorical prowess. The reader is plainly to understand that this is being represented as Socrates' own speech.*

Is Plato the dialogue's author? Aristotle, who cites it twice—not indeed naming Plato as author, but in the same way that he often cites Plato's works, as well known to the reader—gives powerful testimony that he is. Modern scholars' doubts have rested in large part on their inability to conceive what purpose Plato could have had in writing it. One purpose could be satirical, to show by exaggeration how trivial an accomplishment these rhetorical tours-de-force were; better, since Socrates' speech is in fact a highly skilled oration of the genre intended (with all the overblown praise of Athens and the selective attention to history that that entails), is to think it may show (as indeed the Phaedrus *claims) how very much better a skilled philosopher is at the composition of speeches than the usual rhetorical 'expert'. Another ground for doubt has been found in the fact that Socrates carries his story of the Athenians' prowess down to the so-called Corinthian war of 395–387, whose dead he is officially memorializing—long after Socrates' death in 399. But that may only remind us that Plato's, and the ancients', literary conventions are not our own.*

Menexenus was a prominent member of the Socratic circle: he is reported as present for the conversation on Socrates' last day (Phaedo), and he is one of the two young men Socrates questions about friendship in Lysis.

J.M.C.

SOCRATES: Where is Menexenus coming from? The market place?   234

MENEXENUS: Yes, Socrates—the Council Chamber, to be exact.

SOCRATES: You at the Council Chamber? Why? I know—you fancy that you're finished with your schooling and with philosophy, and intend to turn to higher pursuits. You think you're ready for them now. At your   b
age, my prodigy, you're undertaking to govern us older men, so that your family may carry on with its tradition of providing someone to look after us.

MENEXENUS: Socrates, with your permission and approval I'll gladly hold public office; otherwise I won't. Today, however, I went to the Chamber because I heard that the Council was going to select someone to speak over our war-dead. They are about to see to the public funeral, you know.

SOCRATES: Certainly I do. Whom did they choose?

MENEXENUS: Nobody. They put if off until tomorrow. But I think Archinus or Dion will be chosen.

SOCRATES: Indeed, dying in war looks like a splendid fate in many ways, Menexenus. Even if he dies a pauper, a man gets a really magnificent   c
funeral, and even if he was of little account, he gets a eulogy too from the lips of experts, who speak not extempore but in speeches worked up long beforehand. They do their praising so splendidly that they cast a spell over our souls, attributing to each individual man, with the most varied and beautiful verbal embellishments, both praise he merits and praise he   235
does not, extolling the city in every way, and praising the war-dead, all our ancestors before us, and us ourselves, the living. The result is, Menexenus, that I am put into an exalted frame of mind when I am praised by them. Each time, as I listen and fall under their spell, I become a different   b
man—I'm convinced that I have become taller and nobler and better looking all of a sudden. It often happens, too, that all of a sudden I inspire greater awe in the friends from other cities who tag along and listen with me every year. For they are affected in their view of me and the rest of the city just as I am: won over by the speaker, they think the city more wonderful than they thought it before. And this high-and-mighty feeling remains with me more than three days. The speaker's words and the sound of his voice sink into my ears with so much resonance that it is only with   c
difficulty that on the third or fourth day I recover myself and realize where I am. Until then I could imagine that I dwell in the Islands of the Blessed. That's how clever our orators are.

Translated by Paul Ryan.

MENEXENUS: You're forever making fun of the orators, Socrates. This time, though, I don't think that the one who's chosen is going to have an easy time of it; the selection is being made at the last minute, so perhaps the speaker will be forced practically to make his speech up as he goes.

d   SOCRATES: Nonsense, my good man. Every one of those fellows has speeches ready-made, and, besides, even making up this kind of speech as you go isn't hard. Now if he were obliged to speak well of the Athenians among the Peloponnesians or the Peloponnesians among the Athenians, only a good orator could be persuasive and do himself credit; but when you're performing before the very people you're praising, being thought to speak well is no great feat.

MENEXENUS: You think not, Socrates?

SOCRATES: No, by Zeus, it isn't.

e   MENEXENUS: Do you think that *you* could deliver the speech, if that were called for, and the Council were to choose you?

SOCRATES: In fact, Menexenus, there would be nothing surprising in my being able to deliver it. I happen to have no mean teacher of oratory. She is the very woman who has produced—along with a multitude of other good ones—the one outstanding orator among the Greeks, Pericles, son of Xanthippus.

MENEXENUS: What woman is that? But obviously you mean Aspasia?

236   SOCRATES: Yes, I do—her and Connus, son of Metrobius. These are my two teachers, he of music, she of oratory. Surely it's no surprise if a man with an upbringing like that is skilled in speaking! But even someone less well educated than I—a man who learned music from Lamprus and oratory from Antiphon the Rhamnusian[1]—even he, despite these disadvantages, could do himself credit praising Athenians among Athenians.

MENEXENUS: And what would you have to say if the speech were yours to make?

SOCRATES: On my own, very likely nothing; but just yesterday in my

b   lesson I heard Aspasia declaim a whole funeral oration on these same dead. For she heard that the Athenians, just as you say, were about to choose someone to speak. Thereupon she went through for me what the speaker ought to say, in part out of her head, in part by pasting together some bits and pieces thought up before, at the time when she was composing the funeral oration which Pericles delivered, as, in my opinion, she did.

MENEXENUS: And can you remember what Aspasia said?

SOCRATES: I *think* I can. Certainly I was taught it by the lady herself—

c   and I narrowly escaped a beating every time my memory failed me.

MENEXENUS: So why don't you go ahead and repeat it?

SOCRATES: I'm afraid my teacher will be angry with me if I divulge her speech.

---

1. Lamprus was a respected musician, and Thucydides called Antiphon the foremost orator in Athens. Socrates' broad ironical point is that no one could have more accomplished teachers than these two.

MENEXENUS: Have no fear, Socrates. Speak. I shall be very grateful, whether you're pleased to recite Aspasia's speech or whosoever it is. Only speak.

SOCRATES: But perhaps you will laugh at me if I seem to you, old as I am, to go on playing like a child.

MENEXENUS: Not at all, Socrates. In any case, just speak the speech.

SOCRATES: Well, certainly you're a man I'm so bound to gratify that I would even be inclined to do so if you asked me to take off my clothes and dance—especially since we are alone. All right, listen. To begin with she spoke, I think, on the dead themselves—as follows:

"As for deeds, these men have just received at our hands what they deserve,[2] and with it they are making the inevitable journey, escorted at the outset communally by the city and privately by their families. Now we must render them in words the remaining recognition that the law appoints for them and duty demands. For when deeds have been bravely done, it is through an eloquent speech that remembrance and honor accrue to their doers from the hearers. Clearly, what is required is a speech that will praise the dead as they deserve but also gently admonish the living, urging their sons and brothers to imitate the valor of these men, and consoling their fathers, their mothers and any of their grandparents who may remain alive.

"Well then, what speech on our part would display that effect? Where would it be right for us to begin our praise of brave men, who in their lives gladdened their families and friends through their valor and by their death purchased safety for their survivors? I think it appropriate to present their praises in an order the same as that in which they became brave— the order of nature: they became brave by being sons of brave fathers. Let us, therefore, extoll first their noble birth, second their rearing and educa- tion. After that, let us put on view the deeds they performed, showing that they were noble and worthy of their birth and upbringing.

"The nobility of these men's origin is rooted in that of their ancestors. The latter were not immigrants and did not, by arriving from elsewhere, make these descendants of theirs live as aliens in the land, but made them children of the soil, really dwelling and having their being in their ancestral home, nourished not, as other peoples are, by a stepmother, but by a mother, the land in which they lived. Now they lie in death among the familiar places of her who gave them birth, suckled them, and received them as her own. Surely it is most just to celebrate the mother herself first; in this way the noble birth of these men is celebrated at the same time.

"Our land is indeed worthy of being praised not merely by us but by all of humanity. There are many reasons for that, but the first and greatest is that she has the good fortune to be dear to the gods. The quarrel of the

---

2. The remains of the dead have been exposed to view, mourned, and carried in procession to the tomb, where the speech is being delivered.

d gods who disputed over her and the verdict that settled it bear witness to what we say.[3] How could it not be just for all humankind to praise a land praised by the gods? The second commendation that is due her is that in the age when the whole earth was causing creatures of all kinds— wild animals and domestic livestock—to spring up and thrive, our land showed herself to be barren of savage beasts and pure. Out of all the animals she selected and brought forth the human, the one creature that towers over the others in understanding and alone acknowledges justice and the gods.

e "The fact that everything that gives birth is supplied with the food its offspring needs is weighty testimony for this assertion that the earth hereabouts gave birth to these men's ancestors and ours. For by this sign it can be seen clearly whether or not a woman has really given birth: she is foisting off an infant not her own, if she does not have within her the wellsprings of its nourishment. The earth here, our mother, offers precisely this as sufficient testimony that she has brought forth humans. She first

238 and she alone in that olden time bore food fit for humans, wheat and barley, which are the finest and best nourishment for the human race, because she really was the mother of this creature. And such testimonies are to be taken more seriously on earth's behalf than a woman's, inasmuch as earth does not mimic woman in conceiving and generating, but woman earth.

"She was not miserly with this grain; she dispensed it to others too. Later she brought olive oil to birth for her children, succor against toil. And when she had nourished them and brought them to their youthful

b prime, she introduced the gods to rule and teach them. They (it is fitting to omit their names on an occasion like this: we know them) equipped us for living, by instructing us, earlier than other peoples, in arts for meeting our daily needs, and by teaching us how to obtain and use arms for the defense of the land.

"With the birth and education I have described, the ancestors of these men lived under a polity that they had made for themselves, of which it

c is right to make brief mention. For a polity molds its people; a goodly one molds good men, the opposite bad. Therefore I must show that our ancestors were molded in a goodly polity, thanks to which both they and the present generation—among them these men who have died—are good men. For the polity was the same then and now, an aristocracy; we are now governed by the best men and, in the main, always have been since that remote age. One man calls our polity democracy, another some other

d name that pleases him; in reality, it is government by the best men along with popular consent. We have always had kings; at one time they were

3. In myth Athena and Posidon vied for sovereignty of Athens. On the grounds that Athena's gift of the olive tree was more valuable than the salt-water spring Posidon had made gush forth on the Acropolis, the twelve gods appointed by Zeus to arbitrate the dispute awarded the sovereignty to her.

hereditary, later elected.[4] Yet in most respects the people have sovereign power in the city; they grant public offices and power to those who are thought best by them at a given time, and no one is excluded because of weakness or poverty or obscurity of birth, nor is anyone granted honors because of the corresponding advantages, as happens in other cities. There is, rather, one standard: he who is thought wise or good exercises power and holds office.

"The reason we have this polity is our equality in birth. The other cities have been put together from people of diverse origin and unequal condition, so that their polities also are unequal—tyrannies and oligarchies. Some of their inhabitants look on the others as slaves, while the latter look on the former as masters. We and our fellows-citizens, all brothers sprung from one mother, do not think it right to be each other's slaves or masters. Equality of birth in the natural order makes us seek equality of rights in the legal and defer to each other only in the name of reputation for goodness and wisdom.

"Because of this splendid polity of ours, the fathers of these men—our fathers—and the men themselves, brought up in complete freedom and well-born as they were, were able to display before all humanity, in both the private and the public spheres, many splendid deeds. They thought that they were obliged to fight on the side of freedom both for Greeks against Greeks and against barbarians for Greece as a whole. My time is too brief to narrate as the matter deserves how they defended their country against Eumolpus and the Amazons and even earlier invaders, or how they defended the Argives against the Cadmeans and the sons of Heracles against the Argives.[5] Besides, poets have already hymned the valorous exploits of the ancients in splendid song and made them known to all; so if we should try to elaborate the same subjects in prose, we would perhaps finish a clear second.

"I think it best to pass those deeds by for that reason as well as because they already have a reward worthy of them. But in regard to deeds for which no poet has yet received glory worthy of worthy themes, and which remain in virgin state[6]—those I think I ought to mention with praise and

---

4. After the monarchy was abolished at Athens, one of the nine principal administrative officials, called archons, was the "king archon." He was concerned for the most part with religious functions.

5. Eumolpus was defeated at Eleusis by the legendary Athenian king Erechtheus. According to legend, the Amazons, when they invaded Athens, were defeated by Theseus, who also led the Athenians in forcing Thebes, founded by Cadmus, to return the Argive dead after the war of the Seven Against Thebes. The Sons of Heracles were supposed to have been pursued by their father's enemy Eurystheus, who ruled cities in the part of the Peloponnese that is often referred to, somewhat loosely, as Argos. When they took refuge in Athens, he marched against them and was defeated and killed by the Athenians.

6. Reading *en mnēsteia(i)* in c4.

woo out of seclusion for others to put into choral odes and poems of other kinds in a manner that befits the men who performed them.

d   Here are the first among the deeds I mean. When the Persians held dominion over Asia and were trying to enslave Europe, the sons of this land checked them—our fathers, whose valor it is both right and necessary to mention first in praise. Clearly one who is to praise it well must contemplate it after he has, in thought, been transported into that time when the whole of Asia was already subject to a third Persian king. Cyrus, the first of them, when by his keen spirit he liberated his fellow citizens, the Persians,

e   enslaved the Medes, their masters, at the same time and became lord over the rest of Asia as far as Egypt; his son over as much of Egypt and Libya as it was possible to penetrate. Darius, third of the line, with his land forces set the bounds of his sway as far as Scythia, and with his ships

240 gained so much control over the sea and its islands that no one presumed to oppose him. The minds of all humankind were in bondage: so many, such great and warlike, peoples had the realm of Persia enslaved.

"Now Darius denounced us and the Eretrians. On the pretext that we had plotted against Sardis he dispatched five hundred thousand men in transport and combat ships, with three hundred ships of war, and ordered Datis, their commander, to come back with the Athenians and Eretrians in tow if he wanted to keep his head on his shoulders.

b   "Datis sailed to Eretria, against men who were the most highly esteemed in warfare of the Greeks of that time and were quite numerous besides. He overpowered them in three days. He also scoured their whole country to keep anyone from escaping. This he accomplished in the following way: his soldiers proceeded to the border of Eretria's territory and posted themselves at intervals from sea to sea; they then joined hands and passed

c   through the entire country, so that they would be able to tell the king that no one had escaped them.

"Datis and his force left Eretria and came ashore at Marathon with the same intention, confident that it would be easy for them to force the Athenians under the same yoke as they had the Eretrians and lead them captive too. Even though the first of these operations had been accomplished and the second was underway, none of the Greeks came to aid either the Eretrians or the Athenians except the Lacedaemonians—and

d   they arrived on the day after the battle. All the others were panic-stricken and lay low, cherishing their momentary safety.

"By being transported into that situation, I say, one might realize just how great the valor really was of those men who withstood the might of the barbarians[7] at Marathon, chastened the arrogance of all Asia, and were first to erect a trophy[8] over the barbarians. They showed the way and

7. I.e., as usual in classical Greek, the Persians. Similarly, "king" below refers to the king of Persia.

8. I.e., win a battle; trophies, usually consisting of a suit of enemy armor on a stake, were erected at battle sites by the army still in possession of the field after the action.

taught the rest that Persian power is not invincible and that there is no multitude of men and mass of money that does not give way to valor. I declare that those men were fathers not only of our bodies but of our freedom, ours and that of everyone on this continent. For it was with eyes on that deed that the Greeks dared to risk the battles for their deliverance that followed—pupils of the men who fought at Marathon.

"So the highest rank in honor must be assigned to them by my speech, but the second to the men who fought and won at sea off Salamis and at Artemisium.[9] For one could give a lengthy account of those men, too— the kind of assaults they withstood on land and sea, and how they fought them off. But I shall mention what I think is their finest achievement: they accomplished the successor to the task accomplished at Marathon. The men there showed the Greeks only that a few of them could fight off many barbarians by land; by sea there was still doubt, and the Persians had a reputation for invinciblity because of their numbers, wealth, skill, and strength. This in particular is what merits praise in the men who fought the sea battles of those times: they freed the Greeks from this second terror and made them stop fearing preponderance in ships and men. So it turns out that the other Greeks were educated by both—by those who fought at Marathon and those who took part in the naval battle at Salamis: as pupils of the former by land and the latter by sea, they lost their habit of fearing the barbarians.

"And of the exploits for the deliverance of Greece that at Plataea was, I maintain, the third, both in number and in valor—at last an effort shared by both the Lacedaemonians and the Athenians.

"So all the men in those battles fought off a very great and formidable danger. They are being eulogized for their valor now by us, and will be eulogized in the future by posterity. Afterwards, though, many Greek cities were still subject to the barbarian, and it was reported that the king himself had a new attempt on the Greeks in mind. Therefore, it is right for us to mention those, too, who, by cleansing the sea and driving from it the entire barbarian force, brought to completion what their predecessors had done for our deliverance. These were the men who fought in the naval battle at Eurymedon, those who made the expedition to Cyprus, and those who sailed to Egypt and many other places. They must be mentioned with gratitude, because they instilled fear in the king and forced him to ponder his own safety rather than plot the destruction of the Greeks.

"Well, this war against the barbarians was endured to the end by the whole city in defense of ourselves and our fellow speakers of Greek. But when peace prevailed and the city was held in honor, there came upon her what people generally inflict on the successful: jealousy and—through jealousy—ill-will. And that involved her, reluctantly, in fighting against Greeks. When war had broken out, the Athenians did battle with the

9. During the second Persian invasion of the Greek mainland, by Darius' son Xerxes in 480–479.

Lacedaemonians at Tanagra for the freedom of the Boeotians, and although
b   the issue of the battle was unclear, the action that followed was decisive.
For the Lacedaemonians withdrew and abandoned those whom they had
come to aid, but our men were victorious at Oenophyta two days later
and justly restored those who were unjustly in exile. They were the first
after the Persian War to fight for the freedom of Greeks in the new way—
c   against Greeks; and since they proved to be brave men and liberated those
to whose aid they came, they were the first to be buried in this tomb with
civic honors.

"Later, when a great war[10] had broken out, and all the Greeks attacked
our city, ravaged her land, and made sorry recompense for the services
she had done them, our countrymen, who had been victorious over them
at sea and had captured their Lacedaemonian leaders on Sphacteria, spared
d   the latter, sent them home, and made peace, even though they could have
killed them. They thought that against men of their own race it is right to
make war as far as victory rather than bring the common interests of Greece
to ruin through resentment against one city, but against the barbarians it
is right to make total war. The men who fought in that war and now lie
here deserve praise, because they showed that if anyone maintained that
in the former war, the one against the barbarians, any other people were
braver than the Athenians, that was not true. By prevailing when Greece
e   was in discord, by getting the better of the foremost among the other
Greeks, they showed on this occasion that they could conquer by themselves those with whom they had once conquered the barbarians in a
common effort.

"After this peace a third war[11] broke out—a war that defied all expecta-
243   tions and was terrible. Many brave men who died in it lie here. Many fell
on Sicilian shores after they had set up a great many trophies in battles
for the freedom of the people of Leontini. Bound by oaths, they had sailed
to those parts to defend them, but when their city found herself thwarted
on account of the length of the voyage and could not reinforce them, they
gave out and came to grief. Their enemies, even though they fought on
the other side, have more praise for their self-control and valor than have
the friends of other men. Many fell, too, in naval battles on the Hellespont,
b   after capturing all the enemy ships in one engagement,[12] and coming off
victorious in many others.

"As for my saying that the war was terrible and defied all expectations,
what I mean is that the other Greeks arrived at such a pitch of jealous
rivalry against our city that they brought themselves to send an embassy

---

10. The reference is to the first part (432–421) of the Peloponnesian War, called the
Archidamian War after a Spartan, i.e., Lacedaemonian, king.

11. This "third war" (counting the Persian War as the first) is the second and final part
of the Peloponnesian War, which broke out when the Athenians sent an expedition to
Sicily in 415 and which lasted until 404.

12. The battle of Cyzicus, in 410.

to their worst enemy, the king, whom they had as our allies expelled in a common effort, to bring him back on their own, a barbarian against Greeks, and to muster everyone, Greeks and barbarians, against our city.

"And at just that point her strength and valor shone bright. For when her enemies supposed that she was already beaten, and when her ships were blockaded at Mytilene, the citizens themselves embarked and went to the rescue with sixty ships. After they had, as everyone agrees, behaved most heroically in overcoming their enemies and rescuing their friends, they met with undeserved calamity: their dead were not picked up from the sea and do not lie here.[13] We ought to remember and praise those men forever, because by their valor we won not only that naval engagement, but also the rest of the war. For it was through them that the opinion gained currency that our city could never be defeated in war, not even by all mankind. And that belief was true. We were overcome by our own quarrels, not by other men; by them we remain undefeated to this day, but we conquered ourselves and suffered defeat at our own hands.

"Afterwards, when tranquillity reigned and we were at peace with our neighbors, there was civil war[14] among us, fought in such a way that, if people *had* to engage in internal strife, no one would pray for his city to be stricken in any other. So readily and naturally—so much contrary to the expectations of the other Greeks—did the citizens from the Piraeus and those from the city deal with each other! So moderately did they bring the war against the men at Eleusis to a conclusion!

"And the sole cause for all that was their genuine kinship, which provided them, not in word but in fact, with a firm friendship based on ties of blood. We must also remember those who died at each other's hands in that war and try to reconcile them in ceremonies such as today's by what means we have—prayers and sacrifices—praying to the gods below who have power over them, since we ourselves are reconciled as well. For they did not lay hands on each other through wickedness or enmity, but through misfortune. And we, the living, are witnesses of this ourselves, since we, who are of the same stock, have forgiven each other for what we did and for what we suffered.

"After that we got general peace, and the city enjoyed tranquillity. She forgave the barbarians; she had done them harm, and they gave as good as they got. But the Greeks aroused her indignation, because she recalled the thanks they had returned for the good she had done them—by making common cause with the barbarians, stripping her of the ships that had once been their salvation, and dismantling walls once sacrificed by us to

c

d

e

244

b

c

---

13. Failure to pick up the dead and rescue the wounded from the sea after the battle of Arginusae, in 406, caused widespread resentment against the generals in charge.

14. This "civil war" was fought in 403 to restore the Athenian democracy by ousting the oligarchy of the "Thirty Tyrants," who had seized power with Spartan help at the end of the Peloponnesian War. The conclusion of the civil war, referred to just below, came about through the defeat of the Thirty at Eleusis, where they had retreated.

keep theirs from falling.[15] The city formed a policy of no longer protecting Greeks from being enslaved, either by each other or by barbarians, and conducted herself accordingly. So, since this was our policy, the Lacedae-

d   monians, thinking that we, the champions of freedom, had fallen and all they had to do now was enslave the other Greeks, set about that very task.

"And why should I prolong the tale? From here on I wouldn't be speaking of things that happened in the past to former generations. We ourselves know how the foremost among the Greeks—the Argives and the Boeotians and Corinthians—came, in a state of panic, to feel a need for our city, and— wonder of wonders!—even the king reached such a point of perplexity that his deliverance came full circle to arising from nowhere other than this city, which he had kept zealously trying to destroy.

e   "In fact, if one should wish to lay a just charge against our city, one would rightly blame her only by saying that she is always too compassionate and solicitous of the underdog. And during this time in particular, she was not able to persevere and stick to the policy she had decided on—namely,

245 to aid against enslavement none of the cities that had treated her people unfairly. On the contrary, she relented, came to the rescue, and released the Greeks from slavery by coming to their aid herself, with the result that they remained free until they once more enslaved themselves. On the other hand—out of respect for the trophies at Marathon and Salamis and Plataea—she could not stomach aiding the king in person; but merely by allowing exiles and mercenaries to assist him, she was, by common consent, his salvation. And after she had rebuilt her walls and fleet, she took the

b   war upon herself, when she was forced to do so, and fought with the Lacedaemonians in the Parians' behalf.

"The king came to fear our city, when he saw that the Lacedaemonians were giving up the war at sea. Out of a wish to disengage himself, he demanded, as his price for continuing to fight on our side and that of the other allies, the Greeks on the Asian mainland whom the Lacedaemonians had previously made over to him.[16] He did so because he believed that

c   we would refuse and give him an excuse for disengaging. He was mistaken about the other allies; the Corinthians, the Argives, the Boeotians, and the rest were willing to hand them over to him and made a sworn treaty on terms that if he would give them money, they would hand over the Greeks on the mainland. We alone could not bring ourselves to betray them or swear the oath. That is how firm and sound the high-mindedness and liberality of our city are, how much we are naturally inclined to hate the

d   barbarians, through being purely Greek with no barbarian taint. For people

15. In response to Xerxes' invasion, the Athenians abandoned their city walls to destruction and took to the "wooden walls" of their ships, which were instrumental in defeating the Persians at Salamis. Now Sparta had exacted the destruction of both walls and ships in the peace terms that ended the Peloponnesian War.

16. This probably refers to the terms under which the Spartans brought Persia into the Peloponnesian War against Athens in 412.

who are barbarians by birth but Greeks by law—offspring of Pelops, Cadmus, Aegyptus, Danaus and many others—do not dwell among us.[17] We dwell apart—Greeks, not semibarbarians. Consequently, our city is imbued with undiluted hatred of foreignness.

"For all that, we found ourselves once again isolated, because we refused to commit a shameful and sacrilegious deed by betraying Greeks to barbarians. So we arrived in the same circumstances that had led to our defeat before, but this time, with divine help, we managed the war better: we disengaged ourselves while still in possession of our ships, walls, and colonies. That is how glad the enemy, too, were to make peace! But we lost brave men in this war also, victims of rough terrain at Corinth and treason at Lechaeum. Brave, too, were those who extricated the king from his difficulties and banished the Lacedaemonians from the sea. I remind you of those men, and it is fitting for you to praise them with me and do them honor.

"And these, in truth, were the deeds of the men who lie here and of others who have died for Athens. Many fine words have been spoken about them, but those that remain unsaid are a great deal more numerous and finer still; many days and nights would not suffice for one who sets out to complete the enumeration. Therefore we must remember the fallen, and every man, just as in war, must encourage their descendants not to desert the ranks of their ancestors and not to yield to cowardice and fall back. So then, I myself both so encourage you today, sons of brave men, and in the future, whenever I meet any of you, I will remind you and exhort you to do your utmost to be as brave as can be.

"On this occasion, though, it is my duty to repeat the words that our fathers commanded us to report to those left at home every time they were about to put their lives at risk, in case they lost them. I will tell you what I heard from them and what—judging by what they said then—they would gladly say to you now, if only they could. Whatever I report you must imagine you are hearing from them in person. And this is what they said:

"'Sons, the present circumstance itself reveals that you are sprung from brave fathers. Free to live on ignobly, we prefer to die nobly rather than subject you and your descendants to reproach and bring disgrace on our fathers and all our ancestors. We consider the life of one who has brought disgrace on his own family no life, and we think that no one, human being or god, is his friend, either on the earth or beneath it after his death.

"'Therefore, you must remember what we say and do whatever you do to the accompaniment of valor, knowing that without it all possessions and all ways of life are shameful and base. For neither does wealth confer

17. Many Greek cities had adventurers from abroad mixed up in their foundation legends, such as Pelops from Asia Minor at Mycenae, Cadmus from Phoenicia at Thebes, and Aegyptus and Danaus from Egypt and Libya at Argos.

distinction on one who possesses it with cowardice (the riches of a man like that belong to another, not himself) nor do bodily beauty and strength, when they reside in a worthless and cowardly man, seem to suit him. On the contrary, they seem out of character; they show up the one who has them for what he is and reveal his cowardice. Moreover, all knowledge

247   cut off from rectitude and the rest of virtue has the look of low cunning, not wisdom.

"'For these reasons, make it your business from beginning to end to do your absolute utmost always in every way to surpass us and our ancestors in glory. If you do not, be sure that if we excel you in valor, our victory, as we see it, brings us shame, but if we are excelled by you, our defeat brings happiness. And the surest way to bring about our defeat and your

b   victory would be if you would prepare yourselves not to abuse and waste the good repute of your ancestors, because you are aware that for a man with self-respect nothing is more disgraceful than to make himself honored not through himself, but through his ancestors' glory. Honors that come from ancestors are a noble and magnificent treasure for their descendants, but it is shameful and unmanly to enjoy the use of a treasure of wealth and honors and fail to hand it on to the following generation because of a lack of acquisitions and public recognition on one's own part. And if

c   you will live as we advise you to live, you will come to us as friends to friends, when your destiny conveys you here; but if you have neglected our advice and behaved as cowards, no one will welcome you. So ends what is to be reported to our sons.

"'And as for those of our fathers and mothers who still live, one ought ceaselessly to encourage them to bear the sorrow, should it fall to their lot, as easily as they can, instead of joining them in lamentations. For they

d   will stand in no need of a stimulus for grief; the misfortune that has befallen them will be enough to provide that. A better course is to try to heal and soothe them, by reminding them that the gods have answered their most earnest prayers. For they prayed for their sons to live not forever, but bravely and gloriously. And that—the greatest of boons—is what they received. It is not easy for a mortal to have *everything* in his life turn out as he would have it.

"'If they bear their sorrows courageously, they will seem to be really fathers of courageous sons—and just as courageous themselves; but if they

e   succumb to grief, they will provide grounds for suspicion that either they are not our fathers or the people who praise us are mistaken. Neither of these must happen. On the contrary, they above all must be our encomiasts in action, by showing themselves to be true men, with the look of truly being the fathers of true men. *Nothing too much* has long been thought an excellent adage—because it is, in truth, excellent. For that man's life is best arranged for whom all, or nearly all, the things that promote happiness

248   depend on himself. Such a man does not hang from other men and necessarily rise or fall in fortune as they fare well or badly; he is the temperate, he is the brave and wise man. He above all, when wealth and children

come and when they go, will pay heed to the adage: because he relies on himself, he will be seen neither to rejoice nor to grieve *too much*.

"'That is the sort of men we expect our fathers to be, the sort we wish them to be, and the sort we say they are. It is, moreover, how we now comport ourselves—neither too much vexed nor too fearful if the time of our death is upon us. And we beg our fathers and mothers to pass the rest of their lives with these same sentiments. We want them to know that they will give us no special pleasure by singing dirges and wailing over us. On the contrary, if there is among the dead any perception of the living, that is how they would most displease us—by doing themselves injuries and bearing their sorrows heavily. They would please us most by bearing them lightly and with moderation. By that time our lives will have come to the conclusion that is noblest for human beings, so that it is more fitting to celebrate them than to lament them. But by caring for our wives and children and nourishing them, and by turning their minds to the concerns of the living, they would most readily forget their troubles and live more nobly, more uprightly, and more in harmony with our wishes.

"'That is enough to report from us to our parents. As for the city—we would exhort her to care for our parents and children, educating the latter decently and cherishing the former in their old age as they deserve, if we did not, in fact, know that she will care for them well enough with no exhortation from us.'

"Children and parents, the dead commanded me to report those words, and I report them with all my heart. And on my own part, in these men's name I beg their sons to imitate them, and I beg their fathers to be confident about themselves, knowing that we will, as individuals and as a community, cherish you in your old age and care for you, anywhere any one of us comes upon any one of you. No doubt you yourselves are aware of the concern shown by the city: she has made laws relating to the families of men who have died in war, and she takes care of their children and parents. More than in the case of other citizens, it is the official duty of the highest magistracy to see to it that their fathers and mothers are protected from injustice. The city herself assists in bringing up their children, eager to keep their orphaned condition as hidden from them as it can be. She assumes the role of father to them while they are still children. When they attain manhood, she decks each of them out in hoplite's armor and sends him out on his life's business, showing him and reminding him of his father's pursuits, by giving him the tools of his father's valor and, at the same time, allowing him, for the sake of the omen, to go for the first time to his ancestral hearth, there to rule in might, arrayed in arms.[18]

18. During the festival called the Great Dionysia, before the competition in tragedy which formed part of it, grown sons of men who had been killed in war were presented to the people in the theater, dressed in hoplite armor, and put in charge of their household and property.

"The dead themselves she never fails to honor: every year she herself celebrates for all publicly the rites that are celebrated for each in private, and in addition she holds contests in athletic prowess and horsemanship and in music and poetry of every kind. Quite simply, for the dead she 249c stands as son and heir, for their sons as a father, for their parents as a guardian; she takes complete and perpetual responsibility for all of them.

"With this in mind, you ought to bear your sorrow more patiently; in that way you would best please both the dead and the living and would most easily heal and be healed. And now that you and all the others have, according to the custom, publicly lamented the dead, take your departure."

d   There you have it, Menexenus—the speech of Aspasia of Miletus.

MENEXENUS: By Zeus, Socrates, your Aspasia is indeed lucky if, woman though she be, she can compose speeches like that one.

SOCRATES: If you doubt it, come to class with me and hear her speak.

MENEXENUS: I have often talked with Aspasia, and I know what she is like, Socrates.

SOCRATES: Well then, don't you admire her and aren't you grateful to her for her speech now?

MENEXENUS: Yes, Socrates, I'm very grateful for that speech—to her or e   whoever it was who recited it to you. Furthermore, I'm grateful to him who recited it to me, for that and many other favors besides.

SOCRATES: Very well, but make sure you don't give me away, so that I may report to you many fine, statesmanlike speeches from her in the future.

MENEXENUS: Don't worry. I won't. Just be sure to report them.

SOCRATES: Yes, I'll be sure to.

CLITOPHON

Socrates is in Clitophon's bad books because he has been unable to satisfy Clitophon's thirst for virtue. It was Socrates himself, with his rousing exhortations to virtue, who stimulated this desire in Clitophon and caused him to enter the Socratic milieu in search of the knowledge that he needed next: a philosophical understanding of virtue itself, especially justice. With Socrates and Socrates' friends, his search always ended in dead ends, and he concluded that the Socratic project had to be pursued at a deeper level, in open discussions with Thrasymachus and anybody else who might help.

It comes as quite a surprise to see a Platonic dialogue in which Socrates is the target of attack and fails to have the last word, especially considering that the criticisms he leaves unanswered are delivered by an associate of Thrasymachus, the radical thinker whose views are rejected in Plato's Republic. Even considering the rich variety of the Platonic corpus, Clitophon is an oddity, indeed an enigma.

One of the most interesting features of the dialogue is the Socratic exhortation to virtue (407b–408c), a version of the speeches with which Socrates repeatedly harangued his fellow Athenians. The ideas in this exhortation have parallels in Plato's Apology and Euthydemus, the Alcibiades, Aeschines' Alcibiades (fragments), Xenophon's Memoirs of Socrates (IV.ii), and other works, including no doubt the lost Exhortation dialogues of Aristippus of Cyrene and Antisthenes of Athens. The rhetoric of Socrates' exhortation in Clitophon is paralleled in Xenophon's Memoirs of Socrates (I.v). Although his enthusiasm for this style of exhortation is rather sarcastically expressed, Clitophon focuses his criticism on what comes next, or rather, on what fails to come next: a properly philosophical understanding of the nature of justice and what it accomplishes. The remarkable thing is that Clitophon argues in the same dialectical way that Socrates does in Plato's Socratic dialogues; Socrates is hoist with his own petard, and Clitophon is the Socratic hero of the piece.

But why is Socrates the villain? Does the author align himself with the rhetorical tradition in rejecting the entire Socratic legacy as a dead end? Or is he a spokesman for Plato and his dialectical attempt to establish the Socratic way of thinking on deeper and better foundations than those built upon by competing followers of Socrates? Might the author even be Plato himself? All these questions remain open.

Xenophon seems to have read Clitophon; if so, his reply in Socrates' defense (Memoirs of Socrates I.iv.1) would date it to the second quarter of the fourth *century* B.C.—*during Plato's lifetime. The dialogue is a carefully contrived pamphlet, not a fragment or a draft.*

D.S.H.

406   SOCRATES: We have recently been informed that Clitophon the son of Aristonymos, in discussion with Lysias, has been criticizing the conversations and speeches of Socrates, while greatly praising the instruction of Thrasymachus.[1]

CLITOPHON: Whoever told you that, Socrates, misrepresented what I said to Lysias about you. Though it's true that I didn't praise you for some things, I did praise you for others. Since you're obviously scolding me right now, though you're pretending you don't care, I'd be very glad to tell you myself what I said—especially since we happen to find ourselves alone—so you won't so readily suppose that I have anything against you. In fact, you probably didn't hear the truth, which is why I think you're being needlessly hard on me. So[2] if you'd let me speak freely, I'd gladly do so—I want to tell you what I said.

407   SOCRATES: By all means; it would be shameful for me not to submit to you when your intention is to help me; for clearly, once I know my good and bad points, I will make it my practice to pursue and develop the former while ridding myself of the latter to the extent that I am able.

CLITOPHON: Listen, then. Socrates, when I was associating with you I was often struck with amazement by what you said. You appeared to me to rise above all other men with your magnificent speeches when you reproached mankind and, like a god suspended above the tragic stage, chanted[3] the following refrain:

b   O mortals, whither are you borne? Do you not realize that you
         are doing none of the things you should?![4] You men spare no
         pains in procuring wealth for yourselves, but you neither see to it[5]
         that your sons, to whom you are leaving this wealth, should know
         how to use it justly, nor do you find them teachers of justice (if
         justice can be taught), nor anybody to exercise and train them ade-
         quately (if it is acquired by exercise and training)—nor indeed
         have you started by undergoing such treatment yourselves!

Translated by Francisco J. Gonzalez.

1. Lysias was a famous orator in Athens (*Phaedrus* 227a ff.); Thrasymachus, a teacher of rhetoric (*Phaedrus* 266c), appears in *Republic* (336b ff.) in a hostile light.

2. Reading *dē* instead of *de* in a12.

3. Accepting the conjecture *humnois* in a8.

4. Placing a question mark after *prattontes* in b2.

5. Accepting the supplement *oute phrontizete* after *paradōsete* in b4.

But when you see that you and your children have had a thorough education in grammar, gymnastics and the arts—which you consider to be a complete education in virtue—and that you still have turned out to be no good at using wealth, how can you fail to despise our present education, and seek those who will rescue you from this lack of culture?! Yet it is this dissonance, this carelessness, not dancing the wrong measures to the lyre, that makes measure and harmony disappear between brother and brother, city and city, as they oppose each other, clash and fight, inflicting and suffering the utmost horrors of war.

You say that men are unjust because they want to be, not because they are ignorant or uneducated. But then you have the effrontery to say, on the other hand, that injustice is shameful and hateful to the gods. Well, then, how could anyone willingly choose such an evil?! "Perhaps he is defeated by pleasure," you say. But isn't this defeat involuntary if conquering is voluntary? Thus every way you look at it, the argument shows that injustice is involuntary, and that every man privately and every city publicly must devote to this matter greater care than is presently the norm.

When, Socrates, I hear you say such things time and time again, I'm very impressed and I praise you to the skies; and also when you go on to the next point, that those who discipline the body while neglecting the soul are doing something else of the same sort, neglecting that which should rule while busying themselves with that which should be ruled; and also when you say that it's better to leave unused what you don't know how to use: if someone doesn't know how to use his eyes or his ears or his whole body, it would be better for him not to use it all, whether for seeing or hearing or anything else, rather than use it in some haphazard way. In fact, the same applies to skills; for someone who doesn't know how to use his own lyre will hardly be able to use his neighbor's lyre, nor will someone who doesn't know how to use the lyre of others be capable of using his own lyre, nor any other instrument or possession whatsoever. Your speech delivers a wonderful coup de grace when it concludes that someone who doesn't know how to use his soul is better off putting his soul to rest and not living at all rather than leading a life in which his actions are based on nothing but personal whim. If for some reason he must live, it would be better for such a man to live as a slave than to be free, handing over the rudder of his mind, like that of a ship, to somebody else who knows that skill of steering men which you, Socrates, often call politics, the very same skill, you say, as the judicial skill and justice.

I dare say I never objected nor, I believe, ever will object to these arguments, nor to many other eloquent ones like them, to the effect that virtue is teachable and that more care should be devoted to one's self than to anything else. I consider them to be extremely beneficial and extremely

effective in turning us in the right direction; they can really rouse us as if
we'd been sleeping. I was therefore very interested in what would come
next after such arguments; at first I asked not you, Socrates, but your
companions and fellow enthusiasts, or friends, or whatever we should call
their relationship to you. And I first questioned those who are thought by
d   you to be really something; I asked them what argument would come next
and put my case to them in a style somewhat like your own:

O you most distinguished gentlemen, what are we actually[6] to
make of Socrates' exhorting of us to pursue virtue? Are we to believe that this is all there is, and that it is impossible to pursue the
matter[7] further and grasp it fully? Will this be our life-long work,
e   simply to convert to the pursuit of virtue those who have not yet
been converted so that they in turn may convert others? Even if
we agree that this is what a man should do, should we not also
ask Socrates, and each other, what the next step is? How should
we begin to learn what justice is? What do we say?
It's as if we were children with no awareness of the existence of
such things as gymnastics and medicine, and somebody saw this
and exhorted us to take care of our bodies and reproached us, saying that it's shameful that we devote such care to cultivating
wheat, barley, vines and all the other things which we work hard
to acquire for the sake of the body, while we fail to discover any
409   skill or other means of making the body itself as good as possible,
even though such skills exist. Now, if we were to ask the man
who gave us this exhortation, "Which skills are you talking
about?," he would presumably reply, "Gymnastics and medicine."
Now what about us? What do we say is the skill which concerns
the virtue of the soul? Let's have an answer.

The man who appeared the most formidable among your companions
answered these questions by telling me that this skill is "the very skill
b   which you hear Socrates talking about, namely, justice itself." Then I said,
"Don't just give me the name; try it this way. Medicine is surely a kind
of skill. It has two results: it produces other doctors in addition to those
who are already doctors, and it produces health. Of these, the second result
is not itself a skill, but rather the product of a skill, the product we call
'health'; the skill itself is what teaches and what's taught. Likewise, carpentry has as its results a house and carpentry itself; the first is the product
while the second is what's taught. Let's assume that one result of justice
c   is also to produce just men, just as in the case of each of the skills a goal

6. Reading *nun* in d2 as enclitic.
7. Accepting the emendation *estin* for *eni* in d4.

is to produce men with that skill—but what, then, are we to call the other thing, the product which the just man produces for us? Tell me."

He, I think, replied, "the beneficial," somebody else said, "the appropriate," someone else, "the useful" and someone else, "the advantageous." But[8] I returned to the point and said, "All those words, such as 'acting correctly', 'advantageously', 'usefully' and the like, are to be found in each of the skills as well. When asked, however, what these all aim at, each skill will mention some product peculiar to itself. So, for example, when carpentry uses the words 'well', 'properly' and 'appropriately', it is speaking of the production of wooden artifacts, which are products distinct from the skill itself. What, then, is the peculiar product of justice? Give me that sort of answer."

Finally, Socrates, one of your friends answered—and he really seemed quite clever in saying this—that the product peculiar to justice and not shared by any of the other skills is to produce friendship within cities. When questioned, he said that friendship is always good and never bad. When questioned further, he wouldn't allow that what we call the "friendships" of children and animals are really friendships, since he was led to the conclusion that such relationships are more often harmful than good. So in order to avoid saying that this is true of friendship, he claimed that these relationships are not friendships at all and that those who call them that are wrong; instead, real and true friendship is most precisely *agreement*. When asked whether he considered this agreement to be shared belief or knowledge, he rejected the former suggestion since he was forced to admit that many men's shared beliefs are harmful, whereas he had agreed that friendship is entirely good and is the product of justice; so he said that agreement is the same, being knowledge, not belief.

Now by the time we reached this point in the argument, having really made no progress, the bystanders were able to take him to task and say that the argument had gone around in a circle back to where it began.

"Medicine too," they said, "is a sort of agreement, as is every skill, and they all can say what they're *about*. But what you call 'justice' and 'agreement' has no idea what it's aiming at, and so it's not clear what its product could be."

So, Socrates, finally I asked you yourself these questions and you told me that the aim of justice is to hurt one's enemies and help one's friends. But later it turned out that the just man never harms anyone, since everything he does is for the benefit of all.

When I had endured this disappointment, not once or twice but a long time, I finally got tired of begging for an answer. I came to the conclusion that while you're better than anyone at turning a man towards the pursuit of virtue, one of two things must be the case: either this is all you can do, nothing more—as might happen with any other skill, for example, when someone who's not a pilot rehearses a speech in praise of the pilot's skill

8. Reading *de* instead of *dē* in c3.

as being something of great worth to men; the same could also be done for any other skill. And someone might accuse you of being in the same position with justice, that your ability to praise it so well does not make you any more knowledgeable about it. Now that's not my own view, but there are only two possibilities: either you don't know it, or you don't wish to share it with me.

410d   And this is why, I suppose, I go[9] to Thrasymachus and to anyone else I can: I'm at a loss. But if you're finally ready to stop exhorting me with speeches—I mean, if it had been about gymnastics that you were exhorting me, saying that I must not neglect my body, you would have proceeded to give me what comes next after such an exhortation, namely, an explanation of the nature of my body and of the particular kind of treatment this

e   nature requires—that's the kind of thing you should do now.

Assume that Clitophon agrees with you that it's ridiculous to neglect the soul itself while concerning ourselves solely with what we work hard to acquire for its sake. Suppose now that I have also said all the other things which come next and which I just went through. Then, please, do as I ask and I won't praise you before Lysias and others for some things while criticizing you for others, as I do now. For I will say this, Socrates, that while you're worth the world to someone who hasn't yet been converted to the pursuit of virtue, to someone who's already been converted you rather get in the way of his attaining happiness by reaching the goal of virtue.

9. Reading *poreuomai* in c7.

REPUBLIC

The Republic's *ancient subtitle—On Justice—much understates the scope of the work. It begins as a discussion of the nature of justice, much in the manner of 'Socratic' dialogues like* Laches *or* Charmides, *with Socrates examining and refuting successive views of his interlocutors on this subject. But in book II he renews the inquiry, now agreeing to cease examining and refuting the opinions of others, and to present his own account. He will say what justice really is and show that people who are truly and fully just thereby lead a better, happier life than any unjust person could. The horizon lifts to reveal ever-expanding vistas of philosophy. Socrates presents his views on the original purposes for which political communities—cities—were founded, the basic principles of just social and political organization, and the education of young people that those principles demand (books II, III, and V). He decides that a truly just society requires philosophic rulers—both men and women—living in a communistic 'guardhouse' within the larger community. The need for such rulers leads him on to wider topics. He discusses the variety and nature (and proper regimentation) of human desires, and the precise nature of justice and the other virtues—and of the corresponding vices—both in the individual person's psychology and in the organization of political society (IV, VIII, IX). He explains the nature of knowledge and its proper objects (V–VII): The world revealed by our senses—the world of everyday, traditional life—is, he argues, cognitively and metaphysically deficient. It depends upon a prior realm of separately existing Forms, organized beneath the Form of the Good and graspable not by our senses but only through rigorous dialectical thought and discussion, after preparation in extended mathematical studies. There is even a discussion of the basic principles of visual and literary art and art criticism (X). All this is necessary, Socrates says, finally to answer the basic question about justice— not what it is, but why it must make the just person live a good, happy life, and the unjust person a bad, miserable one.*

Speaking throughout to no identified person—that is, directly to the reader—Socrates relates a conversation he took part in one day in the Athenian port city of Piraeus. All the others present, a considerable company, represent historical personages: among them were the noted sophist and teacher of oratory, Thrasymachus, and Glaucon and Adeimantus, Plato's brothers. Glaucon is an ambitious, energetic, 'manly' young man, much interested in public affairs and drawn to the life of politics. An intelligent and argumentative person, he scorns ordinary pleasures and aspires to 'higher' things. Always especially attracted by such people, it was with him that Socrates had gone down to

971

Piraeus in the first place. Adeimantus, equally a decent young man, is less driven, less demanding of himself, more easily satisfied and less gifted in philosophical argument. After book I Socrates carries on his discussion first with one, then with the other of these two men. The conversation as a whole aims at answering to their satisfaction the challenge they jointly raise against Socrates' conviction that justice is a preeminent good for the just person, but Socrates addresses different parts of his reply to a different one of them. (To assist the reader, we have inserted the names of the speakers at the tops of the pages of the translation.)

Though in books II–X Socrates no longer searches for the truth by criticizing his interlocutors' ideas, he proceeds nonetheless in a spirit of exploration and discovery, proposing bold hypotheses and seeking their confirmation in the first instance through examining their consequences. He often emphasizes the tentativeness of his results, and the need for a more extensive treatment. Quite different is the main speaker in the late dialogues Sophist, Statesman, Philebus, and Laws—whether Socrates himself, or a visitor from Elea or Athens: there, we get confident, reasoned delivery of philosophical results assumed by the speaker to be well established.

J.M.C.

Book I

327   I went down to the Piraeus yesterday with Glaucon, the son of Ariston. I wanted to say a prayer to the goddess,[1] and I was also curious to see how they would manage the festival, since they were holding it for the first time. I thought the procession of the local residents was a fine one and that the one conducted by the Thracians was no less outstanding. After we had said our prayer and seen the procession, we started back towards

b   Athens. Polemarchus saw us from a distance as we were setting off for home and told his slave to run and ask us to wait for him. The slave caught hold of my cloak from behind: Polemarchus wants you to wait, he said. I turned around and asked where Polemarchus was. He's coming up behind you, he said, please wait for him. And Glaucon replied: All right, we will.

c   Just then Polemarchus caught up with us. Adeimantus, Glaucon's brother, was with him and so were Niceratus, the son of Nicias, and some others, all of whom were apparently on their way from the procession.

Polemarchus said: It looks to me, Socrates, as if you two are starting off for Athens.

It looks the way it is, then, I said.

Do you see how many we are? he said.

Translated by G.M.A. Grube, revised by C.D.C. Reeve.

1. The Thracian goddess Bendis, whose cult had recently been introduced in the Piraeus, the harbor town of Athens.

I do.

Well, you must either prove stronger than we are, or you will have to stay here.

Isn't there another alternative, namely, that we persuade you to let us go?

But could you persuade us, if we won't listen?

Certainly not, Glaucon said.

Well, we won't listen; you'd better make up your mind to that.

Don't you know, Adeimantus said, that there is to be a torch race on   328
horseback for the goddess tonight?

On horseback? I said. That's something new. Are they going to race on horseback and hand the torches on in relays, or what?

In relays, Polemarchus said, and there will be an all-night festival that will be well worth seeing. After dinner, we'll go out to look at it. We'll be joined there by many of the young men, and we'll talk. So don't go; stay.

It seems, Glaucon said, that we'll have to stay.   b

If you think so, I said, then we must.

So we went to Polemarchus' house, and there we found Lysias and Euthydemus, the brothers of Polemarchus, Thrasymachus of Chalcedon, Charmantides of Paeania, and Clitophon the son of Aristonymus. Pole-   c
marchus' father, Cephalus, was also there, and I thought he looked quite old, as I hadn't seen him for some time. He was sitting on a sort of cushioned chair with a wreath on his head, as he had been offering a sacrifice in the courtyard. There was a circle of chairs, and we sat down by him.

As soon as he saw me, Cephalus welcomed me and said: Socrates, you don't come down to the Piraeus to see us as often as you should. If it were still easy for me to walk to town, you wouldn't have to come here; we'd   d
come to you. But, as it is, you ought to come here more often, for you should know that as the physical pleasures wither away, my desire for conversation and its pleasures grows. So do as I say: Stay with these young men now, but come regularly to see us, just as you would to friends or relatives.

Indeed, Cephalus, I replied, I enjoy talking with the very old, for we should ask them, as we might ask those who have travelled a road that we too will probably have to follow, what kind of road it is, whether rough   e
and difficult or smooth and easy. And I'd gladly find out from you what you think about this, as you have reached the point in life the poets call "the threshold of old age."[2] Is it a difficult time? What is your report about it?

By god, Socrates, I'll tell you exactly what I think. A number of us, who   329
are more or less the same age, often get together in accordance with the old saying.[3] When we meet, the majority complain about the lost pleasures

---

2. *Iliad* xxii.60, xxiv.487; *Odyssey* xv.246, 348, xxiii.212.

3. "God ever draws together like to like" (*Odyssey* xvii.218).

they remember from their youth, those of sex, drinking parties, feasts, and the other things that go along with them, and they get angry as if they had been deprived of important things and had lived well then but are now hardly living at all. Some others moan about the abuse heaped on

b   old people by their relatives, and because of this they repeat over and over that old age is the cause of many evils. But I don't think they blame the real cause, Socrates, for if old age were really the cause, I should have suffered in the same way and so should everyone else of my age. But as it is, I've met some who don't feel like that in the least. Indeed, I was once present when someone asked the poet Sophocles: "How are you as far as

c   sex goes, Sophocles? Can you still make love with a woman?" "Quiet, man," the poet replied, "I am very glad to have escaped from all that, like a slave who has escaped from a savage and tyrannical master." I thought at the time that he was right, and I still do, for old age brings peace and freedom from all such things. When the appetites relax and cease to importune us, everything Sophocles said comes to pass, and we escape

d   from many mad masters. In these matters and in those concerning relatives, the real cause isn't old age, Socrates, but the way people live. If they are moderate and contented, old age, too, is only moderately onerous; if they aren't, both old age and youth are hard to bear.

I admired him for saying that and I wanted him to tell me more, so I

e   urged him on: When you say things like that, Cephalus, I suppose that the majority of people don't agree, they think that you bear old age more easily not because of the way you live but because you're wealthy, for the wealthy, they say, have many consolations.

That's true; they don't agree. And there is something in what they say, though not as much as they think. Themistocles' retort is relevant here. When someone from Seriphus insulted him by saying that his high reputa-

330   tion was due to his city and not to himself, he replied that, had he been a Seriphian, he wouldn't be famous, but neither would the other even if he had been an Athenian. The same applies to those who aren't rich and find old age hard to bear: A good person wouldn't easily bear old age if he were poor, but a bad one wouldn't be at peace with himself even if he were wealthy.

Did you inherit most of your wealth, Cephalus, I asked, or did you make it for yourself?

What did I make for myself, Socrates, you ask. As a money-maker I'm

b   in a sort of mean between my grandfather and my father. My grandfather and namesake inherited about the same amount of wealth as I possess but multiplied it many times. My father, Lysanias, however, diminished that amount to even less than I have now. As for me, I'm satisfied to leave my sons here not less but a little more than I inherited.

The reason I asked is that you don't seem to love money too much. And those who haven't made their own money are usually like you. But those

c   who have made it for themselves are twice as fond of it as those who haven't. Just as poets love their poems and fathers love their children, so those who have made their own money don't just care about it because it's useful, as other people do, but because it's something they've made themselves. This makes them poor company, for they haven't a good word to say about anything except money.

That's true.

It certainly is. But tell me something else. What's the greatest good you've received from being very wealthy?   d

What I have to say probably wouldn't persuade most people. But you know, Socrates, that when someone thinks his end is near, he becomes frightened and concerned about things he didn't fear before. It's then that the stories we're told about Hades, about how people who've been unjust here must pay the penalty there—stories he used to make fun of—twist his soul this way and that for fear they're true. And whether because of   e
the weakness of old age or because he is now closer to what happens in Hades and has a clearer view of it, or whatever it is, he is filled with foreboding and fear, and he examines himself to see whether he has been unjust to anyone. If he finds many injustices in his life, he awakes from sleep in terror, as children do, and lives in anticipation of bad things to come. But someone who knows that he hasn't been unjust has sweet good   331
hope as his constant companion—a nurse to his old age, as Pindar[4] says, for he puts it charmingly, Socrates, when he says that when someone lives a just and pious life

> *Sweet hope is in his heart,*
> *Nurse and companion to his age.*
> *Hope, captain of the ever-twisting*
> *Minds of mortal men.*

How wonderfully well he puts that. It's in this connection that wealth is most valuable, I'd say, not for every man but for a decent and orderly one. Wealth can do a lot to save us from having to cheat or deceive someone   b
against our will and from having to depart for that other place in fear because we owe sacrifice to a god or money to a person. It has many other uses, but, benefit for benefit, I'd say that this is how it is most useful to a man of any understanding.

A fine sentiment, Cephalus, but, speaking of this very thing itself, namely, justice, are we to say unconditionally that it is speaking the truth   c
and paying whatever debts one has incurred? Or is doing these things sometimes just, sometimes unjust? I mean this sort of thing, for example: Everyone would surely agree that if a sane man lends weapons to a friend and then asks for them back when he is out of his mind, the friend shouldn't return them, and wouldn't be acting justly if he did. Nor should anyone be willing to tell the whole truth to someone who is out of his mind.

4. Frg. 214 (Snell).

d   That's true.

Then the definition of justice isn't speaking the truth and repaying what one has borrowed.

It certainly is, Socrates, said Polemarchus, interrupting, if indeed we're to trust Simonides at all.[5]

Well, then, Cephalus said, I'll hand over the argument to you, as I have to look after the sacrifice.

So, Polemarchus said, am I then to be your heir in everything?

You certainly are, Cephalus said, laughing, and off he went to the sacrifice.

Then tell us, heir to the argument, I said, just what Simonides stated
e   about justice that you consider correct.

He stated that it is just to give to each what is owed to him. And it's a fine saying, in my view.

Well, now, it isn't easy to doubt Simonides, for he's a wise and godlike man. But what exactly does he mean? Perhaps you know, Polemarchus, but I don't understand him. Clearly, he doesn't mean what we said a moment ago, that it is just to give back whatever a person has lent to you, even if he's out of his mind when he asks for it. And yet what he has lent
332   to you is surely something that's owed to him, isn't it?

Yes.

But it is absolutely not to be given to him when he's out of his mind?

That's true.

Then it seems that Simonides must have meant something different when he says that to return what is owed is just.

Something different indeed, by god. He means that friends owe it to their friends to do good for them, never harm.

I follow you. Someone doesn't give a lender back what he's owed by giving him gold, if doing so would be harmful, and both he and the lender
b   are friends. Isn't that what you think Simonides meant?

It is.

But what about this? Should one also give one's enemies whatever is owed to them?

By all means, one should give them what is owed to them. And in my view what enemies owe to each other is appropriately and precisely—something bad.

It seems then that Simonides was speaking in riddles—just like a poet!—when he said what justice is, for he thought it just to give to each what
c   is appropriate to him, and this is what he called giving him what is owed to him.

What else did you think he meant?

Then what do you think he'd answer if someone asked him: "Simonides, which of the things that are owed or that are appropriate for someone or

---

5. Simonides (c. 548–468 B.C.), a lyric and elegiac poet, was born in the Aegean island of Ceos.

something to have does the craft[6] we call medicine give, and to whom or what does it give them?"

It's clear that it gives medicines, food, and drink to bodies.

And what owed or appropriate things does the craft we call cooking give, and to whom or what does it give them?

It gives seasonings to food.   d

Good. Now, what does the craft we call justice give, and to whom or what does it give it?

If we are to follow the previous answers, Socrates, it gives benefits to friends and does harm to enemies.

Simonides means, then, that to treat friends well and enemies badly is justice?

I believe so.

And who is most capable of treating friends well and enemies badly in matters of disease and health?

A doctor.

And who can do so best in a storm at sea?   e

A ship's captain.

What about the just person? In what actions and what work is he most capable of benefiting friends and harming enemies?

In wars and alliances, I suppose.

All right. Now, when people aren't sick, Polemarchus, a doctor is useless to them?

True.

And so is a ship's captain to those who aren't sailing?

Yes.

And to people who aren't at war, a just man is useless?

No, I don't think that at all.

Justice is also useful in peacetime, then?

It is.   333

And so is farming, isn't it?

Yes.

For getting produce?

Yes.

And shoemaking as well?

Yes.

For getting shoes, I think you'd say?

Certainly.

Well, then, what is justice useful for getting and using in peacetime?

Contracts, Socrates.

And by contracts do you mean partnerships, or what?

I mean partnerships.

---

6. Here and in what follows "craft" translates *technē*. As Socrates conceives it a *technē* is a disciplined body of knowledge founded on a grasp of the truth about what is good and bad, right and wrong, in the matters of concern to it.

Is someone a good and useful partner in a game of checkers because
b   he's just or because he's a checkers player?

Because he's a checkers player.

And in laying bricks and stones, is a just person a better and more useful
partner than a builder?

Not at all.

In what kind of partnership, then, is a just person a better partner than
a builder or a lyre-player, in the way that a lyre-player is better than a
just person at hitting the right notes?

In money matters, I think.

Except perhaps, Polemarchus, in using money, for whenever one needs
to buy a horse jointly, I think a horse breeder is a more useful partner,
c   isn't he?

Apparently.

And when one needs to buy a boat, it's a boatbuilder or a ship's captain?

Probably.

In what joint use of silver or gold, then, is a just person a more useful
partner than the others?

When it must be deposited for safekeeping, Socrates.

You mean whenever there is no need to use them but only to keep them?

That's right.

Then it is when money isn't being used that justice is useful for it?
d   I'm afraid so.

And whenever one needs to keep a pruning knife safe, but not to use
it, justice is useful both in partnerships and for the individual. When you
need to use it, however, it is skill at vine pruning that's useful?

Apparently.

You'll agree, then, that when one needs to keep a shield or a lyre safe
and not to use them, justice is a useful thing, but when you need to use
them, it is soldiery or musicianship that's useful?

Necessarily.

And so, too, with everything else, justice is useless when they are in
use but useful when they aren't?

It looks that way.

e   In that case, justice isn't worth much, since it is only useful for useless
things. But let's look into the following point. Isn't the person most able
to land a blow, whether in boxing or any other kind of fight, also most
able to guard against it?

Certainly.

And the one who is most able to guard against disease is also most able
to produce it unnoticed?

So it seems to me, anyway.

And the one who is the best guardian of an army is the very one who
334   can steal the enemy's plans and dispositions?

Certainly.

Whenever someone is a clever guardian, then, he is also a clever thief.

Probably so.

If a just person is clever at guarding money, therefore, he must also be clever at stealing it.

According to our argument, at any rate.

A just person has turned out then, it seems, to be a kind of thief. Maybe you learned this from Homer, for he's fond of Autolycus, the maternal grandfather of Odysseus, whom he describes as better than everyone at lying and stealing.[7] According to you, Homer, and Simonides, then, justice seems to be some sort of craft of stealing, one that benefits friends and harms enemies. Isn't that what you meant?

No, by god, it isn't. I don't know any more what I did mean, but I still believe that to benefit one's friends and harm one's enemies is justice.

Speaking of friends, do you mean those a person believes to be good and useful to him or those who actually are good and useful, even if he doesn't think they are, and similarly with enemies?

Probably, one loves those one considers good and useful and hates those one considers bad and harmful.

But surely people often make mistakes about this, believing many people to be good and useful when they aren't, and making the opposite mistake about enemies?

They do indeed.

And then good people are their enemies and bad ones their friends?

That's right.

And so it's just to benefit bad people and harm good ones?

Apparently.

But good people are just and able to do no wrong?

True.

Then, according to your account, it's just to do bad things to those who do no injustice.

No, that's not just at all, Socrates; my account must be a bad one.

It's just, then, is it, to harm unjust people and benefit just ones?

That's obviously a more attractive view than the other one, anyway.

Then, it follows, Polemarchus, that it is just for the many, who are mistaken in their judgment, to harm their friends, who are bad, and benefit their enemies, who are good. And so we arrive at a conclusion opposite to what we said Simonides meant.

That certainly follows. But let's change our definition, for it seems that we didn't define friends and enemies correctly.

How did we define them, Polemarchus?

We said that a friend is someone who is believed to be useful.

And how are we to change that now?

Someone who is both believed to be useful and is useful is a friend; someone who is believed to be useful but isn't, is believed to be a friend but isn't. And the same for the enemy.

b

c

d

e

335

7. *Odyssey* xix.392–98.

According to this account, then, a good person will be a friend and a bad one an enemy.

Yes.

So you want us to add something to what we said before about justice, when we said that it is just to treat friends well and enemies badly. You want us to add to this that it is just to treat well a friend who is good and to harm an enemy who is bad?

b Right. That seems fine to me.

Is it, then, the role of a just man to harm anyone?

Certainly, he must harm those who are both bad and enemies.

Do horses become better or worse when they are harmed?

Worse.

With respect to the virtue[8] that makes dogs good or the one that makes horses good?

The one that makes horses good.

And when dogs are harmed, they become worse in the virtue that makes dogs good, not horses?

Necessarily.

Then won't we say the same about human beings, too, that when they c are harmed they become worse in human virtue?

Indeed.

But isn't justice human virtue?

Yes, certainly.

Then people who are harmed must become more unjust?

So it seems.

Can musicians make people unmusical through music?

They cannot.

Or horsemen make people unhorsemanlike through horsemanship?

No.

Well, then, can those who are just make people unjust through justice?

d In a word, can those who are good make people bad through virtue?

They cannot.

It isn't the function of heat to cool things but of its opposite?

Yes.

Nor the function of dryness to make things wet but of its opposite?

Indeed.

Nor the function of goodness to harm but of its opposite?

Apparently.

---

8. I.e., *aretē*. *Aretē* is broader than our notion of virtue, which tends to be applied only to human beings, and restricted to good sexual behavior or helpfulness on their part to others. *Aretē* could equally be translated "excellence" or "goodness." Thus if something is a knife (say) its *aretē* or "virtue" as a knife is that state or property of it that makes it a good knife—having a sharp blade, and so on. So with the virtue of a man: this might include being intelligent, well-born, or courageous, as well as being just and sexually well-behaved.

And a just person is good?

Indeed.

Then, Polemarchus, it isn't the function of a just person to harm a friend or anyone else, rather it is the function of his opposite, an unjust person?

In my view that's completely true, Socrates.

If anyone tells us, then, that it is just to give to each what he's owed   e
and understands by this that a just man should harm his enemies and benefit his friends, he isn't wise to say it, since what he says isn't true, for it has become clear to us that it is never just to harm anyone?

I agree.

You and I shall fight as partners, then, against anyone who tells us that Simonides, Bias, Pittacus, or any of our other wise and blessedly happy men said this.

I, at any rate, am willing to be your partner in the battle.

Do you know to whom I think the saying belongs that it is just to benefit   336
friends and harm enemies?

Who?

I think it belongs to Periander, or Perdiccas, or Xerxes, or Ismenias of Corinth, or some other wealthy man who believed himself to have great power.[9]

That's absolutely true.

All right, since it has become apparent that justice and the just aren't what such people say they are, what else could they be?

While we were speaking, Thrasymachus had tried many times to take over the discussion but was restrained by those sitting near him, who   b
wanted to hear our argument to the end. When we paused after what I'd just said, however, he couldn't keep quiet any longer. He coiled himself up like a wild beast about to spring, and he hurled himself at us as if to tear us to pieces.

Polemarchus and I were frightened and flustered as he roared into our midst: What nonsense have you two been talking, Socrates? Why do you act like idiots by giving way to one another? If you truly want to know   c
what justice is, don't just ask questions and then refute the answers simply to satisfy your competitiveness or love of honor. You know very well that it is easier to ask questions than answer them. Give an answer yourself, and tell us what you say the just is. And don't tell me that it's the right, the beneficial, the profitable, the gainful, or the advantageous, but tell me   d
clearly and exactly what you mean; for I won't accept such nonsense from you.

His words startled me, and, looking at him, I was afraid. And I think that if I hadn't seen him before he stared at me, I'd have been dumbstruck. But as it was, I happened to look at him just as our discussion began to exasperate him, so I was able to answer, and, trembling a little, I said: e

9. The first three named are notorious tyrants or kings, the fourth a man famous for his extraordinary wealth.

Don't be too hard on us, Thrasymachus, for if Polemarchus and I made an error in our investigation, you should know that we did so unwillingly. If we were searching for gold, we'd never willingly give way to each other, if by doing so we'd destroy our chance of finding it. So don't think that in searching for justice, a thing more valuable than even a large quantity of gold, we'd mindlessly give way to one another or be less than completely serious about finding it. You surely mustn't think that, but rather—as I do— that we're incapable of finding it. Hence it's surely far more appropriate for us to be pitied by you clever people than to be given rough treatment.

337

When he heard that, he gave a loud, sarcastic laugh. By Heracles, he said, that's just Socrates' usual irony. I knew, and I said so to these people earlier, that you'd be unwilling to answer and that, if someone questioned *you*, you'd be ironical and do anything rather than give an answer.

That's because you're a clever fellow, Thrasymachus. You knew very well that if you ask someone how much twelve is, and, as you ask, you

b   warn him by saying "Don't tell me, man, that twelve is twice six, or three times four, or six times two, or four times three, for I won't accept such nonsense," then you'll see clearly, I think, that no one could answer a question framed like that. And if he said to you: "What are you saying, Thrasymachus, am I not to give any of the answers you mention, not even if twelve happens to be one of those things? I'm amazed. Do you want me to say something other than the truth? Or do you mean something

c   else?" What answer would you give him?

Well, so you think the two cases are alike?

Why shouldn't they be alike? But even if they aren't alike, yet seem so to the person you asked, do you think him any less likely to give the answer that seems right to him, whether we forbid him to or not?

Is that what you're going to do, give one of the forbidden answers?

I wouldn't be surprised—provided that it's the one that seems right to me after I've investigated the matter.

What if I show you a different answer about justice than all these—and

d   a better one? What would you deserve then?

What else than the appropriate penalty for one who doesn't know, namely, to learn from the one who does know? Therefore, that's what I deserve.

You amuse me, but in addition to learning, you must pay a fine.

I will as soon as I have some money.

He has some already, said Glaucon. If it's a matter of money, speak, Thrasymachus, for we'll all contribute for Socrates.

I know, he said, so that Socrates can carry on as usual. He gives no

e   answer himself, and then, when someone else does give one, he takes up the argument and refutes it.

How can someone give an answer, I said, when he doesn't know it and doesn't claim to know it, and when an eminent man forbids him to express the opinion he has? It's much more appropriate for you to answer, since

you say you know and can tell us. So do it as a favor to me, and don't   338
begrudge your teaching to Glaucon and the others.

While I was saying this, Glaucon and the others begged him to speak.
It was obvious that Thrasymachus thought he had a fine answer and that
he wanted to earn their admiration by giving it, but he pretended that he
wanted to indulge his love of victory by forcing me to answer. However,
he agreed in the end, and then said: There you have Socrates' wisdom; he   b
himself isn't willing to teach, but he goes around learning from others and
isn't even grateful to them.

When you say that I learn from others you are right, Thrasymachus,
but when you say that I'm not grateful, that isn't true. I show what gratitude
I can, but since I have no money, I can give only praise. But just how
enthusiastically I give it when someone seems to me to speak well, you'll
know as soon as you've answered, for I think that you will speak well.

Listen, then. I say that justice is nothing other than the advantage of the   c
stronger. Well, why don't you praise me? But then you'd do anything to
avoid having to do that.

I must first understand you, for I don't yet know what you mean. The
advantage of the stronger, you say, is just. What do you mean, Thrasymachus? Surely you don't mean something like this: Polydamus, the pancra-
tist,[10] is stronger than we are; it is to his advantage to eat beef to build up
his physical strength; therefore, this food is also advantageous and just
for us who are weaker than he is?   d

You disgust me, Socrates. Your trick is to take hold of the argument at
the point where you can do it the most harm.

Not at all, but tell us more clearly what you mean.

Don't you know that some cities are ruled by a tyranny, some by a
democracy, and some by an aristocracy?

Of course.

And in each city this element is stronger, namely, the ruler?

Certainly.

And each makes laws to its own advantage. Democracy makes democratic laws, tyranny makes tyrannical laws, and so on with the others. And   e
they declare what they have made—what is to their own advantage—to
be just for their subjects, and they punish anyone who goes against this
as lawless and unjust. This, then, is what I say justice is, the same in all
cities, the advantage of the established rule. Since the established rule is   339
surely stronger, anyone who reasons correctly will conclude that the just
is the same everywhere, namely, the advantage of the stronger.

Now I see what you mean. Whether it's true or not, I'll try to find
out. But you yourself have answered that the just is the advantageous,
Thrasymachus, whereas you forbade that answer to me. True, you've
added "of the stronger" to it.

10. The *pancration* was a mixture of boxing and wrestling.

b   And I suppose you think that's an insignificant addition.

It isn't clear yet whether it's significant. But it is clear that we must investigate to see whether or not it's true. I agree that the just is some kind of advantage. But you add that it's *of the stronger*. I don't know about that. We'll have to look into it.

Go ahead and look.

We will. Tell me, don't you also say that it is just to obey the rulers?

I do.

c   And are the rulers in all cities infallible, or are they liable to error?

No doubt they are liable to error.

When they undertake to make laws, therefore, they make some correctly, others incorrectly?

I suppose so.

And a law is correct if it prescribes what is to the rulers' own advantage and incorrect if it prescribes what is to their disadvantage? Is that what you mean?

It is.

And whatever laws they make must be obeyed by their subjects, and this is justice?

Of course.

d   Then, according to your account, it is just to do not only what is to the advantage of the stronger, but also the opposite, what is not to their advantage.

What are you saying?

The same as you. But let's examine it more fully. Haven't we agreed that, in giving orders to their subjects, the rulers are sometimes in error as to what is best for themselves, and yet that it is just for their subjects to do whatever their rulers order? Haven't we agreed to that much?

I think so.

e   Then you must also think that you have agreed that it is just to do what is disadvantageous to the rulers and those who are stronger, whenever they unintentionally order what is bad for themselves. But you also say that it is just for the others to obey the orders they give. You're terribly clever, Thrasymachus, but doesn't it necessarily follow that it is just to do the opposite of what you said, since the weaker are then ordered to do what is disadvantageous to the stronger?

340   By god, Socrates, said Polemarchus, that's quite clear.

If you are to be his witness anyway, said Clitophon, interrupting.

Who needs a witness? Polemarchus replied. Thrasymachus himself agrees that the rulers sometimes order what is bad for themselves and that it is just for the others to do it.

That, Polemarchus, is because Thrasymachus maintained that it is just to obey the orders of the rulers.

He also maintained, Clitophon, that the advantage of the stronger is
b   just. And having maintained both principles he went on to agree that the

stronger sometimes gives orders to those who are weaker than he is—in other words, to his subjects—that are disadvantageous to the stronger himself. From these agreements it follows that what is to the advantage of the stronger is no more just than what is not to his advantage.

But, Clitophon responded, he said that the advantage of the stronger is what the stronger believes to be his advantage. This is what the weaker must do, and this is what he maintained the just to be.

That isn't what he said, Polemarchus replied.

It makes no difference, Polemarchus, I said. If Thrasymachus wants to put it that way now, let's accept it. Tell me, Thrasymachus, is this what you wanted to say the just is, namely, what the stronger believes to be to his advantage, whether it is in fact to his advantage or not? Is that what we are to say you mean?

Not at all. Do you think I'd call someone who is in error stronger at the very moment he errs?

I did think that was what you meant when you agreed that the rulers aren't infallible but are liable to error.

That's because you are a false witness in arguments, Socrates. When someone makes an error in the treatment of patients, do you call him a doctor in regard to that very error? Or when someone makes an error in accounting, do you call him an accountant in regard to that very error in calculation? I think that we express ourselves in words that, taken literally, do say that a doctor is in error, or an accountant, or a grammarian. But each of these, insofar as he is what we call him, never errs, so that, according to the precise account (and you are a stickler for precise accounts), no craftsman ever errs. It's when his knowledge fails him that he makes an error, and in regard to that error he is no craftsman. No craftsman, expert, or ruler makes an error at the moment when he is ruling, even though everyone will say that a physician or a ruler makes errors. It's in this loose way that you must also take the answer I gave earlier. But the most precise answer is this. A ruler, insofar as he is a ruler, never makes errors and unerringly decrees what is best for himself, and this his subject must do. Thus, as I said from the first, it is just to do what is to the advantage of the stronger.

All right, Thrasymachus, so you think I'm a false witness?

You certainly are.

And you think that I asked the questions I did in order to harm you in the argument?

I know it very well, but it won't do you any good. You'll never be able to trick me, so you can't harm me that way, and without trickery you'll never be able to overpower me in argument.

I wouldn't so much as try, Thrasymachus. But in order to prevent this sort of thing from happening again, define clearly whether it is the ruler and stronger in the ordinary sense or in the precise sense whose advantage you said it is just for the weaker to promote as the advantage of the stronger.

I mean the ruler in the most precise sense. Now practice your harm-doing and false witnessing on that if you can—I ask no concessions from you—but you certainly won't be able to.

c   Do you think that I'm crazy enough to try to shave a lion or to bear false witness against Thrasymachus?

You certainly tried just now, though you were a loser at that too.

Enough of this. Tell me: Is a doctor in the precise sense, whom you mentioned before, a money-maker or someone who treats the sick? Tell me about the one who is really a doctor.

He's the one who treats the sick.

What about a ship's captain? Is a captain in the precise sense a ruler of sailors or a sailor?

A ruler of sailors.

We shouldn't, I think, take into account the fact that he sails in a ship,

d   and he shouldn't be called a sailor for that reason, for it isn't because of his sailing that he is called a ship's captain, but because of his craft and his rule over sailors?

That's true.

And is there something advantageous to each of these, that is, to bodies and to sailors?

Certainly.

And aren't the respective crafts by nature set over them to seek and provide what is to their advantage?

They are.

And is there any advantage for each of the crafts themselves except to be as complete or perfect as possible?

e   What are you asking?

This: If you asked me whether our bodies are sufficient in themselves, or whether they need something else, I'd answer: "They certainly have needs. And because of this, because our bodies are deficient rather than self-sufficient, the craft of medicine has now been discovered. The craft of medicine was developed to provide what is advantageous for a body." Do you think that I'm right in saying this or not?

You are right.

342   Now, is medicine deficient? Does a craft need some further virtue, as the eyes are in need of sight, and the ears of hearing, so that another craft is needed to seek and provide what is advantageous to them? Does a craft itself have some similar deficiency, so that each craft needs another, to seek out what is to its advantage? And does the craft that does the seeking need still another, and so on without end? Or does each seek out what is

b   to its own advantage by itself? Or does it need neither itself nor another craft to seek out what is advantageous to it, because of its own deficiencies? Is it that there is no deficiency or error in any craft? That it isn't appropriate for any craft to seek what is to the advantage of anything except that of which it is the craft? And that, since it is itself correct, it is without either fault or impurity, as long as it is wholly and precisely the craft that it is?

Consider this with the preciseness of language you mentioned. Is it so or not?

It appears to be so.

Medicine doesn't seek its own advantage, then, but that of the body? c

Yes.

And horse-breeding doesn't seek its own advantage, but that of horses? Indeed, no other craft seeks its own advantage—for it has no further needs—but the advantage of that of which it is the craft?

Apparently so.

Now, surely, Thrasymachus, the crafts rule over and are stronger than the things of which they are the crafts?

Very reluctantly, he conceded this as well.

No kind of knowledge seeks or orders what is advantageous to itself, then, but what is advantageous to the weaker, which is subject to it. d

He tried to fight this conclusion, but he conceded it in the end. And after he had, I said: Surely, then, no doctor, insofar as he is a doctor, seeks or orders what is advantageous to himself, but what is advantageous to his patient? We agreed that a doctor in the precise sense is a ruler of bodies, not a money-maker. Wasn't that agreed?

Yes.

So a ship's captain in the precise sense is a ruler of sailors, not a sailor?

That's what we agreed. e

Doesn't it follow that a ship's captain or ruler won't seek and order what is advantageous to himself, but what is advantageous to a sailor, his subject?

He reluctantly agreed.

So, then, Thrasymachus, no one in any position of rule, insofar as he is a ruler, seeks or orders what is advantageous to himself, but what is advantageous to his subject, that on which he practices his craft. It is to his subject and what is advantageous and proper to it that he looks, and everything he says and does he says and does for it.

When we reached this point in the argument, and it was clear to all that his account of justice had turned into its opposite, instead of answering, 343 Thrasymachus said: Tell me, Socrates, do you still have a wet nurse?

What's this? Hadn't you better answer *my* questions rather than asking *me* such things?

Because she's letting you run around with a snotty nose, and doesn't wipe it when she needs to! Why, for all she cares, you don't even know about sheep and shepherds.

Just what is it I don't know?

You think that shepherds and cowherds seek the good of their sheep b and cattle, and fatten them and take care of them, looking to something other than their master's good and their own. Moreover, you believe that rulers in cities—true rulers, that is—think about their subjects differently than one does about sheep, and that night and day they think of something besides their own advantage. You are so far from understanding about c justice and what's just, about injustice and what's unjust, that you don't

realize that justice is really the good of another, the advantage of the stronger and the ruler, and harmful to the one who obeys and serves. Injustice is the opposite, it rules the truly simple and just, and those it rules do what is to the advantage of the other and stronger, and they make the one they serve happy, but themselves not at all. You must look at it
d   as follows, my most simple Socrates: A just man always gets less than an unjust one. First, in their contracts with one another, you'll never find, when the partnership ends, that a just partner has got more than an unjust one, but less. Second, in matters relating to the city, when taxes are to be paid, a just man pays more on the same property, an unjust one less, but when the city is giving out refunds, a just man gets nothing, while an
e   unjust one makes a large profit. Finally, when each of them holds a ruling position in some public office, a just person, even if he isn't penalized in other ways, finds that his private affairs deteriorate because he has to neglect them, that he gains no advantage from the public purse because of his justice, and that he's hated by his relatives and acquaintances when he's unwilling to do them an unjust favor. The opposite is true of an unjust man in every respect. Therefore, I repeat what I said before: A person of
344 great power outdoes everyone else. Consider him if you want to figure out how much more advantageous it is for the individual to be just rather than unjust. You'll understand this most easily if you turn your thoughts to the most complete injustice, the one that makes the doer of injustice happiest and the sufferers of it, who are unwilling to do injustice, most wretched. This is tyranny, which through stealth or force appropriates the property of others, whether sacred or profane, public or private, not little by little, but all at once. If someone commits only one part of injustice and
b   is caught, he's punished and greatly reproached—such partly unjust people are called temple-robbers,[11] kidnappers, housebreakers, robbers, and thieves when they commit these crimes. But when someone, in addition to appropriating their possessions, kidnaps and enslaves the citizens as well, instead of these shameful names he is called happy and blessed, not
c   only by the citizens themselves, but by all who learn that he has done the whole of injustice. Those who reproach injustice do so because they are afraid not of doing it but of suffering it. So, Socrates, injustice, if it is on a large enough scale, is stronger, freer, and more masterly than justice. And, as I said from the first, justice is what is advantageous to the stronger, while injustice is to one's own profit and advantage.
d   Having emptied this great flood of words into our ears all at once like a bath attendant, Thrasymachus intended to leave. But those present didn't let him and made him stay to give an account of what he had said. I too begged him to stay, and I said to him: After hurling such a speech at us, Thrasymachus, do you intend to leave before adequately instructing us
e   or finding out whether you are right or not? Or do you think it a small

___

11. The temples acted as public treasuries, so that a temple robber is much like a present-day bank robber.

matter to determine which whole way of life would make living most worthwhile for each of us?

Is *that* what I seem to you to think? Thrasymachus said.

Either that, or else you care nothing for us and aren't worried about whether we'll live better or worse lives because of our ignorance of what you say you know. So show some willingness to teach it to us. It wouldn't be a bad investment for you to be the benefactor of a group as large as ours. For my own part, I'll tell you that I am not persuaded. I don't believe   345 that injustice is more profitable than justice, not even if you give it full scope and put no obstacles in its way. Suppose that there *is* an unjust person, and suppose he *does* have the power to do injustice, whether by trickery or open warfare; nonetheless, he doesn't persuade me that injustice is more profitable than justice. Perhaps someone here, besides myself, feels   b the same as I do. So come now, and persuade us that we are wrong to esteem justice more highly than injustice in planning our lives.

And how am I to persuade you, if you aren't persuaded by what I said just now? What more can I do? Am I to take my argument and pour it into your very soul?

God forbid! Don't do that! But, first, stick to what you've said, and then, if you change your position, do it openly and don't deceive us. You see, Thrasymachus, that having defined the true doctor—to continue examining the things you said before—you didn't consider it necessary later to keep   c a precise guard on the true shepherd. You think that, insofar as he's a shepherd, he fattens sheep, not looking to what is best for the sheep but to a banquet, like a guest about to be entertained at a feast, or to a future sale, like a money-maker rather than a shepherd. Shepherding is concerned only to provide what is best for that which it is set over, and it is itself   d adequately provided with all it needs to be at its best when it doesn't fall short in any way of being the craft of shepherding. That's why I thought it necessary for us to agree before[12] that every kind of rule, insofar as it rules, doesn't seek anything other than what is best for the thing it rules and cares for, and this is true both of public and private kinds of rule. But do you think that those who rule cities, the true rulers, rule willingly?   e

I don't think it, by god, I know it.

But, Thrasymachus, don't you realize that in other kinds of rule no one wants to rule for its own sake, but they ask for pay, thinking that their ruling will benefit not themselves but their subjects? Tell me, doesn't every craft differ from every other in having a different function? Please don't   346 answer contrary to what you believe, so that we can come to some definite conclusion.

Yes, that's what differentiates them.

And each craft benefits us in its own peculiar way, different from the others. For example, medicine gives us health, navigation gives us safety while sailing, and so on with the others?

---

12. See 341e–342e.

Certainly.

And wage-earning gives us wages, for this is its function? Or would
b you call medicine the same as navigation? Indeed, if you want to define
matters precisely, as you proposed, even if someone who is a ship's captain
becomes healthy because sailing is advantageous to his health, you
wouldn't for that reason call his craft medicine?

Certainly not.

Nor would you call wage-earning medicine, even if someone becomes
healthy while earning wages?

Certainly not.

Nor would you call medicine wage-earning, even if someone earns pay
while healing?
c No.

We are agreed, then, that each craft brings its own peculiar benefit?

It does.

Then whatever benefit all craftsmen receive in common must clearly
result from their joint practice of some additional craft that benefits each
of them?

So it seems.

And we say that the additional craft in question, which benefits the
craftsmen by earning them wages, is the craft of wage-earning?

He reluctantly agreed.

Then this benefit, receiving wages, doesn't result from their own craft,
d but rather, if we're to examine this precisely, medicine provides health,
and wage-earning provides wages; house-building provides a house, and
wage-earning, which accompanies it, provides a wage; and so on with the
other crafts. Each of them does its own work and benefits the thing it is
set over. So, if wages aren't added, is there any benefit that the craftsman
gets from his craft?

Apparently none.
e But he still provides a benefit when he works for nothing?

Yes, I think he does.

Then, it is clear now, Thrasymachus, that no craft or rule provides for
its own advantage, but, as we've been saying for some time, it provides
and orders for its subject and aims at its advantage, that of the weaker,
not of the stronger. That's why I said just now, Thrasymachus, that no
one willingly chooses to rule and to take other people's troubles in hand
347 and straighten them out, but each asks for wages; for anyone who intends
to practice his craft well never does or orders what is best for himself—
at least not when he orders as his craft prescribes—but what is best for
his subject. It is because of this, it seems, that wages must be provided to
a person if he's to be willing to rule, whether in the form of money or
honor or a penalty if he refuses.

What do you mean, Socrates? said Glaucon. I know the first two kinds
of wages, but I don't understand what penalty you mean or how you can
call it a wage.

Then you don't understand the best people's kind of wages, the kind that moves the most decent to rule, when they are willing to rule at all. Don't you know that the love of honor and the love of money are despised, and rightly so?

I do.

Therefore good people won't be willing to rule for the sake of either money or honor. They don't want to be paid wages openly for ruling and get called hired hands, nor to take them in secret from their rule and be called thieves. And they won't rule for the sake of honor, because they aren't ambitious honor-lovers. So, if they're to be willing to rule, some compulsion or punishment must be brought to bear on them—perhaps that's why it is thought shameful to seek to rule before one is compelled to. Now, the greatest punishment, if one isn't willing to rule, is to be ruled by someone worse than oneself. And I think that it's fear of this that makes decent people rule when they do. They approach ruling not as something good or something to be enjoyed, but as something necessary, since it can't be entrusted to anyone better than—or even as good as—themselves. In a city of good men, if it came into being, the citizens would fight in order *not to rule*, just as they do now in order to rule. There it would be quite clear that anyone who is really a true ruler doesn't by nature seek his own advantage but that of his subject. And everyone, knowing this, would rather be benefited by others than take the trouble to benefit them. So I can't at all agree with Thrasymachus that justice is the advantage of the stronger—but we'll look further into that another time. What Thrasymachus is now saying—that the life of an unjust person is better than that of a just one—seems to be of far greater importance. Which life would you choose, Glaucon? And which of our views do you consider truer?

I certainly think that the life of a just person is more profitable.

Did you hear all of the good things Thrasymachus listed a moment ago for the unjust life?

I heard, but I wasn't persuaded.

Then, do you want us to persuade him, if we're able to find a way, that what he says isn't true?

Of course I do.

If we oppose him with a parallel speech about the blessings of the just life, and then he replies, and then we do, we'd have to count and measure the good things mentioned on each side, and we'd need a jury to decide the case. But if, on the other hand, we investigate the question, as we've been doing, by seeking agreement with each other, we ourselves can be both jury and advocates at once.

Certainly.

Which approach do you prefer? I asked.

The second.

Come, then, Thrasymachus, I said, answer us from the beginning. You say that complete injustice is more profitable than complete justice?

I certainly do say that, and I've told you why.

Well, then, what do you say about this? Do you call one of the two a virtue and the other a vice?

Of course.

That is to say, you call justice a virtue and injustice a vice?

That's hardly likely, since I say that injustice is profitable and justice isn't.

Then, what exactly do you say?

The opposite.

That justice is a vice?

No, just very high-minded simplicity.

d   Then do you call being unjust being low-minded?

No, I call it good judgment.

You consider unjust people, then, Thrasymachus, to be clever and good?

Yes, those who are completely unjust, who can bring cities and whole communities under their power. Perhaps, you think I meant pickpockets? Not that such crimes aren't also profitable, if they're not found out, but they aren't worth mentioning by comparison to what I'm talking about.

e   I'm not unaware of what you want to say. But I wonder about this: Do you really include injustice with virtue and wisdom, and justice with their opposites?

I certainly do.

That's harder, and it isn't easy now to know what to say. If you had declared that injustice is more profitable, but agreed that it is a vice or shameful, as some others do, we could have discussed the matter on the basis of conventional beliefs. But now, obviously, you'll say that injustice is fine and strong and apply to it all the attributes we used to apply to

349   justice, since you dare to include it with virtue and wisdom.

You've divined my views exactly.

Nonetheless, we mustn't shrink from pursuing the argument and looking into this, just as long as I take you to be saying what you really think. And I believe that you aren't joking now, Thrasymachus, but are saying what you believe to be the truth.

What difference does it make to you, whether *I* believe it or not? It's *my account* you're supposed to be refuting.

It makes no difference. But try to answer this further question: Do you

b   think that a just person wants to outdo someone else who's just?

Not at all, for he wouldn't then be as polite and innocent as he is.

Or to outdo someone who does a just action?

No, he doesn't even want to do that.

And does he claim that he deserves to outdo an unjust person and believe that it is just for him to do so, or doesn't he believe that?

He'd want to outdo him, and he'd claim to deserve to do so, but he wouldn't be able.

That's not what I asked, but whether a just person wants to outdo an

c   unjust person but not a just one, thinking that this is what he deserves?

He does.

What about an unjust person? Does he claim that he deserves to outdo a just person or someone who does a just action?

Of course he does; he thinks he deserves to outdo everyone.

Then will an unjust person also outdo an *unjust* person or someone who does an *unjust* action, and will he strive to get the most he can for himself from everyone?

He will.

Then, let's put it this way: A just person doesn't outdo someone like himself but someone unlike himself, whereas an unjust person outdoes both like and unlike.   d

Very well put.

An unjust person is clever and good, and a just one is neither?

That's well put, too.

It follows, then, that an unjust person is like clever and good people, while the other isn't?

Of course that's so. How could he fail to be like them when he has their qualities, while the other isn't like them?

Fine. Then each of them has the qualities of the people he's like?

Of course.

All right, Thrasymachus. Do you call one person musical and another   e
nonmusical?

I do.

Which of them is clever in music, and which isn't?

The musical one is clever, of course, and the other isn't.

And the things he's clever in, he's good in, and the things he isn't clever in, he's bad in?

Yes.

Isn't the same true of a doctor?

It is.

Do you think that a musician, in tuning his lyre and in tightening and loosening the strings, wants to outdo another musician, claiming that this is what he deserves?

I do not.

But he does want to outdo a nonmusician?

Necessarily.

What about a doctor? Does he, when prescribing food and drink, want to outdo another doctor or someone who does the action that medicine pre-   350
scribes?

Certainly not.

But he does want to outdo a nondoctor?

Yes.

In any branch of knowledge or ignorance, do you think that a knowledge-able person would intentionally try to outdo other knowledgeable people or say something better or different than they do, rather than doing or saying the very same thing as those like him?

994

Thrasymachus/Socrates

Well, perhaps it must be as you say.

And what about an ignorant person? Doesn't he want to outdo both a
b knowledgeable person and an ignorant one?

Probably.

A knowledgeable person is clever?

I agree.

And a clever one is good?

I agree.

Therefore, a good and clever person doesn't want to outdo those like
himself but those who are unlike him and his opposite.

So it seems.

But a bad and ignorant person wants to outdo both his like and his opposite.

Apparently.

Now, Thrasymachus, we found that an unjust person tries to outdo
those like him and those unlike him? Didn't you say that?

I did.

c And that a just person won't outdo his like but his unlike?

Yes.

Then, a just person is like a clever and good one, and an unjust is like
an ignorant and bad one.

It looks that way.

Moreover, we agreed that each has the qualities of the one he resembles.

Yes, we did.

Then, a just person has turned out to be good and clever, and an unjust
one ignorant and bad.

Thrasymachus agreed to all this, not easily as I'm telling it, but reluc-
d tantly, with toil, trouble, and—since it was summer—a quantity of sweat
that was a wonder to behold. And then I saw something I'd never seen
before—Thrasymachus blushing. But, in any case, after we'd agreed that
justice is virtue and wisdom and that injustice is vice and ignorance, I
said: All right, let's take that as established. But we also said that injustice
is powerful, or don't you remember that, Thrasymachus?

I remember, but I'm not satisfied with what you're now saying. I could
make a speech about it, but, if I did, I know that you'd accuse me of
e engaging in oratory. So either allow me to speak, or, if you want to ask
questions, go ahead, and I'll say, "All right," and nod yes and no, as one
does to old wives' tales.

Don't do that, contrary to your own opinion.

I'll answer so as to please you, since you won't let me make a speech.
What else do you want?

Nothing, by god. But if that's what you're going to do, go ahead and
do it. I'll ask my questions.

Ask ahead.

351 I'll ask what I asked before, so that we may proceed with our argument
about justice and injustice in an orderly fashion, for surely it was claimed

that injustice is stronger and more powerful than justice. But, now, if justice is indeed wisdom and virtue, it will easily be shown to be stronger than injustice, since injustice is ignorance (no one could now be ignorant of that). However, I don't want to state the matter so unconditionally, Thrasymachus, but to look into it in some such way as this. Would you say that it is unjust for a city to try to enslave other cities unjustly and to hold them in subjection when it has enslaved many of them?

Of course, that's what the best city will especially do, the one that is most completely unjust.

I understand that's your position, but the point I want to examine is this: Will the city that becomes stronger than another achieve this power without justice, or will it need the help of justice?

If what you said a moment ago stands, and justice is cleverness or wisdom, it will need the help of justice, but if things are as I stated, it will need the help of injustice.

I'm impressed, Thrasymachus, that you don't merely nod yes or no but give very fine answers.

That's because I'm trying to please you.

You're doing well at it, too. So please me some more by answering this question: Do you think that a city, an army, a band of robbers or thieves, or any other tribe with a common unjust purpose would be able to achieve it if they were unjust to each other?

No, indeed.

What if they weren't unjust to one another? Would they achieve more?

Certainly.

Injustice, Thrasymachus, causes civil war, hatred, and fighting among themselves, while justice brings friendship and a sense of common purpose. Isn't that so?

Let it be so, in order not to disagree with you.

You're still doing well on that front. So tell me this: If the effect of injustice is to produce hatred wherever it occurs, then, whenever it arises, whether among free men or slaves, won't it cause them to hate one another, engage in civil war, and prevent them from achieving any common purpose?

Certainly.

What if it arises between two people? Won't they be at odds, hate each other, and be enemies to one another and to just people?

They will.

Does injustice lose its power to cause dissension when it arises within a single individual, or will it preserve it intact?

Let it preserve it intact.

Apparently, then, injustice has the power, first, to make whatever it arises in—whether it is a city, a family, an army, or anything else—incapable of achieving anything as a unit, because of the civil wars and differences it creates, and, second, it makes that unit an enemy to itself and to what is in every way its opposite, namely, justice. Isn't that so?

Certainly.

And even in a single individual, it has by its nature the very same effect. First, it makes him incapable of achieving anything, because he is in a state of civil war and not of one mind; second, it makes him his own enemy, as well as the enemy of just people. Hasn't it that effect?

Yes.

And the gods too are just?

Let it be so.

b   So an unjust person is also an enemy of the gods, Thrasymachus, while a just person is their friend?

Enjoy your banquet of words! Have no fear, I won't oppose you. That would make these people hate me.

Come, then, complete the banquet for me by continuing to answer as you've been doing. We have shown that just people are cleverer and more capable of doing things, while unjust ones aren't even able to act together, c   for when we speak of a powerful achievement by unjust men acting together, what we say isn't altogether true. They would never have been able to keep their hands off each other if they were completely unjust. But clearly there must have been some sort of justice in them that at least prevented them from doing injustice among themselves at the same time as they were doing it to others. And it was this that enabled them to achieve what they did. When they started doing unjust things, they were only halfway corrupted by their injustice (for those who are all bad and completely unjust are completely incapable of accomplishing anything). These are the things I understand to hold, not the ones you first maintained. d   We must now examine, as we proposed before,[13] whether just people also live better and are happier than unjust ones. I think it's clear already that this is so, but we must look into it further, since the argument concerns no ordinary topic but the way we ought to live.

Go ahead and look.

I will. Tell me, do you think there is such a thing as the function of a horse? e   I do.

And would you define the function of a horse or of anything else as that which one can do only with it or best with it?

I don't understand.

Let me put it this way: Is it possible to see with anything other than eyes?

Certainly not.

Or to hear with anything other than ears?

No.

Then, we are right to say that seeing and hearing are the functions of eyes and ears?

Of course.

What about this? Could you use a dagger or a carving knife or lots of 353   other things in pruning a vine?

13. See 347e.

Of course.

But wouldn't you do a finer job with a pruning knife designed for the purpose than with anything else?

You would.

Then shall we take pruning to be its function?

Yes.

Now, I think you'll understand what I was asking earlier when I asked whether the function of each thing is what it alone can do or what it does better than anything else.

I understand, and I think that this is the function of each.   b

All right. Does each thing to which a particular function is assigned also have a virtue? Let's go over the same ground again. We say that eyes have some function?

They do.

So there is also a virtue of eyes?

There is.

And ears have a function?

Yes.

So there is also a virtue of ears?

There is.

And all other things are the same, aren't they?

They are.

And could eyes perform their function well if they lacked their peculiar   c
virtue and had the vice instead?

How could they, for don't you mean if they had blindness instead of sight?

Whatever their virtue is, for I'm not now asking about that but about whether anything that has a function performs it well by means of its own peculiar virtue and badly by means of its vice?

That's true, it does.

So ears, too, deprived of their own virtue, perform their function badly?

That's right.

And the same could be said about everything else?   d

So it seems.

Come, then, and let's consider this: Is there some function of a soul that you couldn't perform with anything else, for example, taking care of things, ruling, deliberating, and the like? Is there anything other than a soul to which you could rightly assign these, and say that they are its peculiar function?

No, none of them.

What of living? Isn't that a function of a soul?

It certainly is.

And don't we also say that there is a virtue of a soul?

We do.

Then, will a soul ever perform its function well, Thrasymachus, if it is   e
deprived of its own peculiar virtue, or is that impossible?

It's impossible.

Doesn't it follow, then, that a bad soul rules and takes care of things badly and that a good soul does all these things well?

It does.

Now, we agreed that justice is a soul's virtue, and injustice its vice?

We did.

Then, it follows that a just soul and a just man will live well, and an unjust one badly.

Apparently so, according to your argument.

And surely anyone who lives well is blessed and happy, and anyone

354   who doesn't is the opposite.

Of course.

Therefore, a just person is happy, and an unjust one wretched.

So be it.

It profits no one to be wretched but to be happy.

Of course.

And so, Thrasymachus, injustice is never more profitable than justice.

Let that be your banquet, Socrates, at the feast of Bendis.

Given by you, Thrasymachus, after you became gentle and ceased to give me rough treatment. Yet I haven't had a fine banquet. But that's my

b   fault not yours. I seem to have behaved like a glutton, snatching at every dish that passes and tasting it before properly savoring its predecessor. Before finding the answer to our first inquiry about what justice is, I let that go and turned to investigate whether it is a kind of vice and ignorance or a kind of wisdom and virtue. Then an argument came up about injustice being more profitable than justice, and I couldn't refrain from abandoning the previous one and following up on that. Hence the result of the discus-

c   sion, as far as I'm concerned, is that I know nothing, for when I don't know what justice is, I'll hardly know whether it is a kind of virtue or not, or whether a person who has it is happy or unhappy.

Book II

357   When I said this, I thought I had done with the discussion, but it turned out to have been only a prelude. Glaucon showed his characteristic courage on this occasion too and refused to accept Thrasymachus' abandonment of the argument. Socrates, he said, do you want to seem to have persuaded us that it is better in every way to be just than unjust, or do you want

b   truly to convince us of this?

I want truly to convince you, I said, if I can.

Well, then, you certainly aren't doing what you want. Tell me, do you think there is a kind of good we welcome, not because we desire what comes from it, but because we welcome it for its own sake—joy, for example, and all the harmless pleasures that have no results beyond the joy of having them?

Certainly, I think there are such things.

And is there a kind of good we like for its own sake and also for the sake of what comes from it—knowing, for example, and seeing and being healthy? We welcome such things, I suppose, on both counts.

Yes.

And do you also see a third kind of good, such as physical training, medical treatment when sick, medicine itself, and the other ways of making money? We'd say that these are onerous but beneficial to us, and we wouldn't choose them for their own sakes, but for the sake of the rewards and other things that come from them.

There is also this third kind. But what of it?

Where do you put justice?

I myself put it among the finest goods, as something to be valued by anyone who is going to be blessed with happiness, both because of itself and because of what comes from it.

That isn't most people's opinion. They'd say that justice belongs to the onerous kind, and is to be practiced for the sake of the rewards and popularity that come from a reputation for justice, but is to be avoided because of itself as something burdensome.

I know that's the general opinion. Thrasymachus faulted justice on these grounds a moment ago and praised injustice, but it seems that I'm a slow learner.

Come, then, and listen to me as well, and see whether you still have that problem, for I think that Thrasymachus gave up before he had to, charmed by you as if he were a snake. But I'm not yet satisfied by the argument on either side. I want to know what justice and injustice are and what power each itself has when it's by itself in the soul. I want to leave out of account their rewards and what comes from each of them. So, if you agree, I'll renew the argument of Thrasymachus. First, I'll state what kind of thing people consider justice to be and what its origins are. Second, I'll argue that all who practice it do so unwillingly, as something necessary, not as something good. Third, I'll argue that they have good reason to act as they do, for the life of an unjust person is, they say, much better than that of a just one.

It isn't, Socrates, that I believe any of that myself. I'm perplexed, indeed, and my ears are deafened listening to Thrasymachus and countless others. But I've yet to hear anyone defend justice in the way I want, proving that it is better than injustice. I want to hear it praised *by itself*, and I think that I'm most likely to hear this from you. Therefore, I'm going to speak at length in praise of the unjust life, and in doing so I'll show you the way I want to hear you praising justice and denouncing injustice. But see whether you want me to do that or not.

I want that most of all. Indeed, what subject could someone with any understanding enjoy discussing more often?

Excellent. Then let's discuss the first subject I mentioned—what justice is and what its origins are.

They say that to do injustice is naturally good and to suffer injustice bad, but that the badness of suffering it so far exceeds the goodness of doing it that those who have done and suffered injustice and tasted both, but who lack the power to do it and avoid suffering it, decide that it is 359   profitable to come to an agreement with each other neither to do injustice nor to suffer it. As a result, they begin to make laws and covenants, and what the law commands they call lawful and just. This, they say, is the origin and essence of justice. It is intermediate between the best and the worst. The best is to do injustice without paying the penalty; the worst is to suffer it without being able to take revenge. Justice is a mean between these two extremes. People value it not as a good but because they are b   too weak to do injustice with impunity. Someone who has the power to do this, however, and is a true man wouldn't make an agreement with anyone not to do injustice in order not to suffer it. For him that would be madness. This is the nature of justice, according to the argument, Socrates, and these are its natural origins.

We can see most clearly that those who practice justice do it unwillingly c   and because they lack the power to do injustice, if in our thoughts we grant to a just and an unjust person the freedom to do whatever they like. We can then follow both of them and see where their desires would lead. And we'll catch the just person red-handed travelling the same road as the unjust. The reason for this is the desire to outdo others and get more and more. This is what anyone's nature naturally pursues as good, but nature is forced by law into the perversion of treating fairness with respect.

The freedom I mentioned would be most easily realized if both people had the power they say the ancestor of Gyges of Lydia possessed. The d   story goes that he was a shepherd in the service of the ruler of Lydia. There was a violent thunderstorm, and an earthquake broke open the ground and created a chasm at the place where he was tending his sheep. Seeing this, he was filled with amazement and went down into it. And there, in addition to many other wonders of which we're told, he saw a hollow bronze horse. There were windowlike openings in it, and, peeping in, he saw a corpse, which seemed to be of more than human size, wearing e   nothing but a gold ring on its finger. He took the ring and came out of the chasm. He wore the ring at the usual monthly meeting that reported to the king on the state of the flocks. And as he was sitting among the others, he happened to turn the setting of the ring towards himself to the inside of his hand. When he did this, he became invisible to those sitting 360   near him, and they went on talking as if he had gone. He wondered at this, and, fingering the ring, he turned the setting outwards again and became visible. So he experimented with the ring to test whether it indeed had this power—and it did. If he turned the setting inward, he became invisible; if he turned it outward, he became visible again. When he realized this, he at once arranged to become one of the messengers sent to report to the king. And when he arrived there, he seduced the king's wife, attacked b   the king with her help, killed him, and took over the kingdom.

Let's suppose, then, that there were two such rings, one worn by a just and the other by an unjust person. Now, no one, it seems, would be so incorruptible that he would stay on the path of justice or stay away from other people's property, when he could take whatever he wanted from the marketplace with impunity, go into people's houses and have sex with anyone he wished, kill or release from prison anyone he wished, and do all the other things that would make him like a god among humans. Rather his actions would be in no way different from those of an unjust person, and both would follow the same path. This, some would say, is a great proof that one is never just willingly but only when compelled to be. No one believes justice to be a good when it is kept private, since, wherever either person thinks he can do injustice with impunity, he does it. Indeed, every man believes that injustice is far more profitable to himself than justice. And any exponent of this argument will say he's right, for someone who didn't want to do injustice, given this sort of opportunity, and who didn't touch other people's property would be thought wretched and stupid by everyone aware of the situation, though, of course, they'd praise him in public, deceiving each other for fear of suffering injustice. So much for my second topic.

As for the choice between the lives we're discussing, we'll be able to make a correct judgment about that only if we separate the most just and the most unjust. Otherwise we won't be able to do it. Here's the separation I have in mind. We'll subtract nothing from the injustice of an unjust person and nothing from the justice of a just one, but we'll take each to be complete in his own way of life. First, therefore, we must suppose that an unjust person will act as clever craftsmen do: A first-rate captain or doctor, for example, knows the difference between what his craft can and can't do. He attempts the first but lets the second go by, and if he happens to slip, he can put things right. In the same way, an unjust person's successful attempts at injustice must remain undetected, if he is to be fully unjust. Anyone who is caught should be thought inept, for the extreme of injustice is to be believed to be just without being just. And our completely unjust person must be given complete injustice; nothing may be subtracted from it. We must allow that, while doing the greatest injustice, he has nonetheless provided himself with the greatest reputation for justice. If he happens to make a slip, he must be able to put it right. If any of his unjust activities should be discovered, he must be able to speak persuasively or to use force. And if force is needed, he must have the help of courage and strength and of the substantial wealth and friends with which he has provided himself.

Having hypothesized such a person, let's now in our argument put beside him a just man, who is simple and noble and who, as Aeschylus says, doesn't want to be believed to be good but to be so.[1] We must take

---

1. In *Seven Against Thebes*, 592–94, it is said of Amphiaraus that "he did not wish to be believed to be the best but to be it." The passage continues with the words Glaucon quotes below at 362a–b.

c

d

e

361

b

c   away his reputation, for a reputation for justice would bring him honor
and rewards, so that it wouldn't be clear whether he is just for the sake
of justice itself or for the sake of those honors and rewards. We must strip
him of everything except justice and make his situation the opposite of
an unjust person's. Though he does no injustice, he must have the greatest
reputation for it, so that he can be tested as regards justice unsoftened by
his bad reputation and its effects. Let him stay like that unchanged until
d   he dies—just, but all his life believed to be unjust. In this way, both will
reach the extremes, the one of justice and the other of injustice, and we'll
be able to judge which of them is happier.

Whew! Glaucon, I said, how vigorously you've scoured each of the men
for our competition, just as you would a pair of statues for an art competition.

I do the best I can, he replied. Since the two are as I've described, in
any case, it shouldn't be difficult to complete the account of the kind of
life that awaits each of them, but it must be done. And if what I say sounds
e   crude, Socrates, remember that it isn't I who speak but those who praise
injustice at the expense of justice. They'll say that a just person in such
circumstances will be whipped, stretched on a rack, chained, blinded with
fire, and, at the end, when he has suffered every kind of evil, he'll be
impaled, and will realize then that one shouldn't want to be just but to
362 be believed to be just. Indeed, Aeschylus' words are far more correctly
applied to unjust people than to just ones, for the supporters of injustice
will say that a really unjust person, having a way of life based on the truth
about things and not living in accordance with opinion, doesn't want
simply to be believed to be unjust but actually to be so—

> *Harvesting a deep furrow in his mind,*
b   *Where wise counsels propagate.*

He rules his city because of his reputation for justice; he marries into any
family he wishes; he gives his children in marriage to anyone he wishes;
he has contracts and partnerships with anyone he wants; and besides
benefiting himself in all these ways, he profits because he has no scruples
about doing injustice. In any contest, public or private, he's the winner
and outdoes his enemies. And by outdoing them, he becomes wealthy,
benefiting his friends and harming his enemies. He makes adequate sacri-
c   fices to the gods and sets up magnificent offerings to them. He takes better
care of the gods, therefore, (and, indeed, of the human beings he's fond
of) than a just person does. Hence it's likely that the gods, in turn, will
take better care of him than of a just person. That's what they say, Socrates,
that gods and humans provide a better life for unjust people than for
just ones.

d   When Glaucon had said this, I had it in mind to respond, but his brother
Adeimantus intervened: You surely don't think that the position has been
adequately stated?

Why not? I said.

The most important thing to say hasn't been said yet.

Well, then, I replied, a man's brother must stand by him, as the saying goes.[2] If Glaucon has omitted something, you must help him. Yet what he has said is enough to throw me to the canvas and make me unable to come to the aid of justice.

Nonsense, he said. Hear what more I have to say, for we should also fully explore the arguments that are opposed to the ones Glaucon gave, the ones that praise justice and find fault with injustice, so that what I take to be his intention may be clearer.

e

When fathers speak to their sons, they say that one must be just, as do all the others who have charge of anyone. But they don't praise justice itself, only the high reputations it leads to and the consequences of being thought to be just, such as the public offices, marriages, and other things Glaucon listed. But they elaborate even further on the consequences of reputation. By bringing in the esteem of the gods, they are able to talk about the abundant good things that they themselves and the noble Hesiod and Homer say that the gods give to the pious, for Hesiod says that the gods make the oak trees

363

b

> *Bear acorns at the top and bees in the middle*
> *And make fleecy sheep heavy laden with wool*

for the just, and tells of many other good things akin to these. And Homer is similar:

> *When a good king, in his piety,*
> *Upholds justice, the black earth bears*
> *Wheat and barley for him, and his trees are heavy with fruit.*
> *His sheep bear lambs unfailingly, and the sea yields up its fish.*[3]

c

Musaeus and his son make the gods give the just more headstrong goods than these.[4] In their stories, they lead the just to Hades, seat them on couches, provide them with a symposium of pious people, crown them with wreaths, and make them spend all their time drinking—as if they thought drunkenness was the finest wage of virtue. Others stretch even further the wages that virtue receives from the gods, for they say that someone who is pious and keeps his promises leaves his children's children and a whole race behind him. In these and other similar ways, they praise

d

2. See *Odyssey* xvi.97–98.

3. The two last quotations are from *Works and Days* 232 ff. and *Odyssey* xix.109–13, omitting 110, respectively.

4. Musaeus was a legendary poet closely associated with the mystery religion of Orphism.

justice. They bury the impious and unjust in mud in Hades; force them to carry water in a sieve; bring them into bad repute while they're still alive, and all those penalties that Glaucon gave to the just person they

e   give to the unjust. But they have nothing else to say. This, then, is the way people praise justice and find fault with injustice.

Besides this, Socrates, consider another form of argument about justice and injustice employed both by private individuals and by poets. All go on repeating with one voice that justice and moderation are fine things,

364   but hard and onerous, while licentiousness and injustice are sweet and easy to acquire and are shameful only in opinion and law. They add that unjust deeds are for the most part more profitable than just ones, and, whether in public or private, they willingly honor vicious people who have wealth and other types of power and declare them to be happy. But they dishonor and disregard the weak and the poor, even though they

b   agree that they are better than the others.

But the most wonderful of all these arguments concerns what they have to say about the gods and virtue. They say that the gods, too, assign misfortune and a bad life to many good people, and the opposite fate to their opposites. Begging priests and prophets frequent the doors of the rich and persuade them that they possess a god-given power founded on

c   sacrifices and incantations. If the rich person or any of his ancestors has committed an injustice, they can fix it with pleasant rituals. Moreover, if he wishes to injure some enemy, then, at little expense, he'll be able to harm just and unjust alike, for by means of spells and enchantments they can persuade the gods to serve them. And the poets are brought forward as witnesses to all these accounts. Some harp on the ease of vice, as follows:

> *Vice in abundance is easy to get;*
d   > *The road is smooth and begins beside you,*
> *But the gods have put sweat between us and virtue,*

and a road that is long, rough, and steep.[5] Others quote Homer to bear witness that the gods can be influenced by humans, since he said:

> *The gods themselves can be swayed by prayer,*
> *And with sacrifices and soothing promises,*
e   > *Incense and libations, human beings turn them from their purpose*
> *When someone has transgressed and sinned.*[6]

And they present a noisy throng of books by Musaeus and Orpheus, offspring as they say of Selene and the Muses, in accordance with which

---

5. *Works and Days* 287–89, with minor alterations.
6. *Iliad* ix.497–501, with minor alterations.

they perform their rituals.[7] And they persuade not only individuals but whole cities that the unjust deeds of the living or the dead can be absolved or purified through ritual sacrifices and pleasant games. These initiations, as they call them, free people from punishment hereafter, while a terrible fate awaits those who have not performed the rituals.

When all such sayings about the attitudes of gods and humans to virtue and vice are so often repeated, Socrates, what effect do you suppose they have on the souls of young people? I mean those who are clever and are able to flit from one of these sayings to another, so to speak, and gather from them an impression of what sort of person he should be and of how best to travel the road of life. He would surely ask himself Pindar's question, "Should I by justice or by crooked deceit scale this high wall and live my life guarded and secure?" And he'll answer: "The various sayings suggest that there is no advantage in my being just if I'm not also thought just, while the troubles and penalties of being just are apparent. But they tell me that an unjust person, who has secured for himself a reputation for justice, lives the life of a god. Since, then, 'opinion forcibly overcomes truth' and 'controls happiness,' as the wise men say, I must surely turn entirely to it.[8] I should create a façade of illusory virtue around me to deceive those who come near, but keep behind it the greedy and crafty fox of the wise Archilochus."[9]

"But surely," someone will object, "it isn't easy for vice to remain always hidden." We'll reply that nothing great is easy. And, in any case, if we're to be happy, we must follow the path indicated in these accounts. To remain undiscovered we'll form secret societies and political clubs. And there are teachers of persuasion to make us clever in dealing with assemblies and law courts. Therefore, using persuasion in one place and force in another, we'll outdo others without paying a penalty.

"What about the gods? Surely, we can't hide from them or use violent force against them!" Well, if the gods don't exist or don't concern themselves with human affairs, why should we worry at all about hiding from them? If they do exist and do concern themselves with us, we've learned all we know about them from the laws and the poets who give their genealogies—nowhere else. But these are the very people who tell us that the gods can be persuaded and influenced by sacrifices, gentle prayers, and offerings. Hence, we should believe them on both matters or neither. If we believe them, we should be unjust and offer sacrifices from the fruits of our injustice. If we are just, our only gain is not to be punished by the gods, since we lose the profits of injustice. But if we are unjust, we get the

365

b

c

d

e

366

---

7. It is not clear whether Orpheus was a real person or a mythical figure. His fame in Greek myth rests on the poems in which the doctrines of the Orphic religion are set forth.

8. The quotation is attributed to Simonides, whom Polemarchus cites in Book I.

9. Archilochus of Paros (c. 756–716 B.C.) was an iambic and elegiac poet who composed a famous fable about the fox and the hedgehog.

profits of our crimes and transgressions and afterwards persuade the gods by prayer and escape without punishment.

"But in Hades won't we pay the penalty for crimes committed here, either ourselves or our children's children?" "My friend," the young man will say as he does his calculation, "mystery rites and the gods of absolution have great power. The greatest cities tell us this, as do those children of
b   the gods who have become poets and prophets."

Why, then, should we still choose justice over the greatest injustice? Many eminent authorities agree that, if we practice such injustice with a false façade, we'll do well at the hands of gods and humans, living and dying as we've a mind to. So, given all that has been said, Socrates, how
c   is it possible for anyone of any power—whether of mind, wealth, body, or birth—to be willing to honor justice and not laugh aloud when he hears it praised? Indeed, if anyone can show that what we've said is false and has adequate knowledge that justice is best, he'll surely be full not of anger but of forgiveness for the unjust. He knows that, apart from someone of godlike character who is disgusted by injustice or one who has gained
d   knowledge and avoids injustice for that reason, no one is just willingly. Through cowardice or old age or some other weakness, people do indeed object to injustice. But it's obvious that they do so only because they lack the power to do injustice, for the first of them to acquire it is the first to do as much injustice as he can.

And all of this has no other cause than the one that led Glaucon and me to say to you: "Socrates, of all of you who claim to praise justice, from the original heroes of old whose words survive, to the men of the present
e   day, not one has ever blamed injustice or praised justice except by mentioning the reputations, honors, and rewards that are their consequences. No one has ever adequately described what each itself does of its own power by its presence in the soul of the person who possesses it, even if it remains hidden from gods and humans. No one, whether in poetry or in private conversations, has adequately argued that injustice is the worst thing a soul can have in it and that justice is the greatest good. If you had treated
367 the subject in this way and persuaded us from youth, we wouldn't now be guarding against one another's injustices, but each would be his own best guardian, afraid that by doing injustice he'd be living with the worst thing possible."

Thrasymachus or anyone else might say what we've said, Socrates, or maybe even more, in discussing justice and injustice—crudely inverting their powers, in my opinion. And, frankly, it's because I want to hear the
b   opposite from you that I speak with all the force I can muster. So don't merely give us a theoretical argument that justice is stronger than injustice, but tell us what each itself does, because of its own powers, to someone who possesses it, that makes injustice bad and justice good. Follow Glaucon's advice, and don't take reputations into account, for if you don't deprive justice and injustice of their true reputations and attach false ones to them, we'll say that you are not praising them but their reputations

and that you're encouraging us to be unjust in secret. In that case, we'll   c
say that you agree with Thrasymachus that justice is the good of another,
the advantage of the stronger, while injustice is one's own advantage and
profit, though not the advantage of the weaker.

You agree that justice is one of the greatest goods, the ones that are
worth getting for the sake of what comes from them, but much more so
for their own sake, such as seeing, hearing, knowing, being healthy, and   d
all other goods that are fruitful by their own nature and not simply because
of reputation. Therefore, praise justice as a good of that kind, explaining
how—because of its very self—it benefits its possessors and how injustice
harms them. Leave wages and reputations for others to praise.

Others would satisfy me if they praised justice and blamed injustice in
that way, extolling the wages of one and denigrating those of the other.
But you, unless you order me to be satisfied, wouldn't, for you've spent
your whole life investigating this and nothing else. Don't, then, give us   e
only a theoretical argument that justice is stronger than injustice, but show
what effect each has because of itself on the person who has it—the one
for good and the other for bad—whether it remains hidden from gods
and human beings or not.

While I'd always admired the natures of Glaucon and Adeimantus, I
was especially pleased on this occasion, and I said: You are the sons of a   368
great man, and Glaucon's lover began his elegy well when he wrote,
celebrating your achievements at the battle of Megara,

> *Sons of Ariston, godlike offspring of a famous man.*

That's well said in my opinion, for you must indeed be affected by the
divine if you're not convinced that injustice is better than justice and yet
can speak on its behalf as you have done. And I believe that you really
are unconvinced by your own words. I infer this from the way you live,   b
for if I had only your words to go on, I wouldn't trust you. The more I
trust you, however, the more I'm at a loss as to what to do. I don't see
how I can be of help. Indeed, I believe I'm incapable of it. And here's my
evidence. I thought what I said to Thrasymachus showed that justice is
better than injustice, but you won't accept it from me. On the other hand,
I don't see how I can refuse my help, for I fear that it may even be impious
to have breath in one's body and the ability to speak and yet to stand idly
by and not defend justice when it is being prosecuted. So the best course
is to give justice any assistance I can.   c

Glaucon and the others begged me not to abandon the argument but to
help in every way to track down what justice and injustice are and what
the truth about their benefits is. So I told them what I had in mind:
The investigation we're undertaking is not an easy one but requires keen
eyesight. Therefore, since we aren't clever people, we should adopt the   d
method of investigation that we'd use if, lacking keen eyesight, we were
told to read small letters from a distance and then noticed that the same

letters existed elsewhere in a larger size and on a larger surface. We'd consider it a godsend, I think, to be allowed to read the larger ones first and then to examine the smaller ones, to see whether they really are the same.

That's certainly true, said Adeimantus, but how is this case similar to

e   our investigation of justice?

I'll tell you. We say, don't we, that there is the justice of a single man and also the justice of a whole city?

Certainly.

And a city is larger than a single man?

It is larger.

Perhaps, then, there is more justice in the larger thing, and it will be easier to learn what it is. So, if you're willing, let's first find out what sort

369 of thing justice is in a city and afterwards look for it in the individual, observing the ways in which the smaller is similar to the larger.

That seems fine to me.

If we could watch a city coming to be in theory, wouldn't we also see its justice coming to be, and its injustice as well?

Probably so.

And when that process is completed, we can hope to find what we are looking for more easily?

b   Of course.

Do you think we should try to carry it out, then? It's no small task, in my view. So think it over.

We have already, said Adeimantus. Don't even consider doing anything else.

I think a city comes to be because none of us is self-sufficient, but we all need many things. Do you think that a city is founded on any other principle?

No.

And because people need many things, and because one person calls

c   on a second out of one need and on a third out of a different need, many people gather in a single place to live together as partners and helpers. And such a settlement is called a city. Isn't that so?

It is.

And if they share things with one another, giving and taking, they do so because each believes that this is better for himself?

That's right.

Come, then, let's create a city in theory from its beginnings. And it's our needs, it seems, that will create it.

It is, indeed.

d   Surely our first and greatest need is to provide food to sustain life.

Certainly.

Our second is for shelter, and our third for clothes and such.

That's right.

How, then, will a city be able to provide all this? Won't one person have to be a farmer, another a builder, and another a weaver? And shouldn't we add a cobbler and someone else to provide medical care?

All right.

So the essential minimum for a city is four or five men?

Apparently.   e

And what about this? Must each of them contribute his own work for the common use of all? For example, will a farmer provide food for everyone, spending quadruple the time and labor to provide food to be shared by them all? Or will he not bother about that, producing one quarter the food in one quarter the time, and spending the other three quarters, one in   370 building a house, one in the production of clothes, and one in making shoes, not troubling to associate with the others, but minding his own business on his own?

Perhaps, Socrates, Adeimantus replied, the way you suggested first would be easier than the other.

That certainly wouldn't be surprising, for, even as you were speaking it occurred to me that, in the first place, we aren't all born alike, but each of us differs somewhat in nature from the others, one being suited to one task, another to another. Or don't you think so?   b

I do.

Second, does one person do a better job if he practices many crafts or— since he's one person himself—if he practices one?

If he practices one.

It's clear, at any rate, I think, that if one misses the right moment in anything, the work is spoiled.

It is.

That's because the thing to be done won't wait on the leisure of the doer, but the doer must of necessity pay close attention to his work rather than treating it as a secondary occupation.   c

Yes, he must.

The result, then, is that more plentiful and better-quality goods are more easily produced if each person does one thing for which he is naturally suited, does it at the right time, and is released from having to do any of the others.

Absolutely.

Then, Adeimantus, we're going to need more than four citizens to provide the things we've mentioned, for a farmer won't make his own plough, not if it's to be a good one, nor his hoe, nor any of his other farming tools. Neither will a builder—and he, too, needs lots of things. And the same is   d true of a weaver and a cobbler, isn't it?

It is.

Hence, carpenters, metal workers, and many other craftsmen of that sort will share our little city and make it bigger.

That's right.

Yet it won't be a huge settlement even if we add cowherds, shepherds, and other herdsmen in order that the farmers have cows to do their plough-
e ing, the builders have oxen to share with the farmers in hauling their materials, and the weavers and cobblers have hides and fleeces to use.

It won't be a small one either, if it has to hold all those.

Moreover, it's almost impossible to establish a city in a place where nothing has to be imported.

Indeed it is.

So we'll need yet further people to import from other cities whatever is needed.

Yes.

And if an importer goes empty-handed to another city, without a cargo of the things needed by the city from which he's to bring back what his
371 own city needs, he'll come away empty-handed, won't he?

So it seems.

Therefore our citizens must not only produce enough for themselves at home but also goods of the right quality and quantity to satisfy the requirements of others.

They must.

So we'll need more farmers and other craftsmen in our city.

Yes.

And others to take care of imports and exports. And they're called merchants, aren't they?

Yes.

So we'll need merchants, too.

Certainly.

And if the trade is by sea, we'll need a good many others who know
b how to sail.

A good many, indeed.

And how will those in the city itself share the things that each produces? It was for the sake of this that we made their partnership and founded their city.

Clearly, they must do it by buying and selling.

Then we'll need a marketplace and a currency for such exchange.

Certainly.

c If a farmer or any other craftsman brings some of his products to market, and he doesn't arrive at the same time as those who want to exchange things with him, is he to sit idly in the marketplace, away from his own work?

Not at all. There'll be people who'll notice this and provide the requisite service—in well-organized cities they'll usually be those whose bodies are weakest and who aren't fit to do any other work. They'll stay around the
d market exchanging money for the goods of those who have something to sell and then exchanging those goods for the money of those who want them.

Then, to fill this need there will have to be retailers in our city, for aren't those who establish themselves in the marketplace to provide this service of buying and selling called retailers, while those who travel between cities are called merchants?

That's right.

There are other servants, I think, whose minds alone wouldn't qualify them for membership in our society but whose bodies are strong enough for labor. These sell the use of their strength for a price called a wage and hence are themselves called wage-earners. Isn't that so?   e

Certainly.

So wage-earners complete our city?

I think so.

Well, Adeimantus, has our city grown to completeness, then?

Perhaps it has.

Then where are justice and injustice to be found in it? With which of the things we examined did they come in?

I've no idea, Socrates, unless it was somewhere in some need that these   372 people have of one another.

You may be right, but we must look into it and not grow weary. First, then, let's see what sort of life our citizens will lead when they've been provided for in the way we have been describing. They'll produce bread, wine, clothes, and shoes, won't they? They'll build houses, work naked and barefoot in the summer, and wear adequate clothing and shoes in the   b winter. For food, they'll knead and cook the flour and meal they've made from wheat and barley. They'll put their honest cakes and loaves on reeds or clean leaves, and, reclining on beds strewn with yew and myrtle, they'll feast with their children, drink their wine, and, crowned with wreaths, hymn the gods. They'll enjoy sex with one another but bear no more children than their resources allow, lest they fall into either poverty or war.   c

It seems that you make your people feast without any delicacies, Glaucon interrupted.

True enough, I said, I was forgetting that they'll obviously need salt, olives, cheese, boiled roots, and vegetables of the sort they cook in the country. We'll give them desserts, too, of course, consisting of figs, chickpeas, and beans, and they'll roast myrtle and acorns before the fire, drinking moderately. And so they'll live in peace and good health, and when they   d die at a ripe old age, they'll bequeath a similar life to their children.

If you were founding a city for pigs, Socrates, he replied, wouldn't you fatten *them* on the same diet?

Then how should I feed these people, Glaucon? I asked.

In the conventional way. If they aren't to suffer hardship, they should recline on proper couches, dine at a table, and have the delicacies and desserts that people have nowadays.   e

All right, I understand. It isn't merely the origin of a city that we're considering, it seems, but the origin of a *luxurious* city. And that may not be a bad idea, for by examining it, we might very well see how justice and injustice grow up in cities. Yet the true city, in my opinion, is the one we've described, the healthy one, as it were. But let's study a city with a

373   fever, if that's what you want. There's nothing to stop us. The things I
      mentioned earlier and the way of life I described won't satisfy some people,
      it seems, but couches, tables, and other furniture will have to be added,
      and, of course, all sorts of delicacies, perfumed oils, incense, prostitutes,
      and pastries. We mustn't provide them only with the necessities we
      mentioned at first, such as houses, clothes, and shoes, but painting and
      embroidery must be begun, and gold, ivory, and the like acquired. Isn't
      that so?

b   Yes.
      Then we must enlarge our city, for the healthy one is no longer adequate.
      We must increase it in size and fill it with a multitude of things that go
      beyond what is necessary for a city—hunters, for example, and artists or
      imitators, many of whom work with shapes and colors, many with music.
      And there'll be poets and their assistants, actors, choral dancers, contrac-
      tors, and makers of all kinds of devices, including, among other things,
      those needed for the adornment of women. And so we'll need more ser-

c   vants, too. Or don't you think that we'll need tutors, wet nurses, nannies,
      beauticians, barbers, chefs, cooks, and swineherds? We didn't need any
      of these in our earlier city, but we'll need them in this one. And we'll also
      need many more cattle, won't we, if the people are going to eat meat?
      Of course.
      And if we live like that, we'll have a far greater need for doctors than

d   we did before?
      Much greater.
      And the land, I suppose, that used to be adequate to feed the population
      we had then, will cease to be adequate and become too small. What do
      you think?
      The same.
      Then we'll have to seize some of our neighbors' land if we're to have
      enough pasture and ploughland. And won't our neighbors want to seize
      part of ours as well, if they too have surrendered themselves to the endless
      acquisition of money and have overstepped the limit of their necessities?

e   That's completely inevitable, Socrates.
      Then our next step will be war, Glaucon, won't it?
      It will.
      We won't say yet whether the effects of war are good or bad but only
      that we've now found the origins of war. It comes from those same desires
      that are most of all responsible for the bad things that happen to cities
      and the individuals in them.
      That's right.
      Then the city must be further enlarged, and not just by a small number,
      either, but by a whole army, which will do battle with the invaders in

374   defense of the city's substantial wealth and all the other things we men-
      tioned.
      Why aren't the citizens themselves adequate for that purpose?
      They won't be, if the agreement you and the rest of us made when we
      were founding the city was a good one, for surely we agreed, if you

remember, that it's impossible for a single person to practice many crafts or professions well.

That's true.

Well, then, don't you think that warfare is a profession?   b

Of course.

Then should we be more concerned about cobbling than about warfare?

Not at all.

But we prevented a cobbler from trying to be a farmer, weaver, or builder at the same time and said that he must remain a cobbler in order to produce fine work. And each of the others, too, was to work all his life at a single trade for which he had a natural aptitude and keep away from all the others, so as not to miss the right moment to practice his own work well.   c Now, isn't it of the greatest importance that warfare be practiced well? And is fighting a war so easy that a farmer or a cobbler or any other craftsman can be a soldier at the same time? Though no one can become so much as a good player of checkers or dice if he considers it only as a sideline and doesn't practice it from childhood. Or can someone pick up a shield or any other weapon or tool of war and immediately perform adequately in an infantry battle or any other kind? No other tool makes   d anyone who picks it up a craftsman or champion unless he has acquired the requisite knowledge and has had sufficient practice.

If tools could make anyone who picked them up an expert, they'd be valuable indeed.

Then to the degree that the work of the guardians is most important, it   e requires most freedom from other things and the greatest skill and devotion.

I should think so.

And doesn't it also require a person whose nature is suited to that way of life?

Certainly.

Then our job, it seems, is to select, if we can, the kind of nature suited to guard the city.

It is.

By god, it's no trivial task that we've taken on. But insofar as we are able, we mustn't shrink from it.

No, we mustn't.   375

Do you think that, when it comes to guarding, there is any difference between the nature of a pedigree young dog and that of a well-born youth?

What do you mean?

Well, each needs keen senses, speed to catch what it sees, and strength in case it has to fight it out with what it captures.

They both need all these things.

And each must be courageous if indeed he's to fight well.

Of course.

And will a horse, a dog, or any other animal be courageous, if he isn't spirited? Or haven't you noticed just how invincible and unbeatable spirit is, so that its presence makes the whole soul fearless and unconquerable?   b

I have noticed that.

The physical qualities of the guardians are clear, then.

Yes.

And as far as their souls are concerned, they must be spirited.

That too.

But if they have natures like that, Glaucon, won't they be savage to each other and to the rest of the citizens?

By god, it will be hard for them to be anything else.

c   Yet surely they must be gentle to their own people and harsh to the enemy. If they aren't, they won't wait around for others to destroy the city but will do it themselves first.

That's true.

What are we to do, then? Where are we to find a character that is both gentle and high-spirited at the same time? After all, a gentle nature is the opposite of a spirited one.

Apparently.

If someone lacks either gentleness or spirit, he can't be a good guardian. Yet it seems impossible to combine them. It follows that a good guardian

d   cannot exist.

It looks like it.

I couldn't see a way out, but on reexamining what had gone before, I said: We deserve to be stuck, for we've lost sight of the analogy we put forward.

How do you mean?

We overlooked the fact that there *are* natures of the sort we thought impossible, natures in which these opposites are indeed combined.

Where?

You can see them in other animals, too, but especially in the one to which we compared the guardian, for you know, of course, that a pedigree

e   dog naturally has a character of this sort—he is gentle as can be to those he's used to and knows, but the opposite to those he doesn't know.

I do know that.

So the combination we want is possible after all, and our search for the good guardian is not contrary to nature.

Apparently not.

Then do you think that our future guardian, besides being spirited, must also be by nature philosophical?

376   How do you mean? I don't understand.

It's something else you see in dogs, and it makes you wonder at the animal.

What?

When a dog sees someone it doesn't know, it gets angry before anything bad happens to it. But when it knows someone, it welcomes him, even if it has never received anything good from him. Haven't you ever wondered at that?

I've never paid any attention to it, but obviously that is the way a dog behaves.

Surely this is a refined quality in its nature and one that is truly philo-   b
sophical.

In what way philosophical?

Because it judges anything it sees to be either a friend or an enemy, on
no other basis than that it knows the one and doesn't know the other. And
how could it be anything besides a lover of learning, if it defines what is
its own and what is alien to it in terms of knowledge and ignorance?

It couldn't.

But surely the love of learning is the same thing as philosophy or the
love of wisdom?

It is.

Then, may we confidently assume in the case of a human being, too,
that if he is to be gentle toward his own and those he knows, he must be
a lover of learning and wisdom?   c

We may.

Philosophy, spirit, speed, and strength must all, then, be combined in
the nature of anyone who is to be a fine and good guardian of our city.

Absolutely.

Then those are the traits a potential guardian would need at the outset.
But how are we to bring him up and educate him? Will inquiry into that
topic bring us any closer to the goal of our inquiry, which is to discover
the origins of justice and injustice in a city? We want our account to be   d
adequate, but we don't want it to be any longer than necessary.

I certainly expect, Glaucon's brother said, that such inquiry will further
our goal.

Then, by god, Adeimantus, I said, we mustn't leave it out, even if it
turns out to be a somewhat lengthy affair.

No, we mustn't.

Come, then, and just as if we had the leisure to make up stories, let's
describe in theory how to educate our men.

All right.   e

What will their education be? Or is it hard to find anything better than
that which has developed over a long period—physical training for bodies
and music and poetry for the soul?

Yes, it would be hard.

Now, we start education in music and poetry before physical training,
don't we?

Of course.

Do you include stories under music and poetry?

I do.

Aren't there two kinds of story, one true and the other false?

Yes.

And mustn't our men be educated in both, but first in false ones?   377

I don't understand what you mean.

Don't you understand that we first tell stories to children? These are
false, on the whole, though they have some truth in them. And we tell
them to small children before physical training begins.

That's true.

And that's what I meant by saying that we must deal with music and poetry before physical training.

All right.

You know, don't you, that the beginning of any process is most important, especially for anything young and tender? It's at that time that it is
b   most malleable and takes on any pattern one wishes to impress on it.

Exactly.

Then shall we carelessly allow the children to hear any old stories, told by just anyone, and to take beliefs into their souls that are for the most part opposite to the ones we think they should hold when they are grown up?

We certainly won't.

Then we must first of all, it seems, supervise the storytellers. We'll select their stories whenever they are fine or beautiful and reject them when they
c   aren't. And we'll persuade nurses and mothers to tell their children the ones we have selected, since they will shape their children's souls with stories much more than they shape their bodies by handling them. Many of the stories they tell now, however, must be thrown out.

Which ones do you mean?

We'll first look at the major stories, and by seeing how to deal with them, we'll see how to deal with the minor ones as well, for they exhibit the same pattern and have the same effects whether they're famous or
d   not. Don't you think so?

I do, but I don't know which ones you're calling major.

Those that Homer, Hesiod, and other poets tell us, for surely they composed false stories, told them to people, and are still telling them.

Which stories do you mean, and what fault do you find in them?

The fault one ought to find first and foremost, especially if the falsehood isn't well told.

For example?

When a story gives a bad image of what the gods and heroes are like,
e   the way a painter does whose picture is not at all like the things he's trying to paint.

You're right to object to that. But what sort of thing in particular do you have in mind?

First, telling the greatest falsehood about the most important things doesn't make a fine story—I mean Hesiod telling us about how Uranus behaved, how Cronus punished him for it, and how he was in turn punished by his own son.[10] But even if it were true, it should be passed over
378   in silence, not told to foolish young people. And if, for some reason, it has to be told, only a very few people—pledged to secrecy and after sacrificing not just a pig but something great and scarce—should hear it, so that their number is kept as small as possible.

Yes, such stories are hard to deal with.

10. See Hesiod, *Theogony* 154–210, 453–506.

And they shouldn't be told in our city, Adeimantus. Nor should a young   b
person hear it said that in committing the worst crimes he's doing nothing
out of the ordinary, or that if he inflicts every kind of punishment on an
unjust father, he's only doing the same as the first and greatest of the gods.

No, by god, I don't think myself that these stories are fit to be told.

Indeed, if we want the guardians of our city to think that it's shameful
to be easily provoked into hating one another, we mustn't allow *any* stories
about gods warring, fighting, or plotting against one another, for they   c
aren't true. The battles of gods and giants, and all the various stories of
the gods hating their families or friends, should neither be told nor even
woven in embroideries. If we're to persuade our people that no citizen
has ever hated another and that it's impious to do so, then *that's* what
should be told to children from the beginning by old men and women;
and as these children grow older, poets should be compelled to tell them
the same sort of thing. We won't admit stories into our city—whether   d
allegorical or not—about Hera being chained by her son, nor about Hephaestus being hurled from heaven by his father when he tried to help
his mother, who was being beaten, nor about the battle of the gods in
Homer. The young can't distinguish what is allegorical from what isn't,
and the opinions they absorb at that age are hard to erase and apt to
become unalterable. For these reasons, then, we should probably take the
utmost care to insure that the first stories they hear about virtue are the   e
best ones for them to hear.

That's reasonable. But if someone asked us what stories these are, what
should we say?

You and I, Adeimantus, aren't poets, but we *are* founding a city. And
it's appropriate for the founders to know the patterns on which poets must   379
base their stories and from which they mustn't deviate. But we aren't
actually going to compose their poems for them.

All right. But what precisely are the patterns for theology or stories
about the gods?

Something like this: Whether in epic, lyric, or tragedy, a god must always
be represented as he is.

Indeed, he must.

Now, a god is really good, isn't he, and must be described as such?   b
What else?

And surely nothing good is harmful, is it?

I suppose not.

And can what isn't harmful do harm?

Never.

Or can what does no harm do anything bad?

No.

And can what does nothing bad be the cause of anything bad?

How could it?

Moreover, the good is beneficial?

Yes.

It is the cause of doing well?

Yes.

The good isn't the cause of all things, then, but only of good ones; it isn't the cause of bad ones.

c   I agree entirely.

Therefore, since a god is good, he is not—as most people claim—the cause of everything that happens to human beings but of only a few things, for good things are fewer than bad ones in our lives. He alone is responsible for the good things, but we must find some other cause for the bad ones, not a god.

That's very true, and I believe it.

Then we won't accept from anyone the foolish mistake Homer makes

d   about the gods when he says:

> *There are two urns at the threshold of Zeus,*
> *One filled with good fates, the other with bad ones. . . .*

and the person to whom he gives a mixture of these

> *Sometimes meets with a bad fate, sometimes with good,*

but the one who receives his fate entirely from the second urn,

> *Evil famine drives him over the divine earth.*

e   We won't grant either that Zeus is for us

> *The distributor of both good and bad.*

And as to the breaking of the promised truce by Pandarus, if anyone tells us that it was brought about by Athena and Zeus or that Themis and Zeus were responsible for strife and contention among the gods, we will not

380   praise him. Nor will we allow the young to hear the words of Aeschylus:

> *A god makes mortals guilty*
> *When he wants utterly to destroy a house.*[11]

And if anyone composes a poem about the sufferings of Niobe, such as the one in which these lines occur, or about the house of Pelops, or the tale of Troy, or anything else of that kind, we must require him to say that these things are not the work of a god. Or, if they are, then poets must look for the kind of account of them that we are now seeking, and

11. The first three quotations are from *Iliad* xxiv.527–32. The sources for the fourth and for the quotation from Aeschylus are unknown. The story of Athena urging Pandarus to break the truce is told in *Iliad* iv.73–126.

say that the actions of the gods are good and just, and that those they punish are benefited thereby. We won't allow poets to say that the punished   b
are made wretched and that it was a god who made them so. But we will allow them to say that bad people are wretched because they are in need of punishment and that, in paying the penalty, they are benefited by the gods. And, as for saying that a god, who is himself good, is the cause of bad things, we'll fight that in every way, and we won't allow anyone to say it in his own city, if it's to be well governed, or anyone to hear it either—whether young or old, whether in verse or prose. These stories   c
are not pious, not advantageous to us, and not consistent with one another.

I like your law, and I'll vote for it.

This, then, is one of the laws or patterns concerning the gods to which speakers and poets must conform, namely, that a god isn't the cause of all things but only of good ones.

And it's a fully satisfactory law.

What about this second law? Do you think that a god is a sorcerer, able to appear in different forms at different times, sometimes changing himself   d
from his own form into many shapes, sometimes deceiving us by making us think that he has done it? Or do you think he's simple and least of all likely to step out of his own form?

I can't say offhand.

Well, what about this? If he steps out of his own form, mustn't he either change himself or be changed by something else?   e

He must.

But the best things are least liable to alteration or change, aren't they? For example, isn't the healthiest and strongest body least changed by food, drink, and labor, or the healthiest and strongest plant by sun, wind, and the like?

Of course.   381

And the most courageous and most rational soul is least disturbed or altered by any outside affection?

Yes.

And the same account is true of all artifacts, furniture, houses, and clothes. The ones that are good and well made are least altered by time or anything else that happens to them.

That's right.

Whatever is in good condition, then, whether by nature or craft or both,   b
admits least of being changed by anything else.

So it seems.

Now, surely a god and what belongs to him are in every way in the best condition.

How could they fail to be?

Then a god would be least likely to have many shapes.

Indeed.

Then does he change or alter himself?

Clearly he does, if indeed he is altered at all.

Would he change himself into something better and more beautiful than himself or something worse and uglier?

c   It would have to be into something worse, if he's changed at all, for surely we won't say that a god is deficient in either beauty or virtue.

Absolutely right. And do you think, Adeimantus, that anyone, whether god or human, would deliberately make himself worse in any way?

No, that's impossible.

Is it impossible, then, for gods to want to alter themselves? Since they are the most beautiful and best possible, it seems that each always and unconditionally retains his own shape.

That seems entirely necessary to me.

d   Then let no poet tell us about Proteus or Thetis, or say that

> The gods, in the likeness of strangers from foreign lands,
> Adopt every sort of shape and visit our cities.[12]

Nor must they present Hera, in their tragedies or other poems, as a priestess collecting alms for

> the life-giving sons of the Argive river Inachus,[13]

or tell us other stories of that sort. Nor must mothers, believing bad stories
e   about the gods wandering at night in the shapes of strangers from foreign lands, terrify their children with them. Such stories blaspheme the gods and, at the same time, make children more cowardly.

They mustn't be told.

But though the gods are unable to change, do they nonetheless make us believe that they appear in all sorts of ways, deceiving us through sorcery?

Perhaps.

382   What? Would a god be willing to be false, either in word or deed, by presenting an illusion?

I don't know.

Don't you know that a *true* falsehood, if one may call it that, is hated by all gods and humans?

What do you mean?

I mean that no one is willing to tell falsehoods to the most important part of himself about the most important things, but of all places he is most afraid to have falsehood there.

I still don't understand.

---

12. *Odyssey* xvii.485–86.

13. Inachus was the father of Io, who was persecuted by Hera because Zeus was in love with her. The source for the part of the story Plato quotes is unknown.

That's because you think I'm saying something deep. I simply mean   b
that to be false to one's soul about the things that are, to be ignorant and
to have and hold falsehood there, is what everyone would least of all
accept, for everyone hates a falsehood in that place most of all.

That's right.

Surely, as I said just now, this would be most correctly called true
falsehood—ignorance in the soul of someone who has been told a falsehood. Falsehood in words is a kind of imitation of this affection in the
soul, an image of it that comes into being after it and is not a pure falsehood.
Isn't that so?   c

Certainly.

And the thing that is really a falsehood is hated not only by the gods
but by human beings as well.

It seems so to me.

What about falsehood in words? When and to whom is it useful and
so not deserving of hatred? Isn't it useful against one's enemies? And
when any of our so-called friends are attempting, through madness or
ignorance, to do something bad, isn't it a useful drug for preventing them?
It is also useful in the case of those stories we were just talking about, the
ones we tell because we don't know the truth about those ancient events   d
involving the gods. By making a falsehood as much like the truth as we
can, don't we also make it useful?

We certainly do.

Then in which of these ways could a falsehood be useful to a god?
Would he make false likenesses of ancient events because of his ignorance
of them?

It would be ridiculous to think that.

Then there is nothing of the false poet in a god?

Not in my view.

Would he be false, then, through fear of his enemies?

Far from it.   e

Because of the ignorance or madness of his family or friends, then?

No one who is ignorant or mad is a friend of the gods.

Then there's no reason for a god to speak falsely?

None.

Therefore the daemonic and the divine are in every way free from
falsehood.

Completely.

A god, then, is simple and true in word and deed. He doesn't change
himself or deceive others by images, words, or signs, whether in visions
or in dreams.

That's what I thought as soon as I heard you say it.   383

You agree, then, that this is our second pattern for speaking or composing
poems about the gods: They are not sorcerers who change themselves, nor
do they mislead us by falsehoods in words or deeds.

I agree.

So, even though we praise many things in Homer, we won't approve of the dream Zeus sent to Agamemnon, nor of Aeschylus when he makes
b   Thetis say that Apollo sang in prophecy at her wedding:

> *About the good fortune my children would have,*
> *Free of disease throughout their long lives,*
> *And of all the blessings that the friendship of the gods would bring me,*
> *I hoped that Phoebus' divine mouth would be free of falsehood,*
> *Endowed as it is with the craft of prophecy.*
> *But the very god who sang, the one at the feast,*
> *The one who said all this, he himself it is*
> *Who killed my son.*[14]

Whenever anyone says such things about a god, we'll be angry with him,
c   refuse him a chorus,[15] and not allow his poetry to be used in the education of the young, so that our guardians will be as god-fearing and godlike as human beings can be.

I completely endorse these patterns, he said, and I would enact them as laws.

Book III

386   Such, then, I said, are the kinds of stories that I think future guardians should and should not hear about the gods from childhood on, if they are to honor the gods and their parents and not take their friendship with one another lightly.

I'm sure we're right about that, at any rate.

What if they are to be courageous as well? Shouldn't they be told stories that will make them least afraid of death? Or do you think that anyone
b   ever becomes courageous if he's possessed by this fear?

No, I certainly don't.

And can someone be unafraid of death, preferring it to defeat in battle or slavery, if he believes in a Hades full of terrors?

Not at all.

Then we must supervise such stories and those who tell them, and ask them not to disparage the life in Hades in this unconditional way, but rather to praise it, since what they now say is neither true nor beneficial
c   to future warriors.

We must.

---

14. In *Iliad* ii.1–34, Zeus sends a dream to Agamemnon to promise success if he attacks Troy immediately. The promise is false. The source for the quotation from Aeschylus is unknown.

15. I.e., deny him the funding necessary to produce his play.

Then we'll expunge all that sort of disparagement, beginning with the following lines:

> *I would rather labor on earth in service to another,*
> *To a man who is landless, with little to live on,*
> *Than be king over all the dead.*[1]

and also these:

> *He feared that his home should appear to gods and men*   d
> *Dreadful, dank, and hated even by the gods.*[2]

and

> *Alas, there survives in the Halls of Hades*
> *A soul, a mere phantasm, with its wits completely gone.*[3]

and this:

> *And he alone could think; the others are flitting shadows.*[4]

and

> *The soul, leaving his limbs, made its way to Hades,*
> *Lamenting its fate, leaving manhood and youth behind.*[5]

and these: 387

> *His soul went below the earth like smoke,*
> *Screeching as it went . . .*[6]

and

1. *Odyssey* xi.489–91. Odysseus is being addressed by the dead Achilles in Hades.

2. *Iliad* xx.64–65. The speaker is the god of the underworld—who is afraid that the earth will split open and reveal that his home is dreadful, etc.

3. *Iliad* xxiii.103–4. Achilles speaks these lines as the soul of the dead Patroclus leaves for Hades.

4. *Odyssey* x.495. Circe is speaking to Odysseus about the prophet Tiresias.

5. *Iliad* xvi.856–57. The words refer to Patroclus, who has just been mortally wounded by Hector.

6. *Iliad* xxiii.100–101. The soul referred to is Patroclus'.

> *As when bats in an awful cave*
> *Fly around screeching if one of them falls*
> *From the cluster on the ceiling, all clinging to one another,*
> *So their souls went screeching . . .*[7]

b   We'll ask Homer and the other poets not to be angry if we delete these
passages and all similar ones. It isn't that they aren't poetic and pleasing
to the majority of hearers but that, the more poetic they are, the less they
should be heard by children or by men who are supposed to be free and
to fear slavery more than death.

Most certainly.

And the frightening and dreadful names for the underworld must be
struck out, for example, "Cocytus" and "Styx,"[8] and also the names for
c   the dead, for example, "those below" and "the sapless ones," and all those
names of things in the underworld that make everyone who hears them
shudder. They may be all well and good for other purposes, but we are
afraid that our guardians will be made softer and more malleable by
such shudders.

And our fear is justified.

Then such passages are to be struck out?

Yes.

And poets must follow the opposite pattern in speaking and writing?

Clearly.

Must we also delete the lamentations and pitiful speeches of famous
d   men?

We must, if indeed what we said before is compelling.

Consider though whether we are right to delete them or not. We surely
say that a decent man doesn't think that death is a terrible thing for
someone decent to suffer—even for someone who happens to be his friend.

We do say that.

Then he won't mourn for him as for someone who has suffered a terrible fate.

Certainly not.

We also say that a decent person is most self-sufficient in living well
e   and, above all others, has the least need of anyone else.

That's true.

Then it's less dreadful for him than for anyone else to be deprived of
his son, brother, possessions, or any other such things.

Much less.

Then he'll least give way to lamentations and bear misfortune most
quietly when it strikes.

---

7. *Odyssey* xxiv.6–9. The souls are those of the suitors of Penelope, whom Odysseus
has killed.

8. "Cocytus" means river of wailing or lamenting; "Styx" means river of hatred or
gloom.

Certainly.

We'd be right, then, to delete the lamentations of famous men, leaving them to women (and not even to good women, either) and to cowardly men, so that those we say we are training to guard our city will disdain   388
to act like that.

That's right.

Again, then, we'll ask Homer and the other poets not to represent Achilles, the son of a goddess, as

> *Lying now on his side, now on his back, now again*
> *On his belly; then standing up to wander distracted*
> *This way and that on the shore of the unharvested sea.*

Nor to make him pick up ashes in both hands and pour them over his head, weeping and lamenting in the ways he does in Homer. Nor to   b
represent Priam, a close descendant of the gods, as entreating his men and

> *Rolling around in dung,*
> *Calling upon each man by name.*[9]

And we'll ask them even more earnestly not to make the gods lament and say:

> *Alas, unfortunate that I am, wretched mother of a great son.*[10]   c

But, if they do make the gods do such things, at least they mustn't dare to represent the greatest of the gods as behaving in so unlikely a fashion as to say:

> *Alas, with my own eyes I see a man who is most dear to me*
> *Chased around the city, and my heart laments*

or

> *Woe is me, that Sarpedon, who is most dear to me, should be*
> *Fated to be killed by Patroclus, the son of Menoetius . . .*[11]   d

If our young people, Adeimantus, listen to these stories without ridiculing them as not worth hearing, it's hardly likely that they'll consider the things

9. The last three references and quotations are to *Iliad* xxiv.3–12, *Iliad* xviii.23–24, and *Iliad* xxii.414–15, respectively.

10. *Iliad* xviii.54. Thetis, the mother of Achilles, is mourning his fate among the Nereids.

11. *Iliad* xxii.168–69 (Zeus is watching Hector being pursued by Achilles), and *Iliad* xvi.433–34.

described in them to be unworthy of mere human beings like themselves
or that they'll rebuke themselves for doing or saying similar things when
misfortune strikes. Instead, they'll feel neither shame nor restraint but
groan and lament at even insignificant misfortunes.

e   What you say is completely true.

Then, as the argument has demonstrated—and we must remain persuaded by it until someone shows us a better one—they mustn't behave
like that.

No, they mustn't.

Moreover, they mustn't be lovers of laughter either, for whenever anyone
indulges in violent laughter, a violent change of mood is likely to follow.

So I believe.

Then, if someone represents worthwhile people as overcome by laughter,
we won't approve, and we'll approve even less if they represent gods
389   that way.

Much less.

Then we won't approve of Homer saying things like this about the gods:

> And unquenchable laughter arose among the blessed gods
> As they saw Hephaestus limping through the hall.[12]

According to your argument, such things must be rejected.

b   If you want to call it mine, but they must be rejected in any case.

Moreover, we have to be concerned about truth as well, for if what we
said just now is correct, and falsehood, though of no use to the gods, is
useful to people as a form of drug, clearly we must allow only doctors to
use it, not private citizens.

Clearly.

Then if it is appropriate for anyone to use falsehoods for the good of
the city, because of the actions of either enemies or citizens, it is the rulers.
But everyone else must keep away from them, because for a private citizen
c   to lie to a ruler is just as bad a mistake as for a sick person or athlete not
to tell the truth to his doctor or trainer about his physical condition or for
a sailor not to tell the captain the facts about his own condition or that of
the ship and the rest of its crew—indeed it is a worse mistake than either
of these.

That's completely true.

d   And if the ruler catches someone else telling falsehoods in the city—

> Any one of the craftsmen,
> Whether a prophet, a doctor who heals the sick, or a maker of spears[13]

12. *Iliad* i.599–600.
13. *Odyssey* xvii.383–84.

—he'll punish him for introducing something as subversive and destructive to a city as it would be to a ship.

He will, if practice is to follow theory.

What about moderation? Won't our young people also need that?

Of course.

And aren't these the most important aspects of moderation for the majority of people, namely, to obey the rulers and to rule the pleasures of drink, sex, and food for themselves?   e

That's my opinion at any rate.

Then we'll say that the words of Homer's Diomedes are well put:

> *Sit down in silence, my friend, and be persuaded by me.*

and so is what follows:

> *The Achaeans, breathing eagerness for battle,*
> *Marched in silence, fearing their commanders.*

and all other such things.

Those *are* well put.

But what about this?

> *Wine-bibber, with the eyes of a dog and the heart of a deer*[14]

and the rest, is it—or any other headstrong words spoken in prose or poetry by private citizens against their rulers—well put?   390

No, they aren't.

I don't think they are suitable for young people to hear—not, in any case, with a view to making them moderate. Though it isn't surprising that they are pleasing enough in other ways. What do you think?

The same as you.

What about making the cleverest man say that the finest thing of all is when

> *The tables are well laden*
> *With bread and meat, and the winebearer*   b
> *Draws wine from the mixing bowl and pours it in the cups.*

or

---

14. The last three citations are, respectively, *Iliad* iv.412, where Diomedes rebukes his squire and quiets him; *Iliad* iii.8 and iv.431, not in fact (in our Homer text) adjacent to one another or the preceding; and *Iliad* i.225 (Achilles is insulting his commander, Agamemnon).

Death by starvation is the most pitiful fate.[15]

Do you think that such things make for self-control in young people? Or
what about having Zeus, when all the other gods are asleep and he alone
c   is awake, easily forget all his plans because of sexual desire and be so
overcome by the sight of Hera that he doesn't even want to go inside but
wants to possess her there on the ground, saying that his desire for her
is even greater than it was when—without their parents' knowledge—
they were first lovers? Or what about the chaining together of Ares and
Aphrodite by Hephaestus[16]—also the result of sexual passion?

No, by god, none of that seems suitable to me.

But if, on the other hand, there are words or deeds of famous men, who
d   are exhibiting endurance in the face of everything, surely they must be
seen or heard. For example,

> *He struck his chest and spoke to his heart:*
> *"Endure, my heart, you've suffered more shameful things than this."*[17]

They certainly must.

Now, we mustn't allow our men to be money-lovers or to be bribable
with gifts.

e   Certainly not.

Then the poets mustn't sing to them:

> *Gifts persuade gods, and gifts persuade revered kings.*[18]

Nor must Phoenix, the tutor of Achilles, be praised as speaking with
moderation when he advises him to take the gifts and defend the Achaeans,
but not to give up his anger without gifts.[19] Nor should we think such
things to be worthy of Achilles himself. Nor should we agree that he was
such a money-lover that he would accept the gifts of Agamemnon or
391   release the corpse of Hector for a ransom but not otherwise.

It certainly isn't right to praise such things.

It is only out of respect for Homer, indeed, that I hesitate to say that it
is positively impious to accuse Achilles of such things or to believe others
who say them. Or to make him address Apollo in these words:

---

15. Odysseus in *Odyssey* ix.8–10; *Odyssey* xii.342 (Eurylochus urges the men to slay the
cattle of Helios in Odysseus' absence).

16. *Odyssey* viii.266 ff.

17. *Odyssey* xx.17–18. The speaker is Odysseus.

18. The source of the passage is unknown. Cf. Euripides, *Medea* 964.

19. *Iliad* ix.602–5.

> *You've injured me, Farshooter, most deadly of the gods;*
> *And I'd punish you, if I had the power.*[20]

Or to say that he disobeyed the river—a god—and was ready to fight it,
or that he consecrated hair to the dead Patroclus, which was already   b
consecrated to a different river, Spercheius. It isn't to be believed that he
did any of these. Nor is it true that he dragged the dead Hector around
the tomb of Patroclus or massacred the captives on his pyre.[21] So we'll
deny that. Nor will we allow our people to believe that Achilles, who was   c
the son of a goddess and of Peleus (the most moderate of men and the
grandson of Zeus) and who was brought up by the most wise Chiron,
was so full of inner turmoil as to have two diseases in his soul—slavishness
accompanied by the love of money, on the one hand, and arrogance towards
gods and humans, on the other.

That's right.

We certainly won't believe such things, nor will we allow it to be said
that Theseus, the son of Posidon, and Pirithous, the son of Zeus, engaged
in terrible kidnappings,[22] or that any other hero and son of a god dared   d
to do any of the terrible and impious deeds that they are now falsely said
to have done. We'll compel the poets either to deny that the heroes did
such things or else to deny that they were children of the gods. They
mustn't say both or attempt to persuade our young people that the gods
bring about evil or that heroes are no better than humans. As we said
earlier, these things are both impious and untrue, for we demonstrated   e
that it is impossible for the gods to produce bad things.[23]

Of course.

Moreover, these stories are harmful to people who hear them, for everyone will be ready to excuse himself when he's bad, if he is persuaded that
similar things both are being done now and have been done in the past by

> *Close descendants of the gods,*
> *Those near to Zeus, to whom belongs*
> *The ancestral altar high up on Mount Ida,*
> *In whom the blood of daemons has not weakened.*[24]

For that reason, we must put a stop to such stories, lest they produce in
the youth a strong inclination to do bad things.   392

20. *Iliad* xxii.15, 20.

21. The last four references are to *Iliad* xxi.232 ff., *Iliad* xxiii.141–52, *Iliad* xxiv.14–18, and
Iliad xxiii.175, respectively.

22. According to some legends, Theseus and Pirithous abducted Helen and tried to
abduct Persephone from Hades.

23. See 380d ff.

24. Thought to be from Aeschylus' lost play *Niobe*.

Absolutely.

Now, isn't there a kind of story whose content we haven't yet discussed? So far we've said how one should speak about gods, heroes, daemons, and things in Hades.

We have.

Then what's left is how to deal with stories about human beings, isn't it?

Obviously.

But we can't settle that matter at present.

Why not?

Because I think we'll say that what poets and prose-writers tell us about the most important matters concerning human beings is bad. They say that many unjust people are happy and many just ones wretched, that injustice is profitable if it escapes detection, and that justice is another's good but one's own loss. I think we'll prohibit these stories and order the poets to compose the opposite kind of poetry and tell the opposite kind of tales. Don't you think so?

I know so.

But if you agree that what I said is correct, couldn't I reply that you've agreed to the very point that is in question in our whole discussion?

And you'd be right to make that reply.

Then we'll agree about what stories should be told about human beings only when we've discovered what sort of thing justice is and how by nature it profits the one who has it, whether he is believed to be just or not.

That's very true.

This concludes our discussion of the content of stories. We should now, I think, investigate their style, for we'll then have fully investigated both what should be said and how it should be said.

I don't understand what you mean, Adeimantus responded.

But you must, I said. Maybe you'll understand it better if I put it this way. Isn't everything said by poets and storytellers a narrative about past, present, or future events?

What else could it be?

And aren't these narratives either narrative alone, or narrative through imitation, or both?

I need a clearer understanding of that as well.

I seem to be a ridiculously unclear teacher. So, like those who are incompetent at speaking, I won't try to deal with the matter as a whole, but I'll take up a part and use it as an example to make plain what I want to say. Tell me, do you know the beginning of the *Iliad*, where the poet tells us that Chryses begs Agamemnon to release his daughter, that Agamemnon harshly rejects him, and that, having failed, Chryses prays to the god against the Achaeans?

I do.

You know, then, that up to the lines:

> And he begged all the Achaeans
> But especially the two sons of Atreus, the commanders of the army,[25]

the poet himself is speaking and doesn't attempt to get us to think that the speaker is someone other than himself. After this, however, he speaks as if he were Chryses and tries as far as possible to make us think that the speaker isn't Homer but the priest himself—an old man. And he composes pretty well all the rest of his narrative about events in Troy, Ithaca, and the whole *Odyssey* in this way.

That's right.

Now, the speeches he makes and the parts between them are both narrative?

Of course.

But when he makes a speech as if he were someone else, won't we say that he makes his own style as much like that of the indicated speaker as possible?

We certainly will.

Now, to make oneself like someone else in voice or appearance is to imitate the person one makes oneself like.

Certainly.

In these passages, then, it seems that he and the other poets effect their narrative through imitation.

That's right.

If the poet never hid himself, the whole of his poem would be narrative without imitation. In order to prevent you from saying again that you don't understand, I'll show you what this would be like. If Homer said that Chryses came with a ransom for his daughter to supplicate the Achaeans, especially the kings, and after that didn't speak as if he had become Chryses, but still as Homer, there would be no imitation but rather simple narrative. It would have gone something like this—I'll speak without meter since I'm no poet: "And the priest came and prayed that the gods would allow them to capture Troy and be safe afterwards, that they'd accept the ransom and free his daughter, and thus show reverence for the god. When he'd said this, the others showed their respect for the priest and consented. But Agamemnon was angry and ordered him to leave and never to return, lest his priestly wand and the wreaths of the god should fail to protect him. He said that, before freeing the daughter, he'd grow old in Argos by her side. He told Chryses to go away and not to make him angry, if he wanted to get home safely. When the old man heard this, he was frightened and went off in silence. But when he'd left the camp he prayed at length to Apollo, calling him by his various titles and reminding him of his own services to him. If any of those services had been found pleasing, whether

---

25. *Iliad* i.15–16.

it was the building of temples or the sacrifice of victims, he asked in return that the arrows of the god should make the Achaeans pay for his tears."

b   That is the way we get simple narrative without imitation.

I understand.

Then also understand that the opposite occurs when one omits the words between the speeches and leaves the speeches by themselves.

I understand that too. Tragedies are like that.

c   That's absolutely right. And now I think that I can make clear to you what I couldn't before. One kind of poetry and story-telling employs only imitation—tragedy and comedy, as you say. Another kind employs only narration by the poet himself—you find this most of all in dithyrambs. A third kind uses both—as in epic poetry and many other places, if you follow me.

Now I understand what you were trying to say.

Remember, too, that before all that we said that we had dealt with *what* must be said in stories, but that we had yet to investigate *how* it must be said.

Yes, I remember.

d   Well, this, more precisely, is what I meant: We need to come to an agreement about whether we'll allow poets to narrate through imitation, and, if so, whether they are to imitate some things but not others—and what things these are, or whether they are not to imitate at all.

I divine that you're looking into the question of whether or not we'll allow tragedy and comedy into our city.

Perhaps, and perhaps even more than that, for I myself really don't know yet, but whatever direction the argument blows us, that's where we must go.

Fine.

Then, consider, Adeimantus, whether our guardians should be imitators

e   or not. Or does this also follow from our earlier statement that each individual would do a fine job of one occupation, not of many, and that if he tried the latter and dabbled in many things, he'd surely fail to achieve distinction in any of them?

He would indeed.

Then, doesn't the same argument also hold for imitation—a single individual can't imitate many things as well as he can imitate one?

No, he can't.

Then, he'll hardly be able to pursue any worthwhile way of life while

395 at the same time imitating many things and being an imitator. Even in the case of two kinds of imitation that are thought to be closely akin, such as tragedy and comedy, the same people aren't able to do both of them well. Did you not just say that these were both imitations?

I did, and you're quite right that the same people can't do both.

Nor can they be both rhapsodes and actors.

True.

Indeed, not even the same actors are used for tragedy and comedy. Yet

b   all these are imitations, aren't they?

They are.

And human nature, Adeimantus, seems to me to be minted in even smaller coins than these, so that it can neither imitate many things well nor do the actions themselves, of which those imitations are likenesses.

That's absolutely true.

Then, if we're to preserve our first argument, that our guardians must be kept away from all other crafts so as to be the craftsmen of the city's freedom, and be exclusively that, and do nothing at all except what contributes to it, they must neither do nor imitate anything else. If they do imitate, they must imitate from childhood what is appropriate for them, namely, people who are courageous, self-controlled, pious, and free, and their actions. They mustn't be clever at doing or imitating slavish or shameful actions, lest from enjoying the imitation, they come to enjoy the reality. Or haven't you noticed that imitations practiced from youth become part of nature and settle into habits of gesture, voice, and thought?

I have indeed.

Then we won't allow those for whom we profess to care, and who must grow into good men, to imitate either a young woman or an older one, or one abusing her husband, quarreling with the gods, or bragging because she thinks herself happy, or one suffering misfortune and possessed by sorrows and lamentations, and even less one who is ill, in love, or in labor.

That's absolutely right.

Nor must they imitate either male or female slaves doing slavish things.

No, they mustn't.

Nor bad men, it seems, who are cowards and are doing the opposite of what we described earlier, namely, libelling and ridiculing each other, using shameful language while drunk or sober, or wronging themselves and others, whether in word or deed, in the various other ways that are typical of such people. They mustn't become accustomed to making themselves like madmen in either word or deed, for, though they must know about mad and vicious men and women, they must neither do nor imitate anything they do.

That's absolutely true.

Should they imitate metal workers or other craftsmen, or those who row in triremes, or their time-keepers, or anything else connected with ships?

How could they, since they aren't to concern themselves with any of those occupations?

And what about this? Will they imitate neighing horses, bellowing bulls, roaring rivers, the crashing sea, thunder, or anything of that sort?

They are forbidden to be mad or to imitate mad people.

If I understand what you mean, there is one kind of style and narrative that someone who is really a gentleman would use whenever he wanted to narrate something, and another kind, unlike this one, which his opposite by nature and education would favor, and in which he would narrate.

Which styles are those?

Well, I think that when a moderate man comes upon the words or actions of a good man in his narrative, he'll be willing to report them as if he were that man himself, and he won't be ashamed of that kind of imitation. He'll imitate this good man most when he's acting in a faultless and

d   intelligent manner, but he'll do so less, and with more reluctance, when the good man is upset by disease, sexual passion, drunkenness, or some other misfortune. When he comes upon a character unworthy of himself, however, he'll be unwilling to make himself seriously resemble that inferior character—except perhaps for a brief period in which he's doing something good. Rather he'll be ashamed to do something like that, both because he's unpracticed in the imitation of such people and because he can't stand to shape and mold himself according to a worse pattern. He despises this

e   in his mind, unless it's just done in play.

That seems likely.

He'll therefore use the kind of narrative we described in dealing with the Homeric epics a moment ago. His style will participate both in imitation and in the other kind of narrative, but there'll be only a little bit of imitation in a long story? Or is there nothing in what I say?

That's precisely how the pattern for such a speaker must be.

397   As for someone who is not of this sort, the more inferior he is, the more willing he'll be to narrate anything and to consider nothing unworthy of himself. As a result, he'll undertake to imitate seriously and before a large audience all the things we just mentioned—thunder, the sounds of wind, hail, axles, pulleys, trumpets, flutes, pipes, and all the other instruments, even the cries of dogs, sheep, and birds. And this man's style will consist

b   entirely of imitation in voice and gesture, or else include only a small bit of plain narrative.

That too is certain.

These, then, are the two kinds of style I was talking about.

There are these two.

The first of these styles involves little variation, so that if someone provides a musical mode and rhythm appropriate to it, won't the one who speaks correctly remain—with a few minor changes—pretty well within

c   that mode and rhythm throughout?

That's precisely what he'll do.

What about the other kind of style? Doesn't it require the opposite if it is to speak appropriately, namely, all kinds of musical modes and all kinds of rhythms, because it contains every type of variation?

That's exactly right.

Do all poets and speakers adopt one or other of these patterns of style or a mixture of both?

Necessarily.

d   What are we to do, then? Shall we admit all these into our city, only one of the pure kinds, or the mixed one?

If my opinion is to prevail, we'll admit only the pure imitator of a decent person.

And yet, Adeimantus, the mixed style is pleasant. Indeed, it is by far the most pleasing to children, their tutors, and the vast majority of people.

Yes, it is the most pleasing.

But perhaps you don't think that it harmonizes with our constitution, because no one in our city is two or more people simultaneously, since each does only one job.

Indeed, it doesn't harmonize.

And isn't it because of this that it's only in our city that we'll find a cobbler who is a cobbler and not also a captain along with his cobbling, and a farmer who is a farmer and not also a juror along with his farming, and a soldier who is a soldier and not a money-maker in addition to his soldiering, and so with them all?

That's true.

It seems, then, that if a man, who through clever training can become anything and imitate anything, should arrive in our city, wanting to give a performance of his poems, we should bow down before him as someone holy, wonderful, and pleasing, but we should tell him that there is no one like him in our city and that it isn't lawful for there to be. We should pour myrrh on his head, crown him with wreaths, and send him away to another city. But, for our own good, we ourselves should employ a more austere and less pleasure-giving poet and storyteller, one who would imitate the speech of a decent person and who would tell his stories in accordance with the patterns we laid down when we first undertook the education of our soldiers.

That is certainly what we'd do if it were up to us.

It's likely, then, that we have now completed our discussion of the part of music and poetry that concerns speech and stories, for we've spoken both of what is to be said and of how it is to be said.

I agree.

Doesn't it remain, then, to discuss lyric odes and songs?

Clearly.

And couldn't anyone discover what we would say about them, given that it has to be in tune with what we've already said?

Glaucon laughed and said: I'm afraid, Socrates, that I'm not to be included under "anyone," for I don't have a good enough idea at the moment of what we're to say. Of course, I have my suspicions.

Nonetheless, I said, you know that, in the first place, a song consists of three elements—words, harmonic mode, and rhythm.

Yes, I do know that.

As far as words are concerned, they are no different in songs than they are when not set to music, so mustn't they conform in the same way to the patterns we established just now?

They must.

Further, the mode and rhythm must fit the words.

Of course.

And we said that we no longer needed dirges and lamentations among our words.

We did, indeed.

e   What are the lamenting modes, then? You tell me, since you're musical.

The mixo-Lydian, the syntono-Lydian, and some others of that sort.

Aren't they to be excluded, then? They're useless even to decent women, let alone to men.

Certainly.

Drunkenness, softness, and idleness are also most inappropriate for our guardians.

How could they not be?

What, then, are the soft modes suitable for drinking-parties?

The Ionian and those Lydian modes that are said to be relaxed.

399   Could you ever use these to make people warriors?

Never. And now all you have left is the Dorian and Phrygian modes.

I don't know all the musical modes. Just leave me the mode that would suitably imitate the tone and rhythm of a courageous person who is active in battle or doing other violent deeds, or who is failing

b   and facing wounds, death, or some other misfortune, and who, in all these circumstances, is fighting off his fate steadily and with self-control. Leave me also another mode, that of someone engaged in a peaceful, unforced, voluntary action, persuading someone or asking a favor of a god in prayer or of a human being through teaching and exhortation, or, on the other hand, of someone submitting to the supplications of another who is teaching him and trying to get him to change his mind, and who, in all these circumstances, is acting with moderation and self-control, not with arrogance but with understanding, and is content with

c   the outcome. Leave me, then, these two modes, which will best imitate the violent or voluntary tones of voice of those who are moderate and courageous, whether in good fortune or in bad.

The modes you're asking for are the very ones I mentioned.

Well, then, we'll have no need for polyharmonic or multistringed instruments to accompany our odes and songs.

It doesn't seem so to me at least.

Then we won't need the craftsmen who make triangular lutes, harps,

d   and all other such multistringed and polyharmonic instruments.

Apparently not.

What about flute-makers and flute-players? Will you allow them into the city? Or isn't the flute the most "many-stringed" of all? And aren't the panharmonic instruments all imitations of it?[26]

Clearly.

The lyre and the cithara are left, then, as useful in the city, while in the country, there'd be some sort of pipe for the shepherds to play.

That is what our argument shows, at least.

---

26. The instrument here is the *aulos*, which was not really a flute but a reed instrument. It was especially good at conveying emotion.

Well, we certainly aren't doing anything new in preferring Apollo and   e
his instruments to Marsyas and his.[27]

By god, it doesn't seem as though we are.

And, by the dog, without being aware of it, we've been purifying the
city we recently said was luxurious.

That's because we're being moderate.

Then let's purify the rest. The next topic after musical modes is the
regulation of meter. We shouldn't strive to have either subtlety or great
variety in meter. Rather, we should try to discover what are the rhythms
of someone who leads an ordered and courageous life and then adapt the
meter and the tune to his words, not his words to them. What these   400
rhythms actually are is for you to say, just as in the case of the modes.

I really don't know what to say. I can tell you from observation that
there are three basic kinds of metrical feet out of which the others are
constructed, just as there are four in the case of modes. But I can't tell you
which sort imitates which sort of life.

Then we'll consult with Damon as to which metrical feet are suited to   b
slavishness, insolence, madness, and the other vices and which are suited
to their opposites. I think I've heard him talking about an enoplion, which
is a composite metrical phrase (although I'm not clear on this), and also
about dactylic or heroic meter, which he arranged, I don't know how, to
be equal up and down in the interchange of long and short. I think he
called one foot an iambus, another a trochee, assigning a long and a short   c
to both of them. In the case of some of these, I think he approved or
disapproved of the tempo of the foot as much as of the rhythm itself, or
of some combination of the two—I can't tell you which. But, as I said,
we'll leave these things to Damon, since to mark off the different kinds
would require a long argument. Or do you think we should try it?

No, I certainly don't.

But you can discern, can't you, that grace and gracelessness follow good
and bad rhythm respectively?

Of course.

Further, if, as we said just now, rhythm and mode must conform to the   d
words and not vice versa, then good rhythm follows fine words and is
similar to them, while bad rhythm follows the opposite kind of words,
and the same for harmony and disharmony.

To be sure, these things must conform to the words.

What about the style and content of the words themselves? Don't they
conform to the character of the speaker's soul?

Of course.

And the rest conform to the words?

---

27. After Athena had invented the *aulos*, she discarded it because it distorted her features
to play it. It was picked up by the satyr Marsyas, who was foolish enough to challenge
Apollo (inventor of the lyre) to a musical contest. He was defeated, and Apollo flayed him
alive. Satyrs were bestial in their behavior and desires—especially their sexual desires.

Yes.

Then fine words, harmony, grace, and rhythm follow simplicity of char-
e acter—and I do not mean this in the sense in which we use "simplicity"
as a euphemism for "simple-mindedness"—but I mean the sort of fine and
good character that has developed in accordance with an intelligent plan.

That's absolutely certain.

And must not our young people everywhere aim at these, if they are
to do their own work?

They must, indeed.

Now, surely painting is full of these qualities, as are all the crafts similar
401 to it; weaving is full of them, and so are embroidery, architecture, and the
crafts that produce all the other furnishings. Our bodily nature is full of
them, as are the natures of all growing things, for in all of these there is
grace and gracelessness. And gracelessness, bad rhythm, and disharmony
are akin to bad words and bad character, while their opposites are akin
to and are imitations of the opposite, a moderate and good character.

Absolutely.

b Is it, then, only poets we have to supervise, compelling them to make
an image of a good character in their poems or else not to compose them
among us? Or are we also to give orders to other craftsmen, forbidding
them to represent—whether in pictures, buildings, or any other works—
a character that is vicious, unrestrained, slavish, and graceless? Are we to
allow someone who cannot follow these instructions to work among us,
c so that our guardians will be brought up on images of evil, as if in a
meadow of bad grass, where they crop and graze in many different places
every day until, little by little, they unwittingly accumulate a large evil in
their souls? Or must we rather seek out craftsmen who are by nature able
to pursue what is fine and graceful in their work, so that our young people
will live in a healthy place and be benefited on all sides, and so that
something of those fine works will strike their eyes and ears like a breeze
that brings health from a good place, leading them unwittingly, from
d childhood on, to resemblance, friendship, and harmony with the beauty
of reason?

The latter would be by far the best education for them.

Aren't these the reasons, Glaucon, that education in music and poetry
is most important? First, because rhythm and harmony permeate the inner
part of the soul more than anything else, affecting it most strongly and
bringing it grace, so that if someone is properly educated in music and
e poetry, it makes him graceful, but if not, then the opposite. Second, because
anyone who has been properly educated in music and poetry will sense
it acutely when something has been omitted from a thing and when it
hasn't been finely crafted or finely made by nature. And since he has the
right distastes, he'll praise fine things, be pleased by them, receive them
into his soul, and, being nurtured by them, become fine and good. He'll
402 rightly object to what is shameful, hating it while he's still young and
unable to grasp the reason, but, having been educated in this way, he will

welcome the reason when it comes and recognize it easily because of its kinship with himself.

Yes, I agree that those are the reasons to provide education in music and poetry.

It's just the way it was with learning how to read. Our ability wasn't adequate until we realized that there are only a few letters that occur in all sorts of different combinations, and that—whether written large or small[28]—they were worthy of our attention, so that we picked them out eagerly wherever they occurred, knowing that we wouldn't be competent readers until we knew our letters.

True.

And isn't it also true that if there are images of letters reflected in mirrors or water, we won't know them until we know the letters themselves, for both abilities are parts of the same craft and discipline?

Absolutely.

Then, by the gods, am I not right in saying that neither we, nor the guardians we are raising, will be educated in music and poetry until we know the different forms of moderation, courage, frankness, high-mindedness, and all their kindred, and their opposites too, which are moving around everywhere, and see them in the things in which they are, both themselves and their images, and do not disregard them, whether they are written on small things or large, but accept that the knowledge of both large and small letters is part of the same craft and discipline?

That's absolutely essential.

Therefore, if someone's soul has a fine and beautiful character and his body matches it in beauty and is thus in harmony with it, so that both share in the same pattern, wouldn't that be the most beautiful sight for anyone who has eyes to see?

It certainly would.

And isn't what is most beautiful also most loveable?

Of course.

And a musical person would love such people most of all, but he wouldn't love anyone who lacked harmony?

No, he wouldn't, at least not if the defect was in the soul, but if it was only in the body, he'd put up with it and be willing to embrace the boy who had it.

I gather that you love or have loved such a boy yourself, and I agree with you. Tell me this, however: Is excessive pleasure compatible with moderation?

How can it be, since it drives one mad just as much as pain does?

What about with the rest of virtue?

No.

Well, then, is it compatible with violence and licentiousness?

Very much so.

b

c

d

e

403

---

28. See 368c–d.

Can you think of a greater or keener pleasure than sexual pleasure?

I can't—or a madder one either.

But the right kind of love is by nature the love of order and beauty that has been moderated by education in music and poetry?

That's right.

Therefore, the right kind of love has nothing mad or licentious about it?

No, it hasn't.

Then sexual pleasure mustn't come into it, and the lover and the boy
b   he loves must have no share in it, if they are to love and be loved in the right way?

By god, no, Socrates, it mustn't come into it.

It seems, then, that you'll lay it down as a law in the city we're establish-ing that if a lover can persuade a boy to let him, then he may kiss him, be with him, and touch him, as a father would a son, for the sake of what is fine and beautiful, but—turning to the other things—his association
c   with the one he cares about must never seem to go any further than this, otherwise he will be reproached as untrained in music and poetry and lacking in appreciation for what is fine and beautiful.

That's right.

Does it seem to you that we've now completed our account of education in music and poetry? Anyway, it has ended where it ought to end, for it ought to end in the love of the fine and beautiful.

I agree.

After music and poetry, our young people must be given physical training.

Of course.

In this, too, they must have careful education from childhood throughout
d   life. The matter stands, I believe, something like this—but you, too, should look into it. It seems to me that a fit body doesn't by its own virtue make the soul good, but instead that the opposite is true—a good soul by its own virtue makes the body as good as possible. How does it seem to you?

The same.

Then, if we have devoted sufficient care to the mind, wouldn't we be right, in order to avoid having to do too much talking, to entrust it with the detailed supervision of the body, while we indicate only the general
e   patterns to be followed?

Certainly.

We said that our prospective guardians must avoid drunkenness, for it is less appropriate for a guardian to be drunk and not to know where on earth he is than it is for anyone else.

It would be absurd for a guardian to need a guardian.

What about food? Aren't these men athletes in the greatest contest?

They are.
404   Then would the regimen currently prescribed for athletes in training be suitable for them?

Perhaps it would.

Yet it seems to result in sluggishness and to be of doubtful value for health. Or haven't you noticed that these athletes sleep their lives away and that, if they deviate even a little from their orderly regimen, they become seriously and violently ill?

I have noticed that.

Then our warrior athletes need a more sophisticated kind of training. They must be like sleepless hounds, able to see and hear as keenly as possible and to endure frequent changes of water and food, as well as summer and winter weather on their campaigns, without faltering in   b health.

That's how it seems to me, too.

Now, isn't the best physical training akin to the simple music and poetry we were describing a moment ago?

How do you mean?

I mean a simple and decent physical training, particularly the kind involved in training for war.

What would it be like?

You might learn about such things from Homer. You know that, when his heroes are campaigning, he doesn't give them fish to banquet on, even though they are by the sea in the Hellespont, nor boiled meat either. Instead, he gives them only roasted meat, which is the kind most easily   c available to soldiers, for it's easier nearly everywhere to use fire alone than to carry pots and pans.

That's right.

Nor, I believe, does Homer mention sweet desserts anywhere. Indeed, aren't even the other athletes aware that, if one's body is to be sound, one must keep away from all such things?

They're right to be aware of it, at any rate, and to avoid such things.

If you think that, then it seems that you don't approve of Syracusan   d cuisine or of Sicilian-style dishes.

I do not.

Then you also object to Corinthian girlfriends for men who are to be in good physical condition.

Absolutely.

What about the reputed delights of Attic pastries?

I certainly object to them, too.

I believe that we'd be right to compare this diet and this entire life-style to the kinds of lyric odes and songs that are composed in all sorts of modes and rhythms.   e

Certainly.

Just as embellishment in the one gives rise to licentiousness, doesn't it give rise to illness in the other? But simplicity in music and poetry makes for moderation in the soul, and in physical training it makes for bodily health?

That's absolutely true.

And as licentiousness and disease breed in the city, aren't many law
405   courts and hospitals opened? And don't medicine and law give themselves
solemn airs when even large numbers of free men take them very seriously?

How could it be otherwise?

Yet could you find a greater sign of bad and shameful education in a
city than that the need for skilled doctors and lawyers is felt not only by
inferior people and craftsmen but by those who claim to have been brought
up in the manner of free men? Don't you think it's shameful and a great
b   sign of vulgarity to be forced to make use of a justice imposed by others,
as masters and judges, because you are unable to deal with the situation yourself?

I think that's the most shameful thing of all.

Yet isn't it even more shameful when someone not only spends a good
part of his life in court defending himself or prosecuting someone else
but, through inexperience of what is fine, is persuaded to take pride in
c   being clever at doing injustice and then exploiting every loophole and
trick to escape conviction—and all for the sake of little worthless things
and because he's ignorant of how much better and finer it is to arrange
one's own life so as to have no need of finding a sleepy or inattentive judge?

This case is even more shameful than the other.

And doesn't it seem shameful to you to need medical help, not for
wounds or because of some seasonal illness, but because, through idleness
d   and the life-style we've described, one is full of gas and phlegm like a
stagnant swamp, so that sophisticated Asclepiad doctors are forced to come
up with names like "flatulence" and "catarrh" to describe one's diseases?

It does. And those certainly are strange new names for diseases.

Indeed, I don't suppose that they even existed in the time of Asclepius
himself. I take it as a proof of this that his sons at Troy didn't criticize
e   either the woman who treated Eurypylus when he was wounded, or
Patroclus who prescribed the treatment, which consisted of Pramnian wine
with barley meal and grated cheese sprinkled on it, though such treatment
406   is now thought to cause inflammation.[29]

Yet it's a strange drink to give someone in that condition.

Not if you recall that they say that the kind of modern medicine that
plays nursemaid to the disease wasn't used by the Asclepiads before Herodicus. He was a physical trainer who became ill, so he mixed physical
training with medicine and wore out first himself and then many others
b   as well.

How did he do that?

By making his dying a lengthy process. Always tending his mortal
illness, he was nonetheless, it seems, unable to cure it, so he lived out his
life under medical treatment, with no leisure for anything else whatever.
If he departed even a little from his accustomed regimen, he became

29. See *Iliad* xi.580 ff., 828–36, and 624–50.

completely worn out, but because his skill made dying difficult, he lived into old age.

That's a fine prize for his skill.

One that's appropriate for someone who didn't know that it wasn't   c
because he was ignorant or inexperienced that Asclepius failed to teach this type of medicine to his sons, but because he knew that everyone in a well-regulated city has his own work to do and that no one has the leisure to be ill and under treatment all his life. It's absurd that we recognize this to be true of craftsmen while failing to recognize that it's equally true of those who are wealthy and supposedly happy.

How is that?

When a carpenter is ill, he expects to receive an emetic or a purge from   d
his doctor or to get rid of his disease through surgery or cautery. If anyone prescribed a lengthy regimen to him, telling him that he should rest with his head bandaged and so on, he'd soon reply that he had no leisure to be ill and that life is no use to him if he has to neglect his work and always be concerned with his illness. After that he'd bid good-bye to his doctor,   e
resume his usual way of life, and either recover his health or, if his body couldn't withstand the illness, he'd die and escape his troubles.

It is believed to be appropriate for someone like that to use medicine in this way.

Is that because his life is of no profit to him if he doesn't do his work?   407
Obviously.

But the rich person, we say, has no work that would make his life unlivable if he couldn't do it.

That's what people say, at least.

That's because you haven't heard the saying of Phocylides that, once you have the means of life, you must practice virtue.[30]

I think he must also practice virtue before that.

We won't quarrel with Phocylides about this. But let's try to find out whether the rich person must indeed practice virtue and whether his life is not worth living if he doesn't or whether tending an illness, while it is an obstacle to applying oneself to carpentry and the other crafts, is no   b
obstacle whatever to taking Phocylides' advice.

But excessive care of the body, over and above physical training, is pretty well the biggest obstacle of all. It's troublesome in managing a household, in military service, and even in a sedentary public office.

Yet the most important of all, surely, is that it makes any kind of learning,   c
thought, or private meditation difficult, for it's always imagining some headaches or dizziness and accusing philosophy of causing them. Hence, wherever this kind of virtue is practiced and examined, excessive care of the body hinders it, for it makes a person think he's ill and be all the time concerned about his body.

30. Phocylides of Miletus was a mid-sixth-century elegiac and hexameter poet best known for his epigrams.

It probably does.

Therefore, won't we say that Asclepius knew this, and that he taught medicine for those whose bodies are healthy in their natures and habits but have some specific disease? His medicine is for these people with these habits. He cured them of their disease with drugs or surgery and then ordered them to live their usual life so as not to harm their city's affairs. But for those whose bodies were riddled with disease, he didn't attempt to prescribe a regimen, drawing off a little here and pouring in a little there, in order to make their life a prolonged misery and enable them to produce offspring in all probability like themselves. He didn't think that he should treat someone who couldn't live a normal life, since such a person would be of no profit either to himself or to the city.

The Asclepius you're talking about was quite a statesman.

Clearly. And don't you see that because he was a statesman his sons turned out to be good men at Troy, practicing medicine as I say they did? Don't you remember that they "sucked out the blood and applied gentle potions" to the wound Pandarus inflicted on Menelaus, but without prescribing what he should eat or drink after that, any more than they did for Eurypylus?[31] They considered their drugs to be sufficient to cure men who were healthy and living an orderly life before being wounded, even if they happened to drink wine mixed with barley and cheese right after receiving their wounds. But they didn't consider the lives of those who were by nature sick and licentious to be profitable either to themselves or to anyone else. Medicine isn't intended for such people and they shouldn't be treated, not even if they're richer than Midas.

The sons of Asclepius you're talking about were indeed very sophisticated.

Appropriately so. But Pindar and the tragedians don't agree with us.[32] They say that Asclepius was the son of Apollo, that he was bribed with gold to heal a rich man, who was already dying, and that he was killed by lightning for doing so. But, in view of what we said before, we won't believe this. We'll say that if Asclepius was the son of a god, he was not a money-grubber, and that if he was a money-grubber, he was not the son of a god.

That's right. But what do you say about the following, Socrates? Don't we need to have good doctors in our city? And the best will surely be those who have handled the greatest number of sick and of healthy people. In the same way, the best judges will be those who have associated with people whose natures are of every kind.

I agree that the doctors and judges must be good. But do you know the kind I consider to be so?

If you'll tell me.

---

31. *Iliad* iv.218–19.

32. Cf. Aeschylus *Agamemnon* 1022 ff., Euripides *Alcestis* 3, Pindar *Pythians* 3.55–58.

I'll try. But you ask about things that aren't alike in the same question. In what way?

The cleverest doctors are those who, in addition to learning their craft, have had contact with the greatest number of very sick bodies from childhood on, have themselves experienced every illness, and aren't very healthy by nature, for they don't treat bodies with their bodies, I suppose—if they did, we wouldn't allow their bodies to be or become bad. Rather they treat the body with their souls, and it isn't possible for the soul to treat anything well, if it is or has been bad itself.

That's right.

As for the judge, he *does* rule other souls with his own soul. And it isn't possible for a soul to be nurtured among vicious souls from childhood, to associate with them, to indulge in every kind of injustice, and come through it able to judge other people's injustices from its own case, as it can diseases of the body. Rather, if it's to be fine and good, and a sound judge of just things, it must itself remain pure and have no experience of bad character while it's young. That's the reason, indeed, that decent people appear simple and easily deceived by unjust ones when they are young. It's because they have no models in themselves of the evil experiences of the vicious to guide their judgments.

That's certainly so.

Therefore, a good judge must not be a young person but an old one, who has learned late in life what injustice is like and who has become aware of it not as something at home in his own soul, but as something alien and present in others, someone who, after a long time, has recognized that injustice is bad by nature, not from his own experience of it, but through knowledge.

Such a judge would be the most noble one of all.

And he'd be good, too, which was what you asked, for someone who has a good soul is good. The clever and suspicious person, on the other hand, who has committed many injustices himself and thinks himself a wise villain, appears clever in the company of those like himself, because he's on his guard and is guided by the models within himself. But when he meets with good older people, he's seen to be stupid, distrustful at the wrong time, and ignorant of what a sound character is, since he has no model of this within himself. But since he meets vicious people more often than good ones, he seems to be clever rather than unlearned, both to himself and to others.

That's completely true.

Then we mustn't look for the good judge among people like that but among the sort we described earlier. A vicious person would never know either himself or a virtuous one, whereas a naturally virtuous person, when educated, will in time acquire knowledge of both virtue and vice. And it is someone like that who becomes wise, in my view, and not the bad person.

I agree with you.

Then won't you legislate in our city for the kind of medicine we mentioned and for this kind of judging, so that together they'll look after those
410   who are naturally well endowed in body and soul? But as for the ones
whose bodies are naturally unhealthy or whose souls are incurably evil,
won't they let the former die of their own accord and put the latter to death?

That seems to be best both for the ones who suffer such treatment and
for the city.

However, *our* young people, since they practice that simple sort of music
and poetry that we said produces moderation, will plainly be wary of
coming to need a judge.

That's right.

And won't a person who's educated in music and poetry pursue physical
b   training in the same way, and choose to make no use of medicine except
when unavoidable?

I believe so.

He'll work at physical exercises in order to arouse the spirited part of
his nature, rather than to acquire the physical strength for which other
athletes diet and labor.

That's absolutely right.

Then, Glaucon, did those who established education in music and poetry
c   and in physical training do so with the aim that people attribute to them,
which is to take care of the body with the latter and the soul with the
former, or with some other aim?

What other aim do you mean?

It looks as though they established both chiefly for the sake of the soul.

How so?

Haven't you noticed the effect that lifelong physical training, unaccompanied by any training in music and poetry, has on the mind, or the effect
of the opposite, music and poetry without physical training?

What effects are you talking about?

d   Savagery and toughness in the one case and softness and overcultivation
in the other.

I get the point. You mean that those who devote themselves exclusively
to physical training turn out to be more savage than they should, while
those who devote themselves to music and poetry turn out to be softer
than is good for them?

Moreover, the source of the savageness is the spirited part of one's
nature. Rightly nurtured, it becomes courageous, but if it's overstrained,
it's likely to become hard and harsh.

So it seems.

And isn't it the philosophic part of one's nature that provides the cultiva-
e   tion? If it is relaxed too far, it becomes softer than it should, but if properly
nurtured, it is cultivated and orderly.

So it is.

Now, we say that our guardians must have both these natures.

They must indeed.

And mustn't the two be harmonized with each other?

Of course.

And if this harmony is achieved, the soul is both moderate and coura-
geous?   411

Certainly.

But if it is inharmonious, it is cowardly and savage?

Yes, indeed.

Therefore, when someone gives music an opportunity to charm his
soul with the flute and to pour those sweet, soft, and plaintive tunes we
mentioned through his ear, as through a funnel, when he spends his whole
life humming them and delighting in them, then, at first, whatever spirit
he has is softened, just as iron is tempered, and from being hard and
useless, it is made useful. But if he keeps at it unrelentingly and is beguiled
by the music, after a time his spirit is melted and dissolved until it vanishes,   b
and the very sinews of his soul are cut out and he becomes "a feeble
warrior."[33]

That's right.

And if he had a spiritless nature from the first, this process is soon
completed. But if he had a spirited nature, his spirit becomes weak and
unstable, flaring up at trifles and extinguished as easily. The result is
that such people become quick-tempered, prone to anger, and filled with
discontent, rather than spirited.   c

That's certainly true.

What about someone who works hard at physical training and eats well
but never touches music or philosophy? Isn't he in good physical condition
at first, full of resolution and spirit? And doesn't he become more courageous than he was before?

Certainly.

But what happens if he does nothing else and never associates with the   d
Muse? Doesn't whatever love of learning he might have had in his soul soon
become enfeebled, deaf, and blind, because he never tastes any learning or
investigation or partakes of any discussion or any of the rest of music and
poetry, to nurture or arouse it?

It does seem to be that way.

I believe that someone like that becomes a hater of reason and of music.
He no longer makes any use of persuasion but bulls his way through every
situation by force and savagery like a wild animal, living in ignorance and
stupidity without either rhythm or grace.   e

That's most certainly how he'll live.

It seems, then, that a god has given music and physical training to
human beings not, except incidentally, for the body and the soul but for
the spirited and wisdom-loving parts of the soul itself, in order that these
might be in harmony with one another, each being stretched and relaxed
to the appropriate degree.   412

33. *Iliad* xvii.588.

It seems so.

Then the person who achieves the finest blend of music and physical training and impresses it on his soul in the most measured way is the one we'd most correctly call completely harmonious and trained in music, much more so than the one who merely harmonizes the strings of his instrument.

That's certainly so, Socrates.

Then, won't we always need this sort of person as an overseer in our city, Glaucon, if indeed its constitution is to be preserved?

b   It seems that we'll need someone like that most of all.

These, then, are the patterns for education and upbringing. Should we enumerate the dances of these people, or their hunts, chases with hounds, athletic contests, and horse races? Surely, they're no longer hard to discover, since it's pretty clear that they must follow the patterns we've already established.

Perhaps so.

All right, then what's the next thing we have to determine? Isn't it which of these same people will rule and which be ruled?

c   Of course.

Now, isn't it obvious that the rulers must be older and the ruled younger?

Yes, it is.

And mustn't the rulers also be the best of them?

That, too.

And aren't the best farmers the ones who are best at farming?

Yes.

Then, as the rulers must be the best of the guardians, mustn't they be the ones who are best at guarding the city?

Yes.

Then, in the first place, mustn't they be knowledgeable and capable, and mustn't they care for the city?

d   That's right.

Now, one cares most for what one loves.

Necessarily.

And someone loves something most of all when he believes that the same things are advantageous to it as to himself and supposes that if it does well, he'll do well, and that if it does badly, then he'll do badly too.

That's right.

Then we must choose from among our guardians those men who, upon examination, seem most of all to believe throughout their lives that they

e   must eagerly pursue what is advantageous to the city and be wholly unwilling to do the opposite.

Such people would be suitable for the job at any rate.

I think we must observe them at all ages to see whether they are guardians of this conviction and make sure that neither compulsion nor magic spells will get them to discard or forget their belief that they must do what is best for the city.

What do you mean by discarding?

I'll tell you. I think the discarding of a belief is either voluntary or involuntary—voluntary when one learns that the belief is false, involuntary in the case of all true beliefs.   413

I understand voluntary discarding but not involuntary.

What's that? Don't you know that people are voluntarily deprived of bad things, but involuntarily deprived of good ones? And isn't being deceived about the truth a bad thing, while possessing the truth is good? Or don't you think that to believe the things that are is to possess the truth?

That's right, and I do think that people are involuntarily deprived of true opinions.

But can't they also be so deprived by theft, magic spells, and compulsion?   b

Now, I don't understand again.

I'm afraid I must be talking like a tragic poet! By "the victims of theft" I mean those who are persuaded to change their minds or those who forget, because time, in the latter case, and argument, in the former, takes away their opinions without their realizing it. Do you understand now?

Yes.

By "the compelled" I mean those whom pain or suffering causes to change their mind.

I understand that, and you're right.

The "victims of magic," I think you'd agree, are those who change their mind because they are under the spell of pleasure or fear.   c

It seems to me that everything that deceives does so by casting a spell.

Then, as I said just now, we must find out who are the best guardians of their conviction that they must always do what they believe to be best for the city. We must keep them under observation from childhood and set them tasks that are most likely to make them forget such a conviction or be deceived out of it, and we must select whoever keeps on remembering   d
it and isn't easily deceived, and reject the others. Do you agree?

Yes.

And we must subject them to labors, pains, and contests in which we can watch for these traits.

That's right.

Then we must also set up a competition for the third way in which people are deprived of their convictions, namely, magic. Like those who lead colts into noise and tumult to see if they're afraid, we must expose our young people to fears and pleasures, testing them more thoroughly than gold is tested by fire. If someone is hard to put under a spell, is   e
apparently gracious in everything, is a good guardian of himself and the music and poetry he has learned, and if he always shows himself to be rhythmical and harmonious, then he is the best person both for himself and for the city. Anyone who is tested in this way as a child, youth, and adult, and always comes out of it untainted, is to be made a ruler as well   414
as a guardian; he is to be honored in life and to receive after his death the most prized tombs and memorials. But anyone who fails to prove himself

in this way is to be rejected. It seems to me, Glaucon, that rulers and guardians must be selected and appointed in some such way as this, though we've provided only a general pattern and not the exact details.

It also seems to me that they must be selected in this sort of way.

b   Then, isn't it truly most correct to call these people complete guardians, since they will guard against external enemies and internal friends, so that the one will lack the power and the other the desire to harm the city? The young people we've hitherto called guardians we'll now call *auxiliaries* and supporters of the guardians' convictions.

I agree.

How, then, could we devise one of those useful falsehoods we were talking about a while ago,[34] one noble falsehood that would, in the best case, persuade even the rulers, but if that's not possible, then the others in the city?

What sort of falsehood?

Nothing new, but a Phoenician story which describes something that has happened in many places. At least, that's what the poets say, and they've persuaded many people to believe it too. It hasn't happened among us, and I don't even know if it could. It would certainly take a lot of persuasion to get people to believe it.

You seem hesitant to tell the story.

When you hear it, you'll realize that I have every reason to hesitate.

Speak, and don't be afraid.

d   I'll tell it, then, though I don't know where I'll get the audacity or even what words I'll use. I'll first try to persuade the rulers and the soldiers and then the rest of the city that the upbringing and the education we gave them, and the experiences that went with them, were a sort of dream, that in fact they themselves, their weapons, and the other craftsmen's tools

e   were at that time really being fashioned and nurtured inside the earth, and that when the work was completed, the earth, who is their mother, delivered all of them up into the world. Therefore, if anyone attacks the land in which they live, they must plan on its behalf and defend it as their mother and nurse and think of the other citizens as their earthborn brothers.

It isn't for nothing that you were so shy about telling your falsehood.

415   Appropriately so. Nevertheless, listen to the rest of the story. "All of you in the city are brothers," we'll say to them in telling our story, "but the god who made you mixed some gold into those who are adequately equipped to rule, because they are most valuable. He put silver in those who are auxiliaries and iron and bronze in the farmers and other craftsmen. For the most part you will produce children like yourselves, but, because

b   you are all related, a silver child will occasionally be born from a golden parent, and vice versa, and all the others from each other. So the first and most important command from the god to the rulers is that there is nothing that they must guard better or watch more carefully than the mixture of

34. See 382a ff.

metals in the souls of the next generation. If an offspring of theirs should be found to have a mixture of iron or bronze, they must not pity him in any way, but give him the rank appropriate to his nature and drive him out to join the craftsmen and farmers. But if an offspring of these people is found to have a mixture of gold or silver, they will honor him and take him up to join the guardians or the auxiliaries, for there is an oracle which says that the city will be ruined if it ever has an iron or a bronze guardian." So, do you have any device that will make our citizens believe this story?

I can't see any way to make them believe it themselves, but perhaps there is one in the case of their sons and later generations and all the other people who come after them.

I understand pretty much what you mean, but even that would help to make them care more for the city and each other. However, let's leave this matter wherever tradition takes it. And let's now arm our earthborn and lead them forth with their rulers in charge. And as they march, let them look for the best place in the city to have their camp, a site from which they can most easily control those within, if anyone is unwilling to obey the laws, or repel any outside enemy who comes like a wolf upon the flock. And when they have established their camp and made the requisite sacrifices, they must see to their sleeping quarters. What do you say?

I agree.

And won't these quarters protect them adequately both in winter and summer?

Of course, for it seems to me that you mean their housing.

Yes, but housing for soldiers, not for money-makers.

How do you mean to distinguish these from one another?

I'll try to tell you. The most terrible and most shameful thing of all is for a shepherd to rear dogs as auxiliaries to help him with his flocks in such a way that, through licentiousness, hunger, or some other bad trait of character, they do evil to the sheep and become like wolves instead of dogs.

That's certainly a terrible thing.

Isn't it necessary, therefore, to guard in every way against our auxiliaries doing anything like that to the citizens because they are stronger, thereby becoming savage masters instead of kindly allies?

It is necessary.

And wouldn't a really good education endow them with the greatest caution in this regard?

But surely they have had an education like that.

Perhaps we shouldn't assert this dogmatically, Glaucon. What we can assert is what we were saying just now, that they must have the right education, whatever it is, if they are to have what will most make them gentle to each other and to those they are guarding.

That's right.

Now, someone with some understanding might say that, besides this education, they must also have the kind of housing and other property

that will neither prevent them from being the best guardians nor encourage
d   them to do evil to the other citizens.

That's true.

Consider, then, whether or not they should live in some such way as
this, if they're to be the kind of men we described. First, none of them
should possess any private property beyond what is wholly necessary.
Second, none of them should have a house or storeroom that isn't open for
all to enter at will. Third, whatever sustenance moderate and courageous
e   warrior-athletes require in order to have neither shortfall nor surplus in
a given year they'll receive by taxation on the other citizens as a salary
for their guardianship. Fourth, they'll have common messes and live together like soldiers in a camp. We'll tell them that they always have gold
and silver of a divine sort in their souls as a gift from the gods and so
have no further need of human gold. Indeed, we'll tell them that it's
impious for them to defile this divine possession by any admixture of
such gold, because many impious deeds have been done that involve the
417 currency used by ordinary people, while their own is pure. Hence, for
them alone among the city's population, it is unlawful to touch or handle
gold or silver. They mustn't be under the same roof as it, wear it as jewelry,
or drink from gold or silver goblets. In this way they'd save both themselves
and the city. But if they acquire private land, houses, and currency themselves, they'll be household managers and farmers instead of guardians—
b   hostile masters of the other citizens instead of their allies. They'll spend
their whole lives hating and being hated, plotting and being plotted against,
more afraid of internal than of external enemies, and they'll hasten both
themselves and the whole city to almost immediate ruin. For all these
reasons, let's say that the guardians must be provided with housing and
the rest in this way, and establish this as a law. Or don't you agree?

I certainly do, Glaucon said.

Book IV

419 And Adeimantus interrupted: How would you defend yourself, Socrates,
he said, if someone told you that you aren't making these men very happy
and that it's their own fault? The city really belongs to them, yet they
derive no good from it. Others own land, build fine big houses, acquire
furnishings to go along with them, make their own private sacrifices to
the gods, entertain guests, and also, of course, possess what you were
talking about just now, gold and silver and all the things that are thought
to belong to people who are blessedly happy. But one might well say that
your guardians are simply settled in the city like mercenaries and that all
420 they do is watch over it.

Yes, I said, and what's more, they work simply for their keep and get
no extra wages as the others do. Hence, if they want to take a private trip
away from the city, they won't be able to; they'll have nothing to give to

their mistresses, nothing to spend in whatever other ways they wish, as people do who are considered happy. You've omitted these and a host of other, similar facts from your charge.

Well, let them be added to the charge as well.

Then, are you asking how we should defend ourselves?   b

Yes.

I think we'll discover what to say if we follow the same path as before. We'll say that it wouldn't be surprising if these people were happiest just as they are, but that, in establishing our city, we aren't aiming to make any one group outstandingly happy but to make the whole city so, as far as possible. We thought that we'd find justice most easily in such a city and injustice, by contrast, in the one that is governed worst and that, by observing both cities, we'd be able to judge the question we've been inquiring into for so long. We take ourselves, then, to be fashioning the happy   c
city, not picking out a few happy people and putting them in it, but making the whole city happy. (We'll look at the opposite city soon.[1])

Suppose, then, that someone came up to us while we were painting a statue and objected that, because we had painted the eyes (which are the most beautiful part) black rather than purple, we had not applied the most beautiful colors to the most beautiful parts of the statue. We'd think it reasonable to offer the following defense: "You mustn't expect us to paint the eyes so beautifully that they no longer appear to be eyes at all, and   d
the same with the other parts. Rather you must look to see whether by dealing with each part appropriately, we are making the whole statue beautiful." Similarly, you mustn't force us to give our guardians the kind of happiness that would make them something other than guardians. We know how to clothe the farmers in purple robes, festoon them with gold   e
jewelry, and tell them to work the land whenever they please. We know how to settle our potters on couches by the fire, feasting and passing the wine around, with their wheel beside them for whenever they want to make pots. And we can make all the others happy in the same way, so that the whole city is happy. Don't urge us to do this, however, for if we do, a farmer wouldn't be a farmer, nor a potter a potter, and none of the   421
others would keep to the patterns of work that give rise to a city. Now, if cobblers become inferior and corrupt and claim to be what they are not, that won't do much harm to the city. Hence, as far as they and the others like them are concerned, our argument carries less weight. But if the guardians of our laws and city are merely believed to be guardians but are not, you surely see that they'll destroy the city utterly, just as they alone have the opportunity to govern it well and make it happy.

If we are making true guardians, then, who are least likely to do evil to the city, and if the one who brought the charge is talking about farmers and banqueters who are happy as they would be at a festival rather than   b
in a city, then he isn't talking about a city at all, but about something else.

---

1. This discussion is announced at 445c, but doesn't begin until Book VIII.

With this in mind, we should consider whether in setting up our guardians we are aiming to give them the greatest happiness, or whether—since our aim is to see that the city as a whole has the greatest happiness—we must compel and persuade the auxiliaries and guardians to follow our other
c policy and be the best possible craftsmen at their own work, and the same with all the others. In this way, with the whole city developing and being governed well, we must leave it to nature to provide each group with its share of happiness.

I think you put that very well, he said.

Will you also think that I'm putting things well when I make the next point, which is closely akin to this one?

Which one exactly?

Consider whether or not the following things corrupt the other workers,
d so that they become bad.

What things?

Wealth and poverty.

How do they corrupt the other workers?

Like this. Do you think that a potter who has become wealthy will still be willing to pay attention to his craft?

Not at all.

Won't he become more idle and careless than he was?

Much more.

Then won't he become a worse potter?

Far worse.

And surely if poverty prevents him from having tools or any of the other things he needs for his craft, he'll produce poorer work and will
e teach his sons, or anyone else he teaches, to be worse craftsmen.

Of course.

So poverty and wealth make a craftsman and his products worse.

Apparently.

It seems, then, that we've found other things that our guardians must guard against in every way, to prevent them from slipping into the city unnoticed.

What are they?

422 Both wealth and poverty. The former makes for luxury, idleness, and revolution; the latter for slavishness, bad work, and revolution as well.

That's certainly true. But consider this, Socrates: If our city hasn't got any money, how will it be able to fight a war, especially if it has to fight against a great and wealthy city?

b Obviously, it will be harder to fight one such city and easier to fight two.

How do you mean?

First of all, if our city has to fight a city of the sort you mention, won't it be a case of warrior-athletes fighting against rich men?

Yes, as far as that goes.

Well, then, Adeimantus, don't you think that one boxer who has had the best possible training could easily fight two rich and fat nonboxers?

Maybe not at the same time.

Not even by escaping from them and then turning and hitting the one who caught up with him first, and doing this repeatedly in stifling heat and sun? Wouldn't he, in his condition, be able to handle even more than two such people?

That certainly wouldn't be surprising.

And don't you think that the rich have more knowledge and experience of boxing than of how to fight a war?

I do.

Then in all likelihood our athletes will easily be able to fight twice or three times their own numbers in a war.

I agree, for I think what you say is right.

What if they sent envoys to another city and told them the following truth: "We have no use for gold or silver, and it isn't lawful for us to possess them, so join us in this war, and you can take the property of those who oppose us for yourselves." Do you think that anyone hearing this would choose to fight hard, lean dogs, rather than to join them in fighting fat and tender sheep?

No, I don't. But if the wealth of all the cities came to be gathered in a single one, watch out that it doesn't endanger your nonwealthy city.

You're happily innocent if you think that anything other than the kind of city we are founding deserves to be called *a city*.

What do you mean?

We'll have to find a greater title for the others because each of them is a great many cities, not *a* city, as they say in the game. At any rate, each of them consists of two cities at war with one another, that of the poor and that of the rich, and each of these contains a great many. If you approach them as one city, you'll be making a big mistake. But if you approach them as many and offer to give to the one city the money, power, and indeed the very inhabitants of the other, you'll always find many allies and few enemies. And as long as your own city is moderately governed in the way that we've just arranged, it will, even if it has only a thousand men to fight for it, be the greatest. Not in reputation; I don't mean that, but the greatest in fact. Indeed, you won't find a city as great as this one among either Greeks or barbarians, although many that are many times its size may seem to be as great. Do you disagree?

No, I certainly don't.

Then this would also be the best limit for our guardians to put on the size of the city. And they should mark off enough land for a city that size and let the rest go.

What limit is that?

I suppose the following one. As long as it is willing to remain *one* city, it may continue to grow, but it cannot grow beyond that point.

That is a good limit.

Then, we'll give our guardians this further order, namely, to guard in every way against the city's being either small or great in reputation instead of being sufficient in size and one in number.

At any rate, that order will be fairly easy for them to follow.

And the one we mentioned earlier is even easier, when we said that, if an offspring of the guardians is inferior, he must be sent off to join the other citizens and that, if the others have an able offspring, he must join
d   the guardians. This was meant to make clear that each of the other citizens is to be directed to what he is naturally suited for, so that, doing the one work that is his own, he will become not many but one, and the whole city will itself be naturally one not many.

That *is* easier than the other.

These orders we give them, Adeimantus, are neither as numerous nor as important as one might think. Indeed, they are all insignificant, provided, as the saying goes, that they guard the one great thing, though I'd rather
e   call it sufficient than great.

What's that?

Their education and upbringing, for if by being well educated they become reasonable men, they will easily see these things for themselves, as well as all the other things we are omitting, for example, that marriage, the having of wives, and the procreation of children must be governed as
424 far as possible by the old proverb: Friends possess everything in common.

That would be best.

And surely, once our city gets a good start, it will go on growing in a cycle. Good education and upbringing, when they are preserved, produce good natures, and useful natures, who are in turn well educated, grow up even better than their predecessors, both in their offspring and in other
b   respects, just like other animals.

That's likely.

To put it briefly, those in charge must cling to education and see that it isn't corrupted without their noticing it, guarding it against everything. Above all, they must guard as carefully as they can against any innovation in music and poetry or in physical training that is counter to the established order. And they should dread to hear anyone say:

> People care most for the song
> That is newest from the singer's lips.[2]

Someone might praise such a saying, thinking that the poet meant not
c   new songs but new ways of singing. Such a thing shouldn't be praised, and the poet shouldn't be taken to have meant it, for the guardians must beware of changing to a new form of music, since it threatens the whole system. As Damon says, and I am convinced, the musical modes are never changed without change in the most important of a city's laws.

You can count me among the convinced as well, Adeimantus said.

2. *Odyssey* i.351–52, slightly altered.

Then it seems, I said, that it is in music and poetry that our guardians must build their bulwark.   d

At any rate, lawlessness easily creeps in there unnoticed.

Yes, as if music and poetry were only play and did no harm at all.

It is harmless—except, of course, that when lawlessness has established itself there, it flows over little by little into characters and ways of life. Then, greatly increased, it steps out into private contracts, and from private contracts, Socrates, it makes its insolent way into the laws and government, until in the end it overthrows everything, public and private.   e

Well, is that the way it goes?

I think so.

Then, as we said at first, our children's games must from the very beginning be more law-abiding, for if their games become lawless, and the children follow suit, isn't it impossible for them to grow up into good and law-abiding men?   425

It certainly is.

But when children play the right games from the beginning and absorb lawfulness from music and poetry, it follows them in everything and fosters their growth, correcting anything in the city that may have gone wrong before—in other words, the very opposite of what happens where the games are lawless.

That's true.

These people will also discover the seemingly insignificant conventions their predecessors have destroyed.

Which ones?

Things like this: When it is proper for the young to be silent in front of their elders, when they should make way for them or stand up in their   b presence, the care of parents, hair styles, the clothes and shoes to wear, deportment, and everything else of that sort. Don't you agree?

I do.

I think it's foolish to legislate about such things. Verbal or written decrees will never make them come about or last.

How could they?

At any rate, Adeimantus, it looks as though the start of someone's education determines what follows. Doesn't like always encourage like?   c

It does.

And the final outcome of education, I suppose we'd say, is a single newly finished person, who is either good or the opposite.

Of course.

That's why I wouldn't go on to try to legislate about such things.

And with good reason.

Then, by the gods, what about market business, such as the private contracts people make with one another in the marketplace, for example, or contracts with manual laborers, cases of insult or injury, the bringing   d of lawsuits, the establishing of juries, the payment and assessment of whatever dues are necessary in markets and harbors, the regulation of market, city, harbor, and the rest—should we bring ourselves to legislate about any of these?

It isn't appropriate to dictate to men who are fine and good. They'll easily

e   find out for themselves whatever needs to be legislated about such things.

Yes, provided that a god grants that the laws we have already described are preserved.

If not, they'll spend their lives enacting a lot of other laws and then amending them, believing that in this way they'll attain the best.

You mean they'll live like those sick people who, through licentiousness, aren't willing to abandon their harmful way of life?

That's right.

426   And such people carry on in an altogether amusing fashion, don't they? Their medical treatment achieves nothing, except that their illness becomes worse and more complicated, and they're always hoping that someone will recommend some new medicine to cure them.

That's exactly what happens to people like that.

And isn't it also amusing that they consider their worst enemy to be the person who tells them the truth, namely, that until they give up drunkenness, overeating, lechery, and idleness, no medicine, cautery, or surgery,

b   no charms, amulets, or anything else of that kind will do them any good?

It isn't amusing at all, for it isn't amusing to treat someone harshly when he's telling the truth.

You don't seem to approve of such men.

I certainly don't, by god.

Then, you won't approve either if a whole city behaves in that way, as we said. Don't you think that cities that are badly governed behave exactly like this when they warn their citizens not to disturb the city's whole

c   political establishment on pain of death? The person who is honored and considered clever and wise in important matters by such badly governed cities is the one who serves them most pleasantly, indulges them, flatters them, anticipates their wishes, and is clever at fulfillling them.

Cities certainly do seem to behave in that way, and I don't approve of it at all.

What about those who are willing and eager to serve such cities? Don't

d   you admire their courage and readiness?

I do, except for those who are deceived by majority approval into believing that they are true statesmen.

What do you mean? Have you no sympathy for such men? Or do you think it's possible for someone who is ignorant of measurement not to believe it himself when many others who are similarly ignorant tell him

e   that he is six feet tall?

No, I don't think that.

Then don't be too hard on them, for such people are surely the most amusing of all. They pass laws on the subjects we've just been enumerating and then amend them, and they always think they'll find a way to put a stop to cheating on contracts and the other things I mentioned, not realizing that they're really just cutting off a Hydra's head.[3]

Yet that's all they're doing.

427

I'd have thought, then, that the true lawgiver oughtn't to bother with that form of law or constitution, either in a badly governed city or in a well-governed one—in the former, because it's useless and accomplishes nothing; in the latter, because anyone could discover some of these things, while the others follow automatically from the ways of life we established.

What is now left for us to deal with under the heading of legislation?   b

For us nothing, but for the Delphic Apollo it remains to enact the greatest, finest, and first of laws.

What laws are those?

Those having to do with the establishing of temples, sacrifices, and other forms of service to gods, daemons, and heroes, the burial of the dead, and the services that ensure their favor. We have no knowledge of these things, and in establishing our city, if we have any understanding, we won't be persuaded to trust them to anyone other than the ancestral guide. And   c
this god, sitting upon the rock at the center of the earth,[4] is without a doubt the ancestral guide on these matters for all people.

Nicely put. And that's what we must do.

Well, son of Ariston, your city might now be said to be established. The   d
next step is to get an adequate light somewhere and to call upon your brother as well as Polemarchus and the others, so as to look inside it and see where the justice and the injustice might be in it, what the difference between them is, and which of the two the person who is to be happy should possess, whether its possession is unnoticed by all the gods and human beings or not.

You're talking nonsense, Glaucon said. You promised to look for them yourself because you said it was impious for you not to come to the rescue of justice in every way you could.   e

That's true, and I must do what I promised, but you'll have to help.

We will.

I hope to find it in this way. I think our city, if indeed it has been correctly founded, is completely good.

Necessarily so.

Clearly, then, it is wise, courageous, moderate, and just.

Clearly.

Then, if we find any of these in it, what's left over will be the ones we haven't found?

Of course.   428

---

3. The Hydra was a mythical monster. When one of its heads was cut off, two or three new heads grew in its place. Heracles had to slay the Hydra as one of his labors.

4. I.e., on the rock in the sanctuary at Delphi, which was believed to be the navel or center of the earth.

Therefore, as with any other four things, if we were looking for any one of them in something and recognized it first, that would be enough for us, but if we recognized the other three first, this itself would be sufficient to enable us to recognize what we are looking for. Clearly it couldn't be anything other than what's left over.

That's right.

Therefore, since there are four virtues, mustn't we look for them in the same way?

Clearly.

b   Now, the first thing I think I can see clearly in the city is wisdom, and there seems to be something odd about it.

What's that?

I think that the city we described is really wise. And that's because it has good judgment, isn't it?

Yes.

Now, this very thing, good judgment, is clearly some kind of knowledge, for it's through knowledge, not ignorance, that people judge well.

Clearly.

But there are many kinds of knowledge in the city.

Of course.

Is it because of the knowledge possessed by its carpenters, then, that the city is to be called wise and sound in judgment?

c   Not at all. It's called skilled in carpentry because of that.

Then it isn't to be called wise because of the knowledge by which it arranges to have the best wooden implements.

No, indeed.

What about the knowledge of bronze items or the like?

It isn't because of any knowledge of that sort.

Nor because of the knowledge of how to raise a harvest from the earth, for it's called skilled in farming because of that.

I should think so.

Then, is there some knowledge possessed by some of the citizens in the city we just founded that doesn't judge about any particular matter but about the city as a whole and the maintenance of good relations, both d   internally and with other cities?

There is indeed.

What is this knowledge, and who has it?

It is guardianship, and it is possessed by those rulers we just now called complete guardians.

Then, what does this knowledge entitle you to say about the city?

That it has good judgment and is really wise.

Who do you think that there will be more of in our city, metal-workers e   or these true guardians?

There will be far more metal-workers.

Indeed, of all those who are called by a certain name because they have some kind of knowledge, aren't the guardians the least numerous?

By far.

Then, a whole city established according to nature would be wise because of the smallest class and part in it, namely, the governing or ruling one. And to this class, which seems to be by nature the smallest, belongs a share of the knowledge that alone among all the other kinds of knowledge   429
is to be called wisdom.

That's completely true.

Then we've found one of the four virtues, as well as its place in the city, though I don't know how we found it.

Our way of finding it seems good enough to me.

And surely courage and the part of the city it's in, the part on account of which the city is called courageous, aren't difficult to see.

How is that?

Who, in calling the city cowardly or courageous, would look anywhere   b
other than to the part of it that fights and does battle on its behalf?

No one would look anywhere else.

At any rate, I don't think that the courage or cowardice of its other citizens would cause the city itself to be called either courageous or cowardly.

No, it wouldn't.

The city is courageous, then, because of a part of itself that has the power to preserve through everything its belief about what things are to be feared, namely, that they are the things and kinds of things that the lawgiver   c
declared to be such in the course of educating it. Or don't you call that courage?

I don't completely understand what you mean. Please, say it again.

I mean that courage is a kind of preservation.

What sort of preservation?

That preservation of the belief that has been inculcated by the law through education about what things and sorts of things are to be feared. And by preserving this belief "through everything," I mean preserving it and not abandoning it because of pains, pleasures, desires, or fears. If you   d
like, I'll compare it to something I think it resembles.

I'd like that.

You know that dyers, who want to dye wool purple, first pick out from the many colors of wool the one that is naturally white, then they carefully prepare this in various ways, so that it will absorb the color as well as possible, and only at that point do they apply the purple dye. When something is dyed in this way, the color is fast—no amount of washing,   e
whether with soap or without it, can remove it. But you also know what happens to material if it hasn't been dyed in this way, but instead is dyed purple or some other color without careful preparation.

I know that it looks washed out and ridiculous.

Then, you should understand that, as far as we could, we were doing something similar when we selected our soldiers and educated them in music and physical training. What we were contriving was nothing other   430
than this: That because they had the proper nature and upbringing, they

would absorb the laws in the finest possible way, just like a dye, so that
their belief about what they should fear and all the rest would become so
fast that even such extremely effective detergents as pleasure, pain, fear,
and desire wouldn't wash it out—and pleasure is much more potent than

b any powder, washing soda, or soap. This power to preserve through everything the correct and law-inculcated belief about what is to be feared and
what isn't is what I call courage, unless, of course, you say otherwise.

I have nothing different to say, for I assume that you don't consider the
correct belief about these same things, which you find in animals and
slaves, and which is not the result of education, to be inculcated by law,
and that you don't call it courage but something else.

c That's absolutely true.

Then I accept your account of courage.

Accept it instead as my account of *civic* courage, and you will be right.
We'll discuss courage more fully some other time, if you like. At present,
our inquiry concerns not it but justice. And what we've said is sufficient
for that purpose.

You're quite right.

There are now two things left for us to find in the city, namely, modera-

d tion[5] and—the goal of our entire inquiry—justice.

That's right.

Is there a way we could find justice so as not to have to bother with
moderation any further?

I don't know any, and I wouldn't want justice to appear first if that
means that we won't investigate moderation. So if you want to please me,
look for the latter first.

e I'm certainly willing. It would be wrong not to be.

Look, then.

We will. Seen from here, it is more like a kind of consonance and harmony
than the previous ones.

In what way?

Moderation is surely a kind of order, the mastery of certain kinds of
pleasures and desires. People indicate as much when they use the phrase
"self-control" and other similar phrases. I don't know just what they mean
by them, but they are, so to speak, like tracks or clues that moderation
has left behind in language. Isn't that so?

Absolutely.

Yet isn't the expression "self-control" ridiculous? The stronger self that
does the controlling is the same as the weaker self that gets controlled, so

431 that only one person is referred to in all such expressions.

Of course.

---

5. The Greek term is *sōphrosunē*. It has a very wide meaning: self-control, good sense,
reasonableness, temperance, and (in some contexts) chastity. Someone who keeps his
head under pressure or temptation possesses *sōphrosunē*.

Nonetheless, the expression is apparently trying to indicate that, in the soul of that very person, there is a better part and a worse one and that, whenever the naturally better part is in control of the worse, this is expressed by saying that the person is self-controlled or master of himself. At any rate, one praises someone by calling him self-controlled. But when, on the other hand, the smaller and better part is overpowered by the larger, because of bad upbringing or bad company, this is called being self-defeated or licentious and is a reproach.

Appropriately so.

Take a look at our new city, and you'll find one of these in it. You'll say that it is rightly called self-controlled, if indeed something in which the better rules the worse is properly called moderate and self-controlled.

I am looking, and what you say is true.

Now, one finds all kinds of diverse desires, pleasures, and pains, mostly in children, women, household slaves, and in those of the inferior majority who are called free.

That's right.

But you meet with the desires that are simple, measured, and directed by calculation in accordance with understanding and correct belief only in the few people who are born with the best natures and receive the best education.

That's true.

Then, don't you see that in your city, too, the desires of the inferior many are controlled by the wisdom and desires of the superior few?

I do.

Therefore, if any city is said to be in control of itself and of its pleasures and desires, it is this one.

Absolutely.

And isn't it, therefore, also moderate because of all this?

It is.

And, further, if indeed the ruler and the ruled in any city share the same belief about who should rule, it is in this one. Or don't you agree?

I agree entirely.

And when the citizens agree in this way, in which of them do you say moderation is located? In the ruler or the ruled?

I suppose in both.

Then, you see how right we were to divine that moderation resembles a kind of harmony?

How so?

Because, unlike courage and wisdom, each of which resides in one part, making the city brave and wise respectively, moderation spreads throughout the whole. It makes the weakest, the strongest, and those in between—whether in regard to reason, physical strength, numbers, wealth, or anything else—all sing the same song together. And this unanimity, this agreement between the naturally worse and the naturally better as to

b

c

d

e

432

which of the two is to rule both in the city and in each one, is rightly
called moderation.

b   I agree completely.

All right. We've now found, at least from the point of view of our present
beliefs, three out of the four virtues in our city. So what kind of virtue is
left, then, that makes the city share even further in virtue? Surely, it's clear
that it is justice.

That is clear.

Then, Glaucon, we must station ourselves like hunters surrounding a
wood and focus our understanding, so that justice doesn't escape us and
vanish into obscurity, for obviously it's around here somewhere. So look
c   and try eagerly to catch sight of it, and if you happen to see it before I
do, you can tell me about it.

I wish I could, but you'll make better use of me if you take me to be a
follower who can see things when you point them out to him.

Follow, then, and join me in a prayer.

I'll do that, just so long as you lead.

I certainly will, though the place seems to be impenetrable and full of
shadows. It is certainly dark and hard to search through. But all the same,
we must go on.

d   Indeed we must.

And then I caught sight of something. Ah ha! Glaucon, it looks as though
there's a track here, so it seems that our quarry won't altogether escape us.

That's good news.

Either that, or we've just been stupid.

In what way?

Because what we are looking for seems to have been rolling around at
our feet from the very beginning, and we didn't see it, which was ridiculous
of us. Just as people sometimes search for the very thing they are holding
e   in their hands, so we didn't look in the right direction but gazed off into
the distance, and that's probably why we didn't notice it.

What do you mean?

I mean that, though we've been talking and hearing about it for a long
time, I think we didn't understand what we were saying or that, in a way,
we were talking about justice.

That's a long prelude for someone who wants to hear the answer.

433   Then listen and see whether there's anything in what I say. Justice, I
think, is exactly what we said must be established throughout the city
when we were founding it—either that or some form of it. We stated, and
often repeated, if you remember, that everyone must practice one of the
occupations in the city for which he is naturally best suited.

Yes, we did keep saying that.

Moreover, we've heard many people say and have often said ourselves
that justice is doing one's own work and not meddling with what isn't
b   one's own.

Yes, we have.

Then, it turns out that this doing one's own work—provided that it comes to be in a certain way—is justice. And do you know what I take as evidence of this?

No, tell me.

I think that this is what was left over in the city when moderation, courage, and wisdom have been found. It is the power that makes it possible for them to grow in the city and that preserves them when they've grown for as long as it remains there itself. And of course we said that   c
justice would be what was left over when we had found the other three.

Yes, that must be so.

And surely, if we had to decide which of the four will make the city good by its presence, it would be a hard decision. Is it the agreement in belief between the rulers and the ruled? Or the preservation among the soldiers of the law-inspired belief about what is to be feared and what isn't? Or the wisdom and guardianship of the rulers? Or is it, above all,   d
the fact that every child, woman, slave, freeman, craftsman, ruler, and ruled each does his own work and doesn't meddle with what is other people's?

How could this fail to be a hard decision?

It seems, then, that the power that consists in everyone's doing his own work rivals wisdom, moderation, and courage in its contribution to the virtue of the city.   e

It certainly does.

And wouldn't you call this rival to the others in its contribution to the city's virtue justice?

Absolutely.

Look at it this way if you want to be convinced. Won't you order your rulers to act as judges in the city's courts?

Of course.

And won't their sole aim in delivering judgments be that no citizen should have what belongs to another or be deprived of what is his own?

They'll have no aim but that.

Because that is just?

Yes.

Therefore, from this point of view also, the having and doing of one's own would be accepted as justice.   434

That's right.

Consider, then, and see whether you agree with me about this. If a carpenter attempts to do the work of a cobbler, or a cobbler that of a carpenter, or they exchange their tools or honors with one another, or if the same person tries to do both jobs, and all other such exchanges are made, do you think that does any great harm to the city?

Not much.

But I suppose that when someone, who is by nature a craftsman or some other kind of money-maker, is puffed up by wealth, or by having a majority of votes, or by his own strength, or by some other such thing, and attempts   b
to enter the class of soldiers, or one of the unworthy soldiers tries to enter

that of the judges and guardians, and these exchange their tools and honors, or when the same person tries to do all these things at once, then I think you'll agree that these exchanges and this sort of meddling bring the city to ruin.

Absolutely.

Meddling and exchange between these three classes, then, is the greatest harm that can happen to the city and would rightly be called the worst

c   thing someone could do to it.

Exactly.

And wouldn't you say that the worst thing that someone could do to his city is injustice?

Of course.

Then, that exchange and meddling is injustice. Or to put it the other way around: For the money-making, auxiliary, and guardian classes each to do its own work in the city, is the opposite. That's justice, isn't it, and makes the city just?

d   I agree. Justice is that and nothing else.

Let's not take that as secure just yet, but if we find that the same form, when it comes to be in each individual person, is accepted as justice there as well, we can assent to it. What else can we say? But if that isn't what we find, we must look for something else to be justice. For the moment, however, let's complete the present inquiry. We thought that, if we first tried to observe justice in some larger thing that possessed it, this would make it easier to observe in a single individual.[6] We agreed that this larger thing is a city, and so we established the best city we could, knowing well

e   that justice would be in one that was good. So, let's apply what has come to light in the city to an individual, and if it is accepted there, all will be well. But if something different is found in the individual, then we must go back and test that on the city. And if we do this, and compare them

435 side by side, we might well make justice light up as if we were rubbing fire-sticks together. And, when it has come to light, we can get a secure grip on it for ourselves.

You're following the road we set, and we must do as you say.

Well, then, are things called by the same name, whether they are bigger or smaller than one another, like or unlike with respect to that to which that name applies?

Alike.

Then a just man won't differ at all from a just city in respect to the form

b   of justice; rather he'll be like the city.

He will.

But a city was thought to be just when each of the three natural classes within it did its own work, and it was thought to be moderate, courageous, and wise because of certain other conditions and states of theirs.

6. See 368c ff.

That's true.

Then, if an individual has these same three parts in his soul, we will expect him to be correctly called by the same names as the city if he has the same conditions in them.   c

Necessarily so.

Then once again we've come upon an easy question, namely, does the soul have these three parts in it or not?

It doesn't look easy to me. Perhaps, Socrates, there's some truth in the old saying that everything fine is difficult.

Apparently so. But you should know, Glaucon, that, in my opinion, we will never get a precise answer using our present methods of argument—although there is another longer and fuller road that does lead to such an   d answer. But perhaps we can get an answer that's up to the standard of our previous statements and inquiries.

Isn't that satisfactory? It would be enough for me at present.

In that case, it will be fully enough for me too.

Then don't weary, but go on with the inquiry.

Well, then, we are surely compelled to agree that each of us has within himself the same parts and characteristics as the city? Where else would   e they come from? It would be ridiculous for anyone to think that spiritedness didn't come to be in cities from such individuals as the Thracians, Scythians, and others who live to the north of us who are held to possess spirit, or that the same isn't true of the love of learning, which is mostly associated with our part of the world, or of the love of money, which one might say   436 is conspicuously displayed by the Phoenicians and Egyptians.

It would.

That's the way it is, anyway, and it isn't hard to understand.

Certainly not.

But this *is* hard. Do we do these things with the same part of ourselves, or do we do them with three different parts? Do we learn with one part, get angry with another, and with some third part desire the pleasures of food, drink, sex, and the others that are closely akin to them? Or, when we set out after something, do we act with the whole of our soul, in each case? This is what's hard to determine in a way that's up to the standards   b of our argument.

I think so too.

Well, then, let's try to determine in that way whether these parts are the same or different.

How?

It is obvious that the same thing will not be willing to do or undergo opposites in the same part of itself, in relation to the same thing, at the same time. So, if we ever find this happening in the soul, we'll know that we aren't dealing with one thing but many.   c

All right.

Then consider what I'm about to say.

Say on.

Is it possible for the same thing to stand still and move at the same time in the same part of itself?

Not at all.

Let's make our agreement more precise in order to avoid disputes later on. If someone said that a person who is standing still but moving his hands and head is moving and standing still at the same time, we wouldn't consider, I think, that he ought to put it like that. What he ought to say is that one part of the person is standing still and another part is moving.
d   Isn't that so?

It is.

And if our interlocutor became even more amusing and was sophisticated enough to say that whole spinning tops stand still and move at the same time when the peg is fixed in the same place and they revolve, and that the same is true of anything else moving in a circular motion on the same spot, we wouldn't agree, because it isn't with respect to the same parts of themselves that such things both stand still and move. We'd say
e   that they have an axis and a circumference and that with respect to the axis they stand still, since they don't wobble to either side, while with respect to the circumference they move in a circle. But if they do wobble to the left or right, front or back, while they are spinning, we'd say that they aren't standing still in any way.

And we'd be right.

No such statement will disturb us, then, or make us believe that the same thing can be, do, or undergo opposites, at the same time, in the same
437   respect, and in relation to the same thing.

They won't make me believe it, at least.

Nevertheless, in order to avoid going through all these objections one by one and taking a long time to prove them all untrue, let's hypothesize that this is corrrect and carry on. But we agree that if it should ever be shown to be incorrect, all the consequences we've drawn from it will also be lost.

We should agree to that.
b   Then wouldn't you consider all the following, whether they are doings or undergoings, as pairs of opposites: Assent and dissent, wanting to have something and rejecting it, taking something and pushing it away?

Yes, they are opposites.

What about these? Wouldn't you include thirst, hunger, the appetites
c   as a whole, and wishing and willing somewhere in the class we mentioned? Wouldn't you say that the soul of someone who has an appetite for a thing wants what he has an appetite for and takes to himself what it is his will to have, and that insofar as he wishes something to be given to him, his soul, since it desires this to come about, nods assent to it as if in answer to a question?

I would.

What about not willing, not wishing, and not having an appetite? Aren't these among the very opposites—cases in which the soul pushes and drives things away?

Of course.   d

Then won't we say that there is a class of things called appetites and that the clearest examples are hunger and thirst?

We will.

One of these is for food and the other for drink?

Yes.

Now, insofar as it is thirst, is it an appetite in the soul for more than that for which we say that it is the appetite? For example, is thirst thirst for hot drink or cold, or much drink or little, or, in a word, for drink of a certain sort? Or isn't it rather that, where heat is present as well as thirst, it causes the appetite to be for something cold as well, and where cold for   e something hot, and where there is much thirst because of the presence of muchness, it will cause the desire to be for much, and where little for little? But thirst itself will never be for anything other than what it is in its nature to be for, namely, drink itself, and hunger for food.

That's the way it is, each appetite itself is only for its natural object, while the appetite for something of a certain sort depends on additions.

Therefore, let no one catch us unprepared or disturb us by claiming that   438 no one has an appetite for drink but rather good drink, nor food but good food, on the grounds that everyone after all has appetite for good things, so that if thirst is an appetite, it will be an appetite for good drink or whatever, and similarly with the others.

All the same, the person who says that has a point.

But it seems to me that, in the case of all things that are related to something, those that are of a particular sort are related to a particular sort of thing, while those that are merely themselves are related to a thing   b that is merely itself.

I don't understand.

Don't you understand that the greater is such as to be greater than something?

Of course.

Than the less?

Yes.

And the much greater than the much less, isn't that so?

Yes.

And the once greater to the once less? And the going-to-be greater than the going-to-be less?

Certainly.

And isn't the same true of the more and the fewer, the double and the half, heavier and lighter, faster and slower, the hot and the cold, and all   c other such things?

Of course.

And what about the various kinds of knowledge? Doesn't the same apply? Knowledge itself is knowledge of what can be learned itself (or whatever it is that knowledge is of), while a particular sort of knowledge is of a particular sort of thing. For example, when knowledge of building

d houses came to be, didn't it differ from the other kinds of knowledge, and so was called knowledge of building?

Of course.

And wasn't that because it was a different sort of knowledge from all the others?

Yes.

And wasn't it because it was of a particular sort of thing that it itself became a particular sort of knowledge? And isn't this true of all crafts and kinds of knowledge?

It is.

Well, then, this is what I was trying to say—if you understand it now— when I said that of all things that are related to something, those that are merely themselves are related to things that are merely themselves, while those that are of a particular sort are related to things of a particular sort.

e However, I don't mean that the sorts in question have to be the same for them both. For example, knowledge of health or disease isn't healthy or diseased, and knowledge of good and bad doesn't itself become good or bad. I mean that, when knowledge became, not knowledge of the thing itself that knowledge is of, but knowledge of something of a particular sort, the result was that it itself became a particular sort of knowledge, and this caused it to be no longer called knowledge without qualification, but—with the addition of the relevant sort—medical knowledge or whatever.

I understand, and I think that that's the way it is.

Then as for thirst, wouldn't you include it among things that are related

439 to something? Surely thirst is related to . . .

I know it's related to drink.

Therefore a particular sort of thirst is for a particular sort of drink. But thirst itself isn't for much or little, good or bad, or, in a word, for drink of a particular sort. Rather, thirst itself is in its nature only for drink itself.

Absolutely.

Hence the soul of the thirsty person, insofar as he's thirsty, doesn't wish

b anything else but to drink, and it wants this and is impelled towards it.

Clearly.

Therefore, if something draws it back when it is thirsting, wouldn't that be something different in it from whatever thirsts and drives it like a beast to drink? It can't be, we say, that the same thing, with the same part of itself, in relation to the same, at the same time, does opposite things.

No, it can't.

In the same way, I suppose, it's wrong to say of the archer that his hands at the same time push the bow away and draw it towards him.

We ought to say that one hand pushes it away and the other draws it towards him.

Absolutely.   c

Now, would we assert that sometimes there are thirsty people who don't wish to drink?

Certainly, it happens often to many different people.

What, then, should one say about them? Isn't it that there is something in their soul, bidding them to drink, and something different, forbidding them to do so, that overrules the thing that bids?

I think so.

Doesn't that which forbids in such cases come into play—if it comes into play at all—as a result of rational calculation, while what drives and drags them to drink is a result of feelings and diseases?   d

Apparently.

Hence it isn't unreasonable for us to claim that they are two, and different from one another. We'll call the part of the soul with which it calculates the rational part and the part with which it lusts, hungers, thirsts, and gets excited by other appetites the irrational appetitive part, companion of certain indulgences and pleasures.

Yes. Indeed, that's a reasonable thing to think.   e

Then, let these two parts be distinguished in the soul. Now, is the spirited part by which we get angry a third part or is it of the same nature as either of the other two?

Perhaps it's like the appetitive part.

But I've heard something relevant to this, and I believe it. Leontius, the son of Aglaion, was going up from the Piraeus along the outside of the North Wall when he saw some corpses lying at the executioner's feet. He had an appetite to look at them but at the same time he was disgusted and turned away. For a time he struggled with himself and covered his face, but, finally, overpowered by the appetite, he pushed his eyes wide   440 open and rushed towards the corpses, saying, "Look for yourselves, you evil wretches, take your fill of the beautiful sight!"

I've heard that story myself.

It certainly proves that anger sometimes makes war against the appetites, as one thing against another.

Besides, don't we often notice in other cases that when appetite forces someone contrary to rational calculation, he reproaches himself and gets angry with that in him that's doing the forcing, so that of the two factions   b that are fighting a civil war, so to speak, spirit allies itself with reason? But I don't think you can say that you've ever seen spirit, either in yourself or anyone else, ally itself with an appetite to do what reason has decided must not be done.

No, by god, I haven't.

What happens when a person thinks that he has done something unjust? Isn't it true that the nobler he is, the less he resents it if he suffers hunger,   c cold, or the like at the hands of someone whom he believes to be inflicting this on him justly, and won't his spirit, as I say, refuse to be aroused?

That's true.

But what happens if, instead, he believes that someone has been unjust to him? Isn't the spirit within him boiling and angry, fighting for what he believes to be just? Won't it endure hunger, cold, and the like and keep
d   on till it is victorious, not ceasing from noble actions until it either wins, dies, or calms down, called to heel by the reason within him, like a dog by a shepherd?

Spirit is certainly like that. And, of course, we made the auxiliaries in our city like dogs obedient to the rulers, who are themselves like shepherds of a city.

You well understand what I'm trying to say. But also reflect on this further point.
e   What?

The position of the spirited part seems to be the opposite of what we thought before. Then we thought of it as something appetitive, but now we say that it is far from being that, for in the civil war in the soul it aligns itself far more with the rational part.

Absolutely.

Then is it also different from the rational part, or is it some form of it, so that there are two parts in the soul—the rational and the appetitive—instead of three? Or rather, just as there were three classes in the city that
441 held it together, the money-making, the auxiliary, and the deliberative, is the spirited part a third thing in the soul that is by nature the helper of the rational part, provided that it hasn't been corrupted by a bad upbringing?

It must be a third.

Yes, provided that we can show it is different from the rational part, as we saw earlier it was from the appetitive one.

It isn't difficult to show that it is different. Even in small children, one can see that they are full of spirit right from birth, while as far as rational calculation is concerned, some never seem to get a share of it, while the
b   majority do so quite late.

That's really well put. And in animals too one can see that what you say is true. Besides, our earlier quotation from Homer bears it out, where he says,

He struck his chest and spoke to his heart.[7]

For here Homer clearly represents the part that has calculated about better
c   and worse as different from the part that is angry without calculation.

That's exactly right.

---

7. See 390d, and note.

Well, then, we've now made our difficult way through a sea of argument. We are pretty much agreed that the same number and the same kinds of classes as are in the city are also in the soul of each individual.

That's true.

Therefore, it necessarily follows that the individual is wise in the same way and in the same part of himself as the city.

That's right.

And isn't the individual courageous in the same way and in the same part of himself as the city? And isn't everything else that has to do with virtue the same in both?

Necessarily.

Moreover, Glaucon, I suppose we'll say that a man is just in the same way as a city.

That too is entirely necessary.

And we surely haven't forgotten that the city was just because each of the three classes in it was doing its own work.

I don't think we could forget that.

Then we must also remember that each one of us in whom each part is doing its own work will himself be just and do his own.

Of course, we must.

Therefore, isn't it appropriate for the rational part to rule, since it is really wise and exercises foresight on behalf of the whole soul, and for the spirited part to obey it and be its ally?

It certainly is.

And isn't it, as we were saying, a mixture of music and poetry, on the one hand, and physical training, on the other, that makes the two parts harmonious, stretching and nurturing the rational part with fine words and learning, relaxing the other part through soothing stories, and making it gentle by means of harmony and rhythm?

That's precisely it.

And these two, having been nurtured in this way, and having truly learned their own roles and been educated in them, will govern the appetitive part, which is the largest part in each person's soul and is by nature most insatiable for money. They'll watch over it to see that it isn't filled with the so-called pleasures of the body and that it doesn't become so big and strong that it no longer does its own work but attempts to enslave and rule over the classes it isn't fitted to rule, thereby overturning everyone's whole life.

That's right.

Then, wouldn't these two parts also do the finest job of guarding the whole soul and body against external enemies—reason by planning, spirit by fighting, following its leader, and carrying out the leader's decisions through its courage?

Yes, that's true.

And it is because of the spirited part, I suppose, that we call a single individual courageous, namely, when it preserves through pains and pleasures the declarations of reason about what is to be feared and what isn't.

That's right.

And we'll call him wise because of that small part of himself that rules in him and makes those declarations and has within it the knowledge of what is advantageous for each part and for the whole soul, which is the community of all three parts.

Absolutely.

And isn't he moderate because of the friendly and harmonious relations between these same parts, namely, when the ruler and the ruled believe in common that the rational part should rule and don't engage in civil

d   war against it?

Moderation is surely nothing other than that, both in the city and in the individual.

And, of course, a person will be just because of what we've so often mentioned, and in that way.

Necessarily.

Well, then, is the justice in us at all indistinct? Does it seem to be something different from what we found in the city?

It doesn't seem so to me.

If there are still any doubts in our soul about this, we could dispel them

e   altogether by appealing to ordinary cases.

Which ones?

For example, if we had to come to an agreement about whether someone similar in nature and training to our city had embezzled a deposit of gold or silver that he had accepted, who do you think would consider him to

443 have done it rather than someone who isn't like him?

No one.

And would he have anything to do with temple robberies, thefts, betrayals of friends in private life or of cities in public life?

No, nothing.

And he'd be in no way untrustworthy in keeping an oath or other agreement.

How could he be?

And adultery, disrespect for parents, and neglect of the gods would be more in keeping with every other kind of character than his.

With every one.

And isn't the cause of all this that every part within him does its own

b   work, whether it's ruling or being ruled?

Yes, that and nothing else.

Then, are you still looking for justice to be something other than this power, the one that produces men and cities of the sort we've described?

No, I certainly am not.

Then the dream we had has been completely fulfilled—our suspicion that, with the help of some god, we had hit upon the origin and pattern

c   of justice right at the beginning in founding our city.[8]

8. See 432c–433b.

Absolutely.

Indeed, Glaucon, the principle that it is right for someone who is by nature a cobbler to practice cobblery and nothing else, for the carpenter to practice carpentry, and the same for the others is a sort of image of justice—that's why it's beneficial.

Apparently.

And in truth justice is, it seems, something of this sort. However, it isn't concerned with someone's doing his own externally, but with what is inside him, with what is truly himself and his own. One who is just does   d not allow any part of himself to do the work of another part or allow the various classes within him to meddle with each other. He regulates well what is really his own and rules himself. He puts himself in order, is his own friend, and harmonizes the three parts of himself like three limiting notes in a musical scale—high, low, and middle. He binds together those parts and any others there may be in between, and from having been many things he becomes entirely one, moderate and harmonious. Only   e then does he act. And when he does anything, whether acquiring wealth, taking care of his body, engaging in politics, or in private contracts—in all of these, he believes that the action is just and fine that preserves this inner harmony and helps achieve it, and calls it so, and regards as wisdom the knowledge that oversees such actions. And he believes that the action that destroys this harmony is unjust, and calls it so, and regards the belief that oversees it as ignorance.   444

That's absolutely true, Socrates.

Well, then, if we claim to have found the just man, the just city, and what the justice is that is in them, I don't suppose that we'll seem to be telling a complete falsehood.

No, we certainly won't.

Shall we claim it, then?

We shall.

So be it. Now, I suppose we must look for injustice.

Clearly.

Surely, it must be a kind of civil war between the three parts, a meddling   b and doing of another's work, a rebellion by some part against the whole soul in order to rule it inappropriately. The rebellious part is by nature suited to be a slave, while the other part is not a slave but belongs to the ruling class. We'll say something like that, I suppose, and that the turmoil and straying of these parts are injustice, licentiousness, cowardice, ignorance, and, in a word, the whole of vice.

That's what they are.

So, if justice and injustice are really clear enough to us, then acting justly, acting unjustly, and doing injustice are also clear.   c

How so?

Because just and unjust actions are no different for the soul than healthy and unhealthy things are for the body.

In what way?

Healthy things produce health, unhealthy ones disease.

Yes.

And don't just actions produce justice in the soul and unjust ones in-
d   justice?

Necessarily.

To produce health is to establish the components of the body in a natural
relation of control and being controlled, one by another, while to produce
disease is to establish a relation of ruling and being ruled contrary to nature.

That's right.

Then, isn't to produce justice to establish the parts of the soul in a natural
relation of control, one by another, while to produce injustice is to establish
a relation of ruling and being ruled contrary to nature?

Precisely.

Virtue seems, then, to be a kind of health, fine condition, and well-being
e   of the soul, while vice is disease, shameful condition, and weakness.

That's true.

And don't fine ways of living lead one to the possession of virtue,
shameful ones to vice?

Necessarily.

So it now remains, it seems, to inquire whether it is more profitable to
445 act justly, live in a fine way, and be just, whether one is known to be so
or not, or to act unjustly and be unjust, provided that one doesn't pay the
penalty and become better as a result of punishment.

But, Socrates, this inquiry looks ridiculous to me now that justice and
injustice have been shown to be as we have described. Even if one has
every kind of food and drink, lots of money, and every sort of power to
rule, life is thought to be not worth living when the body's nature is ruined.
b   So even if someone can do whatever he wishes, except what will free him
from vice and injustice and make him acquire justice and virtue, how can
it be worth living when his soul—the very thing by which he lives—is
ruined and in turmoil?

Yes, it is ridiculous. Nevertheless, now that we've come far enough to
be able to see most clearly that this is so, we mustn't give up.

That's absolutely the last thing we must do.
c   Then come here, so that you can see how many forms of vice there are,
anyhow that I consider worthy of examination.

I'm following you, just tell me.

Well, from the vantage point we've reached in our argument, it seems
to me that there is one form of virtue and an unlimited number of forms
of vice, four of which are worth mentioning.

How do you mean?

It seems likely that there are as many types of soul as there are specific
types of political constitution.

How many is that?
d   Five forms of constitution and five of souls.

What are they?

One is the constitution we've been describing. And it has two names. If one outstanding man emerges among the rulers, it's called a kingship; if more than one, it's called an aristocracy.

That's true.

Therefore, I say that this is one form of constitution. Whether one man emerges or many, none of the significant laws of the city would be changed, if they followed the upbringing and education we described.

Probably not.

Book V

This is the kind of city and constitution, then, that I call good and correct,   449
and so too is this kind of man. And if indeed this is the correct kind, all the others—whether as city governments or as organizations of the individual soul—are bad and mistaken. Their badness is of four kinds.

What are they? he said.

I was going to enumerate them and explain how I thought they developed out of one another,[1] but Polemarchus, who was sitting a little further away than Adeimantus, extended his hand and took hold of the latter's   b
cloak by the shoulder from above. He drew Adeimantus towards him, while he himself leaned forward and said something to him. We overheard nothing of what he said except the words "Shall we let it go, or what?"

We certainly won't let it go, Adeimantus said, now speaking aloud.

And I asked: What is it that you won't let go?

You, he said.

For what reason in particular?   c

We think that you're slacking off and that you've cheated us out of a whole important section of the discussion in order to avoid having to deal with it. You thought we wouldn't notice when you said—as though it were something trivial—that, as regards wives and children, anyone could see that the possessions of friends should be held in common.[2]

But isn't that right, Adeimantus?

Yes it is. But this "right," like the other things we've discussed, requires an explanation—in this case, an explanation of the manner in which they are to be held in common, for there may be many ways of doing this. So don't omit telling us about the particular one you mean. We've been   d
waiting for some time, indeed, for you to tell us about the production of children—how they'll be produced and, once born, how they'll be brought up—and about the whole subject of having wives and children in common. We think that this makes a considerable difference—indeed all the difference—to whether a constitution is correct or not. So now, since you are beginning to describe another constitution before having adequately

---

1. This task is taken up in Book VIII.
2. See 423e–424a.

discussed these things, we are resolved, as you overheard, not to let you
450   off until you explain all this as fully as the rest.

Include me, Glaucon said, as a partner in this resolution.

In fact, Socrates, Thrasymachus added, you can take this as the resolution
of all of us.

What a thing you've done, I said, in stopping me! What an argument
you've started up again from the very beginning, as it were, about the
constitution! I was delighted to think that it had already been described
and was content to have these things accepted as they were stated before.
You don't realize what a swarm of arguments you've stirred up by calling
b   me to account now. I saw the swarm and passed the topic by in order to
save us a lot of trouble.

Well, said Thrasymachus, are we here to search for gold[3] or to listen to
an argument?

The latter, I said, but within reason.

It's within reason, Socrates, Glaucon said, for people with any understanding to listen to an argument of this kind their whole life long. So
don't mind about us, and don't get tired yourself. Rather, tell us at length
what your thoughts are on the topic we inquired about, namely, what the
c   common possession of wives and children will amount to for the guardians
and how the children will be brought up while they're still small, for the
time between birth and the beginning of education seems to be the most
difficult period of all. So try to tell us what the manner of this upbringing
must be.

It isn't an easy subject to explain, for it raises even more incredulity
than the topics we've discussed so far. People may not believe that what
we say is possible or that, even if it could be brought about, it would be
for the best. It's for this reason that I hesitated to bring it up, namely, that
d   our argument might seem to be no more than wishful thinking.

Then don't hesitate, for your audience isn't inconsiderate, incredulous,
or hostile.

Are you trying to encourage me by saying that?

I am.

Well, you're doing the opposite. Your encouragement would be fine, if
I could be sure I was speaking with knowledge, for one can feel both
secure and confident when one knows the truth about the dearest and
most important things and speaks about them among those who are them-
e   selves wise and dear friends. But to speak, as I'm doing, at a time when
one is unsure of oneself and searching for the truth, is a frightening and
451   insecure thing to do. I'm not afraid of being laughed at—that would be
childish indeed. But I am afraid that, if I slip from the truth, just where
it's most important not to, I'll not only fall myself but drag my friends

---

3. A proverbial expression applied to those who neglect the task at hand for some
more fascinating but less profitable pursuit.

down as well. So I bow to Adrastea[4] for what I'm going to say, for I suspect that it's a lesser crime to kill someone involuntarily than to mislead people about fine, good, and just institutions. Since it's better to run this risk among enemies than among friends, you've well and truly encouraged me!   b

Glaucon laughed and said: Well, Socrates, if we suffer from any false note you strike in the argument, we'll release you and absolve you of any guilt as in a homicide case: your hands are clean, and you have not deceived us. So take courage and speak.

I will, for the law says that someone who kills involuntarily is free of guilt when he's absolved by the injured party. So it's surely reasonable to think the same is true in my case as well.

With that as your defense, speak.

Then I'll have to go back to what should perhaps have been said in   c
sequence, although it may be that this way of doing things is in fact right and that after the completion of the male drama, so to speak, we should then go through the female one—especially as you insist on it so urgently.

For men born and educated as we've described there is, in my opinion, no right way to acquire and use women and children other than by following the road on which we started them. We attempted, in the argument, to set up the men as guardians of the herd.

Yes.

Then let's give them a birth and rearing consistent with that and see   d
whether it suits us or not.

How?

As follows: Do we think that the wives of our guardian watchdogs should guard what the males guard, hunt with them, and do everything else in common with them? Or should we keep the women at home, as incapable of doing this, since they must bear and rear the puppies, while the males work and have the entire care of the flock?

Everything should be in common, except that the females are weaker   e
and the males stronger.

And is it possible to use any animals for the same things if you don't give them the same upbringing and education?

No, it isn't.

Therefore, if we use the women for the same things as the men, they must also be taught the same things.

Yes.   452

Now, we gave the men music and poetry and physical training.

Yes.

Then we must give these two crafts, as well as those having to do with warfare, to the women also to use in the same way as the men use them.

That seems to follow from what you say.

---

4. Adrastea was a kind of Nemesis, a punisher of pride. The "bow to Adrastea" is a kind of apology for the sort of behavior that might otherwise spur her to take action.

But perhaps much of what we are saying, since it is contrary to custom, would incite ridicule if it were carried out in practice as we've described.

It certainly would.

What is the most ridiculous thing that you see in it? Isn't it obviously the women exercising naked in the palestras with the men? And not just the young women, but the older ones too—like old men in gymnasiums

b who, even though their bodies are wrinkled and not pleasant to look at, still love to do physical training.

Yes, that would look really ridiculous as things stand at present.

But surely, now that we've started to speak about this, we mustn't fear the various jokes that wits will make about this kind of change in music and poetry, physical training, and—last but not least—in bearing arms

c and riding horses.

You're right.

And now that we've begun to speak about this, we must move on to the tougher part of the law, begging these people not to be silly (though that is their own work!) but to take the matter seriously. They should remember that it wasn't very long ago that the Greeks themselves thought it shameful and ridiculous (as the majority of the barbarians still do) for even men to be seen naked and that when the Cretans and then the Lacedaemonians began the gymnasiums, the wits of those times could

d also have ridiculed it all. Or don't you think so?

I do.

But I think that, after it was found in practice to be better to strip than to cover up all those parts, then what was ridiculous to the eyes faded away in the face of what argument showed to be the best. This makes it clear that it's foolish to think that anything besides the bad is ridiculous or to try to raise a laugh at the sight of anything besides what's stupid or

e bad or (putting it the other way around) it's foolish to take seriously any standard of what is fine and beautiful other than the good.

That's absolutely certain.

However, mustn't we first agree about whether our proposals are possible or not? And mustn't we give to anyone who wishes the opportunity to question us—whether in jest or in earnest—about whether female human

453 nature *can* share all the tasks of that of the male, or none of them, or some but not others, and to ask in which class the waging of war belongs? Wouldn't this, as the best beginning, also be likely to result in the best conclusion?

Of course.

Shall we give the argument against ourselves, then, on behalf of those who share these reservations, so that their side of the question doesn't fall by default?

b There's no reason not to.

Then let's say this on their behalf: "Socrates and Glaucon, there's no need for others to argue with you, for you yourselves, when you began to found your city, agreed that each must do his own work in accordance with his nature."

And I think we certainly did agree to that.

"Can you deny that a woman is by nature very different from a man?"

Of course not.

"And isn't it appropriate to assign different work to each in accordance with its nature?"

Certainly.

"How is it, then, that you aren't mistaken and contradicting yourselves when you say that men and women must do the same things, when their natures are so completely separate and distinct?"

Do you have any defense against that attack?

It isn't easy to think of one on the spur of the moment, so I'll ask you to explain the argument on our side as well, whatever it is.

This and many other such things, Glaucon, which I foresaw earlier, were what I was afraid of, so that I hesitated to tackle the law concerning the possession and upbringing of women and children.

By god, it doesn't seem to be an easy topic.

It isn't. But the fact is that whether someone falls into a small diving pool or into the middle of the biggest ocean, he must swim all the same.

He certainly must.

Then we must swim too, and try to save ourselves from the sea of argument, hoping that a dolphin will pick us up or that we'll be rescued by some other desperate means.[5]

It seems so.

Come, then. Let's see if we can find a way out. We've agreed that different natures must follow different ways of life and that the natures of men and women are different. But now we say that those different natures must follow the same way of life. Isn't that the accusation brought against us?

That's it exactly.

Ah! Glaucon, great is the power of the craft of disputation.

Why is that?

Because many fall into it against their wills. They think they are having not a quarrel but a conversation, because they are unable to examine what has been said by dividing it up according to forms. Hence, they pursue mere verbal contradictions of what has been said and have a quarrel rather than a conversation.

That does happen to lots of people, but it isn't happening to us at the moment, is it?

It most certainly is, for it looks to me, at any rate, as though we are falling into disputation against our will.

How?

---

5. See Herodotus, *Histories* 1.23–24 for the story of Arion's rescue by the dolphin.

We're bravely, but in a quarrelsome and merely verbal fashion, pursuing the principle that natures that aren't the same must follow different ways of life. But when we assigned different ways of life to different natures and the same ones to the same, we didn't at all examine the form of natural difference and sameness we had in mind or in what regard we were distinguishing them.

No, we didn't look into that.

c   Therefore, we might just as well, it seems, ask ourselves whether the natures of bald and long-haired men are the same or opposite. And, when we agree that they are opposite, then, if the bald ones are cobblers, we ought to forbid the long-haired ones to be cobblers, and if the long-haired ones are cobblers, we ought to forbid this to the bald ones.

That would indeed be ridiculous.

And aren't we in this ridiculous position because at that time we did not introduce every form of difference and sameness in nature, but focused on the one form of sameness and difference that was relevant to the particular ways of life themselves? We meant, for example, that a male

d   and female doctor have souls of the same nature. Or don't you think so?

I do.

But a doctor and a carpenter have different ones?

Completely different, surely.

Therefore, if the male sex is seen to be different from the female with regard to a particular craft or way of life, we'll say that the relevant one must be assigned to it. But if it's apparent that they differ only in this respect, that the females bear children while the males beget them, we'll say that there has been no kind of proof that women are different from

e   men with respect to what we're talking about, and we'll continue to believe that our guardians and their wives must have the same way of life.

And rightly so.

Next, we'll tell anyone who holds the opposite view to instruct us in this: With regard to what craft or way of life involved in the constitution

455   of the city are the natures of men and women not the same but different?

That's a fair question, at any rate.

And perhaps he'd say, just as you did a moment ago, that it isn't easy to give an immediate answer, but with enough consideration it should not be difficult.

Yes, he might say that.

Shall we ask the one who raises this objection to follow us and see whether we can show him that no way of life concerned with the manage-

b   ment of the city is peculiar to women?

Of course.

"Come, now," we'll say to him, "give us an answer: Is this what you meant by one person being naturally well suited for something and another being naturally unsuited? That the one learned it easily, the other with difficulty; that the one, after only a brief period of instruction, was able

to find out things for himself, while the other, after much instruction, couldn't even remember what he'd learned; that the body of the one adequately served his thought, while the body of the other opposed his. Are there any other things besides these by which you distinguished those   c
who are naturally well suited for anything from those who are not?"

No one will claim that there are any others.

Do you know of anything practiced by human beings in which the male sex isn't superior to the female in all these ways? Or must we make a long story of it by mentioning weaving, baking cakes, and cooking vegetables, in which the female sex is believed to excel and in which it is most ridiculous of all for it to be inferior?   d

It's true that one sex is much superior to the other in pretty well everything, although many women are better than many men in many things. But on the whole it is as you say.

Then there is no way of life concerned with the management of the city that belongs to a woman because she's a woman or to a man because he's a man, but the various natures are distributed in the same way in both creatures. Women share by nature in every way of life just as men do, but in all of them women are weaker than men.   e

Certainly.

Then shall we assign all of them to men and none to women?

How can we?

We'll say, I suppose, that one woman is a doctor, another not, and that one is musical by nature, another not.

Of course.

And, therefore, won't one be athletic or warlike, while another is unwarlike and no lover of physical training?   456

I suppose so.

Further, isn't one woman philosophical or a lover of wisdom, while another hates wisdom? And isn't one spirited and another spiritless?

That too.

So one woman may have a guardian nature and another not, for wasn't it qualities of this sort that we looked for in the natures of the men we selected as guardians?

Certainly.

Therefore, men and women are by nature the same with respect to guarding the city, except to the extent that one is weaker and the other stronger.

Apparently.

Then women of this sort must be chosen along with men of the same sort to live with them and share their guardianship, seeing that they are   b
adequate for the task and akin to the men in nature.

Certainly.

And mustn't we assign the same way of life to the same natures?

We must.

We've come round, then, to what we said before and have agreed that it isn't against nature to assign an education in music, poetry, and physical training to the wives of the guardians.

Absolutely.

c   Then we're not legislating impossibilities or indulging in mere wishful thinking, since the law we established is in accord with nature. It's rather the way things are at present that seems to be against nature.

So it seems.

Now, weren't we trying to determine whether our proposals were both possible and optimal?

Yes, we were.

And haven't we now agreed that they're possible?

Yes.

Then mustn't we next reach agreement about whether or not they're optimal?

Clearly.

Should we have one kind of education to produce women guardians, then, and another to produce men, especially as they have the same natures

d   to begin with?

No.

Then, what do you think about this?

What?

About one man being better and another worse. Or do you think they're all alike?

Certainly not.

In the city we're establishing, who do you think will prove to be better men, the guardians, who receive the education we've described, or the cobblers, who are educated in cobblery?

Your question is ridiculous.

e   I understand. Indeed, aren't the guardians the best of the citizens?

By far.

And what about the female guardians? Aren't they the best of the women?

They're by far the best.

Is there anything better for a city than having the best possible men and women as its citizens?

There isn't.

And isn't it music and poetry and physical training, lending their support

457   in the way we described, that bring this about?

Of course.

Then the law we've established isn't only possible; it is also optimal for a city?

Yes.

Then the guardian women must strip for physical training, since they'll wear virtue or excellence instead of clothes. They must share in war and the other guardians' duties in the city and do nothing else. But the lighter parts must be assigned to them because of the weakness of their sex. And the man who laughs at naked women doing physical training for the sake of what is best is "plucking the unripe fruit"[6] of laughter and doesn't know, it seems, what he's laughing at or what he's doing, for it is and always will be the finest saying that the beneficial is beautiful, while the harmful is ugly.

Absolutely.

Can we say, then, that we've escaped one wave of criticism in our discussion of the law about women, that we haven't been altogether swept away by laying it down that male and female guardians must share their entire way of life, and that our argument is consistent when it states that this is both possible and beneficial?

And it's certainly no small wave that you've escaped.

You won't think that it's so big when you get a look at the next one.

Tell me about it, and I'll decide.

I suppose that the following law goes along with the last one and the others that preceded it.

Which one?

That all these women are to belong in common to all the men, that none are to live privately with any man, and that the children, too, are to be possessed in common, so that no parent will know his own offspring or any child his parent.

This wave is far bigger than the other, for there's doubt both about its possibility and about whether or not it's beneficial.

I don't think that its being beneficial would be disputed or that it would be denied that the common possession of women and children would be the greatest good, if indeed it is possible. But I think that there would be a lot of disagreement about whether or not it is possible.

There could very well be dispute about both.

You mean that I'll have to face a coalition of arguments. I thought I'd escape one of them, if you believed that the proposal was beneficial, and that I'd have only the one about whether or not it's possible left to deal with.

But you didn't escape unobserved, so you have to give an argument for both.

Well, then, I'll have to accept my punishment. But do me this favor. Let me, as if on a holiday, do what lazy people do who feast on their own thoughts when out for a solitary walk. Instead of finding out how something they desire might actually come about, these people pass that over, so as to avoid tiring deliberations about what's possible and what isn't. They assume that what they desire is available and proceed to arrange the rest, taking pleasure in thinking through everything they'll do when they have what they want, thereby making their lazy souls even lazier. I'm getting soft myself at the moment, so I want to delay consideration

---

6. Plato is here adapting a phrase of Pindar, "plucking the unripe fruit of wisdom," frg. 209 (Snell).

of the feasibility of our proposal until later. With your permission, I'll assume that it's feasible and examine how the rulers will arrange these matters when they come to pass. And I'll try to show that nothing could be more beneficial to the city and its guardians than those arrangements. These are the things I'll examine with you first, and I'll deal with the other question later, but only if you'll permit me to do it this way.

You have my permission, so carry on with your examination.

c   I suppose that our rulers and auxiliaries—if indeed they're worthy of the names—will be willing to command and to obey respectively. In some cases, the rulers will themselves be obeying our laws, and in others, namely, the ones we leave to their discretion, they'll give directions that are in the spirit of our laws.

Probably so.

Then you, as their lawgiver, will select women just as you did men, with natures as similar to theirs as possible, and hand them over to the men. And since they have common dwellings and meals, rather than
d   private ones, and live together and mix together both in physical training and in the rest of their upbringing, they will, I suppose, be driven by innate necessity to have sex with one another. Or don't you think we're talking about necessities here?

The necessities aren't geometrical but erotic, and they're probably better than the others at persuading and compelling the majority of people.

That's right. But the next point, Glaucon, is that promiscuity is impious
e   in a city of happy people, and the rulers won't allow it.

No, for it isn't right.

Then it's clear that our next task must be to make marriage as sacred as possible. And the sacred marriages will be those that are most beneficial.

Absolutely.

How, then, will they be most beneficial? Tell me this, Glaucon: I see
459   that you have hunting dogs and quite a flock of noble fighting birds at home. Have you noticed anything about their mating and breeding?

Like what?

In the first place, although they're all noble, aren't there some that are the best and prove themselves to be so?

There are.

Do you breed them all alike, or do you try to breed from the best as much as possible?

I try to breed from the best.

And do you breed from the youngest or the oldest or from those in
b   their prime?

From those in their prime.

And do you think that if they weren't bred in this way, your stock of birds and dogs would get much worse?

I do.

What about horses and other animals? Are things any different with them?

It would be strange if they were.

Dear me! If this also holds true of human beings, our need for excellent rulers is indeed extreme.

It does hold of them. But what of it?   c

Because our rulers will then have to use a lot of drugs. And while an inferior doctor is adequate for people who are willing to follow a regimen and don't need drugs, when drugs are needed, we know that a bolder doctor is required.

That's true. But what exactly do you have in mind?

I mean that it looks as though our rulers will have to make considerable use of falsehood and deception for the benefit of those they rule. And we said that all such falsehoods are useful as a form of drug.[7]   d

And we were right.

Well, it seems we were right, especially where marriages and the producing of children are concerned.

How so?

It follows from our previous agreements, first, that the best men must have sex with the best women as frequently as possible, while the opposite is true of the most inferior men and women, and, second, that if our herd is to be of the highest possible quality, the former's offspring must be reared but not the latter's. And this must all be brought about without   e
being noticed by anyone except the rulers, so that our herd of guardians remains as free from dissension as possible.

That's absolutely right.

Therefore certain festivals and sacrifices will be established by law at which we'll bring the brides and grooms together, and we'll direct our poets to compose appropriate hymns for the marriages that take place. We'll leave the number of marriages for the rulers to decide, but their aim   460
will be to keep the number of males as stable as they can, taking into account war, disease, and similar factors, so that the city will, as far as possible, become neither too big nor too small.

That's right.

Then there'll have to be some sophisticated lotteries introduced, so that at each marriage the inferior people we mentioned will blame luck rather than the rulers when they aren't chosen.

There will.

And among other prizes and rewards the young men who are good in war or other things must be given permission to have sex with the women   b
more often, since this will also be a good pretext for having them father as many of the children as possible.

That's right.

And then, as the children are born, they'll be taken over by the officials appointed for the purpose, who may be either men or women or both, since our offices are open to both sexes.

7. See 382c ff. and 414b ff.

Yes.

I think they'll take the children of good parents to the nurses in charge
c   of the rearing pen situated in a separate part of the city, but the children
of inferior parents, or any child of the others that is born defective, they'll
hide in a secret and unknown place, as is appropriate.

It is, if indeed the guardian breed is to remain pure.

And won't the nurses also see to it that the mothers are brought to the
rearing pen when their breasts have milk, taking every precaution to insure
that no mother knows her own child and providing wet nurses if the
d   mother's milk is insufficient? And won't they take care that the mothers
suckle the children for only a reasonable amount of time and that the care
of sleepless children and all other such troublesome duties are taken over
by the wet nurses and other attendants?

You're making it very easy for the wives of the guardians to have
children.

And that's only proper. So let's take up the next thing we proposed.
We said that the children's parents should be in their prime.

True.

Do you share the view that a woman's prime lasts about twenty years
e   and a man's about thirty?

Which years are those?

A woman is to bear children for the city from the age of twenty to the
age of forty, a man from the time that he passes his peak as a runner until
he reaches fifty-five.

461   At any rate, that's the physical and mental prime for both.

Then, if a man who is younger or older than that engages in reproduction
for the community, we'll say that his offense is neither pious nor just, for
the child he begets for the city, if it remains hidden, will be born in darkness,
through a dangerous weakness of will, and without the benefit of the
sacrifices and prayers offered at every marriage festival, in which the
priests and priestesses, together with the entire city, ask that the children
of good and beneficial parents may always prove themselves still better
b   and more beneficial.

That's right.

The same law will apply if a man still of begetting years has a child
with a woman of child-bearing age without the sanction of the rulers.
We'll say that he brings to the city an illegitimate, unauthorized, and
unhallowed child.

That's absolutely right.

However, I think that when women and men have passed the age of
having children, we'll leave them free to have sex with whomever they
wish, with these exceptions: For a man—his daughter, his mother, his
c   daughter's children, and his mother's ancestors; for a woman—her son
and his descendants, her father and his ancestors. Having received these
instructions, they should be very careful not to let a single fetus see the
light of day, but if one is conceived and forces its way to the light, they
must deal with it in the knowledge that no nurture is available for it.

That's certainly sensible. But how will they recognize their fathers and daughters and the others you mentioned?

They have no way of knowing. But a man will call all the children born in the tenth or seventh month after he became a bridegroom his sons, if they're male, and his daughters, if they're female, and they'll call him father. He'll call their children his grandchildren, and they'll call the group to which he belongs grandfathers and grandmothers. And those who were born at the same time as their mothers and fathers were having children they'll call their brothers and sisters. Thus, as we were saying, the relevant groups will avoid sexual relations with each other. But the law will allow brothers and sisters to have sex with one another if the lottery works out that way and the Pythia[8] approves.

That's absolutely right.

This, then, Glaucon, is how the guardians of your city have their wives and children in common. We must now confirm that this arrangement is both consistent with the rest of the constitution and by far the best. Or how else are we to proceed?

In just that way.

Then isn't the first step towards agreement to ask ourselves what we say is the greatest good in designing the city—the good at which the legislator aims in making the laws—and what is the greatest evil? And isn't the next step to examine whether the system we've just described fits into the tracks of the good and not into those of the bad?

Absolutely.

Is there any greater evil we can mention for a city than that which tears it apart and makes it many instead of one? Or any greater good than that which binds it together and makes it one?

There isn't.

And when, as far as possible, all the citizens rejoice and are pained by the same successes and failures, doesn't this sharing of pleasures and pains bind the city together?

It most certainly does.

But when some suffer greatly, while others rejoice greatly, at the same things happening to the city or its people, doesn't this privatization of pleasures and pains dissolve the city?

Of course.

And isn't that what happens whenever such words as "mine" and "not mine" aren't used in unison? And similarly with "someone else's"?

Precisely.

Then, is the best-governed city the one in which most people say "mine" and "not mine" about the same things in the same way?

It is indeed.

What about the city that is most like a single person? For example, when one of us hurts his finger, the entire organism that binds body and soul together into a single system under the ruling part within it is aware of

---

8. The priestess of Apollo at Delphi.

d   this, and the whole feels the pain together with the part that suffers. That's
     why we say that the man has a pain in his finger. And the same can be
     said about any part of a man, with regard either to the pain it suffers or
     to the pleasure it experiences when it finds relief.

     Certainly. And, as for your question, the city with the best government
     is most like such a person.

     Then, whenever anything good or bad happens to a single one of its
     citizens, such a city above all others will say that the affected part is its
e   own and will share in the pleasure or pain as a whole.

     If it has good laws, that must be so.

     It's time now to return to our own city, to look there for the features
     we've agreed on, and to determine whether it or some other city possesses
     them to the greatest degree.

     Then that's what we must do.

     What about those other cities? Aren't there rulers and people in them,
463 as well as in ours?

     There are.

     Besides fellow citizens, what do the people call the rulers in those
     other cities?

     In many they call them despots, but in democracies they are called just
     this—rulers.

     What about the people in our city? Besides fellow citizens, what do they
     call their rulers?

b   Preservers and auxiliaries.

     And what do they in turn call the people?

     Providers of upkeep and wages.

     What do the rulers call the people in other cities?

     Slaves.

     And what do the rulers call each other?

     Co-rulers.

     And ours?

     Co-guardians.

     Can you tell me whether a ruler in those other cities could address some
     of his co-rulers as his kinsmen and others as outsiders?

     Yes, many could.

     And doesn't he consider his kinsman to be his own, and doesn't he
c   address him as such, while he considers the outsider not to be his own?

     He does.

     What about your guardians? Could any of them consider a co-guardian
     as an outsider or address him as such?

     There's no way he could, for when he meets any one of them, he'll hold
     that he's meeting a brother or sister, a father or mother, a son or daughter,
     or some ancestor or descendant of theirs.

     You put that very well. But tell me this: Will your laws require them
     simply to use these kinship names or also to do all the things that go along
d   with the names? Must they show to their "fathers" the respect, solicitude,

and obedience we show to our parents by law? Won't they fare worse at the hands of gods and humans, as people whose actions are neither pious nor just, if they do otherwise? Will these be the oracular sayings they hear from all the citizens from their childhood on, or will they hear something else about their fathers—or the ones they're told are their fathers—and other relatives?

The former. It would be absurd if they only mouthed kinship names without doing the things that go along with them.   e

Therefore, in our city more than in any other, they'll speak in unison the words we mentioned a moment ago. When any one of them is doing well or badly, they'll say that "mine" is doing well or that "mine" is doing badly.

That's absolutely true.

Now, didn't we say that the having and expressing of this conviction is closely followed by the having of pleasures and pains in common?   464

Yes, and we were right.

Then won't our citizens, more than any others, have the same thing in common, the one they call "mine"? And, having that in common, won't they, more than any others, have common pleasures and pains?

Of course.

And, in addition to the other institutions, the cause of this is the having of wives and children in common by the guardians?

That more than anything else is the cause.

But we agreed that the having of pains and pleasures in common is the greatest good for a city, and we characterized a well-governed city in terms of the body's reaction to pain or pleasure in any one of its parts.   b

And we were right to agree.

Then, the cause of the greatest good for our city has been shown to be the having of wives and children in common by the auxiliaries.

It has.

And, of course, this is consistent with what we said before, for we said somewhere that, if they're going to be guardians, they mustn't have private houses, property, or possessions, but must receive their upkeep from the other citizens as a wage for their guardianship and enjoy it in common.[9]   c

That's right.

Then isn't it true, just as I claimed, that what we are saying now, taken together with what we said before, makes even better guardians out of them and prevents them from tearing the city apart by not calling the same thing "mine"? If different people apply the term to different things, one would drag into his own house whatever he could separate from the others, and another would drag things into a different house to a different wife and children, and this would make for private pleasures and pains   d
at private things. But our people, on the other hand, will think of the same

9. See 416d ff.

things as their own, aim at the same goal, and, as far as possible, feel pleasure and pain in unison.

Precisely.

And what about lawsuits and mutual accusations? Won't they pretty well disappear from among them, because they have everything in common except their own bodies? Hence they'll be spared all the dissension that arises between people because of the possession of money, children, and families.

e

They'll necessarily be spared it.

Nor could any lawsuits for insult or injury justly occur among them, for we'll declare that it's a fine and just thing for people to defend themselves against others of the same age, since this will compel them to stay in good physical shape.

That's right.

465

This law is also correct for another reason: If a spirited person vents his anger in this way, it will be less likely to lead him into more serious disputes.

Certainly.

But an older person will be authorized to rule and punish all the younger ones.

Clearly.

And surely it's also obvious that a younger person won't strike or do any sort of violence to an older one or fail to show him respect in other ways, unless the rulers command it, for there are two guardians sufficient to prevent him from doing such things—shame and fear. Shame will prevent him from laying a hand on his parents, and so will the fear that the others would come to the aid of the victim, some as his sons, some as his brothers, and some as his fathers.

b

That's the effect they'll have.

Then, in all cases, won't the laws induce men to live at peace with one another?

Very much so.

And if there's no discord among the guardians, there's no danger that the rest of the city will break into civil war, either with them or among themselves.

Certainly not.

I hesitate to mention, since they're so unseemly, the pettiest of the evils the guardians would therefore escape: The poor man's flattery of the rich, the perplexities and sufferings involved in bringing up children and in making the money necessary to feed the household, getting into debt, paying it off, and in some way or other providing enough money to hand over to their wives and household slaves to manage. All of the various troubles men endure in these matters are obvious, ignoble, and not worth discussing.

c

d

They're obvious even to the blind.

They'll be free of all these, and they'll live a life more blessedly happy than that of the victors in the Olympian games.

How?

The Olympian victors are considered happy on account of only a small part of what is available to our guardians, for the guardians' victory is even greater, and their upkeep from public funds more complete. The victory they gain is the preservation of the whole city, and the crown of victory that they and their children receive is their upkeep and all the necessities of life. They receive rewards from their own city while they live, and at their death they're given a worthy burial.   e

Those are very good things.

Do you remember that, earlier in our discussion, someone—I forget who—shocked us by saying that we hadn't made our guardians happy, that it was possible for them to have everything that belongs to the citizens, yet they had nothing? We said, I think, that if this happened to come up   466 at some point, we'd look into it then, but that our concern at the time was to make our guardians true guardians and the city the happiest we could, rather than looking to any one group within it and molding it for happiness.[10]

I remember.

Well, then, if the life of our auxiliaries is apparently much finer and better than that of Olympian victors, is there any need to compare it to the lives of cobblers, farmers, or other craftsmen?   b

Not in my opinion.

Then it's surely right to repeat here what I said then: If a guardian seeks happiness in such a way that he's no longer a guardian and isn't satisfied with a life that's moderate, stable, and—as we say—best, but a silly, adolescent idea of happiness seizes him and incites him to use his power to take everything in the city for himself, he'll come to know the true wisdom of   c Hesiod's saying that somehow "the half is worth more than the whole."[11]

If he takes my advice, he'll keep to his own life-style.

You agree, then, that the women and men should associate with one another in education, in things having to do with children, and in guarding the other citizens in the way we've described; that both when they remain in the city and when they go to war, they must guard together and hunt together like dogs and share in everything as far as possible; and that by   d doing so they'll be doing what's best and not something contrary either to woman's nature as compared with man's or to the natural association of men and women with one another.

I agree.

Then doesn't it remain for us to determine whether it's possible to bring about this association among human beings, as it is among animals, and to say just how it might be done?

You took the words right out of my mouth.

10. See 419a ff.
11. *Works and Days* 40.

e   As far as war is concerned, I think it's clear how they will wage it.
        How so?
        Men and women will campaign together. They'll take the sturdy children
with them, so that, like the children of other craftsmen, they can see what
they'll have to do when they grow up. But in addition to observing, they
can serve and assist in everything to do with the war and help their mothers
467   and fathers. Haven't you noticed in the other crafts how the children of
potters, for example, assist and observe for a long time before actually
making any pots?
        I have indeed.
        And should these craftsmen take more care in training their children
by appropriate experience and observation than the guardians?
        Of course not; that would be completely ridiculous.
b   Besides, every animal fights better in the presence of its young.
        That's so. But, Socrates, there's a considerable danger that in a defeat—
and such things are likely to happen in a war—they'll lose their children's
lives as well as their own, making it impossible for the rest of the city
to recover.
        What you say is true. But do you think that the first thing we should
provide for is the avoidance of all danger?
        Not at all.
        Well, then, if people will probably have to face some danger, shouldn't
it be the sort that will make them better if they come through it successfully?
        Obviously.
        And do you think that whether or not men who are going to be warriors
observe warfare when they're still boys makes such a small difference that
c   it isn't worth the danger of having them do it?
        No, it does make a difference to what you're talking about.
        On the assumption, then, that the children are to be observers of war,
if we can contrive some way to keep them secure, everything will be fine,
won't it?
        Yes.
        Well, then, in the first place, their fathers won't be ignorant, will they,
about which campaigns are dangerous and which are not, but rather as
d   knowledgeable about this as any human beings can be?
        Probably so.
        Then they'll take the children to some campaigns and not to others?
        Correct.
        And they'll put officers in charge of them whose age and experience
qualifies them to be leaders and tutors?
        Appropriately so.
        But, as we say, the unexpected often occurs.
        Indeed.
        With this in mind, we must provide the children with wings when
they're small, so that they can fly away and escape.

What do you mean?   e

We must mount them on horses as early as possible—not on spirited or aggressive horses, but on very fast and manageable ones—and when they've learned to ride, they must be taken to observe a war. In this way, they'll get the best look at their own work and, if the need arises, make the securest possible escape to safety, following their older guides.

I think you're right.

What about warfare itself? What attitude should your soldiers have to   468
each other and to the enemy? Are my views about this right or not?

First, tell me what they are.

If one of them leaves his post or throws away his shield or does anything else of that sort through cowardice, shouldn't he be reduced to being a craftsman or farmer?

Certainly.

And shouldn't anyone who is captured alive be left to his captors as a gift to do with as they wish?

Absolutely.   b

But don't you think that anyone who distinguishes himself and earns high esteem should, while still on the campaign, first be crowned with wreaths by each of the adolescents and children who accompany the expedition?

I do.

And what about shaken by the right hand?

That too.

But I suppose that you wouldn't go this far?

Namely?

That he should kiss and be kissed by each of them.

That most of all. And I'd add this to the law: As long as the campaign lasts, no one he wants to kiss shall be allowed to refuse, for then, if one of them happens to be in love with another, whether male or female, he'll   c
be all the more eager to win the rewards of valor.

Excellent. And we've already stated that, since he's a good person, more marriages will be available to him, and he'll be selected for such things more frequently than the others, so that he'll beget as many children as possible.

Yes, we did say that.

Indeed, according to Homer too, it is just to honor in such ways those young people who are good, for he says that Ajax, when he distinguished himself in battle, "was rewarded with the long cut off the backbone." And   d
that's an appropriate honor for a courageous young man, since it will both honor him and increase his strength.

That's absolutely right.

Then we'll follow Homer in these matters at least. And insofar as good people have shown themselves to be good, we'll honor them at sacrifices and all such occasions with hymns, "seats of honor, meats, and well-filled

cups of wine,"[12] and in all the other ways we mentioned, so that, in addition
e   to honoring good men and women, we'll continue to train them.

That's excellent.

All right. And as for those who died on the campaign, won't we say,
first of all, that, if their deaths were distinguished, they belong to the
golden race?

That above all.

And won't we believe with Hesiod that, whenever any of that race die,
they become

469   *Sacred daemons living upon the earth,*
            Noble spirits, protectors against evil, guardians of articulate mortals?[13]

We'll certainly believe that.

Then we'll inquire from the god[14] what kind of distinguished funeral
we should give to daemonic and godlike people, and we'll follow his instructions.

Of course.

And for the remainder of time, we'll care for their graves and worship
at them as we would at those of daemons. And we'll follow the same rites
b   for anyone whom we judge to have lived an outstandingly good life,
whether he died of old age or in some other way.

That is only just.

Now, what about enemies? How will our soldiers deal with them?

In what respect?

First, enslavement. Do you think it is just for Greeks to enslave Greek
cities, or, as far as they can, should they not even allow other cities to do
so, and make a habit of sparing the Greek race, as a precaution against
c   being enslaved by the barbarians?

It's altogether and in every way best to spare the Greek race.

Then isn't it also best for the guardians not to acquire a Greek slave and
to advise the other Greeks not to do so either?

Absolutely. In that way they'd be more likely to turn against the barbarians and keep their hands off one another.

What about despoiling the dead? Is it a good thing to strip the dead of
anything besides their armor after a victory? Or don't cowards make this
d   an excuse for not facing the enemy—as if they were doing something of
vital importance in bending over a corpse? And haven't many armies been
lost because of such plundering?

12. The last two quotations are from *Iliad* vii.321 and viii.162, respectively.

13. *Works and Days* 122.

14. Apollo. See 427b.

Indeed, they have.

Don't you think it's slavish and money-loving to strip a corpse? Isn't it small-minded and womanish to regard the body as your enemy, when the enemy himself has flitted away, leaving behind only the instrument with which he fought? Or do you think such behavior any different from that of dogs who get angry with the stone that hits them and leave the thrower alone?   e

It's no different at all.

Then may our soldiers strip corpses or refuse the enemy permission to pick up their dead?

No, by god, they certainly may not.

Moreover, we won't take enemy arms to the temples as offerings, and if we care about the goodwill of other Greeks, we especially won't do this with *their* arms. Rather we'd be afraid of polluting the temples if we   470 brought them such things from our own people, unless, of course, the god tells us otherwise.

That's absolutely right.

What about ravaging the land of the Greeks and burning their houses? Will your soldiers do things of this sort to their enemies?

I'd like to hear *your* opinion about that.

Well, I think they should do neither of these things but destroy the year's harvest only. Do you want me to tell you why?   b

Of course.

It seems to me that as we have two names, "war" and "civil war," so there are two things and the names apply to two kinds of disagreements arising in them. The two things I'm referring to are what is one's own and akin, on the one hand, and what's foreign and strange, on the other. The name "civil war" applies to hostilities with one's own, while "war" applies to hostilities with strangers.

That's certainly to the point.

Then see whether this is also to the point: I say that the Greek race is its own and akin, but is strange and foreign to barbarians.   c

That's right.

Then when Greeks do battle with barbarians or barbarians with Greeks, we'll say that they're natural enemies and that such hostilities are to be called war. But when Greeks fight with Greeks, we'll say that they are natural friends and that in such circumstances Greece is sick and divided into factions and that such hostilities are to be called civil war.   d

I, at any rate, agree to think of it that way.

Now, notice that, wherever something of the sort that's currently called civil war occurs and a city is divided, if either party ravages the land of the others and burns their houses, it's thought that this is abominable and that neither party loves their city, since otherwise they'd never have ravaged their very nurse and mother. However, it *is* thought appropriate for the victors to carry off the harvest of the vanquished. Nonetheless, their

attitude of mind should be that of people who'll one day be reconciled
e   and who won't always be at war.

This way of thinking is far more civilized than the other.

What about the city you're founding? It is Greek, isn't it?

It has to be.

Then, won't your citizens be good and civilized?

Indeed they will.

Then, won't they love Greece? Won't they consider Greece as their own
and share the religion of the other Greeks?

Yes, indeed.

Then won't they consider their differences with Greeks—people who
471   are their own—not as war but as civil war?

Of course.

And won't they quarrel like people who know that one day they'll
be reconciled?

Certainly.

Then they'll moderate their foes in a friendly spirit, not punish them
with enslavement and destruction, for they're moderators, not enemies.

That's right.

And being Greeks, they won't ravage Greece or burn her houses, nor
will they agree that in any of her cities all the inhabitants—men, women,
and children—are their enemies, but that whatever differences arise are
caused by the few enemies that any city inevitably contains. Because of
this, because the majority are friendly, they won't ravage the country or
b   destroy the houses, and they'll continue their quarrel only to the point at
which those who caused it are forced to pay the penalty by those who
were its innocent victims.

I agree that this is the way our citizens must treat their enemies, and
they must treat barbarians the way Greeks currently treat each other.

Then shall we also impose this law on the guardians: Neither ravage
c   the country nor burn the houses?

Consider it imposed. And let's also assume that this law and its predecessors are all fine. But I think, Socrates, that if we let you go on speaking
about this subject, you'll never remember the one you set aside in order
to say all this, namely, whether it's possible for this constitution to come
into being and in what way it could be brought about. I agree that, if it
existed, all the things we've mentioned would be good for the city in
which they occurred. And I'll add some that you've left out. The guardians
would be excellent fighters against an enemy because they'd be least likely
to desert each other, since they know each other as brothers, fathers, and
d   sons, and call each other by those names. Moreover, if their women joined
their campaigns, either in the same ranks or positioned in the rear to
frighten the enemy and in case their help should ever be needed, I know
that this would make them quite unbeatable. And I also see all the good
things that they'd have at home that you've omitted. Take it that I agree
e   that all these things would happen, as well as innumerable others, if this

kind of constitution came into being, and say no more on that subject. But rather let's now try to convince ourselves that it is possible and how it is possible, and let the rest go.

This is a sudden attack that you've made on my argument, and you show no sympathy for my delay. Perhaps you don't realize that, just as I've barely escaped from the first two waves of objections, you're bringing the third—the biggest and most difficult one—down upon me. When you see and hear it, you'll surely be completely sympathetic, and recognize that it was, after all, appropriate for me to hesitate and be afraid to state and look into so paradoxical a view.

The more you speak like that, the less we'll let you off from telling us how it's possible for this constitution to come into being. So speak instead of wasting time.

Well, then, we must first remember that we got to this point while trying to discover what justice and injustice are like.

We must. But what of it?

Nothing. But if we discover what justice is like, will we also maintain that the just man is in no way different from the just itself, so that he is like justice in every respect? Or will we be satisfied if he comes as close to it as possible and participates in it far more than anyone else?

We'll be satisfied with that.

Then it was in order to have a model that we were trying to discover what justice itself is like and what the completely just man would be like, if he came into being, and what kind of man he'd be if he did, and likewise with regard to injustice and the most unjust man. We thought that, by looking at how their relationship to happiness and its opposite seemed to us, we'd also be compelled to agree about ourselves as well, that the one who was most like them would have a portion of happiness most like theirs. But we weren't trying to discover these things in order to prove that it's possible for them to come into being.

That's true.

Do you think that someone is a worse painter if, having painted a model of what the finest and most beautiful human being would be like and having rendered every detail of his picture adequately, he could not prove that such a man could come into being?

No, by god, I don't.

Then what about our own case? Didn't we say that we were making a theoretical model of a good city?[15]

Certainly.

So do you think that our discussion will be any less reasonable if we can't prove that it's possible to found a city that's the same as the one in our theory?

Not at all.

15. See 369a–c.

Then that's the truth of the matter. But if, in order to please you, I must also be willing to show how and under what conditions it would most be possible to found such a city, then you should agree to make the same concessions to me, in turn, for the purposes of this demonstration.

Which ones?

473

Is it possible to do anything in practice the same as in theory? Or is it in the nature of practice to grasp truth less well than theory does, even if some people don't think so? Will you first agree to this or not?

I agree.

Then don't compel me to show that what we've described in theory can come into being exactly as we've described it. Rather, if we're able to discover how a city could come to be governed in a way that most closely approximates our description, let's say that we've shown what you ordered us to show, namely, that it's possible for our city to come to be. Or wouldn't

b you be satisfied with that? *I* would be satisfied with it.

So would I.

Then next, it seems, we should try to discover and point out what's now badly done in cities that keeps them from being governed in that way and what's the smallest change that would enable our city to reach our sort of constitution—one change, if possible, or if not one, two, and if not two, then the fewest in number and the least extensive.

c That's absolutely right.

There is one change we could point to that, in my opinion, would accomplish this. It's certainly neither small nor easy, but it is possible.

What is it?

Well, I've now come to what we likened to the greatest wave. But I shall say what I have to say, even if the wave is a wave of laughter that will simply drown me in ridicule and contempt. So listen to what I'm going to say.

Say on.

Until philosophers rule as kings or those who are now called kings and leading men genuinely and adequately philosophize, that is, until political

d power and philosophy entirely coincide, while the many natures who at present pursue either one exclusively are forcibly prevented from doing so, cities will have no rest from evils, Glaucon, nor, I think, will the human race. And, until this happens, the constitution we've been describing in

e theory will never be born to the fullest extent possible or see the light of the sun. It's because I saw how very paradoxical this statement would be that I hesitated to make it for so long, for it's hard to face up to the fact that there can be no happiness, either public or private, in any other city.

Socrates, after hurling a speech and statement like that at us, you must expect that a great many people (and not undistinguished ones either) will cast off their cloaks and, stripped for action, snatch any available

474 weapon, and make a determined rush at you, ready to do terrible things. So, unless you can hold them off by argument and escape, you really will pay the penalty of general derision.

Well, you are the one that brought this on me.

And I was right to do it. However, I won't betray you, but rather defend you in any way I can—by goodwill, by urging you on, and perhaps by being able to give you more appropriate answers than someone else. So, with the promise of this assistance, try to show the unbelievers that things are as you say they are.   b

I must try it, then, especially since you agree to be so great an ally. If we're to escape from the people you mention, I think we need to define for them who the philosophers are that we dare to say must rule. And once that's clear, we should be able to defend ourselves by showing that the people we mean are fitted by nature both to engage in philosophy and to rule in a city, while the rest are naturally fitted to leave philosophy   c
alone and follow their leader.

This would be a good time to give that definition.

Come, then, follow me, and we'll see whether or not there's some way to set it out adequately.

Lead on.

Do you need to be reminded or do you remember that, if it's rightly said that someone loves something, then he mustn't love one part of it and not another, but he must love all of it?[16]

I think you'll have to remind me, for I don't understand it at all.   d

That would be an appropriate response, Glaucon, for somebody else to make. But it isn't appropriate for an erotically inclined man to forget that all boys in the bloom of youth pique the interest of a lover of boys and arouse him and that all seem worthy of his care and pleasure. Or isn't that the way you people behave to fine and beautiful boys? You praise a snub-nosed one as cute, a hook-nosed one you say is regal, one in between is well proportioned, dark ones look manly, and pale ones are children of the gods. And as for a honey-colored boy, do you think that this very term   e
is anything but the euphemistic coinage of a lover who found it easy to tolerate sallowness, provided it was accompanied by the bloom of youth? In a word, you find all kinds of terms and excuses so as not to reject   475
anyone whose flower is in bloom.

If you insist on taking me as your example of what erotically inclined men do, then, for the sake of the argument, I agree.

Further, don't you see wine-lovers behave in the same way? Don't they love every kind of wine and find any excuse to enjoy it?

Certainly.

And I think you see honor-lovers, if they can't be generals, be captains, and, if they can't be honored by people of importance and dignity, they put up with being honored by insignificant and inferior ones, for they desire the whole of honor.   b

Exactly.

Then do you agree to this or not? When we say that someone desires something, do we mean that he desires everything of that kind or that he desires one part of it but not another?

---

16. See 438a–b.

We mean he desires everything.

Then won't we also say that the philosopher doesn't desire one part of wisdom rather than another, but desires the whole thing?

Yes, that's true.

And as for the one who's choosy about what he learns, especially if he's young and can't yet give an account of what is useful and what
c   isn't, we won't say that he is a lover of learning or a philosopher, for we wouldn't say that someone who's choosy about his food is hungry or has an appetite for food or is a lover of food—instead, we'd say that he is a bad eater.

And we'd be right to say it.

But the one who readily and willingly tries all kinds of learning, who turns gladly to learning and is insatiable for it, is rightly called a philosopher, isn't he?

d   Then many strange people will be philosophers, for the lovers of sights seem to be included, since they take pleasure in learning things. And the lovers of sounds are very strange people to include as philosophers, for they would never willingly attend a serious discussion or spend their time that way, yet they run around to all the Dionysiac festivals, omitting none, whether in cities or villages, as if their ears were under contract to listen to every chorus. Are we to say that these people—and those who learn
e   similar things or petty crafts—are philosophers?

No, but they are *like* philosophers.

And who are the true philosophers?

Those who love the sight of truth.

That's right, but what exactly do you mean by it?

It would not be easy to explain to someone else, but I think that you will agree to this.

To what?

Since the beautiful is the opposite of the ugly, they are two.
476   Of course.

And since they are two, each is one?

I grant that also.

And the same account is true of the just and the unjust, the good and the bad, and all the forms. Each of them is itself one, but because they manifest themselves everywhere in association with actions, bodies, and one another, each of them appears to be many.

That's right.

So, I draw this distinction: On one side are those you just now called lovers of sights, lovers of crafts, and practical people; on the other side are
b   those we are arguing about and whom one would alone call philosophers.

How do you mean?

The lovers of sights and sounds like beautiful sounds, colors, shapes, and everything fashioned out of them, but their thought is unable to see and embrace the nature of the beautiful itself.

That's for sure.

In fact, there are very few people who would be able to reach the beautiful itself and see it by itself. Isn't that so?

Certainly.   c

What about someone who believes in beautiful things, but doesn't believe in the beautiful itself and isn't able to follow anyone who could lead him to the knowledge of it? Don't you think he is living in a dream rather than a wakened state? Isn't this dreaming: whether asleep or awake, to think that a likeness is not a likeness but rather the thing itself that it is like?

I certainly think that someone who does that is dreaming.

But someone who, to take the opposite case, believes in the beautiful itself, can see both it and the things that participate in it and doesn't believe that the participants are it or that it itself is the participants—is he living   d
in a dream or is he awake?

He's very much awake.

So we'd be right to call his thought knowledge, since he knows, but we should call the other person's thought opinion, since he opines?

Right.

What if the person who has opinion but not knowledge is angry with us and disputes the truth of what we are saying? Is there some way to console him and persuade him gently, while hiding from him that he isn't   e
in his right mind?

There must be.

Consider, then, what we'll say to him. Won't we question him like this? First, we'll tell him that nobody begrudges him any knowledge he may have and that we'd be delighted to discover that he knows something. Then we'll say: "Tell us, does the person who knows know something or nothing?" You answer for him.

He knows something.

Something that is or something that is not?[17]

Something that is, for how could something that is not be known?   477

Then we have an adequate grasp of this: No matter how many ways we examine it, what is completely is completely knowable and what is in no way is in every way unknowable?

A most adequate one.

Good. Now, if anything is such as to be and also not to be, won't it be intermediate between what purely is and what in no way is?

Yes, it's intermediate.

Then, as knowledge is set over what is, while ignorance is of necessity set over what is not, mustn't we find an intermediate between knowledge

---

17. Because of the ambiguity of the verb *einai* ("to be"), Socrates could be asking any or all of the following questions: (1) "Something that exists or something that does not exist?" (existential "is"); (2) "Something that is beautiful (say) or something that is not beautiful?" (predicative "is"); (3) "Something that is true or something that is not true?" (veridical "is").

and ignorance to be set over what is intermediate between what is and
b   what is not, if there is such a thing?

Certainly.

Do we say that opinion is something?

Of course.

A different power from knowledge or the same?

A different one.

Opinion, then, is set over one thing, and knowledge over another, according to the power of each.

Right.

Now, isn't knowledge by its nature set over what is, to know it as it is? But first maybe we'd better be a bit more explicit.

How so?

c   Powers are a class of the things that are that enable us—or anything else for that matter—to do whatever we are capable of doing. Sight, for example, and hearing are among the powers, if you understand the kind of thing I'm referring to.

I do.

Here's what I think about them. A power has neither color nor shape nor any feature of the sort that many other things have and that I use to distinguish those things from one another. In the case of a power, I use
d   only what it is set over and what it does, and by reference to these I call each the power it is: What is set over the same things and does the same I call the same power; what is set over something different and does something different I call a different one. Do you agree?

I do.

Then let's back up. Is knowledge a power, or what class would you put it in?

It's a power, the strongest of them all.

e   And what about opinion, is it a power or some other kind of thing?

It's a power as well, for it is what enables us to opine.

A moment ago you agreed that knowledge and opinion aren't the same.

How could a person with any understanding think that a fallible power is the same as an infallible one?

478   Right. Then we agree that opinion is clearly different from knowledge.

It is different.

Hence each of them is by nature set over something different and does something different?

Necessarily.

Knowledge is set over what is, to know it as it is?

Yes.

And opinion opines?

Yes.

Does it opine the very thing that knowledge knows, so that the knowable and the opinable are the same, or is this impossible?

It's impossible, given what we agreed, for if a different power is set over something different, and opinion and knowledge are different powers, then the knowable and the opinable cannot be the same.

                                                              b

Then, if what is is knowable, the opinable must be something other than what is?

It must.

Do we, then, opine what is not? Or is it impossible to opine what is not? Think about this. Doesn't someone who opines set his opinion over something? Or is it possible to opine, yet to opine nothing?

It's impossible.

But someone who opines opines some one thing?

Yes.

Surely the most accurate word for that which is not isn't "one thing" but "nothing"?

                                                              c

Certainly.

But we had to set ignorance over what is not and knowledge over what is?

That's right.

So someone opines neither what is nor what is not?

How could it be otherwise?

Then opinion is neither ignorance nor knowledge?

So it seems.

Then does it go beyond either of these? Is it clearer than knowledge or darker than ignorance?

No, neither.

Is opinion, then, darker than knowledge but clearer than ignorance?

It is.

Then it lies between them?

                                                              d

Yes.

So opinion is intermediate between those two?

Absolutely.

Now, we said that, if something could be shown, as it were, to be and not to be at the same time, it would be intermediate between what purely is and what in every way is not, and that neither knowledge nor ignorance would be set over it, but something intermediate between ignorance and knowledge?

Correct.

And now the thing we call opinion has emerged as being intermediate between them?

It has.

Apparently, then, it only remains for us to find what participates in both being and not being and cannot correctly be called purely one or the other, in order that, if there is such a thing, we can rightly call it the opinable, thereby setting the extremes over the extremes and the intermediate over the intermediate. Isn't that so?

                                                              e

It is.

Now that these points have been established, I want to address a question
479   to our friend who doesn't believe in the beautiful itself or any form of the
beautiful itself that remains always the same in all respects but who does
believe in the many beautiful things—the lover of sights who wouldn't
allow anyone to say that the beautiful itself is one or that the just is one
or any of the rest: "My dear fellow," we'll say, "of all the many beautiful
things, is there one that will not also appear ugly? Or is there one of those
just things that will not also appear unjust? Or one of those pious things
that will not also appear impious?"

    There isn't one, for it is necessary that they appear to be beautiful in a
b   way and also to be ugly in a way, and the same with the other things you
asked about.

    What about the many doubles? Do they appear any the less halves
than doubles?

    Not one.

    So, with the many bigs and smalls and lights and heavies, is any one
of them any more the thing someone says it is than its opposite?

    No, each of them always participates in both opposites.

    Is any one of the manys what someone says it is, then, any more than
it is not what he says it is?

    No, they are like the ambiguities one is entertained with at dinner parties
or like the children's riddle about the eunuch who threw something at a
c   bat—the one about what he threw at it and what it was in,[18] for they are
ambiguous, and one cannot understand them as fixedly being or fixedly
not being or as both or as neither.

    Then do you know how to deal with them? Or can you find a more
appropriate place to put them than intermediate between being and not
being? Surely, they can't *be* more than what is or *not be* more than what
is not, for apparently nothing is darker than what is not or clearer than
d   what is.

    Very true.

    We've now discovered, it seems, that the many conventions of the major-
ity of people about beauty and the others are rolling around as intermediates between what is not and what purely is.

    We have.

    And we agreed earlier that anything of that kind would have to be called
the opinable, not the knowable—the wandering intermediate grasped by
the intermediate power.

    We did.

    As for those who study the many beautiful things but do not see the
e   beautiful itself and are incapable of following another who leads them to

---

18. The riddle seems to have been: A man who is not a man saw and did not see a bird
that was not a bird in a tree (lit., a piece of wood) that was not a tree; he hit (lit., threw
at) and did not hit it with a stone that was not a stone. The answer is that a eunuch
with bad eyesight saw a bat on a rafter, threw a pumice stone at it, and missed.

it, who see many just things but not the just itself, and so with everything—these people, we shall say, opine everything but have no knowledge of anything they opine.

Necessarily.

What about the ones who in each case study the things themselves that are always the same in every respect? Won't we say that they know and don't opine?

That's necessary too.

Shall we say, then, that these people love and embrace the things that knowledge is set over, as the others do the things that opinion is set over? Remember we said that the latter saw and loved beautiful sounds and colors and the like but wouldn't allow the beautiful itself to be anything?

We remember, all right.

We won't be in error, then, if we call such people lovers of opinion rather than philosophers or lovers of wisdom and knowledge? Will they be angry with us if we call them that?

Not if they take my advice, for it isn't right to be angry with those who speak the truth.

As for those who in each case embrace the thing itself, we must call them philosophers, not lovers of opinion?

Most definitely.

Book VI

And so, Glaucon, I said, after a somewhat lengthy and difficult discussion, both the philosophers and the nonphilosophers have revealed who they are.

It probably wouldn't have been easy, he said, to have them do it in a shorter one.

Apparently not. But for my part, I think that the matter would have been better illuminated if we had only it to discuss and not all the other things that remain to be treated in order to discover the difference between the just life and the unjust one.

What's our next topic?

What else but the one that's next in order? Since those who are able to grasp what is always the same in all respects are philosophers, while those who are not able to do so and who wander among the many things that vary in every sort of way are not philosophers, which of the two should be the leaders in a city?

What would be a sensible answer to that?

· We should establish as guardians those who are clearly capable of guarding the laws and the ways of life of the city.

That's right.

And isn't it clear that the guardian who is to keep watch over everything should be keen-sighted rather than blind?

Of course it's clear.

Do you think, then, that there's any difference between the blind and those who are really deprived of the knowledge of each thing that is? The latter have no clear model in their souls, and so they cannot—in the manner of painters—look to what is most true, make constant reference to it, and

d   study it as exactly as possible. Hence they cannot establish here on earth conventions about what is fine or just or good, when they need to be established, or guard and preserve them, once they have been established.

No, by god, there isn't much difference between them.

Should we, then, make these blind people our guardians or rather those who know each thing that is and who are not inferior to the others, either in experience or in any other part of virtue?

It would be absurd to choose anyone but philosophers, if indeed they're not inferior in these ways, for the respect in which they are superior is pretty well the most important one.

Then shouldn't we explain how it is possible for someone to have both

485   these sorts of qualities?

Certainly.

Then, as we said at the beginning of this discussion, it is necessary to understand the nature of philosophers first,[1] for I think that, if we can reach adequate agreement about that, we'll also agree that the same people *can* have both qualities and that no one but they should be leaders in cities.

How so?

Let's agree that philosophic natures always love the sort of learning that makes clear to them some feature of the being that always is and does not

b   wander around between coming to be and decaying.

And further, let's agree that, like the honor-lovers and erotically inclined men we described before,[2] they love all such learning and are not willing to give up any part of it, whether large or small, more valuable or less so.

That's right.

Consider next whether the people we're describing must also have this

c   in their nature.

What?

They must be without falsehood—they must refuse to accept what is false, hate it, and have a love for the truth.

That's a reasonable addition, at any rate.

It's not only reasonable, it's entirely necessary, for it's necessary for a man who is erotically inclined by nature to love everything akin to or belonging to the boy he loves.

That's right.

And could you find anything that belongs more to wisdom than truth does?

Of course not.

---

1. See 474b–c.
2. See 474c–475c.

Then is it possible for the same nature to be a philosopher—a lover of wisdom—and a lover of falsehood?   d

Not at all.

Then someone who loves learning must above all strive for every kind of truth from childhood on.

Absolutely.

Now, we surely know that, when someone's desires incline strongly for one thing, they are thereby weakened for others, just like a stream that has been partly diverted into another channel.

Of course.

Then, when someone's desires flow towards learning and everything of that sort, he'd be concerned, I suppose, with the pleasures of the soul itself by itself, and he'd abandon those pleasures that come through the body— if indeed he is a true philosopher and not merely a counterfeit one.

That's completely necessary.   e

Then surely such a person is moderate and not at all a money-lover. It's appropriate for others to take seriously the things for which money and large expenditures are needed, but not for him.

That's right.

And of course there's also this to consider when you are judging whether   486 a nature is philosophic or not.

What's that?

If it is at all slavish, you should not overlook that fact, for pettiness is altogether incompatible with a soul that is always reaching out to grasp everything both divine and human as a whole.

That's completely true.

And will a thinker high-minded enough to study all time and all being consider human life to be something important?

He couldn't possibly.

Then will he consider death to be a terrible thing?   b

He least of all.

Then it seems a cowardly and slavish nature will take no part in true philosophy.

Not in my opinion.

And is there any way that an orderly person, who isn't money-loving, slavish, a boaster, or a coward, could become unreliable or unjust?

There isn't.

Moreover, when you are looking to see whether a soul is philosophic or not, you'll look to see whether it is just and gentle, from youth on, or savage and hard to associate with.

Certainly.

And here's something I think you won't leave out.   c

What?

Whether he's a slow learner or a fast one. Or do you ever expect anyone to love something when it pains him to do it and when much effort brings only small return?

No, it couldn't happen.

And what if he could retain nothing of what he learned, because he was full of forgetfulness? Could he fail to be empty of knowledge?

How could he?

Then don't you think that, if he's laboring in vain, he'd inevitably come to hate both himself and that activity in the end?

Of course.

Then let's never include a forgetful soul among those who are sufficiently
d   philosophical for our purposes, but look for one with a good memory.

Absolutely.

Now, we'd certainly say that the unmusical and graceless element in a person's nature draws him to lack of due measure.

Of course.

And do you think that truth is akin to what lacks due measure or to what is measured?

To what is measured.

Then, in addition to those other things, let's look for someone whose thought is by nature measured and graceful and is easily led to the form of each thing that is.

Of course.

Well, then, don't you think the properties we've enumerated are compatible with one another and that each is necessary to a soul that is to have
e   an adequate and complete grasp of that which is?
487   They're all completely necessary.

Is there any objection you can find, then, to a way of life that no one can adequately follow unless he's by nature good at remembering, quick to learn, high-minded, graceful, and a friend and relative of truth, justice, courage, and moderation?

Not even Momus[3] could find one.

When such people have reached maturity in age and education, wouldn't you entrust the city to them and to them alone?

And Adeimantus replied: No one would be able to contradict the things you've said, Socrates, but on each occasion that you say them, your hearers
b   are affected in some such way as this. They think that, because they're inexperienced in asking and answering questions, they're led astray a little bit by the argument at every question and that, when these little bits are added together at the end of the discussion, great is their fall, as the opposite of what they said at the outset comes to light. Just as inexperienced checkers players are trapped by the experts in the end and can't make a
c   move, so they too are trapped in the end and have nothing to say in this different kind of checkers, which is played not with disks but with words. Yet the truth isn't affected by this outcome. I say this with a view to the present case, for someone might well say now that he's unable to oppose you as you ask each of your questions, yet he sees that of all those who take up philosophy—not those who merely dabble in it while still young

---

3. Momus is a personification of blame or censure.

in order to complete their upbringing and then drop it, but those who
continue in it for a longer time—the greatest number become cranks, not   d
to say completely vicious, while those who seem completely decent are
rendered useless to the city because of the studies you recommend.

When I'd heard him out, I said: Do you think that what these people
say is false?

I don't know, but I'd be glad to hear what you think.

You'd hear that they seem to me to speak the truth.

How, then, can it be true to say that there will be no end to evils in our   e
cities until philosophers—people we agree to be useless—rule in them?

The question you ask needs to be answered by means of an image
or simile.

And you, of course, aren't used to speaking in similes!

So! Are you making fun of me now that you've landed me with a claim
that's so hard to establish? In any case, listen to my simile, and you'll
appreciate all the more how greedy for images I am. What the most decent   488
people experience in relation to their city is so hard to bear that there's
no other single experience like it. Hence to find an image of it and a defense
for them, I must construct it from many sources, just as painters paint
goat-stags by combining the features of different things. Imagine, then,
that something like the following happens on a ship or on many ships.
The shipowner is bigger and stronger than everyone else on board, but
he's hard of hearing, a bit short-sighted, and his knowledge of seafaring   b
is equally deficient. The sailors are quarreling with one another about
steering the ship, each of them thinking that he should be the captain,
even though he's never learned the art of navigation, cannot point to
anyone who taught it to him, or to a time when he learned it. Indeed, they
claim that it isn't teachable and are ready to cut to pieces anyone who
says that it is. They're always crowding around the shipowner, begging
him and doing everything possible to get him to turn the rudder over to   c
them. And sometimes, if they don't succeed in persuading him, they execute the ones who do succeed or throw them overboard, and then, having
stupefied their noble shipowner with drugs, wine, or in some other way,
they rule the ship, using up what's in it and sailing in the way that people
like that are prone to do. Moreover, they call the person who is clever at
persuading or forcing the shipowner to let them rule a "navigator," a
"captain," and "one who knows ships," and dismiss anyone else as useless.   d
They don't understand that a true captain must pay attention to the seasons
of the year, the sky, the stars, the winds, and all that pertains to his craft,
if he's really to be the ruler of a ship. And they don't believe there is any
craft that would enable him to determine how he should steer the ship,
whether the others want him to or not, or any possibility of mastering this   e
alleged craft or of practicing it at the same time as the craft of navigation.
Don't you think that the true captain will be called a real stargazer, a
babbler, and a good-for-nothing by those who sail in ships governed in
that way, in which such things happen?   489

I certainly do.

I don't think that you need to examine the simile in detail to see that the ships resemble cities and their attitude to the true philosophers, but you already understand what I mean.

Indeed, I do.

Then first tell this simile to anyone who wonders why philosophers aren't honored in the cities, and try to persuade him that there would be

b   far more cause for wonder if they were honored.

I will tell him.

Next tell him that what he says is true, that the best among the philosophers are useless to the majority. Tell him not to blame those decent people for this but the ones who don't make use of them. It isn't natural for the captain to beg the sailors to be ruled by him nor for the wise to knock at the doors of the rich—the man who came up with that wisecrack made a mistake. The natural thing is for the sick person, rich or poor, to knock at

c   the doctor's door, and for anyone who needs to be ruled to knock at the door of the one who can rule him. It isn't for the ruler, if he's truly any use, to beg the others to accept his rule. Tell him that he'll make no mistake in likening those who rule in our cities at present to the sailors we mentioned just now, and those who are called useless stargazers to the true captains.

That's absolutely right.

Therefore, it isn't easy for the best ways of life to be highly esteemed by people who, as in these circumstances, follow the opposite ways. By far the greatest and most serious slander on philosophy, however, results

d   from those who profess to follow the philosophic way of life. I mean those of whom the prosecutor of philosophy declared that the greatest number are completely vicious and the most decent useless. And I admitted that what he said was true, didn't I?

Yes.

And haven't we explained why the decent ones are useless?

Yes, indeed.

Then, do you next want us to discuss why it's inevitable that the greater number are vicious and to try to show, if we can, that philosophy isn't

e   responsible for this either?

Certainly.

Then, let's begin our dialogue by reminding ourselves of the point at which we began to discuss the nature that someone must have if he is to become a fine and good person. First of all, if you remember, he had to

490 be guided by the truth and always pursue it in every way, or else he'd really be a boaster, with no share at all in true philosophy.

That's what was said.

And isn't this view completely contrary to the opinions currently held about him?

It certainly is.

Then, won't it be reasonable for us to plead in his defense that it is the nature of the real lover of learning to struggle toward what is, not to

remain with any of the many things that are believed to be, that, as he
moves on, he neither loses nor lessens his erotic love until he grasps the   b
being of each nature itself with the part of his soul that is fitted to grasp
it, because of its kinship with it, and that, once getting near what really
is and having intercourse with it and having begotten understanding and
truth, he knows, truly lives, is nourished, and—at that point, but not
before—is relieved from the pains of giving birth?

That is the most reasonable defense possible.

Well, then, will such a person have any part in the love of falsehood,
or will he entirely hate it?

He'll hate it.   c

And if truth led the way, we'd never say, I suppose, that a chorus of
evils could ever follow in its train.

How could it?

But rather a healthy and just character, with moderation following it.

That's right.

What need is there, then, to marshal all over again from the beginning
the members of the philosophic nature's chorus in their inevitable array?
Remember that courage, high-mindedness, ease in learning, and a good
memory all belong to it. Then you objected, saying that anyone would be
compelled to agree with what we said, but that, if he abandoned the   d
argument and looked at the very people the argument is about, he'd say
that some of them were useless, while the majority had every kind of vice.
So we examined the reason for this slander and have now arrived at the
point of explaining why the majority of them are bad. And it's for this
reason that we've again taken up the nature of the true philosophers and
defined what it necessarily has to be.

That's true.   e

We must now look at the ways in which this nature is corrupted, how
it's destroyed in many people, while a small number (the ones that are
called useless rather than bad) escape. After that, we must look in turn at
the natures of the souls that imitate the philosophic nature and establish
themselves in its way of life, so as to see what the people are like who   491
thereby arrive at a way of life they are unworthy of and that is beyond
them and who, because they often strike false notes, bring upon philosophy
the reputation that you said it has with everyone everywhere.

In what ways are they corrupted?

I'll try to enumerate them for you if I can. I suppose that everyone would
agree that only a few natures possess all the qualities that we just now
said were essential to becoming a complete philosopher and that seldom
occur naturally among human beings. Or don't you think so?   b

I certainly do.

Consider, then, the many important ways in which these few can be corrupted.

What are they?

What will surprise you most, when you hear it, is that each of the things
we praised in that nature tends to corrupt the soul that has it and to drag

it away from philosophy. I mean courage, moderation, and the other things we mentioned.

That does sound strange.

c   Furthermore, all the things that are said to be good also corrupt it and drag it away—beauty, wealth, physical strength, relatives who are powerful in the city, and all that goes with these. You understand what I have in mind?

I do, and I'd be glad to learn even more about it.

If you correctly grasp the general point I'm after, it will be clear to you, and what I've said before won't seem so strange.

What do you want me to do?

d   We know that the more vigorous any seed, developing plant, or animal is, the more it is deficient in the things that are appropriate for it to have when it is deprived of suitable food, season, or location. For the bad is more opposed to the good than is the merely not good.

Of course.

Then it's reasonable to say that the best nature fares worse, when unsuitably nurtured, than an ordinary one.

It is.

Then won't we say the same thing about souls too, Adeimantus, that
e   those with the best natures become outstandingly bad when they receive a bad upbringing? Or do you think that great injustices and pure wickedness originate in an ordinary nature rather than in a vigorous one that has been corrupted by its upbringing? Or that a weak nature is ever the cause of either great good or great evil?

No, you're right.

Now, I think that the philosophic nature as we defined it will inevitably
492   grow to possess every virtue if it happens to receive appropriate instruction, but if it is sown, planted, and grown in an inappropriate environment, it will develop in quite the opposite way, unless some god happens to come to its rescue. Or do you agree with the general opinion that certain young people are actually corrupted by sophists—that there are certain sophists with significant influence on the young who corrupt them through private teaching? Isn't it rather the very people who say this who are the greatest sophists of all, since they educate most completely, turning young and
b   old, men and women, into precisely the kind of people they want them to be?

When do they do that?

When many of them are sitting together in assemblies, courts, theaters, army camps, or in some other public gathering of the crowd, they object very loudly and excessively to some of the things that are said or done and approve others in the same way, shouting and clapping, so that the
c   very rocks and surroundings echo the din of their praise or blame and double it. In circumstances like that, what is the effect, as they say, on a young person's heart? What private training can hold out and not be swept away by that kind of praise or blame and be carried by the flood wherever

it goes, so that he'll say that the same things are beautiful or ugly as the crowd does, follow the same way of life as they do, and be the same sort of person as they are?

He will be under great compulsion to do so, Socrates.

And yet we haven't mentioned the greatest compulsion of all.

What's that?

It's what these educators and sophists impose by their actions if their words fail to persuade. Or don't you know that they punish anyone who isn't persuaded, with disenfranchisement, fines, or death?

They most certainly do.

What other sophist, then, or what private conversations do you think will prevail in opposition to these?

I don't suppose that any will.

No, indeed, it would be very foolish even to try to oppose them, for there isn't now, hasn't been in the past, nor ever will be in the future anyone with a character so unusual that he has been educated to virtue in spite of the contrary education he received from the mob—I mean, a human character; the divine, as the saying goes, is an exception to the rule. You should realize that if anyone is saved and becomes what he ought to be under our present constitutions, he has been saved—you might rightly say—by a divine dispensation.

I agree.

Well, then, you should also agree to this.

What?

Not one of those paid private teachers, whom the people call sophists and consider to be their rivals in craft, teaches anything other than the convictions that the majority express when they are gathered together. Indeed, these are precisely what the sophists call wisdom. It's as if someone were learning the moods and appetites of a huge, strong beast that he's rearing—how to approach and handle it, when it is most difficult to deal with or most gentle and what makes it so, what sounds it utters in either condition, and what sounds soothe or anger it. Having learned all this through tending the beast over a period of time, he calls this knack wisdom, gathers his information together as if it were a craft, and starts to teach it. In truth, he knows nothing about which of these convictions is fine or shameful, good or bad, just or unjust, but he applies all these names in accordance with how the beast reacts—calling what it enjoys good and what angers it bad. He has no other account to give of these terms. And he calls what he is compelled to do just and fine, for he hasn't seen and cannot show anyone else how much compulsion and goodness really differ. Don't you think, by god, that someone like that is a strange educator?

I do indeed.

Then does this person seem any different from the one who believes that it is wisdom to understand the moods and pleasures of a majority gathered from all quarters, whether they concern painting, music, or, for that matter, politics? If anyone approaches the majority to exhibit his poetry or some other piece of craftsmanship or his service to the city and gives them mastery over him to any degree beyond what's unavoidable, he'll be under Diomedean compulsion, as it's called, to do the sort of thing of which they approve. But have you ever heard anyone presenting an argument that such things are truly good and beautiful that wasn't absolutely ridiculous?

e   No, and I don't expect ever to hear one.

Keeping all this in mind, recall the following question: Can the majority in any way tolerate or accept the reality of the beautiful itself, as opposed to the many beautiful things, or the reality of each thing itself, as opposed

494   to the corresponding many?

Not in any way.

Then the majority cannot be philosophic.

They cannot.

Hence they inevitably disapprove of those who practice philosophy?

Inevitably.

And so do all those private individuals who associate with the majority and try to please them.

Clearly.

Then, because of all that, do you see any salvation for someone who is by nature a philosopher, to insure that he'll practice philosophy correctly to the end? Think about what we've said before. We agreed that ease in

b   learning, a good memory, courage, and high-mindedness belong to the philosophic nature.

Yes.

And won't someone with a nature like that be first among the children in everything, especially if his body has a nature that matches that of his soul?

How could he not be?

Then I suppose that, as he gets older, his family and fellow citizens will want to make use of him in connection with their own affairs.

Of course.

Therefore they'll pay court to him with their requests and honors, trying

c   by their flattery to secure for themselves ahead of time the power that is going to be his.

That's what usually happens, at any rate.

What do you think someone like that will do in such circumstances, especially if he happens to be from a great city, in which he's rich, well-born, good-looking, and tall? Won't he be filled with impractical expectations and think himself capable of managing the affairs, not only of the Greeks, but of the barbarians as well? And as a result, won't he exalt himself to great

d   heights and be brimming with pretension and pride that is empty and lacks understanding?

He certainly will.

And if someone approaches a young man in that condition and gently tells him the truth, namely, that that there's no understanding in him, that he needs it, and that it can't be acquired unless he works like a slave to attain it, do you think that it will be easy for him to listen when he's in the midst of so many evils?

Far from it.

And even if a young man of that sort somehow sees the point and is guided and drawn to philosophy because of his noble nature and his kinship with reason, what do you think those people will do, if they believe that they're losing their use of him and his companionship? Is there anything they won't do or say to him to prevent him from being persuaded? Or anything they won't do or say about his persuader—whether plotting against him in private or publicly bringing him into court—to prevent him from such persuasion?

There certainly isn't.

Then, is there any chance that such a person will practice philosophy?

None at all.

Do you see, then, that we weren't wrong to say that, when someone with a philosophic nature is badly brought up, the very components of his nature—together with the other so-called goods, such as wealth and other similar advantages—are themselves in a way the cause of his falling away from the philosophic way of life?

I do, and what we said was right.

These, then, are the many ways in which the best nature—which is already rare enough, as we said—is destroyed and corrupted, so that it cannot follow the best way of life. And it is among these men that we find the ones who do the greatest evils to cities and individuals and also—if they happen to be swept that way by the current—the greatest good, for a petty nature will never do anything great, either to an individual or a city.

That's very true.

When these men, for whom philosophy is most appropriate, fall away from her, they leave her desolate and unwed, and they themselves lead lives that are inappropriate and untrue. Then others, who are unworthy of her, come to her as to an orphan deprived of the protection of kinsmen and disgrace her. These are the ones who are responsible for the reproaches that you say are cast upon philosophy by those who revile her, namely, that some of those who consort with her are useless, while the majority deserve to suffer many bad things.

Yes, that is indeed what is said.

And it's a reasonable thing to say, for other little men—the ones who are most sophisticated at their own little crafts—seeing that this position, which is full of fine names and adornments, is vacated, leap gladly from those little crafts to philosophy, like prisoners escaping from jail who take refuge in a temple. Despite her present poor state, philosophy is still more high-minded than these other crafts, so that many people with defective natures desire to possess her, even though their souls are cramped and spoiled by the mechanical nature of their work, in just the way that their bodies are mutilated by their crafts and labors. Isn't that inevitable?

e

495

b

c

d

e

It certainly is.

Don't you think that a man of this sort looks exactly like a little bald-headed tinker who has come into some money and, having been just released from jail, has taken a bath, put on a new cloak, got himself up as a bridegroom, and is about to marry the boss's daughter because she is poor and abandoned?

496   They're exactly the same.

And what kind of children will that marriage produce? Won't they be illegitimate and inferior?

They have to be.

What about when men who are unworthy of education approach philosophy and consort with her unworthily? What kinds of thoughts and opinions are we to say they beget? Won't they truly be what are properly called sophisms, things that have nothing genuine about them or worthy of being called true wisdom?

That's absolutely right.

Then there remains, Adeimantus, only a very small group who consort with philosophy in a way that's worthy of her: A noble and well brought-up character, for example, kept down by exile, who remains with philosophy

b   according to his nature because there is no one to corrupt him, or a great soul living in a small city, who disdains the city's affairs and looks beyond them. A very few might be drawn to philosophy from other crafts that they rightly despise because they have good natures. And some might be held back by the bridle that restrains our friend Theages[4]—for he's in every way qualified to be tempted away from philosophy, but his physical illness

c   restrains him by keeping him out of politics. Finally, my own case is hardly worth mentioning—my daemonic sign[5]—because it has happened to no one before me, or to only a very few. Now, the members of this small group have tasted how sweet and blessed a possession philosophy is, and at the same time they've also seen the madness of the majority and realized, in a word, that hardly anyone acts sanely in public affairs and that there is no ally with whom they might go to the aid of justice and survive, that

d   instead they'd perish before they could profit either their city or their friends and be useless both to themselves and to others, just like a man who has fallen among wild animals and is neither willing to join them in doing injustice nor sufficiently strong to oppose the general savagery alone. Taking all this into account, they lead a quiet life and do their own work. Thus, like someone who takes refuge under a little wall from a storm of dust or hail driven by the wind, the philosopher—seeing others filled with lawlessness—is satisfied if he can somehow lead his present life free from injustice and impious acts and depart from it with good hope, blameless

e   and content.

4. See the *Theages*.

5. See Plato, *Apology* 31c–32a, where Socrates explains that his *daimonion* has kept him out of politics.

Well, that's no small thing for him to have accomplished before de-   497
parting.

But it isn't the greatest either, since he didn't chance upon a constitution
that suits him. Under a suitable one, his own growth will be fuller, and
he'll save the community as well as himself. It seems to me that we've
now sensibly discussed the reasons why philosophy is slandered and why
the slanderer is unjust—unless, of course, you have something to add.

I have nothing to add on that point. But which of our present constitutions do you think is suitable for philosophers?

None of them. That's exactly my complaint: None of our present constitu-   b
tions is worthy of the philosophic nature, and, as a result, this nature is
perverted and altered, for, just as a foreign seed, sown in alien ground, is
likely to be overcome by the native species and to fade away among them,
so the philosophic nature fails to develop its full power and declines into
a different character. But if it were to find the best constitution, as it is   c
itself the best, it would be clear that it is really divine and that other natures
and ways of life are merely human. Obviously you're going to ask next
what the best constitution is.

You're wrong there; I wasn't going to ask that, but whether it was
the constitution we described when we were founding our city or some
other one.

In the other respects, it is that one. But we said even then[6] that there must
always be some people in the city who have a theory of the constitution, the
same one that guided you, the lawgiver, when you made the laws.   d

We did say that.

Yes, but we didn't emphasize it sufficiently, for fear of what your objections have made plain, namely, that its proof would be long and difficult.
And indeed what remains is by no means easy to go through.

What's that?

How a city can engage in philosophy without being destroyed, for all
great things are prone to fall, and, as the saying goes, fine things are really
hard to achieve.

Nevertheless, to complete our discussion, we'll have to get clear   e
about this.

If anything prevents us from doing it, it won't be lack of willingness
but lack of ability. At least you'll see how willing *I* am, for notice again
how enthusiastically and recklessly I say that the manner in which a city
ought to take up the philosophic way of life is the opposite of what it does
at present.

How?

At present, those who study philosophy do so as young men who have
just left childhood behind and have yet to take up household management
and money-making. But just when they reach the hardest part—I mean   498
the part that has to do with giving a rational account—they abandon it

6. See 412a–b.

and are regarded as fully trained in philosophy. In later life, they think
they're doing well if they are willing to be in an invited audience when
others are doing philosophy, for they think they should do this only as a
sideline. And, with a few exceptions, by the time they reach old age, their
eagerness for philosophy is quenched more thoroughly than the sun of
b   Heraclitus, which is never rekindled.[7]

What should they do?

Entirely the opposite. As youths and children, they should put their
minds to youthful education and philosophy and take care of their bodies
at a time when they are growing into manhood, so as to acquire a helper
for philosophy. As they grow older and their souls begin to reach maturity,
they should increase their mental exercises. Then, when their strength
begins to fail and they have retired from politics and military service, they
should graze freely in the pastures of philosophy and do nothing else—I
c   mean the ones who are to live happily and, in death, add a fitting destiny
in that other place to the life they have lived.

You seem to be speaking with true enthusiasm, Socrates. But I'm sure
that most of your hearers, beginning with Thrasymachus, will oppose you
with even greater enthusiasm and not be at all convinced.

Don't slander Thrasymachus and me just as we've become friends—not
d   that we were enemies before. We won't relax our efforts until we either
convince him and the others or, at any rate, do something that may benefit
them in a later incarnation, when, reborn, they happen upon these arguments again.

That's a short time you're talking about!

It's nothing compared to the whole of time. All the same, it's no wonder
that the majority of people aren't convinced by our arguments, for they've
never seen a *man* that fits our *plan* (and the rhymes of this sort they have
heard are usually intended and not, like this one, the product of mere
e   chance). That is to say, they've never seen a man or a number of men who
themselves rhymed with virtue, were assimilated to it as far as possible,
499   and ruled in a city of the same type. Or do you think they have?

I don't think so at all.

Nor have they listened sufficiently to fine and free arguments that search
out the truth in every way for the sake of knowledge but that keep away
from the sophistications and eristic quibbles that, both in public trials and
in private gatherings, aim at nothing except reputation and disputation.

No, they haven't.

It was because of this, because we foresaw these difficulties, that we
were afraid. Nonetheless, we were compelled by the truth to say that no
b   city, constitution, or individual man will ever become perfect until either
some chance event compels those few philosophers who aren't vicious

---

7. Aristotle (*Meteorologica* 355a14) reports Heraclitus as believing that "the sun is new
every day": the sun not only sets at night, it ceases to exist, being replaced by a totally
new sun the next morning.

(the ones who are now called useless) to take charge of a city, whether they want to or not, and compels the city to obey them, or until a god inspires the present rulers and kings or their offspring with a true erotic love for true philosophy. Now, it cannot be reasonably maintained, in my view, that either of these things is impossible, but if it could, we'd be justly ridiculed for indulging in wishful thinking. Isn't that so?   c

It is.

Then, if in the limitless past, those who were foremost in philosophy were forced to take charge of a city or if this is happening now in some foreign place far beyond our ken or if it will happen in the future, we are prepared to maintain our argument that, at whatever time the muse of   d philosophy controls a city, the constitution we've described will also exist at that time, whether it is past, present, or future. Since it is not impossible for this to happen, we are not speaking of impossibilities. That it is *difficult* for it to happen, however, we agree ourselves.

That's my opinion, anyway.

But the majority don't share your opinion—is that what you are going to say?

They probably don't.

You should not make such wholesale charges against the majority, for they'll no doubt come to a different opinion, if instead of indulging your love of victory at their expense, you soothe them and try to remove their   e slanderous prejudice against the love of learning, by pointing out what you mean by a philosopher and by defining the philosophic nature and way of life, as we did just now, so that they'll realize that you don't mean   500 the same people as they do. And if they once see it your way, even you will say that they'll have a different opinion from the one you just attributed to them and will answer differently. Or do you think that anyone who is gentle and without malice is harsh with someone who is neither irritable nor malicious? I'll anticipate your answer and say that a few people may have such a harsh character, but not the majority.

And, of course, I agree.

Then don't you also agree that the harshness the majority exhibit towards   b philosophy is caused by those outsiders who don't belong and who've burst in like a band of revellers, always abusing one another, indulging their love of quarrels, and arguing about human beings in a way that is wholly inappropriate to philosophy?

I do indeed.

No one whose thoughts are truly directed towards the things that are, Adeimantus, has the leisure to look down at human affairs or to be filled with envy and hatred by competing with people. Instead, as he looks at and studies things that are organized and always the same, that neither   c do injustice to one another nor suffer it, being all in a rational order, he imitates them and tries to become as like them as he can. Or do you think that someone can consort with things he admires without imitating them?

I do not. It's impossible.

Then the philosopher, by consorting with what is ordered and divine and despite all the slanders around that say otherwise, himself becomes

d   as divine and ordered as a human being can.

That's absolutely true.

And if he should come to be compelled to put what he sees there into people's characters, whether into a single person or into a populace, instead of shaping only his own, do you think that he will be a poor craftsman of moderation, justice, and the whole of popular virtue?

He least of all.

And when the majority realize that what we are saying about the philosopher is true, will they be harsh with him or mistrust us when we say that

e   the city will never find happiness until its outline is sketched by painters who use the divine model?

They won't be harsh, if indeed they realize this. But what sort of sketch

501   do you mean?

They'd take the city and the characters of human beings as their sketching slate, but first they'd wipe it clean—which isn't at all an easy thing to do. And you should know that this is the plain difference between them and others, namely, that they refuse to take either an individual or a city in hand or to write laws, unless they receive a clean slate or are allowed to clean it themselves.

And they'd be right to refuse.

Then don't you think they'd next sketch the outline of the constitution?

Of course.

b   And I suppose that, as they work, they'd look often in each direction, towards the natures of justice, beauty, moderation, and the like, on the one hand, and towards those they're trying to put into human beings, on the other. And in this way they'd mix and blend the various ways of life in the city until they produced a human image based on what Homer too called "the divine form and image" when it occurred among human beings.[8]

That's right.

They'd erase one thing, I suppose, and draw in another until they'd made characters for human beings that the gods would love as much

c   as possible.

At any rate, that would certainly result in the finest sketch.

Then is this at all persuasive to those you said were straining to attack us—that the person we were praising is really a painter of constitutions? They were angry because we entrusted the city to him: Are they any calmer, now that they've heard what we had to say?

They'll be much calmer, if they have any moderation.

Indeed, how could they possibly dispute it? Will they deny that philoso-

d   phers are lovers of what is or of the truth?

That would be absurd.

8. See, for example, *Iliad* i.131.

Or that their nature as we've described it is close to the best?

They can't deny that either.

Or that such a nature, if it follows its own way of life, isn't as completely good and philosophic as any other? Or that the people we excluded are more so?

Certainly not.

Then will they still be angry when we say that, until philosophers take control of a city, there'll be no respite from evil for either city or citizens, and the constitution we've been describing in theory will never be completed in practice?

They'll probably be less angry.

Then if it's all right with you, let's not say that they'll simply be less angry but that they'll become altogether gentle and persuaded, so that they'll be shamed into agreeing with us, if nothing else.

It's all right with me.

Let's assume, therefore, that they've been convinced on this point. Will anyone dispute our view that the offspring of kings or rulers could be born with philosophic natures?

No one would do that.

Could anyone claim that, if such offspring are born, they'll inevitably be corrupted? We agree ourselves that it's hard for them to be saved from corruption, but could anyone claim that in the whole of time not one of them could be saved?

How could he?

But surely one such individual would be sufficient to bring to completion all the things that now seem so incredible, provided that his city obeys him.

One would be sufficient.

If a ruler established the laws and ways of life we've described, it is surely not impossible that the citizens would be willing to carry them out.

Not at all.

And would it be either astonishing or impossible that others should think as we do?

I don't suppose it would.

But I think our earlier discussion was sufficient to show that these arrangements are best, if only they are possible.

Indeed it was.

Then we can now conclude that this legislation is best, if only it is possible, and that, while it is hard for it to come about, it is not impossible.

We can.

Now that this difficulty has been disposed of, we must deal with what remains, namely, how the saviors of our constitution will come to be in the city, what subjects and ways of life will cause them to come into being, and at what ages they'll take each of them up.

Indeed we must.

It wasn't very clever of me to omit from our earlier discussion the troublesome topics of acquiring wives, begetting children, and appointing

e

502

b

c

d

rulers, just because I knew that the whole truth would provoke resentment and would be hard to bring about in practice, for as it turned out, I had to go through these matters anyway. The subject of women and children has been adequately dealt with, but that of the rulers has to be taken up again from the beginning. We said, if you remember, that they must show themselves to be lovers of their city when tested by pleasure and pain and that they must hold on to their resolve through labors, fears, and all other adversities. Anyone who was incapable of doing so was to be rejected, while anyone who came through unchanged—like gold tested in a fire— was to be made ruler and receive prizes both while he lived and after his death. These were the sort of things we were saying while our argument, afraid of stirring up the very problems that now confront us, veiled its face and slipped by.

That's very true; I do remember it.

We hesitated to say the things we've now dared to say anyway. So let's now also dare to say that those who are to be made our guardians in the most exact sense of the term must be philosophers.

Let's do it.

Then you should understand that there will probably be only a few of them, for they have to have the nature we described, and its parts mostly grow in separation and are rarely found in the same person.

What do you mean?

You know that ease of learning, good memory, quick wits, smartness, youthful passion, high-mindedness, and all the other things that go along with these are rarely willing to grow together in a mind that will choose an orderly life that is quiet and completely stable, for the people who possess the former traits are carried by their quick wits wherever chance leads them and have no stability at all.

That's true.

On the other hand, people with stable characters, who don't change easily, who aren't easily frightened in battle, and whom one would employ because of their greater reliability, exhibit similar traits when it comes to learning: They are as hard to move and teach as people whose brains have become numb, and they are filled with sleep and yawning whenever they have to learn anything.

That's so.

Yet we say that someone must have a fine and goodly share of both characters, or he won't receive the truest education, honors, or rule.

That's right.

Then, don't you think that such people will be rare?

Of course.

Therefore they must be tested in the labors, fears, and pleasures we mentioned previously. But they must also be exercised in many other subjects—which we didn't mention but are adding now—to see whether they can tolerate the most important subjects or will shrink from them like the cowards who shrink from other tests.

It's appropriate to examine them like that. But what do you mean by the most important subjects?

Do you remember when we distinguished three parts in the soul, in order to help bring out what justice, moderation, courage, and wisdom each is?

If I didn't remember that, it wouldn't be just for me to hear the rest.

What about what preceded it?

What was that?

We said, I believe, that, in order to get the finest possible view of these   b
matters, we would need to take a longer road that would make them plain to anyone who took it but that it was possible to give demonstrations of what they are that would be up to the standard of the previous argument.[9] And you said that that would be satisfactory. So it seems to me that our discussion at that time fell short of exactness, but whether or not it satisfied you is for you to say.

I thought you gave us good measure and so, apparently, did the others.

Any measure of such things that falls short in any way of that which   c
is is not good measure, for nothing incomplete is the measure of anything, although people are sometimes of the opinion that an incomplete treatment is nonetheless adequate and makes further investigation unnecessary.

Indeed, laziness causes many people to think that.

It is a thought that a guardian of a city and its laws can well do without.

Probably so.

Well, then, he must take the longer road and put as much effort into learning as into physical training, for otherwise, as we were just saying, he will never reach the goal of the most important subject and the most   d
appropriate one for him to learn.

Aren't these virtues, then, the most important things? he asked. Is there anything even more important than justice and the other virtues we discussed?

There is something more important. However, even for the virtues themselves, it isn't enough to look at a mere sketch, as we did before, while neglecting the most complete account. It's ridiculous, isn't it, to strain every nerve to attain the utmost exactness and clarity about other things of little value and not to consider the most important things worthy of the greatest exactness?   e

It certainly is. But do you think that anyone is going to let you off without asking you what this most important subject is and what it concerns?

No, indeed, and you can ask me too. You've certainly heard the answer often enough, but now either you aren't thinking or you intend to make trouble for me again by interrupting. And I suspect the latter, for you've often heard it said that the form of the good is the most important thing   505
to learn about and that it's by their relation to it that just things and the others become useful and beneficial. You know very well now that I am

9. See 435d.

going to say this, and, besides, that we have no adequate knowledge of
it. And you also know that, if we don't know it, even the fullest possible
knowledge of other things is of no benefit to us, any more than if we
acquire any possession without the good of it. Or do you think that it is
any advantage to have every kind of possession without the good of it?

b   Or to know everything except the good, thereby knowing nothing fine
or good?

No, by god, I don't.

Furthermore, you certainly know that the majority believe that pleasure
is the good, while the more sophisticated believe that it is knowledge.

Indeed I do.

And you know that those who believe this can't tell us what sort of
knowledge it is, however, but in the end are forced to say that it is knowledge of the good.

And that's ridiculous.

c   Of course it is. They blame us for not knowing the good and then turn
around and talk to us as if we did know it. They say that it is knowledge
of the good—as if we understood what they're speaking about when they
utter the word "good."

That's completely true.

What about those who define the good as pleasure? Are they any less
full of confusion than the others? Aren't even they forced to admit that
there are bad pleasures?

Most definitely.

So, I think, they have to agree that the same things are both good and
bad. Isn't that true?

d   Of course.

It's clear, then, isn't it, why there are many large controversies about this?

How could it be otherwise?

And isn't this also clear? In the case of just and beautiful things, many
people are content with what are believed to be so, even if they aren't
really so, and they act, acquire, and form their own beliefs on that basis.
Nobody is satisfied to acquire things that are merely believed to be good,
however, but everyone wants the things that really *are* good and disdains
mere belief here.

That's right.

e   Every soul pursues the good and does whatever it does for its sake. It
divines that the good is something but it is perplexed and cannot adequately grasp what it is or acquire the sort of stable beliefs it has about
other things, and so it misses the benefit, if any, that even those other
things may give. Will we allow the best people in the city, to whom we

506   entrust everything, to be so in the dark about something of this kind and
of this importance?

That's the last thing we'd do.

I don't suppose, at least, that just and fine things will have acquired
much of a guardian in someone who doesn't even know in what way they

are good. And I divine that no one will have adequate knowledge of them until he knows this.

You've divined well.

But won't our constitution be perfectly ordered, if a guardian who knows these things is in charge of it?   b

Necessarily. But, Socrates, you must also tell us whether you consider the good to be knowledge or pleasure or something else altogether.

What a man! It's been clear for some time that other people's opinions about these matters wouldn't satisfy you.

Well, Socrates, it doesn't seem right to me for you to be willing to state other people's convictions but not your own, especially when you've spent so much time occupied with these matters.   c

What? Do you think it's right to talk about things one doesn't know as if one does know them?

Not as if one knows them, he said, but one ought to be willing to state one's opinions as such.

What? Haven't you noticed that opinions without knowledge are shameful and ugly things? The best of them are blind—or do you think that those who express a true opinion without understanding are any different from blind people who happen to travel the right road?

They're no different.

Do you want to look at shameful, blind, and crooked things, then, when you might hear illuminating and fine ones from other people?   d

By god, Socrates, Glaucon said, don't desert us with the end almost in sight. We'll be satisfied if you discuss the good as you discussed justice, moderation, and the rest.

That, my friend, I said, would satisfy me too, but I'm afraid that I won't be up to it and that I'll disgrace myself and look ridiculous by trying. So let's abandon the quest for what the good itself is for the time being, for even to arrive at my own view about it is too big a topic for the discussion we are now started on. But I am willing to tell you about what is apparently an offspring of the good and most like it. Is that agreeable to you, or would you rather we let the whole matter drop?   e

It is. The story about the father remains a debt you'll pay another time.

I wish that I could pay the debt in full, and you receive it instead of just the interest. So here, then, is this child and offspring of the good. But be careful that I don't somehow deceive you unintentionally by giving you an illegitimate account of the child.[10]   507

We'll be as careful as possible, so speak on.

I will when we've come to an agreement and recalled some things that we've already said both here and many other times.

Which ones?   b

---

10. Throughout, Socrates is punning on the word *tokos*, which means either a child or the interest on capital.

We say that there are many beautiful things and many good things, and so on for each kind, and in this way we distinguish them in words.

We do.

And beauty itself and good itself and all the things that we thereby set down as many, reversing ourselves, we set down according to a single form of each, believing that there is but one, and call it "the being" of each.

That's true.

And we say that the many beautiful things and the rest are visible but not intelligible, while the forms are intelligible but not visible.

That's completely true.

c   With what part of ourselves do we see visible things?

With our sight.

And so audible things are heard by hearing, and with our other senses we perceive all the other perceptible things.

That's right.

Have you considered how lavish the maker of our senses was in making the power to see and be seen?

I can't say I have.

Well, consider it this way. Do hearing and sound need another kind of thing in order for the former to hear and the latter to be heard, a third

d   thing in whose absence the one won't hear or the other be heard?

No, they need nothing else.

And if there are any others that need such a thing, there can't be many of them. Can you think of one?

I can't.

You don't realize that sight and the visible have such a need?

How so?

Sight may be present in the eyes, and the one who has it may try to use it, and colors may be present in things, but unless a third kind of thing is present, which is naturally adapted for this very purpose, you know that

e   sight will see nothing, and the colors will remain unseen.

What kind of thing do you mean?

I mean what you call light.

You're right.

Then it isn't an insignificant kind of link that connects the sense of sight

508 and the power to be seen—it is a more valuable link than any other linked things have got, if indeed light is something valuable.

And, of course, it's very valuable.

Which of the gods in heaven would you name as the cause and controller of this, the one whose light causes our sight to see in the best way and the visible things to be seen?

The same one you and others would name. Obviously, the answer to your question is the sun.

And isn't sight by nature related to that god in this way?

Which way?

Sight isn't the sun, neither sight itself nor that in which it comes to be, namely, the eye.   b

No, it certainly isn't.

But I think that it is the most sunlike of the senses.

Very much so.

And it receives from the sun the power it has, just like an influx from an overflowing treasury.

Certainly.

The sun is not sight, but isn't it the cause of sight itself and seen by it?

That's right.

Let's say, then, that this is what I called the offspring of the good, which the good begot as its analogue. What the good itself is in the intelligible realm, in relation to understanding and intelligible things, the sun is in the visible realm, in relation to sight and visible things.   c

How? Explain a bit more.

You know that, when we turn our eyes to things whose colors are no longer in the light of day but in the gloom of night, the eyes are dimmed and seem nearly blind, as if clear vision were no longer in them.

Of course.

Yet whenever one turns them on things illuminated by the sun, they see clearly, and vision appears in those very same eyes?   d

Indeed.

Well, understand the soul in the same way: When it focuses on something illuminated by truth and what is, it understands, knows, and apparently possesses understanding, but when it focuses on what is mixed with obscurity, on what comes to be and passes away, it opines and is dimmed, changes its opinions this way and that, and seems bereft of understanding.

It does seem that way.

So that what gives truth to the things known and the power to know to the knower is the form of the good. And though it is the cause of   e knowledge and truth, it is also an object of knowledge. Both knowledge and truth are beautiful things, but the good is other and more beautiful than they. In the visible realm, light and sight are rightly considered sunlike, but it is wrong to think that they are the sun, so here it is right to think of knowledge and truth as goodlike but wrong to think that either   509 of them is the good—for the good is yet more prized.

This is an inconceivably beautiful thing you're talking about, if it provides both knowledge and truth and is superior to them in beauty. You surely don't think that a thing like that could be pleasure.

Hush! Let's examine its image in more detail as follows.

How?   b

You'll be willing to say, I think, that the sun not only provides visible things with the power to be seen but also with coming to be, growth, and nourishment, although it is not itself coming to be.

How could it be?

Therefore, you should also say that not only do the objects of knowledge owe their being known to the good, but their being is also due to it, although the good is not being, but superior to it in rank and power.

c   And Glaucon comically said: By Apollo, what a daemonic superiority!

It's your own fault; you forced me to tell you my opinion about it.

And I don't want you to stop either. So continue to explain its similarity to the sun, if you've omitted anything.

I'm certainly omitting a lot.

Well, don't, not even the smallest thing.

I think I'll have to omit a fair bit, but, as far as is possible at the moment, I won't omit anything voluntarily.

Don't.

d   Understand, then, that, as we said, there are these two things, one sovereign of the intelligible kind and place, the other of the visible (I don't say "of heaven" so as not to seem to you to be playing the sophist with the name).[11] In any case, you have two kinds of thing, visible and intelligible.

Right.

It is like a line divided into two unequal sections.[12] Then divide each section—namely, that of the visible and that of the intelligible—in the same ratio as the line. In terms now of relative clarity and opacity, one subsection of the visible consists of images. And by images I mean, first,

---

11. The play may be on the similarity of sound between *ouranou* ("of heaven") and *horatou* ("of the visible"). More likely, Socrates is referring to the fact that *ouranou* seems to contain the word *nou*, the genitive case of *nous* ("understanding"), and relative of *noētou* ("of the intelligible"). If he said that the sun was sovereign of heaven, he might be taken to suggest in sophistical fashion that it was sovereign of the intelligible and that there was no real difference between the good and the sun.

12. The line is illustrated below:

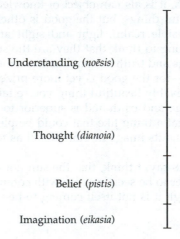

Understanding (*noēsis*)

Thought (*dianoia*)

Belief (*pistis*)

Imagination (*eikasia*)

shadows, then reflections in water and in all close-packed, smooth, and   e
shiny materials, and everything of that sort, if you understand.   510

I do.

In the other subsection of the visible, put the originals of these images, namely, the animals around us, all the plants, and the whole class of manufactured things.

Consider them put.

Would you be willing to say that, as regards truth and untruth, the division is in this proportion: As the opinable is to the knowable, so the likeness is to the thing that it is like?

Certainly.   b

Consider now how the section of the intelligible is to be divided.

How?

As follows: In one subsection, the soul, using as images the things that were imitated before, is forced to investigate from hypotheses, proceeding not to a first principle but to a conclusion. In the other subsection, however, it makes its way to a first principle that is *not* a hypothesis, proceeding from a hypothesis but without the images used in the previous subsection, using forms themselves and making its investigation through them.

I don't yet fully understand what you mean.

Let's try again. You'll understand it more easily after the following   c
preamble. I think you know that students of geometry, calculation, and the like hypothesize the odd and the even, the various figures, the three kinds of angles, and other things akin to these in each of their investigations, as if they knew them. They make these their hypotheses and don't think it necessary to give any account of them, either to themselves or to others, as if they were clear to everyone. And going from these first principles through the remaining steps, they arrive in full agreement.   d

I certainly know that much.

Then you also know that, although they use visible figures and make claims about them, their thought isn't directed to them but to those other things that they are like. They make their claims for the sake of the square itself and the diagonal itself, not the diagonal they draw, and similarly with the others. These figures that they make and draw, of which shadows   e
and reflections in water are images, they now in turn use as images, in seeking to see those others themselves that one cannot see except by means of thought.   511

That's true.

This, then, is the kind of thing that, on the one hand, I said is intelligible, and, on the other, is such that the soul is forced to use hypotheses in the investigation of it, not travelling up to a first principle, since it cannot reach beyond its hypotheses, but using as images those very things of which images were made in the section below, and which, by comparison to their images, were thought to be clear and to be valued as such.

I understand that you mean what happens in geometry and related   b
sciences.

Then also understand that, by the other subsection of the intelligible, I mean that which reason itself grasps by the power of dialectic. It does not consider these hypotheses as first principles but truly as hypotheses—but as stepping stones to take off from, enabling it to reach the unhypothetical first principle of everything. Having grasped this principle, it reverses itself and, keeping hold of what follows from it, comes down to a conclusion without making use of anything visible at all, but only of forms themselves,

c   moving on from forms to forms, and ending in forms.

I understand, if not yet adequately (for in my opinion you're speaking of an enormous task), that you want to distinguish the intelligible part of that which is, the part studied by the science of dialectic, as clearer than the part studied by the so-called sciences, for which their hypotheses are first principles. And although those who study the objects of these sciences are forced to do so by means of thought rather than sense perception, still,

d   because they do not go back to a genuine first principle, but proceed from hypotheses, you don't think that they understand them, even though, given such a principle, they are intelligible. And you seem to me to call the state of the geometers thought but not understanding, thought being intermediate between opinion and understanding.

Your exposition is most adequate. Thus there are four such conditions in the soul, corresponding to the four subsections of our line: Understanding for the highest, thought for the second, belief for the third, and imaging

e   for the last. Arrange them in a ratio, and consider that each shares in clarity to the degree that the subsection it is set over shares in truth.

I understand, agree, and arrange them as you say.

Book VII

514   Next, I said, compare the effect of education and of the lack of it on our nature to an experience like this: Imagine human beings living in an underground, cavelike dwelling, with an entrance a long way up, which is both open to the light and as wide as the cave itself. They've been there since childhood, fixed in the same place, with their necks and legs fettered, able to see only in front of them, because their bonds prevent them from turning their heads around. Light is provided by a fire burning far above

b   and behind them. Also behind them, but on higher ground, there is a path stretching between them and the fire. Imagine that along this path a low wall has been built, like the screen in front of puppeteers above which they show their puppets.

I'm imagining it.

Then also imagine that there are people along the wall, carrying all kinds of artifacts that project above it—statues of people and other animals,

c   made out of stone, wood, and every material. And, as you'd expect, some

515   of the carriers are talking, and some are silent.

It's a strange image you're describing, and strange prisoners.

They're like us. Do you suppose, first of all, that these prisoners see anything of themselves and one another besides the shadows that the fire casts on the wall in front of them?

How could they, if they have to keep their heads motionless through-out life?   b

What about the things being carried along the wall? Isn't the same true of them?

Of course.

And if they could talk to one another, don't you think they'd suppose that the names they used applied to the things they see passing before them?[1]

They'd have to.

And what if their prison also had an echo from the wall facing them? Don't you think they'd believe that the shadows passing in front of them were talking whenever one of the carriers passing along the wall was doing so?

I certainly do.

Then the prisoners would in every way believe that the truth is nothing   c other than the shadows of those artifacts.

They must surely believe that.

Consider, then, what being released from their bonds and cured of their ignorance would naturally be like, if something like this came to pass.[2] When one of them was freed and suddenly compelled to stand up, turn his head, walk, and look up toward the light, he'd be pained and dazzled and unable to see the things whose shadows he'd seen before. What do you think he'd say, if we told him that what he'd seen before was inconse-   d quential, but that now—because he is a bit closer to the things that are and is turned towards things that are more—he sees more correctly? Or, to put it another way, if we pointed to each of the things passing by, asked him what each of them is, and compelled him to answer, don't you think he'd be at a loss and that he'd believe that the things he saw earlier were truer than the ones he was now being shown?

Much truer.

And if someone compelled him to look at the light itself, wouldn't his eyes hurt, and wouldn't he turn around and flee towards the things he's   e able to see, believing that they're really clearer than the ones he's being shown?

He would.

And if someone dragged him away from there by force, up the rough, steep path, and didn't let him go until he had dragged him into the sunlight, wouldn't he be pained and irritated at being treated that way? And when he came into the light, with the sun filling his eyes, wouldn't he be unable   516 to see a single one of the things now said to be true?

---

1. Reading *parionta autous nomizein onomazein* in b5.
2. Reading *hoia tis an eiē phusei, ei* in c5.

He would be unable to see them, at least at first.

I suppose, then, that he'd need time to get adjusted before he could see things in the world above. At first, he'd see shadows most easily, then images of men and other things in water, then the things themselves. Of these, he'd be able to study the things in the sky and the sky itself more easily at night, looking at the light of the stars and the moon, than during
b   the day, looking at the sun and the light of the sun.

Of course.

Finally, I suppose, he'd be able to see the sun, not images of it in water or some alien place, but the sun itself, in its own place, and be able to study it.

Necessarily so.

And at this point he would infer and conclude that the sun provides the seasons and the years, governs everything in the visible world, and is
c   in some way the cause of all the things that he used to see.

It's clear that would be his next step.

What about when he reminds himself of his first dwelling place, his fellow prisoners, and what passed for wisdom there? Don't you think that he'd count himself happy for the change and pity the others?

Certainly.

And if there had been any honors, praises, or prizes among them for the one who was sharpest at identifying the shadows as they passed by and who best remembered which usually came earlier, which later, and
d   which simultaneously, and who could thus best divine the future, do you think that our man would desire these rewards or envy those among the prisoners who were honored and held power? Instead, wouldn't he feel, with Homer, that he'd much prefer to "work the earth as a serf to another, one without possessions,"[3] and go through any sufferings, rather than share their opinions and live as they do?

e   I suppose he would rather suffer anything than live like that.

Consider this too. If this man went down into the cave again and sat down in his same seat, wouldn't his eyes—coming suddenly out of the sun like that—be filled with darkness?

They certainly would.

And before his eyes had recovered—and the adjustment would not be quick—while his vision was still dim, if he had to compete again with
517 the perpetual prisoners in recognizing the shadows, wouldn't he invite ridicule? Wouldn't it be said of him that he'd returned from his upward journey with his eyesight ruined and that it isn't worthwhile even to try to travel upward? And, as for anyone who tried to free them and lead them upward, if they could somehow get their hands on him, wouldn't they kill him?

They certainly would.

---

3. *Odyssey* xi.489–90.

This whole image, Glaucon, must be fitted together with what we said | b
before. The visible realm should be likened to the prison dwelling, and
the light of the fire inside it to the power of the sun. And if you interpret
the upward journey and the study of things above as the upward journey
of the soul to the intelligible realm, you'll grasp what I hope to convey,
since that is what you wanted to hear about. Whether it's true or not, only
the god knows. But this is how I see it: In the knowable realm, the form
of the good is the last thing to be seen, and it is reached only with difficulty.
Once one has seen it, however, one must conclude that it is the cause of
all that is correct and beautiful in anything, that it produces both light | c
and its source in the visible realm, and that in the intelligible realm it
controls and provides truth and understanding, so that anyone who is to
act sensibly in private or public must see it.

I have the same thought, at least as far as I'm able.

Come, then, share with me this thought also: It isn't surprising that the
ones who get to this point are unwilling to occupy themselves with human
affairs and that their souls are always pressing upwards, eager to spend
their time above, for, after all, this is surely what we'd expect, if indeed
things fit the image I described before. | d

It is.

What about what happens when someone turns from divine study to
the evils of human life? Do you think it's surprising, since his sight is still
dim, and he hasn't yet become accustomed to the darkness around him,
that he behaves awkwardly and appears completely ridiculous if he's
compelled, either in the courts or elsewhere, to contend about the shadows
of justice or the statues of which they are the shadows and to dispute
about the way these things are understood by people who have never
seen justice itself? | e

That's not surprising at all.

No, it isn't. But anyone with any understanding would remember that | 518
the eyes may be confused in two ways and from two causes, namely, when
they've come from the light into the darkness *and* when they've come from
the darkness into the light. Realizing that the same applies to the soul,
when someone sees a soul disturbed and unable to see something, he
won't laugh mindlessly, but he'll take into consideration whether it has
come from a brighter life and is dimmed through not having yet become
accustomed to the dark or whether it has come from greater ignorance
into greater light and is dazzled by the increased brilliance. Then he'll
declare the first soul happy in its experience and life, and he'll pity the
latter—but even if he chose to make fun of it, at least he'd be less ridiculous | b
than if he laughed at a soul that has come from the light above.

What you say is very reasonable.

If that's true, then here's what we must think about these matters:
Education isn't what some people declare it to be, namely, putting knowl-
edge into souls that lack it, like putting sight into blind eyes. | c

They do say that.

But our present discussion, on the other hand, shows that the power to learn is present in everyone's soul and that the instrument with which each learns is like an eye that cannot be turned around from darkness to light without turning the whole body. This instrument cannot be turned around from that which is coming into being without turning the whole soul until it is able to study that which is and the brightest thing that is,

d   namely, the one we call the good. Isn't that right?

Yes.

Then education is the craft concerned with doing this very thing, this turning around, and with how the soul can most easily and effectively be made to do it. It isn't the craft of putting sight into the soul. Education takes for granted that sight is there but that it isn't turned the right way or looking where it ought to look, and it tries to redirect it appropriately.

So it seems.

Now, it looks as though the other so-called virtues of the soul are akin to those of the body, for they really aren't there beforehand but are added

e   later by habit and practice. However, the virtue of reason seems to belong above all to something more divine, which never loses its power but is either useful and beneficial or useless and harmful, depending on the way

519   it is turned. Or have you never noticed this about people who are said to be vicious but clever, how keen the vision of their little souls is and how sharply it distinguishes the things it is turned towards? This shows that its sight isn't inferior but rather is forced to serve evil ends, so that the sharper it sees, the more evil it accomplishes.

Absolutely.

However, if a nature of this sort had been hammered at from childhood and freed from the bonds of kinship with becoming, which have been fastened to it by feasting, greed, and other such pleasures and which, like

b   leaden weights, pull its vision downwards—if, being rid of these, it turned to look at true things, then I say that the same soul of the same person would see these most sharply, just as it now does the things it is presently turned towards.

Probably so.

And what about the uneducated who have no experience of truth? Isn't it likely—indeed, doesn't it follow necessarily from what was said before— that they will never adequately govern a city? But neither would those who've been allowed to spend their whole lives being educated. The former

c   would fail because they don't have a single goal at which all their actions, public and private, inevitably aim; the latter would fail because they'd refuse to act, thinking that they had settled while still alive in the faraway Isles of the Blessed.

That's true.

It is our task as founders, then, to compel the best natures to reach the study we said before is the most important, namely, to make the ascent and see the good. But when they've made it and looked sufficiently, we

d   mustn't allow them to do what they're allowed to do today.

What's that?

To stay there and refuse to go down again to the prisoners in the cave and share their labors and honors, whether they are of less worth or of greater.

Then are we to do them an injustice by making them live a worse life when they could live a better one?

You are forgetting again that it isn't the law's concern to make any one class in the city outstandingly happy but to contrive to spread happiness throughout the city by bringing the citizens into harmony with each other through persuasion or compulsion and by making them share with each other the benefits that each class can confer on the community.[4] The law produces such people in the city, not in order to allow them to turn in whatever direction they want, but to make use of them to bind the city together.

That's true, I had forgotten.

Observe, then, Glaucon, that we won't be doing an injustice to those who've become philosophers in our city and that what we'll say to them, when we compel them to guard and care for the others, will be just. We'll say: "When people like you come to be in other cities, they're justified in not sharing in their city's labors, for they've grown there spontaneously, against the will of the constitution. And what grows of its own accord and owes no debt for its upbringing has justice on its side when it isn't keen to pay anyone for that upbringing. But we've made you kings in our city and leaders of the swarm, as it were, both for yourselves and for the rest of the city. You're better and more completely educated than the others and are better able to share in both types of life. Therefore each of you in turn must go down to live in the common dwelling place of the others and grow accustomed to seeing in the dark. When you are used to it, you'll see vastly better than the people there. And because you've seen the truth about fine, just, and good things, you'll know each image for what it is and also that of which it is the image. Thus, for you and for us, the city will be governed, not like the majority of cities nowadays, by people who fight over shadows and struggle against one another in order to rule—as if that were a great good—but by people who are awake rather than dreaming, for the truth is surely this: A city whose prospective rulers are least eager to rule must of necessity be most free from civil war, whereas a city with the opposite kind of rulers is governed in the opposite way."

Absolutely.

Then do you think that those we've nurtured will disobey us and refuse to share the labors of the city, each in turn, while living the greater part of their time with one another in the pure realm?

It isn't possible, for we'll be giving just orders to just people. Each of them will certainly go to rule as to something compulsory, however, which is exactly the opposite of what's done by those who now rule in each city.

4. See 420b–421c, 462a–466c.

This is how it is. If you can find a way of life that's better than ruling for the prospective rulers, your well-governed city will become a possibil-

521   ity, for only in it will the truly rich rule—not those who are rich in gold but those who are rich in the wealth that the happy must have, namely, a good and rational life. But if beggars hungry for private goods go into public life, thinking that the good is there for the seizing, then the well-governed city is impossible, for then ruling is something fought over, and this civil and domestic war destroys these people and the rest of the city as well.

That's very true.

b   Can you name any life that despises political rule besides that of the true philosopher?

No, by god, I can't.

But surely it is those who are not lovers of ruling who must rule, for if they don't, the lovers of it, who are rivals, will fight over it.

Of course.

Then who will you compel to become guardians of the city, if not those who have the best understanding of what matters for good government and who have other honors than political ones, and a better life as well?

No one.

Do you want us to consider now how such people will come to be in

c   our city and how—just as some are said to have gone up from Hades to the gods—we'll lead them up to the light?

Of course I do.

This isn't, it seems, a matter of tossing a coin, but of turning a soul from a day that is a kind of night to the true day—the ascent to what is, which we say is true philosophy.

Indeed.

Then mustn't we try to discover the subjects that have the power to

d   bring this about?

Of course.

So what subject is it, Glaucon, that draws the soul from the realm of becoming to the realm of what is? And it occurs to me as I'm speaking that we said, didn't we, that it is necessary for the prospective rulers to be athletes in war when they're young?

Yes, we did.

Then the subject we're looking for must also have this characteristic in addition to the former one.

Which one?

It mustn't be useless to warlike men.

If it's at all possible, it mustn't.

Now, prior to this, we educated them in music and poetry and physi-

e   cal training.

We did.

And physical training is concerned with what comes into being and dies, for it oversees the growth and decay of the body.

Apparently.

So it couldn't be the subject we're looking for.

No, it couldn't.

Then, could it be the music and poetry we described before?

But that, if you remember, is just the counterpart of physical training. It educated the guardians through habits. Its harmonies gave them a certain harmoniousness, not knowledge; its rhythms gave them a certain rhythmical quality; and its stories, whether fictional or nearer the truth, cultivated other habits akin to these. But as for the subject you're looking for now, there's nothing like that in music and poetry.

Your reminder is exactly to the point; there's really nothing like that in music and poetry. But, Glaucon, what is there that does have this? The crafts all seem to be base or mechanical.

How could they be otherwise? But apart from music and poetry, physical training, and the crafts, what subject is left?

Well, if we can't find anything apart from these, let's consider one of the subjects that touches all of them.

What sort of thing?

For example, that common thing that every craft, every type of thought, and every science uses and that is among the first compulsory subjects for everyone.

What's that?

That inconsequential matter of distinguishing the one, the two, and the three. In short, I mean number and calculation, for isn't it true that every craft and science must have a share in that?

They certainly must.

Then so must warfare.

Absolutely.

In the tragedies, at any rate, Palamedes is always showing up Agamemnon as a totally ridiculous general. Haven't you noticed? He says that, by inventing numbers, he established how many troops there were in the Trojan army and counted their ships and everything else—implying that they were uncounted before and that Agamemnon (if indeed he didn't know how to count) didn't even know how many feet he had? What kind of general do you think that made him?

A very strange one, if that's true.

Then won't we set down this subject as compulsory for a warrior, so that he is able to count and calculate?

More compulsory than anything. If, that is, he's to understand anything about setting his troops in order or if he's even to be properly human.

Then do you notice the same thing about this subject that I do?

What's that?

That this turns out to be one of the subjects we were looking for that naturally lead to understanding. But no one uses it correctly, namely, as something that is really fitted in every way to draw one towards being.

What do you mean?

I'll try to make my view clear as follows: I'll distinguish for myself the things that do or don't lead in the direction we mentioned, and you must study them along with me and either agree or disagree, and that way we may come to know more clearly whether things are indeed as I divine.

Point them out.

I'll point out, then, if you can grasp it, that some sense perceptions *don't* summon the understanding to look into them, because the judgment of sense perception is itself adequate, while others encourage it in every way to look into them, because sense perception seems to produce no sound result.

You're obviously referring to things appearing in the distance and to *trompe l'oeil* paintings.

You're not quite getting my meaning.

Then what do you mean?

The ones that don't summon the understanding are all those that don't go off into opposite perceptions at the same time. But the ones that do go off in that way I call *summoners*—whenever sense perception doesn't declare one thing any more than its opposite, no matter whether the object striking the senses is near at hand or far away. You'll understand my meaning better if I put it this way: These, we say, are three fingers—the smallest, the second, and the middle finger.

That's right.

Assume that I'm talking about them as being seen from close by. Now, this is my question about them.

What?

It's apparent that each of them is equally a finger, and it makes no difference in this regard whether the finger is seen to be in the middle or at either end, whether it is dark or pale, thick or thin, or anything else of that sort, for in all these cases, an ordinary soul isn't compelled to ask the understanding what a finger is, since sight doesn't suggest to it that a finger is at the same time the opposite of a finger.

No, it doesn't.

Therefore, it isn't likely that anything of that sort would summon or awaken the understanding.

No, it isn't.

But what about the bigness and smallness of fingers? Does sight perceive them adequately? Does it make no difference to it whether the finger is in the middle or at the end? And is it the same with the sense of touch, as regards the thick and the thin, the hard and the soft? And do the other senses reveal such things clearly and adequately? Doesn't each of them rather do the following: The sense set over the hard is, in the first place, of necessity also set over the soft, and it reports to the soul that the same thing is perceived by it to be both hard and soft?

That's right.

And isn't it necessary that in such cases the soul is puzzled as to what this sense means by the hard, if it indicates that the same thing is also

soft, or what it means by the light and the heavy, if it indicates that the
heavy is light, or the light, heavy?

Yes, indeed, these are strange reports for the soul to receive, and they   b
do demand to be looked into.

Then it's likely that in such cases the soul, summoning calculation and
understanding, first tries to determine whether each of the things announced to it is one or two.

Of course.

If it's evidently two, won't each be evidently distinct and one?

Yes.

Then, if each is one, and both two, the soul will understand that the
two are separate, for it wouldn't understand the inseparable to be two,
but rather one.   c

That's right.

Sight, however, saw the big and small, not as separate, but as mixed up
together. Isn't that so?

Yes.

And in order to get clear about all this, understanding was compelled
to see the big and the small, not as mixed up together, but as separate—
the opposite way from sight.

True.

And isn't it from these cases that it first occurs to us to ask what the
big is and what the small is?

Absolutely.

And, because of this, we called the one the intelligible and the other
the visible.

That's right.   d

This, then, is what I was trying to express before, when I said that some
things summon thought, while others don't. Those that strike the relevant
sense at the same time as their opposites I call summoners, those that
don't do this do not awaken understanding.

Now I understand, and I think you're right.

Well, then, to which of them do number and the one belong?

I don't know.

Reason it out from what was said before. If the one is adequately seen
itself by itself or is so perceived by any of the other senses, then, as we
were saying in the case of fingers, it wouldn't draw the soul towards being.
But if something opposite to it is always seen at the same time, so that   e
nothing is apparently any more one than the opposite of one, then something would be needed to judge the matter. The soul would then be
puzzled, would look for an answer, would stir up its understanding, and
would ask what the one itself is. And so this would be among the subjects
that lead the soul and turn it around towards the study of that which is.   525

But surely the sight of the one does possess this characteristic to a
remarkable degree, for we see the same thing to be both one and an
unlimited number at the same time.

Then, if this is true of the one, won't it also be true of all numbers?

Of course.

Now, calculation and arithmetic are wholly concerned with numbers.

That's right.

b   Then evidently they lead us towards truth.

Supernaturally so.

Then they belong, it seems, to the subjects we're seeking. They are compulsory for warriors because of their orderly ranks and for philosophers because they have to learn to rise up out of becoming and grasp being, if they are ever to become rational.

That's right.

And our guardian must be both a warrior and a philosopher.

Certainly.

Then it would be appropriate, Glaucon, to legislate this subject for those who are going to share in the highest offices in the city and to persuade them to turn to calculation and take it up, not as laymen do, but staying

c   with it until they reach the study of the natures of the numbers by means of understanding itself, nor like tradesmen and retailers, for the sake of buying and selling, but for the sake of war and for ease in turning the soul around, away from becoming and towards truth and being.

Well put.

Moreover, it strikes me, now that it has been mentioned, how sophisticated the subject of calculation is and in how many ways it is useful for

d   our purposes, provided that one practices it for the sake of knowing rather than trading.

How is it useful?

In the very way we were talking about. It leads the soul forcibly upward and compels it to discuss the numbers themselves, never permitting anyone to propose for discussion numbers attached to visible or tangible bodies. You know what those who are clever in these matters are like: If, in the course of the argument, someone tries to divide the one itself, they laugh

e   and won't permit it. If you divide it, they multiply it, taking care that one thing never be found to be many parts rather than one.

That's very true.

Then what do you think would happen, Glaucon, if someone were to

526   ask them: "What kind of numbers are you talking about, in which the one is as you assume it to be, each one equal to every other, without the least difference and containing no internal parts?"

I think they'd answer that they are talking about those numbers that can be grasped only in thought and can't be dealt with in any other way.

b   Then do you see that it's likely that this subject really is compulsory for us, since it apparently compels the soul to use understanding itself on the truth itself?

Indeed, it most certainly does do that.

And what about those who are naturally good at calculation or reasoning? Have you already noticed that they're naturally sharp, so to speak, in all subjects, and that those who are slow at it, if they're educated and exercised in it, even if they're benefited in no other way, nonetheless improve and become generally sharper than they were?

That's true.

Moreover, I don't think you'll easily find subjects that are harder to learn or practice than this.   c

No, indeed.

Then, for all these reasons, this subject isn't to be neglected, and the best natures must be educated in it.

I agree.

Let that, then, be one of our subjects. Second, let's consider whether the subject that comes next is also appropriate for our purposes.

What subject is that? Do you mean geometry?

That's the very one I had in mind.

Insofar as it pertains to war, it's obviously appropriate, for when it   d
comes to setting up camp, occupying a region, concentrating troops, deploying them, or with regard to any of the other formations an army adopts in battle or on the march, it makes all the difference whether someone is a geometer or not.

But, for things like that, even a little geometry—or calculation for that matter—would suffice. What we need to consider is whether the greater and more advanced part of it tends to make it easier to see the form of the good. And we say that anything has that tendency if it compels the   e
soul to turn itself around towards the region in which lies the happiest of the things that are, the one the soul must see at any cost.

You're right.

Therefore, if geometry compels the soul to study being, it's appropriate, but if it compels it to study becoming, it's inappropriate.

So we've said, at any rate.

Now, no one with even a little experience of geometry will dispute that   527
this science is entirely the opposite of what is said about it in the accounts of its practitioners.

How do you mean?

They give ridiculous accounts of it, though they can't help it, for they speak like practical men, and all their accounts refer to doing things. They talk of "squaring," "applying," "adding," and the like, whereas the entire subject is pursued for the sake of knowledge.   b

Absolutely.

And mustn't we also agree on a further point?

What is that?

That their accounts are for the sake of knowing what always is, not what comes into being and passes away.

That's easy to agree to, for geometry *is* knowledge of what always is.

Then it draws the soul towards truth and produces philosophic thought by directing upwards what we now wrongly direct downwards.

As far as anything possibly can.

c   Then as far as *we* possibly can, we must require those in your fine
city not to neglect geometry in any way, for even its by-products are
not insignificant.

What are they?

The ones concerned with war that you mentioned. But we also surely
know that, when it comes to better understanding any subject, there is a
world of difference between someone who has grasped geometry and
someone who hasn't.

Yes, by god, a world of difference.

Then shall we set this down as a second subject for the young?

Let's do so, he said.

And what about astronomy? Shall we make it the third? Or do you dis-
d   agree?

That's fine with me, for a better awareness of the seasons, months, and
years is no less appropriate for a general than for a farmer or navigator.

You amuse me: You're like someone who's afraid that the majority will
think he is prescribing useless subjects. It's no easy task—indeed it's very
difficult—to realize that in every soul there is an instrument that is purified
and rekindled by such subjects when it has been blinded and destroyed
e   by other ways of life, an instrument that it is more important to preserve
than ten thousand eyes, since only with it can the truth be seen. Those
who share your belief that this is so will think you're speaking incredibly
well, while those who've never been aware of it will probably think you're
talking nonsense, since they see no benefit worth mentioning in these
subjects. So decide right now which group you're addressing. Or are your
528 arguments for neither of them but mostly for your own sake—though you
won't begrudge anyone else whatever benefit he's able to get from them?

The latter: I want to speak, question, and answer mostly for my own sake.

Then let's fall back to our earlier position, for we were wrong just now
about the subject that comes after geometry.

What was our error?

After plane surfaces, we went on to revolving solids before dealing with
solids by themselves. But the right thing to do is to take up the third
b   dimension right after the second. And this, I suppose, consists of cubes
and of whatever shares in depth.

You're right, Socrates, but this subject hasn't been developed yet.

There are two reasons for that: First, because no city values it, this
difficult subject is little researched. Second, the researchers need a director,
for, without one, they won't discover anything. To begin with, such a
director is hard to find, and, then, even if he could be found, those who
c   currently do research in this field would be too arrogant to follow him. If
an entire city helped him to supervise it, however, and took the lead in
valuing it, then he would be followed. And, if the subject was consistently
and vigorously pursued, it would soon be developed. Even now, when it
isn't valued and is held in contempt by the majority and is pursued by

researchers who are unable to give an account of its usefulness, nevertheless, in spite of all these handicaps, the force of its charm has caused it to
develop somewhat, so that it wouldn't be surprising if it were further
developed even as things stand.

The subject *has* outstanding charm. But explain more clearly what you   d
were saying just now. The subject that deals with plane surfaces you took
to be geometry.

Yes.

And at first you put astronomy after it, but later you went back on that.

In my haste to go through them all, I've only progressed more slowly.
The subject dealing with the dimension of depth was next. But because it
is in a ridiculous state, I passed it by and spoke of astronomy (which deals
with the motion of things having depth) after geometry.   e

That's right.

Let's then put astronomy as the fourth subject, on the assumption that
solid geometry will be available if a city takes it up.

That seems reasonable. And since you reproached me before for praising
astronomy in a vulgar manner, I'll now praise it your way, for I think it's
clear to everyone that astronomy compels the soul to look upward and   529
leads it from things here to things there.

It may be obvious to everyone except me, but that's not my view about it.

Then what *is* your view?

As it's practiced today by those who teach philosophy, it makes the soul
look very much downward.

How do you mean?

In my opinion, your conception of "higher studies" is a good deal too
generous, for if someone were to study something by leaning his head
back and studying ornaments on a ceiling, it looks as though you'd say
he's studying not with his eyes but with his understanding. Perhaps you're   b
right, and I'm foolish, but I can't conceive of any subject making the soul
look upward except one concerned with that which is, and that which is
is invisible. If anyone attempts to learn something about sensible things,
whether by gaping upward or squinting downward, I'd claim—since
there's no knowledge of such things—that he never learns anything and
that, even if he studies lying on his back on the ground or floating on it   c
in the sea, his soul is looking not up but down.

You're right to reproach me, and I've been justly punished, but what
did you mean when you said that astronomy must be learned in a different
way from the way in which it is learned at present if it is to be a useful
subject for our purposes?

It's like this: We should consider the decorations in the sky to be the
most beautiful and most exact of visible things, seeing that they're embroidered on a visible surface. But we should consider their motions to fall
far short of the true ones—motions that are really fast or slow as measured   d
in true numbers, that trace out true geometrical figures, that are all in

relation to one another, and that are the true motions of the things carried along in them. And these, of course, must be grasped by reason and thought, not by sight. Or do you think otherwise?

Not at all.

Therefore, we should use the embroidery in the sky as a model in the study of these other things. If someone experienced in geometry were to come upon plans very carefully drawn and worked out by Daedalus or some other craftsman or artist, he'd consider them to be very finely executed, but he'd think it ridiculous to examine them seriously in order to find the truth in them about the equal, the double, or any other ratio.

How could it be anything other than ridiculous?

Then don't you think that a real astronomer will feel the same when he looks at the motions of the stars? He'll believe that the craftsman of the heavens arranged them and all that's in them in the finest way possible for such things. But as for the ratio of night to day, of days to a month, of a month to a year, or of the motions of the stars to any of them or to each other, don't you think he'll consider it strange to believe that they're always the same and never deviate anywhere at all or to try in any sort of way to grasp the truth about them, since they're connected to body and visible?

That's my opinion anyway, now that I hear it from you.

Then if, by really taking part in astronomy, we're to make the naturally intelligent part of the soul useful instead of useless, let's study astronomy by means of problems, as we do geometry, and leave the things in the sky alone.

The task you're prescribing is a lot harder than anything now attempted in astronomy.

And I suppose that, if we are to be of any benefit as lawgivers, our prescriptions for the other subjects will be of the same kind. But have you any other appropriate subject to suggest?

Not offhand.

Well, there isn't just one form of motion but several. Perhaps a wise person could list them all, but there are two that are evident even to us.

What are they?

Besides the one we've discussed, there is also its counterpart.

What's that?

It's likely that, as the eyes fasten on astronomical motions, so the ears fasten on harmonic ones, and that the sciences of astronomy and harmonics are closely akin. This is what the Pythagoreans say, Glaucon, and we agree, don't we?

We do.

Therefore, since the subject is so huge, shouldn't we ask them what they have to say about harmonic motions and whether there is anything else besides them, all the while keeping our own goal squarely in view?

What's that?

That those whom we are rearing should never try to learn anything incomplete, anything that doesn't reach the end that everything should reach—the end we mentioned just now in the case of astronomy. Or don't you know that people do something similar in harmonics? Measuring audible consonances and sounds against one another, they labor in vain, just like present-day astronomers.

531

Yes, by the gods, and pretty ridiculous they are too. They talk about something they call a "dense interval" or quartertone—putting their ears to their instruments like someone trying to overhear what the neighbors are saying. And some say that they hear a tone in between and that *it* is the shortest interval by which they must measure, while others argue that this tone sounds the same as a quarter tone. Both put ears before understanding.

b

You mean those excellent fellows who torment their strings, torturing them, and stretching them on pegs. I won't draw out the analogy by speaking of blows with the plectrum or the accusations or denials and boastings on the part of the strings; instead I'll cut it short by saying that these aren't the people I'm talking about. The ones I mean are the ones we just said we were going to question about harmonics, for they do the same as the astronomers. They seek out the numbers that are to be found in these audible consonances, but they do not make the ascent to problems. They don't investigate, for example, which numbers are consonant and which aren't or what the explanation is of each.

c

But that would be a superhuman task.

Yet it's useful in the search for the beautiful and the good. But pursued for any other purpose, it's useless.

Probably so.

Moreover, I take it that, if inquiry into all the subjects we've mentioned brings out their association and relationship with one another and draws conclusions about their kinship, it does contribute something to our goal and isn't labor in vain, but that otherwise it is in vain.

d

I, too, divine that this is true. But you're still talking about a very big task, Socrates.

Do you mean the prelude, or what? Or don't you know that all these subjects are merely preludes to the song itself that must also be learned? Surely you don't think that people who are clever in these matters are dialecticians.

e

No, by god, I don't. Although I have met a few exceptions.

But did it ever seem to you that those who can neither give nor follow an account know anything at all of the things we say they must know?

My answer to that is also no.

Then isn't this at last, Glaucon, the song that dialectic sings? It is intelligible, but it is imitated by the power of sight. We said that sight tries at last to look at the animals themselves, the stars themselves, and, in the end, at the sun itself. In the same way, whenever someone tries through

532

argument and apart from all sense perceptions to find the being itself of each thing and doesn't give up until he grasps the good itself with

b   understanding itself, he reaches the end of the intelligible, just as the other reached the end of the visible.

Absolutely.

And what about this journey? Don't you call it dialectic?

I do.

Then the release from bonds and the turning around from shadows to statues and the light of the fire and, then, the way up out of the cave to the sunlight and, there, the continuing inability to look at the animals, the plants, and the light of the sun, but the newly acquired ability to look at

c   divine images in water and shadows of the things that are, rather than, as before, merely at shadows of statues thrown by another source of light that is itself a shadow in relation to the sun—all this business of the crafts we've mentioned has the power to awaken the best part of the soul and lead it upward to the study of the best among the things that are, just as, before, the clearest thing in the body was led to the brightest thing in the

d   bodily and visible realm.

I accept that this is so, even though it seems very hard to accept in one way and hard not to accept in another. All the same, since we'll have to return to these things often in the future, rather than having to hear them just once now, let's assume that what you've said is so and turn to the song itself, discussing it in the same way as we did the prelude. So tell us: what is the sort of power dialectic has, what forms is it divided into, and what paths does it follow? For these lead at last, it seems, towards

e   that place which is a rest from the road, so to speak, and an end of journeying for the one who reaches it.

533   You won't be able to follow me any longer, Glaucon, even though there is no lack of eagerness on my part to lead you, for you would no longer be seeing an image of what we're describing, but the truth itself. At any rate, that's how it seems to me. That it is really so is not worth insisting on any further. But that there is some such thing to be seen, *that* is something we must insist on. Isn't that so?

Of course.

And mustn't we also insist that the power of dialectic could reveal it only to someone experienced in the subjects we've described and that it cannot reveal it in any other way?

That too is worth insisting on.

b   At any rate, no one will dispute it when we say that there is no other inquiry that systematically attempts to grasp with respect to each thing itself what the being of it is, for all the other crafts are concerned with human opinions and desires, with growing or construction, or with the care of growing or constructed things. And as for the rest, I mean geometry and the subjects that follow it, we described them as to some extent grasping what is, for we saw that, while they do dream about what is, they are unable to command a waking view of it as long as they make use of hypotheses that they leave untouched and that they cannot give any account of. What mechanism could possibly turn any agreement into knowledge when it begins with something unknown and puts together the conclusion and the steps in between from what is unknown?

None.

Therefore, dialectic is the only inquiry that travels this road, doing away with hypotheses and proceeding to the first principle itself, so as to be secure. And when the eye of the soul is really buried in a sort of barbaric bog, dialectic gently pulls it out and leads it upwards, using the crafts we described to help it and cooperate with it in turning the soul around. From force of habit, we've often called these crafts sciences or kinds of knowledge, but they need another name, clearer than opinion, darker than knowledge. We called them thought somewhere before.[5] But I presume that we won't dispute about a name when we have so many more important matters to investigate.

Of course not.

It will therefore be enough to call the first section knowledge, the second thought, the third belief, and the fourth imaging, just as we did before. The last two together we call opinion, the other two, intellect. Opinion is concerned with becoming, intellect with being. And as being is to becoming, so intellect is to opinion, and as intellect is to opinion, so knowledge is to belief and thought to imaging. But as for the ratios between the things these are set over and the division of either the opinable or the intelligible section into two, let's pass them by, Glaucon, lest they involve us in arguments many times longer than the ones we've already gone through.

I agree with you about the others in any case, insofar as I'm able to follow.

Then, do you call someone who is able to give an account of the being of each thing dialectical? But insofar as he's unable to give an account of something, either to himself or to another, do you deny that he has any understanding of it?

How could I do anything else?

Then the same applies to the good. Unless someone can distinguish in an account the form of the good from everything else, can survive all refutation, as if in a battle, striving to judge things not in accordance with opinion but in accordance with being, and can come through all this with his account still intact, you'll say that he doesn't know the good itself or any other good. And if he gets hold of some image of it, you'll say that it's through opinion, not knowledge, for he is dreaming and asleep throughout his present life, and, before he wakes up here, he will arrive in Hades and go to sleep forever.

Yes, by god, I'll certainly say all of that.

Then, as for those children of yours whom you're rearing and educating in theory, if you ever reared them in fact, I don't think that you'd allow

5. See 511d–e.

them to rule in your city or be responsible for the most important things while they are as irrational as incommensurable lines.

Certainly not.

Then you'll legislate that they are to give most attention to the education that will enable them to ask and answer questions most knowledgeably?

e   I'll legislate it along with you.

Then do you think that we've placed dialectic at the top of the other subjects like a coping stone and that no other subject can rightly be placed above it, but that our account of the subjects that a future ruler must learn
535   has come to an end?

Probably so.

Then it remains for you to deal with the distribution of these subjects, with the question of to whom we'll assign them and in what way.

That's clearly next.

Do you remember what sort of people we chose in our earlier selection of rulers?[6]

Of course I do.

In the other respects, the same natures have to be chosen: we have to select the most stable, the most courageous, and as far as possible the most graceful. In addition, we must look not only for people who have a noble
b   and tough character but for those who have the natural qualities conducive to this education of ours.

Which ones exactly?

They must be keen on the subjects and learn them easily, for people's souls give up much more easily in hard study than in physical training, since the pain—being peculiar to them and not shared with their body— is more their own.

That's true.

c   We must also look for someone who has got a good memory, is persistent, and is in every way a lover of hard work. How else do you think he'd be willing to carry out both the requisite bodily labors and also complete so much study and practice?

Nobody would, unless his nature was in every way a good one.

In any case, the present error, which as we said before explains why philosophy isn't valued, is that she's taken up by people who are unworthy of her, for illegitimate students shouldn't be allowed to take her up, but only legitimate ones.

How so?

d   In the first place, no student should be lame in his love of hard work, really loving one half of it, and hating the other half. This happens when someone is a lover of physical training, hunting, or any kind of bodily labor and isn't a lover of learning, listening, or inquiry, but hates the work involved in them. And someone whose love of hard work tends in the opposite direction is also lame.

6. See 412b ff.

That's very true.

Similarly with regard to truth, won't we say that a soul is maimed if it hates a voluntary falsehood, cannot endure to have one in itself, and is greatly angered when it exists in others, but is nonetheless content to accept an involuntary falsehood, isn't angry when it is caught being ignorant, and bears its lack of learning easily, wallowing in it like a pig?

Absolutely.

And with regard to moderation, courage, high-mindedness, and all the other parts of virtue, it is also important to distinguish the illegitimate from the legitimate, for when either a city or an individual doesn't know how to do this, it unwittingly employs the lame and illegitimate as friends or rulers for whatever services it wants done.

That's just how it is.

So we must be careful in all these matters, for if we bring people who are sound of limb and mind to so great a subject and training, and educate them in it, even justice itself won't blame us, and we'll save the city and its constitution. But if we bring people of a different sort, we'll do the opposite, and let loose an even greater flood of ridicule upon philosophy.

And it would be shameful to do that.

It certainly would. But I seem to have done something a bit ridiculous myself just now.

What's that?

I forgot that we were only playing, and so I spoke too vehemently. But I looked upon philosophy as I spoke, and seeing her undeservedly besmirched, I seem to have lost my temper and said what I had to say too earnestly, as if I were angry with those responsible for it.

That certainly wasn't my impression as I listened to you.

But it was mine as I was speaking. In any case, let's not forget that in our earlier selection we chose older people but that that isn't permitted in this one, for we mustn't believe Solon[7] when he says that as someone grows older he's able to learn a lot. He can do that even less well than he can run races, for all great and numerous labors belong to the young.

Necessarily.

Therefore, calculation, geometry, and all the preliminary education required for dialectic must be offered to the future rulers in childhood, and not in the shape of compulsory learning either.

Why's that?

Because no free person should learn anything like a slave. Forced bodily labor does no harm to the body, but nothing taught by force stays in the soul.

That's true.

Then don't use force to train the children in these subjects; use play instead. That way you'll also see better what each of them is naturally fitted for.

---

7. Athenian statesman, lawgiver, and poet (c. 640–560).

That seems reasonable.

Do you remember that we stated that the children were to be led into war on horseback as observers and that, wherever it is safe to do so, they should be brought close and taste blood, like puppies?

I remember.

In all these things—in labors, studies, and fears—the ones who always show the greatest aptitude are to be inscribed on a list.

b   At what age?

When they're released from compulsory physical training, for during that period, whether it's two or three years, young people are incapable of doing anything else, since weariness and sleep are enemies of learning. At the same time, how they fare in this physical training is itself an important test.

Of course it is.

And after that, that is to say, from the age of twenty, those who are chosen will also receive more honors than the others. Moreover, the subjects they learned in no particular order as children they must now bring to-
c   gether to form a unified vision of their kinship both with one another and with the nature of that which is.

At any rate, only learning of that sort holds firm in those who receive it.

It is also the greatest test of who is naturally dialectical and who isn't, for anyone who can achieve a unified vision is dialectical, and anyone who can't isn't.

I agree.

Well, then, you'll have to look out for the ones who most all have this ability in them and who also remain steadfast in their studies, in war,
d   and in the other activities laid down by law. And after they have reached their thirtieth year, you'll select them in turn from among those chosen earlier and assign them yet greater honors. Then you'll have to test them by means of the power of dialectic, to discover which of them can relinquish his eyes and other senses, going on with the help of truth to that which by itself is. And this is a task that requires great care.

What's the main reason for that?

Don't you realize what a great evil comes from dialectic as it is cur-
e   rently practiced?

What evil is that?

Those who practice it are filled with lawlessness.

They certainly are.

Do you think it's surprising that this happens to them? Aren't you sympathetic?

Why isn't it surprising? And why should I be sympathetic?

Because it's like the case of a child brought up surrounded by much wealth and many flatterers in a great and numerous family, who finds
538   out, when he has become a man, that he isn't the child of his professed parents and that he can't discover his real ones. Can you divine what the

attitude of someone like that would be to the flatterers, on the one hand, and to his supposed parents, on the other, before he knew about his parentage, and what it would be when he found out? Or would you rather hear what I divine about it?

I'd rather hear your views.

Well, then, I divine that during the time that he didn't know the truth, he'd honor his father, mother, and the rest of his supposed family more than he would the flatterers, that he'd pay greater attention to their needs, be less likely to treat them lawlessly in word or deed, and be more likely to obey them than the flatterers in any matters of importance.

Probably so.

When he became aware of the truth, however, his honor and enthusiasm would lessen for his family and increase for the flatterers, he'd obey the latter far more than before, begin to live in the way that they did, and keep company with them openly, and, unless he was very decent by nature, he'd eventually care nothing for that father of his or any of the rest of his supposed family.

All this would probably happen as you say, but in what way is it an image of those who take up arguments?

As follows. We hold from childhood certain convictions about just and fine things; we're brought up with them as with our parents, we obey and honor them.

Indeed, we do.

There are other ways of living, however, opposite to these and full of pleasures, that flatter the soul and attract it to themselves but which don't persuade sensible people, who continue to honor and obey the convictions of their fathers.

That's right.

And then a questioner comes along and asks someone of this sort, "What is the fine?" And, when he answers what he has heard from the traditional lawgiver, the argument refutes him, and by refuting him often and in many places shakes him from his convictions, and makes him believe that the fine is no more fine than shameful, and the same with the just, the good, and the things he honored most. What do you think his attitude will be then to honoring and obeying his earlier convictions?

Of necessity he won't honor or obey them in the same way.

Then, when he no longer honors and obeys those convictions and can't discover the true ones, will he be likely to adopt any other way of life than that which flatters him?

No, he won't.

And so, I suppose, from being law-abiding he becomes lawless.

Inevitably.

Then, as I asked before, isn't it only to be expected that this is what happens to those who take up arguments in this way, and don't they therefore deserve a lot of sympathy?

Yes, and they deserve pity too.

Then, if you don't want your thirty-year-olds to be objects of such pity, you'll have to be extremely careful about how you introduce them to arguments.

That's right.

And isn't it one lasting precaution not to let them taste arguments while they're young? I don't suppose that it has escaped your notice that, when
b   young people get their first taste of arguments, they misuse it by treating it as a kind of game of contradiction. They imitate those who've refuted them by refuting others themselves, and, like puppies, they enjoy dragging and tearing those around them with their arguments.

They're excessively fond of it.

Then, when they've refuted many and been refuted by them in turn, they forcefully and quickly fall into disbelieving what they believed before.
c   And, as a result, they themselves and the whole of philosophy are discredited in the eyes of others.

That's very true.

But an older person won't want to take part in such madness. He'll imitate someone who is willing to engage in discussion in order to look for the truth, rather than someone who plays at contradiction for sport. He'll be more sensible himself and will bring honor rather than discredit
d   to the philosophical way of life.

That's right.

And when we said before that those allowed to take part in arguments should be orderly and steady by nature, not as nowadays, when even the unfit are allowed to engage in them—wasn't all that also said as a precaution?

Of course.

Then if someone continuously, strenuously, and exclusively devotes himself to participation in arguments, exercising himself in them just as he did in the bodily physical training, which is their counterpart, would that be enough?
e   Do you mean six years or four?

It doesn't matter. Make it five. And after that, you must make them go down into the cave again, and compel them to take command in matters of war and occupy the other offices suitable for young people, so that they won't be inferior to the others in experience. But in these, too, they must be tested to see whether they'll remain steadfast when they're pulled this
540 way and that or shift their ground.

How much time do you allow for that?

Fifteen years. Then, at the age of fifty, those who've survived the tests and been successful both in practical matters and in the sciences must be led to the goal and compelled to lift up the radiant light of their souls to what itself provides light for everything. And once they've seen the good itself, they must each in turn put the city, its citizens, and themselves in
b   order, using it as their model. Each of them will spend most of his time

with philosophy, but, when his turn comes, he must labor in politics and rule for the city's sake, not as if he were doing something fine, but rather something that has to be done. Then, having educated others like himself to take his place as guardians of the city, he will depart for the Isles of the Blessed and dwell there. And, if the Pythia agrees, the city will publicly establish memorials and sacrifices to him as a daemon, but if not, then as a happy and divine human being.

Like a sculptor, Socrates, you've produced ruling men that are completely fine.

And ruling women, too, Glaucon, for you mustn't think that what I've said applies any more to men than it does to women who are born with the appropriate natures.

That's right, if indeed they are to share everything equally with the men, as we said they should.

Then, do you agree that the things we've said about the city and its constitution aren't altogether wishful thinking, that it's hard for them to come about, but not impossible? And do you also agree that they can come about only in the way we indicated, namely, when one or more true philosophers come to power in a city, who despise present honors, thinking them slavish and worthless, and who prize what is right and the honors that come from it above everything, and regard justice as the most important and most essential thing, serving it and increasing it as they set their city in order?

How will they do that?

They'll send everyone in the city who is over ten years old into the country. Then they'll take possession of the children, who are now free from the ethos of their parents, and bring them up in their own customs and laws, which are the ones we've described. This is the quickest and easiest way for the city and constitution we've discussed to be established, become happy, and bring most benefit to the people among whom it's established.

That's by far the quickest and easiest way. And in my opinion, Socrates, you've described well how it would come into being, if it ever did.

Then, isn't that enough about this city and the man who is like it? Surely it is clear what sort of man we'll say he has to be.

It is clear, he said. And as for your question, I think that we have reached the end of this topic.

Book VIII

Well, then, Glaucon, we've agreed to the following: If a city is to achieve the height of good government, wives must be in common, children and all their education must be in common, their way of life, whether in peace or war, must be in common, and their kings must be those among them who have proved to be best, both in philosophy and in warfare.

We have agreed to that, he said.

Moreover, we also agreed that, as soon as the rulers are established,
b   they will lead the soldiers and settle them in the kind of dwellings we
described, which are in no way private but common to all. And we also
agreed, if you remember, what kind of possessions they will have.

I remember that we thought that none of them should acquire any of
the things that the other rulers now do but that, as athletes of war and
guardians, they should receive their yearly upkeep from the other citizens
c   as a wage for their guardianship and look after themselves and the rest
of the city.[1]

That's right. But since we have completed this discussion, let's recall
the point at which we began the digression that brought us here, so that
we can continue on the same path from where we left off.

That isn't difficult, for, much the same as now, you were talking as if
you had completed the description of the city.[2] You said that you would
class both the city you described and the man who is like it as good, even
d   though, as it seems, you had a still finer city and man to tell us about.
544 But, in any case, you said that, if this city was the right one, the others were
faulty. You said, if I remember, that there were four types of constitution
remaining that are worth discussing, each with faults that we should
observe, and we should do the same for the people who are like them.
Our aim was to observe them all, agree which man is best and which
worst, and then determine whether the best is happiest and the worst
most wretched or whether it's otherwise. I was asking you which four
constitutions you had in mind when Polemarchus and Adeimantus inter-
b   rupted.[3] And that's when you took up the discussion that led here.

That's absolutely right.

Well, then, like a wrestler, give me the same hold again, and when I
ask the same question, try to give the answer you were about to give before.

If I can.

I'd at least like to hear what four constitutions you meant.

c   That won't be difficult since they're the ones for which we have names.
First, there's the constitution praised by most people, namely, the Cretan
or Laconian.[4] The second, which is also second in the praise it receives, is
called oligarchy and is filled with a host of evils. The next in order, and
antagonistic to it, is democracy. And finally there is genuine tyranny,
surpassing all of them, the fourth and last of the diseased cities. Or can
you think of another type of constitution—I mean another whose form is
distinct from these? Dynasties and purchased kingships and other constitu-

---

1. See 414d–20b.
2. See 445c–e.
3. See 449b ff.
4. I.e., the Spartan constitution.

tions of that sort, which one finds no less among the barbarians than   d
among the Greeks, are somewhere intermediate between these four.

At any event, many strange ones are indeed talked about.

And do you realize that of necessity there are as many forms of human
character as there are of constitutions? Or do you think that constitutions
are born "from oak or rock"[5] and not from the characters of the people
who live in the cities governed by them, which tip the scales, so to speak,
and drag the rest along with them?   e

No, I don't believe they come from anywhere else.

Then, if there are five forms of city, there must also be five forms of the
individual soul.

Of course.

Now, we've already described the one that's like aristocracy, which is
rightly said to be good and just.

We have.   545

Then mustn't we next go through the inferior ones, namely, the victory-
loving and honor-loving (which corresponds to the Laconian form of constitution), followed by the oligarchic, the democratic, and the tyrannical, so
that, having discovered the most unjust of all, we can oppose him to the
most just? In this way, we can complete our investigation into how pure
justice and pure injustice stand, with regard to the happiness or wretchedness of those who possess them, and either be persuaded by Thrasymachus
to practice injustice or by the argument that is now coming to light to
practice justice.   b

That's absolutely what we have to do.

Then, just as we began by looking for the virtues of character in a
constitution, before looking for them in the individual, thinking that they'd
be clearer in the former, shouldn't we first examine the honor-loving
constitution? I don't know what other name there is for it, but it should
be called either timocracy or timarchy. Then shouldn't we examine an
individual who is related to that constitution, and, after that, oligarchy
and an oligarchic person, and democracy and a democratic person? And
finally, having come to a city under a tyrant and having examined it,   c
shouldn't we look into a tyrannical soul, trying in this way to become
adequate judges of the topic we proposed to ourselves?

That would be a reasonable way for us to go about observing and
judging, at any rate.

Well, then, let's try to explain how timocracy emerges from aristocracy.
Or is it a simple principle that the cause of change in any constitution is
civil war breaking out within the ruling group itself, but that if this group—
however small it is—remains of one mind, the constitution cannot be   d
changed?

Yes, that's right.

5. See e.g. *Odyssey* xix.163.

      How, then, Glaucon, will our city be changed? How will civil war arise, either between the auxiliaries and the rulers or within either group? Or do you want us to be like Homer and pray to the Muses to tell us "how

e   civil war first broke out?"[6] And shall we say that they speak to us in tragic tones, as if they were in earnest, playing and jesting with us as if we were children?

      What will they say?

546   Something like this. "It is hard for a city composed in this way to change, but everything that comes into being must decay. Not even a constitution such as this will last forever. It, too, must face dissolution. And this is how it will be dissolved. All plants that grow in the earth, and also all animals that grow upon it, have periods of fruitfulness and barrenness of both soul and body as often as the revolutions complete the circumferences of their circles. These circumferences are short for the short-lived, and the opposite for their opposites.[7] Now, the people you have educated to be leaders in your city, even though they are wise, still won't, through calcula-

b   tion together with sense perception, hit upon the fertility and barrenness of the human species, but it will escape them, and so they will at some time beget children when they ought not to do so. For the birth of a divine creature, there is a cycle comprehended by a perfect number. For a human being, it is the first number in which are found root and square increases, comprehending three lengths and four terms, of elements that make things like and unlike, that cause them to increase and decrease, and that render

c   all things mutually agreeable and rational in their relations to one another. Of these elements, four and three, married with five, give two harmonies when thrice increased. One of them is a square, so many times a hundred. The other is of equal length one way but oblong. One of its sides is one hundred squares of the rational diameter of five diminished by one each or one hundred squares of the irrational diameter diminished by two each. The other side is a hundred cubes of three. This whole geometrical number controls better and worse births.[8] And when your rulers, through ignorance of these births, join brides and grooms at the wrong time, the children

---

6. An adaptation of *Iliad* xvi.112–13.

7. The reference is to the fertility and gestation periods of different species of plants and animals and their (supposedly related) life spans.

8. The human geometrical number is the product of 3, 4, and 5 "thrice increased," multiplied by itself three times, i.e., $(3\cdot4\cdot5)^4$ or 12,960,000. This can be represented geometrically as a square whose sides are 3600 or as an oblong or rectangle whose sides are 4800 and 2700. The first is "so many times a hundred," viz. 36 times. The latter is obtained as follows. The "rational diameter" of 5 is the nearest rational number to the real diagonal of a square whose sides are 5, i.e., to $\sqrt{50}$. This number is 7. Since the square of 7 is 49, we get the longer side of the rectangle by diminishing 49 by 1 and multiplying the result by 100. This gives 4800. The "irrational diameter" of 5 is $\sqrt{50}$. When squared, diminished by 2, and multiplied by 100 this, too, is 4800. The short side, "a hundred cubes of three," is 2700.

will be neither good natured nor fortunate. The older generation will   d
choose the best of these children but they are unworthy nevertheless, and
when they acquire their fathers' powers, they will begin, as guardians, to
neglect us Muses. First, they will have less consideration for music and
poetry than they ought, then they will neglect physical training, so that
your young people will become less well educated in music and poetry.
Hence, rulers chosen from among them won't be able to guard well the   e
testing of the golden, silver, bronze, and iron races, which are Hesiod's
and your own.[9] The intermixing of iron with silver and bronze with gold
that results will engender lack of likeness and unharmonious inequality, 547
and these always breed war and hostility wherever they arise. Civil war,
we declare, is always and everywhere 'of this lineage'."[10]

And we'll declare that what the Muses say is right.

It must be, since they're Muses.

What do the Muses say after that?   b

Once civil war breaks out, both the iron and bronze types pull the
constitution towards money-making and the acquisition of land, houses,
gold, and silver, while both the gold and silver types—not being poor,
but by nature rich or rich in their souls—lead the constitution towards
virtue and the old order. And thus striving and struggling with one another,
they compromise on a middle way: They distribute the land and houses
as private property, enslave and hold as serfs and servants those whom
they previously guarded as free friends and providers of upkeep, and
occupy themselves with war and with guarding against those whom   c
they've enslaved.

I think that is the way this transformation begins.

Then, isn't this constitution a sort of midpoint between aristocracy
and oligarchy?

Absolutely.

Then, if that's its place in the transformation, how will it be managed after
the change? Isn't it obvious that it will imitate the aristocratic constitution in
some respects and oligarchy in others, since it's between them, and that d
it will also have some features of its own?

That's right.

The rulers will be respected; the fighting class will be prevented from
taking part in farming, manual labor, or other ways of making money; it
will eat communally and devote itself to physical training and training for
war; and in all such ways, won't the constitution be like the aristocratic one?

Yes.

On the other hand, it will be afraid to appoint wise people as rulers, on
the grounds that they are no longer simple and earnest but mixed, and   e
will incline towards spirited and simpler people, who are more naturally

9. See *Works and Days* 109–202.
10. See e.g. *Iliad* vi.211.

548 suited for war than peace; it will value the tricks and stratagems of war and spend all its time making war. Aren't most of these qualities peculiar to it?

Yes.

Such people will desire money just as those in oligarchies do, passionately adoring gold and silver in secret. They will possess private treasuries and storehouses, where they can keep it hidden, and have houses to enclose them, like private nests, where they can spend lavishly either on women

b or on anyone else they wish.

That's absolutely true.

They'll be mean with their own money, since they value it and are not allowed to acquire it openly, but they'll love to spend other people's because of their appetites. They'll enjoy their pleasures in secret, running away from the law like boys from their father, for since they've neglected the true Muse—that of discussion and philosophy—and have valued physical training more than music and poetry, they haven't been educated by

c persuasion but by force.

The constitution you're discussing is certainly a mixture of good and bad.

Yes, it is mixed, but because of the predominance of the spirited element, one thing alone is most manifest in it, namely, the love of victory and the love of honor.

Very much so.

This, then, is the way this constitution would come into being and what it would be like, for, after all, we're only sketching the shape of the constitution in theory, not giving an exact account of it, since even from

d a sketch we'll be able to discern the most just and the most unjust person. And, besides, it would be an intolerably long task to describe every constitution and every character without omitting any detail.

That's right.

Then who is the man that corresponds to this constitution? How does he come to be, and what sort of man is he?

I think, said Adeimantus, that he'd be very like Glaucon here, as far as the love of victory is concerned.

In that respect, I said, he might be, but, in the following ones, I don't think his nature would be similar.

e Which ones?

He'd be more obstinate and less well trained in music and poetry, though he's a lover of it, and he'd love to listen to speeches and arguments, though he's by no means a rhetorician. He'd be harsh to his slaves rather than merely looking down on them as an adequately educated person does.

549 He'd be gentle to free people and very obedient to rulers, being himself a lover of ruling and a lover of honor. However, he doesn't base his claim to rule on his ability as a speaker or anything like that, but, as he's a lover of physical training and a lover of hunting, on his abilities and exploits in warfare and warlike activities.

Yes, that's the character that corresponds to this constitution.

Wouldn't such a person despise money when he's young but love it more and more as he grows older, because he shares in the money-loving nature and isn't pure in his attitude to virtue? And isn't that because he lacks the best of guardians?   b

What guardian is that? Adeimantus said.

Reason, I said, mixed with music and poetry, for it alone dwells within the person who possesses it as the lifelong preserver of his virtue.

Well put.

That, then, is a timocratic youth; he resembles the corresponding city.

Absolutely.   c

And he comes into being in some such way as this. He's the son of a good father who lives in a city that isn't well governed, who avoids honors, office, lawsuits, and all such meddling in other people's affairs, and who is even willing to be put at a disadvantage in order to avoid trouble.

Then how does he come to be timocratic?

When he listens, first, to his mother complaining that her husband isn't one of the rulers and that she's at a disadvantage among the other women as a result. Then she sees that he's not very concerned about money and that he doesn't fight back when he's insulted, whether in private or in   d public in the courts, but is indifferent to everything of that sort. She also sees him concentrating his mind on his own thoughts, neither honoring nor dishonoring her overmuch. Angered by all this, she tells her son that his father is unmanly, too easy-going, and all the other things that women repeat over and over again in such cases.   e

Yes, Adeimantus said, it's like them to have many such complaints.

You know, too, I said, that the servants of men like that—the ones who are thought to be well disposed to the family—also say similar things to the son in private. When they see the father failing to prosecute someone who owes him money or has wronged him in some other way, they urge the son to take revenge on all such people when he grows up and to be more of a man than his father. The boy hears and sees the same kind of   550 things when he goes out: Those in the city who do their own work are called fools and held to be of little account, while those who meddle in other people's affairs are honored and praised. The young man hears and sees all this, but he also listens to what his father says, observes what he does from close at hand, and compares his ways of living with those of the others. So he's pulled by both. His father nourishes the rational part   b of his soul and makes it grow; the others nourish the spirited and appetitive parts. Because he isn't a bad man by nature but keeps bad company, when he's pulled in these two ways, he settles in the middle and surrenders the rule over himself to the middle part—the victory-loving and spirited part— and becomes a proud and honor-loving man.

I certainly think that you've given a full account of how this sort of man comes to be.

Then we now have the second constitution and the second man.   c

We have.

Then shall we next talk, as Aeschylus says, of "another man ordered like another city,"[11] or shall we follow our plan and talk about the city first?

We must follow our plan.

And I suppose that the one that comes after the present constitution is oligarchy.

And what kind of constitution would you call oligarchy?

The constitution based on a property assessment, in which the rich rule,
d   and the poor man has no share in ruling.

I understand.

So mustn't we first explain how timarchy is transformed into oligarchy?

Yes.

And surely the manner of this transformation is clear even to the blind.

What is it like?

The treasure house filled with gold, which each possesses, destroys the constitution. First, they find ways of spending money for themselves, then they stretch the laws relating to this, then they and their wives disobey the laws altogether.

They would do that.

And as one person sees another doing this and emulates him, they make
e   the majority of the others like themselves.

They do.

From there they proceed further into money-making, and the more they value it, the less they value virtue. Or aren't virtue and wealth so opposed that if they were set on a scales, they'd always incline in opposite directions?

That's right.

So, when wealth and the wealthy are valued or honored in a city, virtue
551 and good people are valued less.

Clearly.

And what is valued is always practiced, and what isn't valued is neglected.

That's right.

Then, in the end, victory-loving and honor-loving men become lovers of making money, or money-lovers. And they praise and admire wealthy people and appoint them as rulers, while they dishonor poor ones.

Certainly.

Then, don't they pass a law that is characteristic of an oligarchic constitution, one that establishes a wealth qualification—higher where the constitution is more oligarchic, less where it's less so—and proclaims that those
b   whose property doesn't reach the stated amount aren't qualified to rule? And they either put this through by force of arms, or else, before it comes to that, they terrorize the people and establish their constitution that way. Isn't that so?

Of course it is.

11. Perhaps an adaptation of *Seven Against Thebes* 451.

Generally speaking, then, that's the way this kind of constitution is established.

Yes, but what is its character? And what are the faults that we said it contained?   c

First of all, the very thing that defines it is one, for what would happen if someone were to choose the captains of ships by their wealth, refusing to entrust the ship to a poor person even if he was a better captain?

They would make a poor voyage of it.

And isn't the same true of the rule of anything else whatsoever?

I suppose so.

Except a city? Or does it also apply to a city?

To it most of all, since it's the most difficult and most important kind of rule.

That, then, is one major fault in oligarchy.   d

Apparently.

And what about this second fault? Is it any smaller than the other?

What fault?

That of necessity it isn't one city but two—one of the poor and one of the rich—living in the same place and always plotting against one another.

By god, that's just as big a fault as the first.

And the following is hardly a fine quality either, namely, that oligarchs probably aren't able to fight a war, for they'd be compelled either to arm and use the majority, and so have more to fear from them than the enemy, or not to use them and show up as true oligarchs—few in number—on   e
the battlefield. At the same time, they'd be unwilling to pay mercenaries, because of their love of money.

That certainly isn't a fine quality either.

And what about the meddling in other people's affairs that we condemned before? Under this constitution, won't the same people be farmers, money-makers, and soldiers simultaneously? And do you think it's right for things to be that way?   552

Not at all.

Now, let's see whether this constitution is the first to admit the greatest of all evils.

Which one is that?

Allowing someone to sell all his possessions and someone else to buy them and then allowing the one who has sold them to go on living in the city, while belonging to none of its parts, for he's neither a money-maker, a craftsman, a member of the cavalry, or a hoplite, but a poor person without means.

It is the first to allow that.   b

At any rate, this sort of thing is not forbidden in oligarchies. If it were, some of their citizens wouldn't be excessively rich, while others are totally impoverished.

That's right.

Now, think about this. When the person who sells all his possessions was rich and spending his money, was he of any greater use to the city in the ways we've just mentioned than when he'd spent it all? Or did he merely seem to be one of the rulers of the city, while in truth he was neither ruler nor subject there, but only a squanderer of his property?

That's right. He seemed to be part of the city, but he was nothing but

c   a squanderer.

Should we say, then, that, as a drone exists in a cell and is an affliction to the hive, so this person is a drone in the house and an affliction to the city?

That's certainly right, Socrates.

Hasn't the god made all the winged drones stingless, Adeimantus, as well as some wingless ones, while other wingless ones have dangerous stings? And don't the stingless ones continue as beggars into old age, while

d   those with stings become what we call evildoers?

That's absolutely true.

Clearly, then, in any city where you see beggars, there are thieves, pickpockets, temple-robbers, and all such evildoers hidden.

That is clear.

What about oligarchic cities? Don't you see beggars in them?

Almost everyone except the rulers is a beggar there.

e   Then mustn't we suppose that they also include many evildoers with stings, whom the rulers carefully keep in check by force?

We certainly must.

And shall we say that the presence of such people is the result of lack of education, bad rearing, and a bad constitutional arrangement?

We shall.

This, then, or something like it, is the oligarchic city. It contains all these evils and probably others in addition.

That's pretty well what it's like.

Then, let's take it that we've disposed of the constitution called oligar-

553   chy—I mean the one that gets its rulers on the basis of a property assessment—and let's examine the man who is like it, both how he comes to be and what sort of man he is.

All right.

Doesn't the transformation from the timocrat we described to an oligarch occur mostly in this way?

Which way?

The timocrat's son at first emulates his father and follows in his footsteps. Then he suddenly sees him crashing against the city like a ship against a

b   reef, spilling out all his possessions, even his life. He had held a generalship or some other high office, was brought to court by false witnesses, and was either put to death or exiled or was disenfranchised and had all his property confiscated.

That's quite likely.

The son sees all this, suffers from it, loses his property, and, fearing for his life, immediately drives from the throne in his own soul the honor-loving and spirited part that ruled there. Humbled by poverty, he turns greedily to making money, and, little by little, saving and working, he amasses property. Don't you think that this person would establish his appetitive and money-making part on the throne, setting it up as a great king within himself, adorning it with golden tiaras and collars and girding it with Persian swords?

I do.

He makes the rational and spirited parts sit on the ground beneath appetite, one on either side, reducing them to slaves. He won't allow the first to reason about or examine anything except how a little money can be made into great wealth. And he won't allow the second to value or admire anything but wealth and wealthy people or to have any ambition other than the acquisition of wealth or whatever might contribute to getting it.

There is no other transformation of a young man who is an honor-lover into one who is a money-lover that's as swift and sure as this.

Then isn't this an oligarchic man?

Surely, he developed out of a man who resembled the constitution from which oligarchy came.

Then let's consider whether he resembles the oligarchic constitution?

All right.

Doesn't he resemble it, in the first place, by attaching the greatest importance to money?

Of course.

And, further, by being a thrifty worker, who satisfies only his necessary appetites, makes no other expenditures, and enslaves his other desires as vain.

That's right.

A somewhat squalid fellow, who makes a profit from everything and hoards it—the sort the majority admires. Isn't this the man who resembles such a constitution?

That's my opinion, anyway. At any rate, money is valued above everything by both the city and the man.

I don't suppose that such a man pays any attention to education.

Not in my view, for, if he did, he wouldn't have chosen a blind leader for his chorus and honored him most.[12]

Good. But consider this: Won't we say that, because of his lack of education, the dronish appetites—some beggarly and others evil—exist in him, but that they're forcibly held in check by his carefulness?

Certainly.

Do you know where you should look to see the evildoings of such people?

Where?

---

12. Plutus, the god of wealth, is represented as being blind.

To the guardianship of orphans or something like that, where they have ample opportunity to do injustice with impunity.

True.

And doesn't this make it clear that, in those other contractual obligations, where he has a good reputation and is thought to be just, he's forcibly holding his other evil appetites in check by means of some decent part of

d   himself? He holds them in check, not by persuading them that it's better not to act on them or taming them with arguments, but by compulsion and fear, trembling for his other possessions.

That's right.

And, by god, you'll find that most of them have appetites akin to those of the drone, once they have other people's money to spend.

You certainly will.

Then someone like that wouldn't be entirely free from internal civil war and wouldn't be one but in some way two, though generally his better

e   desires are in control of his worse.

That's right.

For this reason, he'd be more respectable than many, but the true virtue of a single-minded and harmonious soul far escapes him.

I suppose so.

Further, this thrifty man is a poor individual contestant for victory in a city or for any other fine and much-honored thing, for he's not willing to

555 spend money for the sake of a fine reputation or on contests for such things. He's afraid to arouse his appetites for spending or to call on them as allies to obtain victory, so he fights like an oligarch, with only a few of his resources. Hence he's mostly defeated but remains rich.

That's right.

Then have we any further doubt that a thrifty money-maker is like an

b   oligarchic city?

None at all.

It seems, then, that we must next consider democracy, how it comes into being, and what character it has when it does, so that, knowing in turn the character of a man who resembles it, we can present him for judgment.

That would be quite consistent with what we've been doing.

Well, isn't the city changed from an oligarchy to a democracy in some such way as this, because of its insatiable desire to attain what it has set before itself as the good, namely, the need to become as rich as possible?

In what way?

c   Since those who rule in the city do so because they own a lot, I suppose they're unwilling to enact laws to prevent young people who've had no discipline from spending and wasting their wealth, so that by making loans to them, secured by the young people's property, and then calling those loans in, they themselves become even richer and more honored.

That's their favorite thing to do.

So isn't it clear by now that it is impossible for a city to honor wealth and at the same time for its citizens to acquire moderation, but one or the other is inevitably neglected?   d

That's pretty clear.

Because of this neglect and because they encourage bad discipline, oligarchies not infrequently reduce people of no common stamp to poverty.

That's right.

And these people sit idle in the city, I suppose, with their stings and weapons—some in debt, some disenfranchised, some both—hating those who've acquired their property, plotting against them and others, and longing for a revolution.   e

They do.

The money-makers, on the other hand, with their eyes on the ground, pretend not to see these people, and by lending money they disable any of the remainder who resist, exact as interest many times the principal sum, and so create a considerable number of drones and beggars in the city.   556

A considerable number indeed.

In any case, they are unwilling to quench this kind of evil as it flares up in the city, either in the way we mentioned, by preventing people from doing whatever they like with their own property or by another law which would also solve the problem.

What law?

The second-best one, which compels the citizens to care about virtue by prescribing that the majority of voluntary contracts be entered into at the lender's own risk, for lenders would be less shameless then in their pursuit   b
of money in the city and fewer of those evils we were mentioning just now would develop.

Far fewer.

But as it is, for all these reasons, the rulers in the city treat their subjects in the way we described. But as for themselves and their children, don't they make their young fond of luxury, incapable of effort either mental or physical, too soft to stand up to pleasures or pains, and idle besides?   c

Of course.

And don't they themselves neglect everything except making money, caring no more for virtue than the poor do?

Yes.

But when rulers and subjects in this condition meet on a journey or some other common undertaking—it might be a festival, an embassy, or a campaign, or they might be shipmates or fellow soldiers—and see one another in danger, in these circumstances are the poor in any way despised by the rich? Or rather isn't it often the case that a poor man, lean and   d
suntanned, stands in battle next to a rich man, reared in the shade and carrying a lot of excess flesh, and sees him panting and at a loss? And don't you think that he'd consider that it's through the cowardice of the poor that such people are rich and that one poor man would say to another

e
when they met in private: "These people are at our mercy; they're good for nothing"?

I know very well that's what they would do.

Then, as a sick body needs only a slight shock from outside to become ill and is sometimes at civil war with itself even without this, so a city in the same condition needs only a small pretext—such as one side bringing in allies from an oligarchy or the other from a democracy—to fall ill and to fight with itself and is sometimes in a state of civil war even without any external influence.

557
Absolutely.

And I suppose that democracy comes about when the poor are victorious, killing some of their opponents and expelling others, and giving the rest an equal share in ruling under the constitution, and for the most part assigning people to positions of rule by lot.

Yes, that's how democracy is established, whether by force of arms or because those on the opposing side are frightened into exile.

Then how do these people live? What sort of constitution do they have? It's clear that a man who is like it will be democratic.

b

That is clear.

First of all, then, aren't they free? And isn't the city full of freedom and freedom of speech? And doesn't everyone in it have the license to do what he wants?

That's what they say, at any rate.

And where people have this license, it's clear that each of them will arrange his own life in whatever manner pleases him.

It is.

Then I suppose that it's most of all under this constitution that one finds people of all varieties.

c

Of course.

Then it looks as though this is the finest or most beautiful of the constitutions, for, like a coat embroidered with every kind of ornament, this city, embroidered with every kind of character type, would seem to be the most beautiful. And many people would probably judge it to be so, as women and children do when they see something multicolored.

They certainly would.

d
It's also a convenient place to look for a constitution.

Why's that?

Because it contains all kinds of constitutions on account of the license it gives its citizens. So it looks as though anyone who wants to put a city in order, as we were doing, should probably go to a democracy, as to a supermarket of constitutions, pick out whatever pleases him, and establish that.

e
He probably wouldn't be at a loss for models, at any rate.

In this city, there is no requirement to rule, even if you're capable of it, or again to be ruled if you don't want to be, or to be at war when the others are, or at peace unless you happen to want it. And there is no requirement in the least that you not serve in public office as a juror, if you happen to want to serve, even if there is a law forbidding you to do so. Isn't that a divine and pleasant life, while it lasts?   558

It probably is—while it lasts.

And what about the calm of some of their condemned criminals? Isn't that a sign of sophistication? Or have you never seen people who've been condemned to death or exile under such a constitution stay on at the center of things, strolling around like the ghosts of dead heroes, without anyone staring at them or giving them a thought?

Yes, I've seen it a lot.

And what about the city's tolerance? Isn't it so completely lacking in   b small-mindedness that it utterly despises the things we took so seriously when we were founding our city, namely, that unless someone had transcendent natural gifts, he'd never become good unless he played the right games and followed a fine way of life from early childhood? Isn't it magnificent the way it tramples all this underfoot, by giving no thought to what someone was doing before he entered public life and by honoring him if only he tells them that he wishes the majority well?   c

Yes, it's altogether splendid!

Then these and others like them are the characteristics of democracy. And it would seem to be a pleasant constitution, which lacks rulers but not variety and which distributes a sort of equality to both equals and unequals alike.

We certainly know what you mean.

Consider, then, what private individual resembles it. Or should we first inquire, as we did with the city, how he comes to be?

Yes, we should.

Well, doesn't it happen like this? Wouldn't the son of that thrifty oligarch be brought up in his father's ways?   d

Of course.

Then he too rules his spendthrift pleasures by force—the ones that aren't money-making and are called unnecessary.

Clearly.

But, so as not to discuss this in the dark, do you want us first to define which desires are necessary and which aren't?

I do.

Aren't those we can't desist from and those whose satisfaction benefits us rightly called necessary, for we are by nature compelled to satisfy them both? Isn't that so?   e

Of course.

So we'd be right to apply the term "necessary" to them?   559

We would.

What about those that someone could get rid of if he practiced from youth on, those whose presence leads to no good or even to the opposite? If we said that all of them were unnecessary, would we be right?

We would.

Let's pick an example of each, so that we can grasp the patterns they exhibit.

We should do that.

Aren't the following desires necessary: the desire to eat to the point of
b   health and well-being and the desire for bread and delicacies?

I suppose so.

The desire for bread is necessary on both counts; it's beneficial, and unless it's satisfied, we die.

Yes.

The desire for delicacies is also necessary to the extent that it's beneficial to well-being.

Absolutely.

What about the desire that goes beyond these and seeks other sorts of foods, that most people can get rid of, if it's restrained and educated while they're young, and that's harmful both to the body and to the reason and
c   moderation of the soul? Would it be rightly called unnecessary?

It would indeed.

Then wouldn't we also say that such desires are spendthrift, while the earlier ones are money-making, because they profit our various projects?

Certainly.

And won't we say the same about the desire for sex and about other desires?

Yes.

And didn't we say that the person we just now called a drone is full of such pleasures and desires, since he is ruled by the unnecessary ones,
d   while a thrifty oligarch is ruled by his necessary desires?

We certainly did.

Let's go back, then, and explain how the democratic man develops out of the oligarchic one. It seems to me as though it mostly happens as follows.

How?

When a young man, who is reared in the miserly and uneducated manner we described, tastes the honey of the drones and associates with wild and dangerous creatures who can provide every variety of multicolored pleasure in every sort of way, this, as you might suppose, is the beginning
e   of his transformation from having an oligarchic constitution within him to having a democratic one.

It's inevitable that this is how it starts.

And just as the city changed when one party received help from like-minded people outside, doesn't the young man change when one party of his desires receives help from external desires that are akin to them and of the same form?

Absolutely.

And I suppose that, if any contrary help comes to the oligarchic party within him, whether from his father or from the rest of his household, who exhort and reproach him, then there's civil war and counterrevolution
560   within him, and he battles against himself.

That's right.

Sometimes the democratic party yields to the oligarchic, so that some of the young man's appetites are overcome, others are expelled, a kind of shame rises in his soul, and order is restored.

That does sometimes happen.

But I suppose that, as desires are expelled, others akin to them are being nurtured unawares, and because of his father's ignorance about how to bring him up, they grow numerous and strong.   b

That's what tends to happen.

These desires draw him back into the same bad company and in secret intercourse breed a multitude of others.

Certainly.

And, seeing the citadel of the young man's soul empty of knowledge, fine ways of living, and words of truth (which are the best watchmen and guardians of the thoughts of those men whom the gods love), they finally occupy that citadel themselves.

They certainly do.   c

And in the absence of these guardians, false and boastful words and beliefs rush up and occupy this part of him.

Indeed, they do.

Won't he then return to these lotus-eaters and live with them openly? And if some help comes to the thrifty part of his soul from his household, won't these boastful words close the gates of the royal wall within him to prevent these allies from entering and refuse even to receive the words of older private individuals as ambassadors? Doing battle and controlling things themselves, won't they call reverence foolishness and moderation   d cowardice, abusing them and casting them out beyond the frontiers like disenfranchised exiles? And won't they persuade the young man that measured and orderly expenditure is boorish and mean, and, joining with many useless desires, won't they expel it across the border?

They certainly will.

Having thus emptied and purged these from the soul of the one they've possessed and initiated in splendid rites, they proceed to return insolence, anarchy, extravagance, and shamelessness from exile in a blaze of torch-   e light, wreathing them in garlands and accompanying them with a vast chorus of followers. They praise the returning exiles and give them fine names, calling insolence good breeding, anarchy freedom, extravagance magnificence, and shamelessness courage. Isn't it in some such way as this that someone who is young changes, after being brought up with necessary desires, to the liberation and release of useless and unneces-   561 sary pleasures?

Yes, that's clearly the way it happens.

And I suppose that after that he spends as much money, effort, and time on unnecessary pleasures as on necessary ones. If he's lucky, and his frenzy doesn't go too far, when he grows older, and the great tumult within him has spent itself, he welcomes back some of the exiles, ceases b   to surrender himself completely to the newcomers, and puts his pleasures on an equal footing. And so he lives, always surrendering rule over himself to whichever desire comes along, as if it were chosen by lot. And when that is satisfied, he surrenders the rule to another, not disdaining any but satisfying them all equally.

That's right.

And he doesn't admit any word of truth into the guardhouse, for if someone tells him that some pleasures belong to fine and good desires
c   and others to evil ones and that he must pursue and value the former and restrain and enslave the latter, he denies all this and declares that all pleasures are equal and must be valued equally.

That's just what someone in that condition would do.

And so he lives on, yielding day by day to the desire at hand. Sometimes he drinks heavily while listening to the flute; at other times, he drinks only water and is on a diet; sometimes he goes in for physical training;
d   at other times, he's idle and neglects everything; and sometimes he even occupies himself with what he takes to be philosophy. He often engages in politics, leaping up from his seat and saying and doing whatever comes into his mind. If he happens to admire soldiers, he's carried in that direction, if money-makers, in that one. There's neither order nor necessity in his life, but he calls it pleasant, free, and blessedly happy, and he follows it for as long as he lives.

e   You've perfectly described the life of a man who believes in legal equality.

I also suppose that he's a complex man, full of all sorts of characters, fine and multicolored, just like the democratic city, and that many men and women might envy his life, since it contains the most models of constitutions and ways of living.

That's right.

Then shall we set this man beside democracy as one who is rightly
562   called democratic?

Let's do so.

The finest constitution and the finest man remain for us to discuss, namely, tyranny and a tyrannical man.

They certainly do.

Come, then, how does tyranny come into being? It's fairly clear that it evolves from democracy.

It is.

And doesn't it evolve from democracy in much the same way that
b   democracy does from oligarchy?

What way is that?

The good that oligarchy puts before itself and because of which it is established is wealth, isn't it?

Yes.

And its insatiable desire for wealth and its neglect of other things for the sake of money-making is what destroyed it, isn't it?

That's true.

And isn't democracy's insatiable desire for what it defines as the good also what destroys it?

What do you think it defines as the good?

Freedom: Surely you'd hear a democratic city say that this is the finest thing it has, so that as a result it is the only city worth living in for someone who is by nature free.   c

Yes, you often hear that.

Then, as I was about to say, doesn't the insatiable desire for freedom and the neglect of other things change this constitution and put it in need of a dictatorship?

In what way?

I suppose that, when a democratic city, athirst for freedom, happens to get bad cupbearers for its leaders, so that it gets drunk by drinking more than it should of the unmixed wine of freedom, then, unless the rulers are   d
very pliable and provide plenty of that freedom, they are punished by the city and accused of being accursed oligarchs.

Yes, that is what it does.

It insults those who obey the rulers as willing slaves and good-for-nothings and praises and honors, both in public and in private, rulers who behave like subjects and subjects who behave like rulers. And isn't it inevitable that freedom should go to all lengths in such a city?   e

Of course.

It makes its way into private households and in the end breeds anarchy even among the animals.

What do you mean?

I mean that a father accustoms himself to behave like a child and fear his sons, while the son behaves like a father, feeling neither shame nor fear in front of his parents, in order to be free. A resident alien or a foreign visitor is made equal to a citizen, and he is their equal.   563

Yes, that is what happens.

It does. And so do other little things of the same sort. A teacher in such a community is afraid of his students and flatters them, while the students despise their teachers or tutors. And, in general, the young imitate their elders and compete with them in word and deed, while the old stoop to the level of the young and are full of play and pleasantry, imitating the young for fear of appearing disagreeable and authoritarian.   b

Absolutely.

The utmost freedom for the majority is reached in such a city when bought slaves, both male and female, are no less free than those who bought them. And I almost forgot to mention the extent of the legal equality of men and women and of the freedom in the relations between them.

What about the animals? Are we, with Aeschylus, going to "say whatever it was that came to our lips just now" about them?   c

Certainly. I put it this way: No one who hasn't experienced it would believe how much freer domestic animals are in a democratic city than anywhere else. As the proverb says, dogs become like their mistresses;

horses and donkeys are accustomed to roam freely and proudly along the streets, bumping into anyone who doesn't get out of their way; and all
d   the rest are equally full of freedom.

You're telling me what I already know. I've often experienced that sort of thing while travelling in the country.

To sum up: Do you notice how all these things together make the citizens' souls so sensitive that, if anyone even puts upon *himself* the least degree of slavery, they become angry and cannot endure it. And in the end, as you know, they take no notice of the laws, whether written or unwritten,
e   in order to avoid having any master at all.

I certainly do.

This, then, is the fine and impetuous origin from which tyranny seems to me to evolve.

It is certainly impetuous. But what comes next?

The same disease that developed in oligarchy and destroyed it also develops here, but it is more widespread and virulent because of the general permissiveness, and it eventually enslaves democracy. In fact, excessive action in one direction usually sets up a reaction in the opposite direction. This happens in seasons, in plants, in bodies, and, last but not
564 least, in constitutions.

That's to be expected.

Extreme freedom can't be expected to lead to anything but a change to extreme slavery, whether for a private individual or for a city.

No, it can't.

Then I don't suppose that tyranny evolves from any constitution other than democracy—the most severe and cruel slavery from the utmost freedom.

Yes, that's reasonable.

But I don't think that was your question. You asked what was the disease
b   that developed in oligarchy and also in democracy, enslaving it.

That's true.

And what I had in mind as an answer was that class of idle and extravagant men, whose bravest members are leaders and the more cowardly ones followers. We compared them to stinged and stingless drones, respectively.

That's right.

Now, these two groups cause problems in any constitution, just as phlegm and bile do in the body. And it's against them that the good doctor
c   and lawgiver of a city must take advance precautions, first, to prevent their presence and, second, to cut them out of the hive as quickly as possible, cells and all, if they should happen to be present.

Yes, by god, he must cut them out altogether.

Then let's take up the question in the following way, so that we can see what we want more clearly.

In what way?

Let's divide a democratic city into three parts in theory, this being the way that it is in fact divided. One part is this class of idlers, that grows
d   here no less than in an oligarchy, because of the general permissiveness.

So it does.

But it is far fiercer in democracy than in the other.

How so?

In an oligarchy it is fierce because it's disdained, but since it is prevented from having a share in ruling, it doesn't get any exercise and doesn't become vigorous. In a democracy, however, with a few exceptions, this class is the dominant one. Its fiercest members do all the talking and acting, while the rest settle near the speaker's platform and buzz and refuse to tolerate the opposition of another speaker, so that, under a democratic constitution, with the few exceptions I referred to before, this class manages everything.   e

That's right.

Then there's a second class that always distinguishes itself from the majority of people.

Which is that?

When everybody is trying to make money, those who are naturally most organized generally become the wealthiest.

Probably so.

Then they would provide the most honey for the drones and the honey that is most easily extractable by them.

Yes, for how could anyone extract it from those who have very little?

Then I suppose that these rich people are called drone-fodder.

Something like that.

The people—those who work with their own hands—are the third class. They take no part in politics and have few possessions, but, when   565
they are assembled, they are the largest and most powerful class in a democracy.

They are. But they aren't willing to assemble often unless they get a share of the honey.

And they always do get a share, though the leaders, in taking the wealth of the rich and distributing it to the people, keep the greater part for themselves.

Yes, that is the way the people get their share.   b

And I suppose that those whose wealth is taken away are compelled to defend themselves by speaking before the people and doing whatever else they can.

Of course.

And they're accused by the drones of plotting against the people and of being oligarchs, even if they have no desire for revolution at all.

That's right.

So in the end, when they see the people trying to harm them, they truly do become oligarchs and embrace oligarchy's evils, whether they want to   c
or not. But neither group does these things willingly. Rather the people act as they do because they are ignorant and are deceived by the drones, and the rich act as they do because they are driven to it by the stinging of those same drones.

Absolutely.

And then there are impeachments, judgments, and trials on both sides.

That's right.

Now, aren't the people always in the habit of setting up one man as their special champion, nurturing him and making him great?

They are.

d   And it's clear that, when a tyrant arises, this special leadership is the sole root from which he sprouts.

It is.

What is the beginning of the transformation from leader of the people to tyrant? Isn't it clear that it happens when the leader begins to behave like the man in the story told about the temple of the Lycean Zeus[13] in Arcadia?

What story is that?

That anyone who tastes the one piece of human innards that's chopped up with those of other sacrificial victims must inevitably become a wolf.

e   Haven't you heard that story?

I have.

Then doesn't the same happen with a leader of the people who dominates a docile mob and doesn't restrain himself from spilling kindred blood? He brings someone to trial on false charges and murders him (as tyrants so often do), and, by thus blotting out a human life, his impious tongue and lips taste kindred citizen blood. He banishes some, kills others, and drops hints to the people about the cancellation of debts and the redistribu-

566   tion of land. And because of these things, isn't a man like that inevitably fated either to be killed by his enemies or to be transformed from a man into a wolf by becoming a tyrant?

It's completely inevitable.

He's the one who stirs up civil wars against the rich.

He is.

And if he's exiled but manages, despite his enemies, to return, doesn't he come back as a full-fledged tyrant?

Clearly.

And if these enemies are unable to expel him or to put him to death by

b   accusing him before the city, they plot secretly to kill him.

That's usually what happens at least.

And all who've reached this stage soon discover the famous request of the tyrant, namely, that the people give him a bodyguard to keep their defender safe for them.

That's right.

And the people give it to him, I suppose, because they *are* afraid for his safety but aren't worried at all about their own.

c   That's right.

And when a wealthy man sees this and is charged with being an enemy of the people because of his wealth, then, as the oracle to Croesus put it, he

13. Zeus the wolf-god.

> *Flees to the banks of the many-pebbled Hermus,*
> *Neither staying put nor being ashamed of his cowardice.*

He wouldn't get a second chance of being ashamed.

That's true, for if he was caught, he'd be executed.

He most certainly would.

But, as for the leader, he doesn't lie on the ground "mighty in his might,"[14] but, having brought down many others, he stands in the city's chariot, a complete tyrant rather than a leader.   d

What else?

Then let's describe the happiness of this man and of the city in which a mortal like him comes to be.

Certainly, let's do so.

During the first days of his reign and for some time after, won't he smile in welcome at anyone he meets, saying that he's no tyrant, making all sorts of promises both in public and in private, freeing the people from debt, redistributing the land to them and to his followers, and pretending   e
to be gracious and gentle to all?

He'd have to.

But I suppose that, when he has dealt with his exiled enemies by making peace with some and destroying others, so that all is quiet on that front, the first thing he does is to stir up a war, so that the people will continue to feel the need of a leader.

Probably so.

But also so that they'll become poor through having to pay war taxes, for that way they'll have to concern themselves with their daily needs and   567
be less likely to plot against him.

Clearly.

Besides, if he suspects some people of having thoughts of freedom and of not favoring his rule, can't he find a pretext for putting them at the mercy of the enemy in order to destroy them? And for all these reasons, isn't it necessary for a tyrant to be always stirring up war?

It is.

And because of this, isn't he all the more readily hated by the citizens?   b

Of course.

Moreover, don't the bravest of those who helped to establish his tyranny and who hold positions of power within it speak freely to each other and to him, criticizing what's happening?

They probably do.

Then the tyrant will have to do away with all of them if he intends to rule, until he's left with neither friend nor enemy of any worth.

Clearly.

He must, therefore, keep a sharp lookout for anyone who is brave, large-minded, knowledgeable, or rich. And so happy is he that he must be the

14. See *Iliad* xvi.776.

c   enemy of them all, whether he wants to be or not, and plot against them
until he has purged them from the city.

That's a fine sort of purge!

Yes, for it's the opposite of the one that doctors perform on the body.
They draw off the worst and leave the best, but he does just the opposite.

Yet I expect he'll have to do this, if he's really going to rule.

d   It's a blessedly happy necessity he's bound by, since it requires him
either to live with the inferior majority, even though they hate him, or not
to live at all.

Yet that's exactly his condition.

And won't he need a larger and more loyal bodyguard, the more his
actions make the citizens hate him?

Of course.

And who will these trustworthy people be? And where will he get
them from?

They'll come swarming of their own accord, if he pays them.

Drones, by the dog! All manner of foreign drones! That's what I think
e   you're talking about.

You're right.

But what about in the city itself? Wouldn't he be willing . . .

Willing to what?

To deprive citizens of their slaves by freeing them and enlisting them
in his bodyguard?

He certainly would, since they'd be likely to prove most loyal to him.

What a blessedly happy sort of fellow you make the tyrant out to be,
if these are the sort of people he employs as friends and loyal followers
568   after he's done away with the earlier ones.

Nonetheless, they're the sort he employs.

And these companions and new citizens admire and associate with him,
while the decent people hate and avoid him.

Of course.

It isn't for nothing, then, that tragedy in general has the reputation of
being wise and that Euripides is thought to be outstandingly so.

Why's that?

Because among other shrewd things he said that "tyrants are wise who
associate with the wise." And by "the wise" he clearly means the sort of
b   people that we've seen to be the tyrant's associates.

Yes. And he and the other poets eulogize tyranny as godlike and say
lots of other such things about it.

Then, surely, since the tragic poets are wise, they'll forgive us and those
whose constitutions resemble ours, if we don't admit them into our city,
since they praise tyranny.

c   I suppose that the more sophisticated among them will.

And so I suppose that they go around to other cities, draw crowds, hire
people with fine, big, persuasive voices, and lead their constitutions to
tyranny and democracy.

They do indeed.

And besides this, they receive wages and honors, especially—as one might expect—from the tyrants and, in second place, from the democracies, but the higher they go on the ascending scale of constitutions, the more their honor falls off, as if unable to keep up with them for lack of breath.

Absolutely.

But we digress. So let's return to that fine, numerous, diverse, and ever-changing bodyguard of the tyrant and explain how he'll pay for it.

Clearly, if there are sacred treasuries in the city, he'll use them for as long as they last, as well as the property of the people he has destroyed, thus requiring smaller taxes from the people.

What about when these give out?

Clearly, both he and his fellow revellers—his companions, male or female—will have to feed off his father's estate.

I understand. You mean that the people, who fathered the tyrant, will have to feed him and his companions.

They'll be forced to do so.

And what would you have to say about this? What if the people get angry and say, first, that it isn't just for a grown-up son to be fed by his father but, on the contrary, for the father to be fed by his son; second, that they didn't father him and establish him in power so that, when he'd become strong, they'd be enslaved to their own slave and have to feed both him and his slaves, along with other assorted rabble, but because they hoped that, with him as their leader, they'd be free from the rich and the so-called fine and good people in the city; third, that they therefore order him and his companions to leave the city, just as a father might drive a son and his troublesome fellow revellers from his house?

Then, by god, the people will come to know what kind of creature they have fathered, welcomed, and made strong and that they are the weaker trying to drive out the stronger.

What do you mean? Will the tyrant dare to use violence against his father or to hit him if he doesn't obey?

Yes—once he's taken away his father's weapons.

You mean that the tyrant is a parricide and a harsh nurse of old age, that his rule has become an acknowledged tyranny at last, and that—as the saying goes—by trying to avoid the frying pan of enslavement to free men, the people have fallen into the fire of having slaves as their masters, and that in the place of the great but inappropriate freedom they enjoyed under democracy, they have put upon themselves the harshest and most bitter slavery to slaves.

That's exactly what I mean.

Well, then, aren't we justified in saying that we have adequately described how tyranny evolves from democracy and what it's like when it has come into being?

We certainly are, he said.

Book IX

571   It remains, I said, to consider the tyrannical man himself, how he evolves
from a democrat, what he is like when he has come into being, and whether
he is wretched or blessedly happy.

Yes, he said, he is the one who is still missing.

And do you know what else I think is still missing?

What?

I don't think we have adequately distinguished the kinds and numbers
of our desires, and, if that subject isn't adequately dealt with, our entire
b   investigation will be less clear.

Well, isn't now as fine a time as any to discuss the matter?

It certainly is. Consider, then, what I want to know about our desires.
It's this: Some of our unnecessary pleasures and desires seem to me to be
lawless. They are probably present in everyone, but they are held in check
by the laws and by the better desires in alliance with reason. In a few
people, they have been eliminated entirely or only a few weak ones remain,
c   while in others they are stronger and more numerous.

What desires do you mean?

Those that are awakened in sleep, when the rest of the soul—the rational,
gentle, and ruling part—slumbers. Then the beastly and savage part, full
of food and drink, casts off sleep and seeks to find a way to gratify itself.
You know that there is nothing it won't dare to do at such a time, free of
all control by shame or reason. It doesn't shrink from trying to have sex
d   with a mother, as it supposes, or with anyone else at all, whether man,
god, or beast. It will commit any foul murder, and there is no food it
refuses to eat. In a word, it omits no act of folly or shamelessness.

That's completely true.

On the other hand, I suppose that someone who is healthy and moderate
with himself goes to sleep only after having done the following: First, he
rouses his rational part and feasts it on fine arguments and speculations;
e   second, he neither starves nor feasts his appetites, so that they will slumber
and not disturb his best part with either their pleasure or their pain, but
572   they'll leave it alone, pure and by itself, to get on with its investigations,
to yearn after and perceive something, it knows not what,[1] whether it is
past, present, or future; third, he soothes his spirited part in the same way,
for example, by not falling asleep with his spirit still aroused after an
outburst of anger. And when he has quieted these two parts and aroused
the third, in which reason resides, and so takes his rest, you know that it
is then that he best grasps the truth and that the visions that appear in
b   his dreams are least lawless.

Entirely so.

---

1. Reading *kai* before *aisthanesthai* in a2.

However, we've been carried away from what we wanted to establish, which is this: Our dreams make it clear that there is a dangerous, wild, and lawless form of desire in everyone, even in those of us who seem to be entirely moderate or measured. See whether you think I'm talking sense and whether or not you agree with me.

I do agree.

Recall, then, what we said a democratic man is like. He was produced by being brought up from youth by a thrifty father who valued only those desires that make money and who despised the unnecessary ones that aim   c
at frivolity and display. Isn't that right?

Yes.

And by associating with more sophisticated men, who are full of the latter desires, he starts to indulge in every kind of insolence and to adopt their form of behavior, because of his hatred of his father's thrift. But, because he has a better nature than his corrupters, he is pulled in both directions and settles down in the middle between his father's way of life and theirs. And enjoying each in moderation, as he supposes, he leads a life that is neither slavish nor lawless and from having been oligarchic he   d
becomes democratic.

That was and is our opinion about this type of man.

Suppose now that this man has in turn become older and that *he* has a son who is brought up in *his* father's ethos.

All right.

And further suppose that the same things that happened to his father now happen to him. First, he is led to all the kinds of lawlessness that those who are leading him call freedom. Then his father and the rest of   e
the household come to the aid of the middle desires, while the others help the other ones. Then, when those clever enchanters and tyrant-makers have no hope of keeping hold of the young man in any other way, they contrive to plant in him a powerful erotic love, like a great winged drone, to be the leader of those idle desires that spend whatever is at hand. Or do you think that erotic love is anything other than an enormous drone   573
in such people?

I don't think that it could be anything else.

And when the other desires—filled with incense, myrrh, wreaths, wine, and the other pleasures found in their company—buzz around the drone, nurturing it and making it grow as large as possible, they plant the sting of longing in it. Then this leader of the soul adopts madness as its body-guard and becomes frenzied. If it finds any beliefs or desires in the man   b
that are thought to be good or that still have some shame, it destroys them and throws them out, until it's purged him of moderation and filled him with imported madness.

You've perfectly described the evolution of a tyrannical man.

Is this the reason that erotic love has long been called a tyrant?

It looks that way.

Then doesn't a drunken man have something of a tyrannical mind?   c

Yes, he has.

And a man who is mad and deranged attempts to rule not just human beings, but gods as well, and expects that he will be able to succeed.

He certainly does.

Then a man becomes tyrannical in the precise sense of the term when either his nature or his way of life or both of them together make him drunk, filled with erotic desire, and mad.

Absolutely.

This, then, it seems, is how a tyrannical man comes to be. But what way does he live?

d   No doubt *you're* going to tell *me*, just as posers of riddles usually do.

I am. I think that someone in whom the tyrant of erotic love dwells and in whom it directs everything next goes in for feasts, revelries, luxuries, girlfriends, and all that sort of thing.

Necessarily.

And don't many terrible desires grow up day and night beside the tyrannical one, needing many things to satisfy them?

Indeed they do.

Hence any income someone like that has is soon spent.

Of course.

e   Then borrowing follows, and expenditure of capital.

What else?

And when everything is gone, won't the violent crowd of desires that has nested within him inevitably shout in protest? And driven by the stings of the other desires and especially by erotic love itself (which leads all of them as its bodyguard), won't he become frenzied and look to see

574   who possesses anything that he could take, by either deceit or force?

He certainly will.

Consequently, he must acquire wealth from every source or live in great pain and suffering.

He must.

And just as the pleasures that are latecomers outdo the older ones and steal away their satisfactions, won't the man himself think that he deserves to outdo his father and mother, even though he is younger than they are— to take and spend his father's wealth when he's spent his own share?

Of course.

And if they won't give it to him, won't he first try to steal it from them

b   by deceitful means?

Certainly.

And if that doesn't work, wouldn't he seize it by force?

I suppose so.

And if the old man and woman put up a fight, would he be careful to refrain from acting like a tyrant?

I'm not very optimistic about their fate, if they do.

But, good god, Adeimantus, do you think he'd sacrifice his long-loved and irreplaceable mother for a recently acquired girlfriend whom he can

do without? Or that for the sake of a newfound and replaceable boyfriend in the bloom of youth, he'd strike his aged and irreplaceable father, his   c
oldest friend? Or that he'd make his parents the slaves of these others, if he brought them under the same roof?

Yes, indeed he would.

It seems to be a very great blessing to produce a tyrannical son!

It certainly does!

What about when the possessions of his father and mother give out? With that great swarm of pleasures inside him, won't he first try to break   d
into someone's house or snatch someone's coat late at night? Then won't he try to loot a temple? And in all this, the old traditional opinions that he had held from childhood about what is fine or shameful—opinions that are accounted just—are overcome by the opinions, newly released from slavery, that are now the bodyguard of erotic love and hold sway along with it. When he himself was subject to the laws and his father and had   e
a democratic constitution within him, these opinions used only to be freed in sleep. Now, however, under the tyranny of erotic love, he has permanently become while awake what he used to become occasionally while asleep, and he won't hold back from any terrible murder or from any kind of food or act. But, rather, erotic love lives like a tyrant within him, in complete anarchy and lawlessness as his sole ruler, and drives him, as if   575
he were a city, to dare anything that will provide sustenance for itself and the unruly mob around it (some of whose members have come in from the outside as a result of his keeping bad company, while others have come from within, freed and let loose by his own bad habits). Isn't this the life that a tyrannical man leads?

It is indeed.

Now, if there are only a few such men in a city, and the rest of the people are moderate, this mob will leave the city in order to act as a bodyguard to some other tyrant or to serve as mercenaries if there happens   b
to be a war going on somewhere. But if they chance to live in a time of peace and quiet, they'll remain in the city and bring about lots of little evils.

What sort of evils do you mean?

They steal, break into houses, snatch purses, steal clothes, rob temples, and sell people into slavery. Sometimes, if they are good speakers, they become sycophants and bear false witness and accept bribes.

These evils *are* small, provided that there happen to be only a few such people.   c

Yes, for small things are small by comparison to big ones. And when it comes to producing wickedness and misery in a city, all these evils together don't, as the saying goes, come within a mile of the rule of a tyrant. But when such people become numerous and conscious of their numbers, it is they—aided by the foolishness of the people—who create a tyrant. And he, more than any of them, has in his soul the greatest and strongest tyrant of all.   d

Naturally, for he'd be the most tyrannical.

That's if the city happens to yield willingly, but if it resists him, then, just as he once chastised his mother and father, he'll now chastise his fatherland, if he can, by bringing in new friends and making his fatherland and his dear old motherland (as the Cretans call it) their slaves and keeping them that way, for this is surely the end at which such a man's desires are directed.

e   It most certainly is.

Now, in private life, before a tyrannical man attains power, isn't he this sort of person—one who associates primarily with flatterers who are ready to obey him in everything? Or if he himself happens to need anything from other people, isn't he willing to fawn on them and make every gesture of friendship, as if he were dealing with his own family? But once he gets

576   what he wants, don't they become strangers again?

Yes, they certainly do.

So someone with a tyrannical nature lives his whole life without being friends with anyone, always a master to one man or a slave to another and never getting a taste of either freedom or true friendship.

That's right.

Wouldn't we be right to call someone like that untrustworthy?

Of course.

And isn't he as unjust as anyone can be? If indeed what we earlier

b   agreed about justice was right.

And it certainly was right.

Then, let's sum up the worst type of man: His waking life is like the nightmare we described earlier.

That's right.

And he evolves from someone by nature most tyrannical who achieves sole rule. And the longer he remains tyrant, the more like the nightmare he becomes.

That's inevitable, said Glaucon, taking over the argument.

Well, then, I said, isn't the man who is clearly most vicious also clearly most wretched? And isn't the one who for the longest time is most of all

c   a tyrant, most wretched for the longest time? If, that is to say, truth rather than majority opinion is to settle these questions.

That much is certain, at any rate.

And isn't a tyrannical man like a city ruled by a tyrant, a democratic man like a city ruled by a democracy, and similarly with the others?

Of course.

And won't the relations between the cities with respect to virtue and happiness be the same as those between the men?

d   Certainly.

Then how does the city ruled by a tyrant compare to the city ruled by kings that we described first?

They are total opposites: one is the best, and the other the worst.

I won't ask you which is which, since it's obvious. But is your judgment the same with regard to their happiness and wretchedness? And let's not be dazzled by looking at one man—a tyrant—or at the few who surround him, but since it is essential to go into the city and study the whole of it, let's not give our opinion, till we've gone down and looked into every corner.   e

That's right, for it's clear to everyone that there is no city more wretched than one ruled by a tyrant and none more happy than one ruled by kings.

Would I be right, then, to make the same challenge about the individuals, assuming, first, that the person who is fit to judge them is someone who in   577 thought can go down into a person's character and examine it thoroughly, someone who doesn't judge from outside, the way a child does, who is dazzled by the façade that tyrants adopt for the outside world to see, but is able to see right through that sort of thing? And, second, that he's someone—since we'd all listen to him if he were—who is competent to judge, because he has lived in the same house with a tyrant and witnessed his behavior at home and his treatment of each member of his household when he is stripped of his theatrical façade, and has also seen how he behaves when in danger from the people? Shouldn't we ask the person   b who has seen all that to tell us how the tyrant compares to the others in happiness and wretchedness?

That's also right.

Then do you want us to pretend that we are among those who can give such a judgment and that we have already met tyrannical people, so that we'll have someone to answer our questions?

I certainly do.

Come, then, and look at it this way for me: Bearing in mind the resem-   c blance between the city and the man, look at each in turn and describe its condition.

What kinds of things do you want me to describe?

First, speaking of the city, would you say that a tyrannical city is free or enslaved?

It is as enslaved as it is possible to be.

Yet you see in it people who are masters and free.

I do see a few like that, but the whole city, so to speak, and the most decent part of it are wretched, dishonored slaves.

Then, if man and city are alike, mustn't the same structure be in him   d too? And mustn't his soul be full of slavery and unfreedom, with the most decent parts enslaved and with a small part, the maddest and most vicious, as their master?

It must.

What will you say about such a soul then? Is it free or slave?

Slave, of course.

And isn't the enslaved and tyrannical city least likely to do what it wants?

Certainly.

Then a tyrannical soul—I'm talking about the whole soul—will also be least likely to do what it wants and, forcibly driven by the stings of a dronish gadfly, will be full of disorder and regret.   e

How could it be anything else?

Is a tyrannically ruled city rich or poor?

Poor.

578   Then a tyrannical soul, too, must always be poor and unsatisfiable.

That's right.

What about fear? Aren't a tyrannical city and man full of it?

Absolutely.

And do you think that you'll find more wailing, groaning, lamenting, and grieving in any other city?

Certainly not.

Then, are such things more common in anyone besides a tyrannical man, who is maddened by his desires and erotic loves?

How could they be?

It is in view of all these things, I suppose, and others like them, that
b   you judged this to be the most wretched of cities.

And wasn't I right?

Of course you were. But what do you say about a tyrannical man, when you look at these same things?

He's by far the most wretched of all of them.

There you're no longer right.

How is that?

I don't think that this man has yet reached the extreme of wretchedness.

Then who has?

Perhaps you'll agree that this next case is even more wretched.

Which one?

c   The one who is tyrannical but doesn't live a private life, because some misfortune provides him with the opportunity to become an actual tyrant.

On the basis of what was said before, I assume that what you say is true.

Yes, but in matters of this sort, it isn't enough just to assume these things; one needs to investigate carefully the two men in question by means of argument, for the investigation concerns the most important thing, namely, the good life and the bad one.

That's absolutely right.

Then consider whether I'm talking sense or not, for I think our investiga-
d   tion will be helped by the following examples.

What are they?

We should look at all the wealthy private citizens in our cities who have many slaves, for, like a tyrant, they rule over many, although not over so many as he does.

That's right.

And you know that they're secure and do not fear their slaves.

What have they got to be afraid of?

Nothing. And do you know why?

Yes. It's because the whole city is ready to defend each of its individual citizens.

e   You're right. But what if some god were to lift one of these men, his fifty or more slaves, and his wife and children out of the city and deposit him with his slaves and other property in a deserted place, where no free person could come to his assistance? How frightened would he be that he himself and his wife and children would be killed by the slaves?

Very frightened indeed.

And wouldn't he be compelled to fawn on some of his own slaves, promise them lots of things, and free them, even though he didn't want to? And wouldn't he himself have become a panderer to slaves?

579

He'd have to or else be killed.

What if the god were to settle many other neighbors around him, who wouldn't tolerate anyone to claim that he was the master of another and who would inflict the worst punishments on anyone they caught doing it?

I suppose that he'd have even worse troubles, since he'd be surrounded by nothing but vigilant enemies.

b

And isn't this the kind of prison in which the tyrant is held—the one whose nature is such as we have described it, filled with fears and erotic loves of all kinds? Even though his soul is really greedy for it, he's the only one in the whole city who can't travel abroad or see the sights that other free people want to see. Instead, he lives like a woman, mostly confined to his own house, and envying any other citizen who happens to travel abroad and see something worthwhile.

c

That's entirely so.

Then, isn't this harvest of evils a measure of the difference between a tyrannical man who is badly governed on the inside—whom you judged to be most wretched just now—and one who doesn't live a private life but is compelled by some chance to be a tyrant, who tries to rule others when he can't even control himself. He's just like an exhausted body without any self-control, which, instead of living privately, is compelled to compete and fight with other bodies all its life.

d

That's exactly what he's like, Socrates, and what you say is absolutely true.

And so, Glaucon, isn't this a completely wretched condition to be in, and doesn't the reigning tyrant have an even harder life than the one you judged to be hardest?

He certainly does.

In truth, then, and whatever some people may think, a real tyrant is really a slave, compelled to engage in the worst kind of fawning, slavery, and pandering to the worst kind of people. He's so far from satisfying his desires in any way that it is clear—if one happens to know that one must study his whole soul—that he's in the greatest need of most things and truly poor. And, if indeed his state is like that of the city he rules, then he's full of fear, convulsions, and pains throughout his life. And it is like it, isn't it?

e

Of course it is.

And we'll also attribute to the man what we mentioned before, namely, that he is inevitably envious, untrustworthy, unjust, friendless, impious, host and nurse to every kind of vice, and that his ruling makes him even

580

more so. And because of all these, he is extremely unfortunate and goes
on to make those near him like himself.

No one with any understanding could possibly contradict you.

Come, then, and like the judge who makes the final decision, tell me
who among the five—the king, the timocrat, the oligarch, the democrat,
b   and the tyrant—is first in happiness, who second, and so on in order.

That's easy. I rank them in virtue and vice, in happiness and its opposite,
in the order of their appearance, as I might judge choruses.

Shall we, then, hire a herald, or shall I myself announce that the son of
Ariston has given as his verdict that the best, the most just, and the most
c   happy is the most kingly, who rules like a king over himself, and that the
worst, the most unjust, and the most wretched is the most tyrannical, who
most tyrannizes himself and the city he rules?

Let it be so announced.

And shall I add to the announcement that it holds, whether these things
remain hidden from every god and human being or not?

Add it.

Good. Then that is one of our proofs. And there'd be a second, if you
d   happen to think that there is anything in this.

In what?

In the fact that the soul of each individual is divided into three parts,
in just the way that a city is, for that's the reason I think that there is
another proof.

What is it?

This: it seems to me that there are three pleasures corresponding to the
three parts of the soul, one peculiar to each part, and similarly with desires
and kinds of rule.

What do you mean?

The first, we say, is the part with which a person learns, and the second
the part with which he gets angry. As for the third, we had no one special
name for it, since it's multiform, so we named it after the biggest and
e   strongest thing in it. Hence we called it the appetitive part, because of the
intensity of its appetites for food, drink, sex, and all the things associated
with them, but we also called it the money-loving part, because such
581   appetites are most easily satisfied by means of money.

And rightly so.

Then, if we said that its pleasure and love are for profit, wouldn't that
best determine its central feature for the purposes of our argument and
insure that we are clear about what we mean when we speak of this
part of the soul, and wouldn't we be right to call it money-loving and
profit-loving?

That's how it seems to me, at least.

What about the spirited part? Don't we say that it is wholly dedicated
to the pursuit of control, victory, and high repute?

b   Certainly.

Then wouldn't it be appropriate for us to call it victory-loving and honor-loving?

It would be most appropriate.

Now, it is clear to everyone that the part with which we learn is always wholly straining to know where the truth lies and that, of the three parts, it cares least for money and reputation.

By far the least.

Then wouldn't it be appropriate for us to call it learning-loving and philosophical?

Of course.

And doesn't this part rule in some people's souls, while one of the other parts—whichever it happens to be—rules in other people's?

That's right.

And isn't that the reason we say that there are three primary kinds of people: philosophic, victory-loving, and profit-loving?

That's it precisely.

And also three forms of pleasure, one assigned to each of them?

Certainly.

And do you realize that, if you chose to ask three such people in turn to tell you which of their lives is most pleasant, each would give the highest praise to his own? Won't a money-maker say that the pleasure of being honored and that of learning are worthless compared to that of making a profit, if he gets no money from them?

He will.

What about an honor-lover? Doesn't he think that the pleasure of making money is vulgar and that the pleasure of learning—except insofar as it brings him honor—is smoke and nonsense?

He does.

And as for a philosopher, what do you suppose he thinks the other pleasures are worth compared to that of knowing where the truth lies and always being in some such pleasant condition while learning? Won't he think that they are far behind? And won't he call them really necessary, since he'd have no need for them if they weren't necessary for life?

He will: we can be sure of that.

Then, since there's a dispute between the different forms of pleasure and between the lives themselves, not about which way of living is finer or more shameful or better or worse, but about which is more pleasant and less painful, how are we to know which of them is speaking most truly?

Don't ask me.

Look at it this way: How are we to judge things if we want to judge them well? Isn't it by experience, reason, and argument? Or could anyone have better criteria than these?

How could he?

Consider, then: Which of the three men has most experience of the pleasures we mentioned? Does a profit-lover learn what the truth itself is

like or acquire more experience of the pleasure of knowing it than a
b philosopher does of making a profit?

There's a big difference between them. A philosopher has of necessity
tasted the other pleasures since childhood, but it isn't necessary for a profit-
lover to taste or experience the pleasure of learning the nature of the things
that are and how sweet it is. Indeed, even if he were eager to taste it, he
couldn't easily do so.

Then a philosopher is far superior to a profit-lover in his experience of
both their pleasures.
c   He certainly is.

What about an honor-lover? Has he more experience of the pleasure of
knowing than a philosopher has of the pleasure of being honored?

No, for honor comes to each of them, provided that he accomplishes
his aim. A rich man is honored by many people, so is a courageous one
and a wise one, but the pleasure of studying the things that are cannot be
tasted by anyone except a philosopher.
d   Then, as far as experience goes, he is the finest judge of the three.

By far.

And he alone has gained his experience in the company of reason.

Of course.

Moreover, the instrument one must use to judge isn't the instrument of
a profit-lover or an honor-lover but a philosopher.

What instrument is that?

Arguments, for didn't we say that we must judge by means of them?

Yes.

And argument is a philosopher's instrument most of all.

Of course.

Now, if wealth and profit were the best means of judging things, the
e praise and blame of a profit-lover would necessarily be truest.

That's right.

And if honor, victory, and courage were the best means, wouldn't it be
the praise and blame of an honor-lover?

Clearly.

But since the best means are experience, reason, and argument . . .

The praise of a wisdom-lover and argument-lover is necessarily truest.

Then, of the three pleasures, the most pleasant is that of the part of the
583 soul with which we learn, and the one in whom that part rules has the
most pleasant life.

How could it be otherwise? A person with knowledge at least speaks
with authority when he praises his own life.

To what life and to what pleasure does the judge give second place?

Clearly, he gives it to those of a warrior and honor-lover, since they're
closer to his own than those of a money-maker.

Then the life and pleasure of a profit-lover come last, it seems.

Of course they do.

These, then, are two proofs in a row, and the just person has defeated the   b
unjust one in both. The third is dedicated in Olympic fashion to Olympian
Zeus the Savior. Observe then that, apart from those of a knowledgeable
person, the other pleasures are neither entirely true nor pure but are like a
shadow-painting, as I think I've heard some wise person say. And yet, if this
were true, it would be the greatest and most decisive of the overthrows.

It certainly would. But what exactly do you mean?

I'll find out, if I ask the questions, and you answer.   c

Ask, then.

Tell me, don't we say that pain is the opposite of pleasure?

Certainly.

And is there such a thing as feeling neither pleasure nor pain?

There is.

Isn't it intermediate between these two, a sort of calm of the soul by
comparison to them? Or don't you think of it that way?

I do.

And do you recall what sick people say when they're ill?

Which saying of theirs do you have in mind?

That nothing gives more pleasure than being healthy, but that they
hadn't realized that it was most pleasant until they fell ill.   d

I do recall that.

And haven't you also heard those who are in great pain say that nothing
is more pleasant than the cessation of their suffering?

I have.

And there are many similar circumstances, I suppose, in which you find
people in pain praising, not enjoyment, but the absence of pain and relief
from it as most pleasant.

That may be because at such times a state of calm becomes pleasant
enough to content them.

And when someone ceases to feel pleasure, this calm will be painful   e
to him.

Probably so.

Then the calm we described as being intermediate between pleasure
and pain will sometimes be both.

So it seems.

Now, is it possible for that which is neither to become both?

Not in my view.

Moreover, the coming to be of either the pleasant or the painful in the
soul is a sort of motion, isn't it?

Yes.

And didn't what is neither painful nor pleasant come to light just now
as a calm state, intermediate between them?   584

Yes, it did.

Then, how can it be right to think that the absence of pain is pleasure
or that the absence of pleasure is pain?

There's no way it can be.

Then it isn't right. But when the calm is next to the painful it appears pleasant, and when it is next to the pleasant it appears painful. However, there is nothing sound in these appearances as far as the truth about pleasure is concerned, only some kind of magic.

That's what the argument suggests, at any rate.

b   Take a look at the pleasures that don't come out of pains, so that you won't suppose in their case also that it is the nature of pleasure to be the cessation of pain or of pain to be the cessation of pleasure.

Where am I to look? What pleasures do you mean?

The pleasures of smell are especially good examples to take note of, for they suddenly become very intense without being preceded by pain, and when they cease they leave no pain behind. But there are plenty of other examples as well.

That's absolutely true.

Then let no one persuade us that pure pleasure is relief from pain or c   that pure pain is relief from pleasure.

No, let's not.

However, most of the so-called pleasures that reach the soul through the body, as well as the most intense ones, are of this form—they are some kind of relief from pain.

Yes, they are.

And aren't the pleasures and pains of anticipation, which arise from the expectation of future pleasures or pains, also of this form?

They are.

d   Do you know what kind of thing they are and what they most resemble?

No, what is it?

Do you believe that there is an up, a down, and a middle in nature?

I do.

And do you think that someone who was brought from down below to the middle would have any other belief than that he was moving upward? And if he stood in the middle and saw where he had come from, would he believe that he was anywhere other than the upper region, since he hasn't seen the one that is truly upper?

By god, I don't see how he could think anything else.

And if he was brought back, wouldn't he suppose that he was being e   brought down? And wouldn't he be right?

Of course.

Then wouldn't all this happen to him because he is inexperienced in what is really and truly up, down, and in the middle?

Clearly.

Is it any surprise, then, if those who are inexperienced in the truth have unsound opinions about lots of other things as well, or that they are so disposed to pleasure, pain, and the intermediate state that, when they descend to the painful, they believe truly and are really in pain, but that, 585   when they ascend from the painful to the intermediate state, they firmly

believe that they have reached fulfillment and pleasure? They are inexperienced in pleasure and so are deceived when they compare pain to painlessness, just as they would be if they compared black to gray without having
experienced white.

No, by god, I wouldn't be surprised. In fact, I'd be very surprised if it
were any other way.

Think of it this way: Aren't hunger, thirst, and the like some sort of   b
empty states of the body?

They are.

And aren't ignorance and lack of sense empty states of the soul?

Of course.

And wouldn't someone who partakes of nourishment or strengthens
his understanding be filled?

Certainly.

Does the truer filling up fill you with that which is less or that which
is more?

Clearly, it's with that which is more.

And which kinds partake more of pure being? Kinds of filling up such
as filling up with bread or drink or delicacies or food in general? Or the
kind of filling up that is with true belief, knowledge, understanding, and,
in sum, with all of virtue? Judge it this way: That which is related to what
is always the same, immortal, and true, is itself of that kind, and comes   c
to be in something of that kind—this is more, don't you think, than that
which is related to what is never the same and mortal, is itself of that
kind, and comes to be in something of that kind?

That which is related to what is always the same is far more.

And does the being of what is always the same participate more in being
than in knowledge?

Not at all.

Or more than in truth?

Not that either.

And if less in truth, then less in being also?

Necessarily.

And isn't it generally true that the kinds of filling up that are concerned
with the care of the body share less in truth and being than those concerned   d
with the care of the soul?

Yes, much less.

And don't you think that the same holds of the body in comparison to
the soul?

Certainly.

And isn't that which is more, and is filled with things that are more,
really more filled than that which is less, and is filled with things that
are less?

Of course.

Therefore, if being filled with what is appropriate to our nature is pleasure, that which is more filled with things that are more enjoys more really

e   and truly a more true pleasure, while that which partakes of things that are less is less truly and surely filled and partakes of a less trustworthy and less true pleasure.

That's absolutely inevitable.

586   Therefore, those who have no experience of reason or virtue, but are always occupied with feasts and the like, are brought down and then back up to the middle, as it seems, and wander in this way throughout their lives, never reaching beyond this to what is truly higher up, never looking up at it or being brought up to it, and so they aren't filled with that which really is and never taste any stable or pure pleasure. Instead, they always look down at the ground like cattle, and, with their heads bent over the dinner table, they feed, fatten, and fornicate. To outdo others in these

b   things, they kick and butt them with iron horns and hooves, killing each other, because their desires are insatiable. For the part that they're trying to fill is like a vessel full of holes, and neither it nor the things they are trying to fill it with are among the things that are.

Socrates, you've exactly described the life of the majority of people, just like an oracle.

Then isn't it necessary for these people to live with pleasures that are mixed with pains, mere images and shadow-paintings of true pleasures? And doesn't the juxtaposition of these pleasures and pains make them

c   appear intense, so that they give rise to mad erotic passions in the foolish, and are fought over in just the way that Stesichorus tells us the phantom of Helen was fought over at Troy by men ignorant of the truth?

Something like that must be what happens.

And what about the spirited part? Mustn't similar things happen to someone who satisfies it? Doesn't his love of honor make him envious and his love of victory make him violent, so that he pursues the satisfaction

d   of his anger and of his desires for honors and victories without calculation or understanding?

Such things must happen to him as well.

Then can't we confidently assert that those desires of even the money-loving and honor-loving parts that follow knowledge and argument and pursue with their help those pleasures that reason approves will attain the truest pleasures possible for them, because they follow truth, and the

e   ones that are most their own, if indeed what is best for each thing is most its own?

And indeed it is best.

Therefore, when the entire soul follows the philosophic part, and there is no civil war in it, each part of it does its own work exclusively and is just, and in particular it enjoys its own pleasures, the best and truest

587   pleasures possible for it.

Absolutely.

But when one of the other parts gains control, it won't be able to secure its own pleasure and will compel the other parts to pursue an alien and untrue pleasure.

That's right.

And aren't the parts that are most distant from philosophy and reason the ones most likely to do this sort of compelling?

They're much more likely.

And isn't whatever is most distant from reason also most distant from law and order?

Clearly.

And didn't the erotic and tyrannical desires emerge as most distant from these things?   b

By far.

And weren't the kingly and orderly ones least distant?

Yes.

Then I suppose that a tyrant will be most distant from a pleasure that is both true and his own and that a king will be least distant.

Necessarily.

So a tyrant will live most unpleasantly, and a king most pleasantly.

Necessarily.

Do you know how much more unpleasant a tyrant's life is than a king's?

I will if you tell me.

There are, it seems, three pleasures, one genuine and two illegitimate, and a tyrant is at the extreme end of the illegitimate ones, since he flees both law and reason and lives with a bodyguard of certain slavish pleasures. But   c
it isn't easy, all the same, to say just how inferior he is to a king, except perhaps as follows. A tyrant is somehow third from an oligarch, for a democrat was between them.

Yes.

Then, if what we said before is true, doesn't he live with an image of pleasure that is third from an oligarch's with respect to truth?[2]

He does.

Now, an oligarch, in turn, is third from a king, if we identify a king and an aristocrat.   d

Yes, he's third.

So a tyrant is three times three times removed from true pleasure.

Apparently so.

It seems then, on the basis of the magnitude of its number, that the image of tyrannical pleasure is a plane figure.

Exactly.

But then it's clear that, by squaring and cubing it, we'll discover how far a tyrant's pleasure is from that of a king.

It is clear to a mathematician, at any rate.

Then, turning it the other way around, if someone wants to say how far a king's pleasure is from a tyrant's, he'll find, if he completes the calculation, that a king lives seven hundred and twenty-nine times more   e

---

2. Third because the Greeks always counted the first as well as the last member of a series, e.g. the day after tomorrow was the third day from today.

pleasantly than a tyrant and that a tyrant is the same number of times more wretched.

That's an amazing calculation of the difference between the pleasure and pain of the two men, the just and the unjust.

588

Yet it's a true one, and one appropriate to human lives, if indeed days, nights, months, and years are appropriate to them.

And of course they are appropriate.

Then, if a good and just person's life is that much more pleasant than the life of a bad and unjust person, won't its grace, fineness, and virtue be incalculably greater?

By god, it certainly will.

b   All right, then. Since we've reached this point in the argument, let's return to the first things we said, since they are what led us here. I think someone said at some point that injustice profits a completely unjust person who is believed to be just. Isn't that so?

It certainly is.

Now, let's discuss this with him, since we've agreed on the respective powers that injustice and justice have.

How?

By fashioning an image of the soul in words, so that the person who says this sort of thing will know what he is saying.

c   What sort of image?

One like those creatures that legends tell us used to come into being in ancient times, such as the Chimera, Scylla, Cerberus, or any of the multitude of others in which many different kinds of things are said to have grown together naturally into one.

Yes, the legends do tell us of such things.

Well, then, fashion a single kind of multicolored beast with a ring of many heads that it can grow and change at will—some from gentle, some from savage animals.

d   That's work for a clever artist. However, since words are more malleable than wax and the like, consider it done.

Then fashion one other kind, that of a lion, and another of a human being. But make the first much the largest and the other second to it in size.

That's easier—the sculpting is done.

Now join the three of them into one, so that that they somehow grow together naturally.

They're joined.

Then, fashion around them the image of one of them, that of a human being so that anyone who sees only the outer covering and not what's

e   inside will think it is a single creature, a human being.

It's done.

Then, if someone maintains that injustice profits this human being and that doing just things brings no advantage, let's tell him that he is simply saying that it is beneficial for him, first, to feed the multiform beast well and make it strong, and also the lion and all that pertains to him; second, to starve and weaken the human being within, so that he is dragged along 589 wherever either of the other two leads; and, third, to leave the parts to bite and kill one another rather than accustoming them to each other and making them friendly.

Yes, that's absolutely what someone who praises injustice is saying.

But, on the other hand, wouldn't someone who maintains that just things are profitable be saying, first, that all our words and deeds should insure that the human being within this human being has the most control; second, that he should take care of the many-headed beast as a farmer does his b animals, feeding and domesticating the gentle heads and preventing the savage ones from growing; and, third, that he should make the lion's nature his ally, care for the community of all his parts, and bring them up in such a way that they will be friends with each other and with himself?

Yes, that's exactly what someone who praises justice is saying.

From every point of view, then, anyone who praises justice speaks truly, and anyone who praises injustice speaks falsely. Whether we look at the matter from the point of view of pleasure, good reputation, or advantage, a praiser of justice tells the truth, while one who condemns it has nothing c sound to say and condemns without knowing what he is condemning.

In my opinion, at least, he knows nothing about it.

Then let's persuade him gently—for he isn't wrong of his own will— by asking him these questions. Should we say that this is the original basis for the conventions about what is fine and what is shameful? Fine things are those that subordinate the beastlike parts of our nature to the human— or better, perhaps, to the divine; shameful ones are those that enslave the d gentle to the savage? Will he agree or what?

He will, if he takes my advice.

In light of this argument, can it profit anyone to acquire gold unjustly if, by doing so, he enslaves the best part of himself to the most vicious? If he got the gold by enslaving his son or daughter to savage and evil men, it wouldn't profit him, no matter how much gold he got. How, then, e could he fail to be wretched if he pitilessly enslaves the most divine part of himself to the most godless and polluted one and accepts golden gifts in return for a more terrible destruction than Eriphyle's when she took 590 the necklace in return for her husband's soul?[3]

A much more terrible one, Glaucon said. I'll answer for him.

And don't you think that licentiousness has long been condemned for just these reasons, namely, that because of it, that terrible, large, and multiform beast is let loose more than it should be?

Clearly.

And aren't stubbornness and irritability condemned because they inharmoniously increase and stretch the lionlike and snakelike part? b

3. Eriphyle was bribed with a golden necklace by Polynices to persuade her husband, Amphiaraus, to join the "Seven Against Thebes." He was killed. See *Odyssey* xi.326–27; Pindar, *Nemean* 9.16 ff.

Certainly.

And aren't luxury and softness condemned because the slackening and loosening of this same part produce cowardice in it?

Of course.

And aren't flattery and slavishness condemned because they subject the spirited part to the moblike beast, accustoming it from youth on to being insulted for the sake of the money needed to satisfy the beast's insatiable appetites, so that it becomes an ape instead of a lion?

c   They certainly are.

Why do you think that the condition of a manual worker is despised? Or is it for any other reason than that, when the best part is naturally weak in someone, it can't rule the beasts within him but can only serve them and learn to flatter them?

Probably so.

Therefore, to insure that someone like that is ruled by something similar to what rules the best person, we say that he ought to be the slave of that best person who has a divine ruler within himself. It isn't to harm the

d   slave that we say he must be ruled, which is what Thrasymachus thought to be true of all subjects, but because it is better for everyone to be ruled by divine reason, preferably within himself and his own, otherwise imposed from without, so that as far as possible all will be alike and friends, governed by the same thing.

Yes, that's right.

This is clearly the aim of the law, which is the ally of everyone. But it's also our aim in ruling our children, we don't allow them to be free until we establish a constitution in them, just as in a city, and—by fostering their best part with our own—equip them with a guardian and ruler similar

591   to our own to take our place. Then, and only then, we set them free.

Clearly so.

Then how can we maintain or argue, Glaucon, that injustice, licentiousness, and doing shameful things are profitable to anyone, since, even though he may acquire more money or other sort of power from them, they make him more vicious?

There's no way we can.

Or that to do injustice without being discovered and having to pay the penalty is profitable? Doesn't the one who remains undiscovered become

b   even more vicious, while the bestial part of the one who is discovered is calmed and tamed and his gentle part freed, so that his entire soul settles into its best nature, acquires moderation, justice, and reason, and attains a more valuable state than that of having a fine, strong, healthy body, since the soul itself is more valuable than the body?

That's absolutely certain.

Then won't a person of understanding direct all his efforts to attaining

c   that state of his soul? First, he'll value the studies that produce it and despise the others.

Clearly so.

Second, he won't entrust the condition and nurture of his body to the irrational pleasure of the beast within or turn his life in that direction, but neither will he make health his aim or assign first place to being strong, healthy, and beautiful, unless he happens to acquire moderation as a result. Rather, it's clear that he will always cultivate the harmony of his body for the sake of the consonance in his soul. d

He certainly will, if indeed he's to be truly trained in music and poetry.

Will he also keep order and consonance in his acquisition of money, with that same end in view? Or, even though he isn't dazzled by the size of the majority into accepting their idea of blessed happiness, will he increase his wealth without limit and so have unlimited evils?

Not in my view.

Rather, he'll look to the constitution within him and guard against e disturbing anything in it, either by too much money or too little. And, in this way, he'll direct both the increase and expenditure of his wealth, as far as he can.

That's exactly what he'll do.

And he'll look to the same thing where honors are concerned. He'll willingly share in and taste those that he believes will make him better, 592 but he'll avoid any public or private honor that might overthrow the established condition of his soul.

If that's his chief concern, he won't be willing to take part in politics.

Yes, by the dog, he certainly will, at least in his own kind of city. But he may not be willing to do so in his fatherland, unless some divine good luck chances to be his.

I understand. You mean that he'll be willing to take part in the politics of the city we were founding and describing, the one that exists in theory, for I don't think it exists anywhere on earth. b

But perhaps, I said, there is a model of it in heaven, for anyone who wants to look at it and to make himself its citizen on the strength of what he sees. It makes no difference whether it is or ever will be somewhere, for he would take part in the practical affairs of that city and no other.

Probably so, he said.

Book X

Indeed, I said, our city has many features that assure me that we were 595 entirely right in founding it as we did, and, when I say this, I'm especially thinking of poetry.

What about it in particular? Glaucon said.

That we didn't admit any that is imitative. Now that we have distinguished the separate parts of the soul, it is even clearer, I think, that such poetry should be altogether excluded. b

What do you mean?

Between ourselves—for *you* won't denounce me to the tragic poets or any of the other imitative ones—all such poetry is likely to distort the thought of anyone who hears it, unless he has the knowledge of what it is really like, as a drug to counteract it.

What exactly do you have in mind in saying this?

I'll tell you, even though the love and respect I've had for Homer since I was a child make me hesitate to speak, for he seems to have been the first teacher and leader of all these fine tragedians. All the

c   same, no one is to be honored or valued more than the truth. So, as I say, it must be told.

That's right.

Listen then, or, rather, answer.

Ask and I will.

Could you tell me what imitation in general is? I don't entirely understand what sort of thing imitations are trying to be.

Is it likely, then, that *I'll* understand?

That wouldn't be so strange, for people with bad eyesight often see

596   things before those whose eyesight is keener.

That's so, but even if something occurred to me, I wouldn't be eager to talk about it in front of you. So I'd rather that you did the looking.

Do you want us to begin our examination, then, by adopting our usual procedure? As you know, we customarily hypothesize a single form in connection with each of the many things to which we apply the same name. Or don't you understand?

I do.

Then let's now take any of the manys you like. For example, there are

b   many beds and tables.

Of course.

But there are only two forms of such furniture, one of the bed and one of the table.

Yes.

And don't we also customarily say that their makers look towards the appropriate form in making the beds or tables we use, and similarly in the other cases? Surely no craftsman makes the form itself. How could he?

There's no way he could.

Well, then, see what you'd call *this* craftsman?

c   Which one?

The one who makes all the things that all the other kinds of craftsmen severally make.

That's a clever and wonderful fellow you're talking about.

Wait a minute, and you'll have even more reason to say that, for this same craftsman is able to make, not only all kinds of furniture, but all plants that grow from the earth, all animals (including himself), the earth itself, the heavens, the gods, all the things in the heavens and in Hades beneath the earth.

d   *He'd* be amazingly clever!

You don't believe me? Tell me, do you think that there's no way any craftsman could make all these things, or that in one way he could and in another he couldn't? Don't you see that there is a way in which you yourself could make all of them?

What way is that?

It isn't hard: You could do it quickly and in lots of places, especially if you were willing to carry a mirror with you, for that's the quickest way of all. With it you can quickly make the sun, the things in the heavens, the earth, yourself, the other animals, manufactured items, plants, and everything else mentioned just now.   e

Yes, I could make them appear, but I couldn't make the things themselves as they truly are.

Well put! You've extracted the point that's crucial to the argument. I suppose that the painter too belongs to this class of makers, doesn't he?

Of course.

But I suppose you'll say that he doesn't truly make the things he makes. Yet, in a certain way, the painter does make a bed, doesn't he?

Yes, he makes the appearance of one.

What about the carpenter? Didn't you just say that he doesn't make the form—which is our term for the being of a bed—but only *a* bed?   597

Yes, I did say that.

Now, if he doesn't make the being of a bed, he isn't making that which is, but something which is like that which is, but is not it. So, if someone were to say that the work of a carpenter or any other craftsman is completely that which is, wouldn't he risk saying what isn't true?

That, at least, would be the opinion of those who busy themselves with arguments of this sort.

Then let's not be surprised if the carpenter's bed, too, turns out to be a somewhat dark affair in comparison to the true one.

All right.   b

Then, do you want us to try to discover what an imitator is by reference to these same examples?

I do, if you do.

We get, then, these three kinds of beds. The first is in nature a bed, and I suppose we'd say that a god makes it, or does someone else make it?

No one else, I suppose.

The second is the work of a carpenter.

Yes.

And the third is the one the painter makes. Isn't that so?

It is.

Then the painter, carpenter, and god correspond to three kinds of bed?

Yes, three.

Now, the god, either because he didn't want to or because it was neces-sary for him not to do so, didn't make more than one bed in nature, but   c
only one, the very one that is the being of a bed. Two or more of these have not been made by the god and never will be.

Why is that?

Because, if he made only two, then again one would come to light whose form they in turn would both possess, and *that* would be the one that is the being of a bed and not the other two.

That's right.

d   The god knew this, I think, and wishing to be the real maker of the truly real bed and not just *a* maker of *a* bed, he made it to be one in nature.

Probably so.

Do you want us to call him its natural maker or something like that?

It would be right to do so, at any rate, since he is by nature the maker of this and everything else.

What about a carpenter? Isn't he the maker of a bed?

Yes.

And is a painter also a craftsman and maker of such things?

Not at all.

Then what do you think he does do to a bed?

He imitates it. He is an imitator of what the others make. That, in my

e   view, is the most reasonable thing to call him.

All right. Then wouldn't you call someone whose product is third from the natural one an imitator?

I most certainly would.

Then this will also be true of a tragedian, if indeed he is an imitator. He is by nature third from the king and the truth, as are all other imitators.

It looks that way.

We're agreed about imitators, then. Now, tell me this about a painter. Do you think he tries in each case to imitate the thing itself in nature or

598   the works of craftsmen?

The works of craftsmen.

As they are or as they appear? You must be clear about that.

How do you mean?

Like this. If you look at a bed from the side or the front or from anywhere else is it a different bed each time? Or does it only appear different, without being at all different? And is that also the case with other things?

That's the way it is—it appears different without being so.

Then consider this very point: What does painting do in each case? Does

b   it imitate that which is as it is, or does it imitate that which appears as it appears? Is it an imitation of appearances or of truth?

Of appearances.

Then imitation is far removed from the truth, for it touches only a small part of each thing and a part that is itself only an image. And that, it seems, is why it can produce everything. For example, we say that a painter can paint a cobbler, a carpenter, or any other craftsman, even though he

c   knows nothing about these crafts. Nevertheless, if he is a good painter and displays his painting of a carpenter at a distance, he can deceive children and foolish people into thinking that it is truly a carpenter.

Of course.

Then this, I suppose, is what we must bear in mind in all these cases. Hence, whenever someone tells us that he has met a person who knows all the crafts as well as all the other things that anyone else knows and that his knowledge of any subject is more exact than any of theirs is, we must assume that we're talking to a simple-minded fellow who has apparently encountered some sort of magician or imitator and been deceived into thinking him omniscient and that the reason he has been deceived is that he himself can't distinguish between knowledge, ignorance, and imitation.

That's absolutely true.

Then, we must consider tragedy and its leader, Homer. The reason is this: We hear some people say that poets know all crafts, all human affairs concerned with virtue and vice, and all about the gods as well. They say that if a good poet produces fine poetry, he must have knowledge of the things he writes about, or else he wouldn't be able to produce it at all. Hence, we have to look to see whether those who tell us this have encountered these imitators and have been so deceived by them that they don't realize that their works are at the third remove from that which is and are easily produced without knowledge of the truth (since they are only images, not things that are), or whether there is something in what these people say, and good poets really do have knowledge of the things most people think they write so well about.

We certainly must look into it.

Do you think that someone who could make both the thing imitated and its image would allow himself to be serious about making images and put this at the forefront of his life as the best thing to do?

No, I don't.

I suppose that, if he truly had knowledge of the things he imitates, he'd be much more serious about actions than about imitations of them, would try to leave behind many fine deeds as memorials to himself, and would be more eager to be the subject of a eulogy than the author of one.

I suppose so, for these things certainly aren't equally valuable or equally beneficial either.

Then let's not demand an account of any of these professions from Homer or the other poets. Let's not ask whether any of them is a doctor rather than an imitator of what doctors say, or whether any poet of the old or new school has made anyone healthy as Asclepius did, or whether he has left any students of medicine behind as Asclepius did his sons. And let's not ask them about the other crafts either. Let's pass over all that. But about the most important and most beautiful things of which Homer undertakes to speak—warfare, generalship, city government, and people's education—about these it *is* fair to question him, asking him this: "Homer, if you're not third from the truth about virtue, the sort of craftsman of images that we defined an imitator to be, but if you're even second and capable of knowing what ways of life make people better in private or in public, then tell us which cities are better governed because of you, as

Sparta is because of Lycurgus, and as many others—big and small—are because of many other men? What city gives you credit for being a good
e lawgiver who benefited it, as Italy and Sicily do to Charondas, and as we do to Solon? Who gives such credit to you?" Will he be able to name one?

I suppose not, for not even the Homeridae[1] make that claim for him.

Well, then, is any war in Homer's time remembered that was won
600 because of his generalship and advice?

None.

Or, as befits a wise man, are many inventions and useful devices in the crafts or sciences attributed to Homer, as they are to Thales of Miletus and Anacharsis the Scythian?[2]

There's nothing of that kind at all.

Then, if there's nothing of a public nature, are we told that, when Homer was alive, he was a leader in the education of certain people who took pleasure in associating with him in private and that he passed on a Homeric
b way of life to those who came after him, just as Pythagoras did? Pythagoras is particularly loved for this, and even today his followers are conspicuous for what they call the Pythagorean way of life.

Again, we're told nothing of this kind about Homer. If the stories about him are true, Socrates, his companion, Creophylus,[3] seems to have been an even more ridiculous example of education than his name suggests, for they tell us that while Homer was alive, Creophylus completely ne-
c glected him.

They do tell us that. But, Glaucon, if Homer had really been able to educate people and make them better, if he'd known about these things and not merely about how to imitate them, wouldn't he have had many companions and been loved and honored by them? Protagoras of Abdera, Prodicus of Ceos,[4] and a great many others are able to convince anyone who associates with them in private that he wouldn't be able to manage his household or city unless they themselves supervise his education, and
d they are so intensely loved because of this wisdom of theirs that their disciples do everything but carry them around on their shoulders. So do you suppose that, if Homer had been able to benefit people and make them more virtuous, his companions would have allowed either him or Hesiod to wander around as rhapsodes? Instead, wouldn't they have clung

---

1. The Homeridae were the rhapsodes and poets who recited and expounded Homer throughout the Greek world.

2. Thales of Miletus is the first philosopher we know of in ancient Greece. He is said to have predicted the solar eclipse of 585 B.C. Anacharsis, who lived around 600 B.C., is credited with beginning Greek geometry and with being able to calculate the distance of ships at sea.

3. Creophylus is said to have been an epic poet from Chios. His name comes from two words meaning "meat" and "race" or "kind." A modern equivalent would be "meathead."

4. Protagoras and Prodicus were two of the most famous fifth-century sophists.

tighter to them than to gold and compelled them to live with them in their homes, or, if they failed to persuade them to do so, wouldn't they have followed them wherever they went until they had received sufficient education?

It seems to me, Socrates, that what you say is entirely true.

Then shall we conclude that all poetic imitators, beginning with Homer, imitate images of virtue and all the other things they write about and have no grasp of the truth? As we were saying just now, a painter, though he knows nothing about cobblery, can make what seems to be a cobbler to those who know as little about it as he does and who judge things by their colors and shapes.

That's right.

And in the same way, I suppose we'll say that a poetic imitator uses words and phrases to paint colored pictures of each of the crafts. He himself knows nothing about them, but he imitates them in such a way that others, as ignorant as he, who judge by words, will think he speaks extremely well about cobblery or generalship or anything else whatever, provided—so great is the natural charm of these things—that he speaks with meter, rhythm, and harmony, for if you strip a poet's works of their musical colorings and take them by themselves, I think you know what they look like. You've surely seen them.

I certainly have.

Don't they resemble the faces of young boys who are neither fine nor beautiful after the bloom of youth has left them?

Absolutely.

Now, consider this. We say that a maker of an image—an imitator—knows nothing about that which is but only about its appearance. Isn't that so?

Yes.

Then let's not leave the discussion of this point halfway, but examine it fully.

Go ahead.

Don't we say that a painter paints reins and a mouth-bit?

Yes.

And that a cobbler and a metal-worker makes them?

Of course.

Then, does a painter know how the reins and mouth-bit have to be? Or is it the case that even a cobbler and metal-worker who make them don't know this, but only someone who knows how to use them, namely, a horseman?

That's absolutely true.

And won't we say that the same holds for everything?

What?

That for each thing there are these three crafts, one that uses it, one that makes it, and one that imitates it?

Yes.

Then aren't the virtue or excellence, the beauty and correctness of each manufactured item, living creature, and action related to nothing but the use for which each is made or naturally adapted?

They are.

It's wholly necessary, therefore, that a user of each thing has most experience of it and that he tell a maker which of his products performs well or badly in actual use. A flute-player, for example, tells a flute-maker about the flutes that respond well in actual playing and prescribes what
e   kind of flutes he is to make, while the maker follows his instructions.

Of course.

Then doesn't the one who knows give instructions about good and bad flutes, and doesn't the other rely on him in making them?

Yes.

Therefore, a maker—through associating with and having to listen to the one who knows—has right opinion about whether something he makes
602 is fine or bad, but the one who knows is the user.

That's right.

Does an imitator have knowledge of whether the things he makes are fine or right through having made use of them, or does he have right opinion about them through having to consort with the one who knows and being told how he is to paint them?

Neither.

Therefore an imitator has neither knowledge nor right opinion about whether the things he makes are fine or bad.

Apparently not.

Then a poetic imitator is an accomplished fellow when it comes to wisdom about the subjects of his poetry!

Hardly.

Nonetheless, he'll go on imitating, even though he doesn't know the good or bad qualities of anything, but what he'll imitate, it seems, is what
b   appears fine or beautiful to the majority of people who know nothing.

Of course.

It seems, then, that we're fairly well agreed that an imitator has no worthwhile knowledge of the things he imitates, that imitation is a kind of game and not something to be taken seriously, and that all the tragic poets, whether they write in iambics or hexameters, are as imitative as they could possibly be.

That's right.

c   Then is this kind of imitation concerned with something that is third from the truth, or what?

Yes, it is.

And on which of a person's parts does it exert its power?

What do you mean?

This: Something looked at from close at hand doesn't seem to be the same size as it does when it is looked at from a distance.

No, it doesn't.

And something looks crooked when seen in water and straight when seen out of it, while something else looks both concave and convex because our eyes are deceived by its colors, and every other similar sort of confusion is clearly present in our soul. And it is because they exploit this weakness in our nature that *trompe l'oeil* painting, conjuring, and other forms of trickery have powers that are little short of magical.

That's true.

And don't measuring, counting, and weighing give us most welcome assistance in these cases, so that we aren't ruled by something's looking bigger, smaller, more numerous, or heavier, but by calculation, measurement, or weighing?

Of course.

And calculating, measuring, and weighing are the work of the rational part of the soul.

They are.

But when this part has measured and has indicated that some things are larger or smaller or the same size as others, the opposite appears to it at the same time.

Yes.

And didn't we say that it is impossible for the same thing to believe opposites about the same thing at the same time?[5]

We did, and we were right to say it.

Then the part of the soul that forms a belief contrary to the measurements couldn't be the same as the part that believes in accord with them.

No, it couldn't.

Now, the part that puts its trust in measurement and calculation is the best part of the soul.

Of course.

Therefore, the part that opposes it is one of the inferior parts in us.

Necessarily.

This, then, is what I wanted to get agreement about when I said that painting and imitation as a whole produce work that is far from the truth, namely, that imitation really consorts with a part of us that is far from reason, and the result of their being friends and companions is neither sound nor true.

That's absolutely right.

Then imitation is an inferior thing that consorts with another inferior thing to produce an inferior offspring.

So it seems.

Does this apply only to the imitations we see, or does it also apply to the ones we hear—the ones we call poetry?

It probably applies to poetry as well.

However, we mustn't rely solely on a mere probability based on the analogy with painting; instead, we must go directly to the part of our

d

e

603

b

5. See 436b–c.

thought with which poetic imitations consort and see whether it is inferior
c   or something to be taken seriously.

Yes, we must.

Then let's set about it as follows. We say that imitative poetry imitates
human beings acting voluntarily or under compulsion, who believe that,
as a result of these actions, they are doing either well or badly and who
experience either pleasure or pain in all this. Does it imitate anything apart
from this?

Nothing.

Then is a person of one mind in all these circumstances? Or, just as he
was at war with himself in matters of sight and held opposite beliefs about
d   the same thing at the same time, does he also fight with himself and engage
in civil war with himself in matters of action? But there is really no need
for us to reach agreement on this question now, for I remember that we
already came to an adequate conclusion about all these things in our
earlier arguments, when we said that our soul is full of a myriad of such
oppositions at the same time.[6]

And rightly so.

It *was* right, but I think we omitted some things then that we must
e   now discuss.

What are they?

We also mentioned somewhere before[7] that, if a decent man happens
to lose his son or some other prized possession, he'll bear it more easily
than the other sorts of people.

Certainly.

But now let's consider this. Will he not grieve at all, or, if that's impossible, will he be somehow measured in his response to pain?

The latter is closer to the truth.

Now, tell me this about him: Will he fight his pain and put up more
604   resistance to it when his equals can see him or when he's alone by himself
in solitude?

He'll fight it far more when he's being seen.

But when he's alone I suppose he'll venture to say and do lots of things
that he'd be ashamed to be heard saying or seen doing.

That's right.

And isn't it reason and law that tells him to resist his pain, while his
b   experience of it tells him to give in?

True.

And when there are two opposite inclinations in a person in relation to
the same thing at the same time, we say that he must also have two parts.

Of course.

6. See 439c ff.

7. See 387d–e.

Isn't one part ready to obey the law wherever it leads him?

How so?

The law says, doesn't it, that it is best to keep as quiet as possible in misfortunes and not get excited about them? First, it isn't clear whether such things will turn out to be good or bad in the end; second, it doesn't make the future any better to take them hard; third, human affairs aren't worth taking very seriously; and, finally, grief prevents the very thing   c
we most need in such circumstances from coming into play as quickly as possible.

What are you referring to?

Deliberation. We must accept what has happened as we would the fall of the dice, and then arrange our affairs in whatever way reason determines to be best. We mustn't hug the hurt part and spend our time weeping and wailing like children when they trip. Instead, we should always accustom our souls to turn as quickly as possible to healing the disease and putting the disaster right, replacing lamentation with cure.   d

That would be the best way to deal with misfortune, at any rate.

Accordingly, we say that it is the best part of us that is willing to follow this rational calculation.

Clearly.

Then won't we also say that the part that leads us to dwell on our misfortunes and to lamentation, and that can never get enough of these things, is irrational, idle, and a friend of cowardice?

We certainly will.

Now, this excitable character admits of many multicolored imitations. But a rational and quiet character, which always remains pretty well the   e
same, is neither easy to imitate nor easy to understand when imitated, especially not by a crowd consisting of all sorts of people gathered together at a theater festival, for the experience being imitated is alien to them.

Absolutely.   605

Clearly, then, an imitative poet isn't by nature related to the part of the soul that rules in such a character, and, if he's to attain a good reputation with the majority of people, his cleverness isn't directed to pleasing it. Instead, he's related to the excitable and multicolored character, since it is easy to imitate.

Clearly.

Therefore, we'd be right to take him and put him beside a painter as his counterpart. Like a painter, he produces work that is inferior with respect to truth and that appeals to a part of the soul that is similarly inferior rather than to the best part. So we were right not to admit him   b
into a city that is to be well-governed, for he arouses, nourishes, and strengthens this part of the soul and so destroys the rational one, in just the way that someone destroys the better sort of citizens when he strengthens the vicious ones and surrenders the city to them. Similarly, we'll say that an imitative poet puts a bad constitution in the soul of each individual

by making images that are far removed from the truth and by gratifying
c   the irrational part, which cannot distinguish the large and the small but
believes that the same things are large at one time and small at another.

That's right.

However, we haven't yet brought the most serious charge against imitation, namely, that with a few rare exceptions it is able to corrupt even
decent people, for that's surely an altogether terrible thing.

It certainly is, if indeed it can do that.

Listen, then, and consider whether it can or not. When even the best of
us hear Homer or some other tragedian imitating one of the heroes sorrow-
ing and making a long lamenting speech or singing and beating his breast,
d   you know that we enjoy it, give ourselves up to following it, sympathize
with the hero, take his sufferings seriously, and praise as a good poet the
one who affects us most in this way.

Of course we do.

But when one of us suffers a private loss, you realize that the opposite
happens. We pride ourselves if we are able to keep quiet and master our
grief, for we think that this is the manly thing to do and that the behavior
e   we praised before is womanish.

I do realize that.

Then are we right to praise it? Is it right to look at someone behaving
in a way that we would consider unworthy and shameful and to enjoy
and praise it rather than being disgusted by it?

No, by god, that doesn't seem reasonable.

606   No, at least not if you look at it in the following way.

How?

If you reflect, first, that the part of the soul that is forcibly controlled in
our private misfortunes and that hungers for the satisfaction of weeping
and wailing, because it desires these things by nature, is the very part that
receives satisfaction and enjoyment from poets, and, second, that the part
of ourselves that is best by nature, since it hasn't been adequately educated
either by reason or habit, relaxes its guard over the lamenting part when
it is watching the sufferings of somebody else. The reason it does so is
b   this: It thinks that there is no shame involved for it in praising and pitying
another man who, in spite of his claim to goodness, grieves excessively.
Indeed, it thinks that there is a definite gain involved in doing so, namely,
pleasure. And it wouldn't want to be deprived of that by despising the
whole poem. I suppose that only a few are able to figure out that enjoyment
of other people's sufferings is necessarily transferred to our own and that
the pitying part, if it is nourished and strengthened on the sufferings of
others, won't be easily held in check when we ourselves suffer.

c   That's very true.

And doesn't the same argument apply to what provokes laughter? If
there are any jokes that you yourself would be ashamed to tell but that
you very much enjoy hearing and don't detest as something evil in comic
plays or in private, aren't you doing the same thing as in the case of what

provokes pity? The part of you that wanted to tell the jokes and that was held back by your reason, for fear of being thought a buffoon, you then release, not realizing that, by making it strong in this way, you will be led into becoming a figure of fun where your own affairs are concerned.

Yes, indeed.

And in the case of sex, anger, and all the desires, pleasures, and pains   d that we say accompany all our actions, poetic imitation has the very same effect on us. It nurtures and waters them and establishes them as rulers in us when they ought to wither and be ruled, for that way we'll become better and happier rather than worse and more wretched.

I can't disagree with you.

And so, Glaucon, when you happen to meet those who praise Homer   e and say that he's the poet who educated Greece, that it's worth taking up his works in order to learn how to manage and educate people, and that one should arrange one's whole life in accordance with his teachings, you should welcome these people and treat them as friends, since they're as good as they're capable of being, and you should agree that Homer is the   607 most poetic of the tragedians and the first among them. But you should also know that hymns to the gods and eulogies to good people are the only poetry we can admit into our city. If you admit the pleasure-giving Muse, whether in lyric or epic poetry, pleasure and pain will be kings in your city instead of law or the thing that everyone has always believed to be best, namely, reason.

That's absolutely true.

Then let this be our defense—now that we've returned to the topic of poetry—that, in view of its nature, we had reason to banish it from the   b city earlier, for our argument compelled us to do so. But in case we are charged with a certain harshness and lack of sophistication, let's also tell poetry that there is an ancient quarrel between it and philosophy, which is evidenced by such expressions as "the dog yelping and shrieking at its master," "great in the empty eloquence of fools," "the mob of wise men that has mastered Zeus,"[8] and "the subtle thinkers, beggars all." Nonetheless, if   c the poetry that aims at pleasure and imitation has any argument to bring forward that proves it ought to have a place in a well-governed city, we at least would be glad to admit it, for we are well aware of the charm it exercises. But, be that as it may, to betray what one believes to be the truth is impious. What about you, Glaucon, don't you feel the charm of the pleasure-giving Muse, especially when you study her through the eyes of Homer?   d

Very much so.

Therefore, isn't it just that such poetry should return from exile when it has successfully defended itself, whether in lyric or any other meter?

Certainly.

---

8. Reading *Dia sophōn* in c1.

Then we'll allow its defenders, who aren't poets themselves but lovers of poetry, to speak in prose on its behalf and to show that it not only gives pleasure but is beneficial both to constitutions and to human life. Indeed, we'll listen to them graciously, for we'd certainly profit if poetry were

e shown to be not only pleasant but also beneficial.

How could we fail to profit?

However, if such a defense isn't made, we'll behave like people who have fallen in love with someone but who force themselves to stay away from him, because they realize that their passion isn't beneficial. In the same way, because the love of this sort of poetry has been implanted in us by the upbringing we have received under our fine constitutions, we are well disposed to any proof that it is the best and truest thing. But if

608 it isn't able to produce such a defense, then, whenever we listen to it, we'll repeat the argument we have just now put forward like an incantation so as to preserve ourselves from slipping back into that childish passion for poetry which the majority of people have. And we'll go on chanting that such poetry is not to be taken seriously or treated as a serious undertaking with some kind of hold on the truth, but that anyone who is anxious about the constitution within him must be careful when he hears it and must

b continue to believe what we have said about it.

I completely agree.

Yes, for the struggle to be good rather than bad is important, Glaucon, much more important than people think. Therefore, we mustn't be tempted by honor, money, rule, or even poetry into neglecting justice and the rest of virtue.

After what we've said, I agree with you, and so, I think, would anyone else.

c And yet we haven't discussed the greatest rewards and prizes that have been proposed for virtue.

They must be inconceivably great, if they're greater than those you've already mentioned.

Could anything really great come to pass in a short time? And isn't the time from childhood to old age short when compared to the whole of time?

It's a mere nothing.

Well, do you think that an immortal thing should be seriously concerned

d with that short period rather than with the whole of time?

I suppose not, but what exactly do you mean by this?

Haven't you realized that our soul is immortal and never destroyed?

He looked at me with wonder and said: No, by god, I haven't. Are you really in a position to assert that?

I'd be wrong not to, I said, and so would you, for it isn't difficult.

It is for me, so I'd be glad to hear from you what's not difficult about it.

Listen, then.

Just speak, and I will.

Do you talk about good and bad?

I do.

And do you think about them the same way I do?   e

What way is that?

The bad is what destroys and corrupts, and the good is what preserves and benefits.

I do.

And do you say that there is a good and a bad for everything? For example, ophthalmia for the eyes, sickness for the whole body, blight for grain, rot for wood, rust for iron or bronze. In other words, is there, as I   609 say, a natural badness and sickness for pretty well everything?

There is.

And when one of these attaches itself to something, doesn't it make the thing in question bad, and in the end, doesn't it disintegrate it and destroy it wholly?

Of course.

Therefore, the evil that is natural to each thing and the bad that is peculiar to it destroy it. However, if they don't destroy it, nothing else will, for the good would never destroy anything, nor would anything   b neither good nor bad.

How could they?

Then, if we discover something that has an evil that makes it bad but isn't able to disintegrate and destroy it, can't we infer that it is naturally incapable of being destroyed?

Probably so.

Well, what about the soul? Isn't there something that makes it bad?

Certainly, all the things we were mentioning: Injustice, licentiousness, cowardice, and lack of learning.   c

Does any of these disintegrate and destroy the soul? Keep your wits about you, and let's not be deceived into thinking that, when an unjust and foolish person is caught, he has been destroyed by injustice, which is evil in a soul. Let's think about it this way instead: Just as the body is worn out, destroyed, and brought to the point where it is a body no longer by disease, which is evil in a body, so all the things we mentioned just now reach the point at which they cease to be what they are through their own peculiar evil, which attaches itself to them and is present in them. Isn't that so?   d

Yes.

Then look at the soul in the same way. Do injustice and the other vices that exist in a soul—by their very presence in it and by attaching themselves to it—corrupt it and make it waste away until, having brought it to the point of death, they separate it from the body?

That's not at all what they do.

But surely it's unreasonable to suppose that a thing is destroyed by the badness proper to something else when it is not destroyed by its own?

That is unreasonable.

Keep in mind, Glaucon, that we don't think that a body is destroyed by the badness of food, whether it is staleness, rottenness, or anything   e

else. But if the badness of the food happens to implant in the body an evil proper to a body, we'll say that the body was destroyed by its own evil, namely, disease. But, since the body is one thing and food another, we'll
610   never judge that the body is destroyed by the badness of food, unless it implants in it the body's own natural and peculiar evil.

That's absolutely right.

By the same argument, if the body's evil doesn't cause an evil in the soul that is proper to the soul, we'll never judge that the soul, in the absence of its own peculiar evil, is destroyed by the evil of something else. We'd never accept that *anything* is destroyed by an evil proper to something else.

That's also reasonable.

Then let's either refute our argument and show that we were wrong, or, as long as it remains unrefuted, let's never say that the soul is destroyed by a fever or any other disease or by killing either, for that matter, not
b   even if the body is cut up into tiny pieces. We mustn't say that the soul is even close to being destroyed by these things until someone shows us that these conditions of the body make the soul more unjust and more impious. When something has the evil proper to something else in it, but its own peculiar evil is absent, we won't allow anyone to say that it is
c   destroyed, no matter whether it is a soul or anything else whatever.

And you may be sure that no one will ever prove that the souls of the dying are made more unjust by death.

But if anyone dares to come to grips with our argument, in order to avoid having to agree that our souls are immortal, and says that a dying man does become more vicious and unjust, we'll reply that, if what he says is true, then injustice must be as deadly to unjust people as a disease,
d   and those who catch it must die of it because of its own deadly nature, with the worst cases dying quickly and the less serious dying more slowly. As things now stand, however, it isn't like that at all. Unjust people do indeed die of injustice, but at the hands of others who inflict the death penalty on them.

By god, if injustice were actually fatal to those who contracted it, it wouldn't seem so terrible, for it would be an escape from their troubles. But I rather think that it's clearly the opposite, something that kills other
e   people if it can, while, on top of making the unjust themselves lively, it even brings them out at night. Hence it's very far from being deadly to its possessors.

You're right, for if the soul's own evil and badness isn't enough to kill and destroy it, an evil appointed for the destruction of something else will hardly kill it. Indeed, it won't kill anything at all except the very thing it is appointed to destroy.

"Hardly" is right, or so it seems.

Now, if the soul isn't destroyed by a single evil, whether its own or something else's, then clearly it must always be. And if it always is, it
611   is immortal.

Necessarily so.

So be it. And if it is so, then you realize that there would always be the same souls, for they couldn't be made fewer if none is destroyed, and they couldn't be made more numerous either. If anything immortal is increased, you know that the increase would have to come from the mortal, and then everything would end up being immortal.

That's true.

Then we mustn't think such a thing, for the argument doesn't allow it, nor must we think that the soul in its truest nature is full of multicolored variety and unlikeness or that it differs with itself.   b

What do you mean?

It isn't easy for anything composed of many parts to be immortal if it isn't put together in the finest way, yet this is how the soul now appeared to us.

It probably isn't easy.

Yet our recent argument and others as well compel us to believe that the soul *is* immortal. But to see the soul as it is in truth, we must not study it as it is while it is maimed by its association with the body and other evils—which is what we were doing earlier—but as it is in its pure state,   c
that's how we should study the soul, thoroughly and by means of logical reasoning. We'll then find that it is a much finer thing than we thought and that we can see justice and injustice as well as all the other things we've discussed far more clearly. What we've said about the soul is true of it as it appears at present. But the condition in which we've studied it is like that of the sea god Glaucus, whose primary nature can't easily be made out by those who catch glimpses of him. Some of the original parts   d
have been broken off, others have been crushed, and his whole body has been maimed by the waves and by the shells, seaweeds, and stones that have attached themselves to him, so that he looks more like a wild animal than his natural self. The soul, too, is in a similar condition when we study it, beset by many evils. That, Glaucon, is why we have to look somewhere else in order to discover its true nature.

To where?

To its philosophy, or love of wisdom. We must realize what it grasps   e
and longs to have intercourse with, because it is akin to the divine and immortal and what always is, and we must realize what it would become if it followed this longing with its whole being, and if the resulting effort lifted it out of the sea in which it now dwells, and if the many stones and   612
shells (those which have grown all over it in a wild, earthy, and stony profusion because it feasts at those so-called happy feastings on earth) were hammered off it. Then we'd see what its true nature is and be able to determine whether it has many parts or just one and whether or in what manner it is put together. But we've already given a decent account, I think, of what its condition is and what parts it has when it is immersed in human life.

We certainly have.

And haven't we cleared away the various other objections to our argument without having to invoke the rewards and reputations of justice, as
b   you said Homer and Hesiod did?[9] And haven't we found that justice itself
is the best thing for the soul itself, and that the soul—whether it has the
ring of Gyges or even it together with the cap of Hades[10]—should do
just things?

We have. That's absolutely true.

Then can there now be any objection, Glaucon, if in addition we return
to justice and the rest of virtue both the kind and quantity of wages that
c   they obtain for the soul from human beings and gods, whether in this life
or the next?

None whatever.

Then will you give me back what you borrowed from me during the discussion?

What are you referring to in particular?

I granted your request that a just person should seem unjust and an
unjust one just, for you said that, even if it would be impossible for these
things to remain hidden from both gods and humans, still, this had to be
granted for the sake of argument, so that justice itself could be judged in
d   relation to injustice itself. Don't you remember that?

It would be wrong of me not to.

Well, then, since they've now been judged, I ask that the reputation
justice in fact has among gods and humans be returned to it and that we
agree that it does indeed have such a reputation and is entitled to carry
off the prizes it gains for someone by making him seem just. It is already
clear that it gives good things to anyone who is just and that it doesn't
deceive those who really possess it.

e   That's a fair request.

Then won't you first grant that it doesn't escape the notice of the gods
at least as to which of the two is just and which isn't?

We will.

Then if neither of them escapes the gods' notice, one would be loved
by the gods and the other hated, as we agreed at the beginning.

That's right.

And won't we also agree that everything that comes to someone who
is loved by gods, insofar as it comes from the gods themselves, is the best
613   possible, unless it is the inevitable punishment for some mistake he made
in a former life?

Certainly.

Then we must suppose that the same is true of a just person who falls
into poverty or disease or some other apparent evil, namely, that this will

---

9. See 357–367e.

10. The ring of Gyges is discussed at 359d–360a. The cap of Hades also made its
wearer invisible.

end well for him, either during his lifetime or afterwards, for the gods never neglect anyone who eagerly wishes to become just and who makes himself as much like a god as a human can by adopting a virtuous way of life.

It makes sense that such a person not be neglected by anyone who is like him.

And mustn't we suppose that the opposite is true of an unjust person?

Definitely.

Then these are some of the prizes that a just person, but not an unjust one, receives from the gods.

That's certainly my opinion.

What about from human beings? What does a just person get from them? Or, if we're to tell the truth, isn't this what happens? Aren't clever but unjust people like runners who run well for the first part of the course but not for the second? They leap away sharply at first, but they become ridiculous by the end and go off uncrowned, with their ears drooping on their shoulders like those of exhausted dogs, while true runners, on the other hand, get to the end, collect the prizes, and are crowned. And isn't it also generally true of just people that, towards the end of each course of action, association, or life, they enjoy a good reputation and collect the prizes from other human beings?

Of course.

Then will you allow me to say all the things about them that you yourself said about unjust people? I'll say that it is just people who, when they're old enough, rule in their own cities (if they happen to want ruling office) and that it is they who marry whomever they want and give their children in marriage to whomever they want. Indeed, all the things that you said about unjust people I now say about just ones. As for unjust people, the majority of them, even if they escape detection when they're young, are caught by the end of the race and are ridiculed. And by the time they get old, they've become wretched, for they are insulted by foreigners and citizens, beaten with whips, and made to suffer those punishments, such as racking and burning, which you rightly described as crude. Imagine that I've said that they suffer all such things, and see whether you'll allow me to say it.

Of course I will. What you say is right.

Then these are the prizes, wages, and gifts that a just person receives from gods and humans while he is alive and that are added to the good things that justice itself provides.

Yes, and they're very fine and secure ones too.

Yet they're nothing in either number or size compared to those that await just and unjust people after death. And these things must also be heard, if both are to receive in full what they are owed by the argument.

Then tell us about them, for there aren't many things that would be more pleasant to hear.

b

c

d

e

614

b

It isn't, however, a tale of Alcinous that I'll tell you but that of a brave Pamphylian man called Er, the son of Armenias, who once died in a war.[11] When the rest of the dead were picked up ten days later, they were already putrefying, but when he was picked up, his corpse was still quite fresh. He was taken home, and preparations were made for his funeral. But on the twelfth day, when he was already laid on the funeral pyre, he revived and, having done so, told what he had seen in the world beyond. He said that, after his soul had left him, it travelled together with many others

c until they came to a marvellous place, where there were two adjacent openings in the earth, and opposite and above them two others in the heavens, and between them judges sat. These, having rendered their judgment, ordered the just to go upwards into the heavens through the door on the right, with signs of the judgment attached to their chests, and the unjust to travel downward through the opening on the left, with signs of

d all their deeds on their backs. When Er himself came forward, they told him that he was to be a messenger to human beings about the things that were there, and that he was to listen to and look at everything in the place. He said that he saw souls departing after judgment through one of the openings in the heavens and one in the earth, while through the other two souls were arriving. From the door in the earth souls came up covered with dust and dirt and from the door in the heavens souls came down

e pure. And the souls who were arriving all the time seemed to have been on long journeys, so that they went gladly to the meadow, like a crowd going to a festival, and camped there. Those who knew each other exchanged greetings, and those who come up from the earth asked those who came down from the heavens about the things there and were in turn questioned by them about the things below. And so they told their stories

615 to one another, the former weeping as they recalled all they had suffered and seen on their journey below the earth, which lasted a thousand years, while the latter, who had come from heaven, told about how well they had fared and about the inconceivably fine and beautiful sights they had seen. There was much to tell, Glaucon, and it took a long time, but the main point was this: For each in turn of the unjust things they had done and for each in turn of the people they had wronged, they paid the penalty ten times over, once in every century of their journey. Since a century is

b roughly the length of a human life, this means that they paid a tenfold penalty for each injustice. If, for example, some of them had caused many deaths by betraying cities or armies and reducing them to slavery or by participating in other wrongdoing, they had to suffer ten times the pain they had caused to each individual. But if they had done good deeds and had become just and pious, they were rewarded according to the same scale. He said some other things about the stillborn and those who had

c lived for only a short time, but they're not worth recounting. And he also

---

11. Books ix–xi of the *Odyssey* were traditionally referred to as the tales of Alcinous.

spoke of even greater rewards or penalties for piety or impiety towards gods or parents and for murder with one's own hands.

For example, he said he was there when someone asked another where the great Ardiaeus was. (This Ardiaeus was said to have been tyrant in some city in Pamphylia a thousand years before and to have killed his aged father and older brother and committed many other impious deeds as well.) And he said that the one who was asked responded: "He hasn't arrived here yet and never will, for this too was one of the terrible sights we saw. When we came near the opening on our way out, after all our sufferings were over, we suddenly saw him together with some others, pretty well all of whom were tyrants (although there were also some private individuals among them who had committed great crimes). They thought that they were ready to go up, but the opening wouldn't let them through, for it roared whenever one of these incurably wicked people or anyone else who hadn't paid a sufficient penalty tried to go up. And there were savage men, all fiery to look at, who were standing by, and when they heard the roar, they grabbed some of these criminals and led them away, but they bound the feet, hands, and head of Ardiaeus and the others, threw them down, and flayed them. Then they dragged them out of the way, lacerating them on thorn bushes, and telling every passer-by that they were to be thrown into Tartarus, and explaining why they were being treated in this way." And he said that of their many fears the greatest each one of them had was that the roar would be heard as he came up and that everyone was immensely relieved when silence greeted him. Such, then, were the penalties and punishments and the rewards corresponding to them.

Each group spent seven days in the meadow, and on the eighth they had to get up and go on a journey. On the fourth day of that journey, they came to a place where they could look down from above on a straight column of light that stretched over the whole of heaven and earth, more like a rainbow than anything else, but brighter and more pure. After another day, they came to the light itself, and there, in the middle of the light, they saw the extremities of its bonds stretching from the heavens, for the light binds the heavens like the cables girding a trireme and holds its entire revolution together. From the extremities hangs the spindle of Necessity, by means of which all the revolutions are turned. Its stem and hook are of adamant, whereas in its whorl[12] adamant is mixed with other kinds of material. The nature of the whorl was this: Its shape was like that of an ordinary whorl, but, from what Er said, we must understand its structure as follows. It was as if one big whorl had been made hollow by being thoroughly scooped out, with another smaller whorl closely fitted into it, like nested boxes, and there was a third whorl inside the second, and so on, making eight whorls altogether, lying inside one another, with their rims appearing as circles from above, while from the back they formed

d

e

616

b

c

d

---

12. A whorl is the weight that twirls a spindle.

e   one continuous whorl around the stem, which was driven through the
center of the eighth. The first or outside whorl had the widest circular rim;
that of the sixth was second in width; the fourth was third; the eighth was
fourth; the seventh was fifth; the fifth was sixth; the third was seventh;
and the second was eighth. The rim of the largest was spangled; that of
617 the seventh was brightest; that of the eighth took its color from the seventh's
shining on it; the second and fifth were about equal in brightness, more
yellow than the others; the third was the whitest in color; the fourth was
rather red; and the sixth was second in whiteness. The whole spindle
turned at the same speed, but, as it turned, the inner circles gently revolved
in a direction opposite to that of the whole. Of the whorls themselves, the
eighth was the fastest; second came the seventh, sixth, and fifth, all at the
b   same speed; it seemed to them that the fourth was third in its speed of
revolution; the fourth, third; and the second, fifth. The spindle itself turned
on the lap of Necessity. And up above on each of the rims of the circles
stood a Siren, who accompanied its revolution, uttering a single sound,
one single note. And the concord of the eight notes produced a single
harmony. And there were three other beings sitting at equal distances
from one another, each on a throne. These were the Fates, the daughters
c   of Necessity: Lachesis, Clotho, and Atropos. They were dressed in white,
with garlands on their heads, and they sang to the music of the Sirens.
Lachesis sang of the past, Clotho of the present, and Atropos of the future.
With her right hand, Clotho touched the outer circumference of the spindle
and helped it turn, but left off doing so from time to time; Atropos did
the same to the inner ones; and Lachesis helped both motions in turn, one
d   with one hand and one with the other.

When the souls arrived at the light, they had to go to Lachesis right
away. There a Speaker arranged them in order, took from the lap of
Lachesis a number of lots and a number of models of lives, mounted a
high pulpit, and spoke to them: "Here is the message of Lachesis, the
maiden daughter of Necessity: 'Ephemeral souls, this is the beginning of
another cycle that will end in death. Your daemon or guardian spirit will
not be assigned to you by lot; you will choose him. The one who has the
e   first lot will be the first to choose a life to which he will then be bound
by necessity. Virtue knows no master; each will possess it to a greater or
less degree, depending on whether he values or disdains it. The responsibility lies with the one who makes the choice; the god has none.'" When he
had said this, the Speaker threw the lots among all of them, and each—
with the exception of Er, who wasn't allowed to choose—picked up the
one that fell next to him. And the lot made it clear to the one who picked
it up where in the order he would get to make his choice. After that, the
models of lives were placed on the ground before them. There were far
618 more of them than there were souls present, and they were of all kinds,
for the lives of animals were there, as well as all kinds of human lives.
There were tyrannies among them, some of which lasted throughout life,
while others ended halfway through in poverty, exile, and beggary. There

were lives of famous men, some of whom were famous for the beauty of their appearance, others for their strength or athletic prowess, others still for their high birth and the virtue or excellence of their ancestors. And there were also lives of men who weren't famous for any of these things. b And the same for lives of women. But the arrangement of the soul was not included in the model because the soul is inevitably altered by the different lives it chooses. But all the other things were there, mixed with each other and with wealth, poverty, sickness, health, and the states intermediate to them.

Now, it seems that it is here, Glaucon, that a human being faces the greatest danger of all. And because of this, each of us must neglect all other subjects and be most concerned to seek out and learn those that will c enable him to distinguish the good life from the bad and always to make the best choice possible in every situation. He should think over all the things we have mentioned and how they jointly and severally determine what the virtuous life is like. That way he will know what the good and bad effects of beauty are when it is mixed with wealth, poverty, and a particular state of the soul. He will know the effects of high or low birth, d private life or ruling office, physical strength or weakness, ease or difficulty in learning, and all the things that are either naturally part of the soul or are acquired, and he will know what they achieve when mixed with one another. And from all this he will be able, by considering the nature of the soul, to reason out which life is better and which worse and to choose accordingly, calling a life worse if it leads the soul to become more unjust, better if it leads the soul to become more just, and ignoring everything e else: We have seen that this is the best way to choose, whether in life or death. Hence, we must go down to Hades holding with adamantine determination to the belief that this is so, lest we be dazzled there by wealth and other such evils, rush into a tyranny or some other similar 619 course of action, do irreparable evils, and suffer even worse ones. And we must always know how to choose the mean in such lives and how to avoid either of the extremes, as far as possible, both in this life and in all those beyond it. This is the way that a human being becomes happiest. b

Then our messenger from the other world reported that the Speaker spoke as follows: "There is a satisfactory life rather than a bad one available even for the one who comes last, provided that he chooses it rationally and lives it seriously. Therefore, let not the first be careless in his choice nor the last discouraged."

He said that when the Speaker had told them this, the one who came up first chose the greatest tyranny. In his folly and greed he chose it without adequate examination and didn't notice that, among other evils, he was fated to eat his own children as a part of it. When he examined at c leisure, the life he had chosen, however, he beat his breast and bemoaned his choice. And, ignoring the warning of the Speaker, he blamed chance, daemons, or guardian spirits, and everything else for these evils but himself. He was one of those who had come down from heaven, having lived his previous life under an orderly constitution, where he had participated in virtue through habit and without philosophy. Broadly speaking, indeed,

d   most of those who were caught out in this way were souls who had come down from heaven and who were untrained in suffering as a result. The majority of those who had come up from the earth, on the other hand, having suffered themselves and seen others suffer, were in no rush to make their choices. Because of this and because of the chance of the lottery, there was an interchange of goods and evils for most of the souls. However, if someone pursues philosophy in a sound manner when he comes to live

e   here on earth and if the lottery doesn't make him one of the last to choose, then, given what Er has reported about the next world, it looks as though not only will he be happy here, but his journey from here to there and back again won't be along the rough underground path, but along the smooth heavenly one.

Er said that the way in which the souls chose their lives was a sight

620 worth seeing, since it was pitiful, funny, and surprising to watch. For the most part, their choice depended upon the character of their former life. For example, he said that he saw the soul that had once belonged to Orpheus choosing a swan's life, because he hated the female sex because of his death at their hands, and so was unwilling to have a woman conceive and give birth to him. Er saw the soul of Thamyris[13] choosing the life of a nightingale, a swan choosing to change over to a human life, and other musical animals doing the same thing. The twentieth soul chose the life

b   of a lion. This was the soul of Ajax, son of Telamon.[14] He avoided human life because he remembered the judgment about the armor. The next soul was that of Agamemnon, whose sufferings also had made him hate the human race, so he changed to the life of an eagle. Atalanta[15] had been assigned a place near the middle, and when she saw great honors being given to a male athlete, she chose his life, unable to pass them by. After her, he saw the soul of Epeius, the son of Panopeus, taking on the nature

c   of a craftswoman.[16] And very close to last, he saw the soul of the ridiculous Thersites clothing itself as a monkey.[17] Now, it chanced that the soul of

13. Thamyris was a legendary poet and singer, who boasted that he could defeat the Muses in a song contest. For this they blinded him and took away his voice. He is mentioned at *Iliad* ii.596–600.

14. Ajax is a great Homeric hero. He thought that he deserved to be awarded the armor of the dead Achilles, but instead it went to Odysseus. Ajax was maddened by this injustice and finally killed himself because of the terrible things he had done while mad. See Sophocles, *Ajax*.

15. Atalanta was a mythical huntress, who would marry only a man who could beat her at running. In most versions of the myth, losers were killed.

16. Epeius is mentioned at *Odyssey* viii.493 as the man who helped Athena make the Trojan Horse.

17. Thersites is an ordinary soldier who criticizes Agamemnon at *Iliad* ii.211–77. Odysseus beats him for his presumption and is widely approved for doing so.

Odysseus got to make its choice last of all, and since memory of its former sufferings had relieved its love of honor, it went around for a long time, looking for the life of a private individual who did his own work, and with difficulty it found one lying off somewhere neglected by the others. He chose it gladly and said that he'd have made the same choice even if he'd been first. Still other souls changed from animals into human beings, or from one kind of animal into another, with unjust people changing into wild animals, and just people into tame ones, and all sorts of mixtures occurred.

d

After all the souls had chosen their lives, they went forward to Lachesis in the same order in which they had made their choices, and she assigned to each the daemon it had chosen as guardian of its life and fulfiller of its choice. This daemon first led the soul under the hand of Clotho as it turned the revolving spindle to confirm the fate that the lottery and its own choice had given it. After receiving her touch, he led the soul to the spinning of Atropos, to make what had been spun irreversible. Then, without turning around, they went from there under the throne of Necessity and, when all of them had passed through, they travelled to the Plain of Forgetfulness in burning, choking, terrible heat, for it was empty of trees and earthly vegetation. And there, beside the River of Unheeding, whose water no vessel can hold, they camped, for night was coming on. All of them had to drink a certain measure of this water, but those who weren't saved by reason drank more than that, and as each of them drank, he forgot everything and went to sleep. But around midnight there was a clap of thunder and an earthquake, and they were suddenly carried away from there, this way and that, up to their births, like shooting stars. Er himself was forbidden to drink from the water. All the same, he didn't know how he had come back to his body, except that waking up suddenly he saw himself lying on the pyre at dawn.

e

621

b

And so, Glaucon, his story wasn't lost but preserved, and it would save us, if we were persuaded by it, for we would then make a good crossing of the River of Forgetfulness, and our souls wouldn't be defiled. But if we are persuaded by me, we'll believe that the soul is immortal and able to endure every evil and every good, and we'll always hold to the upward path, practicing justice with reason in every way. That way we'll be friends both to ourselves and to the gods while we remain here on earth and afterwards—like victors in the games who go around collecting their prizes—we'll receive our rewards. Hence, both in this life and on the thousand-year journey we've described, we'll do well and be happy.

c

d

TIMAEUS

Timaeus offers the reader a rhetorical display, not a philosophical dialogue. In a stage-setting conversation, Socrates reviews his own previous day's exposition of the institutions of the ideal city (apparently those of the Republic*), but the remainder of the work is taken up by Timaeus' very long speech describing the creation of the world. Other works in the Platonic corpus similarly consist of a single speech: not to mention the* Apology, *the same is true of* Critias (Timaeus' *incomplete companion piece) and* Menexenus. *But* Timaeus' *speech is unique among them in having extensive philosophical content: here we get philosophy, but grandiose and rhetorically elaborate cosmic theorizing, not the down-to-earth dialectical investigation of most of Plato's philosophical works. For a parallel one has to look to* Phaedrus, *where Socrates' two speeches on erotic love, especially the second, similarly deck out philosophical theses in brilliant, image-studded rhetorical dress.*

Timaeus, who appears to be a dramatic invention of Plato's, comes from Southern Italy, noted for its Greek mathematicians and scientists. He bases his cosmology on the Platonic division, familiar for example from Phaedo *and* Republic, *between eternal, unchanging 'Forms' and their unstable 'reflections' in the physical, perceptible world of 'becoming'. But he introduces a creator god, the 'demiurge' (Greek for 'craftsman'), who crafts and brings order to the physical world by using the Forms as patterns—Timaeus does not conceive the Forms as themselves shaping the world. And he develops the theory of a 'receptacle' underlying physical things, onto which, as onto a featureless plastic stuff, the Formal patterns are imposed. In these terms, and emphasizing mathematical relationships as the basis for cosmic order, Timaeus sets out the foundations of the sciences of astronomy, physics, chemistry, and physiology, including the physiology and psychology of perception, ending with a classification of the diseases of body and soul and provisions for their treatment. Timaeus was a central text of Platonism in later antiquity and the Middle Ages—it was almost the only work of Plato's available in Latin—and the subject of many controversies. Did Timaeus' creation story mean that the world was created in time—or did it merely tell in temporal terms a story of the world's eternal dependence on a higher reality, the Forms? Did the demiurge really stand apart from those realities in designing it, or were they in fact simply the contents of his own divine mind? Timaeus was central to debates on these and other questions of traditional Platonism.*

Most scholars would date Timaeus *among Plato's last works, though a minority argue for a date in the 'middle period', closer to* Republic, *which it* seems certainly to postdate. Plato, as author of the work, is responsible for all Timaeus' theories. How far do they represent his own philosophical convictions at the time he wrote? Timaeus himself emphasizes—in effect, because of the great distance, literal and metaphorical, separating us from the heavens, on which the rest of the world depends—that we cannot have more than a 'likely story', not the full, transparent truth, about the physical details of the world's structure. It may be instructive to work out detailed theories, but he offers them as no more than reasonable ways in which the creator might have proceeded in designing the world. Moreover, according to the Phaedrus, rhetorically skilled speakers will base what they say on the full philosophical truth, but will vary and embellish it as needed to attract and hold their hearers' attention and to persuade them to accept what is essential in it. Timaeus may be Plato's spokesman, but if Plato attended to the Phaedrus's strictures on rhetoric in composing his speech, one should exercise more than ordinary caution in inferring from what Timaeus says to details of Plato's own commitments even on matters of philosophical principle. In what Timaeus says about 'being' and 'becoming', the Forms and 'reflections', the 'demiurge' and the 'receptacle', and the arguments he offers on these subjects, what belongs to the rhetorical embellishment—intended to impress Socrates and his other listeners—and what is the sober truth, as Plato now understands it? The dialogue forces these questions on us, but gives no easy answers.

J.M.C.

SOCRATES: One, two, three ... Where's number four, Timaeus? The four   17
of you were my guests yesterday and today I'm to be yours.

TIMAEUS: He came down with something or other, Socrates. He wouldn't have missed our meeting willingly.

SOCRATES: Well then, isn't it for you and your companions to fill in for your absent friend?

TIMAEUS: You're quite right. Anyhow, we'll do our best not to come up   b
short. You did such a fine job yesterday hosting us visitors that now it wouldn't be right if the three of us didn't go all out to give you a feast in return.

SOCRATES: Do you remember all the subjects I assigned to you to speak on?

TIMAEUS: Some we do. And if there are any we don't—well, you're here to remind us. Better still, if it's not too much trouble, why don't you take a few minutes to go back through them from the beginning? That way they'll be the more firmly fixed in our minds.

SOCRATES: Very well. I talked about politics yesterday and my main   c
point, I think, had to do with the kind of political structure cities should

Translated by Donald J. Zeyl.

have and the kind of men that should make it up so as to be the best possible.

TIMAEUS: Yes, Socrates, so you did, and we were all very satisfied with your description of it.

SOCRATES: Didn't we begin by separating off the class of farmers and all the other craftsmen in the city from the class of those who were to wage war on its behalf?

TIMAEUS: Yes.

d   SOCRATES: And we followed nature in giving each person only one occupation, one craft for which he was well suited. And so we said that only those whose job it was to wage war on everyone's behalf should be the guardians of the city. And if some foreigner or even a citizen were to go

18   against the city to cause trouble, these guardians should judge their own subjects lightly, since they are their natural friends. But they should be harsh, we said, with the enemies they encountered on the battlefield.

TIMAEUS: Yes, absolutely.

SOCRATES: That's because—as I think we said—the guardians' souls should have a nature that is at once both spirited and philosophical to the highest degree, to enable them to be appropriately gentle or harsh as the case may be.

TIMAEUS: Yes.

SOCRATES: What about their training? Didn't we say that they were to be given both physical and cultural training, as well as training in any other appropriate fields of learning?

TIMAEUS: We certainly did.

b   SOCRATES: Yes, and we said, I think, that those who received this training shouldn't consider gold or silver or anything else as their own private property. Like the professionals they are, they should receive from those under their protection a wage for their guardianship that's in keeping with their moderate way of life. And we said that they should share their expenses and spend their time together, live in one another's company, and devote their care above all to excellence, now that they were relieved of all other occupations.

TIMAEUS: Yes, we said that as well.

c   SOCRATES: And in fact we even made mention of women. We said that their natures should be made to correspond with those of men, and that all occupations, whether having to do with war or with the other aspects of life, should be common to both men and women.

TIMAEUS: That, too, was discussed.

SOCRATES: And what did we say about the procreation of children? We couldn't possibly forget that subject, because what we said about it was so unusual. We decided that they should all have spouses and children in common and that schemes should be devised to prevent anyone of them

d   from recognizing his or her own particular child. Everyone of them would believe that they all make up a single family, and that all who fall within their own age bracket are their sisters and brothers, that those who are older, who fall in an earlier bracket, are their parents or grandparents, while those who fall in a later one are their children or grandchildren.

TIMAEUS: You're right. That really was an unforgettable point.

SOCRATES: And surely we also remember saying, don't we, that to make their natures as excellent as possible right from the start, the rulers, male and female, should secretly arrange marriages by lot, to make sure that good men and bad ones would each as a group be separately matched up with women like themselves? And we said that this arrangement wouldn't create any animosity among them, because they'd believe that the matching was due to chance?

TIMAEUS: Yes, we remember.

SOCRATES: And do we also remember saying that the children of the good parents were to be brought up, while those of the bad ones were to be secretly handed on to another city? And that these children should be constantly watched as they grew up, so that the ones that turned out deserving might be taken back again and the ones they kept who did not turn out that way should change places with them?

TIMAEUS: We did say so.

SOCRATES: So now, Timaeus, are we done with our review of yesterday's talk—at least with its main points—or are we missing some point we made then? Have we left anything out?

TIMAEUS: Not a thing, Socrates. This is exactly what we said.

SOCRATES: All right, I'd like to go on now and tell you what I've come to feel about the political structure we've described. My feelings are like those of a man who gazes upon magnificent looking animals, whether they're animals in a painting or even actually alive but standing still, and who then finds himself longing to look at them in motion or engaged in some struggle or conflict that seems to show off their distinctive physical qualities. I felt the same thing about the city we've described. I'd love to listen to someone give a speech depicting our city in a contest with other cities, competing for those prizes that cities typically compete for. I'd love to see our city distinguish itself in the way it goes to war and in the way it pursues the war: that it deals with the other cities, one after another, in ways that reflect positively on its own education and training, both in word and deed—that is, both in how it behaves toward them and how it negotiates with them. Now on these matters, Critias and Hermocrates, I charge myself with being quite unable to sing fitting praise to our city and its men. That this should be so in my case isn't at all surprising. But I have come to have the same opinion of the poets, our ancient poets as well as today's. I have no disrespect for poets in general, but everyone knows that imitators as a breed are best and most adept at imitating the sort of things they've been trained to imitate. It's difficult enough for any one of them to do a decent job of imitating in performance, let alone in narrative description, anything that lies outside their training. And again, I've always thought that sophists as a class are very well versed in making long speeches and doing many other fine things. But because they wander from one city to the next and never settle down in homes of their own, I'm afraid their representations of those philosopher-statesmen would simply miss their mark. Sophists are bound to misrepresent whatever these leaders accomplish on the battlefield when they engage any of their enemies, whether in actual warfare or in negotiations.

So that leaves people of your sort, then. By nature as well as by training you take part in both philosophy and politics at once. Take Timaeus here.

20   He's from Locri, an Italian city under the rule of excellent laws. None of his compatriots outrank him in property or birth, and he has come to occupy positions of supreme authority and honor in his city. Moreover, he has, in my judgment, mastered the entire field of philosophy. As for Critias, I'm sure that all of us here in Athens know that he's no mere layman in any of the areas we're talking about. And many people whose testimony must surely be believed assure us that Hermocrates, too, is

b   well qualified by nature and training to deal with these matters. Already yesterday I was aware of this when you asked me to discuss matters of government, and that's why I was eager to do your bidding. I knew that if you'd agree to make the follow-up speech, no one could do a better job than you. No one today besides you could present our city pursuing a war that reflects her true character. Only you could give her all she requires. So now that I'm done speaking on my assigned subject, I've turned the tables and assigned you to speak on the subject I've just described. You've

c   thought about this together as a group, and you've agreed to reciprocate at this time. Your speeches are your hospitality gifts, and so here I am, all dressed up for the occasion. No one could be more prepared to receive your gifts than I.

HERMOCRATES: Yes indeed, Socrates, you won't find us short on enthusiasm, as Timaeus has already told you. We don't have the slightest excuse for not doing as you say. Why, already yesterday, right after we had left here and got to Critias' guest quarters where we're staying—and even

d   earlier on our way there—we were thinking about this very thing. And then Critias brought up a story that goes back a long way. Tell him the story now, Critias, so he can help us decide whether or not it will serve the purpose of our assignment.

CRITIAS: Yes, we really should, if our third partner, Timaeus, also agrees.

TIMAEUS: Of course I do.

CRITIAS: Let me tell you this story then, Socrates. It's a very strange one, but even so, every word of it is true. It's a story that Solon, the wisest of

e   the seven sages once vouched for. He was a kinsman and a very close friend of my great-grandfather Dropides. Solon himself says as much in many places in his poetry. Well, Dropides told the story to my grandfather Critias, and the old man in his turn would tell it to us from memory. The story is that our city had performed great and marvelous deeds in ancient times, which, owing to the passage of time and to the destruction of human life, have vanished. Of all these deeds one in particular was magnificent.

21   It is this one that we should now do well to commemorate and present

to you as our gift of thanks. In so doing we shall also offer the goddess a hymn, as it were, of just and true praise on this her festival.[1]

SOCRATES: Splendid! Tell me, though, what was that ancient deed our city performed, the one that Solon reported and old Critias told you about? I've never heard of it. They say it really happened?

CRITIAS: I'll tell you. It's an ancient story I heard from a man who was no youngster himself. In fact, at the time Critias was pretty close to ninety years old already—so he said—and I was around ten or so. As it happened, it was the day of the presentation of children during the Apaturia.[2] On this occasion, too, we children got the customary treatment at the feast: our fathers started a recitation contest. Many compositions by many different poets were recited, and many of us children got to sing the verses of Solon, because they were new at the time. Now someone, a member of our clan, said that he thought that Solon was not only the wisest of men in general, but that his poetry in particular showed him to be the most civilized of all the poets. (The man may have been speaking his mind, or else he may have just wanted to make Critias feel good.) And the old man—how well I remember it—was tickled. He grinned broadly and said, "Yes, Amynander, it's too bad that Solon wrote poetry only as a diversion and didn't seriously work at it like the other poets. And too bad that he never finished the story he'd brought back home with him from Egypt. He was forced to abandon that story on account of the civil conflicts and all the other troubles he found here when he returned. Otherwise not even Hesiod or Homer, or any other poet at all would ever have become more famous than he. That's what *I* think, anyhow." "Well, Critias? What story was that?" asked the other. "It's the story about the most magnificent thing our city has ever done," replied Critias, "an accomplishment that deserves to be known far better than any of her other achievements. But owing to the march of time and the fact that the men who accomplished it have perished, the story has not survived to the present." "Please tell us from the beginning," said the other, "What was this 'true story' that Solon heard? How did he get to hear it? Who told him?"

"In Egypt," Critias began, "in that part of the Delta where the stream of the Nile divides around the vertex there is a district called the Saïtic. The most important city of this district is Saïs. (This is in fact also the city from which King Amasis came.) This city was founded by a goddess whose name was 'Neith' in Egyptian and (according to the people there) 'Athena' in Greek. They are very friendly to Athens and claim to be related to our people somehow or other. Now Solon said that when he arrived there the people began to revere him. Furthermore, he said that when he asked those priests of theirs who were scholars of antiquity about ancient times,

---

1. The goddess is Athena, patron deity of Athens; the conversation is presumably taking place at the celebration of the Panathenaic Festival in Athens.

2. The Apaturia was celebrated in Athens in October–November of each year. The presentation of children took place on the third day.

he discovered that just about every Greek, including himself, was all but completely ignorant about such matters. On one occasion, wanting to lead them on to talk about antiquity, he broached the subject of our own ancient history. He started talking about Phoroneus—the first human being, it is

b said—and about Niobe, and then he told the story of how Deucalion and Pyrrha survived the flood. He went on to trace the lines of descent of their posterity, and tried to compute their dates by calculating the number of years which had elapsed since the events of which he spoke. And then one of the priests, a very old man, said, 'Ah, Solon, Solon, you Greeks are ever children. There isn't an old man among you.' On hearing this, Solon said, 'What? What do you mean?' 'You are young,' the old priest replied, 'young in soul, every one of you. Your souls are devoid of beliefs about antiquity handed down by ancient tradition. Your souls lack any learning

c made hoary by time. The reason for that is this: There have been, and there will continue to be, numerous disasters that have destroyed human life in many kinds of ways. The most serious of these involve fire and water, while the lesser ones have numerous other causes. And so also among your people the tale is told that Phaethon, child of the Sun, once harnessed his father's chariot, but was unable to drive it along his father's course. He ended up burning everything on the earth's surface and was destroyed himself when a lightning bolt struck him. This tale is told as a

d myth, but the truth behind it is that there is a deviation in the heavenly bodies that travel around the earth, which causes huge fires that destroy what is on the earth across vast stretches of time. When this happens all those people who live in mountains or in places that are high and dry are much more likely to perish than the ones who live next to rivers or by the sea. Our Nile, always our savior, is released and at such times, too, saves us from this disaster. On the other hand, whenever the gods send floods of water upon the earth to purge it, the herdsmen and shepherds

e in the mountains preserve their lives, while those who live in cities, in your region, are swept by the rivers into the sea. But here, in this place, water does not flow from on high onto our fields, either at such a time or any other. On the contrary, its nature is always to rise up from below. This, then, explains the fact that the antiquities preserved here are said to be the most ancient. The truth is that in all places where neither inordinate

23 cold nor heat prevent it, the human race will continue to exist, sometimes in greater, sometimes in lesser numbers. Now of all the events reported to us, no matter where they've occurred—in your parts or in ours—if there are any that are noble or great or distinguished in some other way, they've all been inscribed here in our temples and preserved from antiquity on. In your case, on the other hand, as in that of others, no sooner have you achieved literacy and all the other resources that cities require, than there again, after the usual number of years, comes the heavenly flood. It sweeps

b upon you like a plague, and leaves only your illiterate and uncultured people behind. You become infants all over again, as it were, completely unfamiliar with anything there was in ancient times, whether here or in your own region. And so, Solon, the account you just gave of your people's lineage is just like a nursery tale. First of all, you people remember only one flood, though in fact there had been a great many before. Second, you are unaware of the fact that the finest and best of all the races of humankind once lived in your region. This is the race from whom you yourself, your whole city, all that you and your countrymen have today, are sprung, c thanks to the survival of a small portion of their stock. But this has escaped you, because for many generations the survivors passed on without leaving a written record. Indeed, Solon, there was a time, before the greatest of these devastating floods, when the city that is Athens today not only excelled in war but also distinguished itself by the excellence of its laws in every area. Its accomplishments and its social arrangements are said to have been the finest of all those under heaven of which we have re- d ceived report.'

"When Solon heard this he was astounded, he said, and with unreserved eagerness begged the priests to give him a detailed, consecutive account of all that concerned those ancient citizens. 'I won't grudge you this, Solon,' the priest replied. 'I'll tell you the story for your own benefit as well as your city's, and especially in honor of our patron goddess who has founded, nurtured and educated our cities, both yours and ours. Yours she founded first, a thousand years before ours, when she had received e from Earth and Hephaestus the seed from which your people were to come. Now our social arrangement, according to the records inscribed in our sacred documents, is eight thousand years old. Nine thousand years ago, then, did these fellow citizens of yours live, whose laws and whose finest achievement I'll briefly describe to you. At another time we'll go 24 through all the details one by one at our leisure and inspect the documents themselves.

"'Let's compare your ancient laws with ours today. You'll discover many instances that once existed among you, existing among us today. First, you'll find that the class of priests is marked off and separated from the other classes. Next, in the case of the working class, you'll find that each group—the herdsmen, the hunters and the farmers—works independently, without mixing with the others. In particular, I'm sure you've noticed that b our warrior class has been separated from all the others. It's been assigned by law to occupy itself exclusively with matters of war. Moreover, the style of armor used is that of shields and spears, which we were the first among the peoples of Asia to use for arming ourselves. The goddess instructed us just as she first instructed you in the regions where you live. Moreover, as for wisdom, I'm sure you can see how much attention our way of life here has devoted to it, right from the beginning. In our study c of the world order we have traced all our discoveries, including prophecy and health-restoring medicine, from those divine realities to human levels, and we have also acquired all the other related disciplines. This is in fact nothing less than the very same system of social order that the goddess first devised for you when she founded your city, which she did once she had chosen the region in which your people were born, and had discerned that the temperate climate in it throughout the seasons would bring forth

d   men of surpassing wisdom. And, being a lover of both war and wisdom, the goddess chose the region that was likely to bring forth men most like herself, and founded it first. And so you came to live there, and to observe laws such as these. In fact your laws improved even more, so that you came to surpass all other peoples in every excellence, as could be expected from those whose begetting and nurture were divine.

"'Now many great accomplishments of your city recorded here are awe-

e   inspiring, but there is one that surely surpasses them all in magnitude and excellence. The records speak of a vast power that your city once brought to a halt in its insolent march against the whole of Europe and Asia at once—a power that sprang forth from beyond, from the Atlantic ocean. For at that time this ocean was passable, since it had an island in it in front of the strait that you people say you call the 'Pillars of Heracles.' [3] This island was larger than Libya and Asia combined, and it provided passage to the other islands for people who traveled in those days. From

25 those islands one could then travel to the entire continent on the other side, which surrounds that real sea beyond. Everything here inside the strait we're talking about seems nothing but a harbor with a narrow entrance, whereas that really is an ocean out there and the land that embraces it all the way around truly deserves to be called a continent. Now on this Isle of Atlantis a great and marvelous royal power established itself, and ruled not only the whole island, but many of the other islands and parts of the continent as well. What's more, their rule extended even inside the

b   strait, over Libya as far as Egypt, and over Europe as far as Tyrrhenia.[4] Now one day this power gathered all of itself together, and set out to enslave all of the territory inside the strait, including your region and ours, in one fell swoop. Then it was, Solon, that your city's might shone bright with excellence and strength, for all humankind to see. Preeminent among all others in the nobility of her spirit and in her use of all the arts of war,

c   she first rose to the leadership of the Greek cause. Later, forced to stand alone, deserted by her allies, she reached a point of extreme peril. Nevertheless she overcame the invaders and erected her monument of victory. She prevented the enslavement of those not yet enslaved, and generously freed all the rest of us who lived within the boundaries of Heracles. Some time

d   later excessively violent earthquakes and floods occurred, and after the onset of an unbearable day and a night, your entire warrior force sank below the earth all at once, and the Isle of Atlantis likewise sank below the sea and disappeared. That is how the ocean in that region has come

3. The strait of Gibraltar.

4. South of the Mediterranean the empire extended across North Africa to the western frontier of Egypt. To the north it included Europe as far east as central Italy.

to be even now unnavigable and unexplorable, obstructed as it is by a layer of mud at a shallow depth,[5] the residue of the island as it settled.'"

What I've just related, Socrates, is a concise version of old Critias' story, as Solon originally reported it. While you were speaking yesterday about politics and the men you were describing, I was reminded of what I've just told you and was quite amazed as I realized how by some supernatural chance your ideas are on the mark, in substantial agreement with what Solon said. I didn't want to say so at the time, though. Because it had been so long ago, I didn't remember Solon's story very well. So I realized that I would first have to recover the whole story for myself well enough, and then to tell it that way. That's why I was so quick to agree to your assignment yesterday. The most important task in situations like these is to propose a speech that rewards people's expectations, and so I thought that we would be well supplied if I gave this one. And that's how—as Hermocrates has already said—the moment I left here yesterday, I began to repeat the story to him and to Timaeus as it came back to me. After I left them I concentrated on it during the night and recovered just about the whole thing. They say that the lessons of childhood have a marvelous way of being retained. How true that is! In my case, I don't know if I'd be able to recall everything I heard yesterday, but I'd be extremely surprised if any part of this story has gotten away from me, even though it's been a very long time since I heard it. What I heard then gave me so much childlike pleasure—the old man was so eager to teach me because I kept on asking one question after another—that the story has stayed with me like the indelible markings of a picture with the colors burnt in. Besides, I told the whole story to Timaeus and Hermocrates first thing this morning, so that not just I, but they, too, would have a supply of material for our speech.

I've said all this, Socrates, to prepare myself to tell Solon's story now. I won't just give you the main points, but the details, one by one, just the way I heard it. We'll translate the citizens and the city you described to us in mythical fashion yesterday to the realm of fact, and place it before us as though it is ancient Athens itself. And we'll say that the citizens you imagined are the very ones the priest spoke about, our actual ancestors. The congruence will be complete, and our song will be in tune if we say that your imaginary citizens are the ones who really existed at that time. We'll share the task among us, and we'll all try our best to do justice to your assignment. What do you think, Socrates? Will this do as our speech, or should we look for another to replace it?

SOCRATES: Well, Critias, what other speech could we possibly prefer to this one? We're in the midst of celebrating the festival of the goddess, and this speech really fits the occasion. So it couldn't be more appropriate. And of course the fact that it's no made-up story but a true account is no

---

5. Reading *kata bracheos* in d5.

small matter. How and where shall we find others to celebrate if we let these men go? We've no choice. Go on with your speech, then, and good

27 luck! It's my turn now to sit back and listen to your speeches that pay back mine of yesterday.

CRITIAS: All right, Socrates, what do you think of the plan we've arranged for our guest gift to you? We thought that because Timaeus is our expert in astronomy and has made it his main business to know the nature of the universe, he should speak first, beginning with the origin of the universe, and concluding with the nature of human beings. Then I'll go next, once I'm in possession of Timaeus' account of the origin of human beings

b   and your account of how some of them came to have a superior education. I'll introduce them, as not only Solon's account but also his law would have it, into our courtroom and make them citizens of our ancient city— as really being those Athenians of old whom the report of the sacred records has rescued from obscurity—and from then on I'll speak of them as actual Athenian citizens.

SOCRATES: Apparently I'll be getting a complete, brilliant banquet of speeches in payment for my own. Very well then, Timaeus, the task of being our next speaker seems to fall to you. Why don't you make an invocation to the gods, as we customarily do?

c   TIMAEUS: That I will, Socrates. Surely anyone with any sense at all will always call upon a god before setting out on any venture, whatever its importance. In our case, we are about to make speeches about the universe—whether it has an origin or even if it does not[6]—and so if we're not to go completely astray we have no choice but to call upon the gods and goddesses, and pray that they above all will approve of all we have

d   to say, and that in consequence we will, too. Let this, then, be our appeal to the gods; to ourselves we must appeal to make sure that you learn as easily as possible, and that I instruct you in the subject matter before us in the way that best conveys my intent.

As I see it, then, we must begin by making the following distinction: What is *that which always is* and has no becoming, and what is *that which*

28 *becomes*[7] but never is? The former is grasped by understanding, which involves a reasoned account. It is unchanging. The latter is grasped by opinion, which involves unreasoning sense perception. It comes to be and passes away, but never really is. Now everything that comes to be[8] must of necessity come to be by the agency of some cause, for it is impossible for anything to come to be without a cause. So whenever the craftsman[9]

6. Reading *ei gegonen ē kai agenes estin* in c5.

7. Omitting *aei* in a1.

8. "Becoming" and "coming to be" here as elsewhere translate the same Greek word, *genesis*, and its cognates; the Greek word does not say, as English "comes to be" does, that once a thing has come to be, it now *is*, or has *being*.

9. Greek *dēmiourgos*, also sometimes translated below as "maker" (40c2, 41a7) or "fashioner" (69c3)—whence the divine "Demiurge" one reads about in accounts of the *Timaeus*.

looks at what is always changeless and, using a thing of that kind as his model, reproduces its form and character, then, of necessity, all that he so completes is beautiful. But were he to look at a thing that has come to be and use as his model something that has been begotten, his work will lack beauty.

Now as to the whole universe[10] or world order [*kosmos*]—let's just call it by whatever name is most acceptable in a given context—there is a question we need to consider first. This is the sort of question one should begin with in inquiring into any subject. Has it always existed? Was there no origin from which it came to be? Or did it come to be and take its start from some origin? It has come to be. For it is both visible and tangible and it has a body—and all things of that kind are perceptible. And, as we have shown, perceptible things are grasped by opinion, which involves sense perception. As such, they are things that come to be, things that are begotten. Further, we maintain that, necessarily, that which comes to be must come to be by the agency of some cause. Now to find the maker and father of this universe [*to pan*] is hard enough, and even if I succeeded, to declare him to everyone is impossible. And so we must go back and raise this question about the universe: Which of the two models did the maker use when he fashioned it? Was it the one that does not change and stays the same, or the one that has come to be? Well, if this world of ours is beautiful and its craftsman good, then clearly he looked at the eternal model. But if what it's blasphemous to even say is the case, then he looked at one that has come to be. Now surely it's clear to all that it was the eternal model he looked at, for, of all the things that have come to be, our universe is the most beautiful, and of causes the craftsman is the most excellent. This, then, is how it has come to be: it is a work of craft, modeled after that which is changeless and is grasped by a rational account, that is, by wisdom.

Since these things are so, it follows by unquestionable necessity that this world is an image of something. Now in every subject it is of utmost importance to begin at the natural beginning, and so, on the subject of an image and its model, we must make the following specification: the accounts we give of things have the same character as the subjects they set forth. So accounts of what is stable and fixed and transparent to understanding are themselves stable and unshifting. We must do our very best to make these accounts as irrefutable and invincible as any account may be. On the other hand, accounts we give of that which has been formed to be like that reality, since they are accounts of what is a likeness, are themselves likely, and stand in proportion to the previous accounts, i.e., what being is to becoming, truth is to convincingness. Don't be surprised then, Socrates, if it turns out repeatedly that we won't be able to produce accounts on a great many subjects—on gods or the coming to be of the universe—that are completely and perfectly consistent and accurate. Instead, if we can

b

c

29

b

c

10. *Ouranos*, i.e., "heaven."

come up with accounts no less likely than any, we ought to be content, keeping in mind that both I, the speaker, and you, the judges, are only

d   human. So we should accept the likely tale on these matters. It behooves us not to look for anything beyond this.

SOCRATES: Bravo, Timaeus! By all means! We must accept it as you say we should. This overture of yours was marvellous. Go on now and let us have the work itself.

TIMAEUS: Very well then. Now why did he who framed this whole

e   universe of becoming frame it? Let us state the reason why: He was good, and one who is good can never become jealous of anything. And so, being free of jealousy, he wanted everything to become as much like himself as was possible. In fact, men of wisdom will tell you (and you couldn't do

30 better than to accept their claim) that this, more than anything else, was the most preeminent reason for the origin of the world's coming to be. The god wanted everything to be good and nothing to be bad so far as that was possible, and so he took over all that was visible—not at rest but in discordant and disorderly motion—and brought it from a state of disorder to one of order, because he believed that order was in every way better than disorder. Now it wasn't permitted (nor is it now) that one who is

b   supremely good should do anything but what is best. Accordingly, the god reasoned and concluded that in the realm of things naturally visible no unintelligent thing could as a whole be better than anything which does possess intelligence as a whole, and he further concluded that it is impossible for anything to come to possess intelligence apart from soul. Guided by this reasoning, he put intelligence in soul, and soul in body, and so he constructed the universe. He wanted to produce a piece of work that would be as excellent and supreme as its nature would allow. This, then, in keeping with our likely account, is how we must say divine

c   providence brought our world into being as a truly living thing, endowed with soul and intelligence.

This being so, we have to go on to speak about what comes next. When the maker made our world, what living thing did he make it resemble? Let us not stoop to think that it was any of those that have the natural character of a part, for nothing that is a likeness of anything incomplete could ever turn out beautiful. Rather, let us lay it down that the universe resembles more closely than anything else that Living Thing of which all other living things are parts, both individually and by kinds. For that Living Thing comprehends within itself all intelligible living things, just

d   as our world is made up of us and all the other visible creatures. Since the god wanted nothing more than to make the world like the best of the intelligible things, complete in every way, he made it a single visible living

31 thing, which contains within itself all the living things whose nature it is to share its kind.

Have we been correct in speaking of *one* universe, or would it have been more correct to say that there are many, in fact infinitely many universes? There is but one universe, if it is to have been crafted after its model. For that which contains all of the intelligible living things couldn't ever be one of a pair, since that would require there to be yet another Living Thing, the one that contained those two, of which they then would be parts, and then it would be more correct to speak of our universe as made in the likeness, now not of those two, but of that other, the one that contains them. So, in order that this living thing should be like the complete Living Thing in respect of uniqueness, the Maker made neither two, nor yet an infinite number of worlds. On the contrary, our universe came to be as the one and only thing of its kind, is so now and will continue to be so in the future.

Now that which comes to be must have bodily form, and be both visible and tangible, but nothing could ever become visible apart from fire, nor tangible without something solid, nor solid without earth. That is why, as he began to put the body of the universe together, the god came to make it out of fire and earth. But it isn't possible to combine two things well all by themselves, without a third; there has to be some bond between the two that unites them. Now the best bond is one that really and truly makes a unity of itself together with the things bonded by it, and this in the nature of things is best accomplished by proportion. For whenever of three numbers which are either solids[11] or squares the middle term between any two of them is such that what the first term is to it, it is to the last, and, conversely, what the last term is to the middle, it is to the first, then, since the middle term turns out to be both first and last, and the last and the first likewise both turn out to be middle terms, they will all of necessity turn out to have the same relationship to each other, and, given this, will all be unified.

So if the body of the universe were to have come to be as a two dimensional plane, a single middle term would have sufficed to bind together its conjoining terms with itself. As it was, however, the universe was to be a solid, and solids are never joined together by just one middle term but always by two. Hence the god set water and air between fire and earth, and made them as proportionate to one another as was possible, so that what fire is to air, air is to water, and what air is to water, water is to earth. He then bound them together and thus he constructed the visible and tangible universe. This is the reason why these four particular constituents were used to beget the body of the world, making it a symphony of proportion.[12] They bestowed friendship[13] upon it, so that, having come

---

11. "Solids" are cubes (e.g., $2 \times 2 \times 2$, or 8).

12. A simple example of a proportionate progression that satisfies Plato's requirements in 32a might be that of 2, 4, 8. So: 2:4::4:8 (the first term is to the middle what the middle is to the last, the last term is to the middle what the middle is to the first); 4:2::8:4 or 4:8::2:4 (the middle term turns out to be first and last and the first and last terms turn out to be middles). Since, however, the body of the world is three-dimensional, its components must be represented by "solid" numbers (see previous note). This will require two middle terms.

13. Compare *Gorgias* 508a: ". . . Wise men claim that partnership and friendship . . . hold together heaven and earth . . . and that is why they call this universe a *world-order* . . ."

together into a unity with itself, it could not be undone by anyone but the one who had bound it together.

Now each one of the four constituents was entirely used up in the process of building the world. The builder built it from all the fire, water, air and earth there was, and left no part or power of any of them out. His intentions in so doing were these: First, that as a living thing it should be as whole and complete as possible and made up of complete parts. Second, that it should be just one universe, in that nothing would be left over from which another one just like it could be made. Third, that it should not get old and diseased. He realized that when heat or cold or anything else that possesses strong powers surrounds a composite body from outside and attacks it, it destroys that body prematurely, brings disease and old age upon it and so causes it to waste away. That is why he concluded that he should fashion the world as a single whole, composed of all wholes, complete and free of old age and disease, and why he fashioned it that way. And he gave it a shape appropriate to the kind of thing it was. The appropriate shape for that living thing that is to contain within itself all the living things would be the one which embraces within itself all the shapes there are. Hence he gave it a round shape, the form of a sphere, with its center equidistant from its extremes in all directions. This of all shapes is the most complete and most like itself, which he gave to it because he believed that likeness is incalculably more excellent than unlikeness. And he gave it a smooth round finish all over on the outside, for many reasons. It needed no eyes, since there was nothing visible left outside it; nor did it need ears, since there was nothing audible there, either. There was no air enveloping it that it might need for breathing, nor did it need any organ by which to take in food or, again, expel it when it had been digested. For since there wasn't anything else, there would be nothing to leave it or come to it from anywhere. It supplied its own waste for its food. Anything that it did or experienced it was designed to do or experience within itself and by itself. For the builder thought that if it were self-sufficient, it would be a better thing than if it required other things.

And since it had no need to catch hold of or fend off anything, the god thought that it would be pointless to attach hands to it. Nor would it need feet or any support to stand on. In fact, he awarded it the movement suited to its body—that one of the seven motions which is especially associated with understanding and intelligence. And so he set it turning continuously in the same place, spinning around upon itself. All the other six motions he took away, and made its movement free of their wanderings. And since it didn't need feet to follow this circular path, he begat it without legs or feet.

Applying this entire train of reasoning to the god that was yet to be, the eternal god made it smooth and even all over, equal from the center, a whole and complete body itself, but also made up of complete bodies. In its center he set a soul, which he extended throughout the whole body, and with which he then covered the body outside. And he set it to turn in a circle, a single solitary universe, whose very excellence enables it to keep its own company without requiring anything else. For its knowledge of and friendship with itself is enough. All this, then, explains why this world which he begat for himself is a blessed god.

As for the world's soul, even though we are now embarking on an account of it *after* we've already given an account of its body, it isn't the case that the god devised it to be younger than the body. For the god would not have united them and then allow the elder to be ruled by the younger. We have a tendency to be casual and random in our speech, reflecting, no doubt, the whole realm of the casual and random of which we are a part. The god, however, gave priority and seniority to the soul, both in its coming to be and in the degree of its excellence, to be the body's mistress and to rule over it as her subject.

The components from which he made the soul and the way in which he made it were as follows: In between the *Being* that is indivisible and always changeless, and the one that is divisible and comes to be in the corporeal realm, he mixed a third, intermediate form of being, derived from the other two. Similarly, he made a mixture of the *Same*, and then one of the *Different*, in between their indivisible and their corporeal, divisible counterparts. And he took the three mixtures and mixed them together to make a uniform mixture, forcing the Different, which was hard to mix, into conformity with the Same. Now when he had mixed these two together with Being, and from the three had made a single mixture, he redivided the whole mixture into as many parts as his task required,[14] each part remaining a mixture of the Same, the Different, and of Being. This is how he began the division: first he took one portion away from the whole, and then he took another, twice as large, followed by a third, one and a half times as large as the second and three times as large as the first. The fourth portion he took was twice as large as the second, the fifth three times as large as the third, the sixth eight times that of the first, and the seventh twenty-seven times that of the first.

After this he went on to fill the double and triple intervals by cutting off still more portions from the mixture and placing these between them, in such a way that in each interval there were two middle terms, one exceeding the first extreme by the same fraction of the extremes by which it was exceeded by the second, and the other exceeding the first extreme by a number equal to that by which it was exceeded by the second. These connections produced intervals of 3/2, 4/3, and 9/8 within the previous intervals. He then proceeded to fill all the 4/3 intervals with the 9/8 interval, leaving a small portion over every time. The terms of this interval of the portion left over made a numerical ratio of 256/243. And so it was that the mixture, from which he had cut off these portions, was eventually completely used up.

c

35

b

36

b

---

14. In order to establish in the soul, through connected geometrical proportions, the source of the harmonious order it needs to impart to the three-dimensional body of the world, and in particular to the heaven and the bodies it contains.

Next, he sliced this entire compound in two along its length, joined the
c   two halves together center to center like an X, and bent them back in a
circle, attaching each half to itself end to end and to the ends of the other
half at the point opposite to the one where they had been joined together.
He then included them in that motion which revolves in the same place
without variation, and began to make the one the outer, and the other
the inner circle. And he decreed that the outer movement should be the
movement of *the Same*, while the inner one should be that of *the Different*.[15]
He made the movement of the Same revolve toward the right by way of
the side, and that of the Different toward the left by way of the diagonal,
d   and he made the revolution of the Same, i.e., the uniform, the dominant
one in that he left this one alone undivided, while he divided the inner
one six times, to make seven unequal circles.[16] His divisions corresponded
to the several double and triple intervals, of which there were three each.
He set the circles to go in contrary directions: three to go at the same
speed, and the other four to go at speeds different from both each other's
and that of the other three. Their speeds, however, were all proportionate
to each other.

Once the whole soul had acquired a form that pleased him, he who
e   formed it went on to fashion inside it all that is corporeal, and, joining
center to center, he fitted the two together. The soul was woven together
with the body from the center on out in every direction to the outermost
limit of the universe, and covered it all around on the outside. And,
revolving within itself, it initiated a divine beginning of unceasing, intelligent life for all time. Now while the body of the universe had come to be
as a visible thing, the soul was invisible. But even so, because it shares in
37   reason and harmony, the soul came to be as the most excellent of all the
things begotten by him who is himself most excellent of all that is intelligible
and eternal.

Because the soul is a mixture of the Same, the Different and Being (the
three components we've described), because it was divided up and bound
together in various proportions, and because it circles round upon itself,
then, whenever it comes into contact with something whose being is scatter-
able or else with something whose being is indivisible, it is stirred throughout its whole self. It then declares what exactly that thing is the same as,
b   or what it is different from, and in what respect and in what manner, as
well as when, it turns out that they are the same or different and are

15. The outer band is the circle responsible for the constant daily rotation of the fixed
stars—hence for the "movement of *the Same*." The inner band is the circle responsible
for contrary movements in the Zodiac of the seven "wandering" stars (moon and sun,
plus the five planets known to the ancients)—hence for the "movements of *the Different*."
16. These circles or bands are the ones responsible for the individual movements in the
Zodiac respectively of moon, sun, Mercury, Venus, Mars, Jupiter, and Saturn, the seven
"wanderers" (see 38c–d). The sun, Venus, and Mercury are the three mentioned just
below as going "at the same speed" (see 38d).

characterized as such. This applies both to the things that come to be, and to those that are always changeless. And when this contact gives rise to an account that is equally true whether it is about what is different or about what is the same, and is borne along without utterance or sound within the self-moved thing, then, whenever the account concerns anything that is perceptible, the circle of the Different goes straight and proclaims it throughout its whole soul. This is how firm and true opinions and convictions come about. Whenever, on the other hand, the account concerns   c
any object of reasoning, and the circle of the Same runs well and reveals it, the necessary result is understanding and knowledge. And if anyone should ever call that in which these two arise, not soul but something else, what he says will be anything but true.

Now when the Father who had begotten the universe observed it set in motion and alive, a thing that had come to be as a shrine for the everlasting gods, he was well pleased, and in his delight he thought of making it more like its model still. So, as the model was itself an everlasting Living Thing,   d
he set himself to bringing this universe to completion in such a way that it, too, would have that character to the extent that was possible. Now it was the Living Thing's nature to be eternal, but it isn't possible to bestow eternity fully upon anything that is begotten. And so he began to think of making a moving image of eternity: at the same time as he brought order to the universe, he would make an eternal image, moving according to number, of eternity remaining in unity. This number, of course, is what we now call "time."

For before the heavens came to be, there were no days or nights, no   e
months or years. But now, at the same time as he framed the heavens, he devised their coming to be. These all are parts of time, and *was* and *will be* are forms of time that have come to be. Such notions we unthinkingly but incorrectly apply to everlasting being. For we say that it *was* and *is* and *will be*, but according to the true account only *is* is appropriately said   38
of it. *Was* and *will be* are properly said about the becoming that passes in time, for these two are motions. But that which is always changeless and motionless cannot become either older or younger in the course of time— it neither ever became so, nor is it now such that it has become so, nor will it ever be so in the future. And all in all, none of the characteristics that becoming has bestowed upon the things that are borne about in the realm of perception are appropriate to it. These, rather, are forms of time that have come to be—time that imitates eternity and circles according to number. And what is more, we also say things like these: that what has   b
come to be *is* what has come to be, that what is coming to be *is* what is coming to be, and also that what will come to be *is* what will come to be, and that what is not *is* what is not. None of these expressions of ours is accurate. But I don't suppose this is a good time right now to be too meticulous about these matters.

Time, then, came to be together with the universe so that just as they were begotten together, they might also be undone together, should there

ever be an undoing of them. And it came to be after the model of that
c   which is sempiternal, so that it might be as much like its model as possible.
For the model is something that has being for all eternity, while it, on the
other hand, has been, is, and shall be for all time, forevermore. Such was
the reason, then, such the god's design for the coming to be of time, that
he brought into being the Sun, the Moon and five other stars, for the
begetting of time. These are called "wanderers," and they came to be in
order to set limits to and stand guard over the numbers of time. When
the god had finished making a body for each of them, he placed them into
d   the orbits traced by the period of the Different—seven bodies in seven
orbits. He set the Moon in the first circle, around the earth, and the Sun
in the second, above it. The Dawnbearer (the Morning Star, or Venus) and
the star said to be sacred to Hermes (Mercury) he set to run in circles that
equal the Sun's in speed, though they received the power contrary to its
power. As a result, the Sun, the star of Hermes and the Dawnbearer alike
overtake and are overtaken by one another. As for the other bodies, if I
were to spell out where he situated them, and all his reasons for doing
e   so, my account, already a digression, would make more work than its
purpose calls for. Perhaps later on we could at our leisure give this subject
the exposition it deserves.

Now when each of the bodies that were to cooperate in producing time
had come into the movement prepared for carrying it and when, bound
by bonds of soul, these bodies had been begotten with life and learned
their assigned tasks, they began to revolve along the movement of the
39   Different, which is oblique and which goes through the movement of the
Same, by which it is also dominated.[17] Some bodies would move in a larger
circle, others in a smaller one, the latter moving more quickly and the
former more slowly. Indeed, because of the movement of the Same, the
ones that go around most quickly appeared to be overtaken by those going
more slowly, even though in fact they were overtaking them. For as it
revolves, this movement gives to all these circles a spiral twist, because
b   they are moving forward in two contrary directions at once. As a result,
it makes that body which departs most slowly from it—and it is the fastest
of the movements—appear closest to it.

And so that there might be a conspicuous measure of their relative
slowness and quickness with which[18] they move along in their eight revolutions, the god kindled a light in the orbit second from the earth, the light
that we now call the Sun. Its chief work would be to shine upon the whole
universe and to bestow upon all those living things appropriately endowed
and taught by the revolution of the Same and the uniform, a share in
c   number. In this way and for these reasons night-and-day, the period of a
single circling, the wisest one, came to be. A month has passed when the

17. Reading *iousan . . . kratoumenēn* in a1–2.
18. Accepting the emendation *kath'ha* in b3.

Moon has completed its own cycle and overtaken the Sun; a year when the Sun has completed its own cycle.

As for the periods of the other bodies, all but a scattered few have failed to take any note of them. Nobody has given them names or investigated their numerical measurements relative to each other. And so people are all but ignorant of the fact that time really is the wanderings of these bodies, bewilderingly numerous as they are and astonishingly variegated. It is none the less possible, however, to discern that the perfect number of time brings to completion the perfect year at that moment when the relative speeds of all eight periods have been completed together and, measured by the circle of the Same that moves uniformly, have achieved their consummation. This, then, is how as well as why those stars were begotten which, on their way through the universe, would have turnings. The purpose was to make this living thing as like as possible to that perfect and intelligible Living Thing, by way of imitating its sempiternity.

Prior to the coming to be of time, the universe had already been made to resemble in various respects the model in whose likeness the god was making it, but the resemblance still fell short in that it didn't yet contain all the living things that were to have come to be within it. This remaining task he went on to perform, casting the world into the nature of its model. And so he determined that the living thing he was making should possess the same kinds and numbers of living things as those which, according to the discernment of Intellect, are contained within the real Living Thing. Now there are four of these kinds: first, the heavenly race of gods; next, the kind that has wings and travels through the air; third, the kind that lives in water; and fourth, the kind that has feet and lives on land. The gods he made mostly out of fire, to be the brightest and fairest to the eye.[19] He made them well-rounded, to resemble the universe, and placed them in the wisdom of the dominant circle [i.e., of the Same], to follow the course of the universe. He spread the gods throughout the whole heaven to be a true adornment [*kosmos*] for it, an intricately wrought whole. And he bestowed two movements upon each of them. The first was rotation, an unvarying movement in the same place, by which the god would always think the same thoughts about the same things. The other was revolution, a forward motion under the dominance of the circular carrying movement of the Same and uniform. With respect to the other five motions, the gods are immobile and stationary, in order that each of them may come as close as possible to attaining perfection.

This, then, was the reason why all those everlasting and unwandering stars—divine living things which stay fixed by revolving without variation in the same place—came to be. Those that have turnings and thus wander in that sort of way came to be as previously described.

d

e

40

b

---

19. These are the fixed stars, i.e., those other than the moon, sun, and planets, which have already been created (cf. below, 40b).

The Earth he devised to be our nurturer, and, because it winds around
c   the axis that stretches throughout the universe, also to be the maker and
guardian of day and night. Of the gods that have come to be within the
universe, Earth ranks as the foremost, the one with greatest seniority.

To describe the dancing movements of these gods, their juxtapositions
and the back-circlings and advances of their circular courses on themselves;
to tell which of the gods come into line with one another at their conjunc-
tions and how many of them are in opposition, and in what order and at
which times they pass in front of or behind one another, so that some are
occluded from our view to reappear once again, thereby bringing terrors
d   and portents of things to come to those who cannot reason—to tell all this
without the use of visible models would be labor spent in vain. We will
make do with this account, and so let this be the conclusion of our discussion of the nature of the visible and generated gods.

As for the other spiritual beings [*daimones*], it is beyond our task to know
and speak of how they came to be. We should accept on faith the assertions
of those figures of the past who claimed to be the offspring of gods. They
must surely have been well informed about their own ancestors. So we
e   cannot avoid believing the children of gods, even though their accounts
lack plausible or compelling proofs. Rather, we should follow custom and
believe them, on the ground that what they claim to be reporting are
matters of their own concern. Accordingly, let us accept their account of
how these gods came to be and state what it is.

Earth and Heaven gave birth to Ocean and Tethys, who in turn gave
birth to Phorcys, Cronus and Rhea and all the gods in that generation.
41   Cronus and Rhea gave birth to Zeus and Hera, as well as all those siblings
who are called by names we know. These in turn gave birth to yet another
generation. In any case, when all the gods had come to be, both the
ones who make their rounds conspicuously and the ones who present
themselves only to the extent that they are willing, the begetter of this
universe spoke to them. This is what he said:

"O gods, works divine whose maker and father I am, whatever has
come to be by my hands cannot be undone but by my consent.[20] Now
b   while it is true that anything that is bound is liable to being undone, still,
only one who is evil would consent to the undoing of what has been well
fitted together and is in fine condition. This is the reason why you, as
creatures that have come to be, are neither completely immortal nor exempt
from being undone. Still, you will not be undone nor will death be your
portion, since you have received the guarantee of my will—a greater, more
sovereign bond than those with which you were bound when you came
to be. Learn now, therefore, what I declare to you. There remain still three
kinds of mortal beings that have not yet been begotten; and as long as
they have not come to be, the universe will be incomplete, for it will still
c   lack within it all the kinds of living things it must have if it is to be

---

20. Accepting the emendation *theiōn* and the supplement <*ta*> before *di' emou* in a7.

sufficiently complete. But if these creatures came to be and came to share in life by my hand, they would rival the gods. It is you, then, who must turn yourselves to the task of fashioning these living things, as your nature allows. This will assure their mortality, and this whole universe will really be a completed whole. Imitate the power I used in causing you to be. And to the extent that it is fitting for them to possess something that shares our name of 'immortal', something described as divine and ruling within those of them who always consent to follow after justice and after you, I shall begin by sowing that seed, and then hand it over to you. The rest of   d the task is yours. Weave what is mortal to what is immortal, fashion and beget living things. Give them food, cause them to grow, and when they perish, receive them back again."

When he had finished this speech, he turned again to the mixing bowl he had used before, the one in which he had blended and mixed the soul of the universe. He began to pour into it what remained of the previous ingredients and to mix them in somewhat the same way, though these were no longer invariably and constantly pure, but of a second and third grade of purity. And when he had compounded it all, he divided the mixture into a number of souls equal to the number of the stars and assigned each soul to a star. He mounted each soul in a carriage, as it   e were, and showed it the nature of the universe. He described to them the laws that had been foreordained: They would all be assigned one and the same initial birth, so that none would be less well treated by him than any other. Then he would sow each of the souls into that instrument of time suitable to it, where they were to acquire the nature of being the most   42 god-fearing of living things, and, since humans have a twofold nature, the superior kind should be such as would from then on be called "man." So, once the souls were of necessity implanted in bodies, and these bodies had things coming to them and leaving them, the first innate capacity they would of necessity come to have would be sense perception, which arises out of forceful disturbances. This they all would have. The second would be love, mingled with pleasure and pain. And they would come to have fear and spiritedness as well, plus whatever goes with having these emotions, as   b well as all their natural opposites. And if they could master these emotions, their lives would be just, whereas if they were mastered by them, they would be unjust. And if a person lived a good life throughout the due course of his time, he would at the end return to his dwelling place in his companion star, to live a life of happiness that agreed with his character. But if he failed in this, he would be born a second time, now as a woman.   c And if even then he still could not refrain from wickedness, he would be changed once again, this time into some wild animal that resembled the wicked character he had acquired. And he would have no rest from these toilsome transformations until he had dragged that massive accretion of fire-water-air-earth into conformity with the revolution of the Same and uniform within him, and so subdued that turbulent, irrational mass by means of   d reason. This would return him to his original condition of excellence.

Having set out all these ordinances to them—which he did to exempt himself from responsibility for any evil they might afterwards do—the god proceeded to sow some of them into the Earth, some into the Moon, and others into the various other instruments of time. After the sowing, he handed over to the young gods the task of weaving mortal bodies. He had them make whatever else remained that the human soul still needed

e to have, plus whatever goes with those things. He gave them the task of ruling over these mortal living things and of giving them the finest, the best possible guidance they could give, without being responsible for any evils these creatures might bring upon themselves.

When he had finished assigning all these tasks, he proceeded to abide at rest in his own customary nature. His children immediately began to attend to and obey their father's assignment. Now that they had received the immortal principle of the mortal living thing, they began to imitate the craftsman who had made them. They borrowed parts of fire, earth,

43 water and air from the world, intending to pay them back again, and bonded together into a unity the parts they had taken, but not with those indissoluble bonds by which they themselves were held together. Instead, they proceeded to fuse them together with copious rivets so small as to be invisible, thereby making each body a unit made up of all the components. And they went on to invest this body—into and out of which things were to flow—with the orbits of the immortal soul. These orbits, now bound within a mighty river, neither mastered that river nor were mastered by it, but tossed it violently and were violently tossed by it. Consequently

b the living thing as a whole did indeed move, but it would proceed in a disorderly, random and irrational way that involved all six of the motions.[21] It would go forwards and backwards, then back and forth to the right and the left, and upwards and downwards, wandering every which way in these six directions. For mighty as the nourishment-bearing billow was in its ebb and flow, mightier still was the turbulence produced by the disturbances caused by the things that struck against the living things.

c Such disturbances would occur when the body encountered and collided with external fire (i.e., fire other than the body's own) or for that matter with a hard lump of earth or with the flow of gliding waters, or when it was caught up by a surge of air-driven winds. The motions produced by all these encounters would then be conducted through the body to the soul, and strike against it. (That is no doubt why these motions as a group came afterwards to be called "sensations," as they are still called today.)[22] It was just then, at that very instant, that they produced a very long and

d intense commotion. They cooperated with the continually flowing channel

21. Timaeus is here describing the uncontrolled movements of a new-born animal. He goes on to describe the confusion produced in its soul by its first sensations.

22. It is not clear what etymological point involving the word *aisthēseis* (sensations) Plato wants to make here. Perhaps he thinks (incorrectly) that *aisthēsis* is etymologically related to *aïssein*, "to shake."

to stir and violently shake the orbits of the soul. They completely bound that of the Same by flowing against it in the opposite direction, and held it fast just as it was beginning to go its way. And they further shook the orbit of the Different right through, with the result that they twisted every which way the three intervals of the double and the three of the triple, as well as the middle terms of the ratios of 3/2, 4/3 and 9/8 that connect them.[23] [These agitations did not undo them, however,] because they cannot be completely undone except by the one who had bound them together. They mutilated and disfigured the circles in every possible way so that the circles barely held together and though they remained in motion, they moved without rhyme or reason, sometimes in the opposite direction, sometimes sideways and sometimes upside down—like a man upside down, head propped against the ground and holding his feet up against something. In that position his right side will present itself both to him and to those looking at him as left, and his left side as right. It is this very thing—and others like it—that had such a dramatic effect upon the revolutions of the soul. Whenever they encounter something outside of them characterizable as *same* or *different*, they will speak of it as "the same as" something, or as "different from" something else when the truth is just the opposite, so proving themselves to be misled and unintelligent. Also, at this stage souls do not have a ruling orbit taking the lead. And so when certain sensations come in from outside and attack them, they sweep the soul's entire vessel along with them. It is then that these revolutions, however much in control they seem to be, are actually under their control. All these disturbances are no doubt the reason why even today and not only at the beginning, whenever a soul is bound within a mortal body, it at first lacks intelligence. But as the stream that brings growth and nourishment diminishes and the soul's orbits regain their composure, resume their proper courses and establish themselves more and more with the passage of time, their revolutions are set straight, to conform to the configuration each of the circles takes in its natural course. They then correctly identify what is the same and what is different, and render intelligent the person who possess them. And to be sure, if such a person also gets proper nurture to supplement his education, he'll turn out perfectly whole and healthy, and will have escaped the most grievous of illnesses. But if he neglects this, he'll limp his way through life and return to Hades uninitiated and unintelligent.

But this doesn't happen until later. Our present subject, on the other hand, needs a more detailed treatment. We must move on to treat the prior questions—the ones that deal with how bodies came to be, part by part, as well as the soul. What were the gods' reasons, what was their plan when they caused these to be? In discussing these questions we shall hold fast to what is most likely, and proceed accordingly.

23. See 36b above.

    Copying the revolving shape of the universe, the gods bound the two divine orbits into a ball-shaped body, the part that we now call our head. This is the most divine part of us, and master of all our other parts. They then assembled the rest of the body and handed the whole of it to the head, to be in its service. They intended it to share in all the motions there

e   were to be. To keep the head from rolling around on the ground without any way of getting up over its various high spots and out of the low, they gave it the body as a vehicle to make its way easy. This is the reason why the body came to have length and grow four limbs that could flex and extend themselves, divinely devised for the purpose of getting about. Holding on and supporting itself with these limbs, it would be capable of

45   making its way through all regions, while carrying at the top the dwelling place of that most divine, most sacred part of ourselves. This is how as well as why we have all grown arms and legs. And considering the front side to be more honorable and more commanding than the back, the gods gave us the ability to travel for the most part in this direction. Human beings no doubt ought to have the front sides of their bodies distinguishable from and dissimilar to their backs, and so the gods began by setting the

b   face on that side of the head, the soul's vessel. They bound organs inside it to provide completely for the soul, and they assigned this side, the natural front, to be the part that takes the lead.

    The eyes were the first of the organs to be fashioned by the gods, to conduct light. The reason why they fastened them within the head is this. They contrived that such fire as was not for burning but for providing a gentle light should become a body, proper to each day. Now the pure fire inside us, cousin to that fire, they made to flow through the eyes: so they made the eyes—the eye as a whole but its middle in particular—close-

c   textured, smooth and dense, to enable them to keep out all the other, coarser stuff, and let that kind of fire pass through pure by itself. Now whenever daylight surrounds the visual stream, like makes contact with like and coalesces with it to make up a single homogeneous body aligned with the direction of the eyes. This happens wherever the internal fire strikes and presses against an external object it has connected with. And because this body of fire has become uniform throughout and thus uni-

d   formly affected, it transmits the motions of whatever it comes in contact with as well as of whatever comes in contact with it, to and through the whole body until they reach the soul. This brings about the sensation we call "seeing." At night, however, the kindred fire has departed and so the visual stream is cut off. For now it exits only to encounter something unlike itself. No longer able to bond with the surrounding air, which now has lost its fire, it undergoes changes and dies out. So it not only stops seeing, but even begins to induce sleep. For when the eyelids—which the gods

e   devised to keep eyesight safe—are closed, they shut in the power of the internal fire, which then disperses and evens out the internal motions, and when these have been evened out, a state of quietness ensues. And if this quietness is deep, one falls into an all but dreamless sleep. But if some fairly strong motions remain, they produce images similar in kind and in number to the kind of motions they are, and the kind of regions in which they remain—images which, though formed within, are recalled upon waking as external objects.

And so there is no longer any difficulty in understanding how images are produced in mirrors or in any other smooth reflecting surfaces. On such occasions the internal fire joins forces with the external fire, to form on the smooth surface a single fire which is reshaped in a multitude of ways. So once the fire from the face comes to coalesce with the fire from sight on the smooth and bright surface, you have the inevitable appearance of all images of this sort. What is left will appear as right, because the parts of the fire from sight connect with the opposite parts of the fire from the face, contrary to the usual manner of encounter. But, on the other hand, what is right does appear as right, and what is left as left whenever light switches sides in the process of coalescing with the light with which it coalesces. And this happens whenever the mirror's smooth surface is curled upwards on both sides, thereby bending the right part of the fire from sight towards the left, and the left part towards the right. And when this same smooth surface is turned along the length of the face [i.e., vertically], it makes the whole object appear upside down, because it bends the lower part of the ray toward the top, and the upper part toward the bottom.

Now all of the above are among the auxiliary causes employed in the service of the god as he does his utmost to bring to completion the character of what is most excellent. But because they make things cold or hot, compact or disperse them, and produce all sorts of similar effects, most people regard them not as auxiliary causes, but as the actual causes of all things. Things like these, however, are totally incapable of possessing any reason or understanding about anything. We must pronounce the soul to be the only thing there is that properly possesses understanding. The soul is an invisible thing, whereas fire, water, earth and air have all come to be as visible bodies. So anyone who is a lover of understanding and knowledge must of necessity pursue as primary causes those that belong to intelligent nature, and as secondary all those belonging to things that are moved by others and that set still others in motion by necessity. We too, surely, must do likewise: we must describe both types of causes, distinguishing those which possess understanding and thus fashion what is beautiful and good, from those which, when deserted by intelligence, produce only haphazard and disorderly effects every time.

Let us conclude, then, our discussion of the accompanying auxiliary causes that gave our eyes the power which they now possess. We must next speak of that supremely beneficial function for which the god gave them to us. As my account has it, our sight has indeed proved to be a source of supreme benefit to us, in that none of our present statements about the universe could ever have been made if we had never seen any stars, sun or heaven. As it is, however, our ability to see the periods of

day-and-night, of months and of years, of equinoxes and solstices, has led
to the invention of number, and has given us the idea of time and opened
b   the path to inquiry into the nature of the universe. These pursuits have
given us philosophy, a gift from the gods to the mortal race whose value
neither has been nor ever will be surpassed. I'm quite prepared to declare
this to be the supreme good our eyesight offers us. Why then should we
exalt all the lesser good things, which a non-philosopher struck blind
would "lament and bewail in vain"?[24] Let us rather declare that the cause
and purpose of this supreme good is this: the god invented sight and gave
it to us so that we might observe the orbits of intelligence in the universe
c   and apply them to the revolutions of our own understanding. For there
is a kinship between them, even though our revolutions are disturbed,
whereas the universal orbits are undisturbed. So once we have come to
know them and to share in the ability to make correct calculations according
to nature, we should stabilize the straying revolutions within ourselves
by imitating the completely unstraying revolutions of the god.

Likewise, the same account goes for sound and hearing—these too are
the gods' gifts, given for the same purpose and intended to achieve the
same result. Speech was designed for this very purpose—it plays the
d   greatest part in its achievement. And all such composition as lends itself
to making audible musical sound[25] is given in order to express harmony,
and so serves this purpose as well. And harmony, whose movements are
akin to the orbits within our souls, is a gift of the Muses, if our dealings
with them are guided by understanding, not for irrational pleasure, for
which people nowadays seem to make use of it, but to serve as an ally in
the fight to bring order to any orbit in our souls that has become unharmonized, and make it concordant with itself. Rhythm, too, has likewise been
e   given us by the Muses for the same purpose, to assist us. For with most
of us our condition is such that we have lost all sense of measure, and are
lacking in grace.

Now in all but a brief part of the discourse I have just completed I have
presented what has been crafted by Intellect. But I need to match this
account by providing a comparable one concerning the things that have
48   come about by Necessity. For this ordered world is of mixed birth: it is
the offspring of a union of Necessity and Intellect. Intellect prevailed over
Necessity by persuading it to direct most of the things that come to be
toward what is best, and the result of this subjugation of Necessity to wise
persuasion was the initial formation of this universe. So if I'm to tell the
story of how it really came to be in this way, I'd also have to introduce
the character of the Straying Cause—how it is its nature to set things adrift.
b   I shall have to retrace my steps, then, and, armed with a second starting
point that also applies to these same things, I must go back once again to

24. A near-quotation from Euripides, *Phoenician Women*, 1762.
25. Reading *phōnēs* in d1.

the beginning and start my present inquiry from there, just as I did with my earlier one.

We shall of course have to study the intrinsic nature of fire, water, air and earth prior to the heaven's coming to be, as well as the properties they had then. So far no one has as yet revealed how these four came to be. We tend to posit them as the elemental "letters" of the universe and tell people they are its "principles" on the assumption that they know what fire and the other three are. In fact, however, they shouldn't even be compared to syllables. Only a very unenlightened person might be expected to make such a comparison. So let me now proceed with my treatment in the following way: for the present I cannot state "the principle" or "principles" of all things, or however else I think about them, for the simple reason that it is difficult to show clearly what my view is if I follow my present manner of exposition. Please do not expect me to do so then. I couldn't convince even myself that I could be right to commit myself to undertaking a task of such magnitude. I shall keep to what I stated at the beginning, the virtue of likely accounts, and so shall try right from the start to say about things, both individually and collectively, what is no less likely than any—more likely, in fact, than what I have said before.[26] Let us therefore at the outset of this discourse call upon the god to be our savior this time, too, to give us safe passage through a strange and unusual exposition, and lead us to a view of what is likely. And so let me begin my speech again.

The new starting point in my account of the universe needs to be more complex than the earlier one. Then we distinguished two kinds, but now we must specify a third, one of a different sort. The earlier two sufficed for our previous account: one was proposed as a model, intelligible and always changeless, a second as an imitation of the model, something that possesses becoming and is visible. We did not distinguish a third kind at the time, because we thought that we could make do with the two of them. Now, however, it appears that our account compels us to attempt to illuminate in words a kind that is difficult and vague. What must we suppose it to do and to be? This above all: it is a *receptacle* of all becoming— its wetnurse, as it were.

However true that statement may be, we must nevertheless describe it more clearly. This is a difficult task, particularly because it requires us to raise a preliminary problem about fire and the other three:

It is difficult to say of each of them—in a way that employs a reliable and stable account—which one is the sort of thing one should really call *water* rather than *fire*, or which one one should call some one of these rather than just any and every one of them. What problem, then, do they present for us to work through in likely fashion? And then how and in what manner are we to go on to speak about this third kind?

---

26. Accepting the insertion of <*tōn*> after *mallon de* in d3.

First, we see (or think we see) the thing that we have just now been
c   calling *water* condensing and turning to stones and earth. Next, we see
this same thing dissolving and dispersing, turning to wind and air, and
air, when ignited, turning to fire. And then we see fire being condensed
and extinguished and turning back to the form of air, and air coalescing
and thickening and turning back into cloud and mist. When these are
compressed still more we see them turning into flowing water, which we
see turning to earth and stones once again. In this way, then, they transmit
their coming to be one to the other in a cycle, or so it seems. Now then,
d   since none of these appears ever to remain the same, which one of them
can one categorically assert, without embarrassment, to be some particular
thing, *this* one, and not something else? One can't. Rather, the safest course
by far is to propose that we speak about these things in the following way:
what we invariably observe becoming different at different times—fire for
example—to characterize that, i.e., fire, not as "this," but each time as
"what is such," and speak of water not as "this," but always as "what is
such." And never to speak of anything else as "this," as though it has
e   some stability, of all the things at which we point and use the expressions
"that" and "this" and so think we are designating something. For it gets
away without abiding the charge of "that" and "this," or any other expression that indicts them of being stable. It is in fact safest not to refer to it
by any of these expressions. Rather, "what is such"—coming around like
what it was, again and again—*that's* the thing to call it in each and every
case. So fire—and generally everything that has becoming—it is safest to
call "what is altogether such." But that *in* which they each appear to keep
coming into being and *from* which they subsequently pass out of being,
50   *that's* the only thing to refer to by means of the expressions "that" and
"this." A thing that is some "such" or other, however,—hot or white, say,
or any one of the opposites, and all things constituted by these—should
be called none of these things [i.e., "this" or "that"].[27]

27. An alternative translation of 49c7–50a4 has been proposed by H. F. Cherniss (*Am.
J. of Philol.* 75, 113 ff.):

> Since these thus never appear as severally identical, concerning which of them could
> one without shame firmly assert that this is any particular thing and not another? It
> is not possible, but by far the safest way is to speak of them on this basis: What we
> ever see coming to be at different times in different places, for example fire, not to
> say "this is fire," but "what on any occasion is such and such is fire," nor "this is
> water," but "what is always such and such is water," nor ever "[this]," as if it had
> some permanence, "is some other" of the things that we think we are designating as
> something when by way of pointing we use the term "this" or "that." For it slips
> away and does not abide the assertion of "that" and "this" or any assertion that indicts
> them of being stable. But [it is safest] not to speak of these as severally distinct but
> so to call the such and such that always recurs alike in each and all cases together,
> for example [to call] that which is always such and such fire, and so with everything

I must make one more effort to describe it, more clearly still. Suppose you were molding gold into every shape there is, going on non-stop re-molding one shape into the next. If someone then were to point at one of them and ask you, "What *is* it?," your safest answer by far, with respect b to truth, would be to say, "gold," but never "triangle" or any of the other shapes that come to be in the gold, as though it *is* these, because they change even while you're making the statement. However, that answer, too, should be satisfactory, as long as the shapes are willing to accept "what is such" as someone's designation. This has a degree of safety.

Now the same account, in fact, holds also for that nature which receives all the bodies. We must always refer to it by the same term, for it does not depart from its own character in any way. Not only does it always receive all things, it has never in any way whatever taken on any character- c istic similar to any of the things that enter it. Its nature is to be available for anything to make its impression upon, and it is modified, shaped and reshaped by the things that enter it. These are the things that make it appear different at different times. The things that enter and leave it are imitations of those things that always are, imprinted after their likeness in a marvellous way that is hard to describe. This is something we shall pursue at another time. For the moment, we need to keep in mind three types of things: that which comes to be, that in which it comes to be, and d that after which the thing coming to be is modeled, and which is the source of its coming to be. It is in fact appropriate to compare the receiving thing to a mother, the source to a father, and the nature between them to their offspring. We also must understand that if the imprints are to be varied, with all the varieties there to see, this thing upon which the imprints are to be formed could not be well prepared for that role if it were not itself devoid of any of those characters that it is to receive from elsewhere. For e if it resembled any of the things that enter it, it could not successfully copy their opposites or things of a totally different nature whenever it were to receive them. It would be showing its own face as well. This is why the thing that is to receive in itself all the elemental kinds must be totally devoid of any characteristics. Think of people who make fragrant ointments. They expend skill and ingenuity to come up with something just like this [i.e., a neutral base], to have on hand to start with. The liquids that are to receive the fragrances they make as odorless as possible. Or think of people who work at impressing shapes upon soft materials. They emphatically refuse to allow any such material to already have some definite shape. Instead, they'll even it out and make it as smooth as it can be. In the same 51

---

that comes to be; and, on the other hand, that in which these severally distinct characteristics are ever and anon being manifested as they come to be in it and out of which
again they are passing away, it is safest to designate it alone when we employ the
word "this" or "that" but what is of any kind soever, hot or white or any of the
contraries and all that consist of these, not in turn to call it any of these.

way, then, if the thing that is to receive repeatedly throughout its whole self the likenesses of the intelligible objects, the things which always are[28]— if it is to do so successfully, then it ought to be devoid of any inherent characteristics of its own. This, of course, is the reason why we shouldn't call the mother or receptacle of what has come to be, of what is visible or perceivable in every other way, either earth or air, fire or water, or any of their compounds or their constituents. But if we speak of it as an invisible

b   and characterless sort of thing, one that receives all things and shares in a most perplexing way in what is intelligible, a thing extremely difficult to comprehend, we shall not be misled. And in so far as it is possible to arrive at its nature on the basis of what we've said so far, the most correct way to speak of it may well be this: the part of it that gets ignited appears on each occasion as fire, the dampened part as water, and parts as earth or air in so far as it receives the imitations of these.

   But we must prefer to conduct our inquiry by means of rational argument. Hence we should make a distinction like the following: Is there such a thing as a Fire *by itself*? Do all these things of which we always say that

c   each of them is something "by itself" really exist? Or are the things we see, and whatever else we perceive through the body, the only things that possess this kind of actuality, so that there is absolutely nothing else besides them at all? Is our perpetual claim that there exists an intelligible Form for each thing a vacuous gesture, in the end nothing but mere talk? Now we certainly will not do justice to the question before us if we dismiss it, leaving it undecided and unadjudicated, and just insist that such things

d   exist, but neither must we append a further lengthy digression to a discourse already quite long. If, however, a significant distinction formulated in few words were to present itself, that would suit our present needs best of all. So here's how I cast my own vote: If understanding and true opinion are distinct, then these "by themselves" things definitely exist—these Forms, the objects not of our sense perception, but of our understanding only. But if—as some people think—true opinion does not differ in any way from understanding, then all the things we perceive through our

e   bodily senses must be assumed to be the most stable things there are. But we do have to speak of understanding and true opinion as distinct, of course, because we can come to have one without the other, and the one is not like the other. It is through instruction that we come to have understanding, and through persuasion that we come to have true belief. Understanding always involves a true account while true belief lacks any account. And while understanding remains unmoved by persuasion, true belief gives in to persuasion. And of true belief, it must be said, all men have a share, but of understanding, only the gods and a small group of people do.

52   Since these things are so, we must agree that that which keeps its own form unchangingly, which has not been brought into being and is not

---

28. Accepting the insertion of *noētōn* before *pantōn* in a1.

destroyed, which neither receives into itself anything else from anywhere else, nor itself enters into anything else anywhere, is one thing. It is invisible—it cannot be perceived by the senses at all—and it is the role of understanding to study it. The second thing is that which shares the other's name and resembles it. This thing can be perceived by the senses, and it has been begotten. It is constantly borne along, now coming to be in a certain place and then perishing out of it. It is apprehended by opinion, which involves sense perception. And the third type is space, which exists always and cannot be destroyed. It provides a fixed state for all things that come to be. It is itself apprehended by a kind of bastard reasoning that does not involve sense perception, and it is hardly even an object of conviction. We look at it as in a dream when we say that everything that exists must of necessity be somewhere, in some place and occupying some space, and that that which doesn't exist somewhere, whether on earth or in heaven, doesn't exist at all.

b

We prove unable to draw all these distinctions and others related to them—even in the case of that unsleeping, truly existing reality—because our dreaming state renders us incapable of waking up and stating the truth, which is this: Since that for which an image has come to be is not at all intrinsic to the image, which is invariably borne along to picture something else, it stands to reason that the image should therefore come to be *in* something else, somehow clinging to being, or else be nothing at all. But that which really is receives support from the accurate, true account—that as long as the one is distinct from the other, neither of them ever comes to be in the other in such a way that they at the same time become one and the same, and also two.

c

d

Let this, then, be a summary of the account I would offer, as computed by my "vote." There are being, space, and becoming, three distinct things which existed even before the universe came to be.

Now as the wetnurse of becoming turns watery and fiery and receives the character of earth and air, and as it acquires all the properties that come with these characters, it takes on a variety of visible aspects, but because it is filled with powers that are neither similar nor evenly balanced, no part of it is in balance. It sways irregularly in every direction as it is shaken by those things, and being set in motion it in turn shakes them. And as they are moved, they drift continually, some in one direction and others in others, separating from one another. They are winnowed out, as it were, like grain that is sifted by winnowing sieves or other such implements. They are carried off and settle down, the dense and heavy ones in one direction, and the rare and light ones to another place.

e

53

That is how at that time the four kinds were being shaken by the receiver, which was itself agitating like a shaking machine, separating the kinds most unlike each other furthest apart and pushing those most like each other closest together into the same region. This, of course, explains how these different kinds came to occupy different regions of space, even before the universe was set in order and constituted from them at its coming to

be. Indeed, it is a fact that before this took place the four kinds all lacked
b   proportion and measure, and at the time the ordering of the universe was
undertaken, fire, water, earth and air initially possessed certain traces of
what they are now. They were indeed in the condition one would expect
thoroughly god-forsaken things to be in. So, finding them in this natural
condition, the first thing the god then did was to give them their distinctive
shapes, using forms and numbers.

Here is a proposition we shall always affirm above all else: The god
fashioned these four kinds to be as perfect and excellent as possible, when
they were not so before. It will now be my task to explain to you what
c   structure each of them acquired, and how each came to be. My account
will be an unusual one, but since you are well schooled in the fields of
learning in terms of which I must of necessity proceed with my exposition,
I'm sure you'll follow me.

First of all, everyone knows, I'm sure, that fire, earth, water and air
are bodies. Now everything that has bodily form also has depth. Depth,
moreover, is of necessity comprehended within surface, and any surface
bounded by straight lines is composed of triangles. Every triangle, more-
d   over, derives from two triangles, each of which has one right angle and
two acute angles. Of these two triangles, one [the isosceles right-angled
triangle] has at each of the other two vertices an equal part of a right angle,
determined by its division by equal sides; while the other [the scalene
right-angled triangle] has unequal parts of a right angle at its other two
vertices, determined by the division of the right angle by unequal sides.
This, then, we presume to be the originating principle of fire and of the other
bodies, as we pursue our likely account in terms of Necessity. Principles yet
more ultimate than these are known only to the god, and to any man he
may hold dear.

e   We should now say which are the most excellent four bodies that can
come to be. They are quite unlike each other, though some of them are
capable of breaking up and turning into others and vice-versa. If our
account is on the mark, we shall have the truth about how earth and fire
and their proportionate intermediates [water and air] came to be. For we
shall never concede to anyone that there are any visible bodies more
excellent than these, each conforming to a single kind. So we must wholeheartedly proceed to fit together the four kinds of bodies of surpassing
excellence, and to declare that we have come to grasp their natures well
enough.

54   Of the two [right-angled] triangles, the isosceles has but one nature,
while the scalene has infinitely many. Now we have to select the most
excellent one from among the infinitely many, if we are to get a proper
start. So if anyone can say that he has picked out another one that is more
excellent for the construction of these bodies, his victory will be that of a
friend, not an enemy. Of the many [scalene right-angled] triangles, then,
we posit as the one most excellent, surpassing the others, that one from
[a pair of] which the equilateral triangle is constructed as a third figure.

Why this is so is too long a story to tell now. But if anyone puts this   b
claim to the test and discovers that it isn't so, his be the prize, with our
congratulations. So much, then, for the selection of the two triangles out
of which the bodies of fire and the other bodies are constructed—the [right-
angled] isosceles, and [the right-angled] scalene whose longer side squared
is always triple its shorter side squared [i.e., the half-equilateral].

At this point we need to formulate more precisely something that was
not stated clearly earlier. For then it appeared that all four kinds of bodies
could turn into one another by successive stages.[29] But the appearance is
wrong. While there are indeed four kinds of bodies that come to be from   c
the [right-angled] triangles we have selected, three of them come from
triangles that have unequal sides, whereas the fourth alone is fashioned
out of isosceles triangles. Thus not all of them have the capacity of breaking
up and turning into one another, with a large number of small bodies
turning into a small number of large ones and vice-versa. There are three
that can do this. For all three are made up of a single type of triangle, so
that when once the larger bodies are broken up, the same triangles can
go to make up a large number of small bodies, assuming shapes appropriate
to them. And likewise, when numerous small bodies are fragmented into   d
their triangles, these triangles may well combine to make up some single
massive body belonging to another kind.

So much, then, for our account of how these bodies turn into one another.
Let us next discuss the form that each of them has come to have, and the
various numbers that have combined to make them up.

Leading the way will be the primary form [the tetrahedron], the tiniest
structure, whose elementary triangle is the one whose hypotenuse is twice
the length of its shorter side. Now when a pair of such triangles are
juxtaposed along the diagonal [i.e., their hypotenuses] and this is done
three times, and their diagonals and short sides converge upon a single   e
point as center, the result is a single equilateral triangle, composed of six
such triangles. When four of these equilateral triangles are combined, a
single solid angle is produced at the junction of three plane angles. This,   55
it turns out, is the angle which comes right after the most obtuse of the
plane angles.[30] And once four such solid angles have been completed, we
get the primary solid form, which is one that divides the entire circumference [sc. of the sphere in which it is inscribed] into equal and similar parts.

The second solid form [the octahedron] is constructed out of the same
triangles which, however, are now arranged in eight equilateral triangles
and produce a single solid angle out of four plane angles. And when
six such solid angles have been produced, the second body has reached
its completion.

Now the third body [the icosahedron] is made up of a combination of
one hundred and twenty of the elementary triangles, and of twelve solid   b

29. Cf. 49b–c.

30. The solid angle is the conjunction of three 60° plane angles, totalling 180°.

angles, each enclosed by five plane equilateral triangles. This body turns out to have twenty equilateral triangular faces. And let us take our leave of this one of the elementary triangles, the one that has begotten the above three kinds of bodies and turn to the other one, the isosceles [right-angled] triangle, which has begotten the fourth [the cube]. Arranged in sets of four whose right angles come together at the center, the isosceles triangle produced a single equilateral quadrangle [i.e., a square]. And when six of

c   these quadrangles were combined together, they produced eight solid angles, each of which was constituted by three plane right angles. The shape of the resulting body so constructed is a cube, and it has six quadrangular equilateral faces.

One other construction, a fifth, still remained, and this one the god used for the whole universe, embroidering figures on it.[31]

Anyone following this whole line of reasoning might very well be puzzled about whether we should say that there are infinitely many worlds

d   or a finite number of them. If so, he would have to conclude that to answer, "infinitely many," is to take the view of one who is really "unfinished" in things he ought to be "finished" in. He would do better to stop with the question whether we should say that there's really just one world or five and be puzzled about that. Well, our "probable account" answer declares there to be but one world, a god—though someone else, taking other things into consideration, will come to a different opinion. We must set him aside, however.

Let us now assign to fire, earth, water and air the structures which have just been given their formations in our speech. To earth let us give the

e   cube, because of the four kinds of bodies earth is the most immobile and the most pliable—which is what the solid whose faces are the most secure must of necessity turn out to be, more so than the others. Now of the [right-angled] triangles we originally postulated, the face belonging to those that have equal sides has a greater natural stability than that belonging to triangles that have unequal sides, and the surface that is composed of the two triangles, the equilateral quadrangle [the square], holds its position with greater stability than does the equilateral triangle, both in

56   their parts and as wholes. Hence, if we assign this solid figure to earth, we are preserving our "likely account." And of the solid figures that are left, we shall next assign the least mobile of them to water, to fire the most mobile, and to air the one in between. This means that the tiniest body belongs to fire, the largest to water, and the intermediate one to air—and also that the body with the sharpest edges belongs to fire, the next sharpest to air, and the third sharpest to water. Now in all these cases the body that has the fewest faces is of necessity the most mobile, in that it, more than any other, has edges that are the sharpest and best fit for cutting in

b   every direction. It is also the lightest, in that it is made up of the least

---

31. The dodecahedron, the remaining one of the regular solids. It approaches most nearly a sphere in volume—the shape of the universe, on Timaeus' story.

number of identical parts. The second body ranks second in having these same properties, and the third ranks third. So let us follow our account, which is not only likely but also correct, and take the solid form of the pyramid that we saw constructed as the element or the seed of fire. And let us say that the second form in order of generation is that of air, and the third that of water.

Now we must think of all these bodies as being so small that due to their small size none of them, whatever their kind, is visible to us individu- c ally. When, however, a large number of them are clustered together, we do see them in bulk. And in particular, as to the proportions among their numbers, their motions and their other properties, we must think that when the god had brought them to complete and exact perfection (to the degree that Necessity was willing to comply obediently), he arranged them together proportionately.

Given all we have said so far about the kinds of elemental bodies, the following account [of their transformations] is the most likely: When earth d encounters fire and is broken up by fire's sharpness, it will drift about— whether the breaking up occurred within fire itself, or within a mass of air or water—until its parts meet again somewhere, refit themselves to- gether and become earth again. The reason is that the parts of earth will never pass into another form. But when water is broken up into parts by fire or even by air, it could happen that the parts recombine to form one corpuscle of fire and two of air. And the fragments of air could produce, e from any single particle that is broken up, two fire corpuscles. And con- versely, whenever a small amount of fire is enveloped by a large quantity of air or water or perhaps earth and is agitated inside them as they move, and in spite of its resistance is beaten and shattered to bits, then any two fire corpuscles may combine to constitute a single form of air. And when air is overpowered and broken down, then two and one half entire forms of air will be consolidated into a single, entire form of water.

Let us recapitulate and formulate our account of these transformations as follows: Whenever one of the other kinds is caught inside fire and gets 57 cut up by the sharpness of fire's angles and edges, then if it is reconstituted as fire, it will stop getting cut. The reason is that a thing of any kind that is alike and uniform is incapable of effecting any change in, or being affected by, anything that is similar to it. But as long as something involved in a transformation has something stronger than it to contend with, the process of its dissolution will continue non-stop. And likewise, when a few of the smaller corpuscles are surrounded by a greater number of bigger b ones, they will be shattered and quenched. The quenching will stop when these smaller bodies are willing to be reconstituted into the form of the kind that prevailed over them, and so from fire will come air, and from air, water. But if these smaller corpuscles are in process of turning into these and one of the other kinds encounters them and engages them in battle, their dissolution will go on non-stop until they are either completely squeezed and broken apart and escape to their own likes, or else are defeated, and, melding from many into one, they are assimilated to the kind that prevailed over them, and come to share its abode from then on.

c   And, what is more, as they undergo these processes, they all exchange their territories: for as a result of the Receptacle's agitation the masses of each of the kinds are separated from one another, with each occupying its own region, but because some parts of a particular kind do from time to time become unlike their former selves and like the other kinds, they are carried by the shaking towards the region occupied by whatever masses they are becoming like to.

These, then, are the sorts of causes by which the unalloyed primary bodies have come to be. Now the fact that different varieties are found within their respective forms is to be attributed to the constructions of

d   each of the elementary triangles. Each of these two constructions did not originally yield a triangle that had just one size, but triangles that were both smaller and larger, numerically as many as there are varieties within a given form. That is why when they are mixed with themselves and with each other they display an infinite variety, which those who are to employ a likely account in their study of nature ought to take note of.

Now as for motion and rest, unless there is agreement on the manner and the conditions in which these two come to be, we will have many

e   obstacles to face in our subsequent course of reasoning. Although we have already said something about them, we need to say this as well: there will be no motion in a state of uniformity. For it is difficult, or rather impossible, for something to be moved without something to set it in motion, or something to set a thing in motion without something to be moved by it. When either is absent, there is no motion, but [when they are present] it is quite impossible for them to be uniform. And so let us always presume that rest is found in a state of uniformity and to attribute motion to non-

58   uniformity. The latter, moreover, is caused by inequality, the origin of which we have already discussed.[32]

We have not explained, however, how it is that the various corpuscles have not reached the point of being thoroughly separated from each other kind by kind, so that their transformations into each other and their movement [toward their own regions] would have come to a halt. So let us return to say this about it: Once the circumference of the universe has comprehended the [four] kinds, then, because it is round and has a natural tendency to gather in upon itself, it constricts them all and allows no empty

b   space to be left over. This is why fire, more than the other three, has come to infiltrate all of the others, with air in second place, since it is second in degree of subtlety, and so on for the rest. For the bodies that are generated from the largest parts will have the largest gaps left over in their construction, whereas the smallest bodies will have the tiniest. Now this gathering, contracting process squeezes the small parts into the gaps inside the big ones. So now, as the small parts are placed among the large ones and the smaller ones tend to break up the larger ones while the larger tend to

32. The reference is unclear. Cf. perhaps 52e.

cause the smaller to coalesce, they all shift, up and down, into their own respective regions. For as each changes in quantity, it also changes the position of its region. This, then, is how and why the occurrence of non-uniformity is perpetually preserved, and so sets these bodies in perpetual motion, both now and in the future without interruption.

Next, we should note that there are many varieties of fire that have come to be. For example, there is both flame and the effluence from flame which, while it doesn't burn, gives light to the eyes. And then there is the residue of flame which is left in the embers when the flame has gone out. The same goes for air. There is the brightest kind that we call "aether," and also the murkiest, "mist" and "darkness." Then there are other, name-less sorts which result from inequality among the triangles. The varieties of water can first of all be divided into two groups, the liquid and the liquifiable. Because the former possesses water parts that are not only unequal but also small, it turns out to be mobile, both in itself and when acted upon by something else. This is due to its non-uniformity and the configuration of its shape. The other type of water, composed of large and uniform kinds, is rather more immobile and heavy, compacted as it is by its uniformity. But when fire penetrates it and begins to break it up, it loses its uniformity, and once that is lost it is more susceptible to motion. When it has become quite mobile it is spread out upon the ground under pressure from the air surrounding it. Each of these changes has its own name: "melting" for the disintegration of its bulk and "flowing" for the spreading on the ground. But when, conversely, the fire is expelled from it, then, since the fire does not pass into a void, pressure is exerted upon the surrounding air, which in turn compresses the still mobile liquid mass into the places previously occupied by the fire and mixes it with itself. As it is being compressed, the mass regains its uniformity now that fire, the agent of non-uniformity, has left the scene, and it resettles into its own former state. The departure of the fire is called "cooling," and the compression that occurs when the fire is gone is called "jelling." Of all these types of water that we have called liquifiable, the one that consists of the finest, the most uniform parts and has proved to be the most dense, one that is unique in its kind and tinged with brilliant yellow, is gold, our most precious possession, filtered through rocks and thereby compacted. And gold's offshoot, which because of its density is extremely hard and has a black color, is called adamant. Another has parts that approximate gold and comes in more than one variety. In terms of density, it is in one way denser than gold and includes a small, fine part of earth, so that it is harder. But it is actually lighter than gold, because it has large gaps inside of it. This, it turns out, is copper, one variety of the bright, jelled kinds of water. Whenever the earth part of the mixture separates off again from the rest in the passage of time, this part, called verdigris, becomes visible by itself.

As for going further and giving an account of other stuffs of this sort along the lines of the likely stories we have been following, that is no complicated matter. And should one take a break and lay aside accounts

d   about the things that always are, deriving instead a carefree pleasure from
     surveying the likely accounts about becoming, he would provide his life
     with a moderate and sensible diversion. So shall we, then, at this time
     give free rein to such a diversion and go right on to set out the next
     likelihoods on these subjects, as follows:

     Take now the water that is mixed with fire. It is fine and liquid and on
     account of its mobility and the way it rolls over the ground it is called
     "liquid." It is soft, moreover, in that its faces, being less firm than those
     of earth, give way to it. When this water is separated from its fire and air
e   and is isolated, it becomes more uniform, and it is pressed together into
     itself by the things that leave it. So compacted, the water above the earth
     which is most affected by this change turns to hail, while that on earth
     turns to ice. Some water is not affected quite so much, being still only half
     compacted. Such water above the earth becomes snow while that on the
     earth becomes what is called "frost," from dew that is congealed.

     Now most of the varieties of water which are mixed with one another
60   are collectively called "saps," because they have been filtered through
     plants that grow out of the earth. Because they are mixed, each of them
     has its own degree of non-uniformity. Many of these varieties are nameless,
     though four of them, all with fire in them, are particularly conspicuous
     and so have been given names. First, there is wine, which warms not only
     the body but the soul as well. Second, there are the various oils, which
     are smooth and divide the ray of sight and for that reason glisten, appearing
     bright and shiny to the eye: these include resin, castor oil, olive oil and
b   others that share their properties. And third, there is what is most com-
     monly called honey, which includes all that relaxes the taste passages of
     the mouth back to their natural state, and which by virtue of this property
     conveys a sense of sweetness. Fourth, there is what has been named tart
     juice, quite distinct from all the other saps. It is a foamy stuff, and is caustic
     and hence hazardous to the flesh.

     As for the varieties of earth, first, such earth as has been filtered through
     water turns into a stony body in something like the following way: When
     the water that is mixed with it disintegrates in the mixing process, it is
c   transformed into the form of air, and, once it has turned into air, it thrusts
     its way upwards toward its own region. And since there is no void above
     it, it pushes aside the air next to it. And when this air, heavy as it is, is
     pressed and poured around the mass of earth, it squeezes it hard and
     compresses it to fill the places vacated by the recently formed air. When
     so compressed by air, earth is insoluble in water and constitutes itself as
     stone. The more beautiful kind of stone is stone that is transparent and
     made up of equal and uniform parts; the uglier kind is just the opposite.
d   Second, there is the kind of earth from which moisture has been completely
     expelled by a swiftly burning fire and which thus comes to have a rather
     more brittle constitution than the first kind of earth. This is a kind to which
     the name "pottery" has been given. Sometimes, however, moisture gets
     left in and we get earth that is made liquifiable by fire. When it has cooled

it turns to stone that is black in color (i.e., lava). Then, thirdly, there are the two varieties of earth that both alike are the residue of a mixture of a great quantity of water. They are briny, made up of the finest parts of earth, and turn out to be semi-solid and water soluble again. One of these is soda, a cleansing agent against oil and dirt; the other is salt, which is well suited to enhance various blends of flavor and has, not unreasonably, proven itself to be a stuff pleasing to the gods.

There are also compounds of earth and water which are soluble by fire but not by water.[33] These are compacted in this way for the following sort of reason: Neither air nor fire will dissolve masses of earth, because air and fire consist of parts that by nature are smaller than are the gaps within earth. They thus pass without constraint through the wide gaps of a mass of earth, leaving it intact and undissolved. But since the parts of water are naturally bigger, they must force their way through, and in so doing they undo and dissolve the earth. For water alone can in this way dissolve earth that isn't forcibly compressed, but when earth is compressed nothing but fire can dissolve it. That is because fire is the only thing left that can penetrate it. So also, only fire can disperse water that has been compressed with the greatest force, whereas both fire and air can disperse water that is in a looser state. Air does it by entering the gaps, and fire by breaking up the triangles. The only way in which air that has been condensed under force can be broken up is into its elemental triangles, and even when it is not forcibly compressed only fire can dissolve it.

So as for these bodies that are mixtures of earth and water, as long as the gaps within a given mass of earth are occupied by its own water which is tightly packed within the gaps, the water parts that come charging upon it from the outside have no way of getting into the mass and so flow around the whole of it, leaving it undissolved. The fire parts, however, do penetrate the gaps within the water parts and hence as fire they do to water[34] what water did to earth. They alone, it turns out, cause this body, this partnership of earth and water to come apart and become fluid. These compounds of earth and water include not only bodies that have less water in them than earth, such as glass and generally all stone formations that can be called liquifiable, but also bodies that have more water than earth, namely all those that have the consistency of wax or of incense.

We have now pretty much completed our presentation of the kinds of bodies that are distinguished by their multifarious shapes, their combinations and their intertransformations. Now we must try to shed some light on what has caused them to come to have the properties they do. First, we need at every step in our discourse to appeal to the existence of sense perception, but we have so far discussed neither the coming to be of flesh, or of what pertains to flesh, nor the part of the soul that is mortal. It so

---

33. I.e., glass, wax, and similar bodies; see below.
34. Accepting the conjecture *hudōr* at b5.

d   happens, however, that we cannot give an adequate account of these
    matters without referring to perceptual properties, but neither can we give
    an account of the latter without referring to the former, and to treat them
    simultaneously is all but impossible. So we must start by assuming the
    one or the other, and later revisit what we have assumed. Let's begin by
    taking for granted for now the existence of body and soul. This will allow
    our account of these properties to succeed the account we've just given
    of the elemental kinds.

        First, then, let us see what we mean when we call fire *hot*. Let's look at
    it in this way: We notice how fire acts on our bodies by dividing and
e   cutting them. We are all well aware that the experience is a sharp one.
    The fineness of fire's edges, the sharpness of its angles, the minuteness of
    its parts and the swiftness of its motion—all of which make fire severely
62 piercing so that it makes sharp cuts in whatever it encounters—must be
    taken into consideration as we recall how its shape came to be. It is this
    substance, more than any other, that divides our bodies throughout and
    cuts them up into small pieces, thereby giving us the property (as well as
    the name [*kermatizein*]) that we now naturally call *hot* [*thermon*].

        What the opposite property is, is quite obvious; we should not, however,
    keep anything left out of our account. As the larger parts of the moisture
    surrounding our bodies penetrate our bodies and push out the smaller
    parts, but are unable to take up the places vacated by those smaller parts,
b   they compress the moisture within us and congeal it by rendering it in a
    state of motionlessness in place of a state of moving non-uniformity, by
    virtue of the uniformity and compression so introduced. But anything
    which is being unnaturally compressed has a natural tendency to resist
    such compression, and pushes itself outward, in the opposite direction.
    This resistance, this shaking is called "shivering" and "chill," and the
    experience as a whole, as well as what brings it about, has come to have
    the name *cold*.

        Hard we call whatever our flesh gives way to; *soft*, whatever gives way
    to our flesh. And this is how they are relative to each other. Whatever stands
c   upon a small base tends to give way. The form composed of quadrangles,
    however, is the least liable to being displaced because its bases are very
    secure, and that which is compacted to its maximum density is particularly
    resistant to being displaced.

        Heavy and *light* can be most clearly explained if we examine them in
    conjunction with what we call *above* and *below*. It is entirely wrong to hold
    that there are by nature two separate regions, divorced from and entirely
    opposite one another, the one the region "below," toward which anything
    that has physical mass tends to move, and the other the region "above"
    toward which everything makes its way only under force. For given that
d   the whole heaven is spherical, all the points that are situated as extremes
    at an equal distance from the center must by their nature be extremes of
    just the same sort, and we must take it that the center, being equidistant
    from the extremes, is situated at the point that is the opposite to all the

extremes. Now if this is the universe's natural constitution, which of the points just mentioned could you posit as "above" or "below" without justly giving the appearance of using totally inappropriate language? There is no justification for describing the universe's central region either as a natural "above" or a natural "below," but just as "at the center." And the region at the circumference is, to be sure, not the center, but neither is one of its parts so distinguished from any other that it is related to the center in a specific way more so than any of the parts opposite to it. What contrary terms could you apply to something that is by nature all alike in every direction? How could you think to use such terms appropriately? If, further, there is something solid and evenly balanced at the center of the universe, 63 it could not move to any of the extreme points, because these are all alike in all directions. But if you could travel around it in a circle, you would repeatedly take a position at your own antipodes and call the very same part of it now the part "above," and then the part "below." For the whole universe, as we have just said, is spherical, and to say that some region of it is its "above," and another its "below," makes no sense. The origin of these terms and the subjects to which they really apply, which explain how we have become accustomed to using them in dividing the world as a whole in this way, we must resolve by adopting the following supposition: b Imagine a man stepping onto that region of the universe that is the particular province of fire, where the greatest mass of fire is gathered together, and toward which other fire moves. Imagine, further, that he has the power to remove some parts of the fire and place them on scales. When he raises the beam and drags the fire into the alien air, applying force to it, clearly c the lesser quantity of fire somehow gives way to his force more easily than the greater. For when two things are raised by one and the same exertion, the lesser quantity will invariably yield more readily and the greater (which offers more resistance) less readily, to the force applied. And so the large quantity will be described as *heavy* and moving *downward*, and the small one as *light* and moving *upward*. Now this is the very thing we must detect ourselves doing in our own region. When we stand on the earth and weigh out one earth-like thing against another, and sometimes some earth itself, we drag these things by force, contrary to their natural tendency, into the alien air. While both of them tend to cling to d what is akin to them, nevertheless the smaller one will yield sooner and more readily than the larger one to the force we apply that introduces it into the alien stuff. Now this is what we call *light*, and the region into which we force it to go we call *above*; their opposites we call *heavy* and *below*. Now the things [having any of these designations] necessarily differ relatively to one another, because the various masses of the elemental kinds of body occupy opposite regions: what in one region is light, heavy, below or above will all be found to become, or to be, directly opposite to, e or at an angle to, or in any and every different direction from, what is light, heavy, below or above in the opposite region. In fact, this is the one thing that should be understood to apply in all these cases: the path towards its own kind is what makes a thing moving along it "heavy" and the region into which it moves, "below," whereas the other set of terms ["light" and "above"] are for things behaving the other way. This, then, concludes our account of what causes [things to have] these properties.

As for *smooth* and *rough*, I take it that anyone could discern the explanation of those properties and communicate it to someone else: roughness results from the combination of hardness with non-uniformity, while
64   smoothness is the result of uniformity's contribution to density.

The most important point that remains concerning the properties that have a common effect upon the body as a whole, pertains to the causes of pleasures and pains in the cases we have described as well as all cases in which sensations are registered throughout the bodily parts, sensations which are also simultaneously accompanied by pains and pleasures in those parts. With every property, whether perceived or not, let us take up the question of the causes of pleasure or pain in the following way, recalling
b   the distinction made in the foregoing between what is easily moved and what is hard to move. This is the way in which we must pursue all that we intend to comprehend. When even a minor disturbance affects that which is easily moved by nature, the disturbance is passed on in a chain reaction with some parts affecting others in the same way as they were affected, until it reaches the center of consciousness and reports the property that produced the reaction. On the other hand, something that is hard to move remains fixed and merely experiences the disturbance without
c   passing it on in any chain reaction. It does not disturb any of its neighboring parts, so that in the absence of some parts passing on the disturbance to others, the initial disturbance affecting them fails to move on into the living thing as a whole and renders the disturbance unperceived. This is true of our bones and hair and of the other mostly earth-made parts that we possess. But the former is true of our sight and hearing in particular, and this is due to the fact that their chief inherent power is that of air and of fire.

This, then, is what we should understand about pleasure and pain: an
d   unnatural disturbance that comes upon us with great force and intensity is painful, while its equally intense departure, leading back to the natural state, is pleasant. One that is mild and gradual is not perceived, whereas the opposite is the case with the opposite disturbance. Further, one that occurs readily can be completely perceived, more so than any other, though neither pleasure nor pain is involved. Take, for example, those involved in the act of seeing. Earlier[35] we described the ray of sight as a body that comes into being with the daylight as an extension of ourselves. The cuttings, the burnings and whatever else it undergoes don't cause any
e   pains in it, nor does the return to its former state yield any pleasures. Its perceptions are the more vivid and clear the more it is affected and the greater the number of things it encounters and makes contact with, for there is absolutely no violence involved when it is severed [by the cutting

35. At 45c.

and burning, etc.] and reconstituted. Bodies consisting of larger parts, on the other hand, won't easily give way to what acts upon them. They pass on the motions they receive to the entire body, and so they do get pleasures and pains—pains when they are alienated from their natural condition and pleasures when they are once again restored to it. All those bodies 65 which experience only gradual departures from their normal state or gradual depletions but whose replenishments are intense and substantial are bodies that are unaware of their depletions but not of their replenishments, and hence they introduce very substantial pleasures in the mortal part of the soul but not any pains. This is clear in the case of fragrances. But all those bodies whose alienations are intense while their restorations to their former states are but gradual and slow, pass on motions that are entirely b contrary to those mentioned just before. Again, this clearly turns out to be the case when the body suffers burns or cuts.

We have now pretty much covered those disturbances that affect the whole body in a common way, as well as all the terms that have come to be applied to the agents that produce them. We must now try to discuss, if we can, those that take place in our various particular parts, and, as before, their causes, which lie in the agents that produce them. First, then, c we need to shed what light we can on what we left untreated earlier when we talked about tastes, and these are the properties specifically connected to the tongue. It seems that these, too, in common with most other properties, come about as a result of contractions and dilations, but apart from that, these tongue-related properties seem rather more than any of the others to involve roughness and smoothness. Now as earth-like parts penetrate the area around the tiny vessels that act as testers for the tongue and reach down to the heart, they impact upon the moist, soft flesh of the d tongue and are melted away. In the process they contract the vessels and dry them up. When they tend to be rather rough, we taste them as *sour*; when less rough, as *tangy*. Things that rinse the vessels and wash the entire area around the tongue are all called *bitter* when they do so to excess and so assault the tongue as to dissolve some of it, as soda actually can do. e When they are not as strong as soda and effect only a moderate rinsing, they taste *salty* to us. They have none of the harsh bitterness, and we find them rather agreeable. Things that absorb the heat of the mouth, by which they are also worn smooth, are ignited and in their turn return their fire to that which made them hot. Their lightness carries them up to the senses in the head, as they cut any and everything they come up against. Because 66 this is what they do, things of this sort have all been called *pungent*. On the other hand, there are those things which have been refined by the process of decomposition and which then intrude themselves into the narrow vessels. These are proportioned both to the earth parts and those of air that are contained within the vessels, so that they agitate the earth and air parts and cause them to be stirred one around the other. As these are being stirred, they surround one another, and, as parts of one sort intrude themselves into parts of another, they make hollows which envelop b   the parts that go inside. So when a hollow envelope of moisture, whether earthy or pure, as the case may be, is stretched around air, we get moist vessels of air, hollow spheres of water. Some of these, those that form a transparent enclosure consisting of a pure moisture are called "bubbles"; those, on the other hand, whose moisture is earthy and agitates and rises upward all at once are called by the terms "effervescence" and "fermentation." That which causes these disturbances is called *acid* to the taste.

c   There is a disturbance that is the opposite of all the ones we have just discussed, one that is the effect of an opposite cause. Whenever the composition of the moistened parts that enter the vessels of the tongue is such that it is congruent with the natural condition of the tongue, these entering parts make smooth and lubricate the roughened parts and in some cases constrict while in others they relax the parts that have been abnormally dilated or contracted. They decisively restore all those parts back to their natural position. As such, they prove to be a cure for the violent disturbances [just discussed], being fully pleasant and agreeable to one and all, and are called *sweet*.

d   So much for the subject of tastes. As for the power belonging to the nostrils, there are no types within it. This is because a smell is always a "half-breed." None of the elemental shapes, as it happens, has the proportions required for having any odor. The vessels involved in our sense of smell are too narrow for the varieties of earth and water parts, yet too wide for those of earth and air. Consequently no one has ever perceived any odor coming from these elemental bodies. Things give off odors when they

e   either get damp or decay, or melt or evaporate; for when water changes to air or air to water, odors are given off in the transition. All odors collectively are either vapor or mist, mist being what passes from air to water, and vapor what passes from water to air, and this is why odors as a group turn out to be finer than water, yet grosser than air. Their character becomes clear when one strains to draw one's breath through something that obstructs one's breathing. There will be no odor that filters through. All that comes through is just the breath itself, devoid of any odor.

67   These variations among odors, then, form two sets, neither of which has a name, since they do not consist of a specific number of simple types. Let us draw the only clear distinction we can draw here, that between the *pleasant* and the *offensive*. The latter of these irritates and violates the whole upper body from the top of the head to the navel, while the former soothes that area and welcomes it back to its natural state.

b   A third kind of perception that we want to consider is hearing. We must describe the causes that produce the properties connected with this perception. In general, let us take it that sound is the percussion of air by way of the ears upon the brain and the blood and transmitted to the soul, and that hearing is the motion caused by the percussion that begins in the head and ends in the place where the liver is situated. And let us take it that whenever the percussion is rapid, the sound is *high-pitched*, and that the slower the percussion, the lower the pitch. A regular percussion produces a uniform, smooth sound, while a contrary one produces one that is *rough*. A forceful percussion produces a *loud* sound, while a contrary one produces one that is *soft*. But we must defer discussion of harmonization in sounds to a later part of our discourse.

c

The fourth and remaining kind of perception is one that includes a vast number of variations within it, and hence it requires subdivision. Collectively, we call these variations *colors*. Color is a flame which flows forth from bodies of all sorts, with its parts proportional to our sight so as to produce perception. At an earlier point in our discourse we treated only the causes that led to the origination of the ray of sight;[36] now, at this point, it is particularly appropriate to provide a well-reasoned account of colors.

d

Now the parts that move from the other objects and impinge on the ray of sight are in some cases smaller, in others larger than, and in still other cases equal in size to, the parts of the ray of sight itself. Those that are equal are imperceptible, and these we naturally call *transparent*. Those that are larger contract the ray of sight while those that are smaller, on the other hand, dilate it, and so are "cousin" to what is cold or hot in the case of the flesh, and, in the case of the tongue, with what is sour, or with all those things that generate heat and that we have therefore called "pungent." So *black* and *white*, it turns out, are properties of contraction and dilation, and are really the same as these other properties, though in a different class, which is why they present a different appearance. This, then, is how we should speak of them: *white* is what dilates the ray of sight, and *black* is what does the opposite.

e

Now when a more penetrating motion of a different type of fire pounces on the ray of sight and dilates it right up to the eyes, and forces its way through the very passages within the eyeballs and melts them, it discharges from those passages a glob of fire and water which we call a tear. The penetrating motion itself consists of fire, and as it encounters fire from the opposite direction, then, as the one fire leaps out from the eyes like a lightning flash and the other enters them but is quenched by the surrounding moisture, the resulting turmoil gives rise to colors of every hue. The disturbance so produced we call "dazzling," and that which produces it we name *bright* and *brilliant*.

68

On the other hand, the type of fire that is intermediate between white and bright is one that reaches the moisture in the eyes and blends with it, but is not brilliant. As the fire shines through the moisture with which it is mixed, it yields the color of blood, which we call *red*. And when bright is mixed with red and white, we get *orange*. But it would be unwise to state the proportions among them, even if one could know them. It is impossible, even approximately, to provide a proof or a likely account on these matters.

b

36. See 45b–d.

c   Now red mixed with black and white is of course *purple*. When this combination is burnt further and more black is mixed with it, we get *violet*. *Gray* is a mixture of black and white, and the mixture of orange and gray produces *amber*. *Beige* comes from white mixed with orange. White combined with bright and immersed in a saturated black produces a *cobalt blue* color, which, when blended with white, becomes *turquoise*. A mixture

d   of amber with black yields *green*. As for the other hues, it should be fairly clear from the above cases by what mixtures they are to be represented in a way that preserves our "likely story." But if anyone in considering these matters were to put them to an actual test, he would demonstrate his ignorance of the difference between the human and the divine. It is god who possesses both the knowledge and power required to mix a plurality into a unity and, conversely, to dissolve a unity into a plurality, while no human being could possess either of these, whether at the present time or at any time in the future.

e   And so all these things were taken in hand, their natures being determined then by necessity in the way we've described, by the craftsman of the most perfect and excellent among things that come to be, at the time when he brought forth that self-sufficient, most perfect god. Although he did make use of the relevant auxiliary causes, it was he himself who gave their fair design to all that comes to be. That is why we must distinguish two forms of cause, the divine and the necessary. First, the divine, for

69   which we must search in all things if we are to gain a life of happiness to the extent that our nature allows, and second, the necessary, for which we must search for the sake of the divine. Our reason is that without the necessary, those other objects, about which we are serious, cannot on their own be discerned, and hence cannot be comprehended or partaken of in any other way.

We have now sorted out the different kinds of cause, which lie ready for us like lumber for carpenters. From them we are to weave together the remainder of our account. So let us briefly return to our starting point and quickly proceed to the same place from which we arrived at our

b   present position.[37] Let us try to put a final "head" on our account, one that fits in with our previous discussion.

To repeat what was said at the outset, the things we see were in a condition of disorderliness when the god introduced as much proportionality into them and in as many ways—making each thing proportional both to itself and to other things—as was possible for making them be commensurable and proportionate. For at the time they had no proportionality at all, except by chance, nor did any of them qualify at all for the names we now use to name them, names like *fire, water*, etc. All these

c   things, rather, the god first gave order to, and then out of them he proceeded to construct this universe, a single living thing that contains within itself all living things, mortal or immortal. He himself fashioned those that were

---

37. Cf. 31b–32c and 48b, 48e–49a, respectively.

divine, but assigned his own progeny the task of fashioning the generation of those that were mortal.

They imitated him: having taken the immortal origin of the soul, they proceeded next to encase it within a round mortal body [the head], and to give it the entire body as its vehicle. And within the body they built another kind of soul as well, the mortal kind, which contains within it those dreadful but necessary disturbances: pleasure, first of all, evil's most powerful lure; then pains, that make us run away from what is good; besides these, boldness also and fear, foolish counselors both; then also the spirit of anger hard to assuage, and expectation easily led astray. These they fused with unreasoning sense perception and all-venturing lust, and so, as was necessary, they constructed the mortal type of soul. In the face of these disturbances they scrupled to stain the divine soul only to the extent that this was absolutely necessary, and so they provided a home for the mortal soul in another place in the body, away from the other, once they had built an isthmus as boundary between the head and the chest by situating a neck between them to keep them apart. Inside the chest, then, and in what is called the trunk they proceeded to enclose the mortal type of soul. And since one part of the mortal soul was naturally superior to the other, they built the hollow of the trunk in sections, dividing them the way that women's quarters are divided from men's. They situated the midriff between the sections to serve as a partition. Now the part of the mortal soul that exhibits manliness and spirit, the ambitious part, they settled nearer the head, between the midriff and the neck, so that it might listen to reason and together with it restrain by force the part consisting of appetites, should the latter at any time refuse outright to obey the dictates of reason coming down from the citadel. The heart, then, which ties the veins together, the spring from which blood courses with vigorous pulse throughout all the bodily members, they set in the guardhouse. That way, if spirit's might should boil over at a report from reason that some wrongful act involving these members is taking place—something being done to them from outside or even something originating from the appetites within—every bodily part that is sensitive may be keenly sensitized, through all the narrow vessels, to the exhortations or threats and so listen and follow completely. In this way the best part among them all can be left in charge.

The gods foreknew that the pounding of the heart (which occurs when one expects what one fears or when one's spirit is aroused) would, like all such swelling of the passions, be caused by fire. So they devised something to relieve the pounding: they implanted lungs, a structure that is first of all soft and without blood and that secondly contains pores bored through it like a sponge. This enables it to take in breath and drink and thereby cool the heart, bringing it respite and relaxation in the heat. That, then, is why they cut the passages of the windpipe down to the lungs, and situated the lungs around the heart like padding, so that when spirit within the heart should reach its peak, the heart might pound against something that gives way to it and be cooled down. By laboring less, it might be better able to join spirit in serving reason.

e   The part of the soul that has appetites for food and drink and whatever else it feels a need for, given the body's nature, they settled in the area between the midriff and the boundary toward the navel. In the whole of this region they constructed something like a trough for the body's nourishment. Here they tied this part of the soul down like a beast, a wild one, but one they could not avoid sustaining along with the others if a mortal race were ever to be. They assigned it its position there, to keep it ever feeding at its trough, living as far away as possible from the part that takes counsel, and making as little clamor and noise as possible, thereby

71   letting the supreme part take its counsel in peace about what is beneficial for one and all. They knew that this part of the soul was not going to understand the deliverances of reason and that even if it were in one way or another to have some awareness of them, it would not have an innate regard for any of them, but would be much more enticed by images and phantoms night and day. Hence the god conspired with this very tendency

b   by constructing a liver, a structure which he situated in the dwelling place of this part of the soul. He made it into something dense, smooth, bright and sweet, though also having a bitter quality, so that the force of the thoughts sent down from the mind might be stamped upon it as upon a mirror that receives the stamps and returns visible images. So whenever the force of the mind's thoughts could avail itself of a congenial portion of the liver's bitterness and threaten it with severe command, it could then frighten this part of the soul. And by infusing the bitterness all over the liver, it could project bilious colors onto it and shrink the whole liver,

c   making it wrinkled and rough. It could curve and shrivel up the liver's lobe and block up and close off its receptacles and portal fissures, thereby causing pains and bouts of nausea. And again, whenever thought's gentle inspiration should paint quite opposite pictures, its force would bring respite from the bitterness by refusing to stir up or to make contact with a nature opposite to its own. It would instead use the liver's own natural

d   sweetness on it and restore the whole extent of it to be straight and smooth and free, and make that portion of the soul that inhabits the region around the liver gracious and well behaved, conducting itself with moderation during the night when, seeing that it has no share in reason and understanding, it practices divination by dreams. For our creators recalled their father's instruction to make the mortal race as excellent as possible, and so, redeem-

e   ing even the base part of ourselves in this way, they set the center of divination here, so that it might have some grasp of truth.

        The claim that god gave divination as a gift to human folly has good support: while he is in his right mind no one engages in divination, however divinely inspired and true it may be, but only when his power of understanding is bound in sleep or by sickness, or when some sort of possession works a change in him. On the other hand, it takes a man who has his wits about him to recall and ponder the pronouncements produced by this state of divination or possession, whether in sleep or while awake. It takes such a man to thoroughly analyze any and all visions that are seen, to determine how and for whom they signify some future, past or present good or evil. But as long as the fit remains on him, the man is incompetent to render judgment on his own visions and voices. As the ancient proverb well puts it, "Only a man of sound mind may know himself and conduct his own affairs." This is the reason why it is customary practice to appoint interpreters to render judgment on an inspired divination. These persons are called "diviners" by some who are entirely ignorant of the fact that they are expositors of utterances or visions communicated through riddles. Instead of "diviners," the correct thing to call them is, "interpreters of things divined."

This, then, explains why the liver's nature is what it is, and why it is situated in the region we say—it is for the purpose of divination. Now while each creature is still alive, an organ of this sort will display marks that are fairly clear, but once its life has gone, the organ turns blind and its divinations are too faint to display any clear marks. Moreover, the neighboring organ situated on its left turns out to have a structure which is meant to serve the liver in keeping it bright and clean continuously, like a dust cloth provided for wiping a mirror, placed next to it and always available. Hence, whenever impurities of one sort or another, the effects of bodily illnesses, turn up all around the liver, the spleen, a loosely-woven organ with hollow spaces that contain no blood, cleans them all away and absorbs them. In consequence it becomes engorged with the impurities it has cleaned off, swells to great size and festers. Later, when the body's cleansing is complete, the swelling subsides, and the spleen once again shrinks back to its normal size.

So, as for our questions concerning the soul—to what extent it is mortal and to what extent divine; where its parts are situated, with what organs they are associated, and why they are situated apart from one another— that the truth has been told is something we could affirm only if we had divine confirmation. But that our account is surely at least a "likely" one is a claim we must risk, both now and as we proceed to examine the matter more closely. Let that be our claim, then.

Our next topic must be pursued along the same lines. This was to describe how the rest of the body came to be.[38] The following train of reasoning should explain its composition best of all. The creators of our race knew that we were going to be undisciplined in matters of food and drink. They knew that our gluttony would lead us to consume much more than the moderate amount we needed. So, to prevent the swift destruction of our mortal race by diseases and to forestall its immediate, premature demise, they had the foresight to create the lower abdomen, as it's called, as a receptacle for storing the excess food and drink. They wound the intestines round in coils to prevent the nourishment from passing through

38. Cf. 61c.

so quickly that the body would of necessity require fresh nourishment just as quickly, thereby rendering it insatiable. Such gluttony would make our whole race incapable of philosophy and the arts, and incapable of heeding the most divine part within us.

b   As for flesh and bones and things of that nature, this is how it is. The starting point for all these was the formation of marrow. For life's chains, as long as the soul remains bound to the body, are bound within the marrow, giving roots for the mortal race. The marrow itself came to be out of other things. For the god isolated from their respective kinds those primary triangles which were undistorted and smooth and hence, owing to their exactness, were particularly well suited to make up fire, water, air

c   and earth. He mixed them together in the right proportions, and from them made the marrow, a "universal seed" contrived for every mortal kind. Next, he implanted in the marrow the various types of soul and bound them fast in it. And in making his initial distribution, he proceeded immediately to divide the marrow into the number and kinds of shapes that matched the number and kinds of shapes that the types of soul were to possess, type by type. He then proceeded to mold the "field," as it were,

d   that was to receive the divine seed, making it round, and called this portion of the marrow, "brain." Each living thing was at its completion to have a head to function as a container for this marrow. That, however, which was to hold fast the remaining, mortal part of the soul, he divided into shapes that were at once round and elongated, all of which he named "marrow." And from these as from anchors he put out bonds to secure the whole soul and so he proceeded to construct our bodies all around this marrow, beginning with the formation of solid bone as a covering for the whole of it.

e   This is how he constructed bone. He sifted earth that was pure and smooth, kneaded it and soaked it with marrow. Next, he set this mixture in fire, and then dipped it in water, then back in fire, followed by water again. By moving it this way repeatedly from the one and then back to the other, he made it insoluble by both. He made use of this material in shaping a round, bony globe to enclose the brain, and left it with a narrow

74   passage out. From the material he then proceeded to mold vertebrae to enclose marrow of the neck and back, and set them in place one underneath another, beginning with the head and proceeding along the whole length of the trunk, to function as pivots. And so, to preserve all of the seed, he fenced it in with a stony enclosure. In this enclosure he made joints, employing in their case the character of the Different situated between them to allow them to move and to flex.

b   Moreover, the god thought that bone as such was rather too brittle and inflexible, and also that repeatedly getting extremely hot and cold by turns would cause it to disintegrate and to destroy in short order the seed within it. That is why he contrived to make sinews and flesh. He bound all the limbs together with sinews that could contract and relax, and so enabled the body to flex about the pivots and to stretch itself out. The flesh he made as a defense against summer's heat and as protection against winter's cold. And, as protection against injuries, too, he made the flesh so that it would give way softly and gently to bodies like the felted coverings we wear. He made it to contain within itself a warm moisture that would come out as perspiration during summertime, when, by moistening the body on the outside, it would impart the body's own coolness to the whole of it. And conversely, in wintertime this moisture would provide an adequate defense, by means of this fire, against the frost which surrounds it and attacks it from outside. Such were the designs of him who molded us like wax: he made a mixture using water, fire and earth, which he adjusted together, and created a compound of acid and brine, a fermented mixture which he combined with the previous mixture, and so he formed flesh, sappy and soft. The sinews he made out of a mixture of bone and unfermented flesh, to make up a single yellow stuff whose character was intermediate between them both. That is the reason the sinews came to have a stretchier and tougher character than flesh, yet softer and more moist than bone. With these the god wrapped the bones and the marrow. First he bound the bones to each other with sinews, and then he laid a shroud of flesh upon them all.

All those bones that had more soul than others he proceeded to wrap in a very thin layer of flesh, while those that contained less he wrapped in a very thick layer of very dense flesh. And indeed, at the joints of the bones, where it appeared that reason did not absolutely require the presence of flesh, he introduced only a thin layer of flesh, so that the ability of the joints to flex would not be impeded, a condition that would have made it very difficult for the bodies to move. A further reason was this: if there were a thick layer of flesh there, packed extremely densely together, its hardness would cause a kind of insensibility, which would make thinking less retentive and more obscure. This he wanted to prevent.

This explains why thighs and calves, the area around the hips, arms (both upper and lower), and all other bodily parts where there are no joints as well as all the internal bones, are all fully provided with flesh. It is because they have only small amounts of soul in their marrow, and so are devoid of intelligence. On the other hand, all those bodily parts that do possess intelligence are less fleshy, except perhaps for a fleshy thing—the tongue, for example—that was created to be itself an organ of sensation. But in most cases it is as I said. For there is no way that anything whose generation and composition are a consequence of Necessity can accommodate the combination of thick bone and massive flesh with keen and responsive sensation. If these two characteristics had not refused their concomitance, our heads above all else would have been so constituted as to possess this combination, and the human race, crowned with a head fortified with flesh and sinews would have a life twice, or many more times as long, a healthier and less painful life than the one we have now. As it was, however, our makers calculated the pros and cons of giving our race greater longevity but making it worse, versus making it better, though less long-lived, and

c

d

e

75

b

c

decided that the superior though shorter life-span was in every way preferable for everyone to the longer but inferior one. This is why they capped
the head with a sparse layer of bone—and not with flesh and sinew, given
that the head has no joints. For all these reasons, then, the head has turned
out to be more sensitive and intelligent but also, in every man's case, much
d   weaker than the body to which it is attached. With this in mind the god
thus positioned sinews at the very edge of the head, around the neck, and
welded them uniformly. To these sinews he fastened the ends of the
jawbones underneath the face. The other sinews he shared out among all
the limbs, fastening joint to joint.

Our makers fitted the mouth out with teeth, a tongue and lips in their
e   current arrangement, to accommodate both what is necessary and what
is best: they designed the mouth as the entry passage for what is necessary,
and as the exit for what is best: for all that comes in and provides nourishment for the body is necessary, while that stream of speech that flows out
through the mouth, that instrument of intelligence, is the fairest and best
of all streams.

Moreover, the head couldn't be left to consist of nothing but bare bone,
in view of the extremes of seasonal heat and cold. On the other hand, any
mass of flesh with which it might be veiled couldn't be allowed to make
76   it dull and insensitive, either. And so, an outer layer, disproportionately
large (the thing we now call "skin"), was separated off from the flesh [of
the upper body] that wasn't drying out completely. The moisture in the
area of the brain enabled this layer to draw together toward itself and
grow so as to envelop the head all around. Coming up under the sutures,
this moisture watered it, and closed it together upon the crown, drawing
it together in a knot, as it were. The sutures varied considerably, owing
to the effect of the revolutions [in the head][39] and of the nourishment taken:
the greater the conflict among these revolutions, the more numerous the
b   sutures—the lesser the conflict, the less numerous they were.

Now the divine part [the brain] began to puncture this whole area of
skin all around with its fire. Once the skin was pierced and the moisture
had exuded outward through it, all that was purely wet and hot went
away. The part that was compounded of the same stuff that the skin was
made up of, caught up by this motion, was stretched to a great length
outside this skin, no thicker than the punctured hole [through which it
passed]. However, it moved slowly, and so the surrounding air pushed it
c   back inside to curl underneath the skin and take root there. This is the
process by which hair has come to grow on the skin. Hair is something
fibrous, made of the same stuff as the skin, though harder and more dense
due to the felting effect of the cooling process: once a hair separates off
from skin, it is cooled and so gets felted together.

With this stuff, then, our maker made our heads bushy, availing himself
of the causal factors just described. His intention was that this, not bare

39. Cf. 43a ff.

flesh, ought to provide a protective covering for the part of the head that   d
holds the brain: it was light, and just right for providing shade in summer,
and shelter in winter, without obstructing or interfering with the head's
sensitivity in any way.

Sinew, skin and bone were interwoven at the ends of our fingers and
toes. The mixture of these three was dried out, resulting in the formation
of a single stuff, a piece of hard skin, the same in every case. Now these
were merely auxiliary causes in its formation—the preeminent cause of
its production was the purpose that took account of future generations:
our creators understood that one day women and the whole realm of wild   e
beasts would one day come to be from men, and in particular they knew
that many of these offspring would need the use of nails and claws or
hoofs for many purposes.[40] This is why they took care to include nails
formed in a rudimentary way in their design for humankind, right at the
start. This was their reason, then, and these the professed aims that guided
them in making skin, hair and nails grow at the extremities of our
limbs.

So all the parts, all the limbs of the mortal living thing came to constitute
a natural whole. Of necessity, however, it came about that he lived his life   77
surrounded by fire and air, which caused him to waste away and be
depleted, and so to perish. The gods, therefore, devised something to
protect him. They made another mixture and caused another nature to
grow, one congenial to our human nature though endowed with other
features and other sensations, so as to be a different living thing. These
are now cultivated trees, plants and seeds, taught by the art of agriculture
to be domesticated for our use. But at first the only kinds there were were   b
wild ones, older than our cultivated kinds. We may call these plants "living
things" on the ground that anything that partakes of life has an incontest-
able right to be called a "living thing."[41] And in fact, what we are talking
about now partakes of the third type of soul, the type that our account
has situated between the midriff and the navel. This type is totally devoid
of opinion, reasoning or understanding, though it does share in sensation,
pleasant and painful, and desires. For throughout its existence it is completely passive, and its formation has not entrusted it with a natural ability
to discern and reflect upon any of its own characteristics, by revolving
within and about itself, repelling movement from without and exercising   c
its own inherent movement. Hence it is alive, to be sure, and unmistakably
a living thing, but it stays put, standing fixed and rooted, since it lacks
self-motion.

All these varieties were planted by our masters, to whom we are subject,
to nourish us. Having done that, they proceeded to cut channels throughout

---

40. See below, 90e–92c.

41. The word for living things here, *zōa* (which is often appropriately translated "animals"), is cognate with Timaeus' word for "life." His point is that because plants have
"life" (*zēn*), they are appropriately called *zōa*, even though they are not animals.

our bodies, like water pipes in a garden, so that our bodies could be irrigated, as it were, by an oncoming stream. First, they cut two blood

d   veins, channels hidden underneath the skin where the flesh joins it, to go down either side of the back—the body is a twofold thing, with a right and a left side. They situated these veins alongside the spine, and between them they placed the life-giving marrow as well, to give it its best chance to flourish, and to allow the bloodstream, which courses downhill, to flow readily from this region and uniformly irrigate the other parts of the body.

e   They next split these veins in the region of the head, and wove them through one another, crossing them in opposite directions. They diverted the veins from the right toward the left side of the body, and those from the left toward the right, so that they, together with the skin, would act as a bond to keep the head fastened to the body, seeing that there were no sinews attached to the crown to enclose the head all around. They did this especially to make sure that the stimulations received by the senses, coming from either side of the body, might register clearly upon the body as a whole.

     From here the gods proceeded to fashion the irrigation system in the

78 following way. We'll come to see it more easily if we can first agree on this point: whatever is made up of smaller parts holds in larger parts, while what consists of larger parts is incapable of holding in smaller parts. Of all the elemental kinds, fire is made up of the smallest parts, and that is the reason it can pass through water, earth and air, and any of their compounds. Nothing can hold it in. Now we must apply the same point

b   to our belly. When food and drink descend into it, it holds them in, but it cannot hold in air and fire, consisting as they do of smaller parts than it does. And so the god availed himself of fire and air to conduct moisture from the belly to the [two] veins. He wove together an interlaced structure of air and fire, something like a fish trap. At its entrance it had a pair of funnels, one of which in turn he subdivided into two. And from the funnels he stretched reeds, as it were, all around throughout the structure, right

c   to its extremities. All the interior parts of this network he made of fire; the funnels and the shell he made of air.

     He took this structure and set it around the living thing which he had fashioned, in the following way. The funnel part he inserted into the mouth, and, consisting as it did of two funnels, he let one of them descend into the lungs down the windpipe, and the other alongside the windpipe into the belly. He made a split in the first one and assigned each of its parts a common outlet by way of the nostrils, so that when the one part fails to

d   provide passage by way of the mouth, all of its currents also might be replenished from that one. The shell, the other part of the trap, he made to grow around the hollow part of the body, and he made this whole thing now flow together onto the funnels [compressing them]—gently, because they are made of air—now, when the funnels flow back [expanding again], he made the interlaced structure sink into and through the body—a relatively porous thing—and pass outside again.[42] The interior rays of fire [inside the shell], bound from side to side, he made to follow the air as it passed in both directions. This process was to go on non-stop for as long as the mortal living thing holds together; and this, of course, is the phenomenon to which the name-giver (so we claim) assigned the names of *inhalation* and *exhalation*. This entire pattern of action and reaction, irrigating and cooling our bodies, supports their nutrition and life. For whenever the internal fire, united with the breath that passes in or out, follows it along, it surges up and down continually and makes its way through and into the belly, where it gets hold of the food and drink. These it dissolves or breaks up into tiny parts, which it then takes through the outbound passages along which it is advancing, and transfers them into the [two] veins, as water from a spring is transferred into water pipes. And so it causes the currents of the veins to flow through the body as through a conduit.

Let us, however, take another look at what happens in respiration. What explains its having the character that it now actually has? It is this. Since there is no void into which anything that is moving could enter, and since the air we breathe out does move out, away from us, it clearly follows that this air doesn't move into a void, but pushes the air next to it out of its place. As this air is pushed out, it drives out the air next to it, and so on, and so inevitably the air, displaced all around, enters the place from which the original air was breathed out and refills that place, following hard on the breath. This all takes place at once, like the rotation of a wheel, because there is no such thing as a void. Consequently even as the breath is being discharged, the area of the chest and the lungs fills up again with the air that surrounds the body, air that goes through the cycle of displacement and penetrates the porous flesh. And again, when the air is turned back and passes outward through the body, it comes round to push respiration inward by way of the mouth and the nostrils.

How did these processes get started? The explanation, we must suppose, is this: in the case of every living thing, its inner parts that are close to the blood and the veins are its hottest parts—an inner spring of fire inside it, as it were. This, of course, is what we've been comparing to the interlaced structure of a fish trap; it is entirely woven of fire, we said, and extended throughout its middle, while the rest of it, the external parts, are woven of air. Now it is beyond dispute that what is hot has a natural tendency to move outward into its own proper region, toward that which is akin to it. In this case there are two passages out, one out through [the pores of] the body, and the other out through the mouth and nose. So whenever hot air rushes out the one passage, it pushes air around into the other, and the air so pushed around gets hot as it encounters the fire, while the

e

79

b

c

d

e

42. As 79c–e seems to show, Timaeus appears to envisage the "shell" as an envelope of air surrounding the exterior of the torso, being drawn through the interstices of the body into the interior and then pushed out again, as breathing takes place.

air that passes out is cooled down. Now as the temperature changes and the air that enters by way of one or the other of the passages gets hotter, the hotter air is more inclined to return by way of the passage it entered, since it moves toward what is like itself, and so it pushes air around to and through the other passage. This air is affected the same way, and produces the same effect every time; and so, due to both these principles it produces an oscillation back and forth, thereby providing for inhalation and exhalation to occur.

80   In this connection we should pursue along these lines an inquiry into the causes of the phenomena associated with medical cupping, and of swallowing, as well as of the motion of all projectiles that are dispatched into the air and along the ground. We should also investigate all sounds, whether fast or slow—sounds that appear to us as high pitched or low. Sometimes, when the motion they produce in us as they move towards us lacks conformity, these sounds are inharmonious; at other times, when the motion does have conformity, the sounds are harmonious. [What happens in the latter case is this.] The slower sounds catch up with the motions

b   of the earlier and quicker sounds as these are already dying away and have come to a point of conformity with the motions produced by the slower sounds that travel later. In catching up with them, the slower sounds do not upset them, even though they introduce another motion. On the contrary, they graft onto the quicker movement, now dying away, the beginning of a slower one that conforms to it, and so they produce a single effect, a mixture of high and low. Hence the pleasure they bring to fools and the delight they afford—by their expression of divine harmony in mortal movement—to the wise.

c   And what is more, every kind of water current, even the descent of a thunderbolt as well as that marvellous "attraction" exercised by amber and by the lodestone, in all these cases there is no such thing as a force of attraction. As any careful investigator will discover, there is no void; these things push themselves around into each other; all things move by exchanging places, each to its own place, whether in the process of combination or of dissolution. He will discover that these "works of wizardry" are due to the interactive relationships among these phenomena.

d   The phenomenon of respiration, which provided the occasion for this account, is a case in point. The above are the principles and causes to which it owes its existence, as we have said before. The fire cuts up the food [in our bellies] and as it follows the breath it oscillates inside us. As the oscillation goes on, the fire pumps the cut-up bits of food from the belly and packs them into the veins. This is the mechanism by which the streams of nourishment continue to flow throughout the bodies of all living things. The bits of food, freshly cut up and derived from things like

e   themselves—from fruits or from vegetables which the god had caused to grow for this very purpose, to serve us as food—come to have a variety of colors as a result of being mixed together, but a reddish color pervading them predominates, a character that is the product of the cutting and staining action of fire upon moisture. This is why the color of the liquid that flows in our bodies looks the way we've described; this liquid we call *blood*, which feeds our flesh and indeed our whole bodies. From this source the various parts of our bodies are watered and so replenish the supports of the depleted areas. Now both processes, the replenishment and the depletion, follow the manner of the movement of anything within the universe at large: everything moves toward that which is of its own kind. In this case, our external environment continually wastes us away and distributes our bulk by dispatching each [elemental] kind toward its own sort. The ingredients in our blood, then, having been chopped up inside us and encompassed by the individual living thing as by the frame of the universe, of necessity imitate the universe's motion. And so, as each of the fragmented parts inside moves toward its own kind, it replenishes once again the area just then depleted. In every case, whenever there is more leaving a body than flowing in [to replenish it], it diminishes; whenever less, the body grows. So while a living thing's constitution is still young, and its elemental triangles are "fresh from the slips," as it were, the triangles are firmly locked together, even though the frame of its entire mass is pliable, seeing that it has just lately been formed from marrow and nourished with milk. Now when the triangles that constitute the young living thing's food and drink enter its body from the outside and are enveloped within it, the body's own new triangles cut and prevail over these others, which are older and weaker than they are. The living thing is thus nourished by an abundance of like parts, and so made to grow big. But when the roots of the triangles are slackened as a result of numerous conflicts they have waged against numerous adversaries over a long period of time, they are no longer able to cut up the entering food-triangles into conformity with themselves. They are themselves handily destroyed by the invaders from outside. Every living thing, then, goes into decline when it loses this battle, and it suffers what we call "old age." Eventually the interlocking bonds of the triangles around the marrow can no longer hold on, and come apart under stress, and when this happens they let the bonds of the soul go. The soul is then released in a natural way, and finds it pleasant to take its flight. All that is unnatural, we recall, is painful while all that occurs naturally is pleasant. This is true of death as well: a death that is due to disease or injury is painful and forced, while a death that comes naturally, when the aging process has run its course, is of all deaths the least distressing—a pleasant, not a painful death.

How diseases originate is, I take it, obvious to all. Given that there are four kinds of stuff out of which the body has been constructed—earth, fire, water and air—it may happen that some of these unnaturally increase themselves at the expense of the others. Or they may switch regions, each leaving its own and moving into another's region. Or again, since there is in fact more than one variety of fire and the other stuffs, it may happen that a given bodily part accommodates a particular variety that is not appropriate for it. When these things happen, they bring on conflicts and

diseases. For when any of these unnatural occurrences and changes take
b   place, bodily parts that used to be cold become hot, or those that are dry
go on to become moist, and so with light and heavy, too. They undergo
all sorts of changes in all sorts of ways. Indeed, it is our view that only
when that which arrives at or leaves a particular bodily part is the same
as that part, consistent, uniform and in proper proportion with it, will the
body be allowed to remain stable, sound and healthy. On the other hand,
anything that causes offense by passing beyond these bounds as it arrives
or departs will bring on a multiplicity of altered states, and an infinity of
diseases and degenerations.

Furthermore, since there is a class of secondary structures to be found
c   in nature, anyone who intends to understand diseases will have a second
set of subjects to study. Since marrow and bone, flesh and sinew are
composed of the elemental stuffs—from which blood also has been formed,
though in a different way—most of the diseases are brought on in the
manner just described. But the most serious and grievous diseases are
contracted when the process of generation that led to the formation of
these structures is reversed. When this happens, they degenerate. It is
natural for flesh and sinews to be formed from blood, the sinew from the
d   fiber (which is of its own kind) and the flesh from the part of the blood
that congeals when the sinew is separated from it. And the sticky and oily
stuff that in its turn emerges from the sinew and the flesh both glues the
flesh to the bone and feeds the marrow-encompassing bone itself, so causing it to grow. And because the bone is so dense, the part of this stuff that
filters through, consisting as it does of the purest, smoothest and oiliest
e   kind of triangles, forms droplets inside the bone and waters the marrow.
And when this is the way it actually happens in each case, health will
generally result.

Disease, however, will result if things happen the other way around.
For when flesh that is wasting away passes its waste back into the veins,
the veins will contain not only air but also an excess of blood of great
variety. This blood will have a multitude of colors and bitter aspects, and
even acidic and salty qualities, and will contain bile and serum and phlegm
of every sort. These are all back-products and agents of destruction. To
83   begin with, they corrupt the blood itself, and then also they do not supply
the body any further with nourishment. They move everywhere throughout the veins, no longer keeping to the order of natural circulation. They
are hostile to one another, since none receives any advantage from any
other, and they wage a destructive and devastating war against the constituents of the body that have stayed intact and kept to their posts.

Now as the oldest part of the flesh wastes away, it resists assimilation.
It turns black as a result of being subjected to a prolonged process of
b   burning, and because it is thoroughly eaten up it is bitter, and so it launches
a severe attack against any part of the body that has not yet been destroyed.
Sometimes the bitterness is largely refined away, and then the black color
acquires an acidic quality that replaces the bitter. At other times, though,

the bitterness is steeped in blood, and then it comes to have more of a reddish color, and when the black is mixed with this, it becomes a grass-like green. Further, when the flesh that is disintegrated by the fire of the inflammation is fairly young, the color that is mixed with the bitterness is a yellowish orange. Now the name "bile," common to all these varieties, was given to them either by doctors, possibly, or else by someone who had the ability to look at a plurality of unlike things and see in them a single kind that deserves to be called by a single name. As for everything that can be called a variety of bile, each has its own distinctive definition, depending on its color. In the case of serum, some of it, the watery part of the blood, is benign while that which is a part of the black, acid bile is malignant when heat causes it to be mixed with a salty quality. This kind of thing is called acid phlegm. Furthermore, when the stuff that comes from the disintegration of young, tender flesh is exposed to air and blown up with wind and enveloped in moisture, bubbles form as a result, each one too small to be seen though collectively amounting to a visible mass. These bubbles look white, as foam begins to form. All this disintegration of tender flesh reacting with air is what we call white phlegm. Newly formed phlegm, furthermore, has a watery part which consists of perspiration and tears, as well as any other impurities that are discharged every day. So whenever the blood, instead of being replenished in the natural way by nutrients from food and drink, derives its volume from opposite sources, contrary to nature's way, all these things, it turns out, serve as instruments of disease.

Now when a certain part of the flesh is decomposed by disease, as long as the foundations of the flesh remain intact, the effect of the calamity is only half of what it would otherwise be, for there is still a chance of an easy recovery. But when the stuff that binds the flesh to the bones becomes diseased and no longer nourishes the bone or binds the flesh to the bone because it is now separated from flesh and bone as well as from sinews,[43] it turns from being slick and smooth and oily to being rough and briny, shriveled up in consequence of its bad regimen. When this occurs, all the stuff that this happens to crumbles away back into the flesh and the sinew, and separates from the bone. The flesh, which collapses with it away from its roots, leaves the sinews bare and full of brine. And the flesh itself succumbs back into the bloodstream, where it works to aggravate the previously mentioned diseases.

Severe as these bodily processes are, those disorders that affect the more basic tissues are even more serious. When the density of the flesh prevents the bone from getting enough ventilation, the bone gets moldy, which causes it to get too hot. Gangrene sets in and the bone cannot take in its nourishment. It then crumbles and, by a reverse process, is dissolved into that nourishment which, in its turn, enters the flesh, and as the flesh lands in the blood it causes all of the previously mentioned diseases to become

c

d

e

84

b

c

43. Reading *au to ex ekeinōn hama kai neurōn* in a2.

more virulent still. But the most extreme case of all is when the marrow becomes diseased, either as a result of some deficiency or some excess. This produces the most serious, the most critically fatal diseases, in which all the bodily processes are made to flow backwards.

d Further, there is a third class of diseases, which we should think of as arising in three ways. (a) One way is from air, (b) another from phlegm and (c) the third from bile. (a) When the lungs, the dispensers of air to the body, are obstructed by humors, they do not permit a clear passage. At some places the air cannot get in, while at others more than the appropriate amount gets in. In the former case, there will be parts of the body that don't get any breath and so begin to decay, while in the latter case the air forces its way through the veins and twists them together like strands. It makes its way into the central region of the body, the region that contains the midriff, where it is shut in, thereby causing the body to waste away.

e These factors produce countless painful diseases, often accompanied by profuse perspiration. And often, when flesh disintegrates inside the body, air is produced there, but is unable to get out. This air then causes just as much excruciating pain as the air that comes in from outside. The pain is most severe when the air settles around the sinews and the veins there and causes them to swell, thereby stretching backwards the "back stays" (the great sinews of the shoulder and arm) and the sinews attached to them. It is from this phenomenon of stretching, of course, that the diseases called *tetanus* ("tension") and *opisthotonus* ("backward stretching") have received their names. These diseases are difficult to cure. In fact, the onset

85 of a fever affords the best prospects for relief from such ailments.

(b) Now as for the white phlegm, as long as it is trapped in the body, it is troublesome because of the air in its bubbles. But if it finds a vent to the outside of the body, it is gentler, even though it does deck the body with white, leprous spots and engenders the corresponding diseases. If it is mixed with black bile and the mixture is sprayed against the divine circuits in the head, thereby throwing them into confusion, the effect is

b fairly mild if it comes during sleep, but should it come upon someone while awake, it is much harder to shake off. Seeing that it is a disease of the sacred part of our constitution, it is entirely just that it should be called the "sacred" disease (i.e., epilepsy).

Acid and salty phlegm is the source of all those diseases that come about by passage of fluids. These disorders have been given all sorts of different names, in view of the fact that the bodily regions into which the fluids flow are quite diverse.

(c) All inflammations in the body (so called from their being burned or

c "set aflame") are caused by bile. When bile finds a vent to the outside, it boils over and sends up all sorts of tumors, but when it is shut up inside, it creates many inflammatory diseases. The worst occurs when the bile gets mixed with clean blood and disrupts the disposition of the blood's fibers, which are interspersed throughout the blood. These fibers act to preserve a balance of thinness and thickness, i.e., to prevent both the blood from getting so liquid, due to the body's heat, that it oozes out from the body's pores, and, on the other hand, its getting so dense that it is sluggish and hardly able to circulate within the veins. The fibers, then, by virtue of their natural composition, preserve the appropriate state between these conditions. And even after death, when the blood cools down, if the fibers are [extracted from the blood and] collected, the residue will still be completely runny, while if they are left in the blood, they, along with the surrounding cold, congeal it in no time. Given, then, that the fibers have this effect upon the blood, though the bile—which originated as primitive blood and then from flesh was dissolved into blood again—is hot and liquid at first as a little of it invades the blood, it congeals under the effect of the fibers, and as it congeals and is forced to extinguish its heat it causes internal cold and shivering. But as more of it flows in, it overpowers the fibers with its own heat. It boils over and shakes them up into utter confusion. And if it proves capable of sustaining its power to the end, it penetrates to the marrow and burns it up, thereby loosening the cables that hold the soul there, like a ship, and setting the soul free. But when there is rather little of it and the body resists its dissolution, the bile is itself overpowered and is expelled either by way of the body as a whole or else it is compressed through the veins into the lower or upper belly, and is expelled from the body like an exile from a city in civil strife, so bringing on diarrhea, dysentery and every disease of that kind. Bodies afflicted mostly by an excess of fire will generate continuous states of heat and fevers; those suffering from an excess of air produce fevers that recur every day; while those that have an excess of water have fevers that recur only every other day, given that water is more sluggish than air or fire. Bodies afflicted by an excess of earth, the most sluggish of the four, are purged within a fourfold cycle of time and produce fevers that occur every fourth day, fevers that are hard to get over.

The foregoing described how diseases of the body happen to come about. The diseases of the soul that result from a bodily condition come about in the following way. It must be granted, surely, that mindlessness is the disease of the soul, and of mindlessness there are two kinds. One is madness, and the other is ignorance. And so if a man suffers from a condition that brings on either one or the other, that condition must be declared a disease.

We must lay it down that the diseases that pose the gravest dangers for the soul are excessive pleasures and pains. When a man enjoys himself too much or, in the opposite case, when he suffers great pain, and he exerts himself to seize the one and avoid the other in inopportune ways, he lacks the ability to see or hear anything right. He goes raving mad and is at that moment least capable of rational thought. And if the seed of a man's marrow grows to overflowing abundance like a tree that bears an inordinately plentiful quantity of fruit, he is in for a long series of bursts of pain, or of pleasures, in the area of his desires and their fruition. These severe pleasures and pains drive him mad for the greater part of his life,

d

e

86

b

c

d   and though his body has made his soul diseased and witless, people will think of him not as sick, but as willfully evil. But the truth about sexual overindulgence is that it is a disease of the soul caused primarily by the condition of a single stuff which, due to the porousness of the bones, flows within the body and renders it moist. And indeed, just about every type of succumbing to pleasure is talked about as something reproachable, as though the evils are willfully done. But it is not right to reproach people

e   for them, for no one is willfully evil. A man becomes evil, rather, as a result of one or another corrupt condition of his body and an uneducated upbringing. No one who incurs these pernicious conditions would will to have them.

      And as for pains, once again it is the body that causes the soul so much trouble, and in the same ways. When any of a man's acid and briny phlegms or any bitter and bilious humors wander up and down his body

87   without finding a vent to the outside and remain pent up inside, they mix the vapor that they give off with the motion of the soul and so are confounded with it. So they produce all sorts of diseases of the soul, some more intense and some more frequent than others. And as they move to the three regions of the soul, each of them produces a multitude of varieties of bad temper and melancholy in the region it attacks, as well as of recklessness and cowardice, not to mention forgetfulness and stupidity. Further-

b   more, when men whose constitutions are bad in this way have bad forms of government where bad civic speeches are given, both in public and in private and where, besides, no studies that could remedy this situation are at all pursued by people from their youth on up, that is how all of us who are bad come to be that way—the products of two causes both entirely beyond our control. It is the begetters far more than the begotten, and the nurturers far more than the nurtured, that bear the blame for all this. Even so, one should make every possible effort to flee from badness, whether with the help of one's upbringing, or the pursuits or studies one undertakes, and to seize its opposite. But that is the subject for another speech.

c   The counterpart to the subject just dealt with, i.e., how to treat our bodies and states of mind and preserve them whole, is one that it is now fitting and right to give its turn. After all, good things have more of a claim to be the subject of our speech than bad things. Now all that is good is beautiful, and what is beautiful is not ill-proportioned. Hence we must take it that if a living thing is to be in good condition, it will be well-proportioned. We can perceive the less important proportions and do some figuring about them, but the more important proportions, which are of

d   the greatest consequence, we are unable to figure out. In determining health and disease or virtue and vice no proportion or lack of it is more important than that between soul and body—yet we do not think about any of them nor do we realize that when a vigorous and excellent soul is carried about by a too frail and puny frame, or when the two are combined in the opposite way, the living thing as a whole lacks beauty, because it is lacking in the most important of proportions. That living thing, however, which finds itself in the opposite condition is, for those who are able to observe it, the most beautiful, the most desirable of all things to behold. Imagine a body which lacks proportion because its legs are too long or something else is too big. It is not only ugly but also causes itself no end of troubles. As its parts try to cooperate to get its tasks done it frequently tires itself out or gets convulsive, or, because it lurches this way and that, it keeps falling down. That's how we ought to think of that combination of soul and body which we call the living thing. When within it there is a soul more powerful than the body and this soul gets excited, it churns the whole being and fills it from inside with diseases, and when it concentrates on one or another course of study or inquiry, it wears the body out. And again, when the soul engages in public or private teaching sessions or verbal battles, the disputes and contentions that then occur cause the soul to fire the body up and rock it back and forth, so inducing discharges which trick most so-called doctors into making misguided diagnoses. But when, on the other hand, a large body, too much for its soul, is joined with a puny and feeble mind, then, given that human beings have two sets of natural desires—desires of the body for food and desires of the most divine part of us for wisdom—the motions of the stronger part will predominate, and amplify their own interest. They render the functions of the soul dull, stupid and forgetful, thereby bringing on the gravest disease of all: ignorance.

From both of these conditions there is in fact one way to preserve oneself, and that is not to exercise the soul without exercising the body, nor the body without the soul, so that each may be balanced by the other and so be sound. The mathematician, then, or the ardent devotee of any other intellectual discipline should also provide exercise for his body by taking part in gymnastics, while one who takes care to develop his body should in his turn practice the exercises of the soul by applying himself to the arts and to every pursuit of wisdom, if he is to truly deserve the joint epithets of "fine and good." And the various bodily parts should also be looked after in this same way, in imitation of the structure of the universe. For since the body is heated and cooled inside by things that enter it and is dried and moistened by things outside of it and made to undergo the consequent changes by both of these motions, it will happen that when a man subjects his body to these motions when it has been in a state of rest, the body is overcome and brought to ruin. But if he models himself after what we have called the foster-mother and nurse of the universe and persistently refuses to allow his body any degree of rest but exercises and continually agitates it through its whole extent, he will keep in a state of natural equilibrium the internal and the external motions. And if the agitation is a measured one, he will succeed in bringing order and regularity to those disturbances and those elemental parts that wander all over the body according to their affinities in the way described in the account we gave earlier about the universe. He will not allow one hostile element to position itself next to another and so breed wars and diseases in the body.

89   Instead, he will have one friendly element placed by another, and so bring
      about health.
         Now the best of the motions is one that occurs within oneself and is
      caused by oneself. This is the motion that bears the greatest kinship to
      understanding and to the motion of the universe. Motion that is caused
      by the agency of something else is less good. Worst of all is the motion
      that moves, part by part, a passive body in a state of rest, and does so by
      means of other things. That, then, is why the motion induced by physical
      exercise is the best of those that purify and restore the body. Second is
      that induced by the rocking motion of sea travel or travel in any other
 b   kind of conveyance that doesn't tire one out. The third type of motion is
      useful in an occasional instance of dire need; barring that, however, no
      man in his right mind should tolerate it. This is medical purging by means
      of drugs. We should avoid aggravating with drugs diseases that aren't
      particularly dangerous. Every disease has a certain makeup that in a way
      resembles the natural makeup of living things. In fact, the constitution of
      such beings goes through an ordered series of stages throughout their life.
      This is true of the species as a whole, and also of its individual members,
 c   each of which is born with its allotted span of life, barring unavoidable
      accidents. This is because its triangles are so made up, right from the
      beginning, as to have the capacity to hold up for a limited time beyond
      which life cannot be prolonged any further. Now diseases have a similar
      makeup, so that when you try to wipe them out with drugs before they
      have run their due course, the mild diseases are liable to get severe, and
      the occasional ones frequent. That is why you need to cater to all such
      diseases by taking care of yourself to the extent you are free and have the
 d   time to do that. What you should not do is aggravate a stubborn irritation
      with drugs.
         Let these remarks suffice, then, on the subject of the living thing as a
      whole and its bodily parts, and how a man should both lead and be led
      by himself in order to have the best prospects for leading a rational life.
      Indeed, we must give an even higher priority to doing our utmost to make
      sure that the part that is to do the leading is as superbly and perfectly as
 e   possible fitted for that task. Now a thoroughgoing discussion of these
      matters would in and of itself be a considerable task, but if we treat it as
      a side issue, in line with what we have said before, it may not be out of
      turn to conclude our discourse with the following observations.
         There are, as we have said many times now, three distinct types of soul
      that reside within us, each with its own motions. So now too, we must
      say in the same vein, as briefly as we can, that any type which is idle and
      keeps its motions inactive cannot but become very weak, while one that
90   keeps exercising becomes very strong. And so we must keep watch to
      make sure that their motions remain proportionate to each other.
         Now we ought to think of the most sovereign part of our soul as god's
      gift to us, given to be our guiding spirit. This, of course, is the type of
      soul that, as we maintain, resides in the top part of our bodies. It raises

us up away from the earth and toward what is akin to us in heaven, as though we are plants grown not from the earth but from heaven. In saying this, we speak absolutely correctly. For it is from heaven, the place from which our souls were originally born, that the divine part suspends our head, i.e., our root, and so keeps our whole body erect. So if a man has become absorbed in his appetites or his ambitions and takes great pains to further them, all his thoughts are bound to become merely mortal. And so far as it is at all possible for a man to become thoroughly mortal, he cannot help but fully succeed in this, seeing that he has cultivated his mortality all along. On the other hand, if a man has seriously devoted himself to the love of learning and to true wisdom, if he has exercised these aspects of himself above all, then there is absolutely no way that his thoughts can fail to be immortal and divine, should truth come within his grasp. And to the extent that human nature can partake of immortality, he can in no way fail to achieve this: constantly caring for his divine part as he does, keeping well-ordered the guiding spirit that lives within him, he must indeed be supremely happy. Now there is but one way to care for anything, and that is to provide for it the nourishment and the motions that are proper to it. And the motions that have an affinity to the divine part within us are the thoughts and revolutions of the universe. These, surely, are the ones which each of us should follow. We should redirect the revolutions in our heads that were thrown off course at our birth,[44] by coming to learn the harmonies and revolutions of the universe, and so bring into conformity with its objects our faculty of understanding, as it was in its original condition. And when this conformity is complete, we shall have achieved our goal: that most excellent life offered to humankind by the gods, both now and forevermore.

And now indeed, it seems, we have all but completed our initial assignment, that of tracing the history of the universe down to the emergence of humankind. We should go on to mention briefly how the other living things came to be—a topic that won't require many words. By doing this we'll seem to be in better measure with ourselves so far as our words on these subjects are concerned.

Let us proceed, then, to a discussion of this subject in the following way. According to our likely account, all male-born humans who lived lives of cowardice or injustice were reborn in the second generation as women. And this explains why at that time the gods fashioned the desire for sexual union, by constructing one ensouled living thing in us as well as another one in women. This is how they made them in each case: There is [in a man] a passage by which fluids exit from the body, where it receives the liquid that has passed through the lungs down into the kidneys and on into the bladder and expels it under pressure of air. From this passage they bored a connecting one into the compacted marrow that runs from the head along the neck through the spine. This is in fact the marrow that

b

c

d

e

91

b

44. See 43a–44a.

we have previously called "seed."[45] Now because it has soul in it and had now found a vent [to the outside], this marrow instilled a life-giving desire for emission right at the place of venting, and so produced the love of procreation. This is why, of course, the male genitals are unruly and self-willed, like an animal that will not be subject to reason and, driven crazy by its desires, seeks to overpower everything else. The very same causes

c   operate in women. A woman's womb or uterus, as it is called, is a living thing within her with a desire for childbearing. Now when this remains unfruitful for an unseasonably long period of time, it is extremely frustrated and travels everywhere up and down her body. It blocks up her respiratory passages, and by not allowing her to breathe it throws her into extreme emergencies, and visits all sorts of other illnesses upon her until finally

d   the woman's desire and the man's love bring them together, and, like plucking the fruit from a tree, they sow the seed into the ploughed field of her womb, living things too small to be visible and still without form. And when they have again given them distinct form, they nourish these living things so that they can mature inside the womb. Afterwards, they bring them to birth, introducing them into the light of day.

That is how women and females in general came to be. As for birds, as a kind they are the products of a transformation. They grow feathers instead of hair. They descended from innocent but simpleminded men,

e   men who studied the heavenly bodies but in their naiveté believed that the most reliable proofs concerning them could be based upon visual observation. Land animals in the wild, moreover, came from men who had no tincture of philosophy and who made no study of the universe whatsoever, because they no longer made use of the revolutions in their heads but instead followed the lead of the parts of the soul that reside in the chest. As a consequence of these ways of theirs they carried their forelimbs and their heads dragging towards the ground, like towards like. The tops of their heads became elongated and took all sorts of shapes,

92   depending on the particular way the revolutions were squeezed together from lack of use. This is the reason animals of this kind have four or more feet. The god placed a greater number of supports under the more mindless beings, so that they might be drawn more closely to the ground. As for the most mindless of these animals, the ones whose entire bodies stretch out completely along the ground, the gods made them without feet, crawl-

b   ing along the ground, there being no need of feet anymore. The fourth kind of animal, the kind that lives in water, came from those men who were without question the most stupid and ignorant of all. The gods who brought about their transformation concluded that these no longer deserved to breathe pure air, because their souls were tainted with transgressions of every sort. Instead of letting them breathe rare and pure air, they shoved them into water to breathe its murky depths. This is the origin of fish, of all shellfish, and of every water-inhabiting animal. Their justly

---

45. At 73c1; 74a4.

due reward for their extreme stupidity is their extreme dwelling place. c
These, then, are the conditions that govern, both then and now, how all
the animals exchange their forms, one for the other, and in the process
lose or gain intelligence or folly.

And so now we may say that our account of the universe has reached
its conclusion. This world of ours has received and teems with living
things, mortal and immortal. A visible living thing containing visible ones,
perceptible god, image of the intelligible Living Thing,[46] its grandness,
goodness, beauty and perfection are unexcelled. Our one universe, indeed
the only one of its kind, has come to be.

46. Cf. 30c, d and 39e.

CRITIAS

At the beginning of Timaeus, *Socrates, Critias, Timaeus, and Hermocrates agree to an exchange of speeches. For the entertainment of the others on the previous day, Socrates had explained the institutions of the* Republic's *ideal city. But a truly satisfying account of their excellence would require more than that 'theoretical' description: we need to see them fully in effect, functioning in a city's actual life—especially in wartime, the most severe test of a city's mettle. Critias (an Athenian) offers to do this, on the supposition that the Athens of nine thousand years before was governed by the institutions of Socrates' city, as a myth from Egypt that he has heard recited has suggested to him. (This Critias is either Plato's mother's cousin—the Critias of* Charmides, Protagoras, *and* Eryxias— *or that cousin's grandfather.) He will tell the tale of ancient Athens' war with the inhabitants of Atlantis, an island then located in the Atlantic Ocean near the entrance to the Mediterranean sea. Under their kings, the technologically advanced Atlantids had conquered Europe as far as Italy, and Africa up to the border of Egypt, and it fell to the freedom-loving, well-governed Athenians to defeat these interlopers and save the Mediterranean peoples from outside domination. At the successful conclusion of the war, Atlantis itself was destroyed in an earthquake and sank into the sea, carrying its inhabitants and all the warriors of Athens—its adult male population—to their deaths.*

The Timaeus *itself is taken up with Timaeus' preliminary account of the creation of the world, down to that of human beings, whose paragon specimens are the men of Athens at the time of the Atlantic war. Having heard that account, Critias now tells the tale of the conflict between Athens and Atlantis (or rather the introductory part of it—Plato left the dialogue incomplete, without reaching the war). To all appearances, Critias' speech would have completed the agenda agreed to at the outset; however, near the beginning of* Critias, *Socrates seems confusingly to suggest that the fourth personage of the dialogue, Hermocrates, an historical general and statesman of Syracuse, will have a turn to speak after that, though he does not indicate at all what his subject would be. If that marks an alteration of Plato's plan, he evidently never carried it out.*

J.M.C.

106   TIMAEUS: What a pleasure it is, Socrates, to have completed the long march of my argument. I feel the relief of the traveler who can rest after

Translated by Diskin Clay.

a long journey. Now I offer my prayer to that god who had existed long before in reality, but who has now been created in my words. My prayer is that he grant the preservation of all that has been spoken properly; but that he will impose the proper penalty if we have, despite our best intentions, spoken any discordant note. For the musician who strikes the wrong note the proper penalty is to bring him back into harmony. To assure, then, that in the future we will speak as we should concerning the origin of the gods we pray that he will grant the best and most perfect remedy—understanding. And, now that we have offered our prayer, we will keep our agreement and hand over to Critias the speech that is to follow ours in its proper sequence.

CRITIAS: Very well, Timaeus. I will accept the task, but I will make the same plea as you made at the beginning of your speech, when you asked for our sympathy and understanding on account of the magnitude of the argument you were undertaking. I make this same entreaty now too, but I ask to be granted even greater understanding for what I am going to say. And I must admit that I realize that what I am pleading for is self-indulgent and a less polite request than it should be. But I must make it nonetheless. Now, who in his senses would undertake to maintain that your speech was not an excellent speech? As for the speech you are about to hear, I must somehow bring home to you the fact that it requires greater indulgence, given the difficulty of my subject. It is easier, Timaeus, for someone to give the impression that he is a successful speaker when he speaks of gods to an audience of mortals. The audience's lack of experience and sheer ignorance concerning a subject they can never know for certain provide the would-be speaker with great eloquence. We know how we stand when it comes to our knowledge of the gods. To make my meaning plainer, let me ask you to follow me in this illustration.

It is inevitable, I suppose, that everything we have all said is a kind of representation and attempted likeness. Let us consider the graphic art of the painter that has as its object the bodies of both gods and men and the relative ease and difficulty involved in the painter's convincing his viewers that he has adequately represented the objects of his art. We will observe first that we are satisfied if an artist is able to represent—even to some small extent—the earth and mountains and rivers and forests and all of heaven and the bodies that exist and move within it, and render their likeness; and next that, since we have no precise knowledge of such things, we do not examine these paintings too closely or find fault with them, but we are content to accept an art of suggestion and illusion for such things, as vague and deceptive as this art is. But, when a painter attempts to create a likeness of our bodies, we are quick to spot any defect, and, because of our familiarity and life-long knowledge, we prove harsh critics of the painter who does not fully reproduce every detail. We must view the case of speeches as precisely the same. We embrace what is said about the heavens and things divine with enthusiasm, even when what is said is quite implausible; but we are nice critics of what is said of mortals and human beings.

Now, with these reflections in mind, which I have offered for the present
e   occasion, if we are unable to speak fully and fittingly in representing our
theme, we deserve your sympathy. You must realize that human life is
no easy subject for representation, but is rather one of great difficulty, if
108   we are to satisfy people's opinions. I wanted to remind you of this, Socrates,
to make my plea not for less but for greater sympathy and understanding
as you listen to what I am about to say. If you find that I made a just
claim on this favor, grant it with good will.

SOCRATES: Why, Critias, would we hesitate to grant it? Let this favor of
ours be granted to Hermocrates as well who will follow you as the third
to speak. It is clear that a little later, when it comes his turn to speak he
b   will make the same entreaty as have you and Timaeus. So to make it
possible for him to invent another preamble and not compel him to repeat
what Timaeus and Critias have said, let him speak when his turn comes,
knowing that he has our sympathy. But now, my dear Critias, I must
caution you about the attitude of your audience in this theater: the first
of the poets to compete in it put on such a glorious performance that you
will need a great measure of sympathy if you are going to be able to
compete after him.

HERMOCRATES: The injunction you made to Critias here applies to me,
c   Socrates, as well. But, even so, Critias, the faint hearted have never yet set
up a victory monument. You must march bravely forward to encounter
your speech, and, as you invoke Paeon[1] and the Muses, display in your
hymn of praise the bravery of your ancient citizens.

CRITIAS: Dear Hermocrates, you stand last in rank, but, since there is
someone standing in front of you, you are still confident. That courage is
needed, you will discover yourself, when you take my place. But I must
d   pay attention to your exhortation and encouragement, and, in addition to
the gods you just named, invoke the other gods and make a special prayer
to Mnemosyne.[2] The success or failure of just about everything that is most
important in our speech lies in the lap of this goddess. For, if we can
sufficiently recall and relate what was said long ago by the priests and
brought here to Athens by Solon, you the audience in our theater will
find, I am confident, that we have put on a worthy performance and
acquitted ourselves of our task. So much said. Now we must act. Let us
delay no more.

e   We should recall at the very beginning that, in very rough terms, it was
some nine thousand years since the time when a war is recorded as having
broken out between the peoples dwelling outside the pillars of Heracles[3]
and all those dwelling within. This war I must now describe. Now they

1. Apollo, the Healer.
2. The mother of the nine Muses and the goddess of memory.
3. The Straits of Gibraltar.

said that this city of Athens was the ruler of the [Mediterranean] peoples and fought for the duration of the entire war. They said, too, that the kings of the island of Atlantis were the rulers of the other peoples. This island, as we were saying,[4] was at one time greater than both Libya and Asia combined.[5] But now because of earthquakes it has subsided into the great Ocean and has produced a vast sea of mud that blocks the passage of mariners who would sail into the great Ocean from Greek waters and for this reason it is no longer navigable.   109

In its progress, our tale will describe, as if it were unrolled, the many barbarian nations and all the different Greek peoples of that time, encountering them as they emerge from place to place. It is first necessary at the beginning of this tale to describe the condition of the Athenians of that age and the adversaries with whom they waged war: their respective power and their respective constitutions. But of these themes, pride and place must go to the condition of Athens before this war.

At one time, the gods received their due portions over the entire earth region by region—and without strife. To claim that gods did not recognize what was proper to each would not be fitting, nor would it be right to say that, although they recognized what belonged by just title to others, some would attempt to take possession of this for themselves—in open strife. But, as they received what was naturally theirs in the allotment of justice, they began to settle their lands. Once they had settled them, they began to raise us as their own chattel and livestock, as do shepherds their sheep. But they did not compel us by exerting bodily force on our bodies, as do shepherds who drive their flocks to pasture by blows, but rather, by what makes a creature turn course most easily; as they pursued their own plans, they directed us from the stern, as if they were applying to the soul the rudder of Persuasion. And in this manner they directed everything mortal as do helmsmen their ships.

Now, as the gods received their various regions lot by lot, they began to improve their possessions. But, in the case of Hephaestus and Athena, since they possessed a common nature, both because she was his sister of the same father and because they had entered the same pursuits in their love of wisdom and the arts, they both received this land as their portion in a single lot, because it was congenial to their character and was naturally suited to them in its excellence and intelligence. And they fashioned in it good men sprung from the land itself and gave them a conception of how to govern their society. The names of these first inhabitants have been preserved, but their deeds have perished on account of the catastrophes that befell those who succeeded them and the long passage of time intervening.

b

c

d

---

4. See *Timaeus* 24e–25d.

5. For Critias' contemporaries Asia was defined by the Nile and the Hellespont, and Libya enclosed the entire coast of Saharan Africa west of the Nile. Thus, with Europe, these were the other two parts of the known world.

Those of their race who survived these successive destructions were, as I said before,[6] left as an illiterate mountain people who had only heard the tradition of the names of the rulers of their country and beyond these only little of their deeds. Now, they were pleased to give their descendants
e   the names of these rulers, even though they were unaware of their ancestors' virtues and institutions—except for some dim legends concerning each of them. Then, for many generations, these survivors and their children lived in distress for their survival and gave thought to their needs;
110   they spoke only of supplying these needs, and had no interest in the events of the distant past. For it is in the train of Leisure that Mythology and Inquiry into the Past arrive in cities, once they have observed that in the case of some peoples the necessities of life have been secured, but not before.

This is why the names of the ancients have been preserved but not their deeds. I make this claim and cite as my evidence the statement of Solon, who said that, in their account of the war of that time, the Egyptian priests gave for the most part names such as Cecrops and Erechtheus, and
b   Erichthonius, and Erysichthon,[7] and the names of most of the others which have come down in tradition before the generation of Theseus. And the same is true of the names of the women. Consider too the attributes of the goddess Athena and her statue. At that time the military training of women and men was common. For this reason the people of that time fashioned the statue of the goddess as armed to reflect that ancient custom—an indication that all the female and male creatures that live together
c   in a flock can very well pursue in common, as much as is possible, the special talents that are suited to each species.

Now, at that time, the other classes of citizens who dwelt in our city were engaged in manufacture and producing food from the earth, but the warrior class that had originally been separated from them by god-like men lived apart. They had all that was appropriate to their training and
d   education. None of them had any private possession, but they thought of all their possessions as the common property of all, and they asked to receive nothing from the other citizens beyond what they needed to live. Their activities were all of the activities that were spoken of yesterday, when the guardians proposed by our theory were discussed.

The report of the Egyptian priests concerning our territory was plausible and true. First of all, at that time its boundaries extended to the Isthmus of Corinth, and, on the mainland to the north, they extended to the summits of Cithaeron and Parnes. And, descending to the east, the boundaries
e   extended down to the region of Oropus to the north and they were defined by the Asopus river down to the sea. In its great fertility our land far surpassed every other, for it was then capable of supporting a great army of men who did not work the land. There is impressive evidence for this

6. *Timaeus* 22d ff.
7. Mythical figures in the early history of Athens and Attica, the first three as kings.

excellence. What has now survived of this land can rival any other land in the variety and quality of its crops and the pasture it offers all species of animals. But, at that time, our land produced all this not only of high quality but in great abundance. You might ask how this is credible and how our present land could possibly be called a vestige of our earlier land.

111

From the interior this entire land extends a great distance into the sea, as if it jutted out as a promontory. It so happens that the entire basin of the sea that surrounds falls off precipitously. Many and great were the floods that occurred in the space of nine thousand years—for this is the number of years between that time and the present—and during this succession of natural disasters the soil was washed down from the high places. It did not form any considerable alluvial deposits, as in other regions, but it disappeared into the deep, as in flood after flood it was continuously washed into the sea from all sides. What actually remains is like our small and barren islands, and, compared to the land it once was, Attica of today is like the skeleton revealed by a wasting disease, once all the rich topsoil has been eroded and only the thin body of the land remains. But in that age our land was undiminished and had high hills with soil upon them; what we now call the Rocky Barrens were covered with deep rich soil. And in the mountains there were dense forests of which there still survives clear evidence. Some of our mountains can now grow just barely enough for bees, but it was not so long ago that [lofty trees grew there].[8] There can still be found intact rafters cut from trees that were felled and brought down to be used for the greatest building projects. And there were many trees that were cultivated for their fruit and they provided limitless fodder for flocks of sheep and goats.

b

c

Every year there was a harvest of Zeus-sent rain. It was not lost, as it is now, as it flows off the hard surface of the ground into the sea, but the deep soil absorbed the rain and it stored it away as it created a reservoir with a covering of clay soil above it; and, as it distributed the water it had absorbed from the high places into its hollows, it produced an abundant flow of water to feed springs and rivers throughout every region of the country. There are even today some sacred monuments at these ancient springs that are evidence of the truth of what we are now saying about our country.

d

This was the nature of the countryside. The land was cultivated with great skill, as we can reasonably conjecture, by farmers who were farmers in the true sense of the word and who devoted themselves to this single occupation—but farmers who had an eye for beauty and were of a truly noble nature, and who in addition possessed a most fertile land and water in abundance, and above this land a climate and seasons that were most temperate.

e

As for the city itself, it was laid out at that time in a plan that I will now describe. First of all, the acropolis was very different then than it is

---

8. There is a lacuna of a few words here in the mss.

112   now. A single night of torrential rain stripped the acropolis of its soil
       and reduced it to bare limestone in a storm that was accompanied by
       earthquakes. Before the destructive flood of Deucalion, this was the third
       such cataclysmic storm. In the past, the acropolis extended to the Eridanus
       and Ilisus and held within its circuit the Pnyx and Mt. Lycabettus that
       faces the Pnyx. It was entirely covered by soil and, except for some small
   b   outcroppings, level on top. Outside the acropolis and under its slopes
       there lived the class of artisans and those of the farmers who worked the
       neighboring land. But on the heights the class of warriors lived in isolation,
       as if they belonged to a single household, around the sanctuary of Athena
       and Hephaestos, which they had enclosed by a single garden wall. On the
       far northern edge of the acropolis they inhabited common dwellings and
       ate together in common messes in buildings they had constructed for their
       winter quarters. And they had a supply of all that was needed for their
   c   communal institutions—both in buildings for themselves and for the
       priests. They made no use of gold or silver—possessions they never had
       any need of. But, in pursuing a mean between ostentation and servility,
       they built for themselves tasteful houses and they grew old in them in the
       company of their grandchildren; and for generation after generation they
       passed these dwellings down to descendants who were like themselves.
       As for the south of the acropolis, when they left their orchards, gymnasia,
       and common messes, as they would for the summer season, they converted
       it to these uses.
   d   There was a single spring in the location of the present acropolis, but
       it has been choked by the debris of the earthquakes [of that night], and
       its waters now flow only in a trickle about the circuit wall. But it provided
       the men of that age with an abundant supply of water, since it was situated
       in a location that made it neither too cold in the winter nor too hot in
       the summer.
          This was the manner of their life: they were the guardians of their own
       citizens and the leaders of the rest of the Greek world, which followed
       them willingly. And they kept their population stable as far as they could—
       both of men and women—for generation after generation, maintaining the
       population of those who had reached military age or were still of military
       age at close to twenty thousand at most.
   e   Such, to conclude, was the character of this people and such was their
       life generation after generation as they directed the life of their city and
       of Greece with justice. Their fame for the beauty of their bodies and for
       the variety and range of their mental and spiritual qualities spread through
       all of Asia and all of Europe. And the consideration in which they were
       held and their renown was the greatest of all the nations of that age.
          As for the state of those who went to war against them and the origins
       of that state, we will now openly reveal its history to you our friends, as
       the common property of friends, if we have not lost the memory of what
113   we heard when we were still boys. I must explain one small point before
       I enter into my history so that you will not be astonished as you hear

Greek names frequently used for people who are not Greek. You will now learn the origins of these names. Solon, when he was contemplating his own poetic version of this legend and was inquiring into the meaning of these names, discovered that his Egyptian sources had been the first to record them, once they had translated their meaning into their own language. He, in his turn, recovered the meaning of each of these names and recorded it as he translated them into Greek. These very manuscripts were in the possession of my grandfather and they now remain in my possession. When I was a boy, I studied them carefully. Consequently, do not be astonished if you hear names that sound like Greek names; you now know their explanation.

b

What follows, approximately, was the introduction to the long account I heard then. As I said before concerning the distribution of lands among the gods, in some regions they divided the entire earth into greater apportionments and in others into lesser apportionments, as they established sanctuaries and sacrifices for themselves. So it was that Posidon received as one of his domains the island of Atlantis and he established dwelling places for the children he had fathered of a mortal woman in a certain place on the island that I shall describe.

c

Now seaward, but running along the middle of the entire island, was a plain which is said to have been the loveliest of all plains and quite fertile. Near this plain in the middle of the island and at about fifty stades'[9] distance was a uniformly low and flat hill. Now, there lived on this hill one of the people of this island who had originally sprung up from the earth. His name was Evenor and he dwelt there with his wife Leucippe. They had an only child, a daughter by the name of Clito. When this girl grew to marriageable age, both her mother and father died. It was then that Posidon conceived a desire for her and slept with her. To make the hill on which she lived a strong enclosure he broke it to form a circle and he created alternating rings of sea and land around it. Some he made wider and some he made more narrow. He made two rings of land and three of sea as round as if he had laid them out with compass and lathe.

d

They were perfectly equidistant from one another. And so the hill became inaccessible to humans. For at that time ships and the art of navigation had not yet come into existence.

e

And the god himself greatly beautified the island he had created in the middle to make it a dwelling suitable for a god. Because he was a god, he did this with little effort. He drew up two subterranean streams into springs. One gushed out in a warm fountain and the other in a cold fountain. And from the earth he produced all varieties of crops that were sufficient to his island. He sired five pairs of twin sons and he raised them to manhood. He divided the entire island of Atlantis into ten districts: to the first born of the first set of twins he gave as his portion the dwelling

9. There are three units of measure in Critias' description of the island: the foot, the *plethron* (100 feet), and the stade (600 feet).

114   of his mother and the circular island, since it was the largest and the best.
And he made him king over the others. The other sons he made governors
and to each of these he gave the rule over many men and a great extent
of land.

And he gave each of his sons names. To the son who was oldest and
king he gave the name from which the entire island and its surrounding
sea derive their names, because he was the first of the kings of that time.
His name was Atlas; the island is called Atlantis and the sea Atlantic after

b   him. To the twin born after him, who had received as his portion the cape
of the island facing the pillars of Heracles opposite what is now called the
territory of Gadira after this region, he gave the name that translates into
Greek as Eumelos, but in the language of Atlantis, it is Gadirus. It would
seem that he gave his name to the region of Cadiz. The two brothers of
the second set of twins he called Ampheres and the Euaemon. To the third
set he gave the name Mneseas to the first-born and Autochthon to the

c   second-born. Of the fourth set Elasippus was the first-born, Mestor the
second. For the fifth set he gave the name Azaes to the first-born and the
name Diaprepes to the second. Now all of these sons inhabited the island,
as did their sons and descendants over many generations. They were the
rulers of many other islands in the Atlantic and, as I have said,[10] they
even extended their rule into the Mediterranean as near to us as Etruria
and Egypt.

d   The race of Atlas increased greatly and became greatly honored. And
they maintained their kingdom through many generations, as the oldest
king would hand his kingship on to his oldest son. They amassed more
wealth than had ever been amassed before in the rule of any previous
kings or could easily be amassed after them. And they provided for everything that was needed, both in the city and in the rest of the island. For

e   their empire brought them many imports from outside, and the island
itself provided most of what was needed for their livelihood. First, there
were the mines that produced both hard and fusible ore. And in many
regions of the island they exploited that metal which is now only a name
to us, but which was then more than a name—*oreichalkos*.[11] In that age it
was valued only less than gold. And the island provided all trees to be
hewn and worked by builders and this in great abundance. It also produced
abundant animal life, both domestic and wild. In addition to these there
was a great population of elephants. There was pasture land for the other
animals who graze in marshlands and along lakes and rivers and on

115   mountainsides and plains, and there was plenty for them and for this the
greatest of animals, which consumes the most fodder.

The island produced in addition all the aromatic plants the earth produces now—sweet smelling roots and greens, herbs, trees, and gums from

10. *Timaeus* 25a–b.
11. "Mountain copper" or yellow copper ore.

flowers and fruits as well, and they flourished there. The island also produced the domesticated crop of grains on which we live and all the other crops on which we depend for our food. It also produced the kinds of crops we call "pulse" and the trees that give us our drink, food, and oils— and the crop that sprung up for the sake of our entertainment and pleasure, is hard to preserve, and comes from tree tops; it produced the side dishes we offer the weary guest as a relief after he has eaten his fill and that refresh him after dinner. All of these did that sacred island once bear in that age under a fostering sun—products lovely, marvelous, and of abundant bounty. And they took all these products from the earth and from their proceeds they constructed their sanctuaries and their palaces, their harbors and their ship-sheds, and they improved the rest of their land according to the plan I will now describe.

    First, they constructed bridges joining the rings of sea, which surrounded the ancient metropolis, making a road out from the palace and in to the palace. Their first project was to build a palace in the dwelling of the god and of their ancestors. One king inherited the project from his predecessor, and, as he improved on the beauty of what had already been improved, he would surpass to the extent of his resources what his predecessor had been able to achieve. They continued this progress until they had created for themselves a dwelling astonishing in its size and in its manifold beauty. And starting at the sea they excavated a canal three plethra in width, one hundred feet in depth, and fifty stades in length up to the outermost sea ring. They then made passage from the sea into the interior possible by opening a channel into the sea ring that was wide enough for the largest ships to sail into it as if it were a harbor. And, as for the land rings that separated the rings of sea, they pierced them at the point of the bridges, and thus joined them by water. The resulting canal was wide enough for a single trireme to sail through as it passed into a ring of water. They constructed a roof over the channel to protect the passage of ships, for the walls of the canal through the land rings were high enough from the sea to the bridge above to allow ships to pass under. The largest of the water rings into which the passage from the sea had been excavated was three stades in width and the next land ring was equal to it. Of the next rings of water and land, the ring of water was two stades wide and, as in the first case, the land ring was equal to it as well. And, finally, the ring of water running around the island in the middle was a stade wide.

    The island where the palace was located had a diameter of five stades. They threw up an unbroken stone circuit wall around this island, and they also walled the land rings, and the bridge, which was a plethron wide. They built towers and gates at the point where the bridges crossed over the rings of water. They quarried stone from under the circular island that formed the center ring and from the inner and outer land rings as well. There were three colors of stone: white, black, and red. As they quarried this stone, they fashioned ship sheds for two ships in the rock roofed by the stone of the quarry itself.

b   Some of their buildings they constructed of stones of uniform color. But
to delight themselves they made of others a tapestry of stones of different
colors, variegating the colors to bring out their natural charm. And they
invested the entire circuit wall of the outermost land ring with bronze, as
if the bronze revetment were a bright dye. The interior of the land wall
they invested with tin. And the wall surrounding the acropolis itself they
c   invested with *oreichalkos*, which glittered like darting fire.

I will now describe the palace buildings erected within the acropolis.
At its center was the shrine of Clito and Posidon. It was kept consecrated
and no one was permitted to enter it. It was surrounded by a wall of gold.
It was here that Posidon and Clito first begot and produced the race of
the ten kings. It was to this shrine that each of the ten divisions came to
offer their first fruits to each of these original kings in a yearly festival.
The temple of Posidon was in this area. It was one stade long, three plethra
d   wide, and of a height that appeared to be proportional to its length and
width, but it had something barbaric about its appearance. They invested
the entire exterior of the temple with silver, except for the acroteria, which
they gilded with gold. The interior presented a roof of solid ivory inlaid
with gold, silver, and *oreichalkos;* and they plated all the other areas of the
temple with this same metal—the cella walls, the interior columns, and
the floors. They placed gold statues within the temple. There was a statue
e   of Posidon standing in a chariot with a team of six winged horses. This
statue was so tall that his head touched the rafter of the temple roof; there
were a hundred Nereids riding dolphins and arranged in a circle about
him, for men of that age thought that the Nereids were a hundred in
number; and there were many other statues inside which were the offerings
of private individuals.

Outside and surrounding the temple there stood gold statues of all the
descendants of the ten kings and their wives and many other dedications
of great size made by the kings and private individuals who came from
the city of Atlantis itself and from the subject peoples elsewhere. There
117   was an altar on the same scale as the temple and its workmanship was
equally lavish. The palace was magnificent in its monumental architecture
and it was worthy of the greatness of their empire and the adornment of
the temple and shrines.

They drew their water from two springs—a spring of cold water and a
spring of hot water. Both had an abundant flow and in the amazing natural
freshness and quality of its waters each had its own use. They built fountain
houses around them and plantations of trees suitable to the temperature
b   of the waters. And they also built reservoirs around the springs. Some
they left open, but to the north they covered the reservoirs to convert them
to warm baths. The reservoirs of the kings were separate from those of
the rest of the population. Some reservoirs were reserved for the use of
women, others for watering horses and other draft animals, and each they
fashioned appropriately to its use. The overflow they channeled into the
grove of Posidon, where, thanks to the fertility of the soil, there grew all

varieties of trees of extraordinary beauty and height. They also irrigated the outer land rings by means of canals that crossed over along the bridges joining them.

Here there were constructed numerous shrines to numerous gods and c the land was laid out for many orchards and gymnasia. There were gymnasia for men on each of the two ring islands and tracks for horses were set apart as well. And, remarkably, through the middle of the greatest of the islands they laid out a separate race course for horses, one stade wide, and it extended in a circle around the entire island. Located on each side of the central race course were quarters for the palace guard.

The garrison of the most reliable soldiers was established on the smaller d of the ring islands, the island situated nearest to the acropolis. And quarters were built on the acropolis for the most reliable soldiers of all, surrounding the palaces of the kings themselves. The ship-sheds were filled with triremes and all the fittings needed for triremes, and all were in good working order. Such, then, were the buildings they constructed around the [dwellings of the] kings themselves.

Now, once you had crossed over the three rings of water, you would come to a circuit wall that began at the sea and surrounded the greatest e of the land rings on all sides at a uniform distance of fifty stades from the greatest land ring and its harbor. It began at the point where the channel had been dug through to the sea. The entire area within was settled by a dense population whose houses were crowded close together. The waterway into the interior and the greatest harbor was teeming with ships and crowds of merchants who had arrived from all over the world and whose voices and bustle produced a commotion and hubbub that could be heard day and night.

I have recalled this description of the capital and the ancient dwelling of the kings pretty much as it was told [to Solon] at that time. But now I 118 must attempt to recall the nature of the rest of the country and the manner in which it was improved. To begin with, the priests said that the entire country was very high and that it rose sheer from the sea. The entire plain that surrounded the capital was itself surrounded by a ring of mountains that sloped down as far as the sea. The plain was smooth and level and entirely rectangular. On its long sides it extended for three thousand stades and, as measured from the sea, it was over two thousand stades across. The slope of the island was to the south and it was protected from the b northerly winds. The mountains surrounding the plain were legendary for their number and size and beauty. None of the mountain ranges that exist today can compare with them. They contained on their slopes and in their valleys many populous and wealthy villages. And they contained rivers and lakes and meadows that supplied enough to feed all the animals there, both domesticated and wild. In their abundance and variety, the shrubs and trees were plentiful for all kinds of constructions and uses.

I will now relate how this plain had been developed by nature, and by c many kings and over a long period of time. For the most part, the plain was naturally rectangular, regular, and oblong. Where it was not perfectly straight and even they evened it out by excavating a Great Canal around it. As described, its depth and width and length provoke disbelief, since it was the work of human hands and so vast when compared to the other building projects. Nevertheless, I must repeat precisely what we heard then. The Great Canal was excavated to the depth of a plethron, it measured

d   a stade wide along its entire length, and as it framed the entire plain it came to a total length of ten thousand stades. As it received the flow of water that came off the mountains, and as this water circulated and reached the city on two sides, the trench allowed the water to flow out to the sea. Towards the interior, canals were cut in straight lines from the city over the plain a hundred feet broad at most and these emptied their waters into the Great Canal facing the sea. These were spaced at an interval of a hundred stades. They also cut horizontal connecting channels linking one

e   canal with another and with the city, and it is by these canals that they transported timber and the other products of the land on barges from the mountains to the city.

They harvested their crops twice a year. In the winter season they relied on the water of Zeus-sent rains, and in the summer season they used the waters stored in the earth drawing it into their canal system to irrigate the crops.

Now, as for the numbers of the men of the plain who were fit to serve in the army: each military district was assigned to contribute one com-

119   mander. The area of each district was as much as a hundred stades. The total of these districts came to sixty thousand. And as far as the population of the mountainous regions and the rest of the country goes, it was said to be too large to calculate. But, counted by regions and villages, all men fit for military service were assigned to one of the sixty thousand military districts and they served under the commander of each district. In times of war each commander was assigned to have in readiness a sixth part of the complement of a war chariot as a contribution to a force of ten thousand

b   chariots; and in addition, two horses and two riders, a pair of horses without a chariot, with its complement of two riders, a runner, a rider who could fight on foot armed with a small shield, and serving as a charioteer a rider who could mount either horse, two hoplites, two archers, and two sling men; three light armed soldiers with stones and three with javelins. He also had to contribute four sailors to the crews manning twelve thousand ships. These were the principles for raising an army in the royal city. The formulas varied in the nine other cities, and it would take a long time to describe them.

c   The original ordering of powers and honors in Atlantis was as follows. Within his own patrimony and in his own city, each of the ten kings held power over the inhabitants and over most of the laws, and he could punish or put to death whomever he wished. But, as for their common empire and federation, the kings were regulated by the laws of Posidon as these had been passed down by tradition and according to an inscription which the first kings had cut on a stele of *oreichalkos*. This inscription was placed in the middle of the island in the sanctuary of Posidon. Here in every fifth or sixth year, and in alternating sequence, it was their custom to gather. To both the even and to the odd they accorded an equal share. Once they had assembled, they deliberated on matters of common concern and held an assize to determine if anyone of them had broken the law, and they gave judgment. Whenever they were about to declare judgment, they first offered one another pledges in this manner: as all ten kings were alone in the sanctuary of Posidon, where bulls had been allowed to run free, they joined in prayer to ask the god to be allowed to capture the bull which would be the most acceptable offering to him. They pursued the bulls with staffs and nooses—but with no iron weapon, and they led the bull they had captured to the stele.[12] There they slaughtered it on the crest of the stele and let its blood spill down over the inscription. In addition to the laws written on the stele there was an oath inscribed calling terrible curses down upon those who broke them. And, when they had then sacrificed the bull following this ritual, they would burn all the limbs of the bull and, mixing his blood in a mixing-bowl, they would pour a clot of his blood over the head of each of them, and, once they had scrubbed the stele clean, they would bring the remaining blood over to the fire.

After this, they would draw the blood from the mixing-bowl into gold pouring vessels. Pouring the blood over the fire they would take an oath to render justice according to the laws inscribed on the stele and to punish anyone who had violated these laws since last they met. They swore that in the future they would not willingly violate any of the provisions of the inscription and that they would neither rule nor obey a ruler if either they or he did not issue commands that were in conformity with the laws of their father. When each of the kings had made this oath and engaged both himself and his descendants, they drank and dedicated their pouring-vessels in the sanctuary of the god. And, once they had finished with their dinner and everything else they had to do and night had fallen and the fire about the sacrificial offerings had subsided, they all put on a deep blue robe of the most splendid appearance and, sitting on the ground next to the embers of the sacrificial victim, at night, they put out the fire still flickering in the sanctuary and judged anyone accused of violating any of their laws and were judged themselves. Once they had passed judgment, when day dawned, they recorded their judgments on a gold tablet which they dedicated as a memorial offering along with their robes.

There were many other particular laws concerning the prerogatives of each of the kings, but the most important of these were those forbidding them to bear arms against one another and commanding them to help one another should anyone in any of their cities make an attempt to overturn the divine family; that they should deliberate together, as had their

12. A block or slab, of the sort to be inscribed with a record of victories, dedications, treaties, decrees, etc.

d   ancestors before them, over their decisions concerning war and their other actions, but that they should cede leadership to the royal family of Atlantis; and, finally, that the king should have power to put none of his kinsmen to death, if he could not obtain the approval of the majority of the ten kings.

      Now, this was the power, so great and so extraordinary, that existed in that distant region at that time. This was the power the god mustered and brought against these [Mediterranean] lands. It was said that his pretense

e   was something like what I shall describe. For many generations and as long as enough of their divine nature survived, they were obedient unto their laws and they were well disposed to the divinity they were kin to. They possessed conceptions that were true and entirely lofty. And in their attitude to the disasters and chance events that constantly befall men and in their relations with one another they exhibited a combination of mildness and prudence, because, except for virtue, they held all else in disdain and thought of their present good fortune of no consequence. They bore their vast wealth of gold and other possessions without difficulty, treating them

121   as if they were a burden. They did not become intoxicated with the luxury of the life their wealth made possible; they did not lose their self-control and slip into decline, but in their sober judgment they could see distinctly that even their very wealth increased with their amity and its companion, virtue. But they saw that both wealth and concord decline as possessions become pursued and honored. And virtue perishes with them as well.

      Now, because these were their thoughts and because of the divine nature that survived in them, they prospered greatly as we have already related. But when the divine portion in them began to grow faint as it was often

b   blended with great checkers of mortality and as their human nature gradually gained ascendancy, at that moment, in their inability to bear their great good fortune, they became disordered. To whoever had eyes to see they appeared hideous, since they were losing the finest of what were once their most treasured possessions. But to those who were blind to the true way of life oriented to happiness it was at this time that they gave the semblance of being supremely beauteous and blessed. Yet inwardly they were filled with an unjust lust for possessions and power. But as Zeus, god of the gods, reigning as king according to law, could clearly see this state of affairs, he observed this noble race lying in this abject

c   state and resolved to punish them and to make them more careful and harmonious as a result of their chastisement. To this end he called all the gods to their most honored abode, which stands at the middle of the universe and looks down upon all that has a share in generation. And when he had gathered them together, he said . . .

MINOS

Socrates and a friend try to find a definition of 'law'. While his friend thinks that laws are whatever is decided upon in various cities, Socrates argues that laws reveal a certain reality, the truth of how civilized life should be regulated. This reality is common and unchanging, and has been grasped best of all in the ancient Cretan legal system. It was King Minos, under the tutelage of Zeus, who established these laws for the benefit of the Cretans; he was a hero of legislation, and one must not believe the slanders heaped upon him by Athenian dramatists.

The assumptions and techniques of argument in Minos *are thoroughly Platonic; indeed, it is a sort of preface to Plato's* Laws. *It explains why the* Laws *begins with the story that Minos was the divinely inspired law-giver of Crete, which is the starting point of a discussion about legislation between three old men on their way from Cnossus (the capital city of Minos) to the Idaean cave (where Minos was said to have learned about legislation from Zeus). In* Minos, *bodies of laws are conceived as written texts which can be true or false, a conception shared by Plato, who also held that legal texts benefit from literary elaboration (*Laws *718c–723d). Proper laws express the reality of social life, a reality which is as enduring as the ideal city which the three old men sketch in* Laws—*the best possible social, political, and legal system under which people can live in cities in permanent peace and stability. Although* Minos *was probably written after* Laws, *it adopts an earlier conception of politics as the skill of herding human beings, the conception discussed and rejected in Plato's* Statesman.

The Greek word for law is nomos, *which is also used for custom or an established usage or practice. Socrates' friend in* Minos *attempts to define* nomos *as something* nomizomenon *(the present passive participle of the related verb* nomizō)—*that is, 'accepted'. Indeed,* nomizō *has a wide range of uses, including 'practice', 'have in common or customary use', 'enact', 'treat, consider as', 'accept the idea that', 'hold the customary or conventional belief that', 'believe, hold'. Most of these uses, and the translation of* nomizomenon *by 'accepted', fit rather more easily with* nomos *conceived as custom than as written law.*

From the formal point of view, Minos *is composed of dry Academic dialectic together with a literary-historical excursus. The classic example of such an excursus is the Atlantis myth in Plato's* Timaeus *and* Critias, *and there are other examples in* Alcibiades, Second Alcibiades, Hipparchus, *and probably in the (now mostly lost) Socratic dialogues of Antisthenes and Aeschines. The*

Academic dialectic of Minos *is a good example of the way questions were dis-*
cussed in the mid-fourth-century Academy, the dialectic studied in Aristotle's
Topics *and* Sophistical Refutations. *The combination of dialectic and ex-*
cursus in Minos *is very similar to that in* Hipparchus, *as is the skepticism to-*
ward the values implicit in Athenian popular culture and history; many schol-
ars conclude that they are the work of the same author, probably writing soon
after the middle of the fourth century B.C.

D.S.H.

313   SOCRATES: Law—in our view, what is it?

FRIEND: What sort of laws are you asking about?

SOCRATES: Well, now! Is it possible that law differs from law in this very
respect of being law? Think about the question I'm actually asking you.
If I had asked: "What is gold?," then if you had asked me in the same
way: "What sort of gold am I referring to?," I reckon that your question
would have been incorrect. For surely gold does not differ at all from gold

b   nor stone from stone in respect of being stone or in respect of being gold.
And so law too, I suppose, does not differ at all from law—they are all
the same thing. Each of them is law alike, not one more, another less.
What I am asking, then, is just this—the global question: what is law? If
you have an answer to hand, say it.

FRIEND: What else would law be, Socrates, but what is accepted?

SOCRATES: And so speech, in your view, is what is spoken, or sight what

c   is seen, or hearing what is heard? Or is speech one thing, what is spoken
another, sight one thing, what is seen another, hearing one thing, what is
heard another—and so law one thing, what is accepted another? Is that
so, or what is your view?

FRIEND: They are two different things, as it now seems to me.

SOCRATES: Law, then, is not what is accepted.

FRIEND: I don't think so.

SOCRATES: So what can law be? Let's investigate the question as follows.
Suppose someone had asked us about what we said just now: "Since you

314   say it is by sight that what is seen is seen, what is this sight by which such
things are seen?" We would have replied to him: "That form of sense
perception which reveals such things through the eyes." And if he had
asked us another question: "Well, now: since it is by hearing that what is
heard is heard, what is this hearing?," we would have replied to him:
"That form of sense perception which reveals sounds to us through our
ears." So, then, if he were to ask us: "Since it is by law that what is accepted
is accepted, what is this law by which such things are accepted? Is it a

b   form of perception or revealing, as what is learned is learned by the

Translated by Malcolm Schofield.

revelations of knowledge? Or is it a form of discovery, as what is discovered is discovered—for example, facts about health and sickness by medicine, or the intentions of the gods (as the diviners say) by divination: for a skill is surely in our view a discovery of things, is it not?

FRIEND: Certainly.

SOCRATES: Which among these alternatives, then, would we be most inclined to suppose law to be?

FRIEND: The resolutions and decrees themselves, in my own view. What else could one say that law is? So it looks as though the answer to your global question about law has to be: resolution of a city.

SOCRATES: Political judgment, it appears, is what you call law.

FRIEND: I do.

SOCRATES: And perhaps this is a good answer. But maybe we'll get a better one in the following way. Do you call certain people wise?

FRIEND: I do.

SOCRATES: Aren't the wise wise in virtue of wisdom?

FRIEND: Yes.

SOCRATES: Well then, aren't the just just in virtue of justice?

FRIEND: Certainly.

SOCRATES: And aren't the law-abiding law-abiding in virtue of law?

FRIEND: Yes.

SOCRATES: And the lawless lawless by virtue of lawlessness?

FRIEND: Yes.

SOCRATES: And the law-abiding are just?

FRIEND: Yes.

SOCRATES: And the lawless unjust?

FRIEND: Unjust.

SOCRATES: Aren't justice and law something very fine?

FRIEND: That is so.

SOCRATES: But injustice and lawlessness are something very shameful?

FRIEND: Yes.

SOCRATES: And the one preserves cities and everything else, but the other destroys and subverts them?

FRIEND: Yes.

SOCRATES: Then we must think about law as something that is fine, and seek it as something good.

FRIEND: Obviously.

SOCRATES: Now we said that law is resolution of a city?

FRIEND: We did say so.

SOCRATES: Well, now: is it not the case that some resolutions are admirable, others wicked?

FRIEND: It is.

SOCRATES: Yet law was not wicked?

FRIEND: No.

SOCRATES: It is not correct, then, to reply in such unqualified terms that law is resolution of a city.

FRIEND: Not in my view.

SOCRATES: It would not be in order, then, to take it that a wicked resolution is law.

FRIEND: No indeed.

SOCRATES: But still, it is quite apparent to me for my part that law is a kind of judgment. And since it is not the wicked judgment, is it not quite obvious by now that it is the admirable, given that law is judgment?

FRIEND: Yes.

SOCRATES: But what is admirable judgment? Is it not true judgment?

315   FRIEND: Yes.

SOCRATES: Now isn't true judgment discovery of reality?

FRIEND: It is.

SOCRATES: Then ideally law is discovery of reality.

FRIEND: How is it, Socrates, if law is discovery of reality, that we do not always make use of the same laws on the same matters, assuming we have discovered reality?

SOCRATES: Ideally, nevertheless, law is discovery of reality. So it must
b   be that any human beings who do not always make use of the same laws, as appears to be the case with us, are not always capable of discovering what ideally the law does discover—reality. Let's have a look and see whether it actually does become quite clear to us from our inquiry whether we always make use of the same laws, or different ones at different times, and whether all make use of the same laws, or different people different ones.

FRIEND: That's not difficult to determine, Socrates: the same people do not always make use of the same laws, and different people make use of different ones. For example, with us there is no law providing for human sacrifice—indeed it is unholy, whereas the Carthaginians make such sacri-
c   fices as something that is holy and lawful for them, and in fact some of them sacrifice even their own sons to Cronus, as perhaps you have heard yourself. And it is not just foreigners who make use of different laws from us, but those people in Lycia and the descendants of Athamas perform the sacrifices they perform even though they are Greeks. You know about ourselves too, I imagine, from what you have heard yourself, the sorts of laws we made use of in the past with regard to those who died, slaughtering
d   sacred victims before the corpse was carried out and sending for urn women. Again, those who lived in still earlier times used to bury their dead right there in the house. We do none of these things. One could give thousands of such examples—there is ample room to prove that we do not always make use of the same laws as we ourselves recognize, nor do people make use of the same laws as one another.

SOCRATES: Look, my friend, it wouldn't be at all surprising if what you say was correct but went over my head. So long as you express your views
e   in lengthy speeches in your own style and I do too in my turn, I don't think we'll ever reach any agreement. But if the inquiry is made a common

enterprise, maybe we would agree. So join in a common inquiry with me, asking questions of me if you like, or answering them if you would rather.

FRIEND: Socrates, I'm willing to answer whatever you like.

SOCRATES: Right, then: do you accept that just things are unjust and unjust things just, or that the just are just and the unjust unjust?

FRIEND: I accept that the just are just and the unjust unjust.

SOCRATES: Now are they accepted as such among all people as they are here?

FRIEND: Yes.

SOCRATES: So among the Persians as well?

FRIEND: Among the Persians as well.

SOCRATES: Always, I suppose.

FRIEND: Always.

SOCRATES: Are things which pull down the scale more accepted here as heavier, and those which pull it down less as lighter, or the opposite?

FRIEND: No, those which pull it down more as heavier, those less as lighter.

SOCRATES: And is this the case in Carthage and in Lycia as well?

FRIEND: Yes.

SOCRATES: Things that are fine are accepted as fine everywhere, it appears, and things that are shameful as shameful, and not the shameful as fine or the fine as shameful.

FRIEND: That is so.

SOCRATES: Therefore, to generalize to all cases, what is so is accepted as being so, not what is not so, both among us and among all other people.

FRIEND: That is my view.

SOCRATES: Then anyone who mistakes what is so mistakes what is accepted.

FRIEND: When you express things this way, Socrates, these things do seem to be accepted always both by us and by the others. But when I consider that we are constantly turning the laws upside down, I cannot be persuaded.

SOCRATES: Perhaps you do not take into consideration that when we move the pieces at checkers they remain the same pieces. But look at the question with me in the following way. Have you ever come across a treatise on health for the sick?

FRIEND: I have.

SOCRATES: Then you know what skill it is that this is the treatise of?

FRIEND: I do know—medicine.

SOCRATES: Don't you call those who possess knowledge of these matters doctors?

FRIEND: I agree.

SOCRATES: Do people who possess knowledge accept the same things on the same matters, or do different people accept different things?

FRIEND: The same things, in my view.

316

b

c

d

SOCRATES: Is it simply that the Greeks accept the same things as the Greeks on the matters they know about, or do foreigners too accept the same things, agreeing among themselves and with the Greeks?

FRIEND: I would suppose it definitely has to be the case that those who know agree in accepting the same things, both Greeks and foreigners.

SOCRATES: Well answered. And won't they always agree?

FRIEND: Yes, always.

SOCRATES: And don't the doctors in their treatises on health write what
e   they accept as being so?

FRIEND: Yes.

SOCRATES: Then these treatises of the doctors are medical, and laws of medicine.

FRIEND: Medical, to be sure.

SOCRATES: So farming treatises too are laws of farming?

FRIEND: Yes.

SOCRATES: And whose are the treatises and accepted ideas on working a garden?

FRIEND: Gardeners.

SOCRATES: Then these are our laws of gardening.

FRIEND: Yes.

SOCRATES: Formulated by people who know how to manage a garden?

FRIEND: Obviously.

SOCRATES: And it is the gardeners who have the knowledge?

FRIEND: Yes.

SOCRATES: And whose are the treatises and accepted ideas on preparing a meal?

FRIEND: Cooks.

SOCRATES: Then these are the laws of cookery?

FRIEND: Cookery.

317   SOCRATES: Formulated, as it appears, by people who know how to manage the preparation of a meal?

FRIEND: Yes.

SOCRATES: And it is the cooks who have the knowledge, as they claim?

FRIEND: Yes, they have the knowledge.

SOCRATES: Very well. But then, whose are the treatises and accepted ideas on administration of a city? Isn't it those who know how to manage cities?

FRIEND: In my view it is.

SOCRATES: And does anyone possess this knowledge except those who are skilled in politics and kingship?

FRIEND: Those it is.

SOCRATES: Then these writings which people call laws are treatises on
b   politics—treatises by kings and good men.

FRIEND: What you say is true.

SOCRATES: Then surely those who possess knowledge will not write different things at different times on the same matters?

FRIEND: No.

SOCRATES: Nor yet will they ever change one set of accepted ideas for another on the same matters?

FRIEND: Certainly not.

SOCRATES: So if we see anyone doing this anywhere, shall we say that those who do it are in possession of knowledge, or not in possession?

FRIEND: Not in possession.

SOCRATES: And won't we also say that whatever is correct is the accepted idea in each sphere, whether in medicine or in cookery or in gardening?

FRIEND: Yes.

SOCRATES: And whatever is not correct, we shall never again say that it is the accepted idea?

FRIEND: Never again.

SOCRATES: Then it proves to be unlawful.

FRIEND: It must be.

SOCRATES: And in treatises on what is just and unjust and in general on the organization of a city and on how one should administer a city, isn't what is correct a law of royal skill? But not what is not correct, although it is taken to be law by those who don't know. That is unlawful.

FRIEND: Yes.

SOCRATES: Then we were correct in agreeing that law is discovery of reality.

FRIEND: It seems so.

SOCRATES: Now to a further point that we need to note carefully on the topic. Who has knowledge of how to distribute seed over land?

FRIEND: A farmer.

SOCRATES: Does he distribute appropriate seed for each sort of land?

FRIEND: Yes.

SOCRATES: Then the farmer is a good apportioner of it, and his laws and distributions are correct in this sphere?

FRIEND: Yes.

SOCRATES: And who is a good apportioner of notes in songs?[1] Whose laws are correct here?

FRIEND: The laws of the flautist and the lute-player.

SOCRATES: Then the person whose laws are most authoritative in this sphere is the person whose command of flute-playing is best.

FRIEND: Yes.

SOCRATES: And who is best at distributing nourishment for human bodies? Is it not the person who distributes it appropriately?

FRIEND: Yes.

SOCRATES: Then his distributions and laws are best, and the person whose laws are most authoritative in this sphere is also the best apportioner.

FRIEND: Certainly.

SOCRATES: Who is this person?

FRIEND: A trainer.

c

d

e

318

1. Conjecturally deleting *kai ta axia neimai* in d8–9.

SOCRATES: He is supreme at driving a human herd?[2]

FRIEND: Yes.

SOCRATES: And who is supreme at driving a herd of sheep? What is his name?

FRIEND: A shepherd.

SOCRATES: Then it is the laws of the shepherd that are best for the sheep.

FRIEND: Yes.

SOCRATES: And the laws of the cowherd for cattle?

FRIEND: Yes.

SOCRATES: And whose laws are best for human souls? Isn't it those of the king? Agreed?

FRIEND: I do agree.

b SOCRATES: You're doing well in your answers. Can you now say who in antiquity proved himself a good lawgiver in the sphere of laws of flute-playing? Perhaps you don't call him to mind—would you like me to remind you?

FRIEND: Certainly.

SOCRATES: Isn't it said to be Marsyas, and his boyfriend Olympus the Phrygian?[3]

FRIEND: What you say is true.

SOCRATES: Now their flute tunes are absolutely divine, and alone stir

c and make manifest those who are in need of the gods—and to this day there are still only these, because they are divine.

FRIEND: That is so.

SOCRATES: And who among the ancient kings is said to have proved himself to be a good lawgiver, so that even to this day his accepted provisions remain in force, because they are divine?

FRIEND: I cannot call him to mind.

SOCRATES: Don't you know which of the Greeks make use of the most ancient laws?

FRIEND: Are you referring to the Spartans, and Lycurgus the lawgiver?

SOCRATES: But that is not yet three hundred years ago, perhaps, or a

d little more than that. Where do the best of their accepted provisions come from? Do you know?

FRIEND: People say from Crete.

SOCRATES: So among the Greeks it is the Cretans who make use of the most ancient laws?

FRIEND: Yes.

SOCRATES: Then do you know who were their good kings? Minos and Rhadamanthus, the sons of Zeus and Europa: these laws were theirs.

2. Accepting a conjectural deletion of *tou sōmatos* in a1–2.

3. Marsyas was said to have invented a form of music for wind instruments (such as the *aulos*, here conventionally but misleadingly translated "flute"). Olympus was credited with bringing this music from the Near East to Greece and developing it further.

FRIEND: People certainly claim that Rhadamanthus was a just man, Socrates; but they say Minos was savage and harsh and unjust.

SOCRATES: My good friend, you are telling a theatrical Attic version of the story.

FRIEND: Well, isn't that what they say about Minos?

SOCRATES: Not Homer and Hesiod. Yet they are more persuasive than all the tragedians put together—who are the people you are listening to if this is what you are saying.

FRIEND: And what is it that Homer and Hesiod say about Minos?

SOCRATES: I will tell you, so that you won't commit impiety along with the mass of people. There cannot be anything more impious than this, nor anything over which one should take more precautions, than being mistaken in word and deed with regard to gods, and in second place, with regard to divine humans. You should always exercise very great forethought, when you are about to criticize or praise a man, to ensure that you don't speak incorrectly. This is why you should learn to distinguish admirable from wicked men. For god vents his anger when anyone criticizes someone similar to himself, or praises someone whose condition is opposite to his own; the former is the good man. For you really mustn't think that there are sacred stones and pieces of wood and birds and snakes, but not humans.[4] A good human being is the most sacred of all of these, and one who is wicked the most defiled.

So now I will speak about Minos, and how Homer and Hesiod sing his praises, with this purpose in mind: that you, as a human and the son of a human, may not be mistaken in what you say about a hero who is son of Zeus. Homer when telling us about Crete and how there are many men in it and "ninety cities," says:

> *Among them is Cnossus, a great city, where Minos*
> *was King in the ninth season, having converse with great Zeus.*[5]

This, then, is how Homer sings the praises of Minos: briefly expressed— but Homer composed nothing like it for any of the heroes. That Zeus is a sophist and that this art of his is something altogether excellent, he makes clear here as well as in many other places. For he means that during the ninth year Minos got together with Zeus to discuss things, and went regularly to be educated by Zeus as though he were a sophist. So the fact that Homer assigns this privilege of being educated by Zeus to no one among the heroes but to Minos is extraordinary praise. And in the book of the dead in the *Odyssey* he represents Minos, not Rhadamanthus, as giving judgment with a golden scepter.[6] He does not represent

4. Reading *toi* for *ti* in a5.
5. *Odyssey* xix.178–79.
6. *Odyssey* xi.568–71.

Rhadamanthus as giving judgment in this passage, nor as associated with Zeus in any passage. For this reason I say that Minos beyond all others has had his praises sung by Homer.

To be the son of Zeus and then to be the only one educated by Zeus is praise that cannot be exceeded. For this verse, "was king in the ninth season, having converse with great Zeus" indicates that Minos was an

e associate of Zeus. "Converses" are discussions, and someone who "has converse" is an associate in discussions. In other words, every nine years Minos would go into the Cave of Zeus, partly to learn and partly to demonstrate what he had learned from Zeus in the preceding ninth year. There are those who suppose that someone who "has converse" is a drinking and partying companion of Zeus, but one may use the following as

320 evidence that those who make this supposition talk nonsense. Of all the many human beings there are, Greeks and foreigners, none abstain from drinking sessions and the sort of partying there is when wine is present except Cretans and in second place Spartans, who have learned it from the Cretans. In Crete it is one of the laws Minos laid down that people are not to drink together to the point of drunkenness. And indeed it is clear that what he accepted as admirable he laid down as accepted practice

b also for his own citizens. For Minos would surely not have accepted one thing but done something different from what he accepted, like a dishonest person. His form of association was as I say, through discourses for education into virtue. This is why he laid down for his own citizens those laws which have made Crete happy for all time, and Sparta from when she began to make use of them, because they are divine.

c Rhadamanthus was a good man: he had been educated by Minos. But he had been educated not in the art of kingship as a whole, but in one subsidiary to it, confined to presiding in law courts; that is why he was said to be a good judge. Minos used him as watcher over the law in the town, but Talos in the rest of Crete. Talos used to tour the villages three times a year, preserving a watch over the law in them by having the laws written on bronze tablets: this is why he was called "bronze."

d Hesiod too has said some things akin to these with regard to Minos. After making mention of his name he says

> *Who proved to be most kingly of mortal kings, and ruled over most of the people in the countryside, holding the scepter of Zeus—with which he exercised kingship also over cities.*[7]

He means by "the scepter of Zeus" nothing other than the education he received from Zeus, by means of which he governed Crete.

e FRIEND: Why, then, Socrates, has this rumor about Minos as someone who was uneducated and harsh ever been spread about?

SOCRATES: Because of something over which you, my good friend, will take precautions, if you are sensible, and so will anyone else who cares for a good reputation: never to fall out with any man who is skilled

---

7. Hesiod frg. 144 (Merkelbach-West).

in poetry. The poets have great power where reputation is concerned, whichever mode—eulogy or abuse—they adopt in writing about people. Which was the mistake Minos made in waging war on this city, where as well as many other forms of wisdom there are poets of every kind, who compose tragedy as well as every other kind of poetry. Tragedy is an ancient form here, not beginning with Thespis as some suppose nor with Phrynichus:[8] if you care to consider the matter you will find it to be a very ancient discovery, made in this very city. Tragedy is that form of poetry which most delights the populace and which most seduces the soul. So it is in tragedy that we torture Minos and take vengeance upon him for that tribute he compelled us to pay.[9] This, then, was the mistake Minos made, in falling out with us. And that is why, to answer your question, he has come to have a worse and worse reputation. He was good and lawabiding, as we said at the outset, a good apportioner. And the greatest indication of this is that his laws are unaltered: that shows how well he did at discovering reality as regards habitation of a city.

FRIEND: In my view, Socrates, the account you have given is a likely one.

SOCRATES: Now if what I say is true, is it your view that the Cretans, who are citizens of Minos and Rhadamanthus, make use of the most ancient laws?

FRIEND: They seem to.

SOCRATES: Then these two have proved to be the best lawgivers among the ancients, apportioners and shepherds of men, just as Homer said that the good general was "shepherd of the people."[10]

FRIEND: Certainly.

SOCRATES: Please, now, by Zeus god of friendship: if someone were to ask us what are these things that the good lawgiver and apportioner for the body distributes to the body to make it better, we would say if we were to reply well and briefly: food and hard work, building it up with the one, and exercising and constituting the body itself with the other.

FRIEND: Quite correct.

SOCRATES: If then after this he were to ask us: "Whatever then are those things that the good lawgiver and apportioner distributes to the soul to make it better?," what reply would we make if we are not to be ashamed both of ourselves and of our mature years?

FRIEND: I don't any more know what to say.

SOCRATES: Yet it really is a disgrace to the soul in each of us that it plainly doesn't know what in it constitutes goodness and badness for it, whereas what constitutes goodness and badness for the body, and for other things, is something it has already considered.

321

b

c

d

---

8. Thespis was the first playwright to win a prize at the Athenian festival of Dionysus, about 535 B.C. Phrynichus was a tragic playwright active in the early fifth century.

9. According to legend, after Minos defeated the Athenians, he exacted a tribute every nine years of seven maidens and seven young men, whom he imprisoned in the Labyrinth, eventually to be devoured by the Minotaur, the 'bull of Minos'.

10. *Iliad* i.263, *Odyssey* iv.532, and elsewhere.

LAWS

This work, Plato's longest and a product of his last years, was left unpublished at his death, perhaps because he felt it still needed revision. Plato's associate Philip of Opus is said to have transcribed it for publication. It seems to be complete as it stands.

Three elderly gentlemen, all apparently fictional—Clinias from Crete, Megillus, a Spartan, and an unnamed Athenian—begin a journey on foot from Cnossus in Crete to the shrine of Zeus' birthplace on Mount Ida. The Athenian begins a conversation on 'laws and constitutions' (which continues till the end of book III) by querying the central purpose of his Cretan and Spartan friends' famously similar civic institutions: the optimal conduct of war, as Clinias maintains. As one might expect in an Athenian, this strikes him as too narrow and exclusive a focus on one aspect of civic life, and that a secondary one: wars are undertaken to make secure the activities of peacetime. Laws should indeed see to the training of citizens in the virtues of wartime, but also, and even more, in those of peace. A broader and culturally deeper education and range of experience are needed to produce truly good human beings. Athens itself, however, had been ruined by its predilection for the personal freedoms provided by democratic institutions; the best laws would follow the Cretan and Spartan lead by establishing strong civic authority and discipline, but they would aim at the fullest possible development of all the human virtues.

At the end of book III Clinias reveals that he is one of ten commissioners entrusted with establishing the laws for a new city being founded in Crete, and the conversation continues, with the Athenian now offering his advice on the laws that will be needed to achieve this objective. Since these are to be citizens of a free, self-governing state, the laws must have 'preambles' that explain the purposes for which they are instituted, so as to gain the willing acquiescence of those to whom they apply: commands backed by threats (contained in the bare text of the law) are otherwise not appropriately addressed to a free person (book IV). And it is in the preliminary discussion and preambles to the laws set out in the following books—running the gamut from family law and education to administrative, trade, property, and criminal law—that we find the philosophical core of the dialogue's jurisprudence and social and political theory.

Of special note are the theory of punishment and its legitimate purposes in book IX and the elaborate argument in book X to prove the existence of gods and to establish the law forbidding behavior that denies them due deference and enacting the appropriate punishments for infractions.

Understandably, most people nowadays read the Laws *for its theoretical ideas more than for any practical applications. Scholars debate whether the constitution of* Laws *replaces—and implicitly criticizes—the constitution of* Republic, *with its rule by philosopher-kings essentially untrammeled by law. And they compare—and contrast—the accounts of the rule of law and its philosophical basis given in* Statesman *and* Laws. *But Plato's Academy was not merely an institute for higher education and for research in mathematics, the sciences, philosophy, and ethical and political thought; Plato and his associates were called upon also for concrete advice about 'laws and constitutions' in reforming existing states and founding new ones. In writing* Laws *Plato was perhaps not engaging in pure constitutional and legislative theory, as in* Statesman *and* Republic. *In considering* Laws *in relation to these other works, one should bear in mind this context of possible practical applications.*

J.M.C.

Book I

ATHENIAN: Tell me, gentlemen, to whom do you give the credit for establishing your codes of law? Is it a god, or a man?   624

CLINIAS: A god, sir, a god—and that's the honest truth. Among us Cretans it is Zeus; in Sparta—which is where our friend here hails from—they say it is Apollo, I believe. Isn't that right?

MEGILLUS: Yes, that's right.

ATHENIAN: You follow Homer, presumably, and say that every ninth year Minos used to go to a consultation with his father Zeus,[1] and laid down laws for your cities on the basis of the god's pronouncements?   b

CLINIAS: Yes, that's our Cretan version, and we add that Minos' brother, Rhadamanthus—doubtless you know the name—was an absolute paragon of justice. We Cretans would say that he won this reputation because of the scrupulously fair way in which he settled the judicial problems of his day.   625

ATHENIAN: A distinguished reputation indeed, and one particularly appropriate for a son of Zeus. Well then, since you and your companion have been raised under laws with such a splendid ancestry, I expect you will be quite happy if we spend our time together today in a discussion about constitutions and laws, and occupy our journey in a mutual exchange of views. I've heard it said that from Cnossus to Zeus' cave and shrine is quite a long way, and the tall trees along the route provide shady resting-places which will be more than welcome in this stiflingly hot weather. At   b

---

Translated by Trevor J. Saunders. Text: Budé, bks. I–VI ed. E. des Places, VII–XII ed. A. Diès, Paris (1951, 1956).

1. *Odyssey* xix.178–79. Minos was a legendary king of Crete.

our age, there is every excuse for having frequent rests in them, so as to refresh ourselves by conversation. In this way we shall come to the end of the whole journey without having tired ourselves out.

c   CLINIAS: And as you go on, sir, you find tremendously tall and graceful cypress trees in the sacred groves; there are also meadows in which we can pause and rest.

ATHENIAN: That sounds a good idea.

CLINIAS: It is indeed, and it'll sound even better when we see them. Well then, shall we wish ourselves *bon voyage*, and be off?

ATHENIAN: Certainly. Now, answer me this. You have meals which you eat communally; you have a system of physical training, and a special type of military equipment. Why is it that you give all this the force of law?

CLINIAS: Well, sir, I think that these customs are quite easy for anyone to understand, at any rate in our case. You see the Cretan terrain in general
d   does not have the flatness of Thessaly: hence we usually train by running (whereas the Thessalians mostly use horses), because our land is hilly and more suited to exercise by racing on foot. In this sort of country we have to keep our armor light so that we can run without being weighed down, and bows and arrows seem appropriate because of their lightness. All these Cretan practices have been developed for fighting wars, and that's
e   precisely the purpose I think the legislator intended them to serve when he instituted them. Likely enough, this is why he organized the common meals, too: he observed that when men are on military service they are all obliged by the pressure of events, for their own protection, to eat together throughout the campaign. In this, I think, he censured the stupidity of ordinary men, who do not understand that they are all engaged in a never-ending lifelong war against all other states. So, if you grant the
626   necessity of eating together for self-protection in war-time, and of appointing officers and men in turn to act as guards, the same thing should be done in peace-time too. The legislator's position would be that what most men call 'peace' is really only a fiction, and that in cold fact all states are by nature fighting an undeclared war against every other state. If you see things in this light, you are pretty sure to find that the Cretan legislator established all these institutions of ours, both in the public sphere and the private, with an eye on war, and that this was the spirit in which he gave
b   us his laws for us to keep up. He was convinced that if we don't come out on top in war, nothing that we possess or do in peace-time is of the slightest use, because all the goods of the conquered fall into the possession of the victors.

ATHENIAN: You certainly have had a splendid training, sir! It has, I think, enabled you to make a most penetrating analysis of Cretan institutions. But explain this point to me rather more precisely: the definition you gave
c   of a well-run state seems to me to demand that its organization and administration should be such as to ensure victory in war over other states. Correct?

CLINIAS: Of course, and I think our companion supports my definition.

MEGILLUS: My dear sir, what other answer could one possibly make, if one is a Spartan?

ATHENIAN: But if this is the right criterion as between states, what about as between villages? Is the criterion different?

CLINIAS: Certainly not.

ATHENIAN: It is the same, then?

CLINIAS: Yes.

ATHENIAN: Well now, what about relations between the village's separate households? And between individual and individual? Is the same true?

CLINIAS: The same is true.

ATHENIAN: What of a man's relations with himself—should he think of *himself* as his own enemy? What's our answer now?   d

CLINIAS: Well done, my Athenian friend! (I'd rather not call you 'Attic', because I think it is better to call you after the goddess,[2] as you deserve.) You have made the argument clearer by expressing it in its most elementary form. Now you will find it that much easier to realize that the position we took up a moment ago is correct: not only is everyone an enemy of everyone else in the public sphere, but each man fights a private war against himself.

ATHENIAN: You *do* surprise me, my friend. What do you mean?   e

CLINIAS: This, sir, is where a man wins the first and best of victories— over himself. Conversely, to fall a victim to oneself is the worst and most shocking thing that can be imagined. This way of speaking points to a war against ourselves within each one of us.

ATHENIAN: Now let's reverse the argument. You hold that each one of us is either 'conqueror of' or 'conquered by' himself: are we to say that   627 the same holds good of household, village and state? Or not?

CLINIAS: You mean that they are individually either 'conquerors of' or 'conquered by' themselves?

ATHENIAN: Yes.

CLINIAS: This again is a good question to have asked. Your suggestion is most emphatically true, particularly in the case of states. Wherever the better people subdue their inferiors, the state may rightly be said to be 'conqueror of' itself, and we should be entirely justified in praising it for its victory. Where the opposite happens, we must give the opposite verdict.

ATHENIAN: It would take too long a discussion to decide whether in fact   b there *is* a sense in which the worse element could be superior to the better, so let's leave that aside. For the moment, I understand your position to amount to this: sometimes evil citizens will come together in large numbers and forcibly try to enslave the virtuous minority, although both sides are members of the same race and the same state. When they prevail, the state may properly be said to be 'inferior to' itself and to be an evil one; but

2. Athena, goddess of wisdom and patron of Athens in Attica.

when they are defeated, we can say it is 'superior to' itself and that it is a good state.

c   CLINIAS: That's a paradoxical way of putting it, sir, but it is impossible to disagree.[3]

ATHENIAN: But now wait a minute. Let's look at this point again: suppose a father and mother had several sons—should we be surprised if the majority of these brothers were unjust, and the minority just?

CLINIAS: By no means.

ATHENIAN: We could say that if the wicked brothers prevail the whole
d   household and family may be called 'inferior to' itself, and 'superior to' itself if they are subdued—but it would be irrelevant to our purpose to labor the point. The reason why we're now examining the usage of the common man is not to pass judgment on whether he uses language properly or improperly, but to determine what is essentially right and wrong in a given law.

CLINIAS: Very true, sir.

MEGILLUS: I agree—it's been nicely put, so far.

ATHENIAN: Let's look at the next point. Those brothers I've just mentioned—they'd have a judge, I suppose?

CLINIAS: Of course.

e   ATHENIAN: Which of these judges would be the better, the one who put all the bad brothers to death and told the better ones to run their own lives, or the one who put the virtuous brothers in command, but let the scoundrels go on living in willing obedience to them? And we can probably add a third and even better judge—the one who will take this single
628   quarrelling family in hand and *reconcile* its members, without killing any of them; by laying down regulations to guide them in the future, he will be able to ensure that they remain on friendly terms with each other.

CLINIAS: Yes, this judge—the legislator—would be incomparably better.

ATHENIAN: But in framing these regulations he would have his eye on the exact opposite of war.

CLINIAS: True enough.

ATHENIAN: But what about the man who brings harmony to the state?
b   In regulating its life, will he pay more attention to external war, or internal? This 'civil' war, as we call it, does break out on occasion, and is the last thing a man would want to see in his own country; but if it did flare up, he would wish to have it over and done with as quickly as possible.

CLINIAS: He'll obviously pay more attention to the second kind.

ATHENIAN: One side might be destroyed through the victory of the other, and then peace would follow the civil war; or, alternatively, peace and friendship might be the result of reconciliation. Now, which of these results

---

3. Clinias is struck by the paradox that when 'inferior' numbers conquer, the state is morally 'superior', and when 'superior' numbers conquer, it is morally 'inferior'.

would you prefer, supposing the city then had to turn its attention to a
foreign enemy?   c

CLINIAS: Everybody would prefer the second situation to the first, so far
as his own state was concerned.

ATHENIAN: And wouldn't a legislator have the same preference?

CLINIAS: He certainly would.

ATHENIAN: Now surely, every legislator will enact his every law with
the aim of achieving the greatest good?

CLINIAS: Of course.

ATHENIAN: The greatest good, however, is neither war nor civil war
(God forbid we should ever need to resort to either of them), but peace
and goodwill among men. And so the victory of a state over itself, it
seems, does not after all come into the category of ideals; it is just one of   d
those things in which we've no choice. You might just as well suppose
that the sick body which has been purged by the doctor was therefore in
the pink of condition, and disregard the body that never had any such
need. Similarly, anyone who takes this sort of view of the happiness of a
state or even an individual will never make a true statesman in the true
sense—if, that is, he adopts foreign warfare as his first and only concern;
he'll become a *genuine* lawgiver only if he designs his legislation about
war as a tool for peace, rather than his legislation for peace as an instrument   e
of war.

CLINIAS: What you say, sir, has the air of having been correctly argued.
Even so, I shall be surprised if our Cretan institutions, and the Spartan
ones as well, have not been wholly orientated towards warfare.

ATHENIAN: Well, that's as may be. At the moment, however, there's no   629
call for a stubborn dispute on the point. What we need to do is to conduct
our inquiry into these institutions dispassionately, seeing that we share
this common interest with their authors. So keep me company in the
conversation I'm going to have. Let's put up Tyrtaeus,[4] for example, an
Athenian by birth who became a citizen of Sparta. He, of all men, was
particularly concerned with what we are discussing. He said:

'I'd not mention a man, I'd take no account of him,

no matter' (he goes on) 'if he were the richest of men, no matter if he had   b
a huge number of good things' (he enumerated pretty nearly all of them)
'unless his prowess in war were beyond compare.' Doubtless you too have
heard the lines; Megillus here knows them backwards, I expect.

---

4. Tyrtaeus (mid-seventh century) was noted for his poems in praise of courage in
war. The Athenian quotes the first line of the poem verbatim and then summarizes the
next nine; at 629e he gives a somewhat adapted quotation of lines 11 and 12. For the
whole poem see J. M. Edmonds, *Elegy and Iambus* (Loeb), vol. I, pp. 74–77.

MEGILLUS: I certainly do.

CLINIAS: And they have certainly got as far as Crete: they were brought across from Sparta.

ATHENIAN: Now then, let's jointly ask our poet some such question as
c   this: 'Tyrtaeus, you are a poet, and divinely inspired. We are quite sure of your wisdom and virtue, from the special commendation you have bestowed on those who have particularly distinguished themselves in active service. On this point we—Megillus here, Clinias of Cnossus and I—find ourselves, we think, emphatically in agreement with you; but we want to be quite clear that we are talking about the same people. Tell us: do you clearly distinguish, as we do, two sorts of war? Or what?' I fancy
d   that in reply to this even a man far less gifted than Tyrtaeus would state the facts of the case and say 'Two'. The first would be what we all call 'civil' war, and as we were saying just now, this is the most bitterly fought of all; and we shall all agree, I think, in making the other type of war the one we fight when we quarrel with our foreign enemies from outside the state, which is a much less vicious sort of war than the other.

CLINIAS: I agree.

ATHENIAN: 'Well now, Tyrtaeus, which category of soldiers did you shower with your praises and which did you censure? Which was the type of war they were fighting, that led you to speak so highly of them? The war fought against foreign enemies, it would seem—at any rate, you
e   have told us in your verses that you have no time for men who cannot "stand the sight of bloody butchery

> *and do not attack in close combat with the foe."'*

So here is the next thing we'd say: 'It looks as if you reserve your special praise, Tyrtaeus, for those who fight with conspicuous gallantry in external war against a foreign enemy.' I suppose he'd agree to this, and say 'Yes'?

CLINIAS: Surely.

ATHENIAN: However, while not denying the courage of those soldiers,
630 we still maintain that those who display conspicuous gallantry in *total* war are very much more courageous. We have a poet to bear witness to this, Theognis,[5] a citizen of Megara in Sicily, who says:

> *'Cyrnus, find a man you can trust in deadly feuding:*
> *He is worth his weight in silver and gold.'*

---

5. Theognis (late sixth century) belonged to the landed gentry of Megara (probably the Megara near Athens, in spite of what is said here). He wrote lively, indignant poems from a conservative point of view about the social and political changes of his day. Some 1400 lines of his work survive: see J. M. Edmonds, *Elegy and Iambus* (Loeb), vol. I, pp. 216–401. The Athenian quotes lines 77–78.

Such a man, in our view, who fights in a tougher war, is far superior to
the other—to just about the same degree as the combination of justice,   b
self-control and good judgment, reinforced by courage, is superior to courage alone. In civil war a man will never prove sound and loyal unless he
has every virtue; but in the war Tyrtaeus mentions there are hordes of
mercenaries who are ready to dig their heels in and die fighting,[6] most of
whom, apart from a very small minority, are reckless and insolent rogues,
and just about the most witless people you could find. Now, what conclusion does my argument lead to? What is the point I am trying to make
clear in saying all this? Simply that in laying down his laws every legislator   c
who is any use at all—and especially your legislator here in Crete, duly
instructed by Zeus—will never have anything in view except the highest
virtue. This means, in Theognis' terms, 'loyalty in a crisis'; one might call
it 'complete justice'. The virtue that Tyrtaeus praised so highly is indeed
a noble one, and has been appropriately celebrated by the poet, but strictly
speaking, in order of merit it comes only fourth.   d

CLINIAS: And that, sir, is to reduce our Cretan legislator to the status of
a failure.

ATHENIAN: No, my dear fellow, it is not. The failure was entirely on our
part. We were quite wrong to imagine that when Lycurgus and Minos[7]
established the institutions of Sparta and this country the primary end
they had in view was invariably warfare.

CLINIAS: But what ought we to have said?

ATHENIAN: We had no particular axes to grind in our discussion, and I
think we ought to have told the honest truth. We ought not to have said
that the legislator laid down his rules with an eye on only a part of virtue,   e
and the most trivial part at that. We should have said that he aimed at
virtue in its entirety, and that the various separate headings under which
he tried to frame the laws of his time were quite different from those
employed by modern legal draftsmen. Each of these invents any category
he feels he wants, and adds it to his code. For instance, one will come up
with a category on 'Inheritances and Heiresses', another with 'Assault',
and others will suggest other categories *ad infinitum*. But we insist that the
correct procedure for framing laws, which is followed by those who do   631
the job properly, is precisely the one we have just embarked upon. I am
delighted at the way you set about explaining your laws: you rightly
started with *virtue,* and explained that this was the aim of the laws the
legislator laid down. However, you did say that he legislated entirely by
reference to only one part of virtue, and the most inconsiderable part at
that. Now there I thought you were wrong: hence all these additional

6. See Tyrtaeus 16–18.
7. Traditional founders of the Spartan and Cretan constitutions.

remarks. So what is this distinction I could have wished to hear you draw
b   in your argument? Shall I tell you?

CLINIAS: Certainly.

ATHENIAN: 'Now, Sir,' you ought to have said, 'it is no accident that the
laws of the Cretans have such a high reputation in the entire Greek world.
They are sound laws, and achieve the happiness of those who observe
them, by producing for them a great number of benefits. These benefits
fall into two classes, "human" and "divine." The former depend on the
c   latter, and if a city receives the one sort, it wins the other too—the greater
include the lesser; if not, it goes without both. Health heads the list of the
lesser benefits, followed by beauty; third comes strength, for racing and
other physical exercises. Wealth is fourth—not "blind" wealth,[8] but the
clear-sighted kind whose companion is good judgment—and good judgment itself is the leading "divine" benefit; second comes the habitual self-
control of a soul that uses reason. If you combine these two with courage,
d   you get (thirdly) justice; courage itself lies in fourth place. All these take
a natural precedence over the others, and the lawgiver must of course
rank them in the same order. Then he must inform the citizens that the
other instructions they receive have these benefits in view: the "human"
benefits have the "divine" in view, and all these in turn look towards
reason, which is supreme. The citizens join in marriage; then children,
e   male and female, are born and reared; they pass through childhood and
later life, and finally reach old age. At every stage the lawgiver should
supervise his people, and confer suitable marks of honor or disgrace.
Whenever they associate with each other, he should observe their pains,
632   pleasures and desires, and watch their passions in all their intensity; he
must use the laws themselves as instruments for the proper distribution
of praise and blame. Again, the citizens are angry or afraid; they suffer
from emotional disturbances brought on by misfortune, and recover from
them when life is going well; they have all the feelings that men usually
experience in illness, war, poverty or their opposites. In all these instances
b   the lawgiver's duty is to isolate and explain what is good and what is bad
in the way each individual reacts. Next, the lawgiver must supervise the
way the citizens acquire money and spend it; he must keep a sharp eye
on the various methods they all employ to make and dissolve (voluntarily
or under duress) their associations with one another, noting which methods
are proper and which are not; honors should be conferred upon those who
c   comply with the laws, and specified penalties imposed on the disobedient.
When the lawgiver comes to the final stages of organizing the entire life
of the state, he must decide what honors should be accorded the dead and
how the manner of burial should be varied. His survey completed, the
author of the legal code will appoint guardians (some of whom will have

---

8. Plutus, the god of wealth, was traditionally represented as blind.

rational grounds for their actions, while others rely on "true opinion"), so that all these regulations may be welded into a rational whole, demonstrably inspired by considerations of justice and self-restraint, not of wealth and ambition.' That is the sort of explanation, gentlemen, that I should have liked you to give, and still want now—an explanation of how all these conditions are met in the laws attributed to Zeus and the Pythian Apollo, which Minos and Lycurgus laid down. I wish you could have told me why the system on which they are arranged is obvious to someone with an expert technical—or even empirical—knowledge of law, while to laymen like ourselves it is entirely obscure.

CLINIAS: Well then, sir, where do we go from here?

ATHENIAN: I think we ought to go back and start again. As before, we should consider first the activities that promote courage; then, if you like, we'll work through the other kinds of virtue, one by one. We'll take the way we deal with the first as a model, and try to while away the journey by discussing the others in the same way. Then after dealing with virtue as a whole, we shall show, God willing, that the regulations we have just listed had this in view.

MEGILLUS: A splendid idea! Our friend here is an admirer of Zeus, so try examining him, to start with.

ATHENIAN: I'll try to examine not only him, but you and myself as well— we all have a stake in the discussion. Tell me, then, you two: do we maintain that the common meals and gymnastic exercises have been invented by your legislator for the purpose of war?

MEGILLUS: Yes.

ATHENIAN: What about a third such institution, and a fourth? To make a full list like this will probably be the right procedure in the case of the other 'parts' of virtue, too (or whatever the right terminology is: no matter, so long as one's meaning is clear).

MEGILLUS: I—and any Spartan, for that matter—would mention the legislator's invention of hunting as the third item.

ATHENIAN: Let's have a shot at adding a fourth, and a fifth too, if we can.

MEGILLUS: Well, I might try to add a fourth: the endurance of pain. This is a very conspicuous feature of Spartan life. You find it in our boxing matches, and also in our 'raids', which invariably lead to a severe whipping. There is also the 'Secret Service',[9] as it is called, which involves a great deal of hard work, and is a splendid exercise in endurance. In winter, its members go barefoot and sleep without bedclothes. They dispense with orderlies and look after themselves, ranging night and day over the whole country. Next, in the 'Naked Games', men display fantastic endurance, contending as they do with the full heat of summer. There are a great

d

e

633

b

c

---

9. An official organization of young Spartans, who had the job of keeping the Spartan slave class (helots) in subjection.

many other practices of the same kind, but if you produced a detailed list it would go on pretty well forever.

ATHENIAN: You've put it all very well, my Spartan friend. But what is
d   to be our *definition* of courage? Are we to define it simply in terms of a fight against fears and pains only, or do we include desires and pleasures, which cajole and seduce us so effectively? They mold the heart like wax—even the hearts of those who loftily believe themselves superior to such influences.

MEGILLUS: Yes, I think so—the fight is against all these feelings.

ATHENIAN: Now, if we remember aright what was said earlier on, our friend from Cnossus spoke of a city and an individual as 'conquered by' themselves. Isn't that right?

CLINIAS: Surely.

e   ATHENIAN: Well, shall we call 'bad' only the man who is 'conquered by' pains, or shall we include the victim of pleasures as well?

CLINIAS: The term 'bad' we apply, I think, to the victim of pleasures even more than to the other. When we say that a man has been shamefully 'conquered by' himself, we are all, I fancy, much more likely to mean someone defeated by pleasures than by pains.

634   ATHENIAN: But the legal code of those lawgivers (inspired as they are by Zeus and Apollo) certainly did not envisage a courage with one hand tied behind its back, able to hit out on the left, but powerless in face of the cunning and seductive blandishments from the right. Surely it was supposed to resist in both directions?

CLINIAS: Yes, both, I think.

ATHENIAN: We ought to mention next what practices exist in your two cities that give a man a taste of pleasure rather than teach him how to avoid it—you remember how a man could not avoid pains, but was surrounded by them, and then forced, or persuaded by awards of honor, to
b   get the better of them. Now where in your codes of law is the institution that does the same for pleasure? Could you say, please, what institution you have that makes one and the same body of citizens courageous in face of pains and of pleasures alike, so that they conquer where they ought to conquer and never fall victims to these their most intimate and dangerous enemies?

MEGILLUS: I was certainly able to point to a good many laws that were
c   designed to counteract pains, stranger, but I doubt if I should find it so easy to give striking and clear examples in the case of pleasures. I might have some success, perhaps, in finding minor cases.

CLINIAS: No more would I be able to find an obvious illustration of this sort of thing in the laws of Crete.

ATHENIAN: My dear sirs, this should not surprise us. (I hope, by the way, that if in his desire to discover goodness and truth any of us is led to criticize some legal detail in the homeland of either of his companions,

we shall receive such criticism from each other tolerantly and without truculence.)

CLINIAS: You have put it quite fairly, my Athenian friend. We must do
as you say.

ATHENIAN: Truculence, Clinias, would be hardly the thing for men of   d
our age.

CLINIAS: No indeed.

ATHENIAN: The criticisms people bring against the way Sparta and Crete
are run may be right or wrong: that is another issue. At any rate, I am
probably better able than either of you to report what most people generally
say. However, granted that your codes of law have been composed with
reasonable success, as indeed they have been, one of the best regulations
you have is the one which forbids any young man to inquire into the
relative merits of the laws; everyone has to agree, with one heart and   e
voice, that they are all excellent and exist by divine *fiat;* if anyone says
differently, the citizens must absolutely refuse to listen to him. If an old
man has some point to make about your institutions, he must make such
remarks to an official, or someone of his own age when no young man
is present.

CLINIAS: That's absolutely right, sir—you must be a wizard! You are far
removed in time from the legislator who laid down these laws, but I
think you have hit on his intentions very nicely, and state them with   635
perfect accuracy.

ATHENIAN: Well, there are no young men here now. In view of our age,
the legislator surely grants us the indulgence of having a private discussion
on these topics without giving offense.

CLINIAS: So be it: don't hesitate to criticize our laws. There is no disgrace
in being told of some blemish—indeed, if one takes criticism in good part,
without being ruffled by it, it commonly leads one to a remedy.   b

ATHENIAN: Splendid. But criticism of your laws is not what I propose:
that can wait until we have scrutinized them exhaustively. I shall simply
mention my difficulties. Among all the Greek and foreign peoples who have
come to my knowledge, you are unique in that you have been instructed by
your lawgiver to keep away from the most attractive entertainments and
pleasures, and to refrain from tasting them. Yet when it came to pains and
fears, your legislator reckoned that if a man ran away from them on every
occasion from his earliest years and was then faced with hardships, pains   c
and fears he could not avoid, he would likewise run away from any
enemies who *had* received such a training, and become their slaves. I think
this same lawgiver ought to have taken this same line in the case of
pleasures too. He ought to have said to himself: 'If our citizens grow up
without any experience of the keenest pleasures, and if they are not trained
to stand firm when they encounter them, and to refuse to be pushed into
any disgraceful action, their fondness for pleasure will bring them to the   d

same bad end as those who capitulate to fear. Their slavery will be of a different kind, but it will be more humiliating: they will become the slaves of those who are able to stand firm against the onslaughts of pleasure and who are past-masters in the art of temptation—utter scoundrels, sometimes. Spiritually, our citizens will be part slave, part free, and only in a limited sense will they deserve to be called courageous and free.' Just consider this argument: do you think it has any relevance at all?

e   CLINIAS: Yes, I think it has, at first blush. But it is a weighty business, and to jump to confident conclusions so quickly may well be childish and naive.

ATHENIAN: Well then, Clinias and our friend from Sparta, let's turn to the next item we put on the agenda: after courage, let's discuss self-control. We found, in the case of war, that your two political systems were superior to those of states with a more haphazard mode of government. Where's

636   the superiority in the case of self-control?

MEGILLUS: That's rather a difficult question. Still, I should think the common meals and the gymnastic exercises are institutions well calculated to promote both virtues.

ATHENIAN: Well, my friends, I should think the real difficulty is to make political systems reflect in practice the trouble-free perfection of theory. (The human body is probably a parallel. One cannot rigidly prescribe a given regimen for a given body, because any regimen will invariably turn

b   out, in some respects, to injure our bodies at the same time as it helps them in others.) For instance, these gymnastic exercises and common meals, useful though they are to a state in many ways, are a danger in their encouragement of revolution—witness the example of the youth of Miletus, Boeotia and Thurii. More especially, the very antiquity of these practices seems to have corrupted the natural pleasures of sex, which are common to man and beast. For these perversions, your two states may well be the

c   first to be blamed, as well as any others that make a particular point of gymnastic exercises. Circumstances may make you treat this subject either light-heartedly or seriously; in either case you ought to bear in mind that when male and female come together in order to have a child, the pleasure they experience seems to arise entirely naturally. But homosexual intercourse and lesbianism seem to be unnatural crimes of the first rank, and are committed because men and women cannot control their desire for pleasure. It is the Cretans we all hold to blame for making up the story

d   of Ganymede:[10] they were so firmly convinced that their laws came from Zeus that they saddled him with this fable, in order to have a divine 'precedent' when enjoying that particular pleasure. That story, however, we may dismiss, but not the fact that when men investigate legislation, they

10. A handsome boy carried off to be Zeus' companion and cupbearer: see Homer, *Iliad* xx.231 ff.

investigate almost exclusively pleasures and pains as they affect society and the character of the individual. Pleasure and pain, you see, flow like two springs released by nature. If a man draws the right amount from the right one at the right time, he lives a happy life; but if he draws unintelligently at the wrong time, his life will be rather different. State and individual and every living being are on the same footing here.

MEGILLUS: Well, sir, I suppose that what you say is more or less right; at any rate, we're baffled to find an argument against it. But in spite of that I still think the legislator of Sparta is right to recommend a policy of avoiding pleasure (our friend here will come to the rescue of the laws of Cnossus, if he wants to). The Spartan law relating to pleasures seems to me the best you could find anywhere. It has completely eliminated from our country the thing which particularly prompts men to indulge in the keenest pleasures, so that they become unmanageable and make every kind of a fool of themselves: drinking parties, with all their violent incitements to every sort of pleasure, are not a sight you'll see anywhere in Sparta, either in the countryside or in the towns under her control. None of us would fail to inflict there and then the heaviest punishment on any tipsy merry-maker he happened to meet; he would not let the man off even if he had the festival of Dionysus as his excuse. Once, I saw men in that condition on wagons in your country, and at Tarentum, among our colonials, I saw the entire city drunk at the festival of Dionysus. *We* don't have anything like that.

ATHENIAN: My Spartan friend, all this sort of thing is perfectly laudable in men with a certain strength of character; it is when they cannot stop themselves that it becomes rather silly. A countryman of mine could soon come back at you tit for tat by pointing to the easy virtue of your women. There is one answer, however, which in Tarentum and Athens and Sparta too is apparently thought to excuse and justify all such practices. When a foreigner is taken aback at seeing some unfamiliar custom there, the reply he gets on all hands is this: 'There is no need to be surprised, stranger: this is what we do here; probably you handle these things differently.' Still, my friends, the subject of this conversation is not mankind in general but only the merits and faults of legislators. In fact, there is a great deal more we ought to say on the whole subject of drinking: it is a custom of some little importance, and needs a legislator of some little skill to understand it properly. I am not talking about merely drinking wine or totally abstaining from it: I mean *drunkenness*. How should we deal with it? One policy is that adopted by the Scythians and Persians, as well as by the Carthaginians, Celts, Iberians and Thracians—belligerent races, all of them. Or should we adopt your policy? This, as you say, is one of complete abstention, whereas the Scythians and Thracians (the women as well as the men) take their wine neat, and tip it down all over their clothes; in this they reckon to be following a glorious and splendid custom. And the

Persians indulge on a grand scale (though with more decorum) in these and other luxuries which you reject.

638　MEGILLUS: Oh, but my fine sir, when we get weapons in our hands we rout the lot of them.

ATHENIAN: Oh, but my *dear* sir, you must not say that. Many a time an army has been defeated and routed in the past, and will be in the future, without any very obvious reason. Merely to point to victory or defeat in battle is hardly to advance a clear and indisputable criterion of the merits

b　or demerits of a given practice. Larger states, you see, defeat smaller ones in battle, and the Syracusans enslave the Locrians, the very people who are supposed to be governed by the best laws you could find in those parts; the Athenians enslave the Ceians, and we could find plenty of other similar instances. It is by discussing the individual practice itself that we should try to convince ourselves of its qualities: for the moment, we ought to leave defeats and victories out of account, and simply say that such-and-such a practice is good and such-and-such is bad. First, though, listen to my explanation of the correct way to judge the relative value of these practices.

c　MEGILLUS: Well then, let's have the explanation.

ATHENIAN: I think that everyone who sets out to discuss a practice with the intention of censuring it or singing its praises as soon as it is mentioned is employing quite the wrong procedure. You might as well condemn cheese[11] out of hand when you heard somebody praising its merits as a food, without stopping to ask about what effect it has and how it is taken (by which I mean such questions as how it should be given, who should take it, what should go with it, in what condition it should be served, and

d　the state of health required of those who eat it). But this is just what I think we are doing in our discussion. We have only to hear the word 'drunkenness', and one side immediately disparages it while the other praises it—a pointless procedure if there ever was one. Each puts up enthusiastic witnesses to endorse its recommendations: one side thinks that the number of its witnesses clinches the matter, the other points to the sight of the teetotalers conquering in battle—not that the facts of the case are beyond dispute even here. Now, if this is the way we are going

e　to work one by one through the other customs, I for one shall find it goes against the grain. I want to discuss our present subject, drunkenness, by following a different—and, I think, correct—procedure, to see if I can demonstrate the right way to conduct an inquiry into such matters as these in general. Thousands and thousands of states, you see, differ from your pair of states in their view of these things, and would be prepared to fight it out in discussion.

639　MEGILLUS: Certainly, if a correct method of inquiry into such matters is available, we ought not to shy away from hearing what it is.

---

11. Accepting the conjecture of *turous* in c5.

ATHENIAN: Let us conduct the inquiry more or less like this: suppose somebody were to praise goat-keeping, and commended the goat as a valuable article of possession; suppose somebody else were to disparage goats because he had seen some doing damage to cultivated land by grazing on it without a goatherd, and were to find similar fault with every animal he saw under incompetent control or none at all. What do we think of the censure of someone like that? Does it carry any weight at all?

MEGILLUS: Hardly.

ATHENIAN: If a man possesses only the science of navigation, can we say that he will be a useful captain on board a ship, and ignore the question whether he suffers from seasickness or not? Can we say that, or can't we?

b

MEGILLUS: Certainly not, at any rate if, for all his skill, he's prone to the complaint you mention.

ATHENIAN: What about the commander of an army? Is he capable of taking command just by virtue of military skill, in spite of being a coward in face of danger? The 'seasickness' in this case is produced by being, as it were, drunk with terror.

MEGILLUS: Hardly a capable commander, that.

ATHENIAN: And what if he combines cowardice with incompetence?

MEGILLUS: You are describing a downright useless fellow—a commander of the daintiest of dainty women, not of men at all.

ATHENIAN: Take any social gathering you like, which functions naturally under a leader and serves a useful purpose under his guidance: what are we to think of the observer who praises or censures it although he has never seen it gathered together and running properly under its leader, but always with bad leaders or none at all? Given that kind of observer and that kind of gathering, do we reckon that his blame or praise will have any value?

c

MEGILLUS: How could it, when he has never seen or joined any of these gatherings run in the proper way?

d

ATHENIAN: Hold on a moment. There are many kinds of gatherings, and presumably we'd say drinkers and drinking-parties were one?

MEGILLUS: Of course.

ATHENIAN: Has anyone *ever* seen such a gathering run in the proper way? You two, of course, find the answer easy: 'Never, absolutely never'; drinking-parties are just not held in your countries, besides being illegal. But I have come across a great many, in different places, and I have investigated pretty nearly all of them. However, I have never seen or heard of one that was properly conducted throughout; one could approve of a few insignificant details, but most of them were mismanaged virtually all the time.

e

CLINIAS: What are you getting at, sir? Be a little more explicit. As you said, we have no experience of such events, so that even if we did find ourselves at one we would probably be unable to tell off-hand which features were correct and which not.

640

ATHENIAN: Very likely. But you can try to understand from my explanation. You appreciate that each and every assembly and gathering for any purpose whatever should invariably have a leader?

CLINIAS: Of course.

ATHENIAN: We said a moment ago that if it is a case of men fighting, their leader must be brave.

CLINIAS: Yes, indeed.

ATHENIAN: And a brave man, surely, is less thrown off balance by fears than cowards are.

b CLINIAS: That too is true enough.

ATHENIAN: If there were some device by which we could put in charge of an army a commander who was completely fearless and imperturbable, this is what we should make every effort to do, surely?

CLINIAS: It certainly is.

ATHENIAN: But the man we are discussing now is not going to take the lead in hostile encounters as between enemies, but in the peaceful meetings of friends with friends, gathering to foster mutual goodwill.

CLINIAS: Exactly.

c ATHENIAN: But we can assume that this sort of assembly will get rather drunk, so it won't be free of a certain amount of disturbance, I suppose.

CLINIAS: Of course not—I imagine precisely the opposite.

ATHENIAN: To start with, then, the members of the gathering will need a leader?

CLINIAS: Of course they will, more than anybody else.

ATHENIAN: Presumably we should if possible equip them with a leader who can keep his head?

CLINIAS: Naturally.

ATHENIAN: And he should also, presumably, be a man who knows how to handle a social gathering, because his duty is not only to preserve the existing friendliness among its members, but to see that it is strengthened

d as a result of the party.

CLINIAS: Quite true.

ATHENIAN: So, when men become merry with drink, don't they need someone put in charge of them who is sober and discreet rather than the opposite? If the man in charge of the revellers were himself a drinker, or young and indiscreet, he ought to thank his lucky stars if he managed to avoid starting some serious trouble.

CLINIAS: Lucky? I'll say so!

ATHENIAN: Consequently, an attack on such gatherings in cities where

e they are conducted impeccably might not in itself amount to unjustified criticism, provided the critic were attacking the institution itself. But if he abuses the institution simply because he sees every possible mistake being made in running it, he clearly does not realize, first, that this is a case of mismanagement, and secondly that any and every practice will appear in

the same light if it is carried on without a sober leader to control it. Surely
you appreciate that a drunken steersman, or any commander of anything,   641
will always make a total wreck of his ship or chariot or army, or whatever
else he may be directing?

CLINIAS: Yes, sir, there's truth in *that*, certainly. But the next step is for
you to tell us what conceivable benefit this custom of drinking parties
would be to us, given proper management. For instance, to take our example of a moment ago, if an army were properly controlled, its soldiers
would win the war and this would be a considerable benefit, and the same   b
reasoning applies to our other instances. But what solid benefit would it be
to individuals or the state to instruct a drinking party how to behave itself?

ATHENIAN: Well, what solid benefit are we to say it is to the state when
just one lad or just one chorus of them has been properly instructed? If
the question were put like that, we should say that the state gets very little
benefit from just one; but ask in general what great benefit the state derives
from the training by which it educates its citizens, and the reply will be
perfectly straightforward. The good education they have received will
make them good men, and being good they will achieve success in other   c
ways, and even conquer their enemies in battle. Education leads to victory;
but victory, on occasions, results in the *loss* of education, because men
often swell with pride when they have won a victory in war, and this
pride fills them with a million other vices. Men have won many 'Cadmean
victories', and will win many more, but there has never been such a thing
as 'Cadmean education'.[12]

CLINIAS: It looks to us, my friend, as if you mean to imply that passing   d
the time with friends over a drink—provided we behave ourselves—is a
considerable contribution to education.

ATHENIAN: Most certainly.

CLINIAS: Well then, could you now produce some justification for this
view?

ATHENIAN: Justification? Only a god, sir, would be entitled to insist that
this view is correct—there are so many conflicting opinions. But if necessary
I am quite prepared to give my own, now that we have launched into a
discussion of laws and political organizations.

CLINIAS: This is precisely what we are trying to discover — your own   e
opinion of the business we are now debating.

ATHENIAN: Well then, let that be our agenda: you have to direct your
efforts to understanding the argument, while I direct mine to expounding
it as clearly as I can. But first listen to this, by way of preface: you'll find
every Greek takes it for granted that my city likes talking and does a great

---

12. Compare our expression 'Pyrrhic victory', i.e., one which is more disastrous for the
victors than the vanquished. Cadmus, founder of Thebes, sowed the teeth of a dragon;
armed men sprang up and killed each other.

642 deal of it, whereas Sparta is a city of few words and Crete cultivates the intellect rather than the tongue. I don't want to make you feel that I am saying an awful lot about a triviality, if I deal exhaustively and at length with such a limited topic as drinking. In fact, the genuinely correct way to regulate drinking can hardly be explained adequately and clearly except in the context of a correct theory of culture; and it is impossible to explain this without considering the whole subject of education. That calls for a very long discussion indeed. So what do you think we ought to do now? What about skipping all this for the moment, and passing on to some

b other legal topic?

MEGILLUS: As it happens, sir—perhaps you haven't heard—my family represents the interests of your state, Athens, in Sparta. I dare say all children, when they learn they are *proxeni*[13] of a state, conceive a liking for it from their earliest years; each of us thinks of the state he represents as a fatherland, second only to his own country. This is exactly my own

c experience now. When the Spartans were criticizing or praising the Athenians, I used to hear the little children say, 'Megillus, your state has done the dirty on us,' or, 'it has done us proud.' By listening to all this and constantly resisting on your behalf the charges of Athens' detractors, I acquired a whole-hearted affection for her, so that to this day I very much enjoy the sound of your accent. It is commonly said that when an Athenian is good, he is 'very very good', and I'm sure that's right. They are unique in that they are good not because of any compulsion, but spontaneously,

d by grace of heaven; it is all so genuine and unfeigned. So you're welcome to speak as long as you like, so far as I'm concerned.

CLINIAS: I endorse your freedom to say as much as you like, sir: you'll see that when you've heard what I have to say, too. You have probably heard that Epimenides, a man who was divinely inspired, was born hereabouts. He was connected with my family, and ten years before the Persian

e attack he obeyed the command of the oracle to go to Athens,[14] where he performed certain sacrifices which the god had ordered. He told the Athenians, who were apprehensive at the preparations the Persians were making, that the Persians would not come for ten years, and that when they did, they would go back with all their intentions frustrated, after sustaining greater losses than they had inflicted. That was when my ances-tors formed ties of friendship with you Athenians, and ever since then my

643 forebears and I have held you in affection.

ATHENIAN: Well then, on your part you are prepared to listen, apparently; on my side, I am ready and willing to go ahead, but the job will certainly tax my abilities. Still, the effort must be made. To assist the argument, we

---

13. A *proxenos* looked after the interests of a foreign state in his own country.

14. Clinias' chronology is a trifle confused. He thinks that Epimenides, a seer and wonder-worker, lived about 500 B.C., which is 100 years later than his actual date.

ought to take the preliminary step of defining education and its potentialities, because we have ventured on a discussion which is intended to lead us to the god of wine, and we are agreed that education is as it were the route we have to take.

CLINIAS: Certainly let's do that, if you like.

ATHENIAN: I am going to explain how one should describe education: b see if you approve of my account.

CLINIAS: Your explanation, then, please.

ATHENIAN: It is this: I insist that a man who intends to be good at a particular occupation must practice it from childhood: both at work and at play he must be surrounded by the special 'tools of the trade'. For instance, the man who intends to be a good farmer must play at farming, and the man who is to be a good builder must spend his playtime building c toy houses; and in each case the teacher must provide miniature tools that copy the real thing. In particular, in this elementary stage they must learn the essential elementary skills. For example, the carpenter must learn in his play how to handle a rule and plumb-line, and the soldier must learn to ride a horse (either by actually doing it, in play, or by some similar activity). We should try to use the children's games to channel their pleasures and desires towards the activities in which they will have to engage when they are adult. To sum up, we say that the correct way to bring up d and educate a child is to use his playtime to imbue his soul with the greatest possible liking for the occupation in which he will have to be absolutely perfect when he grows up. Now, as I suggested, consider the argument so far: do you approve of my account?

CLINIAS: Of course.

ATHENIAN: But let's not leave our description of education in the air. When we abuse or commend the upbringing of individual people and say that one of us is educated and the other uneducated, we sometimes use this latter term of men who have in fact had a thorough education— one directed towards petty trade or the merchant-shipping business, or e something like that. But I take it that for the purpose of the present discussion we are not going to treat this sort of thing as 'education'; what we have in mind is education from childhood in *virtue,* a training which produces a keen desire to become a perfect citizen who knows how to rule and be ruled as justice demands. I suppose we should want to mark 644 off this sort of training from others and reserve the title 'education' for it alone. A training directed to acquiring money or a robust physique, or even to some intellectual facility not guided by reason and justice, we should want to call coarse and illiberal, and say that it had no claim whatever to be called education. Still, let's not quibble over a name; let's stick to the proposition we agreed on just now: as a rule, men with a correct education become good, and nowhere in the world should education be b despised, for when combined with great virtue, it is an asset of incalculable value. If it ever becomes corrupt, but can be put right again, this is a lifelong task which everyone should undertake to the limit of his strength.

CLINIAS: True. We agree with your description.

ATHENIAN: Here is a further point on which we agreed some time ago:[15] those who can control themselves are good, those who cannot are bad.

CLINIAS: Perfectly correct.

c   ATHENIAN: Let's take up this point again and consider even more closely just what we mean. Perhaps you'll let me try to clarify the issue by means of an illustration.

CLINIAS: By all means.

ATHENIAN: Are we to assume, then, that each of us is a single individual?

CLINIAS: Yes.

ATHENIAN: But that he possesses within himself a pair of witless and mutually antagonistic advisers, which we call pleasure and pain?

CLINIAS: That is so.

ATHENIAN: In addition to these two, he has opinions about the future, whose general name is 'expectations'. Specifically, the anticipation of pain d   is called 'fear', and the anticipation of the opposite is called 'confidence'. Over and against all these we have 'calculation', by which we judge the relative merits of pleasure and pain, and when this is expressed as a public decision of a state, it receives the title 'law'.

CLINIAS: I can scarcely follow you; but assume I do, and carry on with what comes next.

MEGILLUS: Yes, I'm in the same difficulty.

ATHENIAN: I suggest we look at the problem in this way: let's imagine that each of us living beings is a puppet of the gods. Whether we have been constructed to serve as their plaything, or for some serious reason, e   is something beyond our ken, but what we certainly do know is this: we have these emotions in us, which act like cords or strings and tug us about; they work in opposition, and tug against each other to make us perform actions that are opposed correspondingly; back and forth we go across the boundary line where vice and virtue meet. One of these dragging forces, according to our argument, demands our constant obedience, and this is 645   the one we have to hang on to, come what may; the pull of the other cords we must resist. This cord, which is golden and holy, transmits the power of 'calculation', a power which in a state is called the public law; being golden, it is pliant, while the others, whose composition resembles a variety of other substances, are tough and inflexible. The force exerted by law is excellent, and one should always co-operate with it, because although 'calculation' is a noble thing, it is gentle, not violent, and its efforts need assistants, so that the gold in us may prevail over the other substances. If b   we do give our help, the moral point of this fable, in which we appear as

15. See 626e.

puppets, will have been well and truly made; the meaning of the terms 'self-superior' and 'self-inferior'[16] will somehow become clearer, and the duties of state and individual will be better appreciated. The latter must digest the truth about these forces that pull him, and act on it in his life; the state must get an account of it either from one of the gods or from the human expert we've mentioned, and incorporate it in the form of a law to govern both its internal affairs and its relations with other states. A further result will be a clearer distinction between virtue and vice; the light cast on that problem will perhaps in turn help to clarify the subject of education and the various other practices, particularly the business of drinking parties. It may well be thought that this is a triviality on which a great deal too much has been said, but equally it may turn out that the topic really does deserve this extended discussion.

CLINIAS: You are quite right; we certainly ought to give full consideration to anything that deserves our attention in the 'symposium' we are having now.

ATHENIAN: Well then, tell me: if we give drink to this puppet of ours, what effect do we have on it?

CLINIAS: What's your purpose in harking back to that question?

ATHENIAN: No particular purpose, for the moment. I'm just asking, in a general way, what effect is had on something when it is associated with something else. I'll try to explain my meaning even more clearly. This is what I'm asking; does drinking wine make pleasures and pains, anger and love, more intense?

CLINIAS: Very much so.

ATHENIAN: What about sensations, memory, opinions and thought? Do these too become more intense? Or rather, don't they entirely desert a man if he fills himself with drink?

CLINIAS: Yes, they desert him entirely.

ATHENIAN: So he reverts to the mental state he was in as a young child?

CLINIAS: Indeed.

ATHENIAN: And it's then that his self-control would be at its lowest?

CLINIAS: Yes, at its lowest.

ATHENIAN: A man in that condition, we agree, is very bad indeed.

CLINIAS: Very.

ATHENIAN: So it looks as if it's not only an old man who will go through a second childhood, but the drunkard too.

CLINIAS: That's well said, sir.

ATHENIAN: Now, is there any argument that could even begin to persuade us that we ought to venture on this practice, rather than make every possible effort to avoid it?

16. Cf. 620d ff.

CLINIAS: Apparently there is; at any rate, this is what you say, and a minute ago you were ready to produce it.

b   ATHENIAN: A correct reminder; I'm ready still, now that you have both said you would be glad to listen to me.

CLINIAS: We'll be all ears, sir, if only because of your amazing paradox that a man should, on occasions, voluntarily abandon himself to extreme depravity.

ATHENIAN: You mean spiritual depravity, don't you?

CLINIAS: Yes.

ATHENIAN: And what about degradation of the body, my friend—emaciation, disfigurement, ugliness, impotence? Shouldn't we be startled to find

c   a man voluntarily reducing himself to such a state?

CLINIAS: Of course we should.

ATHENIAN: We don't suppose, do we, that those who voluntarily take themselves off to the surgery in order to drink down medicines are unaware of the fact that very soon after, for days on end, their condition will be such that, if it were to be anything more than temporary, it would make life insupportable? We know, surely, that those who resort to gymnasia for vigorous exercises become temporarily enfeebled?

CLINIAS: Yes, we are aware of all this.

ATHENIAN: And of the fact that they go there of their own accord, for the sake of the benefit they will receive after the initial stages?

d   CLINIAS: Most certainly.

ATHENIAN: So shouldn't we look at the other practices in the same light?

CLINIAS: Yes indeed.

ATHENIAN: So the same view should be taken of time spent in one's cups—if, that is, we may think of it as a legitimate parallel.

CLINIAS: Of course.

ATHENIAN: Now if time so spent turned out to benefit us no less than time devoted to the body, it would have the initial advantage over physical exercises in that, unlike them, it is painless.

e   CLINIAS: You're right enough in that, but I'd be surprised if we could discover any such benefit in this case.

ATHENIAN: Then this is the point it looks as if we ought to be trying to explain. Tell me: can we conceive of two roughly opposite kinds of fear?

CLINIAS: Which?

ATHENIAN: These: when we expect evils to occur, we are in fear of them, I suppose?

CLINIAS: Yes.

ATHENIAN: And we often fear for our reputation, when we imagine we

647   are going to get a bad name for doing or saying something disgraceful. This is the fear which we, and I fancy everyone else, call 'shame'.

CLINIAS: Surely.

ATHENIAN: These are the two fears I meant. The second resists pains and the other things we dread, as well as our keenest and most frequent pleasures.

CLINIAS: Very true.

ATHENIAN: The legislator, then, and anybody of the slightest merit, values this fear very highly, and gives it the name 'modesty'. The feeling of confidence that is its opposite he calls 'insolence', and reckons it to be the biggest curse anyone could suffer, whether in his private or his public life.

CLINIAS: True.   b

ATHENIAN: So this fear not only safeguards us in a lot of other crucial areas of conduct but contributes more than anything else, if we take one thing with another, to the security that follows victory in war. Two things, then, contribute to victory: fearlessness in face of the enemy, and fear of ill-repute among one's friends.

CLINIAS: Exactly.

ATHENIAN: Every individual should therefore become both afraid and unafraid, for the reasons we have distinguished in each case.   c

CLINIAS: Certainly.

ATHENIAN: Moreover, if we want to make an individual proof against all sorts of fears, it is by exposing him to fear, in a way sanctioned by the law, that we make him unafraid.

CLINIAS: Evidently we do.

ATHENIAN: But what about our attempts to make a man *afraid*, in a way consistent with justice? Shouldn't we see that he enters the lists against impudence, and give him training to resist it, so as to make him conquer in the struggle with his pleasures? A man has to fight and conquer his   d
feelings of cowardice before he can achieve perfect courage; if he has no experience and training in that kind of struggle, he will never more than half realize his potentialities for virtue. Isn't the same true of self-control? Will he ever achieve a perfect mastery here without having fought and conquered, with all the skills of speech and action both in work and play, the crowd of pleasures and desires that stimulate him to act shamelessly and unjustly? Can he afford *not* to have the experience of all these struggles?

CLINIAS: It would seem hardly likely.

ATHENIAN: Well then, has any god given me a drug to produce fear, so   e
that the more a man agrees to drink of it, the more the impression grows on him, after every draft, that he is assailed by misfortune? The effect would be to make him apprehensive about his present and future prospects, until finally even the boldest of men would be reduced to absolute terror;   648
but when he had recovered from the drink and slept it off, he would invariably be himself again.

CLINIAS: And what drink does that, sir? There's hardly an example we could point to anywhere in the world.

ATHENIAN: No. But if one had cropped up, would a legislator have been able to make any use of it to promote courage? This is the sort of point we might well have put to him about it: 'Legislator—whether your laws are to apply to Cretans or to any other people—tell us this: wouldn't you b   be particularly glad to have a criterion of the courage and cowardice of your citizens?

CLINIAS: Obviously, every legislator would say 'Yes'.

ATHENIAN: 'Well, you'd like a safe test without any serious risks, wouldn't you? Or do you prefer one full of risks?'

CLINIAS: They will all agree to this as well: safety is essential.

ATHENIAN: 'Your procedure would be to test these people's reactions c   when they had been put into a state of alarm, and by encouraging, rebuking and rewarding individuals you would compel them to become fearless. You would inflict disgrace on anyone who disobeyed and refused to become in every respect the kind of man you wanted; you would discharge without penalty anyone who had displayed the proper courage and finished his training satisfactorily; and the failures you would punish. Or would you refuse point-blank to apply the test, even though you had nothing against the drink in other respects?'

CLINIAS: Of course he would apply it, sir.

ATHENIAN: Anyway, my friend, compared with current practice, this training would be remarkably straightforward, and would suit individuals, d   small groups, and any larger numbers you may want. Now if a man retreated into some decent obscurity, out of embarrassment at the thought of being seen before he is in good shape, and trained against his fears alone and in privacy, equipped with just this drink instead of all the usual paraphernalia, he would be entirely justified. But he would be no less justified if, confident that he was already well equipped by birth and breeding, he were to plunge into training with several fellow drinkers. e   While inevitably roused by the wine, he would show himself strong enough to escape its other effects: his virtue would prevent him from committing even one serious improper act, and from becoming a different kind of person. Before getting to the last round he would leave off, fearing the way in which drink invariably gets the better of a man.

CLINIAS: Yes, sir, even he would be prudent enough to do that.

649   ATHENIAN: Let's repeat the point we were making to the legislator: 'Agreed then: there is probably no such thing as a drug to produce fear, either by divine gift or human contrivance (I leave quacks out of account: they're beyond the pale). But is there a drink that will banish fear and stimulate over-confidence about the wrong thing at the wrong moment? What do we say to this?'

CLINIAS: I suppose he'll say 'There is', and mention wine.

ATHENIAN: And doesn't this do just the opposite of what we described a moment ago? When a man drinks it, it immediately makes him more b   cheerful than he was before; the more he takes, the more it fills him with boundless optimism: he thinks he can do anything. Finally, bursting with self-esteem and imposing no restraint on his speech and actions, the fellow loses all his inhibitions and becomes completely fearless: he'll say and do anything, without a qualm. Everybody, I think, would agree with us about this.

CLINIAS: Certainly.

ATHENIAN: Now let's think back again to this point: we said that there were two elements in our souls that should be cultivated, one of them in order to make ourselves supremely confident, its opposite to make our- c selves supremely fearful.

CLINIAS: The latter being modesty, I suppose.

ATHENIAN: Well remembered! But in view of the fact that one has to learn to be courageous and intrepid when assailed by fears, the question arises whether the opposite quality will have to be cultivated in opposite circumstances.

CLINIAS: Probably so.

ATHENIAN: So the conditions in which we naturally become unusually bold and daring seem to be precisely those required for practice in reducing our shamelessness and audacity to the lowest possible level, so that we become terrified of ever venturing to say, suffer, or do anything disgraceful. d

CLINIAS: Apparently.

ATHENIAN: Now aren't we affected in this way by all the following conditions—anger, love, pride, ignorance and cowardice? We can add wealth, beauty, strength and everything else that turns us into fools and makes us drunk with pleasure. However, we are looking for an inexpensive and less harmful test we can apply to people, which will also give us a chance to train them, and this we have in the scrutiny we can make of them when they are relaxed over a drink. Can we point to a more suitable e pleasure than this—provided some appropriate precautions are taken? Let's look at it in this way. Suppose you have a man with an irritable and savage temper (this is the source of a huge number of crimes). Surely, to make contracts with him, and run the risk that he may default, is a more dangerous way to test him than to keep him company during a festival 650 of Dionysus? Or again, if a man's whole being is dominated by sexual pleasures, it is dangerous to try him out by putting him in charge of your wife and sons and daughters; this is to scrutinize the character of his soul at the price of exposing to risk those whom you hold most dear. You could cite dozens of other instances, and still not do justice to the superiority of this wholly innocuous 'examination by recreation'. In fact, I think neither the Cretans nor any other people would disagree if we summed it all up b like this: we have here a pretty fair test of each other, which for cheapness, safety and speed is absolutely unrivaled.

CLINIAS: True so far.

ATHENIAN: So this insight into the nature and disposition of a man's soul will rank as one of the most useful aids available to the art which is concerned to foster a good character—the art of *statesmanship*, I take it?

CLINIAS: Certainly.

Book II

652   ATHENIAN: It looks as if the next question we have to ask is this: is the insight we somehow get into men's natural temperaments the *only* thing in favor of drinking parties? Or does a properly run drinking party confer some other substantial benefit that we ought to consider very seriously? What do we say to this? We need to be careful here: as far as I can see, our argument does tend to point to the answer 'Yes', but when we try to
b   discover how and in what sense, we may get tripped up by it.

CLINIAS: Tell us why, then.

ATHENIAN: I want to think back over our definition of correct education,
653   and to hazard the suggestion now that drinking parties are actually its *safeguard*, provided they are properly established and conducted on the right lines.

CLINIAS: That's a large claim!

ATHENIAN: I maintain that the earliest sensations that a child feels in infancy are of pleasure and pain, and this is the route by which virtue and vice first enter the soul. (But for a man to acquire good judgment, and unshakable correct opinions, however late in life, is a matter of good luck: a man who possesses them, and all the benefits they entail, is perfect.)
b   I call 'education' the initial acquisition of virtue by the child, when the feelings of pleasure and affection, pain and hatred, that well up in his soul are channeled in the right courses before he can understand the reason why. Then when he does understand, his reason and his emotions agree in telling him that he has been properly trained by inculcation of appropriate habits. Virtue is this general concord of reason and emotion. But there is one element you could isolate in any account you give, and this is the
c   correct formation of our feelings of pleasure and pain, which makes us hate what we ought to hate from first to last, and love what we ought to love. Call this 'education', and I, at any rate, think you would be giving it its proper name.

CLINIAS: Yes, sir, we entirely approve of what you have just said about education and that goes for your previous account, too.[1]

ATHENIAN: Splendid. Education, then, is a matter of correctly disciplined feelings of pleasure and pain. But in the course of a man's life the effect wears off, and in many respects it is lost altogether. The gods, however,
d   took pity on the human race, born to suffer as it was, and gave it relief in the form of religious festivals to serve as periods of rest from its labors. They gave us the Muses, with Apollo their leader, and Dionysus; by having these gods to share their holidays, men were to be made whole again, and thanks to them, we find refreshment in the celebration of these festivals. Now, there is a theory which we are always having dinned into our ears: let's see if it squares with the facts or not. It runs like this: virtually all

1. See 643a ff.

young things find it impossible to keep their bodies still and their tongues quiet. They are always trying to move around and cry out; some jump and skip and do a kind of gleeful dance as they play with each other, while others produce all sorts of noises. And whereas animals have no sense of order and disorder in movement ('rhythm' and 'harmony', as we call it), we human beings have been made sensitive to both and can enjoy them. This is the gift of the same gods whom we said were given to us as companions in dancing; it is the device which enables them to be our chorus-leaders and stimulate us to movement, making us combine to sing and dance—and as this naturally[2] 'charms' us, they invented the word 'chorus'.[3] So shall we take it that this point is established? Can we assume that education comes originally from Apollo and the Muses, or not?

CLINIAS: Yes.

ATHENIAN: So by an 'uneducated' man we shall mean a man who has not been trained to take part in a chorus; and we must say that if a man *has* been sufficiently trained, he is 'educated'.

CLINIAS: Naturally.

ATHENIAN: And of course a performance by a chorus is a combination of dancing and singing?

CLINIAS: Of course.

ATHENIAN: And this means that the well-educated man will be able both to sing and dance *well*?

CLINIAS: So it seems.

ATHENIAN: Now let's see just what that word implies.

CLINIAS: What word?

ATHENIAN: We say 'he sings *well*' or 'he dances *well*'. But should we expand this and say 'provided he sings *good* songs and dances *good* dances'? Or not?

CLINIAS: Yes, we should expand it.

ATHENIAN: Now then, take a man whose opinion about what is good is correct (it really *is* good), and likewise in the case of the bad (it really *is* bad), and follows this judgment in practice. He may be able to represent, by word and gesture, and with invariable success, his intellectual conception of what is good, even though he gets no pleasure from it and feels no hatred for what is bad. Another man may not be very good at keeping on the right lines when he uses his body and his voice to represent the good, or at trying to form some intellectual conception of it; but he may be very much on the right lines in his feelings of pleasure and pain, because he welcomes what is good and loathes what is bad. Which of these two will be the better educated musically, and the more effective member of a chorus?

CLINIAS: As far as education is concerned, sir, the second is infinitely superior.

---

2. Reading *hēi dē* in a3.

3. A playful etymology: *choros* (chorus) is derived from *chara* (charm, joy, delight).

ATHENIAN: So if the three of us grasp what 'goodness' is in singing and dancing, we have also a sound criterion for distinguishing the educated man from the uneducated. If we fail to grasp it, we'll never be able to make up our minds whether a safeguard for education exists, or where
e   we ought to look for it. Isn't that so?

CLINIAS: Yes, it is.

ATHENIAN: The next quarry we have to track down, like hounds at a hunt, will be what constitutes a 'good' bodily movement, tune, song and dance. But if all these notions give us the slip and get away, it will be pointless utterly to prolong our discussion of correct education, Greek or foreign.

CLINIAS: Quite.

ATHENIAN: Good. Now, what is to be our definition of a good tune or bodily movement? Tell me—imagine a courageous soul and a cowardly
655 soul beset by one and the same set of troubles: do similar sounds and movements of the body result in each case?

CLINIAS: Of course not. The complexion is different, to start with.

ATHENIAN: You are absolutely right, my friend. But music is a matter of rhythm and harmony, and involves tunes and movements of the body; this means that while it is legitimate to speak of a 'rhythmical' or a 'harmonious' movement or tune, we cannot properly apply to either of them the chorus-masters' metaphor 'brilliantly colored'. But what *is* the appropriate language to describe the movement and melody used to portray the brave
b   man and the coward? The correct procedure is to call those of brave men 'good' and those of cowards 'disgraceful'. But let's not have an inordinately long discussion about the details; can we say, without beating about the bush, that all movements and tunes associated with spiritual or bodily excellence (the real thing or a representation) are good? And conversely bad if they have to do with vice?

CLINIAS: Yes, that's a reasonable proposal. You may assume we agree.

ATHENIAN: Here's a further point: do we all enjoy every type of perfor-
c   mance by a chorus to the same degree? Or is that far from being true?

CLINIAS: As far as it could be!

ATHENIAN: But can we put our finger on the cause of our confusion? Is it that 'good' varies from person to person? Or that it is *thought* to vary, although in point of fact it does not? No one, I fancy, will be prepared to say that dances portraying evil are better than those portraying virtue, or that although other people enjoy the virtuous Muse, his own personal liking is for movements expressing depravity. Yet most men do maintain
d   that the power of music to give pleasure to the soul is the standard by which it should be judged. But this is an insupportable doctrine, and it is absolute blasphemy to speak like that. More likely, though, it's something else that's misleading us.

CLINIAS: What?

ATHENIAN: Performances given by choruses are representations of charac-ter, and deal with every variety of action and incident. The individual performers enact their roles partly by expressing their own characters, partly by imitating those of others. That is why, when they find that the speaking or singing or any other element in the performance of a chorus appeals to their natural character or acquired habits, or both, they can't help applauding with delight and using the term 'good'. But sometimes they find these performances going against the grain of their natural character or their disposition or habits, in which case they are unable to take any pleasure in them and applaud them, and in this case the word they use is 'shocking'. When a man's natural character is as it should be, but he has acquired bad habits, or conversely when his habits are correct but his natural character is vicious, his pleasure and his approval fail to coincide: he calls the performances 'pleasant, but depraved'. Such performers, in the company of others whose judgment they respect, are ashamed to make this kind of movement with their bodies, and to sing such songs as though they genuinely approved of them. But in their heart of hearts, they enjoy themselves.

CLINIAS: You are quite right.

ATHENIAN: Now, does a man's enjoyment of bad bodily movements or bad tunes do him any harm? And does it do him any good to take pleasure in the opposite kind?

CLINIAS: Probably.

ATHENIAN: 'Probably'? Is that all? Surely there *must* be a precise analogy here with the man who comes into contact with depraved characters and wicked people, and who does not react with disgust, but welcomes them with pleasure, censuring them half-heartedly because he only half-realizes, as in a dream, how perverted such a state is: he just cannot escape taking on the character of what he enjoys, whether good or bad—even if he is ashamed to go so far as to applaud it. In fact we could hardly point to a greater force for good—or evil—than this inevitable assimilation of character.

CLINIAS: No, I don't think we could.

ATHENIAN: So, in a society where the laws relating to culture, education and recreation are, or will be in future, properly established, do we imagine that authors will be given a free hand? The choruses will be composed of the young children of law-abiding citizens: will the composer be free to teach them *anything* by way of rhythm, tune and words that amuses him when he composes, without bothering what effect he may have on them as regards virtue and vice?

CLINIAS: That's certainly not sensible; how could it be?

ATHENIAN: But it is precisely this that they are allowed to do in virtually all states—except in Egypt.

CLINIAS: Egypt! Well then, you'd better tell us what legislation has been enacted there.

ATHENIAN: Merely to hear about it is startling enough. Long ago, apparently, they realized the truth of the principle we are putting forward only now, that the movements and tunes which the children of the state are to e practice in their rehearsals must be good ones. They compiled a list of them according to style, and displayed it in their temples. Painters and everyone else who represent movements of the body of any kind were restricted to these forms; modification and innovation outside this traditional framework were prohibited, and are prohibited even today, both in this field and the arts in general. If you examine their art on the spot, you will find that ten thousand years ago (and I'm not speaking loosely: I mean

657 literally ten thousand), paintings and reliefs were produced that are no better and no worse than those of today, because the same artistic rules were applied in making them.

CLINIAS: Fantastic!

ATHENIAN: No: simply a supreme achievement of legislators and statesmen. You might, even so, find some other things to criticize there, but in the matter of music this inescapable fact deserves our attention: it has in fact proved feasible to take the kind of music that shows a natural correctness and put it on a firm footing by legislation.[4] But it is the task of a god,

b or a man of god-like stature; in fact, the Egyptians do say that the tunes that have been preserved for so long are compositions of Isis. Consequently, as I said, if one could get even a rough idea of what constitutes 'correctness' in matters musical, one ought to have no qualms about giving the whole subject systematic expression in the form of a law. It is true that the craving for pleasure and the desire to avoid tedium lead us to a constant search for novelty in music, and choral performances that have been thus consecrated may be stigmatized as out-of-date; but this does not have very much power to corrupt them. In Egypt, at any rate, it does not seem to have had a corrupting effect at all: quite the contrary.

c CLINIAS: So it would seem, to judge from your account.

ATHENIAN: So, equally without qualms, we can surely describe the proper conditions for festive music and performances of choruses more or less like this. When we think things are going well for us, we feel delight; and to put it the other way round, when we feel delight, we come to think that things are going well. Isn't that so?

CLINIAS: It is.

ATHENIAN: In addition, when we are in that state—I mean 'delight'— we can't keep still.

CLINIAS: That's true.

d ATHENIAN: Our youngsters are keen to join the dancing and singing themselves, but we old men think the proper thing is to pass the time as spectators. The delight we feel comes from their relaxation and merrymaking. Our agility is deserting us, and as we feel its loss we are only too pleased to provide competitions for the young, because they can best stir in us the memory of our youth and re-awaken the instincts of our younger days.

CLINIAS: Very true.

4. Deleting *tharrounta* in a7.

ATHENIAN: So we'd better face the fact that there is a grain of truth in   e
contemporary thought on the subject of holiday-makers. Most people say
that the man who delights us most and gives us most pleasure should be
highly esteemed for his skill, and deserves to be awarded first prize,
because the fact that we are allowed to relax on such occasions means that
we ought to lionize the man who gives most people most pleasure, so
that, as I said just now, he deserves to carry off the prize. In theory that's
right, isn't it? And wouldn't it be equally right in practice?   658

CLINIAS: Maybe.

ATHENIAN: Ah, my fine fellow, such a conclusion 'may be' rash! We must
make some distinctions, and examine the question rather like this: suppose
somebody were to arrange a competition, and were to leave its character
entirely open, not specifying whether it was to be gymnastic, artistic or
equestrian. Assume that he gathers together all the inhabitants of the state,
and offers a prize: anyone who wishes should come and compete in giving
pleasure, and this is to be the sole criterion; the competitor who gives the   b
audience most pleasure will win; he has an entirely free hand as to what
method he employs, but provided he excels in this one respect he will be
judged the most pleasing of the competitors and win the prize. What effect
do we think such an announcement would have?

CLINIAS: In what way do you mean?

ATHENIAN: Likely enough, I suppose, one competitor will play the Homer
and present epic poetry, another will sing lyric songs to music, another
will put on a tragedy, and another a comedy; and it will be no surprise
if somebody even reckons his best chance of winning lies in putting on a   c
puppet-show. Now, with all these competitors and thousands of others
entering, can we say which would *really* deserve to win?

CLINIAS: That's an odd question! Who could answer it for you with
authority before hearing the contestants, and listening to them individually
on the spot?

ATHENIAN: Well then, do you want me to give you an equally odd answer?

CLINIAS: Naturally.

ATHENIAN: Suppose the decision rests with the smallest infant children.
They'll decide for the exhibitor of puppets, won't they?

CLINIAS: Of course.   d

ATHENIAN: If it rests with the older children, they will choose the producer
of comedies. Young men, ladies of cultivated taste, and I dare say pretty
nearly the entire populace, will choose the tragedy.

CLINIAS: Yes, I dare say.

ATHENIAN: We old men would probably be most gratified to listen to a
reciter doing justice to the *Iliad* or *Odyssey*, or an extract from Hesiod: we'd
say he was the winner by a clear margin. Who, then, would be the *proper*
winner? That's the next question, isn't it?

CLINIAS: Yes.

ATHENIAN: Clearly you and I are forced to say that the proper winners   e
would be those chosen by men of our vintage. To us, from among all the

customs followed in every city all over the world today, this looks like the best.

CLINIAS: Surely.

ATHENIAN: I am, then, in limited agreement with the man in the street. Pleasure is indeed a proper criterion in the arts, but not the pleasure experienced by anybody and everybody. The productions of the Muse are at their finest when they delight men of high calibre and adequate education—but particularly if they succeed in pleasing the single individ-
659   ual whose education and moral standards[5] reach heights attained by no one else. This is the reason why we maintain that judges in these matters need high moral standards: they have to possess not only a discerning taste,[6] but courage too. A judge won't be doing his job properly if he reaches his verdict by listening to the audience and lets himself be thrown off balance by the yelling of the mob and his own lack of training; nor must he shrug his shoulders and let cowardice and indolence persuade him into a false verdict against his better judgment, so that he lies with
b   the very lips with which he called upon the gods when he undertook office. The truth is that he sits in judgment as a teacher of the audience, rather than as its pupil; his function (and under the ancient law of the Greeks he used to be allowed to perform it) is to throw his weight *against* them, if the pleasure they show has been aroused improperly and illegiti-mately. For instance, the law now in force in Sicily and Italy, by truckling to the majority of the audience and deciding the winner by a show of
c   hands, has had a disastrous effect on the authors themselves, who compose to gratify the depraved tastes of their judges; the result is that in effect *they* are taught by the audience. It has been equally disastrous for the quality of the pleasure felt by the spectators: they ought to come to experience more elevated pleasures from listening to the portrayal of characters invariably better than their own, but in fact just the opposite happens, and they have no one to thank but themselves. Well, then, now that we have finished talking about that, what conclusion is indicated? Let's see if it isn't this—

CLINIAS: What?

d   ATHENIAN: For the third or fourth time, I think, our discussion has come full circle. Once again, education has proved to be a process of attraction, of leading children to accept right principles as enunciated by the law and endorsed as genuinely correct by men who have high moral standards and are full of years and experience. The soul of the child has to be prevented from getting into the habit of feeling pleasure and pain in ways not sanctioned by the law and those who have been persuaded to obey it; he should follow in their footsteps and find pleasure and pain in the

---

5. 'Moral standards' here and 'high moral standards' just below translate *aretē*, else-where normally translated 'virtue.'

6. 'Discerning taste' translates *phronēsis*, elsewhere usually translated 'good judgment' or 'wisdom'—it is one of the four basic virtues Plato recognizes, along with justice, courage, and self-control (or moderation or restraint—*sōphrosunē*).

same things as the old. That is why we have what we call songs, which are really 'charms' for the soul. These are in fact deadly serious devices e
for producing this concord[7] we are talking about; but the souls of the young cannot bear to be serious, so we use the terms 'recreation' and 'song' for the charms, and children treat them in that spirit. We have an analogy in the sick and ailing; those in charge of feeding them try to administer the proper diet in tasty foods and drinks, and offer them un- 660
wholesome items in revolting foods, so that the patients may get into the desirable habit of welcoming the one kind and loathing the other. That is just what the true legislator will persuade (or, failing persuasion, compel) the man with a creative flair to do with his grand and marvelous language: to compose correctly by portraying, with appropriate choreography and musical setting, men who are moderate, courageous and good in every way.

CLINIAS: Good Heavens, sir, do you really think that's how they compose b
nowadays in other cities? My experience is limited, but I know of no such proceeding as you describe, except among us Cretans or in Sparta. In dancing and all the other arts one novelty follows another; the changes are made not by law but are prompted by wildly changing fancies that are very far from being permanent and stable like the Egyptian tastes you're explaining: on the contrary, they are never the same from minute c
to minute.

ATHENIAN: Well said, Clinias. But if I gave you the impression that I was speaking of the present day when I referred to the procedure you mention, I expect it was my own lack of clarity in expressing my thoughts that led you astray and caused me to be misunderstood. I was only saying what I want to see happen in the arts, but perhaps I used expressions that made you think I was referring to facts. It always goes against the grain to pillory habits that are irretrievably on the wrong lines, but sometimes one has to. d
So, seeing that we are agreed in approving this custom, tell me this, if you will: is it more prevalent among you Cretans and the Spartans than among the other Greeks?

CLINIAS: Certainly.

ATHENIAN: And what if it became prevalent among the others as well? Presumably we'd say that that was an improvement on present practice?

CLINIAS: Yes, I suppose it would be a tremendous improvement if they adopted the procedure of Crete and Sparta—which is also in accordance with the recommendations you made just now.

ATHENIAN: Now then, let's make sure we understand each other in this e
business. The essence of the entire cultural education of your countries is surely this: you oblige your poets to say that the good man, because he is temperate and just, enjoys good fortune and is happy, no matter whether he is big and strong, or small and weak, or rich, or poor; and that even if he is 'richer than Midas or Cinyras', and has not justice, he is a wretch,

7. See 653b.

and lives a life of misery. 'I'd not mention a man', says your poet,[8] and how right he is, and 'I'd take no account of him', even if all his actions
661   and possessions were what people commonly call 'good', if he were without justice, nor even if, with a character like that, he 'attacked in close combat with the foe'. If he is unjust, I wouldn't want him to 'stand the sight of bloody butchery' nor 'outdo in speed the north wind of Thrace', nor ever achieve any of the things that are generally said to be 'good'. You see, these things men usually call 'good' are misnamed. It is commonly said that health comes first, beauty second, and wealth third. The list goes on
b   indefinitely: keen sight and hearing, and acute perception of all the objects of sensation; being a dictator and doing whatever you like; and the seventh heaven is supposed to be reached when one has achieved all this and is made immortal without further ado. You and I, presumably, hold that all these things are possessions of great value to the just and pious, but that to the unjust they are a curse, every one of them, from health all the way
c   down the list. Seeing, hearing, sensation, and simply being alive, are great evils, if in spite of having all these so-called good things a man gains immortality without justice and virtue in general; but if he survives for only the briefest possible time, the evil is less. I imagine you will persuade or compel the authors in your states to embody this doctrine of mine in the words, rhythms and 'harmonies' they produce for the education of
d   your youth. Isn't that right? Look here, now: my position is quite clear. Although so-called evils are in fact evil for the just, they are good for the unjust; and so-called 'goods', while genuinely good for the good, are evils for the wicked. Let me ask the same question as before: are you and I in agreement, or not?

CLINIAS: In some ways I think we are, but certainly not in others.

ATHENIAN: I expect this is where I sound implausible: suppose a man were to enjoy health and wealth and permanent absolute power—and, if
e   you like, I'll give him enormous strength and courage as well, and exempt him from death and all the other 'evils', as people call them. But suppose he had in him nothing but injustice and insolence. It is obvious, I maintain, that his life is wretchedly *un*happy.

CLINIAS: True, that's precisely where you fail to convince.

ATHENIAN: Very well, then, How should we put it now? If a man is
662   brave, strong, handsome, and rich, and enjoys a life-long freedom to do just what he wants to, don't you think—if he is unjust and insolent—that his life will inevitably be a disgrace? Perhaps at any rate you'd allow the term 'disgrace'?

CLINIAS: Certainly.

ATHENIAN: Will you go further, and say he will live 'badly'?[9]

---

8. Tyrtaeus: see 629a and note. The Athenian makes further brief quotations from the same poem. Midas and Cinyras, kings of Phrygia and Cyprus respectively, were notorious for extreme wealth.

9. The expression is ambiguous: it may mean 'miserably' or 'wickedly'. In his reply, Clinias is thinking of the first meaning.

CLINIAS: No, we'd not be so ready to admit that.

ATHENIAN: What about going further still, and saying he will live 'unpleasantly and unprofitably'?

CLINIAS: How could we possibly be prepared to go as far as that?

ATHENIAN: 'How'? My friend, it looks as if it would be a miracle if we ever harmonized on this point: at the moment your tune and mine are scarcely in the same key. To me, these conclusions are inescapably true— in fact, my dear Clinias, rather more true and obvious than that Crete is an island. If I were a lawgiver, I should try to compel the authors and every inhabitant of the state to take this line; and if anybody in the land said that there are men who live a pleasant life in spite of being scoundrels, or that while this or that is useful and profitable, something else is more just, I should impose pretty nearly the extreme penalty. There are many other things I should persuade my citizens to say, which would flatly contradict what Cretans and Spartans maintain nowadays, apparently— to say nothing of the rest of the world. Zeus and Apollo! Just you imagine, my fine fellows, asking these gods who inspired your laws, 'Is the life of supreme justice also the life that gives most pleasure? Or are there two kinds of life, one being "the supremely just," the other "the most pleasurable"?' Suppose they replied 'There are two.' If we knew the right question to ask, we might perhaps pursue the point: 'Which category of men should we call the most blessed by heaven? Those who live the supremely just life, or the most pleasurable?' If they said 'Those who live the most pleasurable life', then that would be, for them, a curious thing to say. However, I am unwilling to associate the gods with such a statement; I prefer to think of it in connection with forefathers and lawgivers. So let's suppose those first questions have been put to a forefather and lawgiver, and that he has replied that the man who lives the life of greatest pleasure enjoys the greatest happiness. This is what I'd say then: 'Father, didn't you want me to receive as many of the blessings of heaven as I could? Yet in spite of that you never tired of telling me to order my life as *justly* as possible'. In taking up that kind of position our forefather or lawgiver will, I think, appear in rather an odd light: it will look as if he cannot speak without contradicting himself. However, if he declared that the life of supreme justice was the most blessed, I imagine that everybody who heard him would want to know what splendid benefit, superior to pleasure, was to be found in this kind of life. What was there in it that deserved the commendation of the law? Surely, any benefit a just man got out of it would be *inseparable* from pleasure? Look: are we to suppose that fame and praise from gods and men are fine and good, but unpleasant (and vice versa in the case of notoriety)? ('My dear legislator,' we'd say, 'of course not'.) Or, if you neither injure another nor are injured yourself by someone else, is that unpleasant, in spite of being fine and good? Is the opposite pleasant, but disgraceful and wicked?

CLINIAS: Certainly not.

ATHENIAN: So the argument that does not drive a wedge between 'pleasant' on the one hand and 'just' and 'fine' and 'good' on the other, even if it achieves nothing else, will do something to persuade a man to live a just and pious life. This means that any teaching which denies the truth of all this is, from the lawgiver's standpoint, a complete disgrace and his worst enemy. (Nobody would willingly agree to do something which would not bring him more pleasure than pain.)

Looking at a thing from a distance makes nearly everyone feel dizzy, especially children; but the lawgiver will alter that for us, and lift the fog

c   that clouds our judgment: somehow or other—by habituation, praise, or argument—he will persuade us that our ideas of justice and injustice are like pictures drawn in perspective. Injustice looks pleasant to the enemy of justice,[10] because he regards it from his own personal standpoint, which is unjust and evil; justice, on the other hand, looks *un*pleasant to him. But from the standpoint of the just man the view gained of justice and injustice is always the opposite.

CLINIAS: So it seems.

ATHENIAN: And which of these judgments are we to say has a better claim to be the correct one? The judgment of the worse soul or the better?

d   CLINIAS: That of the better, certainly.

ATHENIAN: Then it is equally certain that the unjust life is not only more shocking and disgraceful, but also in fact less pleasant, than the just and holy.

CLINIAS: On this argument, my friends, it certainly looks like it.

ATHENIAN: But just suppose that the truth had been different from what the argument has now shown it to be, and that a lawgiver, even a mediocre one, had been sufficiently bold, in the interests of the young, to tell them a lie. Could he have told a more useful lie than this, or one more effective

e   in making everyone practice justice in everything they do, willingly and without pressure?

CLINIAS: Truth is a fine thing, and it is sure to prevail, but to persuade men of it certainly seems no easy task.

ATHENIAN: Yes, but what about that fairy story about the Sidonian?[11] That was well-nigh incredible, but it was easy enough to convince men of it, and of thousands of other similar stories.

CLINIAS: What sort of stories?

ATHENIAN: The sowing of the teeth and the birth of armed men from

664   them. This remarkable example shows the legislator that the souls of the young can be persuaded of anything; he has only to try. The only thing he must consider and discover is what conviction would do the state most good; in that connection, he must think up every possible device to ensure that as far as possible the entire community preserves in its songs and stories and doctrines an absolute and lifelong unanimity. But if you see the matter in any other light, have no hesitation in disputing my view.

10. Accepting the conjecture of *enantiōi* in c3.

11. Cadmus. See 641c and note.

CLINIAS: No, I don't think either of us would be able to dispute that.   b

ATHENIAN: Then it will be up to me to introduce the next point. I maintain that our choruses—all three of them—should charm the souls of the children while still young and tender, and uphold all the admirable doctrines we have already formulated, and any we may formulate in the future. We must insist, as the central point of these doctrines, that the gods say the best life does in fact bring most pleasure. If we do that, we shall be telling   c
the plain truth, and we shall convince those whom we have to convince more effectively than if we advanced any other doctrine.

CLINIAS: Yes, one has to agree with what you say.

ATHENIAN: To start with, it will be only right and proper if the children's chorus (which will be dedicated to the Muses) comes on first to sing these doctrines with all its might and main before the entire city. Second will come the chorus of those under thirty, which will call upon Apollo Paean[12] to bear witness that what they say is true, and pray that he will vouchsafe   d
to convince the young. Thirdly, there must be the songs of those between thirty and sixty. That leaves the men who are older than this, who are, of course, no longer up to singing; but they will be inspired to tell stories in which the same characters will appear.

CLINIAS: You mention these three choruses, sir: what are they? We are not very clear what you mean to say about them.

ATHENIAN: But the greater part of the discussion we have had so far has been precisely for their sake!

CLINIAS: We still haven't seen the point. Could you try to elucidate   e
still further?

ATHENIAN: If we remember, we said at the beginning of our discussion[13] that all young things, being fiery and mettlesome by nature, are unable to keep their bodies or their tongues still—they are always making uncoordinated noises and jumping about. No other animal, we said, ever develops a sense of order in either respect; man alone has a natural ability to   665
do this. Order in movement is called 'rhythm', and order in the vocal sounds—the combination of high and low notes—is called 'harmony'; and the union of the two is called 'a performance by a chorus'. We said that the gods took pity on us and gave us Apollo and the Muses as companions and leaders of our choruses; and if we can cast our minds back, we said that their third gift to us was Dionysus.

CLINIAS: Yes, of course we remember.

ATHENIAN: Well, we've mentioned the choruses of Apollo and the Muses; the remaining one, the third, must be identified as belonging to Dionysus.   b

CLINIAS: What! You had better explain yourself: a chorus of elderly men dedicated to Dionysus sounds a weird and wonderful idea, at any rate at first hearing. Are men of more than thirty and even fifty, up to sixty, really going to dance in honor of Dionysus?

12. The god of healing.
13. See 653d ff.

ATHENIAN: You are absolutely right—to show how this could be reasonable in practice does need, I think, some explanation.

CLINIAS: It certainly does.

ATHENIAN: Are we agreed on the conclusions we have reached so far?

c   CLINIAS: Conclusions about what?

ATHENIAN: About this—that every man and child, free-man and slave, male and female—in fact, the whole state—is in duty bound never to stop repeating to each other the charms[14] we have described. Somehow or other, we must see that these charms constantly change their form; at all costs they must be continually varied, so that the performers always long to sing the songs, and find perpetual pleasure in them.

CLINIAS: Agreed: that's exactly the arrangement we want.

d   ATHENIAN: This last chorus is the noblest element in our state; it carries more conviction than any other group, because of the age and discernment of its members. Where, then, should it sing its splendid songs, if it is to do most good? Surely we are not going to be silly enough to leave this question undecided? After all, this chorus may well prove to be consummate masters of the noblest and most useful songs.

CLINIAS: No; if that's really the way the argument is going, we certainly can't leave this undecided.

ATHENIAN: So what would be a suitable method of procedure? See if this will do.

CLINIAS: What, then?

e   ATHENIAN: As he grows old, a man becomes apprehensive about singing; it gives him less pleasure, and if it should happen that he cannot avoid it, it causes him an embarrassment which grows with the increasingly sober tastes of his advancing years. Isn't that so?

CLINIAS: Indeed it is.

ATHENIAN: So naturally he will be even more acutely embarrassed at standing up and singing in front of the varied audience in a theater. And if men of that age were forced to sing in the same condition as members of choruses competing for a prize—lean and on a diet after a course of voice-training—then of course they would find the performance positively unpleasant and humiliating, and would lose every spark of enthusiasm.

666   CLINIAS: Yes, that would be the inevitable result.

ATHENIAN: So how shall we encourage them to be enthusiastic about singing? The first law we shall pass, surely, is this: children under the age of eighteen are to keep off wine entirely. We shall teach them that they must treat the violent tendencies of youth with due caution, and not pour fire on the fire already in their souls and bodies until they come to undertake the real work of life. Our second law will permit the young man under

b   thirty to take wine in moderation, but he must stop short of drunkenness and bibulous excesses. When he reaches his thirties, he should regale himself at the common meals, and invoke the gods; in particular, he should

14. See 659e.

summon Dionysus to what is at once the play-time and the prayer-time of the old, which the god gave to mankind to help cure the crabbiness of age. This is the gift he gave us to make us young again: we forget our peevishness, and our hard cast of mind becomes softer and grows more malleable, just like iron thrust in a fire. Surely any man who is brought into that frame of mind would be ready to sing his songs (that is 'charms', as we've called them often enough) with more enthusiasm and less embarrassment? I don't mean in a large gathering of strangers, but in a comparatively small circle of friends.

CLINIAS: Certainly.

ATHENIAN: As a method of inducing them to join us in our singing, there wouldn't be anything you could particularly object to in this.

CLINIAS: By no means.

ATHENIAN: But what sort of philosophy of music will inspire their songs? Obviously, it will have to be one appropriate to the performers.

CLINIAS: Of course.

ATHENIAN: And the performers are men of almost divine distinction. What notes would be appropriate for them? Those produced by the choruses?

CLINIAS: Well, sir, we Cretans, at any rate—and the same goes for the Spartans—would hardly be up to singing any song except those we learned to sing by growing familiar with them in our choruses.

ATHENIAN: Naturally enough. In cold fact, you have failed to achieve the finest kind of song. You organize your state as though it were a military camp rather than a society of people who have settled in towns, and you keep your young fellows together like a herd of colts at grass. Not a man among you takes his own colt and drags him, furiously protesting, away from the rest of the herd; you never put him in the hands of a private groom, and train him by combing him down and stroking him. You entirely fail to lavish proper care on an education which will turn him out not merely a good soldier but a capable administrator of a state and its towns. Such a man is, as we said early on, a better fighter than those of Tyrtaeus, precisely because he does not value courage as the principal element in virtue: he consistently relegates it to *fourth* place wherever he finds it, whether in the individual or the state.

CLINIAS: I suspect, sir, you are being rather rude about our legislators again.

ATHENIAN: If I am, my dear fellow, it is entirely unintentionally. But if you don't mind, we ought to follow where the argument leads us. If we know of any music that is of finer quality than the music of choruses and the public theaters, we ought to try to allocate it to these older people. They are, as we said, embarrassed at the other kind; but music of the highest quality is just what they are keen to take part in.

CLINIAS: Yes, indeed.

ATHENIAN: The most important point about everything that has some inherent attractive quality must be *either* this very quality *or* some kind of

'correctness' *or* (thirdly) its usefulness. For instance, I maintain that eating
and drinking and taking nourishment in general are accompanied by the
c particular attractive quality that we might call pleasure; as for their usefulness and 'correctness', we invariably speak of the 'wholesomeness' of
the foods we serve, and in their case the most 'correct' thing in them is
precisely this.

CLINIAS: Quite.

ATHENIAN: An element of attractiveness—the pleasure we feel—goes
with the process of learning, too. But what gives rise to its 'correctness'
and usefulness, its excellence and nobility, is its accuracy.

CLINIAS: Exactly.

ATHENIAN: What about the arts of imitation, whose function is to produce
d likenesses? When they succeed in doing this, it will be quite proper to say
that the pleasure—if any—that arises out of and accompanies that success
constitutes the attractive quality of these arts.

CLINIAS: Yes.

ATHENIAN: Generally speaking, I suppose, the 'correctness' in such cases
would depend not so much on the pleasure given, as on the accurate
representation of the size and qualities of the original?

CLINIAS: Well put.

ATHENIAN: So pleasure would be the proper criterion in one case only.
A work of art may be produced with nothing to offer by way of usefulness
e or truth or accuracy of representation (or harm, of course). It may be
produced solely for the sake of this element that normally accompanies
the others, the attractive one. (In fact, it is when this element is associated
with none of the others that it most genuinely deserves the name 'pleasure'.)

CLINIAS: You mean only harmless pleasure?

ATHENIAN: Yes, and it is precisely this that I call 'play', when it has no
particular good or bad effect that deserves serious discussion.

CLINIAS: Quite right.

ATHENIAN: And we could conclude from all this that no imitation at all
should be judged by reference to incorrect opinions about it or by the
criterion of the pleasure it gives. This is particularly so in the case of
668 every sort of equality. What is equal is equal and what is proportional is
proportional, and this does not depend on anyone's opinion that it is so,
nor does it cease to be true if someone is displeased at the fact. Accuracy,
and nothing else whatever, is the only permissible criterion.

CLINIAS: Yes, that is emphatically true.

ATHENIAN: So do we hold that all music is a matter of representation
and imitation?

CLINIAS: Of course.

ATHENIAN: So when someone says that music is judged by the criterion
of pleasure, we should reject his argument out of hand, and absolutely
b refuse to go in for such music (if any were ever produced) as a serious
genre. The music we ought to cultivate is the kind that bears a resemblance
to its model, beauty.

CLINIAS: Very true.

ATHENIAN: These people, then, who are anxious to take part in the finest possible singing, should, apparently, look not for a music which is sweet, but one which is correct; and correctness, as we said, lies in the imitation and successful reproduction of the proportions and characteristics of the model.

CLINIAS: It does indeed.

ATHENIAN: This is certainly so in the case of music: everyone would admit that all musical compositions are matters of imitation and representation. In fact, composers, audiences and actors would register universal agreement on this point, wouldn't they?

CLINIAS: Certainly.

ATHENIAN: So it looks as if a man who is not to go wrong about a given composition must appreciate what it is, because failure to understand its nature—what it is trying to do and what in fact it is a representation of—will mean that he gets virtually no conception of whether the author has achieved his aim correctly or not.

CLINIAS: No, virtually none, naturally.

ATHENIAN: And if he cannot gauge the correctness of the composition, surely he won't be able to judge its moral goodness or badness? But this is all rather obscure. Perhaps this would be a clearer way of putting it.

CLINIAS: What?

ATHENIAN: There are, of course, thousands of representations that strike the eye?

CLINIAS: Yes.

ATHENIAN: Now, imagine someone who didn't know the character of each of the objects that are imitated and represented. Would he ever be able to estimate the correctness of the finished article? This is the sort of point I have in mind: does it preserve the overall proportions of the body and the position of each of its various parts? Does it hit off the proportions exactly and keep the parts in their proper positions relative to one another? And what of their colors and contours? Have all these features been reproduced higgledy-piggledy? Do you think that if a man did not know the character of the creature represented he would ever be able to assess these points?

CLINIAS: Of course not.

ATHENIAN: What if we knew that the thing molded or painted is a man, and that all his parts with their colors and contours have been caught by the artist's skill? Suppose a man knows all that; is he without further ado necessarily ready to judge whether the work is beautiful or falls short of beauty in some respect?

CLINIAS: In that case, sir, pretty well all of us would be judges of the quality of a representation.

ATHENIAN: You have hit the nail on the head. So anyone who is going to be a sensible judge of any representation—in painting and music and every other field—should be able to assess three points: he must know, b   first, *what* has been represented; second, how *correctly* it has been copied; and then, third, the *moral value* of this or that representation produced by language, tunes and rhythms.

CLINIAS: Apparently so.

ATHENIAN: We ought not to fail to mention the peculiar difficulty about music, which is discussed much more than any other kind of artistic representation and needs much more careful handling than all the others. A man who goes wrong on this subject will suffer a good deal of harm
c   because he feels attracted to evil dispositions; and his mistake is very difficult to detect, because the authors hardly have the same degree of creative ability as the actual Muses. The Muses would never make the ghastly mistake of composing the speech of men to a musical idiom suitable for women, or of fitting rhythms appropriate to the portrayal of slaves and slave-like people to the tune and bodily movements used to represent free men (or again of making rhythms and movements appropriate to free men accompany a combination of tune and words that conflicted with those rhythms). Nor would they ever mix up together into one production
d   the din of wild animals and men and musical instruments and all kinds of other noises and still claim to be representing a unified theme. But human authors, in their silly way, jumble all these things together into complicated combinations; in Orpheus' words, anyone 'whose delight in life is in its springtime', will find them a rich source of amusement. And in the midst of all this confusion, he will find that the authors also divorce
e   rhythm and movement from the tune by putting unaccompanied words into meter, and rob tune and rhythm of words by using stringed instruments and pipes on their own without singers. When this is done, it is extraordinarily difficult to know what the rhythm and harmony without speech are supposed to signify and what worthwhile object they imitate and represent. The conclusion is inevitable: such practices appeal to the taste of the village idiot. It is this fondness for speed and dexterity (as in
670 reproducing the noises of wild animals) which prompts the use of pipes and lyre otherwise than as an accompaniment to dancing and singing. Using either instrument on its own is in fact sheer showmanship that has nothing to do with art. But enough of theory: what we are considering is not what sort of music our citizens over thirty and fifty should avoid, but what sort they should go in for. I think our argument so far seems to point
b   to the conclusion that the fifty-year-olds who have the duty of singing must have enjoyed an education that reached a higher standard than the music of choruses. They must, of course, have a nice appreciation of rhythms and harmonies and be able to understand them. Otherwise how could a man assess the correctness of the tunes, and tell whether the Dorian mode was appropriate or not in a given case, or judge whether the author has set the tunes to the right rhythm or not?

CLINIAS: Clearly he couldn't.

ATHENIAN: The belief of the general public, that they can form an adequate judgment of merit and demerit in matters of harmony and rhythm, is

laughable: they have only been drilled into singing to the pipes and march-
ing in step, and they never stop to think that they do all this without the   c
smallest understanding of it. In fact, every tune with the right elements
is correct, but if it has the wrong ones, it is faulty.

CLINIAS: Inevitably.

ATHENIAN: What about the man who doesn't even understand what the
elements are? As we said, will he ever be able to decide that any aspect
of the piece is correct?

CLINIAS: No, how could he?

ATHENIAN: So it looks as if once again we are discovering that it is
virtually indispensable for these singers of ours (who are not only being
encouraged to sing but *compelled* to do it in a willing spirit, if I may put   d
it like that), to have been educated up to at least this point: they should
each be able to follow the notes of the tunes and the basic units of rhythm,
so that they may examine the harmonies and rhythms and select those
that men of their age and character could appropriately sing. If that is
how they sing, they will give themselves harmless pleasure, and at the
same time stimulate the younger generation to adopt virtuous customs   e
with the proper enthusiasm. Assuming the education of these singers
reaches that level, they will have pursued a more advanced course of
training than will be given to ordinary men, or even the authors themselves.
The author is more or less obliged to have a knowledge of rhythm and
harmony, but there is no necessity for him to be able to assess the third
point—whether the imitation is a morally good one or not. The men we
are talking about, however, must be equally competent in all three fields,
so that they can isolate the primary and secondary degrees of goodness;   671
otherwise they will never prove capable of charming the young in the
direction of virtue.

ATHENIAN: Our argument has done its level best: we have to consider
whether it has succeeded in its original intention of showing that our
defense of Dionysus' chorus was justified. A gathering like that, of course,
inevitably gets increasingly rowdier as the wine flows more freely. (In fact,
our initial assumption in the present discussion of this business was that
such a tendency is unavoidable.)   b

CLINIAS: Yes, it is unavoidable.

ATHENIAN: Everyone is taken out of himself and has a splendid time;
the exuberance of his conversation is matched only by his reluctance to
listen to his companions, and he thinks himself entitled to run their lives
as well as his own.

CLINIAS: He certainly does.

ATHENIAN: And didn't we say that when this happens the souls of the
drinkers get hot and, like iron in a fire, grow younger and softer, so that
anyone who has the ability and skill to mold and educate them, finds them   c
as easy to handle as when they were young? The man to do the molding
is the same one as before—the good lawgiver. When our drinker grows
cheerful and confident and unduly shameless and unwilling to speak and

keep quiet, to drink and sing, at the proper times, the lawgiver's job will
be to lay down drinking laws which will be able to make this fellow willing
d   to mend his ways; and to do battle with this disgraceful over-confidence
as soon as it appears, they will be able to send into the arena, with the
blessing of justice, this divine and splendid fear we have called 'modesty'
and 'shame'.[15]

CLINIAS: Exactly.

ATHENIAN: The cool-headed and sober should guard and co-operate with
these laws by taking command of those who are not sober; fighting the
enemy without cool-headed leaders is actually *less* dangerous than fighting
drink without such help as this. If a man cannot show a willing spirit and
e   obey these commanders and the officials of Dionysus (who are upwards
of sixty years of age), the dishonor he incurs must equal or even exceed
that incurred by the man who disobeys the officials of the god of war.

CLINIAS: Precisely.

ATHENIAN: So, if they drank and made merry like that, the revelers who
took part in the proceedings would surely benefit? They would go their
way on better terms with each other than they were before, instead of
loathing each other, which is what happens nowadays; and this would be
672 because they had rules to regulate the whole of their intercourse and had
followed every instruction given by the sober to the tipsy.

CLINIAS: Precisely—if indeed the party were to go as you describe.

ATHENIAN: So let's not abuse the gift of Dionysus any longer in the old
unqualified terms, saying that it is bad and does not deserve to be received
into the state. One could, indeed, enlarge on its benefits even more. But
in front of the general public I would be chary of mentioning the *main*
benefit conferred by the gift, because people misconstrue and misunder-
b   stand the explanation.

CLINIAS: What is the benefit?

ATHENIAN: There is a little-known current of story and tradition[16] which
says that Dionysus was robbed of his wits by his stepmother Hera, and
that he gets his revenge by stimulating us to Bacchic frenzies and all the
mad dancing that results; and this was precisely the reason why he made
us a present of wine. This sort of story, however, I leave to those who see
no danger in speaking of the gods in such terms. But I am quite certain
c   of this: no animal that enjoys the use of reason in its maturity is ever born
with that faculty, or at any rate with it fully developed. During the time
in which it has not yet attained its characteristic level of intelligence, it is
completely mad: it bawls uncontrollably, and as soon as it can get on its
feet it jumps about with equal abandon. Let's think back: we said that this
situation gave rise to music and gymnastics.

15. 646e ff.
16. Cf. Euripides, *Cyclops*, 3.

CLINIAS: We remember, of course.

ATHENIAN: And also that this was the source of man's appreciation of   d
rhythm and harmony, and Apollo and the Muses and Dionysus were the
gods who co-operated to implant it in us.

CLINIAS: Yes, indeed.

ATHENIAN: In particular, it seems that according to the common story
wine was given to men as a means of taking vengeance on us—it was
intended to drive us insane. But our interpretation is entirely the opposite:
the gift was intended to be a medicine and to produce reverence in the
soul, and health and strength in the body.

CLINIAS: Yes, sir, that's a splendid recapitulation of the argument.

ATHENIAN: We are now half-way through our examination of singing   e
and dancing. Shall we carry on with the other half in whatever way
recommends itself, or shall we pass it over?

CLINIAS: What halves do you mean? Where do you put your dividing-
line?

ATHENIAN: We found that singing and dancing, taken together,
amounted, in a sense, to education as a whole. One part of it—the vocal
part—was concerned with rhythms and 'harmonies'.

CLINIAS: Yes.

ATHENIAN: The second part concerned the movement of the body. Here
too we had rhythm, a feature shared with the movement of the voice; but
the body's movements were its own particular concern, just as in the other   673
half the tune was the special job of the vocal movements.

CLINIAS: True enough.

ATHENIAN: When the sound of the voice penetrates the soul, we took
that to be an education in virtue, and we hazarded the term 'music' to
describe it.

CLINIAS: And quite rightly.

ATHENIAN: When the movements of the body, which we described as
'dancing in delight', are such as to result in a fine state of physical fitness,
we ought to call the systematic training which does this 'gymnastics'.

CLINIAS: Exactly.

ATHENIAN: So much, then, for music, which is roughly the half of the   b
subject of choruses that we said we had examined and finished with; so
that's that. Shall we discuss the other half? Or what method should we
follow now?

CLINIAS: Really, my dear fellow! You are having a conversation with
Cretans and Spartans, and we have discussed music thoroughly—leaving
gymnastics still to come. What sort of answer do you think you'll get to
that question, from either of us?

ATHENIAN: I should say that question was a pretty unambiguous answer.   c
I take it that your question, as I said, amounts in fact to a reply, an order
even, to finish off our examination of gymnastics.

CLINIAS: You understand me perfectly: do just that.

ATHENIAN: Yes, I must. Of course, discussing a subject so familiar to you both is not very difficult. You see, you have had much more experience of this particular skill than of the other.

CLINIAS: True enough.

d ATHENIAN: Again, the origin of this form of recreation too lies in the fact that every animal has the natural habit of jumping about. The human animal, as we said, acquired a sense of rhythm, and that led to the birth of dancing. The tune suggested rhythm and awakened the memory of it, and out of the union of the two was born choral singing and dancing as a recreation.

CLINIAS: Exactly.

ATHENIAN: We have already discussed one of these two; now we are going to set about the discussion of the other.

CLINIAS: Yes, indeed.

e ATHENIAN: However, if you are agreeable, let's give our discussion of the use of drink its final flourish.

CLINIAS: What flourish do you mean?

ATHENIAN: Suppose a state takes this practice we are now discussing sufficiently seriously to control it by a set of rules and use it to cultivate moderate habits; suppose it permits a similar enjoyment of other pleasures on the same principle, seeing it simply as a device for mastering them. In each and every case, our method will be the one that must be followed. But if the state treats a drink as recreation pure and simple, and anybody

674 who wants to can go drinking and please himself when and with whom he does it, and do whatever else he likes at the same time, then my vote would be in favor of never allowing this state or individual to take wine at all. I would go further than Cretan and Spartan practice: I would support the law of the Carthaginians, which forbids anyone on military service to take a drink of wine, and makes water the only permissible beverage during the entire campaign. As for civilians, it forbids slaves, male and

b female, ever to touch wine; it forbids magistrates during their year of office; steersmen and jurymen on duty are absolutely prohibited from touching it, and so too is any councillor who is going to take part in an important discussion; nobody at all is permitted to drink wine during the day, except for reasons of training or health, nor at night if they intend to procreate children (this prohibition applying to men and women alike); and one could point to a great many other situations in which any sensible

c person with a respect for the law would find it proper not to drink wine. This kind of approach would mean that no state would need many vines and as part of the regulations covering agriculture in general and the whole question of diet, the production of wine in particular would be restricted to the most modest quantities. With your permission, gentlemen, let's take that as the final flourish to our discussion of wine.

CLINIAS: Splendid! Permission granted.

Book III

ATHENIAN: We can take that as settled, then. But what about political 676
systems? How are we to suppose they first came into existence? I feel sure
that the best and easiest way to see their origins is this.

CLINIAS: What?

ATHENIAN: To use the same method that we always have to adopt when
we look into a state's moral progress or decline.

CLINIAS: What method have you in mind?

ATHENIAN: We take an indefinitely long period of time and study the
changes that occur in it.   b

CLINIAS: How do you mean?

ATHENIAN: Look, do you think you could ever grasp how long it is that
states have existed and men have lived under some sort of political organization?

CLINIAS: No, not very easily.

ATHENIAN: But at any rate you realize it must be an enormously long time?

CLINIAS: Yes, I see *that*, of course.

ATHENIAN: So surely, during this period, thousands upon thousands of
states have come into being, while at least as many, in equally vast numbers, c
have been destroyed? Time and again each one of them has adopted every
type of political system. And sometimes small states have become bigger,
and big ones have grown smaller; superior states have deteriorated and
bad ones have improved.

CLINIAS: Inevitably.

ATHENIAN: Let's try to pin down just why these changes took place, if
we can; then perhaps we shall discover how the various systems took root
and developed.

CLINIAS: Admirable! Let's get down to it. You must do your best to
explain your views, and we must try to follow you.

ATHENIAN: Do you think there is any truth in tradition?   677

CLINIAS: What sort of tradition do you mean?

ATHENIAN: This: that the human race has been repeatedly annihilated
by floods and plagues and many other causes, so that only a small fraction
of it survived.

CLINIAS: Yes, of course, all that sort of thing strikes everyone as entirely credible.

ATHENIAN: Now then, let's picture just one of this series of annihilations—
I mean the effect of the flood.

CLINIAS: What special point are we to notice about it?

ATHENIAN: That those who escaped the disaster must have been pretty   b
nearly all hill-shepherds—a few embers of mankind preserved, I imagine,
on the tops of mountains.

CLINIAS: Obviously.

ATHENIAN: Here's a further point: such men must have been in general unskilled and unsophisticated. In particular, they must have been quite innocent of the crafty devices that city-dwellers use in the rat-race to do each other down; and all the other dirty tricks that men play against one another must have been unknown.

CLINIAS: Quite likely.

c   ATHENIAN: And we can take it, can't we, that the cities that had been built on the plains and near the sea were destroyed root-and-branch?

CLINIAS: Yes, we can.

ATHENIAN: So all their tools were destroyed, and any worthwhile discovery they had made in politics or any other field was entirely lost? You see, my friend, if their discoveries had survived throughout at the same level of development as they have attained today, it is difficult to see what room there can ever have been for any new invention.

d   CLINIAS: The upshot of all this, I suppose, is that for millions of years these techniques remained unknown to primitive man. Then, a thousand or two thousand years ago, Daedalus and Orpheus and Palamedes made their various discoveries, Marsyas and Olympus pioneered the art of music, Amphion invented the lyre, and many other discoveries were made by other people. All this happened only yesterday or the day before, so to speak.

ATHENIAN: How tactful of you, Clinias, to leave out your friend, who really was born 'yesterday'!

CLINIAS: I suppose you mean Epimenides?

e   ATHENIAN: Yes, that's the man. His discovery, my dear fellows, put him streets ahead of all the other inventors. Hesiod had foreshadowed it in his poetry long before, but it was Epimenides who achieved it in practice, so you Cretans claim.[1]

CLINIAS: We certainly do claim that.

ATHENIAN: Perhaps we can describe the state of mankind after the cataclysm like this: in spite of a vast and terrifying desolation, plenty of fertile land was available, and although animals in general had perished it happened that some cattle still survived, together with perhaps a small stock of goats. They were few enough, but sufficient to maintain the correspond-
678   ingly few herdsmen of this early period.

CLINIAS: Agreed.

ATHENIAN: But at the moment we are talking about the state, and the business of legislation and political organization. Is it conceivable that any trace at all of such things survived—even, so to speak, in the memory?

---

1. Epimenides' 'magic brew' was believed to have been inspired by Hesiod's mention (*Works and Days* 40-41) of the virtue of mallow and asphodel. For Epimenides, see 642d ff. and note.

CLINIAS: Of course not.

ATHENIAN: So out of those conditions all the features of our present-day life developed: states, political systems, technical skills, laws, rampant vice and frequent virtue.

CLINIAS: What do you mean?

ATHENIAN: My dear sir, can we really suppose that the men of that period, who had had no experience of city life in all its splendor and squalor, ever became totally wicked or totally virtuous? b

CLINIAS: A good point. We see what you mean.

ATHENIAN: So it was only as time went on, and the numbers of the human race increased, that civilization advanced and reached its present stage of development?

CLINIAS: Exactly.

ATHENIAN: The process was probably not sudden, but gradual, and took a considerable time.

CLINIAS: Yes, that's perfectly plausible. c

ATHENIAN: I imagine men were all numbed with fear at the prospect of descending from the hills to the plains.

CLINIAS: Naturally enough.

ATHENIAN: And what a pleasure it must have been to see each other, there being so few of them at that time! However, pretty well all vehicles they might have used to visit each other by land or sea had been destroyed, and the techniques used to construct them had been lost, so that I suppose they found getting together none too easy. They suffered from a scarcity d of timber, because iron, copper and mineral workings in general had been overlaid with sludge and had been lost to sight, so that it was virtually impossible to refine fresh supplies of metal. Even if there was the odd tool left somewhere on the mountains, it was quickly worn down to nothing by use. Replacements could not be made until the technique of mining sprang up again among men.

CLINIAS: True.

ATHENIAN: And how many generations later did that happen, on our calculation?

CLINIAS: A good many, obviously. e

ATHENIAN: Well then, during that period, or even longer, all techniques that depend on a supply of copper and iron and so on must have gone out of use?

CLINIAS: Of course.

ATHENIAN: For several reasons, then, war and civil war alike came to an end.

CLINIAS: How so?

ATHENIAN: In the first place, men's isolation prompted them to cherish and love one another. Second, their food supply was nothing they needed 679 to quarrel about. Except perhaps for a few people in the very early stages, there was no shortage of flocks and herds, which is what men mostly lived on in that age. They always had a supply of milk and meat, and could always add to it plenty of good food to be got by hunting. They also had an abundance of clothes, bedding, houses, and equipment for cooking and other purposes. (Molding pottery and weaving, skills that have no need

b of iron, were a gift from God to men—his way, in fact, of supplying them with all that kind of equipment. His intention was that whenever the human race was reduced to such a desperate condition it could still take root and develop.) Because of all this, they were not intolerably poor, nor driven by poverty to quarrel with each other; but presumably they did not grow rich either, in view of the prevailing lack of gold and silver. Now the community in which neither wealth nor poverty exists will generally

c produce the finest characters because tendencies to violence and crime, and feelings of jealousy and envy, simply do not arise. So these men were *good*, partly for that very reason, partly because of what we might call their 'naïveté'. When they heard things labeled 'good' or 'bad', they were so artless as to think it a statement of the literal truth and believe it. This lack of sophistication precluded the cynicism you find today: they accepted as the truth the doctrine they heard about gods and men, and lived their lives in accordance with it. That is why they were the sort of people we have described.

d   CLINIAS: Megillus and I, at least, agree with your account.

ATHENIAN: If we compare them with the era before the flood and with the modern world, we shall have to say that the many generations which lived in that way were inevitably unskilled and ignorant of techniques in general, and particularly of the military devices used on land and sea nowadays. They must also have been innocent of the techniques of warfare

e peculiar to city-life—generally called 'lawsuits' and 'party-strife'—in which men concoct every possible device to damage and hurt each other by word and deed. Weren't our primitive men simple and manlier and at the same time more restrained and upright in every way? We have already explained why.

CLINIAS: Yes, you're quite right.

ATHENIAN: Let's remind ourselves that this reconstruction, and the con-

680 clusions we shall draw from it, are supposed to make us appreciate how early man came to feel the need of laws, and who their lawgiver was.

CLINIAS: Well reminded!

ATHENIAN: Presumably they felt no need for legislators, and in that era law was not yet a common phenomenon. Men born at that stage of the world cycle[2] did not yet have any written records, but lived in obedience to accepted usage and 'ancestral' law, as we call it.

---

2. A 'cycle' is apparently thought of as the interval between one cosmic upheaval (e.g. the flood) and the next.

CLINIAS: Quite likely.

ATHENIAN: But this is already a political system, of a sort.

CLINIAS: What sort?

ATHENIAN: Autocracy—the name which everyone, I believe, uses for the   b
political system of that age. You can still find it in many parts of the world
today, both among Greeks and non-Greeks. I suppose this is what Homer
is describing in his account of the household of the Cyclopes:[3]

> No laws, no councils for debate have they:
> They live on the tips of lofty mountains
> In hollow caves; each man lays down the law
> To wife and children, with no regard for neighbor.

   c

CLINIAS: That poet of yours sounds as if he was a charming fellow. I
have gone through other verses of his, and very polished they were too.
Not that I know his work to any great extent—we Cretans don't go in for
foreign poetry very much.

MEGILLUS: But we at Sparta do, and we think Homer is the prince of
epic poets, even though the way of life he describes is invariably Ionian   d
rather than Spartan. In this instance he certainly seems to bear you out when
he points in his stories to the wild life of the Cyclopes as an explanation of
their primitive customs.

ATHENIAN: Yes, he does testify in my favor. So let's take him as our
evidence that political systems of this kind do sometimes develop.

CLINIAS: Very well.

ATHENIAN: And they arise among these people who live scattered in
separate households and individual families in the confusion that follows
the cataclysms. In such a system the eldest member rules by virtue of   e
having inherited power from his father or mother; the others follow his
lead and make one flock like birds. The authority to which they bow is
that of their patriarch: they are governed, in effect, by the most justifiable
of all forms of kingship.

CLINIAS: Yes, of course.

ATHENIAN: The next stage is when several families amalgamate and form
larger communities. They turn their attention to agriculture, initially in   681
the foot-hills, and build rings of dry stones to serve as walls to protect
themselves against wild animals. The result now is a single large unit, a
common homestead.

CLINIAS: I suppose that's quite probable.

ATHENIAN: Well then, isn't this probable too?

CLINIAS: What?

---

3. *Odyssey* ix.112–15.

ATHENIAN: As these original relatively tiny communities grew bigger, each of the small constituent families lived under its own ruler—the eldest
b member—and followed its own particular customs which had arisen because of its isolation from the others. The various social and religious standards to which people had grown accustomed reflected the bias of their ancestors and teachers: the more restrained or adventurous the ancestor, the more restrained or adventurous would be the character of his descendants. Consequently, as I say, the members of each group entered the larger community with laws peculiar to themselves, and were ready to impress their own inclinations on their children and their children's children.

CLINIAS: Naturally.

c ATHENIAN: And of course each group inevitably approved of its own laws and looked on those of other people with rather less favor.

CLINIAS: Exactly.

ATHENIAN: So it looks as if we have unwittingly stumbled on the origin of legislation.

CLINIAS: We certainly have.

ATHENIAN: At any rate the next and necessary step in this amalgamation is to choose some representatives to review the rules of all the families, and to propose openly to the leaders and heads of the people—the 'kings',
d so to speak—the adoption of those rules that particularly recommend themselves for common use. These representatives will be known as lawgivers, and by appointing the leaders as officials they will create out of the separate autocracies a sort of aristocracy, or perhaps kingship. And while the political system passes through this transitional stage they will administer the state themselves.

CLINIAS: Yes, that sort of change would certainly come about by stages.

ATHENIAN: So we can now go on to describe the birth of a third type of political system, one which in fact admits *all* systems and all their modifications and exhibits equal variety and change in the actual states as well.

e CLINIAS: What type is this?

ATHENIAN: The one which Homer too listed as the successor of the second. This is how he describes the origin of the third:[4] 'He founded Dardania'—I think this is how it goes—'when holy Ilium,

> *A town upon the plain for mortal men, had not been built:*
> *For still they lived upon the lower slopes of many-fountained Ida.'*

682 He composed these lines, as well as those about the Cyclopes, under some sort of inspiration from God. And how true to life they are! This is because

---

4. *Iliad* xx.216–18. 'He' is Dardanus; Ilium is Troy.

poets as a class are divinely gifted and are inspired when they sing, so that with the help of Graces and Muses they frequently hit on how things really happen.

CLINIAS: They do indeed.

ATHENIAN: Let's carry on with the story we are telling: it may suggest something to our purpose. I take it this is what we ought to do?

CLINIAS: Of course.

ATHENIAN: Ilium was founded, according to us, when men had descended from the hills to a wide and beautiful plain. They built their city on a hill of moderate height near several rivers which poured down from Ida above.

CLINIAS: So the story goes.

ATHENIAN: I suppose we may assume that this descent of theirs took place many ages after the flood?

CLINIAS: Yes, naturally, many ages later.

ATHENIAN: I mean that apparently the disaster we've just described must have been forgotten to a quite remarkable degree if they founded their city on the lower reaches of several rivers flowing down from the mountains, and put their trust in hills that were none too high.

CLINIAS: Yes, a clear proof that they were far removed in time from any such experience.

ATHENIAN: With the increase in the human population many other cities, one supposes, were already being founded.

CLINIAS: Naturally.

ATHENIAN: These cities also mounted an expedition against Ilium, probably by sea as well, because by then all mankind had overcome its fear and had taken to ships.

CLINIAS: So it seems.

ATHENIAN: And after a siege of about ten years the Achaeans sacked Troy.

CLINIAS: Indeed they did.

ATHENIAN: They besieged Ilium for ten years, and during this period the domestic affairs of the individual attackers took a turn for the worse. The younger generation revolted, and the ugly and criminal reception they gave the troops when they returned to their own cities and homes led to murder, massacre and expulsion on a large scale. When the exiles came back again they adopted a new name, and were now known as Dorians instead of Achaeans, in honor of Dorieus, who had rallied them while they were in exile. A full and exhaustive account of subsequent events can be found in your traditional Spartan stories.

MEGILLUS: Of course.

ATHENIAN: When we were starting to discuss legislation, the question of the arts and drinking cropped up, and we made a digression.[5] But now

5. At 636e ff.

we really do have a chance to come to grips with our subject. As if God himself were guiding us, we've come back to the very point from which

683   we digressed: the actual foundation of Sparta. You maintained that Sparta was established on the right lines, and you said the same of Crete, because it has laws that bear a family resemblance to Sparta's. We have had a rather random discussion about various foundations and political systems, but we have achieved at least this much: we have watched the first, second and third type of state being founded in succession over a vast period of time, and now we discover this fourth state (or 'nation', if you like) whose historical foundation and development we are tracing down to its maturity

b   today.[6] After all this, perhaps we can get some idea of what was right and wrong in the way these foundations were established. Can we see what kind of laws are responsible for continued preservation of the features that survive and the ruin of those that collapse? What detailed alterations will produce happiness in a state? If we can understand all this, Clinias and Megillus, we shall have to discuss the whole business all over again: it will be like making a fresh start. However, we may be able to find some fault in our account so far.

c   MEGILLUS: Well, sir, if some god were to give us his word that if we do make a second attempt to look at the problem of legislation, we shall hear an account of at least the quality and length of the one we have just had, I for one would willingly extend our journey, and the present day would seem not a moment too long—though it is in fact more or less the day when the Sun-god turns past summer towards winter.

ATHENIAN: So it looks as if we must press on with the investigation.

MEGILLUS: Certainly.

ATHENIAN: Let's imagine that we are living at the time when the territory

d   of Sparta, Argos and Messene, and the districts nearby, had in effect come under the control of your ancestors, Megillus. Their next decision, or so the story goes, was to split their forces into three and establish three states—Argos, Messene and Sparta.

MEGILLUS: That's quite right.

ATHENIAN: Temenus became king of Argos, Cresphontes of Messene, and Procles and Eurysthenes of Sparta.

MEGILLUS: True.

ATHENIAN: And all their contemporaries swore to them that they would

e   go to their help if anybody tried to subvert their thrones.

MEGILLUS: Precisely.

ATHENIAN: Now when a monarchy is overthrown (and indeed when any other type of authority has been destroyed at any time) surely no one but

---

6. The four are: (1) single families under autocratic rule, (2) collections of families under aristocratic rule, (3) the cities of the plains (e.g. Troy) with various constitutions, (4) a league of such cities, now to be discussed.

the rulers themselves are to blame? That was the line we took when the subject cropped up a little time ago—or have we forgotten by now?

MEGILLUS: No, of course not.

ATHENIAN: So now we can put our thesis on a firmer footing, because it looks as if our study of history has led us to the same conclusion as before. This means we shall carry on our investigation on the basis of the actual facts rather than conjecture. The facts are, of course, as follows: each of the three royal families, and each of the three royal states they ruled, exchanged oaths in accordance with mutually binding laws which they had adopted to regulate the exercise of authority and obedience to it. The kings swore never to stiffen their rule as the nation continued down the years; the others undertook, provided the rulers kept to their side of the bargain, never themselves to overthrow the kingships nor tolerate an attempt to do so by others. The kings would help the kings and peoples if they were wronged, and the peoples would help the peoples and the kings likewise. That's right, isn't it?

MEGILLUS: Certainly.

ATHENIAN: Now whether it was the kings or someone else who laid down laws for this political system thus established in the three states, the crucial provision, surely, was this—

MEGILLUS: What?

ATHENIAN: Whenever a given state broke the established laws, an alliance of the other two would always be there to take the field against it.

MEGILLUS: Obviously.

ATHENIAN: Of course, most people only ask their legislators to enact the kind of laws that the population in general will accept without objection. But just imagine asking your trainer or doctor to give you pleasure when he trains or cures your body!

MEGILLUS: Exactly.

ATHENIAN: In fact, you often have to be satisfied if you can restore your body to health and vigor without undue pain.

MEGILLUS: True.

ATHENIAN: In another respect too the people of that time were particularly well placed to make legislation a painless process.

MEGILLUS: What respect?

ATHENIAN: Their legislators' efforts to establish a certain equality of property among them were not open to one particularly damaging accusation which is frequently made in other states. Suppose a legal code is being framed and someone adopts the policy of a change in the ownership of land and a cancellation of debts, because he sees that this is the only way in which equality can be satisfactorily achieved. 'Hands off fundamentals' is the slogan everybody uses to attack a legislator who tries to bring in that kind of reform, and his policy of land-redistribution and remission of debts earns him only curses. It's enough to make any man despair. So here is another tremendous advantage the Dorians enjoyed: the absence of resentment. No one could object to the way the land was parceled out, and large long-standing debts did not exist.

MEGILLUS: True.

ATHENIAN: Then why on earth, my friends, did this foundation and its legislation turn out such a dismal failure?

685   MEGILLUS: What do you mean by that? What's your objection?

ATHENIAN: Three states were founded but in two of them the political system and the legal code were quickly corrupted. Only the third settlement survived—that of your state, Sparta.

MEGILLUS: A pretty difficult problem you're posing!

ATHENIAN: Nevertheless, it demands our attention. So now let's look into it, and while away the journey, as we said when we set out, by amusing ourselves with laws—it's a dignified game and it suits our time

b   of life.

MEGILLUS: Of course. We must do as you say.

ATHENIAN: No laws could form a better subject for our investigation than those by which these states have been administered. Or are there any bigger or more famous states whose foundation we might examine?

MEGILLUS: No, it's not easy to think of alternatives.

ATHENIAN: Well then, it's pretty obvious that they intended the arrange-

c   ments they made to protect adequately not only the Peloponnese but the Greeks in general against any possible attack by non-Greeks—as for example occurred when those who then lived in the territory of Ilium trusted to the power of the Assyrian empire, which Ninos had founded, and provoked the war against Troy by their arrogance. You see, a good deal of the splendor of the Assyrian empire still remained, and the dread of its united organization was the counterpart in that age of our fear of the Great King of Persia today. The Assyrians had a tremendous grudge

d   against the Greeks: Troy, which was part of the Assyrian empire, had been captured for a second time.[7] To meet such dangers the Dorian army formed a single unified body, although at that period it was distributed among the three states under the command of the kings (who were brothers, being sons of Hercules). It seemed to be excellently conceived and equipped— better even than the army which sailed against Troy. For a start, people thought the sons of Hercules were, as commanders, a cut above the grand-

e   sons of Pelops;[8] secondly, they rated the prowess of the army itself higher than that of the expedition which went to Troy. After all, they calculated, *that* had consisted of Achaeans, the very people the Dorians had defeated. So may we take it that this was the nature and purpose of the arrangements they made?

7. For the first capture, see *Iliad* v.640.

8. Agamemnon and Menelaus, who led the expedition against Troy.

MEGILLUS: Certainly.

ATHENIAN: And for various reasons they probably expected these ar-   686
rangements would be permanent and last a long time. They had been
comrades in a great many toils and dangers in the past, and now they
had been brought under the control of a single family (the kings being
brothers); and they had also consulted a large number of prophets, notably
Apollo's at Delphi.

MEGILLUS: Yes, that's probable enough, of course.

ATHENIAN: But apparently these large expectations evaporated pretty   b
quickly, except, as we said a minute ago, in the case of just one small part
of the alliance—your state, Sparta. And right up to the present day Sparta
has never stopped fighting the other two members. But if they had done
as they intended and had agreed on a common policy, their power would
have been irresistible, militarily speaking.

MEGILLUS: It certainly would.

ATHENIAN: So just how did their plans misfire? This is surely a problem
we ought to look into: why was such a vast and tremendous organization
unlucky enough to be destroyed?

MEGILLUS: True: this is the right direction to look. Neglect these, and   c
you'll never find any other laws or political systems preserving (or eliminating) such remarkable and important features.

ATHENIAN: What a stroke of luck! It looks as if we've somehow got on
to a crucial point.

MEGILLUS: No doubt about it.

ATHENIAN: Well now, my fine fellow, what hackneyed thoughts we've
been having, without realizing it! When people see some tremendous
achievement, they always think to themselves, 'What terrific results it
would have led to, if someone had known how to set about putting it to   d
proper use!' Here and now, perhaps our ideas on the topic we are discussing are just as wrong and unrealistic as anybody else's who looks at
anything in that sort of way.

MEGILLUS: Well really, what *do* you mean? What are we supposed to
think you're driving at when you say that?

ATHENIAN: I was poking fun at no one but myself, my friend. I was
thinking about the army we are discussing and it occurred to me how
splendid it was and what a marvellous tool (as I said) had been put into
the hands of the Greeks—if only someone had put it to the proper use at
the time!

MEGILLUS: And you were quite right and sensible in everything you said,   e
and we heartily agreed with you—equally rightly and sensibly.

ATHENIAN: Maybe so. Still, my view is that everyone who sets eyes on
something big and strong and powerful immediately gets the feeling that
if the owner knew how to take advantage of its size and scale he would
get tremendous results and be a happy man.

687   MEGILLUS: And this again is surely right and proper. Or do you see it differently?

ATHENIAN: Well now, just consider what criteria a man ought to employ if he is going to be 'right' to give such praise in an individual case. What about the one we are discussing, for a start? Suppose those who undertook the organization of the army in that age had known their job: somehow, they would have succeeded in it—but the question is *how*. They ought, of course, to have consolidated their army and kept it on a permanent footing; this would have ensured them their own freedom while they ruled over anybody else they liked, and in general it would have enabled them to

b   do whatever they or their children wanted all over the world, among Greeks and non-Greeks indifferently. This is what men would praise them for, isn't it?

MEGILLUS: It is indeed.

ATHENIAN: Again, anyone who notices a case of great wealth or exceptional family distinction or something like that takes precisely the same line. He assumes that just because a man enjoys these advantages his every wish will be granted—or at any rate most of them, and the most important ones.

MEGILLUS: Quite likely.

c   ATHENIAN: Now then, this shows that there is one specific desire common to all mankind. Isn't this the upshot of our discussion?

MEGILLUS: What desire?

ATHENIAN: That events should obey whatever orders one feels like giving—invariably, if possible, but failing that, at least where human affairs are concerned.

MEGILLUS: Very true.

ATHENIAN: So seeing that this is the constant wish of us all, right from childhood to old age, isn't it inevitably what we are always *praying* for too?

MEGILLUS: Of course.

d   ATHENIAN: And I suppose our prayers on behalf of those whom we love will be for precisely what they themselves pray for on their own behalf?

MEGILLUS: Certainly.

ATHENIAN: A man who is a father loves the child who is his son?

MEGILLUS: Of course.

ATHENIAN: Yet there is a good deal in the son's prayers that the father will beg the gods never to grant.

MEGILLUS: You mean when the son who prays is still young and irresponsible?

ATHENIAN: Yes, and I'm thinking too of when the father is senile or even

e   unduly impulsive because of second childhood, and has lost all sense of what is right and proper. He gets into the same state as Theseus when he dealt with Hippolytus, who died so wretchedly,[9] and his prayers become very vehement indeed. But if the son understands the situation, do you think he will join in his father's prayers, given those circumstances?

MEGILLUS: I know what you mean. Your point, I take it, is that you should demand your own way in your prayers only if your wishes are supported by your rational judgment—and this, a rational outlook, should be the object of the prayers and efforts of us all, states and individuals alike.

ATHENIAN: It should indeed, and in particular—let me remind myself— it should always be the aim of a state's legislator when he frames the provisions of his laws. And I remind *you* again—to recollect the beginning of our discussion—of what you two recommended: you said that the good legislator should construct his entire legal code with a view to war;[10] for my part, I maintained that this was to order him to establish his laws with an eye on only one virtue out of the four. I said he ought to keep virtue as a whole in mind but especially and preeminently the virtue that heads the list—judgment and wisdom, and a strength of mind such that desires and appetites are kept under control. Our discussion has come full circle, and being the speaker at the moment I make the same point as before. You can treat it as a joke if you like, but if you prefer, you can take it seriously: I maintain that, if you lack wisdom, praying is a risky business, because you get the opposite of what you want. If you like to suppose that I am in earnest, do so: I'm confident that if you follow the line of argument we opened up a moment ago you'll soon discover that the cause of the ruin of the kings and the whole enterprise was not cowardice nor a lack of military expertise in the commanders or in those whose role it was to obey them. The disaster was caused by every other sort of vice, and in particular ignorance about mankind's most vital concerns. And if that was true then it is even more so today; and precisely the same will be true in the future. If you like, I'll try to press on with the next stages in the argument and develop the point. As you are my friends, I'll do my very best to make it clear.

CLINIAS: To make a speech in your praise, sir, would be a tasteless thing to do. Our actions rather than our words will show our regard for you: we shall give you our closest attention. This is the best way to tell whether a gentleman approves or not.

MEGILLUS: Well said, Clinias. Let's do as you say.

CLINIAS: And so we shall, God willing. Now let's have your explanation.

ATHENIAN: Well then, to go back on to the track of the argument, we maintain that crass ignorance destroyed that great empire, and that it has

688

b

c

d

e

---

9. Hippolytus' stepmother Phaedra falsely accused him of sexual misconduct towards herself; Theseus, her husband, prayed for the death of his son. The prayer was granted, but then Theseus discovered Hippolytus' innocence.

10. 625d ff.

a natural tendency to produce precisely the same results today. If this is so, it means that the legislator must try to inspire states with as much good sense as possible, and eradicate folly, as far as he can.

CLINIAS: Obviously.

689   ATHENIAN: So what kind of ignorance would deserve the title 'crass'? See if you agree with my description. I suggest this kind.

CLINIAS: What?

ATHENIAN: The kind involved when a man thinks something is fine and good, but loathes it instead of liking it, and conversely when he likes and welcomes what he believes is wicked and unjust. I maintain that this disaccord between his feelings of pleasure and pain and his rational judgment constitutes the very lowest depth of ignorance. It is also the most

b   'crass', in that it affects the most extensive element in the soul (the element that experiences pleasure and pain, which corresponds to the most extensive part of a state, the common people). So when the soul quarrels with knowledge or opinion or reason, its natural ruling principles, you have there what I call 'folly'. This applies both to the state in which people disobey their rulers and laws, and to the individual, when the fine principles in which he really believes prove not only ineffective but actually harmful. It's all these examples of ignorance that I should put down as

c   the worst kind of discord in a state and individual, not the mere professional ignorance of a workman. I hope you see what I mean, gentlemen.

CLINIAS: We do, my friend, and we agree with what you say.

ATHENIAN: So let's adopt this as an agreed statement of policy: no citizens who suffer from this kind of ignorance should be entrusted with any degree of power. They must be reproved for their ignorance, even if their ability to reason is outstanding and they have worked hard at every nice

d   accomplishment that makes a man quick-witted. It is those whose characters are at the other extreme who must be called 'wise', even if, as the saying is, 'they cannot read, they cannot swim'; and it is these sensible people who must be given the offices of state. You see, my friends, without concord, how could you ever get even a glimmer of sound judgment? It's out of the question. But we should be entirely justified in styling the greatest and most splendid concord of all 'the greatest wisdom'. Anyone who lives a rational life shares in this wisdom, but the man who lacks it will invariably turn out to be a spendthrift and no savior to the city—

e   quite the reverse, because he suffers from this particular kind of ignorance. So as we said just now, let's adopt this as the statement of our views.

CLINIAS: Adopted it is.

ATHENIAN: Now, I take it that states must contain some people who govern and others who are governed?

CLINIAS: Naturally.

690   ATHENIAN: Good. Well then, what titles are there to either rank? Can we count them? (I mean both in the state and in the family, in each case

irrespective of size.) One claim, surely, could be made by father and mother; and in general the title of parents to exercise control over their children and descendants would be universally acknowledged, wouldn't it?

CLINIAS: Of course.

ATHENIAN: Close behind comes the title of those of high birth to govern those of low birth. Next in order comes our third demand: that younger people should consent to be governed by their elders.

CLINIAS: Certainly.

ATHENIAN: The fourth is that slaves should be subject to the control of   b
their masters.

CLINIAS: No doubt about it.

ATHENIAN: And I suppose the fifth is that the stronger should rule and the weaker should obey.

CLINIAS: A pretty compelling claim to obedience, that!

ATHENIAN: Yes, and one which prevails throughout the animal kingdom—by decree of nature, as Pindar of Thebes once remarked.[11] But it looks as if the most important claim will be the sixth, that the ignorant man should follow the leadership of the wise and obey his orders. In spite of you, my clever Pindar, what I'd called the 'decree of nature' is in fact   c
the rule of law that governs willing subjects, without being imposed by force; I'm certainly not prepared to say it's *un*natural.

CLINIAS: Quite right.

ATHENIAN: And we persuade a man to cast lots, by explaining that this, the seventh title to authority, enjoys the favor of the gods and is blessed by fortune. We tell him that the fairest arrangement is for him to exercise authority if he wins, but to be subject to it if he loses.

CLINIAS: That's very true.

ATHENIAN: 'So you see, O legislator' (as we might jocularly address   d
someone who sets about legislation with undue optimism), 'you see how many titles to authority there are, and how they naturally conflict with each other. Now here's a source of civil strife we've discovered for you, which you must put to rights. First, though, join us in trying to find out how the kings of Argos and Messene went astray and broke these rules, and so destroyed themselves and the power of Greece, for all its splendor at that time. Wasn't it because they didn't appreciate the truth of Hesiod's   e
remark that the half is often greater than the whole?[12] He thought that when it is harmful to get the whole, and the half is enough, then enough is *better* than a feast, and is the preferable alternative.'

CLINIAS: True enough.

---

11. The Athenian alludes to a few lines of a poem now largely lost (frg. 109 Snell): cf. 714e and 890a.

12. *Works and Days* 40.

ATHENIAN: So where do we suppose this destructive process invariably starts? Among kings or people?

691   CLINIAS: Most instances suggest that this is probably a disease of kings whose life of luxury has made them arrogant.

ATHENIAN: So it is clear that it was the kings of that era who were first infected by the acquisitive spirit in defiance of the law of the land. The precise point to which they had given their seal of approval by their word and oath became the ground of their disagreement, and this lack of harmony (which is, in our view, the 'crassest' stupidity, though it looks like wisdom) put the whole arrangement jarringly off key and out of tune: hence its destruction.

CLINIAS: Quite likely.

b   ATHENIAN: Very well. Then what precautions ought a contemporary legislator to have taken in his code to nip this disease in the bud? God knows, the answer's not difficult nowadays, and the point is quite simple to understand—though if anyone had foreseen the problem then, assuming it was possible to do so, he'd have been wiser than we are.

MEGILLUS: What do you mean?

ATHENIAN: Hindsight, Megillus! In the perspective of today it's easy to understand what should have been done then, and once understood it's equally easy to explain.

MEGILLUS: You'd better be even clearer than that.

ATHENIAN: The clearest way of putting it would be this.

MEGILLUS: What?

c   ATHENIAN: If you neglect the rule of proportion and fit excessively large sails to small ships, or give too much food to a small body, or too high authority to a soul that doesn't measure up to it, the result is always disastrous. Body and soul become puffed up: disease breaks out in the one, and in the other arrogance quickly leads to injustice. Now, what are we getting at? Simply this: the mortal soul simply does not exist, my friends, which by dint of its natural qualities will ever make a success of

d   supreme authority among men while it is still young and responsible to no one. Full of folly, the worst of diseases, it inevitably has its judgment corrupted, and incurs the enmity of its closest friends; and once that happens, its total ruin and the loss of all its power soon follow. A first-class lawgiver's job is to have a sense of proportion and to guard against this danger. Nowadays it is a reasonable guess that this was in fact done at that time. However, it looks as if there was. . .

MEGILLUS: What?

ATHENIAN: . . . some god who was concerned on your behalf and saw what was going to happen. He took your single line of kings and split it into two,[13] so as to restrict its powers to more reasonable proportions. After

13. Procles and Eurysthenes, the first kings of Sparta, were the twin sons of Aristodemus.

that, a man[14] who combined human nature with some of the powers of a   e
god observed that your leadership was still in a feverish state, so he blended
the obstinacy and vigor of the Spartans with the prudent influence of age   692
by giving the twenty-eight elders the same authority in making important
decisions as the kings. Your 'third savior'[15] saw that your government was
still fretting and fuming with restless energy, so he put a kind of bridle
on it in the shape of the power of the ephors[16]—a power which came very
close to being held by lot. This is the formula that turned your kingship
into a mixture of the right elements, so that thanks to its own stability it
ensured the stability of the rest of the state. If things had been left to the
discretion of Temenus and Cresphontes and the legislators of that time,   b
whoever in fact they were, not even Aristodemus' part[17] would have survived. You see, they were tiros in legislation: otherwise it would never
have occurred to them to rely on oaths[18] to restrain the soul of a young
man who had taken over power from which a tyranny could develop. But
the fact is that God has demonstrated the sort of thing a position of authority
ought to have been then and should be now, if it is to have any prospects
of permanency. As I said before, we don't need any great wisdom to   c
recognize all this now—after all, it's not difficult to see the point if you
have a historical example to go by. But if anyone had seen all this then,
and had been able to control the various offices and produce a single
authority out of the three, he would have saved all the splendid projects
of that age from destruction, and neither the Persians nor anyone else
would ever have sent a fleet to attack Greece, contemptuously supposing
that we were people who counted for very little.

CLINIAS: That's true.

ATHENIAN: After all, Clinias, the way the Greeks repulsed them was a   d
disgrace. In saying this, I don't mean that those who won the battles of
that war by land and sea did not do so magnificently. By 'disgrace' I mean
that, to start with, only one of those three states fought to defend Greece.
The other two were rotten to the core. One of them[19] even hindered Sparta's
attempts to help the defense, and fought her tooth and nail, while the   e
other, Argos (which used to be paramount when the territory was first

14. Lycurgus, who created the Spartan Council of Elders.

15. The expression 'third savior' is proverbial, and refers to the custom of offering Zeus
the Savior the third libation at banquets. Plato probably means Theopompus, a king of
Sparta in the eighth century.

16. Five annually elected officials who in addition to wide executive and judicial powers
exercised close control over the conduct of the kings.

17. I.e., Sparta: see 683c ff. and 684e ff.

18. See 684a.

19. Messene. Cf. 698c–e.

divided up), although called upon to repel the barbarian, ignored the request and failed to contribute to the defense. A detailed history of the course of that war would have some pretty ugly charges to make against Greece: indeed, there is no reason why it should report that Greece made any defense at all. If it hadn't been for the joint determination of the

693 Athenians and the Spartans to resist the slavery that threatened them, we should have by now virtually a complete mixture of the races—Greek with Greek, Greek with barbarian, and barbarian with Greek. We can see a parallel in the nations whom the Persians lord it over today: they have been split up and then horribly jumbled together again into the scattered communities in which they now live. Well now, Clinias and Megillus, why are we making these accusations against the so-called 'statesmen' and legislators of that day and this? Because if we find out *why* they went

b wrong we shall discover what different course of action they ought to have followed. That is what we were doing just now, when we said that legislation providing for powerful or extreme authority is a mistake. One should always remember that a state ought to be free and wise and enjoy internal harmony, and that this is what the lawgiver should concentrate on in his legislation. (It ought not to surprise us if several times before now we

c have decided on a number of other aims and said *they* were what a lawgiver should concentrate on, so that the aims proposed never seem to be the same from minute to minute. When we say that the legislator should keep self-control or good judgment or friendship in view, we must bear in mind that all these aims are the same, not different. Nor should we be disconcerted if we find a lot of other expressions of which the same is true.)

CLINIAS: Yes, when we think back over the argument we'll certainly try to remember that. But you wanted to explain what the legislator ought to aim at in the matter of friendship and good judgment and liberty. So tell

d us now what you were going to say.

ATHENIAN: Listen to me then. There are two mother-constitutions, so to speak, which you could fairly say have given birth to all the others. Monarchy is the proper name for the first, and democracy for the second. The former has been taken to extreme lengths by the Persians, the latter by my country; virtually all the others, as I said, are varieties of these two. It is absolutely vital for a political system to combine them, *if* (and this is of course the point of our advice, when we insist that no state formed

e without these two elements can be constituted properly)—*if* it is to enjoy freedom and friendship applied with good judgment.

CLINIAS: Of course.

ATHENIAN: One state was over-eager in embracing only the principle of monarchy, the other in embracing only the ideal of liberty; neither has achieved a balance between the two. Your Spartan and Cretan states have done better, and time was when you could say much the same of the

694 Athenians and Persians, but things have changed since then. Let's run through the reasons for this, shall we?

CLINIAS: Yes, of course—if, that is, we mean to finish what we have set out to do.

ATHENIAN: Then let's listen to the story. Under Cyrus, the life of the Persians was a judicious blend of liberty and subjection, and after gaining their own freedom they became the masters of a great number of other people. As rulers, they granted a degree of liberty to their subjects and put them on the same footing as themselves, with the result that soldiers felt more affection for their commanders and displayed greater zeal in the   b face of danger. The king felt no jealousy if any of his subjects was intelligent and had some advice to offer; on the contrary, he allowed free speech and valued those who could contribute to the formulation of policy; a sensible man could use his influence to help the common cause. Thanks to freedom, friendship, and the practice of pooling their ideas, during that period the Persians made progress all along the line.

CLINIAS: It does rather look as if that was the situation in the period you describe.

ATHENIAN: So how are we to explain the disaster under Cambyses, and   c the virtually complete recovery under Darius?[20] To help our reconstruction of events, shall we have a shot at some inspired guessing?

CLINIAS: Yes, because this topic we've embarked on will certainly help our inquiry.

ATHENIAN: My guess, then, about Cyrus, is that although he was doubt-less a good commander and a loyal patriot, he never considered, even superficially, the problem of correct education; and as for running a house-hold, I'd say he never paid any attention to it at all.

CLINIAS: And what interpretation are we to put on a remark like that?

ATHENIAN: I mean that he probably spent his entire life after infancy on   d campaign, and handed over his children to the women to bring up. These women reared them from their earliest years as though they were already Heaven's special favorites and darlings, endowed with all the blessings that implies. They wouldn't allow anyone to thwart 'their Beatitudes' in anything, and they forced everybody to rhapsodize about what the children said or did. You can imagine the sort of person they produced.

CLINIAS: And a fine old education it must have been, to judge from your account.

ATHENIAN: It was a womanish education, conducted by the royal harem.   e The teachers of the children had recently come into considerable wealth, but they were left all on their own, without men, because the army was preoccupied by wars and constant dangers.

CLINIAS: That makes sense.

---

20. Cambyses, son of Cyrus, was King of Persia from 529 to 521. 'Disaster' refers to the military failures of his reign, his tyrannical madness, and the short-lived seizure of his throne by Gomates (see 695b and note). Cambyses was succeeded by Darius (521-486), who followed the prudent policies described in 695c–d. See Herodotus, III, 61 ff.

ATHENIAN: The children's father, for his part, went on accumulating herds and flocks for their benefit—and many a herd of human beings too, quite apart from every other sort of animal; but he didn't know that his intended heirs were not being instructed in the traditional Persian discipline. This discipline (the Persians being shepherds, and sons of a stony soil) was a tough one, capable of producing hardy shepherds who could camp out and keep awake on watch and turn soldier if necessary. He just didn't notice that women and eunuchs had given his sons the education of a Mede[21] and that it had been debased by their so-called 'blessed' status. That is why Cyrus' children turned out as children naturally do when their teachers have never corrected them. So, when they succeeded to their inheritance on the death of Cyrus, they were living in a riot of unrestrained debauchery. First, unwilling to tolerate an equal, one of them killed the other; next, he himself, driven out of his senses by liquor and lack of self-control, was deprived of his dominions by the Medes and 'the Eunuch' (as he was then called), to whom the idiot Cambyses was an object of contempt.[22]

CLINIAS: So the story goes, and it seems probable enough.

ATHENIAN: And it goes on, I think, to say that the empire was regained for the Persians by Darius and 'the Seven'.

CLINIAS: Certainly.

ATHENIAN: Now let's carry on with this story of ours and see what happened. Darius was no royal prince, and his upbringing had not encouraged him to self-indulgence. When he came and seized the empire with the aid of the other six, he split it up into seven divisions, of which some faint outlines still survive today. He thought the best policy was to govern it by new laws of his own which introduced a certain degree of equality for all; and he also included in his code regulations about the tribute promised to the people by Cyrus. His generosity in money and gifts rallied all the Persians to his side, and stimulated a feeling of community and friendship among them; consequently his armies regarded him with such affection that they added to the territory Cyrus had bequeathed at least as much again. But Darius was succeeded by Xerxes, whose education had reverted to the royal pampering of old. ('Darius'—as perhaps we'd be entitled to say to him—'you haven't learned from Cyrus' mistake, so you've brought up Xerxes in the same habits as Cyrus brought up Cambyses.') So Xerxes, being a product of the same type of education, naturally had a career that closely reproduced the pattern of Cambyses' misfortunes. Ever since then, hardly any king of the Persians has been genuinely 'great', except in style and title. I maintain that the reason for

21. I.e., an education of extreme luxury.
22. Gomates impersonated Cambyses' dead brother in order to seize the kingdom.

this is not just bad luck, but the shocking life that the children of dictators   696
and fantastically rich parents almost always lead: no man, you see, however
old or however young, will ever excel in virtue if he has had this sort of
upbringing. We repeat that this is the point the legislator must look out
for, and so must we here and now. And in all fairness, my Spartan friends,
one must give your state credit for at least this much: rich man, poor man,
commoner and king are held in honor to the same degree and are educated
in the same way, without privilege, except as determined by the supernatural instructions you received from some god when your state was   b
founded.[23] A man's exceptional wealth is no more reason for a state to
confer specially exalted office on him than his ability to run, his good
looks, or his physical strength, in the absence of some virtue—or even if
he *has* some virtue, if it excludes self-control.

MEGILLUS: What do you mean by that, sir?

ATHENIAN: Courage, I take it, is one part of virtue.

MEGILLUS: Of course.

ATHENIAN: So now that you've heard the story, use your own judgment:
would you be glad to have as a resident in your house or as a neighbor
a man who in spite of considerable courage was immoderate and licentious?

MEGILLUS: Heaven forbid!   c

ATHENIAN: Well then, what about a skilled workman, knowledgeable in
his own field, but unjust?

MEGILLUS: No, I'd never welcome him.

ATHENIAN: But surely, in the absence of self-control, justice will never
spring up.

MEGILLUS: Of course not.

ATHENIAN: Nor indeed will the 'wise' man we put forward just now,[24]
who keeps his feelings of pleasure and pain in tune with right reason and
obedient to it.

MEGILLUS: No, he certainly won't.

ATHENIAN: Now here's another point for us to consider, which will help
us to decide whether civic distinctions are, on a given occasion, conferred   d
correctly or incorrectly.

MEGILLUS: And what is that?

ATHENIAN: If we found self-control existing in the soul in isolation from
all other virtue, should we be justified in admiring it? Or not?

MEGILLUS: I really couldn't say.

ATHENIAN: A very proper reply. If you had opted for either alternative
it would have struck an odd note, I think.

MEGILLUS: So my reply was all right, then.

---

23. 624a ff. and 691d ff.
24. 689d ff.

ATHENIAN: Yes. But if you have something which in itself deserves to be admired or execrated, a mere additional element isn't worth talking
e   about: much better pass it over and say nothing.

MEGILLUS: Self-control is the element you mean, I suppose.

ATHENIAN: It is. And in general, whatever benefits us most, when this element is added, deserves the highest honor, the second most beneficial thing deserves the second highest honor, and so on: as we go down the list, everything will get in due order the honor it deserves.

697   MEGILLUS: True.

ATHENIAN: Well then, shan't we insist again[25] that the distribution of these honors is the business of the legislator?

MEGILLUS: Of course.

ATHENIAN: Would you prefer us to leave the entire distribution to his discretion and let him deal with the details of each individual case? But as we too have something of a taste for legislation, perhaps you'd like us to try our hands at a three-fold division and distinguish the most important class, then the second and the third.

MEGILLUS: Certainly.

b   ATHENIAN: We maintain that if a state is going to survive to enjoy all the happiness that mankind can achieve, it is vitally necessary for it to distribute honors and marks of disgrace on a proper basis. And the proper basis is to put spiritual goods at the top of the list and hold them—provided the soul exercises self-control—in the highest esteem; bodily goods and advantages should come second, and third those said to be provided by property and wealth. If a legislator or a state ever ignores these guide-
c   lines by valuing riches above all or by promoting one of the other inferior goods to a more exalted position, it will be an act of political and religious folly. Shall we take this line, or not?

MEGILLUS: Yes, emphatically and unambiguously.

ATHENIAN: It was our scrutiny of the political system of the Persians that made us go into this business at such length. Our verdict was that their corruption increased year by year; and the reason we assign for this is that they were too strict in depriving the people of liberty and too energetic
d   in introducing authoritarian government, so that they destroyed all friend-ship and community of spirit in the state. And with that gone, the policy of rulers is framed not in the interests of their subjects the people, but to support their own authority: let them only think that a situation offers them the prospect of some profit, even a small one, and they wreck cities and ruin friendly nations by fire and sword; they hate, and are hated in return, with savage and pitiless loathing. When they come to need the
e   common people to fight on their behalf, they discover the army has no loyalty, no eagerness to face danger and fight. They have millions and

25. Cf. 631e ff.

millions of soldiers—all useless for fighting a war, so that just as if manpower were in short supply, they have to hire it, imagining that mercenaries and foreigners will ensure their safety. Not only this, they inevitably become so stupid that they proclaim by their very actions that as compared with gold and silver everything society regards as good and valuable is in their eyes so much trash.

698

MEGILLUS: Exactly.

ATHENIAN: So let's have done with the Persians. Our conclusion is that the empire is badly run at the moment because the people are kept in undue subjection and the rulers excessively authoritarian.

MEGILLUS: Precisely.

ATHENIAN: Next we come to the political system of Attica. We have to demonstrate, on the same lines as before, that complete freedom from all authority is infinitely worse than submitting to a moderate degree of control.

b

At the time of the Persian attack on the Greeks—on virtually everyone living in Europe, is perhaps a better way of putting it—we Athenians had a constitution, inherited from the distant past, in which a number of public offices were held on the basis of four property-classes. Lady Modesty was the mistress of our hearts, a despot who made us live in willing subjection to the laws then in force. Moreover, the enormous size of the army that was coming at us by land and sea made us desperately afraid, and served to increase our obedience to the authorities and the law. For all these reasons we displayed a tremendous spirit of co-operation. You see, about ten years before the battle of Salamis, Datis had arrived at the head of a Persian army; he had been sent by Darius against the Athenians and the Eretrians with explicit instructions to make slaves of them and bring them home, and he had been warned that failure would mean death. With his vast numbers of soldiers, Datis made short work of the Eretrians, whom he completely overpowered and captured. He then sent to Athens a blood-curdling report that not a single Eretrian had got away—propaganda which asked us to believe that Datis' soldiers, hand in hand in a long line, had combed over every inch of Eretria. Well, whatever the truth or otherwise of this tale, it terrified the Greeks; the Athenians were particularly scared, and they sent off envoys in all directions, but no one was prepared to help them except the Spartans—who were, however, prevented by the Messenian war, which was going on at that time, or perhaps by some other distraction (I'm not aware of any information being given on the point). However that may be, the Spartans arrived at Marathon one day too late for the battle. After this, reports of vast preparations and endless threats on the part of the king came thick and fast. The years went by, and then we were told that Darius was dead, but that his son, young and impetuous, had inherited the kingdom and was determined not to give up the invasion. The Athenians reckoned that all these preparations were directed against themselves, because of what had happened at Marathon;

c

d

e

699

and when they heard of the canal that had been dug through Athos, the bridging of the Hellespont and the huge number of Xerxes' ships, they calculated that neither land nor sea offered any prospects of safety. No one, they thought, would come to help them. They remembered the previous attack and the success of the Persians in Eretria: no one had assisted
b the Athenians then, no one had faced the danger by fighting at their side. On land they expected the same thing to happen this time; and as for the sea, they realized that escape by this route was out of the question, in view of the thousand or more ships coming to the attack. They could think of only one hope, and a thin, desperate hope it was; but there was simply no other. Their minds went back to the previous occasion, and they reflected how the victory they won in battle had been gained in equally desperate
c circumstances. Sustained by this hope, they began to recognize that no one but they themselves and their gods could provide a way out of their difficulties. All this inspired them with a spirit of solidarity. One cause was the actual fear they felt at the time, but there was another kind too, encouraged by the traditional laws of the state. I mean the 'fear' they had learned to experience as a result of being subject to an ancient code of laws. In the course of our earlier discussion[26] we have called this fear 'modesty' often enough, and we said that people who aspire to be good must be its slave. A coward, on the other hand, is free of this particular kind of fear and never experiences it. And if 'ordinary' fear had not overtaken the cowards on that occasion, they would never have combined to defend themselves or protected temples, tombs, fatherland, and friends and rela-
d tives as well, in the way they did. We would all have been split up and scattered over the face of the earth.

MEGILLUS: Yes, sir, you are quite right, and your remarks reflect credit both on your country and yourself.

ATHENIAN: No doubt, Megillus; and it is only right and proper to tell you of the history of that period, seeing that you've been blessed with your ancestors' character. Now then, you and Clinias, consider: have these remarks of ours any relevance at all to legislation? After all, this is the object of the exercise—I'm not going through all this simply for the story.
e Look: in a way, we Athenians have had the same experience as the Persians. They, of course, reduced the people to a state of complete subjection, and we encouraged the masses to the opposite extreme of unfettered liberty, but the discussion we have had serves well enough as a pointer to the next step in the argument, and shows us the method to follow.

700 MEGILLUS: Splendid! But do try to be even more explicit about what you mean.

ATHENIAN: Very well. When the old laws applied, my friends, the people were not in control: on the contrary, they lived in a kind of 'voluntary slavery' to the laws.

26. At 647a, 671d.

MEGILLUS: Which laws have you in mind?

ATHENIAN: I'm thinking primarily of the regulations about the music of
that period (music being the proper place to start a description of how
life became progressively freer of controls). In those days Athenian music
comprised various categories and forms. One type of song consisted of   b
prayers to the gods, which were termed 'hymns'; and there was another
quite different type, which you might well have called 'laments'. 'Paeans'
made up a third category, and there was also a fourth, called a 'dithyramb'
(whose theme was, I think, the birth of Dionysus). There existed another
kind of song too, which they thought of as a separate class, and the name
they gave it was this very word that is so often on our lips: 'nomes'[27] ('for
the lyre', as they always added). Once these categories and a number of
others had been fixed, no one was allowed to pervert them by using one
sort of tune in a composition belonging to another category. And what was   c
the authority which had to know these standards and use its knowledge in
reaching its verdicts, and crack down on the disobedient? Well, certainly
no notice was taken of the catcalls and uncouth yelling of the audience,
as it is nowadays, nor yet of the applause that indicates approval. People
of taste and education made it a rule to listen to the performance with
silent attention right through to the end; children and their attendants and
the general public could always be disciplined and controlled by a stick.   d
Such was the rigor with which the mass of the people was prepared to
be controlled in the theatre, and to refrain from passing judgment by
shouting. Later, as time went on, composers arose who started to set a
fashion of breaking the rules and offending good taste. They did have a
natural artistic talent, but they were ignorant of the correct and legitimate
standards laid down by the Muse. Gripped by a frenzied and excessive
lust for pleasure, they jumbled together laments and hymns, mixed paeans
and dithyrambs, and even imitated pipe tunes on the lyre. The result
was a total confusion of styles. Unintentionally, in their idiotic way, they   e
misrepresented their art, claiming that in music there are no standards of
right and wrong at all, but that the most 'correct' criterion is the pleasure
of a man who enjoyed the performance, whether he is a good man or not.
On these principles they based their compositions, and they accompanied
them with propaganda to the same effect. Consequently they gave the
ordinary man not only a taste for breaking the laws of music but the
arrogance to set himself up as a capable judge. The audiences, once silent,   701
began to use their tongues; they claimed to know what was good and
bad in music, and instead of a 'musical meritocracy', a sort of vicious
'theatrocracy' arose. But if this democracy had been limited to gentlemen
and had applied only to music, no great harm would have been done; in
the event, however, music proved to be the starting point of everyone's
conviction that he was an authority on everything, and of a general

---

27. The Greek word is *nomoi*, which also means 'laws'. Cf. 722d, 775b, 799e.

disregard for the law. Complete license was not far behind. The conviction
b   that they *knew* made them unafraid, and assurance engendered effrontery.
You see, a reckless lack of respect for one's betters is effrontery of peculiar
viciousness, which springs from a freedom from inhibitions that has gone
much too far.

MEGILLUS: You're absolutely right.

ATHENIAN: This freedom will then take other forms. First people grow
unwilling to submit to the authorities, then they refuse to obey the admonitions of their fathers and mothers and elders. As they hurtle along towards
the end of this primrose path, they try to escape the authority of the laws;
c   and the very end of the road comes when they cease to care about oaths
and promises and religion in general. They reveal, reincarnated in themselves, the character of the ancient Titans[28] of the story, and thanks to
getting into the same position as the Titans did, they live a wretched life
of endless misery. Again I ask: what's the purpose of saying all this? My
tongue has been galloping on and obviously I ought to curb it constantly;
I must keep a bridle in my mouth and not let myself be carried away by
d   the argument so as to 'take a toss from the hoss', as the saying is. Let me
repeat the question: what's the point of this speech I've made?

MEGILLUS: Well asked!

ATHENIAN: The point is one we've made before.

MEGILLUS: What?

ATHENIAN: We said [29] that a lawgiver should frame his code with an eye
on three things: the freedom, unity and wisdom of the city for which he
legislates. That's right, isn't it?

MEGILLUS: Certainly.

e   ATHENIAN: That was why we selected two political systems, one authoritarian in the highest degree, the other representing an extreme of liberty;
and the question is now, which of these two constitutes correct government? We reviewed a moderate authoritarianism and a moderate freedom,
and saw the result: tremendous progress in each case. But when either the
Persians or the Athenians pushed things to extremes (of subjection in the
one case and its opposite in the other), it did neither of them any good at all.

702   MEGILLUS: You're quite right.

ATHENIAN: We had precisely the same purpose when we looked at the
settlement of the Dorian forces, Dardanus' dwellings in the foothills, the
foundation by the sea, and the original survivors of the flood; earlier, we
discussed music and drink from the same point of view, as well as other
topics before that. The object was always to find out what would be the
b   ideal way of administering a state, and the best principles the individual

28. Children of Heaven and Earth, long-standing enemies ultimately overthrown by the
Olympian gods.
29. See 693b.

can observe in running his own life. But has it been worth our while? I wonder, Clinias and Megillus, if there's some test of this that we could set ourselves?

CLINIAS: I think I can see one, sir. As luck would have it, I find that all the subjects we have discussed in our conversation are relevant to my needs here and now. How fortunate that I've fallen in with you and Megillus! I won't keep you in the dark about my position—indeed, I think that meeting you is a good omen for the future. The greater part of Crete is attempting to found a colony, and has given responsibility for the job to the Cnossians; and the state of Cnossus has delegated it to myself and nine colleagues. Our brief is to compose a legal code on the basis of such local laws as we find satisfactory, and to use foreign laws as well—the fact that they are not Cretan must not count against them, provided their quality seems superior. So what about doing me—and you—a favor? Let's take a selection of the topics we have covered and construct an imaginary community, pretending that we are its original founders. That will allow us to consider the question before us, and it may be that I'll use this framework for the future state.

ATHENIAN: Well, Clinias, that's certainly welcome news! You may take it that I for my part am entirely at your disposal, unless Megillus has some objection.

CLINIAS: Splendid!

MEGILLUS: Yes, I too am at your service.

CLINIAS: I'm delighted you both agree. Now then, let's try—initially only in theory—to found our state.

Book IV

ATHENIAN: Well, now, how should we describe our future state? I don't mean just its name: I'm not asking what it's called now, nor what it ought to be called in the future. (This might well be suggested by some detail of the actual foundation or by some spot nearby: perhaps a river or spring or some local gods will give the new state their own style and title.) This is my real question: is it to be on the coast, or inland?

CLINIAS: The state I was talking about a moment ago, sir, is approximately eighty stades[1] from the sea.

ATHENIAN: Well, what about harbors? Are there any along the coast on that side of the state, or are they entirely absent?

CLINIAS: No, sir. The state has harbors in that direction which could hardly be bettered.

ATHENIAN: A pity, that. What about the surrounding countryside? Does it grow everything or are there some deficiencies?

---

1. Nine or ten miles.

CLINIAS: No, it grows practically everything.

ATHENIAN: Will it have some nearby state for a neighbor?

CLINIAS: Absolutely none—that's just why it's being founded. Ages ago, there was a migration from the district, which has left the land deserted for goodness knows how long.

ATHENIAN: What about plains and mountains and forests? How is it off for each of these?

d   CLINIAS: Very much like the rest of Crete in general.

ATHENIAN: Rugged rather than flat, you mean?

CLINIAS: Yes, that's right.

ATHENIAN: Then the state will have tolerably healthy prospects of becoming virtuous. If it were going to be founded near the sea and have good harbors, and were deficient in a great number of crops instead of growing everything itself, then a very great savior indeed and lawgivers of divine stature would be needed to stop sophisticated and vicious characters developing on a grand scale: such a state would simply invite it. As it is, we can take comfort in those eighty stades. Even so, it lies nearer the sea than it should, and you say that it is rather well off for harbors, which makes

705   matters worse; but let's be thankful for small mercies. For a country to have the sea nearby is pleasant enough for the purpose of everyday life, but in fact it is a 'salty-sharp and bitter neighbor'[2] in more senses than one. It fills the land with wholesaling and retailing, breeds shifty and deceitful habits in a man's soul, and makes the citizens distrustful and hostile, not only among themselves, but also in their dealings with the world outside. Still, the fact that the land produces everything will be

b   some consolation for these disadvantages, and it is obvious in any case that even if it does grow every crop, its ruggedness will stop it doing so in any quantity; if it yielded a surplus that could be exported in bulk, the state would be swamped with the gold and silver money it received in return—and this, if a state means to develop just and noble habits, is pretty nearly the worst thing that could happen to it, all things considered (as we said, if we remember, earlier in our discussion).

CLINIAS: Of course we remember, and we agree that our argument then was right, and still is now.

c   ATHENIAN: The next point is this: how well is the surrounding district supplied with timber for building ships?

CLINIAS: There are no firs or pines worth mentioning, and not much by way of cypress, though you'll find a small quantity of plane and Aleppo pine, which is, of course, the standard material shipwrights must have to construct the interior parts of a boat.

ATHENIAN: That too is a feature of the country which will do it no harm.

CLINIAS: Oh?

---

2. Apparently in part a quotation from Alcman, a Spartan poet of the seventh century. See D. A. Campbell, *Greek Lyric* (Loeb), vol. II, pp. 468–69.

ATHENIAN: It's a good thing that a state should find it difficult to lower itself to copy the wicked customs of its enemies.

CLINIAS: And what on earth has been said to prompt *that* remark?

ATHENIAN: My dear sir, cast your mind back to the beginning of our discussion and watch what I'm up to. Do you remember the point we made about the laws of the Cretans having only one object, and how in particular the two of you asserted that this was warfare? I took you up on the point and argued that in so far as such institutions were established with virtue as their aim, they were to be approved; but I took strong exception to their aiming at only a part of virtue instead of the whole. Now it's your turn: keep a sharp eye on this present legislation, in case I lay down some law which is not conducive to virtue, or which fosters only a part of it. I'm going on the assumption that a law is well enacted only if it constantly aims, like an archer, at that unique target which is the only object of legislation to be invariably and uninterruptedly attended by some good result; the law must ignore everything else (wealth or anything like that), if it happens not to meet the requirements I have stipulated. This 'disgraceful copying of enemies' to which I was referring occurs when people live by the sea and are plagued by such foes as Minos, who once forced the inhabitants of Attica to pay a most onerous tribute (though of course in saying this I've no wish at all to hark back to our old grudges against you).[3] Minos exercised tremendous power at sea, whereas the Athenians had not yet acquired the fighting ships they have today, nor was their country so rich in supplies of suitable timber that they could readily construct a strong fleet; consequently they couldn't turn themselves into sailors at a moment's notice and repel the enemy by copying the Cretan use of the sea. Even if they *had* been able to do that, it would have done them more good to lose seven boys over and over again rather than get into bad habits by forming themselves into a navy. They had previously been infantrymen, and infantrymen can stand their ground; but sailors have the bad habit of dashing at frequent intervals and then beating a very rapid retreat indeed back to their ships. They see nothing disgraceful at all in a craven refusal to stand their ground and die as the enemy attacks, nor in the plausible excuses they produce so readily when they drop their weapons and take to their heels—or, as they put it, 'retreat without dishonor'. This is the sort of terminology you must expect if you make your soldiers into sailors; these expressions are not 'beyond praise' (far from it): men ought never to be trained in bad habits, least of all the citizen-elite. Even from Homer, I suspect, you can see that this is bad policy. He has Odysseus pitching into Agamemnon for ordering the ships to be put to sea just when the Achaeans were being hard put to it in their fight with the Trojans. In his anger, Odysseus says to him:

3. The Athenians killed Androgeos, son of Minos, King of Crete, who then exacted a tribute of seven girls and seven boys as victims for the Minotaur, a Cretan monster.

e
> *Why bid the well-benched ships be put to sea,*
> *When in our ears the noise of battle rings?*
> *Do you want the Trojans' dearest wish fulfilled,*
> *and utter ruin send us to the grave?*
> *Put the ships to sea, and watch the Achaeans*
> *buckle to the fight! No: they'll scuttle off*
> *and shrink away from battle. The advice you give*
> *will mean the end of us.*[4]

707   So Homer too realized that it is bad tactics to have triremes lined up at sea in support of infantry in the field. This is the sort of habit-training that will soon make even lions run away from deer. And that's not all. When a state which owes its power to its navy wins a victory, the bravest soldiers never get the credit for it, because the battle is won thanks to the skill of

b   steersman, boatswain and rower and the efforts of a motley crowd of ragamuffins, which means that it is impossible to honor each individual in the way he deserves. Rob a state of its power to do that, and you condemn it to failure.

CLINIAS: I suppose that's more or less inevitable. But in spite of that, sir, it was by fighting at sea at Salamis against the barbarians that the Greeks saved their country—according to us Cretans, anyway.

c   ATHENIAN: Yes, that's what most people say, Greek and non-Greek alike. Still, my friend, we—Megillus here and myself—are arguing in favor of two battles fought on land: Marathon, which first got the Greeks out of danger, and Plataea, which finally made them really safe. We maintain that these battles *improved* the Greeks, whereas the fighting at sea had the opposite effect. I hope this isn't too strong language to use about battles that at the time certainly helped to ensure our survival (and I'll concede you the battle at Artemisium as well as the one at Salamis). That's all very

d   well, but when we examine the natural features of a country and its legal system, our ultimate object of scrutiny is of course the quality of its social and political arrangements. We do not hold the common view that a man's highest good is to survive and simply continue to exist. His highest good is to become as virtuous as possible and to continue to exist in that state as long as life lasts. But I think we've already taken this line before.

CLINIAS: Of course.

ATHENIAN: Then we need consider only one thing: is the method we are following the same as before? Can we assume it is the best way to found a state and legislate for it?

CLINIAS: Yes, it's by far the best.

e   ATHENIAN: Now for the next point. Tell me, what people will you be settling? Will your policy be to accept all comers from the whole of Crete, on the grounds that the population in the individual cities has exceeded

---

4. *Iliad* xiv.96–102.

the number that can be supported by the land? I don't suppose you're taking all comers from the Greeks in general—though in fact I notice that some settlers from Argos and Aegina and other parts of Greece have come to settle in your country. But tell me what you intend on this occasion: where do you think your citizen body will come from this time?

CLINIAS: They will probably come from all over Crete; as for the other Greeks, I imagine settlers from the Peloponnese will be particularly welcome. You are quite right in what you said just now, that there are some here from Argos: they include the Gortynians, the most distinguished of the local people, who hail from the well-known Gortyn in the Peloponnese.

ATHENIAN: So it won't be all that easy for the Cretan states to found their colony. The emigrants, you see, haven't the unity of a swarm of bees: they are not a single people from a single territory settling down to form a colony with mutual goodwill between themselves and those they have left behind. Such migrations occur because of the pressures of land-shortage or some similar misfortune: sometimes a given section of the community may be obliged to go off and settle elsewhere because it is harassed by civil war, and on one occasion a whole state took to its heels after being overcome by an attack it could not resist. In all these cases to found a state and give it laws is, in some ways, comparatively easy, but in others it's rather difficult. When a single people speaks the same language and observes the same laws you get a certain feeling of community, because everyone shares the same religious rites and so forth; but they certainly won't find it easy to accept laws or political systems that differ from their own. Sometimes, when it's bad laws that have stimulated the revolt, and the rebels try in their new home to keep to the same familiar habits that ruined them before, their reluctance to toe the line presents the founder and lawgiver with a difficult problem. On the other hand, a miscellaneous combination of all kinds of different people will perhaps be more ready to submit to a new code of laws—but to get them to 'pull and puff as one' (as they say of a team of horses) is very difficult and takes a long time. There's no escaping it: founding a state and legislating for it is a superb test that separates the men from the boys.

CLINIAS: I dare say; but what do you mean? Please be a little clearer.

ATHENIAN: My dear fellow, now that I'm going back to considering legislators again, I think I'm actually going to insult them: but no matter, so long as the point is relevant. Anyway, why should I have qualms about it? It seems true of pretty nearly all human affairs.

CLINIAS: What are you getting at?

ATHENIAN: I was going to say that no man ever legislates at all. Accidents and calamities occur in a thousand different ways, and it is they that are the universal legislators of the world. If it isn't pressures of war that overturn a constitution and rewrite the laws, it's the distress of grinding poverty; and disease too forces us to make a great many innovations, when plagues beset us for years on end and bad weather is frequent and prolonged. Realizing all these possibilities, you may jump to conclusions b   and say what I said just now, that no mortal ever passes any law at all, and that human affairs are almost entirely at the mercy of chance. Now of course this same view could equally plausibly be taken of the profession of the steersman or doctor or general—but at the same time there's another point that could be made about all these examples, and with no less justification.

CLINIAS: What?

ATHENIAN: That the all-controlling agent in human affairs is God, assisted by the secondary influences of 'chance' and 'opportunity'. A less uncom-

c   promising way of putting it is to acknowledge that there must be a third factor, namely 'skill', to back up the other two. For instance, in a storm the steersman may or may not use his skill to seize any favorable opportunity that may offer. I'd say it would help a great deal if he did, wouldn't you?

CLINIAS: Yes.

ATHENIAN: So the same will apply in the other cases too, and legislation in particular must be allowed to play the same role. If a state is to live in happiness, certain local conditions must be present, and when all these coincide, what the community needs to find is a legislator who understands the right way to go about things.

CLINIAS: Very true.

d   ATHENIAN: So a professional man in each of the fields we've enumerated could hardly go wrong if he prayed for conditions in which the workings of chance needed only to be supplemented by his own skill.

CLINIAS: Certainly.

ATHENIAN: And all the other people we've instanced would of course be able to tell you what conditions they were praying for, if you asked them.

CLINIAS: Of course.

ATHENIAN: And I fancy a legislator would do just the same.

CLINIAS: I agree.

e   ATHENIAN: 'Well now, legislator,' let's say to him, 'tell us your requirements. What conditions in the state we are going to give you will enable you to run it properly on your own from now on?' What's the right answer to a question like that? (We're giving the legislator's answer for him, I take it.)

CLINIAS: Yes.

ATHENIAN: Then this is what he'll say: 'Give me a state under the absolute control of a dictator, and let the dictator be young, with a good memory, quick to learn, courageous, and with a character of natural elevation. And

710 if his other abilities are going to be any use, his dictatorial soul should also possess that quality which was earlier agreed to be an essential adjunct to all the parts of virtue.'

CLINIAS: I think the 'essential adjunct' our companion means, Megillus, is self-control. Right?

ATHENIAN: Yes, Clinias—but the everyday kind, not the kind we speak of in a heightened sense, when we compel self-control to be good judgment

as well. I mean the spontaneous instinct that flowers earlier in life in children and animals and in some cases succeeds in imposing a certain restraint in the search for pleasure, but fails in others. We said that if this quality existed in isolation from the many other merits we are discussing,   b
it was not worth consideration. You see my point, I take it.

CLINIAS: Of course.

ATHENIAN: This is the innate quality our dictator must have, in addition to the others, if the state is going to get, as quickly and efficiently as possible, a political system that will enable it to live a life of supreme happiness. You see, there is no quicker or better method of establishing a political system than this one, nor could there ever be.

CLINIAS: Well sir, how can a man convince himself that he is talking   c
sense in maintaining all this? What arguments are there for it?

ATHENIAN: It's easy enough, surely, to see that the very facts of the case make the doctrine true.

CLINIAS: What do you mean? If we were to get a dictator, you say, who is young, restrained, quick to learn, with a retentive memory, courageous and elevated—

ATHENIAN: —and don't forget to add 'lucky' too, in this one point: he should be the contemporary of a distinguished lawgiver, and be fortunate enough to come into contact with him. If that condition is fulfillled, God   d
will have done nearly all that he usually does when he wants to treat a state with particular favor. The next best thing would be a pair of such dictators; the third best would be several of them. The difficulties are in direct proportion to the numbers.

CLINIAS: It looks as if your position is this: the best state will be the product of a dictatorship, thanks to the efforts of a first-rate legislator and a well-behaved dictator, and this will be the quickest and easiest way to bring about the transformation. The second best will be to start with an oligarchy—is that your point, or what?—and the third to start with   e
a democracy.

ATHENIAN: Certainly not. The ideal starting point is dictatorship, the next best is constitutional kingship, and the third is some sort of democracy. Oligarchy comes fourth, because it has the largest number of powerful people, so that it admits the growth of a new order only with difficulty. And we maintain, of course, that such a growth takes place when circumstances throw up a genuine lawgiver who comes to share a degree of power with the most influential persons in the state. Where the most influential element   711
is both extremely powerful and numerically as small as it could be, as in a dictatorship, you usually get a rapid and trouble-free transition.

CLINIAS: How? We don't understand.

ATHENIAN: We've made the point more than once, I think. Perhaps you two have not so much as seen a state under the control of a dictator.

CLINIAS: No, and I don't particularly want to, either.

ATHENIAN: Still, suppose you did: you'd notice something we remarked   b
on just now.

CLINIAS: What's that?

ATHENIAN: That when a dictator wants to change the morals of a state, he doesn't need to exert himself very much or spend a lot of time on the job. He simply has to be the first to set out on the road along which he wishes to urge the citizens—whether to the practice of virtue or vice— and give them a complete moral blueprint by setting his own personal

c   example; he must praise and commend some courses of action and censure others, and in every field of conduct he must see that anyone who disobeys is disgraced.

CLINIAS: And why should we expect the citizens to obey, with such alacrity, a man who combines persuasion with compulsion like that?

ATHENIAN: My friends, there's no quicker or easier way for a state to change its laws than to follow the leadership of those in positions of power; there is no other way now, nor will there be in the future, and we shouldn't let anyone persuade us to the contrary. Actually, you see, it's not simply

d   this that is impossible or difficult to achieve. What *is* difficult, and a very rare occurrence in the history of the world, is something else; but when it does occur, the state concerned reaps the benefit on a grand scale— indeed, there's no blessing that will pass it by.

CLINIAS: What occurrence do you mean?

ATHENIAN: A situation in which an inspired passion for the paths of restraint and justice guides those who wield great power. The passion may seize a single supreme ruler, or perhaps men who owe their power

e   to exceptional wealth or high birth; or you may get a reincarnation of Nestor, who, superior as he was to all mankind for the vigor of his speech, is said to have put them in the shade even more by his qualities of restraint. In Trojan times, they say, such a paragon did exist, but he is certainly unheard of today. Still, granted someone like that did in fact exist in the past or is going to in the future, or is alive among us now, blessed is the life of this man of moderation, and blessed they who listen to the words

712 that fall from his lips. And whatever the form of government, the same doctrine holds true: where supreme power in a man joins hands with wise judgment and self-restraint, there you have the birth of the best political system, with laws to match; you'll never achieve it otherwise. So much for my somewhat oracular fiction! Let's take it as established that though in one sense it is difficult for a state to acquire a good set of laws, in another sense nothing could be quicker or easier—granted, of course, the conditions I've laid down.

CLINIAS: How so?

b   ATHENIAN: What about pretending the fiction is true of your state, Clinias, and having a shot at making up its laws? Like children, we old men love a bit of make-believe.

CLINIAS: Yes, what are we waiting for? Let's get down to it.

ATHENIAN: Let us therefore summon God to attend the foundation of the state. May he hear our prayers, and having heard, come graciously and benevolently to help us settle our state and its laws.

CLINIAS: May he come indeed.

ATHENIAN: Well now, what political system do we intend to impose on the state?

CLINIAS: Please be a little more explicit about what you really mean by that question. Do you mean we have to choose between a democracy, an oligarchy, and an aristocracy? Presumably you're hardly contemplating a dictatorship—or so we'd think, at any rate.

ATHENIAN: Well then, which of you would be prepared to answer first and tell us which of these terms fits the political system of your homeland?

MEGILLUS: Isn't it right and proper for me to answer first, as the elder?

CLINIAS: Perhaps so.

MEGILLUS: Very well. When I consider the political system in force at Sparta, sir, I find it impossible to give you a straight answer: I just can't say what one ought to call it. You see, it really does look to me like a dictatorship (it has the ephors, a remarkably dictatorial institution), yet on occasions I think it gets very close to being run democratically. But then again, it would be plain silly to deny that it is an aristocracy; and there is also a kingship (held for life), which both we and the rest of the world speak of as the oldest kingship of all. So when I'm asked all of a sudden like this, the fact is, as I said, that I can't distinguish exactly which of these political systems it belongs to.

CLINIAS: I'm sure I'm in the same predicament as you, Megillus. I find it acutely difficult to say for sure that the constitution we have in Cnossus comes into any of these categories.

ATHENIAN: And the reason, gentlemen, is this: you really do operate constitutions worthy of the name. The ones we called constitutions just now are not really that at all: they are just a number of ways of running a state, all of which involve some citizens living in subjection to others like slaves, and the state is named after the ruling class in each case. But if that's the sort of principle on which your new state is to be named, it should be called after the god who really does rule over men who are rational enough to let him.

CLINIAS: What god is that?

ATHENIAN: Well, perhaps we ought to make use of this fiction a little more, if we are going to clear up the question at issue satisfactorily.

CLINIAS: Yes, that will be the right procedure.

ATHENIAN: It certainly will. Well now, countless ages before the formation of the states we described earlier,[5] they say there existed, in the age of Cronus, a form of government and administration which was a great success, and which served as a blueprint for the best run of our present-day states.

CLINIAS: Then I think we simply must hear about it.

ATHENIAN: Yes, I agree. That's just why I introduced it into the discussion.

---

5. Accepting the conjecture of *anerōtētheis* in e4.

CLINIAS: You were quite right to do so, and seeing how relevant it is,
c   you'll be entirely justified in giving a systematic account of what happened.

ATHENIAN: I must try to meet your wishes. The traditional account that
has come down to us tells of the wonderfully happy life people lived then,
and how they were provided with everything in abundance and without
any effort on their part. The reason is alleged to be this: Cronus was of
course aware that human nature, as we've explained,[6] is never able to take
complete control of all human affairs without being filled with arrogance
d   and injustice. Bearing this in mind, he appointed kings and rulers for our
states; they were not men, but beings of a superior and more divine order—
spirits. We act on the same principle nowadays in dealing with our flocks
of sheep and herds of other domesticated animals: we don't put cattle in
charge of cattle or goats in charge of goats, but control them ourselves,
because we are a superior species. So Cronus too, who was well-disposed
to man, did the same: he placed us in the care of the spirits, a superior
order of beings, who were to look after our interests—an easy enough
e   task for them, and a tremendous boon to us, because the result of their
attentions was peace, respect for others, good laws, justice in full measure,
and a state of happiness and harmony among the races of the world. The
story has a moral for us even today, and there is a lot of truth in it: where
the ruler of a state is not a god but a mortal, people have no respite from
toil and misfortune. The lesson is that we should make every effort to
imitate the life men are said to have led under Cronus; we should run our
public and our private life, our homes and our cities, in obedience to what
714 little spark of immortality lies in us, and dignify these edicts of reason
with the name of 'law'. But take an individual man, or an oligarchy, or
even a democracy, that lusts in its heart for pleasure and demands to have
its fill of everything it wants—the perpetually unsatisfied victim of an evil
greed that attacks it like the plague—well, as we said just now, if a power
like that controls a state or an individual and rides roughshod over the
laws, it's impossible to escape disaster. This is the doctrine we have to
b   examine, Clinias, and see whether we are prepared to go along with it—
or what?

CLINIAS: Of course we must go along with it.

ATHENIAN: You realize that some people maintain that there are as many
different kinds of laws as there are of political systems? (And of course
we've just run through the many types of political systems there are
popularly supposed to be.) Don't think the question at issue is a triviality:
it's supremely important, because in effect we've got back to arguing about
the criteria of justice and injustice. These people take the line that legislation
c   should be directed not to waging war or attaining complete virtue, but to
safeguarding the interests of the established political system, whatever
that is, so that it is never overthrown and remains permanently in force.

6. See 691c.

They say that the definition of justice that measures up to the facts is best formulated like this.

CLINIAS: How?

ATHENIAN: It runs: 'Whatever serves the interest of the stronger'.

CLINIAS: Be a little more explicit, will you?

ATHENIAN: The point is this: according to them, the element in control at any given moment lays down the law of the land. Right?

CLINIAS: True enough.

ATHENIAN: 'So do you imagine,' they say, 'that when a democracy has   d
won its way to power, or some other constitution has been established (such as dictatorship), it will ever pass any laws, unless under pressure, except those designed to further its own interests and ensure that it remains permanently in power? That'll be its main preoccupation, won't it?'

CLINIAS: Naturally.

ATHENIAN: So the author of these rules will call them 'just' and claim that anyone who breaks them is acting 'unjustly', and punish him?

CLINIAS: Quite likely.

ATHENIAN: So this is why such rules will always add up to 'justice'.

CLINIAS: Certainly, on the present argument.

ATHENIAN: We are, you see, dealing with one of those 'claims to au-   e
thority'.[7]

CLINIAS: What claims?

ATHENIAN: The ones we examined before, when we asked who should rule whom. It seemed that parents should rule children, the elder the younger, and the noble those of low birth; and there was a large number of other titles to authority, if you remember, some of which conflicted with others. The claim we're talking about now was certainly one of these: we said, I think, that Pindar turned it into a law of nature—which meant that he 'justified the use of force extreme', to quote his actual words.[8]   715

CLINIAS: Yes, those are the points that were made.

ATHENIAN: Now look: to which side in the dispute should we entrust our state? In some cities, you see, this is the sort of thing that has happened thousands of times.

CLINIAS: What?

ATHENIAN: When offices are filled competitively, the winners take over the affairs of state so completely that they totally deny the losers and the losers' descendants any share of power. Each side passes its time in a narrow scrutiny of the other, apprehensive lest someone with memories   b
of past injustices should gain some office and lead a revolution. Of course, our position is that this kind of arrangement is very far from being a genuine political system; we maintain that laws which are not established for the good of the whole state are bogus laws, and when they favor

---

7. See 690a ff.

8. See 690b and note.

particular sections of the community, their authors are not citizens but party-men; and people who say those laws have a claim to be obeyed are wasting their breath. We've said all this because in your new state we

c aren't going to appoint a man to office because of his wealth or some other claim like that, say strength or stature or birth. We insist that the highest office in the service of the gods must be allocated to the man who is best at obeying the established laws and wins *that* sort of victory in the state; the man who wins the second prize must be given second rank in that service, and so on, the remaining posts being allocated in order on the same system. Such people are usually referred to as 'rulers', and if I have

d called them 'servants of the laws' it's not because I want to mint a new expression but because I believe that the success or failure of a state hinges on this point more than on anything else. Where the law is subject to some other authority and has none of its own, the collapse of the state, in my view, is not far off; but if law is the master of the government and the government is its slave, then the situation is full of promise and men enjoy all the blessings that the gods shower on a state. That's the way I see it.

e CLINIAS: By heaven, sir, you're quite right. You've the sharp eye of an old man for these things.

ATHENIAN: Yes, when we're young, we're all pretty blind to them; old age is the best time to see them clearly.

CLINIAS: Very true.

ATHENIAN: Well, what now? I suppose we should assume our colonists have arrived and are standing before us. So we shall have to finish off the topic by addressing them.

CLINIAS: Of course.

ATHENIAN: Now then, our address should go like this: 'Men, according to the ancient story, there is a god who holds in his hands the beginning

716 and end and middle of all things, and straight he marches in the cycle of nature. Justice, who takes vengeance on those who abandon the divine law, never leaves his side. The man who means to live in happiness latches on to her and follows her with meekness and humility. But he who bursts with pride, elated by wealth or honors or by physical beauty when young and foolish, whose soul is afire with the arrogant belief that so far from needing someone to control and lead him, he can play the leader to others—

b there's a man whom God has deserted. And in his desolation he collects others like himself, and in his soaring frenzy he causes universal chaos. Many people think he cuts a fine figure, but before very long he pays to Justice no trifling penalty and brings himself, his home and state to rack and ruin. Thus it is ordained. What action, then, should a sensible man take, and what should his outlook be? What must he *avoid* doing or thinking?'

CLINIAS: This much is obvious: every man must resolve to belong to those who follow in the company of God.

c ATHENIAN: 'So what conduct recommends itself to God and reflects his wishes? There is only one sort, epitomized in the old saying "like approves of like" (excess apart, which is both its own enemy and that of due proportion). In our view it is God who is preeminently the "measure of all things," much more so than any "man," as they say.[9] So if you want to recommend yourself to someone of this character, you must do your level best to make your own character reflect his, and on this principle the moderate man is God's friend, being like him, whereas the immoderate and unjust man is not like him and is his enemy; and the same reasoning applies to the other vices too.

'Let's be clear that the consequence of all this is the following doctrine (which is, I think, of all doctrines the finest and truest): If a good man sacrifices to the gods and keeps them constant company in his prayers and offerings and every kind of worship he can give them, this will be the best and noblest policy he can follow; it is the conduct that fits his character as nothing else can, and it is his most effective way of achieving a happy life. But if the wicked man does it, the results are bound to be just the opposite. Whereas the good man's soul is clean, the wicked man's soul is polluted, and it is never right for a good man or for God to receive gifts from unclean hands—which means that even if impious people do lavish a lot of attention on the gods, they are wasting their time, whereas the trouble taken by the pious is very much in season. So this is the target at which we should aim—but what "missiles" are we to use to hit it, and what "bow" is best carried to shoot them? Can we name these "weapons"? The first weapon in our armory will be to honor the gods of the underworld next after those of Olympus, the patron-gods of the state; the former should be allotted such secondary honors as the Even and the Left, while the latter should receive superior and contrasting honors like the Odd.[10] That's the best way a man can hit his target, piety. After these gods, a sensible man will worship the spirits, and after them the heroes. Next in priority will be rites celebrated according to law at private shrines dedicated to ancestral gods. Last come honors paid to living parents. It is meet and right that a debtor should discharge his first and greatest obligation and pay the debt which comes before all others; he must consider that all he has and holds belongs to those who bore and bred him, and he is meant to use it in their service to the limit of his powers. He must serve them first with his property, then with hand and brain, and so give to the old people what they desperately need in view of their age: repayment of all that anxious care and attention they lavished on him, the longstanding "loan" they made him as a child. Throughout his life the son must be very careful to watch his tongue in addressing his parents, because there is a very heavy penalty for careless and ill-considered language; Retribution, messenger of Justice, is the appointed overseer of these things. If his parents get angry, he must submit to them, and whether they satisfy their anger

9. Protagoras, a philosopher and sophist of the fifth century, maintained that 'man is the measure of all things'.

10. A reference to the Pythagorean list of opposites: Odd, Even; Right, Left; Male, Female; Good, Bad; and a number of others.

in speech or in action, he must forgive them; after all, he must reflect, it's natural enough for a father to get very angry if he thinks he's being harmed by his own son. When the parents die, the most modest burial will be best, and the ceremonies should not be more elaborate than custom demands nor

e inferior to those with which his forefathers laid their own parents to rest. Year by year he should honor the departed by similar acts of devotion;

718 he will honor them best by never failing to provide a perpetual memorial to them, spending on the dead a proper proportion of the money he happens to have available. If we do that, and live in accordance with these rules, each of us will get the reward we deserve from the gods and such beings as are superior to ourselves, and live in a spirit of cheerful confidence for most of the years of our life.'

The laws themselves will explain the duties we owe to children, relatives, friends and fellow citizens, as well as the service heaven demands we render to foreigners; they will tell us the way we have to behave in the company of each of these categories of people, if we want to lead a full

b and varied life without breaking the law. The laws' method will be partly persuasion and partly (when they have to deal with characters that defy persuasion) compulsion and chastisement; and with the good wishes of the gods they will make our state happy and prosperous. There are a

c number of other topics which a legislator who thinks as I do simply must mention, but they are not easily expressed in the form of a law. So he should, I think, put up to himself and those for whom he is going to legislate an example of the way to deal with the remaining subjects, and when he has explained them all as well as he can, he should set about laying down his actual code of laws. So what's the particular form in which such topics are expressed? It's none too easy to confine one's exposition of them to a single example, but let's see if we can crystallize our ideas by looking at the matter rather like this.

CLINIAS: Tell us what you have in mind.

ATHENIAN: I should like the citizens to be supremely easy to persuade along the paths of virtue; and clearly this is the effect the legislator will try to achieve throughout his legislation.

d CLINIAS: Of course.

ATHENIAN: It occurs to me that the sort of approach I've just explained,[11] provided it is not made to totally uncouth souls, will help to make people more amenable and better disposed to listen to what the lawgiver recommends. So even if the address has no great effect but only makes his listener a trifle easier to handle, and so that much easier to teach, the legislator should be well pleased. People who are anxious to attain moral excellence with all possible speed are pretty thin on the ground and it isn't easy to find them: most only go to prove the wisdom of Hesiod's remark that the

e road to vice is smooth and can be traveled without sweating, because it is very short; but 'as the price of virtue', he says,

11. Reading *toi nundē* in d2.

> *The gods have imposed the sweat of our brows,*
> *And long and steep is the ascent that you have to make*
> *And rough, at first; but when you get to the top,*   719
> *Then the rugged road is easy to endure.*[12]

CLINIAS: It sounds as if he hit off the situation very well.

ATHENIAN: He certainly did. But after this discussion I'm left with certain impressions which I want to put forward for your consideration.

CLINIAS: Do so, then.

ATHENIAN: Let's have a word with the legislator and address him like this: 'Tell us, legislator, if you were to discover what we ought to do and   b
say, surely you'd tell us?'

CLINIAS: Of course.

ATHENIAN: 'Now didn't we hear you saying a few minutes ago[13] that a legislator ought not to allow the poets to compose whatever happened to take their fancy? You see, they'd never know when they were saying something in opposition to the law and harming the state.'

CLINIAS: You're quite right.

ATHENIAN: Well, then, if we took the poets' side and addressed the legislator, would this be a reasonable line to take?

CLINIAS: What?

ATHENIAN: This: 'There is an old proverb, legislator, which we poets   c
never tire of telling and which all laymen confirm, to the effect that when a poet takes his seat on the tripod of the Muse, he cannot control his thoughts. He's like a fountain where the water is allowed to gush forth unchecked. His art is the art of representation, and when he represents men with contrasting characters he is often obliged to contradict himself, and he doesn't know which of the opposing speeches contains the truth. But for the legislator, this is impossible: he must not let his law say two   d
different things on the same subject; his rule has to be "one topic, one doctrine." For example, consider what you said just now. A funeral can be extravagant, inadequate or modest, and your choice falls on one of these three—the moderate—which you recommend with unqualified praise. But if I were composing a poem about a woman of great wealth and how she gave instructions for her own funeral, I should recommend the elaborate   e
burial; a poor and frugal character, on the other hand, would be in favor of the cheap funeral, while the moderate man of moderate means would recommend accordingly. But you ought not to use the term "moderate" in the way you did just now: you must say what "moderate" means and how big or small it may be. If you don't, you must realize that a remark such as you made still has some way to go before it can be a law.'

12. *Works and Days* 287–92.
13. See 656c ff.

CLINIAS: That's quite right.

ATHENIAN: So should the legislator whom we appoint skip any such announcement at the beginning of his laws? Is he to say without ceremony what one should and should not do, and simply threaten the penalty for disobedience before passing on to the next law, without adding to his statutes a single word of encouragement or persuasion? It's just the same with doctors, you know, when we're ill: one follows one method of treatment, one another. Let's recall the two methods, so that we can make the same request of the legislator that a child might make of its doctor, to treat him as gently as possible. You want an example? Well, we usually speak, I think, of doctors and doctors' assistants, but of course we call the latter 'doctors' too.

b   CLINIAS: Certainly.

ATHENIAN: And these 'doctors' (who may be free men or slaves) pick up the skill empirically, by watching and obeying their masters; they've no systematic knowledge such as the free doctors have learned for themselves and pass on to their pupils. You'd agree in putting 'doctors' into these two categories?

CLINIAS: Of course.

c   ATHENIAN: Now here's another thing you notice. A state's invalids include not only free men but slaves too, who are almost always treated by other slaves who either rush about on flying visits or wait to be consulted in their surgeries. This kind of doctor never gives any account of the particular illness of the individual slave, or is prepared to listen to one; he simply prescribes what he thinks best in the light of experience, as if he had precise knowledge, and with the self-confidence of a dictator. Then he dashes off on his way to the next slave-patient, and so takes off his

d   master's shoulders some of the work of attending the sick. The visits of the free doctor, by contrast, are mostly concerned with treating the illnesses of free men; *his* method is to construct an empirical case-history by consulting the invalid and his friends; in this way he himself learns something from the sick and at the same time he gives the individual patient all the instruction he can. He gives no prescription until he has somehow gained the invalid's consent; then, coaxing him into continued cooperation, he

e   tries to complete his restoration to health. Which of the two methods do you think makes a doctor a better healer, or a trainer more efficient? Should they use the *double* method to achieve a *single* effect, or should the method too be single—the less satisfactory approach that makes the invalid more recalcitrant?

CLINIAS: The double, sir, is much better, I think.

ATHENIAN: Would you like us to see how this double method and the single work out when applied to legislation?

CLINIAS: Yes, I'd like that very much.

ATHENIAN: Well then, in heaven's name, what will be the first law our legislator will establish? Surely the first subject he will turn to in his

regulations will be the very first step that leads to the birth of children in 721
the state.

CLINIAS: Of course.

ATHENIAN: And this first step is, in all states, the union of two people
in the partnership of marriage?

CLINIAS: Naturally.

ATHENIAN: So the correct policy for every state will probably be to pass
marriage laws first.

CLINIAS: No doubt about it.

ATHENIAN: Now then, to start with, let's have the simple form. It might
run more or less like this:

> A man must marry between the ages of thirty and thirty-five. b
> If he does not, *he must* be punished by fines and disgrace—

and the fines and disgrace will then be specified. So much for the simple
version of the marriage law; this will be the double version:

> A man must marry between the ages of thirty and thirty-five, reflecting
> that there is a sense in which nature has not only somehow endowed
> the human race with a degree of immortality, but also planted in us all
> a longing to achieve it, which we express in every way we can. One c
> expression of that longing is the desire for fame and the wish not to lie
> nameless in the grave. Thus mankind is by nature a companion of
> eternity, and is linked to it, and will be linked to it, forever. Mankind
> is immortal because it always leaves later generations behind to preserve
> its unity and identity for all time: it gets its share of immortality by
> means of procreation. It is never a holy thing voluntarily to deny oneself
> this prize, and he who neglects to take a wife and have children does d
> precisely that. So if a man obeys the law he will be allowed to go his
> way without penalty, but
> If a man disobeys, and reaches the age of thirty-five without having
> married, *he must* pay a yearly fine

(of a sum to be specified; that ought to stop him thinking that life as a
bachelor is all cakes and ale),

> *and be* deprived too of all the honors which the younger people in the
> state pay to their elders on the appropriate occasions.

When one has heard this law and compared it with the other, one can
judge whether in general laws should run to at least twice the length by e
combining persuasion and threats, or restrict themselves to threats alone
and be of 'single' length only.

MEGILLUS: The Spartan instinct, sir, is always to prefer brevity. But if I
were asked to sit in judgment on these statutes and say which of the two
I'd like to see committed to writing in the state, I'd choose the longer one, 722
and my choice would be precisely the same for every law drafted in the

alternative versions of which you've given us specimens. Still, I suppose
Clinias here too must approve this present legislation, seeing that it's his
state that is contemplating the adoption of laws modeled on it.

CLINIAS: You've put it all very well, Megillus.

ATHENIAN: However, it would be pretty fatuous to spend our time talking
b   about the length or brevity of the text: it's high quality that we should
value, I think, not extreme brevity or length. One of the kinds of laws we
mentioned just now is twice as valuable for practical purposes as the other,
but that's not all: as we said a little while ago, the two types of doctors
were an extremely apt parallel:[14] A relevant point here is that no legislator
ever seems to have noticed that in spite of its being open to them to use
two methods in their legislation, compulsion and persuasion (subject to
the limitations imposed by the uneducated masses), in fact they use only
c   one. They never mix in persuasion with force when they brew their laws,
but administer compulsion neat. As for myself, my dear sirs, I can see a
third condition that should be observed in legislation—not that it ever is.

CLINIAS: What condition do you mean?

ATHENIAN: Providentially enough, the point is brought out by the very
conversation we've had today. Since we began to discuss legislation dawn
has become noon and we've reached this splendid resting-place; we've
d   talked about nothing but laws—and yet I suspect it was only a moment
ago that we really got round to framing any, and that everything we've
said up till now has been simply legislative preamble. Now why have I
pointed this out? I want to make the point that the spoken word, and in
general all compositions that involve using the voice, employ 'preludes'
(a sort of limbering up, so to speak), and that these introductions are
artistically designed to aid the coming performance. For instance, the
'nomes' of songs to the harp, and all other kinds of musical composition,
e   are preceded by preludes of fantastic elaboration. But in the case of the
real 'nomes',[15] the kind we call 'administrative', nobody has ever so much
as breathed the word 'prelude' or composed one and given it to the world;
the assumption has been that such a thing would be repugnant to nature.
But in my opinion the discussion we've had indicates that it is perfectly
natural; and this means that the laws which seemed 'double' when I
described them a moment ago are not really 'double' in the straightforward
sense the term suggests: it's just that they have *two elements*, 'law' and
'preface to law'. The 'dictatorial prescription', which we compared to the
723   prescriptions of the 'slavish' doctors, is the law pure and simple; and the
part that comes before it, although in point of fact 'persuasive' (as Megillus
put it), nevertheless has a function, analogous to that of a preamble in a
speech. It seems obvious to me that the reason why the legislator gave

14. The point seems to be that in the case of the doctors, one kind of treatment was
'*much* better' (720e) than the other (not simply twice as good). In other words, if you
double the length of your laws, you *more* than double their value.

15. I.e., laws, the Greek word *nomoi* meaning both 'laws' and 'melodies'.

that entire persuasive address was to make the person to whom he promul-
gated his law accept his orders—the law—in a more co-operative frame
of mind and with a correspondingly greater readiness to learn. That's why,
as I see it, this element ought properly to be termed not the 'text' of the   b
law, but the 'preamble'. So after all that, what's the next point I'd like
made? It's this: the legislator must see that both the permanent body of
laws and the individual sub-divisions are always supplied with preambles.
The gain will be just as great as it was in the case of the two specimens
we gave just now.

CLINIAS: As far as I'm concerned, I'd certainly instruct our lawgiver,
master of his art though he is, to legislate in no way but that.

ATHENIAN: Yes, Clinias, I think you're right to agree that all laws have   c
their preambles and that the first task must be to preface the text of
each part of the legal code with the appropriate introduction, because the
announcement it introduces is important, and it matters a great deal
whether it is clearly remembered or not. However, we should be wrong
to demand that both 'major' laws and minor rules should *invariably* be   d
headed by a preface. Not every song and speech, after all, needs this
treatment. (They all have introductions in the nature of the case, but it's
not always appropriate to use them.) Still, the decision in all these cases
must be left to the discretion of the orator or singer or legislator.

CLINIAS: I think all this is very true. But let's not waste any more time
delaying, sir. Let's get back to our theme and make a fresh start, if you
are agreeable, on the subject you dealt with before, when you were not
professing to compose in preamble form; let's go over the topic again
('second time lucky', as they say in games), on the understanding that we   e
are not talking at random, as we did just now, but composing a preface;
and we should begin by agreeing that this is what we are doing. We've
heard enough said just now about the worship of the gods and the services
to be rendered to our ancestors;[16] let's try to deal with the subsequent
topics until you think the entire preface has been adequately put together.
Then you will go on to work through the actual laws.

ATHENIAN: So our feeling at the moment is that we have already produced   724
an adequate preface about the gods and the powers below them, and about
parents living and dead. Your instructions now, I think, are that I should,
as it were, take the covers off the remainder of the preface.

CLINIAS: Certainly.

ATHENIAN: Well now, the next thing is this: how far should a man
concentrate or relax the efforts he devotes to looking after his soul, his
body, and his property? This is a suitable topic, and it will be to the mutual   b
advantage of both speaker and listeners to ponder it and so perfect their
education as far as they can. So beyond a shadow of a doubt here's the
next subject for explanation and the next topic to listen to.

CLINIAS: You're quite right.

---

16. See 715e–718a.

Book V

726   ATHENIAN: Everyone who was listening to the address just now about the gods and our dearly beloved ancestors, should now pay attention.

Of all the things a man can call his own, the holiest (though the gods are holier still) is his soul, his most intimate possession. There are two elements that make up the whole of every man. One is stronger and superior, and acts as master; the other, which is weaker and inferior, is a slave; and so a man must always respect the master in him in preference to the slave. Thus when I say that next after the gods—our masters—and

727   their attendant spirits, a man must honor his soul, my recommendation is correct. But hardly a man among us honors it in the right way: he only thinks he does. You see, nothing that is evil can confer honor, because to honor something is to confer marvelous benefits upon it; and anyone who reckons he is magnifying his soul by flattery or gifts or indulgence, so that he fails to make it better than it was before, may *think* he is honoring it, but in fact that is not what he is doing at all. For instance, a person has

b   only to reach adolescence to imagine he is capable of deciding everything; he thinks he is honoring his soul if he praises it, and he is only too keen to tell it to do what it likes. But our present doctrine is that in doing this he is not honoring but harming it; whereas we are arguing that he should honor it next after the gods. Similarly when a man thinks that the responsibility for his every fault lies not in himself but in others, whom he blames for his most frequent and serious misfortunes, while exonerating himself,

c   he doubtless supposes he is honoring his soul. But far from doing that, he is injuring it. Again, when he indulges his pleasures and disobeys the recommendations and advice of the legislator, he is not honoring his soul at all, but dishonoring it, by filling it with misery and repentance. Or, to take the opposite case, he may not brace himself to endure the recommended toils and fears and troubles and pains, and simply give up; but his surrender confers no honor on his soul, because all such conduct brings

d   disgrace upon it. Nor does he do it any honor if he thinks that life is a good thing no matter what the cost. This too dishonors his soul, because he surrenders to its fancy that everything in the next world is an evil, whereas he should resist the thought and enlighten his soul by demonstrating that he does not really know whether our encounter with the gods in the next world may not be in fact the best thing that ever happens to us. And when a man values beauty above virtue, the disrespect he shows his soul is total and fundamental, because he would argue that the body

e   is more to be honored than the soul—falsely, because nothing born on earth is to be honored more than what comes from heaven; and anyone who holds a different view of the soul does not realize how wonderful is this possession which he scorns. Again, a man who is seized by lust to

728   obtain money by improper means and feels no disgust in the acquisition,

will find that in the event he does his soul no honor by such gifts—far from it: he sells all that gives the soul its beauty and value for a few paltry pieces of gold; but all the gold upon the earth and all the gold beneath it does not compensate for lack of virtue.

To sum up, the legislator will list and classify certain things as disgraceful and wicked, and others as fine and good; everyone who is not prepared to make all efforts to refrain from the one kind of action and practice the other to the limits of his power must be unaware that in all such conduct he is treating his soul, the most holy possession he has, in the most disrespectful and abominable manner. You see, practically no one takes into account the greatest 'judgment', as it is called, on wrongdoing. This is to grow to resemble men who are evil, and as the resemblance increases to shun good men and their wholesome conversation and to cut oneself off from them, while seeking to attach oneself to the other kind and keep their company. The inevitable result of consorting with such people is that what you do and have done to you is exactly what *they* naturally do and say to each other. Consequently, this condition is not really a 'judgment' at all, because justice and judgment are fine things: it is mere punishment, suffering that follows a wrongdoing. Now whether a man is made to suffer or not, he is equally wretched. In the former case he is not cured, in the latter he will ultimately be killed to ensure the safety of many others.

To put it in a nutshell, 'honor' is to cleave to what is superior, and, where practicable, to make as perfect as possible what is deficient. Nothing that nature gives a man is better adapted than his soul to enable him to avoid evil, keep on the track of the highest good, and when he has captured his quarry to live in intimacy with it for the rest of his life.

For those reasons the soul has been allotted the second rank of honor;[1] third—as everyone will realize—comes the honor naturally due to the body. Here again it is necessary to examine the various reasons for honoring it, and see which are genuine and which are false; this is the job of a legislator, and I imagine he will list them as follows. The body that deserves to be honored is not the handsome one or the strong or the swift—nor yet the healthy (though a good many people would think it was); and it is certainly not the one with the opposite qualities to all these. He will say that the body which achieves a mean between all these extreme conditions is by far the soundest and best-balanced, because the one extreme makes the soul bold and boastful, while the other makes it abject and groveling.

The same is true of the possession of money and goods: its value is measured by the same yardstick. Both, in excess, produce enmity and feuds in private and public life, while a deficiency almost invariably leads to slavery.

No one should be keen on making money for the sake of leaving his children as rich as possible, because it will not do them any good, or the state either. A child's fortune will be most in harmony with his

1. The first rank has been given to the gods (726e–727a).

circumstances, and superior to all other fortunes, if it is modest enough not to attract flatterers, but sufficient to supply all his needs; to our ears such a fortune strikes exactly the right note, and it frees our life from anxiety. Extreme modesty, not gold, is the legacy we should leave our children. We imagine that the way to bequeath them modesty is to rebuke them when they are immodest, but that is not the result produced in the young when people admonish them nowadays and tell them that youth must show respect to everyone. The sensible legislator will prefer to instruct the older men to show respect to their juniors, and to take especial care not to let any young man see or hear them doing or saying anything disgraceful: where the old are shameless the young too will inevitably be disrespectful to a degree. The best way to educate the younger generation (as well as yourself) is not to rebuke them but patently to practice all your life what you preach to others.

If a man honors and respects his relatives, who all share the worship of the family gods and have the same blood in their veins, he can reasonably expect to have the gods of birth look with benevolence on the procreation of his own children. And as for friends and companions, you will find them easier to get on with in day-to-day contact if you make more of their services to you and esteem them more highly than they do, and put a smaller value on your own good turns to your friends and companions than they do themselves. In dealings with the state and one's fellow citizens, the best man by far is the one who, rather than win a prize at Olympia or in any of the other contests in war and peace, would prefer to beat everyone by his reputation for serving the laws of his country—a reputation for having devoted a lifetime of service to them with more distinction than anyone else.

As to foreigners, one should regard agreements made with them as particularly sacrosanct. Practically all offenses committed as between or against foreigners are quicker to attract the vengeance of God than offenses as between fellow citizens. The foreigner is not surrounded by friends and companions, and stirs the compassion of gods and men that much more, so that anyone who has the power to avenge him comes to his aid more readily; and that power is possessed preeminently by the guardian spirit or god, companion of Zeus the God of Strangers, who is concerned in each case. Anyone who takes the smallest thought for the future will therefore take great care to reach the end of his days without having committed during his life any crime involving foreigners. The most serious of offenses against foreigners or natives is always that affecting suppliants; the god the victim supplicated and invoked when he won his promise becomes a devoted protector of his suppliant, who can consequently rely on the promise he received never to suffer without vengeance being taken for the wrongs done to him.

We've now dealt fairly thoroughly with a man's treatment of his parents, himself and his own possessions, and his contacts with the state, his friends, his relatives, foreigners and countrymen. The next question for consideration is the sort of person he must be himself, if he is to acquit himself with distinction in his journey through life; it's not the influence of law that we're concerned with now, but the educational effect of praise and blame, which makes the individual easier to handle and better disposed towards the laws that are to be established.

Truth heads the list of all things good, for gods and men alike. Let   c
anyone who intends to be happy and blessed be its partner from the start, so that he may live as much of his life as possible a man of truth. You can trust a man like that, but not the man who is fond of telling deliberate lies (and anyone who is happy to go on producing falsehoods in *ignorance* of the truth is an idiot). Neither state is anything to envy: no one has any friends if he is a fool or cannot be trusted. As the years go by he is recognized for what he is, and in the difficulties of old age as life draws to its close he isolates himself completely; he has just about as much contact   d
with his surviving friends and children as with those who are already dead.

A man who commits no crime is to be honored; yet the man who will not even allow the wicked to do wrong deserves more than twice as much respect. The former has the value of a single individual, but the latter, who reveals the wickedness of another to the authorities, is worth a legion. Anyone who makes every effort to assist the authorities in checking crime should be declared to be the great and perfect citizen of his state, winner of the prize for virtue.

The same praise should also be given to self-control and good judg-   e
ment, and to all the other virtues which the possessor can communicate to others as well as displaying in his own person. If a man does so communicate them, he should be honored as in the top rank; if he is prepared to communicate them but lacks the ability, he must be left in second place; but if he is a jealous fellow and churlishly wants to monopolize his virtues, then we should certainly censure him, but without   731
holding the virtue itself in less esteem because of its possessor—on the contrary, we should do our best to acquire it. We want everyone to compete in the struggle for virtue in a generous spirit, because this is the way a man will be a credit to his state—by competing on his own account but refraining from fouling the chances of others by slander. The jealous man, who thinks he has to get the better of others by being rude about them, makes less effort himself to attain true virtue and discourages his competitors by unfair criticism. In this way he hinders the whole state's struggle   b
to achieve virtue and diminishes its reputation, in so far as it depends on him.

Every man should combine in his character high spirit with the utmost gentleness, because there is only one way to get out of the reach of crimes committed by other people and which are dangerous or even impossible to cure: you have to overcome them by fighting in self-defense and rigidly punishing them, and no soul can do this without righteous indignation.   c
On the other hand there are some criminals whose crimes are curable, and

the first thing to realize here is that every unjust man is unjust against his will. No man on earth would ever deliberately embrace any of the supreme evils, least of all in the most precious parts of himself—and as we said, the truth is that the most precious part of every man is his soul. So no one will ever voluntarily accept the supreme evil into the most valuable part of himself and live with it throughout his life. No: in general, the

d   unjust man deserves just as much pity as any other sufferer. And you may pity the criminal whose disease is curable, and restrain and abate your anger, instead of persisting in it with the spitefulness of a shrew; but when you have to deal with complete and unmanageably vicious corruption, you must let your anger off its leash. That is why we say that it must be the good man's duty to be high-spirited or gentle as circumstances require.

     The most serious vice innate in most men's souls is one for which

e   everybody forgives himself and so never tries to find a way of escaping. You can get some idea of this vice from the saying that a man is in the nature of the case 'his own best friend', and that it is perfectly proper for him to have to play this role. It is truer to say that the cause of each and every crime we commit is precisely this excessive love of ourselves, a love which blinds us to the faults of the beloved and makes us bad judges of

732 goodness and beauty and justice, because we believe we should honor our own ego rather than the truth. Anyone with aspirations to greatness must admire not himself and his own possessions, but acts of justice, not only when they are his own, but especially when they happen to be done by someone else. It's because of this same vice of selfishness that stupid people are always convinced of their own shrewdness, which is why we think we know everything when we are almost totally ignorant, so that

b   thanks to not leaving to others what we don't know how to handle, we inevitably come to grief when we try to tackle it ourselves. For these reasons, then, every man must steer clear of extreme love of himself, and be loyal to his superior instead; and he mustn't be put off by shame at the thought of abandoning that 'best friend'.

     There is a certain amount of more detailed but no less useful advice which one hears often enough, and one should go through it to oneself by way of reminder. (Where waters ebb, there is always a corresponding flow, and the act of remembering is the 'flow' of thought that has drained away.)

c   So then: excessive laughter and tears must be avoided, and this is the advice every man must give to every other; one should try to behave decently by suppressing all extremes of joy and grief, both when one's guardian angel brings continued prosperity and when in times of trouble our guardians face difficulties as insurmountable as a high, sheer cliff. We should always have the hope that the blessings God sends will decrease

d   the troubles that assail us, change our present circumstances for the better, and make us lucky enough to see our good fortune always increase. These are the hopes that every man should live by; he must remember all this advice and never spare any effort to recall it vividly to his own mind and that of others, at work and in leisure time alike.

Now then, from the point of view of religion, we've expounded pretty thoroughly what sort of activities we should pursue and what sort of person the individual ought to be; but we have not yet come down to the purely secular level. But we must, because we are addressing men, not gods.

Human nature involves, above all, pleasures, pains, and desires, and no mortal animal can help being hung up dangling in the air (so to speak) in total dependence on these powerful influences. That is why we should praise the noblest life—not only because it enjoys a fine and glorious reputation, but because (provided one is prepared to try it out instead of recoiling from it as a youth) it excels in providing what we all seek: a predominance of pleasure over pain throughout our lives. That this result is guaranteed, if it is tried out in the correct manner, will be perfectly obvious in an instant. But what is 'correctness' here? One should consider this point in the light of the following thesis. We have to ask if one condition suits our nature while another does not, and weigh the pleasant life against the painful with that question in mind. We want to have pleasure; we neither choose nor want pain; we prefer the neutral state if we are thereby relieved of pain, but not if it involves the loss of pleasure. We want less pain and more pleasure, we do not want less pleasure and more pain; but we should be hard put to it to be clear about our wishes when faced with a choice of two situations bringing pleasure and pain in the same proportions. These considerations of number or size or intensity or equality (or their opposites) which determine our wishes all influence or fail to influence us whenever we make a choice. This being inevitably the way of things, we want a life in which pleasures and pains come frequently and with great intensity, but with pleasure predominating; if pains predominate, we reject that life. Similarly when pleasures and pains are few and small and feeble: if pain outweighs pleasure, we do not want that life, but we do when pleasure outweighs pain. As for the 'average' life, which experiences only moderate pleasures or pains, we should observe the same point as before: we desire it when it offers us a preponderance of pleasure (which we enjoy), but not when it offers us a preponderance of pain (which we abhor). In that sense, then, we should think of all human lives as bound up in these two feelings, and we must think to what kind of life our natural wishes incline. But if we assert that we want anything outside this range, we are talking out of ignorance and inexperience of life as it is really lived.

So when a man has considered his likes and dislikes, what he would willingly do and what not, and adopted that as a working rule to guide him in choosing what he finds congenial and pleasant and supremely excellent, he will select a life that will enable him to live as happily as a man can. So what are these lives, and how many are there, from which he must make this choice? Let us list them: there is the life of self-control for one, the life of wisdom for another, and the life of courage too; and let us treat the healthy life as another. As opposed to these, we have another four lives—the licentious, the foolish, the cowardly and the diseased. Now anyone who knows what the life of self-control is like will describe it as 734 gentle in all respects, with mild pleasures and pains, light appetites, and desires without frenzy; the licentious life he will say is violent through and through, involving extreme pleasures and pains, intense and raging appetites and desires of extreme fury. He will say that in the life of self-control the pleasures outweigh the pains, and in the licentious life the pains exceed the pleasures, in point of size, number and frequency. That b is why we inevitably and naturally find the former life more pleasant, the latter more painful, and anyone who means to live a pleasant life no longer has the option of living licentiously. On the contrary, it is already clear (if our present position is correct) that if a man is licentious it must be without intending to be. It is either because of ignorance or lack of self-control, or both, that the world at large lives immoderately. The healthy and unhealthy life should be regarded in the same way: they both offer pleasures and c pains, but the pleasures outweigh the pains in the healthy life, vice versa in the unhealthy. But what we want when we choose between lives is not a predominance of pain: we have chosen as the pleasanter life the one where pain is the weaker element. And so we can say that the self-controlled, the wise and the courageous, experience pleasure and pain with less intensity and on a smaller and more restricted scale than the profligate, the fool and the coward. The first category beats the second on the score of pleasure, d while the second beats the other when it comes to pain. The courageous man does better than the coward, the wise man than the fool; so that, life for life, the former kind—the restrained, the courageous, the wise and the healthy—is pleasanter than the cowardly, the foolish, the licentious and the unhealthy.

To sum up, the life of physical fitness, and spiritual virtue too, is not only pleasanter than the life of depravity but superior in other ways as well: it makes for beauty, an upright posture, efficiency and a good reputation, so e that if a man lives a life like that it will make his whole existence infinitely happier than his opposite number's.

At this point we may stop expounding the preface to the laws, it being now complete. After the 'prelude' should come the 'tune',[2] or (more accurately) a sketch of a legal and political framework. Now it is impossible, when dealing with a web or any piece of weaving, to construct the warp 735 and the woof from the same stuff: the warp must be of a superior type of material (strong and firm in character, while the woof is softer and suitably workable). In a rather similar way it will be reasonable to distinguish between the authorities who are going to rule in a city and the citizens whose education has been slighter and less testing. You may assume, you

---

2. A pun: the Greek *nomos* means both 'tune' and 'law'. Cf. 722d–e.

see, that there are two elements in a political system: the installation of individuals in office, and equipping those officials with a code of laws.

But before all that, here are some further points to notice. Anyone who takes charge of a herd of animals—a shepherd or cattle-man or breeder of horses or what have you—will never get down to looking after them without first performing the purge appropriate to his particular animal-community: that is, he will weed out the unhealthy and inferior stock and send it off to other herds, and keep only the thoroughbreds and the healthy animals to look after. He knows that otherwise he would have to waste endless effort on sickly and refractory beasts, degenerate by nature and ruined by incompetent breeding, and that unless he purges the existing stock these faults will spread in any herd to the animals that are still physically and temperamentally healthy and unspoilt. This is not too serious in the case of the lower animals, and we need mention it only by way of illustration, but with human beings it is vitally important for the legislator to ascertain and explain the appropriate measures in each case, not only as regards a purge, but in general. To purge a whole state, for instance, several methods may be employed, some mild, some drastic; and if a legislator were a dictator too he'd be able to purge the state drastically, which is the best way. But if he has to establish a new society and new laws without dictatorial powers, and succeeds in administering no more than the mildest purge, he'll be well content even with this limited achievement. Like drastic medicines, the best purge is a painful business: it involves chastisement by a combination of 'judgment' and 'punishment',[3] and takes the latter, ultimately, to the point of death or exile. That usually gets rid of the major criminals who are incurable and do the state enormous harm. The milder purge we could adopt is this. When there is a shortage of food, and the underprivileged show themselves ready to follow their leaders in an attack on the property of the privileged, they are to be regarded as a disease that has developed in the body politic, and in the friendliest possible way they should be (as it will tactfully be put) 'transferred to a colony'. Somehow or other everyone who legislates must do this in good time; but our position at the moment is even more unusual. There's no need for us here and now to have resort to a colony or arrange to make a selection of people by a purge. No: it's as though we have a number of streams from several sources, some from springs, some from mountain torrents, all flowing down to unite in one lake. We have to apply ourselves to seeing that the water, as it mingles, is as pure as possible, partly by draining some of it off, partly by diverting it into different channels. Even so, however you organize a society, it looks as if there will always be trouble and risk. True enough: but seeing that we are operating at the moment on a theoretical rather than a practical level, let's suppose we've recruited our citizens and their purity meets with our approval. After all, when we

b

c

d

e

736

b

---

3. See 728b–c.

c   have screened the bad candidates over a suitable period and given them
every chance to be converted, we can refuse their application to enter and
become citizens of the state; but we should greet the good ones with all
possible courtesy and kindness.

We should not forget that we are in the same fortunate position as the
Heraclids when they founded their colony: we noticed[4] how they avoided
vicious and dangerous disputes about land and cancellations of debts and
distribution of property. When an old-established state is forced to resort
d   to legislation to deal with these problems, it finds that both leaving things
as they are and reforming them are somehow equally impossible. The only
policy left them is to mouth pious hopes and make a little cautious progress
over a long period by advancing a step at a time. (This is the way it can
be done. From time to time some of the reformers should be themselves
great land-owners and have a large number of debtors; and they should
be prepared, in a philanthropic spirit, to share their prosperity with those
debtors who are in distress, partly by remitting debts and partly by making
e   land available for distribution. Their policy will be a policy of moderation,
dictated by the conviction that poverty is a matter of increased greed rather
than diminished wealth. This belief is fundamental to the success of a
state, and is the firm base on which you can later build whatever political
737 structure is appropriate to such conditions as we have described. But when
these first steps towards reform falter, subsequent constitutional action in
any state will be hard going.) Now as we say, such difficulties do not
affect us. Nevertheless, it's better to have explained how we could have
escaped them if they had. Let's take it, then, that the explanation has been
given: the way to escape those difficulties is through a sense of justice
b   combined with an indifference to wealth; there is no other route, broad
or narrow, by which we can avoid them. So let's adopt this principle as
a prop for our state. Somehow or other we must ensure that the citizens'
property does not lead to disputes among them—otherwise, if people have
longstanding complaints against each other, anyone with any sense at all
will not go any further with organizing them, if he can help it. But when,
as with us now, God has given a group of people a new state to found,
in which so far there is no mutual malice—well, to stir up ill-will towards
each other because of the way they distribute the land and houses would
be so criminally stupid that no man could bring himself to do it.

c   So what's the correct method of distribution? First, one has to determine
what the total number of people ought to be, then agree on the question
of the distribution of the citizens and decide the number and size of the
subsections into which they ought to be divided; and the land and houses
must be divided equally (so far as possible) among these subsections. A
d   suitable total for the number of citizens cannot be fixed without considering
the land and the neighboring states. The land must be extensive enough

4. See 684d–e.

to support a given number of people[5] in modest comfort, and not a foot more is needed. The inhabitants should be numerous enough to be able to defend themselves when the adjacent peoples attack them, and contribute at any rate some assistance to neighboring societies when they are wronged. When we have inspected the land and its neighbors, we'll determine these points and give reasons for the action we take; but for the moment let's just give an outline sketch and get on with finishing our legislation.

Let's assume we have the convenient number of five thousand and forty farmers and protectors of their holdings, and let the land with its houses be divided up into the same number of parts, so that a man and his holding always go together. Divide the total first by two, then by three: you'll see it can be divided by four and five and every number right up to ten. Everyone who legislates should have sufficient appreciation of arithmetic to know what number will be most use in every state, and why. So let's fix on the one which has the largest number of consecutive divisors. Of course, an infinite series of numbers would admit all possible divisions for all possible uses, but our 5040 admits no more than 59 (including 1 to 10 without a break), which will have to suffice for purposes of war and every peacetime activity, all contracts and dealings, and for taxes and grants.

Anyone who is legally obliged to understand these mathematical facts should try to deepen his understanding of them even in his spare time. They really are just as I say, and the founder of a state needs to be told of them, for the following reasons. It doesn't matter whether he's founding a new state from scratch or reconstructing an old one that has gone to ruin: in either case, if he has any sense, he will never dream of altering whatever instructions may have been received from Delphi or Dodona or Ammon[6] about the gods and temples that ought to be founded by the various groups in the state, and the gods or spirits after whom the temples should be named. (Alternatively, such details may have been suggested by stories told long ago of visions or divine inspiration, which somehow moved people to institute sacrifices with their rituals—either native or taken from Etruria or Cyprus or some other country—so that on the strength of these reports they consecrated statues, altars, temples and sites of oracles, providing each with its own sacred plot of land.) The legislator must not tamper with any of this in the slightest detail. He must allocate to each division of citizens a god or spirit or perhaps a hero, and when he divides up the territory he must give these priority by setting aside plots of land for them, endowed with all the appropriate resources. Thus when the different divisions gather together at fixed times they will have an opportunity of satisfying their various needs, and the citizens will

5. Reading *posous* in d1 with accent on the second syllable.

6. There were sites of prestigious oracles of Apollo at Delphi, Zeus at Dodona in northwest Greece, and the Egyptian god Ammon at the oasis of Siwa in the Libyan desert.

e   recognize and greet each other at the sacrifices in mutual friendship—and there can be no greater benefit for a state than that the citizens should be well-known one to another. Where they have no insight into each other's characters and are kept in the dark about them, no one will ever enjoy the respect he merits or fill the office he deserves or obtain the legal verdict to which he is entitled. So every citizen of every state should make a particular effort to show that he is straightforward and genuine, not shifty, and try to avoid being hoodwinked by anyone who is.

739   The next move in this game of legislation is as unusual as going 'across the line' in checkers, and may well cause surprise at first hearing. But reflection and experience will soon show that the organization of a state is almost bound to fall short of the ideal. You may, perhaps—if you don't know what it means to be a legislator without dictatorial powers—refuse to countenance such a state; nevertheless the right procedure is to describe not only the ideal society but the second and third best too, and then leave

b   it to anyone in charge of founding a community to make a choice between them. So let's follow this procedure now: let's describe the absolutely ideal society, then the second-best, then the third. On this occasion we ought to leave the choice to Clinias, but we should not forget anyone else who may at some time be faced with such a choice and wish to adopt for his own purposes customs of his native country which he finds valuable.

c   You'll find the ideal society and state, and the best code of laws, where the old saying 'friends' property is genuinely shared' is put into practice as widely as possible throughout the entire state. Now I don't know whether in fact this situation—a community of wives, children and all property—exists anywhere today, or will ever exist, but at any rate in such a state the notion of 'private property' will have been by hook or by crook completely eliminated from life. Everything possible will have been done to throw into a sort of common pool even what is by nature 'my own',

d   like eyes and ears and hands, in the sense that to judge by appearances they all see and hear and act in concert. Everybody feels pleasure and pain at the same things, so that they all praise and blame with complete unanimity. To sum up, the laws in force impose the greatest possible unity on the state—and you'll never produce a better or truer criterion of an absolutely perfect law than that. It may be that gods or a number of the children of gods inhabit this kind of state: if so, the life they live there,

e   observing these rules, is a happy one indeed. And so men need look no further for their ideal: they should keep this state in view and try to find the one that most nearly resembles it. This is what we've put our hand to, and if in some way it could be realized, it would come very near immortality and be second only to the ideal. Later, God willing, we'll describe a third best. But for the moment, what description should we give of this second-best state? What's the method by which a state like this is produced?

First of all, the citizens must make a distribution of land and houses;
740   they must not farm in common, which is a practice too demanding for

those born and bred and educated as ours are. But the distribution should be made with some such intention as this: each man who receives a portion of land should regard it as the common possession of the entire state. The land is his ancestral home and he must cherish it even more than children cherish their mother; furthermore, Earth is a goddess, and mistress of mortal men. (And the gods and spirits already established in the locality must be treated with the same respect.)

Additional measures must be taken to make sure that these arrangements are permanent: the number of hearths established by the initial distribution must always remain the same; it must neither increase nor decrease. The best way for every state to ensure this will be as follows: the recipient of a holding should always leave from among his children only *one* heir to inherit his establishment. This will be his favorite son, who will succeed him and give due worship to the ancestors (who rank as gods) of the family and state; these must be taken to include not only those who have already passed on, but also those who are still alive. As for the other children, in cases where there are more than one, the head of the family should marry off the females in accordance with the law we shall establish later; the males he must present for adoption to those citizens who have no children of their own—priority to be given to personal preferences as far as possible. But some people may have no preferences, or other families too may have surplus offspring, male or female; or, to take the opposite problem, they may have too few, because of the onset of sterility. All these cases will be investigated by the highest and most distinguished official we shall appoint. He will decide what is to be done with the surpluses or deficiencies, and will do his best to discover a device to keep the number of households down to 5040. There are many devices available: if too many children are being born, there are measures to check propagation; on the other hand, a high birthrate can be encouraged and stimulated by conferring marks of distinction or disgrace, and the young can be admonished by words of warning from their elders. This approach should do the trick, and if in the last resort we are in complete despair about variations from our number of 5040 households, and the mutual love of wives and husbands produces an excessive flow of citizens that drives us to distraction, we have that old expedient at hand, which we have often mentioned before. We can send out colonies of people that seem suitable, with mutual goodwill between the emigrants and their mother-city. By contrast, we may be flooded with a wave of diseases or by the ravages of wars, so that bereavements depress the citizens far below the appointed number. In this event we ought not to import citizens who have been brought up by a bastard education, if we can help it; but not even God, they say, can grapple with necessity.

So let's pretend our thesis can talk and gives us this advice: 'My dear sirs, don't ignore the facts and be careless enough to undervalue the concepts of likeness, equality, identity and agreement, either in mathematics or in any other useful and productive science. In particular, your first task now is

b

c

d

e

741

b

to keep to the said number as long as you live; you must respect the upper limits of the total property which you originally distributed as being reasonable, and not buy and sell your holdings among yourselves. The lot by which they were distributed is a god, so there will be no support for you there, or from the legislator either. And there are two warnings
c the law has for the disobedient: (A) You may choose or decline to take part in the distribution, but if you do take part you must observe the following conditions: (i) you must acknowledge that the land is sacred to all the gods; (ii) after priests and priestesses have offered prayers for that intention at the first, second and third sacrifices,

> 1. Anyone buying or selling his allotted land or house
> *must suffer* the penalty appropriate to the crime.[7]

You are to inscribe the details on pieces of cypress wood and put these
d written records on permanent deposit in the temples. (B) You must appoint the official who seems to have the sharpest eyes to superintend the observance of the rule, so that the various contraventions may be brought to your notice and the disobedient punished by the law and the god alike. What a boon this rule is to all the states that observe it, given the appropriate arrangements, no wicked men—as the saying goes—will ever understand; such knowledge is the fruit of experience and virtuous habits. Such arrange-
e ments, you see, involve very little by way of profit-making, and there is no need or opportunity for anyone to engage in any of the vulgar branches of commerce (you know how a gentleman's character is coarsened by manual labor, which is generally admitted to be degrading), and no one will presume to rake in money from occupations such as that.'

All these considerations suggest a further law that runs like this: no
742 private person shall be allowed to possess any gold or silver, but only coinage for day-to-day dealings which one can hardly avoid having with workmen and all other indispensable people of that kind (we have to pay wages to slaves and foreigners who work for money). For these purposes, we agree, they must possess coinage, legal tender among themselves, but valueless to the rest of mankind. The common Greek coinage is to be used for expeditions and visits to the outside world, such as when a man has
b to be sent abroad as an ambassador or to convey some official message; to meet these occasions the state must always have a supply of Greek coinage. If a private individual should ever need to go abroad, he should first obtain leave of the authorities, and if he returns home with some surplus foreign money in his pocket he must deposit it with the state and take local money to the same value in exchange.

> 2. If he is found keeping it for himself,
> *it must* be confiscated by the state.

---

7. In this translation the laws making up the legal code proposed for Clinias' city are set off from the surrounding text and numbered consecutively.

3. If anyone who knows of its concealment fails to report it, *he must* be liable to a curse and a reproach (and so must the importer),   c and in addition be fined in a sum not less than that of the foreign currency brought in.

When a man marries or gives in marriage, no dowry whatsoever must be given or received. Money must not be deposited with anybody whom one does not trust. There must be no lending at interest, because it will be quite in order for the borrower to refuse absolutely to return both interest and principal.

The best way to appreciate that these are the best policies for a state to follow is to examine them in the light of the fundamental aim. Now we   d maintain that the aim of a statesman who knows what he's about is not in fact the one which most people say the good legislator should have. They'd say that if he knows what he's doing his laws should make the state as huge and as rich as possible; he should give the citizens gold mines and silver mines, and enable them to control as many people as possible by land and sea. And they'd add, too, that to be a satisfactory legislator he must want to see the state as good and as happy as possible.   e But some of these demands are practical politics, and some are not, and the legislator will confine himself to what can be done, without bothering his head with wishful thinking about impossibilities. I mean, it's pretty well inevitable that happiness and virtue should come hand in hand (and this is the situation the legislator will want to see), but virtue and great wealth are quite incompatible, at any rate great wealth as generally understood (most people would think of the extreme case of a millionaire, who will of course be a rogue into the bargain). In view of all this, I'll never   743 concede to them that the rich man can become really happy without being virtuous as well: to be extremely virtuous and exceptionally rich at the same time is absolutely out of the question. 'Why?' it may be asked. 'Because,' we shall reply, 'the profit from using just *and* unjust methods is more than twice as much as that from just methods alone, and a man who refuses to spend his money either worthily or shamefully spends only half the sum laid out by worthwhile people who are prepared to spend on worthy purposes too.[8] So anyone who follows the opposite policy   b will never become richer than the man who gets twice as much profit and makes half the expenditures. The former is a good man; the latter is not actually a rogue so long as he uses his money sparingly, but on some occasions[9] he is an absolute villain; thus, as we have said, he is *never* good. Ill-gotten and well-gotten gains plus expenditure that is neither just nor unjust, when a man is also sparing with his money, add up to wealth; the absolute rogue, who is generally a spendthrift, is quite impoverished. The

8. I.e., as well as on 'neutral' objects.
9. I.e., when he *makes* money (by dishonest means).

c   man who spends his money for honest ends and uses only just methods
to come by it, will not easily become particularly rich or particularly poor.
Our thesis is therefore correct: the very rich are not good; and if they are
not good, they are not happy either.'

The whole point of our legislation was to allow the citizens to live
supremely happy lives in the greatest possible mutual friendship. How-
d   ever, they will never be friends if injuries and lawsuits arise among them
on a grand scale, but only if they are trivial and rare. That is why we
maintain that neither gold nor silver should exist in the state, and there
should not be much money made out of menial trades and charging
interest, nor from prostitutes; the citizens' wealth should be limited to the
products of farming, and even here a man should not be able to make so
much that he can't help forgetting the real reason why money was invented
(I mean for the care of the soul and body, which without physical and
e   cultural education respectively will never develop into anything worth
mentioning). That's what has made us say more than once that the pursuit
of money should come last in the scale of value. Every man directs his
efforts to three things in all, and if his efforts are directed with a correct
sense of priorities he will give money the third and lowest place, and his
soul the highest, with his body coming somewhere between the two. In
particular, if this scale of values prevails in the society we're now describing, then it has been equipped with a good code of laws. But if any of the
744   laws subsequently passed is found giving pride of place to health in the
state rather than the virtue of self-control, or to wealth rather than health
and habits of restraint, then quite obviously its priorities will be wrong.
So the legislator must repeatedly try to get this sort of thing straight in
his own mind by asking 'What do I want to achieve?' and 'Am I achieving
it, or am I off target?' If he does that, perhaps he'll complete his legislation
by his own efforts and leave nothing to be done by others. There's no
other way he could possibly succeed.

b   So when a man has drawn his lot, he must take over his holding on the
terms stated.[10] It would have been an advantage if no one entering the
colony had had any more property than anyone else; but that's out of the
question, and some people will arrive with relatively large fortunes, others
with relatively little. So for a number of reasons, and especially because
the state offers equality of opportunity, there must be graded property-
classes, to ensure that offices and taxes and grants may be arranged on
the basis of what a man is worth. It's not only his personal virtues or his
ancestors' that should be considered, or his physical strength or good
c   looks: what he's made of his wealth or poverty should also be taken into
account. In short, the citizens must be esteemed and given office, so far
as possible, on exactly equal terms of 'proportional inequality', so as to
avoid ill-feeling. For these reasons four permanent property-classes must

10. See 741b–c.

be established, graded according to wealth: the 'first', 'second', 'third', and 'fourth' classes, or whatever other names are employed. A man will either keep his original classification, or, when he has grown richer or poorer   d
than he was before, transfer to the appropriate class.

In view of all this, the next law I'd pass would be along the following lines. (We maintain that if a state is to avoid the greatest plague of all— I mean civil war, though civil disintegration would be a better term— extreme poverty and wealth must not be allowed to arise in any section of the citizen-body, because both lead to both these disasters. That is why the legislator must now announce the acceptable limits of wealth and poverty.) The lower limit of poverty must be the value of the holding   e
(which is to be permanent: no official nor anyone else who has ambitions to be thought virtuous will ever overlook the diminution of any man's holding). The legislator will use the holding as his unit of measure and allow a man to possess twice, thrice, and up to four times its value. If anyone acquires more than this, by finding treasure-trove or by gift or by a good stroke of business or some other similar lucky chance which presents   745
him with more than he's allowed, he should hand over the surplus to the state and its patron deities, thereby escaping punishment and getting a good name for himself.

> 4. If a man breaks this law,
> *anyone* who wishes may lay information and be rewarded with half the amount involved, the other half being given to the gods; and besides this the guilty person must pay a fine equivalent to the surplus out of his own pocket.

The total property of each citizen over and above his holding of land should be recorded in a public register kept in the custody of officials legally appointed for that duty, so that lawsuits on all subjects—in so far   b
as they affect property—may go smoothly because the facts are clear.

After this, the legislator's first job is to locate the city as precisely as possible in the center of the country, provided that the site he chooses is a convenient one for a city in all other respects too (these are details which can be understood and specified easily enough). Next he must divide the country into twelve sections. But first he ought to reserve a sacred area for Hestia, Zeus and Athena (calling it the 'acropolis'), and enclose its boundaries; he will then divide the city itself and the whole country into   c
twelve sections by lines radiating from this central point. The twelve sections should be made equal in the sense that a section should be smaller if the soil is good, bigger if it is poor. The legislator must then mark out five thousand and forty holdings, and further divide each into two parts; he should then make an individual holding consist of two such parts coupled so that each has a partner near the center or the boundary of the state as the case may be. (A part near the city and a part next to the boundary should form one holding, the second nearest the city with the   d
second from the boundary should form another, and so on.) He must

apply to the two parts the rule I've just mentioned about the relative quality of the soil, making them equal by varying their size. He should also divide the population into twelve sections, and arrange to distribute among them as equally as possible all wealth over and above the actual holdings (a comprehensive list will be compiled). Finally, they must allocate
e   the sections as twelve 'holdings' for the twelve gods, consecrate each section to the particular god which it has drawn by lot, name it after him, and call it a 'tribe'. Again, they must divide the city into twelve sections in the same way as they divided the rest of the country; and each man should be allotted two houses, one near the center of the state, one near the boundary. That will finish off the job of getting the state founded.

But there's a lesson here that we must take to heart. This blueprint as a whole is never likely to find such favorable circumstances that every
746 single detail will turn out precisely according to plan. It presupposes men who won't turn up their noses at living in such a community, and who will tolerate a moderate and fixed level of wealth throughout their lives, and the supervision of the size of each individual's family as we've suggested. Will people really put up with being deprived of gold and other things which, for reasons we went into just now, the legislator is obviously going to add to his list of forbidden articles? What about this description of a city and countryside with houses at the center and in all directions round about? He might have been relating a dream, or modeling a state
b   and its citizens out of wax. The ideal impresses well enough, but the legislator must reconsider it as follows (this being, then, a *reprise* of his address to us).[11] 'My friends, in these talks we're having, don't think it has escaped me either that the point of view you are urging has some truth in it. But I believe that in every project for future action, when you are displaying the ideal plan that ought to be put into effect, the most satisfactory procedure is to spare no detail of absolute truth and beauty.
c   But if you find that one of these details is impossible in practice, you ought to put it on one side and not attempt it: you should see which of the remaining alternatives comes closest to it and is most nearly akin to your policy, and arrange to have that done instead. But you must let the legislator finish describing what he really wants to do, and only then join him in considering which of his proposals for legislation are feasible, and which
d   are too difficult. You see, even the maker of the most trivial object must make it internally consistent if he is going to get any sort of reputation.'

Now that we've decided to divide the citizens into twelve sections, we should try to realize (after all, it's clear enough) the enormous number of divisors the subdivisions of each section have, and reflect how these in turn can be further subdivided and subdivided again until you get to 5040.[12] This is the mathematical framework which will yield you your

11. See 739a ff.

12. 5040 = 12 × 420. A 'section' (420) has many divisors (including all numbers from 1 to 7), and several (e.g. 12, 15, 20) can be conveniently subdivided. Division of all the 12

brotherhoods, local administrative units, villages, your military companies and marching-columns, as well as units of coinage, liquid and dry measures, and weights. The law must regulate all these details so that the proper proportions and correspondences are observed. And not only that: the legislator should not be afraid of appearing to give undue attention to detail. He must be bold enough to give instructions that the citizens are not to be allowed to possess any equipment that is not of standard size. He'll assume it's a general rule that numerical division in all its variety can be usefully applied to every field of conduct. It may be limited to the complexities of arithmetic itself, or extended to the subtleties of plane and solid geometry; it's also relevant to sound, and to motion (straight up or down or revolution in a circle). The legislator should take all this into account and instruct all his citizens to do their best never to operate outside that framework. For domestic and public purposes, and all professional skills, no single branch of a child's education has such an enormous range of applications as mathematics; but its greatest advantage is that it wakes up the sleepy ignoramus and makes him quick to understand, retentive and sharpwitted; and thanks to this miraculous science he does better than his natural abilities would have allowed. These subjects will form a splendidly appropriate curriculum, *if* by further laws and customs you can expel the spirit of pettiness and greed from the souls of those who are to master them and profit from them. But if you fail, you'll find that without noticing it you've produced a 'twister' instead of a man of learning—just what can be seen to have happened in the case of the Egyptians and Phoenicians, and many other races whose approach to wealth and life in general shows a narrowminded outlook. (It may have been an incompetent legislator who was to blame for this state of affairs, or some stroke of bad luck, or even some natural influences that had the same effect.)

And that's another point about the choice of sites, Clinias and Megillus, that we mustn't forget. Some localities are more likely than others to produce comparatively good (or bad) characters, and we must take care to lay down laws that do not fly in the face of such influences. Some sites are suitable or unsuitable because of varying winds or periods of heat, others because of the quality of the water; in some cases the very food grown in the soil can nourish or poison not only the body but the soul as well. But best of all will be the places where the breeze of heaven blows, where spirits hold possession of the land and greet with favor (or disfavor) the various people who come and settle there. The sensible legislator will ponder these influences as carefully as a man can, and then try to lay down laws that will take account of them. This is what you must do too, Clinias. You're going to settle a territory, so here's the first thing you have to attend to.

CLINIAS: Well said, sir. I must follow your advice.

---

sections, if carried far enough, will ultimately give you 5040. The brotherhoods and units mentioned just below would be subdivisions of the tribes (a tribe = 420 citizens).

Book VI

751   ATHENIAN: Well then, now that I've got all that off my chest, your next
job will be to appoint officials for the state.

CLINIAS: It certainly will.

ATHENIAN: There are two stages involved in organizing a society.[1] First
you establish official positions and appoint people to hold them: you decide
how many posts there should be and how they ought to be filled. Then
b   each office has to be given its particular laws: you have to decide which
laws will be appropriate in each case, and the number and type required.
But before we make our choice, let's pause a moment and explain a point
that will affect it.

CLINIAS: And what's that?

ATHENIAN: This. It's obvious to anyone that legislation is a tremendous
task, and that when you have a well constructed state with a well-framed
legal code, to put incompetent officials in charge of administering the code
is a waste of good laws, and the whole business degenerates into farce.
c   And not only that: the state will find that its laws are doing it damage
and injury on a gigantic scale.

CLINIAS: Naturally.

ATHENIAN: Now let's notice the relevance of this to your present society
and state. You appreciate that if your candidates are to deserve promotion
to positions of power, their characters and family background must have
been adequately tested, right from their childhood until the moment of
d   their election. Furthermore, the intending electors ought to have been well
brought up in law-abiding habits, so as to be able to approve or disapprove
of the candidates for the right reasons and elect or reject them according
to their deserts.[2] But in the present case we are dealing with people who
have only just come together and don't know each other—and they're
uneducated too. So how could they ever elect their officials without going wrong?

CLINIAS: It's pretty well impossible.

ATHENIAN: But look here, 'once in the race, you've no excuses', as the
saying is. That's just our predicament now: you and your nine colleagues,
e   you tell us, have given an undertaking to the people of Crete to turn your
752   energies to founding this state; I, for my part, have promised to join in
with this piece of fiction I'm now relating. Seeing that I've got on to telling
a story, I'd be most reluctant to leave it without a head: it would look a
grim sight wandering about like that!

CLINIAS: And a fine story it's been, sir.

ATHENIAN: Surely, but I also intend to give you actual help along those
lines, so far as I can.

---

1. Cf. 735a; after the preliminaries of 735b–750e, the Athenian now resumes his discussion of political offices.

2. Deleting *te* in c9 and reading *pros to* in d1.

CLINIAS: Then let's carry out our program, certainly.

ATHENIAN: Yes, we shall, God willing, if we can keep old age at bay for long enough.

CLINIAS: 'God willing' can probably be taken for granted.   b

ATHENIAN: Of course. So let's be guided by him and notice something else.

CLINIAS: What?

ATHENIAN: That we'll find we've been pretty bold and foolhardy in launching this state of ours.

CLINIAS: What's made you say that? What have you in mind?

ATHENIAN: I'm thinking of the cheerful way we're legislating for people who'll be new to the laws we've passed, without bothering how they'll ever be brought to accept them. It's obvious to us all, Clinias, even if we're   c
not very clever, that at the start they won't readily accept any at all. Ideally, we'd remain on the spot long enough to see people getting a taste of the laws while they're still children; then when they've grown up and have become thoroughly accustomed to them, they can take part in the elections to all the offices of the state. If we can manage that (assuming acceptable ways and means are available), then I reckon that the state would have a firm guarantee of survival when its 'schooldays' are over.

CLINIAS: That's reasonable enough.   d

ATHENIAN: So let's see if we can find ways and means. Will this do? I maintain, Clinias, that of all the Cretans, the citizens of Cnossus have a special duty. They must not be content with simply doing all that religion demands for the mere soil of your settlement: they must also take scrupulous care to see that the first officials are appointed by the best and safest methods. And it's absolutely vital to give your best attention to choosing,   e
first of all, Guardians of the Laws. (Less trouble need be taken over the other officials.)

CLINIAS: So can we find a reasonable way of going about it?

ATHENIAN: Yes. 'Sons of Crete' (I say), 'as the Cnossians take precedence over your many cities, they should collaborate with the newly arrived settlers in choosing a total of thirty-seven men from the two sides, nineteen from the settlers, the rest from Cnossus itself'—the gift of the Cnossians   753
to this state of yours, Clinias. They should include you in the eighteen, and make you yourself a citizen of the colony, with your consent (failing which, you'll be gently compelled).

CLINIAS: But why on earth, sir, haven't you, and Megillus too, enrolled as joint administrators?

ATHENIAN: Ah, Clinias, Athens is a high and mighty state, and so is Sparta; besides, they're both a long way off. But it's just the right thing for you and the other founders, and what I said a moment ago of you   b
applies equally to them. So let's take it we've explained how to deal with the present situation. But as time goes on and the constitution has become established, the election of these officials should be held more or less as follows. Everyone who serves in the cavalry or infantry, and has fought in the field while young and strong enough to do so, should participate.

c   They must proceed to election in the temple which the state considers to be the most venerable; each elector should place on the altar of the god a small tablet on which he has written the name of the person he wishes to vote for, adding the candidate's father, tribe, and deme; and he should append his own name with the same details. For at least thirty days anyone who wishes should be allowed to remove any tablet bearing a name he finds objectionable and put it on display in the market-place. Then the

d   officials must exhibit to the state at large the three hundred tablets that head the list; on the basis of this list the voters must then again record their nominations, and the hundred names that lead this second time must be publicly displayed as before. On the third occasion anyone who wishes should walk between the victims of a sacrifice and record which of these three hundred he chooses. The thirty-seven who receive most votes must then submit to scrutiny and be declared elected.

e   Well then, Clinias and Megillus, who will make all these arrangements about these officials in our state, and their scrutiny? We can surely appreciate that as the state apparatus is as yet only rudimentary such people have to be on hand; but they could hardly be available before any officials at all have been appointed. Even so, we must have them, and these two hundred persons mustn't be feeble specimens, either, but men of the highest caliber. As the proverb says, 'getting started is half the battle', and a *good*

754 beginning we all applaud. But in my view a good start is more than 'half', and no one has yet given it the praise it deserves.

       CLINIAS: That's quite true.

       ATHENIAN: So as we acknowledge the value of a good beginning, let's not skip discussion of it in this case. Let's get it quite clear in our own minds how we can tackle it. I've no particular points to make, except one, which is vitally relevant to the situation.

       CLINIAS: And what's that?

       ATHENIAN: Apart from the city which is founding it, this state we are

b   about to settle has, so to speak, no father or mother. I'm quite aware, of course, that many a foundation has quarreled repeatedly with its founder-state, and will again, but in the present circumstances we have, as it were, the merest infant on our hands. I mean, any child is going to fall out with his parents sooner or later, but while he's young and can't help himself, he loves them and they love him; he's forever scampering back to his family and finding his only allies are his relatives. That's exactly the way

c   I maintain our young state regards the citizens of Cnossus and how they regard it, in virtue of their role as its guardians. I therefore repeat what I said just now—there's no harm in saying a good thing twice—that the citizen of Cnossus should choose colleagues from among the newly arrived colonists and take charge of all these arrangements; they should choose at least a hundred of them, the oldest and most virtuous they can find; and they themselves should contribute another hundred. They should enter the new state and collaborate in seeing that the officials are designated

d   according to law, and after designation, scrutinized. When they've done all that, the citizens of Cnossus should resume living in Cnossus and leave the infant state to work out its own salvation and flourish unaided.

The duties for which the members of the body of thirty-seven should be appointed are as follows (not only here and now, but permanently): first, they are to act as Guardians of the Laws; second, they are to take charge of the documents in which each person has made his return to the officials of his total property. (A man may leave four hundred drachmas undeclared if he belongs to the highest property-class, three hundred if to the second, two hundred if to the third, and one hundred if he belongs to the fourth.)

5. If anyone is found to possess anything in addition to the registered sum,
the entire surplus should be confiscated by the state,

and on top of that anyone who wants to should bring a charge against him—and an ugly, discreditable and disgraceful charge it will be, if the man is convicted of being enticed by the prospect of gain to hold the laws in contempt. The accuser, who may be anyone, should accordingly enter a charge of 'money-grubbing' against him, and prosecute in the court of the Law-Guardians themselves.

6. If the defendant is found guilty,
he must be excluded from the common resources of the state, and when a grant of some kind is made, he must go without and be limited to his holding; and for as long as he lives his conviction should be recorded for public inspection by all and sundry.

A Law-Guardian must not hold office for longer than twenty years; he should be not less than fifty years old on appointment, and if he is appointed at sixty, his maximum tenure must be ten years, and so on. And if a man survives beyond seventy, he should no longer expect to hold such an important post as membership of this board.

That gives us three duties to assign to the Guardians of the Laws. As the legal code is extended, every new law will give this body of men additional duties to perform, over and above the ones we've mentioned.

Now for the election of the other officials, one by one.

Next, then, we have to elect Generals and their aides-de-camp, so to speak: Cavalry-Commanders, Tribe-Leaders, and controllers of the tribal companies of infantry ('Company-Commanders' will be a good name for these officers, which is in fact what most people do call them).

Generals. The Guardians of the Laws must compile a preliminary list of candidates, restricted to citizens, and the Generals should then be elected from this list by all those who have served in the armed forces at the proper age, or are serving at the time. If anybody thinks that someone not on the preliminary list is better qualified than someone who is, he must name his proposed substitute, and say whom he should replace; then, having sworn his oath, he must propose the alternative candidate.

Whichever of the two the voting favors should be a candidate in the election. The three candidates who receive most votes should become Generals and take over the organization of military affairs, after being scrutinized in the same way as the Guardians of the Laws.

e *Company-Commanders.* The elected Generals should make their own preliminary list of twelve Company-Commanders, one for each tribe; the counternominations, the election and the scrutiny must be conducted as they were for the Generals themselves.

The Elections. For the moment, before a council and executive committees have been chosen, your assembly must be convened by the Guardians of the Laws in the holiest and most capacious place they can find; and they must seat the heavy-armed soldiers, the cavalry, and finally all other ranks, in separate blocks. The Generals and Cavalry-Commanders should be

756 elected by the whole assembly, the Company-Commanders by the shieldbearers, and their Tribe-Leaders by the entire cavalry; as for light-armed troops, archers, or whatever other ranks there may be, the appointment of their leaders should be left to the Generals' discretion.

Cavalry-Commanders. That will leave us with the appointment of the Cavalry-Commanders. The preliminary list must be drawn up by the same persons as drew up the list of Generals, and the election and counterproposals should be conducted in the same way; the cavalry must hold

b the election watched by the infantry, and the two candidates with the most votes must become leaders of the entire mounted force.

Disputed Votes. Votes may be disputed no more than twice. If anyone contests the vote on the third occasion, the tellers must decide the issue by voting among themselves.

   The council should have thirty dozen members, as three hundred sixty will be a convenient number for subdivision. The total will be divided

c into four sections of ninety, this being the number of members to be elected from each property-class. The first step in the election is to be compulsory for all: everyone must take part in the nomination of members of the highest class, and anybody who neglects his duty must pay the approved fine. When the nominations are completed, the names must be noted down.

   On the next day, using the same procedure as before, they will nominate members of the second class.

   On the third day, nominating for Councillors from the third class will

d be optional, except for voters of the first three classes: voters of the fourth and lowest class will be exempted from the fine if they do not care to make a nomination.

   The fourth day will see the nomination for representatives of the fourth and lowest class; everyone must take part, but voters of the third and fourth class who do not wish to nominate should not be fined—unlike voters of the second and first classes, who must be fined treble and quadruple the standard fine respectively if they do not make a nomination.

On the fifth day the officials must display to the entire citizen body the names duly noted down, and on the basis of these lists every man must cast his vote or pay the standard fine. One hundred eighty must be selected from each property-class, and half of them finally chosen by lot. These, after scrutiny, are to be Councillors for the year.

A system of selection like that will effect a compromise between a monarchical and a democratic constitution, which is precisely the sort of compromise a constitution should always be. You see, even if you proclaim that a master and his slave shall have equal status, friendship between them is inherently impossible. The same applies to the relations between an honest man and a scoundrel. Indiscriminate equality for all amounts to *in*equality, and both fill a state with quarrels between its citizens. How correct the old saying is, that 'equality leads to friendship'! It's right enough and it rings true, but what *kind* of equality has this potential is a problem which produces ripe confusion. This is because we use the same term for two concepts of 'equality', which in most respects are virtual opposites. The first sort of equality (of measures, weights and numbers) is within the competence of any state and any legislator: that is, one can simply distribute equal awards by lot. But the most genuine equality, and the best, is not so obvious. It needs the wisdom and judgment of Zeus, and only in a limited number of ways does it help the human race; but when states or even individuals do find it profitable, they find it very profitable indeed. The general method I mean is to grant much to the great and less to the less great, adjusting what you give to take account of the real nature of each—specifically, to confer high recognition on great virtue, but when you come to the poorly educated in this respect, to treat them as they deserve. We maintain, in fact, that statesmanship consists of essentially this—strict justice. This is what we should be aiming at now, Clinias: this is the kind of 'equality' we should concentrate on as we bring our state into the world. The founder of any other state should also concentrate on this same goal when he frames his laws, and take no notice of a bunch of dictators, or a single one, or even the power of the people. He must always make *justice* his aim, and this is precisely as we've described it: it consists of granting the 'equality' that unequals deserve to get. Yet on occasion a state as a whole (unless it is prepared to put up with a degree of friction in one part or another) will be obliged to apply these concepts in a rather rough and ready way, because complaisance and toleration, which always wreck complete precision, are the enemies of strict justice. You can now see why it was necessary to avoid the anger of the man in the street by giving him an equal chance in the lot (though even then we prayed to the gods of good luck to make the lot give the right decisions). So though force of circumstances compels us to employ both sorts of equality, we should employ the second, which demands good luck to prove successful, as little as possible.

e

757

b

c

d

e

758

So much, my friends, for the justification of our policy, which is the policy a state must follow if it means to survive. The state is just like a ship at sea, which always needs someone to keep watch night and day: as it is steered through the waves of international affairs, it lives in constant peril of being captured by all sorts of conspiracies. Hence the need of an

b   unbroken chain of authority right through the day and into the night and then on into the next day, guard relieving guard in endless succession. But a large body will never be able to act quickly enough, and most of the time we have to leave the majority of council members free to live their private lives and administer their own establishments. We must therefore divide the members of the council into twelve groups, one for

c   each month, and have them go on guard by turns. They must be available promptly, whenever anyone from abroad or from within the state itself approaches them wishing to give information or inquire about those topics on which a state must arrange to answer the questions of other states and receive replies to its own. They must be particularly concerned with the

d   constant revolutions of all kinds that are apt to occur in a state; if possible, they must prevent them, but failing that they must see that the state gets to know as soon as possible, so that the outbreak can be cured. That is why this executive committee has to be in charge of convening and dissolving not only statutory meetings but also those held in some national emergency. The authority that should see to all this—a twelfth of the council— will of course be *off* duty for eleven-twelfths of the year: it's the section of the council *on* duty that must co-operate with other officials and keep a watchful eye on the state.

e   That will be a reasonable arrangement for the city, but what about the rest of the country? How should it be superintended and organized? Well now, the entire city and the entire country have been divided into twelve sections; there are the roads of the central city; there are houses, public buildings, harbors, the market, and fountains; there are, above all, sacred enclosures and similar places. Shouldn't all these things have officials appointed to look after them?

CLINIAS: Naturally.

759 ATHENIAN: We can say, then, that the temples should have Attendants and Priests and Priestesses. Next, there are the duties of looking after streets and public buildings, ensuring that they reach the proper standards, stopping men and animals doing them damage, and seeing that conditions both in the suburbs and the city itself are in keeping with a civilized life. All these duties require three types of officials to be chosen: the 'City-Wardens' (as they will be called) will be responsible for the points we've just mentioned, and the 'Market-Wardens' for the correct conduct of the market.

b   Priests or Priestesses of temples who have hereditary priesthoods should not be turned out of office. But if (as is quite likely in a new foundation) few or no temples are thus provided for, the deficiencies must be made good by appointing Priests and Priestesses to be Attendants in the temples of the gods. In all these cases the appointments should be made partly by election and partly by lot, so that a mixture of democratic and non-democratic methods in every rural and urban division may lead to the greatest possible feeling of solidarity. In electing Priests, one should leave it to the god himself to express his wishes, and allow him to guide the luck of the draw. But the man whom the lot favors must be screened to see that he is healthy and legitimate, reared in a family whose moral standards could hardly be higher, and that he himself and his father and mother have lived unpolluted by homicide and all such offenses against heaven.

They must get laws on all religious matters from Delphi, and appoint Expounders of them; that will provide them with a code to be obeyed. Each priesthood must be held for a year and no longer, and anyone who intends to celebrate our rites in due conformity with religious law should not be less than sixty years old. The same rules should apply to Priest-esses too.

There should be three[3] Expounders. The tribes will be arranged in three sets of four, and every man should nominate four persons, each from the same set as himself; the three candidates who receive most votes should be scrutinized, and nine names should then be sent to Delphi for the oracle to select one from each group of three. Their scrutiny, and the requirement as to age, should be the same as in the case of the Priests; these three must hold office for life, and when one dies the group of four tribes in which the vacancy occurs should make nominations for a replacement.

The highest property-class must elect Treasurers to control the sacred funds of each temple, and to look after the temple-enclosures and their produce and revenues; three should be chosen to take charge of the largest temples, two for the less large, and one for the very small. The election and scrutiny of these officials should be conducted as it was for the Generals.

So much by way of provision for the holy places.

As far as practicable, nothing should be left unguarded. The protection of the city is to be the business of the Generals, Company-Commanders, Cavalry-Commanders, Tribe-Leaders and members of the Executive—and the City-Wardens and Market-Wardens too, once we have them elected and satisfactorily installed in office. The whole of the rest of the country should be protected as follows. Our entire territory has been divided as exactly as possible into twelve equal sections, and every year one tribe must be allocated by lot to each of them. Every tribe must provide five 'Country-Wardens' or 'Guards-in-Chief', each of whom will be allowed to choose from his own tribe[4] twelve young men who must be not younger than twenty-five nor older than thirty. The effect of the lot will be that each group will take a different section every month, so that they all get experience and knowledge of the entire country. The guards and their

3. Reading *treis* in d5.

4. Alternatively, " . . . 'Guards-in-Chief', who will be allowed to choose from their own tribe . . ." On the translation in the text there will be 60 assistant guards; on this alternative translation, 12.

officers in charge are to hold their respective commissions for two years.
Starting from the original sections (i.e., districts of the country) assigned
d   by lot, the Guards-in-Chief are to take their groups round in a circle,
transferring them each month to the next district on the right ('on the
right' should be understood to mean 'to the East'). But it's not enough
that as many of the guards as possible should get experience of the country
at only one season of the year: we want them to add to their knowledge
of the actual territory by discovering what goes on in every district at
every season. So their leaders for the time being should follow up the first
e   year by spending a second leading them back through the various districts,
moving this time to the left. For the third year, a tribe must choose other
Country-Wardens, and five new Guards-in-Chief, each in charge of
twelve assistants.

While stationed in the various districts, their duties should be as follows.
To start with, they must see that the territory is protected against enemies
as thoroughly as possible. They must dig ditches wherever necessary, and
excavate trenches and erect fortifications to check any attempt to harm the
761 land and the livestock. They will requisition the beasts of burden and
slaves of the local residents for these purposes, and employ them at their
discretion, picking as far as possible times when they are not required for
their normal duties. The wardens must arrange that the enemy would be
impeded at every turn, whereas movement by our own side (by men or
beasts of burden or cattle) would be facilitated; and they must see that
every road is as easy for the traveler as can be managed.

The rain God sends must do the countryside good, not harm, so the
b   wardens must see that the water flowing off the high ground down into
any sufficiently deep ravines between the hills is collected by dikes and
ditches, so that the ravines can retain and absorb it, and supply streams
and springs for all the districts in the countryside below, and give even
the driest of spots a copious supply of pure water. As for water that springs
from the ground, the wardens must beautify the fountains and rivers that
c   form by adorning them with trees and buildings; they must use drains to
tap the individual streams and collect an abundant supply, and any grove
or sacred enclosure which has been dedicated nearby must be embellished
by having a perennial flow of water directed by irrigation into the very
temples of the gods. The young men should erect in every quarter gymnasia
for themselves and senior citizens, construct warm baths for the old folk,
and lay up a large stock of thoroughly dry wood. All this will help to
d   relieve invalids, and farmers wearied by the labor of the fields—and it
will be a much kinder treatment than the tender mercies of some fool of
a doctor.

All these and similar projects will beautify and improve a district, and
permit some welcome recreation into the bargain. The Wardens' really
serious duties should be as follows. Each squad of sixty must protect its
own district not only from enemies, but from those who profess to be
e   friends. If a slave or a free man injures a neighbor or any other citizen,

the Wardens must try the case brought by the plaintiff. The five leaders should deal with the trivial cases on their own authority, but in the more important cases (when one man sues another for any sum up to three minas) they should sit in judgment with one group of twelve assistants as a bench of seventeen. Apart from the officials whose decisions (like those of kings) are final, no judge shall hold court, and no official shall fill his position, without being liable to be called to account for his actions. The Country-Wardens are to be no exception, if they treat the people in their care at all high-handedly by giving them unfair orders or by trying   762 to grab and remove any agricultural equipment without permission, or allow their palms to be greased, or go so far as to deliver unjust verdicts. For giving way to boot-lickers they must be publicly disgraced. When the actual injury they have done to an inhabitant of their district does not exceed one mina in value, they should voluntarily submit to a trial before the villagers and neighbors. Whenever larger sums are involved (or even   b smaller sums, if the accused is not prepared to submit to trial because he's confident that by moving to a fresh district every month he will get away and 'get off' too), the injured party should file suit against him in the common courts.

7. If the plaintiff wins the day,
then this elusive fellow who was not prepared to pay a penalty with a good grace must pay him double the amount at issue.

The way of life of the Country-Wardens and their officers during their two years on duty will be something like this. First, in every district of the country there should be communal restaurants, at which everyone will   c have to eat together.

8. If a Warden fails to turn up at these meals even for one day, or sleeps away from his quarters at night, except on the express orders of his superiors or because of some unavoidable necessity,
the five leaders may post his name in the market-place as a deserter from his post; if they do, he will have to bear the disgrace of having turned traitor to the state, and everyone who happens to meet him will be entitled to give him a beating if he wants to, without being punished for it.

If one of the actual officers goes so far as to commit this sort of offense,   d all his fifty-nine colleagues must look into the business.

9. If one of them notices (or is told) what is going on and fails to bring a case,
the same laws should be invoked against him, and he must be punished with greater severity than his juniors: that is, he is to be stripped of his right to exercise any authority over the young.

The Guardians of the Laws should keep a sharp eye on these offenses and try to stop them being committed at all; failing that, they must see that the proper penalties are inflicted.

e   No one will ever make a commendable master without having been a servant first; one should be proud not so much of ruling well but of serving well—and serving the laws above all (because this is the way we serve the gods), and secondly, if we are young, those who are full of years and honor. It is vital that everyone should be convinced that this rule applies to us all. The next point, then, is that when someone who has joined the Country-Wardens gets to the end of his two years, he ought to be no stranger to a meager daily ration of uncooked food. In fact, after being selected, the groups of twelve assistant Wardens must assemble with the
763 five officers and resolve that, being servants, they will not possess other servants and slaves for themselves, nor employ the attendants of other people (the farmers and villagers) for their own private needs, but only for public tasks. With that exception, they must expect to double as their own servants and fend for themselves; and on top of all that they must reckon to investigate the entire country, summer and winter, in arms, to
b   protect and get to know every district in succession. Everyone should be closely familiar with his own country: probably no study is more valuable. This is the real reason why the youths must go in for hunting with dogs, and other types of chase—quite apart from the pleasure and profit that everyone gets out of such activities.

So much for these 'secret-service men' or 'Country-Wardens' (call them
c   what you will), and their regimen—a regimen into which everyone who means to play his part in keeping his country safe must throw himself heart and soul.

The next election on our list was that of the Market-Wardens and City-Wardens. There are to be three of the latter, who will divide the twelve sections of the city into three groups, and like their counterparts (the Country-Wardens), will look after the roads, both the streets within the city boundaries and the various routes that extend into the capital from
d   the country; and they must also supervise the buildings, to see that they are constructed to the statutory standards. In particular, they must ensure that the water which the Guards-in-Chief have transmitted and sent on to them in good condition reaches the fountains pure and in sufficient quantities, so that it enhances the beauty and amenities of the city. So these officials too must be men of some caliber, with time to go in for public affairs, which means that every citizen nominating City-Wardens must confine his choice to members of the highest property-class. When
e   they have held the election and produced a short list of six candidates with the most votes, the officials responsible are to select three of them by lot; and these, after scrutiny, should hold office in accordance with the laws provided for them.

Next, five Market-Wardens must be elected from the first and second property-classes. In general, their election should be conducted as for the

City-Wardens: ten should be selected from the list of candidates by voting, and then five selected by lot, who after due scrutiny should be appointed to office. (Voting is compulsory for all in every election, and everyone who fails in his duty and is denounced to the authorities should be fined 764 fifty drachmas and get the reputation of being a scoundrel. Attendance at the assembly (the general meeting of the state) is to be optional, except for members of the first and second property-classes, who will be fined ten drachmas if their absence from such a meeting is proved. But the third and fourth classes will not be forced to attend and should not be subject to any penalty unless the authorities, for some pressing reason, instruct everyone to come.) To get back to the Market-Wardens: they are to maintain b due order in the market, and look after the temples and fountains, to see that no one damages them. They must punish anyone who commits an offense, a slave or foreigner by whipping him and putting him in chains; but if a native citizen misbehaves himself in this way, the Market-Wardens should be authorized to decide the case on their own and fine the culprit up to a hundred drachmas, the limit being increased to two hundred if they sit in association with the City-Wardens. In their own sphere, the c City-Wardens too should have the same power of fining and punishing, and inflict fines up to one mina on their own, and up to two minas in association with the Market-Wardens.

The right thing to do next will be to appoint officials in charge of (A) culture and (B) physical training—two categories of them in each case, one (1) to handle the educational side and the other (2) to organize competitions. By (1) 'education officials' the law means superintendents of gymnasia and schools, who see that they are decently run, supervise the d curriculum and organize such related matters as the attendance and accommodation of the boys and girls. (2) 'Officials in charge of competitions' means judges of competitors in athletics and contests of the arts (there being here again two categories (AB) of officials, one for the arts, one for athletics). (B2) Men and horses in athletic contests can have the same judges, but (A2) in the arts, choruses should properly have (A2a) one set of judges, while solo dramatic performances (given by reciters of poetry, e lyre-players, pipe-players and such people) ought to have another (A2b). So I suppose a good start will be to select (A2a) the authority to supervise children, men and girls as they enjoy themselves in choruses by dancing and every other type of cultural activity. One official, who is to be not less than forty years old, will suffice, and one of not less than thirty (A2b) will 765 also be enough to present the solo performances and give an adequate decision between the contestants. The Chief Organizer of the Choruses (A2a) must be chosen in some such way as this. All those who are keen on such things should attend the election meeting and be liable to a fine if they don't (this is a point for the Guardians of the Laws to decide), whereas others who do not wish to attend should not be compelled. In b proposing their choice the electors should confine themselves to the experts, and in the scrutiny there must be only one reason for accepting or rejecting the candidate the lot has favored: that he is experienced or inexperienced as the case may be. One of the ten nominees with the most votes must be selected by lot, scrutinized, and be in charge of the choruses for the year according to law. Similarly with the year's entrants for solo performances and combined pieces on the pipes: only after the application of the same criterion should the candidate (A2b) favored by the lot take charge of them and decide between them, having referred the decision in his own case to

c   his judges. Next, (B2) Umpires for athletic contests and exercises of horses and men must be chosen from the second and also the third property-class; it will be compulsory for members of the first three classes to take part in the election, but the lowest class may be let off without a fine. The Umpires should number three, chosen by lot from the twenty candidates who head the poll, and duly sanctioned by the scrutineers.

d   If anyone is judged and found wanting in the scrutiny after being drawn by lot for any office, another person must be chosen in his place by the same methods, and his scrutiny conducted in the same way.

    The remaining official in this field is the director of the entire education of the boys and girls. Here too there should be one official in charge under the law. He must be not younger than fifty years old, and the father of legitimate children—preferably both sons and daughters, though either

e   alone will do. The chosen candidate himself and those who choose him should appreciate that this is by far the most important of all the supreme offices in the state. Any living creature that flourishes in its first stages of growth gets a tremendous impetus towards its natural perfection and the final development appropriate to it, and this is true of both plants and

766 animals (tame and wild), and men too. Man is a 'tame' animal, as we put it, and of course if he enjoys a good education and happens to have the right natural disposition, he's apt to be a most heavenly and gentle creature; but his upbringing has only to be inadequate or misguided and he'll become the wildest animal on the face of the earth. That's why the legislator should not treat the education of children cursorily or as a secondary matter; he should regard the right choice of the man who is going to be in charge of the children as something of crucial importance, and appoint

b   as their Minister the best all-round citizen in the state. So all the officials except the council and members of the Executive[5] should meet at the temple of Apollo and hold a secret ballot, each man voting for whichever Guardian of the Laws he thinks would make the best Minister of Education. The one who attracts the largest number of votes should be scrutinized by the officials who have elected him, the Guardians of the Laws standing

c   aside. The Minister should hold office for five years, and in the sixth he should be replaced by his successor after an election held under the same rules.

    If any public official dies in office and there are more than thirty days of his tenure left to run, the officials concerned must follow the same

5. See 758a ff.

procedure as before and appoint a replacement. If a guardian of orphans dies, the relatives on both the mother's and the father's side (as far as the children of first cousins), provided they are living in the state, should appoint a successor within ten days, or be fined a drachma for every day they let pass without appointing the children's new guardian.

Of course, any state without duly established courts simply ceases to *be* a state. If a judge is silent, and (as in arbitration) has no more to say than the litigants in a preliminary hearing he'll never be able to come to a satisfactory decision on the cases before him. That's why a large bench finds it difficult to return good verdicts—and so does a small one, if its members are of poor caliber. The point in dispute between the parties must always be made crystal clear, and leisurely and repeated interrogation over a period of time helps a lot to clarify the issues. That is the justification for making litigants bring their charges initially before a court of neighbors, who will be their friends and understand best the actions which provoke the dispute. If a litigant is dissatisfied with the judgment of this court, he may apply to a second, but if the first two courts are both unable to settle the argument, the verdict of the third must close the case.

In a sense, to establish a court is to elect officials. Every official, you see, sometimes has to set up as a judge as well; and a judge, although strictly he has no official position, becomes in a way an official of considerable importance during the day on which he sits in judgment and gives his verdict. So on the assumption that judges too are officials, let's specify what judges will be appropriate, the disputes they will decide, and how many should sit on each case. The court appointed by the common choice of the litigants themselves for their own private cases should have absolute authority. Cases may be brought before the other courts for two reasons: one private person may charge another with having done him wrong, and bring him to court so that the issue can be decided; or someone may believe that one of the citizens is acting against the public interests and wish to come to the community's assistance. Now we must specify the character and identity of the judges.

First, let's set up a common court for all private persons who are contesting an issue with each other for the third time. It is to be formed in some such way as this. All officials whose tenure lasts for a year or longer should assemble in a single temple on the day just before the new year opens in the month after the summer solstice; then, after swearing to the god, they must offer him their choicest fruit, so to speak: each board of officials should contribute one judge, the man who appears to be the outstanding member of his board and seems likely to judge the cases of his fellow citizens during the coming year in the best and most god-fearing manner. When the judges have been chosen, their scrutiny should be conducted before their very electors, and if any one of them is rejected, a replacement should be chosen under the same rules. Those who pass the scrutiny are to sit in judgment on the cases of the litigants who refuse to accept the decision of the other courts. They are to vote openly, and it will be

d

e

767

b

c

d

e

compulsory for the Councillors and the other officials who elected the judges to watch and listen to the trials; others may attend if they wish.

If anyone accuses a man of having knowingly returned a false verdict, he must go to the Guardians of the Laws to prefer the charge.

10. If the accused is found guilty as charged,
he will have to pay to the injured party half the damages awarded; if he is thought to deserve a stiffer punishment, his judges must calculate the additional penalty he should suffer or additional fine he ought to pay to the state and his prosecutor.

768   As for charges of crimes against the state, the first need is to let the man in the street play his part in judging them. A wrong done to the state is a wrong done to all its citizens, who would be justifiably annoyed if they were excluded from deciding such cases. But although we should allow the opening and closing stages of this kind of trial to be in the hands of the people, the detailed examination should be conducted by three of the highest officials, chosen by agreement between prosecutor and defendant. If they are unable to reach agreement themselves, the council should decide between their respective choices.

b   Everyone should have a part to play in private suits too, because anyone excluded from the right to participate in trying cases feels he has no stake in the community whatever. Hence we must also have courts organized on a tribal basis, where the judges, being chosen by lot as occasion arises, will give their verdicts uncorrupted by external pressures. But the final decision in all these cases is to be given by that other court which deals

c   with litigants who cannot settle their case either before their neighbors or in the tribal courts, and which for their benefit has been made (we claim) as incorruptible a court as can be assembled by human power.

So much for our courts (and we admit that to call their members either 'officials' or 'non-officials' without qualification raises difficulties of terminology). We've given a sort of superficial sketch, which in spite of including a number of details, nevertheless omitted a good many, because a better place for presenting an exact legal procedure and classification of suits

d   will be towards the end of our legislation. So this theme may be dismissed till we are finishing off. We have already explained most of the rules for establishing official posts, but we still can't get a completely clear and exact picture of every individual detail of the entire constitutional organization of the state: for that, we need to take every single topic in proper sequence and go through the whole subject from beginning to end. So far, then,

e   we've described the election of officials, and that brings us to the end of our introduction. Now to start the actual legislation: there's no need to postpone or delay it any longer.

CLINIAS: I very much approve of your introduction, sir, and I'm even more impressed by the way you've rounded it off so that it leads into the opening of the next theme.

ATHENIAN: So far, then, these ideas we old men have been tossing about   769
have given us splendid sport.

CLINIAS: Splendid indeed, but I fancy you really meant they were 'a
splendid challenge for men in their prime of life'.

ATHENIAN: I dare say. But here's another point. I wonder if you agree
with me?

CLINIAS: What about? What point?

ATHENIAN: You know how painting a picture of anything seems to be
a never-ending business. It always looks as if the process of touching up   b
by adding color or relief (or whatever it's called in the trade) will never
finally get to the point where the clarity and beauty of the picture are
beyond improvement.

CLINIAS: Yes, I too get much the same sort of impression, though only
from hearsay—I've never gone in for that sort of skill.

ATHENIAN: Well, you haven't missed anything. But we can still use this
passing mention of it to illustrate the next point. Suppose that one day
somebody were to take it into his head to paint the most beautiful picture   c
in the world, which would never deteriorate but always improve at his
hands as the years went by. You realize that as the painter is not immortal,
he won't achieve anything very permanent by lavishing such care and
attention on his picture unless he leaves some successor to repair the
ravages of time? Won't his successor also have to be able to supplement
deficiencies in his master's skill and improve the picture by touching it up?[6]

CLINIAS: True.

ATHENIAN: Well then, don't you think the legislator will want to do   d
something similar? First of all he'll want to write his laws and make them
as accurate as he can; then as time goes on and he tries to put his pet
theories into practice—well, do you think there's any legislator so stupid
as not to realize that his code has many inevitable deficiencies which must
be put right by a successor, if the state he's founded is to enjoy a continuous   e
improvement in its administrative arrangements, rather than suffer a decline?

CLINIAS: Yes, I think—indeed I'm sure—that this is the sort of thing any
legislator will want to do.

ATHENIAN: So if a legislator were able to discover a way of doing this—
that is, if by instruction or pointing to concrete examples he could make
someone else understand (perfectly or imperfectly) how to keep laws in
good repair by amending them—I suppose he'd never give up explaining
his method until he'd got it across?

CLINIAS: Of course.   770

ATHENIAN: So isn't this what you two and I ought to be doing now?

CLINIAS: What do you mean?

ATHENIAN: Now that we (in the evening of life) are on the point of
framing laws, for which we have guardians already chosen (our juniors),

---

6. Deleting *eis to prosthen* in c6.

oughtn't we to combine our law-giving with an attempt to turn *them* into law-'givers' as well as law-'guardians', as far as we can?

b   CLINIAS: Of course we ought, assuming we're up to it.

ATHENIAN: Anyhow, we ought to try, and do our level best.

CLINIAS: Certainly.

ATHENIAN: Let's address them as follows: 'Colleagues and protectors of our laws, we shall—inevitably—leave a great many gaps in every section of our code. However, we shall certainly take care to outline a sort of sketch of the complete system with its main points, and it will be your
c   job to take this sketch and fill in the details. You ought to hear what your aims should be when you do this. Megillus and Clinias and I have mentioned it to each other more than once, and we are agreed that our formula is a good one. We want you to be sympathetic to our way of thinking and become our pupils, keeping in view this aim which the three of us are unanimous a giver and guardian of laws should have. The central point on which we agree amounted to this. "Our aim in life should be
d   goodness and the spiritual virtue appropriate to mankind. There are various things that can assist us: it may be some pursuit we follow, a particular habit, or something we possess; we may get help from some desire we have or some opinion we hold or some course of study; and all this is true of both male and female members of the community, young or old. Whatever the means, it's this aim we've described that we must all strain every muscle to achieve throughout our lives. No man, whoever he is,
e   should ever be found valuing anything else, if it impedes his progress—not even, in the last resort, the state. Rather than have the state tolerate the yoke of slavery and be ruled by unworthy hands, it may be absolutely necessary to allow it to be destroyed, or abandon it by going into exile. All that sort of hardship we simply have to endure rather than permit a change to the sort of political system which will make men worse." This, then, is the agreed statement; now it's up to you to consider this double
771   aim of ours and censure the laws that can do nothing to help us; but you must commend and welcome the effective ones with enthusiasm, and cheerfully live as they dictate. You must have no truck with other pursuits which aim at different "goods" (as people call them).'

The best way to start the next section of our code will be to deal with matters of religion. First, we should go back to the figure of 5040 and
b   reflect again how many convenient divisors we found both in this total and its subdivision the tribe (which is one-twelfth of the total, as we specified, i.e., exactly the product of twenty-one multiplied by twenty). Our grand total is divisible by twelve, and so is the number of persons in a tribe (420) and in each case this subdivision must be regarded as holy, a gift of God, corresponding to the months of the year and the revolution of the universe. This is exactly why every state is guided by innate intuition to give these fractions the sanction of religion, though in some cases the divisions have been made more correctly than in others and the religious
c   backing has proved more successful. So for our part we claim that we had

every justification for preferring 5040, which can be divided by every number from one to twelve, except eleven (a drawback that's very easily cured: one way to remedy it is simply to omit two hearths). The truth of this could be demonstrated very briefly in any idle moment. So let's trust to the rule we've just explained, and divide our number along those lines. We must allocate a god, or child of a god, to each division and subdivision of the state and provide altars and the associated equipment; we must establish two meetings per month for the purposes of sacrifice, one in each of the twelve tribes into which the state is divided, and another in each of the twelve local communities that form the divisions of each tribe. This arrangement is intended to ensure, first, that we enjoy the favor of the gods and heaven in general, and secondly (as we'd be inclined to stress[7]) that we should grow familiar and intimate with each other in every kind of social contact.

You see, when people are going to live together as partners in marriage, it is vital that the fullest possible information should be available about the bride and her background and the family she'll marry into. One should regard the prevention of mistakes here as a matter of supreme importance—so important and serious, in fact, that even the young people's recreation must be arranged with this in mind. Boys and girls must dance together at an age when plausible occasions can be found for their doing so, in order that they may have a reasonable look at each other; and they should dance naked, provided sufficient modesty and restraint are displayed by all concerned.

The controllers and organizers of the choruses should be in charge of all these arrangements and maintain due order; and in conjunction with the Guardians of the Laws they will settle anything we leave out. As we said, it's inevitable that a legislator will omit the numerous details of such a topic; those who administer his laws from year to year will have to learn from experience and settle the details by annual refinements and amendments, until they think they've made the rules and procedures sufficiently precise. In the case of sacrifices and dances, a reasonable and adequate period to allow for experiment, in general and in detail, will be ten years. So long as the original legislator is alive, the various officials should bring him into the consultations, but when he is dead they must use their own initiative in putting up to the Guardians of the Laws proposals for remedying the deficiencies in their respective spheres. This process should continue until every detail is thought to have received its final polish. After that, they must assume that the rules are immutable, and observe them along with the rest of the code which the legislator laid down and imposed on them originally. Not a single detail should be altered, if they can help it; but if they ever believe that the force of circumstances has become irresistible, they must consult all the officials, the entire citizen body and all the oracles of the gods. If the verdict is unanimously in favor,

7. See 738b–e.

then they may amend, but never in any other conditions whatever; the law will be that the opposition must always win the day.

To resume, then: when a man of twenty-five has observed others and been observed by them and is confident that he has found a family offering someone to his taste who would make a suitable partner for the procreation
e   of children, he should get married, and in any case before he reaches thirty. First, however, he ought to hear the correct method of trying to find a suitable and congenial partner. As Clinias says, the appropriate preface should stand at the head of every law.

CLINIAS: Well reminded, sir—and at just the right moment in our conversation, I fancy.

ATHENIAN: Quite so. 'My boy,' let's say to this son of a good family,
773 'you must make a marriage that will be approved by sensible folk. They will advise you not to be over keen to avoid marrying into a poor family or to seek to marry into a rich one; other things being equal, you should always prefer to marry somewhat beneath you. That will be best both for the state and the union of your two hearths and homes, because it is infinitely better for the virtue of a man and wife if they balance and complement each other than if they are both at the same extreme. If a man
b   knows he's rather headstrong and apt to be too quick off the mark in everything he does, he ought to be anxious to ally himself to a family of quiet habits, and if he has the opposite kind of temperament he should marry into the opposite kind of family. One general rule should apply to marriage: we should seek to contract the alliance that will benefit the state, not the one that we personally find most alluring. Everyone is naturally drawn to the person most like himself, and that puts the whole state off
c   balance, because of discrepancies in wealth and character, and these in turn generally lead, in most states, to results we certainly don't want to see in ours.'

If we give explicit instructions in the form of a law—'no rich man to marry into a rich family, no powerful person to marry into a powerful house, the headstrong must be forced to join in marriage with the phlegmatic and the phlegmatic with the headstrong'—well, it's ludicrous, of course,
d   but it will also annoy a great many people who find it hard to understand why the state should be like the mixture in a mixing-bowl. When you pour in the wine it seethes furiously, but once dilute it with the god of the teetotalers, and you have a splendid combination which will make you a good and reasonable drink. Very few people have it in them to see that the same principle applies to the alliance that produces children. For these reasons we are forced to omit such topics from our actual laws. However, we must resort to our 'charms'[8] and try to persuade everybody
e   to think it more important to produce well-balanced children than to marry his equal and never stop lusting for wealth. Anyone who is set on enriching

8. See 659e.

himself by his marriage should be headed off by reproaches rather than compelled by a written law.

So much for marriage: these exhortations should be added to our previous account of how we should become partners in eternity by leaving a line of descendants to serve God forever in our stead.[9] A correctly composed preface would have all that and more to say about the obligation to marry.

774

11. If anyone disobeys (except involuntarily), and unsociably keeps himself to himself so that he is still unmarried at the age of thirty-five, *he must* pay an annual fine: one hundred drachmas if he belongs to the highest property-class, seventy if to the second, sixty if to the third, and thirty if to the fourth; the sum to be consecrated to Hera.

b

12. If he refuses to pay his annual fine, *his debt* must be increased ten times.

(The fine is to be collected by the treasurer of the goddess.

13. If he fails to collect it, *he will* have to owe the sum himself.

Every treasurer must give an account of himself in this respect at the scrutiny.) So much for the financial penalty to be paid by anyone refusing to marry, but

12. (cont.) *he should* also be barred from receiving the respect due to him from his juniors, none of whom should ever readily take the slightest notice of him. If the bachelor tries to chastise a man, everyone should take the victim's side and protect him.

14. If a bystander fails to give the victim help, *the law* should see that he gets the reputation of being a rotten, lily-livered citizen.

c

We've already discussed dowries,[10] but we ought to repeat that even if the poor do have to marry and give in marriage on limited resources, it will not affect their prospects of a long life one way or the other, because in this state no one will go without the necessities of life. Nor will wives be so inclined to give themselves airs, and their husbands will be less humiliated by kowtowing to them for financial reasons. If a man obeys this law, so much to his credit.

d

15. If he does not, and gives or receives more than fifty drachmas for the trousseau in the case of the lowest property-class (or more than a hundred or a hundred and fifty or two hundred according to class),

9. See 721b–d.
10. See 742c.

he must owe as much again to the treasury, and the amount given or received must be dedicated to Hera and Zeus.

e   16. The treasurers of these gods are to exact these sums in the same way as we said the treasurers of Hera had to collect the fines in every case of refusal to marry,
or pay out of their own pockets.

The right to make a valid betrothal should rest initially with the bride's father, secondly with her grandfather, thirdly with her brothers by the same father. If none of these is available, the right should belong to the relatives on the mother's side in the same order. If any exceptional misfortune occurs, the nearest relatives shall be authorized to act in conjunction with the girl's guardians.

775   That leaves us with the pre-marriage sacrifices and any other relevant rites that should be performed before, during or after the wedding. A citizen should ask the Expounders about these matters, and be confident that if he does as they tell him, everything will be in order.

As for the wedding-feast, neither family should invite more than five friends of both sexes, and the number of relatives and kinsmen from either side should be limited similarly. No one should incur expense beyond his means: that is, no more than a mina in the case of the wealthiest class,
b   half a mina for the next and so on down the scale according to class. Everyone should commend the man who obeys the regulation, but

17. The Guardians of the Laws must chastise the disobedient as a philistine who has never been trained to appreciate the melodies[11] of the Muses of marriage.

To drink to the point of inebriation is improper whatever the place (except at the feasts of the god who made us the gift of wine), and it's dangerous too, especially if you want to make your marriage a success. On the day of their wedding particularly, when they are at a turning-point
c   in their lives, bride and groom ought to show restraint, so as to make as sure as they can (it being practically impossible to tell the day or night in which by the favor of God conception will take place) that any child they may have should have parents who were sober when they conceived him. Apart from that, children should not be conceived when the parents' bodies are in a state of drunken relaxation; the fetus should be compactly formed and firmly planted, and its growth should be orderly and undisturbed. But when he's drunk a man reels about all over the place and bumps into
d   things, and a raging passion invades his body and soul; this means that as a sower of his seed a drunkard will be clumsy and inefficient, and he'll produce unbalanced children who are not to be trusted, with devious

11. 'Nomes': the same pun as in 700b, 722d–e.

characters, and in all probability with misshapen bodies too. That's why all the year round, throughout his life (but particularly during the age of procreation), a man must take great care to do nothing to injure his health, if he can help it, and nothing with any hint of insolence or injustice, which will inevitably rub off on to the souls and bodies of his children, and produce absolutely degenerate creatures who have been stamped with the   e
likeness of their father. At the very least, he must shun such vices on the day of his wedding and the following night, because if a human institution gets off to a good and careful start, there is a sort of divine guarantee that it will prosper.

The bridegroom must regard one of the two homes included in the lot   776
as the nest in which he will bring up his brood of young; here he must be married, after leaving his father and mother, and here he must make his home and become the breadwinner for himself and his children. You see, when people feel the need of absent friends, the ties that bind them are strengthened, but when they overdo it and are too much together so that they're not apart long enough to miss each other, they drift apart. That's why the newly-weds must leave their father and mother and the wife's relatives in the old home and live somewhere else, rather as if they had gone off to a colony; and each side should visit, and be visited by,   b
the other. The young couple should produce children and bring them up, handing on the torch of life from generation to generation, and always worshipping the gods in the manner prescribed by law.

Now for the question of property: what will it be reasonable for a man to possess? Mostly, it's not difficult to see what it would be, and acquire it; but slaves offer difficulties at every turn. The reason is this. The terms   c
we employ are partly correct and partly not, in that the actual language we use about slaves is partly a reflection and partly a contradiction of our practical experience of them.

MEGILLUS: Oh? What do you mean? We don't yet see your point, sir.

ATHENIAN: No wonder, Megillus. The Spartan helot-system is probably just about the most difficult and contentious institution in the entire Greek world;[12] some people think it's a good idea, others are against it (though less feeling is aroused by the slavery to which the Mariandynians have   d
been reduced at Heraclea, and by the race of serfs to be found in Thessaly). Faced with these and similar cases, what should our policy be on the ownership of slaves? The point I happened to bring up in my discussion of the subject, and which naturally made you ask what I meant, was this: we know we'd all agree that a man should own the best and most docile slaves he can get—after all, many a paragon of a slave has done much more for a man than his own brother or son, and they have often been

---

12. The Spartan helots were a numerous class of state serfs, in part the descendants of the original non-Doric population conquered by the Dorian settlers (c. 1000 B.C.); see 633b above.

e   the salvation of their masters' persons and property and entire homes. We know quite well, don't we, that some people do tell such stories about slaves?

MEGILLUS: Certainly.

ATHENIAN: And don't others take the opposite line, and say that a slave's soul is rotten through and through, and that if we have any sense we won't trust such a pack at all? The most profound of our poets actually
777 says (speaking of Zeus) that

> *If you make a man a slave, that very day*
> *Far-sounding Zeus takes half his wits away.*[13]

Everyone sees the problem differently, and takes one side or the other. Some people don't trust slaves as a class in anything: they treat them like animals, and whip and goad them so that they make the souls of their slaves three times—no, a thousand times—more slavish than they were. Others follow precisely the opposite policy.

MEGILLUS: True.

b   CLINIAS: Well then, sir, in view of this conflict of opinion, what should we do about our own country? What's our line on the possession of slaves, and the way to punish them?

ATHENIAN: Look here, Clinias: the animal 'man' quite obviously has a touchy temper, and it looks as if it won't be easy, now or in the future, to persuade him to fall neatly into the two categories (slave and freeman master) which are necessary for practical purposes. Your slave, therefore,
c   will be a difficult beast to handle. The frequent and repeated revolts in Messenia, and in the states where people possess a lot of slaves who all speak the same language, have shown the evils of the system often enough; and we can also point to the various crimes and adventures of the robbers who plague Italy, the 'Rangers', as they're called. In view of all this you may well be puzzled to know what your general policy ought to be. In fact, there are just two ways of dealing with the problem open to us: first,
d   if the slaves are to submit to the condition without giving trouble, they should not all come from the same country or speak the same tongue, as far as it can be arranged; secondly, we ought to train them properly, not only for their sakes but above all for our own. The best way to train slaves is to refrain from arrogantly ill-treating them, and to harm them even less (assuming that's possible) than you would your equals. You see, when a man can hurt someone as often as he likes, he'll soon show whether or not his respect for justice is natural and unfeigned and springs from a
e   genuine hatred of injustice. If his attitude to his slaves and his conduct towards them are free of any taint of impiety and injustice, he'll be splendidly effective at sowing the seeds of virtue. Just the same can be said of

---

13. *Odyssey* xvii.322–23.

the way in which any master or dictator or person in any position of authority deals with someone weaker than himself. Even so, we should certainly punish slaves if they deserve it, and not spoil them by simply giving them a warning, as we would free men. Virtually everything you say to a slave should be an order, and you should never become at all familiar with them—neither the women nor the men. (Though this is how a lot of silly folk do treat their slaves, and usually only succeed in spoiling them and in making life more difficult—more difficult, I mean, for the slaves to take orders and for themselves to maintain their authority.)

CLINIAS: You're quite right.

ATHENIAN: So now that the citizen has been supplied with a sufficient number of suitable slaves to help him in his various tasks, the next thing will be to outline a housing-plan, won't it?

CLINIAS: Certainly.

ATHENIAN: Our state is new, and has no buildings already existing, so it rather looks as if it will have to work out the details of its entire architectural scheme for itself, particularly those of the temples and city walls. Ideally, Clinias, this subject would have been dealt with before we discussed marriage, but as the whole picture is theoretical anyway, it's perfectly possible to turn to it now, as we are doing. Still, when we put the scheme into practice, we'll see to the buildings, God willing, *before* we regulate marriage, and marriage will then crown our labors in this field. But here and now, let's just give a swift sketch of the building program.

CLINIAS: By all means.

ATHENIAN: Temples should be built all round the marketplace and on high ground round the perimeter of the city, for purposes of protection and sanitation. Next to them should be administrative offices and courts of law. This is holy ground, and here—partly because the legal cases involve solemn religious issues, partly because of the august divinities whose temples are nearby—judgment will be given and sentence received. Among these buildings will be the courts in which cases of murder, and all other crimes which deserve the death penalty, may properly be heard.

As for city walls, Megillus, I'd agree with the Spartan view that they should be left lying asleep and undisturbed in the ground. My reasons? As the poet neatly puts it, in those words so often cited, 'a city's walls should be made of bronze and iron, not stone'.[14] Besides, what fools people would take us for, and rightly, if we sent our young men out into the countryside every year to excavate trenches and ditches and various structures to ward off the enemy and stop them coming over the boundaries at all[15]—and then were to build a wall round the city! A wall never contributes anything to a town's health, and in any case is apt to encourage a certain softness in the souls of the inhabitants. It invites them to take refuge behind

778

b

c

d

e

779

14. We do not know the poet referred to, but the sentiment is fairly common: see e.g. Aeschylus, *Persians* 349.

15. See 760e.

it instead of tackling the enemy and ensuring their own safety by mounting guard night and day; it tempts them to suppose that a foolproof way of protecting themselves is to barricade themselves in behind their walls and gates, and then drop off to sleep, as if they were brought into this world for a life of luxury. It never occurs to them that comfort is really to be won by the sweat of the brow, whereas the only result of such disgusting luxury and idleness is a fresh round of troubles, in my view. However, if

b   men are to have a city wall at all, the private houses should be constructed right from the foundations so that the whole city forms in effect a single wall: that is, all the houses should be easy to defend because they present to the street a regular and unbroken front. A whole city looking like a single house will be quite a pretty sight, and being easy to guard it will be superior to any other for safety. The job of seeing that the buildings

c   always keep to the original scheme should properly belong to their occupants, but the City-Wardens should keep an eye on them and even impose fines to force any negligent person to do his duty. They should also supervise all the sanitary arrangements of the town and stop any private person encroaching on public land by buildings or excavations. The same officials must take particular care to see that rainwater flows away properly, and in general they must make all the appropriate arrangements inside and outside the city. To deal with all these points, and to supplement any other

d   deficiency in the law (which cannot be exhaustive), the Guardians of the Laws are to make additional rules in the light of experience.

So much for these buildings, together with those round the marketplace, and gymnasia and all the schools: they are now ready and waiting to be entered, and the theaters are prepared for the arrival of their audiences. Now let's pass on to the next item in our legislation, the time after the wedding.

CLINIAS: By all means.

e   ATHENIAN: Let's suppose the ceremony is over, Clinias; between then and the birth of a child there may well be a complete year. Now, in a state which sets its sights higher than others, how this year is to be spent by a bride and groom (you remember we broke off when we got to this point) is not the easiest thing in the world to specify. We've had knotty problems like this before, but the common man will find our policy this time more difficult to swallow than ever. However, we should never shrink from speaking the truth as we see it, Clinias.

CLINIAS: Of course.

780   ATHENIAN: Take someone who proposes to promulgate laws to a state about the correct conduct of the public life of the community. What if he reckons that *in principle* one ought not to use compulsion—even in so far as one *can* use it in private affairs? Suppose he thinks that a man ought to be allowed to do what he likes with the day, instead of being regulated at every turn. Well, if he excludes private life from his legislation, and expects that the citizens will be prepared to be law-abiding in their public life as a community, he's making a big mistake. Now, what's made me say this? It's because we

are going to assert that our newly-marrieds ought to attend communal meals   b
no more and no less than they did before their wedding. I know that this
custom of eating together caused eyebrows to be raised when it was introduced in your parts of the world, but I suppose it was dictated by war or
some other equally serious emergency that pressed hard on a small people
in a critical situation. But once you had had this enforced experience of communal meals, you realized just how much the custom contributed to your
security. It must have been in some such way that the practice of communal   c
feeding established itself among you.

CLINIAS: That sounds plausible enough.

ATHENIAN: As I was saying, it was once an astonishing custom and some
people were apprehensive about imposing it. But if a legislator wanted to
impose it today, he wouldn't have half so much trouble. But the custom
points to another measure, which would probably prove equally successful,
if tried. Today, it's absolutely unheard-of, and that's what makes the legislator 'card his wool into the fire', as the saying is, and make so many efforts
fruitlessly. This measure is neither easy to describe nor simple in execution.   d

CLINIAS: Well then, sir, what's the point you're trying to make? You
seem to be awfully reluctant to tell us.

ATHENIAN: Listen to me, then: let's not waste time lingering over this
business. The blessings that a state enjoys are in direct proportion to the
degree of law and order to be found in it, and the effects of good regulations
in some fields are usually vitiated to the extent that things are controlled
either incompetently or not at all in others. The point is relevant to the
subject in hand. Thanks to some providential necessity, Clinias and Megil-   e
lus, you have a splendid and—as I was saying—astonishing institution:
communal meals for men. But it is entirely wrong of you to have omitted   781
from your legal code any provision for your women, so that the practice
of communal meals for them has never got under way. On the contrary,
half the human race—the female sex, the half which in any case is inclined
to be secretive and crafty, because of its weakness—has been left to its
own devices because of the misguided indulgence of the legislator. Because
you neglected this sex, you gradually lost control of a great many things
which would be in a far better state today if they had been regulated by
law. You see, leaving women to do what they like is not just to lose *half*   b
the battle (as it may seem): a woman's natural potential for virtue is inferior
to a man's, so she's proportionately a greater danger, perhaps even twice
as great. So the happiness of the state will be better served if we reconsider
the point and put things right, by providing that all our arrangements
apply to men and women alike. But at present, unhappily, the human race
has not progressed as far as that, and if you're wise you won't breathe a   c
word about such a practice in other parts of the world where states do
not recognize communal meals as a public institution at all. So when it
comes to the point, how on earth are you going to avoid being laughed
to scorn when you try to force women to take their food and drink in
public? There's nothing the sex is likely to put up with more reluctantly:

women have got used to a life of obscurity and retirement, and any attempt
to force them into the open will provoke tremendous resistance from them,
d   and they'll be more than a match for the legislator. Elsewhere, as I said,
the very mention of the correct policy will be met with howls of protest.
But perhaps this state will be different. So if you want our discussion
about political systems to be as complete as theory can ever be, I'd like to
explain the merits and advantages of this institution—that is, if you are
equally keen to listen to me. If not, then let's skip it.

CLINIAS: No, no, sir: we're very anxious to hear the explanation.

ATHENIAN: Let's listen, then. But don't be disconcerted if I appear to be
e   starting a long way back. We've time to spare, and there's no compelling
reason why we shouldn't look into the business of legislation from all
possible angles.

CLINIAS: You're quite right.

ATHENIAN: Let's go back to what we said at the beginning.[16] Here's
something that everyone must be perfectly clear about: *either* mankind had
782   absolutely no beginning in time and will have no end, but always existed
and always will, *or* it has existed for an incalculably long time from its
origin.

CLINIAS: Naturally.

ATHENIAN: Well, now we may surely assume that in every part of the
world cities have been formed and destroyed, and all sorts of customs
have been adopted, some orderly, some not, along with the growth of
every sort of taste in food, solid and liquid. And the various changes in the
seasons have developed, which have probably stimulated a vast number of
b   natural changes in living beings.

CLINIAS: Of course.

ATHENIAN: Well, we believe, don't we, that at a certain point virtues
made their appearance, not having existed before, and olives likewise, and
the gifts of Demeter and Kore,[17] which Triptolemus, or whoever it was,
handed on to us? So long as these things did not exist, we can take it that
animals resorted to feeding on each other, as they do now?

CLINIAS: Certainly.

c   ATHENIAN: We observe, of course, the survival of human sacrifice among
many people today. Elsewhere, we gather, the opposite practice prevailed,
and there was a time when we didn't even dare to eat beef, and the
sacrifices offered to the gods were not animals, but cakes and meal soaked
in honey and other 'pure' offerings like that. People kept off meat on the
grounds that it was an act of impiety to eat it, or to pollute the altars of
the gods with blood. So at that time men lived a sort of 'Orphic'[18] life,

16. See 676a ff.

17. Grains.

18. The Orphics held that a human soul could be reborn in the body of another human
being or an animal, and the soul of an animal in another animal or a human being.
Hence they strictly prohibited killing and meat-eating.

keeping exclusively to inanimate food and entirely abstaining from eating   d
the flesh of animals.

CLINIAS: So it's commonly said, and it's easy enough to believe.

ATHENIAN: Then the question naturally arises, why have I related all this
to you now?

CLINIAS: A perfectly correct assumption, sir.

ATHENIAN: Now then, Clinias, I'll try to explain the next point, if I can.

CLINIAS: Carry on, then.

ATHENIAN: Observation tells me that all human actions are motivated
by a set of three needs and desires. Give a man a correct education, and   e
these instincts will lead him to virtue, but educate him badly and he'll
end up at the other extreme. From the moment of their birth men have a
desire for food and drink. Every living creature has an instinctive love of
satisfying this desire whenever it occurs, and the craving to do so can fill
a man's whole being, so that he remains quite unmoved by the plea that
he should do anything except satisfy his lust for the pleasures of the body,
so as to make himself immune to all discomfort. Our third and greatest   783
need, the longing we feel most keenly, is the last to come upon us: it is
the flame of the imperious lust to procreate, which kindles the fires of
passion in mankind. These three unhealthy instincts must be canalized
away from what men call supreme pleasure, and *towards* the supreme good.
We must try to keep them in check by the three powerful influences of
fear, law, and correct argument; but in addition, we should invoke the
help of the Muses and the gods who preside over competitions, to smother   b
their growth and dam their tide.

The topic which should come after marriage, and before training and
education, is the birth of children. Perhaps, as we take these topics in
order, we shall be able to complete each individual law as we did before,
when we approached the question of communal meals—I mean that when
we've become intimate with our citizens, perhaps we shall be able to see
more clearly whether such gatherings should consist of men only or
whether, after all, they should include women. Similarly, when we've won
control of certain institutions that have never yet been controlled by law,   c
we'll use them as 'cover', just as other people do, with the result I indicated
just now: thanks to a more detailed inspection of these institutions, we
may be able to lay down laws that take account of them better.

CLINIAS: Quite right.

ATHENIAN: So let's bear in mind the points we've just made, in case we
find we need to refer to them later on.

CLINIAS: What points in particular are you telling us to remember?

ATHENIAN: The three impulses we distinguished by our three terms: the
desire for 'food' (I think we said) and 'drink', and thirdly 'sexual stimu-   d
lation'.

CLINIAS: Yes, sir, we'll certainly remember, just as you tell us.

ATHENIAN: Splendid. Let's turn our attention to the bridal pair, and
instruct them in the manner and method by which they should produce

children. (And if we fail to persuade them, we'll threaten them with a law or two.)

CLINIAS: How do you mean?

ATHENIAN: The bride and groom should resolve to present the state with
e   the best and finest children they can produce. Now, when human beings
co-operate in any project, and give due attention to its planning and execution, the results they achieve are always of the best and finest quality; but
if they act carelessly, or are incapable of intelligent action in the first place,
the results are deplorable. So the bridegroom had better deal with his wife
and approach the task of begetting children with a sense of responsibility,
and the bride should do the same, especially during the period when no
784 children have yet been born to them. They should be supervised by women
whom we have chosen[19] (several or only a few—the officials should appoint
the number they think right, at times within their discretion). These women
must assemble daily at the temple of Eileithuia[20] for not more than a third
of the day, and when they have convened each must report to her colleagues
any wife or husband of childbearing age she has seen who is concerned
with anything but the duties imposed on him or her at the time of the
b   sacrifices and rites of their marriage. If children come in suitable numbers,
the period of supervised procreation should be ten years and no longer.
But if a couple remain childless throughout this period, they should part,
and call in their relatives and the female officials to help them decide terms
of divorce that will safeguard the interests of them both. If some dispute
arises about the duties and interests of the parties, they must choose ten
c   of the Guardians of the Laws as arbitrators, and abide by their decisions
on the points referred to them. The female officials must enter the homes
of the young people and by a combination of admonition and threats try
to make them give up their ignorant and sinful ways. If this has no effect,
they must go and report the case to the Guardians of the Laws, who must
resort to sterner methods. If even the Guardians prove ineffective, they
should make the case public and post up the relevant name, swearing on
their oath that they are unable to reform so-and-so.

d   18. (a) Unless the person whose name is posted up succeeds in convicting
         in court those who published the notice,
         he must be deprived of the privilege of attending weddings and parties
         celebrating the birth of children.

         19. If he persists in attending,
         anyone who wishes should chastise him by beating him, and not be pun-
         ished for it.

19. No such women have been mentioned. (In other ways too the state of the text
hereabouts suggests a lack of revision.)

20. Goddess of childbirth.

18. (b) If a woman misbehaves and her name is posted up, and she fails to win the day in court,
the same regulations are to apply to her too: she must be excluded from female processions and distinctions, and be forbidden to attend weddings and parties celebrating the birth of children.

20. When children have been produced as demanded by law, if a man   e
has intercourse with another woman, or a woman with another man, and the other party is still procreating,
they must suffer the same penalty as was specified for those who are still having children.

21. After the period of child-bearing, the chaste man or woman should be highly respected;
the promiscuous should be held in the opposite kind of 'repute' (though *dis*repute would be a better word).

When the majority of people conduct themselves with moderation in   785
sexual matters, no such regulations should be mentioned or enacted; but if there is misbehavior, regulations should be made and enforced after the pattern of the laws we've just laid down.

Our first year is the beginning of our whole life, and every boy's and girl's year of birth should be recorded in their family shrines under the heading 'born'. Alongside, on a whitened wall, should be written up in every brotherhood the sequence-numbers of the officials who facilitate the numbering of the years. The names of the living members of the brother-   b
hood should be inscribed nearby, and those of the deceased expunged.

The age limits for marriage shall be: for a girl, from sixteen to twenty (these will be the extreme limits specified), and for a man, from thirty to thirty-five. A woman may hold office from the age of forty, a man from thirty. Service in the armed forces shall be required of a man from twenty to sixty. As for women, whatever military service it may be thought necessary to impose (after they have finished bearing children) should be performed up to the age of fifty; practicable and appropriate duties should be specified for each individual.

Book VII

ATHENIAN: Now that the boys and girls have been born, I suppose their   788
education and training will be the most suitable topic to deal with next. This is not something we can leave on one side: that would be out of the question. However, we shall clearly do better to confine our remarks to advice and instruction, and not venture on precise regulations. In the privacy of family life, you see, a great many trivial activities never get publicity, and under the stimulus of feelings of pleasure or pain or desire   b

they can all too easily fly in the face of the lawgiver's recommendations and produce citizens whose characters are varied and conflicting, which is a social evil. Now although these activities are so trivial and so common that one cannot decently arrange to punish them by law, they do tend to undermine the written statutes, because men get into the habit of repeatedly
c   breaking rules in small matters. That's why in spite of all the difficulties of legislating on such points, we can't simply say nothing about them. But I must try to clarify my point by showing you some samples, as it were. At the moment, I expect it looks as if I'm rather concealing my meaning.

CLINIAS: You're quite right, it does.

ATHENIAN: I take it we were justified in asserting that if an education is to qualify as 'correct', it simply must show that it is capable of making our souls and bodies as fine and as handsome as they can be?

CLINIAS: Of course.

d   ATHENIAN: And I suppose (to take the most elementary requirement), that if a person is going to be supremely good-looking, his posture must be as erect as possible, right from his earliest years?

CLINIAS: Certainly.

ATHENIAN: Well now, we observe, don't we, that the earliest stages of growth of every animal are by far the most vigorous and rapid? That's why a lot of people actually maintain that in the case of man, the first five years of life see more growth than the next twenty.

CLINIAS: That's true.

789   ATHENIAN: But we're aware that rapid growth without frequent and appropriately graded exercises leads to a lot of trouble for the body?

CLINIAS: Yes, indeed.

ATHENIAN: And isn't it precisely when a body is getting most nourishment that it needs most exercise?

CLINIAS: Good Heavens, sir, are we going to demand such a thing of new-born babies and little children?

ATHENIAN: No—I mean even earlier, when they're getting nourishment in their mother's body.

CLINIAS: What's that you say? My dear sir! Do you really mean in the womb?

b   ATHENIAN: Yes, I do. But it's hardly surprising you haven't heard of these athletics of the embryo. It's a curious subject, but I'd like to tell you about it.

CLINIAS: Do so, of course.

ATHENIAN: It's something it would be easier to understand in Athens, where some people go in for sport more than they should. Not only boys, but some elderly men as well, rear young birds and set them to fight one
c   another. But they certainly don't think just pitting them one against another will give such creatures adequate exercise. To supplement this, each man keeps birds somewhere about his person—a small one in the cup of his hand, a larger one under his arm—and covers countless stades in walking

about, not for the sake of his own health, but to keep these animals in good shape. To the intelligent person, the lesson is obvious: all bodies find it helpful and invigorating to be shaken by movements and joltings of all kinds, whether the motion is due to their own efforts or they are carried on a vehicle or boat or horse or any other mode of conveyance. All this enables the body to assimilate its solid and liquid food, so that we grow healthy and handsome and strong into the bargain. In view of all this, can we say what our future policy should be? If you like, we could lay down precise rules (and how people would laugh at us!): (1) A pregnant woman should go for walks, and when her child is born she should mold it like wax while it is still supple, and keep it well wrapped up for the first two years of its life. (2) The nurses must be compelled under legal penalty to contrive that the children are always being carried to the country or temples or relatives, until they are sturdy enough to stand on their own feet. (3) Even then, the nurses should persist in carrying the child around until it's three, to keep it from distorting its young limbs by subjecting them to too much pressure. (4) The nurses should be as strong as possible, and there must be plenty of them—and we could provide written penalties for each infringement of the rules. But no! That would lead to far too much of what I mentioned just now.

CLINIAS: You mean . . .

ATHENIAN: . . . the tremendous ridicule we'd provoke. And the nurses (women and slaves, with characters to match) would refuse to obey us anyway.

CLINIAS: Then why did we insist that the rules should be specified?

ATHENIAN: For this reason. A state's free men and masters have quite different characters to the nurses', and there's a chance that if they hear these regulations they may be led to the correct conclusion: the state's general code of laws will never rest on a firm foundation as long as private life is badly regulated, and it's silly to expect otherwise. Realizing the truth of this, they may themselves spontaneously adopt our recent suggestions as rules, and thereby achieve the happiness that results from running their households and their state on proper lines.

CLINIAS: Yes, that's all very reasonable.

ATHENIAN: Still, let's not abandon this style of legislation yet. We started to talk about young children's bodies: let's use the same sort of approach to explain how to shape their personalities.

CLINIAS: Good idea.

ATHENIAN: So let's take this as our basic principle in both cases: all young children, and especially very tiny infants, benefit both physically and mentally from being nursed and kept in motion, as far as practicable, throughout the day and night; indeed, if only it could be managed, they ought to live as though they were permanently on board ship. But as that's impossible, we must aim to provide our new-born infants with the closest possible approximation to this ideal.

Here's some further evidence, from which the same conclusions should be drawn: the fact that young children's nurses, and the women who cure Corybantic conditions,[1] have learned this treatment from experience and have come to recognize its value. And I suppose you know what a mother does when she wants to get a wakeful child to sleep. Far from keeping

e him still, she takes care to move him about, rocking him constantly in her arms, not silently, but humming a kind of tune. The cure consists of *movement*, to the rhythms of dance and song; the mother makes her child *'pipe down'* just as surely as the music of the *pipes* bewitches the frenzied Bacchic reveler.[2]

CLINIAS: Well then, sir, have we any particular explanation for all this?

ATHENIAN: The reason's not very hard to find.

CLINIAS: What is it?

ATHENIAN: Both these conditions are a species of fear, and fear is the result

791 of some inadequacy in the personality. When one treats such conditions by vigorous movement, this external motion, by canceling out the internal agitation that gives rise to the fear and frenzy, induces a feeling of calm and peace in the soul, in spite of the painful thumping of the heart experienced by each patient. The result is very gratifying. Whereas the wakeful children are sent to sleep, the revelers (far from asleep!), by being set to dance to the music of the pipes, are restored to mental health after their

b derangement, with the assistance of the gods to whom they sacrifice so propitiously. This explanation, brief as it is, is convincing enough.

CLINIAS: Yes, indeed.

ATHENIAN: Well then, seeing how effective these measures are, here's another point to notice about the patient.[3] Any man who has experienced terrors from his earliest years will be that much more likely to grow up timid. But no one will deny that this is to train him to be a coward, not a hero.

CLINIAS: Of course.

c ATHENIAN: Contrariwise, we'd agree that a training in courage right from infancy demands that we overcome the terrors and fears that assail us?

CLINIAS: Exactly.

ATHENIAN: So we can say that exercising very young children by keeping them in motion contributes a great deal towards the perfection of one aspect of the soul's virtue.

CLINIAS: Certainly.

ATHENIAN: Further, good humor and bad humor will be a conspicuous element in a good or bad moral character respectively.

---

1. Frenzied pathological states accompanied by a strong desire to dance, popularly supposed to be caused by the Corybantes, spirits in attendance on the goddess Cybele. The condition was cured homoeopathically by the *disciplined* music and dancing of Corybantic ritual.

2. Reading *bakcheiōn* in e3 with acute accent on the second syllable.

3. Reading *autois* in b6.

CLINIAS: Of course.

ATHENIAN: So how can we instil into the new-born child, right from the start, whichever of these two characteristics we want? We must try to indicate how far they are within our control, and the methods we have to use. | d

CLINIAS: Quite so.

ATHENIAN: I belong to the school of thought which maintains that luxury makes a child bad-tempered, irritable, and apt to react violently to trivial things. At the other extreme, unduly savage repression turns children into cringing slaves and puts them so much at odds with the world that they become unfit to be members of a community.

CLINIAS: So how should the state as a whole set about bringing up children who are as yet unable to understand what is said to them or respond to any attempt to educate them? | e

ATHENIAN: More or less like this. Every new-born animal is apt to give a sort of loud yell—especially the human child, who in addition to yelling is also exceptionally prone to tears.

CLINIAS: He certainly is.

ATHENIAN: So if a nurse is trying to discover what a child wants, she judges from these reactions to what it is offered. Silence, she thinks, means she is giving it the right thing, whereas crying and bawling indicate the wrong one. Clearly these tears and yells are the child's way of signaling his likes and dislikes—and ominous signs they are, too, because this stage lasts at least three years, and that's quite a large part of one's life to spend badly (or well). | 792

CLINIAS: You're right.

ATHENIAN: Now don't you two think that a morose and ungenial fellow will on the whole be a more of a moaner and a grumbler than a good man has any right to be? | b

CLINIAS: Yes, *I* think so, at any rate.

ATHENIAN: Well then, suppose you do your level best during these years to shelter him from distress and fright and any kind of pain at all. Shouldn't we expect that child to be educated into a more cheerful and genial disposition?

CLINIAS: Certainly, and especially, sir, if one surrounded him with lots of pleasures. | c

ATHENIAN: Now here, my dear sir, is just where Clinias no longer carries me with him. That's the best way to ruin a child, because the corruption invariably sets in at the very earliest stages of his education. But perhaps I'm wrong about this: let's see.

CLINIAS: Tell us what you mean.

ATHENIAN: I mean that we're now discussing a topic of great importance. So you too, Megillus, see what your views are, and help us to make up our minds. My position is this: the right way of life is neither a single-minded pursuit of pleasure nor an absolute avoidance of pain, but a genial (the word I used just now) contentment with the state between those | d extremes—precisely the state, in fact, which we always say is that of God himself (a conjecture that's reasonable enough, supported as it is by the statements of the oracles). Similarly if one of *us* aspires to live like a god, this is the state he must try to attain. He must refuse to go looking for pleasure on his own account, aware that this is not a way of avoiding pain; nor must he allow anyone else to behave like that, young or old,

e   male or female—least of all newly-born children, if he can help it, because that's the age when habits, the seeds of the entire character, are most effectively implanted. I'd even say, at the risk of appearing flippant, that all expectant mothers, during the year of their pregnancy, should be supervised more closely than other women, to ensure that they don't experience frequent and excessive pleasures, or pains either. An expectant mother should think it important to keep calm and cheerful and sweet-tempered throughout her pregnancy.

793   CLINIAS: There's no need to ask Megillus which of us two has made the better case, sir. I agree with you that everyone should avoid a life of extreme pleasure and pain, and always take the middle course between them. Your point has been well and truly put, and you've heard it well and truly endorsed.

ATHENIAN: Admirable, Clinias! Well then, here's a related point that the three of us should consider.

CLINIAS: What's that?

ATHENIAN: That all the rules we are now working through are what
b   people generally call 'unwritten customs', and all this sort of thing is precisely what they mean when they speak of 'ancestral law'. Not only that, but the conclusion to which we were driven a moment ago was the right one: that although 'laws' is the wrong term for these things, we can't afford to say *nothing* about them, because they are the bonds of the entire social framework, linking all written and established laws with those yet to be passed. They act in the same way as ancestral customs dating from time immemorial, which by virtue of being soundly established and in-
c   stinctively observed, shield and protect existing written law. But if they go wrong and get 'out of true'—well, you know what happens when carpenters' props buckle in a house: they bring the whole building crashing down, one thing on top of another, stays and superstructure (however well built) alike—all because the original timberwork has given way. So you see, Clinias, this is what we have to bear in mind in thoroughly binding your state together while it is still a new foundation; we must do our best
d   not to omit anything, great or small, whether 'laws', 'habits' or 'institutions', because they are all needed to bind a state together, and the permanence of the one kind of norm depends on that of the other. So we ought not to be surprised to see a flood of apparently unimportant customs or usages making our legal code a bit on the long side.

CLINIAS: You're quite right, and we'll keep the point in mind.

ATHENIAN: Up to the age of three the early training of a boy or girl will
e   be helped enormously by this regimen, provided it is observed punctili-

ously and systematically. In the fourth, fifth, sixth and even seventh year of life, a child's character will need to be formed while he plays; we should now stop spoiling him, and resort to discipline, but not such as to humiliate him. We said, in the case of slaves,[4] that discipline should not be enforced so high-handedly that they become resentful, though on the other hand we mustn't spoil them by letting them go uncorrected; the same rule should apply to free persons too. When children are brought together, they discover more or less spontaneously the games which come naturally to them at that age. As soon as they are three, and until they reach the age of six, all children must congregate at the village temples—the children of each village to assemble at the same place. They should be kept in order and restrained from bad behavior by their nurses, who should themselves be supervised, along with their groups as a whole, by the twelve women elected for the purpose, one to be in charge of one group for a year at a time, the allocations to be made by the Guardians of the Law. The twelve must be elected by the women in charge of supervising marriage, one must be chosen from each tribe, and they must be of the same age as their electors. The woman allotted to a given tribe will discharge her duties by visiting the temple daily and punishing any cases of wrongdoing. She may use a number of state slaves to deal with male and female slaves and aliens on her own authority; however, if a citizen disputes his punishment, she must take the case to the City-Wardens, but if he does not dispute it, she may punish him too on her own authority. When the boys and girls have reached the age of six, the sexes should be separated; boys should spend their days with boys, and girls with girls. Each should attend lessons. The males should go to teachers of riding, archery, javelin-throwing and slinging—and the females too, if they are agreeable, may attend at any rate the lessons, especially those in the use of weapons. In this business, you see, pretty nearly everyone misunderstands the current practice.

CLINIAS: How so?

ATHENIAN: People think that where the hands are concerned right and left are *by nature* suited for different specialized tasks—whereas of course in the case of the feet and the lower limbs there is obviously no difference in efficiency at all. Thanks to the silly ideas of nurses and mothers we've all been made lame-handed, so to speak. The natural potential of each arm is just about the same, and the difference between them is our own fault, because we've habitually misused them. Of course, in activities of no consequence—using the left hand for the lyre and the right for the plectrum and so on—it doesn't matter in the slightest. But to take these examples as a model for other activities too, when there's no need, is pretty stupid. The Scythian practice is an illustration of this: a Scythian doesn't use his left hand exclusively to draw his bow and his right hand exclusively to fit in the arrow, but uses both hands for both jobs indifferently. There are

4. See 777d ff.

a lot of other similar examples to be found—in driving chariots, for instance, and other activities—from which we can see that when people train the left hand to be weaker than the right they are going *against* nature. As we said, that doesn't matter when it's a case of *plectra* of horn and similar instruments. But it matters enormously when one has to use iron weapons of war (javelins, arrows or whatever), and it matters most of all when you have to use your weapons in fighting hand to hand. And what a difference there is between a man who has learned this lesson and one who has not, between the trained and the untrained fighter! You know how a trained pancratiast or boxer or wrestler can fight on his left, so that when his opponent makes him change over and fight on that side, he doesn't stagger round as though he were lame, but keeps his poise. And I reckon we have to suppose that precisely the same rule applies to the use of weapons and to all other activities: when a man has two sets of limbs for attack and defense, he ought to leave neither of them idle and untrained if he can help it. In fact, if you were born with the body of a Geryon or a Briareus, you ought to be able to throw a hundred shafts with your hundred hands. All these points should come under the supervision of the male and female officials, the latter keeping an eye on the training the children get at play, the former superintending their lessons. They must see that every boy and girl grows up versatile in the use of both hands and both feet, so that they don't ruin their natural abilities by their acquired habits, so far as they can be prevented.

In practice, formal lessons will fall into two categories, physical training for the body, and cultural education to perfect the personality. Physical training can be further subdivided into two branches: dancing and wrestling. Now when people dance, they are either acting the words of the composer, and a dignified and civilized style is their prime concern, or they are aiming at physical fitness, agility and beauty. In this case they are preoccupied with bending and stretching in the approved fashion, so that each limb and other part of the body can move with its own peculiar grace—a grace which is then carried over and infused into dancing in general. As for wrestling, the kind of trick introduced as part of their technique by Antaeus and Cercyon because of their wretched obsession with winning, and the boxing devices invented by Epeius and Amycus, are absolutely useless in a military encounter and don't merit the honor of being described.[5] But if the legitimate maneuvers of *regular* wrestling—extricating the neck and hands and sides from entanglement—are practiced for the sake of strength and health with a vigorous desire to win and without resort to undignified postures, then they are extremely useful, and we mustn't neglect them. So when we reach the proper place in our legal code we must tell the future teachers to present all this kind of

5. E.g. dropping on to the ground in wrestling (Antaeus), and the use of gloves in boxing (Amycus).

instruction in an attractive way, and the pupils to receive it with gratitude. Nor should we omit to mention the chorus-performances that may appropriately be imitated: for instance, here in Crete the 'games in armor' of the Curetes,[6] and those of the Dioscuri[7] in Sparta. And at Athens our Virgin Lady,[8] I believe, charmed by the pleasure of performing in a chorus, and disapproving of empty hands in recreation, thought she should perform the dance only when arrayed in full armor. Our boys and girls should imitate her example wholeheartedly, and prize the gift which the goddess has made them, because it increases their fighting skill and embellishes their festivals. Young boys, right from the early stages up to the age of military service, should be equipped with weapons and horses whenever they parade and process in honor of any god; and when they supplicate the gods and sons of gods they must dance and march in step, sometimes briskly, sometimes slowly. Even contests and preliminary heats, if they are to prove their worth in war and peace to the state and private households, must be conducted with these purposes in view and no other. Other kinds of physical exercise, Megillus and Clinias, whether serious or by way of recreation, are beneath the dignity of a gentleman.

    I've now pretty well described the sort of physical education which needed to be described, as I said early on.[9] So there it is, in all its detail. If you know of a better system than that, let's have it.

    CLINIAS: No sir, if we cry off these ideas of yours a better program of competitions and physical training won't be easy to find.

    ATHENIAN: The next subject is the gifts of Apollo and the Muses. When we discussed this before,[10] we thought we'd exhausted the topic, and that physical training alone remained for discussion. But it's clear now that a number of points were omitted—points which everyone ought in fact to hear first. So let's go through them in order.

    CLINIAS: Yes, they should certainly be mentioned.

    ATHENIAN: Listen to me then. You've done that before, of course, but such a curious eccentricity calls for extreme caution in the speaker and his audience. You see, I'm going to spin a line that almost makes me afraid to open my mouth; still, I'll pluck up my courage and go ahead.

    CLINIAS: What is this thesis of yours, sir?

    ATHENIAN: I maintain that no one in any state has really grasped that children's games affect legislation so crucially as to determine whether the laws that are passed will survive or not. If you control the way children play, and the same children always play the same games under the same

---

6. Cretan spirits who protected the infant Zeus.

7. Castor and Pollux.

8. Athena.

9. See 673b ff.

10. In Books I–II.

rules and in the same conditions, and get pleasure from the same toys, you'll find that the conventions of adult life too are left in peace without alteration. But in fact games are always being changed and constantly modified and new ones invented, and the younger generation never enthuses over the same thing for two days running. They have no permanent agreed standard of what is becoming or unbecoming either in deportment

c or their possessions in general; they worship anyone who is always introducing some novelty or doing something unconventional to shapes and colors and all that sort of thing. In fact, it's no exaggeration to say that this fellow is the biggest menace that can ever afflict a state, because he quietly changes the character of the young by making them despise old things and value novelty. That kind of language and that kind of outlook is—again I say it—the biggest disaster any state can suffer. Listen: I'll tell you just how big an evil I maintain it is.

d CLINIAS: You mean the way the public grumbles at old-fashioned ways of doing things?

ATHENIAN: Exactly.

CLINIAS: Well, you won't find us shutting our ears to that kind of argument—you couldn't have a more sympathetic audience.

ATHENIAN: So I should imagine.

CLINIAS: Go on then.

ATHENIAN: Well now, let's listen to the argument with even greater attention than usual, and expound it to each other with equal care. Change, we shall find, except in something evil, is extremely dangerous. This is true of seasons and winds, the regimen of the body and the character of

e the soul—in short, of everything without exception (unless, as I said just now, the change affects something evil). Take as an example the way the body gets used to all sorts of food and drink and exercise. At first they upset it, but then in the course of time it's this very regimen that is responsible for its putting on flesh. Then the regimen and the flesh form

798 a kind of partnership, so that the body grows used to this congenial and familiar system, and lives a life of perfect happiness and health. But imagine someone forced to change again to one of the other recommended systems: initially, he's troubled by illnesses, and only slowly, by getting used to his new way of life, does he get back to normal. Well, we must suppose that precisely the same thing happens to a man's outlook and personality.

b When the laws under which people are brought up have by some heaven-sent good fortune remained unchanged over a very long period, so that no one remembers or has heard of things ever being any different, the soul is filled with such respect for tradition that it shrinks from meddling with it in any way. Somehow or other the legislator must find a method of bringing about this situation in the state. Now here's my own solution of the problem. All legislators suppose that an alteration to children's

c games really is just a 'game', as I said before, which leads to no serious or genuine damage. Consequently, so far from preventing change, they feebly give it their blessing. They don't appreciate that if children introduce novelties into their games, they'll inevitably turn out to be quite different people from the previous generation; being different, they'll demand a different kind of life, and that will then make them want new institutions and laws. The next stage is what we described just now as the biggest evil that can affect a state—but not a single legislator takes fright at the prospect.   d Other changes, that affect only deportment, will do less harm, but it is a very serious matter indeed to keep changing the criteria for praising or censuring a man's moral character, and we must take great care to avoid doing so.

CLINIAS: Of course.

ATHENIAN: Well then, are we still happy about the line we took earlier, when we said that rhythms and music in general were means of representing the characters of good men and bad? Or what?   e

CLINIAS: Yes, our view remains exactly the same.

ATHENIAN: So our position is this: we must do everything we possibly can to distract the younger generation from wanting to try their hand at presenting new subjects, either in dance or song; and we must also stop pleasure-mongers seducing them into the attempt.

CLINIAS: You're absolutely right.

ATHENIAN: Now, does any of us know of a better method of achieving   799 such an object than that of the Egyptians?

CLINIAS: What method is that?

ATHENIAN: To *sanctify* all our dances and music. The first job will be to settle the festivals by drawing up the year's program, which should show the dates of the various holidays and the individual gods, children of gods, or spirits in whose honor they should be taken. Second, it has to be decided what hymn should be sung at the various sacrifices to the gods and the type of dancing that should dignify the ritual in question. These decisions   b should be taken by some authority or other, and then the whole body of the citizens together should ratify them by sacrificing to the Fates and all the other gods, and by pouring a libation to consecrate the various songs to their respective divinities and other powers.

22. If anybody disobeys and introduces any different hymns or dances in honor of any god,
the priests and priestesses, in association with the Guardians of the Laws, will have the backing of sacred and secular law in expelling him.

23. If he resists expulsion,
he must be liable to a charge of impiety for the rest of his life at the hands of anyone who wishes to bring it.

CLINIAS: And serve him right.

ATHENIAN: Now seeing that we've got on to this topic, we must watch   c our step and behave ourselves.

CLINIAS: How do you mean?

ATHENIAN: No young man, much less an old one, on seeing or hearing anything paradoxical or unfamiliar, is ever going to brush aside his doubts all in a hurry and reach a snap decision about it. More probably, like a traveler who has come to a crossroads, alone or with others, and is rather uncertain about the right road, he'll pause, and put the problem to himself or his companions; and he won't continue his journey until he's pretty sure of his direction and bearings. That's precisely what we must do now. Our discussion has led us to a legal paradox, and naturally we must go into it in details and not—at our age—rashly claim to pontificate in such an important field off the cuff.

CLINIAS: You're absolutely right.

ATHENIAN: So we won't hurry over the problem, and only when we've looked into it properly shall we draw any firm conclusions. Still, there's no point in being deterred from completing the formal presentation of these 'laws' we're dealing with now, so let's press on till we get to the end of them. God willing, the completion of the whole exposition may perhaps point to an adequate solution of our present problem.

CLINIAS: You've put it very well, sir; let's do as you say.

ATHENIAN: So let's assume we've agreed on the paradox: our songs have turned into 'nomes' (apparently the ancients gave some such name to tunes on the lyre—perhaps they had some inkling of what we're saying, thanks to the intuition of someone who saw a vision either in his sleep or while awake). However that may be, let's adopt this as our agreed policy: no one shall sing a note, or perform any dance-movement, other than those in the canon of public songs, sacred music, and the general body of chorus performances of the young—any more than he would violate any other 'nome' or law. If a man obeys, he shall go unmolested by the law; but if he disobeys, the Guardians of the Laws and the priests and priestesses must punish him, as we said just now. Can we accept this as a statement of policy?

CLINIAS: We can.

ATHENIAN: Then how could one put these rules in proper legal form, without being laughed to scorn? Well now, there's a new point we ought to notice: in this business, the safest method is to sketch a few model rules. Here's one for you: imagine a sacrifice has been performed and the offerings burnt as demanded by law and someone standing in a private capacity near the altar and offerings—a son or brother, say—breaks out into the most extreme blasphemy: wouldn't his words fill his father and his other relations with alarm and despondency and forebodings of despair? Isn't that what we'd expect?

CLINIAS: Of course.

ATHENIAN: But it is hardly an exaggeration to say that in our corner of the world this is exactly what happens in pretty nearly every state. When an official has performed a public sacrifice, a chorus—or rather a mob of

choruses—arrives and takes up position not far from the altar and some-   d
times right next to it. Then they swamp the holy offerings with a flood of
absolute blasphemy. With words and rhythms and music of the most
morbid kind they work up the emotions of their audience to a tremendous
pitch, and the prize is awarded to the chorus which succeeds best in
making the community burst into tears—the very community which has
just offered sacrifice. Well, that's certainly a 'nome' on which we must
pass an unfavorable verdict, isn't it? If there is ever any real need for the
public to listen to such lugubrious noises, on days that are unclean and   e
unlucky, it will be much better, and entirely appropriate, to hire some
foreign choruses to sing such songs (just as one hires mourners to accompany funerals with Carian dirges). In particular, the costume appropriate
for such funeral dirges will not be garlands or trappings of gilt, but—to
polish off the topic as quickly as possible—quite the opposite kind of thing.
I merely repeat the question we're always asking ourselves: are we happy
to adopt this, for a start, as one of our model rules of singing?

CLINIAS: What?

ATHENIAN: The rule of auspicious language. This is the characteristic   801
that is absolutely vital for our kind of song. Or shall I simply lay down
the rule without repeating the question?

CLINIAS: Lay it down by all means: your law's been approved without
a single vote against it.

ATHENIAN: After auspicious language, then, what will be the second law
of music? Surely this: that the gods to whom we sacrifice should always
be offered our prayers.

CLINIAS: Of course.

ATHENIAN: And the third law, I suppose, will be this: poets should
appreciate that prayers are requests for something from the gods, so they
must take great care that they never inadvertently request an evil under   b
the impression that it is a benefit. What a ludicrous calamity it would be
to offer that kind of prayer!

CLINIAS: It certainly would.

ATHENIAN: Now didn't our remarks a short time ago[11] persuade us that
'Gold and Silver, the gods of Wealth, ought to have neither temple nor
home in our state'?

CLINIAS: Absolutely.

ATHENIAN: So what lesson can we say this doctrine holds for us? Surely
this: that authors in general are quite unable to tell good from bad. We   c
conclude that a composer who embodies this error in his words or even
in his music, and who produces mistaken prayers, will make our citizens
pray improperly when it comes to matters of importance—and, as we
were saying, we shan't find many more glaring mistakes than that. So can
we establish this as one of our model laws of music?

---

11. See 727e ff., 741e ff.

CLINIAS: What?

d   ATHENIAN: That a poet should compose nothing that conflicts with society's conventional notions of justice, goodness and beauty. No one should be allowed to show his work to any private person without first submitting it to the appointed assessors and to the Guardians of the Laws, and getting their approval. (In effect, we've got our assessors already appointed—I mean the legislators we chose to regulate the arts, and the person we elected as Minister of Education.) Well then, here's the same question yet again: are we satisfied to adopt this as our third principle and our third model law? Or what do you think?

CLINIAS: Of course we'll adopt it.

e   ATHENIAN: The next point is that it will be proper to sing hymns and panegyrics, combined with prayers, in honor of the gods. After the gods, we may similarly give the spirits and heroes their meed of praise, and pray to each of them as appropriate.

CLINIAS: Certainly.

ATHENIAN: And the next law, which should be adopted quite ungrudgingly, will run as follows: deceased citizens who by their physical efforts or force of personality have conspicuous and strenuous achievements to their credit, and who have lived a life of obedience to the laws, should be regarded as proper subjects for our panegyrics.

CLINIAS: Of course.

802   ATHENIAN: But to honor a man with hymns and panegyrics during his lifetime is to invite trouble: we must wait until he has come to the end of the course after running the race of life successfully. (Men and women who have shown conspicuous merit should qualify for all these honors without distinction of sex.)

The following arrangements should be made with regard to singing and dancing. Among the works we've inherited from the past there are a great many grand old pieces of music—dances too, for occasions when we want to exercise our bodies—from which we should not hesitate to choose those

b   suitable and appropriate for the society we are organizing. Censors of at least fifty years of age should be appointed to make the selection, and any ancient composition that seems to come up to standard should be approved; absolutely unsuitable material must be totally rejected, and substandard pieces revised and re-arranged, on the advice of poets and musicians. (Although we shall exploit the creative talents of these people, we

c   shan't—with rare exceptions—put our trust in their tastes and inclinations. Instead, we shall interpret the wishes of the lawgiver and arrange to *his* liking our dancing and singing and chorus performances in general.) Music composed in an undisciplined style is always infinitely improved by the imposition of form, even if that makes it less immediately attractive. But music doesn't *have* to be disciplined to be pleasant. Take someone who has right from childhood till the age of maturity and discretion grown familiar with a controlled and restrained style of music. Play him some

d   of the other sort, and how he'll loathe it! 'What vulgar stuff!' he'll say.

Yet, if he's been brought up to enjoy the strong appeal of popular music, it's the disciplined kind he'll call frigid and repellent. So as I said just now, on the score of pleasure or the lack of it, neither type is superior nor inferior to the other. The difference is simply this: the one musical environment is invariably a good influence, the other a bad.

CLINIAS: Well said!

ATHENIAN: In addition, we shall have to distinguish, in a rough and ready way, the songs suitable for men and those suitable for women, and give each its proper mode and rhythm. It would be terrible if the words failed to fit the mode, or if their meter were at odds with the beat of the music, which is what will happen if we don't match properly the songs to each of the other elements in the performance—elements which must therefore be dealt with, at any rate in outline, in our legal code. One possibility is simply to ensure that the songs men and women sing are accompanied by the rhythms and modes imposed by the words in either case; but our regulations about female performances must be more precise than this and be based on the natural difference between the sexes. So an elevated manner and courageous instincts must be regarded as characteristic of the male, while a tendency to modesty and restraint must be presented—in theory and law alike—as a peculiarly feminine trait.

Now to deal with how this doctrine should be taught and handed on. What method of instruction should we use? Who should be taught, and when should the lessons take place? Well, you know that when a shipwright is starting to build a boat, the first thing he does is to lay down the keel as a foundation and as a general indication of the shape. I have a feeling my own procedure now is exactly analogous. I'm trying to distinguish for you the various ways in which our character shapes the kind of life we live; I really am trying to 'lay down the keel', because I'm giving proper consideration to the way we should try to live—to the 'character-keel' we need to lay if we are going to sail through this voyage of life successfully. Not that human affairs are worth taking very seriously—but take them seriously is just what we are forced to do, alas. Still, perhaps it will be realistic to recognize the position we're in and direct our serious efforts to some suitable purpose. My meaning?—yes, you'd certainly be right to take me up on that.

CLINIAS: Exactly.

ATHENIAN: I maintain that serious matters deserve our serious attention, but trivialities do not; that all men of good will should put God at the center of their thoughts; that man, as we said before,[12] has been created as a toy for God; and that this is the great point in his favor. So every man and every woman should play this part and order their whole life accordingly, engaging in the best possible pastimes—in a quite different frame of mind to their present one.

CLINIAS: How do you mean?

803

b

c

d

e

12. See 644d ff.

ATHENIAN: The usual view nowadays, I fancy, is that the purpose of serious activity is leisure—that war, for instance, is an important business, and needs to be waged efficiently for the sake of peace. But in cold fact neither the immediate result nor the eventual consequences of warfare ever turn out to be *real* leisure or an education that really deserves the name—and education is in our view just about the most important activity of all. So each of us should spend the greater part of his life at peace, and

e   that will be the best use of this time. What, then, will be the right way to live? A man should spend his whole life at 'play'—sacrificing, singing, dancing—so that he can win the favor of the gods and protect himself from his enemies and conquer them in battle. He'll achieve both these aims if he sings and dances in the way we've outlined; his path, so to speak, has been marked out for him and he must go on his way confident that the poet's words are true.

804

> Some things, Telemachus, your native wit will tell you,
> And Heaven will prompt the rest. The very gods, I'm sure,
> Have smiled upon your birth and helped to bring you up.[13]

And those *we* bring up, too, must proceed in the same spirit. They must expect that although our advice is sound as far as it goes, their guardian deity will make them further suggestions about sacrifices and dancing—

b   telling them the various divinities in whose honor they should hold their various games, and on what occasions, so as to win the gods' good will and live the life that their own nature demands, puppets that they are, mostly, and hardly real at all.

MEGILLUS: That, sir, is to give the human race a very low rating indeed.

CLINIAS: Don't be taken aback, Megillus. You must make allowances for me. I said that with my thoughts on God, and was quite carried away. So, if you like, let's take it that our species is *not* worthless, but something

c   rather important.

To resume, then. So far, we have provided for the public gymnasia and the state schools to be housed in three groups of buildings at the center of the city; similarly, on three sites in the suburbs, there should be training grounds for horses, and open spaces adapted for archery and the discharge of other long-range missiles, where the young may practice and learn these skills. Anyway, if we haven't explained all this adequately before, let's do so now, and put our requirements into legal form.

d   Foreign teachers should be hired to live in these establishments and provide the pupils with complete courses of instruction in both military and cultural subjects. Children must not be allowed to attend or not attend school at the whim of their father; as far as possible, education must be

---

13. *Odyssey* iii.26–28.

compulsory for 'every man and boy' (as the saying is), because they belong to the state first and their parents second.

Let me stress that this law of mine will apply just as much to girls as to boys. The girls must be trained in precisely the same way, and I'd like to make this proposal without any reservations whatever about horse-riding or athletics being suitable activities for males but not for females. You see, although I was already convinced by some ancient stories I have heard, I now know for sure that there are pretty well countless numbers of women, generally called Sarmatians, round the Black Sea, who not only ride horses but use the bow and other weapons. There, men and women have an equal duty to cultivate these skills, so cultivate them equally they do. And while we're on the subject, here's another thought for you. I maintain that if these results can be achieved, the state of affairs in our corner of Greece, where men and women do *not* have a common purpose and do *not* throw all their energies into the same activities, is absolutely stupid. Almost every state, under present conditions, is only half a state, and develops only half its potentialities, whereas with the same cost and effort, it could double its achievement. Yet what a staggering blunder for a legislator to make!

CLINIAS: I dare say. But a lot of these proposals, sir, are incompatible with the average state's social structure. However, you were quite right when you said we should give the argument its head, and only make up our minds when it had run its course. You've made me reproach myself for having spoken. So carry on, and say what you like.

ATHENIAN: The point I'd like to make, Clinias, is the same one as I made a moment ago, that there might have been something to be said against our proposal, if it had not been proved by the facts to be workable. But as things are, an opponent of this law must try other tactics. We are not going to withdraw our recommendation that so far as possible, in education and everything else, the female sex should be on the same footing as the male. Consequently, we should approach the problem rather like this. Look: if women are *not* to follow absolutely the same way of life as men, then surely we shall have to work out some other program for them?

CLINIAS: Inevitably.

ATHENIAN: Well then, if we deny women this partnership we're now prescribing for them, which of the systems actually in force today shall we adopt instead? What about the practice of the Thracians and many other peoples, who make their women work on the land and mind sheep and cattle, so that they turn into skivvies indistinguishable from slaves? Or what about the Athenians and all the other states in that part of the world? Well, here's how we Athenians deal with the problem: we 'concentrate our resources', as the expression is, under one roof, and let our women take charge of our stores and the spinning and wool-working in general. Or we could adopt the Spartan system, Megillus, which is a compromise. You make your girls take part in athletics and you give them a compulsory

e

805

b

c

d

e

806

education in the arts; when they grow up, though dispensed from working wool, they have to 'weave' themselves a pretty hard-working sort of life which is by no means despicable or useless: they have to be tolerably efficient at running the home and managing the house and bringing up children—but they *don't* undertake military service. This means that even if some extreme emergency ever led to a battle for their state and the lives

b of their children, they wouldn't have the expertise to use bows and arrows, like so many Amazons, nor could they join the men in deploying any other missile. They wouldn't be able to take up shield and spear and copy Athena,[14] so as to terrify the enemy (if nothing more) by being seen in some kind of battle-array gallantly resisting the destruction threatening their native land. Living as they do, they'd never be anything like tough enough to imitate the Sarmatian women, who by comparison with such

c femininity would look like men. Anyone who wants to commend your Spartan legislators for this state of affairs, had better get on with it: I'm not going to change *my* mind. A legislator should go the whole way and not stick at half-measures; he mustn't just regulate the men and allow the women to live as they like and wallow in expensive luxury. That would be to give the state only half the loaf of prosperity instead of the whole of it.

MEGILLUS: What on earth are we to do, Clinias? Are we going to let our visitor run down Sparta for us like this?

d CLINIAS: Yes, we are. We told him he could be frank, and we must give him his head until we've properly worked through every section of our legal code.

MEGILLUS: Very well.

ATHENIAN: So I suppose I should try to press straight on with the next topic?

CLINIAS: Naturally.

ATHENIAN: Now that our citizens are assured of a moderate supply of necessities, and other people have taken over the skilled work, what will

e be their way of life? Suppose that their farms have been entrusted to slaves, who provide them with sufficient produce of the land to keep them in modest comfort; suppose they take their meals in separate messes, one for themselves, another nearby for their families, including their daughters and their daughters' mothers; assume the messes, are presided over by officials, male and female as the case may be, who have the duty of dismissing their respective assemblies after the day's review and scrutiny

807 of the diners' habits; and that when the official and his company have poured libations to whatever gods that day and night happen to be dedicated, they all duly go home. Now, do such leisured circumstances leave them no pressing work to do, no genuinely appropriate occupation? Must each of them get plumper and plumper every day of his life, like a fatted

---

14. A reference to 796b–c.

beast? No: we maintain that's *not* the right and proper thing to do. A man who lives like that won't be able to escape the fate he deserves; and the fate of an idle fattened beast that takes life easy is usually to be torn to pieces by some other animal—one of the skinny kind, who've been emaciated by a life of daring and endurance. (Our ideal, of course, is unlikely to be realized *fully* so long as we persist in our policy of allowing individuals to have their own private establishments, consisting of house, wife, children and so on.[15] But if we could ever put into practice the second-best scheme we're now describing, we'd have every reason to be satisfied.) So we must insist that there is something left to do in a life of leisure, and it's only fair that the task imposed, far from being a light or trivial one, should be the most demanding of all. As it is, to dedicate your life to winning a victory at Delphi or Olympia keeps you far too busy to attend to other tasks; but a life devoted to the cultivation of every physical perfection *and* every moral virtue (the only life worth the name) will keep you at least twice as busy. Inessential business must never stop you taking proper food and exercise, or hinder your mental and moral training. To follow this regimen and to get the maximum benefit from it, the whole day and the whole night is scarcely time enough.

In view of this, every gentleman must have a timetable prescribing what he is to do every minute of his life, which he should follow at all times from the dawn of day until the sun comes up at the dawn of the next. However, a lawgiver would lack dignity if he produced a mass of details about running a house, especially when he came to the regulations for curtailing sleep at night, which will be necessary if the citizens are going to protect the entire state systematically and uninterruptedly. Everyone should think it a disgrace and unworthy of a gentleman, if any citizen devotes the whole of any night to sleep; no, he should always be the first to wake and get up, and let himself be seen by all the servants. (It doesn't matter what we ought to call this kind of thing—either 'law' or 'custom' will do.) In particular, the mistress of the house should be the first to wake up the other women; if she herself is woken by some of the maids, then all the slaves—men, women and children—should say 'How shocking!' to one another, and so too, supposing they could, should the very walls of the house. While awake at night, all citizens should transact a good proportion of their political and domestic business, the officials up and down the town, masters and mistresses in their private households. By nature, prolonged sleep does not suit either body or soul, nor does it help us to be active in all this kind of work. Asleep, a man is useless; he may as well be dead. But a man who is particularly keen to be physically active and mentally alert stays awake as long as possible, and sets aside for sleep only as much time as is necessary for his health—and that is only a little, once that little has become a regular habit. Officials who are wide awake

15. Reading *nun ei* in b3.

at night in cities inspire fear in the wicked, whether citizens or enemies, but by the just and the virtuous they are honored and admired; they benefit themselves and are a blessing to the entire state. And an additional advantage of spending the night in this way will be the courage thus inspired in individual members of the state.

d When dawn comes up and brings another day, the children must be sent off to their teachers. Children must not be left without teachers, nor slaves without masters, any more than flocks and herds must be allowed to live without attendants. Of all wild things, the child is the most unmanageable: an unusually powerful spring of reason, whose waters are not

e yet canalized in the right direction, makes him sharp and sly, the most unruly animal there is. That's why he has to be curbed by a great many 'bridles', so to speak. Initially, when he leaves the side of his nurse and mother, and is still young and immature, this will be his tutor's duty, but later on it will devolve on his instructors in the various subjects—subjects which will be an extra discipline in themselves. So far, he will be treated as a young gentleman deserves. However, both the boy and his tutor or teacher must be punished by any passing gentleman who finds either of them misbehaving, and here the child must be treated as though he were a slave.

24. Any passer-by who fails to inflict due punishment,
must for a start be held in the deepest disgrace, and the Guardian of

809 the Laws who has been put in charge of the young must keep under observation this fellow who has come across miscreants of the kind we mentioned and has either failed to inflict the necessary punishment, or not inflicted it in the approved fashion.

Our sharp-eyed and efficient supervisor of the education of the young must redirect their natural development along the right lines, by always setting them on the paths of goodness as embodied in the legal code.

b But how will the law itself adequately convey its teaching to this Guardian? So far, the instruction he has had from the law has been cursory and obscure, because only a selection of topics has been covered. But nothing, as far as possible, should be omitted; the Guardian should have every point explained to him so that he in turn may enlighten and educate others. Now, the business of choruses has already been dealt with: we've seen what types of song and dance should be selected or revised, and then consecrated. But what type of *prose* works should be put in front of your pupils? How should they be presented? Now here, my dear Director of

c Youth, is something we've not explained. Of course, we've told you what military skills they must practice and learn, but what about (a) literature, (b) playing the lyre, (c) arithmetic? We stipulated that they must each understand enough of these subjects to fight a war and run a house and administer a state; for the same reasons they must acquire such knowledge about the heavenly bodies in their courses—sun, moon and stars—as will

help them with the arrangements that every state is forced to make in this   d
respect. You ask what arrangements we are referring to? We mean that
the days must be grouped into months, and the months into years, in such
a way that the seasons, along with their various sacrifices and festivals,
may each receive proper recognition by being duly observed in their natural
sequence. The result will be to keep the state active and alert, to render
the gods due honor, and to make men better informed on these matters.
All this, my friend, has not yet been adequately explained to you by the   e
legislator. So pay attention to the points which are going to be made next.

We said that you have insufficient information about literature, for a
start. Now, what's our complaint against the instructions you were given?
It's simply that you've not yet been told whether a *complete* mastery of
the subject is necessary before one can become a decent citizen or whether
one shouldn't attempt it at all; and similarly in the case of the lyre. Well,
we maintain that these subjects do have to be tackled. About three years
will be a reasonable time for a child of ten to spend on literature, and a
further three years, beginning at the age of thirteen, should be spent on   810
learning the lyre. These times must be neither shortened nor lengthened:
neither the child nor its father must be allowed to extend or curtail these
periods of study out of enthusiasm for, or distaste of, the curriculum; that
will be against the law.

25. Cases of disobedience must be punished by disqualification from
the school prizes we shall have to describe a little later.

First, though, you yourself must grasp just what must be taught by the
teachers and learned by the pupils in those periods of time. Well, the   b
children must work at their letters until they are able to read and write,
but any whose natural abilities have not developed sufficiently by the end
of the prescribed time to make them into quick or polished performers
should not be pressed.

The question now arises of the study of written works which the authors
have not set to music. Although some of these works are in meter, others
lack any rhythmical pattern at all—they are writings that simply reproduce
ordinary speech, unadorned by rhythm and music. Some of the many   c
authors of such works have left us writings that constitute a danger. Now,
my splendid Guardians of the Laws, how are you going to deal with these
works? What will be the right instructions for the lawgiver to give you
about coping with them? I reckon he's going to be very much at a loss.

CLINIAS: What is the difficulty you're talking about, sir? It looks as if
you're faced by a genuine personal problem.

ATHENIAN: Your assumption is quite right, Clinias. But the two of you
are my partners in legislation, and I'm obliged to tell you when I think I
anticipate a difficulty and when I do not.

CLINIAS: Oh? What makes you bring up that aspect of the business at   d
this point? What's the matter?

ATHENIAN: I'll tell you: the idea of contradicting many thousands of voices. That's always difficult.

CLINIAS: Well, bless my soul! Do you really imagine that your existing legislative proposals flout popular prejudices in just a few tiny details?

ATHENIAN: Yes, that's fair comment. The point you're making, I take it, is that although a lot of people set their face against the path we are following in our discussion, just as many are enthusiastic about it (or even

e   if they *are* fewer in number, they're not inferior in quality)—and you're telling me to rely on the support of the latter and proceed with boldness and resolution along the legislative path opened up for us by our present discussion, and not to hang back.

CLINIAS: Naturally.

ATHENIAN: Best foot forward, then. Now, what I say is this. We have a great many poets who compose in hexameters and trimeters and all the standard meters; some of these authors try to be serious, while others aim at a comic effect. Over and over again it's claimed that in order to educate young people properly we have to cram their heads full of this stuff; we

811 have to organize recitations of it so that they never stop listening to it and acquire a vast repertoire, getting whole poets off by heart. Another school of thought excerpts the outstanding work of all the poets and compiles a treasury of complete passages, claiming that if the wide knowledge of a fully informed person is to produce a sound and sensible citizen, these extracts must be committed to memory and learned by rote. I suppose you're now pressing me to be quite frank and show these people where they are right and where they've gone wrong?

CLINIAS: Of course.

b   ATHENIAN: Well then, in a nutshell, what sort of estimate will do them all justice? I imagine everybody would agree if I put it rather like this. Each of these authors has produced a lot of fine work, and a lot of rubbish too—but if that's so, I maintain that learning so much of it puts the young at risk.

CLINIAS: So what recommendation would you give the Guardian of the Laws?

ATHENIAN: What about?

CLINIAS: The model work that will enable him to decide what material

c   all the children may learn, and what not. Tell us, without any hesitation.

ATHENIAN: My dear Clinias, I suspect I've had a bit of luck.

CLINIAS: How's that?

ATHENIAN: Because I haven't got far to look for a model. You see, when I look back now over this discussion of ours, which has lasted from dawn up till this very moment—a discussion in which I think I sense the inspiration of heaven—well, it's come to look, to my eyes, just like a literary composition. Perhaps not surprisingly, I was overcome by a feeling of

d   immense satisfaction at the sight of my 'collected works', so to speak, because, of all the addresses I have ever learned or listened to, whether in verse or in this kind of free prose style I've been using, it's *these* that have impressed me as being the most eminently acceptable and the most entirely appropriate for the ears of the younger generation. So I could hardly commend a better model than this to the Guardian of the Laws in charge of education. Here's what he must tell the teachers to teach the children, and if he comes across similar and related material while working through prose writings, or the verse of poets, or when listening to unwritten compositions in simple prose that show a family resemblance to our discussion today, he must on no account let them slip through his fingers, but have them committed to writing. His first job will be to compel the teachers to learn this material and speak well of it, and he must not employ as his assistants any teachers who disapprove of it; he should employ only those who endorse his own high opinion, and entrust them with the teaching and education of the children. That, then, is my doctrine on literature and its teachers, so let me finish there.

CLINIAS: Well, sir, as far as I can judge from our original program, we've not strayed off the subjects we set out to discuss. But is our general policy the right one, or not? I suspect it would be difficult to say for sure.

ATHENIAN: That, Clinias, as we have often remarked, is something which will probably become clearer of its own accord when we've completely finished expounding our laws.

CLINIAS: True enough.

ATHENIAN: After the teacher of literature, surely, we have to address the lyre-master?

CLINIAS: Of course.

ATHENIAN: Now when we allocate these masters the duties of teaching this instrument and giving instruction in the subject in general, I think we ought to remember the line we took earlier.

CLINIAS: What line do you mean?

ATHENIAN: We said[16] I think, that the sixty-year-old singers of Dionysus should be persons who are particularly sensitive to rhythm and the way in which 'harmonies' are constructed, so that when faced with good or vicious musical representations, and the emotions aroused by them, they may be able to select the works based on good representation and reject those based on bad. The former they should present and sing to the community at large, so as to charm the souls of the young people, encouraging each and every one of them to let these representations guide them along the path that leads to virtue.

CLINIAS: You're absolutely right.

ATHENIAN: With this object in view, here's how the lyre-master and his pupil must employ the notes of their instruments. By exploiting the fact that each string makes a distinct sound, they must produce notes that are identical in pitch to the words being sung. The lyre should not be used to play an elaborate independent melody: that is, its strings must produce no notes except those of the composer of the melody being played; small

16. See 644b ff. and 669b ff.

intervals should not be combined with large, nor quick tempo with slow,
e   nor low notes with high. Similarly, the rhythms of the music of the lyre
must not be tricked out with all sorts of frills and adornments. All this
sort of thing must be kept from students who are going to acquire a
working knowledge of music in three years, without wasting time. Such
conflict and confusion makes learning difficult, whereas the young people
should above all be swift learners, because they have a great many important compulsory subjects laid down for them as it is—and in due time, as
our discussion progresses, we shall see what these subjects are. But all
these musical matters should be controlled, according to his brief, by our
official in charge of education. As regards the actual singing, and the
words, we have explained earlier what tunes and style of language the
813   chorus-masters must teach: we said—remember?—that these things should
be consecrated and each allocated to a suitable festival, so as to benefit
society by the welcome pleasure they give.

CLINIAS: Here again you've spoken the truth —

ATHENIAN: — the whole truth and nothing but the truth! So these are
the regulations the person appointed as our Director of Music must adopt
and enforce: let's wish him the best of luck in his task.

b   We, however, must supplement our previous regulations about dancing
and the training of the body in general. We've filled in the gaps in our
tuition in the case of music, so now let's deal with physical training in the
same way. Both boys and girls, of course, must learn to dance and perform
physical exercises?

CLINIAS: Yes.

ATHENIAN: So it won't come amiss if we provide dancing masters for
the boys and dancing mistresses for the girls, so as to facilitate practice.

CLINIAS: Agreed.

c   ATHENIAN: So now let's summon once again the official that has the
hardest job of all—the Director of Children. He'll be in charge both of
music and of physical training, so he won't get much time off.

CLINIAS: How then will a man of his advancing years be able to supervise
so much?

ATHENIAN: There is no problem here, my friend. The law has already
given him permission, which it will not withdraw, to recruit as assistant
supervisors any citizens he may wish, of either sex. He will know whom
d   to choose, and a sober respect for his office and a realization of its importance will make him anxious not to choose wrongly, because he'll be
well aware that only if the younger generation has received and goes on
receiving a correct education shall we find everything is 'plain sailing',
whereas if not—well, it would be inappropriate to describe the consequences, and as the state is young we shall refrain from doing so, out of
respect for the feelings of the excessively superstitious.

Well then, on these topics too—I mean dances and the entire range of
movements involved in physical training—we have already said a great

deal. We are establishing gymnasia for all physical exercises of a military kind—archery and deployment of missiles in general, skirmishing, heavy-armed fighting of every variety, tactical maneuvers, marches of every sort, pitching camp, and also the various disciplines of the cavalryman. In all these subjects there must be public instructors paid out of public funds; their lessons must be attended by the boys and men of the state, and the girls and women as well, because they too have to master all these techniques. While still girls, they must practice every kind of dancing and fighting in armor; when grown women, they must play their part in maneuvering, getting into battle formation and taking off and putting on weapons, if only to ensure that if it ever proves necessary for the whole army to leave the state and take the field abroad, so that the children and the rest of the population are left unprotected, the women will at least be able to defend them. On the other hand—and this is one of those things we can't swear is impossible—suppose a large and powerful army, whether Greek or not, were to force a way into the country and make them fight a desperate battle for the very existence of the state. It would be a disaster for their society if its women proved to have been so shockingly ill-educated that they couldn't even rival female birds, who are prepared to run every risk and die for their chicks fighting against the most powerful of wild animals. What if, instead of that, the women promptly made off to temples and thronged every altar and sanctuary, and covered the human race with the disgrace of being by nature the most lily-livered creatures under the sun?

CLINIAS: By heaven, sir, no state in which that happened could avoid disgrace—quite apart from the damage that would be caused.

ATHENIAN: So let's lay down a law to the effect that women must not neglect to cultivate the techniques of fighting, at any rate to the extent indicated. These are skills which all citizens, male and female, must take care to acquire.

CLINIAS: That gets my vote, at least.

ATHENIAN: Now for wrestling. We've partly dealt with this already, but we haven't described what in my eyes is its most important feature. But it's not easy to find words to explain it unless at the same time someone gives an actual demonstration with his body. So we'll postpone a decision on this point till we can support our statements with concrete examples and prove, among other points we've mentioned, that of all physical movements, those involved in our kind of wrestling are the most closely related to those demanded in warfare, and in particular that we should practice wrestling for the sake of military efficiency, rather than cultivate the latter in order to be better wrestlers.

CLINIAS: You're right in that, at least.

ATHENIAN: So let's accept what we've said so far as an adequate statement of what wrestling can do for a man. The proper term for most of the other movements that can be executed by the body as a whole is 'dancing'. Two varieties, the decent and the disreputable, have to be distinguished. The

first is a representation of the movements of graceful people, and the aim is to create an effect of grandeur; the second imitates the movements of unsightly people and tries to present them in an unattractive light. Both have two subdivisions. The first subdivision of the decent kind represents handsome, courageous soldiers locked in the violent struggles of war; the second portrays a man of temperate character enjoying moderate pleasures
815   in a state of prosperity, and the natural name for this is 'dance of peace'. The dance of war differs fundamentally from the dance of peace, and the correct name for it will be the 'Pyrrhic'. It depicts the motions executed to avoid blows and shots of all kinds (dodging, retreating, jumping into the air, crouching); and it also tries to represent the opposite kind of motion, the more aggressive postures adopted for shooting and discharging javelins and delivering various kinds of blows. In these dances, which portray fine
b   physiques and noble characters, the correct posture is maintained if the body is kept erect in a state of vigorous tension, with the limbs extended nearly straight. A posture with the opposite characteristics we reject as *not* correct. As for the dance of peace, the point we have to watch in every chorus-performer is this: how successfully—or how disastrously—does he keep up the fine style of dancing to be expected from men who've been brought up under good laws? This means we'd better distinguish the
c   dubious style of dancing from the style we may accept without question. So can we define the two? Where should the line be drawn between them? 'Bacchic' dances and the like, which (the dancers allege) are a 'representation' of drunken persons they call Nymphs and Pans and Sileni and Satyrs, and which are performed during 'purifications' and 'initiations', are something of a problem: taken as a group, they cannot be termed either 'dances of peace' or 'dances of war', and indeed they resist all attempts to label them. The best procedure, I think, is to treat them as separate from 'war-
d   dances' and 'dances of peace', and put them in a category of their own which a statesman may ignore as outside his province. That will entitle us to leave them on one side and get back to dances of peace and war, both of which undeniably deserve our attention.

Now, what about the non-combatant Muse? The dances she leads in honor of the gods and children of gods will comprise one broad category of dances performed with a sense of well-being. This is how we shall
e   distinguish between the two forms this feeling may take: (1) the particularly keen pleasure felt by people who have emerged from trouble and danger to a state of happiness; (2) the quieter pleasures of those whose past good fortune has not only continued but increased. Now, take a man in either of these situations. The greater his pleasure the brisker his body's movements; more modest pleasures make his actions correspondingly less brisk. Again, the more composed the man's temperament, and the tougher he has been
816   trained to be, the more deliberate are his movements; on the other hand, if he's a coward and has not been trained to show restraint, his actions are wilder and his postures change more violently. And in general, when

a man uses his voice to talk or sing, he finds it very difficult to keep his body still. This is the origin of the whole art of dancing: the gestures that express what one is saying. Some of us make gestures that are invariably in harmony with our words, but some of us fail. In fact, one has only to reflect on many other ancient terms that have come down to us, to see   b
that they should be commended for their aptness and accuracy. One such term describes the dances performed by those who enjoy prosperity and seek only moderate pleasures: it's just the right word, and whoever coined it must have been a real musician. He very sensibly gave all such dances the name '*emmeleiai*',[17] and established two categories of approved dancing, the 'war-dance' (which he called 'Pyrrhic') and 'dance of peace' ('*emme-*   c
leiai'), thus giving each its apt and appropriate title. The lawgiver should give an outline of them, and the Guardian of the Laws should see where they are to be found; then, after hunting them out, he must combine the dance-sequences with the other musical elements, and allocate each sacrifice and feast in the calendar the style of dance that is appropriate. After thus consecrating the whole list of dances, he must henceforth refrain from altering any feature either of the dancing or the singing: the same state and the same citizens (who should all be the same sort of people, as   d
far as possible), should enjoy the same pleasures in the same fashion: that is the secret of a happy and a blessed life.

So much for the way men of superior physique and noble character should perform in choruses of the kind we've prescribed. We are now obliged to examine and pronounce on the misshapen bodies and degraded outlook of those performers who have turned to producing ludicrous and comic effects by exploiting the opportunities for humorous mimicry offered by dialogue, song and dance. Now anyone who means to acquire a discern-   e
ing judgment will find it impossible to understand the serious side of things in isolation from their ridiculous aspect, or indeed appreciate anything at all except in the light of its opposite. But if we intend to acquire virtue, even on a small scale, we can't be serious and comic too, and this is precisely why we must learn to recognize buffoonery, to avoid being trapped by our ignorance of it into doing or saying anything ridiculous when there's no call for it. Such mimicry must be left to slaves and hired aliens, and no one must ever take it at all seriously. No citizen or citizeness must be found learning it, and the performances must always contain some new twist. With that law, and that explanation of it, humorous   817
amusements—usually known as 'comedy'—may be dismissed.

But what about our 'serious' poets, as they're called, the tragedians? Suppose some of them were to come forward and ask us some such question as this: 'Gentlemen, may we enter your state and country, or not? And may we bring our work with us? Or what's your policy on this point?' What would be the right reply for us to make to these inspired geniuses?   b

---

17. The key to the sequence of thought is that 'in harmony' (816a) = *emmelōs*.

This, I think: 'Most honored guests, we're tragedians ourselves, and our tragedy is the finest and best we can create. At any rate, our entire state has been constructed so as to be a "representation" of the finest and noblest life—the very thing we maintain is most genuinely a tragedy. So we are poets like yourselves, composing in the same *genre,* and your competitors as artists and actors in the finest drama, which true law alone has the

c   natural powers to "produce" to perfection (of that we're quite confident). So don't run away with the idea that we shall ever blithely allow you to set up stage in the market-place and bring on your actors whose fine voices will carry further than ours. Don't think we'll let you declaim to women and children and the general public, and talk about the same practices as we do but treat them differently—indeed, more often than not, so as virtually to contradict us. We should be absolutely daft, and so would any

d   state as a whole, to let you go ahead as we've described before the authorities had decided whether your work was fit to be recited and suitable for public performance or not. So, you sons of the charming Muses, first of all show your songs to the authorities for comparison with ours, and if your doctrines seem the same as or better than our own, we'll let you produce your plays; but if not, friends, that we can never do.'

e   So as regards chorus performances in general and the question of learning a part in them, custom will march hand in hand with law—dealing with slaves and their masters separately, if you are agreeable.

CLINIAS: How could we fail to agree, at any rate for the moment?

ATHENIAN: For gentlemen three related disciplines still remain: (1) computation and the study of numbers; (2) measurements of lines, surfaces and solids; (3) the mutual relationship of the heavenly bodies as they

818   revolve in their courses. None of these subjects must be studied in minute detail by the general public, but only by a chosen few (and who they are, we shall say when the time comes, when our discussion is drawing to a close). But what about the man in the street? It would certainly be a disgrace for him to be ignorant of what people very rightly call the 'indispensable rudiments'; but it will be difficult—impossible, even—for him to make a minute study of the entire subject. However, we can't dispense with the basic necessities, which was probably the point in the mind of the coiner

b   of that saying about God, to the effect that 'not even God will be found at odds with necessity'[18]—presumably divine necessities, because if you interpret the remark as referring to necessities in the mortal realm, as do most people who quote such things, it's by far the most naive remark that could be made.

CLINIAS: Well, then, sir, what necessities, divine rather than the other sort, are relevant to these studies?

---

18. Perhaps the poet Simonides (late sixth and early fifth century); see D. A. Campbell, *Greek Lyric* (Loeb), vol. III, pp. 434–37.

ATHENIAN: These, I think: the necessities of which at least *some* practical and theoretical knowledge will always be essential for every god, spirit or hero who means to take charge of human beings in a responsible fashion. A man, at any rate, will fall a long way short of such godlike standards if he can't recognize one, two and three, or odd and even numbers in general, or hasn't the faintest notion how to count, or can't reckon up the days and nights, and is ignorant of the revolutions of the sun and moon and the other heavenly bodies. It's downright stupid to expect that anyone who wants to make the slightest progress in the highest branches of knowl- edge can afford to ignore any of these subjects. But what parts of them should be studied, and how intensively, and when? Which topics should be combined, and which kept separate? How will they be synthesized? These are the first questions we have to answer, and then with these preliminary lessons to guide us we may advance to the remaining studies. This is the natural procedure enforced by the necessity with which we maintain no god contends now, or ever will.

CLINIAS: Yes, sir, those proposals of yours, put like that, seem natural and correct.

ATHENIAN: They certainly are, Clinias, but such a preliminary statement of them is difficult to put into legal form. If you like, we'll postpone more precise legislation till later.

CLINIAS: It looks to us, sir, as if you're deterred by the way our country- men commonly neglect this sort of subject. But your fears are quite ground- less, so try to tell us what you think, without keeping anything back on that account.

ATHENIAN: I am indeed deterred, for the reasons you mention, but I am even more appalled at those who have actually undertaken those studies, but in the wrong manner. Total ignorance over an entire field is never dangerous or disastrous; much more damage is done when a subject is known intimately and in detail, but has been improperly taught.

CLINIAS: You're right.

ATHENIAN: So we should insist that gentlemen should study each of these subjects to at least the same level as very many children in Egypt, who acquire such knowledge at the same time as they learn to read and write. First, lessons in calculation have been devised for tiny tots to learn while they are enjoying themselves at play: they divide up a given number of garlands or apples among larger or smaller groups, and arrange boxers or wrestlers in an alter- nation of 'byes' and 'pairs', or in a sequence of either, and in the various further ways in which 'byes' and 'pairs' naturally succeed each other. An- other game the teachers play with them is to jumble up bowls of gold and bronze and silver and so on, or distribute whole sets of one material. In this way, as I indicated, they make the uses of elementary arithmetic an integral part of their pupils' play, so that they get a useful introduction to the art of marshaling, leading and deploying an army, or running a household; and in general they make them more alert and resourceful persons. Next, the d   teacher puts the children on to measuring lengths, surfaces and solids—a study which rescues them from the deep-rooted ignorance, at once comic and shocking, that all men display in this field.

CLINIAS: What sort of ignorance do you mean, in particular?

ATHENIAN: My dear Clinias, even I took a very long time to discover mankind's plight in this business; but when I did, I was amazed, and could scarcely believe that human beings could suffer from such swinish
e   stupidity. I blushed not only for myself, but for Greeks in general.

CLINIAS: Why so? Go on, sir, tell us what you're getting at.

ATHENIAN: I'll explain—or rather, I'll make my point by asking you a few questions. Here's a simple one: you know what's meant by a 'line', I suppose?

CLINIAS: Of course.

ATHENIAN: Very well. What about 'surface'?

CLINIAS: Surely.

ATHENIAN: You appreciate that these are two distinct things, and that 'volume' is a third?

CLINIAS: Naturally.

ATHENIAN: And you regard all these as commensurable?

CLINIAS: Yes.

ATHENIAN: And one length, I suppose, is essentially expressible in terms
820   of another length, one surface in terms of another surface, and one volume in terms of another volume?

CLINIAS: Exactly.

ATHENIAN: Well, what if some of these can't be thus expressed, either 'exactly' or approximately. What if some can, and some cannot, in spite of your thinking they *all* can? What do you think of your ideas on the subject now?

CLINIAS: They're worthless, obviously.

ATHENIAN: What about the relationship of line and surface to volume, or surface and line to each other? Don't all we Greeks regard them as in some sense commensurable?

b   CLINIAS: We certainly do.

ATHENIAN: But if, as I put it, 'all we Greeks' believe them to be commensurable when fundamentally they are *in*commensurable, one had better address these people as follows (blushing the while on their behalf): 'Now then, most esteemed among the Greeks, isn't this one of those subjects we said[19] it was disgraceful not to understand—not that a knowledge of the basic essentials was much to be proud of?'

CLINIAS: Of course.

ATHENIAN: Now there are a number of additional and related topics
c   which are a fertile breeding-ground for mistakes similar to those we've mentioned.

19. Reading *ephamen* in b5.

CLINIAS: What sort of topics?

ATHENIAN: The real relationship between commensurables and in-commensurables. We must be very poor specimens if on inspection we can't tell them apart. These are the problems we ought to keep on putting up to each other, in a competitive spirit, when we've sufficient time to do them justice; and it's a much more civilized pastime for old men than checkers.

CLINIAS: Perhaps so. Come to think of it, checkers is not radically different   d
from such studies.

ATHENIAN: Well, Clinias, I maintain that these subjects are what the younger generation should go in for. They do no harm, and are not very difficult: they can be learned in play, and so far from harming the state, they'll do it some good. But if anyone disagrees, we must listen to his case.

CLINIAS: Of course.

ATHENIAN: However, although obviously we shall sanction them if that proves to be their effect, we shall reject them if they seem to disappoint our expectations.

CLINIAS: Obviously indeed. No doubt about it.   e

ATHENIAN: Well then, sir, so that our legal code shall have no gaps, let's regard these studies as an established but independent part of the desired curriculum—independent, that is, of the rest of the framework of the state, so that they can be 'redeemed' like 'pledges', in case the arrangements fail to work out to the satisfaction of us the depositors or you the pledgees.

CLINIAS: Yes, that's a fair way to present them.

ATHENIAN: Next, consider astronomy. Would a proposal to teach it to the young meet with your approval, or not?

CLINIAS: Just tell us what you think.

ATHENIAN: Now here's a very odd thing, that really is quite intoler-able.   821

CLINIAS: What?

ATHENIAN: We generally say that so far as the supreme deity and the universe are concerned, we ought not to bother our heads hunting up explanations, because that is an act of impiety. In fact, precisely the opposite seems to be true.

CLINIAS: What's your point?

ATHENIAN: My words will surprise you, and you may well think them out of place on the lips of an old man. But it's quite impossible to keep quiet about a study, if one believes it is noble and true, a blessing to society and pleasing in the sight of God.   b

CLINIAS: That's reasonable enough, but what astronomy are we going to find of which we can say all that?

ATHENIAN: My dear fellows, at the present day nearly all we Greeks do the great gods—Sun and Moon—an injustice.

CLINIAS: How so?

ATHENIAN: We say that they, and certain other heavenly bodies with them, never follow the same path. Hence our name for them: 'planets.'[20]

c   CLINIAS: Good heavens, sir, that's absolutely right. In the course of my life I've often seen with my own eyes how the Morning and the Evening Star, and a number of others, never describe the same course, but vary from one to another; and we all know that the sun and moon always move like that.[21]

ATHENIAN: Megillus and Clinias, this is precisely the sort of point about the gods of the heavens that I am insisting our citizens and young men d   must study, so as to learn enough about them all to avoid blasphemy, and to use reverent language whenever they sacrifice and offer up their pious prayers.

CLINIAS: Right enough—if it's possible, in the first place, to acquire the knowledge you mention. On the assumption that investigation will enable us to correct any errors in our present statements, I too agree that this subject must be studied, in view of its grandeur and importance. So do your level best to convince us of the case you're making, and we'll try to follow you and take in what you say.

e   ATHENIAN: My point is not an easy one to appreciate, but it's not unduly difficult either, and won't take up a lot of time, as I'll prove to you by my ability to keep my explanation brief—even though it wasn't so very long ago, when I was no youngster, that I heard of these things. If the subject were difficult, I'd never be able to explain it to you, old men that we all are.

822   CLINIAS: You're right. But what is this subject you say is so wonderful, so suitable for young men to learn, yet unknown to us? Try to tell us that much about it, at any rate, as clearly as you can.

ATHENIAN: Yes, try I must. This belief, my dear fellows, that the moon and sun and other heavenly bodies do in fact 'wander', is incorrect: precisely the opposite is true. Actually, each of them perpetually describes just one fixed orbit, although it is true that to all appearances its path is always changing. b   Further, the quickest body is wrongly supposed to be the slowest, and vice versa. So if the facts are as stated, and we are in error, we're no better than spectators at Olympia would be, if they said that the fastest horse in the race or the fastest long-distance runner was the slowest, and the slowest the fastest, and composed panegyrics and songs extolling the loser as the winner. I don't suppose the praises showered on the runners would be at all apt or welcome to them—they're only men, after all! At Olympia, such c   a mistake would be merely ludicrous. But what are we to think of the

20. Greek *planēta*, lit. 'wanderers'.
21. Reading *tauta* in c5.

analogous theological errors we're committing nowadays? In this field such mistakes are not funny at all; and it certainly gives the gods no pleasure to have us spread false rumors about them.

CLINIAS: Very true—if you're right about the facts.

ATHENIAN: So if we can prove I *am* right, all such topics as these must be studied to the level indicated, but in the absence of proof they must be left alone. May we adopt this as agreed policy?

CLINIAS: Certainly.   d

ATHENIAN: So it's high time to call a halt to our regulations about the subjects to be studied in the educational curriculum, and turn our attention to hunting and all that sort of thing. Here too we must adopt the same procedure as before, because the legislator's job is not done if he simply lays down laws and gets quit of the business. In addition to his legislation, he must provide something else, which occupies a sort of no-man's land between admonition and law. This is a point, of course, that we've come across often enough as we talked of this and that, as for instance when   e we dealt with the training of very young children. We hold that although education at that level is certainly the sort of topic on which suggestions are needed, it would be plain silly to think of these suggestions as formal laws. Even when the actual laws and the complete constitution have been thus formally committed to writing, you don't exhaust the praises of a supremely virtuous citizen by saying 'Here's a good man for you, a devoted and utterly obedient servant of the laws'. Your praise will be more comprehensive if you can say, 'He's a good man because he has given a lifetime of unswerving obedience to the written words of the legislator, whether they took the form   823 of a law, or simply expressed approval or disapproval'. There is no truer praise of a citizen than that. The real job of the legislator is not only to write his laws, but to blend into them an explanation of what he regards as respectable and what he does not, and the perfect citizen must be bound by these standards no less than by those backed by legal sanctions.

We can cite our present subject as a kind of witness to demonstrate the point more clearly. You know how 'hunting' takes a great many forms,   b almost all of which are nowadays covered by this one term. There is a variety of ways of hunting water animals, and the same goes for the birds of the air, and the animals that live on land too—and not only the wild ones, either: we also have to take into account the hunting of men, not merely by their enemies in war (such as the raids carried out by robbers and the pursuit of army by army), but by their lovers, who 'pursue' their quarry for many different reasons, some admirable, some execrable. When the legislator comes to lay down his laws about hunting he cannot   c leave all this unexplained, but neither can he produce a set of menacing regulations by imposing rules and punishments for all cases. So how are we going to tackle this kind of thing? He—the legislator—having asked himself 'Are these suitable exercises and activities for the young, or not?', must then approve or condemn the various forms of hunting. The young men, for their part, must listen to the lawgiver and obey him, without being seduced by the prospect of pleasure or deterred by vigorous effort;

d   and they should pay much more attention to carrying out warm recommendations than to the detailed threats and punishment of the formal law.

With those preliminaries, we may now put in due form our approval or disapproval of the various forms of hunting, commending the kind that is a good influence on the younger generation and censuring the other sort. So let's now follow up with a talk to the young people, and address them in this idealistic vein:

e   'Friends, we hope you'll never be seized by a desire or passion to fish in the sea or to angle or indeed to hunt water animals at all; and don't resort to creels, which a lazybones will leave to catch his prey whether he's asleep or awake. We hope you never feel any temptation to capture men on the high seas and take to piracy, which will make you into brutal hunters and outlaws; and we hope it never so much as occurs to you to turn thief in town or country. Nor should any young man ever be seduced by a fancy to trap birds—away with such an uncivilized desire! That leaves

824 only land animals for the athletes of our state to hunt and capture. Now sometimes this is done by what is called "night-hunting," when the participants, sluggards that they are, take it in turn to sleep. This sort of hunting is *not* to be recommended, nor is the sort that offers periods of rest from exertion, where the savage strength of the animals is subdued by nets and traps, rather than because a hunter who relishes the fight has got the better of them. All men who wish to cultivate the "divine"[22] courage have only one type of hunting left, which is the best: the capture of four-footed animals with the help of dogs and horses and by your own exertions, when you hunt in person and subdue all your prey by chasing and striking them and hurling weapons at them.'

This address may be taken as an explanation of what we approve and condemn in this entire business. Here's the actual law:

(1) No one should restrain these genuinely 'holy' hunters from taking their hounds where they like and as they like; but the night-trapper, who relies on nets and snares, must not be allowed by anyone, at any time or place, to hunt his prey.

(2) The fowler is not to be restrained on fallow-land or on the mountain side, but any passer-by should chase him off cultivated or holy ground.

(3) The fisherman is to be allowed to fish anywhere except in harbors and sacred rivers, ponds and lakes, provided only that he does not make the water turbid by using noxious juices.

So here's where we have to say that our regulations about education are finally complete.

CLINIAS: That's good news!

22. See 631b–d.

Book VIII

ATHENIAN: Now then, the next job is to enlist the aid of the oracles 　828
reported from Delphi to draw up a program of festivals to be established
by law, and discover what sacrifices the state will find it 'meet and right'
to offer and which gods should receive them. It will probably be within
our own discretion to decide the number and the occasions.

CLINIAS: Yes, I dare say the number will be up to us.

ATHENIAN: So let's deal with that first. There are to be no less than three 　b
hundred and sixty-five of them, so as to ensure that there is always at
least one official sacrificing to some god or spirit on behalf of the state,
its citizens and their property. The Expounders, Priests, Priestesses and
Prophets are to hold a meeting with the Guardians of the Laws and fill in
the details the legislator has inevitably omitted (in fact, this same combined
board will also have to spot where such deficiencies exist in the first place).
The law will provide for twelve festivals in honor of the twelve gods who 　c
give their names to the individual tribes. Every month the citizens should
sacrifice to each of these gods and arrange chorus performances and cultural and gymnastic contests, varied according to the deity concerned and
appropriate to the changing seasons of the year; and they must divide
festivals for women into those that must be celebrated in the absence of
men, and those that need not be. Further, they must not confuse the cult
of the gods of the underworld with that of the 'heavenly' gods (as we
must style them) and their retinue. They are to keep the two kinds of
celebration separate, and put the former by law in the twelfth month,
which is sacred to Pluto. Men of battle should feel no horror for such a 　d
god as this—on the contrary, they should honor him as a great friend of
the human race. The union of body and soul, you see, can never be superior
to their separation (and I mean that quite seriously).

There's a further point they will have to appreciate if they are going to
allocate these events satisfactorily. Although on the score of leisure-time
and abundance of all necessities our state has no rivals at the present day,
it still has to live the *good* life, just like the individual person; and the first 　829
requirement for a happy life is to do yourself no injury nor allow any to
be done to you by others. Of course, the first half of the requirement
presents no great problem; the difficulty lies in becoming strong enough
to be immune to injury—and the one and only thing that brings such
immunity is complete virtue. The same applies to a state: if it adopts the
ways of virtue, it can live in peace; but if it is wicked, war and civil war
will plague it. That's the situation in a nutshell, and it means that each
and every citizen must undertake military training in peace-time, and not 　b
leave it till war breaks out. So a state that knows its business should reserve
at least one day per month (and more than one, if the authorities think
fit) for military maneuvers, to be held without regard for the weather,
come rain come shine. Men, women and children should participate, and
the authorities will decide from time to time whether to take them out on

maneuvers *en masse* or in sections. They must never fail to mount a program of wholesome recreation, accompanied by sacrifices; and the program ought to include 'war-games' which should simulate the conditions of
c   actual fighting as realistically as possible. On each field-day they should distribute prizes and awards of merit, and compose speeches in commendation or reproof of each other according to the conduct of individuals not only in the contests but in daily life too: those who are deemed to have acquitted themselves particularly well should be honored, while the failures should be censured. But not everyone should produce such compositions. For a start, a composer must be at least fifty years old, and he must not be one of those people who for all their poetical and musical competence have not a single noble or outstanding achievement to their credit. The
d   compositions that ought to be sung (even if in terms of art they leave something to be desired) are those of citizens who have achieved a high standard of conduct and whose personal merits have brought them distinction in the state. The official in charge of education, together with the other Guardians of the Laws, are to select them and grant them alone the privilege of giving their Muses free rein; other people are to be entirely forbidden. No one should dare to sing any unauthorized song, not even if it is sweeter
e   than the hymns of Orpheus or of Thamyras.[1] Our citizens must confine themselves to such pieces as have been given the stamp of approval and consecrated to the gods, and to compositions which on the strength of their authors' reputation are judged to be suitable vehicles for commendation or censure. (I intend the same regulations to apply to men and women alike, both as regards military excursions and freedom to compose unsupervised.)

The legislator should think things over and employ this sort of analogy: 'Let's see, now, once I've organized the state as a whole, what sort of
830   citizen do I want to produce? *Athletes* are what I want—competitors against a million rivals in the most vital struggles of all. Right?' 'Very much so', one would reply, correctly. Well then, if we were training boxers or pancratiasts or competitors in some other similar contest should we go straight into the ring unprepared by a daily work-out against an opponent? If we were boxers, surely we'd have spent days on end *before* the contest in strenuous practice, learning how to fight, and trying out all those maneu-
b   vers we intended to use when the time came to fight to win? We'd come as close as we could to the real conditions of the contest by putting on practice-gloves instead of thongs, so as to get as much practice as possible in delivering and dodging punches. And if we ran particularly short of sparring partners then we'd go to the trouble of hanging up a lifeless dummy to practice against; and we certainly wouldn't be put off by the idiots who might laugh at us. Come to that, if one day we ran out of sparring
c   partners completely, living or otherwise, and had no one to practice with

---

1. Orpheus' singing was said to be able to charm animals and trees and even rocks. Thamyras was a bard who boasted that not even the Muses could rival his music.

at all, we'd go so far as to box against our own shadows—shadow-boxing with a vengeance! After all, how else can you describe a practice-session in which you just throw punches at the air?

CLINIAS: No, sir, there's no other term for it than the one you've just used.

ATHENIAN: Very well. So when the fighting force of our state comes to brace itself to face the most important contest of all—to fight for life and   d
children and property and the entire state—is it really to be after less intensive training than combatants such as these have enjoyed? Is our citizens' legislator going to be so scared that their practice against each other may look silly to some people that he will neglect his duty? I mean his duty of instructing that maneuvers on a small scale, without arms, should be held every day, if possible (and for this purpose he should arrange teams to compete in every kind of gymnastic exercise), whereas the 'major' exercises, in which arms are carried, should be held not less than once per month. The citizens will compete with each other throughout the entire country, to see who is best at occupying positions and laying   e
ambushes, and they must reproduce the conditions of every kind of battle (that will give them *real* practice, because they will be aiming at the closest possible approximation to the *real* targets).[2] And they should use missiles that are moderately dangerous: we don't want the competitions they hold against each other to be entirely unalarming, but to inspire them with fear and do something to reveal the brave man and the coward; and the legisla-tor should confer honors or inflict disgrace as appropriate, so as to prepare   831
the whole state to be an efficient fighter in the real struggle that lasts a lifetime. In fact, if anyone is killed in such circumstances, the homicide should be regarded as involuntary, and the legislator should decree that the killer's hands are clean when once he has been purified according to law. After all, the lawgiver will reflect, even if a few people do die, others who are just as good will be produced to replace them, whereas if fear dies (so to speak), he'll not be able to find in all these activities a yardstick to separate the good performers from the bad—and that would be a bigger disaster for the state than the other.   b

CLINIAS: Yes, sir, we'd agree that this is the sort of law that every state should pass and observe.

ATHENIAN: Now we all know, don't we, the reason why this kind of teamwork and competition is not to be found in any state at the present time, except on a very modest scale indeed? I suppose we'd say it was because the masses and their legislators suffer from ignorance?

CLINIAS: Maybe so.

ATHENIAN: Not a bit of it, my dear Clinias! We ought to say there are   c
two causes, and pretty powerful ones at that.

CLINIAS: What are they?

---

2. The translation of this parenthesis is something of a paraphrase of some difficult and obscure Greek.

ATHENIAN: The first is a passion for wealth which makes men unwilling to devote a minute of their time to anything except their own personal property. This is what every single citizen concentrates on with all his heart and soul; his ruling passion is his daily profit and he's quite incapable of worrying about anything else. Everyone is out for himself, and is very quick off the mark indeed to learn any skill and apply himself to any technique that fills his pocket; anything that doesn't do that he treats with complete derision. So we can treat this as one reason why states are not prepared to undertake this[3] or any other praiseworthy activity in a serious spirit, whereas their insatiable desire for gold and silver makes them perfectly willing to slave away at any ways and means, fair or foul, that promise to make them rich. It doesn't matter whether something is sanctioned by heaven, or forbidden and absolutely disgusting—it's all the same to them, and causes not the slightest scruple, provided it enables them to make beasts of themselves by wallowing in all kinds of food and drink and indulging every kind of sexual pleasure.

CLINIAS: You're quite right.

ATHENIAN: So I've described one cause: let's treat this obsession as the first obstacle that prevents states from following an adequate course of training, either for military or for any other purposes: naturally decent folk are turned into traders or merchant-venturers or just plain servants, and bold fellows are made into robbers and burglars, and become bellicose and overbearing. Quite often, though, they are not naturally corrupt: they're simply unlucky.

CLINIAS: How do you mean?

ATHENIAN: Well, if you have to live out your life with a continual hunger in your soul, aren't you 'unlucky' to a degree? What other term could I use?

CLINIAS: Very well, that's one reason. What's your second, sir?

ATHENIAN: Ah, yes, thank you for jogging my memory.

CLINIAS:[4] According to you, one cause is the insatiable and lifelong acquisitive urge which obsesses us all and stops us undertaking military training in the proper way. All right—now tell us the second.

ATHENIAN: I dare say it looks as if I'm putting off getting round to it because I don't know what to say?

CLINIAS: No, but you do seem to be such a 'good hater' of this sort of character that you're berating it more than the subject in hand requires.

ATHENIAN: That's a very proper rebuke, gentlemen. So you're all ready for the next point, it seems.

CLINIAS: Just tell us, that's all!

ATHENIAN: The cause I want to put forward are those 'non-constitutions' that I've often mentioned earlier in our conversation—democracy, oligarchy and tyranny. None of these is a genuine political system: the best

3. Military exercises.
4. This speech and Clinias' next one are attributed to Megillus in the Budé text.

name for them all would be 'party rule', because under none of them do willing rulers govern willing subjects: that is, the rulers are always willing enough, but they never hold power with the consent of the governed. They hold it by constant resort to a degree of force, and they are never prepared to allow any of their subjects to cultivate virtue or acquire wealth or strength or courage—and least of all will they tolerate a man who can fight. So much for the two main roots of pretty nearly all evil, and certainly the main roots of the evils we're discussing. However, the political system which we are now establishing by law has avoided both of them. Our state enjoys unparalleled leisure, the citizens live free of interference from each other, and I reckon these laws of ours are quite unlikely to turn them into money-grubbers. So it's a reasonable and natural supposition that a political system organized along these lines will be unique among contemporary constitutions in finding room for the military training-cum-sport that we've just described—and described in the detail it deserves, too.

CLINIAS: Splendid.

ATHENIAN: The next thing we have to bear in mind about any athletic contest is this: if it helps us to train for war we must go in for it and put up prizes for the winners, but leave it strictly alone if it does not. Isn't that right? It will be better to stipulate from the start the contests we want, and provide for them by law. First, I take it we should arrange races, and contests of speed in general?

CLINIAS: Yes, we should.

ATHENIAN: At any rate, what makes a man a fine soldier more than anything else is general agility, a ready use of his hands as well as his feet. If he's a good runner, he can make a capture or show a clean pair of heels, and versatile hands will stand him in good stead in tangling with the enemy in close combat, where strength and force are essential.

CLINIAS: Certainly.

ATHENIAN: But if he hasn't any weapons, neither ability will help him as much as it might.

CLINIAS: Of course not.

ATHENIAN: So in our contests the first competitor our herald will summon will be (as now) the single-length runner, and he will come forward armed; we shan't put up any prizes for competitors who are *un*armed. So, as I say, the competitor who intends to run one length will come on first, carrying his arms; second will come the runner over two lengths, and third the middle-distance runner; the long-distance man will come on fourth. The fifth competitor we shall call the 'heavy-armed' runner, from his heavier equipment. We shall start by sending him in full armor over a distance of sixty lengths to some temple of Ares and back. His course will be over comparatively level ground, whereas the other runner,[5] an archer in full archer rig, will run a course of 100 lengths over hills and constantly

5. The runner in a sixth race? The passage is confusingly written. (A 'length' = a 'stade' = about 200 yards; 60 lengths = about 7 miles; 100 lengths = about 11½ miles.)

c   changing terrain to a temple of Apollo and Artemis. While we're waiting
for these runners to return, we'll hold the other contests and finally award
the prizes to the winners of each event.

CLINIAS: Fine.

ATHENIAN: Let's arrange these contests in three groups, one for boys,
one for youths, and one for men. When youths and boys compete as archers
and heavy-armed runners, we shall make the course for youths two-thirds
of the full distance and for the boys one-half. As for females, girls below
d   the age of puberty must enter (naked) for the single-length, double-length,
middle and long-distance races, their competition being confined to the
stadium. Girls from thirteen till the marriage-age must enter till they are
at least eighteen, but not beyond the age of twenty. (They, however, must
put on some suitable clothing before presenting themselves as competitors
in these races.)

So much for men's and women's races; now to deal with trials of strength.
Instead of wrestling and other he-man contests that are the fashion nowa-
e   days, we'll have our citizens fight each other *armed*—man to man, two a
side, and any number per team up to ten. We ought to take our cue from
the authorities in charge of wrestling, who have established criteria which
will tell you whether a wrestler's performance is good or bad. We must
call in the leading exponents of armed combat and ask them to assist us
in framing rules about the blows one needs to avoid or inflict to win in
834   this sort of of contest, and similarly the points we need to look for to
decide the loser. The same set of rules should also apply to the female
competitors (who must be below the age of marriage). To replace the
pancration[6] we shall establish a general contest of light-infantry; the weapons of the competitors are to be bows, light shields, javelins, and stones
cast by hand and sling. Here too we'll lay down rules, and give the honor
of victory to the competitor who reaches the highest standard as defined
by the regulations.

The next thing for which we must provide rules is horse-racing. In Crete,
b   of course, horses are of rather limited use and you don't find very many
of them, so that the comparatively low level of interest in rearing and
racing them is inevitable. No one in this country keeps a team of horses
for a chariot, nor is ever likely to covet such a thing, so that if we established
contests in something so foreign to the local customs, we'd be taken for
c   idiots (and rightly). The way to modify this sport for the local Cretan
terrain is to put up prizes for skill in *riding* the animals—as foals, when
half-grown, and when fully grown. So our law should provide for contests
in which jockeys can compete with each other in these categories; Tribe-
Leaders and Cavalry-Commanders should be entrusted with the job of
deciding the actual courses and deciding which competitor has won (in
full armor, of course: just as in the athletic events, if we established contests
for unarmed competitors we'd be failing in our duty as legislators). And

---

6. A form of wrestling-cum-boxing that permitted kicking and choking as well.

since your Cretan is no fool at archery and javelin-throwing in the saddle,   d
people should amuse themselves by competing in this sort of contest too.
As for women, there's no point in making it legally compulsory for them
to join in all this, but if their previous training has got them into the habit,
and girls and young women are in good enough shape to take part without
hardship, then they should be permitted to do so and not discouraged.

   That brings us to the end of our discussion of competitions and the
teaching of physical training, and we've seen what strenuous efforts are   e
involved in the contests and the daily sessions with instructors. In fact,
we've also dealt pretty thoroughly with the role of the arts, although
arrangements about reciters of poetry and similar performers, and the
chorus-competitions obligatory at festivals, can wait till the gods and the
minor deities have had their days and months and years allocated to them;
then we can decide whether festivals should be held at two-year or four-
year intervals, or whether the gods suggest some other pattern. On these   835
occasions we must also expect the various categories of competitions in
the arts to be held. This is the province of the stewards of the games, the
Minister of Education and the Guardians of the Laws, who should all meet
as an ad hoc committee and produce their own regulations about the date
of each chorus-competition and dance, and specify who should compete
and who may watch. The original legislator has often enough explained
the sort of thing each of these performances should be, and has dealt with   b
the songs, the spoken addresses and the musical styles that accompany
the rhythmical movements of the dancers. His successors must emulate
his example in their own legislation and match the right contests with the
right sacrifices at the right times, and so provide festivals at which the
state may make merry.

   ATHENIAN: It's not difficult to see how to cast these and similar matters
in the form of a law, and making this or that alteration won't help or harm
the state very much. But now for something which is not a triviality at
all. It's a point on which it is difficult to convince people, and God himself
is really the only person to do it—supposing, that is, we could in fact   c
somehow get explicit instructions from him. Since that's impossible, it
looks as if we need some intrepid mortal, who values frankness above all,
to specify the policy he believes best for the state and its citizens, give a
firm 'no' to our most compelling passions, and order his audience of
corrupted souls to observe standards of conduct in keeping with, and
implied by, the whole organization of the state. There will be no one to
back him up. He'll walk alone, with reason alone to guide him.

   CLINIAS: What new topic is this, sir? We don't see what you're getting at.   d

   ATHENIAN: That's not surprising. Well, I'll try to put the point more
explicitly. When I came to discuss education, I envisaged young men and
women associating with each other on friendly terms. Naturally enough,
I began to feel some disquiet. I wondered how one would handle a state
like this, with everyone engaged on a life-long round of sacrifices and
festivals and chorus-performances, and the young men and women well-   e

nourished and free of those demanding and degrading jobs that damp down lust so effectively. Reason, which is embodied in law as far as it can be, tells us to avoid indulging the passions that have ruined so many people. So how will the members of *our* state avoid them? (Actually, most

836   desires may well be kept in check by the regulations we have already framed. If so, we needn't be surprised. After all, the law against excessive wealth will do a great deal to encourage self-control, and the educational curriculum is full of sound rules designed for the same purpose. The officials too, who have been rigorously trained to watch this point closely, and to keep the young people themselves under constant surveillance, will do something to restrain ordinary passions, as far as any man can.) But

b   there are *sexual* urges too—of boys and girls and heterosexual love among adults. What precautions should one take against passions which have had a such a powerful effect on public and private life? What's the remedy that will save us from the dangers of sex in each? It's a great problem, Clinias. We're faced with the fact that though in several other respects Crete in general and Sparta give us pretty solid help when we frame laws that flout common custom, in affairs of the heart (there's no one listening,

c   so let's be frank) they are totally opposed to us. Suppose you follow nature's rule and establish the law that was in force before the time of Laius.[7] You'd argue that one may have sexual intercourse with a woman but not with men or boys. As evidence for your view, you'd point to the animal world, where (you'd argue) the males do not have sexual relations with each other, because such a thing is unnatural. But in Crete and Sparta your argument would not go down at all well, and you'd probably persuade nobody. However, another argument is that such practices are incompatible with what in our view should be the constant aim of the

d   legislator—that is, we're always asking 'which of our regulations encourages virtue, and which does not?' Now then, suppose in the present case we agreed to pass a law that such practices are desirable, or not at all *un*desirable—what contribution would they make to virtue? Will the spirit of courage spring to life in the soul of the seduced person? Will the soul of the seducer learn habits of self-control? No one is going to be led astray by that sort of argument—quite the contrary. Everyone will censure the

e   weakling who yields to temptation, and condemn his all-too-effeminate partner who plays the role of the woman. So who on earth will pass a law like that? Hardly anyone, at any rate if he knows what a genuine law really is. Well, how do we show the truth of this? If you want to get these

837   things straight, you have to analyze the nature of friendship and desire and 'love', as people call it. There are two separate categories, plus a third which is a combination of both. But one term covers all three, and that causes no end of muddle and confusion.

   CLINIAS: How's that?

---

7. In myth, Laius (Oedipus' father) abducted his host Pelops' son, thus inaugurating homosexual attachments between men and teenage boys.

ATHENIAN: When two people are virtuous and alike, or when they are equals, we say that one is a 'friend' of the other; but we also speak of the poor man's 'friendship' for the man who has grown rich, even though they are poles apart. In either case, when the friendship is particularly ardent, we call it 'love'.

CLINIAS: Yes, we do.   b

ATHENIAN: And a violent and stormy friendship it is, when a man is attracted to someone widely different to himself, and only seldom do we see it reciprocated. When men are alike, however, they show a calm and mutual affection that lasts a lifetime. But there is a third category, compounded of the other two. The first problem here is to discover what this third kind of lover is really after. There is the further difficulty that he himself is confused and torn between two opposing instincts: one tells him to enjoy his beloved, the other forbids him. The lover of the body,   c hungry for his partner who is ripe to be enjoyed, like a luscious fruit, tells himself to have his fill, without showing any consideration for his beloved's character and disposition. But in another case physical desire will count for very little and the lover will be content to gaze upon his beloved without lusting for him—a mature and genuine desire of soul for soul. That body should sate itself with body he'll think outrageous; his reverence and respect for self-control, courage, high principles and good judgment will make him want to live a life of purity, chaste lover with chaste beloved.   d This combination of the first two is the 'third' love we enumerated a moment ago.

So there's your list of the various forms love can take: should the law forbid them all, and keep them out of our community? Or isn't it obvious that in our state we'd want to see the virtuous kind spring up—the love that aims to make a young man perfect? It's the other two we'll forbid, if we can. Or what *is* our policy, Megillus, my friend?

MEGILLUS: Indeed, sir, I heartily endorse what you've said on the subject.   e

ATHENIAN: So it looks as if I've won you over, my dear fellow, as I guessed I would, and there's no call for me to inquire what line the law of Sparta takes on this topic: it is enough to note your assent to my argument. Later on I'll come back to the subject and try to charm Clinias also into agreeing with me. Let's assume you've both conceded my point, and press on with our laws without delay.

MEGILLUS: Fair enough.

ATHENIAN: I want to put the law on this subject on a firm footing, and   838 at the moment I'm thinking of a method which is, in a sense, simplicity itself. But from another point of view, nothing could be harder.

MEGILLUS: What are you getting at?

ATHENIAN: We're aware, of course, that even nowadays most men, in spite of their general disregard for the law, are very effectively prevented from having relations with people they find attractive. And they don't refrain reluctantly, either—they're more than happy to.

MEGILLUS: What circumstances have you in mind?

ATHENIAN: When it's one's brother or sister whom one finds attractive.
b And the same law, unwritten though it is, is extremely effective in stopping a man sleeping—secretly or otherwise—with his son or daughter, or making any kind of amorous approach to them. Most people feel not the faintest desire for such intercourse.

MEGILLUS: That's perfectly true.

ATHENIAN: So the desire for this sort of pleasure is stifled by a few words?

MEGILLUS: What words do you mean?

ATHENIAN: The doctrine that 'these acts are absolutely unholy, an abomination in the sight of the gods, and that nothing is more revolting'. We
c refrain from them because we never hear them spoken of in any other way. From the day of our birth each of us encounters a complete unanimity of opinion wherever we go; we find it not only in comedies but often in the high seriousness of tragedy too, when we see a Thyestes on the stage, or an Oedipus or a Macareus, the clandestine lover of his sister.[8] We watch these characters dying promptly by their own hand as a penalty for their crimes.

d MEGILLUS: You're right in this, anyway, that when no one ventures to challenge the law, public opinion works wonders.

ATHENIAN: So we were justified in what we said just now. When the legislator wants to tame one of the desires that dominate mankind so cruelly, it's easy for him to see his method of attack. He must try to make everyone—slave and free, women and children, and the entire state without any exception—believe that this common opinion has the backing of reli-
e gion. He couldn't put his law on a securer foundation than that.

MEGILLUS: Very true. But how on earth it will ever be possible to produce such spontaneous unanimity—

ATHENIAN: I'm glad you've taken me up on the point. This is just what I was getting at when I said I knew of a way to put into effect this law of ours which permits the sexual act only for its natural purpose, procreation, and forbids not only homosexual relations, in which the human race is deliberately murdered, but also the sowing of seeds on rocks and stone,
839 where it will never take root and mature into a new individual; and we should also have to keep away from any female 'soil' in which we'd be sorry to have the seed develop. At present, however, the law is effective only against intercourse between parent and child, but if it can be put on a permanent footing and made to apply effectively, as it deserves to, in other cases as well, it'll do a power of good. The first point in its favor is that it is a *natural* law. But it also tends to check the raging fury of the sexual instinct that so often leads to adultery; it discourages excesses in
b food and drink, and inspires men with affection for their own wives. And there are a great many other advantages to be gained, if only one could get this law established.

8. Thyestes had intercourse with his own daughter; Oedipus married his own mother.

But suppose some impatient young man were standing here, bursting
with seed, and heard us passing this law. He'd probably raise the echoes
with his bellows of abuse, and say our rules were stupid and unrealistic.
Now this is just the sort of protest I had in mind when I remarked that I
knew of a very simple—and yet very difficult—way of putting this law   c
into effect permanently. It's easy to see that it *can* be done, and easy to
see *how*: if the rule is given sufficient religious backing, it will get a grip
on every soul and intimidate it into obeying the established laws. But in
fact we've reached a point where people still think we'd fail, even granted
those conditions. It's just the same with the supposed impossibility of the
common meals: people see no prospect of a whole state keeping up the   d
practice permanently. The proven facts of the case in your countries do
nothing to convince your compatriots that it would be natural to apply
the practice to women. It was this flat disbelief that made me remark on
the difficulty of turning either proposal into an established law.

MEGILLUS: You're absolutely right.

ATHENIAN: Even so, I could put up quite a convincing case for supposing
that the difficulties are not beyond human powers, and can be overcome.
Do you want me to try to explain?

CLINIAS: Of course.

ATHENIAN: When will a man find it easier to keep off sex, and do as he's   e
told in a decent and willing spirit? When he's not neglected his training
and is in the pink of condition, or when he's in poor shape?

CLINIAS: He'll find it a great deal easier if he's in training.

ATHENIAN: Now of course we've all heard the story of how Iccus of   840
Tarentum set about winning contests at Olympia and elsewhere. He was
so ambitious to win, they say, and his expertise was strengthened by a
character of such determination and self-discipline, that he never had a
woman or even a boy during the whole time he was under intensive
training. In fact, we are told very much the same about Crison, Astylus,
Diopompus, and a great many others. And yet, Clinias, their characters
were far less well educated than the citizens you and I have to deal with,
and physically they were much lustier.   b

CLINIAS: Yes, you're right—our ancient sources are quite definite that
these athletes did in fact do as you say.

ATHENIAN: Well then, they steeled themselves to keep off what most
people regard as sheer bliss, simply in order to win wrestling matches
and races and so forth. But there's a much nobler contest to be won than
that, and I hope the young people of our state aren't going to lack the
stamina for it. After all, right from their earliest years we're going to tell
them stories and talk to them and sing them songs, so as to charm them,   c
we trust, into believing that this victory is the noblest of all.

CLINIAS: What victory?

ATHENIAN: The conquest of pleasure. If they win this battle, they'll have
a happy life—but so much the worse for them if they lose. That apart, the

fear that the act is a ghastly sin will, in the end, enable them to tame the passions that their inferiors have tamed before them.

CLINIAS: Quite likely.

d ATHENIAN: So thanks to the general corruption, that's the predicament we've got into at this point in our consideration of the law about sex. My position, therefore, is that the law must go ahead and insist that our citizens' standards should not be lower than those of birds and many other wild animals which are born into large communities and live chaste and unmarried, without intercourse, until the time comes for them to breed. At

e the appropriate age they pair off; the male picks a wife, and female chooses a husband, and forever afterwards they live in a pious and law-abiding way, firmly faithful to the promises they made when they first fell in love. Clearly our citizens ought to reach standards higher than the animals'. But if they are corrupted by seeing and hearing how most other Greeks and non-Greeks go in for 'free' love on a grand scale, they may prove unable to keep themselves in check. In that case, the law-guardians must turn themselves into law-makers and frame a second law for people to observe.

841 CLINIAS: So if they find it impossible to enforce the ideal law now proposed, what other law do you advise them to pass?

ATHENIAN: The second best, Clinias, obviously.

CLINIAS: Namely?

ATHENIAN: My point is that the appetite for pleasures, which is very strong and grows by being fed, can be *starved* (you remember) if the body is given plenty of hard work to distract it. We'd get much the same result if we were incapable of having sexual intercourse without feeling ashamed; our shame

b would lead to infrequent indulgence, and infrequent indulgence would make the desire less compulsive. So in sexual matters our citizens ought to regard privacy—though not complete abstinence—as a decency demanded by usage and unwritten custom, and lack of privacy as disgusting. That will establish a second legal standard of decency and indecency—not the ideal standard, but the next to it. People whose characters have been corrupted (they form a single group we call the 'self-inferior') will be made prisoners

c of three influences that will compel them not to break the law.

CLINIAS: What influences do you mean?

ATHENIAN: Respect for religion, the ambition to be honored, and a mature passion for spiritual rather than physical beauty. 'Pious wishes!' you'll say; 'what romance!' Perhaps so. But if such wishes were to come true, the world would benefit enormously.

However, God willing, perhaps we'll succeed in imposing one or other of

d two standards of sexual conduct. (1) Ideally, no one will dare to have relations with any respectable citizen woman except his own wedded wife, or sow illegitimate and bastard seed in courtesans, or sterile seed in males in defiance of nature. (2) Alternatively, while suppressing sodomy entirely, we might insist that if a man does have intercourse with any woman (hired or procured in some other way) except the wife he wed in holy marriage with the blessing of the gods, he must do so without any other man or woman

e

getting to know about it. If he fails to keep the affair secret, I think we'd be right to exclude him by law from the award of state honors, on the grounds that he's no better than an alien. This law, or 'pair' of laws, as perhaps we should say, should govern our conduct whenever the sexual urge and the passion of love impel us, wisely or unwisely, to have intercourse.   842

MEGILLUS: Speaking for myself, sir, I'd be very glad to adopt this law of yours. Clinias must tell us his view on the subject himself.

CLINIAS: I'll do that later, Megillus, when I think a suitable moment has arrived. For the nonce, let's not stop our friend from going on to the next stage of his legislation.

MEGILLUS: Fair enough.

ATHENIAN: Well then, this is the stage we've reached now. We can assume   b
that communal meals have been established (a thing that would be a problem in other countries, we notice, but not in Crete, where no one would think of doing anything else). But how should they be organized? On the Cretan model, or the Spartan? Or is there some third type that would suit us better than either? I don't think this is a difficulty, and there's not much to be gained from settling the point. The arrangements we have made are quite satisfactory as they are.

The next question is the organization of a food-supply in keeping with   c
our communal meals. In other states the sources of supply are many and varied—in fact, at least twice as many as in ours, because most Greeks draw on both the land and the sea for their food, whereas our citizens will use the land alone. For the legislator, this makes things simpler. It's not just that half the number of laws or even substantially fewer will do,   d
but they'll be more suitable laws for gentlemen to observe. Our state's legislator, you see, need not bother his head very much about the merchant-shipping business, trading, retailing, inn-keeping, customs duties, mining, money-lending and compound interest. Waving aside most of these and a thousand other such details, he'll legislate for farmers, shepherds, bee-keepers, for the protectors of their stock and the supervisors of their equip-   e
ment. His laws already cover such major topics as marriage and the birth and rearing of children, as well as their education and the appointment of the state's officials, so the next topic to which he must turn in his legislation is their food, and the workers who co-operate in the constant effort to produce it.

Let's first specify the 'agricultural' laws, as they're called. The first law— sanctioned by Zeus the Protector of Boundaries—shall run as follows:

No man shall disturb the boundary stones of his neighbor, whether fellow citizen or foreigner (that is, when a proprietor's land is on the boundary of the state), in the conviction that this would be 'moving the immovable'[9] in the crudest sense. Far better that a man should want to   843
try to move the biggest stone that does not mark a boundary, than a small

---

9. A proverbial expression of disapproval for fundamental social and political change. Cf. 684e.

one separating friend's land from foe's, and established by an oath sworn to the gods. Zeus the God of Kin is witness in the one case, Zeus the Protector of Foreigners in the other. Rouse him in either capacity, and the most terrible wars break out. If a man obeys the law he will escape its penalties, but if he holds it in contempt he is to be liable to two punishments,

b the first at the hands of the gods, the second under the law. No man, if he can help it, must move the boundary stones of his neighbor's land, but if anyone does move them, any man who wishes should report him to the farmers, who should take him to court.

26. If anyone is found guilty of such a charge,
he must be regarded as a man who has tried to reallocate land, whether clandestinely or by force; and the court must bear that in mind when assessing what penalty he should suffer or what fine he should pay.

Next we come to those numerous petty injuries done by neighbor to neighbor. The frequent repetition of such injuries makes feelings run high, so that relations between neighbors become intolerably embittered. That's

c why everyone should do everything he can to avoid offending his neighbor; above all, he must always go out of his way to avoid all acts of encroachment. Hurting a man is all too easy, and we all get the chance to do that; but it's not everyone who is in a position to do a good turn.

27. If a man oversteps his boundaries and encroaches on his neighbor's land,
he should pay for the damage, and also, by way of cure for such uncivilized
d and inconsiderate behavior, give the injured party a further sum of twice that amount.

In all these and similar cases the Country-Wardens should act as inspectors, judges and assessors (the entire divisional company in the graver cases, as indicated earlier,[10] and the Guards-in-Chief in the more trivial).

28. If a man lets his cattle graze on someone else's land,
these officials must inspect the damage, reach a decision, and assess the penalty.

e 29. If anyone takes over another man's bees, by making rattling noises to please and attract them, so that he gets them for himself,
he must pay for the injury he has done.

30. If anyone burns his own wood without taking sufficient precautions to protect his neighbor's,
he must be fined a sum decided by the officials.

10. See 761d–e.

31. If when planting trees a man fails to leave a suitable gap between
them and his neighbor's land,
the same regulation is to apply.

These are points that many legislators have dealt with perfectly adequately, and we should make use of their work rather than demand that
the grand architect of our state should legislate on a mass of trivial details
that can be handled by any run-of-the-mill lawgiver. For instance, the   844
water supply for farmers is the subject of some splendid old-established
laws—but there's no call to let them overflow into our discussion! It is
fundamental that anyone who wants to conduct a supply of water to his
own land may do so, provided his source is the public reservoirs and he
does not intercept the surface springs of any private person. He may
conduct the water by any route he likes, except through houses, temples
and tombs, and he must do no damage beyond the actual construction of
the conduit. But in some naturally dry districts the soil may fail to retain   b
the moisture when it rains, so that drinking water is in short supply. In
that case the owner must dig down to the clay, and if he fails to strike
water at that depth he should take from his neighbors sufficient drinking
water for each member of his household. If the neighbors too are short of
water, he should share the available supply with them and fetch his ration
daily, the amount to be fixed by the Country-Wardens. A man may injure   c
the farmer or householder next door on higher ground by blocking the
flow of rainwater; on the other hand he may discharge it so carelessly as
to damage the man below. If the parties are not prepared to co-operate in
this matter, anyone who wishes should report the matter to an official—
a City-Warden in the city, and a Country-Warden in the country—and
obtain a ruling as to what each side should do. Anyone refusing to abide
by the ruling must take the consequences of being a grudging and ill-   d
tempered fellow:

32. If found guilty,
he should pay twice the value of the damage to the injured party as a
penalty for disobeying the officials.

Everyone should take his share of the fruit harvest on roughly the
following principles. The goddess of the harvest has graciously bestowed
two gifts upon us, (a) the fruit which pleases Dionysus so much, but which
won't keep, and (b) the produce which nature has made fit to store. So
our law about the harvest should run as follows.

33. Anyone who consumes any part of the coarse crop of grapes or figs,
whether on his own land or another's, before the rising of Arcturus[11]   e
ushers in the vintage,
must owe

---

11. The autumn equinox.

(a) fifty drachmas, to be presented to Dionysus, if he takes the fruit from his own trees,

(b) one hundred if from his neighbor's, and

(c) sixty-six and two-thirds drachmas if from anyone else's trees.

If a man wants to gather in the 'dessert' grapes or figs (as they are called nowadays), he may do so whenever and however he likes, provided they come from his own trees; but

34. (a) if he takes them from anyone else's trees, without permission, *he must* be punished in accordance with the provisions of the law which forbids the removal of any object except by the depositor.[12]

(b) If a slave fails to get the landowner's permission before touching any of this kind of fruit, *he must* be whipped, the number of lashes to be the same as the number of grapes in the bunch or figs picked off the fig tree.

845

A resident alien may buy dessert fruit and gather it in as he wishes. If a foreigner on a visit from abroad feels inclined to eat some fruit as he travels along the road, he may, if he wishes, take some of the dessert crop gratis, for himself and one attendant, as part of our hospitality. But foreigners must be prevented by law from sharing with us the 'coarse' and similar fruits.

b

35. If a foreigner, master or slave, touches such fruit in ignorance of the law,

(a) *the slave* is to be punished with a whipping;

(b) *the free* man is to be dismissed with a warning and told to stick to the crop that is unsuitable to be kept in store in the form of raisins, wine, or dried figs.

There should be nothing to be ashamed of in helping oneself inconspicuously to apples and pears and pomegranates and so on, but

c

36. (a) if a man under thirty is caught at it, *he should* be cuffed and driven off, provided he suffers no actual injury.

A citizen should have no legal redress for such an assault on his person. (A foreigner is to be entitled to a share of these fruits too, on the same terms as he may take some of the dessert grapes and figs.) If a man *above* thirty years of age touches some fruits, consuming them on the spot and taking none away with him, he shall share them all on the same terms as the foreigner, but

(b) if he disobeys the law, *he should* be liable to be disqualified from competing for awards of merit, if anyone draws the attention of the assessors to the facts when the awards are being decided.

d

12. This offense is thus brought under the umbrella of the general law mentioned in 842e–843b.

Water is the most nourishing food a garden can have, but it's easily fouled, whereas the soil, the sun and the winds, which co-operate with the water in fostering the growth of the plants that spring up out of the ground, are not readily interfered with by being doctored or channeled off or stolen. But in the nature of the case, water is exposed to all these hazards. That is why it needs the protection of a law, which should run   e as follows.

If anyone deliberately spoils someone else's water supply, whether spring or reservoir, by poisons or excavations or theft, the injured party should take his case to the City-Wardens and submit his estimate of the damage in writing.

37. Anyone convicted of fouling water by magic poisons
should, in addition to his fine, purify the spring or reservoir, using whatever method of purification the regulations of the Expounders[13] prescribe as appropriate to the circumstances and the individuals involved.

A man may bring home any crop of his own by any route he pleases,   846 provided he does no one any damage, or, failing that, benefits to at least three times the value of the damage he does his neighbor. The authorities must act as inspectors in this business, as well as in all other cases when someone uses his own property deliberately to inflict violent or surreptitious damage on another man or some piece of his property without his permission. When the damage does not exceed three minas, the injured party must report it to the magistrates and obtain redress; but if he has a larger claim to bring against someone, he must get his redress from the culprit by taking the case to the public courts.   b

38. If one of the officials is judged to have settled the penalties in a biased fashion,
he must be liable to the injured person for double the damages.

Offenses committed by the authorities in handling any claim should be taken to the public courts by anyone who may wish to do so. (There are thousands of procedural details like this that must be observed before a penalty can be imposed: the complaint has to be lodged, the summonses issued and served in the presence of two witnesses, or whatever the proper   c number is. All this sort of detail must not be left to look after itself, but it is not important enough for a legislator who is getting on in years. Our younger colleagues must settle these points, using the broad principles laid down by their predecessors as a guide for their own detailed regulations, which they must apply as need arises. They must thus proceed by trial and error until they think they have got a satisfactory set of formalities, and once the process of modification is over, they should finalize their rules of procedure and render them lifelong obedience.)

13. For these officials, see 759d–e.

d   As for craftsmen in general, our policy should be this. First, no citizen of our land nor any of his servants should enter the ranks of the workers whose vocation lies in the arts and crafts. A citizen's vocation, which demands a great deal of practice and study, is to establish and maintain good order in the community, and this is not a job for part-timers. Following

e   two trades or two callings efficiently—or even following one and supervising a worker in another—is almost always too difficult for human nature. So in our state this must be a cardinal rule: no metal worker must turn to carpentry and no carpenter must supervise workers in metal instead of practicing his own craft. We may, of course, be met with the excuse that

847 supervising large numbers of employees is more sensible—because more profitable—than just following one's own trade. But no! In our state each individual must have one occupation only, and that's how he must earn his bread. The City-Wardens must have the job of enforcing this rule.

> 39. If a citizen born and bred turns his attention to some craft instead of to the cultivation of virtue,
> *the City-Wardens* must punish him with marks of disgrace and dishonor until they've got him back on the right lines.

> 40. If a foreigner follows two trades,
> *the Wardens* must punish him by prison or fines or expulsion from the

b   state, and so force him to play one role, not many.

As for craftsmen's pay, and cases of refusal to take delivery of their work, or any other wrong done to them by other parties or by them to others, the City-Wardens must adjudicate if the sum at issue does not exceed fifty drachmas; if more, the public courts must decide the dispute as the law directs.

In our state no duties will have to be paid by anyone on either imports or exports. No one must import frankincense and similar foreign fragrant

c   stuff used in religious ritual, or purple and similar dyes not native to the country, or materials for any other process which only needs imports from abroad for inessential purposes; nor, on the other hand, is anyone to export anything that it is essential to keep in the state. The twelve Guardians of the Laws next in order of seniority after the five eldest must act as inspectors and supervisors in this entire field. But what about arms and other military

d   equipment? Well, if we ever need, for military purposes, some technique, vegetable product, mineral, binding material or animal that has to be obtained from abroad, the *state* will receive the goods and pay for them, and the Cavalry-Commanders and the Generals are to be in charge of importing them and exporting other goods in exchange. The Guardians of the Laws will lay down suitable and adequate regulations on the subject. Nowhere in the whole country and whole state are these—or any other—

e   goods to be retailed for profit.

It looks as if the right way to organize the food supply and distribute agricultural produce will be to adopt something like the regulations in force in Crete. Every citizen must divide each crop into twelve parts corresponding to the twelve periods in which it is consumed. Take wheat or barley, for instance (though the same procedure must be followed for all the other crops too, as well as for any livestock there may be for sale in 848 each district): each twelfth part should be split proportionately into three shares, one for the citizens, one for their slaves, and the third for workmen and foreigners in general (i.e., communities of resident aliens in need of the necessities of life, and occasional visitors on some public or private business). It should be necessary to sell only this third share of all the necessities of life; there should be *no* necessity to sell any part of the other b two. So what will be the right way to arrange the division? It's obvious, for a start, that the shares we allocate will in one sense be equal, but in another sense unequal.

CLINIAS: What do you mean?

ATHENIAN: Well, the land will grow a good crop of one thing and a bad crop of another. That's inevitable, I take it.

CLINIAS: Of course.

ATHENIAN: None of the three shares—for masters, slaves and foreigners—must be better than the others: when the distribution is made, each group should be treated on an equal footing and get the same share. Each citizen must take his two shares and distribute them at his discretion to the slaves c and free persons in his charge (quality and quantity being up to him). The surplus should be distributed by being divided up according to the number of animals that have to be supported by the produce of the soil, and rationed out accordingly.

Next, the population should have houses grouped in separate localities. This entails the following arrangements. There should be twelve villages, one in the middle of each of the twelve divisions of the state; in each d village the settlers should first select a site for a market-place with its temples for gods and their retinue of spirits. (Local Magnesian gods, and sanctuaries of other ancient deities who are still remembered, must be honored as they were in earlier generations.) In each division they must establish shrines of Hestia, Zeus, Athena, and the patron deity of the district; after this their first job must be to build houses on the highest ground in a circle round these temples, so as to provide the garrison with e the strongest possible position for defense.

Thirteen groups of craftsmen must be formed to provide for all the rest of the territory. One should be settled in the central city and the others distributed all round it on the outskirts in twelve further sub-groups corresponding to the twelve urban districts; and the categories of craftsmen useful to farmers must be established in each village. They must all be under the supervision of the chief Country-Wardens, who must decide the number and type required in each district and say where they should settle in order to prove their full worth to the farmers and cause them as little trouble as possible. Similarly the board of City-Wardens must assume 849 permanent responsibility for the craftsmen in the city.

The detailed supervision of the market must naturally be in the hands of the Market-Wardens. Their first job is to ensure that no one does any damage to the temples round the marketplace; secondly, to see whether people are conducting their business in an orderly or disorderly fashion, and inflict punishment on anyone who needs it. They must ensure that every commodity the citizens are required to sell to the aliens is sold in
b the manner prescribed by law. The law will be simply this. On the first day of the month the agents (the foreigners or slaves who act for the citizens) must produce the share that has to be sold to the aliens, beginning with the twelfth part of corn. At this first market an alien must buy corn and related commodities to last him the whole month. On the tenth day the respective parties must buy and sell a whole month's supply of liquids.
c The third[14] market should be on the twentieth, when they should hold a sale of the livestock that individuals find they need to buy or sell, and also of all the equipment or goods sold by the farmers, and which aliens cannot get except by purchase—skins, for example, and all clothing, woven material, felt, and all that sort of thing. But these goods (and barley and wheat ground into flour and every other kind of food) should never be
d bought by, or sold to, a citizen or his slave through *retail* channels. The proper place for 'retail' trading (as it's generally called) in corn and wine is the foreigners' market, where foreigners are to sell these goods to craftsmen and their slaves; and when the butchers have cut up the animals, it is to foreigners that they must dispose of the meat. Any foreigner who wishes may buy any kind of firewood wholesale any day from the district agents and sell it to other foreigners whenever he likes and in whatever
e quantity he pleases.

All other goods and equipment needed by various people should be brought to the general market and put up for sale in the place allotted them. (The Guardians of the Laws and the Market-Wardens, in conjunction with the City-Wardens, will have marked out suitable spaces and decided where each article is to be sold.) Here they must exchange money for goods and goods for money, and never hand over anything without getting something in return; anyone who doesn't bother about this and trusts the other party must grin and bear it whether or not he gets
850 what he's owed, because for such transactions there will be no legal remedy. If the amount or value of the object bought or sold is greater than is allowed by the law which forbids increase or diminution of a man's property above or below a given limit, the excess must immediately be registered with the Guardians of the Laws; but if there is a deficiency, it must be cancelled. The same rules are to apply to the registration of the property of resident aliens.

Anyone who wishes may come to live in the state on specified conditions. (a) There will be a community of foreigners open to anyone willing and
b able to join it. (b) The alien must have a skill and (c) not stay longer than

14. Reading *tritē* in b8.

twenty years from the date of registration. (d) He need pay no alien-tax, even a small one (apart from behaving himself), nor any tax on any purchase or sale. (e) When his time has expired, he is to collect his possessions and depart. (f) If during this period he has distinguished himself for some notable service to the state, and is confident he can persuade the council and the assembly to grant his request for an official extension of his stay, either temporarily or for life, he should present himself and make out his case; and he must be allowed to enjoy to the full whatever concessions the state grants him. (g) Children of resident aliens must be craftsmen, and (h) their period of residence must be deemed to have started when they reach the age of fifteen. On these conditions they may stay for twenty years, after which they must depart to whatever destination they like. If they wish to stay longer, they may do so provided they obtain permission as already specified. (i) Before a departing alien leaves he must cancel the entries that he originally made in the records kept in the custody of the officials.

Book IX

ATHENIAN: Next, in accordance with the natural arrangement of our legal code, will come the legal proceedings that arise out of all the occupations we have mentioned up till now. To some extent, so far as agricultural affairs and related topics are concerned, we have already listed the acts that should be prosecuted, but the most serious have yet to be specified. Our next task is to enumerate these one by one, mentioning what penalty each should attract and to which court it should be assigned.

CLINIAS: That's right.

ATHENIAN: The very composition of all these laws we are on the point of framing is, in a way, a disgrace: after all, we're assuming we have a state which will be run along excellent lines and achieve every condition favorable to the practice of virtue. The mere idea that a state of this kind could give birth to a man affected by the worst forms of wickedness found in other countries, so that the legislator has to anticipate his appearance by threats—this, as I said, is in a way a disgrace. It means we have to lay down laws against these people, to deter them and punish them when they appear, on the assumption that they will certainly do so. However, unlike the ancient legislators, we are not framing laws for heroes and sons of gods. The lawgivers of that age, according to the story told nowadays, were descended from gods and legislated for men of similar stock. But we are human beings, legislating in the world today for the children of humankind, and we shall give no offense by our fear that one of our citizens will turn out to be, so to speak, a 'tough egg', whose character will be so 'hard-boiled' as to resist softening; powerful as our laws are, they may not be able to tame such people, just as heat has no effect on tough beans. For their dismal sake, the first law I shall produce will deal with robbery from temples, in case anyone dares to commit this crime. Now in view of the correct education our citizens will have received, we should hardly want any of them to catch this disease, nor is there much reason to expect that they will. Their slaves, however, as well as foreigners and the slaves of foreigners, may well make frequent attempts at such 854 crimes. For their sake principally—but still with an eye on the general weakness of human nature—I'll spell out the law about robbery from temples, and about all the other similar crimes which are difficult or even impossible to cure.

Following the practice we agreed earlier, we must first compose preambles, in the briefest possible terms, to stand at the head of all these laws. Take a man who is incited by day and kept awake at night by an evil impulse which drives him to steal some holy object. You might talk to him and exhort him as follows:

b   'My dear fellow, this evil impulse that at present drives you to go robbing temples comes from a source that is neither human nor divine. It is a sort of frenzied goad, innate in mankind as a result of crimes of long ago that remained unexpiated; it travels around working doom and destruction, and you should make every effort to take precautions against it. Now, take note what these precautions are. When any of these thoughts enters your head, seek the rites that free a man from guilt; seek the shrines of the gods who avert evil, and supplicate them; seek the company of men c   who have a reputation in your community for being virtuous. Listen to them as they say that every man should honor what is fine and just—try to bring yourself to say it too. But run away from the company of the wicked, with never a backward glance. If by doing this you find that your disease abates somewhat, well and good; if not, then you should look upon death as the preferable alternative, and rid yourself of life.'

These are the overtures we make to those who think of committing all these impious deeds that bring about the ruin of the state. When a man obeys us, we should silently omit the actual law; but in cases of disobedience, we must change our tune after the overture and sing this resounding strain:

d   41. If a man is caught thieving from a temple and is (a) a foreigner or slave,
        a brand of his misfortune shall be made on his face and hands, and he shall be whipped, the number of lashes to be decided by his judges. Then he shall be thrown out beyond the boundaries of the land, naked.

(Perhaps paying this penalty will teach him restraint and make him a better man: after all, no penalty imposed by law has an evil purpose, but e   generally achieves one of two effects: it makes the person who pays the penalty either more virtuous or less wicked.)

(b) If a citizen is ever shown to be responsible for such a crime—to have perpetrated, that is, some great and unspeakable offense against the

gods or his parents or the state,
the penalty is death.

The judge should consider him as already beyond cure; he should bear in mind the kind of education and upbringing the man has enjoyed from his earliest years, and how after all this he has still not abstained from acts of the greatest evil. But the very tiniest of evils will be what the offender suffers, indeed, he will be of service to others, by being a lesson to them   855
when he is ignominiously banished from sight beyond the borders of the state. And if the children and family escape taking on the character of the father, they should be held in honor and win golden opinions for the spirit and persistence with which they have shunned evil and embraced the good.

In a state where the size and number of the farms are to be kept permanently unaltered, it would not be appropriate for the state to confiscate the property of any of these criminals. But if a man commits a crime and is thought to deserve a penalty in money, then provided he possesses a surplus over and above the basic equipment of his farm, he must pay his   b
fine. The Guardians of the Laws must scrutinize the registers and discover the precise facts in these cases, and make an exact report to the court on each occasion, so as to prevent any farm becoming unworked because of a shortage of money. If a man appears to deserve a stiffer fine, and if some of his friends are not prepared to bail him out by contributing the money to set him free, his punishment should take the form of a prolonged period of imprisonment (which should be open to public view), and various humiliations. But no one, no matter what his offense, is ever to be deprived   c
of his citizen rights completely, not even if he has gone into exile beyond our frontiers for it. The penalties we impose will be death, imprisonment, whipping, or various degrading postures (either standing or sitting), or being rusticated and made to stand before temples on the boundaries of the state; and payments of money may be made in certain cases which we have just mentioned, where such a punishment is appropriate. In cases involving the death penalty the judges are to be the Guardians of the Laws, sitting in conjunction with the court whose members are selected by merit from the officials of the previous year. The method of bringing   d
these cases to court, the serving of the summonses and similar procedural details must be the concern of the legislators who succeed us; what *we* have to do is legislate about the voting. The vote should be taken openly, but before this our judges should have ranged themselves according to seniority and sat down close together facing the prosecutor and defendant; all citizens who have some spare time should attend and listen carefully to such trials. First, the prosecutor should deliver a single speech, then the   e
defendant; the most senior judge should follow these addresses by cross-questioning, and continue until he has gone into the arguments in sufficient detail. One by one, the other judges should follow the most senior and work through any points on which either litigant has left him dissatisfied by some kind of error or omission. A judge who feels no such dissatisfaction

should hand on the interrogation to his colleague. All the judges should
856 endorse those arguments that appear pertinent by appending their signatures and then depositing the documents on the altar of Hestia. The next
day they must reconvene in the same place, and after similar interrogation
and examination again append their signatures to the depositions. Having
followed this procedure three times, after giving due consideration to the
evidence and witnesses, each judge should cast a sacred vote, swearing
in the name of Hestia to give, as far as lies in him, a judgment just and
true. In this way they should conclude this category of trial.

b   We come next, after these matters of religion, to cases of political subver-
sion. We should treat as the biggest enemy of the entire state the man who
makes the laws into slaves, and the state into the servant of a particular
interest, by subjecting them to the diktat of mere men. This transgressor
of the law uses violence in all that he does and stirs up sedition. Second
in the scale of wickedness, in our estimation, should come the holder of
some high state office, who while not an accessory to any such crimes,
nevertheless fails to detect them and exact the vengeance of his fatherland
c   (or, if he does detect them, holds back through cowardice). Every man
who is any good at all must denounce the plotter to the authorities and
take him to court on a charge of violently and illicitly overthrowing the
constitution. The court should consist of the same judges as for robbers
from temples, and the procedure of the entire trial should be the same as
it was for them, a majority vote being sufficient for the death penalty.

As a rule, penalties and disgrace incurred by a father should not be
d   passed on to any of his children, except where a man's father, grandfather
and great-grandfather have all in turn been sentenced to death. The state
should deport such cases to the state and city from which their family
originally came; and they should take their property with them, apart from
all the basic equipment of their farm. Next, sons of citizens who have more
than one son over ten years of age should be nominated by their father
or grandfather on either the mother's or the father's side. Ten of them
should be chosen by lot, and the names of those whom the lot selects
e   should be reported to Delphi. The god's choice should then be installed
as heir to the abandoned property—and he, we hope, will have better luck.

CLINIAS: Splendid.

ATHENIAN: The same regulations about the judges that should try the
case, and the procedure to be followed at the trial, will apply in yet a third
instance, when a man is brought to court on a charge of treason. In the
857 same way, a single law should apply to all three cases and decide whether
the children of these criminals (traitor, temple-robber, and the violent
wrecker of the laws of the state) should remain in their fatherland or leave it.

Again, a single law and legal penalty should apply to every thief, no
matter whether his theft is great or small:

42. (a) *he must* pay twice the value of the stolen article, if he loses the
day and has sufficient surplus property over and above his farm with
which to make the repayment.

(b) if he has not,
he must be kept in prison until he pays up or persuades the man who
has had him convicted to let him off.

43. If a man is convicted of stealing from *public* sources, b
he shall be freed from prison when he has either persuaded the state to
let him off or paid back twice the amount involved.

CLINIAS: How on earth can we be serious, sir, in saying that it makes no
odds whether his theft is large or small, or whether it comes from sacred
or secular sources? And what about all the other different circumstances
of a theft? Shouldn't a legislator vary the penalties he inflicts, so that he
can cope with the various *categories* of theft?

ATHENIAN: That's a good question, Clinias: I have been walking in my
sleep, and you have bumped into me and woken me up. You have re- c
minded me of something that has occurred to me before, that the business
of establishing a code of law has never been properly thought out—as we
can see from the example that has just cropped up. Now, what am I getting
at? It wasn't a bad parallel we made, you know, when we compared all
those for whom legislation is produced today to slaves under treatment
from slave doctors.[1] Make no mistake about what would happen, if one
of those doctors who are innocent of theory and practice medicine by rule
of thumb were ever to come across a gentleman doctor conversing with d
a gentleman patient. This doctor would be acting almost like a philosopher,
engaging in a discussion that ranged over the source of the disease and
pushed the inquiry back into the whole nature of the body. But our other
doctor would immediately give a tremendous shout of laughter, and his
observations would be precisely those that most 'doctors' are always so
ready to trot out. 'You ass,' he would say, 'you are not treating the patient,
but tutoring him. Anybody would think he wanted to become a doctor
rather than get well again.' e

CLINIAS: And wouldn't he be right to say that?

ATHENIAN: Perhaps he would—if he were to bear in mind this further
point, that anyone who handles law in the way we are now, *is* tutoring
the citizens, not imposing laws on them. Wouldn't it be equally right to
say that?

CLINIAS: Perhaps so.

ATHENIAN: However, at the moment, we are in a fortunate position.

CLINIAS: How do you mean?

ATHENIAN: I mean the lack of any necessity to legislate. We are simply 858
carrying out our own review of every kind of political system and trying
to see how we could put into effect the absolutely ideal kind, as well as
the least good sort that would still be acceptable. This is particularly true
of our legislation, where it looks as if we have a choice: either we can
examine ideal laws, if we want to, or again, if we feel like it, we can look

1. See 719e–720e.

at the minimum standard we are prepared to put up with. So we must choose which course we want to take.

CLINIAS: This is a ridiculous choice to give ourselves, my friend: it's not
b   as if we were legislators forced by some irresistible necessity to legislate at a minute's notice, without being allowed to put the business off till tomorrow. We, God willing, can do as bricklayers do, or workmen starting some other kind of erecting. We can gather our materials in no particular order and then select—and select at leisure—the items which are appropriate for the forthcoming construction. Our assumption should be, therefore, that we are constructing something, but not under any constraint; we work at our convenience and spend part of the time preparing our material, part of the time fitting it together. So it would be quite fair to
c   describe our penal code as already partially laid down, while other material for it lies ready to hand.

ATHENIAN: At any rate, Clinias, this will be the more realistic way to conduct our review of legislation. Well then, may we please notice this point that concerns legislators?

CLINIAS: What point?

ATHENIAN: I suppose literary compositions and written speeches by many other authors are current in our cities, besides those of the legislator?

CLINIAS: Of course they are.

ATHENIAN: To whose writings ought we to apply ourselves? Are we to
d   read the poets and others who have recorded in prose or verse compositions their advice about how one should live one's life, to the neglect of the compositions of the legislators? Or isn't it precisely the latter that deserve our closest attention?

CLINIAS: Yes, it certainly is.

ATHENIAN: And I suppose the legislator, alone among writers, is to be denied permission to give advice about virtue and goodness and justice? Is he alone to be prevented from explaining their nature and how they should be reflected in our conduct, if we aim to be happy?

CLINIAS: No, of course not.

e   ATHENIAN: Then is it really more scandalous in the case of Homer and Tyrtaeus and the other poets to have composed in writing[2] bad rules for the conduct of life, but less so for Lycurgus and Solon, and all others who have turned legislator and committed their recommendations to writing? The proper view, surely, is this: a city's writings on legal topics should turn out, on being opened, to be the finest and best of all those it has in
859 circulation; the writings of other men should either sound in harmony with them, or provoke ridicule by being out of tune. So what *is* the style in which a state's laws ought to be written, in our opinion? Should the regulations appear in the light of a loving and prudent father and mother? Or should they act the tyrant and the despot, posting their orders and

---

2. For Tyrtaeus, see 629a and note. Lycurgus was the traditional founder of the Spartan constitution. Solon legislated for Athens in 594 and wrote poems justifying his measures.

threats on walls and leaving it at that? Clearly, then, at this stage, we must decide whether we are going to try to talk about laws in the right spirit. Succeed or no, we shall at any rate show our good intentions. If we take   b
this course and have to face some difficulties *en route*, then let's face them. Good luck to us, and God willing, we shall succeed.

CLINIAS: You've put it splendidly. Let's do as you suggest.

ATHENIAN: In the first place, we must continue the attempt we've just made: we must scrutinize our law about robbers of temples, theft in general, and every variety of crime. We should not let it daunt us if in the full spate of our legislation we find that although we have settled some matters,   c
our inquiry into others has still to be completed. We are still aiming at the status of legislators, but we haven't achieved it yet; perhaps eventually we may succeed. So now let's look at these topics I've mentioned—if, that is, you are prepared to look at them in the way I have explained.

CLINIAS: Certainly we are prepared.

ATHENIAN: Now, on the whole subject of goodness and justice, we ought to try to see quite clearly just where we agree, and where there are differences of opinion between us. Again, how far do ordinary men agree? What differences are there between *them*? (Naturally, we should claim that we wanted there to be at least a small 'difference between' us and ordinary men!)   d

CLINIAS: What sort of 'differences between us' have you in mind when you say that?

ATHENIAN: I'll try to explain. When we talk about justice in general— just men, just actions, just arrangements, we are, after a fashion, unanimous that all these things are 'good'. One might insist that even if just men happen to be shocking in their physical appearance, they are still preeminently 'good' because of their supremely just character. No one would think a man was talking nonsense in saying that.   e

CLINIAS: Wouldn't that be right?

ATHENIAN: Perhaps. But if everything that has the quality of justice is 'good', we ought to note that we include in that 'everything' even the things done *to* us, which are about as frequent, roughly speaking, as the things *we* do to others.

CLINIAS: What now, then?

ATHENIAN: Any just action we do has the quality of being 'good' roughly in proportion to the degree to which it has the quality of justice.

CLINIAS: Indeed.

ATHENIAN: So surely, anything done *to* us, which has the quality of   860
justice, is to that extent agreed to be 'good'? This wouldn't involve our argument in any contradiction.

CLINIAS: True.

ATHENIAN: If we agree that something done to us is just, but at the same time shocking, the terms 'just' and 'good' will be in conflict with each other—the reason being that we have termed 'just' actions 'most shameful'.

CLINIAS: What are you getting at?

ATHENIAN: It's not difficult to understand. The injunctions of the laws we laid down a little while ago would seem to be in flat contradiction to what we are saying now.

CLINIAS: How so?

b ATHENIAN: Our ruling was, I think, that the temple-robber and the enemy of properly established laws would suffer a 'just' death. But then, on the brink of establishing a great many such rules, we held back. We saw ourselves becoming involved with penal suffering of infinite variety and on a grand scale. Of all sufferings, these were particularly just; but they were also the particularly shocking ones. Thus, surely, one minute we shall find 'just' and 'good' invariably turning out to be the same, and the next moment discover they are opposites.

CLINIAS: Likely enough.

c ATHENIAN: This is the source of the inconsistency in the language of the ordinary man: he destroys the unity of the terms 'good' and 'just'.

CLINIAS: That is indeed how it looks, sir.

ATHENIAN: Now, Clinias, we ought to examine our own position again. How far is it consistent in this business?

CLINIAS: Consistent? What consistency do you mean?

ATHENIAN: Earlier in our discussion I think I have said quite categorically—or if I haven't before, assume I'm saying it now—that . . .

CLINIAS: What?

d ATHENIAN: . . . all wicked men are, in all respects, *unwillingly* wicked. This being so, my next argument necessarily follows.

CLINIAS: What argument?

ATHENIAN: That the unjust man is doubtless wicked; but that the wicked man is in that state only against his will. However, to suppose that a voluntary act is performed involuntarily makes no sense. Therefore, in the eyes of someone who holds the view that injustice is involuntary, a man who acts unjustly would seem to be doing so against his will. Here and now, that is the position *I* have to accept: I allow that no one acts unjustly

e except against his will. (If anyone with a disputatious disposition or a desire to attract favorable notice says that although there *are* those who are unjust against their will, even so many men do commit unjust acts voluntarily, I would reject his argument and stick to what I said.) Well then, how am I to make my own arguments consistent? Suppose the two of you, Clinias and Megillus, were to ask me, 'If that's so, sir, what advice have you for us about laying down laws for the city of the Magnesians? Do we legislate, or don't we?' 'Of course we legislate', I'd say, and you'd ask: 'Are you going to make a distinction for the Magnesians between voluntary and involuntary acts of injustice? Shall we impose stiffer penal-

861 ties on voluntary wrongdoing and acts of injustice, and smaller penalties on the involuntary? Or shall we treat them all on an equal footing, on the grounds that there simply is no such thing as an act of voluntary injustice?'

CLINIAS: You are perfectly right, sir. So what use shall we make of this position we have just taken up?

ATHENIAN: That's a good question. First of all, we shall make this use of it—

CLINIAS: What?

ATHENIAN: Let's cast our minds back. A few minutes ago we were quite right to say that in the matter of justice we were in a state of great muddle and inconsistency. With that in mind, we may go back to asking questions of ourselves. 'We have not yet found a way out of our confusion in these things. We have not defined the difference between these two categories of wrongs, voluntary and involuntary. In all states, every lawgiver who has ever appeared treats them as distinct, and the distinction is reflected in his laws. Now, is the position we took up a moment ago to overrule all dissent, like a decision handed down from God? Shall we make just this one assertion and dismiss the topic, without adducing any reasons to show that our position is correct?' Impossible. What we must do, before we legislate, is somehow make clear that there *are* two categories, but that the distinction between them is a different one. Then, when one imposes the penalty on either, everybody will be able to appreciate the arguments for it, and make some kind of judgment whether it is the appropriate penalty to have imposed or not.

CLINIAS: We think you state the position fairly, sir. We must do one of two things, either stop insisting that unjust acts are always involuntary, or, before going any further, demonstrate its validity by means of a preliminary distinction.

ATHENIAN: The first of the two alternatives, denying the proposition when I believe it to represent the truth, is absolutely unacceptable to me. I should be breaking the laws of both God and man. But if the two things do not differ by virtue of being 'voluntary' and 'involuntary', how *do* they differ? What other factor is involved? That is what we have to try, somehow or other, to show.

CLINIAS: It is surely impossible, sir, to approach the problem in any other way.

ATHENIAN: So this is what we shall try to do. Look: when citizens come together and associate with each other, they obviously inflict many *injuries*; and to these the terms 'voluntary' and 'involuntary' can be freely applied.

CLINIAS: Of course.

ATHENIAN: But no one should describe all these injuries as acts of injustice, and conclude that therefore the unjust acts committed in these cases of injury fall into two categories, (a) involuntary (because if we add them all up, you see, the involuntary injuries are no less numerous and no less great than the voluntary ones), and (b) voluntary *as well*. Rather than do that, consider the next step I am going to take in my argument: am I on to something or just driveling? My position, Clinias and Megillus, is not that, if someone hurts someone else involuntarily and without intending it, he is acting unjustly but involuntarily. I will not legislate so as to make this an involuntary act of injustice. Ignoring its relative seriousness or triviality, I shall refuse to put down such an injury under the heading of 'injustice' at all. Indeed, if my view is sustained, we shall often say of a

b

c

d

e

862

b   benefactor that 'he is committing the injustice of conferring a benefit'—an
improper benefit. You see, my friends, in effect we should not simply call
it 'just' when one man bestows some object on another, nor simply 'unjust'
when correspondingly he takes it from him. The description 'just' is applicable only to the benefit conferred or injury inflicted by someone with a
just character and outlook. This is the point the lawgiver has to watch; he
must keep his eyes on these two things, injustice and injury. He must use

c   the law to exact damages for damage done, as far as he can; he must
restore losses, and if anyone has knocked something down, put it back
upright again; in place of anything killed or wounded, he must substitute
something in a sound condition. And when atonement has been made by
compensation, he must try by his laws to make the criminal and the victim,
in each separate case of injury, friends instead of enemies.

CLINIAS: So far, so good.

ATHENIAN: Now to deal with unjust injuries (and gains too, as when one
man's unjust act results in a gain for someone else). The cases that are
curable we must cure, on the assumption that the soul has been infected
by disease. We must, however, state what general policy we pursue in
our cure for injustice.

CLINIAS: What is this policy?

d   ATHENIAN: This: when anyone commits an act of injustice, serious or
trivial, the law will combine instruction and constraint, so that in the future
either the criminal will never again dare to commit such a crime voluntarily,
or he will do it a very great deal less often; and in addition, he will pay
compensation for the damage he has done. This is something we can
achieve only by laws of the highest quality. We may take action, or simply
talk to the criminal; we may grant him pleasures, or make him suffer; we
may honor him, we may disgrace him; we can fine him, or give him gifts.
We may use absolutely *any* means to make him hate injustice and embrace

e   true justice—or at any rate not hate it. But suppose the lawgiver finds a
man who's beyond cure—what legal penalty will he provide for this case?
He will recognize that the best thing for all such people is to cease to
live—best even for themselves. By passing on they will help others, too:
first, they will constitute a warning against injustice, and secondly they

863 will leave the state free of scoundrels. That is why the lawgiver should
prescribe the death penalty in such cases, by way of punishment for their
crimes—but in no other case whatever.

CLINIAS: In one way, what you have said seems eminently reasonable.
However, we should be glad to hear a clearer explanation of two points:
first, the difference between injustice and injury, and secondly the various
senses of 'voluntary' and 'involuntary' that you distinguished so elaborately in the course of your argument.

b   ATHENIAN: I must try to meet your request and explain these points.
Doubtless in the course of conversation you make at least this point to
each other about the soul: one of the constituent elements (whether 'part'
or 'state' is not important) to be found in it is 'anger', and this innate

impulse, unruly and difficult to fight as it is, causes a good deal of havoc by its irrational force.

CLINIAS: Yes, indeed.

ATHENIAN: The next point is the distinction we make between 'pleasure' and 'anger'. We say Pleasure wields her power on the basis of an opposite kind of force; she achieves whatever her will desires by persuasive deceit that is irresistibly compelling.[3]

CLINIAS: Quite right.

ATHENIAN: Thirdly, we would be saying nothing but the truth if we   c
named ignorance as a cause of wrongdoing. The lawgiver would, in fact, do a better job if he divided ignorance into two: (1) 'simple' ignorance, which he would treat as the cause of trivial faults, (2) 'double' ignorance, which is the error of a man who is not only in the grip of ignorance but on top of that is convinced of his own wisdom, believing that he has a thorough knowledge of matters of which, in fact, his ignorance is total. When such ignorance is backed up by strength and power, the lawgiver will treat it as the source of serious and barbarous wrongdoing; but when   d
it lacks power, he will treat the resultant faults as the peccadilloes of children and old men. He will of course regard these deeds as offenses, and will legislate against these people as offenders, but the laws will be of the most gentle character, full of understanding.

CLINIAS: Your proposals are perfectly reasonable.

ATHENIAN: Most of us agree that some people are 'conquerors of' their desire for pleasure and feelings of anger, while others are 'conquered' by them. And that is in fact the situation.

CLINIAS: It certainly is.

ATHENIAN: But we have never heard anyone say that some people are 'conquerors of' their ignorance, while others are 'conquered by' it.

CLINIAS: Very true.   e

ATHENIAN: But we do say that each of these influences often prompts every man to take the opposite course to the one which attracts him and which he *really* wishes to take.

CLINIAS: Yes, times without number.

ATHENIAN: May I now clearly distinguish for you, without elaboration, what in my view the terms 'just' and 'unjust' mean. My general description of injustice is this: the mastery of the soul by anger, fear, pleasure, pain, envy and desires, whether they lead to any actual damage or not. But no   864
matter how states or individuals think they can achieve the good, it is a conception of what the good is that should govern every man and hold sway in his soul, even if he is a little mistaken. If it does, every action done in accordance with it, and any part of a man's nature that becomes subject to such control, we have to call 'just', and best for the entire life of mankind—and this in spite of the popular belief that damage done in such circumstances is an 'involuntary' injustice. However, we are not

3. Reading *biaiou* in b8.

engaging now in a captious dispute about terminology. But since it has
b   become clear that there are three kinds of basic faults, we ought first to
impress these upon our memory even more firmly. Our first kind is a
painful one, and we call it anger and fear.

CLINIAS: Yes.

ATHENIAN: The second kind consists of pleasures and desires. The third,
which is a distinct category, consists of hopes and opinion—a mere shot
at the truth about the supreme good.[4] If we divide this last category twice,[5]
we get three types; and that makes, according to our present argument,
a total of five in all. We must enact different laws for the five kinds, and
we must have two main categories.

c   CLINIAS: And what are these?

ATHENIAN: The first category covers every occasion when crimes are
committed openly with violence; secondly, we have crimes that take place
under cover of darkness, involving secrecy and fraud. Sometimes we find
a combination of both methods, in which case our laws will have to be
very harsh indeed, if they are going to do their job.

CLINIAS: Of course.

d   ATHENIAN: Now let's go back to the point where we started to digress,
and carry on with our enactment of the legal code. Our regulations about
those who pillage from the gods, and about traitors, had, I think, already
been made; we had also dealt with those who do violence to the laws in
order to subvert the existing constitution. A man who commits one of
these crimes might be suffering from insanity, or be as good as insane
either because of disease, or the effects of advanced senility, or because
he is still in the years of childhood.

44. (a) If clear proof of any of these states is ever shown to the judges
selected in each case, on the submission of either the criminal or his
counsel, and in the opinion of the court the man was in that condition
e   when he committed his crime,
he must pay, without fail, simple recompense for any damage he may
have inflicted on anyone, but the other details of the penalty should be
waived,
(b) if he has killed someone and his hands are polluted by murder,
he must depart to a place in another country and live there in exile for
a year.

45. If he comes back before the legally appointed time, or even puts a
foot into any part of his native country,

---

4. Reading . . . *kai doxēs, tou alēthous peri to ariston ephesis, triton* . . . in b7.

5. Assuming that the 'third' category here is equivalent to that of 'ignorance' as a cause
of wrongdoing (863c–d), the reference here is to the 'simple' and 'double' forms of
ignorance there noted, of which the latter was divided into that 'with power' and that
'without power'. That would yield 'three types', as the Athenian goes on to say here.

he must be imprisoned in the public jail by the Guardians of the Laws for two years, after which he shall be released.

The start we have made points the way forward: we need not scruple   865
to lay down a comprehensive set of laws that will cover every category of murder. First we should deal with those committed with the use of force, but unintentionally:

46 A. If anyone has unintentionally killed a man who is not an enemy
(a) in a contest or public games—whether death occurs immediately, or later as a result of the wounds,
(b) in war similarly,
(c) in military training, whether in javelin-exercises without the protec-   b
tion of armor, or when some weapons are being carried in imitation of wartime usage,
the offender shall be free of pollution when he has been purified in accordance with the relevant law from Delphi.
(d) All doctors, if their patient dies as an unintended result of their treatment,
are to be free of pollution according to law.
B. If one man kills another by his own act, but unintentionally,
(α) by his own hand,
   (i) without weapons, or
   (ii) by tool, weapon, administration of food or drink, application of fire or cold, or deprivation of air, whether
(β) (i) he does the deed himself, or   c
   (ii) through the agency of others,
in all cases it must be reckoned his own act and he must pay penalties as under:
If he kills
(a) a slave,
he must indemnify the dead man's master against the damage, reflecting what the loss would be if his own slave had been killed.
C. If he fails to indemnify the master,
he must pay a penalty of twice the value of the dead man, the judges making an estimate of it, and he must resort to greater and more numerous purifications than those who have killed in contests; and such expounders as are chosen by the oracle are to be in charge of these purifica-   d
tions.
B. cont. (b) If he kills a slave of his own,
let him purify himself, and be quit of the murder according to law.
(c) If he kills a free man, inadvertently,
he must undergo the same purifications as the killer of a slave.

He should not take lightly an old story that comes from our collection of ancient tales. It runs as follows: Having lived in the full proud spirit of freedom, the man murdered by violence, freshly dead, turns his fury on e   the person responsible. The dead man is full of fear and loathing at his own violent sufferings; he abominates the sight of his own murderer going about localities once familiar to himself; to the full limit of his powers he visits his own anguish on the perpetrator of the crime, the man and his deeds; and his allies are the memories that haunt the murderer. Therefore

> D. (a) *A killer* must keep clear of his victim for all the seasons of an entire year, by staying away from the dead man's usual haunts and the whole of his native country.
>
> (b) If the deceased is a foreigner,

866

> *the killer* should keep clear of the foreigner's homeland as well for an identical period.
>
> If a man obeys this law without demur, the deceased's next of kin, who will take note of his compliance with these requirements, will grant him pardon and will be entirely correct to live on peaceable terms with him.
>
> E. If the killer disobeys,
>
> (a) by daring to enter temples and perform sacrifices, polluted as he is, and then
>
> (b) by refusing to complete the above-mentioned period abroad,

b

> *the deceased's* next of kin must prosecute the killer on a charge of murder. In case of conviction, all penalties are to be doubled.
>
> F. If the next of kin does not prosecute the crime,
>
> *the pollution* must be deemed to have arrived at his own door, owing to the murdered man's supplications for atonement. Anyone who wishes may bring a charge against the next of kin and force him to keep away from his native country for five years, according to law.
>
> G. (a) If a foreigner kills a foreigner who is living in the state,

c

> *anyone* who wishes should prosecute under the same laws.
>
> (b) If the killer is
>
> > (i) a resident alien,
>
> *he must* go abroad for a year;
>
> > (ii) a non-resident alien,
>
> *he must* keep away, for the whole of his life, from the country that lays down these laws, in addition to performing the purifications; this is to apply whether he kills (1) a non-resident alien, (2) a resident alien, or (3) a citizen.
>
> H. If he returns
>
> (a) illegally,
>
> *the Guardians of the Laws* must punish him by death, and if he has any property, they must present it to his victim's nearest relative;
>
> (b) unintentionally,

d

> > (i) being shipwrecked on the coast,
>
> *he must* camp out where the sea washes by his feet and await an opportunity to sail away;
>
> > (ii) being forcibly brought in overland by someone,
>
> *the first* official of the state that comes across him must set him free and dispatch him unharmed beyond the border.

If someone kills a free man by his own hand, but the deed is done in anger, we must first make an internal distinction within this type of crime. Anger is common to (1) those who kill a man by blows or similar means, owing to a sudden impulse: here the action is immediate, there is no previous intention to kill, and regret for the deed follows at once; (2) those who have been stung by insults or opprobrious actions and who pursue their vengeance until, some time later, they kill somebody: they *intend* to kill, and the deed causes no repentance. So it looks as if we have to establish two categories of murder; broadly speaking, both are done in anger, but a proper description would be 'falling somewhere midway between "voluntary" and "involuntary" '; however, each type comes closer to one or other of these extremes. The man who nurses his anger and takes his vengeance later—not suddenly, on the spur of the moment, but with premeditation—approximates to the voluntary murderer. The man whose anger bursts forth uncontrollably, whose action is instant, immediate, and without premeditation, resembles the involuntary killer. Yet even so, he is not an entirely involuntary killer: he only resembles one. It is therefore sometimes difficult to categorize murders done under the influence of anger, and to know whether to treat them in law as voluntary or involuntary. The best course, which corresponds most closely to reality, is to classify them both under what they most resemble, and to distinguish them by the presence or absence of premeditation. We should lay down comparatively severe penalties for those who have killed in anger and with premeditation, and lighter ones for those who have killed on the spur of the moment without previous intent. Something which resembles a greater evil should attract a greater punishment, whereas a lesser penalty should be visited on that which resembles a lesser evil. This, then, is the course our laws should take.

CLINIAS: Indeed it is.

ATHENIAN: Then let's go back to our subject and carry on as follows:

47 A. If someone kills a free man with his own hand, and the deed is done in a fit of anger, without previous intent,
his penalty should in general be that appropriate to a man who has killed without anger; but in addition he should be obliged to go into exile for two years, by way of a curb for his anger.
B. If a man kills in anger, but with premeditation,
his penalty should in general be that inflicted in the previous instance; but his exile should be for three years as against the other's two, the period of punishment being longer because of the greater violence of his passion.

In such cases, regulations for the return from exile should run as follows. (It is not easy to make hard and fast rules: sometimes the fiercer criminal as defined by the law may turn out easier to manage, whereas the man who is supposedly more manageable may turn out to be a more difficult case, having committed a murder with some savagery; the other, e   conversely, may have dispatched his victim without brutality. However, my account does describe the cases you'll find are typical.)

The Guardians of the Laws should act as assessors of all these points, and when the period of exile prescribed for either category has come to an end, they should send twelve of their number, as judges, to the borders of the country. During the time that has elapsed these twelve should have made a still more exact investigation into what the exiles did, so as to decide whether to grant pardon and permission to return; and the exiles are bound to acquiesce in the judgment of these authorities.

868   C. (a) If a returned exile of either category is ever again overcome by anger and commits the same offense,
he must go into exile and never come back.
(b) If he does come back,
his penalty will be the same as that imposed on the foreigner who returns [46H].
D (a) If a man kills his own slave,
he must purify himself.
(b) If he kills another's slave, in anger,
he must pay double damages to the owner.
E. If a killer in any category flouts the law and in his unpurified state pollutes the market-place, the sports stadium, and other holy places,

b   *anyone who wishes* should prosecute both the killer and the relative of the dead man who allows the killer to do this, and compel the relative to exact payment of twice the fine and the other expenses; and the prosecutor shall be legally entitled to take for himself the money so paid.
F. (a) If a slave kills his own master, in anger,
the relatives of the deceased shall treat the killer in whatever way they

c   like (except that under no circumstances whatever may they let him go on living), and be free of pollution.
(b) If a slave murders a free man who is not his master, in anger,
his master shall deliver him up to the relatives of the deceased, who will be obliged to kill him, the manner of the execution being within their discretion.
G. (This is a rare occurrence, but not unknown.)
(a) If a father or mother kills a son or daughter in anger by beating them or by using some other form of violence,
the murderers must undergo the same purifications as apply in the other

d   cases, and go into exile for three years.
(b) When they come back, the female killer must be separated from her husband and the male from his wife, and they must have no more children; and they must never again share hearth and home with those whom they have robbed of a son or brother, or join in religious ceremonies with them.
H. If someone is impious enough to disobey these regulations,
he shall be liable to a charge of impiety at the hands of anyone who wishes.

e   I. (a) If a man kills his wedded wife in a fit of anger, or a wife her husband,

they must undergo the same purifications and spend three years in exile.
(b) On his return, a person who has done such a deed must never join
his children in religious ceremonies nor eat at the same table with them.
J. If the parent or the child disobeys,
he shall equally be liable to a charge of impiety at the hands of anyone
who wishes.
K. If in anger
(a) a brother kills a brother or a sister, or
(b) a sister kills a brother or a sister,
the same purifications and periods of exile as applied to parents and
children should be specified as applying in these cases too. (That is, they
should never share hearth and home with the brothers whom they have
deprived of their fellow brothers nor with parents whom they have
deprived of children, nor join in religious ceremonies with them.)
L. If anyone disobeys this law,
he will be subject to the relevant law of impiety already laid down, as   869
is only right and proper.
M. If anyone gets into such an ungovernable temper with his parents
and begetters that in his insane fury he dares to kill one of them, and
(a) is let off responsibility for murder by a voluntary statement of the
deceased before death,
he must perform the same purifications as those who commit involuntary
murder; and when he has followed the rest of the procedure prescribed
for those cases, he may be considered purified.
(b) If he is not let off,

the perpetrator of such a crime will be indictable under many laws. He   b
will be subject to the most huge penalties for assault, and likewise for
impiety and temple-robbery—he has plundered the shrine that is his parent's body, and deprived it of life. Consequently if one man could die
many times, the murderer of his father or mother who has acted in anger
would deserve to die the death over and over again. To this one killer no
law will allow the plea of self-defense; no law will permit him to kill his   c
father or mother, who brought him into the world. The law will instruct
him to put up with all manner of suffering before he does such a thing.
But what other penalty than death could the law appropriately lay down
for this criminal? The law, then, should run:

(b) cont.
the penalty for the murderer of a father or mother is to be death.
N. (a) If a brother kills his own brother in a political brawl or some
similar circumstances, in self-defense when his victim had struck first,
he should be regarded as free of pollution (as though he had killed   d
an enemy).
(b) The same applies if
(i) a citizen kills a citizen, or
(ii) a foreigner kills a foreigner.

(c) If in self-defense
    (i) a citizen kills a foreigner, or
    (ii) a foreigner kills a citizen,
the culprit should be in the same position with regard to the freedom from pollution, and likewise if
    (iii) a slave kills a slave.
O. If however a slave, in self-defense, kills a free man, *he should* be subject to the same laws as the parricide [47M].

P. The regulations stated about the acquittal from responsibility for murder granted by a father are to apply to every acquittal in such cases (when, that is, one man voluntarily absolves another of responsibility, on the grounds that the murder has been committed involuntarily): *the criminal* must undergo the purifications and spend one year away from the country according to law.

Let this more or less suffice as a description of involuntary murders, which involve violence and anger. Our next task is to speak of voluntary murders, which are premeditated and spring from sheer injustice—the lack of control over the desire for pleasure and over one's lusts and jealous feelings.

CLINIAS: True.

ATHENIAN: First of all, we ought again to make as complete a list as possible of these sources of crime.

870   The chief cause is lust, which tyrannizes a soul that has gone wild with desire. This lust is most usually for money, the object of most men's strongest and most frequent longing. Because of the innate depravity of men and their misdirected education, money has the power to produce in them a million cravings that are impossible to satisfy—all centering on the endless acquisition of wealth. The cause of this incorrect education is the pernicious praise given to wealth by the public opinion of Greeks and non-Greeks alike. In fact, wealth takes only third place in the scale of goodness;[6] but they make it preeminent, to the ruination of posterity and themselves. The best and the noblest policy for all cities to follow is to tell the truth about wealth, namely that it exists to serve the body, just as the body should be the servant of the soul. Although the ends which wealth naturally serves are indeed 'good', wealth itself will take third place, coming after the perfection of the soul and the body. Taking, therefore, this argument as our guide, we shall find that the man who means to be happy should not seek simply to be wealthy, but to be wealthy in a way consistent with justice and self-control. Murders needing still more murders in expiation would not occur in cities that had taken this lesson to heart. But as things are, as we said when we embarked on this topic, we have here one cause, and an extremely prominent cause at that, of the most serious charges of deliberate murder.

6. See the lists at 697b ff. and 743e.

Second, an ambitious cast of mind: this breeds feelings of jealousy, which are dangerous companions to live with, particularly for the person who actually feels jealous, but potentially harmful to the leading citizens of the state as well.

In the third place, many a murder has been prompted by the cowardly   d
fears of a guilty man. When a man is committing some crime, or has already committed it, he wants no one to know about it, and if he cannot eliminate a possible informer in any other way, he murders him.

These remarks should constitute the preface applying to all these crimes. In addition, we must tell the story which is so strongly believed by so many people when they hear it from those who have made a serious study of such matters in their mystic ceremonies. It is this:

Vengeance is exacted for these crimes in the after-life, and when a man returns to this world again he is ineluctably obliged to pay the penalty   e
prescribed by the law of nature—to undergo the same treatment as he himself meted out to his victim, and to conclude his earthly existence by encountering a similar fate at the hands of someone else.

If a man obeys and heartily dreads such a penalty after merely hearing the overture, there is no need to play over the relevant law. But in case   871
of disobedience the following law should be stated in writing:

48 A. (a) If a man by his own hand viciously kills a fellow citizen, with premeditation,
he must be excluded from the places where people usually gather, and not pollute temples or market or harbors or any other common place of assembly, *whether or not* someone makes a proclamation against the culprit in these terms. (The reason is that the law itself makes the proclamation. It makes a permanent and public proclamation on behalf of the whole state, and always will.)
B. If a man fails in his duty to prosecute the culprit or bar him by   b
proclamation, and is a relative (no more distant than a cousin) of the deceased on either the father's side or the mother's,
the pollution, together with the enmity of the gods, should arrive at his own door. (The curse imposed by the law turns the edict of heaven against him.) He must be subject to prosecution at the hands of any man who wishes to take vengeance for the deceased, and the man who thus wishes to take vengeance must scrupulously perform all the appropriate ablutions and all the other ritual details the god prescribes   c
for such cases; and when he has published the proclamation, he must go and make the criminal submit to the imposition of the penalty, under the law.

It is easy for a legislator to demonstrate that all this should be accompanied by a number of prayers and sacrifices to those gods who make it their business to prevent murders occurring in society. The Guardians of the Laws, in association with expounders, soothsayers, and the god, should   d
rule who these gods are to be, and specify the procedure for bringing such

cases that would be most in harmony with the requirements of religion; they should then follow it themselves in bringing these cases to court, which should be the same as the one given final authority over temple-robbers.[7]

48 A. cont.

(b) If a man is found guilty,

he must be punished by death and be deprived of burial in the country of his victim. (In this way we can show he has not been forgiven, and avoid impiety.)

C. (a) If the defendant makes off and refuses to submit to trial,

he must remain in exile permanently.

(b) If such a person sets foot within the country of the murdered man,[8]

e   *the first* of the relatives of the deceased who comes across him, or indeed any citizen, should either

(i) kill him with impunity, or

(ii) tie him up, and hand him over to the judges who tried the case for them to carry out the execution.

D. When a man undertakes a prosecution, he should immediately demand sureties from the accused. The latter must duly provide his sureties, who must be deemed, in the eyes of the judges who constitute the court in these cases, to be credit-worthy; and these three credit-worthy sureties must pledge themselves to produce the accused at his trial. If a man refuses, or is unable, to produce sureties,

the authorities must arrest him and keep him bound and under guard, so that they can produce him at the hearing of the case.

872   E. If a man does not actually kill with his own hands, but simply plans the murder, and although responsible for it by virtue of plotting arrangements, continues to live in the state with his soul polluted by homicide, his trial for this crime should proceed along the same lines as before, except as regards the bail. If he is convicted,

he may be granted burial in his native land, but the other details of the punishment should conform with the regulations previously laid down for this category.[9]

F. These same regulations about the actual commission and mere plotting of a murder should apply when

(a) (i) foreigners prosecute foreigners,

(ii) citizens prosecute foreigners and foreigners citizens, and

b   (iii) slaves prosecute slaves.

(b) But an exception should be made in the business of the surety. Just as it was said [48D.] that *actual* murderers should provide sureties, the person who proclaims the ban arising from the murder should simultaneously demand sureties in these cases too [48F(a)(i-iii)].

---

7. 855c–856a.

8. Reading *toutōn* in d7.

9. That is, for those who *do* kill with their own hand.

G. If a slave intentionally kills a free man, whether he did the deed himself or planned it, and is convicted,
the public executioner should haul him off in the direction of the deceased's grave to a point from which the culprit can see the tomb. He should then scourge him, giving as many strokes as the successful prosecutor instructs. If the homicide survives the scourging, he is to be executed.   c
H. If a man kills an innocent slave, fearing that he will inform against his own shocking and disgraceful conduct, or prompted by some similar motive,
he should submit to trial, when a slave has died in these circumstances, precisely as he would have submitted to trial for murder if he had killed a citizen.

Certain crimes, which may occur, make the mere composition of laws for them an unpleasant and distasteful business, but it is impossible to   d
omit them from our code. I mean deliberate and wholly wicked murders of relatives, whether the murderer commits the crime in person or merely plots it. Generally speaking, these killings occur in states that are badly administered or have a defective system of education, but occasionally one of them might crop up even in a country where one would hardly look for it. What we have to do is to repeat our explanation of a moment ago, hoping that anyone who hears it will be more willing and able to avoid committing murders that are absolutely the most detestable in the sight of Heaven. The 'myth', or 'explanation', or whatever the right word is, has come down to us in unambiguous terms from the lips of priests of long ago.   e
Justice stands on guard to exact vengeance for the spilling of the blood of relatives; she operates through the law we have just mentioned, and her decree is that a man who has done something of this kind is obliged to suffer precisely what he has inflicted. If ever a man has murdered his father, in the course of time he must suffer the same fate from violent treatment at the hands of his children. A matricide, before being reborn, must adopt the female sex, and after being born a woman and bearing children, be dispatched subsequently by them. No other purification is available when common blood has been polluted; the pollution resists   873
cleansing until, murder for murder, the guilty soul has paid the penalty and by this appeasement has soothed the anger of the deceased's entire line.
Thus the fear of such vengeance, exacted by the gods, should hold a man in check. But this is the law the human legislator will lay down in case some people should be overwhelmed by the terrible misfortune of committing such a crime:

I. (a) If they should dare to tear the soul from the body of their father, mother, brothers or children, deliberately and with premeditation,
the proclamations of banishment from places of public resort, and the sureties, should be identical to those detailed in previous cases.   b

(b) If a man is convicted of such a murder, having killed one of the aforementioned persons,
the court-assistants and the officials shall execute him, and throw him out, naked, at a specified place where three roads meet outside the city. All the officials, on behalf of the entire state, must take a stone and throw it at the head of the corpse, and thus purify the entire state. After this, they must carry the corpse to the borders of the land and eject it, giving it no burial, as the law instructs.

c

But what about the killer of the person who is, above all, his 'nearest and dearest', as the expression is? What penalty ought he to undergo? I am talking about the man who kills *himself*, who (1) uses violence to take his fate out of the hands of destiny, (2) is not acting in obedience to any legal decision of his state, (3) whose hand is not forced by the pressure of some excruciating and unavoidable misfortune, (4) has not fallen into some irremediable disgrace that he cannot live with, and (5) imposes this unjust judgment on himself in a spirit of slothful and abject cowardice. In general, what ritual observances should take place with regard to purification and interment in this case, are matters known to God; the relatives must seek guidance from expounders and the relevant laws, and act in these instances according to their instructions. But

d

49. (a) People who perish in this way must be buried individually, with no one to share their grave.
(b) They must be buried in disgrace on the boundaries of the twelve territorial divisions, in deserted places that have no name.
(c) The graves must not be identifiable, either by headstone or title.

e

50. (a) If a beast of burden or any other animal kills anyone (except when the incident occurs while they are competing in one of the public contests),
  (i) *the relatives* must prosecute the killer for murder;
  (ii) *the next of kin* must appoint some Country-Wardens (whichever ones he pleases, and as many as he likes), and they must try the case:
  (iii) if the animal is found guilty,
they must kill it and throw it out beyond the frontiers of the country.
(b) If some inanimate object causes loss of human life (but not if it is a stroke of lightning or some similar weapon wielded by God—it must be one of the other things that kill a man by falling on him, or because he falls on it),

874

  (i) *the next of kin* must appoint the nearest neighbor to sit in judgment on the object, and thus effect the purification of himself and the deceased's entire line;
  (ii) *the condemned* object must be thrown over the frontiers, in the way specified in the case of animals.

51. If someone is found dead, and the killer is not known and cannot be discovered by diligent efforts to trace him,

the proclamations should be the same as laid down in former cases, being made, however, against 'the murderer': when the prosecutor has established his case, he must give notice in the market-place to the killer and convicted murderer of so-and-so, that he must not enter holy places nor any part of the country of the deceased; he must threaten that if he does turn up and is recognized, he will be executed, denied burial, and his body ejected from the country of his victim.   b

So much, then, for the law on that sort of murder. In the following conditions, however, it will be right to regard the killer as innocent:

52. (a) If he catches a thief entering his home at night to steal his goods, and kills him,
he shall be innocent.
(b) If he kills a footpad in self-defense,   c
he shall be innocent.
(c) If anyone sexually violates a free woman or boy,
he may be killed with impunity by the victim of the violence, or by the victim's father or brothers or sons.
(d) If a husband discovers his wedded wife being raped and kills the attacker,
the law will regard him as innocent.
(e) If a man kills someone while saving the life of his father (provided the latter is not committing a crime), or while rescuing his mother or children or brothers, or the mother of his children,
he shall be completely innocent.   d

ATHENIAN: Let us assume we have completed our legislation concerning the training and education that the soul needs during a man's life (a life that is worth the living if these needs are met, but not if they are not), and the penalties that should apply in cases of death by violence. We have discussed, too, the training and education of the body, and the related topic in this case is the violent treatment, voluntary or involuntary, of one man by another. So far as we can, we must distinguish the various categories, see how many there are, and say what penalties will be appropriate for each. It looks as if this could properly form the next subject of our legislation.   e

Even the biggest bungler you could find among would-be legislators will put cases of wounding and mutilation immediately after cases of murder. Woundings ought to be distinguished as murders were: some are inflicted involuntarily, some in anger, some through fear, while others are committed voluntarily and with premeditation. A preliminary address must be given about all these categories as follows:

It is vital that men should lay down laws for themselves and live in obedience to them; otherwise they will be indistinguishable from wild   875
animals of the utmost savagery. The reason is this: no man has sufficient natural gifts *both* to discern what benefits men in their social relationships

and to be constantly ready and able to put his knowledge to the best practical use. The first difficulty is to realize that the proper object of true political skill is not the interest of private individuals but the common good. This is what knits a state together, whereas private interests make
b   it disintegrate. If the public interest is well served, rather than the private, then the individual and the community alike are benefited.

The second difficulty is that even if a man did get an adequate theoretical grasp of the truth of all this, he might then attain a position of absolute control over a state, with no one to call him to account. In these circumstances he would never have the courage of his convictions; he would never devote his life to promoting the welfare of the community as his first concern, making his private interests take second place to the public good. His human nature will always drive him to look to his own advantage and the lining of his own pocket. An irrational avoidance of pain and
c   pursuit of pleasure will dominate his character, so that he will prefer these two aims to better and more righteous paths. Blindness, self-imposed, will ultimately lead the man's whole being, and the entire state, into a morass of evil. But if ever by the grace of God some natural genius were born, and had the chance to assume such power, he would have no need of laws to control him. Knowledge is unsurpassed by any law or regulation;
d   reason, if it is genuine and really enjoys its natural freedom, should have universal power: it is not right that it should be under the control of anything else, as though it were some sort of slave. But as it is, such a character is nowhere to be found, except a hint of it here and there. That is why we need to choose the second alternative, law and regulation, which embody general principles, but cannot provide for every individual case.

I have pointed this out because we are now going to settle the penalty or fine to be imposed on someone who has wounded or harmed someone else. Anyone could quite easily and properly take us up on any point and
e   ask: 'What attacker, what wound, what victim do you mean? How was the attack made, and when? The circumstances of these cases differ in a thousand and one different ways.' Now to leave all these details to the judgment of the courts is impracticable, and equally impracticable to leave them none. In every case, however, one point in particular simply must be left to the courts: in each separate instance, they must decide whether the crime did in fact take place, or not. But on the other hand it is hardly
876   feasible to produce laws oneself to cover every case, serious or trivial; one can scarcely leave the courts no discretion at all about the fine or punishment that ought to be imposed on a criminal of this kind.

CLINIAS: Well, then, where do we go from here?

ATHENIAN: We conclude that some details ought to be left to the courts, but not others; these should be regulated by the legislator.

CLINIAS: Which points, then, ought to be in the legal code, and which ought to be referred to the judgment of the courts?

ATHENIAN: In this connection, here's the next thing to notice: sometimes
b   we find in a state that the juries are useless, dumb things; the individual

jurymen keep their opinions a mystery known only to themselves and give their decisions by secret ballot. It's even more serious when so far from keeping silent when they hear a case they make a tremendous disturbance as though they were in a theatre, and hurl shouts of applause or disapproval at the speaker on either side in turn. All this puts the state at large into an awkward predicament. It is a wretched business to be forced to lay down laws for courts of that type, but if one is forced, the right thing to do is to hand over to them the assessment of penalties only in very trivial cases, providing for the majority in explicit laws of one's own— if, that is, one ever does legislate for a state organized in this way. But in a country where the regulation of the courts is as satisfactory as can be achieved and the jurymen-to-be have received a good education and been examined by all kinds of tests, it is right and proper to grant them complete discretion on all points to do with the punishments or fines that convicted criminals should suffer. In the present case we cannot be blamed if we leave to their discretion the most frequent and important points that arise, because they are points which even inadequately educated jurymen could grasp and apply when they have to give each individual crime a penalty appropriate both to the damage done and to the wickedness which is at the root of the actual deed. We believe, in fact, that the people for whom we are legislating may well turn out quite conspicuously able judges of these matters, so we should leave most decisions to them. Even so, in enacting earlier parts of our legal code, we mentioned the practice of sketching some examples of penalties—models for the judges to imitate, to stop them exceeding the due limits of justice. We suited the action to the word; it was the right course then and it is the right course now, as I once again resume our legislation.

Our law on wounding, then, should be written in the following terms:

53 A. If a man deliberately intends to kill a fellow citizen (unless the latter is one of those whose death is sanctioned by the law [52(a-e)]), and wounds him without being able to kill him, no pity should be wasted on the man who has inflicted a wound with that sort of intention: he should be treated with no more respect than a killer, and made to stand trial for murder.

But we should have due respect for the luck that has saved him from total ruin, and for his guardian angel too, who in pity for the attacker and the wounded man has stopped the injury of the latter from proving fatal, and prevented the disastrous ill luck of the former from bringing a curse down upon his head. We should duly thank his guardian spirit and not obstruct its wishes:

53 A. cont.
He who has inflicted the wound shall be spared the death penalty, but he must suffer life-long banishment to some neighboring state, with full freedom to enjoy all the income from his property; he must pay full

compensation for whatever injury he has done the wounded man, the sum to be assessed by the court that tries the case. (The court will consist of the same people who would have tried him for murder if his victim had died of the wounds sustained.)

B. If with similar premeditation

(a) a child wounds his parents, or

(b) a slave wounds his master,

death is to be the penalty.

C. If similarly

(a) a brother wounds a brother or a sister, or

(b) a sister wounds a brother or a sister,

c   and is convicted of wounding with premeditation,

death is to be the penalty.

D If with intent to kill

(a) a wife wounds her husband, or

(b) a husband wounds his wife,

he or she must go into permanent exile. If they have sons or daughters who are still in their minority, the trustees must administer their property in trust, and care for the children as though they were orphans. If the offspring are adult, they should themselves take possession of the property, and be under no obligation to support the exile.[10] If anyone

d   who succumbs to such misfortune is childless, the relatives of the exile, as far as the children of the cousins on both the male and female side, must hold a meeting, and in consultation with the Guardians of the Laws appoint an heir for this property, the 5040th in the state.

(They should look at the matter in the following light: none of the 5040 farms belongs to its occupant or his family in general as much as to the state, which is entitled to it not only as a piece of public property but also

e   as its own private possession; and the state ought to do its best to keep its own properties as holy and prosperous as possible.) Therefore:

54. When one of the properties falls away from this condition of holiness and prosperity to such an extent that the possessor leaves no children to succeed him, being unmarried, or married but childless, and meets his end convicted of

(a) (i) deliberate murder, or

(ii) some other crime against gods or citizens for which the death penalty is specifically laid down by law, or if

(b) someone without male issue goes into permanent exile,

first of all, this property must be cleansed and purified according to law;

878   then the relatives must hold the meeting we mentioned just now, and in consultation with the Guardians of the Laws pick out a family that has the best reputation for virtue of all the families in the state and is

---

10. Reading *mē* for *ēdē* in c6.

at the same time fortunate enough to have produced several children. One of these they must adopt on behalf of the deceased's father and forebears, who will receive him as their son; from them he will take his name, which should be an omen of good fortune. The relatives should pray that as a result of his adoption he will bring them children, and guard the hearth and look after the family affairs, both sacred and secular, with greater success than his adoptive father enjoyed. In this   b way they should install him, according to law, as heir to the property. (c) When such disasters as we have mentioned [54.(a,b)] overwhelm the sinner,

they should let him lie nameless in his grave, childless and deprived of his family estate.

We can see that it is not universally true that one district extends right up to the boundary of another. In some cases there is a no man's land in between, which will extend so as to touch either boundary and occupy an intermediate position between the two. This, we said,[11] was true of an act done in anger: it falls somewhere between voluntary and involuntary. Our regulations concerning wounding inflicted in anger should therefore run as follows:

55 A. If a man is found guilty, and   c
(a) the wound turns out to be curable,
he must pay double damages;
(b) if it is incurable,
he must pay quadruple damages.
(c) If he has inflicted a wound which, though curable, makes the wounded man feel acutely embarrassed and ashamed,
he must pay triple damages.
B. If one man wounds another and injures not only his victim but the state, by rendering him unable to defend his fatherland against the enemy,
he must, in addition to the other penalties, make restitution to the state for the loss it has sustained, viz. he must perform not only his own military service but that of the incapacitated person as well by serving   d in the army on his behalf.
C. If he fails so to serve,
he shall be liable under the law to a charge of evading military service, at the hands of anyone who wishes.
A. cont. The assessment of the damages, double, triple, or quadruple, must be made by the judges who found him guilty.
D. If one relative wounds another in any of these ways,
the fellow clansmen and close relatives, male and female, as far as sons of cousins on both the male and female side, must hold a meeting, and   e

11. See 866d–867c.

when they have reached their verdict, they must entrust the assessment to the natural parents. If the assessment is challenged, the assessment of the relatives on the male side must be taken as final. If they cannot agree themselves, they must, in the end, hand over the matter to the Guardians of the Laws.

E. When children inflict this kind of wound on their parents, it is essential for the judges to be parents over sixty years of age who have children of their own and not merely adopted ones. If a man is found guilty, *these judges* must decide whether a man who could do such a thing as this should die, or whether the penalty should be something even more severe,[12] or perhaps something a trifle less severe. None of the relations of the culprit should act as a judge, not even if he is of the age required by law.

879

F. (a) If a slave wounds a free man in anger,
the owner must hand him over to the wounded man, who may treat him in whatever way he likes.

(b) If the owner fails to hand him over,
he must remedy the damage himself.

(c) If anyone alleges that the affair is the result of collusion between the slave and the wounded party, he must contest the point at law. If he does not win the case,
he must pay triple damages.

If he does win, he must prosecute the author of the collusion with the slave on a charge of kidnapping.

56. If anyone involuntarily wounds someone else,

b   *he must* pay simple damages. (No legislator is capable of regulating the workings of chance.) The judges are to be the same as those appointed to try children who wound their parents; and they will have the duty of assessing the amount of the damages.

ATHENIAN: All the injuries we have so far mentioned involve the use of violence, and so too do the various kinds of assault. In these cases, the point that every man, woman and child should bear in mind is this:

Age is always very much more highly regarded than youth, and this is

c   so both among the gods and among men, if they intend to live in security and happiness. Therefore, the assault of an older man by a younger in public is a disgusting sight, and the gods hate to see it. No young man who is struck by an old man should ever make a fuss, but put up with his bad temper, and so establish a claim to similar respect when he himself grows old.

Our law, then, should run as follows:

Everyone in our community must show, by his words and actions, respect for his senior. A man should avoid crossing any person (male or female) who is twenty years older than himself, regarding him or her in the same way as he would his father or mother. For the sake of the gods

12. Such as deprivation of burial.

of birth, he must always keep himself from striking anyone old enough   d
to have been his parent. Similarly, he must refrain from striking a foreigner,
whether the latter is a long-established resident or a recent immigrant. He
must never go so far as to punish such a person by hitting him, either by
attacking him first, or in self-defense.

   57 A. (a) If he thinks the foreigner is unruly and insolent in an attack
   on himself, and needs to be punished, he must arrest him and take
   him, without hitting him, to the court of the City-Wardens, so that the
   foreigner may learn to banish all thoughts of ever striking a citizen again.   e
   The City-Wardens must take the man and interrogate him, with proper
   respect for the god who is the protector of foreigners. If in fact the
   foreigner seems to have been in the wrong in striking the citizen,
   the City-Wardens must put a stop to this unruliness, so characteristic of
   a foreigner; they must give him as many strokes of the lash as will equal
   the number of blows he himself inflicted.
   (b) If he is not in the wrong,
   they must warn and rebuke the man who made the arrest, and dismiss
   the pair of them.
   B. If one man strikes another who
   (a) is about the same age, or
   (b) is older, but has no children,
   whether the attacker is an old man striking an old man, or a young man   880
   striking a young man, the man attacked must defend himself by natural
   means—with his own bare hands, without a weapon. But if a man over
   forty years of age has the face to fight someone, whether
      (i) he strikes the first blow, or
      (ii) fights in self-defense,
   he will get the reputation of being an uncivilized boor with the manners
   of a slave, and this ignominious punishment will serve him right.

A man who is easily persuaded by these words of exhortation will give
us no trouble; but stubborn people, who ignore the preamble, ought to be
ready to take more notice of the following regulations:

   C. If anyone strikes a man twenty years or more his senior, any bystander,   b
   if he is neither of the same age nor younger than the combatants, should
   separate them,
   or be treated under the law as a wretched coward. If he is of the same
   age as the person attacked, or younger, he should go to his assistance
   as if it were his own brother or father being wronged, or some still more
   senior relative.
   D. In addition, the man who dares to strike his senior as defined[13] must
   stand trial for assault. If he loses the case,

---

13. I.e., someone twenty years older.

c   *he must* be imprisoned for not less than a year. If the court fixes a longer imprisonment, the period it decides on shall stand.

E. If a foreigner, or a resident alien, strikes a man twenty years or more his senior, the same regulation [57C] about assistance from passers-by shall be enforced in the same way as before.

(a) A man found guilty of such a charge, if he is a foreigner not resident in the state,

must pay his penalty by spending two years in prison.

(b) If it is a resident alien who is in breach of these regulations,

he must go to prison for three years, except that the court may specify
d   a longer period by way of penalty.

F. The passer-by who comes across any of these cases of assault and does not give assistance as required by law

must be fined: a member of the first property-class one hundred drachmas, a member of the second fifty drachmas, a member of the third thirty drachmas, and a member of the fourth twenty drachmas. The court in such cases is to consist of the Generals, Company-Commanders, Tribe-Leaders and Cavalry-Commanders.

Some laws, it seems, are made for the benefit of honest men, to teach them the rules of association that have to be observed if they are to live
e   in friendship; others are made for those who refuse to be instructed and whose naturally tough natures have not been softened enough to stop them turning to absolute vice. It will be they who have prompted the points I am just going to make, and it is for their benefit that the lawgiver will be compelled to produce his laws, although he would wish never to find any occasion to use them. Consider a man who will dare to lay hands on his father or mother or their forebears by way of violent assault. He will fear neither the wrath of the gods above nor the punishments said to
881   await him in the grave; he will hold the ancient and universal tradition in contempt, on the strength of his 'knowledge' in a field where he is in fact a total ignoramus. He will therefore turn criminal, and will stand in need of some extreme deterrent. Death, however, is not an extreme and final penalty; the sufferings said to be in store for these people in the world to come are much more extreme than that. But although the threat of these sufferings is no idle one, it has no deterrent effect at all on souls like these. If it did, we should never have to deal with assaults on mothers, and
b   wicked and presumptuous attacks on other forebears. I conclude, therefore, that the punishments men suffer for these crimes here on earth while they are alive should as far as possible equal the penalties beyond the grave.

Our next enactment, then, should run as follows:

G. If a man who is not in the grip of insanity dares to strike his father or mother, or their father or mother, the first point is that the passer-by must render assistance as provided in former cases.

(a)(i) If the resident alien renders assistance,

he shall be invited to a front seat at the games;

(ii) if he does not render assistance,

he must go into permanent exile from the land.

(b)(i) If the non-resident alien renders assistance,   c

he shall be commended.

(ii) If he does not render assistance,

he must be reprimanded.

(c)(i) If a slave renders assistance,

he shall be set free.

(ii) If he does not render assistance,

he must receive a hundred strokes of the lash.

If the crime was committed in the market-place, the whipping should be administered by the Market-Wardens; if in the city but not in the market, by the City Warden in residence; if somewhere in the country-side, by the chief Country-Wardens.

(d) Everyone of citizen birth who passes by, whether man, woman or child, must shout 'you wicked monster' at the attacker, and repel him.   d

If the passer-by makes no attempt to repel him,

he must be liable under the law to a curse from Zeus, guardian of the family and protector of parents.

H. If a man is convicted of an assault on his parents,

he must be permanently rusticated from the city to some other part of the country, and be banned from all sacred places.

I. (a) If he returns to the city,

he must be punished by death,

(b) If he does not keep away from sacred places,

the Country-Wardens must punish him by a whipping, and by any other method at their discretion.

J. (a) If any free man eats or drinks in company with such a person, or associates with him in some other similar fashion, even by deliberately   e

failing to cut him on meeting,

he must not enter any temple, or market-place, or any part of the city, before he has been purified, bearing in mind that he has come into contact with a misfortune that brings a curse upon a man.

K. If he disobeys the law and in defiance of it pollutes temples and city, *any official* who discovers the fact and does not take the man to court will find that this is one of the most serious charges against him at his scrutiny.[14]

L. If a slave strikes a free man, foreigner or citizen, the passer-by who   882

does not render assistance

must pay the penalty prescribed for his property-class.

M. The passers-by in conjunction with the person attacked must bind the slave and hand him over to his victim; the victim must take him,   b

put him in chains, and give him as many strokes of the whip as he likes,

---

14. At the end of their term officials had to submit to an examination of their conduct in office before being discharged; see 945e–947b.

provided he does not diminish the value of the slave to his master; he should then hand him over to the latter's legal ownership. This legal ownership must be subject to the following provision. Any slave who has struck a free man, other than on the orders of the officials, must be

c   tied up; his master must receive him from the assaulted person and not release him before the slave persuades his victim that he deserves to live free of constraint.

The same regulations should apply in all cases (a) of women against each other, (b) of women against men, and (c) of men against women.

Book X

884   ATHENIAN: So much for cases of assault. Now let's state a single comprehensive rule to cover acts of violence. It will run more or less like this. No one may seize or make off with other people's property, nor use any of his neighbor's possessions without getting the permission of the owner. Contempt for this principle has always been (and still is and always will be) the source of all the evils just mentioned. But there are other acts of violence, too, of which the worst are the insolence and outrageous actions of the young. These actions are most serious when they affect sacred objects; and the damage is particularly grave when it is done to sacred property that also belongs to the public, or is held in common by the

885   members of a sub-division of the state, such as a tribe or some similar association. Second, and second in order of gravity, comes wanton damage to sacred objects that are privately owned, particularly tombs; third come attacks (apart from those already dealt with) on parents. A fourth category of outrageous conduct is when someone ignores the wishes of the authorities and seizes or removes or uses something belonging to them without their permission; and any violations of the civil rights of the private citizen which demand legal redress will constitute a fifth class. We have to frame a comprehensive law that will cover each individual case. As for robbery from temples, whether clandestine or open and violent, we have already specified in general terms the appropriate punishment;[1] but our statement

b   of the penalty for offensive remarks about the gods or outrageous actions against their interests should be prefaced by these words of exhortation:

No one who believes in gods as the law directs ever voluntarily commits an unholy act or lets any lawless word pass his lips. If he does, it is because of one of three possible misapprehensions: either, as I said, he believes (1) the gods do not exist, or (2) that they exist but take no thought for the human race, or (3) that they are influenced by sacrifices and supplications and can easily be won over.

c   CLINIAS: So what's the right thing for us to do or say to these people?

---

1. See 854d ff.

ATHENIAN: My friend, let's listen to the ridicule and scorn with which I imagine they put their case.

CLINIAS: What ridicule?

ATHENIAN: They'll probably go in for bantering, and address us like this: 'Gentlemen of Athens, of Sparta and of Crete, you are quite right. Some of us are indeed absolute atheists, whereas others do believe in such gods as you describe. So we demand of you what you yourselves demanded of the laws, that before you resort to threats and bullying, you should try   d to convince us by argument and cogent proofs that gods do exist, and that they are in fact above being seduced by gifts into turning a blind eye to injustice. But you see, it's precisely in these and similar terms that we hear them spoken of by the most highly thought-of poets and orators and prophets and priests and thousands of other people too. That's why most of us make little effort to avoid crime, but commit it first and try to put   e things right afterwards. So from lawgivers who profess to use the velvet glove rather than the iron fist we claim the right to be tackled by persuasion first. Even if, when you state your case for the existence of gods, your elegance of expression is only marginally superior to your opponents', persuade us that your argument is a better expression of the *truth*, and then perhaps we'll believe you. Isn't that fair enough? Well then, try to reply to our challenge.'

CLINIAS: Well sir, don't you think that the gods' existence is an easy truth to explain?

ATHENIAN: How?   886

CLINIAS: Well, just look at the earth and the sun and the stars and the universe in general; look at the wonderful procession of the seasons and its articulation into years and months! Anyway, you know that all Greeks and all foreigners are unanimous in recognizing the existence of gods.

ATHENIAN: My dear sir, when I think of the contempt these scoundrels will probably feel for us, I'm overcome with embarrassment—no, I withdraw that word: let's say they 'alarm' me—because you don't appreciate the real grounds of their opposition to you. You think it's just because they can't resist temptation and desire that they are attracted to the godless life.   b

CLINIAS: What other reason could there be, sir?

ATHENIAN: A reason which you two, living rather off the beaten track as you do, simply wouldn't appreciate. It will have completely passed you by.

CLINIAS: What are you talking about now?

ATHENIAN: A form of ignorance that causes no end of trouble, but which passes for the height of wisdom.

CLINIAS: How do you mean?

ATHENIAN: In Athens a number of written works are current which are not found in your states (which are, I understand, too well run to tolerate   c them). The subject of these writings (some of which are in verse, others in prose) is theology. The most ancient accounts, after relating how the primitive substances—the sky and so on—came into being, pass rapidly on to a description of the birth of the gods and the details of how once born they subsequently treated each other. On some subjects, the antiquity of these works makes them difficult to criticize, whatever their influence—good or bad—on their audience; but when it comes to the respect and

d   attention due to parents, I for one shall never recommend them either as a good influence or as a statement of the honest truth. Still, there's no need to bother with this old material: we may freely allow it to be arranged and recounted in any way the gods find amusing. But the principles of our modern pundits do need to be denounced as a pernicious influence. Just look at the effects of their arguments! When you and I present our proofs for the existence of gods and adduce what you adduced—sun, moon, stars and earth—and argue they are gods and divine beings, the

e   proselytes of these clever fellows will say that these things are just earth and stones, and are incapable of caring for human affairs, however much our plausible rhetoric has managed to dress them up.

CLINIAS: Even if it were unique, sir, that theory you've just described would make trouble. But as similar doctrines in fact exist in their thousands, the situation is even worse.

ATHENIAN: What now, then? What's our reply? What must we do? It's as though we were on trial before a bench of godless judges, defending

887   ourselves on a charge arising out of our legislation. 'It's monstrous,' they say to us, 'that you should pass laws asserting that gods exist.' Shall we defend ourselves? Or shall we ignore them and get back to our legislation, so that the mere preface doesn't turn out longer than the actual code? You see, if we're going to postpone passing the appropriate legislation until we've proved properly to those with a taste for impiety all the points they insisted we had to cover, so that they feel uneasy and begin to find their views going sour on them, our explanation will be anything but brief.

b   CLINIAS: Even so, sir, as we've often said in the comparatively short time we've been talking, there's no reason at the moment to prefer a brief explanation to a full one: after all, no one's 'breathing down our neck' (as they say). It would be an awful farce, if we appeared to be putting brevity first and quality second. It's vital that somehow or other we should make out a plausible case for supposing that gods do exist, that they are good, and that they respect justice more than men do. Such a demonstration would constitute just about the best and finest preamble our penal code

c   could have. So let's overcome our reluctance and unhurriedly exert what powers of persuasion we have in this field, devoting ourselves wholeheart-edly to a full exposition of our case.

ATHENIAN: How keen and insistent you are! I take it you're suggesting we should now offer up a prayer for the success of our exposition, which we certainly can't delay any longer.

Well now, how *can* one argue for the existence of gods without getting angry? You see, one inevitably gets irritable and annoyed with these people

d   who have put us to the trouble, and continue to put us to the trouble, of composing these explanations. If only they believed the stories which they had as babes and sucklings from their nurses and mothers! These almost literally 'charming' stories were told partly for amusement, partly in full earnest; the children heard them related in prayer at sacrifices, and saw acted representations of them—a part of the ceremony a child always loves to see and hear; and they saw their own parents praying with the utmost seriousness for themselves and their families in the firm conviction that their prayers and supplications were addressed to gods who really did exist. At the rising and setting of the sun and moon the children saw and heard Greeks and foreigners, in happiness and misery alike, all prostrate at their devotions; far from supposing gods to be a myth, the worshippers believed their existence to be so sure as to be beyond suspicion. When some people contemptuously brush aside all this evidence without a single good reason to support them (as even a half-wit can see) and oblige us to deliver this address—well, how could one possibly admonish them and at the same time teach them the basic fact about gods, their existence, without using the rough edge of one's tongue? Still, we must make the best of it: we don't want both sides maddened at once, they by their greed for pleasure, we by our anger at their condition. So our address to men with such a depraved outlook should be calm, and run as follows. Let's use honeyed words and abate our anger, and pretend we're addressing just one representative individual.

'Now then, my lad, you're still young, and as time goes on you'll come to adopt opinions diametrically opposed to those you hold now. Why not wait till later on to make up your mind about these important matters? The most important of all, however lightly you take it at the moment, is to get the right ideas about the gods and so live a good life:—otherwise you'll live a bad one. In this connection, I want first to make a crucial and irrefutable point. It's this: you're not unique. Neither you nor your friends are the first to have held this opinion about the gods. It's an illness from which the world is never free, though the number of sufferers varies from time to time. I've met a great many of them, and let me assure you that none of them who have been convinced early in life that gods do not exist have ever retained that belief into old age. However, it is true that some men (but not many) do persist in laboring under the impression either that although the gods exist they are indifferent to human affairs, or alternatively that they are not indifferent but can easily be won over by prayers and sacrifices. Be guided by me: you'll only see this business in its truest light if you wait to gather your information from all sources, particularly the legislator, and then see which theory represents the truth. In the meantime, don't venture any impiety where gods are concerned. You may take it that it will be up to your lawgiver, now and in the future, to try to enlighten you on precisely these topics.'

CLINIAS: So far, sir, that's very well said.

ATHENIAN: Certainly, Megillus and Clinias, but what an amazing doctrine we've got involved in, without noticing it!

CLINIAS: What doctrine do you mean?

e   ATHENIAN: I mean the one which many people regard as the highest
truth of all.

CLINIAS: Please be more explicit.

ATHENIAN: Some people, I believe, account for all things which have
come to exist, all things which are coming into existence now, and all
things which will do so in the future, by attributing them either to nature,
art, or chance.

CLINIAS: Isn't that satisfactory?

889   ATHENIAN: Oh, I expect they've got it more or less right—they're clever
fellows. Still, let's keep track of them, and see what's really implied in the
theories of that school of thought.

CLINIAS: By all means.

ATHENIAN: The facts show—so they claim—that the greatest and finest
things in the world are the products of nature and chance, the creations
of art being comparatively trivial. The works of nature, they say, are grand
and primary, and constitute a ready-made source for all the minor works
constructed and fashioned by art—*art*efacts, as they're generally called.

CLINIAS: How do you mean?

b   ATHENIAN: I'll put it more precisely. They maintain that fire, water, earth
and air owe their existence to nature and chance, and in no case to art,
and that it is by means of these entirely inanimate substances[2] that the
secondary physical bodies—the earth, sun, moon and stars—have been
produced. These substances moved at random, each impelled by virtue
of its own inherent properties, which depended on various suitable amal-
gamations of hot and cold, dry and wet, soft and hard, and all other
haphazard combinations that inevitably resulted when the opposites were
c   mixed. This is the process to which all the heavens and everything that is
in them owe their birth, and the consequent establishment of the four
seasons led to the appearance of all plants and living creatures. The cause
of all this, they say, was neither intelligent planning, nor a deity, nor art,
but—as we've explained—nature and chance. Art, the brain-child of these
living creatures, arose later, the mortal child of mortal beings; it has pro-
d   duced, at a late stage, various amusing trifles that are hardly real at all—
mere insubstantial images of the same order as the arts themselves (I mean
for instance the productions of the arts of painting and music, and all their
ancillary skills). But if there are in fact some techniques that produce worthwhile results, they are those that *co-operate* with nature, like medicine
and farming and physical training. This school of thought maintains that
government, in particular, has very little to do with nature, and is largely
e   a matter of art; similarly legislation is never a natural process but is based
on technique, and its enactments are quite artificial.

CLINIAS: What are you driving at?

ATHENIAN: My dear fellow, the first thing these people say about the
gods is that they are artificial concepts corresponding to nothing in nature;

2. Or possibly, 'by these entirely inanimate agencies' (i.e., nature and chance).

they are legal fictions, which moreover vary very widely according to the different conventions people agree on when they produce a legal code. In particular, goodness according to nature and goodness according to the law are two different things, and there is no natural standard of justice at all. On the contrary, men are always wrangling about their moral standards and altering them, and every change introduced becomes binding from the moment it's made, regardless of the fact that it is entirely artificial,   890 and based on convention, not nature in the slightest degree. All this, my friends, is the theme of experts—as our young people regard them—who in their prose and poetry maintain that anything one can get away with by force is absolutely justified. This is why we experience outbreaks of impiety among the young, who assume that the kind of gods the law tells them to believe in do not exist; this is why we get treasonable efforts to convert people to the 'true natural life', which is essentially nothing but a life of conquest over others, not one of service to your neighbor as the law enjoins.

CLINIAS: What a pernicious doctrine you've explained, sir! It must be   b the ruin of the younger generation, both in the state at large and in private families.

ATHENIAN: That's very true, Clinias. So what do you think the legislator ought to do, faced with such a long-established thesis as this? Is he simply to stand up in public and threaten all the citizens with punishment if they don't admit the existence of gods and mentally accept the law's description of them? He could make the same threat about their notions of beauty and justice and all such vital concepts, as well as about anything that encourages virtue or vice; he could demand that the citizens' belief and   c actions should accord with his written instructions, and insist that anyone not showing the proper obedience to the laws must be punished either by death, or by a whipping and imprisonment, deprivation of civic rights, or by being sent into exile a poorer man. But what about *persuading* them? When he establishes a legal code for his people, shouldn't he try to talk them into being as amenable as he can make them?

CLINIAS: Certainly, sir. If even limited persuasion can be applied in this   d field, no legislator of even moderate ability should shrink from making the effort. On the contrary, he should argue 'till the cows come home', as the saying is, to back up the old doctrine that the gods exist, and to support the other arguments you ran through just now. In particular, he should defend law itself and art as either part of nature or existing by reason of some no less powerful agency—being in fact, to tell the truth, creations of reason. That, I think, is the point you're making, and I agree.

ATHENIAN: Really, Clinias, you *are* enthusiastic! But when these themes   e are presented as you suggest, in addresses composed for a popular audience, aren't they found rather difficult to understand? And don't the addresses tend to go on for ever?

CLINIAS: Well, sir, we put up with one long discussion, about inebriation in the cause of culture, so surely we can tolerate another, about theology

and so forth. And of course this helps intelligent legislation tremendously,
891   because legal instructions, once written down, remain fixed and permanent,
ready to stand up to scrutiny forever. So there's no reason for alarm if at
first they make difficult listening, because your slow learner will be able
to go back again and again and examine them. Nor does their length,
provided they're useful, justify any man in committing what seems to me,
at least, an impiety: I mean refusing to facilitate these explanations as best
he can.

MEGILLUS: Yes, sir, I entirely approve of what Clinias says.

b   ATHENIAN: As well you may, Megillus, and we must do as he suggests.
Of course, if this sort of argument had not been disseminated so widely
over pretty well the entire human race, there would be no call for arguments
to prove the existence of gods. But in present circumstances we've no
choice. When the most important laws are being trampled under foot by
scoundrels, whose duty is it to rush to their defense, if not the legislator's?

MEGILLUS: Nobody's.

c   ATHENIAN: Now then, Clinias, you must take your share in the explanation, so tell me your opinion again. I assume the upholder of this doctrine
thinks of fire and water, earth and air as being the first of all substances,
and this is precisely what he means by the term 'nature'; soul, he thinks,
was derived from them, at a later stage. No, I do more than 'assume': I'd
say he argues the point explicitly.

CLINIAS: True.

ATHENIAN: Now then, by heaven, haven't we discovered the fountain-
head, so to speak, of the senseless opinions of all those who have ever
undertaken investigation into nature? Scrutinize carefully every stage in
d   their argument, because it will be crucial if we can show that these people
who have embraced impious doctrines and lead others on are using falla-
cious arguments rather than cogent ones—which I think is in fact the case.

CLINIAS: You're right, but try to explain their error.

ATHENIAN: Well, it looks as if we have to embark on a rather unfamiliar
line of argument.

CLINIAS: Don't hesitate, sir. I realize you think we'll be straying outside
legislation if we attempt such an explanation, but if this is the only way
e   to reach agreement that the beings currently described as gods in our law
are properly so described, then this, my dear sir, is the kind of explanation
we must give.

ATHENIAN: So it looks as if I must now argue along rather unfamiliar lines.
Well then, the doctrine which produces an impious soul also 'produces', in
a sense, the soul itself, in that it denies the priority of what was in fact
the first cause of the birth and destruction of all things, and regards it as
a later creation. Conversely, it asserts that what actually came later, came
first. That's the source of the mistake these people have made about the
real nature of the gods.

892   CLINIAS: So far, the point escapes me.

ATHENIAN: It's the *soul*, my good friend, that nearly everybody seems
to have misunderstood, not realizing its nature and power. Quite apart

from the other points about it, people are particularly ignorant about its birth. It is one of the *first* creations, born long before all physical things, and is the chief cause of all their alterations and transformations. Now if that's true, anything closely related to soul will necessarily have been created before material things, won't it, since soul itself is older than matter?   b

CLINIAS: Necessarily.

ATHENIAN: Opinion, diligence, reason, art and law will be prior to roughness and smoothness, heaviness and lightness. In particular, the grand and primary works and creations, precisely *because* they come in the category 'primary', will be attributable to art. Natural things, and nature herself— to use the mistaken terminology of our opponents—will be secondary products from art and reason.

CLINIAS: Why do you say 'mistaken'?   c

ATHENIAN: When they use the term 'nature', they mean the process by which the primary substances were created. But if it can be shown that soul came first, not fire or air, and that it was one of the first things to be created, it will be quite correct to say that soul is preeminently natural. This is true, provided you can demonstrate that soul is older than matter, but not otherwise.

CLINIAS: Very true.

ATHENIAN: So this is precisely the point we have to tackle next?   d

CLINIAS: Of course.

ATHENIAN: It's an extremely tricky argument, and we old men must be careful not to be taken in by its freshness and novelty, so that it eludes our grasp and makes us look like ridiculous fools whose ambitious ideas lead to failure even in little things. Just consider. Imagine the three of us had to cross a river in spate, and I were the younger and had plenty of experience of currents. Suppose I said, 'I ought to try first on my own   e account, and leave you two in safety while I see if the river is fordable for you two older men as well, or if not, just how bad it is. If it turns out to be fordable, I'll then call you and put my experience at your disposal in helping you to cross; but if in the event it cannot be crossed by old men like yourselves, then the only risk has been mine.' Wouldn't that strike you as fair enough? The situation is the same now: the argument ahead runs too deep, and men as weak as you will probably get out of your depth. I want to prevent you novices in answering from being dazed and dizzied by a stream of questions, which would put you in an undignified   893 and humiliating position you'd find most unpleasant. So this is what I think I'd better do now: first I'll ask questions of myself, while you listen in safety; then I'll go over the answers again and in this way work through the whole argument until the soul has been thoroughly dealt with and its priority to matter proved.

CLINIAS: We think that's a splendid idea, sir. Please act on your suggestion.

ATHENIAN: Come then, if ever we needed to call upon the help of God,   b it's now. Let's take it the gods have been most pressingly invoked to assist the proof of their own existence, and let's rely on their help as if it were a rope steadying us as we enter the deep waters of our present theme. Now when I'm under interrogation on this sort of topic, and such questions as the following are put to me, the safest replies seem to be these. Suppose someone asks 'Sir, do all things stand still, and does nothing move? Or is precisely the opposite true? Or do some things move, while others are

c   motionless?' My reply will be 'I suppose some move and others remain at rest.' 'So surely there must be some *space* in which the stationary objects remain at rest, and those in motion move?' 'Of course.' 'Some of them, presumably, will do so in one location, others in several?' 'Do you mean', we shall reply, 'that "moving in one location" is the action of objects which are able to keep their centers immobile? For instance, there are circles which are said to "stay put" even though as a whole they are revolving.' 'Yes.' 'And we appreciate that when a disk revolves like that, points near and far from the center describe circles of different radii in the same time;

d   their motion varies according to these radii and is proportionately quick or slow. This motion gives rise to all sorts of wonderful phenomena, because these points simultaneously traverse circles of large and small circumference at proportionately high or low speeds—an effect one might have expected to be impossible.' 'You're quite right.' 'When you speak of motion in many locations I suppose you're referring to objects that are always leaving one spot and moving on to another. Sometimes their motion involves only one point of contact with their successive situations, some-

e   times several, as in rolling.

'From time to time objects meet; a moving one colliding with a stationary one disintegrates, but if it meets other objects traveling in the opposite direction they coalesce into a single intermediate substance, half one and half the other.' 'Yes, I agree to your statement of the case.' 'Further, such combination leads to an increase in bulk, while their separation leads to diminution—so long as the existing states of the objects remain unimpaired; but if either combination or separation entails the abolition of the existing state, the objects concerned are destroyed.'

894   'Now, what conditions are always present when anything is produced? Clearly, an initial impulse grows and reaches the second stage and then the third stage out of the second, finally (at the third stage) presenting percipient beings with something to perceive. This then is the process of change and alteration to which everything owes its birth. A thing exists as such so long as it is stable, but when it changes its essential state it is completely destroyed.'

So, my friends, haven't we now classified and numbered all forms of

b   motion, except two?

CLINIAS: Which two?

ATHENIAN: My dear chap, they are the two which constitute the real purpose of every question we've asked.

CLINIAS: Try to be more explicit.

ATHENIAN: What we really had in view was soul, wasn't it?

CLINIAS: Certainly.

ATHENIAN: The one kind of motion is that which is permanently capable of moving other things but not itself; the other is permanently capable of moving *both* itself *and* other things by processes of combination and separation, increase and diminution, generation and destruction. Let these stand as two further distinct types in our complete list of motions.   c

CLINIAS: Agreed.

ATHENIAN: So we shall put ninth the kind which always imparts motion to something else and is itself changed by another thing. Then[3] there's the motion that moves both itself and other things, suitable for all active and passive processes and accurately termed the source of change and motion in all things that exist. I suppose we'll call that the tenth.

CLINIAS: Certainly.

ATHENIAN: Now which of our (roughly) ten motions should we be justi-fied in singling out as the most powerful and radically effective?   d

CLINIAS: We can't resist the conclusion that the motion which can generate itself is infinitely superior, and all the others are inferior to it.

ATHENIAN: Well said! So shouldn't we correct one or two inaccuracies in the points we've just made?

CLINIAS: What sort of inaccuracy do you mean?

ATHENIAN: It wasn't quite right to call that motion the 'tenth'.

CLINIAS: Why not?

ATHENIAN: It can be shown to be first, in ancestry as well as in power; the next kind—although oddly enough a moment ago we called it 'ninth'—   e
we'll put second.

CLINIAS: What are you getting at?

ATHENIAN: This: when we find one thing producing a change in another, and that in turn affecting something else, and so forth, will there ever be, in such a sequence, an original cause of change? How could anything whose motion is transmitted to it from something else be the *first* thing to effect an alteration? It's impossible. In reality, when something which has set itself moving effects an alteration in something, and that in turn effects something else, so that the motion is transmitted to thousands upon thousands of things one after another, the entire sequence of their   895
movements must surely spring from some initial principle, which can hardly be anything except the change effected by self-generated motion.

CLINIAS: You've put it admirably, and your point must be allowed.

ATHENIAN: Now let's put the point in a different way, and once again answer our own questions: 'Suppose the whole universe were somehow to coalesce and come to a standstill—the theory which most of our philoso-pher-fellows are actually bold enough to maintain—which of the motions we have enumerated would inevitably be the first to arise in it?' 'Self-   b
generating motion, surely, because no antecedent impulse can ever be transmitted from something else in a situation where no antecedent im-pulse exists. Self-generating motion, then, is the source of all motions, and

---

3. Inserting *te* after *heautēn* in c4.

the primary force in both stationary and moving objects, and we shan't be able to avoid the conclusion that it is the most ancient and the most potent of all changes, whereas the change which is produced by something else and is in turn transmitted to other objects, comes second.'

CLINIAS: You're absolutely right.

c   ATHENIAN: So now we've reached this point in our discussion, here's another question we should answer.

CLINIAS: What?

ATHENIAN: If we ever saw this phenomenon—self-generating motion— arise in an object made of earth, water or fire (alone or in combination) how should we describe that object's condition?

CLINIAS: Of course, what you're really asking me is this: when an object moves itself, are we to say that it is 'alive'?

ATHENIAN: That's right.

CLINIAS: It emphatically is alive.

ATHENIAN: Well then, when we see that a thing has a soul, the situation is exactly the same, isn't it? We have to admit that it is alive.

CLINIAS: Yes, exactly the same.

d   ATHENIAN: Now, for heaven's sake, hold on a minute. I suppose you'd be prepared to recognize three elements in any given thing?

CLINIAS: What do you mean?

ATHENIAN: The first point is what the object actually *is*, the second is the definition of this, and the third is the name. And in addition there are two questions to be asked about every existing thing.

CLINIAS: Two?

ATHENIAN: Sometimes we put forward the mere name and want to know the definition, and sometimes we put forward the definition and ask for the name.

CLINIAS: I take it the point we want to make at the moment is this.

ATHENIAN: What?

e   CLINIAS: In general, things can be divided into two, and this is true of some numbers as well. Such a number has the *name* 'even' and its *definition* is 'a number divisible into two equal parts'.

ATHENIAN: Yes, that's the sort of thing I mean. So surely, in either case— whether we provide the name and ask for the definition or give the defini- tion and ask for the name—we're referring to the same object? When we *call* it 'even' and *define* it as 'a number divisible into two', it's the same thing we're talking about.

CLINIAS: It certainly is.

896   ATHENIAN: So what's the definition of the thing we call the soul? Surely we can do nothing but use our formula of a moment ago: 'motion capable of moving itself'.

CLINIAS: Do you mean that the entity which we all *call* 'soul' is precisely that which is *defined* by the expression 'self-generating motion'?

ATHENIAN: I do. And if this is true, are we still dissatisfied? Haven't we got ourselves a satisfactory proof that soul is identical with the original source of the generation and motion of all past, present and future things and their contraries? After all, it has been shown to be the cause of all change and motion in everything. b

CLINIAS: Dissatisfied? No! On the contrary, it has been proved up to the hilt that soul, being the source of motion, is the most ancient thing there is.

ATHENIAN: But when one thing is put in motion by another, it is never thereby endowed with the power of independent self-movement. Such derived motion will therefore come second, or as far down the list as you fancy relegating it, being a mere change in matter that quite literally 'has no soul'.

CLINIAS: Correctly argued.

ATHENIAN: So it was an equally correct, final and complete statement of the truth, when we said that soul is prior to matter, and that matter c came later and takes second place. Soul is the master, and matter its natural subject.

CLINIAS: That is indeed absolutely true.

ATHENIAN: The next step is to remember our earlier admission that if soul were shown to be older than matter, the spiritual order of things would be older than the material.

CLINIAS: Certainly.

ATHENIAN: So habits, customs, will, calculation, right opinion, diligence d and memory will be prior creations to material length, breadth, depth and strength, if (as is true) soul is prior to matter.

CLINIAS: Unavoidably.

ATHENIAN: And the next unavoidable admission, seeing that we are going to posit soul as the cause of *all* things, will be that it is the cause of good and evil, beauty and ugliness, justice and injustice and all the opposites.

CLINIAS: Of course.

ATHENIAN: And surely it's necessary to assert that as soul resides and e keeps control anywhere where anything is moved, it controls the heavens as well.

CLINIAS: Naturally.

ATHENIAN: One soul, or more than one? I'll answer for you both: more than one. At any rate, we must not assume fewer than two: that which does good, and that which has the opposite capacity.

CLINIAS: That's absolutely right.

ATHENIAN: Very well, then. So soul, by virtue of its own motions, stirs into movement everything in the heavens and on earth and in the sea. The names of the motions of soul are: wish, reflection, diligence, counsel, 897 opinion true and false, joy and grief, cheerfulness and fear, love and hate. Soul also uses all related or initiating motions which take over the secondary movements of matter and stimulate everything to increase or diminish, separate or combine, with the accompanying heat and cold, heaviness and lightness, roughness and smoothness, white and black, bitter and sweet.

These are the instruments soul uses, whether it cleaves to divine reason
b   (soul itself being, if the truth were told, a divinity), and guides everything
to an appropriate and successful conclusion, or allies itself with unreason
and produces completely opposite results. Shall we agree this is the case,
or do we still suspect that the truth may be different?

CLINIAS: By no means.

ATHENIAN: Well then, what kind of soul may we say has gained control
of the heavens and earth and their entire cycle of movement? Is it the
rational and supremely virtuous kind, or that which has neither advantage?
c   Would you like our reply to run like this?

CLINIAS: How?

ATHENIAN: 'If, my fine fellow' (we should say) 'the whole course and
movement of the heavens and all that is in them reflect the motion and
revolution and calculation of reason, and operate in a corresponding fashion, then clearly we have to admit that it is the best kind of soul that cares
for the entire universe and directs it along the best path.'

CLINIAS: True.

ATHENIAN: 'If however these things move in an unbalanced and disorga-
d   nized way, we must say the evil kind of soul is in charge of them.'

CLINIAS: That too is true.

ATHENIAN: 'So what is the nature of rational motion?' Now this, my
friends, is a question to which it is difficult to give an answer that will
make sense, so you're justified here in calling me in to help with your reply.

CLINIAS: Good.

ATHENIAN: Still, in answering this question we mustn't assume that
mortal eyes will ever be able to look upon reason and get to know it
adequately: let's not produce darkness at noon, so to speak, by looking at
e   the sun direct. We can save our sight by looking at an *image* of the object
we're asking about.

CLINIAS: How do you mean?

ATHENIAN: What about selecting from our list of ten motions the one
which reason resembles, and taking that as our image? I'll join you in
recalling it, and then we'll give a joint answer to the question.

CLINIAS: Yes, that's probably your best method of explanation.

ATHENIAN: Do we still remember at any rate this from the list of points
we made earlier, that all things are either in motion or at rest?

CLINIAS: Yes, we do.

ATHENIAN: And some of those in motion move in a single location, others
898 in a succession of locations?

CLINIAS: That is so.

ATHENIAN: Of these two motions, that taking place in a single location
necessarily implies continuous revolution round a central point, just like
wheels being turned on a lathe; and this kind of motion bears the closest
possible affinity and likeness to the cyclical movement of reason.

CLINIAS: What do you mean?

ATHENIAN: Take reason on the one hand, and motion in a single location on the other. If we were to point out that in both cases the motion was determined by a single plan and procedure and that it was (a) regular, (b) uniform, (c) always at the same point in space, (d) around a fixed center, (e) in the same position relative to other objects, and were to illustrate both by the example of a sphere being turned on a lathe, then no one could ever show us up for incompetent makers of verbal images.

CLINIAS: You're quite right.

ATHENIAN: Now consider the motion that is never uniform or regular or at the same point in space or round the same center or in the same relative position or in a single location, and is neither planned nor organized nor systematic. Won't that motion be associated with every kind of unreason?

CLINIAS: Absolutely true, it will.

ATHENIAN: So now there's no difficulty in saying right out that since we find that the entire cycle of events is to be attributed to soul, the heavens that we see revolving must necessarily be driven round—we have to say—because they are arranged and directed *either* by the best kind of soul *or* by the other sort.

CLINIAS: Well, sir, judging from what has been said, I think it would be rank blasphemy to deny that their revolution is produced by one or more souls blessed with perfect virtue.

ATHENIAN: You've proved a most attentive listener, Clinias. Now attend to this further point.

CLINIAS: What?

ATHENIAN: If, in principle, soul drives round the sun, moon and the other heavenly bodies, does it not impel each individually?

CLINIAS: Of course.

ATHENIAN: Let's take a single example: our results will then obviously apply to all the other heavenly bodies.

CLINIAS: And your example is . . .?

ATHENIAN: . . . the sun. Everyone can see its body, but no one can see its soul—not that you could see the soul of any other creature, living or dying. Nevertheless, there are good grounds for believing that we are in fact held in the embrace of some such thing though it is totally below the level of our bodily senses, and is perceptible by reason alone. So by reason and understanding let's get hold of a new point about the soul.

CLINIAS: What?

ATHENIAN: If soul drives the sun, we shan't go far wrong if we say that it operates in one of three ways.

CLINIAS: And what are they?

ATHENIAN: Either (a) the soul resides within this visible spherical body and carries it wherever it goes, just as *our* soul takes us around from one place to another, or (b) it acquires its own body of fire or air of some kind (as certain people maintain), and impels the sun by the external contact of body with body, or (c) it is entirely immaterial, but guides the sun along its path by virtue of possessing some other prodigious and wonderful powers.

CLINIAS: Yes, it must necessarily be by one of these methods that the soul manages the universe.

ATHENIAN: Now, just wait a minute. Whether we find that it is by stationing itself in the sun and driving it like a chariot, or by moving it from outside, or by some other means, that this soul provides us all with light, every single one of us is bound to regard it as a god. Isn't that right?

b   CLINIAS: Yes, one would be absolutely stupid not to.

ATHENIAN: Now consider all the stars and the moon and the years and the months and all the seasons: what can we do except repeat the same story? A soul or souls—and perfectly virtuous souls at that—have been shown to be the cause of all these phenomena, and whether it is by their living presence in matter that they direct all the heavens, or by some other means, we shall insist that these souls are gods. Can anybody admit all this and still put up with people who deny that 'everything is full of gods'?[4]

c   CLINIAS: No sir, nobody could be so mad.

ATHENIAN: Now then, Megillus and Clinias, let's delimit the courses of action open to anyone who has so far refused to believe in gods, and get rid of him.

CLINIAS: You mean . . .

ATHENIAN: . . . *either* he should demonstrate to us that we're wrong to posit soul as the first cause to which everything owes its birth, and that our subsequent deductions were equally mistaken, *or*, if he can't put a better case than ours, he should let himself be persuaded by us and live the rest of his life a believer in gods. So let's review the thesis we argued

d   for the existence of gods against the non-believers: was it cogent or feeble?

CLINIAS: Feeble, sir? Not in the least.

ATHENIAN: Very well. So far as atheists are concerned, we may regard our case as complete. Next we have to use some gentle persuasion on the man who believes in gods but thinks they are unconcerned about human affairs. 'My splendid fellow,' we'll say, 'your belief in the existence of gods probably springs from a kind of family tie between you and the gods that draws you to your natural kin and makes you honor them and recognize their existence. What drives you to impiety is the good fortune of scoundrels

e   and criminals in private and public life—which in reality is not good fortune at all, although it is highly admired as such by popular opinion and its misplaced enthusiasms: poetry and literature of every kind invest it with a pernicious glamour. Or perhaps you observe men reaching the

900   end of their lives, full of years and honor, leaving behind them their children's children, and your present disquiet is because you've discovered

---

4. A remark attributed to Thales (*c.* 600 B.C.), traditionally the first philosopher.

(either from hearsay or personal observation) a few of the many ghastly acts of impiety which (you notice) are the very means by which some of these people have risen from humble beginnings to supreme power and dictatorships. The result is that although by virtue of your kinship with the gods you'd clearly be reluctant to lay such things at their door, your mental confusion and your inability to find fault with them has brought   b you to your present predicament where you believe they exist, but despise and neglect human affairs. Now, we want to prevent your thoughts from becoming more impious than they are already: let's see if argument will ward off the disease while it is still in its early stages. We must also try to make use of the original thesis we argued so exhaustively against the absolute atheist, by linking the next step in the exposition on to it.' So you, Clinias and Megillus, must do what you did before: take the young man's   c place and answer on his behalf. If any difficulty crops up in the argument, I'll take over from you two as I did just now, and conduct you across the river.

CLINIAS: Good idea. You play your part, and we'll carry out your suggestions to the best of our ability.

ATHENIAN: Still, perhaps it won't be too difficult to show our friend that gods are just as attentive to details as to important matters—more so, in fact. You see, he was here a moment ago and heard that their special job—   d an expression of their perfect virtue—is to watch over the universe.

CLINIAS: Yes, he certainly did hear that said.

ATHENIAN: The next thing is for our opponents to join us in asking this question: what particular virtue have we in mind when we agree that the gods are good? Now then: don't we regard moderation and the possession of reason as a mark of virtue, and their opposites as marks of vice?

CLINIAS: We do.

ATHENIAN: What about courage and cowardice? Are we agreed they   e come under virtue and vice respectively?

CLINIAS: Certainly.

ATHENIAN: And we'll label the one set of qualities 'disgraceful' and the other 'admirable'?

CLINIAS: Yes, we must.

ATHENIAN: And if the base qualities are characteristic of anyone, they are characteristic of us; the gods, we shall say, are *not* affected by them, either radically or slightly.

CLINIAS: No one would disagree with that either.

ATHENIAN: Well, then, shall we regard neglect and idleness and riotous living as part of the soul's virtue? Or what's your view?

CLINIAS: Really!

ATHENIAN: As part of vice, then?

CLINIAS: Yes.

ATHENIAN: So it's the opposite qualities that will be ascribed to virtue?   901

CLINIAS: Right.

ATHENIAN: Very well then. In our view all idle and thoughtless bons vivants will be just the kind of people the poet said were 'like nothing so much as stingless drones'.[5]

CLINIAS: Very apt, that.

ATHENIAN: So we mustn't say that God has precisely the sort of character he himself detests, and we mustn't allow any attempt to maintain such a view.

CLINIAS: Of course not; it would be intolerable.

b   ATHENIAN: Take someone who has the special job of looking after some particular sphere of action, and who is preoccupied with his major duties to the neglect of the small. Could we possibly commend him, except for reasons that would ring quite hollow? Let's consider the point in this light: doesn't this sort of conduct—divine or human—fall into two categories?

CLINIAS: Two categories, do we say?

ATHENIAN: *Either* a man thinks it makes no difference to his job as a whole if he neglects the details, *or* important though they are, he nevertheless lives

c   in idleness and self-indulgence and neglects them. Or is there some other possible reason for his neglecting them? (Of course, if it is simply *impossible* to look after everything, and a god or some poor mortal fails to take care of something when he has not the strength and therefore the ability, no question of positive neglect of either major or minor duties will arise.)

CLINIAS: No, of course not.

ATHENIAN: Now let our two opponents answer the questions of the three

d   of us. They both admit gods exist, but one thinks they can be bought off, the other that they are careless about details. 'First of all, do you both admit that the gods know and see and hear everything, and that nothing within the range of our senses or intellect can escape them? Is this your position, or what?

CLINIAS: 'It is.'

ATHENIAN: 'And also, that they can do anything which is within the power of mortals and immortals?'

CLINIAS: Yes, of course they'll agree to that too.

e   ATHENIAN: Further, the five of us have already agreed that the gods are good—supremely so, in fact.

CLINIAS: Emphatically.

ATHENIAN: So surely, given they're the sort of beings we've admitted, it's absolutely impossible to agree that they do anything out of sloth and self-indulgence. Among us mortals, you see, laziness springs from coward-ice, and sloth from laziness and self-indulgence.

CLINIAS: That's very true.

ATHENIAN: Then no god neglects anything because of sloth and laziness, because no god, presumably, suffers from cowardice.

CLINIAS: You're quite right.

---

5. *Works and Days* 304.

ATHENIAN: Now if in fact they do neglect the tiny details of the universe, 902
the remaining possibilities are surely these: *either* they neglect them because
they know that no such detail needs their attention, *or*—well, what other
explanation could there be, except a lack of knowledge?

CLINIAS: None.

ATHENIAN: So, my dearest sir, are we to interpret you as saying that the
gods are ignorant, and display negligence where it is necessary to be
solicitous, because they don't *know*? Or alternatively that they realize the
necessity, but do what the most wretched of men are said to do, namely
fail in their duty because they are somehow overcome by temptation or
pain, even though they know that there are better options than the one b
they've in fact chosen?

CLINIAS: Indeed not.

ATHENIAN: Now surely human life has something to do with the world
of the soul, and man himself is the most god-fearing of all living creatures,
isn't he?

CLINIAS: I dare say.

ATHENIAN: And we regard all mortal creatures as possessions of gods,
like the universe as a whole.

CLINIAS: Of course.

ATHENIAN: So whether you argue these possessions count for little or
much in the sight of the gods, in neither case would it be proper for our c
owners to neglect us, seeing how very solicitous and good they are. You
see, there's another point we ought to consider here.

CLINIAS: What?

ATHENIAN: It's a point about perception and physical strength. Aren't
they essentially at opposite poles, so far as ease and difficulty are concerned?

CLINIAS: What do you mean?

ATHENIAN: Although little things are more difficult to see or hear than
big, they are much easier, when there are only a few of them, to carry or
control or look after.

CLINIAS: Yes, much easier. d

ATHENIAN: Take a doctor who has been given the entire body to treat.
Will he ever get good results if he neglects the individual limbs and tiny
parts, in spite of being willing and able to look after the major organs?

CLINIAS: No, never.

ATHENIAN: Nor yet will helmsmen or generals or householders, nor
'statesmen' or anybody of that ilk, succeed in major day-to-day matters if
they neglect occasional details. You know how even masons say the big e
stones don't lie well without the small ones.

CLINIAS: Of course.

ATHENIAN: So let's not treat God as less skilled than a mortal craftsman,
who applies the same expertise to all the jobs in his own line whether
they're big or small, and gets more finished and perfect results the better
he is at his work. We must not suppose that God, who is supremely wise,

903   and willing and able to superintend the world, looks to major matters
        but—like a faint-hearted lazybones who throws up his hands at hard
        work—neglects the minor, which we established were in fact *easier* to
        look after.

        CLINIAS: No sir, we should never entertain such notions about gods. It's
        a point of view that would be absolutely impious and untrue.

        ATHENIAN: Well, it looks to me as if we've given a pretty complete answer
        to this fellow who's always going on about the negligence of heaven.

        CLINIAS: Yes, we have.

   b   ATHENIAN: At any rate, our thesis has forced him to admit he was wrong.
        But I still think we need to find a form of words to *charm* him into agreement.

        CLINIAS: Well, my friend, what do you suggest?

        ATHENIAN: What we say to the young man should serve to convince him
        of this thesis: 'The supervisor of the universe has arranged everything
        with an eye to its preservation and excellence, and its individual parts
        play appropriate active or passive roles according to their various capaci-
        ties. These parts, down to the smallest details of their active and passive
        functions, have each been put under the control of ruling powers that have
   c   perfected the minutest constituents of the universe. Now then, you perverse
        fellow, one such part—a mere speck that nevertheless constantly contri-
        butes to the good of the whole—is you, you who have forgotten that
        nothing is created except to provide the entire universe with a life of
        prosperity. You forget that creation is not for your benefit: *you* exist for
        the sake of the universe. Every doctor, you see, and every skilled craftsman
        always works for the sake of some end-product as a whole; he handles
        his materials so that they will give the best results in general, and makes
   d   the parts contribute to the good of the whole, not vice versa. But you're
        grumbling because you don't appreciate that your position is best not only
        for the universe but for you too, thanks to your common origin. And since
        a soul is allied with different bodies at different times, and perpetually
        undergoes all sorts of changes, either self-imposed or produced by some
        other soul, the divine checkers-player has nothing else to do except promote
        a soul with a promising character to a better situation, and relegate one
        that is deteriorating to an inferior, as is appropriate in each case, so that
   e   they all meet the fate they deserve.'

        CLINIAS: How do you mean?

        ATHENIAN: I fancy I could explain how easy it could be for gods to
        control the universe. Suppose that in one's constant efforts to serve its
        interests one were to mold all that is in it by *transforming* everything (by
        turning fire into water permeated by soul, for instance), instead of produc-
        ing variety from a basic unity or unity from variety, then after the first or
904   second or third stage of creation everything would be arranged in an
        infinite number of perpetually changing patterns.[6] But in fact the supervisor
        of the universe finds his task remarkably easy.

        ───────────

        6. Deleting *mē* in e4.

CLINIAS: Again, what do you mean?

ATHENIAN: This. Our King saw (a) that all actions are a function of soul and involve a great deal of virtue and a great deal of vice, (b) that the combination of body and soul, while not an eternal creation like the gods sanctioned by law, is nevertheless indestructible (because living beings could never have been created if one of these two constituent factors had been destroyed), (c) that one of them—the good element in soul—is   b
naturally beneficial, while the bad element naturally does harm. Seeing all this he contrived a place for each constituent where it would most easily and effectively ensure the triumph of virtue and the defeat of vice throughout the universe. With this grand purpose in view he has worked out what sort of position, in what regions, should be assigned to a soul to match its changes of character; but he left it to the individual's acts of will to determine the *direction* of these changes. You see, the way we react   c
to particular circumstances is almost invariably determined by our desires and our psychological state.

CLINIAS: Likely enough.

ATHENIAN: So all things that contain soul change, the cause of their change lying within themselves, and as they change they move according to the ordinance and law of destiny. Small changes in unimportant aspects of character entail small horizontal changes of position in space, while a substantial decline into injustice sets the soul on the path to the depths of   d
the so-called "under"world, which men call "Hades" and similar names, and which haunts and terrifies them both during their lives and when they have been sundered from their bodies. Take a soul that becomes particularly full of vice or virtue as a result of its own acts of will and the powerful influence of social intercourse. If companionship with divine virtue has made it exceptionally divine, it experiences an exceptional change of location, being conducted by a holy path to some superior place elsewhere. Alternatively, opposite characteristics will send it off to live in   e
the opposite region. And in spite of your belief that the gods neglect you, my lad, or rather young man,

This is the sentence of the gods that dwell upon Olympus[7]

—to go to join worse souls as you grow worse and better souls as you grow better, and alike in life and all the deaths you suffer to do and be done by according to the standards that birds of a feather naturally apply   905
among themselves. Neither you nor anyone else who has got into trouble will ever be able to run fast enough to boast that he has escaped this sentence—a sentence to which the judges have attached special importance, and which should take every possible care to avoid. Make yourself ever so small and hide in the depths of the earth, or soar high into the sky: this

7. *Odyssey* xix.43.

sentence will be ever at your heels, and either while you're still alive on
b   earth or after you've descended into Hades or been taken to some even
more remote place, you'll pay the proper penalty of your crimes. You'll
find the same is true of those whom you imagine have emerged from
misery to happiness because you've seen them rise from a humble position
to high estate by acts of impiety, or some similar wickedness. These actions,
it seemed to you, were like a mirror which reflected the gods' total lack
of concern. But you didn't appreciate how the role of the gods contributes
to the total scheme of things. What a bold fellow you must be, if you think
c   you've no need of such knowledge! Yet without it no one will ever catch
so much as a glimmer of the truth or be able to offer a reasoned account
of happiness or misery in life. So if Clinias here and this whole group of
old men convince you that you don't really understand what you're saying
about the gods, then the divine assistance will be with you. But it may be
that you need some further explanation, so if you have any sense you'll
d   listen while we address our third opponent.

Now as far as I'm concerned, we've proved, not too inadequately, that
gods exist and care for mankind. However, there remains the view that
they can be bought off by the gifts of sinners. No one should ever assent
to this thesis, and we must fight to the last ditch to refute it.

CLINIAS: Well said. Let's do as you suggest.

ATHENIAN: Look—in the name of the gods themselves!—*how* would they
e   be bought off, supposing they ever were? What would they have to be?
What sort of being would do this? Well, if they are going to run the entire
universe forever, presumably they'll have to be rulers.

CLINIAS: True.

ATHENIAN: Now then, what sort of ruler do the gods in fact resemble?
Or rather, what rulers resemble them? Let's compare small instances with
great, and see what rulers will serve our purpose. What about drivers of
competing teams of horses, or steersmen of boats in a race? Would they
be suitable parallels? Or we might compare the gods to commanders of
armies. Again, it could be that they're analogous to doctors concerned
906 to defend the body in the war against disease, or to farmers anxiously
anticipating the seasons that usually discourage the growth of their crops,
or to shepherds. Now since we've agreed among ourselves that the universe
is full of many good things and many bad as well, and that the latter
outnumber the former, we maintain that the battle we have on our hands
is never finished, and demands tremendous vigilance. However, gods and
spirits are fighting on our side, the gods and spirits whose chattels we
b   are. What ruins us is injustice and senseless aggression; what protects us
is justice and sensible moderation—virtues that are part of the spiritual
characteristics of the gods, although one can find them quite clearly residing
among us too, albeit on a small scale. Now there are some souls living on
earth in possession of ill-gotten gains, who in their obviously brutish way
throw themselves before the souls of their guardians (whether watch-dogs,
shepherds, or masters of the utmost grandeur) and by wheedling words

and winning entreaties try to persuade them of the truth of the line put about by scoundrels—that they have the right to feather their nest with impunity at mankind's expense. But I suppose our view is that this vice   c we've named—acquisitiveness—is what is called 'disease' when it appears in flesh and blood, and 'plague' when brought by the seasons or at intervals of years; while if it occurs in the state and society, the same vice turns up under yet another name: 'injustice'.

CLINIAS: Certainly.

ATHENIAN: Thus anyone who argues that gods are always indulgent to   d the unjust man and the criminal, provided they're given a share in the loot, must in effect be prepared to say that if wolves, for instance, were to give watch-dogs a small part of their prey, the dogs would be appeased by the gift and turn a blind eye to the plundering of the flock. Isn't this what people are really suggesting when they say that gods can be squared?

CLINIAS: It certainly is.

ATHENIAN: So consider all those guardians we instanced a moment ago. Can one compare gods to any of them, without making oneself ridiculous? What about steersmen who are turned from their course 'by libations and   e burnt offerings',[8] and wreck both the ship and its crew?

CLINIAS: Of course not.

ATHENIAN: And presumably they are not to be compared to a charioteer lined up at the starting point who has been bribed by a gift to throw the race and let others win.

CLINIAS: No sir, to describe the gods like that would be a scandalous comparison.

ATHENIAN: Nor, of course, do they stand comparison with generals or doctors or farmers, or herdsmen, or dogs beguiled by wolves.

CLINIAS: What blasphemy! The very idea!   907

ATHENIAN: Now aren't all the gods the most supreme guardians of all, and don't they look after our supreme interests?

CLINIAS: Very much so.

ATHENIAN: So are we really going to say that these guardians of the most valuable interests, distinguished as they are for their personal skill in guarding, are inferior to dogs, or the mere man in the street, who'll never abandon justice, in spite of the gifts that the unjust immorally press upon him?

CLINIAS: Of course not. That's an intolerable thing to say. There's no sort   b of impiety that men won't commit, but anyone who persists in this doctrine bids fair to be condemned—and with every justification—as the worst and most impious of the impious.

ATHENIAN: Can we now say that our three theses—that the gods exist, that they are concerned for us, and that they are absolutely above being corrupted into flouting justice—have been adequately proved?

CLINIAS: Certainly, and we endorse these arguments of yours.

8. *Iliad* ix.500.

c　ATHENIAN: Still, I fancy that being so anxious to get the better of these scoundrels, we've put our case rather polemically. But what prompted this desire to come out on top, my dear Clinias, was a fear that the rogues should think that victory in argument was a license to do as they please and act on any and every theological belief they happen to hold. Hence our anxiety to speak with some force. However, if we've made even a small contribution to persuading those fellows to hate themselves and

d　cherish the opposite kind of character, then this preface of ours to the law of impiety will have been well worth composing.

CLINIAS: Well, there is that hope. But even without those results, the lawgiver will not be at fault for having discussed such a topic.

ATHENIAN: Now then, after the preface we'll have a form of words that convey the purpose of our laws—a general promulgation to all the ungodly that they should abandon their present habits in favor of a life of piety. Then in cases of disobedience the following law of impiety should apply:

e　Anyone who comes across a case of impiety of word or deed should go to the aid of the law by alerting the authorities. The first officials to be notified should bring the matter, in due legal form, before the court appointed to try this category of case.

> 58. If an official who hears of the incident fails to perform this duty, *he must* himself be liable to a charge of impiety at the hands of anyone who wishes to champion the cause of the laws.

When verdicts of 'guilty' are returned, the court is to assess a separate penalty for each impious act of each offender. Imprisonment is to apply

908　in all cases. (The state will have three prisons: (1) a public one near the market-place for the general run of offenders, where large numbers may be kept in safe custody, (2) one called the 'reform center', near the place where the Nocturnal Council[9] assembles, and (3) another in the heart of the countryside, in a solitary spot where the terrain is at its wildest; and the title of this prison is somehow to convey the notion of 'punishment'.)

Now since impiety has three causes, which we've already described,

b　and each is divided into two kinds, there will be six categories of religious offenders worth distinguishing; and the punishment imposed on each should vary in kind and degree. Consider first a complete atheist: he may have a naturally just character and be the sort of person who hates scoundrels, and because of his loathing of injustice is not tempted to commit it; he may flee the unjust and feel fondness for the just. Alterna-

c　tively, besides believing that all things are 'empty of' gods, he may be a prey to an uncontrollable urge to experience pleasure and avoid pain, and he may have a retentive memory and be capable of shrewd insights. Both these people suffer from a common failing, atheism, but in terms of the harm they do to others the former is much less dangerous than the latter.

9. See 961 ff.

The former will talk with a complete lack of inhibition about gods and sacrifices and oaths, and by poking fun at other people will probably, if he continues unpunished, make converts to his own views. The latter holds the same opinions but has what are called 'natural gifts': full of cunning d and guile, he's the sort of fellow who'll make a diviner and go in for all sorts of legerdemain; sometimes he'll turn into a dictator or a demagogue or a general, or a plotter in secret rites; and he's the man who invents the tricks of the so-called 'sophists'. So there can be many different types of atheist, but for the purpose of legislation they need to be divided into two e groups. The dissembling atheist deserves to die for his sins not just once or twice but many times, whereas the other kind needs simply admonition combined with incarceration. The idea that gods take no notice of the world similarly produces two more categories, and the belief that they can be squared another two. So much for our distinctions.

59. (a) Those who have simply fallen victim to foolishness and who do not have a bad character and disposition
should be sent to the reform center by the judge in accordance with the 909 law for a term of not less than five years, and during this period no citizen must come into contact with them except the members of the Nocturnal Council, who should pay visits to admonish them and ensure their spiritual salvation.
(b) When his imprisonment is over, a prisoner who appears to be enjoying mental health should go and live with sensible people; but if appearances turn out to have been deceptive, and he is reconvicted on a similar charge, *he should be* punished by death.

There are others, however, who in addition to not recognizing the existence of gods, or believing they are unconcerned about the world or can be bought off, become subhuman. They take everybody for fools, and many a man they delude during his life; and then by saying after his death that b they can conjure up his spirit, and by promising to influence the gods through the alleged magic powers of sacrifices and prayers and charms, they try to wreck completely whole homes and states for filthy lucre.

60. If one of these people is found guilty,
the court must sentence him to imprisonment as prescribed by law in the prison in the center of the country; no free man is to visit him at c any time, and slaves must hand him his ration of food fixed by the Guardians of the Laws. When he dies the body must be cast out over the borders of the state unburied.

61. If any free man lends a hand in burying him,
he must be liable to a charge of impiety at the hands of anyone who cares to prosecute.
   If the prisoner leaves children suitable for citizenship, the guardians of orphans must look after them too, from the day of their father's conviction, no less than ordinary orphans. d

All these offenders must be covered by one general law, which by forbidding illegal religious practices will cause most of them to sin less in word and deed against religion, and which in particular will do something to enlighten them. The following comprehensive law should be enacted to deal with all these cases.

No one is to possess a shrine in his own private home. When a man takes it into his head to offer sacrifice, he is to go to the public shrines in order to do so, and he should hand over his offerings to the priests and priestesses responsible for consecrating them; then he, and anyone else he may wish to participate, should join in the prayers. The grounds for these stipulations are as follows. To establish gods and temples is not easy; it's a job that needs to be very carefully pondered if it is to be done properly. Yet look at what people usually do—all women in particular, invalids of every sort, men in danger or any kind of distress, or conversely when they have just won a measure of prosperity: they dedicate the first thing that comes to hand, they swear to offer sacrifice, and promise to found shrines for gods and spirits and children of gods. And the terror they feel when they see apparitions, either in dreams or awake—a terror which recurs later when they recollect a whole series of visions—drives them to seek a remedy for each individually, with the result that on open spaces or any other spot where such an incident has occurred they found the altars and shrines that fill every home and village. The law now stated must be observed not only for all these reasons but also in order to deter the impious from managing to conduct these activities too in secret, by establishing shrines and altars in private houses, calculating to win the favor of the gods on the quiet by sacrifices and prayers. This would make their wickedness infinitely worse, and bring the reproach of heaven both on themselves and on the virtuous people who tolerate them, so that, by a sort of rough justice, the whole state would catch the infection of their impiety. Still, God won't blame the legislator, because this is the law to be enacted:

The possession of shrines in private houses is forbidden. If a man is proved to possess and worship at shrines other than the public ones, and the injustice committed is not an act of serious impiety (whether the possessor is a man or a woman), anyone who notices the fact must lay information before the Guardians of the Laws, who should give orders for the removal of the private shrines to public temples.

62. (a) If the culprits disobey,
they must be punished until they carry out the removal.
(b) But if a man is proved guilty of a serious act of impiety typical of an adult, and not just the peccadillo of a child, either by establishing a shrine on private land or by sacrificing on public land to gods not included in the pantheon of the state,
he must be punished by death for sacrificing with impure hands.

The Guardians of the Laws, after deciding whether the crime was a childish peccadillo or not, must then take the matter straight to court, and exact from the culprits the penalty for their impiety.

Book XI

ATHENIAN: The next subject needing to be reduced to due order will be   913
our transactions with each other. I suppose something like this will serve
as a general rule. Ideally, no one should touch my property or tamper
with it, unless I have given him some sort of permission; and if I am
sensible I shall treat the property of others with the same respect.

Let's take as our first example treasure which someone who was not
one of my ancestors stored away for himself and his family. I should never
pray to the gods to come across such a thing; and if I do, I must not disturb   b
it nor tell the diviners, as they are called, who (I shall find) can always
invent some reason for advising one to remove something deposited in
the ground. The financial benefit I'd get from removing it could never
rival what I'd gain by way of virtue and moral rectitude by leaving it
alone; by preferring to have justice in my soul rather than money in my
pocket, I'd get—treasure for treasure—the better bargain, and for a better
part of myself, too.

'Hands off immovables'[1] is aptly applied to a great many situations, and
this is one of them. And we should put our trust in the traditional view   c
of such conduct—that it injures our descendants. Suppose a man takes no
thought for his children and becomes indifferent to the legislator, and
removes what neither he himself nor his father nor any of his fathers before
him deposited, without the consent of the depositor; suppose he thus
undermines the finest law there is, that simple rule of thumb, formulated
as it was by a man of great nobility,[2] 'Don't pick up what you didn't put
down'—well, when a man treats these *two* legislators[3] so contemptuously   d
and picks up something he had not put down (and sometimes no bagatelle,
either, but a huge treasure trove), what penalty should he suffer? God
knows the penalty of heaven; but the first person to notice such an occurrence in the city should report it to the City-Wardens; if somewhere in
the city's market, to the Market-Wardens; and if in some place in the
country, he should inform the Country-Wardens and their Chiefs. On   914
receiving the information the state should send to Delphi and in submission
to the oracles of the god do whatever he ordains about the objects and
the person who removed them. If the informant is a free man, he should
acquire a reputation for virtue, but

> 63. (a) if a free man fails to inform,
> *he must* get a reputation for vice.

If the informant is a slave, then as a reward he will deservedly be presented
with freedom by the state, which will give[4] his master what he is worth, but

---

1. Cf. 842e and note.
2. Solon.
3. Solon and the Magnesian legislator.
4. Reading *apodidousēs* in a8.

(b) if a slave fails to inform,
he must be punished by death.

b   The natural thing to do next is to apply this same rule to all objects, important or trivial. If a man leaves some piece of his own property somewhere, deliberately or inadvertently, anyone who finds it should let it be, on the assumption that such things are under the protection of the goddess of the wayside, to whom they are consecrated by law.

64. If in defiance of this rule someone picks up an object of no great value and takes it home, and
(a) he is a slave,
he should be soundly beaten by any passer-by who is not less than thirty years of age;
c   (b) if he is a free man,
in addition to being thought ungentlemanly and lawless, he must pay the person who left the article ten times its value.

If one man accuses another of being in possession of some piece of his own property, whether valuable or not, and the accused person admits he has it but denies that it belongs to the complainant, the latter should— if the object has been registered with the authorities according to law— summon the person in possession of it before the authorities, and the
d   possessor must produce it; then if on being presented for inspection it proves to have been recorded in the registers as the property of one of the disputants, the owner must take it and depart; but if it belongs to some other party not present, then whichever disputant furnishes a credit-worthy guarantor should exercise the absent party's right of removal and take the article away on his behalf for delivery into his possession. If on the other hand the article in dispute has not been registered with the authorities, it must be left with the three oldest officials pending settlement of the case;
e   and if it is an animal that is thus kept in safe custody, the loser of the suit must pay the officials for its keep. The officials are to settle the case within three days.
       Anyone who wishes—provided he's in his right mind—may seize his own slave, and (within the permitted limits) treat him as he likes. He may also arrest a runaway slave, in order to stop him escaping, on behalf of a relative or friend. If anyone demands the release of someone who is being taken for a slave and arrested, the captor must let him go, but the releaser must furnish three credit-worthy sureties. On these terms and on no other the man may be released.

65. If a man secures a release except on these conditions, he must be liable to a charge of violence and if convicted,
915   *he must* pay to the captor twice the damages claimed in the suit.

Freedmen too may be arrested if they fail to perform their services to their manumittor, or perform them inadequately. (The services are these: three

times a month a freedman must proceed to the home of his manumittor
and offer to do anything lawful and practicable; and as regards marrying
he must do whatever his former master thinks right.) He must not grow
more wealthy than his manumittor; if he does, the excess must become   b
the property of the master. The freedman must not stay in the state longer
than twenty years, but like the other aliens[5] he must then take all his
property and leave, unless he has gained permission from the authorities
and his manumittor to remain. If a freedman or one of the other aliens
acquires property in excess of the limit allowed the third property-class,[6]
then within thirty days of this event he must pack up and be off, without   c
any right to ask the authorities to extend his stay.

   66. If a freedman disobeys these regulations and is taken to court and
   convicted,
   he must be punished by death and his property confiscated by the state.

Such cases should be tried in the tribal courts, unless the litigants have
previously settled their charges against each other before their neighbors—
that is, judges they have chosen themselves.
   If a man formally seizes as his own any animal or some other piece of   d
property of any other man[7] the person in possession must return it to the
warrantor or donor, provided the latter is suable and solvent, or to the
person who validly transferred it to him by some other procedure. If he
received it from a citizen or a resident alien, he must do so within thirty
days; but if he took delivery from a complete alien, he must return it
within the five months of which the third shall be the month in which the
summer solstice occurs.
   When one person makes an exchange with another by buying or selling,
the transfer must be made by handing over the article in the appointed
part of the market-place (and nowhere else), and by receiving the price   e
on the nail; no payment for delivery later or sale on credit is to be allowed.
If a man exchanges one thing for another in any other place or under any
other arrangement, trusting to the honesty of the other party to the exchange, he must do so on the understanding that when sales are made
other than under the rules now stated the law does not permit him to sue.
(Anyone may collect contributions to clubs on a friendly basis, but if some
disagreement arises over the collection he must do so on the understanding
that in this business no one under any circumstances will be allowed to
go to law.)
   A seller of an article who receives a price of fifty drachmas or more
must be obliged to remain in the state for ten days, and the buyer (in view
of the complaints that people are apt to make in this connection, and so   916

5. See 850a ff.
6. See 744a ff. and 754d ff.
7. Reading *autou* in d1.

that, if necessary, restitution may be made according to law) must be informed of his address. Here are the rules under which legal restitution may be demanded or refused. If someone sells a slave suffering from consumption or stone or strangury or the so-called 'sacred' disease[8] or some other mental or physical complaint that is chronic and difficult to cure and which the ordinary man could not diagnose, and if the purchase was made by a doctor or trainer, or if the facts were pointed out before the time of sale, the buyer shall have no right to return him to the vendor.

b   But if a layman is sold such a slave by a professional, the purchaser may return him within six months, except in the case of the 'sacred' disease, when the period for restitution is to be extended to a year. The case should be heard before a bench of three doctors appointed by joint nomination of the parties, and if the vendor loses he must pay twice the selling price.

c   If a layman sells to a layman there should be a right of restitution and a hearing as in the previous instance, but the loser should pay only the simple price. If the slave is a murderer, and both buyer and seller are aware of the fact, there shall be no right of restitution for the purchase; but if the buyer acted in ignorance he shall have a right of restitution as soon as he realizes the situation, and the case should be tried before the five youngest Guardians of the Laws; if the vendor is judged to have known the facts, he must purify the house of the buyer under the Expounders' rules

d   and pay him three times the price.

Anyone exchanging money for money or for anything else, animate or inanimate, should always give and receive full value as the law directs. Let's do as we did in other parts of our legislation and allow ourselves a preface dealing with the whole range of crimes that arise in this connection.

Everyone should think of adulteration as essentially the same sort of thing as lying and deceit—which in fact people commonly describe as

e   quite respectable. But they are wrong to defend this sort of conduct as 'frequently justified, on appropriate occasions', because what they mean by the 'appropriate' place and occasion they leave vague and indefinite, and their dictum does nothing but harm both to themselves and to others. Now a legislator cannot afford to leave this vague: he must always lay down precise limits, however wide or narrow they may be. So let's define some limits now: a man must tell no lie, commit no deceit, and do no

917   fraud in word or deed when he calls upon the gods, unless he wants to be thoroughly loathed by them—as anyone is who snaps his fingers at them and swears false oaths, or (though they find this less offensive) tells lies in the presence of his superior. Now the 'superiors' of bad men are the good, and of the young their elders (usually)—which means that parents are the superiors of their offspring, men are (of course) the superiors of women and children, and rulers of their subjects. All these people in positions of authority deserve the respect of us all, and the authorities of the state deserve it in particular. This is in fact what prompted these

8. Epilepsy.

remarks. Anyone who is so lacking in respect for men and reverence for   b
the gods as to pull off some swindle of the market-place by swearing oaths
and calling heaven to witness (even though the rules and warnings of the
Market-Wardens stare him in the face), is a liar and a cheat. So in view
of the low level of religious purity and holiness most of us generally
achieve, let me emphasize what a good habit it is to think twice before
taking the names of the gods in vain.

   If any cases of disobedience arise, the following law should be invoked:
the seller of any article in the market must never name two prices for his   c
goods, but only one, and if he doesn't get it, he will (quite rightly) remove
his wares without raising or lowering his price that day; and he must not
push anything he has for sale, or take an oath on its quality.

   67. If a man disobeys these regulations,
   any citizen passing by, provided he is not less than thirty years of age,
   should punish the taker of the oath and beat him with impunity.

   68. If the passer-by ignores these instructions and disobeys them,
   he must be liable to the reproach of having betrayed the laws.

If a man proves to be beyond persuasion by our present address and sells   d
a faulty article, the passer-by who has the knowledge and ability to expose
him should prove his case before the authorities, and, if a slave or resident
alien, may then take the faulty article for himself; a citizen, however, should
dedicate it to the gods of the marketplace.

   69. If a citizen fails to expose the offender,
   he should be pronounced a rogue, as he has cheated the gods.

   70. Anyone discovered selling such adulterated merchandise,
   apart from being deprived of it, must be whipped (one lash for every   e
   drachma of the asking price of the object he was selling), after a herald
   has announced in the market-place the reason why the culprit is going
   to be flogged.

The Market-Wardens and the Guardians of the Laws, having ascertained
from experts the details of the adulterations and malpractices of sellers,
should record in writing rules which specify what vendors must and must
not do; these regulations should then be inscribed on a pillar and displayed
in front of the Market-Wardens' office for the information of those who   918
transact business in the market-place. (As for the City-Wardens, we have
already given an adequate description of their duties, but if it seems some
additional rules are needed, the wardens should consult the Guardians of
the Laws, write out what they think missing, and record both the new
and the old rules of their office on a pillar in front of their quarters.)

   Hard on the heels of tricks of adulteration come the practices of retail
trade. First we should give a word of advice on the whole subject, then
lay down legislation for it. The natural function in the state of retail trading   b
in general is not to do harm, but quite the opposite. When goods of any

kind are distributed disproportionately and unequally, anyone who makes
the distribution equal and even cannot fail to do good. It needs to be stated
that this redistribution, in which money too plays an effective role, is
precisely the purpose the trader is meant to serve. Hired laborers, inn-
keepers and other workmen of varying degrees of respectability all perform

c   the function of satisfying the needs of the community by ensuring an even
distribution of goods. Why then is trading thought to be such a low and
disreputable occupation? Why has it come to be so abused? Let's see if
we can discover the reason, so that we can use our legislation to reform
at any rate some branches of commerce, even if not the whole institution.
This looks like an important task that calls for exceptional resource.

CLINIAS: How do you mean?

ATHENIAN: My dear Clinias, only a small part of mankind—a few highly-
d   educated men of rare natural talent—is able to steel itself to moderation
when assailed by various needs and desires; given the chance to get a lot
of money, it's a rare bird that's sober enough to prefer a modest competence
to wealth. Most people's inclinations are at the opposite pole: their demands
are always violent demands, and they brush aside the opportunity of
modest gain in favor of insatiable profiteering. That's why all branches of
retailing, trade and inn-keeping suffer from abuse and extreme unpopular-
e   ity. Now here's something I'm determined to mention, ludicrous though
it is; it'll never happen, and Heaven help us if it did. But just picture to
yourselves some eminently virtuous men forced for a time to go in for
inn-keeping or retailing or some similar occupation, or some eminently
virtuous women similarly forced by some stroke of fate to take up that
kind of life. We'd soon realize how desirable and pleasing each of these
trades really is, and if they were carried on according to honest standards
we'd value them all as highly as we do our mother or our nurse. But what
happens? A man goes off to some remote point on a road running through
919 the middle of nowhere and sets up his establishment to sell provisions;
he receives the weary traveler with welcome lodging—peace and quiet
for the victim of violent storms, cool refreshment for the sufferer from
stifling heat—but then instead of greeting them as friends and offering
them in addition to his hospitality some gifts as a token of goodwill, he
treats them like so many enemy prisoners that have fallen into his hands,
and holds them up to ransom for a monstrously steep and iniquitous sum.
b   It's these and similar swindles, which are practiced in all branches of the
trade, that have given the occupation of helping the worn-out traveler
such a bad name, and in every case the legislator has to find a remedy.
The old saying is quite right: it's difficult to fight against two enemies,
especially when they are fundamentally different (as with diseases, for
instance, and there are a lot of other examples). Our present battle is a
case in point: it is a battle against two foes, wealth and poverty—wealth
that corrupts our souls by luxury, poverty that drives us by distress into
c   losing all sense of shame. So what remedy for this disease will be open
to an enlightened community? First, it should keep its trading class as

small as possible; second, trade should be made over to a class of people whose corruption will not harm the state unduly; third, some means must be found to prevent those engaging in such activities from slipping too easily into an utterly shameless and small-minded way of life.

d

After these remarks, our law on the subject should run like this, with Heaven's blessing: God is now re-establishing and re-founding Magnesia, and no inhabitant who holds one of the 5040 hearths must ever, willingly or otherwise, become a retailer or a wholesaler, or perform any service whatever for private individuals who are not his equals in status, with the exception of those services that a free man will naturally render to his father and mother and remoter ancestors, and to all free persons older than himself. Of course, it is not easy to lay down in a law precisely what is consistent with the dignity of a free man and what is not, and the point will have to be determined by those who have won distinctions for their aversion to the latter and devotion to the former. Anyone who by some trick goes in for retail trading in a way forbidden to a gentleman should be indicted by anyone who wishes before a court of judges with a high reputation for virtue, on a charge of disgracing his clan.

e

71. If he is judged to be sullying his paternal hearth by following an unworthy calling,
he must be imprisoned for a year and so be taught to refrain from such conduct.

72. If he does not then refrain,
he must be imprisoned for two years, and the period of imprisonment must be doubled indefinitely on each subsequent conviction.

920

Now for a second law: anyone who intends to go in for retail trading must be either a resident alien or a temporary visitor. Thirdly, as a third law, such people must behave with as much virtue and as little vice as possible while they share in the life of the state. To that end, the Guardians of the Laws must not simply be regarded as guardians of those whom it is easy to keep from wickedness and crime thanks to their good birth and education. There are those who do not enjoy such advantages, and need more careful supervision, because they engage in pursuits which are very powerful inducements to vice. So since retail trading is an occupation of great variety and embraces many cognate activities, the Guardians of the Laws must hold a meeting about it, or at any rate about such branches of it as they have concluded are unavoidable and essential to the state, after the others have been eliminated; and just as we ordered in the case of adulteration—a closely connected matter—experts in each branch should be in attendance. The meeting must see what ratio of expenditure to receipts will give the retailer a decent profit, and the ratio arrived at must be recorded in writing, put on display, and then imposed on the various traders by the Market-Wardens, City-Wardens and Country-Wardens.

b

c

Perhaps thus retail trade will benefit the population at large and do minimum harm to those members of society who engage in it.

d   If a man fails to fulfill an agreed contract—unless he had contracted to do something forbidden by law or decree, or gave his consent under some iniquitous pressure, or was involuntarily prevented from fulfilling his contract because of some unlooked-for accident—an action for such an unfulfilled agreement should be brought in the tribal courts, if the parties have not previously been able to reconcile their differences before arbitrators (their neighbors, that is).

The class of craftsmen who have enriched our lives by their arts and skills will have Athena and Hephaestus as its patrons, while Ares and
e   Athena will be patrons of those who protect the products of these craftsmen by skills of a different order—the techniques of defense. (The consecration of this latter class to these gods is perfectly justified, in that both classes are in the continuous service of land and people, the latter by taking the lead in the struggles of war, the former by producing tools and goods in return for pay.) So if they respect their divine ancestors, they will think it a disgrace to break their word in a professional matter.

921   73. If one of the craftsmen culpably fails to complete his work within the stipulated time, out of disrespect for the god from whom he wins his bread, fondly thinking that he can count on the indulgence of the divinity with whom he has some personal relationship,
(a) *first he* will pay a penalty to the god,
(b) *and secondly,* under the provisions of the law applicable to his case, he must owe the price of the works of which he has cheated his employer, and perform his task all over again within the stipulated period, free of charge.

And the law will give the contractor for a work the same advice as it gave
b   a seller, not to take advantage by setting too high a price on his services, but to name their actual value without further ado. The contractor has precisely the same duty, because as a craftsman he knows what the job is worth. In a state of gentlemen a workman must never use his craft, which is at bottom accurate and straightforward, to take 'craft' advantage of laymen, and anyone who is thus imposed upon shall be able to sue the culprit. But if anyone lets a contract to a workman and fails to pay him
c   the price stipulated in a valid legal agreement, and snaps his fingers at those partners in our social framework, Zeus the patron of the state, and Athena, so that his delight at being in pocket wrecks the fundamental bonds of society, then the following law, with the backing of the gods, must reinforce the cohesion of the state:

74. (a) If a man takes delivery of a piece of work and fails to pay for it within the agreed time,
he must be charged double;
(b) if a whole year elapses,

then notwithstanding the rule that loans in general do not bear interest, he must pay an obol per drachma[9] for every month in arrear.   d

Actions in these cases should be brought before the tribal courts.

Now that we have broached the subject of craftsmen in general, we ought in all fairness to glance at those whose job it is to keep us safe in war, such as generals and other experts in military techniques. These persons are just as much craftsmen as ordinary workmen, though of a different kind, so when one of them undertakes some public task, voluntarily or under orders, and performs it well, the law will never tire of praising anyone who pays him the honor he deserves—honor being in effect a   e
military man's pay. But if anyone receives the benefit of some splendid military action and fails to pay that price, the law will censure him. For the benefit of the military, then, let us enact following regulation-cum-commendation, by way of advising rather than compelling the people at large. Those fine men who safeguard the whole state either by exploits of   922
valor or by military expertise must be accorded honor—but honor of the second rank, because the highest honor should be given first and foremost to those who have proved conspicuously conscientious in respecting the written regulations of the good legislator.

ATHENIAN: We've now pretty well completed our provisions for the most important agreements that men make with each other, with the exception of those relating to orphans and the care and attention due to them from their guardians. So now we've more or less provided for the first topic, here's the next thing on which we are obliged to impose some sort of   b
order. All our regulations must start from two basic facts: (a) people at the point of death like to settle their affairs by a will, (b) sometimes, by chance, they die intestate. What a difficult and contentious business it is, Clinias! That's what I had in mind when I said we were 'obliged' to deal with it: to leave it unregulated is quite out of the question. If you allow a will unchallengeable validity whatever condition a man near the end of   c
his life may have been in when he drew it up, he might make any number of mutually inconsistent provisions that contradicted not only the spirit of the laws but also the inclinations of those who survive him, and indeed his own earlier intentions before he set out to make his will. After all, most of us, when we think death is at hand, just go to pieces and can't think straight.

CLINIAS: How do you mean, sir?

ATHENIAN: When a man is about to die, Clinias, he becomes refractory, and keeps harping on a principle that spreads alarm and despondency among legislators.

CLINIAS: How's that?

---

9. I.e., 200 per cent per annum (6 obols = 1 drachma). Cf. 742c for the rule that loans do not bear interest.

ATHENIAN: In his anxiety for complete authority he's apt to express
d   himself with some warmth.

CLINIAS: To what effect?

ATHENIAN: 'Ye gods!' says he, 'it's a fine thing if I'm not going to be
allowed to give—or not give—my own property to anyone I please! Why
shouldn't I give more to one man and less to another depending on whether
they have shown themselves good or bad friends to me? My illnesses,
my old age and all my other various misfortunes have sorted them out
well enough.'

CLINIAS: Well, sir, don't you think that's well said?

e   ATHENIAN: Clinias, my view is that the ancient lawgivers were too easy-
going, and legislated on the basis of a superficial and inadequate appreciation of the human condition.

CLINIAS: How do you mean?

ATHENIAN: My dear fellow, because they feared the line of argument I
have mentioned, they passed the law allowing a man to dispose of his
923 own property in his will exactly as he pleases. But when people have
come to death's door in your state, you and I will make a rather more
appropriate response:

'Friends, you "creatures of a day" in more senses than one, it's difficult
for you in your present circumstances to know the truth about your own
property and also "know yourselves," as the Delphic inscription puts it.
Therefore, I, as legislator, rule that neither you nor this property of yours
b   belongs to yourselves, but to your whole clan, ancestors and descendants
alike; and your clan and its property in turn belong, even more absolutely,
to the state. That being so, I should be reluctant to tolerate someone
worming himself into your good graces when you are smitten with illness
or old age, and wheedling you into making a will that is not for the best.
I shall legislate with a view to nothing except the interest of your clan and
the entire state, relegating (as is only right) that of the individual to second
place. So as you go on your journey, which is the way of all flesh, show
restraint and goodwill towards us: we will look after your affairs for
the future and guard your interests with the utmost care, down to the
c   smallest detail.'

Let that stand by way of preamble and consolation for both the living
and the dying, Clinias. Here's the actual law:

Anyone who settles his property by writing a will should first, if he has
had children, write down the name of that son who in his opinion deserves
to be his heir, and he should also record precisely which, if any, of his
other children he offers for adoption by someone else. If, however, he is still
d   left with one of his sons not adopted into an estate, who will presumably be
dispatched by law to a colony,[10] the father should be permitted to present
him with as much of his property as he likes, apart from the family estate
and all its associated equipment; and if there is more than one son in that

10. Cf. 740e.

position, his father is to distribute his property among them—excluding the estate—in whatever proportion he pleases. But he should not distribute any part of his property to any son who has a home. He should treat a daughter analogously: if she is promised in marriage, he should not let her share his goods, but only if she is not promised. If subsequent to the will one of the sons or daughters is discovered to have come into possession of an estate in Magnesia, he or she should abandon his or her legacy to the testator's heir. If the testator is leaving no male offspring but only female, he should select whichever of his daughters he pleases and in his will provide someone to be a husband for her and a son for himself, and record this person as his heir. And here's another disaster a man should allow for when drawing up his will: if his son (his own or adopted) dies in infancy before he can reach man's estate, the will should specify in writing a child who is to take his place—and who, one hopes, will have better luck. When a man who has no children at all writes a will, he may reserve one tenth of his acquired property and give it to anyone he wishes; all the rest he should leave to his adopted heir, so that in making him his son with the blessing of the law he gains his goodwill by treating him fairly. When a man's children need guardians, and the deceased has made a will and stated in writing the number of guardians he wants his children to have and who they should be (provided they are ready and willing to undertake the office), the choice of guardians put on record in this way should be binding. But if a man dies absolutely intestate or without selecting guardians, then the two nearest relatives on the father's side and the two nearest on the mother's, together with one of the deceased's friends, must be authorized to act as guardians; and the Guardians of the Laws should appoint them for any orphan who stands in such need. Everything to do with guardianship and orphans should be the concern of the fifteen eldest Guardians of the Laws, who should divide themselves by seniority into groups of three, one group to act one year and another the next, until the five terms of office have been completed in rotation; and so far as possible there should be no gaps in the sequence.

When a man dies absolutely intestate and leaves children in need of guardians, these same laws must be brought into operation to relieve their distress. But if he meets with some unforeseen accident and leaves just daughters, he must forgive the lawgiver if he arranges the giving of them in marriage with an eye on only two out of three possible considerations: close kinship, and the security of the estate. The third point, which a father would have taken into account—namely to select from among the entire citizen body someone whose character and habits qualify him to be his own son and his daughter's bridegroom—these considerations, I say, will have to be passed over, because it's impracticable to weigh them. So here's how the best law we can manage in such a field should run. If a man fails to make a will, and leaves only daughters, then on his death (a) a brother on his father's side (or, if without an estate of his own, a brother on his mother's side) should take the daughter and the estate of the deceased.

e

924

b

c

d

e

(b) If there is a brother's son available, but no brother, then if the parties are of a similar age the same procedure is to apply. In the absence of all these, (c) a sister's son is to benefit under the same regulations. (d) Next in line is to be the brother of the deceased's father, next (e) that brother's son, and finally (f) the son of the sister of the deceased's father. And in all cases where a man leaves only female offspring, the succession is to

925 pass through the family according to the same rules of kinship, through brothers and brothers' and sisters' sons, the males in any one generation always taking precedence over the females. As for age, the assessor must determine the propriety or otherwise of the marriage by inspection, viewing the males naked and the females stripped down to the navel. If the family suffers from such a dearth of relatives that not even a grandson either of the deceased's brother or of the son of the deceased's grandfather exists, then in consultation with her guardians the girl may single out of her own free choice any other citizen, provided he does not object, who

b should then become the deceased's heir and the daughter's bridegroom. However, 'flexibility above all': sometimes suitable candidates from within the state itself may be in unusually short supply, so if a girl is hard put to it to find a husband among her compatriots, and has in view someone who has been dispatched to a colony whom she would like to inherit her father's property, then if the man is related to her, he should enter into the estate under the provisions of the law; if he is not of her clan, then provided there are no near kin living in the state, he shall be entitled by

c virtue of the choice of the daughter of the deceased and that of her guardians to marry her and return to his homeland to take over the establishment of the intestate father.

When a man dies intestate and leaves neither male nor female issue, the situation should in general be met by the foregoing law, and a man and a woman from the clan should 'go in harness' and enter into the deserted establishment with full title to the estate. The order of precedence

d on the female side is to be: (a) the deceased's sister, (b) his brother's daughter, (c) the sister's son, (d) the sister of the deceased's father, (e) the daughter of the father's brother, and (f) the daughter of the father's sister. A woman from this list should set up home with a man from the other list according to the degrees of kinship and the demands of religion[11] for which we made provision earlier.

But let's not forget the severity of such laws. It can sometimes be hard for a near relative of the deceased to be instructed to marry his kinswoman, by a law that to all appearances takes no account of the thousands of social

e difficulties that deter people from obeying such instructions in a willing spirit, so that they invariably prefer to put up with anything rather than comply—I mean difficulties like physical or mental illnesses or defects in the man or woman one is told to marry. I dare say some people imagine the lawgiver is not bothered about these things at all, but they're wrong.

11. See 741a–e.

So in the interests of the lawgiver and those for whom he legislates, let's compose a sort of impartial preamble begging those who are subject to the legislator's orders to forgive him if in his concern for the common good he finds it hardly possible to cope with the personal inconvenience   926 experienced by individuals; and the people for whom the lawgiver's regulations are intended should also be forgiven for their occasional understandable inability to carry out the orders which, in all ignorance, he gives them.

CLINIAS: Well then, sir, what would be the most reasonable way of dealing with such cases?

ATHENIAN: It is essential, Clinias, to choose people to arbitrate between laws of that sort and the persons affected by their provisions.

CLINIAS: How do you mean?

ATHENIAN: Sometimes a nephew with a wealthy father might be reluctant to take his uncle's daughter because he fancies his chances and is bent on   b making a better marriage; in another case a man would have no choice but to disobey the law because the instructions devised by the lawgiver would lead to untold trouble—as for instance if they tried to compel him to marry someone suffering from lunacy or some other terrible physical or mental defect that would make the life of the partner not worth living. This policy should be embodied in a law with the following provisions:

If in practice people attack the established laws about wills on any point   c whatever, but especially where a marriage is concerned, and swear that if the legislator were alive and present in person he would never have forced them to either of the courses to which they are in fact being forced (to marry this man or that woman), but one of the relatives or a guardian takes the opposite line, then we must remember that the fifteen Guardians of the Laws have been bequeathed to orphan boys and girls by the legislator to act as their fathers and arbitrate on their behalf; so litigants on any of these matters must go to them to get disputes settled, and carry out their   d decisions as binding. But if a litigant believes that this is too great an authority to be vested in the Guardians of the Laws, he should take them before the court of the Select Judges and get a decision on the points at issue.

75. If he loses the day,
the lawgiver should visit him with censure and disgrace, a punishment which any sensible person will regard as more severe than a huge fine.

The effect of this will be to give our orphan children a sort of second birth.   e We have already described the training and education they should all receive after their first; after this second and parentless birth we have to see that these children who have had the ill luck to be bereaved and made orphans are to be pitied as little as possible for their misfortune. In the first place, the Guardians of the Laws—substitute parents at least as good as the original ones—should lay down rules for them; in particular, we instruct the three Guardians on duty for the year to look after them as though they were their own children; and for the guidance of these officials and the guardians we shall compose a suitable preamble on the education

927   of orphans. And luckily enough, I fancy, we have described already how after death the souls of the departed enjoy certain powers which they use to take an interest in human affairs.[12] The stories which tell of these things are true, but long, so one should trust to the ancient and widely disseminated common traditions on the point, and also take the legislator's word for it that the doctrine is true—unless, of course, one believes them to be arrant fools. Now if this is really the way of things, a guardian should

b   fear, in the first place, the gods above, who are aware how deprived orphans are, and secondly the souls of the departed, whose natural instinct is to watch with particular care over their own children, showing benevolence to people who respect them and hostility to those who treat them badly. And he should also fear the reactions of those who, full of years and honor, are still living, because in a state which thrives under good

c   laws their grandchildren will show them glad and tender affection, and old men have sharp eyes and ears for such things: if you do the right thing by an orphan, they'll be kind to you, whereas they'll soon show you their displeasure if you take advantage of an orphan's exposed position, because they regard orphans as a supreme and sacred trust. A guardian or official with even the slightest sense has a duty to give close attention to all these warnings, and take great care over the training and education of orphans, helping them in every possible way, just as if he were contributing to the good of his own self and family.

    A man who complies with the preface to the law and refrains from any ill-treatment of an orphan will be spared first-hand experience of the

d   legislator's fury against such actions, but

> 76. if a man refuses to comply, and harms a child deprived of its father or mother,
>
> *he must* pay double the damages that he would have to pay for a crime committed against a child with both parents living.

But do we really *need* precise rules to control a guardian's treatment of an orphan, and an official's supervision of a guardian? They already possess a pattern of how to bring up free-born children, in the education they themselves give up their own, and in the way they manage their private

e   possessions—and of course the rules they have to guide them on those matters are pretty exact. If they were not, it would be reasonable to lay down rules of guardianship as a special and separate category, and make an orphan's life different from that of ordinary children by working out a detailed régime of its own. But in fact in our state being an orphan doesn't differ very much from living under one's own father, although in

928   public esteem, and the amount of attention the children get, orphanhood is usually much less desirable. That is why in dealing with this topic— rules about orphans—the law has gone to such lengths in encouraging

---

12. See 865d–e.

and threatening. And here's the sort of threat that will come in very handy indeed. Anyone acting as a guardian of a boy or girl, and any Guardian of the Laws who supervises that guardian by virtue of being appointed to control him, must show this child who has had the misfortune of bereavement no less affection than his own children, and be just as zealously concerned for his ward's property as he is for his own—more so, in fact; and everyone who acts as a guardian will have just that one law to observe   b
on the subject of orphans. But

77. if this law is contravened in such respects,
(a) *a guardian* should be punished by his official,
(b) *an official* should be summoned before the court of Select Judges by the guardian and punished by a fine of twice the damages as estimated by the court.

If a guardian is suspected by the relatives or indeed by any other citizen of neglect or malpractice, he should be summoned before the same court.

78. *He must* be fined four times the sum he is found to have taken, half   c
the fine going to the child and half to the successful prosecutor.

If once he has grown up an orphan concludes that he was badly treated by his guardian, he may bring a suit for incompetent guardianship, provided he does so within five years of its expiry.

79. (a) If a guardian is found guilty,
the court is to estimate what he is to suffer or pay;
(b) if an official is found guilty of injuring the orphan
    (i) through negligence,
the court must assess how much he is to pay to the child;   d
    (ii) by criminal conduct,
then in addition to paying the sum assessed, he must be ejected from the office of Guardian of the Laws,

and the government must supply the state and country with a fresh Guardian of the Laws to take his place.

The bitterness with which fathers quarrel with their children and children with their fathers is often excessive. A father is apt to think that the legislator ought to give him legal authority, if he wishes, to make a public proclamation through a herald that under the provisions of the law his   e
son is his son no longer; for their part, sons believe that if they have a father whose suffering from disease or old age has become a disgrace, they are entitled to prosecute him on a charge of lunacy. Such disputes are usually found where men's characters are irredeemably corrupt, because when the corruption is confined to one party—as when the son is corrupt but not the father, or the other way round—the bad feeling is not sufficient to lead to trouble. Now in any other state a child repudiated by his father would not necessarily find himself a stateless person, but in the case of Magnesia, to which these laws will apply, a man disowned by his

929   father will be obliged to migrate to another country, because the 5040 homes
      cannot be increased even by one. Consequently before this punishment can
      be legally inflicted on him, he must be repudiated not only by his father
      but by the entire clan. Procedure in such cases is to be governed by
      some such law as this: anyone who has the extreme misfortune to want—
      justifiably or not—to expel from the clan the child he has fathered and
      reared, must not be allowed to do so casually and on the spur of the
  b   moment. First of all he must assemble all the relatives on his own side
      and all the relatives of the son on the mother's side, as far as cousins in
      each case, and accuse his son before them, explaining why he deserves to
      be drummed out of the clan by its united action. The son shall have the
      right of reply, to argue that none of these penalties is called for. If the
      father carries his point, and wins the vote of more than half the relatives
  c   (he himself and the mother and the accused son being excluded from the
      voting, as well as those males and females who are not yet of adult age),
      then by this procedure and on these terms he shall be entitled to repudiate
      his son, but in no other way whatever. If some other citizen wishes to
      adopt the repudiated son, no law is to stop him (a young man's character
      is by nature bound to change frequently enough in the course of his life),
      but if after ten years no one has been moved to adopt the disowned person,
  d   the supervisors of surplus children intended for the colony[13] must take
      him too under their wing so that he may be suitably established in the
      same colony as the others.
          Now suppose illness or old age or a cantankerous temper or all three
      make a man more wayward than old men usually are, unbeknown to all
      except his immediate circle; and suppose he squanders the family resources
      on the grounds that he can do as he likes with his own property, so that
      his son is driven to distraction but hesitates to bring a charge of lunacy.
  e   This is the law the son must observe. First of all he must go to the eldest
      Guardians of the Laws and explain his father's misfortune, and they, after
      due investigation, must advise him whether to bring the charge or not. If
      they advise that he should, they must come forward as witnesses for the
      prosecution and plead on his behalf.

          80. If the case is proved,
          the father must lose all authority to manage his own affairs, even in
          trivialities, and be treated like a child for the rest of his days.

          Whenever a man and his wife find it impossible to get on with each other
      because of an unfortunate incompatibility of temperament, the case must
930   come under the control of ten men—middle-aged Guardians of the Laws—
      and ten of the women in charge of marriage, of the same age. Any arrange-
      ments they make which reconcile the couple should stand, but if feelings
      are too exacerbated for that they must do their best to find each some

      13. Cf. 740e.

other congenial partner. It's quite likely that the existing partners are people of rough temper, so one should try to fit them in harness with mates of a more phlegmatic and gentle disposition. And when the quarreling couple have no children or only a few, the procreation of children must be kept in view in the setting up of the new homes; where sufficient children   b
already exist, the divorce and the remarriages should facilitate companionship and mutual help in the evening of life.

If a wife dies and leaves male and female children, we'll lay down a law advising, though not compelling, the husband to bring up his existing children without importing a stepmother; but if there are no children, he must be obliged to remarry so as to beget sufficient children for his home and for the state. If the husband dies, leaving an adequate number of   c
children, their mother should remain in her position and bring them up; but if it is judged that she is too young to live unmarried without injuring her health, her relatives should report the facts to the women in charge of marriages and do whatever seems advisable to both sides; and if there have been no children born as yet, they should bear that in mind too. (The minimum acceptable number of children is to be fixed by law as one of each sex.)   d

Whenever there is no dispute about the parentage of a child, but a ruling is required as to which parent it should follow, the offspring of intercourse between a slave woman and a slave or a free man or a freedman should become the absolute property of the woman's owner; if a free woman has intercourse with a slave, the issue should belong to his master. If a free man has a child by his own slave woman, or a free woman by her own slave, and the facts are crystal clear, the female officials are to send the   e
free woman's child along with its father to another country, and the Guardians of the Laws must similarly send away the free man's child with its mother.

No god or any man with his wits about him will ever advise anyone to neglect his parents. On the contrary, we should be quick to appreciate how very relevant the following preface on the subject of worshipping gods will be to the respect or disrespect in which we hold our father and mother.

Time-honored cult observances all over the world fall into two categories. Man exalts some of the gods because he can see them with his own eyes,   931
others he represents, by setting up statues of them, and believes that his worship of these inanimate 'gods' ensures him the abundant gratitude and benevolence of their real and living counterparts. This means that no one who has living in his house his father or mother, or their mothers and fathers, treasures old and frail, must ever forget that so long as he possesses such a 'shrine' at his hearth and looks after it properly, no other objects of worship will ever do him as much good.

CLINIAS: What do you mean by 'properly'?   b

ATHENIAN: I'll tell you. After all, my friends, such themes are worth a hearing.

CLINIAS: Tell us, then.

ATHENIAN: Our version of the story of Oedipus is that when he was insulted by his sons he called down a curse on them—and you know how people have never stopped relating how the gods heard and answered his prayer. And Amyntor fell into a rage with his son Phoenix and cursed him; Theseus did the same to Hippolytus, and there are thousands of
c similar cases, which all go to show that the gods take the parents' side against the children: no man, you'll find, can curse anyone as effectively as a parent can curse his child; and that's absolutely right. So if it is true that the gods listen to the prayers of fathers or mothers who have been wantonly insulted by their children, isn't it reasonable to suppose that when by contrast the respect we show our parents delights them so much that they pray hard to heaven for a blessing on their children, the gods will be just as ready to listen as before, and grant us it? If not, they'd be conferring blessings unjustly—which we maintain is a peculiarly inappro-
d priate thing for a god to do.

CLINIAS: Very much so.

ATHENIAN: So as we said just now, we must reckon that the most precious object of worship a man can have is his father or grandfather, weak with age, or his mother in a similar condition, because when he honors and respects them God is delighted—if he weren't, he wouldn't listen to their prayers. These 'living shrines', in the shape of our forefathers, affect us
e far more wonderfully than lifeless ones, because when we look after them they invariably join their prayers to ours, whereas if we insult them, they oppose us. As ordinary statues do neither of these things, a man who treats his father and grandfather and so on as they deserve will have objects of worship that are much more effective than any others in winning him the favor of heaven.

CLINIAS: Excellently put.

ATHENIAN: Anyone with his wits about him holds the prayers of his parents in fear and respect, knowing that the cases in which such prayers have been brought to pass have been many and frequent. This being the
932 way of things, a good man will regard his elderly forebears as a veritable god-send, right up till they breathe their last; and when they pass on, they will be sorely missed by the next generation,[14] and be a terror to the wicked. Let everyone be convinced by this argument and do their parents all the honor enjoined by law.

But if even so a man gets the reputation of being deaf to such prefaces, then the right law to pass to deal with him will run as follows.
b If anyone in this state of ours looks after his parents less diligently than he should and fails to carry out their wishes in all respects with more indulgence than he shows to those of his sons and descendants in general, and indeed to his own desires too, the neglected parent must report the fact, either in person or by messenger, to the three most senior Guardians

14. Reading *neois* in a3.

of the Laws and three of the women in charge of marriages. These officials must take the matter in hand, and provided the offender is still a young man under the age of thirty, chastise him with a whipping and imprisonment. (In   c
the case of a woman, the same chastisement may be inflicted until she is forty.) Older persons, if they persist in neglecting (and perhaps actually ill-treating) their parents, should be summoned before a court consisting of the 101 most elderly citizens of the state.

81. If a man is found guilty,
the court is to assess what penalty or fine is to be exacted, and absolutely no fine or penalty that a man can pay must be excluded from consideration.

If ill-treatment prevents a parent from complaining, any free man who   d
discovers the situation should alert the authorities.

82. If he does not,
he must be regarded as a scoundrel and be liable to a suit for damage at the hands of anyone who wishes.

If the informant is a slave, he should be given his freedom; if he belongs to the criminal or his victim, he must be released by the authorities; and if he belongs to some other citizen, the public treasury is to see that the owner is reimbursed. Official action must be taken to stop anyone injuring him in revenge for giving information.

We have already dealt with *fatal* injuries inflicted by the use of drugs,   e
but we have not yet discussed any of the less harmful cases of voluntary and premeditated injury, inflicted by giving food or drink or by applying ointments. Full treatment of the question is hindered by the fact that so far as human beings are concerned, poisoning is of two kinds. First there is the sort we have just explicitly mentioned: the injury a body suffers from some physical substance by natural processes. The other kind is a   933
matter of spells and charms and 'enchantments': not only are the victims persuaded that they are being seriously injured by people with magic influence, but even the perpetrators themselves are convinced that it really is in their power to inflict injury by these methods. It is not easy to know the truth about these and similar practices, and even if one were to find out, it would be difficult to convince others; and it is just not worth the   b
effort to try to persuade people whose heads are full of mutual suspicion, that even if they do sometimes catch sight of a molded waxen figure in a doorway or at a junction of three roads or on their parents' grave, they should ignore it every time, because they cannot be sure these things work. All this means that our law about drugs must be a double law, reflecting the two methods by which poisoning may be attempted. But first, by   c
entreaty, exhortation and advice, we'll explain that no such thing should ever be attempted, that one should not alarm and terrify the common man, like an impressionable child, and that legislators and judges should not be put to the necessity of curing men of such fears. We shall point out for

a start that unless the person who tries to use poison happens to be a diviner or soothsayer, he acts in ignorance of how his spells will turn out, and unless he happens to be an expert in medicine, he acts in ignorance of the effect he will have on the body. So the wording of our law about
d   the use of poisons should be as follows:

83. (a) If a doctor poisons a man without doing either him or any member of his household fatal injury, or injures his cattle or bees (fatally or otherwise), and is found guilty on a charge of poisoning,
he must be punished by death.
(b) If the culprit is a layman,
the court is to decide the proper penalty or fine to be inflicted in his case.

84. (a) If a diviner or soothsayer is deemed to be in effect injuring
e   someone, by spells or incantations or charms or any other poison of that kind whatever,[15]
he must die.
(b) If someone with no knowledge of divination is found guilty of this kind of poisoning,[16]
the same procedure is to be followed as with the other laymen [83.(b)]— that is, the court is to decide what it thinks is the appropriate penalty or fine for him to pay.

When one man harms another by theft or violence and the damage is extensive, the indemnity he pays to the injured party should be large, but smaller if the damage is comparatively trivial. The cardinal rule should be that in every case the sum is to vary in proportion to the damage done, so that the loss is made good. And each offender is to pay an additional
934 penalty appropriate to his crime, to encourage him to reform. Thus if a man has been led to do wrong by the folly of someone else, being over-persuaded because of his youth or some similar reason, his penalty should tend to be light; but it is to be heavier when his offense is due to his own folly and inability to control his feelings of pleasure and pain—as when he has fallen victim to cowardice and fear, or some deep-rooted jealousy or lust or fury. This additional penalty is to be inflicted not because of the crime (what's done can't be undone), but for the sake of the future: we
b   hope that the offender himself and those that observe his punishment will either be brought to loathe injustice unreservedly or at any rate recover appreciably from this disastrous disease. All these reasons and considerations make it necessary for the law to aim, like a good archer, at a penalty that will both reflect the magnitude of the crime and fully indemnify the victim. The judge has the same aim, and when he is faced by his legal duty of assessing what penalty or fine the defendant must pay, he must
c   follow closely in the legislator's footsteps; and the latter must turn himself

15. Reading *haistisinoun* in e1.
16. Reading *ōn tēs* in e3.

into a sort of artist and sketch some specimen measures consistent with his written prescriptions. That, Clinias and Megillus, is the job to which we must now devote our best efforts; we have to describe what type of penalty is called for in all categories of theft and violence—granted, of course, that the gods and children of gods are prepared to see us legislate in this field.

Lunatics must not be allowed to appear in public; their relations must keep them in custody in private houses by whatever means they can improvise.   d

85. If they fail to do so,
they must pay a fine: one hundred drachmas for a member of the highest property-class (whether it is a slave or a free man that he fails to keep an eye on), eighty for a member of the second class, sixty for the third, and forty for the lowest.

There are several kinds of madness, brought on by several causes. The cases we have just mentioned are the result of illness, but there are some people with an unfortunate natural irritability, made worse by poor discipline, who in any trivial quarrel will shout their heads off in mutual abuse. Such a thing is highly improper in a well-run state. So this single law   e
should apply to all cases of defamation: no one is to defame anybody. If you are having an argument you should listen to your opponent's case, and put your own to him and the audience, without making any defamatory remarks at all. When men take to damning and cursing each other and to calling one another rude names in the shrill tones of women, these   935
mere words, empty though they are, soon lead to real hatreds and quarrels of the most serious kind. In gratifying his ugly emotion, anger, and in thus disgracefully stoking the fires of his fury, the speaker drives back into primitive savagery a side of his character that was once civilized by education, and such a splenetic life makes him no better than a wild beast; bitter indeed, he finds, are the pleasures of anger. Besides, on such occasions all men are usually quick to resort to ridicule of their opponents, and no one who has indulged that habit has ever acquired the slightest sense of   b
responsibility or remained faithful to many of his principles. That is why no one must ever breathe a word of ridicule in a temple or at a public sacrifice or at the games or in the marketplace or in court or in any public gathering, and the relevant official must always punish such offenses.

86. If he fails to do so,
he must be disqualified from competing for awards of merit, as being a   c
man who disregards the laws and fails to perform the duties imposed upon him by the legislator.

87. If in other localities someone fails to refrain from abusive language, whether he resorts to it first or by way of reply,
the passer-by, provided he is older than the offender, should lend his

support to the law and eject by force this fellow who has shown such indulgence to anger, that bad companion.

88. If the passer-by fails to do so,
he must be liable to the appointed penalty.

The view we are putting forward now is that when a man is embroiled in a slanging-match he is incapable of carrying on the dispute without d trying to make funny remarks, and when such conduct is motivated by anger we censure it. Well then, what does this imply? That we are prepared to tolerate a comedian's eagerness to raise a laugh against people, provided that when he sets about ridiculing our citizens in his comedies, he is not inspired by anger? Or shall we divide comedy into two kinds, according to whether it is *good-natured* or not? Then we could allow the playful e comedian to joke about something, without anger, but forbid, as we've indicated, anyone whatever to do so if he is in deadly earnest and shows animosity. We must certainly insist on this stipulation about anger; but we still have to lay down by law who ought to receive permission for ridicule and who not. No composer of comedies, or of songs or iambic verse, must ever be allowed to ridicule either by description or by impersonation any citizen whatever, with or without rancor. Anyone who disobeys this rule must be ejected from the country that same day by the presidents of the games.

936   89. If the latter fail to take this action,
they must be fined three hundred drachmas, to be dedicated to the god in whose honor the festival is being held.

Those who have earlier[17] been licensed to compose verse against each other should be allowed to poke fun at people, not in savage earnest, but in a playful spirit and without rancor. The distinction between the two kinds must be left to the minister with overall responsibility for the education of the young; an author may put before the public anything the minister approves of, but if it is censored, the author must not perform it to anyone b personally nor be found to have trained someone else to do so, whether a free man or a slave.

90. If he does,
he must get the reputation of being a scoundrel and an enemy of the laws.

It is not the starving *tout court* or the similarly afflicted who deserve sympathy, but the man who in spite of his moderation or some other virtue or progress towards it, nevertheless experiences some misfortune. That being so, it will be a matter for surprise if a virtuous person, whether slave or free, even if the state and society he lives in is run with only average skill, is ever so grossly neglected as to be reduced to abject poverty.

17. See 816e.

So the legislator will be quite safe if he lays down a law running more or less like this. No one is to go begging in the state. Anyone who attempts to do so, and scrounges a living by never-ending importunities, must be expelled from the market by the Market-Wardens, from the city by the City-Wardens, and from the surrounding country conducted by the Country-Wardens across the border, so that the land may rid itself completely of such a creature.

If a slave man or woman damages any piece of someone else's property, then provided the person who suffers the loss was not himself partly to blame because of inexperience or careless conduct, the slave's owner must either make good the damage in full, or hand over the actual offender. But if the owner counter-claims that the prosecution has been brought as a result of the injured person and the culprit putting their heads together to rob him of his slave, he must sue the allegedly injured party on a charge of collusion. If he wins the day, he is to receive twice the value of the slave as assessed by the court.

91. If he loses,
he must both make good the damage and hand over the slave.

92. If a beast of burden or a horse or dog or some other animal damages a piece of a neighbor's property,
its owner is to pay for the damage on the same basis.

If anyone deliberately refuses to appear as a witness, the person who needs his evidence must serve a summons on him; and on being duly summoned the man is to present himself at the trial. If he knows something and is prepared to testify, he should give evidence accordingly; if he claims he knows nothing, he must swear an oath to three gods, Zeus, Apollo and Themis, to the effect that quite definitely he has no information, and thus be dismissed from the proceedings. If a man is summoned to give evidence and fails to answer the summons, he must be liable by law to a suit for damage. No juryman is to vote in a trial in which he has been put up as a witness and given evidence. A free woman is to be allowed to be a witness and to speak in support of a litigant, provided she is over forty years of age, and to bring prosecutions, provided she has no husband; but if she has a husband living, she must be limited to acting as a witness. Slaves (male and female), and children, should be allowed to support a case by giving evidence, but only in a trial for murder and provided a credit-worthy surety is put up to guarantee their appearance at the trial if their evidence is objected to as false. If either disputant claims someone has borne false witness, he should enter an objection to all or part of the testimony before a verdict in the case is decided on. The objections, under the seal of both parties, should be placed in official custody and produced at the trial for perjury. If anyone is convicted twice on this charge, he may not be *compelled* under any law to bear witness again; if he is convicted a third time, he must never be *allowed* to be a witness in the future; and if he does have the face to give testimony on a further occasion after a third conviction, anyone who wishes should report him to the authorities, who should haul him before a court.

93. If he is found guilty,
he must be punished by death.

When a court decides to throw out evidence on the ground that the winning
d side has triumphed because certain witnesses have perjured themselves, and more than half the evidence is condemned, the suit lost on the strength of it should come up for retrial, and after due inquiry a ruling should be given that the false evidence was, or was not, the decisive influence on the verdict; and this ruling, whichever way it goes, will automatically settle the original action.

Although human life is graced by many fine institutions, most of them have their own evil genius, so to speak, which pollutes and corrupts them. Take justice, for instance, which has civilized so much of our behavior:
e how could it fail to be a blessing to human society? And granted justice is a blessing, can advocacy fail to be a blessing too? But valuable though they are, both these institutions have a bad name. There is a certain kind of immoral practice, grandly masquerading as a 'skill', which proceeds on the assumption that a technique exists—itself, in fact—of conducting one's own suits and pleading those of others,[18] which can win the day regardless of the rights and wrongs of the individual case; and that this skill itself
938 and the speeches composed with its help are available free—free, that is, to anyone offering a consideration in return. Now it is absolutely vital that this skill—if it really is a skill, and not just a knack born of casual trial and error—should not be allowed to grow up in our state if we can prevent it. The lawgiver will have nothing to say to those who obey his command that one should either listen to justice and not contradict her, or leave for some other country; but if anyone disobeys him, the law shall pronounce
b as follows: if anyone seems to be trying to misrepresent to the judges where the course of justice lies, and to enter one plea after another in support of either his own or someone else's case, when equity would call a halt, then anyone who wishes should indict him on a charge of perverse pleading or criminal advocacy. He should be tried in the court of select judges and if he is found guilty the court should decide whether it thinks his motive is avarice or pugnacity.

94. (a) If the court believes his motive is pugnacity,
it must determine how long he must refrain from prosecuting anyone or helping someone else to do so.
(b) If the motive appears to be avarice,
c   (i) *a foreigner* must leave the country and never return, on pain of death;

18. Punctuating with the second dash after *autē* in e5 and a comma after *alloi* in e6.

(ii) *a citizen* must die, for letting a love of money become the obsession of his life.

95. If a man is convicted twice of committing such an offense through pugnacity,
he must die.

Book XII

If a man passes himself off as an ambassador or herald of the state and enters into unauthorized negotiations with a foreign power, or, when actually sent on such a mission, delivers a message other than the one with which he was sent—or contrariwise if he is shown to have misreported, in his capacity as an ambassador or herald, the communications which enemy or friendly states have given him, he must be open to prosecution for violating the law by impiety against the pronouncements and instructions of Hermes and Zeus.   941

96. If he is convicted,
the penalty or fine he must pay will have to be assessed.   b

Theft of property is uncivilized, and robbery with violence an act of brazen insolence. The sons of Zeus take no pleasure in fraud and force, and none of them has ever committed either of these crimes. So no one who commits such an offense should be seduced into believing the lies of poets or other story-tellers: the thief or thug mustn't think 'There's no shame in this—after all, the gods do it themselves.' That is neither plausible nor true, and no one who breaks the law by such an act can possibly be a god or child of gods. The lawgiver is in a much better position to understand these things than all the poets in the world. Anyone who is   c
convinced by this doctrine of ours is a happy man, and long may he so continue; but anyone who refuses to listen should have some such law as this to contend with: all theft of public property, great or small, should attract the same punishment. The greed of the pilferer is just as great as any other thief's—it's only his efficiency that's inferior; whereas anyone who makes off with some valuable object he did not deposit indulges his   d
criminal tendencies to the full. In the eyes of the law, the one deserves a lighter penalty than the other not because of the amount of the theft, but because he is probably curable while the other is not. Thus

97. (a) if anyone successfully prosecutes in court a foreigner or slave on a charge of theft of some piece of public property,
a decision must be reached as to the fine or penalty he should pay in view of the fact that he can probably be cured.
(b) If a citizen, in spite of the education he will have enjoyed, is convicted   942
of plundering or attacking his fatherland, whether he is caught in the

act or not,
he must be punished by death, as being virtually beyond cure.

Military service is a subject on which we need to give a great deal of advice and have a large number of regulations. The vital point is that no one, man or woman, must ever be left without someone in charge of him; nobody must get into the habit of acting alone and independently, either in sham fighting

b or the real thing, and in peace and war alike we must give our constant attention and obedience to our leader, submitting to his guidance even in tiny details. When the order is given we should stand, march, exercise, wash, feed, stay awake at night on duty as guards or messengers, and even in the midst of dangers not pursue the enemy or yield without a sign from our

c commander. In short, we must condition ourselves to an instinctive rejection of the very notion of doing anything without our companions; we must live a life in which we never do anything, if possible, except by combined and united action as members of a group. No better or more powerful or efficient weapon exists for ensuring safety and final victory in war, and never will. This is what we must practice in peacetime, right from childhood—the exercise of authority over others and submission to them in turn. Freedom from

d control must be uncompromisingly eliminated from the life of all men, and of all the animals under their domination.

In particular, all choruses should be calculated to encourage prowess in the field, and for the same reason people must learn to put a brave and cheerful face on it when they have to put up with poor food and drink, extreme cold and heat, and rough bedding. Most important, they must not ruin the natural powers of head and feet by wrapping them round with artificial protection, so discouraging the spontaneous growth of the

e cap and shoes that nature provides. When these two extremities are in sound condition they help to keep the whole body at the peak of efficiency, whereas their ruin is its ruin too. The feet are the most willing servants the body has, and the head is the organ of supreme control, the natural seat of all the principal senses of the body.

943 That's the praise of military life that ought, in my view, to ring in a young man's ears. Here are the regulations. When a man is called up, or detailed for some special duty, he is obliged to perform his military service. If he is a coward and fails to present himself, without the permission of his commanders, a prosecution for failure to serve should be brought before the military authorities after return from the field. Such cases must be judged by the soldiers who have fought in the campaign; the various categories (infantry, cavalry and the other branches of the armed forces) should meet separately, infantrymen being brought before infantrymen,

b cavalrymen before cavalrymen, and the others before their own comrades similarly.

98. If a defendant is found guilty,
(a) *he must* in future be debarred from
(i) competing for any kind of military distinction,

(ii) bringing a charge against anyone else for refusing to perform military service, and

(b) *the court* must assess the additional penalty or fine he is to pay.

Afterwards, when the charges of refusal to serve have been decided, the commanders must reconvene each arm of the forces and in the presence of the candidates' fellow soldiers seek decisions on those applying for awards of distinction. Supporting statements by eye-witnesses and other evidence adduced by the candidates must not relate to any previous campaign, but only to the one they have just fought. The prize in each case is to be a wreath of olive, which the winner should take to the temple of whichever god of war he pleases and dedicate it, suitably inscribed, as life-long evidence that the first, second or third prize was awarded to him.

If a man does go on active service, but returns home before the commanders withdraw the troops, he should be prosecuted on a charge of desertion before the same court as is concerned with refusal of service.

99. If he is found guilty,
the same penalties should apply as before [98].

Naturally, everyone who brings a prosecution ought to be very wary of inflicting an unjustified punishment, whether in cold blood or by accident. Justice is said—and well said—to be the daughter of Respect, and both are the natural scourges of falsehood. So in general we must be careful not to offend against justice, and particularly as regards the abandonment of weapons in the field: we mustn't reproach an enforced abandonment in mistake for an ignominious one, and so inflict penalties as undeserved as the victims are undeserving of them. Although it is by no means easy to tell the two cases apart, a rough and ready distinction must be attempted in the legal code. We can explain the point with the help of a story. If Patroclus had pulled round after being carried to his tent without his weapons (as has happened in thousands of other cases)—the weapons which the poet tells us were presented to Peleus by the gods as a dowry when he married Thetis, and which had been taken by Hector—then it would have been open to all the scoundrels of the time to reproach the son of Menoetius for abandoning his arms.[1] Again, sometimes men have lost their weapons because of being thrown down from a height, or when at sea, or when suddenly caught up by a tremendous onrush of water during their struggles in a storm. There are countless similar circumstances one could plausibly adduce to excuse and palliate a disaster that positively invites denigration. So we must do our best to distinguish the more serious and reprehensible disasters from the other kind, and in a rough and ready way the distinction can be expressed by varying our expressions of rebuke. Thus 'he *abandoned* his shield' can sometimes be properly replaced by 'he

c

d

e

944

b

---

1. See *Iliad* xvi fin., xvii.125 ff., xviii.78 ff. In the Trojan war, Patroclus, son of Menoetius and companion of Achilles, while wearing the armor of Achilles' father Peleus, was killed by Hector.

c   *lost* his weapons'. When you are robbed of your shield with some force,
     you have not 'abandoned' it in the same way as if you had thrown it away
     deliberately: the two cases are fundamentally different. The distinction
     should be written into the legal code in the following terms:

     If a man finds the enemy at his heels and instead of turning round and
     defending himself with the weapons he has, deliberately lets them drop
     or throws them away, preferring a coward's life of shame to the glorious
     and blessed death of a hero, then there should certainly be a penalty for
d   losing his weapons by abandonment. But when he has lost his weapons
     in the other way we've described the judge must not fail to take the fact
     into account. It is the criminal you need to punish, to reform him, not
     someone who's simply been unlucky—that's useless. So what will be the
     right penalty when someone has made good his escape by throwing away
     the weapons that could have protected him? Unfortunately, it's beyond
     the power of man to do the opposite of what people say some god did to
     Caeneus of Thessaly—that is, change him from a woman into a man. If
     only we could inflict the reverse transformation, from man to woman, that
e   would be, in a sense, the most appropriate punishment for a man who
     has thrown away his shield. But what we *can* do is to reward him for
     saving his skin by giving him the closest possible approximation to such
     a penalty: we can make him spend the rest of his days in utter safety, so
     that he lives with his ghastly disgrace for as long as possible. Here's the
     law that will deal with such people:

     100. If a man is convicted on a charge of shamefully dropping his weap-
     ons of war;

945 (a) *no general* or any other army officer must employ him as a soldier
     again, or appoint him to any position whatever;
     (b) *and in addition* to being thus permitted, like the natural coward he
     is, to avoid the risks that only real men can run, the guilty man must
     also pay a sum of money: one thousand drachmas if he belongs to the
     highest property-class, five hundred if to the second, three hundred if
b   to the third, and one hundred if to the lowest.[2]

     101. If an officer disobeys and posts the coward again,
     the officer's Scrutineer is to condemn him to pay the same fine: one
     thousand drachmas if he belongs to the highest property-class, five
     hundred if to the second, three hundred if to the third, and one hundred
     if to the fourth.

     Well then, what will be the proper policy for us to adopt on the subject
     of Scrutineers? So far, we simply have a corps of officials, some appointed
     for a single year by the luck of the draw, others chosen from a preliminary
     slate of selected candidates to serve for several years. What if one of them
     proves so inadequate to the dignity and weight of his office that he gets
     'out of true' and does something crooked? Who will be capable of making

     ───────────────────

     2. In Plato's text the regulation called here 100(b) comes *after* 101.

a man like that go straight again? It is desperately difficult to find someone
of high moral standards to exercise authority over the authorities, so to   c
speak, but try we must. So where are our god-like 'straighteners' to be
found? The point is this: a state has many crucial parts that prevent it
from disintegrating, just as a ship has its stays and bracing ropes and a
body its tendons and associated sinews. (Features of this kind are a very
widespread phenomenon, and in spite of the many different names we
give them in different contexts, they are basically the same sort of thing.)
Now the office of Scrutineer is the single most crucial factor determining
whether a state survives or disintegrates. If the Scrutineers are better men   d
than the officials they scrutinize, and display irreproachable impartiality
and integrity, the entire state and country flourishes and prospers. But if
their investigation of the officials is conducted badly, then the sense of
justice that unites all the interests in the state is destroyed, with the result
that all the officials go their different ways and refuse to pull together any
longer; they fragment the state into lots of smaller states by filling it with   e
the party-strife that so speedily wrecks it. That is why it is absolutely vital
that the moral standards of the Scrutineers should be exemplary. So let's
try to produce these officials by some such procedure as this:

   Every year after the summer solstice the entire state should congregate
in a precinct dedicated jointly to Apollo and the Sun, in order to present
to the god three out of their number. Each citizen is to propose that person,   946
apart from himself, whom he believes to be perfect in every way; the
candidate is to be at least fifty years of age. This preliminary list should
be divided into two halves (on the assumption that the total is an even
number; if not, the person with the fewest votes should be excluded before
the division is made), and the half consisting of those with the most votes
should be selected to proceed to the next stage after the other half with
fewer votes have been eliminated. If some names receive the same number
of votes, so that the selected candidates are too numerous, the excess
should be removed by eliminating the youngest candidates. The selected
candidates that remain should be voted for again until only three are left,   b
each with a different number of votes. If two of them, or all three, attract
equal support, then the decision should be left to chance and the gods of
good luck: the first, second and third choices must be determined by lot,
crowned with olive and given the rewards of their success. Next, a public
proclamation must be made to the effect that the state of the Magnesians,
now by the grace of God securely re-established, presents to the Sun-god
her three best men; and these, her choicest fruits, in accordance with the   c
law of old, she consecrates for the term of their judicial office as a joint
gift to Apollo and the Sun. In the first year twelve such Scrutineers are to
be appointed, each to retain office till the age of seventy-five; thereafter
three more are to be added every year.

   The Scrutineers are to divide all the officials into twelve groups and
look into their conduct by making all such inquiries as are consistent with
the dignity of a gentleman. During their period of office as Scrutineers
they are to live in the precinct of Apollo and the Sun where they were   d

elected. When they have sat in judgment, either privately and individually, or in association with colleagues, on those at the end of their term of office in the service of the state, they must make known, by posting written notice in the market-place, what penalty or fine in their opinion each official ought to pay. Any official who refuses to admit that he has been judged impartially should haul the Scrutineers before the Select Judges, and if he is deemed innocent of the accusations he should accuse the
e   Scrutineers themselves, if he so wishes. But

102. If he is convicted, and
(a) the Scrutineers had decided on death as his penalty,
he must die (a penalty which in the nature of the case cannot be increased); but
(b) if his penalty is one that it is possible to double,
then double he must pay.

Now we ought to hear about the scrutiny of the Scrutineers themselves. What will it be, and how will it be organized?
947   During their lifetime these men, whom the whole state has thought fit to dignify with the highest honors, should sit in the front seat at all the festivals; moreover, when the Greeks assemble to perform sacrifices or see spectacles together, or congregate for other sacred purposes, the leaders of the delegations sent by the state should be chosen from the Scrutineers; and the Scrutineers are to be the only citizens whose heads may be graced by a crown of laurel. They should all be priests of Apollo and the Sun; the chief priesthood should be an annual office, held by the Scrutineer
b   who has come top of the list of those appointed that year—which must be recorded under his name, so as to provide a framework for the calendar for as long as the state endures.
After the death of a Scrutineer, his laying-out, his last journey and his tomb must be on a grander scale than for ordinary citizens. All cloth used must be white, dirges and laments must be banned, and a chorus of fifteen girls and another of fifteen youths must stand one on each side of the bier
c   and sing alternately a kind of hymn of praise to the dead priest, celebrating his glory in song throughout the day. As dawn comes up the following day the bier shall be taken to the tomb escorted by a hundred of the youths who attend the gymnasia, chosen by the relatives of the dead man. In front must go the young men who are as yet unmarried, each rigged out in his own military equipment; the cavalry should bring their horses, the infantry their weapons, and so on. Around the bier itself, towards the front, will be
d   boys chanting the traditional strains, followed by girls, and women who have finished bearing children. The Priests and Priestesses will bring up the rear; they are of course banned from other funerals, but provided the oracle at Delphi also approves, they shall attend this one, as it will not defile them. The Scrutineer's tomb shall be an oblong crypt built of choice[3] stone of the most indestructible kind obtainable; in this, on benches of stone set side by

3. Reading *protimōn* in d7.

side, they will lay him who has gone to his reward. On top of the tomb they   e
will pile a circular mound, and plant a sacred grove of trees around it—
except on one side, to allow for the indefinite extension of the tomb, where
more earth will have to be piled up to cover subsequent burials. Every year
the citizens will hold competitions in the Scrutineers' honor, one athletic,
one equestrian, and one of the arts. All these honors will be bestowed on
Scrutineers whose conduct has borne scrutiny.

If a Scrutineer relies on his election to protect him and goes to the bad,
thus showing he's only too human after all, the law will order a charge
to be brought against him by anyone who feels inclined to prosecute.
The trial should be held in court according to the following procedure.   948
Guardians of the Laws, and all the Scrutineers, active or retired, must sit
in conjunction with the court of the Select Judges, and the charge brought
by the prosecutor against the defendant must be to the effect that 'so-and-
so is a disgrace to his distinctions and his office.'

103. If the defendant is convicted,
he must be ejected from his office, denied the special tomb, and stripped
of the honors he has already received.

104. If the prosecutor fails to win one fifth of the votes,
he must pay a fine of twelve hundred drachmas if he belongs to the
highest property-class, eight hundred if to the second, six hundred if to   b
the third, and two hundred if to the lowest.

Rhadamanthus should be admired for the way in which, according to
report, he decided the suits that came before him. He realized that his
contemporaries were absolutely convinced of the existence of gods—and
not surprisingly, as most people alive then were actually descended from
them, and this is traditionally true of Rhadamanthus himself. I suppose
it was because he thought that no mere man should be given the task of
judging, but only gods, that he managed to make his judgments so swift
and straightforward. Whatever the subject of dispute, he made the litigants
take an oath, a device which enabled him to get through his list of cases   c
rapidly and without making mistakes. Nowadays, however, some people
(as we remarked) don't believe in gods at all, while others believe they
are not concerned about mankind; and there are others—the worst and
most numerous category—who hold that in return for a miserable sacrifice
here and a little flattery there, the gods will help them to steal enormous
sums of money and rescue them from all sorts of heavy penalties. So in
the modern world the legal procedure used by Rhadamanthus will hardly
do. The climate of opinion about the gods has changed, so the law must   d
change too, and a legislator who knows his business ought to abolish the
oaths sworn by each side in a lawsuit. When a man brings a charge against
someone, he should put his accusations in writing without taking an oath;
the defendant should similarly write out his denial and hand it to the
officials unsworn. It would be dreadful, you see, to know quite well, in
view of the frequent lawsuits that occur in the state, that although pretty

e   nearly half our citizens[4] have perjured themselves, they go on mixing with each other at common meals and other public and private gatherings without the slightest qualms.

There should therefore be a law requiring a juryman to take an oath before setting about his job. The law should also apply to anyone who votes in the election of officials to public positions: he must do so either
949   under oath or with a ballot-pebble he has obtained from a temple; so too should the judge of a chorus or any other artistic performance, and also the supervisor or umpire of any athletic or equestrian competition—and indeed the judge in any matter where there is nothing to 'gain' (as it seems to human eyes) from perjury. But whenever there is clearly much to be 'gained' from denials and oaths to back them up, then the question at issue between the disputants must be judged at a trial in which oaths are *not* taken.

And more generally, the presiding officials at a trial are not to give a
b   man a hearing if he tries to win belief by swearing oaths, or imprecating himself or his family, or by grovelling appeals for clemency, or effeminate wailing, but only if he states his lawful claims, and listens to those of the other side, with decency and decorum. Otherwise, the officials will ignore his remarks as irrelevant and instruct him to return to the issue before the court.

c   However, aliens should be entitled, as at present, to offer and accept binding oaths from each other, if they so wish—after all, they're not going to grow old in the state, nor, as a rule, build a nest in it to produce others entitled to live in the country and behave in the same way as themselves. And whenever an alien prosecutes an alien, the trial should be held under the same rules.

Sometimes a free man may defy the state in something not serious enough to deserve a whipping or imprisonment or death—by refusing to take part in a chorus or procession, for instance, or some public ceremony,
d   or to pay some contribution for such communal purposes as a sacrifice in time of peace, or a special levy in war. The first thing to be done in all these cases is to assess the damages; then the culprit is to give a pledge to those officials who have the duty of exacting it under the law of the land. If he still refuses to obey even after the seizure of the pledge, it should be sold and the proceeds confiscated by the state. If a more severe punishment is called for, the official concerned shall impose the appropriate
e   fine on this stubborn fellow and haul him through the courts until he's prepared to do as he's told.

A state which does not go in for trading and whose only source of wealth is the soil is obliged to have some settled policy regarding the foreign travel of its own citizens and the admission of aliens from abroad. The legislator, who has to give advice on these problems, must start by being as persuasive as he can.

---

4. Alternatively, 'half the litigants'.

In the nature of the case, contact between state and state produces a medley of all sorts of characters, because the unfamiliar customs of the 950 visitors rub off on to their hosts—and this, in a healthy society living under sound laws, is an absolute disaster. Most states, however, are not well run at all, so it makes no difference to them if their citizens fraternize with foreigners by welcoming them into the state and by going for trips abroad themselves whenever they feel like it and wherever their wanderlust takes them, whatever their age. On the other hand a policy of complete exclusion and complete refusal to go abroad is just not feasible, and in any case the rest of the world would think us churlish and uncivilized: we'd get the b reputation of being a truculent and surly people who have 'Deportations of Aliens', as the term is—and a brutal one it is, too. Whether the figure you cut in the eyes of others is good or bad, you should never underestimate its importance. You see, people in general don't fall so far short of real goodness that they can't recognize virtue and vice when they see it in others; even wicked people have an uncanny instinct that usually enables even an absolute villain to understand and describe accurately enough c what distinguishes a good man from a bad. That is why most states find it an excellent precept to value their good standing with the rest of the world. But the soundest and most important rule is this: if you mean to be perfect, you should seek to live in good repute only if you are really good in the first place, but not otherwise. And so it will be entirely right and proper if the state we are now founding in Crete wins among men a brilliant and glorious reputation for virtue, and if things go according to plan there is every reason to expect that, out of all the states and countries d which look upon the Sun and the other gods, Magnesia will be one of the few that are well administered.

So what should we do about the admission of aliens and our own journeys to places in foreign countries? First of all, no young person under forty is ever to be allowed to travel abroad under any circumstances; nor is anyone to be allowed to go for private reasons, but only on some public business, as a herald or ambassador or as an observer of one sort or another. (Of course, absence abroad on miliary service in wartime doesn't deserve e to be mentioned in the same breath: it's not one of those journeys which are 'for diplomatic reasons'!) We must send representatives to take part in the sacrifices and games held at Delphi in honor of Apollo and at Olympia in honor of Zeus, and to Nemea and the Isthmus; and we must send as many representatives as we can, the finest and noblest of our citizens, who will do credit to our state in these sacred gatherings of peace, 951 and win it renown to match that of her armies on the field of battle. And when they return, they will tell the younger generation that the social and political customs of the rest of the world don't measure up to their own.

But there are other kinds of observers who should be dispatched, provided the Guardians of the Laws give permission. If any citizen would like to spend rather longer surveying at his leisure the life lived by foreigners, no law should prevent him, because no state will ever be able to live at a

properly advanced level of civilization if it keeps itself to itself and never
b   comes into contact with all the vices and virtues of mankind; nor will it
be able to preserve its laws intact if it just gets used to them without
grasping their raison d'être. In the mass of mankind you'll invariably find
a number—though only a small number—of geniuses with whom it is
worth anything to associate, and they crop up just as often in badly-ruled
c   states as in the well-ruled. So the citizen of a well-run state, provided he's
incorruptible, should go out and range over land and sea to track them
down, so that he can see to the strengthening of the customs of his country
that are soundly based, and the refurbishing of any that are defective.
Without this observation and research a state will never stay at the peak
of perfection; nor will it if the observers are incompetent.

CLINIAS: So how can we ensure that both these requirements are met?

ATHENIAN: Like this. In the first place, anyone who goes observing for
us in this fashion must be over fifty; and since the Guardians of the Laws
are going to send him abroad as a specimen Magnesian, he must be one
of those citizens who have gained a good reputation generally, and particu-
d   larly in war; and on passing sixty he must go off observing no longer.
When he has spent as many of his ten years as he pleases making his
observations, he should come home and present himself before the council
which muses on legislation. (This council,[5] which should consist partly of
young men and partly of old, must have a strict rule to meet daily from
dawn until the sun is well up in the sky. Its membership is to be: (1) those
Priests who have won high distinction, (2) the ten Guardians of the Laws
e   who are currently the most senior, (3) the Minister of Education for the
time being, together with his predecessors in office. No member should
attend alone: each is to bring a young man of his own choice, aged between
thirty and forty. The discussion at their meetings must always center round
952   their own state, the problems of legislation, and any other important point
relevant to such topics that they may discover from external sources.
They must be particularly concerned with those studies which promise,
if pursued, to further their researches by throwing light on legislative
problems that would otherwise remain difficult and obscure. Whichever
of these studies are sanctioned by the older members should be pursued
with all diligence by the younger. If one of the protégés invited to attend
is judged to be inadequate, the whole council is to censure the man who
b   invited him; but any that get a good name should be fostered and watched
with particular care by the state at large, and if they do what's wanted of
them, they are to be specially honored, but if they turn out worse than
most other young men they should suffer correspondingly worse disgrace.)
To this council, then, the observer of foreign customs must proceed as
soon as he gets back. If he has come across people who were able to give
him some information about any problems of legislation or teaching or
education, or if he actually comes back with some discoveries of his own,

5. Apparently the 'Nocturnal' council, which has not yet been announced: see 960b ff.

he should make his report to a full meeting of the council. If he seems to   c
be not a whit better or worse for his journey, he should be congratulated
at any rate for his energy; if he is thought to have become appreciably
better, even higher recognition should be given him during his lifetime,
and after his death he must be paid appropriate honors by authority of
the assembled council. But if it seems that he has returned corrupted, this
self-styled 'expert' must talk to no one, young or old, and provided he
obeys the authorities he may live as a private person; but if not, and

105. he is convicted in court of meddling in some educational or legal   d
question,
he must die.

106. If none of the authorities takes him to court when that is what he
deserves,
it should count as a black mark against them when distinctions are
awarded.

So much for the way foreign travel should be undertaken and the sort
of persons who should venture on it. But what about our duty to welcome
foreign visitors? There are four categories of them worth discussing. Those
in the first turn up every year without fail, usually in summer, with the   e
regularity of migrating birds. Most of them are on business trips in search
of profit, and throughout the summer they 'wing' their way like so many
birds across the sea to foreign parts. They must be received at trading
posts and harbors and in public buildings outside but not far from the
state by officials appointed for the purpose, who should (a) take good care
that none of this category of visitor introduces any novel custom, (b)   953
handle with proper impartiality the lawsuits that affect them, and (c) keep
intercourse with them down to the unavoidable minimum. The second
type are 'observers' in the most basic sense: they come to see the sights,
and to listen, too, at festivals of the arts. All such visitors should be received
in hospitable lodgings near temples, by whose priests and custodians they
are to be looked after and attended to. Then, when they have stayed for
a reasonable length of time, and seen and heard what they came to see
and hear, they should take their leave without having inflicted or suffered
any harm. If anyone injures them, or they injure anyone else, the Priests   b
are to act as judges, provided no more than fifty drachmas are involved.
If the claim is for a greater sum, the trial must be held before the
Market-Wardens.
    The third type of visitor, who arrives from another country on some
matter of state, should be received at public expense, and by no one except
Generals, Cavalry-Commanders and Company-Commanders. Together
with the executive for the time being, the official by whom he is put up
and entertained should have the sole responsibility for him.   c
    Sometimes, though rarely, a fourth kind of visitor arrives. If ever a
counterpart to our own observers comes from a foreign country, we shall

first of all require that he should be not less than fifty years old, and in addition he should profess to be coming to view something whose excellence surpasses that of anything in the rest of the world, or to report on some such feature to another state. Such a man may dispense with invita-

d   tions, and present himself at the doors of the wise and rich, because that is the class of man he is himself. In the full confidence that he is the right sort of guest for such a distinguished host, he should go to the home of (say) the Minister of Education, or of someone who has won an award for virtue. He should spend his time in the company of one or other of these, and after an exchange of information take his leave, duly honored as a friend by friends with fitting presents and tokens of esteem.

These are the laws that should govern the reception of all our visitors

e   from abroad, of either sex, and the dispatch of our own people to other countries. We must show respect for Zeus the God of Strangers, and not keep aliens at arm's length by uncongenial food and offensive sacrifices (like the sons of Old Father Nile do nowadays), or by uncivilized proclamations.

Anyone who stands surety should do so in precise terms, by specifying all the details of the agreement in a written contract, before not less than three witnesses if the sum involved is less than one thousand drachmas,

954 and not less than five in the case of greater sums. (Also, a warrantor[6] is surety for a vendor who is insolvent or cannot be sued, and is to have the same liability in law.)

When a man wants to search someone else's premises, he should do so clad in only his tunic,[7] without a belt, and after swearing to the gods specified by law that he really does expect to find what he's looking for. The other party is to open up his home, including all its sealed and unsealed property, to be searched; if he refuses permission to search to anyone

b   requesting it, the party thus hindered must go to law, giving his estimate of the value of the object he is looking for.

107. If the defendant is convicted,
he must pay double the estimated value as damages.

If the owner of the house happens to be away, the residents must make unsealed property available for search; sealed property should be counter-sealed by the searcher, who should then post anyone he likes to guard it for a period of five days. If the householder stays away for longer than that, the other party should fetch the City-Wardens and make the search, opening up sealed property as well and sealing it up again afterwards in

c   the same way in the presence of the household and the City-Wardens.

Now for cases when title is in dispute. After a certain period has elapsed, it must be no longer possible to challenge the rights of the person in

6. The vendor from whom the vendor bought the object in question.
7. Deleting *ē* in a5.

possession. In Magnesia, of course, dispute about land or houses is out of the question. But as for other possessions, if a man has used something openly in town or market-place or temple, and no one has tried to recover it and claimed to have been looking for it all the time the other man has obviously made no attempt at concealment, then provided the ownership of the one party and the search of the other have continued for a year, d after the expiry of that period no claim for recovery is to be permitted. If a man uses an object openly, not indeed in town or market-place, but in the countryside, and no one confronts him with a claim to it for five years, then on the expiry of that period no one is to be allowed to attempt repossession. If the article is used in a man's town house, the time limit is to be three years; if it is kept in a building in the country, ten years; and if it is used abroad, then there is to be no time limit for recovery at e all, however long the claimant may take to find it.

Sometimes a man may forcibly prevent a litigant or witness from appearing at a trial. If he prevents a slave, his own or another's, the suit should be null and void.

108. If he prevents a free man,
he must be imprisoned for a year and be liable to a suit for kidnapping 955
at the hands of anyone who cares to prosecute, and the suit will be null
in any case.

If a man forcibly prevents a rival competitor from participating in an athletic or cultural or any other contest, anyone who wishes should report the fact to the supervisors of the games, who should set the would-be contestant free to enter the competition. If they prove unable to do so, and the man responsible for the competitor's absence wins, the prize should be awarded to the person prevented from competing, and he should be b recorded as the winner in any temple he pleases.

109. The person who has hindered him must not be allowed to make any dedication or record relating to that contest, and he must be liable to a prosecution for damages whether he wins or loses.

110. If a man receives stolen goods, knowing them to be stolen, *he must* suffer the same penalty as the thief.

111. The penalty for harboring an exile should be death.

Everyone is to have the same friends and enemies as the state.

112. (a) If a man makes a private peace or wages private war with c anyone without the backing of the state,
he too must be punished by death.

If any sectional interest in the state makes peace or war with any parties on its own account, the Generals must haul those responsible for the affairs before a court.

(b) If the defendants are convicted,
death should be the penalty.

Members of the public service should perform their duties without taking bribes. Such a practice must never be extenuated by an approving reference to maxims like 'One good turn deserves another'. It is not easy for an
d   official to reach his decisions impartially and stick to them, and the safest thing he can do is to listen to the law and obey its command to take no gifts for his services.

113. If a man disobeys and is convicted in court,
the only penalty permitted is to be death.

Now to deal with payments to the public treasury. For a variety of reasons, an assessment must be made of each man's property, and the members of the tribes must make a written return of the year's produce to the Country-Wardens. The treasury will thus be able to use whichever
e   of the two methods of exacting payment it finds convenient—that is, every year the authorities will decide to levy a proportion *either* of the sum total of the individual assessments *or* of the revenues accruing that particular year. (Payment for the common meals should be excluded from the calculations.)

The offerings a reasonable man makes to the gods should be on a correspondingly reasonable scale. As the earth and every household's hearth are already sacred to all the gods, no one should consecrate them a second time. The gold and silver that you find in temples and private
956   houses in other states encourage jealousy; ivory, taken as it is from a lifeless body, is an unclean offering; and iron and bronze are instruments of war. A man may offer at the public temples any objects he likes made of wood or stone, provided that in either case it consists of no more than a single piece; if he offers woven material, it should not exceed what one woman can produce in a month. In general, and particularly in the case of woven material, white is the color appropriate to the gods; dyes must not be
b   employed, except for military decorations. The gifts the gods find most acceptable are birds and pictures, provided they do not take a painter more than a single day to complete. All this should serve as a pattern for all our other offerings.

Now that we have described the nature and number of the parts into which the whole state is divided, and done what we can to frame laws for all the most important agreements men make, we're left with the question of legal procedure. The court of first resort will consist of judges— arbitrators, in fact, but 'judges' is really a more appropriate title—chosen
c   by agreement between prosecutor and defendant. If the case is not settled in the first court, the litigants should go and contest it again before the second (composed of villagers and tribesmen, duly divided into twelve groups), but at the risk of an enhanced penalty: if the defendant loses for the second time, he must be mulcted an additional fifth of the penalty

previously assessed and recorded. If he is still aggrieved with his judges and wants to fight the case for the third time, he must take it to the Select Judges, and if he is defeated again, he is to pay one and a half times the original penalty. As for the prosecutor, if he is not prepared to lie down under defeat in the first court, and goes before the second, he should be awarded the extra fifth of the penalty if he wins, but be fined that amount if he loses. If the litigants refuse to acquiesce in the earlier decision and go before the third court, and the defendant loses, he must pay one and a half times the penalty as already stated; if the prosecutor loses, he must be fined one half of it.

But what about the balloting for jurors, and the procedure for making up the juries? What about the appointment of attendants for the various officials, the fixing of times at which the various formalities should be completed, voting methods, adjournments, and all the other similar inescapable details of legal procedure, such as putting cases early or late in the calendar, the enforcement of attendance and of replies to interrogation, and suchlike? Well, we've made the point before, but the truth is all the better for being stated two or even three times. All these minor rules are perfectly easy to invent, and the senior legislator may skip them and leave it to his young successor to fill in the gaps. But although that will be reasonable enough in the case of the courts that are appointed privately, the common public courts, and those that the various officials need to use in the performance of their duties, need a rather different approach. Sensible people in several states have framed a good many decent regulations which our Guardians of the Laws should adapt for the state that we are now founding. The Guardians should examine them and touch them up after trying them out in practice, until they think they have licked each single one into shape; then they should finalize them, ratify them as immutable, and render them lifelong obedience. Then there is the question of the silence of the judges, and the restraint or otherwise of their language, as well as all the other details in which our standards of justice and goodness and decorum differ from those you find in such variety in other states. We've already had something to say on this topic, and we shall have more to say towards the end. The judge who wants to act with proper judicial impartiality should bear all these points in mind and get hold of books in which to study the subject. The study of laws, provided they are good laws, is unsurpassed for its power to improve the student. (It can't be an accident that the name of this god-given and wonderful institution, law, is so suggestive of reason.)[8] And other compositions, such as eulogies or censures in verse or prose, in the latter case either taking written form or being simply spoken during our day-to-day contacts when we indulge in contentious argument or (sometimes thoughtlessly) express our agreement—all these will be measured against a clear criterion: the writings of the legislator, which the good judge will treasure as a kind of antidote

8. *Nomos* ('law') suggests *nous* ('reason').

against the others, so as to ensure his own moral health and that of the
state. He will confirm and strengthen the virtuous in the paths of righteous-
e   ness, and do his best to banish ignorance and incontinence and cowardice
and indeed every sort of injustice from the hearts of those criminals whose
outlook can be cured. However—and this is a point that deserves constant
958 repetition—when a man's soul is unalterably fixed in that condition by
decree of fate, our erudite judges and their advisers will deserve the commendation of the whole state if they cure him by imposing the penalty
of death.

When the suits for the year have been finally decided, the following
laws must apply to the execution of judgment. First of all, immediately
after the voting in each case, and by proclamation of a herald in the hearing
of the judges, the official who has pronounced sentence should assign all
b   the property of the convicted party, except the minimum he must retain,
to the successful prosecutor. If after the expiry of the month following that
in which the case was tried the loser has not settled the business with the
victor to the satisfaction of both, the official who gave judgment must at
the request of the victorious party hand over the goods of the loser. If the
latter lacks the means to pay, and the deficiency amounts to a drachma
or more, he must not be allowed to prosecute other people (they however,
c   being entitled to prosecute *him*), until he has paid his debt in full to his
opponent. If someone who has received an adverse verdict obstructs the
bench that condemned him, the officials thus obstructed should haul him
before the court of the Guardians of the Laws.

> 114. If he is convicted on such a charge,
> *he must* be punished by death,

on the grounds that his conduct is wrecking the entire state and its laws.
Now here's the next point. A man is born and brought up, and begets
and rears his own children in turn; he deals fairly in his business transac-
d   tions, paying the penalty if he has done anyone injury and exacting one
if others have wronged him; and finally, as destiny decrees, after an old
age spent in obedience to the laws, the course of nature will bring him to
the end of his life. So what should we do when a man or woman has
died? First, we must bow to the absolute authority of the Expounders'
instructions about the sacred rites to be observed in honor of the nether
gods and those of this world. No tomb, whether its mound is large or
small, should be constructed anywhere on land that can be farmed; graves
e   must take up space only where nature has made the ground good for
nothing except the reception and concealment of the bodies of the dead
with minimum detriment to the living, because no one, alive or dead, must
ever rob the living of any land which—thanks to the natural fertility of
Mother Earth—will grow food for the human race. The soil must not be
piled higher than five men can manage by working for five days. Stone
slabs must not be made bigger than they need to be to accommodate a

eulogy of the deceased's career of not more than the usual four hexameters.   959
The laying-out at home should not last longer than is necessary to confirm
that the person really is dead and not just in a faint; in average cases, it
will be reasonable for the body to be taken to the tomb after two days.

We should, of course, trust whatever the legislator tells us, but especially
his doctrine that the soul has an absolute superiority over the body, and
that while I am alive I have nothing to thank for my individuality except
my soul, whereas my body is just the likeness of myself that I carry round
with me. This means we are quite right when we say a corpse 'looks like'   b
the deceased. Our real self—our immortal soul, as it is called—departs,
as the ancestral law declares, to the gods below to give an account of itself.
To the wicked, this is a terrifying doctrine, but a good man will welcome
it. And once he's dead, there's not a great deal we can do to help a man:
all his relatives should have helped him while he was still in the land of
the living, so that he could have passed his life in all possible justice and   c
holiness; and then after death he could have escaped the penalty visited
on evil deeds in the life to come. This all goes to show that we should
never squander our last penny, on the fanciful assumption that this lump
of flesh being buried really is our own son or brother or whoever it is we
mournfully think we are burying. We ought to realize that in fact he has
departed in final consummation of his destiny, and that it is our duty to
make the best of what we have and spend only a moderate sum on the
body, which we may now think of as a kind of altar to the gods below,   d
now deserted by its spirit; and as for what is meant by 'moderate' in this
matter, the most respectable ideas will be those of the legislator. The law,
then, should specify a reasonable level of expenditure as follows. In the
case of a member of the highest property-class, the whole funeral should
not cost more than five hundred drachmas; three hundred may be spent
on a member of the second class, two hundred on a member of the third,
and one hundred on a member of the fourth.

The Guardians of the Laws will have to shoulder a great many burdens
and responsibilities, but their overriding duty will be to devote their lives   e
to the care of children and adults and indeed persons of all ages. In
particular, when a man is nearing his end his household should invite one
Guardian to take charge of him, and if the funeral arrangements pass off
decorously and without extravagance, this Guardian-in-charge will get the
credit, but if not, then the blame will be at his door. The laying-out and
other matters should take place according to usage, but usage must be
modified by the following directions of our legislator-statesman. 'Tasteless
though it is to forbid or instruct people to weep over the dead, dirges   960
should be forbidden; and cries of mourning should be allowed only inside
the house. The mourners must not bring the corpse on to the open street
nor make their procession a noisy one, and they must be outside the city
by day-break.' So much for the regulations on the subject. The person who
obeys them will never be punished, but

115. if a man disobeys a single Guardian of the Laws,
he must be punished by them all with whatever penalty recommends itself to their united judgment.

b   The other methods of burying the dead, and the kind of criminals to whom we deny burial, such as parricides, temple-robbers and all similar categories, have already been specified and provided for in the legal code.[9] And that means, I suppose, that we have pretty well come to the end of our legislation.

ATHENIAN: However, even when you have achieved or gained or founded something, you have never quite finished. Only when you have ensured complete and perpetual security for your creation can you reckon to have done everything that ought to have been done. Until then, it's a case of
c   'unfinished business'.

CLINIAS: Well said, sir—but what's the particular point you had in mind in saying that? Could you be a little clearer?

ATHENIAN: Well, you know, Clinias, a lot of old expressions are extraordinarily apt. I'm thinking particularly of the names of the Fates.

CLINIAS: What names?

ATHENIAN: Lachesis for the first, Clotho for the second, and Atropos for the third fulfiller of destiny[10]—the last so called from her likeness to a
d   woman making the threads on her spindle irreversible.[11] That is precisely the situation we want to see in our state and its citizens—not merely physical health and soundness, but the rule of law in their souls and (more important than all that) the preservation of the laws themselves. In fact, it seems to me that the service we've still not done for the laws is to discover how to build into them a resistance to being reversed.

CLINIAS: That's serious, because I don't suppose there's a way of giving anything that sort of property.

e   ATHENIAN: But there is. I see that quite clearly now.

CLINIAS: Well then, we mustn't abandon our task till we've achieved this for the legal code we've expounded. It would be silly to waste our labor on something by failing to construct it on a firm foundation.

ATHENIAN: You're right to encourage me, and you'll find me as keen as you are.

CLINIAS: Splendid! So what is this safety device for our political system and legal code going to be, according to you? And how can we construct it?

961   ATHENIAN: We said[12] that we ought to have in the state a council with the following range of membership. The ten Guardians of the Laws who are currently the eldest were to convene together with all persons who had won awards of distinction and the travelers who had gone abroad to

9. 717e–718a, 872e ff., 908e ff., and 947b ff.

10. Respectively 'the Distributor of Lots', 'the Spinner', and 'the Inflexible One'.

11. Reading *atraktōi* in c9.

12. 951d–952d.

see if they could discover any special method of keeping a legal code intact. When these observers got back safe and sound, they were to be accepted as suitable associates of the council, provided they had first passed the scrutiny of its members. In addition, each member had to bring a young man of at least thirty years of age, but only after selecting him as particularly well qualified by natural abilities and education; on these terms the young man was to be introduced to the other members of the council, and if they approved of him, he was to join them; if not, they were not to breathe a word to anyone about the fact that he was considered, least of all to the rejected candidate himself. The council was to meet before dawn, when people are least beset by other business, public or private. That was more or less the description we gave earlier, wasn't it?

CLINIAS: Certainly it was.

ATHENIAN: So I'm going to resume the subject of this council, and here's the point I want to make about it. I maintain that if one were to lower it as a sort of 'anchor' for the whole state, then provided conditions were suitable, it would keep safe everything we wanted it to.

CLINIAS: How so?

ATHENIAN: Now at this crucial moment, we must strain every muscle to get things right.

CLINIAS: That's a fine sentiment. Now do what you have in mind.

ATHENIAN: The question we have to ask about anything, Clinias, is this: what is it that has the special power of keeping it safe in each of its activities? In a living creature, for instance, this is the natural function of the soul and the head, in particular.

CLINIAS: Again, what's your point?

ATHENIAN: Well, when these two are functioning satisfactorily, they ensure the animal's safety, don't they?

CLINIAS: How so?

ATHENIAN: Because no matter what else is true of either, the soul is the seat of reason and the head enjoys the faculties of sight and hearing. In short, the combination of reason with the highest senses constitutes a single faculty that would have every right to be called the salvation of the animal concerned.

CLINIAS: That's likely enough, I suppose.

ATHENIAN: Of course it is. But *how* do reason and the senses combine to ensure the safety of a ship, in fair weather or foul? Isn't it because captain and crew interpret sense-data by reason, *as embodied in* the expertise captains have, that they keep themselves and the whole ship safe?

CLINIAS: Naturally.

ATHENIAN: We've no need to multiply examples, but take a general in command of his army, or any doctor tending a human body. What will they each aim at, on the assumption that they intend, as they should, to preserve their charges safe and sound? Won't the general aim at victory and control over the enemy, and won't doctors and their attendants aim to keep the body in a healthy condition?

CLINIAS: Of course.

ATHENIAN: Now consider a doctor who can't recognize the state of the body we've just called 'health', or a general who doesn't know what's meant by 'victory' and the other terms we reviewed. Could either of them possibly be judged to have a rational knowledge of his field?

CLINIAS: Of course not.

b ATHENIAN: And if the ruler of a *state* were obviously ignorant of the target at which a statesman should aim, would he really deserve his title 'ruler'? Would he be capable of ensuring the safety of an institution whose purpose he entirely failed to appreciate?

CLINIAS: Certainly not.

ATHENIAN: Well then, in the present circumstances, if our settlement of this territory is to be finished off properly, it looks as if we shall have to provide it with some constituent that understands (a) this target we have mentioned—the target, whatever we find it is, of the statesman, (b) how to hit it, and (c) which laws (above all) and which persons have helpful advice to give and which not. If a state lacks some such constituent, no c one will be surprised to see it staggering from one irrational and senseless expedient to another in all its affairs.

CLINIAS: That's true.

ATHENIAN: So is there any institution or constituent part of our state qualified and prepared to function as an organ of protection? Can we name one?

CLINIAS: No, sir, not with much assurance, anyway. But if guess I must, I think your remarks point to the Council you said just now had to convene during the night.

d ATHENIAN: You've caught my meaning splendidly, Clinias. As the drift of our present argument shows, that body must possess virtue in all its completeness, which means above all that it will *not* take erratic aim at one target after another but keep its eye on one single target and shoot all its arrows at that.

CLINIAS: Certainly.

ATHENIAN: Now we can see why it is hardly surprising that rules and regulations fluctuate so much from state to state: it is because legislation has a different aim in each. Nor is it surprising that in most cases you find that some people think of justice as nothing but the subjection of the state e to the rule of this or that type of person without regard to their vice or virtue, while others think of it as the opportunity to become rich, no matter whether they are thereby enslaved or not; others again are bent hell for leather on a life of 'freedom'. Some legislators keep both ends in view, and their laws have the dual purpose of securing control over other states *and* freedom for their own. The cleverest legislators of all (as they like to think of themselves), so far from aiming at one single end, look not only to these but all others like them, simply because they cannot identify any supremely valuable end to which all others ought, in their view, to contribute.

CLINIAS: Well then, sir, the line we took so long ago was the right one. 963
We said that every detail of our legislation ought to have a *single* end in
view, and the proper name to call it was, I think we agreed, 'virtue'.[13]

ATHENIAN: Yes.

CLINIAS: And I think we maintained that the virtues were four.

ATHENIAN: Indeed we did.

CLINIAS: The leading one, to which not only the other three but everything
else should be orientated, was reason.

ATHENIAN: You take the point admirably, Clinias. Now follow the rest
of the argument. As far as the captain, doctor and general are concerned, b
we have already indicated that their intellect aims at some appropriate
single end. Now it is the turn of the statesman's reason to be investigated.
Let's personify it and ask it the following question: "My good sir, what
aim do *you* have in view? What's your single overriding purpose? The
intelligent doctor can identify his accurately enough, so can't you, with
all your superior wisdom (as I suppose you'd claim), identify yours?" Or
can you two, Clinias and Megillus, answer for him and tell me precisely
what your notion of his aim is, just as I've often given you detailed accounts c
of the notions of many other people on their behalf?

CLINIAS: No, sir, we certainly cannot.

ATHENIAN: What about replying, 'I think he should make every effort
to get an overall understanding of his aim, as well as see it in its various contexts'?

CLINIAS: What contexts, for example?

ATHENIAN: Well, when we said there were four species of virtue, obviously the very fact that there were four meant that each had to be thought
of as somehow distinct from the others.

CLINIAS: Surely.

ATHENIAN: Yet in fact we call them all by a single name. We say courage
is virtue, wisdom is virtue, and the other two similarly, on the ground
that really they are not several things but just one—virtue. d

CLINIAS: Very true.

ATHENIAN: It's not hard to explain how these two 'virtues' and the rest
differ from each other and how each has acquired a different name. The
real problem is this: why, precisely, have we described both of them (as
well as the others) by this *common* term 'virtue'?

CLINIAS: What do you mean?

ATHENIAN: My point is perfectly easy to explain. Shall we let one of us
ask the questions, and the other answer them?

CLINIAS: Again, what do you mean?

ATHENIAN: Here's the question for you to put to me: "Why is it that after e
calling both by the single term 'virtue', in the next breath we speak of
two 'virtues', courage and wisdom?" I'll tell you why. One of them,
courage, copes with fear, and is found in wild animals as well as human

---

13. See 630d–e.

beings, notably in the characters of very young children. The soul, you see, becomes courageous by a purely natural process, without the aid of reason. By contrast, in this absence of reason a wise and sensible soul is out of the question. That is true now, has always been true, and always will be true; the two processes are fundamentally different.

CLINIAS: That's true.

964   ATHENIAN: So there's your explanation of why there are two different virtues. Now it's your turn: you tell me why they are one and the same thing. Your job, you understand, is to tell me why the four of them nevertheless form a unity; and when you have demonstrated that unity, ask me to show you again in what sense they are four.

Next after that we ought to ask ourselves what constitutes adequate knowledge of any object that has a name and a definition: is it enough to know only the name and not the definition? On the contrary, if a man is worth his salt, wouldn't it be a disgrace in him not to understand all these

b   points about a topic so grand and so important?

CLINIAS: Presumably it would.

ATHENIAN: And as for a giver or guardian of laws, and indeed anyone who thinks of his own virtue as superior to the rest of the world's, and has won awards for his achievement, *is* there anything more important than the qualities we are now discussing—courage, restraint, justice and wisdom?

CLINIAS: Of course not.

ATHENIAN: So in such circumstances what role should the expounders, teachers and lawgivers—the guardians of the rest of the community—

c   play when a criminal needs enlightenment and instruction, or perhaps correction and punishment? Should they not prove better than anyone else at giving him a full explanation and description of the effects of virtue and vice? Or is some poet-visitor to the state, or some self-styled 'educationalist', going to put up a better show than the winner of the palm for every kind of virtue? Where there are no efficient and articulate guardians with an adequate understanding of virtue, it will be hardly

d   surprising if the state, precisely because it is unguarded, meets the fate of so many states nowadays.

CLINIAS: No, hardly surprising at all, I suppose.

ATHENIAN: Well then, shall we carry out these proposals, or what? Shall we make sure our guardians are more highly qualified than the man in the street to explain what virtue is, and to put it into practice? How else could our state function like the head and sense of a wise man, now that it possesses within itself something analogous to protect it?

CLINIAS: Where is this resemblance, sir? How do we draw such a comparison?

e   ATHENIAN: Obviously the state itself corresponds to the trunk, and the junior guardians, chosen for their natural gifts and the acuteness of their mental vision, live as it were at the summit and survey the whole state; they store up in their memory all the sensations they receive while on

965   guard, and act as reporters for their elder colleagues of everything that

takes place in the state; and the old men—we could compare them to the intellect, for their high wisdom in so many vital questions—take advantage of the assistance and advice of their juniors in debating policy, so that the joint efforts of both ranks effectively ensure the safety of the entire state. Now is this the sort of organization we want to see, or some other? Should the state, in fact, keep all its citizens on the same level, without giving some a more specialized training and education than others?

CLINIAS: My dear sir! That's quite impracticable.

ATHENIAN: Then we have to pass on to a more advanced education than the one we described earlier. b

CLINIAS: Perhaps so.

ATHENIAN: What about the education we touched on a moment ago? Would that answer our needs?

CLINIAS: Certainly it would.

ATHENIAN: Didn't we say that a really skilled craftsman or guardian in any field must be able not merely to see the many individual instances of a thing, but also to win through to a knowledge of the single central concept, and when he's understood that, put the various details in their proper place in the overall picture?

CLINIAS: We did, and rightly.

ATHENIAN: So what better tool can there be for a penetrating investigation c of a concept than an ability to look beyond the many dissimilar instances to the single notion?

CLINIAS: Probably none.

ATHENIAN: 'Probably!' No, my dear fellow, this is most *certainly* the surest method we can follow, no matter who we are.

CLINIAS: I trust you, sir, and I agree, so let's carry on with the discussion on that basis.

ATHENIAN: So it looks as if we have to compel the guardians of our divine foundation to get an exact idea of the common element in all the d four virtues—that factor which, though single, is to be found in courage, restraint, justice and wisdom, and thus in our view deserves the general title 'virtue'. This element, my friends, if only we have the will, is what we must grip until we can explain adequately the essence of what we have to contemplate, whether it is a single entity, a composite whole, or both, or whatever. If this point eludes us, can we ever expect to attain virtue—when we can't say whether it comprises a great number of things e or just four, or whether it is a unity? Never—not if we believe our own advice, anyway, and we'll have to ensure the growth of virtue in the state by some other means. But if in the circumstances we decide we ought to abandon the attempt entirely, abandon it we must.

CLINIAS: No, sir, in the name of the gods of hospitality, we must never abandon such a project: you seem to us to be absolutely right. So now then: how is one to tackle the problem?

ATHENIAN: Let's postpone the question of method. The first thing we 966 have to settle and decide among ourselves is whether the attempt should be made at all.

CLINIAS: Indeed it should, if possible.

ATHENIAN: Well then, do we take the same line about goodness and beauty? Should the guardians know no more than that both these terms are a plurality, or should they understand the senses in which they are unities?

CLINIAS: It looks as if they are more or less obliged to comprehend that too—how they are unities.

b   ATHENIAN: But what if they understood the point, but couldn't find the words to demonstrate it?

CLINIAS: How absurd! That's the condition of a slave.

ATHENIAN: Well then, isn't our doctrine going to be the same about all serious questions? If our guardians are going to be *genuine* guardians of the laws they must have *genuine* knowledge of their real nature; they must be articulate enough to explain the real difference between good actions and bad, and capable of sticking to the distinction in practice.

CLINIAS: Naturally.

c   ATHENIAN: And surely one of the finest fields of knowledge is theology, on which we've already lavished a great deal of attention. It's supremely important to appreciate—so far as it's given to man to know these things —the existence of the gods and the obvious extent of their power. The man in the street may be forgiven if he simply follows the voice of the law, but if any intended guardian fails to work hard to master every theological proof there is, we must certainly not grant *him* the same indulgence; in other words, we must never choose as a Guardian of the Laws

d   anyone who is not preternaturally gifted or has not worked hard at theology, or allow him to be awarded distinctions for virtue.

CLINIAS: It's fair enough, as you say, that the idle or incompetent in this business should never be allowed to get anywhere near such honors.

ATHENIAN: Now we know, don't we, that among the arguments we've already discussed, there are two in particular which encourage belief in the gods?

CLINIAS: Which two are they?

ATHENIAN: One is the point we made about the soul, when we argued that

e   it is far older and far more divine than all those things whose movements have sprung up and provided the impulse which has plunged it into a perpetual stream of existence. Another argument was based on the systematic motion of the heavenly bodies and the other objects under the control of reason, which is responsible for the order in the universe. No one who has contemplated all this with a careful and expert eye has in fact ever degenerated into

967   such ungodliness as to reach the position that most people would expect him to reach. They suppose that if a man goes in for such things as astronomy and the essential associated disciplines, and sees events apparently happening by necessity rather than because they are directed by the intention of a benevolent will, he'll turn into an atheist.

CLINIAS: Well, what would happen, in fact?

ATHENIAN: Today, as I said, the situation is quite different from the time when thinkers regarded these bodies as inanimate. Even then, men were

b   overcome with wonder at them, and those who studied them really closely got an inkling of the accepted doctrines of today, that such remarkably accurate predictions about their behavior would never have been possible if they were inanimate, and therefore irrational; and even in those days there were some[14] who had the hardihood to stick their neck out and assert it was reason that imposed regularity and order on the heavens. However, these same thinkers went sadly astray over the soul's natural priority to matter: regarding soul as a recent creation, they turned the universe upside down, so to speak, and their own theories to boot. They concluded from the evidence of their eyes that all the bodies that move across the heavens were mere collections of stone and earth and many other kinds of inanimate matter—inanimate matter which nevertheless initiated a chain of causation responsible for all the order in the universe. These views brought down on the philosophers' heads a great many accusations of atheism, and provoked a lot of hostility; poets, in particular, joined in the chorus of abuse and among other inanities compared the philosophers to bitches baying at the moon. But today, as I said, the situation is fundamentally different.

CLINIAS: How so?

ATHENIAN: No mortal can ever attain a truly religious outlook without risk of relapse unless he grasps the two doctrines we're now discussing: first, that the soul is far older than any created thing, and that it is immortal and controls the entire world of matter; and second (a doctrine we've expounded often enough before) that reason is the supreme power among the heavenly bodies. He also has to master the essential preliminary studies, survey with the eye of a philosopher what they have in common, and use them to frame consistent rules of moral action; and finally, when a reasoned explanation is possible, he must be able to provide it. No one who is unable to acquire these insights and rise above the level of the ordinary virtues will ever be good enough to govern an entire state, but only to assist government carried on by others. And that means, Clinias and Megillus, that we now have to consider whether we are going to add yet another law to the code we've already expounded, to the effect that the Nocturnal Council of the Authorities, duly primed by the course of studies we've described, shall be constituted the legal protector of the safety of the state. Or is there some alternative course for us to take?

CLINIAS: Oh, but my dear sir, there's no question of refusing to add this law, if we can manage it, even if our success is only partial.

ATHENIAN: Then let's make every effort to win the struggle. I've had a lot of experience of such projects and have studied the field for a long time, so I'll be more than happy to help you—and perhaps I shall find others to join me.

CLINIAS: Well, sir, we must certainly stick to the path on which—it is hardly an exaggeration to say—God himself is guiding us. But the question to which we need an answer at the moment is this: what will be the correct procedure on our part?

---

14. Presumably Anaxagoras (mid fifth century) in particular. Cf. *Phaedo* 97b ff.

ATHENIAN: Megillus and Clinias, it is impossible to lay down the council's activities until it has been established. Its curriculum must be decided by those who have already mastered the necessary branches of knowledge— and only previous instruction and plenty of intimate discussion will settle such matters as that.

CLINIAS: How so? How are we supposed to understand *that* remark?

d ATHENIAN: First of all, of course, we shall have to compile a list of candidates qualified for the office of guardian by age, intellectual attainments, moral character and way of life. Then there's the question of what they have to learn. It is difficult to find out this for oneself, and it is not easy either to discover somebody else who has already done so and learn from him. Quite apart from that, it will be a waste of time to produce written regulations about the order in which the various subjects should be tackled and how long should be spent on each, because even the stu-

e dents, until they have thoroughly absorbed a subject, won't realize why it comes at just that point in the curriculum. So although it would be a mistake to treat all these details as inviolable secrets, it would be fair to say that they ought not to be divulged beforehand, because advance disclosure throws no light at all on the questions we're discussing.

CLINIAS: Well then, sir, if that's the case, what are we to do?

ATHENIAN: My friends, we must 'chance our arm', as the saying is. If we are prepared to stake the whole constitution on a throw of 'three sixes'

969 or 'three ones', then that's what we'll have to do, and I'll shoulder part of the risk by giving a full explanation of my views on training and education, which we've now started to discuss all over again. However, the risk is enormous and unique. So I bid you, Clinias, take the business in hand: establish the state of the Magnesians (or whatever other name God adopts for it), and if you're successful you'll win enormous fame; at

b any rate you'll never lose a reputation for courage that will dwarf all your successors'. And if, my good companions, if this wonderful council of ours can be formed, then the state must be entrusted to it, and practically no modern legislator will want to oppose us. We thought of our combined metaphor of head and intellect, which we mentioned a moment ago, as idealistic dreaming[15]—but it will all come true, provided the council mem-

c bers are rigorously selected, properly educated, and after the completion of their studies lodged in the citadel of the country and made into guardians whose powers of protection we have never seen excelled in our lives before.

MEGILLUS: My dear Clinias, judging from what we've heard said, either we'll have to abandon the project of founding the state or refuse to let our visitor leave us, and by entreaties and every ruse we can think of enroll him as a partner in the foundation of the state.

d CLINIAS: You're quite right, Megillus. That's what I'm going to do. May I enlist your help too?

MEGILLUS: You may indeed.

15. See 961d and 964e–965a.

EPINOMIS

As its name indicates, Epinomis *is an addition or appendix to the* Laws *(Nomoi in Greek). Clinias, Megillus, and the Athenian visitor reconvene at some unspecified time after their conversation in the* Laws. *Their purpose is to discuss the nature of wisdom—the copestone of human fulfillment and happiness—and, more particularly, the studies by which it is to be attained. Instruction in these must be given to the members of the governing Council of their proposed new city of Magnesia, charged as the Council is with knowing in detail the overall aim of law and how to maintain in perpetuity laws and practices that achieve it. At the end of the* Laws, *it was agreed that these matters could not usefully be explained in advance; the thing to do was actually to establish a city having the right laws, educate and select a Council, and leave to them the further legislation about their successors' education. Now, going back on that, the Athenian agrees to explain what the necessary studies are and to legislate about them. It turns out, surprisingly perhaps, that though certain preliminary studies are also needed, wisdom is constituted solely by the knowledge of astronomy—of the single, mathematically unified system of the constant movements of the heavenly bodies (assumed, of course, to be rotating round the earth). Knowing that, the Council members will know the principle of order needed to organize correctly the whole of human life, both individually and socio-politically.*

This discrepancy (and there are others) already suggests that Plato was not the author of this work. This is generally accepted in current scholarship. There is ancient testimony that its author was in fact Philip of Opus, who is also said to have 'transcribed' the Laws, *presumably from wax tablets in which Plato left the work at his death because he was still revising it. If so, it presents one of the first 'Platonisms', very close to Plato's own time, carrying forward the 'spirit' of Plato's work while giving selective and distorting emphases to various elements within it.*

J.M.C.

CLINIAS: My friend, all three of us—you, I and Megillus here—have   973
come to do what we agreed: to consider what account we ought to give
in explaining the nature of wisdom, as well as to discuss the course of

Translated by Richard D. McKirahan, Jr. Text: L. Tarán, *Academica: Plato, Philip of Opus, and the Pseudo-Platonic Epinomis*, American Philosophical Society, Philadelphia, 1975.

studies that we say makes a person who engages in thought as wise as a
b human can be. And rightly so, since although we have set out in detail
everything else that has to do with legislation, we have neither stated nor
discovered the most important thing: what a mortal must learn in order
to be wise. We must not abandon this now, since to do so would be to
leave largely unachieved the goal of our labors, which was to make things
clear from start to finish.

ATHENIAN VISITOR: That is a good idea, Clinias, but I fear you are about
c to hear an account that is strange, though yet in a way not strange: the
human race is, as a rule, neither blessed nor happy. Many people, through
their experience in life, offer this same account. Pay attention then and
consider closely whether you find that I too, following them, am correct
on this point. I claim that people cannot become blessed and happy; there
are but a few exceptions to this rule. (I limit this claim to the duration of
our lives. Those who strive to live as nobly as they can during their life
and at their end to die a noble death have a good hope of attaining after
d they die everything for which they have striven.) I am not saying anything
clever, but only what we all know in some way, both Greeks and foreigners:
from the start the terms of life are harsh for every living thing. First we
have to go through the stage of being embryos. Then we have to be born
974 and then be brought up and educated, and we all agree that every one of
these stages involves countless pains. In fact, if we don't count hardships,
but only what everyone would consider tolerable, the time involved turns
out to be quite brief—a period round about the middle of a person's life,
which is thought to provide a kind of breathing-space. But then old age
quickly overtakes us and tends to make anyone who takes his whole life
into account unwilling ever to go through life again, unless he is full of
childish thoughts.

b What proof do I have of this? That what we are now investigating points
in this direction. We are investigating how to become wise, as if this
capacity were found in everyone. But it takes to its heels whenever anyone
achieves any expertise in any of the so-called arts or branches of wisdom
or in any of the other fields usually considered to be sciences—which
suggests that none of them deserves the title of wisdom about these human
concerns. On the other hand, while the soul is strongly convinced and
c divines that it is somehow its nature to have wisdom, it is wholly unable
to find out what this is, and when and how it is attained. In these circumstances, isn't our difficulty about wisdom entirely appropriate, and our
investigation as well? This turns out to be a larger project than any of us
expect who are capable of examining themselves and others intelligently
and consistently through arguments of all kinds and sorts. Shall we not
agree that this is so?

d CLINIAS: Perhaps we shall, my friend, since over time we have come to
share your hope that we may reach the full truth in these matters.

ATHENIAN: First we must go through all the other subjects that are called
sciences but that do not make those who understand and possess them

wise. After getting these out of the way, we will try to identify the ones we need, and then learn them.

To begin, let us consider how it is that the sciences that have to do with the first needs of a mortal race are most necessary and truly first, but also how it happens that those who have knowledge of them, though in early times they were considered wise, nowadays are not reputed for wisdom, but rather are reproached for such knowledge. We shall identify them and show that virtually everyone with an ambition for a reputation of having developed into as good a person as possible avoids them in order to acquire wisdom and practice it.

First there is the knowledge that has to do with animals' eating one another. The story goes that this is what has made it customary to eat some kinds of animals while entirely keeping us from eating others. May the men of former times be kindly to us, as indeed they are; but let the first persons we leave aside be the experts at the knowledge just mentioned. Next, the production of barley meal and wheat flour, in combination with the knowledge of how to use them for nourishment, though it is a noble and excellent pursuit, will never succeed in making anyone completely wise, since this very thing—labelling production as wisdom—would lead to disgust at the products themselves. Nor will cultivation of the entire earth make anyone completely wise: it is clearly not by art but by a natural capacity we have from God that we have all put our hands to working the earth. Moreover, neither will the "weaving together" of dwellings, or construction as a whole, or the art of making all kinds of furnishings and implements, which includes bronze-working, building, molding and weaving, as well as the manufacture of all instruments. This knowledge has practical utility for the masses, but it is not because it is thought to confer virtue that it is called knowledge. Nor does the art of hunting in all its various forms make anyone noble and wise, though it has come to have many forms and involves great skill. Nor do prophetic inspiration or the ability to interpret divine messages have this effect in the least. The prophet only knows what he says; he does not understand if it is true.

We now see that these arts enable us to possess the necessities of life, but that none of them makes anyone wise. Next in order is a kind of play, which is mostly imitative and in no way serious. Its practitioners make use of many instruments and many bodily gestures—and not wholly becoming ones at that. This includes skills that employ words, all the arts of the Muses, and the genres of visual representation, which are responsible for producing many varied figures in many media, both wet and dry. But the imitative art makes no one wise in any of these things, even those who practice their craft with the utmost seriousness.

Now that all these subjects have been dealt with, the next group turns out to be kinds of defense, which come in many different forms and which benefit many people. The chief and most widespread of these, the art of war, which is known as military strategy, has the highest reputation for utility, but requires the greatest amount of good luck and is granted to

976   people through courage more than wisdom. The art called medicine too
      is surely a defense, in this case against all the ravages the climate inflicts
      upon animals through cold, unseasonable heat, and other things of the
      sort. But none of these arts is distinguished for wisdom of the truest
      sort. They lack measure, are carried along by opinion, and proceed by
      guesswork. We will also call both sea-captains and sailors defenders, but
      no one should encourage us by proclaiming any single one of these men
  b   wise. No one could know the anger or friendship of the wind, even though
      the art of sailing would find this knowledge most agreeable. Nor are those
      men wise who claim to be defenders in lawsuits by virtue of their speaking
      ability. Their attention to people's characters is based on memory and rote
      acquaintance with opinion, and they stray wide of the truth about what
      is genuinely just.
         As a candidate for the reputation of wisdom there still remains a certain
      strange ability, which most would call not wisdom, but a natural gift. Some
  c   people easily learn whatever they are learning and accurately remember a
      great number of things, and some can call to mind what is useful for each
      person—what would be fitting if it were to take place—and quickly bring
      it about. When we notice such people, some will regard all these traits as
      a natural gift, while others will call them wisdom and still others a natural
      agility of mind. But no intelligent person will ever be willing to call anyone
      genuinely wise for having any of them.
         But surely there must turn out to be some science whose possession
      makes a wise person genuinely wise and not merely wise by reputation.
  d   Let us see, then. We are tackling an extremely difficult subject—to discover
      a different science from the ones we have discussed, one which may be
      both genuinely and plausibly called wisdom, and which will make its
      possessor neither vulgar nor foolish, but a wise and good citizen of his
      city, a just ruler and subject, and in tune with himself and the world as
      well. First let us identify this science. Of all the sciences that now exist,
      which one would render humans the most unintelligent and senseless of
      living things if it completely disappeared from the human race or had not
  e   been developed? In point of fact, it is not at all hard to identify. If we
      compare, so to speak, one science with another, we will see that the one
      that has given the gift of number would have this effect upon the entire
      mortal race.
         It is God himself, I believe, and not some good fortune that saves us by
      making us this gift. But I must say which god I mean, though it will seem
977   strange, though yet in a way not strange. How can we keep from believing
      that what causes all things that are good for us is also the cause of the
      good that is by far the greatest, namely, wisdom? So, Megillus and Clinias,
      what god am I speaking of with such solemnity? Uranus (i.e., the heaven),
      the god whom above all others it is most just to pray to and to honor, as
      all the other divinities and gods do. We will unanimously agree that he
      has been the cause of all other good things for us. But we declare that he
      is really the one who gave us number too, and he will continue to give
  b   it, supposing that we are willing to follow him closely. If we come to

contemplate him in the right way—whether we prefer to call him Cosmos or Olympus or Heaven [Uranus]—let us call him as we like, but let us notice carefully how by decorating himself and making the stars revolve in himself through all their orbits, he brings about the seasons and provides nourishment for all. Together with the entirety of number, he also furnishes, we would insist, everything else that involves intelligence and everything that is good. But this is the greatest thing, for a person to receive from him the gift of numbers and go on to examine fully the entire revolution of the heavens.

Next, let us return to a point made a little while ago and recall that we   c
were very right to observe that if the human race were deprived of number, we would never come to be intelligent in anything. We would be animals unable to give a rational account, and our soul would never obtain the whole of virtue. An animal that does not know two and three or odd and even, one that is completely ignorant of number, could never give an account of the things it has grasped by the only means available to it— perception and memory. But while nothing prevents it from possessing   d
the remainder of virtue—courage and moderation—no one deprived of the ability to give a true account can ever become wise, and anyone lacking wisdom, which is the greatest part of all virtue, can never become completely good or, in consequence, happy. Thus it is altogether necessary to employ number as a basis, though why this is necessary would require a still longer account than all I have said. But we will also be right in stating the present point, that regarding the achievements attributed to the other arts, the ones we recently surveyed when we allowed all the arts to exist,   e
not a single one remains. They are all completely eliminated when we take away the science of number.

If we reflect upon the arts, we might well suppose that there are a few purposes for which the human race needs numbers—although even this concession is important. Further, if we contemplate the divine and the mortal elements in the generated world, we will discover reverence for the divine and also number in its true nature. But even so, not every one   978
of us will yet understand either how great a power intimate knowledge of the whole of number can confer upon us (since in addition to what I have mentioned, all musical phenomena clearly require movement and sounds that are based on number), or—the most important thing—that number causes all good things. We must also understand well that it causes no evil that may occur. By contrast, movement that is irrational, disorderly, unseemly, unrhythmical and inharmonious is wholly lacking in number, as is everything that shares in any evil. This is how anyone who is going   b
to die happy must think. And as regards justice, goodness, beauty, and all such things, without knowledge no one who has attained true opinion will ever give a numerical account that is at all likely to persuade either himself or anyone else.

Now let us go on to take up this very topic, number. How did we learn to count? How did we come to have the concepts of one and two? The   c
Universe has endowed us with the natural capacity to have concepts,

whereas many other living things lack even the capacity to learn from the
Father how to count. With us humans, the first thing God caused to dwell
in us was the capability to understand what we are shown, and then he
proceeded to show us, and he still does. And of the things he shows us,
taken one by one, what can we behold more beautiful than the day? Later,
d   when we come to see the night, everything appears different to our vision.
Since Heaven never stops making these bodies ply their course night after
night and day after day, he never stops teaching humans one and two,
until even the slowest person learns well enough to count. For each of us
who sees them will also form the concepts of three, four, and many. Out
of these many, God made a unit by constructing a moon which goes
through its course sometimes appearing larger and sometimes smaller,
e   thus always revealing each day as different until fifteen days and nights
have passed. This *is* a period, if one is willing to treat the entire cycle as
a unit. As a result, even the stupidest of the animals God has endowed
with the ability to learn is able to learn it. Every living being that can has
become quite knowledgeable in numbers this far [i.e., up to fifteen] and
979   in these numbers, by considering each thing individually. Next, for the
purpose of reckoning on each occasion all things in relation to one another
as numbers[1] and also for a purpose which I regard as greater—after creating
the moon, waxing and waning as we said, God established months in
relation to the year, and so all the living beings who could began to
comprehend number in relation to number, with the blessing of Good
Fortune. Thanks to these celestial events we have crops, the earth bears
food for all living things, and the winds that blow and the rains that fall
b   are not violent or without measure. If on the contrary anything turns out
for the worse, we must not blame God, but humans, for not rightly managing their own lives.

Now in our inquiry about Laws we found that the other things that are
best for humans are easy to know, and that we are all competent both to
understand what we are told and to act on that basis, as long as we know
what is likely to be advantageous and the reverse. Indeed, we found then
c   and we still maintain that none of the other pursuits is particularly difficult,
but how to become good people is an extremely difficult problem. Also,
to acquire everything else that is good—property in the right amount and
a body of the right sort—is, as the saying goes, both possible and not
difficult. Further, everyone will grant that the soul should be good, and
as to how it should be good, everyone says it must be just, moderate,
brave, and wise as well. But when it comes to the precise form of wisdom
d   it must have, as we have recently shown in detail, there is no longer any
agreement, at least among the many. But as a matter of fact we have just
now discovered over and above all the former kinds of wisdom one that
is by no means insignificant, at least in that anyone who masters the
material we have outlined is guaranteed a reputation for wisdom. But are

1. Thus extending the concept of number to include ratios.

those who know these things really wise and good? This is precisely what requires a satisfactory account.

CLINIAS: How right you were, my friend, to say that you were setting out to say important things on important subjects!

ATHENIAN: Indeed, they are not trivial, Clinias. But—and this is even   e
more difficult—I am attempting to say things that are wholly and universally true.

CLINIAS: I agree completely. But even so, please don't get weary of telling me your ideas.

ATHENIAN: Of course, but don't you two get tired of listening, either.

CLINIAS: Don't worry—and I am speaking on behalf of the two of us.

ATHENIAN: Very well. We must begin from the beginning. In the first   980
place, it appears that above all we must find a single name, if we can, for this thing we hold to be wisdom. If we simply cannot do this, our second objective will be to determine what and how many kinds of wisdom a person must know in order to be wise according to our account.

CLINIAS: Please go on.

ATHENIAN: The next point is that no one can blame the lawgiver for fashioning an account of the gods that is finer and better than those given up to now, engaging, so to speak, in noble play and honoring the gods, and   b
for him to pass his whole life celebrating them with hymns of happiness.

CLINIAS: Well said, my friend! I hope that this is the goal of your laws, that people will sing hymns to the gods and live purer lives, and then meet with the end that is at once best and finest.

ATHENIAN: What are we saying, then, Clinias? Does it seem that by singing hymns to the gods we are honoring them greatly, praying that we will be led to say the finest and best things about them? Is this what you mean, or something else?

CLINIAS: Precisely that. But pray to the gods with confidence and state   c
the account that it occurs to you to offer about the fine things that concern the gods and goddesses.

ATHENIAN: This will happen if God himself guides me. Only please join in my prayer.

CLINIAS: Please go on to the next point.

ATHENIAN: Since people in the past have failed badly in describing the generation of gods and living things, it appears that I must begin by constructing an account based on my previous one, taking up again my   d
attack on impious accounts,[2] and declaring that there are gods who care for all things, great and small, who are inexorable in matters of justice. I suppose you remember, Clinias, since you have even received a written record. What we said then was quite true. The most important point was that as a whole, soul is older than any body. Do you recall? You surely must remember. For what is superior, older and more godlike is obviously   e
so in relation to what is inferior, younger and less honorable, and what

---

2. *Laws* x; for the point noted just below, see 891e ff., 896a ff.

rules or leads is in every way older than what is ruled or led. Let us accept
981   this point, then, that soul is older than body. But if this is so, the first step
in our first account of generation will be more plausible. Let us take it,
then, that the beginning of our beginning is more seemly and that we are
taking exactly the right steps in approaching the most important part of
wisdom, the generation of gods.

CLINIAS: Anyone must grant that we are stating these matters the best
we can.

ATHENIAN: Next, when a soul and a body come together to form a single
structure and produce a single form, do we assert that this is most truly
said to be a living thing, in virtue of its nature?

CLINIAS: Yes.

b   ATHENIAN: So this kind of thing is most correctly called a living being?

CLINIAS: Indeed.

ATHENIAN: We must identify solid bodies, five in number on the most
plausible account, from which the things that are finest and best can be
fashioned. The remaining kind of entity, all of it, has but a single form,
for soul, the truly most divine type of entity, is the only thing that could
possibly have no body or be without any color at all. This is the only entity
c   naturally suited for fashioning and creating, while body, we maintain, is
suited for being fashioned, for becoming, and being seen. The former type
(let us say it again, since it should not be stated just once) is naturally
suited to be invisible, and intelligent and intelligible as well, sharing in
memory and calculation that involves the vicissitudes of odd and even.
There being five bodies, then, we declare that they are fire, water, air,
earth, and ether, and that each of the many and varied kinds of living
things is brought to perfection with one of these playing the chief role.

But we need to learn this for each kind individually, as follows. As the
d   first kind we discuss, let us take up the earthy one. This includes all
humans, and in addition all living things with many legs and those with
none, and all that move and the ones that are stationary, held fast by roots.
What makes this a single kind, we should believe, is the fact that although
all kinds of living beings are composed of all the five bodies, the greatest
part of this kind is made of earth with its solid nature.

We ought further to suppose there is a second, different kind of living
thing that comes to be and moreover is visible. Its largest portion is fire,
e   but it has portions of earth and air along with small amounts of all the
rest. This is why we should declare that from these bodies arise visible
living things of all kinds. We must further suppose that the kinds of living
things in the heavens—which is what we should claim the divine stars to
be—have come to be, endowed with the finest body and the best and
happiest soul. But as to their destiny, which might be either of two sorts,
we must allow opinion a role. Either they are all entirely and of absolute
982   necessity indestructible, immortal and divine, or else each of them is content to possess such a vast length of life that they could never possibly
demand more.

To repeat, let us first suppose that these are two kinds of living things, that both are visible, the one made entirely, as it might seem, of fire, the other of earth, and that the earthy kind moves in disorder, while the one of fire moves in perfect order. Now what moves in disorder (which is exactly how the kind of living things around us behaves for the most part) we ought to consider unintelligent. But if something has an orderly path b in the heavens we should treat that as powerful evidence of its intelligence. For if it always proceeds in its course uniformly and without variation, and always acts and is affected in the same way, it gives ample evidence of intelligent life. The necessity of the soul that possesses intelligence is far the most powerful of all necessities. For it is a ruler, not a subject, and so ordains its decrees. When a soul reaches the best decision in accordance c with the best intelligence, the result, which is truly to its mind, is perfectly unalterable. Not even adamant could ever be mightier or more unalterable. Truly, three Fates hold fast whatever has been decided through the best counsel by each and all of the gods, and guarantee that it is brought to pass. Humans should admit as evidence of the intelligence of the stars and this entire movement of theirs, the fact that they always do the same things, because they are doing what was decided an astonishingly long time ago and do not change their decision back and forth, sometimes doing d one thing and at others doing something else, wandering and changing their orbits. This opinion of ours is the exact opposite of what most people believe—that because they do the same things uniformly they do not possess soul. The crowd has followed the fools in supposing that the human race is intelligent and alive because it undergoes change, whereas the divine is unintelligent because it remains in the same orbits. But in fact anyone could have adopted views that are finer, better and acceptable, e and could have understood that whatever always operates uniformly, without variation, and through the same causes is for that very reason to be regarded as intelligent. Such a person could also understand that this is the nature of the stars, the finest of all things to behold, and further that moving through their march and dance, the finest and most magnificent dance there is, they bring to pass what all living things need.

In fact, we are right to say they possess soul. First, consider their size. 983 They are not as small as they appear; the mass of each is inconceivably large. This point should be accepted with confidence since it is based on adequate proofs. For we can correctly reason that the sun is larger than the earth, and indeed, all the moving stars have an amazing size. How can any being cause so vast a mass to revolve always in the same period? I declare that God is the cause and that it could never be otherwise. For b nothing could ever come to be alive except through God, as we have shown. And since God is capable of this, it is perfectly easy for him first to make any body and any mass of material into a living being and then make it move however he thinks best. I hope the single account I am now stating may hold true for them all. Unless a soul is attached to each of them or even *in* each, earth, heaven and all the stars and all the masses made c of these things cannot move with such precision in their annual, monthly and daily courses, making all that takes place turn out good for us all.

Since man is so sorry a thing, it is important to avoid speaking nonsense and to be clear in what we say. If anyone is going to identify as causes certain bodies in rushing movement, or kinds of matter or anything of the sort, he will not succeed in saying anything clear. As for the account we

d have given, we really must take it up again, to see whether it is reasonable or wholly deficient. We hold first that there are two kinds of entities, soul and body, and many individuals of each kind, each one different from others of its kind and from those of the other kind, and there is no third kind of entity found in anything. Second, that soul is superior to body: we shall hold that the former is intelligent, the latter not, the one rules, the other is ruled, the one is the cause of everything, the other the cause of nothing that takes place. And so it is the height of folly and absurdity

e to say that the things in the heavens have arisen through the agency of anything else and are not the products of both soul and body, as we hold. If our theories about all the celestial beings are to win out, and if it is to appear convincing that they are all divine, we must suppose them to be one of two things. Either they are themselves gods and it is perfectly correct to celebrate them in hymns, or we must suppose them to be likenesses of

984 gods, something like images of them, made by the gods themselves, for their creators were not unintelligent or of little worth. As we have declared, we must suppose them to be one of these two things, and once we do this, we must honor them above all images. Assuredly no other image will ever appear more beautiful or more widely shared by all humans than these, let alone established in better locations or surpassing them in

b purity, awe, and their whole manner of life, since they have been made superior in all these ways.

Concerning the gods let us go no further. Now that we have identified the two kinds of living things that are visible to us, of which we declare that one is immortal, while all the other, the earthy kind, is mortal, let us try with the greatest accuracy that plausible opinion permits to describe the three intermediate kinds which fall in between the two already discussed. After fire let us take up ether. We may suppose that soul fashions

c living things out of it which (like the other kinds of living things) are for the most part characterized by that substance, but which also possess smaller amounts of the other kinds in order to bond them together. After ether, soul fashions a different kind of living things out of air, and a third out of water. After creating them all, it is plausible that soul filled the entire heaven with living things, employing each according to its character, since all share in life. These are the second, third, fourth and fifth kinds

d of living things, beginning from the visible gods and ending up with us humans.

As to the gods—Zeus, Hera and all the rest—we may legislate as we like, the same law holding for each, and we must treat this principle as firmly established. But as to the first gods, those that are visible, greatest, most honored, and most sharply seeing everywhere, we must declare that these are the stars together with all the celestial phenomena we perceive. After them and next in order beneath them are *daimons*. The kind made of air, which occupies the third, middle, position, is responsible for mediation between gods and humans, and should be highly honored in our prayers for bringing words of good tiding. Both these kinds of living beings—the one made of ether and the next in order, the one made of air—are wholly imperceptible. Even when they are close by we cannot see them. They have a wonderful intelligence, being of kinds that learn quickly and have good memories, and we should say that they know all our thoughts and both love those of us who are noble and good and hate those who are extremely evil, since already with these kinds we are discussing beings that experience pain. (By contrast, God, who enjoys the perfection of divine nature, is removed from pain and pleasure, and is entirely occupied in thinking and knowing.) Since the heaven is completely filled with living beings, we should say that they communicate with one another and with the highest gods about all humans and all other things. They do so through the movements of the middle ranks of living beings, which are wafted lightly towards the earth and also towards the whole heaven. It would be correct to represent the fifth kind of living thing, that made of water, as a demigod made of that substance, sometimes seen, sometimes hidden and invisible, provoking wonder through its dim appearance.

These five kinds of beings really are living things, and some of them have had various types of encounters with humans, whether through dreams in sleep or in audible communications through divine voices or prophecies to certain people whether healthy or ill or even at the point of death. The resulting beliefs affect both individuals and communities and have been the origin of many religious rites for many people and will be in the future as well. Anyone who legislates on all these matters and has even the least intelligence will never dare to make innovations and turn his own city towards a piety which lacks any clear foundation. On the other hand, in his complete lack of knowledge he will not forbid what ancestral law has declared about sacrifices, since it is impossible for mortals to have knowledge about such things.

On the same reasoning, the worst people are those that do not dare to declare to us the gods that really do appear to us, or to reveal them as being other gods, ones who do not receive worship or the honors they are due. But in fact, this is exactly what is taking place. It is as if at some point one of us had seen a sun or a moon coming into existence and looking down at us all, and through some inability failed to report it, and further was not eager to do his part to bring them from their dishonored state into a place of honor and make them conspicuous, and also to institute festivals and sacrifices for them and to determine their periods of longer or, in several cases, shorter years, setting apart a time for each of them.

Wouldn't such a person himself, as well as anyone else who was aware of the situation, agree that it would be right to call him evil?

CLINIAS: Absolutely so, my friend, most evil.

ATHENIAN: But, my dear Clinias, I want you to know that this is precisely my situation now.

CLINIAS: What do you mean?

ATHENIAN: There are eight powers [i.e., orbits] of the celestial beings, that are brothers of one another. I myself have observed them. This is no

b   special accomplishment; others can do it easily too. Three of them are the ones we mentioned a little while ago:[3] those belonging to the sun, to the moon, and to all the stars. But there are five more. Now regarding all these orbits and the beings which move in them (whether they move of their own accord or proceed in their courses borne on chariots), none of us must ever rashly suppose that some of them are gods and others are not or that some are legitimate while others are what it is wrong for any of us even

c   to utter. Instead, we must declare and assert that they are all brothers and have brothers' shares. We must not attribute the year to one of them and the month to another, while refusing to assign to the rest any share or any time in which it completes its own orbit, contributing to the perfection of the visible cosmos established by the most divine law of all.

Anyone who is happy began by being struck with awe at this cosmos, and then conceived a passion for learning all that a mortal can, believing

d   that this is how to live the best and most fortunate life and that when he dies he will go to places where virtue is at home. Further, once he is really and truly initiated and has achieved perfect unity and a share of the one true wisdom, he continues for the rest of his days as an observer of the fairest things that sight can see.

e   The next thing is to say how many and who these gods are. For we must make it clear that we never go back on our word. In fact, I insist with certainty on just the following. I repeat that they are eight, and of the eight, three have been discussed and five still remain. The fourth orbit and period of revolution and the fifth as well are nearly equal in speed to the sun, neither faster nor slower overall. Of these three, the one with sufficient intelligence must be the leader. These three orbits belong to the sun, the morning star, and a third body which I cannot call by name since its name is not known. The reason is that the first person to observe them

987   was a foreigner. Egypt and Syria have a marvelously beautiful summer season. In consequence it was an ancient practice there that led people to reflect on these matters for the first time. They were always observing the entire totality of the visible stars, as it were, since their part of the world has no clouds or rain. From there, after being closely examined for thousands of years, in fact an infinite time, this knowledge spread everywhere including Greece. Therefore we must be bold and enact this into law. It is clearly not for people of intelligence to hold some divine things in dishonor and

3. 978c–979a.

others in honor. As to why they have not got names, this is the reason   b
that should be given. Instead, they have taken as their appellations the
names of [the traditional] gods. The morning star, which is also the evening
star, is accounted as Aphrodite's star [i.e., Venus], a name highly appropriate for a Syrian law-giver to choose. The star that more or less accompanies both the sun and Aphrodite's is Hermes' [Mercury]. We have yet to
speak of three more orbits that move to the right[4] like the moon and the
sun. But we should mention one, the eighth, which above all should be
called the cosmos. It moves in the opposite direction to all the others and
carries them, as should be obvious even to humans who know a little
about these things. But all that we know well we must tell, and we are   c
telling it. For to anyone with even a small amount of understanding that
is correct and divine, what is genuinely wisdom appears to be somewhat
along these lines. Of the remaining three stars, one is particularly slow,
and some call it by the name "Cronus' " [Saturn]. The next slowest we
should call Zeus' [Jupiter], and the next one Ares' [Mars]; this one has the
reddest color of them all. None of this is hard to comprehend if someone   d
explains it, but once a person learns it, we say, he must believe it.

Every Greek ought to bear in mind that the location we Greeks possess
is absolutely best for virtue. Its merit is that it is intermediate between
winter and summer. Since our summer is inferior to the summer in those
other places, as we said, we were late in coming to observe the ordering
of these gods. But let us take it for granted that whatever Greeks receive
from foreigners they improve in the end—a point that we must suppose   e
holds for the present subject in particular. In fact, it is difficult to find out
all these things for certain, but there is high and good hope that even   988
though the tradition about all these gods and also their worship have come
from abroad, the Greeks, on account of their forms of education, the oracles
from Delphi, and their whole legally codified system of worship, will
succeed in worshiping them better and in a real sense more justly.

Let no Greek ever fear that being mortal we should never concern
ourselves with the divine. We should have quite the opposite thought; the
divine [i.e., the cosmos] is never without intelligence nor is it at all ignorant   b
of human nature, but it knows that if it teaches we will follow along and
learn what we are taught. And of course it knows that the very thing that
it teaches us and that we learn is number and how to count. If it did not
know this it would be the least intelligent thing of all. It would really not
"know itself," as the proverb goes, if it were angry at those who are able
to learn and did not instead rejoice without envy along with the ones who
become good through God's help.

Now it makes much good sense that when humans first had thoughts   c
about how the gods came to be and what they were like and what deeds
they did once they came to be, what they said was not acceptable or
pleasing to sensible people. Nor were the later accounts, in which fire,

---

4. I.e., from West to East.

water and the other bodies were declared oldest and the wonderful soul younger, and which also maintained that that motion was superior and more valuable which belongs to body and which body produces in itself by heat, cold, and all things of that sort, and that the soul does not move

d both body and soul itself. But now, when we say that it is no surprise that if a soul comes to be in a body it causes both the body and itself to move and revolve, on no account does our soul disbelieve that it has the capacity to make any weight revolve, no matter how large. Therefore, since as we now claim, soul is the cause of the whole cosmos, and all good things have causes that are good, while evil things have different causes, which

e are evil, it is no wonder that soul is the cause of every orbit and motion, and the best kind of soul causes orbits and motions that tend toward the good, while the opposite kind of soul causes those that tend toward the opposite. It follows that the good must always have defeated and must always defeat the evil.

All that we have said is in accord with Justice, who takes vengeance on the unholy. Consequently, getting back to the object of our investigation,

989 we cannot but believe that the good person, at least, is wise. But as for the wisdom for which we have long been searching, let us see whether we can discover any discipline or art such that ignorance of it would make us lack all judgment about justice. In fact, I think we can. Let me say what it is. I shall try to make clear to you how it dawned upon me as I searched high and low. The cause of our failure is that we do not practice the most

b important part of virtue in the right way. What I just said seems to me to indicate this strongly. For no one will ever persuade us that there is a more important part of virtue for mortals than reverence towards the gods, although it must be admitted that through ignorance of the worst kind this quality has been absent from the people with the best natures.

Such natures hardly ever occur, but if they do they are an outstanding benefit. For a soul that possesses both quickness and slowness in a mild and moderate degree will tend to be good-natured. It will be inclined towards courage, readily induced to moderation, and—the most important

c feature in such cases—since it will be good at learning and remembering, it can greatly enjoy these activities, and so will have a love of learning. These are not easily produced, but when they are born and are nurtured and trained in the necessary way, it is absolutely right for such people to be able to hold the inferior majority in subjection by thinking, doing and saying all that concerns the gods in the right ways at the right times, not hypocritically performing sacrifices and purification rites for violations

d against gods and humans, but in truth honoring virtue. In fact, honoring virtue is the single most important thing for the entire city. Now we hold that this segment of the population is by nature best suited to authority and is capable of learning the noblest and finest studies, if anyone will teach them. But no one could do so unless God leads the way. Indeed, if someone were to teach, but not in the right way, it would be better not to learn. Even so, it follows from what I am now saying that people with this kind of nature, the best, must learn these things and that I must tell them to.

I must try, then, to give a detailed account of what those things are, what they are like, and how to learn them, given my ability as a speaker and the ability of those who can hear me: what things a person is to learn about reverence towards the gods and how he is to learn them. When you hear what it is, you will find it strange. I say its name is astronomy, an answer no one would ever expect through unfamiliarity with the subject. People do not know that the true astronomer must be the wisest person. I do not mean anyone practicing astronomy the way Hesiod did and everyone else of that sort, by observing risings and settings of stars, but the one who has observed seven of the eight circuits, each of them completing its own orbit in a way no one can easily contemplate who is not endowed with an extraordinary nature. We have now said what we must learn. We shall go on to state, as we say, how we must and should learn it. My first point is the following.

The moon completes its circuit most quickly, bringing the month [the new moon] and before it the full moon. Next we must attain knowledge of the sun, which brings the solstices as it completes its entire circuit, and then the planets that accompany it [i.e., Venus and Mercury]. To avoid repeating ourselves many times about the same things, since the remaining orbits which we discussed earlier are not easy to understand, we should make continuous efforts in preparing for this knowledge the people whose natures can understand it, to teach them many preliminary subjects and accustom them to learning when they are boys and youths. For this reason they need to study mathematics.

First and foremost is the study of numbers in their own right, as opposed to numbers that possess bodies. This is the study of the entire nature and properties of odd and even—all that number contributes to the nature of existing things. After learning this, next in order is what goes by the extremely silly name of geometry [literally, "earth measurement"]. In fact, it is absolutely clear that this subject is the assimilation by reference to plane surfaces of numbers that are not by nature similar to one another. That this miracle is of divine, not human origin should be obvious to anyone who can understand it. After this is the study of numbers with three factors, which are similar in virtue of their nature as solids. Another art, called stereometry by those acquainted with it, assimilates numbers that are dissimilar. But what people who look into these matters and understand them find divine and miraculous is how nature as a whole molds sorts and kinds according to each proportion, with reference to the power that is always based on the double and the power opposite to this [the half]. The first sequence of the double is the one carried out in numbers in the ratio one to two [i.e., the sequence 1, 2, 4, . . .]. The sequence determined by squares [sc. of these numbers: the sequence 1, 4, 16, . . .] is the double of this. Double of *this* is the one [the sequence 1, 8, 64, . . .] that reaches what is solid and tangible, after proceeding from one to eight.[5] The sequence that gives the mean of the double involves both the mean that exceeds the smaller and is exceeded by the larger by an equal amount [i.e., the arithmetic mean], and the mean that exceeds one of the extremes by the same fraction of that extreme as the fraction of the other extreme by which it is exceeded by that extreme [i.e., the harmonic mean].

b   (The means of 6 in relation to 12 are determined by the ratios 3:2 and 4:3.)[6] The sequence based on both of these means has been granted to the human race by the blessed choir of the Muses and has bestowed upon us the use of concord and symmetry to promote play in the form of rhythm and harmony.

Let us take it that all these things are as we have said. But what is the point of learning them? To ascertain this we must refer to the divine element in the generated world, which consists of the finest and most divine sort of visible things God has permitted humans to observe. No

c   one who has observed them can ever claim to have learned them in any easy way that does not involve the sciences that I just described. In addition, in all our discussions we must fit the individual to the species by asking questions and refuting errors. This method is the first and finest touchstone for humans to use, whereas all the tests that are not genuine but pretend to be so involve everyone in totally useless labor. We must also have an

d   accurate knowledge of how time brings to pass all celestial events precisely. If we do, then everyone who has confidence in the truth of our account that soul is both older and more divine than body should believe that the saying "all things are full of gods" is entirely right and sufficient, and further that we are never slighted through the forgetfulness or neglect of our superiors.

In all these studies, though, the following point must be kept in mind: anyone who comprehends each of them through the right method is greatly benefited in doing so; otherwise, it is better to call on God for help. The

e   right method is this—I must say this much at least. To the person who learns in the right way it will be revealed that every diagram and complex system of numbers, and every structure of harmony and the uniform pattern of the revolution of the stars are a single thing applying to all these phenomena. And it *will* be revealed to anyone who learns correctly, as we

992   say, fixing his eye on unity. To one who studies these subjects in this way, there will be revealed a single natural bond that links them all. But anyone who is going to pursue these studies in any other way must "call on Good

---

5. This last sequence, formed by cubing the numbers in the first sequence, represents three dimensions, the "solid and tangible." (Likewise, the first and second sequences represent one and two dimensions, respectively.) In reaching it, we have passed through the previous two sequences; that is, the generation of three dimensions presupposes that of one and two dimensions.

6. The arithmetic mean of 6 and 12 is 9, the harmonic mean is 8, and 9:6 = 3:2 and 8:6 = 4:3; also 12:9 = 4:3 and 12:8 = 3:2.

Fortune for help," as we say too. For without them, no one in cities will ever become happy. This is the right way, this is the upbringing, these are the studies. Whether they are difficult, whether they are easy, this is the way we must proceed.

It is not right to neglect the gods once it is obvious that our story about them all has been told in the right way and blessed by Good Fortune. Anyone who has grasped all these things in this way I say is truly the wisest. I maintain also, both in jest and in earnest, that when any of these people fulfills his destiny by dying (if indeed he still exists in death), he will no longer be affected by a multitude of perceptions as he is now but will participate in a destiny of unity. Having become one from many, he will be happy, most wise, and blessed—whether in his blessed state he dwells on continents or islands [the Isles of the Blest]—and he will enjoy this fortune forever. And whether he lives his life engaging in these pursuits in private or in public, the gods will grant him to experience the same things in the same way. But as to what we asserted at the outset, the identical account is now at hand again, and it is genuinely true—that with but a few exceptions, humans are incapable of becoming perfectly blessed and happy. This has been stated correctly. Only those who are by nature godlike and moderate, who also possess the rest of virtue, and have understood all the subjects connected with the blessed science [astronomy] (and we have stated what these are) have obtained and possess all the gifts of the divinity in adequate measure.

In private we say and in public we enact into law that the highest offices must be bestowed upon those individuals who have mastered these studies in the right way, with much labor, and have arrived at the fullness of old age. The others must obey them and speak in praise of all gods and goddesses. Now that we have come to know this wisdom well enough and have tested it, we are all bound, most rightly, to urge the Nocturnal Council to pursue it.

LETTERS

The biographer Diogenes Laertius tells us that Thrasyllus included in his edition of Plato thirteen letters alleging to have been written by him. These are the letters presented here, in Thrasyllus' numbering. Apart from two insignificant ones indicating no presumed date, they all profess to be from the last two decades of Plato's life. Most of them show him deeply and personally involved in the politics of Syracuse, the most important Greek city of Sicily, then engaged in a protracted struggle with Carthage to preserve Greek hegemony in the island, or at least its eastern half. The general Dionysius had established himself as 'tyrant' of the previously democratic Syracuse, being succeeded in 367/6 by his son Dionysius II, to whom Letters I, II, III, and XIII are addressed. Plato had visited the court of Dionysius I in about 387, and according to these Letters he had formed a close friendship there with the tyrant's young brother-in-law, Dion—later an influential figure in his government—of whose intellectual and moral qualities he held a high opinion. According to the account of Letter VII, by far the longest and most interesting of the series, Dion shared Plato's ideals of government—presumably those expressed in Republic. With the accession of the younger Dionysius, a young man who showed an interest in philosophical matters, Dion saw an opportunity, with the help of Plato's instruction in philosophy, to win Dionysius over to abandoning his tyranny for a rule of the 'best' laws under free institutions. Thus—still according to the Letters—Plato returned to Syracuse in 367 or 366 to carry out his and Dion's purpose of establishing there the magnanimous rule of a 'philosopher-king'. But Dionysius proved less tractable than Dion had expected; within four months, fearing him as a rival, he banished Dion to Greece, and Plato himself returned to Athens not long afterwards, the grand project a shambles. He came back a third time some four years later, at Dionysius' urging, in the hope at least of restoring Dion to Dionysius' good graces. At that too he failed. The rest of the story—Dion's successful expedition to take Syracuse in 357, effectively ending Dionysius' rule, and his eventual murder in 354 in the factional fighting that ensued—can be read in Plutarch's Life of Dion.

Are these letters, or any of them, genuine? We have no way of knowing for sure. We have no record of any Platonic letters existing before the end of the third century B.C., some one hundred fifty years or more after the nominal date of composition. We know that many such 'letters' of famous personages originated as exercises in the schools of rhetoric in later times, and others were forged for various reasons. Our manuscripts report a doubt (perhaps going back to Thrasyllus) about Letter XII's authenticity, and from their content *others can hardly be by Plato. Letter VII, the least unlikely to have come from Plato's pen, contains much tantalizing information about Plato's views about philosophy which if genuine could be of some significance for working out his final positions. The author reiterates in bold language his commitment to Forms, and, drawing upon an elaborate theory about the means of arriving at philosophical truth and the defectiveness of language to express it, he explains why he would never write any philosophical treatise. If not by Plato, Letter VII must have been written about when it says it was—not long after Dion's death in 354—and by someone close enough to Plato to be confident of writing about philosophy in a way that could convince a discriminating audience that included Greek philosophers in Southern Italy that the author was indeed Plato.*

J.M.C.

I

PLATO TO DIONYSIUS, WELFARE.   309

During all the time that I was with you administering your empire and enjoying your confidence above all others, you got the benefits and I the slanders. But I endured them, grievous as they were, because I knew that men would not think me a willing accomplice in any of your more barbarous acts. For all who are associated with you in your government are my witnesses, many of whom I myself have defended and saved from no little injury. And although I have held the highest authority and have protected your city on numerous occasions, you have deported me with less consideration than you ought to show in sending away a beggar who had been with you for the same length of time. I shall therefore in the future consult my own interests with less trust in mankind, and you, tyrant that you are, will live without friends.

The bearer of this letter, Bacchius, is bringing you the pretty gold that you gave for my departure. It was not enough for my traveling expenses, nor could I use it for any other need. The offer of it did you great dishonor, and its acceptance would do me almost as much, therefore I refuse it. No doubt it makes little difference to you whether you get or give such a trifle as this, so take it back and use it to serve some other friend as you have served me; I have had enough of your attentions.

A line of Euripides comes appropriately to my mind: "Thou'lt pray for such a helper at thy side."[1] Let me remind you also that most of the other tragic poets, when they bring in a tyrant who is being assassinated, make him cry out: "O wretched me! for lack of friends I die." But no one has

Translated by Glenn R. Morrow.

1. Frg. 956.

ever portrayed him as dying for lack of money. And these other lines, too,
make sense to sensible men:

> It is not gold, though a shining rarity in mortals' hopeless life,
> Nor gems, nor silver couches, that brighten the eyes of men,
> Nor broad and self-sufficient fields laden with the harvest,
> But the approving thought of upright men.

b   Farewell. May you realize how much you have lost in me and so conduct
yourself better toward others.

II

Plato to Dionysius, Welfare.

Archedemus[1] tells me you think that not only I but my friends also
should keep quiet about you and refrain from saying or doing anything
to your discredit, Dion alone excepted. This very statement, that you except
c   Dion, shows that I have no power over my friends; for if I could control
you and Dion and the others as you suggest, it would be much better for
us, I maintain, and for all the other Greeks. As it is, I am conspicuous in
showing willingness to follow my own precept. But I say this without
implying that there is any truth in the reports of Cratistolus and Polyxenus,
d   one of whom told you, I hear, that while at Olympia he heard many of
my companions speak ill of you. He must have much sharper hearing
than I, for I heard nothing of the sort. But this is what you must do, I
think, in the future; whenever you hear anything like this said of one of
us, write and inquire of me, and I will tell you the truth without shame
or hesitation.

So far as the relations between you and me are concerned the situation
e   is this. We are both known to practically every Greek, and our connection
with each other is no secret. Remember, too, that it will be no secret to
future generations, for those who hear of it will be as great in number as
our friendship has been long continued and open. What do I mean by
saying this now? Let me begin with a general truth. It is a law of nature
that wisdom and great power go together; they exert a mutual attraction
and are forever seeking to be united. And men love to converse with one
another about them, and to listen to what the poets say. For example,
311   when men talk of Hiero and Pausanias the Lacedaemonian, they like to
recall Simonides' connection with them and what he said and did. Likewise
they usually celebrate together Periander of Corinth and Thales of Miletus,
Pericles and Anaxagoras, and again Croesus and Solon, as wise men, with

---

1. See *Letters* III, 319a, and VII, 339a, 349d.

Cyrus, as ruler. In the same strain the poets couple Creon and Tiresias,   b
Polyeidus and Minos, Agamemnon and Nestor, Odysseus and Palamedes.
And our early ancestors, if I am not mistaken, linked Prometheus with
Zeus in much the same manner. Of these men some are sung about as
coming together in conflict, others for friendship; and some as being friends
at one time and enemies at another, and agreeing in some things and
disagreeing in others. I say all this to show you that when we are dead,   c
men will still talk about us, and we must have a care for their opinions.
It is necessary, I think, that we should be concerned about the future, since
it is the nature of an utterly slavish man to give it no thought, whereas
men of superior virtue do everything in their power to have themselves
well spoken of after they are dead. This very attitude is to me an indication
that the dead have some perception of what is going on here; for superior
minds divine that this is so, while those of no account deny it; and of these   d
two the intimations of good men are the more worthy of credence. It is
my belief that the men whom I have mentioned above would be only too
eager, if it were possible to rectify their associations with one another so
as to have a better account given of them than is now current. This is still
possible for us, please God; if there has been any fault in our past relations
we can still correct it by our words and actions; for the account which will
be given of true philosophy, and the reputation that it will enjoy, will be   e
better or worse, I say, according as we act nobly or basely. Indeed we can
show no greater piety than to act always with this concern, nor greater
impiety than to neglect it.

Shall I tell you then what we ought to do and what justice requires?
When I came to Sicily my reputation was high among philosophers, and
I came to Syracuse to make you my witness, so that philosophy might   312
gain favor with the multitude. In this I failed ingloriously, as is well known.
But I deny that the cause was what many persons might think. Instead,
it is because you showed that you did not quite trust me, but desired to
send me away and summon others to find out from them what my purposes
were, apparently mistrusting me. Many people thereupon bruited it about
that you held me in contempt and were interested in other things. This,   b
as you know, was the general report. Hear now what in consequence you
ought to do, and this will answer your question how you and I should
behave towards each other. If you feel nothing but contempt for philosophy, then let it alone; or if from your own studies or from the teachings
of others you have found better doctrines than mine, give them your
allegiance. But if, as I think, you favor my principles, then you ought to
honor them and me in particular. Now, as at the beginning, if you lead I
will follow. If you honor me, I will honor you; if not, I will keep silent.   c
Furthermore, if you take the lead in honoring me, you will get the reputation of honoring philosophy; and the very fact that you once were considering other philosophers will bring you commendation from many persons
as being yourself a philosopher. But if I pay you honor without any honor

from you, it will look as if I had my eyes on your money, and we know that this attitude has an evil name among men. In short, if you honor me it will be a tribute to us both; if I honor you, it will bring us both disgrace.

d   Enough of these matters. The sphere is not correct. Archedemus will explain it to you when he comes. And upon that other question of weightier and more sublime import about which you say you have difficulties, let him by all means enlighten you. According to his report, you say that the nature of "the first" has not been sufficiently explained. I must speak of this matter to you in enigmas, in order that if anything should happen to these tablets "in the recesses of the sea or land," whoever reads them may

e   not understand our meaning. It is like this. Upon the king of all do all things turn; he is the end of all things and the cause of all good. Things of the second order turn upon the second principle, and those of the third order upon the third. Now the soul of man longs to understand what sort of things these principles are, and it looks toward the things that are akin to itself, though none of them is adequate; clearly the king and the other

313   principles mentioned are not of that sort. The soul thereupon asks, What then is the nature of these principles? This is the question, O son of Dionysius and Doris, that causes all the trouble; or rather, this it is that produces in the soul the pains of childbirth, from which she must be delivered, or she will never really attain truth. You yourself once told me, under the

b   laurel trees in your garden, that you understood this matter, having found the answer yourself; and I replied that if you thought so, you had spared me many words. I said, however, that I had never met anyone who had discovered this truth, and that most of my own study was devoted to it. Perhaps you once heard something from someone and providentially started on the track of the answer, but then, thinking you had it safe, neglected to fix fast the proofs of it, which now dart here and there[2] about some object of your fancy, whereas the reality itself is quite different. You

c   are not alone in this experience; I assure you that everyone at first hearing is affected in just this way, and though some have more difficulty than others, there is almost no one who escapes with but little effort.

Considering thus our past and our present circumstances, we can fairly say we have found the answer to the question in your letter about our relations toward each other. For now that you are conversing with other

d   philosophers and are testing my doctrines, both by themselves and by comparing them with others, these teachings will take root this time, if your examination is sincere, and you will become attached both to them and to me.

Now how can this and all else that I have mentioned be brought about? It was quite proper of you to send Archedemus to me; do likewise in the future, for when he reaches you and gives you my answers you may still have difficulties. You will then send Archedemus back to me, if you are well advised, and he will return to you, like a good merchant. After you

2. Reading *a(i)ttousi* in b7.

have done this two or three times and have thoroughly examined the answers I send to you, I shall be much surprised if the matters which are now troubling you do not appear in an altogether different light. So be bold and inquire of me in this way; for you could not order, nor could Archedemus secure for you, any nobler or diviner merchandise.

Only take care that these letters do not fall into the hands of uninstructed men. Nothing, I dare say, could sound more ridiculous to the multitude than these sayings, just as to gifted persons nothing could be more admirable and inspiring. One must talk about them and hear them expounded again and again, perhaps for many years, and even then their gold is with the utmost difficulty separated and refined. The most surprising thing about it is this: many a man of able understanding and tenacious memory has become old in the hearing of these doctrines and has told me that after more than thirty years of hearing them expounded, after examining them and testing them in every way, those points which at the beginning seemed most doubtful he now thinks to be the clearest and most self-evident of all, while the matters he then thought most credible are now quite the contrary. Keep this in mind and take care that you have no occasion in the future to feel remorse for now exposing these doctrines unworthily. The best precaution is not to write them down, but to commit them to memory; for it is impossible that things written should not become known to others. This is why I have never written on these subjects. There is no writing of Plato's, nor will there ever be; those that are now called so come from an idealized and youthful[3] Socrates. Farewell and heed my warning; read this letter again and again, then burn it.

Enough of these matters. You were surprised that I sent Polyxenus to you; but about him as well as Lycophron and the other men now at your court, I repeat the opinion that I have long had; you are far superior to them in dialectic, both by natural aptitude and by your method of disputation; and none of them lets himself be defeated intentionally, as some people suppose, but only because he cannot help it. You seem, however, to have dealt with them quite fairly and rewarded them properly. But enough, and more than enough, about such men. As for Philistion,[4] if you still need him, by all means keep him there; but if it is possible, release him and let Speusippus have his services. Speusippus joins me in this request, and Philistion also assured me that he would be glad to come to Athens if you would let him go. You did well to release the man from the rock quarries; and my petition about Hegesippus, the son of Ariston, and his family is easy to grant, for you wrote me that if anyone ever tried to do him or them an injury and you knew of it you would prevent it. The truth should be told about Lysiclides; he is the only man who has come from Sicily to Athens who has not given a distorted report of the relations

3. Alternatively, 'modernized'.
4. A doctor.

between us; he continues, as always, to put the best interpretation upon what happened.

III

<small>PLATO TO DIONYSIUS, GREETINGS.</small>

Is this the most appropriate way to address you, or should I wish you
b   welfare, as I usually do in letters to my friends? You yourself, so I am told by those who were with you on the embassy to Delphi, addressed the god with this fawning expression, writing, they say,

Greetings to you! May you continue the pleasant life of the tyrant!

c   For my part I should not address such an exhortation even to a man, far less to a god. To God it would be enjoining something contrary to nature, since the divine has its seat far removed from pleasure and pain; and as for man, pleasure and pain more often do harm, by breeding stupidity, forgetfulness, folly, and insolence in his soul. But enough from me on the subject of salutations; read this and make whatever use you please of it.

d   Not a few persons have reported to me that you are telling it about among the ambassadors to your court that once, when I heard you announce your intention to resettle the Greek cities in Sicily and relieve Syracuse by changing your government from a tyranny to a kingship, I dissuaded you, you say, though you were very eager; but that now I am instructing Dion
e   to do these very things, and thus we are using your own ideas to wrest your empire from you. You know best whether you gain anything by such tales; in any case you are doing me wrong in telling the exact opposite of what happened. I have been slandered enough by Philistides and numerous other persons before the mercenaries and the people of Syracuse, because I was living in the citadel; and those outside, if any mistake was made, blamed it all on me, saying that you obeyed me in all things. You yourself
316   know quite well that on political matters I willingly labored with you on only a few things at the beginning, when I thought I could do some good. Besides other minor matters, I did considerable work on the preambles to the laws, i.e., on those parts distinct from what you or someone else has added. For I hear that some of you have since been revising them; but which parts are mine and which yours will be obvious to anyone who is able to judge of my character.[1] But as I have just said, I don't need to be further misrepresented, either to the people of Syracuse or to anyone else whom these words of yours may influence; rather I need to be defended
b   against those earlier charges as well as against these graver and more malicious ones that have since appeared. Since, then, I am accused on two counts, I must make a twofold defense and show, first, that it was reason-

---

1. Alternatively, "to recognize my style."

able of me to avoid taking part in your affairs of state, and secondly, that it was not my advice that prevented you, as you say, and stood in your way when you were going to resettle the Greek cities. So now hear first my defense on the former of these two points.

I came to Syracuse at the joint invitation of you and Dion. The latter was an old and well-tried friend of mine, of mature age and settled character; and these qualities, as any man with a grain of sense can see, were absolutely necessary for advising upon problems as important as yours were at that time. You, on the contrary, were quite young, with almost no experience in the affairs with which you should have been acquainted, and were quite unknown to me. Shortly after—whether it was a man, or God, or chance working through you that was responsible—Dion was banished. Do you think that I could then co-operate with you in state affairs, when I had lost my wise colleague and saw the foolish one left, a ruler only in his own imagination, in reality being ruled by the crowd of unscrupulous men around him? What was my duty under those conditions? Was it not to do what I did, i.e., to let public affairs alone from that time on, protecting myself against the slanders of those who envied me, and trying above all to make you [and Dion] friends again, if possible, despite the differences that had arisen to separate you? You yourself can testify that this is the end for which I never ceased to labor. Eventually, though with difficulty, we came to an agreement. Since you had a war on your hands, I was to take ship for home; but after peace had been brought about, both Dion and I were to return to Syracuse and you were to summon us. These are the facts of my first visit to Syracuse and my safe return home.

When peace had come you sent for me a second time, not, however, in accordance with our agreement, for you invited me only, promising to recall Dion later. On this account I refused to come, much to Dion's displeasure, for he thought it would be better for me to come as you commanded. A year later a trireme arrived with letters from you, the main import of which was that if I would come, Dion's affairs would be settled in accordance with my desires, but the contrary if I did not. I hesitate to say how many letters at that time came from you and from others in Italy and Sicily who wrote at your request, and to how many of my friends and acquaintances they were sent, all urging in the strongest terms that I accede to your request and go. Thus it seemed to everyone, beginning with Dion, that I ought to take ship without hesitation. I kept protesting to them that I was old, and insisting that you would not be strong enough to resist those who were slandering me and wished to make us enemies. For I saw then as I see now that a great and swollen fortune, whether the possessor be a private person or a monarch, generally produces an equally numerous and mighty progeny of talebearers and companions in shameless pleasures; this is the worst result of wealth or power of any sort. Nevertheless I dismissed all these thoughts and came to you, determined that no friend of mine should ever be able to claim that he had lost all his goods when they could have been saved by my efforts. Upon my arrival (you know,

e   of course, all that happened thereafter) I demanded, in accordance with
     the promises made in your letters, first that you recall Dion and make him
     your friend—urging that friendship which, if you had then listened to me,
     would probably have been better for you and for Syracuse and for the
     rest of Greece than what we now have, or so my inner oracle tells me. In
     the second place I asked that Dion's property be held by his family, instead
318 of being apportioned among the executors whose names I need not men-
     tion. Furthermore, I thought that my presence with you made it more
     rather than less obligatory upon you to continue the annual revenues
     you had been sending to Dion. Failing in each of these requests, I asked
     permission to depart. Your next move was to urge me to remain for the
     year, saying that you would sell the whole of Dion's property and send
     half the proceeds to Corinth, retaining the other half there in Syracuse for
b   Dion's son. I could mention many promises that you made and did not
     keep, but they are numerous and I must be brief. After you had sold all
     his property and without Dion's consent (though you had said you would
     not sell it without his consent), then, my fine friend, you put the colophon
     on all your broken promises. You hit upon a scheme that was neither
     honorable nor fitting, nor just nor advantageous, to frighten me into ignor-
     ing what was going on so that I would not even ask for the dispatch of
c   Dion's money. After you had banished Heraclides (an act which neither
     I nor the people of Syracuse thought just), the fact that I had joined with
     Theodotes and Eurybius in begging you not to do this you took as a
     sufficient pretext and said that it had long been clear that I cared nothing
     for you, but only for Dion and his friends and followers; and that now
     when accusations had been made against Heraclides and Theodotes, who
d   were friends of Dion, I was doing all in my power to keep them from
     being punished.
         But enough of our partnership in political affairs. If you noted in me
     any other evidences of estrangement from you, you may rightly explain
     them in the same way. What would you expect? Any reasonable man
     would properly think me a knave if I had been seduced by the greatness
     of your power to desert an old comrade and guest-friend in the distress
     that you had brought him to (and a man in no way inferior to you, if I
e   may say so) and had chosen you who were the cause of his wrongs, and
     had fallen in with all your plans, evidently for the sake of money; for no
     one would have thought there was any other reason for such a change in
     me, if I had so changed. It is these events, brought about by you as I have
     described, that are responsible for the estrangement and wolf-friendship
     between us.
         And now comes, almost as an immediate consequence of the foregoing,
     my statement on the second point on which I said I should have to defend
319 myself. Attend carefully and see if you can detect any falsehood or untruth
     in what I say. I declare that about twenty days before my departure from
     Syracuse for home, when Archedemus and Aristocritus were with us in
     the garden, you brought against me the same reproach that you now make,

that I cared more for Heraclides and all the rest than I did for you. In their presence you asked me whether I remembered advising you, when I first arrived, to resettle the Greek cities. I admitted that I remembered it, and said I still thought that was the best policy. And I must remind you, Dionysius, of what was said immediately afterwards. I asked, as you remember, whether this was all my advice, or whether there was something more; and you replied, with considerable anger and derision, as you thought (whence it has come about that what you then derided is no longer a dream but a reality),[2] and said, with a very forced laugh, "I remember well;[3] you told me to get an education, or leave all these projects alone." I replied that your memory was excellent. "And this education," you said, "was to be in geometry, was it not?" I refrained from giving the reply that occurred to me, fearing lest a little word might narrow my prospect of sailing home, to which I was then looking forward with confidence.

Now the reason for all I have said is this: don't slander me by saying that I would not allow you to resettle the Greek cities destroyed by barbarians, or to relieve the people of Syracuse by changing your tyranny into a kingship. No lie you could possibly tell about me would be less appropriate; and there is more and even clearer evidence that I could submit for examination, if ever there should be a competent inquiry into the matter, that it was I who urged you to these projects and you who refused to undertake them. And it is not hard to show that they were the best things that could have been done for you and the people of Syracuse and all Sicily.

And now, my friend, if you deny that you have said any of these things that you said, that is all the justice I ask; but if you agree that you said them, then follow the wise example of Stesichorus, imitate his recantation, and change your lies to truth.

IV

Plato to Dion of Syracuse, Welfare.

I think my good will towards your enterprise has been evident from the beginning, as well as my earnest desire to see it brought to completion, for no other reason than admiration for noble deeds. For I deem it right that the men who really possess virtue and exemplify it in their conduct should receive the glory that is due them. All has gone well so far, thank God, but the greatest contest lies ahead. Strength, courage, and cleverness are qualities in which others also may win distinction; but to be

---

2. Dionysius' contempt for the ideal of a philosophical ruler, it is implied, brought about the victory of Dion and the triumph (or so it seemed at the time) of Plato's political ideals.

3. Accepting the emendation *eu memnēmai* in c1, and taking it as a part of the tyrant's reply.

preeminent above others in truthfulness, justice, high-mindedness, and
c the grace of conduct which these virtues express—this is what would by
general consent be expected of those who profess to honor these traits of
character. What I say is obvious; nevertheless we must keep reminding
ourselves that these men (you know whom I mean) ought to stand out so
that the rest of mankind will be as children in comparison. We must make
it manifest that we are really the sort of men we say we are, particularly
d since, by God's help, it can easily be done. Other men have to travel far
and wide if they are to become known; but the events of which you are
the center are such that the whole world, to speak somewhat boastfully,
has its eyes upon one place, and upon you especially in that place. You
are the object of universal interest; make ready, then, to eclipse Lycurgus
and Cyrus and anyone else deemed preeminent in character and statesmanship, especially since many people (indeed most people) here are saying
e that with Dionysius out of the way your cause will in all likelihood come
to ruin through your ambitions and those of Heraclides, Theodotes, and
the other notables. May no such dissension arise; but if it does, you must
321 show that you can heal it and all will be well. You will no doubt smile at
my saying this, for you are yourself aware of the danger. But I have noticed
that competitors in the games are spurred on by the shouts of the children,
and still more by those of their friends, when they think that the cheering
springs from sincerity and good will. Be you then the contestants, and
write us when we can help you.

b   Matters here are almost the same as when you were with us. Write us
also what you have done or are doing, since we hear many reports but
know nothing surely. Letters have just now come to Lacedaemon and
Aegina from Theodotes and Heraclides, but as I said, though we hear
many rumors from the people here,[1] we know nothing. Remember that
some persons think you are not sufficiently obliging; don't forget that one
c must please men if one would do anything with them, whereas self-will
is fit only for solitude. Good luck!

V

PLATO TO PERDICCAS,[2] WELFARE.
   I have advised Euphraeus, as you wrote me, to look studiously after
your interests, and it is right that I should give you also the proverbial
"holy counsel" of a friend on the various matters you mention, and
d particularly as to the use you should now make of Euphraeus. The man
can be of service to you in many ways, but most of all in supplying what
you now lack, for you are young and there are not many who can counsel

---

1. Accepting the emendation *akouontes per tōn tēide* in b4–5.
2. Perdiccas III, elder brother of Philip and king of Macedon from 364 to 359.

young men about it. Constitutions, like species of animals, have each their own language—democracy one, oligarchy another, and monarchy still another. Many persons would say they know these languages, but for the most part, and with rare exceptions, they fall short of understanding them. The constitution that speaks its own language to gods and men, and suits its actions to its words, always prospers and survives; but it goes to ruin if it imitates another. Now in this Euphraeus can perhaps be of most use to you, though he will be a manly aid in other respects as well; I believe that he can search out the words appropriate to monarchy as well as any man in your service. Use him, then, for this, and you will not only profit yourself but confer upon him a very great benefit.

    If anyone hears this and says, "Plato apparently claims to know what is good for a democracy, but though he is at liberty to speak in the assembly and give it his best advice, he has never yet stood up and said a word," you can answer by saying, "Plato was born late in the life of his native city, and he found the demos advanced in years and habituated by former advisers to many practices incompatible with the advice he would give. Nothing would be sweeter to him than to give advice to the demos as to a father, if he did not think he would be risking danger in vain and accomplish nothing. He would do the same about advising me, I know. If we seemed to him incurable, he would bid us a long farewell and refrain from advising about me or my affairs." Good luck!

VI

PLATO TO HERMIAS AND ERASTUS AND CORISCUS,[1] WELFARE.
    It is evident to me that some god has graciously and generously prepared good luck for you, if you receive his gift properly. For you are living as neighbors to one another and each of you needs what the others can best supply. Hermias should know that his power for all purposes has its greatest support not in the number of his horses or other equipment of war, nor in the gold he adds to his treasury, but in steadfast friends of solid character. And to Erastus and Coriscus I say, "old as I am," that they need to supplement their knowledge of the Ideas—that noble doctrine— with the knowledge and capacity to protect themselves against wicked and unjust men. They are inexperienced, since they have spent a great part of their lives with us, among men of moderation and good will; this is why I said they need some power to protect them, that they may not be forced to neglect the true wisdom and concern themselves more than is fitting with that which is worldly and necessary. Now this power that

---

1. Hermias was tyrant of Atarneus and Assos in the Troad; Erastus and Coriscus were members of the Academy.

they need Hermias apparently possesses, both as a natural gift (so far as one
323　may judge without knowing him), and as an art perfected by experience.

What is the point of these remarks? To you, Hermias, since I have known
Erastus and Coriscus longer than you have, I solemnly declare and bear
witness that you will not easily find more trustworthy characters than
these neighbors of yours, and I therefore advise you to make it a matter
of central importance to attach yourself to them by every honorable means.
Coriscus and Erastus in their turn I advise to hold fast to Hermias and to
b　try to develop this mutual alliance into a bond of friendship. If ever any
one of you should seem to be weakening this union (for nothing human
is altogether secure), send a letter to me and my friends declaring the
grievance; for unless the injury be very grave, I believe your sense of justice
and your respect for us will make the words that we may send more
efficacious than any incantation would be in binding up the wound and
causing you to grow together again into friendship and fellowship as
c　before. If all of us, you and we alike, according to our several abilities and
opportunities, apply our wisdom to the preservation of this bond, the
prophecies I have just uttered will come true. What will happen if we do
not, I will not say, for I am prophesying only what is good, and I declare
that with God's help we shall bring all these things to a good issue.

Let this letter be read, if possible, by all three of you gathered together,
otherwise by twos, and as often as you can in common. Adopt it as a just
d　and binding law and covenant, taking a solemn oath—in gentlemanly
earnest, but with the playfulness that is the sister of solemnity—in the
name of the divine letter of all things present and to come, and in the
name of the lordly father of this governor and cause, whom we shall all
some day clearly know, in so far as the blessed are able to know him, if
we truly live the life of philosophy.

VII

PLATO TO THE FRIENDS AND FOLLOWERS OF DION, WELFARE.

You have written me that I must consider your aims as identical with
those that Dion had, and you therefore urge me to co-operate with you
324　as much as I can, both in word and in deed. My answer is that if your
views and purposes are really the same as his, I agree to join with you; if
not, I shall have to consider the matter further. What his principles and
ambitions were I can tell you, I may say, not from conjecture, but from
certain knowledge. For when I first came to Syracuse, being then about
forty years of age, Dion was of the age that Hipparinus is now; and it was
b　then that he came to the opinions which he continued to hold until the
end; the Syracusans, he thought, ought to be free and live under the best
of laws. It would not then be surprising if some divine power should bring
Hipparinus also to the same mind that Dion had about government. To

learn the way in which these convictions come about is instructive to young and old alike; and since the present occasion seems appropriate, I will try to describe how they originated in my own case.

When I was a young man I had the same ambition as many others: I thought of entering public life as soon as I came of age. And certain happenings in public affairs favored me, as follows. The constitution we then had, being anathema to many, was overthrown; and a new government was set up consisting of fifty-one men, two groups—one of eleven and another of ten—to police the market place and perform other necessary duties in the city and the Piraeus respectively, and above them thirty other officers with absolute powers. Some of these men happened to be relatives and acquaintances of mine, and they invited me to join them at once in what seemed to be a proper undertaking. My attitude toward them is not surprising, because I was young. I thought that they were going to lead the city out of the unjust life she had been living and establish her in the path of justice, so that I watched them eagerly to see what they would do. But as I watched them they showed in a short time that the preceding constitution had been a precious thing. Among their other deeds they named Socrates, an older friend of mine whom I should not hesitate to call the justest man of that time, as one of a group sent to arrest a certain citizen[1] who was to be put to death illegally, planning thereby to make Socrates willy-nilly a party to their actions. But he refused, risking the utmost danger rather than be an associate in their impious deeds. When I saw all this and other like things of no little consequence, I was appalled and drew back from that reign of injustice.[2] Not long afterwards the rule of the Thirty was overthrown and with it the entire constitution; and once more I felt the desire, though this time less strongly, to take part in public and political affairs. Now many deplorable things occurred during those troubled days, and it is not surprising that under cover of the revolution too many old enmities were avenged; but in general those who returned from exile[3] acted with great restraint. By some chance, however, certain powerful persons brought into court this same friend Socrates, preferring against him a most shameless accusation, and one which he, of all men, least deserved. For the prosecutors charged him with impiety, and the jury condemned and put to death the very man who, at the time when his accusers were themselves in misfortune and exile, had refused to have a part in the unjust arrest of one of their friends.

The more I reflected upon what was happening, upon what kind of men were active in politics, and upon the state of our laws and customs, and the older I grew, the more I realized how difficult it is to manage a city's affairs rightly. For I saw it was impossible to do anything without friends

1. Leon of Salamis. See *Apology* 32c–d.
2. Alternatively, "from those evil men."
3. Supporters of the democracy.

and loyal followers; and to find such men ready to hand would be a piece of sheer good luck, since our city was no longer guided by the customs and practices of our fathers, while to train up new ones was anything but easy. And the corruption of our written laws and our customs was

e   proceeding at such amazing speed that whereas at first I had been full of zeal for public life, when I noted these changes and saw how unstable everything was, I became in the end quite dizzy; and though I did not cease to reflect how an improvement could be brought about in our laws

326   and in the whole constitution, yet I refrained from action, waiting for the proper time. At last I came to the conclusion that all existing states are badly governed and the condition of their laws practically incurable, without some miraculous remedy and the assistance of fortune; and I was forced to say, in praise of true philosophy, that from her height alone was it possible to discern what the nature of justice is, either in the state or in

b   the individual, and that the ills of the human race would never end until either those who are sincerely and truly lovers of wisdom come into political power, or the rulers of our cities, by the grace of God, learn true philosophy.

Such was the conviction I had when I arrived in Italy and Sicily for the first time. When I arrived and saw what they call there the "happy life"— a life filled with Italian and Syracusan banquets, with men gorging themselves twice a day and never sleeping alone at night, and following all the

c   other customs that go with this way of living—I was profoundly displeased. For no man under heaven who has cultivated such practices from his youth could possibly grow up to be wise—so miraculous a temper is against nature—or become temperate, or indeed acquire any other part of virtue. Nor could any city enjoy tranquillity, no matter how good its laws,

d   when its men think they must spend their all on excesses, and be easygoing about everything except the feasts and the drinking bouts and the pleasures of love that they pursue with professional zeal. These cities are always changing into tyrannies, or oligarchies, or democracies, while the rulers in them will not even hear mention of a just and equitable constitution.

These, plus the conviction previously mentioned, were my thoughts on

e   coming to Syracuse—a coming which may have been mere coincidence, but which seems to have been the work of some higher power laying then the foundation for what has since come to pass with respect to Dion and Syracuse; and for still further misfortunes, too, I fear, unless you now obey

327   the advice which I am giving for the second time. How can I say that my coming to Sicily then was the beginning of it all? In my association with Dion, who was then a young man, I imparted to him my ideas of what was best for men and urged him to put them into practice; and in doing so I was in a way contriving, though quite unwittingly, the destruction of the tyranny that later came to pass. For Dion was in all things quick to learn, especially in the matters upon which I talked with him; and he listened with a zeal and attentiveness I had never encountered in any

b   young man, and he resolved to spend the rest of his life differently from most Italians and Sicilians, since he had come to love virtue more than pleasure and luxury. For this reason his way of life was more than annoying to those who guided themselves by the practices of tyranny, until the death of Dionysius. After that event he conceived that these convictions which he himself had got from proper instruction might arise in others besides himself; and observing that they were in fact making their appearance in the minds of some, at least, of his associates, he thought that by the help of the gods Dionysius himself might be counted among this number; and if this should happen, it would mean an incalculably blessed life for the tyrant himself and the other Syracusans. Furthermore, he thought that by all means I should come to Syracuse as soon as possible and become a partner in his plans, for he recalled our conversations together and how effectively they had aroused in him the desire for a life of nobility and virtue. If now he could arouse this desire in Dionysius, as he was attempting to do, he had high hopes of establishing throughout the land a true and happy life, without the massacres and deaths and the other evils that have come to pass. With this just purpose in mind Dion persuaded Dionysius to send for me, and he himself wrote urging me by all means to come at once before certain others came in contact with Dionysius and diverted him to a less worthy ideal of life. His petition, though too long to give in full, was as follows: "What better opportunity can we expect," he said, "than the situation which Providence has presented us with?" He mentioned the empire in Italy and Sicily, his own power in it, the youth of Dionysius, and the eager interest he was showing in philosophy and culture; Dion's nephews and other relatives, he said, could be easily persuaded to accept the life and doctrine that I have always taught, and would be a very strong additional influence upon Dionysius; so that now, if ever, might we confidently hope to accomplish that union, in the same persons, of philosophers and rulers of great cities.

These and many other like arguments he addressed to me. For my own part I felt a certain anxiety, since one never knows how young men will turn out, for their desires arise quickly and often change to their contraries; but Dion's character, I knew, was steadfast by nature and he had already reached middle age. Consequently I weighed the question and was uncertain whether or not to yield to his urging and undertake the journey. What tipped the scales eventually was the thought that if anyone ever was to attempt to realize these principles of law and government, now was the time to try, since it was only necessary to win over a single man and I should have accomplished all the good I dreamed of. This, then, was the "bold" purpose I had in setting forth from home, and not what some persons ascribed to me. Above all I was ashamed lest I appear to myself as a pure theorist, unwilling to touch any practical task—and I saw that I was in danger of betraying Dion's hospitality and friendship at a time of no little real danger to him. Suppose he should be killed or banished by Dionysius and his other enemies and should come to me in his exile and say, "Here I am, Plato, a fugitive, not because I lacked hoplites or

horsemen to ward off my enemies, but only for need of the persuasive words by which, as I well know, you are always able to turn young men towards goodness and justice and make them friends and comrades of
e   one another. This weakness which you could have remedied is the cause of my being here in exile from Syracuse. But my own misfortune is a small part of your dishonor. You are always praising philosophy, and saying she is held in little esteem by the rest of mankind; but in betraying me now have you not, by neglecting this opportunity, also betrayed her? If
329 we had happened to be living in Megara you would certainly have come as a helper in answer to my call, or you would consider yourself the most trifling of men. And now do you think you can escape the charge of cowardice by pleading the length of the journey, the greatness of the voyage and its fatigue? Far from it." To words of this sort what respectable answer could I give? None. And so from motives as rational and just as
b   is humanly possible I departed, giving up for those reasons my occupations here, which are not without dignity, to live under a tyranny seemingly unsuited both to my doctrines and to me. In so going I discharged my obligation to Zeus Xenios[4] and cleared myself of reproach from philosophy, which would have been dishonored if I had incurred disgrace through softness or cowardice.

When I arrived—to make the story short—I found the court of Dionysius full of faction and of malicious reports to the tyrant about Dion. I defended
c   him as well as I could, but I was able to do very little; and about the fourth month Dionysius, charging Dion with plotting against the tyranny, had him put aboard a small vessel and exiled in disgrace. Thereupon we friends of Dion were all afraid that one of us might be accused and punished as an accomplice in Dion's conspiracy. About me there even went abroad in Syracuse a report that I had been put to death by Dionysius as the cause
d   of all that had happened. But Dionysius, seeing how we all felt, and apprehensive lest our fears might lead to something even graver, treated us all kindly, and me especially he reassured, telling me to have no fear and earnestly begging me to remain; for there was no honor for him in my leaving, he said, but only in my remaining. For this reason he made a great pretense of begging me, but we know that the requests of tyrants are mingled with compulsion. He devised a means for preventing my
e   departure by bringing me inside the citadel and lodging me there, whence no ship's captain would have dared to take me away without a messenger sent from Dionysius himself commanding him to do so, still less if Dionysius had forbidden it. Nor would any merchant or guard along the roads leading out of the country have let me pass alone, but would have taken me in charge at once and brought me back to Dionysius, especially since
330 another report had already got abroad, contrary to the earlier one, that Dionysius was wonderfully fond of Plato. What in fact was the situation? With the passage of time Dionysius, I must truly say, did become more

4. Zeus the protector of strangers, the guardian of the obligations of hospitality.

and more attached to me as he became more familiar with my manner and character; but he wanted me to praise him more than I did Dion and value his friendship more highly, and he was marvelously persistent towards this end. How this could best have come about, if at all, was through his becoming my disciple and associating with me in discourse about philosophy; but he shrank from this, for the intriguers had made him fear that he would be entrapped, so that Dion would have accomplished his purposes. I put up with all this, however, holding fast to the original purpose for which I had come, hoping that he might somehow come to desire the philosophic life; but I never overcame his resistance.

These, then, were the circumstances that account for my first visit to Sicily and occupied the time of my sojourn there. Afterwards I came home, only to return again at the urgent summons of Dionysius. Why I returned and what I did, with the explanation and justification of my actions, I will go into later for the benefit of those who wonder what my purpose was in going a second time. But in order that these incidental matters may not usurp the chief place in my letter, I will first advise what is to be done in the present circumstances. This, then, is what I have to say.

When one is advising a sick man who is living in a way injurious to his health, must one not first of all tell him to change his way of life and give him further counsel only if he is willing to obey? If he is not, I think any manly and self-respecting physician would break off counseling such a man, whereas anyone who would put up with him is without spirit or skill. So too with respect to a city: whether it be governed by one man or many, if its constitution is properly ordered and rightly directed, it would be sensible to give advice to its citizens concerning what would be to the city's advantage. But if it is a people who have wandered completely away from right government and resolutely refuse to come back upon its track and instruct their counselor to leave the constitution strictly alone, threatening him with death if he changes it, and order him instead to serve their interests and desires and show them how they can henceforth satisfy them in the quickest and easiest way—any man, I think, who would accept such a role as adviser is without spirit, and he who refuses is the true man. These are my principles; and whenever anyone consults me on a question of importance in his life, such as the making of money, or the care of his body or soul, if it appears to me that he follows some plan in his daily life or is willing to listen to reason on the matters he lays before me, I advise him gladly and don't stop with merely discharging my duty. But a man who does not consult me at all, or makes it clear that he will not follow advice that is given him—to such a man I do not take it upon myself to offer counsel; nor would I use constraint upon him, not even if he were my own son. Upon a slave I might force my advice, compelling him to follow it against his will; but to use compulsion upon a father or mother is to me an impious act, unless their judgment has been impaired by disease. If they are fixed in a way of life that pleases them, though it may not please me, I should not antagonize them by useless admonitions,

nor yet by flattery and complaisance encourage them in the satisfaction of desires that I would die rather than embrace. This is the principle which a wise man must follow in his relations towards his own city. Let him
d   warn her, if he thinks her constitution is corrupt and there is a prospect that his words will be listened to and not put him in danger of his life; but let him not use violence upon his fatherland to bring about a change of constitution. If what he thinks is best can only be accomplished by the exile and slaughter of men, let him keep his peace and pray for the welfare of himself and his city.

In this way, then, I venture to advise you, as Dion and I used to advise Dionysius, first of all to make his daily life such as to give him the greatest
e   possible mastery over himself and win him loyal friends and followers. In so doing, we said, he might avoid his father's experience when, after taking over many great cities in Sicily that had been laid waste by the barbarians, he was unable at their resettlement to establish loyal governments in them. For he had no comrades to head these governments, neither among foreigners, nor among his own brothers whom he had trained in
332   their youth (since they were younger than himself) and raised from private to royal station and from poverty to great wealth. None of these was he able, either by persuasion or by teaching, by benefits conferred or by ties of kinship, to make an associate in his empire. In this respect he was seven times weaker than Darius, who had neither brothers to rely upon, nor persons trained by himself, but only those who helped him to overthrow
b   the Mede and the Eunuch. He distributed among them seven provinces, each one greater than all Sicily, and he found them to be loyal, for they did not attack him or one another; and in so doing he set an example of what a good lawgiver and king should be, for he established laws that have kept the Persian empire to this day. We have another example in the Athenians, who took over the protection of a number of Hellenic cities threatened by barbarians. Though the Athenians had not themselves settled these cities but took them over already established, yet they maintained
c   their power over them for seventy years because of the friends they made in each of them. But Dionysius, though he united all Sicily into a single city (for he knew that he could trust no one), was scarcely able to survive, for he was poor in friends and loyal followers, and the possession or lack of these is the best indication of a man's virtue or vice.

This is the advice that Dion and I gave to Dionysius, since his father's
d   neglect had resulted in his being without culture and unused to associations appropriate to his position. We said that once embarked upon the course just mentioned[5] he should induce others among his relatives and companions to become friends and partners in the pursuit of virtue; but above all to become a friend to himself, for in this respect he was incredibly deficient. We did not say it thus openly, for that would not have been safe, but made veiled references to his weakness, striving by our words to show

5. Accepting the emendation *epi tauta* at d3, with no lacuna in d2.

him that everyone must do this who would save himself and the people
over whom he rules, whereas any other course will accomplish his ruin
and theirs. Let him take the path we pointed out and perfect himself in
wisdom and self-control; then if he should resettle the deserted cities of
Sicily, and bind them together with such laws and constitutions as would
make them friendly to himself and to one another and a mutual help
against the barbarians, he would have an empire not twice but actually
many times as powerful as his father's had been; he would be ready to
inflict upon the Carthaginians a far heavier defeat than they had suffered
in the days of Gelon, instead of paying tribute to these barbarians as he
was doing at present under the agreement his father had made.

These were the words of exhortation we addressed to Dionysius—we
who were conspiring against him, according to the reports that were current
on all sides. These reports finally prevailed with Dionysius, as you know,
bringing exile to Dion and fear to us his friends. But—to jump to the end
of the many events of this short time—when Dion returned from the
Peloponnesus and Athens he indeed taught Dionysius a lesson. And then
when he had delivered the people of Syracuse and twice restored their
city to them, they felt towards Dion exactly as Dionysius had. For at the
time when Dion was endeavoring to educate Dionysius and form him into
a king worthy of the office, making himself thus a partner in all Dionysius'
life, Dionysius was giving ear to the slanderers who said that Dion was
conspiring against the tyrant in all that he was doing. The studies he
enjoined were obviously intended, they said, to bewitch the mind of Dionysius so that he would neglect his kingdom and entrust it to Dion, who
would then make it his own and treacherously banish Dionysius from
power. These suspicions against Dion prevailed then as they did later
when circulated among the Syracusans; but their triumph was an unnatural
one and puts to shame those who were the cause of it. What sort of triumph
it was you ought to hear, you who have asked for my help in the present
crisis. I, an Athenian citizen, a friend of Dion and his ally, came to the
tyrant in order to bring about friendship, not war, between them; but the
slanderers worsted me in this contest. And when Dionysius tried by honors
and gifts to persuade me to take his side and affirm that his banishment
of Dion had been proper, he failed utterly, as you know. Later Dion came
home bringing with him two brothers from Athens, friends whom he had
acquired not through philosophy, but by way of that facile comradeship
which is the basis of most friendship, and which is cultivated by hospitality
and mystic rites and initiation into secrets; because of these associations
and the service they had rendered Dion in returning to Syracuse, these
two men who came with him had become his comrades. But when they
arrived in Sicily and saw how Dion was being slandered among the people
of Syracuse whom he had liberated, and was being accused of plotting to
become a tyrant, not only did they betray their comrade and host, but
they became as it were his murderers, since they stood by with arms in
their hands to assist his assassins. The shame and impiety of their action

b I mention only, without dwelling upon it; many others will make it their theme both now and in time to come. But I cannot pass over what is said about Athens, that these men brought dishonor on their city. Remember that he also was an Athenian who refused to betray this same Dion when by doing so he could have had money and honors in abundance. He had become Dion's friend not through vulgar fellowship, but through common liberal culture; and this alone should a sensible man trust, rather than kinship of soul or body. Therefore I say that these two who murdered

c Dion were not worthy of bringing their city into discredit, for they were never men of any consequence.

I have said all this for the purpose of advising Dion's friends and relatives; and to all that has been said I add the same advice and the same doctrine that I have given twice before. Do not subject Sicily nor any other state to the despotism of men, but to the rule of laws; this at least is my doctrine. For despotic power benefits neither rulers nor subjects, but is

d an altogether deadly experience for themselves, their children, and their children's children; and no one grasps at the prizes it offers except petty and illiberal souls who know nothing of the divine and human goods that are now and for all time good and just. This is the doctrine that I endeavored to bring home, first to Dion, next to Dionysius, and now for the third time do so to you. Listen to me then, in the name of Zeus the Savior, to whom this third libation belongs. Consider Dionysius and Dion, of whom one

e was deaf to my teachings and now lives ignobly, and the other listened to me and died nobly; for it is altogether noble and right to suffer whatever may come while aiming at the highest for oneself or one's city. None of us can avoid death, nor if any man could would he be happy, as people think; for there is nothing worth mentioning that is either good or bad to

335 creatures without souls, but good and evil exist only for a soul, either joined with a body or separated from it. And we must always firmly believe the sacred and ancient words declaring to us that the soul is immortal, and when it has separated from the body will go before its judges and pay the utmost penalties. Therefore we must count it a lesser evil to suffer great wrongs and injustices than to do them, though this is

b a saying that the avaricious man, who is poor in the goods of the soul, will not give ear to; or if he does, laughs it into silence, as he thinks, and goes about like a wild beast snatching from every quarter whatever he thinks will furnish him meat or drink or the satisfaction of that slavish and graceless pleasure incorrectly called after Aphrodite. He is blind and does not see what defilement his plunderings involve, nor how great an evil attaches to each wicked act—a defilement which the evildoer necessarily drags with him as he goes up and down the earth and follows his

c dishonorable and utterly wretched path to the world below.

Now Dion had accepted this and other similar teachings of mine, and I may rightly be as indignant at his murderers as at Dionysius. Both parties have done infinite wrong to me and, I may say, to all mankind—the first two in striking down a man whose purpose was to realize justice, the

other in refusing to have anything to do with justice, though he possessed
every resource for making it prevail throughout his domain. If in his empire d
there had been brought about a real union of philosophy and power, it
would have been an illustrious example to both Greeks and barbarians,
and all mankind would have been convinced of the truth that no city nor
individual can be happy except by living in company with wisdom under
the guidance of justice, either from personal achievement of these virtues
or from a right training and education received under God-fearing rulers.
This is the center of my grievance against Dionysius; the other injuries e
that he has done to me are trivial in comparison. And he who murdered
Dion has unknowingly produced the same result. For of Dion I know, as
surely as a man can know anything about his fellow men, that if he had
held the power he would not have been diverted from using it for the
following purposes. First of all, with regard to Syracuse,[6] his native city, 336
after having cleansed her of her servitude and put on her the garment of
freedom, he would have made every effort to adorn her citizens with the
best and most suitable laws. Then he would have turned with ardor to the
next task, that of resettling all Sicily and liberating her from the barbarians,
driving out some of them and subjugating others, a thing he could have
done more easily than Hiero. Such deeds accomplished by a man of justice
and courage and temperance and philosophy would have produced in the b
multitude the same respect for virtue which, if Dionysius had listened to
me, would have made its saving appearance, one may say, among all
mankind. But now some daemon or avenging deity has fallen upon us,
and through disrespect for law and the gods, and worst of all, through
the audacity of ignorance—that soil in which all ills are rooted and grow,
to produce in the end a bitter fruit for those who have planted them—
such ignorance has a second time overturned all our plans and brought
them to naught.

But on this our third trial let us avoid saying anything of ill omen. In c
spite of previous misfortunes, I advise you, the friends of Dion, to imitate
his love for his country and his sober way of living and to try to carry
out, under better auspices, these plans of his; and what they were you
have clearly heard me explain. If there is anyone in your number who is
incapable of living in the Dorian fashion like your fathers and follows the
"Sicilian life" of the slayers of Dion, do not ask his help nor imagine that d
he will act loyally or dependably. But summon others to help you in
resettling all Sicily and equalizing her laws. Summon them not only from
Sicily herself, but from the whole of the Peloponnesus; and do not fear
even Athens, for Athens also has citizens preeminent in virtue who abhor
the shameless audacity of those who slay their hosts. But if these projects
I have mentioned must be deferred, because you are now hard pressed
by the many and diverse factions daily sprouting in your midst, then e
anyone to whom the gods have given a modicum of right opinion must

6. Accepting the emendation *ē epi tode. Surakousas* in a1.

know that there can be no end to the evils of faction until the party that has gained the victory in these battles and in the exiling and slaughtering of fellow citizens forgets its wrongs and ceases trying to wreak vengeance upon its enemies. If it controls itself and enacts laws for the common good, considering its own interests no more than those of the vanquished, the defeated party will be doubly constrained, by respect and by fear, to follow the laws—by fear because the other party has demonstrated its superior force, and by respect because it has shown that it is able and willing to conquer its desires and serve the law instead. In no other way can a city that is rent by factions bring its disorders to an end, but it will continue to be divided within itself by strife and enmity, hatred and distrust.

Whenever, then, the victors desire to save their city, they must enter into counsel with themselves and first of all select the most eminent Greeks they can discover—old men, with wives and children at home, descended from a long line of illustrious ancestors and each of them possessing a fair amount of property (fifty such men will be enough for a city of ten thousand)—and these they must induce, by personal entreaties and by all the honors at their disposal, to leave home and come to their aid; and when they have come they must direct them to make laws, binding them upon oath to award no more to the victors than to the vanquished, but to consider only the equal and common good of the whole city. And then when the laws have been laid down everything depends upon this. If the victors show themselves more eager than the vanquished to obey the laws, then everything will be safe, happiness will abound, and all these evils will take their flight. But let no one who refuses to abide by these principles call upon me or anyone else for support. These proposals are akin to those that Dion and I tried to accomplish for the benefit of Syracuse, but second best. The best were those that we earlier tried to effect with the aid of Dionysius himself [goods to be common to all]. But fortune is mightier than men and shattered our plans. Now it is for you to try to bring them about with better luck, and may divine favor attend your efforts.

This, then, is my advice and admonition, and the account of my first visit to Dionysius. As to my later journey across the water, whoever is interested can learn from what follows that it was a reasonable and proper venture. The early part of my first stay in Syracuse passed as I have described it above before giving my advice to the relatives and friends of Dion. After the events described, I made every effort to persuade Dionysius to let me depart, and we came to an agreement that when peace was restored (war was then going on in Sicily) and when Dionysius had made his empire more secure, he would recall both Dion and me. He also asked Dion to consider himself not as having been exiled, but only banished.[7] On these conditions I promised that I would return. After peace was restored he sent for me, but Dion he asked to wait another year; me, however, he urged most strongly to come. Dion consented, and even

---

7. Banishment did not involve the confiscation of the condemned person's property.

entreated me to set sail; in fact there were many reports coming from Sicily that Dionysius had now once more conceived a great desire for philosophy, and this was why Dion persistently urged me not to disobey the summons. But as for me, though I knew that philosophy often affects young men in this way, yet it seemed to me safer, for the present at least, to say farewell   c
to my plans and let Dion and Dionysius alone; and I offended both of them by replying that I was an old man, and that what they were doing now did not at all accord with the agreement we had made. Now it seems that after this, Archytas visited Dionysius (for before my departure I had established relations of friendship and hospitality between Archytas and his Tarentine friends and Dionysius), and that there were certain other   d
persons who had learned something from Dion, and others who had learned from them; and being full of these half-understood doctrines, they were apparently trying to converse with Dionysius about them as if he had mastered all my thought. Now he is not without natural capacity for learning, and besides is extraordinarily vain; and no doubt he was pleased to have these questions addressed to him, and ashamed to have it discovered that he had learned nothing during my stay. For these reasons he   e
came to desire a clearer understanding, and at the same time his ambition spurred him on. (Why he did not learn from me during my first visit, I have described above.) When, therefore, I had got safely home and had, as I have just said, disregarded his summons to return, Dionysius' chief ambition, I think, was to prevent anyone from supposing that I had refused to come to his court because I had a contempt for his nature and character   339
and was displeased with his way of living. I must tell the truth, and put up with it if anyone, after hearing what happened, despises my philosophy and esteems the tyrant's intelligence. Dionysius summoned me a third time, sending a trireme to ease the journey for me, and with it certain Sicilian acquaintances of mine, among them Archedemus, one of the associates of Archytas and a man whom, as he knew, I valued the most highly   b
of all men in Sicily. These all brought me the same story of the marvelous progress Dionysius was making in philosophy. He knew of my feelings towards Dion and of Dion's desire to have me embark and go to Syracuse; so he wrote me a very lengthy letter, evidently composed with these facts in view. The beginning of it was about as follows: "Dionysius to Plato," then the customary salutations, and immediately afterwards, "If you come   c
at once to Syracuse as we have requested, first of all the issues that concern Dion will be settled in whatever way you desire (for I know you will desire only what is fair and I agree to this); but if not, none of these questions, whether touching Dion's person or any other matter, will be settled to your liking." Such were his words; to give the rest of the letter would take too much space and would not be pertinent here. Other letters kept coming to me from Archytas and the Tarentines praising Dionysius'   d
philosophy and saying that if I did not come now the friendship I had brought about between them and Dionysius, a friendship which was of no little importance to their state, would be broken off. Now when the

summons had taken on this character, with my friends in Sicily and Italy pulling me and those at Athens almost pushing me away with their urging,

e the same consideration occurred to me as before, that I ought not to betray my friends and followers in Tarentum. Besides, I thought, it is not an unusual thing that a young man of native intelligence who has overheard some talk of lofty matters should be seized by a love for an ideal of life. I ought then to test the situation clearly to see on which side the truth lay, and by no means to give up in advance and expose myself to the blame

340 that would rightly fall upon me if these reports should really be true. I set off, therefore, under cover of this reasoning, though with many fears and forebodings of evil, as can well be understood. "The third time to the Savior," runs the proverb;[8] and my third journey at least confirmed its truth, for by good luck I again came off safely; and next to God I thank Dionysius for it, because there were many determined to destroy me, but he prevented them and showed a certain respect for me and my position.

b When I arrived, I thought my first task was to prove whether Dionysius was really on fire with philosophy, or whether the many reports that came to Athens were without foundation. Now there is a certain way of putting this to the test, a dignified way and quite appropriate to tyrants, especially to those whose heads are full of half-understood doctrines, which I saw at once upon my arrival was particularly the case with Dionysius. You must picture to such men the extent of the undertaking, describing what

c sort of inquiry it is, with how many difficulties it is beset, and how much labor it involves. For anyone who hears this, who is a true lover of wisdom, with the divine quality that makes him akin to it and worthy of pursuing it, thinks that he has heard of a marvelous quest that he must at once enter upon with all earnestness, or life is not worth living; and from that time forth he pushes himself and urges on his leader without ceasing, until he has reached the end of the journey or has become capable of doing without

d a guide and finding the way himself. This is the state of mind in which such a man lives; whatever his occupation may be, above everything and always he holds fast to philosophy and to the daily discipline that best makes him apt at learning and remembering, and capable of reasoning soberly with himself; while for the opposite way of living he has a persistent hatred. Those who are really not philosophers but have only a coating of opinions, like men whose bodies are tanned by the sun, when they see how much learning is required, and how great the labor, and how orderly

e their daily lives must be to suit the subject they are pursuing, conclude that the task is too difficult for their powers; and rightly so, for they are

341 not equipped for this pursuit. But some of them persuade themselves that they have already sufficiently heard the whole of it and need make no further effort. Now this is a clear and infallible test to apply to those who love ease and are incapable of strenuous labor, for none of them can ever

---

8. See 334d above.

blame his teacher, but only himself, if he is unable to put forth the efforts that the task demands.

It was in this fashion that I then spoke to Dionysius. I did not explain everything to him, nor did he ask me to, for he claimed to have already a sufficient knowledge of many, and the most important, points because of what he had heard others say about them. Later, I hear, he wrote a book on the matters we talked about, putting it forward as his own teaching, not what he had learned from me. Whether this is true I do not know. I know that certain others also have written on these same matters; but who they are they themselves do not know. So much at least I can affirm with confidence about any who have written or propose to write on these questions, pretending to a knowledge of the problems with which I am concerned, whether they claim to have learned from me or from others or to have made their discoveries for themselves: it is impossible, in my opinion, that they can have learned anything at all about the subject. There is no writing of mine about these matters, nor will there ever be one. For this knowledge is not something that can be put into words like other sciences; but after long-continued intercourse between teacher and pupil, in joint pursuit of the subject, suddenly, like light flashing forth when a fire is kindled, it is born in the soul and straighway nourishes itself. And this too I know: if these matters are to be expounded at all in books or lectures, they would best come from me. Certainly I am harmed not least of all if they are misrepresented. If I thought they could be put into written words adequate for the multitude, what nobler work could I do in my life than to compose something of such great benefit to mankind and bring to light the nature of things for all to see? But I do not think that the "examination," as it is called, of these questions would be of any benefit to men, except to a few, i.e., to those who could with a little guidance discover the truth by themselves. Of the rest, some would be filled with an ill-founded and quite unbecoming disdain, and some with an exaggerated and foolish elation, as if they had learned something grand.

Let me go into these matters at somewhat greater length, for perhaps what I am saying will become clearer when I have done so. There is a true doctrine that confutes anyone who has presumed to write anything whatever on such subjects, a doctrine that I have often before expounded, but it seems that it must now be said again. For every real being, there are three things that are necessary if knowledge of it is to be acquired: first, the name; second, the definition; third, the image; knowledge comes fourth, and in the fifth place we must put the object itself, the knowable and truly real being. To understand what this means, take a particular example, and think of all other objects as analogous to it. There is something called a circle, and its name is this very word we have just used. Second, there is its definition, composed of nouns and verbs. "The figure whose extremities are everywhere equally distant from its center" is the definition of precisely that to which the names "round," "circumference," and "circle" apply. Third is what we draw or rub out, what is turned or destroyed;

but the circle itself to which they all refer remains unaffected, because it is different from them. In the fourth place are knowledge (*epistēmē*), reason (*nous*), and right opinion (which are in our minds, not in words or bodily shapes, and therefore must be taken together as something distinct both from the circle itself and from the three things previously mentioned); of

d   these, reason is nearest the fifth in kinship and likeness, while the others are further away. The same thing is true of straight-lined as well as of circular figures; of color; of the good, the beautiful, the just; of body in general, whether artificial or natural; of fire, water, and all the elements; of all living beings and qualities of souls; of all actions and affections. For

e   in each case, whoever does not somehow grasp the four things mentioned will never fully attain knowledge of the fifth.

These things, moreover, because of the weakness of language, are just as much concerned with making clear the particular property of each object

343   as the being of it. On this account no sensible man will venture to express his deepest thoughts in words, especially in a form which is unchangeable, as is true of written outlines. Let us go back and study again the illustration just given. Every circle that we make or draw in common life is full of characteristics that contradict the "fifth," for it everywhere touches a straight line, while the circle itself, we say, has in it not the slightest element belonging to a contrary nature. And we say that their names are by no

b   means fixed; there is no reason why what we call "circles" might not be called "straight lines," and the straight lines "circles," and their natures will be none the less fixed despite this exchange of names. Indeed the same thing is true of the definition: since it is a combination of nouns and verbs, there is nothing surely fixed about it. Much more might be said to show that each of these four instruments is unclear, but the most important point is what I said earlier: that of the two objects of search—the particular

c   quality and the being of an object—the soul seeks to know not the quality but the essence, whereas each of these four instruments presents to the soul, in discourse and in examples, what she is not seeking, and thus makes it easy to refute by sense perception anything that may be said or pointed out, and fills everyone, so to speak, with perplexity and confusion. Now in those matters in which, because of our defective training, we are not accustomed to look for truth but are satisfied with the first image suggested to us, we can ask and answer without making ourselves ridicu-

d   lous to one another, being proficient in manipulating and testing these four instruments. But when it is "the fifth" about which we are compelled to answer questions or to make explanations, then anyone who wishes to refute has the advantage, and can make the propounder of a doctrine, whether in writing or speaking or in answering questions, seem to most of his listeners completely ignorant of the matter on which he is trying to speak or write. Those who are listening sometimes do not realize that it is not the mind of the speaker or writer which is being refuted, but these four instruments mentioned, each of which is by nature defective.

By the repeated use of all these instruments, ascending and descending   e
to each in turn, it is barely possible for knowledge to be engendered of
an object naturally good, in a man naturally good; but if his nature is
defective, as is that of most men, for the acquisition of knowledge and the
so-called virtues, and if the qualities he has have been corrupted, then not   344
even Lynceus could make such a man see.[9] In short, neither quickness of
learning nor a good memory can make a man see when his nature is not
akin to the object, for this knowledge never takes root in an alien nature;
so that no man who is not naturally inclined and akin to justice and all
other forms of excellence, even though he may be quick at learning and
remembering this and that and other things, nor any man who, though
akin to justice, is slow at learning and forgetful, will ever attain the truth
that is attainable about virtue. Nor about vice, either, for these must be   b
learned together, just as the truth and error about any part of being must
be learned together, through long and earnest labor, as I said at the beginning. Only when all of these things—names, definitions, and visual and
other perceptions—have been rubbed against one another and tested, pupil
and teacher asking and answering questions in good will and without
envy—only then, when reason and knowledge are at the very extremity
of human effort, can they illuminate the nature of any object.[10]

For this reason anyone who is seriously studying high matters will be   c
the last to write about them and thus expose his thought to the envy and
criticism of men. What I have said comes, in short, to this: whenever we
see a book, whether the laws of a legislator or a composition on any other
subject, we can be sure that if the author is really serious, this book does
not contain his best thoughts; they are stored away with the fairest of his
possessions. And if he has committed these serious thoughts to writing,
it is because men, not the gods, "have taken his wits away."[11]   d

To anyone who has followed this discourse and digression it will be
clear that if Dionysius or anyone else—whether more or less able than
he—has written concerning the first and highest principles of nature, he
has not properly heard or understood anything of what he has written
about; otherwise he would have respected these principles as I do, and
would not have dared to give them this discordant and unseemly publicity.
Nor can he have written them down for the sake of remembrance; for
there is no danger of their being forgotten if the soul has once grasped   e
them, since they are contained in the briefest of formulas. If he wrote them,
it was from unworthy ambition, either to have them regarded as his own
ideas, or to show that he had participated in an education of which he
was unworthy if he loved only the reputation that would come from having   345

9. Lynceus, one of the Argonauts, was proverbial for his keenness of vision.
10. Accepting the emendation *sunteinontōn* at b7.
11. *Iliad* vii.360.

shared in it. Now if Dionysius did indeed come to understand these matters from our single conversation, how that happened, "God wot," as the Thebans say. For as I said, I went through the matter with him once only, never afterwards. Whoever cares to understand the course of subsequent events should consider why it was that we did not go over the matter a second or a third time, or even oftener. Was it that Dionysius, after this

b   one hearing, thought he understood well enough and really did understand, either because he had already found these principles himself or had previously learned them from others? Or did he think that what I said was of no value? Or, a third possibility, did he realize that this teaching was beyond him, and that truly he would not be able to live in constant pursuit of virtue and wisdom? If he thought my teachings of no value he contradicts many witnesses who say the opposite and who are probably much more capable judges of such matters than Dionysius. And if he had already discovered or learned these doctrines and regarded them as fitted

c   for educating a liberal mind, how—unless he is a very strange creature indeed—could he have so lightly brought ignominy upon their teacher and guardian? But this is what he did, as I shall now tell you.

Shortly after the above occurrence, although Dionysius had previously allowed Dion to retain possession of his property and to enjoy its revenues, he gave orders to Dion's stewards not to send anything more to the Peloponnesus, as if he had completely forgotten his letter, saying that this property belonged not to Dion but to Dion's son, who was his nephew

d   and under his legal guardianship. Matters then had come to this, in so short a time. From this action I saw precisely the character of Dionysius' desire for philosophy, and in spite of myself I was indignant, and with good reason. It was summer at the time, and ships were leaving the port. Though it was clear to me that I ought not to be more angry with Dionysius than with myself and the others who had compelled me to come a third

e   time to this strait of Scylla, "To measure again the length of deadly Charybdis,"[12] yet I thought I ought to tell Dionysius that it was impossible for me to remain after this scurvy treatment of Dion. He tried to placate me and begged me to remain, thinking it would not go well with him if I should set out immediately as the personal bearer of this news; but when he could not persuade me, he said that he would himself make the

346 preparations for my departure. For in my anger I thought of going on board one of the vessels ready to set sail and suffering the consequences, whatever they might be, of being detained, since it was clearly evident that I had done no wrong but was the victim of wrongdoing. Seeing that nothing could induce me to remain, he devised a scheme for keeping me until the ships could no longer leave port. The following day he came to me with this persuasive speech: "Let us dispose of this matter of Dion

b   and Dion's property which has been the cause of frequent disagreement between you and me. For your sake I will do this for Dion. Let him have

12. *Odyssey* xii.428.

his property and live in the Peloponnesus, not as an exile, but as one permitted to return here as soon as he and I and you his friends have come to an understanding—all this upon condition that he is not to conspire against me; you and your relatives and the relatives of Dion here shall be sureties to me, and he shall give you pledges of good faith. Let the property he takes be deposited in the Peloponnesus and at Athens in the keeping of any persons you please, and let Dion enjoy the revenues from it, but   c be without power to dispose of the principal without your consent. For it will be a large sum and I have little faith that if he had this wealth at his disposal he would act justly towards me; but in you and your friends I have more confidence. See now whether these proposals please you, and if they do, stay for the year on these terms and when spring comes depart   d with this property. Dion, I know, will be very grateful to you if you do this for him."

I was angered when I heard this proposal, nevertheless I said I would consider the matter and bring him my opinion on it the following day. This then was agreed upon. Later, when I had got to my own quarters and was thinking the matter over, I found myself in great perplexity; but this was the dominant thought in my deliberations: "Beware! Dionysius   e may not intend to keep a single one of his promises; but what if he should write to Dion after I have gone, telling him what he has just said to me? And should persuade a number of Dion's friends to write also, intimating plausibly that it was not his refusal but mine that prevented his doing what he promised, and making me out altogether indifferent to Dion's interests? Besides this, if he does not want to see me go and, without issuing definite orders to any ship's captain, should let it be generally   347 known, as he easily could, that he was unwilling for me to sail, would any captain take me as a passenger, even if I could get out of the palace of Dionysius?" For besides the other disadvantages of my situation, I was living in the garden surrounding the palace, and the gatekeeper would not have let me out without an express command from Dionysius. "But if I remain for the year, I can write to Dion what my situation is and what I am doing; and then if Dionysius keeps any part of his promises, what I have done will not seem altogether ridiculous," for the property of Dion,   b if estimated rightly, was probably worth not less than a hundred talents. "On the other hand, if the contrary comes to pass,[13] as is most likely, I don't see what course I can then take. Nevertheless, it seems that I must probably hold out one more year and put these schemes of Dionysius to the test of events."

Having come to this decision, I told Dionysius the next day that I had decided to remain. "But," I said, "you must not think that I can bind Dion.   c Let us send him a joint letter explaining the agreement we have just made and ask whether its terms satisfy him, telling him that if he is not satisfied and wishes to modify them in any way to write us at once; and in the

13. Reading *apemphainonta* in b3.

meantime I ask that you take no new steps affecting him." These were my words and these were the terms we agreed upon, almost exactly as I have stated them. Now the boats had set sail and it was no longer possible for

d me to leave, when Dionysius mentioned to me that half the property should be Dion's and half his son's. He said he was going to sell it and give me half the proceeds to take to Dion; the other half he would keep here for the son, for this was clearly the most equitable procedure. I was stunned by this statement, but thought it foolish to make any further protest; yet I did say that we should await the letter from Dion and advise him of these new conditions. Immediately thereafter he sold the whole of Dion's

e property in the most audacious manner, selling it on whatever terms and to whomever he pleased, and said not a word to me about it. And likewise I refrained from saying anything more to him about Dion's affairs, for I thought any further effort would be useless.

This then was the result of my efforts in aid of philosophy and my friends. From this time on Dionysius and I lived, I like a bird looking out

348 of its cage and longing to fly away, he scheming how to frighten me[14] without turning over any of Dion's property; yet before all Sicily we professed to be friends.

Now Dionysius, contrary to the practice of his father, tried to reduce the pay of his older mercenaries. The soldiers, infuriated, gathered in a

b mob and declared they would not permit it. He tried to hold out against them by closing the gates of the citadel, but they straightway moved against the walls, chanting a barbarian war cry; and this so frightened Dionysius that he yielded and granted even more than they demanded to the peltasts assembled there. Now a rumor quickly got about that Heraclides had been the cause of all this disturbance. Upon hearing it, Heraclides took flight and concealed himself; and Dionysius, being at a loss how to apprehend

c him, summoned Theodotes to the palace garden, where I happened to be walking at the time. I do not know what else they talked about, for I could not hear them; but I know and recall what Theodotes said to Dionysius in my presence. "Plato," he said, "I am trying to persuade Dionysius here that if I can bring Heraclides before us to answer the charges that have just been made against him, and if in consequence it seems necessary for him to leave Sicily, to let[15] him take his wife and child and sail to the

d Peloponnesus and live there, enjoying the revenue from his property so long as he does no harm to Dionysius. I have already summoned him and will do so now again, and one or the other of these messages should bring him. And I ask and beseech Dionysius, if he should happen upon Heraclides anywhere, either here or in the country, to do nothing more

e than banish him from the land during his present displeasure. Do you consent to this?" he asked, turning to Dionysius. "I consent," he said;

14. See *Letter* III, 318b.
15. Reading *axioun* in c9.

"even if he should be found in your own house he will suffer nothing beyond what you have said." The evening of the following day Eurybius and Theodotes came to me in haste, greatly troubled. Theodotes spoke for them. "Plato," he said, "you were a witness yesterday to the promise Dionysius made to you and me about Heraclides?" "Indeed I was," I replied. "But now," he continued, "there are peltasts running all about trying to take Heraclides, and it is likely that he is somewhere near here. You must with all speed go with us to Dionysius," he said. So we set out, and when we came into his presence the two men stood weeping silently, and I said: "They are afraid that you have changed your mind regarding Heraclides and are acting contrary to what was agreed upon yesterday. For it appears that he has taken refuge nearby." At this he became angry and turned various colors, as is the way with an angry man. Falling before him, Theodotes seized his hand and implored him, with tears in his eyes, not to do such a thing. "Cheer up, Theodotes," I interrupted, trying to encourage him; "Dionysius will not presume to do anything contrary to the promise he made yesterday." And Dionysius looked at me and, like a true tyrant, "To you," he said, "I made no promise whatever." "By the gods," I replied, "you at least made a promise, not to do what Theodotes is now imploring you not to do." With these words I turned and went out. After this Dionysius continued to hunt for Heraclides, while Theodotes sent messengers warning him to flee; and though Tisias and a band of peltasts were sent in pursuit, Heraclides, it was reported, having a few hours the start of them, got safely into Carthaginian territory.

After this, Dionysius conceived that my resistance to his long-standing plot not to restore Dion's money could now be plausibly made the ground for enmity toward me. His first step was to send me out of the citadel on the pretext that the women were to hold a ten-day sacrifice in the garden where I dwelt, and directed me to live outside during this period at the home of Archedemus. While I was there Theodotes sent for me and poured out his complaints and his anger against Dionysius for what he had done. When Dionysius heard that I had visited Theodotes he used this as another pretext, similar to the earlier one, for quarreling with me. He sent to inquire whether I had in fact visited Theodotes at his invitation. "Certainly," I replied. "Then he bade me say," said the messenger, "that you are not doing right in always preferring Dion and Dion's friends to himself." After this message he never again summoned me back to the palace, it being now clear that I was the friend of Heraclides and Theodotes, and consequently his enemy, and he knew also that I was not pleased at the complete dissipation of Dion's goods. From that time on, then, I lived outside the acropolis among the mercenaries. Some of the rowers in the fleet were from Athens and fellow citizens of mine; they and others came to me with the report that I had an evil name among the peltasts and that some of them were threatening to kill me if they ever got hold of me. I began then to plan the following means of escape. I sent letters to Archytas and my other friends in Tarentum telling them of my plight, and they found some

pretext for an embassy from their city, dispatching Lamiscus, one of their
b number, with a thirty-oared vessel. When he arrived he besought Dionysius
on my behalf, saying that I wished to depart and begging him not to
prevent it. Dionysius complied and released me, giving me travel money;
but for Dion's property I made no further demand, nor did anyone deliver
it to me.

Upon my return to the Peloponnesus I encountered Dion among the
spectators at Olympia and recounted to him what had occurred. Calling
upon Zeus to witness, he straightway summoned me and my relatives
c and friends to prepare for vengeance against Dionysius, demanding satisfaction to me for breach of hospitality (these were his words and this is
what he thought), and to himself for his unjust dismissal and exile. When
I heard this I told him to call upon my friends, if they wished to help him.
"But as for me," I said, "you and the others compelled me, in a way, to
become a guest at the table and hearth of Dionysius and a participant in
his sacrifices; and he perhaps believed, from the many reports circulated
against me, that I was plotting with you against him and the tyranny—
d yet he did not put me to death, but respected my person. Nor am I any
longer at the age for helping anyone carry on war, though I am with
you if ever you desire one another's friendship and wish to accomplish
something good. But as long as you are intent on harm, look elsewhere
for your allies." I said this in disgust at my Sicilian "adventure" and its
lack of success. But they did not listen to me; and in failing to heed
my attempts at reconciliation they are themselves responsible for all the
misfortunes that have come upon them. None of them would ever have
e occurred, humanly speaking, if Dionysius had restored his property to
Dion or become fully reconciled with him, for I would have been willing
and easily able to restrain Dion; but as it is they have attacked one another
and brought about universal disaster.

351   Dion's purpose, however, with respect to his native city and to the power
he sought for himself and his friends, was exactly what I should say any
moderate man, myself or anyone else, ought to have; such a man would
think of enjoying great power and honor only because he is conferring
great benefits. I do not mean such benefits as are conferred by an impecunious agitator, lacking in self-control, the weak victim of his passions, who
enriches himself and his partisans and his city by organizing plots and
b conspiracies, and puts to death the men of wealth on the pretext that
they are enemies, and distributes their property, and charges his fellow
conspirators and followers not to blame him if they are poor; nor do I
mean the honors enjoyed by a man who "benefits" his city in this way,
by dividing the goods of the few among the many by public decree, or
who, as head of a great city ruling over many lesser ones, unjustly assigns
c the wealth of the smaller ones to his own city. Neither Dion nor anyone
else in his right mind would seek power for these ends, power that would
be a plague to himself and his family for all time; but rather would seek
it for the purpose of creating, without murder or bloodshed, the best and

most just constitution and system of laws. This is what Dion was aiming at, preferring to be the victim of wickedness rather than the agent of it, though he endeavored to protect himself. In spite of all this he fell, just as he had come to the summit of triumph over his enemies. There is nothing surprising in what he experienced. For although a good man who is also prudent and sagacious cannot be altogether deceived about the character of wicked men, it would not be surprising if he should suffer the misfortune of the skilled captain who, though not unaware of the approach of a storm, may not foresee its extraordinary and unexpected violence, and be swamped by its force. This is the mistake that Dion made. Those who caused him to fall were men whom he well knew to be villains, but he did not suspect the depths of their ignorance and villainy and greed. By this error he is fallen, and Sicily is overwhelmed with grief.

    The advice I have to offer you in the present state of affairs has mostly been given, and let that suffice. Why I undertook the second voyage to Sicily I thought I ought to explain, because of the strange and improbable nature of these events. If then they appear more plausible as I have described them, and if it has been made evident that there were sufficient motives for what happened, this account will have properly accomplished its purpose.

VIII

Plato to the Relatives and Friends of Dion, Welfare.

    What principles you must follow if you are really to fare well I will do my best to explain to you. And I hope that my advice will be of advantage not only to you (though to you, of course, first of all), but secondly to everyone in Syracuse, and thirdly even to your enemies and adversaries— except anyone of them who has done an unholy deed;[1] for such acts are irremediable and a man can never wash away their stain. Give your thought, then, to what I say.

    Since the fall of the tyranny you have had nothing but dissension throughout all Sicily, one party desiring to get its power back, the other to make final the suppression of the tyranny. In such circumstances the multitude always think the right counsel is to recommend those measures that will do their enemies the most harm and their friends the most good. But it is by no means easy to do great harm to others without bringing many other evils upon oneself. We have a clear example of this close at hand. Only look at what has happened right here in Sicily, with one party attempting to act upon that principle and the other defending itself against their actions; the story of these events, if you should tell it to others, would give them many useful lessons, though of such instruction there is hardly

d

e

352

b

c

d

e

---

1. I.e., those who connived in the murder of Dion.

any need. On the other hand, a policy that would benefit all concerned, friends and foes alike, or do as little harm as possible to both—this is not easy to see, nor to carry out when it is seen; and to counsel such a policy, or attempt to explain it, seems like making a prayer. By all means, then let it be a prayer—for the gods should be first in every man's words and thoughts—and may it be fulfilled when it declares unto us some such word as follows.

353

Now you and your enemies have been ruled almost continuously from the beginning of the war by a single family, a family that your ancestors put in power at a time when they were in the direst peril and there was imminent danger that all of Hellenic Sicily would be overrun by the Carthaginians and become barbarian territory. For then it was that to save Sicily they chose Dionysius, a young and brilliant warrior, to take charge of the military actions for which he had an aptitude, and Hipparinus as his elder and counselor, making them, as they say, "generals with full power."[2] Was it God and divine chance that saved the city? Or the valor of these leaders? Or both luck and leadership together with the efforts of the citizens? Think what you will; in any case, the city was saved for that generation. It is right that everyone should feel gratitude to these saviors for the qualities they displayed; and if in later times the tyrants misused in any way the gift the city had bestowed upon them, for these misdeeds they have in part paid the penalty and should make even further atonement. But what penalties would it necessarily be right to impose in the present state of their affairs? If you were able to get rid of them easily, and without great toil and danger, or if they could easily regain their power, there would be no occasion for offering the advice that I am going to give. As it is, however, both of your factions ought to reflect and call to mind how often each party has been in high hopes, and has thought almost always that it lacked only a little of being able to do what it liked, and that this little has repeatedly turned out to be the cause of great and innumerable disasters. The limit is never reached; but what seems to be the end of an old difficulty always involves the beginning of a new one, and in this endless round there is danger that both the tyrannical party and the democratic party will be completely destroyed; and eventually, if things take their natural course (which God forbid!), the whole of Sicily will have practically lost the Greek language and will have come under the empire and dominion of the Phoenicians or the Opici.

b

c

d

e

This is a prospect which should incite every Hellene to search for a remedy with all his might. If anyone has an apter or a better plan than the one I am going to offer, let him bring it forth and he will rightly be called a loyal Hellene. What now appears best to me I will try to explain in all frankness and set it forth with just and impartial reasoning. I am speaking in the fashion of an arbitrator between two parties at law, the one a former tyrant, the other his former subject, and proffering to each

354

2. Accepting the correction *stratēgous* in b3.

of them my well-known counsel. Now, as always, I advise the tyrant to shun his name and the reality it stands for, and to change his government to a kingship if he can. That he can is shown by the action of that wise and good man, Lycurgus, who, seeing that his own relatives in Argos and Messene were becoming tyrants instead of kings and in both cases destroying both themselves and their cities, was filled with apprehension both for his house and his native city, and instituted as a remedy the office of the Elders and that of the Ephors as the saving bond of the kingly power. By such means this kingship has been signally secure through all these generations, since law became the lord and king of men, not men tyrants over the laws.

Now this is the point of my present recommendation to you all: let those who are aiming at tyrannical power shun and flee from what senseless and insatiate men call happiness; let them try to change into the form of kings and subject themselves to kingly laws, thus acquiring the highest honors from their willing subjects and from the laws. Likewise I advise those who cherish the ways of freedom and shun the yoke of slavery as something evil, to beware lest by an excessive and ill-timed thirst for freedom they fall into the affliction of their ancestors, the excessive anarchy they experienced as a result of their unmeasured passion for liberty. For the Sicilians before the reign of Dionysius and Hipparinus lived happily, as they thought, faring sumptuously and ruling their rulers; they it was who, without any legal judgment, stoned to death the ten generals who preceded Dionysius, in order not to be subject to any master, not even justice and the law, but to be altogether and absolutely free. This is why tyranny came upon them. Both servitude in excess and liberty in excess are very great evils, but in due measure both are great goods. Due measure is found in obedience to God, the absence of measure in obedience to men. And the god of wise men is the law; of foolish men, pleasure.

Since this is so, I call upon the friends of Dion to say to all Syracusans that what I advise is his and my joint counsel. I shall be the interpreter of what he would say if he were alive and able to speak to you now. Well, then, someone may say, what words does Dion's counsel contain for us about our present situation? These:

"First of all, men of Syracuse, accept laws that you think will not arouse your desires and turn your thoughts toward money-making and wealth. Of the three goods—soul, body, and wealth—your laws must give the highest honor to the excellence of the soul, the second place to that of the body, as subordinate to the excellence of the soul, and the third and lowest rank to wealth, since it serves both body and soul. The sacred tradition that ranks them in this order might rightly be made a positive law among you, since it makes truly happy those who live by it; whereas the doctrine that the rich are the happy ones is a foolish saying of women and children, a miserable doctrine in itself, bringing misery upon all who follow it. Put to trial these words about law and you will see by the event that my advice is sound; experience seems to be the truest test of any matter.

d "Having received laws of this sort, then, since Sicily is in grave danger and neither you nor your adversaries are clearly superior in force, it would without question be just and expedient for all of you to strike a compromise—both for those of you who wish to avoid the rigor of absolute rule and for those who are bent on regaining their power. It was their ancestors, remember, who in their time saved the Hellenes from the barbarians and made it possible for us now to be discussing a constitution; for if the Greeks had been defeated then, there would be no opportunity for deliberation nor any basis for hope. So now let the one party have the freedom they desire, but under the government of a king; and let the other have their office,

e but let it be a responsible kingship, the laws punishing kings and citizens alike if they disobey.

   "Now with a steadfast and wholehearted adherence to all these conditions, and with God's help, appoint [three] kings: first, my son, in double gratitude for my father's services and my own (as my father in his time

356 saved the city from the barbarians, I have twice freed it from tyrants, as you yourselves can bear witness); secondly, him who has the same name as my father and is the son of Dionysius, in gratitude for the help he has just rendered your cause, as well as because of his upright character; for though he is the son of a tyrant, he is voluntarily liberating the city and gaining for himself and his house undying honor in place of an ephemeral and unjust tyranny. Thirdly, invite him who is now head of the army of

b your enemies—Dionysius the son of Dionysius—to become king of the Syracusans as willing king of a willing city, if, through fear of misfortune and pity for his native city and its neglected temples and tombs, he shows himself willing to exchange his power for that of a king, in order that his city may not be completely ruined by this civil strife and fall a rich prize to the barbarians.

   "Let these then be your kings, three in number. Whether you invest them with the authority of the Spartan kings or agree upon some more limited powers for them, install them in something like the following

c manner. I have already said this to you on a former occasion, but it is well that you hear it again. If the family of Dionysius and Hipparinus is willing to end the present disorders for the salvation of Sicily and gain enduring honors for themselves and their houses on these terms, then, as I have said, summon ambassadors with full authority to effect a reconciliation. Let these ambassadors be whoever and as many as they please, chosen from persons here, or abroad, or both. When they have come together, let

d them begin by drawing up laws and a constitution providing that the kings shall have authority over religious and all other matters appropriate to former benefactors of the city, but that matters of war and peace shall be under the control of five-and-thirty guardians of the laws ruling in conjunction with the assembly and council. There should be various courts of justice for various offenses, but offenses involving death or exile should be judged by the thirty-five, in conjunction with other select judges chosen each year from the officeholders of the preceding year (one from each

office, namely that officer who showed himself the best and justest); these   e
should for the ensuing year judge all cases involving the death or imprisonment or exiling of citizens. But a king should not be permitted to act as judge
in such cases, since like a priest he is to remain undefiled by bloodshed or
imprisonment or exile.   357

"This is what I planned to accomplish for you when I was alive, and
this is still my earnest desire. If avenging deities in the guise of friends
had not prevented me, I should have carried out this plan, after conquering
my enemies with your help. Then, if everything had gone as I desired, I
should have resettled the rest of Sicily and driven out the barbarians that
now possess it, with the exception of those who made common cause with
us in fighting for freedom against the tyranny, and I should have restored to   b
their ancient and ancestral homes the former inhabitants of those Hellenic
regions. So now I advise all parties to adopt these same purposes as your
common aids, and to work and summon everybody to work with you for
their realization, and to regard anyone who refuses as your common enemy. These aims are not impossible of accomplishment, for what is already
in two minds, and readily appears the most feasible to those who have
reflected upon it, can hardly be called impossible by any man of understanding. By the "two minds" I mean that of Hipparinus, the son of Diony-   c
sius, and that of my own son; when these two have come to an agreement,
I think all others in Syracuse who care for their city will give their assent.

"Now offer honor and prayers to all the gods and to all other beings to
whom, with the gods, honor belongs, persuading and exhorting friends
and opponents gently but unceasingly, until the plans that I have just
described, like the dreams that God sends to waking men, have been   d
brought to visible and happy realization."

IX

PLATO TO ARCHYTAS OF TARENTUM,[1] WELFARE.

Archippus and Philonides and their companions have come to me with
the letter you gave them and have brought me news of you. Their mission to   e
the city they accomplished with no difficulty, since it was not a burdensome
matter. But as to you, they reported that you think it a heavy trial not to
be able to get free from the cares of public life. It is indeed one of the
sweetest things in life to follow one's own interests, especially when they   358
are such as you have chosen; practically everyone would agree. But this
also you must bear in mind, that none of us is born for himself alone; a
part of our existence belongs to our country, a part to our parents, a part
to our other friends, and a large part is given to the circumstances that

---

1. Pythagorean philosopher and mathematician, who was also a leading statesman of
his native city, in southern Italy. Plato visited there shortly before 388 B.C.

command our lives. When our country calls us to public service it would,
b I think, be unnatural to refuse; especially since this means giving place to unworthy men, who enter public life for motives other than the best.

Enough of this. As for Echecrates, I am taking care of him and will do so in the future, both for your sake and the sake of his father Phrynion as well as for the young man himself.

X

PLATO TO ARISTODORUS, WELFARE.

c I hear from Dion that you are one of his most trusted followers and have been so from the beginning, manifesting the most philosophical of the philosophical virtues; for to be steadfast, loyal, and dependable—this, I say, is true philosophy; whereas all other learning, and all cleverness directed to any other end than this, I call—and I think rightly—mere ornaments. Farewell; hold fast to these virtues that you have thus far manifested.

XI

d PLATO TO LAODAMAS, WELFARE.

I have written you before that the matters you have mentioned will all be greatly advanced if you yourself can come to Athens; but since you say that is impossible, the next best thing would be, as you write, that I
e or Socrates[1] should come to you, if we can. But Socrates is ill with strangury, and it would be unseemly for me to come and not accomplish what you summoned me for. For my part I have little hope that it can be done, though to explain why would require another and longer letter giving all the reasons; and besides, at my time of life I have not the bodily strength for travel and for all the dangers that one encounters both by land and by sea, and at present all the circumstances of travel are full of danger. I can, however, give you and the leaders of your colony a piece of advice
359 which, when I have spoken it, "may seem trifling," to quote Hesiod, but is hard to take. If they think[2] that a constitution can ever be well established by the enactment of laws, of whatever sort they may be, without some authority in the city to look after the daily life of the citizens and to insure that both free men and slaves live in a temperate and manly fashion, they are thinking wrongly. This could be done, however, if you have at hand
b men worthy of exercising such authority; but if you lack an educator, then

---

1. This is the younger Socrates, who figures as one of the personages in the *Statesman*.
2. Accepting the emendation *oiontai* in a3.

you have neither teachers nor learners, as I see it, and no course is left but to pray to the gods. Indeed most cities in the past have been similarly established and later attained good government under the force of circumstances brought on by war or other enterprises of the city, when a man of nobility and character has appeared and exercised great power. In the meantime you must and should ardently desire this to happen; but reflect on what I have said and do not act lightly, thinking that success is within your grasp. Good luck!

c

XII

PLATO TO ARCHYTAS OF TARENTUM,[1] WELFARE.

I am overjoyed at receiving the treatises that have come from you and am filled with admiration for their author, who seemed to me a man worthy of his ancient ancestors. These ancestors are said to have been Myrians, and to have been among the Trojans who emigrated under Laomedon. Good men they were, according to the accepted legend. As to the writings of mine about which you wrote, they are not yet completed, but I am sending them to you as they are. We are agreed that they ought to be guarded, so I need not admonish you on that point.

d

e

(Some have contended that this letter is not Plato's.)[2]

XIII

PLATO TO DIONYSIUS, TYRANT OF SYRACUSE, WELFARE.

360

Let this beginning of my letter be likewise a sign to you that it comes from me.[3] Once when you were feasting the young men from Locri you arose and came over to me (your couch being at some distance from mine) and greeted me with a phrase that was both friendly and neatly turned, as it seemed to me. The man lying next to me (and a fair youth he was) thought so too, for he said: "I suppose, Dionysius, that you have got much wisdom from Plato?" "And much else besides," you said; "for from the very minute I sent for him, and by the very fact that I had sent for him, I was the gainer." So let us preserve this opinion and endeavor always to increase our usefulness to one another. It is for this very purpose that I am sending you some Pythagorean writings and some *Divisions,* and also a man whom we thought, you remember, that both you and Archytas, if Archytas comes to you, could use to advantage. His name is Helicon, his

b

c

1. See note to 357d above.
2. This notation is found in our best manuscripts, and may go back to Thrasyllus.
3. Because of its salutation "Welfare," for the usual "Greetings": see *Letter* III, 315a.

family is of Cyzicus, and he is a disciple of Eudoxus[4] and well versed in all that eminent man's doctrines. Moreover he has been associated with one of the pupils of Isocrates and with Polyxenus, one of the followers of Bryson. But, what is rarer with such men, he is pleasant to meet, seemingly

d not difficult, but easy and mild mannered. I put it thus cautiously, for it is a man I am giving my opinion of; and though man has his good qualities, he is, with rare exceptions and in the greater part of his actions, quite changeable. I had my fears and doubts even about this man, so I not only conversed with him myself but also made inquiry among his fellow citizens, and nobody had anything to say against him. But look him over yourself and be on your guard. Above all, if you can in any way find leisure for it, take lessons from him as part of your studies in philosophy.

e If not, have him instruct someone else so that when you do have leisure you can learn and thereby add to your character and your good name. In this way I shall continue to be of help to you. But enough of this.

361 As for the things you wrote me to send you, I have had the Apollo executed and Leptines is bringing it to you, the work of a good young sculptor whose name is Leochares. There was another piece in his shop that I thought very charming, and I therefore bought it to give to your wife, for she looked after me, both in health and in sickness, in a manner that did honor both to me and to you. Give it to her, then, if you think it fitting. I am also sending twelve jars of sweet wine and two jars of honey

b for the children. I arrived too late for the fig harvest, and the myrtle berries that were laid by have spoiled. We shall look after them better next time. Leptines will tell you about the plants.

The money for these purchases and for certain payments to the city I procured from Leptines, telling him (what I thought was quite proper as well as true) that the money we spent in fitting out the Leucadian ship, about sixteen minae, came from my funds. So I got this sum from him,

c have made use of it, and have sent these objects to you. Now hear how it stands with respect to your funds here at Athens, and mine. I will make use of your money, as I told you, just as I do that of my other friends; but I am using it as sparingly as I can, and only so much as seems necessary or just or proper, not to me only, but to your agent. My own situation is this. Four daughters were left by my nieces (who died at the time when

d you bade me wear a crown, you remember, but I refused), one of marriageable age, another eight years old, another a little over three, and the other not yet one. My friends and I must provide dowries for them, at least for those who are married during my lifetime; the others we may leave out of account. Nor need I provide for those whose fathers may become richer than I am; but at present I am the wealthiest, and it was I who, with the help of Dion and other friends, provided dowries for their mothers. The

e oldest of these girls is to marry Speusippus, whose sister's daughter she is. For her I will require at most thirty minae; that is a reasonable wedding

---

4. Eudoxus of Cnidus, one of the foremost mathematicians of the fourth century, had moved his school from Cyzicus to Athens and merged it with the Academy.

portion for us to give. Moreover, if my mother should die I should need almost ten minae for building her tomb. These are about all my obligations at present. If any other private or public expense comes up because of my visit to you, I will endeavor to make the expenditure as little as possible; but what I cannot avoid will have to be at your charge, as I told you must be the case.

Now a word regarding your funds at Athens and their expenditure. In the first place, if it should ever be necessary for me to fit out a chorus or anything of the sort, you have no guest-friend here who would advance the money, as we thought. Furthermore, if some matter of great importance to you should arise such that you would be benefited immediately if an expenditure were made but injured if it were not made or were delayed until word had come from you, the situation would be not only damaging but humiliating for you. I found this out myself when, wishing to send you some other and more costly articles that you had written for, I sent Erastus to Andromedes the Aeginetan, upon whom, as your guest-friend, you told me to draw if I needed money. He replied, as was only human and natural, that he had formerly advanced money for your father but had had difficulty in collecting it; so now he would give a small sum, but no more. And so I got it from Leptines, who deserves to be praised, not because he gave, but because he gave willingly; and in all else that he has done and said about you he has shown the quality of his friendship. I ought to report such things, as well as matters of an opposite sort, to show how I think this or that man is disposed towards you. And so I shall be frank with you about your money; since it is only right, and since moreover I can speak from experience of the men who surround you. Whenever your men bring in their reports, they hesitate to mention any matter that they think involves expense, for fear of your displeasure. You must therefore compel them to form the habit of speaking about these things as well as other matters; for it is your duty to know everything, so far as possible, and pass judgment and not shrink from any facts. This will be the best of all ways of enhancing your authority. To make expenditures rightly and to repay debts properly is a good thing in many ways, and even furthers the acquisition of money, as you yourself will see more and more. Then do not allow those who profess to be looking out for your interests to give you a bad name; for there is no advantage nor honor in being known as difficult in money matters.

And now I would say something about Dion. About the other matters at issue I can say nothing as yet, until the letters come which you say you are sending me; but on the subject which you forbade me to mention to him, though I have not mentioned nor spoken about it, I have tried to find out how he would take it if you carried out your design, and it seemed to me he would be not a little indignant. In every other respect Dion's attitude toward you, as shown in his words and actions, is quite temperate.

To Cratinus, the brother of Timotheus and my friend, let us give a hoplite breastplate, one of the light kind for foot soldiers; and to the daughters of Cebes three full-length chitons, not the expensive Amorgian ones, but

362

b

c

d

e

363

linen ones of Sicilian make. You are probably familiar with the name of Cebes, for he figures in the Socratic writings as taking part with Simmias in a discussion with Socrates about the soul. He is an intimate friend and well disposed towards us all.

363b   You no doubt recall the sign that distinguishes the letters I write that are seriously intended from those that are not. Still I would have you attend carefully and keep it in mind; for there are many who ask me to write whom it is not easy to refuse openly. Those that are seriously meant begin with "God"; those less seriously with "gods."

The ambassadors also asked me to write you, and quite properly; for they have everywhere been sounding your praises and mine, not least of c   all Philagrus, the one who had a sore hand, you remember. Philaedes, who has just returned from the Great King, also spoke of you. If it had not required too long a letter I should have written you what he said; but as it is you must ask Leptines.

If you send the breastplate or anything else that I have mentioned, and have no one you wish to send it by, give it to Tyrillus; for he is always traveling back and forth, and is a friend of mine, accomplished in philosophy and other matters. He is the son-in-law of Tison, who was civic magistrate at the time when I set sail.

Farewell, study your philosophy, and try to interest the other young d   men in it. Give my greetings to your fellow students of the spheres. Instruct Aristocritus and the rest that if any book or letter comes from me, they are to have it brought at once to your attention and to remind you to pay heed to its contents. And now do not neglect to repay Leptines the money he advanced, but do it promptly so that others, seeing your treatment of him, may be more willing to oblige you.

e   Iatrocles, whom I set free at the same time as Myronides, is traveling with the things I am now sending you. Put him in your pay, since he bears you good will, and use him for any service you wish. Preserve this letter, or an abstract of it, and take it to heart.[5]

---

5. Accepting the deletion of *ho* in e5.

DEFINITIONS

Definitions is a dictionary of about 185 philosophically significant terms. Many intellectuals in ancient Greece developed definitions: mathematicians, natural philosophers, educators such as Prodicus, and also Socrates, who believed that knowing correct definitions of ethical ideas would make people morally better. But it was Plato who urged a systematic approach to definition by collection and division in his Phaedrus *and practiced it in his* Sophist *and* Statesman. *The Academic enterprise of definition by division was satirized in a comedy of about 350* B.C., *in which members of Plato's Academy cogitated over the definition of 'pumpkin' (Epicrates, frg. 11 Edmonds). Diogenes the Cynic ridiculed the Academic definition of 'man' as 'featherless, two-footed animal' by plucking a chicken and saying, "Here's Plato's man!"*

Many philosophers after Plato were also interested in definitions: his nephew and successor as head of the Academy, Speusippus, was credited with a work called Definitions, *and in a list of Aristotle's works we find "Definitions (in thirteen books)" and "Definitions prefixed to the* Topics *(in seven books)." Theophrastus wrote three books of* Definitions, *and Chrysippus the Stoic wrote many large books of and about definitions. Certain similarities between definitions in the present collection and Aristotelian and Stoic definitions have inclined some scholars to regard* Definitions *as a late and eclectic work, but these similarities are perhaps better explained by the fact that Aristotle and the Stoics both made use of fourth-century Academic ideas in working out their own philosophical positions.*

What we find in Definitions *is probably a tiny selection of all the definitions formulated and discussed in Plato's Academy in the middle years of the fourth century. These definitions were used in dialectical discussions, of the kind familiar to us from Aristotle's* Topics *and* Sophistical Refutations. *The definition of 'man' at 415a as 'featherless, two-footed, flat-fingernailed animal' could be a response to Diogenes' chicken, and other definitions are probably dialectical as well. Some are drawn directly from Plato's dialogues, such as the definition of 'sophist' at 415c, from* Sophist *231d.*

The individual definitions were probably coined by members of the Academy in the fourth century B.C., *but we cannot know who edited them into the present collection. Indeed,* Definitions *seems to consist of two separate collections. The first collection is organized into the three branches of philosophy recognized by Plato's Academy and by the Stoics: philosophy of nature (411 a–c), ethics (411d–414a), philosophy of knowledge and language (414a–e). The second collection (from 'utility' at 414e onward) has no such internal organization and contains independent definitions of many of the terms defined in the first collection. Certainly Plato is not to be regarded as the editor of all or part of* Definitions, *and the ascription to "Plato" probably signifies nothing more than "school of Plato." Some ancient scholars guessed at Speusippus as their author, probably incorrectly.*

Since reference works and collections such as Definitions *are not written in ordinary prose, they are especially liable to corruption in the course of transmission. That is why this translation involves a particularly high degree of guesswork, both about the text itself and about its proper construal. Some definitions have probably fallen out accidentally, and some may possibly have been interpolated by later ancient scribes and scholars.*

D.S.H.

411 ἀΐδιον (*aïdion*), eternal: existent at all times, including past and present, without being destroyed.

θεός (*theos*), god: immortal living being, self-sufficient for happiness; eternal being, the cause of the nature of goodness.

γένεσις (*genesis*), becoming: change into being; coming to participate in being; passing into existence.

ἥλιος (*hēlios*), sun: the only celestial fire which is visible to the same people from dawn to

b dusk; the daylight star; the largest eternal living creature.

χρόνος (*chronos*), time: the motion of the sun, the measure of its course.

ἡμέρα (*hēmera*) day: the journey of the sun, from rising to setting; the light opposed to the night.

ἕως (*heōs*), dawn: the beginning of the day; first light of the sun.

μεσημβρία (*mesēmbria*), midday: the time at which the shadows of bodies are all at their shortest.

δείλη (*deilē*), sunset: the end of the day.

νύξ (*nux*), night: the darkness opposed to day; the absence of the sun.

τύχη (*tuchē*), luck: passage from the unclear to the unclear; spontaneous cause of a supernatural event.

γῆρας (*gēras*), old age: deterioration of a living thing due to the passage of time.

πνεῦμα (*pneuma*), wind: movement of air in the region of the earth.

ἀήρ (*aēr*), air: the element to which every spatial motion is natural.

οὐρανός (*ouranos*), sky: the body which surrounds all perceptible things except the uppermost air itself.

ψυχή (*psuchē*), soul: that which moves itself; the cause of vital processes in living creatures.

δύναμις (*dunamis*), ability: that which produces results on account of itself.

ὄψις (*opsis*), vision: the state of being able to discern bodies.

ὀστοῦν (*ostoun*), bone: marrow hardened by heat.

Translated by D. S. Hutchinson.

στοιχεῖον (*stoicheion*), element: that which complex things are composed of and resolved into.

d ἀρετή (*aretē*), virtue: the best disposition; the state of a mortal creature which is in itself praiseworthy; the state on account of which its possessor is said to be good; the just observance of the laws; the disposition on account of which he who is so disposed[1] is said to be perfectly excellent; the state which produces faithfulness to law.

φρόνησις (*phronēsis*), practical wisdom: the ability which by itself is productive of human happiness; the knowledge of what is good and bad; the knowledge that produces happiness;[2] the disposition by which we judge what is to be done and what is not to be done.

δικαιοσύνη (*dikaiosunē*), justice: the unanimity of the soul with itself, and the good discipline of the parts of the soul with respect to each other and concerning each other; the state that distributes to each person according to what is deserved; the state on account of which its possessor chooses what appears to him to be just; the state underlying a law-abiding way of life; social equality; the state of obedience to the laws.

σωφροσύνη (*sōphrosunē*), self-control: moderation of the soul concerning the desires and pleasures that normally occur in it; harmony and good discipline in the soul in respect of normal pleasures and pains; concord of the soul in respect of ruling and being ruled; normal personal independence; good discipline in the soul; rational agreement within the soul about what is admirable and contemptible; the state by which its possessor chooses and is cautious about what he should.

ἀνδρεία (*andreia*), courage: the state of the soul which is unmoved by fear; military confidence; knowledge of the facts of warfare; self-restraint in the soul about what is fearful and terrible; boldness in obedience to wisdom; being intrepid in the face of death; the state which stands on guard over correct thinking in dangerous situations; force which counterbalances danger; force of fortitude in respect of virtue; calm in the soul about what correct thinking takes to be frightening or encouraging things; the preservation of fearless[3] beliefs about the terrors and experience of warfare; the state which cleaves to the law.

ἐγκράτεια (*enkrateia*), self-restraint: the ability to endure pain; obedience to correct thinking; the unbeatable ability of the conceptions of correct thinking.

αὐτάρκεια (*autarkeia*), self-sufficiency: perfect possession of good things; the state in respect of which those who have it are masters of themselves.

412

b

---

1. Omitting *echon* in d3.

2. Reading *epistēmē poiētikē eudaimonias·* after *kakōn* in d6 (a misprint in Burnet).

3. Accepting the conjecture *adeilon* for *adēlon* in b1.

ἐπιείκεια (*epieikeia*), fairness: ced-
ing one's rights and advantages;
moderation in agreements; the
good discipline of a rational
soul in respect of what is
c   admirable and contemptible.
καρτερία (*karteria*), fortitude:
endurance of pain for the sake
of what is admirable; endurance
of labor for the sake of what is
admirable.
θάρσος (*tharsos*), confidence: not
foreseeing anything bad; being
undisturbed by the presence of
something bad.
ἀλυπία (*alupia*), painlessness: the
state in respect of which we are
not subject to suffering pain.
φιλοπονία (*philoponia*), industrious-
ness: the state which accomplishes what one has proposed;
voluntary fortitude; irreproachable state in respect of labor.
αἰδώς (*aidōs*), modesty: voluntarily
drawing back from reckless
behavior, according to what is
right and seems best; voluntarily holding to what is best;
being cautious to avoid justified
d   criticism.
ἐλευθερία (*eleutheria*), freedom: being in control of one's life; having sole authority in all respects;
power to do what one likes in
life; being unsparing in using
and possessing property.
ἐλευθεριότης (*eleutheriotēs*), liberality: the proper state in respect
of money-making; appropriate
expenditure[4] and saving of
property.
πραότης (*praiotēs*), even temper:
suppression of the impulse

caused by anger; an harmonious
blend of the soul.
κοσμιότης (*kosmiotēs*), decorum:
voluntary submission to what
seems best; being disciplined in
moving the body.
εὐδαιμονία (*eudaimonia*), success in
life: the good composed of all
goods; an ability which suffices
for living well; perfection in respect of virtue; resources sufficient for a living creature.
μεγαλοπρέπεια (*megaloprepeia*),
magnificence: being estimable,
according to the correct reasoning of the most dignified of
men.[5]
ἀγχίνοια (*anchinoia*), quick wit:
talent of the soul which enables
its possessor to hit upon what is
necessary in each case; mental
penetration.
χρηστότης (*chrēstotēs*), honesty:
moral sincerity, together with intelligence; excellence of character.
καλοκαγαθία (*kalokagathia*), moral
perfection: the state which decides to do the best things.
μεγαλοψυχία (*megalopsuchia*), mag-
nanimity: nobility in dealing
with events; magnificence of
soul, together with reason.
φιλανθρωπία (*philanthrōpia*), love
of humanity, or kindness: the
easy-going character state of
being friendly to people; the
state of being helpful to people;
the trait of gratefulness; memory, together with helpfulness.
εὐσέβεια (*eusebeia*), piety: justice
concerning the gods; the ability
to serve the gods voluntarily;   41᠄
the correct conception of the

4. Accepting the conjecture *proesis* for *prosthesis* in d4–5.
5. Accepting the conjecture *tou semnotatou* in e2–3.

honor due to gods; knowledge of the honor due to gods.

ἀγαθόν (*agathon*), good: that which is for its own sake.

ἀφοβία (*aphobia*), fearlessness: the state in which we are not subject to fear.

ἀπάθεια (*apatheia*), passionlessness: the state in which we are not subject to passions.

εἰρήνη (*eirēnē*), peace: a quiet period in respect of military conflict.

ῥᾳθυμία (*rāithumia*), laziness: inertia of the soul; having no passion in the spirited part.

δεινότης (*deinotēs*), cleverness: the disposition which enables its possessor to hit upon his particular objective.

φιλία (*philia*), friendship: agreeing about what is admirable and just; deciding on the same way of life; having the same views about moral decision and moral b conduct; agreeing on a way of life; sharing on the basis of benevolence; sharing in rendering and accepting favors.

εὐγένεια (*eugeneia*), nobility: the virtue of a noble character; a soul well cultivated in words and deeds.

αἵρεσις (*hairesis*), selection: correct evaluation.

εὔνοια (*eunoia*), benevolence: kindliness of a man towards another.

οἰκειότης (*oikeiotēs*), kinship: sharing in the same descent.

ὁμόνοια (*homonoia*), agreement: sharing everything that is on one's mind;[6] harmony of thoughts and assumptions.

ἀγάπησις (*agapēsis*), contentment: welcoming everything.

πολιτική (*politikē*), political skill: the knowledge of what is admirable and useful; the knowledge of how to produce justice in a city. c

ἑταιρία (*hetairia*), camaraderie: the friendship among people of the same age formed by keeping company with each other.

εὐβουλία (*euboulia*), good counsel: the inborn virtue of reasoning.

πίστις (*pistis*), faith: the conception[7] that things are as they appear to one; firmness of character.

ἀλήθεια (*alētheia*), truth, veracity: the correct state expressed in affirmation and denial; knowledge of truths.

βούλησις (*boulēsis*), will: wanting, based on correct reason; reasonable desire; natural desire, based on reason.

συμβούλευσις (*sumbouleusis*), consultation: advice to another person about conduct, how he should conduct himself.

εὐκαιρία (*eukairia*), good timing: hitting upon the right time to do something or have something done to one. d

εὐλάβεια (*eulabeia*), caution: being on guard against what is bad; being sure to be on guard.

τάξις (*taxis*), order: functional similarity in all the mutual elements of a whole; due proportion in a society; cause of all the mutual elements of a whole; due proportion in respect of learning.[8]

---

6. Accepting the conjecture *tōn en nōi ontōn* for *tōn ontōn* in b8.

7. Accepting a conjectural transposition of *orthē* from c4 to c6.

8. Reading *summetria pros to mathein* in d4.

πρόσεξις (*prosexis*), attention: the effort the soul makes to learn something.

εὐφυΐα (*euphuïa*), talent: speed in learning; good natural[9] inheritance; natural virtue.

εὐμάθεια (*eumatheia*), cleverness: the mental talent to learn quickly.

δίκη (*dikē*), judgment, trial: authoritative declaration about a disputed matter; dispute[10] about whether or not there has been

e   injustice.

εὐνομία (*eunomia*), law-abidingness: obedience to good laws.

εὐφροσύνη (*euphrosunē*), cheerfulness: joy in doing what a temperate man does.

τιμή (*timē*), honor: the gift of good things given for virtuous deeds; the dignity conferred by virtue; dignified bearing; the cultivation of one's dignity.

προθυμία (*prothumia*), zeal: manifestation of an active will.

χάρις (*charis*), charity: voluntary beneficence; giving up something good which is of service at an opportune moment.

ὁμόνοια (*homonoia*), concord: opinion shared between those who govern and those who are governed about how to govern and be governed.

πολιτεία (*politeia*), republic: community of many men, self-sufficient for living successfully; community of many under the

414   rule of law.

πρόνοια (*pronoia*), foresight, providence: preparation for some future event.

βουλή (*boulē*), deliberation: investigation about what would be beneficial in the future.

νίκη (*nikē*), victory: ability triumphant in a competition.

εὐπορία (*euporia*), inventiveness: good judgment which triumphs over something said.

δωρεά (*dōrea*), gift: exchange of favors.

καιρός (*kairos*), opportunity: the ideal time for something beneficial; the time that contributes to obtaining something good.

μνήμη (*mnēmē*), memory: disposition of the soul which guards over the truth which resides in it.

ἔννοια (*ennoia*), reflection: intense thinking.

νόησις (*noēsis*), intuition: the starting point of knowledge.

ἁγνεία (*hagneia*), piety: caution about mistakes with respect to the gods; paying service, in a normal way, to the honor of a god.

μαντεία (*manteia*), divining: the knowledge which predicts events without proof.

μαντική (*mantikē*), divination: the knowledge which contemplates the present and future of mortal beings.

σοφία (*sophia*), wisdom: non-hypothetical knowledge; knowledge of what always exists; knowledge which contemplates the cause of beings.

φιλοσοφία (*philosophia*), philosophy: desire for the knowledge of what always exists; the state which contemplates the truth,

---

9. Reading *phuseōs* in d6.

10. Accepting the conjectural restoration *Dikē ˙ apophasis . . . pragmatos˙ amphisbētēsis peri tou adikein ē mē.*

what makes it true; cultivation
of the soul, based on correct
reason.

ἐπιστήμη (*epistēmē*), knowledge:
conception of the soul which
cannot be dislodged by reason-
c   ing; ability to conceive one or
more things which cannot be
dislodged by reasoning; true
argument which cannot be
dislodged by thinking.

δόξα (*doxa*), opinion: conception
which is open to persuasion by
reason; fluctuation in reasoning;
the thinking which is led by
reason to the false as well as the
true.

αἴσθησις (*aisthēsis*), perception:
fluctuation in the soul; movement of the mind via the body;[11]
an announcement for the benefit
of human beings, from which
arises a non-rational ability in
the soul to recognize things
through the body.

ἕξις (*hexis*), state: disposition of
the soul on account of which
people are said to be of a
d   certain sort.

φωνή (*phōnē*), voiced sound: an
emission of thought through the
mouth.

λόγος (*logos*), speech: voice
articulated in letters capable of
indicating each existing thing;
linguistic sound compounded
of nouns and verbs, without
music.

ὄνομα (*onoma*), noun: uncom-
pounded linguistic sound expressing both what is predicated
in the essence and everything
which is not said of a thing in
its own right.

διάλεκτος (*dialektos*), language,
linguistic expression: human
sound with letters; a common
sign which is expressive,
without music.

συλλαβή (*sullabē*), syllable: articulation of the human voice that can
be written.

ὅρος (*horos*), definition: something
said, comprised of genus and
differentia.   e

τεκμήριον (*tekmērion*), evidence:
proof of the non-evident.

ἀπόδειξις (*apodeixis*), proof: true
argument reasoning to a conclusion; argument that declares
something through what is
previously known.

στοιχεῖον φωνῆς (*stoicheion phōnēs*),
element of voiced sound: uncom-
pounded voiced sound, the
reason that the other voiced
sounds are voiced sounds.

ὠφέλιμον (*ōphelimon*), utility: what
causes something to be well off;
what causes good.

συμφέρον (*sumpheron*), beneficial:
what conduces to the good.

ἀγαθόν (*agathon*), good: what
causes the preservation of
beings; the cause toward which
everything tends, from which
is derived what should be
chosen.

σῶφρον (*sōphron*), self-controlled:
being orderly in the soul.

δίκαιον (*dikaion*), just: prescription
of law which produces justice.   415

ἑκούσιον (*hekousion*), voluntary:
what produces its own action;
what is chosen for itself; what is
achieved with thinking.

ἐλεύθερον (*eleutheron*), free: what
rules itself.

---

11. Moving the semicolon from after *kinēsis* to after *sōmatos* in c5, and deleting
psuchēs.

μέτριον (*metrion*), moderate: in between excess and insufficiency, satisfying the strictures of skill.

μέτρον (*metron*), measure: the mean between excess and insufficiency.

ἆθλον ἀρετῆς (*athlon aretēs*), prize of virtue: the reward worth choosing for its own sake.

ἀθανασία (*athanasia*), immortality: the eternal duration of a living substance.[12]

ὅσιον (*hosion*), holy: service to a god which is agreeable to the god.

ἑορτή (*heortē*), festival: time that is sacred by law.

ἄνθρωπος (*anthrōpos*), man: wingless, two-footed, flat-fingernailed animal; the only being capable of acquiring

b   rational knowledge.

θυσία (*thusia*), sacrifice: offering of a victim to a god.

εὐχή (*euchē*), prayer: request by men to the gods for what is good or seems good.

βασιλεύς (*basileus*), king: an officer who is legally beyond accountability; an officer of a political organization.

ἀρχή (*archē*), command: being in charge of everything.

ἐξουσία (*exousia*), legal authority: discretionary power granted by law.

νομοθέτης (*nomothetēs*), lawgiver: the maker of the laws under which a city is to be governed.

νόμος (*nomos*), law: political judgment of many people, not limited to a certain time.

ὑπόθεσις (*hypothesis*), hypothesis: indemonstrable first principle;

summary of the principal points in a discourse.

ψήφισμα (*psēphisma*), decree: political judgment limited to a certain time.

πολιτικός (*politikos*), statesman: one who knows how to organize a city.

πόλις (*polis*), city-state: the place of residence of a number of men who follow decisions made in common; a number of men being under the same law.

πόλεως ἀρετή (*poleōs aretē*), virtue of a city: the establishment of a good constitution.

πολεμική (*polemikē*), military skill: having experience of war.

συμμαχία (*summachia*), military alliance: community of warring parties.

σωτηρία (*sōtēria*), preservation: keeping safe and sound.

τύραννος (*turannos*), dictator: an officer of a city who rules according to his own ideas.

σοφιστής (*sophistēs*), sophist: paid hunter of rich and distinguished young men.

πλοῦτος (*ploutos*), wealth: having sufficient possessions to live happily; an abundance of property which conduces to happiness.

παρακαταθήκη (*parakatathēkē*), deposit: something given on trust.

κάθαρσις (*katharsis*), purification: the separation of the worse from the better.

νικᾶν (*nikan*), being victorious: prevailing in a conflict.

ἀγαθὸς ἄνθρωπος (*agathos anthrōpos*), good person: the sort of person who can achieve what is good for a human being.

---

12. Accepting the emendation *ousias empsuchou aïdios monē* in a8.

σώφρων (*sōphrōn*), self-controlled: person having moderate desires.

ἐγκρατής (*enkratēs*), self-restrained: one who overpowers the parts of the soul when they are contrary to right reason.

σπουδαῖος (*spoudaios*), excellent: he who is completely good; he who has the virtue proper to human beings.

σύννοια (*sunnoia*), worry: an irrational and disturbing thought.

δυσμαθία (*dusmathia*), stupidity: slowness in learning.

δεσποτεία (*despoteia*), rule over slaves: just authority which is accountable to nobody.

ἀφιλοσοφία (*aphilosophia*), lack of philosophy: the state whose possessor is a hater of argument.

φόβος (*phobos*), fear: consternation of the soul in expectation of something bad.

θυμός (*thumos*), passion: forceful impulse of the non-rational part of the soul, without being ordered by reasoning and thought.[13]

ἔκπληξις (*ekplēxis*), consternation: fear in the expectation of something bad.

κολακεία (*kolakeia*), flattery: keeping company for the sake of pleasure, without considering what is best; the state of socializing for pleasure in excess of what is moderate.

ὀργή (*orgē*), anger: the urging of the passionate part of the soul for vengeance.

ὕβρις (*hubris*), assault: injustice driving one to dishonor someone.

ἀκρασία (*akrasia*), lack of self-restraint: the violent state,

without correct reasoning, which is oriented towards what seems to be pleasant.

ὄκνος (*oknos*), laziness: running away from labor; cowardice which paralyzes impulses.

ἀρχή (*archē*), origin: first cause of being.

διαβολή (*diabolē*), slander: the alienation of friends by speech.

καιρός (*kairos*), opportunity: the time it is appropriate to do each thing or undergo it.

ἀδικία (*adikia*), injustice: the state of despising the laws.

ἔνδεια (*endeia*), poverty: being short of goods.

αἰσχύνη (*aischunē*), shame: fear in expectation of bad reputation.

ἀλαζονεία (*alazoneia*), pretentiousness: the state which makes those who lack a good or goods pretend to have it or them.

ἁμαρτία (*hamartia*), error: an action against correct reasoning.

φθόνος (*phthonos*), envy: being distressed by the goods of one's friends, either present or past.

ἀναισχυντία (*anaischuntia*), shamelessness: the state of the soul which endures dishonor for the sake of profit.

θρασύτης (*thrasutēs*), temerity: excessive boldness in face of dangers which one should not face.

φιλοτιμία (*philotimia*), vanity: the state of the soul which is lavish with every expense without thinking.

κακοφυΐα (*kakophuïa*), bad nature: badness in nature and an error of what is natural; disease of what is natural.

ἐλπίς (*elpis*), hope: the expectation of good.

13. Emending *nous taxeōs* to *kai nou taxeōs* in e6.

416   μανία (*mania*), madness: the state which is destructive of true conception.

λαλιά (*lalia*), talkativeness: irrational lack of self-restraint in speech.

ἐναντιότης (*enantiotēs*), contrariety: the greatest distance between objects of the same genus which fall under some difference.

ἀκούσιον (*akousion*), involuntary: what is accomplished without thinking.

παιδεία (*paideia*), education: the ability that is of service to the soul.

παίδευσις (*paideusis*), educating: bestowing education.

νομοθετική (*nomothetikē*), legislative skill: knowledge of how to produce a good city.

νουθέτησις (*nouthetēsis*), admonition: speech which blames with judgment; speech for the sake of keeping someone from a mistake.

βοήθεια (*boētheia*), help: the prevention of something bad, either present or about to happen.

κόλασις (*kolasis*), chastisement: treatment given to a soul concerning a past mistake.

δύναμις (*dunamis*), ability: superiority in word or deed; the state which makes its possessor be able; natural strength.

σῴζειν (*sōizein*), save: to keep safe and sound.

ON JUSTICE

Socrates discusses with a friend several disjointed questions about justice. He makes the following points: it is speech that decides what is just and unjust (though that does not answer the question what the just is); the same acts can be just or unjust, depending on the situation; justice is knowledge of the right time to do things; people who are unjust are unwillingly unjust. All these are familiar Socratic ideas, presented in an unusually bald and unattractive format.

On Justice verges on incoherence because of its brevity and abrupt transitions. One explanation might be that it is not an original work, but is excerpted or adapted from earlier Socratic literature. The argument that the same actions (even deceiving and stealing) are sometimes just and sometimes unjust, depending on the situation, is urged by Socrates in Xenophon, Memoirs of Socrates *IV.ii.12–20, and Plato has Socrates use a similar argument for situational ethics (*Republic *331b–d). Xenophon often adapted earlier Socratic texts, in this case apparently the same text or texts as the author or compiler of* On Justice.

That Socrates argued for the propriety of deceiving and stealing was one of the complaints urged by Polycrates in his Accusation of Socrates, *written in 393/2 B.C. (a speech now lost but whose contents can be partly inferred from the various replies it provoked, especially the* Apology *of Libanius, the fourth century A.D. teacher of rhetoric). If Polycrates was replying to a Socratic source excerpted or adapted by the author of* On Justice, *we can only guess which it was, but the most attractive possibility is a (now lost) dialogue by Antisthenes called* On Law *or* On Rightness and Justice.

*Plato's influence can be felt at one point only: when Socrates argues, apparently needlessly, that since people are unwillingly unjust their unjust conduct must also be unwilling, the author is insisting on a point that Plato felt he needed to insist on at the end of his life (*Laws *860c–e). If the dialogue was intended to support Plato's view, it can be dated to after the middle of the fourth century B.C., perhaps well after.*

Some manuscripts of On Justice *list as speakers 'Socrates, Friend', others say 'Socrates, Anonymous', and one says 'Socrates, Clinias'; that Socrates is a speaker is clear from the dialogue itself, but the other three appellations are evidently guesses by later scholars. So it seems to have been transmitted during antiquity without any indication of who the speakers were. The same is true of the dialogue labeled* On Virtue; *these two dialogues also lack titles of a normal Platonic sort and may be among those said in ancient lists of Platonic works to*

*be 'without a heading'. In this translation, we have decided to call the un-
known interlocutor 'Friend'.*

D.S.H.

372   SOCRATES: Can you tell us what the just is, or don't you think it's worthwhile to discuss this?

FRIEND: I think it would be very worthwhile.

SOCRATES: What is the just, then?

FRIEND: Well, what could it be, if not what's established as just by custom?

SOCRATES: That's not the way to answer. If you were to ask me what an
eye is, I'd tell you it's what we see with; and if you demand that I prove
it, I'll prove it. And if you ask me what "soul" is the name of, I'll tell you
it's what we think with. And if, again, you ask me what voice is, I'll answer
that it's what we converse with. In this same way, now tell me what the
just is, by referring to how we use it, like I've now done with these
other things.

FRIEND: I can't possibly answer you that way.

SOCRATES: Well, since you can't do it that way, would it perhaps be
easier for us to discover it in this sort of way? Now, when we want to
distinguish what's longer and what's shorter, with what do we examine
them? Isn't it with a measuring-stick?

FRIEND: Yes.

373   SOCRATES: Besides the measuring-stick, what skill do we use? Isn't it skill
in measuring?

FRIEND: Right, skill in measuring.

SOCRATES: And what about distinguishing what's light and what's heavy?
Don't we do that with a scale?

FRIEND: Yes.

SOCRATES: Besides the scale, what skill do we use? Isn't it skill in
weighing?

FRIEND: Definitely.

SOCRATES: Well, then, when we want to distinguish what's just and
what's unjust, what instrument do we use to examine them? And, besides
this instrument, what skill do we use in dealing with them? Or doesn't
this way make it clear to you either?

FRIEND: No.

SOCRATES: Well, let's start again. Whenever we disagree about what's
larger and what's smaller, who are the ones who decide between us? Aren't
they the ones who measure?

FRIEND: Yes.

b   SOCRATES: And whenever we disagree about number, about many and
few, who are the ones who decide? Aren't they the ones who count?

FRIEND: Obviously.

Translated by Andrew S. Becker.

SOCRATES: Whenever we disagree with each other about what's just and what's unjust, to whom do we go? Who are those who decide between us in each case? Tell me.

FRIEND: Are you talking about judges, Socrates?

SOCRATES: Well done! Now go on and try to tell me this: What are the measurers doing when they decide about what's large and what's small? They're measuring, aren't they?

FRIEND: Yes.

SOCRATES: And when the weighers decide about what's heavy and what's light, aren't they weighing?

FRIEND: Of course they're weighing.

SOCRATES: And when the counters decide about many and few, they're counting, aren't they?

FRIEND: Yes.

SOCRATES: And when the judges decide about what's just and what's   c
unjust, what are they doing? Answer me.

FRIEND: I can't.

SOCRATES: Say "they're speaking."

FRIEND: Yes.

SOCRATES: Then is it by speaking that they decide between us, whenever the judges decide about what's just and what's unjust?

FRIEND: Yes.

SOCRATES: And it was by measuring that the measurers decided about what's small and what's large, since it was with a measuring-stick that these things were decided.

FRIEND: That's right.

SOCRATES: Again, it was by weighing that the weighers decided about what's heavy and what's light, since it was with a scale that these things were decided.

FRIEND: It was.

SOCRATES: Again, it was by counting that the counters decided about   d
many and few, since it was by number that these things were decided.

FRIEND: That's right.

SOCRATES: Yes, and, as we agreed a moment ago, it's by speaking that the judges decide between us about what's just and what's unjust, since it was with speech that these things were decided.

FRIEND: Well said, Socrates.

SOCRATES: Yes, because it was truly said: speech, as it seems, decides what's just and what's unjust.

FRIEND: It certainly seems so.

SOCRATES: What could the just and the unjust possibly be? Suppose someone asked us: "Since a measuring-stick, skill in measuring, and a measurer decide what's larger and what's smaller, what are "larger" and "smaller"?" We might tell him that "larger" is what exceeds and "smaller" is what's exceeded. Or: "Since a scale, skill in weighing, and a weigher   e
decide what's heavy and what's light, what are "heavy" and "light"?" We

might tell him that "heavy" is what sinks down in the balance, and "light" is what rises up. In this way, then, if someone should ask us: "Since speech, skill in judging, and a judge decide what's just and what's unjust for us, what could "just" and "unjust" possibly be?" How can we answer him? Are we still unable to tell him?

FRIEND: We're unable.

SOCRATES: Do you think people do unjustice willingly or unwillingly?
374   What I mean is this: Do you think that people act unjustly and are unjust willingly or unwillingly?

FRIEND: Willingly, I'd say, Socrates, for they're wicked.

SOCRATES: Then do you think that people are wicked and unjust willingly?

FRIEND: Definitely. Don't you?

SOCRATES: No, at least not if we're to trust the poet.

FRIEND: What poet?

SOCRATES: The one who said: "No one is willingly wicked, nor unwillingly blessed."[1]

FRIEND: But, you know, Socrates, the old saying holds true, that singers tell many lies.

b   SOCRATES: But I'd be surprised if this singer lied about this. If you have the time, let's consider whether he tells the truth, or lies.

FRIEND: Well, I do have the time.

SOCRATES: Then which do you think is just, lying or telling the truth?

FRIEND: Telling the truth, obviously.

SOCRATES: Lying, then, is unjust?

FRIEND: Yes.

SOCRATES: And which do you think is just, deceiving or not deceiving?

FRIEND: Not deceiving, certainly.

SOCRATES: Deceiving, then, is unjust?

FRIEND: Yes.

SOCRATES: Well, then, which is just, harming or helping?

FRIEND: Helping.

SOCRATES: Harming, then, is unjust?

FRIEND: Yes.

c   SOCRATES: So, telling the truth, not deceiving, and helping are just, but lying, harming, and deceiving are unjust.

FRIEND: Yes, by Zeus, definitely.

SOCRATES: Even in the case of enemies?

FRIEND: Certainly not!

SOCRATES: Then is harming enemies just, and helping them unjust?

FRIEND: Yes.

SOCRATES: And isn't harming enemies just, even if you deceive them?

FRIEND: It must be.

---

1. Epicharmus of Syracuse, an early comic poet (frg. 7).

SOCRATES: What about lying to deceive and harm them? Isn't this just?

FRIEND: Yes.

SOCRATES: Well, then, you say that helping friends is just, don't you?

FRIEND: Definitely.

SOCRATES: By not deceiving them, or by deceiving them, if it's for their benefit?

FRIEND: Even deceiving them, by Zeus.

SOCRATES: But, while it's just to help people by deceiving them, certainly it's not just to help them by lying? What if we help them by lying?

FRIEND: It would be just even if we lied.

SOCRATES: Then, as it seems, both lying and telling the truth are just and unjust.

FRIEND: Yes.

SOCRATES: And not deceiving and deceiving are just and unjust.

FRIEND: I guess so.

SOCRATES: Both harming and helping are just and unjust.

FRIEND: Yes.

SOCRATES: So all these sorts of things, it appears, are both just and unjust.

FRIEND: So it seems to me.

SOCRATES: Listen, then. I have a right and a left eye, don't I, just like other people?

FRIEND: Yes.

SOCRATES: A right and a left nostril?

FRIEND: Definitely.

SOCRATES: And a right and a left hand?

FRIEND: Yes.

SOCRATES: Although you call these by the same name, you say some are right and some are left. If I ask you which is which, wouldn't you be able to say that these on this side are right and these on the other are left?

FRIEND: Yes.

SOCRATES: Then let's get back to our point. Although you call those acts by the same name, you say that some are just and some are unjust. Can you say which are just and which are unjust?

FRIEND: Well, I suppose that each of these acts turns out to be just if and when we should do them, but unjust if we shouldn't.

SOCRATES: Good for you! Then does the person who does each of these acts, when he should, do what's just, while the person who does them, when he shouldn't, does what's unjust?

FRIEND: Yes.

SOCRATES: And isn't he himself just, the one who does what's just, but the one who does what's unjust is himself unjust?

FRIEND: That's right.

SOCRATES: Now, who can perform surgery and cauterize and reduce swelling, if and when he should?

FRIEND: A doctor.

375b   SOCRATES: Because he knows how, or for some other reason?
        FRIEND: Because he knows how.
        SOCRATES: And who can cultivate and plow and plant when he should?
        FRIEND: A farmer.
        SOCRATES: Because he knows how, or because he doesn't?
        FRIEND: Because he knows how.
        SOCRATES: Isn't this true for the other cases as well? The one who knows
how can do what he should, if and when he should, but the one who
doesn't know how can't?
        FRIEND: So it is.
        SOCRATES: And what about lying and deceiving and giving help? Can
the one who knows how do each of these acts when he should and at the
right time, but the one who doesn't know how can't?
c   FRIEND: That's true.
        SOCRATES: But the person who does them when he should is just?
        FRIEND: Yes.
        SOCRATES: And he does them because of his knowledge.
        FRIEND: How else?
        SOCRATES: Then a just person is just because of his knowledge.
        FRIEND: Yes.
        SOCRATES: Isn't the unjust person unjust for the opposite reason?
        FRIEND: So it seems.
        SOCRATES: And the just person is just because of his wisdom.
        FRIEND: Yes.
        SOCRATES: The unjust person is unjust, then, because of his ignorance.
        FRIEND: I guess so.
        SOCRATES: So it looks like justice is what our ancestors handed down to
us as wisdom, and injustice is what they handed down to us as ignorance.
d   FRIEND: I guess so.
        SOCRATES: Are people ignorant willingly or unwillingly?
        FRIEND: Unwillingly.
        SOCRATES: So they're also unjust unwillingly?
        FRIEND: It seems so.
        SOCRATES: Are unjust people wicked?
        FRIEND: Yes.
        SOCRATES: So they're wicked and unjust unwillingly?
        FRIEND: Absolutely.
        SOCRATES: And they act unjustly because they're unjust?
        FRIEND: Yes.
        SOCRATES: So, unwillingly?
        FRIEND: Of course.
        SOCRATES: Clearly what's done willingly doesn't happen unwillingly.
        FRIEND: It couldn't.
        SOCRATES: And acting unjustly comes about because there is injustice.
        FRIEND: Yes.
        SOCRATES: And injustice is unwilled.

FRIEND: Unwilled, yes.
SOCRATES: Then they act unjustly and are unjust and wicked unwillingly.
FRIEND: Unwillingly, it seems.
SOCRATES: Then in that case the singer didn't lie.
FRIEND: I guess not.

ON VIRTUE

How can a man become virtuous? If virtue can be taught, there must be teachers of it; yet there don't seem to be any—even the famous virtuous men of Athens failed to teach virtue to their own sons, let alone to anyone else. Nor is virtue a natural gift, for if it were there would be trainers dedicated to recognizing and fostering it, as with horse trainers and athletics coaches. The remaining alternative is that those who enjoy it have the gods to thank, not their nature, nor their educators.

Whole passages from Plato's Meno *reappear, more or less unchanged, in this dry little dialogue: 377b–378c ≈* Meno *93d–94e. This apparent plagiarism offends the sensibilities of modern scholars, but surely the author had no wish to conceal the borrowings from* Meno; *on the contrary, his use of themes and passages from* Meno *and other well-known Platonic dialogues is a way of citing them and drawing support from authoritative sources for his thesis. That thesis was not common ground in Plato's Academy; Plato's own position was far more nuanced than our author's, and Xenocrates, a student of Plato and the third head of the Academy, wrote a work (now lost) affirming that* Virtue Can Be Transmitted, *perhaps in response to the question asked by Socrates in* Meno, *whether virtue can be taught. If the dialogue was part of a debate internal to the Old Academy, then it can be dated to the latter half of the fourth century* B.C., *when Aristotle as well as Xenocrates addressed the question. Or else the dialogue may have been directed against the Stoics, who claimed that virtue can be taught and that its foundation lies in human nature; if so, it might date from the middle of the third century* B.C., *a time when Arcesilaus, as head of the Academy, was placing new emphasis on Plato's written works and drawing skeptical and anti-Stoical lessons from them.*

The view espoused at the end of On Virtue, *that virtue comes about by divine allotment, not only echoes Socrates' comments at the end of Plato's* Meno; *it is of a piece with Plato's view that philosophers should rule and that their rule might come about by divine allotment (Letter VII 326a–b,* Republic *473c–d). Theological support for this view of god is given by Plato at* Laws *715e–716d. Aristotle also uses some of the imagery and expressions found at the end of* On Virtue *(Eudemian Ethics 1246b37–1247a13 and 1248b3–7, Nicomachean Ethics 1145a20–29, Politics 1284a3–11).*

Most manuscripts of On Virtue *list as speakers 'Socrates, Friend', but two say 'Socrates, Meno', and one says 'Socrates, Hippotrophus [Horse-trainer]'; that Socrates is a speaker is clear from the dialogue itself, but the other three appellations are evidently guesses by later scholars. So it seems to have been transmitted during antiquity without any indication of who the speakers were. The same is true of the dialogue labeled* On Justice; *these two dialogues also lack titles of a normal Platonic sort and may be among those said in ancient lists of Platonic works to be 'without a heading'. In this translation, we have decided to call the unknown interlocutor 'Friend'.*

D.S.H.

SOCRATES: Can virtue be taught? If not, do men become good by nature, or in some other way? 376

FRIEND: I can't give you an answer right now, Socrates. b

SOCRATES: Well now, let's consider it. Tell me, if someone wanted to become good with the virtue that makes expert chefs good, how would he do it?

FRIEND: By learning from good chefs, obviously.

SOCRATES: Good. Now if he wanted to become a good doctor, to whom would he go to become a good doctor?

FRIEND: That's obvious—to one of the good doctors.

SOCRATES: And if he wanted to become good with the virtue that makes expert builders good? c

FRIEND: To one of the builders.

SOCRATES: And if he had wanted to become good with the virtue that makes men wise and good, where must he go to learn it?

FRIEND: This virtue, too, if it *can* be learned, I suppose he'd have to learn from good men. Where else?

SOCRATES: Then tell me, who were the good men of our city? Let's consider if these are the ones who make men good.

FRIEND: Thucydides, Themistocles, Aristides, and Pericles. d

SOCRATES: Can we name a teacher for each of them?

FRIEND: No, we can't; I haven't heard of any.

SOCRATES: Well then, can we name a student, either a foreigner or a citizen, or anybody else, either free or slave, who is reputed to have become wise and good by associating with these men?

FRIEND: I haven't heard of anybody.

SOCRATES: Might they not have been too jealous to share their virtue with other men?

FRIEND: Maybe.

SOCRATES: Just as chefs, doctors and builders are jealous—that way they won't have any rivals. For it isn't profitable for them to have many rivals or to live among many similar professionals. Is it similarly unprofitable for good men to live among men like themselves?

FRIEND: Probably.

Translated by Mark Reuter.

SOCRATES: But aren't they just, as well as good?

FRIEND: Yes.

SOCRATES: Does it profit someone to live not among good, but among bad men?

FRIEND: I can't tell you.

SOCRATES: Well, can you tell me this—whether it's the business of good men to harm, and of bad men to help or *vice versa*?

FRIEND: *Vice versa.*

377 SOCRATES: The good, therefore, help, and the evil harm?

FRIEND: Yes.

SOCRATES: Is there anyone who wants to be harmed rather than be helped?

FRIEND: Of course not.

SOCRATES: Therefore, no one wants to live among bad rather than good men.

FRIEND: That's right.

SOCRATES: Therefore, no good man will be too jealous to make another man good and similar to himself.

FRIEND: Apparently not, according to that argument.

SOCRATES: Have you heard that Cleophantus was the son of Themistocles?

FRIEND: I've heard that.

SOCRATES: Isn't it obvious that Themistocles would not have begrudged his son becoming the best—Themistocles, a man who wouldn't have begrudged that to anyone, if he really was good, which he was, as we admit.

b   FRIEND: Yes.

SOCRATES: Did you realize that Themistocles taught his son to be an expert horseman—he could ride standing upright on his horse, he could throw a javelin from this position, and he could perform many other remarkable feats—his father taught him and made him an expert in many other things that require good teachers. Haven't you heard that from the older generation?

FRIEND: I have.

c   SOCRATES: So no one could criticize his son's natural ability as bad.

FRIEND: Not rightly, at least from what you say.

SOCRATES: What about this? Have you ever heard anyone—young or old—say that Cleophantus, the son of Themistocles, was a wise and good man in the way that his father was wise?

FRIEND: Never.

SOCRATES: Are we to suppose, then, that he wanted to teach his son those things, but he didn't want to make him better than any of his neighbors in the wisdom that he himself enjoyed, if virtue can indeed be taught?

d   FRIEND: That isn't very likely.

SOCRATES: And yet he was just the sort of teacher of virtue that you suggested. But let's consider another man, Aristides, who raised Lysimachus. He gave his son the best Athenian education in matters which require teachers, but he made him no better than anyone else. Both you and I know this, for we've spent time with him.

FRIEND: Yes.

SOCRATES: And you know that Pericles, too, raised his sons Paralus and Xanthippus—in fact, I think you were in love with one of them. As you know, he taught them horsemanship—and they were as good as any Athenian—the liberal arts, and athletic games; he brought them up to be as good as anyone at every skill for which there are teachers; and yet he didn't want to make them good men?   e

FRIEND: But perhaps they would have been, Socrates, if they hadn't died young.

SOCRATES: You're coming to the aid of your boyfriend, which is fair enough. But if virtue were teachable and if it were possible to make men good, Pericles would certainly have made his sons expert in his own virtue rather than in the liberal arts or athletic games. But it doesn't seem to   378 be teachable, since Thucydides, as well, raised two sons, Melesias and Stephanus, and you cannot say about them what you said about the sons of Pericles, for you know very well that one lived to a ripe old age, and the other much longer. Indeed, their father taught them well, especially to be the finest wrestlers in Athens. He sent one to Xanthias and the other to Eudorus—weren't they supposed to be the finest wrestlers of the day?

FRIEND: Yes.

SOCRATES: So it's clear that he would never have taught his sons what   b he had to spend money on, when he could have made them good without spending anything—wouldn't he have taught them to be good, if it could be taught?

FRIEND: That seems likely.

SOCRATES: But perhaps Thucydides was a commoner, and he didn't have many friends among the Athenians and their allies? No, but he was from a great household, and he was able to do great things here in Athens and in other Greek cities. So, if virtue could be taught, he would have found   c someone—either locally or abroad—who could have made his sons good, if he himself didn't have the time because of his political affairs. No, my friend, it looks as if virtue can't be taught.

FRIEND: No, probably not.

SOCRATES: Well then, if virtue isn't teachable, are men naturally good? If we examine this in the following way, perhaps we might find out. Now then, do we think that good horses have particular natures?

FRIEND: They do.

SOCRATES: And aren't there some men who have a skill by which they   d know the natures of the good horses, those physically fit for racing and mentally spirited or else lethargic?

FRIEND: Yes.

SOCRATES: What, then, is this skill? What name does it have?

FRIEND: Horsemanship.

SOCRATES: And likewise for hunting dogs, is there some skill by which men can discern the good and bad natures of the dogs?

FRIEND: There is.

SOCRATES: What is it?

FRIEND: Huntsmanship.

SOCRATES: And what about gold and silver? Do we think there are money-changers who separate the good coins from the bad by looking at them?

e   FRIEND: There are.

SOCRATES: What do you call them?

FRIEND: Assayers.

SOCRATES: And again athletic coaches know by looking which traits of the human body are good or bad for each of the events, and in older or younger boys which are going to be their most valuable traits, where they have high hopes for them to succeed in what their bodies can perform well.

FRIEND: That's true.

SOCRATES: Which of these is more important for cities: good horses, good
379 dogs, and so on, or good men?

FRIEND: Good men.

SOCRATES: Well? Don't you think, if men had innate characters good for virtue, that people would make every effort to recognize them?

FRIEND: Very likely.

SOCRATES: Now can you tell me which skill is dedicated to, and capable of judging, the natural qualities of good men?

FRIEND: No, I can't.

SOCRATES: And yet it would surely be worth a great deal, as would those
b   who possess it, for they could show us which of the young, while still boys, are going to be good. We would take them and guard them in the acropolis at public expense, like silver, only more carefully, so that no harm would come to them, from battle or any other danger. They would be stored up for the city as guards and benefactors when they came of age.

But really, I dare say that it's neither by nature nor by teaching that men become virtuous.

c   FRIEND: How then do you suppose, Socrates, that they become virtuous, if it's neither by nature nor teaching? How else could they become good?

SOCRATES: I don't think it's very easy to explain this. My guess, however, is that the possession of virtue is very much a divine gift and that men become good just as the divine prophets and oracle-mongers do. For they become what they are neither by nature nor skill: it's through the inspiration of the gods that they become what they are. Likewise, good men announce
d   to their cities the likely outcome of events and what is going to happen, by the inspiration of god, much better and much more clearly than the fortune-tellers. Even the women, I think, say that this sort of man is divine, and the Spartans, whenever they applaud someone in high style, say that he is divine. And often Homer uses this same compliment, as do other poets. Indeed, whenever a god wishes a city to become successful, he places good men in it, and whenever a city is slated to fail, the god takes the good men away from that city. So it seems that virtue is neither teachable nor natural, but comes by divine allotment to those who possess it.

DEMODOCUS

What has come down to us under the title Demodocus *seems to be a combination of two separate works: a monologue (addressed to Demodocus) which argues against collective decision-making (part I), and a trilogy of dialogues which raise doubts about three elements of common sense (parts II–IV). The trilogy may have been among the Platonic works said in antiquity to be 'without a heading', together with* On Justice *and* On Virtue. *At some point a scribe seems to have attached the trilogy to the end of* Demodocus I *by accident, which caused all subsequent copies to have the expanded format.*

In Demodocus I, *Socrates refuses Demodocus' request to give advice on a matter soon to be discussed in a public meeting. He argues instead that the whole collective decision procedure (offering advice, listening to advice, and deciding the question by voting) is absurd. Both the content (which overlaps with that of* Sisyphus) *and the style of argument (which proceeds largely by dilemma) are Platonic enough, though the monologue form is unusual. The addressee, Demodocus, also appears in* Theages, *where he agrees with Socrates that advice is something sacred. The piece is probably later than mid-fourth century* B.C., *perhaps much later.*

In Demodocus II–IV, *the narrator (we are probably meant to assume that he is Socrates) reports three conversations, between unnamed third parties, which call into question certain principles of common sense; he is left in doubt about these principles, a doubt which the reader is expected to share. The common-sense principles are plausible, but arguments in the other direction are developed in order to balance their plausibility and leave the reader with an open mind. This is a technique practiced by adherents of the Academy under the sceptical philosopher Arcesilaus and after, which suggests that the dialogues are from the middle of the third century* B.C., *or later.*

D.S.H.

I

You invite me,[1] Demodocus, to give you advice on the matters you are 380 meeting to discuss; but I am inclined rather to ask what is the point of your assembly and of the readiness of those who think to give you advice and of the vote which each of you intends to cast.

Translated by Jonathan Barnes.

1. The speaker is not named, but is apparently intended to be taken as Socrates.

Suppose, on the one hand, that it is impossible to give good and informed advice on the matters you are meeting to discuss: then surely it is ridiculous
b   to meet to discuss matters on which it is impossible to give good advice. Suppose, on the other hand, that it *is* possible to give good and informed advice on such matters: then surely it would be absurd if there were no knowledge on the basis of which it is possible to give good and informed advice on these matters—and if there *is* some knowledge on the basis of which it is possible to give good advice about such matters, then there must be some people who in fact know how to give good advice on such matters; and if there *are* some people who know how to give advice on
c   the matters you are meeting to discuss, then necessarily in your own case either you know how to give advice on these matters, or you do not know how to do so, or else some of you know and others do not know. Now if you all know, why do you still need to meet to discuss the question? Each one of you is competent to give advice. If none of you know, then how can you discuss the question? And what will you gain from this assembly
d   if you *cannot* discuss the question? If some of you know and others do not know, and if the latter need advice, then—supposing that it is possible for a man of sense to give advice to those who are uninformed—surely *one* man is enough to give advice to those of you who lack knowledge?[2] For presumably those who know how to give advice all give the same advice, so that you ought to hear one man and then be done with it. But this is not what you are actually doing: rather, you want to hear several advisers. You are assuming that those who are undertaking to give you advice do not know about the matters on which they are giving advice; for if you assumed that your advisers did know, then you would be
381 satisfied when you had heard just one of them. Now it is surely absurd to meet to hear people who do not know about these matters, with the thought that you will thereby gain something.

This, then, is what perplexes me about your assembly. As for the readiness of those who think to give you advice, there is the following perplexity.

Suppose that, although they are giving advice on the same matters, they do not give the same advice: then how can all of them be giving sound advice if they are not giving the advice given by someone who gives good
b   advice? And is it not absurd for people to be ready to give advice on matters about which they are uninformed? For if they are informed they will not choose to give advice which is not good. But if they give the same advice, why need they all give advice? It will be enough for one of them to give this advice.[3] Now surely it is absurd to be ready to do something which will gain nothing. Thus the readiness of those who are uninformed cannot fail to be absurd, given what it is; while men of sense will not be
c   ready in such a case, knowing as they do that any one of their number

---

2. Accepting two emendations in d4: adding *ouk* before *epistamenois*; changing *humin* to *humōn*.

3. Emending *ta auta* to *tauta* in b5.

will have the same effect if he gives advice as he ought to. Hence I am at a loss to discover how[4] the readiness of those who think to give you advice can be anything but ridiculous.

I am particularly perplexed to grasp the point of the votes which you intend to cast. Are you judging men who know how to give advice?—No more than one of them will give advice, nor will they give different advice on the same matters. Hence you will not need to cast any votes about them. Or[5] are you judging men who are uninformed and do not give the advice they should?—You ought not to allow such people, any more than madmen, to give advice. But if you are going to judge neither the informed nor the uninformed, then who *are* you judging?

In any case, why need other men give you advice at all if you are competent to judge such matters? And if you are not competent, what is the point of your votes? Surely it is ridiculous for you to meet to take advice, which implies that you need advice and are *not* yourselves competent, and then, having met, to think that you ought to vote, which implies that you *are* competent to judge. For it can hardly be the case that as individuals you are ignorant and yet having met you become wise; or that in private you are perplexed and yet having come to the same place you are no longer perplexed but become competent to see what you ought to do— all this without learning from anyone or finding things out for yourselves. This is the most extraordinary thing of all: given that you cannot see what ought to be done, you will not be competent to judge anyone who gives you good advice on these matters. Nor will this adviser of yours, being just one man, say that he will teach you to see[6] what you ought to do and also to judge those who give you bad or good advice, given that he has so little time and you are so numerous—this would plainly be no less extraordinary than the previous supposition. But if neither the meeting nor your adviser makes you competent to judge, what is the use of your votes?

Surely your meeting is inconsistent with your voting and your voting with the readiness of your advisers? For your meeting implies that you are not competent but need advisers, while the casting of votes implies that you do not need advisers but *are* capable of judging and of giving advice. And the readiness of your advisers implies that they have knowledge, while your casting votes implies that the advisers do not have knowledge.

Moreover, suppose that, after you had voted and after he had given you advice on whatever you were voting about, someone were to ask whether you knew if the goal for the sake of which you intended to put into action what you had voted on would come about: I do not think that you would say that you did know. Again, if the goal for the sake of which

d

e

382

b

c

---

4. Replacing the question mark after *sumbouleuein* in c4 with a comma.
5. Accepting the emendations of *alla* to *ē* in d1, and *ē* to *alla* in d2.
6. Adding *kai sunoran* after *didaxein* in a3.

you intend to act were to come about, do you know that it would be in your interest? I do not think that either you or your adviser would say that you do. And if someone were to ask you further whether[7] you thought that any man knew anything of these matters, I do not think you would admit that you did.

d   Now when the sort of matters about which you are giving advice are unclear to you, and when the voters and the advisers are uninformed, it stands to reason, as you yourselves will agree, that men often lose confidence and change their minds about whatever they took advice on and voted about. But such a thing ought not to happen to good men. For they know what the matters on which they are giving advice are like, and that those whom they have persuaded will surely attain[8] the goal for the sake of which they give advice, and that neither they nor those whom they

e   have persuaded will ever change their minds.

Thus I thought that it was proper[9] for a sensible man to give advice on topics of this sort and not on the matters on which you invite me to give advice. For advice on the former topics ends in success, nonsense on the latter in failure.

II

I witnessed a man upbraiding his companion because he believed the plaintiff when he had not heard the defendant but only the plaintiff. He said that he was doing something appalling: he was condemning the man

383   in advance[10] when he had neither witnessed the affair himself nor heard the man's friends who had witnessed it and whose words he might reasonably trust; and, without hearing both sides he had rashly trusted[11] the plaintiff. Justice required hearing the defendant, too, as well as the plaintiff, before giving praise or blame. How could anyone decide a case fairly or

b   judge men properly if he had not heard both parties? As with purple, or with gold coins, so with arguments it was good to judge by comparison. And why was time allotted to both parties, or why did the jurors swear to hear both impartially, unless the lawgiver had thought that cases would be more justly and better judged by the jurors in this way?

"You seem to me not even to have heard the popular saying."

c   "Which one?" he asked.

" 'O, never judge in a case until you have heard both the stories'.[12] This would hardly circulate so widely if it were not a right and proper saying.

7. Emending *de* to *d'ei* in c6, and replacing the question mark in c7 with a comma.

8. Emending *huparchei* to *huparxei* in d7.

9. Emending *axioun* to *axion* in e2.

10. Reading *prokatagignōskōn* in e9.

11. Emending *episteuse* to *pisteusas* in a3.

12. Hesiod, frg. 338 Merkelbach-West.

So I advise you," he said, "in the future not to blame or praise men so rashly."

His companion replied that it seemed quite clear to him that it would be absurd if it were impossible to tell whether one speaker was speaking truly or falsely and yet possible to tell whether two speakers were; or if it were impossible to learn from someone who spoke the truth and yet possible to be instructed in the same matters by the same man together with someone else who spoke falsely; or if one man who spoke correctly and truly could not make clear what he was saying and yet two men, one of whom spoke falsely and not correctly, could make clear what the man who spoke correctly could not make clear.

"I am perplexed," he said, "by the following point too: how will they ever make the matter clear? By being silent or by speaking? If they make it clear by being silent, then there will be no need to hear either, let alone both. If they both make it clear by speaking and yet certainly do not both speak together (each is required to speak in turn), how can they both make it clear at the same time? If they are both to make it clear at the same time, then they will speak at the same time—and this is not allowed. Hence if they make it clear by speaking, it can only be that each of them makes it clear by speaking, and that when each of them speaks, each of them then makes it clear. Hence one will speak first and the other second, and one will make it clear first and the other second. Yet if each in turn makes the same thing clear, why do you still need to hear the later speaker? The matter will already have been cleared up by the man who spoke first. Moreover," he said, "if both make it clear, then surely each of them makes it clear. For if one of a pair does not make something clear, how could they both make it clear? But if each of them makes it clear, plainly the one who[13] speaks first will also make it clear first. So isn't it possible to tell how things stand after listening to him alone?"[14]

When I heard them I myself was perplexed and could not come to a judgment—though the others who were present said that the first man spoke the truth. So help me with the matter if you can:[15] when one man speaks can you assess what he says, or do you need his opponent too if you are to know whether he is telling the truth? Or is it unnecessary to hear both sides? What do you think?

III

The other day someone was criticizing a man because he had been unwilling to trust him and lend him money. The man who was being criticized was defending himself, and someone else who was present asked the critic

13. Adding *hos* before *erei* in a4.
14. Replacing the period in a5 with a question mark.
15. Placing a comma after *echeis* in b1.

whether it was the man who did not trust him and lend him money who was in the wrong. "Or haven't *you* gone wrong," he said, "in not persuading him to lend to you?"

"Where did I go wrong?," he replied.

"Who seems to you to go wrong," he said, "—someone who fails to get what he wanted or someone who gets it?"

"Someone who fails," he replied.

"And you failed," he said, "since you wanted the loan, whereas he wanted not to give it and didn't fail in that."

"Yes," he replied, "but, granted that he didn't give me the money, *where* did I go wrong?"

"Well," he said, "if you asked him for what you ought not to have

d   asked, then surely you realize that you were in the wrong, whereas he, who did not give it, was in the right. And if you asked him for what you ought to have asked, then surely in failing to get it you must have gone wrong."

"Perhaps," he replied. "But surely he was wrong in not trusting me?"

"Well," he said, "if you had dealt with him as you should, you would not have gone wrong at all, would you?"

"No indeed."

"In fact, then, you didn't deal with him as you should."

"Apparently not," he said.

"So if he wasn't persuaded because you didn't deal with him as you

e   should, how can you justly criticize him?"

"I can't say."

"And can't you say either that one needn't be considerate to people who behave badly?"

"I can certainly say that," he replied.

"But don't those who don't treat people as they should seem to you to behave badly?"

"They do," he replied.

"Then what did he do wrong if he wasn't considerate to you when you behaved badly?"

"Nothing at all, it seems," he said.

"Then why on earth," he said, "do men criticize one another in this way, blaming people they have not persuaded for not having been per-suaded but never criticizing themselves in the least for not having per-

385   suaded them?"

Someone else who was present said: "Suppose you've behaved well to someone and helped him, and then when you ask him to behave in the same way to you he refuses—surely in these circumstances you might reasonably blame him?"

"The man you are asking to behave in the same way," he said, "is either able or unable to behave fairly towards you, isn't he? If he's not able to, surely you're not making a fair request in asking him to do what he's not able to do; and if he *is* able to, how did you fail to persuade such a man?

b   How can it be fair for people to say such things?"

"Damn it," he replied, "he ought to criticize such conduct in order that in future he'll behave better towards him—and his other friends, too, who have heard his criticisms."

"Do you think that people behave better," he asked, "if they hear someone speaking properly and making proper requests or if they hear someone going wrong?"

"Someone speaking properly," he replied.

"But you thought that he was not making a proper request?"

"True," he said.

"Then surely people won't behave better when they hear such criticisms?"

"No, they won't," he replied.

"Then what is the point of such reproaches?"   c

He said that he could not find an answer.

IV

Someone was accusing a man of naïveté because he was quick to trust anyone who spoke to him.

"It's reasonable to trust your fellow citizens and your relations; but to trust men you've never seen or heard before, when you're well aware that most men are rogues and liars—that's no small sign of simplicity."   d

One of those present said: "I thought that you would esteem someone who grasped things quickly, no matter what they were, rather than someone who did so slowly?"

"Indeed I do," the first man replied.

"Then why do you criticize him," he asked, "if he is quick to trust anyone who speaks the truth?"

"But I'm not criticizing him for that," he replied; "rather, it's because he's quick to trust people who don't tell the truth."

"But suppose he had taken longer to give his trust and hadn't trusted just anybody, and had then been deceived[16]—wouldn't you have criticized him all the more?"

"I would," he replied.

"Because he was slow to trust and didn't trust just anybody?"   e

"Of course not," he replied.

"No," he said, "I'm sure you don't think it's right to criticize a man for that reason, but rather because he trusts people who say what's not trustworthy?"

"Yes indeed," he said.

"Do you think then," he said, "that it's *not* right to criticize him for being slow to trust people and for not trusting just anybody, but that it *is* right to criticize him for being quick to trust and for trusting just anybody?"

"No, I don't," he replied.

---

16. Accepting the emendation of *ēitiato* to *ēpatato* in d7.

"Then why are you criticizing him?" he asked.

"Because he's wrong to trust just anybody and to trust them quickly, before considering the question."

386   "But if he trusted them slowly before considering the question he wouldn't be wrong?"

"Of course he would," he replied "—in that case he'd be just as wrong. I think, rather, that he shouldn't trust just anybody."

"If you think that he shouldn't trust just anybody," he said, "then surely he shouldn't be quick to trust strangers? Rather, you think that he should first consider whether they're telling the truth?"

"I do," he replied.

"And if they're friends and relations, needn't he consider whether they're telling the truth?"

"I should say that he does need to," he replied.

"For perhaps even some of *these* people say what's not trustworthy?"

"Yes indeed," he replied.

b   "Then why," he said, "is it reasonable to trust your friends and relations rather than just anybody?"

"I can't say," he replied.

"Again, if you should trust your relations[17] rather than just anybody, shouldn't you also think them more trustworthy[18] than just anybody?"

"Of course," he replied.

"Then if they're relations of some people and strangers to others, surely you'll have to think them more trustworthy than themselves?[19] For you shouldn't think that relations and strangers are equally trustworthy, or so you say."

"I can't accept that," he replied.

"Equally," he said, "some will trust[20] what they say and others will deem it untrustworthy, and neither party will be wrong."

"That too is absurd," he replied.

c   "Again," he said, "if relations say the same thing as just anybody, surely what they say will be equally trustworthy or untrustworthy?"

"Necessarily so," he replied.

"Then shouldn't you give equal trust to anyone who says these things when he says them?"

"That's plausible," he replied.

While they argued in this way I was perplexed as to who on earth I should and shouldn't trust, and whether I should trust the trustworthy and people who know what they're talking about, or rather relations and acquaintances. What do you think about this?

17. Deleting *ou* in b2.

18. Accepting the emendation of *ouk apistous* to *ou kai pistous* in b3–4.

19. Accepting the emendation of *autōi* to *autōn* in b6.

20. Accepting the emendation of *pisteuousin* to *pisteusousin* in b10.

SISYPHUS

Are some people better than others at thinking about what course of action to follow? Sisyphus certainly assumes so. He stayed behind in Pharsalus a day longer than expected in order to meet with the governing authorities to help them in their deliberations. But Socrates is puzzled about what deliberation can really be, and he wonders how it differs from mere guesswork. By the end of the dialogue, it becomes clear that Sisyphus does not know the first thing about deliberating, and Socrates offers to delve into it again with him.

Sisyphus thinks that deliberating is trying to find out the best course of action. But Socrates argues that this cannot be right—if you are in a position to deliberate about something, you must already understand that subject, and if you understand it, you won't try to find it out; unlike inquiry, which presupposes ignorance, meaningful deliberation presupposes knowledge. Since the objects of deliberation are in the future and not yet in determinate existence, deliberation risks being a shot in the dark unless it is aimed at something definite. What target should it be aimed at? What kind of knowledge is presupposed? The dialogue does not tell us, but surely its author (probably a follower of Plato writing in mid-fourth-century B.C.*) means to encourage his readers toward Platonic philosophy and its central target—Goodness itself. At roughly the same time, in his* Protrepticus, *or* Exhortation to Philosophy *(a work surviving only in fragments), Aristotle was also arguing that political judgment needs a foundation in speculative philosophy (B46–51).*

Aristotle investigated the concept of deliberation in his lectures on ethics, where several passages indicate that this topic had been discussed in Plato's Academy, apparently in much the same terms as in Sisyphus. *Of Plato's own works, the most relevant are* Meno, *which raises the paradox that one cannot try to find out either what one knows or what one doesn't know (80d–e), and* Euthydemus, *which mentions two related paradoxes in the course of illustrating the difference between mere logic-chopping and real philosophy (275e–277c).*

We find in Sisyphus *certain notable anachronisms which place it firmly in the fourth century* B.C.*—not the fifth, when Socrates actually lived. Sisyphus of Pharsalus in Thessaly was a contemporary of Plato, not of Socrates, and played a prominent role in local affairs. Stratonicus of Athens, whom the author gratuitously mentions at the beginning of the dialogue, was a renowned performing musician and teacher of the first third of the fourth century, whom Socrates could scarcely have known. And when Socrates asks, "Where is Callistratus?" (388c), he seems to refer to Callistratus of Aphidna, a prominent Athenian*

*politician who was on the run from a death sentence for several years after
362. So the author must have intended his dialogue to resonate with a contemporary mid-fourth-century audience. Plato's* Meno *suggests by certain bio-
graphical details that it is directed against the rival educational philosophy
offered by Isocrates in Athens, and the same may well be true of* Sisyphus.
*Isocrates undertook to make his students good at deliberating, without taking
what he regarded as the useless detour of Platonic philosophy, and held that
"likely opinion about useful things is far better than exact knowledge of useless
things" (*Helen *5). Isocrates also declared, "I regard a man as wise whose opinions enable him to hit upon the best course in most cases" (*Antidosis *271), a
conception of wise deliberation that is called into question in* Sisyphus.

D.S.H.

387b SOCRATES: We waited a long time for you yesterday as well, Sisyphus,
before Stratonicus' show, so that you could join us in hearing a real master
giving a performance full of splendid material, both in theory and in
practice; but after we gave up thinking you were coming, we went to hear
the man by ourselves.

SISYPHUS: Yes, that's absolutely right—some business arose, you see,
c which was fairly urgent, so I couldn't ignore it. Our authorities were in
conference yesterday, so they required me to join their deliberations; and
if the authorities summon any of us to join their deliberations, we citizens
of Pharsalus are legally bound to comply.

SOCRATES: Well, it's a splendid thing to obey the law, and also to be
considered a good deliberator by one's fellow citizens—as you yourself
are considered to be one of the good deliberators in Pharsalus. Still, I'm
not in a position to take issue with you about good deliberation, Sisyphus,
d at the moment; that, I think, would call for a lot of leisure and a long
argument—but I'd like to propose a discussion with you about deliberation
itself, first of all, about what it is.

What could deliberation itself be? Could you tell me that?—not how to
do it well or badly or splendidly, but just what sort of thing deliberation
itself is? Surely you could do that quite easily, being such a good deliberator
yourself? I hope I'm not being too inquisitive by questioning you on
the subject.

SISYPHUS: Can it really be that you don't know what deliberation is?

e SOCRATES: Indeed I don't, Sisyphus, at least if it differs at all from what's
done by a man who lacks understanding on some matter calling for action,
guessing his answer by divining or making it up: he says whatever comes

Translated by David Gallop.

into his head, just like people who play odds-and-evens; they have no idea, of course, whether they're holding an even or an odd number of things in their hands, yet when they say which it is, they hit upon the truth. Perhaps deliberation is also something like that: someone who has no understanding of what he's deliberating about is just lucky in what he says, and hits upon the truth. If it's something like that, then I do know roughly what deliberation is; but if it's not like that, then I don't understand it at all.

SISYPHUS: But surely, it's not like being utterly and completely ignorant of some matter, but like being familiar with part of it, while not yet understanding the rest.

SOCRATES: Perhaps you mean that deliberation is—Heaven help me! I feel as if I'm almost divining your view about good deliberation—do you mean it's something like this? Someone is trying to find out what would be the best course of action to take, and doesn't yet clearly understand it, but is rather in the process of thought, as it were? Is that more or less what you mean?

SISYPHUS: Yes, it is.

SOCRATES: Which do people try to find out—matters which they know, or ones which they don't know?

SISYPHUS: Both.

SOCRATES: When you say that people try to find out both—things they do know as well as things they don't—perhaps you mean something like this: one might, for example, be acquainted with Callistratus—know who he was—yet not know where he was to be found.[1] Is that what you mean by trying to find out both?

SISYPHUS: Yes, it is.

SOCRATES: Now you wouldn't try to find out the former, knowing Callistratus, at least if you knew him?

SISYPHUS: Of course not.

SOCRATES: But you might try to find out where he was.

SISYPHUS: Yes, I think you might.

SOCRATES: Nor, again, would you try to discover where the man was to be found, if you knew that; in that case, you would go and find him right away, wouldn't you?

SISYPHUS: Yes.

SOCRATES: Apparently, then, it isn't things which people know that they try to find out, but things they don't know.

But that argument may strike you as captious, Sisyphus, put forward not with a view to the truth of the matter, but merely as a debating point. If so, look at it this way, and see if you agree with what was just said. You know, don't you, what happens in geometry: the diagonal is unknown to geometers, yet there's no question whether it is or is not a diagonal— that's not what they're trying to find out at all—but rather, how long it

---

1. Accepting the deletion of *ouch hostis eiē ho Kallistratos* in c6.

is in relation to the sides of the areas it bisects. Isn't *that* what they're trying to find out about the diagonal?

SISYPHUS: I believe so.

SOCRATES: And that *is* something unknown, isn't it?

SISYPHUS: Absolutely.

SOCRATES: Or again, take the doubling of the cube. You know, don't you, that geometers try to find out, by reasoning, how big it is? As for the cube itself, they don't try to find out whether it's a cube or not. That much they know, don't they?

SISYPHUS: Yes.

389   SOCRATES: Or again, consider the upper air. You surely know that what Anaxagoras and Empedocles and all the rest of the cosmologists are trying to find out is whether it's infinite or finite.

SISYPHUS: Yes.

SOCRATES: But they don't ask whether it is air, do they now?

SISYPHUS: Of course not.

SOCRATES: In all such cases, then, our conclusion is as follows: nobody can ever try to find out anything that he knows, only what he doesn't know. Would you agree with me about that?

SISYPHUS: I would.

b   SOCRATES: Now isn't this what deliberation seemed to us to be—somebody trying to find out the best course to follow in matters requiring him to take action?

SISYPHUS: Yes.

SOCRATES: And we thought that deliberation was trying to find out something concerning practical matters, didn't we?

SISYPHUS: Yes, of course.

SOCRATES: So now it's time for us to consider what it is that prevents people from finding out what they're trying to find out.

SISYPHUS: I think it is.

c   SOCRATES: And what should we say it is that prevents them, if not incomprehension?

SISYPHUS: Let's look into it, for Heaven's sake.

SOCRATES: Absolutely!—we must let out every reef, as they say, and raise full cry.

So now let's examine the following question together: do you think it's possible for a man to deliberate about music if he has no knowledge of music, and knows neither how to play the cithara nor how to perform any other kind of music?

SISYPHUS: No, I don't.

d   SOCRATES: And what about military or nautical expertise? Would someone who knew neither of those subjects be able to deliberate at all about what he should do in either field? Would he be able to deliberate about how to command a force or captain a vessel if he lacked all knowledge of military or nautical matters?

SISYPHUS: No.

SOCRATES: And would you expect the same to hold in all other fields? It is quite impossible for someone who doesn't understand something either to know or to deliberate about what he doesn't understand.

SISYPHUS: I agree.

SOCRATES: But it *is* possible to try to find out what one doesn't know; isn't that right?

SISYPHUS: Certainly.

SOCRATES: Then trying to find out can no longer be identified with deliberating.

SISYPHUS: Why not?

SOCRATES: Because what one tries to find out is evidently something one doesn't know, whereas apparently no human being can deliberate about what he doesn't know. Wasn't that what we just said?

SISYPHUS: It certainly was.

SOCRATES: And isn't that what you Pharsalians were doing yesterday, trying to find out the best things for your city to do, yet not knowing them? Because if you knew them, you surely wouldn't still have been trying to find them out—just as we don't try to find out anything else we already know, do we?

SISYPHUS: No, we don't.

SOCRATES: And if one doesn't know something, Sisyphus, which do you think one should do: try to find it out or learn it?

SISYPHUS: Learn it, for Heaven's sake; that's what *I* think.

SOCRATES: And there you're right. But tell me, is it for the following reason that you think one should learn it rather than try to find it out? One can discover it more quickly and easily by learning it from those who understand it, than by trying to find it out on one's own, when one doesn't know it. Or is there some other reason?

SISYPHUS: No, that is the reason.

SOCRATES: Well then, why did you people take the trouble to deliberate yesterday on matters you don't understand, and try to find out the best course of action for the city to take? Why weren't you learning those things, rather, from someone who understands them, so that you could take the best course of action for the city? Instead, it seems to me that you spent the whole day yesterday sitting there, making things up and divining about matters you didn't understand, instead of taking the trouble to learn them—I mean those who govern your city, including you.

Perhaps you'll say that I've been jesting at your expense merely for the sake of having a discussion, but that you think nothing has been seriously proved. Yet you'll certainly have to take this next point seriously, Sisyphus. Suppose it be granted that there is such a thing as deliberation; suppose it does not, as was discovered just now, prove identical with sheer incomprehension,[2] guesswork, or making things up, no different, but just using a grander name for it. In that case, don't you think there's a difference

e

390

b

c

---

2. Accepting the conjecture *anepistēmosunē* in c4.

between some people and others with respect to deliberating well or being good deliberators, just as some people differ from others in all other areas of expertise—as, for example, some carpenters differ from others, or some
d   doctors from others, or some pipers from others, or as tradesmen in general differ from one another?[3] Just as those experts differ in their respective skills, don't you think the same applies to deliberating—that there's a difference between some people and others?

SISYPHUS: Yes, I do.

SOCRATES: Now tell me, don't all those who deliberate either well or badly deliberate about things that are going to exist in the future?

SISYPHUS: Certainly.

SOCRATES: And what's in the future doesn't exist yet. Isn't that right?

SISYPHUS: Of course.

e   SOCRATES: Because otherwise, presumably, it wouldn't *still* be going to exist in the future, but would exist already, wouldn't it?

SISYPHUS: Yes.

SOCRATES: And if it doesn't exist yet, it hasn't yet[4] come into being either.

SISYPHUS: No, it hasn't.

SOCRATES: But if it hasn't even yet come into being, then it doesn't yet possess any nature of its own either, does it?

SISYPHUS: None at all.

SOCRATES: Then those who deliberate well and those who do it badly are all deliberating about matters that neither exist nor have come into being nor possess any nature, whenever they deliberate about what's in the future. Isn't that right?

SISYPHUS: It does appear to be.

SOCRATES: Now do you think it's possible for anyone to hit upon the nonexistent either well or badly?

SISYPHUS: What do you mean by that?

SOCRATES: I'll show you what I'm suggesting. Consider a number of
391   archers. How would you distinguish which of them was a good marksman and which was a poor one? That's not hard to tell, is it? You would presumably ask them to aim at some target.

SISYPHUS: Certainly.

SOCRATES: And the one who most often succeeded in hitting the target you would judge the winner?

SISYPHUS: I would.

SOCRATES: But if there were no target set up for them to aim at, and each
b   just shot wherever he pleased, how could you distinguish between the good marksman and the poor one?

SISYPHUS: I couldn't.

---

3. Placing a question-mark after *diapherousin* in 390d2, and a comma after *technais* in d3.

4. Conjecturing *oupō* for *houtōs* in e2.

SOCRATES: And wouldn't you also be at a loss to distinguish good deliberators from bad ones, if they didn't understand what they were deliberating about?

SISYPHUS: I would.

SOCRATES: And if those who deliberate are deliberating about matters in the future, they're deliberating about matters that don't exist, aren't they?

SISYPHUS: Absolutely.

SOCRATES: And it's impossible, isn't it, for anyone to hit upon the nonexistent. How do you think anyone could ever hit upon what doesn't exist?   c

SISYPHUS: It can't be done.

SOCRATES: And since it's impossible to hit upon the nonexistent, no one who's deliberating about the nonexistent could actually hit upon it. For the future is something that doesn't exist, isn't it?

SISYPHUS: So I believe.

SOCRATES: Then since nobody can hit upon what's in the future, no human being can actually be good or bad at deliberation.

SISYPHUS: Apparently not.

SOCRATES: Nor can one person be either a better or a worse deliberator than another, if one cannot, in fact, be more or less successful at hitting upon the nonexistent.

SISYPHUS: Indeed not.   d

SOCRATES: So what standard could people possibly have in mind when they call certain people good or bad deliberators? Don't you think, Sisyphus, that it would be worth delving into this again some time?

HALCYON

Socrates tells his devoted friend Chaerephon the legend of Halcyon, who was transformed by some heavenly power into a sea bird, the better to search for her much-beloved husband, who had drowned at sea. Chaerephon doubts the truth of the legend, but Socrates argues that his doubt is unfounded; we are ignorant of the limits of divine power, which is unimaginably greater than human power and has shown itself to be capable of tremendous things.

The topic and the setting of this lyrical little dialogue appear to be derived from a passage in Plato's Phaedrus *where Socrates also interprets a legend about the transformation of human beings into animals (258e–259d). The association between cosmos, heaven, nature, and divine power is characteristic of Platonism in later times, as is the skeptical stress on the limits of human knowledge, and the affinity between human beings and other animals. The dialogue is elaborately cultivated, both in vocabulary and composition, and is a good example of the artificial style called 'Asiatic' by later critics. It was probably composed between 150 B.C. and 50 A.D.*

The ending of Halcyon *contains a sly allusion to the story of the two wives of Socrates, Xanthippe and Myrto, both of whom, he hopes, will be as devoted to him as Halcyon was to her husband. This story of the bigamy of Socrates goes back to the fourth century B.C. at least.*

Although many manuscripts attribute Halcyon *to Plato and an ancient book list records it as being among the works incorrectly ascribed to him, it has virtually disappeared from the Platonic corpus. This is because it was later attributed to Lucian, the second-century A.D. orator and dialogue writer, probably by Byzantine scholars who noticed similarities with the methods and themes of Lucian. When the corpus of Platonic works was established for modern times in the sixteenth-century edition of Henri Étienne (Stephanus),* Halcyon *was not printed, and it has normally not been printed in other modern editions of Plato. It is nowadays usually printed only in editions of the Lucianic corpus.*

D.S.H.

CHAEREPHON: Socrates, what was that voice that reached us from way   1
down along the beach, under the headland? It was so sweet to my ears!
What creature can it be that makes that sound? Surely creatures that live
in the sea are silent.

SOCRATES: It's a sort of sea bird, Chaerephon, called the halcyon, much
given to lamenting and weeping. There is an ancient account about this
bird, which was handed down as a myth by men of old. They say that it
was once a woman, the daughter of Aeolus the son of Hellen, who ached
with love and lamented the death of her wedded husband, Ceyx of Trachis,
the son of Eosphorus the Dawn Star—a handsome son of a handsome
father. And then, through some act of divine will, she grew wings like a
bird and now flies about the sea searching for him, since she could not
find him when she wandered all over the face of the earth.

CHAEREPHON: Is it Halcyon that you're referring to? I had never heard   2
the voice before; it really did strike me as something exotic. Anyway, the
creature certainly does produce a mournful sound. About how big is
it, Socrates?

SOCRATES: Not very large. Yet great is the honor she has been given by
the gods because of her love for her husband. For it's when the halcyons
are nesting that the cosmos brings us what are called the 'halcyon days'
in mid-winter, days distinguished for their fair weather—today is an especially good example. Don't you see how bright the sky above is and how
the whole sea is calm and tranquil, like a mirror, so to speak?

CHAEREPHON: You're right; today does seem to be a halcyon day, and
yesterday was much like it. But by the gods, Socrates! How can we actually
believe those ancient tales, that once upon a time birds turned into women
or women into birds? All that sort of thing seems utterly impossible.

SOCRATES: Ah, my dear Chaerephon, we seem to be utterly short-sighted   3
judges of what is possible or impossible—we make our assessment according to the best of our human ability, which is unknowing, unreliable, and
blind. Many things which are feasible seem, to us, not feasible, and many
things which are attainable seem unattainable—often because of our inexperience, and often because of the childish folly in our minds. For in fact
all human beings, even very old men, really do seem to be as foolish as
children, since the span of our lives is small indeed, no longer than childhood when compared with all eternity. My good friend, how could people
who know nothing about the powers of the gods and divinities, or of
nature as a whole, possibly tell whether something like this is possible
or impossible?

Did you notice, Chaerephon, how big a storm we had the day before
yesterday? Someone pondering those lightning flashes and thunderbolts
and the tremendous force of the winds might well be struck by fear; one
might have thought the whole inhabited world was actually going to
collapse. But a little later there was an astounding restoration of fair weather   4

Translated by Brad Inwood. Text: M. D. MacLeod, *Luciani Opera* (Oxford, 1987), vol. IV.

which has lasted right up to the present moment. Do you think, then, that it is a greater and more laborious task to conjure up this kind of fair weather out of such an overwhelming storm and disturbance and to bring the entire cosmos into a state of calm, than it is to reshape a woman's form and turn it into a bird's? Even our little children who know how to model such things out of clay or wax can easily work them into all kinds of shapes, all out of the same material. Since the divinity possesses great power, incomparably greater than ours, perhaps all such things are actually very easy for it. After all, how much greater than yourself would you say that the whole of heaven is?

5   CHAEREPHON: Socrates, who among men could imagine or find words for anything of the sort? Even to say it is beyond human attainment.

SOCRATES: When we compare people with each other, do we not see that there are vast differences in their abilities and inabilities? Adult men, when compared to mere infants who are five or ten days old, have an amazing superiority in their ability at virtually all the practical affairs of life, those carried out by means of our sophisticated skills as well as those carried out by means of the body and soul; these things cannot, as I said, even

6   cross the minds of young children. And how immeasurably superior is the physical strength of one man grown to full size, compared to them, for one man could easily vanquish thousands of such children; and it is surely natural that in the initial stages of life men should be utterly helpless and incapable of anything. When one person, as it seems, is so far superior to another, how are we to suppose that the powers of the whole heaven would appear, compared with our powers, to those who are capable of grasping such matters? Perhaps indeed many people will think it plausible that, just as the size of the cosmos surpasses the form of Socrates or Chaerephon, so its power and wisdom and intelligence will to the same degree surpass our condition.

7   For you and me and many others like us, many things are impossible which are quite easy for others to do. For as long as they lack the knowledge, it is more impossible that people who cannot play the flute should do so or that the illiterate should read or write, than it is to make women out of birds or birds out of women. Nature virtually tosses into a honeycomb an animal which is footless and wingless; then she gives it feet and wings, adorns it with all kinds of variegated and beautiful colors and so produces a bee, wise producer of heavenly honey; and from mute and lifeless eggs she shapes many species of winged, walking and water-dwelling animals,

8   using (as some say) the sacred arts of the vast aether. We are mortal and utterly trivial, unable to see clearly either great or small matters and in the dark about most of the things which happen to us; so we could not possibly make any reliable claim about the mighty powers of the immortals, whether as regards halcyons or as regards nightingales.[1]

----

1. Legend tells that Procne and Philomela were also turned into birds, one into a nightingale, the other into a swallow.

O bird of musical lamentations, I shall pass on to my children the far-famed myth about your songs just as I received it from my ancestors, and I shall sing frequently to my wives, Xanthippe and Myrto, of your piety and loving devotion to your husband, with special emphasis on the honor you received from the gods. Will you too do something like this, Chaerephon?

CHAEREPHON: That would certainly be appropriate, Socrates, and what you say is a double exhortation to the bond between husbands and wives.

SOCRATES: Well, now it's time to bid farewell to Halcyon, and go on to the city from Cape Phaleron.

CHAEREPHON: Certainly; let's do so.

ERYXIAS

Socrates falls into conversation with Erasistratus, and the talk turns to the topic of wealth and virtue. If the wealthiest person is whoever possesses what is of the greatest value, then those who possess the skill of practical wisdom must be the wealthiest, argues Socrates. Eryxias rejects this line of thinking, but when he asserts that it is good to be materially prosperous, he is defeated by Critias' argument that having money is not always a good thing. Socrates shows that Eryxias' common-sense ideas about money are confused; money has only conventional value and is no more useful, for providing ourselves with what our bodies need, than the skills which a teacher can communicate to others. In a subtle argument addressed to Critias, Socrates concludes that money cannot be considered useful at all, even when it is needed to obtain something of value. The final paradox: if money is useful, whoever has the most of it must be in the worst condition; if he wasn't in a very bad condition, he wouldn't need a lot of money and he wouldn't find it useful.

In between the arguments about wealth runs another theme, a discussion about the nature of philosophical argument: What is the difference between serious philosophical arguments and intellectual games? What is the difference between philosophical arguments and quarrels? Is it the argument or the speaker that carries credibility? Is philosophy a matter of personal commitment or a diverting performance?

Together these two themes constitute a meditation on the way of life embraced by Socrates and like-minded philosophers. Outwardly poor but inwardly rich, they support themselves by teaching others their wisdom, a wisdom that increases the value to them and their students of all that they come across and make use of in life. Their skill lies in their arguments, which they take seriously but not to the point of quarrelling, arguments to which they give credence and are personally committed.

Many of the ideas in Eryxias are Socratic commonplaces, and some have parallels in Plato. Socrates prayed, "May I consider the wise man rich. As for gold, let me have as much as a moderate man could bear and carry with him" (Phaedrus 279c). It is better to know how to use things than to possess them, he argues in advocating philosophy in Euthydemus. But the influence of Plato on the unknown author of Eryxias is probably strongest in the dialogue's literary composition, which is as subtle as many of Plato's own 'Socratic' dialogues. Scholars have noticed parallels to Stoic and sceptic ideas in Eryxias and have tried to draw chronological conclusions. But the only secure evidence is the gymnasiarch of 399a, holder of an office that took that form at some date

between 337 and 318 B.C. *The dialogue must be of that date or later, and it*
may have been written in the Academy, which provided a fertile ground for the
later development of Stoicism and scepticism.

D.S.H.

I happened to be strolling about in the Stoa of Zeus the Liberator with   392
Eryxias, from the deme Stiria, when Critias and Erasistratus, the nephew
of Phaeax (Erasistratus' son), came up to us. Erasistratus, it turned out,
was just recently back from Sicily and other places nearby. When he came
to me he said, "Greetings, Socrates."   b

"The same to you," I replied. "Well now, anything worth reporting to
us from Sicily?"

"Certainly. But would you care to sit down first? I walked from Megara
yesterday and now I'm exhausted."

"By all means, if that's what you want."

"What would you like to hear first about the situation over there? What
the Sicilians are up to, or what attitude they're taking towards our city?
Personally, I think that in their feelings towards us they're like wasps. If
you stir them up and get them angry just a little at a time they become   c
unmanageable; you have to drive them out by attacking their nest. That's
what the Syracusans are like. Unless we make it our business to go to
their city with a very large force, there's no chance they will ever submit
to us. Half-measures can only make them angrier, and then they'll be
extremely hard to deal with. In fact they've just now sent envoys to us,
and I think they intend to trick our city somehow."

While we were talking the Syracusan envoys happened to pass by.   d
Erasistratus pointed to one of them and said, "That man over there, Socrates, is the wealthiest in all Sicily and Italy. He must be, since he has such
an enormous amount of land at his disposal that he could easily farm a
huge tract if he wanted to. This land of his is unlike any other, in Greece
at any rate. And he also has plenty of the other things that make you
wealthy—slaves, horses, gold, and silver."

When I saw that he was getting ready to babble on about the man's   393
possessions, I asked him, "But, Erasistratus, what sort of reputation does
he have in Sicily?"

"People think that he's the wickedest of all the Sicilians and Italians,
and he really is. He's even more wicked than he is wealthy, so if you
wanted to ask any Sicilian who he thinks is the wickedest man, and who
is the wealthiest, everyone will say the same thing: he is."

I thought that what Erasistratus was talking about was no small matter;
on the contrary, it's what people consider to be of the very highest
importance, namely virtue and wealth. So I asked him, "Who's wealthier,   b

Translated by Mark Joyal.

a man who has one talent[1] of silver, or a man who has a field worth two talents?"

"The man with the field, I suppose."

"By the same argument, if someone had clothes or blankets or other things worth yet more than our Sicilian fellow's property, he would be wealthier." Erasistratus agreed. "And if someone were to give you a choice between these two, which would you want?"

c   "I would choose the most valuable of them."

"Do you think that choice would make you wealthier?"

"I do."

"So as it stands we think that whoever possesses the most valuable things is the wealthiest person?"

"Yes."

"Then healthy people would be wealthier than sick people, since health is a more valuable possession than the sick man's property. Everyone, at

d   any rate, would prefer to be healthy and possess little money than to be sick and possess the Great King's[2] fortune, since they obviously believe that health is more valuable. After all, nobody would ever choose in favor of health unless he thought it was preferable to wealth."

"Of course not."

"Again, if something else should seem more valuable than health, the one who possessed this would be the wealthiest person."

"Yes."

"And suppose someone were to come up to us now and ask, 'Can

e   you tell me, Socrates, Eryxias, and Erasistratus, what the most valuable possession for a person is? Is it the thing whose possession would enable him to make the best decisions about how he could most effectively manage both his own affairs and those of his friends?' What would we say this thing is?"

"In my view, Socrates, prosperity is a person's most valuable possession."

"That's not a bad answer at all. But would we consider the most prosperous people in the world to be the most successful?"

"Yes, I believe so."

"And wouldn't the most successful people be the ones who make the fewest errors in handling their own affairs and those of others, while doing the most things right?"

"Exactly."

394   "So those who know what's bad and what's good, and what a person should and shouldn't do, would have the greatest success and make the fewest errors?" Erasistratus accepted this too. "As it is, then, the same men are apparently the wisest, the most successful, the most prosperous, and the wealthiest, since it turns out that wisdom is the most valuable possession."

---

1. Accepting the emendation *talanton hen* in b2.
2. The king of Persia, proverbially wealthy.

"Yes."

Eryxias interrupted: "But Socrates, how could it be any advantage to this person if he were wiser than Nestor but didn't have the things he needed for day to day living—food, drink, clothing, and other things of that kind? What help could wisdom be? How could he be the wealthiest, since he might as well be a beggar if he has none of the basic necessities?"

b

I thought that Eryxias made a lot of sense, and answered, "But would this happen to the person who possessed wisdom but lacked these necessities? And if someone possessed the house of Poulytion, and it was full of gold and silver, would he need nothing?"

c

"Why yes! He might very well sell his possessions at once and obtain in exchange whatever he actually needed for his day to day existence, or even spend hard currency, in exchange for which he could acquire those items and then have a good supply of everything right away."

"True—provided that the other people actually wanted a house like Poulytion's more than our friend's wisdom. And yet if they were the sort of people who put greater stock in the man's wisdom and what it produces, the wise man would be able to sell it much more easily, if it was the case that he needed and wanted to sell it and its products. Do people actually feel such a powerful compulsion to have the use of a house, and does it make such a great difference in a person's life to live in a house like Poulytion's rather than in a small and humble dwelling, while the use of wisdom has little value, and it doesn't make much difference whether a person is wise or ignorant in things that really matter? Do people despise wisdom and refuse to pay for it, and are there many who need and want to purchase the cypress wood in Poulytion's house and marble from Mt. Pentelicon? At any rate, if a person were a navigator or a doctor skilled at his profession, or were able to have a successful practice in some other profession along those lines, he would be valued more highly than every one of the greatest material possessions. And what about the person who can offer good advice about how to achieve success, both for himself and for someone else—wouldn't he be able to sell this skill, if that's what he wanted to do?"

d

e

Eryxias broke in, looking annoyed as though someone had done something wrong to him: "If you had to tell the truth, Socrates, would you really claim that you're wealthier than Callias, the son of Hipponicus?[3] I'm sure you'd agree that you're no less intelligent in all the most important things, indeed wiser; but that hasn't made you any wealthier."

395

"Maybe, Eryxias, you think these arguments we're now discussing are just a game, since, as you suppose, they have no reality, like pieces in backgammon which you can move to gain an advantage over your opponents so that they have no move they can make to counter yours. Now maybe with regard to wealth, too, you think that the true situation is no

b

---

3. One of the wealthiest men in Athens, noted for his lavish spending on the sophists. See *Apology* 20a; the events of *Protagoras* take place in his house.

more one way than another, and that some arguments are of the same kind, no more true than false. If a person offered these arguments he could get the better of his opponents in claiming that the wisest are in our view

c   also the wealthiest, even though what he was saying was false while his opponents were speaking the truth. Perhaps this isn't surprising; it's as if two men were talking about letters: one claims that the name 'Socrates' begins with an 'S,' the other that it begins with an 'A'; and the argument that the name begins with an 'A' proves stronger than the argument that it begins with an 'S'."

Eryxias cast a glance around at the people who were there, laughing and blushing as though he had not been present at the earliest discussions,

d   and said: "Socrates, I thought that our arguments shouldn't be the kind that can't persuade any of the people here and provide some benefit to them. Who in his right mind could ever be persuaded that the wisest are the wealthiest? What we should be discussing, since we're talking about wealth, is under what conditions it's an admirable thing to be wealthy and under what conditions it's a disgraceful thing, and just what kind of thing wealth is, whether it's good or bad."

e   "All right, I'll be careful from now on; and thank you for your good advice. But since you're introducing the problem, why don't you venture to tell us yourself whether you consider it good or bad to be wealthy?— especially since you don't think that our earlier arguments dealt with this subject."

"Well then, I think it's good to be wealthy."

He wanted to go on speaking, but Critias interrupted and said: "Tell me, Eryxias, *do* you consider it a good thing to be wealthy?"

"I certainly do. I'd be crazy if I didn't; and I'm sure the whole world would agree with me about this."

396   "But I also think I could convince everybody that for some people, being wealthy is a bad thing. Yet if it really were good, it wouldn't appear bad to some of us."

Then I said to them: "If the two of you couldn't agree over who is the greater authority on expert horsemanship, and I happened to know about horses, I'd try to put a stop to your quarrel. After all, I'd be ashamed if I were there and didn't do all I could to prevent your quarrelling; likewise

b   if you couldn't agree about anything else at all and were likely to go away as enemies instead of friends unless you came to an understanding. But as it is your disagreement is over something which you're bound to deal with throughout your whole life, and it makes a big difference whether you should consider it useful or not. What's more, the Greeks don't think it's any ordinary thing; they hold it in the highest regard—at any rate,

c   that's why the first thing that fathers advise their sons to consider, as soon as they think their sons have reached the age when they have their wits about them, is how they will become wealthy, since a man who has possessions is worth something, but one who doesn't is worthless. Now if this is taken so seriously, and you see eye to eye on other things but differ over such an important matter—on top of that, not over whether wealth is black or white, or light or heavy, but whether it's good or bad—that you actually become the worst of enemies if you argue over what's good and what's bad, even though you're really the closest friends and relatives—well, as far as I can, I'm not going to ignore you while you're carrying on your argument. If I could explain the situation to you and put a stop to your dispute, I would. But in fact, since I can't do that, and since each of you thinks he can make the other agree with him, I'm ready to help you all I can to come to an agreement about wealth. So try to make us agree with you, Critias, as you had undertaken to do."

"As I intended, I'd like to ask Eryxias if he thinks there are just and unjust people."

"I most certainly do."

"Then do you think injustice is a good thing or a bad thing?"

"A bad thing."

"Do you think a man would be behaving unjustly or not if he were to pay money to commit adultery with his neighbor's wife, when in fact both the city and its laws forbid it?"

"To my mind he would be acting unjustly."

"So if the unjust man who wanted to do this were wealthy and able to spend money on it, he would commit the crime. But if he weren't wealthy and didn't have the resources to spend, he simply wouldn't be able to carry out what he wanted; and then there'd be no crime at all. It follows that this man would be better off if he weren't wealthy, since he would have less chance of carrying out what he wanted when what he wanted was wrong.

"And here's something else: would you say that being sick is bad or good?"

"Bad."

"Now then, do you think that some people are weak-willed?"

"Yes."

"Then if it were better for the weak-willed person's health to stay away from food, drink, and the other things that people regard as pleasurable, but he wasn't able to do this because of his weakness, would it be better for him if he didn't have the means to acquire them, rather than if he had a superabundance of what he needed? For in that case he wouldn't have the opportunity to go wrong, no matter how much he wanted to."

I was thinking that Critias had conducted this conversation so effectively that if it weren't for the embarrassment Eryxias was feeling in front of everyone there, he might very well have stood up and hit Critias. Eryxias thought that something important had been taken from him, since it had become apparent to him that his earlier opinions about wealth were wrong. I realized that he was feeling like this and was worried that it might lead to insults and antagonism, so I said: "Just a couple of days ago this very

argument was being used in the Lyceum by a wise man named Prodicus,
d   from Ceos.[4] The people who were there thought he was talking such
nonsense that he couldn't convince any of them that he was speaking the
truth. As a matter of fact a very outspoken young man came up and sat
beside Prodicus. He began to laugh and jeer at him and provoke him; he
wanted Prodicus to explain what he was saying. What's more, his standing
among the audience was much higher than Prodicus'."

Erasistratus said, "Would you like to give us a report of the conversation?"

e   "By all means, provided I can remember it. I think it went something
like this.

"The young man asked him in what respect he thought wealth was bad
and in what respect good. Prodicus responded as you did just now: 'It's
good for gentlemen, the people who know in what situations they should
use their property; but it's bad for those who are wicked and ignorant.
The situation is the same with everything else as well: the nature of the
things people deal in inevitably reflects the people themselves. I think
that Archilochus'[5] poem said it well: "Men's thoughts are like the things
they encounter." '

398   " 'In that case,' the young man said, 'suppose someone were to make
me skilled in the same thing that good men are skilled in. He's bound at
the same time to make everything else good for me as well. Yet *that* wasn't
the point of his efforts, since he was concentrating on the thing at which
he has made me skilled rather than ignorant. It's as if someone now were
to make me skilled in letters: he would necessarily make the other things
that have to do with letters good for me; and likewise with music too. It's
b   the same story when he makes me good: inevitably he's made the other
things good for me too.'

"To these analogies Prodicus didn't offer his agreement, yet he went
along with the young man's initial remark.

" 'Do you think,' the young man said, 'that doing good things is just
like building a house, that it's the work of human hands? Or do things
have to go on being the very same as they were at the outset, whether
bad or good?'

"Prodicus, I think, was now suspicious about where their argument was
c   headed. So to avoid being defeated by the young man in full view of
everyone who was there—though he thought it made no difference if this
happened while they were alone—he gave a very shrewd response, that
doing good things is the work of human hands.

" 'Do you think,' the young man said, 'that excellence can be taught, or
is it innate?'

4. A professional educator (sophist); see *Protagoras* 315d, 337a ff. The Lyceum was a
public space just outside the walls of Athens.

5. Early seventh-century-B.C. composer of iambic and elegiac poems. The line quoted
is in frg. 70 Edmonds (Loeb) *Elegy and Iambus*, vol. 2.

" 'I believe it can be taught,' Prodicus said.

" 'Do you think a person would be foolish if he supposed that by praying to the gods he could become skilled in letters or music or could gain some other expertise, which he could only possess by learning from another person or by finding it out for himself?'

" 'Yes, I do.'

" 'So, Prodicus,' the young man said, 'whenever you pray to the gods for success and good things, you're praying on those occasions for nothing other than to become a gentleman, since it's the case that things are actually good for gentlemen, but bad for mediocre people. But if excellence really can be taught, it would appear that you're praying for nothing other than to be taught what you don't know.'

"I told Prodicus that I thought he was under a serious delusion if it turned out that he was wrong in supposing that we receive from the gods what we pray for at the same time that we pray for it. 'Although you sometimes hurry to the Acropolis and pray to the gods and beg them to give you good things, you don't know that they can give you what you're begging for. It's the same as if you were to go to the doors of a schoolteacher and implore him to give you skill in letters without any effort on your part, so that after you had received it you too would immediately be able to do the work that a schoolteacher does.'

"While I was saying this Prodicus, annoyed that his prayers to the gods might appear useless, began to go after the young man in order to defend himself; he meant to offer the same arguments that you did a moment ago. But then the supervisor of the gymnasium came up and told him to leave. He thought that Prodicus' discussions weren't suitable for young ears, and if they weren't suitable, they must be wicked.

"The reason I've recounted this is so that you may observe how people feel about philosophy. If Prodicus were here arguing as he was, you would all think he was so mad that he should even be expelled from the gymnasium, whereas just now you seem to have conducted your argument so extremely well, Critias, that you not only convinced everyone here but also made your opponent agree with you. It's clearly like the situation in lawcourts: if two people were to offer the same testimony—one with the reputation of a gentleman, the other of a wicked man—the jurors would remain unconvinced by the wicked man's testimony, but might possibly even do the opposite to what he wanted. But if the one who had the reputation of a gentleman were to say the same things, his words would be judged to be absolutely true. Perhaps the attitude your listeners have taken towards you and Prodicus is like this. They thought that Prodicus was a sophist and a charlatan, but they think you are an important man who is involved in the affairs of our city.[6] They also believe that they should not concentrate on the argument itself but rather on the character of the people who are arguing."

d

e

399

b

c

---

6. Accepting the conjectural deletion of *kai* before *andra* in c4.

"Why, Socrates, *you* may not be serious about what you're saying, but in my opinion Critias is clearly on to something important."

d   "Rest assured I'm absolutely serious. But since the two of you carried on your discussion so effectively, why not put the final touch on it as well?[7] I think there's something left for you to investigate, since there seemed to be agreement at least on the point that wealth is good for some and bad for others. All that's left now is to examine what wealth itself is; unless you first determine this you won't even be able to reach an agree-

e   ment on whether it's bad or good. I'm ready to give you as much help as I can to complete your investigation, so it's up to the one who claims that wealth is good to explain his position to us."

"My own opinion about wealth is no different from everyone else's: wealth is the possession of a lot of property. And I'm sure that Critias here also has the same opinion about wealth."

"In that case, then, you would *still* be left to consider what property is in order to avoid the appearance a bit later of arguing about this all over

400   again. Let me illustrate this with the Carthaginians, who use the following kind of currency. In a small piece of leather something roughly the size of a stater[8] is tied up, but no one knows what this is except the people who did the tying. Then when this is sealed they put it into circulation, and the person who has the largest number of these is considered to have the most property and to be the wealthiest. Yet if any Greek had a tremendous amount of this currency, he wouldn't be any wealthier than if he had a lot of pebbles which he took from the hill. In Lacedaemon they

b   put iron into circulation according to weight, and what's more, the useless kind.[9] The person who has a large weight of this kind of iron is considered wealthy, yet elsewhere such a possession is worthless. In Ethiopia they use engraved stones which a Lacedaemonian would find useless. And among the Scythian nomads anyone who possessed the house of Poulytion would be considered no wealthier than an owner of Mount Lycabettus would be considered by us.

c   "So clearly, each of these things cannot be property since some of the people who possess them seem no wealthier because of it. Yet each of them really is property for some people, and these people are wealthy because of their possession of it; but for others neither is it property nor does it make them wealthier. Likewise the same things are not beautiful and ugly to everybody, but rather different things strike different people in different ways.

d   "If, then, we should wish to investigate why it is that houses are not property in the eyes of the Scythians but they are to us, or why leather is property to the Carthaginians but not to us, or why iron is property to

---

7. Accepting the emendation *epetelesaton* in d2.

8. A coin; the Athenian stater was 17.5 grams of silver.

9. Accepting the conjectural deletion of *tou sidērou* in b1.

the Lacedaemonians but not to us, wouldn't our findings be precisely like that? Let me elaborate. Suppose someone in Athens had a thousand talents in weight of the stones found in the marketplace. Since we have no use for these stones, is there any reason why we should consider him any wealthier because he has them?"

"Apparently not."

"But suppose he had the same weight of lychnite,[10] would we say that he was in fact very wealthy?"

"Of course."

"Is it because the one thing is useful to us while the other is useless?"

"Yes."

"And that's also why among the Scythians houses are not property, because the Scythians have no use for a house; nor would a Scythian prefer the finest house over a heavy leather coat, since the one thing is useful to him while the other isn't. Again, we don't think that the Carthaginian coinage is property, since we couldn't possibly obtain from it what we need, as we do with silver; therefore it would be useless to us."

"Fair enough."

"It follows that everything that turns out to be useful to us is property, while everything useless is not."

In response to this Eryxias said: "How can that be, Socrates? When we're dealing with one another don't we engage in talking and looking[11] and many other things? Would we consider these property? They *do* seem useful. But even so we haven't gained an impression of what property is. Everyone has pretty well agreed that something must be useful if it's going to be property, but since not all useful things are property, what kinds of useful things *are*?"

"What[12] if we were to pursue the question again through a comparison with drugs, which were invented for ending illnesses? Would we have a better chance of finding what we're looking for, namely, what it is that we treat as property and for what purpose the possession of property was invented? Possibly that approach would make it clearer to us. Now it appears that everything which is property must also be useful, and that what we call property is a species of these useful things. Therefore what we still have to do is consider for what use property is useful to use. For instance, all things which we use for work are useful, of course, just as all things that have life are animals, but of these animals we call one species man. Now suppose someone were to ask us what would have to be done away with so that we wouldn't need medicine or medical instruments. Our response would be, if illnesses were removed from the body and didn't occur at all, or if they were removed as soon as they did occur.

10. Parian marble; or else a red precious stone.
11. Accepting the emendation *blepein* in a2.
12. Assigning these two paragraphs to Socrates instead of Eryxias.

Therefore it seems that medicine is the science which is useful for removing illnesses.

d   "But if someone were then to ask us what would have to be removed so that we wouldn't need property, would we have an answer? If we don't, let's start over again along these lines: if a person could live without food and drink, and not go hungry or thirsty, what need would he have of these things, or of money or anything else to provide himself with them?"

"None, I suppose."

"It's the same with other things, too. If we had no need of the things that we presently require to take care of our bodies, heat and cold for

e   instance, and everything else too which the body lacks but requires, then what passes for property would be useless to us, since no one would have any need at all of the things for whose sake we want property. The result for us would be satisfaction, as far as the persistent desires and needs of the body are concerned. So if it's to care for the body's needs that the possession of property is useful, and if these needs were taken out of our way, we wouldn't have any need for property, and property might not even exist at all."

"It looks like it."

"Then the things which are useful for that business appear to us, I suppose, to be property."

Eryxias agreed with this, but he was becoming seriously confused by the argument.

402   "What about this way of looking at it? Would we say that the same thing can be sometimes useful, but sometimes useless, for one specific purpose?"

"No, I don't think so. Instead, if we were to have any need of the thing for that one purpose, then I do think it's useful, but if we don't, then it isn't."

"So if we were able to make a gold statue without using fire, we wouldn't have any need of fire for that purpose. And if we didn't have any need

b   of fire, it wouldn't be useful to us either. The same argument applies to other things as well."

"It seems so."

"And so it would appear that whatever isn't needed when something is being done is also not useful to us in that particular case."

"That's right."

"Then if it should turn out one day that we were able to put an end to the body's needs so that it no longer had any, and we could do this without silver, gold, and other things of that kind which we don't actually use for the body (in the way that we use food, drink, clothing, blankets and houses), then it would appear that silver, gold, and other such things

c   wouldn't even be useful to us for this particular purpose, provided that the body's needs can one day be removed without using them."

"You're right."

"Then it would appear that these things aren't property to us either if they aren't useful, though they would be things which enable us to obtain what is useful."

"Socrates, I could never be convinced that gold, silver, and other things like them are not property, as you say. I'm *certainly* convinced that the things which are useless to us are not property, and that property ranks among the most useful things besides.[13] But I'm not persuaded that these things are not actually useful to us for living, since we can obtain what we require by means of them."

d

"Come on then, what would we say to this? Are there any teachers of music, letters, or some other skill, who obtain what they require for themselves by receiving compensation in return for their teaching?"

"There are."

"So it's with this skill of theirs that these people can obtain what they require, by receiving something in return for that skill in the same way that we receive things in return for gold and silver."

e

"Yes."

"But if it's with this that they obtain what they use for living, then it would actually be useful in itself for living. We did say, didn't we, that property is useful because with it we're able to obtain what we require for the body?"

"Yes we did."

"So if these skills are classified as useful for this purpose, then it appears they are property, for the same reason that gold and silver are property. It's clear too that those who possess these skills are wealthier. Yet a little earlier[14] we were having a lot of trouble accepting the argument that these are the wealthiest people. Based on the agreement we've just reached, however, it would have to follow that the more skillful are sometimes wealthier. For instance, if someone were to ask us whether we thought a horse is useful to everybody, wouldn't you answer that it's useful to those who know how to use a horse, but not to those who don't?"

403

"I would."

"And by the same argument medicine also isn't useful to everybody, but only to the person who knows how to use it?"

"Yes."

"Is it the same with everything else too?"

"Apparently."

b

"Then gold, silver, and the other things generally regarded as property would be useful only to the one who knows how they should be used?"

"Right."

"Now weren't we under the impression earlier[15] that it took a gentleman to know when and how to use each of these things?"

"We were."

---

13. Accepting the emendations *toutois* for *touto* and *ta chrēmata* for *chrēmata ta chrēsima* in d1.

14. 394a–395d.

15. 397e.

"Then these things would be useful only to gentlemen, since they're the ones who know how they should be used. But if these are useful only to them, then to them alone, it seems, would these things be property. It
c   appears, moreover, that if someone were to take a person who knew nothing about riding a horse and who owned horses which were useless to him, and then made him knowledgeable about horses, he would have made him at the same time wealthier too, since he has taken what was previously useless to this man and made it useful. For by giving the man some knowledge he's instantly made him wealthy."

"It seems so."

"And yet I'm sure I could also swear on Critias' behalf that he's not convinced by any of these arguments."

d   "I'm certainly not. In fact I'd be crazy if I were. But go on and finish your argument that the things generally accepted as money—silver, gold, and other such things—are not property. You can't imagine how much I admire these arguments of yours as I'm listening to you relate them right now."

"I think, Critias, that you enjoy listening to me in the same way that you enjoy listening to the rhapsodes who sing Homer's poems: you don't think a word of it is true. But come on, what would we say to this? Would
e   you say that some things are useful for housebuilders when they are constructing a house?"

"Yes, I think so."

"Would we say that those things are useful which they use[16] for this construction—stones, bricks, boards, and that kind of thing? Or are these things also useful, the tools they used to build the house and with which they provided themselves with the boards and the stones, and likewise the tools for *these* tools?"

"I suppose that all the things involved in the operation are useful."

"Isn't this the case with all other activities? Not only are these things themselves useful which we use for each of our tasks, but also those by which we acquire these things and without which our work couldn't be done?"

"Exactly."

"Then likewise the things with which these last things were made, and
404   anything that came before them, and, again, the things with which these were made, and once more the things that preceded them, on and on endlessly—do all these things inevitably appear useful for the production of our work?"

"Yes, that might well be the case."

"Now what if a person possessed food, drink, clothing, and whatever else he's likely to use for his body, would he have any additional need for gold, silver, or anything else with which to acquire them, seeing that he already possesses them?"

16. Accepting the emendation *katachrōinto* in e4.

"I doubt it."

"Do you suppose a situation could occur when a man would need none b
of these things for the use of his body?"

"No, I don't."

"Now if these things were to appear useless for this purpose, wouldn't
it follow that they can never appear useful? After all it was a basis of
our discussion that things could not be sometimes useful, but sometimes
useless, for one specific purpose."

"Well, in that respect, at least, our arguments may be in agreement: if
these things should ever be useful for this purpose, they would never turn
out also to be useless. As it is, for doing certain things ... c

... some for doing wicked things, others for doing good things?"[17]

"Yes, I would say so."

"Can something wicked be useful for the purpose of doing something
good?"

"No, I don't think so."

"Would we say that those acts are good which a person performs virtu-
ously?"

"Yes."

"Can a person learn anything which is taught orally, if he's completely
deprived of his ability to hear somebody else?"[18]

"No, by Zeus, I don't think so."

"So it would appear that hearing is to be classified as useful for virtue, d
since virtue can be taught through the sense of hearing and we make use
of this sense for learning."

"Yes."

"Since medicine can put an end to a person's illness, it seems that
sometimes medicine also may be classified as useful for virtue, if a person
can acquire the sense of hearing through medicine."

"That may be so."

"And again, if we were to obtain medicine in exchange for property,
property would obviously be useful for virtue too." e

"Yes, that's quite true."

"Likewise also the means by which we obtain the property?"

"Absolutely."

"Do you suppose that a person could obtain money by wicked and
disgraceful means, and in return get hold of the medical knowledge by
which he would be able to hear after having been unable to hear, and that
he could make use of that same ability for excellence or for other things
of a similar kind?"

"I certainly think so."

17. Some words seem to have been lost in the transmission of the text. Possibly Critias
claims that for doing certain things, certain items are always useful: then Socrates asks
if some items can be useful for doing wicked things, others for doing good things.

18. Accepting the conjectural deletion of *ē* (and the comma before it) in c8.

"Surely nothing wicked could be useful for virtue."

"No, it couldn't."

"Then those things by which we obtain what is useful for one purpose or another are not necessarily also useful for that same purpose. Otherwise bad things would sometimes appear to be useful for a good purpose. Perhaps this will make it clearer. If things are useful for one purpose or another, and this purpose couldn't come into existence unless those things existed beforehand, tell me, what would you say about that? Can ignorance be useful for knowledge, or sickness for health, or wickedness for virtue?"

"I don't think so."

"Yet on this we would agree, that knowledge can't belong to a person if ignorance didn't exist in him beforehand, that health can't belong to him if sickness didn't exist in him beforehand, and that excellence can't belong to him if wickedness didn't exist in him beforehand."

b   "Yes, I suppose we would."

"Then it would appear that those things which are required for the creation of something else are not necessarily also useful for that thing. Otherwise it would seem that ignorance is useful for knowledge, sickness for health, and wickedness for virtue."

Critias was finding it very hard to go along with these arguments, that not everything we had mentioned could be property. When I realized that it would be—as the saying goes—as easy to persuade him as it is to boil

c   a stone, I said: "Let's forget about those arguments, since we can't agree whether or not useful things and property are the same. But what would we say about this? Would we consider a person to be more prosperous and better if his physical requirements and his requirements for day to day living were extremely numerous, or if they were as few and simple as possible? Maybe the best way to look at it would be to compare the

d   person with himself by considering whether his condition is better when he is sick or when he is healthy."

"We certainly don't have to consider *that* for very long."

"No doubt it's because everybody easily recognizes that the healthy person's condition is superior to the sick person's. Now then, in what circumstance would we have a greater need for all kinds of things, when we're ill or when we're healthy?"

"When we're ill."

e   "So it's when we're in the worst condition that we have the most powerful and most numerous desires and needs, as far as physical pleasures are concerned?"

"Yes."

"And just as a person is in the best condition when he himself has the fewest requirements of that kind, can the same reasoning apply to two people, where one's desires and needs are powerful and numerous, while the other's are few and gentle? For example, consider anybody at all who is a gambler, or a drunkard, or else a glutton—all such conditions amount to nothing but desires."

"Exactly."

"But all these desires are nothing but the need for something; and those who have the greatest needs are in a worse condition than those who have no needs at all or as few as possible."

406

"As far as I'm concerned, people like that are certainly in a very bad state; the more they need the worse off they are."

"And so do we think that things can't be useful for some purpose unless we need them for that purpose?"

"That's right."

"Then if we suppose that these things are useful for taking care of the body's needs, mustn't we also require them for this purpose?"

"I think so."

"So the person who possesses the largest number of useful things for this purpose would also appear to *require* the largest number of things for this purpose, since he's bound to require all the things that are useful."

"That's how it seems to me."

"According to this argument, at least, it appears that those who have a lot of property must also need many of the things required to take care of the body, since property was seen as useful for this purpose. So the wealthiest people would necessarily appear to us to be in the worst condition, since they are in need of the greatest number of these things."

AXIOCHUS

Axiochus has come close to dying and was shaken by the experience, despite being familiar with arguments that used to make him laugh at death and at those who feared it. Socrates is summoned to his bedside to administer his usual consolations, of which he has a wide selection. Eventually some of them have the desired effect, and Axiochus welcomes the prospect of death as the release of his divine soul to a better place. He collects his thoughts, and Socrates goes on his way.

This dialogue is an unconventional version of a very conventional genre—the consolation letter. Typical examples include Seneca's Consolation for Marcia *and* Consolation for Polybius *and Plutarch's* Consolation for His Wife. *The Plutarchean* Consolation for Apollonius *is a sort of treasury of consolation arguments, and there are echoes and reflections of the genre in Cicero's* Tusculan Disputations *I and III, as well as in many other ancient sources, indicating its continuous popularity from at least the third century* B.C. *to the end of the pagan world, before being adapted by Christian writers. Every philosophical school produced arguments of consolation, especially Stoicism, and many letters of consolation freely borrowed arguments from all possible sources, whether or not the ideas were mutually consistent.*

It should therefore come as no surprise to see Socrates urging on Axiochus a wide variety of mutually incompatible consolations, including rhetorical and Cynic commonplaces as well as Epicurean, Stoic, and Platonic arguments. Some authors of this genre seem to have been less concerned with whether the arguments were true than with whether they were reassuring: "there are also some authors of consolation letters who combine all these kinds of consolation—for one man is moved by one sort, another by another—like the way I threw them all together in my Consolation, *for my soul was in a fever and I tried everything to cure it" (Cicero,* Tusculan Disputations *III.76).*

The strategy of Axiochus seems to be derived from Plato's Apology, *where Socrates says that death is either a permanent loss of consciousness or a transition to somewhere else. The arguments which are effective for Axiochus are Stoic (370b–d) and Platonic (371a–372a); "whether above or below, Axiochus, you ought to be happy, if you have lived piously." But the Cynic harangues and commonplaces (366d–369b) seem to make little impression, and the Epicurean arguments (365d–e and 369b–370b) are quite over his head.*

What makes Axiochus unconventional is that it is not a letter addressed to someone who has been bereaved, but a dialogue with somebody who is about to lose his own life, a situation in which the problematic emotion is not grief but

1734

fear. The author, probably a Platonist writing between 100 B.C. *and 50* A.D., *has borrowed characters from earlier Socratic writings to clothe the* consolatio *in the guise of a Socratic dialogue.*

D.S.H.

While I was on my way to the Cynosarges and getting near the Ilisus, I heard the voice of someone shouting, "Socrates, Socrates!" When I turned around to find out where it was coming from, I saw Clinias the son of Axiochus, running toward the Callirhoe,[1] together with Damon the musician, and Charmides the son of Glaucon.[2] (Damon was Clinias' music teacher; Charmides and Clinias were companions, and in love with one another.) So I decided to turn off the main road to meet up with them and get together as quickly as possible. With tears in his eyes, Clinias said:

"Socrates, now's your chance to show off the wisdom they're always saying you have! My father has been unwell for a while,[3] and is near the end of his life; and he's miserable on his deathbed, even though he used to laugh at people who had a phobia about death, and tease them a little. So come and reassure him in your usual way, so that he may meet his fate without complaining, and so that I and the rest of the family can also perform the proper rituals."

"Well, Clinias, you won't find me refusing such a reasonable request, especially since what you ask involves religion. Let's go; if that's the situation, speed is essential."

"Just seeing you, Socrates, will revive him; in fact he's often before managed to rally from this condition."

After hurrying along the wall to the Itonian gates—he lived near the gates by the Amazon column—we found that Axiochus had already collected his senses and was strong in body, though weak in spirit, very much in need of consolation, sobbing and groaning, again and again, as well as weeping and clapping his hands. I looked down at him and said:

"Axiochus, what's all this? Where's your former self-confidence, and your constant praise of manly virtues, and that unshakable courage of yours? You're like a feeble athlete who put on a brave show in training exercises and lost the actual contest! Consider who you are—a man of such an advanced age, who listens to reason, and, if nothing else, an Athenian!—don't you realize that life is a kind of sojourn in a foreign land (indeed, that's a commonplace, on everybody's lips), and that those who

364

b

c

d
365

b

Translated by Jackson P. Hershbell.

1. The Cynosarges was a gymnasium outside the Athenian city wall; the Ilisus was a river in whose stream bed was a spring called Callirhoe.

2. Axiochus was the uncle of the famous Alcibiades; Clinias and Charmides, both remarkably handsome young men, appear in *Euthydemus* and *Charmides*, respectively, as members of the Socratic circle.

3. Accepting the conjectural deletion of *aiphnidiou*.

have led a decent life should go to meet their fate cheerfully, almost singing a paean of praise? Being so faint-hearted and unwilling to be torn from life is childish and inappropriate for someone old enough to think for himself."

c   "True enough, Socrates, I think you're right. And yet, somehow or other, now that I'm very close to that awful moment, all those powerful and impressive arguments mysteriously lose their strength and I can't take them seriously; and a certain fear remains which assails my mind in various forms: that I will lose this light of day and these good things, and will lie somewhere or other, unseen and forgotten, rotting, and turning into maggots and wild beasts."

d   "In your distraction, Axiochus, you're confusing sensibility with insensibility, without realizing it. What you say and do involves internal self-contradiction; you don't realize that you're simultaneously upset by your loss of sensations and pained by your decay and the loss of your pleasures—as if by dying you entered into another life, instead of lapsing into the utter insensibility that existed before your birth. Just as during the government of Draco or Cleisthenes there was nothing bad at all that concerned you (because you did not exist then for it to concern you), nor will anything

e   bad happen to you after your death (because you will not exist later for it to concern you).

       "Away, then, with all such nonsense! Keep this in mind: once the compound is dissolved and the soul has been settled in its proper place, the body which remains, being earthly and irrational, is not the human person. For each of us is a soul, an immortal living being locked up in a mortal

366   prison; and Nature has fashioned this tent for suffering—its pleasures are superficial, fleeting, and mixed with many pains; but its pains are undiluted, long-lasting, and without any share of pleasure. And while the soul is forced to share with the sense organs their diseases and inflammations and the other internal ills of the body (since it is distributed among its pores), it longs for its native heavenly aether, nay, thirsts after it, striving

b   upwards in hopes of feasting and dancing there. Thus being released from life is a transition from something bad to something good."

       "Well, Socrates, if you think that living is bad, why do you remain alive? Especially since you puzzle your brain about these things and you're much cleverer than most of us."

       "Axiochus, you don't give a true account of me; you think, like most Athenians, that just because I'm an inquirer I'm also an expert on something. I wish I knew these ordinary things, so far am I from knowing the

c   extraordinary ones! My remarks are but echoes of the wise Prodicus,[4] some purchased for half a drachma, others for two, and still others for four. (That fellow teaches nobody for free and is always repeating the saying of Epicharmus:[5] "One hand washes the other"—give something and take

4. Prodicus of Ceos was a philosopher and teacher; see *Protagoras* 315d, 337a ff.
5. A fifth-century-B.C. comic poet.

something.) Anyway, just recently he gave a performance at the house of Callias son of Hipponicus,[6] in which he denounced living, so much so that I came within a hair's-breadth of writing it off; and since then, Axiochus, my soul has wanted to die."

"What did he have to say?"

"I'll tell you what I remember: What part of a lifetime is without its   d portion of misery? Doesn't the baby begin his life in pain, and cry from the first moment of birth? Certainly he lacks no occasion for suffering; hunger and thirst and cold and heat and hard knocks distress him, and he can't yet say what the problem is; crying is his only way of expressing discomfort. When he reaches the age of seven, after having endured much physical pain, he is set upon by tyrannical tutors, teachers, and trainers;   e and as he grows older there are scholars, mathematicians and military instructors, all a great crowd of despots. When he is enrollled among the Ephebes there is the Commander, and fear of beatings; then comes the   367 Lyceum and the Academy and the gymnasium-masters with their canings and excessive punishments; and his entire youth[7] is spent under Supervisors of Young Men and the Committee for Young Men of the Council of the Areopagus.[8]

"After he's free of all that, worries immediately steal upon him, and considerations about his career in life present themselves to him. And the earlier troubles seem like child's play, the bogey-men of babies, so to speak, compared with the later ones: military campaigns, wounds, and constant battles.

"Then old age creeps upon you unawares, into which flows everything   b in nature that is mortal and life-threatening. And unless you repay your life quickly, like a debt, nature stands by like a money-lender, taking security, sight from one man, hearing from another, and often both. And if you survive that, you'll be paralyzed, mutilated, crippled. Some people are physically in their prime in great old age—and their old minds enter a second childhood.

"And that is why[9] the gods, who understand the human condition, give   c a quick release from life to those[10] they hold in highest regard. For example, Agamedes and Trophonius, who built the temple of the Pythian god, after praying for the best thing that might happen to them, fell asleep and never woke up. And there were also the sons of the Argive priestess,[11] for whom

---

6. Callias was a wealthy Athenian noted for his patronage of philosophers (*Apology* 20a); the events in Plato's *Protagoras* and Xenophon's *Symposium* take place in his house.

7. Reading *chronos* in a2.

8. Ephebes were members of an Athenian military college established in the late fourth century B.C.

9. Reading *dia* for *kai* before *touto* in b7.

10. Omitting *kai* in c1.

11. Omitting *Hēras* in c5.

their mother likewise prayed for some reward from Hera for their piety, since when the team of mules was late they yoked themselves to the cart and took her to the temple; that night after their mother's prayer they passed away.

d   "It would take too long to go through the works of the poets, who prophesy with inspired voices the events of life while deploring life itself. I shall quote only one of them, the most important one, who said,

> *Such is the way the gods spun life for unfortunate mortals,*
> *that we live in unhappiness,*

and,

> *Since among all creatures that breathe on earth and crawl on it*
> *there is not anywhere a thing more dismal than man is.*

e   "And what does he say about Amphiaraus?

368

> *Whom Zeus of the aegis loved in his heart, as did Apollo,*
> *with every favor, but he never came to the doorsill of old age.*[12]

"And he who bids us,[13] 'Sing a dirge for the newly born; he faces so much misery'—what do you think of that? But I'll stop now, so as not to break my promise and lengthen my speech by mentioning other examples.

"What pursuit or trade has anyone ever chosen without criticizing it b   and chafing at its conditions? Shall we discuss the jobs of tradesmen and laborers, toiling from dawn to dusk, barely able to provide for their needs, deploring their lot and spoiling all their sleepless nights with lamentation and tears? Well, shall we talk about the job of the merchant, who sails through so many perils and is, as Bias has shown, neither among the dead nor the living: terrestrial man throws himself into the sea as if he were c   amphibious, and is entirely at the mercy of chance. Well, is farming a pleasant occupation? Really! Isn't it just one big blister, as they say, which always finds an excuse for pain? Now it's drought, now it's too much rain, now it's blight, now it's too much heat or frost, that makes the farmer weep.

"Well, how about highly respected politics? (I'm skipping over many cases.) How many dreadful things is it dragged through, feverishly quivering and throbbing, sometimes with joy, sometimes with painful failure, d   worse than a thousand deaths? How could anyone be happy living for the masses, when he is whistled for and lashed, like the electorate's pet

---

12. *Iliad* xxiv.525–26 and xvii.446–47 and *Odyssey* xv.245–46, respectively (translations by R. Lattimore).

13. Euripides, in his lost play *Cresphontes* (frg. 452 Dindorf).

horse, driven from office, jeered, fined, and killed?[14] Well then, Mr. Politician Axiochus, how did Miltiades die? How did Themistocles die? How did Ephialtes die?[15] How did the ten commanders recently die, when I refused to refer the question to the people?[16] I didn't think it was proper for me to preside over a mad mob, yet on the next day the party of Theramenes and Callixenus suborned the presiding officers of the meeting and secured a condemnation against the men without a trial. Indeed, you and Euryptolemus were the only ones to defend them, of the thirty thousand citizens in the Assembly."

"That's quite right, Socrates, and since then I've had enough of the speaker's platform, and I think that nothing is more irksome than politics. That's clear to everyone involved. You speak, of course, as a distant observer, but those of us who go through the experience know it perfectly well. The electorate, my dear Socrates, is an ungrateful, fickle, cruel, malicious, and boorish thing: a club, so to speak, of violent fools, drawn from the rabble in the street. And he who associates himself with it is even more contemptible by far."

"Well, Axiochus, since you regard the most reputable calling of all as more to be rejected than all the others, what are we to think of life's other pursuits? Shall we not escape from them?

"Once I also heard Prodicus say that death concerns neither the living nor those who have passed away."

"What do you mean, Socrates?"

"As far as the living are concerned, death does not exist; and the dead do not exist. Therefore death is of no concern to you now, for you are not dead, nor, if something should happen to you, will it concern you, for you will not exist. To be upset for Axiochus, about what neither does nor will concern Axiochus, is pointless distress, just as if you were to be upset about Scylla, or the Centaur, which, as far as you're concerned, neither exist now, nor will exist later, after your death. What is fearful exists for those who exist; how could it exist for those who don't?"

"You've taken those clever ideas from the nonsense that everybody's talking nowadays, like all this tomfoolery dreamed up for youngsters. But it distresses me to be deprived of the goods of life, even if you marshal arguments more persuasive than those, Socrates. My mind doesn't understand them and is distracted by the fancy talk; they go in one ear and out the other; they make for a splendid parade of words, but they miss the mark. My suffering is not relieved by ingenuity; it's satisfied only by what can come down to my level."

"That's because, Axiochus, you're confusing the perception of fresh evils with the deprivation of goods, without realizing it, forgetting that you

14. Omitting *eleoumenon* in d4.

15. Three fifth-century-B.C. leaders under the Athenian democracy.

16. The naval commanders at Arginusae were illegally prosecuted en masse; cf. Xenophon, *Memoirs of Socrates* I.1.18, and Plato, *Apology* 32a–c.

370   will have died. What distresses someone who is deprived of good things is having them replaced by bad things, and someone who doesn't exist cannot even conceive of the deprivation. How could anyone feel distress whose condition provides no awareness of anything distressing? If you hadn't started out, Axiochus, by ignorantly supposing, somehow or other, that the dead also have some sensation, you could never have been alarmed by death. But in fact you refute yourself; because you're afraid to be deprived of your soul, you invest this deprivation with a soul of its own; and you dread the absence of perception, but you think you will perceptually grasp this perception that is not to be.

b   "As well as many other fine arguments for the immortality of the soul, a mortal nature would surely not have risen to such lofty accomplishments that it disdains the physical superiority of wild animals, traverses the seas, builds cities, establishes governments, and looks up at the heavens and sees the revolutions of the stars, the courses of sun and moon, their risings and settings, their eclipses and swift restorations, the twin equinoxes and

c solstices, and Pleiades storms, summer winds, torrential downpours, and the violent course of tornadoes, and establishes for all eternity a calendar of the states of the universe, unless there really were some divine spirit in the soul which gives it comprehension and insight into such vast subjects.

   "And so, Axiochus, you pass away, not into death, but into immortality, nor will you have good things taken from you, but a purer enjoyment of

d them, nor pleasures mixed with the mortal body, but entirely undiluted by pains. For once you are released from this prison cell, you will set forth yonder, to a place free from all struggle, grief, and old age, a tranquil life untroubled by anything bad, resting in undisturbed peace, surveying Nature and practicing philosophy, not for a crowd of spectators, but in the bountiful midst of Truth."

e   "Your argument has converted me to the opposite point of view. I no longer have any fear of death—I almost long for it, if I may imitate the orators and use a hyperbole. I have traveled[17] the upper regions for ages past and shall complete the eternal and divine circuit. I was being weak, but I've got a grip on myself and become a new man."

371   "Then perhaps you'd like another argument, which was related to me by Gobryas, a Persian sage: he said that his grandfather Gobryas (who, when Xerxes made his crossing, was sent to Delos to guard the island sanctuary where two deities were born) learned from some bronze tablets, which Opis and Hecaërge had brought from the Hyperboreans, that the soul, after its release from the body, goes to the Place Unseen, to a dwelling beneath the earth. Here the palace of Pluto is not inferior to the court of

b Zeus, since the earth occupies the center of the universe and the vault of heaven is spherical, and half of this sphere fell to the celestial gods, and the other half to the gods under the earth, some of them brothers, others children of brothers. The gates on the way to Pluto's palace are protected

17. Accepting the emendation *meteōroporō* or *-polō* in e3.

by iron bolts and bars. When the gates swing open, the river Acheron, and then the river Cocytus, receives those who are to be ferried across to Minos and Rhadamanthus, in what is called the Plain of Truth. There sit judges who interrogate everyone who arrives about what kind of life he has lived and what sorts of activities he engaged in while he dwelled in his body. It is impossible to lie.

"Now those who were inspired by a good daemon during their lifetimes go to reside in a place for the pious, where the ungrudging seasons teem with fruits of every kind, where fountains of pure water flow, where all sorts of meadows bloom with many kinds of flowers, with philosophers discoursing, poets performing, dances in rings, musical concerts, delightful drinking-parties and self-furnished feasts, undiluted freedom from pain and a rich diet of pleasure; nor does fierce cold or heat ever occur, but through it wafts a temperate breeze, infused with the gentle rays of the sun.

"There is a certain place of honor for those who are initiated, and there they perform their sacred rites. Why should you not be the first in line for this privilege, you who are 'kin to the gods'? Legend tells us that Heracles and Dionysus, before their descents into the realm of Hades, were initiated in this world, and supplied by the Eleusinian goddess[18] with courage for their journeys yonder.

"But those who have wasted their lives in wickedness are led by the Erinyes to Erebus and Chaos through Tartarus, where there is a place for the impious, and the ceaseless water-fetching of the Danaids, the thirst of Tantalus, the entrails of Tityus eternally devoured and regenerated, and the never-resting stone of Sisyphus, whose end of toil is a new beginning. Here, too, are people being licked clean by wild beasts, set on fire constantly by the Avengers, and, tortured with every kind of torture, consumed by everlasting punishment.

"That is what I heard from Gobryas, but you must decide for yourself, Axiochus. I am moved by argument, and I know only this for sure: every soul is immortal, and also, when removed from this place, free from pain. So whether above or below, Axiochus, you ought to be happy, if you have lived piously."

"I'm too embarrassed to say anything to you, Socrates. I'm so far from fearing death that now I actually passionately desire it. That's how much I've been affected by this argument, as well as by the one about the heavens. Now I despise life, since I'm moving to a better home.

"And now I'd like to go over what you've said, quietly and by myself. But after midday, Socrates, please visit me."

"I will do what you ask. And now I'll go back to my walk to the Cynosarges, where I was going when I was summoned here."

---

18. Demeter, whose cult at Eleusis was the most important of the Greek mystery cults; those initiated there were promised a happy survival in the underworld after death.

EPIGRAMS

Before Socrates enticed him into philosophy—so an ancient tradition goes—
Plato was active for a time as a composer of tragedies and dithyrambs (Diony-
sian choral songs). If that is true, nothing of his work in those genres survives.
Even apart from his sometimes very poetical prose, for example in Socrates' sec-
ond speech of Phaedrus, *we do, however, have evidence of Plato's work as a*
poet. A number of "epigrams" attributed to him—poems suitable for inscrip-
tion on a funerary monument or for other dedicatory purposes—survive in one
or both of two collections of short Greek poems dating from medieval times, the
"Palatine" and "Planudean" Anthologies. The edition of J. M. Edmonds, which
we follow, prints seventeen poems from these sources, plus an eighteenth—in
praise of the comic poet Aristophanes—that Olympiodorus (sixth century A.D.
neo-Platonist philosopher) quotes as Plato's (as does Thomas Magister in his
Life of Aristophanes). *The first ten poems are also quoted as Plato's work in*
Diogenes Laertius' life of Plato, and many of the eighteen are quoted under
Plato's name by one or more additional ancient authors. They are all in the
form of elegiac couplets (a dactyllic hexameter, the meter of the Homeric epics,
followed by a dactyllic pentameter), mostly a single couplet each (but numbers
4, 5, 7, 11, and 13 are double couplets, and 3 consists of three).

The first two poems are addressed to a young man, as it seems a student of
astronomy, named Astēr (or perhaps only affectionately so called by his ad-
mirer)—a Greek word for 'star'. Diogenes Laertius reports that the third was
actually inscribed on the tomb at Syracuse of its dedicatee, Plato's friend and
associate in Syracusan political affairs, Dion (prominent in so many of the Pla-
tonic Letters). *The Anthologies also give other attributions than to Plato in*
the case of some four of these poems, and Plato's authorship has reasonably
been doubted in other cases as well. It is odd to find Plato in numbers 4 and 6
speaking in erotic terms of Agathon and Phaedrus as desirable youths—these
are historical persons appearing as characters in Plato's dialogues on eros, but
they were two decades Plato's senior; and one notes that the object of the poet's
affection in number 8, Xanthippe, has the same name as Socrates' wife. None-
theless, there seems no reason to doubt that some of these poems—above all
number 3, and perhaps others, including especially 1, 2, and 7—are actually
by him.

For ease of identification we add for each poem (except the last) its position
in Hermann Beckby's edition of the Anthologia Graeca *(Munich, 1957).*

J.M.C.

1

You gaze at the stars, my Star; would that I were Heaven, that I might look at you with many eyes!

Greek Anthology vii 669

2

Even as you shone once the Star of Morning among the living, so in death you shine now the Star of Evening among the dead.

Greek Anthology vii 670

3

The Fates decreed tears to Hecuba and the women of Troy right from their birth;[1] but for you, Dion, the gods spilled your widespread hopes upon the ground after you had triumphed in the doing of noble deeds. And so in your spacious homeland you lie honored by your fellow citizens, O Dion, you who made my heart mad with love.

Greek Anthology vii 99

4

Now, when I have but whispered that Alexis is beautiful, he is the observed of all observers. O my heart, why show dogs a bone? You'll be sorry for it afterwards: was it not so that we lost Phaedrus?

Greek Anthology vii 100

5

My mistress is Archeanassa of Colophon, on whose very wrinkles there is bitter love. Hapless are all you who met such beauty on its first voyage; through what a burning did you pass!

Greek Anthology vii 217

6

When I kiss Agathon my soul is on my lips, where it comes, poor thing, hoping to cross over.

Greek Anthology v 78

Translated by J. M. Edmonds, revised by John M. Cooper. Text: *Elegy and Iambus* (Harvard University Press, Loeb Classical Library, 1931), vol. II.

1. Reading *tote* in line 2.

7

I throw the apple at you, and if you are willing to love me, take it and share your girlhood with me; but if your thoughts are what I pray they are not, even then take it, and consider how short-lived is beauty.[2]

Greek Anthology v 79

8

I am an apple; one who loves you throws me at you. Say yes, Xanthippe; we fade, both you and I.

Greek Anthology v 80

9

We are Eretrians of Euboea,[3] but we lie near Susa, alas, how far from home!

Greek Anthology vii 259

10

A man who found some gold left a noose, and the one who did not find the gold he had left tied on the noose he found.

Greek Anthology ix 44

11

I, Laïs, who laughed so disdainfully at Greece and once kept a swarm of young lovers at my door, dedicate this mirror to the Paphian[4]—for I do not wish to see me as I am, and cannot see me as I was.

Greek Anthology vi 1

12

This man was pleasing to foreigners and dear to his fellow citizens— Pindar, servant of the melodious Muses.

Greek Anthology vii 35

---

2. The apple was dear to Aphrodite; to throw an apple at someone was to declare one's love; to catch and hold it, to show one's acceptance.

3. They were deported to Susa, King Darius' capital, by the Persians in 490 B.C. See also no. 13.

4. I.e., Aphrodite; the poem was inscribed on a mirror for dedication by Laïs to her.

13

We once left the sounding waves of the Aegean to lie here amidst the plains of Ecbatana. Fare thee well, renowned Eretria, our former country. Fare thee well, Athens, Euboea's neighbor. Fare thee well, dear Sea.

Greek Anthology vii 256

14

I am the tomb of a ship's captain; the tomb opposite is a farmer's: for beneath the land and beneath the sea is the same place of Death.

Greek Anthology vii 265

15

Sailors, be safe, by sea and on land; I would have you know that the tomb you pass is a shipwrecked man's.

Greek Anthology vii 269

16

Some say there are nine Muses. How thoughtless! Look at Sappho of Lesbos; she makes a tenth.

Greek Anthology ix 506

17

When Cypris saw Cypris at Cnidus, "Alas!" said she; "where did Praxiteles see me naked?"[5]

Greek Anthology xvi 162

18

The Graces, seeking for themselves a shrine that would not fall, found the soul of Aristophanes.

---

5. Cypris is Aphrodite, of whom there was a famous nude statue by Praxiteles at Cnidus.

ABBREVIATIONS OF TITLES

Alcibiades	Alc.	Laches	Lch.
Second Alcibiades	2Alc.	Laws	L.
Apology	Ap.	Letters	Ltr.
Axiochus	Ax.	Lysis	Ly.
Charmides	Chrm.	Menexenus	Mx.
Clitophon	Clt.	Meno	M.
Cratylus	Cra.	Minos	Min.
Critias	Criti.	Parmenides	Prm.
Crito	Cri.	Phaedo	Phd.
Definitions	Def.	Phaedrus	Phdr.
Demodocus	Dem.	Philebus	Phlb.
Epigrams	Epgr.	Protagoras	Prt.
Epinomis	Epin.	Republic	R.
Eryxias	Eryx.	Rival Lovers	Riv.
Euthydemus	Euthd.	Sisyphus	Sis.
Euthyphro	Euthphr.	Sophist	Sph.
Gorgias	Grg.	Statesman	Stm.
Halcyon	Hal.	Symposium	Smp.
Hipparchus	Hppr.	Theaetetus	Tht.
Greater Hippias	G.Hp.	Theages	Thg.
Lesser Hippias	L.Hp.	Timaeus	Ti.
Ion	Ion	On Virtue	Virt.
On Justice	Just.		

"+" = "and following." For example, "R. 327a+" means "*Republic* 327a and following"; i.e., section 327a plus one or more of the sections immediately following.

INDEX

A

Abaris: Chrm. 158b
Abdera: Prt. 309c; R. 10.600c
abortion: R. 5.461c; Tht.149d
Academy: Ax. 367a; Ly. 203a
Acarnania(ns): Euthd. 271c
Acesimbrotus: Cra. 394c
Achaeans: Alc. 112b; L. 3.682d+,
    3.685e, 3.706d+; R. 3.389e, 3.390e,
    3.393+
Achaemenes: Alc. 120e
Acharnae: Grg. 495d
Achelous: Phdr. 230b, 263d
Acheron: Ax. 371b; Phd. 112e, 113d
Acherousian Lake: Phd. 113+
Achilles: Ap. 28c; Cra. 428c; G.Hp.
    292e; L.Hp. 363b, 364b+, 364e, 365b,
    369a+, 370b, 370e+, 371a+, 371d; Ion
    535b; Prt. 340a; R. 3.388a+, 3.390e+,
    3.391c; Smp. 178a, 179e+, 180a, 208d,
    221c
Acragas: Thg. 127e
acropolis of Athens: Criti. 112a; Eryx.
    398e; Euthphr. 6b; M. 89b
acropolis of Atlantis: Criti. 115d, 116c+
acropolis of Syracuse: Ltr. 3.315e,
    7.329e, 7.348a, 7.349d, 7.350a
acropolis of the model city: L. 5.745,
    6.778c
actors: *see* theater
Acumenus: Phdr. 227a, 268a, 269a; Prt.
    315c; Smp. 176b
Acusilaus: Smp. 178b
Adeimantus, son of Ariston: interlocu-
    tor in *Parmenides* (126a+) and *Repub-
    lic* (1.328a, 2.362d+, 2.376d+,
    4.419a+, 5.449b+, 6.487a+, 8.548d+);
    Ap. 34a; Prm. 126a+; R. 1.327c,
    2.362d, 2.368a, 2.368d, 2.376d, 4.419,
    5.449b+, 6.487a, 8.548d

Adeimantus, son of Cepis: Prt. 315e
Adeimantus, son of Leucolophides:
    Prt. 315e
Admetus: Smp. 179b, 208d
Adonis, gardens of: Phdr. 276b
adoption: L. 9.878a+, 11.923c+, 11.929c
Adrastea: R. 5.451a; *see also* Destiny,
    law of
Adrastus: Phdr. 269a
adultery: Eryx. 396e–397a; L. 6.784e,
    8.841d+; R. 461a; Smp. 181e
advice/adviser: Alc. 106c–107e, 108e–
    109c, 113b, 116d, 125e–126a, 127d;
    2Alc. 144e–145c; Def. 413c; Dem.
    380a–382e; Eryx. 394e; Ltr. 5.322a+,
    7.330c+; Prt. 313a+; Thg. 122a–122c
Aeacus: Alc. 121b; Ap. 41a; G.Hp. 292e;
    Grg. 523e+, 526c+, 526e; Thg. 124c
Aeantodorus: Ap. 34a
Aegean Sea: Epgr. 13
Aegina (nymph): Grg. 526e
Aegina/Aeginetan (place): Alc. 121b;
    Cra. 433a; Grg. 511d; L. 4.708a; Ltr.
    4.321b, 13.362b; Phd. 59c
Aegisthus: Thg. 124c
Aegyptus: Mx. 245d
Aeneas: Lch. 191a+
Aeolus: Halc. 1
Aeschines: Ap. 33e; Phd. 59b
Aeschylus: Smp. 180a; quoted: Euthd.
    291d; Phd. 108a; R. 2.361b, 2.361e–
    362a, 3.380a, 3.381d, 3.383b, 3.391e,
    8.550c, 8.563c
Aesop's fables: Alc. 123a; Phd. 60c+,
    61b+
aether: Ax. 366a; Epin. 981c, 984d+;
    Halc. 7; Phd. 98c, 109c, 111b; Ti. 58d
Aexone: Lch. 197c; Ly. 204e
Agamedes: Ax. 367c
Agamemnon: Ap. 41b; Cra. 395a+;
    L. 4.706d; L.Hp. 370b+; Ltr. 2.311b;

E

H

L

M

O

Symposium (176a+; his speech, 180c–185c); Smp. 176a, 193b; Prt. 315e

Pausanias of Sparta: Ltr. 2.311a

payment: Alc. 119a; Ap. 20a; Ax. 366c; Cra. 384b, 391b+; Def. 415c; Eryx. 394e, 402d; Euthd. 304a+; G.Hp. 281b, 282b+, 285b, 300c; Grg. 515e, 519c, 520c; Hppr. 228c; L. 7.804d, 11.921b+; Lch. 186c+; M. 91b+; Prt. 310d+, 311d+, 328b, 349a; R. 1.337d; Riv. 135c; Sph. 223a, 231d, 233b; Thg. 121d, 127a, 127c–128a; Tht. 167d; Virt. 378b; *see also* wage earner(s)

peace: Alc. 107d, 107e+, 108d, 109a; 2Alc. 144e; Def. 413a; L. 1.626a, 1.628c+, 7.803d+, 7.814e+, 8.829a+, 12.955b+; Stm. 307e

Pegasuses: Phdr. 229d

Peleus: L. 12.944a; R. 3.391c; Thg. 124c

Pelopidae: L. 3.685d; Mx. 245d; R. 2.380a

Peloponnesus: L. 3.685b; Ltr. 7.333b, 7.336d, 7.343c, 7.346c, 7.348c, 7.350b; Mx. 235d

Pelops: Cra. 395c; G.Hp. 293b; Mx. 245d; *see also* Pelopidae

Penelope: Alc. 112b; Ion 535b; Phd. 84a

Penia: Smp. 203b+

Pentelicon: Eryx. 394e

people, the: Alc. 110e–112a; Ax. 369a; L. 3.700a, 6.768b; Min. 318e; Mx. 238d; *see also* many, the (contrasted with the few, etc.); multitude, the

Peparethians: Alc. 116d

peras: *see* limit(ed)

perception: Ax. 369e–370a; Def. 411c, 414c; L. 10.902c; Ltr. 7.344b; Min. 314a–314b; Phd. 65, 79; Phlb. 35a, 38b+; R. 6.507c+, 7.523b+; Tht. 151e+, 154b+, 156, 157e+, 159+, 160c+, 163+, 165b+, 166a+, 179c, 181d+, 182e, 184b+, 185+, 191b, 192+; *see also* pleasure(s); sensation; sense(s)

Perdiccas II: Grg. 470d, 471a+; R. 1.336a; Thg. 124d

Perdiccas III: Ltr. 5.321c+

Periander: Ltr. 2.311a; R. 1.336a; Thg. 124c–124e

Pericles: Alc. 104b, 105b, 118c–119a, 122b, 124c; 2Alc. 143e–144b; Grg. 455e, 472b, 503c, 515d+, 519a; Ltr. 2.311a; M. 94a, 94b; Mx. 235e, 236b; Phdr. 269a, 269e+; Prt. 314e, 315a, 320a, 328c, 329a; Smp. 221c, 215e; Thg. 126a; Virt. 376c–376d, 377d–378a

perjury: L. 11.916e+, 11.937b+, 12.943e; Phlb. 65c; Smp. 183b; *see also* oaths

Persephone: L. 6.782b; *see also* Phersephone

Perseus: Alc. 120e

Persia, king of: Alc. 120a, 120c, 120e–121e, 123b–123e; Ap. 40e; Eryx. 393d; Euthd. 274a; Grg. 470e, 524e; Ltr. 13.363b; Ly. 209d; M. 78d; Mx. 241d, 241e; R. 8.553c; Sph. 230d; Stm. 264c

Persia/Persian(s): Alc. 120a, 120c, 121c, 121d–122c, 123b–123e; Ax. 371a; Chrm. 158a; L. 1.637d+, 1.642d+, 3.692c+, 3.693a, 3.693d, 3.694a+, 3.694c+, 3.695a, 3.697c+, 3.698b+, 4.707b+; L.Hp. 368c; Lch. 191c; Ltr. 7.332a+; Min. 316a; Mx. 239d+, 241b, 243b, 244d

personal identity: Smp. 207d; Tht. 159b+

persuasion: Alc. 114b–114d; G.Hp. 304b; Grg. 453+, 454e; L. 4.719e+, 4.722b+, 10.885d; Phdr. 260; Phlb. 58a; Sph. 222c+; Stm. 304c+; *see also* belief

Phaeax: Eryx. 392a

Phaedo, referred to: Ltr. 13.363a

Phaedo: interlocutor in (57a+, 89b+, 102b+) and narrator of (59c+) *Phaedo*; Phd. 117d

Phaedondas: Phd. 59c

Phaedrus: interlocutor in *Phaedrus* (227a+) and *Symposium* (176d+, 194d, 199c; his speech, 178a–180b); Epgr. 4; Phdr. 228+, 234c+, 236d+, 242a, 243d, 244a, 258e, 276e; Prt. 315c; Smp. 176c, 176d, 177a+, 178–180

Phaenarete: Alc. 131e; Tht. 149a

Phaethon: Ti. 22c

Phaleron: Halc. 8; Smp. 172a

Q

V

W

A Note on the Type

The text and minor headings of this book are set in Palatino, a typeface designed by the great typographer Hermann Zapf in 1948 and first released for use in 1950. Originally created as a commercial face, Palatino has nonetheless won wide acceptance for book work. The major headings are set in Michelangelo, a titling font which Zapf designed to accompany Palatino. Like all of Zapf's many designs, Palatino and Michelangelo possess the essential qualities of clearness, beauty, and character.

The jacket type is Trajan, a titling face designed by Carol Twombly and first made available in 1989, with Centaur, designed by Bruce Rogers and first used in 1915.

Composition by WorldComp